THE PAN PACIFIC HOTEL
Vancouver

The D1441747 85 8690

photo: Stefan Schulhof

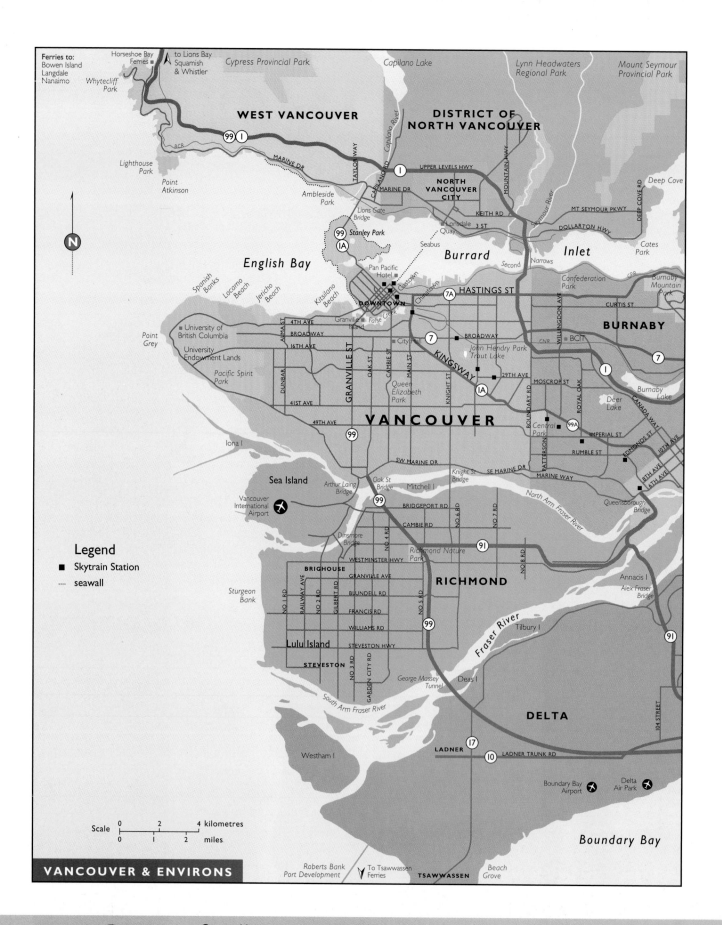

VANCOUVER & ENVIRONS

Legend
- ■ Skytrain Station
- ···· seawall

Scale
0 — 2 — 4 kilometres
0 — 1 — 2 miles

THE PAN PACIFIC HOTEL
Vancouver

Greater Vancouver enjoys a splendid setting in British Columbia's southwest. Nearly two million people live here by the broad waters of the Fraser River, with the Coast Mountains a spectacular backdrop. Placed dramatically on Burrard Inlet, with panoramic views on all sides and world-famed

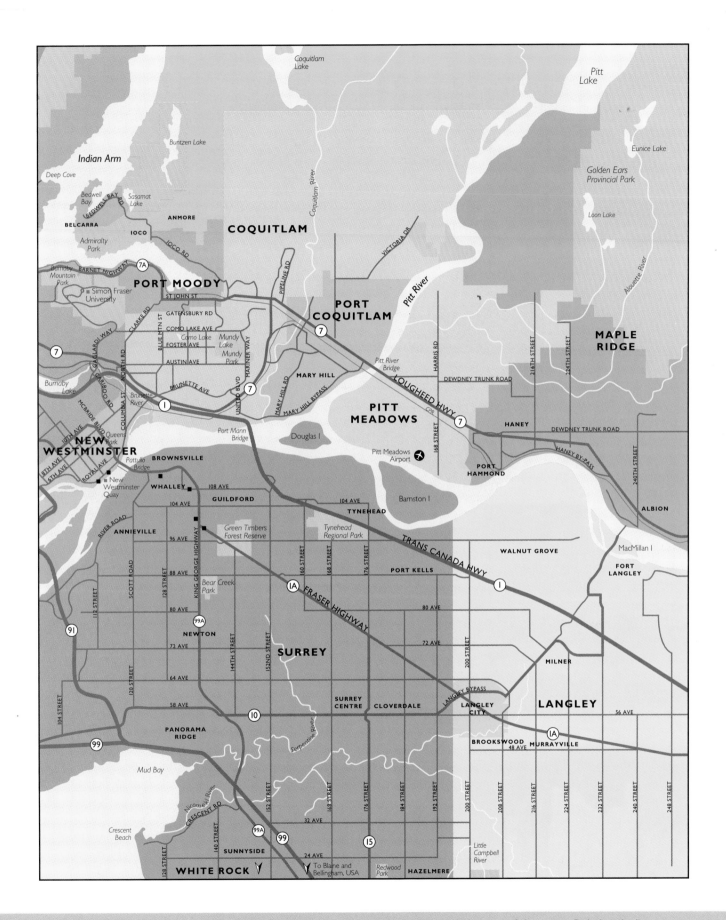

Stanley Park a few minutes away, the Pan Pacific Hotel Vancouver is perfectly sited to take advantage of the setting. Right beside the famous five sails of Canada Place, the Vancouver Trade and Convention Centre, and next to the city's busy cruise ship terminal, the Pan Pacific Hotel Vancouver has been greeting national and international travellers since the 1986 Centennial of the City of Vancouver.

A building owned by <u>Equitable Real Estate Investment Corporation</u> was home for research for the 1976 <u>The Vancouver Book.</u> Twenty years later, a building owned by Equitable was home for research for <u>The Greater Vancouver Book!</u> <u>Equitable</u> is proud to have been chosen by the publishers of both these extraordinarily useful books, filled with so many fascinating features. A fact for many decades: an office in any of the several downtown <u>Equitable</u> locations is an excellent choice.

Call us at (604) 683 7571

325 Howe Street

Shelly Building

Vancouver Block

Photos: Jim Jorgenson

Enjoy!

Chuck Davis

the Greater

vancouver

book an urban encyclopaedia

Chuck Davis Editor in Chief

Linkman Press

THIS BOOK IS DEDICATED TO MY FATHER, GEORGE DAVIS
(1905–1969). WITH VIRTUALLY NO FORMAL EDUCATION,
BUT BLESSED WITH UNQUENCHABLE CURIOSITY, HE BECAME
A CONSTANT READER. WHEN I WAS A LIST-LOVING KID, HE
TOLD ME ONE DAY, "CHARLIE, ONE OF THESE DAYS YOU'RE
GOING TO MAKE A LIST OF ALL YOUR LISTS." HE WOULD HAVE
LOVED THE GREATER VANCOUVER BOOK—*Chuck Davis, 1997*

Published by: **The Linkman Press***
15032–97th Avenue, Surrey B.C. V3R 8K2
   *A Division of Linkman Press Ltd.

Editor in Chief: Chuck Davis
Managing Editor: John Cochlin
Project Manager/Comptroller: Kathy Cochlin
Production Coordinator: Lawrence Boxall
Editor: Julian Beder
Associate Editors: Constance Brissenden,
   Iain Hiscoe, Jack Vermee
Book Designer and Picture Editor: Robin Ward
Typeset in Garamond and Gill Sans by
   Lawrence Boxall

**Produced by CODA Print Communications for
The Linkman Press**
   Electronic Pre-press: CODA
   Cartography: Xanthe Willer
   Color Separations: John McCluskey, ChromaTech
   Printed in Canada by Mitchell Press, Vancouver

Canadian Cataloguing in Publication Data
Main entry under title:
The Greater Vancouver Book: an urban encyclopaedia
   Includes index
   ISBN 1-896846-00-9
   1. Vancouver Metropolitan Area (B.C.)
   I. Davis, Chuck, 1935-
FC3847.3.G73 1996   971.1'33   C96-901034-6
F1089.5.V22G73 1996

Picture credits:
All pictures in this book are copyright ©. None can
be reproduced without written permission from the
copyright holder (noted after each picture caption)

Most of the photographs are reproduced with the
kind permission of **Pacific Press Limited,** publisher of *The Vancouver Sun* (vs) and *The Province* (vp)

Historical photographs are reproduced courtesy of
City of Vancouver Archives (cva). Other pictures are
by Robin Ward (rw) and other acknowledged sources

frontispiece: *the Lions Gate Bridge and Vancouver
city centre seen from West Vancouver, 1990.* vs

*The publishers of The Greater Vancouver Book
welcome comments and updates—write, fax or
phone The Linkman Press; phone 604 588 5465
fax 604 588 5558, email linkman@uniserve.com*

**Linkman
Press**

Tel 731-2126 Fax 733-3938
info@codacom.com
http://www.codacom.com

Sponsors of The Greater Vancouver Book

WITHOUT THE HELP of the many companies and individuals below, this book would not have been possible . . . or would have cost five times as much. Their sponsorship of articles and other material in the book is terrific testament to their interest in and affection for Greater Vancouver. They have given you a resource that thousands of people will use for many years. From the Linkman Press to all our Sponsors, many thanks!

650 C-ISL Radio • AAA Horse & Carriage • Ace Cycle • Air Canada • Air Transat Holidays • Alberta Distillers • Anvil Auto Glass • Association of Professional Engineers & Geoscientists of B.C. • B.C. Film Commission • B.C. Medical Association • B.C. Rail • B.C. Trade & Investment • B.C. Forestry Association • BC Gas • B.C. Hydro • B.C. Pavilion Corporation • B.C. & Yukon Hotels Association • BC Transit • Beatty Street Bar & Grill • Bentall Corporation • Birks Family Foundation • Bishop's Restaurant • Boston Pizza • Bridges Restaurant & Pub • Buy & Sell Press • C.H. Cates & Sons • Canada Mortgage & Housing Corporation • Canada Wide Magazines • Canfor Corporation • Canadian Imperial Bank of Commerce • Canadian Pacific Hotels • Can-Dive Construction • Capilano Suspension Bridge • Capt. Billy's Magical Tours • CBC Stereo 105.7 • Canadian Tour Guide Association • Central Heat Distribution • Charlie Mayrs • Chouinard & Company • Christopher Richardson • City of Burnaby • City of Langley • City of North Vancouver • City of Port Coquitlam • City of Richmond • City of Surrey • CN IMAX Theatre at Canada Place • CODA Print Communications • Cohen Family • Colin Ryan • Concord Pacific Developments • Contacts Target Marketing • Croden Personnel Consultants • Dairyworld Foods • Dal Richards • David Roels • Dome Advertising • Don Cassie • Don Docksteader Motors • Douglas & McIntyre • Douglas Lake Cattle Ranch • Downs/Archambault Architects • DUECK GM on Marine • Duthie Books • Earls Restaurants • Elephant and Castle • Environment Canada • Equitable Real Estate Investment Corp. • Festival Cinemas • Finning Limited • The Flag Shop • Forest Alliance of B.C. • Four Seasons Hotel • Fraser Downs at Cloverdale • Freeway Chrysler Dodge • General Paint • Geoffrey Dodds • Georgia Tiedemann • Georgian Court Hotel • Gerry P. Prefontaine • Goethe Institute • Greater Vancouver Regional District • Griffiths Gibson Ramsay Productions Ltd. • Grouse Mountain Resorts • H.Y. Louie • Harbour Air • Hastings Park • Hemlock Printers • Hong Kong Merchants Association • Hotel Vancouver • Hudson's Bay Company • Hunky Bill's • Hyatt Regency Hotel • IKON Office Solutions • Imperial Parking • Information Services Vancouver • Janet Bingham • Jantzen Canada • Jeff Veniot • Jentash Marketing • Jordans Carpets • Kate Walker & Co. • Keen Engineering • KVOS TV Ltd. • Labatt Breweries • Laing Properties • The Landis • Liberty Investments • Lignum Ltd. • Lisogar Construction • Literacy B.C. • The Loewen Group • The Lookout • Lower Mainland Nissan Dealers • McDonald's Restaurants • McLeod Restorations • MacMillan Bloedel • Mainstream Broadcasting • Marathon Developments Inc. • Middlegate Honda • Ministry of Municipal Affairs • Mohawk Oil • Molson Indy • Mountain Equipment Co-op • Mr. Fireworks • Native Brotherhood of B.C. • North Shore Credit Union • Odlum Brown • The Old Spaghetti Factory • Oppenheimer Bros. & Co. Ltd. • Orpheum • Overwaitea Foods • Pacific Press Ltd. • Pacific Yachting • Palmer Jarvis Advertising • Pan Pacific Hotel Vancouver • Parsons Brown • Pitman Business College • Playboard Magazine • Port of Vancouver • Princess Cruises • Princeton Developments • The Province • Purdy's Chocolates • Queen Elizabeth Theatre • Ralph's Radio • Richmond Chinese Community Society • Rocky Mountaineer Railtours • Roedde House • Roxy Cabaret • Science World • Seaspan International • Serviceworks Distribution • Sev Morin • Sharon Furlotte-Unruh • Simon Fraser University • Sing Tao Newspapers • Society of Notaries of B.C. • Sprite Computer Systems • Taconite • Taiwan Entrepreneurs & Investors Assn. • Teahouse/Seasons Restaurants • The Torresan Group • Tourism Vancouver • Thomson & Page • Tilbury Cement • Tobi Sales • Tourism Vancouver • Umberto's • Urbanics Consultants • VanCity Savings Credit Union • Vancouver Airport Authority • Vancouver Aquarium • Vancouver Area Newspaper Network • Vancouver Board of Trade/World Trade Centre • Vancouver Pioneers • Vancouver Sun • Vancouver Stock Exchange • Vancouver Trolley Company • Walker & Co. • Waterfront Centre Hotel • The Westin Bayshore Hotel • Weyerhaeuser Canada • Western International Communications • White Spot Restaurants • William Parton Agencies • William Tell Restaurant • Windsor Plywood • M.K. Wong & Associates • Xerox of Canada • Z 95.3 FM • Zlotnik Lamb & Co.

Contents

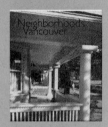

TOMORROW THERE WILL be 110 more residents in Greater Vancouver than there are today. Since we began working on this book nearly four years ago the population of the Vancouver metropolitan area has grown by more than 120,000 and demographers say there will be two million of us by 2001. That rapidly growing population—many of its members newcomers unfamiliar with the city—is one reason the Linkman Press is publishing this book.

But even people born somewhere in Greater Vancouver or like me, born elsewhere but having spent years here, should find this book useful and interesting. Hundreds of people have been involved in it and their collective experience and researches far exceed the knowledge any one person could have. I came here as a kid more than 50 years ago and have written extensively about it since, yet I've learned a great deal that is new to me from the hundreds of articles gathered here. There is much more to the city and its surroundings than you might imagine.

It's the diversity, color and interest, conflict and constant change energizing Greater Vancouver that prompted me to conceive of the book. Something of this is touched on by Hugh J.M. Johnston, a professor of history at Simon Fraser University, in a short introduction to a book that appeared a few months before this one. In *The Pacific Province: A History of British Columbia,* Professor Johnston writes, "In Eastern Canada many towns and villages achieved a staid and rooted look within a couple of generations, but that does not seem to have happened to British Columbia: the population has been too transient, the influx of immigrants too continuous, and the racial and ethnic mix too diverse. From the moment in the eighteenth century when outsiders first saw possibilities here, British Columbia has attracted a restless population of opportunists . . ." Vancouver can certainly be described as restless. Many don't like restlessness. They flee the city, if they can. Then there are the rest of us.

The *Greater Vancouver Book* was born in July 1967 on a scrap of paper on which I had written a sudden idea: "should do urban almanac on Vancouver." That eventually led, in 1976, to the 500-page *Vancouver Book,* published by J.J. Douglas Ltd. of North Vancouver. A continuing and gratifying public interest over the years eventually led, albeit a full 21 years later, to the present book. A more detailed description of how the 1967 idea turned into the 1997 book is given on page 852.

The books are alike, yet different. The idea behind both is the same: answer as many questions about the area as possible, or at the least tell where information can be found. But in 1976 the focus was on Vancouver itself; this time around it's broader, covering all of Greater Vancouver, more than 20 different areas. There is a lot of new material, the major example being the

"Greater Vancouver Hall of Fame." Of all the chapters in the book this is the one of which I'm proudest. Writer Constance Brissenden has done a marvellous job bringing us thumbnail biographies of 500 notable people of our past. This has never been done here before. What Constance did was so good we're planning a separate book by her. It will include more names.

One of the items we decided not to repeat this time around is a listing of current elected officials. We've made other changes too: the phrase "Ethnic Groups" as a chapter heading disappears to be replaced by the "Peoples of Greater Vancouver." One of the results of writing about ethnic groups is that you may neglect—as we did in 1976—to write about your own. (Surely it's other people who are ethnic!) So this time around people who trace their ancestry to the U.K. get space too. We changed the "Churches" title, as well: that description doesn't comfortably include ashrams, temples, synagogues and other places where Greater Vancouverites worship.

Many new kinds of listings and expanded versions of original listings played their part in making this new book bigger. And why is the book so big? I regret it's so small. When managing editor (and business partner and friend) John Cochlin and I sat down in 1993 to plan the book we ended up with more than 1,200 pages of material. That turned out to be financially and technically impossible. So, many things didn't get in. An example: Alan Twigg's article on local authors; it is one-quarter its submitted length and hundreds of deserving writers and books had to be dropped. Max Wyman's history of dance in this area was 4,000 truly excellent words—unfortunately we had room for just 1,400. Gary Bannerman wrote a whole book on cruise ships—how could he possibly squeeze their story onto one page?

And so it went. We haven't completely thrown in the sponge, however: Alan Twigg's original article—expanded even further—will make a nice book of its own and a similar destiny is in store for Michael Walsh's article on locally-made movies. As well, a CD-ROM version of this book is forthcoming and thanks to the awesome capacity of the CD we'll be able to drop in the long versions of many of these items and still have room for much else.

Speaking of Michael Walsh and Max Wyman—and Sandra McKenzie and Denny Boyd and G.P.V. and Helen B. Akrigg and Cynthia Crampton and Ray Chatelin and more than a dozen others—one of the most gratifying aspects of this new book is that many of its contributors were in the original book too.

Another original contributor was the award-winning designer of the 1976 book, Mike Yazzolino. In a wonderful coincidence Mike, who moved back to California many years ago, happened to be in Victoria on assignment in April, 1996. We got together for a terrific lunch and reminiscence and I was able to tell him the design torch had been passed along to Robin Ward whose cover for the new version is a kind of homage to Mike's original.

A pleasant circumstance unique to this book is that it was introduced with its own music! So far as we know this is the first time a book's publication has been celebrated with a specially commissioned orchestral work. We asked composer Michael Conway Baker for a concerto (featuring the oboe) and he gave us a splendid one titled *Vancouver Variations.* More detail about that on page 852.

We thank them in more detail elsewhere but our corporate and other sponsors made this book possible. Without them it would have cost you more than $125 . . . if you had bought it at all, which at that price is unlikely! This is another unique aspect of *The Greater Vancouver Book:* it is an encyclopedia made possible through corporate support.

About our publishing company name: a "linkman" was a fellow who, in England before the days of street lighting, carried a torch (or "link") to light people's way. If you emerged from the pub or the theatre or a party into the dark of night you'd give this guy a few pennies to light your way home. The books of the Linkman Press, of which this is the first, are designed to light your way—and with the Vancouver metropolitan area getting bigger and more crowded and more complex everyday, the more help its citizens can get the better. Think of the *Greater Vancouver Book* as what historians call a *vade mecum,* a book for ready reference (the Latin means literally "go with me"). This isn't a coffee table book—it's meant to be used.

An example: in an article written for us on some special trees in Greater Vancouver, Carol DeFina writes: "When passing the little triangular park created by the intersection of Kingsway, 15th Avenue and Fraser Street, slow down to enjoy a magnificent specimen of tree of heaven (*Ailanthus altissima* Swingle). This one has a particularly large spreading canopy. Its smooth, grey bark resembles that of a beech. It has large compound leaves and, in midsummer, small yellow-green flowers in clusters." Now, a more unlikely route than Kingsway along which to find a "tree of heaven" is hard to imagine. I've driven by that particular corner hundreds of times but after reading Carol's reference did slow down to enjoy looking at that tree. I'd never "seen" it before. And it is splendid.

I took the advice given in that article and went to Gerald Straley's book, *Trees in Vancouver,* to read more about the tree of heaven. There are several in the region but Straley, too, particularly cites the Kingsway specimen. The tree is originally from China. The one on Kingsway is a female. And in eastern North American cities the tree of heaven is considered a weed!

So yet another tiny morsel of interest (and in this case pleasure) has been added to my own store of knowledge about the city. We wish the same sort of result for you as you read—and reread—this book. Enjoy!

—*Chuck Davis*
April 1997 Vancouver, B.C. 49.16 N 123.07 W

The Marine Building has been a beloved symbol of Vancouver since 1930. Even today, with taller, later buildings looming above, its charm and beauty have not diminished. Extensive restoration work in recent years has assured—at a cost of more than $20 million—many more years of service for the building. McLeod Restorations Ltd., in a three-year project, performed a complete exterior facade restoration including repair and restoration of the terra cotta and repair, restoration and the pinning back of the brick facade. vs

Acknowledgements

Fɪʀsᴛ ᴀɴᴅ ᴇᴀsɪʟʏ ꜰᴏʀᴇᴍᴏsᴛ, thanks go to John Cochlin, business partner and friend, whose astonishing array of abilities made this book possible. My awe for John's energy, imagination and robust work ethic is genuine. As Linkman Press evolves into a major Canadian publisher, it will be John Cochlin who makes it happen. Kathy Cochlin kept the books, the faith and her sense of humor, and was the one in 1993 who said, "Why don't you do the *Vancouver Book* again?"

Thanks a million to all of our writers. You have collaborated on a book unique in Canada, one that will entertain, amuse and inform thousands of people for a lot of years. Special gratitude goes to the two dozen people who contributed both to the original book 21 years ago and to this one.

Thanks to the people in sponsors' offices who said "Yes," from the first, Ted Schellenberg at BC Gas, through to the 200th, Graeme Stamp at Marathon Realty (now Marathon Developments). Without sponsors this book would never have left the launch pad.

To Fin Anthony, who found many of those sponsors, and who came up with so many innovative sales and marketing ideas, thanks. Fin also named the book—adapted from the title of the 1976 version, which was suggested by its publisher, Scott McIntyre. Patricia Prince was a cheerily relentless seeker of sponsors. Thanks to Robin Ward whose design and picture editing brought it all together. To our editing crew led by Julian Beder and including Jack Vermee, Iain Hiscoe and Constance Brissenden, our deep appreciation. Lawrence Boxall, our production manager, saved our skins a hundred times with his knowledge of papers and inks and formatting and much else. He was joined in the latter, frantic stages of production by Shirley Vercruysse.

To Dr. Yosef Wosk, who loved this idea and helped us make it work, and who became a friend, our thanks. The same to Michael Conway Baker, whose "Vancouver Variations," inspired by the book, was a musically luscious tribute to the city . . . and thanks to Penny Baker for a dozen good reasons. (Writer Ben D'Andrea suggested the music's name. *Grazie,* Ben!) Thanks, Norman Young, for good advice, great reminiscences and your help with the April 30, 1996, Orpheum concert, and thanks, too, to Rae Ackerman and Pat Kostyk of Vancouver Civic Theatres. A special tip of the hat to Marty Zlotnik who made the concert possible, and to CBC Stereo producer Karen Wilson and her staff, emcee Jurgen Gothe, special guests Denny Boyd and Norm Grohmann (a friend for nearly 50 years) and Judy Taylor of the Vancouver Public Library Board. Thanks, Dave Roels, for the memorable photos of that memorable evening. And it was Gail McDermott who had the idea to launch the book with a piece of music.

And, speaking of the Vancouver Public Library, thanks, director Madge Aalto and all your staff. Thank you, city archivist Sue Baptie and your dedicated staff, and the Friends of the Vancouver City Archives. To Xanthe Willer, cartographer, and Stefan Schulhof and Vance Hanna, photographers, thank you! John Ward and Gordon Hill of Equitable Real Estate Investment Corp. were our friendly landlords in the handsome Rogers Building for three years. It's nice to be able to renew my gratitude to Ernie Fladell—to whom the first book was dedicated—and to Ernie's wife, Judy Fladell. They're two of my dearest friends. And *gracias* to Annie Fladell for getting us some key city neighborhood information. Gary Bannerman was hugely helpful on land and sea. Jean Hyatt believed when it mattered.

Many thanks to remarkable Rick Antonson, president and CEO of Tourism Vancouver, and his remarkable staff, especially Heather Chapman, Elvira Quarin (now retired), Tracey Corbett and Tammy Culpin. Thanks to Don Babick, publisher of *The Vancouver Sun* and *The Province,* Ian Haysom, former editor in chief of *The Vancouver Sun* and his successor, John Cruickshank; thanks, too, to Sue Dudley in John's office, to former Pacific Press promotion lady Lynne Munro and Pacific Press' Don MacLachlan and to Debbie Millward and her staff at Pacific Press Library; to Bruce Macdonald for valuable advice on neighborhood boundaries; Red Robinson, Rick Honey, Dave Abbott (and Ingrid Abbott, too), Jim McGraw, Jim Nielsen, Rafe Mair, Dal Richards, Art Jones, Hal Wake and the staff of CBC Radio's Early Edition, and Dave Berner for stimulating interviews and generous mentions; Joy Metcalfe, Mac Parry, Peter Clough, Archie Rollo and Hugh Pickett for super plugs; Judy Oberlander for your stewardship of SFU's Urban Conversations series; to mine hosts Michael Seelig, Nathan Divinsky and Peter Horwood at Bridges Restaurant; Imbi Harding at UBC's campus planning and development for that excellent data on the university's buildings; Ron Stanaitis, editor of the Vancouver Board of Trade's newsletter, *Sounding Board,* for your enthusiasm and your coverage (and thanks, too, to Ray Torresan and Lyndon Grove for the fine ad they designed for us).

For their encouragement, our gratitude to Vancouver city councillors Sam Sullivan, Nancy Chiavario, Gordon Price, Maggie Ip and Don Bellamy . . . and especially to Sam, for finding us a willing worker in Kirstin Brundin, whose three months with us were busy fun at a badly needed time. We were really lucky with office help: Lesley Lyon came in as a volunteer and we ended up hiring her not least for her cheerfulness. Victoria Rutigliano was another office whiz. And thanks to Mayor Philip Owen and Muriel Honey, then of the mayor's staff, for favors rendered. Richard Mulcaster and Barbara Oates at the Vancouver Foundation, thank you, thank you. It was Barbara who suggested we make the CD-ROM version of this book available to B.C.'s 2,160 schools and libraries, an idea we eagerly adopted.

Special thanks to Alan Stubbs at MacMillan Bloedel for advice on paper and to Alan Twigg and Katja Pantzar at *B.C. Book World* for that super profile. Huge thanks to Charlie Giordano, head of the journalism department at Kwantlen University College. Thanks to you, several of your students have their first bylines outside the college. Special thanks to student Hettie Phillips, for coordinating the others, and to Nicole Smith, who spent her practicum with us and suggested (then wrote) the article on the Peace Arch. Good luck in your careers to Shawn Logan, Jaime McCulloch, Amy Williams, Jake Adams, Tracey Holmes, Mike Ecker, John Lucas, Byron Churchill, Lee Toop, Sara Reeves, Lori Wallis, Mandy Boatwright, Carey Gillette, Ian Jacques, Kelly Bland, Angie Poss, Amy Johal (thanks for finding the poem *Vancouver,* Amy!), John Bennett and instructor Clive Court. GVRD chair (and Richmond mayor) Greg Halsey-Brandt was enthusiastic and supportive; Crawford Kilian gave us good CD-ROM advice; and Jeff Veniot and Bill Sampson of Capt. Billy's Magical Tours did work beyond the call of duty in nosing out the area's plaques and monuments.

Thanks to Eleanor Yuen for her links to the Chinese community, to Jean Hyatt for believing, and Kate Walker of Kate Walker & Co. for invaluable advice on the book trade. Paul Clough of Imperial Parking now has a permanent parking space in our hearts. And thanks to Robert Watt, chief herald of Canada, for yeoman work in assembling the coats of arms of Greater Vancouver for the book. Thanks to Mark Andrew of the Hyatt Regency Hotel and Ellie Teano, and to Mark's staff at Fish & Co. Restaurant. Peter Armstrong, of the *Rocky Mountaineer,* that trip to Banff was a welcome break. Thanks to Tom Tevlin of the Forest Alliance of British Columbia for favors rendered; to Linkman Press' legal eagle Rosalyn Manthorpe, ol' buddy Bruce Mason of SFU's Information Services and to Ken Mennell, who runs that service; to New Westminster historian Archie Miller; to Patrick Reid (then chair of the Port of Vancouver) for his marketing suggestions; to Rob Craig and the staff at Stratford Technologies for an Internet introduction; and to Enrico Diano for the same.

Vancouver AM Club speakers were often sources for information in the book. So thanks to Ray Greenwood, Conrad Gregoire, John Allen, Marguerite Ford, Geoffrey Dodds, Dave Duprey, Jim Jorgensen, Peter Ladner, Bea Leinbach, Kate Brown, Su-Marie Baird, Jan Culkins, Bunny Parton and all the rest of the mob. Thanks, also, to Barbara Rogers, crack researcher and genealogist; Sandy Gilmer at Business in Vancouver; Irene Sleeman, hall-of-fame researcher; UBC President Dr. David Strangway, as well as UBC's Dr. Charles Slonecker and Peter Ufford; longtime friend Phil Boname of Urbanics, who seems to know everybody and who got me through an important door; engineer extraordinaire Bogue Babicki; Environment Canada's Harm Dhillon, who sees the international potential of the book, and Jim Gilmore, now retired from the B.C. Medical Association; Doreen Braverman of the Flag Shop and husband Jack; Barbara Brink for good advice; Brian Butters, former editor in chief at the *Province*; Karl Crosby of Contacts Target Marketing; two of my favorite book people, Celia Duthie and Nick Hunt of Duthie Books, their 4th Avenue store manager Dave Kerfoot, my book guru for a couple of decades, and their Robson Street manager, James Bryner.

Thanks to Gil Evans, Eila Loughlin, Cynthia Crampton and Hazel Smith of Information Services Vancouver for encouragement, friendship and great assistance; to Chuck Gosbee, former head of communications at the Vancouver School Board; to Bud Elsie and his successor Deb Trouton, David Cadman, Martin Van Driel, Paisley Moscovich and Dan Donnelly at the GVRD. Thanks to Scott Macrae at Vancouver city hall for prompt and cordial response to requests for information and for getting me excited about the possibilities of the Internet. And thanks to Betty and Rolly Fox for their thoughtful cooperation in our preparation of the article on Terry Fox. The suggestion to have a history of local engineering in the book came from Janet Benjamin; thanks to Stanley Kwok for some excellent advice and leads; and thank you to Steven Crombie and his staff, especially Stephen Fergacs and Connie Bagshaw, at UBC's Information Office.

And for a myriad of other reasons our thanks go to: Dave Adair of Mount Pleasant Neighborhood House; Sadru Ahmed, president of Jentash Marketing; editor Marlyn Graziano and reporter Doug Alexander of *The Now;* Susan Anderson, Alice Niwinski, Shirley Chan and Carol Broomhall, all with the City of Vancouver; Dr. Alan Stewart Andree of the Vancouver Consular Corps; Al Arnason, a standout among our writers for his dedication; Alan Artibise, then with the International Centre for Sustainable Cities; Joan Athey of CBC Public Relations and George Laverock, CBC producer; Ace Cycle's Evelyn Atkinson, Engine 374 champion; Herb Auerbach, public art enthusiast;

continued on page 854

History

As we hurtle uncertainly toward the vast gates of a new millennium, it is time to admit that Vancouver has, like any grand lady, been shamelessly lying about its age. In the year of this book's birth, we admit to being 110 years old, having been officially spanked into squalling life by a bill of incorporation signed into law April 6, 1886.

After Lieutenant-Governor J.W. Cornett signed that pretentious scrap of legislative paper, the wisest thing he did was to get out of the way, to let the evolution of our city, which was 1,000 millennia old back then, continue.

What we have now, what we boast about, was shaped and defined a million years ago by the greatest architectural force in history, the Ice Age. Beginning a million years ago, and lasting until 10,000 years ago, this area was covered by an incomprehensibly big ice pack, ice a mile thick, ice that reached as high as the peaks of The Lions. Billions of tons of ice pressed down relentlessly on the malleable land, compressing it, grinding it, carving it into what would become its random beauty. It shaped our central peninsula. It ground the sharp peaks of the Coast Mountains, giving them their soft, gracious contours and, as an afterthought, left the slopes that would be the North Shore. The ice spat out hundreds of tiny bits that would become the Gulf Islands and left ruts that would become rivers.

When the ice moved on, it left the grid that would, in the majestic slowness of nature's time, become one of the great cities of the world.

In contrast to what nature did in its leisurely pace, the subsequent efforts of man were puny and filled with error. In fact, it took the corrective work of what is usually viewed as a terrible tragedy, the Great Fire of June 13, 1886, to wipe out the first mistake and provide a fresh start. The ugly shacktown that was Vancouver of 1886 had been built with too much urgency and too little vision. It deserved burning down and it was only from the three feet of smoking ashes that a better town emerged. And if you are looking for unsung heroes, sing of 14 good, practical men who declined to take a justified day off work.

The morning after the fire the mayor, 10 aldermen, the clerk, the chief constable and one concerned citizen gussied up in their finest suits, held a city council meeting in a one-pole tent thrown up in the smoky dawn by alderman L.A. Hamilton at the corner of Carrall and Water streets. A hand-printed sign on the tent said City Hall but the real message was, Still in Business. The first order of business, the approval of funds for a fire-wagon. The second, a stiffer set of building codes.

Twelve hours after the 20-minute fire that wiped out the old town, the sound of hammer and saw announced that the building of the new one was under way. And this time they would get it right.

By nightfall, wagons from New Westminster and Moodyville were rumbling into the desolate scene, bearing good neighbors, food, medical supplies and lumber for the new begining. In three days, a new clothing store and public hall had been built. Within three months, 400 new houses went up. By the end of 1886, the new town had 8,000 residents, 23 hotels, 51 shops, nine saloons and one church. Life had sprung from fire and ice.

—Denny Boyd

facing page: Granville Street at 37th Avenue, c. 1895. cva
above: Vancouver's temporary City Hall after the Great Fire of 1886. cva

Chronology of Greater Vancouver

The history and heritage of Oppenheimer is that of Western Canada, inseparable and interdependent. Established in 1858, the Company is the oldest operating food broker in Canada and the oldest company in Greater Vancouver.

Chronology of Greater Vancouver
Hilary Blair

1791 Jul 5 Spanish explorer Lt. Jose Maria Narvaez anchors west of Point Grey and explores the mouth of the Fraser River, Burrard Inlet and Indian Arm.

1792 Jun 13 Capt. George Vancouver explores and charts Burrard Inlet and adjacent waters. **June 21** Vancouver rendezvous with Spanish Capts. Galiano and Valdes near Point Grey.

1808 Jul 2 Simon Fraser reaches the mouth of the Fraser River and lands at the native village of Musqueam.

1824 Dec 16 A Hudson Bay Co. (HBC) expedition led by chief trader James McMillan arrives at the Fraser River near Derby (later the site of the first Fort Langley).

1827 Aug 1 Construction on the first Fort Langley is begun by the HBC.

1829 Salmon curing for commercial export begins at Fort Langley with the help of native women.

1831 Some 300 barrels of salted salmon—including 100 barrels for Hawaii—are shipped abroad from Fort Langley. Trade with Hawaii is later expanded to include Fraser River shingles and timber. A number of Hawaiians (called "kanakas") settle in the Fraser Valley and marry native women.

1832 Despite American competition 2,500 beaver skins are traded at Fort Langley. Twenty skins buy a gun, two buy a blanket.

1839 Fort Langley moves to its present location and begins provisioning the Pacific Coastal Russian colonies with foodstuffs including salmon, pork, beef and butter.

1840 Apr 11 The new Fort Langley burns down and a third is begun, will be completed in 1841. This is the present fort although it is now much reconstructed.

1841 Sep The first missionary to visit the Lower Mainland, Catholic priest Father Modeste Demers, journeys to Fort Langley. Several thousand native people from usually hostile groups mingle to hear him.

1847 Winter During the harsh winter of 1847-48 natives at Fort Langley save many HBC cattle by sheltering them in their own houses.

1848 Fort Langley's salmon production surpasses furs in value and the HBC post becomes the largest fish exporter on the Pacific coast.

facing page: Vancouver City Hall and totem pole, Stanley Park. vs, rw

1853 Alexander McLean and his family begin farming beside the Pitt River with 50 milk cows, the first to be taken up the Fraser.

1856 Apr 16 Gov. Douglas announces the discovery of gold in British Columbia, in 1857 will proclaim the Crown's control of mineral rights on the mainland and require miners to take out licences.

1858 Apr 25 The first boatload of gold seekers arrives from San Francisco. • **Jun 30** The last fur brigade arrives at Fort Langley. Thereafter brigades travel to Hope where steamers serving the gold rush carry the furs directly to Victoria. • **Nov 19** British Columbia (that is, the mainland) is proclaimed a British Crown colony in the Big House at Fort Langley. James Douglas, already governor of the Vancouver Island colony, is sworn in as governor. • **Also in 1858** Capt. William Irving arrives in Queensborough and forms a riverboat company to build sternwheelers for Fraser River traffic.

1859 Feb 14 Queensborough is proclaimed as the site of the new capital of British Columbia. • **Mar** Robert Burnaby, private secretary to Col. Moody of the Royal Engineers, explores the region north of Queensborough. Burnaby Lake is named after him. • **May 1** St. John the Divine Anglican, the first permanent church in the new colony, is consecrated at Derby. With no local sawmills the church is built of imported California redwood. • **Jun 13** Surgeon Charles Wood inspects a coal seam on the south shore of Burrard Inlet discovered by officers of the HMS *Plumper*, a surveying vessel. The stretch of water is named Coal Harbour. • **Jul 20** The name of British Columbia's capital is changed from Queensborough to New Westminster at Queen Victoria's request. Her personal involvement leads locals to dub the new capital the Royal City. • **Oct 11** A grant of £160 is given to build a school for the Royal Engineers' children at Sapperton, our first school. • **Also in 1859** The Royal Engineers begin to build a road north to Burrard Inlet to provide an ice-free harbor in case the Fraser freezes. North Rd. still exists. • Delta's first white settlers begin clearing land on Annacis Island and on the south shore of the Fraser. • The Coast Meridian Rd. (168th St.) is built to aid further surveys.

1860 Jul 17 New Westminster is incorporated making it the oldest incorporated municipality west of Ontario. • **Dec 11** Twelve children from the Musqueam reserve are baptized by Father Leon Fouquet O.M.I. • **Also in 1860** False Creek Trail (now Kingsway) opens between New Westminster and False Creek. • William Holmes is the first non-native resident of what will become Burnaby, settling on the Brunette River on North Rd.. • King Farris Lumber Co. opens a

mill and begins logging in the Green Timbers area of Surrey. As such companies clear land farmers move in. • The first church in White Rock is a Catholic church built by the Semiahmoo people on their reserve. • J.A. Homer establishes a sawmill near New Westminster. By the late 1860s the centre for sawmilling shifts to Burrard Inlet. • Capt. G.H. Richards names the eastern end of Burrard Inlet Port Moody after Col. R.C. Moody of the Royal Engineers.

1861 Jan The sternwheeler *Maria*, en route to Hope, sticks fast in river ice during a snow storm. The native wife of a crew member follows native trails to Fort Langley to summon help. It takes two more days to effect a rescue by which time 50 of the 200 passengers freeze to death. • **Jan 10** Col. Moody names Lulu Island for Lulu Sweet, an American actress who has appeared in theatrical performances for the Royal Engineers in New Westminster. • **Feb 13** The first issue of New Westminster's *British Columbian* newspaper appears. • **Winter** The North Arm Trail along the Fraser is built to provide access to New Westminster should the river freeze. It does, to a depth of over half-a-metre from Lulu Island to Hope. Ice hockey is played on it (for the first time in B.C.). • **Also in 1861** A great potlatch is held on MacMillan Island near Fort Langley. About 4,000 native people come from throughout the Fraser Valley. • The Hyack Volunteer Fire Brigade is organized in New Westminster. The first fire engine, a horse-drawn tank, arrives from San Francisco in 1863.

1862 Feb Construction begins on the first Royal Columbian Hospital in New Westminster. Patients will pay $5 a week. • **Sep** The Mc-Cleerys settle on the north bank of the Fraser and begin to farm on part of what is now the McCleery Golf Course. • **Nov 3** Chartres Brew, justice of the peace at New Westminster, records the preemption claim of the "three greehorns." • **Also in 1862** Construction begins on the New Westminster house of William Irving, riverboat captain. It is now a historic centre. • Hugh McRoberts constructs a home on Sea Island and becomes the first non-native settler in present-day Richmond. • A stone obelisk is erected to mark the spot on the 49th parallel at Point Roberts from which all survey work proceeds eastwards.

1863 Jun Pioneer Sawmills, the first industrial plant on Burrard Inlet, begins operations on the North Shore. Logs are hauled over skid roads by oxen. Water to power the mill is brought by flume from Lynn Creek. • **Aug 12** The first cargo of lumber from Pioneer Mills goes to New Westminster on the steamboat *Flying Dutchman*. • **Nov 11 or 14** Col. Moody leaves for England. Offered land grants, most of his Royal Engineers and their families stay on and settle throughout the Lower Mainland.

1864 Jan 21 The first session of the legislative council of the colony of British Columbia is held in New Westminster, Sir James Douglas presiding. (He will retire in April.) • **Apr 20** Gov. Douglas' successor, Frederick Seymour, arrives in New Westminster to take up residence. • **May** Gov. Seymour invites the native people along the Fraser to Victoria Day celebrations at New Westminster. Nearly 3,000 respond. • **Fall** Sam Brighouse buys 270 hectares on Lulu Island, runs a dairy farm and raises stock and thoroughbreds. • **Nov 4** The first foreign-bound lumber cargo from Burrard Inlet leaves for Australia on the *Ellen Lewis*. • **Also in 1864** Father Fouquet vaccinates about 4,000 natives against smallpox, almost the entire native population of the Fraser Valley. • W.P. Foster preempts land on the northern tip of Annacis Island where he later establishes a sugar beet farm. • Elsinger Brown preempts land on the Fraser's south bank opposite New Westminster. By 1910 Brownsville is an established community.

1865 Jan Sewell Moody buys the faltering Pioneer Mills on the North Shore, renames it Burrard Inlet Lumber Mills and builds the first substantial export business on the mainland for lumber and spars. • **Apr 18** The Collins Overland Telegraph Co. completes the mainland's first telegraph line following many of the early trails in the Lower Mainland en route from California to Alaska. The first message over the new line is of U.S. President Abraham Lincoln's assassination. • **May** Some 6,000 natives arrive in 1,000 canoes at New Westminster for Victoria Day celebrations at the invitation of Gov. Seymour. • **Jun 19** Rev. Ebenezer Robson, a Methodist minister, travels from New Westminster to hold the first Christian service for non-natives on Burrard Inlet; he preaches to 15 men at Moody's Mill. • **Aug 15** The New Westminster Library is established with books donated by the Royal Engineers. • **Also in 1865** The Sisters of St. Anne establish a day school for girls in New Westminster. • Douglas Rd. is completed running from New Westminster to the inlet just west of the present day Second Narrows Bridge. Oliver Hocking opens a hotel at the end of the road. The following year it has become known as the Brighton Hotel, a favorite summer vacation spot for New Westminsterites.

1866 Mar 1 Oliver Hocking is made deputy collector of customs at Burrard Inlet. Now captains of ships docking there no longer need to walk through the woods to New Westminster to obtain their papers. • **Aug 6** The Crown colonies of Vancouver Island and British Columbia are united and will be known as British Columbia.

The capital, until 1868, is New Westminster. • **Also in 1866** An unscheduled ferry service is established across Burrard Inlet by "Navvy Jack" Thomas. The vessel is a rowboat.

1867 Jan 24 The first session of British Columbia's new legislative council opens at Sapperton, New Westminster. • **May 20** A Crown grant of Lot 185 (now Vancouver's West End) is given to the "three greenhorns" for payment of £114, 11s. 8d. • **Jun 18** Stamp's Mill goes into production at what is now the foot of Dunlevy St. in Vancouver. It will be competition for Moody's Mill across the inlet. • **Jul 1** Confederation (British Columbia will not join until 1871). • **Jul 9** Postal service is established in William Ladner's house at Ladner's Landing, the only steamer stop between Victoria and New Westminster. Ladner would row out to passing steamers to pick up and dispatch the local mail. • **Jul** Lewis's weekly stage service, New Westminster to Brighton Hotel, begins. • **Sep** John "Gassy Jack" Deighton starts a saloon just west of Stamp's Mill. • **Also in 1867** The steamer *Sea Foam* is brought from Fraser River service to run as a ferry between Moody's Mill, Stamp's Mill and New Brighton (later called Hastings Townsite and the terminus of Douglas Rd. from New Westminster). • Jerry Rogers begins to log in today's Kitsilano area at "Jerry's Cove" which becomes known as Jericho. • Hugh Burr purchases land east of Moody's Mill on the North Shore. Making deliveries by boat he supplies the mill with milk from his dairy farm, the first on the inlet. • "Navvy Jack" Thomas begins a gravel operation at the mouth of the Capilano. A certain type of gravel is still known in Vancouver as "navvy jack" gravel.

1868 Jul 18 The first marriage among the non-native immigrant population of Burrard Inlet occurs between Ada Young and Peter Plant. It is performed at Moody's Mill by the Rev. Edward White. • **Aug 8** The purchase by William and Thomas Ladner of 164 hectares each on the banks of the Chilukthan Slough is recorded at New Westminster. • **Also in 1868** "Sew" Moody builds a second mill, this one steam-driven, and installs the latest machinery. Until 1875 Moody's Mill will take spars out of Lynn Valley for ships masts. Some are 21 metres long and 4 metres in diameter without a knot in them. • With the help of Father Durieu native chiefs of the Lower Fraser petition the B.C. government against the reduction of their reserves. Their most productive land has been taken from them and given to non-native settlers.

1869 Jan 15 The first Masonic Lodge on the inlet is established at Moody's Mill. The officers are all connected with the mill. Downstairs the Mechanics' Institute opens as a library and read-

ing room and occasional place of worship. • **May 31** Stamp's Mill is sold by its English founders to a San Francisco group, is renamed Hastings Mill in 1870. • **Jun 29** The colonial government grants licences to "Gassy Jack" and Ebenezer Brown to open saloons on Burrard Inlet. • **Nov** Mrs. Phelps, a singer and "poetess", performs at Moodyville. • **Also in 1869** Maximilien Michaud who has walked to the Pacific coast from Eastern Canada buys the Brighton Hotel at Hastings Townsite and renames it the Hastings Hotel.

1870 Jan 29 A boat race is held between crews from Burrard Inlet and New Westminster over a four-kilometre course between Moody's Mill and Hastings Mill. • **Mar 10** Granville, known colloquially as Gastown, comes officially into being with government approval of the townsite surveyed in February. • **May 4** New Westminster's first May Queen is crowned, seated on a fire engine and drawn by four horses to Sapperton cricket field. The festival has been held every year since. • **Also in 1870** A small union church is built in South Vancouver to serve worshippers of several denominations—Anglicans, Methodists and Presbyterians. Their ministers take turns in leading the worship. As each denomination can afford to, it builds its own church. • Alexander Ewen, a New Westminster fishmonger and entrepreneur, establishes the first commercial salmon cannery in British Columbia on the Fraser at Annieville, five kilometres below New Westminster.

1871 Jul 20 Burrard Inlet celebrates British Columbia's entry into Confederation with a day of races and sports. • **Also in 1871** Jonathan Miller is appointed constable for Granville. He lives in a cottage with a small jail in the backyard, next to "Gassy Jack's" saloon.

1872 Feb The first school in Vancouver opens on Hastings Mill grounds. In the following year it becomes the Granville School. • **Apr 24** "Gassy Jack" Deighton hoists the first Canadian flag to fly in Burrard Inlet over Deighton House in Gastown. • **Aug 15** New Westminster becomes a city. (It incorporated as a municipality in 1860.) • **Oct 2** The first bridge opens over False Creek. • **Also in 1872** The name Moodyville is adopted for the North Shore settlement growing up around Moody's Mill. • John Jessop, B.C.'s first superintendent of schools, suggests endowment lands be set aside for a university. • Construction begins on the Yale Wagon Rd. between New Westminster and Yale. It will be completed in 1874 and link the Lower Mainland to the Interior. • B.C.'s first recorded earthquake occurs near White Rock, estimated at about magnitude 7 on the Richter scale.

1873 Apr 26 The District of Langley is incorpo-

They traveled the goldfields continually, surveying their claims, and often collecting payment in gold dust. The Oppenheimers founded the first wholesale grocery in Vancouver making them the city's premier commercial establishment, importing food and provisions, tobacco, and sundries. By the 1950s the Company was jointly managed by David Oppenheimer (third generation), who was responsible for the brokerage of perishable produce, and by Ernest Krieger, who was responsible for foods.

rated with James Mackie as the first reeve. • **Dec 22** Moody's steam-powered mill burns to the ground, is quickly rebuilt with lumber and bricks purchased from Hastings Mill and will eventually be known as the most extensive mill north of Puget Sound. • **Also in 1873** John Sullivan Deas, a free black man from Carolina, opens a cannery on what will later be called Deas Island. Deas sells out in 1878 and leaves B.C. • The *Eleanora*, built from a scow and powered by an engine from a threshing machine, begins service as a ferry across Burrard Inlet. The engine is later fastened with chains attached to a buoy so it can be located if it falls through the hull in mid-trip. Locals nickname it the "Sudden Jerk." • "Navvy Jack" Thomas builds the first house in what will become West Vancouver on his waterfront property and marries the daughter of a Squamish chief. (The house was moved and still stands, much altered, at 1768 Argyle St.) • **1874** William Eaton is the first person to preempt land on Bowen Island. • Ladner Trunk Rd. (then called Kirkland Rd.) is built by John Kirkland with predominantly Chinese labor. It's a 21-kilometre "corduroy" (cedar log) road.

1875 Mar 17 Edwin and Ann Woodward arrive at the Point Atkinson light station as the first lightkeepers. Ann is the first white woman in West Vancouver and their third child, James Atkinson Woodward, is the first white child born there (April 25, 1876). • **Apr 22** Queen Victoria gives royal assent to an act passed in the B.C. legislative assembly denying the vote to Chinese and native people. • **Fall** Classes begin in Delta's first one-room schoolhouse, Trenant School, at Ladner's Landing. • **Nov 4** Sewell Moody embarks on the S.S. *Pacific* for a trip to San Francisco. He and everyone else on board is lost when the ship sinks in a storm. • **Also in 1875** Jerry Rogers locates a logging camp near present day Douglas Park. He logs selectively for 2,000 fir masts, each 45 metres long, for the navies of Russia, France and Holland.

1876 Jul A road is built between Granville and Hastings, now called Hastings St. • **Sep 14** Gov. Gen. Lord Dufferin visits the Lower Mainland and Cariboo gold fields, the first visit by a governor general. • **Also in 1876** The Rev. Charles Tate and the Rev. Thomas Derrick, Methodist missionaries, dedicate an Indian mission church at Granville, the village's first church.

1877 Fall The Burrard Inlet-Lillooet cattle trail, begun in 1873, is completed.

1878 May Manoah Steves and his family settle on the southwestern tip of Lulu Island, an area later called Steveston. • **Jul 20** Volume 1, No. 1, of the inlet's first newspaper, the *Moodyville Tickler*, appears. It will have a very short life. • **Also in 1878** Thomas Ladner builds the Delta

Cannery at Ladner's Landing and processes up to 15,000 48-pound cases a year. • Gold is discovered in the Seymour River and claims are staked in the mountains above and on Lynn Creek although little gold is found. • The first prisoners arrive at the new B.C. Penitentiary built on the Royal Engineers' Sapperton site.

1879 Oct 4 Port Moody is named the official terminus of the transcontinental railway. • **Nov 10** Incorporation of the Municipalities of Surrey and Delta and the Township of Richmond.

1881 Apr 15 The maiden voyage of the *Senator*, a steam tug built at Moodyville, ferrying passengers and mail (and occasionally cattle) across Burrard Inlet. • **May 15** St. James Anglican Church at Granville is consecrated. • **Also in 1881** The first municipal hall is built at Surrey Centre. It will be used until 1912 then used during Surrey's annual fall fair as the poultry building and an unofficial museum. The building is now part of the Surrey Museum. • Surveys begin in Port Moody for the CPR railway line.

1882 Feb 4 Electricity is installed at Moodyville. The mayor and council of Victoria make a special trip to see the electric lights, the first north of San Francisco. • **Also in 1882** Spratt's Oilery, a floating fish oil plant and cannery, is established in Coal Harbour. It uses dynamite to catch herring. • St. John the Divine Anglican Church is floated across the river to Maple Ridge from Derby. Built in 1859 it is still active, the oldest functioning church in B.C.

1883 Feb 2 The first sale of Port Moody lots is held at New Westminster. By March there will be 11 houses there. • **Mar 12** The *Duke of Abercorn* unloads its first shipment of rails destined for the CPR from Cardiff at Port Moody. In October a locomotive arrives, also by ship. • **Also in 1883** A stage line begins a regular service between New Westminster and Port Moody using the North Rd. Passengers then take a ferry into Port Moody. • John Irving of New Westminster buys out the HBC ships and forms the Canadian Pacific Navigation Co. In January 1901 it will be sold to the Canadian Pacific Steamship Co.

1884 Mar 17 The *K de K* steam ferry, built for $2,000, begins the first ferry service between New Westminster and Brownsville on the south bank of the Fraser. Tickets range from 10¢ for a child, sheep, calf or pig to $2.50 for a horse-drawn threshing machine. • **Mar** A post office opens at Granville. • **Jun 20** A Roman Catholic church is consecrated at Ustlawn village, the native mission village in North Vancouver, and named Sacred Heart. It becomes (and remains) a familiar landmark replacing a tiny chapel built in 1868 by those people of the Squamish nation

who had converted to Catholicism. A second spire is added in 1910 when renovations are made and the church is rededicated as St. Paul's. • **Aug 6** William Van Horne, general manager of the CPR, visits Granville. (On September 16 Van Horne will ask CPR directors to choose Granville as the line's western terminus and recommends it be renamed Vancouver.) • **Also in 1884** A massive cantilever bridge to carry the CPR across the Fraser at Lytton arrives in sections at Port Moody by ship from Britain. • A forest fire sweeps through the future West Vancouver from Hollyburn to Eagle Harbour. • Canoe Pass School opens in Delta with Frederick Howay (later to become well known as a judge, orator and historian) as the first teacher. • Huge, knot-free beams, 34 metres by 70 centimetres square are shipped to Beijing's Imperial Palace from Burrard Inlet sawmills. • An anti-potlatch law is passed although it fails to stop the practice central to northwest coast native culture. The law stays in place until 1951.

1885 Jul 20 An act to restrict and regulate Chinese immigration into Canada receives royal assent. Among other restrictions it imposes a head tax of $50 and is the first of many enactments to discriminate against Vancouver's large Chinese population. The result (intended): many men who pioneered in the gold fields of B.C. or worked to build the CPR cannot bring over their families from China to join them. • **Oct 6** A resolution of Richmond council provides that white labor only will be employed on municipal works contracts. Similar resolutions are passed in many Greater Vancouver municipalities in the late 19th century. • **Also in 1885** Lauchlan A. Hamilton, CPR surveyor, begins to lay out the Vancouver townsite. There are 400 residents when the CPR announces Vancouver will be the railway's terminus in preference to Port Moody. • Charles Henry Cates settles in Moodyville and begins hauling stone in a 72-metre steam scow called *Spratt's Ark*. He later acquires two tugs and begins ship-building and towboating. • The first church in Surrey, Christ Church Anglican near Cloverdale, is built in seven weeks. • The first public wharf is built near Steveston at London's Landing. The *Telephone* is the first regular steamboat service calling daily at points on both banks of the South Arm en route to New Westmins-ter.

1886 Jan 15 The first issue of Vancouver's first newspaper the *Vancouver Weekly Herald and North Pacific News*. • **Apr 6** The town of Granville is incorporated as the City of Vancouver. • **May 1** Jonathan Miller becomes the first postmaster of Vancouver. He is also returning officer in Vancouver's 1886 civic election. • **May 10** The first meeting of Vancouver's first city

The two divisions operated independently and separated in 1961, leaving Oppenheimer responsible for all non-perishable food products. On January 1st, 1981 Charlie Trimble, a ten year employee, bought the Company with a vision of a Western Canada organization. On January 1st, 1993 Larry Martin, Rick Stefani, and Jennifer Trimble bought the company.

council. The first piece of business: a petition to lease from the federal government a 400-hectare military reserve to be used by the city as a park. Today it's Stanley Park. • **Jun 13** A swift, furious fire destroys Vancouver in a time variously reported between twenty and forty-five minutes. Rebuilding begins almost immediately. • **Jul 4** The first scheduled CPR transcontinental passenger train reaches Port Moody after travelling for 5 days, 19 hours. It is one minute late. • **Jul 13** Vancouver city council passes by-law No. 258 to regulate the use of bicycles which must henceforth not exceed 8 mph. •

Jul 26 The first inward cargo to the port of Vancouver arrives: tea from China. • **Jul 30** Vancouver's first fire engine, the *M.A. MacLean,* a 2,250 kilogram steam pumper, arrives in town, but there are no horses to pull it. • **Sep 1** Vancouver's first bank, the Bank of British Columbia (no connection with today's), opens on the site of today's SkyTrain Waterfront Station. • **Sep 13** The St. Andrew's and Caledonian Society of Vancouver is formed.

1887 Feb A white mob attacks and wrecks a Chinese camp in False Creek. These and other disturbances lead to the suspension of the city charter and the dispatch of special constables from Victoria. • **Mar 16** The First Baptist Church of Vancouver opens on Cordova St. • **Apr** Vancouver's first band concert is held at the Methodist Church on Water St. opening with *The Maple Leaf Forever.* • **May 16** Official opening of the first Hotel Vancouver. • **May 23** The first CPR passenger train arrives in Vancouver from Montreal. The choice of Vancouver as the Pacific terminus for the CPR ensures the town's dominant role in southwestern B.C. New Westminster, Victoria and small centres of settlement are gradually eclipsed. A furious Port Moody, the original terminus, sees a slump in business and population. • **Jun 13-14** S.S. *Abyssinia,* chartered by the CPR, arrives from the Orient with a cargo of tea, silk and mail bound for London, England. This marks the beginning of the trans-Pacific/trans-Atlantic trade using the new railway. • **Jul 1** Vancouver is made a customs port of entry. • **Aug 8** The first electric lights are turned on in Vancouver. • **Dec 14** The Vancouver Reading Room opens (in April 1889, it will become a free library). • **Also in 1887** The Salvation Army begins in Vancouver with four ladies known as the "Hallelujah Lassies." • Hugh Boyd, a Richmond farmer and its first warden, is awarded a medal for the best wheat grown in the British Empire. • Surrey appoints E.T. Wade as its first police constable. A year later they buy him handcuffs and a gun. • Gihei Kuno, a Japanese fisherman, visits Steveston. He settles in the area and sends an invitation to other

young men from his village which had lost much of its fishing grounds to Osaka. Many of his countrymen follow him. • There is a typhoid outbreak in Delta due partly to river pollution caused by salmon canneries. There were about 16 canneries operating in the Lower Fraser.

1888 Feb 7 Local 226 (Vancouver) of the International Typographical Union receives its charter. • **Jul 5** St. Luke's Hospital is opened in Vancouver by Mayor David Oppenheimer and consecrated by the Ven. Archdeacon Woods. Here Sister Frances Redmond ran B.C.'s first nurses training school and Vancouver's first social services centre. • **Jul 26** The first steamer on the West Coast, the *Beaver,* runs aground on Prospect Point. • **Sep 27** Stanley Park is officially opened, Mayor David Oppenheimer presiding. • **Also in 1888** The Delta Agricultural Society is founded for the purpose of holding an annual agricultural fair. A harness-racing track is built on the fairgrounds. • Moodyville's steamer *Eliza* is making five round trips a day from Moodyville to Vancouver and one to Hastings. The fare is 25¢ each way. With increased access North Shore population begins to grow.

1889 Jan 4 The first Granville St. Bridge opens. • **Mar 5** The first banquet of the Vancouver Board of Trade is held in the Hotel Vancouver at a cost of $12.50 per plate including a quart bottle of Mumm's Extra Dry Champagne. • **Mar 26** The first water into Vancouver is brought from the Capilano River by pipeline under the First Narrows. • **Sep 28** The windjammer *Titania* departs Steveston with canned salmon for direct shipment to Britain, the first ship to do so. Earlier, local canneries have imported and exported via Victoria. • Vancouver's first city hospital opens, a wooden building at Beatty St. and Cambie, with 35 beds. • **Nov 16** The Union Steamship Co. is formed from the consolidation of the Moodyville Ferry Co. and Burrard Inlet Towing Co. • **Also in 1889** The Trades and Labour Council is formed for the purpose of establishing a nine-hour work day. • Bridges connect Lulu and Sea Islands with the mainland. These and other early bridges suffer repeated damage from floods and ice. • The first New Westminster Salmonbellies lacrosse team is formed. • The Marpole midden, largest known in North America to that date, is discovered.

1890 Jan 4 The new North Arm bridge collapses due to ice pressure in the the Fraser. • **Jan** Vancouver's first high school opens under principal Robert Law. • **Mar 22** Adoption of constitution and rules of B.C. Amateur Lacrosse Assn. • **Jun 28** Opening of Vancouver's electric streetcar system following a test run on June 26 from Granville St. Bridge to Union and Westminster (Main) Sts. • **Nov 12** The first ship-

ment of raw sugar, 225 tonnes, arrives on board the S.S. *Abyssinia* from the Philippines for the B.C. Sugar refinery. • **Also in 1890** The Burrard Inlet Bridge and Tunnel Co. is formed. Its charter gives it the right to construct a tunnel under the First Narrows and a bridge over the Second Narrows, both for foot, carriage, street railway and railway purposes. Because of a financial depression the charter fell into disuse.

1891 Jan 2 Electric street lights are switched on in New Westminster, from a power plant fuelled by sawdust. • **Jan 14** Lt. Gov. Hugh Nelson proclaims the former military reserve in Burnaby to be Central Park and sets it aside for recreation. (The park has been named after Central Park in New York where Mrs. Oppenheimer, wife of Vancouver's mayor, was born.) • **Feb 9** Grand opening of Vancouver Opera House on Granville St., built by the CPR. • **Mar 10** H.O. Bell-Irving forms the Anglo-British Columbia Packing Co. • **Apr 28** The CPR's *Empress of India* arrives in the city for the first time. • **Jun 12** The Ross McLaren Sawmills at Millside (later known as Fraser Mills), built in 1889, finally begins operations in earnest. • **Jul 1** The Douglas border crossing, named after Sir James Douglas, is established. • **Aug 22** Municipality of Coquitlam incorporated. • **Aug 29** First councillors for North Vancouver District sworn in. Moodyville decides not to be a part of the new municipality which stretches from Horseshoe Bay to Deep Cove. C.J.P. Phibbs is the first district reeve. • **Sep 21** Sarah Bernhardt stars in *Fedora* at the Vancouver Opera House. • E.H. Wall of New York demonstrates the Edison gramophone for the first time in Vancouver at Manor House. • **Sep 26** Squatter Sam Greer shoots and wounds Deputy Sheriff Armstrong who has been sent to evict him from his home near Kitsilano Beach. • At Brockton Point the first British Columbia Amateur Athletic Meet is held. • **Oct 1** The inaugural run from Vancouver to New Westminster of Canada's first interurban line, the Westminster and Vancouver Tramway Co. • **Nov 27** Great Northern Railroad from Seattle reaches the south shore of the Fraser at New Westminster. (The new interurban line then transported the freight from New Westminster to Vancouver). • **Also in 1891** The Great Northern Cannery is built near Sandy Cove in West Vancouver where the fisheries research station now stands. It operates until 1969. • There are now 13,000 residents in Vancouver. In six years it has grown from a population of 400. • Richmond's Minoru Chapel is built, the first church on Lulu Island. In 1967 it was relocated and restored in Minoru Park and later designated a heritage building. It is now an interdenominational chapel used mainly for weddings and funerals. • The first telephone line in Richmond is installed at a Steveston store. Messengers are sent from the store to fetch the person for whom the call is intended while the caller waits.

1892 Feb 15 Financing is obtained from J.C. Keith for a road to be built from Howe Sound to Indian Arm on the North Shore. Work begins but the depression halts it and the slash trail deteriorates. • **Mar 3** Charles Woodward opens his first store selling dry goods near Main and Hastings in Vancouver. • **Apr 30** The first election is held in the new municipality of South Vancouver. W.J. Brewer is elected first reeve. • **Sep 22** A provincial order-in-council is signed creating the Municipality of Burnaby. • **Oct 10** Women's Christian Temperance Union children's home opens at Dunsmuir and Homer in Vancouver. • **Nov 4** The first New Westminster Farmers' Market opens attended by reeves and pioneer settlers from throughout the Fraser Valley. • **Nov 15** First assizes held in Vancouver with Judge McCreight presiding. • **Dec 5** The Terminal City Club is formed in Vancouver. • **Also in 1892** James Machin is appointed the first librarian of the Vancouver City Library. • The B.C. Fisheries Commission orders the clean-up of industrial pollution, mainly fish offal, from the Fraser River canneries. Delta's dairying industry will benefit as a result.

1893 Jun 9 Canadian-Australasian service inaugurated with the steamer *Miowera*. • **Oct 6** The HBC opens a new store at Georgia and Granville. • **Also in 1893** The Fraser River Fishermen's Protective Assn. is established. In the late 19th century the Fraser was fished by sail and oar-powered gill-net boats owned mostly by canneries. • A wharf is built at the southern end of No. 5 Rd., Richmond and becomes known as Woodward's Landing. There is a twice-weekly boat to New Westminster. • Land held by Mr. Austin (now the Vancouver Golf Club on Austin Rd.) is assessed for tax purposes at $20 per acre.

1894 Jan 17 Maj. T.O. Townley administers oath to men at a theatre on Pender St. inaugurating No. 5 Co. of the B.C. Brigade of Garrison Artillery. • **Jan 22** First Burnaby school opens in the Edmonds neighborhood. • **May 16** St. Paul's Hospital is founded with 20 beds. • **May** The Fraser floods and many families in the delta area are moved. There is some loss of life and much damage to dykes, bridges and railway lines. Some canneries are swept away. The valley is paralyzed for a week. After the floods it is found that the deep channel of the Lower Fraser has shifted from the Delta to the Richmond side, and Canoe Pass (where there were canneries) begins to silt up. Thus Ladner loses prominence in the canning industry to Steveston but the delta soil is greatly

enriched and produces better vegetables. • **Aug** The cornerstone of Christ Church Cathedral in Vancouver is laid. • **Oct 12** A party of hikers climb a North Vancouver mountain and upon shooting a blue grouse there decide to call it Grouse Mountain. • **Also in 1894** Mrs. Thomson establishes the first kindergarten in Vancouver on Georgia St. • Alfred Wallace establishes a boat-building operation in his backyard. He later moves it to False Creek, then to North Vancouver.

1895 Jan 6 Gen. William Booth, founder of the Salvation Army, visits Vancouver. • **Aug 2** Delta Creamery's first shipment of butter reaches Vancouver Island. • **Fall** Richmond bores to find artesian water but by 300 metres none is found and the project is abandoned. Residents and canneries rely on Fraser River water taken at very low tide, collect rain water or import water from the mainland. • **Also in 1895** The Vancouver Lawn Tennis Club is formed. • The first letter-boxes are installed on Vancouver streets.

1896 Oct 26 Vancouver council sets 25 as maximum number of cows per owner within city limits. • **Nov 7** Burnaby hires its first law enforcer —at $2 a day—to police rowdyism, notify owners of swine running at large and enforce the wide tire by-law for wagons. He is dismissed for lack of funds in April 1897. • **Also in 1896** Fort Langley is closed by the HBC.

1897 Jan 3 The Vancouver city chain gang goes on strike protesting work on clearing lanes. • **Apr 15** The B.C. Electric Railway Co. forms and takes control of the interurban tram system which it operates until October 23, 1953. • **Aug 2** The "movies" come to Vancouver with an Ethiopticon Kinetoscope moving picture exhibition at Market Hall in Vancouver together with Edison's "wonder speaking phonograph." • **Oct 2** News of the death September 19 on the Skagway Trail of former Vancouver mayor Fred Cope reaches the city. • **Oct 21** Pauline Johnson reads her poetry at Homer St. Methodist Church. Sir Charles Tupper, until three months earlier Canada's prime minister, is in the audience. • **Also in 1897** Alexander McDonald Paterson comes to Delta to run the Paterson farm called Inverholme. He later serves as Delta's reeve for 28 years. The Inverholme schoolhouse (now preserved on Deas Island) was built in 1909 on the Paterson farm. • There are nearly 2,000 Japanese fishermen on the Lower Fraser, about one third of the total fishing population. The Steveston Fishermen's Assn. is organized to represent them. • This is a bonanza year for the fishing industry: as many as 14 ships line up at Steveston's wharves to load canned sockeye for European markets. The catch exceeds the canning industry's capacity and

surplus fish (for which the fishermen are not paid) are tossed into the Fraser to rot.

1898 Mar 1 Crofton House School (for girls) established. • **Mar 26** The first edition of the *Province* daily newspaper is published (the paper had started as a weekly in Victoria in 1896) and on March 28 the newspaper office installs Vancouver's first long-distance telephone line. • **Jun 24** Vancouver papers report lady cyclists following the new "bloomer" fashion are finding it hard to get admission to respectable places while wearing them. • **Jul 1** Single scull championship of the world is held in Vancouver harbour. Jake Gandaur beats Vancouverite R.V. Johnston. • **Aug 6** The first pay telephones in Vancouver are installed at English Bay. Cost: 5¢. • **Sep 10/11** The entire downtown section of New Westminster is burned in a great fire, including almost all the commercial section. Hundreds are left homeless. • **Oct 7** Canada's first motion picture theatre opens on Cordova St. • **Also in 1898** The Nine O'Clock Gun is placed at Brockton Point. (Another source says 1894.) • Vancouver city now has 25,000 residents.

1899 Jan 22 Bishop Durieu consecrates St. Paul's Boarding School on the Mission reserve in North Vancouver. Natives there help fund and build the school. It was demolished in 1959. • **Jul 6** Vancouver aldermen in carriages tour city sewer works under construction. • **Jul 16** The cornerstone of Holy Rosary Cathedral is laid by Archbishop Langevin of St. Boniface. • **Jul 29** The first council meeting is held in Burnaby's first municipal hall, a small wooden structure built at a cost of $906. It's at the corner of Vancouver Rd. (Kingsway) and Edmonds. • **Oct 24** Seventeen Vancouver volunteers are among 60 men from B.C. who leave on a CPR train to join the Canadian contingent going to the Boer War. Mayor Garden presents each man with $25 on behalf of the citizens. • **Also in 1899** W.H. Armstrong introduces Vancouver to its first horseless carriage, a steam-driven automobile. • Vancouver High School affiliates with McGill University and takes the name of Vancouver College. • St. John the Divine, the first church in Burnaby, is built in what is now Central Park. It burns down in 1904 and another is built on the same site in 1905. • Fraser River canneries pack more than 300,000 cases of salmon reflecting the Fraser's position as one of the world's most important salmon rivers. • Francis Caulfeild, recently arrived from England, settles at Skunk Cove, later renamed Caulfeild, where he plans a village in keeping with the beautiful surroundings and in which the whole waterfront is reserved as a public park. Caulfeild builds a water system served by Cypress Falls and by 1909 is offering lots for summer homes. • J.M. Fromme is the first homesteader in Lynn Valley. • The B.C. Fishermen's Union is established.

1900 May 10 First meeting of the recently incorporated Japanese Fishermen's Benevolent Society (Dantai) at the Phoenix Cannery in Steveston. • **May 12** The ferry *North Vancouver* begins operation as the first ferry with a regular service between North Vancouver and the south shore of Burrard Inlet. It was later renamed *North Vancouver No. 1*. After many adventures the boat becomes a private residence and is beached on a small island near Tofino. • **Jun 9** John Oliver begins his political career as MLA for Delta. • **Jul 1** There is a fishermen's strike on the Lower Fraser. Overfishing by Americans is partly to blame for depleted salmon stocks as fish traps are still legal in Washington State (until 1934). During the strike there is hostility between the white fishermen's union and the Japanese fishermen who live in cannery houses and depend on the canneries for food. Four hundred armed soldiers arrive to protect the Japanese. • **Oct 26** The collector of votes in Vancouver, Thomas Cunningham, refuses to put Japanese, including naturalized citizens, on the voters list. • **Nov 1** A ball is held at the Hotel Vancouver by Mrs. Shimizu in honor of Her Imperial Majesty, the Empress of Japan. • **Also in 1900** At the turn of the century fish canneries are largely responsible for the ethnic diversity in the delta area. Chinese men, often brought to Canada as indentured laborers by a "China boss," butcher and can the fish; native and Japanese women clean the fish and fill the cans; native, Japanese and European men fish. More than 200 cannery and fishery workers are needed to process 1200 cases a day (26,000 kilograms). • The Japanese Fishermen's Chapel Hospital is by 1900 financed by the Japanese Fishermen's Assn. The Japanese Hospital cares for both whites and Japanese and charges a membership fee of just $8 per family. • Cannery owners form the Fraser River Salmon Canners Assn. to protect their interests against dissatisfied fishermen. • The Dewdney Trunk Rd. is built on the north bank of the Fraser. • The North Pacific Lumber Co. on Burrard Inlet at Barnet is active. One of the largest mills in the British Empire, its log booms are towed down the coast from northern B.C. where the company has timber rights. • Burnaby's population is about 400—Vancouver's is more than 25,000.

1901 Jul 23 Mr. and Mrs. B.T. Rogers' housewarming party at their new mansion Gabriola on Davie St. • **Sep 30** Vancouver's first royal visit begins with arrival of the Duke and Duchess of Cornwall and York (later George V and Queen Mary). Events include opening of the new drill hall and a visit to Hastings Sawmill. • **Also in 1901** The census records 365 people living in

North Vancouver and the British Columbia Directory describes the area as a "suburban townsite." • A peak year for salmon. Forty-nine canneries operate on the Lower Fraser and nearly a million cases are packed. • Moodyville Mill closes after being the largest single source of export income for B.C. for 20 years. It is cheaper to move the mill to the source of logs than the other way around.

1902 Jan 20 The Royal Brewing Co. takes over a small brewery at Cedar Cottage and starts brewing heavy English ale. • **Mar 29** Grand Master F.M. Young of B.C. Grand Lodge of Masons lays the cornerstone of the Vancouver Free Library • **May 27** Vancouver's baseball team beats University of California team 4-2 at Powell St. grounds. • **May** B.C. Packers Assn. assumes control of, and consolidates 30 Fraser River canneries. Alexander Ewen becomes its first president. • **Jul 1** Operated by the CPR principally to serve the canneries, the first passenger train arrives in Steveston. Three years later the BCER takes over the line and converts it to electricity from steam. The line becomes known as the "Sockeye Limited" although it is not used to export the canned salmon as the canneries still prefer shipping by boat. The railway serves Steveston for 50 years. • **Sep 12** Woodward's department store opens at Hastings and Abbott Sts. • **Oct 31** The Pacific cable is completed from Vancouver to Brisbane, Australia with the first message sent by Sir Sandford Fleming. • **Also in 1902** Capitol Hill in Burnaby is logged by L.I. Dundas using oxen. • The *Britannia* is added to Capt. John Cates' Howe Sound ferry service, newly named the Terminal Steamship Co. Built in the shipyard of his brother George E. Cates in False Creek, the *Britannia* can carry several hundred passengers and has plush covered seats. • The District of North Vancouver opens its first school at 4th and Chesterfield and the influx of new residents means two teachers are needed. • Peter Larson builds the Hotel North Vancouver on West Esplanade. It serves as the community centre where public gatherings are held and from 1906 is the site of spectacular Dominion Day celebrations which draws crowds even from Vancouver. • Canada's first permanent cinema is believed to be the Edison Electric Theatre opened in Vancouver by John A. Schulberg.

1903 Jan 6 Vancouver Business College opens. • **Mar 10** The Fraser River Sawmills company is formed and operates out of the old Ross McLaren mill in Port Coquitlam. It grows to become the largest lumber shipper in the British Empire. • **Summer** A steel cable suspension bridge, the first commercial tourist attraction in North Vancouver, is built over the Capilano Canyon. A tea-house will be added in 1911. •

Fall The first North Vancouver District municipal hall is built at the corner of First St. and Lonsdale Ave. Since incorporation in 1891 the council has been meeting in various buildings in Vancouver except for one obligatory meeting a year in the district. • **Oct 1** The Carnegie Library opens at Hastings and Main. • **Dec 17** Transmission of electricity to Vancouver begins from BCER's hydro plant on Indian Arm. A three-kilomtre tunnel through Eagle Mountain from Lake Coquitlam to Buntzen Lake ensures a continuous supply of water. • **Also in 1903** Royal Vancouver Yacht Club formed. • The first taxi is driven in Vancouver by H. Hooper. • The recession ended, North Vancouver District council at last raises enough money to rebuild the Capilano and Seymour bridges, destroyed 10 years earlier. • Ladner's Landing changes its name to Ladner. Ladner was never incorporated as a town or village but has always been a part of Delta. It has never had a government of its own and has no official boundaries. • A new railway line connects Cloverdale and Port Guichon near Ladner making it possible to travel from Brownsville in North Surrey to Victoria by railway. An existing line takes passengers from Brownsville to Cloverdale and a rail-car ferry plies between Port Guichon and Sidney, Vancouver Island whence a line runs to Victoria. The trains are infrequent and often very late. • The population of Delta is 2,000; 350 of those are Chinese, mostly cannery workers, who live in a Chinatown along the dyke.

1904 Jan 20 The Canadian government disallows the B.C. Act Restricting Chinese Immigration. • **May 20** A small schoolhouse with 18 pupils is opened in Lynn Valley. • **Jun** Konstantin von Alvensleben, a Prussian financier nicknamed "Alvo", arrives in the city. He makes a living first by painting barns, repairing fish nets and shooting ducks and geese which he sells to the Vancouver Club at 35¢ each. He becomes a stock promoter, makes a fortune, and is a prominent social figure. • **Jul 23** The first bridge to span the Fraser is opened. It joins New Westminster to Brownsville (North Surrey). Hailed as the engineering feat of the century and built for $1 million by the provincial government it carries trains on the lower span and vehicles and pedestrians on the upper, just wide enough for two hay wagons to pass. • **Sep 10** Bill Miner masterminds Canada's first train robbery at Silverdale, west of Mission. • **Nov** St. Andrews Presbyterian Church is built on Lower Keith Rd. in North Vancouver and Rev. J.D. Gillam becomes the first minister of any denomination to settle on the North Shore. The church later relocates to 10th St. and St. Georges, becoming St. Andrews United in 1926 when the Methodist and Presbyterian congregations amalgamate. • **Also in 1904** Frank and Fred Begg start the first auto dealership in Vancouver and the first gasoline-powered car is bought by industrialist John Hendry. • Frank Kerr opens the first movie house in New Westminster. He frequently has to glue the film together when it breaks. • The Steveston Land and Oil Co. is formed to drill for oil on Lulu Island. By 1906 reserves sufficient to pay for the expensive screening out of the fine silt have not been found. But Steveston will be lighted by natural gas for many years. • Charles Cates builds a wharf in North Vancouver and handles cargo from California destined for the Klondike.

1905 Jan Vancouver High School (later King Edward) opens. • **Jul 10** The first buildings are erected for Colony Farm (later Essondale). The farm later supplies the nearby "hospital of the mind" (Riverview) and wins contests across Canada for its produce and livestock. It closes in 1983. • **Labour Day** The first auto club race around Stanley Park. Eleven cars start, five finish; all the finishers are Oldsmobiles. • **Also in 1905** The first bathhouse is built by the park board at English Bay at a cost of $6,000. • McDowell's Drug Store opens next to McMillan's Grocery at First St. and Lonsdale in North Vancouver. It will continue to be run by the same family until 1973. • A tract of land between White Rock and Crescent Beach (formerly Blackie's Spit) is named Ocean Park by Surrey pioneer H.T. Thrift. He buys the land on behalf of a wealthy Winnipeg philanthropist who wishes to develop it for the Methodist Episcopal church.

1906 Apr 16 The Police Mutual Benefit Assn. of Vancouver is organized. • **May 1** The telephone comes to North Vancouver making a difference to the ferry system: until the ferry terminal hooked up to the new line the wharfinger had used a system of calls with a horn to let consignees know when their goods arrive. Two toots for McMillan's, three for Larson's Hotel, a long and two shorts for the *Express* (newspaper) and two long toots for the butcher. • **Jul 3** Chief Joe Capilano of the Squamish Nation travels to London to present a petition to King Edward VII concerning aboriginal land rights. He goes with Cowichan and Cariboo chiefs and they are received hospitably by the King and Queen. Chief Capilano reports they are warned such matters might take as much as five years to settle. • **Jul 21** The *Chehalis* is sunk by the *Princess Victoria* near Brockton Point. Eight lives are lost. • **Aug 15** Electricity becomes commonly available to North Vancouver after a cable is laid across the Second Narrows. • **Aug 22** Vancouver's Canadian Club is formed. An inaugural luncheon is held September 25 at the Hotel Vancouver

with Gov. Gen. Earl Grey as guest of honor. • **Sep 3** Street cars begin operation in North Vancouver and will serve the area for 40 years. • **Also in 1906** David Spencer opens his first store. • Alfred Wallace opens a shipyard in North Vancouver. Under various names (Burrard Dry Dock, Versatile Pacific etc.) it becomes the North Shore's largest industry, building scores of ships during both world wars. • Richmond school districts merge and a Richmond school board is formed. • Another huge salmon run. About this time the Smith butchering machine is introduced. It takes the place of a 30-man gang of Chinese cannery workers, and will come to be nicknamed the "Iron Chink." Other technological changes include solderless cans and, instead of sail and oars, two-stroke gasoline engines for the fishing fleet. • B.C. Packers control 50 per cent of the Fraser canning industry.

1907 Feb 2 Surrey's John Oliver becomes leader of the opposition in the B.C. legislature after the first provincial election to be run on party lines. • **Apr 12** The Vancouver Stock Exchange is incorporated by an act of the provincial legislature. • **Apr** Chief Joe Capilano is threatened by authorities with a charge of "inciting the Indians to revolt" after he reports statements he says were made by King Edward VII at their meeting. • **May 13** The small, central core of North Vancouver's business and industry breaks away and forms its own municipality, the City of North Vancouver. • **Spring** John Lawson, known as the "Father of West Vancouver," settles his family in "Navvy Jack" Thomas's house, which becomes known as Hollyburn. Lawson is instrumental in getting West Vancouver to secede from North Vancouver and serves as councillor, reeve and postmaster while managing his real estate business. • **Jun 10** The newly constituted District of North Vancouver holds its first meeting in Lynn Valley Schoolhouse. A new municipal hall on Lynn Valley Rd. will be completed in 1911. • **Jun 13** The Presbyterian Theological College, Westminster Hall, is founded. • **Jun 24** Formation of the Jericho Country Club. • **Aug 8** Train robber Bill Miner escapes from the penetentiary in New Westminster. In 1911 he held up a train in Georgia, was caught, and died in jail there in 1913. • **Sep 7** Anti-oriental riots erupt in Vancouver's Chinatown and Japantown. • **c.1907** The first gas station in Canada opens at Cambie and Smithe Sts. • **Also in 1907** Japanese residents of Vancouver build an arch to honor the visit of His Imperial Highness Prince Fushimi. • The first community hall in Surrey, Tynehead Hall, is built.

1908 Mar 19 The first Vancouver Horse Show is held at the Drill Hall. • **Jun** The first hospital to serve the North Shore is opened, a tiny six-bed

facility at St. Andrews and 15th St. • **Sep 9** The British Columbia Refining Co. Ltd. in Port Moody is incorporated. It refines oil shipped from California. • **Nov 1** The federal ministry of defence renews the lease of Stanley Park to Vancouver for 99 years, renewable. • **Also in 1908** The University of British Columbia is founded. • Municipality of Point Grey is formed. • First tourist bus service in Stanley Park. • Shaughnessy Heights is subdivided by CPR. • The sale of opium is prohibited. • Grand Blvd. in North Vancouver is cleared and planted with shrubs by the North Vancouver Land and Improvement Co. It is conveyed to the City of North Vancouver for parkland around which a high income residential area is planned. • Members of the B.C. Mountaineering Club make the first known ascent of Mt. Seymour on the North Shore. • Richmond builds its first high school at Bridgeport. With four rooms it is considered huge. The first graduating class will be in 1911. • The Surrey police force is formed, responsible for welfare issues, collecting poll and business taxes and investigating local crime. • New Westminster Salmonbellies lacrosse team win their first national prize, the Minto Cup. • The largest agriculture fair ever held in the province is opened in New Westminster. By this time Fraser Valley fruit is being canned and shipped all over the world.

1909 Jan 7 The first export shipment of grain is made out of Vancouver. • **Mar 15** The first freight train travels the new Great Northern Railway track along the White Rock foreshore precipitating real estate speculation and a building boom. A customs post is opened at White Rock. • **Mar 29** Longshoremen strike for higher pay. They want 35¢ an hour for day work and 40¢ an hour for night work. • **Jun** The first moving picture theatre opens in North Vancouver at Larson's Pavilion. • **Aug 21** Minoru Race Track, named after King Edward's Epsom Derby winner, opens in Richmond with 7,000 people on hand. Minoru closes during World War I, re-opens in 1920 as Brighouse Park. Minoru was also the site of polo games and boxing matches. • **Sep 6** Gov. Gen. Earl Grey officially opens the new Granville St. Bridge. • **Sep 28** The first contingent of 110 French Canadians from Quebec's lumber industry arrives by train to work at Fraser Mills. Their residential settlement, built with company help, becomes known as Maillardville, named after community leader Father Maillard. • **Sep** The St. Andrews and Caledonian Society begins a group in North Vancouver for Scottish dancing. • **Oct** The first bank in Surrey, a branch of the Bank of Montreal, opens in Cloverdale. • **Nov 8** The West Vancouver Transportation Co. begins a ferry service across the inlet with the 35-passenger *West Vancouver*. The pier is at the foot of 17th St. on land owned by John Lawson (one of the company's founders), now called John Lawson Park. • **Also in 1909** English Bay pier is built. • Founding of the Chinese Benevolent Assn. • Vancouver's first skyscraper, the Dominion Trust Building at Hastings and Cambie, is completed. It is still there. Its architect slips on the stairs and falls to his death down the building's central core. • The Great Northern Railway line is completed through South Langley. • The Interurban railway is extended from Eburne in Richmond to New Westminster. • The Caulfeild subdivision on the North Shore is completed and lots go on sale for summer homes. • Wigwam Inn is built by German financier "Alvo" von Alvensleben. By 1913 it is popular enough to have daily boat service provided by the sternwheeler *Skeena*. • Richmond enters into an agreement to have its water supply piped from New Westminster's reservoir after many years of unsuccessful drilling to find its own water. • The North Pacific Lumber mill at Barnet is destroyed by fire. A modern plant is constructed to handle 150,000 board feet a day. Separate accommodation is built for Caucasian, Chinese, and Sikh workers, and Barnet, although a part of Burnaby, becomes a company townsite. Closed during the Depression it re-opens as Kapoor Sawmill and operates until 1964.

1910 Mar 12 An explosion at a dynamite plant on Bowen Island kills five workers and is felt in Nanaimo. • **Mar 25** The first airplane flight west of Winnipeg takes place at Minoru Park in Richmond with 3,500 spectators on hand. Flying a Curtiss pusher biplane is pilot Charles K. Hamilton. On March 26 Hamilton flies from Minoru to New Westminster and back. He later challenges a racehorse to a one-mile race which, much to Hamilton's embarrassment, the horse wins by ten seconds. • **Apr 20** A man in Surrey is fined $10 for speeding in his 1907 Marion car. He was travelling at 12 mph. • **May 14** Streetcar service is extended northeast along the new Lynn Valley Rd. in North Vancouver. The fare from the foot of Lonsdale for the five kilometre run is 5¢. • **Jun** The North Vancouver Yacht Club holds its first long distance race for the Cates Cup, won by W.S. Buttar's *Ysidro*. • **Jul** A man is fined $25 for driving an automobile over 10 mph in North Vancouver. • **Aug 16** The first Vancouver Exhibition (later the PNE) begins at Hastings Park, officially opened by Prime Minister Sir Wilfrid Laurier. It runs until August 21. • **Aug** Maj. Gen. Baden-Powell visits North Vancouver and inspects local Boy Scouts. • **Sep** North Vancouver General Hospital moves into new quarters at Twelfth St. east of Lonsdale. It has two storeys, six bedrooms and an operating

theatre. • **Oct 3** Formal opening of the Fraser Valley branch of the B.C. Electric Railway, New Westminster to Chilliwack. •
Oct All-night street lighting begins in North Vancouver. • **Nov 23** HMCS *Rainbow*, Canada's first cruiser on the Pacific Coast, makes her maiden voyage into Vancouver. • **Dec 12** Hastings Townsite taxpayers vote to join Vancouver. • **Also in 1910** From 1910 to 1918 the City of South Vancouver exists as a separate municipality. • Fraser Mills becomes the Canadian Western Lumber Co.. It grows to become the biggest lumber company in the British Empire. • North Vancouver High School opens. For many years it is the only high school on the North Shore; moves to its own building at 23rd and St. Georges in 1924. • There are six hotels in Steveston doing a thriving business during the fishing season from May to October. Their bars offer the first drink of the day free. There is even a bar situated beside the dyke for the convenience of fishermen. • Car dealer H. Hooper makes a record automobile trip from Chilliwack to New Westminster in two hours and ten minutes. • Henry and Grace Ceperley build Fairacres at Deer Lake. In 1922, after Grace's death and in accordance with her wishes, Henry sells the house and uses the money to build Ceperley Playground in Stanley Park.

1911 Feb 24 The first Vancouver Automobile, Motor Boat and Accessory Exhibition opens. •
Feb 27 *North Vancouver Ferry No. 3* is launched from Wallace Shipyards, the first self-propelled boat of any size to be built in North Vancouver. • **Feb** George Cunningham opens his first drug store at Denman and Nelson. • **Jun 24** The first nine holes of the Vancouver Golf Club in Coquitlam open for play. The club house is the old Austin farm house with a dormitory for golfers who miss the last tram back to Vancouver or New Westminster. • **Jun** The *Sea Foam* is added to the West Vancouver Transportation Co.'s ferry fleet with a capacity of 60 passengers. Sometimes it tows freight barges hauling West Vancouver residents' furniture and effects. •
Jul 11 Wallace Shipyards in North Vancouver is destroyed by fire but rebuilt almost immediately. • **Jul** North Vancouver Tennis Club holds its opening tournament on its courts at 23rd and Lonsdale, the site of the present recreation centre. • **Sep 15** The greatest bank vault robbery in North American history to that time occurs in New Westminster with the theft of more than a quarter of a million dollars. • **Oct 18** The first elementary school in West Vancouver opens for classes in, says one source, the Presbyterian tent. There are 14 pupils. • **Dec 12** A new municipal hall opens in Burnaby. • **Dec 20** Frank Patrick from Nelson opens the Denman Arena, Canada's

first artificial (and the world's largest) ice rink. • **Dec** The Lonsdale Theatre opens in North Vancouver. • **Also in 1911** The CPR builds Piers A and B. • The first suffrage convention is held in Vancouver at O'Brien Hall with Mayor Louis Taylor as chairman. • The first Vancouver Girl Guide Troop is started by Miss P. James. • Essondale's Colony Farm is considered the best in the West, yielding 637 tonnes of crops and 91,000 litres of milk. The farm provides therapy as well as food for its patients. • The Burnaby Lake Interurban line starts operation. • A Japanese school is established in Steveston by the Japanese Fishermen's Benevolent Society. It has instruction in Japanese and a Japanese curriculum. • Japanese settlers begin growing strawberries in Surrey. The nearby community hall comes to be called "Strawberry Hill." The berries are sent to canneries in New Westminster and Vancouver. • A resolution is passed by Surrey council to close the Serpentine and Nicomekl Rivers to navigation in order to construct dams for land reclamation. The era of steam boats and log booms on these rivers comes to an end. • A one-room school opens in White Rock. (Another source says 1910.) • The North Shore Iron Works is formed from a company merger. It is one of the largest industrial concerns on the North Shore, described as "Shipbuilders, Boilermakers, Iron and Brass Founders and General Engineers."

1912 Jan 28 Vancouver Ald. Pettipiece addresses a crowd at the Powell St. grounds on unemployment. The meeting is broken up by mounted police. • **Feb 27** The Pacific Great Eastern Railway(PGE) is incorporated to build and operate a railway from North Vancouver to Prince George. North Vancouver hopes thereby to become the major railway terminus on the West Coast and capture the import/export business from the prairies. The PGE is named after and partly funded by Britain's Great Eastern Railway. • **Mar15** Incorporation of the Municipality of West Vancouver. • **Apr 6** The first municipal election in West Vancouver. Charles Nelson is elected reeve. • **Apr 8** The West Vancouver ferry service is taken over by the municipality. It runs at a loss until 1924. By 1929 the ferries are one of West Vancouver's leading assets. • **Apr 21** A public memorial service is held at the Vancouver Opera House in aid of widows and orphans of the seamen of the *Titanic*, lost on April 14. • **Apr 24** Billy Stark is the pilot for the first passenger flight in B.C. Passenger James Hewitt, a *Province* reporter, is flown for 10 kilometres and eight minutes, soaring up to 180 metres. The plane travels at 65 kph and Hewitt rides on a board strapped to the lower wing. • **May 6** The King Edward VII Memorial Fountain in

Stanley Park is unveiled. Today the fountain is beside the Vancouver Art Gallery. • **May 24** The first parachute jump in Canada is made in Richmond's Minoru Park by Charles Saunders. • **May 30** Cedar Cottage property owners vote for annexation with Vancouver. • **May** Enrolment commences of the 6th Field Engineers of North Vancouver under the command of Maj. J. P. Fell. The unit becomes a training and recruitment depot in the two world wars and itself sees action on D-Day. • **Jul 16** "Splash Day" in Burnaby celebrates the completion of the municipal waterworks system. • **Jul 24** The BCER holds its first annual picnic at Hastings Park. • **Sep 2** A temporary jail with 25 inmates is opened at Oakalla Prison Farm at Deer Lake. The main structure will be completed in 1914. A number of executions are carried out there. • **Sep 14** Lynn Canyon Park is opened and the 6th Field Engineers of North Vancouver make their first appearance as an honor guard. • **Sep 18** The visit of the Duke and Duchess of Connaught who officially open the court house (now Vancouver Art Gallery) and the Connaught Bridge. The latter, now gone, is never called Connaught by locals who prefer "Cambie Street Bridge." Mayor Findlay wears the new gold civic chain of office for the first time at a reception given for the duke and duchess by Jonathan Rogers. • **Sep** West Vancouver opens its first municipal hall. • **Dec 7** The first exhibition of the North Vancouver Kennel Club. • **Dec 12** Richmond's town hall burns to the ground. A new town hall will be built in Brighouse in 1919. • **Also in 1912** The Board of Harbour Commissioners is formed to monitor traffic on the North Arm of the Fraser. • The Clachan (Gaelic for meeting place) Tea Room is built at Dundarave in West Vancouver and run by Jessie and Helen Stevenson. In 1914 a second floor allows for overnight guests. Later it becomes a restaurant and is now called the Beach House at Dundarave Pier. • The present Point Atkinson lighthouse is built. Lighthouse Park was originally set aside as a timber preserve to provide fuel for the lighthouse and its steam fog alarm. Thus the park has never been logged and retains many of its original native trees and plants. • A real estate boom boosts Burnaby's population in four years from 800 to 15,000. • The Burnaby branch of the Victorian Order of Nurses is formed to provide community nursing care at a time when there are few doctors and a rapidly expanding population. • Surrey opens a spacious new municipal hall. • Burnaby's new municipal hall is built. It is shared by the RCMP from 1935 to 1956, then by the library. It will be torn down in 1972. • Imperial Oil builds a storage and shipping plant on the north side of Capitol Hill. • Charlie

Chaplin and Stan Laurel perform in Vancouver with a music hall troupe from England, "Karno's Comedians."

1913 Jan The *North Vancouver Express* is published as the *North Shore Press*. • **Mar 7** Poet Pauline Johnson dies in Vancouver. Her ashes are scattered on Siwash Rock. • **Mar 8** Vancouver's Rotary Club is organized. • **Mar 11** Port Moody incorporates as a city and civic elections are held April 3. P.D. Roe is elected the first mayor by acclamation. • **Apr 18** The City of Port Coquitlam Inauguration Day celebrating its incorporation as a city, having seceded from the District of Coquitlam. Baseball's Athletic Park is dedicated. It will be renamed Capilano Stadium in 1942. The first admission prices are 25-50¢. • **May 16** An act of parliament creates the Vancouver Harbour Commission. • **May** The North Vancouver Rowing Club is launched. • **Jun 18** The Fraser Valley Milk Producers Assn. is formed. • **Jul 12** The Pacific Hwy. opens, runs from the Fraser River bridge to the U.S. border. A new customs office opens at the border in a tent, later in a permanent wooden building. • **Jul 31** Alys Bryant, a visiting American aviatrix, is the first woman in Canada to make a solo flight, at Minoru Park in Richmond. • **Jul** North Vancouver city hall at First and Lonsdale is remodelled as a post office. Council moves to temporary quarters in the Keith Block. • **Aug** A slide at Hell's Gate prevents a record sockeye run from reaching its spawning grounds. Massive amounts of rock are accidentally blasted into the Fraser River during construction of the Canadian Northern Railway. Leads to the decimation of the 1917 salmon run: Fraser canning industry badly affected; many canneries close. • **Sep** The recently paved Vancouver Rd. is renamed Kingsway and opened with great fanfare and a parade of automobiles. • **Nov 8** The doors of the "elegant and vast" new Birks store open at Georgia and Granville in Vancouver. • **Dec 4** An Ayrshire cow, Flossie, is given an award by the Canadian Ayrshire Breeders Assn. for producing 53,000 kilograms of milk and 200 kilograms of butterfat over 314 consecutive days. Flossie is owned by the Shannon brothers of Cloverdale. • **Also in 1913** The World Building (now known as the old Sun Tower) is completed. • Conservative Hall, later called Dundarave Hall, is built on Marine Dr. in West Vancouver and used for community social activities. In its 80-year lifespan it has also served as a cabaret, a church, a furniture store and restaurant. • The Campbell River Lumber Co. builds a mill in White Rock about a mile east of the railway station. In addition to being a holiday resort White Rock flourishes as a lumber town until 1929 when the mill closes because of a log shortage. • A subscription to one of Van-

couver's newspapers brings a bonus: a building lot in White Rock. • West Vancouver builds a ferry terminal at the foot of 14th St. In 1989 it becomes a designated heritage structure with exhibition space for community displays. • C.H. Cates Ltd. is incorporated. Cates Tugs is controlled by the Cates family until 1992 when it is bought by U.S. entrepreneur Dennis Washington, owner of the Montana-based Washington Corporation. • Hollyburn School opens, the first purpose-built school in West Vancouver. • Natives of Kitsilano Indian reserve sell their 29 hectares to the Government for $218,750. The land is valued at $2 million when divided into residential lots.

1914 Jan Imperial Oil Co. relocates its refinery to Ioco, an acroym for Imperial Oil Co.. After 1915 a company town is built here. • **Mar 2** St. David's Day banquet given by Welsh community at Pender Hall. • **Apr** The *Komgata Maru* incident in Vancouver. • **May 19** Myrtle and Alex Philip arrive at Alta Lake and begin building Rainbow Lodge, the first fishing/vacation lodge of any size in the Whistler area. The new PGE railway brings guests and supplies. • **Jun 11** The Pageant of Vancouver begins—a huge two-day musical-historical extravaganza at the Horse Show Building. • **Aug 21** The first troop train leaves Vancouver for the war in Europe. • **Aug** Food merchants in North Vancouver sell out as hoarding begins because of the war. • **Oct 20** The Vancouver School of Pharmacy is established. • **Oct 27** Port Coquitlam city hall is opened. With additions and renovations, the building is still in use. • **Nov 13** Col. Albert Whyte, agent for the developers of White Cliff City in West Vancouver, requests the area be renamed Whytecliff. • **Nov 20** A "French cabaret" is held at the Avenue Theatre in aid of the Women's Employment League. • **Fall** New Westminster raises the 47th, 121st and the 131st Battalions. • **Dec 1** A luncheon is given by owners and officers of Russian Volunteer Fleet S.S. *Novgorod* for "commercial interests" of the city. The menu includes *consomme Czar Nicholas avec petites pates*. • **Also in 1914** Naval gun emplacements are built in Stanley Park. • Dundarave Pier is built in West Vancouver but is too exposed for a ferry service. • Baron von Mackensen who had built a "castle" at Port Kells in Surrey is arrested on suspicion of being a German spy. Before the war he has hosted community Christmas parties but in 1914 has raised the German flag over his "castle." After the war he is deported. • The third (and present) CPR station opens. • Construction of a new White Rock pier begins. It is 190 metres long but a further 295 metres will be added in 1915. Later it is shut down because of deterioration and will not be reconstructed until 1977. • The Pacific Construction Co. takes over shipbuilding yards in Port Coquitlam. It builds several wooden ships during World War I and is one of the Lower Mainland's four largest shipyards. However, it is unable to adapt to building steel ships in the post-war years. • The Canadian Northern Railway builds a line across Lulu Island from Queensborough to Steveston. A few years later peat fires destroy much of the railway. • The Panama Canal opens shortening the distance by sea from Vancouver to London, England from 23,000 to 14,000 kilometres.

1915 Spring To avoid violating American neutrality a Seattle company named British Pacific Engineering builds submarines for Russia at top-secret plants in Burnaby and Vancouver. Once completed the hulls are dismantled and shipped to St. Petersburg for re-assembly. • **Jun** A sports ground is opened at Mahon Park in North Vancouver. • Wallace Shipyards and the North Shore Iron Works get contracts for high-explosive shells for the war. • **Jul 1** The first Georgia St. Viaduct is opened. • **Jul 30** White Rock's newly extended pier is officially opened. • **Aug 11** The North Shore's Marine Dr. is opened by Premier Richard McBride allowing access to previously secluded areas such as Caulfeild. • **Aug 26** North Vancouver city hall relocates in the old Central School whose staff and pupils have moved to the new Queen Mary's School. Council intends it as a temporary structure but meets there for many years. It is now Presentation House, home of North Vancouver's museum, a theatre and a photographic gallery. • **Aug 28** The first Canadian Northern (later Canadian National) train arrives in the city. • **Sep 30** UBC opens in Fairview. • **Also in 1915** Granville Island, once a sandbar in False Creek, is opened to industry. • Vancouver Millionaires win the Stanley Cup in the Denman Arena, led by the scoring of Cyclone Taylor. • Moodyville joins the City of North Vancouver. The following year the abandoned sawmill is destroyed by fire.

1916 Mar 8 Sock Day in Vancouver. The IODE has asked for socks for men at the front. • **Apr 26** A Canadian Club luncheon is held in the Hotel Vancouver to commemorate the April 22, 1915 Battle of Ypres. • **May 4** The first convocation for conferring of degrees is held by UBC at the Hotel Vancouver. • **Jun** The first issue of BCER's *Buzzer*. • **Labour Day** Two PGE trains collide in West Vancouver. One of them, the *No. 2*, built in 1910 in Philadelphia, is restored and is now at the West Coast Railway Heritage Park near Squamish. • **Sep** An application by Miss Rose Peers for membership in the North Vancouver Board of Trade creates controversy. However, she is finally accepted as the first female member. • **Also in 1916** Vancouver aldermen vote to open civic offices to women. •

The first grain elevator is built in Vancouver. • The people of the Squamish Nation who have lived on Howe Sound, the Squamish River and Burrard Inlet migrate to the inlet for jobs and consolidate into one band. The Halkomelem people of the Burrard reserve who have a different Coast Salish language do not join them although the two groups have many links. • West Vancouver begins its municipal bus service which becomes known as the "Blue Buses." • The first annual regatta is held at Dundarave Pier in West Vancouver.

1917 Feb 2 The *Mabel Brown* is launched at Wallace Shipyards in North Vancouver, the first of a series of wartime wooden ships reinforced with steel girders. • **May 17** The *War Dog* is launched by Wallace Shipyards, their first steel steamer and the first steel ocean-going freighter to be built on Burrard Inlet. • **Jun** A BCER strike. • **Aug 29** The Migratory Birds Convention Act is given royal assent. Before the act a good hunter could take up to 2,000 birds a year in the Fraser delta and earn a comfortable income selling waterfowl to the local market. • **Also in 1917** Robert Dollar (latterly of Everett, Wash.) builds a large lumber and shingle mill at Dollarton. (Another source gives 1918.) He builds houses for his workers and the $15 a month rent includes (at first) water, electricity and wood. • Prohibition begins. • Vancouver Chief of Police McLennan and a passing boy are killed in a raid on a cocaine den. • Helen Emma MacGill, Canada's first woman judge, is appointed to the bench of the juvenile court in Vancouver. • A massive snowslide blocks the PGE railway line and cuts off the Whistler Valley for six weeks.

1918 Feb The vessel *War Puget* is launched, the first for Lyall Shipyards of North Vancouver. • **Mar 6** "Honest John" Oliver, a farmer from Delta, is elected premier of B.C. and will die in office in 1927. (Oliver had become premier in 1917 when Harlan Brewster retired because of ill-health, was elected in his own right in 1918.) • **Apr** Daylight saving time goes into effect for the first time. (The first season ends October 26, 1918.) • **May 14** A fire in Steveston destroys three canneries, three hotels, numerous residences and much of the business district. • **May 18** The first grain shipment out of Vancouver via the Panama Canal. • **May** The provincial government takes over the PGE railway on the North Shore when it runs into financial trouble. The service has become unreliable and the railway has shown no sign of attempting to complete the Howe Sound portion of its track. • **Jun** An eight-day strike at North Shore shipyards followed by a streetcar strike and a postal workers strike in July. • **Sep 24** Port Coquitlam holds a sale of property for arrears of taxes but there are not

many buyers and the city retains ownership of much of the land, gradually sells it off in the 1920s. Other municipalities find themselves in similar situations. • **Sep 9** The Surrey Board of Trade is established. • **Oct 24** The *Princess Sophia* sinks in Lynn Canal with a loss of 343 lives. • **Nov 11** Greater Vancouver celebrates Armistice and the end of the Great War. • **Nov 15** Vancouver city health officers order continuation of a ban on church services, theatre openings and late shopping during a serious influenza epidemic. • **Dec 7** Earthquake tremors stop the clock on the Vancouver Block. • **Also in 1918** A four-cycle heavy duty marine engine is developed by Easthope Brothers of Vancouver for the Fraser River fishing industry. Costing about $150 the engines soon become standard.

1919 Jan 30 The Native Daughters of B.C. is formed. • **Mar 3** U.S. pilot Eddie Hubbard flies the first sack of Canadian airmail to Seattle. • **Jun 3** A general strike begins in Vancouver. At its height more than 10,000 workers are on strike including some civic employees. • **Jun** Strikes close shipyards and halt streetcars in North Vancouver• **Jul 19** A Great Peace Celebration and Parade are held including a Thanksgiving service in Stanley Park led by Premier Pattullo and Mayor Gale. • **Sep 22** Edward, Prince of Wales, visits Vancouver. There is a civic reception and a military ball in the arena in the evening with tickets at $5. He visits other areas of Greater Vancouver and opens the New Westminster Exhibition. • **Also in 1919** Japanese employment in the fishing industry in the Lower Fraser reaches its highest level with 3,267 licences, about half of those issued. In 1922 fishing licences to "other than white, British subjects and Indians" are cut by up to 40 per cent. The Japanese fishermen take their case to court and win but the government enacts legislation to allow the discrimination to continue. The case goes to the Privy Council in England in 1929. The fishermen win but only half remain by this time. • In 1919-20 a commercial fishing licence for the Fraser River costs $5. • Capt. Ernest Hoy makes the first airmail delivery across the Rockies—from Richmond to Golden, Calgary and Lethbridge. • Eggs at the Farmers' Market in New Westminster cost $1 a dozen. Times are good for Surrey farmers as prices forced up by the war have not yet fallen.

1920 Jan A traffic count on the Fraser River bridge reveals more than 13,000 trains—passenger, freight and mixed—crossed during the previous year (an average of more than 35 a day). By comparison, 65 automobiles per hour is the highest count for the upper span. • **Feb 4** Don and Phyllis Munday of North Vancouver are married. By 11:00 a.m. they are climbing one of the local mountains. This celebrated mountaineering couple climb many peaks together in the Coast Range and Rockies and put Mt. Waddington (highest peak entirely within B.C.) on the map. • **Feb** The firemen of North Vancouver strike for more pay. Fire Chief Sparks and his entire force are dismissed. • **Apr 9** A memorial to Japanese-Canadian soldiers who died in World War I is dedicated in Stanley Park. • **Aug 5** Fire destroys much of downtown Port Coquitlam. It is believed to have started above the firehall in the residence of the fire/police chief. • **Oct 17** The first transcontinental flight in Canada arrives in Richmond from Halifax after 10 days of travel. • **Dec** The Union Steamship Co. buys the boats and the Bowen Island resort of the Terminal Steam Navigation Co. (owned by Capt. John Cates) and continues the Howe Sound service. On summer weekends as many as 5,000 passengers board the boats. • **Also in 1920** Horseshoe Bay is a summer destination for many campers, picnickers and weekend fishermen who travel by train for a 50¢ fare on a regular 30-minute service. Summer cabins—often wood frames covered with canvas—are built during the summer and rented out. • An oil well is drilled in Surrey to a depth of 366 metres before it is abandoned. Several attempts in subsequent years to strike oil also meet with failure.

1921 Jan 1 The Polar Bear Club swim is started by Peter Pantages. (Another source says 1920.) • **Mar 25** The Capitol Theatre opens on Granville St. • **May 24** Grand opening of the largest dance pavilion in B.C. at the Union Steamship Co.'s Bowen Island resort. The pavilion accommodates 800 people and the moonlight dance cruises from Vancouver are notorious for their rowdyism. In the daytime, however, the resort is a popular destination for employee, church, municipal and other group day outings as well as vacationers for many years. • **Jul** 700 tourists camp in Central Park in Burnaby. These "autoists" come from as far away as Eastern Canada and the U.S. and the municipality considers putting in "shower baths" and laundry "wash houses." The camp closes about 1927. • **Sep 6** The Peace Arch is dedicated. • **Sep** Burrard Dry Dock (formerly Wallace Shipyards) launches the *Princess Louise* for the CPR, an all-B.C. product. A new joiner shop has to be built to cope with large amounts of work on this passenger vessel. • **Oct 28** The Coquitlam River causes extensive flooding in Port Coquitlam. Several businesses and St. Catherine's Church are swept downstream. The church and the barber shop come to rest on a sandbar. • **Nov 21** The Vancouver Electrical Show opens at the Drill Hall. • **Also in 1921** The old sternwheeler *Skeena* is still plying the Fraser with passengers and freight though more people travel by train. The vessel is pow-

ered now by gas rather than wood. • Richmond wins top prizes for its agricultural produce at the Vancouver and Victoria Exhibition. On these occasions both the quality and the diversity of produce—grain, forage crops, vegetables, berries, tree fruits and dairy—are evident. Richmond becomes the cranberry capital of North America. • The intersection of Edmonds and Kingsway is becoming the business and municipal centre of Burnaby.

1922 Jan 1 At 2:00 a.m. motor vehicles in British Columbia change from driving on the left to driving on the right hand side of the street. • **Feb 4** Joe Fortes, celebrated English Bay lifeguard, dies. His funeral at Holy Rosary Cathedral is perhaps the most heavily attended in Vancouver history with thousands outside the packed church. • **Mar 13** The *Vancouver Province* begins broadcasting a "radiophone" program of news and music from a transmitter in the Merchant's Exchange Building. • **Mar 22** The *Weekly Optimist* of Delta begins publishing. • **May 1** Richmond's first May Queen, Violet Thompson, is crowned at Brighouse (formerly Minoru) Park. • **Fall** Sumas Lake is pumped dry and the fertile land beneath reclaimed for farming. It will become the richest, most efficient dairy, berry and hop-growing region of the province. • **Oct 28** In the "Great Trek," more than a thousand UBC students parade through downtown streets then march to the uncompleted campus at Point Grey to dramatize the need for buildings. • **Also in 1922** A memorial to poet Pauline Johnson is unveiled in Stanley Park. • Electric power comes at last to West Vancouver after seven years of appeals. • Pacific Stages Transport begins a bus route from Vancouver to Port Moody and Port Coquitlam. Later the service is extended to Haney and eventually becomes Pacific Stage Lines (PSL).

1923 Feb 27 The *Surrey Gazette*, a weekly, begins publication. • **Feb** The three North Shore municipalities urge the Port of Vancouver to develop grain handling facilities on the North Shore. • **Jul 1** A new Chinese immigration act comes into effect virtually banning Chinese immigration to Canada. Only four kinds of Chinese immigrants are allowed: diplomats, children born in Canada, students and merchants. Only 44 Chinese enter Canada during the next 24 years. Chinese-Canadians long refer to July 1 as "Humiliation Day" and many refuse to join in Dominion Day celebrations. • **Jul** U.S. President Warren Harding visits Vancouver. Premier John Oliver and Mayor Tisdall host a lunch in his honor at the Hotel Vancouver. Harding dies August 2 in Washington, mere days after his visit and a shocked Vancouver commissions a monument in his honor. Created

by Charles Marega, it's in Stanley Park. • **Sep 3** A banquet is held to commemorate the completion of the cement surfacing of the Pacific Hwy. from the Fraser River bridge to the American border. There is an opening ceremony and dancing on the highway in the evening. • **Sep 4** West Vancouver High School opens in the Hollyburn Elementary School building. • **Oct 1** The first ship of the Canadian government mercantile marine leaves Vancouver with grain bound for Britain. • **Dec 5** Radio is used for the first time in a Vancouver mayoralty election campaign. Candidate Owen gives a ten minute speech over station CJCE. • **Also in 1923** The first buses are purchased and placed on the Grandview Hwy. route in Vancouver. • Burnaby gets its first fire truck, a Model T Ford converted in his garage by mechanic (and fire truck driver) Bill Banks. He later converts a 12-cylinder Packard limousine. • The federal government passes the Chinese Exclusion Act whereby Chinese immigration is prohibited. The act will not be repealed until 1947 and then only wives and children under 18 of Canadian citizens are admitted. • Coquitlam joins the Greater Vancouver Water Board. Annual rates are introduced: 75¢ for houses without bath, $1.15 for houses with. • Ocean Park gets its first post office. It is featured in Ripley's *Believe it or Not* as the smallest in the world. People write from distant places just to get the postmark. • PSL and the B.C. Rapid Transit Co., subsidiaries of BCER, begin regular passenger service in the Fraser Valley.

1924 Apr 27 The cenotaph at Vancouver's Victory Square is unveiled by Mayor Owen. • **Jun 25** A Tyee potlatch is held during a 10-day visit by the British fleet. • **Jun 21** The *Lady Alexandra,* flagship of Union Pacific's new excursion fleet, arrives from Scotland. With accommodation for 1,400 picnickers she is on the Howe Sound to Bowen Island run until 1953. Then, moored in Vancouver harbor and renamed the *Princess Louise II,* she serves as a restaurant until new American owners tow her to California. • **Also in 1924** Janet Smith, a Scottish domestic, is murdered in a Shaughnessy mansion touching off a fascinating case involving high society and charges of police and official negligence. • The rumrunner *Beryl* is hijacked in the Gulf of Georgia. • Lansdowne Track in Richmond opens, named for a former governor general. The peat bog on which the track is built acts like a sponge and horses are known to run slower at high tide. The grandstands hold 4,000 people with a further 1,000 seats in the club house. • A Union Steamship Co. store is built in Snug Cove on Bowen Island. It is now a heritage building and part of Crippen Regional Park. • Miss Gladys Davies becomes the first woman councillor in West Vancouver. A co-proprietor of the Blue Dragon Inn at Horseshoe Bay, she drives a Model-T Ford. • Radio CFXC, predecessor of CJOR, begins broadcasting out of a coat closet in New Westminster.

1925 Feb 7 Eleven petty officers and men, returning to the Imperial Japanese ship *Idzumo,* drown in fog-choked Burrard Inlet after their small ship's boat collides with a barge. A memorial service is held February 11 at Wesley Church. • **May 7** The *Beaver* memorial at Prospect Point is unveiled. • **Jun 10** An inaugural service is held at St. Andrews Presbyterian to celebrate the formation of the United Church. • **Aug 11** An 18,000 tonne floating dry dock at Burrard Dry Dock in North Vancouver is opened by J.H. King, federal minister of public works. • **Sep** The Vancouver Oil Refinery is established at First and Bewicke in North Vancouver. • **Nov 7** The first Second Narrows bridge opens over the protests of shipping experts. 3,000 cars cross on opening day. Its lift-span, allowing ships to pass, is built at the south end of the span and not in the centre where there is deeper water. This is to cut costs but proves to be a mistake. • **Also in 1925** The UBC campus opens at Point Grey. • Burnaby's first fire department, made up of volunteers, is formed in South Burnaby. The chief of police also acts as fire chief. • By special arrangement with the HBC, 4-point blankets are sold to tourists for $18 a pair at the gas station at Fry's Corner (junction of Fraser and Pacific Hwys. in Surrey). • Arthur Whalley opens a service station, general store and soft drink stand in Surrey. When PSL opens a bus stop there they call it Whalley's Corner. The name Whalley is officially adopted in 1948.

1926 Jan 27 The West Vancouver Town Planning Commission is created and bans the construction of temporary waterfront shacks and unsightly summer camps. Industry is also banned and West Vancouver becomes a residential suburb of Vancouver. • **Apr 9** The *West Vancouver News* begins publishing. • **May** Howard and Alma Fletcher open West Vancouver's first theatre, the Hollyburn, on Marine Dr. near 18th St. • **Sep 30** Vancouver Women's Building at Thurlow and Alberni dedicated. • **Nov 20** Vancouver's first big show of radio receiving sets opens in the winter garden at English Bay pier. • **Nov** A tea party opens the Grouse Mountain Chalet. Industrialist W.C. Shelly sees the potential of the mountain as a recreation area and has the first log chalet built—without a nail—by Scandinavian craftsmen. It is made with yellow cedar taken from the mountain slopes and is accessible by car via a toll road, an extension of Mountain Hwy., completed in 1924. The chalet burns down in 1962. • **Also in 1926** A park at

Whytecliff Point opens, called Rockcliffe at first. A tea-room with a dance floor is built about where the present lookout is. • Road access to Horseshoe Bay and Whytecliff opens. • Hollyburn Lodge on Hollyburn Mountain is built by three Scandinavians—Oscar Pearson, Ole Anderson and Andrew Israels—to promote the recreational potential of the mountain. They haul up lumber salvaged from the old Naismith Mill buildings a mile down the mountainside. • Whistler's first sawmill is built by the Barr brothers on Green Lake. At its peak it employs up to 50 men and gives the PGE more business than any other stop on the line.

1927 Feb The Kitsilano Branch Library, first branch library in B.C., is opened. • **Mar 7** Golden Ears Provincial Park is created. • **Apr 26** Arctic explorer Roald Amundsen visits Vancouver, tells of his dirigible flight over the North Pole. • **May 7** Official opening of the Hotel Georgia. • **May** A 9 pm curfew is introduced in North Vancouver city as vandalism gets out of hand. Hood Point Estates Ltd. is formed to develop an exclusive summer community on Bowen Island. **Jul 1** Gleneagles Golf Course, built on part of the old Larson estate in West Vancouver, opens for play. • **Jul 4** CPR Piers B and C officially open as part of Diamond Jubilee festivities. • **Nov 8** The inaugural performance in the new (present) Orpheum Theatre in Vancouver. • **Dec 14** The first high school building in West Vancouver opens. Inglewood High School has modern facilities such as two machine shops and an auditorium/gymnasium. • **Also in 1927** Two-car streetcars go into service in Vancouver. • The HBC gets Vancouver's first postage meter. • The North Burnaby Public Library opens with 125 books. • The family firm of H.Y. Louie Co. is incorporated with five employees. It becomes an important drugstore and wholesale grocery business, employing 2,000 people by 1986. • Burnaby's volunteer firemen are paid $3 per man for each fire attended and for time spent manning the firehall in 12-hour shifts. Their first fire truck is a converted 1927 Packard truck. • The Richmond Athletic Club is formed by Pete Rolston. The club includes football, tennis, badminton and softball teams. • Phil Jackman, last surviving member of the Royal Engineers, dies.

1928 Jan 1 St. Francis in the Wood Church in Caulfeild, West Vancouver, is consecrated. It was designed by Henry A. Stone, a local resident, businessman and early benefactor of the Vancouver Art Gallery. • **Mar** Fenwick Fatkin stages a display of daffodils in the community hall at Bradner in conjunction with local growers. • **Apr 23** The *Norwich City* strikes the Second Narrows Bridge. It is the 18th major bridge mishap in three years. Shipping interests take

the Burrard Inlet Tunnel and Bridge Co. to court maintaining the bridge is a hazard to navigation. The Privy Council finds against the bridge company but the bridge remains. • **May 7** The 28-metre *St. Roch* is launched by Burrard Dry Dock. Built for the RCMP of Douglas fir and Australian "iron bark" and reinforced to withstand ice pressure it is designed as an arctic supply and patrol vessel. • **Jun 16** Nat Bailey opens a drive-in hotdog barbecue stand on Granville at 67th Ave. In 1933 Bailey's White Spot No. 1 restaurant opens at the same location. • **Aug 25** A statue of poet Robert Burns is unveiled in Stanley Park. • **Sep 14** Thousands of citizens welcome home Percy Williams, gold medallist in track at the 1928 Olympics. • **Oct 20** Vancouver's first talking motion picture, *Mother Knows Best,* opens at the Capitol. • **Nov 29** The North Vancouver section of the PGE railway closes. It begins losing money soon after the road to Horseshoe Bay opens in 1926. • **Also in 1928** Crystal Pool is opened. • Fishermen stage a strike over salmon prices, idling more than 1,500 boats. • The last of the Fraser River riverboats stops running, superseded by vehicular traffic. • The last stand of timber is logged at Green Timbers in Surrey. • The first traffic lights in Vancouver go up at Carrall and Hastings. • After shipping knocks out the aerial telephone cable, a submarine cable is laid to link Vancouver with West Vancouver. • Japanese residents of Steveston build a Buddhist temple. Earlier plans had met with opposition from other residents. • The CPR ferry service from Steveston to Sidney, Vancouver Island begins. Fog, ice, and flood hamper the service. • **1929 Jan 2** The first meeting of new city council following amalgamation of Vancouver with South Vancouver and Point Grey. • **Jan** Ballantyne pier opens. • **Feb 7** Colored motion pictures (without artificial tinting) are shown for the first time in Vancouver at the Kodak store on Granville St. • **Jul** The provincial exhibition buildings in New Westminster burn down. • **Aug 7** The first annual B.C. High Schools Olympiad at Hastings Park opens. • **Sep1** Boeing opens an aircraft factory at Coal Harbour. • **Sep 10** The Rt. Hon. Winston Churchill opens the provincial exhibition in New Westminster which has improvised with circus tents due to the July fire. Churchill also visits the largest logging company in B.C., the A & L at Maple Ridge. • **Dec 18** Burnaby's first ornamental street lighting is turned on illuminating Hastings St. from Boundary to Gilmore. • **Also in 1929** Hastings Mill is demolished. • Gov. Gen. and Lady Willingdon visit Burnaby.

1930 • **May 3** Premier Simon Fraser Tolmie opens Capilano Bridge in West Vancouver and Marine Dr. is classified as a primary highway. •

May Dominion Bridge Co. opens its Burnaby plant which produces steel for Vancouver's Marine Building, the Alberta Wheat Pool and Second Narrows Bridge repairs. • **Jul 28** Hastings Mill store, Vancouver's oldest building and a survivor of the Great Fire of 1886, is towed to Pioneer Park. • **Sep 13** After an accident in April in which the *Losmar* tears away the south span of the Second Narrows Bridge the *Pacific Gatherer* finishes the job by taking out the fixed centre span. No attempt is made to reconstruct the bridge. In 1932 the Burrard Inlet Tunnel & Bridge Co. goes bankrupt and ownership of the bridge eventually passes to the Crown. The bridge is closed for four years. Despite all the accidents there have been no injuries. • **Oct** The Marine Building is completed. • **Nov 22** Spencer's holds a giant toy parade with Santa Claus and a retinue of story-book people. The previous day Vancouver's first "Lillybet" dolls, modelled after Princess Elizabeth, arrive in a toy shipment. • **Also in 1930** The Fraser Hwy. becomes part of the Trans-Canada Hwy. • Richmond becomes a member of the Greater Vancouver Water Board. The municipality has been plagued over the years with broken, corroded or frozen pipes as it endeavors to transport fresh water across bridges or over the bed of the Fraser to Sea and Lulu Islands. • All Japanese students in Steveston are allowed to attend general schools as well as being able to attend Japanese language schools after-hours. The Japanese community of Steveston had contributed funds for Lord Byng School in 1929. • A world record for egg-laying is set by No Drone, No. 5H, a hen from the Whiting farm in Surrey. She has laid 357 eggs in 365 days. No Drone is preserved for posterity and her stuffed form put on display at the World Poultry Congress in Rome, Italy in 1934. In 1954 she is presented by the Whiting family to the Langley Museum. • As a form of unemployment relief Surrey council gives one day's work a week to single men and two days work to married men as long as weather conditions permit and until the sum of $10,000 has been used up. • McKenzie Derrick, later McKenzie Barge and Marineways, opens for business on Dollarton Hwy. in North Vancouver. • Burnaby's first annual Better Baby Contest is held to promote child welfare. Judges are the medical health officer and the school board doctor. • Burnaby Town Planning Commission is established. • The Carnegie Corporation of New York donates funds for a bookmobile and library administration services in the Fraser Valley. After the funds are exhausted valley residents, despite the Depression, vote to pay a new tax to continue the service and the first regional library in North America is born—the Fraser Valley Union

Library—later the Fraser Valley Regional Library. • 200 skeletons are found in the ancient Marpole midden.

1931 Jan 10 Lt.-Gov. Bruce opens the old Hastings Mill store museum. • **Mar 19** The Franciscan Sisters of the Atonement begin a mission to Japanese residents of Steveston and run a nursery, a Sunday school and English classes. The mission goes with the Japanese from Steveston who are interned at Greenwood during World War II. • **Jul 1** The cornerstone is laid for St. Andrews Wesley Church in Vancouver. • **Jul 12** The Crescent Hotel in White Rock is selling fresh crab salad for 50¢. • **Jul 22** Opening of the Vancouver Airport and Seaplane Harbour. • **Aug 15** The official opening of the Kitsilano salt-water swimming pool. Kits Pool becomes the largest of its kind in North America. • **Oct 5** The Vancouver Art Gallery opens. • **Oct 10** West Vancouver agrees to sell 1,600 hectares to a syndicate called British Pacific Properties for $75,000, about $47 a hectare. • **Oct** A plebiscite approves sales of beer by the glass in North Vancouver City. Strikers at Fraser Mills protesting repeated wage roll-backs are dispersed by mounted police. • **Nov 5** The first annual Provincial Ploughing Match is held under the auspices of the Delta Farmers' Institute at A.D. Paterson's farm near Ladner. There is a horseshoe pitching contest (Ladner vs Langley Prairie) for the David Spencer Shield. The banquet and entertainment costs $1. • **Dec** Greater Vancouver residents form the Common Good Cooperative Society to engage in a "war against poverty." A self-help society, it operates a store, grows food on vacant land and helps many through the worst of the Depression. The credit union movement in B.C. is an offshoot of the society. • **Also in 1931** St. George's Private School for boys opens. • Vancouver Golf Club entrance fee is $100, dues are $6 a month. Caddies earn about 75¢ for four hours work. The dues are reduced during the Depression to $1 a month and 20¢ each time you play.

1932 Spring The Bradner Flower Show is attended by huge crowds with a grand concert and dance in the evening. • **Apr 13** Paderewski gives a recital in the Vancouver Arena. • **May 4** A large demonstration by the unemployed occurs at Vancouver city hall. • **Jul 1** Official opening of the Burrard St. Bridge. • **Aug 20** Vancouver beer parlors can open from 9.30 am to 11.30 pm. • **Oct** Commencement of building of the British Properties in West Vancouver which at the height of the Depression gives 150 local men steady employment. • **Dec 25** Greater Vancouverites listen to the first Christmas radio message from the sovereign as George V speaks from Sandringham. •

Dec The Municipality of Burnaby, battered by the Depression, goes into receivership—until 1942. The District of North Vancouver also goes into receivership, followed by the City of North Vancouver in January, 1933. • **Also in 1932** The *Richmond Review* newspaper begins publication. • Mrs. J.R. Paton wins first prize for her griddle scones at the Surrey Agricultural Fair. In 1936 she wins second prize for her Scotch Oat Cakes. • From 1932 to 1968 the M.V. *Scenic,* the only floating post office in the British Empire, is known as the Burrard Inlet T.P.O. (Travelling Post Office.) • Farmers from the drought-stricken prairies load their families into old vehicles and come west. Many squat on land in Surrey and some of those eventually buy land and become established.

1933 Jan 27 Blackburn's Farmer's Market, with more than 40 stalls, opens at Seymour and Robson in Vancouver. • **Jun 9** Vancouver city council allows men to go "topless" on city beaches. • **Jul 3** Burnaby police are called out when "over 100" unemployed interfere with a sheriff's order to evict a family from its house in the 4200-block Eton. • **Aug 10** Mrs. Victor Spencer introduces her eldest daughter Louise at a "fete" at Aberthau, their Point Grey residence. Guests mingle under a specially erected marquee. • **Aug 14** J.S. Woodsworth, leader of the CCF (Co-Operative Commonwealth Confederation, precursor of the NDP) speaks to crowds in the arena about the new party. • **Sep 21** The first Vancouver Folksong and Dance Festival opens. • **Dec 13** Voters approve a First Narrows Bridge scheme in a plebiscite. • **Also in 1933** Dan Sewell of Horseshoe Bay converts a Briggs and Stratton household appliance motor to his boats and begins one of the first power boat and sports fishing operations on the coast.

1934 Jan 5 The Vancouver Library Board accepts city council help to reopen the library's reading room, closed for most of 1933 for lack of funds. • **Jan 19** Prime Minister R.B. Bennett speaks to the board of trade's 47th anniversary dinner at the Hotel Vancouver. Among his words, "Canada is a world example of successful weathering of this depression." • **Jul 8** The first performance of the Vancouver Symphony Orchestra is held in Malkin Bowl. • **Jul 13** Coquitlam councillor Thomas Douglas is shot dead at his North Rd. gas station. Because he is a socialist some think the murder has political overtones. • **Sep** First radio broadcasts of local lacrosse games. • **Nov** A newly reconstructed Second Narrows Bridge opens. • **Also in 1934** Howard Rodgers operates a water taxi and rescue boat from Horseshoe Bay, running mercy missions for the Britannia Mines. • Convicts in the B.C. Penitentiary refuse to work unless given wages, then go on a rampage destroying prison property. It is the first disturbance of any note at the prison and presages many tumultuous years ahead. • Minnekhada Lodge in Coquitlam is built as a country retreat and hunting lodge by Eric W. Hamber, later lieutenant-governor of B.C. It is acquired in 1958 by Col. Clarence Wallace, a former lieutenant govenor. It is now managed by the GVRD.

1935 Jan 21 The Hastings Park Forum roof collapses. • **Jan** A severe snow and ice storm together with flooding hits the Fraser Valley, cutting communication and transportation links and causing much other damage. • **Feb 4** *West Vancouver No. 5* ferry sinks after colliding with the CPR *Princess Alice* off Prospect Point. A woman passenger loses her life. • **Mar 1** The B.C. Provincial Police take over from the Burnaby municipal police until August, 1950 when the RCMP take over. • **Mar** Standard Oil purchases 22 hectares of land at the north foot of Willingdon in Burnaby for a refinery. • **Apr 15** A Grand Rally of Scouts and Guides at Hastings Park welcomes Lord and Lady Baden-Powell. Horse chestnut trees on 17th St. are planted by West Vancouver Boy Scouts in honor of the Baden-Powell visit. • **Apr 23** Relief camp men parade and demonstrate in the HBC store. Mayor McGeer reads the riot act in Victory Square. • **Jun 3** One thousand unemployed men board freight cars in Vancouver to begin the "On to Ottawa" trek protesting conditions for the unemployed. • **Summer** The Kitsilano Showboat starts, a forum for amateur talent continuing to this day. • **Sep** A horseshoe pitch opens in Burnaby's Central Park. It has been built by residents on relief or working out delinquent taxes. • **Nov 11** The foundation stone of St. James Anglican Church in Gastown is laid.

1936 Jan 31 Mount Seymour Provincial Park, then only 274 hectares, is opened. During World War II conscientious objectors are put to work building a road up to the developing ski area. • **May 24** Civic Golden Jubilee celebrations marking the city's 50th birthday open in Vancouver. • **Jul 18** Opening of a Chinese Carnival Village at Pender and Carrall, Chinatown's part in jubilee celebrations. • **Aug 20** Unveiling of the Capt. Vancouver statue at Vancouver city hall and presentation by the lord mayor of London of the civic mace. Denman Arena in Vancouver burns down. • **Aug 29** Formal opening of the Seaforth Armouries in Vancouver by Gov. Gen. Lord Tweedsmuir. • **Dec 1** Civic wards are abolished in Vancouver. • **Also in 1936** Lost Lagoon fountain, a jubilee project, begins to play. • The Capilano Golf and Country Club opens in West Vancouver. • Farmers in the Fraser Valley send fruit, vegetables and clothing to prairie farmers

afflicted by drought.

1937 Mar 24 Helena Gutteridge of the CCF becomes the first woman ever elected to Vancouver city council. • **Mar 31** Construction begins on the Lions Gate Bridge, then the longest suspension bridge in the British Empire, to give better access to the British Properties. More than 300 men are employed in the construction. • **May 12** A Coronation Day (George VI and Queen Elizabeth) service is held at Brockton Point. • **Jun 16** The federal government announces a contract for eleven Blackburn "Shark" warplanes to be built by Boeing at Coal Harbour for the RCAF • **Jul 19** Sliced bread comes to Vancouver, 8¢ a loaf. • **Aug 4** The Oak movie theatre opens with great fanfare at Kingsway and Marlborough—tickets are 25¢ for adults and 10¢ for children. Hailed as a masterpiece of *art moderne* it operates until 1968. • **Sep** Mr. A.E. Crickmay shoots a 105-kilogram bear at 234 East 15th St. in North Vancouver. • **Nov 14** The Vancouver Golf Club clubhouse burns to the ground. • **Nov 15** Opening of the Pattullo Bridge at New Westminster. It charges tolls until 1952.

1938 Jun 19 On "Bloody Sunday" Vancouver police using clubs and tear gas evict unemployed men from the post office after a six-week occupation. Protesting B.C.'s stoppage of relief, groups of unemployed men also occupy the art gallery and the Hotel Georgia. • **Oct 1-9** Air Travel Week is proclaimed to mark the establishment of Vancouver to Winnipeg airmail service by Trans Canada Airlines (TCA). • **Oct 22** Mart Kenney and his Western Gentlemen instruct dancers at the Hotel Vancouver in a new dance craze, the Lambeth Walk. • **Nov 12** The Lions Gate Bridge is opened to traffic without ceremony. It is officially opened May 26, 1939 by King George VI and his wife, Queen Elizabeth. The bridge costs more than five million dollars and carries a 25¢ automobile toll. • **Also in 1938** Coquitlam opens its first high school and students no longer have to travel to New Westminster. • The Ford Motor Co. builds an assembly plant in Burnaby. During World War II it produces military vehicles. It is demolished in 1988 to make way for Station Square.

1939 Apr 1 The first transcontinental passenger air service (Vancouver to Montreal) is inaugurated by TCA with ceremonies at Sea Island, Richmond. • **May 25** The third (and present) Hotel Vancouver is opened. George VI and Queen Elizabeth stay overnight. On the 27th local Chinese hold a street dance to celebrate the royal visit. • **Sep 10** Nine days after World War II begins German-speaking citizens pledge their loyalty at a mass meeting in Moose Hall. • **Sep** Vancouver Harbour is put under the control

of the Royal Canadian Navy. Gun emplacements are built under the First Narrows Bridge and at Ferguson Point, Point Grey, Steveston and Point Atkinson. All shipping passing into Vancouver Harbour must stop and report to naval launches. • **Oct 11** Dr. L.S. Klinck, UBC president, opens the city's first public aquarium at the old English Bay Bathhouse. The star exhibit is Oscar the Octopus. Manager of the aquarium is an American named Ivar Haglund who later moves to Seattle and opens a restaurant called Ivar's Acres of Clams. • **Also in 1939** Steelhead Lodge in Coquitlam, a secluded getaway for Hollywood stars, is built by Canadian movie stunt man Karl Jacobs. Some of the present streets in the River Springs neighborhood are named for famous visitors: Gable, Novak and Flynn. • Steveston votes to stay "dry." • Soon after the start of World War II Richmond's Japanese residents, among others, raise money for the national defence fund. • B.C. Electric ends its daily milk run for Fraser Valley farmers.

1940 Feb Canada's first all-Chinese-language school is dedicated at 571 E. Georgia St. • **Apr 11** Greater Vancouver shipyards begin to build corvettes and minesweepers for action in the Atlantic. Some passenger ships are converted. • **May** The first May Day festival in Coquitlam. • **Jul 8** The first British war evacuee children arrive in Vancouver. • **Jul 22** Elementary Training School No. 8, part of the Commonwealth Air Training Plan, begins training its first batch of pilots. • **Aug 6** The first season of "Theatre Under the Stars" begins in Stanley Park's Malkin Bowl. The program features *The Geisha, As You Like It*, and *Midsummer Night's Dream*. Reserved seats are 50¢, unreserved 25¢. • **Oct 16** The official opening of King George VI Hwy. at Peace Arch Park. • **Nov 10** "Cap" Hobbis opens his first bicycle store in New Westminster. He later owns 12 Cap's Bicycle shops throughout the Lower Mainland and establishes a bicycle museum at the first store. • **Also in 1940** In the 1940s the Boeing Aircraft factory in Richmond employs about 5,000 people producing parts for the B-29 Superfortress. • In the 1940s peat moss is extracted from Delta's Burns Bog by the U.S. government for the manufacture of magnesium fire bombs. • During the war years many single women from the prairies come to work in Fraser River canneries. They live in company bunkhouses each of which has a matron in charge. Many of the women marry local fishermen and stay on. • Benedictine monks buy the old Ceperley Mansion at Burnaby's Deer Lake for use as a seminary. • Kingsway is widened to four lanes.

1941 Jan 31 The first orders are given to West Coast shipyards for 9,100 tonne cargo ships to convey war materiel and food to war-torn

Europe. Working against time the shipyards build new facilities and hire thousands of workers from all walks of life throughout the West. Most shipyards work 24 hours a day, seven days a week. The West Coast climate allows work to continue year-round and Lower Mainland shipyards build more than half the ships Canada supplies to the war effort. • **Feb 28** Vancouver's new YMCA building opens • **Apr 23** Burrard Dry Dock lays the keel of the SS *Fort St. James,* the first of its North Sands 9,100 tonne cargo vessels. It takes nine months to complete. The last North Sands ship, begun in March of 1943, takes three-and-a-half months. Despite thousands of workers new to the shipbuilding industry mass production techniques quickly enable the formation of an efficient workforce. • **May 18** One thousand Air Raid Precaution (ARP) volunteers put on a public demonstration at Mahon Park in North Vancouver. Chief Warden G. Robert Bates makes the mock air raid as realistic as possible—complete with low-flying bomber and incendiary devices. • **Jul 19** The first twilight horse races at Hastings Park. • **Jul 29** A mass victory meeting is held at Brockton Point. There is community singing led by Sir Ernest MacMillan with the Kitsilano Boys Band and Spencer's Remnants Pipe Band. • **Aug 16** A Narvaez Pageant is held in West Vancouver to commemorate the 150th anniversary of the sighting of this shore by the Spanish explorer. • **Aug 26** The first *Sun* Free Salmon Derby takes place with its headquarters at Dan Sewell's marina at Horseshoe Bay. • **Aug** The first annual civic picnic in North Vancouver. • **Nov 9** The Westminster Regiment sails for overseas service. • **Dec 10** Iwatichi Sugiyama, a naturalized British subject, is the only Japanese to vote in Vancouver civic elections. • **Dec 14** Gas masks go on sale to the general public. School children do their part by learning to study with them on and taking part in drills. • **Dec 18-20** Gracie Fields performs at Exhibition Gardens. • **Also in 1941** The liner *Awatea* sails from Vancouver with a Canadian contingent for Hong Kong. • Semiahmoo Park is established in White Rock with land leased from the Semiahmoo Indian band. The band later protests unfair terms in its agreement with the municipality. • Surrey municipality owns so much land from unpaid taxes during the Depression it gives away lots to generate tax revenue from them. • Einar Neilson founds Lieban, a retreat for artists and intellectuals on Bowen Island. • In Greater Vancouver four out of five homes do not have all of the following: a car, a telephone, a radio and a vacuum cleaner.

1942 Jan 14 Ottawa announces all Japanese are to be removed from the West Coast to government camps. • **Jan 22** The federal government announces plans for an RCAF storage depot on the Kitsilano Indian reserve west of Burrard St. Bridge. • **Apr 1** Japanese-Canadians begin to be moved from the West Coast to internment camps in the interior and points east. The government "takes into custody" 1,337 of their fishboats as well as houses and other property. The owners receive little or no compensation. • **Aug 24** The Wartime Prices and Trade Board begins the issue of ration books covering purchase of sugar, coffee and tea. • **Sep 30** The first group of women workers is hired by Burrard Dry Dock in North Vancouver. At the peak of war-time activity 1,000 of the yard's 13,000 workforce are women. • **Nov 6** A bomb partially destroys one of the courthouse lions. The culprit is never found. • **Dec 21** Butter is rationed. • **Also in 1942** To fill the gap left by the departure of the Japanese-Canadian workforce many people come from the prairies which is slower to recover from the Depression. The fishing industry is declared an essential service during the war and workers are exempt from conscription. Convicts are released to work on the fishboats. • The Dollar Mill at Dollarton closes. • Much of Surrey's strawberry crop is lost with the departure of the Japanese farmers to internment camps. • Burnaby comes out of receivership and once again can elect a reeve and council.

1943 Mar 2 RCAF war ace Buzz Beurling, "King of the Air over Malta," visits the city. • **Mar 18** The *Fort Columbia,* the first of the Victory ships, is begun by Burrard Dry Dock. With oil-fired boilers they are cheaper to run than coal-fired North Sands ships although some Victory ships are built to run on either. Thirty-four Victory ships are built in 26 months by Burrard Dry Dock. • **May 15** The 33rd Annual Exhibition of the B.C. Society of Fine Arts opens at the Vancouver Art Gallery. Six Emily Carr paintings at $50 each are among those exhibited. • **Jun** Burnaby endorses a "closed shop" for civic employees—the third municipality in Canada to do so and the first in B.C. • **Sep 13** The West Vancouver Park Board is established. • **Also in 1943** Kitsilano Beach is used for rehearsing commando beach assaults.

1944 Jan 6 A strike at B.C. Electric lasts to Jan 26. Streetcars stop. • **Mar 6** New and tighter rationing of gasoline begins as AA ration books are issued. • **May 2** Local Doukhobors hold a prayer vigil on the courthouse steps for 13 of their brethren in Oakalla. • **Jul** International Artists' Film Corp. signs a 20-year lease with Burnaby for a 10-hectare production location on Canada Way near Willingdon. • **Aug 14** Vancouver city council adopts Odessa, USSR as a sister city. • **Aug 15** Radio station CKNW begins broadcasting 24 hours a day. It also begins news on the hour, another Canadian radio first. Official sign-on is Sep. 1. • **Sep** A forest fire sweeps down Black Mountain in West Vancouver covering 11 square kilometres and is finally stopped just 275 metres above Eagle Harbour. • **Oct16** The RCMP ship *St. Roch* arrives in Vancouver from Halifax via the Northwest Passage, the first ship to have sailed the passage in both directions. The outward journey has taken 28 months but the return only 86 days, which also makes the *St. Roch* the first to sail the passage in a single season. • **Oct 21** (Trafalgar Day) HMCS *Discovery* is officially opened on Deadman's Island. • **Also in 1944** Surrey school teachers ask for a pay raise. Students with summer jobs in war industries are making more than their teachers. • Les Gilmore of Richmond harvests 2,250 bushels of potatoes per hectare, the highest yield per hectare in Canada.

1945 Mar 6 The freighter *Greenhill Park* explodes in Vancouver Harbour killing eight men and breaking hundreds of downtown windows. • **Apr 30/May 1** Fire destroys Capilano Stadium in Vancouver. • **May 6** We celebrate the end of the European war. • **May 16** Prime Minister Mackenzie King opens the federal election campaign with a speech from Vancouver broadcast over Radio CBR. • **May 22** The first veteran moves into the newly completed veterans' homes. • **Aug 14** World War II ends with VJ Day. • **Dec** Burrard Dry Dock lets go the last of its female workers. The union cries discrimination but the war has ended and women are expected to make way for the returning men. At its peak Burrard Dry Dock is building eight 9,100 tonne cargo ships at the same time. • **Also in 1945** The United Fishermen and Allied Workers Union is organized. • The first double chairlift in North America is constructed on Grouse Mountain running from the top of Skyline Rd. to a village of more than 100 cabins used by local residents as weekend retreats. Later the Cut chairlift is built connecting the village to the top of the mountain. • The Vancouver Park Board is criticized about the "segregation of coloured races at the Crystal Pool" and the board agrees to desegregate the pool. • Lansdowne Race Track is sold to the B.C. Turf and Country Club. It closes from 1949-1955, permanently closes in 1960. The stables and track continue to be used as training facilities. • The first Cloverdale Rodeo.

1946 Apr 30 As its part in the civic Diamond Jubilee (60th anniversary) celebrations the Vancouver Park Board hosts a dinner at the pavilion for nine "Jubilarians," all born in Vancouver in 1886 after incorporation. • **May** The first sail-past of the West Vancouver Yacht Club (at Sandy Cove). • **Jun 23** An earthquake felt mostly on

Vancouver Island stops the clock on the Vancouver Block, a repeat of 1918. • **Jul 1** This Dominion Day is the first national holiday since the end of the war and Vancouver celebrates with a spectacular parade in the world's largest outdoor theatre built at Brockton Point. 250,000 people attend. Steveston holds its first Salmon Festival and Sophie Kuchma, the first Salmon Queen, is crowned. • **Aug 30** The Cascades Drive-In Theatre opens in Burnaby. Cars arrive two hours before the showing of *Home in Indiana* is to begin. Closed in 1980, the site is now occupied by the Cascade Village condominium development. • **Sep 19** C.D. Howe officiates at a ceremony in honor of the arrival of the first plane from Australia and establishment of an air route around the world through the Commonwealth. • **Dec 10** West Vancouver votes to discontinue the ferry service to Vancouver. • **Also in 1946** Veterans occupy the old (second) Hotel Vancouver for a hostel because of an extreme housing shortage. • A year of shortages everywhere. In Cloverdale and White Rock alone 264 people are waiting for telephones. • Troll's Restaurant opens in Horseshoe Bay. (A new building will be erected in 1963.) • In 1946 visitors to Bowen Island reach an all-time high of 101,000.

1947 Jan 31 Mayor McGeer officiates at sod-turning ceremonies for the new Schara Tzedeck Synagogue on Oak St., a memorial to Jewish war veterans. • **Feb 10** The last ferry (*No. 6*) runs to West Vancouver then returns to the downtown terminal. • **Feb** Publication of *Under the Volcano* by Malcolm Lowry. Written in obscurity in a squatter's shack in Dollarton, North Vancouver, it is later acclaimed one of the great books of modern literature and a movie is made in 1984. Lowry returns to England in 1954 and dies there in 1957. • **Mar 31** Eburne Post Office in Richmond, opened in 1892, closes. • **Apr 27** The last streetcar, *No. 157*, retires from service in North Vancouver; B.C. Electric has gradually replaced them with buses. • **Apr 28** A TCA Lockheed Lodestar disappears near Chilliwack with 15 people on board. It is not found until 1994. • **May** The 1923 Chinese Exclusion Act is repealed but only dependents of Canadian citizens are allowed in. Chinese are not able to immigrate to Canada on the same basis as other immigrants until 1967. • **Spring** Chinese and East Indians are given the provincial franchise which means they can also vote in federal elections. • **Jun 30** The ward system is abolished in Burnaby. • **Labour Day** A potlatch is held at McMillan Island reserve near Fort Langley. As in 1861 native people come from all over the Lower Mainland as do many non-natives. (The law prohibiting potlatches was not repealed until 1951.)

• **Dec 3** The old Lumberman's Arch is demolished. Originally erected at Pender and Hamilton for the 1912 visit of the Duke of Connaught was moved to Stanley Park and dedicated on August 29, 1919 to its designer, Captain G.P. Bowie, who was killed at Ypres on July 7, 1915. • **Also in 1947** Woodwards is now the fourth-largest department store chain in Canada and run by "Chunky" (Charles) Woodward, grandson of the founder. Thirty years later the fourth generation of Woodwards will enter the family business. • Surrey becomes a member of the Greater Vancouver Water District.

1948 Apr 14 The HBC store begins operation of the first two-way escalators in Vancouver. The event makes the newspapers. • **Apr 26** Vancouver's first boat show opens. • **May 24** Flooding of the Fraser isolates Greater Vancouver from the rest of the country for days as both railways and the Trans-Canada Hwy. are cut. Barnston Island is flooded and cattle have to be removed. In Richmond, which has had more warning, only 30 metres of dyke is broken. Premier Johnson declares a state of emergency. 16,000 people lose their homes, ten die and the damage is estimated at $17 million. • **Oct 3** Hallelujah Point in Stanley Park is officially named to commemorate the work of the Salvation Army in B.C. 1887-1947. • **Dec** Eaton's purchases David Spencer's. • **Also in 1948** The first television signal reaches Vancouver with broadcasts received from Seattle. • Westlake Lodge on Hollyburn Mountain installs rope tows. Lift tickets are $1.50. • Sixty thousand daffodil bulbs are planted along Stanley Park Causeway, a gift from Holland to thank Canadian soldiers for helping to liberate their country from the Nazis. • The Surrey Parks Commission is established. • Bus service begins in Burnaby which now has many paved roads. • The George Derby Veteran's Rehabilitation Centre opens in Burnaby. • Cloverdale Rodeo is enlarged but postponed to Labour Day because of the Fraser floods.

1949 Mar 24 Henry Blair, Vancouver's last surviving "Father of Incorporation" signatory of January 15, 1886, dies. • **Apr 14** An earthquake in Surrey. Buildings rock, pictures swing and golfers see undulations of the ground but no damage is reported. • **May 31** The new labour temple opens on Broadway. • **Jun 25** Sod is turned for a Woodwards store at Park Royal in West Vancouver, part of the first drive for shopping centres in Canada. • **Aug 15** Kingsway re-opens as a six-lane highway between Vancouver and New Westminster. • **Nov 2** A civic banquet is given at the Hotel Vancouver for Prime Minister Nehru of India. • **Nov 11** Kerrisdale Arena officially opens. • **Nov 26** The Capilano River, swollen by a violent rainstorm,

sweeps away a large section of Marine Dr. the only road link to West Vancouver. A hastily-built Bailey bridge is also destroyed and, writes historian Bruce Ramsey, the municipality is cut off for ten days. • **Also in 1949** Japanese and natives given the provincial franchise. Native people had lost the vote in 1872. • The *Lady Alexandra* excursion boat plies between White Rock and Victoria. The trip (one-way) takes about three hours. • The Matsumoto family purchases a small shipyard on Dollarton Hwy. in North Vancouver, builds fishboats and fire-fighting boats for Mexico. The company is sold in 1988 to Pacific Western Shipbuilders. • A crisis in Surrey's poultry business sees egg prices dropping and producers going out of business. The British market is gone and the American overloaded. Poultrymen demand a floor price for eggs. The provincial government establishes a poultry marketing board. • Four European starlings are sighted in Surrey. Since then the starling population has spread throughout the Lower Mainland. (European starlings are first introduced into North America in 1890 in New York's Central Park and spread across the continent from there.) • Japanese families begin returning to Greater Vancouver.

1950 Feb The Crescent Beach Hotel burns down. • **Mar 15** A new passenger terminal opens at Vancouver airport. • **Apr 13** The Ridge Theatre opens. • **May** Patricia Kronebusch becomes Cloverdale's first Rodeo Queen. • **Spring** Vandals paint White Rock's white rock black enraging citizens who have to pay for the clean-up. • **Aug 29** Eccles-Rand Ltd. personnel check out Vancouver's first atomic bomb shelter which their firm has built in an unidentified Shaughnessy backyard. • **Sep 1** Park Royal shopping centre opens, the first regional shopping centre in Canada. Originally on the north side of Marine Dr. it later expands to the south. • **Sep 17** The last run of Vancouver's street car *No. 124*, an open-air observation car which, with famed conductor Teddy Lyons, has shown tourists the city since 1910. • **Sep 30** Over the protests of local people a B.C. Electric tram makes the last run between New Westminster and Chilliwack. A settlement is made in which B.C. Electric contributes to the cost of establishing bus transportation. Businesses complain mail is slower. • **Sep** Fall assizes open with the first Chinese juror, Jack Chan, on jury duty. • **Nov 11** The West Vancouver Memorial Library opens. An earlier library had been opened in 1921 but closed during the Depression. • **Nov** Sargit Singh and Bob Bose of Surrey win the Canadian championship in potato judging at the Royal Winter Fair in Toronto. • **Also in 1950** Irving House is purchased by the City of New Westminster for use as a historic centre. • A modern sewage plant is installed at White Rock and 1,200 homes and businesses are connected with the disposal plant. • Four-room Gleneagles School, the first in the area, opens near Horseshoe Bay. • The *Vancouver Sun* establishes Camp Gates on Bowen Island for its paper carriers and names it after Herb Gates, the circulation manager. • Thirteen kilometres of double-lane road to the top of Mt. Seymour is completed. • The first diesel train comes to White Rock. In the 1950s there are three trains a day (9 am, 1 pm and 9 pm) and residents set their watches by them.

1951 May 1 The RCMP take over the policing of Surrey with a cost-sharing agreement between the federal and municipal governments. • **May 11** Demonstration at the Hotel Vancouver of the latest weapon in the war against impaired drivers: the "Drunkometer". • **Aug** Postal zones are introduced into Vancouver. • **Oct 20** Greater Vancouver enjoys a visit by Princess Elizabeth and Prince Philip. • **Dec** High tides and gale-force winds combine to flood 480 hectares of farmland to a depth of 1.5 metres between the Serpentine and Nicomekl rivers. Repairs cost about $20,000 and the land suffers lower productivity for the next few years because of salt residue. • **Also in 1951** The Black Ball ferries begin a service between Gibsons and Horseshoe Bay with the MV *Machigonne* (passengers only) and the MV *Quillyute*. • The Lougheed Hwy. is completed accelerating development on the north shore of the Fraser.

1952 Feb 7 A 21-gun salute is fired at Brockton Point to mark the accession to the throne of Elizabeth II. • **Feb 12** Tolls are finally removed from Pattullo Bridge. • **Jul 15** The new (and present) Lumberman's Arch is dedicated. • **Jul** Kerrisdale switches to trolley buses. (The first Interurban tram arrived there July 4, 1905.) • **Sep 4** The UBC Law Building is opened by Prime Minister Louis St. Laurent. • **Oct 30** Burnaby General Hospital opens. • **Also in 1952** Lots in West Vancouver's British Properties sell for between $2,000 and $5,000.

1953 Spring A Women's Institute convention in Cloverdale passes a resolution calling for a national health scheme to give complete coverage for all Canadians. • **Oct15** The Trans-Mountain oil pipeline from Edmonton to Vancouver is completed. • **Oct 23** The Burnaby Lake Interurban tram line closes after 42 years, replaced by a bus service. Charlie Martin, the first conductor on the original 1911 run comes out of retirement to act as conductor for the last tram run. • **Oct 29** Cinemascope makes its Vancouver debut at the Capitol with a showing of *The Robe*. • **Nov 19** The old New Westminster city hall closes and a new one opens on Royal Ave. •

Dec 9 The first Chinese Lions Club in North America is organized in Vancouver's Chinatown. • **Dec 17** Vancouver's first television station, CBUT, goes on the air. • **Also in 1953** Vancouver Town Planning Commission is formed. • The Benedictine monk's priory at Deer Lake becomes an abbey. Father Eugene Medved is the first abbott. • Gillnet fishermen on the Fraser object to a government proposal to close the river to commercial fishing above Pattullo Bridge by mid-September each year. 650 gillnetters are licensed to fish above the bridge, many of them Surrey residents. Their livelihood affects Surrey's economy. • Nylon nets are introduced to the Fraser River fishing industry. They are stronger, lighter and more durable than the linen nets used previously. • The Black Ball ferries begin service between Nanaimo and Horseshoe Bay. • Imperial Oil decides to phase out its company townsite at Ioco as workers retire, die or move away.

1954 Feb 4 The present Granville St. Bridge opens. • **Jun 23** Vancouver voters approve a six-day shopping week. • **Jul** Vancouver's first cocktail bar opens in the Sylvia Hotel. • **Aug 7** The "Miracle Mile" at the British Empire Games at Empire Stadium. Roger Bannister of England beats John Landy of Australia in the first race in which two racers run the mile in under four minutes. • **Aug 25** The 45-bed Peace Arch Hospital opens in White Rock after six years of planning and fund-raising by local residents. • **Aug** The B.C. Lions work out for the first time at Empire Stadium. • **Oct12** The RCMP ship *St. Roch* returns to Vancouver after being the first ship to circumnavigate North America. (In 1974 the *St. Roch* became the centrepiece of an Historic Site, adjacent to and now administered by the Vancouver Maritime Museum.) • **Nov 19** Cleveland Dam is dedicated and named after Dr. E.A. Cleveland, first commissioner of the Greater Vancouver Water District, which oversees the development of the water system. • **Also in 1954** Richmond converts to a dial exchange from a manual telephone system. • Land expropriations begin on Sea Island as Vancouver International Airport expands. • TCA (now Air Canada) introduces a fleet of Lockheed Super-Constellations for its Vancouver to Montreal flights. They carry 63 passengers as well as mail and freight and travel at 550 kilometres an hour. • The Surrey Co-op is now a multi-million dollar business. Other industries in Surrey include Cloverdale Paint, Perlite Industries and Green Valley Fertilizer. The major farm products are vegetables, hay, berries and potatoes. There are mink and nutria ranches, chicken, turkey and dairy farms and plant nurseries. • Completion of a 1,150-kilometre crude oil pipeline from Edmonton to Trans-Mountain's facility in Burnaby.

1955 Mar 15 Langley city is incorporated as a separate municipality. • **Apr 24** The last day of streetcar operation in Vancouver. • **Jun 3** Canadian Pacific Airlines inaugurates the first service between Vancouver and Amsterdam over the North Pole. The 7,800-kilometre journey takes 18 hours. • **Jul 22** The first industrial park in Canada is built on Annacis Island by Grosvenor International, owned by the Duke of Westminster. • **Nov 26** The Montreal Alouettes and Edmonton Eskimos meet in the first Grey Cup played in Vancouver. Montreal wins. • The *Clifford J. Rogers*, the world's first container ship, leaves Vancouver with her first shipment bound for the Yukon. • **Also in 1955** The laying of gas pipes begins in Surrey as B.C. Electric promises natural gas distribution for the Fraser Valley at Vancouver prices. At Port Mann B.C. Electric builds the "largest gas turbine in the world" to generate electricity from natural gas. • Cloverdale changes over to dial telephones. • Lions Gate Bridge is sold to the provincial government for $6 million, about half its appraised value. • Fort Langley is established as a national historic park and reconstruction begins. The storehouse is the only surviving building and is restored as the trading store. It is possibly the oldest intact structure in B.C.

1956 Jan 16 Hastings East Community Centre is opened. • **Apr 3** A bank robbery shoot-out at Cariboo Trail shopping centre in Coquitlam leaves one robber dead and a policeman injured. It is thought to be the first time a machine-gun has been used in a local bank robbery. • **Jun 15** Stanley Park Aquarium opens with the ribbon cut by fisheries minister James Sinclair. It develops into the third largest aquarium in North America. • **Jun 22** Burnaby's stylish new municipal hall opens near Deer Lake in the geographical centre of the municipality. • **Jun 27** Bill Haley and the Comets play to an estimated 6,000 at a concert in Kerrisdale Arena with Red Robinson as emcee. • **Aug 13** Letter carrier service begins in White Rock. • **Dec 5** The first Hungarian refugees arrive in Vancouver. • **Dec 7** The Black Ball Ferry Co. makes its inaugural run to Bowen Island after the Union Steamship franchise is cancelled. • **Also in 1956** Burnaby Library is formally established. • The PGE Railway (now BC Rail) is completed from Squamish to Horseshoe Bay along Howe Sound, and the Horseshoe Bay to North Vancouver section is rebuilt. • A new community centre opens in Cloverdale, four years after the old "Opera House" burned down.

1957 Apr 15 The City of White Rock is incorporated after breaking away from Surrey. It is named for the large granite rock on the beach, a relic of the Ice Age. • **Jul 1** The Oak St. Bridge opens, a vital link to Vancouver for Richmond.

Tolls are charged until 1964. • **Nov 1** A new main Vancouver Public Library building opens at Burrard and Robson. • **Nov 4** A new passenger facility opens at Vancouver airport. • **Also in 1957** The Upper Levels Hwy. is completed on the North Shore. • A mosquito control board is formed in Surrey. "The mosquitoes are still fighting back." • For the sake of practicality road names in Surrey become road numbers and much colorful local history is lost. • The Burnaby Historical Society is formed and becomes the driving force behind the creation of the archives, museum and heritage advisory committee. • Completion of the first gas pipeline to Vancouver.

1958 Jan The Esco Co. establishes its first Canadian alloy steel foundry in Port Coquitlam —its accessibility to the mainline of the CPR facilitates the export of the finished product. • **Apr 19** Professional baseball tickets are sold on Sunday for the first time in Vancouver at Capilano Stadium. On April 28 the Supreme Court of Canada upholds B.C.'s approval of a Vancouver City Charter by-law amendment permitting Sunday sports. Newspapers call it the end of the biggest public issue of the decade. • **May 28** The P & O Line's *Chusan* arrives in port. One observer notes it is an historic event, re-establishing passenger vessel links with the Orient which had lapsed for almost 20 years with the last voyages of the great CPR *Empress* liners. • **Jun 17** The new Second Narrows Bridge collapses during construction. Eighteen workmen and one rescue worker die and 20 more are injured. In 1995 the bridge is renamed in their and other workers' honor. It is now officially the Ironworkers Memorial Second Narrows Crossing. • **Jul 1** Premier W.A.C. Bennett announces B.C. will establish its own ferry service between Vancouver Island and the mainland. The move is prompted by labor strife in both the Black Ball and Canadian Pacific ferry systems. • **Jul** Princess Margaret opens the reconstructed Fort Langley almost 100 years after B.C. is proclaimed a colony there. • **Aug 13** The park board closes Vancouver beaches because of pollution. • **Aug 30** Ferry service between Vancouver and North Vancouver ends—until the start-up of the Seabus 19 years later. • **Summer** A 30-metre-high Kwakiutl totem-pole is raised in front of Vancouver's new Maritime Museum in honor of the centennial of the founding of the colony of British Columbia, November 19, 1858. • **Oct 5** The Surrey Centennial Museum opens. W.E. Ireland, provincial archivist, is there with his wife, a descendant of Eric Anderson, a Surrey pioneer whose log cabin is now a part of the museum. • **Oct** The hula hoop craze hits Greater Vancouver. • **Also in 1958** Shaughnessy Golf Course

negotiates a long-term lease for part of the Musqueam Indian reserve with the department of Indian affairs. The natives protest the terms once they learn of them and in 1985 a Supreme Court of Canada decision upholds a $10 million award to the band because the department has not acted in the best interests of the natives. • The largest roller coaster in Canada is built at the PNE grounds. • The Interurban era closes with the last train leaving Marpole for Steveston. • Brighouse Race Track in Richmond is sold for development. • 8,000 people celebrate B.C.'s centennial at a barbecue atop Burnaby Mountain. A pavilion is built there as a centennial project.

1959 Jan A four-day Chinese New Year celebration is held in Vancouver's Chinatown for the first time, sponsored by Chinese-Canadian businessmen. • **Mar 16** The *Lake Atlin* is the first vessel to berth at the newly completed National Harbours Board Centennial Pier. • **May 6** The official opening of Oakridge shopping centre. • **May 23** The Deas Island Tunnel opens for traffic (it will be officially opened by Queen Elizabeth on July 15). Tolls are collected until 1964. • **Jun 11** Dedication and opening of Vancouver Maritime Museum. • **Jul 3** McCleery Public Golf Course opens. • **Jul 5** The Queen Elizabeth Theatre opens. • **Jul** Westwood Motorsport Park opens in Coquitlam, at the time the only European-style race track in Canada. It closes in 1990. • **Also in 1959** More than 1,000 people attend the funeral of Andy Paul, Squamish leader, at North Vancouver's Mission reserve. He has been honored by Pope Pius XII in 1955 for his contribution to the church and to the native people of Canada. Paul is active for many years in the native land-claims question and is the founder of the North American Indian Brotherhood. • Surrey Memorial Hospital opens.

1960 May 3 Nitobe Memorial Gardens at UBC opens. • **May 19** Unveiling of the Lord Stanley statue in Stanley Park by Gov. Gen. Georges Vanier. • **Aug 25** Premier W.A.C. Bennett opens the present Second Narrows Bridge. The cantilevered span of the main arch, at 330 metres, is at the time the second longest in Canada. • **Also in 1960** A B.C. government-owned ferry service begins between Tsawwassen and Victoria. Within a year it takes over the Black Ball Ferries operation in Horseshoe Bay. • Two new freeways pass through Surrey. Charlie Perkins stands guard over his ivy-covered fir tree, directly in the path of Hwy. 401. As he has dedicated the tree to fallen comrades in World War I the public outcry results in the engineers curving the road around it. • The Garibaldi Lift Co. is formed to develop Whistler as a ski mountain. There is no road, no hydro, no water supply and no money at the time. • Brentwood Mall opens in Burnaby.

At 12 hectares it is the largest of its kind in B.C. at the time.

1961 Jan 15 The Coquitlam River floods again prompting an extensive dyking and drainage program. • **May 3** An 11-day B.C. International Trade Fair opens at Exhibition Park. • **Jun 5** Beginning of direct distance dialing. • **Aug** The B.C. government approves the take-over of the British Columbia Electric Co. as a Crown corporation. Dr. Gordon Shrum is the first chairman. • **Dec** The Christmas Carol Ships tradition begins. • **Also in 1961** Surrey municipal employees go on strike for the first time.

1962 Feb 26 The Queen Elizabeth Playhouse opens. • **May 30** There is a near riot at the Forum as Prime Minister Diefenbaker addresses a rowdy crowd at an election rally. • **Jun 18** Greater Vancouver native people vote in their first federal election after Parliament extends the franchise to them in 1960. • **Jun 18** The first Grouse Mountain chalet burns down. • **Jun 25** The Haida section of Totem Park at UBC opens. • **Oct 12** Typhoon Frieda does thousands of dollars worth of damage in Greater Vancouver. Gusts reach 125 kph at the Sea Island weather station. Windows of downtown department stores are blown out and 3,000 trees blow down in Stanley Park. • **Dec 10** The old Union Steamship Hotel on Bowen Island is demolished and the resort closed down. • **Also in 1962** Austrian ski area consultant Willy Schaeffler reports favorably on Whistler's potential as a world-class ski area. • Trinity Junior College is opened in Langley by the Evangelical Free Church of America with 17 students.

1963 Apr 2 Tolls come off the Lions Gate Bridge. • **Apr 18** The Iona Island sewage treatment plant opens in Richmond. • **Summer** The First Vancouver Sea Festival. • **Sep** Killarney Community Centre opens. • **Nov 26** A memorial service is held at UBC for assassinated U.S. President John F. Kennedy. • **Also in 1963** Pollution coming down the Nicomekl and Serpentine Rivers puts an end to oyster farming at Crescent Beach which has flourished for decades.

1964 Feb The new Grandview Community Centre is opened by Mrs. Eric Hamber. • **May 29** Vancouver's Mayor Bill Rathie and park board chairman George Wainborn drive the last spike in the Stanley Park miniature railway. • **Jun 12** The Port Mann Bridge opens. Its construction is unique in North America and at the time it was the most expensive piece of highway in Canada. • **Aug** The Beatles visit Vancouver. • **Sep 16** U.S. President Lyndon B. Johnson, Prime Minister Lester B. Pearson and Premier W.A.C. Bennett meet at Peace Arch Park to sign the Columbia River Treaty. • **Oct 6** The British Columbia Institute of Technology is opened by Premier

W.A.C. Bennett. • **Nov 19** The New Westminster Museum opens. • **Nov 29** Thousands welcome home the B.C. Lions from their 34-24 Grey Cup win over Hamilton. • **Also in 1964** Grouse Mountain Resorts Ltd. is formed and the following year a decision is made to build Canada's largest aerial tramway and a new chalet. Grouse Mountain Ski School later becomes Canada's biggest. • The Deas Island Tunnel is renamed George Massey Tunnel. Tolls are removed from the tunnel and the Oak St. Bridge. **1965 Sep 9** Simon Fraser University opens on Burnaby Mountain. Designed by Arthur Erickson and Geoffrey Massey, it is built within two years. 2,500 students enrol. • **Also in 1965** The Fraser River Harbour Commission replaces the New Westminster Harbour Board. Now all municipalities adjoining the river send representatives to the new commission which deals with issues like water pollution and industrial growth. • The Bentall 1 office tower is completed in downtown Vancouver. • Richmond Square shopping mall opens. • Surrey adopts the concept of "five towns" within the municipality: Guildford, Whalley, Cloverdale, Newton and Sunnyside. • Grace MacInnis of Vancouver becomes B.C.'s first woman MP. Her father, J.S. Woodsworth, was the founder of the CCF, forerunner of the NDP. **1966 Feb 15** The first ski lifts open to the public on Whistler Mountain. • **Feb** Richmond General Hospital opens. • **Nov 25** Grey Cup riot in Vancouver. • **Dec 15** The first Grouse Mountain skyride is opened by Premier W.A.C. Bennett. It carries 50 passengers. The busy Premier Bennett opens Centennial Fountain, built on the Georgia St. side of the Vancouver Art Gallery, to commemorate the union of the Crown colonies of British Columbia and Vancouver Island in 1866. • **Also in 1966** North Vancouver Recreation Centre opens at 23rd and Lonsdale, jointly funded by the city and district as a centennial project. • Guildford shopping centre opens in Surrey. **1967 Mar 26** A big anti-Vietnam War protest in Vancouver. On the same day there is a Super Human Be-In in Stanley Park. • **Apr 15** Big peace march in Vancouver. • **May 17** The Canadian Lacrosse Hall of Fame opens in New Westminster. • **Jun 1** The first McDonald's restaurant in Canada opens in Richmond at 7120 No. 3 Rd. It is take-out only and hamburgers cost 18¢ • **Jun 10** The first "Miles for Millions" walk in Vancouver in aid of the Third World. The Ceperley Mansion at Deer Lake opens as the Burnaby Art Gallery. • **Jun** The Greater Vancouver Regional District (GVRD) is incorporated. • **Jul 4** Chief Dan George of North Vancouver's Burrard band moves a crowd of more than 30,000 people to silence with his eloquent "Lament for Confederation" at Empire Stadium. • **Jul 30** 212 bathtubs

enter the first Nanaimo to Vancouver bathtub race. • **Oct 19** Citizens parade on Pender St. to protest city council's plan for a freeway through the Chinese residential area. There is additional vigorous protest on November 23 at a city hall meeting. The plan is eventually abandoned. • **Dec 1** French language radio starts in Vancouver with the opening broadcast of CBUF-FM. • **Also in 1967** The North Vancouver Youth Band, founded in 1939, wins five first-place trophies at the National Band Competition, an unprecedented achievement. • A federal law is passed allowing Chinese immigrants to be admitted under the same rules as all other immigrants. • The Grandview-Douglas Hwy. in Burnaby is renamed Canada Way in honor of Canada's centennial. • Greenpeace, now the world's largest environmental organization, begins in a home in the Dunbar area, with a group calling itself the "Don't Make a Wave Committee." **1968 Feb** The Surrey Centennial Fine Arts Centre opens with a production of *Brigadoon*. Subsequently the Surrey Arts Council is formed. • **Mar 12** The founding meeting of TEAM, The Electors Action Movement, at Grandview Community Centre. • **Mar** A civic parade for Canadian ski champion Nancy Greene who has won an Olympic gold medal for the women's giant slalom. • **Apr 26** Premier Bennett and city archivist Maj. J.S. Matthews dedicate New Brighton Park. • **May 20** West Vancouver is "twinned" with the Montreal suburb of Verdun. • **Jul 18** The Bank of British Columbia opens in Vancouver. It is Canada's tenth chartered bank. • **Aug** The Granville St. Theatre Row beautification project opens. • **Sep 11** The inaugural Japan Air Lines Tokyo to Vancouver flight. • **Sep 22** Vancouver's Community Arts Council sponsors a walking tour of Gastown to stimulate interest in preserving the historic area. • **Oct 25** Vancouver's first "northside" international airport terminal is officially opened by Paul Hellyer, minister of transport. (It had been open for business since September 10.) • **Oct 26** The Centennial Museum and the H.R. MacMillan Planetarium open at Vanier Park. • **Nov 25** Students end a three-day occupation of the administration building at SFU. The police charge 104 people. • **Dec 12** The Arthur Erickson-designed MacMillan Bloedel building opens on W. Georgia St. • **Also in 1968** The Richmond Arts Centre and Brighouse Centre Library open. • A martial arts centre is opened in Steveston. • Whistler Mountain Ski School begun. • Heli-skiing begins at Whistler. **1969 Feb 23** The first scheduled hovercraft service in Canada begins between Vancouver and Nanaimo. • **Mar 31** Vancouver is granted its first legal coat of arms and badge. • **Mar** The new YWCA building on Burrard opens. • **Apr 27**

"Town fool" Joachim Foikis spends the last of his Canada Council grant on a party for skid road residents in Gastown. • **Apr** A 4.8 km causeway to the man-made island of Roberts Bank in Delta opens to provide access to a deep-sea port being developed to ship Alberta and B.C. coal to Japan. • **May 2** Surrey's municipal council holds a meeting in the original town hall which has become part of the museum. Since 1881 Surrey's population has grown from a few hundred to more than 90,000. • **Jul 21** The *Sun* and *Province* newspapers issue special supplements commemorating man's first moonwalk the previous day. • **Sep 25** Lougheed mall opens. • **Dec 1** Vancouver gets a National Hockey League franchise. • **Dec 6** The Bloedel Conservatory and Plaza opens and *Knife-Edge (Two-Piece)*, a sculpture by Henry Moore, is unveiled. • **Also in 1969** Vancouver's Elaine "Mighty Mouse" Tanner retires from competitive swimming at age 18 having set five world records and won three Olympic medals. She is the best woman swimmer in Canadian history. • West Vancouver's cannery near Sandy Cove closes. The site is purchased by the federal government for the Pacific coast fisheries research station. • Vancouver International Airport announces it can handle "jumbo jets," Boeing 747s. • Judith Forst, born in Fraser Mills, Coquitlam, is awarded a five-year contract with the Metropolitan Opera Assn. of New York and becomes a world-renowned mezzo-soprano. • Jimmy Christmas, mayor of Coquitlam, dies in office after almost 25 years as mayor. • Delta's second municipal hall, built in 1913, becomes the Delta Museum and Archives. • The last pick-up of milk cans in Surrey. From now on milk from dairy farms goes by tanker truck. • Bill Vander Zalm becomes mayor of Surrey. • Swangard Stadium, named for journalist Erwin Swangard, is built in Burnaby's Central Park. **1970 Apr 7** Jana Jorgenson, an 18-year old Centennial High School student from Coquitlam, wins the Miss Teen Canada contest. • **Apr 30** The first CP Rail computer-commanded coal train from Alberta reaches Delta's new Roberts Bank superport. • **Oct 9** The new Vancouver Canucks make their NHL debut at the Coliseum against Los Angeles Kings. (Kings win 3-1.) • **Oct** Vancouver police and hostel dwellers from Jericho clash on 4th Ave. • **Nov 3** Vancouver city council approves sale of land for multi-purpose development in Champlain Heights, the last large undeveloped tract in Vancouver. • **Also in 1970** The liner *Oronsay* is quarantined on arrival in Vancouver with typhoid among passengers. • Chief Dan George from North Vancouver's Burrard reserve gets an Oscar nomination for Best Supporting Actor in *Little Big Man*. He was chief of the Burrard band for 12 years and an honorary chief of the Squamish Nation. He dies on September 23, 1981 at 82. • Alberta Co-op's poultry processing plant locates in Port Coquitlam marking the start of the Kingsway Ave. industrial park development. The operation processes 25,000 chickens in an eight-hour day.

1971 Jan 8 Seaspan International is chosen as the new name after the merger of Vancouver Tugboats and Island Tug and Barge. The North Vancouver company operates tugs and specialty barges from Alaska to Mexico. • **Jan 15** Vancouver gets title to the old Shaughnessy Golf Course lands to be developed as Van Dusen Botanical Display Garden. • **Feb** Gastown and Chinatown are designated historic sites by the provincial government. • **Mar 4** Prime Minister Pierre Trudeau marries Margaret Sinclair at St. Stephen's Catholic Church in Lynn Valley, North Vancouver. • **Apr** The railway through White Rock (now called the Burlington Northern) ends its passenger service. A few years later a "fast-bus" commuter service by B.C. Hydro links White Rock with Vancouver. • **Jun 23** Vancouver mayor Tom Campbell visits the "Four Seasons" site (at the entrance to Stanley Park) and spars with young people squatting there. • **Jun 28** The new Georgia/Dunsmuir Viaduct opens. • **Jul 20** A special pageant at Empire Stadium marks the centennial of B.C.'s entry into Confederation. • **Aug 7** A Gastown riot leads to charges of police over-reaction. The inquiry is headed by Mr. Justice T.A. Dohm. • **Sep 26** Official opening of the Stanley Park seawall. Special guest is the Hon. H.H. Stevens, present as an MP in 1914 when the park board and federal government authorize constructon of the first section of the wall. • **Oct 6** Thousands of Greater Vancouver high school students protest the planned Amchitka atomic blast, outside the U.S. Consulate in Vancouver. • **Oct 29** *Greenpeace Too* sails from Vancouver for Amchitka. • **Nov 19** Heritage Village (now Burnaby Village Museum) is opened by Gov. Gen. Roland Michener.

1972 Mar 18 The first purpose-built martial arts centre, or dojo house, outside Japan opens in Steveston. • **Jun 10** Elek Imredy's *Girl in Wet Suit* sculpture is unveiled on a rock off Stanley Park. • **Aug 30** Coquitlam NDP MLA Dave Barrett becomes premier-elect of B.C. • **Oct** The Capilano fish hatchery near Cleveland Dam opens. Before the dam was built the Capilano River produced 1,000 to 2,000 coho salmon annually. Twenty years later the hatchery is returning to the river annually half a million coho, from two to three million chinook and 20,000 steelhead trout. • **Dec 29** The City of Vancouver Archives opens at Vanier Park. • **Also in 1972** A roe herring fishery begins on

the Lower Fraser for the Japanese market. At $3,350 a tonne it is a lucrative business. • Cypress Lodge, on the west side of Alta Lake at Whistler, is bought by the Canadian Youth Hostels Assn. • Construction of Capilano College on Purcell Way in North Vancouver begins. The college has begun to offer courses in 1968 in portables on the grounds of West Vancouver Secondary School.

1973 Mar 13 The National Harbours Board announces construction of a large container facility for the port. • **Apr 1** Vancouver city takes over the Jericho defence lands for a new 29-hectare park. • **Jun 18** Traffic barriers go up in Vancouver's West End. A 1996 study shows they have greatly reduced accidents. • **Summer** Burnaby hosts Canada's Summer Games. Preparations include the creation of a 2,200-metre rowing course on Burnaby Lake, then one of only three such competitive courses in North America. • **Oct 15** The Vancouver East Cultural Centre opens in what had been a church. • **Also in 1973** Wakayama, Japan becomes the sister city of Richmond. Mio-mura, a village in the same prefecture, is the native home of many of Steveston's earliest Japanese immigrants. • Establishment of the Agricultural Land Reserve restricting development on farm land. • Karen Magnussen, who trains first at Kerrisdale Arena, then at the North Shore Winter Club, wins the World Women's Figure Skating Championship for the second year in a row, in addition to her silver medal in the 1972 Winter Olympics in Japan. She is awarded the Order of Canada and the Freedom of the District of North Vancouver. A North Vancouver arena is subsequently named after her.

1974 Jan 15 Knight St. Bridge opens. It replaces the Fraser St. Bridge which closes February 10. • **Jan 22** A portion of Granville St. closes to automobile traffic for conversion to a pedestrian mall. • **Mar 19** City council votes to buy the Orpheum Theatre for use as a new concert hall. • **Jun 21** The inaugural run of the refurbished steam locomotive *Royal Hudson* from North Vancouver to Squamish. • **Oct 16** Opening of the *St. Roch* National Historic Site at the Vancouver Maritime Museum. It is 30 years after its return from its historic voyage through the Northwest Passage and some of the former crew are on hand for the ceremonies.

1975 Jan 27 The last wall of the old Birks Building comes down to make way for the Vancouver Centre development. • **Feb** Construction begins at Kingsway and Boundary on B.C. Tel headquarters, a building nicknamed "the Boot" because of its design. • **Jun** Mrs. Otto Koerner turns the sod near Building 14 at Vanier Park to mark the start of construction of the new Community Music School home. The False Creek seawall is finished.

Burnaby hosts Canada's Summer Games. Preparations include the creation of a 2,200-metre rowing course on Burnaby Lake

• **Sep 6** The Resort Municipality of Whistler is established by the provincial legislature. The unique designation takes account of the special problems faced by the developing resort. • **Oct 9** Cypress Provincial Park is created in West Vancouver. • **Also in 1975** A riot at B.C. Penitentiary; hostage Mary Steinhauser is killed.

1976 May 15 Arthur Laing Bridge officially opens, named after a native son of Richmond who becomes a cabinet minister under Pierre Trudeau, later a senator. • **May 27** Habitat, a UN Conference on Human Settlements, convenes in Vancouver. It runs to Jun 11. A successful alternate conference, Habitat Forum, run by Alan Clapp, is held at Jericho Beach Park. • **May 31** UBC's Museum of Anthropology, around since 1947, moves into a stunning new building designed by Arthur Erickson. • **Dec 15** Grouse Mountain Resorts' "Superskyride" is opened by Premier Bill Bennett, more than doubling the uphill capacity. • **Also in 1976** Vancouver's Greg Joy wins the Olympic silver in high jump.

1977 Apr 2 Vancouver's restored Orpheum Theatre opens as the new home of the Vancouver Symphony Orchestra. • **May** One of the largest state-of-the-art electronic automatic telephone exchanges ever put into operation by BC Tel (to that date) begins service in Whalley. • **Jun 17** The SeaBus makes its inaugural run. • **Sep 14** Lansdowne Park shopping mall opens in Richmond. • **Also in 1977** Michael J. Fox, 16, a student at Burnaby Central Senior High School, takes his first professional acting job in a CBC television series, *Leo and Me*. • Rainbow Lodge at Whistler burns down after 63 years of operation. • Burnaby's Christmas hockey tournament for junior teams features 98 teams and 1,600 players. It has become the largest event of its kind in the world and is listed in the *Guinness*

Book of World Records. Many talented players are produced by Burnaby's hockey program.
1978 Jan 1 Canada's first native Indian citizenship judge, Marjorie Cantryn, swears in 30 new Canadians in Whalley. • **May 14** George B. Tocher and a navigator set out for Hawaii from West Vancouver in a native-style log canoe to prove Hawaiians could have originated in B.C. • **Oct** Taylor's Shoe Store in Ladner closes after 66 years. Begun as a harness repair shop the business switches to shoes when automobiles begin to replace horses. • The new New Westminster Library opens. • **Also in 1978** The world's first children's festival is held at Vanier Park, will later be copied by New York, Boston and cities in Australia and Europe. • The Gastown Steam Clock (forced to run on electricity since its installation in 1977) begins running on steam.
1979 Jun 16 Richmond celebrates 100 years since incorporation. In August Richmond hosts the three-day 1979 B.C. Summer Games, the first to include disabled athletes. • **Jul 12** Granville Island Public Market opens. • **Aug 6** Surrey council "invites one and all" to its 100th Birthday Party Centennial week at Bear Creek Park. • **Aug 16** Coquitlam Centre opens. • **Sep 8** Vancouver Whitecaps win the NASL Soccer Bowl in New York defeating the Tampa Bay Rowdies 2-1. 100,000 fans greet the team on its return. • **Oct 27** The last scheduled passenger train departs from the 1912 CPR station at the foot of Granville St. • **Dec 16** The Steveston Museum opens in a 1905 building, formerly a bank, then a doctor's office. The Steveston Historical Society also operates a post office there. • **Also in 1979** Surrey has become "Vancouver's bedroom" as more than 50 per cent of its residents work elsewhere. In 1879 almost everyone who lives in Surrey works there. • Vancouver's new courthouse and Robson Square complex, designed by Arthur Erickson, is completed. • White Rock's first International Sandcastle-building Competition. The event is discontinued in the 1980s because of the rowdiness of some sightseers. • North Vancouver High School closes having served the community for 69 years. Upon the closure of the school the new gym, named after principal Mickey McDougall, becomes part of the North Vancouver Recreation Cente.
1980 Apr 12 One-legged runner Terry Fox of Coquitlam begins his cross-country "Marathon of Hope" to raise money for cancer research. • **May 18** The eruption of Mount St. Helens in Washington state rattles windows in Greater Vancouver. • **Summer** Greater Vancouver brewery workers go on strike. Thirsty residents block border crossings on evenings and weekends. • **Dec** Blackcomb Mountain, Whistler's neighboring mountain, opens for skiing. • **Also in 1980** The

B.C. Penitentiary in New Westminster is closed for good. • The nine-kilometre Stanley Park seawall is completed. Much of it was built or supervised by master stonemason Jimmy Cunningham who has hefted thousands of the 45-kilogram blocks into place over 32 years. • The Boeing plant on Sea Island is demolished. It was built in 1939 for the production of Canso and Catalina and later B-29 Superfortress aircraft. At the peak of production it employed 6,000 people. • Large numbers of trespassers picking hallucinogenic mushrooms become a nuisance for Surrey farmers. One farmer solves the problem by pasturing a young bull on his land and posting conspicuous notices to "Beware of the Bull."
1981 Apr 1 Kwantlen College in Richmond opens. • **Jun** A new floating dock arrives at Burrard Dry Dock from Japan. • **Spring** CUPE members strike and garbage piles up at tennis courts and other makeshift sites throughout Greater Vancouver. • **Jul 5** The Devonshire Hotel is brought down by a controlled explosion. • **Sep 13** More than 880 Canadian communities hold 10-km runs in the first Terry Fox Run to raise money for cancer research. • **Sep 25** A new courthouse opens on Begbie Square in New Westminster. • **Oct17** Vancouver police break up a Ku Klux Klan rally celebrating the assassination of Egyptian leader Anwar Sadat. It is the first Klan activity in the city for nearly 50 years. • **Oct** The national edition of the *Globe and Mail* is extended to Vancouver via its satellite printing network. • **Also in 1981** Study of the Fraser River estuary pollution problems results in the Fraser River Estuary Management Program. • Zool Suleman, a Richmond High School student, wins the top Canadian debating championship. • Richmond receives 188 days of rain in 1981, the highest annual level since 1939. Farms produce only 56 per cent of normal yield. • St. Paul's Indian Catholic Church in North Vancouver is designated a National Historic Site. • Dr. Louis Miranda receives the honorary degree of doctor of laws from SFU for being the initiator of the Squamish Nation's written language program in 1975.
1982 Jan 14 Mass-murderer Clifford Olson pleads guilty to the murder of 11 Vancouver-area children and is sentenced to life imprisonment. • **Apr 24** The first peace march against nuclear arms in Vancouver. The annual event grows to be the largest of its kind in North America with up to 100,000 participants. • **Nov 14** Inflation of the 255-tonne B.C. Place Stadium fabric dome, largest of its kind in the world. • **Also in 1982** The Vancouver Food Bank starts as a temporary facility for needy people. By 1989 there are six depots distributing to 15,000 people every month. • Douglas College moves

to downtown New Westminster. • London Farm, restored by the Richmond Historical and Museum Society, opens to the public. • A $15 million addition to Richmond General Hospital is completed. • Surrey Co-op goes into receivership when a demand loan is called in by the B.C. Central Credit Union. A long strike in 1977 and the building of two shopping malls (on borrowed money) had led to financial troubles.
1983 Mar 3 The Surrey Food Bank begins distributing food to the unemployed and needy, operating out of store front premises in the Evergreen Mall at Fraser Hwy. and 152nd St. • **Mar 9** The Royal Yacht *Britannia* sails into Vancouver with the Queen and Prince Philip. At B.C. Place the Queen invites the world to Expo 86. • **Apr 5** The Surrey Festival of Dance, the largest festival of its type in North America, begins, runs to May 7. There are classes in Irish, Polynesian, Highland, ballet, tap, stage and jazz dancing. • **Jun 19** Premier Bill Bennett opens Canada's first domed stadium, the 60,000-seat B.C. Place. • **Jun 29** The *North Shore News* reports none of the five North Shore shipyards (Burrard Yarrows, Vancouver Shipyards, BelAire, Allied and Matsumoto) has any new shipbuilding contracts on the books. It is expected 2,500 workers will be unemployed by July. • **Aug 10** A Solidarity rally at Empire Stadium is held by more 40,000 public-private-sector workers to protest the Social Credit government's restraint policy. • **Oct 8** Official opening of the *Samson V* Maritime Museum. • **Oct 23** The Kuan Yin Temple in Richmond is dedicated. Built by the International Buddhist Society it is the first architecturally authentic Buddhist temple in North America. • **Nov 15** The *Columbian*, B.C.'s oldest newspaper, ceases publication. It had run for 123 years in New Westminster, Victoria and Coquitlam. • **Nov 27** Toronto Argonauts defeat B.C. Lions 18-17 in Vancouver to win the Grey Cup for the first time in 31 years. • **Also in 1983** The M.V. *Terry Fox* is built by Burrard Yarrows in North Vancouver, which has become a world leader in building ice-breakers. • The Vancouver Art Gallery relocates to the newly refurbished 1916 courthouse. • The federal government purchases B.C. Packers harbor in Steveston. To be known as Paramount Harbour it is to accommodate 700 commercial fishing vessels. • Three Richmond men, Lloyd Yodogawa, Dan Milkovich and Grant Kuramoto are gold medallists in judo at the Canada Winter Games. Also Jim Kojima, "Mr. Judo," is named to the Order of Canada for his 40-year-involvement in judo as participant, referee, coach and organizer.
1984 Mar 28 A seven-week strike begins at the *Vancouver Sun* and *Province* newspapers. • **May 25** A "Shame the Johns" operation begins

in Vancouver in an attempt to drive prostitutes' clients from the West End. • **Jun 9** Granville Island lager beer first goes on sale. • **Sep 18** Pope John Paul II makes the first papal visit ever to Vancouver and the Lower Mainland. • **Sep 29** Richmond's Gateway Theatre opens. • **Nov 16** Michael Jackson and his brothers, "The Jackson Five," attract more than 100,000 fans to B.C. Place grossing several million and setting a new Vancouver entertainment record for a three-night stand. • **Also in 1984** Evangelist Billy Graham speaks to 46,000 people at BC Place Stadium. • Karim Rajani, a student at McNair High School in Richmond, is the Canadian National Debating Champion. • Woodwards becomes the first major Vancouver department store to open on Sundays. • The recession results in the largest Surrey tax sale list on record. A total of 633 properties go up for sale for delinquent taxes. • Bryan Adams, from North Vancouver becomes a global superstar with his album *Reckless*.

1985 Jan Hall's Prairie School in South Surrey celebrates its 100th anniversary. It was built on its current site, 18035 8th Ave., in the fall of 1884 and opened for classes in January 1885 with teacher John C. McLennan and 15 students. • **Mar 21** Rick Hansen, paralyzed as a result of an accident begins his around-the-world "Man in Motion" tour by wheelchair. • **Mar 27** Maillardville shopping centre in Coquitlam is destroyed by fire. • **Jun 1** Weldwood of Canada closes its sawmill in South Westminster. Shortage of Douglas fir logs leads the company to consolidate its operations in Squamish. • **Jun 17** The mess hall of the Point Atkinson Second World War II military base in West Vancouver re-opens as Phyllis Munday House for use as a nature house by West Vancouver Girl Guides. Phyllis Munday, a well-known mountaineer, had a life-long association with the guide movement. • **Aug 2** The light at the Stanley Park war memorial commemorating the Japanese-Canadian contribution during World War I is turned back on. It had been extinguished since December 8, 1941. Much decorated veteran Masumi Mitsui, the last surviving Japanese-Canadian World War I veteran, re-lights it. Mitsui dies in 1987 on April 22, one year before Ottawa issues an official apology to Japanese-Canadians for the injustices done to them during World War II. • **Dec 11** Opening of SkyTrain, Vancouver's Advanced Light Rapid Transit system. It follows the same route through Burnaby as the old Interurban tramline. • **Also in 1985** Burrard Dry Dock (formerly Wallace Shipyards) becomes Versatile Pacific Shipyards. • B.C. Lions win the Grey Cup and the street in front of the football club's Whalley headquarters is renamed Lions Way. • The one B.C. Packers

cannery at Steveston cans more salmon in 1985 (11 million kilograms, with a further 5.5 million kilograms frozen) than all the Steveston canneries together in the boom year of 1901 (7 million kilograms). Unlike the earlier period when canneries owned the boats most of the fishboats are now owner-operated. Steveston remains the largest commercial fishing harbor in Canada. • Figures on farm production in 1985 show Surrey's largest farm acreage is in the production of vegetables and fruits. There are 16,500 head of cattle and 845 full-time farmers. • A dwarf-tossing contest at the Flamingo Hotel in Whalley leads to newspaper stories and comment all over North America. • Former Surrey mayor and MLA Bill Vander Zalm and his wife Lillian begin construction of Fantasy Gardens in Richmond. • A downtown revitilization program begins at Horseshoe Bay. • Capers, a natural food store and restaurant, opens at Dundarave in West Vancouver. • Construction begins on the New Westminster Quay. • Burnaby's Ismaili Jamatkhana and Centre opens, the first such purpose-built centre in Canada. • Trinity Western College becomes a university. The only private university in B.C. it stresses leadership, excellence and Christian ethics.

1986 Feb 19 The Lions Gate Bridge is illuminated, a gift from the Guinness family who built the bridge. • **Apr 6** The City of Vancouver celebrates its 100th birthday. • **May 2** Vancouver plays host to the world as Expo 86 opens. • **Jun 27** The Newton Youth Centre opens. • **Jul 19** Westminster Quay Public Market opens. The old city market closes the following February. • **Aug 7** Bill Vander Zalm is sworn in as premier of B.C. • **Summer** SkyBridge construction begins to allow the extension of SkyTrain across the Fraser into Surrey. • **Sep 22** The Alex Fraser Bridge opens linking Delta with New Westminster. • **Oct 13** Expo 86 closes. Attendance, originally projected at 14 million, has topped 22 million. • **Nov 26** The Bank of B.C. sells all its assets to the Hongkong Bank of Canada for an undisclosed price. • **Also in 1986** Joe Fortes, English Bay's first lifeguard, who died in 1922, is named "Citizen of the Century" by the Vancouver Historical Society. He is credited with more than 100 rescues. • Restoration begins of the 1888 CPR Roundhouse as a Vancouver centennial project. • Sun Yat-Sen Gardens opens in Chinatown. • White Spot's original restaurant on Granville St. is destroyed by fire. • Metrotown shopping centre in Burnaby opens. • Lonsdale Quay opens in North Vancouver. • New border facilities are opened at the Pacific Hwy. port of entry in Surrey, a $13 million project which will be the main clearing port for freight trucks. • Burnaby becomes a sister city

to Loughborough in England where Robert Burnaby is buried.

1987 • **Mar 15** West Vancouver celebrates its 75th anniversary. • **May 22** Rick Hansen completes his 26-month around-the-world "Man in Motion" tour when he wheels his chair into Oakridge shopping centre—from which he had started. • **Jul 26** The Federation Cup, the Women's World Team Tennis Championship, is held at Hollyburn Country Club in West Vancouver. It is the first time the Cup has been played in Canada in its 25-year history. • **Oct 15** Queen Elizabeth II opens the Commonwealth Leaders' Conference in Vancouver. • **Also in 1987** Surrey buys the Kodak Bowl from Expo 86, moves it to the Surrey Fair Grounds and renames it the Stetson Bowl. There is seating for 4,200 with room for an equal number of portable seats. • Expo's flagpole, the world's tallest at 84 metres is purchased by Guildford Town Centre's Chev-Olds dealership which is renamed Flag Chev-Olds. Measuring 12 by 24 metres, the flag can be seen from 6 kilometres away. • The Vancouver Trade and Convention Centre opens on the former Expo 86 Canadian Pavilion site. • Surrey is granted a new coat of arms which is presented by an official of the Queen's royal household from London. • The Easthope Brothers Steveston shop closes. For 90 years the company has built marine engines used by B.C.'s fishing fleet.

1988 Apr 23 The Metrotown Save-on-Foods roof collapses during opening ceremonies only minutes after Mayor Copeland has directed evacuation. There are no fatalities. • **Jun** While the prairies suffer from drought, a record rainfall in the Fraser Valley: 144 milimetres. • **Also in 1988** Surrey's Farm Fair celebrates its 100th birthday and changes its name to the Cloverdale Exhibition. • Steveston Buddhist church celebrates its 60th anniversary of the faith's presence. • A Cree language course is offered in the Guildford Park continuing education program. Buffalo Child, a full-blooded Cree, is to be the teacher. • Ray Murao of the Steveston Kendo Club wins Best Fighting Spirit award at World Kendo Tournament. • The vacant Expo site is sold to Li Ka-shing of Hong Kong in one of the largest real estate deals in Canadian history. • B.C. Tel reports 40 per cent of all new homes built in B.C. in 1988 are located in Surrey.

facing page, clockwise from top left:
Chinese Carnival Village, 1936; post office riot, 1938; the last run of Vancouver Streetcar No. 124, 1950; Birks building, built 1912–13, demolished 1974–75; Carrall Street, 1886, before the Great Fire. vca, vp, vp, vp, vca

Sponsored by Oppenheimer Bros.

1989 May 5 SFU opens a downtown Vancouver campus in the historic Spencer building on W. Hastings St., known as the Harbour Centre Campus. • **May 6** Science World opens in the former Expo Preview Centre. • **May 25** Richmond's Bridgepoint Harbour Market opens. • **Jun 3** Garry Point Park in Steveston opens, one of many development projects carried out in Steveston in the late 1980s, some of them controversial. • **Jul** Hwy. 91, the east-west freeway across Lulu Island in Richmond, is completed. The B.C. Summer Games are held in Surrey with 4,000 athletes from all over the province. • **Fall** Cannell Studios locates in North Vancouver. • **Also in 1989** The Whalley All Stars compete in the final baseball game of the Senior Little League World Series. They lose to the defending champions from Taiwan. • The old Lafarge gravel pit in Coquitlam opens as a recreation complex, the 40 hectare Town Centre Park. • Langley joins the GVRD. • The Port of Vancouver handles more imports/exports than any other port in North America; it handles more lumber, grain and coal than any other in Canada. Thirty per cent of exports now go to Japan, almost as much as to the U.S. More than 3,000 foreign vessels dock there in 1989. • The 750-hectare Pacific Spirit Park is created from part of the UBC Endowment Lands. • Dragon boat races in False Creek begin. Today it's a two-weekend event called the Canadian International Dragon Boat Festival.

1990 Mar 16 SkyTrain service to Scott Rd. Station in Surrey begins. • **Apr 15** The Canada Customs building at Pacific Hwy. border crossing is closed for a few hours for safety checks after earthquake tremors shake it. There is minimal damage. • **Midsummer** A multicultural arts festival held at Bear Creek Park in Surrey is the first of its kind in Western Canada. • **Labour Day** The first Molson Vancouver Indy Race takes place on a 2.65 kilometre track around the B.C. Place Stadium. One track-worker is killed while push-starting a disabled vehicle. • **Also in 1990** Vancouver is now North America's third largest film production centre surpassed only by Los Angeles and New York. • The blue box recycling system begins. • 1,200 independent truckers protesting their wages block access to the border for freight trucks. • In Surrey, Barnston Island dairy farmers see a water supply project fail because costs for water supplied from the Indian reserve hook-up are more than the farmers will pay. • Bryan Adams receives the Order of British Columbia and becomes a Member of the Order of Canada. • Westwood Motorsport Park in Coquitlam closes.

1991 Mar 6 The new Bob Prittie Metrotown Branch of the Burnaby Public Library officially

Vancouver hosts a summit meeting between Bill Clinton and Boris Yeltsin

opens. • **Apr 2** Rita Johnson, MLA for Newton in Surrey, becomes Canada's first female premier when she becomes Social Credit's interim party leader after Bill Vander Zalm resigns. • **Jun 30** Oakalla Prison Farm on Burnaby's Deer Lake closes after 79 years. • **Dec** South Surrey's new ice arena opens. It is the only Olympic size arena in B.C. • **Also in 1991** The restoration of the oldest brick building in Vancouver, the Oppenheimer Bros. grocery warehouse at Columbia and Powell, by its new owner, rock star Bryan Adams.

1992 Jan Britannia Heritage Shipyard in Steveston is declared a National Historic Site. Built in 1889-90 as a cannery and converted into a shipyard in 1918 it is the oldest surviving collection of cannery/shipyard buildings on the Fraser. • **May 23** Burnaby's centennial parade to Swangard Stadium with fireworks from atop the BC Tel building. • **Jun 20** The Burnaby Centennial Quilt is unveiled at the Bob Prittie Library in Metrotown. Celebrating Burnaby's history it has taken 18 seniors one year to create. • **Sep 22** The District of Burnaby turns 100 and becomes the City of Burnaby. • **Nov** Richmond's new cultural centre opens. Included in the complex are the new Brighouse Library, Richmond Museum and Archives, an art gallery and a cafeteria. • **Dec** The North Vancouver division of Versatile Pacific Shipyards lays off its last employees. The company would have celebrated its 100th anniversary in 1994. (The Victoria division closes in 1994.) • **Also in 1992** Chief Joe Mathias of the Squamish Nation signs on behalf of the First Nations of B.C. at the B.C. Treaty Commission signing. The agreement between the federal and provincial governments and B.C.'s First Nations establishes a process to negotiate modern-day treaties.

1993 Jan 15 Woodward's, a retail institution in Greater Vancouver for more than 90 years, closes its original downtown store at Hastings and Abbott. The demise of the company follows in June. However, the famous big "W" sign atop the store is a landmark which the people of Vancouver are reluctant to lose. It stays aloft long after the building is put to other uses. • **Mar 27** The restored Parker carousel is set in motion in Burnaby's Village Museum. Built in 1912 in Kansas

it has given pleasure to PNE Playland visitors for more than 50 years. • **Apr 3** Vancouver is the venue for a two-day summit meeting between Presidents Bill Clinton of the United States and Boris Yeltsin of Russia. • **Aug 4** Woodward Place in New Westminster is renamed Royal City Centre. • **Also in 1993** The largest Fraser River salmon return since 1913.

1994 April Vancouver awarded NBA franchise. • **June** Ninety local teams compete in the Canadian International Dragon Boat Festival, together with many other Canadian and international teams. • **Jun 14** Vancouver Canucks lose the Stanley Cup to the New York Rangers in the seventh game of a seven-game series. After the game a crowd riots in downtown Vancouver smashing shop windows and looting. • **Jun 25** The Gulf of Georgia Cannery in Steveston celebrates its 100th birthday and re-opens to the public with new exhibits commemorating Canada's West Coast fishing industry. • **Jun 29** At Vancouver Shipyards in North Vancouver Premier Michael Harcourt announces an $800 million overhaul of the B.C. ferry system including construction of three high-speed catamarans for the Horseshoe Bay to Nanaimo run. The ships, carrying 200 passenger vehicles each, will be built in B.C. • **Jul 1** West Vancouver Museum and Archives opens in Gertrude Lawson House. • **Aug 24** A fire at the Alberta Wheat Pool dock forces closure of the Second Narrows Bridge for six hours and the evacuation of the PNE due to potential danger of explosion. • **Sep 17** GM Place opens in downtown Vancouver. • **Sep 18** Point Atkinson Lighthouse in West Vancouver is designated a National Historic Site. • **Sep** The crash site is discovered on Mt. Cheam near Chilliwack of a TCA Lockheed Lodestar that disappeared on April 28, 1947 with 15 people on board. • **Oct. 17** • Vancouver's NBA Grizzlies play first game at GM Place. • **Nov 27** The B.C. Lions defeat Baltimore 26-23 to win the Grey Cup before hometown fans in Vancouver. It is the Lions' first Grey Cup victory in nine years and the third in their 40-year history. • **Also in 1994** After founding and operating Grace Hospital for 65 years the Salvation Army withdraws and the facility's name is changed to British Columbia Women's Hospital and Health Centre.

1995 Jan 1 Matsqui and Abbotsford merge, to be known as the City of Abbotsford.

Compiled with assistance from Shirley Mooney and Chuck Davis.

For events from 1995 on, see the article "1995-1997 . . . and stuff keeps right on happening" by Shane McCune.

Before Narvaez
Norman Newton

THE HISTORY OF VANCOUVER begins, as it should, in myth. A legend states, "In earlier times this Fraser River resembled an enormous dish that stored up food for all mankind . . ." In the beginning, there were no deciduous trees, only evergreens; there were only clams and mussels in the sea, since the more highly developed fish had not yet appeared; and there were no mammals at all. Then God created groups of people in various places, and one of these he settled at Musqueam (now on the outskirts of Vancouver, just off Southwest Marine Drive).

After man degenerated from his first state and became wicked, a hero appeared out of the western sea. He went through the disordered land, re-establishing civil society and turning various persons or creatures, most of them ill-disposed, to stone. These stone images may still be unearthed, the story continues, though it is dangerous to find them.

The legend may refer to the stone images of the Marpole culture. This culture, named after the Vancouver suburb in which its relics were first found, seems to have been the true ancestor of that village civilization encountered by such explorers as Narvaez and Fraser. According to the archaeologists, it was preceded by a much simpler culture. It began to flower around 200 B.C., coming to its end, or perhaps just changing into the culture the explorers found, about 500 A.D.

The class structure was a kind of democratic aristocracy. The gentlefolk were expected to have better table manners than the vulgar, to be generous in their attitude towards the commoners who depended on them, to be modest except on those ceremonial occasions when a recital of ancient rights was required, and to be virtuous in their sexual lives. Had they shown in daily life the formal hauteur expected of Haida and Tsimshian chiefs, they would have been thought overbearing and pretentious.

The evidence indicates that the Marpole people lived in large plank houses and used dugout canoes. Their wooden artifacts have perished and what we have are some of their tools, copper ornaments and fine stone carvings which display, says art historian Paul S. Wingert, "a mastery that is not surpassed or often duplicated in the Indian arts north of Mexico." Similar stone carvings have been found on Vancouver Island and the Gulf Islands, up the Fraser Valley, along the valley of the Columbia, and as far north as Alaska. We have some knowledge of the art styles and material culture of the Marpole people,

> # The class structure was a kind of democratic aristocracy. The gentlefolk were expected to have better table manners ...to be generous in their attitude towards the commoners ...

but only a sketchy idea of their beliefs. From the evidence of one burial, copper was a metal of great symbolic importance. In that burial, two women had been killed and buried with a young chief, presumably to accompany him into the other world.

At the time of the first European explorers the area of greatest settlement was on the southern shore of Point Grey, near Sea Island, where there were three villages, arranged in a semicircle around a little bay. The largest of these contained 76 shed-roofed houses, set end to end, and constructed of rough-hewn planks. They were a kind of row housing, made up of a number of units, each with some 6 metres of frontage and 18 metres of depth. There were no connecting doors between them. In some cases the entire complex was surrounded by a stockade of half-logs. Here and there, close to the houses, were wooden statues or totem poles. However, the class structure was less rigid than the heraldic structures of the Haida and Tsimshian, who were at the centre of "totem pole" culture.

Most of the prominent natural features in the Vancouver area have legends attached to them. In this respect we live in a mythical landscape whose features are as well delineated as those of ancient Greece, Egypt or Mesoamerica. It is enriching, when one sees Siwash Rock, to be reminded that it is the petrified form of T'elch, the devoted husband and father, or to speculate about the hero who landed long ago at Point Grey and the murderous warrior who was turned into a great rock near New Westminster when he attempted to thwart the hero's civilizing mission. (The rock is said to have been buried by engineers when they constructed the approaches to Pattullo Bridge.) Even the stars over Vancouver have a local origin, since this hero created them, too. But the mythology of these peoples, it should be remembered, hid a profound traditional wisdom beneath its charming surface naiveté.

The Linkman Press, publishers of The Greater Vancouver Book, was established in 1993 by Chuck Davis and John Cochlin. The Greater Vancouver Book is the first in what is intended to be a never-ending assortment of books on a variety of subjects. As a fond tribute to and remembrance of the 1976 original, *The Vancouver Book*, The Linkman Press is pleased to sponsor the above article which appeared in the original book.

Aboriginal History Before European Contact
Andrew Scott

THE PADDLERS WHO greeted José Maria Narvaez as he and his crew sailed cautiously into English Bay had a profound knowledge of the place we call Vancouver. They and their ancestors had lived in the area—either year-round or just during the summer months—for hundreds of generations. The mild climate and an abundance of food had allowed them to develop a creative, self-sufficient culture. Their villages and camps dotted the evergreen shorelines. But even by June 1791, when the Spanish strangers first visited them, the rich, complex way of life of the Coast Salish was beginning to change.

No one knows how many human beings occupied the region at the time of the first European contact. Habitation patterns varied dramatically with the season, and two smallpox epidemics (in the 1770s and about 1800, believed to have been spread from tribe to tribe ahead of the Europeans) had reduced the population. An estimate of 3,000 to 5,000 made by Chief August Jack Khahtsahlanough in the 1930s cannot be verified. Bruce Macdonald's fascinating historical atlas, *Vancouver: A Visual History,* identifies numerous seasonal camps and at least five villages established within Vancouver city boundaries over the past 3,000 years. Sixty per cent of them, he noted in 1992, have been obliterated by urban development.

The Musqueam people lived round the mouth of the Fraser River and along the shores of Burrard Inlet and English Bay. The Squamish, whose main villages were beside the Squamish and Cheakamus rivers above the head of Howe Sound, also inhabited Burrard Inlet and English Bay. Most Squamish camps were used only in summer, but some were substantial and may have been populated year-round. The Musqueam spoke Halkomelem, a language used throughout the Fraser Valley, while the Squamish spoke a separate tongue. Still, there was much interaction and marriage between the two nations.

The Kwantlen, whose villages were near New Westminster, controlled territory farther east, and the Tsawwassen lived to the south, in Delta and Richmond. North Vancouver's Burrard band claims descent from a separate Halkomelem-speaking nation, the Tsleil'waututh. Other Coast Salish tribal groups—Cowichan, Saanich, Nanaimo—occupied large seasonal camps while the Fraser River salmon were running.

In 1791 the Squamish nation had three principal habitation sites in what is now Vancouver: Sun'ahk ("inside, at the head"), on the east side of Kitsilano Point; Khwaykhway ("masks"), where Lumberman's Arch now stands in Stanley Park; and Be'yullmough ("good spring water"), at Jericho Beach. Archaeological evidence suggests that Locarno Beach, just west of Jericho, was also an important native site 2,500 to 3,500 years ago. Other Squamish villages were located on the shores of North and West Vancouver.

Mahli and Stsulawh, the two main villages of the Musqueam (Wh'muthkweyum—"people of the grass"), were located at the mouth of the North Arm of the Fraser River, on the site of the current Musqueam Band reserve. The Musqueam have lived there for over 3,000 years, and Mahli and Stsulawh may have had a combined population of over 2,000 in the 18th century. The villagers charmed Dionisio Galiano, commander of one of two tiny Spanish schooners that explored the Vancouver area in the summer of 1792 (and met George Vancouver doing the same thing). "Their liveliness, grace and talent engaged all our attention," he wrote. "They displayed an unequalled affability together with a warlike disposition."

Slightly upriver, along the Marpole foreshore, a five-metre-deep deposit of shell and bone known as the Great Fraser Midden tells a story of human occupation over 3,000 years ago, when this spot was right at the mouth of the river. The residents of Marpole were skilled artists; exquisite stone and bone carvings have been found there. Farther upstream, even older habitations have been identified. On the south shore of the river, east of the Alex Fraser Bridge in Delta municipality, the St. Mungo and Glenrose sites also marked the mouth of the steadily advancing Fraser delta at one time. They are believed to date back over 9,000 years, to the period after the glaciers of the last ice age had retreated from this part of the world.

First Nation oral traditions, combined with the reports of early explorers, provide a fair amount of detail about Vancouver's first inhabitants and their society. Long-standing kinship patterns, which evolved between related communities, determined the social status of individuals, as well as the fishing, hunting and gathering rights of families. At the bottom of the pecking order were slaves, captured in intertribal warfare, who became the property of high-ranking chiefs and performed menial tasks. Formality attended every stage of life. Infant's heads were bound with cedar pads to make the growing skull wedge-shaped as a wide, flat forehead was considered beautiful. The dead, wrapped in blankets or mats, were placed in boxes and lodged on elevated platforms. Decorative and ceremonial items—like dentalia shells, mother-of-pearl, copper, iron and jade—were eagerly traded with neighboring tribes, as were a wide range of foodstuffs, textiles and domestic materials of all kinds.

Simon Fraser, who reached the mouth of the Fraser in 1808 but was chased back upstream by hostile Musqueam warriors, recalled their village as a "fort 1,500 feet [457.2 metres] in length and 90 feet [27.4 metres] in breadth." What he more likely saw was a row of joined cedar plankhouses, the interiors divided by hanging mats to form spacious rooms for family groups. Small smoke- and sweathouses were built separately. Farther up the river valley, Fraser described a six-metre-high structure. "The posts or pillars are nearly 3 feet in diameter at the base," he wrote, "In one of these posts is an oval opening answering the purpose of a door . . . Above, on the outside, are carved a human figure large as life, and there are other figures in imitation of beasts and birds. The fires are in the centre and the smoke goes out an opening at top."

Fraser wrote about the patterned robes that the Fraser Valley people wove, and mentions the little white dogs that were bred and greatly valued for their woolly fur. The cedar canoes, hollowed by adze and fire, then stretched to shape, impressed him; fashioned from single logs, some were 10 metres long. Cedar bark, roots, reeds and animal skins and furs were used to make containers, clothing and other domestic articles. In his journal, Fraser recalls being offered fish oil, sturgeon, dried oysters and raspberries to eat, as well as salmon cooked with hot stones in wooden receptacles.

While the region's early residents subsisted mainly on salmon—catching the life-giving fish with specialized equipment like trawl and dip nets and weirs, then smoking it for winter use—their other food sources were numerous. Deer, elk, bear and goat were hunted with bow and arrow, as were many types of birds, which might also be netted or snared. Seal, porpoise and sturgeon were taken with cleverly designed harpoons, the heads of which were tied to lines and separated from the shafts on contact. Shellfish were gathered, also fruit and berries, edible roots and the wapato or Indian potato, which grew beside the Fraser.

Preserving and storing food in summer enabled people to live comfortably through the wet, cool winters and gave them time to develop distinctive ceremonies and customs. Ritual dances were performed, accompanied by singing and drumming; feasts were held, stories told and games played. Sacred and utilitarian objects were carved from wood, stone and bone. The intertribal, gift-giving tradition of the potlatch, which conferred status and power on the host, was prevalent.

Important ceremonies in the Greater Vancouver area sometimes involved a dancer wearing a feathered costume and a plumed, bug-eyed skhwaykhwey mask. Although skhwaykhwey masks and rattles were found throughout the region, their use, according to old stories, may have originated in Stanley Park, where the mask gave its name to Khwaykhway village. Other tales explained the origins of the land and those who inhabited it, including supernatural beings and animals, and provided everyday events with a dense foundation of myth.

The entire landscape, in fact, was alive with meaning for Vancouver's original inhabitants. That meaning, which lingers on in ancient placenames and in legends of rock and lake and cliff and cove, is still sacred to their descendants. Although their numbers were decimated by European disease and their way of life altered forever by a voracious occupation, Vancouver's First Nations continue to play an essential role in the city's cultural mosaic. The landscape we see today is the same one seen by aboriginal people hundreds, even thousands, of years ago. Their memories, passed down and kept alive by countless generations, connect those who live here now with an older, deeper spirit of the place we call home.

Siwash Rock, Stanley Park. cva

Early Coastal Explorers
Heather Conn

LONG BEFORE 1791, when the first major exploration and charting of waters around Vancouver took place, native people travelled the region by canoe. When Captain James Cook arrived in 1778 at Nootka Sound on Vancouver Island's west coast, the natives believed his crew were transformed fish. "One white man had a real hooked nose," retells Winifred David, whose husband's Mowachaht (Nootka) ancestors greeted Cook's ship and passed down this oral story. "And one of the men was saying to this other guy, he must have been a dog salmon, that guy . . . Look at that one, he's a humpback [salmon]."

Juan Perez in the *Santiago* made the first Spanish voyage to the Northwest Coast in 1774. Like Britain, Spain longed to discover the Northwest Passage. Control of this passage, believed to link the Pacific and Atlantic oceans across the top of North America, promised trade. Dutch, British and French navigation on the Northwest Coast threatened Spain. Russians had already colonized what is now Alaska and their fur trading stimulated coastal exploration in the 1770s. Spaniards had colonized the Pacific Coast near San Francisco and made brief trips farther north. But Spain wanted to boost her sovereignty claim to this region. So between 1774 and 1779, Spain sent three separate expeditions to explore the northern Pacific Coast. That's when Cook arrived at Nootka Sound via the South Pacific and followed the coast from Oregon to Alaska. But no ship had yet reached the Strait of Georgia.

For the next few years, war replaced exploration. Britain fought the American colonies to crush their bid for independence while Spain and France, to support the colonies, maintained ships in the Atlantic. But exploration resumed after the American Revolution ended in 1783. More than 100 trading ships, mostly from Britain and America, arrived at the coast between 1785 and 1792. French ships navigated parts of the coast in 1786. John Meares visited Nootka Sound in 1788 and helped British fur-traders keep an almost constant presence there. This diminished Spain's historical claim to the site, which was still believed to be part of the mainland. In 1789 Alejandro Malaspina received orders to check on Spain's new settlement at Nootka Sound, which he did, and to discover the Northwest Passage, which he did not.

Europeans first ventured into Vancouver's surrounding waters in July 1791. Spanish navigator José Maria Narvaez explored the Strait of Georgia for three weeks. He sailed "a line of water that was more sweet than salty" between what is present-day Point Roberts, Washington and Point Grey. He saw openings in the land but did not realize that these formed the mouths of the Fraser River. Narvaez thought that Point Grey was an island surrounded by other islands, and called "them" Islas de Langara. On his chart of this region Narvaez marked three squares on today's north shore of Burrard Inlet. Evidence indicates that these were native villages, the first recorded dwellings in Greater Vancouver.

In the summer of 1792 British and Spanish ships appeared in the area. Captain George Vancouver, Cook's former apprentice, led his expedition in the sloop *Discovery*. They anchored at Birch Bay, then travelled up Georgia Strait in smaller boats. The Spaniards, who had sailed from Mexico to Nootka, used Narvaez's chart to explore the area. Their two schooners, one under Dionisio Alcala Galiano, anchored off Point Grey. Both nations' expeditions sailed up Burrard Inlet and the east coast of Vancouver Island. Galiano explored Indian Arm, then shared his information with Vancouver, who passed the mouth of the Fraser River but decided that its shoals precluded channel navigation. Vancouver produced meticulous maps of the area between 39° and 52° north latitude. He examined the Strait of Juan de Fuca (whose namesake explorer had wrongly charted the waterway at 47° and 48° north latitude), and realized that it offered no source to the Northwest Passage. Vancouver charted more of this shoreline in one summer than any predecessor. He found Howe Sound "a dreary, comfortless region."

Britain became Spain's ally in the French Revolution. But by 1795 Spain's influence declined and she withdrew from the West Coast. Britain now ruled the region. Today, coastal names still evoke Spain's former glory. Vancouver relied on Spanish charts and never changed original Spanish names. Explorers did not appear again in Vancouver until 1808. That spring, Simon Fraser of the North West Company visited the area to establish trading posts. Navigating the Fraser River, he reached its mouth on July 2, but not the open sea. Two years before, he had approached the Fraser overland, thinking it was the Columbia. But this time he found that the nearby latitude was 49°, which ruled out the Columbia, as its entrance is 46° 20′.

Vancouver's era of coastal exploration ended here as overland travellers—from eastern Hudson's Bay Company sites to the Fraser River Gold Rush—sought furs and gold. They formed the roots of permanent settlement, resulting in the ultimate exclusion of Vancouver's first residents—the native people— from most of their traditional lands.

Archaeology in Greater Vancouver
Roy Carlson

"What are these things, who made them, and how old are they?"

ARCHAEOLOGISTS HAVE BEEN ACTIVE here for more than a century. In 1895 Charles Hill-Tout, a New Westminster teacher, published *Later Prehistoric Man in British Columbia,* which brought together the results of research into the local mounds of earth and clam shells as well as the uses of stone tools found in farmers' fields. Hill-Tout asked, "What are these things, who made them, and how old are they?" Today most of these questions can be answered. There are many professional archaeologists working in the universities and colleges of Greater Vancouver and as consultants employed by environmental firms. The archaeology branch in Victoria oversees the implementation of legislation, issues permits for excavations, and maintains the master file of the thousands of archaeological sites.

The oldest known site in Greater Vancouver area is at the Glenrose Cannery in Surrey. A walk on the beach there reveals both the occasional "pebble tool," a simple artifact made by taking a cobble and hammering it with another rock to remove flakes and form a sharp edge, and the stubs of water-logged posts protruding from the beach deposits. These posts have been interpreted as the remains of a fish weir and dated by radiocarbon to 4,500 years ago. Excavations in the 1970s on the rise of land behind the beach cross-sectioned a deep cultural deposit with the lower layers dating to 8,000 years ago. At that time pebble tools and rather simple flaked stone leaf-shaped knives and spear points were found. The artifacts from Glenrose are very similar to those found on the central coast at Namu dated at 9,700 years, at the Milliken site near Yale at 9,000 years and at the Bear Cove site on northern Vancouver Island at 8,000 years ago. All of these early sites are situated at places where fish or sea mammals could be taken. Shellfish remains are scarce in these early sites whereas sites younger than 5,000 years ago are typically "shell middens" made up of masses of clamshells.

A hundred years ago the area on the North Arm of the Fraser River opposite the east end of Sea Island was the site of a huge shell midden, up to at least 5 metres in depth, which covered 1.8 hectares and was known as either the Marpole site, the Eburne Mound or the Great Fraser Midden. Hill-Tout excavated there as have many archaeologists since his time. The centre of the site is approximately the Fraser Arms Hotel on Marine Drive. Marpole shows a very rich culture with tools made by grinding and polishing stone, ornaments of hand hammered native copper, sculptured stone bowls, and bone and antler carvings indicative of a well-developed ceremonial life. The site was occupied between approximately 2,500 and 1,500 years ago before the extensive delta at the mouth of the Fraser had reached its present size. Other sites of this time period on the Strait of Georgia and lower Fraser show much the same configuration of culture. In Greater Vancouver excavations in such sites have taken place at Locarno Beach, Crescent Beach, Point Grey, at Whalen farm and Beach Grove on Boundary Bay, at the St. Mungo Cannery near the south end of the Alex Fraser Bridge, on the Pitt River and at several sites in Tsawwassen near the ferry dock. Several of these sites pre-date Marpole and show assemblages of artifacts that are transitional in style between Marpole site and the earlier Glenrose assemblages.

The best known excavated late period sites—those that date within the last 1,500 years—are several sites on the Musqueam Reserve, the Belcarra Park site on Indian Arm and parts of the Crescent Beach and Beach Grove sites. There are differences in artifacts found at these later sites, but there are also many continuities from earlier periods. What archaeologists see in the archaeological record is a gradual change from the early flaked stone tools of the pre-5,000 period to the elaborate culture of Marpole times to the culture of the native Salish-speaking peoples who were here at the time of the early explorers.

Exhibits of local archaeological remains can be found in the Museum of Anthropology at UBC and the Museum of Archaeology and Ethnology at SFU. The Vancouver Museum at Vanier Park has a large collection of artifacts from the St. Mungo and Marpole sites, although no artifacts are currently on display.

The department of archaeology at SFU offers an undergraduate major program as well as graduate degrees in archaeology. UBC offers a specialization in archaeology as part of its anthropology programs. Capilano, Douglas, Langara and Kwantlen offer undergraduate courses in B.C. archaeology including evening courses. The Archaeology Society of British Columbia sponsors a monthly lecture at the Vancouver Museum and publishes a newsletter, *The Midden.* Technical publications are available from Archaeology Press at SFU and from UBC Press.

Simon Fraser—Explorer
Barbara Rogers

Simon Fraser, CVA

SIMON FRASER COULD be called the founding father of British Columbia because he built the first colonial trading posts west of the Rockies, enabling the British Crown to eventually claim the land. He is, however, best known for his daring exploration of the great river which bears his name.

Descended from a noble Scottish Highland family, the Lovat Frasers, he was the youngest son of Simon Fraser of Culbokie and Isabel Grant of Duldreggan. In September 1773 the family emigrated to America on the SS *Pearl* and settled in Albany, New York. Simon Jr. was born in the hamlet of Mapleton, Hoosick Township on May 20, 1776, the very eve of the American Revolution. Simon's Loyalist father was captured at the Battle of Bennington and died a prisoner in Albany jail. His widowed mother fled with her family to Canada in 1784.

Uncle John Fraser, a Montreal judge, took charge of Simon's education and when the boy turned 16 secured him a clerical position with the famous North West Company. In 1793 Simon was sent to the Athabascan wilderness to learn his trade at the isolated Peace River Nor'Wester posts. By 1802 he was appointed one of the company's youngest partners. In 1805 he was chosen for the important role of expanding the company's trade to the land beyond the Rockies and to explore the river (then believed to be the Columbia) to its mouth. Between 1805 and 1807 he established the first four forts west of the Rockies at McLeod, Stuart and Fraser Lakes and Fort George. He named this new wilderness domain New Caledonia.

On May 22, 1808, Simon Fraser began the expedition which has been described as one of the greatest explorations in North America—the Fraser River with its whirlpools, treacherous currents and perilous rapids. He set off from Stuart Lake with two clerks, John Stuart and Jules Quesnel, 19 voyageurs and two Indian guides. Fraser's personal qualities of courage, determination, leadership and remarkable insight into human nature would all be tested during the greatest adventure of his life.

The group encountered thousands of First Nations peoples who had never before seen Europeans. Without their hospitality, assistance and guidance the expedition would have been impossible, a fact frequently acknowledged by the explorer. He learned to announce his arrival and intentions by always sending ambassadors ahead to inform the next village.

The river, even more dangerous in the June freshet, presented insurmountable challenges and, once embarked, the towering precipices made it impossible to land. After surviving numerous near drownings and upset canoes even the determined Fraser was, at last, convinced that it was impossible to continue by water.

Reluctantly, he cached the canoes near Leon Creek and continued on foot which brought new trials. At the Black Canyon they were forced to follow Indian guides as they climbed forbidding cliffs using intricate scaffolds, bridges and ladders hundreds of feet above the swirling water. One missed step would be their last.

Entering the Fraser Valley their greatest threat would be *man*. Their sojourn in the Fraser Valley was brief, from June 28 to July 8, but their lives were in constant danger. Without canoes and with few provisions, Fraser was forced to rely on the natives for both. His excitement grew when he learned that the ocean was within a day's travel.

Problems arose at an unidentified "mystery" village near present-day Fort Langley where Fraser was amazed at the size of a communal cedar-plank house 195 metres long and 15 metres broad. At first all was well. The group was hospitably received and the chief promised to lend them his large canoe for the next day's dash to the ocean. The residents were fascinated by the strange visitors' pale skins and blue and grey eyes. They called them Sky People. When the wondrous trade goods were spread out to dry, the young braves watched with avaricious eyes. During the night a few braves helped themselves.

July 2 should have been Fraser's day of triumph. Instead it was a long trying day in which they barely escaped with their lives. The thefts discovered, the culprits were kicked which, though considered an appropriate punishment by Europeans of that era, to the natives was a deadly insult. They resolved to kill the Sky People. The chief refused to lend his canoe. Fraser was aghast. The whole success of his mission depended on obtaining transportation. While he used all his persuasive powers, an almost comical tug-of-war took place for the canoe. Eventually the chief relented and, with some of his men, accompanied Fraser.

At the Kwantlen summer village of Kikait, opposite present day New Westminster, Fraser learned the Kwantlens were at war with the coastal Musqueams. The chief's followers refused to let him embark. Fraser was forced to commandeer the canoe and leave without a guide. Worse, he was unable to honor the native protocol of announcing his arrival and purpose. Consequently, when they arrived at Musqueam they were considered enemies. Villagers ran to fetch their warriors. Curiosity overcoming caution Fraser went ashore to examine a huge community house 457 metres in length. Warned to return to their canoe, they found it abandoned high and dry by the ebbing tide. Their armed Kwantlen pursuers, seeing the group's predicament, closed in, joined by the Musqueam warriors who "began to make their appearance from every direction howling like so many wolves, brandishing their war clubs." The crew desperately dragged their canoe to deep water, threatening their opponents with their firearms. Unable to continue they were forced to turn back up the river.

They paddled at great speed arriving at dawn at the "mystery" village, where they hoped to obtain provisions. The chief refused and demanded the return of his canoe. Fraser reluctantly decided to head back to New Caledonia. Their Kwantlen pursuers then arrived and encouraged the villagers to pillage the visitor's goods. The next few minutes were chaotic. Fraser pretended to be in a great rage, which restored order but once again they were obliged to take the canoe by force, leaving a blanket as payment. The chase was on! The day was to end in even greater disappointment, for when observations were taken, Fraser realized that the river they were on was not the Columbia. All their efforts had been in vain!

But their immediate problem was to extricate themselves from their perilous situation. Fraser's crew paddled all night hoping to beat their pursuers to the next village in order to secure badly needed provisions. However, the chief soon arrived to demand his canoe. The natives became aggressive and violent. The young explorer now found himself in a similar situation to that of Captain Cook in Hawaii, where the outcome was fatal to the great navigator. Fraser described their predicament in the formal language of the day: "It was then, that our situation might really be considered as critical. Placed upon a small sandy Island, few in number without canoes,

without provisions, and surrounded by upwards of 700 barbarians. However, our resolution did not forsake us." Fraser's men were forced to threaten the hostile natives with their guns until they could embark. The chase resumed. For the next two days other, previously friendly riverside villagers, stirred up by their tormenters, joined in the pursuit.

July 6 was yet another trying day. Somewhere between Hope and Yale they came to a large camp of hostile, armed Indians. The natives tried to seize the canoe. In the melee, Fraser's canoe was caught in a strong current which carried the men down some rapids.

With heroic exertions the skillful voyageurs managed to land at the foot of a large hill. Stuart and some of the crew immediately jumped ashore to set up a defence. Their pursuers withdrew but kept watch. By now the crew were half-starved, and exhausted by the continuous paddling and lack of sleep. Traumatized by the non-stop, hostile harassment, some of them refused to re-embark. Almost hysterical with fear they threatened to disperse overland rather than be killed on the water. Fraser jumped ashore to reason with the mutinous crew. In turn he remonstrated, pleaded, threatened, endeavouring to show them the folly of their plan. Eventually, he appealed to their mutual spiritual belief and succeeded in getting everyone to shake hands and take an oath of loyalty: "I solemnly swear before Almighty God that I shall sooner perish than forsake in distress any of our crew during the present voyage." This brief ceremony over, Fraser had everyone change into their best apparel. The Indians were astonished to see their prey in such good spirits, noisily laughing and singing as they paddled away from the Lower Mainland. Awed by this unusual behavior the non-plussed pursuers retreated downriver.

Simon Fraser spent 10 more gruelling years in the fur trade before finally retiring in 1818. He settled on family land in St. Andrews West, near Cornwall, Ontario, where he farmed and operated mills. On June 7, 1820, he married Catherine MacDonell of Leek and they raised five sons and three daughters. Together for 42 years, they died within hours of each other. Simon on August 18, 1862, and Catherine a few hours later on August 19. They were buried in the same grave in the small Catholic cemetery at St. Andrews West.

Over a century after his death, a new Vancouver university searched for a suitable name. Since the Fraser River could be seen from the Burnaby Mountain site, the name "Simon Fraser University" was chosen. At the opening ceremonies, on September 9, 1965, while his kinsman, Lord Lovat, officiated, Simon's second great-grandson, Donald Fraser of Fargo, North Dakota, beamed proudly from the audience.

Simon Fraser University's more than 600 faculty members annually attract $20 million in research funding. In 1989, SFU opened Harbour Centre campus in Vancouver to serve the life-long education needs of people in the downtown area.

Captain George Vancouver
W. Kaye Lamb

CAPTAIN GEORGE VANCOUVER, the first European to explore the inner waters of Burrard Inlet, was born in King's Lynn, Norfolk, on June 22, 1757. He was of Dutch ancestry, descended from the titled Van Coeverden family, whose castle at Coeverden was long an important fortress on the eastern frontier with Germany. Vancouver's great-grandfather married an Englishwoman; his grandfather seems to have spent most of his later years in England. George's father, John Jasper Vancouver, was assistant collector of customs at King's Lynn (actually the functioning official, as the position of collector was a sinecure). His mother, Bridget Berners, came from an old county family that numbered Sir Richard Grenville, of *Revenge* fame, among their ancestors.

King's Lynn was then a busy seaport, and John Jasper had many contacts in maritime and official circles. In 1772, when Cook was preparing to sail on the second of his three great voyages to the Pacific, no doubt it was through those contacts that Jasper was able to bring young George to Cook's attention and have him appointed to the *Resolution*. It was a much sought after position and meant that Vancouver would receive a rigorous training in seamanship, navigation and surveying under Cook and also under William Wales, a noted astronomer, who was serving on the *Resolution*. A decade later, when Vancouver was naming a point on the British Columbia coast after Wales, he noted in his journal that it was to Wales' "kind instruction" that he was indebted "for that information which has enabled me to traverse and delineate these lonely regions."

The chief purpose of Cook's second voyage was to ascertain whether a legendary antarctic continent actually existed. After summer exploration of the Antarctic region, and winter exploration of the South Pacific, in July 1775 the *Resolution* was back in England. But almost immediately Cook began planning for a third voyage, one that would take him on a search for the long sought for Northwest Passage. He once again sailed in the *Resolution,* with Vancouver appointed to her smaller companion, the *Discovery.*

The *Resolution* and *Discovery* returned to England in October 1780, and Vancouver applied for and passed examinations that qualified him for promotion to lieutenant. His first appointment was to the sloop *Martin.* Early in 1782 she was sent to the West Indies Station, where Vancouver was to spend the better part of five years. His last and most important spell of duty there was in the *Europa,* flagship of Commodore Sir

Alan (later Admiral Lord) Gardner, in whom he found a friend and influential patron. It was also in the *Europa* that Vancouver met four young men who were to figure in his own survey of the Northwest Coast—Peter Puget, Joseph Baker, Joseph Whidbey and Zachary Mudge. Vancouver himself rose to be 1st Lieutenant (second-in-command) of the *Europa,* and his friendship with Gardner became doubly important when, not long after the ship returned to England, Gardner became a member of the board of admiralty.

Meanwhile developments were taking place in the maritime fur trade that were to have important consequences for George Vancouver. Russian fur hunters were advancing through the Aleutian Islands toward the mainland of Alaska and its panhandle; farther south, British and American traders were gathering furs along the Northwest Coast. Spain, which claimed exclusive sovereignty over the coast from California to Cook Inlet, became anxious and sent expeditions north from Mexico to explore and to gauge the seriousness of the threat offered by the fur traders. In 1789 Spain decided to occupy Nootka Sound and a fortified post was built there. It was commanded by Estéban José Martinez, an ardent nationalist, who seized three British ships that entered the harbor and imprisoned their crews. The ships were controlled by a partnership that included John Meares, who had himself traded on the coast in 1788.

The first inkling of these events reached London in January 1790. In April Meares, who had hurried home from China, gave an exaggerated account of the damage suffered. Britain demanded satisfaction from Spain (whose claim to sovereignty of the coast was not recognized by Britain) and war became likely. Vancouver had been appointed second-in-command of a projected surveying expedition, but preparations for it were suspended when war threatened. Recalled to combat duty, he was appointed to the *Courageux,* a unit in a powerful squadron that became known as the Spanish Armament. Significantly, Gardner was her captain.

A convention with Spain signed in October ended the war threat and sharpened the focus of the expedition. Vancouver was recalled to London and in December was appointed its commander. He was given three assignments: first, to meet a Spanish commissioner at Nootka and settle the damage claims arising from the 1789 seizures; secondly, to make a detailed survey of the coast from California to Alaska; and, thirdly, to try to ascertain once and for all whether an entry to a Northwest Passage (or a navigable passage that extended far inland) actually existed. The voyage was clearly intended to supplement Cook's voyage of 1778, and to fill in the gaps in his charts occasioned by the bad weather that had driven him offshore.

There has been a Hotel Vancouver in the city for more than 100 years. The first opened May 16, 1887, just one week before the first transcontinental passenger train arrived in Vancouver. The second, much larger, hotel—a spectacular addition to the growing city's skyline—replaced it in 1916. And in 1939 the present magnificent hotel opened to immediate fame when the touring King George VI and Queen Elizabeth were first guests in the luxuriously-appointed Royal Suite.

Vancouver's ships were the *Discovery*, 337 tons (not Cook's ship of the same name—a new vessel specially purchased and outfitted), and the much smaller *Chatham*. They sailed from Falmouth on April 1, 1791, and followed Cook's route to the Northwest Coast—the Cape of Good Hope, Australia (the southwest corner of which Vancouver was the first to explore), New Zealand, Tahiti and Hawaii. It was a year-long voyage; the ships reached the coast of California in April 1792 and entered the Strait of Juan de Fuca in June.

The Spanish commissioner Vancouver was to meet at Nootka was Juan Francisco de la Bodega y Quadra, commander of the forces based on San Blas, Mexico. No stranger to the Northwest Coast, Quadra had made a remarkable voyage of discovery north to Alaska in 1775 in the tiny schooner *Sonora*. The *Daedalus*, a transport, bringing supplies and additional instructions from the admiralty, was to meet Vancouver at Nootka. Naturally he was anxious to see the instructions before opening negotiations with Quadra, and to allow time for a late arrival of the *Daedalus* he decided to spend some weeks in exploration.

The admiralty thought the survey of the coast could probably be completed in two seasons, but due largely to Vancouver's attention to detail, it actually required three. His survey plan has been aptly described as being "rendered infallible by its simplicity"—he would endeavor to trace every foot of the continental shore, a strategy that would be time-consuming, but which should prevent any bay or inlet of consequence from being overlooked.

The 1792 season (the most interesting of the three from a regional point of view) was shortened by the necessity of meeting Quadra, but Vancouver nevertheless made important discoveries. The first of these was Puget Sound, the entrance to which the Spanish had noted but not entered. Vancouver was surprised to find it required a month to sort out its maze of channels and islands. He also noted the survey could be carried out only by the ships' boats; even the *Chatham*, let alone the *Discovery*, was too large for the task. This determined the basic pattern of the Vancouver survey: the large ships would anchor in a suitable haven and the boats would then fan out to examine the adjacent coastline in detail.

Birch Bay was one such anchorage, and it was from it that two boats, commanded by Vancouver and Puget, set out on the survey that would include the inner waters of Burrard Inlet. On June 13, 1792, they passed through the First Narrows and spent the rest of the day ascertaining the extent of the inlet. They camped for the night on the shore opposite the entrance to Indian Arm, and left in the morning to resume the pursuit of the continental shore, which they carried as far north as Jervis Inlet and Texada Island.

When returning to the ships at Birch Bay, Vancouver was astonished to find two small Spanish ships at anchor near Point Grey, and he was chagrined to learn that in 1791 a schooner commanded by José Maria Narvaez had traced the coastline some distance beyond the point at which he himself had turned back. In spite of this disappointment, cordial relations were soon established between the British and Spanish commanders, who agreed to cooperate in continuing the survey.

All went well until the ships reached the northern end of Georgia Strait, where they encountered islands and channels that must have reminded Vancouver of Puget Sound. The crisis came when they were faced with the formidable Arran Rapids, at the entrance to Bute Inlet. Fortunately Vancouver had been sending Lieutenant James Johnstone on scouting expeditions that had extended far beyond the point reached by the ships. On the last of these Johnstone had reached Queen Charlotte Strait, and he was convinced that it had an outlet to the ocean. Vancouver decided to follow a route suggested by Johnstone's surveys, which took the ships through Discovery Passage, Johnstone Strait and Queen Charlotte Strait. When he reached the Pacific, Vancouver made a second major discovery—he had established the insularity of Vancouver Island. He then turned northward and carried the coastal survey as far as Burke Channel. Presently a trading ship brought word that the *Daedalus* had arrived, and he sailed for Nootka immediately.

Vancouver and Quadra became friends, but they were unable to resolve the difficulties that had arisen from the 1789 seizures. The *Daedalus* had not brought Vancouver the promised additional instructions, and Quadra was handicapped by uncertainties about the desirable extent of Spanish sovereignty and the future of Nootka. All they could do was agree to refer the points at issue back to their respective governments in Madrid and London. There were no personal hard feelings; a permanent souvenir of their friendship might have resulted when Quadra asked Vancouver to name "some port or Island after us both" and Vancouver responded by naming "our place of meeting" Quadra and Vancouver's Island; but this unwieldy name was soon shortened by popular usage to Vancouver Island. It was one of more than 400 place names bestowed by Vancouver in the course of his voyage, a high proportion of which still survive in their original or a modified form.

Vancouver sailed south to California, where the *Discovery* was the first foreign vessel to enter San Francisco harbor, and thence to Monterey, where he enjoyed a last visit with Quadra.

Today's Hotel Vancouver, a Heritage Building, is renowned for its distinctive green copper roof, exterior carvings, modern conference facilities, and 550 elegant guest rooms, including 44 suites and the famed five-bedroom Royal Suite. In 1996 a complete renovation of the main lobby and lower shopping arcade was completed, with dramatic results: a spacious display of timeless elegance in a thoroughly modern downtown hotel. The hotel's staff of more than 500 assures guests of prompt, efficient and friendly service.

The *Chatham* joined him, and they sailed for the Hawaiian Islands to spend the winter in the milder climate.

The spring of 1793 found the ships back on the Northwest Coast, ready to resume their survey. They met in Burke Channel, worked their way northward, explored Observatory Inlet and Portland Canal, and ended the season by circumnavigating Revillagigedo Island, in Alaska. This last survey nearly ended in disaster, as the ship's boat commanded by Vancouver was subjected to much the most dangerous attack by Indians suffered by the expedition. It was beaten off with casualties limited to two men wounded, but Vancouver admitted frankly that he had failed to take proper defensive precautions. In his own words, relations with the Indians had been so uniformly friendly that "apprehensions of any molestation from them were totally done away with."

The end of the survey season found the ships heading once more for California and then Hawaii. Vancouver liked the islands and the islanders liked him. He developed two ambitions: first, to try to induce the various chiefs to refrain from the inter-island warfare that caused death and destruction, and secondly, to persuade the chiefs to cede the islands to Great Britain. His first ambition was never realized, but in 1794 Kamehameha and the district chiefs of the island of Hawaii did cede the lands within their control. This interesting agreement was never followed up in any effective way in London; Britain was preoccupied by more pressing matters closer to home, notably the Napoleonic wars.

For the third and final survey season Vancouver decided to work southward instead of northward. This survey, which was entirely in what is now Alaska, began in Cook Inlet and ended in a bay near the southern tip of Baranof Island, which Vancouver named Port Conclusion. The return of the last of the ships' boats was celebrated in a modest way, but one hardly in keeping with the conclusion of one of the greatest surveying ventures which, incidentally, had proven once and for all that the Northwest Passage did not exist within the vast extent of coastline it had examined.

After a call at Nootka the ships began the long homeward voyage, which was made by way of California, Valparaiso, Cape Horn and St. Helena. There the *Chatham* was detached on special duty, and it was the *Discovery,* travelling with a convoy she had encountered, that reached the Shannon, in Ireland, on September 12, 1795, and the Thames a month later. The *Chatham* joined her there in November. Since leaving Falmouth in 1791 the ships had sailed about 105,000 kilometres. Of the 180 men who sailed with the expedition, all but five returned safely—a remarkable score for the time, and one that reflected the efforts Vancouver made to care for his crews.

Vancouver's health was failing and he soon retired to Petersham, on the outskirts of London. The admiralty instructed him to prepare his journal for publication—a formidable assignment in which he was assisted by his brother John. The published version, half a million words in length, was within a hundred pages of completion when Vancouver died on May 12, 1798, at the early age of 40. He was buried in the churchyard of St. Peter's, Petersham, and over the years has not been forgotten. A wreath from the mayor and council of the City of Vancouver is laid on the grave each year on the anniversary of his death.

Appropriately the city has arranged to have the grave cared for by the Petersham and Ham Sea Scout Group.

Captain George Vancouver. cva

There are three splendid restaurants in the Hotel Vancouver, and guests enjoy 24-hour room service and valet parking. The hotel has a modern health club with glass-covered pool, a sun deck, patio, Jacuzzi, fitness equipment, fitness consultants and massage therapist. For conferences, 32,500 square feet of meeting space is available with a capacity of up to 1,500 people, including two grand ballrooms. The Hotel Vancouver regularly earns the prestigious CAA/AAA Four Diamond Award of Excellence.

HMS *Discovery*
W. Kaye Lamb

HMS DISCOVERY, COMMANDED by Captain Vancouver on his great voyage to the Northwest Coast in 1791-95, was the sixth ship in the Royal Navy to bear the name, which dates from 1665. While under construction as a merchant ship in a Thames yard, she was purchased in November 1789 by the Admiralty, which was looking for a ship suitable "for surveying in Remote Parts." Launched and named in December, she was moved to Deptford Dockyard for outfitting.

She was a surprisingly small ship, only 29 metres long and 337 tons, but size could be dangerous in survey work on a complicated coastline. Rated as a sloop, the *Discovery* was ship-rigged on Vancouver's voyage. Her complement was 100, plus sundry supernumeraries; with the crew crammed into her small hull for four years, it is not surprising that problems of discipline and morale sometimes arose.

Outfitting at Deptford was well advanced when it was interrupted in April 1790 by the Nootka Sound crisis. Spain had seized British ships at Nootka in 1789, and when full details were known in London war with Spain became probable. The crisis lasted until late October; in the interval the *Discovery* served as a receiving ship for newly enlisted seamen.

The Nootka crisis sharpened the focus of her mission, which now centered on the Northwest Coast of America, the area that had been in contention with Spain. Vancouver was to endeavor to arrive at a diplomatic settlement with a Spanish emissary at Nootka, after which he was to survey the coast from 30° to 60° north latitude—from southern California to Cook Inlet, in Alaska. Incidentally he was to keep a sharp outlook for any inlet that might lead to the fabled Northwest Passage. The *Discovery* and her smaller companion, the armed tender *Chatham,* sailed from Falmouth on April 1, 1791, and reached the California coast, by way of the Cape of Good Hope, Australia, New Zealand, Tahiti and Hawaii, a year later. They entered the Strait of Juan de Fuca on April 30, 1792.

Three summers were devoted to the coastal survey; the intervening winters were spent in the kinder climate of Hawaii. The survey—one of the most remarkable of its kind—ended in August 1794 at a harbor on Baranof Island to which Vancouver gave the appropriate name of Port Conclusion. The long homeward passage was made by way of Valparaiso, Cape Horn and St. Helena. After a call at the Shannon, in Ireland, the *Discovery* returned to the Thames in October 1795. The distance

> She was a surprisingly small ship …but size could be dangerous in survey work on a complicated coastline. Rated as a sloop, the *Discovery* was ship-rigged on Vancouver's voyage. Her complement was 100 …with the crew crammed into her small hull for four years, it is not surprising that problems of discipline and morale sometimes arose

she had travelled since she left England in 1791 has been estimated at 105,000 kilometres.

Until early in 1798 she lay idle at Deptford. She was then moved to the yard that had built her for conversion into a bomb ship, which meant that the light armament she had carried for surveying was replaced with heavier guns. Her only moment of military glory came in April 1801, when she was part of the force under Nelson that attacked Copenhagen. Thereafter she was laid up much of the time, and she was finally paid off at Sheerness in December 1805. In 1808 the dockyard there reduced her to the lowly service of a convict hulk. In this capacity she served for 10 years at Sheerness and a further 15 years at Woolwich. Thence she was moved once more to Deptford, where she was broken up. Demolition was completed in February 1834.

The only contemporary depiction of the *Discovery* as Vancouver knew her appears to be the line engraving in Vancouver's *Voyage of Discovery,* after a sketch by Zachary Mudge, one of her midshipmen. This shows her ashore on a reef in Queen Charlotte Strait, in August 1792. An etching by E. W. Cooke shows her as a convict hulk.

(There is an excellent scale model of *Discovery* in the Hotel Vancouver.)

A Brief History of Greater Vancouver

VanCity

1996 marked the 50th anniversary of Vancouver City Savings Credit Union. Fifty years ago, 14 charter members came together in Vancouver with a unique vision. They wanted to create a community credit union, a grass roots financial institution providing financial services not available through the large banks of the day. VanCity pioneers saw their credit union grow and flourish. Today, VanCity has more than 230,000 members, 33 branches and a long and proud history of innovation and community involvement.

A Brief History of Greater Vancouver
Chuck Davis

Envision the span of human occupation in this area—say, 8,000 years—as a city block. The events described herein happened within a few footsteps. Articles elsewhere describe that long pre-European occupation, and explorations by Narvaez (1791), Vancouver and Galiano (1792) and Fraser (1808). Our "modern" story begins in the winter of 1824 with the Hudson's Bay Company setting up a network of fur-trading posts on the Pacific slope.

A party of 40 men led by chief factor James McMillan reached what is now the Langley area December 16, 1824. They approached from the west, entering the Nicomekl River from its mouth on Boundary Bay, paddling through what is now Surrey, then portaging to the Salmon River. They entered the Fraser River about 50 kilometres from its mouth, then carried on north into the interior. But McMillan noted the location and chose a prominent tree, nicknamed the Hudson's Bay Tree, to remind him of it. Two-and-a-half years later, aboard the *Cadboro,* he was back by the tree with 25 men and instructions to build in the area. It was July 27, 1827.

That date is as good as any to mark the beginning of Greater Vancouver. (Fort construction began a few days later.)

The Kwantlen people left their winter villages at the mouth of the Brunette River to take up fur trading around the fort. In 1832 Fort Langley shipped out more than 2,000 beaver pelts. Then salted salmon became a major industry. By the late 1840s the fort was the largest fish exporter on the Pacific Coast, with Hawaii a major market. The original fort was abandoned in 1839 and a new one built 35 kilometres upstream, the present site. Next, farming became an important source of income. Thirty years after its establishment, Fort Langley was thriving.

Everything changed in 1858 following announcement of the discovery of gold on the Fraser River. That news travelled quickly to California. Within weeks 25,000 American prospectors flooded in, prompting an alarmed James Douglas, the governor of the colony of Vancouver Island, to declare the mainland a British colony, too. The proclamation was made at Fort Langley November 19, 1858.

To ensure control of the new colony by Britain and discourage any thoughts of American expansion, a small detachment of Royal Engineers had been sent for to show the flag and build roads. The first 25 "sappers" arrived from England November

facing page: Downtown Vancouver, 1994. vs

25, 1858 under the command of Col. Richard Moody. (The Engineers get their nickname from an old word, sap, a spade used in digging trenches.) Their settlement came to be called Sapperton. Today it's a New Westminster neighborhood.

Richard Moody is the most important figure in Greater Vancouver's early history. He selected the routes for our first roads, the sites for the first military reserves and the location of our first city. Moody was alarmed by Fort Langley's strategically poor location on the south side of the river, with its "back" to the Americans. Calling on the advice of his officers he picked a more suitable site a little farther to the west and on the north bank. Called Queensborough at first, in tribute to Queen Victoria, it would become—at the suggestion of the Queen herself—New Westminster. (Because it was named by the Queen, New Westminster dubbed itself The Royal City.) It became the capital of the mainland colony, supplanting Fort Langley. Victoria was the capital of the colony of Vancouver Island. In 1866, when the two colonies were united, New Westminster became capital of both. But in 1868 Victoria regained the title.

In 1859 Moody had a trail built through the forest from New Westminster to ice-free Burrard Inlet; today, as North Road, it's the boundary between Burnaby and Coquitlam. Not long after, he set aside a government reserve for a townsite that would come to be called Hastings. Superimposed on a city map today, Hastings Townsite would extend south all the way from Burrard Inlet to 29th Avenue between Nanaimo Street and Boundary Road. (A fascinating graphic account by Bruce Macdonald, in his book *Vancouver: A Visual History,* shows the process of the city's physical changes over the years in maps and photographs. Macdonald's book is an indispensable guide to the story of the city's growth.)

People began to settle in what we know now as Burnaby and Delta. A dairy farm with 50 milk cows was established on the Pitt River. The False Creek Trail, closely following a very old native-built trail, was opened in 1860 between New Westminster and False Creek. Today's Kingsway follows its route fairly closely. A school for the sappers' children was built, and the first permanent church went up. (Oddly, there were no local sawmills yet, so St. John the Divine Anglican, consecrated May 1, 1859 at Derby, near Fort Langley, was built of imported California redwood!)

In 1861 the first newspaper (New Westminster's *British Columbian*) appeared; in 1862 the first real hospital was built; a telegraph line went in in 1865 (its first message the assassination of U.S. president Abraham Lincoln); postal service began in 1867, and so did the first regular transportation service between New Westminster and Burrard Inlet . . . by stagecoach!

Brothers Fitzgerald and Samuel McCleery arrived September 26, 1862 and set up a farm in what would become the city of Vancouver. (And their farm would become a public golf course.) A month later a Yorkshire potter named John Morton saw a chunk of Burrard Inlet coal on display in a New Westminster shop window and wondered if near that coal there might be fine clay suitable for pottery. There was clay, but of a quality suitable only for bricks, and so Morton and two associates preempted 550 acres—at a price equivalent to $1.01 an acre—with a view to becoming brickmakers. (They spent, some thought, far too much money for the remote "Brickmaker's Claim," and one newspaper report derisively described them as "three greenhorn Englishmen.") The "three greenhorns" built a cabin near the north foot of today's Burrard Street and began to raise cows. The property they had selected, now the West End of Vancouver, made two of them wealthy, one of them (John Morton) very much so.

The native people, the original inhabitants of this bountiful corner of the world, found their occupation of the land ended, after thousands of years, with numbing speed.

The trees that once thickly covered the Lower Mainland were magnificent: one mighty specimen was recorded at 300 feet, about the height of the Marine Building. With all that splendid wood standing around, it wasn't long before intensive logging began. In 1862 two men, George Scrimgeour and T.W. Graham, preempted land for a sawmill on the north shore of Burrard Inlet and built Pioneer Mills. The mill sent a shipload of lumber to Australia in 1864, the earliest export of lumber from Burrard Inlet to a foreign port.

In June 1867 on the south shore of Burrard Inlet, Edward Stamp began—with British financing—Vancouver's first major industry. Stamp's mill (it was at the north foot of today's Dunlevy Street) built a flume from Trout Lake to its sawmill to sustain its steam-driven machinery.

Confederation came in 1867, creating a new country away to the east called Canada, and naturally inspiring thoughts it might eventually stretch from sea to sea. That was the same year a talkative former riverboat captain, Yorkshire-born John Deighton, with a complexion of "muddy purple," had a vision, although his wasn't so lofty. Deighton paddled into Burrard Inlet on the last day of September with his native wife, her mother, her cousin, a yellow dog, two chairs and a barrel of whiskey and jovially greeted the men who worked at Stamp's mill. The canny Deighton knew the nearest drink for these thirsty fellows was a five-kilometre row east up the inlet to the Engineers' North Road, then a 15-kilometre walk along that rude trail through the forest, the elk and the bears to

New Westminster. (Encounters with bears were not at all uncommon those days.) He announced to the mill workers they could have all they could drink if they helped him build a bar. The Globe Saloon was up within 24 hours. The locals had a nickname for Deighton, endlessly and garrulously confident of the area's future. They called him "Gassy Jack." That led, the story goes, to the area around his saloon—a gathering spot for mill-workers and visiting sailors—being nicknamed, in turn, "Gastown." There are other theories for the origin of the name, one associated with a nearby pocket of natural gas.

The irascible mill manager Edward Stamp had a falling out with his English investors and left. The operation, quickly under new ownership, became the Hastings Mill. This was, as historian W. Kaye Lamb has written, "the nucleus around which the city of Vancouver grew up in the 1880s."

Our wood would become famous around the world. There are immensely long, knot-free beams in the Imperial Palace in Beijing, China, cut from Burrard Inlet lumber by famed Jerry Rogers and his men. Forestry brought quick prosperity to the Lower Mainland. By 1875 a village that had sprung up around the north shore mill—now owned by an American named Sewell Moody, no relation to the colonel, and called Moodyville in his honor—could boast the inlet's first library, the first school and, in 1882, the first electric lights on the Pacific coast north of San Francisco. The mayor and city council of Victoria came over to watch them being turned on.

For all our progress in creating new places and in settlement and construction and industry, we were still backward when it came to human rights: on April 22, 1875 Queen Victoria gave Royal Assent to an act passed in the B.C. legislature denying the vote to Chinese and native people, a decision in force for more than 70 inglorious years.

Meanwhile, the boundaries of Greater Vancouver commenced to be drawn. The first entry, in 1873, a big one, was called the District of Langley, for a Hudson's Bay Company director. In 1874 Maple Ridge was created, the outcome of a meeting held in a dairy farm—also called Maple Ridge, for a long, beautiful ridge of the trees, more than three kilometres of them along the Fraser River. Huge chunks of the map were filled in in 1879 with the creation, all on November 10th, of Surrey, Delta and Richmond. Their populations numbered in the mere hundreds at the time.

Scattered settlements had been made in other places all over the Lower Mainland. Brothers William and Thomas Ladner had settled in the Fraser River lowland in 1868. Their farms grew into the pioneer settlement of Ladner's Landing. The

1959: VanCity pioneered the concept of an "open mortgage" which could be paid off by members without penalty at any time.

Granville (Gastown), circa 1884. cva

rumpled little settlement that had coalesced around Gassy Jack's saloon and the Hastings Mill got the formal name Granville Townsite in 1870. The first recorded white settler on Bowen Island was Charlie Dagget, who logged there in 1872. In May of 1878 Manoah Steves and his family settled on the southwestern tip of Lulu Island, an area later called Steveston.

In 1871 British Columbia, assured by Canada that its entry would bring it the railway, joined Confederation. Now British Columbians were also Canadians. If they had known that the railway would not reach them for another 15 years, they might not have been so willing to join! Port Moody, at the eastern end of Burrard Inlet, was in a fever of speculation as the Canadian Pacific Railway (CPR) line grew nearer. The little settlement had been announced as the railway's Pacific terminus. (It's a slightly bizarre fact of local history that the first CPR locomotive arrived here by sea!) But Port Moody's optimism was misplaced. A CPR official had come out for a closer look at the location and gone back with a melancholy secret: the eastern end of Burrard Inlet was too shallow for the ocean-going ships that were part of the railway's global shipping plans. In August of 1884 the dynamic and forceful William Van Horne, general manager of the railway, visited Granville. A little more than a month later, he asked CPR directors to choose it as the line's western terminus, instead of Port Moody. They agreed. When the announcement was eventually made, the people of Port Moody erupted in rage at what they considered an act of betrayal and began a series of law suits. None was successful.

There was an even weightier factor in the decision to move a little farther along the inlet. "The CPR," as David Mitchell writes in this book, "was anxious to develop a sizable new townsite . . . since the official Pacific terminus was to be at Port Moody, the railway's property entitlements from the government of Canada ended there. As a result the CPR secretly entered into negotiations with the provincial government of British Columbia for Crown land on Burrard peninsula. An initial request for 11,000 acres was rejected but a counter-offer of 6,000 acres was

agreed upon, subject to an extension of the rail line from Port Moody to a new CPR terminus 'in the immediate vicinity of Coal Harbour and English Bay . . .' The CPR would become the dominant private landowner in the new townsite."

William Van Horne is also responsible for the city's name. The legend, likely true, is that an excited Van Horne was rowed around what became Stanley Park by the CPR's local land commissioner Lauchlan Hamilton—another version has realtor Alexander Wellington Ross at the oars—and exclaimed that the city was destined to be a great one and must have a name commensurate with its greatness. Nobody would know where "Granville" was, Van Horne told whoever was rowing, but everyone knew of Captain Vancouver's Pacific explorations. The town's new name was in use early: the first issue of the city's first newspaper, the *Vancouver Weekly Herald and North Pacific News,* preceded incorporation by three months.

In 1885 Hamilton began to lay out the Vancouver townsite. A plaque at the northwest corner of Hamilton and Hastings streets marks his starting place.

When the CPR announced Vancouver would be the railway's terminus, the town's population was about 400. (Four years after the railway arrived, it was 13,000.) Incorporation came April 6, 1886 at a modest ceremony in Jonathan Miller's house. A civic election followed quickly. A month later the first piece of business at the first meeting of Vancouver's first city council, presided over by its first mayor, Malcolm Maclean, was the drafting of a petition to lease from the federal government a 1,000-acre military reserve to be used by the city as a park. That became Stanley Park.

The tiny city, a ramshackle tumble of stumps, brush and crude wooden buildings was little more than two months old on June 13, 1886 when a swift and furious fire—started when a sudden freak squall blew in sparks from clearing fires to the west—destroyed it in a time recalled as anywhere from 20 to 45 minutes. The Great Fire left a pitiful scattering of buildings.

Rebuilding began within hours, this time with brick, and while the fire's embers were still smoking.

Less than a month later (July 4, 1886) the first scheduled CPR transcontinental passenger train reached a still cranky Port Moody and, also in July, the first inward cargo to the port of Vancouver—tea from China—arrived. Then Vancouver's first bank, the Bank of British Columbia (no connection with today's), opened. The first CPR passenger train to arrive in Vancouver, famous little #374, chugged in in May of 1887, adorned with a large photograph of Queen Victoria. The first passenger to step down onto the platform was a 22-year-old Welshman named Jonathan Rogers who would become a prominent Vancouver developer and philanthropist. A band began to play a triumphant ditty called *See, the Conquering Hero Comes.* Rogers later laughingly admitted he thought they were playing it for him. The first train was followed a month later by the arrival from Japan of the CPR-chartered S.S. *Abyssinia* with a cargo of tea, silk and mail bound for London. The *Abyssinia's* arrival marked the beginning of the trans-Pacific, trans-Atlantic trade using the new railway. It left no doubt the little city was going to thrive.

But not without tensions. The same year, 1887, a white mob attacked and wrecked a Chinese camp in False Creek. (A contractor had hired Chinese laborers for work at 75 cents a day when white laborers were asking $2.) Special constables had to be brought in from Victoria and the city's charter was briefly suspended.

Intolerance has been a constant in our history from the beginning, sometimes with official sanction: in July of 1885 an act to restrict and regulate Chinese immigration into Canada received royal assent. It was the first of many enactments to discriminate against the area's large Chinese population, another of which was to impose a head tax of $50. The result (intended) was that Chinese men could not afford to bring their families over to join them. Later that same year a resolution of Richmond Council provided that white labor only would be employed on municipal works contracts. Similar resolutions were passed in many Greater Vancouver municipalities in the late 19th century.

Electricity came to Vancouver in 1887.

With the population on the north shore increasing, a group of locals applied to the provincial government to incorporate, and on August 10, 1891 the District of North Vancouver was born. Moodyville was invited to be in the new municipality but refused. (Years later it would join North Vancouver City.) The district was huge: it stretched along the north shore all the way from Horseshoe Bay to Deep Cove. The population was sparse, a few hundred.

Later in 1891 Coquitlam was created. Two men named Ross and McLaren had built Fraser Mills, the largest mill in B.C. at the time, capable of producing 200,000 board feet of lumber in a 10-hour shift. Coquitlam had grown up around it.

Settlers had been establishing homes in the area north of New Westminster, writes historian Pixie McGeachie, and they "decided their tax money should be used for their roads and services instead of going to Victoria." Burnaby was born on September 22, 1892. That was the same year the municipality of South Vancouver was created. Greater Vancouver's population now was more than 20,000.

The first of the area's several "secessions" was next. Property owners in North Vancouver's lower Lonsdale area felt they had little in common with the loggers of Capilano and Lynn Valley, and decided to incorporate separately as a city. When North Vancouver City was carved out of the surrounding district in 1907 it had almost 2,000 residents and 53 businesses, a bank, two hotels and a school. Electric service and the telephone had arrived the year before.

In 1912 the western part of the district would break away to form another municipality, West Vancouver, with a population of 700. Some 28 kilometres of ruggedly handsome shoreline had been attracting people from the southern shores of the inlet, vacationers who pitched tents here during the summer months as relief from the "busy haunts of man." A regular ferry service across the inlet had been started in 1909 by an entrepreneur named John Lawson, called by some "the father of West Vancouver." That triggered a real estate boom.

Meantime Vancouver had been having an unbroken boom of its own for 20 years, with the railway bringing in new arrivals every day. The city's population leaped from 13,709 to 29,000 in the 10 years between 1891 and 1901 . . . and then it began to explode. The CPR's first Hotel Vancouver opened just before the railway arrived. The company—which was reaping a bonanza from sales of its property—built the lavish Opera House where Sarah Bernhardt would perform in 1891. Stanley Park was officially opened, the B.C. Sugar Refinery was gaining new markets, the first Granville Street bridge leaped bravely across False Creek and The Vancouver Board of Trade launched itself with a banquet in which every attendee got a full dinner and a bottle of fine champagne. Tab: $12.50. The Terminal City Club, a private club for monied businessmen, began. Electric streetcars began to clang along city streets, leading quickly to the famed Interurban lines to Burnaby, Steveston, New Westminster and the Fraser Valley. The first of the CPR's Empress line of ocean liners pulled into port. Canneries

1977: VanCity launched a fully-automated inter-branch computer system, giving members on-line access to their accounts at any VanCity branch.

at Steveston were shipping salmon everywhere, setting a record in 1901 with 16 million pounds. With all this growth and new sophistication there were occasional reminders it could still be a raw, largely untamed place: there were more anti-Asiatic riots in 1907, a Vancouver by-law restricted the number of cows that could be kept within city limits, and Burnaby's first law enforcer included among his regular duties the reporting of swine running loose.

Culture was not confined to Sarah Bernhardt. The movies got here in 1897, and Pauline Johnson read her poetry here to an attentive audience that included a visiting ex-prime minister, Sir Charles Tupper. We got pay telephones in 1898.

Growth became almost frenzied. Boosterism bordering on arrogance is reflected in the newspapers of the time. A banner across Granville Street proclaimed, in what we would now view as a politically incorrect rhyme, "In 1910 Vancouver then will have 100,000 men." It did, and more.

Newspaper rivalry was keen here, with as many as four dailies fighting for circulation. Louis D. Taylor's *World* was flourishing, to put it mildly. In 1912 he built a tower to house it, at the time the tallest building in the British Empire. Taylor—who would set a record (seven times) for being elected mayor that still stands—boasted that the *World* carried more display advertising than any other newspaper in North America. Most of it was for real estate. The *Province*, which had started in Vancouver in 1898, was doing pretty well for itself, too. One edition of the era had no fewer than 60 full pages of realtors' advertisements. Among the more aggressive land peddlers was the Prussian Gustav Konstantin von Alvensleben, one of the great characters in Vancouver history.

The opening of the Panama Canal in 1914 would prove beneficial to Vancouver, considerably shortening ocean journeys between British Columbia and Europe and spurring the port's growth in grain exports. Today we ship more grain than any other Canadian port.

Greater Vancouver's educational life took a leap forward in 1915 with the establishment of the University of British Columbia—even though UBC would take many years to finally settle in at Point Grey, spurred by a "Great Trek" in 1922 of more than a thousand impatient students, angry at being cooped up in the "Fairview huts."

The year 1915 also saw the opening of a new CPR station at the north foot of Granville Street and the creation of an industrial enclave from soil dredged out of False Creek, piled onto a mudflat, and proudly named Granville Island. The effervescence of the era is captured in the premiere that same year of a frothy little musical show set in Vancouver and called *Fifty Years Forward.* One of its predictions for Vancouver in 1965 was a lady mayor. After more than 90 civic elections, it hasn't happened yet.

Prosperity and growth was not confined, of course, to the biggest guy on the Greater Vancouver block. On the north shore of Burrard Inlet the Pacific Great Eastern Railway (PGE) had started regular passenger service in 1914 between North Vancouver and Whytecliff near Horseshoe Bay. It was a small beginning in its torturously slow progress into the province's interior. Wallace Shipyards in North Vancouver was building boats and saw a leap in orders during World War I. Marine Drive on the North Shore opened to traffic in 1915, the same year White Rock's famous pier was built. (White Rock, by the way, was flourishing as a lumber centre.) Imperial Oil moved its refinery to what became the Ioco area in 1914, and started a townsite there. Further east, Robert Dollar began his mill at Roche Point on Indian Arm. In Hammond a mill built in 1916 is still there, Maple Ridge's largest employer. Just to the west of Maple Ridge, a new addition to the Greater Vancouver map was created in 1914 with Pitt Meadows. (The map would now stay unaltered for decades until Langley City's 1955 breakaway from the township.)

Bowen Island and Horseshoe Bay had become flourishing summertime haunts. In 1921 a dance hall, the largest in B.C., was built on Bowen, allowing 800 people to shimmy at once. Radio broadcasting began, adding to the fun. The Pacific Highway opened down to the border crossing at Douglas, which made it easier to drive to Bellingham and Seattle . . . and easier for visiting Americans to drive up. By the late 1920s more than 300,000 of them were doing just that every year.

By 1928 the population of the Lower Mainland outside Vancouver was over 150,000. More than 80,000, however, were residents of the municipalities of South Vancouver and Point Grey, both of which decided in 1928 to amalgamate with Vancouver. When newly elected mayor W. H. Malkin walked into his office January 2, 1929 he was the chief executive of a city that had, overnight, grown in population by more than 50 per cent to become the third largest in Canada.

Malkin, whose wholesale grocery firm was a city institution for decades, is one of a handful of pre-World War II Vancouver mayors whose names many still remember. Men like McBeath, Findlay, Buscombe and Collins have faded from memory, while Malkin, Taylor, Oppenheimer and Tisdall are still recalled. Preeminent among all the mayors, however, was the remarkable, the ebullient, the unstoppable Gerald Grattan McGeer. Gerry McGeer blew into office in 1935, burying L.D. Taylor by more than 20,000 votes. "McGeer," writes Donna

Jean McKinnon in this book, "was voted into office on a mandate to fight crime, and to do away with slot machines, gambling, book-making, white slavery and corruption in the police force. True to his promise, he confiscated 1,000 slot machines in his first week." McGeer used all that zeal and vigor and not a little cunning to force through the location in 1936 of a new city hall at 12th and Cambie in the Mount Pleasant area. At the time many thought that remote location—so far from the city's business district—was ridiculous. His 1935 reading of the Riot Act at Victory Square, to dispel a mob of angry unemployed workers, splits local opinion along partisan lines to this day.

The Great Depression was no rougher on or kinder to Greater Vancouver than elsewhere. There were breadlines and demonstrations at city halls. A fellow named Woodsworth came to town to talk about a new political party called the Co-Operative Commonwealth Federation (CCF). Greater Vancouver residents formed the Common Good Cooperative Society to engage in a "war against poverty." It ran a store, grew food on vacant land and helped give birth to the credit union movement in B.C. In 1935 a thousand unemployed men boarded freight cars in Vancouver to begin an "On to Ottawa" trek. Burnaby, West Vancouver and both North Vancouvers went into receivership and were run by public trustees for a time.

Not all the news was gloomy during the Depression years: in May 1930 Dominion Bridge opened a plant in Burnaby to produce steel for construction. In 1931 the Vancouver Art Gallery opened. So did St. George's private school for boys. At Vancouver Golf Club during the lean times, dues were reduced from $6 a month to $1.

In 1935 the ward system ended in Vancouver. Despite several indications since that a slight majority of the city's residents favor going back to the system—which would guarantee representation from all city areas—craftily worded questions on the subject have succeeded in avoiding a true test at the polls. The Non-Partisan Association (NPA), which has dominated city politics with a few lapses since the early 1930s, and which opposes the ward system, won all 10 council seats in the 1996 civic election. What Paul Tennant wrote for *The Vancouver Book* back in 1976 could go unchanged today: " . . . politically active persons are not a cross section of the population . . . persons and groups of little education and low income still tend to avoid civic politics. Those who are active in Vancouver politics are mostly from the professional-managerial category and more often than not live west of Main Street . . ." Vancouver is the only large Canadian city without a ward system. It might prove in practice no better than the at-large system, but a chance to test their relative merits seems unlikely.

In October 1931 West Vancouver agreed to sell 4,000 acres of its mountainsides to a syndicate called British Pacific Properties. That turned out to be a landmark decision. To lure property buyers to its extensive new holdings, the syndicate (controlled by the Guinness Brewing Company) offered to build a bridge across the First Narrows. The fact that the road leading to the bridge would cut through the middle of Stanley Park made a lot of locals furious, but the work it would provide—not to mention the economic benefits to follow—made the decision inevitable: Lions Gate Bridge (costing $6 million) opened to traffic in November 1938. It brought an immediate boost to the fortunes of the North Shore.

And it foretold one of the great themes of the area's history: the growth of suburban Vancouver. The 1941 census showed the metropolitan population had increased to more than 400,000, with about 70 per cent of us in Vancouver itself. Ten years later the relevant figures would be 590,000 and 58 per cent.

World War II yanked Vancouver out of the Great Depression, as it would do elsewhere. Local shipyards began to build corvettes and minesweepers. The Boeing Aircraft factory in Richmond took on 5,000 people to produce parts for B-29s. The newly incorporated Wartime Housing Limited began building rental units for war industry workers. WHL built nearly 800 homes on the North Shore.

In early 1942 in the wake of the December 7, 1941 Japanese bombing of Pearl Harbor, local Japanese-Canadians were herded into holding areas at Hastings Park and then removed to government camps in the Interior. Their fishboats, homes and other property were "taken into custody." The owners received little or no compensation. A light in a Stanley Park monument built to honor Japanese-Canadian soldiers who had fought bravely and with high casualties in World War I was extinguished. Masumi Mitsui, the last surviving Japanese-Canadian World War I veteran, would relight the flame in 1985.

World War II changed the lives of women, as it would do elsewhere. Single women from the Prairies came to work in Fraser River canneries during the war. Many of them married local fishermen and stayed on. Out of a work force of 13,000, a thousand women worked at busy Burrard Dry Dock where, at the war's height, 34 "Victory" ships were built in 26 months. (When victory was announced in 1945, some women at Burrard found themselves in tears knowing their jobs had ended and that, despite a fight by their union to keep them on, the returning men would necessarily put them out of work.)

A remarkable success story began during the war when an imaginative fellow named Bill Rea started radio station CKNW. Rea realized local people wanted war news, so from the day the station signed on (August 15, 1944) he started hourly newscasts and stayed on the air 24 hours a day. No one else was doing that, and it immediately made this little New Westminster-based station noted and, eventually, dominant in local radio. It helped NW to have a late-night disc jockey named Jack Cullen, a broadcasting phenomenon whose 50th anniversary as a broadcaster occurred as this book was being completed.

The 1940s also brought us Canada's first drive-in theatre, two-way escalators in the Hudson's Bay store and, in 1948, on a tiny smattering of grey flickering screens the first television signal: a college football game played in Seattle. Chinese and East Indians were given the provincial vote in 1947, with Japanese and native Indians winning it in 1949.

What did the 1950s bring us: further expansion at Vancouver airport with CP Air beefing up its flights across the Pacific, inaugurating flights to Amsterdam and introducing jet aircraft; the Lougheed Highway; the Upper Levels Highway; completion of the PGE Railway (now BC Rail) from Squamish to Horseshoe Bay; a provincially owned Lions Gate Bridge; the Oak Street Bridge; death to the streetcar and the Interurban; a new phenomenon for Canada, a "shopping centre," at Park Royal; another, called an "industrial park," on Annacis Island; still another, the world's first "container ship," an initiative of the White Pass & Yukon Railway; atomic bomb shelters; an oil pipeline from Edmonton; Cleveland Dam; the Deas Island (George Massey) Tunnel; an end to ferry service between Vancouver and North Vancouver, balanced by an announcement of a new ferry service between the Lower Mainland and Vancouver; the B.C. Lions.

We got a big new central branch for the Vancouver Public Library at Robson and Burrard, where it would stay long after it had become too small for what it held; our own television station in late 1953 when CBUT, the CBC's local channel, signed on. CBUT brought us world-wide publicity the following year when it broadcast the "Miracle Mile" at the British Empire Games at Empire Stadium, the first sports event broadcast live to all of North America. Some saw a weakening in our moral fibre in the decade with the approval of, first, a six-day shopping week; second, the opening of Vancouver's first cocktail bar in the Sylvia Hotel; and, third, rock 'n roll when an incredibly loud little band called Bill Haley and the Comets starred in a 1956 show hosted by an incredibly fast-talking young disc jockey named Red Robinson. There was tragedy in 1958 with the collapse during construction of a new Second Narrows Bridge. Nineteen men died.

Next, for the first time in just over 40 years, the Greater Vancouver map changed, with the creation in 1955 of Langley City as a separate municipality. Two years later White Rock broke away from Surrey to become a haven for sun-seekers and retirees.

Suburban growth continued. By 1961 the metropolitan Vancouver population had climbed to more than 800,000, double the figure of 20 years earlier, pushing Vancouver's share of the population down to 46 per cent.

In the 1960s we gained Nitobe Memorial Gardens, the Second Narrows Bridge, the 401 freeway, Whistler as a ski resort, direct distance dialing and provincial ownership of the British Columbia Electric Co. We greeted the Queen Elizabeth Playhouse, the first Vancouver Sea Festival, the Grey Cup, bathtub races, French-language radio and the Beatles. BCIT opened, as did the Grouse Mountain Skyride, Whistler's first ski-lifts, the Port Mann bridge and, in Richmond, the Iona Island Sewage Treatment Plant.

We lost the Lyric Theatre and Bowen Island's Union Steamship Hotel to obsolescence and the first Grouse Mountain chalet to fire.

Midway through the 1960s Simon Fraser University opened in Burnaby. The decade was marked here as elsewhere by protests against the war in Vietnam, peace rallies and marches. A new kind of people called "hippies" appeared and made Vancouver's West 4th Avenue their neighborhood. Protest flared up in 1967 when Strathcona residents—many of them Chinese who had lived there for decades—squelched a freeway through their neighborhood. The world's preeminent environmental activist group, Greenpeace, was born in a Dunbar neighborhood living room. The era of protest would continue into the 1970s with hippies clashing with Mayor "Tom Terrific" Campbell, and thousands of high school students demonstrating against U.S. atomic-bomb tests on Alaska's Amchitka Island.

Grace MacInnis of Vancouver became B.C.'s first female member of parliament, and Surrey elected as mayor one Bill Vander Zalm. The Canadian Lacrosse Hall of Fame opened, so did the Bank of British Columbia and, in Richmond, so did the first McDonald's restaurant in Canada (with hamburgers at 18 cents). Vancouver's Community Arts Council sponsored a walking tour of Gastown to stimulate interest in preserving the historic area. The Centennial Museum and the H.R. MacMillan Planetarium opened at Vanier Park. Swangard Stadium was built in Burnaby. The Canucks would play their first game in 1970.

The Greater Vancouver Regional District was incorporated in 1967, bringing a new level and a new kind of government to the Lower Mainland. In 1971 the census showed the metropolitan population had topped the million mark. (One remarkable finding of that census was that Delta's population had tripled in 10 years.) A tiny part of that million was little Lions Bay, incorporated in 1971 with a population just over 1,000. And 1971 was the year even tinier Fraser Mills, population under 200, was absorbed into Coquitlam.

Canada's economic links to the Pacific Rim were boosted with the opening of a coal port at Delta's Roberts Bank in the 1970s. The city's infrastructure expanded with a new Georgia/Dunsmuir Viaduct, the Knight Street Bridge, a big container facility for the port, an archives building named for the late city archivist, Major J.S. Matthews, and the Stanley Park seawall. A 1974 experiment, the Granville Mall, is still being tinkered with. Continuing growth at Vancouver International Airport made a new link necessary: Arthur Laing Bridge opened. Post-secondary education came to the North Shore with the opening of Capilano College. Grand new traditions began with the inauguration of the Royal Hudson steam train run from North Vancouver to Squamish, the launch of the world's first children's festival and the opening of the stunning Museum of Anthropology at UBC, architect Arthur Erickson's greatest Vancouver creation. Erickson and his associates would change the face of downtown in 1979 with the new courthouse and Robson Square complex.

Change was frequent in this decade: a small church in the city's East End turned into the Vancouver East Cultural Centre; the old Orpheum Theatre was bought by the city and became a home for the Vancouver Symphony Orchestra. Shaughnessy Golf Course changed to Van Dusen Botanical Gardens. The venerable old Birks Building came down, despite protests, to be replaced by an office/retail complex called Vancouver Centre. The Gastown Steam Clock, the world's first, began to pipe up, and is today likely the single most-photographed object in Greater Vancouver. An era could honestly be said to have ended when the last scheduled passenger train pulled out of the old CPR station on Cordova Street on October 27, 1979, just over 92 years since the first had pulled into town. (Today, the handsome old building is home to offices, shops, snack bars and the SeaBus terminal.) A rare phenomenon occurred as the 1970s ended: an initiative by the federal government turned into a smashing success with Granville Island's conversion to a site for a big public market, and a range of handsome shops, restaurants and offices.

Whistler became a Resort Municipality in 1975, the only one with that designation in B.C., and West Vancouver gained the dramatic Cypress Provincial Park. A Coquitlam MLA named Dave Barrett was elected premier, and Canada's first Native Indian citizenship judge was appointed. A 1976 United Nations conference called Habitat focussed on the supply of fresh water

to millions in the undeveloped world. In sports, the Vancouver Whitecaps won the NASL Soccer Bowl. A new member of the Greater Vancouver Regional District popped up in 1979 as the Village of Belcarra, where Burrard Inlet meets Indian Arm.

By 1981 two-thirds of Greater Vancouver's population lived outside the central city. The 1981 census was sobering for Vancouver: it showed a drop in absolute numbers, with 12,000 fewer people in the city since the '71 census. Most of the suburbs were leaping ahead: Langley Township had more than doubled in population in a decade, Surrey grew by more than 50 per cent, Richmond by more than 55. Delta was now five times bigger than it had been 20 years earlier. Only New Westminster joined Vancouver: its population dropped 10 per cent during the 1970s.

To open the 1980s, Terry Fox captured the hearts of the entire nation with his courageous attempt to run across Canada. Annual Terry Fox runs raise millions of dollars for the fight against cancer.

The B.C. Penitentiary in New Westminster closed. A new courthouse went up in New Westminster, and an old hotel, the Devonshire, was imploded in Vancouver. Also blown up, but in the opposite direction, was the fabric dome of B.C. Place Stadium. Premier Bill Bennett opened it in June 1983. Kwantlen College opened in Richmond and Douglas College moved to downtown New Westminster. The Vancouver Art Gallery relocated to a refurbished 1916 courthouse.

A 1981 peace march against nuclear arms in Vancouver became an annual event, the largest of its kind in North America, with up to 100,000 participants. A "temporary" facility called the Vancouver Food Bank opened. By 1989, it had grown to six depots distributing to 15,000 people every month.

Under the dome in 1983 Queen Elizabeth invited the world to Expo 86. Enthusiasm for the world exposition was tempered by nagging unemployment, with, among other gloomy news, word that none of five shipyards on the North Shore had any new shipbuilding contracts pending. The Social Credit government's restraint policy inspired a "Solidarity" rally at Empire Stadium, at which more than 40,000 public and private sector workers aired their protests.

The City of Vancouver celebrated its 100th birthday in 1986, and opened its doors on May 2 to more than 21 million Expo visitors. The success of the Granville Island Public Market inspired similar ventures at New Westminster Quay, at Lonsdale Quay in North Vancouver and in Richmond's Bridge Point Harbour Market. SkyTrain, Vancouver's advanced light rapid transit system opened. Two new bridges sprang across the Fraser: SkyBridge (to carry SkyTrain into Surrey) and the Alex

Fraser Bridge. Burnaby's vast Metrotown complex opened. So did the SunYat-Sen Gardens in Chinatown and the Vancouver Trade and Convention Centre in the former Expo 86 Canada Pavilion site. VTCC is now booking conventions well into the 21st century. A "Shame the Johns" operation began in Vancouver in an attempt to drive prostitutes' clients from the West End. It simply drove them elsewhere.

After 123 years *The Columbian,* B.C.'s oldest newspaper, stopped. Pope John Paul II made the first papal visit ever to Vancouver and the Lower Mainland, which didn't prevent Woodward's from becoming the first major Vancouver department store to open on Sundays.

New stars were created in the 1980s: Rick Hansen began his around-the-world Man-in-Motion Tour by wheelchair to raise millions for research into spinal cord injury. Cross-country runner Steve Fonyo duplicated Terry Fox's fund raising ability at first, then ran into severe personal roadblocks. North Vancouver singer Bryan Adams, who once washed dishes at the Tomahawk Grill, became—and remains—a global superstar. In other cultural news, a dwarf-tossing contest at the Flamingo Hotel in Surrey's Whalley neighborhood made headlines. The B.C. Lions won the Grey Cup again.

Surrey's Bill Vander Zalm won election as premier. Surrey made more headlines in 1988 when B.C. Tel reported that 40 per cent of all new homes built in B.C. that year were located there. Other big economic news as the decade wound down: it was announced that the Port of Vancouver was now handling more imports/exports than any other port in North America; and that 30 per cent of those exports were going to Japan.

The vacant Expo site was sold to Li Ka-shing of Hong Kong in one of the biggest real estate deals in Canadian history, for a price many believe was a fantastic bargain. Li's Concord Pacific development is transforming the site into the largest urban project in North America.

More 1989 openings: Simon Fraser University's downtown campus; Science World; Highway 91; and Cannell Studios in North Vancouver. Local movie audiences delighted in seeing familiar landmarks in big-budget Hollywood movies filmed here. Vancouver is now North America's third largest film production centre, after Los Angeles and New York. We got a big new urban park, too, with the 750-hectare Pacific Spirit Park, created from part of the UBC Endowment Lands.

The 1987 addition of the brand-new Village of Anmore and the 1989 inclusions of Langley and Maple Ridge completed the map of the Greater Vancouver Regional District.

The 1990s began with a roar as the first "Indy" race took place in downtown Vancouver, the start of what has become an annual event. What was gained in the city was lost in Coquitlam when Westwood Motorsport Park closed after 30 years. SkyTrain service was extended to Scott Road station in Surrey.

Small blue plastic bins began showing up at residential curbsides as recycling caught on.

Big news in the 1990s was Canada's first female premier (Rita Johnson, MLA for Newton in Surrey, who was chosen after Bill Vander Zalm resigned.) The Bob Prittie Metrotown Branch of the Burnaby Public Library opened. There were conspicuous deletions in the decade: Oakalla Prison Farm; Versatile Pacific Shipyards (due to celebrate its 100th anniversary in 1994) and Woodward's, a retail institution.

The Canucks lost the Stanley Cup in the final game of the 1994 season, a nail-biting blazer of a series that led to frustrated fans rioting downtown. The B.C. Lions gained their third Grey Cup in '94, defeating Baltimore. The Lions were in trouble in late 1996 with the departure of chief coach Joe Paopao and lukewarm response to a season tickets drive.

The world's largest LSD (and other 'designer drugs') factory was raided in Port Coquitlam, and its head, a long-sought U.S. fugitive, was nabbed by the RCMP.

One thing that stopped happening in the 1990s was the trend to Vancouver having an increasingly smaller share of the metropolitan population: 1995 estimates show the central city's population had increased by more than 107,000 since 1981—a 26 per cent jump! "Our city," says Larry Beasley, Vancouver's director of central area planning, "is emerging as an unbelievably unique place. We have tens of thousands of citizens who have elected to move back into the city." It's expected 1996 census figures will show a net increase in the downtown residential population for the first time in decades.

Some of the concerns we face in the closing years of the 20th century (eloquently detailed in Stephen Hume's epilogue in this book) have a familiar ring. We have been living with them for up to 100 years: ethnic tension, crime, pollution, traffic, drugs, unemployment, labor unrest, taxes, a deteriorating infrastructure . . . but at the same time we enjoy a climate that is always tolerable and very often wonderful, a physical setting envied by many, a level of energy that makes living here exciting, an increasingly cosmopolitan flavor to our streets, a thriving cultural life, an array of excellent restaurants, a level of literacy higher than anywhere else in Canada and a passionate interest, unique in its intensity in this country, in the unforeseeable power, and maybe glory, of the electronic information world.

One prediction can safely be made about our future: it will be extraordinarily interesting.

Gassy Jack
Donna Jean MacKinnon

VANCOUVER'S EARLIEST NAME came thanks to a saloon keeper. John "Gassy Jack" Deighton, born in Hull, Yorkshire, on the North Sea near the mouth of the Humber, started out as a steamship operator in the late 1850s, but bad health (painful swelling of his legs and feet) forced him to take up another line of work. He opened a bar in New Westminster that thrived on the traffic going to and from the Cariboo Gold Rush of 1862.

By 1867 the rush was over and the businesses that had profited from it began to close down. Meanwhile, on the south shore of Burrard Inlet, Captain Edward Stamp had opened a sawmill. In September Deighton rowed to the Stamp's Mill site with his native wife, "with little more than $6 in his pocket, a few sticks of furniture, a yellow dog and a bottle of whiskey." He was 36. With the help of the thirsty sawmill workers, for whom the nearest drink was nearly 25 kilometres away in New Westminster, Deighton built the Globe Saloon within 24 hours of his arrival. The small wooden shack stood just west of the mill at what is now the intersection of Carrall and Water streets, where Vern Simpson's statue of Gassy Jack stands today. "I can assure you it was a lonesome place when I came here first," he wrote his brother, Tom, in England. "Surrounded by Indians, I dare not look outdoors after dark. There was a friend of mine, about a mile distant, found with his head cut in two."

Business, despite such perils, was very good, but to discourage competition Jack let on that things were tough, something he got away with for more than a year. Soon enough, there were a number of other saloons and hotels in the area, but Jack's saloon continued to be the busiest and most popular. Jack attracted the custom of the loggers and longshoremen, even if he was strict at kicking them out each night at 10:30, telling them they had to get their sleep. But he was always ready for a story and, it is said, got his nickname because of his own gift of the gab.

The little community that grew up around Jack's saloon had to be torn down when a townsite called Granville was established and a five-corner intersection was laid out, but he bought a nearby lot and built a hotel (with bar) called Deighton House. It became so busy that he invited his brother to come out from England and work with him. Around the same time, following the death of his first wife (whose name is not recorded), Jack took up with her 12-year-old niece Qua-hail-ya, also known as Madeline or Matrine. In 1871 they had a

> ## "I can assure you it was a lonesome place when I came here first…Surrounded by Indians, I dare not look outdoors after dark. There was a friend of mine, about a mile distant, found with his head cut in two."

son, Richard, who was quite simple-minded and came to be derisively nicknamed the "Earl of Granville."

Jack's brother Tom and sister-in-law Emma came out from England, but Jack and Emma didn't get along. His personal difficulties and an improvement in his health persuaded Jack to move to New Westminster, where he returned to steamboating on the Fraser on the vessel *Onward*. Tom and Emma were left in charge of the hotel, and an 1874 advertisement in the *Mainland Guardian* makes reference to the "newly constructed and commodious Hotel . . . The establishment is replete with all the comforts of a home. The large and comfortable parlors, single and double bedrooms, extensive dining-rooms are furnished in every respect with care, and are under the experienced management of Mrs. Thos. Deighton."

During a visit to Granville another round of furious namecalling between Jack and Emma was the last straw. Emma ended by throwing hotel china at Jack, saying he didn't have it in him to have been Richard's father (as an indignant Jack wrote to a friend, "She hated the little Earl of Granville, you know, and she spread the rumour that I didn't have the tackle to father him"), and scorning him because of his own illegitimacy. ("I was my father's son by another woman.") After that incident Tom and Emma moved to Victoria and never returned. Jack took charge of the hotel again and made renovations in anticipation of increased business from the construction of a new road, but fell ill again and died soon after at the age of 44 on May 29, 1875. Qua-hail-ya was disinherited, and Richard died before Jack's meagre estate (about $300) was probated.

Jack's body was transported to New Westminster, where it lay in an unmarked grave for 97 years until the Gassy Jack Memorial Fund was established and a headstone erected in 1972.

The Great Fire
Chuck Davis

FIRES IN THE NEW TOWNS OF the late 1800s were not uncommon; what made Vancouver's unique was its speed. A city of about 1,000 wooden buildings was destroyed in less than 45 minutes, some say as little as 20. Details vary in the accounts of eyewitnesses, but all agree it happened with stunning suddenness. "Vancouver didn't burn," said one eyewitness, "it exploded."

It was June 13, 1886, a Sunday. A small crew of Canadian Pacific Railway men was keeping an eye on clearing fires set the day before. "The fire started between Hamilton and Granville streets," volunteer fireman Hugh Campbell told the city archivist in 1931. "The CPR were clearing the land, and the fire got away from them." The reason it got away was a freakish squall, a sudden blast of wind from the west. The wind was strong enough to take the coal hulk *Robert Kerr,* anchored off Deadman's Island, and push her, dragging her anchor, down to the Hastings Sawmill at the foot of Dunlevy Street. (There, providentially enough, the *Kerr* served as a refuge for people jumping into the inlet to escape the fury of the fire.) The wind blew big trees over . . . and blew flames and burning debris right into the sprawling tinder-dry collection of homely wooden buildings that was the two-month-old City of Vancouver.

Someone who saw the ominous and rising clouds of smoke began furiously ringing the bell of St. James' Church at Powell and Westminster Road (now Main Street). For many that was the first warning of the fire. Then came the alarmed shouts of men, running ahead of the flames to escape and warn the town. But the fire overtook them, leaping from treetop to treetop in the heavily forested area south of Hastings, and descended with a roar on the defenceless little town. (A fire-fighting steam pump purchased by the city would not arrive until August. Fire-fighters had only axes, shovels and buckets.)

Men dropped before their companions' eyes and were consumed in the fire; a mother and her child were found dead at the bottom of a well into which they had leaped for safety, smothered when the flames consumed the oxygen above. The heat was ferocious—the bell of St. James that had warned so many was turned to a molten lump of slag when the church in its turn burst into flame. (The melted bell can be seen today at the Vancouver Museum.) And the fire was erratic: roofs of buildings distant from the flames, like the Presbyterian Church, caught fire when other buildings much closer to the inferno were still untouched.

. . . the bell of St. James turned to a molten lump of slag when the church in its turn burst into flame.

People tried desperately to save what they could, but the speed of the fire made that virtually impossible: one woman waded into the waters of the inlet with her sewing machine, which was all she saved; Sunday School teacher L.Z. Hall was left with only his Bible. Lauchlan Hamilton, the CPR land commissioner and city alderman, dashed to his office, collected "the most valuable papers," shoved them in a sheaf under his arm and ran into a cauldron of fire, "breathing air as hot as cinders." When he reached safety, he saw that the papers, still under his arm, were charred black.

In the midst of the tragedy there was, as always, a comic touch. Dr. H.E. Langis lamented the loss of his anatomical specimen, a human skeleton. It was found under the ruins of his office. "Do you know what they said when they picked it up? They said, 'This poor fellow must have been very sick before he died—look, his bones are all wired together.' "

The death toll is uncertain. A figure as high as 28 has been cited, but an informal inquest held the next day noted only eight confirmed deaths. Many dead could have been burned up without a trace—and the nature of the town was such that there were many transients, whose names would not have been known.

Mayor Malcolm Maclean wired Prime Minister Macdonald for assistance ("Our city in ashes . . ."), and received a prompt hand-written response promising $5,000. Help from surrounding towns was swift and generous. In *Vancouver, Milltown to Metropolis* Alan Morley writes: "Doctors and women collected medical supplies and bandages, food, clothing and household goods were donated, and by 6 o'clock in the evening an unending relief caravan was crawling over the Westminster Road and in sight of Vancouver. It passed crowds of refugees making their way to the hospitality of the neighboring communities, where every door was open to them. By 3 o'clock in the morning, lumber wagons were jolting in from the Fraser communities; nails and tools were unloaded by the light of lanterns and the flickering of still-burning stumps. By daylight, tents and building frames stood in the dawn, with the smoke curling around them and the ashes puffing wherever a man trod.

"In 20 minutes, Vancouver had been wiped off the earth. In 12 hours, it was rising again."

James Skitt Matthews and the Vancouver City Archives
Donna Jean MacKinnon

MAJOR J. S. MATTHEWS—adventurer, innovator, and first archivist of the City of Vancouver—was born September 7, 1878, in Wales. He was a natural archivist, keeping meticulous track of his activities and of those around him who he thought were making an impact on society.

It was a short step for him to start collecting general historical material from others in Vancouver. As the collection grew, he developed his own cataloguing systems, in the end amassing many thousands of photographs and hundreds of civic records and personal papers.

After graduating from grammar school in Auckland, New Zealand, he worked as a timber clerk. In 1898 he sailed for the United States "to make his fortune." After arriving in San Francisco, Matthews moved north along the West Coast, staying briefly in Tacoma, Seattle and Victoria. There he met Valentia Maud Boscawen, his fiancée, who arrived from New Zealand. They came to Vancouver, fell in love with the city and its surroundings, and decided to make it their home.

Imperial Oil—the first oil company in British Columbia—installed Canada's first gas pump in Vancouver. Matthews' work for the pioneering firm began in 1899 and during his 20 years with it he worked as a clerk, a travelling salesman and manager of various aspects of the provincial operation.

The Matthews family doubled in 1900 with the arrival of twins James and Herbert, and the next year their third son Hugh was born. In 1902 Matthews fell ill with typhoid and was in Vancouver General Hospital for three months. There he met the woman who years later would become his second wife.

After recovering, Matthews was frequently out of town because of his work for Imperial Oil, or on militia duty during the miners' strike in Nanaimo in 1913. He had joined a local militia unit in 1903 but when war broke out was transferred to the regular armed forces, serving in Europe from February 1916 to May 1918. Matthews led the first and second waves of a trench attack near Ypres, becoming something of a hero. Later he was invited to take tea at Windsor Castle because of his development of "fire cubes," eventually used by the British army. Matthews also served as the deputy returning officer in Belgium during the Canadian federal election of 1917. By the end of the war he was a major—a title he used until his death.

Matthews returned to Vancouver in 1918 to an estranged wife, but before their divorce was able to persuade Maud to accompany him on a tour for the federal government to promote the sale of Liberty Bonds. Two years later he married Emily Eliza Edwards, his nurse of nearly 20 years earlier. Incidentally, Emily is credited as the co-founder of the City of Vancouver Archives, but little is known about her.

After the war Matthews began his own business as a scow-owner and tug operator, taking as business partner his younger son Hugh. Two years later Hugh was killed in an elevator accident at work. In 1924 Matthews closed the towing business, briefly managed Canada Western Cordage, then retired.

With his working days at an end, Major Matthews began to devote himself to collecting and recording Vancouver history. He ran unsuccessfully for the park board in 1927 and 1928, when he was also director of the Arts, Historical and Scientific Society (predecessor to the museum).

After filling every available space in their Kits Point home with city memorabilia, Matthews obtained space in the attic of city hall—a room that came to be called the Deserted Chamber. There, in those early days of the archives, he worked in a cold, dark and dirty room. He called it a disgrace, and enlisted the support of public figures for a better location. The archives moved several times—to the Holden Building on East Hastings Street, the new city hall and then to the main library—before finally relocating to its current location in Vanier Park.

For many years Matthews was embroiled in controversy with the library board over the ownership and organization of the documents he had collected. The city's position was that official recognition of the archives in 1932, along with an honorarium to Matthews of $30 a month, amounted to city ownership of the material. Matthews disagreed and moved the collection back to his house. After weeks of wrangling, he was appointed city archivist and returned the material to city hall.

The city archives has evolved with donations from a number of families and organizations in the city in addition to Matthews' own collection and transcriptions of interviews with native leaders and European settlers. As a result of his efforts, Vancouver became the first city in Canada to erect a municipal archives building, a striking structure half-submerged in the earth at Vanier Park. Appropriately it was named in Major Matthews' honor. He died in 1970 at the age of 92.

The archives is now part of the city clerk's department. It houses original records of the city going back to 1886 as well as records and photographs donated by private individuals and organizations and prominent families. As a civic facility, it is open for public research on topics such as genealogy, architecture, neighborhoods and social issues.

Major J.S. Matthews—adventurer, innovator, and first archivist of the City of Vancouver. cva

First Election
Donna Jean MacKinnon

THE FIRST VANCOUVER civic election, May 3, 1886, was a crooked affair and, though the "good guy" won, only the chaos of the Great Fire saved it from being declared null and void.

There were two candidates for mayor—Richard H. Alexander, the manager of the Hastings Sawmill, and Malcolm Alexander MacLean, recently arrived and virtually unknown in Vancouver, who was approached and persuaded to run.

It was an "anybody but Alexander" campaign and about forty men cajoled and concocted the election results in favor of MacLean that day. Those who worked at Hastings Sawmill were "sore" at Alexander as he was arrogant and a bit of a tyrant as well. A few days before the election, at a strike at Hastings Sawmill, Alexander, threatening the workers and revealing contemporary racism, said he could run the mill more cheaply by using native and Chinese labor and that Canadians were "North American Chinamen" anyway.

Alexander's arrogance didn't make his employees inclined to vote for him, and retaliating forces went to work to ensure he didn't win the election. Vancouver pioneer Mr. Haywood told the story, "We wanted to put MacLean in and we did. There was a lot of people who voted who did not have a vote. Lots of people stopping in hotels had no qualifications." Hoteliers went along with the ruse to exaggerate the number of tenants in their rooms and also backdated receipts so that more pro-MacLean people could satisfy the residency requirement.

The Hastings Sawmill people coerced the Chinese employees and sent them up to vote for Alexander. But there were a lot of anti-Alexander navvies (laborers) hanging around Granville on election day and they threatened the Chinese and prevented them from voting.

At the end of the day, 499 votes had been cast and MacLean was elected by a margin of 17 votes. The citizens were said to have been so excited that they "took him in the back seat of a buggy and hauled him all over what there was of the little town."

Before a judgement could be made on the validity of the election, however, the Great Fire of June 13, 1886, occurred. In the confusion that followed, the protestations were dropped and Mayor MacLean went on to become elected for a second term.

London Drugs was established in 1945 when entrepreneur Sam Bass opened a thousand-square-foot drug-store in Vancouver. By its 50th birthday in 1995 the company had grown to a chain of 43 stores and had become a household name in the nearly 30 major markets it serves. Acquired by B.C.-owned and operated H.Y. Louie Group in 1976, London Drugs today employs more than 5,000 people and serves millions of people every year. Today, London Drugs stores carry more than 33,000 different products!

The Origins of Stanley Park
Heather Conn

IN 1863 THE COAL HARBOUR PENINSULA, which makes up most of today's Stanley Park, became a military reserve. Surveyed by Colonel Moody's Royal Engineers, the thick-timbered region commanded a view of the First Narrows entrance to Burrard Inlet. Americans had made the colony nervous with a military occupation of the San Juan Islands in the Gulf of Georgia only four years earlier. To ensure British control of the harbor entrance, a similar military reserve was established directly across the inlet on the north shore.

Natives had hunted and gathered for centuries in what is now Stanley Park. Coal Harbour once teemed with herring, its beaches rich with clams. Whales entered the bight to feed. Cougars roamed the forests. The peninsula's first roads were paved in 1888 with seashells from the Salish peoples' middens. These mounds of cultural debris covered almost two hectares and were up to 2.5 metres deep. One was a seasonal campsite for one of the largest Squamish villages. It later lay abandoned after a smallpox epidemic broke out between 1888 and 1892. Deadman's Island became an isolation site and burial ground for disease victims. The island's Douglas firs and red cedars also held Squamish and Musqueam bentwood boxes which contained their dead.

The area's first white settler, a Scottish calico printer named Jimmy Sievewright, set up a camp in 1858 with friends at the site of today's Second Beach. Portuguese ship-jumper Peter Smith, who settled at Brockton Point, used the island to render blubber from whales caught in the harbor. In 1859 Francis Brockton, chief engineer on HMS *Plumper,* discovered coal nearby. *Plumper's* captain, George Henry Richards, named the waters Coal Harbour.

In the early 1860s a Squamish village of four homes and a lodge—called Whoi-Whoi, meaning "masks" or "great village"—stood at the site of today's Lumberman's Arch. It hosted huge potlatches, attended by thousands of native people.

In May 1868 John "Gassy Jack" Deighton applied unsuccessfully to lease land to start a fishery in what is now Stanley Park. Five logging companies operated in the forests of the park-to-be. (Large stumps in today's park still bear the notches from loggers' springboards used for standing support while wielding a crosscut saw.) Most of today's trails in Stanley Park owe their start to logging, where they began as skid roads. Even before the area was declared a park, Lauchlan A. Hamilton,

land agent for the Canadian Pacific Railway, and a Vancouver alderman, surveyed its first roads. The perimeter road of today's park is virtually identical to Hamilton's original routing.

Vancouver newspapers began to discuss the future of the military reserve, which was no longer needed for defence, as a park. But the major initiative for the transformation came from a powerful land speculator, Arthur Wellington Ross. A park of untouched forest offered a valuable drawing card for realtors whose property was near. Ross co-owned adjacent property with H.F. Ceperley, head of one of Vancouver's most successful real estate companies, Ross and Ceperley.

Ross pitched his vision for a park to his friend, the influential William Van Horne of the CPR, even boating him around the reserve for a first-hand look. Van Horne agreed to speak to well-placed people in Ottawa, and he and Ross then talked to Alderman Hamilton, who speedily brought the idea before the city council.

The first resolution of Vancouver's first city council was a request to the federal government on May 12, 1886, to grant the First Narrows Military Reserve to the city as a park. A year later, the federal government established Stanley Park on a leasehold basis.

Mayor David Oppenheimer officially opened the park on September 17, 1888, declaring it a place where Vancouver's 6,000 inhabitants could "spend some time amid the beauties of nature away from the busy haunts of men." Several weeks earlier Oppenheimer had written to the CPR's Sir Donald Smith in Montreal asking him to name the park on behalf of Vancouver. Smith asked Governor General Lord Stanley to allow the park to be called by his family name and he agreed. Lord Stanley dedicated the park on October 29, 1889, during the first visit to Vancouver of a Governor General. An observer wrote: "Lord Stanley threw his arms to the heavens, as though embracing within them the whole of one thousand acres of primeval forest, and dedicated it to the use and enjoyment of peoples of all colours, creeds, and customs, for all time."

THE WESTIN BAYSHORE
Vancouver

Heralded at the time as the most luxurious hotel built, The Westin Bayshore opened its doors March 27, 1961 at a cost of $6 million. Then called the Bayshore Inn, the hotel has since grown to 517 rooms. The Westin Bayshore has been home to many travellers, including a six-month stay in 1972 of Howard Hughes. The Westin Bayshore continues to develop for the future to become Vancouver's premier residential area—and with a new address: 1601 Bayshore Drive.

Rafe Remembers
Rafe Mair

IT'S LIKE A SCOTTISH CLAN—you can't join, you must be born to it. I was. On a New Year's Eve many winters ago in old Grace Hospital I became a Vangcouverite. It might have been called Rafe Hospital if Grace McCarthy hadn't beaten me out. (Oh, you mean Grace was named after the hospital, not the other way around?)

Yes, Vangcouver has a "g" in it and it's Kitsil"eye"no and Capil"eye"no. That's one way you tell the natives. The other is by the eternally smug look they have—especially when the newcomer is from Toronto and says "sawassen" as if that's how you pronounced the name of the ferry terminal.

My early memories are somewhat jumbled. I remember Mayor Telford in an open car near Stanley Park on King George V's Silver Jubilee throwing toffee suckers out for the kids. It was then that I first thought politics must be fun.

And I remember Gerry McGeer—our Gerry. He was more famous than Mackenzie King—who I thought must be King of Canada with the name reversed in the style of Quebeckers.

facing page: *Brockton Point, Stanley Park, circa 1940.* cva
below: *Lord Stanley, after whom the park was named.* cva

Gerry McGeer was the only true mayor Vancouver ever had, with the possible exception of Tom "Terrific" Campbell, because he made people know about Vancouver. I remember when, after an absence of several years, McGeer ran for mayor again after the war. His slogan, and only campaign promise, was "Gerry's Back." He won in a huge landslide.

And there was Teddy Lyons, the conductor on the open-air streetcar that took tourists around the city. He was every kid's hero. He nearly got me away from politics to streetcar conducting but then B.C. Electric got rid of those wonderful streetcars for those damn buses.

I remember when the King and Queen came—somehow my cousin Hugh and I got ahold of some medals to wear. God knows where because the last war a Mair fought in was in New Zealand in the 1880s. But the Royal couple went by so fast that I don't think the King even saw me and my medals.

Then came the war. One Sunday morning the newsboys came down the street shouting "Extra, Extra! War Declared. Read all about it!" This led to many hardships. I had to weed our "Victory Garden" ensuring a lifelong dislike of horticulture. We collected silver paper from cigarette boxes—Export were best because they had cards with navy ships on them. Liquor was rationed—my Dad had 8 teetotalers' ration cards. War was rough.

Politics meant "Green" which always bothered me because blue was my favorite color. Then my Dad told me it was Howard Green, the perpetual MP from Point Grey. And there was Ian Mackenzie MP, later senator, who was always mocked so brilliantly in the Stearman Hardware ads in the *Province* classified section, which many read before the main sections.

I remember well the drinking clubs which were the only watering holes before cocktail bars were permitted by W.A.C. Bennett (who himself was a "dry," which didn't prevent him from helping Cap Capozzi form Calona wines). As the great wit Barry Mather said, "the Pacific Athletic Club is no more noted for athletes than the Arctic Club is for Eskimos."

Politicians came and went. Tom Campbell wanted to jail hippies under the War Measures act. W.A.C. was elected on the promise not to nationalize the B.C. Electric then promptly did just that. The first Vancouver boy to become premier, Dave Barrett, came and went quickly—it just seemed such a long time. And I moved to Kamloops, finally got into politics, first as an alderperson then as MLA and cabinet minister, then returned to my roots to talk to the people I love. Vangcouverites.

There was no place like it when I grew up here—there's no place like it now.

The Marine Building
Murray Forster

IT BEGAN WITH Lt. Commander J.W. Hobbs, vice-president of the Toronto bond-trading house, G.A. Stimson. After the Panama Canal began operating in 1914 Hobbs—who was president of Hobbs Bros. Ltd., ship owners—realized Vancouver had the potential to become a major west coast port, a sea route to Europe as well as a gateway to the Orient. And Vancouver's marine-related businesses would need offices near the waterfront—near the immigration buildings, the customs house, the Canadian Pacific and the Canadian National steamship terminals.

Hobbs dreamed of a skyscraper—a building that would put Vancouver on the international shipping map. It was conceived by its architects as a great crag of a building, "rising from the sea, clinging with sea flora and fauna, in sea-green flashed with gold." What resulted is a world masterpiece of Art Deco architecture. Hobbs found a site at the foot of Burrard Street that would give his tower spectacular views of the harbor and the North Shore mountains. He hired a local firm, McCarter and Nairne, to create his vision. McCarter, the engineer, jumped at the chance to design his first skyscraper. Nairne, the architect, inspired by New York City's Chrysler Building, was excited at the chance to create his own dazzling Art Deco showpiece.

He envisioned the 27-metre-long lobby (the "Grand Concourse") as a cavernous Mayan temple filled to the brim with treasures. Junior architects designed a huge array of sea creatures: snails, skate, crabs, turtles, carp, scallops and sea horses swam and frolicked over the walls and polished brass doors. Even the numbers on the large lobby clock were represented by sea creatures. Transportation was an important theme too, so Nairne had his team produce designs of trains, ships, automobiles and aircraft including zeppelins. Vancouver's position as a sea and rail connection was represented by ships and speeding trains. Famous ships like the *Golden Hind,* the *Resolution,* the *Beaver* and the *Empress of Japan* are shown in murals, and the stained glass over the entranceway paid tribute to Captain Vancouver with his ship, the *Discovery,* on the horizon.

There was a renewed interest in ancient mythology in the late 1920s, and Nairne picked up on that too: the 12 signs of the zodiac are worked into the floor. The original floor was made of corkoid, or "battleship linoleum," manufactured in Scotland by a firm that specialized in producing similar floors for luxury ocean liners. In 1989 the floor was replaced and replicated in marble.

Construction of the 25-storey building by E.J. Ryan Contracting began in mid-March 1929 when Vancouver mayor W.H. Malkin blew a blast from a golden whistle, setting in motion a steam shovel that began the excavation.

And then, midway through construction, came the Wall Street crash. J.W. Hobbs' tenacity was greater than the Great Depression, and everyone pressed on. When the Marine Building opened in October 1930 (at a cost of $2.3 million, $1.1 million over budget), it was the talk of the town. It was, for more than a decade, the tallest building in the British Empire.

Uniformed doormen stood by massive brass doors opening onto the dazzling lobby, and five sailor-suited young women waited to escort passengers in five high-speed (700 feet per minute at a time when the average was 150) elevators. The walls of the elevators were inlaid with 12 varieties of British Columbia hardwood.

The aura of affluence projected by the magnificent new structure intimidated some Depression-battered Vancouverites. But early tenants included the Vancouver Merchants' Exchange—which had contracted for a minimum of 10 years tenancy, The Vancouver Board of Trade, the Bank of Montreal and others. The architects themselves moved in, and were tenants for many years.

Still, almost everyone associated with the structure lost their shirts. Hobbs' dream had turned into a financial nightmare. For several years only the first four floors had tenants. In 1933 Stimson and Co. failed, and the Marine Building was sold to the Guinness family of Ireland for $900,000, little more than a third of its cost. A Guinness executive, A.J. Taylor, was put in charge of the building. He and his wife lived in the lavish two-storey, three-level penthouse. But Mona Taylor was afraid of heights, and the Taylors moved out. (One of the subsequent tenants of the penthouse was an eccentric widow who treated her grandchildren to rides on a Shetland pony that pranced around the balcony!)

The Marine Building is now co-owned by Princeton Developments Ltd., OMERS Realty Corporation and Confederation Life Insurance Company. Paul Merrick Architects made alterations and improvements that respected the fine old tradition of Vancouver's most treasured building. McLeod Restorations Ltd., in a three-year project, performed a complete exterior facade restoration including repair and restoration of the terra cotta and repair, replacement and the pinning back of the brick facade. From the mid-1980s on, nearly $20 million has been spent to restore the building to its original glory.

See the spine of this book for a photograph of the building.

MCLEOD RESTORATIONS LTD.
Masonry Preservation Specialists

McLeod Restorations began in 1974 when Gordon McLeod founded McLeod Masonry Ltd. The company expanded into restoration work and since 1979 has, as McLeod Restorations, been busy—using unique and tradition-respecting methods—in repair and restoration of historic buildings and facades. Projects include the Marine Building, Sinclair Centre, the Vancouver Art Gallery, Ballantyne Pier, the Orpheum, Sun Yat-Sen Gardens, Cathedral Place, the Spencer Building, Queen Elizabeth Theatre and Christ Church Cathedral.

Who Killed Janet Smith?
Ed Starkins

ON THE AFTERNOON of July 26, 1924 the Point Grey municipal police were summoned to 3851 Osler Avenue in Shaughnessy Heights, the home of F.L. Baker, a socially prominent exporter of pharmaceutical drugs, to investigate the apparent suicide of Janet Smith, the Baker family's 22-year-old Scottish nursemaid.

Wong Foon Sing, the houseboy at the Osler residence, told the police he had been alone in the house with Janet Smith since 9 A.M. Around noon, while peeling potatoes in the kitchen, he had heard a loud noise which sounded like a car backfiring in the street. He had hurried downstairs to find the nursemaid lying on the floor of the basement laundry room with blood oozing from a bullet wound above her right eye. A .45-calibre revolver lay at her side. Wong then telephoned the Pender Street office of F.L. Baker, who had rushed home, taken a brief look at the body and called the police.

At a coroner's inquest, two doctors who had examined Janet Smith's remains testified that it was unlikely that a bullet wound would have caused the massive damage that had occurred to the woman's skull. Moreover, they had found unusual burn marks on Smith's torso, and a mysterious stain on her index finger. The Point Grey police witnesses, however, saw nothing suspicious about the death of the Bakers' nursemaid. Their testimony helped determine the inquest finding that Janet Smith had either committed suicide or had accidentally shot herself.

Within days, several Shaughnessy Heights nursemaids came forward to dispute this verdict. In interviews with the local press, they insisted that Janet Smith had been an intelligent, easygoing and untroubled young woman who had no reason to take her own life. Unsettling rumors began to spread throughout the city suggesting that Smith had been killed, and possibly raped, by a member of Vancouver's high society, and that police officials had been bribed to cover up the crime.

On September 9, after five days of often sensational testimony, a second coroner's jury decided that Janet Smith had been murdered by persons unknown. Six months later, after intense speculation in Canadian and British newspapers, no arrests had been made. The mystery of the Scottish Nightingale seemed ready to fade from public view.

Then, on March 20, 1925, a group of vigilantes dressed in the hooded apparel of the Ku Klux Klan kidnapped Wong Foon Sing from the front lawn of the Baker house. For six weeks, he was shackled to the floor of an attic room in Point Grey, and subjected to frequent beatings, death threats, and other forms of intimidation to force him to tell what he knew about the Smith murder.

On May 1, the British Columbia Provincial Police announced that a delirious Wong Foon Sing had been found wandering late at night along a lonely stretch of Marine Drive. Shortly after taking Wong into custody, the police charged him with the murder of Janet Smith. To anyone familiar with the details of the Smith case, the accusation seemed absurd. Attorney General A.M. Manson soon confided to a newspaper reporter that he knew that the houseboy was innocent, but that the Crown wanted to use his trial to flush out the real murderer, an admission which persuaded a Vancouver grand jury to order Fong released for lack of evidence.

On June 17, the Wong Foon Sing affair took another startling turn as kidnapping charges were laid against Point Grey reeve J.A. Paton, police chief Hiram Simpson and four police constables. Also accused were three Canadian Detective Agency "operatives" who had worked for the municipality.

Reeve Paton and his colleagues did not bother to protest their innocence. Instead, they accused A.M. Manson of having sanctioned the kidnapping. The attorney general, they claimed, had met with a representative from Point Grey while Wong was in captivity. Manson denied these accusations on the floor of the British Columbia legislature, but not without damage to his political career. While the private detectives who had been on the city payroll received prison sentences, charges against the Point Grey officials were eventually dropped.

By the summer of 1925, the Janet Smith case had become a staple item in the British tabloid press. In Vancouver, one heard rumors of bribery, political interference, drug smuggling and the decadent behavior of the rich and powerful.

One of the more provocative murder theories asserted that Janet Smith was killed when she inadvertently became involved in a violent romantic quarrel between Jack Nichol, the playboy son of Lieutenant-Governor W.G. Nichol, and Lucille McRae, daughter of general and multimillionaire A.D. McRae. Lucille McRae was said to have lashed out at Smith in a jealous rage, causing her to slip on a wet floor and fracture her skull on a plumbing fixture.

Although Scotland Yard officials privately informed British Columbia authorities that F.L. Baker had operated a major drug smuggling ring in London in 1920-1923, no arrests were made in the Janet Smith case. In January 1926, Wong Foon Sing returned to China, ending the police investigation into one of Canada's most intriguing murder mysteries.

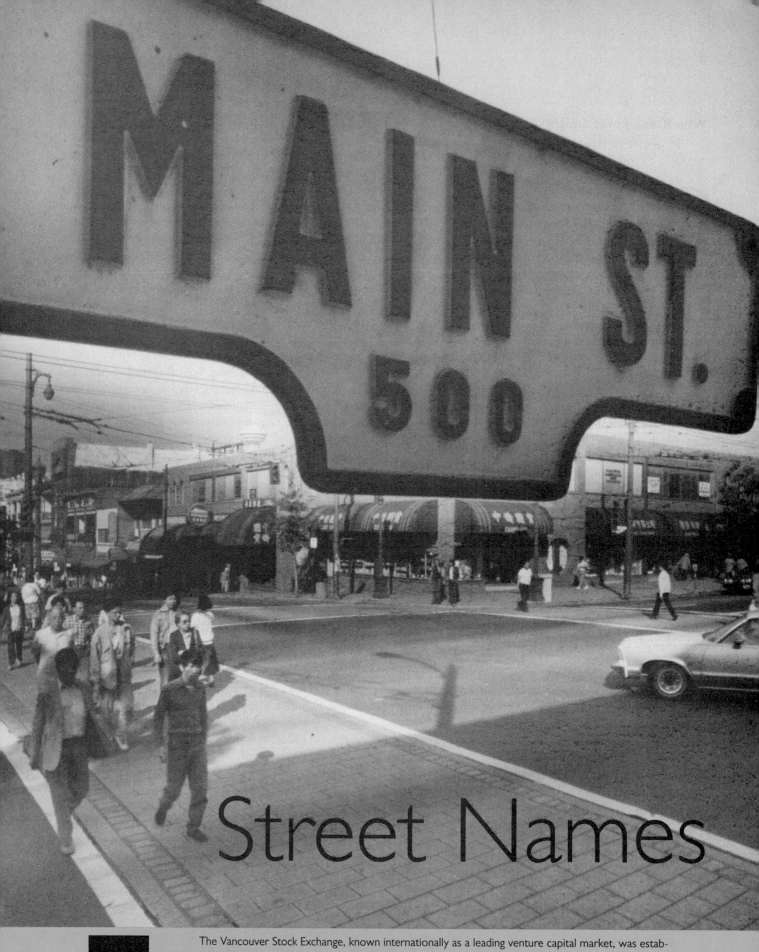

Street Names

The Vancouver Stock Exchange, known internationally as a leading venture capital market, was established in 1907 as a central marketplace for the resource-based economy emerging in Western Canada. Most of the early companies who sought financing through VSE facilities were involved in the burgeoning mining industry, and the VSE is still recognized as "Canada's mining exchange." Today, oil and gas and an increasing number of junior industrial and high-technology firms also turn to the VSE for capital.

Street Names
Derlang Ansager

STREET NAMES TEND TO give a lopsided view of local history: in the early years of a municipality they often commemorate business people (Flavelle, Ewen, Taylor, Hendry, Lonsdale, Keith, Dollarton), Canadian Pacific Railway officials (Matthews, Beatty, Cambie, Hamilton, Angus, Salsbury, Whyte), companies (Mainland, Ambassador), military men (Pender, Richards, Odlum, Alberni, French), politicians (numberless examples) or those who combine politics and business (Dunsmuir, Prior, Oppenheimer).

Women get short shrift (with Greene, Grafton and Magnussen notable exceptions) unless they're the wives (Martha, St. Anne) or daughters (Marguerite, Princess, Wenonah) of prominent men. First Nations people are certainly not ignored in names on local maps but at street level (with the exception of streets on the property of the Musqueam Indian Band) their ranks are thin. And where in Greater Vancouver is there a street, even in Chinatown, named for a prominent Chinese?

Newer places like Whistler happily broaden their approach and many newer street names take note of local topographical features . . . although a cynic has said that today's new developments tend to be named for the things removed (trees, for example) to make room for the development!

Pioneers and their families often give their names to streets in the areas they opened up: Powell, Lawson, Draycott, Fromme, Gatensbury, Vidal, Cornish, Fleming, Irvine, McLean, MacLean, Richardson, Avison, Ladner, Mackie, McBride, Roper, Springer, Lynas, Morton . . . Historical events (and oddities) play a role: check Ian Chunn's or Beverly McPherson's articles on Smuggler's Cove, Leg-in-Boot Square, Eddington Street, Adanac, Leonora, Senator and Minoru, for example.

Sometimes streets are named in bunches: after World War II there was a housing crisis so almost 50 hectares of empty land were quickly developed in Vancouver near Grandview Highway and Boundary Road. Alderman Halford Wilson, chair of the civic street naming commitee, announced in 1948 that the new streets would be named after wartime personalities, locations, battles and events. That gave us: Worthington and Falaise Avenues, Dieppe, Anzio, Mons, Normandy, Seaforth and Maida Drives, and Vimy and Matapan Crescents. Falaise and Malta Place completed the set. (Donald and

facing page: Main and Pender, Vancouver, 1987. vp

Jack Worthington were soldiers, sons of a former alderman.)

Then there are all those "provincial streets." Dr. Israel W. Powell, an early settler and city benefactor (after whom Powell Street is named) was responsible for naming streets after Canadian provinces, from Columbia to Prince Edward (excluding Alberta and Yukon, named later). Recreation has not been ignored: in 1952 city council approved naming streets in Fraserview after well-known golf courses across North America. The following streets derive their names from that decision: Seigniory, Leaside, Uplands, Bonnacord, Scarboro, Bonnyvale, Brigadoon and Bobolink. In 1935 the Quilchena Golf Club gave up its land and the CPR's Land Department subdivided it, naming streets to commemorate the following: Brackenridge (former city engineer), Edgar (Civic Zoning Appeal Board member), Haggart (former building inspector), McMullen (former CPR solicitor), McBain (CPR land agent) and Townley (first land registrar).

A very important pioneer figure in the naming of many streets was CPR land commissioner Lauchlan A. Hamilton. There's a plaque in his honor at the southwest corner of Hamilton and Hastings Streets, commemorating the 1885 start of his street-creating and naming work. Years later in response to a request for details from a historian, Hamilton wrote "I had a free hand in the property lying south of False Creek [Fairview] so there I was able to adopt the modern system of naming avenues 1st, 2nd, 3rd etc, and the streets I called after trees as Alder Street, Birch Street, Cedar Street, etc., preserving them as [much] as possible according to the arrangement of the alphabet." After selecting the names he handed them to his draughtsman, but forgot to mention they were to be arranged in alphabetical order. When Point Grey and South Vancouver were settled the avenue-numbering scheme was extended and eventually stretched as far as the North Arm of the Fraser River.

A naming competition for streets on the University of British Columbia campus was held in 1924. The successful suggestion by Joseph E. Fagan was largely based on names of other Canadian universities (Allison, Dalhousie, Knox) except for Wesbrook Crescent, named for Frank Wesbrook, UBC's first president. There are several streets in northeast Vancouver and north Burnaby (Yale, Oxford, McGill, Cambridge, etc.) named for universities.

Further information on the origins of street names in Greater Vancouver is welcome. Any future editions of *The Greater Vancouver Book* would benefit from an expansion of this colorful and interesting material. See the address for Linkman Press at the front of the book. A book by Elizabeth Walker was in progress as this book went to press.

Street Names of Greater Vancouver
Ian Chunn

WHISTLER

Alta Lake Road Named for the lake; a settlement there was a stop on the Pacific Great Eastern Railway.

Ambassador Crescent Gunnar Vogel owned a company called Ambassador Developments.

Beaver Lane Beavers once dammed Crabapple Creek.

Buckhorn Drive, Place Named for the nearby Buckhorn Ranch.

Cheakamus Way Named for the glacier, the lake, and the river by Bayshores developers Andy McGregor, Dennis Paul and Greg Pantages.

Corrie Drive Corrie Peak is south of Cheakamus Lake; Corrie Creek flows into the lake.

Crabapple Drive Named for Crabapple Creek.

Deerhorn Place During construction of Emerald Estates, six or seven deer a day would wander down and stare at the bulldozers.

Drifter Way, Place In the higher part of the development, snow drifted in during winter.

Eagle Drive This and other golf terms (Par Road, Fairway Drive and Street, Andrews Way and so on) are found in a development of Bob Bishop and Tom Good's, next to the Arnold Palmer-designed Whistler Golf Course.

Easy Street Al Davis, a Beat Generation survivor who drove a bulldozer, appreciated the idea of government support for the building of the subdivision and proclaimed they would all be living on Easy Street

Emerald Drive, Place Named for the color of the adjacent lake.

Fissile Lane Fissile Glacier and Fissile Mountain are visible to the south.

Fitzsimmons Road Named for the glacier and the creek that flows into Green Lake.

Garibaldi Way In 1890 British naval surveyor Captain George Henry Richards named the mountain, after which the street is named, for Italian patriot Giuseppe Garibaldi.

Horstman Place Harry Horstman was a trapper and prospector who settled here; he also left his name on a glacier and a creek.

Lorimer Road An established name long predating the Whistler development.

Mons Road BC Rail (then the PGE) had reached this point when the battle of Mons was fought during World War I. Vimy is farther up the line.

Mountview Drive A fine vantage point taking in a number of peaks, including Mt. Currie.

Nancy Greene Drive Named for the Olympic skier.

Needles Drive Pine needles 30 centimetres

deep blew everywhere as the houses were being built.

Rainbow Drive A glacier beyond Alta Lake is the source of the name for Rainbow Lodge, where Myrtle (Tapley) Philip and her husband Alec lived. Known to some as "Deadhorse Drive," because a horse belonging to one of the developers was buried in a field cleared two years later for Rainbow Drive. It's said the municipality needs to come around every so often and fill in a soft spot in the road!

Sarajevo Drive Named for the Olympic ski site by developers John and Kay Taylor and Dick Baxter.

St. Anton Way Named, like Aspen, Squaw Valley, and Lake Placid, for great places to ski—some of which have also been sites for the Olympics. Developer Ted Russell chose this name, along with the others in Alta Vista, including the family name given to Archibald Way.

Tapley Place The Tapleys had a farm and a sawmill. They built Rainbow Lodge.

Toad Hollow Bob Bishop, a realtor and developer, and Bernie Brown, a Squamish pharmacist, gave names to the streets in the Nesters development.

Toni Sailer Lane Toni Sailer skied for Canada in the Olympics.

Watson Way Vancouver lawyer Garry Watson built a cottage on some property and put in a 70-metre street with the help of some friends.

Wedgeview Place High up this dead-end road you can see Wedge Mountain.

Whistler Way Whistler Village names came from the government of B.C. Whistler's own name comes from the sound the marmots make; Whistler was once Alta Lake and the mountain used to be London Mountain.

HOWE SOUND

Argyle Avenue A street named, like Bruce, Chatham, Fox, Pitt, and Rosebery, for statesmen.

Clarke Drive Brigadier General R.P. Clarke was a founder of Gleneagles Company.

Dufferin Avenue Named after one of Canada's Governors General (Grey, Minto and Lorne are other examples).

Keith Road For 69 years the family of James Cooper Keith owned Passage Island at the entrance to Howe Sound.

Odlum Court In 1912 Major General Victor Odlum owned two lots on which he put a cottage; he added to it over the years and between 1945 and 1955 it was the family home.

Raleigh Street A street named, like Wellington and Wolseley, for military and naval leaders.

Reid Road Named for a pioneer family.

BOWEN ISLAND

Adams Road George Adams (d. 1955) was a contractor who built Vancouver's Carnegie

Library, early parts of the Vancouver General Hospital and the W.H. Malkin warehouse, now the Old Spaghetti Factory. He bought lot 492 at Tunstall Bay, built a house and moved there with his family in 1939. He also built a summer camp for *Vancouver Sun* carriers on the property in 1950 (named Camp Gates in honor of circulation manager Herb Gates).

Arbutus Point Road Arbutus Point is a subdivision on the former property of Fred Malkin.

Cowan Road George H. Cowan (1858-1935) was a Vancouver lawyer who, in 1896, while campaigning to represent Burrard for the federal Liberal Conservative Party, was very impressed by the southeast tip of Bowen Island. He bought Harry Lee's 46 hectares in 1899 and by 1917 had more than 400 hectares on which he built cottages for family and friends.

Dorman Road Jacob Dorman (1858-1939) was born in Constantinople where his father was an engineer for the British government. He joined the army in India and came to Canada in 1885 with his wife and two sons. He was a pipefitter in Yale for the Canadian Pacific Railway and came to Vancouver in 1886. In 1890 he preempted 65 hectares on Bowen then sold the title to the Royal City Planing Mill. He bought more land, then let it go when he moved back to England in 1895. In 1900 he was back in Vancouver and in 1905 he settled on Bowen. While always planning to open a hotel on his property, he never had enough money to realize that dream.

Finisterre Road Finisterre is the tidal island off Hood Point, whose name comes from the Norman word for 'Land's End' in England.

Grafton Road Caroline Susanna Grafton (d. 1914), a widow from London, came to Canada with her daughter in 1886 to join her three sons. Thomas and David preempted 65 hectares in 1889 and later Mrs. Grafton, with William and David, bought another 190 hectares near Trout Lake, now named after the family. In 1914, at the age of 80, she decided to visit England again, and did not survive the sinking of the *Empress of Ireland* when the ship was rammed in the St. Lawrence, near Rimouski, by the collier *Storstad*.

Green Road Robert Green (d. 1914), hailed originally from Lanceville, Nova Scotia. In 1899 he acquired 65 hectares. A farmer, canner and logger, he was often away and the household was managed by his wife, Matilda Jane Horne (1866-1913), from Truro, N.S. Both were school trustees.

Hood Point Road In 1860 Captain George Henry Richards named Hood Point, Mount Gardner, Cape Roger Curtis and Collingwood Channel after naval officers in the battle won by Earl Howe and Rear Admiral James Bowen on June 1, 1794, against the new French Republic.

Howe Road Named for the naval hero Admiral the Right Honourable Richard Scrope, Earl Howe.

Humming Bird Lane Croft and Angus, a Chemainus lumber company, sold its interest in land near Tunstall Bay to the Victoria Lumber and Manufacturing Company in 1889. Chief owner of the company was J.A. Humbird of Wisconsin.

Leonora Road The *Leonora* was a tug owned by Burrard Inlet Towing when it was taken over by the Union Steamship Company in 1889.

Miller Road Isaac Miller, from Huron County in Ontario, had a dairy in Vancouver. He bought property that he and his wife began parcelling out to sons, daughters and relatives, and the spot became known as Miller's Landing. Eldest son George (1882-1968) began to subdivide the property in 1909 and went on to success in politics from 1929 to 1957, as alderman, mayor of Vancouver (1937-38) and MLA (1952-54).

Robinson Road Jack and Muriel Robinson came to Bowen in 1946 and set up a cottage industry as weavers. Tourists brought by the Union Steamship Company to the Bowen Inn, travelled to the Weave Shop for tea. In 1957 the hotel was closed; when business declined the Robinsons left.

Senator Road The *Senator*, a Moodyville ferry, was another of the boats taken over by Union Steamship from Burrard Inlet Towing in 1889.

Smugglers Cove Road During Prohibition in the 1920s rum-runners frequented the bays of Bowen Island; one keeps the name of Smugglers Cove to this day.

Tunstall Road George C. Tunstall (1866-1950) came to Vancouver in 1887 then moved to the Kootenays and travelled for the Hamilton Powder Company, selling explosives to the mines. After representing the Nobel Powder Company of Scotland in Australia for a few years, he returned to B.C. and helped to start Western Explosives in 1908. Its plant was located at Tunstall Bay.

WEST VANCOUVER

Bellevue Avenue Named for the subdivision next to Dundarave.

Caulfeild Court, Drive, Place Francis William Caulfeild, aged 54, bought a sizeable piece of property in 1898 and laid out a village following the contours of the hills and using wild animal paths for trails. A general store and post office were established as was a wharf for Captain John Cates's ships. Building lots were put on the market in 1909.

Inglewood Avenue Named for the Ontario town, home to John Lawson's brother-in-law, William Charles Thompson.

Kew Road, Kew Cliff Road Edward "Holy Joe"

Collett had land at the cove till 1913. Quinton James Trotter renamed it Kew after the "Q" in his name and Kew Gardens in London.

Lawson Avenue John Lawson, the "Father of West Vancouver," came west from Ontario as a conductor with the CPR. He arrived in Vancouver in 1903 and bought John "Navvy Jack" Thomas' land in 1906. West Van's first Presbyterian services were held in his house in 1908. He was influential in getting the pier built at the foot of 17th Street, organized the first school, was the first postmaster (the post office was in his house) and donated waterfront land for the city hall in 1912. He served as reeve in 1913.

Leyland Street J.B. Leyland served as reeve from 1920-30.

Nelson Avenue Charles Nelson, one of the petitioners for the incorporation of the municipality, was a pharmacist whose business was located in the West End.

Odlum Court Professor Edward Odlum bought land in 1906; his son, Major General Victor Odlum, was a soldier, newspaper publisher and diplomat who gave the estate Rockcliffe Park to UBC (the land was along Marine Drive between Caulfeild and Whytecliff).

Palmerston Avenue This British prime minister is remembered along with other statesmen like Beaconsfield, Asquith, Pitt, Peel, Salisbury, Balfour, Rosebery and Gladstone.

Taylor Way Alfred James Towle Taylor was an engineer and investment entrepreneur. In London he managed to get the attention of W.S. Eyre and Lord Southborough, who represented the Guinness family's Iveagh Trust. In 1931 the Guinness' British Pacific Properties purchased the area we know as the British Properties today.

NORTH VANCOUVER (CITY)

Capilano Road An anglicized version of the name Ki-ap-a-la-no, chief of the Squamish tribe in 1859 when Captain Richards of the *Plumper* arrived to investigate a dispute. The name may be an honorific or a family name meaning "the people of Kiap," or "restored to life."

Fell Avenue James Pemberton Fell, an Englishman, was a chief shareholder in the Lonsdale Estate, one of the first divisions of land on the North Shore. He was also a colonel and the original commander of the Sixth Field Company, North Vancouver, 1912.

Hendry Avenue John Hendry was a manufacturer born in 1843 in New Brunswick. His interests in timber and sawmilling were complemented by his directorship on the Vancouver, Westminster and Yukon Railway.

Keith Road James Cooper Keith was a shareholder in the North Vancouver Land and Improvement Company and one of the prime instigators of the movement for incorporation of

the municipality in 1891. He was also active in undertaking the ferry service.

Kennedy Avenue Thomas Leslie Kennedy, a city alderman, was born in 1866 in New Brunswick and came to the North Shore in 1893. There he "engaged in logging operations," and built the first wharf at the foot of Lonsdale Avenue. He went up to the Klondike in 1901 and returned in 1905 with enough money to set himself up as a contractor. He built the Esplanade, First and Third streets, and the northern end of Lonsdale Avenue. Kennedy Lake, a source of the city's water, was a find of his.

Larson Road Pete Larson built the Hotel North Vancouver in 1902.

Lonsdale Avenue Heywood Heywood-Lonsdale, an Englishman related to J.P. Fell, was one of the chief shareholders in Lonsdale Estate.

MacKay Avenue Named for George G. MacKay, a director of the Burrard Inlet Railway and Ferry Company and a man closely connected to the incorporation of North Vancouver.

Mahon Avenue The principal shareholder in the North Vancouver Land and Improvement Company was J. Mahon, who sent his brother Edward to be the president and active member of Mahon, McFarland and Mahon.

Moody Avenue Sewell Prescott "Sue" Moody came to Victoria with his brother from Maine in 1859. He bought the mill on Burrard Inlet. After 1865 it was known as "Moody's Mill," and he lived there until his untimely death aboard the ill-fated *SS Pacific* en route to California in 1875.

NORTH VANCOUVER (DISTRICT)

Allan Road Named after Thomas Allan, former partner with J.M. Fromme.

Barrow Street Named for John and Janet Barrow, the parents of Wilhelmina (Barrow) Cates, who married Charles H. Cates, founder of C.H. Cates and Sons.

Boundary Road The boundary line between North Van City and the District of North Vancouver. Allan Road was formerly Boundary Road, as it was the eastern boundary of Moody's Mill's timber lease.

Chamberlain Drive Named after the English statesman, Rt. Hon. Joseph Chamberlain.

Church Road St. Clement's Anglican Church was here before it was moved to Institute Road as an annex to the new church.

Dollarton Highway In 1912 Robert Dollar, famous in the world of California shipping, established the Canadian Robert Dollar Company and set up a sawmill and dock on a 30-hectare site on the North Arm. The Dollar Fleet, with its famous $ insignia, sailed out of Burrard Inlet and, as a community grew around the mill, the name was changed to Dollarton.

Draycott Road, Place, Park, Gardens Walter

Mackay Draycott, born in Leicestershire in 1883, came to Canada in 1907 and Vancouver in 1911. After serving as a topographer in World War I he returned to North Vancouver where he was a justice of the peace, a school trustee, a collector, writer and informed historical resource. This "wayfaring scribe" lived to be 102. A sculpture of him rests in Pioneer Park, Lynn Valley.

Duval Road J.M.S. Duval, the writer and publisher of the *Industrial News* in the 1880s in Victoria, lived on this road.

Dempsey Road Dempsey was a Vancouver Land Agent.

Fromme Road Julius Martin Fromme, born in 1857 in Nova Scotia, came to Port Moody in 1883. He was the foreman of the Hastings Mill for ten years and then moved to the North Shore and formed the Lynn Valley Lumber Company. The first settler and founder of Lynn Valley, he later became reeve of the district.

Lowry Lane Named for author Malcolm Lowry. From his squatter's shack in what is now Cates Park he could look across Burrard Inlet and see the Shell sign with the "S" burned out glowing infernally through the night . . .

Lynn Valley Road Formerly the Pipeline Road, as the North Vancouver water pipe was imbedded along it from the Lynn Creek intake to North Vancouver City.

Magnussen Place Named for Karen Magnussen, Olympic skater.

Mill Street Named for the Upper Saw Mill—the First Mill—off Dempsey Road.

Nancy Greene Way Named after Nancy Greene, Olympic skier.

Viney Road Named for Captain Viney of the North Vancouver Ferry Service.

Whitely Court Named for Margaret Whitely, Lynn Valley's first teacher, who arrived in 1904.

PORT MOODY

Clarke Road, Street James Anthony Clarke was born in 1834 in New Brunswick and went to sea in 1856. In 1865 he came ashore in Portland with malaria and the ague, and came up to Canada. In command of Governor F. Seymour's yacht *Leviathan* for seven years, he dwelt in Langley where he was one of the petitioners for its 1872 incorporation. In 1883 he moved to Port Moody where he owned land; there he built the Elgin House Hotel to house CPR workers at $7 a week. The hotel was destroyed by fire in 1887.

Douglas Street James Douglas, the Hudson Bay Company's chief factor in 1851, became the second governor of Vancouver Island and the first governor of the Colony of British Columbia.

Elgin Street Lord Elgin was a British diplomat at the time John Murray Jr. was naming the streets of Port Moody.

Flavelle Drive Aird Flavelle, whose father had done well in Ontario in produce and cold storage, came out with H.R. MacMillan in 1910 to investigate lumber investments. He returned from Ontario in 1911 and in 1912 bought the Emerson Lumber Company with R.F. Thurston.

Grant Street Duncan B. Grant was one of the first pioneer merchants to open a store in Port Moody; he became postmaster as well.

Henry Street John Murray Jr.'s younger brother, who died in infancy in 1874.

Hugh Street One of the Murray brothers, born in 1856 in Southampton.

Ioco Road Imperial Oil Company, established in Ontario in 1880, set up shop in Burnaby in 1912. In 1914 they moved to the present Ioco site because of deep anchorage, fresh water and cheaper land. A townsite was developed adjacent to the plant.

Jane Street Named for John Murray Jr.'s mother.

Kyle Street William Black Kyle married John Murray Jr.'s sister Sarah in 1881.

Mary Street Named for Mary Murray, John Murray Jr.'s sister, who married Charles McDonough in 1882 and moved to Nanaimo.

Murray Street John Murray Sr. (1831-1905) of Scottish background was born in Netby, Ireland. A lance-corporal in the Royal Engineers he and his wife Jane Fuller (d. 1896) were the first settlers in Port Moody. From 1863 he was a boatbuilder and in 1875 became the lighthouse keeper on Behrens Island in Victoria Harbour. He returned to Port Moody in 1883 to manage the Rocky Point Hotel. His son John Murray Jr. (1859-1942), known as "Mr. Port Moody," was responsible for naming the streets of the municipality.

St. Andrews Street What is now the United Church was built in 1900 and moved nearby in 1912 to allow for the construction of additions. The old site was used for parishioner Robert Abernethy's tennis court.

St. John's Street Possibly named for John Murray Jr. or his father. In 1899 the Anglican church was built on a lot donated by Captain Clarke.

Williams Street William was another Murray brother, born in Sapperton in 1866.

COQUITLAM

Austin Avenue W.R. Austin ran the Blue Mountain Ranch on the site of what is now the Vancouver Golf Club. He later moved to Kamloops.

Blue Mountain Street Named after W.R. Austin's ranch.

Coast Meridian Road This road marks the survey line laid out by Joseph Trutch for the Royal Engineers. Its baseline runs due north from the first survey post east of Boundary Bay on the 49th parallel. It was used for surveying unregistered land in the Fraser Valley.

Como Lake Road In 1893 the road was laid from North Road to Lillian for $5 a chain. In 1894 the west end was built for logging.

Delestre Avenue Father Delestre ran the convent school Notre Dame de Lourdes in Maillardville.

Erskine Street Bob Erskine ran a blacksmith shop that burned in the 1920 fire.

Finnigan Street Father Finnigan offered mass in Port Coquitlam from 1934; he then bought a lot on which Our Lady of the Assumption Catholic Church was built.

Gatensbury Street Ernest Edgar Gatensbury was a pioneer who set up the Como Lake Greenhouses. Born in Derbyshire in 1870 he settled in Coquitlam in 1910. When the greenhouses failed following a freak weather accident, he went to work for the Fraser Mills from 1922-39.

Johnson Street The Johnsons—with the Waltons— were the first homesteaders in east Coquitlam. Their house was complete by 1910.

MacIntosh Street Johnny and Alec were two of Coquitlam's original settlers.

Mundy Street George Munday (the correct spelling), an Owen Sound lather and brickmaker born in 1869, put in a "homestead entry" for 60 hectares in 1888. This was granted in 1895 while he was still living with his wife Constance Jane in Sapperton. The street, lake and park all misspell his name.

Pipeline Road Old Pipeline Road was a trail that ran over Dawes Hill.

Poirier Street The Poiriers were one of the families who came from Quebec to work in the mills in 1910.

PORT COQUITLAM

Atkins Avenue This Irish family moved to Australia, then New Zealand and came to Victoria in 1859. In 1868 all but "Ned" (Edmund A., b. 1843) returned to Australia. Ned married a native herbalist named Susan; in 1891 he became councillor, in 1897 reeve (for seven years). He spent 13 years on the school board and in 1912 was a justice of the peace.

Davies Avenue Charles S. Davies came from England in 1909 and was a contractor and builder on such projects as the city hall and the Commercial Hotel. He served in World War I and was postmaster in 1923. Director of the *Coquitlam Star*, he also served on council for 30 years, nine of them as mayor.

Fox Street James Fox came to Coquitlam as a foreman with the CPR in 1885. A farmer, he served as a councillor from 1891 to 1910.

Galer Way Roger C. Galer was born in Suffolk in 1874. A mason, he came to Port Coquitlam in 1907 and started a shoe store. A councillor as early as 1913, he went on to become president of the board of trade and mayor from 1924-46.

Grant Avenue General R.E. Grant was "Captain Jack," Col. R.C. Moody's senior captain. It was he who refused to make the first cut at Mary Hill, arguing that New Westminster was a better site for the capital of the new mainland colony.

Irvine Avenue R.D. Irvine was the first Coquitlam municipal clerk from 1891 to 1899. He was also one of the earliest teachers in the area.

Kelly Avenue R.D. Kelly, with his father-in-law Col. Scott, built the first hotel in Westminster Junction, the Junction Hotel. It was popular in the early 1900s and housed the first post office; Kelly was the first postmaster. His hall on Dewdney Trunk Road, "Kelly's Hall," served as the municipal hall between 1890 and 1913. From 1891 to 1897 Kelly served as the first reeve.

Kilmer Street City engineer John Kilmer was born in Ontario in 1861; he came west to join the Trail of '98. From 1900 to 1906 he was Vancouver's assistant city engineer; in 1912 Coquitlam's supervising engineer; and in 1913 Port Coquitlam engineer.

Langan Avenue Councillor John Langan was a director of the *Coquitlam Star,* the first newspaper in the municipality.

Lobb Avenue Named for councillor C.F. Lobb.

Mars Street James Mars, born in Scotland in 1870, came to Coquitlam via Manitoba. With his brother Arthur, who brought his family to Coquitlam in 1896, he kept a general store. James was reeve from 1911-13 and was then acclaimed mayor. He fought at Vimy Ridge in the 131st Battalion and, once back home, was a justice of the peace. Arthur was mayor in 1919.

Marshall Avenue M. Marshall was an Agricultural Society member and an early settler.

McLean Avenue Captain Alexander McLean settled at Pitt Meadows in 1851. His son Donald, Coquitlam's first pioneer, preempted land about six kilometres north, near De Bouille Slough in 1881, and became a successful dairy farmer.

Nacht Avenue Alderperson and realtor Ronald Nacht, from Saskatchewan, was a strong supporter of the Coquitlam Sports Complex.

Pitt River Road A need for land accessibility when the Fraser froze convinced Governor Douglas to have roads constructed; in 1859 North Road was put through and in 1862 the Pitt River Road completed. It was named for the statesman.

Richardson Road William Richardson came from the eastern U.S. He set up a ranch across the river in Pitt Meadows.

Routley Avenue John Manning Routley, a Scot who emigrated to Langley, had two sons, Thomas J. and William. Thomas ran a fish store in Coquitlam, was a councillor as early as 1916 and a school trustee between 1920 and 1926.

William had an interest in the Coquitlam Hotel and hauled freight as well.

Rowland Street Jacob "Jake" Rowland came to Coquitlam with his family in 1894 as CPR agent for the Junction. He was later postmaster and part owner of the Junction Hotel.

Tuohey Avenue W. Tuohey, who came to Port Coquitlam in 1929, was a school trustee through the 1930s and was responsible for preparations for the 1939 Royal Visit. He is also remembered for his service to the Royal Canadian Legion.

Welcher Avenue Dennis Eugene Welcher was born in Michigan in 1859 and came to Coquitlam around 1896. A logger and farmer he was reeve in 1909-10 and a Port Coquitlam alderman from 1913-15.

Wilson Avenue Alderman W. Wilson ran a stagecoach from Westminster Junction to the second dam on Coquitlam Lake.

PITT MEADOWS

Advent Road A large group of Seventh Day Adventists settled in the area before 1920.

Baynes Road Baynes was an early resident.

Bonson Road This was the Pitt Meadows Road but it was later named after Robert F. Bonson, the first road foreman in the municipality. Sternwheelers from Fort Langley stopped at Bonson's Landing to load produce for the New Westminster market.

Davison Road Tom Davison was a trustee in the municipality.

Fenton Road Charles Fenton, who came from Ireland and returned to Britain to serve in World War I, was a councillor with the municipality.

Ford Road S.H. Ford, a certified seed potato grower, was reeve in the late 1920s.

Harris Road Wellington Jeffers Harris came with his family by boat from New Westminster and settled on higher lands (avoiding the annual floods) in 1873. He preempted the land in 1874 and was a commissioner from 1893. He was Pitt Meadows' first reeve and worked hard to create a dyking system. He later became a member of the legislative assembly.

Kennedy Road Named for a family that has lived in Pitt Meadows since 1910.

McMyn Road W.R. McMyn served on the first council and again from 1916-19; he was also on the school board.

McNeil Road Archbishop McNeil of the Holy Rosary Cathedral bought land in the No. 2 Dyke Area in 1911. The land became known as "the Archbishop's Subdivision."

McQuarrie Road Alex McQuarrie from Nova Scotia was one of those who settled on the land purchased by Archbishop McNeil.

Mitchell Road Robert Mitchell was a school trustee.

Park Road William James Park preempted prop-

erty in 1905. He built a log house and later a frame building and established a sawmill that sold ties as well as telegraph poles and cordwood to the CPR. A signatory to the petition to create the municipality, he became its first clerk in 1914. A reeve through the 1930s, he served the municipality for 29 years.

Reichenbach Road W.T. Reichenbach was a soldier-settler.

Richardson Road William Richardson came to the area in 1882 from Ontario by way of the U.S. (taking a wagon train to Seattle). He settled up the Pitt River and built a tug with partner George Mouldy. The two used the tug to pull two scowloads of sturgeon each week from Pitt Lake. A member of the first council, he served for many years.

Rippington Road Sydney T. Rippington was a councillor and president of the Farmer's Institute. A soldier-settler, he also co-founded the local Legion Branch.

Woolridge Road C.R. Woolridge was a councillor with the municipality.

MAPLE RIDGE

Abernethy Lane, Way George Abernethy was a partner with Nelson Lougheed in Abernethey and Lougheed, a lumber and milling concern. The firm, headquartered north of Webster's Corners, had its own railroad to bring fir, cedar and spruce in from the camps to make into lumber, shingles and moldings.

Baker Road Now 240th Street, the road was named for Peter Baker who changed his name from Ferdinand Boulanger when he left Quebec for California and then B.C. in his search for gold. He bought land on the Fraser River next to the first settler in Albion ("East Haney"), Samuel Robertson.

Blackstock Street Farmer Robert Blackstock was reeve of Maple Ridge in 1889, 1897-99.

Calligan Avenue Named (and misspelled) after Thomas Haney's father-in-law D. Callaghan.

Cliff Avenue This street runs along the partially filled-in northern rim of the gash left in the hillside after a chunk of land 400 metres long slid into the Fraser between Hammond and Haney. William Edge of Langley died in the tidal wave that resulted and wharves and bridges were mowed down.

Derby Street Derby was the name of the town to be built just west of Fort Langley that was, at one point, to become the capital of the Colony of British Columbia.

Hammond Road English brothers John (b. 1836) and William (b. 1843) had been settlers in the area since 1862. They developed a commercial area (as did Haney) as the CPR arrived in the 1880s. A wharf was built here to handle ship traffic to Victoria (Port Hammond was established in 1883). John Hammond brought in the first named varieties of orchard stock in the district.

Hampton Street William Hampton came with John Laity from Cornwall, by way of Denver, in 1879. He settled on land he bought from the Hammond brothers.

Haney By-pass, Place Thomas H. Haney, a Cape Bretoner, went to school in Ontario and became a brickmaker. He came to Maple Ridge in 1876 where he bought riverfront acreage and used the rich local clay deposits to start a flourishing brickmaking business. A councillor as early as 1877, Thomas put in 14 years of community service. Port Haney was established in 1882. Thomas Haney died in 1916.

Howison Avenue In 1876 William Justice Howison was Maple Ridge's first postmaster and in 1882, George Howison was reeve.

Laity Street John Laity travelled with William Hampton from Cornwall in 1879 and bought almost 50 hectares from the Hammond brothers. Laity Street connected the school, church, stores and post office of Nelson's Landing to the homesteads north of the municipality. Reeve in 1892-93 and 1908, John Laity raised sheep and prize cattle and poultry.

McFarlane Avenue J.C. McFarlane married the daughter of John McIvor the former HBC cooper whose farm gave Maple Ridge its name. McFarlane was reeve from 1910-13.

McIntosh Avenue Mr. McIntosh was one of the first registered lot holders on the North Lillooet River. The river's name was changed in 1914 to Alouette to avoid confusion with the Lillooet of the Interior.

Purdey Avenue Mr. Purdey owned a brickworks in Maple Ridge.

St. Anne Avenue Named for the patron saint of Thomas Haney's wife Ann.

Selkirk Avenue Charles Selkirk homesteaded on the Lillooet (Alouette) River from 1898 and started what became known as Frenchman's Mill. His brother James, a partner in the Selkirk and Pelletier Mill (manufacturing shingle bolts from 1907), became reeve in 1910.

Stephens Street Joseph Stephens was reeve in 1894.

Tyner Avenue The Tyner sawmill opened around 1905 at River Road and Hinch (now 225th). It was bought by Abernethy and Lougheed in 1912.

LANGLEY

Douglas Court Sir James Douglas was the first governor of British Columbia.

Duncan Way William Duncan was born in Scotland in 1882 and was a commercial fisher living in the valley from 1911. At the far east end of River Road he established the Duncan Fishing

Bar. He was famous for having landed a 330-kilogram sturgeon.

Ferguson Road Now 100th Avenue, the street was named for Munro Ferguson (who married Annie Merryfield). Born in New Brunswick in 1860 the son of a senator and a judge's daughter, he homesteaded from 1885. The couple raised a family of nine children on the farm.

Jackman Road Philip Jackman (1835-1927) was born in Devon and came to B.C. as one of the Royal Engineers in 1859. He built the road to False Creek on a private contract. For nine years he was New Westminster's one-man police force; his Black Maria was a wheelbarrow. With his wife Sara Ann Lovegrove he homesteaded on a quarter-section (65 hectares) in Langley, ran a store, surveyed for the railway and was reeve. He was also a fisheries officer for 14 years. He gave the name "Aldergrove" to the locale, perhaps inspired by his wife's maiden name.

Mackie Street James W. Mackie came from Banffshire in Scotland in the early 1870s and settled on the Salmon River. He was Langley's first reeve in 1873 and was re-elected as warden in 1874 and 1875.

Marr Street Ben Marr (who married Isabel Drew) was a doctor in Fort Langley who kept horses. He did dental work and performed veterinary services as well.

Matheson Road Donald and Flora were early settlers.

Mavis Avenue Alex Mavis bought the site of the HBC store in Fort Langley in 1888.

McBride Street Arthur McBride was made warden of the B.C. Penitentiary in 1878 but was suspended in 1894 following a Royal Commission into prison operations. His son Richard, born in New Westminster in 1870, became B.C.'s first native-born premier and at 33 its youngest. "Glad-hand Dick," a Conservative, exploited anti-Asian sentiment and bashed Ottawa effectively enough to stay in office for a dozen years. He established the provincial university and oversaw legislation requiring that B.C. timber be processed here. He resigned in 1915 and died not long after.

McDonald Road Archibald McDonald was the HBC's strict but fair chief trader at Fort Langley. He developed the salmon export industry there.

Michaud Court M. Michaud came from Quebec to B.C. by way of Wisconsin arriving in 1878. An uncle, Maximilian, was already here as was a brother who had bought the New Brighton (later Hastings) Hotel in 1865. Michaud had almost 250 hectares in Langley Prairie.

Morrison Road Ken Morrison (1831-1900) from the Isle of Lewis was a former HBC employee who came to Fort Langley as a soldier in 1853 but soon deserted. Caught, he worked in the

fort's cooperage and then left to try the Cariboo. He returned to Fort Langley and preempted 65 hectares where he had been discovered after deserting. There he and his wife Lucy Allard operated a stopping house for miners. In 1873 he was a councillor for Langley.

Mufford Court Thomas Mufford was a Cornish tin miner born in 1838. He worked in the U.S. before settling in Fort Langley in 1885.

Nash Avenue John Angus Nash and his wife Alice left their English farm to come to Canada in 1895. They tried Bellingham as well but returned to Canada in 1900, where they farmed and shipped cream to Lynden, Washington. They were instrumental in building the Lutheran church and John served as a councillor in Langley. He died in 1945; she died in 1949.

Taylor Road John James Taylor was a settler and signatory to the petition in 1872 requesting the creation of the municipality of Langley.

Telegraph Trail Following the failure of the first attempt to lay a cable across the Atlantic floor, plans were made for the development of an overland line. The Collins Overland Telegraph would reach Europe by way of B.C., Alaska and Siberia. In 1865 Governor Seymour commissioned a sleigh road from the tidewater to Yale, using old HBC routes, to set up the telegraph. Running from New Westminster through Langley, Matsqui and Chilliwack to Hope, the trail was less than four metres wide and was effectively useless for the carriage of goods and people. The first message to leave the Fraser Valley, sent by Seymour to London, read: "Weather beautiful. All well and Indians perfectly quiet."

Williams Road Alexander and William Williams were early settlers and signatories to the 1872 petition that led to incorporation in 1873.

WHITE ROCK

Coldicutt Avenue Thomas Davis Coldicutt (1879-1970) came to Canada from Birmingham in 1900 to participate in the Klondike Gold Rush. In 1908 he moved from New Westminster to east Burnaby where he is remembered by Coldicutt Street. From 1909 he was a councillor and in 1912 he became involved in real estate. He donated 90 hectares for Central Park and secured the money to build Kingsway. In 1912 he bought a home in Crescent Beach; in 1932 he bought 200 hectares and built homes, a villa with lodges, a stable and tennis courts. These are today's Ocean Ridge townhouses.

Kerfoot Road W.D. Kerfoot was an editor and manager of the *Semiahmoo Sun*.

O'Hara Lane Municipal engineer James F. O'Hara retired in 1922.

Oxenham Avenue James Oxenham (d. 1944) came from Ontario and married Emily Jane

Bridges in High River, where they had four of their nine children. Their general store in White Rock, where James was postmaster, was an 1887 structure that lasted until the 1960s at Coast Meridian Road and Old McLellan.

Roper Avenue Robert Roper came to B.C. in 1885 from Kansas with sons John and Laben. John (d. 1932) was a logger who, with Fred Philp and Henry Thrift, built White Rock's first school. In 1900 the Ropers bought 65 hectares at the highest point in town and put up the first building in the vicinity. When the 65 hectares were subdivided the road allowance passing the Roper home was given their name.

Stevens Street Vancouver-based H.H. Stevens was interested in real estate and owned property in White Rock. He was a member of R.B. Bennett's cabinet in the 1930s, was instrumental in establishing what became Granville Island and later became a senator.

Thrift Avenue Henry Thomas Thrift (1852-1947) came to Canada in 1874 and was a brickmaker in Yale in 1882. He became Surrey municipal clerk in 1883 and got a school going that year as well. In 1905 he donated land for Hazelmere United Church and in 1910 he donated land for a new school.

Vidal Street James Henry "Harry" Vidal camped and pioneered from 1903; in 1905 he cleared a site and built one house. Later, he put up another. A realtor, he also wrote for the *Columbian*. His wife, who later became known as "Granny Vidal," founded the town's swimming association, its scout troop and other clubs.

SURREY

Boothroyd, Pike, Stayte Road *160th Street* George Boothroyd built a house for himself in 1873 in Surrey Centre without the benefit of any roads to bring in the lumber. He was a councillor in 1882 and often thereafter. William Pike was also on council. Mr. Stayte farmed along the road.

Bose, Peck, Medd Road *64th Avenue* Henry Bose came to Surrey in 1890 at the age of 22 and established the successful Meadow Ridge Farm. He was reeve for five years, a police magistrate for 35 and the president of the Surrey Cooperative for 25 years. Peck and Medd farmed along the road as well.

Boundary Road *0 Avenue* In 1858 some of the Royal Engineers had a base camp at White Rock from which they built two-and-a-half kilometres of good road along the beach and through the Semiahmoo Indian Reserve. Working with a party from the U.S. the engineers placed further markers along a survey line to the east, forming a border trail where 0 Avenue runs today.

Brown Road *32nd Avenue* Surrey's early settlers included many people named Brown. Near the road were David W. Brown whose sons planted the trees in Redwood Park; his brother Archie; and William Brown who sold Surrey produce in Victoria and brought supplies back by boat for the settlers.

Campbell River Road *8th Avenue* The road follows the Campbell River, named by the Royal Engineers for Archibald Campbell, a U.S. representative on the International Boundary Commission.

Clover Valley Road, Pacific Highway *176th Street* William Shannon named the district Clover Valley in the 1870s. For a long time the road ended at the Nicomekl River as sternwheelers could carry the freight from there. By 1913 with the growing importance of the automobile, the road was gravelled, opened south to the U.S. and renamed the Pacific Highway. Paved in 1923 the road benefited from a planting effort by the Kiwanis Club of Vancouver, who put in 1,150 ornamental trees as a gesture towards hiding some ugly clearcuts left by decamped lumber companies.

Colebrook Road Colebrook was the name of J.J. Brown's farm.

Gilley Street The Gilley brothers ran an important lumber outfit.

Hall's Prairie Road *184th Street* In 1845 Sam Hall settled in southeast Surrey with his native wife. He murdered her and died in the New Westminster jail. The road was the best connection from the Old Yale Road to the U.S. in the days of horse and wagon.

Hjorth Road *104th Avenue* In 1885 the Norwegian Hans Christian Hjorth was the first of a number of fishermen to move up from Fraser River shacks to lots on what has become 104th Avenue. He returned to his native country in 1900 but his name stuck.

Johnston Road *152nd Street* James Johnston with sons Isaac and William came to Surrey in 1866 and preempted land along what has become 152nd Street and 64th Avenue. The year after Surrey became a municipality in 1879, Isaac was elected councillor. John Johnston won the contract for making the trail from the settlement in 1884; the road took years to complete.

Kells Road *196th Street* This road marks Surrey's eastern boundary. Two men, both named Henry Kells, preempted land on the Fraser River and established Port Kells. Though it never became the busy port they had hoped for, industry and residences occupy the space today.

Kennedy, Davis, Holt Road *88th Avenue* In 1860 James Kennedy became the first person to preempt land in the area that became Surrey. Davis received money for work done on the road near his farm and Holt farmed along the road as well.

Kensington, Mud Bay, Bradshaw, *40th Avenue* H.T. Thrift named part of Hall's Prairie District Kensington Prairie; the road ran to Mud Bay in the west; and Mr. Bradshaw owned a farm alongside the road.

King George VI Highway, Bergstrom Road *136th Street* George VI was King in 1940 when the highway linking Vancouver with the Peace Arch to the U.S. was opened. Bergstrom farmed along 136th Street near Bear Creek Park, site of the Arts Centre today.

Latimer Road *192nd Street* J. Latimer settled on the east side of Surrey and served on its second council. The road once marked Surrey's eastern boundary but an unclaimed 800-metre strip between Surrey and Langley came to Surrey in 1881, before moving its boundary that much further east.

McLellan, New McLellan, Milton, Shannon, Dullay, Roberts Road *56th Avenue* A.J. McLellan was contractor for 13 miles of the road. It ran northeast from the Serpentine River through Surrey Centre; an 1890s continuation of the original road going east became known as New McLellan. A Mr. J.C. McLellan was the first school teacher in Hazelmere and was also a road foreman. Albert Milton dwelt next to and worked on the road; Tom Shannon was the first warden after Surrey was incorporated; and Dullay and Roberts also farmed along the road.

North Bluff Road *16th Avenue* George Vancouver noted "high white sand cliffs falling perpendicularly into the sea." A south bluff is on the U.S. side of the border and the north bluff is near Ocean Park on the Canadian side.

Sandell, Stevenson Road *128th Street* Swedish sailor Nels Peter Andersson jumped ship in 1887 and settled at what is now the corner of 96th Avenue and 128th Street. Fearing discovery he changed his name to Sandell, married, and farmed happily in Surrey until 1901, when he moved to Burnaby. Ben Stevenson came to Surrey in 1887 aged 17 and worked on his brother's farm for ten years before buying his own 97 hectares on Wade Road (44th Avenue) at Mud Bay. Public-spirited, he donated land for Ocean Park's first school, carried mail from New Westminster to the Elgin Hotel and allowed people from the Coqualeetza Reserve to use his land for a summer camp.

Scott Road *120th Street* In 1873 Col. J.T. Scott contracted to build a wagon road south to the Semiahmoo Trail from the Fraser River settlement of Brownsville. He had not finished the work by 1875 so the contract was completed by someone else the following year. The name remained however.

Sullivan Street In 1903 Thomas Sullivan and his brother Henry acquired the timber rights to the land at Johnston and Bose; this became the Sullivan District. Surrey Shingle Manufacturing was

---

With the implementation January 29, 1990, of the Vancouver Computerized Trading (VCT) system, the Vancouver Stock Exchange became the first North American exchange to have converted from a traditional trading floor structure to a fully automated trading environment. After several software and hardware upgrades and six international sales of the system, VCT continues to win accolades. Today more than 200 VCT terminals are located in brokerage firms in Vancouver, Alberta, Toronto and Montreal.

established in the small hamlet that sprang up. Tom also developed the Sullivan and Hyland Lumber Company. He served three terms as councillor and was reeve for ten years.

NEW WESTMINSTER

Cunningham Street Thomas Cunningham, born in Ulster in 1837, came to Victoria in July of 1859. In New Westminster he opened a hardware and general store. Later as an MLA he voted in favour of union with Canada. In 1885 he opened Pelham Gardens at Third Avenue and Fourth Street. He grew prize-winning fruit and served as provincial horticulturalist. His son James, born in 1867, owned and operated (with partner Alex Ewen) the New Westminster Gas Company, supplying the city with gaslight for streets and residences from 1886. With the advent of electricity in the 1890s, the company dwindled in importance.

Fader Street Elijah J. Fader was involved in a number of concerns including the Pitt Lake Brick and Cement Company. He had the Russell Hotel (now the College Place Hotel) built in 1908; at that time it was the last word in elegance, a place where the "new tango" enlivened tea dances around the end of World War I.

Gifford Street Thomas Gifford was a Scottish jeweller who established himself here in 1887. He was elected to the provincial legislature in 1902 where he served for 16 years.

McBride Boulevard Arthur McBride was first warden of the B.C. Penitentiary and his son Richard the first native-born premier of B.C. Lord Grey is reputed to have said of Richard when the latter was visiting England, "I like the look of that picturesque buffalo McBride."

Moody Street Col. R.C. Moody (1813-1887) commanded the Royal Engineers at Sapperton; their task was to survey, clear land, build roads and lay out what was to be the new capital of the Colony of British Columbia.

Rickman Place Reginald J. Rickman came to the province in 1882 and worked as a manager of the B.C. Mills. He served as lieutenant with the New Westminster Rifles for seven years.

BURNABY

Armstrong Avenue William J. Armstrong built one of Queensborough's first buildings, a grocery store and residence. He helped to form the B.C. Coal Mining Company to mine Coal Harbour. J.C. Armstrong was a strong advocate in favor of the creation of the municipality of Burnaby in 1892.

Cariboo Road "Cariboo Jack," a returned miner, built a shack alongside the "pleasure path" that ran from New Westminster to the foot of Burnaby Lake in early 1859.

Curtis Street Mr. Curtis was an employee of Burnaby at the time of the street's opening.

Douglas Road James Douglas was the first governor of the Colony of British Columbia.

Duthie Avenue Settler William Dothy (d. 1911) opened a post office in 1909 at Broadway and Bainbridge. His name was pronounced "duthie."

Edmonds Street Named by D.C. Patterson after Henry Valentine Edmonds who owned much of the property along this street. Edmonds' brother-in-law was John A. Webster who pushed hard for the interurban line.

Ellesmere Avenue The street's name was Ross but to avoid confusion with nearby Rosser was renamed, probably after the Duke of Ellesmere.

Gaglardi Way "Flyin' Phil" Gaglardi was the highways minister in successive W.A.C. Bennett governments.

Gilmore Avenue Hugh B. Gilmour was MPP when Hastings Street opened through north Burnaby. A mechanical engineer by training he had been a master mechanic for the CPR in Calgary in 1883 before working his way west. He managed the Watrous Engine Works then went on to become alderperson and, later, MPP (1901-03). In 1912 the principal of Gilmour Avenue School, Mr. Griffiths, got city clerk Arthur G. Moore to declare an official spelling of the name; Moore, not knowing the background, gave it the spelling we know today.

Holdom Avenue Walter John Holdom came to Burnaby in 1909 and became a developer and insurance agent; some of the lots he sold were on Capitol Hill. In 1916 he became a Burnaby councillor and Holdom Avenue was named during his tenure.

Joyce Street Early settler Peregrine Joyce had a fruit orchard frequently raided by neighborhood children. His unpopularity was also manifested in the oft-played practical joke in which the signs of his and the Collingwood stations on the B.C. Electric Railway would be switched around.

Lougheed Highway Nelson Lougheed, a partner in the logging firm Abernethy and Lougheed, became minister of public works. (He pronounced his name "lawheed.")

McKay Avenue Carpenter Alexander McKay had acreage which ran from the tramline to Vancouver Road (Kingsway). He gave 10 metres of property on its eastern border as part of a right-of-way to Kingsway. Mr. Keefer, who owned the adjoining land to the east, gave the other half of what became McKay Avenue. There was a McKay station on the tramline.

Patterson Avenue Dugald Campbell Patterson (born Paterson) came to Victoria, where he married Frances Mabel Webb in 1890 (Frances Avenue in that city is named after her). They homesteaded in Burnaby from 1894 and Patterson's Landing became Patterson Station after Dugald built an interurban stop (resurrected on

the SkyTrain route). Patterson was one of the founders of Central Park and developed southeast Burnaby. To avoid confusion with another developer he doubled the "t's" in his last name. First postmaster of the Burnaby district of Edmonds, he was a school trustee in 1912-13.

Phillips Avenue George Phillips was an early settler who lived east of the avenue.

Rosser Avenue Named for General Rosser, former chief engineer of the CPR in 1881.

Royal Oak Avenue Many spots in the Empire were named to recall the pollard oak that Charles II hid in after his defeat at Winchester in 1651. The Royal Oak Hotel, built by Levi Morris in 1892, was served by a tramline stop.

Rumble Street John Rumble was a Burnaby councillor from 1903-08 and 1910-11.

Sanderson Way Thomas F. Sanderson came to Canada from Edinburgh by way of Chile and was an accountant at a northern cannery before becoming chief accountant at the Hastings Mill. A keen lawn bowler his property on Inman had a manicured lawn used by fellow enthusiasts. The Sanderson trophy is awarded by the B.C. Lawn Bowling Association.

Sperling Avenue Rochford Henry Sperling (b. 1876) was educated at Eton and Faraday House and came to Canada in 1896. He was the general manager of the B.C. Electric Railway and developed real estate as well. Sperling Avenue used to be the Pole Line Road; it ran from Hastings to Johnston (now Broadway) and was named for the high-potential power lines of the BCER carrying energy from Buntzen Lake to the substation at Gilley Avenue near Edmonds.

Springer Avenue Ben Springer came to B.C. in 1863 and was manager of the Moodyville sawmills. His wife was one of the first teachers in Vancouver's first school.

Sprott Street Charles Sprott was councillor from 1895-1904 and reeve from 1904-05.

RICHMOND

Blundell Road The Blundells owned greenhouses. The B.C. Electric Railway had a stop at their property.

Cooney Road E.O. Cooney was a Richmond councillor.

Ewen Road First president of B.C. Packers, Alexander Ewen operated several canneries and ranched and farmed on 260 hectares of Lulu Island.

Garratt Court, Drive B.W. Garratt was reeve from 1893-95.

Grauer Street Jacob Grauer from Württemberg set up as a butcher in Vancouver in 1886. In 1895 he moved to 120 hectares in Eburne on Sea Island's northeast tip. His butcher shop became a focus for the community and the Grauer farm prospered, its products widely known under the Frasea Farms trademark. The land was expropriated for the airport in 1952. Jacob Grauer's son Rudolph M. Grauer was reeve from 1930-49.

Hunt Street E. Hunt was reeve in 1907.

Lynas Lane A pioneer family.

Minoru Boulevard, Court Minoru was King Edward VII's Epsom Derby winner. A group of investors built a race track in Richmond and named it after the horse. The track's excellent surface could become sponge-like depending on the tide, affecting racing times by as much as a second.

Oliver Court, Drive George Oliver was a road contractor and builder and William was a road overseer.

Rees Road In 1880 at age 16 Rice Victor Rees, from Wales, jumped ship and settled on the South Arm of the Fraser. He went on to serve the community in the capacity of school trustee.

St. Albans Road This Anglican mission was closed in 1912 and re-established in 1925. The parish hall was built in 1926.

Sexsmith Road J.W. Sexsmith was an early settler on Lulu Island. He was one of those who signed the petition to incorporate in 1879. For two years from 1882 he ran the small steamboat *Alice* up the river to New Westminster. Reeve in 1887, 1890 and 1892, he also served as school trustee and postmaster.

Steveston Highway Manoah Steves came to Richmond in 1877 from New Brunswick. William Ladner showed him around Delta and Steves settled on the southwest tip of Lulu Island. His son, William Herbert Steves, bought the land that would become the Steveston townsite and ran the journal the *Steveston Enterprise*.

Trites Road Frank Trites built and managed a boardinghouse in Steveston and ran a general store. He worked in hotels and farming, and later in real estate. He served as councillor, 1907-11.

Udy Road The Udy Stables were established for race horses.

DELTA

Arthur Drive James and William Arthur were two early settlers in Delta.

Chehalis Way The *Chehalis* was a tug of the Bell-Irving syndicate (Anglo-British Columbia Packing Company) used in fishing operations.

Chisholm Street Donald C. Chisholm bought seven hectares of land near the Delta Cannery in 1882. With Thomas McNeely and William H. Ladner he subdivided the townsite. Chisholm, who had a saloon on Front Street in New Westminster, played the largest part in the founding of Ladner; his was the acreage that became the principal part of the first townsite.

Hume Avenue Mr. Hume was the next settler after the Ladners. He preempted land on Chalucthan Slough and built a shack there. Away on business, he caught smallpox and died.

Ladner Trunk Road William H. (b. 1826) and Thomas E. (b. 1836) came from Cornwall and tried Wisconsin and California before coming to B.C. with the Fraser River Gold Rush in 1858. They married sisters Mary and Edney Booth and became the first settlers in Delta. By 1868 they had just over 460 hectares.

Lyon Road American Joseph Lyon was the general mechanic and superintendent of operations at the Delta Cannery.

Todd Place J.H. Todd of Victoria's J.H. Todd and Sons was a cannery owner.

Trenant Street Thomas Ladner's farm, named for the place in Cornwall where his father had been a tenant farmer.

Wadham Drive Edward A. Wadhams built a salmon cannery on land he bought from William Ladner. He also had a cannery at Point Roberts. He developed a salmon trap that could withstand all but the strongest storms because its piles had been driven in with a pile-driver instead of a maul.

VANCOUVER

Most of the material in this section was researched by Beverly MacPherson of the Vancouver City Archives, with additional research by Chuck Davis.

Abbott Street One of the original streets of Vancouver, surveyed in 1885 or 1886. Henry Abbott was the first general superintendent of the CPR'S Pacific division.

Adanac Street In 1928 Alderman J. DeGraves of the street-naming committee recommended to the Town Planning Commission that Union Street be changed to Adanac, which is Canada spelled backwards.

Agnes Street Mrs. Agnes Fowler donated the property at Dumfries and West 22nd Avenue where St. Margaret's Church was built.

Alberni Street Don Pedro Alberni was a captain of infantry in the Spanish army and commander of the first military post in B.C.

Alvin Narod Mews A short street in the area of Mainland, Cambie and Pacific Boulevard, this was named in 1995 for the well-known developer.

Angus Drive R.B. Angus was a director of the CPR and a member of the original syndicate that built the railway. In 1938 the street gained the notorious reputation of being a lovers' lane and city electrician Thomas Martin complained that "Cupid is breaking more street lights than hearts." Remedies and suggestions ranged from "No Necking" signs to designating the drive as "a street reserved for spooning."

Arbutus Street Named by Lauchlan Hamilton after the arbutus tree, indigenous to certain coast districts of the Lower Mainland and Vancouver Island. The area was still forest in 1909 and swamp-like conditions made it impassable until about 1924-25, when sand from False Creek was used as fill and a plank sidewalk installed.

Atlantic Street Formerly Grove Avenue and Bayview Street it was renamed in the early 1900s. Major J.S. Matthews, city archivist 1931-70, considered it "a thoughtless appellation without historic meaning or significance."

Austrey Avenue In the early days the streets in South Vancouver were named after pioneers who had settled the area. Austrey may be derived from "Österreich," the Austrian name for Austria.

Avison Avenue In Stanley Park, and named for Henry Avison, the first employee of the Vancouver Park Board. He cut the first trails and roadways in Stanley Park. Avison and his family lived in the park in the 1880s.

Balaclava Street Shown as Richards Street on the official map of Vancouver in 1886. The Hon. A.N. Richards was the second lieutenant-governor of B.C. (1876-81). In 1907 the name was changed to Balaclava (British headquarters during the Crimean War) to avoid confusion with another Richards Street named after Captain George Richards of HMS *Plumper*.

Baker's Clearing (Also known as Hallelujah Point or Nine O'Clock Gun) Johnnie Baker was one of the first sawyers at the Hastings Mill and the pioneer who cleared land at this site.

Beach Avenue In 1898 Beach Avenue was the only street south of Robson open from Granville to Denman.

Beatty Street Named after Sir Edward W. Beatty of the Beatty Steamship lines. He was also a former president of the CPR.

Bentall Street Named in 1953 after Charles Bentall, president of Dominion Construction.

Bidwell Street Named by Hamilton in 1886. This should have been Bedwell, after Edward Parker Bedwell, second master of HMS *Plumper* which surveyed Burrard Inlet in June 1859.

Bill Curtis Plaza This Yaletown spot was named in October, 1994, for the longtime Vancouver city engineer.

Bismarck Street Originally named after Otto von Bismarck, the German "iron" chancellor of the 19th century. During World War I it was renamed Kitchener Street.

Black Trail (now Kingsway) So named because a fire ran through the area in the early 1860s after the first simple track had been cut.

Blanca Street Named in 1912, although the street had been surveyed in 1886, for the Spanish foreign minister Conde de Floridablanca.

Blenheim Street Shown as Cornwall Street on the official map of 1902. The name was changed by city council in 1907 because of another

Cornwall Street named in 1901 in honor of Lieutenant-Governor Clement F. Cornwall.

Boulder Corner A site at the northwest corner of Carrall and Cordova streets where the Boulder Hotel and bar stood. Later the Royal Bank of Canada occupied a building there.

Boundary Road The dividing line between Burnaby and Vancouver which at 45th Avenue reaches more than 120 metres high.

Boundary Street The boundary between District Lot 192 and the CPR grant. In 1907 the name was changed to Trafalgar Street.

Broadway Originally 9th Avenue in Hamilton's scheme the name was changed in May 1909 as a result of enormous real estate expansion. There were a number of Americans involved in the real estate boom and it was felt that Broadway (after Broadway in New York City) would, in Major Matthews' words, "help promote some mysterious advantage."

Broughton Street Named after William Robert Broughton who commanded HMS *Chatham*, companion ship of Captain Vancouver's vessel, the *Discovery*. He pronounced it "Brawton."

Bryn Mawr The highest point of Point Grey's plateau and reputedly the place "where sunshine and fresh air meet." *Brynmawr* is Welsh for "great hill."

Burnaby Street Named by Hamilton in 1886 after Robert Burnaby, secretary to Col. R.C. Moody of the Royal Engineers in the 1860s.

Burrard Street Named by Hamilton. An explanation for the northeast slant of West End streets is apparently found in Royal Engineer survey notes of 1863. They show a compass variation of 22.15 degrees. The angles of West End streets, it seems, relate to magnetic north, whereas other streets are aligned to true north. Named after Burrard Inlet, itself named by Capt. Vancouver after a navy friend, Sir Henry Burrard.

Bute Street Named after Bute Inlet, itself named for the Marquis of Bute, a friend of King George III.

Cambie Street Named by Hamilton in 1886 for H.J. Cambie, first division engineer of the CPR. It was the dividing line on the west between the old Granville Townsite and the CPR Townsite. The attractive median on Cambie was designed, without city council approval, by imported planner Harland Bartholomew.

Cameron Avenue In Point Grey, this street was named for John Angus Cameron who put through most of Point Grey's roads.

Cardero Street After Don José Cordero, one of the officers of the *Mexicana*. (The street name has been misspelled.)

Carlisle Street Named in 1886 after the first fire chief, John H. Carlisle.

Carnarvon Street Named in honor of Lord Carnarvon.

Carrall Street Named after the Hon. Senator R.W. Carrall, one of the British Columbia delegates to Ottawa in 1869 to arrange terms of confederation.

Cemetery Road A colloquial name for the road (now part of Kingsway) from Westminister Road to the Mountain View Cemetery.

Chilco Street In 1886 when Hamilton was choosing street names some names were picked at random from maps. Street names such as Chilco, Seaton (now Hastings, west of Burrard) and Nicola were named after lakes.

Clark Drive The street was named for Ephram J. Clark, who donated land to the city in 1889 for parkland (today's Clark Park). This was once Percival Street.

Clough Street Edgar Clough was a nephew of John Clough, lamplighter of Vancouver.

Commercial Drive The heart of Vancouver's "Little Italy;" there was an unsuccessful campaign in the early 1980s to change the name to Via Garibaldi. This was Park Drive until 1911.

Comox Street Chosen by Hamilton in 1886 from a provincial map. At that time Comox was of relatively greater geographical importance.

Cooperage Way A Granville Island street that recalls the days when the island was an industrial beehive of activity, and when the famous Sweeney Cooperage made thousands of barrels for use in industry.

Cordova Street This was once Vancouver's main street. Supposed to be pronounced "CORdova" not "CorDOva." A reminder of the Spanish era, when in 1790 the Spanish named Esquimalt Puerto de Cordova.

Cornett Street Named in 1951 for J.W. Cornett, mayor of Vancouver, 1941-46.

Cornish Street A pioneer Marpole family.

Cornwall Street The Duke and Duchess of Cornwall and York visited the city in 1901.

Crowley Drive Everett Crowley, famous for his successful opposition to the poll tax, was the founder of Avalon Dairy.

Davie Street Alexander Edmund Batson Davie was premier of B.C. in 1887. In December of 1898 Davie Street, where Burrard crossed it, was a muddy ditch, probably seven-and-a-half metres wide and less than one metre deep.

Denman Street Named in honor of Admiral Denman, hero of the bloodiest naval action ever fought on the coast of British Columbia. "Sent on a punitive expedition against a rebellious Vancouver Island tribe, he conducted a bombardment that destroyed 9 villages and 64 canoes."

Discovery Street This short street was named for Capt. Vancouver's ship. It was once called Imperial Street.

Douglas Road Named for the first governor of colonial British Columbia.

Drake Street Named by Hamilton in 1886 in honor of Mr. Justice Herbert Drake of the supreme court. One of the four blind end streets—Dunsmuir, Smythe, Helmcken, Drake - which Hamilton was obliged to make on account of a previous survey plan set up in 1882.

Dunbar Street Shown on the official map of Vancouver in 1886. The street name originated when the province subdivided the land between English Bay and 16th Avenue and likely commemorates Charles Dunbar, a real estate promoter and owner of much property. It was carried south when Point Grey Municipality changed the name of Clere Road in 1912. One source says the street "may have been named for the battle of Dunbar, 1650."

Dunlevy Street Vancouver's first industry, the Hastings Sawmill, was at what is now the north foot of this street. Peter C. Dunlevy was a Cariboo rancher and hotel owner.

Dunsmuir Street Named by Hamilton in 1886. He explained: "The large plan of the city was prepared by myself in the office of the Esquimalt and Nanaimo Railway, Victoria. Mr. Dunsmuir, the head of that corporation, was good enough to give me room in that Victoria office."

Dupont Street Named for Major Dupont of Victoria. Dupont Street was Vancouver's first Chinese district; their homes extended from around the south end of Carrall Street to about as far as Columbia Street The name was changed in 1907 to Pender Street, which already existed to the west. Dupont earned an "unsavory" reputation as an early red-light district.

Earles Street Henry Earle was an early settler.

Eddington Drive In 1930 the Canadian Pacific Land Department proposed to subdivide vacant land adjoining the Quilchena Golf Course. W.B. Young, assistant city engineer, had been reading a book on astronomy by a famous British scientist, Sir Arthur Eddington, and applied the name to the thoroughfare.

Edgar Crescent Named for longtime zoning board member R.M. Edgar.

Elk Lane A three-block-long lane between Whyte Avenue and McNicholl Avenue. There was formerly an "elk yard" located there.

Eveleigh Street A tiny street in the heart of Downtown unknown to many locals. It was named for Sydney Morgan Eveleigh, of whom we could learn nothing more.

Fleming Street John Fleming was a pioneer plasterer and contractor who came to B.C. in 1886 and took up residence at Cedar Cottage in 1897.

Frances Street Named in 1929 after Sister Frances, a pioneer nurse at St. Luke's Home and St. James Church on Cordova Street.

Fraser Street Originally known as the North Arm Road to Granville, it was one of the more important pioneer trails.

French Street Sir John French, commander-in-chief of the British Army in 1914.

Front Street One of the first streets named in Vancouver, it was one of the four streets of the Granville Townsite and is known today as Water Street

Gale Street R.H. Gale was mayor of Vancouver from 1918 to 1921.

Galiano Road Lieutenant Dionisio Galiano was an officer in command of the Spanish exploratory vessels *Sutil* and *Mexicano,* which dropped anchor off the Spanish Banks and met Captain Vancouver.

Garden Drive James F. Garden was mayor of Vancouver from 1898 to 1900.

Gartley Street Ernest Gartley was a pioneer powder man in charge of blowing up stumps to level trails and roadways.

Gavin Street J.J. Gavin was a city alderman in 1892.

George Street This street has an unusual naming story: it was originally Godfrey Street, named for George Godfrey. Then they changed it from his last name to his first. Why? And who was George Godfrey? We don't know.

Georgia Street The crew of Captain Vancouver's vessel, the *Discovery,* named the Gulf of Georgia after King George III. Hamilton named the street after the gulf.

Gibson Street One version has it that Gibson was named for G.F. Gibson, former city comptroller; another that it was for a Moses Gibson. Another former "Boundary Avenue," because it was the western edge of the old Hastings Townsite, it was renamed in 1911 when the townsite was annexed.

Glendalough Place Named in 1956 for the old family home of city councillor Anna Sprott. The meaning is "lake in the glen."

Gore Avenue Considering the odd angle of this street (its two parallel neighbors, Main to the west, Dunlevy to the east, run straight), it's ironic it was named for W.S. Gore, once surveyor- general for B.C. Gore Avenue is an old "skid road," once used to take logs down to the inlet.

Granville Street A reminder of the old townsite name, named in turn for the colonial secretary of the time, Lord Granville. Plank sidewalks were first laid in 1886 and in 1906 electric lighting replaced the old arc-lights. South Granville was once named Centre Street.

Graveley Street In the city's East End, Graveley was named for financier Walter E. Graveley. There is a famous photo taken the day after the Great Fire of 1886 showing Graveley lying on the ground reading while the blackened city smolders in the distance.

Great Northern Way Named in 1960 in honor of the Great Northern Railway which provided much of the land for this thoroughfare.

Greenlees Street Named in 1959 after Richmond's centennial baby—David Jones Greenlees, born January 1, 1958, at 1:01 a.m.

Griffiths Way One of Vancouver's newest streets, this short stretch was named for Frank Griffiths, Sr., the late broadcasting executive and owner of the Vancouver Canucks.

Guelph Street The early pioneers named streets to honor the Royal family as a token of their loyalty. The family name of Queen Victoria was Guelph. There is a town of Guelph in Ontario.

Haggart Street Andrew Haggart was a building inspector.

Hamilton Street Named after himself by Hamilton in 1886. See the introduction to this article. On a bank at the southwest corner of Hamilton and Hastings is a plaque indicating the spot at which Hamilton began his survey.

Haro Street Named in 1886 by Sub-Lieutenant Manuel Quimper, commander of the confiscated British sloop *Princess Royal*. Don Gonzales de Lopez de Haro was a central figure in the 1789 troubles at Nootka which ended with the British takeover of Spanish territory.

Hastings Street Named for the first town on Burrard Inlet, Hastings Townsite, which was named for Rear Admiral George Fowler Hastings, Commander of Her Majesty's Coast Squadron, 1836-1869. The sawmill begun by Captain Stamp became Hastings Sawmill and the trail leading to it became Hastings Street. It was laid out as the main trunk road to the townsite and in 1892 was among the first streets paved. In 1911 Hastings Townsite was annexed by the city and the street kept its name.

Heatley Avenue Edward Davis Heatley was an early agent of the Hastings Sawmill Company in London, England.

Helmcken Street, Drive John S. Helmcken came to British Columbia as surgeon for the HBC and was a vigorous opponent of the province's entry into confederation. He favored annexation to the United States. He was Governor James Douglas' son-in-law.

Homer Street J.A.R. Homer was a member of the mainland legislature from 1864 to 1866 and in 1881 was MP for New Westminster. He was British Columbia's first lumber exporter.

Hornby Street Named in 1886 after Hornby Island which in turn was named after Rear Admiral Phipps Hornby, C.B., commander-in-chief of the flagship HMS *Asia.*

Howe Street Named by Hamilton in 1886 in honor of Admiral Lord Howe, the 18th-century naval commander.

Inverness Street Originally called Thomas Street for a member of the pioneer Edmonds family, it was changed to Inverness in 1910 .

Jackson Street R.E. Jackson was a Victoria lawyer.

Janes Road Named after the first Westminster-to-Vancouver stage owner and driver.

Jervis Street Named in honor of Admiral Sir John Jervis, who defeated the Spanish fleet in 1787. Hamilton applied the name in 1886. The admiral pronounced it "JARvis."

Joyce Road Mr. Joyce was a partner of George Kerr, road foreman and engineer for South Vancouver.

Kaye Road Alex Kaye came to Vancouver in 1907 and was a federal assayer until his 1951 death.

Keefer Street George Keefer was a contractor for the CPR and the Capilano Water Works. Years after the Great Fire of 1886, Keefer, in charge of a slash-burning crew, said it was his fault it began.

Kerrisdale Avenue Named in 1910 at the request of Mrs. McKinnon whose family had settled in that area in 1897. Kerrisdale was named after their home in Scotland, Kerry's Dale.

King George Highway Originally named the Peace Arch Highway. On October 18, 1939, a committee of prominent men from the Lower Mainland approached Surrey council and successfully petitioned to rename the route King George VI Highway.

Kingsway A local newspaper wrote on October 1, 1913: "The new highway between Vancouver and New Westminster passing through South Vancouver and Burnaby, is now complete . . . It is a broad, magnificent road, and by none will it be more appreciated than motorists, who, to the number of six hundred made the trip between the two cities on the day the road was opened." There is a famous London highway of this name, and it is thought our Kingsway is named for that one. (See also Black Trail).

Laburnum Street Named after the tree, by the CPR in 1909, when the land behind Kitsilano Beach was opened.

Lakewood Drive So named because, according to E.B. Hermon (an early surveyor), its southern end led to the then-wooded Trout Lake.

Lalande Street Named for Abraham Lalande, a prominent real estate agent in the 1900s. Now called 54th Avenue

Lansdowne Street Originally named in honor of the Marquis of Lansdowne, Governor General of Canada. In 1907 it was renamed Waterloo Street when a number of street names were changed to commemorate battles.

Leg-in-Boot Square This curiously named spot

was so named because a boot containing part of a human leg washed ashore close to Lamey's Mill on the southern shore of False Creek, near here, during the 1880s. The boot was hung from a pole beside police headquarters for a week, but no one claimed or identified it.

Le Roi Street This street was named by Alderperson Frank Woodside, for many years secretary of the B.C. Chamber of Mines. Le Roi was the name of a mine near Rossland, B.C.

Locarno Crescent Named at the time when the Locarno Pact (1925) meant peace to a war-weary world. Locarno is a town in Switzerland.

Lord Street Named in 1952 for a former civic official, Judge A.E. "Art" Lord.

McBain Street G.W. McBain was a CPR land agent.

Macdonald Street Shown on the 1886 map of the city. In 1938 a controversy developed over the spelling of the name, with many spelling it "McDonald." The question was soon settled since the street was originally named for Prime Minister Sir John A. Macdonald.

MacLean Drive Malcolm Alexander MacLean was the first mayor of Vancouver, 1886-87.

McMullen Avenue S.E. McMullen was with the CPR legal department.

McNicholl Avenue David McNicholl was a senior vice president of the CPR.

McSpadden Street Col. George McSpadden was a Vancouver alderman.

Main Street Main Street has been known by several names including False Creek Road and Westminster Road. In July,1910, the present name was applied.

Mainland Street So named on account of the Mainland Transfer Company, a large truck and dray company located there early in the 1900s.

Marguerite Avenue In Shaughnessy Heights, and named for the daughter of Lord Shaughnessy, president of the CPR.

Marshall Street A short street running into John Hendry Park. Thomas Marshall was a plumber. Legend has it that many streets in this area were named for working-class folk.

Martha Street The wife of John A. Webster, a very early settler on Burrard Inlet.

Matthews Avenue W.D. Matthews was a director of the CPR. The street was named when Shaughnessy was cleared by the CPR land department and offered for sale.

Menchion Quay The Menchion shipyard was a landmark for many years on Coal Harbour.

Midlothian Street One of five street names (the others being Peveril, Denmont, Nigel and Talisman) said to have been chosen by Willie Young, a former city engineer, from names used by Sir Walter Scott in his Waverly novels, one of which was *The Heart of Midlothian*.

Morton Street A short street at English Bay, off Davie and Denman streets. John Morton landed nearby in 1862 and was the first settler in the West End. The street was named around 1920.

Montgomery Street S.J. Montgomery was secretary of the Board of Works from 1907 to 1944.

Narvaez Drive The name was adopted March 6, 1941, on the recommendation of the Town Planning Commission. The street looks down on the waters first navigated by the Spanish explorer José Maria Narvaez in the summer of 1791.

Neal Street Named in 1958 for W.M. Neal, former chair and president of the CPR.

Nelson Street Named by Hamilton in 1886 for Senator Hugh Nelson, a pioneer of the 1862 Cariboo Gold Rush, lieutenant-governor of B.C., senator and, in 1868, a delegate to the abortive Yale convention where the entry of B.C. into Confederation was first considered.

Nicola Street Named in 1886 by Hamilton: "I was acquainted with Nicola in the Upper Country, but whether the name was adopted for that reason entirely, or partially a compromise between Nicola and Nicholas Hamilton, my grandfather, who was commonly known to the Hamilton clan as 'Old Nick!' is unclear."

Norquay Street John Norquay was premier of Manitoba in its pioneer days.

Oak Street One of the "tree streets." It was a gravel road subject to washouts and floods until 1952 when plans for paving were approved.

Oben Street Phillip Oben cleared the forest in the western section of the West End in 1890.

Odlum Street Professor Edward Odlum was one of Grandview's early residents and a member of city council in 1892.

Ogden Avenue I.G. Ogden was vice president in charge of finance for the CPR. Another source says it was for trapper and HBC chief factor Peter Skene Ogden, which is unlikely.

Oliver Crescent Named in 1951 for the Hon. John Oliver, premier of B.C. (1918-27) and known as "Honest John."

Oppenheimer Avenue Named in 1898 for David Oppenheimer, mayor of Vancouver 1888-91. The family pronounces the name "AWpen-HYmer."

Paton Street Named in 1958 for J.S. Paton, former Point Grey reeve and Vancouver alderman.

Pender Street Named after Commander Daniel Pender, a British naval officer and surveyor.

Pendrell Street Believed to be named in honor of Pendrell, hydrographer of HMS *Plumper*.

Peters Road Named after an early settler who established himself in the woods at the corner of the North Arm Road (now Granville Street south) and Peters Road (now 64th Avenue).

Pierce Street Lt. Thomas Pierce of the Royal

Marines figured in a momentous episode in West Coast history. On March 28th, 1795, he accepted the surrender of this country from the Spanish on behalf of the British Crown.

Pound Street Named after Reeve Pound of South Vancouver.

Powell Street Named after Dr. Israel Wood Powell who, among other good works, donated the site of the first city hall. Powell River was also named after him.

Price Street An early municipal official of South Vancouver, Spencer Robinson, related the naming of Price Street: "Mr. Price lived on the same street, Price Street, and owned acreage . . . He was the first janitor of Carleton School."

Princess Street Originally went from Main Street to the city's eastern boundary. One of the first settlers established the name before 1890: "Princess Street! I named Princess Street; they called it Dupont Street, but we did not like the name so we changed it . . ." It was supposedly in honor of Annie, a "princess-like" daughter of the Ramage family, who had six sisters. The Seven Sisters, a grove of trees in Stanley Park, was named as a tribute to them.

Prior Street Lt. Col. Edward G. Prior was the commander of the Fifth Regiment Canadian Garrison Artillery, an MP, then premier of B.C. from November 1902 to June 1903.

Quadra Street Don Juan Francisco de la Bodega y Quadra was the Spanish diplomat charged with completing the Nootka Convention with Capt. Vancouver that established Britain's claim to the West Coast.

Quilchena Crescent An Indian name meaning "many waters." In 1925 the Quilchena Golf Club occupied the area, which had many creeks, and the name was retained when it was subdivided.

Rae Avenue Named after George Rae, reeve of South Vancouver.

Raymur Avenue Capt. J.A. Raymur was the first manager of Hastings Sawmill after it was sold by the founder, Capt. Edward Stamp.

Renfrew Street Named by alderman Frank E. Woodside, probably after the B.C. town.

Rhodes Street Cecil Rhodes was the wealthy South African.

Richards Street An earlier street was so named in honor of Lieutenant-Governor A.N. Richards. The name was changed due to duplication (see Balaclava Street). The Downtown street retained its name, which commemorates Capt. George Richards of HMS *Plumper*.

Robinson Street At one time there was a single house on the street and a Mr. Robinson lived in it. He tacked a board with "Robinson" painted on it to a post to indicate where he lived and that was how the name came to be applied.

Robson Street Named by Hamilton in 1886 for

the Hon. John Robson, MPP, provincial secretary in 1883, and premier of B.C., 1889-92.

Roundhouse Mews A reminder that the CPR once had extensive works in this area. The "roundhouse," still here, was used to service the railway's locomotives. Engine 374 that brought the first passenger train into the city in May, 1887, is on display here.

Salsbury Drive W.F. Salsbury was an alderman and the first CPR treasurer in Vancouver.

Sasamat Street Named in 1887 by the surveyor general. Sasamat is said to be the Spanish version of the native name for Burrard Inlet, or Indian Arm off the inlet. Some believe it derives its name from an Indian word meaning "cool place."

Seacombe Road Named about 1910 for Edward Seacombe who cut the trail. Now known as Prince Edward Street

Seaton Street The original name, until 1915, for the tiny stretch of Hastings Street west of Burrard. Originally named by Hamilton in 1886 after a lake chosen at random from a B.C. map.

Semlin Drive The Hon. Charles Semlin was premier of B.C., 1898-1900.

Seymour Street Hamilton named Seymour Street after Frederick Seymour, governor of British Columbia, 1864-67. He pronounced his name "seemer."

Shannon Road Now 57th Avenue West. William Shannon was a pioneer in 1863 on the North Arm of the Fraser River.

Short Street A block-long street in Kitsilano which connected Cypress Street to the Kitsilano Indian Reserve. Renamed Greer Street in 1920 in honor of Sam Greer's beach and changed again in 1952 to Fleming Street

Smithe Street Originally named in 1886 after the Hon. William Smythe, premier of B.C. 1883-87. Despite the spelling of the former premier's name, the street became Smithe.

Spencer Street Spencer Robinson served as a councillor for the Municipality of South Vancouver in 1909.

Sperling Street R.H. Sperling was a manager of the BCER.

Station Street When, in April 1923, city engineer F.L. Fellows drew up plans for the proposed Canadian National and Great Northern railways' passenger stations, he found himself with a nameless street. Since it led to the stations he thought Station Street would be a good name.

Stephen Street Named in honor of Lord Mount Stephen, former president of the CPR.

Stewart Street Named for a Mr. Stewart, chief engineer in the public works department, "a very nice fellow with a Vandyke beard."

Tanner Street Named for an early settler who owned a lot of property off Joyce Road. He never held civic office but took a keen interest in public affairs.

Taylor Street Louis D. Taylor was mayor of Vancouver, holding office for a total of 11 years (1910-11, 1915, 1925-28, 1931-34).

Tecumseh Avenue A Shawnee Indian chief killed during the War of 1812 while fighting on the British side.

Templeton Street William Templeton was mayor of Vancouver in 1897.

Terry Fox Way The late Terry Fox was the courageous young Coquitlam man who lost a leg to cancer, yet began an epic run across Canada to raise funds for cancer research. His run was cut short by a recurrence of the disease. See the article on page 402.

Terminal Avenue Named in 1923 by city engineer F.L. Fellows.

Thistle Street A block-long street between Cornwall and Kitsilano Beach. Until 1930 no one lived there because the land had been used as fill for the Imperial Street sewer and the area was a three-metre-deep hole below street level.

Thurlow Street Named in 1886 by Hamilton after Thurlow Island, itself named for Baron Thurlow, an eminent British jurist.

Tisdall Street Named for Charles Edward Tisdall, mayor of Vancouver, 1922-23.

Todd Street Running into Slocan Park this short street commemorates Eric Todd, a South Vancouver municipal engineer.

Tolmie Street Named after Dr. William Fraser Tolmie, an HBC official and Victoria pioneer. His son Simon Fraser Tolmie was premier of B.C., 1928-33.

Townley Street Thomas O. Townley was mayor of Vancouver in 1901.

Trafalgar Street In 1907 alderman J.H. Calland was entertaining when the question of street names arose. Someone suggested using battle names. On September 30, 1907, city council accepted Calland's proposal. Victoria Road became Point Grey Road, Campbell Street became Alma Road (Crimean War), Richards Street became Balaclava (Crimean War), Cornwall—the second street with that name—became Blenheim (Battle of Blenheim), Lansdowne became Waterloo and the old Boundary Street that divided District Lot 192 and the CPR grant became Trafalgar.

Trutch Street Sir Joseph W. Trutch was the first lieutenant-governor of B.C., 1871-76.

Union Street This was once Barnard Street, after Sir Frank Stillman Barnard, lieutenant governor. The name was often confused with Burrard and so was changed in 1913.

Venables Street Named in 1886; the reason is still a mystery. Perhaps it honors Captain Cavendish Venables who tried to preempt land as a military grant at Bella Coola in 1862.

Roundhouse Mews … The roundhouse was used to service the railway's locomotives

Vernon Drive The Hon. Forbes George Vernon was chief commissioner of lands and works in Victoria after 1876.

Vivian Street Named for William T. Vivian who settled in Vancouver in 1886. His daughter Jennie was the first child born (1892) in Collingwood.

Walden Street Named in 1910 for Henry Wright Walden who "owned, well, blocks and blocks, was a very large taxpayer, from 25th Avenue up on Main Street. They said he was the largest taxpayer in South Vancouver."

Walker Street Named between 1900 and 1906 after a Mr. Walker, municipal clerk of the Municipality of South Vancouver.

Water Street One of the first four streets named in the old Granville Townsite.

Wenonah Street Named for Mayor J.W. Cornett's daughter.

Whyte Avenue Sir William Whyte of Winnipeg was vice president of the CPR western lines.

Wilson Road Originally a stopping place for the CPR steam train to Steveston, where they dumped flour, baled hay, groceries and barrels of petroleum for use on the logging skid roads. Now 41st Avenue East. Charles Wilson was an early alderman.

Winter Street Named after Thomas Winters, the only police officer in the Municipality of South Vancouver in 1906.

Wylie Street Named for alderman P. Wylie (1901-1902) who was also city street superintendent for several years.

Yale Street James Murray Yale, an important early HBC official, did much to make Fort Langley economically important. Yale, B.C., is named for him and, by extension, so is Vancouver's trendy Yaletown area.

Yew Street One of the "tree streets" named by Hamilton. The *Province* of January 7, 1938, printed a cartoon depicting a lady lost in dense Vancouver fog. The lady: (groping) "Is this Yew?" A gentleman: "Your guess is as good as mine, lady, but I think it's me—how about yourself?"

York Street Named, like Cornwall Street, in honor of the Duke and Duchess of Cornwall and York who visited the city in 1901.

Place Names

Place Names of the Lower Mainland

Philip G.P.V. and Helen B. Akrigg

Alice Lake Lake north of Squamish named after the wife of Charles Rose, who came to the area in the 1880s.

Ambleside Morris Williams, who settled here in 1912, had earlier lived in Ambleside in the Lake District, England.

Anmore Village north of Ioco named by F.J. Lancaster, a local "part-time homesteader," after his wife Annie and a daughter Leonore. From their names he coined "Annore," which locals modified into "Anmore."

Annacis Island Originally Annance's Island, named after François Annance, a Hudson's Bay Company clerk, who was with chief factor James McMillan when he sailed up the Fraser River in 1827 and founded Fort Langley.

Barnet James MacLaren, an Ottawa lumberman who opened a sawmill here, named the settlement after his mother, whose maiden name was Elizabeth Barnet.

Barnston Island After George Barnston, a clerk with Chief Factor McMillan when he founded Fort Langley in 1827.

Belcarra Judge Norman Bole, the Irishman who gave Belcarra this Gaelic name, said that it meant "the fair land of the sun."

Black Mountain The mountain was covered with charred trees when its name was adopted in the early 1860s.

Blackie Spit After Walter Black, who was New Westminster's first blacksmith. Black bought the spit in 1875.

Boundary Bay The international boundary intersects the bay.

Bowen Island James Bowen was master of Howe's flagship, *Queen Charlotte*. One of many features in Howe Sound named after ships or officers that served under Admiral Lord Howe when, in 1794, he won his great victory, "The Glorious First of June."

Brackendale After Thomas Hirst Bracken, first postmaster here (1906-12).

Brighouse After Sam Brighouse, who arrived in B.C. in 1862. That year he, John Morton and William Hailstone ("The Three Greenhorns") purchased "The Brickmakers' Claim," today Vancouver's West End. In 1864 Brighouse established a ranch on Lulu Island.

Bridgeport "Bridge" after the two bridges which at the end of 1889 linked Richmond with the mainland. "Port" reflected the hopes of the locals when the connection was built.

facing page: Sikh parade, Surrey, 1994. vs

Britannia Beach Takes its name from the Britannia Range behind it. Captain G.H. Richards, R.N., named the mountains after HMS *Britannia,* which served in the Battle of St. Vincent (1797) and the Battle of Trafalgar (1805).

British Properties In the early 1930s Britain's wealthy Guinness family secured rights to this area from the Municipality of West Vancouver. The Lions Gate Bridge was built as part of the Guinness scheme to develop "The British Properties," a name which was officially recognized by the provincial government in 1979, long after it appeared on district maps.

Brockton Point In 1859 Francis Brockton, chief engineer of surveying vessel *Plumper,* discovered coal in COAL HARBOUR.

Brownsville Named after Ebenezer Brown, who came to B.C. during the Fraser Gold Rush. He farmed here and ran a very respectable saloon in NEW WESTMINSTER. Brownsville was located opposite New Westminster, and was once connected to it by ferry.

Brunette River Descriptive of the stream's brownish water, and named around 1860 by William Holmes, the first settler in Burnaby. Peat gives the water its color.

Buntzen Lake After Johannes Buntzen, a native of Denmark who became in 1897 the first general manager of the B.C. Electric Railway Company.

Burkeville After Stanley Burke, president of Boeing Aircraft Company of Canada in 1943, when this wartime housing estate was established on Sea Island for workers in the aircraft factories. The name was chosen in a competition among Boeing employees.

Burnaby This city gets its name from Burnaby Lake, which lies within its borders. The lake was named after Robert Burnaby. Born in 1828, the fourth son of a Leicestershire parson, Burnaby spent his early years working in the Customs House in London. In 1858 he came to British Columbia with a letter of introduction from Sir Edward Bulwer-Lytton, the British secretary of state for the colonies. He was appointed private secretary to Colonel Moody of the Royal Engineers. Burnaby became closely associated with the survey of this area, and the lake was named after him. A person who knew Burnaby in B.C. described him as a "myrthful active honest pleasant little fellow." After leaving Moody's service, Robert Burnaby engaged in various business enterprises, chiefly in Victoria. He returned to England in 1874, and died there in 1878. It is ironic that so minor a figure has his name given to one of the province's largest urban areas.

Burquitlam A manufactured name consisting of the first syllable of "Burnaby" and the last two syllables of "Coquitlam."

Burrard Inlet In June 1792 Captain George Vancouver named this inlet Burrards Channel, after his friend Sir Harry Burrard (1765–1840), who had served with him aboard HMS *Europa* in the West Indies in 1785. Burrard was commander-in-chief of the Mediterranean Fleet from 1823 to 1826. The Spaniards, who explored the inlet about the same time as Vancouver, named it Boca de Floridablanca, after the Conde de Floridablanca, the Spanish prime minister of the day.

Canoe Passage During the gold rush of 1858 miners, seeking to elude naval patrols checking for mining licences, sneaked into the Fraser River by this minor entrance. Probably such traffic was limited to canoes.

Capilano River "Capilano" is the anglicized form of a personal name that originally came from the Nanoose area but, through marriage, is now held by men of mixed Squamish and Musqueam background. The last Chief Capilano, who died in about 1870, had a home beside the river which now bears his name.

Caulfeild Francis William Caulfeild, an English gentleman and first town planner of West Vancouver loved the beautiful wild flowers, woods and beaches in this area. In 1899 he bought the land between Cypress Creek and Point Atkinson and proceeded to lay out a village. Disliking the North American grid where straight streets and avenues intersect at right angles, he laid out a village of the English type with winding lanes following the natural contours of the wooded slopes. Francis Caulfeild died in 1934, aged about ninety.

Cheakamus River In the Squamish language *cheakamus* means "salmon weir place."

Cleveland Dam Named in 1954 after E.A. Cleveland, first chief commissioner of the Greater Vancouver Water District.

Cloverdale The first settler, William Shannon, arrived here in 1875 and found wild clover growing luxuriantly. Accordingly he named the area Clover Valley. When a settlement grew up, it took the name of Cloverdale.

Coal Harbour After the discovery here, in 1859, of seams of coal ranging in thickness from 10 to 38 centimetres. (See BROCKTON POINT.)

Como Lake. Possibly named after beautiful Lake Como in northern Italy, but just as possibly after Como, a Kanaka (Hawaiian) who was in the party that sailed up the Fraser with chief factor McMillan in 1827 to found Fort Langley. It has been suggested that Como is a compound: "Co" for Coquitlam, and "mo" for Port Moody.

Coquitlam From the Halkomelem word meaning "stinking of fish slime." During a great winter famine the Coquitlam people sold themselves into slavery to the more numerous and prosper-

ous Kwantlen tribe. The new slaves, while butchering large quantities of salmon for their masters, got covered with fish slime—hence the name.

Dam Mountain The mountain was named in 1894 because of its view over a waterworks dam on the Capilano River.

Deadman Island There are various Deadman Islands in B.C., indicating a place where the natives left their dead.

Deas Island After John Sullivan Deas, a mulatto tinsmith who owned a cannery here in the 1870s. A "W. Deas" is listed among the Royal Engineers, who served in British Columbia between 1858 and 1863, and evidence suggests the two men may be identical.

Deeks Creek After John F. Deeks, whose Deeks Sand & Gravel Company started its operations here on Howe Sound in 1908.

Deer Lake In 1867 Charles Seymour opened a "wayside house" on Douglas Road, close to where the Royal Engineers had established a game reserve on the Oakalla prison site. This became a popular rendezvous for deer hunters.

Derby Reach This stretch of the Fraser River is the only survival of "Derby," the name given to Fort Langley when it was expected to become the capital of the new mainland Crown Colony of British Columbia. The name honored the prime minister of Britain, the Earl of Derby.

Dollarton After Captain Robert Dollar, who owned a lumber mill here. Born in Scotland in 1844, Dollar is chiefly remembered today because of his Dollar Steamship Line, a major one in its day.

Douglas This border crossing-point, adjacent to Blaine, is named after Benjamin Douglas, a pioneer settler.

Douglas Island Originally Manson Island, after Donald Manson, a member of the expedition which founded nearby Fort Langley in 1827. However, after Governor Douglas had purchased the island and presented it to his daughter Cecilia, it became known as Douglas Island.

Dundarave An early resident, Russell Macnaghten, professor of Greek at the University of British Columbia, named this part of West Vancouver after Dundarave Castle in Scotland, the ancestral home of Clan Macnaghten. Dundarave, which should rhyme with "have," comes from a Gaelic word having reference to a two-oared boat.

Eburne After W.H. Eburne, farmer and storekeeper, who became the first postmaster here in 1892. In 1916 the mainland portion of Eburne was renamed MARPOLE.

Edmonds After Henry Valentine Edmonds, born in Ireland in 1837, one of the original promoters

of the Vancouver-New Westminster interurban railway.

Elsje Point Pronounced "El-shuh." This point, at the end of the Vancouver Maritime Museum's breakwater, commemorates Mrs. W.M. Armstrong, née Elsje de Ridder, a former trustee of the Vancouver Museum. Through extraordinary effort Elsje Armstrong secured for the museum the adjacent Heritage Harbor. An accomplished woman, she was also a founder of the nearby Vancouver Academy of Music.

English Bay This and nearby SPANISH BANKS commemorate the meeting of the English (under Captain Vancouver) and the Spanish (under Galiano and Valdes) in this area in June 1792.

English Bluff Immediately south lies Boundary Bluff, where the international boundary meets the Pacific. English Bluff got its name because it lay on the British side of the line.

Ewen Slough After Alexander Ewen, an early cannery owner. A dour Scot, he was reputed never to have laughed.

Essondale After Dr. Henry Esson Young, who was provincial secretary when the provincial mental hospital was established here. As minister of education from 1907 to 1916, Dr. Young was responsible for the founding of the University of British Columbia.

Fairview Named by Lauchlan A. Hamilton, the Canadian Pacific Railway land commissioner. An 1891 newspaper advertisement announced that "the clearing of the Land being nearly completed in that new and beautifully situated part of the VANCOUVER TOWNSITE known as FAIRVIEW," the CPR was prepared to sell lots there.

False Creek Named by Captain G.H. Richards, R.N., in the late 1850s, presumably because, despite its promising entrance, this small inlet soon ended in mud flats. (In England the word "creek" is used for any narrow indentation in a coast.)

Fannin Range North of Vancouver. After John Fannin (1839-1904), the first curator of the Provincial Museum, Victoria.

Ferguson Point After Alfred Graham Ferguson, the first chairman of the Vancouver Parks Board. (Since Ferguson was an American, the swearing-in ceremony was tactfully omitted.) He died in San Francisco in 1903.

Fisherman's Cove Named around 1888, when some Newfoundland fishermen and their families settled here.

Fort Langley After Thomas Langley, for many years a director of the Hudson's Bay Company. He died in 1829. In October 1824 the HBC's Governor Simpson sent chief factor James McMillan on a reconnaissance of the lower Fraser Valley, with a view to establishing a post there. Later, in 1827, McMillan founded Fort Lan-

gley. The original fort was abandoned in 1837 and a new post (the present Fort Langley) was built several kilometres upstream, where the land was better for agriculture. The Crown Colony of British Columbia was proclaimed at Fort Langley in 1858, but the capital was soon moved to New Westminster. Fort Langley then went into slow decline. The HBC closed its store here in 1896 and the buildings of the old fort rotted away. Restoration of the fort began in 1957-58 as part of the celebration of British Columbia's centennial.

Fraser River After Simon Fraser (1776-1862).

Furry Creek. After Oliver Furry, trapper and prospector, who in 1898 staked claims to rich copper deposits close to Britannia Beach.

Gastown After the Hastings Mill was built on the south shore of Burrard Inlet in 1867, a colorful character named "Gassy Jack" Deighton opened a saloon there. The little settlement that grew up around Deighton's establishment became known as Gastown. For a time the name was accepted and appeared on the British Admiralty chart for the area. In 1870, however, the inhabitants renamed their community Granville, in honor of Earl Granville, the British secretary for the colonies.

Georgia Strait This is the euphonious Grand Canal de Nuestra Senora del Rosario la Marinera of the Spanish explorers. Captain Vancouver wrote that it was on June 4, 1792, the same day that he proclaimed British sovereignty over the northwest Pacific Coast beyond Cape Mendocino, that he "honoured" this "interior sea" with the name of the Gulf of Georgia. The honor lay in the fact that "Georgia" was derived from the name of King George III. On November 27, 1858, Captain G.H. Richards, R.N., wrote to the hydrographer of the navy that he had modified the name to Georgia Strait, which he deemed more appropriate.

Gleneagles The Gleneagles subdivision, formed around 1927, took the name of an adjacent golf course. The latter was named after the Gleneagles links in Perthshire, England.

Goat Mountain Mountain north of Vancouver named in 1894 by hunters who had shot two mountain goats there.

Golden Ears This name for the peaks on MOUNT BLANSHARD was used as early as 1862, when Commander R.C. Mayne, R.N., wrote of "the beautiful peaks known as Golden Ears."

Granville Island After the British secretary for the colonies, the second Earl Granville appointed December 10, 1868.

Grouse Mountain Named in 1894, when climbed by a party which included E.A. Cleveland, who later became chief commissioner of the Greater

Vancouver Water District. They called it "Grouse Mountain" because of the blue grouse they had shot on it.

Guildford The directors of Grosvenor Laing, the developer of the town centre, used the name of Guildford in Surrey, England, where their company had its headquarters.

Haney After Thomas Haney (1841-1916), who settled here in 1876. The settlement was originally known as Haney's Landing, and later as Port Haney. With the increasing importance of roads, the centre of Haney moved up from the river to the highway.

Hazelmere H.J. Thrift, a pioneer here, said he named the place not so much because he came from Hazelmere in England as because his farm had both a thick growth of hazel bush and a small pond or "mere."

Hollyburn Mountain West Vancouver's first colonial settler, John Lawson, planted holly by the side of the "burn" (a Scottish word for a stream) flowing across his property. Putting the two words together, he coined "Hollyburn" as the name for his home.

Horseshoe Bay Named because of its shape.

Howe Sound Named by Captain Vancouver after Admiral Richard Scrope, Earl Howe. He won his most famous victory in 1794, in the battle that has gone down in the annals of the Royal Navy as "The Glorious First of June." On that day Howe not only defeated a superior French fleet but captured seven of its ships. The King presented him with a sword with a diamond-studded hilt valued at 3,000 guineas.

Indian Arm Explored in June 1792 by the Spanish, who met a few Indians here. They learned that the natives applied the name SASAMAT to Indian Arm and area.

Ioco The first letters of the Imperial Oil Company, which owns the large refinery here.

Iona Island Called McMillan Island after a pioneer settler, Donald McMillan (1848-1901), until he renamed it Iona, after the island where St. Columba in 563 began christianizing the Scots.

Jericho Takes its name from Jeremiah ("Jerry") Rogers (1818-79). As early as 1864 or 1865 he sent axemen from his base at Jerry's Cove (Jericho) to fell the giant trees that once grew on POINT GREY.

Kerrisdale In 1905, when B.C. Electric built a station on its Steveston interurban line at what is now West 41st Avenue in Vancouver, the company's general manager called on a young Scottish couple named MacKinnon, who had recently settled in the district, and invited Mrs. MacKinnon to name the new station. Her choice, "Kerrysdale," after her home in Scotland, soon became Kerrisdale.

Kitsilano Around 1905 when the Canadian Pacific Railway was looking for a name for its new Vancouver subdivision, it approached a local ethnologist, Professor Charles Hill-Tout. He suggested "Kitsilano," an anglicized form of the name of a Squamish man who had lived in Stanley Park in the mid 1800s. The name is held today by a descendant.

Kwomais Point This feature on Boundary Bay has a Halkomelem name meaning "dog face."

Ladner After William and Thomas Ladner, who took up land here in 1868. Born in Cornwall, the brothers came to B.C. in 1858. They prospected in the Cariboo, ran packtrains and were merchants there before turning to farming here.

Langara Preserves the name the Spanish navigator Eliza gave to Point Grey in 1791. His Punta de Langara was named in honor of the Spanish admiral Don Juan de Langara.

Langley Takes its name from nearby FORT LANGLEY.

Lions, The These landmark mountains were known by the Indians as Chee-chee-yoh-hee, meaning "The Twins." The first colonial settlers called them "Sheba's Paps" (breasts). Around 1890 Judge Gray, noting their resemblance to crouching lions, suggested that the entrance to Vancouver Harbour be called "The Lions' Gate."

Locarno Park Commemorates the pact, supposed to outlaw wars, signed in 1925 in Locarno, Switzerland.

Lonsdale This part of North Vancouver is named after Arthur Heywood-Lonsdale of Shavington Hall, Shropshire, England, who with a kinsman once owned the waterfront between Moodyville and the Capilano River.

Lost Lagoon Named by the native poet Pauline Johnson, who enjoyed canoeing here. The lagoon was "lost" in that, before the Stanley Park causeway was built in 1912, it drained into Coal Harbour at low tide, and so briefly ceased to exist.

Lulu Island Gallantly named by Colonel R.C. Moody of the Royal Engineers after a young actress, Lulu Sweet, who was a member of the first theatrical company to visit British Columbia. A Victorian newspaper said of her performance, "Miss Lulu's dancing was most chaste and beautiful. She was fairly smothered with bouquets and loudly encored."

Lynn Creek After John Linn (note the spelling), one of the Royal Engineers who came to British Columbia in 1859. After the contingent was disbanded in 1863 the officers returned to England, but most of the sappers, including Linn, remained in B.C. He lived with his family at the mouth of this creek and died in 1876.

Maillardville After Father Edmond Maillard, O.M.I., a native of St. Malo, Brittany. He was placed in charge of the Parish of Our Lady of Lourdes, founded in 1909 to minister to the needs of the French-Canadians brought out from Quebec to work in the Fraser Mills. He died in France in 1966, aged 86.

Marpole Formerly called EBURNE, but renamed Marpole in 1916. After Richard Marpole (1850-1920) who, after early railway experience in England, came out to Canada and worked under contract for the Canadian Pacific Railway. In 1886 he became superintendent of construction and operation for the CPR's Pacific Division.

Mary Hill The Royal Engineers, who saw this hill as a good site for a citadel to protect New Westminster in the event of an American invasion, named it after the wife of their colonel, Richard Moody.

Milner After Viscount Milner (1854-1925), British statesman and colonial administrator.

Minnekhada Park and Lodge This Sioux name meaning "water rattling by," was given by an American who farmed here before World War I. The "Scottish hunting lodge," built in 1934 by E.W. Hamber (lieutenant-governor of B.C., 1936-40), passed to Clarence Wallace (lieutenant-governor, 1950-55). The GVRD now owns both the park and the lodge.

Minoru Park In about 1909 a racetrack named Minoru Park was opened here. Minoru was a famous racehorse owned by King Edward VII.

Mitchell Island After the first man to farm on the island, Alex Mitchell.

Mount Blanshard In 1859 Captain G.H. Richards, R.N., named this mountain behind Haney after Richard Blanshard, first governor of Vancouver Island (1850-51).

Mount Burke Named by Captain G.H. Richards, R.N., about 1860, probably after Edmund Burke (1730-97), the famous statesman, orator and author.

Mount Fromme After J.M. Fromme, "Father of Lynn Valley," who in 1899 built the first house in the valley. From 1924 to 1929 he was the reeve of North Vancouver District. He died, aged 83, in 1941.

Mount Garibaldi After the Italian patriot and soldier Giuseppe Garibaldi (1807-82). The name was conferred by Captain Richards, R.N., of surveying vessel *Plumper* in about 1860. A story goes that the name owes something to there being an Italian sailor aboard the ship when the mountain was in view on Garibaldi's birthday. (Also Garibaldi Provincial Park.)

Mount Seymour After Frederick Seymour, governor of the Crown Colony of British Columbia. He died of acute alcoholism aboard HMS *Sparrowhawk* at Bella Coola in 1869.

Mount Strachan This mountain north of Hollyburn is named after Admiral Sir Richard Strachan (pronounced "Strawn"). In 1805 he won a brilliant victory over the French, capturing four of their ships.

Musqueam Simon Fraser, in his account of his hostile reception at the mouth of the Fraser River, notes that "here we had the good fortune to escape the cruelty of the Musquiamme." Musqueam means "place of iris-like plants." The Musqueam people lived for centuries at the mouth of the Fraser River.

New Westminster Fort Langley on the south bank of the Fraser River was too vulnerable to American attack. Colonel Richard Moody advised Governor Douglas that the capital of the new Colony of British Columbia should be moved to where New Westminster now stands. Moody favored the name "Queenborough," but Douglas wanted "Queensborough." A request was then sent to London that the Queen herself choose the name of the new capital. Her Majesty decided on "New Westminster." Aware of Queen Victoria's role, the people of New Westminster take pride in its unofficial name, "The Royal City."

Newton After a pioneer New Westminster settler and harness-maker. His real name was Villeneuve but, being in an anglophone community, he changed it to Newton (which, like Villeneuve, means "new town").

Nicomekl River Preserves the name of an Indian tribe that once lived in the area but was wiped out by smallpox, probably in about 1770.

Noon Breakfast Point Lt. Peter Puget, of Captain Vancouver's company, applied this name to a small point near the tip of Point Grey in 1792. It was adopted officially in 1981.

Oakridge This name began with the construction in 1949 of the Oakridge Trolley Bus Garage at the corner of Oak Street and West 41st Avenue.

Ocean Park Chosen in about 1910 by the Rev. W.P. Goard for his Ocean Park Syndicate, comprising prominent Lower Mainland Methodists seeking land for recreational and educational purposes.

Pacific Spirit Park In April 1989 the provincial government transferred title to 763 hectares of undeveloped land from the UNIVERSITY ENDOWMENT LANDS to the GVRD to form a park. Sherry Sakamoto won a competition to provide a name. She chose the name to signify "Gateway to the Pacific and spiritual ground to becoming one with nature."

Pitt River "Pitt's River" is first mentioned in 1827, in the journal of James McMillan, the founder of Fort Langley. Apparently he named it in honor of William Pitt the Younger (1759-1806), prime minister of Britain during much of the Napoleonic Wars.

Point Atkinson Named by Captain Vancouver after an unidentified "particular friend." He may have been Thomas Atkinson, master of HMS *Victory* during the Battle of Trafalgar.

Point Garry At the southwest tip of Lulu Island, named after Nicholas Garry, deputy governor of the Hudson's Bay Company, 1822-35. The name was given by Captain Aemilius Simpson of the HBC's maritime service in 1827, when he brought the schooner *Cadboro* into the mouth of the Fraser, the first colonial vessel to enter the river.

Point Grey Named by Captain Vancouver "in compliment to my friend Captain George Grey of the Navy," who commanded HMS *Victory* at the Battle of St. Vincent in 1797. The Spaniards, arriving a year before Vancouver, had named it Punta de Langara. To the Indians it was Ulksen ("The Nose").

Point Roberts Named by Captain Vancouver after his "esteemed friend," Lt. Henry Roberts. Roberts, a gifted cartographer, had served with Vancouver on Captain Cook's second and third voyages of discovery. Originally Roberts was to command the Royal Navy's 1791 expedition to explore this coast. Only when Roberts was unavailable did that historic commission pass to Captain Vancouver.

Port Coquitlam See COQUITLAM.

Port Guichon After Laurent Guichon (1836-1902). French by birth, he joined the Cariboo Gold Rush of 1862 and subsequently ranched in the Interior. In 1883 he began farming a large tract of land here in the Fraser delta. The "port," once a steamboat halt, is now silted in.

Port Hammond After John Hammond, a farmer, and his brother William Hammond, a civil engineer, young Englishmen who owned the

New Westminster, circa 1860. cva

In 1986 the Buy&Sell opened its phone lines to receive international ads, making it the easiest and fastest way to place an ad in any country in the world. Buy&Sell Vancouver was the world's original free ad newspaper, and a founding member of the Free Ads Paper International Association, spanning virtually every major city in the world from Moscow to Los Angeles. Mike Abbott, owner of the Vancouver Buy&Sell, is Honorary President of F.A.P.I.A., a lifetime appointment.

townsite at the time of the building of the Canadian Pacific Railway.

Port Mann After Donald Mann of the firm Mackenzie and Mann, the builders of the Canadian Northern Railway. Port Mann was originally intended to be the railway's Pacific terminus. Mann was knighted in 1911. His railway became part of the Canadian National Railway in 1923.

Port Moody Named in 1860 after Colonel Richard Clement Moody (1813-87), commanding officer of the "Columbia Detachment" of the Royal Engineers (6 officers and 158 NCOs and men) that served in B.C. from 1858 to 1863. Colonel Moody returned to Britain when his detachment was disbanded, and rose to the rank of major-general.

Prospect Point This Stanley Park viewpoint was known in the nineteenth century as "Observation Point."

Porteau An adaptation of the French porte d'eau, meaning "watergate." The name was suggested in about 1908 by a Mr. Newberry of the Deeks Sand and Gravel Company.

Queensborough This community has taken a name once proposed for NEW WESTMINSTER.

Reifel Island This island, formerly known as Smoky Tom Island, was purchased in 1929 by George C. Reifel. When the Canadian Wildlife Service bought much of the island in 1972, George H. Reifel donated the rest of the island to form the Reifel Bird Sanctuary.

Richmond Hugh McRoberts, who had come to B.C. from Australia, established Richmond Farm here in 1861. The farm's name was chosen by one of McRoberts' daughters, who selected the name of a favorite place in Australia.

Sapperton The Royal Engineers (traditionally called "sappers"), who were sent out to B.C. in 1858-59, had their original camp beside the townsite of NEW WESTMINSTER. Colonel Moody coined the name "Sapperton" for this base. When members of the corps settled here, they kept the name of Sapperton for their village.

Sasamat Lake The Spanish explorers noted that Sasamat was the native name for the Indian Arm area. It actually was the name of an early Indian village at the mouth of the Seymour River, and can be translated as "lazy people."

Semiahmoo Bay Preserves the name of a subgroup of the Strait's Salish people. A claim has been made that semiahmoo means "half moon."

Shaughnessy The Canadian Pacific Railway named this subdivision after Thomas George Shaughnessy (1853-1923), an American railroader recruited in 1882 over a glass of Milwaukee beer as general purchasing agent for the CPR. Shaughnessy was president of the CPR from 1898 to 1918, he was knighted in 1901 and became Lord Shaughnessy in 1916.

Siwash Rock The original Squamish name for this landmark means "standing up." There is a native legend about how three supernatural brothers ("Transformers") came this way in a canoe and changed a bather into the rock. In early years settlers called this "Ninepins Rock." Its present name (Siwash) is a Chinook jargon word derived from the French sauvage and applied to any native.

Spanish Banks Commemorates Captain Vancouver's meeting, on June 22, 1792, with two Spanish ships, the brig Sutil commanded by Galiano and the schooner Mexicana commanded by Valdes. Actually he found the Spaniards riding at anchor a little south and west of Point Grey.

Squamish Takes its name from the local Indian nation. No meaning is known for squamish.

Stanley Park Well before there was any Vancouver this area, then called Coal Peninsula (see COAL HARBOUR), was set aside as a military reservation for fortifications that could defend the entrance to Burrard Inlet against an American invasion. In October 1889 Lord Stanley of Preston, Governor General of Canada, dedicated the new park which took his name.

Steveston In 1887 Manoah Steves, a New Brunswicker, settled on Lulu Island. In 1889 W.H. Steves, his eldest son, laid out part of the farm in townlots. It was first planned to name the village simply Steves, but this soon became the more formal Steveston.

Strathcona This East Vancouver community bears the name of Donald Alexander Smith, later Lord Strathcona and Mount Royal (1820-1914), who amassed a fortune through his connections with the Hudson's Bay Company and the Canadian Pacific Railway.

Sturgeon Park Named by Captain Vancouver "in consequence of our having purchased of the natives some excellent fish of that kind."

Surrey "The Corporation of Surrey" was created by Letters Patent issued on November 10, 1879. The new municipality probably owes its name to the fact that it lies south across the Fraser from NEW WESTMINSTER, just as in England the County of Surrey lies south across the Thames from Westminster.

Tilbury Island After Tilbury, England, where a fort once stood on the Thames downstream from London.

Tsawwassen Preserves the name of the local Indian band. The Halkomelem word means "facing seaward."

Tynehead Originally "Tinehead," since the head of the Serpentine River is here, but converted into Tynehead by analogy with the River Tyne in the north of England.

University Endowment Lands The University Endowment Act of 1907 provided for some 810,000 hectares of provincial lands to be set aside to produce revenue for the new University of British Columbia. The scheme was never really implemented. The present tiny UEL residential district in Point Grey is a vestige of the plan, which actually never contributed to the university's finances.

Vancouver After Captain George Vancouver of the Royal Navy who, from April 1792 until late 1794, with HMS Discovery and the tender Chatham made his historic survey of the mainland coast of the Pacific Northwest. When, in 1884, the Canadian Pacific Railway decided to have its Pacific terminus at Coal Harbour and not at Port Moody, W.C. Van Horne, the railroad's general manager, refused to accept either Granville, the new name of Gastown, or Liverpool, the name mooted for what is now the West End. Said Van Horne, ". . . this eventually is destined to be a great city in Canada. We must see that it has a name that will designate its place on the map of Canada. Vancouver it shall be, if I have the ultimate decision." And Vancouver it became, a distinctive name, but confusing to those who quite logically expect the City of Vancouver to be situated on Vancouver Island.

Westham Island Named by Harry Trim, an Englishman from Westham in Sussex.

Whalley After Arthur Whalley, who settled here with his family in 1925. The earlier name of Whalley's Corner, shortened to Whalley, was adopted by the community in 1948.

Whistler Takes its name from Whistler Mountain (formerly London Mountain). Whistler Mountain is named after the numerous whistlers (marmots) living on its slopes. Whistler post office was opened in 1976.

White Rock Named for a large, glacially deposited white rock on the beach. An Indian legend has it that the rock was hurled across Georgia Strait by a young chief who had promised his beloved to make their home where the white rock landed.

Whytecliff An Admiralty survey named the promontory White Cliff Point, but in 1914 a real estate developer, Colonel Albert Whyte, persuaded the Pacific Great Eastern Railway (now B.C. Rail) to name its station here not White Cliff but Whytecliff.

Willingdon Heights After the Marquis of Willingdon (1866-1941), Governor General of Canada (1926-31).

Woodward's Landing After Nathaniel Woodward, who settled here with his son Daniel in 1874.

Yennadon E.W. Prowse named this settlement near Haney after his grandfather's former home, Yennadon Manor, a beautiful place on Dartmoor in England.

Neighborhoods
Vancouver

Rocking on your front porch in the stillness of a cool summer evening, inhaling the fragrance of fresh lilac. Greeting a clerk from a local store by name as he bicycles by on a delivery. Leaning over your backyard fence in the yearly ritual of giving your neighbor a jar of raspberry jam from your garden. Walking up the block to catch the streetcar and chatting with a neighbor on the ride down to Stanley Park. Strolling to church with your family in your Sunday best and afterwards spending a peaceful afternoon back on the front porch.

Neighborhood life in Vancouver was fundamentally different in the days before the Great War, before the automobile, before television. Today's homes have turned inward behind curtains and locked doors, away from traffic noise and the eyes of strangers, towards the television set.

Vancouver's neighborhoods first began to develop as a series of separate and distinct villages around the street car stations most people depended on for transportation.

Where are these neighhorhoods today? The arrival of the automobile in this city, increased bureaucratic centralization, and the zoning of land into large residential, commercial and industrial areas have each had their effect. The result is a more homogeneous city of continuous streets, nameless commercial strips and vast bedroom areas.

In many parts of the city this has created an identity crisis. Consider how many people living between 16th Avenue and 41st Avenue and Cambie and Fraser believe or even know that they are supposed to be living in a place called "Riley Park." It is no surprise that many parts of Vancouver lack a sense of community and place. In a recent survey many Vancouverites could only identify their own "neighborhood" as the East End—an area containing half of the whole city!

We have lost many of our neighborhoods (Vancouver's citizens have been looking for them without success in the present landscape), and a more promising place to look is in the city's past and, with the help of City Plan, in the city's future.

If we look into Vancouver's past for neighborhoods, we can find as an example the Cedar Cottage of 1910. Here was a small but thriving village, centred on Cedar Cottage Road with Cedar Cottage School facing down the street toward the Cedar Cottage Interurban Station at the other end. Businesses on this main street, including the Cedar Cottage Theatre and Cedar Cottage Pharmacy, were surrounded by homes that were all within walking distance. From there outwards in every direction was undeveloped land. In old Cedar Cottage you knew when you crossed its threshold and you knew when you arrived at its centre. You certainly can't do that any more. Today there is an absence of discernable boundaries, and we no longer name businesses, buildings, parks, schools, streets and institutions after the places they occupy.

In order to look into Vancouver's future for neighborhoods, consider the results of City Plan. Between 1992 and 1995 Vancouver citizens, business people and city hall administrators worked together to create "a shared vision for the future of Vancouver." The outcome was that "Vancouverites want a city of neighborhoods . . . villages within a city, each with its own identity." A city with a diverse economy and jobs close to home, with transit, walking and bikes—not cars—as a priority.

It seems Vancouverites would like the best of small town country living contained within their city, while retaining most of the advantages that life in a humming metropolis has to offer. They want to blend the best of Vancouver's past with the best of current city life to create an even better future. All with citizen input.

The purpose of City Plan was to set directions to guide the city over the subsequent 30 years. The directions have been set, and the critical part is the next step: "citizens, council and staff working together to fill in the details."

If you are interested in getting back Vancouver's neighborhoods, remember "citizen input" means *your* input.

—*Bruce Macdonald*

facing page: *Heritage homes at 1100 block, Comox Street overlooking Nelson Park in the West End. The historic block was saved in 1996 after a neighborhood preservation campaign.* rw
above: *Edwardian porch detail, 2300 Birch Street, Fairview.* rw

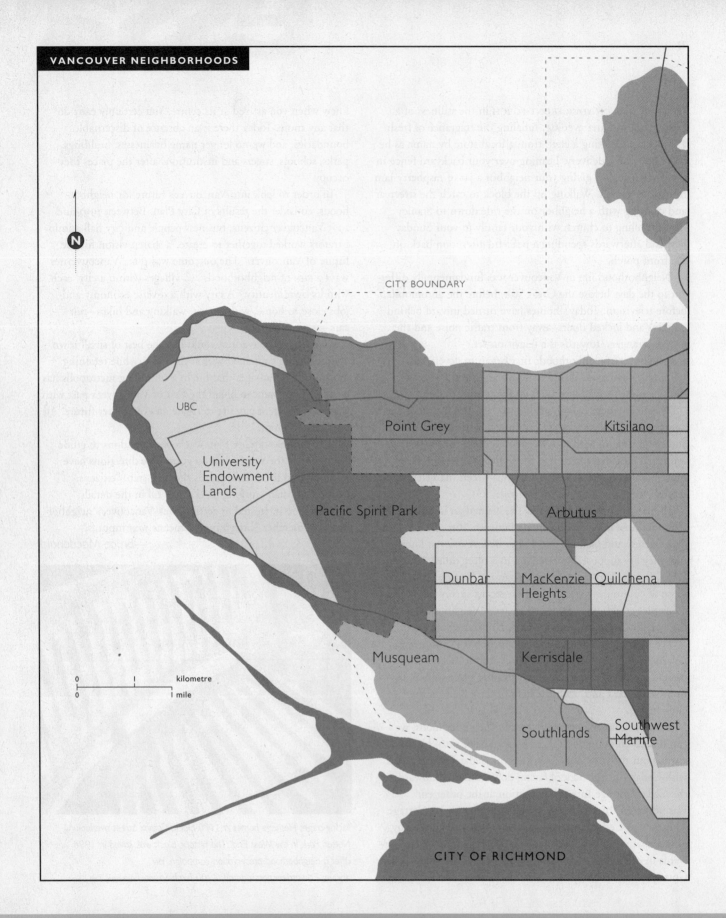

CITY BOUNDARY

UBC

Point Grey

Kitsilano

University
Endowment
Lands

Pacific Spirit Park

Arbutus

Dunbar

MacKenzie
Heights

Quilchena

0   1   kilometre
0   1 mile

Musqueam

Kerrisdale

Southlands

Southwest
Marine

CITY OF RICHMOND

Thomson & Page Ltd. was founded in 1929 by Melvin S. Thomson and Lawrence Page. Mr. Page left the company in the mid-1930s and Ronald Wilson became a silent partner. Thomson & Page began as appliance and electrical retailers, would later expand into records, stereos, television sets and VCRs. When Mr. Thomson decided to retire in 1975, the store was purchased by Jim and Peggy Knauer. Jim Knauer introduced Canada's first "furniture Gallery," featuring the Drexel Heritage Furniture line in 1979.

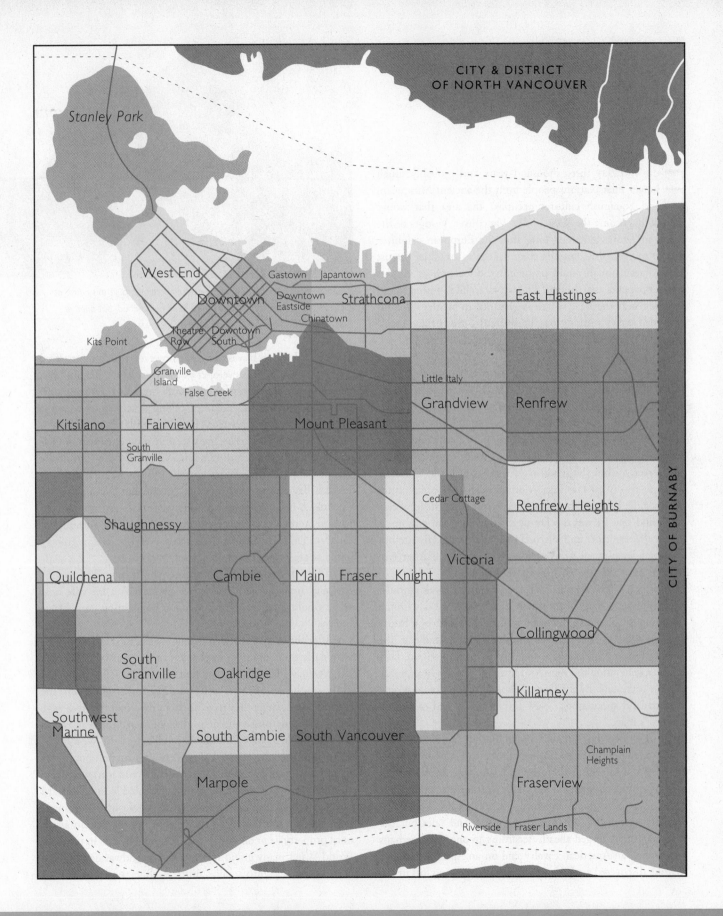

CITY & DISTRICT
OF NORTH VANCOUVER

Stanley Park

West End

Gastown   Japantown

Downtown

Downtown
Eastside

Strathcona

East Hastings

Chinatown

Theatre
Row

Downtown
South

Kits Point

Granville
Island

False Creek

Little Italy

Grandview   Renfrew

Kitsilano   Fairview

Mount Pleasant

South
Granville

Cedar Cottage

Renfrew Heights

Shaughnessy

Quilchena

Cambie   Main   Fraser   Knight

Victoria

Collingwood

South
Granville

Oakridge

Killarney

Southwest
Marine

South Cambie   South Vancouver

Champlain
Heights

Marpole

Fraserview

Riverside   Fraser Lands

CITY OF BURNABY

Today, Thomson & Page concentrates on fine furnishings and accessories, featuring Drexel Heritage, Pennsylvania House and Stickley, and upholstery specialists like Highland House, Burton James, Holt and Temple. Thomson & Page also offers complete interior design service, with design consultants to assist in planning entire projects or the choice of a single piece. This is a family business, in the same location since 1929, with Jeff Knauer representing the third generation of the family involved in Thomson & Page.

West End
Ed Starkins

Thomas A. Fee, a noted turn-of-the-century architect, built this house at Gilford and Comox streets. It has since been demolished, but another Fee house still stands at 1119 Broughton Street. cva

F OR AT LEAST three thousand years and probably much longer First Nations people from the ancient Musqueam and Squamish cultures occupied the area that would eventually become the West End of Vancouver. Vestiges of the native millennia remained long after the European colonization of the British Columbia coast. In the 1930s Chief August Jack Khatsalanough could point out the location of villages and settlements that he had known as a child, among them Staytook near the Beach Avenue entrance to Stanley Park. In 1932 road crews working on the Burrard Street bridge paved over the ruins of Chip-kaay-am, Chief George's potlatch house.

In 1862 three Englishmen, John Morton, Samuel Brighouse and William Hailstone paid $550.75 for District Lot 185, a 218 hectare parcel of land with boundaries nearly identical to those of the modern West End. Morton became the first European to live in the neighborhood when he built a cabin on a cliff overlooking Coal Harbour, half a block south of modern Burrard Street, within the shadows of what is now the Guinness Tower at 1055 West Hastings. Morton, who had been a potter in Yorkshire, England, began making bricks from the local clay but found that he was too far away from potential customers in New Westminster and Victoria to earn a profit. His attempt to start a small farm proved equally unsuccessful. After two years he left to start a business in Abbotsford.

Morton, Brighouse and Hailstone began to speak enthusiastically about a "City of Liverpool" that would one day stretch from English Bay to Coal Harbour but their vision of a future metropolis did little more than earn them the nickname of "the three greenhorns." Morton and his partners had, in fact, arrived a generation too soon for District Lot 185 to be of much value as real estate. By the 1880s, although they had sold several acres to land speculators, "New Liverpool" existed only on a surveyor's map.

In 1885 when the Canadian Pacific Railway announced that it was extending its transcontinental line to Granville at Coal Harbour the "greenhorns" surrendered nearly a third of their holdings to the company in return for a promise from the CPR to shift part of its operations into District Lot 185. This extraordinary agreement did little to promote land sales but the partners gamely forged ahead. According to one story, perhaps apocryphal, an American cavalry raid on an Apache village in Arizona discovered a stack of pamphlets advertising lots in the Brighouse Estates. It was the CPR, however, which set itself up as the first real estate developer in the West End when, in 1888, the company began to sell high-priced homes to company officials and other affluent citizens along a section of Georgia Street that became known as "Blueblood Alley."

While the CPR enclave grew steadily the slopes west of Nelson and south of Burrard remained empty. By the turn of the century summertime crowds travelled to the bathing beach at English Bay on the newly opened Robson and Denman streetcar line. A few blocks west of Granville the streetcar entered a forlorn landscape of brush and tree stumps before turning left on Denman Street where there were several houses, a grocery and a confectioners' shop.

In June 1900 James S. Matthews, who became Vancouver's first city archivist went blackberry picking with his wife near what would later be the intersection of Thurlow and Davie Streets.

"After the evening meal, we went too far, or sat too long, for with darkness coming on, we could not find our way back. No lights were visible; all was darkness when night fell. All the area of the southern slope west of Burrard Street was wilderness; the stumps stood where they have been cut off when the trees were felled; the underbrush and debris had all been cleared away and it was possible to walk, or rather scramble over, the West End."

By 1901 the long-awaited West End construction boom was under way, reaching its peak between 1907 and 1910 when row after row of two-storey frame houses appeared west of Burrard Street. Near English Bay wealthy citizens built luxurious mansions making the West End the chief venue for the city's rich until property went on sale in Shaughnessy Heights in 1909. By World War I many grand homes from the Edwardian era had been subdivided into smaller units. Architectural survivors of the West End's brief gilded age include the B.T. Rogers mansion (1902), Lord Roberts School (1906) and the Manhattan Apartments (1908), the West End's first apartment block.

Over the next half century the West End enjoyed a reputation as a congenial, relaxed and affordable neighborhood. During the 1930s David Savage, a *Vancouver News Herald* reporter, lived in the Buchan Hotel at 1906 Haro, paying $40 a month for a large room with maid service and three meals a day. Savage recalled:

"The West End was a gracious place of beautiful old houses and mellow gardens. It was a place for the very young, starting out at very low wages, and the very old, surviving on often very small pensions. Both wanted something cheap, and the West End was cheap."

Savage and his friend Noel Robinson, a *Province* reporter, were among the genteel Bohemians who frequented parties and afternoon teas at the Haro Street homes of Lilavati, an Indian dancer, and her husband Jack Jacquillard, a Princeton graduate. The young left-wing writers of the New Frontier Club, including the poet Dorothy Livesay, met at the English Bay Bath House, now a community centre.

Until the mid-1950s the tallest building in the West End was the eight-storey Sylvia Hotel. Post-war construction projects were mainly limited to squat three-storey walkups which often had a small penthouse straddling the rooftop. In 1956 city council, attentive to the complaints of downtown businessmen who had been losing trade to suburban shopping centres, rezoned the West End to allow significantly higher population density. Artists' renderings made the proposed high rise architecture look classy and attractive. To avoid overcrowding, broad areas of open space, determined by a mathematical formula, would surround each new structure.

By 1972 when investors' enthusiasm for high rise construction fizzled the West End was no longer a cozy neighborhood of few pretensions. During a 13-year period developers had built more than 220 high rises, several of them 20-storey Bauhaus cell blocks containing 200 or more suites. Few apartment dwellers enjoyed views of the bay and the mountains; most simply looked out at the people living across the way.

Despite many protests the era of monolith building claimed much of the traditional architecture of the West End. Typical of lost heritage structures was the Simpson Block, a patterned brownstone building with arched porticos and wood-paneled interiors built at the corner of Denman and Davie in 1912. Some buildings, notably the Thomas A. Fee house (1904) at 1119 Broughton, have survived with extensive modifications.

By the 1970s automobile traffic plagued the West End's once-quiet streets. City planners blocked off many intersections with shrubbery, trees and benches but on summer nights bumper-to-bumper traffic circled the 1200-blocks of Pendrell and Davie Streets as hundreds of curious motorists came to stare at and occasionally consort with local prostitutes. In the mid-'80s a citizens' organization known as "Shame the Johns" began silent curbside vigils to interfere with the sex trade. Eventually the provincial government obtained a court order forcing prostitutes from neighborhood streets.

According to federal census data the population of the West End remained static during the 1980s: there were 36,950 residents in 1981, 37,190 in 1991—a change of .6 per cent. By the end of the decade the neighborhood had experienced considerable "gentrification" recording a 28 per cent increase in residents with incomes over $70,000 per annum and a 20 per cent drop among those with incomes of less than $10,000. During the same period there had been a 61.3 per cent growth in the number of privately owned dwellings. Housing conditions reflected the "two-tier" economy as deteriorating, ill-maintained buildings, many of them from the 1956-1972 period, stood next to luxury condominiums. During the 1980s the rental cost of apartment units in the West End rose steadily, averaging $701 per month in 1991.

The West End has always been a highly transient neighborhood: 72 per cent of its residents moved between 1985 and 1991. Many were low income earners who left the area permanently but the most significant exodus was among persons of retirement age. In the 1980s there was nearly a 20 per cent decline in the number of residents over the age of 55. In 1991 49.7 per cent of West Enders were between the ages of 20 and 40.

The West End, 1973. vp

Central Business District
Chris McBeath

IF ONE THING could characterize downtown Vancouver, it would be its relationship to the water. Through every decade since the city's inception the harbor has fuelled commercial activity, bearing witness to a city skyline that has evolved to a forest of glass and steel where virgin timber once soared.

Vancouver's Central Business District, bordered by Stanley Park, the West End and Cambie Street, lies nestled between the Burrard Inlet and False Creek. Presently its centre covers a 10-block business and retailing radius from the Georgia and Granville intersection, but with over 405 hectares of downtown urban renewal under way, refurbished neighborhoods such as Yaletown, cosmopolitan Robson Street, historic Gastown and Coal Harbour are pulling the city's hub to its perimeters.

In the 1860s and 1870s all activity focussed along bustling Burrard Inlet. Settlers staked land claims for $1 per acre. Canoes paddled up to Water Street's floating boardwalks. Prospectors gathered supplies enroute to the Kootenays, and later to the Klondike Gold Rush. And busy sawmills, lining the waterfront, supplied lumber to ships bound for California, Australia, Asia and Europe. At one time, the mill at the foot of Dunlevy Street (called Luk'luk'i by the Salish meaning "grove of beautiful trees") provided the masts and spars for most of the world's sailing ships.

It was the powerful Canadian Pacific Railway which charted Vancouver's future, and by the time the city was incorporated in 1886, the railway had already secured land grants which comprised one-quarter of what is now this city, including the entire downtown peninsula. Lauchlan Hamilton, the CPR's first land commissioner, driving his stake into the earth at Hastings and Hamilton, began laying out and naming the downtown's streets.

Wherever tracks were laid, communities grew, businesses boomed and real estate prices spiralled upwards. Downtown lots that sold for less than $300 in March, changed hands for $1,000 in May and parcels "out in the woods" at Hornby and Georgia were listed at $620.

Even the Great Fire of 1886, reducing the township to ashes, did little to halt its growth. Rebuilding began as stumps still smouldered. Within months, signs of the disaster had all but disappeared and by New Year's Day, 1887, there were 14 office blocks and civic buildings, 23 hotels, 51 stores, 9 saloons, a church, a livery stable, a miller and a wharf, with more construction under way as far west as Thurlow.

Five months later on May 23, 1887, Engine No. 374, CPR's first transcontinental train, steamed into the western terminus at the foot of Howe Street. A week later the *Abyssinia* sailed into harbor, her cargo of oriental silks and teas destined for Europe. With CPR's new harborfront West-East link, they reached London via New York within record-setting time and Vancouver's role as a "trading gateway to the Pacific Rim" was secured.

While the gentry gravitated to Hastings Street west of Burrard (known then as Seaton Street), building mansions and private clubs, the city's hard-working commercial district flourished around Gastown, Cordova and East Hastings streets, where evidence can still be seen of its once grand Victoria-era hotels, warehouses and specialty shops.

But as CPR's influence took hold, a shift was inevitable. CPR cut Granville Street through from Burrard Inlet to False Creek, spent $200,000 to clear and pave Hastings and Pender streets, developed the ritzy West End and, by 1887, had built its imposing Hotel Vancouver on the highest point of land, 42.7 metres above sea level where Eaton's now stands. The hotel was relocated to its present site in the thirties. In 1893, when the Hudson Bay Company left Cordova Street to set up shop opposite the hotel, on a $2,250 plot on which it still stands, it signalled an East-West retailing rivalry which was to last, in earnest, until World War I.

On June 28, 1890, Vancouver's first streetcar rattled a rectangular route along Main, Cordova, Granville and Pender streets. Finally the busy waterfront and popular Gastown were connected to the newly emerging business area along tree-lined Granville. Slowly the heart of the city moved west, leaving an area which Statistics Canada today designates as the lowest-income postal district in Canada.

By the turn of the century, Vancouver's population was doubling every five years, reaching 120,847 in 1911. Real estate agents multiplied from a modest 50 to a fervent 650 in less than a decade, outnumbering grocery stores three to one. Land prices rocketed. Motor cars (driven on the left side of the street until January 1, 1922) became a common sight. Around 1907, at the foot of Cambie near Smithe, Imperial Oil opened the first gas station in the Dominion of Canada.

By 1912 the central business district was fully developed, flanked by comfortable residential neighborhoods and accessed by electric streetcars carrying 100,000 passengers a day. Flamboyant, high-rolling speculators financed a freewheeling stock exchange. The post office at Granville and Hastings handled the fourth largest volume in Canada, and Vancouver's fire

department on Seymour near Robson, the first to be motorized in the country, was ranked among the world's best, matched only by Leipzig, Germany and London, England.

The Vancouver Block Office Tower (whose clock stopped in the 1918 and 1946 earthquakes), the World Tower and Dominion Trust Building each boasted the title of tallest building in the British Empire in its time, and the stately courthouse at Georgia and Howe reflected the city's growing stature. Vancouver's infrastructure included 58 kilometres of streets, nearly 40 kilometres of wooden sidewalks, electric, water and sewerage systems, a number of factories, a five-storey hotel, two newspapers, two cathedrals, 12,000 telephones and a new opera house on Granville advertising seats from 25 cents. By 1927 furnished apartments at Burrard and Thurlow rented for $45-80 per week and the Rogers Building, opened in 1911, had sold for an unprecedented one million dollars.

Growth and gaiety came to an abrupt halt after the Wall Street Crash in 1929. The destitute thronged downtown streets in search of work, joined daily by hundreds of the unemployed who rode the rods west. Receiving relief payments of 20 cents a day and living in "hobo jungles" (shanty towns) beneath the four-lane Georgia Viaduct and along the False Creek flats, they soon earned Vancouver the unwelcome title of "Hobo Capital of Canada." World War II pulled the city out of depression, but it would be nearly 20 years before the Vancouver downtown core would renew its rapid expansion.

Traffic congestion was a fundamental issue in post-war city planning. During the decade of the Roaring Twenties the number of cars catapulted from 650 to 36,500. The city's first traffic light blinked on October 18, 1928, at the corner of Hastings and Main and an innovation called parking meters were installed in 1946, charging one nickel for one hour's parking. A deteriorating transit system compounded the congestion problem and, in spite of a population that had doubled to 800,000 between 1946 and 1964, transit use halved.

The issue peaked in the mid-sixties, when conservationists defeated a freeway proposal that would have cut through the historic heart of the city. Pro-developers, however, succeeded in reorganizing the downtown core around massive Pacific Centre, the flagship project for a 20-year rejuvenation program for central Vancouver. It cued the $160 million Robson Square complex, the restoration of a rundown Gastown, the distinctive white-domed B.C. Place Stadium, the Sinclair Centre heritage project, the less-than-successful refit of Granville Street into a pedestrian mall which, unexpectedly, breathed new life into Robson Street (now the hottest retail strip in the city), as well as a revamped transportation system.

Expo 86, celebrating Vancouver's centennial, spurred further development. Its legacies such as Canada Place are city landmarks, and the lingering benefits of significantly higher international visitor counts and a broadening, culturally diverse population and investment base are reshaping the downtown core for the new millennium.

Unlike many urban centres, downtown Vancouver has a vibrant residential population base. Almost 50,000 people live on its doorstep with forecasts indicating growth of an additional 80,000 within 20 years. Increases of 60,000 in the city's workforce are also anticipated, reaching 230,000 by 2006. Add to this the 500,000 people and 300,000 vehicles that already enter and leave the downtown core almost daily, plus the astounding fact that nearly 98 per cent of downtown's rush-hour comprises passenger cars, and it becomes apparent why a walk-to-work, pedestrian-oriented philosophy is vital to maintain a healthy city core.

The Greenways Plan—linking the city's parks and walkways with greenery—is helping to defray mounting pollution counts from vehicular traffic and, coupled with new bicycle pathways, seawall walkways and restrictive one-way systems, is a key component of much downtown development.

In the past decade Vancouver has racked up over $3 billion in construction annually. Eighteen major downtown projects are under way or recently completed, including the $160 million General Motors Place arena, the $100 million Library Square, the $24.5 million Ford Centre for the Performing Arts and the $8.6 million Pacific Space Centre. Projects such as the Bentall Group's fifth tower on Burrard will contribute to the district's 74,320 sq. metre annual average of new office space, while ventures such as university "satellite" campuses and sophisticated retail outlets along Hastings Street are redefining the downtown core.

Along the once industrial north shore of False Creek, the former Expo 86 site, Concord Pacific Developments, owned by Hong Kong billionaire Li Ka-Shing, is undertaking the largest private redevelopment in North America. In a 15-year project estimated to cost in excess of $3 billion, 82.5 hectares are being transformed into nearly 1.2 million sq. metres of mixed office, retail and residential space for 15,000 people, including 1.7 hectares of parkland and the preservation of the historic Round House for Engine No. 374.

Along Coal Harbour and the Bayshore Lands, Marathon Developments (the name for the new company created when C.P. Limited sold Marathon Realty) holds tenure on much of downtown's prime real estate. Marathon is lifting the CP tracks after more than a century to make way for a 20-year

Designed for the maximum comfort of the traveller, Hyatt Regency guestrooms offer contemporary and spacious designs and many have spectacular views of the inner harbor, the North Shore mountains or Vancouver's beautiful skyline.

redevelopment of 19 hectares of land. The mixed use project includes offices, a hotel and the first residential neighborhood on Burrard Inlet. Plans call for 2,240 residences, 185,800 sq. metres of commercial and retailing space, and almost 7 hectares of parks and open space including a 3.2-hectare waterfront park.

Zoning changes are creating new high-density residential neighborhoods such as Crosstown, an artist's colony on the fringes of Gastown, and the 8-hectare International Village nearby. And in downtown south, between the Burrard and Granville bridges, the density ratio is slated to be three times greater than the West End, giving rise to a vigorous Downtown Eastside Residents Association (DERA), formed to protect the interests of its many long-time, low-income residents in hotels such as the Austin, the California and the Ambassador.

Asian interests own over 20 per cent of downtown Vancouver and, financing two-thirds of its major development projects, they signal a new type of business leadership. Although resource-rich corporate giants in fishing, foresty, real estate and mining are still prominent, most economic growth is in the service-related industries: finance, insurance, retail, hi-tech and hospitality.

Tourism has ballooned over the last ten years with convention delegates, cruise ship arrivals and visitor counts climbing to unprecedented highs. In 1994 visitors topped 6.3 million, of which an estimated 148,609 convention delegates alone spent $168 million, inciting fierce competition between Greystone Properties Ltd., Concord Pacific and Marathon Developments to provide enlarged convention facilities.

For all its bustle and new construction, Vancouver's relationship to the water continues to mark its prosperity. As salt air sweeps through downtown streets and seaviews peek through canyons of glass, Vancouver is clean, safe and ranked as one of the most livable, urban centres in the world, as if fulfilling the vision of Captain Vancouver when he wrote in his log: "It requires only to be enriched by the industry of man with villages, mansions, cottages and other buildings to render it the most lovely country that can be imagined."

right, top: Georgia and Granville, looking west, circa 1905 (the original Hotel Vancouver is on the left) cva; bottom: The BC Hydro Building, the city's finest office tower when opened in 1957, converted to residential use in 1994. vp facing page, top: Georgia Street, seen from the dome of Vancouver Art Gallery, 1993; bottom: Hastings Street at Victory Square, 1994. vs

Over the years the Hyatt has played host to many dignitaries, including H.R.H. Prince Charles, Prime Ministers Jean Chretien, Brian Mulroney and Pierre Trudeau, U.S. President Bill Clinton, then Vice President George Bush, and Russian leader Mikhail Gorbachev.

In the heart of downtown, the Hyatt Regency Vancouver is within walking distance of all major attractions, including world famous Stanley Park and Vancouver's newest stadium, GM Place.

Strathcona
John Atkin

Heatley and Georgia, Strathcona, 1957. vp

A SPIT OF LAND in Burrard Inlet, just east of Main Street at the foot of Dunlevy Avenue, is the birthplace of both Vancouver and its first neighborhood—Strathcona. This former native campsite, called Kumkumalay, meaning "big leaf maple trees," was chosen by Captain Edward Stamp as the site for his new sawmill in 1865. The rag-tag collection of shacks and cottages around the Hastings Mill quickly developed into a residential area that moved south and east away from the mill.

In the beginning Strathcona was simply known as the East End. This referred to an area that took in everything east of Main to Campbell Avenue and from Burrard Inlet to False Creek. At that time, False Creek was four times its present size; at high tide its waters lapped at the pilings of buildings on Pender Street and extended east to Clark Drive. The Strathcona of today is bounded by Hastings, Campbell, Gore, Atlantic and Prior streets.

Strathcona has always been known as a cosmopolitan neighborhood and the student body at Strathcona Elementary, one of Vancouver's oldest schools, provided a good indication of this diversity. School enrolment in the 1930s included Japanese (who made up almost half the student population), Chinese, Italians, Jews, and a smattering of Scandinavians, Russians, Ukrainians and blacks along with many others. While there were no strict boundaries within the neighborhood, many of the Japanese lived on the north side of Hastings Street, while the Italian community primarily occupied Union and Prior streets. Between these two groups were the Ukrainian Hall, built in 1928 at Hawks and Pender, and one block west at Heatley, the Schara Tzedeck Synagogue. The 1908 Fountain Chapel on Jackson at Prior (previously the German, then Norwegian, Lutheran Church) was the spiritual home for Vancouver's small black population. The growing Chinese population lived on the edges of Chinatown.

It was because of its mixture of housing and industry, and the fact that it was the entry point to the city for successive waves of immigrants, that the East End name came to have a derogatory meaning and, by the 1950s, planners had declared it a slum for demolition, despite evidence to the contrary.

By 1967, despite protests, 15 blocks of the neighborhood had already been acquired and cleared for urban redevelopment when the city announced a freeway to downtown. Strathcona residents were horrified by plans to use the blocks in between Union and Prior for the freeway, connected via a new Georgia Viaduct to the larger network of roads that were to carve up the downtown.

The outcry from the general public, community activists and professionals was loud and clear about the lack of public consultation and the amount of destruction the new roads would cause. In the end the Georgia and Dunsmuir street viaducts were the only pieces of the system to be constructed; they were opened in 1972 to a city uninterested in freeways.

From the protests and struggle to save the neighborhood, Strathcona has emerged with a strong sense of identity and pride, not found in many of Vancouver's neighborhoods. It is a place where residents meet as they walk to the corner store, exercise the dog or practise Tai Chi in the park. The street-end parks are meeting places to talk or sit and read in the sunshine. The jumble of buildings are squeezed onto narrow lots, so close to each other that their gutters sometimes touch, and in a mixture of styles and colors that is uniquely Strathcona. Flower gardens overflow the front yards onto the sidewalks and the backyards are used for intensive vegetable gardening. Apartment buildings, houses, and corner stores (which provide for the day-to-day needs of residents and become meeting places and provide community bulletin boards) exist side by side, a form of development that communities across North America are now trying to duplicate. What planners of the 1950s saw as disorder is today becoming the model for the new "urban villages."

Yet its inner-city location means that Strathcona has its own set of problems, such as pressures from nearby prostitution and drug dealing. Some see the inevitable onset of gentrification as another problem, as the neighborhood grows in popularity due to its proximity to downtown. The architecture, which accounts for a good deal of Strathcona's charm, is some of Vancouver's oldest and most fragile. Unsympathetic renovation, demolition and incompatible new construction could endanger the delicate balance that exists in the neighborhood.

But as before Strathcona will not only survive, but thrive, continuing to be a healthy community and a special place to live.

Hastings/Sunrise
Bruce Macdonald

FOR CENTURIES if not millennia the sheltered bay at the northern edge of the district of Hastings/Sunrise provided a natural stopping point, Khanamoot, for local native peoples beaching canoes on their way to pick berries or hunt deer and elk in the productive grounds surrounding Deer Lake and Burnaby Lake. This old trail led all the way to the Kwantlen settlements on the Fraser River where the gold rush town of New Westminster was to appear suddenly in 1859. From there in 1863 Colonel Moody of the Royal Engineers decided Khanamoot was the logical place for a future saltwater port to develop. He supervised the creation of a government town reserve that became known as the Hastings Townsite. Today the district of Hastings/Sunrise comprises the northern half of this original reserve, occupying the northeast corner of Vancouver, the area east of Nanaimo Street and north of Broadway. The word "Sunrise" was not associated with the region south of 1st Avenue until the 1940s, when a new subdivision named Sunrise Ridge was built and a nearby park was named Sunrise Park.

In 1865, during the construction of the second sawmill on Burrard Inlet, the Colony of British Columbia upgraded the old native trail to a stagecoach road and the Brighton Hotel was built at Khanamoot as a seaside resort for holidaying residents of New Westminster.

In 1869 the site was renamed Hastings after Rear Admiral Hastings of the British naval fleet stationed on the Pacific coast and the first subdivision lots in the future Vancouver were put up for sale. Sawmills and shingle mills were built and in the following decades the Hastings Townsite was logged over for its giant cedar, fir and hemlock. A real town never developed there, however, even after the Canadian Pacific Railway came steaming right through it en route to Gastown. Despite its slow and humble development, Hastings still earned a significant spot in the history of Vancouver as the site of the city's first road, hotel, wharf, post office, museum and subdivision.

In 1888 the province designated 65 hectares just to the south of Hastings as a park for the "recreation and enjoyment of the public." Although its use strayed from that of a "park"—as a horse racetrack, an amusement park, sports facilities and buildings for the Pacific National Exhibition replaced the original creeks and forest—in 1994 the province finally recommitted itself to the future redevelopment of Hastings Park as a major East Side park. 1997 would be the PNE's last year at Hastings Park.

Hastings earned a significant spot in Vancouver history as site of the city's first road, hotel, wharf, post office, museum and subdivision

Significant residential development of the Hastings Townsite began only after Vancouver spread outwards to the area around 1911, the year the landowners of the Hastings Townsite voted 1,200 to 1 to join the City of Vancouver. Then the stump clearing and road building began in earnest, and large landowners such as John Hendry, the owner of the Hastings Sawmill, and Joe Martin, the former premier of British Columbia, sold off their holdings to thousands of working-class people. The building boom took off in the 1920s and by the end of the 1940s most of the available land was covered with single family housing. Despite the complete industrial development of the waterfront, at the old site of Khanamoot and Brighton a new park was created and New Brighton outdoor pool was opened in 1936.

The year 1954 saw Hastings/Sunrise's debut on the national and international scene with the construction of the largest sports stadium in Canada at Exhibition Park—Empire Stadium —for the main site of the British Empire Games. Today a large bronze statue of two runners, Roger Bannister and John Landy, depicts the Games' most spectacular event, the Miracle Mile. Empire Stadium then became the home for the newly formed B.C. Lions football team.

Since the 1890s the centrepiece of the Hastings/Sunrise district has been Hastings Park, located at the crossroads of a number of major transportation routes. Here the CPR enters Vancouver, the Trans-Canada Highway is carried across Burrard Inlet by the Second Narrows Bridge, and a Canadian National Railway tunnel emerges to lead to a rail bridge across the Inlet. The south end of the CNR bridge is near the Alberta Wheat Pool elevator, the largest oceanside elevator in the world.

Hastings Park became the home of professional hockey in British Columbia in 1970 as the Vancouver Canucks joined the national hockey league and, in 1974, it became the home for Vancouver's professional soccer team, now the 86ers. Despite this, no sporting event ever drew as continuous and deafening a response from an audience as Elvis Presley in 1957 and the Beatles in 1965, when they strained to be heard above audiences at Empire Stadium committed to non-stop screaming.

Collingwood and Renfrew
Bruce Macdonald

THE FIRST MODERN EFFORT by humans to alter the forested landscape that blanketed the districts of Collingwood and Renfrew was made in 1861. That year Colonel Richard Moody oversaw the building of a military trail along an old native trail leading to English Bay from New Westminster. Colonel Moody then selected for himself some of the choicest land along this trail—the 114 hectares that today make up the heart of downtown Collingwood. At the time there was not a single colonial settler in what is now Vancouver. The appeal to Colonel Moody was probably the shallow lake that ran for about a kilometre in the low valley along the north side of his False Creek Trail, now Kingsway. In 1863, just before returning to England permanently, Moody laid out a large government townsite for a future saltwater port on Burrard Inlet. The southern border of the Hastings Townsite touched the northern limit of his own property in Collingwood. Today this is 29th Avenue, the dividing point between the Renfrew and Collingwood areas.

The earliest known settler in today's Collingwood was George Wales in 1878. Wales paid $1 per acre for 221 acres (89.4 hectares) bounded today by Wales Street, Kingsway and 45th Avenue. In the 1880s stagecoaches travelled what would become Kingsway as they moved through the vast forest between Gastown and New Westminster. The first business set up in the districts of Collingwood and Renfrew was the Collingwood Inn, a roadhouse catering to stagecoaches, one block east of the present intersection of Kingsway and Joyce.

Until the 1890s the inhabitants of the Collingwood and Renfrew districts were predominantly ducks, geese, loons, beaver, black bears, cougars, wolves and deer. The most interesting features of the landscape were Moody's large lake just south of the present Skytrain route in the centre of the future Collingwood and three small lakes caused by beaver dams along the present Grandview Highway in the Renfrew area. Although no sign of these lakes exists today, for pioneers the waterfowl that flocked to them were enjoyed for their meat and the "snow white breasts" of the loons were coveted for hat trimmings.

The neighborhood became known as Collingwood in 1891 following construction of an interurban tramway between the cities of Vancouver and New Westminster—the first interurban system in North America. The tramway ran along the present Skytrain route with the Collingwood East station about halfway between the two cities. From here the neighborhood's first road was built, Joyce Road. By most accounts the name "Collingwood" originated with some of the owners of the tramway company who came from Collingwood, Ontario. The sparsely populated region around Collingwood was organized into the Municipalities of South Vancouver and Burnaby in 1892.

When the two-room East Vancouver School was built in 1896, it was able to accommodate all the students in Collingwood—there were just 30. The building survives today on a corner of the Collingwood School grounds and has the distinction of being the oldest school building in Vancouver. A number of Collingwood's main streets were named after the families of the school's first students, such as the Battison brothers (Battison Road) and Florence Earle (Earles Road). The secretary of the first school board was A. Joyce (Joyce Road) and the first child born in the area in 1892 was Jennie Vivian (Vivian Road).

By 1913 Collingwood was a fast-growing town centred along Joyce Street and spreading in both directions from the interurban station, but still far away from the other small towns sprouting along the rail line. The surrounding area was semi-agricultural with many small orchards, ranches and farms. As automobiles came into use, the commercial buildings along Kingsway near Joyce began to form a new town centre. Most of the settlement of the Renfrew district took place in the 1920s and the 1940s.

Because Collingwood was relatively isolated in its early days, the residents of Collingwood developed a strong sense of community and a devout loyalty to their local school. While many other institutions and establishments have come and gone in Collingwood, Carleton School has proven to be a cornerstone of stability and pride for the neighborhood.

Renfrew for decades was the unpopulated southern half of the old Hastings Townsite and it became part of the City of Vancouver in 1911. Collingwood became part of Vancouver when the Municipality of South Vancouver joined the City of Vancouver in 1929. Houses have since filled in the open land that surrounded Collingwood making the boundaries of the original community indiscernible. The interurban was closed in 1954 after 63 years. However, the 1986 construction of the Skytrain along the old interurban route resulted in a new wave of settlement into lowrise and highrise apartment buildings near the station stops, echoing the original settlement of the area.

Killarney and Champlain Heights
Bruce Macdonald

STRETCHING SOUTH from Kingsway along Boundary Road to the Fraser River, the districts of Killarney and Champlain Heights formed the last corner of Vancouver to be urbanized. From the arrival of the first settler in 1868, until just after the World War II, the area was essentially wild land with scattered agricultural operations.

The first modern settler was William Rowling in 1868. Rowling was given District Lot 268 along the Fraser River as a grant for his British military service. His work as a surveyor in the Royal Engineers included marking out the border between British Columbia and the Washington Territory in 1859. By the 1880s the Rowling family's landholdings had expanded to include all of the 3.5 kilometres of Fraser River shoreline in the Killarney district. In 1878 George Wales became the first settler in the northern half of modern Killarney when he took up District Lot 50—221 acres (89.4 hectares) for $1 an acre. In 1888 all of the land in the district between Wales' and Rowlings' property was auctioned off to eight buyers as eight 65-hectare lots. In the 1890s the first two roads were built along the northern boundaries of these properties, No. 1 Road (now 45th Avenue) and No. 2 Road (now 54th Avenue). This area was to remain very rural with scattered farms until after World War II. The 8-hectare F.R. Stewart fruit ranch established in the 1890s produced fruit for the Vancouver market before the Okanagan fruit industry was developed.

Other Killarney pioneers are remembered by the early street names and other landmarks. The Vivian family (Vivian Creek) lived in a landmark stone house at Vivian Road and No. 2 Road. Jennie Vivian, born in 1892, was the first child born between Collingwood and the Rowlings' holdings. Her brothers later became well known as the developers of the Vivian Diesel Engine. George Kerr (Kerr Road) and his partner A. Joyce (Joyce Road) had a market garden on No. 1 Road. The Doman family farmed on Doman Road and George Wales lived on Wales Road. In 1906 Jeremiah Crowley started a dairy at the Avalon Ranch on Wales Road. His son carried on the business and served as a member of the parks board for years. Today he is remembered by Everett Crowley Park, Killarney district's largest park. This park is the former site of a creek and waterfall leading into a deep ravine used for years as a city land fill site. The Crowley family still operates the Avalon Dairy out of the 1908 family home at 5805 Wales Road, now the oldest dairy in British Columbia.

In 1909 an interurban line was opened along the Fraser River from Marpole to New Westminster. Combined with the dredging of the mouth of the North Arm of the Fraser in 1915, this made Killarney's riverfront lands suitable for the establishment of large industries. Over time many of the industries that originated in False Creek relocated to the banks of the Fraser River. In Killarney the huge Dominion Mills alone employed almost 1,000 workers near the foot of Boundary Road by the 1920s. One of the few large homes ever built in this area in the old days was the 1911 home built at 3358 South East Marine Drive for the president of the Dominion Creosoting Company, William Harvey. This company produced creosoted wood to make bridges, docks, railway ties and the wooden blocks used to pave city streets.

As a way to provide employment during the Depression of the 1930s, relief workers were used to clear the land for the Fraserview Golf Course, Vancouver's first public golf course. Before it was opened in 1935, permits were given to cold and hungry local residents to cut firewood and to use the land for vegetable gardens. The swamps south of Killarney Park were a natural place to pick salmonberries, huckleberries, blueberries, blackberries and a few cranberries.

In the early decades the closest town centre to the sparsely populated Killarney district was Collingwood on its northern edge. For people in Collingwood the area was always just the outer region of Collingwood and only became known as Killarney in the 1950s. Near Killarney Street, Killarney High School opened in 1957 and the Killarney Community Centre in 1963. The southerly part became known as Champlain Heights after the old farms south of 54th Avenue gave way to houses, apartments and a shopping centre beginning in 1960. In the 1980s most of the remaining land to the southeast was developed with townhouses.

Jean Crowley, Avalon Dairy. vp

Sunset, Victoria and Fraserview
Bruce Macdonald

THE SUNSET, VICTORIA AND FRASERVIEW districts occupy the south-facing slope of Vancouver overlooking the North Arm of the Fraser River and Richmond's Lulu Island, part of the large delta formed by the river. The northern limit is 41st Avenue, from Ontario Street in the west to the Fraserview Golf Course in the east. The name Sunset was applied to the western section in 1967, following the naming of the Sunset Nurseries, Sunset Park and Sunset Community Centre at 52nd Avenue.

According to Musqueam tradition, the village of Tsukhulehmulth once occupied a site on the Vancouver shore of the Stalo (Fraser River) just to the east of Mitchell Island. An ancient trail ran along the high ground just above the Fraser River floodplain from Musqueam village eastwards, past Tsukhulehmulth to Musqueam settlements at what later became Sapperton in New Westminster. After the establishment of the first local non-native settlement at Sapperton in 1859 during the gold rush, the old riverside trail was officially upgraded to the North Arm Trail in 1863. Vancouver's south central slope remained uninhabited by permanent settlers until the construction of the North Arm wagon road in 1875 made farming more viable. This road, following the route of present-day Fraser Street, connected the rich farmland along the Fraser River to their markets in the sawmills and logging camps on Burrard Inlet. The following year customers in New Westminster became more accessible when the old riverside trail was upgraded to a road (later called River Road, then South East Marine Drive).

The first substantial settlers were Charles Cridland, his wife and stepson, Henry Eburne, in 1875. They bought 65 hectares at the western foot of the new North Arm Road. Across the road to the east William Daniels did the same in 1876 and the following year John Daniels took up similar acreage to the west of the Cridlands. Farming and then logging were the main activities through to the 1880s. In 1891 a small group of pioneers established the Municipality of South Vancouver in the rural and vacant land that stretched six kilometres from Vancouver's city limits at 16th Avenue to the Fraser River. In 1898 the first South Vancouver municipal hall was built on Fraser Street at Wilson Road (now 41st Avenue).

In 1905 Fraser Street was extended to bridge the Fraser River into Richmond, and in 1909 the streetcar line was brought down the hill to meet the new east-west interurban line along

The fertile land along the Fraser developed with ... Chinese vegetable gardens ...

the Fraser River to New Westminster. This helped to stimulate frenzied residential home construction in the relatively undeveloped uplands between 1909 and 1913. The commercial village of South Hill sprang up along Fraser Street centred between 41st and 49th avenues and at 64th Avenue and Main Street the much smaller settlement of Grimmett appeared.

The fertile land along the Fraser River had been quickly developed with farms and "Chinese vegetable gardens" that supplied most Vancouver families with fresh vegetables delivered door to door by horse-drawn wagon. Later these developed into "truck gardens" operated by Chinese and Sikh settlers. Many residents grew their own vegetables and fruit trees and kept farm animals. A honey competition and goat show were the highlights of the 5th annual South Vancouver Horticultural Association and Farmers' Institute Exhibition and Fair in 1920.

Gradually industries such as sawmills began to replace the farmland between the rail line and the Fraser River and by the 1950s all of the flat farmland had been taken over by large industrial operations. Returning war veterans created a shortage of housing in Vancouver and the federal government responded by building 1,100 homes in one large subdivision in the early 1950s. They called it Fraserview after the golf course that had been built to the east of it in 1935, and its curved streets were named after famous golf courses from around the world.

After decades of being cut off by industrial development from its beautiful riverfront shoreline, Vancouver's first large scale residential development of land along the Fraser River began in the 1980s. In the new Riverside neighborhood east of the foot of Victoria Drive, apartments and townhouses now command sweeping views over the Fraser River. Meanwhile on Main Street near 49th Avenue, the interesting ethnic shopping district was officially named the Punjabi Market. It features East Indian fabric and jewellery stores, bakeries and restaurants.

Knight Street became a more distinct dividing point between the western Sunset and eastern Victoria and Fraserview districts after the building of the Knight Street Bridge in 1974. This new thoroughfare over the Fraser River to Richmond opened up both areas to increased commerce and development.

Cedar Cottage and Kensington
Bruce Macdonald

Trout Lake, 1993. vp

Cedar cottage is the district centred on Victoria Drive north of Kingsway, and Kensington is the district centred on Knight Street south of Kingsway. Cedar Cottage has always been proud to be the only neighborhood in Vancouver to have a lake. The words "East Vancouver" are not often associated with the word "beach," let alone a place to tan and swim in the summer or sometimes skate in the winter. Trout Lake's brief shoreline is a delight for the stroller and the home of unusual sights for Vancouver: a living peat bog, stunted pine trees, migrating ducks and a variety of other interesting birds.

Until the 1860s Trout Lake was a natural home to families of beaver and huge flocks of waterfowl. In 1863 John Hall hiked down the old Indian trail from New Westminster to stake out the lake and its surrounding acreage for himself. In 1867 he sold it to Walter Blackie and for a time it was referred to as "Blackie's Lake." The first industry built in Vancouver, the Hastings Sawmill, arranged for the water rights to the lake and built a flume from the lake to its sawmill to sustain its steam-driven machinery. In 1878 the owners of the mill bought the land, but in 1884 innocently sold it to Israel Powell, a government insider who knew about the coming of the transcontinental railway. Later it became the property of Aldene Hamber, the daughter of Hastings Sawmill owner John Hendry, and her husband Eric Hamber, a future lieutenant-governor of British Columbia. In 1926 they donated the lake and surrounding land to the city on the condition it be named after John Hendry.

The district's first substantial building was the Gladstone Inn, a stagecoach stop built for Gastown pioneer Joe Mannion in 1871 at the corner of what is now Gladstone Street and Kingsway. This stop on the dirt road from Gastown to New Westminster was operated by Thomas Deighton, the brother of Gastown's earliest pioneer, John "Gassy Jack" Deighton. In the 1870s Mannion acquired 65 hectares centred on Kingsway as did another Gastown pioneer immediately to the west, postmaster Jonathan Miller (Miller Street bears his name). When local loggers and Fraser River farmers assembled to form a municipality in 1891, they met at the Gladstone Inn and picked the name "South Vancouver." In 1886 Jonathan Miller sold 14 hectares of his land to Arthur Wilson, the present southeast corner of Knight and Kingsway. Here Wilson built a cottage amid a grove of cedar trees and started the Cedar Cottage Nursery.

Cedar Cottage as a district began in 1891 as a remote stop on the new interurban line to New Westminster and took its name from the Cedar Cottage Nursery. The original owners of the site where the village began to grow were L.A. Agassiz, of Agassiz, B.C., and William Brewer, after whom nearby Brewer's Park is named. In 1892 Brewer was elected the first reeve of South Vancouver. Cedar Cottage was located outside what was then Vancouver's southern border at 16th Avenue.

By 1910 Cedar Cottage was a small rural town five kilometres from Vancouver. Most residents had apple or cherry trees in their yards and many kept a few cows, goats or chickens. The town centre boasted Marfew Hall, "the largest hall in South Vancouver," a new movie theatre showing silent films, a Bank of Hamilton and a small roller coaster. Cedar Cottage's existence as an independent rural village was not unlike the story of its roller coaster—new and exciting but rather short-lived.

The coaster disappeared before the depression of 1913, and the population dropped as men went off to fight in the Great War, leaving the main street half deserted. By the 1920s automobiles began to erode the monopoly on pedestrian traffic resulting from the tram stop, favoring the evolution of Kingsway as the main shopping area. Small industries began to replace the stores on Cedar Cottage's main street as the urban sprawl of Vancouver overran the area and dissolved its formerly distinct boundaries. In 1929 Cedar Cottage literally became part of Vancouver when South Vancouver was absorbed by its larger neighbor.

The pre-war boom also saw house construction spill over Kingsway southwards to the hillside above 33rd Avenue. Here grew Kensington Heights, commanding a broad view northward to the city skyline, the harbor and the North Shore mountains. The surrounding district of Kensington didn't fill up until after the World War II.

In Cedar Cottage and Kensington one important constant has been Trout Lake. Area residents continue to picnic there, swim and enjoy walking around it.

Grandview
Bruce Macdonald

THE EARLIEST known mention of the Grandview area appears in Pauline Johnson's *Legends of Vancouver*. Johnson relays a story from Chief Joe Capilano about the first Chief Capilano, who in about 1820 wounded a giant seal in False Creek with a special elk-bone spear and pursued it into the area. In the late 1850s during the gold rush Chief Joe Capilano himself shot 13 elk in the future Grandview—perhaps the last herd of elk in Vancouver—and canoed the meat to market in Victoria.

Native people identified the region near the north foot of today's Victoria Drive by its enormous cedar trees, calling it Khupkhahpay'ay, the Squamish word for cedar tree. Cedar trees were an extremely important element in the lives of native people, providing materials for the making of homes, canoes, tools, mats, cordage, baskets and clothing. Here a small creek emptied into a bay of Burrard Inlet that later became known as Cedar Cove. In the 1890s the first industry established on the bay was the Cedar Cove Brewery, followed by the Cedar Cove Saw and Planing Mills.

A few years after the gold rush, all the land along Grandview's uninhabited coastline became the property of three land speculators: Victoria's Henry Crease, the first attorney general of the colony of British Columbia and later a supreme court justice; Henry Holbrook, the mayor of New Westminster; and John Graham, B.C.'s secretary of the treasury. Holbrook sold out to Israel Powell (Powell Street is named after him), and Powell, Crease and Graham all made fortunes after the Canadian Pacific Railway was built through their property in the 1880s. In 1871 the remainder of Grandview was acquired by the Hastings Sawmill company, which immediately cut down all the valuable fir and hemlock trees, and built a flume through Grandview to carry water from Trout Lake to its sawmill near Gastown.

One of the prominent early developers was E.J. Clark (hence Clark Drive) who donated a city block in 1899 for Clark's Park, the second park in Vancouver after Stanley Park. Grandview remained completely unsettled until the construction of the interurban line to New Westminster in 1891 made its hectares of stumps accessible to Vancouver workers. One of the earliest residents, proud of the prospect of the city from his yard, nailed up a sign "Grand View" at the interurban stop (near today's intersection of Commercial Drive and 1st Avenue) in about 1892. The first road built along the rail line was named Park Drive (renamed Commercial Drive in 1911) because it headed-straight to Clark's Park at 14th Avenue. Few homes had been

A few years after the gold rush, all the land along Grandview's coastline became the property of three land speculators

built before 1906, when local landowner and promoter Professor Edward Odlum (Odlum Drive bears his name) built a large house with an octagonal corner tower at 1774 Grant Avenue at the beginning of a tremendous growth spurt. By 1912 the centre of Grandview was completely covered in new homes within walking distance of the shops on Commercial Drive, forming a distinct village kilometres from the rest of Vancouver. This separateness was a factor in the area's ongoing sense of uniqueness. Residents were predominantly of British ancestry, as indicated in such local names as Britannia High School, Queen Victoria Elementary and Victoria Drive.

On the waterfront new industrial plants and port facilities soon jammed Grandview's shoreline. A few years later Grandview lost all of its western shoreline on False Creek when the earth removed for the Grandview railway cut was used to fill in False Creek all the way from Clark Drive to Main Street. Over the following decades the commercial strip along Hastings Street gradually grew eastwards from downtown and westwards from beyond Nanaimo Street to converge on Commercial Drive, while industrial buildings spread from the waterfront south to Hastings and along Clark Drive from the False Creek railyards. Since the war almost all the houses west of Commercial Drive and north of Hastings have been torn down and replaced with apartment buildings.

Grandview's uniqueness lies in the tremendous diversity of its people, housing and land use. The community is focused on the Drive (Commercial Drive), a fascinating collection of ethnic restaurants and food stores, funky coffee bars and hangouts, unusual clothing stores and street activity. Just off the Drive are small parks, the Vancouver East Cultural Centre, and the fully equipped Britannia Community Centre. The Britannia Centre boasts an ice rink, large swimming pool, sauna, weight room, gymnasiums, library, meeting rooms and a daycare facility.

To the west are new apartment buildings, to the east houses from the pre-World War I building boom, to the north manufacturers and wholesalers, and to the south, Trout Lake, the Skytrain and Broadway corridor. Nearby on the edge of Grandview are the Italian Cultural Centre, the Croatian Cultural Centre and Chinatown—all contributing to a robust mix unique in Vancouver.

Fairview
Bruce Macdonald

Granville Island, 1936. vp

I N THE 1860s the First Nations people living in the village of Sun'ahk near today's Granville Island were the only residents of Fairview. Their fishing weir at the mouth of the tidal bay formed by the sandbar (that would eventually be transformed into Granville Island) screened the outflowing waters and trapped a daily supply of fresh fish.

In the 1870s, after logging camps were established and skid roads were laid through the woods under the direction of Jerry Rogers, the heavy timber in the surrounding forest was cut down to feed the Hastings Sawmill. Teams of oxen dragged the exceptionally fine logs down the Fairview Slopes to tidewater at King's Landing and Mackie's Landing, now the False Creek foot of today's Granville and Cambie streets.

There was a lull in further development until the summer of 1887, when the Canadian Pacific Railway's Lauchlan Hamilton rowed his wooden canoe south across the cool clear waters of False Creek to pitch his tent on the forested south slope. While carving road survey lines through the bush and looking back across the water at the brand new city of Vancouver rising against the backdrop of the imposing North Shore mountain range, he determined that the new subdivision should be called "Fairview." This wilderness was soon made accessible with the opening of the Granville Street Bridge in 1889. In 1891 the completion of the Cambie Street Bridge and the new Fairview Beltline streetcar service heralded the beginning of house construction on the slopes. Accommodation was needed for the people working in the new sawmills, shingle mills and other industries sprouting around False Creek. Today the only restored buildings from this era are Sir John and Lady Reid's Fairview House, circa 1889, at 1151 West 8th Avenue and the 1894 Hodson Manor, now relocated to 1254 West 7th Avenue.

As downtown Vancouver filled up, Fairview became the chosen site for the new Vancouver High School, the new Vancouver General Hospital and the Model School, all finished in 1905. The False Creek shoreline became jammed with smokestack industries while the building boom that peaked in 1912 resulted in construction of homes on most of the remaining lots in Fairview. In 1913 the Vancouver Beavers, the city's immensely popular pro baseball team, moved to the new Athletic Park near the foot of Granville, and in 1915 the new University of British Columbia opened its doors next to the general hospital. The Great War brought many wartime industries to the area, and by 1918 shipbuilding on False Creek was Vancouver's largest industry.

After the war, apartment buildings began replacing the homes between Granville and Oak streets. This trend, as well as the retention of industry and the development of Granville Street, Cambie Street and Broadway as the main commercial strips, continued into the 1960s, at which point many industries began to relocate to the suburbs. For decades Vancouverites heated their homes with the enormous amounts of sawdust generated by the sawmills along False Creek. For decades they also endured the side effects of the sawmill's beehive burners—having to navigate through heavy fogs and frequently clean off soot sticking to curtains and walls.

Radical change came in the 1970s, when almost all of Fairview's waterfront area was transformed with modern redevelopment into an open area market and cultural centre on Granville Island, and lowrise apartments along the shore, featuring Fairview's largest park. In the 1980s virtually all the original homes on the Fairview Slopes and the rest of Fairview were torn down and replaced with apartments.

Today Fairview is crowned by highrise buildings spread along the Broadway corridor as it runs east-west through its centre. Just south of the centre of Broadway the Vancouver General Hospital complex provides one of the largest medical establishments in North America. In west Fairview the upscale shops of Granville Street are the focus, while the eastern rim features the City Square Shopping Centre across from City Hall. Fairview's False Creek oceanfront is rimmed by the popular seawall, a favorite route for pedestrians to amble their way to one of the city's favorite destinations, Granville Island. Here the Granville Island Market and the mix of fine restaurants, arts facilities, house boats, marinas, shops and old industries attract many tourists as well.

From various points along False Creek pedestrians can take the Aquabus water-taxi to quickly gain access to the West End's Aquatic Centre, English Bay, Yaletown, Science World, B.C. Place Stadium, G.M. Place, or be within walking distance of the library, the Queen Elizabeth Theatre, the Ford Centre for the Performing Arts, Gastown and Chinatown.

Mount Pleasant
Bruce Macdonald

FOR UNTOLD CENTURIES the site of Mount Pleasant was a dense forest diagonally bisected by an ancient trail travelled by First Nations peoples and wildlife such as deer, bear and elk. On its southern edge was an opening in the forest where a beaver dam had backed up a creek forming a large swamp.

In 1860 Colonel Moody's Royal Engineers improved the trail for better access to the new naval reserves set aside on English Bay. The purpose was to provide advance notice of any naval attack by Americans on the new capital of the Colony of British Columbia at New Westminster, and to provide access to ice-free Burrard Inlet if the Fraser ever froze over. An open swampy area was a landmark on the trip through the dark forest and soon was named the "Tea Swamp" after its Labrador tea, a small plant used by pioneers to brew tea.

In 1869 the visionary H.V. Edmonds, clerk of the municipal council in New Westminster, acquired all of the land north of today's Broadway in the future Mount Pleasant, believing that the natural harbor would someday be home to the terminus of a transcontinental railway. During the 1870s a rickety bridge was built across False Creek and the Hastings Sawmill acquired the remaining land in the area and chopped down the heavy timber for use in its mill. In the early 1880s the only substantial building was the Junction Inn (at the intersection of today's Kingsway and Fraser), one of a series of stagecoach roadhouses on the old trail to New Westminster that was upgraded and renamed the Westminster Road in 1884.

In 1887, as Edmonds had foreseen, the railway created spectacular growth in the newly named boomtown of Vancouver. A year later a new bridge was built south across False Creek and he decided to develop his land holdings on the Westminster Road (today's Kingsway), naming the new subdivision after his wife's birthplace in Ireland, Mount Pleasant. At the crest of a hill above False Creek a hub was formed where a supply of fresh water—Brewery Creek—intersected with the first east-west through road, 7th Avenue, Westminster Road and the only road south from Vancouver, today's Main Street.

Mount Pleasant developed into Vancouver's first suburb while the rest of Vancouver outside the downtown core remained a logged over forest crisscrossed by skid roads. By the end of the 1800s Brewery Creek had been home to the Reifel brother's San Francisco Brewery, Charles Doering's Vancouver Breweries, "the largest on the Pacific Coast," and Thorpe & Company Soda Water Works—producers of Ginger Beer, Kola

Champagne, Iron Brew and Sarsaparilla. On either side of the mouth of Brewery Creek were two slaughterhouses and on the creek bank at 12th Avenue was the Vancouver Tannery, where leather was made from the animal skins. The hides were tanned with wagonloads of hemlock bark brought up from forests to the south along the only through street, the dirt road that evolved into Fraser Street. Today the notable survivors of this period are the unique brick and stone Vancouver Breweries building at 6th Avenue and Scotia Street, and the 1888 Thomas Clark House at 243 East 5th Avenue—the oldest house in Mount Pleasant.

In 1891 the arrival of streetcar service was a further spur to growth, and by the turn of the century Mount Pleasant was a well-formed small town with its own stores, fire hall, fruit tree nurseries, greenhouses, Methodist, Presbyterian and Baptist churches and hundreds of fine new homes. In the middle of its main intersection was a bandstand where the Mount Pleasant Band played on Sunday afternoons to appreciative townsfolk observing the Sabbath. Children on their way to the school at Kingsway and Broadway would sometimes see beavers at work building a dam or bears feeding on blackberries. The only settlement from the outer edge of town at 16th Avenue to the Fraser River, kilometres away, was one small group of houses at 20th Avenue where a couple of families by the name of Hicks lived. The sophisticated residents of Mount Pleasant got a kick out of referring to the area as "Hicksville."

By the beginning of World War I the population of Vancouver was five times larger than it had been just 15 years before and the formerly distinct village of Mount Pleasant became embedded in the urban sprawl being made possible by the mobility of the newly introduced automobile. But there was no denying the prosperity of the times. The tall landmark Lee Building at Broadway and Main soared skyward in 1912 followed in 1916 by the grand new post office at 15th and Main (now Heritage Hall, the home of community organizations and a meeting hall for local events). There were many successful new businesses such as Calladine's Grocery, recalled by local historian Claude Douglas. Douglas was born in Mount Pleasant and grew up at 117 West 10th Avenue. Today this house is one of the Davis Houses, Mount Pleasant's best-known group of restored homes. Douglas recalls Calladine's Grocery with memories of "sawdust covered floors, great sacks of meal, potatoes, sugar and beans. The crunching sound of the old fire-engine-red coffee grinder and its permeating aroma. The great rounds of cheeses, so mellow. All shepherded by clerks in chaste white aprons." This was in the days before customers served themselves in grocery stores, when the Safeway chain in

Westminister Avenue (Main Street) looking north from 6th Avenue,
circa 1891. vpl

Vancouver went by the name Piggly Wiggly.

Progress also brought the loss of half of Mount Pleasant's oceanfront land and the elimination of the mouth of Brewery Creek during World War I, when the tidal flats of False Creek were filled in from Main Street eastwards a dozen blocks to Clark Drive. The new area of flat land provided a site for two large, new railway terminals and their railyards right at the tail end of the great era of railway building.

Mount Pleasant was the birthplace of one of the city's most colorful mayors, Gerry McGeer, who made sure the new city hall constructed during his term in 1936 was built in Mount Pleasant at 12th and Cambie. McGeer, also an MLA, MP and a senator, grew up on the edge of the old Tea Swamp, where he had tended his father's cows as a barefooted youth. Another nationally known figure was Percy Williams, the sprinter who put Vancouver on the world's sports map for the first time by winning the gold medals in the 100-metre and 200-metre races at the 1928 Olympics. He lived for many years at the southeast corner of 12th Avenue and Columbia Street.

Mount Pleasant retained its mix of industry near False Creek and its commercial zone on Main Street surrounded by houses and churches until the 1950s. In the 1960s many low-rise apartment buildings were built around the old village core and False Creek industry overran the residential part of the northwest sector. This speeded the shift of Mount Pleasant from a community of long-term homeowners in single family houses well aware of their past, to a district of predominantly short-term tenants in suites and apartments with very little sense of what had gone before. Now a few oldtimers with fond memories of the earlier decades remain amidst a growing number of younger people interested in Mount Pleasant's heritage, and

the restoration and retention of its older structures—some of the oldest in the city.

The 1990s have brought Mount Pleasant the groundswell of rebuilding that has already swept around the rest of False Creek, leaving completely transformed neighborhoods in its wake. First was Kitsilano, then Granville Island, Fairview, Yaletown, the end of False Creek, False Creek north and the rim of Chinatown. In Mount Pleasant, the first of Vancouver's artist live/work studios began to appear in the early 1990s. The upgrading of homes to much higher standards is spreading slowly eastwards from the more prosperous western section.

Mount Pleasant is also a community experiencing a resurgence of community spirit. Residents have banded together to address local concerns, resulting in the creation of Vancouver's first neighborhood crime prevention office in 1994, a Mount Pleasant Area Network and a new Mount Pleasant Neighborhood House. The presence of numerous artists living in the community is apparent in a number of ways, from the founding and development of Vancouver's annual Fringe Festival and the funding of a community artist in residence, to the Western Front performance/media facility and the proliferation of artist live/work studios along the former route of Brewery Creek. The western section of Mount Pleasant south of Broadway has recently become revitalized with the restoration of many heritage homes, some from the 1890s, and with historic plaques along the new Mount Pleasant Walkway. The old business core has received heritage revitalization funds and the local business owner's Commercial Improvement Society has enhanced Main Street with many features to emphasize its heritage. The revitalized Lee Building is still the landmark that marks the centre of Old Mount Pleasant.

Oakridge
Michael Kluckner

B Y THE TIME of the Great Depression, Vancouver was solidly developed southwards as far as King Edward Avenue. East of the Canadian Pacific Railway's land boundary at Ontario Street, houses interspersed with vacant lots extended south towards the Fraser River; to the west, in the 1920s, lots in Kerrisdale and Shaughnessy had found ready buyers. The CPR, whose land holdings had become the city's desirable west side, was very careful to balance the supply of lots against the demand, and opened up new areas only when its earlier neighborhoods were well established.

Left vacant for future growth was the land between Oak and Ontario south of King Edward Avenue. Only golf courses—the 1912 Shaughnessy links at 37th and Oak and the 1926 Langara links southeast of 49th and Cambie—intruded their groomed presence into the marshy alder scrub which had replaced the logged-off forest. Down narrow Oak Street ran the No. 17 streetcar, a notably bumpy line established in 1912 to connect Marpole with the built-up city. Cambie Street was graded only as far south as Little Mountain.

Although it delayed opening the area between Oak and Ontario for housing, the CPR did sell tracts of land to a number of civic and private institutions. Western Residential Schools purchased property to the east of Shaughnessy Golf Course and erected two large boarding schools—Braemar and Langara—in the Tudor style of the architects Maclure and Fox. Langara, at 4949 Heather Street, survives today as an RCMP training facility. Shaughnessy Hospital opened on Oak Street in 1919; it was followed in the late 1920s by the Salvation Army's Grace Hospital, and in the late 1930s by St. Vincent's Hospital at 33rd and Heather. The area south of 41st Avenue remained bushland, and was sufficiently remote for the Vancouver Gun Club's rifle range, which operated there until the early 1950s.

As prosperity returned in the late 1930s, the CPR planned to open its property to development, but World War II intervened. Instead the land between Heather and Cambie south of 37th became an army training camp, dubbed "Little Aldershot," for the duration of the war years.

The name "Oakridge" was first applied to B.C. Electric's new trolley depot at 41st and Oak, which opened in 1949. The new trolleys replaced the poorly maintained streetcar system; one of the more symbolic casualties was the "teeth-rattler" No. 17 line, which had its last run in April 1952. Oak Street, so

> ...the land between Heather and Cambie south of 37th became "Little Aldershot," an army training camp, for the duration of the war years

dusty and bumpy that "no Saskatchewan road could be worse," was repaved as soon as the old tram tracks were ripped up.

The stage was set for the creation of a new Oakridge community. After the war the city's Jewish community moved from its former Strathcona enclave and began to settle along Oak Street. The Jewish Community Centre was erected at the corner of 41st and Oak, and the blocks to the east soon became Vancouver's Jewish neighborhood.

In postwar Vancouver a new style of suburbia became fashionable—wider streets, open landscaping, and low-lying, wood-sided bungalows and split-levels. In the heyday of this style the CPR made plans to subdivide the 112 hectares bounded by Oak, Cambie, 41st and 57th. Announced in 1955, the Oakridge community featured 24-metre-wide single family housing lots, many on curving streets, and a small apartment area, next to which was proposed a large shopping mall with Woodward's department store as the anchor tenant.

The Oakridge Shopping Centre opened in 1959 and instantly attracted customers from the surrounding neighborhoods; it contributed, at least in the short term, to the decline of the old shopping areas in Kerrisdale, south Main Street and especially Marpole. Within twenty years, however, the Oakridge mall had itself been left behind, as new malls opened throughout the region and shoppers ranged farther and farther afield. To regain its customers, Oakridge was extensively renovated in 1984. More apartments have been added to the surrounding blocks, making them popular with seniors.

Although it was one of the last areas of Vancouver to be developed, Oakridge has been substantially redeveloped already. The original houses in the area were quite luxurious in their day but too small for the expansive lifestyles of the late 1980s and 1990s. New, large homes in the area have found wealthy buyers, including many Chinese attracted to the local schools and convenient location. Oakridge today is a luxurious family area, an extension eastward of Kerrisdale and Shaughnessy rather than one westward from the Main Street and South Vancouver neighborhoods.

Riley Park/South Cambie
Bruce Macdonald

A 1945 plan for a stadium at Little Mountain, twin city hall buildings and a boulevard on Cambie Street. VS

RILEY PARK/SOUTH CAMBIE AND MOUNT PLEASANT are the only districts in Vancouver situated half in the East End, half on the West Side. Ontario Street forms the boundary just west of Main Street that is the north-south zero point of the street hundred block system and the former boundary between the municipalities of Point Grey and South Vancouver. The section of the district on the West Side was part of the land granted to the Canadian Pacific Railway and formed part of the Municipality of Point Grey from 1908 to 1929. Most of this land remained vacant until the late 1940s. Appropriately the name South Cambie originates with Cambie Street, named after Henry Cambie, the engineer in charge of the western division of the CPR. East of Ontario Street, Riley Park district was part of the Municipality of South Vancouver from 1892 to 1929, named after the former municipal clerk of South Vancouver, Clark Riley.

The district of Riley Park/South Cambie is dominated by Little Mountain, physically the highest point of Vancouver, occupying its geographical centre and commanding a 360-degree view of the whole city.

In its earlier days as a vast forest the district's most distinguishing feature was the old "beaver meadow," now Douglas Park, which served as an elk pasture until the gold rush of 1858 brought about the extinction of elk in Greater Vancouver.

The first modern settler in the Riley Park/South Cambie area was William Mackie, a pioneer logger and old Cariboo gold miner. In 1874 Mackie marked off and claimed the 65 hectares centred on the former elk pasture. The next year Jeremiah Rogers built a skid road up to Little Mountain to access the fine timber that crowned the summit. He set up his logging camp at the pasture—lush forage for his oxen. The innovative Rogers rigged the skid road into a logging tramway using an old steam tractor engine in the first use of mechanized logging in the B.C. forest industry. After the timber had been removed, the rich soil of the former oxen pasture became the site of a small milk ranch. By the 1910s the cow pasture had become a Chinese vegetable farm while houses sprang up on the less fertile ground surrounding it. In 1926, surrounded by houses, the four city blocks were designated as Douglas Park.

The year 1874 also marked the cutting of the first modern trail through Riley Park/South Cambie. Funded by the provincial government, the False Creek Trail ran diagonally from what is now Marpole, past the foot of Little Mountain to Gas-town. This first north-south route in Vancouver was abandoned the next year when the trail was upgraded to a wagon road along a different route. It was repositioned to the present Fraser Street and called the "North Arm Waggon Road," since its purpose was to provide a land route to Gastown for the produce of the farms along the North Arm of the Fraser River. The junction where this road intersected the old Westminster Road (now Kingsway) became the site of the first local business establishment, a stagecoach roadhouse called the Junction Inn. After the newly created City of Vancouver acquired land for a cemetery on the North Arm Road at what is now 33rd Avenue, the future Fraser Street became known as Cemetery Road. Riley Park/South Cambie had more dead residents than live ones until Main Street was extended southwards from Mount Pleasant and the streetcar village of Hillcrest was built out in the forest of stumps near 30th Avenue in about 1910.

Many of the streets laid out at this time were surfaced with crushed slate from quarries on Little Mountain. In the 1920s one of these open pit mines was converted into the main water reservoir for Vancouver and the surrounding area was made into a park renamed Queen Elizabeth Park in 1940. Another of the open pits was transformed into a beautiful sunken garden, now a tourist attraction and a favorite summer-time site for wedding party photographs. In 1957 professional baseball came to nearby Capilano Stadium and in 1960 Percy Norman Pool opened in Riley Park next door to the stadium. In 1969 Little Mountain was crowned with the Bloedel Conservatory, a geodesic-domed indoor garden of exotic plants and birds from all over the world. Nearby Main Street runs down the centre of Riley Park/South Cambie and by 25th Avenue features the Antique Row shopping area.

Marpole
Michael Kluckner

THE GEOGRAPHY OF FARMLAND, the Fraser River and the markets of New Westminster and Vancouver made Marpole a strategic crossroads over a century ago. Even today, when aviation and housing have replaced farmland and the north arm of the river is less important for commerce than it once was, the region's traffic still passes through and plays a large role in determining Marpole's future.

During previous millennia, the Marpole area was home to natives who, for much the same reasons as the Europeans, established communities along the shore. The grassy banks of the river offered sites for villages, notably at Mahli near the mouth of the river, where in 1808 the threat of a conflict turned Simon Fraser back towards the British Columbia Interior, and at the site known as the Great Fraser Midden, between Granville and Hudson south of 75th Avenue. The latter commanded the fork in the river where the Middle Arm splits from the North Arm around Sea Island. History records a trail running eastward along the river from Mahli, following the approximate route of today's Marine Drive.

The first European settlers, the McRoberts and McCleery families, saw potential farms on the grassy delta lands of Sea Island and the adjoining bank of the river, now the Southlands flats, and occupied the area in the years following the Cariboo Gold Rush of 1862. Fitzgerald and Samuel McCleery got their first good look at the area in the spring of 1863, when they were hired by the colonial government and spent three months clearing River Road, now Marine Drive, from the government seat at New Westminster to Mahli.

The Southlands, Sea Island and Richmond farmers of the early years had no need for a north-south route to Burrard Inlet, as no market existed for produce there until the early 1880s. Instead they used the river to reach customers at New Westminster. Although George Garypie and James Mackie had preempted Marpole's riverfrontage in the 1860s, it wasn't until the arrival of Harry Eburne in the early 1870s that settlement began and a community started to take shape. Eburne opened a store near the foot of Hudson Street, next to a Methodist church, built in 1871, which served the nearby farming community. Soon after, the store became the local post office for the "Eburne" community.

The future Marpole nonetheless remained isolated until 1885, when Canadian Pacific Railway crews cut a new North Arm Road, now Granville Street, southwards through the for-est to the Fraser River. Four years later, a San Francisco company erected a bridge from the eastern end of Sea Island, near the Arthur Laing bridge's southern footings, to the north bank of the river at Eburne's store. Slowly the area began to grow. Once a second bridge joined Sea Island to Richmond, the store relocated to the former, which became the local hub of activity and assumed the name Eburne. A cannery opened there, a hotel attracted travellers, and the Vancouver side of the river lapsed into comparative unimportance, being known in the early years of the 20th century only as Eburne Station.

The "station" part of the name came from the completion, in the summer of 1902, of the Vancouver & Lulu Island Railway, usually called the "Sockeye Limited," running along today's Arbutus Corridor between False Creek and the Fraser River to the foot of Oak Street, where a trestle bridge crossed to Richmond; the rails then proceeded through the countryside to Steveston's salmon canneries. As the railway by-passed Eburne, most Sea Island residents travelled to Eburne Station and walked across the North Arm bridge to their homes.

Business people were quick to realize the industrial potential of the Marpole riverfrontage and, in the early years of the 20th century, established sawmills and shingle mills along the waterfront. B.C. Electric Railway opened the area to further development in 1909 by extending an interurban line along the north side of the river from Eburne Station to New Westminster.

This nearby employment prompted house building on the narrow streets south of the CPR land boundary at Park Drive—a street grid which only partially matches that of the surrounding city. To connect these new settlers with Vancouver by a route other than the Steveston-Vancouver interurban, B.C. Electric laid a streetcar line between Marine Drive and Fairview along Oak Street. Eburne Station soon had a thriving shopping area along Bridge Street (now Hudson) at Marine.

In the palmy, prosperous days before World War I, an optimistic investor built the Grand Central Hotel at the northeast corner of Hudson and Marine. Out in the bushland to the north, attracted by its sunny southern exposure, a few wealthy individuals established country estates on large properties, including Charles Gardner Johnson at "Oakherst" at 57th and Oak, Dr. Duncan Bell-Irving at 1312 West 57th Avenue, William McKenzie at 1196 West 59th Avenue, and B.T. Rogers at "Shannon" at 57th and Granville.

With the Sea Island side of the river known as Eburne, "Eburne Station" lacked a distinct identity. In 1916 the community was renamed Marpole, after the former western superintendent of the CPR who was then retired and living on Marpole Avenue in Shaughnessy Heights.

As in much of the rest of Vancouver, Marpole's great expectations foundered on the reefs of economic depression, first in 1913 and then in the Great Depression of the 1930s. The Grand Central Hotel found a new use from 1917 until 1965 as the Provincial Home for Incurables, mainly tuberculosis patients; its shingle-covered staff house on Hudson survives today as a community corrections facility. A number of the large estate houses were converted to rooming houses or institutions, most notably the 1912 home of J.M. McCallan at the northeast corner of 67th and Hudson, which in 1927 became Vancouver's first Children's Hospital. Industrial employment at the mills and factories along the river remained strong, however, especially during the 1920s, and Marpole's small lots filled up with modest bungalows. One rural holdout was the Shannon dairy, founded in 1912 on cleared land south of the "Shannon" estate, which continued in operation until the early 1950s.

In the 1920s car-owning Vancouverites discovered the scenic loop through Point Grey along newly paved Marine Drive and Granville Street. Their appetites were slaked by a young entrepreneur named Nat Bailey, who sold snack food to motorists off the back of a truck at Lookout Point on Marine Drive; in the summer of 1928 he established a permanent restaurant in a small log hut at 67th and Granville, calling it the White Spot Barbecue. Over the years, it grew into a large dining room, but many patrons preferred to eat their "Triple-O" burgers in their cars. In the 1950s and 1960s this White Spot was the hottest drive-in in the city—the centre of the car culture—for everyone below legal drinking age. Those of drinking age patronized another Marpole institution—the Fraser Arms Hotel at the foot of Granville. The White Spot lost its flagship when the original restaurant burned down in the mid-1980s.

The car ownership which supported the White Spot eventually doomed the old, tightly knit Marpole community. Housing expanded into Richmond, and the need for new roads for the new commuters rendered the old Marpole-Eburne swingspan obsolete. When the Oak Street bridge opened in June 1957, traffic suddenly moved several blocks to the east, and the business district along Hudson and Marine went into a swift decline. The city rezoned the old part of Marpole south of 70th for apartments, and in the 1960s lowrise, stucco-covered walk-ups replaced the old houses. Businesses migrated to Granville Street. A final blow, visually at least, was the ramps for the new Arthur Laing bridge, built in 1975 once again to connect Marpole with Eburne; this time, however, it led to the Vancouver International Airport, rather than to a farming community.

Throughout all the change and disruption, Marpole's community spirit has stayed strong, epitomized by the refit of Firehall No. 22 at 70th and Hudson for seniors' and neighborhood programs. Two other pieces of Marpole's heritage have recently garnered public support: in 1990 the city purchased the old Children's Hospital and began its restoration as a residence for seniors; five years later the city granted a 60-year lease to the Marpole Museum and Historical Society for the Colbourne House, a tiny, gambrel-roofed farmhouse at 8743 South West Marine Drive. In population, Marpole today is very close to the city average in the age and income of its residents but has more renters than the average.

The next Marpole battle will likely involve the businesses on Granville Street, as they struggle to maintain their on-street parking in the face of the trend towards transit-only lanes along regional transportation corridors. In Marpole, which is still a strategic crossroads for the Lower Mainland, some things haven't changed.

Nat Bailey, who founded White Spot Restuarants at 67th and Granville in 1928. vp

South West Marine Drive
Michael Kluckner

SOUTH WEST MARINE DRIVE is one of Vancouver's neighborhoods of golf courses, mansions and wonderful views—a "Millionaires' Row." The oldest estates overlooking the river date to the 1910s, when the area was quite rural, while the blocks of housing east of Marine and south of Maple Grove Park in most cases date from after World War II. Many of the small ranchers there have been replaced by larger homes.

Marine Drive was originally the crooked North Arm Trail. In the spring of 1863 the colonial government hired the McCleery brothers to improve and extend it from the population centre at New Westminster to the Mahli and Musqueam villages. They completed the three-month job in June, after which Fitzgerald and Samuel McCleery settled on the Southlands flats. Samuel McCleery's 1891 farmhouse at 2610 South West Marine survived until 1977.

Renamed River Road, the old North Arm Trail became Marine Drive at the dawn of the automobile age, in 1911, when Point Grey municipal council straightened and black-topped it. Touted as "the greatest panoramic driveway on the coast," Marine Drive was envisaged as part of a scenic loop of Point Grey, with Granville Street, paved from 25th Avenue to Marpole in 1910, forming the north-south leg. One of the early settlers of Marine Drive, at 2250, was a man named W.O. Webster, the Vancouver distributor for Gray-Dort motorcars— the remoteness of the area demanded car ownership, which required money, which ensured exclusivity.

Maple Grove Park at Yew and Marine was dedicated initially as Bowser Park just before World War I, when houses began to appear in the blocks south of 49th Avenue. Point Grey council decided not to remove the enormous stumps left in the park from old logging operations, so that children could imagine the size of Vancouver's original forest.

The first Marine Drive residents purchased acreages and on them built substantial, self-contained estates, often with their own wells and electric dynamos. The earliest was "Southlands," built in 1910 for the wholesale grocer W.H. Malkin on property bounded by Balaclava, Blenheim, Marine and the Von Alvensleben property at 43rd Avenue (now Crofton House). The most remote estate was near the tip of Point Grey, built in 1912 by the lawyer E.P. Davis and now known as Cecil Green Park.

The first houses on the "Millionaire's Row" stretch of Marine between Marpole and Maple Grove Park were erected just west of Yew Street in about 1912-14 for the president and vice president of the Vancouver Lumber Company, John Tucker and his son-in-law Edward Knight. The Tuckers erected the stone-foundationed Arts & Crafts-style house at 2280 South West Marine, partially visible down a long, rhododendron-lined driveway. The Knights' house, at 2326, is a hipped-roof Tudor with very tall chimneys. Both houses are best viewed from the flats below, along Macdonald Street or from the McCleery golf course. Another pre-World War I house is 2194 South West Marine, a Maclure & Fox design for Herbert Barton.

The next set of houses date to the early 1920s. Their occupants were a "who's who" of Vancouver, including George Kidd, the general manager of B.C. Electric Railway, at 2136 (demolished), the Hastings Street clothier William Dick at 2000 (demolished), and Gordon Farrell, the long-time president of B.C. Telephone, in the twin-gabled house at 1890. Blythe Rogers, the eldest son of B.C. Sugar founder B.T. Rogers, built the stylish Tudor originally called "Knole" at the northwest corner of 57th and Marine in 1919, shortly before his death at the age of twenty-six. Down below Marine at 57th Avenue, the Marine Drive Golf Club laid out links on Samuel McCleery's old farm, and farther west at Blenheim Street, the Point Grey Golf Club took over the former Mole farm.

The two houses which established Marine Drive's reputation for a rather garish ostentation were financed by brewery and liquor money in the early 1930s. Harry Reifel's "Rio Vista," a Spanish Colonial Revival house at 2170 South West Marine, with a tessellated "Pompeiian" indoor pool and spectacular gardens, was the first; the larger "Casa Mia" at 1920 was erected for Harry's brother George, the namesake of the waterfowl sanctuary on Westham Island. Another son of B.T. Rogers, Philip, built the French Provincial-style mansion at 2010 during what was known elsewhere as the Great Depression.

Subdivisions of the original properties along the Marine Drive bluff have reduced the estate-like quality of the area. On the flats below, reached by following Angus Drive down the hill to the riverbank, new houses occupy land that, until the 1980s, was home to blackberry thickets and some gardeners' cottages and greenhouses for the big homes above. The impression today, looking from the river's edge back towards Marine Drive, is of a row of very large houses set cheek-by-jowl along the ridge—impressive, but a far cry from the old days.

Kerrisdale
Kayce White

Growing up in Kerrisdale had a magical, storybook quality

A COMFORTABLE, HISTORIC WESTSIDE neighborhood stretching from Blenheim to Granville Street and Angus Drive, and from 41st Avenue to the North Arm of the Fraser River, Kerrisdale is among the most stable communities in Canada. At most social events, chances are you'll meet several residents who were born, educated and married in Kerrisdale and who until a few years ago might reasonably have planned to retire there. Families scattered when soaring real estate prices spurred the sale and demolition of older houses once passed from generation to generation. Gone were the days when parents knew the name of every child on the street, and children might expect to be students in the same schools their grandparents had attended. Growing up in Kerrisdale had a magical, storybook quality about it, said a district businessman. "I've lived here all my life and my wife and I were childhood sweethearts. All our friends seemed to expect we'd get married when we finished school and that's exactly what we did."

While talk of redevelopment is standard at social gatherings, the continuous change seems to have had little impact on Kerrisdale's affluence or stability. Statistics Canada ranks the neighborhood as one of the most affluent in North America. In 1986, average household income was $59,474, almost twice as high as the $32,403 average for Vancouver city. Of the slightly more than 5,000 dwelling units, more than 60 per cent are owner occupied. Among the 12,000-plus community inhabitants, there are fewer low-income households (10 per cent compared to 26 per cent city wide) and single parent families (10.5 per cent compared to 15.6 per cent).

However, Kerrisdale has changed considerably through extensive redevelopment. In 1988-89, amid considerable controversy, approximately 500 permanent residents were dispersed when a number of low-rise rental apartments were demolished to make way for intended condominium developments. Today, some of the sites still remain vacant.

Kerrisdale can be seen as a village with almost every service, supply outlet and recreational facility a community needs: a broad range of restaurants and shops; equipment rental; recreational and cultural facilities; elementary, secondary and private schools; daycare centres; health and fitness centres. There is a major public library; a seniors' centre; two swimming pools; two major golf courses; a skating rink, an arena and a bowling club. Various service organizations and services promote social welfare and business opportunities. A society devoted to historical research and preservation of historic buildings has attracted more than 150 members.

There are more than 20 financial institutions on West 41st Avenue, the main business strip which, in some residents' view, is a tad more banks than the community actually needs. On the same street is a unique green grocer, J.B. Hoy Produce, a family-operated store where operators wear white smocks to set out the veggies. The Koo family first set up the shop in 1925, and eventually assured themselves a permanent spot by buying the building. On the same street, among cafes ranging from fast to fancy, is a burger-and-milkshake joint, The Red Onion, that belongs in an old-fashioned village.

Kerrisdale began taking shape more than 130 years ago, five years before Confederation and more than nine years before British Columbia became a Canadian province. In the 1860s the Magees, Moles, Shannons and McCleerys were neighbors whose names are interwoven with Kerrisdale's history. Hugh Magee, known as "the pig-headed Irishman," started a farm just below Marine Drive at Balaclava. Henry Mole, known for his forthright nature, homesteaded on land where the Point Grey Golf Club now is located; William Shannon, a former Cariboo freight hauler, farmed on land adjacent to West 57th Avenue, close to the present Shannon Park. Irish immigrant brothers Sam and Fitzgerald McCleery made their way here via the Fraser after failing to hit pay dirt in Cariboo gold fields. On September 26, 1862 Sam and Fitz preempted a meadow and built a homesteader cabin at 49th and Marine Crescent, now McCleery Park, where their descendants farmed until 1956. In 1985 the Kerrisdale Historical Society erected a memorial cairn at the site.

Kerrisdale originally was the name of a tram station at Wilson Road (now 41st Avenue) and West Boulevard; the community was part of Point Grey municipality which merged with Vancouver in 1929. In 1905 B.C. Electric Railway manager R.H. Sterling asked area resident Mrs. William MacKinnon to name the tram station. She adapted the name Kerrisdale from her old family home, Kerrydale, in Gairloch, Scotland.

Tracks were laid to connect Kerrisdale to Dunbar and, by 1912, to downtown Vancouver. By the 1920s Kerrisdale had become an integral part of Vancouver city. At the same time, because of the central focus of shops, transportation and community facilities, it retained its sense as a separate—and charming—village.

Shaughnessy
Ed Starkins

MANY AREAS OF VANCOUVER have had a close historical connection with the Canadian Pacific Railway but nowhere has the CPR influence been more strongly felt than in Shaughnessy Heights. The neighborhood was named in honor of CPR president Sir Thomas Shaughnessy. Its principal streets bear the names of his daughter, Marguerite, and several early members of the company board of directors: Angus, Marpole, Hosmer, Osler and Nanton.

Shaughnessy Heights was once part of District Lot 526, a 2,428 hectare land grant assigned to CPR officials Donald Smith and Richard Angus in 1885 but later transferred to the direct control of the railway. For many years the CPR did little with this vast domain which was too far from the Vancouver townsite to have much value as real estate. The company set aside a small area of land to grow vegetables and flowers for its hotels and transcontinental trains and, in 1888, helped to finance the construction of the North Arm Road, later Granville Street, south to the Fraser River. In the early 1900s the CPR began to sell lots in the Fairview and Kitsilano districts at the English Bay end of District Lot 526. To the south, beyond 12th Avenue, was a wasteland covered by brush and tree stumps.

In 1907 Richard Marpole, general superintendent of the CPR, announced that the company planned to create an exclusive suburb for Vancouver's upper class citizens on the hilly slopes south of False Creek. The Montreal landscape architect Frederick Todd and his assistant, L.E. Davick, a Danish engineer, were placed in charge of the $2 million project which was to include such amenities as a lawn bowling club, golf course and tennis courts. The design of Shaughnessy Heights reflected Todd's enthusiasm for the "garden city" concept of urban landscaping. The homes of the rich were surrounded by hedgerows and broad lawns. Tree-lined boulevards followed the contours of the local terrain, ascending to the Crescent, a circular drive of expensive property situated on the highest ground in the neighborhood.

In the summer of 1909 an army of 1200 workers began to cut roads, build sidewalks and lay sewer lines in the 101 hectare CPR fiefdom. When the first lots went on sale a year later Vancouver's wealthier citizens were quick to abandon their former haunts in the West End. By 1914 there were 243 households in Shaughnessy Heights, 80 per cent of which were listed in the Vancouver social register.

The pre-World War I "golden age" of Shaughnessy Heights home construction included a variety of architectural styles: 18th century Georgian townhouses, Spanish colonial haciendas, federal style homes, Cape Cod cottages and oversized California bungalows. The favored society architects of the period were Samuel Maclure of Victoria and his Vancouver partner C.C. Fox, designers of such classic Tudor revival homes as Rosemary, constructed in 1913 at 3689 Selkirk for A.E. Tulk, a distillery owner. Tulk named his mansion after his only daughter but most early Shaughnessyites gave their homes whimsical names such as the British gentry might have preferred: Bonnie Blink, Welcome Holme, Greyshott, Glen Brae, Grey Gables, Greencroft.

By 1920 the society pages of Vancouver newspapers were an intimate chronicle of the lives of Shaughnessy residents as they moved through an endless whirl of balls, dances, yacht parties, charity meetings and afternoon teas. Social standing in "CPR Heaven" was often determined by the status of the guests invited to one's home, at Ardor, Maj. Gen. "Jack" Stewart, a railway contractor with political connections, was host to such notables as the Dukes of Windsor and Kent; Misak Aivazaoff, a Russian émigré, entertained the pianist Sergei Rachmaninoff and members of the dispossessed Russian nobility in Villa Russe at 3390 the Crescent.

In the early '20s the high point of the Shaughnessy social calendar was the New Year's Eve costume ball at Hycroft, residence of Gen. Alexander Duncan McRae, the multi-millionaire cannery owner. Built in the style of a palatial ante-bellum Southern mansion, Hycroft was famous for its downstairs ballroom where the floorboards were packed with dried seaweed to give dancers greater bounce. (Glen Brae has a similar floor.) On the grounds outside were three gardens, an enormous greenhouse, riding stables, tennis courts and a guest house. The interior of the mansion reflected General McRae's aristocratic tastes with a wine cellar, mirrored bar and a variety of dens, drawing rooms and solaria. The general's household servants went about their work in hidden passageways that ran parallel to the McRae family's well-appointed quarters.

Shaughnessy Heights was developed in three stages over a twenty-year period. Most of the lots in so-called First or Old Shaughnessy, extending from 16th Avenue to King Edward Ave., were sold by 1914. By then work crews were clearing the land south to 37th Avenue for Second Shaughnessy, which was completed in 1929. The expansion into Third Shaughnessy, between King Edward and 41st Avenue, did not begin until 1926.

In the early stages of Shaughnessy Heights' development the CPR took steps to assure that the provincial legislature, rather than the Municipality of Point Grey, controlled local zoning regulations—an arrangement made possible by the unusual number of political and financial leaders who resided in the neighborhood. In 1911 the British Columbia legislature passed the first local zoning law, followed in 1922 by the Shaughnessy Heights Building Restriction Act which prohibited the division of single family dwellings into apartments or housekeeping rooms. Most CPR deeds of sale contained their own single-family clauses as well as restrictive covenants forbidding the re-sale of property to Jews and Orientals.

During the Depression years the homes of many Shaughnessy Heights residents were either repossessed by the CPR or placed on the market for a fraction of their original value. (Cynical observers referred to the once affluent neighborhood as Poverty Hill and Mortgage Heights.) Appraised at $75,000 in 1920, Glen Brae, the William Lamont Tait mansion at 1690 Matthews, sold in 1939 for $7,500 and was later used as a kindergarten and nursing home. Today this ornate old mansion has been transformed into Canuck Place, a hospice for children. Rosemary was turned into a convent. Hycroft became a military hospital.

In 1942 wartime housing shortages prompted the federal government to issue an order-in-council allowing Shaughnessy homes to be split up into smaller units. In 1955, when the order-in-council expired, the Shaughnessy Heights Property Owners' Association led the campaign to return to the pre-war period of single family homes. Eventually the provincial government decided that it would not change the status of existing multiple family dwellings but that any properties that lapsed into single family use for more than a month would be zoned that way permanently.

Despite the complaints of local residents, Vancouver real estate developers showed little reluctance to break up the old manorial properties, a process made easier when the provincial building restriction legislation expired in 1970. In 1975 the CPR constructed condominiums and townhouses on the former Shaughnessy Golf Course, setting aside 22 hectares for the VanDusan Botanical Gardens.

According to the federal census of 1991 the average household income in Shaughnessy Heights declined by 10 per cent between 1980 and 1990 from $112,106 to $102,933. (During the same period, average Vancouver household incomes rose by 4.5 per cent.)

In 1991, 58 per cent of Shaughnessy Heights residents had a university education compared to 34 per cent in Vancouver as a whole. Seventy-six per cent owned their homes (40 per cent in Vancouver). In 1991 it cost $913 to rent the average Shaughnessy Heights apartment ($707 in the rest of the city).

The population of Shaughnessy Heights remained static during the 1980s; there were 9,345 residents in 1981; 9,035 in 1991—a decline of 3.3 per cent. From 1980 to 1990 Shaughnessy Heights witnessed a 25 per cent drop in the number of residents under the age of 25 and a 55 per cent increase among people in their early 40s—a possible demographic effect of the aging baby-boom population.

"Glen Brae", Shaughnessy's most spectacular mansion, was designed in 1910 to evoke its owner's native Scotland (its glazed bricks and cast iron gate posts were imported from Glasgow). Today it's Canuck Place. rw

Kitsilano and Arbutus Ridge
Michael Kluckner

SINCE IT WAS FIRST SETTLED around the turn of the 20th century, Kitsilano has been home to a very diverse cross-section of Vancouver's population. Throughout its history, the homes of the wealthy have stood next to rental apartments, and workers' cottages occupied streets near popular bathing beaches. In the early days, the two factors which created this diversity were the pretty English Bay waterfront on the one hand and industrial False Creek on the other. Since the 1970s Kitsilano's proximity to the white-collar jobs of downtown Vancouver has boosted prices on both the surviving cottages and the mansions.

In the 19th century the English Bay waterfront was the scene of small logging operations, supplied by skid roads and logging railways extending back into the hills of Mackenzie Heights, and a cannery at the foot of Bayswater Street. The large parcels of surveyed property on the south side of the bay were bought, sold and traded among Vancouver's early speculators, but there were too few customers to support any real-estate development until late in the 1890s, when a few homes began to appear on the muddy streets west of Granville Street and the Fairview Slopes streetcar line. Workers' cottages and tenements occupied the lowlands within an easy walk of the sawmills and sash-and-door factories on False Creek.

At the time, natives lived in a village called Sun'ahk, facing into False Creek near the Kitsilano side of the Burrard Bridge; in 1869 they had been granted a tiny reservation around the village, bounded roughly by First Avenue, Chestnut and the Burrard Bridge right-of-way. Although eight years later the land grant was doubled to include part of Kitsilano Point, in 1901 the Provincial Government decided to displace the native community, which broke up, some members going to Squamish, some to the Capilano reserve. A decade later the reservation was abandoned and considered to be a future industrial reserve.

Also displaced was the first white settler, Sam Greer, who lived on Kitsilano Beach from 1882 till 1890, when he lost a dispute with the Canadian Pacific Railway over title to the land. Greer went to jail for shooting and wounding the sheriff who had come to evict him, and the CPR publicized plans for a deep-sea terminus on Kitsilano Point. However, the company soon abandoned the plans and turned its thoughts to residential development. After consulting with Professor Charles Hill-Tout, the CPR decided in 1905 to name the new area after Chief Khahtsahlanough, whose grandson August Jack was a resident of Sun'ahk.

Meanwhile Vancouverites flocked by rowboat, and on foot from Granville Street, to camp at Greer's Beach, as it had become known. To service the beach community and open the area for settlement, the CPR leased its trestle across False Creek and right-of-way along English Bay to the B.C. Electric Railway Company, which started a regular streetcar service in 1905. Permanent occupants of the new area included a few brave souls who had built homes along the beach: the earliest was a realtor named Theodore Calland, who built the mansion "Edgewood" in 1902 (demolished) just west of the Trafalgar Street CPR boundary, and the MacGowan family, who built in 1904 at 2575 Cornwall.

A number of other fine estates were erected on the Kitsilano hillside and along the beach in the years before World War I: the Rorison house at 3148 Point Grey Road, in about 1960; the Ells house on the triangle of Point Grey Road and York Avenue, in 1908, now converted into condominiums; "Killarney" at Point Grey Road and Bayswater, now the site of an apartment building of the same name, in 1908 by Sam Greer's daughter; the Stearman house at First Avenue and Larch in 1908; the Logan house at 2530 Point Grey Road in 1909; and "Seagate Manor," at the foot of Macdonald Street, in 1912 (demolished).

On nearby blocks, land was subdivided into 10-metre lots and sold to builders catering to middle-class home-buyers. The CPR itself developed Kitsilano Point for housing in 1909. By the time of the outbreak of World War I, most of the slope above the beach was occupied by houses, mainly two or two-and-a-half storeys in the "Vancouver Box" or Craftsman styles, interspersed here and there with the occasional rowhouse or apartment building.

Another streetcar line, extending from Granville Bridge along 4th Avenue to Alma, was completed in 1909, opening up more land. Block after block of wooden houses were thrown up between 4th and 9th (named Broadway in 1912). A more exclusive subdivision of grand, Craftsman-style homes was marketed by James Quiney north of 4th Avenue and west of Blenheim. To meet the population boom, new schools opened —West Fairview, on the north side of 4th between Yew and Vine, in 1907 (demolished); Henry Hudson at Cornwall and Cypress in 1911; General Gordon at 6th at Bayswater in 1912; Lord Tennyson at 10th and Cypress in 1913; Bayview at Collingwood and 7th in 1914; and Kitsilano High at 10th and Trafalgar in 1917.

The eastern end of Kitsilano was dominated less by aesthetic and family concerns and more by its proximity to industry. The blocks of Cypress and Cedar (now Burrard Street) near the beach were home to Vancouver's Sikh community before World War I; nearby employers included the B.C. Electric's interurban car shops near the Kitsilano trestle, the sawmills, and a number of businesses served by the B.C. Electric rail line, including the Reifels' Vancouver Brewery at 12th and Yew and the metal shops on Granville Island.

The fate of the former Indian reservation, coveted by industry but used during World War II as an RCAF Equipment Depot, was only decided in 1956, when the Parkview Towers apartment building went up at Chestnut and Cornwall. Over the next 20 years institutions, including the Maritime Museum, the Vancouver Museum, the Planetarium, the Southam Observatory, the Vancouver Archives and the Vancouver School of Music, occupied the land; grassy swards beloved of kite fliers extended to the windy point.

Most of the old estates, and many single-family homes, converted into rooming houses during World War II and stayed that way through the 1950s and into the 1960s, by which time Kitsilano was very popular with university students. Following city council's 1954 decision to rezone the slope above the beach for apartments, few owners maintained the old houses, leading to the deterioration of the neighborhood. With this affordable housing, the nearby beach, and vacant shops on 4th Avenue, Kitsilano was the perfect home for Vancouver's hippie community of the sixties and seventies.

Many who moved to the area at that time established themselves and, with their new-found wealth from well-paying downtown jobs, bought and restored houses and became the yuppies of the 1980s. Kitsilano is today quite a wealthy area with a young, mobile population. Although many single-family houses have been demolished, or converted into strata units, there is still a "heritage" feeling clinging to many of its tree-lined streets.

Unlike Kitsilano, the Arbutus Ridge area south of 16th Avenue is more homogeneous. Lying between the interurban tracks and the CPR's boundary at Trafalgar Street, the area was largely bypassed by development, which sought more desirable properties on higher ground. Only in the late 1930s did the blocks north of King Edward Avenue become popular for "starter houses," usually hipped-roof, stuccoed bungalows with octagon windows near the front door. The process continued after World War II with much the same kind of houses, many of which have since been replaced by newer generations of "Vancouver Specials." The most prominent

survivor from the immediate post-war years is the block of shops at 16th and Arbutus, with the distinctive Ridge Theatre and bowling alley.

South and west of King Edward Avenue as far as the Quilchena hillside at 33rd, the land was marshy bushland known as Consumption Hollow, Asthma Flats or Johnston's Farm. It was leased in 1925 to the Quilchena Golf Club, which had a clubhouse at 29th and Maple Crescent, and a small interurban station for golfing passengers! After the club moved to Richmond in 1960, housing development commenced. Prince of Wales School, the Arbutus Club, Arbutus Gardens, and a few private-care hospitals took large blocks of land, while rancher-style houses filled the adjoining, winding streets (Valley Drive, cutting diagonally across the area, follows part of the route of an 1870s-era logging railway). The Arbutus Village shopping centre and housing complex, completed in the 1970s, were the last pieces fitted into the puzzle.

One thing that Arbutus Ridge shares with Kitsilano is a Greek presence; in the former, it is the Greek Orthodox church on Valley Drive, which superseded the Greek community's earlier church—now Kits House at 7th and Vine. Since the 1950s, Vancouver's Greek commercial area has been the blocks of Broadway west of Macdonald.

Arbutus at 33rd Avenue, looking north east to Quilchena Golf Course, circa 1930. vs

Point Grey
Michael Kluckner

MUCH OF POINT GREY's exclusivity today results from its location as the westernmost of Vancouver's neighborhoods, bordering on its north side English Bay and on its west and southwest Pacific Spirit Park. Like its adjoining community, Dunbar, Point Grey was to have been part of a western-spreading city extending all the way to the University of British Columbia and Point Grey (the tip of the peninsula) itself. But the University Endowment Lands were never developed as envisaged and, after decades of debate, were declared parkland in the 1980s.

Point Grey was named for Captain George Grey, a friend of Captain Vancouver. The British, along with Spanish navigators whose presence is remembered in the name Spanish Banks, visited in the early 1790s a forested peninsula that for centuries had been home to native people. At Jericho Beach, a village known as Ee'yullmough stood at the edge of a meadow of mossy grass, hemmed in by enormous Douglas firs and hemlocks that were later known as "the best spars in the world."

The Europeans who arrived in the mid-19th century quickly set to work logging the Point Grey slopes, and floated the boomed logs through First Narrows to the Hastings Mill. Although most of Point Grey was leased in 1865 to the mill, the colonial government recognized the area's strategic importance by establishing Government Reserves at the Point and along Jericho; the former became the University of B.C., while the latter is now the site of Jericho Park, the School for the Deaf and Blind and the Jericho army base.

Jericho is a corruption of "Jerry's Cove" or of "Jerry & Co.," named for Jeremiah Rogers, the most successful of the contract loggers working for the Hastings Mill. His logging camp stood near the old Indian village. Whalers briefly used the cove in the 1870s. A few dairy farmers followed the loggers, and pastured their cows amongst the stumps and bracken. A building at Belmont and Sasamat, selling feeds and general merchandise on the main floor and housing the proprietors in the bay-windowed upstairs rooms, opened in 1905 and soon became the post office and meeting place for what was generally known as the Langara district. In the 1910s and 1920s families camped along the beach there in the summertime.

In 1908 Point Grey "seceded" from South Vancouver and became a municipality in its own right.

On the grassy meadow at Jericho in 1892, a handful of enterprising golfers under the leadership of Dr. Duncan Bell-Irving

The remoteness of the Government Reserve made it suitable for a school for wayward youth...

set up a nine-hole course, later expanded across Fourth Avenue to comprise eighteen, which is considered to be the first links established west of the Mississippi. The links were abandoned at the outbreak of the World War II and the land reverted to military uses. The old clubhouse burned down in 1948.

The remoteness of the Government Reserve made it suitable for a school for wayward youth: the Jericho Boys' Industrial School, which opened in 1904 at 4100 West 4th Avenue. Civilization, in the form of the 4th Avenue streetcar, did not arrive at Alma Street for another five years, by which time Point Grey's first large house, called Aberthau and now operating as a community centre at 4397 West 2nd Avenue, was under construction. The subsequent expansion of the streetcar system in 1912 up the gentle grade of 10th Avenue to Sasamat, north on Sasamat to 4th, and along 4th to Drummond Drive opened the area to housing development, creating the middle-class neighborhood of single-family houses which survives today. Another grand early home was that of Philip Gilman, built in 1913 at Jericho Beach; known now as Brock House, it operates as a seniors' centre and restaurant next to the Royal Vancouver Yacht Club.

In 1929 Point Grey, along with South Vancouver immediately to the east, amalgamated with the City of Vancouver.

The Government Reserve at Jericho provided a strategic site for an air station in the early 1920s. Flying boats operating from the beach chased rumrunners, mapped the coastline, and dogged illegal immigrants during the next 20 years, then during the war years performed anti-submarine reconnaissance.

The remaining flying boat hangars had a final moment of glory during the 1976 Habitat Forum conference, but burned or were razed soon thereafter. One of the barracks for the old air station became the Jericho Youth Hostel in 1971. The Canadian Forces army base continues in operation in the mid 1990s, but future plans for the land there probably include complete redevelopment as housing.

Like much of the west side of Vancouver, Point Grey's streets have witnessed the demolition of many of the small, older homes from the 1920s and 1930s and their replacement by much larger single family ones. Ironically the oldest survivor of all is actually a recent arrival to the area: the Hastings Mill store, built in about 1865 on Vancouver's downtown waterfront, was moved in 1930 to Pioneer Park at the foot of Alma Street.

Dunbar/Southlands
Rita Woodman

ARCHAEOLOGICAL DATA INDICATE native people occupied this area for at least 2,000 years before the arrival of Europeans. The first homesteaders, in 1863, were Fitzgerald and Sam McCleery. The McCleery farm, now McCleery golf course, was the first operating farm in Vancouver, and the farmhouse, built in 1873, was the first permanent dwelling in the Vancouver area.

Dunbar/Southlands was part of the old Municipality of Point Grey. The area had been logged, but land for development was available only in Marpole and Kerrisdale. Most of the land was a mass of fallen, burned timber and was held by the Canadian Pacific Railway and the provincial government.

The origin of the name Dunbar is sometimes attributed to Charles Trott Dunbar, general agent for the Union Land Company of St. Paul, Minnesota, who came to Vancouver in 1888. He invested largely in real estate, and owned and controlled considerable property in the city. In 1906 a Vancouver newspaper reported he was promoting Dunbar Heights and "selling lots like hotcakes." However, the name's origin is earlier, for in 1886 it already appears on a map of Vancouver. Another suggestion is that the area was named after the Battle of Dunbar in 1650, in association with other battle-named streets in the area—Trafalgar, Balaclava, Blenheim, Waterloo and Alma. These names, however, were given by the city council in 1907 in substitution for Boundary, Richards, Cornwall, Lansdowne and Campbell, which were in use elsewhere in the city.

In 1912 a section of the UBC lands was subdivided and laid out on town-planning principles. The fact the university was to be established nearby was undoubtedly responsible in large part for the early development (and type of development) of the Dunbar/Southlands area. By 1919 the municipality was earning a reputation as a well-controlled area with regulations outlining building and landscaping. At that time a third of Point Grey's municipal revenue came from CPR land taxes. By 1927 three streetcar routes served the area.

When Point Grey amalgamated with Vancouver in 1929, it was agreed Vancouver would respect the area's restrictive zoning by-laws. The first land development of any consequence occurred in the mid-1920s, and some of the homes built during this period are still standing. Dunbar/Southlands consists almost entirely of single family dwellings and there are no highrises. There are "castle" homes scattered throughout, with two fine examples on West 39th Avenue just west of Dunbar.

The area is noted for its beautiful gardens, and the park board has planted many flowering trees along the streets. In some parts the trees meet overhead, forming archways several blocks long. There are many parks, the largest being Memorial Park West on Dunbar between 31st and 33rd avenues. Dunbar Community Centre opened here in 1950 after a spirited community drive for funds. At Musqueam Park one can plunge into the forest and follow Tin Can Creek, where salmon still spawn each fall.

The churches have followed the area's development. Knox Presbyterian started in 1910. It later became part of the United Church and changed its name to Knox United. Immaculate Conception Church began in 1924 and St. Philip's Anglican in 1925. Dunbar Heights United also dates from these years.

Within 15 minutes of downtown Vancouver, at the mouth of the Fraser River, there's a serene pastoral retreat where horses and waterfowl mingle with high-tech development and historical landmarks. No other major Canadian city has country living so close by. It's not uncommon to hear the cries of blue herons, red-tailed hawks and bald eagles as you clip-clop along a country road on your horse. You'll also pass opulent new homes next to old rustic dwellings, as the area is still zoned for limited agriculture.

Spring cherry blossoms, among the best in the city, herald the beginning of the planting, pruning, and sowing season for spectacular English country gardens. Great pride is taken in creating these postcard-quality blooms.

Southlands Riding Club, incorporated in 1943 and home to some of Canada's finest equestrians, sits on just over seven hectares in the heart of the community. The clubhouse, once an abandoned fisherman's net storage hut on Deering Island was dismantled and carried piece by piece, by members on horseback, to its present site. Today cyclists, joggers, walkers and riders enjoy the wonderful river trail along the Fraser leading to Pacific Spirit Park, with its meandering trails under giant cedar and firs. Two-thousand-year-old Camosun Bog, a unique wetland within the park, can be reached by a boardwalk path beginning at Camosun and 19th Avenue. The bog is revered by the Musqueam people as a portal to the spirit world.

The entire Dunbar/Southlands covers an expanse from 16th Avenue to the Fraser River, and from Camosun Street east to Blenheim. It encompasses the Musqueam reserve, Celtic and Deering Islands, plus two public and three championship-rated private golf courses. This area contains some of the highest-priced real estate in Canada.

With additional material by Elfleda Wilkinson and Glenda Guttman.

University Endowment Lands
Kerry Gold

THE AREA KNOWN as the University Endowment Lands is actually a patchwork of jurisdictions that include University Hill, the Pacific Spirit Regional Park and the University of British Columbia. The fact that the bulk of the University Endowment Lands is a forested 763-hectare park—almost twice the size of Stanley Park—is nothing short of a miracle considering the series of lofty development proposals throughout its history.

Any schemes to fully develop the area were permanently laid to rest in April 1989, when the enormous forest was turned over to the GVRD for safekeeping. However, the path to preservation was a tumultuous one, and the university's proposal to transform almost 30 per cent of its 402-hectare campus into market housing is a sign that the status quo is by no means a foregone conclusion.

The University Endowment Lands will undergo perhaps its greatest change in the next 20 years as density climbs and a large, new community develops. But the wide open shores of Point Grey Peninsula make the area one of the Lower Mainland's most cherished locations, and opposition to development of market housing is already brewing.

The 202 hectares that comprise the provincially administered University Hill contain housing that ranges from low-rent student accommodation to $10-million mansions. There are 2,400 full-time University Hill residents living on the fringes of UBC campus which is located in the southwest corner of the peninsula. UBC has a student population of 35,000 and a residential population of 800 already living in a 10-hectare development called Hampton Place. Once UBC transforms a proposed 100 undeveloped hectares into more market housing, up to 12,000 more people could live on the campus. For the purposes of the GVRD, the entire area is known as electoral area A.

The GVRD is working to regenerate Pacific Spirit Regional Park, once a thriving ecosystem of giant old-growth species including western red cedar, western hemlock, Douglas fir, sitka spruce and yew. This last stand of urban forest is an anomaly, considering the amount of ravaging it has withstood since it was first inspected by British military men charting the coast for sites for military reserves to protect the new colony.

Although already home to Musqueam natives, the forest had caught the imagination of Colonel Moody of the Royal Engineers, who was in charge of establishing military reserves along Burrard Inlet. Moody established the reserves, and went on to establish himself as director of the B.C. and Vancouver Island Spar Lumber and Saw Mill Company, precursor to Hastings Sawmill. The mill was granted a 21-year timber lease in 1865, part of which included today's Pacific Spirit Regional Park.

The fragmented remains of old skids used to transport heavy timber down to Wreck Beach can be found today in the mossy blanket of forest floor. Despite active logging between 1861 and 1891, the forest was by no means clear-cut. Unintentionally the sawmill logged selectively because trees were often too difficult to reach and some had too many knots and branches. Enough trees were left to generate a new crop, and the chopping continued piecemeal throughout the turn of the century.

In 1908 the government established the legal and financial framework for the University of British Columbia. A University Loan Act was passed that set aside almost 810,000 hectares of land in the Interior as an endowment for the new university. All that was needed was a location. In 1910 the province appointed a site commission that toured British Columbia in May and June of that year before choosing Point Grey.

By 1911 it was clear the endowment wasn't attracting the buyers the government had anticipated. The University Loan Act was revised and the allotted land was swapped for 1,174 hectares of land adjacent to the 222-hectare university site. Lots were to be surveyed and cut up, intended for residential sales that would underwrite the university's burgeoning costs. In 1912 the entire Endowment Lands, where Pacific Spirit Regional Park is today, were proposed for residential or commercial development. Only 56.5 hectares were to be retained as park land. Fortunately this plan, like others to follow, was never realized.

The construction of UBC did, however, become reality, despite what many locals may have thought at the time. UBC officially opened a make-shift school on September 30, 1915, at its Fairview campus near Vancouver General Hospital, with a student body of 379 students. Construction of the science building had begun at the Point Grey site but was halted when World War I broke out. The war ended, and almost a decade passed and students were still trudging to classes in Fairview's ramshackle buildings, originally intended as a temporary wartime measure. So limited was space that some classes were held in the basement of a nearby church.

By 1922 the student body had grown by 21 per cent, and the students had had enough. They staged a full-blown publicity campaign called "Build the University" that culminated in an event known today as the "Great Trek." On October 28 almost 1,200 students marched from Fairview campus to downtown,

Clock Tower, UBC, 1980. vs

their procession along the dirt trail that led through the forest to the unfinished site. Newspapers published pictures of students forming a gigantic human "UBC" on the science building grounds. Later a small group travelled to Victoria, carrying a 56,000-name petition to cabinet. Legislators got the message loud and clear, and by 1925 the doors of a permanent university officially opened.

The construction of UBC was not without its problems, wrought by the school's relatively remote location. The area was still undeveloped and only a dirt trail connected UBC to the rest of the city, making transportation of construction materials a hefty expense for builders.

In the end B.C. Electric Railway constructed a rail line to the university that formed an arch over Marine Drive. An aerial tramway, powered by a donkey engine, connected a wharf to the Point Grey clifftops. Below the cliffs, tons of Nelson Island granite were shipped in by barge to the wharf and hoisted up by tramway. Newspapers predicted the $10,000 project would be in use 25 years down the road; but it was dismantled as soon as construction was completed.

In 1930 the university cleared 120 hectares between Chancellor Boulevard and Spanish Banks for development. However, the Depression had struck, and plans were subverted. UBC couldn't afford to build the infrastructure necessary for market housing development, and in the 1930s they returned control of the endowment lands to the province. Today aged stands of red alder cover the site that was cleared. By 1955 more than half of the undeveloped Crown land remained, due to the Depression and war shortages of the 1940s.

Attempts in the sixties and seventies to transform the beleaguered forest into housing projects triggered outrage among an increasingly environmentally aware community. Resident Iva Mann had fought to save the forested remains of the peninsula since 1951. Her efforts began when a white dogwood at the rear of her property was cut down during one of government's many subdivision attempts. Mann couldn't save the tree, but the incident was pivotal in sparking her environmental interest. By 1970 she was working with a residents' group called the Regional Park Committee as well as B.C. Outdoor Recreation, transforming the old logging skid trails into suitable hiking trails. The idea was to make the forested area accessible, and therefore desirable, to the public.

The designation of Pacific Spirit Regional Park was finally announced on December 1988, by Premier Bill Vander Zalm. The City of Vancouver also contributed property east of Camosun that forms part of the 2,000-year-old Camosun Bog. A series of park trails was named "Iva Mann Walk," in honor of her efforts—although Mann refuses to take full credit, modestly insisting the long-standing battle was a collective effort.

Another drawn-out appeal to the province was resolved in March 1995. For the past 70 years residents have been officially classified as living in "unorganized territory," administered out of an on-site office by 21 provincial employees, including an area manager. Unlike their neighbors in Vancouver, the residents on Crown land have no mayor, no council and no municipal elections. At issue was whether the residents, who pay civic-type taxes to the province, would incorporate as a municipality called University Hill, or maintain the status quo. For six years proponents of incorporation petitioned the province to hold a referendum to put the question to rest one way or the other. Incorporation would give the 2,400 residents more control over zoning, development and taxation, they argued.

After much door-to-door campaigning and information meetings held at a local church, 65 per cent of residents voted March 4, 1995, against the community becoming a separate municipality. The vote was 599 to 318 to remain under the authority of the ministry of municipal affairs.

The University Endowment Lands has sustained a quiet, suburban-like atmosphere since early loggers and developers fist set foot on its shores. Nudists wishing for seclusion still make the steep trek down a trail near UBC's Gate 6 to Wreck Beach, as they've done since the early seventies. And school field trips and out-of-towners flock to UBC's Nitobe and Botanical gardens, Totem Park, the anthropological museum and Pacific Spirit Regional Park. As for the substantial market housing proposed for UBC campus, the GVRD is creating the campus' first community plan. The GVRD and UBC will consult with faculty, staff, students, environmental groups, businesses, residents and the general public on that ever-present, ever-pressing issue of University Endowment Lands development.

Neighborhoods
GVRD

Before World War II, communities developed in the Lower Mainland around historic crossroads and strategic spots for river navigation. Always, their existence depended on some kind of local industry—brick making at Clayburn, fish packing and boat building at Steveston, farming at Cloverdale-and the people who lived in the town and in the surrounding countryside focused their attention inward, towards the main street, the post office and, often, the movie house, the cafe and the beer parlor in the hotel.

The shared purpose of so many residents meant that there was also something of a shared vision of the town's activities and future. Some communities also had strong ties of language and culture—many of the farms in the Fraser Valley were settled by migrants from England; Japanese fisherman and their families put a distinctive stamp on Fraser River fish camps like Annieville and towns like Steveston; the Finns of Finn Slough along the river in south Richmond created a unique community tied more to the water than to the land.

Trips to the metropolis were rare. Although car ownership gradually grew during the Twenties and Thirties, from one car for every twelve people in 1922 to one in seven in 1936 (far below the United States where, for example, in Seattle in 1928, there was one car for every three people), operating costs were still quite high, and many families used their vehicles just for Saturday shopping and Sunday drives.

A new attitude toward the automobile after the Second World War redefined the nature of communities out in the countryside. Traffic was beginning to become "regional," although in the early 1950s the idea of highways bypassing country towns was dismissed as "absurd," because "most of the traffic is heading for town anyway." But with the completion of the Highway One Freeway in the mid 1960s, and extensive improvements to the Lougheed Highway, everything began to change.

First, many people bought into new subdivisions on the outskirts of the old country towns because they wanted affordable space and could now drive easily to their jobs elsewhere in the region. Secondly, many municipal councils rezoned large areas for shopping malls, such as Richmond Centre, Coquitlam Centre, Surrey Centre, and Langley's Willowbrook; in most cases this economic rivalry was too much for the old town centres, which lost customers to the malls. Old businesses relocated, others closed, and the main streets slipped into a decline. The Whalley Commercial area, now the centre of Surrey City, was one casualty; Haney's main street along the Lougheed has struggled since the 1970s; Langley's old downtown along the Fraser Highway is attempting to reverse a decade-long skid with a "heritage" refit.

Not surprisingly, the residents in these new suburbs did not share interests with their neighbors to the same extent as in the old days. Often, both adults in a family worked elsewhere, so a sense of belonging to a community was slower to develop. People might shop on the way home from work, or at the mall thirty miles away, or even in the United States if it suited their fancy.

Residents of these new subdivisions are more inclined to find common ground through schools and recreation rather than through the commerce which used to anchor the old towns. Certainly, the new communities are more homogeneous in their age groups and income levels than were the old ones—young families with children over here, seniors behind the wall over there. As a result, some communities develop identity only in crises, such as a crime wave, or unwelcome redevelopment plans, especially the encroachment of high-density housing into what had previously been a single-family preserve. Sometime they are united only in what they don't want, as in the oft-heard Langley statement: "We don't want to become like Walnut Grove!"

—Michael Kluckner

facing page: Columbia Street, New Westminster, 1890. vpl
above: Richmond, 1994. vs

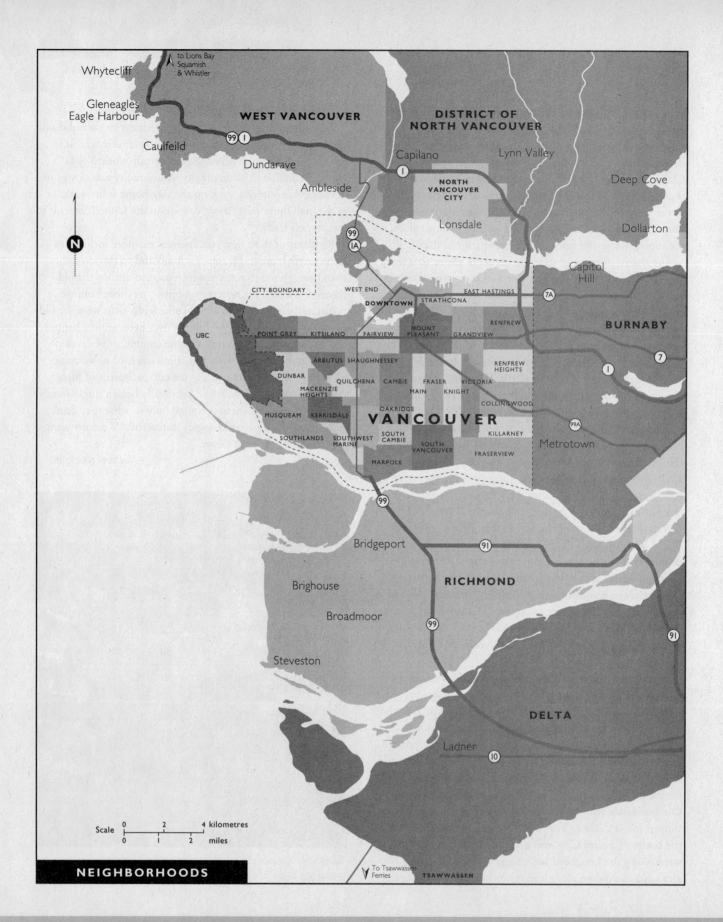

to Lions Bay
Squamish
& Whistler

Whytecliff

Gleneagles
Eagle Harbour

Caulfeild

WEST VANCOUVER

**DISTRICT OF
NORTH VANCOUVER**

Dundarave

99 1

Capilano

Lynn Valley

Deep Cove

Ambleside

1

**NORTH
VANCOUVER
CITY**

Dollarton

N

99
1A

Lonsdale

Capitol
Hill

CITY BOUNDARY

WEST END

EAST HASTINGS

7A

DOWNTOWN

STRATHCONA

POINT GREY   KITSILANO   FAIRVIEW

MOUNT
PLEASANT

RENFREW

BURNABY

UBC

GRANDVIEW

7

ARBUTUS SHAUGHNESSEY

RENFREW
HEIGHTS

1

DUNBAR

QUILCHENA   CAMBIE   FRASER   VICTORIA

MACKENZIE
HEIGHTS

MAIN   KNIGHT

COLLINGWOOD

99A

MUSQUEAM   KERRISDALE

OAKRIDGE

VANCOUVER

KILLARNEY

Metrotown

SOUTHLANDS   SOUTHWEST
MARINE

SOUTH
CAMBIE

SOUTH
VANCOUVER

FRASERVIEW

MARPOLE

99

Bridgeport

91

Brighouse

RICHMOND

Broadmoor

99

91

Steveston

DELTA

Ladner

10

Scale   0   2   4 kilometres

0   1   2   miles

To Tsawwassen
Ferries

TSAWWASSEN

NEIGHBORHOODS

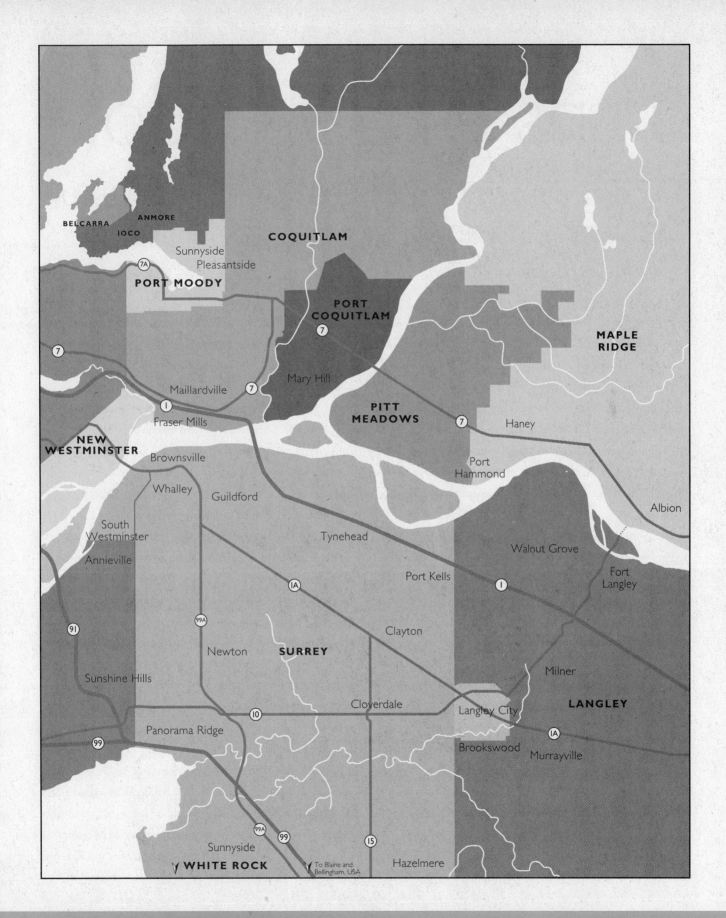

BELCARRA
ANMORE
IOCO
Sunnyside
Pleasantside
PORT MOODY
COQUITLAM
PORT COQUITLAM
Mary Hill
Maillardville
Fraser Mills
NEW WESTMINSTER
Brownsville
PITT MEADOWS
Haney
Port Hammond
MAPLE RIDGE
Albion
Whalley
Guildford
South Westminster
Annieville
Tynehead
Port Kells
Walnut Grove
Fort Langley
Clayton
Newton
SURREY
Milner
LANGLEY
Sunshine Hills
Cloverdale
Langley City
Panorama Ridge
Brookswood
Murrayville
Sunnyside
WHITE ROCK
To Blaine and Bellingham, USA
Hazelmere

Independent research shows that VAN Network newspapers are read by more than one million adults each week. No other single newspaper company delivers more readers or households than VAN Network.

Signs of Splendor

Official Symbolism of the Municipalities of the Greater Vancouver Regional District

Robert D. Watt, Chief Herald of Canada

SHARP-EYED MOTORISTS, travelling around the Lower Mainland of British Columbia will every once in a while pass a site featuring one of the official emblems of the surrounding municipality. It might be the south wall sculpture of the Delta coat of arms on the municipal hall, or the flag of Burnaby flying at Library Square in Metrotown, the armorial welcome sign to the District of North Vancouver on Highway 1 north of the Second Narrows Bridge or the flags of Richmond and Vancouver which mark the entrance to the airport.

The story of these official emblems, and the others in the Region is a fascinating one. It begins in the mid 19th century with the first European settlements and the first incorporated municipality, the City of New Westminster, and unfolds virtually up to the present, as increasing numbers of maturing communities move to express their identity through one of the most beautiful of our visual traditions—heraldry. Naturally, the various elements that make up these symbols are often a direct expression of local history, local economies and geographic situation. As a group, these symbols are both diverse and colorful; collectively they can aptly be described as emblems of splendor for it is very often the eye-popping local vistas of mountain peaks, seaside and riverside outlooks, rich delta and valley lands and forested slopes which are given pride of place in the designs.

For over a century and a quarter, a mix of legal requirements and civic pride together with the need to identify property and services has given rise to these symbols. Some have roots which span the whole period, others are only a year or two old. Well over half of them are not only in daily use, but have added significance as symbols granted by the Crown in recognition of the importance of these communities nationally, as well as locally. These coats of arms, which are borne by 70 per cent of the municipalities which are full members of the GVRD, and which include those with over 90 per cent of the regional population, represent the greatest concentration of such municipal symbols anywhere in Canada.

The objective of this short essay is to provide a ready reference to the content of these symbols with a brief review of their history. By way of introduction, these symbols are of two types; those which are lawfully granted coats of arms, granted by the Crown and described in an internationally recognized written language as well as an interpretive pictorial form. The oldest of these, granted from 1967 to 1988, were issued by the Crown's traditional heraldic officers, headquartered in London or Edinburgh.

In 1988, heraldry was patriated to Canada and a Canadian Heraldic Authority established as part of the Governor General's office. Since then, all lawful heraldry granted to Canadian corporations or individuals flows from this office. The second group of official symbols are non heraldic; logos or wordmarks designed by graphic artists and others and adopted by resolution of a particular Council. As the use of heraldry has spread across the GVRD, this type of emblem has become less common.

Hudson's Bay Company

Following a Dream *In the mid-1600s the fur trade in Canada was booming. But reaching the pelt rich regions north of the Great Lakes meant a massive return trek by canoe along the St. Lawrence River—until two enterprising traders, Medard Chouart Sieur des Groseilliers and Pierre Radisson, realized that sailing into Hudson Bay would make the furs easier to get to. They took their proposal to King Charles II of England in 1665. Three years later, they left England for Hudson's Bay.*

THE COMPANY OF ADVENTURERS

The Hudson's Bay Company was formed on May 2, 1670. On that day, King Charles II of England signed a Royal Charter and awarded it to the 18 courtier-investors who were the "Company of Adventurers of England Tradeing into Hudson's Bay". The vast territory included the provinces of Ontario and Quebec north of the Laurentian watershed and west of the Labrador boundary, the whole of Manitoba, most of Saskatchewan, the southern half of Alberta, and a large portion of the Northwest Territories; in all a great basin of 1,486,000 square miles, comprising 38.7% of what is today Canada. In the earliest days, the Company's trade was conducted almost entirely by the canoe routes that flowed into the Bay for which their company was named. But pressure grew to expand further with overland routes into the west. Explorers such as Henry Kelsey, the first European to journey into the prairies, helped bring trade and goods even further afield.

THE FIGHT TO SURVIVE

The business pages of modern newspapers are filled with stories of hostile takeovers. But takeovers today are never as hostile as they were in the early days of the Hudson's Bay Company. The riches from the fur trade were vast. And the fight that raged for control of the fur trade was long and bitter. In addition to Rupert's House, the original for Radisson and Groseilliers built on the shores of James Bay, the Company added other outposts to serve as centres of trade. These forts came under constant attack and were raided from both land and sea. Although the forts were repeatedly burned to the ground they were rebuilt each time. Through it all, the Company of Adventurers always managed to maintain at least one fort on the shores of Hudson's Bay and James Bay. Finally, in 1697, the Treaty of Ryswick was signed in Europe. The raiding stopped and the Hudson's Bay Company was able to conduct its growing business in peace.

AN UNIMAGINABLE COLLECTION

"Saleshops" were established outside Hudson's Bay Company forts, stocked with a wide variety of goods. The most elaborate, opened in 1881 in Winnipeg, was three storeys high and offered an almost unimaginable collection of riches, including Russian caviar, silk lingerie and musical instruments. It was a glittering taste of what was to come, as the Hudson's Bay Company soon opened similar stores from coast to coast. Today The Bay is the largest, as well as the oldest, department store chain in Canada.

THE CITY OF BURNABY

The coat of arms draws together elements from Burnaby's natural and historical heritage. The shield represents its situation at the heart of the Lower Mainland. The blue of Burrard Inlet on the north and the Fraser River in the south is separated by the gold of the land, symbolizing the riches of nature and those created by human endeavor. The eagle, symbol of the spirit of the whole community, is at the centre, representing the rich natural attributes of Burnaby Mountain and its wildlife. Its wings are decorated with water symbols; one each for Deer Lake and Burnaby Lake, referring to the geographic centre of the District and the increasing interest in the preservation of heritage landscapes.

The crest blends symbols honoring Burnaby's past with others representing civic government. The dominant colors, red and white, are the national colors of Canada and are also those featured in the 16th century coat of arms of Robert Burnaby's ancestors. The "crown" of silver stones with red masonry is the ancient heraldic emblem for municipal corporations. It is decorated with a heraldic stylization of strawberry flowers, 'fraises', referring to the strawberry farms once found throughout the municipality. They now symbolize the market gardens on the South Slope riverside lands. The fraises are also the main element in the arms of the Fraser Clan of which Simon Fraser was an illustrious member. The lion is taken directly from the Burnaby family arms, honoring the City's namesake and the efforts of all the pioneers. This idea is emphasized by having the lion uphold the City's flag.

The two deer as supporters representing the natural heritage of the City are male and female. Honoring the men and women who have helped create and preserve Burnaby, they are made distinctive from other supporters elsewhere in Canada by adding the collars of red rhododendrons, the municipal flower. They stand on a compartment of grass, representing the City's lands. The motto continues the sentiment found on the first District Seal dating from 1892, the year of incorporation, providing a link with the heritage represented in the original symbol.

CITY OF COQUITLAM

The coat of arms of the District, now the City of Coquitlam, was granted to permanently commemorate the centennial of incorporation on 25 July 1891. When the former District of Coquitlam was incorporated as the City of Coquitlam on 1 December 1992, the coat of arms was affirmed for continued use.

The predominant colors of blue and white were chosen for aesthetic reasons, although the blue does refer to the rivers which define several of the municipal boundaries. In the shield, the wavy blue bars with the gold centre have two meanings; firstly referring to the Fraser River and the gold rush which led to the first European settlement in the area, secondly to the Coquitlam and Pitt Rivers and to the wealth generated from the riverside location. The blue fleur-de-lys honors the French Canadian lumber workers and their families who established Maillardville in 1909, the District's first large settlement. In the upper part of the shield, the crenellated line represents the Royal Engineers who built the first roads in the community in the early 1860s. The dogwoods emphasize that Coquitlam is a British Columbian community and bring into the coat of arms the existing corporate emblem. Between the dogwoods is a silver fraise, a stylized strawberry flower, the plant badge of the Clan Fraser and a reference to Simon Fraser, who named the great river which is Coquitlam's southern boundary and the trade route for some of its early lumber and agricultural products.

The crest repeats the symbols contained in the upper part of the shield but arranged to form a Coquitlam coronet.

Two gold Clydesdale stallions were chosen as supporters, to represent the role of horsepower in the development of the early lumber industry and land clearing. They are made distinctive to the District through the addition of blue fraises at the shoulder of the horses. The horses stand on a compartment of grass, representing the City's lands.

The motto, ANIMUS FLUMINUM VIRES POPULI, "The Spirit of the River The Strength of the People" combines an expression of the City's geographic situation with its aspiration and strengths.

CORPORATION OF DELTA

In 1969, Delta replaced its earlier emblem with a new logo, a stylized version of the Greek letter "Delta" featuring at the apex a "bow on" view of an ocean-going freighter in reference to the new bulk loading facility at Roberts Bank.

The new coat of arms was developed by a committee of Council headed by then Mayor Ernest Burnett and the design synthesized important elements of the history, geography and economy of the municipality.

The shield is particularly striking and is patterned very closely on the Delta logo designed by Robert Miller in 1969. The green field represents Delta's rich farmlands. In the centre, the silver disc represents the sun, enclosed by the silver triangle, referring to the Greek letter.

The crest is composed of the red and white mural coronet, symbolizing a Canadian district municipality and the upper half of a silver ship's wheel, for water based commerce.

The two silver horses represent Delta's foundation industry, agriculture, and its ongoing importance to the community as well as the corporation's strength. Each horse is distinguished by collars and medallions referring to two industries, grain growing and fishing.

The compartment symbolizes the municipality; green fields bordered by the Sea and the River and includes symbols for the Fraser and Boundary Bay.

The motto invites citizens to conserve and strengthen Delta's special qualities.

The coat of arms has been widely used to identify Delta's property and services. When the new municipal hall was completed June 5, 1994, computers were used by designers to create a magnificent one-storey high relief sculpture in concrete of the coat of arms on the exterior wall of the Council Chamber. It is easily visible from Highway 10 to motorists en route to the ferry terminal at Tsawwassen.

THE CITY OF LANGLEY

Langley City's coat of arms was designed between August and October 1994, incorporating a number of themes, notably the concept of the community as a crossroads.

The shield embodies this central idea with the field of red set with a gold cross and square symbolizing the intersection of the old Yale Road and the British Columbia Electric Railway. The foundation settlement of Innes Corners is marked by the blue star, the traditional symbol in Scottish heraldry for persons with the surname Innes. The star also emphasized the concept of the centre and spirit of the City.

The crest features the mural coronet to signify a municipal corporation, decorated with a frieze of maple leaves and dogwood flowers for British Columbia and Canada. Above it is a canoe, shown in portage fashion and colored ermine, representing the early fur trade and the James MacMillan (Hudson's Bay Co.) expedition of 1824, the first recorded European travel across what is now the City. Rising up from the canoe is a black lion, from the Scottish heraldry for MacMillan, an animal renowned also as a symbol of strength of purpose. Here, it also represents the spirit of the community and the determination of citizens to defend the City's interests signalled by the City's flag.

In the compartment, the grass represents the lands and original fields of the City, the lilies, the special natural heritage of the region and the blue and white bars, the Nicomekl river. The elk also refers to the natural heritage of the City with the mare honoring pioneers and the horsepower used in early agriculture and industry. The garbs or wheat sheaves on the collars recall Langley Prairie and agriculture with the cogwheel on the mare's collar a symbol of industry. The bezants, or gold coins, are the traditional symbol of commerce.

The motto, suggested by the Committee, STRENGTH OF PURPOSE SPIRIT OF COMMUNITY, summarizes the spirit and character of the City.

The flag is a banner of the arms and is held by the mare in the coat of arms.

CITY OF NEW WESTMINSTER

The coat of arms for the City of New Westminster was developed by the writer in 1991 based on Council's wish that the grant respect the content of the City's existing emblem as far as possible. Consequently, the changes to the shield were limited to technical adjustments with the color of the cross being fixed as blue and the symbols in the quarters colored in pure heraldic colors where possible. In the crest, a wreath is included in red and white, Canada's national colors, which were also used to color the mural crown. The grizzly bear, which was dark brown in 1860, became gold. The lions remained red, as they had been for 122 years, but they now wore gold collars and medallions. The medallion of the lion on the left featured the Royal Crown, a special grant recommended by the Governor General and approved by the Queen to recognize New Westminster as the "Royal City" chosen by Queen Victoria as the name of the capital of the Crown Colony of British Columbia. On the right, the medallion shows a black anvil, referring to the world famous ceremonial Hyack Anvil Battery. The compartment of forested hills above the waters of the Fraser, representing the City's dramatic location, was a new element. The motto remained as chosen in 1860, "IN GOD WE TRUST".

Two Patents, for the City's coat of arms and flag and for the badge of the New Westminster Police Department, were presented by Governor General Ramon Hnatyshyn at a special ceremony at City Hall October 26, 1992, during a visit celebrating the 125th anniversary of Confederation and the Silver Jubilee of the Canadian Honours system. During the ceremony, several New Westminster residents received decorations personally from the Governor General who also presented Mayor Betty Toporowski with the first of the new City flags. Thus, 122 years after incorporation, B.C.'s first capital was granted a coat of arms which enshrined a good part of its symbolic heritage.

CITY OF NORTH VANCOUVER

The young Salish artist, Susan Sparrow, now Susan Point, whose representation of a salmon and a bear are embedded in the coat of arms for the City of North Vancouver, was a guest of honor at the 1982 ceremony of presentation. Copies of her print, featuring the two representations, were presented to Lieutenant-Governor Henry Bell-Irving and to Conrad Swan, York Herald.

The arms were strongly based not on any existing corporate symbolism but on a fresh interpretation of the City's history and geography.

In the shield, the twin peaks of the Lions rise above the waves of the harbor, indicating the City's geographic position on the North Shore. The late 19th century sailing ship represents maritime-based commerce and the first ships to bring industry and settlers to Moodyville, the original Victorian settlement. The mountain lion heads are an ancient symbol of strength but are portrayed here using the local cougar rather than the stylized heraldic lion of Europe. They underline the significance of the mountains which are a famous local landmark.

The crest, above the shield, repeats the maple leaf and dogwood circlet found in the crest of Richmond and adds a wood grouse in reference to Grouse Mountain whose base forms a main part of the City's site. The sprig of salal in its beak refers to the rich natural heritage of the City.

The black bear and salmon supporters symbolize the environment, the economy and links between the First Nations and European peoples. Traditionally, the bear and salmon were important in the ceremonial life of the Salish people; each carries about its neck a unique example of Salish art, the spindle whorl used in the native spinning process. The whorls represent domestic arts, one carved with a bear, the other with a salmon.

The compartment of the forest and sea represents the twin foundations of the City's prosperity.

THE DISTRICT OF NORTH VANCOUVER

The coat of arms for the District of North Vancouver was designed by the writer working with the Centennial Committee and with comments from District Council.

The coat of arms preserved some of the symbolic themes in use since 1891 but introduced a significant number of new ideas.

Uniquely among the existing coats of arms in the Region, the shield of the District is highly stylized, almost abstract. The District landscape is symbolized with the snow-capped forested mountains beneath a blue sky and the curving lines of the mountain streams and rivers flowing down to meet the waters of the harbor.

The crest is a 19th century sailing ship, representing sea-going commerce and recalling the ships shown on the first corporate seal. The ship flies two flags, the ensign in use by Canadian merchant ships at the time of incorporation in 1891 and a special pennant in the District colors of blue, white and green.

The silver bear and deer represent the riches of the District's natural environment entrusted to citizens for preservation. In the original grant of 16 October 1990, these supporters wore collars of salal leaves and berries. In a supplementary Letters Patent of 18 December 1990, the collars were changed to be composed of maple leaves and dogwood flowers placed with the salal to honor Canada and British Columbia.

The compartment shows forested slopes underlining the importance of forest based wealth and the beauty of the forest environment and the waters of the sea. The representation of the Salish salmon in gold honors the First Peoples.

The motto, MONTES RIVIQUE NOBIS INSPIRANT, "The Mountains and Their Streams are our Inspiration," summarizes the design and the District heritage. It was developed by the writer and translated by Graham L. Anderson.

THE CITY OF PORT COQUITLAM

When completed, the arms of the City of Port Coquitlam took the place of the previous emblem which dated back to the time of incorporation March 7, 1913. The motto, BY COMMERCE AND INDUSTRY WE PROSPER, was an obvious choice for an expansionist and visionary community just before World War I.

The shield blends the themes of native and natural heritage and the railway. The central band or heraldic fess used a special edge implying a conifer twig that was originally developed by a Finnish heraldic artist. Overall, the fess can be seen as a pathway, with the edge representing the City's green spaces and the continuing wealth and amenities flowing from local forests. The railway was highlighted through the use of the twin bands of gold, color of commerce and the red steam locomotive wheel. The name of the river from which the City takes its name, Coquitlam, meaning little red fish, is celebrated in the upper part of the shield.

The crest is set on a wreath of two of the City's official heraldic colors, white and green. It is composed of a mural coronet, emblem for municipal government, set with six anchors, three visible, which represent ships and maritime commerce and refer to the Port in the City's name.

The compartment on which the supporters stand is the grass of the City lands. The beaver supporters, colored in the gold of commerce to echo the motto, are taken directly from the old emblem on City Hall. They have patriotic and thematic meaning as Canada's national animal and a symbol of industry as well as an important part of the City's own heritage of symbols. The collar on the left hand supporter alludes to the Royal Crown in the old emblem. The City's floral emblem, the azalea, is featured as the other collar. A Salish spindle whorl hangs from each collar, carved with a representation of a silver salmon honoring the Stahlo People.

The City's original motto is preserved on a scroll above. The Coat of Arms Committee proposed the new motto to set out a new goal for the City's people.

THE CITY OF PORT MOODY

Port Moody was a creation of the Canadian Pacific Railway and was chosen as the Pacific terminus of the C.P.R. in the 1880s. This historic beginning is a principal focus of the coat of arms. The shield is white and across the centre is a broad band of black with an edge to simulate railway ties bearing two gold lines, symbolizing the railway. Above, the three Douglas fir trees represent the City's lumber industry and beautiful forest setting. At the base of the shield, the blue clipper ship recalls the early ships that brought railway iron and other supplies to the port and formed a large part of maritime-based commerce.

Above the shield, the triple towered silver coronet is the special symbol chosen by Lord Lyon to refer to a Canadian city. Above it is the silver bandtailed pigeon, one of the most beautiful local birds, emblematic of the City's natural heritage. This is also recalled by the supporters; on the left, a silver stag with gold hooves and antlers and on the right, a silver cougar. Both have maple leaf collars to honor Canada's national colors. The deer's collar has a Salish spindle whorl pendant with a salmon design, to represent the local First Nations heritage and the cougar's collar has a pendant featuring a gold railway spike. This underlines Port Moody's railway heritage celebrated annually in "Golden Spike Days". The compartment is a visual metaphor for the City's Burrard Inlet harbor framed by forested ridges.

The motto describes the City's fortune and heritage.

The shield of the arms has been featured on a series of civic flags, with fields of different colors. One of these flags is used by the City generally, the others by various departments.

CITY OF RICHMOND

The predominant colors, blue and gold, of the coat of arms for the City of Richmond were those which had already been accepted as official colors for some time. The gold of the shield referred to the rich delta lands which were the foundation of so much of Richmond's early wealth. The central wavy bar of blue symbolizes the Fraser River and the delta waters surrounding the municipality. The three salmon on the blue wavy pale represent the most common species in the waters around Richmond and also recall the community's historic and continuing association with the fishing industry.

The crest, above the helmet, is composed of two parts; a circlet of red maple leaves and dogwood flowers honoring Canada and British Columbia and a dove with a sprig of olive in its beak, an idea borrowed from the emblem of West Vancouver developed in 1936. The rising dove symbolizes the land rising from the river recalling the biblical story of Noah and referring to reclamation of delta lands by early settlers.

The supporters at either side of the shield are representations of the goddess Fortuna, bearer of prosperity and increase, often shown holding a cornucopia, as a giver of abundance. The cornucopia is a particularly important part of Richmond's symbolic heritage as it was the central element on the Township's corporate seal for decades. Its reappearance in the coat of arms underlines the long-standing importance of agriculture in Richmond's economy. The supporter on the viewer's right has a red ribbon at her neck, embroidered with white roses, a reference to the arms of Richmond in Yorkshire, the namesake of the Canadian municipality. The grassy compartment at the base of the shield which is set with blueberry bushes represents the farmlands of the community and its claim to be the blueberry capital of the world.

The motto, Child of the Fraser, is adapted from the opening line of a poem by local resident Thomas Kidd entitled "Lulu Island." The Committee felt it was an apt summary of Richmond's geographic and economic nature and, more subtly, recalled the year of the grant, which was the International Year of the Child.

THE CITY OF SURREY

For much of its history, Surrey had used the beaver as a corporate emblem. The coat of arms for Surrey was developed by a Committee of Council in 1986-1987, which chose a design that has a beaver as the central element but added many new references to the symbol, combining an interesting mix of geographic, historical and economic allusions.

It was noteworthy that green and gold representing the land and economic wealth were chosen as the dominant colors. In the shield, a gold beaver was placed at the centre, as the historic emblem of the Corporation. On either side were two wavy bars of white and blue, representing the two main rivers in the municipality, the Serpentine and Nicomekl. In the upper part of the shield, five gold stars were set, one for each of Surrey's five historic town centres. At the base of the shield was a representation of the Peace Arch monument, symbolizing Surrey's southern border at the international boundary.

The crest contained a single element, a Salish canoe, in gold, recalling the local First Nations and, particularly, their famous trading route, the Semiahmoo Trail in the southern part of Surrey near the Nicomekl.

The supporters, on the left a thoroughbred horse and on the right a farm horse, symbolize the historic recreational and agricultural role of horses in the development of Surrey and its present day amenities. The thoroughbred's steel collar and pendant feature, for the first time in heraldry, binary digits which are the basis of computer language. They, and the communications tower, salute the community's growing technological sector. The farm horse wears a collar set with ermine spots, a reference to the heraldry of Surrey's English namesake, with a pendant of a gold fir tree, to honor the community's forest landscapes. The compartment is set with a unique collection of local plants and flowers; trilliums, maidenhair ferns, easter lilies and pink fawn lilies, representing the riches of the natural environment. The motto, PROGRESS THROUGH DIVERSITY, was chosen by the Committee to refer to an optimum approach for human and economic development.

CITY OF VANCOUVER

The 1901 visit to Vancouver of the Duke of Cornwall, later King George V, sparked a desire for change in the City's symbol. The Mayor of the day, Major T.O. Townley, asked a local artist and resident of Mount Pleasant, James Blomfield, to prepare sketches.

Blomfield's design preserved nothing of the previous badge, designed by Alderman Lauchlan Hamilton, except the motto although the supporters at either side of the shield, a fisherman and lumberjack, did reflect Hamilton's feeling about important local industries. The shield (in heraldic language, Barry wavy Argent and Azure on a pile Gules a caduceus Or) was meant to represent Vancouver's magnificent harbor site and its world wide commerce. The ship's sail and mural crown in the crest, above the shield, were designed to indicate this was the emblem of a municipal government and a seaport.

Thanks to steady advocacy by former City Clerk Ronald Thompson in the 1950s and 1960s, Council decided to petition the Crown to have its emblem granted as lawful heraldry. The new arms, which were assigned by Letters Patent on 31 March 1969, issued by the heralds at the College of Arms in London, were based very heavily on the Blomfield design of 1903. Among the changes: the central "V" or pile, has become green, instead of red. On it, the caduceus of Mercury was replaced by a Kwakiutl totem pole, one of the most familiar and most dramatic of the art forms of the West Coast First Nations. The upper part of the shield was colored gold and this new area is set with two dogwood flowers. Finally, the word air was added to the motto, acknowledging the increasing role of air transport in the City's history. Overall, the representation of the symbol painted on the Patent showed a more contemporary styling for the various elements, notably the fisherman and the logger.

The coat of arms has been widely used. A fine decorative version, a sculpture by the late Elek Imredy, is displayed in the Council Chamber

THE DISTRICT OF WEST VANCOUVER

In 1936 the then Curator of the Vancouver City Museum contacted all
the municipal clerks in the region asking them to send an example of the
municipal "crest" or seal to be used in a special museum display. In the
case of West Vancouver, this request led directly to a contest to develop
a proper emblem, a competition won by Albert Bibbs. His design used
symbols evocative of the situation and natural beauty of the municipality:
birds, the sea and a ship with blue and white representing the harbor and
the sky.

West Vancouver's new coat of arms was granted by Letters Patent of
November 1, 1986. This document was presented March 15, 1987 at a
splendid ceremony on the exact anniversary of incorporation—March 15,
1912—in the auditorium of West Vancouver High School. Dr. Conrad
Swan made his third official visit to the Region as York Herald, proclaiming
the Patent in the presence of Lieutenant-Governor Robert G. Rogers. A
special highlight of the ceremony was the unveiling of a magnificent armorial sculpture in polychromed wood by local artist Dennis Sedlacek. This
sculpture is on permanent display on the east wall of the Council Chamber
in the municipal hall.

The new coat of arms is centred around the shield designed by Albert
Bibbs, with the only changes being minor embellishments of gold on the
ship. The motto also, Consilio et Animis - "By Wisdom and Courage", was
the one proposed by Bibbs as a compliment to the municipal council of
the day. Important new elements were added to the earlier emblem. The
silver cougars with their collars of fir and golden cones represent the varied fauna and flora found throughout the District. The rocky compartment
symbolizes West Vancouver's rocky shoreline with the mountain streams
flowing across it to meet the waters of Burrard Inlet. The crest blends
Bibb's circlet of maple leaves and dogwoods, an idea borrowed by at least
two other municipalities, with a heraldic pun on one of the municipality's
historic names, Holly burn, using flames and holly leaves.

CITY OF WHITE ROCK

The City Council of the City of White Rock was the first municipality in
Canada to request a grant of arms from the newly established Canadian
Heraldic Authority. When the Authority was less than two weeks old, then
Mayor Gordon Hogg submitted Council's request on June 16, 1988.

The Patent itself was completed February 16, 1992 to commemorate
the 35th anniversary of the City's incorporation April 15, 1957. This milestone anniversary was marked April 10 by a visit of Governor General
Ramon Hnatyshyn and his wife. During the visit, a special ceremony was
held at First United Church.

In the shield, blue and white, the colors of the sea and sky predominate
and the City's oceanside landmark, the great White Rock, rises above the
waters of the Bay. Above it is a Salish salmon symbolizing the riches of the
natural landscape and honoring the Semiahmoo People, the first inhabitants
of the area.

In the crest, the crown is the traditional heraldic symbol for civic government. In this case, it is ornamented with silver maple leaves and stars to
indicate White Rock's proximity to the international boundary. Above, the
gold demi-sun testifies to White Rock's mild, sunny climate and its attractions as a resort.

The supporters, a mermaid and merman, honor the men and women
who created the City as well as the spirit of the sea. The mermaid wears
a medallion featuring the masks of tragedy and comedy, as an emblem of
White Rock's cultural life and a floral crown, a symbol of the City's gardens. The merman's medallion shows a steam locomotive wheel, representing transportation heritage. At the base, the compartment is of sea
sand featuring sandcastles, representing informal recreation on the City's
magnificent beach and White Rock's legendary sandcastle competition.
Between the castles is a medallion showing the City's famous pier.

The motto, which was one of the Committee's earliest choices,
expresses important characteristics and aspirations of the City.

Whistler
Constance Brissenden

HISTORICALLY, WHISTLER IS A PLACE turned inside out. Once one of the most isolated spots north of Vancouver, it's now only two hours away by car. Once a summer resort known as Alta Lake, it's now a winter resort (although summer is again coming on strong) named after a rodent. It once offered remote wilderness for a handful of residents; now it's a mecca for more than one million skiers annually. With a permanent population of 7,000, Whistler swells to nearly 30,000 people at peak times.

The original inhabitants of the area were Coast Salish people to the south and Interior Salish to the north. They criss-crossed the area via an overland route, the basis for today's Highway 99. In 1858 Hudson's Bay Company employees J.W. Mackey and Major William Downie were the first Europeans to travel this overland route.

After the Fraser Gold Rush of 1859 subsided, some prospectors stayed on, establishing a farming community in Pemberton, north of today's Whistler Resort. By 1873 a horse trail was hand cut to Pemberton along the Pemberton Trail. Upgraded in 1877 by the B.C. government for $38,000, the route was only a metre wide along rocky cliffs. It was soon declared a failure.

In 1885 Norwegians, the first European settlers in the Squamish Valley, were flooded out. In 1888 the first homes were built in Brackendale and, in 1902, the Bracken Arms Hotel opened. Logging soon surpassed farming as the area's main industry.

Development was slow, and attracted hardy men who liked to hunt, ride and fish. Women also made their mark. Decked out in the ankle-brushing skirts of the pre-World War I era, Myrtle Philip hiked, rode and fished better than most men. Together with husband, Alex, the 22-year-old Myrtle left Vancouver in 1912 in search of untrammelled wilderness.

When the couple arrived at Alta Lake—site of present-day Whistler—there was no road and no railway. The trip began aboard the ferry *Bowena* to Squamish, then by two-horse buckboard stage to Brackendale. Hiking north, it was two days before they reached Alpha Lake and John Millar's one-room cabin. Millar, an eccentric Texas-born cowboy, put up the Philips for $1 each including room and board. Millar Creek Road in Whistler's commercial suburb, Function Junction, is named after him.

The Philips settled at Alta Lake, 1.5 kilometres north, the highest lake in the valley. In 1914 they opened Rainbow Lodge,

soon recognized as the most popular summer resort west of the Rockies. Along with the lodge, Myrtle ran a general store for more than 30 years before retiring. Husband Alex was noted for his romance novels.

Sadly, Rainbow Lodge was destroyed by fire in 1978. Myrtle (1890-1985) remained active in the community. The Myrtle Philip Elementary School and Myrtle Philip Recreation Centre are named in her honor.

Until the early 1960s Whistler Resort was the dream of a few. Back country cabins marked the small community of Alta Lake, where condos and resort homes now crowd. Only the most devoted made the arduous seven-hour journey over rugged B.C. Hydro access roads. The area had its first paved road in 1964, 50 years after the Pacific Great Eastern Railway (now BC Rail) blasted its way through.

The resort was born in 1965, when the first lift was introduced on London Mountain. Lacking the zing of a Vail or Aspen, the name was soon changed to Whistler Mountain, inspired by the whistler marmot that frequents its rocky outcrops. Inaugural ski runs at Whistler Creek opened in 1965, built by the Garibaldi Lift Company, later renamed the Whistler Mountain Ski Corporation. Franz's Run, named after founder and first president Franz Wilhelmsen, still exists.

Investors originally planned to develop the north side of the mountain with gondola and facilities, where Whistler Village is today. Mineral claims forced the lift company to develop Whistler Creek on the west side instead.

At the site of today's Whistler Village, a dump existed, visited primarily by black bears. Bears are still numerous in the area, and are often relocated or shot when their numbers grow too large.

By the 1970s line-ups of 500 skiers, queuing for hours at the lifts, were commonplace. Whistler was a haphazard place, with shacks patched together to accommodate ski fanatics. Soon modern pioneers like Al Raine, former head coach of Canada's ski team and husband of Olympic gold medallist Nancy Greene, pointed out the obvious: Whistler was heading for disaster without a long-term development plan.

The plan was soon a reality. The Resort Municipality of Whistler, British Columbia's first and only resort designation, complete with a long-term planning vision, was created in 1975.

The north side of Whistler Mountain, as well as Blackcomb Mountain, opened in 1980. Two friendly rivals, the Whistler Mountain Ski Corporation and Intrawest Development Corporation (which manages Blackcomb Mountain), now compete for skiers.

Since 1975 more than $1.5 billion has been invested in the

development of Whistler Resort. Intrawest has invested more than $70 million in Blackcomb Mountain amenities since 1986. In 1992 Nippon Cable purchased a 23 per cent interest in Whistler Mountain for $25 million. Also in 1992 Whistler Mountain Ski Corporation invested $600,000 in trail development, removing 40,000 cubic metres of rock. Five kilometres of new trails resulted, serviced by Redline chair on Whistler Creek. Further development included high-speed gondola systems for both mountains.

The payoff? Whistler Resort is consistently ranked the number one ski resort in North America.

In addition to Whistler Village (opened in 1980), with its hotels, restaurants, pubs, shops, Whistler Conference Centre, banks and tour companies, a second adjacent "village" is now being built. Whistler North began construction in 1993. It will take 10 years to complete expansion of the 60-acre site with condominiums, shops, grocery, liquor store, medical clinic, library, chapel, two hotels, three lodges, offices and recreation cultural centre.

In 1982 work was begun on Blackcomb Benchlands, the area around the base of Blackcomb Mountain. It is now a mix of hotels, shops, restaurants, condominiums and golf course. The Black Market, centred in and around Chateau Whistler and the base of Blackcomb Mountain, is Blackcomb Benchlands' shopping area.

Whistler has more than a dozen residential "neighborhoods," including Alta Lake Road, Bayshores, Whistler Creek, Whistler Highlands, Nordic Estates, Alta Vista, Blueberry Hill, Brio, Whistler Village, Whistler Village North, Blackcomb Benchlands, Horstman Estates, White Gold Estates, Nesters Square, Whistler Cay, Alpine Meadows and Emerald Estates.

With the growth of the year-round population, schools, recreation complexes, medical, fire, library and postal services have been added. Given its proximity to Vancouver, the pressures of year-round residency are already adding to the stresses of development and tourism.

Also important to the community is Function Junction, a retail/industrial area three kilometres south of Whistler. Taking advantage of its proximity to the Village, Function Junction offers everything from cappuccinos to Canadiana furniture to cellular telephone sales and leasing.

Whistler Resort attracted more than 1.3 million visitors in the 1993/94 year—590,000 visitors in summer 1993 and 715,000 visitors in winter 1993-94. It generated $440 million in tourist expenditures, making it third only to Vancouver and Victoria in terms of expenditures generated by a provincial tourism destination.

Chateau Whistler, 1990. vs

With the most ski in/ski out accommodations of any mountain recreation resort in North America, it has 16,800 bed units situated within 365 metres of the lifts. Ski in/ski out accommodation represents more than 52 per cent of all existing bed units within the boundaries of the Resort Municipality of Whistler.

With 32,000 bed units now developed, the resort has reached 61 per cent of total construction levels approved by the 1988 Comprehensive Development Plan. As of 1995, more than 20,000 bed units remain undeveloped within municipal boundaries.

Active advertising campaigns over the past decade have also made Whistler an increasingly popular summer destination.

Total 1994 summer season accommodation occupancies moved to an average of 54 per cent, a growth of seven percentage points over the record 1993 summer season levels. Peak season occupancy (July 1-August 31, 1994) grew to an average of 73 per cent, a nine per cent gain over 1993 peak season levels. These record summer occupancy levels resulted in the generation of more than 235,000 room nights.

Whistler is now in the midst of a construction boom that some feel is turning the resort into a skiers' Disneyworld. Its very success is forcing the resort to face a host of tough issues—from labor and housing shortages to crime control and the provision of adequate community amenities. At the top of the list is the urgent necessity to provide adequate, affordable housing for its thousands of minimum-wage seasonal workers. How it handles this and other issues will determine its continued popularity and prosperity.

Lions Bay
Max Wyman

FROM ITS BEGINNINGS IN 1956 as little more than a developer's pipe-dream, Lions Bay has survived bankruptcy, hurricanes and devastating debris torrents to celebrate, in 1996, 25 years as the GVRD's smallest and most dramatically sited municipality.

Nestled in a steeply raked bowl of second-growth forest, overlooking Howe Sound and overlooked by the majestic twin peaks of The Lions, the village (480 homes, population approximately 1,500 in late 1995) is located 11 kilometres north of Horseshoe Bay.

When North Vancouver resident R.A. (Bob) Nelson purchased the land in 1956, Lions Bay was accessible only by water. The community consisted of a few summer cottages and an open space known as St. Mark's picnic grounds. But Nelson's dream of a complete residential community coincided with the extension of the Pacific Great Eastern (today BC Rail) line from West Vancouver to Squamish in 1956 and the construction of the Seaview (today Sea-to-Sky) Highway two years later. Lots in the first subdivision went on sale in January 1958, and construction of the first home in Lions Bay was begun by Charles and Mary Coltart that spring; they needed a special permit to transport building materials over the unfinished highway. Situated on the waterfront, the house was a cathedral-ceiling, modernist structure of cedar and glass that set the tone for much of the later architecture in the village.

In 1959 a property owners' association was formed, while Nelson looked after garbage collection, water supply and maintenance. However, in October 1962 eight homes in the fledgling community were damaged when Typhoon Freda tore through the Sound, and lot sales slowed so much between 1962 and 1965 that the development went into receivership.

Slowly, however, the community took on the accoutrements of a municipality. In 1966 the Lions Bay Water Improvement District was created, an umbrella agency that not only collected and distributed the water from the mountainside but also dealt with garbage, recreational facilities and fire protection. When a massive flood in Harvey Creek severely damaged creekside homes in September 1969, a report commissioned by the Improvement District and Dawson Developments (which had taken over from Nelson) discovered that the primary causes of the flood were abnormally heavy rainfall, a land slippage that had dammed the creek and inadequate construction and maintenance of logging roads. In response to a demand from the Improvement District, all logging licences in the Harvey Creek basin area were subsequently cancelled. In 1970 a fire that destroyed a village home prompted the Lions Bay Property Owners' Association to acquire a fire truck (staffed by the newly created Lions Bay Volunteer Fire Department).

Late in 1970 a plebiscite on incorporation drew more than the requisite 60 per cent majority from the 250 residents, and in the spring of 1971 Lions Bay became a village municipality. Some members of the GVRD board felt such a small community should not be allowed one of only 57 GVRD votes.

However, it was a significant step ahead for Lions Bay. To qualify as a municipality, it needed a village address, so in 1971 a village complex was built: fire hall, fire truck storage, a council room, village office, kitchen and community hall-cum-gym. Allan (Curly) Stewart was elected mayor by acclamation, and villagers elected their first four-member council.

The change in status marked a new spurt of growth. The Lions Bay Store was established in 1971, and a year later a post office was opened. New home starts increased dramatically, and in 1977 Lions Bay Elementary School (covering playschool, kindergarten and grades one to three) was opened. The same year, Lions Bay Cablevision brought full cable TV service, and the provincial government provided an ambulance on permanent service in the village. The last large parcel of land was rezoned in 1981 into 100 single-family lots, and a bus service linking Lions Bay with the rest of the Lower Mainland was introduced in 1987.

The village's location on the steep mountainside leaves it prone to natural disaster. In 1983 two teenage boys died and five homes were destroyed or damaged when a debris torrent poured tons of mud and logs down Alberta Creek. The creek was subsequently channelized with a concrete lining. Floods and mudslides from time to time create delays and closures on the Sea-to-Sky Highway.

However, for many residents these disadvantages are more than counterbalanced by the quality of life. A solid infrastructure of well-organized and maintained public works, along with fire and ambulance services augmented by a highly skilled search and rescue team, underpins a close and thriving social scene based on volunteer involvement in a host of community activities. Volunteerism is at the essence of Lions Bay's success as a community. In 1972 Lions Bay was one of the first villages in British Columbia to formulate a community plan built on resident input, and that process of community consultation has been maintained—nowhere more visibly than in the lengthy, community-wide preparations for celebrating and commemorating the 25th anniversary in 1996.

Bowen Island
Peter Broronkay

The steamer Lady Alexandra *passing Point Atkinson, West Vancouver on the way to Bowen Island, circa 1925.* vp

AN IMPOSING ROCKY intrusion stands guard at the entrance to Howe Sound. Here grew 1,000-year-old western red cedars before colonial settlement in the late 19th century. Cougars ran wild, while the fiord was graced by humpback whales. The first known human inhabitants were the Salish and Squamish peoples who used the island as a meeting place. The Squamish named the island Xwlil xhwm, meaning "fast drumming ground." In 1794 the Spanish became the first Europeans to sail by the island's rocky coastline, when Narvaez named it the Isle of Apodaca after Sebastian Ruiz de Apodaca (1754–1835), a Spanish aristocrat, naval officer and colonial administrator. Subsequently it was renamed after Rear-Admiral James Bowen (1751–1835) by Captain George Henry Richards in 1860. Bowen never visited the island. The honor was in recognition of his wartime efforts in defeating a French fleet on June 1, 1794, while serving Admiral Howe.

The first recorded non-native settler on Bowen was Charlie Dagget, a logger who moved from Point Grey in 1872. Within 30 years, Bowen supported agriculture, fishing, logging, shingle manufacturing and dynamite production. The dynamite plant was located at present-day Tunstall Bay due to its remote but accessible location from the sound. This precaution was warranted as there was a series of fatal explosions, one of which was powerful enough to be felt 40 kilometres away in Nanaimo. Today the dynamite plant's brick fireplace base still stands along the beach. Mannion Bay contributed to the economic activity on the island, with abundant clay deposits for use in high-quality bricks needed for the active construction industry in Vancouver. This bay was also a resting spot for whaling ships that operated until virtually all humpbacks were slaughtered in the sound by 1907. Later, brick and dynamite production gave way to recreational activities, while logging and agriculture remain to this day on a smaller scale.

Beginning in 1900, the vision of Captain John A. Cates transformed Bowen Island into a picnic destination for Vancouverites. Cates loved Bowen Island and wanted others to see and experience the beauty of the place. His efforts made Bowen Island a resort destination for decades. The Cates family was also responsible for the construction of the *Britannia,* the ship that brought many thousands of visitors to the island.

Hundreds of people would arrive in Snug Cove, where they could find "ample shade in the deep woods." Under Captain Cates' direction, 300 fruit trees were planted and infrastructure put in place for the tourists. Promotional literature stated "where can we go to get out of the heat? Go to Bowen Island, where there is a cool sea breeze, fine shady trees, good water, good bathing and one of the finest cafes on the coast.

Cates expanded the attractions to include a hotel renowned for its clay tennis courts, tournaments and lawn bowling. These new amenities were enjoyed at the end of World War I by many reunited families.

In 1920 Captain Cates sold the business to the Union Steamship Company of B.C., and moved to the province's Interior. However, his love of the area caused him to return in 1924 to construct a house and run a hotel at Crescent Beach.

The Union Steamship Company took over the promotion of tourism to the island and their brochures stated that "it's just fourteen miles to this lovely isle, with its shady beaches, grassy slopes, wooded trails and mountains—where the Spirit of Recreation reigns supreme." Under the Union's direction, a dance pavilion with a capacity of 800 people was added in 1921, and it became an integral part of the "Happy Isle" activities. Three years later, *Lady Alexandra* became the star of ships sailing to Bowen, as it allowed for 1,400 passengers to cruise and dance all the way from Vancouver to Snug Cove. Visitors mostly boarded in downtown Vancouver, as the road to Horseshoe Bay was not opened until 1928.

The village of Snug Cove developed under the steamship company's direction, and in 1941 a Canadian Pacific Railway subsidiary purchased a controlling share of the Union and determined policy for the next 14 years.

Visitors to the island continued to increase until 1946, reaching a record of 101,000, but the peak was followed by a downturn. The decline may have been because of the preference of Vancouverites to go automobile cruising, increased costs or the failed attempt at creating the "Evergreen Park Resort." This planned resort in 1956 was to make Bowen Island "one of North America s most luxurious resorts," but the proposal was met with scepticism by island residents. Rules were changed so that boaters were able to land at the Union wharf only if they dined at the Union hotel. An imposing gate was erected at the entrance to the Union's road that gave a sense of exclusiveness that was not in line with the residents' community spirit. By this time the merry Saturday night cruises belonged to a bygone era, and the dance pavilion was closed. Also the beautiful monkey puzzle tree on the Bowen Inn grounds was chopped down on instructions from Union management, which to this day remains a sore point among long-time residents of the island.

Eventually in the late 1950s and early 1960s, the resort buildings were dismantled, and the resort properties along with the picnic and camping grounds were subdivided and sold as residential lots. The island's growing population was rewarded in 1983 by a GVRD initiative that created Crippen Regional Park out of the remaining 259 hectares of the old Union Steamship property. Glen Crippen was a senior consulting engineer who owned the property before the GVRD purchase.

The new residential subdivisions and the growth of Vancouver contributed to the increase in island population. By 1996 the population was estimated at close to 2,500, with a surge during summer cottage months that increases the total to more than 4,000. Residents have a strong community spirit that is likely strengthened by the geography and social interaction between ferry commuters. Wildlife still abounds on the island, including deer, bald eagles and heron. In 1995 a black bear happily swam to the island but his holiday was cut short when he was caught, transported and released off the Coquihalla Highway.

In recent political history, the island turned down a 1991 referendum on municipal status. The island remains unincorporated and under the jurisdiction of the GVRD. There is now renewed interest in a referendum on the same issue. Administration also falls under the provincial government body, The Islands Trust, that has a mandate "to preserve and protect" the island. The Official Community Plan attempts to control future growth and pegs the population ceiling at 7,200, which may be reached when the allowable building areas are developed. Probably half the non-retired adults on the island commute to work in the Lower Mainland.

The nature of recreational activity on the island has been transformed over the years but remains an important part of the island way of life. Outdoor opportunities in Crippen Regional Park allow for hiking trails in varying ecosystems, and non-motorized boating on Killarney Lake. Hikers may also traverse Crown land to Mount Gardner to enjoy the panoramic view of Georgia Strait. Privacy may be found at Apodaca Provincial Park, a secluded waterfront lot accessible by boat. Popular public beaches are located in Mannion Bay and Bowen Bay, while two marinas at Snug Cove cater to the water sport enthusiasts. Bowen Island Tours maintains a link with the island's past by organizing day trips that include hiking, a picnic lunch, optional kayaking and a cottage brewery tour.

BOWEN ISLAND FACTS • Population near 2,500 in 1996. • 5,260 hectares, with 37 kilometers of coastline. • Mount Gardner is the highest peak at 719 metres. • Ferry crossing takes 20 minutes from Horseshoe Bay. BC Ferries operate between 5:45 A.M. and 9:45 P.M. with additional services of a private taxi boat to 11:30 P.M., except Saturday and Sunday to 12:30 A.M. • Housing is mainly detached single family, with a country cottage atmosphere. • The elementary educational system in Snug Cove is part of the West Vancouver School District. High school students either commute to West Vancouver, or take part in a new private initiative—the Island Pacific School—with emphasis on outdoor pursuits for grades seven to nine. • 911 activates an emergency response including an on-island ambulance service, a taxi boat to Horseshoe Bay and a waiting ambulance for transport to Lions Gate Hospital in North Vancouver. • Other facilities include an RCMP detachment, a volunteer fire department and a library affiliated with West Vancouver's Memorial Library.

facing page: Bowen Island, 1954. vp

West Vancouver
Kerry McPhedran

Y OU HAVE TO LOVE a community that routinely serves draft beer in a pie bakery, cappuccino by the library's fireplace and pancakes in the Hollyburn Funeral Home's parking lot every June for the Community Day Pancake Breakfast. Flapjacks to die for.

Yet West Van, as locals call their village-minded corridor community that stretches along 28 kilometres of shoreline and up the south slopes of the 100-million-year-old Coast Mountains, is missed by most tourists, who veer off onto the Upper Levels Highway bound for Whistler or the Horseshoe Bay ferry terminal.

This is ironic. For although the Spanish explorer José Maria Narvaez and Captain George Vancouver also sailed right by in 1791 and 1792, West Vancouver really began as a popular summer holiday destination.

From the 1880s to the 1900s men and women canoed and eventually ferried across from Vancouver to picnic or camp in the fresh air upwind from what was literally "the Big Smoke" in those early land-clearing and logging days. Every May to September a "tent city" sprang up along the shore from present-day Ambleside village to 23rd Street.

By 1886 smart speculators had already bought up most of future West Vancouver. James Blake preempted the first 65 hectares in 1872. A succession of firsts quickly followed. In 1873 the first white resident, Navvy Jack Thomas, a Welsh deserter from the Royal Navy, and his wife Row-i-a (grandaughter of Chief Ki-ep-i-lan-o after whom the Capilano River was named) moved in. Their house still stands in Ambleside. It is the oldest continuously inhabited residence in the Lower Mainland. In 1874 the first lighthouse was built at Point Atkinson.

By 1912 the place was humming, thanks to a regular ferry service that started in 1909, triggering a small real estate boom and relieving many families from the grim row across the treacherous tides of First Narrows to attend church in Vancouver. Waterfront lots in what was then called "West Capilano" went for $4,500; others for as little as $450. The District of West Vancouver was incorporated on March 15, 1912.

From that seaside hamlet with a 1912 summer population of around 1,500, West Vancouver has grown to a municipality of nearly 42,000. A curious mix of old summer cottages, modest homes and multimillion-dollar waterfront estates, West Vancouver has no industry and no tourist attractions beyond the

The restored Lawson House, West Vancouver, 1994. vs

Park Royal Hotel and those that drew the first tourists: beaches, forests, mountain trails and ski slopes.

West Vancouver's largest source of revenue is property taxes and its biggest business is the municipality itself. West Van has its own police force and its own beloved "Blue Bus" system—as of February, 1996, the first transit system in Canada to be totally wheelchair-accessible. With 27 per cent of the population over 60 (a 54 per cent increase in the past 10 years), this is good thinking.

West Vancouverites can also lay claim to reading more library books and earning more per capita than any other Canadians. They spend a chunk of it in Canada's first shopping mall, Park Royal, built in 1950 on lands leased from Squamish Indian Reserve No. 5. (The December, 1996 winning of more than $13 million in the 6/49 lottery by restaurateur Gary Troll will raise that per capita figure even higher!)

The *Vancouver Sun*'s award-winning editorial cartoonist Len Norris delighted in spoofing West Van's slope-side living. A resident himself, Norris drew genteel West Vancouverites (who conveniently peopled such real places as Tiddley Cove) gardening with one leg shorter than the other or grumbling about the Pacific Great Eastern Railway (now BC Rail)—the initials PGE corrupted to mean "Past God's Endurance."

Long before the PGE first connected North and West Van on New Year's Day, 1914, the earliest known settlement was a Coast Salish village at Sandy Cove. Europeans settled in their own string of small, self-contained west-to-east communities. Ambleside commemorates its "father of West Vancouver" in John Lawson Park. Dundarave was named for the Scottish home of R.E. Macnaghten (and the streets named for British prime ministers).

Caulfeild owes its bucolic setting and spelling to Francis William Caulfeild, an English gentleman and scholar who laid out the village "according to the contours of nature," including the paths of wild animals and cows. Now only a street, Belle-vue was once a subdivision adjoining Dundarave. Dubbed "Vancouver's premier suburb," Bellevue's ads promised "A lot in Bellevue is a joy forever; two lots is rapture."

Further west Colonel Albert Whyte pressed for the 1914 spelling change from White Cliff City to Whytecliff. Only a few families lived in Horseshoe Bay year-round until Dan Sewell arrived in 1931 and opened his marina and the Whyte-cliff Lodge. (Electricity had arrived in 1922; direct telephone to Vancouver in 1928. But by 1930 only 48 of West Van's 100 kilo-metres of road were paved. Many streets still lack sidewalks and longtime residents prefer it that way.)

In 1926 West Van's council lowered the boom on what little logging and fish canning remained. The 1926 town planning act banned any new industry, opting for an exclusively resi-dential municipality with minimum lot sizes. (The Millerd family ran the Great Northern Cannery, built in 1891, until 1967. It is now the site of Enviroment Canada's Pacific Research Laboratories.)

West Van's new policy ultimately saved its goose. It caught the eye of Ireland's wealthy Guinness family during the Depression. The Guinness' British Pacific Syndicate paid less than $50 a hectare for 1,600 scenic hectares on Hollyburn Ridge to develop as the prestigious British Properties around the Capilano Golf and Country Club.

In 1938 they built the $6 million Lions Gate Bridge in order to increase lot sales. (Fifty years after the start of construction Guiness would add lights as an Expo 86 gift.) The familiar British slogan "Guinness is good for you" could well have become West Van's civic motto. King George VI and Queen Elizabeth drove across in 1939 to officially open the British Empire's longest suspension bridge. By 1947 the ferries had stopped. The little 1913 ferry building became a bus depot, then a community gallery.

It was individual houses that ultimately put West Van on the map. From 1945 to 1975 West Vancouver was a centre of award-winning Canadian residential design (inspired by the natural landscape) that culminated in the approach recognized as the West Coast Style. There are literally hundreds of modern hous-es by such designers and architects as C.B.K. Van Norman, John Porter, Ned Pratt, Arthur Erickson, Fred Hollingsworth and Ron Thom.

In 1959 rezoning of some 20 hectares permitted 78 high-den-sity apartments in Ambleside. The Crescent Apartments (1961) was West Van's first highrise condominium. Some along the waterfront—notably Villa Maris, aka the "Pink Palace"—are in Miami pastels.

West Van is changing. New neigborhoods have spread across the so-called "Land Above the Upper Levels." West Van's beloved 15-block seawall connects lively Ambleside and two-block long Dundarave, the latter still crowned by the British Properties—once exclusive to the point of racism but now pep-pered with the Mandarin, Cantonese, German and Iranian accents of new residents.

There are still familiar landmarks of West Van's heritage, many listed in the *West Vancouver Heritage Inventory.* Among them: Caulfeild's charming St. Francis-in-the-Woods Anglican Church (with Willian Morris windows) and Gertrude Lawson's house (now the West Vancouver Museum and Archives), built of stone carried as ship's ballast from New Zealand.

Other bits of West Van's history survive. Chief Joe Capilano, who travelled to London in 1906 to discuss Indian land rights with King Edward VII, overlooks Park Royal from his Keith Road mausoleum. A grove of eight apple trees and one cherry tree near the sixth hole of Gleneagles Golf Course are remnants of the Peter Larson Ranch. The leafy canopy of horse chestnut trees on 17th Street was planted in 1934 by Boy Scouts to com-memorate the visit of Lord Baden-Powell.

Best of all, enthusiastic residents still exercise a pioneer sense of fun. Each year they head like happy lemmings for both the Capilano River Duck Race that sends 30,000 yellow rubber duckies bobbing down the Capilano for charity, and the Coho Festival, which celebrates the return of the salmon that spawn up the same river. They fish and stroll the three ferry-less piers.

Citizenry block off Marine Drive at the drop of a hat—and do so for the August Dundarave Hoe Down, June's Commu-nity Day Parade and on Remembrance Day. Veterans march, Harvards fly overhead, the band plays, tears are shed, wreaths laid and tea and cookies served in the library for all. Around that stone memorial, as Bruce Ramsey notes in A *Place of Excellence,* his chronicle of West Vancouver, have stood medal-bedecked men who saw service in Canada's Northwest Rebel-lion, India's Northwest Frontier, the Zulu campaigns leading to the Boer War, World War I and World War II, as well as Korea, the Suez, Vietnam, Cyprus and Bosnia. For all the changes West Vancouver is still a good place to return home to.

North Vancouver City
Hilary Blair

IT WAS CALLED the "Ambitious City" during its first few years. Property owners in North Vancouver's lower Lonsdale area, who felt they had little in common with the farmers and loggers of Capilano and Lynn Valley, decided their interests would be better served by incorporation as a city, which duly took place on May 13, 1907. When the 1,012-hectare North Vancouver City was carved out of the surrounding district, it had almost 2,000 residents and possessed 53 businesses, a bank, two hotels and a school. It also took with it the municipal hall, the water system, the ferry and equipment for fire-fighting and road-making. In return it paid some of the district's outstanding liabilities. The following year a tiny six-bed hospital opened at St. Andrews and 15th; three blocks farther east Grand Boulevard was laid out and an exclusive residential area planned.

The unofficial community centre in those days was Peter Larson's Hotel North Vancouver, built in 1902 on beachfront property just west of Lonsdale. As well as entertaining Vancouver's elite for Sunday afternoon socials, its grounds were the site for July 1st celebrations. Large crowds gathered, including many from across the Inlet, to watch foot races, bronco busting and canoe races against local native teams. The highlight was watching a trapeze artist parachute to safety from a hot-air balloon. The festivities ended, then as now, with an off-shore fireworks display. Larson's pavilion was used for dances, concerts and political meetings, and in 1909 the first motion picture theatre in North Vancouver opened there.

By 1910 there were 5,000 residents, a board of trade, a high school—and land prices had soared. In 1911 Wallace's Shipyard and McDougall-Jenkins Engineers (later North Shore Iron Works) both had a part in building *Ferry No. 3,* the first self-propelled boat of any size to be launched in North Vancouver. By then Charles Cates had expanded his cargo-handling wharf into a boat repair facility and added a sawmill, and his tug and piledriver were in constant use. C.H. Cates and Sons is presently one of only two Port of Vancouver businesses to own its own land (the other is B.C. Sugar). There were at least 12 lumber and shingle companies operating in the city and district by 1911.

Commercial and retail businesses in lower Lonsdale kept pace with industry. Real estate, insurance and banking were strongly represented, reflecting North Vancouver's interest in land development. By 1914 Paine Hardware had moved to its present location at 90 Lonsdale. There were medical and postal services, and a local newspaper, which shared a building with McMillan's grocery. In 1915 the 255 hectares of Moodyville joined the city, which then took on its present shape.

The number of recreational opportunities in the city also increased. In 1911 the North Vancouver tennis club held its first tournament at 23rd and Lonsdale, and farther down Lonsdale a theatre was opened. The St. Andrews and Caledonian Society had already started a Scottish Country Dance group and sponsored a Burns Supper, and local boy scouts had received a visit from Major-General Baden-Powell. The North Vancouver beaches were an attraction for Vancouver residents, but the burgeoning summer tent colony, which stretched from Moodyville to St. Paul's Mission Church, became a health concern for city council. Another draw for picnickers was the Pacific Great Eastern rail service, which, by mid-1914, extended as far as Whytecliff station in West Vancouver.

The ambitious building boom of the early days was curtailed by the general financial depression of 1913. Then came World War I, and Wallace Shipyards and North Shore Iron Works were given contracts to manufacture high-explosive shells. It was a harbinger of things to come. During both world wars the North Vancouver waterfront was a hive of industrial activity, vital to the war effort. In 1917 Wallace's launched the *Mabel Brown* and five other steel-reinforced wooden ships. It also built three steel steam-powered freighters; *War Dog* was the first such ship built in Canada. Lyall Shipyards, newly established nearby, built wooden ships throughout World War I.

Despite a certain prosperity brought by the war, North Vancouver City was not immune to the worldwide post-war social unrest. There was a rash of strikes by shipyard workers and streetcar and postal workers even before the war's end, and in 1920 Fire Chief Sparks and his entire force struck—and were dismissed. Nor was the city insulated from the 1918 influenza epidemic, which closed schools and public places.

The years between the wars saw big changes along the whole North Vancouver waterfront and recreational use was virtually squeezed out. Many businesses turned to the export trade as the potential of the Panama Canal was realized. Grain elevators were built close to the site of Sewell Moody's wharf. In addition to shipbuilding and repairs, there were lumber and shingle mills, log-booming grounds, oil refineries, a fish cannery and, tucked in among them, the local yacht club and a sea scout base. During this period Wallace Shipyards became Burrard Dry Dock, having acquired the first floating dry-dock on the Pacific Coast. It built the *Princess Louise* for the Canadian Pacific Railway and the *St. Roch* for the RCMP.

But the seeming prosperity of the 1920s rested on a fragile

The City of North Vancouver was incorporated in 1907 as a 13-square-kilometre area surrounding the commercial district on Lonsdale Avenue. Today the city economy no longer relies on logging but on tourism, high technology, retail businesses, a growing film industry and waterfront industries like shipbuilding and towing. As the heart of North Vancouver, the city offers residents convenient access to downtown culture, a beautiful harbor setting and a doorway to the super natural wilderness behind.

Indian Reserve, North Vancouver, 1888, showing the original St. Paul's Church. CVA

base. The Great Depression saw the city follow the district into receivership in 1933, from which the city only emerged in 1944. Inflated real estate values, excessive borrowing, heavy investment in the failed bridge company and falling export prices due to poor world economic conditions were cited. Although the district and city were run by the same commissioner, there was no attempt to amalgamate the two.

Despite wartime privations, World War II initiated an industrial boom for the city. Unemployment was a thing of the past, and thousands of workers from all walks of life, and from all over the West, were quickly turned into efficient shipbuilding workforces by the application of mass production techniques. Burrard Dry Dock built mostly cargo ships to supply war-torn Europe and established another yard on the south side of the Inlet. At its peak it was building eight 10,000-ton cargo ships at the same time, and employing 13,000 workers, eight per cent of them women. Lower Mainland shipyards, working round the clock, built more than half the ships that Canada supplied to the war effort.

The 1950s and 1960s were a time of suburban growth and reconstruction, aided, in part, by easy access over the new Second Narrows Bridge. The 1951 census showed the city's population at more than 15,000, and housing starts took off. Clarence Wallace (son of the Wallace Shipyard's founder) was now lieutenant-governor. In 1957 the Upper Levels Highway was completed, forging high-speed road links from the city in an east-west direction—while at the other end of the municipality, the PGE Railway was finally completed to northern B.C. The war had challenged many prejudices, in the city as elsewhere in Canada, and in 1959 more than a thousand people attended the funeral, at St. Paul's Indian Catholic Church, of Squamish native leader Andy Paull, who had been honored by

the Pope for his contribution to the Church and the native peoples of Canada. The North Vancouver Recreation Centre at 23rd and Lonsdale opened in 1966—a jointly funded Centennial project by the city and district.

In the post-war period Burrard Dry Dock modernized and acquired other shipyards, becoming the largest on Canada's west coast. It went through a number of name changes, pioneered the construction of self-unloading log barges, refitted cruise ships and the BC Ferries fleet, as well as launching icebreaker *Terry Fox* in 1983. But by that time shipbuilding was in the doldrums and, in 1992, just short of its 100th anniversary, Versatile Pacific (as it was then called) laid off its last North Vancouver workers.

Although the city's once thriving shipbuilding industry was in decline, the Port of Vancouver had become the busiest on the Pacific Coast. In 1977 the Seabus had opened, joining the city to Vancouver by ferry once more. Also in the seventies was the inaugural run of the refurbished *Royal Hudson* passenger train and the old Central School/municipal hall opened as Presentation House, with a museum, archives, a gallery and theatre space. Lower Lonsdale was renovated with Lonsdale Quay and Waterfront Park completed in time to welcome Expo 86 visitors. At the eastern end of the city the North Shore Studios opened in the late eighties and the municipality also became home to many high-tech companies.

The residential community lives and plays around the commercial and industrial heartland of North Vancouver City, which also continues to be a bedroom suburb of Vancouver. Events throughout the year encourage a community spirit, and those at Waterfront Park recall a bygone era, when, almost on the same spot, Peter Larson's hotel played host to city residents and visitors alike.

District of North Vancouver
Chuck Davis

THE FIRST LOCAL PEOPLE to greet Captain Vancouver when he entered Burrard Inlet lived on the North Shore. "We passed the situation," Vancouver later wrote, "whence the Indians had first visited us the preceding day, which was a small border of low marshy land on the northern shore, intersected by several creeks of fresh water . . . Most of their canoes were hauled up into the creeks . . . None of their habitations could be discovered, whence we concluded that their village was within the forest."

Seventy years were to pass before the Inlet's people were to see white men again, but when they came in 1862 they came to stay. Contractors T.W. Graham and George Scrimgeour pre-empted land for a sawmill on the north shore of the Inlet more than six kilometres east of First Narrows. They immediately began to build Pioneer Mills, the first industrial plant on Burrard Inlet. Water to power the mill was got from Lynn Creek, more than three kilometres distant, and logs were hauled in by oxen. Cedar trees in Lynn Valley were magnificent, among the largest in the world. They were cut and sent flying down to the harbor in huge flumes. In December 1863, five months after it began, and facing relentless competition from mills closer to its markets (New Westminster and Vancouver Island), Pioneer Mills—along with a million feet of cut timber lying in the nearby woods—was up for sale. The next owner, John Oscar Smith, a New Westminster grocer, had no better success and sold the plant (which he'd renamed Burrard Inlet Mills) in January 1865. Smith accomplished something of historical note during his ownership: on November 9, 1864, he oversaw the first international shipment of goods out of Burrard Inlet: 277,500 feet of lumber to Adelaide, Australia.

The man who bought the mill from Smith was Sewell Prescott Moody, a Maine-born American and a seasoned lumberman. He was a tough and able administrator, and made an immediate change in the mill's fortunes. (There was another change, too: the area around the mill began to be called Moodyville. Moody himself went to live in Victoria.) Renaming the operation Burrard Inlet Lumber Mills, he began to ship wood out in greater and greater quantities. "By God, he was a good lumberman," a contemporary noted. "Kind of a tall, lanky sort of a guy. He would go through the woods like a blooming deer. But a teetotaler. No booze in Moodyville. The guys would have to go over to Gassy Jack's in Gastown . . ." Tragedy struck in 1875 when "Sue" Moody left for a trip to San Francisco

aboard SS *Pacific*. Off Cape Flattery the *Pacific* struck another vessel and sank. Moody was among those drowned. A piece of the ship's wreckage, on which Moody had scrawled his name and the message "All lost" washed up weeks later on the shore in Victoria within sight of his home. The mill carried on without its dynamic boss, finally closing in 1901.

In his diary for June 19, 1865, the Rev. Ebenezer Robson, a New Westminster Methodist minister, noted: "Rode out to Burrard Inlet, and crossing over in a canoe preached to 15 persons at Moody and Co.'s mills after supper; good attention and invitation to come again . . . This was the first sermon on the inlet." The Inlet's first marriage was performed July 18, 1868, when Ada Young was married to Peter Plant in a ceremony performed by the Rev. Edward White.

Communication between the two shores of the inlet was maintained by a succession of ferries, although "ferry" is perhaps too imposing a word for Navvy Jack's rowboat. In 1866 Jack, a gravel merchant, began to row people across the Inlet for a small fee. You could shout across the water to fetch him.

With the North Shore's population increasing, a group of locals got together to apply to the provincial government to incorporate, and on August 10, 1891, the District of North Vancouver was born. The first meeting of the municipal council (with Reeve C.J.P. Phibbs presiding) took place 19 days later in councillor Tom Turner's house near the foot of Lonsdale. The petitioners had hoped to include Moodyville within the new municipality, but the mill's executives refused. Even so, the district was huge: it stretched along the North Shore all the way from Horseshoe Bay to Deep Cove. The population was sparse, a few hundred.

More substantial craft than Navvy Jack's rowboat had begun providing cross-Inlet travel, and by 1900 a scheduled service began with a new vessel, the *North Vancouver*, built expressly for the job. Many of the passengers were heading for scenic hikes or skiing on Grouse Mountain, or a scary stroll across the Capilano Suspension Bridge. Detailed descriptions of the interesting years of ferry service on the Inlet—so important to the history of the district—can be found in two books, *Ferry Across the Inlet*, by former master James Barr, and the informal *Echoes of the Ferries*, by J. Rodger Burnes. *North Vancouver Ferry No. 5* is around to this day as the Seven Seas Restaurant. (By the time the fondly recalled ferry service ended on August 30, 1958, more than 112 million passengers had been carried.)

The *No. 5* was one of many vessels built at Wallace Shipyards, which quickly became a prominent industrial centre on the North Shore. But this prize, begun in 1903 by English-born

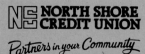

Lumber ships, Moodyville, 1872. cva

Alfred Wallace, was later lost when residents and merchants around Lonsdale petitioned to have a separate place hived off from the district. The newly created City of North Vancouver took the biggest share of the North Shore's population, retail and industrial strength (including Wallace's busy yards) when it was incorporated on May 13, 1907. In 1912 the Municipality of West Vancouver was created, and the district lost still more ground . . . and more tax base. Then tiny Moodyville joined the city in 1915. The Dollar Mill was established in 1916 at Roche Point on Indian Arm. Started by shipping magnate Robert Dollar, the mill was a major employer for many years but closed in 1942. By the 1921 census, while still physically large, the district had a population of 2,950, little more than a third of the city's.

It wasn't until 1925 that a bridge was built across the Inlet, a span designed to carry both trains and automotive traffic. This first Second Narrows Bridge meant someone driving from Vancouver could now reach the North Shore in about 20 minutes. On the day it opened, November 7, more than 3,000 cars drove over it. The creation of the bridge encouraged businessman W.C. Shelly (a baker made prosperous by his famous "4X Bread") to create Grouse Mountain Highway and Scenic Resort. One year after the bridge's opening, the resort's chalet opened with a tea party. Mount Seymour's development took a little longer: the Alpine Club of Canada conducted a ski tour of Seymour in 1929, and vigorous development followed. The new bridge had been badly designed: its lift-span was over shallow water at the south end rather than over the deep central channel. The span was put out of commission so often by ships colliding with it (once disabling the bridge for more than four

years!) that it earned the sour nickname "Bridge of Sighs."

Then came the Great Depression. Like many struggling places in North America, the District of North Vancouver—its tax base hammered by the loss to the city of major industries and the lucrative ferry service—collapsed in 1932 into bankruptcy. One old-timer recalled jigging for salmon in local streams to have something for dinner. Some 75 per cent of landowners saw their property revert to the municipality for unpaid taxes. The district was placed under the control of a commissioner, Charles Tisdall, and would not have representative government again until 1951.

The North Shore's fortunes began to revive in 1939 after the 1938 opening of the Lions Gate Bridge, and war-propelled industrial activity revived the sagging economy. By the 1941 census the district's population had grown to nearly 6,000 to the city's 9,000; by 1951 it had ballooned to nearly 14,500 and 10 years later was at 39,000, some 15,000 *more* than the City. (A recurring theme in the years since the two North Vans separated is the desire to get them back together again. It hasn't happened yet.)

The 1958 opening of a new Second Narrows Bridge sparked another surge in growth. Today the district, with a population of 82,000, is thriving. There isn't room on these two pages to tell all its colorful and busy history. In 1990 a lavishly illustrated book appeared titled *Reflections: A Celebration of the District of North Vancouver's Centennial.* There, people like John Linn, Emily Patterson, Malcolm Lowry, Walter Draycott, Chief Dan George, Chief Capilano Joe, song-writing Bentley C. Hilliam, Alfred Wallace, Captain James Van Bramer, Ron Andrews, Karen Magnussen and others are treated at greater length.

Port Moody
Jarvis Whitney

THE EARLY HISTORY of the Port Moody area was dominated by two events: the 1858 gold rush on the Fraser and the 1886 arrival of the first transcontinental train. With the sudden appearance of thousands of gold prospectors in the Fraser Valley and the need to develop a back-door defence for the burgeoning town of New Westminster, the Royal Engineers—commanded by Col. Richard Moody, after whom Port Moody was named in 1859—were directed to clear a trail from the new capital of British Columbia to Burrard Inlet. The trail, later known as North Road, would allow ships anchored in Burrard Inlet to unload military supplies and personnel if New Westminster were attacked from the south. No attack occurred. But a town, at first no more than a cluster of tents and shacks, began to grow, spurred on by several land grants to some of the Royal Engineers.

One of them was John Murray, who eventually owned about half the town. His son, also named John, later was responsible for many street names—Murray, John, George, William, Henry, Jane, Mary, etc. The main thoroughfare, St. John Street, is a misnomer: John Jr.—police officer, alderman and general mover and shaker—in error put "St." in front of, instead of behind, "John." So the official survey gave the street the name it has today. (The late Major J.S. Matthews, the Vancouver archivist, supposedly said when he heard of the street name: "Johnny Murray was no saint.")

Port Moody had its "15 minutes of fame" in 1879 when it was officially named western terminus for the Canadian Pacific Railway, the transcontinental line promised in 1871 by Prime Minister Sir John A. Macdonald to entice British Columbia into Confederation. The first passenger train from Montreal arrived in Port Moody at noon on July 4, 1886, with about 150 passengers after a 139-hour trip across 4,655 kilometres.

Speculation caused by the imminent arrival of the railway had been rampant; in 1885 a man bought a lot at Clarke and Queen Streets for $15 and sold it later the same year for $1,000. Port Moody was expected to be the biggest town in the West. But William Van Horne decided the company would extend its rail line from Port Moody to a new terminus several kilometres farther west, newly named Vancouver—the railway's executives had determined Port Moody's narrow shelf of land between water and hillside to be insufficient for expansion. There was amazement and anger when the decision became known, and unsuccessful lawsuits were launched. The near-ecstasy of the

first train's arrival in Port Moody soon faded. A cairn in Port Moody commemorates the "Completion of the Canadian Pacific Railway." There is no cairn for William Van Horne! Port Moody's population was static at 250 for nearly 20 years.

J.S. Emerson built a sawmill for cutting cedar in 1905. Records show 125 men were employed there: 34 white men, 80 Chinese, five Japanese and six Hindus. At about the same time several oil refineries opened, followed in 1915 by the large Imperial Oil Company development just outside the Port Moody boundary. In 1913 Port Moody was incorporated as a city. The present city hall was built and Perry A. Roe, the owner of a local sawmill, became the first mayor.

Port Moody was primarily a mill town, full of the smoke and whine of lumber being cut into boards and shingles. If you walked down a street in the early 1920s, you would see mostly private homes with gardens in the back and laundry on the lines. There were five or six general stores selling everything from shoes to steak, three hotels, two gas stations, an elementary school and one police officer. There were no firefighters. When one of the sawmills caught fire, a series of shore whistles was blown and everyone hastened down to help fight the fire.

With the outbreak of World War II, people were able to find steady employment. After the war the town began to spread out and meet surrounding towns as they grew. Port Moody joined the suburbs. In the following decades the process continued as large companies like Andrés Wines, Gulf Oil, Weldwood, Interprovincial Steel, Reichold Chemicals and Pacific Coast Terminals opened up plants in the Port Moody area.

Port Moody has little room to grow and has remained relatively small with a 1995 population of 20,000. The city has had a modicum of industry over the years but is chiefly a serene bedroom suburb of Vancouver.

However, the city has not forgotten its railway heritage. It celebrates Golden Spike Days every year around Canada Day, with events including railway hand-car races as well as bathtub races, fireworks, a street fair and a triathlon.

Many people come to Port Moody now not to watch trains but to watch birds. Its 40-hectare Shoreline Park draws birdwatchers to a four-kilometre trail where 125 species have been recorded. Besides loons, cormorants, herons, eagles, geese, warblers and other birds, there are black bears, coyotes, foxes, raccoons and black-tailed deer. The Inlet also occasionally hosts killer, false killer and grey whales. And coho and chum salmon can be seen from the trail when they spawn in Noons Creek.

With additional material by H.C. Flinn.

Coquitlam
Hazel Postma

THE NAME COQUITLAM comes from the Salish word *kwayhquitlum,* referring to a small salmon, vital to the existence of the Coast Salish, the area's first inhabitants. In 1863 Col. R.C. Moody's Royal Engineers pushed through a trail they called the North Road from New Westminster to the shores of ice-free Burrard Inlet. North Road still exists, is one of the municipality's busiest roads and serves as the Coquitlam-Burnaby boundary.

Frank Ross and James McLaren built Fraser Mills in 1887, the largest mill in B.C. at the time. Fraser Mills formed the nucleus of the district and by 1908 the town boasted 20 houses, a store, post office, hospital, office block, barber shop, pool hall and four police officers.

On August 22, 1891, the District of Coquitlam, covering almost 18,000 hectares, was born. R.B. Kelly was the first reeve and schoolmaster R.D. Irvine was the first district clerk. Jean Baptiste Dicaire, who had arrived in 1904 from Quebec, returned home in 1909 to fetch some of his compatriots. Some 110 arrived and a townsite named Maillardville, after a young French oblate, Father Maillard, grew up north of the mill.

From the beginning Coquitlam was a multicultural community, home to Europeans, East Indians, Chinese and Japanese. Community spirit was fostered through baseball, hockey, lacrosse, the formation of a French-Canadian band and many religious festivities. Industry began with companies like the Dominion Match Factory and a paper plant on North Road. And, reflecting one of the area's economic mainstays, a farmer's market flourished in the early 1900s.

The Walton and Johnson families were the first to homestead east Coquitlam while Obe and Bertha Pollard homesteaded in northeast Coquitlam near Minnekhada Farms—an area transformed into a regional park in 1981. The area's first school opened in 1905 with Dorothy Eldridge teaching 29 pupils. Millside School, for the children of millworkers, opened in 1907. The first volunteer fire brigade was formed in 1912.

Riverview Psychiatric Hospital opened as Colony Farm in 1910, operating out of a hay barn on 404 hectares. Sixty patients were admitted the first year, working on the farm to provide food for themselves and staff. By 1950 Riverview was home to 6,000 patients and employed many Coquitlam residents. Today it has been greatly downsized.

The effects of the Great Depression hit the area hard. Fraser Mills laid off most of its workers, and by 1931 wage reductions resulted in a bitter strike. Police were called to control strikers but Maillardville rallied around its people, establishing soup kitchens with donations from Chinese sympathizers, Fraser Valley farmers and fishers. Six weeks later the strike was over. Workers received few gains and many of the leaders were blacklisted. However the strike provided the impetus for the later unionization of Fraser Mills.

Residents were shocked when district councillor Tommy Douglas was gunned down in his North Road gas station in July, 1934. Douglas had run provincially for the United Front, a Socialist party, and speculation at the time centred on a political assassination.

World War II brought prosperity as wages rose, business flourished and women entered the workforce. Life grew easier and Coquitlam's people began to develop the social, cultural and recreational life of their community.

Then disaster struck in late May, 1948, when the Fraser River flooded much of Fraser Mills and parts of Maillardville. Eight days later the west dike at Riverview's Colony Farms broke—children took to the water, fishing from flat-bottomed boats while older siblings helped with sandbag duty. Dead cattle floated downstream from Fraser Valley farms.

The completion of the Lougheed Highway in 1953 brought more residents and led to the formation of neighborhoods like Harbour Chines and Ranch Park. In 1959 Westwood Motorsport Park opened, the only European-style racing circuit in Canada. Thirty-one years later it closed and the provincial government sold the land for residential development.

In 1972 Coquitlam MLA Dave Barrett led the NDP to victory and became premier of British Columbia. In the 1970s population growth shifted north to Eagle Ridge and in 1979 that growth was acknowledged with the opening of the big Coquitlam Centre Mall. Throughout the 1980s more retail and commercial outlets opened and residents poured into the area. In 1989 a 4,500-house development on the Westwood Plateau began, driving Coquitlam's population to more than 80,000. New firehalls were built and the Poirier Library opened. In 1991 the Town Centre Stadium opened in time for the district's 100th anniversary and its metamorphosis into a city. During the early 1990s Coquitlam hosted the B.C. Summer Games and the B.C. Special Olympics. Currently Coquitlam plans a cultural centre and new civic and public safety buildings in its town centre, joining an aquatic centre, Douglas College and a new secondary school.

Port Coquitlam
Hazel Postma

PORT COQUITLAM'S FIRST INHABITANTS were Salish Indians who fished along the banks of the Fraser, Pitt and Coquitlam rivers. They hunted the forested hills, while the rivers and marshy lowlands provided them with waterfowl.

The first settlers arrived in 1853, among them Alexander McLean, who moved his family to a clearing along the Pitt River after being flooded out of Ladner. He was followed seven years later by the Atkins family from Ireland. Atkins, son Ned and twin brothers Romulus and Remus settled on 65 hectares east of Mary Hill. By 1864 only the McLeans, Atkins and George Black actually lived in the area, although other land was owned by speculators.

In 1868 the Atkins left for Hawaii, but Ned, who had married a local Indian woman, stayed although it was nearly 20 years before the city began to grow, sparked by the completion of the Canadian Pacific Railway spur line in 1886 from the western edge of Coquitlam River along the Fraser River to New Westminster.

The little station at the end of the spur was named Westminster Junction and marked the birth of today's modern city. The station became the nucleus of a village with the Junction Hotel, housing the post office in its lobby, as its hub.

In 1892, a year after Westminster Junction and surrounding lands on the Coquitlam River as far as North Road were incorporated as the District of Coquitlam, the first school opened at the corner of Mary Hill Road and Wilson Street. Known as the Junction School, its 12 students were taught in one room by Miss Dixon. The owner of the Junction Hotel—and postmaster—R.B. Kelly, became the District of Coquitlam's first reeve with council meetings held at his hotel.

By the turn of the century, the 200 residents were joined by new settlers, attracted by the electricity and running water brought down Pipeline Road from Coquitlam Lake. Westminster Junction began to emerge as a trading and political centre of the sprawling district.

Logging joined farming as the main occupations after A.R. Millard, working with F.W. Greer and a Mr. Laflamme, began logging forests along the Coquitlam and Pitt rivers and on Burke Mountain.

In 1911 the CPR, prompted by the imminent opening of the Panama Canal, announced plans to create a major shipyard at Westminster Junction complete with marshalling yards and an industrial complex. Residents envisioned a bright future of factory work and steady wages although a few protested the loss of good agricultural land. Speculators poured into the area, buying large tracts of land and subdividing them into 10-metre lots that were snapped up by eager investors. A new bridge was built over the Pitt River, a second set of tracks was laid alongside the first CPR line, electric transmission lines doubled and scores of homes and shops were built.

Westminster Junction residents decided to go it alone and on March 7, 1913, Mayor James Mars announced the formation of the City of Port Coquitlam, City of Rivers and Mountains. Its population of 1,500 took as its motto "By Commerce and Industry We Prosper."

Prosperity was elusive, however, and expansion ground to a halt two years later. By 1915 land was reverting to the city for unpaid taxes. The shipyard closed in 1918 and timber from the building was floated across the Pitt River and used as paving for sidewalks.

Fires in 1920 destroyed half the buildings along Dewdney Trunk Road and the following year more buildings and a bridge were lost when the Coquitlam River flooded. By the end of 1921 Port Coquitlam was virtually bankrupt and council had to sell the city's fire engine! A bad move, because a year later fire wiped out another section of downtown.

For the next three decades Port Coquitlam slumbered, awaking finally in the 1950s to a period of steady growth that continues today.

Many residents work and play within the city boundaries, taking advantage of the rail, water and trucking terminals, industrial parks and shopping malls, as well as health, educational and recreational facilities.

A flourishing downtown has a refurbished City Hall and plaza as its focal point with a provincial courthouse set to open in 1996. Residents of nearby townhouses and condominiums enjoy shops and restaurants, cafes and craft stores, while the Coquitlam River is just two blocks away.

Bisected by the Lougheed Highway, the city includes farms and golf courses on the north side, industrial parks and Colony Farm to the south. Nestled between the Pitt and Coquitlam rivers is the Kwayhquitlum Indian Reserve.

The 17-kilometre PoCo Trail is a popular walking and cycling trail that meanders through the heart of the city, along river dykes and forested slopes, while the Chelsea Nature Reserve is a popular destination for families, as are the numerous neighborhood parks and playgrounds. In June 1995 the city's new aquatic facility opened just a few yards from Hyde Creek, a spawning ground for salmon.

With more than 45,000 citizens, the City of Port Coquitlam recorded the second highest growth rate in B.C. between 1994 and 1995. New residents are attracted by the small-town atmosphere and pictorial setting. The City's Downtown Core is rejuvenating with new commercial and residential developments. New businesses that have chosen to locate in the city contributed to the 54 per cent growth in employment between 1981 and 1991, twice the rate of growth in the Greater Vancouver region as a whole.

The Fraser flood of 1894. cva

Pitt Meadows
Chris Campbell

FOR MANY YEARS in Pitt Meadows history, water was something to be feared. True, it was an early version of the freeway, with boat-traffic scuttling back and forth, and has been useful for Pitt residents through the years as a source of food. But the benefits were often washed away by occasional bursts of temper from the rivers which surround the town. Every 15 years or so Pitt Meadows residents receive a cranky wake-up call from their neighboring rivers, swamping the banks on three sides and turning the town into Atlantis. Modern dyking has lulled the current generation, but there is still a great deal of power lurking in the waters surrounding today's malls and subdivisions. Sixty per cent of Pitt Meadows land is devoted to agricultural purposes.

The Hudson Bay Company's James McMillan and his party searched the area in the 1820s, and McMillan named the nearby river the Pitt. The grassy flood plains through which the river flowed eventually became known as Pitt Meadows.

Natives from the Fraser Valley and the coast were the first to use the land. They gathered in the fall to host grand potlatches to honor good seasons of hunting and fishing. First Nations people such as the Katzies were attracted to the area because of the bounty the water offered. (Today many of the Katzie are involved in commercial fishing.) For early white settlers, the land was fine for grazing and the making of hay, but only when the flood waters receded. The trick was to capitalize on the opportunity quickly when the water went away. Attempts were made at dyking, but the great Fraser flood of 1894 destroyed the best-laid plans of these men.

The town is flanked by the Pitt River along the west and the mighty Fraser River to the south. The smaller Alouette River stretches along the north. The town fits neatly into the corner where the two big rivers meet, on land dominated by flood plain mixed with higher elevations.

Up until about 1914, the handiest means of transportation to Pitt Meadows was by boat: ferries carried people and horses back and forth across the rivers. There was train service but, for sheer numbers served, the ferries were paramount. Early isolation was heightened by the town's lack of its own post office until 1908. And children had to walk more than six kilometres to Maple Ridge to go to school until Pitt Meadows' first school was built in 1909. That was the same year the first telephone was installed. Electric light didn't arrive until 1928.

Pitt Meadows seemed not to mind being isolated: it petitioned to break away from Maple Ridge in 1896, before finally incorporating in 1914.

Again in 1921 and 1935 devastating floods occurred. Each time new and better dykes were built. By 1948 Pitt Meadows residents were ready to do battle again in a week where the water won the battle, but eventually lost the war. On May 24 of that year, with more than 40 kilometres of dyking in place, the dyke along the Alouette suddenly gave way and 2,800 hectares of land were under water. Residents pulled together to hold onto their homes in a struggle that helped define the community's history and spirit. The Pitt Meadows Council took charge, while farmers evacuated cattle and people moved to higher ground. A Flood Fighter Organization formed and set up base camp in the recreation hall, with the army and navy delivering massive loads of sand to fill bags. The goal was to save the area not yet flooded. The Women's Institute of Pitt Meadows ran a kitchen around the clock, brewing vats of coffee and frying up food for the flood crews, sometimes 300 meals a day. At night the dyke exits glowed with floodlights until June 3, when people literally stood on the banks to hold the sandbags in place . . . and cheered with relief when the water finally began to ebb.

Making the best of an unchangeable situation, Pitt Meadows farmers began harvesting cranberry fields in the 1960s. Blueberries had been picked since 1942 in the community, but local agriculture has always been dominated by dairying, and, for a time, peat harvesting.

The nearby Pitt-Addington Marsh Wildlife Management Area is more than 2,800 hectares in size, and lies along a major bird migration route. It's a unique mix of marsh, raised bog, forest and intertidal mudflats, and home to muskrat, beaver, coyotes, deer and the occasional black bear.

Pitt Meadows Airport accommodates twin-engine and small executive aircraft, helicopters and float planes. Since 1984 the annual value of building permits in Pitt Meadows has risen 55 per cent per year on average, making it one of Greater Vancouver's fastest growing regions.

Maple Ridge
Chris Campbell

Maple Ridge is large, an umbrella for a series of smaller, distinct neighborhoods—seven in all—each with its own history. The name comes from the farm of one of the community's first settlers, John McIvor, who called his dairy farm "Maple Ridge," inspired by a long ridge of beautiful maples, stretching more than three kilometres along the Fraser River. It was at McIvor's farm that the first council gathered in the fall of 1874 to forge a new community out of dense forest, swamps and swarms of mosquitoes.

Directly across the Fraser was Fort Langley and the Hudson's Bay Company post. Eventually the most curious, including several HBC employees, crossed the Fraser to settle in different parts of this rolling land. The most obvious choice was to stay close to the river. Most engaged in logging activity, which is still an important industry with a string of mills along the river. Others went into dairy farming.

With the arrival of the railway Maple Ridge slowly, some might say painfully on such wild land, spread out into seven different communities.

Haney was named for Thomas Haney, a visionary who established a brickyard in the 1880s using the area's unique red clay and who predicted the railway would soon slice through the riverfront where he owned land.

A post office, a train station, a wharf and stores were all quickly established on the banks of the Fraser. Residents included farmers who began to specialize. Farming brought a large contingent of Japanese settlers, who grew strawberries and eventually branched out into greenhouses.

Haney became a busy centre of activity, and over the decades moved up the sloping river banks to flatter land. The Lougheed Highway lead to the development of Haney into a centre of government and what is now downtown Maple Ridge.

During the early period of settlement Hammond, slightly farther west along the river, rivalled Haney. William and John Hammond ran cattle and settled on land formerly occupied by the Katzie people. (The Katzies live today on a nearby reserve.) The riverfront increase in economic activity helped attract the railway, a key to the area's future. Hammond itself developed three hotels and several boarding houses, a bank and later a lumber mill. Today the mill, built in 1916, is Maple Ridge's largest employer. But, on the whole, Hammond—bypassed by the Lougheed—didn't keep pace with Haney, and today is considered more a residential area.

In contrast to these two riverfront communities, other areas developed at a different pace. Albion offered many a chance to catch bountiful amounts of fish in the Fraser. The area was full of strong workers but, other than a community hall and a few stores, did not establish itself as a centre. Some of its people built boats (an industry which remains today) and logged.

Farther east is Whonnock, a community that had its own centre and was cut off from Haney because of a lack of roads. This isolation forged a distinct identity, with a post office, stores, train station and school, and an attitude of self-dependence. Whonnock's people fished, went to school and church, shopped and lived a separate existence from the rest of Maple Ridge.

Even farther east is the community of Ruskin, in the midst of rich forests and with access to the Stave River. Ruskin has more of a connection with Mission, to the east, than Haney. Its thriving sawmills employed enough workers to form the core of a distinct community.

All the communities mentioned so far are riverfront-based. The area of Yennadon, based in the northern area near Golden Ears Mountain, developed more slowly. Settlement was horribly difficult, with swamps that made use of horses impossible, with oxen preferred for farming. Socializing was rudimentary because of the wild terrain, but slowly a community formed with farms and a few sawmills.

The seventh, and perhaps most colorful area, was Webster's Corner, east of Yennadon and close to Kanaka Creek. A small group of settlers tamed the wild land, before the arrival of Finnish people produced several important landmarks and a definite identity. The Abernethy-Lougheed logging company eventually set up shop in this community, providing a sound economic base.

Langley Township
Bob Groeneveld

THE BEGINNING of Langley is integrally linked to the beginning of British Columbia. The area was "discovered" by a party of Hudson Bay Company explorers, led by James McMillan, who struck out from Fort Astoria on November 18, 1824, to find a suitable location for a trading post on the Fraser River. McMillan's group reached Mud Bay on December 13 and followed the Nicomekl River to an area near today's Portage Park (53rd Avenue and 204th Street). From there the group portaged across Langley Prairie to the Salmon River where Trinity Western University is located today, following a route that became known as the Smuggler's Road (later renamed Glover Road). In 1827 McMillan returned to set up his fort at Derby Reach (the site is marked by a cairn at Derby Reach Regional Park). McMillan was replaced as the fort's chief factor by Archibald McDonald, who was in turn followed by James Murray Yale.

By 1838 the fort had become too small and was rebuilt upriver. Destroyed by fire in 1840, it was rebuilt once again at the site of the current National Historic Park. In addition to the fort itself, many of the names associated with it are preserved throughout Langley, primarily through street names: Yale, 1840s postmaster Ovid Allard and B.C. Governor James Douglas among them. Responding to problems caused by a huge population influx (primarily Americans) during the Fraser Gold Rush, Fort Langley was the site of the declaration of B.C. as a Crown Colony on November 19, 1858. The fort was the colony's first capital until just after Christmas when, against James Douglas' wishes, Col. R.C. Moody chose Queensborough (New Westminster) because the fort on the south side of the Fraser River would be too hard to defend against American attack.

Langley Township was incorporated as a municipality in 1873; James Mackie was the first reeve (mayor). The area filled up quickly through the latter part of the century. John Jolly (reeve, 1883) came from Australia. Paul Murray came from northern Scotland to set up at Murray's Corner (now Murrayville). Joseph Michaud arrived from France to settle in Langley Prairie (which became Langley City after the 1955 secession). George Blair came from Ireland to settle in Milner. Henry Davis, another Irishman, built many of the roads which were named after his fellow pioneers. The Medds left England

facing page: Fort Langley, 1971. vs

for Ontario and eventually ended up in the Livingston area. David William Poppy, another Englishman, was reeve from 1908-1913 and again from 1919-1923. His son D.W. Poppy served as reeve from 1956 into the 1970s. The family settled on Otter Road (originally Warwhoop Road, renamed after Col. W.D. Otter, a prairie Indian fighter not believed to ever have set foot in Langley). The Mufford family, also still prominent in the area, came from England via the California gold fields. Among those who settled in Aldergrove (originally Alder Grove) were the Jackmans, the Shortreeds, the Murchisons, and in the County Line district, the Vanettas.

Most of the names of the pioneers are preserved in names of districts, geographical features (such as Murray Creek) and roads, although the latter have been obscured in two ways: street and avenue numbers have replaced most of the names in the municipality and many of the names that remain honor not pioneers, but local boys killed in World War I. (An example is Carvolth Road, which has become 200th Street and one of the most prominent streets in the area—it was named after a young man who had lived in Langley only a few weeks before joining the armed forces and going overseas to his death.)

The aboriginal people of the area were Stalo (which is a Halkomelem word meaning "river") of the Kwantlen band; they still live on McMillan Island next to Fort Langley.

Fort Langley was the economic centre of Langley Township for many years, followed by Murrayville and then Milner through the turn of the century and into the 1920s. When Langley Prairie took over as the business centre through the Dirty Thirties, business people there began to express concern about the taxes they were paying compared to the amount actually spent within their community. By the 1950s the unrest had grown enough to become a popular movement and Langley Prairie split off on its own to become Langley City in 1955.

In the past five years Langley Township's population has grown 19 per cent to nearly 81,000. Huge influxes have occurred in the Walnut Grove and Murrayville areas, and a decision is pending on whether Brookswood or Willoughby will be next to undergo massive development. While a large part of the local economy is rurally inclined (it is the horse capital of B.C., for example, and poultry farming accounted for $170 million in 1995), there are important industrial areas such as those in North West Langley and the Gloucester Estates north of Aldergrove. Langley Township has an airport and numerous tourist attractions, including the National Historic Park in Fort Langley and the Greater Vancouver Zoological Centre (formerly the Vancouver Game Farm) next to Aldergrove.

Langley City
Bob Groeneveld

The name of the new municipality became a bone of contention for some, a source of confusion for many

THE CITY OF LANGLEY is a distinct and separate municipality from its neighbor, the Township of Langley. The City of Langley was born of dissent. Township reeve (mayor) George Brook's adamant "Not a nickel for streetlights for Langley Prairie!" in the early 1950s became the watchword for discontented business people who, some of them since the early 1930s, had been fighting to secede from the township.

The dissidents were upset that the political clout of the Langley Prairie community, quickly becoming the commercial and business centre of Langley, did not match its economic importance (Langley Prairie accounted for 20 per cent of Langley's tax base). Rumblings had been heard as far back as the early thirties, but a significant move toward Langley Prairie independence came December 7th, 1950, when Langley Board of Trade president Richard Langdon publicly supported secession.

A secessionist campaign was led by a committee of prominent residents and business professionals. On September 24, 1954, when put to the vote, they succeeded in drawing 85 per cent of Langley Prairie's approximately 900 taxpayers to their side. Brook's words, emphasizing the disparity between tax dollars collected and spent in Langley Prairie, had provided the final wedge to officially split four square miles, with a total population of 2,025, from Langley Township. Langley City was born on March 15th, 1955.

The name of the new municipality became a bone of contention for some, and a source of confusion for many. Some Langley Township community leaders who had opposed the secession now were angry that the dissidents stuck with Langley. Some felt the new town should be named after Adam Innes, a prominent homesteader. The area was even named Innes Corners before it became known as Langley Prairie in 1911, when the post office was transferred there. Innes lived approximately where Glover Road (then the Smuggler's Trail) meets Fraser Highway (Yale Road) today. Innes also was a major player in the incorporation of the original Langley as a municipality in 1873, and was its second reeve, serving for seven one-year terms between 1874 and 1887.

As a community, Innes Corners/Langley Prairie did not become an important entity until around 1910, when the first Interurban (B.C. Electric Railway) train rumbled through what is today's city core. The area first came to the attention of Europeans in 1824 when James McMillan, scouting for a location for a new Hudson's Bay Company post, came up the Nicomekl River in three roomy bateauxs. He followed an ancient native portage route (hence "Portage Park" at the foot of 204th Street) to the Salmon River. In his diary, he wrote that the plain he crossed, "with the weighty rain is becoming so soft and miry that in several places it resembles a swamp." Following the Salmon River north they arrived at the Fraser. It would be three years, however before the first permanent British settlement on the Lower Mainland of B.C. would be established at the Derby Reach site.

Fort Langley was to play an important role in the establishment of the entire surrounding area, including Innes Corners/Langley Prairie/City of Langley. Two thousand acres of the best farmland between the Nicomekl and Salmon rivers was taken up by the Hudson's Bay Company farm, and was not subdivided until the 1880s. Pioneers were forced to homestead outside that area, and some of the best available land was on the prairie to the south, of which James McMillan wrote, "The soil here appears to be very rich, is a black mould, the remains of a luxurious crop of fern and grass lies on the ground." Among the earliest homesteaders, arriving before 1880, were brothers Adam and William Innes, Henry Wark, Maximillian Michaud, Thomas Henry Cudlipp, Alexander Murchison and James Mackie.

From its 1955 incorporation with a population of just over 2,000, the City of Langley has grown to almost 23,000. Near the eastern end of the Greater Vancouver Regional District, it has the third greatest retail activity in all of Greater Vancouver. Citizens enjoy more than 120 hectares of park land, and an abundance of recreational opportunities, including the Douglas Recreation Centre, walking trails along the meandering Nicomekl River floodplain, 13 developed neighborhood parks, a championship golf course (and a Par 3 planned), a new twin ice arena, as well as a swimming pool, indoor and outdoor bowling greens and the recently constructed senior resources centre—all within six square hectares. There are several educational institutions in the City, one of which is Kwantlen University College, which not only offers the courses you would expect but also a horticultural program ranked the best in the country.

The heart of the city is currently undergoing a major transformation, with several projects taking place simultaneously.

CITY OF
Langley

"Complete, Compact Community" accurately describes the City of Langley, which has emerged as a substantial commercial centre and housing destination for the Lower Mainland and Fraser Valley alike since its incorporation. In 1996 the City was designated as a Regional Town Centre by the GVRD and boasts healthy industrial and commercial sectors, with more than 1,600 businesses. The City's official motto, "Strength of Purpose and Spirit of Community" reflects the aspirations of this progressive community.

White Rock
Sandra McKenzie

THOUGH OFFICIALLY a part of the District of Surrey (incorporated in 1879) until its establishment as a city in 1957, the seaside community of White Rock has always had its own raffish identity as a resort town; the poor man's Carmel. Its sweeping, sandy beach, following the shallow curve of Semiahmoo Bay (the name is derived from a Coast Salish word, meaning "half moon"), its 487-metre pier, the railroad tracks that run along the shoreline and, of course, the giant white boulder that gives the community its name, have conjured images of summer for Lower Mainlanders for more than a century.

About that famous rock just east of the pier: according to romantic legend, the boulder was tossed onto the beach by the son of a Salish sea-god who fell in love with a Cowichan princess. When both mortal and immortal parents objected to their union, the angry scion threw the boulder across the waves, and then, with his bride in his arms, followed the boulder to the shores of Semiahmoo Bay, where they made their home. Actually the last ice age deposited the great granite landmark, which owes its distinctive coloration to layers of sun-bleached guano and several coats of white paint—at least four a year, with regular touch-ups after grad parties.

The original town site was homesteaded in 1886 by a family named Smith, who promptly subdivided their property and sold the lots. By 1887 the British Columbia Directory was promoting Semiahmoo Bay as the "Naples of B.C.," predicting that it would one day become "a popular resort . . . Bathing facilities are the best that could be desired."

The first mention of White Rock appeared in the 1891 Directory, under the entry for Blaine. By the 1901 edition White Rock has grown to comprise a wharf, hotel and store, all built by the Royal City Planing Mills Company of New Westminster. In 1909 the Great Northern Railway rerouted its services between New Westminster and Washington State to cut across the shoreline, making White Rock a point of entry for customs and immigration, and providing easy access to its beaches for Vancouverites. Within three years the town was being promoted as a resort area, complete with daily commuter trains running to New Westminster and Vancouver.

The skeleton of present-day White Rock began to emerge in 1913, when the Campbell River Lumber Company opened, employing 250 men. The town gained a floating pier, a new railway depot and customs office, a tea room, concert hall and waterworks. In 1914 the federal government promised a fixed

> By 1887 the British Columbia Directory was promoting Semiahmoo Bay as the "Naples of B.C.," predicting it would one day become a popular resort . . . bathing facilities are the best

wharf and pier; an electric light system was installed, and two streetcar lines connected the peninsula to Seattle.

By the 1920s White Rock boasted two lumber mills, two churches, a school, stores and a government wharf to serve a year-round population of 800, swelling to 4,000 during the summer. A housing shortage in Vancouver during World War II led to a real estate boom, bumping the population to 7,000 by 1950.

By the 1970s the Burlington Northern had ended its 80 years of passenger service, and the customs and immigration office had moved east, closer to the Blaine and Douglas border crossings. The town, though still a popular beach destination, was looking a little shabby around the edges.

In 1979 a wild idea concocted by friends Tom Kirstein, a chartered accountant, and Chip Barrett, an architect, led to the revitalization of the community. Why not, they wondered aloud, hold a sandcastle competition.

Thus was born a new, though short-lived chapter in White Rock's legend: The Great Canadian Open Sandcastle Competition. With prizes amounting to $10,000, and scores of teams competing, the annual event drew international attention, attracting crowds estimated at 150,000 to the waterfront. Alas, by 1987, community dismay at the crush of people, the inevitable unruly elements, and rising police costs forced the cancellation of the competition.

But sandcastles did succeed in once again focusing attention on White Rock as a sun-and-sand nirvana that is also within convenient commuting distance of Vancouver. Today White Rock's population stands at 17,500. Expensive pastel condos line the bluff above the well-groomed beach, where restaurants cheek-by-jowl cater to a variety of culinary and ethnic tastes. Amtrak trains whiz past the old station house, now an art gallery and museum. White Rock's former reputation as the poor man's Carmel seems dispelled forever.

Surrey
Marlyn Graziano

IT WAS A BARGAIN! It was in 1860 that Governor James Douglas first offered land for sale in the area that was to become Surrey. The price: $1 an acre. More than a century and a quarter later, the average price of a residential lot in Surrey ranged from $115,000 to $120,000 depending on its location. But while Surrey may be the place to be in the 1990s, it wasn't always that way.

Many of Surrey's first settlers were lured to British Columbia by the promise of gold in the Cariboo. Their sights set on amassing fortunes, they didn't stop in Surrey on their way through. But eventually some of the unsuccessful prospectors who found themselves drifting back down the Fraser River stopped in what was to become Surrey.

It was not an easy place to open up. In the late 1800s Surrey was a vast wilderness of tall timber, lush alder bottom and swampy lowlands. It posed many challenges, not the least of which included the clearing of land for farming and roads.

In the centuries before the settlers descended on the area, Coastal Indian nations used the waterways as their main form of transportation. An account of the Royal Kwantlen, by John Pearson and J.M. Reitz, recounts the story of Punnis, a chief of a small Kwantlen village, Kikait, who in July 1827 attempted to ambush the British after Whattlekainum, chief of Ska-iametl (capital of the Kwantlen empire), learned that a Hudson's Bay Company schooner, the *Cadboro,* was sailing up the Fraser.

The natives were quick to mount a defence but were overawed by the size of the schooner. Three decades later the village attracted some of the earliest colonial settlers in Surrey. Ebenezer Brown built the first hotel in 1861 as well as the wharf that became known as Brown's Landing. The transformation of Kikait into present-day Brownsville, in North Surrey, occurred in little more than fifty years.

Surrey was incorporated on November 10, 1879, and the first council meeting held on January 12, 1880. Thomas Shannon was the first warden.

Cloverdale was the business centre of early Surrey and the historical nature of that community survives. Surrey's second municipal hall was built in Cloverdale in 1912 (the first hall had been erected in nearby Surrey Centre in 1881). Cloverdale was also where, in 1904, Surrey's "Opera House" was built. Grand though the name was, the building was just a community hall, but it was well used, recalls Fern Treleaven in *The*

Surrey Story: "There was no radio, no movies; and apart from the annual tour of the Chautauqua Troupe, no professional entertainment. Folks made their own."

The site of Surrey's local government remained in Cloverdale until 1962, when a new hall was built on Highway 10, near the junction with King George Highway.

And, yes, Surrey, was named for the British county of Surrey. Treleaven describes the naming of the municipality: "When a group of men gathered to talk about forming this municipality, an Englishman among them looked across the Fraser River at New Westminster and remembered his old home. In England, the city of old Westminster lies across a river from the county of Surrey. Since all the founding fathers were of British descent, there was no argument when H.J. Brewer suggested that Surrey be the name of this municipality."

Situated between the Fraser River on the north, the Canada-U.S. border on the south, the City of Langley on the east and the Municipality of Delta and the Pacific Ocean to the west, Surrey's environmental attributes have become a source of pride—and a source of more than a few battles between preservationists and those who would see the city developed. But in the 1800s Surrey's geography was a formidable foe for early settlers. The Nicomekl and Serpentine rivers were the first and long preferred transportation routes, as road building was difficult. Clearing the trees and brush was just one problem; once built, routes through the muddy lowlands were often impassable.

But the pioneers persevered and the population grew. Logging, canning, farming and mills were the primary businesses in the late 1800s. But one of the most important undertakings was the crossing of the Fraser River, bridging the gap as it were, between Surrey and New Westminster.

Reeve John Armstrong accomplished that enterprise in 1883, and the next year the small ferry *K de K* made its first transriver voyage. Five years later it was replaced by *The Surrey,* a larger ferry that linked the two cities until the first bridge was built between them in 1904. Vehicles travelled on a temporary deck constructed above the railway bridge until the Pattullo Bridge was built in 1937. Named for Premier Thomas Dufferin Pattullo, the bridge was truly a gateway for growth.

One attractive and historically interesting corner of Surrey is Crescent Beach, where traces of native use go back for more than a thousand years. It was once called Blackie's Spit, after an early resident. There was a busy oyster-farming industry here until 1963, when pollution in the Nicomekl and Serpentine rivers put an end to the industry. (The rivers are recov-

SkyTrain and office development, Surrey, 1994. vp

ering, with salmon runs increasing nicely.) Crescent Beach is occasionally visited by gardeners who collect the seaweed that thickly coats stretches of the shore. B.C. author Ann Blades, who grew up in this area, wrote affectionately about it in *The Cottage at Crescent Beach,* The Neighborhood Association has run Camp Alexandra here for many years.

The population of Surrey swelled to about 15,000 by 1940, but the war years saw the start of a boom that hasn't yet stopped.

Once the Pattullo was built, growth spread in North and South Surrey as people continued to pour into the area. Surrey began to change; although its farming roots remained strong, industry began to develop. Policing was handed over to the RCMP, and the Surrey detachment eventually became the largest in the country, with 335 members and 115 municipal employees. That's a far cry from the early days when Surrey boasted one constable. (The force was tripled in 1937 after the Pattullo Bridge opened.)

In 1991 British Columbia became the first province with a woman at the head of its government and she hailed from Surrey. Rita Johnston—Surrey's second woman councillor—achieved her political groundbreaking in the wake of the resignation of Premier Bill Vander Zalm. (Coincidentally, the pair had served together on Surrey council, which Vander Zalm had led as mayor.)

Johnston, the MLA for Surrey-Newton, was instrumental in bringing SkyTrain to Surrey—a move that heralded the municipality's arrival as the GVRD's second city centre. The resulting business boom and change in image will help mold Surrey as it enters the 21st century. Indeed, Surrey's population is expected to eclipse that of Vancouver as it moves toward becoming the urban giant of the South Fraser area.

Surrey's significance as a major player in the Lower Mainland was not lost on the council of the day and the municipality officially became a city on September 11, 1993.

The next year SkyTrain arrived in Whalley. The rapid transit route and the residential and commercial developments that accompany its three Whalley stations are integral to Surrey's new city centre.

And as the 1990s draw to a close, the geography that once posed such difficulties for settlers is now considered a precious resource to be preserved. Fully one-third of Surrey's land mass is protected as park land or green space, hence Surrey's reputation as the "City of Parks." Now home to about 300,000 people (and little sign that growth will slow in the coming years) Surrey faces the challenge of growing up without forgetting its roots.

The City of Surrey is recognized as one of the most efficient local governments in the province of British Columbia, and has received numerous national and international awards for its creative and innovative delivery of services. Our corporate culture and our response to our citizens' needs is defined by the question "How can we do it better?"

New Westminster

Archie Miller and Valerie Francis,
with added material by Lori Pappajohn

Dominion Day, 1898, New Westminster. vpl

NEW WESTMINSTER SITS proudly on the banks of the Fraser River—a city sited on a hill for reasons of defence and political authority. The city's name was chosen by Queen Victoria, hence its nickname, The Royal City. It was briefly the capital of what we now call the Province of British Columbia, and for many years was the mercantile centre of the Fraser Valley. New Westminster takes pride in its past and its evolving future.

New Westminster, Canada's oldest incorporated city west of the Great Lakes, is a mere 9.6-square kilometres in size. It traces its roots to the discovery of gold on the Thompson River in the 1850s. Soon the Fraser River was giving up this precious metal and thousands of miners and prospectors headed to the region. In 1858 the newly formed Colonial government, under Governor James Douglas, requested assistance from the Colonial Office in England. Thus were sent the Columbia Detachment of Royal Engineers, under Col. R.C. Moody. The sappers, as they were known, were to maintain law and order, establish routes of communication, build roads into the interior, bring "civilization" to this frontier, and locate, survey and establish a town destined to be the capital city of the new Colony of British Columbia. The site they chose and the city they laid out was New Westminster.

In describing the site, Col. Moody wrote in 1859: "There is abundance of room and convenience of every description requisite in a seaport and the capital of a great country. There are great facilities for communication by water, as well as by future great trunk railways into the interior . . . the low lands (which will be most coveted as commercial sites, docks, quays, etc.) . . . are close adjoining and easily made available."

In the early 1860s New Westminster (incorporated in 1860) was the premier city on the mainland, and the main port of call for a fleet of sternwheelers transporting gold seekers, supplies and equipment to the interior gold fields. But over time the gold rush moved on and the capital moved to Victoria in 1868.

In 1870 the city's population gathered on the cricket grounds and celebrated the crowning of New Westminster's first May Queen, an event credited with maintaining citizen morale and ensuring the city's survival. May Day became a symbol of hope and of the rebirth of spring. Today the celebration, which marked its 125th Anniversary in 1995, is the longest continuing event of its type in the British Commonwealth.

In the 1870s and 1880s the little town and its citizens forged on, maintaining a position of commercial and economic importance. Industry began to call the city home, with major sites dedicated to fish, lumber, shipbuilding, farm produce of all types, food processing, international trade and general commerce. The coming of the railway in 1886 was a further spur to development: within a 15-year period, New Westminster was connected to the rest of the continent by three leading railways—and connected to the rest of the Lower Mainland with electric tramlines from Vancouver to Chilliwack.

During the early years of New Westminster, another city grew within it. One of Canada's first and largest Chinatowns was once located at the foot of 10th Street. At one time this community boasted 1,000 residents. Now, nothing remains.

With the arrival of the railways came a real estate boom. Prosperous citizens hired architects such as Samuel Maclure, Charles Clow or George Grant to design their homes. New Westminster became known as a City of Homes because of the grandeur of the houses gracing its hillside. Although many of these homes were later demolished and replaced by apartments, some remain, especially in the Queens Park historic neighborhood.

In the early 1860s New Westminster was the premier city on the mainland, and the main port of call for a fleet of sternwheelers transporting gold seekers to the interior

Twice a year, homes are open to the public for viewing—for a spring tour and for winter parlor concerts, both sponsored by the New Westminster Heritage Preservation Society.

Henderson's Directory of 1889 outlined some of the important activities of the period. "The city is the centre of the fresh fish and fish canning industry. There are 12 canning establishments on the river within 14 miles of the city, and two establishments for shipping and freezing fresh fish. The city is surrounded by extensive tracts of valuable timber, has three large saw mills, and a large and very complete sash, door, and furniture factory; there is also a woolen mill (the only one in the province)." *William's Directory* of 1891 further demonstrates the impact of the city: " . . . four distinct lines of river steamers find constant employment between the city and the agricultural settlements, and this, of course, implies a large volume of business for merchants and shippers."

By 1898 New Westminster was the mercantile centre of the Fraser Valley, with a flourishing city market. Its main street, Columbia, was lined with impressive brick stores and offices. Then disaster struck. On September 10, 1898 the downtown commercial core of the city was destroyed by fire. Again the citizens picked up the pieces and rebuilt their town.

In this century Columbia Street was, for a time, renowned in North America as The Miracle Mile for its commercial value and productivity. If a business was located on "The Mile," it was virtually guaranteed success. The waterfront was home to a well-known array of businesses such as Royal City and Broder's Canning, Webb and Gifford, Belyea, Brackman Ker Milling, B.C. Electric Railway, Buckerfield's, Cunningham Trapp, Canadian Fishing, Canadian Pacific Railway, Gilley Brothers, Kraft, Westminster Paper, Mohawk Lumber and Pacific Coast Terminals.

The waterfront, once jammed with paddlewheel steamboats, sailing ships and globe-trotting freighters, is now home to thousands of residents in modern residential complexes. The area that used to be docks, warehouses and mills features a garden-lined boardwalk linking residences and the Inn at the Quay with Westminster Quay Public Market. Fresh fish, vegetables, bread and pies straight from the oven and a variety of restaurants and shops enliven this popular site. Riverfront visitors can stroll the boardwalk and watch tugs and barges at work on the river or take a boat tour up the Fraser River to historic Fort Langley.

SkyTrain, with stops at 22nd Street, New Westminster and Columbia, now links The Royal City to Vancouver, Burnaby and Surrey and has spurred much development in its wake.

A visit to New Westminster's museums offers a variety of possibilities, including a riverboat captain's home from 1865 (and one of B.C.'s oldest residences) at the beautifully preserved Irving House Historic Centre; a vast collection of memorabilia and information from Western Canada's oldest city at the New Westminster Museum/Archives; stories, photographs and artifacts from our maritime heritage, including the last steam-powered paddlewheeler to operate on the Fraser River, now restored as the Samson V Maritime Museum; the history of Canada's Official Summer Sport at the Canadian Lacrosse Hall of Fame; and our military family tree and heroic efforts through two world wars and other conflicts at the Museum of the Royal Westminster Regiment.

Still on the drawing board but planned for a waterfront location—the Fraser River Discovery Centre, an interactive facility exploring the river that is such an important part of New Westminster's past, present and future. The centre is expected to become one of the top tourist attractions in the Lower Mainland. Scheduled to open before the year 2000, the multimillion-dollar facility will celebrate the province's largest river, and its economic, environmental, cultural and historical importance.

Throughout the year New Westminster's museums and its many community groups organize a variety of special events and activities. There are community events for Heritage Week, May Day, the Hyack Festival, The Hyack Anvil Battery salute, FraserFest, and throughout the Christmas season. There are tours of the city's beautiful homes, walking tours of its streets and cemetery, and programming throughout the year, all dedicated to the history of The Royal City.

As Col. Moody expressed in a letter home to England in 1859, "The site is not only convenient in every respect but it is agreeable and striking in aspect. Viewed from the Gulf of Georgia across the meadows and entering the Fraser, the far distant giant mountains forming a dark background—the City would appear throned, Queen-like and shining in the glory of the midday sun—it is a most important spot."

Burnaby
Pixie McGeachie

Burnaby boosters, 1952. vp

Aﬆ﬇ﬆ THE Colony of British Columbia was officially established in 1858, a hand-picked contingent of Royal Engineers was sent out from England to survey and map areas along the Fraser River and to set up military reserves. With axes, crosscut saws and stumping powder, they cleared kilometres of trails from New Westminster to Port Moody. Today these hard-won routes form Burnaby's main arterial systems: Kingsway, Canada Way, Marine Drive and North Road.

The Royal Engineers, under the command of Colonel R.C. Moody, also had the task of surveying and laying out district lots in New Westminster and what was to become Burnaby. Assisting Moody was Robert Burnaby, who had come from England to set up a commission merchant business but was, for a short time, appointed by Governor James Douglas as Moody's aide and secretary. Burnaby volunteered to join a small party searching for a lake talked about by the local natives. Despite foul weather, the party reached the lake which Moody named Burnaby Lake.

As settlers started to establish homes north of New Westminster, they decided their tax money should be used for their roads and services instead of going to Victoria. They formed a committee and applied for a municipal charter which they received on September 22, 1892. It seemed a good idea to call the municipality Burnaby, after the lake.

A provisional administration was formed and Burnaby was divided into five wards. Charles R. Shaw headed the first council. The municipality's first election by ballot, held in January 1893, brought in Nicolai Schou as reeve. Schou, editor of Vancouver's *News-Advertiser,* was returned as reeve for 10 years before his death in 1903.

With the advent in 1891 of the Central Park interurban line between New Westminster and Vancouver, cluster communities began to form and grow beside the tracks. Power for the system was generated at the powerhouse located at Griffiths Avenue and Kingsway. The line's first roadmaster, Roderick Sample, and his wife Minnie, ran a 15-room boarding house near the powerhouse to accommodate the tram line's staff.

With a ready supply of prime timber and the pioneers' need for lumber to build homes and businesses, Burnaby became a logging centre. Sawmills sprang up on the shores of the lakes and logging outfits laid down skid roads to enable them to drag logs to the mills or to waterways that led to New Westminster's mills. The mill at Barnet on Burrard Inlet developed into a

small townsite and one of the largest processors and exporters of lumber in the British Empire.

The loggers left behind them huge stumps and masses of tangled debris. Settlers wanting to cultivate the land were faced with the backbreaking task of clearing it.

Burnaby's next phase after the logging era was agricultural. Fruit and vegetable farms, turkey and chicken farms, pig farms, dairies and nurseries thrived. Strawberries grown in Burnaby were considered better than most and received a higher price. Many of the fruit and vegetable pickers were Chinese who travelled up from New Westminster as the seasons required.

One prominent Burnaby strawberry grower was Bernard Hill, who paid $10 an acre for land abutting the southwest end of Burnaby Lake. He first cleared enough land on which to build an eight-room house for his wife and children. The Hills shipped eight rooms of furniture from their home in England around Cape Horn to Vancouver at a cost of $12.50. Many early settlers in B.C. sent their possessions on ships which used the furniture as ballast on their way to pick up lumber for European markets.

In 1895, three years after arriving in Burnaby, Hill moved his family into their new home. The furniture was brought from Vancouver by a team of 16 oxen, at a carting cost of $12.00. Over the years, Hill cleared almost 10 hectares out of the forest and successfully grew strawberries and other small fruits.

Burnaby's first one-room school opened at Edmonds and Douglas Road (Canada Way) in 1894. One teacher, Ellen Lister, taught all grades for a decade.

The first churches to go up in Burnaby were the Presbyterian Church and the Anglican St. John the Divine, in the Central Park area. Both churches succumbed to fire, but the latter was rebuilt in 1906 and still stands on Kingsway across from Central Park.

While a few large homes with all the amenities of the times were built in Burnaby by early residents, most houses con-

City of Burnaby

Burnaby's evolution from a suburb of Vancouver to a mature and dynamic urban centre in its own right is now complete. To mark its Centennial, Burnaby officially became a City on September 22, 1992. Burnaby's growth is directed to four town centres: Edmonds, Lougheed, Brentwood and the largest, Metrotown. These centres provide a full range of services, jobs, housing, entertainment and recreational activities for residents and visitors.

structed by and for incoming residents were modest structures that lacked running water, electricity and indoor plumbing. There was plenty of wood for heating and cooking but it had to be cut down and dried before burning. Coal oil lamps were the only source of night light so a trip to the outhouse after dark was something to be put off as long as possible.

Real estate developers expected to get a boost in sales when the Burnaby Lake interurban line was activated on June 12, 1911. Subdivisions were planned for land abutting the lake, but widespread unemployment and an impending world war scuttled the whole idea.

In 1911, when the first police committee was struck, two mounted policemen were hired and $250 was earmarked for the purchase of two horses. The next year three more policemen and a "gaoler" were hired, a patrol wagon was purchased and telephones were installed in police headquarters in the municipal hall at Kingsway and Edmonds.

Concerts were staged during World War I to raise money to buy comforts for men overseas. The Girl Guides, formed in Burnaby in 1914, rolled bandages, knitted socks, sponsored a bed in the Royal Columbian Hospital and printed a newspaper, *News from Home,* that was sent to local men at the Front.

During the twenties, Burnaby welcomed several amenities: a sewer system was initiated, street lighting was gradually installed along the main streets, the first gas mains were laid, and transportation was enhanced by the Blue Funnel Line of buses running along Kingsway to Vancouver. In 1925 Burnaby crowned its first May Queen, Ruth Bearn. On Saturdays 15 cents admitted adults to silent movies at the Central Park and Heights theatres while children got in for a nickel.

The effects of the 1929 Wall Street stock market crash reached Burnaby, increasing unemployment and stepping up demand for relief money. One bright spot in the 1930s was the slow influx of industries into Burnaby: Dominion Bridge, Van Burn Brick and Glass Company, Ford Motor Company of Canada and Shell Oil Company. While companies like these increased Burnaby's tax base, their presence did not solve the municipality's dilemma caused by insufficient funds to keep up with relief payment demands.

With finances completely drained, Burnaby was administered from 1933 to 1942 by the provincial government through a commissioner.

The first five years after World War II ended in 1945 brought to Burnaby a phenomenal 57 per cent increase in population. A burst of residential construction and commercial enterprise began then and has never stopped. With plenty of prime land available for development, Burnaby has evolved from a bedroom community to a vibrant city.

In 1950 Burnaby General Hospital took in its first patients. The sixties brought in the Trans-Canada Highway through Burnaby's central valley; Brentwood Shopping Centre opened, the biggest of its kind in the province at that time; Simon Fraser University took shape on top of Burnaby Mountain; the British Columbia Institute of Technology opened its doors; and the municipality purchased buildings at the northeast end of Deer Lake and dedicated them as an Art Gallery and a Community Arts Centre.

As commercial ventures continued to move into Burnaby, agricultural pursuits disappeared and the municipality entered the third phase in its growth—business and industry. Industrial centres such as Lake City attracted a growing number of tenants, Discovery Park opened up a central site for technology development, and shopping malls were built throughout the municipality.

In 1971 Burnaby marked the centennial of Confederation by creating Burnaby Village Museum, a turn-of-the-century village replica which has become a tourist attraction and a learning resource for school groups.

Co-hosting the 1973 Summer Games with New Westminster took months of planning and the efforts of hundreds of Burnaby citizens. After the games were over, Burnaby inherited more than a million dollars worth of sports facilities including a 2,200-metre rowing course in Burnaby Lake, one of only three such competitive courses in North America at the time.

The influx of residents and businesses accelerated in south Burnaby when the rapid transit SkyTrain, following the old interurban route from Vancouver to New Westminster, began operating in 1986. Along the line just east of Central Park, Metrotown Centre mushroomed to include highrise apartments, multiple-dwelling complexes, office towers and a huge shoppers' destination. An integral part of the centre is the Robert Prittie Memorial Library, a striking design by James K.M. Cheng Architects.

Burnaby has been fortunate to have planners with wisdom and foresight to preserve natural green space for recreation. The city encompasses more than 100 parks and open spaces ranging from small neighborhood grassy areas to large expanses such as the Burnaby Mountain conservation area and the perimeter parks around both Deer and Burnaby lakes.

Today more than 175,000 people live in Burnaby, the third-largest city in British Columbia. The city's Official Community Plan envisions a capacity population of 180,000. The 200 people who made up Burnaby's population just over 100 years ago would be amazed.

With 20 per cent of its land being preserved for parks and open space, Burnaby places the highest priority on protecting ecologically important areas and providing space for recreation. An agreement with Simon Fraser University to dedicate the sides of Burnaby Mountain as parkland contributes to this legacy. Construction of new facilities, like the Shadbolt Centre for the Arts in Deer Lake Park, will ensure Burnaby continues to grow as a vibrant, livable community well into the next century.

Richmond
Dean Pelkey

AN ISLAND CITY set in the mouth of the Fraser River, Richmond has grown up from its days as a sleepy-eyed farming community. With a population of 145,000 people, Richmond is a booming urban centre with a multicultural feel that reflects its Asian nickname as a land of prosperity. But the Richmond of today—with gleaming highrise towers reaching skyward toward the international jets landing at nearby Vancouver International Airport—retains traces of its past.

Founded on the twin pillars of farming and fishing, Richmond still contains some of the best farmland in the Lower Mainland with more than 4,800 hectares preserved in the agricultural land reserve. Cranberries have emerged as the dominant crop for farming in the 1990s. In Steveston, Richmond hosts the largest fishing fleet on Canada's West Coast.

Richmond, which attained city status in 1990, is made up of a group of islands at the mouth of the Fraser River with a total area of 133 sq. kilometres. The largest of these, Lulu Island, is home to the bulk of the city's population, while the second largest, Sea Island, hosts the Vancouver International Airport and the tiny community of Burkeville.

As on much of the West Coast, the first people to roam Richmond were natives, in this case the Musqueam people, who fished and hunted throughout the Fraser delta. Although the band lived on the mainland on the Fraser River's North Arm, they crossed the islands hunting and trapping beaver, muskrat, mink and other game. The islands also provided them with a source of wild blueberries and other fruit.

This fertile delta soil and a lack of large trees made the islands ideal for farming and attracted the first white settlers.

Initially Lulu Island was known on Fraser River maps simply as Island No. 1. But in 1863 Colonel Richard Moody, commander of the Corps of Royal Engineers, decided to name the island after Lulu Sweet, a popular entertainer from San Francisco, passing through with her troupe en route to a show in Victoria.

Hugh McRoberts arrived on Sea Island in 1861, building a dyke around his farm to keep the sea at bay. He was soon followed by other pioneer families: the McNeelys, who began a farm on the south side of Lulu Island, and the Ferrises.

Thomas Kidd arrived in 1874, staking out a 65-hectare farm, also on Lulu Island. He was followed in 1879 by the Blair brothers—John and Arch—who between them built a 136-hectare farm.

But it was with the arrival of Manoah Steves and his family in 1878 that Lulu Island truly began its path to prosperity. In 1879 Steves and 24 of his neighbors successfully petitioned to incorporate the islands as the Township of Richmond.

Many of Richmond's pioneer families are remembered today in the names of the city's schools: Thomas Kidd, Samuel Brighouse, James Gilmore, R.M. Grauer, James McKinney and Manoah Steves. Many of the same names pop up as local politicians. Hugh Boyd became Richmond's first reeve (mayor). He was succeeded by Kidd in an 1881 election. Kidd later became the community's first member of the provincial legislative assembly.

While Steveston enjoyed growth brought by the fishing industry, the rest of Richmond was making a name for itself in agriculture. The Frasea Dairy Farm on Sea Island was Richmond's largest dairy farm. Established in 1922 by Jake Grauer, the farm at one time had 500 cows. In 1954 the farm closed down because of the expansion of the Vancouver International Airport. A last remnant of that farm, an aging barn, was torn down in 1993, when the airport began to build its third runway.

Surrounded as they are by the Fraser River, farmers in Richmond's early days fought constantly to keep the river at bay—a battle they didn't always win.

The first dykes were built by Hugh McRoberts to protect his Sea Island farm and other farmers soon followed. But the dykes failed to prevent the first major flood in 1894, when water rushed over the north Richmond dyke, destroying crops and washing out roads. Dykes were rebuilt, but floods struck again in 1905 and 1948. The last major flood was in 1952, when a flood box in Finn Slough washed out.

In 1968 the city reached an agreement with the provincial government to share the cost of building and maintaining the dykes, removing the care of the dykes away from individual landowners. Today the dykes that surround Lulu Island not only protect against flooding but are an important part of the city's recreational trail system.

While farming and fishing provided the early livelihood for the people of Richmond, horse racing provided the entertainment. Although the name Minoru Park lives on today as Richmond's largest public park, the moniker was originally applied to a horse track on the present park site at the turn of the century. Named after King Edward's Epsom Derby-winning steed, Minoru Park attracted 7,000 people on its opening day on August 21, 1909.

Minoru Park closed when World War I broke out, but reopened after the war as Brighouse Park. The track proved so profitable that a second, Lansdowne Park, was built north of

City of
RICHMOND

Richmond is seven years older than Vancouver. Originally settled by farmers in the 1860s it was first incorporated in 1879, and then reincorporated as a city in 1990. The first flight in B.C. was made from Richmond in 1910. In 1995 just under 12 million passengers passed through Vancouver International Airport, now located on Sea Island in Richmond, and it is projected this figure will almost double in the next 20 years.

Westminster Highway on what is now Lansdowne Park shopping centre. Horse racing faltered in 1941 with the closure of Brighouse Park, as crowds fell during World War II and because of the opening of a new track at Hastings Park, on the PNE grounds in Vancouver. Lansdowne closed in the mid-1960s.

Aircraft played an early and vital role in Richmond's development. The city was host to a series of aviation firsts: the province's first passenger flight in 1912, the first female passenger in Canada flew from Richmond, and the first flight over the Rocky Mountains left from Richmond.

The original airport was a 16-hectare piece of land south of what is now Alexandra Road that was leased to the City of Vancouver. In 1928 planning began for a new airport, with Sea Island selected as the site, a decision made by Vancouver Mayor W.H. Malkin and the Vancouver Board of Trade. Vancouver paid $300,000 for 192 hectares and another $300,000 for runways and hangars.

In 1931 Sea Island Airport opened, with the old Richmond airport returning to farmland. The arrival in 1946 of the first scheduled overseas airline, Australian National Airways (which later became Qantas), signalled a new age for the airport, and its name was changed to Vancouver International Airport in 1948, ensuring Richmond's status as the "Gateway to the West."

Following on the heels of the airport's creation came Burkeville, an anomaly of a settlement built virtually at the eastern tip of Vancouver International Airport's main runway. Burkeville was a child of World War II, built to house workers at Boeing's Sea Island plant and named after Boeing president Stanley Burke. About 328 homes were originally built, and most still remain, housing about 700 people.

Throughout the post-war years, Richmond enjoyed steady growth, transforming from an agricultural community to a bedroom community of Vancouver as farms gave way to housing subdivisions and commercial development.

In 1956 Richmond's population was 26,000. That increased to 43,323 in 1961 and reached 62,121 in 1971. Then the boom began, as Richmond grew to 96,154 people in 1986, jumped to 126,624 in 1991 and was nearing the 150,000 mark in 1996.

Because Richmond is an island, its growth is highly dependent on transportation links to the mainland. In 1957 the Oak Street Bridge was built. By 1962, Highway 99 and the George Massey Tunnel (originally named the Deas Island Tunnel) were also completed, providing a continuous link between the U.S. border and Vancouver through Richmond.

In 1974 the Knight Street Bridge was built over the Fraser's North Arm, replacing the Fraser Street Bridge. The Arthur Laing Bridge was built the following year, connecting Sea Island to Granville Street. The completion of the No. 2 Road Bridge in 1993 added the most recent link to Lulu Island.

With the building boom of the 1970s and 1980s, so too came a change to the ethnic mix of Richmond's population. Until 1961, 60 per cent of the city's population were of British descent. By 1986 the number of people claiming a British heritage had fallen to 27 per cent, while those of Chinese descent made up 8 per cent of the population and 5.6 per cent had an Indo-Pakistani heritage.

Between 1980 and 1988 immigrants from Hong Kong, Taiwan, and China accounted for 23 per cent of all foreign immigrants coming to Richmond.

Likewise, in 1971 83 per cent of the city's population listed English as their first language; by 1991 that had fallen to 69 per cent. By this time Richmond declared itself Canada's first multicultural city, and began offering city services in a variety of languages.

These years also saw Richmond emerge as a centre of high-technology in the Lower Mainland. Led by world-renowned MacDonald Dettwiler and Associates, more than 300 high-tech companies set up shop in Richmond during the 1980s. Many specialized in computers, software development, satellite technology, space and aeronautics.

Richmond, 1991. vp

More than 50 square miles in area and surrounded on three sides by the Fraser River Estuary, Richmond lies seven miles south of Vancouver City Centre and 20 miles north of the U.S. border. A leading manufacturing and distribution centre in Western Canada, Richmond's key economic activities revolve around technology-based companies, the tourism and hospitality industries, airport-related businesses and retail trade.

Steveston
Don Hunter

Gulf of Georgia Cannery National Historic Site, Steveston, 1993. vs

I N 1878 MARTHA STEVES and her six children climbed down from the steam sidewheeler *Enterprise* in the South Arm of the Fraser River, into a rowboat. Awaiting them ashore, on the southwest tip of Lulu Island, was Martha's husband Manoah, a native of New Brunswick who had come west from their Ontario home a year earlier and, liking what he saw, bought 121 hectares on which he would start a dairy farm.

Ten years later Manoah's son, William Herbert, bought more land and laid out a townsite he named Steves. (Its birth was announced on July 31, 1889, in the *Victoria Colonist*.) The town would eventually be renamed Steveston and would become (and remains) the biggest commercial fishing port in Canada.

By 1890 Steveston was a full-blown boom town with a fishing season population of 10,000 cramming the sidewalks and enjoying the pleasures, innocent and otherwise, of its hotels and opera house, saloons and bawdy houses, its opium dens and gambling tables. With more than a dozen canneries operating on the banks of the Fraser, it was home to an industry whose labels became familiar around the globe. The Phoenix Cannery was the first to open in the mid 1880s. It was destroyed by fire in 1896 but, true to its name, reopened in 1898.

At the same time a stable population of dairy, vegetable and fruit farmers continued the building of a society that would flourish and become a significant part of the bigger and still burgeoning City of Richmond, which takes up most of Lulu Island.

Pain often accompanies growth, and Steveston had its share over the years, from floods like that of 1894, which saw whole canneries disappear under the force of the Fraser's spring freshet, to the great fire of 1918, which razed the Chinese and Japanese sections south of Moncton Street, leaving 600 homeless, and the 1900 strike over the price of fish. Before the strike ended in July the workers found themselves facing a Vancouver militia company of the Duke of Connaught's Own Rifles.

In 1942 Steveston suffered its hardest blow with an event that will always be a matter of controversy. In the wake of the December 7, 1941 attack by Japanese forces on the U.S. naval base at Pearl Harbor, the federal government ordered the removal from the coast of all persons of Japanese ancestry, on the grounds that they were potential spies or saboteurs. This involved the majority of Steveston's permanent population. They lost their property—houses and fishboats—and spent the next several years in internment camps and on farms in the B.C. Interior and in Alberta. Enrollment at Lord Byng school dropped from 500 students to 137. It was only in 1988 that a compensation package settlement was reached with the federal government. Money from the redress funds paid for Steveston's Japanese Canadian Cultural Centre, opened in 1992. However, most of the internees did not return to Steveson. The much-reduced Japanese presence remains with the local Buddhist church and the internationally recognized Martial Arts Centre.

Of the industry that brought Steveston its heyday, only one cannery remains active—B.C. Packers' Imperial Cannery, which started in 1893. Yet, despite the decline of the canneries, the fishing industry has sustained Steveston; the harbor is still home to about 1,000 seiners, gillnetters and trollers of the south coast fleet. And Steveston is still a vital, bustling place; a delightful modern waterfront community intent on preserving its heritage for the benefit of resident and visitor alike.

The main and traditional business section occupies three blocks west on Moncton Street from No. 1 Road, with busy sidestreets north and south. One short block south of Moncton is a chic, newish waterfront stretch of boutiques, galleries, stores and restaurants sitting over the Fraser River. Salmon, crab, prawns and other Pacific pleasures are sold directly from the boats that caught them.

Take a walk up Moncton Street to 3811, in the centre of the business district, where the village's history is protected and preserved in the compact Steveston Museum, which is also an operating post office. The building was prefabricated in 1906 in New Westminster, and was first occupied by the Northern Bank.

The restored Gulf of Georgia Cannery, the biggest of them all in its day(1894-1979), is now a public site under the protection of Heritage Canada. The nearby Britannia Heritage Shipyard is also being dramatically revitalized.

Actively involved in preserving Steveston's heritage is Harold Steves, a member of Richmond council since 1968 and a former New Democratic member (1972-75) of the provincial legislature, and a great-grandson of Manoah Steves.

Steveston's strong cultural links with Japan were forged in 1887 with the arrival of the first of many Japanese settlers, a carpenter from the village of Mio in the prefecture of Wakayama. 1996 marked the 50th anniversary of the annual July 1st Salmon Festival and parade. Originally a sports day fundraiser, this event draws crowds to Steveston from across the Lower Mainland to enjoy the family entertainment and activities.

Point Roberts
Carol Woodman

MY WEEKEND RETREAT, a cedar cabin on Point Roberts, was built in 1952 by a woman from Burnaby who knew absolutely nothing about building. The lot cost $200—$10 down and $10 a month. She commuted on weekends, taking the ferry from Steveston to Ladner and driving by gravel road to her site. Log by log she constructed the cabin, while using a tent for her home and the ocean for bathing. "Anyone who can read can build a house," she said. This spirit still prevails on a 12.5 square kilometre peninsula, in Northwest Washington, just 30 minutes out of Vancouver.

In 1846 the 49th parallel, already established as the Canada-U.S. border east of the Rockies, was extended to the Pacific coast (with a dip south to include all of Vancouver Island within Canada). One result of that extension was the creation of a tiny U.S. (Washington State) peninsula south of Tsawwassen.

This little blip of land has become a favored spot for seasonal Canadian residents. The shallowness of the bay allows the sun to warm long stretches of exposed sand, and incoming tides create a huge, warm bathtub where small children can play safely. It's one of the top 15 beaches in the U.S.

Native Indians used this spit occasionally as they crossed the Strait or were blown off course. The first settlers were Icelandic farmers. Farming was marginal; fishing was excellent. Before fish traps were outlawed in the 1930s, fishing was the main industry, and canneries and taverns provided the main source of employment, although during prohibition rum-running was profitable.

After World War II Canadians looking for fun visited Point Roberts to drink beer at two of the largest taverns in America, The Reef and Breakers. They picnicked, drank beer and bought cheap property. Around 1949 most of the residents wanted to secede: they shopped in, and bought their papers, groceries and gas, from Canada, and services were provided by Canada including the Delta fire brigade. B.C. Telephone serviced the area until 1988. One big factor for staying American was access to the Fraser River salmon runs.

The year 1959 was pivotal for "The Point." The Deas Island (Massey) Tunnel opened and "Boozing Canadians Leave Point Roberts a Hangover," read headlines in a Vancouver paper as thousands could now drive directly for "Sudsday" beer. A famous bumper sticker read "Sunday Services at the Breakers." X-rated

> The first settlers were Icelandic farmers. Farming was marginal; fishing was excellent …fishing was the main industry, and canneries and taverns provided the main source of employment, although during prohibition rum-running was profitable

movies came next and residents were worried that their little spit was becoming "Sin City." An International Joint Committee ran a feasibility study to see if Point Roberts could become a national park and concluded only Canada would benefit. Lighthouse Park's 7 hectares, with a boat launch, campsites and picnic areas served residents and visitors.

Water was always the problem. Wells went dry in the summer, and Canadians often brought their own water to cabins. In 1964 a water system was installed, but during the drought of 1973, water was a contentious issue. Signs read "Canadians Go Home," and "disaster area." Unless water for drinking and emergencies was supplied by Delta, the water board threatened to cut off the 850 Canadian residents. Truckloads of water from Blaine alleviated the problem temporarily. Permanent water from Canada became available in 1986.

Water brought development, but there are no sewers. Septic systems determine what and where you can build. Three golf courses are planned and Point Roberts now has a marina, small airport, two taverns, restaurants, gas bars, a marketplace, an art gallery, clothing store, bike shop, hairdresser and a monthly newspaper. The five real estate offices still sell mostly to Canadians, and two sheriffs zealously monitor crime. Customs is open 24 hours, has a PACE lane and cameras to read licence plates.

Movie industry employees have discovered it's an easy commute for the dozens of movies shooting in Vancouver. But where else can Canadians drive 30 minutes out of Vancouver, hop in their boat, put down a crab trap, catch a salmon and have a barbecue for the neighbors on a crime-free, quiet spit of land where properties are relatively inexpensive? That's Point Roberts.

Delta

Marlyn Graziano

Stretching from the Fraser River to the Strait of Georgia and the shores of Boundary Bay up to Scott Road, where it meets its urban neighbor Surrey, the Municipality of Delta possesses some of the richest farmland and most environmentally significant areas in the Lower Mainland.

The municipality's three distinct residential communities—Ladner, Tsawwassen and North Delta—are divided physically by large tracts of agricultural land and the 2,226-hectare Burns Bog, touted as the largest domed peat bog on the west coast of the Americas. (For more on the bog, see Shane McCune's article.)

The early settlers who arrived on the Fraser River delta confronted marshland and forest, and toiled to dyke, drain and clear the land that held so much promise for farming.

Delta's early days are most often linked with the Ladner name. The municipality's best-known pioneers—brothers William and Thomas Ladner—settled in the Fraser River lowland in 1868. Their farms grew into the pioneer settlement of Ladner's Landing, where the community of Ladner now sits on the shores of the Fraser River.

But according to the Delta Museum and Archives, James Kennedy was the first to preempt land in the municipality, doing so in 1859. Over the next few years, he worked at clearing a trail southward from his farm near Brownsville (in Surrey across from New Westminster), helping to open up North Delta. Kennedy's mark is left on many parts of modern North Delta, where the area near Scott Road and 88th Avenue bears his name. Nonetheless, most of the early stories of Delta begin with the Ladner brothers, enterprising Cornishmen who dyked their land to take advantage of its agricultural richness.

Drainage was a continual problem, not just for farming but for transportation as well. The earliest settlers used the inland waterways as transportation routes, as road conditions remained poor, especially during the rainy seasons. The soft peat of Burns Bog, which separates Ladner from North Delta, was some of the most difficult to overcome.

Construction of a government wharf in 1873 allowed Ladner's Landing to become a centre of commerce, where farmers could access passing steamers to ship their goods to other parts of the province.

The area that later became Tsawwassen—named for the native peoples who first inhabited the area—began as a resort community, where beachfront cottages were built along the shores of Boundary Bay. The wetlands of the bay form an important link in the Pacific Flyway—an international migration route used each year by millions of birds.

Delta was incorporated in 1879 and its first elected council met on January 12, 1880, with William Ladner as reeve. The commercial importance of Ladner's Landing continued, and the site became the seat of the municipal government, with the first municipal hall built on Elliott Street in 1883.

In 1878 the Tsawwassen Indian Reserve was established, allotting 243 hectares to the descendants of Delta's first people. Not much is known of the natives' early history, but they were a coastal people who depended mainly on fishing for their survival.

While agriculture remained an important industry in the new municipality, the richness of salmon stocks in the Fraser River soon resulted in a new enterprise, and canneries began to spring up throughout the area. By the end of the 1880s there were over a dozen canneries in operation.

Thomas Ladner was not one to miss an opportunity and was one of four partners to build the Delta Cannery in 1878, near Ladner's Landing. In North Delta the construction of a cannery on Gunderson Slough in 1870 gave rise to a small Norwegian community that came to be known as Annieville. The slough is named after Norwegian pioneer Jacob Gunderson, who arrived in 1897 to work at the Anglo-British Columbia Cannery.

Some say Annieville was named after a Mrs. Laidlaw, whose husband owned the cannery, others say it was named after the wife of pioneer James Symes. The latter version, as told by long-time Annieville resident Edward Erickson, is the more colorful one: on a trip across the Fraser River to New Westminster, the slough was clogged with bullrushes and the crew of a skiff debated how to get through the reeds. According to Erickson, when someone asked who was going to pull the boat through the reeds, the answer came (in a strong Norse accent), "Oh, Annie vill."

The canneries attracted many ethnic workers, including Chinese and natives, and for a while, Ladner had its own Chinatown, the scene of a spectacular fire in July 1929. The settlement stretched along the riverfront and consisted of about 15 buildings. Half of Chinatown was destroyed in the blaze, which was reported in the *Ladner Optimist,* the local newspaper: "Fanned by a tremendous wind, the fire burned like lightning through the dry wood and the damage was all done before firefighting equipment from Vancouver could reach the scene. Calls for help came soon after the blaze was discovered. Its origin is unknown."

As drainage improved, so did Delta's roads, and once the automobile made its appearance, the municipality grew in leaps and bounds. The post-war residential boom in the Lower Mainland filtered into Delta. Growth was further fuelled by the opening of the Pattullo Bridge in 1937, which made North Delta accessible to the thousands of post-war workers who found Vancouver too expensive to call home.

It wasn't until 1958, however, that a fixed link was built between Ladner and Richmond. Until then, river crossings were made via the Ladner-Woodward's Landing ferry. In April 1958 Ladner was connected to Lulu Island via the Deas Island Tunnel (later renamed the George Massey Tunnel). Six sections comprising 663 metres of concrete and steel were sunk to construct the tunnel, which was opened to traffic later that spring. Queen Elizabeth II did the official honors in July.

The Queen was welcomed by about 3,000 people at the tunnel. Others had gathered along the route which the Queen drove with Prince Philip; crowds cheered from Kennedy Heights and Delta Private Hospital, where patients sat outside in chairs. Premier and Mrs. W.A.C. Bennett were the first to greet the royal couple when they arrived at the south entrance to open the $21-million tunnel. From the reviewing stand, Queen Elizabeth cut a blue ribbon that stretched across the roadway. Later the silver scissors she had used were officially presented to her by the premier, to whom she gave a 10-cent piece in observance of an old superstition regarding gifts of knives and scissors.

Delta entered the modern industrial age in May 1953, when the Duke of Westminster, one of Britain's wealthiest peers, unveiled his plans for a multi-million dollar industrial project on Annacis Island. The following decades saw industry flock to Delta, not only to Annacis but to the Tilbury area along River Road, where improved highway systems gave businesses access to Vancouver and the U.S.

Growth—industrial and residential—has not been an easy issue for Delta, sandwiched as it is between Vancouver and Surrey, where expansion south of the Fraser River has brought with it ever-increasing commuter traffic. For that reason, construction of the Alex Fraser Bridge—which opened September 22, 1986, and linked North Delta with Richmond and New Westminster—is the subject of much debate by local residents, who openly wonder if it is a blessing or a curse.

Tsawwassen drew national attention in the spring and summer of 1989, when the now-infamous Tsawwassen Developments controversy raged. Residents banded together to fight the housing proposal along the shores of Boundary Bay, but the battle divided the community, pitting newcomers against oldtimers. The controversy stretched into the longest public hearing in the country's history until the pro-ject was finally sunk by council. The proposal had been debated at a 25-session public hearing that lasted from May 1 to July 17. Over 400 speakers were heard and 3,700 written submissions received.

Then federal environment minister Lucien Bouchard got into the act, calling for a moratorium on development around Boundary Bay. The debate about preservation of the wetlands along the bay continues through the 1990s, as does the push to prevent development in Burns Bog.

Highway approaches to the Alex Fraser Bridge, opened in 1986. vp

Environment

MOHAWK

Mohawk, established in 1960, is a different kind of oil company. The company has been providing Western Canadian motorists with environmentally responsible products for more than a decade. Cleaner burning fuel products include ethanol-blended gasolines, diesel with ECA (Emission Control Additive), propane, natural gas and M85 (methanol). Mohawk collects and, through a unique process, hydrotreats the used oil

Greater Vancouver residents have solid reasons for believing ours is a sophisticated, cosmopolitan place, but to much of the world its chief importance is as a gateway to a vast, natural world.

Our greatest treasure lies around us in the mountains, sea, rivers, lakes and forests, not in what we've built. We don't have the Louvre or the British Museum; we have one of the world's richest salmon rivers. Instead of the Leaning Tower of Pisa we have mountain ranges with flower meadows in summer and skiing in winter. No Taj Mahal, but an inland sea offering unrivalled cruising, fishing and watersports.

Compared with much of the more populated world, our environment remains reasonably clean, green and inviting, despite a long history of friction between the conservationists on the one hand, and the resource industries and developers on the other.

The 400-hectare Stanley Park is the most famous symbol of Vancouver. Ask a first-time visitor what tops his or her itinerary, and odds are it will be Stanley Park first, and maybe Grouse Mountain or Cypress Bowl next.

Almost all of the Lower Fraser Valley was logged, much of it by settlers hacking fields out of forests. More recently a push for more golf courses threatened such ecologically sensitive areas as Boundary Bay and some forested slopes above West Vancouver.

But reasonable compromises seem to be getting more popular. Dozens of municipal, regional and provincial parks provide habitat for smaller wildlife, from hummingbirds and hawks to cottontails and coyotes. The coyote is a story in itself. This small, wily animal has adapted marvellously to the influx of humans, and its clan is more numerous now than it was a century ago. Major new parks and ecological reserves are on the way as the fast-growing population of Greater Vancouver demands more wild and semi-wild green spaces for outdoor recreation and breaks from the pressures of urban living.

Public awareness of environmental issues has expanded dramatically and shows itself in many ways, from recycling programs for householders' bottles, cans and paper to bans on trash-burning (and cigarette-burning) in public places.

As recently as the 1950s and 1960s the air quality of Greater Vancouver was heavily affected by the fumes from the many coal- and sawdust-fuelled furnaces, and by the smoke that poured from the infamous "beehive" waste burners at sawmills dotted around the Lower Mainland.

The buildup of smoke caused some monumental fogs on winter nights. Once I tried to drive home by following the tail-lights of a motorist who seemed to be going in the right direction—and ended up in his driveway. Such mystery trips have been largely eliminated with the switch to heating with oil, natural gas and electricity, and the virtual elimination of sawmill waste burners.

In many parts of the world there is a move to make the economy better serve our environment, rather than sacrificing environmental quality to make extraction of natural resources more profitable. For years we have been told by politicians and industrialists that the economy must keep growing at all costs or the good times will wither and die. But for the new millennium, the movers and shakers are beginning to realize that the key word is *sustainability*.

The concept is simply to reduce consumption of even a renewable resource like trees so there can always be a steady flow of timber to the mills—with enough natural forest left untouched to support all the other, non-consumptive uses.

Tourism is our fastest-expanding industry, but it won't prosper if all our valleys and mountainsides are stripped bare to feed non-sustainable industry.

It's taken a while, but there are strong indications that the people of Greater Vancouver are getting their environmental priorities straight. We just have to be sure officialdom gets the message.

—*Tony Eberts*

facing page: The West End and the North Shore mountains, 1994. vs
above: Land speculators celebrate the felling of "Alex Russel's big tree," cut down in February 1886 on the present site of the Hudson's Bay store at Georgia and Granville. The tree was 310 feet tall. cva

Weather in Greater Vancouver
Phil Reimer

FROM MY PERSPECTIVE, I've always thought of Greater Vancouver weather as theatre. Vancouver Island is the balcony, Georgia Strait the orchestra seating, Greater Vancouver a vibrant stage of entertainment and our local mountains the backdrop.

Aren't we lucky?

Yes, we have weather problems—pollution, especially at certain times of the year, is a concern—but overall we are weather winners. From the Pacific Ocean through the Juan de Fuca and Georgia Straits, the winds flush out our air from time to time. (Weather stations in Burrard Inlet record calm for 20 to 43 per cent of the year.) Our mountain backdrop provides a place to play and the rains and snows fill our watersheds.

The people in Tsawwassen and White Rock take great delight in looking toward Vancouver and seeing the rain while they enjoy a bit of sunshine and cloud. The extreme south and western part of Greater Vancouver has one-third the amount of rain recorded on the North Shore. On the other hand it's impossible to downhill ski in White Rock. One rule of thumb is an increase of 100 millimetres of rain per year for every 100 metres of elevation.

More than three times as much rain falls on Hollyburn, Grouse and Seymour on the North Shore as falls on Richmond (up to 3,000 millimetres versus 1,100 millimetres or so). At the Lions, back in the mountain watershed, it is estimated that annual rainfalls of 5,000 millimetres are common. Tsawwassen, on the other hand, is in the "rain shadow" of the Olympics (clouds meeting the Olympics have been drained on the western slopes) and enjoys clear, dry air.

It is difficult to forecast weather in Vancouver. Take a look at our topography. We go from sea level to mountains in a few kilometres, we're next to an ocean, a strait and the mountains of Vancouver Island. Even Washington's Olympia range affects our weather.

The simple fact that we live here has an effect on our weather. It is warmer in the air above roads, buildings and concentrations of people. The temperature dips by a degree or two Celsius over such undeveloped areas as Stanley Park, Queen Elizabeth Park and Langara Golf Course compared with, say, the intersection of Georgia and Burrard. There is, believe it or not, a diagonal "warm arm along Kingsway," as one meteorology text puts it. With its mixture of urbanization and wilderness, the North Shore shows this effect best, with a core of heat above the foot of Lonsdale Avenue while the stream beds of the Capilano and Seymour rivers and Lynn Creek keep the air above them cold. As housing advances up Hollyburn, Grouse and Seymour we can expect to see the scenic mountaintop snowcap recede.

There is never any shortage of opinion that air pollution is getting worse over any major city. In Vancouver, though, there is good news: visible pollution has declined to the point where Vancouver International Airport is recording one-quarter to one-third the number of foggy days experienced in the 1940s. Much of the 90 days of fog the city used to get consisted of water vapor condensing around airborne particles from coal, wood and sawdust-burning furnaces in homes and industry. The sawmills that once ringed the south shore of False Creek burned off sawdust in "tepee" or "beehive" furnaces until the 1960s. The fog we still experience from 20 to 30 days a year is relatively pure and white—if just as hard to see through!

Then there's wind. The term "Squamish winds" has become a generic term for outflow air currents: winds that blow out of a valley or channel, often at speeds up to 100 kilometres per hour. Howe Sound is a north-south channel that can serve as an outlet for cold Arctic air that often sits over the province's interior in winter. In Howe Sound the speed of the winds is exaggerated by the tightness of the channel. The waters off Squamish itself are known as the best windsurfing location in B.C. because of the frequency and magnitude of these winds.

And there's rain. Vancouver's longest wet spell began January 6, 1953, and ended 29 days later. There was rain recorded on every one of those 29 days. (But Victoria beat that in 1986 with 33 days in a row!) But Vancouver is not Canada's wettest major city. Nor is it the second wettest. Nor even the third. In fact no fewer than five cities in Canada have average annual precipitation higher than Vancouver's paltry 1,113 millimetres. Every major city from Quebec City eastward to St. John's gets more annual precipitation than Vancouver.

So the best and worst thing about living in Greater Vancouver is the weather. (Allan Fotheringham once called Vancouver the Canadian city with the best climate and the worst weather.) When it's good, it's great. You hate to have someone you care for depart without seeing the city on one of those sensationally clear, sharp-focus days when the mountains look close enough to touch, when English Bay is white with sails beating against the wind and there are just enough clouds for a Technicolor sunset. Those days can come anytime, even in February. They come as welcome surprises, gifts from above. They affirm the decisions so many of us made either to move to Vancouver or stay here. It was here that houses with glass walls to bring the

A fog bank drifting into Burrard Inlet partially obscures the Lions Gate Bridge and the city centre, 1995 vs

outdoors inside first appeared in Canada. Where else in Canada would anyone want to bring the environment indoors?

We have, however, had our moments.

The lower Fraser River was known to freeze regularly during our grandparents' lifetimes. A new bridge between Lulu and Sea Islands in Richmond collapsed under pressure from ice floes in 1890. There was ice on the Fraser during Vancouver's worst recorded winter storm in January, 1935—enough to close sawmills and resist attempts to dynamite passageways for boats. Today heat and air pollution from increasing urbanization in the Lower Mainland seldom allow the mighty Fraser to freeze.

We've been keeping weather records here for more than a century: the Royal Engineers began recording weather in New Westminster in 1859 and the Royal City became a meteorological station in 1874. Vancouver began keeping weather records in 1898.

On August 9, 1960, Vancouver experienced its hottest day ever. The day's high was 33.3 degrees Celsius. On January 21, 1935, we had more than 43 centimetres of snow with gale winds and a minus 26 degrees Celsius temperature.

We've had our share of weather related disasters, with well-known examples being Typhoon Freda and the 1894 and 1948 Fraser Valley floods.

Freda hit just after midnight on October 13, 1962, with winds over 100 kilometres per hour, and lasted about four hours. Seven people were killed, a fifth of all the trees in Stanley Park were blown down, houses and buildings were damaged and the Lower Mainland was darkened from Horseshoe Bay to Hope.

On May 28, 1948, British Columbia's worst flood on record occurred, along the lower Fraser River. The toll: ten deaths, $300 million in damage, 200 families left homeless, rail service disrupted for two weeks and more than 80 bridges washed away.

Weather wisdom on the West Coast varies. Those travelling over Lions Gate Bridge note that if you can see Vancouver Island, it's going to rain and if you can't see the island, it's raining. Some believe that if the insects are flying low the humidity is high; others will tell you that if the seagulls are walking on the sand instead of flying, rain is at hand.

Meanwhile rain or shine, this is a TV weatherperson's dream. Never a dull moment.

Recreation in the Fraser River Basin
Kim Joslin

BEAUTIFUL BRITISH COLUMBIA, with its abundance of natural areas, provides a playground for numerous recreational activities. Each year people from all over flock to the province to enjoy leisurely pursuits in the mountains, on rivers, lakes and the ocean. But as the population grows and development pressures increase, especially in the Greater Vancouver area, this natural experience is threatened.

Environment Canada, through its Fraser River Action Plan, commissioned a study in 1994 to determine the value that British Columbians themselves place on recreational experiences. The study focussed on water-based recreational activities in the Fraser River basin—on or around the Fraser River itself, its tributaries like the Nechako, Thompson, Coquitlam and Pitt rivers, its lakes and streams.

Recreational activities on or around water prove to be very popular. One in four British Columbians takes part in activities such as hiking, river rafting, swimming and camping in the Fraser basin. They spend an average of 24 days per year enjoying our natural wilderness through these pastimes. In comparison to the province as a whole, even more Greater Vancouver residents take part in these activities. About one in three participate in recreational activities in the Fraser basin, averaging 22 days a year.

Hiking and backpacking, biking, water-skiing and windsurfing are done most frequently, in terms of the number of trips taken. But relaxing at a cabin or on the beach, biking and windsurfing are the activities on which British Columbians spend the most time. People living in the Greater Vancouver area tend to participate in hiking and backpacking, fishing and camping most often.

Favorite areas for recreational activity are the Lower Fraser and South Thompson regions. The Lower Fraser is the most popular region for canoeing, kayaking, sailing, salmon and steelhead fishing, hiking and backpacking. The South Thompson is favored for motorboating, swimming and sunbathing, picnicking and camping.

British Columbians taking part in these activities are willing to pay to maintain this experience, above and beyond the cost of actually undertaking these activities. On average they are willing to pay between $15 and $30 per activity, per outing. That amounts to a whopping $750 million each year that they are willing to part with in order to preserve their outdoor experiences. Greater Vancouver residents place a higher value than

Outrigger canoe, Vancouver, 1993. vs

average on these activities because they've seen the loss of natural areas to a greater extent than other British Columbians.

The Fraser River basin's natural bounty is definitely worth preserving! And, it seems, we are willing to pay to do so.

Environment Canada
Environnement Canada
FRASER RIVER ACTION PLAN
PLAN D'ACTION DU FRASER

The Fraser River with its tributaries, comprising Canada's fifth largest river system, drains a basin the size of Great Britain. The Fraser is one of the most productive salmon rivers in the world, and more than 300 species of birds and 45 species of mammals live within its basin. More than 80 per cent of British Columbia's Gross Domestic Product is generated within the basin, inhabited in 1996 by 2.5 million people. That population is expected to double by the year 2015.

Environmental Conditions in Greater Vancouver
Tony Eberts

THERE ARE ENCOURAGING trends in Greater Vancouver's air, water and soil qualities, which already compare well with any urban area in the world. Some "problems" might be better classified as issues or controversies. However, there are long-standing disputes, especially in such areas as toxic mill effluents, sewage management, logging near drinking water reservoirs, freeways versus public transport and development of farmland for industry, housing and golf courses.

When you consider that more than half the population of the entire province is concentrated in an area representing less than two per cent of British Columbia and that Greater Vancouver's population is increasing by about 40,000 each year—well, disagreements can hardly come as a surprise.

Woodsmoke is still a problem in many upcountry communities because of large-scale burning of the waste wood left by clearcut logging, but the Vancouver area has outgrown that. Here the battle is against that nasty, brownish haze known as smog, and the chief cause of it is the motor vehicle. On warm, sunny days with little or no wind, polluted air sometimes builds up over the eastern part of Greater Vancouver.

Despite the good effects of the 1990 ban on leaded gasoline, provincial and GVRD monitoring shows that on about 100 days each year some testing stations rate air quality as only fair.

According to environment ministry scientists, computer models of ozone generation (by vehicles, waste burning, natural gas processing and hot sunshine) indicate the situation will change very little during the first decade of the 21st century.

Some cheering statistics: while Vancouver is Canada's third largest city, air quality problems are worse in 10 other major centres. And while some cities (Toronto, for one) have to contend with smog drifting in from other areas, we on the Pacific Coast have only ourselves to deal with.

According to a survey by B.C. Water Management Branch scientists L.G. Swain and G.B. Holms and others, some 900 million cubic metres of gunk (domestic sewage, industrial and milling waste, urban and agricultural runoff) goes into the Fraser River each year from Hope to the estuary.

Frightening as that sounds, the flow of the Fraser (the third-largest river in Canada) is so huge that overall water quality can actually be rated fair to good. And senior government agencies are working on a special Green Plan for protecting the big river and its major salmon runs.

Parts of the estuary now receiving attention include the large Burns Bog in Richmond and Boundary Bay in Delta. Biologists of the Canadian Wildlife Service report that these areas support the greatest numbers of wintering waterfowl, shorebirds and birds of prey in Canada. Burns Bog is a natural wonder—4,000 hectares of swamp, forest, peat and Fraser River foreshore that has resisted dozens of development schemes. Ten times the size of Stanley Park, the bog accommodates much of Vancouver's garbage in one small area, while the rest is home to a wide range of wildlife and a rearing place for young salmon and other fish. Marshlands and undeveloped shoreline along the Fraser are vital to the survival of young salmon and trout.

One of the most emotional disputes involves the clearcut logging that the GVRD water committee allows in the old-growth forests surrounding mountain lake/reservoirs that supply the area's domestic water.

Water quality has fallen sharply, obviously due to increased rapid runoff that washes down silt and other impurities from slopes stripped of forest cover. But instead of suspending the logging and road-building in the watersheds, GVRD officials have chosen to simply treat the dirty water with an expensive chlorination system. One wag has suggested that if Vancouverites don't like dark-colored water, they should ask the loggers to stop chewing tobacco.

Running from West Vancouver to Squamish is scenic Howe Sound, with the Sea to Sky Highway and BC Rail's main line following its rocky shore. Once heavily polluted by rampant effluent of pulp mills, water quality is improving after environmental groups pressured government and the mills.

Some objective viewers of the situation predict that a compromise soon will be struck, just as reasonable compromises are being reached in controlling urban development in prime farmland and creating more parks and wildlife preserves.

Another highly controversial subject is the use of pesticides, especially chemicals broadcast from aircraft. Every time an urban or suburban area is sprayed for the elusive Gypsy Moth, for example, public health officials are bombarded with complaints of mysterious illnesses and invasion of personal rights and liberties.

Agriculture Canada experts insist that the biological pesticide used to save us from the possible (but highly unlikely) invasion of tree-damaging moths has been proven to be totally harmless to humans. Some of the humans respond that the same once was said about DDT. However, government agencies tend toward increasingly strict controls of pesticide use, and regular inspections of agricultural products are turning up no serious problems.

Recycling
Jim Lyon

GREATER VANCOUVER, like big cities everywhere, faces an immense problem in getting rid of household and commercial waste. Each year each one of us creates more garbage. And each year thousands of us come to live in the region to generate even more waste. (The population of the GVRD was expected to grow by roughly 20 per cent or 300,000 people in the 1990s.)

Just think of the stuff we cast out: newspapers, fax paper, cardboard boxes, car tires, batteries, half-empty paint cans, plastic bags and bottles, old mattresses, glass bottles, the plastic frog that croaked on Christmas morning, the VCR that never worked. The list is endless. (It's reckoned, by the way, that the average North American will throw away 600 times his own weight in garbage in a lifetime.)

In 1993, according to the GVRD, we generated over two million tonnes of solid waste—enough to fill B.C. Place Stadium twice over. Planners figured, if this trend wasn't changed, by the year 2000 we'd be generating more than three million tonnes of garbage a year. Landfill sites, where solid waste has traditionally been dumped, wouldn't cope (we're already sending much of our garbage to the Cache Creek landfill site, 300 kilometres away). Both cost and environmental impact would be enormous.

Alarmed by this trend, the provincial government set a goal requiring a 50 per cent per capita reduction in waste disposal by the end of the century. If we're to achieve this goal, we must generate much less waste and we must recycle all that we can.

Waste management is complicated by all the rain Vancouver gets. This increases the chance of contaminants leaching into lakes and streams—unless waste is stored indoors. Also the scarcity of natural clay-bearing soil in the region means there are few potential landfill sites.

In 1991 about 23 per cent of municipal solid waste generated within the GVRD was recovered for recycling. Based on a population of 1.7 million residents at that time the per capita waste generation rate for all GVRD residents was about 860 kilograms per year and the recycling rate was almost 200 kilograms per year.

Between 1988 and 1991 municipal solid waste recycling increased significantly. During that time the quantity of waste generated increased by more than 22 per cent but the amount recovered for recycling increased by almost 300 per cent.

It is estimated that 49 per cent of what is called DCL waste (mostly concrete and asphalt) was recycled in 1991. The remaining 51 per cent was landfilled, mainly in private sites in Delta and Richmond.

More than 210,000 tonnes a year of Greater Vancouver's solid waste is incinerated at the GVRD's state-of-the-art plant in Burnaby. Here steam energy is recovered from the waste burning process and sold to the adjacent paper mill, Paperboard Industries. The facility also recovers about 7,000 tonnes a year of ferrous metal for recycling.

What happens to the materials we put out for recycling?

NEWSPRINT Newsprint is truly recyclable material. After they are collected, newspapers are screened for contaminants like plastic or cardboard. They are then sent to newsprint de-inking plants, one of which is in Coquitlam. This plant essentially adds water to the newspapers, turning them into a slurry of paper fibres from which the ink is then removed. The wet paper, or pulp, is pressed into thick sheets of pure paper pulp. This pulp is sent to local paper manufacturers who then blend the recycled pulp with virgin paper pulp and turn it into new sheets of recycled newsprint. Almost all of this recycled newsprint produced locally is sent to California, where state law requires that newspaper publishers must use newsprint with a minimum of 40 per cent recycled content. Recycled newsprint is also used to produce cat litter or take-out trays.

PLASTICS When plastics were invented, they weren't designed to be recyclable. Each time plastics are remelted and reshaped, they get weaker and the overall quality declines. There are many different types of plastics with different characteristics. You can't recycle a plastic shampoo bottle into a clear pop bottle, for example. You can't remove color from plastic. Once it's colored, an item can be remade only into the same color of plastic or colored black.

There's another problem: because used plastics can't be completely cleaned and sterilized, they can't be turned into food or drink packages. This greatly limits their secondary use. That's why municipal collection programs limit the types of plastic homeowners can discard (usually to milk jugs, which are remelted and made into motor oil jugs or grocery bags, and pop bottles, which are turned into carpets or clothing insulation materials).

In 1994 about 60 tonnes of plastic collected in the City of Vancouver was turned into plastic lumber by Eco-Superwood on Annacis Island. (It's great for park benches.)

ALUMINUM CANS These are remelted and made into new aluminum cans.

TIN CANS They're actually made of steel with an interior tin coating. The tin and steel are separated and are used to make

Tobi Sales began in 1968 with a great asset: a patent on the formula for Spray Kleen, a multi-purpose cleaner formulated by a Lower Mainland chemist. After hard, slogging months of sales to individual stores, company founder Tom Hall fortuitously bumped into a major grocery broker and grabbed the opportunity. He whipped out a ballpoint pen and stained his own suit, then sprayed the stain with Spray Kleen. The stain vanished. The broker was impressed. Spray Kleen had arrived.

Recycling Vancouver, 1993. vp

new tin-coated cans, and any other items normally made from tin or steel.

GLASS BOTTLES AND JARS They are remelted to make new bottles and jars. They are also used as a gravel substitute in road and building construction and in the manufacture of fibreglass.

MOTOR OIL It's been estimated that about five million litres of waste oil is disposed of annually by "do-it-yourselfers" in Greater Vancouver. In 1990 the GVRD and its member municipalities decided to buy only recycled motor oil.

Mohawk Lubricants began operating a used oil re-refining plant in North Vancouver in 1980. Mohawk's used oil division can collect more than 33 million litres a year of used lubricating oil. This equates to 30,000 tonnes of potentially hazardous waste material being removed from the Western Canadian environment every year. Mohawk has a fleet of collection trucks specially designed to retrieve used oil from mines, logging camps, mills, ferries, auto repair shops and gas stations. The company produces a high quality base oil from used oil by distilling and hydrotreating. The re-refined oil is then blended into lubricants which meet or exceed manufacturer's specifications. In 1995 Mohawk was increasing its collection and re-refining capacity.

SCRAP TIRES Each year the region generates about one million scrap tires (10,000 tons), which are incinerated to produce energy for cement making.

LEAD-ACID BATTERIES About 400,000 spent lead-acid batteries are disposed of in the GVRD each year. These are recycled into new batteries.

GYPSUM WALLBOARD About 50,000 tonnes of gypsum wallboard is recycled into new material each year.

CFC RECOVERY PROJECT The GVRD administers a program to recover CFC (chlorofluorocarbon)—an ozone-depleting chemical—from used appliances. CFC is removed by Pierre CFC Recycling and sent to Dupont Chemicals in Ontario, where it is cleaned for re-use. In 1994, 125 kilograms of CFC was removed from more than 1,250 appliances at Vancouver City depots.

OLD REFRIGERATORS B.C. Hydro operates a Power Smart Refrigerator Recovery program. Hydro arranges for the removal of up to two operating fridges free-of-charge, removes the CFC and then delivers the fridges to a scrap metal recycler.

COMPOSTING Several municipalities supply residents with subsidized compost bins so organic waste (otherwise destined for landfills) can be recycled into a usable soil conditioner. The City of Vancouver began the program in 1990. Five years later it had distributed more than 15,000 compost bins ($25 each) to householders, thus diverting about 3,800 tonnes of organic material annually.

The majority of materials recovered from the municipal waste stream are shipped overseas to satisfy the demands of Asian industries for raw resources. Local industries have traditionally used the province's abundant virgin materials to feed their processing and manufacturing facilities.

Much of the success of recycling programs depends on the economics of supply and demand. When world prices for recycled materials are low, municipalities are obliged to give the materials away to companies that arrange for their disposal. When demand is high during an upbeat economic cycle, municipalities negotiate lucrative contracts. (The market price for plastic milk jugs, for example, increased from $230 a tonne to $750 a ton over a two to three year period; old newspapers jumped in value from $50 to $250 a metric tonne in one year in the mid-1990s.)

Apart from its environmental attractiveness, recycling also makes good economic sense. In the mid-1990s the North Shore Recycling Program, jointly funded by the three municipalities there, was collecting 10,000 tonnes of recyclable materials a year and selling them for about $1 million. But that's not the end of it. Since it then cost $69 a tonne to tip materials into landfills (ignoring transportation charges), the municipalities were also saving taxpayers an additional $690,000 a year by diverting recyclable materials.

For more information about recycling in Greater Vancouver, call the Recycling Hotline (732-9253). The GVRD also operates a Compost Hotline (736-2250).

Today, Spray Kleen is bottled in thousands at the plant, but a decision by Tobi Sales in 1972 to make its own bottles was a wise one. It led to the formation of a sister company, Coast Pacific Plastics Ltd., which now makes recycled-plastic bottles not just for Spray Kleen but for clients like General Paint and Recochem. And now a Japanese company has contracted with Coast Pacific to manufacture a plastic component for an innovative sewage-treatment system. Tobi believes in recycling!

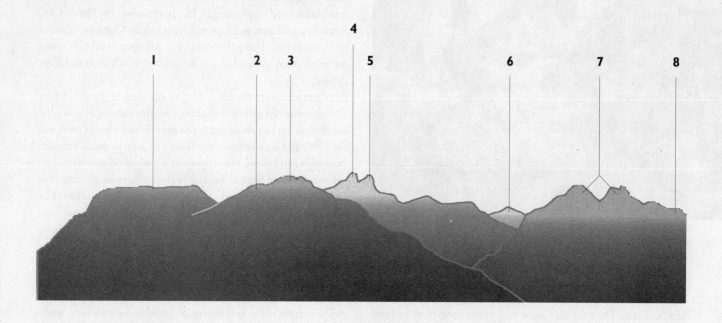

Natural Skyline
Steven Threndyle

FROM PROSPECT POINT in Stanley Park one truly has a front-porch view of the mountains arising from the North Shore of Burrard Inlet. As the eagle flies it's 20 kilometres from the summit plateau of Black Mountain (1) in the west to the alpine bowls and ridges of Mount Seymour (15). These summits before you are not part of a single, contiguous ridge, but are separated from each other by four major valleys: Cypress Creek, the Capilano River, Lynn Valley and the Seymour River. The saltwater Indian Arm of Burrard Inlet separates Mount Seymour from the forested slopes above Coquitlam, such as Burke Mountain. Farther east the Golden Ears group (originally known as "Golden Eyries" because of the local eagle population) dominates the Fraser Valley above Pitt Meadows and Maple Ridge.

Perhaps the most unique characteristic of the North Shore Range is its particular orientation—this seemingly impenetrable wall of forest and rock is oriented in an east-west, as opposed to north-south, direction. From west to east, the

main summits are: (1) Black Mountain—1,217 metres, (2) Mount Hollyburn—1,324 metres, (3) Mount Strachan—1,454 metres, (4) West Lion—1,646 metres, (5) East Lion—1,599 metres, (6) Mount Capilano—1,685 metres, (7) Crown Mountain—1,503 metres, (8) Grouse Mountain—1,211 metres, (9) The Camel—1,495 metres, (10) Cathedral Mountain—1,723 metres, (11) Mount Fromme—1,177 metres, (12) Mount Burwell—1,530 metres, (13) The Needles—1,250 metres, (14) Lynn Peaks—1,000 metres and (15) Mount Seymour—1,450 metres.

The North Shore mountains are not particularly high. In fact only the rocky summits of the West and East Lion (4 and 5, respectively), Crown Mountain and the Camel (9 and 10) are above the treeline. The exposed rock in these peaks consists mainly of a combination of granite, granodiorite, quartz diorite and gabbro. At 20 million years of age the Coast Range is one of North America's youngest mountain ranges. Although pockets of snow can exist year-round on north-facing slopes, there are no glaciers or icefields at this elevation.

Early settlers to Vancouver were as fascinated by the challenge of climbing these mountains as weekend recreationists are today. As the craggiest and most imposing of the North

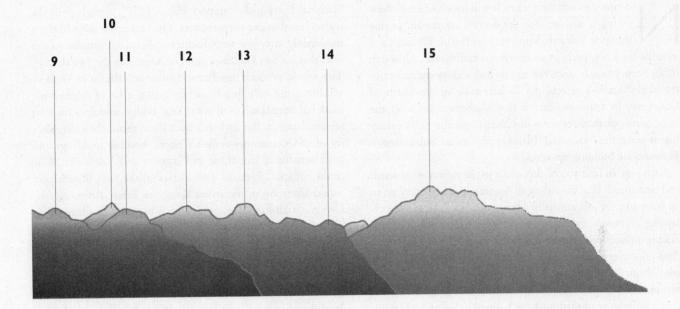

9   10   11   12   13   14   15

Shore mountains, the twin summits of The Lions have produced a considerable body of folklore and legend surrounding early ascents. The earliest recorded climb of the West Lion in 1889 happened almost by accident. A group of hunters following a herd of goats found themselves at the top with no place to go but down. The hunting party was guided by native chief Joe Capilano. One of the members of the hunting team was Doctor Henry Bell-Irving, who asked Capilano if he could time one of the chief's young natives to see how long it would take him to run from the base of the West Lion to the summit. The youth, stripped completely naked, made the round trip ascent and descent in under 20 minutes!

With its steep granitic face the East Lion was believed to be impossible to scale. That did not deter John Latta and his two brothers from setting out to climb the East Lion in 1903. Hearing that climbers often used ropes for mountaineering ascents, they packed one along, but actually had no idea of how to use it. Their technique was to grasp the small shrubs and bushes growing out of the cracks in the rock, a style that would be considered rather poor form today! For good measure the Latta brothers also climbed the West Lion on their way out.

With the formation of the Vancouver Mountaineering Club (later changed to the British Columbia Mountaineering Club) in 1907, the remaining summits of the North Shore were quick to fall. The summer of 1908 must have been a good one for climbing weather, as Mount Seymour, Lynn Peak, Cathedral Mountain, Crown Mountain and the Camel were ascended by BCMC members. With its blocky, granitic formation, the Camel was the first mountain to be ascended using anything approaching standard rock-climbing techniques.

No mention of early mountaineering exploits on the North Shore would be complete without reference to Basil Darling whose climb (in 1908) of the most remote of the North Shore mountains, Cathedral Mountain, is not repeated that often even today. Coast Range mountaineering historian Bruce Fairley notes, "Darling was undoubtedly one of the outstanding mountaineers in all of North America in his time. He made many notable ascents, including the north buttress of the West Lion, and first ascents of Sky Pilot, Golden Ears, Cathedral and other peaks in the Vancouver area. Darling also made early winter attempts on The Lions, ascending the frozen Capilano River in the wee hours by lantern light."

Waiting for the Big One
Daniel Wood

N o one can predict when it will hit or where or how strong it will be. But the experts are certain of one thing: it *will* hit. Southwestern British Columbia is overdue for a big, perhaps an enormous earthquake. Although it has been 50 years since the region had a close encounter of the shaky kind—a strong 7.3 Richter-scale quake north of Courtenay in 1946—the fact is that Vancouver sits atop the most active earthquake zone in Canada and the half-century hiatus since the Vancouver Island quake means subterranean pressures are building up again.

Each year, in fact, 300 quakes occur in the region, most small and unnoticed. But, according to researchers, once every 20 to 50 years a major jolt normally releases this stored pressure, collapsing chimneys, cracking walls, emptying shelves and producing minor landslips as happened in the Courtenay case. And once every 300 to 600 years, this region has been hit by a megathrust quake (8.5+) accompanied by 10- to 20-metre movements along the faultline, landslides and tsunamis on the coast. Were such an earthquake to happen today under Greater Vancouver, the results would be catastrophic. A recent study based on this scenario predicts 10 to 30 per cent of the area's homes would be damaged, 60 to 100 per cent of the older, unreinforced masonry buildings would suffer some degree of collapse, 15 per cent of the highrises would be rendered uninhabitable, many of the bridges and schools would be severely damaged, and thousands would die. It would be the largest natural disaster in Canadian history.

The origin of this danger lies in the Cascadia Subduction Zone, a 1,400 kilometre-long faultline that runs southward from Alaska along the west coast of the Queen Charlotte Islands and Vancouver Island to Oregon. Along this line, three different tectonic plates—the North American Plate, the Pacific Plate and the smaller Juan de Fuca Plate—join together like pieces in a gargantuan puzzle. But the situation is not static. The Pacific Ocean's bottom, spreading eastward at 4.3 centimetres a year (the speed that fingernails grow) is sliding beneath—or subducting—under the westward-drifting continent of North America. Research in the past 20 years has found evidence that this motion is currently stuck. When it is released somewhere along the subducting zone—either offshore like the 1949 quake near the northern tip of the Queen Charlotte Islands that registered 8.0 or inland like the 1872 quake beneath Abbotsford that registered 7.5—the potential for disaster is con-

siderable. A subduction quake off Mexico's coast in 1985 killed 9,000 people, most of them beneath collapsed buildings in Mexico City, 300 kilometres from the epicentre.

There are two scenarios for Greater Vancouver, says the National Earthquake Support Plan (NESP), a study into the region's earthquake preparedness. The first is the most likely: a moderately strong 6 to 7 Richter-scale quake, similar to the ones that hit San Francisco and Los Angeles in the past decade. This would produce significant damage and deaths in Vancouver. Since the 1989 San Francisco quake, a lot of engineering work has been done to upgrade local bridges and dams against seismic hazards. But little has been done about the vulnerability of older, masonry-walled schools, hospital buildings and brick structures like those in Gastown and Yaletown. Some could collapse. Even in a moderate quake, soil liquefaction would likely break the dykes along the Fraser River and the Georgia Strait foreshore, producing widespread flooding. Similar soil liquefaction would also likely affect many structures on reclaimed lands, especially those built on the periphery of False Creek, the Arbutus lowlands, the riverbanks of the Fraser, Sea Island and the Burrard Inlet waterfront all the way to Port Moody. Landslides and underwater slumpages would drop shoreline houses and port facilities. Power, gas and water systems could be affected for days.

The second—and less likely—NESP scenario, based on an 8.5 subduction quake in the Lower Mainland, would produce severe destruction within 100 kilometres of the epicentre. Many buildings would fail. Liquefaction would likely damage the airport, the Fraser Valley dykes, the Massey Tunnel and those bridge supports sunk into loose valley soils. Western sections of the Fraser Valley would flood. Up to 45 per cent of Vancouver's schools would suffer moderate to total collapse. Tsunamis and underwater slumpage would damage shoreline facilities, producing almost inevitable chemical spills, fires and mass evacuations. The death toll would be in the thousands.

The chance of such a catastrophe hitting Vancouver, though real, is extremely remote. Most historic, massive quakes have occurred along the subduction zone west of Vancouver Island and the Queen Charlotte Islands. The last significant quake to jolt Greater Vancouver struck in 1976, a 5.3 Richter-scale fracture 70 kilometres below Pender Island. It knocked people from their beds in White Rock, cut electrical services in Richmond, South Vancouver and the Sechelt Peninsula, and sent residents of West End highrises screaming into the halls as the building swayed for 30 seconds. The bigger 1946 Courtenay quake, much farther distant, dropped some Vancouver chimneys and cornices, emptied some local shelves, swayed buildings and bridges, and frightened everyone. Other occasional quakes over the past century near Vancouver have produced similar effects: no deaths, little damage and a lot of excitement. The fact is that—unlike California where the faults intersect the earth's surface—the plunging Cascadia Subduction Zone heads deeply under Vancouver so that any ruptures there, like the moderate Pender Island quake, lose some of their impact as the vibrations move upward toward the surface. It is the big 1872 Abbotsford quake that makes seismologists, structural engineers and emergency planners worry. Since few lived in the Fraser Valley at the time, its effect was minimal. But reports from that time say that waves a metre high rolled across the solid land and people were thrown to the ground by the force of the shaking. A repeat of that quake today would be a disaster.

The thought of a major historic quake under the Fraser Valley and the recent quakes on North America's west coast have propelled a series of government initiatives in British Columbia. A new emergency response plan now links a dozen different teams of experts—the heavy rescue group, damage assessment engineers, firefighters, communications experts, hazardous materials specialists, the coroner, counselling psychologists—into a network prepared to act quickly in the face of a calamity.

At the preventative level a large number of seismic-upgrading projects in the Vancouver region are either completed or under way. The Cleveland Dam in North Vancouver was brought to the highest seismic code in 1992. The 28 municipal bridges within Vancouver have now all been retrofitted against earthquakes. So have both the Oak Street and the Second Narrows bridges. (The Lions Gate Bridge remains vulnerable and unrepaired since its future is currently uncertain.) The Vancouver School Board is in the early stages of a massive upgrading of the 100 older school buildings at risk—one-third the total in the school system. With most of the unreinforced, brick school buildings in the region under its jurisdiction, Vancouver faces a retrofit bill of $300 million. Vancouver's two major hospitals, both originally housed in fragile, older buildings, are currently moving many of their departments into modern structures. A new $10 million, seismically safe Emergency Operations Centre for Vancouver and adjacent communities is being designed. It will act as the fulcrum of all disaster relief efforts. A new system of three saltwater pumping stations and earthquake-resistant piping is under construction at the periphery of the Vancouver downtown core. This will serve as a back-up in case, as happened in Japan in 1995, water mains break and widespread fires erupt. Corporations, especially those involved with transportation and hazardous materials, have spent millions more to secure their facilities.

But the reality is that when it hits, a major earthquake in the Greater Vancouver area would be a disaster. Most wood-framed homes would ride out the shaking with little serious risk to their occupants. Modern structures, including all highrises and office towers, would remain standing. The old and vulnerable water system would inevitably fail. Gas mains would break and fires would follow. Sections of bridges, port facilities and old masonry-walled buildings would collapse. Train lines, roads and electrical distribution systems would fail. Loose objects within offices, factories and homes would be hurled around. Cornices and chimneys would fall. Glass would fly. Many people would die. Earthquakes search out the most vulnerable sections of a structure. And the Vancouver area has many older buildings that have never been tested in a great quake. The longer the shaking lasts, the worse it will be—as small initial structural failures grow exponentially as the vibrations continue. Someday this will happen here. Nothing can protect Vancouver from things that go bump in the night.

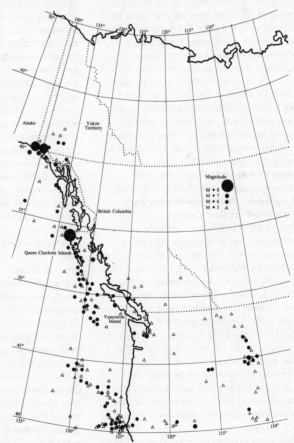

Distribution of significant earthquakes along the northwest coast of North America.

Some Trees of Greater Vancouver
Terri Clark

The Lower Mainland is fortunate in that there are droves of citizens who value trees beyond the present. They plant for the future and we are thankful for that. There are a few tree lovers we should pay special attention to. Their collective efforts, described below, have helped develop the present and future face of the Greater Vancouver area and to them we owe gratitude. Special "must see" trees are listed in the next article.

Stanley Park Forest
Though more than 100 years old as a protected area this 406-hectare preserve offers hope for formerly logged sites. What the visitor sees today is second- and third-growth forest featuring the common West Coast mix of red cedar, Douglas fir and hemlock. Nicely scattered throughout this evergreen quilt are numerous species of deciduous trees like vine maple, big leaf maple and red alder. Few old-growth stands remain; those that do were spared because of their enormous size or remote locations. These monument trees can be discovered just north of the Mounted Squad stables or down the path south of the Hollow Tree leading to Third Beach. Here you'll find the *National Geographic* Tree; the magazine proclaimed it one of the world's largest (almost five metres in diameter) and most ancient trees, as cedars go, at approximately 1,000 years old. Many pathways etch Stanley Park and almost any one of them will lead you to these towering wooden sentinels.

Ornamental Plantings—Stanley Park Pitch-and-Putt Golf Course
Ornamental trees show us a pretty face either in form, flower, leaf, seed or bark. An amazing plantation of such trees exists in and around the Stanley Park Pitch-and-Putt Golf Course. A wonderful old man, Dr. John Yak, whose avocations after his retirement from medicine were botany and ornithology, approached me in the early seventies with a slim, hand-typed book identifying what he described as a "priceless" collection of ornamental trees. Dr. Yak, then about 90, had catalogued each important specimen so that a comprehensive guide would be at the disposal of both the Park Board staff and the public. This first research by Dr. Yak proved an invaluable resource for subsequent publications and articles on this subject.

Specimens to watch for include Sargent's magnolia—looking like enormous pink hankies when in magnificent bloom in early April—which pro-

duces the largest bloom in the magnolia family. Also here are two Wilson's magnolias whose buds are egg-shaped and, when open in May, proffer a lemony scent followed by a purplish-scarlet seed head in autumn. Sprenger's magnolia is here, its late winter, furry flower buds decorating the bare branches before exploding into pinky froth in late March. Also found around the pitch-and-putt pathway is a terrific collection of camellias with colorful blossoms ranging from white to palest pink at their peak from late March to early April. The azaleas and rhododendrons skirting the pitch-and-putt were part of an extensive collection obtained from Ted and Mary Grieg of Royston Nurseries on Vancouver Island. About 4,500 plants are necklaced around the golf course beneath the towering magnolias and evergreens. Of special interest are the *rhododendron auriculatum* hybrids which combine the desirable characteristics of late bloom time in July and August and scent, something not usually found in rhodos. An early evening stroll through this area during the first two weeks in May astounds the park visitor with Italian ice colors combining bloom and foliage. Summer walkers are equally bowled over to see colorful rhodos blooming "out of season." Literally hundreds of further ornamental trees are found here, many around the Park Board administration office at the Beach Avenue entrance to Stanley Park. The building's granite front wall is clothed in a magnificent espaliered specimen of blue atlas cedar which, at more than 30 years of age, reminds us of the powers of pruning. Veils of weeping beech are nearby, next to a small grove of white pine. You'll find a good guide book is necessary, such as Gerald Straley's *Trees of Vancouver* or the Natural History Society's *The Natural History of Stanley Park* with excellent articles by longtime Stanley Park gardener Alleyne Cook. With book in hand you are ready to begin your great tree adventures in Vancouver's first and most-beloved park!

Trees as Gifts
Ever wonder about those superb cherry trees at Stanley Park's entrance? These five spreading specimens of Yoshino cherry trees were a gift to the park in the late 1940s from Japan. They bloom during the last week in March and should be on everyone's guided tour. Another gift of trees came from the Japanese city of Yokohama in 1967; they have since put down their roots on Cambie Street between 41st and 49th Avenues. They are also Yoshino cherry trees and we can't think of a nicer centennial birthday present for Canada. An allee of Katsura trees was donated by the Rotary Club in 1992 and planted in Seaforth Peace Park. The Vancouver Park Board has many tree donation programs serving both

private and corporate needs. These woody gifts of today will grace tomorrow's streets and green spaces.

Queen Elizabeth Park
When first planned this former stone quarry and surrounding land provided a perfect backdrop and environment for an arboretum or plantation of varied species of trees. It is said the sloping hillsides in this jewel of a park contain a specimen of every tree native to Canada. A map and guide to this magnificent collection has yet to be produced but it is often referred to in Gerald Straley's *Trees of Vancouver*. Trees to look for include the giant dogwood, a tree connoisseur's delight and one of the hardest to propagate. The blue spruce, vine maple, western white pine, Lawson cypress, honey locust, the black locust or acacia, golden-twigged ash and amur cork tree are but a few of the treasures awaiting enthusiasts. Queen Elizabeth Park is open all year for those seeking nature's beauty, and in every season you'll discover another surprise.

VanDusen Botanical Display Garden
The former Shaughnessy Golf Course has been transformed into a world-class botanical garden over the past 20 years. The majestic evergreens throughout the site pre-date the garden, and it is on this excellent structure that much of the display's subsequent development was based. Originally designed by the late Bill Livingstone, chief landscaper for the Vancouver Park Board over a splendid 35-year career, the plantings of the last two decades have been conducted under the creative drive and vision of curator Roy Forster whose catholic taste is evident after even a brief stroll in this gorgeous refuge. Special trees include *ginkgo bilbao*, a grove of *sequioadendron giganteum*, *sequioadendron giganteum pendula*, *acer palmatum aralia elata*, *catalpa bignonioides aurea*, *magnolia dawsoniana*, *pyrus salicifolia pendula* and *zelkova serrata*. A new Autumn Colour Garden was opened in 1995 near the hedge maze in VanDusen's southwest corner. Early spring is an excellent time to visit for tree blossoms; visit again in fall when the tints of the harvest season sparkle with crispness. There is an admission charge with reduced rates starting in October.

UBC Botanical Garden
Originally comprising native trees and built in the second decade of the century, this collection was enhanced by exotic specimens following World War II. Campus development infringed on the arboretum but what's left can be observed west of the West Mall, from the Fraser River parkade south to University Boulevard and behind the Ponderosa cafeteria. A detailed map and guide of this area is found in Straley's book. The Asian Garden, part of the UBC Botanical Garden,

Since 1925, Forest Education BC (FEBC) has been working with teachers and students in B.C. to promote understanding of our forests.

offers another adventure in tracking down trees with great, though still young, specimens of maples, magnolias, mountain ash and rhododendrons. UBC's Native Garden proffers nearly all the trees native to British Columbia.

Shaughnessy Crescent

This very large circle of land lies within a roundabout in one of Vancouver's oldest and most prestigious districts, with some homes dating from the 1800s. A walk here with a guide book in hand can be an odyssey of architecture as much as arboriculture. Straley's *Trees of Vancouver* includes a detailed map listing the astonishing variety of trees in this park now tended by the Vancouver Park Board. Highlights include the Japanese snowbell tree, the flowering ash, red horse-chestnut, fringe-tree, English hawthorn, large-leaved linden, copper beech, sourwood, Eddie's white wonder dogwood and the Tree of Heaven to name a few.

Riverview Arboretum

The province's oldest arboretum encompasses the grounds of Riverview Hospital, formerly Essondale Hospital. Developed under the direction of John Davidson, who later started the UBC Botanical Garden and was inspired by Britain's great Kew Gardens, the grounds have remained nearly untouched. Time has rewarded the efforts of those who shaped and planted the land with a splendid collection of trees now in their mature glory. For more than 80 years Riverview Hospital has been home and refuge to patients suffering from mental illness. Many of them labored long and hard to build the grounds as they exist today, their collective efforts serving as both therapy and recreation. For years the patients tended the plants and performed the majority of horticultural duties required in a large park. Many remain here and those who have passed on are buried in the land they tended and loved so well. It is not often that trees are planted with the room needed to reach the full potential of their canopy. A society has been formed to protect this grand arboretum from proposed future development. A trip to the Riverview Lands, located in Coquitlam on more than 100 hectares, should be a requirement for any tree enthusiast. Before your visit pick up a copy of *Riverview Lands*, an excellent guide.

Green Timbers Urban Forest, Surrey

Located at 140th Street and 96th Avenue in Surrey these 260 hectares have become a memorial to what once was a larger natural forest of giant evergreens soaring to 60 metres in height. Green Timbers was, at the turn of the century, the only remaining stretch of virgin forest between San Diego and Vancouver. Tourists would come from all over to view these cathedral-like groves in a 2,031 hectare refuge. Despite proposals to have

Stanley Park, 1984. vp

the forest declared a park, Green Timbers was clear-cut in 1929, with the entire population of trees going to feed a local sawmill. But that was Green Timbers' past. The future started in 1930 when a massive reforestation program was undertaken to renew what had been so precious—an urban forest. Over the ensuing decades groves of native evergreen trees were planted with glorious results. Now administered by the Surrey Parks and Recreation Commission,

Green Timbers is open for the enjoyment and education of all people. It is a mix of remnant woodland and natural regrowth displaying 60-year-old specimens of vine maple, broadleaf maple, western red cedar, hemlock, Douglas fir and grand fir. For further information call the Green Timbers Heritage Society.

Martin Luther said it best about 460 years ago when asked what he would do on the last day of his life. He simply stated, "I would plant a tree."

Forest Education BC is a non-partisan, open association with a broad-based membership and volunteer base dedicated to providing forest education to supplement classroom curricula. Each year FEBC reaches 50,000 students in classrooms and through tours in demonstration forests.

Vancouver's Green Streets
Carol DeFina

VANCOUVER'S FIRST BYLAW relating to the planting of street trees was passed in 1896. In 1916 the responsibility for street planting passed to the Board of Parks and Recreation. In early years the trend was to plant very large trees, such as elm and chestnut, on streets. In the 1950s and 1960s a planting campaign began to add smaller, ornamental trees to the boulevards. Most of these were flowering plum and cherries that still delight Vancouverites each spring with their billowy clouds of blossoms in every shade of pink and white.

Today Vancouver has more than 100,000 trees lining its streets. They add to the beauty and livability of our city, creating a sense of place and an emotional attachment to our neighborhoods. Up to 20 per cent of our street trees are more than 12 metres high—these include maples, chestnuts and elms. Flowering cherries and plums make up another 30 per cent. These trees, unfortunately, have reached their maturity. Many are plagued by disease and are in decline. The Park Board has a remedial program to plant a greater variety of species on our streets. Arboriculture staff plant thousands of trees on our streets every year to compensate for the loss of those in decline and to increase the total number of trees.

Here is a modest sampling of interesting trees to watch for in your travels. Look for the uncommon Japanese Pagoda Tree (*Sophora japonica L.*), also known as the Chinese Scholar Tree, at the foot of Cambie Street at Southeast Marine Drive and along the south side of 12th Avenue, east of Arbutus Street. It is native to China and Korea, with smooth bark and dark green, lacy, compound leaves. In the West End look for a magnificent Caucasian Wingnut (*Pterocaryaa fraxinifolia*) near the southwestern corner of Comox at Chilco. The massive, deeply etched, bulging trunk is its first notable characteristic; then look up and note the long graceful chains of small green nutlets that decorate the tree from summer through fall.

In the little triangular park created by the intersection of Kingsway, 15th Avenue and Fraser Street is a magnificent specimen of Tree of Heaven (*Ailanthus altissima Swingle*). This one has a particularly large spreading canopy. Its smooth, grey bark resembles that of a beech. It has large compound leaves and, in midsummer, small yellow-green flowers in clusters.

Very few conifers have been planted on Vancouver streets, so it is well worth a side trip to see the block planting of the Lawson cypress (*Chamaecyparis lawsoniana erecta*) on the north side of 16th Avenue, east of Arbutus Street. They are an imposing phalanx with their broad, dense pyramidal shape and soft, bright-green foliage. Although some have been infected with root rot caused by a fungus, most are still in good condition.

You can't miss the dramatic brilliance of the chartreuse colored leaves of the Black Locust (*Robinia pseudoacacia Frisia*) found along Yew Street between 3rd and 4th Avenues and on both sides of 8th Avenue from Scotia Street to Prince Edward Street. In the fall their leaves turn a beautiful golden yellow. They are fast becoming a popular choice for street tree planting.

These are just a few of the wonderful and interesting trees that line our boulevards. There are many more to be discovered. The Park Board has a data base of all its street trees. To learn more about a specific street tree, call "Street Trees" at 257-8600, or refer to Gerald Straley's book, *Trees of Vancouver*.

For information on our educational resources, call Forest Education BC's nearest education services representative at 1-888-28-TREES.

Lower Mainland Geology
Roy Wares

Aerial view of the Fraser delta, 1947. vp

THE DYNAMIC GROWTH of Greater Vancouver is a mirror image of its geology and soil. The region's natural destiny was determined by underground activity that began at least 100 million years ago.

Viewed geographically Greater Vancouver straddles the Coast Mountains and the Fraser lowlands of southwest B.C. While the region's geology is a record of events that shaped the earth's subsurface over millions of years, the soil reflects natural forces that left an imprint on the earth's surface over the past 10,000 years: both cast the blueprint for settlement and development.

Over millions of years southwest British Columbia was formed by global movement which stacked slabs of the earth's crust against each other. More than 150 million years ago igneous, granitic rocks were formed by the intrusion of hot, molten rock deep in the earth's crust. More than 80 million years ago the Coast Mountains to the north and west of Vancouver were formed as the granitic rocks progressively were buoyed up in the earth's crust. At the same time the Georgia basin formed between the mountains and what was to become Vancouver Island. Greater Vancouver was formed from sediments deposited approximately 35 million years ago in the younger part of the Georgia basin.

Some 2.5 million years ago when global cooling caused the formation of ice sheets in the Coast Mountains, glacial streams flowed out and over the Greater Vancouver area. When the last ice age began approximately 25,000 years ago, ice streams sculpted the area's landscape. An ice sheet over Greater Vancouver perhaps two kilometres thick deposited a mixture of clay, sand and rock fragments, known as till, on the lowlands.

Until the end of the last ice age approximately 14,000 years ago, Greater Vancouver was submerged below sea level by the great weight of ice. When the ice eventually vanished—about 11,000 years ago—the sea invaded much of the Lower Mainland while the earth's crust gradually emerged from the sea. At the same time great volumes of melting ice water flowed from the mountains and the Interior. Sediment carried down the Fraser River formed an estuary of sand, gravel and mud, which fanned westwards into Georgia Strait.

The process continued. Sediment from the Fraser River delta slowly built—and continues to build—outwards into Georgia Strait. Richmond and Delta are among the habitable areas

facing page: Vancouver treescape. terri clark

formed by such sedimentary deposits. As land rebounded from beneath the sea, a weathering process created Greater Vancouver soils from glacial till, sand and clay. As the climate warmed, superior forests grew in well-drained soil.

Aboriginal groups first formed coastal communities around accessible fish, berries and timber. When European pioneers arrived in the mid-19th century, most of Greater Vancouver was covered by old-growth forest. Grasslands, shrubs and peat bogs covered the Fraser delta.

Settlers who came by boat organized communities close to inlets and creeks which offered safe anchorage, fish and timber. Since cities traditionally grow outwards from an industrial core, areas first to develop have superior soil and access to good timber. Steveston, Burrard Inlet, False Creek and New Westminster developed naturally from geological patterns. New Westminster was an ideal first capital city; situated on the Fraser River, near the upper limit of navigation for seagoing ships, it was easy to defend and close to rich timber resources.

Communities such as Kerrisdale grew around fertile, well-drained soil, accessible by rail and road. As land prices rose many farms and market gardens were swallowed by housing, shopping, schools and recreational facilities. Automobile transport allowed settlers access to other fertile soils which developed as integral communities east and southeast of the original city core.

Greater Vancouver's natural soils have been modified over the years as timber was cut and roads and houses were built. Soils continue to be modified and amended by the planting of non-native species of plants and trees and where construction debris is used as fill. For example, after the natural soil of False Creek was contaminated by industrial waste, it proved an expensive undertaking to revert to natural soil conditions. Many remaining patches of natural soil in Greater Vancouver are in parks which are left in a near-natural state. Stanley Park is a notable example.

B.C.'s Professional Engineers and Geoscientists. For more than 75 years, applying science to meet the needs of British Columbians.

Vancouver: A Garden City
Dagmar Hungerford

THE VANCOUVER AREA has an ideal climate for gardening. The relatively mild winter temperatures and long growing season make it possible for gardeners to grow a large variety of trees, shrubs, flowers and vegetables. Newcomers to the area are amazed at how quickly plants grow and gardens take shape. "If you stick a broom handle into the soil it will soon sprout." This may not be quite true but relatively speaking it is easier to be a gardener here than in many other regions of our country.

Perhaps what most sets our gardens apart from those in colder climates are the varieties of broad-leaved evergreen trees and shrubs we can grow. They dominate many of our landscapes and they form the backbone to our gardens. Laurel, holly and boxwood hedges are our fences. Large collections of flowering rhododendrons in our botanical gardens and home gardens attract visitors from around the world and our indigenous arbutus tree, also an evergreen, with its reddish-brown peeling bark and glossy green leaves, is a distinctive feature of our West Coast landscape.

Winters are more often than not cold, wet and grey but the relatively mild temperatures allow gardeners to flirt with less hardy and unusual trees, shrubs and perennials. The darkest days of the year are brightened by blossoms of the Christmas rose and winter-flowering heathers, and it is not uncommon to see leafy, dark-green Chinese winter vegetables growing from beneath a patch of snow. In January and early February the witch hazel's spider-like yellow flowers brighten the grey winter skies and their sweet fragrance tips us off to the snowdrops and crocuses near bloom at their feet. By mid-April thousands of ornamental flowering cherry trees in full bloom line the city streets to herald the beginning of a new season and by mid-May gardens are once again at their peak.

Garden styles in the Vancouver area are as diverse as its multicultural population. It is not uncommon to see a Mediterranean-style garden with hardy palm trees, figs and eucalyptus bordering onto a Japanese-style garden. Worldwide gardening traditions and ideas have found their way to this area and many gardeners have adopted an eclectic style of gardening, incorporating many styles and plants from around the world into their own little gardens.

Perhaps one common denominator that seems to be influencing the way we garden more than anything else is the water restrictions that have been enforced for the past years. Lawns are being replaced by drought resistant plants and xeriscaping (little or no watering) has become a buzz word. Another fairly recent shift in gardening has been a conscious attempt by home gardeners to garden without the use of chemical herbicides and pesticides, making compost bins a common sight in most gardens.

For many people who live here gardening is a year-round passion. This passion is not only reflected in gardens but also in the many horticultural clubs, botanical gardens and special gardening events that take place all year. Beginner gardeners and newcomers can slot themselves into garden clubs in their area and those with special interests in plants and subjects whether it be cacti, bonsai, fuchsias, mushrooms or begonias can find a horticultural society to suit their needs. For detailed information on clubs and societies call the VanDusen Botanical Library at 878-9274 or obtain a copy of the local gardening book *The Twelve-Month Gardener.*

Although there are garden-related events taking place throughout the year, April and May are the busiest months for plant sales. One of the largest annual plant sales takes place at the University of British Columbia Botanical Garden on Mother's Day. A volunteer group called the FOGS (Friends of the Garden) work all year to put on this fundraiser for the garden. A large variety of unusual perennials, climbers, trees and shrubs are for sale. For new gardeners and newcomers to the area this event gives you a good idea of the plant material that can be grown in this region. Another event that has become a highlight for gardeners is the relatively new annual flower show at VanDusen Botanical Display Garden towards the end of May. This four-day event takes place outdoors on a large stretch of lawn within the grounds of the garden. Many local nurseries and garden centres have display gardens and there are hundreds of exhibits to see. Anything and everything related to gardening is included in this show. It is Vancouver's own "Chelsea Flower Show."

For gardeners who wish to be inspired, the annual garden tour organized by the Vancouver Park Board opens a number of private gardens to the public for a weekend in spring. This is a good way to see the diversity of gardening styles and plant material that can be grown in the Vancouver area.

Whether you live in an apartment or have a large home garden, our mild climate and the large plant material available to us make it possible to have a beautiful and bountiful garden for twelve months of the year.

facing page, top: Heritage home and garden, Deas Island, 1994. vs
bottom: Community garden, East End, 1990. vs

Rivers and Lakes
Moira Farrow

MANY THOUSANDS OF YEARS before the first tree was felled on the site that is now Vancouver, British Columbia's mightiest river—the Fraser—had gouged its way from the Rocky Mountains to the Pacific Ocean. The Fraser traverses 1,375 kilometres from the Rockies to its delta on the Strait of Georgia and drains a basin the size of Great Britain.

Its basin represents just about every type of climatic zone and ecosystem in British Columbia and is home to an abundant diversity of wildlife plus nearly two million people—60 per cent of B.C.'s population. The Fraser is North America's richest salmon river and is the backbone of the province's fishery, contributing 66 per cent of the province's total sockeye salmon catch and 60 per cent of its total pink salmon catch.

However, the river is under stress as millions of tons of pollutants are pumped into it from urban areas and industries. Overfishing and habitat destruction have reduced salmon stocks. And development is non-stop due to the fast-growing population.

To cope with all this change, the Fraser River Action Plan (FRAP) was set up in 1991 with $100 million in federal funds. The objective of FRAP is to rebuild salmon stocks, clean up the environment and protect habitat. Much has been accomplished but much remains to be done.

Today the Fraser delta is home to Vancouver International Airport, Iona Island and Annacis Island sewage treatment plants, Reifel Migratory Bird Sanctuary, four regional parks (Pacific Spirit at Point Grey, Iona Beach in Richmond, Deas Island in the South Arm and Boundary Bay in Delta), and ever-expanding suburbs and shopping centres. It's a volatile mix.

Probably the best known lakes in the city are little ones—Lost Lagoon and Beaver Lake in Stanley Park. Lost Lagoon is artificial, created in 1916 by construction of a causeway. Today its 17 hectares are a paradise for birdlovers and its fountain is endlessly photographed. The water lilies of Beaver Lake flower in dazzling pinks and yellows in August and great blue herons stalk the shoreline. But the lake itself is slowly becoming a swamp.

John Hendry Park in East Vancouver is the site of Trout Lake, which once served as the water source for a sawmill. There are no trout in the lake now, but the park, named after a mill owner, is an oasis of green among city streets.

Burnaby has a network of waterways—river, creeks and lakes—many of which are linked with parks. The 160 hectares of Burnaby Lake, first mapped in 1860, are now the centre of a regional park with nine kilometres of trails, a wildlife sanctuary and nature house. Rowing and canoeing are popular lake sports and there's a viewing tower to watch ducks and great blue herons.

Flowing from the lake is the Brunette River, once heavily polluted, where the Sapperton Fish and Game Club has worked since 1969, to restore salmon stocks with great success. Its name comes from its brown color, caused by the leaching of peat into the river.

About one kilometre southwest of Burnaby Lake is Deer Lake, almost surrounded by a park latticed with trails through woods and meadows. Adult salmon pass through the lake on their way to tributaries where they spawn. The lake acts as a settling pond for pollutants from Still Creek, thereby protecting the "outflowing" Brunette.

The Serpentine River drains most of Surrey and then empties into Mud Bay just north of Crescent Beach. The other major Surrey river is the Nicomekl, which actually rises in Langley and eventually flows into the southern end of Mud Bay. When fur traders paddled up the Nicomekl in 1824, they excitedly reported seeing "thousands of beaver." No such luck these days, but both the Serpentine and the Nicomekl are salmon rivers and the former provides valuable waterfowl habitat near its mouth.

The Salmon River, flanked by farmland as it meanders through Langley, lives up to its name and is one of the most productive coho streams in British Columbia In fact many of the Fraser's richest salmon tributaries clustered between Vancouver and Hope flow through densely populated areas yet they account for a staggering 50 per cent of the Fraser's coho stocks and 100 per cent of its chum. That's why FRAP is working on many of these streams with such projects as planting trees to provide shade and prevent erosion.

Industry has spoiled much of the Coquitlam River, which flows through both Coquitlam and Port Coquitlam into the Fraser just east of the Port Mann Bridge. About 14 kilometres upstream a dam built in 1914 diverted most of the river's water flow for electricity and cut off sockeye salmon from their rearing habitat in Coquitlam Lake. Biologists say the Coquitlam River is one of the most degraded streams in the Lower Mainland with everything from gravel pit operations to dyke construction. But in recent years, thanks to FRAP, much has been done to improve water flow and fish habitat. The Coquitlam's struggling fish are finally getting help.

Also in Coquitlam are several small lakes—Como, Mundy, Lost and Lafarge—in local parks. Hoy Creek, in the midst of suburbia, is also bordered by linear park. In complete contrast in Coquitlam's northern reaches are the rugged mountain lakes, Dennett and Munro, of Burke Mountain Regional Park.

Next door in Port Coquitlam the Pitt River flows from Pitt Lake, the only tidal freshwater lake in the world, into the Fraser River at Douglas Island. Pitt River has several tributaries including the Alouette (the name comes from a native word for wild onion).

The Alouette, which rises 40 kilometres east of Vancouver in Golden Ears Provincial Park and flows through Pitt Meadows and Maple Ridge, is also being helped by FRAP. It's become one of the busiest sport fishing rivers in the Lower Mainland and is a favorite of canoeists.

Also in Maple Ridge lively Kanaka Creek is a raging torrent in wet weather, but its length is almost covered by a linear regional park which provides glorious trail walks.

In Langley the Little Campbell River produces coho, chum, chinook salmon and trout with help from a hatchery. The river enters Semiahmoo Bay near White Rock and a slow-moving stretch of it flows through Campbell Valley Regional Park.

On the North Shore the major stream is the Capilano, which twists and turns through canyons and deep pools for eight kilometres below the 1954-built Cleveland Dam. This section of the river is covered by a regional park where old growth trees make for great hiking territory.

Capilano Lake, formed above the dam, is 5.6 kilometres long and supplies 40 per cent of the Lower Mainland's drinking water. A suspension bridge over one of the Capilano's canyons and a fish hatchery below the dam are major tourist attractions. Within sight of the fishermen often clustered around the river's mouth is a sewage treatment plant.

In North Vancouver, Lynn Creek and the Seymour River flow roughly parallel to each other from the mountains into Burrard Inlet. The lower reaches of Lynn Creek, including another suspension bridge, are mostly parkland. Its upper reaches form the heart of Lynn Headwaters Regional Park, a spectacular wilderness recreation area.

The Seymour River has been dammed about 20 kilometres from its mouth to create Seymour Lake, another of Greater Vancouver's major water reservoirs.

One of the Lower Mainland's warmest lakes, Sasamat, is in Belcarra Regional Park at Burrard Inlet's entrance to Indian Arm. No power boats are allowed on the lake in summer so that it's safe for swimmers. The lake area was added to the park in 1986 and is very popular for group picnics.

One of the few significant watercourses flowing into Howe Sound is Furry Creek and its tributary Middle Creek. The land around both creeks was logged extensively in the 1900s and the upper reaches of Furry Creek were dammed to provide power for Britannia Mine. However, a new golf club across which the creeks run has sparked extensive restoration work and initial plans for a marina on the delta—where gravel beds are important for salmon rearing—have been rejected.

Lynn Canyon, 1995. vs

Burns Bog
Shane McCune

ASK A CLUTCH OF COASTIES to name the Lower Mainland's largest park, and most will come up with Stanley Park, at 400 hectares (1,000 acres) the equal of New York's Central Park.

The most green-spirited might point out, correctly, that Pacific Spirit Park, on the University Endowment Lands, is even bigger, at 750 hectares (1,850 acres).

But the largest green belt in the area is Delta's Burns Bog, at 4,000 hectares the size of 10 Stanley Parks. Occupying a quarter of Delta, south of River Bend and west of Highway 91, it is the largest domed peat bog in North America and one of the largest in the world. It was named after a former owner, Pat Burns of Burns Meat packaging.

The bog is known to biologists around the world, since only three percent of the planet is covered with peatlands. An ancient lake that filled with vegetation over the eons, the bog is choked with trees and bog plants such as sphagnum moss and Labrador tea.

Rain is Burns Bog's only source of water, and its slow evaporation is a major regulator of the region's climate.

The bog covers the largest undeveloped urban area in Canada and the largest wetland in the Fraser River delta. It is home to 24 species of mammals, including beaver, muskrat and Columbian black-tailed deer, 150 species of birds—and the largest garbage dump west of Toronto.

The only protected part is the 60-hectare Delta Nature Reserve. The biggest chunk of Burns Bog, almost 2,300 hectares, is owned by Western Delta Lands Inc., which at various times since the 1970s has sought to develop portions of the bog with a $10 billion superport, a golf course, a 100-room hotel and office complex, and a racetrack. All have been rejected by municipal and/or provincial authorities.

The Burns Bog Conservation Society has been fighting to have the entire area declared an ecological reserve and has been pressing the province to buy the land from WDL. Negotiations broke in the spring of 1996 after the company, owned by the McLaughlin family of Ontario (also owners of Grouse

facing page, clockwise from top left:
Beaver Lake sign; swans, Lost Lagoon;
mist, Lost Lagoon; diver, Capilano River;
skating, Beaver Lake (1945). vs, vp, vs, vs, vp

> The bog covers the largest undeveloped urban area in Canada and the largest wetland in the Fraser River delta. It is home to 24 species of mammals, including beaver, muskrat and Columbian black-tailed deer, 150 species of birds— and the largest garbage dump west of Toronto

Mountain) turned down an offer of $27.5 million.

Over the years the bog has been shaped and altered by both man and nature. Peat-mining in the 1940s gouged huge holes and drainage ditches in the heart of the bog. During World War II, it was controlled by the U.S. Army, which planned to use the peat moss in refining magnesium for artillery shells. Farms have encroached on its periphery and the city of Vancouver dumps its garbage on a landfill in the southern portion. Highway 91, cutting through the eastern edge of the bog, intercepts runoff that once flowed into the bog, and flood control measures designed to protect farms along the Fraser River also prevent the periodic flooding that has watered the bog over the centuries.

The bog has also been the site of serious fires, which can burn underground for months in the methane-rich peat. Major blazes occurred in 1977, 1990 (twice), 1994 and 1996. The 1996 fire covered Greater Vancouver in smoke and ash for two days, destroyed 170 hectares and cost more than $200,000 to extinguish.

Islands of Greater Vancouver
Roger Parton
Additional material *Don Watmough*

THE DIVERSITY OF the region cannot be fully appreciated without a glance at its islands. Like the region itself, they are varied in makeup. Mudflats, sandbars, even mountains are all represented. There are alluvial islands in the Fraser River covered with cottonwood trees, islands in Howe Sound that are little more than barren rock, and islands in Burrard Inlet where parks have been created amidst magnificent surroundings. Some islands are host to small communities or ecological reserves; others are vast industrial parks.

Islands in Greater Vancouver can be placed into two basic categories: islands created by deposits of the Fraser River, and marine islands of Howe Sound and Burrard Inlet. Many were sculpted and shaped by the glaciers of the last ice age, which finally receded about 12,000 years ago. The islands continue to be shaped by the dynamics of nature. Some islands are growing in size due to river silt and sand deposits, while others are shrinking due to erosion.

FRASER RIVER ISLANDS

Lulu Island is the centre of the Municipality of Richmond, all of which is built on islands formed from alluvial sand and silt brought to the coast by the Fraser River. Lulu Island was first settled by whites in 1866 and by 1879, together with 20 other Fraser islands, was incorporated as the Township of Richmond. By the late 19th century, roads joined Lulu Island to Vancouver and New Westminster. (Between Lulu and Sea islands is a small, undyked, marshy island with the charming name of Swishwash Island. Before extensive dyking and ditching to prevent flooding, many of the alluvial islands created by the Fraser River resembled wet, marshy, low-lying Swishwash.)

Lulu Island is noted for its rich agricultural production. The fishing industry is represented also—the southeast corner of Lulu Island is home to Steveston, a vital fishing community in the Lower Mainland. Steveston Island, just offshore, was little more than a sandbar at the turn of the century. A rock jetty was built down the centre of the sandbar to help define the Fraser River shipping channel. The island was later augmented by sand dredged from the river to help maintain depths adequate for shipping. Today it is park-like, and worthy of the local name: Shady Island. It is connected to Steveston by a rock breakwater that is exposed at low tide.

Sea Island, the location of Vancouver International Airport, is especially known to travellers. This large, flat deltaic island

was so named by Captain Richards in 1859, because it was so flat that it was difficult to determine where the sea ended and the land began. The island, like Lulu, is completely dyked. Airport services began there in 1931. Since that time the airport has expanded from 192 hectares to more than 1,600. Sea Island is joined to Vancouver by the Arthur Laing Bridge, a $20 million development. Attached to Sea Island by a causeway is Iona Island, the site of a regional park. As well, since 1973 it has been the site of a sewage plant. The plant handles waste from Richmond, Ladner and Tsawwassen. The deepwater sewage outfall on Iona Island pushes waste out into Georgia Strait, alleviating buildup on the Fraser's Sturgeon Bank. A five-kilometre jetty covers the outfall, and is topped with a walking and cycling pathway. Iona also has several kilometres of beautiful, sandy beach and is a premier birding area.

West of the Arthur Laing Bridge is Richmond Island. This island, owned by Canadian Forest Products and paved from one end to the other, is used primarily for lumber storage.

More tranquil is Deas Island, where Highway 99 actually crosses underneath the Fraser River through the George Massey Tunnel. Massey was a Social Credit MLA who spent years campaigning for the tunnel's construction. It was a vast improvement over the outmoded Ladner ferry! Although partly privately owned, Deas—connected to the mainland by a causeway—is a scenic treat with its quiet trails, pools, pocket beaches and meadows. The GVRD has created a 60-hectare treasure in Deas Island Regional Park, a monument to the Fraser River and its history. In the 1870s Deas Island was the site of one of the busiest canneries on the entire river, and several heritage buildings have been restored. Thousands attend the annual Fraser River Festival here.

Westham Island, in Delta, is renowned for its rich, pastoral farmlands and its dyke. It is possible to follow the winding main road all around the island, then cross by bridge to Reifel Island, home of the Reifel Migratory Bird Sanctuary, where thousands of waterfowl can be seen in winter in their natural habitat. The annual snow goose festival celebrates the week that nearly 30,000 snow geese return each fall from their breeding grounds in Siberia. The earliest marine maps refer to Reifel as "Smoky Tom Island," but the origins of this moniker remain unclear.

Other important grounds for waterfowl on the move are Woodward, Duck, Rose, Barber, Kirkland and Gunn islands, small bits of land east of Westham Island. For the most part, marshes make these islands unsuitable for cultivation. The islands make up the South Arm Marshes Wildlife Management Area. They can be reached only by boat.

Some 294 hectares of Delta's Tilbury Island were purchased

by the provincial government for $14.3 million. Despite the presence of a chemical plant and a storage yard for Canadian National Railway, much of this island on the South Arm of the Fraser River is still farmed. Tilbury is no longer technically an island—it is now joined to the mainland, the channels that once separated it filled with river silt.

Don and Lion Islands are two floodplain islands, recently purchased and turned over to the GVRD for future park use. The rich marshland and forest are home to a variety of fish and wildlife. Lion Island was once the site of a major cannery, and traces of it can be seen. The larger Don Island has some excellent sand beaches which emerge when the tides are low.

Annacis Island is home to a multi-million-dollar industrial estate occupying just over 445 hectares. It was built in 1953 by Britain's Duke of Westminster, and since 1955 has been joined by a causeway to New Westminster. Prior to the development of industry the island was used for farming and fishing. In 1975 a major sewage plant was built here, handling waste from Burnaby, Surrey, Coquitlam, Port Moody, Delta and parts of Richmond. Like adjoining Mitchell Island, its island character is almost completely obscured by buildings, warehouses, roads and bridges.

Poplar Island, just downstream from New Westminster, is almost free of development, a wet marshy forest of cottonwoods. It stands out as an oasis of green in a landscape dominated by factories and sawmills, and provides visual relief to drivers crossing the Queensborough Bridge. It may someday become a park.

Barnston Island is crescent-shaped, nearly five kilometres in length and over three kilometres wide. It is a large flat island of farms encircled by a dyke, topped with a paved road. It is possible to cycle around the island in under an hour, drive around it in less, and casual visitors often do. In 1995, 20 hectares at the northwestern tip of the island were designated a park protected under the new Lower Mainland Nature Legacy Program. At the eastern end of 104th Avenue in Surrey is a tiny free ferry that crosses Parson's Channel to Barnston.

Until recently, 187-hectare Douglas Island—near the junction of the Fraser and Pitt rivers—was the property of Canadian Forest Products. Purchased by the government for $4.5 million, it is an important foreshore marsh and river habitat. Its green space is clearly visible just upstream from the Port Mann Bridge, with a necklace of log booms fringing its shores. Its rich habitat and inaccessibility made it an ideal site for Ducks Unlimited to enhance an area where wildlife could thrive in relative safety, by increasing the ponds and pools.

The last of the Fraser islands as we head upstream are Brae and McMillan islands. The islands are now virtually one island, bisected by Glover Road. The eastern portion (McMillan) is the location of a Kwantlen reserve, and is the terminus for the Albion ferry. A white steepled church on McMillan Island is clearly visible from Fort Langley. The province acquired 167-hectare Brae Island to the west as a future regional park. A walking trail circles Brae, which is reachable from Maple Ridge via the ferry, or by footbridge from the Fort Langley side. A replica paddle wheeler, the *Native,* cruises past the islands upstream of New Westminster and moors at a dock just north of Fort Langley.

MARINE ISLANDS

Granville Island, once a mud flat, reached island status in 1913 through the miracle of dredging. In 1916 it became an industrial centre of the young city. Over time, dredged material was used to transform the island into a peninsula. 1973 saw both acquisition of the island by Central Mortgage and Housing Corp. and the opening of a little waterfront park. The island became public land in 1977, when the federal government bought out all leases on Granville Island. Since that time, it has become host to shops, restaurants and marinas, cultural activities and a famous and thriving public market. Some of the old industrial architecture remains, adding to the charm and excitement of this popular spot, and a fleet of tiny ferries takes visitors across False Creek.

Deadman's Island, so named because it was once the site of native burial grounds (and was later used by white settlers for the same purpose), was the subject of much dispute until 1930, when the federal government granted the city a 99-year lease on the island. Although the condition of the lease was that the land be used as a park, it has been a naval reserve, and closed to the public, since 1944. Currently Deadman's Island, connected to Stanley Park by a controlled bridgeway, and visible from the seawall near the Nine O'Clock Gun, is the subject of a dispute. The Musqueam band claims the land as a burial ground, while naval authorities insist the island is vital to naval training.

Indian Arm remains one of the more beautiful areas of Greater Vancouver. The Arm has become more accessible, but many of its islands remain undeveloped and wooded. The region was recently declared a provincial park that stretches virtually all the way from Deep Cove to Belcarra and up the Arm, making Indian Arm a protected fjord right in our backyard. Indian Arm Marine Provincial Park may one day become one of Greater Vancouver's most outstanding natural attractions. The park is over 20 times the size of Stanley Park, some 9,300 hectares.

Near the entrance to Indian Arm is privately owned Boulder

Island, with a beautiful home and a dock to service it. Nearby Hamber Island (once owned by Lt.-Gov. Eric Hamber), Lone Rock, Grey Rocks and White Rock are also privately owned resident islands . . . completely away from the urban area, yet only a short trip from the heart of the city.

Jug Island, at the northern tip of the Belcarra peninsula, is in essence a large rock placed in the Arm. The island is part of Belcarra Regional Park. There are no facilities, but the island has a fine beach and is a popular stopover for swimmers and boaters. The observant visitor will note the frequent flights of bald eagles overhead. Together with Raccoon Island, the Twin Islands make up part of Indian Arm Provincial Marine Park. The larger of the Twins has a wharf and primitive camping facilities. The two islands, connected by a tombolo spit accessible at low tide, are rich in plant life and covered with pine, hemlock and fir trees. Like Jug and Raccoon islands, the Twins are terrific vantage-points for birders, and small tide pools are interesting to explore.

The largest island in Indian Arm is Croker Island, near the head of the Arm. It was acquired by B.C. Parks as part of the marine park. There are no facilities on the island yet, but scuba divers often dive the "wall" at the island's southern tip. Croker Island overlooks beautiful Granite Falls, which cascades for more than 40 metres over its solid granite face into the clear waters of the fjord's eastern shore. The island is rendered remote by steep cliffs and, like most islands in the region, has no water supply. The lack of fresh water has made development of the Arm islands a slow, difficult process. A small island off Woodlands Settlement is named "Lone Rock." Thanks to a local doctor the island, linked to the mainland by a catwalk, is now a lovely garden with a beautiful home/guest home.

Bowen Island, located at the entrance to Howe Sound, and accessible by a 20-minute ferry ride from Horseshoe Bay, is the most populated island in the Sound. The population in 1996 was nearly 2,500. Bowen is blessed with many natural features, including Crippen Regional Park and a 397-hectare ecological reserve established to preserve the island's extensive ancient hemlock forest. In Crippen Regional Park there are the rocky bluffs of Dorman Point, Killarney Lake, Bridal Falls, a fish hatchery, group picnic area (reservable from GVRD park board) and an extensive trail system. Snug Cove is a delightful place to sit for a spell enjoying the boats and ferries entering and leaving the tiny harbor. See the article on the island's interesting history in this book.

Hutt Island (off the northwest tip of Bowen) is little more than a tree-covered rock, which nonetheless has the interest of quarry operators who want to mine its granite. Bowen's residents are resisting that effort. Farther west of Bowen (and actually part of the Sunshine Coast Regional District) are the eco- logically significant Paisley, Popham and Worlcombe islands. They are virtually undeveloped, and a popular destination for birders and eco-tour groups who study the rich marine life.

Keats Island, opposite Gibson's Landing, is another easy-going, rural-flavored favorite of summer visitors. It is forested, and an ideal spot for picnickers. On its west side is a provincial marine park. Boaters can put down at Plumper Cove, which has a campsite and trails.

North of Bowen is Gambier Island, the largest island in Howe Sound. Although Gambier isn't accessible by car ferry, many summer residences are found on the flatter benches and shorelines. The island has escaped extensive development and remains peaceful and quiet, with only a few roads connecting the small community. Finisterre Island ("Land's End") is a "sometimes" island (an island only when the tide is high). Hermit Island is so named because at the turn of the century it was home to an elderly, eccentric recluse.

Also in Howe Sound are Boyer Island, with some private homes on the south shore, and Anvil Island (named by Captain Vancouver in 1793), where there is a private group camp called Camp Daybreak. With permission you can hike to the top of the island for panoramic views of the Sound.

Passage Island, just offshore of Lighthouse Park in West Vancouver, has a number of private homes that share the island with thousands of gulls. In 1893 Passage Island was purchased for a dollar per acre. A subdivision was developed on the land in the late 1960s. Most of the island is woodland and cliff. Other islets whose main inhabitants are of the feathered variety are Grebe, Bird and Whyte islets, all off the West Vancouver shoreline. Whyte Island, off Whytecliff Park, is also part of an underwater marine park, the first in Canada.

In the heart of West Vancouver's Fisherman's Cove lies Eagle Island. Homes are squeezed onto the tiny island, which the residents access by private runabouts. There was once a hand-cranked, chain-operated communal barge used by commuters to cross the 70 metres to the mainland. Adjacent to Eagle Island is an even smaller islet with a single residence on it. This attractive little lump of land is called Abode Island, but its size and proximity to Eagle Island has led to some residents calling it The Egg. In late 1996 the island was offered for sale for $2.9 million.

facing page, clockwise from top left: Deadman's Island (1908); Snug cove, Bowen Island; aerial view of Croker Island; George Massey Tunnel, Deas Island; Deas slough. vpl, vs, vs, vp, vs

Environment Canada was established June 11, 1971, with a mandate to protect and enhance the quality of the natural environment. The new department was formed by bringing together the Department of Fisheries and Forestry and elements of other departments, including the weather service from Transport Canada; the air pollution control division from Health and Welfare; the water sector from Energy, Mines and Resources; and the Canadian Wildlife Service from Indian and Northern Affairs.

Sergio Marchi, Minister of the Environment, said in 1996: "In this 25th year of Environment Canada's history, the department has many past achievements in which all of us can take pride. It has a future that is equally important." Future goals include: improve ability to predict environmental trends and manage environmental risks effectively; reconcile environmental and economic interests by removing barriers to environmental action; further the capacity of all sections of society to act on their environmental rules and responsibilites.

Birds

Alberta Distillers Limited is a distiller of fine spirits, and an importer of spirits and wine from around the world. One of the key individuals in launching the company fifty years ago was George C. Reifel of Vancouver. It was the Reifel family after whom the Reifel Bird Sanctuary of Ladner, B.C. is named.

Birds of Greater Vancouver
Richard J. Cannings

STRATEGICALLY LOCATED along the West Coast at the mouth of a great river, Vancouver is a magnet to birds and birders alike. About 371 species have been seen in the area, 250 of them occurring annually. The Fraser delta is a globally significant migration stopover and wintering ground for waterfowl and shorebirds, and is clearly the centrepiece of any birding exploration in the Vancouver area. The towering mountains along the North Shore add a diversity of forest habitats right up to the subalpine meadows at their peaks. And few other cities in the world, if any, can boast of so many eagle nests within their boundaries.

BACKYARD BIRDS

As in many North American cities, the birds of urban Vancouver are dominated by a triumvirate of new immigrants—the Rock Dove or common pigeon, the starling and the House Sparrow. All three were brought over to our continent from Europe, where they had evolved in urban and agricultural settings for thousands of years. But Vancouver has its distinctive birds as well. Another immigrant, the Crested Myna, was brought over from China at the turn of the century and prospered in Vancouver until the starling arrived in the 1950s. The jaunty black birds with their punky crests and big white wing patches are becoming a rare sight, but Vancouver is still the only place in North America where they can be seen. Another relatively new arrival is the House Finch, a common sight at backyard feeders, where the males' red plumage and cheery song brighten the cloudy days. These finches moved north from California on their own, following the opening of the coastal forests north.

Perhaps the most conspicuous bird of suburban Vancouver is the Northwestern Crow, a coastal relative of its larger Interior cousin, the American Crow. Crows are opportunistic and omnivorous feeders, and have greatly profited from the switch from intertidal buffet to suburban gardens and garbage. In fall and winter crows assemble in large flocks every evening before going to roost. Easily the most amazing gathering in the province takes place every day near the Willingdon exit on Highway 1 in Burnaby, where about 5,000 to 8,000 crows blacken the buildings and ground as dusk falls.

facing page: Feeding the geese, Stanley Park, 1987. liora beder

A YEAR OF BIRDS
WINTER

The old saying has it that rainy days are good for ducks, and Vancouver birders should take that to heart. Vancouver is simply one of the best places anywhere to watch wintering waterfowl. Thousands of graceful Western Grebes float amid the freighters on English Bay, diving occasionally for a meal of small fish. Rafts of big black Surf Scoters, easy to identify with their heavy, garish pink and yellow bills and white head patches, dive to pull mussels from the bottoms of rocky bays. Handsome Barrow's Goldeneyes, the males with white crescents on their black heads, dive alongside the scoters for smaller mussels. Flocks of American Wigeon carpet grassy parks, grazing the grass like miniature geese. Perhaps the best place to watch ducks at close range is Stanley Park, where freshwater species crowd into Lost Lagoon and sea ducks are plentiful around the seawall.

For a complete wildlife spectacle, however, you can't top Boundary Bay and the Fraser delta. Tens of thousands of ducks, mostly pintail and wigeon, gather there in winter to feast on the food provided by its rich, muddy shallows. Tight necks of Dunlin, a type of sandpiper, perhaps 100,000 in all on the delta, flash white and silver against the dark winter clouds. And of course there are the Snow Geese at Reifel Refuge (see below). Almost 50,000 of these winter-white birds descend on the Fraser delta to gorge on sedges and other vegetation, flying in from Wrangel Island off the coast of eastern Siberia. They arrive in October, shift south to the Skagit delta in midwinter, then return in early spring to refuel before lifting off into the blue April sky for the flight north.

The highlight of the birding winter is the Christmas Bird Count, when hundreds of brave souls actually volunteer to go out into the rain all day to tally the avifauna. Local counts are centred in Vancouver, Ladner, White Rock and Pitt Meadows. The mild weather gives these counts the highest species lists of any in Canada, except for the strong competition from Victoria, of course. For more information call the Federation of B.C. Naturalists (737-3057).

SPRING

Spring in Greater Vancouver means a gradual end to the winter rains, and birders' thoughts turn from ducks to songbirds. Given a bright day in late February, local songbirds such as robins, Bewick's and Winter wrens, Song Sparrows and House Finches are inspired to tune up and start singing. The lengthening days also bring in the first insect eaters from the south; Tree and Violet-green swallows appear on the Fraser delta in late February, signalling the first spring arrivals from south of the Rio Grande.

Alberta Distillers Limited was founded in Calgary, Alberta in 1946 as a company committed to imagination, foresight, and a steadfast dedication to the excellence of its products. Although founded in Alberta, the Corporate Head Office has always been based in the Lower Mainland of British Columbia. The company employs just under 30 people in this province.

Rufous Hummingbirds buzz in from their Mexican wintering grounds in early March, following the pink blooms of salmonberries and wild currants north. A few more species trickle in as the March sun dries out the ground, but the main waves of migrants don't appear until late April. Many pass overhead unseen in the night, but a heavy spring rain will bring them down. Queen Elizabeth Park can be dripping with noisy and colorful birds after a night of rain in late April or early May.

Most of the wintering waterfowl disappear in the middle of April—goldeneyes, grebes and loons to lakes in the Interior, wigeon, pintail and geese up the coast to Alaska. They are replaced by wheeling flocks of sandpipers and plovers passing through in the hundreds of thousands, using the rich delta as a pit stop on their incredible journey from South America to the Arctic.

By the time the hot days of late May settle in, most of the excitement has died down. The bays and mudflats are almost entirely barren of ducks, geese and shorebirds, the tropical migrants gone from backyard gardens, and juvenile robins and starlings are taking over local lawns.

SUMMER

With the winter and spring birds gone, June is a quiet month for Vancouver birders. In fact only about half of the species seen in Vancouver stick around to nest here. This is the songbird month, the best time to relearn all those warbler, flycatcher and sparrow songs forgotten in the winter rains. Long June days mean early June mornings, but you are amply rewarded for getting up and out by 5 A.M. with a stirring dawn chorus from local forested parks as male birds carol out to attract mates. Perhaps the best local sites for a dawn walk are Minnekhada Park in Port Coquitlam and Campbell Valley Park in Langley. Both have a rich variety of coniferous and deciduous forests mixed with wetlands.

By early July the dawn is silent again as birds turn their thoughts from courtship to feeding hungry young. Luckily for birders the first adult sandpipers return from the Arctic in July, still in breeding dress but looking a little worn from all that flying. Their young come through in August, millions of them going all the way to South America on genetic guidance alone. One of the best sites in North America for close-up shorebird watching is the Iona Island sewage lagoons just north of Vancouver International Airport. If you position yourself upwind from the muck, the smell is quite tolerable and the birding is always great!

Midsummer is the best time to explore the high mountain trails of Whistler, Garibaldi and other local areas to see alpine specialties such as ptarmigan, Horned Larks, Gray-crowned

...we need to preserve more natural lands to ensure that our birds will always be there for our children to watch.

Rosy Finches and Pine Grosbeaks.

AUTUMN

As the shorebird migration winds down around Labor Day, the songbird movement reaches a crescendo. Hundreds of tiny birds flit through the woodlands, meadows and backyards of the southern coast. Unfortunately, for the birdwatcher, they are a drabber lot than those that went through in May, garbed in olives, browns and greys. They are quieter in voice as well; their loud, distinctive spring songs replaced by quiet chirps that are difficult to locate and identify. Unlike spring migration, when birds throng in the green, warm lowlands, most of the fall migration happens on mountain ridges, where bountiful berries and bugs help fuel the southward trip. Mountain winds also give a great boost to soaring birds, so local ridges such as Grouse Mountain and Cypress and Mount Seymour Provincial Parks are good spots to watch for southbound hawks and eagles. Groups of Turkey Vultures tilt lazily over Point Roberts, waiting for a tail wind to blow them south. In late September the first waterfowl begin to return from the Interior, and by October all the local bays have their quota of ducks, grebes and loons.

BIRDS IN THE FUTURE

Vancouver is truly a great city in which to enjoy birds of all types. But the disappearance and fragmentation of forests and meadows threaten birds here just as it does elsewhere in the modern world. Lowland forests and meadows are feeling the greatest effects of urban development, and several bird species such as ruffed grouse, meadowlarks, mourning doves and screech owls are becoming harder to find every year. Large urban parks such as Stanley Park and Pacific Spirit Park are wonderful oases of wildlife, but we need to preserve more natural lands to ensure that our birds will always be there for our children to watch. Ordinary citizens can easily help the local birds by following simple rules such as keeping your cats indoors (pet cats are one of the top causes of death in songbirds) and putting your dog on a leash when visiting local parks where waterfowl gather. And, on a positive note, a backyard

facing page, top: Burns Bog landfill, 1989. vp
bottom; Lost Lagoon, Stanley Park, 1993. vp

In 1966, Alberta Distillers Limited acquired Featherstone & Company Limited, importers of fine wines and spirits. This enabled the company to introduce to the Canadian market a broad range of internationally famous brands such as: Lindeman wines from Australia, Mouton Cadet wines from France, Sapporo beer from Japan. Now, itself, owned by Jim Beam Brands out of Chicago, Alberta Distillers Limited also imports brands such as Jim Beam bourbon from the U.S. and Kamora coffee liqueur from Mexico.

feeding station can provide hours of enjoyment and an opportunity to appreciate our bird neighbors even more. If you have any questions about birds, try calling the Vancouver Natural History Society's birding hotline at 737-9910.

THE GEORGE C. REIFEL MIGRATORY BIRD SANCTUARY

The Reifel Refuge, as it is commonly called by birders, is located at the mouth of the Fraser River west of Ladner. It is one of the best local sites for birding, especially for the beginner, since many of its feathered residents are tame enough to get very close looks. Reifel is worth a visit any time of year. Its ponds are full of ducks and shorebirds in early spring, and the diverse shrubs and trees pull in migrant songbirds from kilometres around. Summer is quieter, with most of the waterfowl gone except for the ubiquitous mallards and geese and their families, but birders scan the muddy shores for errant Siberian sandpipers in July and August. The high point of the Reifel year is the Snow Goose festival in early November, when thousands of geese carpet the fields and salt marshes. Midwinter is waterfowl season, but two species of roosting night birds often steal the show—tiny Northern Saw-whet Owls are often found sleeping in the fir trees and this is the only place in the province to see Black-crowned Night-Herons. Call 946-6980 for more information about the sanctuary.

GULLS

Although they are often scorned by the general public as "garbage geese" or worse and lumped in the generic term "sea gulls", gulls are rightfully considered a fascinating group. Their affinity for garbage has certainly made them a successful bunch in the urban world. Besides cleaning up on garbage, they also eat huge quantities of insects, especially craneflies, termites and ants. Eight species of gulls commonly frequent the Vancouver area, most of them only in winter. The 1995 Christmas bird counts in Greater Vancouver tallied almost 45,000 gulls, making them one of the more populous types of birds in the area.

The grey and white adults look superficially similar, but can be identified by a combination of wingtip color, leg color and bill pattern. They take two to four years to get this adult plumage, though, and identification of the mottled brown and grey young birds is usually tackled only by more experienced birders.

The common, big gull that nests on local cliffs and buildings is the Glaucous-winged Gull. Its wingtips are usually grey, pretty much the same shade as its back, and it has the standard yellow bill with red spot. It is the gull of the Pacific Coast from Washington to Alaska, replaced from Oregon south by the darker Western Gull. The two species interbreed in colonies along the Washington coast, and the hybrid offspring with their dark grey wingtips are a major headache for Vancouver birders intent on identifying every gull they see. Glaucous-wings invade city gardens and garbage dumps for food and scavenge on the beaches for anything that looks appetizing. They steal the catches of diving birds and will also kill and eat ducklings. One aggressive individual in Jericho Park even took to stalking and killing pigeons! Most of our local Glaucous-wings nest on Mandarte Island near Sydney, from which they make daily forays to the bog landfill in Delta. The Glaucous-winged Gull is the only gull that is common year-round in the Vancouver area.

Another common gull is the Ring-billed Gull, a medium-sized species with yellow legs, black wingtips and a black ring around its bill. Ring-bills nest in the British Columbia Interior and on the prairies, but a lot of nonbreeding birds hang out on Vancouver beaches in summer, and more are spending the winter there each year. Ring-bills eat a lot of mice and rodents while on their prairie breeding grounds, but Vancouver birds seem more partial to french fries and insects. The Mew Gull is similar to the Ring-billed, but has a plain yellow bill and is present only in winter. It tends to avoid dumps, flocking instead on local playing fields, beaches and farms. A few Mew Gulls nest on coastal lakes in British Columbia, but most spend the summer in the vast northern taiga of Western Canada. The third local gull species with greenish-yellow legs is the California Gull, which is most common in spring and fall. It is a bit larger than the Mew Gull and has a black and red spot on its bill. Most California Gulls breed on the prairies and winter in California.

There are two local gulls with pink legs and black wingtips, the Thayer's Gull and the Herring Gull. The Thayer's is slightly smaller and has dark eyes, while the Herring has lemon-yellow eyes. Thayer's Gulls nest on islands in the Canadian Arctic and winter along the Pacific Coast. Herring Gulls mainly nest on lakes throughout Canada and spend the winter in open interior waters or on the Atlantic Coast; they are outnumbered about ten to one by Thayer's in the Vancouver area.

The smallest gull of Vancouver is the Bonaparte's Gull, a handsome, black-headed bird with white wing flashes and a dancing flight pattern. Named after Charles Bonaparte, a nephew of Napoleon and a well-known 19th century American ornithologist, they are very common along beaches in spring and fall while on their way to nesting lakes in the northern interior. Huge flocks can usually be seen around Mud Bay and in Active Pass in spring, where they feed on shrimp-like crustaceans. In late summer they are particularly attracted to termite swarms over log-covered beaches. Young birds and winter adults lack the distinctive black hood, keeping only a grey smudge behind their eyes.

Alberta Distillers Limited also exports fine spirits to locations all over the world, such as Asia, South Africa, Great Britain, and the United States. The company enjoys a well-earned reputation as a distiller of superior quality spirits, both at home and on the international market.

Insects in Greater Vancouver
Mark L. Winston

MANY OF VANCOUVER's most important insects are similar to its human inhabitants: they came from somewhere else. Honey bees, gypsy moths, cockroaches and crane flies all originated outside of North America, and were carried here by wagons, boats, cars, planes and trains.

Honey bees were deliberately imported to British Columbia by European settlers in the mid-1800s, and have become an important part of our urban environment. Beekeeping is technically not permitted within the city limits of Vancouver, but numerous colonies are comfortably hidden by beekeepers in backyards and gardens, and on rooftops and apartment balconies. These insects pollinate a wide variety of homegrown produce, including fruit trees, squashes, peas, beans and many other garden crops that would not bear fruit without the work of this useful insect. Honey bees do well in the city, and can produce copious honey harvests in addition to performing their crucial pollinating role.

Gypsy moths have been a more recent immigrant, and are Vancouver's most publicized insects. These forest-eating moths originated in Europe and Asia, and regularly arrive today from two directions, eastern North America and Siberia. They may do minor damage to our forests if they become established, but present a major threat to our lumber export industry: importing countries would require fumigation of all B.C. wood products if gypsy moths were declared resident. Vancouver and the surrounding area are the major provincial regions that repeatedly become infested with new moths, because of our port facilities and frequent traffic with Eastern Canada. Thus annual spray programs are conducted to eliminate these incipient infestations. The largest of these was conducted in 1992, when much of the city was sprayed by air with a moth-killing bacteria, and all of Vancouver's residents were media-sprayed with a deluge of newspaper, radio and television stories about gypsy moths.

Cockroaches are another familiar imported resident, in this case originating from various tropical countries. These insects thrive in urban environments because of warm buildings and abundant food they scavenge from garbage bins, unclean cupboards and floors and food processing sites. These most cosmopolitan of insects share Vancouverites' love of restaurants, and can be found dining out in many of our finest food emporiums.

Crane flies came from Europe, and the long-legged, very large adult flies are a noticeable resident in late summer. The adults do no damage, however. It is their larvae, commonly

> Cockroaches, the most cosmopolitan of insects, share Vancouverites' love of restaurants, and can be found dining out in many of our finest food emporiums

called leatherjackets, that feed underground on roots and stems of lawn grass, and can devastate a homeowner's proudly tended lawn in the spring.

Not all of Greater Vancouver's insects came from somewhere else; we can be proud of our local carpenter ants that share many of our homes. These ants burrow in wood to make their nests, and colonies can reach huge sizes if untreated. There probably is not a single home made out of wood that has not been, or will not be, infested with these large ants, and the flights of the winged king and queen reproductive ants are a prominent and sometimes spectacular part of our urban scene. Termites also can be found living in our homes, and can be differentiated from ants by their soft bodies and whitish appearance. Termites also differ from carpenter ants in being truly home-grown; they feed on wood, using bacteria and other organisms living in their guts to digest the tough wood fibres.

Wasps and fleas are two other groups of insects in addition to cockroaches, carpenter ants and termites that provide an excellent business for the abundant population of pest control companies. Wasps are most problematic in late summer, when their nests become large and populous. Wasps are considered harmful because they sting and love snacking on our picnic food, but they actually are beneficial because they eat the larvae of other pest insects. Not much can be said in favor of the flea, however. The local fleas that bite people feed primarily on dogs or cats, but are not averse to a human meal if that becomes available.

One group of Canadian insects is significant for its absence—we have few biting flies and mosquitoes. Our spectacular terrain and heavy rains are responsible for making the Lower Mainland one of the few regions in Canada that are relatively free of these blood-sucking pests. The larvae of these flies require standing water in which to feed and mature, and the area surrounding Vancouver has mostly swiftly flowing streams in which the larvae do not thrive.

Greater Vancouver Marine Life
Murray A. Newman

COASTAL WATERS possess extraordinarily abundant and diverse marine life from microscopic planktonic forms through colorful invertebrates and fishes to giant kelp and whales. Contributing to this abundance is the deeply indented, rocky British Columbia coastline bathed by swiftly moving tidal currents.

Perhaps largely because of its stable, cool temperature the North Pacific has the greatest number of species compared with other temperate oceans. For example, there are about 90 species of starfishes compared with only 20 in the North Atlantic Ocean; six species of Cancer crabs in the North Pacific, only one in the North Atlantic. The continuity of cool temperate conditions over vast geological periods brought about the evolution of a rich fauna adapted to North Pacific conditions. Here species tend to be larger than closely related animals in other oceans. Examples are the giant Pacific octopus (3-metre spread, 45 kilograms), California mussel (20 centimetres long), sunflower star (1 metre in diameter), red sea urchin (12 centimetres in diameter), chinook salmon (30 kilograms) and Pacific halibut (females to 267 centimetres, over 225 kilograms; males to 140 centimetres).

There are great tides along the British Columbia coast creating extensive inter-tidal zones filled with marine organisms. At low tide the mild maritime climate and overlying kelp protect marine animals from dehydration and overheating. Here the beachcomber can find anemones, starfishes, sea urchins, sea cucumbers, crabs of several species, whelks, chitons, marine worms and small fishes such as sculpins and pricklebacks in pools or under rocks.

Vancouver shares the richness of the coast but most of its marine life is invisible since it is far below the surface. As you stare into the water from a dock you see anemones, barnacles, mussels and purple starfish on the pilings together with feather hydroids and some seaweed on which there will be kelp crabs and small decorator crabs. Moon jellyfish with short tentacles and the large orange-brown sea nettles drift along. At low tide you can compare the rocky coast of West Vancouver with the sandy beaches of Spanish Banks, noting the greater diversity and abundance on rocky shores.

Scuba divers see much more. Porteau Cove on Howe Sound and Whytecliff Park in West Vancouver are marine sanctuaries where divers can observe protected underwater habitats. As the divers descend they observe different species at different depths. Between the tides they see red and green anemones, mussels, green urchins and purple starfish. As they go deeper these species are replaced by plumose anemones, red urchins and many starfish species—pink, leather, blood, vermilion and the giant orange sunflower stars. Sometimes, in a cave or crevice or even exposed on the bottom, divers encounter dark red octopuses that quickly seek cover. On the bottom are coon-striped shrimp, orange sea cucumbers and cancer crabs, both red rock and the larger Dungeness crab. In the warmer water above the thermocline in summer, the diver sees small silvery salmon and herring, shiner perch, blackeye gobies and copper rockfish but farther down will see quillback rockfish and striped seaperch in midwater and lingcod, red Irish Lord sculpins, cabezons and occasional wolfeels on the bottom. Over sand or mud there are starry flounders and other flatfishes and skates.

In the deep waters of Vancouver Harbour are dogfish sharks and ratfish and species that people almost never see—little brown sharks, great six-gill sharks, black skates, sculpins of strange shape and appearance, red thornyheads, poachers and eelpouts. The deep water fishes are often black or red and tend to be soft and slimy.

The waters around the city of Vancouver are influenced by the Fraser River which flows into the Strait of Georgia and spreads in a plume over the surface of much of the southern portions of the region. In late springtime when the river is in flood, freshwater sweeps around Point Grey into Vancouver's harbor where occasional freshwater fishes such as carp and sturgeon are found and surf smelt spawn in brackish water along the beaches. Associated with the Fraser River and other streams such as the Capilano, Lynn and Seymour, are salmon runs where young salmon swim out to sea in the springtime and mature salmon return in the summer and autumn. All of the five species of Pacific salmon plus migratory steelhead trout swim through Vancouver waters at one time or another and are sought avidly by both sport and commercial fishermen. In summertime many sport fishing boats can be seen while larger seiners, gill netters and trollers come and go from more distant points.

The Capilano Salmon Hatchery in North Vancouver is a good place to observe salmon. The park itself is very beautiful with the river cascading swiftly though a narrow canyon below the Cleveland Dam. Chinook, coho and steelhead can be seen there. The best times to observe them are: July to October for adult coho, October for Chinook, January to May for young Chinook and year round for young coho and steelhead.

Watching spawning salmon in the autumn is fascinating. All five North American Pacific salmon (there is a sixth species in

Japan) die after they spawn. Some steelhead trout die after they spawn but most survive. Salmon usually undergo great migrations from freshwater to saltwater and back. Associated with these migrations are changes in shape and color, while in the ocean salmon are silvery. As sockeye salmon approach freshwater spawning areas, their bodies turn brilliant red while their heads and tails become green. Male salmon develop big teeth, elongated jaws and hunched backs. The most extreme hunched form are the male pink salmon or "humpbacks."

You can see adult pink salmon in the Jones Creek Spawning Channel near Hope in October during odd-numbered years. Pinks live only two years in southern B.C. waters and runs only occur in odd years.

The Fraser River basin is one of the world's most productive watersheds. The river has never been dammed and has immense salmon runs, the most valuable of which is the famed Adams River Sockeye run. These salmon reach the mouth of the Fraser River in late summer, then return to the Adams in the South Thompson area for spawning in late October. The dominant runs take place every four years—1994, 1998, 2002—when 1.5 to 2.0 million sockeye spawn.

When the salmon are milling around the mouth of the Fraser in August and September, killer whales are often seen in the area. More than 600 of these large black and white dolphins are found along the B.C. coast. They live in four communities: northern resident, southern resident, transient and offshore. Residents and transients have different diets, the former apparently feeding only on fish while transients prefer warm blooded prey such as seals, sea lions and Dall's porpoises. While resident whales are attracted by schools of salmon in the Strait of Georgia, transients are sometimes seen in Vancouver Harbor apparently searching for seals.

Much of our understanding about killer whales, or orcas as they are also called, comes from the photo-identification system used by the late Dr. Michael Bigg. While earlier scientists fired darts with tags into whales, Dr. Bigg carefully photographed most of the orcas along the coast and showed they could be identified by individual marks or scars on their backs and fins.

Killer whales can occasionally be seen from ferry boats crossing the Strait of Georgia, but the best place to observe them is in Johnstone Strait between northern Vancouver Island and the Mainland. During summer, pods of resident killer whales move regularly around the area and can be watched and photographed from tour boats. Dr. John Ford, Vancouver Aquarium's whale scientist, has revealed that the calls of killer whales can be heard with the help of a hydrophone and that call types are arranged in dialects which differ in the various pods.

In the waters around Vancouver other marine mammals can be seen. Many of them follow the migrations of eulachons, herring and salmon, particularly around river mouths. Harbor seals are very common and can be recognized by their spotted coats, large eyes and earless heads. While there are two species of sea lions, the giant Steller sea lions are rare as compared with the California sea lions. Tour boats take tourists out to observe sea lions from the Steveston docks near the mouth of the Fraser River.

The best place to see B.C. marine life is in the Vancouver Aquarium located in Stanley Park. The main exhibits are arranged in a sequence to represent British Columbia aquatic habitats from the open ocean to the headwaters of the Fraser River. Flocks of waterfowl can be seen in Lost Lagoon and the waters around Stanley Park.

Environmental mural, Melville Street, Vancouver, 1993. vp

The Greenpeace Story
Douglas Sagi

IN 1969, A few days after the United States detonated a one-megaton nuclear weapon at Amchitka Island in the Alaskan Aleutians, the Don't Make A Wave Committee was organized in a Vancouver living room containing a small number of people who thought such weapons should not be allowed to make waves through the oceans or atmospheres of the world ever again.

Committee members included Paul Cote, then a UBC law student, Bill Darnell, a field worker for the federal government's Company of Young Canadians, Terry Simmons, a member of the Sierra Club studying at Simon Fraser University and two older men, James Bohlen and Irving Stowe. Bohlen and Stowe had left the United States to protest the Vietnam War as well as the nuclear buildup. Bohlen had once designed rocket engines. Stowe was a Quaker and a lawyer. They talked and argued.

One of the arguments was whether to concentrate the committee's efforts on protesting against another Amchitka test planned for the fall of 1971, or to expand their efforts to fight against all threats to the environment.

"Peace," said Stowe, a gnome-like man in his late fifties as he left one meeting. It was the traditional greeting or farewell of those involved in the peace activist movement.

"Make it a green peace" said Darnell, the youngster from the CYC.

Yellow and green buttons were made up combining the three-pronged nuclear disarmament symbol with the ecology movement's "E" (for the earth) and "O" (for the organisms that live on it) and sold to raise money.

There were fundraising concerts with pop stars Joni Mitchell, Phil Ochs, James Taylor and the rock band Chilliwack taking part. A boat—the 25-metre halibut packer *Phyllis Cormack*—was chartered to head for Amchitka to try to stop the bomb.

The boat, nicknamed *Greenpeace,* was forced by weather to turn back. They raised more money and sent a bigger boat, a converted minesweeper named the *Edgewater Fortune,* which they nicknamed *Greenpeace Too!* (the exclamation point was Stowe's inspiration). *Greenpeace Too!* was also delayed by November's North Pacific weather and the bomb was exploded while the minesweeper was far away.

But when *Greenpeace Too!* returned to New Westminster harbor, what was to become the world's largest, most influential environmental organization was launched.

The Don't Make a Wave Committee changed its name to the Greenpeace Foundation. *Greenpeace III* (originally the *Vega*) sailed to French Polynesia to protest against French nuclear tests in 1972. The *Vega,* a 12.5-metre handmade ketch, belonged to David McTaggart, chair of Greenpeace International from 1969 to 1973. The *Vega* was retired when McTaggart retired after being severely beaten, with others of his crew, during the 1972 protest. Three years later Russian whalers were confronted off the California coast. In Canada Greenpeacers confronted sealers off the East Coast and invaded, by canoe, the Bruce Nuclear Power Station in Lake Huron.

In 1978 Greenpeace bought its own ship, a converted North Sea trawler, the *Sir Williams Hardy,* renamed it the *Rainbow Warrior* and campaigned against whaling in Iceland and Spain.

The organization spread worldwide. In 1979 national Greenpeace organizations in Australia, Canada, France, Holland, New Zealand, the United Kingdom and the United States formed Greenpeace International, which now has headquarters in Amsterdam.

There were protests, boycotts and confrontations around the world throughout the 1980s. Greenpeacers zipped about in inflatable boats, flew a hot-air balloon across Germany, hung a banner from the Ottawa Peace Tower, climbed smokestacks and Mount Rushmore in various environmental causes to save whales and porpoises, to stop nuclear power and nuclear bombs. Some members went to jail.

After the French secret service sunk the original *Rainbow Warrior* in 1985 a second *Warrior* was commissioned (in 1989). Greenpeace operates a fleet of several vessels including converted tugs, fishboats and riverboats. There are organizations in more than 30 countries with total membership of more than five million and a paid staff of 1,000. Greenpeace now spends more than $40 million each year on its activities. Nuclear explosions and whaling are still concerns but major campaigns today are against toxic pollution and the destruction of rainforests.

While the efforts of its members and crews of eco-warriors through the past two decades have occasionally disturbed, if not broken, the peace, the organization is now reassessing its activities. Some current members argue that environmental issues are more complex and require different tactics than in the 1970s. It is possible to mount challenges and present alternatives in the boardrooms of corporations that are now, thanks to the efforts of the eco-warriors, more receptive to the concerns of environmentalists.

Temples of Time in the Greater Vancouver Forest
Ralf Kelman

Greater Vancouver has in its own backyard one of the finest big tree forests and ecological sites in the world. Largely unknown because of a lack of information from the forestry-connected bureaucracies, a treasure-trove of record-breaking forest giants is coming to light in the Lower Mainland area. A caring public alerted in the last two decades to the Stein, Carmanah and Clayoquot heritage big-tree sites would be shocked to learn that they have been kept in the dark about the existence of forests nearby with many trees one thousand to two thousand years old. These include giant western red cedars five metres in diameter or more and Douglas firs as high as 90 metres with trunks four metres in diameter. These trees also include the tallest known western yew still living in what is now the Greater Vancouver watershed.

The *Guinness Book of Records* made our region world famous by featuring the tallest tree ever recorded on the planet. This was a Douglas fir more than 120 metres in height which was located in the Lynn Valley area. This year an excellent book, *Forest Giants of the World Past and Present,* was published by big-tree expert Al Carder of Victoria. Included among the many trees described and pictured is the thickest known western hemlock found anywhere from Oregon to Alaska, located behind Grouse Mountain at Pipeline Pass. It is 2.7 metres in diameter and may be fifteen hundred years old—or older.

A larger forested area from Bowen Island to Kent, Washington including the Fraser Valley lowlands could be called the "Great Vancouver Forest." Skumalasph Island near Deroche has the greatest collection of record black cottonwoods in North America with the top four measuring nine to ten metres in diameter.

Randy Stoltmann, Will Koop and I located and measured many of these trees for Randy's book, *Guide to the Record Trees of British Columbia,* published by the Western Canada Wilderness Committee. Randy said that if you were going to find world record West Coast trees now they would probably be discovered in the Vancouver watershed area. It is vitally important to inventory these watersheds and other local unlogged forests. Standards and guidelines must be developed to protect this great international tree legacy for citizens and visitors for the next millennium and beyond.

The late environmentalist Randy Stoltmann beside giant North Shore tree. rk

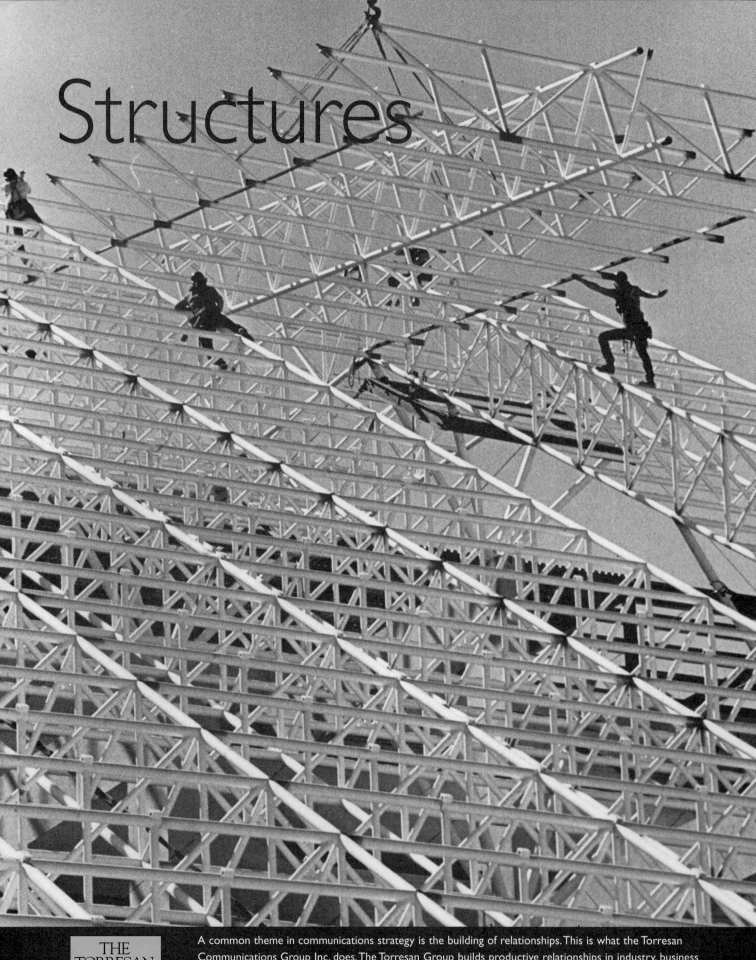

Structures

A common theme in communications strategy is the building of relationships. This is what the Torresan Communications Group Inc. does. The Torresan Group builds productive relationships in industry, business and marketing; it builds relationships for financial development, social programs, and cooperation among public and private sectors and groups with special concerns. The Torresan Group has broad international experience, but remains, at heart, a Vancouver company.

WHILE MANY PEOPLE dwell on the beauty of Greater Vancouver's natural setting, it is the ways in which builders have modified that setting that provide a record of our culture's achievements and aspirations. "Reading" the built environment—the structures, buildings, landscapes and monuments that form our communities—tells us a great deal about ourselves. The structures around us are no more or less than expressions of our cultural values.

Immigrants bring a particular approach to their buildings—and the region's non-natives were all immigrants at one time or another. New arrivals tend to import the ways of building known to them, in an attempt to create a familiar environment in an alien land. We see this in the surviving 19th-century farmhouses of Surrey—such as the Boothroyd and Stewart houses—forms that were familiar in Ontario and California, laced with distant memories of England.

The mercantile carpetbaggers of the early 20th century brought the pretentious Edwardian classicism of Eastern Canada; and new Canadians of our own day often include ages-old Asian elements in their houses of worship (for example, the Buddhist Temple, Sikh Temple and Ismaili Jamatkhana Centre described in this section) and even their shopping centres (such as Richmond's Aberdeen Centre). The first generation builds for survival. Surrounding one's self with familiar images is a means of cultural survival.

Later generations build more lasting monuments: they erect structures that reveal a bolder side of society's aspirations. The former Canadian Pacific Railway Station uses pompous Roman imagery, with a hint of a triumphal arch, to announce Vancouver as its great western terminus and the gateway to Asia. The arch as a symbol of triumph and peace is seen in the Cenotaph in Victory Square, the Peace Arch at the border crossing and the Terry Fox Memorial. Individual egos emerge in office towers such as Louis D. Taylor's conservative World (later Sun) Tower and Dal Grauer's boldly modern B.C. Electric Building.

Changing political values are revealed in the contrast between the aloofness of the former provincial courthouse (now the Vancouver Art Gallery)—a potent symbol of authority built before World War I by the McBride Conservative government—and the accessibility of the Barrett NDP government's courthouse of the 1970s (Robson Square), intended as the people's architecture, so approachable that pedestrians are invited to walk on it!

And what about "ordinary" British Columbians and their housing? Their vision of a promised land, in which everybody could own a house and a lot, is seen in the endless rows of single family properties that line the gridiron blocks of Vancouver's established neighborhoods. They are more stylish, tidier and amply landscaped on the West Side, dominated by business people and professionals who demanded orderly planning; and plainer, less organized, with fewer parks and trees on the East Side, first populated by fiercely independent working people from Britain who shunned taxes and government "interference."

The one-family-per-lot dream has largely evaporated since the emergence of the new Greater Vancouver, metropolis of the Pacific Rim, which first expressed itself fully in Expo 86 (whose legacy of structures includes the spherical Science Centre and the technically sophisticated, if inefficient, SkyTrain). Many people now accept high densities as the price of the global city, and so the central area is rapidly filling up with residential towers and multi-level townhouses. Those who seek space must escape to the suburbs. But now the suburbs are responding by trying to look like the city that spawned them—whether in their polished new public buildings (such as the Metrotown and Newton libraries, or Port Coquitlam's city hall and courthouse), in the pretension and scale of their commercial buildings (the Gateway development in Whalley), or in the increasing density and diminishing open space of their own residential neighborhoods.

As you meet the structures of Greater Vancouver in the articles that follow, enjoy them for what they are, as well as for the hopes and ideals that they express.

—*Harold Kalman*

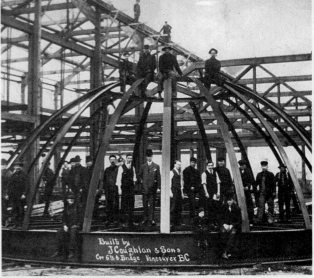

facing page: Spaceframe construction, Law Courts, c.1978. vs

above: Steel dome, courthouse (now Vancouver Art Gallery), 1910. vp

Notable Buildings

It is called *the company that built Vancouver. (Western Living Magazine,* June 1986). Since 1908, the name Bentall has been synonymous with development of landmark buildings and enduring business relationships. Its best known properties are the four towers of Bentall Centre, described by Harold Kalman (Exploring Vancouver, 1978) as *Vancouver's most elegant venture into high rise design.* Within the century, Tower V, the largest project in Bentall's history, will extend Bentall Centre to 2.1. million square feet.

Notable Buildings in Greater Vancouver
Harold Kalman

The following is a selection of buildings, groups of buildings and landscapes of special interest. Many are structures that I particularly like while others are here because of their particular architectural or historical importance. The selection is admittedly arbitrary, and does not give equal representation to all municipalities in the GVRD, but nevertheless runs the gamut of building-types that surround us.

The buildings include some that are old, some that are new, many with ideas that were borrowed and a few whose color is blue. Many represent "high" ("polite") architecture—architect-designed buildings that emulated trends of the time and overtly strove to make important statements. Others are "vernacular" buildings that follow "folk" traditions with little conscious effort at design, yet are just as expressive of the cultures that produced them, although in a more passive way. (These are the "high road" and "low road" buildings identified in *How Buildings Learn,* a fine new book by Stuart Brand, editor of the first *Whole Earth Catalogue*). The thoughtful reader will have little trouble differentiating the two streams.

Much of the information on buildings in Vancouver and the North Shore appears in *Exploring Vancouver,* by Harold Kalman, Ron Phillips and Robin Ward published by UBC Press in 1993. It is used here with the generous permission of Ron Phillips, Robin Ward and the publisher. Additional material has come from the informative heritage inventories that have been prepared by most municipalities (many funded in part by the British Columbia Heritage Trust) as well as published histories of the region's communities, descriptions in architectural periodicals, guides and brochures, and my *A History of Canadian Architecture* (1994). Information on many buildings was kindly provided by architectural firms, municipalities, government agencies and the buildings' occupants. New research for *The Greater Vancouver Book* was undertaken by Meg Stanley. My very warm thanks to all who helped.

VANCOUVER: GASTOWN, CHINATOWN, STRATHCONA, DOWNTOWN EAST SIDE
Byrnes Block
2 Water Street, Vancouver
Elmer H. Fisher, 1886-87
In many ways the symbol of Gastown, this commercial block, resplendent in its pilasters and pediments, rose shortly after the Great Fire of 1886. One of the city's first brick buildings,

facing page: Bentall Centre, 1991. vp

developed by Victoria realtor George Byrnes, it stands on the site of the second saloon of Gassy Jack Deighton, whose chief legacy to Gastown was his nickname. The ornament advertised the relative opulence of the Alhambra Hotel, one of the few in town then charging more than a dollar a night. A dedicated fire truck chaser, architect Fisher soon smelled smoke in Seattle and rebuilt that city's Pioneer Square district after its fire of 1889. The phoenix-like role of the Byrnes Block was repeated in the late 1960s when it became one of the first buildings in Gastown to be rehabilitated—this time by realtor Larry Killam. The face-lift helped to turn around the then-shabby district.

Hotel Europe
43 Powell Street, Vancouver
Parr and Fee, 1908-09
The Hotel Europe was the first reinforced-concrete structure in Vancouver. So foreign was the technology that it had to be built by contractors from Cincinnati, Ohio—the Ferro-Concrete Construction Company, which six years earlier had built the first tall concrete building in the world. Italian-Canadian hotelier Angelo Colari built this flatiron block as the best commercial hotel in town. The flat brick walls and sparse decoration contrast with the ornate Alhambra Hotel (Byrnes Block) across the street. Architects J.E. Parr and Thomas A. Fee developed a highly successful—and pragmatic—Vancouver practice. Many of their plain, glazed-brick commercial buildings remain throughout the Downtown area. The firm advertised that they specialized in the production of buildings that will pay: "*Utilitas* is their motto, and revenue their aim."

Four Sisters Housing Cooperative
133 Powell Street, Vancouver
Davidson and Yuen, 1987
The Downtown Eastside Residents Association (DERA), a community advocacy group that represents the many needy people in this inner-city neighborhood, has been admirably active as a developer. DERA has renovated and built several blocks of what the city calls "social" housing. The Four Sisters Co-op is one of the many success stories. Largely new wood-and-masonry construction and partly rehabilitated warehouse (facing on Alexander Street), the award-winning building was constructed with the help of public-sector funding and is managed by its residents.

Chinese Cultural Centre
50 East Pender Street, Vancouver
James K.M. Cheng, with Romses, Kwan and Associates, 1981
Chinatown remains the focus of Vancouver's strong Chinese-Canadian community, as it has

been for more than a century, although the neighborhood has recently been challenged by commercial centres in Richmond and other suburban areas. The Chinese Cultural Centre was erected to celebrate the community's achievements and reinforce the primacy of Chinatown. The frontispiece of the concrete post-and-beam structure is a traditional gateway, made in China, and erected here after having first been installed at Expo 86. Aspects of the plan follow the principles of *feng shui,* the traditional Chinese practice of topology and geomancy. Behind the Chinese Cultural Centre is the exquisite Dr. Sun Yat-Sen Classical Chinese Garden (Joe Wai, 1986) which recreates the retreat of a scholar of the Ming Dynasty and is based on a prototype in Suzhou, China's "City of Gardens."

Ballantyne Pier
North foot of Heatley Street
1921-23; Musson Cattell Mackey Partnership, 1994-95
Although only a cargo-storage and loading facility for Vancouver's busy port, the original Ballantyne Pier was designed more as a triumphal gateway to the city than a warehouse. Seen by Vancouver Port Corporation as an aging symbol that was inadequate for today's seismic (earthquake) requirements and functional needs, the Pier's storage sheds were mostly demolished and redeveloped with a large new addition that respects (and discreetly recedes from) the restored original facade. A small part of the attractive original concrete structure has been retained inside. The new complex combines a cruise ship terminal on the upper level with general cargo-handling facilities at ground level.

Former American Can Company Building
611 Alexander Street
C.G. Preis, 1925; rehabilitated, Bruno Freschi, 1988
Old and new are superbly mated in this industrial building, built as a container factory and retooled to become a chic design centre. It features showrooms for Vancouver's emerging clothing designers as well as offices and studios occupied by architects and others in the design industry. The original modern reinforced-concrete building, whose large windows are enclosed by spandrels and piers with a soupçon of Gothic and Art Deco, has been enhanced by the insertion of a large internal atrium. The entrance is marked by an elegant filigree tower and spire of steel and glass which contains a new elevator.

St. James's Anglican Church
303 East Cordova Street
Adrian Gilbert Scott, with Sharp and Thompson, 1935-37
This extraordinary church is at once traditional and radical—reflecting its congregation's adherence to the conservative Anglo-Catholic liturgy

while practising an active and liberal program of delivering social services to the area's needy. Designed by a member of the British architectural dynasty founded by cathedral-builder Sir George Gilbert Scott, St. James's provides an ingenious solution to a constricted corner site where it is squeezed between adjacent parish buildings (Clergy House and St. Luke's Home on Cordova Street and the Rectory on Gore Street, all designed by Sharp and Thompson in the 1920s). The overall impression recalls both Romanesque and Gothic churches yet without any literal quotations from historical styles. The central sanctuary is almost Byzantine in feeling with its deep arches supporting a wood ceiling and octagonal tower. The structure is monolithic reinforced concrete with inner and outer walls separated by a 60-centimetre space and internal concrete trusses buttressing the tower. Most radical is the exposed concrete both inside and out, making the building somewhat of a pioneer of the modern movement in Canada.

Sun Tower
100 West Pender Street, Vancouver
W.T. Whiteway, 1911-12
Vancouver has produced several claimants to the title of tallest building in the British Empire (or Commonwealth), among them this 17-storey (84-metre high) skyscraper, which out-reached the previous title-holder, the nearby Dominion Building (207 West Hastings Street, 1908-10). It was eclipsed in turn in 1914 by the Royal Bank of Canada's 20-storey Toronto offices. The Sun Tower was built for the *Vancouver World*—and, for nearly 30 years, occupied by the *Vancouver Sun*. The developer in this case was newspaper publisher and sometime mayor Louis D. Taylor, a man not noted for modesty. The bombastic Beaux-arts copper dome is complemented by nine risqué maidens ("caryatids"), half-way up the building. The slender shaft rises from a broad base, much like Seattle's renowned Smith Tower (1910-14), which boasted of being the tallest building in the world outside New York City. It will soon be overwhelmed by a sea of highrises in adjacent International Village, whose towers are emerging as this is being written.

VANCOUVER: DOWNTOWN AND WEST END
Canada Place
999 Canada Place, Vancouver
Zeidler Roberts Partnership; Musson Cattell Mackey Partnership; Downs/Archambault and Partners, 1983-86
Resplendent with its bright white fabric sails, this cheery harbor landmark—our answer to the renowned Sydney Opera House—was built as the government of Canada's pavilion for Expo

86. It encloses a trade and convention centre and a cruise ship terminal, the latter mostly serving the popular Alaska run. Both uses have already outgrown their space, leading to current discussions over where to build additional facilities. (The new addition to Ballantyne Pier has provided more berths for cruise ships.) The superstructure at the landward end contains the Pan Pacific Hotel and Vancouver's World Trade Centre while a domed IMAX theatre rises at the prow (which is also the name of the restaurant at the end).

Christ Church Cathedral
690 Burrard Street, Vancouver
C.O. Wickenden, 1889-95
The oldest surviving church in the city, this stalwart sandstone structure was built as the Anglican parish church for what was once a residential neighborhood and is now the city's commercial core. The pointed-arched windows, buttresses and steep gabled roof recall the cozy Gothic parish churches of England. This association continues inside with the marvellous timber framework and hammer-beam roof warmly illuminated through superb stained-glass windows. Christ Church became a cathedral in 1929 and a year later the bright and spacious chancel was added (by architects Twizell and Twizell). A generation ago the diocese intended to demolish the cathedral and replace it with an office tower and underground sanctuary. A happier solution was found in the transfer of unused density rights to the adjacent property to the north, giving extra height and bulk to the adjacent Park Place tower (Musson Cattell Mackey Partnership, 1984) and providing the diocese with cash for social programs and building maintenance.

Cathedral Place / Canadian Craft Museum
925 West Georgia Street and 639 Hornby Street, Vancouver
Paul Merrick Architects, 1990-91
Reflecting a building's context is a prime doctrine of Post-Modernism and it's a doctrine well-heeded in this fun-to-visit complex. The name acknowledges Christ Church Cathedral next door. The massing, ornament and sculpted nurses are reminders of the Art Deco Georgia Medical Dental Building which the tower replaced, while the roof and gargoyles respond to the Hotel Vancouver across the street. The lobby offers a delightful potpourri of Art Deco-inspired features. Behind Cathedral Place is the Canadian Craft Museum and its serene grassed cloister (Christopher Phillips and Associates), two gems too often missed by passers-by.

Hotel Vancouver
900 West Georgia Street, Vancouver
Archibald and Schofield, 1928-39

As Canadian as bangers and mash are British, imposing chateau-style hotels were built by the nation's railways in resorts and cities from coast to coast. Inspired by the picturesque castles of France and Scotland, the steep-roofed hotels cater to our fantasies of palatial living. Vancouver's version, resplendent in its gargoyles, Renaissance detail and fine relief sculpture, was built by the Canadian National Railway. Delayed by the Depression it was rushed to completion in 1939 for the Royal Visit of King George VI and Queen Elizabeth. The rival Canadian Pacific Railway co-operatively closed its own, earlier, Hotel Vancouver (on the site of the present Eaton's store, two blocks east), lent the name and entered into a joint-management contract. Today the well-patronized hotel is part of the large chain of Canadian Pacific Hotels and Resorts (as is the new Chateau Whistler).

Robson Square
800-block Robson Street, Vancouver
Arthur Erickson Architects, 1974-79
This extensive complex combines the glass-roofed Law Courts, defined by the distinctive bold shape of its steel space frame, with land-scaped public spaces (Cornelia Hahn Oberlander and Raoul Robillard, landscape architects) that invite public activity on several levels inside and out. The rightist Social Credit provincial government of the early 1970s was determined to build an aggressive 55-storey office tower here. The New Democratic Party government that won the 1973 election dismissed the proposed big-business image by changing architects and architectural programs, laying the tower on its side and producing a low, multi-block courthouse that is symbolically and physically more accessible—so accessible that we can walk on it! All this shows how architecture can provide a powerful political symbol. The classical former courthouse (F.M. Rattenbury, 1906-12) on Georgia Street at the north end of the site was adapted at the same time to become the home of the Vancouver Art Gallery.

Marine Building
355 Burrard Street, Vancouver
McCarter and Nairne, 1929-30
It's "the best Art Deco office building in the world," exclaimed poet laureate and architecture aficionado, the late Sir John Betjeman, to this writer. Encrusted in terracotta ornament, the 21-storey buff-brick building is a monument to Vancouver's maritime presence. Relief panels near the base depict the history of discovery and transportation along the Pacific coast. A frieze featuring waves, sea horses and marine fauna wraps around both fronts of the building. Over the main entrance on Burrard Street a

The story begins in 1908. Charles Bentall, a 24-year-old structural engineer enticed to Canada by a CPR advertisement ("Canada, the land of plenty") arrives in Vancouver with 60 cents in his pocket. He is hired as a draftsman at John Coughlan & Sons (now Canron Inc.), becomes chief structural engineer a year later and in 1911 frames the World Building (now the Sun Tower), the tallest building in the British Empire. He is 29 when he climbs hand-and-foot up the 85-metre, 17-storey World skeleton, examining its integrity on his way

ship's prow sails out of the sunset and Canada geese fly across the sun's rays. Scallops, swirls and zig-zags continue the Art Deco treatment in the bronze grilles. In the dramatic lobby one finds green and blue tiled walls, a beamed ceiling illuminated by lights recessed within ships' prows and colored floor tiles (replaced in kind in a 1989 renovation). The architects' own description reveals how they thought of building and ornament as one:

"The building . . . suggests some great crag rising from the sea, clinging with sea flora and fauna, tinted in sea-green, touched with gold, and at night in winter a dim silhouette piercing the sea mists."

B.C. Electric Building
970 Burrard Street, Vancouver
*Thompson, Berwick and Pratt, 1955-57; reha-
bilitated by Paul Merrick Architects, 1994-95*
Built as the headquarters of the B.C. Electric Company (now B.C. Hydro) this attractive tower was the first highrise building south of Georgia Street. The dynamic collaboration bet-ween B.C. Electric chair Dal Grauer and forward-thinking architect Ned Pratt (ably assisted by Ron Thom and others in his office) produced a tapered, lozenge-shaped tower whose plan placed every desk no farther than five metres from a window and natural light (a poor adver-tisement for the power utility!). The floors are cantilevered from the central concrete service core like branches from a tree, with only slender perimeter columns offering additional support. The blue, green and black mosaic tiles (by B.C. Binning) are an integral part of the design. The building was recently adapted, and the exterior curtain wall replaced, to become a condominium residence called The Electra. The adjacent Dal Grauer Substation (Sharp and Thompson, Berwick, Pratt, 1953-54) is even more uncom-promisingly modernist with the brilliantly colored workings exposed behind a transparent glass wall—which, following a minor explosion, was replaced with opaque glass.

1100-blocks Comox and Pendrell Streets
Vancouver
Various builders and architects, 1890s-1910s; sub-sequent alterations
This block—"Nelson Park South"—boasts the best-preserved collection of early houses in Vancouver. Their survival did not come about by accident. The city began to buy the houses decades ago, intending to demolish them to double the size of adjacent Nelson Park. Times have changed and public open-houses held in 1995 as part of a study of the block's future revealed that the community now values heritage conservation and the retention of affordable housing more than park expansion.

Deferred maintenance has seen many of the houses deteriorate but it now seems likely that the city will commit itself to the long-term preservation and management of the block. The oldest cluster is at 1137-1173 Pendrell (two have been altered), built 1893-97; nos. 1163-69 are verandahed "gable-front" houses with ornate brackets at the second-floor bay windows. The houses at 1110-1122 Comox, built 1904-05, are broad-er in proportions and more classical in detail. The remodelled exterior of 1104 Bute may mask an 1888 house built only two years after the Great Fire.

Orpheum Theatre
884 Granville Street, Vancouver
B. Marcus Priteca; Frederick J. Peters, 1926-27
The 2,800-seat Vancouver outpost of the Chicago-based Orpheum vaudeville circuit was once the largest theatre in Canada and the Pacific Northwest. The lavish interior decorative scheme, derived from the Spanish Baroque, features exuberant arches, tiered columns and interlaced mouldings executed in marble, travertine, cast stone and plaster. Priteca was the chosen architect of the rival Pantages circuit and a master of theatre design; Vancouver's long-demolished Pantages Theatre (1916-17, later the Majestic) was also his. Opened in the year in which "talkies" were introduced, the Orpheum was used more and more for movies. In the early 1970s former owner Famous Players wanted to divide the by-now tired theatre into several small cinemas. With strong community support the city bought the Orpheum and rehabilitated it for use by the Vancouver Symphony Orchestra (Thompson, Berwick, Pratt and Partners, 1975-76). Recent changes to the beautiful auditorium (Architec-tura, begun 1995), driven by acoustic and other functional considerations, have unfortunately compromised the original design.

Terry Fox Memorial
East end of Robson Street, at BC Place
Franklin Allen, 1984
When Coquitlam runner Terry Fox died in 1981, after having to cut short his cross-Canada `Mara-thon of Hope' that raised money for cancer research, communities across Canada rushed to erect memorials to his memory. Vancouver's competition-winning contribution was this curious caricature of a Roman triumphal arch —widely unloved for its lack of a representation of Fox. Popular or not, the Memorial has been credited as the city's first example of Post-Modern ("PoMo") architecture, a style that readmitted historical forms and messages after years of banishment by the dogma of mod-ernism. The pastel-shaded brick, tile, and steel

arch is capped by four fibreglass lions, traditional symbols of strength and heroism. Images etched onto reflective steel plates were subsequently installed within the arch, and public outrage eventually subsided.

Library Square
350 West Georgia Street, Vancouver
Moshe Safdie and Associates; Downs/Archambault and Partners, 1993-95
Vancouverites liken their new public library to the ancient Roman Colosseum, pointing to the look-alike circular walls and tiers of arches, despite architect Safdie's denials. Historical asso-ciations aside the post-modern landmark is a real crowd-pleaser, having been selected in an open competition that included substantial public input. The seven-level library is actually a square inserted within a circle. Acrophobes gingerly cross the elegant bridges that span the atrium and provide access to the serene reading gal-leries along the Homer Street perimeter. The ambitious complex includes a 21-storey federal government office building at the northeast cor-ner, two floors of provincial offices atop the library, retail shops at the southeast corner and three levels of underground parking. All are clad in warm brown precast concrete. The same architects collaborated on the Ford Centre for the Performing Arts (1994-95) across Homer Street, a flashy venue for commercial theatre developed by Toronto impresario Garth Drabinsky.

Sylvia Hotel and Annex
1154 Gilford Street, Vancouver
W.P. White, 1912
1861 Beach Avenue, Vancouver
Henriquez & Partners, 1987
Still popular after all these years, the Sylvia Hotel (and the wildlife inhabiting the vines that ramble over its brick walls) has become an English Bay landmark. Originally built as apartments, the hotel displays timeless classicism that still looks good. Architect Richard Henriquez capitalized on this in his condominium annex whose design partly mimics the Edwardian prototype but peels it away at the corner to allow a bold, glazed, angled extrusion. This witty post-modern solu-tion alludes to the newcomer's historical and contemporary contexts while providing expan-sive suites with superb views of the water.

Pacific Heights Housing Cooperative
1000-block Pacific Street, Vancouver
Roger Hughes, 1983-85
Of the many attempts to preserve a cluster of old West End frame houses while responding to high land prices and the need to intensify devel-opment, this may be the most successful. Eight early residences were moved—first backward to build garages beneath them, then forward

to the top. He gives thanks no lives were lost building it. Life is cheap: no hard hats, no safety precautions, no worker's compensation. From the tower, he looks over the city's incredible building boom—a boom he is a great part of. In 1912 Coughlan advertises that it has erected "every steel frame of importance" in Vancouver, including the dome atop the courthouse (now the Vancouver Art Gallery).

and closer to the street than when originally built and sideways to read as four pairs—and converted into duplexes. One had to be rebuilt entirely. A medium-rise infill building containing stacked two-storey apartments was erected behind them, providing a backdrop. Additional density provided by the city to encourage preservation allowed the creation of 91 units where once there were only eight.

Science World
1455 Quebec Street, Vancouver
1984-86; refitted and extended by Boak Alexander, 1988-89
This shiny sphere, its stainless-steel skin held in place by a white-steel external geodesic frame, is the most evident legacy of Expo 86. It marked the main entrance to Vancouver's much-admired world's fair and served as Expo Centre. The "golfball" was later adapted to become Science World, an immensely popular science centre that attracts hordes of local and touring children and adults. The central domed space contains an Omnimax theatre. Most of the Expo site, which occupied existing and newly filled land along False Creek, was purchased from the province by Hong Kong billionaire Li Ka-Shing and is being developed as Concord Pacific Place, a dense residential community.

VANCOUVER: WEST SIDE AND UBC
Granville Island
Johnston and Duranleau Streets, Vancouver
Begun 1913; rehabilitation plan by Norman Hotson, 1977
Food market, arts and crafts, restaurants, theatres, marine industries, an art college, a brewery, the author's office—all thrive at Granville Island, mostly in rehabilitated industrial buildings that have been well adapted to their new uses. It was developed in the 1970s by Canada (then Central) Mortgage and Housing Corporation which had acquired the tired 15-hectare industrial island from the National Harbours Board. Granville Island has become the region's most successful retail and entertainment emporium. Architects Norman Hotson and Joost Bakker produced an inspired master plan that encouraged the mix of uses and the retention of an industrial vocabulary in building and landscape improvements. They also rehabilitated the former BC Equipment and Wright's Ropes factories to become the Granville Island Public Market (1979-80) while retaining the travelling cranes that hang from the rafters. Nearby Ocean Cement, built around 1920 for Diether's Coal and Building Supplies, and Micon Products (a forge that makes chains) are the last remaining heavy industries.

Vancouver City Hall
453 West 12th Avenue, Vancouver
Townley and Matheson, 1935-36
The City of Vancouver annexed the municipalities of South Vancouver and Point Grey in 1929 and built this new city hall near their common boundary (actually Cambie Street and 16th Avenue) to symbolize the amalgamation. The hard-edged geometry of its dynamic cubic massing resembles the "totalitarian classicism" seen in government buildings of the day from Munich to Moscow. The zig-zag ornament atop the blocks and beneath the windows is vintage Art Deco, although the style is best called "Moderne." A four-storey annex was built to the north in 1968-70 (Townley, Matheson, and Partners).

Walter C. Nichol House
1402 The Crescent, Vancouver
Maclure and Fox, 1912-13
The CPR realized a superb development opportunity by opening Shaughnessy Heights as an exclusive residential enclave for Vancouver's power elite. The area was laid out with curved, tree-lined streets and boulevards by Danish engineer L.E. Davick and Montreal landscape architect Frederick Todd, and the first lots were sold in 1909—just as a new Granville Street Bridge was completed. Many of the city's newly rich fled the West End which was being sullied by apartments and streetcars. Walter Nichol, publisher of the *Province* and subsequently lieutenant-governor of British Columbia, was one of many who chose to build in Shaughnessy. His half-timbered Tudor Revival manor was designed by talented Victoria architect Samuel Maclure and his Vancouver partner C.C. Fox, the darlings of high society. It and its neighbors around The Crescent set a high tone for the area.

Glen Brae (Canuck Place)
1690 Matthews Avenue, Vancouver
Parr and Fee, 1910; rehabilitated by Downs/Archambault and Partners, 1994-95
A pair of domed towers distinguish "Glen Brae"—"Valley by the Mountains"—built by tycoon William Lamont Tait as a reminder of the castles of his native Scotland. The mansion has some remarkable interior features including fine stained-glass windows, exquisite wood and tile finishes and a sprung dance floor on the third floor. The house was bequeathed to the City of Vancouver in 1991—a gift which helped establish the City's Heritage Conservation Foundation—and re-opened in 1995 as Canuck Place (sponsored by hockey's Canuck Foundation), a hospice for children with life-threatening illnesses. The redesigned garden (by Harold Neufeldt) forms a central feature of the children's experience and remains defined by the superb wrought-iron fence made by Walter McFarlane

of Glasgow.

2900-3000-blocks West 5th Avenue, Vancouver
Fred Melton and Cook & Hawkins, 1919-21
The favorite middle-class house in the newly developing suburbs during the 1910s and 1920s was the California bungalow (also called the Arts and Crafts or Craftsman bungalow) which spread from the U.S. in readily available pattern books. Promoted as a home for everybody, the bungalow provided the venue for an informal, servantless lifestyle, with intimate rooms, sleeping porches and no halls. The Kitsilano neighborhood abounds in bungalows. These represent the basic version—a single storey high with a gabled roof, verandah, abundant wood trim and cobblestone or brick posts and chimneys.

Horace G. Barber House
3846 West 10th Avenue, Vancouver
Ross A. Lort, 1936
Architects of the 1930s sought a modern expression by rejecting period styles and simplifying forms. This "Moderne" house, originally white, features sheer concrete walls relieved by asymmetrically placed windows and sparse vertical articulation. The abstract rectilinear geometry parallels some European painting of the day. The house has been rehabilitated and a compatible infill dwelling built at the rear (both by Robert G. Lemon, 1990).

D.H. Copp House
4755 Belmont Avenue, Vancouver
Sharp and Thompson, Berwick, Pratt, 1951
Ron Thom, a partner in Vancouver's premier firm, was a gifted architect with a special talent for houses. In this beautifully sited residence above Spanish Banks he translated his admiration for Frank Lloyd Wright and other modernists into something fresh, exciting, and appropriate to the West Coast. A massive brick chimney acts as a fulcrum from which spread the horizontally composed wood-and-glass wings, exploiting the contours of the terrain. Vancouver and the North Shore retain many of Thom's houses but nearly all are hidden from public view by their maturing landscape settings.

UBC Library
1956 Main Mall, UBC
Begun by Sharp and Thompson, 1923
Several generations of UBC architecture are revealed in the university's main library. The central portion (1923-25) features the stone walls and medievalizing detail of the Collegiate Gothic style originally intended for the entire campus. The wings at either side (Sharp and Thompson, Berwick, Pratt, 1947-48) adopt a cheaper, watered-down version of the style with frame construction and stucco finish. The Sedgewick Undergraduate Library (Rhone and Iredale, 1971-72), located in part beneath Main Mall

---

Newly married, Charles joins the fledgling Dominion Construction Company as assistant general manager, setting aside $100 from his salary each month to purchase shares. Recession and war send Vancouver from boom to bust. In 1912 the city issues development permits for $20 million in construction. In 1915 that plummets to one million. Dominion shareholders sell. Charles buys. By 1920 he is the company's new president. He sells the president's Cadillac and replaces it with a secondhand Ford. The twenties boom. Carpenters earn $7.25

and sprouting conical skylights, represents the mature Vancouver Modernism of its day. And the new first phase of the Walter C. Koerner Library (Aitken Wreglesworth Architects—now part of Architectura—and Arthur Erickson, 1995-96), which closes the composition of the ensemble, will surely be appreciated as a grand statement of the post-modern age. The only campus style that is missing is the early Modernism of the International Style, seen just to the left in the low, adjacent Buchanan Building (Thompson, Berwick, and Pratt, 1956-58, with later additions).

Museum of Anthropology, UBC
6393 Northwest Marine Drive, UBC
Arthur Erickson, 1973-76
The post-and-beam form that characterizes West Coast Modernism is here rendered in concrete. A series of graduated frames, inspired by Kwakwaka'wakw (Kwakiutl) longhouses, encloses the entrance and glass walls of the Massive Carving Gallery. From within they create a dramatic setting for the artifacts, which include huge totem poles displayed against a spectacular backdrop of water and mountains. The lower exhibit and open storage galleries to one side are now balanced by Erickson's Koerner Ceramics Gallery (1970). More totem poles, log houses and native flora fill in the cliffside site, offering a sense of a coastal native village.

First Nations House of Learning
1985 West Mall, UBC
Larry McFarland Architects, 1991-92
Used as a meeting place and support facility for native students, this impressive building has been inspired in its shape and structure by the longhouses of the Coast Salish, while the gabled roof, supported by massive cedar logs, recalls the traditional cedar housing of all coastal native groups. The 280-square-metre Great Hall features carved house posts that support the massive roof beams. Nothing directly imitates the historical sources, yet everything is clearly inspired by them. Architecture has come full circle in a half-century—from denying history in the post-war obsession with Modernism to embracing and reinterpreting it in the post-modern era.

VANCOUVER: EAST SIDE
Collingwood Branch Library
2985 Kingsway, Vancouver
Semmens and Simpson, 1950
The Vancouver Public Library operates 21 branches in addition to its large central library. This is one of the first suburban branches and the oldest to survive unaltered. It is also distinguished for being a design by Semmens and Simpson, the much-admired modernists who also created the previous central library (750 Burrard Street, largely rebuilt to become a retail

emporium by James K.M. Cheng Architects, 1995-96). The Collingwood branch's uncompromising rectilinearity and industrial products (such as the mass-produced steel-sash windows from England) are tempered by local fieldstone and brown-stained wood to produce a regional West Coast version of the modernist style.

Little Mountain Public Housing
33rd to 37th Avenues, between Ontario and Main Streets, Vancouver
Sharp and Thompson, Berwick, Pratt, 1953-54
The post-war baby boom produced a demand for housing and the federal government's new Canada (then Central) Mortgage and Housing Corporation responded by financing rental projects for low-income families. This was Vancouver's first. Architects may have admired the modernist expression but residents would have felt isolated by the sterility of the design, site plan and landscaping, which set the project apart from its neighbors. Newer developments of this kind (La Petite Maison, Champlain Heights) have attempted to integrate the residents physically and psychologically into the community-at-large.

Nat Bailey Stadium
4601 Ontario Street, Vancouver
1946
While many Vancouver baseball fans may long for a major league franchise, Triple-A baseball flourishes in this perfect little ballpark. The 6,500-seat facility was built by Sick's Capilano Brewery who named it Capilano Stadium and donated it to the city. It has since been renamed to honor the late Nat Bailey, founder of the White Spot restaurant chain and an inveterate fan who sponsored the team during lean years. A later owner and brewer, Molson's, called the team the Canadians, after its beer, and the name has stuck.

William H. James House
587 West King Edward Avenue, Vancouver
Probably by Ross A. Lort, 1941
A cozy English Tudor cottage provided the model for this cute fairy-tale residence, one of three put up by builder Brenton T. Lea. (The others are at 3979 West 9th Avenue, Vancouver, and 885 Braeside Avenue, West Vancouver.) The undulating shingle roof convincingly imitates thatching. This portion of King Edward Avenue (25th Avenue) marks the transition from the historically affluent West Side to the more basic amenities of the East Side. To the west the roadway is divided (with boulevard trees and buried services) and picturesquely curves beyond Granville. To the east the roadway narrows and powerlines replace the publicly planted trees. The different landscapes reflect the respective aspirations and tax bills of the former municipalities of Point Grey and South Vancouver.

Bloedel Conservatory
Queen Elizabeth Park, Vancouver
Underwood, McKinley, Cameron, Wilson and Smith, 1969
Futurists inspired by the late American visionary R. Buckminster Fuller have dreamed of creating artificial environments within enormous glazed domes. The Bloedel Conservatory (built shortly after Fuller's spherical U.S. Pavilion at Expo 67) represents a tiny step in that direction. Lush tropical plants and birds thrive beneath the "triodetic" dome assembled from aluminum pipe triangles and 1,500 plexiglas bubbles (designed by Thorson and Thorson, structural engineers). The conservatory sits atop 152-metre-high Little Mountain, the highest point in the city. It and its abandoned basalt quarries have been planted and transformed into Queen Elizabeth Park, a favorite spot for wedding pictures. The nearby decks cover one of two reservoirs on the mountain. The same architects designed the attractive wood restaurant nearby (1972-73).

Value Village
6415 Victoria Drive, Vancouver
McKee and Gray, 1960
In this day of sprawling mega-stores we sometimes forget that the post-war common supermarket represented an ambitious architectural program. The Super-Valu chain, which originally erected and operated this building, developed the best local solution. Large glued-laminated timber arches provide a broad expanse of unobstructed, column-free space. Note the remarkably small metal connectors which bear the full weight of the structure where the arches meet the ground. The building is now a discount outlet that sells used articles.

Vancouver Specials
6100 and 6200 blocks Elgin and Ross Streets, Vancouver
Various builders, 1970s-80s
Around 1970 builders developed a new model for mass-market housing which maximized floor area and site coverage at an attractive price. Principal living and sleeping spaces were located on the second floor, with utility rooms, garage, often an "in-laws suite" on the ground floor, and no basement. The type may have originated in Richmond where the high water table encouraged living high above the damp ground. The "Vancouver specials," as they quickly became known, spread like wildfire throughout the Lower Mainland. They nearly as quickly achieved widespread unpopularity among architects and aesthetes who channelled their reaction to the threat they posed into denouncements of their boring flat fronts, boxy shapes and low-sloped roofs.

---

for an eight-hour day; bricklayers $9. Vancouver boasts 83 millionaires. Bentall is not one of them. To pay off its indebtedness, Bentall's company pays no dividends to shareholders until 1927. During this time Charles executes his single most critical business plan. He redirects company profits and establishes cash reserves to create the New Building Finance Company.

Sikh Temple

8000 Ross Street, Vancouver
Erickson/Massey, 1969-70
This deceptively simple landmark is the central house of worship for Vancouver's large Sikh community. A simple white block is capped by a series of stepped, diagonally interlocked square sections, and crowned by an open steel onion-shaped dome. The design was influenced by the formal geometry of Indian religious symbols. The Khalsa Diwan Society occupies the lower floor. The architectural gem originally stood unpainted and in isolation, but it is now crowded by look-alike additions to the east (1995).

La Petite Maison Housing Cooperative

Talon Square, off Matheson Crescent, Vancouver
Hawthorn/Mansfield/Towers, 1978
Champlain Heights, the name given to this south-eastern corner of Vancouver, was the last unde-veloped acreage within the city limits to be built up. The showcase residential community was planned in the early 1970s with curved roads and cul-de-sacs serving a mix of housing types and income levels. The city retained ownership of the land, leasing it to developers. This stucco-and-wood housing co-op, inspired by the idea of European townhouses around a public square, provides a comfortable, human scale. The first co-op was DeCosmos Village (East 49th at Boundary Road, by Francis Donaldson, 1972). Other projects include subsidized rentals (e.g. 3200-block East 58th Avenue, by David Crinion of CHMC with Downs/Archambault, 1972-73) and market condominiums.

2400 Motel

2400 Kingsway, Vancouver, 1946-47
This period piece belongs in a Raymond Chan-dler novel. Virtually unaltered—from the tall neon sign to the immaculate lawns that could be used as putting greens—the "motor court" offers 65 units on a seven-and-a-half-hectare site. White stucco, green siding and hipped roofs pro-vide a domestic look while the flat-roofed office is a more commercial affair. The project was announced as housing, to obtain scarce post-war resources, but immediately went into use as a motel. Kingsway, the historic road from New Westminster to Vancouver, was a motel strip a generation ago.

Broadway SkyTrain Station

East Broadway and Commercial Drive, Vancouver
Allen Parker and Associates, 1984-85
Expo 86 was a catalyst for a number of regional improvements, most notably SkyTrain, an ALRT (Advanced Light Rail Transit) system linking downtown Vancouver with New Westminster (and subsequently Surrey), partly over the old interurban streetcar right-of-way. Small, driver-less four-car trains, produced in Ontario, ply the route, partly overhead (as here), partly under-ground and partly at grade. The SkyTrain sta-tions adopted a standard appearance featuring tubular-steel hoop trusses that wrap around the station, and metal mesh rather than glazing. Architektengruppen U-Bahn of Vienna served as design consultant for the project.

Kurrajong

1036 Salsbury Street, Vancouver, 1908
Alderman John J. Miller, who was the creative force behind organizing and operating the Pacific National Exhibition, built this ostentatious man-sion which he named after a shrub from his native Australia. The property remains aloof within its reclusive boundary wall and ample landscaping. Kurrajong was one of many substan-tial homes built in this Grandview neighborhood; another is the W.H. Copp House, distinguished by a domed corner turret, at 1110 Victoria Drive (J.P. Malluson, 1910-11).

Vancouver East Cultural Centre

1895 Venables Street, Vancouver
1909; rehabilitated by John Keith-King, 1973, and Derek Neale, 1977
The former Grandview Methodist (subsequently United) Church, which closed its doors in 1967, was adapted to become a theatre, recital hall and community facility for its then culture-starved neighborhood. Founding director Christopher Wootten co-ordinated municipal, provincial and federal support programs to make the ambitious project happen. The intimate audi-ence chamber, with its good sight-lines and acoustics and feeling of warmth, has made "The Cultch" (which can seat up to 350) a popular performing-arts venue that attracts people from far beyond East Vancouver.

Alberta Wheat Pool

North foot of Cassiar Street, Vancouver
C.D. Howe Company, 1927
The ships that are regularly seen at anchor in English Bay include many grain carriers awaiting their turn to load at Burrard Inlet's elevators. The reinforced-concrete terminal elevators are a series of linked silos loaded with prairie wheat that arrives by train (and is "elevated" by con-veyors into bins). The Alberta Wheat Pool is a farmer-owned cooperative that distributes most of that province's grain. This early elevator was designed and built by the engineering firm found-ed in 1916 by C.D. Howe, best known as Cana-da's minister of munitions and supply during World War II. The company was responsible for several others in Vancouver Harbour, including the mammoth, fully automated Saskatchewan Wheat Pool elevator across the water in North Vancouver (1966-68). The harbor's first grain elevator, built in 1914 at the foot of Woodland Drive, was "Stevens' Folly"—the brainchild of local MP H.H. Stevens, who saw the opportunity to the local economy provided by the Panama Canal. The Alberta Wheat Pool has been enhanced by a high-tech, aluminum-clad office addition (Wright Engineers, 1991) whose design responds to that of the brute concrete elevator.

SEA-TO-SKY HIGHWAY: HORSESHOE BAY TO WHISTLER

Union Steamship Company Store

Government Road, Snug Cove, Bowen Island
1924
The Union Steamship Company, which provided passenger and freight service between the com-munities along Burrard Inlet and Howe Sound, built a large resort on Bowen Island in the 1920s, in part to attract traffic to the line. The compa-ny's store on Government Road in Snug Cove survives as a community facility, as do a handful of the 100-odd cabins that were constructed in 1928. The large hotel is gone. Much of the site has been absorbed into the GVRD's Crippen Regional Park, a 243-hectare facility that features lakes, beaches, walking and cycling trails and large picnic areas that retain some of the charac-ter and landscape features of the former resort.

Former PGE Car Shop

West Coast Railway Heritage Park, Government Road, Squamish
1914
The Pacific Great Eastern Railway, now BC Rail, ambitiously began its line from North Vancouver to Prince George in 1913 not knowing it would take more than 40 years to complete. Until 1956 Squamish was the southern terminus and the yard facilities included a large wood-frame car shop, some 24 by 46 metres in plan. In 1991 the car shop—touted as the largest building in the province ever to be moved—was hauled the short distance from the BCR yards to the new West Coast Railway Heritage Park. It forms the centrepiece of the almost-five-hectare railway museum, which features a fine collection of loco-motives and rolling stock representing the rail-ways that have operated in British Columbia.

Concentrator Mill

British Columbia Museum of Mining, Highway 99, Britannia Beach
1921-23
One of the world's richest copper deposits was found high in the mountains behind this site. In the early 1900s the Britannia Copper Syndicate (later renamed) extracted low-grade ore and transported it down the mountain by aerial tramway and electric railway, where it was then crushed and concentrated. The com-pany built a substantial townsite here, some of whose buildings survive as part of the British Columbia Museum of Mining—a provincial and

NBF provides capital to purchase land, finance construction and attract financial partners. It becomes the rock on which the company weathers the Great Depression. In the late thirties two Bentall sons enter the business: Clark, on the construction of Kelowna General Hospital; and the youngest, Bob, as a summer student laborer building the Bay Theatre on Denman Street. In September, 1939, the federal government enlists Bentall's company in Canada's war effort. The company designs and builds a self-propelled cargo landing barge called a

national historic site. The steel, concrete and glass concentrator, a masterpiece of engineering, climbs 61 metres up the side of Britannia Mountain in eight stages. The mine railway entered at the top and deposited the ore into the building. Gravity carried it through the various processing stages and the concentrated ore was then shipped to the company's smelter at Crofton on Vancouver Island. The structure stands in disrepair, used only as an occasional movie set, while the museum tries to secure funds to restore it.

Chateau Whistler Resort
4599 Chateau Boulevard, Upper Village, Whistler
Musson Cattell Mackey, Downs/Archambault and Stockwell Architecture & Planning, 1989
Chateau-style resort hotels in scenic locations were introduced by the CPR in the 1880s with the Banff Springs Hotel. Within a few decades they became the signature pieces of the nation's railways across the country. The Chateau Whistler, operated by Canadian Pacific Hotels and Resorts (although built with offshore money), continues the tradition after more than a half-century hiatus. It revives all the features of the earlier Canadian castles: steep roofs with dormer windows, picturesque massing and memorable service. The contrast between it and the cabins of Whistler's first resort, Rainbow Lodge, show the change in recreational lifestyle brought about by the development of Whistler as a world-class ski centre.

CITY OF NORTH VANCOUVER
Lonsdale Quay Market
123 Carrie Cates Court, North Vancouver
Hotson Bakker Architects, 1985-86
Responding to the success of the Granville Island Public Market—and even retaining the same architects—the Lonsdale Quay Market was developed in an effort to revitalize the lower Lonsdale area. The glazed and galleried interior successfully recalls 19th-century iron-and-glass industrial architecture. The market is also a transportation hub where North Shore bus passengers transfer to and from the SeaBus, initiated in 1977 as an integral ferry link in the region's transit system.

North Vancouver Civic Centre
121 West 14th Street, North Vancouver
Downs/Archambault, 1974
In this municipal hall and library for the City of North Vancouver, designer Barry Downs translated the West Coast residential style into a pair of separate, but integrated, public buildings. The two low, reinforced-concrete structures, partly clad in cedar, nestle in the hillside, looking as if they had grown out of it. Most of the site is given over to park space, leaving the buildings so

understated—perhaps a reflection of the talented architect's modesty—that some visitors have trouble finding them.

Versatile Pacific Shipyard
Lonsdale Avenue and East Esplanade, North Vancouver,
Begun 1912
Shipbuilding was long the mainstay of North Vancouver's economy. Production peaked during World War II when this shipyard (formerly Wallace Shipyards and Burrard Dry Dock) built more than 130 vessels and employed as many as 15,000 people. The yard's many other products include the RCMP schooner *St. Roch* (1928; kept in the Vancouver Maritime Museum, 1905 Ogden Avenue) and several vessels for BC Ferries. Shipbuilding began here in 1906 but a 1911 fire destroyed its first structures. The decaying industrial site contains a wealth of fine structures including lofts, erection shops and derricks. It offers many opportunities for creative re-use —a topical conservation issue—but finding the solution will be a challenge.

St. Paul's Roman Catholic Church
424 West Esplanade, Mission Reserve, North Vancouver
1884, 1909
The French Oblate missionaries came to British Columbia in the 1850s and erected the first chapel here (formerly known as Ustlawn) around 1866. A frame church built in 1884 was enlarged in 1909 to become the present Gothic Revival church. The vertical proportions, culminating in twin spires (formerly the official landmark for ships entering Vancouver Harbour), recall the churches of French-Canada and France, although the wood siding with the "Carpenter's Gothic" ornament is more characteristic of the West Coast. The church was recently restored.

DISTRICT OF NORTH VANCOUVER
Thomas Nye House
3545 Dowsley Court, North Vancouver
Harry Blackadder, 1912
A returning Boer War veteran, Thomas Nye, took district lot 2026 as his grant for military service and made his fortune in the land boom that followed. He promptly lost it by building this imposing Tudor Revival home, known as "Nye's Folly." It remains the centrepiece of the North Lonsdale area, which abounds in fine old houses. The landscaping includes a stone retaining wall and a row of holly trees. The lot has been subdivided allowing two new Tudor-ish houses (Dick Goldhammer, 1989) to be built. Nye's realty office (c. 1909, now a private house) survives at 3311 Lonsdale Avenue. His brother Alfred Nye also received a vet's grant; his fine Craftsman house at 940 Lynn Valley Road (1913) remains in

the family.

Julius M. Fromme House
1466 Ross Road, North Vancouver
1900
Lumberman Fromme built this, the first house in Lynn Valley, facing the skid road used to drag logs from the nearby forest to his mill. A sometime reeve of the district, he built the Fromme Block at 3066-96 Mountain Highway and Lynn Valley Road (1912), a two-storey commercial-and-residential block near the mill operated by his Lynn Valley Lumber Company. Although erected a generation later than the Boothroyd House in Surrey, the Fromme House has the same plain pioneer form—one room deep, called an "I"-house by geographers. (The verandah is a later addition.)

Dollar Mill House
571 Roslyn Boulevard, North Vancouver
c. 1920-24
Robert Dollar's sawmill, the Dollar Mill, was located just south of here. The company built housing for its senior employees. This one survives substantially unchanged—a simple shingle cottage with a projecting entry porch and a "jerkin" roof (a popular 1920s feature). The mill office (c. 1916-20) survives at 518 Beachview Drive, somewhat altered and used as a residence.

WEST VANCOUVER
Ferry Building
101 14th Street, West Vancouver
Thompson and Campbell, 1913
This picturesque clapboard structure was built as the West Vancouver ferry terminal. The Lions Gate Bridge challenged the ferries' viability and service was discontinued in 1947. The terminal was subsequently used by buses and in 1988 it was rehabilitated (Howard/Yano Architects) to become an art gallery. Complemented by the rebuilt pier, water sculpture (by Don Vaughan, 1989) and attractive landscaping, it forms a key component of the Ambleside public waterfront.

John C.H. Porter House
1560 Ottawa Avenue, West Vancouver
J.C.H. Porter, 1948-49
A small group of Vancouver-area architects— including the relatively unknown John Porter— developed a distinctive West Coast Modernism a half-century ago. Since willing clients were hard to find, many of their early buildings were residences for themselves. The principal elements were the use of wood post-and-beam construction, open planning, large areas of glass opening onto the landscape and an attention to detail. Influences included the houses of Frank Lloyd Wright, Japanese architecture and coastal native architecture. Porter's attractive home, which opens onto one of the North Shore's many

lighter. The little craft carries almost 32 tonnes in a test run in False Creek. Over 450 are eventually built. The company constructs the Sea Island base for the RCAF, Sumner Iron Works on East Broadway, the naval station on Deadman Island (now HMCS *Discovery*), and the present causeway at Lost Lagoon. It also builds the Varsity Theatre and 21 Safeway stores.

creeks, uses cedar for its structural members, exterior siding and the low-pitched roof. Winner of a Massey Medal, it was lauded as the "best house in Canada."

St. Francis-in-the-Wood Anglican Church
4797 South Piccadilly, West Vancouver
Harry A. Stone, 1927; Underwood, McKinley, and Cameron, 1957

This charming building, designed to look like an English village church, remains a popular spot for weddings as well as being a place of worship for its suburban parish. The original small sanctuary, illuminated by stained-glass windows by Morris and Company of London, was enclosed by Percy Underwood's A-frame roof some thirty years later at which time the granite-and-cedar parish hall was erected. Piccaddilly was the main street of the picturesque Caulfeild subdivision planned by English university professor and developer Francis Caulfeild.

Point Atkinson Lighthouse
Lighthouse Park, West Vancouver
Colonel William Patrick Anderson, 1911-12

This hexagonal reinforced-concrete lighthouse, characterized by its six external buttresses, guards the outer entrance to Burrard Inlet and Vancouver Harbour. Its two-tone fog horn is very familiar to the many residents within its range. The wood-clad buildings around it remind us that this is one of relatively few lighthouses on the coast to remain staffed. It replaced an earlier lighthouse built in 1875.

Smith House
5030 The Byway, West Vancouver
Erickson/Massey, 1965

Cedar posts, projecting beams and large expanses of glass define four wings that seem to grow upward in a "square spiral" around a central courtyard. The design fuses the natural, "organic" houses of Frank Lloyd Wright with the minimalist houses associated with the International Style, all done with powerful respect for the landscaped site. Architect Arthur Erickson declared: "I wanted the Smith house to reveal the site in the same way that I had found it revealed to me when I first walked onto it." A studio addition (Russell Hollingsworth) was built in 1990.

BURNABY

Bob Prittie Metrotown Burnaby Library and Civic Square
6100 Willingdon Avenue, Burnaby
James K.M. Cheng Architects, 1990-91

This attractive new facility—the main public library for Burnaby—and its adjacent public square are the first components of a large civic complex intended to complement the existing commercial-oriented core of Metrotown. The library is well illuminated by a skylit central atri-um and large windows that open onto the civic green. The two-storey public portion is distinguished from the three-storey administration wing and both are united beneath the sculpted roof, which provides an identifiable image to ground level patrons and to passing travellers on the SkyTrain.

Ismailia Jamatkhana Centre
4010 Canada Way, Burnaby
Bruno Freschi, 1985

The home of Canada's first Ismaili congregation, the Jamatkhana (prayer house) combines Islamic architectural principles with the finest in contemporary design and materials. From the landscaped courtyard the visitor passes through a grand white and red arch into the entrance loggia and finally to the square prayer hall. The building's geometry is based on the square (the plan of the principal spaces) and the octagon—seen in the pavement pattern of the courtyard, the turret-like corner staircases and the richly decorative domes and ceiling coffers. The fortress-like sandstone exterior is plain by comparison. This is the first building of its kind in Canada and a remarkable addition to Greater Vancouver's fine repertoire of religious architecture.

Simon Fraser University
Burnaby Mountain, Burnaby
Begun by Erickson/Massey, 1963-65

SFU was one of many new universities founded across Canada as the baby boomers reached college age. The concept of Arthur Erickson and Geoffrey Massey, with the former as principal designer, was chosen by competition. The linear scheme, sited along the ridge of Burnaby Mountain, organizes the university by use, rather than by faculty or college. The broad Central Mall, designed by Erickson/Massey, is the principal walkway and meeting place. It is covered by a glazed roof supported by deep girders made of Douglas fir beams and steel tie-rods. To either side are the exterior walls of integrated campus buildings, including the W.A.C. Bennett Library (Robert F. Harrison). To the east, up a broad staircase, is the Academic Quadrangle (Zoltan S. Kiss). The planning forces student interaction and was blamed for student unrest in the late 1960s —a tribute to the power of architecture to influence our actions.

Burnaby Art Gallery (Fairacres)
6344 Deer Lake Avenue, Burnaby
Robert Percival Twizell, 1910

Deer Lake provided a scenic setting for gracious pre-war "country" residences of Vancouver and New Westminster's social elite. "Fairacres," a handsome twin-gabled Tudor Revival house, was built by Grace and Henry Ceperly, a Michigan heiress and a Vancouver realtor. Subsequent owners included the brothers of the Benedictine Order who resided here from 1939 to 1955 until they built their present home at Westminster Abbey, Mission. The Municipality of Burnaby bought "Fairacres" for use as the Burnaby Art Gallery, which opened in 1967 as the nucleus of a recreational and cultural complex.

Burnaby Municipal Hall
4949 Canada Way, Burnaby
Fred Hollingsworth, 1956

South Burnaby was the original population and economic centre of Burnaby and so the first municipal hall was built at Kingsway and Edmonds in 1899. By the time the building was outgrown, North Burnaby had become a force to reckon with. Since neither neighborhood would agree to building a new municipal hall on the other's turf, the compromise saw the new facility being located in the geographical centre of Burnaby near Deer Lake. The design was no compromise at all. Fred Hollingsworth, one of the pioneers of the new West Coast style, produced an understated masterpiece of Modernism, a two-storey structure whose crisp rectangular design symbolized Burnaby's progressive leadership.

Overlynn
3755 McGill Street, Burnaby
Maclure and Fox, 1906

North Burnaby developed rapidly in the pre-World War I real estate boom, particularly when it acquired streetcar service to Vancouver in 1913. The Vancouver Heights subdivision was marketed to the wealthy. Some responded including dry-goods merchant Charles J. Peters who retained Maclure and Fox, the firm of talented society architect Samuel Maclure, to design him a grand Tudor Revival manor. The house spent a generation, from 1930, as Seton Academy, a Roman Catholic girls' school. In the 1970s it was overshadowed by the Seton Villa Retirement Centre built on a portion of its original property. "Overlynn" is now leased by British Columbia's Children's Hospital for use as an out-patient clinic. It retains much of its superb interior decorative detail (the first heritage interior in the province to be legally protected) which— true to the arts and crafts tradition—always formed an important part of Maclure's houses.

PORT MOODY

Port Moody City Hall
240 Ioco Road, Port Moody
James K.M. Cheng Architects, 1995

In many early North American communities, formal civic functions and community activities (and sometimes religious worship as well) occurred in the same building. That tradition has been successfully revived in the attractive Port Moody City Hall, the first component in a proposed new town centre. The maple-lined round council

After the war the company introduces the Package Plan: land assembly, design, construction, co-financing and property management. It pioneers the industrial estate concept. On Terminal Avenue between Main and Clark, it packages buildings for General Motors, International Harvester, Canada Packers, Atlas Steel, Firestone and others. On Grandview near Boundary, for Kraft Foods, British Wire Ropes, Heinz, Quaker Oats, RCA Victor, B.F. Goodrich, Imperial Tobacco, Philips and others. It undertakes the $85 million expansion of the Port

chamber doubles as a community theatre, and the committee room in the cupola-like space above is available for private functions. They and the municipal offices are connected to a library by a spacious semi-circular galleria whose arched steel trusses are intended to recall the imagery of railway stations—a reminder that Port Moody was, for a short while, the CPR's western terminus. The entrance and council chamber are directly on axis with a residential-commercial development across loco Road, emphasizing the link between municipal government and the community.

Port Moody Station Museum
2734 Murray Street, Port Moody
1907
The CPR originally chose Port Moody, at the head of Burrard Inlet, as its Pacific terminus but William Van Horne, the line's general manager, recognized the greater commercial and scenic potential of Vancouver. He ordered the line extended down the inlet relegating Port Moody to just another stop along the line. This is the CPR's second station which remained in passenger service until 1978. The Port Moody Heritage Society has restored the building and some of its early functions (e.g. the telegraph office and station agent's kitchen) and maintains exhibits on a number of interesting themes.

NEW WESTMINSTER

Irving House
302 Royal Avenue, New Westminster
1865
Captain William Irving, an early riverboat captain on the Fraser, built this fine residence, described in a newspaper of the day as "the handsomest, the best and most home-like house of which British Columbia can yet boast." The steep roof and central verandahed gable, featuring fine "gingerbread" ornament, certainly distinguished it from the plainer cottages more typical of pioneer days. The house was purchased from descendants of Captain Irving in 1950 by the City of New Westminster at the instigation of the Native Sons and Native Daughters. It has been attractively restored inside and out and is now the home of the Irving House Historic Centre and the New Westminster Museum.

Burr Block and Guichon Block
411-19 and 409 Columbia Street, New Westminster
G.W. Grant, 1892 and 1887
New Westminster, the "Royal City," was British Columbia's first capital, surveyed and carved out of the rainforest by the Royal Engineers beginning in 1859. Columbia Street, along the Fraser River, has always been its main street. The city has suffered many setbacks beginning with the relocation of the capital to Victoria in 1868 and

including major fires and economic collapses. These two commercial buildings, both designed by New West's leading architect of the day, are the only ones to have survived the fire of 1898. They give us a hint of the character of the late 19th century brick structures that lined the street. The four-storey Burr Block is notable for its Romanesque Revival arches and the three-storey Guichon Block for having been the Queen's Hotel, once the city's leading hostelry. Columbia Street remains a tired commercial strip, its retail stores barely showing evidence of the revitalization efforts that have been directed here since its last boom, in the 1950s, when it was known as the "Miracle Mile."

Westminster Quay Public Market
Westminster Quay, New Westminster
Musson Cattell and Partners, 1986
The phasing out of the Pacific Coast Terminals and other docks along New Westminster's waterfront in the 1970s led to a major public-private venture by the British Columbia Development Corporation and the First Capital City Development Corporation. The focus of Westminster Quay is the large public market (with its landmark clock tower) modelled on the success of Granville Island and the Lonsdale Quay in North Vancouver. This was followed by the 125-room Inn at Westminster Quay (1988), the First Capital Place office building and considerable waterfront housing. A handful of historic boats and buildings remind shoppers of the shore's century-and-a-half of European history. The market seems viable but little of the retail traffic spills out onto Columbia Street.

Justice Institute of British Columbia
715 McBride Boulevard, New Westminster
Henriquez & Partners and The IBI Group, 1993-95
The Justice Institute is British Columbia's central training school for police, firefighters, paramedics, corrections officers and other public safety workers. This large new campus features three linked buildings: a triangular one with a central atrium for the classrooms, auditorium, and library; a square one containing a gymnasium and firing range; and a horseshoe-shaped structure between them with offices and cafeteria facing a landscaped courtyard. Its semi-circular form mirrors the course of a former creekbed. Red brick and glass are the dominant materials.

St. Mary the Virgin Anglican Church
121 East Columbia Street, New Westminster
Corporal John C. White, 1865
The Columbia Detachment of Royal Engineers, commanded by Col. R.C. Moody, was instrumental in developing New Westminster and many interior portions of the new Colony of British Columbia, while ensuring peace, order, and good government during the turbulent gold

rush period. Their camp was located here, a mile upriver from New West, in what became known as Sapperton. (The Royal Engineers were known as "sappers.") The detachment was disbanded in 1863 but many sappers stayed here, and they and the governor (who lived nearby at Government House) prayed in St. Mary's Church. It was considerably altered after a fire in 1932 but retains its pioneer-era "Carpenter Gothic" character.

COQUITLAM

Maillardville
Brunette Avenue, between Lougheed Highway and Boileau, Coquitlam
Maillardville is Coquitlam's oldest neighborhood. Settled by French-Canadians working in nearby sawmills, it retains its distinct cultural character, with nearly 15 per cent of its residents having French as their mother tongue. Just north of Brunette Avenue is Laval Square, whose church and social hall retain some Québecois flavor. On the south side of Brunette, across from the old municipal hall, the area around historic Mackin House and a cultural facility known as Place des Arts are being consolidated as Heritage Square.

Minnekhada Lodge
near Oliver Road, Minnekhada Regional Park, Coquitlam
Palmer and Bow, 1934
Begun around 1910 as a farm and expanded in the 1930s to become a country retreat and hunting lodge, this social and architectural anachronism was conceived on the model of an English stately home, albeit rusticated by the realities of British Columbia. The Tudor Revival hunting lodge was built by lumber magnates Eric Hamber and Aldyen Irene (née Hendry) Hamber, who retained the Sioux name given to the farm a generation earlier by lumberman Harry Jenkins. Minnekhada has been home to two lieutenant-governors: Eric Hamber (1936-41) and shipbuilder Clarence Wallace (1950-55). The estate has hosted royalty and boasts a royal suite; Governor General Lord Tweedsmuir and his sons played polo here. The area around the house commands fine views of the Pitt River and retains a Japanese garden. Minnekhada is now the people's palace situated within a regional park that boasts good trails and birdwatching opportunities.

Riverview Hospital
500 Lougheed Highway, Coquitlam
Begun 1910
This extraordinary 99-hectare site, its 169 buildings and its expansive grounds tell the story of nearly a century of mental health-care in British Columbia. Opened in 1910 as the Hospital for the Mind at Mount Coquitlam, and known for many years as Essondale and Colony Farm, it

---

Alberni pulp and paper plant, the wharf and pulp plant at Harmac, the Port Alice townsite and the Henrietta Dam, and the Alberta Wheat Pool extension in Vancouver. Then, in partnership with Great-West Life, it designs an office complex of two towers. The company arranges for an international panel to review the project. The panel recommends the name "Bentall Centre."

was built in the era when fresh air and farming were advocated as good therapy for the mentally ill. For decades the self-contained community produced its own food and power. Some patients lived in the large institutional buildings visible from the Lougheed Highway: the West Lawn (1910-13), Centre Lawn (1923-24), and East Lawn (1929-30) buildings half-way up the hill and the enormous Crease Unit (1930-49) below them. Others lived in domestic-scaled Tudorish "cottages." Current practices encourage patients to return to the larger urban community outside and many buildings are currently vacant or underused. British Columbia Buildings Corporation, which manages the property, is currently seeking appropriate new uses for the Riverview site.

PORT COQUITLAM
Port Coquitlam City Hall
2580 Shaughnessy Street, Port Coquitlam
Toby Russell Buckwell and Partners, 1988
The City of Port Coquitlam responded to growth while acknowledging its past by integrating its 1913 municipal hall with a large and tasteful new addition. The red brick walls and window pattern of the old building (which was thoroughly rehabilitated to today's standards) set the theme for the new wing; the two are connected by a concrete-and-glass entrance and foyer.

MAPLE RIDGE
Maple Ridge Municipal Hall
11995 Haney Place, Maple Ridge
Henriquez and Partners, 1981
Many of Vancouver's suburban municipalities have been formed from a collection of small village centres linked by rural land with the former developing into commercial strips and the latter into tract housing. Maple Ridge is one of these. To provide a needed urban focus it has located its principal community facilities at Haney town centre. (Compare Surrey's Newton and Whalley town centres.) Many of the administrative and recreational amenities are located on a new pedestrian mall located between the Dewdney Trunk Road and a shopping centre to the south. The focus is the municipal hall, a two-storey brick building (designed to accommodate two more floors), set at an angle to be visible from both ends of the mall. The scale relates well to its neighbors. The entrance is emphasized by a flagpole and an arch and parapet that rise above the municipal crest; the semi-circular council chamber (available for use also as a performance space) is clearly expressed as a bulge at the north end. The same architects have designed the Maple Ridge Courthouse (1994) also located on the mall. The popular focus of the mall is not its architecture but rather "The Beast"—the

horse and clocktower created by "builder and fixer" Don Brayford in 1989.

PITT MEADOWS
Pitt Meadows Community Church
12109 Harris Road, Pitt Meadows
c. 1910
Pre-fabricated (also "ready-made" or "knock-down") buildings, popular in the decade before World War I, were promoted as a way of meeting the West's insatiable demand for construction. The most sophisticated system was developed by B.C. Mills, Timber and Trading Company of Vancouver. One-metre-wide insulated sandwich panels were bolted together and the joints covered with vertical batten strips. The Pitt Meadows Community Church is a prefab originally built by a congregation of Seventh Day Adventists. It has been a multi-denominational community church since 1922; today it is used by Anglican and United Church congregations. The intersection of Harris and Ford was the centre of Pitt Meadows in times past; today the area is dominated by new residential development.

LANGLEY / LANGLEY CITY
Fort Langley Community Hall
9167 Glover Road, Fort Langley
Archibald Campbell Hope, 1930-31
We sometimes forget the contributions that volunteer societies make to the quality of life. The Fort Langley Community Improvement Society was formed in 1924 by the Fort Langley Women's Institute, spearheaded by Mrs. Hector Morrison. The organization purchased this, the site of the former Fort Langley municipal hall, for back taxes and built the community hall for the use of area residents. The design is uncompromisingly classical with a pediment supported by Doric pilasters forming the frontispiece of the broad facade. The building remains a community facility and a neighborhood landmark.

BCER Langley Substation
685 256th Street, Langley
H.B. Watson, 1910
The British Columbia Electric Railway (now B.C. Hydro) operated an interurban railway from Vancouver to Chilliwack in 1910—an effective rapid-transit system long before that term was coined. SkyTrain uses a part of the right-of-way through Vancouver, Burnaby, and New Westminster. This was one of five substations in the Fraser Valley that provided electrical power to the line. The reinforced-concrete structure is cast in classical garb, elevating a utilitarian structure to the level of public architecture.

Fort Langley National Historic Park
23433 Mavis, Fort Langley
Begun 1840
A handful of log buildings within a palisade

remind us that the Fraser River was a major thoroughfare for the fur trade long before the area had permanent white settlers. The Hudson's Bay Company established Fort Langley near here, at the head of navigation in 1827, and moved to the present site a dozen years later. Nearly 20 structures stood within the walls in the 1850s, at which time the fort was shipping salmon and cranberries to San Francisco, Hawaii, and Australia while blacksmithing, barrel-making and other economic activities boomed. The Storehouse, built in 1840, is the only survivor of the era. The Big House (built for chief factor James Douglas, later the first governor of British Columbia) and the other buildings are reconstructions built in 1956-58. The site is actively interpreted and well worth a visit.

RICHMOND, DELTA, SURREY, WHITE ROCK
RICHMOND
Thompson Community Centre
6671 Lynas Lane, Richmond
Henriquez Partners Architects, 1995
Is it architecture or is it sculpture? Consistent with architect Richard Henriquez's penchant for making explicit references to his buildings' context, this delightfully whimsical (yet utterly practical) community centre recalls Richmond's historic role as an aviation centre. Its form represents an airplane emerging from a hangar in preparation for take-off. The hangar-like gymnasium, whose roof is supported by two 80-metre-long steel arches (one of which never quite reaches its anchor on the ground), is flanked by a pair of wings whose struts—indoors and out—resemble those of a biplane. The design for a future park on the site reproduces the plan of Richmond with a playground in the far corner to be shaped like Sea Island, site of Vancouver International Airport.

Minoru Chapel
7540 Gilbert Road, Richmond
1891
This city-owned chapel has become an amazingly popular spot for marriages—particularly for couples from Japan who are attracted by the image of a North American country wedding. Built as the Richmond Methodist Church at the corner of Cambie and River Roads, the frame structure features a tower and pointed-arched windows typical of Gothic Revival churches of the time. It was purchased by the municipality, moved to its present site in Pierrefonds Gardens and consecrated in 1968 as a non-denominational church. Minoru was the name of a thoroughbred race horse given to King Edward VII by Emperor Meiji of Japan.

Richmond Town Centre
No. 3 Road
No. 3 Road, between Granville Avenue and

At the time the city is centred well east of Burrard. Bob Bentall convinces the company to build on Burrard and Pender, a location better known for rooming houses and masseuses. "The first tower was a big gamble," Bob recalls. "When we broke ground for it in 1965, we didn't have a single tenant lined up." The centre introduces a new concept to Vancouver: the public plaza. Bentall One is completed in 1967, Bentall Two in 1969.

Bridgeport Road, is suburban strip development at its best—or, some might say, at its worst. The street presents the consumer with virtually continuous commercial frontage. It contains two large shopping centres, Richmond Centre (6551 No. 3 Road) and Lansdowne Park Shopping Centre (5300 No. 3 Road), many smaller "plazas" and countless stores, distinguishable only by their signs, with many separated from the street and the sidewalk by parking lots. Street trees and fancy light standards try to improve the streetscape. The municipality celebrated this shoppers' paradise by building its city hall (6911 No. 3 Road; Allen C. Smith and Associates, 1957) at the south end of the strip. Just off No. 3 Road, Aberdeen Centre (4400 Hazelbridge Way) provides a touch of crowded Hong Kong with small-scale shops and services that cater to the region's new Chinese-Canadians.

Vancouver International Airport
Grant McConachie Way, Richmond
Thompson, Berwick, and Pratt, 1968; Architectura, 1995-96
Vancouver's new role as a major hub on the Pacific Rim has necessitated the construction of a large new international terminal building (on the right) and a much-protested second east-west runway to the north. The "old" airport's textured brown aggregate walls and spiral turrets looked futuristic when the building opened a generation ago. Now it is a pleasant period piece hidden behind a large, new parking garage. Remnants of the original Sea Island airport, which opened in 1931, survive as part of the South Terminal now used for light aircraft.

Burkeville
West of Airport Road, Richmond
McCarter and Nairne, 1943-44
Burkeville was laid out and built by the federal government during World War II to provide 328 houses for workers employed at the Boeing Aircraft plant. It was named for Stanley Burke, president of Boeing. The streets are named after airplane manufacturers. The plain, no-frills dwellings came in several standard sizes. Most have been altered to fit the needs of two generations of residents. After the war Boeing sold the houses to returning veterans. The tightly knit community, already encircled by airport uses, is currently threatened by the intended further expansion of roads and runways.

Finn Slough
South end of No. 4 Road
An early Finnish fishing community established itself here in the 1890s. Fish boats could dock in the slough, close to the somewhat insubstantial houses. In its use and its landscape the area remains much as it was a century ago—even though most of the houses have been rebuilt or renewed. The seemingly disorganized structures on and near the water contrast with the general tidiness of Richmond. As a consequence there is mounting pressure on the municipality to evict the residents, some of whom have shaky title to their land.

Buddhist Temple
9160 Steveston Highway, Richmond
Vincent Kwan, 1983
Two tiers of golden, porcelain-tiled roofs, with flaring eaves and flying dragons along the ridge, provide a striking cap for this very Chinese-looking building—promoted in a brochure as "the most exquisite example of Chinese palatial architecture in North America." Operated by the International Buddhist Society the temple serves regular attendees and is open to the general public for lectures, meditation classes and tea ceremonies. The handsome interior is adorned with fine art and crafts while the courtyard features bonsai plants. Researchers can consult an extensive Buddhist resource library. Architect Kwan also designed the smaller, but somewhat similar, Universal Buddhist Temple (1978) at 525 East 49th Avenue, Vancouver.

Ewen (Keur) Barn
7071 No. 9 Road, Richmond
1893
As part of the Fraser River delta, Richmond's soil is superb for farming. The provincially designated Agricultural Land Reserve has ensured that much remains productive. Unique among the older barns is this 12-sided cattle barn, which holds more than 900 tonnes of hay and feeds 100 head. It was built in 1893 when the property was farmed by the Ewens. For many years this was known as Quilchena Farms, operated as a feed lot by the Keur family. As many as 4,500 head of cattle at a time were fattened here.

Grand Ballroom
Unit 120 -13720 Mayfield Place, Richmond
c. 1990
Would you believe that inside this faceless warehouse, in an area chock full of storage and light industrial uses, can be found the best sprung dance floor in Vancouver? Wendy and Andy Wong saw the potential of the large, column-free space and adapted it for use by the city's keen ballroom dancers—now augmented by line-dancers and two-steppers. [What else? Call the Wongs to find out. 273-3130.] This part of Richmond has many industrial parks of this kind, cheek-by-jowl with working farms (and often overwhelmed by agricultural smells).

Cannery Row
Steveston Waterfront, Richmond
Begun 1880s
The South Arm of the Fraser River was once the salmon-canning centre of British Columbia and a key focus of the West Coast fishing industry. Several historic canneries survive. Some are still used by the fishery although not for canning (the Phoenix Cannery Complex at 4460 Moncton Street; the Paramount Cannery at the foot of Trites Road; and the complex at the New Richmond Canneries at the foot of No. 2 Road, all owned by B.C. Packers). Some have been developed as interpreted historic sites (the Gulf of Georgia Cannery National Historic Site on Moncton Street just west of 3rd Avenue; and Britannia Heritage Shipyard on West Water Road, west of the foot of Trites Road). Others lie derelict (most notably the Pacific Coast Cannery, owned by the federal government, at the western edge of the Paramount Pond complex, 12511 Trites Road). All are on the river side of the present dyke. Collectively the Steveston complex once combined industrial and residential uses in a vibrant waterfront community that included large numbers of Japanese-Canadians. The new commercial development along Bayview attracts large numbers of weekend visitors but its generic Modernism sadly fails to capture the essential spirit of Steveston. A more authentic character can still be found in some of the older stores along Moncton Street.

DELTA
South Delta Baptist Church
1988 56th Street, Tsawwassen, Delta
James K.M. Cheng Architects, 1988
The growth of fundamentalist Christianity in the Fraser Valley has spawned a number of large, new churches catering to suburban residents. This brick church complex, with its glazed belltower and steel roofs, has become a landmark for motorists speeding to the Tsawwassen ferry terminal. The fan-shaped sanctuary seats 1,300 worshippers. Other facilities include a multi-purpose hall, Christian education wing, and administration centre, all organized around an entrance courtyard oriented towards a large parking lot. The different components are strongly connected, reflecting the Baptist community's belief in the church as an all-encompassing sacred and secular lifestyle.

Ladner Village Centre
Delta Street and 48 Avenue, Delta
The area around the little settlement of Ladner's Landing, later known as Ladner, remained rural until the construction of the Massey Tunnel which connected Ladner to Vancouver by a direct highway in 1959. Subsequent development was slowed only by designations under the Agricultural Land Reserve. Ladner village retains some of its small-town look with a number of woodframe commercial buildings clustered around

---

Both are leased quickly. The company begins assembling land for a third tower. Radio hotliner Jack Webster publicly urges that permission to demolish an apartment on the site be denied. Debate rages and the project stalls, but city council finally approves the plan. Bentall Three is completed in 1973. In 1981 Bentall Four is the largest office building in Vancouver (now surpassed). In 1985 the underground concourse is extended to the Burrard ALRT station.

Newton's library is boldly angular, distinguishing itself from the dull sameness of the instant Surrey townscape

the more substantial Tudor Revival former municipal hall (now the Delta Museum and Archives, 4858 Delta Street, designed by A. Campbell Hope and built in 1912). The charming survivors include the former telephone exchange at 4882 Delta Street (1910), a prefabricated structure, the pool hall at 4880 Delta Street (1914) and the Masonic Hall at 4873 Delta Street (1904).

Burrvilla
6920 - 62B Street, Deas Island Regional Park, Delta
1905-06
Deas Island Regional Park, maintained by the GVRD, features tidal marshes, sand dunes, meadows, treed dykes and a number of historic buildings that have been moved to the site. "Burrvilla," a handsome Queen Anne house that once belonged to the Burr Family, came here from the south side of River Road in 1981. The front part is furnished with antiques and collectables, many of which are for sale. Nearby are the one-room Inverholme Schoolhouse built near Boundary Bay in 1909 and used today for special events, and the former Delta Agricultural Hall, a two-storey frame structure built in Ladner in 1894 and now used as a park maintenance building as well as for special displays.

WHITE ROCK
White Rock Museum and Archives
14970 Marine Drive, White Rock
1912
The Great Northern Railway—now the Burlington Northern (BNR)—built its Vancouver-bound tracks from the U.S. along the waterfront through White Rock and Crescent Beach. When passenger service was withdrawn from White Rock in 1975 (it was discontinued entirely in 1981), the BNR gave the station to the city. Since 1991 it has accommodated the White Rock Museum and Archives, a municipal facility which mounts exhibits, serves researchers and operates a gift gallery. Passenger service between Vancou-

ver and Seattle, restored by Amtrak in 1995, passes by the station's door but the train doesn't stop there anymore.

SURREY
Station Tower, Gateway
King George Highway and 108 Avenue, Surrey
Musson Cattell Mackey Partnership, 1994
An "edge city" formed as an amalgamation of small communities, Surrey has no natural city centre. The Whalley area is rapidly becoming Surrey's downtown helped by the construction of Gateway, by Intrawest Development Corporation. The first phase features Station Tower, a massive 18-storey office building that incorporates a SkyTrain station, and Cornerstone, two nearby residential towers (W.M. Moroz Architect Ltd., 1994). Station Tower's geometrical conceit is a square form that appears to be burst egg-like by an internal cylinder, all sheathed in a high-tech Swiss-designed glass curtain wall. Musson Cattell Mackey also created the master plan for Gateway, an eight-hectare site that will eventually accommodate 250,000 square metres of building with a "skyline image" from across the Fraser River.

Christ Church, Surrey Centre
16631 Old McLellan Road, Surrey
Frank W. Macey, 1884
A glimpse of old Surrey can be had by travelling along treed Old McLellan Road—one of the city's few streets to deviate from the grid—up the hill to Christ Church (Anglican) then east to Boothroyd Corners. Christ Church served the early settlers of Surrey Centre, many of them British by birth. With its frame structure, steep roof and Gothic Revival pointed windows, it resembles the Royal Engineers' churches in the Fraser Canyon—no coincidence, since builder William Flood came from Hope. The picturesque graveyard provides another link to Surrey's pioneers. The former Richardson Farm nearby, east of 168 Street at 57 Avenue, completed the picture. Its historic house and sprawling barn were recently demolished and the land filled with a residential subdivision called Richardson Ridge.

Cloverdale Centre
176 Street, between 58A Avenue and 56 Avenue (Highway 10), Surrey
Many separate communities have been absorbed into the large City of Surrey. One of the largest and most distinctive was Cloverdale. Thanks in part to a traffic by-pass a block to the west, 176 Street remains a pedestrian-scaled main street with plain, commercial buildings typical of many British Columbia towns. Buildings such as the former Bank of Montreal (5657-176 Street, 1909) and Duckworth's Dry Goods Store (5741-176 Street, 1926) set the tone. Many are now antique stores. Around the corner at 17675 - 56 Avenue, stands the second Surrey Municipal Hall (C.H.

Clow, 1912), now a seniors' centre, a sturdy Tudor Revival building that resembles the former municipal halls in Ladner, Port Moody and elsewhere in the Lower Mainland.

Stewart Farmhouse
13723 Crescent Road, Surrey
c. 1894
This picturesque cross-gabled house, with its crafted verandah and rooftop finials, is a handsome example of Victorian design. It was built by John and Anne Stewart, he a Scot who came by way of Quebec and California and she a native of Vancouver Island. John settled here in Elgin in 1880 and the Stewarts built their waterfront home after dyking Mud Bay and the Nicomekl River. Many of the farm's outbuildings and landscape features survive, making this city-operated historic site an accessible window on the past.

Newton Library
13795 - 70 Avenue, Surrey
Patkau Architects, 1991
As Surrey grows it is establishing town centres with public and commercial services. Newton, site of a former village, features a library, senior citizens' centre and other amenities connected by a pedestrian spine within a sea of parking lots. The library is a boldly angular structure that distinguishes itself from the dull sameness of the instant Surrey townscape. The inverted gable roof is supported by assertive, angled glued-laminated wood columns and beams. Two of these frames form a portal at the entrance. The canted aluminum box on the roof contains the air-conditioning equipment. The interior features a large, open and naturally illuminated reading room, expansive where the roof rises high and intimate where it dips low.

Peace Arch
Pacific Highway (Highway 99), Surrey
H.W. Corbitt, 1921
The familiar white steel-and-concrete arch at the Canada-U.S. border was an international initiative commemorating the peaceful relationship between our two countries. It was conceived by Sam Hill, president of the Pacific Highway Association, and built with donated labor and materials. It and its lovely park are managed jointly by BC Parks and Washington State Parks. The classical imagery may sit more comfortably in the U.S. (whose federal and state capitols sport a variety of Classical Revival styles) than in Canada (which prefers Gothic and Tudor imagery) but the gesture remains a valid and appreciated one.

facing page: Three generations of Vancouver buildings; Christ Church Cathedral (lower right) with Cathedral Place (left) and the Hotel Vancouver (right), 1992. vs

Meanwhile, after years of retirement and honors, Charles Bentall dies in 1974. The same year the company completes the B.C. Tel building in Burnaby. The company is called in to fast-track the B.C. Pavilion at Expo 86. In 17 short months it completes the $56 million glass pavilion, watertight and on schedule. In 1988 the company restructures. The old Dominion Construction company is split-off, to be operated independently by Clark Bentall. Bob Bentall, president and C.E.O. of the Bentall company since 1985, assumes control of

Bentall Corporation. The first public offering is completed in 1992. On January 1st, 1995, for the first time in its history, the company is led by someone outside the family, Bob Bentall becomes chairman of the board and Mark Shuparski becomes the corporation's president. "The world is changing," Bob Bentall says, "and we are changing with it."

Architects and Architecture of Greater Vancouver
Sean Rossiter

SOME SAY THAT any work of human hands in Vancouver's setting detracts from its natural splendor. But these opinions run in cycles. Captain George Vancouver, upon seeing Burrard Inlet in 1792, thought that it "requires only to be enriched by the industry of man with villages, mansions, cottages, and other buildings to render it the most lovely country that can be imagined . . ."

The dust jacket of Alan Morley's *Vancouver, from Milltown to Metropolis,* published in 1961 to commemorate the city's 75th birthday, shows a painting of Captain Vancouver's statue at city hall in which the captain is pointing toward the city's latest landmark, one of the most ambitious buildings attempted in Vancouver up to then, the three-year-old Main Post Office. It appears to loom at the north end of the old Cambie Bridge, a rickety timber structure with a swinging centre span.

With the Downtown peninsula's tallest structure in 1961 being the B.C. Hydro Building, the North Shore was almost entirely visible from city hall. Of course this cover was meant to depict the metropolis of the book's title. Yet the entire middle ground, False Creek, was still an industrial sewer lined with mills. Vancouver may have been a metropolis, but it was also still a milltown in 1961.

Vancouver did not change much from the eve of World War I to 1966. "In 1913," Morley wrote, "a photograph taken at Hastings and Granville Streets, looking south on Granville, was scarcely distinguishable in its main features from one taken today . . ."

Only 25 years later the same scene had been utterly transformed. In 1986 the north shore of False Creek was the site of Expo 86. If anything, Vancouver has only changed more rapidly since then.

Four building booms, two before World War I and two during the past 30 years, account for the Vancouver depicted on the cover of Morley's book—and the city that, during the early 1990s, was the fastest-growing on the continent outside of the Sun Belt.

The most recent of these booms is the post-Expo 86 Downtown residential boom that continues to fill the empty spaces around the edges of Vancouver's Downtown peninsula and marches northward from False Creek through Yaletown to Chinatown. It will replace the core's onetime industrial areas with highly designed condominium towers that will house many of the 40,000 newcomers flooding into Greater Vancouver annually during the early 1990s.

Each boom had its outstanding architects—more often than not commercial architects working in well-established styles mastered elsewhere and brought with them to a place still under construction. While it was possible to say, as Morley did in 1961, that "Vancouver is the work of one human lifetime," it is also true that it took that long for distinctive architecture to emerge in Vancouver.

That year, 1961, was the turning point. The history of Vancouver architecture consists of everything before Arthur Erickson and everything after. In 1961 Erickson and Woodrow Wilson "Bud" Wood were teaching a more design-oriented architectural approach at the University of Oregon. Erickson was already designing houses in Vancouver that he regarded as experiments; one, for example, entirely out of concrete blocks. Wood became perhaps the most important design mentor at the University of British Columbia's architecture school over three decades.

Ron Thom, the outstanding designer in Vancouver before Erickson, was off to Toronto that year to build Massey College and thus become the first local architect with a national practice. Thom was a protégé of the most influential architect ever to work in Vancouver, C.E. "Ned" Pratt whose firm, Thompson Berwick Pratt & Partners, had by then become the dominant office in the city.

The founders of many of today's important firms were either working for Pratt or about to work for Erickson in 1961. Five

years later Simon Fraser University, the "instant university" designed by Erickson and his partner Geoff Massey on Burnaby Mountain, would for the first time utilize many of the city's talents under the umbrella of Erickson's innovative competition-winning scheme for SFU.

Erickson is the supreme cultural personality ever to emerge in this city. Such a figure is usually the culmination of a slow, time-consuming process of gradual development.

The first generation of Vancouver architects built Gastown and its immediate surroundings in the styles of the time, with the fire-resistant materials mandated by most North American cities. They consisted of load-bearing masonry walls—usually cut stone but brick when available—with heavy timbers used as interior columns and rafters. Most often the style was Italianate with hand-cut lintels and thresholds and elaborate cornices. The Vancouver master of this style was Nathaniel Stonestreet Hoffar, who held two degrees from Washington's Georgetown University. Hoffar was the city's first important architect. He built much of the 300-block of East Cordova (including the Army & Navy Store and the Horne Block) and the Yale Hotel on Granville. Like subsequent key architects of major booms, Hoffar rode the one that ended in 1894 to considerable personal wealth. His descendants owned the shipyard on Coal Harbour where Vancouver's first airplane, the H-1 flying boat, was built. During the 1920s the shipyard became Boeing of Canada.

The next boom, "Vancouver's Golden Years of Growth," lasted from 1907 to 1913. In those six years the financial district along West Hastings that persisted into the 1970s was largely completed. Toward the end of that boom, buildings constructed only blocks from each other successively claimed to be the tallest in the British Empire: first J.S. Helyer's idiosyncratic 13-storey Dominion Trust Building at Hastings and Cambie and then W.T. Whiteway's 17-storey World Building of 1911-12 (now Sun Tower) at Beatty and Pender, financed by Louis D. Taylor, publisher of the *World* and, the city's longest-serving mayor.

Whiteway, from Newfoundland, was an important early century architect in Vancouver. Among his works is The Landing, formerly the Kelly Building, begun in 1905 and rehabilitated by Soren Rasmussen in 1988.

As is still the case it helps for an architect to have steady work from a developer. J.E. Parr & Thomas Fee, the most prolific architects of the pre-World War I boom, built The Orillia (1903, demolished 1985); the Manhattan Apartments on Thurlow at Robson (1907); the first reinforced-concrete structure in

facing page: Cordova Street, c. 1895 (the Army & Navy Store is on the left). cva

Vancouver, the Europe Hotel (1908); the Vancouver Block at 736 Granville (1910) and many other white-tiled buildings along Granville Street. Their patron was W. Lamont Tait, a lumber wholesaler, for whom Parr & Fee did one of the first mansions in Shaughnessy Heights, "Glen Brae" (1911), now the Canuck Place Children's Hospice (renovated 1993-95 by Downs-Archambeault).

Even then, when architects in a city that saw itself as a future Liverpool of the Pacific were imitating Europe, there were the beginnings of a local—or at least regional—style. Carl F. Gould was a Seattle architect who had mastered that city's terracotta material—glazed tiles formed into classical details with weather-resistant qualities appropriate to this climate. When the worldwide collapse of lumber prices in 1910 ended Seattle's boom, Gould and other architects travelled the short distance north to Vancouver where higher prices persisted because of B.C.'s access to British markets. Gould's Rogers Building (1911-12) at 470 Granville is one sumptuous example of what architects from a more sophisticated city could do in booming Vancouver.

The foremost talent to come north—indeed the supreme talent of Vancouver's pre-war boom—was Woodruff Marbury Somervell. Somervell came to Seattle from New York in 1904 to supervise construction of a cathedral, stayed to build several hospitals and a dozen-odd homes on the U.S Register of Historic Places, then brought his romantic Mediterranean styles to Vancouver in 1910. Sugar king B.T. Rogers' mansion, "Shannon" (1912-15); the terracotta Birks Building (1912-13, demolished 1974); and the elegant pair of buildings at Abbott and West Hastings, the Merchant's Bank and the B.C. Electric Railway Company edifice, are Somervell's forgotten legacy. He also left behind the blueprints for the Toronto-Dominion Bank at Hastings and Seymour (built as the Union Bank in 1920) when he went off to World War I.

Somervell's only rival at the height of the 1907-13 boom was Thomas Hooper, whose masterwork is the Winch Building of 1908-09 (now part of Sinclair Centre on Hastings at Granville), the kind of well-financed commercial building that only appears toward the end of a boom. Many feel that Hooper's south facade of Francis Rattenbury's courthouse of 1906-12 (now the featured elevation of Arthur Erickson's Vancouver Art Gallery) is superior to Rattenbury's grander Georgia Street side.

But the pre-World War I boom's most lasting legacy, aside from the buildings, was a firm of architects formed in 1908 that persisted for nearly 80 years. Charles Joseph Thompson was the firm's businessman and George Lister Thornton Sharp its designer-draftsman. Both were capable architects, Thompson

Saanich Commonwealth Place, Eaton Centre Metrotown, Nanaimo General Hospital Renovations, 333 Dunsmuir Office Tower, University of Victoria Student Union Building, Vancouver Hospital LSP II, and the Abbotsford Agricultural Centre. Keen currently has seven offices across Canada.

the nuts-and-bolts chap and Sharp the artist. Sharp and Thompson's future was guaranteed when they won a competition to design the University of British Columbia in 1912. Such civic landmarks as the Vancouver Club (1912-14), the Cenotaph at Victory Square (1924)—on the site of the original courthouse by N.S. Hoffar—and the galleries of the Burrard Bridge (1930-32) all testify to Sharp & Thompson's ability to get work and execute it in a variety of styles.

Sharp and Thompson's first use of concrete as a structural material was for the clergy-house of St. James Anglican parish in 1927; their association with Sir Adrian Gilbert Scott on the parish's third church at Gore and Cordova Streets produced, in Arthur Erickson's estimation, the finest building in Vancouver.

Ned Pratt, a bronze medal winner in pairs rowing at the 1932 Olympics and an engineering student at the University of Toronto, would take the firm to new heights after meeting Thompson in 1937 while courting his daughter Esme. He met his future partner Bob Berwick, also at U of T, at the Thompson tennis court and Berwick persuaded Pratt to switch to architecture.

After a war spent building air force installations along the B.C. coast, Pratt returned to a city little changed from the pre-World War I Vancouver. Sharp & Thompson's great rivals were Townley and Matheson, the leading civic architects, and McCarter and Nairne, the foremost designers of highrise office buildings.

Townley and Matheson, both of whom studied architecture at the University of Pennsylvania, became the city's finest practitioners of the Deco Moderne style, which they applied to the second Stock Exchange Building (1928-29) and Vancouver City Hall (1935-36). They built much of the former Vancouver General Hospital, including its exquisite Children's Health Centre (1944) and its Centennial Pavilion (1956-58) as well as the regrettable Public Safety Building on Main Street.

McCarter Nairne and Partners gave the city its foremost deco skyscrapers, the Marine Building (1931) and the Medical-Dental Building (1929, demolished 1989) on Georgia Street. The new Main Post Office that Capt. Vancouver's statue points to on the cover of Alan Morley's 1961 book was an impressive technical achievement in 1958 (project architect: Bill Leithead), and the firm survived into the 1980s working with distinguished outsiders, such as Victor Gruen of Los Angeles on Pacific Centre (1969-76), the most ambitious construction project undertaken in Vancouver up to that time.

Sharp and Thompson evolved into Thompson Berwick Pratt and Partners, a multi-disciplinary firm that outlasted both of its rivals by producing two generations of great designers who rode the post-war institutional boom in schools, banks, hospitals and transportation facilities. Ned Pratt's TBP&P became known as the West Coast graduate school of architecture, a finishing course for all but a few of the finest architects of Vancouver's last quarter-century.

A few of the "graduates" who founded other major firms include Ron Bain and Ken Burroughs (False Creek South and Lethbridge University for Erickson/Massey); Barry Downs and Richard Archambault (Carnegie Centre, Canada Place); Norman Hotson, Joost Bakker and Mike Geary (Granville Island, 2211 West Fourth); Geoff Massey and Arthur Erickson; and Joe Wai (Sun Yat-sen Chinese Classical Garden).

Among the important TBP&P partners were administrative partner John Dayton, who did Bank of Montreal branches ("Oh, about 150 anyway"); Roy Jessiman (Buchanan Building, UBC); engineer Otto Safir, whom Pratt calls the real author of the B.C. Hydro Building; and Zoltan Kiss (Vancouver International Airport, 1968).

There is a direct line of design influence from Pratt through Ron Thom to Paul Merrick, who developed his own variation of Thom's gothic style, and Brian Hemingway who, with Merrick, won a Governor General's Award for their Officer Training School at CFB Chilliwack. Oddly enough Pratt, one of the first champions of modern architecture in provincial post-war Vancouver, begat a line of romantic architects whose primary design influences, aside from Frank Lloyd Wright, were medieval cathedrals.

Pratt was instrumental in launching the modern era in house design by doing the drawings for artist B.C. Binnings' largely self-designed West Vancouver house in 1940. Pratt's own work is highlighted by the War Memorial Gymnasium at UBC (1947, with Fred Lasserre) and the Dal Grauer Substation on Burrard Street (1954, with Jim White).

Ron Thom was the culmination of the pre-Arthur Erickson era in Vancouver architecture. Many architects are failed artists. Thom was an exceptional artist who turned to architecture—the first of the arts to fully mature in Canada, historian Alan Gowans says—after meeting Richard Neutra during the Los Angeles architect's visit to Vancouver in 1947. Though fundamentally a pupil of Frank Lloyd Wright and an apprentice of Ned Pratt's until 1958, Thom had by then already succeeded in marrying the horizontal Wright house with the West Coast climate to move B.C. residential design into a league of its own. Although Erickson had designed a few houses already, he only began turning out houses incorporating his own ideas around 1961.

By then Ron Thom was off to Toronto. It was as if there had

been some symbolic handoff of design leadership. Each architect would extend the ideas he has explored in house design to bigger and bigger projects; Thom in Ontario, Erickson here. The pressure of such projects as Trent University took their toll on Thom, who drank his way from marriage to marriage and partner to partner. Meanwhile Erickson organized around himself a design and planning talent greenhouse capable of such challenges as the complex that includes Robson Square and Vancouver's new courthouse.

It was Erickson who became the most famous native of Vancouver until Bryan Adams. It was Erickson who completed the process of devising an architecture that was so specific to the city's climate that it could be said to be a Vancouver architecture. Concrete is Erickson's marble, partly because he believes Vancouver's grey climate cannot take bright colors. Glass canopies are an Erickson trademark for the same reason. Feature staircases are Erickson's response to building on slopes, although he covered much of the Robson Square, an essentially horizontal composition, with stairs to give public access to what became, in 1976, Vancouver's central town square. One local masterpiece incorporating these ideas is the Museum of Anthropology at UBC (1973-76).

If, as with Ned Pratt, we calculate Erickson's output as more than buildings, we can foresee his direct influence continuing well into the next century. Its outlines are already apparent. Expo 86 was the turning point for Vancouver as a home for international investment and Erickson's first and second major disciples made significant contributions to that epochal fair.

Bruno Freschi was Expo's planner; with engineer Boque Babicki, who came up with the basic concept, he designed its generic pavilion and left what is now Vancouver's Science Centre as its keynote building. Bing Thom, Erickson's project architect on the Robson Square complex, designed five pavilions (including the award-winning Northwest Territories' entry) for Expo.

Expo was a terrible disappointment for Erickson. His proposal for a retractable-roof theatre at mid-site, with its stage overlooking False Creek, was supplanted by Waisman Dewar Grout's $54 million B.C. Pavilion. After a post-Expo adventure in Los Angeles doing that city's huge Bunker Hill development, Erickson returned for a second career in his hometown, which appropriately included more major buildings for the SFU campus he originated 30 years before.

The architect who rode the 1966-82 boom to commercial success was Frank Musson, whose Musson Cattell Mackey (MCM) firm reoriented Downtown Vancouver from its east-west Georgia Street axis to north-south along Burrard. This change was envisioned by C.B.K. Van Norman, who began the move to that street with his Burrard Building (completed 1957) while simultaneously pushing for the relocation of the Central Library to Burrard. (He lost the commission to Vancouver's finest International Style designers, Semmens and Simpson).

A staff architect from England with Semmens and Simpson and the Bentall family's Dominion Construction firm, Musson and his partner Terry Cattell were natural choices to build Bentall Centre (1966-82), four towers that formed the biggest superblock development in Western Canada. MCM were involved in almost every development from West Georgia to the waterfront, including the Governor General's Award-winning 888 West Hastings (1980); that boom's outstanding commercial building, Park Place (1982); and Canada Place (1985, designed by Toronto's Zeidler-Roberts Partnership with Downs-Archambault).

Vancouver's two biggest firms in 1995 were Aitken-Wreglesworth Associates (AWA) and Waisman Dewar Grout Carter, both founded by Winnipeggers, both numbering at their peaks, 50-odd employees. Winnipeg has long exported the cream of its architects to Vancouver. Both firms did innovative, clean work soon after arriving (AWA's Seimens Building, SFU's Downtown campus; Waisman's Martello Tower apartments in the West End) but lost their edge as their founders became more interested in self-improvement and corporate management programs. In a bid to strengthen its design side AWA engaged Erickson as a consultant and got work at both Lower Mainland universities, including a massive consolidation of UBC's library facilities. But Erickson was not enough to save the big firm. In 1995 Waisman and AWA merged and became Architectura with Clive Grout as chief designer.

The most celebrated pure designer in Vancouver at the time of the mid-nineties slowdown was Richard Henriquez, another ex-Winnipegger. Henriquez, originally from the West Indies, had done innovative work for Rhone & Iredale (Sedgewick Library, UBC, 1971-72) and blossomed on his own with several highly celebrated projects. They included the consolidation of four Downtown heritage buildings into Sinclair Centre (1983-86, with Toby, Russell, Buckwell & Partners); the Sylvia Hotel Extension (1987) and, more recently, a Student Activities Centre gymnasium at UBC, paid for by the students themselves. It sits across a field from Ned Pratt's War Memorial Gym, on an architecturally mediocre campus, as a kind of summary of Vancouver architecture since World War II—and ample evidence that good architecture begets more of the same.

In the workplace Keen Engineering staff have helped us win awards from the Consulting Engineers of British Columbia, the American Society of Heating, Refrigerating, and Air Conditioning Engineers, and BC Hydro Power Smart. Our staff have participated in events such as the Lions Gate Hospital 911 Relay, SFU's Uptown/Downtown Relay, and the Childrens' Hospital Baseball Tournament.

Building Statistics of Greater Vancouver
Jeff Veniot

W<small>E USE THE WORD</small> "opened" rather than "built." Tall or large buildings take a couple of years to construct, so "opened" refers to when it was finished. Building height is from the street level to the top, not including underground parking or any flag poles, masts or radio antennas on top. If the building has a decorative top, the height goes to its peak too. How many floors? From street level to the top, but not mechanical floors, only floors that people can work or live on.

Structure	Opened	Floors	Height
Vancouver			
Harbour Centre, 555 W. Hastings	1977	28	146 m
Royal Centre, 1055 W. Georgia	1973	36	140 m
Park Place, 666 Burrard	1984	35	140 m
Bentall IV, 1055 Dunsmuir	1981	36	137 m
Vancouver Centre, 650 W. Georgia	1977	34	136.5 m
TD Bank Tower, 700 W. Georgia	1972	30	127 m
Granville Square, 200 Granville	1973	30	123 m
Bentall III, 595 Burrard	1974	32	122 m
Landmark Hotel, 1400 Robson	1973	39	120.7 m
Hyatt Hotel, 655 Burrard	1973	34	109.4 m
Wall Garden Centre Hotel, 1088 Burrard	1994	35	102 m
BC Gas, 1111 W. Georgia	1992	24	101.2 m
Hongkong Bank, 885 W.Georgia	1986	23	100.5 m
Paris Place, 199 Keefer Place	1995	32	100.5 m
Coast Plaza at Stanley Park Hotel, 1733 Comox	1968	37	100.2 m
Stock Exchange Tower, 609 Granville	1981	24	100.2 m
Marine Building, 355 Burrard	1930	22	97.8 m
Beach Tower, 1500 Hornby	1993	29	96 m
City Gate, 1188 Quebec	1992	30	93.8 m
Four Seasons Hotel, 791 W. Georgia	1976	24	92.9 m
Cathedral Place, 925 W. Georgia	1991	23	91.4 m
Vancouver Hospital Tower, Laurel Pavilion, 865 W. 12th	1995	17	90.2 m
The Peninsula, 1299 Marina Side Crescent	1996	32	90.2 m
Pacific Point, 1323 Homer	1993	29	89 m
Blue Horizon Hotel, 1225 Robson	1967	30	88.3 m

Structure	Opened	Floors	Height
777 Dunsmuir Street	1990	19	86.2 m
City Crest, 1155 Homer	1993	31	84.7 m
889 Homer	1992	26	83.5 m
IBM Tower, 701 W. Georgia	1975	18	77.7 m
Library Square Tower, 300 W. Georgia	1995	21	74.9 m
805 West Broadway	1974	20	73.1 m
800 Burrard	1983	19	72.2 m
Vancouver City Hall, 453 W. 12th	1936	11	47.5 m
West Vancouver			
338 Taylor Way	1992	23	82.2 m
Shorewood Manor, 2020 Bellevue	1970	20	54.8 m
Ambleside Towers, 1552 Esquimalt	1971	20	54.8 m
District of North Vancouver			
International Plaza Towers, 1979 Marine Drive	1975	26	71.6 m
City of North Vancouver			
The Observatory, 120 W. 2nd	1990	28	91.7 m
Marlborough Tower Apartments, 144 W. 14th	1972	24	67 m
Richmond			
Vancouver International Airport Control Tower	1996	5	64.9 m
Delta Pacific Resort, 10251 St. Edward's Drive	1983	18	57.6 m
Imperial Grand, 7500 Granville	1993	16	46 m
Centre Point, 4 Towers, Lansdowne and Garden City			
8811 Lansdowne	1991	15	45.1 m
8831 Lansdowne	1991	15	45.1 m
8851 Lansdowne	1995	14	45.1 m
8871 Lansdowne	1995	14	45.1 m
Delta Airport Hotel, 3500 Cessna Drive	1973	11	42 m
Travel Lodge Hotel, 3071 St. Edward's Drive	1986	10	36.5 m
Radisson President Hotel, 8181 Cambie	1994	11	34.4 m
Burnaby			
Metro Tower II, 4720 Kingsway	1991	30	99.3 m
Grande Corniche I, 6240 McKay	1987	27	95.7 m
Rogers Cantel Tower, 4710 Kingsway	1989	28	90.8 m
Grande Corniche II, 6220 McKay	1989	25	88.4 m

Structure	Opened	Floors	Height
Arbutus Tower, 4266 Grange	1974	28	84.1 m
The Burlington, 6540 Burlington	1982	26	79.8 m
Concorde Place, 9521 Cardston Crescent	1982	25	71.9 m
Discovery Place I & II, 3980 Carrigan	1984	25	71.9 m
Seton Villa, 3755 McGill	1973	19	54.2 m
New Westminster			
Stirling Place, 719 Princess	1995	24	72.2 m
Berkley Place, 739 Princess	1996	24	72.2 m
The Excelsior, 8 Laguna Court	1991	22	60.9 m
612-5th Avenue	1990	21	59.1 m
Port Moody			
New Port Village, Guildford Way and Ioco Road	1996	20	56 m
Coquitlam			
The Selkirk, 1199 Eastwood	1995	24	71.9 m
The Lakeside, 3070 Guildford Way	1995	23	66.7 m
Parc Laurent, 3071 Glen Drive	1993	22	66.1 m
Port Coquitlam			
PoCo Place, 2755 Lougheed Highway	1981	7	29.8 m
Surrey			
Station Tower, Gateway, 13401 - 108th Avenue	1994	18	72.8 m
Sheraton Inn Guildford, 15263 - 104th Avenue	1992	20	61.2 m
White rock			
Vista Royale Apartments, 15280 North Bluff Road	1972	13	42.3 m

Harbour Centre on Hastings Street, reflected in the mirrored glass of 401 West Georgia. vs

Imperial Parking's stylized "P" logo can be found in 50 North American cities, as well as Southeast Asia. As of March 31, 1996 Impark was a publicly traded company on the Toronto Stock Exchange with annual revenues in excess of $240 million.

Landscape Architecture
Elizabeth Godley

Cambie Boulevard, 1991, now a heritage–designated urban landscape. vs

I N THE LOWER MAINLAND every gas station boasts a strip of Astroturf punctuated by flowers, every office building a tub or two of greenery. Come spring, our thoroughfares burst into blossom with ornamental plum and cherry trees. Our many parks—typically green year-round—are legendary, as are our gardens, replete with a wide range of plants from every corner of the globe.

The mild winters and abundant rainfall have made Greater Vancouver a gardeners' paradise, and the lawns of even the most humble homes are enlivened by shrubbery, often a rhododendron or hydrangea bush.

Perhaps the forgiving climate, coupled with the early immigrants' British disdain for showing off, hobbled the development of landscape architecture in these parts. Whatever the reason, landscaping got off to a shaky start in Vancouver.

The first practitioner was Thomas Mawson, a landscape architect and town planner from Lancashire, England. In 1911 Mawson set up shop on the top floor of the Rogers Building at 470 Granville. He'd come to Vancouver on a cross-Canada lecture tour, and Vancouver's park commissioner immediately hired him to design the lighthouse and underground lifeboat house at Brockton Point.

Mawson also won the competition for developing Lost Lagoon, proposing a formal design of perimeter walkways around a scallop-edged body of water, with four colonnaded recreational buildings at the lagoon's four corners. But the then-park superintendent ignored the plan, opting for a much cheaper, more natural layout. In 1915 Mawson closed his office and, although he returned to work in Banff, Calgary and Ottawa after World War I, he never came back to Vancouver.

Vancouver's leafy and upscale Shaughnessy district, established around 1912 by the Canadian Pacific Railway for the city's well-off families, was planned with the help of Frederick Law Olmsted, the American landscaper who designed Central Park in New York City and major civic parks in Philadelphia, Chicago, Boston and Montreal.

In the twenties horticulturalist Frank Buck acted as adviser to the Municipality of Point Grey. Buck was responsible for landscaping the UBC campus, and oversaw the planting of the silver maples along University Boulevard in 1928.

Vancouver's second professional landscaper was another Englishman, Desmond Muirhead. After graduating from UBC in plant pathology, Muirhead began a landscaping business in Kerrisdale. The firm's work focused on landscape and garden planning for single family homes on 50- and 66-foot lots in Shaughnessy, Point Grey, the University Endowment Lands and West Vancouver's British Properties. Clive Justice, who joined Muirhead's firm in 1953, says that two prevailing modes had dominated landscaping in the fifties: "the 'Seattle large-boulder rockery' on all sloping sites, and 'the pointed and spreading dwarf conifer up against the house foundation' style."

Muirhead introduced the notion of designs and blueprints to Vancouver. Early commissions included the McPhee residence on 49th Avenue near McKenzie, and the Clarence Saba garden between McKenzie and Cedarhurst. These gardens were designed to complement two of the earliest International style homes in Vancouver, by architect Douglas Simpson of Semmens and Simpson.

Most Vancouver-area gardens were heavily influenced by English styles (and to a lesser extent, German) mainly because the climate was similar. Information in British and German how-to books easily adapted to West Coast conditions.

In the 1950s and early 1960s, two firms—Justice & Webb and Tatersfield & Associates—dominated landscape architecture in the region. Among projects completed by Justice & Webb were golf courses (Shaughnessy, Langara, VanDusen and North Richmond), as well as the restoration of Fort Langley. Clive Justice was also instrumental in interesting people in rhododendrons.

John Lantzius' firm also played a major role, working with architects Arthur Erickson and Geoffrey Massey on such projects as Simon Fraser University. Other Lantzius projects included the University of Victoria's Gordon Head campus, housing on the former Langara golf course and massive expansion at UBC.

Landscaping ideas from California began to trickle north, notably the notion of "outdoor living," promulgated by Bob Royston, who taught at the University of California at Berkeley. Sun-decks, planter boxes and private patios with high fence areas began to interrupt the broad swathes of lawn associated with 1950s suburban development.

Many of the landscaped open spaces in Vancouver's downtown core stem from this period: the plaza at the Queen Elizabeth Theatre, the plaza outside Eaton's, and the landscaping around the Bentall buildings.

In the late sixties Art Cowie opened Ecos, the first Vancouver firm to emphasize interdisciplinary planning as a major component of landscape design. Cowie brought together practitioners of a variety of fields to brainstorm major projects all over the province.

The next decade saw the development of Arbutus Village, one of Vancouver's first major projects, which was to set a pattern for the future. From the beginning, the developer, the architects and the landscape architects worked together, creating a new role for the latter.

In the 1970s and 1980s Vancouver gradually established its own identity in landscape architecture. One of the key firms at this time was Don Vaughan & Associates, composed of Vaughan and three Americans—Jeff Philips, Ron Rule and Richard Pavelek. Their projects included Shaughnessy Place (with architects McCarter Nairne); Granville Island (with Hotson Bakker); Shannon Mews (with Erickson Massey); Tumbler Ridge town centre (with TBP Architects); Whistler Town Centre; and the network of urban plazas and fountains built in Vancouver.

Vaughan's company also designed the Discovery Square Sky-Train Station on Burrard (with Alan Parker & Associates) and the Dr. Sun Yat-Sen Garden in Chinatown (with Joe Wai).

The firm changed personnel over the years, with Philips, Rule and Pavelek going on to set up their own companies. Other well-known alumni of the firm are Kim Perry and Jane Durante.

In 1984, when asked to head a team to design the site for Expo 86, Vaughan brought together all his past associates and partners, as well as several others, to tackle the largest landscape project in Vancouver.

In the late 1970s and 1980s landscape architects in the Vancouver area began to rely extensively on native plant material. In earlier decades plant material had to be imported from Europe, but a few far-sighted horticulturalists were now growing salal, Oregon grape, ferns and other local greenery. The use of native plants had been most strongly developed by landscape architect Cornelia Oberlander and architect Arthur Erickson at the UBC Museum of Anthropology. Oberlander and Erickson's interest in integrating landscape with buildings was emphasized again at Robson Square, where a profusion of trailing vines counterpoints the modernist slabs of concrete and glass. That the architect chose to create an urban oasis, rather than another dark tower, underscored Vancouver's idea of itself as a city whose fame rests on its spectacular setting.

By the early nineties the role of the landscape architect had been recognized as an important element in urban design. In the megaprojects at Coal Harbour (Marathon Realty) and on False Creek's north shore (Concord Pacific), landscape architects played an important role as members of the design team.

In 1994 and 1995 Vancouver's planning department acknowledged the importance of the discipline when it commissioned landscape architects to draw up design guidelines for "green ways" and "linear parks," to beautify transitional neighborhoods like Mount Pleasant and the Wall Street area.

Planting trees and shrubs and creating pocket parks is now viewed as one way to humanize the urban jungle, making streets safer by encouraging more pedestrians and enhancing neighborhood pride.

Law Courts, Robson Square, Vancouver, 1990. vp

Monuments and Plaques
Jeff Veniot and Bill Sampson

Rather than try to list all of Greater Vancouver's commemorative monuments and plaques, we have chosen to highlight the more interesting or prominent ones.

Every municipality and veterans' organization has, of course, monuments to honor the war dead—the Victory Square Cenotaph at Hastings and Cambie Streets, for example. And throughout Vancouver many people have honored loved ones by donating park benches, water fountains and even lampposts and have attached markers to them.

Vancouver Centennial and Heritage Plaque Program

For Vancouver's 100th anniversary in 1986 the city introduced 100 oval plaques describing historic events, concentrated in the Chinatown, Gastown and downtown areas. Look up, as many have been placed well up the sides of buildings to prevent them from being taken.

Since the 1970s Vancouver has been designating its heritage buildings for future generations and starting in 1993 began installing distinctive plaques on the properties. The bronze markers incorporate the city crest with a text briefly outlining the building's history and architecture. There are more than 100 plaques now (with more being added), and the heritage department at city hall will provide you with a locations list.

Queen Elizabeth Park

In front of Seasons In The Park restaurant is a marker noting that Russian President Boris Yeltsin and U.S. President Bill Clinton dined there during the 1993 Vancouver Summit. The park has several plaques of note, one for Raoul Wallenberg, the Swedish diplomat who saved thousands of Jewish lives in Hungary during WW II, another honoring the work of the late park board deputy superintendent and chief horticulturalist William "Bill" Livingstone.

Mount Pleasant

On the south side of city hall is a bust of former mayor Gerry McGeer. On the north is a statue of Capt. George Vancouver, sculpted by Charles Marega, with a plaque detailing his 1792 visit. Nearby, at 10th Ave. and Yukon, you'll find the first of many Mount Pleasant Walkway plaques. About half are placed at ground level and the rest on what the neighbors laughingly call tombstones! As you head east on 10th, 11th, 13th, and 14th Aves. you'll find markers describing topics like the origins of Dad's Cookies, Vancouver archivist Maj. Matthews, Percy Williams (the Canadian sports star of the 1928 Olympic Games) and the history of some of the homes

and their former prominent residents.

The 100 block of W. 10th Ave. has seven homes with heritage plaques. The John Davis family, which lives in one of the houses, began in 1973 to restore 166 W. 10th, the oldest (1891) wood frame home in Mount Pleasant. This was the first house to be restored to its original splendor and led to the rejuvenation of the neighborhood.

On the southeast corner of Main and Broadway is a distinctive cairn: complete with pictures and maps, it has information on local "tea swamps," Kingsway, streetcars and Brewery Creek. Vancouver historian Bruce Macdonald penned the text for this and another at 6th and Scotia. A plaque commemorating Vancouver's First Peoples is across the street from the Native Education Centre at 5th and Scotia.

British Columbia Parkway

Following the SkyTrain route the B.C. Parkway has a vast number of monuments, statues and plaques in its parks, gardens and plazas. A big plaque is found on a pillar at Main and Terminal commemorating "100 Years Of Public Transit." On the overpass at the north foot of Main St. is an attractive monument presented in June 1995 by the Shanghai Port Authority. It shows two vigilant lions and commemorates the relationship between Shanghai and Vancouver. At the corner of Clark St. and N. Grandview Hwy. is a statue of Christopher Columbus donated by the city of Genoa, Italy in memory of the Hon. Angelo Branca. Across from the 29th Ave. SkyTrain Station is the German-Canadian Heritage Plaza. Near Swangard Stadium in Central Park is a cairn describing the historic origins of Kingsway and Central Park. Beneath the Royal Oak SkyTrain Station is a plaque honoring those who lost their lives during the initial construction of the rapid transit system. Close by the 22nd St. Station in New Westminster is the Schara Tzedeck Cemetery with a twin obelisk monument commemorating Holocaust victims of World War II.

Along the riverfront near the New Westminster Quay is a potpourri of informational signs describing the history of and present activities on the Fraser River. There is a bust of explorer Simon Fraser and several historic plaques including one telling the Hyack Anvil Battery story. Just up the street at New Westminster city hall a plaque notes the town was the first capital of the province from 1866 to 1868. Historic Irving House Museum is nearby.

Chinatown

At the Dr. Sun Yat-Sen Chinese Cultural Centre is the China Gate which once stood by the Chinese Pavilion at Expo 86. As you walk to a bust of Dr. Sun Yat-Sen behind the centre you pass by large plaques in memory of Chinese-Canadian

veterans of World War II.

Gastown

On the site of the old Hastings Mill at the north foot of Dunlevy St. stands the old mill office and an abstract hard-to-read granite sculpture describing the mill's past. There is, thankfully, a long informational sign nearby on this historic location. On the northwest corner of Dunlevy and Railway Sts. is a city centennial plaque with more information on the mill which opened in 1867. Vern Simpson's *Gassy Jack* statue in Gastown is in Maple Tree Square and sports a plaque recalling a famous maple tree destroyed in the Great Fire of 1886. As you pass the ice cream store on Water St. behind *Gassy Jack* note a large metal sign with information on the Byrnes Block and Jack's second saloon. The Gastown Steam Clock has plaques at its base detailing the history of Gastown and explaining how the clock works.

Pacific National Exhibition and New Brighton Park

This was the 1910 site of Vancouver's first fair. The *Miracle Mile* statue of Roger Bannister and John Landy stands at Renfrew and Hastings Sts. Nearby is a federal government marker reminding us of when Japanese-Canadians were first interned on these grounds, then, in 1942, relocated. The giant Challenger relief map of the province in the B.C. Building has a plaque honoring creator George Challenger. His ashes are interred beneath the plaque. At the south end of the Ironworkers Memorial Second Narrows Bridge are tablets commemorating those who died in 1958 when the bridge collapsed during construction. Just west of the bridge, off Wall St., is New Brighton Park. Look for the "End of the Road" marker plus one on the old Hastings townsite and on a visit by the Royal Engineers in 1863.

Downtown Vancouver

At Hamilton and Hastings Sts. an old plaque describes how the first Canadian Pacific Railway land commissioner, Lauchlan Hamilton, laid out most of the downtown street system from this point in 1885. The old CPR building on Cordova St., now known as Waterfront Station, has historic markers both inside and out, and a plaque commemorating the arrival of the first passenger train on May 23, 1887 is located at the southwest corner of Howe and Cordova Sts. Just to the west of Waterfront Station is Granville Square. The plaza has large plaques describing the history of nearby Canada Place, the harbor and the CPR link from Montreal to Vancouver. Historic Sinclair Centre, very attractively redeveloped from four old buildings, has markers on the Vancouver Pioneers Association, architectural awards and city heritage plaques, one telling the story of the Sinclair Centre clock.

Speaking of clocks, the Birks clock is back at Granville and Hastings—almost where it began. The plaque on the Birks building tells on which corner the famous clock originally stood and where it went before returning here in 1994. To the west note the markers and art deco work both inside and out of the famous Marine Building at 355 Burrard. Teck Lookout Park at Thurlow and Hastings has a plaque describing the *Komagata Maru* incident of 1914. A bust of builder Charles Bentall sits behind the Fountain of the Pioneers at the Bentall Centre towers in the 500-block Burrard. At the Burrard SkyTrain Station is a marker in memory of four workers who died accidentally while constructing a nearby office tower in 1981. Up the street venerable Christ Church Cathedral has a plaque beside each main entry door and at least 20 inside the church (besides superb stained glass windows). Nearby on Hornby St. a marker commemorates the late *Vancouver Sun* columnist Jack Wasserman.

What may be the largest monument in the province is at Robson and Beatty by B.C. Place Stadium in memory of local hero Terry Fox. It shows a picture of Terry and a map of his partial run across Canada. At the south end of Cambie Bridge is a huge red ring gear from the old Connaught (Cambie Street) Bridge while at the north end is a replica of a 1936 "rocket" which stood for years as a symbol of aviation at the first Vancouver Air Terminal.

Canada Place

Nearly 50 informational signs are placed on the promenade around the pier here. Topics include the building itself, Piers B and C, Stanley Park, the Lions mountains, the Lions Gate Bridge, steam ships, cruise ships, maritime history, railroad history, Gastown, Simon Fraser University, marine life, local industries and historic buildings.

Granville St. Starwalk

The Starwalk honors our local entertainment industry. More than 70 plaques have been set into the pavement on Granville between Nelson and Robson Sts. Entertainer Roma Hearn, Ivan Ackery (the late Orpheum Theatre manager), bandleaders Dal Richards and Mart Kenney and singer Bryan Adams are just some of the people honored. The markers are funded and installed by the B.C. Entertainment Hall of Fame Society.

West End

The area bounded by Haro, Barclay, Broughton and Nicola Sts. is designated as Barclay Heritage Square and has many plaques. At the foot of Denman and Davie is a sundial commemorating "the three greenhorns" who in 1862 bought up much of today's West End. Nearby is a plaque honoring Vancouver's first aquarium, located here from 1939 to 1956. Step over to the bath-house and read the plaques describing the New Year's Day Polar Bear Swim and Capt. George Richards's exploration of the area. Across from the bathhouse is a small water fountain and plaque erected in 1927 to honor Joe Fortes, the lifeguard who taught hundreds of children to swim at English Bay. The wonderful old bandstand nearby has markers regarding its history and restoration.

Stanley Park

Historic Malkin Bowl has markers and on the lawn beside it is a large monument to Warren Harding, U.S. President, who visited in 1923. The dining pavilion nearby, a heritage building, is also marked and so is the nearby Air Force Garden of Remembrance. Towards the beluga pool is a large monument in memory of Japanese-Canadians who fought for Canada in World War I.

Across from the Vancouver Rowing Club, also a heritage building, are statues of poet Robert Burns and Gov. Gen. Lord Stanley as well as a monument to Queen Victoria. Hallelujah Point and the statue of sprinter Harry Jerome have plaques as does a concrete slab set in 1863 by the Royal Engineers. The Nine O'Clock Gun carries a descriptive plaque with a second on the Bay downtown store. (The Bay restored the gun barrel and the shelter in 1986). Along the seawall a little farther are the look-out tablets of the Port of Vancouver describing major harbor activities: cruise ship traffic, resource exports, etc. The Brockton Point lighthouse has information markers and nearby is the *Chehalis* monument for the ship sunk in the harbor in 1906. Near the totem-poles is a marker describing the 1865 arrival of pioneer mill owner Edward Stamp. Elek Imredy's 1972 *Girl In Wetsuit* statue is on a large offshore rock near a replica figurehead from the *Empress of Japan*. Across from the children's water park is Lumbermen's Arch, an enormous log placed to honor the province's forestry workers.

The location—on the right side of the park drive at the north foot of Pipeline Rd.—where Stanley Park was declared open by Mayor David Oppenheimer in September 1888 is marked by a 1988 plaque (Lord Stanley made a visit in 1889 to dedicate the park named for him). Three tablets at the south end of the Lions Gate Bridge describe its completion in November 1938, the crossing by King George VI and Queen Elizabeth in May of 1939 and the 1986 lighting of the span. The steamship *Beaver* was wrecked on the rocks below Prospect Point, an event marked with a cairn above. At Ferguson Point is a stone monument into which is carved a likeness of poet Pauline Johnson. This area was the site of a coast defence fort during World War II and is marked with a plaque. Nearby is a tribute to the Com-monwealth forces who served in Burma from 1941 to 1945. On the seawall near Third Beach are plaques describing the Siwash Rock legend. Also nearby is a stone plaque to honor the master stonemason James Cunningham who worked on the seawall for more than 30 years. As you exit the park at Beach Ave. take note of a bust by Charles Marega of David Oppenheimer, Vancouver's second mayor.

Kitsilano to UBC

The Flame of Peace monument at the south end of the Burrard Bridge was a city centennial gift donated by several sponsors. One of the city's most photographed objects is George Norris's stainless steel sculpture of *The Crab* in front of the Centennial Museum and H.R. MacMillan Planetarium in Vanier Park. The plaque explains the significance of the crab and conceals a time capsule. As you walk around the perimeter of the park and to the nearby Maritime Museum look for several monuments and plaques (Elsje Point, the Gate to the North-West Passage, a George Vancouver sculpture, a bust by sculptor Elek Imredy in the City of Vancouver Archives of archivist Maj. J.S. Matthews, the 30-metre tall centennial totem-pole in front of the Maritime Museum, and more).

A cairn donated by lifeguards and dedicated to George Burrows, who supervised Vancouver's beaches and pools from 1931 to 1971, is near the bathhouse at Kitsilano Beach. At the north foot of Trafalgar and Dunbar Sts. are informational signs on "Birds to See on The Point Grey Foreshore." Vancouver's oldest building, the Hastings Mill store, is at Alma and Point Grey Rd. Built in 1865 near Gastown it has been converted to a museum. The Vancouver Youth Hostel near Jericho Beach has a marker describing this former military base and golf course. On a stone by the footpath just west of the Locarno Beach concession stand is a marker to Charles Borden, the "father of B.C. archaeology." His famous excavation on this beach discovered evidence of human occupation dating back more than 3,000 years. At the west end of Spanish Banks is an anchor with text describing the 1791 visit of Spanish pilot Narvaez and the meeting the following year of Valdes, Galiano and Vancouver.

The campus of the University of B.C. occupies more than 400 hectares. Several markers and a monument to Inazo Nitobe of Japan are found at the gardens named in his honor. Just above the rose gardens at the north end of Main Mall is a large bronze map depicting the mountains in the distance. On the Main Mall are the Ladner Carillon and Clock Tower honoring pioneers William and Thomas Ladner and a cairn commemorating the UBC student "Great Trek" of 1922. Along the East Mall many trees have been planted by various graduation classes. The Professor Frank Buck Cairn commemorates the student bodies that financed a number of UBC buildings.

West Vancouver

At the foot of 13th St. in Ambleside Beach is a cairn honoring the first white explorer to visit the Burrard Inlet area (1791), Jose Narvaez. One block west is the old ferry ticket office at Ferry Square where a plaque details how from 1913 to 1947 North Shore residents could catch a ferry across the inlet. On the northeast corner of 17th and Marine Dr. is a large monument carved from an11-tonnne piece of jade extracted from the Cry Lake jade mine near Kutcho Creek, B.C. Just up the street at 680-17th is a plaque honoring Gertrude Lawson; her attractive old home is now the West Vancouver Museum and Archives.

Squamish / Whistler

B.C. Rail's history is indicated by a marker on Hwy. 99 north of Lions Bay. There are several informational signs explaining the history, the subtidal life and the wrecks and reefs found at Porteau Cove Provincial Park. Just north of Britannia Beach are markers on the Britannia Mines and Foulger Creek areas and a plaque honoring Giuseppe Garibaldi after whom Mount Garibaldi is named. At the top of Whistler Mountain are plaques and informational signs on the surrounding area and its wildlife.

North Vancouver

At the foot of Lonsdale Ave. are plaques describing the history of the thriving business district which developed there at the turn of the century and of the ferry traffic across Burrard Inlet from 1893 to 1958. In the northwest corner of the park is "Chiba Garden" with an informational sign describing North Vancouver's association with its sister city of Chiba, Japan. At the western end of Waterfront Park lies Sailor Point where a monument and plaques recognize local maritime history including a tribute to those who gave their lives at sea. Next door to St. Paul's Indian Church, the oldest (1884) surviving mission church in the Vancouver area, is a plaque dedicated by the Squamish Nation honoring all native servicemen who served in the two world wars, Cyprus and Vietnam. On Keith Rd. at Mountain Hwy. is a cairn marking the Lillooet Trail to the Cariboo via Howe Sound in 1877.

Burnaby

A plaque at city hall honors Robert Burnaby and more can be found at Heritage Village next door including one dedicated to the beautifully restored Parker Carousel. Simon Fraser University was opened in 1965 and has various informative plaques and a bust of Mahatma Gandhi in the science complex courtyard. Just below SFU is Burnaby Mountain Park containing the Japanese *Kamui Mintara Playground of the Gods* wooden

sculptures with descriptive tablets.

Port Moody

Col. Richard C. Moody of the Royal Engineers is honored in the area named for him and by a park in New Westminster. St. John St. has a cairn commemorating the CPR's last spike and the first (1886) regular passenger train into Port Moody.

Coquitlam

Maquabeak Park at the north end of the Port Mann Bridge has a plaque in memory of Dorothy Maquabeak Francis who founded the first Native Friendship Centres in Canada. Many markers are found on the grounds of Riverview Hospital where gardens and a large collection of trees indigenous to British Columbia are described in plaques. One of the steepest grades Rick Hansen had to endure on the final day of his epic 1987 wheelchair journey is marked by a sign on Thermal Dr. Blue Mountain Park is now the home of the old CPR station building originally located at Fraser Mills and is marked by an informational sign.

Port Coquitlam

The Terry Fox Library at Wilson Ave. and Mary Hill Rd. has a statue of Terry. His parents, Betty and Rolland Fox, officially opened the library on October 29, 1983. A commemorative plaque was unveiled.

Pitt Meadows

Pitt Meadows Memorial Park honors the Lions International Club for landscape improvements and walkways made possible by them.

Richmond

The road leading to Vancouver International Airport is named in honor of Grant McConachie, Canadian aviation pioneer. Other pilots are remembered on a large marker found on the airport's departures level. A Wall of Coins from Richmond's centennial is in the lobby of city hall and Harry (Silver) Minns is honored with a plaque inside the nearby ice rink for 50 years of amateur sports work. Several thoughtful inscriptions are placed throughout the Chinese gardens of the Buddhist temple at 9160 Steveston Hwy.

Travel west from the south end of No. 3 Rd. along the dyke and stop at London Farm and the Britannia Heritage Shipyard. A time capsule to be opened in 2039 and a marker have been placed in the Steveston Community Centre to give citizens a window on the community of 1989. A large national historic marker on the West Coast fisheries sits by the Gulf of Georgia Cannery and a commemorative plaque honoring the arrival of the first Japanese immigrant is in nearby Garry Point Park.

Delta

Ladner's Landing, the original government wharf and first stop for ships entering the Fraser River,

is marked with a plaque at Elliott and Chisholm Sts. The children of pioneer William Henry Ladner erected a plaque in 1932 on the clock tower beside the museum. He and his brother Thomas Ellis Ladner were the first settlers in the area named for them. Delta pioneers are remembered by a large sculpture beside the hospital in the 4500 block of Harvest Dr.

White Rock / South Surrey

At the junction of Elgin and Crescent Rd. a cairn marks the Semiahmoo Trail, the ancient native travelway linking tribal villages in the White Rock area to the salmon grounds of the Fraser. Nearby in the 13700 block of Crescent Rd. is a plaque on historic Stewart Farmhouse built in 1894. At 148th St. and 20th Ave. is a plaque marking the original 1873 stage coach route, the Semiahmoo Wagon Rd., from New Westminster to the U.S. border. Pope John Paul II had the Semiahmoo Footbridge dedicated to him at Marine Dr. and Stayte Rd.

Surrey / Fort Langley / Chilliwack

Along Zero Ave. from the Peace Arch at the Canada/U.S. border are markers every mile along the 49th parallel. An overpass at the southern 176th St. entrance to Cloverdale is dedicated to a Surrey RCMP officer killed in 1974 while on duty near this site. A block east at Hwy. 10 is a granite tablet marking the 1923 completion of the Pacific Highway. In downtown Cloverdale are various heritage and commemorative sites of note, especially at the entrance to the fairgrounds where a plaque honors the Clover Valley School built in 1882. On the fairgrounds is the Surrey Museum with a marker describing the original municipal hall. Within the city hall/courthouse/police station complex is a cairn honoring other Surrey RCMP officers.

Bear Creek Park has a marker commemorating the Semiahmoo Trail of 1861 and nearby is a sign describing the history of the park. A number of roads in Surrey have heritage markers noting the original street names associated with pioneer settlements or geographical locations. Some locals still use the old names.

A number of plaques are found both in and around Fort Langley, built by the Hudson's Bay Company in 1827 and rebuilt in 1840. At the entrance is a monument and plaque to the SS *Beaver*. Beside the fort is the Langley Centennial Museum. Nearby at the north foot of Glover Rd. is the old CNR station which once sat about 45 metres farther west.

facing page: Queen Victoria monument, Stanley Park; Centennial Rocket, Cambie Bridge; Bannister–Landy statue, Hastings Park. vs, vp, vs

IN·MEMORY·OF
VICTORIA·THE·GOOD
THIS·MONUMENT·IS
ERECTED·BY·THE
SCHOOL·CHILDREN
OF·VANCOUVER·1905

Fountains of Greater Vancouver
Elizabeth Godley

For a region set in a rain forest, the Lower Mainland, particularly Vancouver, boasts an astonishing number of fountains, ponds and reflecting pools. Their suitability in a damp climate has been questioned, notably in 1966 by Aeneas (cct) Bell-Irving, then a Vancouver alderman, who stated: "There is one thing we don't need and that is more fountains, because God has given us a perfectly wonderful supply of rain." Bell-Irving suggested bonfires would be more appropriate.

Despite this, many of the region's fountains and pools give pleasure. Some economically recirculate the water from air-conditioning systems, and the soothing sound of falling water not only masks traffic noise but also reminds urbanites of nature's eternal presence.

VANCOUVER

Lost Lagoon's **Jubilee Fountain,** probably the city's best-known fountain, was designed by Lennox McKenzie (b. 1900), installed in 1936, and restored for Expo in 1986. The fountain was purchased from Chicago, a left-over from that city's world fair. When it was installed, some city residents complained about the expenditure of $35,000 in the depths of the Great Depression. The fountain was just one part of an extensive display to celebrate Vancouver's 50th anniversary. "The original design ... had a large fountain between two smaller ones," McKenzie said in 1980, revealing that he had had to devise an electrical gizmo to produce the effect he was after, "an infinite pattern of colors using just red, blue, green and amber."

In full flow, the **Centennial Fountain** in the 800-block Georgia Street (marble, ceramic and glass tile; 4.5 metres high) pumps more then 1.3 million litres of water an hour. Robert H. Savery, a landscape architect with the provincial department of public works, drew up the basic design, and artist Alex Svoboda, of Conn Art Studios in Toronto, devised the sculpture and mosaics. A gift from the province to commemorate the union of the Crown Colony of Vancouver's (sic) Island with the mainland, the fountain was the subject of much press speculation before its unveiling on December 15, 1966. Entries to a "Feign the Fountain" cartoon contest sponsored by *The Vancouver Sun,* included several mocking depictions of then-Premier W.A.C. Bennett. Carvings on the marble pillars portray "the Earth Goddess Dana . . . holding the cup of healing and friendship," and the Celts, "The ancient

bardic seagoing people, who were the forebears of so many Canadians."

The Queen Victoria memorial (1905, granite, 1.8 metres high) in Stanley Park near the Rowing Club, was designed by James Blomfield (1872-1951). Blomfield, whose father was a renowned supplier of art-glass in Vancouver and Victoria (he installed the commemorative windows for the Victoria Legislature), also designed Vancouver's coat of arms in 1903.

Victory Square drinking fountain (marble/ceramic tile, 1.2 metres high) was donated by Mrs. Donald Stewart, in memory of her son, Norman, killed in World War I. The Stewart family owned Pioneer Laundry, begun in 1890, which merged in 1958 with Nelson Laundries. The fountain was designed by Jack Hambleton (b. 1916, England), who considered himself self-taught, despite some formal training at the Vancouver School of Art.

Joe Fortes Memorial Drinking Fountain in Alexandra Park, (bronze-granite, 2 metres high, 1926) was designed by Charles Marega. Serap-him (Joe) Fortes was Vancouver's first paid lifeguard at English Bay, and gave swimming lessons for 30 years until his death in 1922. The Vancouver Kiwanis Club raised $5,000 for the fountain. Marega also designed the King Edward VII drinking fountain, in the 700-block Hornby. The cement, bronze and ceramic tile fountain, installed in 1912, was donated by the Imperial Order of the Daughters of the Empire and dedicated by Mayor James Finlay. Bronze drinking cups were attached to the fountain but these were quickly stolen. Now only the bronze pins that once held the chained cups remain.

The two-level drinking fountain (for humans and dogs) on the north side of Robson just east of Burrard, was donated as a centennial memorial by Mrs. Theresa Galloway.

Fountain of Time at Vancouver's Public Library, 350 West Georgia, Joseph Montague (b 1955, Montreal), concrete/stone/mosaic. One of the first works of art commissioned under Vancouver's public art policy, this fountain takes its theme from a sixth-century Persian painting. The chute wall is cleverly constructed from sections of concrete pipe.

Salmon Fountain-Shrine at the corner of Abbott and Water in Gastown was designed by Sam Carter, an instructor at the Emily Carr Institute of Art and Design, in 1989.

Queen Elizabeth Plaza fountain (1971, bronze/steel, 6 metres high) was designed by Gerhard Hans Class (b 1924, Germany), as a gift to the city and province from the German-Canadian community. Class' original design was of two granite figures, male and female, representing

immigrants, but money was tight.

The cast-concrete fountain, 601 West Broadway (1980, 6 metres high) was designed by Paul Deggan (b.1932), a West Vancouver artist.

Transcendence at the Thea Koerner Graduate Student Centre, UBC (bronze, 4.2 metres high, 1961), was designed by Jack Harman (b. 1927, Vancouver) and cast at his North Vancouver foundry. This was the sculptor's first commission. When he suggested the design should be larger to balance the bulk of the building behind it, the Koerner family doubled his budget.

Crab at 1100 Chestnut (Vancouver Museum; stainless steel, 6.7 metres high, 1958), was designed by George Norris (b. 1928, Victoria). The work cost $44,000, a gift from the women of Vancouver for Canada's centennial. Waterworks were devised by John Bell, of Bell & Reading Engineers, West Vancouver. The crab in Haida legend protected the harbor, as well as being a sign of the zodiac. Norris, a graduate of the old Vancouver School of Art, designed the fountain's seven water jets to be increased or decreased, depending on the weather or for special occasions such as the Sea Festival.

Flame of Peace fountain, south end of Burrard Bridge (1986) was designed by Sam Carter and Judith Reeve. The landscaping and other additions to this fountain have never been completed.

Twin Fountains 1600 Beach Avenue (copper and steel, 1965) was designed by Lionel Thomas (b. 1915) and commissioned by Block Bros.

Fountain of the Pioneers 500 Burrard St., (silicone bronze, 4 metres high, 1969) was designed by Seattle sculptor George Tsutakawa. In a 1969 *Province* interview, the artist said that a fountain involves three elements: heaven, earth and water. "What really makes a fountain is water, the most elusive and mysterious element of all."

Swedish Fountain VanDusen Gardens (cast bronze, .9 metres high, 1975), by Per Nilsson-Ost, was donated by Swedish community—led by Vancouver real-estate magnate Edwin Albert Alm. Cost was $50,000. Eight bronze panels depict Swedish involvement in British Columbia industry.

Waterfall at 1100 Melville (SunLife Plaza), designed by landscape architects Don Vaughan & Associates.

Waterfall, 1500 West Georgia, 1975. Architect Peter Cardew, then working for Rhone & Iredale, designed this spectacular "wall of water."

Fountain, 475 West Georgia (former B.C. Turf Building). Architect Zoltan Kiss designed this building, which dates from 1976, but believes the fountain was added later.

Fountain/sculpture at Pacific and Beach, designed by Bob Turner, was donated by the

Davis family, scrap-metal merchants as part of Vancouver's 1986 Legacies and Gifts Program. The palm trees, also a gift, were planted later.

Fountain 850 Burrard. This somewhat basic fountain was designed by Eng & Wright, the architects responsible for the building. "We thought it would be a nice place to have a water feature, so we put one in," explains architect Martin Brookner.

Fountain south of 666 Burrard (Park Place), by landscape architect Paul Friedburg (b 1931) of New York. Asked to design "an active, visually attractive, socially relevant plaza that would complement not only Park Place and Christ Church Cathedral, but the city too," Friedburg and his team also had to hide the alley service area and create a garden on top of a three-level underground garage.

Law Courts, Robson Square, the pool and waterfall (completed 1973), were designed by architect Arthur Erickson and landscape architect Cornelia Oberlander. The pool doubles as a holding tank for the building's fire-sprinkler system.

Indoor Fountain Pacific Centre III, (1989) designed by Toronto architect Eb Zeidler: "The fourth wall of the shopping centre couldn't be stores, because of a building next door, so we chose the waterfall as an 'event'" His inspiration was the Villa d'Este, an Italian Renaissance villa just outside Rome dating from 1550, "the first water park, the most wonderful water event ever made."

Fountains, Canada Place (1986) by Eb Zeidler, Toronto architect. One fountain, seen as you enter the atrium, resembles a waterfall; the other, the 'Pacific Rim' fountain, symbolizes Canada's connection with the Orient.

Fountain Blue Horizon Hotel, 1225 Robson. Pavelek & Associates, a Vancouver firm better known as landscape architects, also has an interior-design department, which created this graceful fountain as part of a major facelift for the hotel in 1991. Artist Markian Olynyk designed the glass.

Queen Elizabeth Park's fountain and water features atop the reservoir were designed by landscape architect Bob Royston of San Francisco, father of the post-war "California style," a relaxed, informal approach to landscape. Presented to the city, together with the Bloedel Conservatory and Henry Moore's *Knife Edge,* by Prentice Bloedel in 1969.

Fountain Price Waterhouse building, 601 West Hastings. Architect Graham Tudor and landscape architect Jane Durante designed this fountain. Tudor's interest in mosaics and the zodiac is evident.

Waterfall fountain, on Melville outside Bentall

Centre IV, was designed by landscape architects Vaughan Durante Perry.

Fountain, concrete, 808 Nelson. The building was designed by architects Romses Kwan, but the name of the designer of the fountain has been lost in the mists of time.

No one seems to know who designed the **fountain outside the main library at the University of British Columbia,** where engineering freshmen once were ceremoniously dunked. Frank Buck first landscaped the university grounds.

B.C. Hydro building, 333 Dunsmuir, the **blue-painted steel fountain** was designed by Alberta artist Tony Bloom, who won the commission in a competition. "The complexity was in making it look simple," says Bloom, who was trained as a physicist. The design was inspired by *shishi odoshi,* a bamboo rod that fills with water and swings to the ground with a loud noise, traditionally used in Japanese gardens to scare away deer. A smaller, more traditional fountain in the grounds was designed by landscape architects Durante Kreuk.

Cathedral Place, Dunsmuir and Richards, the reflecting pool forms part of a landscape designed by architect Bruno Freschi, now dean of the school of architecture and planning at the State University of New York at Buffalo, with assistance from landscape architect Jane Durante. It was commissioned by the city. The plaza, which sits atop a B.C. Hydro substation, contains a theatre-in-the-round, which used to be programmed by Vancouver's social planning department. The columns in the plaza double as exhaust fans, and the pool water is part of the substation cooling system.

Fountain, near 1450 Creekside, designed by architect Larry Doyle and built by Pennyfarthing Development Co. in 1987. When Pennyfarthing built their offices, the city granted them a development permit in return for creating public open space nearby. Doyle and Pennyfarthing VP Peter Isler considered adding a gazebo to the little park, but eventually decided on a fountain, thinking it would be less prone to vandalism. Doyle came up with the ziggurat-like design, a concrete core faced with tiles. The fountain boasts a spectacular central jet of water, but electricity bills for its operation became too onerous, and it is turned on only occasionally in summer. In Isler's opinion, fountains are an expensive nuisance.

Fountain at Discovery Square (Burrard SkyTrain Station) was designed by Per Kreuk of landscape architects Vaughan Durante. The initial design called for a larger fountain, but feedback from the public prompted a more subtle approach.

Fountain in the plaza behind 1333 West Broadway was done by landscape architect Christopher Phillips.

Courtyard at 1166 Melville, landscape architects Durante Kreuk took a cue from the nearby wall mural of orca whales, fashioning "a plane of water" to separate the area.

Reflecting pond at 1075 West Georgia, still known as the MacMillan Bloedel Building although the forest company has moved elsewhere, was designed by architect Arthur Erickson. Jets of water were added later.

Water fall at Bayshore Gardens, west of the Bayshore Hotel at Coal Harbour, was designed by Durante Kreuk, who also used pools of water to separate the residential towers on Coal Harbour between Denman and Cardero, and devised a series of connecting pools in the public space to the north.

Fountain in the plaza at 808 Beach, completed in 1993, was designed by landscape architect Jerry Vegelatos. His initial plan was to draw attention to the sloping site and refer to the life-cycle of the salmon by forcing a stream of water uphill. However, the design was modified, and now comprises a sphere of black granite, a stream flowing over small stones, and a cascade of water that splashes into False Creek.

Fountain outside Wall Centre, Burrard Street, was designed by Bruno Freschi and completed in 1995. Originally designed with more jets, the fountain parallels Burrard Street and complements the honey locust trees in the garden behind it.

BURNABY

Fountain at Ismailia Jamatkhana Centre, a mosque at 4010 Canada Way, by architect Bruno Freschi. Lutz Haufschild designed the windows. Water is a symbol of life for Moslems, as it is for many peoples.

Civic Square, Metrotown, water feature designed by landscape architects Durante and Partners and the SWA Group, a California firm.

Burnaby Civic Employees Union Memorial Fountain, 6501 Deer Lake Ave., designed by William Williamson, Westminster Monumental Works, (B.C. granite, 1923). Erected to honor union members killed in World War I, this fountain was originally located on Kingsway near Edmonds at the old Municipal Hall. In 1974, it was moved to Burnaby Village Museum.

Fountain, Royal Oakland Park (1994). A collaboration between Burnaby parks department and landscape architects Durante Kreuk. This fountain, constructed in 1994, contains recycled materials from Oakalla Prison, which once stood on the site.

Jubilee fountain and archway, Earl and Jennie

Lohn Perennial Garden, Central Park (north-east entrance on Kingsway), landscape architect Kate Clark of Burnaby's parks department, (1993). The granite archway once graced the original 1891 Vancouver Club.

WEST VANCOUVER

Landscape architect Don Vaughan designed two fountains for his home municipality. One, **Granite Assemblage,** at the foot of 14th Street (1989, $480,000), doubled as his graduating project at Emily Carr Institute of Art and Design, when Vaughan returned as a mature student, and was inspired both by John Cage's music and the ruins at Olympus, Greece. The other, on Marine Drive at 14th Street, incorporates a chunk of jade that was presented to the municipality by the president of Husky Oil, and makes reference to a stream that once flowed nearby.

RICHMOND

Richmond Cultural Centre, 7700 Minoru Gate, **Fountain,** by Tony O'Regan of CJP Architects, completed in 1994.

SURREY

Surrey Taxation Centre (main entrance), 9755 King George Highway. **Fountain** by Ruth Beer. This fountain's stark simplicity and sharp angular planes contrast sharply with the softer tones of natural brick and wood that surround the entrance to the taxation centre.

NORTH VANCOUVER

City Hall Water feature, 141 West 14th Street. Designed by landscape architects Vaughan Durante around a venerable black-walnut tree (since died), this complex of streams and pools was meant to evoke the North Shore's natural landscape. The original design has been much modified.

Who's Got the Umbrella?, Deep Cove Cultural Centre, 4360 Gallant, Greg Kawczynski (b. 1953, Poland), marble, 1.5 metres by 1.5 metres by 9 metres, 1993. This fountain symbolizes protection for the children of the community. Kawczynski, who immigrated from Poland in 1989 and lives in Deep Cove, presented this fountain to the cultural centre. He travelled to the Leo d'Or mine on northern Vancouver Island himself to get the marble, which was donated.

Capilano Road and Ridgeway abstract fountain by George Norris, (bronze alloy, 1968). This piece was commissioned by the District of North Vancouver.

Joe Fortes Memorial Fountain, designed by Charles Marega, 1926. vs

Charles Marega
Peggy Imredy

ONE OF BRITISH Columbia's most prolific sculptors, Charles Marega (he changed his name from Carlos in the 1920s when he became a Canadian citizen) was born September 24, 1871 in Lucinico, in the commune of Gorizia, then part of the Austro-Hungarian Empire. He received his technical training in plaster work in Mariano, Italy and studied in Vienna and Zurich. In Zurich he worked under Herman Panitz, marrying Panitz's widow Berta (nee Schellenberg) in 1899.

The Maregas arrived in Vancouver in October 1909 en route to California. When they woke up the following day they could see, beneath a brilliant blue sky, a frosting of snow on the mountains across Burrard Inlet. The scene reminded Berta of her beloved Switzerland. They decided to stay.

The timing was excellent: the newspaper announced a memorial gate to be built at the entrance to Stanley Park to honor the late David Oppenheimer, Vancouver's second mayor. The artist approached would be the famous American, Augustus St. Gaudens. Two weeks later the embarrassed committee announced they had learned St. Gaudens had died two years earlier. But they were still willing to spend $40,000 (in 1909 dollars, remember) on the monument.

By the time Marega won the commission in early 1910 the plans were reduced to a bronze bust. Marega was paid $3,000—with a little extra for the granite pedestal. Next the Imperial Order Daughters of the Empire commissioned a fountain in tribute to King Edward VII, who died May 6, 1910. The fountain, bearing a bas-relief of the King's face, now sits on the Hornby Street side of the Vancouver Art Gallery.

His next major commission was in Victoria, where architect F.M. Rattenbury was designing the parliament buildings. Rattenbury's plan for the library wing included 14 statues of famous figures from British Columbia's past. Marega worked on them until 1914, modeling three-foot maquettes which were sent to Victoria where a stone carver turned them into figures nine feet tall.

Marega's training in plaster work drew commissions for ceiling and fireplace ornamentation for Shaughnessy's finest homes. Still visible is the ceiling ornamentation in Alvo Von Alvensleben's mansion, today's Crofton House School for Girls.

During World War I there were no commissions, but Marega busied himself creating small sculptures which he could not sell. He found inspiration in the Canadian soldier and local native people, works which did not appeal to Vancouver's newly rich, who preferred idealized or Grecian-style sculpture.

After the war Marega provided the now-lost plaster work for the Capitol and Strand theatres. After two years in Switzerland, the Maregas returned to Vancouver and rejoined the city's art circles: The Studio Club, British Columbia Society of Fine Art and the British Columbia Art League formed to promote the idea of an art school and gallery. Both Charles and Berta served on committees to set professional standards in exhibitions. The Vancouver School of Decorative and Applied Arts opened in 1925, eventually becoming the Vancouver School of Art (today it's the Emily Carr Institute of Art & Design.) Marega was the sculpture teacher, a part-time position he held until his death.

The late 1920s were busy years for Marega with commissions for the President Warren Harding Memorial in Stanley Park, the Joe Fortes Memorial Fountain at English Bay, ornamental work at the Orpheum Theatre and the plaster work at the lavish Reifel mansion, *Shannon,* at 57th and Granville. He sculpted many of the motifs for the Marine Building.

The Vancouver Art Gallery opened at its Georgia Street location in 1931. Marega was commissioned to create large busts of Michelangelo and DaVinci to flank the entrance, and a frieze of medallions of famous artists. When the gallery moved, and the old building was demolished, the busts and medallions were sent to a garbage dump. Luckily they were rescued. The busts now rest with a private collector in the Fraser Valley. The medallions are in gallery storage.

The Burrard Street bridge, opened in 1932, is decorated with Marega's sculpture (the busts of George Vancouver and Harry Burrard; the city's coat of arms). In 1934 his beloved Berta died. From that time, regardless of his commissions and work, life drained from him. The statue of Captain Vancouver in front of City Hall, and the lions at the Stanley Park entrance to the Lions Gate Bridge were both unveiled during the last year of his life. The lions, his most famous work, ironically represent a discouraging low point in his life. Marega wished to have them cast in bronze, but the builders wanted a cheaper version in concrete.

Marega was 68 when he died March 27, 1939 after teaching a class at the Vancouver School of Art. As was said at his funeral, "There is no need to build him a monument—because of his sculpture he will never be forgotten."

Bridges of Greater Vancouver
Robert Harris

Vancouver's port and marine traffic have been a major factors in the design of local bridges. If for initial economy, a bridge is built low over the water, a movable span must be provided, such as a swing or lift section. About a quarter of Greater Vancouver's bridges still have a movable section. The early bridges were mostly of timber, a plentiful local resource, but their low clearances and short spans made them vulnerable to marine traffic.

Vancouver's first bridges radiated over False Creek from the growing city core to the extensive undeveloped lands to the south and west. These are described going from east to west along False Creek.

Westminster Avenue Trestle
now Main Street 1876–1909/1909–1921
This low timber trestle, 218 metres long, was the first big bridge in the Vancouver area. It was built at the narrows halfway along the original False Creek to carry the road from Granville to the older City of New Westminster. The road, now Kingsway, was laid out by the Royal Engineers as the "False Creek Trail" from New Westminster.

The bridge was widened in 1890 to carry streetcar tracks. In 1909 a steel bascule lift was added. In 1921 the east half of False Creek was filled for yards of the Great Northern (now Burlington Northern) and the Canadian Northern Pacific (now part of Canadian National Railways). The obsolete bridge was removed.

GNR Trestle
over False Creek to Columbia Street Yard on Burrard Inlet c. 1908–1921
The Vancouver, Westminster and Yukon Railway, a subsidiary of the Great Northern, built this bridge to their small yard in downtown Vancouver, between Columbia and Carrall streets. The bridge was removed when the GNR made better yard space by filling the False Creek flats as far west as Main Street.

Georgia Viaduct
1915–72
This was built in 1913–15 for the City of Vancouver to extend Georgia Street over the CPR's Beatty Street yard. It was named the "Hart McHarg" bridge for a World War I hero, but the name did not last.

A classic product of low bidding ($494,000) and meagre supervision, it was never a sound bridge. Streetcar tracks were laid but never used. Every second lamppost was removed to save weight. Much blacktop was used to fill mysterious sags and hollows in the deck. People passing below were injured by falling concrete, and con-

crete spans were propped with timber. The bridge was replaced by the parallel Georgia and Dunsmuir viaducts in 1972, each carrying three lanes of one-way traffic.

Georgia and Dunsmuir Viaducts
1972–
These replaced the crumbling original Georgia Viaduct. The alignments suit the city's downtown one-way street policy, with Georgia eastbound, Dunsmuir westbound. The two structures cost $11.2 million.

Cambie (Connaught) Bridges
1891–1912/1912–1985/1985–
The first bridge was named for the Governor General of the day, but "Cambie" was its usual name, matching the street that it carried. Built for $12,000, the first bridge was a simple piled timber trestle with a trussed timber swing span near the middle.

The next bridge was a four-lane, medium level steel bridge, 1,247 metres long with streetcar tracks, completed in 1911 for $740,000. The concept was similar to the second Granville Bridge (1909). The navigation span was a steel through-truss swing span which the city would open on four hours' notice. In 1953 it opened 79 times. Even in its later years, it was opened once or twice a week. The trusses of the swing span projected through the bridge deck, dividing the two outer lanes from the two inner lanes. This caused many motor vehicle collisions. In April 1915 the creosoted wood deck caught fire, with the collapse of a 24.4 metre steel side span.

The entire Cambie crossing was closed for nine months, starting November 1984, while the present higher six-lane concrete bridge was merged with the existing approaches. The new bridge cost $50 million.

Granville (Street) Bridge
1889–1909/1909–1954/1954–
The first Granville Bridge was a low timber trestle, 732 metres long, giving access to the Marpole/Eburne area via the North Arm Road (now Granville Street). The navigation span, near the north end, was a trussed timber swing span, hogged with wire ropes to a central wooden tower. It was largely designed by the CPR, and cost $16,000. It was a heavier version of the CPR's Kitsilano trestle, immediately to the west. The alignment was directly below the present bridge but extended only from Beach Avenue to 3rd Avenue. In 1891 the bridge was widened on both sides for streetcar tracks, except where the tracks converged for the swing span.

This bridge was replaced in 1909 by a longer, medium-level steel bridge with a through truss swing span. The new bridge extended from Pacific to 4th, east of the original bridge.

The present eight-lane structure was built back

on the original alignment but longer again and 27.4 metres above False Creek. After the bridge opened in 1954, steel plate girders salvaged from the old bridge made barges for constructing the foundations of Oak Street Bridge.

Recent improvements to the bridge include increasing its earthquake resistance, and installing higher curbs and median barriers.

CPR Kitsilano Trestle
1886–1903/1903–1982
Initially the CPR extended as far west as Trafalgar Street on English Bay, requiring a piled timber trestle across the mouth of False Creek. Later a short steel plate girder swing span and adjacent steel through-truss span were installed to conform more closely with the Navigable Waters Protection Act. During World War II, when ships built in False Creek moved to English Bay, the steel truss span was floated aside.

In 1902 B.C. Electric Railway operated the bridge as part of their interurban system to Marpole, and south and east. The bridge was removed in 1982.

Burrard Bridge
1932–
This six-lane highway bridge carries traffic high above False Creek. The bridge piers have provision for a rapid transit vertical lift span beneath the highway deck. To hide the steel superstructure of the main span, an architectural concrete portal with illuminated windows was installed at each end. Cyclists share the sidewalks with pedestrians.

The next 26 bridges, or former bridges, link the Vancouver-New Westminster peninsula with the rest of British Columbia. Starting at the Port Mann Bridge, we make a clockwise tour, ending at the Second Narrows Bridges.

Port Mann Highway Bridge
Fraser River 1964–
This elegant bridge carries the Trans-Canada Highway across the Fraser River at the most stable part of its lower channel, above the two earlier bridges at New Westminster, the apex of the Fraser delta. The high-level centre span is 365.7 metres, framed as a stiffened tied arch, in concept an inverted suspension bridge. Erection of the main span employed balanced cantilevering from the north and south main piers. The two halves of the centre span were suspended by cable tiebacks over temporary steel towers until closure. The bridge is now overcrowded at rush hours.

Fraser River Swing Bridge
New Westminster, originally road/rail, low-level 1904–
This great, $1-million doubledeck bridge was built by the province. It was the first crossing of the lower Fraser River, giving road and rail access south from the Vancouver-New Westminster peninsula to the farmlands of Langley, Surrey and Delta; to the Old Yale Road up the

Fraser Valley; to the Pacific Highway south to Seattle; and to three important railways.

The bridge is a fine example of late 19th century engineering, with pins and eyebars for the main tension members. The steel spans cover 732 metres, plus 2,352 metres of timber approach trestles. The foundations were a major challenge, being driven as much as 43 metres below high water. Nelson Island granite from upcoast was used for facing the pier shafts.

Both road and rail traffic increased steadily over the years. The upper (highway) deck was only one-way width for trucks. In 1937 the upper deck was superseded by the Pattullo Bridge alongside. This released additional load capacity for railway traffic.

The province sold the bridge to Public Works Canada by about 1938. It is now maintained and operated by CNR.

On December 26, 1975, a runaway logging barge, driven by a westerly gale, carried away a 116-metre span of this bridge. Fortunately, Burlington Northern had drawings for a modern 114-metre span recently built at Spokane. This speeded the repair and reopening of this busy but obscure railway bridge.

Pattullo Bridge
Fraser River, New Westminster 1937–
This high-level, four-lane highway bridge is west of the old Fraser River Swing Bridge. The north end springs from the hill on which New Westminster is built, but the lower ground at the south end necessitates long approaches. These were built as light steel truss spans, then encased in concrete. The main span is a tied cantilever arch, giving a clearance of 45.7 metres. Several services have been installed beneath the deck, the heaviest being water mains for the municipalities to the south.

BC Transit SkyBridge
Fraser River, New Westminster 1990–
The SkyBridge, just downstream of Pattullo Bridge, enables commuters from Surrey to avoid the Alex Fraser, Pattullo and Port Mann bridges. It is set skew to the Fraser River to ease the curve coming from New Westminster. It is almost on the line of the original ferry which served the start of the Old Yale Road up the Fraser Valley.

The bridge is cable stayed, like the Alex Fraser, but with the entire deck built of concrete. There are two tracks, enabling SkyTrains to pass on the bridge. With the completion of SkyBridge, the oldest and newest bridges in Greater Vancouver are within sight of each other.

Queensborough Bridge
Lulu Island, low-level road/rail 1891–1913/1913–
The North Arm of the Fraser River was bridged here by the City of New Westminster with a timber highway trestle, connecting the two parts of the city. It was rebuilt in 1913 and 1951 by B.C. Electric Railway for rail access to the industrialized end of Lulu Island. A heavy plate girder swing span takes care of navigation.

The bridge continues in rail freight service to Annacis Island, but was closed to highway traffic in 1960, after the high-level, four-lane Queensborough Bridge was built a little to the west.

Derwent Way Bridge
low-level, road/rail from New Westminster, Annacis Channel, Queensborough, Lulu Island 1955–1986/1986–
This recently reconstructed low-level bridge carries two highway lanes, and a separate rail track. A wide steel girder swing span now provides the navigation opening.

Queensborough Bridge
high-level highway 1960–
The City of New Westminster built this $4-million bridge over the North Arm of the Fraser for access to its suburb of Queensborough at the east end of Lulu Island, and to the Annacis Industrial Estate to the south. It has since become a feeder to Route 91 and the 1986 Alex Fraser (Annacis) Bridge. Queensborough was a toll bridge until bought by the provincial government in November 1966.

Alex Fraser (Annacis) Bridge
high level, Main Channel, Fraser River 1986–
When opened, the 465-metre main span was the worlds longest. The stay cables radiate from two tall concrete towers, founded on large steel pipe piles of similar length. The deck is concrete, laid on steel plate girders. Originally the six-lane deck was restricted to four lanes, the outer lanes being reserved for cyclists and pedestrians. In about a year the bridge had generated sufficient traffic to justify opening all six lanes to vehicles. Pedestrians and cyclists were moved outside the cables.

Annacis Channel East Bridge
1986–
North of Annacis Island, Route 91 crosses Annacis Channel by this medium-level bridge.

Annacis Channel West Bridge
1997–
This three-lane concrete bridge twins the East Bridge. It will elimate the traffic light just north of Annacis Bridge, where Route 91A leaves the road to Queensborough Bridge.

CNR Bridge
low-level, North Arm, Fraser River at Big Bend 1920–
CNR tracks run along the north bank of the Fraser from Sapperton to this bridge; beyond the bridge, on Lulu Island, tracks diverge south and west. There is a steel through-truss swing span.

Knight Street Bridge
North Arm, Fraser River 1974–
This four-lane concrete bridge gives medium-level access above Marine Drive to Lulu Island and both branches of the North Arm of the Fraser at Mitchell Island. There are six lanes as far south as Mitchell Island, where the deck narrows to four lanes.

Construction was balanced cantilever to minimize interference with navigation. The final clearances are 12.2 metres by 79.2 metres over the north channel, and 20.1 by 109.7 metres for the south channel. Innovations included the extensive use of semi-lightweight concrete, and electric heating cables in the deck to minimize de-icing salt in the winter.

Construction took 5 years. The cost, including approaches, was about $15 million. Knight Street Bridge entirely replaced the low-level Fraser Street Bridge 1.6 kilometres to the west, and relieves traffic on Oak Street Bridge. With the completion of the east-west Westminster Highway across Lulu Island, Knight Street Bridge serves Routes 91 and 99 to the south.

Fraser Street Bridge
low-level highway to Mitchell and Lulu islands 1893–1974
This former crossing of the North Arm of the Fraser River connected Fraser Street in Vancouver with No. 5 Road on Lulu Island in Richmond. There was a connection to Mitchell Island en route. The 1905 bridge had a small through-truss swing span, on which the deck was replaced by open steel grating in 1962. Until mechanized in 1948, the bridge was opened by hand. It was obsolete some years before it was replaced by Knight Street Bridge.

Twigg Island Bridge
low-level road/rail 1958–
B.C. Electric Railway built this private road/rail bridge over the north channel of the North Arm to service the Western Canada Steel plant on Twigg Island. The bridge has not been used since 1958. The steel through-trusses, including the swing span, were floated here from the No. 7 Highway Bridge over Pitt River, when the bridge was rebuilt. In turn, the spans had come from the nearby CPR bridge when it was replaced by the present double-track structure.

Oak Street Bridge
high level, North Arm, Fraser River 1957–
This four-lane bridge, on Route 99, also serves Richmond, and was much used to reach Vancouver Airport until completion of the Arthur Laing Bridge in 1975. During the planning, it was the "New Marpole Bridge." With the Middle Arm Bridge, it replaced the old Marpole swing bridge over the North Arm of the Fraser. Tolls were charged until 1959; $1 million was collected in the last year.

Though high enough to avoid interruptions from shipping, it soon became overcrowded at rush hours. The Arthur Laing Bridge to Sea

"When I climbed the timber staircase in that ramshackle old warehouse," Michael Seelig remembers, "and poked my head through a hole in the roofing, I knew immediately we couldn't let the spectacular view of Burrard Bridge and the city skyline slip out of our grasp." He got together with partners Nathan Divinsky and Abe Sacks and, "with the benefit of youth and a blissful ignorance of the industry, we designed a pub, restaurant and wine bistro all under one roof."

Island relieved traffic congestion.

The main spans are heavy steel deck plate girders continuous over three spans of 60.9, 91.4 and 60.9 metres. The deck expansion joints required work. In 1995 two lanes of the bridge were closed alternately for resurfacing the concrete deck. A median barrier and higher curbs were also installed and earthquake resistance enhanced.

Marpole Bridge
low-level rail to Lulu Island 1902–1966/1967–
This CPR crossing carries the Vancouver and Lulu Island Railway over the North Arm of the Fraser River. The bridge and track have long been leased to B.C. Electric Railway (now the Southern Railway of B.C.).

In 1966 the bridge was damaged by a barge. The bridge was rebuilt with full main-line capacity, and a hydraulically operated swing span.

Marpole Bridge
low-level road to Sea and Lulu islands 1889–1901/1901–1957
This bridge, with its tendency to open at inconvenient times, will be familiar to users of Vancouver AMF (Air Mail Field) on Sea Island, now the airfreight and seaplane terminal. (It opened 7,015 times in 1954.) The first bridge served local traffic, mainly farmers and fishermen. It was heavily damaged by river ice in 1890. It was a series of timber through-truss spans, with a steel through-truss for navigation. A similar bridge at the south end continued over the Middle Arm of Fraser River to the north end of No. 3 Road on Lulu Island

The second bridge (1901), with its half-through steel plate girder swing span, was superseded by the Oak Street and Middle Arm bridges, dismantled in 1957. In August 1975 the bridge was replaced by the more direct Arthur Laing Bridge, built higher and longer on the same alignment.

Lulu Island-Sea Island Bridge
1890–c. 1960
The first Middle Arm bridge was built at the north end of No. 3 Road, joining Sea Island to the Bridgeport area of Lulu Island, as an extension of the first Marpole Bridge.

Middle Arm Bridge
low level, Moray Channel 1965–
This two-lane bridge is a short distance south of the preceding bridge, linking the south end of Oak Street Bridge to Sea Island and the airport, as well as serving local traffic. It has a steel plate girder swing span, driven by hydraulic rams.

Dinsmore Bridge
Middle Arm, Fraser River 1969–

facing page, top: BC Transit Skybridge (1990), behind it, the Pattullo Bridge (1937), 1994. vs bottom: The opening of the second Granville Street Bridge, 1909. cva

This two-lane, $845,000 low-level structure connects the densely populated part of Richmond to Sea Island and the airport. It supplements, and is south of, the preceding Middle Arm bridge, and has no movable span.

No. 2 Road Bridge
Middle Arm, Fraser River 1993–
This four-lane road bridge supplements the two preceding bridges over the Middle Arm. It was built by Richmond for $39 million, including approaches. There is no movable span.

Arthur Laing (Hudson Street) Bridge
North Arm, Fraser River 1975–
This is part of a concentration of bridges at the east end of Sea Island. Two parallel independent unpainted steel box girders form the main spans of this four-lane, high-level bridge to Sea Island. It is on the same alignment as its predecessor, the 1899 Marpole Bridge. The problem of traffic flow has been addressed: the length of the several sinuous approaches is much longer than the main spans.

Lions Gate (First Narrows) Bridge
Burrard Inlet 1938–
First Narrows is formed by the delta gravels of Capilano River spreading towards Prospect Point in Stanley Park. The point makes a good high south end to the bridge, but the low flat delta land to the north required the extensive North Viaduct. The bridge was built by Guinness interests and opened in 1938, to assist in developing the upper part of West Vancouver municipality.

Negotiations preceding construction took more than 10 years, with access through Stanley Park almost as contentious as it would be now. When first opened, the bridge had two wide lanes; soon three narrower lanes were laid out, the centre lane for passing. The bridge comprises three suspended spans and a long north viaduct. The main span is 472 metres, with a ship's clearance of 61 metres.

In 1963 the provincial government bought the bridge for $6 million, and soon removed tolls. Overhead lane control signals enabled traffic in the centre lane to be reversed at will.

Modern traffic finds the 2.84 metre lanes narrow; the sidewalks are inadequate for pedestrians and cyclists. Trucks exceeding 13 tonnes are prohibited, as are studded tires. There have been discussions on repairing or replacing the bridge, but no decision had been reached by the end of 1996. At neither end does the provincial government have a free hand: Stanley Park is a Federal Reserve leased directly by the City of Vancouver; the north end crosses Capilano Indian Reserve No. 5.

The Burrard Inlet Tunnel and Bridge Company's Bridge
combined road/rail 1925–1930/1934–1969
The first permanent crossing of Burrard Inlet was at Second Narrows, where the combined deltas of Lynn and Seymour rivers cause a sec-

ond constriction in Burrard Inlet against high ground to the south. Ferry service existed from the earliest times, but the start of the Pacific Great Eastern Railway along the North Shore made a bridge desirable.

The first serious proposal, in 1914, showed a wide combined road/rail bridge having a 177-metre swing span for navigation (the longest in the world) with the deck set high enough to clear the CPR main line at the south end. This was a farsighted plan, since the smaller bridge subsequently built, and rebuilt, was frequently in trouble with shipping.

In 1916 a dam and two sets of locks were proposed for Second Narrows, simplifying the bridging problem, and making the upper harbour into a freshwater lake, with a canal east to Pitt River. This was not built either.

The Burrard Inlet Tunnel and Bridge Company was formed by the North Shore municipalities for the next proposal, resulting in a bridge, a modest version of the 1914 plan, built lower to connect with the CPR tracks. A short bascule span was installed near the south end. This led to barges running under the longer fixed spans, at low tide. Inevitably, a barge got stuck on a rising tide, and dislodged the span. The bridge was closed for more than four years while it was redesigned and rebuilt. The span over the real ships' channel was rebuilt as a 85.3-metre lift span, hoisted between two new steel towers. The new design was more successful; though often hit by shipping, it was never closed for more than 10 days. "Progress" called for an improved crossing. This was done in two stages: on the west side by a high-level road bridge and by a medium-level rail bridge on the east side.

The old bridge could not compete with the convenience of the new; it was closed to highway traffic in 1963, and sold to the CNR for $1.

Second Narrows Highway Bridge
1960–
The new six-lane highway bridge has a cantilevered main span of 350 metres. Construction started in 1956 and ended in 1960. During construction the collapse of the north anchor arm killed 18 men. In 1994 the bridge was renamed The Ironworkers Memorial Bridge. In 1995 its earthquake resistance was upgraded.

CNR Bridge
medium-level rail, Second Narrows 1969–
In 1969 CNR replaced the old BITB rail crossing with a larger, heavier bridge on its east side. This has a vertical lift span which is usually partially raised, allowing free movement of most marine traffic. The CNR passes over the CPR at the south end and continues south through a tunnel to join the CNR main line near Brentwood shopping centre

---

Once the plans for Bridges were on the drawing board, this unlikely trio—Seelig and Divinsky were professors at UBC, Sacks was an industrialist—welcomed two new partners to the consortium: Manny Glaser and George Frankel. They brought with them years of experience in the restaurant industry. The skills of Vancouver's celebrated restaurant designer David Vance completed the picture, and soon the old warehouse was transformed into . . . Bridges! The waterfront restaurant with the wild "eggyolk" exterior was an immediate hit. "We're always moving with the times," says Peter Horwood, who as general manager of Bridges supervises the youthful, enthusiastic staff.

Greater Vancouver Underground
Sandra McKenzie

THE LANDSCAPE BENEATH the sidewalk is one that few of us ever get to explore, though much that affects our daily life happens underground. Here is a mole's eye view of Greater Vancouver.

CPR TUNNEL

The Canadian Pacific Railway tunnel, Vancouver's oldest, was opened in 1932 to eliminate Downtown traffic snarls. It was built by the Northern Construction Company and J.W. Stewart, for $1.6 million. The tunnel is six to 24 metres below the surface and is 1,396 metres in length. It follows an elongated S-curve; starting with the west portal on Burrard Inlet (now the waterfront terminal for SkyTrain), it curves left up Thurlow, and switches back south under Dunsmuir, follows Dunsmuir to Cambie, then curves again almost due south, ending at the east portal near the Georgia Viaduct (now SkyTrain's stadium station).

Though its original use, as a conduit for the CPR transcontinental trains, is now obsolete, the tunnel needed few alterations to route SkyTrain underground—at the stadium station the original single track was widened to accommodate the SkyTrain's dual tracks.

CNR TUNNEL

Connecting the Second Narrows railway bridge with the Burlington Northern line at Gilmore in Burnaby, this train tunnel is more than 45 metres below the surface, more than three kilometres long, eight metres high and five-and-a-half metres wide.

LONSDALE TUNNEL, NORTH VANCOUVER

Below West Esplanade Avenue, west of Lonsdale in North Vancouver, railroad tracks enter a concrete, box-shaped tunnel that passes under the road. The tunnel was originally under the National Harbours Board jurisdiction but is now B.C. Railway-owned. Built in 1928 it is 500 metres long and runs from St. Andrews Avenue to Chesterfield.

B.C. RAILWAY TUNNEL, HORSESHOE BAY, WEST VANCOUVER

Blasted through granite rock right above the ferry terminal, this single-track tunnel replaced more than three kilometres of existing track and eliminated four curves and a timber trestle over Nelson Creek.

CHINATOWN TUNNELS

Extending under Carrall Street and accessed by a winding stairway beneath the Sam Kee Building (the narrowest commercial building in the world) on Pender Street is a tunnel that once held baths, toilets and barber chairs. Other tunnels under Chinatown may once have connected basements.

VANCOUVER HOSPITAL AND HEALTH SCIENCES CENTRE (12TH & OAK SITE)

More than one-and-a-half kilometres of tunnels deliver services and pedestrian traffic beneath the hospital at 12th and Oak. The first link in the system was built in 1912 to connect laundry services with the hospital complex. There is another kilometre-and-a-half or so of pipe tunnel under the hospital's floor.

SHAUGHNESSY HOSPITAL

Now closed, Shaughnessy Hospital's service tunnels contained a central steam plant, pressure reducing stations and service stations, a maintenance shop and a power plant. Also underground were oxygen, water and sewage services. A tunnel joined the main building to the acute-care wing and another connected with the Jean Matheson Pavilion.

POST OFFICE TUNNEL

Built in the late 1950s the tunnel beneath the main post office was obsolete almost before it was completed. It goes from the former CPR depot on Cordova, via Cordova to Richards, from Richards to Dunsmuir and from Dunsmuir to its gaping entrance in the basement of the post office. A two-way conveyor belt carried more than two tonnes of mail per minute from the CPR to the post office. This tunnel, four-and-a-half to 12 metres below the surface and just over two kilometres long, was hand-dug, drilled and blasted (through almost 13 tonnes of sandstone) by Jack Vanim, Art Lemon and their crews at a cost of $1.6 million. Now sealed at its northern (CPR) end, the tunnel was used very briefly before being abandoned.

RESERVOIRS

QUEEN ELIZABETH PARK under the parking area. Two reservoirs with a total capacity of almost 220 million litres.

VANCOUVER HEIGHTS east of Renfrew, north of Hastings. Forty-five million litres, roofed with tennis courts.

CENTRAL PARK on Boundary, between Kingsway and 49th Avenue. Thirty-six million litres.

SASAMAT UNIVERSITY GROUNDS, south of 16th Avenue in the treed area. Capacity is 27 million litres.

NEW WESTMINSTER at 10th and Coquitlam Streets, two reservoirs with a total capacity of more than 113 million litres.

BURNABY MOUNTAIN north of Lake City. Almost 14 million litres.

WHALLEY at 104th Avenue and 146th Street. Thirty-five million litres.

WATER

Vancouver has 1,458 kilometres of water mains and more than 1,609 kilometres of sewers. Many of the major sewer lines were laid in existing creek beds and, through the magic of gravity, fed into the surrounding bodies of water. At one time all waste and rainwater washed into one sewer. These days raw sewage is conveyed by interceptor sewers to the Iona treatment plant.

STEAM

If you see steam rising from a bush on Georgia Street outside the Vancouver Art Gallery, you're looking at one of the supposedly disguised vents in a network of underground steam pipes delivering climate control services (heat or, in the case of air conditioning, steam absorption), domestic hot water and steam for manufacturing purposes to customers of Central Heat Distribution in the Downtown core. The boiler plant is in the former Pacific Press building on Beatty Street. There are about 10.5 kilometres of high-pressure steam pipes between five centimetres and 50 centimetres in diameter running anywhere from one to five metres below street surfaces. Central Heat Distribution heats more than 100 buildings in the Downtown, including B.C. Place, General Motors Place, the new library, major hotels and the Ford Centre.

HYDRO

Beneath the park designed by architect Bruno Freschi, at

Reservoir, Queen Elizabeth Park, 1988. vs

Cathedral Square on Dunsmuir Street across from Holy Rosary Cathedral, lies one of B.C. Hydro's most innovative substations, built to meet long-term electrical load growth. All facilities are fitted below street level in an area measuring 74 metres by 43 metres. A comparable above-ground substation would cover 130 metres by 120 metres. The excavation could hold a six-storey office building.

Power is distributed to customers by underground cables which leave the substation at Richards Street and connect to the existing distribution network via a new duct system. The substation is built for unattended, fully automatic operation. A fibre-optic communications link connects the station to the Dal Grauer substation on Burrard. Six air shafts support the greenhouse-style canopy. There are provisions to extract heated air from the substation and redirect it to enhance plant growth in the park above.

BC GAS

BC Gas was formed in 1988 when Inland Natural Gas acquired the mainland natural gas division of B.C. Hydro. By far the largest natural gas utility in the province, it services about 700,000 residential and corporate customers throughout B.C. via 30,000 kilometres of pipeline, running from the Peace River District through the centre of the province. In the Lower Mainland, storage facilities for Liquefied Natural Gas are in Delta. There are 10,189 kilometres of pipeline transporting and distributing natural gas (exclusive of pipes running to individual customers) throughout the Lower Mainland.

BC TEL

In 1976 when the *Vancouver Book* was published, underground telephone wires were a pretty good idea—good enough, in fact, that many municipalities required new services to be buried. In Vancouver there were about 805 kilometres of underground cable 20 years ago. Today there are thousands of kilometres of cables carrying fibre-optics from Vancouver to Victoria to Nanaimo and back, and thousands more connecting Vancouver to the Okanagan and to northern British Columbia, Eastern Canada and the U.S. In fact so much cable has been laid—mostly underground, though some lines are still carried aerially—that the exact number of kilometres isn't readily determinable.

Locally residents of Concord Pacific Place enjoy security services, environmental control and cable television service thanks to a network of advanced fibre-optics provided by BC Telecom. Eventually, pending federal approval that would allow BC Telecom to hold a broadcast license, B.C. consumers can look forward to interactive video, home-shopping services and more, all brought to us by fibre-optic cables and high-speed satellite communications.

History of Construction
Frank Lillquist

THE CONSTRUCTION INDUSTRY is usually credited with providing the physical structure of a community, but in Vancouver's case a common construction material may have helped provide the political structure. A gravel pit operated at Little Mountain in the 1920s was one of the first major acts of cooperation between Vancouver, South Vancouver and Point Grey, the three separate municipalities that amalgamated into the city in 1929. The three communities needed the aggregate for civic projects and jointly mined rock on the site of what is now the beautiful quarry gardens at Queen Elizabeth Park.

Of course, the history of Vancouver's construction industry goes back a lot further than the 1920s. The first construction in the region was that of First Nations people who built communal log houses in settlements along Burrard Inlet.

Among the first organized construction efforts in the Greater Vancouver area were those of the Royal Engineers based in Sapperton and Fort Langley. Generally associated with the Fraser Canyon Highway, the corps of engineers, architects and tradesmen also surveyed townsites and built schools, churches (New Westminster's first church and school was designed and built by Colonel Moody) and barracks in the mid-1800s.

Bedlam is probably an apt description of construction methods in early Vancouver going by old photographs. Everything from native timber to canvas seemed to have been employed as construction materials, with some brick and stone thrown in. The fire of 1886 swept away much of the early efforts and incidentally prompted a call for more stone buildings.

As the 1800s rolled on things began to get more organized; realtor W. Horne was selling Vancouver building lots from an outdoor operation at Georgia and Granville in 1886. By 1900 the industry was showing signs of civilization when Leslie Wright formed an insurance agency which, as Leslie Wright and Rolfe, went on to write the first contract bond in British Columbia.

In 1879 the original Mechanics' (Builders) Lien Act was passed and in spite of various amendments has successfully defied any effort to fully understand it since. By 1908 Vancouver had passed the first bylaw that made a building permit necessary, although there had been electrical and plumbing inspectors employed by the city since 1893.

With all these civilizing influences, the rough and ready construction industry was ready to start building Vancouver proper.

Early examples include Holy Rosary Cathedral at 646 Richards, completed in 1900 of Gabriola sandstone with granite foundations. Contractor Westinghouse, Church, Kerr & Co. built the Canadian Pacific Railway Station at 601 Cordova from 1912 to 1914. Kelly Bros. and Mitchell Contractors were awarded the contract for the federal building and post office at 701 West Hastings in August of 1905. Five years later they finished the fireproofed steel frame building with granite facade at a construction cost of $600,000—substantially less than a large West Side single family home today.

Photographs of this project being built provide graphic evidence of the changes in construction. During the excavation of the basement and sub-basement there was a gang of men with picks and shovels; today there would be one or two tracked excavators (not steam-shovels, thank you) loading dump trucks.

By 1912 John Coughland and Sons of Vancouver had fabricated 1,250 tons of steel for the tallest building in the British Empire—the 82.3-metre tall World Building, better known today as the heritage Sun Tower. (Typically, some Torontonian had to build a taller one in 1914.)

More elegance came to Vancouver in 1927 with the construction of the much-loved Orpheum Theatre on Granville Street. Built by Northern Construction Company, it cost a cool million, but some of the irreplaceable interior work is beyond price. That includes the ornamental plasterwork done by E.C. MacDougall and Company and George Rush Plastering Company.

Harbingers of the future of Vancouver's major construction projects were the Dominion Agriculture Building (later the RCMP Building, now Heritage Hall), completed at 3102 Main in 1914 and St. Andrews Wesley church at 1012 Nelson completed in 1931-32. Both have stone finishes, but both are reinforced concrete, the material most used to make Vancouver's modern skyline.

With a generally accepted bankruptcy rate of 85 per cent in the construction industry and the family nature of many of the city's early contracting concerns it's safe—and sad—to say that much of the "hands on" history of building a great city is lost. Take the Marine Building, for instance. The design by McCarter Nairne has made it a landmark and the steel installed by Dominion Bridge in 1929 enjoys a rock solid seismic rating to this day. But what subcontractor installed the toilets? The name is lost. And what difficulties did he have to overcome to position the necessaries out of sight behind the art-deco?

Many standout names do remain, however, and they are bound up with Vancouver's history. Just a sampling includes:

Ornamental stonework being prepared for the Credit Foncier building, 1914. cva

- Smith Bros. & Wilson, founded in Grand Forks in 1897, moved its headquarters to Vancouver in 1921. It built such landmarks as the Seaforth Armories, the main post office and the Board of Trade Tower.
- Columbia Bitulithic, founded in 1910 and headquartered in Coquitlam, has built roads throughout the province and is responsible for much of the Vancouver road network (for example, Journal of Commerce records show that on July 30, 1914, the company, then in the Dominion Building, was awarded a $71,815.52 contract to pave Victoria Road from Kingsway to 43rd Avenue).
- Dominion Construction, founded in 1911, is truly synonymous with construction and development in Vancouver. Still owned principally by the Bentall family, the company has branch offices from Toronto to California and a host of related companies. Headquartered in its own massive Bentall Centre on Burrard Street in Vancouver, it has the distinctive "boot" headquarters of B.C. Telephone in Burnaby and many industrial parks to its modern credit.
- Commonwealth Construction, founded in Winnipeg in 1907, built the Vancouver city hall.
- Dominion Bridge, which started out in 1882 to make bridges for the CPR, is still headquartered in the east, but in Van-

couver has contributed the Dominion Building, the Hotel Vancouver, the Lions Gate Bridge and the B.C. Electric (Hydro) Building. The latter is now converted to downtown condominiums, reflecting another era in Vancouver construction—quality renovation.

Many of the successful construction companies around today were founded in the 1950s to take advantage of the baby boom. They are too numerous to mention here, but for a general idea of what they've accomplished look at pictures of the Vancouver skyline about 1959 and compare it with today.

Construction is generally divided into ICI (institutional, commercial and industrial) and residential. The grand and famous usually fall into the ICI category. In Vancouver the watchword in residential construction has always been wood. Styles have gone through phases ranging from two- and three-storey structures to house extended families (and illegal suites), to post-war ranchers on slabs, to split levels to the distinctive "Vancouver special," an oblong configuration designed to make the most of the East Side's 10-metre lots. But they were all mostly wood frames, or "stick built," due obviously to British Columbia's enormous (but not inexhaustible) timber resources. Retired housebuilders and custom millworkers will testify that the quality of lumber available even up to the post-

Today, Tilbury Cement, Ocean Construction Supplies, Rempel Bros. Concrete, Challenge Pumping, Steelhead Aggregates, Pozzolanic International and Construction Aggregates continue that proud tradition, supplying cement, ready-mixed concrete, flyash, sand and gravel, and concrete products to construction projects in all areas of the province.

World War II boom is no longer to be found. A lot of ordinary family homes built in the late 1940s and 1950s had grain matched wooden siding as a matter of course. No wonder that for many years wooden siding was supreme with its only rival-being stucco containing chunks of broken beer bottles.

Wood continues to hold its own as a housebuilding material, but exterior finishes are more likely to be vinyl or metal siding or the new stuccoes, especially on the much debated "monster homes" that are replacing older, more modest dwellings throughout Vancouver neighborhoods. Steel (as in studs, extensively used in commercial projects) and concrete are now challenging wood in the residential field. An interesting aside is that the typical West Coast stick-built house is supposed to be the safest structure to be in during an earthquake, and demonstration homes built in Japan to promote B.C. materials performed well in recent upheavals.

No matter what material is being used, there are some constants to Vancouver construction. Rain has always affected choice of building materials and methods, whether in a single family home or a major highway with the accompanying drainage system. To this day architects consider how a structure's exterior will look wet, excavators pray for rain-free days to finish a dig and roofers cram as much work as possible into the summer months. Keeping the rain out of buildings is also a constant problem, as witnessed by the uproar over leaky condominiums in 1995.

Almost anytime anyone digs a hole in Vancouver, they have to contend with glaciation and a lot of hard sandstone. It's no coincidence that Vancouver has become the shotcrete and anchor capital of the world—shotcrete and anchor being a cost-effective, highly reliable method of shoring that is extensively employed locally.

Geography has always been a determining factor as well. An example is the pre-loading expertise developed because of construction in places with high water tables like Richmond and Queensborough. (Preloading is to heap temporary fill material, usually sand, on a building site and let it sit for a number of months, to compress the natural surface material. It is then removed before construction.) Not to mention the art of building houses without underground basements.

About 75 percent of the construction industry is made up of companies—general contractors and subcontractors—doing less than $5 million annually; they are individually owned or by families or a couple of partners. They are fiercely competitive, as would be expected in a business with an average three per cent return.

They do have associations, however, dedicated to setting standards, recognizing achievement, exchanging technology and speaking to government about the ever-growing list of rules, regulations and bureaucracy involved in building anything these days. The senior existing contractor organization in the Vancouver area is the Amalgamated Construction Association (ACA). Founded in 1966 by an amalgamation of the Vancouver General Contractors Association, the Vancouver Construction Association, the Heavy Construction Association of B.C. and the Victoria Builders Exchange, it was originally intended as a province-wide body. That role is filled by the B.C. Construction Association (BCCA).

Predecessor to them all was the Building and Construction Industries Exchange of B.C. founded in 1928, largely to clean up unscrupulous bidding practices in the city. Prior to that there had been a contractor division in the board of trade and an informal construction club that folded in 1915.

Before the 1980s the majority of Vancouver's major construction achievements (residential excluded) were built by unionized workers mostly represented by the B.C. and Yukon Territory Building Trades Council. The union sector's share of construction work has declined steadily and the majority of work today is performed by the open shop sector. The Independent Contractors and Businesses Association of B.C. was formed in the early 1970s to represent the open shop and the BCCA represents both union and non- union membership.

Segments of the industry have always supported good causes, especially the Variety Club and its works. Then there was the conversion of heritage Glen Brae manor in Shaughnessy into Canuck Place hospice for children. For the volunteers who worked on the project upgrading the 1910 vintage building, it was frustrating work, but rewarding. That wasn't the first instance either. There was also the incredible 19-hour "barn-raising" of Unity House in Tsawwassen when the ACA and the trades council undertook to erect the building during the course of the Variety Club Telethon.

The omissions in this article are legion. Construction is a big industry today—$16 billion annually in British Columbia, employing about 120,000 people according to the Workers' Compensation Board.

Not much has been said about the suppliers to construction and the type of business acumen that made Finning the biggest equipment dealer in the world. Or the innovations of individual companies, the type of which that made Jack Cewe Ltd. a world leader in concrete paving that even the U.S. army relies on.

To sum up for the industry as a whole: whatever the Vancouver construction industry has been asked to do, it built.

From locations throughout Vancouver, the Fraser Valley, and in Victoria, Nanaimo, and Prince George, the company and its more than 800 employees in British Columbia are proud of the part they have played in the building of British Columbia and are working together to build our communities.

Neon!

John Atkin

GREATER VANCOUVER TODAY is awash in the dull, energy-efficient orange glow of its street lights, in contrast to the riot of color and movement that electrified our streets 40 years ago. Granville Street attracted crowds of tourists and gawkers to see one of the world's largest displays of neon. At the peak of neon's popularity in the late 1950s, there was an astonishing one neon sign for every 18 residents in the Lower Mainland—more than 18,000 signs for a population of 345,000!

This great display of light started quietly enough in 1924 when enterprising Granville Street merchants imported the latest in advertising technology, neon signs, from the Claude Neon Company of Paris, France. The world got its first glimpse of this new "liquid light" just before World War I when (depending on which source you read) George Claude either exhibited a small sign using neon gas at the Grand Palais in 1910 or sold a sign to a hair salon in 1912. In 1923 Claude sold two simple blue and red neon signs to a Packard automobile dealer in Los Angeles. They literally stopped traffic.

Claude had seen the commercial potential of a waste product. During experiments to purify oxygen he found himself with an excess of neon, an inert gas. He already knew neon, sealed in a glass tube and excited by electricity, exhibited a pleasant and intense red/orange glow. (Argon, the other principal gas in sign production, produces a blue glow.) Claude set out to achieve a strong and steady light. He succeeded and was granted patents in 1915. Neon, from the Greek *neos* (new), soon came to mean all glass tube signs regardless of the gases used.

Oddly one license ended up in Vancouver among the assets of a bankrupt automobile dealership, Marmon Auto Sales. The potential of the Claude patent was recognized by one of Marmon's creditors, George Sweeny, after local barrister Hugo Ray mentioned seeing an exciting new type of advertising sign in Seattle. Sweeny and other local investors set up a company called Neon Products to produce neon signs for Western Canada. It would eventually become one of the largest sign companies in the world.

Neon signs were eagerly sought after by Vancouver businesses and many small companies ignored Neon Product's exclusive rights. An early newspaper advertisement from Neon Products trumpeted their success by listing 74 "progressive firms" that had already leased neon from them; it also reminded potential customers that Neon Products was still the only company authorized to produce it. But by the time the patent-license

At the peak of neon's popularity in the late 1950s, there were more than 18,000 signs in the Lower Mainland

expired in the early 1930s more than a dozen companies were involved in the production of neon.

All this activity produced some of the most exciting streetscapes in North America. Designers had a heyday creating everything from huge rooftop clocks and loaves of bread to a big red apple for Magee's grocery store. The Sun Tower at Beatty and Pender, with neon tubes outlining the entire building, became a giant sign itself. Pacific Stage Lines had the company name in neon across the front of its buses and house numbers were available in neon for as little as $30.

It's hard to imagine today how the streets must have looked in neon's halcyon days. Remaining examples are often admired for their craftsmanship and artistry yet many were considered by their designers to be modest creations. It's hard to imagine the Niagara Hotel's waterfall sign on Pender as modest but early photographs tell a different story.

By the 1960s abandonment of the inner city for the suburbs meant neon became associated with increasing urban decay. In Vancouver the growing awareness of the city's natural setting and the decline of the business district along Hastings Street meant the glory days of neon were ending. Opinion-makers and civic leaders were making noises about the "neon jungle" and the "hideous spectacle" neon created. Debate reached absurd proportions when one alderperson blamed neon for litter and prostitution problems. Bylaws were passed severely limiting the type and size of sign. The unexpected result: a new lack of ambient light. Few realized the role the color and movement from these signs played in creating the spectacle of a lively street (especially in the rain) and it's not surprising that shortly after the sign bylaws were passed people began discussing the "dying downtown."

In the intervening years the city has come to realize the value of colorful streets and attempts are once again being made to encourage large neon signs, especially along Granville Street. The resurrection of the 1940s Dunn's Tailors sign at their new Granville Street store and the restoration of the Stanley Theatre's marquee illustrate the growing awareness and appreciation of Vancouver's neon heritage. It's a bright idea whose time has come . . . again.

Imperial Parking Limited began in 1962 as a small company with two parking lots in Vancouver, and is now the largest parking management company in Canada. Corporate headquarters are located in one of Vancouver's most beautiful heritage buildings, The Station. Imperial Parking's stylized "P" logo can be found in 50 North American cities, as well as Southeast Asia. As of March 31, 1996 Impark was a publicly traded company on the Toronto Stock Exchange with annual revenues in excess of $240 million.

Designated Heritage Structures and Historical Sites
Robert G. Lemon

In the past year bronze markers have been appearing on some of Vancouver's most distinguished and historic buildings. The triangular shape, blue color and wavy design are drawn from the city crest. Each plaque identifies the building as a heritage building and tells a bit of its history and importance. The plaques are one of the ways Vancouver commemorates its heritage and are the most visible aspect of the story behind the city's designated buildings and its heritage program.

All "Ten of Vancouver's Oldest Buildings" listed by Ron Meyer in the 1976 *Vancouver Book* are still standing. Three remain unprotected despite Meyer's caveat that they "could be destroyed without warning." Surprise demolition could happen back then (and demolition by neglect still does), but not now, as those buildings—indeed all heritage buildings—have been evaluated and listed on the Vancouver Heritage Register. (The register was known until 1994 as the Vancouver Heritage Inventory, which was compiled and adopted by city council in 1986). While being listed doesn't ensure protection, it does afford the first "warning" of pending demolition.

As we learn more about our past—and as interest grows in preserving it—we have a more complete picture of the earliest buildings in the city. It is estimated that there are at least 19 buildings extant dating from the pre-1890 period, nine more than were known in 1976. There are about 59 buildings built by the end of 1895 that are still standing a century later. Of these, 26 (or 44 per cent) have wood framing and cladding, a surprising testament to what is often considered an impermanent material.

Designated buildings and sites are just a part of the overall picture of heritage in Vancouver. Of the more than 2,200 heritage buildings in the city listed in the Vancouver Heritage Register—all having been evaluated for their architectural, historical or contextual value—about 17 per cent are protected through designation. There are 360 buildings on the First Shaughnessy Heritage Inventory (of which 76 are also on the register), lots of character buildings throughout the city's neighborhoods, heritage parks, landscapes, monuments and archaeological sites. Then there are 100 Recent Landmarks, the legacy of our important post-1940 period, and historic interiors will soon be getting much needed attention. Yet more previously unknown or overlooked

buildings come to light every year through the public nomination process and are considered for heritage listing.

The topic of heritage in Vancouver would be a book in itself, but this article will focus on the protected—that is, designated—places in the city.

WHAT IS HERITAGE IN VANCOUVER?
Each city has its own heritage—that is, everything left to us from the past. There are century-old wooden houses in Strathcona, the West End and even a cottage dating from 1888—making it one the oldest houses still standing in the city—in Mount Pleasant. We've got a good stock of buildings from the Edwardian period of the early 20th century, lots of Craftsman bungalows and some excellent buildings, like the Marine Building, from the Art Deco period of the 1920s and 1930s. There is also an impressive collection of buildings from the 1950s and 1960s when Vancouver led the country in modern architecture with a West Coast regional twist. There are many trees and landscapes, monuments and bridges—like the Burrard Bridge—of outstanding heritage value. Varied in style, historic period and setting, they all contribute to the collective legacy of Vancouver's heritage.

HOW IS HERITAGE MANAGED?
Taking care of this range of resources, mostly privately owned, is done in many ways. The City of Vancouver's Heritage Management Plan was established in 1986, Vancouver's centennial year, as the blueprint for looking after the identification, public awareness, conservation and protection of Vancouver's heritage. The plan is administered by the four staff of the Heritage Conservation Program in the Planning Department. Council seeks advice on heritage matters through the Vancouver Heritage Commission, an appointed body of 11 citizens with a range of expertise and interest in heritage.

The Vancouver Heritage Register is the bible—for staff and the public alike—for keeping track of where buildings of heritage value are in the city. This is the list of buildings graded into A, B or C categories depending on their architectural, historical or contextual value. Noting that being "listed" doesn't mean "protected," heritage staff makes use of the various heritage incentives to encourage owners to retain and rehabilitate important buildings in the city. These incentives include the ability to relax regulations of the Zoning and Development bylaw (which can mean allowing more building area for an addition, easing up on yard requirements or reducing the amount of required parking) all in an effort to make retaining the heritage building an attractive alternative to demolition. Other incentives

include "green door" priority processing of heritage development applications, density bonuses and, in the Downtown area, the ability to transfer density (or air rights) from a heritage site to a new development site in certain instances. In exchange for these incentives the owner consents to the building's protection through designation.

HOW DO WE PROTECT HERITAGE?
The 20-year period since the first *Vancouver Book* was published has seen the maturing of the heritage movement. It has also seen the legislation affecting heritage conservation change twice, first in 1977 and then in 1994. Designation remains the primary way that heritage sites are protected. This can be done by the province through provincial designation or by city council through municipal designation. Gastown and Chinatown were deemed heritage areas by provincial designation in 1972 (at the time the city did not have the ability to designate sites itself). There are 133 buildings which continue to be protected by this designation (out of a total of 332 sites in the two historic areas). With the exception of the Roundhouse and Engine 374, the rest of the protected property and buildings in Vancouver are municipally designated.

Simply put, municipal designation is a bylaw which city council enacts to afford protection from alteration or demolition without council approval. There are two categories of designation: schedule A and schedule B (the schedules form part of Heritage bylaw 4837), depending on the extent of the designation. Schedule A buildings have the entire building exterior protected while schedule B buildings have only a specific part protected. For example all of city hall (built in 1936) is protected by being in schedule A, while just the upper two floors of the facade of the Palms Hotel on Granville are protected by being on schedule B. Since 1977 most buildings have become voluntarily designated in exchange for the previously mentioned incentives. Once designated the city provides the bronze heritage plaque to identify the building as protected property and as an important part of Vancouver's heritage.

In October, 1994, the province enacted new heritage legislation which revamped the procedures for heritage designation and introduced a new kind of protection: the Heritage Revitalization Agreement. Overall the new legislation shifted the powers of heritage protection to the local level by creating extensive new heritage conservation sections in the Vancouver charter and the Municipal act (for the rest of B.C.). This makes conservation tools and legislation more readily available at the local level.

The new legislation makes clearer the circumstances where compensation for designation is required, mandates designation proceedings to happen at a public hearing and allows for the protection of interior fixtures and features and landscape elements. Since the new legislation has been in effect, Vancouver has designated 16 heritage buildings.

The Heritage Revitalization Agreement is a new legal tool which enables the city and a property owner to agree on certain variances to the prevailing zoning regulations to assist in the property's revitalization. Its protection is then assured.

WHAT ARE SOME OF THE CITY'S DESIGNATED BUILDINGS AND SITES?

Oldest (and first) designated building:
Hastings Mill Store 1865 • moved 1930

Oldest designated building: original site:
Brynes Block 1887 • 2 Water Street

Youngest designated building:
Gardner House 1958 • 3152 West 49th

First (and only) designated landscape:
Cambie Boulevard

Designated artifact:
Engine 374

Designated sign:
Woodward's "W"

Designated heritage areas:
Gastown, Chinatown

Interiors:
None

WHO ARE SOME OF THE PEOPLE BEHIND THE BUILDINGS?

Michael Lambert has been a proud custodian of the impressive Hotel Vancouver (1939). He helped fund the design fees which got the heritage plaque program off the ground. The magnificent Adamesque Pacific Ballroom has been the venue for the annual Heritage Awards, held in February on Heritage Day.

The Marine Building (1929) was in the capable hands of Princeton Development's general manager Virginia Thurgood. The careful restoration of the brick and terracotta exterior was done under her direction, contributing to its distinction as one of the city's best-loved heritage buildings. (Ms. Thurgood has since joined McLeod Restorations Ltd.)

The city's first designated landscape is largely due to the efforts of Ethel Karmel and the Citizens to Save the Cambie Boulevard. From King Edward Boulevard to Marine Drive the central median of Cambie Boulevard is an important piece of urban planning, envisioned by planner Harland Bartholomew in 1946. It was protected in 1993 and the plaque is located in the central median at 33rd Avenue opposite Queen Elizabeth Park.

Novam Development's president Paolo Pela has a fondness for historic buildings. He also sees the commercial value in their rehabilitation. New life has been given to the majestic Bank of Commerce (1906-08) by Paolo's vision of creating Birks Place. The Birks clock has been relocated right across the street from its original location on Hastings Street.

"Glen Brae" (1910) is one of the city's landmark houses and one of three designated buildings in First Shaughnessy. Through the generosity of the late Elizabeth Wlosinski the house was willed to the city and was the impetus for the creation of the Vancouver Heritage Conservation Foundation. The building is being lovingly restored on the exterior and has been brought up to date for its new use as Canuck Place Children's Hospice.

The University Women's Club has owned Hycroft (1909), another of Shaughnessy's premier buildings, since 1962. They continue to keep it in shape from bottom to top—including the recently restored green tile roof. Inside and out, it is one of the most beautiful buildings in the city.

Since the late 1970s when plans to demolish a stand of historic buildings in the West End were proposed, Janet Bingham has worked tirelessly to save them, starting with the Roedde House (1893). With the help of the Community Arts Council and many others, she was influential in achieving both the creation of the city's only historic house museum and the unique heritage park, Barclay Heritage Square.

John Atkin lives in one of the tiniest designated buildings in the city, one of the four houses on Hawks Avenue (1899-1900). He spearheaded their restoration and continues to be active in heritage, be it the Strathcona Porch Project, Heritage Vancouver or as an award-winning author (*Strathcona—Vancouver's First Neighbourhood*).

The Weeks House (1895) has sat empty for years. Now the last of the heritage houses at Barclay Heritage Square is coming to life as a home away from home for the Friends for Life, under the direction of Lorne Mayencourt.

Historically it's the Randall Building (1929) but since being completely rehabilitated in 1991 it's known as the Cavelti Building. Jeweller Toni Cavelti has succeeded in upgrading a dignified building and adding something modern to cap it all off—a splendid modernist rooftop addition.

The first designated building from the modern era is the Electra, formerly the B.C. Hydro Building (1955-57). Unquestionably a distinctive building on the city's skyline, it has been guided by developer Terry Partington into a new era as a residential building, while preserving its landmark

qualities throughout.

Yaletown is undergoing a transformation and Ron Dick's rehabilitation of the former Stewart and Comrie Warehouse at 1140-1150 Hamilton Street is showing how well it can be done. The previously disfigured facades have been returned to their original character. In exchange for making most of the floor area available for residential use, the building was designated and protected.

The Sylvia Hotel (1911-12) is one of the grand dames of the West End. The accomplished and witty adjacent residential tower (1987), designed in a high post-modern style by Richard Henriquez, shows how new and old can live side by side.

VANCOUVER'S MUNICIPALLY DESIGNATED HERITAGE BUILDINGS

Designated December 1974 (schedule A)

1. *Hastings Mill Store, 1865 • 1575 Alma*
2. *Christ Church Cathedral, 1889-95 690 Burrard*
3. *St. James Church, 1935-37 • 303 East Cordova*
4. *CPR Station, 1912-14 • 601 West Cordova*
5. *Gabriola, 1901 • 1531 Davie*
6. *National Harbours Board, 1905 50 Dunlevy*
7. *Court House, 1906-13 800 West Georgia*
8. *Orpheum Theatre, 1927 • 884 Granville*
9. *Shannon, 1912-13 • 7255 Granville*
10. *Bank of Commerce, 1906-08 640-698 West Hastings*
11. *Old Post Office Building, 1905-10 757 West Hastings*
12. *Credit Foncier Building, 1913-14 850 West Hastings*
13. *Hycroft, 1909 • 1489 McRae*
14. *Heritage Hall, 1914 • 3102 Main*
15. *Glen Brae, 1910 • 1690 Matthews*
16. *St. Andrew's Wesley Church, 1931-33 1012 Nelson*
17. *Sun Tower, 1912 • 100 West Pender*
18. *Holy Rosary Cathedral, 1899-1900 646 Richards*
19. *Aberthau, 1909 • 4397 West 2nd*
20. *Hudson Bay Company Store, 1913 & 1926 640 Granville*

Designated March 1976 (schedule A)

21. *Beatty Street Drill Hall, 1899-1901 620 Beatty*
22. *James England House, 1907 • 2300 Birch*
23. *Marine Building, 1920-30 • 355 Burrard*
24. *Hotel Vancouver, 1929-39 900 West Georgia*
25. *Sylvia Hotel, 1911-12 • 1154 Gilford*
26. *Vancouver Block, 1912 • 736 Granville*
27. *Winch Building, 1909 • 757 West Hastings*

28. *BC Permanent Loan, 1907*
    330 West Pender
29. *Canada Permanent, 1911 • 432 Richards*
30. *Hodson Manor, 1894 & 1903*
    1254 West 7th
31. *Steamboat House, 1890 • 1151 West 8th*
32. *Davis House, 1891 • 166 West 10th*
33. *City Hall, 1936 • 453 West 12th*

Designated December 1976 (schedule A)

34. *Alexandra Park Bandstand, 1915*
    Beach Avenue at Burnaby
35. *St. Paul's Church, 1905 • 1138 Jervis*
36. *First Baptist Church, 1911 • 969 Burrard*
37-40. *Strathcona School, Nos. 2 – 5, 1897*
    594 East Pender
41. *Roedde House, 1893 • 915 West Hastings*
42. *Vancouver Club, 1912-14 • 1415 Barclay*
43. *Ukrainian Orthodox Church, 1950*
    154 East 10th
44. *Hirshfield House, 1910 • 1963 Comox*

Designated December 1976 (schedule B)

45. *Chalmers Church, 1912 • 2801 Hemlock*
46. *Douglas Lodge, 1907 • 2799 Granville*
47. *St. Luke's Home, 1924 • 309 East Cordova*
48. *Palms Hotel, 1890s & 1913 • 869 Granville*
49. *Bank of Commerce, 1929*
    817-819 Granville
50. *Hudson's Bay Insurance Company, 1911 •*
    900 West Hastings

Designated July 1978 (schedule A)

51. *Brock House, 1911 • 3875 Point Grey*

Designated October 1978 (schedule A)

52. *Stanley Park Pavilion, 1911 • Stanley Park*

Designated April 1980 (schedule A)

53. *CN Station and Rooftop Neon Sign,*
    1917-19 • 1150 Station

Designated July 1980 (schedule A)

54. *Coroner's Court, 1932 • 238-240 East*
    Cordova
55. *Firehall No. 2, 1907 • 270 East Cordova*

Designated July 1986 (schedule A)

56. *Dick Building, 1929 • 1482-90 West*
    Broadway
57. *Model School, 1905 • 555 West 12th*
58. *Normal School, 1909 • 555 West 12th*

Designated April 1987 (schedule A)

59-62. *504, 508, 512, 516 Hawks*
    1899-1900

Designated May 1987 (schedule B)

63. *Tudor Manor, 1927-28 • 1311 Beach*

Designated September 1987 (schedule A)

64-65. *2202, 2220 Cypress • 1914*

Designated October 1987 (schedule A)

66. *1096 West 10th • 1922*

Designated February 1988 (schedule A)

67. *883 Broughton • 1903*
68. *889 Broughton • 1903*
69. *891 Broughton • 1903*
70. *1416 Haro • 1909*

71. *1430-32 Haro • 1902*
72. *1436 Haro • 1907*
73. *Barclay Manor, 1890 • 1447 Barclay*
74. *Weeks House, 1985 • 1459 Barclay*
75. *Terminal City Lawn Bowling Club, 1935*
    1650 West 14th
76. *Connaught Park Fieldhouse, 1925*
    2390 West 10th
77. *Memorial Park South Fieldhouse, 1930*
    5950 Prince Albert
78. *Vancouver Rowing Club, 1911*
    Stanley Park

Designated September 1988 (schedule B)

79. *Tellier Tower, 1910-11*
    10-16 East Hastings

Designated September 1988 (schedule A)

80. *Firehall No. 6, 1907 • 1001 Nicola*

Designated May 1989 (schedule A)

81. *Bloomfield House, 1900 • 2532 Columbia*
82. *1642 Stephens • 1911*

Designated August 1989, (schedule A)

83. *3846 West 10th • 1936-37*

Designated August 1990 (schedule A)

84. *117 West 10th • 1895*
85. *140 West 10th • 1910*
86. *144 West 10th • 1894*
87. *148 West 10th • 1908*
88. *150 West 10th • 1907*
89. *156 West 10th • 1894*
90. *2953-55 Ontario • 1907*
91. *989 Bute • 1899*
92. *1235 Nelson • 1931*

Designated August 1990 (schedule B)

93. *Kensington Place 1912 • 1386 Nicola*

Designated September 1990 (schedule A)

94. *2967 West 42nd • 1915*
96. *Fee House 1904 • 1119 Broughton*

Designated January 1991 (schedule A)

96. *2055 West 14th • 1910*

Designated March 1991 (schedule A)

97. *Randall Building, 1929*
    535-565 West Georgia

Designated September 1991 (schedule A)

98. *8264 Hudson • 1912*
99. *835-39 Cambie • 1929*
100. *1037 Matthews • 1913*
101. *Haigler House 1925 • 3537 West 30th*
102-105. *849, 853, 863, 867 Hamilton*
    1895-1900

Designated May 1992 (schedule A)

106. *2740 Yukon • 1913*

Designated July 1992 (schedule A)

107. *1865 West 16th • 1912*

Designated September 1992 (schedule A)

108. *280 East 6th • 1908*
109. *2675 Oak • 1929*

Designated January 1993 (schedule B)

110. *St. George's School 1911-12*
    3851 West 29th

Designated January 1993 (schedule A)

111. *Taylor Manor 1913 • 951 Boundary Road*

Designated April 1993 (schedule A)

112. *Evangelistic Tabernacle 1909-10 • 85*
    East 10th

Designated April 1993 (schedule B)

113. *5709 Wales • 1912*

Designated July 1993 (schedule A)

114. *3358 Southeast Marine Drive • 1911*
115. *3010 West 5th • 1921*

Designated July 1993 (schedule A)

116. *St. Mary's Church Kerrisdale—church building*
    1913 • 2498 West 37th
117. *St. Mary's Church Kerrisdale—parish hall*
    1923 • 2498 West 37th

Designated September 1993 (schedule A)

118. *Central Median of Cambie Street*
    Boulevard • 1940

Designated September 1993 (schedule B)

119. *Jones Tent and Awning 1919*
    2034 West 11th

Designated October 1993 (schedule A)

120. *Toronto Dominion Bank, 1920*
    560-580 West Hastings
121. *330 West 15th • 1912*

Designated November 1993 (schedule A)

122. *B.C. Hydro Building 1955-57 • 970 Burrard*

Designated February 1994 (schedule B)

123. *Gardner House 1958 • 3152 West 49th*

Designated June 1994 (schedule B)

124. *Stewart and Comrie Warehouse 1911 1140-*
    1150 Hamilton

Designated September 1994 (schedule A)

125. *177-179 East Hastings • 1912*

Designated December 1994 (schedule A)

126. *2990 West 5th • 1920*
127. *2216-2218 St. George • 1911*
128. *518 Beatty • 1911*
129. *1050 Nicola • 1909*
130. *Vancouver Public Library 1957*
    750 Burrard (now a retail complex)

Designated March 1995 (schedule A)

131. *6120 Macdonald • 1921*

Designated March 1995 (schedule B)

132. *Japanese Hall and Japanese School*
    1927-28 • 475 Alexander

Designated May 1995 (schedule A)

133. *967 West 8th • 1905*
134. *1178 Hamilton • 1912*
135. *901-911 Homer • 1910*
136. *1183 West 10th • 1907*

Designated June 1995 (schedule A)

137. *2830 West 1st • 1909*
138. *901 West 23rd • 1912*
139. *138 West 10th • 1904*

Designated July 1995 (schedule A)

140. *800 Cassiar • 1912*
141. *Woodward's 1908 various additions*
    101 West Hastings

The essential ingredient of Princeton's success is the building of strong relationships with tenants, suppliers, investors, team members and the people in the communities in which it does business.

Unbuilt Vancouver–City of Destiny
Taras Grescoe

A BRITISH JOURNALIST, paying a visit to a tiny township on Burrard Inlet in 1890, took one look at a handful of waterfront shacks and predicted that one day Vancouver would be the "Constantinople of the West!" Shipping magnates looked at a row of sagging wooden piers on the waterfront and immediately recognized the future "Liverpool of the Pacific!" When Captain George Vancouver nosed his sloop into the inner harbor, he must have dropped his spyglass and cried, "Zounds! The Amsterdam of the Americas!" From the start, Vancouver has been many cities to many people, but common to every booster's hyperbole was a desire to see Burrard Peninsula draped with a metropolis that did some kind of justice to its bracketing river basin and mountain peaks. Whether the goal was to attract settlers from the east, investment from Asia, or tourist dollars from just about anywhere, the Vancouver of the future was to be a shining jewel on the Pacific, studded with glamorous buildings and gossamer spans, all tied up with ribbons of scenic highways.

But first the competition had to be eliminated. Early in the century, Port Moody made a bid to become the chief port on Burrard Inlet by proposing an interurban canal that would cut across Coquitlam and connect the Pacific to the Fraser River. A group of Vancouver-based businesspeople countered with a 1912 plan to build a 15-metre high dam across the Second Narrows, a scheme which, quite incidentally, would have flooded Port Moody. In the same year Richmond, anticipating the opening of the Panama Canal, offered its own modest proposal: a gigantic seaport, with 35 kilometres of oceanfrontage on the west end of Lulu Island. Some speculate that it was only the outbreak of World War I that prevented the Vancouver Board of Trade from dynamiting the dykes and submerging its upstart neighbor.

Gerry McGeer, MP for Vancouver-Burrard in 1933 and for two terms the city's most relentlessly visionary mayor, coined the catch-phrase that would resound through chambers of commerce and tradesmen's clubs for decades, and find echoes in the prefab corridors of Expo 86. "This city of destiny," he thundered to an audience of businesspeople at the height of the depression, "set in such surroundings, would attract enough tourists from the United States to pay off our appalling gold indebtedness." He foresaw a time when a million American tourists would come to the city every year to visit the eighth wonder of the world, a 400-kilometre long scenic driveway that would span Indian Arm, traverse Stanley Park and gird Point Grey. With a nod to the sprawling "jungles" of False Creek—where the barefoot children of Vancouver's 34,000 unemployed were running around in pants made of flour sacks—he promised that with "Canadian labour, Canadian engineering skill and Canadian national credit," realizing his vision would "provide employment for an army of men and cost less than was expended in a single day of fighting on the Western Front."

Since McGeer, nobody has been more obsessed by Vancouver's destiny—and more frustrated by its reality—than Warnett Kennedy. The Glasgow-born architect came to Vancouver in 1952 to create Annacis Island, the first planned industrial community in the country, and stuck around to become an alderman, bête noire of Harry Rankin, the powerful COPE alderman. In his books and magazine articles, Kennedy imagined what he called a "wet village on the west coast" transformed into a megalopolis, where vertical take-off aircraft would take citizens from the roofs of the West End's 100-storey apartment buildings to homes in the suburbs—the peaks of Grouse and Seymour. Key to his vision was the idea that tourists and future residents would come to mountaintop chalets to gaze out over the Fraser Valley's farmlands, which, overdue for a massive flood anyway, would have been left untouched by suburban sprawl.

BRAVE NEW VANCOUVER
In 1931, the same year Aldous Huxley was writing *Brave New World*, the newly created Vancouver Town Planning Commission published a short pamphlet for high school students, describing its goal and methods. "The idea of planning is to prevent waste; it is a scientific attempt to direct the growth of the various components, residential, industrial and business, that go to make up a city along sane, and as far as can be foreseen, permanent lines." Drawing from the Bartholomew Plan of 1929, a massive attempt to make every detail of the urban landscape conform to a sanitary, rational vision of city life, the pamphlet urged the "students of today" to imagine the Vancouver of the future as an orderly place, where houses would be placed on their rectangular lots in a manner pleasing to the eye, where a gridwork of streets was to be serviced by a vast network of streetcars.

Prepared by Harland Bartholomew & Associates, a Saint Louis firm that determined the form of more than 50 other North American cities, the plan described everything from the correct shape of curbs and lampposts to an aesthetically pleasing streetplan for the University Endowment Lands—once the unhygienic forest had been clearcut. Its chief aim was "to deter a haphazard and hodge-podge pattern which, in addition to its other faults, is so unsightly. Not only increased efficiency and orderliness but a more attractive community will naturally result as the Plan is gradually implemented."

Although it was never officially adopted, the 388-page Bartholomew Plan was the Gideon Bible in the top drawer of Planning Department desks for decades, a comforting presence when city planners were assailed by doubt. The fact that it was devised by an American (who was "slightly less interesting than the average bankloan officer," according to one of his contemporaries)—a flatlander whose vision of the ideal city came from planning dozens of Midwestern towns on landlocked plains—didn't seem to bother the civic employees of this mountainous coastal metropolis. And they obviously turned to it often: many of the artist's conceptions of sanely zoned city blocks in the Plan's yellowing pages look suspiciously like present-day streetscapes in Kerrisdale and Dunbar.

Bartholomew's pet project—one he proposed in every city he ever planned for—was never built. He wanted to see a grandiose civic centre on the site of the present-day Aquatic Centre (he initially toyed with the idea of filling in False Creek, but nixed it because of the site's industrial potential), a 13-hectare monument to order that would combine art gallery, museum, library, courthouse and city hall in one location.

Bartholomew and his cohorts were just one in a long line of architects, planners and civic dreamers that sought a home for a monumental civic centre. Theodore Korner, who eventually built the Burrard Street Bridge, won a 1914 design competition with his proposal to place a gigantic complex on what is now the site of the Queen Elizabeth theatre. C.J. Thompson sketched a bird's eye view of an enormous civic auditorium and stadium on Kitsilano Point, neatly obliterating all traces of both the Kitsilano Indian Reserve and a long-standing squatters' camp with a few strokes of his charcoal pencil. A post-war parks commissioner promoted a meandering Georgia Street lined with government buildings.

FAT CITY

The ambitious planners of the fifties and sixties tried to pave the way for a world-class Vancouver—and if many of them had been successful it would have left a city with a core as vibrant and welcoming as downtown Detroit. If it hadn't been for the whining of short-sighted citizens, businessmen from all over the world would now be cruising along a 60-metre wide freeway through the heart of Chinatown, or bolstering the local economy by doing lunch in the penthouse restaurant of the 55-storey tower where Christ Church Cathedral once stood.

If Vancouver today isn't the Fat City that planners of the fifties dreamed of, it certainly isn't for lack of trying. In 1952 the

Lower Mainland Regional Planning Board, predecessor to the GVRD, announced that "within perhaps 50 years the whole area will be, geographically and otherwise, a miniature New York area, with the Burrard Peninsula as its Manhattan." This prediction provoked two reactions: bemused head-shaking from long-time residents of the hundreds of single family homes in the West End; and a cry of "Gee Whiz!"—from the young architects and planners who had enthusiastically swallowed the precepts of the Bartholomew Plan in high school civics classes. The budding technocrats immediately hit the drawing boards, drafting proposals for third crossings, downtown freeways and space needles, the very projects that would add spice to civic politics for decades to come.

A single obstacle stood between Vancouver and its destiny: urban blight. In a 1955 editorial the *Province* warned future world-class architects that this was a hurdle they would one day have to jump: "When decay is ignored, a city deteriorates in the same way as any organism that fails to renew itself. In a city, as in an apple tree, dead wood is unproductive and dangerous. It should be pruned away to make for new growth." The implications were clear: Vancouver was an orchard, low income neighborhoods like Strathcona and Chinatown were the dead wood, and a new generation of gardeners would have to slash and burn so that, one day, the children of the city could enjoy bigger, riper apples.

And how do you like these apples: in 1956, a teenage Arthur Erickson drew up a plan that portrayed the West End as one gigantic apartment building, a stack of monster suites that culminated in 100-storey twin peaks at either end of the downtown. Planners at the department of transport proposed a hovercraft terminal for Deadman's Island, to shuttle passengers from the downtown to the airport. In 1963 the architectural firm Christiani and Nielsen unveiled an image of Coal Harbour with a new island off Stanley Park, part of a $58 million third crossing scheme. Cars were meant to follow a highway along Vancouver's waterfront, veer off onto a four-lane bridge that plunged into Burrard Inlet at a tunnel entrance set into "reclaimed land" off Brockton Point, and re-emerge at the other end of the tunnel on the North Shore.

All of these projects needed space for off-ramps, turnpikes, clover-leaves and toll-booths—in short, a downtown freeway system, one that city hall and the Canadian Pacific Railway had been discussing since the early fifties. In 1967 a San Francisco-based firm concluded that a waterfront freeway would best be served by levelling 600 houses in Strathcona and laying a 10-metre-high overpass over Carrall Street, in the centre of Chinatown. Immediately protest came from every part of the city,

and a crowd of 800 people gathered in city hall to shout down the consultants' proposals. The chairman of the city's planning commission resigned on the spot, and a year later the plan was scrapped. Apparently the spirited editorializing of the local papers in favor of cutting out civic blight with a concrete knife had influenced no one but a handful of architects.

All of which has made developers a little more careful about whose turf they choose to tread on, and the words they pick to describe cherished projects. Mirage's waterfront Casino Proposal, and the PNE's plans to expand Hastings Park, prettied up with delightful artist's renditions and glowing images of poten-

tial benefit to the community, were greeted with widespread public suspicion and eventually died. A new generation of planners seems to have learned its lesson; they're sick of imposing a pre-ordained vision onto a reluctant public, only to have its every detail fought tooth and nail.

Project 200, as visualized in 1970. The unbuilt scheme—for office towers, parking and pedestrian plazas above the CPR tracks—would have stretched from Canada Place to Woodward's Department Store. The proposed waterfront freeway is in the foreground. vs/vp

Government

Vancouver, British Columbia is ranked among the most liveable cities in the world. The kind of political separation of central city and suburbs, so common in American metropolitan areas, is not part of this city's reality. In the Vancouver experience, strong direction has emerged from time to time to deal with spontaneous change in the public understanding of their region in its demographic, economic, political and cultural contexts.

The City of Vancouver, as it is known today, was formed through the amalgamation of the original city and the municipalities of Point Grey and South Vancouver in 1929. The upshot was a major transformation in the scale of the city, its institutions, and its landscape between 1929 and 1937, including the professionalization of the civil service and the institution of a non-partisan form of government. After World War II, thousands of new households were formed by those who had postponed families through depression and wartime. These folks were on a materialistic binge, purchasing houses, appliances, furniture and cars. It was not surprising that they enthusiastically supported a civic administration that produced paved streets and roads, community centres and schools. By the 1950s many aspects of the civic landscape were being transformed, high-rise apartment towers were sprouting in the West End, new bridges and viaducts were constructed into the core, and in the suburbs, gravel roads were transformed by blacktop. Streetcars were replaced by trolley and diesel buses, permitting a massive upgrade of arterial streets. The city's engineering department was the primary agent of the enhancement of its infrastructure.

In the 1960s the consensus upon which the city had been governed broke down. To advise the city on development, U.S. consulting firms were hired and the cures spelled out: construct parkades at public expense to provide subsidized parking for shoppers, build a freeway system linking downtown to suburban municipalities, and redevelop Pacific Centre. Although never formally adopted, it is clear that some of these ideas became the assumed policies of the city, while others were rejected. The members of city council had a clear commitment to the material enhancement of Vancouver. Most were older and conservative in their views. There was a weak mayor and council, elected on an at-large basis and perpetuating small business class interests in the name of non-partisanship. There was a strong professional civic administration that managed the city in a very frugal and efficient manner, focusing on the construction of civic infrastructure, the managing of land, and the maintenance of law and order.

Change was around the corner. As Paul Tennant wrote in 1971: "In retrospect it is clear that by the mid-sixties groups were emerging in Vancouver which, although unorganized and without spokesmen in the beginning, would come to form the opposition to the established order. One of these groups consisted of younger downtown business and professional people; another consisted of volunteer and professional community workers together; another consisted of planners and architects; another consisted of ratepayer groups in more affluent areas; and yet another consisted of UBC academics. These groups were for the most part composed of people who had entered their careers untouched by the values of the NPA and at a time when problems of urban growth and its social effects were becoming highly apparent. From these groups emerged the reform leaders and under their leadership some of the groups began to take positive action to oppose the NPA and the civic bureaucracy."

By 1966 the City of Vancouver was no longer the appropriate scale for planning and administration. Spearheaded by Dan Campbell the provincial government provided for the creation of regional districts. The Greater Vancouver Regional District led the process of cooperatively providing services and regional planning. The GVRD absorbed the water and sewer boards that were founded in the 1920s. But most importantly it tackled the difficult task of providing an overall plan for the region, The Liveable Region Plan of 1975.

Regional districts gain their power through the acceptance of plans and program by a majority of municipalities with a majority of population. It requires consensus. The livable region plan provided for regional town centres such as Metrotown, for light rapid transit and agricultural land reserves. In the Growth Strategies Act of 1995, provision was made for dispute-settlement mechanisms where consensus was impossible among municipalities.

—*Walter G. Hardwick*

above: Mayor Gerry McGeer, 1935, built City Hall (facing page). vs

Vancouver City Services

For a fast and informal look at some Vancouver City government and related activities, read these six pages. Details on subjects like business licences, development permits, the Urban Design Panel, the Vancouver Planning Commission, engineering, secondary suites, liquor licences, etc., etc., and etc. are too complex to deal with in this space. (The city's Internet site totals more than 400 pages!) Call City Hall for information: switchboard 873-7011. A few phone numbers and Internet site addresses are given here. The city has a first-rate local government Web site at http://www.city.vancouver.bc.ca. Much of what's here is adapted from or taken directly from it. A particularly rich page: Vancouver A to Z at commsvcs/planning/atoz/atozindex.html Our thanks to Scott Macrae, the city's director of communications, for his assistance.

A nice feature of the Internet pages is that they give more detail than is possible here. An example is the paragraph on weddings at local parks and beaches. The Web site lists all the locations, shows the rates, rules, etc.

Please note: to save space, the prefix http://www.city.vancouver.bc.ca/ is not shown in the Internet URLs given here. You must add it in front of the Web site addresses shown, unless otherwise indicated.

Annual events in the city A list is on the net at: engsvcs/annualevents.html

Annual reports The city's past annual reports may be viewed at the City of Vancouver Archives.

Archives The City of Vancouver Archives acquires, organizes and preserves Vancouver's historical records. The public is welcome, and research is free. See the article on the archives by Donna Jean McKinnon in this book. 1150 Chestnut Street, just east of the Planetarium. 736-8561. Fax: 736-0626. Web site: ctyclerk/archives/index.html

Artist in residence program Funded by the park board in partnership with Community Centre Associations, providing an opportunity for artists to develop community-focused projects. Call the park board's coordinator of arts and multiculturalism for information: 257-8400. Fax: 257-8427. URL: parks/recreation/air.html

Attendances (1996 unless noted)
B.C. Lions 190,000
H.R. MacMillan Planetarium 180,000
Hastings Park Racecource (live racing attendance 1996) 605,842
International Jazz Festival Vancouver (1993) 300,000
Orpheum Theatre (1995) 310,000
Queen Elizabeth Theatre (1995) 320,000
Science World (1996-97) 530,000
Vancouver 86ers Soccer Club 65,000
Vancouver Aquarium (1995) 915,000
Vancouver Art Gallery 200,000
Vancouver Canadians 336,000
Vancouver Canucks (1995-96) 729,629
Vancouver Children's Festival 80,000
Vancouver Folk Music Festival 30,000
Vancouver Grizzlies (1995-96) 704,489
Vancouver International Film Festival 130,000
Vancouver International Writers Festival 11,222
Vancouver Maritime Museum 110,000
Vancouver Museum 85,000
Vancouver Opera (1995-96) 71,116
Vancouver Playhouse (1995) 113,000
Vancouver Symphony (1995-96) 154,000

B.C. Parkway The parkway is a bike and pedestrian route built by the provincial government, and is generally located under the SkyTrain between Vancouver and New Westminster. The route sometimes uses city streets and sometimes segregated pathways.

Beaches Vancouver beaches are staffed by park board lifeguards from the Victoria Day weekend to Labor Day weekend. Windsurfing board rentals and kayak excursion tours are offered. Information is available from Kits Tower at 738-8535 mid-May to mid-September. Other times of the year call the Vancouver Aquatic Centre, 665-3424. See Lisa Tant's article on beaches in this book. Web site:parks/recreation/beaches

Bench donation program The memorial bench program allows the donor to contribute to the cost of installing a park bench at one of the city's parks or beaches. A brass plaque is attached with copy you supply.
Call 257-8440 for details.

Bicycling City council approved four priority bike corridors (Adanac, Ontario, Off-Broadway and Arbutus Rail) to be developed as part of a bike route network. These routes are designed so that bikes share the road with cars on streets made more bicycle friendly.
Bicycle Hot Line: 871-6070, or
e-mail: transpor@city.vancouver.bc.ca.
Website: engsvcs/transport/cycling/bikepage.html

Block parents Block Watch Vancouver Police Department Block Parent Coordinator: 257-8739.

BlueWays redevelopment along the water's edge has added new waterfront parks and pedestrian and bicycle paths. There is still great potential for water use and preservation. Vancouver has approximately 48 kilometres of shoreline and 1,214 hectares of water space within city limits, compared to 2,023 hectares of park space. It is high time to pay special attention to the water and its use. BlueWays publishes a newsletter. Web site: commsvcs/planning/blueway.htm

Bridgeheads study recommends policies for the development of buildings in the immediate vicinity of the city's major bridges. Emphasis is placed on public views from bridges, the character and identity of the bridge, and the siting of tall buildings adjacent to the Burrard and Granville bridges. engsvcs/transport/transportindex.html (For the history of the city's bridges, see the article by Robert Harris in this book.)

Cargo tonnage (inbound and outbound 1994) 71.5 million tonnes

City directories Directories from past years are available for reading at the City of Vancouver Archives and the Vancouver Public Library.

City Hall is at 453 West 12th Avenue at Cambie Street (postal code V5Y 1V4). The main switchboard is (604) 873-7011. The current City Hall opened December 1, 1936. In March 1976 it was designated a heritage building. (The building's architects were Townley and Matheson.) Each lock plate on the outer doors displays the Vancouver Coat of Arms, and each door knob bears the monogram of the building. The ceiling on the second floor of the rotunda is made of gold leaf from several B.C. mines. The grandfather clock on the third floor was presented to the city in 1986 as a centennial gift from Vancouver's sister city of Yokohama, Japan. The east wing of City Hall, immediately adjacent to the north, was built to provide more room for staff. It was officially opened by HRH Prince Philip on October 29, 1968.

City manager Ken Dobell has held this post since 1990. The City manager is ultimately responsible for the work of all departments and one program (equal employment opportunity) and has close liaison with three other boards over which council has budget control: library, park board and police. The city manager also coordinates the presentation of the city's annual budget.
e-mail: citymanager@city.vancouver.bc.ca
URL: ctyclerk/info_depts_boards/citymanager.html

CityNews A newsletter published twice a year, and sent with tax notices, with general information on city services, bylaw changes, tax payment tips, etc.

CityPlan On June 6, 1995 Council adopted CityPlan as a vision to guide policy decisions, priorities and budgets. See the article by Ann McAfee in this book. For more information: 873-7120, Fax: 873-7889.
E-mail: cityplan@city.vancouver. ba.ca.
Website: commsvcs/commsvcsindex.htm/#CityPlan

CityWeek is published by the communications

division, office of the city clerk. Detailing the week's council and committee meetings, etc., It's posted on the city's home page (http://www. city.vancouver.bc.ca) every Friday. A calendar-style version is faxed to Vancouver media outlets, and posted at City Hall, libraries, community centres, secondary schools, neighborhood houses and health units.

Civic youth strategy On March 28, 1995 council unanimously approved the CYS, a commitment to work in partnership with youth and the larger community on issues affecting youth. CYS is guided by a coalition of municipal government, the Vancouver School Board and youth. The City also has a child and youth advocate. commsvcs/ socialplanning/youth/youthpage.html

Community centre visits (1994) 3,369,543 or 6.4 visits per capita. See Richard von Kleist's article.

Community profiles The city's planning department defines, for planning purposes, 23 neighborhoods: community profiles describe city services and community resources in each of them, and include brief local histories and demographic information. They are an excellent resource. Printed versions of the profiles—with tables, photographs and other information not available on the Internet site—are available from the planning department, 3rd floor, 2675 Yukon Street, 873-7344. See also articles in this book on neighborhoods. (This book's neighborhood boundaries sometimes differ from the city's). community_profiles/index.htm

Composting engsvcs/waste/wastindex.html

Council Vancouver City Council comprises 10 councillors and the mayor, elected for three-year terms. Meetings are televised live on Rogers Cable 4. On November 16, 1996 Philip Owen was re-elected to a second term as mayor and headed a council made up of Jennifer Clarke, Gordon Price, Don Bellamy, George J. Puil, Lynne Kennedy, Nancy A. Chiavario, Sam Sullivan, Daniel Lee, Don Lee and Alan Herbert. The last three are new to council. The mayor's annual salary (1996) is $89,154. Councillors' annual remuneration is $39,278. Every councillor serves as deputy mayor on a monthly rotating basis with an extra stipend for that month of $1,634.

Coyotes The December 1995 issue of *CityNews* reminds us coyotes are an urban phenomenon, too. "Although coyotes eat mainly small mammals such as mice and rats, they will eat domestic pets. Coyotes are generally no threat to people, but should be treated with respect and never fed—most attacks on humans are linked to feeding." Vancouver is involved in a study of urban coyotes. Information: 257-8528.

Crime See Police listings.

Crime Stoppers provides citizens with a vehicle to anonymously supply the police with information about a crime or potential crime of which they have knowledge.

The Crime Stoppers tip line is staffed by trained personnel who receive, process and pass on tip information to investigating officers. Callers are given a code number which is used in all subsequent calls and callers do not have to identify themselves. A reward is offered to anyone providing information which leads to the arrest and charge of a criminal. Rewards may also be paid for information leading to the recovery of stolen property, the seizure of illegal drugs or an arrest on an outstanding warrant. More info: http://www.deepcove.com/ crime_stoppers/. Crime Stoppers has a mugshot page on the Internet! Htp:// www.deepcove. com/crime_ stoppers/mug-shots/suspect1.html

Cruise ship passengers (1995) 596,724

Cruise ship sailings (1995) 283

Cultural affairs The city of Vancouver first invested in the arts in 1893, when the city band requested a grant for its summer concert series. Just over 100 years later, Vancouver invests $6 million annually in more than 100 local non-profit arts organizations.

There are more than 200 non-profit art groups in Vancouver encompassing activities as diverse as classical sitar performances, ballet, fringe plays and art in public spaces. Non-profit art groups spend $70 million annually here and employ 10,000 people.

The office of cultural affairs (OCA), in the city's social planning department, advises city council on art and cultural issues, and develops and administers cultural policy and programs including cultural grants, public art, cultural facilities, the City of Vancouver book award and the transit shelter advertising program.

Cultural grants The city provides grants to Vancouver-based non-profit organizations that create, distribute, display and produce artists' work. For more information, refer to OCA's annual cultural grants brochure.

Public art Since 1990, the city has adopted several policies which encourage artwork in publicly accessible spaces. The public art program provides opportunities for people to experience art in everyday life and for artists and communities to participate in the design, look and feel of our city. *Panorama,* the City of Vancouver's public art newsletter, was launched in 1996 to keep artists and art groups up-to-date on public art happenings and projects. Public art for private development requires major new developments to allocate $0.95 per square foot to public art. See Elizabeth

Godley's article in this book.

Cultural facilities The city owns and operates three theatres through the Vancouver Civic Theatres Department: the 670-seat Vancouver Playhouse; the 2,930-seat multipurpose Queen Elizabeth Theatre; and the Orpheum, a 2,800-seat heritage concert hall. In addition, the Firehall Theatre, Vancouver East Cultural Centre, Vancouver Museum, Planetarium and the Vancouver Art Gallery are all owned by the city and run by non-profit societies. The city has also helped organizations such as the Canadian Craft Museum, Vancouver Cultural Alliance and Vancouver Community Arts Council develop new facilities through an amenity bonusing program.

Growth in the past two decades has created a shortage of facilities. The city is encouraging the development of an arts complex (including a 1,500-seat lyric hall and a 350-seat flexible studio theatre) in the Marathon Coal Harbour redevelopment; shared rehearsal/ production/administration space for the Vancouver Dance Centre and Ballet British Columbia; and affordable artists' studios and live/work space.

City of Vancouver book award The city gives an annual award and $2,000 to the author of an outstanding book that contributes to our understanding of Vancouver's history, unique character and/or the achievements of its residents.

Transit shelter advertising program Advertising is crucial to the success of any enterprise. Through Seaboard Advertising, the city provides Vancouver-based non-profit art organizations access to low-cost bus shelter advertising space.

Dance at dusk Ceperley Park, at the Beach Avenue entrance to Stanley Park, is the site for early evening summer outdoor dancing: Scottish Country Dance, International Folk Dance, Ballroom, Square Dance and so on. No partners are necessary, instruction is free. Park board info: 257-8400. Fax: 257-8427. URL: parks/recreation/dance.html

Disabilities Programs for persons with disabilities include aquatic programs at Stan Stronge, Percy Norman and Britannia pools, and fitness programs at Riley Park Community Centre. See the summer programs listing below for children and youth with disabilities. Info: 257-8400. Fax: 257-8427. URL: parks/sumprog.html

Donations of historical material Ask the City of Vancouver Archives. 736-8561. Fax: 736-0626.

Earthquake preparedness More information can be found in the white pages of your telephone book or by calling the city's risk and emergency management office at 873-7724. The city encourages everyone to become better prepared. See the article on earthquakes by Daniel Wood. URL: corpsvcs/emerg/quakefact.html

E-mail a specific councillor Type clr followed by the councillor's last name followed by @city.vancouver.bc.ca. So, for example, to e-mail councillor Sam Sullivan you'd enter clrsullivan@city.van couver.bc.ca. There are two exceptions: Daniel Lee is cirdslee; Don Lee is drdtlee

E-mail the mayor mayorowen@city.vancouver.bc.ca

E-mail the mayor and all the councillors mayorandcouncil@city.vancouver.bc.ca

Emergencies The Kobe, Japan earthquake and the bombing in Oklahoma City have focused attention on the need to be prepared for disasters, natural or otherwise. The city has an ongoing emergency preparedness program to strengthen its infrastructure, inform residents and train employees to deal with such events. Over the past four years, the city has distributed more than 400,000 pamphlets on how to prepare for an earthquake. These are translated into five languages and are available at community centres, fire halls, and at City Hall. Information about disaster preparedness is also available on the city's home page on the Internet.

Emergency shelters In the event of a disaster, the city would use its 22 community centres to provide emergency shelter, clothing, food and basic medical care to disaster victims. The city currently has about 800 trained volunteers who would help staff the shelters.

Urban search and rescue team Fire and rescue services initiated a three-year project to train a cross-departmental team providing 24-hour urban search and rescue capability in the event of a building or structural collapse.

Post-disaster communications centre The city recognized the need to relocate its Regional 911 and police and fire dispatch systems into a building that will withstand an earthquake. See the entry here titled Radio System, Wide Area.

Seismic upgrading of bridges An $11 million project to seismically upgrade the city's older bridges is in progress. The Grandview Viaduct and the Granville and Burrard bridges have been completed. As a result, these bridges are more likely to withstand an earthquake.

Seismic upgrading of buildings The city has completed a seismic review of city-owned buildings and established priorities for gradual upgrading or replacement. The city has also completed a review of 1,100 privately owned, older, multi-occupancy buildings. This study will help the city to establish response

priorities and also to set policies for long-term upgrading.

Drinking water storage and transmission The engineering services department, in conjunction with other city departments and the Greater Vancouver Regional District (GVRD), is examining the feasibility of a 40-million gallon reservoir to store drinking water. If approved, this project would be part of the 1997-99 waterworks capital plan. To help the water system withstand an earthquake, flexible water couplings are gradually being incorporated into the transmission lines. To improve the reliability of the city's radio control of its water and sewer systems in a disaster, the radio repeater station on Grouse Mountain was replaced with an earthquake-resistant site.

Training and planning The city continues to participate in emergency exercises. These earthquake simulations have helped city departments identify weaknesses in their planning and coordination strategies. The city also offers specialized emergency management courses to selected staff on an ongoing basis and works with the GVRD in coordinated emergency planning.

Emergency centre See the entry here titled Radio System, Wide Area.

Environmental protection This branch is responsible for enforcement of the regional sewer use by-law. Its main functions are to carry out regular inspections and monitor the treatment and discharge to sewers of industrial wastes; search out the source and eliminate the flow of volatile or other hazardous substances entering public or private sewers; advise plant management, consultants and contractors on required waste treatment systems for wet waste industries. This branch also issues waste discharge permits on behalf of the Greater Vancouver Regional District and has increasing involvement in soil contamination assessment of properties. On an as-needed basis, technical support is provided to the Vancouver fire department's HAZMAT (Hazardous Materials) response team. The branch also participates in the city's special office for the environment. enviro.html

Expenditures Total City of Vancouver (1995) $548,742,100.

Faxback A way to get information from the city on your fax machine. Call 871-6266 on a touch-tone phone. Follow the voice prompts.

Filming In 1996, according to entertainment reporter Lynne McNamara, there were 25 feature films, 35 movies of the week and 14 TV series produced in Greater Vancouver.

Fire boats In 1991 the city, in conjunction with the Port of Vancouver and four other municipali-

ties bought five high-speed fire boats. Two are operated by the city and provide water-based firefighting capability.

Fire calls (1994) False alarms or no fire: 7,584. Fires with loss: 1,320. Medical incidents: 25,603.

Fire department See the article by Alex Matches in this book. The Vancouver Fire Department has a Web site at fire/index.html

Firefighting with salt water To ensure adequate water for firefighting, the city is spending $40 million to build three saltwater pumping stations for the downtown peninsula and Kitsilano. The False Creek station was operational by the summer of 1996. A second station, at Hastings and Broughton on Coal Harbour, will be completed by the summer of 1997. This system will be used to augment the fresh water supply system for fighting a large fire in the downtown peninsula. It is also capable of pumping saltwater for firefighting in the event of a failure of the domestic water supply resulting from an earthquake or other cause. More info: fire/info/about/swater. html

Fire trucks Photos of old Vancouver fire department fire trucks can be seen on the Internet at fire/info/gord/photo.html

Freenet Now Vancouver CommunityNet. Web address: http://www.vcn.bc.ca/welcome.html

Garbage collection Vancouver city council has set a goal to reduce the solid waste stream by 50 per cent. More info: 873-7644. URL: engsvcs/ waste/wastindex.html

Gathering place The Gathering Place at 609 Helmcken Street provides social, recreational, educational, health and food services to people living in hotels, hostels and residences, as well as those living on the street, in the Downtown South area. It opened March 20,1995. More than 900 people visit the facility daily.

Gifts for parks program The park board gifts program provides a means for individuals, businesses or organizations to donate funds to the park board to enhance the park system. Popular donations include benches, trees and water fountains, have included picnic tables, rose arbors, sundials, sculpture and other enhancing features. Call the park board: 257-8400. Fax: 257-8427. parks/gifts.html

Greenways are green paths for pedestrians and cyclists. They can be waterfront promenades, urban walks, environmental demonstration trails, heritage walks and nature trails. When the network is complete, no city greenway will be more than a 25-minute walk or a 10-minute bike ride from any residence. The first city-wide greenway project, Ridgeway, is on 37th Avenue between Knight and Granville. It passes VanDusen Gardens, Queen Elizabeth Park and Mountainview Cemetery. It will eventually extend from Pacific

Spirit Park in the UBC endowment lands to Central Park in Burnaby. The plan is available from the planning department (City Hall, East Wing, 2675 Yukon Street, 4th floor) or from engineering on the 6th floor of City Hall. 873-7090 or 873-7305.
URL: commsucs/planning/greenway/htm

Hastings Park restoration program As this book was going to press, the Pacific National Exhibition had one more year (1997) to go at this location. The Hastings Park working committee and the park board prepared a restoration program to shape the park after the PNE's departure. Momiji Garden, built in the park in 1993 to commemorate the internment of Japanese-Canadians during World War II, will receive special attention to overcome traffic noise. Several buildings will be retained (the Coliseum, Agrodome, Garden Auditorium, etc.) while others are doomed: the Pure Foods Bbuilding, Showmart, B.C. Pavilion and the PNE administration building. The huge Challenger Map within the B.C. Pavilion will be saved and relocated. Hastings Park Racetrack will be integrated into the setting. Call the park board: 257-8400. Fax: 257-8427.
URL: parks/hastpk.html

Heywood Bandstand Heywood Bandstand is in Alexandra Park, by English Bay. Concerts are on Sundays from late May through the summer. There's big band, modern jazz, Celtic, light classics, string music, etc. 257-8400. Fax: 257-8427.
URL: parks/recreation/bandstan.html

Hostel The Downtown Vancouver hostel in the city's West End can be reached at 684-7101. The hostel sleeps 220 at rates as low as $17.50 a room.

Hotel occupancy (average) 74.6 per cent

Hotei rooms in vancouver 11,121

Income, average household (1994) $60,262

InfoAction A Vancouver Public Library service (331-3613) that offers document delivery, research and on-line search services to individuals, small businesses and large corporations that need information very quickly. InfoAction will also answer questions on virtually any subject (except case law and patent law) for a base rate of $80 per hour. This includes questions on market research, statistics, and biographical or corporate profiles. InfoAction does not replace the VPL's existing service, providing access to its resources at no charge for visitors to the library who wish to do their own research.

Information Council reports, news releases, public meetings in Vancouver, city job listings and detailed information on the city's various departments and boards can be obtained at City Hall itself, or on the Internet at http://www.city.vancouver.bc.ca. Questions and comments? e-mail: info@city.vancouver.ba.ca

Information systems strategy The city anticipates implementing its own Internet server, providing Internet access to all local area network users, and is examining the potential for a city "broadband" communications system, bringing data, image, and voice communications into a single system.

Internet Vancouver's home page is http://www.city.vancouver.bc.ca. Some Vancouver Public Library branches have terminals where CommunityNet members can view this material and more. More than two dozen computer terminals in VPL's Central Branch are equipped with Netscape browser application software for viewing library information in World Wide Web format. This Web site, which can also be viewed remotely over the Internet, is the first step toward the goal of full Internet access in all VPL branches by Spring, 1997. The Web site address: vpl.vancouver.bc.ca contains information about library services and policies and a virtual tour of the central branch.

Internet technology implementation Since late 1994, the city has provided information to users of the Internet and responded to e-mail follow-ups. Statistics indicate several hundred people a day use the city's World Wide Web site. City staff use the Internet for research into how other governments are addressing common issues, for communication, and for retrieval of technical and product information.

While the number of people using the Internet is still relatively small as a percentage of population, growth is rapid. With one of the most computer-receptive populations in North America, Vancouver can expect the Internet within a few years to become a significant source of information.

Jobs If you're looking for a job with the city: URL: humanresources/jobs/jobspage.html

Kitsilano showboat An annual tradition since 1936 featuring outdoor performances with local amateur performers, held at Kitsilano Pool.

Land area Vancouver covers 113.1 sq. kilometres

Languages (1991 census data)

English 270,405 (59.8 per cent of city population)
Chinese 83,535 (18.5)
Punjabi 10,700 (2.4)
German 9,160 (2.0)
Italian 7,785 (1.7)
French 6,840 (1.5)
Tagalog (Filipino) 6,465 (1.4)
Vietnamese 6,030 (1.3)
Spanish 5,938 (1.3)

Libraries Total Vancouver Public Library system circulation in 1995 was 7,506,994. The number of questions asked librarians: 1,333,922. Visits to the Central Library: 2,304,010. Dial-in connections from home computers 89,654. An excellent

Web site was created by VPL, which includes a tour of the facility. Go to: vpl.vancouver.librarySquare/home.html#Tour. See the articles by Sandra McKenzie in this book.

Lifeguards Ask the park board about attending the Vancouver Lifeguard School. The free program runs from January to April. Other, more specialized courses related to lifeguarding have moderate fees.

Maritime history sources: The Vancouver Maritime Museum (http://www.seawaves.com/vmm.htm), the City of Vancouver Archives, and see several articles in this book.

Mayor For a listing of all Vancouver's mayors, see the article by Donna Jean McKinnon in this book.

Mayor's environmental achievement awards Given for voluntary environmental initiatives that preserve and protect the environment. Awards are announced and presented during Canadian environment week each year.

Multilingual information referral phone service Information on city services is available to Spanish speakers at 871-6464, to Punjabi speakers at 871-6565, to French speakers at 871-6767, to Cantonese or Mandarin speakers at 871-6868 and to Vietnamese speakers at 871-6969. This is a referral service on which voice messages may be left. URL: ctyclerk/intouch/html

Neighborhood emergency response team (NERT) The goal of the emergency preparedness division of Vancouver fire and rescue services is to encourage citizens to achieve 72-hour self-sufficiency, with stored emergency food, water, medical and sanitation supplies. NERT provides training and information.

Neighborhood Histories Source: City of Vancouver Archives. See individual articles in this book.

Neighborhood Integrated Service Teams NISTs work within the extensive network of city services existing in communities—in libraries, recreation centres, community-based policing, fire halls and through engineering with garbage collection, streets and sewers. Fifteen teams cover Vancouver's 23 neighborhoods, collaborating across traditional departmental and agency boundaries. This integrated approach helps them help communities solve problems such as excessive noise and illegal activities. As a result of the NIST initiative, many problems are resolved right in the community.

Neighborhood matching fund A park board program providing matching funds to nonprofit groups who want to improve and develop parks and facilities on park land. Examples include greening a street-end, building a community fence, creating murals, community gardens or orchards, developing natural or historical interpretation, building an information kiosk, etc. Info: 257-8400. Fax: 257-8427. parks/index

Orpheum The December 1995 issue of CityNews announced that after renovations costing $400,000 a new acoustically reflective ceiling at the Orpheum had improved the theatre's sound. See the book *Vancouver's Orpheum: The Life of a Theatre* by Douglas McCallum. theatres/index.html

Painters in the parks If you'd like to paint in Stanley or Queen Elizabeth Park, call the park board for details. (There are reasonable rules and modest fees.) 257-8400. Fax: 257-8427. parks/recreation/artist.html

Park board There are 175 parks in the system, featuring community centres, swimming pools, skating rinks, fitness centres, racquet courts, golf courses, pitch and putt courses, food concessions, marinas, a miniature railway and children's farmyard. The park board also looks after the city's street trees.

The Vancouver board of parks and recreation is at 2099 Beach Avenue. The first resolution of the first city council meeting in 1886 was to petition the federal government for the use of a 1,000-acre military reserve as a park. We know it now as Stanley Park, the city's first and still the largest. The history of the park is told in Richard Steele's books *The Stanley Park Explorer* and *The First One Hundred Years*. See the articles by Kerry McPhedran in this book.

Seven board members are elected by the public and meet weekly. Elected in 1996 were David D. Chesman, Gabriel Yong, Laura L. McDiarmid, Patrick Warren, Duncan R. Wilson, Allan Degenova and Alan P. Fetherstonhaugh.

Picnic sites Picnic sites on park board property are available from May 1 to September 30. There are electrical outlets, kitchens, covered seating, playgrounds and other amenities, although each of the 13 sites differs in its details. Except for schools, scout/guide programs and non-profit groups, there are fees for large picnic groups. Call central recreation services at 257-8482 for info and to book a site.

Playhouse, Vancouver See the article by Mark Leiren-Young in this book. theatres/index.html

Police Said Chief Constable Ray Canuel in 1996, "The introduction of community based policing throughout the city is the department's most significant initiative. Notable achievements to date have been the establishment of neighborhood safety, police and crime prevention offices; work with integrated service teams; and the creation of citizen advisory groups." The Vancouver Police Department has a Web site at: police/ index.html and may be e-mailed at

vpd@wimsey.com. See the article by Gary Hanney in this book.

Citizen Crime Watch Info Vancouver Police Department: 665-2224.

Community Police Offices Citizens can now access police services at:

Police/Community Service Centres, like the Vancouver police-native liaison society storefront project at 239 Main Street; and the Chinatown police community services centre at 18 East Pender. The offices are managed by full-time staff. In addition to police access, they provide professional services through trained counsellors.

Community crime prevention offices Joyce Street community crime prevention office, 5156 Joyce Street; Mount Pleasant community crime prevention office, 672 East Broadway; Broadway Station community crime prevention office, Broadway at Commercial; Little Mountain/Riley Park safer communities office, 3998 Main Street.

Neighborhood Police Offices Neighborhood police use these offices as administrative bases for report writing and other duties. They also work out of these community funded offices to bring crime prevention programs and problem-solving strategies to the neighborhood. They may also handle walk-in crime reports or intelligence. Offices located at:

West End Community Centre, 780 Denman Street.

Waterfront Hotel Community Services Centre, 900 Canada Place Way.

North False Creek Community Police Centre, 1223 Pacific Boulevard.

Gastown Neighborhood Police Office, 12 Water Street.

Strathcona/Hastings North Neighbourhood Police Office, Strathcona Community Centre, 601 Keefer Street.

Downtown Eastside Neighborhood Safety Office, 12 East Hastings.

Britannia Community Centre, 1651 Napier Street.

Police Visitation Programs Established in areas of the city where the community and the police have not felt a strong need for a permanent office. Officers are available for weekly consultation in community centres and other sites on a pre-scheduled basis. There are PVPs at Kensington, Kerrisdale, and Marpole community centres, the West Point Grey Public Library and at the Musqueam police visitation program, 6615 Salish Drive. Non-emergency crime reports are taken from victims and witnesses during these visits, and crime prevention and personal safety advice is given.

Domestic violence and criminal harassment unit Active since February 1996. The unit provides a service to victims from the initial investigation to the trial and beyond.

Direct data entry Direct data entry is replacing a system in which officers' reports were written by hand, then entered into a records management system by civilian data entry clerks. The new system permits timely access right in the officer's car to data for follow-up investigators.

Police board The board governs the actions of the city's police force. There are seven members: the mayor (chair), one member appointed by city council (not a councillor) and five appointed by the provincial cabinet. The board meets monthly.

Police department museum See the article on museums by Kerry McPhedran. police/index. html and e-mail: vpd@wimsey.com

Police and fire department voice mail On July 25, 1995 Council approved funding for a voice mail system for the police and fire departments. The system significantly improves access by community members to their neighborhood patrol officers and specialty sections within the department, and improves service on the 665-3321 report line.

Population (1995 estimate) 521,048. For information on the city's past population figures, see the article by Richard von Kleist in this book.

Queen Elizabeth Theatre theatres/index.html

Questions? The meaty site shown below tells you who to contact at City Hall about, oh, for example, dogs in parks, abandoned vehicles, childcare, civic theatres, noise complaints and dozens of other issues: ctyclerk/info_depts_boards/bbenquiries.html

Radio System, Wide Area In July 1996 a wide area radio system to link emergency services in southwestern B.C. was announced. The system enables communications among the 6,000 police, fire and ambulance personnel who protect two million people in the area. The system will be headquartered at the emergency operations and communications centre, an earthquake-hardened facility to be built at Rupert and Hastings in 1997 and 1998. The 9-1-1 emergency dispatch system will also be moved here.

Rain barrel program The city has designed and manufactured rain barrels for use by residents for garden irrigation. The city subsidizes the cost by 50 per cent. Residential garden irrigation accounts for 40 per cent of domestic summer water consumption. The barrels are manufactured locally, using recycled plastic, and have connections for hoses and faucets to fill watering cans. They weigh 20.5 kilograms and hold 195 litres. Cost: $68. They can be purchased on the 4th floor of City Hall. More info: 871-6144 or 873-7350. See the entry on water conservation in this article.

Recreation spending per capita (1992)
Live sports $77
Live performances $60
Cinema $54
Cable $196

Recycling Hotline Call 327-7573 for information on **Recycling Pickup** or check the Web site: vcs/waste/wastindex.html. There is a map showing garbage and recycling pickup days at: http://www.city.vancouver.bc.ca/engsvcs/gar.gif

Schools More than 56,000 students attend Vancouver public schools. There are 73 elementary schools, 18 primary annexes and 18 secondary schools. The Vancouver school board has a yearly operating budget of more than $350 million and employs more than 3,200 teachers. The students represent more than 100 different language groups. The board has an Internet home-page: http://www.vsb.bc.ca for students, teachers and parents. High school students are helping to expand and improve it. There is also a thriving adult education program: each year, more than 80,000 adults take courses. Elected to school board in 1996: Ken Denike, John Cheng, Bill Brown, Sandy McCormick, Ted Hunt, Bill S.T. Yuen, Barbara Buchanan, John R. Robertson, Mary Salvino Kambas. Vancouver School Board, 1595 West 10th Avenue. 731-1131.

Seawall, Stanley Park The seawall officially opened Sept. 26, 1971. Nine kilometres long, it recently became useable by in-line skaters. You can fish for smelt from the seawall but there are rules relating to times and equipment. See the Stanley Park article in this book. Call the park board for info: 257-8400. Fax: 257-8427.

Services Map A map showing libraries, community centres, police offices, firehalls, health units and other civic facilities. Look for it on the Internet at graphics/mappage.html

Snow removal Call 873-7078 for more info.

Sports The city administers a wide variety of locations where sports are played. For info on baseball, basketball, field sports, fitness centres, golf, horseshoe pitches, ice rinks, indoor and outdoor pools, racquet courts, shuffleboard, tennis and volleyball, call the park board: 257-8400. Web site information on each of these sports is at: parks/recreation/

Street Signs Own a piece of Vancouver by buying street name signs from the city. For info: 873-7341.
Details at: transport/transportindex. html

Summer Programs for Youth and Children with a Disability The park board runs recreational and other programs around the city for children and youth with mental, emotional and intellectual disabilities. Call for info: 257-8400. Fax: 257-8427. URL: parks/sumprog.html

Telephone numbers for the mayor and council members are listed at: ctyclerk/councilmail.html

Theatres theatres/index.html See also specific theatres: Orpheum, Playhouse, Queen Elizabeth, and many references in this book.

Tourist attractions Accommodation, transportation, dining, events and other tourism information is at commsvcs/planning/atoz/tourattract.html which also links to related sites. The city funds an organization, Tourism Vancouver, to run promotion and information programs. Tourism Vancouver is at: Suite 210 - 200 Burrard Street, Vancouver, B.C. V6C 3L6. Tel: (604) 683-2000 Fax: (604) 682-1717, or http://travel.bc.ca/vancouver/new.html. See the article in this book by Tom Poiker.

Trade and Convention Centre Shown on commsvcs/commsvcsindex.html

Traffic signals There are 560 in the city.

Transportation 871-6060 Fax: (604) 873-7255. engsvcs/transport/transportindex.html

Transportation, non-city managed The city reminds residents there are some transportation matters it is NOT responsible for. Among them: BC Transit (bus, SkyTrain and SeaBus routes and schedules: 521-0400); BC Ferries (277-0277); Air Care (775-0103); the Arthur Laing Bridge (federal); the Lions Gate; Second Narrows; Oak Street and Knight Street bridges (provincial: 660-2421); Granville Island (666-6655) and UBC (822-2211).

Transportation Plan Vancouver faces a number of transportation problems. Solutions may include rapid bus corridors along Broadway (the 99B-Line began September 3, from Lougheed Mall to UBC); light rapid transit lines, like SkyTrain; more traffic calming processes; enhanced pedestrian and bicycle access; improved transit to and from downtown; and new formulas to pay for transit. Call 871-6288 for information. engsvcs/transport/transportindex.html or e-mail transportation_plan@ city.vancouver.bc.ca

Trees city.vancouver.bc.ca has a listing regarding protection of trees. See the articles by Terri Clark and Carol DeFina in this book. To promote planting trees on private property, the city, in cooperation with the B.C. Nursery Trades Association and the Tree Canada Foundation, coordinated in 1996 a one-time program to sell 3,000 trees to Vancouver residents at reduced prices. For more on tree programs call the information line at 871-6378.

Vancouver A to Z This is an excellent and richly detailed look at subjects like the ALRT (SkyTrain), assessment and taxation statistics, bicycle paths, bridge dimensions, the Civic Merit Award, and much more. commsvcs/planning/atoz/atozindex.html

Vancouver Artist Residency Award In May 1996 the city presented its first City of Vancouver artist residency award. It provides the use of a city-owned artist live/work studio (on East 4th Ave.) for three years. There is no cost to taxpayers: the site was acquired through a development density bonus. The award's first recipient (unanimously chosen by a panel of artists): Teresa Marshall, a Vancouver-based multimedia artist.

Vancouver CommunityNet Once called Vancouver Freenet this is a free online service run by the Vancouver Community Network Association. Membership is available by a small donation. The list of community organizations linked to CommunityNet is huge: we counted 125 links! http://www.vcn.bc.ca/welcome.html

Vancouver Trends *Vancouver Trends* is a 124-page document produced by the Finance Department. It comprises 170 charts grouped into 10 areas: Setting, People, Economy, Parts of the City, Moving Around, Leisure, Services to People, Services to Property, City Hall and Special Concerns. Copies are available for $7 at Planning, 3rd floor East Wing, 2675 Yukon Street.

Vehicles (inbound, 24 hour average, 1995) 402,645

Water Conservation The city experienced water shortages in the summers of 1990 and 1992. Average household water demand can more than double during the summer, with a great deal of the total water used for lawn sprinkling. The city advises that a lawn needs only about an inch of water a week, about one hour of sprinkling. Household water use on an average summer day in Vancouver: faucets 7 per cent; toilets 20 per cent; dishwashers 2 per cent; bath/showers 18 per cent; laundry 13 per cent; and "outdoors" a full 40 per cent. See the entry on rain barrels in this article.

Waterworks See the GVRD article in this book for the history of water supply to Vancouver. engsvcs/water/index.htm and engsvcs/wwhistory/history.html

Weather intellicast.com/weather/yvr/ This site links you to current weather information from all over the world, including the Vancouver area.

Weddings at Parks and Beaches Wedding ceremonies can be held at park board beaches, parks and picnic sites. For details on locations, rental fees (moderate), hours and capacity, call the park board for info: 257-8400. Fax: 257-8427. parks/weddings.html

Youth See the entry on Civic Youth Strategy.

Vancouver's Coat of Arms and The Mace
Lori L. Wallis & Jake Adams

Mayor Gordon Campbell shows the mace to local school children. vs

THE COAT OF ARMS—During its controversial past Vancouver's coat of arms has been referred to as "a glorious mess" by one former mayor; another proclaimed that "it had more flaws than a dog had fleas." There were enough "fleas" for Britain's College of Arms to refuse to register the design without corrections.

The story goes back to April 6, 1886, the date of Vancouver's incorporation. The city's first coat of arms was designed by Lauchlan A. Hamilton. It was a representation of things that were the lifeblood of the city at that time, depicting a sailing ship, a tree, wooden docks and a train.

Vancouver's second coat of arms was designed by local artist James Blomfield. He prepared several sketches and a design was formally adopted in 1903. The only part of Hamilton's original coat of arms that was incorporated into James Blomfield's creation was the motto, "By sea and land we prosper."

Blomfield's coat of arms pictured a shield meant to represent Vancouver's situation on the sea and its worldwide commerce. The use of the ship's sail and the mural crown on top of the shield indicated Vancouver's status as a seaport. A fisherman and a lumberjack stood at each side of the shield as a representation of two vital industries in the city at that time.

The design was used as Vancouver's official coat of arms until 1969 but was never registered with the College of Heralds because it broke several rules of heraldry. It was this particular coat of arms that was criticized over the years. Several unsuccessful attempts were made to have the coat of arms updated prior to 1969.

Finally Vancouver adopted a new coat of arms on March 31, 1969, which was registered with the College of Heralds in London, England. It differs only in detail from the previous one.

The winged rod of Mercury, entwined with snakes (a sign of prosperity), was replaced by a totem pole of Kwakiutl design that included representations of the eagle, grizzly bear and halibut. The blue waves on the shield have been reduced in number, from seven to four, to make room for the dogwood flowers on a golden background. The dogwood is the provincial flower of British Columbia and the totem pole is one of the most recognizable forms of West Coast native culture.

The helmet on top of the shield was redesigned to include a mantle, which resembles a wavy scarf. The oar and tree branch, which were held by the lumberjack and fisherman in the previous coat of arms, were omitted but the axe remained.

The word "air" was added to the motto, which now reads "By sea, land and air we prosper." It was added to recognize the increasing amount of air travel and transport that marked Vancouver as a major city on the Pacific Rim.

The coat of arms is not a registered trademark although it is registered with the College of Heraldry. Controversies have arisen over the years about the use and misuse of the city's coat of arms. In 1986 debate was sparked because campaign literature used by the Non-Partisan Association bore the city's coat of arms. Some council members at the time believed that gave the impression the City of Vancouver was endorsing NPA candidates.

A decision was made that only official documents of the city can use the coat of arms. It is now the city's policy not to give any person or association permission to use it.

THE MACE

The City of Vancouver mace is a ceremonial staff which symbolizes authority. It is a reproduction of the mace of the City of London, England but instead of the wood used in the shaft of that mace, the shaft of Vancouver's is made from almost three kilograms of silver.

The head of the mace has four compartments: The New Royal Cipher, the Arms of the City of Vancouver, the Arms of the City of London, and the Maple Leaf. The cushion bears the Royal Arms while the arches are exact copies of the original ornate design.

Mayors of Vancouver
Donna-Jean MacKinnon

Malcolm Alexander MacLean 1886–87
(b. Aug. 14, 1844, Tiree, Scotland; arr. Vancouver 1885; d. Apr. 4, 1895, Vancouver)
Though the man who was to be first mayor of Vancouver had only recently moved from Winnipeg and had to be persuaded to run, he grew into his role and established the office of mayor with a combination of pioneer spirit and distinction. MacLean, a realtor, was practically unknown to voters in Vancouver's first election, but he presented himself well, had travelled widely and was not Richard H. Alexander, MacLean's only opponent. Alexander was the unpopular manager of the Hastings Sawmill, the biggest employer in Granville. The city's first election was as honest as could be expected for the time, which is to say, not very. There was chicanery on both sides. MacLean won by 17 votes and "people were so elated that they took him in a buggy and hauled him all over what there was of the little town." Less than a month later the Great Fire of June 13, 1886, destroyed most of Vancouver. Mayor MacLean lost all his possessions but plunged into organizing relief efforts and distributing rations sent from New Westminster. It became obvious he was willing and able to guide the citizens through the crisis. After the initial shock of the fire MacLean called council together in a tent at the northeast corner of Carrall and Water Streets, and resumed the direction of civic affairs "without five cents in the bank, without an assessment roll and without even a chair to sit upon." Challenges to his mayoralty were dropped and he went on to win the next election fair and square. Just one year after the Great Fire, MacLean greeted the first train and the first steamship into Vancouver on behalf of its proud citizens.

David Oppenheimer 1888–91
(b. Jan. 1, 1832, Bleiskastel, Germany; arr. Vancouver 1860; d. Dec. 31, 1897, Vancouver)
Often called the "father" of Vancouver, this wealthy entrepreneur believed public works operations belonged to the taxpayers. During the election campaign of 1888 he promised a sceptical electorate its own water service, public transportation and a sewage system. Within two years, streetcars were running along city streets and a water connection from the Capilano River had been installed. Oppenheimer personally paid the water fees and liberally donated money for the construction of Alexandra Orphanage and the YMCA. He also donated land for city parks including East Park (later Exhibition Park, now

Hastings Park, home for years to the PNE). The second-largest landowner in Vancouver after the Canadian Pacific Railway, Mayor Oppenheimer fostered industrial development when he donated land for B.T. Rogers to build a sugar refinery—the first manufacturing operation in the city. He established the B.C. Electric Railway Company (now B.C. Hydro). Part of the alternative to the West Side, CPR-affiliated business elite led by William Templeton, David Oppenheimer was acclaimed mayor in two of his four single-year terms of office.

Frederick Cope 1892–93
(b. July 9, 1860, Oxford, England; d. Sept. 19, 1897, Yukon)
During Fred Cope's mayoralty Vancouver was experiencing its first economic slowdown and Mayor Cope's efforts were directed to limiting expenses. City staff were laid off and those remaining had pay cutbacks. Because of Mayor Cope's efforts, The Canada-Australia Steam Line began servicing Vancouver, with the first ship (RMS *Minonuera*) arriving in Vancouver on June 8, 1893. He was elected mayor for two consecutive terms.

Robert Alexander Anderson 1894
(b. circa 1858, Belfast, PEI; arr. Vancouver 1887; d. circa 1916, Vancouver)
Anderson was an alderman (1892-93), as well as a realtor. In a decade of slowing financial fortunes in Vancouver, he was fully occupied managing a civic administration with a shrinking budget. He continued layoffs of civic employees begun the year before by Cope. More positively, a temporary relief committee assisted those out of work, a water committee was formed and milk inspections were instituted during his term.

Henry Collins 1895-96
(b. 1844; d. 1904)
Mayor Collins came to Vancouver as a dry-goods merchant and participated in local politics as head of the Board of School Trustees, and as alderman before serving two terms as mayor. It was still an era when royalty and royal visits were revered; Mayor Collins' reception of Chinese statesman Li Hung Chang, Lord and Lady Aberdeen, and the nephew of the king of Italy was believed to be a feather in the cap of the young city and an indication of its growing importance.

William Templeton 1897
(b. 1853, Belleville; arr. Vancouver [Granville] Jan. 4, 1886; d. Jan. 16, 1898, Vancouver)
William Templeton, a butcher, was part of the CPR clique that benefited from the land grant given the company in exchange for making Vancouver its terminus. Despite his electoral victory, this affiliation aroused suspicion among the city's working class, whose contribution to public life

Mayor Collins' reception of the nephew of the king of Italy was believed to be a feather in the cap of the young city

was on the rise. Templeton is said to have been a bad political strategist with an aggressive personality. After failing to win a bid for mayor six years earlier (some say because of a slur he made on opponent David Oppenheimer's accent) he did, however, serve as an alderperson and later as school trustee. After losing his seat to James Garden in a bid for re-election, he purportedly committed suicide by taking an overdose of a sleeping potion.

James Ford Garden 1898–1900
(b. Feb 19, 1847, Upper Woodstock, NB; d. Dec. 8, 1914, Vancouver)
Mayor Garden, elected for three one-year terms in a city perched upon a decade of spectacular growth, had "the respect and confidence of all classes." As well as influencing the physical development of the city, Garden was literally a leader, heading a march of citizens to Deadman's Island to stop Theodore Ludgate from logging it in 1899. The so-called Ludgate Affair began when Mayor Garden read the riot act, defying Ludgate to "chop that tree." He did and was promptly arrested. Years of litigation followed and eventually Ludgate's 25-year lease from the federal government was cancelled, it being determined the property was part of the federal agreement granting Stanley Park to the city in perpetuity. As an engineer Garden's influence on development of the city's infrastructure is obvious. Projects he guided through development include an early streetcar system, sidewalks, road grades and water connections. Mayor Garden also donated the land known today as Garden Park.

Thomas Owen Townley 1901
(b. Aug. 18, 1862, Newmarket, Ont.; d. Mar. 19, 1935, Florida)
During Mayor Townley's year in office the largely British population of Vancouver joined commonwealth nations around the world to mourn the death of Queen Victoria after 63 years as

monarch. Later in 1901 when the Duke and Duchess of Cornwall and York came to Vancouver as part of the Empire Tour, Mayor Townley was said to have been a gracious host to the couple on behalf of the city.

After losing in a bid for a second term he became registrar of land titles in Vancouver, a position he had held previously in New Westminster. He is also remembered as the commander of Vancouver's first militia.

Thomas Fletcher Neelands 1902–03
(b. Mar 8, 1862, Carleton, Ont.; arr. Vancouver [Granville] Mar., 1886; d. Dec. 2, 1944, Vancouver)
Land issues marked Neelands' tenure. After being burned out of the flour and feed business in the Great Fire, he became involved with the Pacific Building Society offering mortgages by lottery to members who paid dues to build up the fund.

While he was mayor the city's recreational facilities improved and expanded with the acquisition of Alexandra and Strathcona Parks (now city hall), as well as Cambie and Powell Street grounds. He also acquired sunbathing rights on English Bay and officiated at the cornerstone laying of the Vancouver Free Library at Main and Hastings (now Carnegie Centre) on March 29, 1902.

Dr. William J. McGuigan 1904
(b. July 18, 1853, Stratford, Ont.; d. Dec. 25, 1908)
McGuigan was said to be a good writer and speaker as well as the most titled man in Vancouver. Ambitious though he was, holding both law and medical degrees, he seems to have given himself wholeheartedly to the development of Vancouver. "There should be no hint of personal ambition," he said, "at the expense of our collective security." While in office Mayor McGuigan oversaw improvements to False Creek that led to the filling in of the portion east of Main about a decade later. His other involvement in civic institutions included work with the B.C. Medical Association, the High School Board and the Free Library Board. His brother Thomas was Vancouver's first city clerk.

Fred Buscombe 1905–06
(b. Sept. 2, 1862, Bodmin, England; d. July 21, 1938)
Glassware merchant Fred Buscombe was a resident of the working-class neighborhood of Mount Pleasant. It was a time when both neighborhood and Downtown commercial development was flourishing. The expansion of streetcar lines to outlying communities allowed working-class families to own homes while working Downtown.

Low water pressure in neighborhoods on the south slopes of False Creek was a hot topic on the campaign trail in these years and Buscombe left his mark on the city by fostering the develop-

ment of the Greater Vancouver Water Board. As the construction boom escalated, white-skinned workers were in short supply and resentment of Asian workers led to ugly incidents of racism. During Buscombe's second term as mayor, council passed a motion asking the federal government to suspend the immigration of East Indians into Canada. This was seven years before the ill-fated *Komagata Maru* passengers were refused entry into Vancouver.

Alexander Bethune 1907-08
(b. Jan. 1, 1852, Peterborough, Ont.; d. June 10, 1947)
Bethune, a shoe merchant, had shown his commitment to the city by serving five years in the role of alderman. During his term as mayor, council asked the federal government for use of the Kitsilano Indian Reserve for city purposes.

Charles Stanford Douglas 1909
(b. Oct. 1, 1852, Madison, Wisconsin, of Scottish ancestry; arr. Vancouver 1889)
Douglas served but a single term after defeating four other candidates. An American-journalist-turned-Vancouver-realtor he officiated at the opening of the first Granville Street Bridge.

Louis Denison Taylor 1910—11
(b. July 22, 1857, Ann Arbor, Michigan; arr. Vancouver Sept. 17, 1896; d. Jun. 4, 1946)
Michigan-born L.D. Taylor was one of the most popular mayors of Vancouver, serving seven times between 1910 and 1934. It was his flamboyance that usually got "L.D." back into office, most often during a period of growth and enthusiasm that followed a nose-to-the-grindstone administration. A tireless promoter of the amalgamation of Point Grey, South Vancouver and Vancouver, he was, however, not in the mayor's chair when amalgamation finally occurred in 1929. That honor went to Mayor Malkin, who slipped into office in between Taylor's two four-year terms. Taylor was called a courageous, capable administrator and initiator of many civic improvements. He opened the airport at Sea Island and supported the development of the city archives. Between periods of public office Taylor published and edited mining newspapers and produced a paper called the *Critic*, essentially an editorial leaflet on contemporary public issues. Being American-born Taylor's property qualifications were challenged twice during his public life. The first came in 1915 when Justice J.J. Clement ruled Taylor lacked property qualifications to serve public office. A by-election a month later returned him. The second challenge came in 1933 but there was no disruption of his term. In that final term, the earliest and harshest years of the Great Depression were stripping Vancouver of its possessions and its dignity. Taylor let it be

known that unemployed men were expected to go to provincial work camps or have their relief payments cut off. But Taylor's image with those who supported him in that stand became tarnished when he suspended chief of police C.E. Edgett for inefficiency. The next mayor-to-be blamed Taylor for bankrupting the city and that (along with an impression that he was too old for the job) was enough to defeat Taylor in the next three elections.

James Findlay 1912
(b. Oct. 5, 1854, Montreal, Que.; arr. Vancouver June, 1887; d. Oct. 19, 1924)
Findlay's background in mining and commerce led to an efficient, business-like civic administration. The monarchy-struck city got a reprieve from the mundane when the Duke and Duchess of Connaught visited in 1912.

Truman Smith Baxter 1913–14
(b. Nov. 24, 1867 on a farm near Carlingford, Fullerton Township, Perth County, Ont.; arr. B.C. 1890; d. Oct. 1956)
Baxter, a former teacher, merchant and Vancouver alderperson (1900, 1905-06, 1912) was unfortunate in coming into office just as the province, and indeed the rest of the country, fell into an economic slump that lasted until the middle years of World War I. All civic departments were reorganized to adapt to the financial crisis and war priorities. At the outbreak of the war city council voted a two per cent cut in pay for civil servants, but also formed a Charities and Relief Committee to look after those most in need. Mayor Baxter claimed it was really his idea, not Gerry McGeer's, to locate the new city hall in Mount Pleasant.

Louis Denison Taylor 1915 (see above)
Malcolm Peter McBeath 1915–17
(b. Dec. 2, 1880, Bruce County, Ont.; arr. Vancouver 1907; d. June 15, 1957)
An alderman in Vancouver from 1912-14, McBeath sat in the mayor's chair for two years immediately after.

Robert Henry Otley Gale 1918–21
(b. 1878, Quebec; d. July 26, 1950)
Gale stepped into the mayor's chair at the end of World War I when housing shortages, economic and social disruption, Spanish flu, the communist revolution in Russia and the general strike in Winnipeg made for a chaotic, reactionary time. Fearful that communist unions would take over workplaces and society in general, the city set up a conciliation committee for settling disputes between itself and its employees, following formation of the Vancouver City Hall Employees Association in 1918. Mayor Gale's greatest achievement was promoting the recognition of Vancouver as a major western port, a more credible claim since the opening of the Panama

Canal in 1914.

Charles Edward Tisdall 1922–23
(b. Apr. 9, 1866, Birmingham, England; arr. Vancouver Apr., 1888; d. Mar. 17, 1936)
When Tisdall stepped into the mayor's chair he became the only mayor selected under the system of proportional representation, in which the candidate for city council getting the most votes became mayor. As an earlier MLA (Conservative), a Park Board member for 15 years and an alderman, Tisdall's popularity and familiarity among the electorate no doubt helped him achieve the highest civic office. These were the first years to show a rise in prosperity since the end of the war, a phenomenon that helped fuel the drive for more schools and parks, and the expansion of port facilities in Vancouver.

William Reid Owen 1924
(b. Nov. 25, 1864, Ontario; arr. Vancouver 1899; d. Mar. 22, 1949, Vancouver)
Vancouver's mayor in the middle of the Roaring Twenties was strongly identified with one of the city's oldest neighborhoods, Mount Pleasant. At the time he became mayor Owen was a realtor and insurance agent there, and earlier had been its first blacksmith. His years in office were the first really good years economically since the post-war slump. Both public and private sources moved to develop recreational facilities and entertainment centres, building parks and golf courses. The number of movie houses grew rapidly. Owen was the first Vancouver mayoralty candidate to use radio in his campaign. He gave a ten-minute speech over station CJCE.

Before becoming mayor, Owen was on the board of directors of the Vancouver General Hospital and held an insurance policy worth $10,000 with the VGH as beneficiary.

Louis Denison Taylor 1925–28 (see above)
William Harold Malkin 1929–30
(b. July 30, 1868, Burslem, Staffordshire, England; arr. Vancouver 1895; d. Oct. 11, 1959)
Sandwiched between L.D. Taylor's double terms of office, merchant and importer William Malkin benefited from public disillusionment with Taylor. He gained the distinction of being the first mayor of Greater Vancouver following amalgamation with Point Grey and South Vancouver in 1929. One of Malkin's campaign slogans during the electoral race in 1928 was: "It's time for a change." Another was: "When you vote for Malkin, you vote for law and order, civic morality and fairness to labor." Malkin established a committee to look into corruption and embezzlement in the city's relief department, worked to bring about changes in civic policy to benefit the working class and wrote a book titled *The Conquest of Poverty*.

Malkin later donated a 2.4 hectare park behind his Kerrisdale home to the city, as well as the money for construction of Malkin Bowl in Stanley Park, the latter dedicated to his late wife Marion.

Louis Denison Taylor 1931–34 (see above)
Gerald Gratton McGeer 1935–36
(b. Jan. 6, 1888, Winnipeg, Man.; arr. Vancouver 1892; d. in office, Aug. 11, 1947, during his second term)
Gerry McGeer's campaign against L.D. Taylor, called the most exciting in the city's history, was really a lot of name-calling with snide intimations about law and order and the lack of it, and managing public dissent. The election itself was a slaughter for Taylor who lost by more than 20,000 votes. McGeer was voted into office on a mandate to fight crime and to do away with slot machines, gambling, book-making, white slavery and corruption in the police force. True to his promise McGeer confiscated 1,000 slot machines in his first week. His extraordinarily zealous and vigorous management style led many to call him a megalomaniac. He was both praised and vilified for his handling of a strike by 2,000 workers from federal government camps. In April, 1935, unemployed men from the camps converged on Vancouver, marched to Victory Square and demanded financial assistance from the city. A delegation paid a call to the mayor. The mayor had them arrested and then went to Victory Square and read the Riot Act, calling on the crowd to disperse. That night, police raided worker headquarters, a riot ensued and police on horseback were called out to control it. This led to a serious fracture in the population. Mayor McGeer, firmly entrenched on the side of the moneyed interests fearful of communist takeover, alienated many would-be supporters who sympathized with the strikers. Meanwhile his proposal to float baby bonds to finance a new city hall opened him to charges of extravagance and corruption, further alienating him from more voters. He won his choice of Strathcona Park at 12th Avenue and Cambie for the city hall but lost a bid for a second term. In 1947 McGeer won the mayoralty again with a huge majority but died in office just six months later. More has been written about Gerry McGeer than about any other of the city's mayors.

George Clark Miller 1937–38
(b. Jan. 9, 1882, Huron County, Ont.; arr. Vancouver 1841 from Manitoba; d. Mar. 17, 1968)
Miller was the first mayor elected under the at-large system, running as an independent. Wards had been done away with by an earlier plebiscite and party politics made its entry into Vancouver government. The strain of deprivation in Vancouver in the 1930s and the indignation of the

public over political showmanship made business-like alderperson Miller a timely candidate. His slogan, "Let's stop bickering and get down to work," may have been easier said than done, but Miller was a realist. He made no extravagant promises and would not promise not to raise taxes. He stood for law and order, and was opposed to civil protests, specifically those by the unemployed or by those against the Spanish Civil War. A decade later when Charles E. Jones died in office (Sept. 1, 1948), Miller took over the mayor's duties until the end of the year.

James Lyle Telford 1939–40
(b. June 21, 1889 on a farm near Valens, Ont.; d. Sept. 27, 1960)
A newcomer to the civic political arena, Telford was, however, no stranger to politics, having represented the CCF in the provincial legislature. In this election he offered "help for the forgotten man," tapping into the frustration of the voters after nearly a decade of poverty. Once elected, Telford resigned from the CCF because he felt civic office should be free of party politics. Despite his obvious working-class following, Telford won the mayoralty with fewer than 2,000 votes in a campaign featuring six other candidates. His challenges to the status quo, his socially unacceptable situation as a divorced man, overall economic improvement and the changed political climate of wartime led to the end of his civic career at the next opportunity.

Jack (Jonathan Webster) Cornett 1941–46
(b. Mar. 10, 1883, Lansdowne, Ont; arr. Vancouver 1907; d. Aug. 19, 1973)
The last reeve of the Municipality of South Vancouver, Cornett (a shoe merchant) was seen as a stable founding-father of modern Vancouver and was trusted to run the city during the disruptive years of World War II. His term was largely taken up with issues of housing and road improvements. He was an active chairman of the city's ARP (Air Raid Precaution Committee). It was not until the war ended and he was in his final year in office that the mayor's efforts came to fruition. Funding for housing improvements from upper levels of government finally came through, allowing the city to undertake a ten-year plan to improve city streets, sidewalks, sewers and lighting, and provide adequate fire protection in the harbor.

Gerald Grattan McGeer 1947 (see above)
Charles E. Jones 1948
(b. Jan. 19, 1881, Whitby, Cheshire, England; arr. Vancouver 1905; d. Sept. 1, 1948, in office)
Already an alderperson when he took over the position of acting mayor after Gerry McGeer died in office, Jones was duly elected the following December. But he too died in office, with former mayor George Miller assuming the duties

for the remainder of that year. Jones lobbied for the development of new industrial areas of the city, the filling-in of False Creek and the accommodation of the automobile with bridges and high-speed thoroughfares.

Charles Edwin Thompson 1949–50
(b. Sept. 17, 1890, Grey County, Ont.;
d. Apr. 19, 1966)
Thompson was a teacher, rancher, automotive dealer and, from 1945 to 1948, an alderman. His apparently contradictory combination of progressive and regressive policies made him a hard character to pin down. He felt that improvements to public transit, roadways and sewer lines as well as efforts to equalize civic taxes should be provided to law-abiding and politically correct citizens. However, civil liberties were impeded during his term through a policy requiring all civic employees to be screened for Communist sympathies.

Frederick J. Hume 1951–58
(b. May 2, 1892, New Westminster, B.C.;
d. Feb. 17, 1967)
This wealthy philanthropist and nine-year mayor of New Westminster donated his salary to charity while he was mayor of Vancouver. Although he won in an election notable for its absence of issues, Mayor Hume was particularly concerned about smog and litter—things generally assumed to have been issues of a later period. While mayor he worked to establish low-rental housing, hoping to do away with slum housing altogether. His community involvement outside civic politics included founding CJOR radio (as CFXC) in 1924 and the ownership and operation of the Vancouver Canucks from 1962 until his death. More than 2,000 people attended his funeral in 1967.

A. Thomas Alsbury 1959–62
(b. 1904, Edinburgh, Scotland; arr. Vancouver 1907; d. July 21, 1990)
Alsbury gained notoriety with his policy of closing board of administration meetings to the public, saying he had "no intention of taking a second look at the policy." Despite his progressive goals and humanitarian interests (he'd worked for the CCF for 24 years before resigning upon election), his abrasive, hard-nosed personal style alienated many would-be supporters and eventually led the Non-Partisan Association (NPA) to reject his candidacy for the mayoralty term of 1963-64. He later became a lively radio commentator on civic and provincial affairs and was involved in improving the lot of senior citizens.

William George Rathie 1963–66
(b. Apr. 1, 1914, Vancouver, B.C.; d. Nov. 26, 1994)
The last in a long line of NPA mayors, and the

first born in Vancouver. Rathie's terms of office coincided with a new emphasis on issues of the urban environment and its livability. As a tax expert and accountant, these were perhaps not the kinds of issues closest to his heart but his contributions were noteworthy. A 20-year program for Vancouver's redevelopment, encompassing transportation, low-cost housing and Downtown revitalization was under consideration and led to, among other things, the new Georgia Viaduct that allowed easier access to the Downtown. Low-cost housing projects including MacLean Park and Skeena Terrace were developed. Rathie got into hot water over the amount paid for renovations to the mayor's office at city hall, something he defended as necessary and fitting to the city's highest office.

Thomas J. Campbell 1967–72
(b. Oct. 5, 1927, Vancouver, B.C.)
Campbell, "Tom Terrific" to the developers who couldn't have asked for a better advocate for their interests at city hall, was an East End boy turned prosperous. Considered a brash upstart, Campbell was chronically absent from council, which didn't stop him from promoting a freeway through Chinatown and the demolition of the Carnegie Centre. He backed the construction of a luxury hotel at the entrance of Stanley Park but it was rejected by voters. It is for his stance during the Gastown riot in the summer of 1971 that Campbell is most remembered. The so-called Battle of Maple Tree Square drew more than 1,000 people to Gastown as a protest against the illegality of marijuana. But police on horseback were called in to break it up, arresting 79 and charging 38. A later judicial inquiry criticized the action, characterizing it as a "police riot."

Art Phillips 1973–76
(b. Sept. 12, 1930, Montreal, Que.)
Art Phillips, who came into the mayor's chair in a landslide victory, was as much an advocate of rehabilitating Gastown as his predecessor had been a detractor. A breath of fresh air, Phillips was one of the founders of TEAM (The Electors Action Movement), an innovative civic political party with a majority on council. He was in a position to implement policies to downsize density in the central business district, undertake local area planning and improve public transit. TEAM tried, but failed, to bring back the ward system of civic government. TEAM enjoyed strong support from Liberal supporters at both the provincial and federal levels and Phillips handily won two consecutive terms of office.

Jack J. Volrich 1977–80
(b. Feb. 27, 1928, Anyox, B.C.)
Lawyer Jack Volrich was a founding member of TEAM but his priorities and outlook seemed

more in keeping with the free-enterprise mayors of previous years. He considered running as an independent in his second bid for office and later still was a member of both the Progressive Conservative and Social Credit parties. Volrich was fiscally conservative and represented both a stabilizing force and a return to the old values in the midst of social ferment. He reintroduced much of the pomp and ceremony to the mayor's office, yet could be wooden and humorless.

Mike Franklin Harcourt 1981–86
(b. Jan. 6, 1943, Edmonton, Alta.)
Although working closely with council members of left-wing COPE (Committee Of Progressive Electors), Mike Harcourt ran as an independent in his bids for mayor. During his terms, civic policies and positions came into focus in terms of their relationship to the provincial (Social Credit) government's policies. Harcourt's mayoralty crystallized grass roots opposition to the provincial government most notably during Solidarity 83, a broad-based protest against provincial cuts to social programs, health and education. Harcourt was mayor during Vancouver's centennial activities but was criticized for his lukewarm response to Expo 86. He later became the leader of the New Democratic Party in B.C. and then premier in a landslide victory over Social Credit.

Gordon Muir Campbell 1986–92
(b. Jan. 12, 1948, Vancouver, B.C.)
Gordon Campbell is a former realtor and business person whose terms in office harkened back to the "good ol' days" of politics where civic government worked more closely with business in fostering development than with the community at large. During his term pro-development by-laws were passed that saw seniors and the poor ousted from rental properties from Kerrisdale to Gastown. Housing shortages led to squatters' protests and demonstrations as conversions to upscale condominiums meant more and more people were unable to find affordable housing. At the end of his second term, Campbell won the leadership of a provincial Liberal party that had gained right-of-centre support in B.C. following the 1991 decimation of Social Credit.

Phillip Owen 1993–
(b. Mar. 12, 1933, Vancouver, B.C.)
Phillip Owen is the first Vancouver mayor elected to a three-year term, a cost-saving measure approved at the last election. It is understandable that the pro-business stance of council has been maintained under his tenure as he was a longtime alderman and member of the NPA (Non-Partisan Association). Some say he is providing routine maintenance for NPA policies implemented under earlier councils but Owen's influence should not be underestimated.

Other Civic Governments
Richard von Kleist

VILLAGE OF ANMORE
Incorporated December 7, 1987
Area: 5 sq. kilometres
Population est. (1996) 900
Government, mayor and four councillors
Council meetings: 2nd and 4th Mondays
Administration: 2697 Sunnyside Road, RR #1
Anmore, B.C. V3H 3C8
Telephone: 469-9877 (fax: 469-0537)
Police: Coquitlam RCMP
Fire: Sasamat Volunteer Fire Department

VILLAGE OF BELCARRA
Incorporated August 22, 1979
Area: 5.6 sq. kilometres
Population est. (1996) 650
Government, mayor and four councillors
Council meetings: every 2nd Monday each
month
Administration: 4084 Bedwell Bay, Belcarra,
B.C. V3H 4P8
Telephone: 939-4411 or 939-4511 (fax: 939-
5034)
Police: Coquitlam RCMP
Fire: Sasamat Volunteer Fire Department

CITY OF BURNABY
Incorporated September 22, 1892 (became a
city September 22, 1992 on its 100th birthday)
Area: 92 sq. kilometres
Population est. (1996) 175,811
Government, mayor and eight councillors
Council meetings: three Mondays per month
Administration: 4949 Canada Way, Burnaby,
B.C. V5G 1M2
Telephone: 294-7944 or (touch-tone info line)
294-7930
Police: RCMP (229 officers)
Fire: Burnaby Fire Department (260 fire
fighters)

CITY OF COQUITLAM
Incorporated July 25, 1891 (became a city
December 1, 1992)
Area: 134 sq. kilometres
Population est. (1996) 100,946
Government, mayor and six councillors
Council meetings: 1st and 3rd Mondays, fol-
lowing Tuesday if Monday a statutory holiday
Administration: 1111 Brunette Avenue,
Coquitlam, B.C. V3K 1E9
Telephone: 664-1400
Police: Coquitlam RCMP (144 officers)
Fire: Coquitlam Fire and Rescue Department
(125 firefighters and personnel)

THE CORPORATION OF DELTA
Incorporated November 10, 1879
Area: 364.3 sq. kilometres

Population est. (1996) 96,870
Government, mayor and six councillors
Council meetings: every Tuesday
Administration: 4500 Clarence Taylor Cres-
cent, Delta, B.C. V4K 3E2
Telephone: 946-4141
Police: Delta Police Department (135 officers)
Fire: Delta Fire Department (130 firefighters)

CITY OF LANGLEY
Incorporated March 15, 1955
Area: 10 sq. kilometres
Population est. (1996) 22,750
Government, mayor and six councillors
Council meetings: once every two weeks
Administration: 5549 204th Street, Langley,
B.C. V3A 1Z4
Telephone: 530-3131
Police: Langley RCMP (120 officers)
Fire: City of Langley Fire Department
(30 firefighters)

TOWNSHIP OF LANGLEY
Incorporated April 26, 1873
Area: 313 sq. kilometres
Population est. (1996) 80,708
Government, mayor and six councillors
Council meetings: 1st, 2nd and 4th Mondays
Administration: 4914 221st Street, Langley,
B.C. V3A 3Z8
Telephone: 534-3211
Police: Langley RCMP (120 officers)
Fire: Township of Langley Fire Department
(182 firefighters)

VILLAGE OF LIONS BAY
Incorporated January 2, 1971
Area: 3 sq. kilometres
Population est. (1996) 1,414
Government, mayor and four councillors
Council meetings: 1st Monday of every
month, following Tuesday if Monday a
statutory holiday
Administration: P.O. Box 141, Lions Bay, B.C.
V0N 2E0
Telephone: 921-9333
Police: RCMP (Squamish) assigned two officers
Fire: Lions Bay Volunteer Fire Department
(20 firefighters)

DISTRICT OF MAPLE RIDGE
Incorporated September 12, 1874
Area: 267 sq. kilometres
Population est. (1996) 59,830
Government, mayor and six councillors
Council meetings: every 2nd Tuesday
each month
Administration: 11995 Haney Place,
Maple Ridge, B.C. V2X 6A9
Telephone: 463-5221
Police: RCMP (83 officers)
Fire: Maple Ridge Volunteer Fire Department
(4 career firefighters, 108 volunteers)

CITY OF NEW WESTMINSTER
Incorporated July 16, 1860, oldest incorporat-
ed municipality west of Ontario (became a city
August 15, 1872)
Area: 22 sq. kilometres
Population est. (1996) 48,000
Government, mayor and six councillors
Council meetings: every Monday
Administration: 511 Royal Avenue, New West-
minster, B.C. V3L 1H9
Telephone: 521-3711
Police: New Westminster Police Service (101
officers)
Fire: New Westminster Fire Department
(90 firefighters)

CITY OF NORTH VANCOUVER
Incorporated May 13, 1907
Area: 12.7 sq. kilometres
Population est. (1996) 41,854
Government, mayor and six councillors
Council meetings: every Monday up to four
Mondays a month; every 2nd Monday in July
and August
Administration: 141 West 14th Street,
North Vancouver, B.C. V7M 1H9
Telephone: 985-7761
Police: RCMP (158 officers)
Fire: City of North Vancouver Fire
Department (44 firefighters)

DISTRICT OF NORTH VANCOUVER
Incorporated August 10, 1891
Area: 178.2 sq. kilometres
Population est. (1996) 81,848
Government, mayor and six councillors
Council meetings: every Monday; in summer
every 2nd Monday
Administration: 355 West Queens. Mailing
address: P.O. Box 86218 North Vancouver,
B.C. V7L 4K1
Telephone: 987-7131
Police: RCMP (158 officers)
Fire: District of North Vancouver Fire Depart-
ment (141 firefighters)

DISTRICT OF PITT MEADOWS
Incorporated April 24, 1914
Area: 80 sq. kilometres
Population est. (1996) 14,500
Government, mayor and six councillors
Council meetings: every Tuesday
Administration: 12007 Harris Road,
Pitt Meadows, B.C. V3Y 2B5
Telephone: 465-5454 (fax: 465-2404)
Police: RCMP
Fire: Pitt Meadows Fire and Rescue

CITY OF PORT COQUITLAM
Incorporated April 18, 1913
Area: 34.8 sq. kilometres
Population est. (1996) 41,854
Government, mayor and six councillors

Council meetings: every 2nd Monday
Administration: 2580 Shaughnessy Street,
Port Coquitlam, B.C. V3C 2A8
Telephone: 944-5411
Police: RCMP
Fire: Port Coquitlam Fire/Rescue
(60 firefighters)

CITY OF PORT MOODY

Incorporated March 7, 1913
Area: 31.92 sq. kilometres
Population est. (1996) 20,459
Government, mayor and six councillors
Council meetings: every 2nd Monday
Administration: 240 Ioco Road, Port Moody,
B.C. V3H 3J3
Telephone: 469-4500
Police: Port Moody Police Department
(30 officers)
Fire: Port Moody Fire Department
(24 firefighters)

CITY OF RICHMOND

Incorporated November 10, 1879 (became
a city December 3, 1990)
Area: 168.1 sq. kilometres
Population est. (1996) 150,000
Government, mayor and eight councillors
Council meetings: every 2nd and 4th Monday,
following Tuesday if Monday a statutory
holiday
Administration: 6911 No. 3 Road,
Richmond, B.C. V6Y 2C1
Telephone: 276-4000
Police: RCMP (161 officers)
Fire: Richmond Fire Department
(239 firefighters)

SURREY CITY

Incorporated November 10, 1879 (became a
city September 11, 1993)
Area: 371.4 sq. kilometres
Population est. (1996) 294,000
Government, mayor and eight councillors
Council meetings: every Monday and Tuesday
Administration: 14245 56th Avenue,
Surrey, B.C. V3X 3A2
Telephone: 591-4011
Police: RCMP (387 officers)
Fire: Surrey Fire Department
(250 firefighters 275 volunteers)

VANCOUVER CITY

Incorporated April 6, 1886
Area: 116.1 sq. kilometres
Population est. (1996) 521,048
Government, mayor and 10 councillors
Council meetings: Tuesdays
Administration: 453 West 12th Avenue,
Vancouver, B.C. V5Y 1V4
Telephone: 873-7011
Police: Vancouver City Police Department
(1,084 officers)

Fire: Vancouver City Fire and Rescue
(642 firefighters)

WEST VANCOUVER MUNICIPALITY

Incorporated March 15, 1912
Area: 98.9 sq. kilometres
Population est. (1996) 41,778
Government, mayor and six councillors
Council meetings: every Monday except 5th
Monday
Administration: 750 17th Street,
West Vancouver, B.C. V7V 3T3
Telephone: 925-7000
Police: West Vancouver Police Department
(76 officers)
Fire: West Vancouver Fire Department
(82 firefighters)

WHISTLER MUNICIPALITY

Incorporated September 6, 1975
Area: 16.5 sq. kilometres
Population est. (1996) 7,200
Government, mayor and six councillors
Council meetings: twice monthly on Mondays
Administration: 4325 Blackcomb Way,
Whistler, B.C. V0N 1B4
Telephone: (toll free) 688-6018 or
(604) 932-5535
Police: RCMP (12 officers)
Fire: Whistler Fire Department
(16 firefighters; 36 volunteer firefighters)

CITY OF WHITE ROCK

Incorporated April 15, 1957
Area: 14 sq. kilometres
Population est. (1996) 17,603
Government, mayor and six councillors
Council meetings: every Monday, following
Tuesday if Monday is a statutory holiday
Administration: 15322 Buena Vista Avenue,
White Rock, B.C. V4B 1Y6
Telephone: 541-2100
Police: RCMP (21 officers)
Fire: White Rock Fire Department
(17 firefighters)

ELECTORAL AREA A (UNIVERSITY ENDOWMENT LANDS, PACIFIC SPIRIT REGIONAL PARK)

Unincorporated
Area: 14 sq. kilometres (includes Pacific Spirit
Regional Park at 7.63 sq. kilometres)
Population est. (1996) 5,503
Administration: GVRD

ELECTORAL AREA C (BOWEN ISLAND, BARNSTON ISLAND, HOWE SOUND, INDIAN ARM)

Unincorporated
Area: 897 sq. kilometres
Population est. (1996) 2,459
(Bowen Island 2,245; all others 214)
Administration: Greater Vancouver Regional
District

*Innovative contemporary housing,
False Creek, 1981.* vs

City Plan
Ann McAfee

I N 1928 HARLAND BARTHOLOMEW submitted Vancouver's first city plan to council with these words: "Few cities possess such a combination of nearby natural resources, a splendid harbor, a terrain ideally suited for urban use, an equable climate, and a setting of great natural beauty." Over the years there have been several plans for Vancouver. The two plans which most clearly defined a comprehensive vision for Vancouver were the 1928 plan prepared by Bartholomew and Associates, a consultant firm from St. Louis, Missouri and CityPlan, a 1995 plan resulting from broad citizen input.

In 1926 the Vancouver Town Planning Commission, a group of nine citizens, Major L.D. Taylor and representatives from the school, harbor, park, and sewer boards hired Harland Bartholomew to prepare a comprehensive town plan for Vancouver.

Bartholomew planned for a city of one million people focused on the "great seaport" of Burrard Inlet. The Fraser River banks and False Creek would be industrial. Businesses would spread evenly over the central business district to "prevent undue traffic congestion." The nearby West End would provide apartments close to jobs.

"The retention of Vancouver as a city of single family homes has always been close to the heart of those engaged in the preparation of the plan." West Point Grey was seen as a "desirable residential district" and "those who gain their livelihood by manual labor could find in the Hastings Townsite and in a replanned South Vancouver a place where they can build modest homes."

The Bartholomew plan was never formally adopted by city council. Nevertheless, over the years much of Bartholomew's vision was realized. Apartments covered the West End. The post-war boom brought new families to South Vancouver.

By the 1970s, well before the city reached Bartholomew's planned one million people, the 1928 vision became obsolete. What had changed?

The Bartholomew plan was prepared by professionals with little input from citizens. Residents now wanted a say in the future of their neighborhoods. Citizens said "no" to a freeway to downtown through Strathcona. Kitsilano residents objected to plans to redevelop the area for apartments.

Through the 1970s and 1980s citizens and city staff worked together to prepare neighborhood plans. As the downtown area grew nearby heavy industry no longer fit around False Creek.

City council initiated imaginative plans to redevelop False Creek for housing and parks.

However, neighborhood and mega-project plans were prepared without an overall vision of Vancouver. By the early 1990s it became clear that the plans did not necessarily fit into the kind of city people wanted. While people said they wanted more rapid transit, no neighborhood plans showed a rapid transit route through their neighborhood.

In January 1992 Mayor Gordon Campbell announced the city "will commence a new city plan. It must be a plan that reflects the Vancouver of today and, even more importantly, that projects a Vancouver for tomorrow". Council wanted the plan to address all issues facing the city and to involve a broad range of people including those who do not normally participate in city planning. This became the mandate of CityPlan.

The process Vancouver used to develop CityPlan was very different from Bartholomew's day. Indeed, the process was so unique that the City of Vancouver won national and international awards for the innovative public process which involved thousands of citizens.

The CityPlan process started in November, 1992 with city council inviting people from all parts of the city—including members of clubs, business associations, resident groups and interested members of the community—to meet in small groups called city circles. Their task was to suggest ideas for Vancouver and how to make them happen.

Over 450 city circles involving some 5,000 people were formed. Youth formed 150 of the circles. More than 70 circles involved multi-cultural groups who participated in languages other than English. The circles worked for three months to prepare ideas. Artists helped the groups display their ideas at a three day "Ideas Fair." Over 10,000 people came to the fair. The ideas raised issues and choices for Vancouver. During 1994 thousands of citizens helped make difficult choices for Vancouver's future. They talked about whether the city should grow or not. They talked about city services and who should pay for them.

During the three year process over 20,000 people actively participated in preparing CityPlan and more than 100,000 people said they "felt involved." In 1995 Vancouver city council adopted CityPlan as a new vision for Vancouver to guide policy decisions, corporate work priorities, budgets and capital plans.

What kind of city is envisioned by CityPlan? CityPlan keeps much of what people like about Vancouver while seeking to accommodate a share of regional growth and recognizing financial constraints.

Downtown Vancouver will continue to be the main office centre for the province. Rather than offices spreading throughout the Burrard peninsula, jobs are concentrated into the downtown core and central Broadway. New housing in False Creek North, Downtown South and Coal Harbour provides opportunities for 50,000 more people to live within walking distance of downtown jobs and activities.

The downtown needs a nearby "fridge" and "closet"—places for food, supplies and equipment to be sorted, stored and distributed. The port also needs backup facilities. Many industrial areas near the downtown area are being redeveloped for new communities. CityPlan keeps the remaining industrial areas—the False Creek flats and the area south of the port—for city-and port-serving uses.

In the past the city's residential areas offered one kind of housing. There were either apartments or there were single-family areas. Neighborhoods seldom offered both family and adult housing. As people's needs changed they had to move to other neighborhoods. CityPlan seeks more choice of housing in each neighborhood. In apartment areas more new units will be designed for families but at higher densities than traditional family housing. In single-family areas there will be more townhouses and apartments to meet the needs of households without children.

In 1928 Bartholomew found residents valued single-family areas. CityPlan participants also valued neighborhood character but they also wanted more choice of housing. The CityPlan solution is to concentrate new development in "neighborhood centres," leaving much of the existing neighborhood intact. The new centres will likely grow from existing shopping streets. They will provide housing choice, more jobs close to where people live and local services to reduce travel distances.

Pollution and congestion are problems facing all growing cities. It is not possible for everyone to commute by car. CityPlan supports GVRD plans to increase transit and provide more opportunities for walking and biking. The region has one rapid transit line—SkyTrain from downtown Vancouver to Surrey. There are plans for new lines along Broadway through Burnaby to Coquitlam, between Coquitlam and New Westminster and from Richmond to downtown Vancouver to be built during the next 30 years.

Over the long term Vancouver's new "neighborhood centres" could be linked by transit to each other and to the downtown core. More immediately, in 1995, city council adopted a "greenways plan" to provide walking and biking routes across the city. Much of the seawall route is in place. Bikeways link the Downtown Eastside via Adanac St. to Boundary Rd., west via Broad-

way to UBC and south via Ontario to the Fraser River. The first new greenway will be the Ridgeway route from Boundary Road across the city, linking Queen Elizabeth Park and Van Dusen Gardens with Pacific Spirit Park on the west.

CityPlan changes the way the city develops and delivers community services. In the past community services were developed and delivered from city hall. CityPlan creates "integrated service teams" which link city staff with neighborhood residents. Community police offices locate staff in the neighborhood to work with residents and businesses. Citizens participate in defining the services they need and in resolving local problems.

CityPlan keeps some of the qualities envisioned by Vancouver's first plan. CityPlan also sets some new directions by:
- increasing housing variety throughout the city to meet people's needs and make better use of existing city services
- locating jobs closer to where people live to reduce travel
- maintaining a diverse economy
- moving people by transit, walking, and biking
- changing the delivery of city services to a neighborhood-based model and
- supporting stronger neighborhoods through the development of neighborhood centres, local character zoning, community-based policing and integrated service teams.

Traditional neighborhood streets—like this one in Grandview, Vancouver—are models for planners' "new urbanism." 1991. vs

History of Planning in Greater Vancouver
Judy Oberlander

GREATER VANCOUVER "is unique both in regards to natural beauty and business prospects," but "is suffering in a special degree from haphazard growth and speculation in real estate, notwithstanding the progress that has taken place in the last few years in regard to the control of sanitary matters and local improvements." So wrote the eminent planner Thomas Adams in his 1915 essay "Report on the Planning of Greater Vancouver." Adams called for a comprehensive plan for Vancouver and its neighboring municipalities and the establishment of a commission to guide this process to "save the taxpayers of the future the heavy expense of remedying evils which are allowed to accumulate as a result of undirected and misdirected growth."

More than 80 years later the issues are similar and dialogue between local governments, community organizations, developers, elected officials and citizens throughout Greater Vancouver continues to focus on the rapid growth of Canada's fastest growing metropolitan area. For the past five years the annual increase in population of more than 40,000 people—equal to the population of Vancouver's West End—means 1.8 million people now live and work in Greater Vancouver.

Adams advocated a comprehensive approach to planning—a "city-functional" approach—with a thorough analysis of social, economic and physical conditions in which each part of a city was designed to serve a particular purpose: residential neighborhoods with services, a civic centre as the focal point for public life, industrial areas well served by transportation, business areas and an overall layout that encouraged links between these functions. Land was to be used efficiently and facilities such as community centres and hospitals were to be easily accessible. These principles guided the planning of Canadian cities, largely reinforced by Thomas Adams' writings. He traveled extensively across the country, was involved in many civic plans and established the Town Planning Institute of Canada in 1919. Greater Vancouver did not escape his attention.

The City of Vancouver was incorporated April 6, 1886. As the largest municipality in the Lower Mainland its planning initiatives influenced the surrounding areas. Other municipalities tended to follow Vancouver's lead as they grew and began to face similar urban issues. Vancouver has desirable features—its magnificent natural setting, its deep-sea port, extensive industrial activity, the terminus of the trans-continental railway, the climate—which have influenced its growth. Originally surveyed by the CPR the topography of Vancouver was largely disregarded and consequently a grid layout continues to dominate the urban landscape, with notable exceptions in areas like Shaughnessy and Champlain Heights. New Westminster was also laid out on a grid pattern (by the Royal Engineers in 1859) and this served as an inspiration for other municipalities.

As the largest municipality in the region Vancouver's planning history provides an insight into local planning initiatives. During the early boom years of the 20th century the city focused its planning efforts on life-safety issues such as fire and sanitation. Little attention was given to overall planning of the city. The layout of new streets was combined with the installation of sewers in Vancouver and Burnaby in the first decade of the century. Building regulations and the development of civic amenities occupied local governments. Comprehensive building regulations in Vancouver came into effect in 1909; Point Grey (which along with South Vancouver amalgamated with Vancouver in 1929) passed a bylaw to regulate lot sizes in 1911; the Vancouver City Park Board and Stanley Park were created in 1888. As in other cities, citizens began to play an active role in the planning of their communities and through the Vancouver Board of Trade the City Planning and Beautifying Association was established. Thomas Adams visited Vancouver in his capacity as town planning adviser to the commission on conservation and through his lectures and writings encouraged the formal planning process. That began with his role as assessor of the Vancouver Civic Centre Competition in 1915. Lobbying for a provincial planning act began in 1917 and in 1925 the Town Planning Act of British Columbia initiated formal planning practices in the province.

The establishment in 1926 of the Vancouver Town Planning Commission marked the beginning of formal planning efforts in the city. Appointed by city council this voluntary commission had nine members—primarily businessmen—with five *ex-officio* members: the mayor and chairmen of the four public authorities (park board, school board, harbor board and the district sewerage and drainage board). At the time the commission served as the city's planning department and consequently its first task was to initiate a comprehensive plan for the city. Harland Bartholomew and Associates, town planning consultants from St. Louis, Missouri, were retained to provide planning services for Vancouver.

Over the next decade Bartholomew and his team were assisted by Horace Seymour, a Canadian town planner who served as the resident engineer for the planning commission. The team surveyed the city, prepared detailed reports on zoning regulations, street design, transportation and transit, public recreation and civic art and conducted meetings with the town planning commission in order to develop a comprehensive plan. It was published in 1928. The following year, when South Vancouver and Point Grey amalgamated with the City of Vancouver, Bartholomew was hired to plan these communities and amend his previous report. In 1944 he returned to Vancouver to assist with new planning initiatives; a 1946 Bartholomew plan for the Lower Fraser River Valley—stretching 4,600 square kilometres from the U.S. border to West Vancouver and Hope.—emphasized his interest in regional planning and a "scheme for control of decentralization."

Public education was an important part of the process and proved to be an important component of these early planning initiatives. Bartholomew's report focused on topics which interested the consultants, and there were some notable omissions such as a discussion of the physical character of Vancouver, housing requirements, social trends and demographics. City council was slow to adopt his recommendations and only portions of Bartholomew's vision became reality. Legacies of his vision, such as the boulevards along Cambie Street and King Edward Avenue and the city's grid pattern, remain today as tangible, if fragmentary, evidence of this master plan.

In the 1928 report the planning commission was seen as the agency to monitor the city's growth and to provide assistance to other civic departments as well as to create links with Burnaby, New Westminster and other municipalities. According to Bartholomew, "it is the duty of the Town Planning Commission as of no other agency to keep careful and accurate records of this growth, testing from time to time the adequacy of the present plan and making necessary readjustments." The commission continued to play an active role in the 1930s and 1940s, and with assistance from various consultants worked with the civic administration to monitor Vancouver's urban development. As the city grew rapidly following World War II there was a need to formalize planning initiatives and as a result a planning department was created in 1951.

The planning commission continued to play an important role in monitoring development but growth in the planning profession and the increased complexity of civic administration gradually changed its mandate. In 1977 it was asked to develop a set of goals for the city. Other municipalities within Greater Vancouver have advisory planning commissions comprised of community volunteers who review development proposals and advise city councils on local developments.

The emphasis on neighborhood planning began in the 1970s with the creation of citizens' planning committees. Different approaches were needed in each neighborhood. Vancouver led the way with plans involving citizens and resulting in specific policies for a diversity of communities—Strathcona, the West End, Grandview and Shaughnessy, for example. The emphasis from the outset was on a two-way planning process with community participation. In the 1980s Vancouver examined how regional planning issues were applied at the neighborhood level and studied their impact on jobs and housing. With changing demographics social issues have assumed a new importance and today municipalities in Greater Vancouver have social planning departments which address matters such as affordable housing, neighborhood services and cultural issues.

The urbanization of the suburbs increased after World War II and in recognition of the need to plan at the regional level the Lower Mainland Regional Planning Board (LMRPB) was created in 1949. Its jurisdiction extended 160 kilometres up the Fraser Valley to Hope. Efficient regional government was gradual and during the 1950s Vancouver tended to dominate the other municipalities where regional planning issues were concerned. Surrounding communities were already linked through special-purpose districts such as the Greater Vancouver Water District or the sewerage and drainage board. These boards facilitated planning initiatives since member municipalities participated in their administration. This requirement continues today, membership on these boards being comprised of elected officials from member municipalities.

The LMRPB was disbanded in 1967 and replaced by regional districts which served a coordination and planning function for groups of municipalities. The provincial government had established the regional district concept in 1965 and the Greater Vancouver Regional District (GVRD) held its first board of directors meeting on July 12, 1967. Today the GVRD is a federation of 18 municipalities and two electoral areas whose membership includes the cities of Burnaby, Coquitlam, Langley, New Westminster, North Vancouver, Port Coquitlam, Port Moody, Richmond, Vancouver, White Rock and Surrey. Districts include Delta, the Township of Langley, Maple Ridge, North Vancouver, Pitt Meadows and West Vancouver, as well as the villages of Anmore, Belcarra and Lions Bay, Electoral area A (University Endowment Lands) and Electoral Area C (Bowen Island).

For a detailed description of the GVRD's many functions see the article on pages 278 to 287.

Greater Vancouver has gained an international reputation for various innovative planning initiatives over the years. A healthy economy, employment opportunities, rapid population increases and the desirability of the West Coast lifestyle have contributed to the region's urban design, the architectur-

CITY OF VANCOUVER
:BRITISH COLUMBIA:
CIVIC CENTRE
PROPOSED DEVELOPMENT OF THE BURRARD STREET SITE
VANCOUVER
TOWN PLANNING COMMISSION
1928

HARLAND BARTHOLOMEW
& ASSOCIATES
CONSULTANTS

Harland Bartholomew's proposed civic centre (to have been built between Burrard and Thurlow, south of Davie Street), 1928. cva

al character of its neighborhoods and general prosperity. The limited land base of the region circumscribed by the mountains, the border and the sea has increased development pressure and created economic challenges for both the public and private sectors. Successful planning initiatives include the rejection of extensive freeway systems, the redevelopment of the south shore of False Creek and the transformation of former industrial lands into town houses and apartments in the mid-1970s, and the creation of eight regional town centres such as Metrotown in Burnaby, Lonsdale in North Vancouver and Haney Town Centre in Maple Ridge. These town centres provide a focal point for higher density residential neighborhoods combined with business and commercial opportunities easily accessible via the regional transit system. They serve as an alternative to the familiar suburban commute into downtown Vancouver and as an effective way to accommodate urban growth and decentralize employment opportunities within the region.

For a detailed look at Vancouver's CityPlan initiative, see the article by Ann McAfee.

Generations of planning in Greater Vancouver have had a great impact on the area. Features include the concentration of major regional attractions like B.C. Place Stadium, GM Place, the new Vancouver Public Library and theatres near transportation nodes in downtown Vancouver, zoning and design guidelines which foster a distinctive character in neighborhoods within each municipality, policies which protect views of the mountains and the water, the retention of industrial lands providing employment opportunities, within Greater Vancouver and an extensive network of parks and open space with public access to water—the ocean, lakes, and rivers—throughout the Lower Mainland.

Vancouver Fire Department
Alex Matches

FROM VERY HUMBLE beginnings in 1886, the Vancouver Fire Department has long been considered one of the finest fire departments to be found anywhere. In 1911 it was deemed one of the world's finest by a committee "as regards to equipment and efficiency," behind only London, England, and Leipzig, Germany. In the 1950s, as the recipient of the National Fire Protection Association's Grand Award for having the most outstanding fire prevention program for 1956, the VFD was described as having "the best fire department on the continent" by the past president of the International Association of Fire Chiefs. And in November 1980 the Canadian Fire Underwriters Survey declared the VFD had achieved Canada's first-ever and only class 1 rating.

When the city was incorporated, its firefighting tools consisted of the citizen's axes, buckets, shovels and ladders, and little else. Although Hastings Mill had an old hand-operated "enjine," it was considered to be "not serviceable."

At city council's second meeting the manager of the local shoe store, Sam Pedgrift, asked them to help fund a fire brigade, but no funds were available. They did, however, pass a by-law providing for the institution of a volunteer brigade. On May 28, 1886, the founding meeting of the Volunteer Fire Brigade took place at George Schetky's men's clothing store, attended by some 40 people. Sam Pedgrift was elected chief of the Volunteer Hose Company No. 1. On June 2, Hook & Ladder Company No. 1 was formed with William Blair elected foreman. George Schetky was elected treasurer with $200 from public subscription, and the volunteers paid dues of "two-bits" a month. It was decided the hose company would wear blue shirts with white trim, so the ladder company picked red shirts with white trim. (They didn't have any equipment, but they wanted to look good!)

The story of the Great Fire of June 13, 1886, has been told many times. A young girl, out on the inlet in a boat said, "It was all over in 45 minutes, a grand but awful sight." Fewer than a dozen buildings survived. The next day, over the still-warm ashes, the rebuilding of the new city was begun with material supplied by the Hastings Mill. Eight days later the city ordered the following equipment from the John D. Ronald Company, of Brussels, Ontario: a 2,728-litre (600-gallon) per-minute Ronald steam pump, 762 metres of hose and four hose reels. The total cost was $6,860, which the manufacturer agreed could be paid over 10 years.

On August 1 the new fire engine and its supporting equipment arrived, and two days later was placed in service "under canvas," until the new firehall was built. The volunteers took the names the Invincible Hose Company No. 1 and the Vancouver Hook & Ladder Company No. 1. A week later the latter volunteers felt their name was an absurdity because they didn't have a hook and ladder, so they became the Reliance Hose Company No. 2.

The first major fire fought by the VFD was at Spratt's Oilery, near midnight on August 11, 1886, and described as "a considerable distance from town" (at the north foot of today's Burrard Street). By the time the volunteers pulled the engine uphill to the site of the fire there wasn't much to save of the abandoned fish processing plant, but they did manage to save a few nearby houses. The newspaper of the day applauded the efforts of the inexperienced firefighters and praised the engine as a "superior article."

An historic event attributed to the fire brigade was the hosting of the city's first-ever public ball, held in Gold's Hall on Water Street, to raise money for the brigade's purchase of uniforms and other expenses. More than 250 attended, the program consisted of 24 dances and a sumptuous banquet.

In October the firehall at 12 Water Street was opened, and it was about this time that Sam Pedgrift left town with the fire brigade's funds, never to be heard from again. Later, in an election, John Howe Carlisle beat John Mateer by one vote to become the new chief, a position he would hold for the next 42 years.

The city installed five 45,460-litre (10,000-gallon) cisterns underground. In May 1887 they were used to fight a large bush fire that could have been a repeat of the fire of 1886. With the new equipment and a shovel corps, the volunteers extinguished the fire. A few days later, on May 23, the volunteers, along with the Hyack volunteers of New Westminster, all in their finest parade uniforms, helped greet the arrival of the first transcontinental train into Vancouver. In June the first "hook & ladder" arrived at No. 1 Firehall.

Chief Carlisle convinced the city of the need for a team of horses so the men could perform more efficiently. In May 1888 horses were purchased for Engine No. 1, named M.A. Maclean in honor of the first mayor. In August a new No. 2 Firehall opened in the 700-block of Seymour Street. By March 1889 water from the North Shore mountains reached Vancouver, and by June the hydrant system was in operation, replacing the cisterns.

By September the first salaries were paid—the chief received $75 per month, the two engineers $60 each, and the two stokers, two drivers and six full-time firefighters $15 each. "Callmen" were paid by the fires attended.

In February 1890, 15 alarm boxes were installed. This was also the first year that records of fire alarms were kept, and that year the department answered 110 alarms. Fire damage was $17,300.

Tragedy struck at 1:30 a.m. on June 5, 1893, with the death of 25-year-old John Smalley, the engine driver from No. 2 Hall, who died when he fell en route to a fire. His was the department's first of 32 on-duty deaths.

The VFD became a fully paid department on July 1, 1893, with three firehalls and 30 firefighters. No. 3 had opened on Broadway, west of Main Street, on November 1, 1892, with a hand-drawn hose reel. No horses, but they had a telephone! When No. 3 got its first horse-drawn hosewagon on October 31, they had to borrow horses from the city water works to pull the wagon.

The period between 1900 and 1910 was known as the "Golden Years." The VFD added seven more firehalls—No.'s 4 through 10—and 20 more pieces of apparatus, including a self-propelled steamer and the first of the motorized rigs. Chief Carlisle gave up his buggy and favorite horse Billy in favor of a two-cylinder McLaughlin touring car in 1907. In spite of criticism he purchased the first three pieces of auto fire equipment offered by the Seagrave Company of Columbus, Ohio, and put them in service in early 1908. Vancouver's fire department, considered in the forefront of firefighting technology, was a "must-see" for visiting fire chiefs. The move to full "automation" was under way.

The first motorized aerial ladder was a 1909 22.8-metre tractor-aerial ladder, first of its type built by the Seagrave Company. It was purchased because of the large number of high buildings being built downtown, like the Dominion Trust Building at Hastings and Cambie, then the tallest in the British Empire.

By 1911 the city had 11 firehalls and 191 firefighters and more equipment was ordered, this time from the American-LaFrance Fire Engine Company, of Elmira, New York. Vancouver took delivery of Canada's first order of this manufacturer's equipment, beginning in 1912, including the department's first motorized pump, a 5,683-litre (1,250-gallon) per-minute engine that remained in service for almost 40 years.

The VFD became fully motorized in 1917, making Vancouver the first major city in Canada and possibly the continent to become so, many years ahead of other large cities. On July 7 the firefighters went on strike for better pay and conditions; city council grudgingly acceded to their demands. From the start of the war in 1914 until the two-platoon system came into effect in 1918, 340 men joined then left the fire department because of the poor conditions and moved on to jobs with better hours and pay. Vancouver's firefighters became the first and only Canadian members of the International Association of Firefighters, headquartered in Washington, D.C., on February 28, 1918. As Local

First fire engine in Kitsilano, 1910. CVA

No. 18, the firefighters continue to be part of the International.

The blackest day in the department's history occurred on May 10, 1918, when No. 11 hosewagon en route to an alarm struck a streetcar at 12th and Commercial, killing four of its crew of five.

During the twenties many important events took place. In 1921 the 17-member Fire Wardens Branch—responsible for inspections, enforcing fire by-laws and investigation of fire scenes—was formed. It replaced a police sergeant who had enforced the fire by-law on a part-time basis for many years.

The worst loss-of-life fire in the city's history occurred at the Royal Alexandra Apartment at Bute and Comox Streets. On a hot July 8, 1927, a painter's job became a nightmare when his varnish and thinners caught fire and turned the building into an inferno in which eight people died.

After many years of trying to get a fireboat for the city, Chief Carlisle proudly watched the launching of the 21,821-litre (4,900-gallon) per-minute J.H. Carlisle, purchased in part by

False Creek property owners. The boat was put in service on September 1, 1928, at No. 16 Station at the south foot of Drake Street.

The following year saw the amalgamation of Point Grey, South Vancouver and the City of Vancouver, which increased the size of the fire department to 250 firefighters and 21 firehalls.

In 1930 the CN Dock fire destroyed the new 305-metre long pier, and in August 1936 the Auditorium fire destroyed the home of Vancouver's Stanley Cup Millionaires in a spectacular four-alarm blaze. The best remembered of them all? The CPR Pier D fire of July 27, 1938, when the entire structure and its contents were destroyed, along with several boxcars and a fire truck.

The fire department added a new component, the "inhalator" crew, the Rescue & Safety Branch, on January 10, 1942. Over the years, the crew would save the lives of many.

On March 6, 1945, many thought the war had come to Vancouver when SS Greenhill Park blew up while loading at CPR Pier B. The explosion in her No. 3 hold rocked the entire downtown area, smashing many windows and killing eight longshoremen. The ship was towed through the harbor to Siwash Rock, where the fire was extinguished.

Tragedy again struck the VFD when, on September 14, 1945, three firefighters were killed in the McMaster Building fire on Homer Street.

In 1951 Vancouver Fireboat No. 2 was placed in service in Burrard Inlet. With a capacity of 90,920 litres (20,000 gallons) per minute, it was said to be the world's most powerful. It proved its worth the following spring when it was instrumental in containing and extinguishing a four-alarm fire at the United Grain Growers Dock. With the fireboat, which was able to reach areas of the fire that land companies could not, the waterfront was saved from a major conflagration. The damage was set at $3 million, but it was estimated that the loss would have surpassed $10 million without the boat.

Throughout the fifties there were many notable fires and incidents, including the collapse of the unfinished Second Narrows Bridge, at which VFD's then-new scuba team spent many hours searching for victims of the accident.

The first five-alarm fire, largest in the history of the department, occurred on July 3, 1960, when fire destroyed the B.C. Forest Products plant and lumber storage facility on False Creek. The fire covered an area equal in size to four city blocks and took many hours to put out. Every available firefighter and piece of equipment was called out, including both fire boats. Twelve firefighters were injured.

The Seventies added many new pieces of apparatus. In 1971, when the J.H. Carlisle was taken out of service, she was replaced by four 6,819-litre (1,500-gallon) per-minute "super pumps" stationed in the firehalls around False Creek, which by then was more easily accessible by land-based fire companies. Then, in 1973, the VFD received Canada's first 28-metre Calavar firefighting platform, which gave firefighters the ability to get up and over many fire scenes because of the rig's articulated column and boom.

With 40 fire deaths 1973 was the worst in the city's history. This terrible toll was partly caused by the lack of sprinkler systems in hotels and rooming houses. Steps were immediately taken to introduce new sprinkler by-laws. The following year the toll was dramatically reduced, and by 1982 deaths by fire were down to eight.

Throughout the 1970s and 1980s, many pieces of fire apparatus were replaced, nine new firehalls were erected and No. 6 was declared a heritage building and renovated. A new Fire Dispatch Centre located at the No. 1 Hall, VFD headquarters, superseded the old Fire Dispatch Office, at 20th and Cambie Street, which had opened in 1931. On May 28, 1986, the members of the department celebrated a "Century of Service."

Cutbacks in manpower in the late 1980s affected manning on fire apparatus and resulted in the decommissioning of Vancouver Fireboat No. 2. It was subsequently sold to the San Francisco Fire Department.

In the fall of 1987 district chiefs became known as "battalion chiefs." With the new fire alarm designations, the VFD's first six-alarm occurred at the Fraser Arms Hotel fire on April 24, 1988. Soon after, pumps were designated "engines," trucks became "ladders" and the articulated platforms (Firebirds) were known as "towers."

Into the 1990s changes continued: the 911 emergency telephone number covered the entire GVRD; the department hired its first female firefighter; fire apparatus became computer-equipped and now have cabs so the crew can ride to alarms in safety; men are now trained to handle hazardous material spills and life-saving defibrillators to aid heart-attack victims. The new training facilities will soon include instructions in confined-space and high-angle rescue. And, lastly, two new fire boats have been put in service to cover waterfront and marine fires in cooperation with three additional fire boats in neighboring fire departments.

From the humble beginnings of the small volunteer fire brigade in 1886, when members volunteered their time and energies for the common good, to today's Vancouver Fire/Rescue Service, the same daring and enthusiasm is shown in putting the "wet stuff on the hot stuff."

facing page: Fire truck crew, Vancouver Fire Department, 1992. vs

Access to Information
Rick Ouston

LOOKING TO GET the goods on a person or property in Greater Vancouver? Information is available, free or at least cheap, from dozens of sources. The following list, while not exhaustive, provides information to get you started. You'll find current addresses and phone numbers in the phone book and unless otherwise noted, most publications are available at larger public libraries. Provincial offices can be called toll-free by dialling 660-2421 and asking to be transferred to the number.

ADOPTIONS in the past have historically been shrouded in secrecy and shame. The B.C. Adoption Reunion Registry, funded by the B.C. government, can help reunite families. ParentFinders does similar work privately.

BANKRUPTCY records are available for the asking from the superintendent of bankruptcy office of the federal consumer and corporate affairs ministry. They are worthwhile checking before lending either money or your heart.

B.C. ASSESSMENT AUTHORITY determines the value of property and buildings for tax purposes. Free public records are maintained in each municipality that reveal the property's assessed value and the owner. An alphabetical list of property owners is also available.

BETTER BUSINESS BUREAU of Vancouver keeps extensive records of questionable business people and practices.

BUSINESS LICENCES are granted by local city halls and recorded by street address. If a company doesn't have a licence, you might wonder about its validity.

CITY DIRECTORIES, unlike the phone book, also list occupants by street name and number. They are available at local libraries.

CORONERS answer one of the most important questions in a person's life: why am I dead? They determine ways to avert similar future deaths. Their records often contain information unavailable from police or the courts.

COURT REGISTRIES grant access to civil supreme court records if someone has been sued, or has sued someone else. They are invaluable for determining assets and business relationships. Files for criminal courts, divorce and young offenders are sealed but criminal files may contain a judge's written ruling, available to the public and often containing important background information. Information sworn to obtain a search warrant is available from the local justice of the peace.

FAMILY TREES can be assembled using the genealogical division of Surrey's Cloverdale branch library. The Church of Jesus Christ of Latter-Day Saints (Mormons) maintains microfiched copies of their historic Salt Lake City genealogical records at its Burnaby Family History Centre.

FINANCIAL DISCLOSURE is demanded of people holding elected office at city halls, school boards and the legislature. They must reveal what they own and what they owe. Records are maintained at individual city halls for civic officials and at the legislative clerk's office for MLAs. These records can be useful for determining possible conflicts of interest.

LAND TITLES OFFICES can tell you who owns a property, who sold it and who holds the mortgages and liens, going back in time. To access records a legal description or property identifier number is needed from the assessment authority.

PHONE LOCATORS help if you have a phone number but don't know who it belongs to. If it's not unlisted, it's in this book, which lists numbers numerically. It's available at libraries.

PUBLIC ACCOUNTS, produced annually by the provincial government, records payments to companies, societies, individuals and civil servants.

PUBLIC COMPANIES, such as those traded on the Vancouver Stock Exchange or those offering partnership units for sale, must file a prospectus and insider trading reports, available at the office of the superintendent of brokers. The VSE also maintains files, including company news releases, available to the public.

PUBLIC INSTITUTIONS like hospitals and colleges must keep a current list of employees and what they earn, available to anyone who asks. Crown corporations like B.C. Hydro also publish employee and compensation lists. The provincial ministry of health reveals lump sums paid to doctors in the medical services commission's financial statements.

REGISTRAR OF COMPANIES offers names of directors and officers of companies and societies, including the registered records office of the company, usually a law firm. Under the provincial Companies act, the "registered in records" office must grant access to several company files to members of the public. Societies in Greater Vancouver also file a Revenue Canada Form T3010—available to the public—containing operating revenue and expenses, and wages of society staff members.

UNIVERSITIES AND COLLEGES maintain lists of experts willing to answer questions from the public in their area of expertise.

For more, see Getting the Goods, *published by New Star Books.*

Vancouver Dog Pound
Faith Bloomfield

DOG CATCHERS. These two words evoke images of large scowling men complete with dangling cigarettes and huge nets skulking around back alleys. They offer doggie treats to vagrant dogs as bribes, luring them away from their families to a certain brutal end. A common image, but an inaccurate one.

Today's dog catchers—animal control officers (ACOs)—are responsible for doing just as their title suggests: controlling animals, specifically dogs. The City of Vancouver Dog Pound's present mandate is the enforcement of the pound by-law and the registration/licensing of all the city's dogs. In a sense the pound, located at 1280 Raymur Avenue, is puppy prison—jail for all canine law-breakers. The original poundkeeper was a man named John Clough, otherwise known as the "One-Armed Jailer." Being in charge of the pound in 1886 was just one of the many roles he played in the new and growing city. (Clough was also the jailer and caretaker of Vancouver's first prison and he kept the city bright as its lamplighter.) The pound changed a great deal when it became a part of city hall and currently it is a division of the permits and licences department. No longer an arm of the police ACOs are often called upon *by* the police to apprehend vicious or nuisance dogs in many high-risk situations.

In Clough's time dogs were just one kind of animal that needed tending. Cows and horses were also common visitors to the premises in those days. As recently as the late 1970s a steer was picked up by the pound at the Fraserview Golf Course after wandering back and forth from Vancouver to the Central Park area in Burnaby for three weeks. The pound officers, unfamiliar with the practice of hitching in an animal, found the cow moving around excessively in the back of their trailer. Soon the cow was halfway out, right in the middle of one of the busiest parts of town—the intersection of Davie and Denman Streets. The Stanley Park Zoo curator was called in to help calm the situation and eventually the steer, whose owner refused to claim him, reached his final destination. Chickens, roosters and rabbits can also sometimes be found in the kennels these days and calls about stray Vietnamese pot-bellied pigs and loose ferrets are also noted.

The pound does not handle live cats but it is not unusual for calls to come in for an ACO to pick up a dead cat from a city street. Cleaning up after dead animals found in public areas in Vancouver is one of the pound's less pleasant responsibilities.

Dogs are rarely put to sleep at the pound, contrary to another all-too-common misconception. In the last few decades less than five per cent of impounded dogs—dogs picked up as loose strays, unregistered and unlicensed—were put to sleep. The ones that are destroyed are found to be unsuitable as pets because of nasty dispositions or health problems. The other 95 per cent or so are either returned to their rightful owners or adopted out to new and hopefully more responsible people.

Licensing has always been a long process for the ACOs as many dog owners refuse to purchase annual tags. In the past pound officers were sworn in every year by the deputy-chief of police as special constables. This allowed them to follow up notices to license with court summonses—an almost weekly occurrence. This policy changed in the 1970s and presently ACOs must rely on the dog owner's honesty. Unfortunately, frequent return house calls are required and some delinquent dog owners must be fined as a last resort.

Long before computers, addresses where licensed dogs lived were hand-written in what was then called a route book. The pound officer always took his book out on the road with him and revised it every time a licence was sold. During the big rush at the start of every year pound officers were known to work through their lunch just to keep their book up to date with all the licences sold. In 1946 just under 17,000 tags were sold and hand-entered by the pound officers. The method advanced slightly in 1973 when a filing system was adopted by the pound and a clerk was hired to process licensing information. In 1977, after a steady increase over the years, the highest number of tags—almost 25,000—were sold and recorded.

In 1987 dog licence sales were finally recorded into a computer program set up by city hall. Now the pound inputs the information itself with about two-thirds of its annual licence sales processed in the first three months of the calendar year. Every dog licence, current and expired, has a constantly updated, four-year history within the pound files, easily accessible to every ACO and pound employee. In 1994 fewer than 16,000 tags were sold. Suggested reasons for the decreases, steady since 1977, are the increasingly high cost of licensing and the opening in that year of the SPCA spay/neuter clinic: fewer puppies being born means fewer dogs licences needed.

As public servants ACOs must enforce the city pound by-law and respond to citizens complaints of dog owners responsible for "poop and scoop" and leash offenses, dogs running at large and numerous vicious-dog infractions. Each violation—past and present—is recorded on the dog's computer record.

At one time the poundkeeper had a permit to carry and use a rifle if a situation demanded such action. In 1974, when a new supervisor arrived at the pound, he returned both the rifle and its ammunition to city hall administrators. Although the rifle was banned the equipment used is still critical, if nowhere near as dangerous. Among ACOs the "weapon" of choice is a throwback from a time when the pound budget was extremely tight. George Masse, poundkeeper from the mid-1940s to 1974, recycled the heavily soiled trolley cable cords discarded by BC Electric, now BC Hydro. Today the ACOs complain that newer ropes, made of the same fibres and slip-knotted like the old ones, don't hold as well. Often a catch pole—an aluminum pole with a cable loop attached to it—is also used to prevent vicious dogs from attacking the attending officer.

In 1987 Vancouver city council gave the pound authority to deal with dangerous dogs by modifying the pound by-law to include a vicious-dog section. The breed-specific amendment declared all pitbulls and pitbull cross breeds vicious, as well as all dogs found to be vicious as a result of an incident and follow-up investigation by the pound. The breed-specific area of the by-law came after a public outcry resulted from increased awareness of vicious attacks by these dogs. The section required owners of these dogs to follow additional rules: besides leashing, vicious dogs must be muzzled and strictly contained.

The public reacts to media portrayals of vicious-dog attacks strongly and in the past a variety of breeds—German shepherds, Doberman pinschers, Saint Bernards, Huskies, etc.—all made "vicious dog of the month" though none were officially deemed vicious until the pitbull scare. Not all the ACOs agree with the breed-specific wording of the section of the by-law and the sentiment often heard around the pound is "there are no bad dogs, just bad owners." In fact in Kitsilano in the early 1970s a pound officer was attacked and bitten—by a man! Historically officers of the pound are victims of violent reactions, both verbal and physical, from the public, as emotions are strained where the family pet is concerned. Pound lore has it that in the 1960s an intoxicated man attacked pound officer Robert Neale after he arrived at the family home with their dog, Snuffy. The dog owner was charged with assault and fined $50 by the magistrate.

There is no "animal control officer school" and every officer has his or her own method of doing the job. As a side-line some officers work outside the pound training championship show dogs and hunting dogs. There have been officers who rely on nothing but sheer patience and will to get dogs to teach themselves. And there was even an officer who "talked" to the dogs, using "psychology" to get the job done. But the only real training ACOs get comes on the job. They are required to know the pound by-law and all health regulations relating to animals. But most essential for a successful career with the pound is a quick sense of timing and a sometimes off-beat sense of humor!

Dog Pounds – GVRD
Faith Bloomfield

WHAT DO VANCOUVER, the City and Township of New Westminster, White Rock, West Vancouver, Langley and Chilliwack all have in common? They are the only areas within Greater Vancouver whose animal control pounds and the Society for the Prevention of Cruelty to Animals are separate entities.

In others areas, including Burnaby, Coquitlam, Port Coquitlam, Maple Ridge, Richmond, Delta, Surrey and North Vancouver—city and district—the responsibility of animal control and municipal by-law enforcement are contracted out to the SPCA.

The mandates for the pound and the SPCA are different. The society is a non-profit organization that, following the Prevention of Cruelty Act (PCA), deals with cruelty issues and undertakes rescues. Animal control agencies follow municipal by-laws unique to each area. The SPCA exists in most of the areas with independent pounds but its responsibility is limited to the protection of animals.

The recently amended PCA enables the SPCA to inspect and investigate any premises where the mistreatment of an animal is suspected. If a situation demands it the act also

SPCA mascot, 1993. vp

gives the society the authority to seize the animal in question and charge the person causing the harm.

Every municipality has its own by-law dealing with licensing, "poop and scoop" and leash rules and impoundings but there are some differences. For the most part a pound's responsibilities are dogs and the enforcement of the pound by-law with no regulations governing cats. Animal control organizations rarely handle cats and, except for Burnaby which has facilities for everything from snakes to livestock, the few that do limit their involvement to adoptions. A number of pound/SPCAs, including Burnaby and Surrey, enforce a large animal by-law although the need is much less than it used to be.

Where the municipal by-laws most often differ is in regard to vicious or dangerous dogs. Each municipality has sections in their by-law describing what constitutes a vicious, or in the case of Delta, a dangerous dog and how they have to be kept. The section is usually breed-specific, concentrating on pitbulls and Staffordshire terriers and dogs crossed with either of these breeds. In fact White Rock's vicious-dog section also includes Rottweilers and Doberman pinschers although this inclusion is currently under review.

Except for Delta all municipalities also have a more general section stating that dogs with the known propensity to attack or who have a history of attacking may be deemed vicious upon investigation. (In Delta the SPCA handles these cases by charging the dog's owner with criminal negligence which may result in a jail term or a $2,000 fine.)

In order to license a vicious/dangerous dog in Delta or Richmond the owner must first purchase liability insurance. A number of other cities charge higher fees for licensing dogs in this category. Whether the by-law is breed-specific or not, all municipalities agree that vicious or dangerous dogs must be properly contained (to varying degrees) and muzzled in public.

There is no specific reason some municipalities have their pounds controlled separately from the SPCA. In White Rock, Vancouver and New Westminster the cities run the animal control branch themselves and in West Vancouver police by-law enforcement officers are responsible. In Langley—city and township—and Chilliwack the contract is bid upon by different organizations including the SPCA and could change with each renewal.

When they are separately run the two organizations often fill each other's gaps and the control and protection of both animals and the public is always maintained.

Leashed resistance. the leader

The Police

GENDIS INC. The conferring of the Order of Canada on Joseph Cohen in 1991 is just one of an astonishing number of accomplishments of a man whose entire life has been one of service. A listing of his directorships, memberships, honors and awards fills four pages—testament to a remarkable individual. Not least among those achievements was the naming of Mr. Cohen as a Freeman of the City of Vancouver in 1980, and his appointment as Honourary Chief of the Vancouver Police Department in 1991.

Police
Gary Hanney

VANCOUVER HAS ITS own police force of just over 1,000 regular members and a support staff of 100 reserves and 269 civilians. The force is directed by a chief and 6 deputy chief constables, each responsible for a division: patrol, operational support, human resources, investigation, support services and management services. Police headquarters is at 2120 Cambie Street, the public information counter and the place to report traffic accidents are at 312 Main Street and the traffic courts are at 190 Alexander Street. Vancouver operates the 911 communications centre for the Lower Mainland, answering all emergency calls for all police, fire and ambulance.

Vancouver policing began in 1885 with one man, Jonathan Miller. He had no uniform but he did have the powers of a constable and was responsible for policing the area bounded by Cambie, Hastings, Carrall and Water Streets. In the 1886 elections his four-cell jail (which was also his cottage) served as polling booth and as council chambers for the first city council meeting. At the time of the Great Fire of 1886 the first Policing Department was formed with Police Chief John Stewart, a sergeant and 2 constables. By 1901 the force had grown to 26 men. By 1912 the force had a chief's car, a detective car, a paddy wagon and an ambulance. (The first police patrol car, a Hudson Speedster, appeared about 10 years later. It was acquired by the city after being seized as a stolen car from Los Angeles. The American insurance company sold it to Vancouver rather than pay for the long drive on gravel roads back to California.) On July 8, 1912, Nancy Harris and Minnie Miller were the first women hired. (Vancouver now has 120 women police officers, in almost all ranks.) In 1929 Vancouver amalgamated with South Vancouver and Point Grey, and the police departments of all three municipalities merged.

Policing has come a long way since the early days; the current focus is on community-based policing: "the police and other services providers in the city working in partnership with the community to address community problems."

Vancouver started up a bicycle squad to put officers back on the street and now have 62 members on bikes. In conjunction with the community and private business, the police have opened up 12 Community Crime Prevention Offices and other police storefronts throughout the city. Six of these are staffed with a

facing page, top: Vancouver Harbor, 1985 and bottom: Vancouver Police Department officers, Granville Street Mall, 1987. vs

police officer and the remainder have members dropping in.

RESERVES

Vancouver operates a 100-member reserve police force which assists regular police on various assignments and works a great deal on traffic duty. Most of their work is on a volunteer basis but they do receive payment for certain duties. Recruiting age for the reserve force ranges from 18 to 55.

TRAINING

The minimum age to become a Vancouver police officer is 19, and some of the qualification requirements include being a Canadian citizen or landed immigrant with a minimum of one year of university or college, and having a good driving history. The three-and-a-half-year program to become a first-class constable starts with basic recruit training at the B.C. Justice Institute. After 14 weeks it's actual on-the-road experience with a senior police officer as a partner and field trainer. The next three years consist of more work at the academy alternating with longer terms on the street.

The Vancouver City Police training section is involved with such programs as refresher courses for the forces, promotion exams, applicants' examinations, in-house courses and roll-call training.

DOG SQUAD

Vancouver's dog squad began in 1957 with four dogs and has grown to 17. All training for this squad is carried out in the city by the Vancouver police's own experts. Their expertise has been recognized by other police forces in B.C. and the western U.S. which send their dogs and handlers to Vancouver for training. The squad has baseball-type collector cards featuring their dogs and handlers. These cards are designed to get a dialogue going between children and all the dog handlers, and come in handy at the many dog shows and events the squad participates in.

MARINE SQUAD

Vancouver has been operating police boats since 1912. The squad patrols more than 160 kilometres of shoreline, from the Second Narrows Bridge to Point Atkinson and along the Fraser River from the Burnaby boundary to the UBC endowment lands. The marine squad is able to cover the large area by trailering their quick-response Zodiac to where it is needed. Their main boat—VPD 99—is the *R. G. McBeath,* commissioned in February, 1995. This specially designed nine-metre aluminum-hull boat is powered by twin 230 h.p. super-turbo diesels and cruises at 30 knots. The main function of the squad is the enforcement of the Canada shipping act, small vessel regulations, the criminal code of Canada and the bylaws of the Vancouver Port Corporation. Other patrol boats in the area include the Coast Guard vessels moored at Kitsilano and Ports

Canada Police and RCMP vessels that patrol the waters outside of Vancouver.

MOUNTED SQUAD

The mounted squad has eight horses stabled in Stanley Park. They patrol the park year-round and at times patrol other areas of the city. In 1909 the first mounted officer was assigned to Stanley Park. One year later the squad was officially formed with 12 horses, and in the next two years it grew to 20 strong. From then on the size of the squad went up and down like a yo-yo until it was disbanded in 1949 to make way for more mechanized transportation. The squad was reinstated in 1951 for a royal visit, using a retired police horse and a borrowed horse. Two years later the mounted squad was again a full unit. In addition to being a very effective mode of transportation in the heavily wooded area of Stanley Park, the horses are very popular with the children and tourists that frequent the park. The squad also trailers their horses to elementary schools for the children to see, and then works the neighboring areas, assisting the patrol division.

PIPE BAND

The Vancouver Police Pipe Band, begun in 1914, is the senior police band in Canada and the third in the world after the Edinburgh and Glasgow police. It is the official civic band for Vancouver. Band members travel to many national and international competitions and parades on their vacation time at their own personal expense. The band has 30 members: 15 are city police, 12 are civilians, two are firefighters and one is a member of the RCMP.

MOTORCYCLE DRILL TEAM

The traffic department operates a motorcycle squad of 31 bikes. Twelve of the Harley-Davidsons are used for the very popular motorcycle drill team, which was formed in 1953. It soon became known as one of the top drill teams in the northwest, performing in numerous cities and municipalities in B.C. and the U.S. The team travels on its own time and is responsible for all the expenses involved.

SCHOOL LIAISON PROGRAM

Crime prevention through education is the aim of this program, and it works. The 15 officers in the program are responsible for all of the 143 schools and 70,000 students in the city. They are each assigned high schools, and are responsible for each of the feeder elementary schools in that area.

Three officers are also assigned to the Safety Patrol Program, which got its start in Vancouver in 1935 as the School Boy Patrol. It is believed to have been the first in North America.

Parent Parking Patrol is relatively new to Vancouver. Three volunteer parents assist with the flow of traffic and students around each school both before and after classes.

VANCOUVER POLICE STOREFRONTS

OPERATION COOPERATION POLICE COMMUNITY SERVICES CENTRE
200 Burrard Street. Telephone: 257-3705. Monday through Friday: 8:00 A.M.-4:00 P.M.

CHINATOWN POLICE COMMUNITY SERVICES CENTRE
18 East Pender Street. Telephone: 688-5030. Tuesday through Saturday: 10:00 A.M.-6:00 P.M.

NATIVE LIAISON SOCIETY STOREFRONT PROJECT
239 Main Street. Telephone: 687-8411. Monday through Friday: 8:30 A.M.-4:30 P.M.

JOYCE STREET COMMUNITY CRIME PREVENTION OFFICE
5156 Joyce Street. Telephone: 665-3406. Tuesday through Friday: 12:00 P.M.-10:00 A.M.

MUSQUEAM POLICE VISITATION PROGRAM
51 Street Hall, 6615 Salish Drive. Wednesdays: 10:00 A.M.-12:00 P.M.

WEST POINT GREY POLICE VISITATION PROGRAM
West Point Grey Community Centre, 4397 West 2nd Avenue. Second and fourth Wednesdays of the month: 7:00 P.M.-9:00 P.M.

KITSILANO VISITATION PROGRAM
Kitsilano Community Centre, 2690 Larch Street. First and third Wednesdays of the month: 7:00 P.M.-9:00 P.M.

STRATHCONA/HASTINGS NORTH NEIGHBORHOOD POLICE OFFICE
Strathcona Community Centre, 601 Keefer Street. Tuesday through Friday: 9:00 A.M.-10:00 A.M. and 3:00 P.M.-4:00 P.M.

KERRISDALE POLICE VISITATION PROGRAM
Kerrisdale Community Centre, 5851 West Boulevard. Saturdays: 9:00 A.M.-10:00 A.M.

DOWNTOWN EASTSIDE NEIGHBORHOOD SAFETY OFFICE
12 East Hastings Street. 9:00 A.M.-5:00 P.M. and some variable hours.

GASTOWN NEIGHBORHOOD POLICE OFFICE
105-12 Water Street. Tuesday through Friday: 9:00 A.M.-12:00 P.M. and 1:00 P.M-4:00 P.M.

MOUNT PLEASANT CRIME PREVENTION OFFICE
72 East Broadway. Monday: 1:00 P.M.-9:00 P.M. Tuesday through Friday: 11:00 A.M.-5:00 P.M.

BRITANNIA COMMUNITY POLICE OFFICE
Britannia Community Centre, 1661 Napier Street. Tuesday through Thursday: 4:00 A.M.-8:00 A.M., Friday: 3:00 P.M-5:00 P.M., Saturday: 12:00 P.M.-4:00 P.M.

WEST END COMMUNITY CENTRE STOREFRONT
870 Denman Street. Monday through Friday: 9:00 A.M.-8:30

P.M. Saturday 9:00 A.M.-5:00 P.M.

NORTH FALSE CREEK COMMUNITY POLICE CENTRE

123 Pacific Boulevard. Monday through Friday: 11:00 A.M.-7:00 P.M.

LITTLE MOUNTAIN/RILEY PARK SAFER COMMUNITIES OFFICE

4438 Main Street. Saturday: 10:00 A.M.-2:00 P.M. Tuesday: 12:00 P.M.-2:00 P.M. Thursday: 4:00 P.M.-8:00 P.M.

GRANVILLE STREET CRIME PREVENTION OFFICE

916 Granville Street. Tuesday through Friday: 10:00 A.M.-3:00 P.M.

KENSINGTON POLICE VISITATION PROGRAM

Kensington Community Centre, 5175 Dumfries Street. Every second Wednesday: 6:30 P.M.-8:30 P.M.

BROADWAY STATION COMMUNITY CRIME

PREVENTION OFFICE

2777 Commercial Drive. Monday: 12:00 P.M.-4:00 P.M.

OTHER POLICE FORCES:

All other cities and municipalities that make up Greater Vancouver have their own police, usually the RCMP, but there are also city (or municipal) police departments in Delta, New Westminster, Port Moody and West Vancouver.

DELTA

The municipality of Delta has its own police force of 137 members. The force is currently located in Ladner in a newly renovated building that used to house both the police and the provincial courts. The first constable for Delta was actually the municipal clerk when he was given additional police duties in 1887. A year later they hired a full time constable but it wasn't until 1891 that he was issued a badge and a revolver.

NEW WESTMINSTER

This city force got its first constable in 1873. Jonathan Morey was paid $30 per month to patrol Columbia Street during the day. In 1879 the police department grew to two members, one for each day and night shift. Among their duties was the lighting of street lamps in the early evening. Their current strength is 101 members with 16 reserve constables.

WEST VANCOUVER

West Vancouver City Police got their start in May, 1912. In the early days the beat was walked on foot or patrolled by an officer on a rented horse or in a taxi. For trips west of town the police rode the bus; for more distant points the constables were provided with a pass on the Pacific Great Eastern Railway. Now the department has a strength of 74 police officers and 14 reserve constables who travel in state-of-the-art transportation.

PORT MOODY

Like a lot of areas, early policing here began with the B.C. Provincial Police. In 1883 Constable Sharp took up office in the old Canadian Pacific Railway station, which also housed his police cells. In 1913 the City of Port Moody was incorporated and so was its police force. Chief Constable Mills moved his one-man department into the new city hall, and took the cells too, installing them in the basement. A few years and moves later the department now sports a new building with 33 police officers and 15 reserves.

RCMP

The RCMP began policing British Columbia on August 15, 1950, when the B.C. Provincial Police force was dissolved and all their duties assumed by the RCMP. This police agency is responsible for all areas of the province except those cities and municipalities that have their own police forces.

In Greater Vancouver the RCMP patrol Burnaby, Coquitlam, Port Coquitlam, Langley, Maple Ridge, North Vancouver, Pitt Meadows, Richmond, Surrey, the UBC endowment lands, the Vancouver International Airport and White Rock. RCMP highway patrols look after Highway 99 (south from Vancouver to the U.S. border), Highway 17 (to the Tsawwassen Ferry Terminal) and Highway 1 (from Capilano Road in North Vancouver to all points east).

Also in Vancouver is the British Columbia "E" Division headquarters for the RCMP. In addition to headquarters personnel, almost 300 RCMP officers are assigned to narcotics, commercial crime, customs and excise, proceeds of crime, immigration and passports, aboriginal policing and other federal jurisdictional areas. They also provide support services, including the forensic laboratory, marine and air services and the bomb squad, to all police in the province.

The RCMP operate the Canadian Police Information Centre (CIPC) in Ottawa, the central computer for all police information in Canada. CPIC is an integrated, automated system which provides police officers with tactical information on crimes and criminals and access to operational police information.

PORTS CANADA POLICE

Another police force that worked in Greater Vancouver was Ports Canada Police. These officers were a federal force under the department of transport, responsible for all harbor areas under the direct control of the Canada Ports Corporation. They patrolled the north and south shores of the Port of Vancouver, Port Moody, Indian Arm and Roberts Bank. The 29 members worked in conjunction with the RCMP and Canada Customs, focussing mainly on organized crime, specifically smuggling. In March 1997 controversy arose over a federal government proposal to discontinue this force and to replace it with contracted private security personnel. The PCP's fate at press time was uncertain, with B.C.'s attorney-general Ujjal Dosanjh protesting the change.

MOTOR VEHICLES

New residents to the province must register their vehicles within 30 days to get B.C. licence plates. A period of six months is allowed to obtain a B.C. driver's licence, unless you have an international driver's licence, in which case a term of one year is given to obtain a new licence. Automobile insurance is compulsory in B.C. and now is sold along with the licence plates for the vehicle. In the Lower Mainland all but brand new vehicles must annually go through the motor vehicle emission-testing stations. In Vancouver and many other areas, illegally parked cars may be impounded during the rush hours, 7:00 A.M. to 9:30 A.M. and 3:00 P.M. to 6:00 P.M., Monday through Friday. Many jurisdictions are implementing special lanes for buses and car or van pools. A provincial law prohibits the use of studded tires except from October 1 to April 30.

British Columbians drive under the point system. Infractions generally bring two or three points against the record of the driver and a fee is set, with more points and higher fees for more serious charges. When nine or ten points are accumulated, the driver stands a good chance of having driving privileges suspended. Fees are calculated by squaring the number of points (for example, a driver with six points pays $36—six times six). The number of points held by a driver is reduced by three each year and all points are eliminated three years from the date of the last conviction.

CHIEF CONSTABLES OF VANCOUVER

John M. Stewart, 1886-1890 • John McLaren, 1890-1895
John M. Stewart, 1896-1901 • Sam North, 1901-1906
C. Chisholm, 1906-1907 • Rufus G. Chamberlain, 1907-1912
C. Mulhern, 1913 • Malcolm McLellan, 1914-1917
W. McRae, 1917-1920 • J. Anderson, 1920-1924
W.W. Long, 1924-1928 • W.J. Bingham, 1929-1931
C.E. Edgett, 1931-1933 • John Cameron, 1933-1934
W.W. Foster, 1935-1939 • D. MacKay, 1939-1945
A.G. McNeill, 1945-1947 • Walter H. Mulligan, 1947-1955
G.J. Archer, 1956-1962 • R.M. Booth, 1962-1968
John R. Fisk, 1968-1974 • Donald R. Winterton, 1974-1981
Robert Stewart, 1981-1991 • William Marshall, 1991-1994
Ray Canuel, 1994-

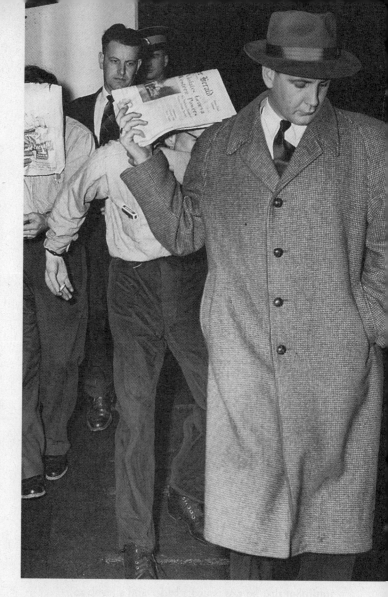

facing page, top: Vancouver police surround a getaway car, 1993. vs
bottom: Ditched getaway car at Willingdon and Grandview Highway after a 90-mile-per-hour chase in 1955; two men later appeared in court (above) charged with armed robbery of a Royal Bank branch, Burnaby. vs

Crime

Greg Middleton

VANCOUVER HAS ALWAYS had a kind of freewheeling, Wild West, buccaneer spirit that created an atmosphere where crime and criminals flourished even before the City of Vancouver existed.

It all started when "Gassy Jack" Deighton paddled into Burrard Inlet and up to the Hastings sawmill. He offered some idle sawmill workers all the whiskey they could drink in a sitting if they would help him build a saloon. About 24 hours later Gassy Jack owned the Globe Saloon, a 3.6-metre by 6-metre shack, the first bar in what was to become downtown Vancouver's notorious skid row—a row of hotels and beer parlors named after the skid road where logs were hauled up to the Hasting Mill.

When Gassy Jack rolled in, the nearest bar was in New Westminster. Gassy Jack's saloon started what was soon to become a rowdy, thriving, rough and tumble shanty town where the province's miners, loggers and fishermen would come to drink and spend their hard-earned money.

Within a year of Gassy Jack having built his saloon a sailor who had been drinking in the bar was brutally murdered. Today half the city's murders still happen within a half-dozen blocks of the corner of Hastings and Main Streets.

By 1869 scenes of drunken debauchery were commonplace along the shores of Burrard Inlet. Two years later, in 1871, citizens of the growing, if ramshackle, town petitioned for more police presence.

Back in 1858 the governor of British Columbia, James Douglas, had proclaimed that the civil and criminal laws of England applied to the growing colony and in March of the following year Chartres Brew was appointed inspector of police and Matthew Baillie Begbie was proclaimed judge. They had wanted to bring 150 trained police officers from the Royal Ulster Constabulary but got only 15 to form a police force for the entire colony. Chartres Brew's brother, Tompkins Brew, was appointed the government-agent and constable of the Township of Granville.

Vancouver didn't get much in the way of law and order until after the 1871 petition from concerned residents. Jonathon Miller soon took over as constable of Granville and what was to become Vancouver.

Despite the growing pressure for a police presence and Miller's efforts the bars along the waterfront were thriving and by 1873 a woman called Birdie was running a bustling bawdy house at what would become the corner of Water and Abbott.

The Hastings Mill area was growing and the merchants of the area hired John Stewart to patrol the streets to keep the patrons of the growing number of saloons and rough hotels in order. The City of Vancouver was finally incorporated in 1886 and Stewart appointed the city's first chief of police. John Clough, the one-armed town drunk, was appropriately hired as jailer because that's where he could most often be found anyway. Little more than a month after Stewart was appointed the newly incorporated town burned down in the great fire of June 13, 1886. After the fire Stewart added a sergeant and two constables as the town was being busily rebuilt.

The years following the Great Fire of 1886, with the railroad coming to the province, were both economic boom times and explosive times for the young city. The Chinese laborers brought in to work the railroad brought opium with them from China. There were an estimated 500 opium users among the Caucasian population alone—considered a terrible problem for a city of only a few thousand people. Youth gangs roamed the streets robbing and terrorizing people and breaking into homes. Prostitution blossomed along Dupont Street—what was eventually to become East Pender Street. Police knew about what was viewed as a public morality problem and made periodic arrests but seemed powerless to do anything to close the brothels.

In 1899 the city had its first police corruption scandal when it was revealed that although the police made periodic raids on the brothels and the madams were fined $50 and each prostitute fined $15, half the fines collected were being paid to the informant who had tipped police to the illegal activity. It turned out that a police department employee was the best and almost only informant.

By 1904 the city had 31 police officers and 27 cells, all of them usually packed to the rafters.

By 1907 the opium problem, public drunkenness, gambling and violence were all growing along with racial tension between the Caucasian and Chinese immigrants. The Chinese were mostly single men and willing to work for less than their white counterparts. In 1907 after rioting whites destroyed much of Chinatown the British Columbia government pressured the federal government to enact the Opium Act. The move came at least partly because opium was associated with the Chinese although the Chinese were for the most part more law abiding and peaceful than their white neighbors.

On March 25, 1912 Const. Lewis Byers responded to a "drunk annoying" call on Powell Street. The drunk had a gun and Byers was shot and killed—the first local police officer killed in the line of duty. Police closed in around a waterfront shack where the drunken Oscar Larsen had holed up. There was a siege that turned into a gun battle. About 25 shots were fired and Larsen was killed.

On May 28, 1913 Const. James Archibald failed to report in. The next day his body was discovered in bushes. He had been shot to death. Near his body was a crude burglar's mask. Acting on tips from informants police surrounded a waterfront shack and arrested Herman Clarke, 25, and Frank Davis, 30. Along with them was found not only the blouse the mask had been cut from but the eyeholes from the mask. They were convicted of murder and hanged.

Drug addiction had become a major problem in the city. The police chief of the day, Malcolm McLennan, was a champion of taking a sympathetic view of the plight of the addicted. Ironically he was shot dead in a gun battle with drug addict Bob Tait in 1917. An innocent passerby, 8-year-old George Robb, was also shot dead. Tait committed suicide before he could be arrested.

1917 also brought prohibition and another boom for the city—one that established it as a major smuggling and bootlegging centre. While booze was illegal south of the border there was a fortune to be made running legally purchased liquor from here to there. More than a few now-prominent Vancouver families made their fortunes in sleek motor yachts making midnight runs from Coal Harbour to the U.S., occasionally coming home full of bullet holes from shots fired by U.S. customs officials. It was dubbed the "overproof navy." Prohibition ended here in 1921.

The 1930s brought poverty to Vancouver in a way it had never seen before with many Canadian broke and homeless riding the rails out to B.C. to get away from the brutal winters of the prairies and Eastern Canada. That immigration of the poor and their problems from east to west continues today.

While World War II brought a kind of prosperity again it also brought its own kinds of problems. Black markets flourished. Extravagantly dressed "zoot suiters," mostly teens too young to serve in the armed forces, hung around on Granville Street with their exaggerated baggy trousers pegged at the ankles, wide lapels and switch-blade knives. Confrontations with soldiers returning on leave were common. The end of the war was also the beginning of the night club era in Vancouver. "Blind pigs" and booze cans, the illegal late-night bars, flourished along with back-room bookmaking. It was also the beginnings of organized crime in the city as U.S. gangsters looked north to get away from increasingly aggressive American law enforcement agencies and members of the Italian,

Sicilian and East European mafias came in with legitimate refugees.

On Feb., 26, 1947 a shootout between some suspected armed robbers and police shocked the city. Det. Percy Hoare and Consts. Oliver Ledingham and Charles Boyles were down by the Great Northern Railway roundhouse at Glen Drive and 5th Avenue when they spotted three suspicious looking men. The two constables walked the three men back toward where Hoare was waiting by his car. Hoare spotted a pistol in the waistband of one of the men and reached for it. The other two pulled guns. In the ensuing gunfight Ledingham and Boyles were shot and killed. Hoare shot and killed one of the gunmen. Another, Harry Medos, was later hanged while a third was finally acquitted on appeal.

By 1950 heroin was becoming a problem in the city. There was an increasing number of addicts and the beginnings of what became a hugely profitable drug trade that was financed by prostitution and supported a growing underworld. But it was mostly confined to a small area of town and the city was still small enough that many of the addicts were known to police. Far more shocking for most people in 1953 was the discovery of the skeletons of two children covered with the remains of a woman's fur coat in Stanley Park. The bodies were those of a girl and a boy between seven and ten years old. Nearby was a hatchet which was later established as the murder weapon. Police had an idea who the children were and who killed them but no proof and the "babes in the woods" case remains one of the city's most disturbing unsolved murders.

By 1955 there was another police corruption scandal. Chief Walter Mulligan fled from a public inquiry, this time over kickbacks from gamblers and bootleggers.

The late 1950s saw the rise of the big legitimate nightclubs like Isy's and the Cave. Vancouver was swinging. The swingers—many of them later to become judges and politicians—went from the supper clubs to after-hours clubs where they rubbed shoulders with gamblers, gangsters and reporters. The '50s is often referred to as Vancouver's "golden era."

The '60s saw the rise of the biker gangs (with names like the Satan's Choice, Coffin Cheaters, and Hell's Rebels) along with the coffee houses, jazz clubs and the beginning of rock and roll. Of the half dozen biker gangs that modelled themselves on the now infamous Hell's Angels from California the most notorious was the Satan's Angels. The biker gang, which was originally based in Burnaby and later took over a Napier Street house as their headquarters, partied throughout the Lower Mainland. Sometimes they entertained other motorcycle clubs like the Devil's Escorts from Kamloops. Often battling it out with rivals the club's reign of terror almost came to an end after club members kidnapped a 20-year-old man in 1968 and subjected him to a night of torture and terror. It was nicknamed the "case of the devil's butler" because one of the bikers was reported to have commented "now we have a butler" when they first grabbed him in a cafe. Ten members of the club were eventually charged and many, including club president David Black, convicted. Black got seven years.

While the bikers got headlines throughout the long trial of 1968 the flower children from San Francisco were drifting north. They took over 4th Ave. and caught the attention of the public and police for much of the early 1970s. Marijuana was seen then as a public menace. A peaceful marijuana smoke-in in Gastown in August of 1971 turned into the Gastown riot and police and hippies fought the "Battle of Jericho" in October as police tried to move hippies camped on the beach. But while the hippies may have sowed the seeds of Vancouver's now multi-million-dollar marijuana industry, underworld groups were busy importing heroin and later cocaine and making fortunes. And the Clark Park Gang was terrorizing East Vancouver. The Clark Park Gang was eventually broken up by a group of baseball-bat wielding Vancouver cops called the Heavy Squad. Meanwhile the once notorious Satan's Angels were taken over by the Hell's Angel's with little fanfare. As the decade drew to a close the most infamous of the drug gangsters, William Faulder "Fats" Robertson, was brought down by police wiretaps. Robertson got 20 years but for importing the new drug on the scene, cocaine, not heroin.

For a short time in the early 1980s, after police broke up some of the big heroin importing syndicates of the '70s, heroin was hard to come by in Vancouver. The drug underworld had virtually collapsed after major undercover operations and mass arrests. There were only a few cafes and beer parlors where heroin could be purchased. But prostitution was flourishing again, now on the streets of the West End, after intense police pressure in the mid-1970s drove the hookers out of the Penthouse and other clubs where they used to hang out. And cocaine had become the drug of choice, at least among the upper class who could afford it.

In 1986 Expo brought the world to our doorstep and a new kind of criminal. Pimps and drug dealers who specialized in cocaine moved up from the U.S. Young Asian street gangs fought with the mostly Hispanic Los Diablos until the police jailed most of the more easily spotted Los Diablos with their distinctive red and black colors. The Hell's Angels were getting rich and fat in near anonymity. Marijuana was being grown in high-tech hydroponic grow-houses. The older European criminals of the '60s and '70s who hadn't been caught and gone to jail were retiring or at least getting respectable. And the Russians, four young men and their associates who spent their days in gyms and their nights in the clubs, had arrived. But more and more of the drugs coming into Vancouver and the huge quantitiies of marijuana grown here were simply being shipped back out again, heading mostly for the eastern U.S. Vancouver was now the Miami of the north.

In the late 1980s triad leaders met with young Asian gang leaders and promised all the heroin they could sell if they would simply stop fighting amongst themselves. The Russians were selling cocaine like it was going out of style. The number of people using the drug intravenously exploded. Overdoses were becoming a daily occurrence. Pimps, some from the U.S. and some from Eastern Canada, fought for control of the streets. On March 17, 1989 "Lucky" David Joseph was gunned down in the Dynasty nightclub in Gastown not far from the site of Gassy Jack Deighton's Globe saloon. On Sept., 7, 1989 the Russian's drug gang was rounded up on charges of conspiring to sell cocaine. More than 13 kilograms of coke valued at $9 million were seized along with machine guns and luxury cars.

The 1990s erupted with a public battle between the upstart Russians and the combined forces of the bikers and one of the Asian gangs. Short of money, the Russians had ripped off both groups by showing up with guns instead of drugs. An associate of the Russians, 23-year-old Ngoc Tung Dang, was machine-gunned in his car. Sergei Filinov, 28, was shot down in broad daylight at a motorcycle dealership less than a month later and his brother Taras, 21, was abducted and killed little more than a year later. The drug charges against the remaining Russians were eventually dropped—partly because several gang members had mysteriously disappeared—but the drug war continued. Bombs went off under the car of one of two remaining brothers who were part of the core group of the gang. They retaliated by shooting up a Hell's Angels clubhouse but were eventually scared out of the country. Later a major drug bust in the U.S. crippled the gang once again and two members committed suicide within months, bringing to an end another violent chapter in Vancouver crime history.

With the growing numbers of people addicted to the huge quanitites of cheap heroin and cocaine that has flooded into the city the number of break-ins, petty theft and theft from cars has risen in recent years. Armed robberies of corner stores, gas stations and video outlets have become commonplace. Drug dealers have so much ill-gotten loot and money laundering has become so big an industry that police set up their own money-laundering business to trap the crooks.

But with the big money in the drug business there is always greed and in the past couple of years a big East Indian drug gang fractured over jealousy. Two brothers, Jim and Ron Dosanjh, were killed within weeks of each other. Unfortunately a completely innocent person was shot after he was mistaken for one of the participants in a botched assasination. Six men were arrested and eventually acquitted after the city's longest and most expensive trial. But even the gangsters recoiled at the killing of an innocent victim. The two men believed responsible for the April 24, 1995 killing of Robert

Glen Olsen have since died of drug overdoses.

While there has always been a Wild West spirit here the criminal underworld tries to remain an underworld and leave others out of their disputes.

below, clockwise from left: Mean streets, Vancouver, 1966; Vancouver Safety Deposit Vaults, robbed by a Montreal gang, 1977 (the gang was nabbed at the airport when their baggage was searched); Skytrain police in action, 1994; Penthouse Cabaret owner, Joe Phillipone, murdered, 1983. vs, vs, vp, vp

Prisons
Stuart Derdeyn

ONCE CONVICTED OF a crime a felon may do time at a federal or provincial detention centre. Following assessment the convicted felon is assigned to a maximum, medium or minimum security location, subject to the type of sentence, previous record, psychological profile and parole probability.

PROVINCIAL DETENTION CENTRES

Individuals convicted of crimes carrying a sentence of less than two years serve out their terms in provincial institutions. Inmates are classified at the institution upon their arrival. There are ten institutions in the Lower Mainland distributed into three administration areas: Vancouver/Burnaby, Fraser Region and Chilliwack. Electronic monitoring programs operate in Surrey and Vancouver.

Any history of B.C. provincial detention centres must include Burnaby's Oakalla Prison Farm, a full-service facility which opened on September 2, 1912. The first inmate was William Daley, sentenced on July 31, 1912 to serve a year of hard labor for stealing some fountain pens valued at over $10. By April 30, 1913, some 328 prisoners had passed through the jail's doors. From 1919 until the abolition of the death penalty in 1959, 44 prisoners were executed by hanging on the Oakalla site. The first execution was that of 25 year-old Alex Ignace on August 29, 1919. Leo Mantha was the last prisoner executed, on April 28, 1959. In 1936 there were several double and even one triple hanging.

Thousands of prisoners passed through the doors of Oakalla —renamed Lower Mainland Regional Correctional Centre in 1970—before it closed on June 30, 1991. Originally designed to house a maximum of 484 prisoners Oakalla's population peaked in 1962-63 at 1,269 inmates. With population averages of 600-plus overcrowding was always a problem. In the institution's final years two nationally-spotlighted events occurred. Thirteen maximum security prisoners escaped on New Year's Day 1988 following a Dec. 27, 1987 uprising and on Nov. 22, 1983 a violent and costly riot took place. Rioters caused more than $150,000 damage in a two-day spree. Oakalla was replaced by the Vancouver Pretrial Services Centre, the Fraser Regional Correctional Centre and the Surrey Pretrial Services Centre.

The Vancouver Pretrial Services Centre opened in 1984. It is a classic remand centre providing facilities for both maximum and medium security and open (minimum) housing for 150 inmates with special provisions for 204 spaces. The building

From 1919 until the abolition of the death penalty in 1959, 44 prisoners were executed by hanging on the Oakalla site

plans include segregation, hostile and observation cells. The centre is the City of Vancouver's only holding facility. The Surrey Pretrial Services Centre opened in 1990 and contains all of the Vancouver centre's features. The Fraser Regional Correctional Centre is the Lower Mainland's only full security institution with the capacity to house 275.

The Lakeside Correctional Centre for Women closed in 1990. The Burnaby Correctional Centre for Women replaced it, housing provincially-sentenced female inmates and those serving federal terms as well. (Previously females serving federal terms were transferred to the P4W [Prison for Women] in Kingston, Ontario.) The facility is an all-level-security prison with an average population of 153 including 28 open security spots.

New Haven Correctional Centre is a borstal-type centre located in Burnaby. New Haven's population is comprised of lower-risk, non-violent inmates, usually in the 18-23 year-old age group. This age limit is not firm and the process of classification is under review. Presently all New Haven inmates are serving six months-plus sentences. Some weekend intermittent sentences are served at New Haven.

Maple Ridge's Alouette River Correctional Centre was originally designed to serve as a treatment centre for specialized substance abuse situations. The camp still carries on most of the drug rehabilitation programs within the provincial system for 150 short-term and indeterminately sentenced inmates. Originally designed to be an open facility the centre was later upgraded to include a medium security centre. Mission's Stave Lake Correctional Centre is a medium security facility for sex offenders. The facility houses about 60 inmates who cannot be blended in with the regular populations of other facilities. The Chilliwack Community Correctional Centre is a halfway house for 34 inmates being held in an open setting. The Ford Mountain Camp is a special facility for 56 inmates requiring customized services ranging from specific care for physically and mentally challenged inmates and sex offenders to safe incarceration for informants.

One of the most interesting developments in the corrections field has been the introduction of technological solutions to lessen the burden on institutions to house inmates. The Electronic Monitoring Services (EMS) operating in Vancouver and Surrey was developed from pilot projects started in 1987, officially coming on-line in 1989. Inmates wear a field monitoring transmitter banded to their ankles for the duration of the sentence. Monitoring signals are broadcast to a field monitoring device attached to the inmate's residential phone line. The signals are sent to the monitoring centre to confirm the inmate is properly located according to the terms of the sentencing arrangement. Felons are referred to the EMS program through three processes: court referrals, classification/re-classification at another institution and sometimes in probation cases. On any given day EMS handles anywhere from 70-175 cases at each centre.

FEDERAL DETENTION CENTRES

Individuals convicted of crimes that carry a sentence of two years or more serve their terms in federal institutions. All federal inmates spend a minimum of eight weeks at the regional reception-assessment centre located on the Matsqui Institution grounds where they will be assessed, classified and then transferred to another federal facility. There are nine federal detention centres in the Lower Mainland. Prior to 1980 the B.C. Penitentiary maximum security prison was the largest facility. The Pen was phased out in 1980, replaced by Kent Prison in Matsqui and other institutions as part of a decentralization plan.

Kent Prison in Agassiz opened in August of 1979. This maximum security institution houses 313 prisoners (original capacity 234). Inmates are kept under a constant level of high surveillance. More that half of the prison population is housed in the protective custody wing, separated from the regular population for the duration of their sentences. On Sunday, January 24, 1988 a riot erupted. Eighty inmates were involved. Three were injured. Another riot in June 1981 caused $100,000 in damages and sparked a massive riot at Matsqui Institution.

Abbotsford's Matsqui Institution opened in May of 1966. This medium security facility houses 362 inmates (original capacity 312). On June 2, 1981, 300 inmates seized control of the institution and set fire to seven prison buildings causing millions of dollars in damages. Actions taken during the riot to rescue eight staff members from a burning roof by Cpl. Patrick Aloysius Kevin McBride led to the corporal receiving his second medal of honor for heroism in the same year from the governor general. The regional reception-assessment centre located on the Matsqui grounds houses 55 inmates.

In January of 1977 Mission Institution opened. It is a full-service medium security facility, the first built as part of the

B.C. Penitentiary decentralization plan. The prison houses 292 inmates (original capacity 230). Agassiz's Mountain Institution opened in July 1962. Designed to house special inmates the facility serves as an incarceration centre for a high percentage of sex offenders. At one time many of the Doukhobors convicted of arson and terrorism in the 1960s were held at this prison. There are 348 inmates (original capacity 322).

The three federal minimum security facilities are Mission's Ferndale Prison with 121 inmates (original capacity 110), opened in November of 1973; Elbow Lakes Work Camp in Harrison Mills opened in December of 1975 with 81 inmates (original capacity 90); and the Sumas Community Correctional Centre, a day parole house with 36 inmates (original capacity 48). These institutions house low-risk inmates and have no secure perimeter fences. (Work and training programs and substance abuse treatment programs are available at all three institutions.)

The regional health centre, adjacent to the Matsqui facility, opened in June of 1972. Prisoners housed here receive special care. They are mentally unstable or disturbed individuals who cannot assimilate well into the regular prison population. The RHC is a multi-level psychiatric facility which functions as a maximum security prison. There are 158 inmates (original capacity 157).

In 1990 the total inmate population for all of the Lower Mainland's federal detention facilities was 1,990. The annual average cost per inmate in the 1993-94 period was $45,753.

YOUTH DETENTION CENTRES

Young offenders convicted under the Young Offenders Act (YOA) serve out their sentences at one of four Lower Mainland institutions. These facilities are broken down into secure (maximum and medium) and open (minimum) designations. Since the introduction of the YOA, the population of incarcerated young offenders increased from 102 in 1974 to 400-plus in 1996. The Burnaby Youth Secure Custody Centre houses 105 inmates serving sentences up to the maximum YOA length of 10 years. Adjacent to the secure centre is the Burnaby Youth Open Custody Centre, including Holly Cottage and a facility at the Maples, housing a total of 47 inmates. An additional 17 inmates are housed in a separate wing of the Burnaby Correctional Centre for Women.

The Fraser Valley region contains the Boulder Bay Youth Secure Custody Centre on Alouette Lake with 33 inmates and Centre Creek camp in Chilliwack with 33 inmates. Centre Creek was originally a forest camp for adult inmates.

Young offenders are classified by the sentencing court although this process is under review. Closing the Burnaby facilities and constructing a new, larger centre to house the growing numbers of convicted young offenders is under review as well.

Prostitution
John Bermingham

THERE ARE CURRENTLY 1,500 prostitutes working in Vancouver. In 1992 the *Vancouver Sun* estimated they generated $63 million in revenues for the local economy. Today vice cops point to a disturbing trend on the city streets—prostitutes and pimps as young as 13 years old with plenty of customers in pursuit. The cops, the lawmakers and the morality crusaders have all tried to expunge prostitution from Vancouver. But they have failed to budge the sex trade which has always found Vancouver to be a bountiful home.

The politicians, the police, the pious and the city's prostitutes were always uneasy bedfellows. After the Great Fire of 1886 Dupont Street (now East Pender) became the brothel bazaar for the city. Many women were imported from China to be lodged in homes run by white madams like Mattie Davis, keeper of the posh house on Dupont. Up the road at Lady Caroline's only judges, lawyers and professional gentlemen were admitted as clientele.

Brothels on Canton and Shanghai streets in Chinatown and those on West Hastings and in Mount Pleasant were so-called "restricted districts"—areas sanctioned by police, making them, in fact, Vancouver's first red-light districts. Police protection money ensured peace and quiet but a *Daily Province* probe in 1906 led to the firing of chief constable Sam North for taking bribes from brothel operators.

Prostitution arrests increased from 20 in 1900 to 500 in 1920. Fines ranged from $15 for the prostitutes to $50 for the keepers. Prisoners' records at Vancouver City Gaol show a third of the prostitutes were former domestic servants who lost their jobs and perhaps had no other alternative livelihood.

In 1939 it was the spread of venereal disease that prompted police chief Col. W.W. Foster to launch yet another crackdown by his "morality squad." While venereal disease rates continued to climb well into the 1970s, the effects of the arrival of AIDS on the prostitute population have not been well documented.

In 1976 the owners and management of the Penthouse Cabaret on Seymour Street were charged with keeping a common bawdy house. The Penthouse Six, as they were called, included Joe Philliponi, a celebrated cabaret figure. In the 1950s and 1960s the Penthouse billed Harry Belafonte, Ella Fitzgerald and Sammy Davis Jr. It was alleged however that, in addition to presenting music, the venue provided a welcome place for 80 to 100 prostitutes to pick up clients each night.

The trial was a sensation. There were undercover tapes,

It seems the city cannot stop the killing of its prostitutes; since 1985 some 60 of them have been murdered

liquor inspectors on the take and stories galore (like how the Japanese Navy "invaded" the Penthouse one steamy summer night in 1975). During the trail Philliponi pleaded for leniency, claiming a conviction "would kill my mother." The trial regaled packed courtrooms for months, before all six finally walked free after successfully appealing the conviction. Fate caught up with Joe Philliponi in 1983 when he was shot dead during a robbery.

In 1979 police seized a little brown book at the apartment of a well-known Vancouver prostitute. In it were the names of 800 men, many of whom constitute a who's who of high society, including a high-ranking member of the B.C. judiciary. Wendy King pleaded guilty to keeping a bawdy house and was fined $1,500. But the notebook was sealed by a B.C. supreme court justice and the names were never revealed.

In recent years local residents have taken to the streets to remove prostitutes from their neighborhoods. For example there was the Mount Pleasant revolt in 1991 during which the Vancouver police published the names of johns nabbed in the area after the city's newspapers refused to do so. In 1984 Concerned Residents of the West End (CROWE), led by former Vancouver Centre MP Pat Carney, fought a street-battle with streetwalkers. Council, led by then-mayor Mike Harcourt, had passed a street-activity bylaw a couple of years before, imposing fines of up to $2,000 for a prostitution conviction. But like so many attempts to legally control prostitution, it failed to stick in the courts. The ensuing protests forced the hookers to simply move elsewhere. Currently the East End and the Downtown Eastside are still the main drags, as they were a century ago.

It seems the city can do nothing to stop the killing of its prostitutes. Since 1985 some 60 prostitutes have been murdered by tricks, pimps or pushers, making Vancouver the most dangerous place in Canada to streetwalk. Police suspect women have died at the hands of at least one serial killer and among those suspected is the infamous Green River Killer, who is still at large.

And finally police say that three out of every four prostitutes in Vancouver are drug addicts, mostly heroin and cocaine abusers. It seems that prostitution in Vancouver has become nastier with age.

Military and Civil Defences, 1859-1948
Peter Moogk

EARLY MILITARY RESERVES AND PUBLIC PARKS

Nature lovers and recreationists should thank officers of the British army and navy who, from 1859 onward, surveyed and reserved land around Burrard Inlet for its defence. From 1859 to 1868, when New Westminster was capital of the mainland Colony of British Columbia, Burrard Inlet was the nearest safe anchorage for warships. The Russians and Americans were potential enemies. The Crimean War had just ended and during the American Civil War there had been congressional bluster about seizing British North America. Similar threats had forced the 1846 cession of the Oregon Territory south of the 49th parallel to the United States.

The name of the colony expressed the imperial government's resolve to hold onto the northern region. Irish-American Fenian raids into British North America from 1866 to 1870 made the American threat believable. Any overland attack from the United States would be a northward thrust across the border. New Westminster had replaced Fort Langley as the administrative capital because it was on high ground on the north bank of the Fraser River—a defensible location with a water barrier against American intruders. British reinforcements could then be transported to the inlet and moved to New Westminster, via the future Kingsway, to aid the defenders.

To accommodate protective gun batteries at the entrance to Burrard Inlet, and at the First Narrows, military and naval reserves were established on Point Grey, at Jericho and at the narrows. Other lots were closed to settlement around the Port Moody-Indian Arm area, where the transcontinental railway was to have its terminus and because the arm was closest to New Westminster. None of these sites was used for its intended purpose before 1914.

The 99-year lease of the Stanley Park reserve to Vancouver in the 1880s (renewed in 1908) set a precedent for deeding other blocks of federal land to the municipalities for public parks or for private construction. The government reserve with rifle range along Kingsway became Central Park; 202 hectares on Point Grey's tip provided the core of the University Endowment Lands, and the military land that once straddled 41st Avenue produced Queen Elizabeth Park. The transfer of the north part of Jericho Beach base to the city in 1969 was yet another gift to Greater Vancouver. Municipal and federal politicians take credit for the resultant parks, although the green space is an inadvertent legacy of military planners. Politi-cians and realtors are insatiable: each transfer has been followed by further lobbying of the federal government to give up more military sites for free or a nominal price. During the "Battles of Jericho" in the 1960s and 1990s newspapers carried statements about "military squatters" who ought to "return [sic] . . . under-utilized lands" to the city for housing and recreation. Military users, who must remain silent on political issues, cannot respond to these claims and lose by default.

THE MILITIA AS SOCIAL INSTITUTION AND IMPERIAL ICON

In appearance Lower Mainland cities are North American communities. This led to a conscious assertion of British identity and imperial pride in the 19th century. Local army reserve units, whose uniforms and traditions copied those of British regiments, affirmed the population's Britishness. Vancouverites had long envied New Westminster, whose rifle regiment dated from the 1860s. Vancouver's militia formation was No. 5 (Artillery) Company organized by citizens in 1893. Young men rushed to enrol: 460 volunteered for the 100-man company, leading to the creation of a second company in 1895. They paraded, with British sailors and marines, on national holidays and during visits by dignitaries and high officers. The militia provided the imperial pageantry that proclaimed Vancouver's preferred identity. The blue or scarlet uniform with white pith helmet and belt was the epitome of Britannic identity. Its emotional significance was revealed in 1899, when Vancouver's gunners were converted to infantry, as the 6th Regiment, Duke of Connaught's Own Rifles. One disgruntled member protested the conversion to a rifleman's drab green-and-black attire with these lines:

> From the radiant brilliance of brass and blue
> To the dull dead black of shoddy and glue,
> The cheapest cloth of the uniform makers,
> For the Sixth Battalion of Undertakers.

In that year 24 infantrymen left Vancouver to fight for the British Empire in South Africa. The Boer War of 1899-1902 revealed the impracticality of the scarlet uniform with white accoutrements; it made British soldiers clear targets for Boer sharpshooters. Light brown or khaki—which provided some camouflage—became the standard color of imperial combat uniforms.

Local enthusiasm for things military endured into the next century. On the eve of World War I there were several Lower Mainland militia units, in addition to the 6th Regiment (DCOR) and New Westminster's infantry regiment: they included the No. 18 Field Ambulance, Army Medical Corps (founded 1909); the 6th Field Company, Canadian Engineers (1910) of North Vancouver; the 72nd Seaforth Highlanders

(1910); No. 19 Company, Army Service Corps (1912); No. 19 Company, Canadian Signal Corps (1912); and the 11th Regiment, Irish Fusiliers of Canada (1913). Unlike Victoria, Vancouver had no resident permanent force units in peacetime. Reservists maintained the area's military traditions.

Until the 1960s there was a social cachet to a military title and uniform. Young men of British and old-Canadian ancestry who worked as clerks, accountants and shop assistants on weekdays could don a tunic and breeches and experience the adventure of military life—in palatably small doses. Summer camps far from home provided teenage boys and bachelors of slender means with a sort of holiday and a chance to indulge in the manly arts of drinking liquor and smoking tobacco while off duty. In the early 1900s militiamen were paid only during summer camps and when they qualified in a special skill, such as signalling. Small remuneration and the cost of mess dues and other deductions tended to exclude married workingmen. Until World War II, officers bought their own uniforms—several orders of dress were required—and a good, private income was a prerequisite for accepting an officer's commission.

Businessmen, senior civil servants, insurance agents and a few professionals provided the militia's officers. The first commander of No. 5 Company, B.C. Battalion of Garrison Artillery (1893), was Thomas Owen Townley, barrister, land registrar and future mayor of Vancouver. The Seaforths' costly Highland regalia meant this regiment's officers came from wealthy families. Militia commissions confirmed the social status of leading citizens. They gloried in being addressed as "Captain," "Major" or "Colonel" and wore scarlet mess-kit at armory dinners, which reproduced the formalities of professional soldiery. The loyal toast, "Gentlemen, the King!" was a signal that smoking was now permitted, while the diners drank port. Wartime experience and medals attesting to bravery in combat were an additional source of prestige. World War I veterans provided most of the senior officers and non-commissioned officers in the 1920s and 1930s.

The butchery of World War I, functional khaki uniforms and the greater emphasis on military proficiency rather than ceremonial pageantry ought to have cooled British Columbians' military ardor; they did not. With fewer than 200,000 inhabitants, Greater Vancouver had 22 militia units in the 1920s. The range of arms extended to artillery and cavalry units with a machine gun corps company located in South Vancouver. The UBC Officers Training Corps (1915) completed the picture. More than 3,000 citizens were part-time soldiers in the army reserve. The permanent forces were now represented by Jericho Beach Air Station, established in 1920. Seaplanes from

Harold McCreath, a 94–year old World War I veteran, Remembrance Day, Victory Square, 1988. vs

Jericho surveyed the coast and provided flight training. Air Force and naval reserve units world appear on the Lower Mainland during World War II.

The army reserve's vitality between the world wars owed something to its social function as well as its practical value. Before electronic home entertainment and the waning of martial and Britannic traditions, the militia was an important patriotic and non-sectarian fraternal association. School cadet corps provided a steady stream of militia recruits and the reserves inducted high school students into manhood. In the 1940s women were incorporated into the services. The white-collar origins of most militia members meant they willingly followed government orders to protect company property and strike-breakers during labor disputes. If British surnames predominated in the nominal rolls of these units, it should be noted that the local population, prior to the 1950s, was overwhelmingly of British origin.

ON GUARD IN WAR

The declaration of war between Great Britain and the Central Powers in August 1914 created panic in British Columbia. Germany's Pacific Ocean squadron of five cruisers was rumored to be sailing toward the West Coast. Against them, Canada had one training cruiser, the *Rainbow*, that had just escorted the *Komagata Maru*, with unwanted East Indian immigrants, out of Canadian waters. Premier Sir Richard McBride augmented this vessel by purchasing two submarines (actually constructed for Chile) in Seattle. Once enemy warships had passed the big guns of Victoria-Esquimalt, they would be unopposed. The Vancouver *Daily Province* pointed out the mainland port's weaknesses: "Vancouver has no fortifications. There are no batteries which could be used for defence," and the militia infantry would be impotent "against a naval force with long-range guns." The federal government's response was to install two 4-inch calibre guns near Siwash Rock in Stanley Park, manned by naval volunteers. Another battery of 60-pounder, long-range field guns from the Cobourg (Heavy) Battery of Ontario was emplaced on Point Grey, near Washout Gully. This was the first time the military reserves had been used for their intended purpose: the protection of Burrard Inlet. These two gun batteries were only temporary, stopgap measures. After the destruction of the German squadron in December 1914, fear subsided and the guns were withdrawn. Reservists and new recruits proceeded overseas to fight in Europe.

In the 1930s Japan was no longer a British ally and was an aggressively expansionist power. The defence of Vancouver against this or another foreign state was not going to be left to last-minute improvisation again. A British coast artillery expert, Major B.D.C. Treatt, assessed the port's needs in 1936 and his report, with a joint staff sub-committee's recommendations, became the basis for planning Vancouver's defences in the event that "the British Empire is at war (U.S.A. neutral) with Japan, alternatively with a coalition of European Powers headed by Germany." The threat of an attack by Japanese armed merchant vessels, submarines, motor torpedo boats and, possibly, by carrier-borne aircraft was taken seriously. In wartime all inbound shipping was to be inspected and cleared before entering the inner harbor. Gun batteries would enforce security regulations and protect the air station, moored vessels and port facilities. Canadian resources during the Great Depression permitted only a beginning in 1938 on the Ferguson Point Battery in Stanley Park, which was to cover detained vessels anchored in English Bay and to provide close-in defence. A three-gun counter-bombardment battery was to be located on Point Grey and close-defence guns were to cover the First Narrows, where a boom with net would act as the harbor's gate. Aircraft patrols would provide an early warning of attack. Ten searchlights along the shoreline would furnish night-time illumination of the maritime approaches. The local Field Brigade, Royal Canadian Artillery (1920), was converted to a coast artillery regiment to man the guns here and on Yorke Island, at the head of the Inside Passage.

The war against Nazi Germany, beginning in September 1939, accelerated construction of the defences. Anti-aircraft batteries, to be coordinated with the coast defence batteries,

were proposed, but Canada did not have the weapons for them. British industry was the traditional source of heavy armaments and, after the Dunkirk evacuation in May-June 1940, all production was needed to re-equip the British forces defending the island kingdom against invasion. B.C. coastal batteries were armed with old weapons already in Canada. When Japanese aircraft attacked Pearl Harbor in December 1941, the inadequacy of the Lower Mainland defences against an aerial attack was apparent to everyone. Blackout curtains were strung across windows and car headlights were painted blue, causing night-time collisions. Hysteria led to the forced evacuation of all Japanese-Canadians from the coast in March 1942.

At their peak in 1942 the Lower Mainland's coastal batteries, from Steveston to Point Atkinson, were manned by 720 gunners, supported by infantry regiments and auxiliary units. Anti-aircraft batteries of 40-mm and 3.7-inch calibre guns appeared at Point Grey, Little Mountain, Ambleside and elsewhere. False alarms were many, but it was the lax observation of port security rules that resulted in the sinking of a ship. Alas, it was one of our own. On September 13, 1943 (the anniversary of the Battle of the Plains of Abraham), a fish-packer blithely entered the inlet, ignoring all signals to identify itself. A warning shot from a 12-pounder gun at the Narrows North Fort ricocheted off the water ahead of the offending vessel and went on to tear through the newly built freighter *Fort Rae,* exiting below the waterline. The sinking craft struggled to return to its birthplace, the Burrard Dry Dock, and settled ingloriously beneath Lions Gate Bridge. The vessel was later patched up and restored to service after causing red faces and recrimination all around.

The receding danger of attack in 1943 brought a gradual reduction in the local defences to release trained personnel for the Canadian Army in Europe, which was now in continuous action. Soon after the war's end in September 1945 the gun batteries were dismantled and closed. Fort Point Grey was the last to go, in 1948, and there, appropriately, is a historic marker at the restored No. 1 Gun position that recalls the battery's history. Complaints about the establishment of Ferguson Point battery and HMCS Discovery, the naval reserve station, in Stanley Park revealed the public's forgetfulness about the park's origins. This is not to begrudge Lord Stanley his namesake or Mayor David Oppenheimer his statue at the park's Beach Avenue entrance. Spare a grateful thought, however, for the likes of Captain George H. Richards and Master Daniel Pender of the Royal Navy as well as Colonel Richard C. Moody, Royal Engineers, for this and for the other parks that we now enjoy.

Legal Resources
Susanna Hughes

Greater Vancouver offers many services to people needing legal advice or assistance. Many of these services are free or inexpensive. The following is a fairly comprehensive listing. For those people who are not sure where to go for assistance, most of the organizations listed will refer callers to the appropriate agency.

COURTS
Provincial Court—Criminal Division
Burnaby, 6263 Deerlake Ave., 660-7130
Coquitlam: 2165 Kelly St., 941-0604
Delta: 4465 Clarence Taylor Cres., 660-3121
Langley: 20389 Fraser Hwy., 530-1164
Maple Ridge: 11960 Haney Pl., 467-1515
New Westminster: Begbie Square, 660-8520
North Vancouver: 200 E. 23rd St., 983-4000
Richmond: 6900 Minoru Blvd., 660-6900
Surrey: 14340-57th Ave., 572-2288
Vancouver: 222 Main St., 660-4200
Vancouver (Traffic): 190 Alexander St., 660-4278
West Vancouver: 1330 Marine Dr., 660-1232
Hears most cases under the Criminal Code, Narcotic Control Act, or other federal criminal legislation, with the exception of the most serious criminal offences. Hears all offences arising under provincial legislation.

Provincial Court—Family and Youth Division
Burnaby: 6263 Deerlake Ave., 660-7130
Coquitlam: 2165 Kelly St., 941-0604
Delta: 4465 Clarence Taylor Cres., 660-3121
Maple Ridge: 11960 Haney Pl., 467-1515
New Westminster: Begbie Square, 660-8522
North Vancouver: 200 E. 23rd St., 983-4000
Richmond: 6931 Granville Ave., 660-4693
Surrey: 14340-57th Ave., 572-2220
Vancouver: 800 Hornby St., 660-8989
West Vancouver: 1330 Marine Dr., 660-1232
Hears almost all family matters except divorce and division of property. Youth Court hears offences arising under the Young Offenders Act. Family court counsellors are available without charge to assist parties involved in family matters.

Provincial Court—Small Claims Division
Burnaby: 6263 Deerlake Ave., 660-7135
Delta: 4465 Clarence Taylor Cres., 660-3121
Maple Ridge: 11960 Haney Pl., 467-1515
New Westminster: Begbie Square, 660-8501
North Vancouver: 200 E. 23rd St., 983-4000
Richmond: 6931 Granville Ave., 775-1215
Surrey: 14340-57th Ave., 572-2210
Vancouver: 800 Hornby St., 660-8989
Hears civil cases involving less than $10,000. Procedures are relatively informal and most cases are handled by the parties themselves,
without lawyers.

Supreme Court of B.C.
New Westminster: Begbie Square, 660-8990
Vancouver: Law Courts, 800 Smithe St., 660-2847
Hears any civil action including family matters. Also hears appeals from Provincial Court. Conducts the most serious criminal trials.

Court of Appeal of B.C.
Vancouver: Law Courts, 800 Smithe St. 660-2858
Hears appeals from the Supreme Court. Appeals from the Court of Appeal of B.C. go to the Supreme Court of Canada.

LEGAL RESOURCES
B.C. Civil Liberties Association
425-815 W. Hastings St., Vancouver, 687-2919
Defends and gives referrals on human rights and civil liberties issues (e.g., freedom of speech and association; privacy and access to information; due process). Active in public education programs, lobbying and infrequent court action. Accepts complaints about discrimination, police misconduct, administrative procedures, prisoners' and children's rights, access to information and invasion of privacy.

B.C. Coalition of People with Disabilities
204-456 W. Broadway, Vancouver, 875-0188
Advocacy Access (toll-free): 1-800-663-1278
Provides individual and group advocacy for people with disabilities.

B.C. Council of Human Rights
406-815 Hornby St., Vancouver, 660-6811
or call toll-free 1-800-663-0876
Provincial agency opposing discrimination on the basis of race, religion, gender, ancestry, place of origin, marital status, mental or physical disability or age. Enforces the B.C. Human Rights Act. Focus is on preventive education programs. The council also assists individual victims of discrimination.

B.C. Courthouse Library Society
Vancouver: Law Courts, 800 Smithe St., 660-2910
New Westminster: Begbie Square, 660-8577
Operates courthouse libraries, open to the public, in the Vancouver and New Westminster Supreme Court buildings.

B.C. Human Rights Coalition
718-744 W. Hastings St., Vancouver, 689-8474
A non-governmental organization which fights discrimination and seeks to improve human rights protection. Provides advocacy services to victims of discrimination or harassment, sponsors public education programs and lobbies to enforce and enhance human rights legislation.

Canadian Human Rights Commission
750-605 Robson St., Vancouver, 666-2251
Government agency administering federal human rights legislation.

Consumer Association of Canada, Consumer Assistance Office
306-198 W. Hastings St., Vancouver, 682-3535
Handles enquiries regarding consumer issues and legislation. Provides individual assistance and referrals for consumer problems.

Consumer Services, Debtor Assistance Branch
5021 Kingsway, Burnaby, 660-3550
Provides financial and related legal advice to people faced with debt problems.

Consumer Services, Investigations Branch
5021 Kingsway, Burnaby, 660-3570
Administers consumer legislation, investigates disputes over unfair or deceptive selling practices.

Consumer Services, Residential Tenancy Branch
400-5021 Kingsway, Burnaby, 660-3400
Information line: 660-3456
Provides information to landlords and tenants on their rights and responsibilities and provides speakers to interested groups. Administers an arbitration system for resolution of most landlord and tenant disputes.

Dial-A-Law
687-4680
or call toll-free 1-800-565-LAWS (5297)
A library of taped messages prepared by the B.C. Branch of the Canadian Bar Association providing practical information on a wide variety of legal topics.

Family Maintenance Enforcement Program
660-3281
or call toll-free 1-800-663-9666
A provincial government program which monitors and enforces spousal and child support payments.

International Self-Counsel Press
1481 Charlotte Rd., North Vancouver, 986-3366
Publishes self-help guides and workbooks on numerous legal and business issues (e.g., divorce and separation agreements, incorporations, wills and estates, small claims procedures, etc.).

Law Courts Education Society
Vancouver: Law Courts, 800 Smithe St., 660-9870
Surrey: 14340-57th Ave., 572-2276
Conducts public education with respect to the court system and offers courthouse tours.

Law Line
Operated by the Legal Services Society (see below). Provides general legal information and referrals over the telephone.

Law Society of B.C.
845 Cambie St., Vancouver, 669-2533
The legal profession's governing body, responsible for the admission, conduct and discipline

of lawyers. Handles complaints about lawyer's conduct.

Law Student's Legal Advice Program (LSLAP)
228-5791
Free legal clinics operated by UBC law students and supervised by lawyers. Clinics at various locations throughout the Lower Mainland provide legal assistance in the following areas: welfare appeals, UIC, family law, landlord/tenant disputes, immigration, wills, small claims, employee/employer disputes, ICBC and motor vehicle claims and minor criminal offences. Specialty clinics are also held on women's and First Nations' issues.

Lawyer Referral Service
845 Cambie St., Vancouver, 687-3221
or call toll-free 1-800-663-1919
Canadian Bar Association service refers callers to participating lawyers who provide an inexpensive 30-minute initial consultation.

Legal Resource Centre
200-1140 W. Pender St., Vancouver, 660-4673
A public library of easy-to-understand legal materials including films and videotapes. Also sponsors legal research and referral workshops for librarians, teachers and interested community groups.

Legal Services Society (Legal Aid)
660-4600
Branch Offices:
Vancouver: 191 Alexander St., 687-1831
Burnaby: 509-5021 Kingsway, 775-2100
Surrey: 105-9180 King George Hwy., 951-2030
Community Law Offices:
Abbotsford: 100-2955 Gladwin Rd., 859-2755
Langley: 21-20189 56th Ave., 530-5811
Maple Ridge: 4-22701 119th Ave., 467-3011
New Westminster: 103-668 Carnarvon St., 524-0381
North Vancouver: 1060 Roosevelt Cr., 985-7138
Port Coquitlam: 300-2232 McAllister Ave., 944-8841
Provides free or inexpensive legal counsel to eligible applicants. Deals primarily with family, criminal or immigration matters. Also offers general legal information.

Native Courtworker & Counselling Association of B.C.
North Vancouver: 404 W. Esplanade (Administration), 985-5355
Vancouver: 50 Powell St., 687-0281
Surrey: 10673 King George Hwy., 589-0511
14340-57th Ave., Surrey (Surrey Courthouse), 572-2293
Provides legal information and advice to native people as well as referrals to legal and other resources. Helps natives in conflict with the law.

OASIS Immigrant Services Centre
Vancouver: 8165 Main St., 324-8186

Surrey: 103-8386 120th St., 590-4667
Provides direct services and programs to Indo-Canadian immigrants (e.g., information, interpretation and referrals for legal and human rights problems).

Office of the Ombudsman of B.C.
202-1275 W. 6th Ave., Vancouver, 660-1366
or call toll-free 1-800-661-3247
Handles complaints about provincial government ministries, Crown agencies, boards or commissions or other provincial government appointees. The ombudsman can investigate and may recommend changes to bureaucratic decisions, actions or practices.

People's Law School (The Public Legal Education Society)
150-900 Howe St., Vancouver, 688-2565
A non-profit society providing public legal education in cooperation with various community organizations. Free law classes are available throughout the Lower Mainland. Topics include property law, wills and estates, landlord and tenant law, immigration, family law, seniors' issues, etc. Self-help booklets and videos are available. Information is available in Cantonese, Japanese, Mandarin, Persian, Polish, Punjabi, Spanish and Vietnamese.

Public Trustee
808 W. Hastings St., Vancouver, 660-4444
A provincial government agency protects the financial affairs of individuals who can't protect themselves legally either by reason of youth or mental incapacity.

Queen's Printer
849 Hornby St., Vancouver, 660-0981
The official bookstore of the B.C. government; provides copies of legislation and other official government publications.

Tenants' Rights Information Line
255-0546 or call toll-free 1-800-665-1185
Hotline with information on tenants' legal rights.

Vancouver Community Legal Assistance Society (VCLAS)
800-1281 W. Georgia St., Vancouver, 685-3425
Provides assistance in civil cases to low-income clients and groups.

Vancouver Gay and Lesbian Centre
1170 Bute St., Vancouver, 684-5307
Offers a library, free legal clinic, counselling, information and referral. All services are confidential.

Vancouver Status of Women
301-1720 Grant St., Vancouver, 255-5511
Provides free legal and general information and counselling specifically for women; referrals to feminist lawyers.

Victims' Information Line
Call toll-free 1-800-563-0808
Offers information and referrals for victims of crime.

Welfare Rights Advocacy Group Society (WRAGS)
1111-6th Ave., New Westminster, 521-6955
Gives advice regarding welfare rights and entitlements; occasionally provides advocacy services for clients.

West Coast LEAF Association (Women's Legal Education and Action Fund)
905-207 W. Hastings St., Vancouver, 684-8772
Promotes equality for women through public education and legal action. Sponsors legal test cases to challenge discrimination against women using the provisions of the Canadian Charter of Rights and Freedoms.

The Law Courts, Vancouver, 1990. vp

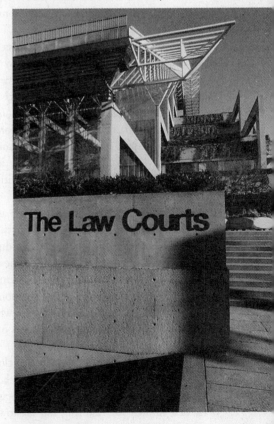

The Consular Corps
Sandra McKenzie

DIPLOMACY IS THE primary vehicle by which nations communicate political concerns, negotiate trade deals, settle disputes and protect the interests of their citizens abroad. At the senior diplomatic level are the embassies or, among the Commonwealth nations, high commissions, located in the host nation's capital. Typically embassies wrangle with high-level contentious political and economic issues such as, say, turbot over-fishing or human rights violations. In Canada 112 nations post ambassadorial staff in Ottawa while another 50 countries oversee their North American interests from embassies in Washington, DC.

At the junior level of the diplomatic community are the consulates, which usually handle the day-to-day bureaucratic and commercial interests of their country. They process visa and passport applications, promote trade and tourism, and provide legal advice and support to their citizens travelling abroad who have run afoul of local law. While embassies are always located in the national capital, consulates are scattered throughout the country's major cities. Montreal has 88 consulates, Toronto 82 and Vancouver 64.

Consulates can be headed by either career diplomats who are citizens of the state they represent or by honorary consuls. Appointing an honorary consul is frequently a cost-saving measure, preserving a diplomatic presence without the overhead of staffing. But sometimes the appointment confers an entree into Canadian political life. Singapore, for example, has former Chief Justice Nathan Nemetz as honorary consul general. Though Mr. Nemetz is not directly involved with consulate work, he does bring high-level political connections to the job.

An honorary consul is a private citizen appointed by a foreign government to represent its interests. In Vancouver 26 consulates are staffed by full-time career diplomats and 38 by Canadian residents. In most instances honorary consuls serve a primarily titular function, leaving the actual business of the post to the professionals. But some appointees play a more direct role. Jeffery Moore, for instance, who is El Salvador's consul in Vancouver, organizes shipments of tools, equipment and school supplies to El Salvador.

While an honorary consul usually has close links, either by birth or business, with the country he or she represents, this is not necessarily the case. Vancouver horologist Raymond Saunders, best known for restoring the Gastown steam clock, is honorary consul for Guinea, a country he has never visited and in which he has no special interests. Saunders sought the job and paid several thousands of dollars for the privilege. While Saunders hasn't divulged the exact amount he paid, the estimated price for an honorary consulship in Western Canada runs as high as $25,000, plus any expenses incurred.

For about the price of a country-club membership, the appointment virtually guarantees an entry to the cocktails-and-canapes circuit. Among the more interesting social and economic doors that suddenly swing open are invitations to dinner with visiting Royals and reserved seats at major events such as the Commonwealth Games. A diplomatic association with a major country can bring in as many as 300 invitations a year. Other perks include diplomatic license plates, which allow the bearer to park darned near anywhere he or she pleases. While an honorary consul may hold dual citizenship (granted at the discretion of the country represented), he or she does not enjoy diplomatic immunity and cannot claim exemption from Canadian law.

In Vancouver the first consulate to be recognized by the Canadian government belonged to Chile, which established its interests here in 1892, naming M.P. Morris as the honorary consul general. Brazil followed Chile's lead in 1915 and in 1920 Belgium became the third country to appoint a consul to Vancouver. In contrast the U.S. waited until 1928 before establishing a consulate here. Great Britain joined ranks after 1930. The most recent arrival on the diplomatic scene is Belize, which established its Vancouver presence in 1995.

What, precisely, were Chile's early interests in a rag-tag town in the Pacific Northwest? The answer, if it exists, is buried deep in the archives in Santiago, though the current Chilean consulate staff speculate that they might have been protecting shipping interests and possibly monitoring the welfare of migrant miners seeking work in British Columbia's copper mines. In any case Chile's Vancouver consulate remained an honorary posting until 1990 when it was upgraded to a full-time, professional office.

Trickier to determine is the size of any given consulate. For diplomatic purposes, consulates are ranked equally. Though the world is currently a relatively quiet place, for security reasons several countries do not publish any personnel details, including staffing figures. However the People's Republic of China, which occupies two buildings on Granville Street, maintains the largest full-time staff.

Longest serving of all local consular officials was Vancouver businessman Frank Bernard, vice-consul for Spain from 1940 to 1989, an astonishing 49 years.

Vancouver's prominence as a centre for diplomatic activity is a recent phenomenon, dating back only to about 1990. In the past six years 20 nations, including former Soviet bloc countries like the Czech Republic, the Slovak Republic, Hungary and Poland, have either established a presence here or have upgraded their operations. According to David Harris, chief of protocol for the provincial government, the reason is Vancouver's geographical position as a meeting point for Asian and European interests. With its relatively balmy climate, Pacific Rim connections and burgeoning high-tech economy, Vancouver has become a door to the world. For countries such as Indonesia, India, Malaysia and South Korea, Vancouver is a gateway to the North American market. Europeans, on the other hand, view it as an opening to Asia.

Some countries have foregone embassies in Ottawa and have, instead, concentrated their resources in Vancouver. Belize, for example, closed its embassy in 1993 and opened an office here in 1995. Singapore, which maintains a full-time consulate staff on the West Coast, relies on a consulate in Manhattan to handle other Canadian affairs.

While the consular offices function primarily as trade and tourism commissions, politics does occasionally rear its head. Invitations to Taiwanese-sponsored events in Vancouver, for example, bring routine reminders from the People's Republic of China consulate that participation could be injurious to international relationships. Though espionage is still a reality of life in the diplomatic corps, it is no longer the growth industry it was during the Cold War. As for diplomatic immunity, it goes with the job for foreign-born consular staff, but it does not mean that transgressions go unpunished. If you break the laws of the host country, you're immediately recalled, your career is ruined and you can expect to feel the full wrath of the law at home, explains a former member of the Canadian foreign service.

Most consulates leave the heavy stuff of crime, punishment and politics to their embassies and concentrate on the business at hand. Panama, for example, oversees the affairs of the 400-plus ships flying the Panamanian flag that pull into Vancouver's ports each year. Mexico keeps busy negotiating trade deals under NAFTA and monitors conditions for migrant agricultural workers who stream north every year. The Polish consulate, under the guidance of author, journalist and diplomat Krzysztof Kasprzyk, has turned the business of issuing passports and visas into a for-profit venture, bringing in revenues of about $400,000 annually to the coffers of the former Soviet Bloc country.

In 1997, dean of the Vancouver consular corps was Lourdes Morales, consul general of the Republic of the Philippines

Vancouver's Consulates and Consulates General:

Consul of Australia	Consul General of Germany	Consul General of the Netherlands
Consul General of Austria	Consul of Ghana	Consul General of New Zealand
Consul of Barbados	Consul of Greece	Consul of Niger
Consul of Belgium	Consul General of Guatemala	Consul General of Norway
Consul of Belize	Consul of Guinea	Consul General of Panama
Consul of Bolivia	Consul of Haiti	Consul General of Peru
Consul General of Brazil	Consul of Hondouras	Consul General of The Philippines
Consul General of Chile	Consul General of Hungary	Consul General of Poland
Consul General of the People's Republic of China	Consul of Iceland	Consul General of Portugal
Consul of Colombia	Consul General of India	Consul of Senegal
Consul General of Costa Rica	Consul General of Indonesia	Consul General of Singapore
Consul of Cote d'Ivoire	Consul General of Italy	Consul of the Slovak Republic
Consul General of the Czech Republic	Consul General of Japan	Consul of South Africa
Consul of Denmark	Consul General of Korea	Consul General of Sri Lanka
Vice Consul of the Dominican Republic	Consul of Lesotho	Consul General of Sweden
Consul of Ecuador	Consul General of Liberia	Consul General of Switzerland
Consul General of El Salvador	Consul General of Luxembourg	Consul General of Thailand
Consul General of Fiji	Consul General of Malaysia	Consul of Tunisia
Consul General of Finland	Consul General of Malta	Consul General of the United Kingdom
Consul General of France	Consul General of Mexico	Consul General of the United States
Consul of Gambia	Consul General of Monaco	Consul of Uruguay
	Consul General of Morocco	

The Post Office
Andrew Scott

VANCOUVER'S FIRST POST OFFICE was not located in Gastown nor anywhere near today's urban centre but in the kitchen of a remote pioneer hotel at the end of the city's first wagon road. Early postal patrons had to hike, ride or row to this spot—now occupied by New Brighton Park next to the looming Alberta Wheat Pool elevators. New Westminster residents—who had enjoyed postal service since 1859—could bounce out by daily stagecoach to two simple hostelries in order to refresh themselves in the ocean and at the bar or take a primitive ferry to Burrard Inlet's nearby lumber mills.

The office on the inlet, which opened July 2, 1869, was the only postal outlet in colonial times within Vancouver's current boundaries. Postmaster Maximilian Michaud, who bought the Brighton Hotel early in 1869 and changed its name to the Hastings, used a grid-lined hammer enclosing the number "28" to cancel the mail. (Only a few envelopes with the "28" postmark are known; an example offered at auction in 1988 sold for over $3,000.) After B.C. joined Confederation in 1871 the post office's unofficial name, Burrard Inlet, was made official. It was renamed Hastings in 1897.

By 1874 the communities surrounding the inlet's two busy mills had grown large enough to require their own postal establishments. An office called Moodyville (the name was changed to North Vancouver in 1902) began service at Sewell Moody's pioneer mill on the north shore of Burrard Inlet on March 1, 1874. One month later the Granville post office opened in the store at Captain Edward Stamp's Hastings Mill located at the top of Dunlevy St. near Gastown. (The 1865 store is the city's oldest building; it was moved in 1930 to a park at the north foot of Alma St.) Henry Harvey, the mill's storekeeper, was the first postmaster. Granville, named after Earl Granville (George Leveson-Gower), Britain's secretary of state for the colonies, is considered the forerunner of the present-day Vancouver post office by most people.

On February 1, 1886 the post office was relocated to the back of Tilley's stationery store which stood on Carrall St. between Powell and Oppenheimer (now Cordova) near Gassy Jack's saloon in Maple Leaf Square. CPR mail clerk John Rooney became postmaster. The city was incorporated on April 6, 1886 and its name changed to Vancouver but the post office continued as Granville until the new cancelling equipment arrived. On May 1 Vancouver post office came into existence. Jonathan Miller took over as postmaster, remaining until September 9, 1908. Miller received a commission on post office revenue but no salary and also served as the fledgling city's collector, jailer, constable, court clerk and government-agent.

June 13, 1886 is Vancouver's most calamitous date. A great fire destroyed Tilley's along with just about every other building in town. Afterwards the post office was briefly housed in a shed at the Royal City Planing Mill which had escaped destruction by virtue of its False Creek site at the foot of Carrall. In July the post office moved to its own building on the north side of Hastings St. near Homer (where 325 West Hastings is located today).

July, 1886 also marked the arrival by train of the first transcontinental shipment of mail over Canadian soil. Up until this time mail from B.C. to eastern Canada had always travelled via the U.S. through San Francisco and other ports. Delivery took weeks, even months. Now a letter could be sent from Montreal to Port Moody in five-and-a-half days.

Vancouver's fast-growing business district was expanding westwards from Main St. to Granville. After less than a year, in June, 1887, the post office joined the shift moving to larger quarters in the three-storey Lady Mount Stephen Block at 309 (now 409) West Hastings. In 1892 postmaster Miller and his staff packed up and relocated yet again, this time to a fine, stone-faced federal office building that used to stand at the southwest corner of Granville and Pender. Here Miller instituted Vancouver's first home delivery service in 1895. Four letter carriers covered the area north of False Creek between Nicola and Campbell Sts.

By the end of the century Vancouver was a vigorous city of 25,000. Streetcars and the electric railway to New Westminster were pushing back the suburbs. Within today's city boundaries post offices had opened at Mount Pleasant (1891), South Vancouver (1893), Epworth (1896, now Cedar Cottage), East End (1897, at Hastings and Gore), West Fairview (1898) and West End (1898, at Burrard and Barclay). Greater Vancouver also saw an explosion of activity with two dozen offices opened west of Langley and the Pitt River before 1900.

In 1910, under postmaster Robert G. MacPherson (a former Vancouver MP), the office moved to the northwest corner of Granville and Hastings where it would stay for 48 years. Its new home had Edwardian baroque dignity, with columns, a clock tower and a granite facade. After 1936 the building underwent a major expansion; a tunnel was built to the CPR station and the lobby richly refurbished in bronze, cedar, terracotta and marble.

Vancouver's first postmen, 1895. cva

for six weeks by 700 unemployed workers demanding federal relief. Rioting by more than 5,000 demonstrators caused considerable damage. Eventually the invaders were ousted by police with tear gas; 39 people were injured and 22 were arrested. In 1986 the building became part of the beautifully restored $38-million Sinclair Centre.

The current post office at 349 W. Georgia St., now known as the Vancouver Mail Processing Plant, was opened in 1958. This $13-million edifice—at the time the largest welded steel structure in the world—is a giant, five-storey machine covering an entire city block. The conveyor system, once state-of-the-art, whips mail from floor to floor, up ramps, down chutes and along three kilometres of whirling belts. Clanking mechanized parcel sorters dump boxes through slots. The building is connected to the CPR station by a conveyor-equipped tunnel but as transport by truck grew more efficient the tunnel became obsolete. By 1965 it wasn't used at all. Neither was the roof pad, designed for helicopter loads of 4.5 tonnes per wheel. Helicopter mail delivery turned out to be too expensive.

During the 1960s and '70s the central post office was the site of almost annual work stoppages and strikes by militant postal unions. Seemingly driven to a frenzy by their mechanized workplace employees fought against further automation. Letter-sorting machinery, however, was introduced in the mid-'70s, at the same time as the postal code. Before this the city was broken into numbered zones for mail sortation.

Today Canada Post employs about 4,500 people in the Vancouver collection area which stretches from Hope to Squamish, including 1,200 at the plant. New A. B. Dick OCR (optical character recognition) machines each scan 25,000 envelopes an hour and read postal or zip codes. The equipment also cancels stamps by ink-jet spray and tags letters with a bar code for further sorting by other locomotive-sized contraptions. Older machinery processes big envelopes and more letter mail. Two million pieces a day are handled on average (six million at Christmas).

Despite the technology the plant's entire third floor is still dedicated to hand-sorting irregular mail. On the fifth floor workers sit at 44 VES (video encoding system) stations reading postal codes from electronic images and keying in data. Three hundred and fifty trucks bring the jumbled proceeds of 4,100 red letterboxes into the second-floor unloading facility then take the day's tidied output to the airport, other cities and a network of local offices. At last count there were 11 postal stations, nine letter-carrier depots and 142 corporate, franchise and retail outlets in Vancouver.

Central post office staff grew from 12 in 1895 to 700 by 1943. Trucks replaced horse-drawn vehicles for transporting bulk mail and steamships carried mail regularly to west coast ports and across the Pacific. Experimental mail flights were attempted in the region as early as 1919 but it wasn't until 1937 that regular intercity and transcontinental air mail services became available from Vancouver (with Trans Canada Airlines).

In 1938 the Vancouver post office was the site of a famous Canadian act of civic disobedience. The building was occupied

The GVRD

The Greater Vancouver Regional District is a voluntary federation of 20 municipalities and two electoral areas that make up our metropolitan region. These communities have chosen to work together through the GVRD to deliver essential services, more economically, efficiently and equitably at a regional level. It is one of 27 regional districts in British Columbia and, with more than 1.8 million residents, a little more than half the population of the province, is the largest.

The Greater Vancouver Regional District
Chuck Davis

O N PLACID MCLEAN POND in Campbell Valley Regional Park a family quietly glides past in a canoe; an injured child is rushed into the emergency ward at Surrey Memorial Hospital; a woman in Burnaby turns on an outside tap to water her lawn; kids play at Richmond's Alderwood Place housing development; a backhoe operator scoops up a load of shattered concrete from a demolished building in downtown Vancouver . . . and as a commercial pops up during an episode of *X-Files,* thousands of people all over the Lower Mainland head for the bathroom. The lives of all these people are affected by activities of the Greater Vancouver Regional District. And decisions by these same people direct, in turn, the activities and future of the GVRD.

The GVRD, incorporated in 1967, is a voluntary federation of 20 municipalities and two electoral areas that make up the metropolitan area of Greater Vancouver. These communities have chosen to work together through the GVRD to deliver essential services more economically, efficiently and equitably at a regional level. It is one of 27 regional districts in British Columbia and, with more than 1.8 million residents, a little more than half the population of the province, is easily the largest.

The late Dan Campbell, minister of municipal affairs in the W.A.C. Bennett government of the early 1960s, and his deputy minister J. Everett Brown, pushed the concept of regional government. Campbell and Brown could be considered the fathers of regional government in B.C. The regional district concept was established by the provincial government in 1965; the first meeting of the GVRD's board of directors was July 12, 1967.

But, in a way, the GVRD's history goes back a lot farther than the creation of regional districts. It starts with water. On March 25, 1889 water flowed through a pipe that led from the Capilano River on the North Shore, snaked across the bottom of First Narrows beneath Burrard Inlet under 20 metres of water and ended in what is now downtown Vancouver on the inlet's south shore. That was the start of what would become, many years later, a regional water system. In that system (started by a private firm but sold in 1891 to the City of Vancouver) was the seed of the idea that became the Greater Vancouver Regional District; the idea that municipalities could provide their infrastructure services better and cheaper

facing page: Upper Capilano watershed, 1992. vs

by working together.

Who are the members? Here's the roll call (with incorporation dates, area in square kilometres and 1996 population estimates):

VILLAGE OF ANMORE
December 7, 1987 (5.0) 900
VILLAGE OF BELCARRA
August 22, 1979 (12.49) 650
CITY OF BURNABY
September 22, 1892 (106.7) 175,811
CITY OF COQUITLAM
July 25, 1892 (152.6) 100,946
DISTRICT OF DELTA
November 10, 1879 (364.3) 96,870
ELECTORAL AREA A (UNIVERSITY ENDOWMENT LANDS)
Unincorporated (14.0) 5,503
ELECTORAL AREA C (BOWEN ISLAND, BARNSTON ISLAND, HOWESOUND AND INDIAN ARM)
Unincorporated (919.1) 3,459
CITY OF LANGLEY
March 15, 1955 (10.2) 22,750
TOWNSHIP OF LANGLEY
April 26, 1873 (317.7) 80,708
VILLAGE OF LIONS BAY
January 2, 1971 (2.9) 1,414
DISTRICT OF MAPLE RIDGE
September 12, 1874 (267.1) 59,830
CITY OF NEW WESTMINSTER
July 16, 1860 (22.0) 47,016
CITY OF NORTH VANCOUVER
May 13, 1907 (12.7) 41,584
DISTRICT OF NORTH VANCOUVER
August 10, 1891 (178.2) 81,848
DISTRICT OF PITT MEADOWS
April 24, 1914 (50.0) 14,500
CITY OF PORT COQUITLAM
March 7, 1913 (31.0) 41,845
CITY OF PORT MOODY
March 7, 1913 (21.0) 20,459
CITY OF RICHMOND
November 10, 1879 (168.1) 150,000
CITY OF SURREY
November 10, 1879 (371.4) 294,000
CITY OF VANCOUVER
April 6, 1886 (116.1) 521,048
DISTRICT OF WEST VANCOUVER
March 15, 1912 (98.9) 41,778

Greater Vancouver Regional District

The GVRD's history starts with water. In March of 1889 a private company laid a pipeline from the Capilano River on the north shore of Burrard Inlet across the inlet to Vancouver. Two years later the City of Vancouver bought the company. Today, the residents and businesses of the metropolitan area consume 400 billion litres of water annually. The foundation for the system was well-planned by Ernest Cleveland, first Commissioner of the Water District.

CITY OF WHITE ROCK

April 15, 1957 (14.0) 17,603

Total 1995 population for the GVRD: 1,819,533.

The GVRD comprises five separate legal entities: the Greater Vancouver Regional District itself; the Greater Vancouver Water District (GVWD, incorp. 1926, became part of the GVRD in 1971); the Greater Vancouver Sewerage and Drainage District (GVSDD, incorp. in 1956, a successor to the Vancouver and District Joint Sewerage and Drainage Board, which had been incorporated in 1914, and became part of the GVRD in 1971); the Greater Vancouver Regional Hospital District (GVRHD, incorp. 1967); and the Greater Vancouver Housing Corporation (GVHC, incorp. 1974). All operate under the umbrella of the GVRD, are in the same offices, have a common administration staff and, except for the housing corporation, virtually the same board of directors.

The GVRD's purpose is to preserve the quality of life in a magnificent region expected to be home to two million people by 2001, three million by 2021. The region's population increases by about 40,000 people annually. That's 110 new residents every day. Rapid growth of that kind calls for serious, long-range planning. And, beginning in the late 1980s, a new element was added: serious, long-range public input.

The GVRD is big business. In 1994 combined capital and operating expenditures and investment activities created a cash flow of more than $600 million. Some 77 per cent of the region's funding comes from member municipalities, 19 per cent from the provincial government, and the rest from licences, fees, etc. The district, in turn, actively seeks ways to generate income: the sale of steam generated from the incineration of garbage, for example, brought in $3.7 million in 1995; air permit fees produced $2.65 million; and parks rental operations brought in nearly $1 million. The current number of GVRD employees is approximately 1,000, the majority of whom work with the sewerage and water divisions. In general, the GVRD's services represent about 14 per cent of a property owner's tax bill. More than 90 per cent of that money is for capital costs for hospitals, water, sewerage and solid waste disposal programs. (The GVRD can't directly levy taxes on property owners.)

The GVRD board is made up of a number of directors (who are mayors and city or municipal councillors), who meet once a month to set policy and vote on decisions. Each community is allowed one vote for every 20,000 people within its boundaries, although no one director can hold more than five votes. As a result, communities with large populations have more than one director. Directors are selected by their respective municipalities, serve one-year terms, and may be re-appointed.

In the two electoral areas, which are unincorporated and do not have councils, regional directors are elected by the voters in those areas to three-year terms. The board elects a chairperson and vice chairperson from among its members.

THE REGIONAL GROWTH MANAGEMENT STRATEGY

On February 10, 1996 the provincial government recognized the GVRD's Liveable Region Strategic Plan as the official growth management strategy for the Greater Vancouver region. This recognition was the result of an innovative program of public involvement and intergovernmental cooperation in regional decision-making, and the legislative provisions of the provincial Growth Strategies Act.

Early in the regional planning process, the public rejected a business-as-usual approach to regional growth that would spread population throughout the Fraser Valley. They rejected it because it would put development pressure on farmland, increase the distance between jobs and housing, cost too much for public services and utilities, and result in worsening air pollution from an increasing dependence on automobile transportation. The plan prescribes a new approach that will conserve the critical resources of the region: land, air, water, energy and financial capital.

The Liveable Region Strategic Plan incorporates policies, growth targets and maps based upon four fundamental strategies:

• protecting the green zone
• building more complete communities
• achieving a compact metropolitan region
• increasing transportation choices

While each of these strategies is an important regional policy change, they are mutually supportive and interdependent.

The Liveable Region Strategic Plan is intended to result in important intergovernmental partnerships to achieve success. Municipal plans will pursue the land use objectives. An agreement with the province will provide transportation investments in accordance with Transport 2021, a regional transportation strategy prepared in conjunction with the Liveable Region Strategic Plan and reflecting the Creating Our Future transportation priorities that place emphasis on walking, cycling and transit over the private automobile.

WATER

In the 1920s Dr. Ernest A. Cleveland, first commissioner of the water district, directed the formation of a water supply system that he envisioned could provide one million people with drinking water. The population at the time was less than a third of that. Dr. Cleveland got us off to a great start! He would be delighted with a visit today to the GVRD's operations centre in Burnaby's Lake City. There, technicians keep an eye on

The population of the GVRD grows by more than 40,000 people a year. Rapid growth of that kind calls for serious, long-range planning. The GVRD board (made up of elected officials from each member municipality) meets once a month to set policy and vote on decisions. One important recent decision was to implement the Livable Region Strategic Plan, a visionary strategy for the region's future. Detailed input from the residents themselves shaped the plan.

wall-sized screens showing an extraordinarily complex, multi-colored array of information: at a glance, they can check water levels in the system's three primary "source lakes" and in its 22 service reservoirs, the status of valves at dozens of points along hundreds of kilometres of supply mains, more than 130 remote terminal units (RTUs), rates of water flow, and much more. (Many of our reservoirs, by the way, like the ones at Little Mountain and Central Park, are topped by tennis courts. Those thick concrete slabs covering the water make great court surfaces.) Four radio channels keep workers in the field in touch with the Lake City operations centre, but thanks to SCADA—Supervisory Control And Data Acquisition, the shorthand name for this complex electronic system—those RTUs allow technicians at the operations centre to open and close distant valves and fill and empty reservoirs with the click of a computer mouse.

Today the GVRD's 1.8 million residents and its businesses consume 400 billion litres of water a year, an average of 600 litres per person per day, enough to fill two-and-a-half bathtubs. As recently as 1990 we were using more than 700 litres a day. That drop, says the GVRD's water conservation office, is because of increasing public knowledge: communication, educational programs and a growing awareness (particularly since well-publicized lawn-sprinkling regulations began in 1992) that the supply of inexpensive water is not limitless. The water originates in three mountainous watersheds surrounding Capilano Lake and Seymour Lake on the North Shore and Coquitlam Lake, north of the city of Coquitlam. The water rights of the first two are owned by the GVRD itself while the water rights to Coquitlam Lake are owned by BC Hydro which sells some of its allotment of water to the GVRD each year to meet demands. Our abundant rain and the snow melt during spring and early summer usually provides an ample supply of water.

Oddly, only about ten per cent of the precipitation can be stored and used by GVRD residents. The rest spills over the tops of the dams or is diverted. Waterworkers like to see rain: it replenishes stocks quickly.

Turbidity in the water (generally during intense rainfall in late autumn) sometimes kicks up silt and may discolor the water in the source lakes. A rare event happened in late 1995 when both Capilano and Seymour Lakes simultaneously experienced turbidity because of landslides. At present there is screening of the water; filtration will start in 2003. Health officials assure the public the water is safe to use but complaints are heard. These turbidity incidents have happened since the formation of the water district, but now they're rarer, and so they're noticed. At this writing (early 1996) Capilano Lake's

level had been lowered and outflow shut down to allow crews to repair the 1995 slide damage, investigate seepage at the eastern side of Cleveland Dam and inspect seismic upgrades to the dam itself that were made in 1992.

Water from the source lakes is soft and slightly acidic, and chlorine (one part per million) is added to disinfect it. (We've been adding chlorine to our water for more than 50 years.) The chlorine dissipates as the water gets farther downstream from the source, and so rechlorination stations will be added throughout the system to make sure the water meets water quality standards.

The water department office explains that it is primarily a gravity-feed system. Normally, pumping is not necessary. However, people above the lakes have to have their water pumped and there are pumps in most municipalities to handle peak flows in the summer. Besides the mountain storage lakes and dams, the distribution network includes more than 20 reservoirs, pump stations and more than 500 kilometres of supply mains. Point Roberts, in Washington State, is also supplied with water by the GVRD. White Rock, in contrast, uses its own independent ground water supply.

Planning for water supply looks decades ahead: it's possible, for example, that because of future population growth and a consequent increase in the amount of water storage needed, a higher Seymour Falls Dam may have to be constructed as early as 2005. Engineers have determined it will be cheaper to build a new higher dam farther downriver than to increase the height of the old one, so if a new dam is built it will submerge the original. The overall GVRD system, including the remaining BC Hydro allotment at Coquitlam Lake, could provide for up to 4.5 million people through provision of more storage facilities. The alternative is to purchase a larger supply from Coquitlam Lake.

The average daily per capita demand for water in the summer months is about 25 per cent higher than in the rest of the year. You may be surprised to learn that lawn watering accounts for about 25 per cent of all water use in the warmer months. That's why there's a such a focus on sprinkling of lawns in the GVRD's four-stage Water Shortage Response Plan: the first stage is just a reminder to be prudent; then, as water levels drop, lawn-watering restrictions go into effect from June 1 to September 30, requiring you to water only on designated days. The third stage limits watering to one day a week. If conditions become extreme, a total ban on watering your lawn is imposed.

We use a lot of water, and it costs a lot to use it. After more than seven years of study and an intensive public consultation program, the GVRD board voted June 29, 1994 to further safe-

A quarter of a million people annually visit the GVRD's Seymour Demonstration Forest, in the District of North Vancouver. Western hemlock, red cedar, Douglas fir and other coniferous trees—many of them a result of reforestation—tower overhead. Cyclists, hikers, picnickers and canoeists enjoy the quiet beauty of the forest, home to more than 100 species of animals, birds and fish. A fish-hatchery here is an interesting and educational experience. And fun, too!

guard Greater Vancouver's drinking water supply. They approved the use of chlorine as a secondary disinfectant and approved further pilot testing of ozone and biological filtration. The decisions came after a lengthy public consultation program. More than 5,000 people participated through meetings, surveys, correspondence, a television forum and a speakers program. And 500,000 households received information about the Drinking Water Treatment Program and the consultation process through newspaper inserts. New water treatment facilities will include primary disinfection and pH adjustment facilities at the Capilano, Seymour and Coquitlam water sources, staged construction of filtration plants at the Seymour and Coquitlam sites, and secondary disinfection stations at GVRD distribution system reservoirs around the region. When construction is completed the region's drinking water will meet standards set by the Canadian Drinking Water Quality guidelines and British Columbia's new Safe Drinking Water Regulations. The GVRD's 1994 annual report predicts that long-range upgrading of the regional water and sewerage systems alone could cost in excess of $2 billion in the next 10 years. (More than $500 million of that will go for secondary treatment of sewage.)

Among projects to be considered by GVRD directors in 1996 is construction of a drinking water filtration plant in North Vancouver at an estimated cost of $150 million. This is a potential public/private partnership project.

Part of the construction budget includes the completion of seismic upgrading for Seymour Falls Dam. Cleveland Dam was upgraded in 1992 and Seymour Falls partially upgraded in 1995. Some of the money being spent on this project may soon start to flow the other way: there is a plan to generate hydro-electric power at Cleveland Dam. Selling it and using some of the off-season surplus water could provide a net annual return to the GVRD of about $1 million.

The GVRD's 5,600-hectare Seymour Demonstration Forest opened in the District of North Vancouver in 1987. It had been closed prior to 1987 because it was part of the region's watershed. The forest, which has been called an outdoor classroom, gets a quarter of a million visitors annually. Most of its trees are coniferous (western hemlock, western red cedar, Douglas fir, etc.) and tower upward in the lower part of a glacier-carved valley between big Lynn Headwaters Regional Park and Mount Seymour Provincial Park. Here you'll see examples of integrated resource management such as timber harvesting, reforestation, fish and wildlife management . . . and recreation, like cycling, hiking, rollerblading, picnicking and canoeing. (Much of the forest here was harvested more than 60 years ago, so

you'll see what a reforested area can look like.) More than 100 species of animals and birds live within the valley and salmon and trout use the Seymour River to spawn. A visit to the volunteer-operated federally-funded hatchery here makes for an interesting and educational stop. Self-guided tours take you past interpretive panels on scenic loop trails, and you can see Seymour Falls Dam and Seymour Lake at the end of an 11-kilometre paved road closed to private vehicles. (A note: visiting the dam and returning is a long walk; a 22-kilometre round trip! At various times organized tours are allowed vehicular access up to the dam. Cyclists and rollerbladers are permitted on weekends.) Supervised summer tours of the normally off-limits watershed areas are available and popular. The four-hour tours involve a walk in old growth forest, information on water quality, storage and conservation, fire protection and so on.

SEWERAGE AND DRAINAGE

Every day nearly a billion litres of sewage and storm runoff flow through municipal sewer systems, then into GVRD trunk lines and next into five treatment plants. Wastewater treatment plants at Annacis Island, Iona Island, Lulu Island, Lions Gate and northwest Langley handle a volume equalling nearly 640 litres per person per day. There are more than 450 kilometres of trunk lines and interceptor sewers to move the waste along. The system is continually being improved, and handled imaginatively: at Iona Island, for example, a $40 million deep-sea outfall built in 1988 not only improved the quality of water at nearby Sturgeon Bank, it served as the foundation for a popular public promenade and cycle path extending four kilometres into Georgia Strait . . . on top of the outfall pipes!

Iona Island's plant opened in 1963. At the time residents of Richmond were really unhappy with the decision to put it there: they wanted Vancouver to keep its own sewage. But, says the GVRD's 1992 annual report, "the tides were against it—Iona was the best location to get a good tidal flushing action." One of the major connectors to the plant is called the High-bury Tunnel, named for the west side street that runs above it. In some places the pipes are 100 metres beneath the surface.

Most wastewater generated in the Lower Mainland receives primary treatment to remove solids. But for treatment plants discharging into the Fraser River secondary treatment facilities are being built to further refine the discharge.

Improvements for secondary treatment at Annacis and Lulu Island Wastewater Treatment Plants are in progress, and scheduled to be complete at the end of 1998. It's estimated that the 360,000 tonnes of concrete to be used in the Annacis Island project would fill 15,000 trucks—enough to line the freeway bumper-to-bumper from Vancouver to Hope, 154 kilometres.

A product called Nutrifor, developed by the University of British Columbia working with the GVRD, is extracted from the nearly one billion litres of sewage and storm runoff that daily flow through the GVRD's 450 kilometres of sewerage pipelines. Trees fertilized by Nutrifor grow faster, and plants grow vigorously. More than 100,000 tonnes of Nutrifor is produced annually, and used widely throughout the province . . . it even helps fertilize poplar tree plantations in the Fraser Valley.

This is the largest single local government capital project ($526 million) ever undertaken in Western Canada. The Lulu Island upgrade seems almost modest at $132 million.

The GVRD's wastewater treatment plants produce 200 tonnes of biosolids every day. But it isn't wasted: it's turned instead into a product called Nutrifor, increasingly in demand to restore depleted soils in British Columbia. The University of British Columbia cooperated with the GVRD in the development of the product. Trees fertilized by Nutrifor are healthy and grow faster, plants and grass grow vigorously. They recycled 100,000 tonnes of the stuff in 1995, and used it in many different places: the Barnet Highway right-of-way has been treated; so has the Cypress Bowl ski hill, Campbell Valley Regional Park, in reclamation of a mine site at Princeton, another at the Highland Valley Copper mine site in the Nicola Valley in the landfill areas in Langley and Coquitlam . . . and poplar plantations in the Fraser Valley. Admire those poplars: you helped grow them!

The department also maintains natural water courses, like the Brunette River and Still Creek, classed as major drainage facilities.

HOSPITAL PLANNING AND DEVELOPMENT

The Greater Vancouver Regional District and the provincial ministry of health are jointly responsible for planning and financing construction and some equipment for hospitals within the Greater Vancouver area. The GVRD contributes 40 per cent of the cost of hospital construction for its 30 area hospitals, the district's single largest budgetary outlay. The province kicks in the other 60 per cent. The hospitals fund a proportion of their equipment needs through donations and their auxiliaries. Work goes on continuously: as this book was being prepared Surrey Memorial Hospital was undergoing dramatic expansion, and as this very article was being written an announcement was made that funds had been approved by the GVRHD for construction of a 70-bed extended-care unit at Zion Park Manor in Cloverdale. (As the average age of our population increases, hundreds of long-term-care beds are being added annually.)

Here's an example of how the regional approach works effectively: 16 hospitals in the GVRD had need to eliminate ozone-depleting chlorofluorocarbons (CFCs) from essential ethylene oxide (EtO) sterilizers. EtO had been used in local hospitals for 20 years for sterilizing instruments and supplies sensitive to heat and moisture. The problem: 88 per cent of the gaseous EtO mixture was CFCs, but—to lessen the impact of CFCs on the ozone layer—federal legislation in 1991 mandated their total elimination by 1996. Then the provincial government quick-

ened the pace with legislation that banned them effective November 1, 1994. Working together, the hospitals and the GVRHD put out tenders for new CFC-free equipment. They had a surprise coming: one of the suppliers who responded to the tender offered a new and unfamiliar technology called "gas plasma." This technology does not use EtO or CFCs and is environmentally friendly. Clinical evaluation followed, and it was found that gas plasma did the same sterilizing job better, far faster and cheaper than EtO. Furthermore, Workers Compensation Board regulations were met. Other hospitals outside the District heard about the results, and asked to join in a group purchase of the new sterilizers. Savings in the first year: $3 million. Annual savings since: $1 million.

One small group within the GVRD starts being interested in you the moment you are born: in March 1993 the Birthing Centre Working Group arranged for a telephone survey of 900 women of childbearing age who lived within the GVRD. The purpose was two-fold: to measure the level of interest in using a birthing centre, and to determine the services preferred. Some 77 per cent of the women surveyed expressed interest in a more family-focused centre, rather than the traditional institutional models. The idea, to quote the BCWG, is to "strengthen and empower families around their own health, so that they become partners rather than passive participants in the health care system." There are as yet no birthing centres in B.C. although there have been recent developments toward the establishment of hospital-based family-centered maternity care models such as labor, delivery, recovery and postpartum rooms that incorporate a birth centre philosophy.

HOUSING

Why is the Greater Vancouver Regional District involved in housing? During the 1970s the member municipalities recognized there was a desperate and growing shortage of affordable rental accommodation to meet the needs of people with lower incomes, sometimes called the "working poor." Some households at the time were paying more than 30 per cent of their gross income on shelter. The federal government created subsidized housing programs administered through the Canada Mortgage and Housing Corporation, but more needed to be done.

Municipally elected officials established the Greater Vancouver Housing Corporation (GVHC), a non-profit subsidiary of the GVRD. The Corporation increased the supply of housing stock throughout the Region by developing subsidized rental housing under the various federal programs available. To minimize a concentration of social housing in any one municipality a regional approach to increasing the rental supply was taken. That resulted in a more equitable distribution through-

The GVRD's single largest budgetary outlay is for hospital construction—$116 million in 1996. There are 30 participating hospitals within the region, and the GVRD contributes 40 per cent of the cost of new construction and purchase of some equipment. Because the hospitals work on a regional basis, savings can be made: a recent example was a group purchase made by 16 of the hospitals of new sterilizing equipment. Annual savings: more than $1 million.

out the Region, and also eliminated the need for separate housing departments in each municipality.

The GVHC provides affordable rental housing for those not likely to be served adequately by the private sector. Alderwood Place in Richmond is a good example: the 48 homes there offer a mix of special needs, seniors and family housing, all with proximity to jobs and transportation services. These lower-income households are assured of rents not exceeding 30 per cent of their gross income. Richmond acquired the land and leases it to the GVHC. The Corporation pays its full share of taxes and utility charges to Richmond.

The GVHC's assets, which include more than 3,000 units, are assessed at approximately a quarter of a billion dollars.

SOLID WASTE

There is a practical side to living in paradise. Someone has to take out the garbage. People in the Greater Vancouver Regional District currently generate about 2.5 million tonnes of solid waste a year. That works out to about 2.2 kilos of solid waste daily for each of us. Of that, about 24 per cent is residential, 37 per cent industrial, commercial and institutional, and 39 per cent generated by demolition, land clearing and construction materials. In descending order of content, solid waste is made up of organic material (kitchen and yard wastes) (32 per cent); paper (32); plastic (9); metal (5); textiles/leather (4); glass (3); and "other" (15 per cent). "Other" includes stuff like drinking boxes, disposable diapers, soil, rocks, furniture, appliances, and so on. Collection of waste from homes and businesses is done by the municipalities and private companies, which channel it into the GVRD's disposal system.

The Cache Creek landfill is a 48-hectare site next to the Trans Canada Highway in an industrial area south of the Village of Cache Creek, northwest of Kamloops. It's the first landfill in Western Canada to be fully designed and operated as an environmentally secure, state-of-the-art landfill facility. Waste from the Lower Mainland is screened—recyclables such as cardboard and ferrous metals are recycled, while hazardous or problem wastes are removed. The landfill was developed by the village and Wastech Services Ltd. for the GVRD and local residents. Since 1989 more than 300,000 tonnes of GVRD garbage has been hauled there.

We're using up disposal sites: six landfills have been closed in the region in the last 20 years. The landfill in Langley City was closed in 1976, that in Coquitlam in 1983, in North Vancouver and Richmond in 1986, and in Langley Township and Maple Ridge three years later. The Port Mann Landfill in Surrey is scheduled to close around 1997.

Solid waste facilities are continually upgraded. Examples of

projects for 1995 included providing new emission monitoring control systems for the Burnaby incinerator and the design of a gas collection system at the Cache Creek Landfill.

More than 30 per cent of the region's waste is recycled. About 20 per cent of what's left is incinerated, and the remainder goes into landfill.

The provincial government requires that all regional districts prepare solid waste management plans showing how a 50 per cent per capita waste reduction goal will be met by the year 2000. It's an ambitious target. The GVRD's plan is to:
- expand residential recycling to include additional materials
- institute "user fee charges" for residential garbage collection, so that those who put out nothing pay nothing, while those who put out, say, 10 bags pay for each
- put more emphasis on backyard composting
- require larger industrial and commercial firms to prepare "waste audit" and waste reduction plans for their operations
- ban from disposal some waste materials from the industrial and commercial sector like newsprint, cardboard and clean wood; companies will be required to recycle them
- put continued pressure on senior governments for more control over packaging and for refundable bottle deposit programs.

As well, there are educational programs for the general public and the industrial, commercial and institutional sector. Residential education programs are developed jointly by the GVRD and member municipalities. And the GVRD monitors and regulates private sector demolition, land clearing and the disposal and recycling of construction waste.

Methane gas is collected from the former Coquitlam Landfill site. They're not just holding their noses, they're selling the gas. A private company collects it and transports it to a newsprint recycling plant in the same neighborhood, which uses it as a substitute energy supply. And about $4 million annually is earned from sale of steam from the GVRD's Burnaby Incinerator. Opened in 1988 at a cost just over $63 million, this is one of the most advanced municipal waste incinerators in North America; it handles about 20 per cent of all the solid waste disposed in the Lower Mainland: 240,000 tonnes of it every year. The District is developing a system for the control of nitrogen oxides emissions from the incinerator, and the intent is to have a functioning treatment system—well within standards mandated by the ministry of environment, lands and parks—installed by July 1996 at an estimated cost of $750,000. The incinerator also produces fly ash (fine particles of ash carried along with the waste gases produced during combustion), which may be treated on-line.

During the 1970s it was recognized some households within the region paid more than 30 per cent of their gross income on shelter. That led to the creation in 1974 of the Greater Vancouver Housing Corporation, a non-profit subsidiary of the GVRD. The Housing Corporation develops subsidized rental housing under federal programs, then locates it carefully to avoid concentrating social housing in any one municipality. Today, the GVHC's assets include more than 3,000 units.

REGIONAL PARKS

Regional parks were created to provide outdoor recreational and educational opportunities across the region that weren't available in municipalities, and to ensure that significant natural landscape features of the region were protected. All GVRD parks are open year-round, and are within easy distance of major urban areas. The parks are generally larger and in a more natural state than municipal parks, which tend to serve local neighborhoods and offer mainly indoor and outdoor sports and athletic activities. And the GVRD's parks serve a region-wide population. (Even beyond: the City of Abbotsford, while not a member of the GVRD, is a member of the parks function.)

In response to strong public support for acquiring and protecting regional wildlife and recreational lands, the GVRD created the Heritage Parkland Acquisition Fund in 1994. At the same time, in cooperation with its member municipalities, the province and other regional districts, GVRD coordinated the Lower Mainland Major Parks Plan. Through this plan, GVRD identified future parkland, conservation and outdoor recreation areas that needed to be acquired. When the province invited the GVRD to become a partner in a section of its Lower Mainland Nature Legacy Program in 1995, GVRD was prepared. Through the program, which nearly quadrupled the amount of parkland in the Lower Mainland, GVRD acquired 2,000 hectares of new land. It was financed by the province, GVRD, the federal ministry of the environment, several municipalities and private enterprise.

The Fraser River component of the nature legacy was particularly impressive. Lands were acquired at Surrey Bend, Douglas Island, Barnston Island, Don and Lion Islands, Brae Island and Colony Farm. New lands were added to Boundary Bay, Belcarra, Minnekhada, Derby Reach, Glen Valley and Iona Beach Regional Parks.

Combined with provincial wildlife reserves along the Fraser, there are now more than 80 kilometres of riverfront for residents to explore.

Today, there are 22 regional parks, covering a total of 11,200 hectares. Much of the new land awaits decisions on trails, facilities and services, restoration and habitat enhancement projects, and projects for disabled users. The busiest is 160-hectare Capilano River Regional Park, in both North Vancouver District and West Vancouver, with spectacular river canyon views and trails, footbridges and viewpoints. The largest is Lynn Headwaters, some 4,685 hectares of North Shore forest with extensive hiking opportunities. The smallest: 6.5 hectare Grant Narrows Regional Park in Pitt Meadows. With its canoe rentals and boat launching facilities, Grant Narrows is a good jumping-off point to explore Widgeon Creek and Widgeon Marsh. Discover the area's plentiful bird life, or admire dramatic mountain and river views as you stroll the nearby dykes to the Pitt Wildlife Management Area and Golden Ears Provincial Park.

Within these parks for all seasons are amenities for year-round recreation and nature interpretation. Facilities are in place for overnight group camping; walking, hiking and equestrian trails; canoeing, fishing, swimming, scuba diving, picnicking ... Boundary Bay Regional Park in Delta features a long, sandy shoreline cherished by swimmers and, when the tide is out, by crabbers! Along with providing for the future with fish hatcheries, wildlife habitat, trail development and community partnerships, the GVRD helps preserve and restore our heritage: in Campbell Valley Regional Park in Langley Township, for example, you'll find the restored 1924 one-room Lochiel Schoolhouse. In Coquitlam, Minnekhada features a rustic 1930s hunting lodge once occupied by vice-regal dignitaries.

Regional parks also offer outdoor special events and nature programs for all ages, and park interpretive specialists will custom design a nature program for any group.

Preserving wildlife habitat while expanding regional parks ranks high on residents' wish lists. This unparalleled blessing of teeming wildlife and serene nature all within easy reach of civic centres is truly remarkable, and the GVRD is committed to maintaining it. Regional park attendance topped five million visits in 1995.

AIR QUALITY

Public feedback is unmistakeable: we all want clean air.

In 1972 the provincial government delegated responsibility for air quality management to the GVRD, creating a regional focus for clean air initiatives. For more than 20 years the GVRD has been responsible for air quality monitoring and the regulation of air pollution sources. In 1994 the GVRD approved the Air Quality Management Plan, the first of its kind in Canada, "to reduce total emissions of sulphur oxides, nitrogen oxides, particulates, carbon monoxide and volatile organic compounds by the year 2000." (Fine particulates pose the greatest public health threat in the region.) The estimated net benefit of this program over the next 25 years is $2.3 billion, from reductions in human mortality and general health improvements.

The GVRD operates an air quality monitoring network, with 40 stations—half of which are continuous analyzers that send readings every 60 seconds to a central location. The daily air quality index is calculated from those readings, and

---

More than 30 per cent of the 2.5 million tonnes of solid waste generated annually by residents and businesses in the Greater Vancouver Regional District is recycled. From that mountain of kitchen and yard wastes, paper, plastic, metal, glass and so on the GVRD generates millions of dollars in income, while lessening damage to the environment. One example: waste burned at the Burnaby Incinerator generates steam, which is sold to industry. Annual income: $4 million.

reproduced in local daily newspapers and broadcasting outlets. The district also operates a mobile air quality monitoring unit (MAMU), used to collect air-quality data not currently covered by the permanent network. The unit is also able to conduct special studies within the region, and to respond to air quality emergencies. A regional by-law controls non-vehicle sources of air pollution and incorporates a polluter-pay system of fees to fund clean air programs. It's serious work, and it's wide-ranging, getting right down to efforts to reduce emissions from paint spray booths and your neighborhood dry cleaner.

There are more than one million motor vehicles in Greater Vancouver. The GVRD works with the provincial government to ensure British Columbians obtain the maximum air-quality benefit through tightened motor-vehicle emission standards for new vehicles. As well, GVRD works with member municipalities to utilize alternative fuels such as propane and natural gas in government vehicles. Since AirCare started in late 1992 (with the GVRD leading the initiative to begin it) there has been a 20-per-cent reduction of vehicle emissions every year. But it's a race to improve those figures even further because of increasing population and vehicle use.

An undeniable fact: nine out of ten GVRD residents blame serious air pollution on motor vehicles, yet the majority of us continue to drive to work alone five days a week instead of taking transit, carpooling, vanpooling, cycling or walking. The GVRD has programs to encourage residents to use transportation alternatives when possible.

STRATEGIC PLANNING

The GVRD's Strategic Planning department provides technical support for the region's environmental protection and growth management policy. Since 1990 the department has led in the preparation of several key regional policies adopted by the GVRD board of directors including the Liveable Region Strategic Plan which provides direction for growth management to the year 2021. The department works closely with member municipalities on the implemention of the plan, and support programs such as Transport 2021. Transport 2021 is a cooperative project involving the provincial ministry of transportation and highways, the ministry of small business, BC Transit, BC Ferries, and staff from the GVRD and its member municipalities. Transport 2021 recommends regional transportation policies, and a network of corridors for public transit and roads. The aim is to have the region's members shape their own transit programs to be consistent with the region's direction of development. The Strategic Planning department also provides local government services for the GVRD's two unincorporated electoral areas.

As well, it coordinates emergency response communications and the 911 telephone system. The 911 system links no fewer than 41 emergency service agencies (police, fire, ambulance, etc.) within the GVRD. In 1995 here's how the figures added up:

- 110 calls an hour
- 2,630 a day
- 960,000 calls in 1995
- Calls expected to top a million in 1996
- 911 can respond within 90 seconds in approximately 150 languages.

PERSONNEL AND LABOUR RELATIONS

The Personnel and Labour Relations department negotiates some 65 collective agreements with unions representing about 14,000 employees of the GVRD and most of its member municipalities. The department also provides both collective bargaining and job evaluation services for most of the members and several related employers, including police and library boards, museums and recreation commissions. And the department offers consulting assistance to member municipalities in managing employment equity and workers' compensation issues.

FINANCE, ADMINISTRATION AND PROPERTIES

Financial planning, treasury, budgeting, purchasing and so on all fall under the FA and P department. And this is where the GVRD budgets get worked out. Here's how the 1996 budget was broken down:

- sewerage $79.5 million
- water $52.9 million
- solid waste and recycling $54.8 million
- hospital $116.6 million
- parks $13.6 million
- air quality $6.5 million
- 911 telephone $4.2 million
- strategic planning $2.8 million
- other (general government, labor relations, municipal radio, electoral areas, Sasamat Fire Department, hospital planning) $6.5 million
- *total*   *$337.4 million*

The separate Greater Vancouver Housing Commission budget is about $32 million.

COMMUNICATIONS AND EDUCATION

This department works with other departments and member municipalities to plan and implement public awareness and education programs, media relations, community relations, public consultation, schools programs and so on. Communications and Education handles thousands of public

Greater Vancouver enjoys fine public parks, and a growing population wants more. The GVRD operates 22 regional parks, generally larger and in a more natural state than municipal parks, with unique recreational and educational opportunities. Strong public support for acquiring and protecting regional wildlife and recreational lands led to the GVRD's partnership with the provincial government in a section of the Lower Mainland Nature Legacy Program. Through that program 2,000 hectares of new parkland were acquired in the GVRD.

GVRD inspector in the First Narrows water tunnel, built in 1932, 400 feet below Burrard Inlet, 1988. vs

enquiries each year, and produces and distributes publications, reports, videos and other information materials. Among its other functions is the production of the GVRD's annual reports. (The 1991 version, which marked the GVRD's 25th anniversary, is particularly rich in historical information and fascinating photographs, such as the construction of Cleveland Dam.)

The Creating our Future vision serves well as an eloquent conclusion to this article: "Greater Vancouver can become the first urban region in the world to combine in one place the things to which humanity aspires on a global basis: a place where human activities enhance rather than degrade the natural environment, where the quality of the built environment approaches that of the natural setting, where the diversity of origins and religions is a source of social strength rather than strife, where people control the destiny of their community, and where the basics of food, clothing, shelter, security and useful activity are accessible to all."

The GVRD is responsible for air quality management in the region. In 1994 the Air Quality Management Plan, the first of its kind in Canada, was instituted to reduce harmful emissions. A 40-station air quality monitoring network is in place, and a mobile unit collects further data throughout the region. The GVRD led the initiative to establish AirCare in 1992; there has been a 20 per cent reduction of vehicle emissions every year since.

Peoples

With five distinct facilities, B.C. Pavilion Corporation is nearly as diverse as the varied peoples that make up the Lower Mainland. Operating B.C. Place Stadium, the Vancouver Trade & Convention Centre, Robson Square Conference Centre, Tradex and the Bridge Studios, we are proud of the selection of activities our facilities provide. Hosting everything from sporting events and consumer shows to international conventions and cultural festivities, the B.C. Pavilion Corporation provides the city's best "people places."

I N JULY, 1877, within sight of the magnificent forests on Haida Gwaii (Queen Charlotte Islands), the first recorded contact between Europeans and indigenous people took place on territory that would later become British Columbia. As a sign of peace and welcome for navigator Juan Perez and his crew the Haida sprinkled feathers on the water by the Spanish vessel. Fifteen years later the Musqueam's first meeting with Capt. George Vancouver in False Creek was just as peaceful but not nearly as poetic: they greeted the British explorer with cooked fish.

Since the first contact between Europeans and the Musqueam at the close of the 18th century the territory at the mouth of the Fraser River that was once inhabited only by the Musqueam, Squamish and other Coast Salish nations has become home to the people of the world. Now called by the name adopted by its European settlers, Vancouver has grown into a cosmopolitan, culturally diverse community.

But it wasn't always that way. Almost from its start as a frontier town in the 1860s Vancouver made Asian newcomers feel unwelcome. About a year after the city's incorporation months of mounting intolerance—given voice in local newspapers—culminated when a mob descended on a Chinese work camp in the West End and chased the inhabitants out of town. Although Chinese Canadians later returned to the city and the incident angered the provincial government enough to send in a special police force to maintain law and order the attack sent out a clear message of intolerance to prospective Asian immigrants. That attitude was reinforced as Vancouver politicians and community groups lobbied for restrictions on Asian immigration and supported retention of laws that prohibited Asian Canadians from full particpation as citizens.

In the late 1940s, however, a massive demographic change started to take place in Vancouver. As refugees from a devastated Europe began arriving, Vancouver's essentially British character and outlook became increasingly less dominant. Immigrants from the Netherlands, Italy, Portugal, Greece, Yugoslavia and Scandinavia were pushed by the lack of opportunity at home and pulled across the Atlantic by a labor shortage caused by the post-war economic boom in Canada. By 1967 all references to ethnicity or country of origin were removed from the Immigration Act and regulations, a move which finally put immigrants from Asia on the same footing as immigrants from European countries. Between 1981 and 1991 some 18 per cent or 28,585 immigrants to the Lower Mainland were from Hong Kong, 14.1 per cent (22,405) from China, 9.3 per cent (14,845) from India, and 6.9 per cent or 10,910 from the Philippines. Immigrants from Great Britain dropped to fifth place at 5.8 per cent or 9,295.

Statistics Canada records 68 ethnicities of people living in the Vancouver region ranging from 20 Haitians as the smallest to the English as the largest at 257,020.

More immigration has helped create a more tolerant, open society in Vancouver. In the 1980s as public officials grappled with cultural diversity, schools began recognizing the importance of teaching tolerance and understanding of cultural diversity by expanding curriculums to include cross-cultural material.

And while a more ethnically diverse population has led to some distinct shopping areas such as Little India at Main and 49th, for the most part immigrants and refugees have dispersed themselves throughout the region. Getting barbecued duck, for example, no longer means having to make the trek to Chinatown but merely of popping into one of several suburban shopping malls, especially in Richmond. Greek, Korean, Japanese, Vietnamese, Chinese, Italian, Thai and South Asian restaurants, to name but a few, can be found not only in Vancouver but throughout the Lower Mainland. In most supermarkets bok choy has become almost as ubiquitous as broccoli.

As Vancouver enters the 21st century its people have grown much more diverse than the city founders could ever have imagined. In a little more than a century Vancouver has been transformed from a British settler society to a multicultural Canadian city that still retains a strong British flavor. The changes over the next century are likely to be as dramatic.

—Kevin Griffin

above: Vancouver Police Pipe Band, 1987. vs
facing page: Chinatown, 1972. vs

First Nations People
Larry Loyie

PRESENT TOTALS of First Nations residents of Greater Vancouver are confusing. Statistics Canada data for 1991 are available, but the numbers, according to urban native organizations, are grossly underestimated. The 1991 census reported that, of a total Vancouver population of 471,844 those with aboriginal origins/First Nations registration was 13,360.

In contrast the United Native Nations Society, representing urban native residents, estimates up to 60,000 First Nations people in the Greater Vancouver area. At present the society is surveying residents of First Nations ancestry, so more accurate figures will soon be available.

According to Barbara Charlie, chair of the Vancouver-Sunshine Coast Aboriginal Management Society, a funder of economic and job creation programs, "Our funding is based on the 1991 census and that census does not reflect the reality of numbers or need."

In 1976, 63.9 per cent of the total native population of British Columbia lived on reserves. This has dropped to 49.7 per cent today. Off-reserve numbers are climbing. In 1976, 36.1 per cent lived off reserve; by 1996 the projected figure is 50.3 per cent. People are moving because the traditional way of providing for one's family no longer exists on reserves.

First Nations people in the area, as across Canada, are waging a battle for survival. According to a 1994 premier's office report, most off-reserve native people live in the Lower Mainland or on Vancouver Island. The report found that 26 per cent of off-reserve First Nations people are jobless; 13 per cent say they can't find work because of discrimination. Native teenagers have babies at four times the rate of the overall population. Twenty per cent of B.C. jail inmates are native, as are 40 per cent of registered users of the needle exchange program. One in ten Canadian women have been abused, but the number jumps to one in three B.C. aboriginal women. A 1995 study by provincial and federal governments found that native life expectancy is 12 years less than that of non-natives. The chance of dying prematurely is twice as high.

Little by little, however, improvements are being made. Attended by thousands, the annual Trout Lake Pow Wow proves that healing is taking place. Traditional gatherings (alcohol and drug free), drumming, dancing, smudges, sweats, talking circles and groups such as Our Elders Speak Wisdom Society and Hey-Way-Noqu Healing Circle for Addictions Society all contribute to the healing process. First Nations people—damaged by cultural dislo-

cation, residential school abuse, loss of language and customs, substance and sexual abuse—come together to relearn traditions.

Elders such as Squamish Chief Simon Baker, born in 1911 on the Capilano reserve, are now being heard. Baker and his wife Emily are recognized as First Nations ambassadors. *Khot-la-cha, The Autobiography of Simon Baker,* compiled and edited by Verna Kirkness, was published in 1994. Elder Vince Stogan from the Musqueam reserve is noted for his efforts to revive native traditions. Honorary doctoral degrees from UBC were given to Baker (1990), Kirkness (1994) and Stogan (1995).

First Nations people are still on the lowest rung of the socio-economic ladder. Because of the residential school system, generations did not have access to high school education. Manual labor continues to be the main type of work done by native people in the Greater Vancouver area.

To compare figures, in the 1991 Canadian census native people stacked up this way: 13 per cent had no income (vs. 9 per cent of the Canadian population); 12 per cent made under $2,000 (vs. 6 per cent); 23 per cent made from $10,000–$19,999 (vs. 6 per cent); 18 per cent made from $20,000–$39,999 (vs. 22 per cent) and 5 per cent made over $40,000 (vs. 15 per cent).

Statistics Canada reported that just over 8 per cent of First Nations people across Canada owned or operated their own business in 1991. Aboriginal Business Canada, which once contributed up to 40 per cent of the start-up cost of approved businesses (with 20 per cent coming from the applicant and an additional 40 per cent from commercial sources), is now "up in the air," hit by the April 1995 federal budget.

In the Greater Vancouver area, bands are making the most of their resources. Both the Burrard and Tsawwassen bands, under chiefs Leonard George and Sharon Bowcott respectively, promote business interests including band-built housing leased to non-native residents. Former Musqueam Chief Wendy Grant, vice chief of the B.C. Region Assembly of First Nations, continues to influence politics and economic development.

Cultural expression by First Nations artists is exploding. Haida artists Bill Reid and Robert Davidson and button blanket maker/clothing designer Dorothy Grant are well known. Among the many others are Salish printmaker/carver/weaver Susan Point, Kwakiutl silver/gold carver Corinne Hunt and Cree painter George Littlechild.

Writers include Metis educator Dr. Howard Adams (*Prisoner of Grass*), Metis poet Gregory Scofield (*Stones for the Medicine Wheel*) and Metis Lee Maracle (*Sojourner's Truth and Other Stories*).

Cree Loretta Todd and Alert Bay-born Barbara Cramner both direct for the National Film Board. Feature films, television series and live theatre provide roles for Greater Vancou-

Squamish canoe, Burrard Inlet, 1992. VS

ver's First Nations actors. A Metis with Cree and Blackfoot heritage, Margo Kane is an award-winning actor/director/playwright (*Moonlodge*). Coast Salish actor/dancer/playwright Evan Tlesla Adams is noted for his Emmy-winning performance in the movie *Lost in the Barrens*. Metis Marie Humber Clements is also one of the city's most diversified actors.

Shuswap Vera Manuel's Storyteller Theatre (*Strength of Indian Women*), Fireweed Productions Society artistic director Cree/Dene Sophie Merasty and the plays of Marie Humber Clements (*Age of Iron*) are noteworthy.

Change is reflected in the educational opportunities provided in Greater Vancouver. Less than a decade ago an institute such as UBC's First Nations House of Learning did not exist. To get as far as high school was a major achievement.

The mandate of the First Nations House of Learning is to make UBC's resources more accessible and improve the university's ability to meet the needs of aboriginal people. The House of Learning is located in The Longhouse, a building that reflects Salish architectural traditions. It serves as a "home away from home" where the campus' estimated 350 First Nations students study and learn in surroundings reflecting their traditions.

The goal of the House of Learning is 1,000 First Nations students by the year 2000. Verna Kirkness, now retired, was a founder and its first director; Jo-ann Archibald is the current director.

Other educational programs of relevance to First Nations students are provided by SFU, BCIT, Capilano College, Douglas College, Emily Carr Institute of Art and Design, Kwantlen College, Vancouver Community College and others. The Native Education Centre runs training programs and prepares students for post-secondary education.

Under the auspices of associations such as the Vancouver Native Housing Society (VNHS) and Lu'ma Native Housing Society, a small portion of the local aboriginal population can find reasonably priced housing. Native housing ensures a higher living standard, crucial to health and well-being. VNHS manages 11 buildings in the East End, with 346 units. Lu'ma has 222 units.

The demand is enormous. The waiting list for VNHS is 2,100 people. Native housing must increase ten-fold as ever-greater numbers move into the area.

In the late 1960s, when women's rights advocate Dr. Rose Charlie established the Indian Homemakers Association of B.C., she started a trend. Originally a cooking and sewing club, it grew into a political force for better living conditions, training and services. Her efforts also led to the creation of the Union of B.C. Indian Chiefs.

A member of the Chehalis Band and Sto:lo Nation, Rose Charlie was president of Indian Homemakers for 28 years, winning the Governor General's award in 1994 for her efforts. The organization has been joined by the Vancouver Aboriginal Child and Family Services Society and the Native Courtworkers and Counselling Association of B.C. and others.

To close on a personal note, we as First Nations people are finally deciding for ourselves what we need to heal and make a better future. While we have much to overcome, through our own efforts we are advancing. Our culture is not closed: I hope that more non-native people will get to know us and understand why we value and are reviving our traditions.

British Isles
Kevin Griffin

As GRIM NEWS about the German advance across Norway filled the front pages of the newspapers in late April, 1940, local English-Canadians gathered to celebrate St. George's Day, in honor of the patron saint of England. They started with a religious ceremony. On Sunday, the 21st of the month, scores of members of various local English societies marched confidently into Christ Church Cathedral carrying flags of famous English battalions, St. George's red cross Standard and the Union Jack while singing "Land of Hope and Glory." Two days later about 300 Vancouverites of English descent gathered in a hotel ballroom for the annual banquet held by the Royal Society of St. George. As the evening's ceremonial highlight nothing could top the Parade of the Roast Beef. Leading the procession was the chef and two helpers who bore 20 kilograms of the steaming sacred meat above their heads. They were followed by a trumpeter and another man carrying almost five kilograms of flaming plum pudding.

At the banquet that evening, the guests ate 68 kilograms of roast beef, many square metres of Yorkshire pudding and 225 grams of prepared mustard. Sated with traditional English fare, the crowd waited for Howard Coulter, the chief toastmaster, to give a speech. Surrounded by the familiar face of King George V1, whose portraits hung on the walls of the ballroom, Coulter looked out on a sea of red roses, the traditional flower associated with St. George. He warmed up the crowd by referring to that "little man with the ridiculous moustache whose real name is Schickelgruber."

"We are not effete," Coulter told the audience, "we can still say to a waiting world that there is a basis in the legend that St. George was the son of God, and the dragon he fought with the evil tongue and fiery breath was the epitomized evil of the world. Again St. George is mounted and out to do battle."

When Coulter gave his inspirational speech in 1940 there were numerous English county, city, regional and cultural organizations in Vancouver. They included: the Royal Society of St. George, the main English-immigrant society in the city and the one which started holding an annual St. George's banquet in 1894; the Vancouver Lodge of Sons and Daughters of England; the Birmingham and Midland Counties Association; and the Shropshire Association. In the 1920s, for example, St. George's Day festivities were preceded by a Shakespeare festival and special city-wide appeals to fly the Union Jack. At the Lancashire Society annual dinners before World War II, more than

350 people could be counted on to attend a Lancashire feast of potato pie and red cabbage. And starting in July, 1940, when the Channel Islands became the only British territory occupied by Nazi Germany, the Channel Islanders' Society became extremely active in holding fundraisers to help refugees from Guernsey and Jersey. When the war was over Channel Islanders held several liberation banquets and feasts, including a garden party where local actors performed *Down Goes the Swastika*, a play about the liberation of Guernsey written by the society's president P.W. Luce.

But by 1955 the thriving pre-war network of English societies and associations had declined. Most eventually merged with the Royal Society of St. George. A similar pattern occurred among those of Scottish, Irish, or Welsh descent in the region: growth in the number and activities of organizations as immigration swelled, then declined as immigrants became Canadians.

In many ways it is almost impossible to write a traditional "ethnic" history of the people of the British Isles in the Lower Mainland. Since the English-speaking people from Great Britain and Ireland were never a minority, except for a brief period when native people outnumbered Europeans in the 1860s, they were never an ethnic group outside the dominant culture. They *were* the dominant culture. Through weight of numbers people from Great Britain and Ireland were able to establish a cultural hegemony over all other ethnocultural groups. They created a colonial settler society with British norms and values, English as the language of commerce and public life and British law and forms of government. Only immigrants who spoke another language or didn't have a British cultural heritage became ethnic groups and had to find accommodation with the dominant British settler society.

And while the English-speaking peoples from the British Isles may not have been an ethnic group in the traditional sense, they certainly had an ethnicity, even if there were very few occasions when any explicit mention was made of it. Those references usually occurred on major festival days: for the English on St. George's Day on April 23; for the Scots on St. Andrew's Day on November 30 or Robert Burns' Day on January 25; and for the Welsh on St. David's Day on March 1. Because the political and historical situation in Ireland divided the native Catholic Irish and Protestant Ulster-Scots, the days when their ethnicity was marked were St. Patrick's Day on March 17 and the Glorious Twelfth on July 12 respectively. But save for those annual feast days, or during periods of conflict in Great Britain and Ireland, newspaper accounts and histories almost never referred to the ethnicity of members of the dominant groups.

So when Malcolm McLean was elected the city's first mayor

in 1886 little was made of the fact that he was from the island of Tyree in Argyleshire, Scotland, spoke Gaelic fluently and had beaten another Scot from Edinburgh, Richard H. Alexander. Or that McLean became the first president of the St. Andrew's and Caledonian Society, the oldest Scottish organization in the city, while being a strong supporter of emigration from Scotland. Nobody thought it odd either that of the 11 council members elected on that first council, three were born in Scotland, one in England and three in Canada of Ulster-Scots descent; the remaining four were born in Ontario or the Maritimes of British stock (or had last names that certainly suggested they had British origins).

From Vancouver's inception as a town in the only British colony on the west coast of the Americas, the British played the pre-eminent role in shaping the region. In many ways the history of the British in Vancouver is the history of the city itself. After the Colony of British Columbia was proclaimed November 19, 1858, at Fort Langley, the Columbia Detachment of the Royal Engineers under Col. R.C. Moody arrived to turn a colony that existed only on paper into a living reality. Sent by the Colonial Office in London the 165-man unit built roads, enforced the colony's laws, laid the groundwork for a civil service and even printed postage stamps. Looking for a capital for the new colony Moody picked a spot on the north side of the Fraser River—named after the Scottish explorer Simon Fraser—so that it might more easily be defended in a war against the Americans. He wanted Queensborough but others thought Prince Albert and Prince Edward more suitable names. To settle the dispute colonial secretary Sir Edward Bulwer Lytton asked Queen Victoria for her opinion. She chose "New Westminster."

The surveying done by Moody and the Royal Engineers laid the backbone of the city's extensive park system by setting aside (for naval purposes) huge chunks of land on Burrard Inlet, including 44.5 hectares at Jericho which became Jericho Park, 315 hectares in Point Grey which became Pacific Spirit Park and 143 hectares on a peninsula by the Downtown which became Stanley Park. A year before the Royal Engineers were disbanded in 1863, three lads from England, John Morton, Samuel Brighouse and William Hailstone, were dubbed the Three Greenhorns for buying 218 hectares in what is now the West End for $550.75, thus becoming some of the first European settlers in what later became know as Vancouver. The city's grid system and recognizable pattern of east/west avenues and north/south streets were based on the work of Lauchlan Alexander Hamilton, a member of the first city council, native of Ontario and grandson of an Ulster man.

As Vancouver grew and prospered in the late 19th and early 20th centuries, it became more British, not less. In 1891 one in five people were born in Great Britain; by 1911 the percentage had increased to one in three. Vancouver's reputation as a British city was so well established that real estate developers marketed the city as the Liverpool of the Pacific or the Glasgow of the northwest. British values and sensibilities also helped shape the region's urban, residential, garden-like landscape. Developers and politicians of British descent were responsible for promoting and building an abundance of affordable single family dwellings, many in an English Tudor or cottage style, for working people rather than apartment buildings as in eastern cities.

While the Canadian Pacific Railway played a major role in shaping the residential look of the city through its vast land holdings, also important was the influence of the B.C. Electric Railway Company. Sold in 1897 to a London-based firm, it became one of the largest privately owned electrical railway companies in the British Empire. By increasing trackage in Vancouver from 21 kilometres in 1900 to 170 kilometres in 1912, the BCER opened up vast chunks of undeveloped land for single family housing. Control of the city's streetcar company in England also symbolized the huge presence British firms had in the life of the region, especially in raising capital for mining and exploration. Even when companies were controlled in B.C. many found it necessary to have a British corporate identity to attract capital. The British link was so strong that regional business people often travelled to London to personally pitch their plans to potential investors or used a British relative for credibility. In 1901, for example, 44 per cent of the heads of major businesses and companies in Vancouver were born in Great Britain and Ireland.

But as English-speaking immigrants from Great Britain and Ireland made Vancouver more British in the early 20th century, they also made the city and region less tolerant of different ethnocultural groups. By stressing the white, Christian and British nature of the dominant groups in the city, Vancouver politicians and community leaders played prominent roles in lobbying for restrictions on Asian immigration from China, Japan and India, and on pressuring Victoria and Ottawa to pass laws discriminating against Canadians of Asian descent. It wasn't that people of British ancestry were any more racist than others; the difference was that in the Vancouver region their control over government, police and the courts meant they could give their prejudices the force of law.

Although the British as a group played a key role in shaping the Lower Mainland, the English, Scots, Welsh and Irish also have their own separate histories. The Scottish St. Andrew's and Caledonian Society, for example, first met on September.

13, 1886, in "Gold's House" at 66 Water Street. For the first year of its life the society met several times in the civic office of Scottish-born Mayor Malcolm McLean. A year after its inception on November 29th, 1887, the society held a grand St. Andrew's Ball in McDonough Hall at the southeast corner of Hastings and Columbia. One newspaper called the event, without a hint of irony in a city barely a year old, "the most brilliant affair in the history of the city." Of the 1,000 people who lived in Vancouver at the time an estimated 400 people braved a rainstorm to attend the ball, which started with dancing at 9:00 P.M. and a dinner two hours later. One account of the ball wryly noted that "what the majority of the dancers did not know about a Scotch reel, would fill a Gaelic prayer book." The annual St. Andrew's Ball became one of the major events in the city's social calendar although not every banquet went off without a hitch. In 1895 the ball committee felt it got a very raw deal and passed a motion that the "supper at the Hotel Vancouver on November 18th was one of the worst the society has ever had since its formation." Because only one-third of the guests got their dinner they vowed only to pay a portion of the bill. Eventually a mediator helped settle the dispute.

By the 1930s, however, the annual Robert Burns Night had overtaken St. Andrew's Day in importance. Local newspapers regularly gave Burns Night considerable positive coverage, including almost a whole page in 1939. That year more than 700 Scots crowded into the Commodore for the annual feast where they heard the haggis (a sheep's stomach stuffed with minced mutton, oatmeal and spices) piped into the hall and addressed with the words of Burns: "Fair fa' your honest sonsie face/Great chieftain o' the pudden race . . ." Behind the head table stood a statue of Burns flanked by the Union Jack and the flag of St. Andrew. Locally the influence of Robert Burns became so widespread that the Chinatown Lions Club eventually organized an annual Burns dinner, complete with haggis served with a sweet and sour sauce.

Another Scottish society which played a prominent role was *An Cumunn Gaidhealch,* The Highland Association. For several years starting in December, 1935, the Highland Association held the B.C. Gaelic Mod, the first annual Gaelic-language music and literary festival outside of the British Isles. Affiliated with the National Mod in Scotland, the B.C. version regularly attracted entrants from all over North America. In 1938 CBC broadcast Scots-Gaelic folk songs from the mod across the country.

Although Scottish sports, language, piping, dancing and cultural groups started locally in the late 19th century, the Scottish community wasn't able to build a community hall until many years later. The first attempt occurred in 1890 when H.O. Bell-

Irving formed a building committee of the St. Andrew's and Caledonian Society and put a downpayment of $350 on two lots at Cambie and Dunsmuir. But the attempt failed and it took Scottish-Canadian groups 65 years until they opened a community hall. On St. Andrew's Day in 1955, 21 Scottish Canadians groups finally opened the United Scottish Cultural Centre at Fir and 12th Avenue in Vancouver. In July, 1986, the centre moved into a new home at 8886 Hudson in Marpole.

The Welsh first started arriving in the region in the 1860s when agents in Liverpool distributed booklets in Aberdare, in South Wales, touting the riches to be had in the Cariboo Gold Rush. In the Lower Mainland the first Welsh society started in 1912 with formation of the Cambrian Society, named after the Cambrian Hills in Wales. In 1929 society members managed to build a community hall at 215 East 17th Avenue, believed to be the only hall built and operated by a Welsh society in North America. Acoustically designed to bring the best out of choir singing, the hall became the home of the annual *Eisteddfod,* a competititive singing and reciting festival, and the *Gymanfa Ganu,* a hymn singing festival. The hall is also one the few places in the region where you can hear Welsh being spoken at its bilingual non-denominational Christian service held once a month.

One of the remarkable stories from the Welsh community occurred on April 12, 1941, when Bob Ito, a Japanese-Canadian boy under 10 years of age, won in one category and came second in another at the annual *Eisteddfod.* During a period of rising animosity to Japanese-Canadians and a little less than a year before Canadians of Japanese descent were uprooted from the West Coast and interned, Ito somehow managed to win a Welsh singing and elocution competition that can trace its roots back more than 1,500 years in Wales.

After World War II the Welsh community raised enough money to send a hand-carved bardic chair to the 1948 Royal National *Eisteddfod* in Bridgend, Wales. Presented annually to the winning bard at the festival, the chair was made from black walnut and white cowhide and combined traditional leeks of Welsh *Eisteddfod* design with a West Coast native design by Bill Calder.

One British group which once had a major public presence in the Lower Mainland were the Orangemen from Northern Ireland. From the late 19th century through the first half of the 20th century Protestant Ulster-Scots held an annual Glorious Twelfth parade through the streets of Vancouver that regularly attracted thousands of people. The parade celebrated the victory of the Protestant King William III over the Roman Catholic James II at the Battle of the Boyne in 1688. And while the day was a festive one for the Protestant Ulster-Scots from Northern Ireland, it was a symbol of sectarian intolerance for Irish Catholics. The Orange Order originated with the Ulster-Scots in Northern Ireland but expanded beyond that limited base in Canada to include many non-Catholic British who believed in Canadian unity under one flag, one language and one school system.

The earliest record of a Glorious Twelfth parade taking place is in July, 1888, when the Loyal Orange Association marched from their meeting space in Vancouver's Keefer's Hall to the wharves where they met fellow Orangemen from New Westminster and Victoria arriving by boat. Over the years the event kept growing in popularity to the point in 1922 when 40 Orange lodges from around the province and more than 5,000 people watched the parade and sports activities in New Westminster. Traditionally the parade was led by a marshall wearing a white plumed hat, sword and riding boots atop a white steed, which was meant to represent King William III when he led his troops in battle. In 1941, however, a minor scandal occurred when local Orangemen were forced to abandon that tradition because nobody could find a white horse. They ended up using a grey one instead. That July, which marked the 251st anniversary of King William's victory, the parade wound its way from the old Cambie Street grounds along Georgia and then along Hastings to Hastings Park.

By the 1950s organizers tried to build interest in the annual event by moving the parade around the region, including holding it along Marine Drive in West Vancouver in 1950. In 1964 the Glorious Twelfth in Vancouver entered its final phase: that year King Billy's white horse was finally replaced by a car. By 1971 interest in the annual parade was petering out as only a few hundred people took part.

An Irish family does hold the distinction of being the first Europeans to build a house on land that later become Vancouver. Hugh McRoberts from Northern Ireland become the first settler on Sea Island and later pre-empted land on the north bank of the Fraser on April 24, 1862. McRoberts' nephews, Samuel and Fitzgerald McCleery from Killyleagh, County Down, built a cabin on the site that September.

The Catholic Irish have played a smaller yet no less significant role than their Protestant counterparts in the life of the region. Starting in the 1880s Irish immigrants, mainly manual and skilled laborers, settled in and around Vancouver after helping to build the Canadian Pacific Railway. But unlike Irish immigrant communities in the U.S., local Irish Catholic settlers never reached the numbers that could hold something as public as a St. Patrick's Day parade.

Sometime either just before or after World War II Irish Catholic immigrants formed the Irish Society, a cultural and social group which remained the main Irish community group through the 1950s. The society held annual St. Patrick's Day dances, picnics at the Peace Arch and fundraising dinners of bacon and cabbage for a dollar per person. Two of the longer lasting groups have been Stage Eireann, a theatrical group, and the Irish Sporting and Cultural Society. In the early 1980s local Irish Canadians managed to start an Irish Centre on Prior Street in Strathcona but political and financial problems forced the centre to close its doors in 1990.

People from the Isle of Man in the Irish Sea have also had a presence in the Lower Mainland since early in the 20th century. The Manx Society became the first Manx organization in the country when it held its first meeting on New Year's Eve, 1908. Society members would regularly gather on the day and sing about *Ellan Vannin*, the Manx name for the Isle of Man, or perform a play in Manx-Gaelic such as *Yn Dooinney Moylee*, (*The Go-Between Man*).

A souvenir from a bygone era; a salvaged Edwardian sign, Vancouver, 1955. vs

Americans
Georgina Bullen

THERE WAS a peaceful, if rather boisterous, American invasion of British Columbia in 1858. It happened in just a few hours on Sunday, April 25, when the American side-wheeler *Commodore* churned into Victoria and disgorged 450 California miners. They were the first of some 25,000 men who arrived, wanting to replenish supplies before crossing the Strait of Georgia to the newly discovered Fraser River gold fields and a chance to strike it rich.

All those Americans made us nervous and in November James Douglas, already governor of the Colony of Vancouver Island, was appointed governor of the Colony of British Columbia to ensure British interests were promoted and American expansionism discouraged.

Americans have influenced our history from the earliest days of European settlement. In 1869 there was gathering support for union with the United States. The proponents wrote President Andrew Johnson, asking for "the Acquisition of this colony by the United States." They foresaw an unrestricted market, growth in population and investment, improvement in mail and communication, less expensive government and protection against foreign enemies. Johnson was (happily for the two-year-old Dominion of Canada) indifferent to the proposal. On July 20, 1871, British Columbia officially entered the Dominion putting an end to any threat, real or imagined, of American annexation of British Columbia.

Americans and American names, habits and customs, however, continued to play a role in the foundation of the new province and the cities that grew and prospered within her boundaries. Vancouver's famed Stanley Park was originally a military reserve guarding against possible American aggression. More benignly, Burnaby's much smaller Central Park was named for the one in New York City, birthplace of the wife of entrepreneur David Oppenheimer. Another New York landmark, Broadway, was the inspiration for changing the name of Vancouver's 9th Avenue in May 1909—partly, it is suspected, to encourage and involve American interests in Vancouver's burgeoning real estate market.

Maine-born Sewell Prescott Moody successfully rescued the bankrupt Burrard Inlet Mills in 1865 and made it a thriving concern. The waterfront area came to be known as Moodyville, renowned for its high-quality timber.

Benjamin Tingley (B.T.) Rogers was born in Pennsylvania and moved to Vancouver in 1889, where he became one of the city's wealthiest men as owner of the B.C. Sugar Refining Company. Rogers and city council negotiated a $30,000 "bonus," 15 tax-free years, a free ten-year water supply as well as a perpetual guarantee of water at ten cents per 4,545 litres—all in return for a promise to hire only white laborers.

Illinois-born Frank W. Hart owned Vancouver's first theatre, first undertaking establishment, first hearse and first silk top hat, and he conducted the first burial in Mountain View cemetery.

Scottish-American philanthropist Andrew Carnegie, whose money sparked construction of dozens of libraries in North America, made Vancouver's Carnegie Library possible with a $50,000 donation. The building still stands at Hastings and Main, used as library and social centre.

Louis D. Taylor, born in Ann Arbor, Michigan, was elected mayor eight times between 1909 and 1931. He was by all accounts irascible, and the story is told that when Teddy Roosevelt and his wife visited Vancouver in 1915, the Board of Trade unwisely did not include Mayor Taylor in the official reception at the CPR station. Undaunted, Taylor boarded the train at an earlier stop, greeted the Roosevelts and whisked the former U.S. president off for a drive around Stanley Park, leaving the Board of Trade reception committee open-mouthed and empty handed. It was L.D. Taylor who made the *Vancouver World* an enormously successful newspaper—and who stretched its resources past the breaking point when he built the World Tower to house it.

In the late 1960s and into the 1970s, many Americans, disenchanted with various aspects of what had become the American way, made their way north. Vietnam War resisters as well as affluent citizens, respected academics and talented artists flocked to Vancouver to escape increased violence, pollution and what many perceived as unhealthy political trends. Many stayed and have enriched Vancouver society.

Among American-born people who have made their mark here: restaurateur Nat Bailey, art curator Alvin Balkind, lumber magnate Prentice Bloedel, archeologist Charles Borden, baseball promoter Bob Brown, MLA Buda Brown, C.H. Cates of tugboat fame, realtor Henry Ceperley, the Army & Navy's Sam Cohen, druggist George Cunningham, fishpacker John Deas, photographer Claud Dettloff, sawmill owner Sewell Moody, the Canadian Pacific Railway's T.G. Shaughnessy and William Van Horne, teacher and critic Warren Tallman, orchestra leader Calvin Winter, Children's Festival founder Ernie Fladell . . . and the first non-native to actually set foot on what would become Greater Vancouver soil, Simon Fraser.

Germans
Sylvia Reinthal

GERMAN SETTLERS WERE part of the first large influx of immigrants to British Columbia in 1857. Most came from southwestern Germany and included shopkeepers, merchants, skilled artisans and craftspeople. They became part of the urban middle class, bringing with them much needed skills and trades, and became prominent in Vancouver's social and political life. German clubs soon sprang up, the members preserving their heritage, language, music and cultural traditions.

There were significant numbers of German immigrants in the early 20th century. Many integrated into local society by marrying into the "old families." German investment bankers and noblemen, barons and counts, entertained lavishly, an era which came to an end because of the international economic crisis prior to World War I.

The war itself turned Germans overnight from much-favored people into vilified enemies. German-Canadians no longer felt at ease speaking in their mother tongue; German-language church services were halted and the federal government suppressed all German newspapers. The post-war census in 1921 showed a decline in British Columbia of nearly 40 per cent of people declaring their German origin, and in public they now spoke English.

During World War II attitudes toward German-Canadians were less hostile, even though all Germans entering Canada after 1922 had to register as enemy aliens. Most of those interned at the outbreak of the war were released as harmless by 1941. This time there were no bitter ethnic tensions, and as early as 1947 Germans were again admitted as immigrants, initially as "displaced persons" who had fled their homes in Eastern Germany.

Some 300,000 German immigrants arrived in the province between 1947 and 1967, many of them skilled tradespeople and most of them with a good education and the command of some school English. They easily merged into the mainstream, and became British Columbia's second largest ethnic group after the British. Successful in business, professions and trades, they persevered and rarely suffered failure. In the post-war era many German-Canadians settled along Vancouver's Fraser Street and in the West End, where they opened small businesses and ethnic restaurants along Robson Street which, at that time, was often called "Robsonstrasse."

According to the 1991 census, 129,950 people of German descent resided in Greater Vancouver. They have German churches of the major denominations, German clubs for recreation and entertainment, German schools and German newspapers to keep the language alive and help adjust to the Canadian way of life. In the region the German community also maintains the German-Canadian Benevolent Society, which looks after several German-Canadian Intermediate Care Homes. Among the many organizations are the German-Canadian Congress, the German-Canadian Baltic Society, the German-Canadian Culture Society, the German-Canadian Business and Professional Association, the Trans-Canada Alliance of the German-Canadians, the Edelweiss Credit Union, the Kolping Society of Vancouver and the Goethe Institute. There is also a German Consulate in Vancouver.

Past and present there are many outstanding and colorful citizens of German origin in Greater Vancouver. The pioneer Dr. John Sebastian Helmcken arrived in 1850 from the Hannover area. For a long time he was the only medical doctor here and children called him affectionately "Doctor Heal My Skin." He married Cecilia Douglas, the future governor's daughter, entered politics and was one of the politicians who brought British Columbia into Confederation.

Agnes Watts, known as "the telethon angel," was born in a small eastern German village near Bunzlau in 1889. She came alone to Victoria, just 19 years old, to work as a nanny. She was the first female employee when Scott Paper opened a mill in New Westminster, and stayed with them for 22 years "rolling toilet paper" and saving every penny. Her great wealth came from her frugality and smart investments in the stock market and real estate. She was one of the most generous patrons of the Variety Club, and gave more than $500,00 to children's projects, for which she was given the Variety Club award by Prince Philip in London in 1987, which she picked up herself.

One of the most colorful and prominent German immigrants is Fritz Ziegler, who came to Vancouver with his parents when he was nine. In 1923 he entered the family chocolate business, the famous Ziegler Chocolates. During the war he was interned but was released after a few years on condition that he not reside in Vancouver. He settled in Fort Langley and, talented and practical as he was, built with his own hands a castle, "Schloss Klipphaus." He lives there today, 93 years old at this writing, with wife Nancy, the great-granddaughter of Canadian Prime Minister Mackenzie Bowell, and entertains people from all over the world.

GOETHE-INSTITUT

The Goethe-Institut Vancouver serves all residents of British Columbia and Alberta interested in German culture and the German language. Films, exhibitions, lectures, and concerts are organized in cooperation with local partners (with most events in English). The library has a substantial selection of German books, newspapers, magazines and videos in both German and English. German classes on all levels are offered in Vancouver as well as referral and consultation for courses at 17 Goethe-Instituts in Germany.

Italians

Ben D'Andrea

A VISITOR TO VANCOUVER'S east side in 1910 reported that a *Piccola Italia,* or Little Italy, had been established in the area around present-day Main Street. Italians in Vancouver then numbered up to a 1,000 or more. Today more than 30,000 Canadians of Italian descent live in the Vancouver area, and parts of Little Italy have sprung up on Commercial Drive and along East Hastings from Nanaimo Street to Burnaby.

Vancouver's first Little Italy emerged from the first wave of Italian immigration to Canada between 1900 and 1914. However, a small number of pioneering Italians were lured here from San Francisco in the 1850s by the Fraser River Gold Rush; some acquired small fortunes. Not until construction began on the Canadian Pacific Railway did Italians arrive here in significant numbers from Eastern Canada. During this period of railway building, Italians began leaving their mark on Vancouver.

Among the many Italians who worked on the CPR was Angelo Calori. His Europe Hotel still stands at the corner of Powell and Alexandra in Gastown. The wooden building Calori bought and rebuilt was one of a very few to survive the Great Fire of 1886. The hotel lobby's marble staircase and brass banister survive as evidence of Calori's success as a hotelier.

Another Italian who left his mark on the city early on was sculptor Charles Marega. Marega came to Vancouver in 1909 and established himself as its first professional sculptor. The concrete lions at the Stanley Park entrance to the Lion's Gate Bridge are his most familiar sculptures. But his work is also in Stanley Park and at Vancouver City Hall, along Beach Avenue and even on the Burrard Street Bridge.

An expanding community of Italians led to the formation of Vancouver's first Italian mutual aid society in 1905. The present Italian Mutual Aid Society, located in the Roma Hall of New Westminster, no longer functions primarily to help immigrants adjust to their new surroundings, but now supports a variety of charitable causes. The diverse cultural and recreational interests of today's Italian-Canadian community are also represented by more than 30 other associations.

To serve the growing Italian community, an Italian-speaking priest was assigned to the Church of the Sacred Heart in 1907. Today Our Lady of Sorrows and St. Helen's in Burnaby serve mainly Italian parishioners. Italian masses are said at several other churches around Greater Vancouver, including Holy Spirit in New Westminster's Queensborough district.

a small number of Italians were lured here in the 1850s by the Fraser River Gold Rush

Vancouver's first Italian newspaper, *L'Italia nel Canada,* appeared in 1911. The contemporary Italian weekly newspaper, *L'Eco d'Italia,* was founded in 1955 and now includes an English section. The Italian community is also represented by radio and television programming. *Radio Amici* is broadcast daily on CJVB radio in Vancouver, and on weekends *Ciao Italia* can be heard on CHMB. On television, *Telitalia* broadcasts daily on the multicultural channel.

Greater Vancouver's current and well-established Italian presence emerged following a second and larger wave of Italian immigration to Canada between 1950 and 1970. (Few Italians have immigrated to Vancouver since 1970.) Post-war Italian newcomers favored settling in large urban areas like Vancouver, where they found work in the local construction industry and established retail businesses ranging from grocery and clothing stores to restaurants.

Vancouver's Italian-Canadians have also gained recognition nation-wide. Among them are the actor Bruno Gerussi, who died in 1995, for years the star of his own television series, *Beachcombers,* and the restaurateur and author Umberto Menghi. But perhaps the most influential member of the Italian-Canadian community was Angelo E. Branca, the lawyer who became a judge of the B.C. Supreme Court and the Court of Appeal. Erected in Branca's memory in Piazza Italia, on Grandview Highway, is a statue of Christopher Columbus donated by the City of Genoa.

Even a brief history of Italians in Greater Vancouver would be incomplete without mentioning the Italian Cultural Centre, located in East Vancouver on Slocan at Grandview Highway. The Centre, built mostly by volunteers, was completed in the summer of 1977. It includes a restaurant, banquet hall, art gallery, daycare centre, television production centre and even an indoor bocce court. Every summer the centre hosts a week-long Italian festival.

Instrumental in the campaign to build this centre was the Italian-born Anna Terrana of Burnaby, now the MP for Vancouver East. On a return visit from Ottawa to attend the Italian National Day celebrations at the centre, Terrana brought greetings to the community from another of Vancouver's prominent Italian-Canadians: Frank Iacobucci, appointed to the Supreme Court of Canada in 1991.

Umberto Menghi arrived in Canada in 1967 and fell in love with the country. In Vancouver he brought the skills and passion of his Tuscan upbringing to a little yellow restaurant called, simply, Umberto's. Now a half-dozen restaurants thrive under his direction in Vancouver and Whistler. (Among his most popular cookbooks is Umberto's Kitchen, displaying the influences of B.C., Tuscany and Northern California.) In 1995 Umberto realized a dream by opening Villa Delia, a cooking school and hotel near Pisa, Tuscany.

French
Claire Hurley

I N 1996 LA JOIE DE VIVRE is alive and well in Vancouver, in the Coquitlam neighborhood known as Maillardville and in the homes of some 55,000 French-Canadians and another 10,000 French-speaking Canadians from France living in British Columbia.

French-Canadians accompanied both Alexander Mackenzie on his 1793 explorations and Simon Fraser in 1805 and 1808. Historically the French presence in B.C. goes back more than 200 years.

In September, 1860, the Oblate Fathers from France began to concentrate their activities on the vast region of the estuaries of the Fraser River. Father Leon Fouquet, a French theologian who had abandoned a brilliant career as a writer in France to work with the natives in Western Canada, was responsible for the construction of two small churches in New Westminster: Saint-Pierre for the white folk and Saint-Charles for the natives.

In 1865 the Marie-Conception and Mainville Sisters opened a school for girls in New Westminster and in 1866 the Oblate Fathers established permanent headquarters in New Westminster. By 1871, when British Columbia joined Confederation, the Catholic Church and its French way of life were solidly implanted in B.C. In 1886 French churches, schools and hospitals were built in Vancouver and around B.C., and in 1887 the Sisters of Saint-Anne opened Saint-Marie Hospital in New Westminster.

The Fraser River Lumber Company owned by A.D. McRae of Winnipeg and Peter Jansen of Nebraska was responsible for bringing many French-Canadians from Quebec. In 1907 tensions between white and Asian workers had led to anti-Asian riots in Vancouver. In 1908 the lumber firm sent French-Canadian Theodore Thereaux, accompanied by Oblate Father Patrick O'Boyle, to Montreal to recruit workers. In September, 1908, some 500 arrived by train at Little Fraser station at the present site of Blue Mountain Park in Coquitlam.

The vibrant community of Maillardville sprang into being with the arrival of the Quebecois. By 1968 68.8 per cent of the Francophones in B.C. had emigrated from their birthplaces in other Canadian provinces. Banks, retail businesses, churches and schools have prospered over the decades in Maillardville.

In 1996 an exciting project was underway in Coquitlam. Two heritage homes, formerly owned by executives of the Fraser Mills Lumber Company, are the locations for the Place des Arts Society (in Ryan House) and the Coquitlam Heritage Society (in Mackin House). In 1996 an educational centre was under construction with funds raised by the Maillardville Heritage Square Campaign. Plans include a glass link connecting the education centre to Ryan House, an outdoor amphitheatre, the moving of the old railway station and an old caboose to the complex, a logging museum, period gardens, walkways and a bicycle path.

French-speaking people newly arrived in the Greater Vancouver region will find a marvellous informational and cultural centre at La Maison de la Francophonie, at 1551 West 7th Avenue in Vancouver. La Maison is the headquarters for Le Centre Culturel Francophone de Vancouver, which has a mandate of promoting French language and francophone culture through cultural, community and educational activities. Le Centre, which has gained an important place within the Vancouver community, sees itself not only as a gathering place for Francophones but also as a centre of attraction for exchanges with other Vancouver cultural communities.

Le Centre is a great place to learn about the variety of community services available to help fulfill the diverse needs of Francophones living in the region. There's a resource centre of services available in French throughout B.C., a "Montreal-style" cafe, outdoor activities and a weekly social gathering on Wednesday evenings. As well the Centre offers language courses in French, English and Spanish, children's classes, community classes and "Virgule," a summer day-camp for children six to 12 years of age.

The demand for French-language classes within the public school system increased during the late 1960s and 1970s. As a result L'Ecole Bilingue opened in September, 1973, in a section of Cecil Rhodes School. L'Ecole Bilingue took over the entire school with its French-immersion program and, in 1996, had an enrollment of 350 students in classes from kindergarten to grade seven. Within the Lower Mainland there are a variety of public schools offering bilingual educational programs.

The Saint-Sacrament Church operates Blessed Sacrament French School, a French-immersion program with 215 students from kindergarten to grade seven.

Media serving French-speaking people within the Greater Vancouver area include the weekly newspaper, *Le Soleil de Colombie,* CBUF-FM radio, CBUFT-TV and RDI (Reseau de l'information) Television. French cuisine is available in many local restaurants although the fare is substantially lighter than tradition would suggest in order to cater to 1990s-style tastes.

Dutch

Albert Van Der Heide

CANADIANS OF DUTCH descent have made their homes in Vancouver and the surrounding area for more than a century, leaving their marks on both the landscape and society. Others of Dutch origin just passed through or lived and worked in this area for a short time only. Among those was explorer Captain George Vancouver whose roots can be traced to the Van Coeverdens, a Dutch family which took its name from a small town on the Dutch-German border. Canadian Pacific Railway's W.C. Van Horne, who accomplished the near impossible with the introduction of modern transportation across Canada, is another. Contractor Andrew Onderdonk of Dutch colonial stock used Chinese labor to build the Yale section of the railroad. Volkert Vedder and his sons arrived here from New York and gave their name to several places in the Chilliwack area.

Shortly after the turn of the century the first Dutch pioneers settled in the area, among them animal protection activist Baroness Van Steenwyk who later formed the Vancouver SPCA. Others who found homes here were Vancouver Symphony director Allard De Ridder, Vancouver Aquarium director Carl Lietze, CCF politician Dorothy Biersteker Steeves, photographer John Vanderpant, orchid grower Jim le Nobel, the Baders of Bader's Dutch Cookies and lawyer Matthew A. Van Roggen who also served as honorary consul of the Netherlands. By the 1920s the Dutch immigrant community had become large enough to organize major social events. In 1926 Holland Society members were instrumental in the institution of the first of British Columbia's 36 Christian Reformed Churches.

Meanwhile local farmers—on Lulu Island, Annacis Island and in Burnaby and Surrey—got acquainted with their Dutch-immigrant neighbors. Although the depression of the 1930s and then World War II put a halt to the community's growth, the infrastructure for the massive Dutch immigration of the 1950s was in place. Early pioneers played an important role in helping newcomers settle in an area that contrasted so much with "the Lowlands."

Among these newcomers was Jan Blom, a Dutch lawyer and investment banker. Earlier he had helped put together a consortium of private Dutch investors with the plan to reclaim a flooded area—2,833 hectares—near Maple Ridge, now known as Pitt Polder. To overcome stringent, post-war Dutch currency controls the group packaged its engineering skills through newly established CBA Engineering and sold know-how in B.C. Ironically the Pitt Polder Company survived for years on CBA's profits from projects such as the Port Mann Bridge, the Keenleyside Dam, and bridges at Golden, Kamloops and Mission. CBA was also involved with the Knight Street and Alex Fraser bridges and other water and hydro contracts. The Dutch investors attracted local participants by the mid-1960s and sold out in 1989.

Numerous Dutch immigrants came to farm but just as many possessed trade-school diplomas. The ten Van Vliet brothers, initially all employed at Van Vliet Construction, built landmarks—Bloedel Conservatory for one—in and around Vancouver and beyond. The Van Vliets were joined by other high-profile Dutch-born engineers, builders and structural-steel fabricators.

The Dutch involvement in forestry was personified by entrepreneur Nick Van Drimmelen who built one of the Cariboo's first integrated lumber operations.

Burnaby is home to the United Flower Growers Co-op which operates Canada's oldest Dutch flower auction. Via this auction nearly 100 nurseries—largely owned by Dutch immigrants—supply potted plants and cut flowers to B.C., the prairies and the U.S. The Dutch presence is also visible through garden centres, landscapers and the supply trade. The largest greenhouse vegetable operation in the area is operated by Dutch immigrants as well.

Part of the fabric of society in the Netherlands has been copied in Canada with Dutch-Canadians not only building Calvinist churches but also starting Christian school systems, operating homes for the aged and the handicapped, providing support services for the mentally ill and even forming a Christian labor union. These institutions now reach beyond the Dutch community. Dutch Roman Catholics blended in with already existing churches, schools and organizations and were emerging in leadership roles by the 1970s. Both groups were instrumental in setting up the Federation of Independent Schools which obtained recognition and some public funding for qualifying schools. In addition quite a few Dutch-Canadaians have entered local and provincial politics.

The B.C. Dutch community of 63,000 is served by Canada's only daily Dutch radio program, aired on CJVB, a station started by Jan Van Bruchem, a Dutch-Canadian. There are also two newspapers: a bi-weekly with three regional editions and a monthly. The Dutch government maintains a consulate general in Vancouver.

Scandinavians
Al Arnason

Accoring to the 1991 census, 107,355 Greater Vancouver people claim at least some Scandinavian and Nordic ancestors. They represent 6.3 per cent of the 1.8 million residents of the Lower Mainland area.

An important recent development is that Norwegian, Swedish and Finnish groups, in the umbrella Scandinavian Community Centre Society, are leasing to purchase the 1.8 hectare Roald Amundsen Centre in Burnaby, and have approached the Danish and Icelandic-Canadian communities to join the society.

Scandinavian and local news is broadcast on the radio program *Coffee Time, Scandinavian Style* on CJVB, which broadcasts in Finnish, Danish, Icelandic, Norwegian and Swedish. *Scandinavian Journey* is a television variety program on the multicultural channel. *Scandinavian Press* is a quarterly magazine of news and features about the five Nordic and Scandinavian nations and emigrants.

The Svenska Kulturforeningen (Swedish Cultural Society) is a Swedish-language group that organizes the annual Lucia Celebration (also called the Festival of Lights) on the Sunday closest to December 13. The Swedish-Canadian Club is a cultural and social group serving Greater Vancouver whose meetings are conducted in English. The Sweden House Society was formed to establish a Swedish Community Centre as part of the Scandinavian Centre in Burnaby. The Swedish-Canadian Rest Home and Manor in Burnaby provides retirement apartments and old-age care.

Swedish Press (*Nya Svenska Pressen*) is a bilingual Swedish/English magazine published monthly in Vancouver and distributed world-wide. It covers matters related to Sweden and Swedes in other countries including Canada and has been published since 1929.

Other groups are the Runeberg Choir, Svenska Herrklubben (Swedish Men's Club) and Svenska Skolan (Swedish School).

More than 500 members belong to the Sons of Norway Sleipner Lodge #8, which meets at the Scandinavian Centre in Burnaby. Sleipner is the eight-legged horse ridden by the Norse god Odin. Varden Lodge #19, New Westminster, meets at the Oddfellows Hall in Burnaby. There are lodges in North Vancouver, Surrey, Maple Ridge, Langley and Chilliwack. Other focal points of the community are Normanna, the Norwegian Rest Home in Burnaby and the First Lutheran Church at 5745 Wales in Vancouver.

Danish-Canadians list 31 organizations as centres of cultural, sports, religious, fraternal and other associations and affiliations. The Surrey-based Danish Community Centre of B.C. since 1962 has been an information coordinator and umbrella group for the community in Greater Vancouver. The Federation of Danish Associations in Canada (Pacific Region) is an umbrella group based in New Westminster for Danish organizations in B.C. and the Yukon. Another prominent group is the Dania Home Society, which operates the retirement complex of suites, cottages and a home in Burnaby.

Many of the original Finnish settlers in Canada emigrated to North America to find religious freedom and to escape from compulsory service in the Russian army. Some were among the first colonial fishermen on the Fraser River.

The most significant Finnish-Canadian organization is the 450-member Finlandia Club, at the Scandinavian Centre in Burnaby. Another is the 150-member Finnish Heritage Society. The Finnish-Canadian Rest Home Association operates two care homes: Finnish Manor in Burnaby and the Finnish-Canadian Rest Home in Vancouver.

The monthly Finnish-language newspaper *Lansirannikon Uutiset* (West Coast News) has a circulation of about 1,200.

Finnish-language church services are held at Finnish Bethel Church in Vancouver, Finnish (Emmaus) Lutheran Church in Burnaby and Finnish Mission Assembly in Surrey.

The primary Icelandic organization is the Icelandic-Canadian Club of British Columbia. The 525-member cultural and social club traces its beginnings to 1908, soon after the first Icelandic settlers arrived here. The group has the largest membership of 13 Icelandic clubs throughout Canada and the United States that are linked through the Icelandic National League of North America, founded in 1919 in Winnipeg. The club has its headquarters at Iceland House in New Westminster. The 3,500-volume SólskinLibrary of Icelandic and English books and the Icelandic Archives of B.C. are located in the building. The club offers Icelandic language classes to the public and scholarships to post-secondary students of Icelandic descent.

Closely linked is Sólskin (Sunshine), a women's group formed in 1917 to aid Icelandic-Canadians serving in World War I. The women run the library and are active as volunteers at the Icelandic Care Home (Hofn). The 64-resident home, not restricted to people of Icelandic descent, is in Vancouver.

Greeks
Ben D'Andrea

A FRASER DELTA fisherman known as "Johnny the Greek" was one of the few Greeks to settle in Greater Vancouver before 1900. A small number of Greek pioneers also worked in the province's sawmills, mines and railroads. But perhaps the best known of Vancouver's first Greek immigrants was Peter Pantages. A member of the Royal Life Saving Society, Peter founded the Polar Bear Club in 1921 and started what has since become an annual event: the New Year's Day swim in English Bay. The Pantages name, however, was first introduced to Vancouver by Peter's uncle, Alexander. The owner of a Seattle-based chain of highly successful vaudeville houses, Alexander built a theatre on Hastings Street.

By the 1920s and 1930s Greek-owned businesses flourished in downtown Vancouver: restaurants, fruit and fish markets, bakeries, shoeshine parlors and even a few Greek "kafenia," or coffee-houses. From a community of about 2,000 in 1927, Greater Vancouver's Greek community has grown today to just over 6,500 members.

The Greeks of Vancouver formally established their community in 1927 by founding their own society: the St. George Orthodox Hellenic Community. In 1930, with the help of money raised by the Womens' Auxiliary founded in 1929, the community built St. George's Greek Orthodox Church at Seventh and Vine in Kitsilano. A Sunday School and a Greek language class were established at the same time.

The creation of the Vancouver or "Gladstone" chapter of AHEPA (Anglo-Hellenic Educational Progressive Association) in 1930 further consolidated the Greek community. AHEPA, the largest Greek Heritage organization in the world, supports a variety of charitable causes. In honor of Canada's centenary in 1967, the Gladstone chapter donated the statue of the Discus Thrower that stands in the courtyard of the Vancouver Museum. The Burnaby chapter of AHEPA was chartered in 1978. Nearly 30 other recreational and region-based Greek organizations in Vancouver are joined under the umbrella of the Hellenic Canadian Congress of B.C. established in 1986.

By the 1950s the Greek community had united around St. George's and transformed Kitsilano into Vancouver's main Greek area. With everything from Greek restaurants and travel agencies to bakeries and a Hellenic Senior Citizens' Drop-In Centre, West Broadway and West Fourth Avenue are the main business areas of Greek Town. West Broadway between MacDonald and Waterloo was also the location for the Greek community's main secular festival, Greek Day. Begun in 1974 and discontinued after 1988, Greek Day has been replaced by two smaller events, a Greek Summer Festival at St. Nicholas-Demetrios Greek Orthodox Church on Boundary Road in East Vancouver and a similar event at the Hellenic Community Center in Kerrisdale.

Three Greek language newspapers currently serve the Greek community. The oldest still publishing is *Acropolis,* a monthly newspaper established in 1974. *Gnome* (Opinion), published semi-monthly with a regular English section, was established in 1988. More recently a monthly newspaper in both Greek and English that originated in Toronto in 1990 appeared in Vancouver in 1993 as the *Greek Canadian Voice.*

The Greek community also has access to Greek radio programming. Established in the early 1970s, *Greek Canadian Memories* broadcasts Sundays on CJVB radio. Established in 1987, the pay radio station HRN (Hellenic Radio Network) offers Greek-language programs, including news direct from Athens, 24 hours a day. HRN has about 3,500 family subscribers province-wide. For the 14 years up to 1993, Vancouver's multicultural television channel broadcast a Greek show several times a week.

The number of Greek immigrants to Vancouver doubled through the 1960s. The new St. George's Greek Orthodox Church on Arbutus Street was completed in 1971 to accommodate the growing community. The adjoining Hellenic Cultural Community Centre opened in 1977. A second church, St. Nicholas-Demetrios, was built in 1984 on Boundary Road to serve the Greek Community in East Vancouver and Burnaby. Established in the mid-1970s, a Greek Christian Evangelical Church currently holds its services in East Vancouver's Culloden Mennonite Brethren Church.

Although Greek immigration to Vancouver has declined steadily since 1968, Vancouver's Greek presence remains strong. And Vancouver's Greek-Canadians have achieved national recognition, particularly in sports. Inducted to the B.C. Sports Hall of Fame in 1967, the well-known diver George Athans Sr., competed in the 1936 Berlin Olympics and won silver and gold medals at the 1950 Empire Games. George Athans Jr. won the world crown for water-skiing in 1973 at Bogota and was inducted to the B.C. Sports Hall of Fame in 1976.

The reason Vancouver has appealed to Greek immigrants is easy to understand. As one woman said while looking out at Vancouver for the first time from the airplane, "What's this? It is so beautiful. It looks like Greece."

Jews in Greater Vancouver
Cyril E. Leonoff

JEWISH PEOPLE have been on the Vancouver scene since the city's earliest days. The first to take up residence was Polish-born Louis Gold, who in 1872 arrived at Granville (Gastown) by tug via the U.S.A. The next year he was joined by his wife Emma and their child "Eddie." The Golds rented premises from "Gassy Jack" Deighton and operated a general merchandise-grocery store on Water Street. Gold was a short man, but he reportedly earned the nickname "Leaping" Louis by springing into the air in the course of some fracas, "swinging his fist mightily and landing with his full weight on his opponent's chin." Such a feat was apparently enough to win the respect of local loggers, longshoremen and sailors whose attitude toward Jews was not always free of prejudice. His wife Emma was a businesswoman, and by 1882 she had established the West End Grocery and Royal City Boot and Shoe stores on Columbia Street, New Westminster.

After the Great Fire of June 1886 destroyed their Vancouver store, the family built the 100-room Gold House, a "strictly first-class" hostelry on Water Street. In 1877 Gold preempted 65 hectares along the North Arm Waggon Road in South Vancouver, leaving him, along with most such landowners in the suburbs, where population was scant, land rich but cash poor. In 1914 Louis' son Edward was elected councillor in South Vancouver, and became reeve the following year. An outspoken, controversial figure, Edward instituted cost-cutting measures by suspending the clerk and other civic employees, and hectic council meetings became an attraction, where "chairs were used as weapons of offense and defense."

Jewish merchants have been associated with the Lower Mainland since gold-rush days. In November 1858 Simon Reinhardt bought one of the first lots at Old Fort Langley (Derby), then projected to be the capital of the new colony of British Columbia. When New Westminster was chosen instead, Meyer, Reinhardt & Co. established there, as did the firm of Levi and Boas, "suppliers to the Cariboo gold fields."

Born in the Saar, Germany, the Oppenheimer brothers, David and Isaac, after business experience in the California gold country, developed a mercantile enterprise to service the Fraser River and Cariboo gold rushes, and later the construction of the Canadian Pacific Railway through the Fraser canyon. Realizing the great potential of the future Vancouver, from 1878 to 1886 David and Isaac and several business associates bought prime land at Coal Harbour, English Bay and a large block east of Carrall Street. In so doing their Vancouver Improvement Company became the largest landowner in town, after the CPR and the Hastings Saw Mill.

David Oppenheimer was undoubtedly the outstanding citizen in Vancouver's formative period. He promoted incorporation of the city, which took place on April 6, 1886. In June Oppenheimer Bros.—today Vancouver's oldest business—built the first wholesale grocery in the city's first brick building, still extant in present-day Gastown. The Great Fire passed over its foundation, then under construction. Upon completion, the building was used as Vancouver's first "city hall." Both David and Isaac were members of the 1887 city council, David being chairman of the finance committee. From 1888 to 1891 David served four terms as mayor, among the most constructive in Vancouver's history.

Mayor Oppenheimer set up the basic civic services: water supply, sewers, fire department, streets, schools, and parks. His civic duties were often intertwined with entrepreneurial investments: the Vancouver Water Works Company, the Vancouver Electric Railway and Light Company, and the Westminster and Vancouver Tramway. He promoted trade far and wide and succeeded in establishing steamship connection between Vancouver and Australia. Oppenheimer also had an active hand in the founding of the B.C. Sugar Refinery. He was a prime mover in forming the city's YMCA, the Alexandra Orphanage, the Vancouver Board of Trade, the British Columbia Exhibition Association, and the Vancouver Club, of which Isaac was president in 1895-96.

As mayor, David Oppenheimer presided over the dedication of Stanley Park on October 29, 1889. He also reserved Burnaby's Central Park along the tramway, calling it after its namesake in his wife's home town, New York City. When in 1911 a bronze-bust memorial sculpted by Charles Marega was unveiled at the English Bay entrance to Stanley Park by Premier Richard McBride, David Oppenheimer was publicly acknowledged as the "father" of Vancouver.

The earliest Jews in Vancouver, originating from Central Europe, had arrived via the United States, the British Empire and the earlier community of Victoria. They soon integrated into the language, way of life and relative affluence of Anglo society. But at the time of Vancouver's formation, events changed the origin and class of the typical Jewish immigrants. Russian persecution, completion of the transcontinental railway, and Canadian policy intended to populate the west all resulted in a flood of immigrants from Eastern Europe. While most of these newcomers settled on the prairies, a trickle found their way to Vancouver. Largely from old-country villages,

Morris J. Wosk, who has lived in Vancouver since 1927, has contributed greatly to its growth and development. He is well known for his philanthropic support around the world of education, health and welfare, industry, commerce, and the arts. Morris was awarded honorary doctorates from Simon Fraser University in 1966, and from the Hebrew University in Jerusalem in 1989. For his outstanding support of Israel he was presented with a Gold Medal by the State of Israel Bonds.

these Jews brought with them their folklore, their ages-old practices of Orthodox Judaism, and the Yiddish language. They settled in the town's working-class Strathcona district. Many were destitute and started out in business as peddlers. Others became storekeepers, or operated as artisans—tailors and shoemakers mostly—along the main business streets of Vancouver's early days—Water, Cordova, and Westminster (Main). Through hard work and mutual assistance almost all eventually gained a better livelihood and higher social standing.

Zebulon Franks was a typical example. A youthful scholar in his home town in the Ukraine, where his father was the rabbi, he witnessed the massacre of his family in a pogrom but escaped across the Austro-Hungarian border. Arriving at Vancouver in 1887, he established a store on Water Street which stocked "hardware, stoves, guns, and every imaginable article—from bucksaws to boots—needed by logger, fisherman, miner and trapper." Named after his wife Yetta, the business operates today as Y. Franks Appliances. Zebulon Franks was the first Jewish religious leader in Vancouver, and the earliest Orthodox services were held in his store.

In 1887, when a tract of land in the forest, now known as Mountain View Cemetery, was procured by the city for burial purposes, a separately fenced section was allotted to the Jewish community. In October 1891 Vancouver's first Jewish congregation Agudas Achim (Congregation of Brothers) celebrated the High Holy Days at the Knights of Pythias Hall on Cordova Street—now part of the Army & Navy store. The press reported on the Orthodox services as if describing an alien civilization: the headline read, "God's Peculiar People." In 1894 with the arrival of Solomon Philo, a German Reform rabbi who had previously ministered to the Victoria congregation, Temple Emanuel of Vancouver was formed. Thus, from the outset, a split developed between the more "Anglicized" Jews and their Yiddish-speaking strictly Orthodox co-religionists.

Samuel Gintzburger, long-term president of Congregation Emanuel, was the leader of Reform Judaism in Vancouver. Arriving from his native Switzerland at the age of 20, in 1887 he purchased 65 hectares on the site of present-day North Vancouver. Gintzburger traded with natives on the west coast of Vancouver Island, hunted seal in the North Pacific and Bering Sea, mined silver in the Kootenay, and joined the gold rush to Atlin. He later served on the first municipal council of West Vancouver, and eventually settled in Vancouver, where he became a real estate, insurance and financial agent, consul of Switzerland, and a citizen of substantial influence.

Another noteworthy person in early Vancouver was Justice Samuel Davies Schultz, a grandson of pioneer Victoria families, who in 1914 was appointed to the Vancouver County Court, the first Jew in Canada named to the bench.

Twenty-five years elapsed before Vancouver's Jewish community managed to build its first synagogue, the Orthodox Sons of Israel, a small wooden building in Strathcona, where the majority of the 250 Jewish families lived. A Hebrew school was also started in a nearby house, which grew into the Vancouver Talmud Torah. A pocket of upper middle-class Jews lived in the affluent West End, but this Reform group remained largely static, and by World War I the more numerous East-European community was predominant. In 1921 a new synagogue named Schara Tzedeck (Gates of Righteousness), seating 600 persons, was consecrated on the site of the first synagogue. A handsome building in traditional Mediterranean style, it is today a heritage landmark, restored for other uses. Nathan Mayer Pastinsky was the spiritual leader, a man of extraordinary sagacity and humanity who worked tirelessly among the immigrant population for 30 years. The Reform congregation suspended its plan to build a synagogue in the West End in order to unite the Jewish community under one roof. Not until 1965 was the Vancouver Reform Congregation reconstituted as Temple Shalom.

By the mid-1930s the Jewish community had grown to 600 families, and the structure of the community was firmly established in the founding of its many core organizations. In 1926 the Council of Jewish Women opened a Neighborhood House in Strathcona, superseded in 1928 by a Jewish Community Centre in Fairview. In 1930 the *Jewish Western Bulletin,* a weekly newspaper, was established. Today the Jewish Federation of Greater Vancouver is the central fund raising and planning agency for the community.

Faced with providing facilities to meet the particular needs of their immigrant group, Vancouver's Jews were often in the forefront of social services. The Hebrew Aid Society was one of the earliest of its kind in Vancouver, assisting needy immigrants with money, food, clothes and shelter, and giving aid to orphanages, hospitals and asylums. In 1924 the Vancouver Jewish Community Chest was organized, and in 1931 became the model for the city-wide organization. The Council of Jewish Women started in 1927 the free Well Baby Clinic, which was later incorporated into the Metropolitan Health Service. Three women who headed much of the cultural and philanthropic work of the community during this period were Rachel Goldbloom, Louise E. Mahrer and Anne Sugarman, who was also a driving force in the Vancouver Folk Festival and a leading Red Cross worker in World War II.

In the mid-1920s and 1930s, most Jewish income earners were

small business people, and a number of the retail merchandise establishments on Hastings and Granville, which had become the principal business streets, were owned by Vancouver Jews. Enterprises such as Wosk's Furniture and Appliance Stores, Toban's Quality Shoe Stores, and Sam Cohen's Army & Navy Department Store became familiar shopping places. Many of Vancouver's Jews resided south of False Creek in the newer districts of Mount Pleasant, Fairview, Shaughnessy and later Kerrisdale and Oakridge. By the end of World War II the Jewish community had completely deserted Strathcona.

With the growth of the second generation, Canadian-born and schooled, a demand arose for a modern congregation without segregation of the sexes and with greater English-speaking content. This led in 1932 to the inauguration of a Conservative congregation, Beth Israel (House of Israel), which reconciles traditional values of Judaism with modern forms, and today is the largest synagogue in the region serving 900 families.

Numerous Jewish stars of vaudeville and radio performed in Vancouver. Benny Kubelsky was playing the Orpheum circuit in 1922, along with the Marx Brothers, and accompanied Zeppo Marx to a Passover service in the home of David Marks, a Vancouver tailor. There he met Marks' daughter Sadie. The couple married in 1927 and in the heyday of radio, under the stage names of Jack Benny and Mary Livingstone, became a world-renowned comedy team. In 1946 the first Jewish home for the aged was opened by comedian and humanitarian Eddie Cantor, who gave a benefit performance in its support. Today this geriatric care facility operates as the Louis Brier Home and Hospital, funded by the legacy of a Yukon pioneer and philanthropist who made his fortune in the Klondike Gold Rush.

The post-war period has seen a many-fold increase in the Jewish population of Vancouver; 25,000 Jews live in Greater Vancouver today. The largest growth has come from a westward migration of second- and third-generation Canadians, particularly from the prairies. These people were graduating in large numbers from the universities as professionals, and arrived looking for new opportunities.

Jews have more recently come to Vancouver from almost every region of the world—the United States, South America, South Africa, the Middle East and the Soviet republics—resulting in a modern, highly cosmopolitan community. Occupations have become diversified to the point where one can nowadays expect to find Jews working in virtually all fields of endeavor.

From 1972 to 1975 a social worker, David Barrett, raised in the East End of Vancouver where his father ran a produce market, led the New Democratic Party in the first social-democratic government in British Columbia. He thus became the first member of the Jewish faith to be elected premier of a Canadian province. In July 1974 Simma Holt, a newspaper reporter, was elected member for Vancouver-Kingsway, becoming the first Jewish woman to serve in the parliament of Canada. Muni Evers, a pharmacist, served seven terms, from 1969 to 1982, as mayor of New Westminster. And Harry Rankin was a perennial alderman of Vancouver. From 1979 to 1988 Nathan T. Nemetz was Chief Justice of British Columbia. Jews have also served as chancellors of the provincial universities.

In contrast to other Canadian cities, there have been few cases of overt anti-Semitism reported in Vancouver. Rather discrimination has been more subtle; there was antipathy toward Jews in the social, fraternal, athletic, and business organizations of the general community, on the faculties of colleges and the university, and in employment. In current times, with equal employment and human rights legislation in place, and attainment by people of all ethnic backgrounds to the highest public offices in the province, discrimination has become infrequent. Reciprocally, Jewish institutions have opened their doors to other races and creeds.

With increasing affluence and the opening of new residential districts in the 1960s and 1970s, the Jewish population has continued to shift southward and westward. Oak Street between 16th and 57th avenues has become the Jewish "main street," where three synagogues, the Talmud Torah day school, the Jewish Community Centre, the Lubavitch Centre, a senior citizens homes and hospital complex, delicatessens and a book store are located.

The 1980s and 1990s have seen a significant shift of population to the suburbs. Recognizable Jewish communities have evolved in Richmond/Delta, the North Shore, Burquest (Burnaby/New Westminster/Coquitlam) and White Rock/South Surrey. Richmond in particular has had a long-time Jewish presence since the 1890s, when pioneer storekeepers Simon Petersky, Louis Rubinowitz and Henry Sisson operated in the fishing village of Steveston. Today Richmond is a bedroom community of professionals and retirees which has three synagogues, a Jewish Community Association, schools, and the Richmond Country Club.

As Jewish people have entered the economic and social mainstream the rate of intermarriage has risen to 50 per cent and concern has been expressed that Jewish distinctiveness and values are eroding. Nevertheless visitors have described Vancouver as having a vibrant Jewish community. Today there are fifteen Jewish congregations in Greater Vancouver, ranging from ultra-Orthodox to Reform.

As owner/manager of a chain of retail stores, hotel builder/operator, and real estate developer Morris Wosk has employed thousands of people. In 1946 he married Dena Heckelman. Dena, an accomplished violinist, is proficient in numerous languages. She was awarded a Gold Medal from the Royal Academy of Music, and in 1987 received the Torch of Learning Award from The Hebrew University. Mr. and Mrs. Wosk have four children—Miriam, Yosef, Mordehai, and Ken—as well as six grandchildren.

Some Other West Europeans
Jacqueline Wood

THE SPANISH

For a people that has never settled in the Lower Mainland in any great number, the Spanish certainly got off to an early start. In fact they were the first Europeans to chart the Northwest coast of North America. These early explorers included Juan Josef Perez Hernandez, who sailed up the coast in 1774 aboard the frigate *Santiago* and sighted the Queen Charlotte Islands; Bruno Hezeta, who in 1775 sighted the mountains of Vancouver Island; Juan Francisco Bodega y Quadra, who in the same year sailed all the way up to Alaska and claimed the coast for Spain; and Don Pedro de Alberni, who gave his name to the inlet on the West Coast of Vancouver Island, and by planting a vegetable garden at Nootka in 1791, became the first European agriculturalist in the province.

The first European to see the site of the future city of Vancouver was the Spanish explorer José Maria Narvaez in 1791.

Since then Spanish immigration has been sporadic at best. In the late 1930s an unknown number of Spanish refugees are believed to have arrived following the Spanish Civil War. To-day there are only about 2,000 Spaniards in the province, of which fewer than 1,000 are thought to live in the Vancouver area. In recent years many Spaniards have even decided to go back to Spain. One reason for that exodus is that Spain has thrived since joining the European Economic Community in 1986.

THE PORTUGUESE

The Portuguese arrived in the province later than the Spanish, but today they're a much larger community. Outside Toronto and Montreal, Vancouver has the largest Portuguese population in the country. At the start of the 1950s there were only about 100 Portuguese in the entire province, now there are an estimated 16,000 Portuguese in the Lower Mainland alone, largely concentrated in East Vancouver, North Vancouver and Richmond.

The first recorded Portuguese immigrant to British Columbia was Antonio G. Quintal from Madeira Island. By chance one day in August 1939 the skipper of a 12-metre English sailboat was looking for a crew member when it docked at the island's harbor. Hired for no pay, Quintal sailed across the Atlantic, passed through the Panama Canal, headed north up the coast and arrived in Vancouver in September 1940. He easily found work in his new homeland, first as a tugboat deckhand and later a ship's pilot. In 1947 he became a Canadian citizen.

But Portuguese immigration really only began after 1953 when the Canadian government encouraged thousands of Por-

The first European to see the site of the future city of Vancouver was Spanish explorer José Maria Narvaez in 1791

tuguese to work in the country's farming and fishing industries. Most of those who came were from the Madeira and Azores islands and wanted to improve their economic situation. Some went to Kitimat and worked in the aluminum industry, others became farm laborers in the Okanagan Valley.

Outside the Okanagan, the largest number of Portuguese reside in Vancouver, especially the city's East End, where the Portuguese Club of Vancouver is located. They have traditionally found work as laborers, carpenters, electricians, factory and service workers, and longshoremen; some eventually became small business owners.

While their economic adjustment was relatively easy, many had problems speaking English. The early pioneers often talked of Portugal in glowing terms to ease their culture shock. Today the community makes an effort to preserve its ethnic identity with year-round cultural events.

THE BELGIANS

Belgians aren't highly visible but they're out there, albeit in small numbers. It is estimated that there are from 3,000 to 5,000 Belgian immigrants in the province, most of whom live in the Vancouver area, but also in the farming areas of Chilliwack and the Okanagan Valley.

The earliest Belgians to come to the province were missionaries. Father Peter de Smet, a Jesuit who began his mission in the Kootenays in 1845, wrote the definitive record of the first impact of white settlement on that area and its inhabitants. In 1928 Leon J. Dupuis was sent by the Belgian Manufacturers' Association to promote trade. He then joined forces with the Honorary Belgian Consul, Leon Ladner, to form a Canadian-Belgian Chamber of Commerce.

Belgian immigrants have traditionally been skilled workers who hoped to improve their job prospects here, business people who wanted to make bigger profits, and war brides from both world wars. Over the past 10 years, however, many of the immigrants have been educated young couples who felt restricted in what they could do in Belgium and appreciate the free enterprise spirit that exists here. Belgians have always merged easily with Canadian society, and ethnic preservation has not been a priority within the community.

Ukrainians
Kevin Griffin

O N THE PRAIRIES, you can hear more Ukrainian spoken on the streets of some towns than in parts of Russified eastern Ukraine. But you won't find that in Vancouver. In the Lower Mainland, rather than outdoors, the Ukrainian-Canadian community lives inside, in family homes, churches and community halls.

Partly that's because of different immigration patterns. The much smaller Ukrainian presence here is due in large measure to Ukrainian agronomist Joseph Oleskin. After a visit to the Prairies in 1885, he left greatly impressed with the fact that a family could get 65 hectares of free land to homestead. But when he visited British Columbia, he thought the mountainous terrain was unsuitable for farming. He published his recommendations to emigrate to the Prairies in a series of widely read and influential articles and pamphlets in the Ukraine. As a result the Lower Mainland received only a handful of the 170,000 Ukrainian immigrants who arrived in the country between 1885 and 1914.

Despite the smaller number of Ukrainian immigrants on the West Coast, the province does hold one unfortunate distinction when it comes to the history of Ukranian-Canadians—the highest number of internment camps (eight) for Ukrainians deemed enemy aliens during World War I. Most Ukrainians in Canada in 1914 were from western Ukraine, then under control of the Austro-Hungarian empire. Despite advice from Great Britain that Ukrainians did not support the Hapsburg empire, the federal government decided to intern 5,000 Ukrainians in 26 camps across the country. Another 80,000 were classed as enemy aliens and regularly had to report their presence to the RCMP. After the war, most of the property and money confiscated was never returned. The issue continued to rankle Ukrainian-Canadians for decades afterwards and led to a national redress movement in the 1980s.

Unlike the farming communities on the Prairies, Ukrainian immigrants in the Lower Mainland tended to be mainly laborers. Rather than arriving with wives and children and putting down roots, many of the region's early Ukrainian immigrants were only here for a short stint before moving on to the U.S. or Eastern Canada in search of better opportunities. The earliest record of Ukrainians in Vancouver dates back to 1908, when the Ukrainian Club for working people opened on Alexander Street. Because many Ukrainian immigrants found themselves working in harsh conditions while building roads and railways or underground in coal mines, they became strong labor and union supporters and helped form the core of the socialist movement on the West Coast.

One of the strongest cultural and political organizations they formed was the Ukrainian Labour-Farm Temple Association. Known for its mandolin orchestra and choir, the ULFTA built a community hall in Strathcona at 805 East Pender in 1928. Twelve years later the hall was one of 108 seized throughout the country by the federal government because of the association's opposition to Canadian involvement in World War II. At the time the ULFTA supported the Soviet Union, which had yet to join the Allied effort against Nazi Germany. By 1943 the federal government removed its ban on the organization, but its members didn't regain control until two years later. To mark the return of their building, Ukrainian-Canadians formed a parade a block and a half long. Everyone clapped wildly when the signal was given to enter the hall's doors, which were decorated with a banner that read: "We are going back to our home." In 1946 the ULFTA changed its name to the Association of United Ukrainian-Canadians.

The seizure and return of the hall was the most dramatic event in the history of Greater Vancouver's Ukrainian-Canadian community. Besides the AUUC, the other strong, secular Ukrainian-Canadian community organization is the Ukrainian-Canadian Congress, a national organization that played a key role in organizing and promoting the countrywide events to mark the centennial of Ukrainian immigration in 1991. As well, many second and third generation Ukrainian-Canadians remain active members of either the Ukrainian Catholic or Orthodox churches.

Thanks to the Ukrainian-Canadian community, one of the most stunning pieces of religious art in the entire Lower Mainland is the nearly 10-metre tall mosaic of the Protection of the Blessed Virgin Mary at the Roman Catholic church of the same name at 560 West 14th in Vancouver. Made from nearly 250,000 pieces of colored glass, the mosaic by Boris Makarenko of New York depicts the Virgin Mary, whose outstretched arms are draped with an Omophor or protective veil. The mosaic refers to the legend of the Virgin Mary appearing with the Omophor over the besieged city of Constantinople in 911 A.D. The story goes that as a result of the vision, the Christian soldiers defending the city were blessed with a victory over the attacking Islamic army.

East and Central Europeans
Jacqueline Wood

As a young boy in Romania, Spiro Floresco enjoyed playing in the shadows of the castle that once belonged to Vlad the Impaler—fictionalized as Dracula. But as a young adult, the shadows were cast by communism and Floresco dreamed of his freedom. In 1968 he risked his life and defected. He slipped through Yugoslavia to Austria, and eventually got to Toronto. There he quickly found work in his field of chemical engineering. Five years later he became a Canadian citizen and finally obtained what was to Floresco the ultimate symbol of freedom, a passport. Today Floresco has two sons and lives with his wife in North Vancouver. He is the producer of East European TV, including the program Teleromania, for Rogers' multicultural channel.

Many East Europeans came to British Columbia during the days of the Iron Curtain, and many of them have similar stories to tell.

THE ROMANIANS
The Romanian community in the Vancouver area was small before the overthrow of dictator Nicolae Ceausescu in December 1989. But there are now anywhere from 10,000 to 15,000 people of Romanian origin living in the Lower Mainland. Most of the new immigrants are highly educated, says Floresco, but unlike the days when he came to Canada, they are finding it hard to find jobs without Canadian work experience.

THE HUNGARIANS
When Soviet tanks rolled towards the University of Sopron in Hungary on November 4, 1956, it was only by a quirk of fate that students from the school of forestry didn't die that day, and instead ended up in Vancouver. About 200 students had been guarding the road to Sopron when it became apparent that a saboteur had removed the firing pins from the Soviet 76 mm guns. One of the Russian soldiers suggested they go home, but instead the students crossed the border into Austria.

After meeting in Europe with the head of the Sopron forestry school, Canada's immigration minister Jack Pickersgill secured the acceptance at UBC of 196 Hungarian students and 24 faculty members. On January 24, 1957, they arrived in Matsqui, then were moved to Powell River. In September 1957 the Sopron Forestry School resumed at UBC, only closing its doors in 1961, when the last of its 140 students had graduated.

Of course, forestry students were not the only refugees to flee the Soviet invasion. At one point in 1957 there were 1,500 Hungarians housed at a camp at the Abbotsford airport.

Throughout the province, however, more than 7,000 refugees came at that time. By 1961 there were 2,200 Hungarians living in Vancouver alone.

Immigrants from Hungary first began arriving in the 1880s; most were laborers and farm workers who got jobs in the province's mines or on the railroads. World War I resulted in some immigration, but in 1921 there were still only 343 Hungarians scattered about the province. The Depression saw another migration of Hungarians, mostly from other parts of North America. This group included factory workers, loggers and many farmers. Many worked at the dairy farms of the Abbotsford-Huntington area, the orchards of the Okanagan Valley or did industrial jobs in Trail and Vancouver. The numbers grew yet again following World War II, but it took the events of 1956 to significantly alter the development of the Hungarian community in the Lower Mainland. There are now about 8,000 Canadians of Hungarian origin living in the Vancouver area.

THE POLES
The first significant wave of Poles arrived in British Columbia early this century—though they came directly from Japan, not Poland. They had been serving with the Russian forces and taken prisoner by the Japanese in the Russo-Japanese War of 1904. Most of them were economic immigrants who didn't want to return to Russian-occupied Poland, and instead settled on farms in the Lower Mainland and on Vancouver Island, or got jobs as railway workers. Combined with a small number of immigrants who arrived in the late 1800s, there were about 1,300 Poles scattered about the province by 1921. In 1926 seven friends started the Polish Friendship Society in Vancouver to maintain the Polish identity, preserve the Polish language and help new arrivals. In 1959 the association opened the Polish Community Centre on Fraser Street.

World War II brought about the second significant wave of Polish immigration. Under Canadian government regulations at the time, Polish war veterans were required to work on a farm for two years—despite the fact that many of them were highly skilled and would later go on to teach in universities or practise other professions.

In the 1970s many Polish seamen abandoned their fishing and grain ships docked in Burrard Inlet and sought asylum. Then in December 1981 Poland's Communist government began its crackdown on the Solidarity trade union and more seamen jumped ship. About 1,000 demonstrators, chanting "Solidarity Forever" marched from Robson Square to Pier B.C.

But Canada's huge refugee backlog in the late 1980s had serious consequences for several hundred Polish refugees in the

About 1,000 demonstrators chanting "Solidarity Forever" marched from Robson Square to Pier B.C.

Lower Mainland. While waiting for a decision on their claims, which were based on being a member or supporter of Solidarity, the Polish government fell and Canada rejected most of the applicants. Even so, today there are at least 20,000 Poles living in the Lower Mainland.

THE CZECHS AND SLOVAKS

Brother Pater Pandosy, an oblate, was one of the earliest settlers to arrive in British Columbia from Bohemia, and helped found the first permanent settlement in the Okanagan in 1859. But the first significant migration occurred at the beginning of this century when laborers, artisans and shopkeepers left underdeveloped areas of Slovakia and Southern Bohemia. Their integration was slow: most were single men who had little education and found English difficult to learn. By contrast, those who came to the province from other parts of Canada were already comfortable in the new society and prospered.

At the outbreak of World War II, the Czechs and Slovaks who were not citizens of Canada and therefore subjects of the Austro-Hungarian Empire were declared enemy aliens. They refused to serve in the Austro-Hungarian army, however, and joined the newly formed Czechoslovak National Association in America, which worked for an independent Czechoslovakia.

The new, democratic Czechoslovakia thrived following the war, and as a result few immigrants arrived here between 1919 and 1938. The Nazi invasion of the country in 1939 changed all that—political leaders, business people, professionals and intellectuals fled. Theodor, Otto, Leon and Walter Koerner were among those who came to British Columbia. Using their background in forestry, the four brothers formed the Alaska Pine and Cellulose Company. Today the Koerners are well known for their generous contributions to our intellectual and cultural institutions.

The next influx of Czechs and Slovaks occurred after August 1968, when the Soviet army invaded the country and put an end to what is known as the Prague Spring. About 1,200 professionals, students, writers, artists and service industry workers, among others, arrived. Today there are about 10,500 Czechs and Slovaks in the Lower Mainland—the majority being Czech. With the end of communism, Czechs and Slo-vaks come to Vancouver mostly as visitors now. In January 1993, Czechoslovakia peacefully split into the Czech Republic and the Slovak Republic.

THE CROATIANS, SERBS, BOSNIANS AND SLOVENES

It goes without saying that the people of the former Yugoslavia are not a tightly knit group in the GVRD. And since the dismemberment of Yugoslavia in 1991, they have became even more divided.

Over the past few years, about 70 per cent of all government-sponsored refugees to the province have been from the former Yugoslavia. Following the outbreak of war, a small group of Bosnian Muslims came to the province, but since then most of the refugees have been Bosnian Serbs—coming at the rate of 200 to 400 a year. (Through others are arriving from the region as independents or though family reunification.)

In earlier migrations Croatians, Serbs and Slovenes came as laborers, farmers and fishermen whose ethnic activity was based on their distinct national cultures and not that of a united Yugoslavia.

The Croatians make up the largest group in the province. In the 1890s a few families from the U.S. settled in the Ladner area and near Ladysmith at Oyster Harbour. A few hundred laborers and fishermen also arrived from the U.S. at the beginning of this century. In the 1920s and 1930s more came, this time directly from Croatia. In 1935 a Croatian Cultural Hall was built, but it closed in 1946. A large number of political refugees entered Canada following the war, including some professionals, business people, and many political activists who opposed the communist influence of Tito. In 1969, with the help of Croatian Muslims, a church was completed on East 1st Avenue in Vancouver.

The first Serb migrants, mostly single laborers, were also small in number and came via the United States. But after 1923 they chose to come here directly instead of going to the U.S. After World War II many Serbian political refugees arrived, some from German POW camps. A little later, once the communist government was installed, people from the skilled, professional and business classes largely settled in Vancouver. The small community's cultural life is centred around the Serbian Orthodox Church.

Early Slovene settlement was disrupted by World War I, for like the Croatians, Slovenes were treated as enemy aliens by Canada. Despite considerable hardship, a few hundred people settled here and by 1929 a branch of the Slovenian Society was opened in Vancouver. After 1945 the community changed slightly with the addition of artists and professionals. Today Slovenes rarely migrate here.

Japanese
Carol Baker and Naomi Uranishi

THE MOST VISIBLE Japanese in Vancouver today are the visitors who frequent the downtown hotels, such sites of interest as the Capilano Suspension Bridge and the numerous Japanese restaurants and shops on Robson and Alberni Streets. Vancouver has about 300 Japanese restaurants. Japan Air Lines, which has been flying into Vancouver since 1968, runs 12 flights a week in summer from Tokyo to Vancouver (about eight-hours' flying time). After Hawaii, Australia and Switzerland, Canada is the holiday destination of choice for the Japanese. About 250,000 visited Vancouver last year. Many of these were single young women.

That's quite a different situation from a century and a quarter ago when most of the Japanese arriving in Vancouver were single young men. They did not come to sightsee, shop, snap photos nor take home the prestige of having studied English in Canada. They came to work toward their dreams of riches, hoping to find a better life for themselves and their families.

Japan had been isolated from the world for a long time when in 1870 the new Meiji regime declared that, "During youth, it is positively necessary to view foreign countries . . . knowledge shall be sought throughout the world, so that the welfare of the empire may be promoted."

The first Japanese immigrant was Manzo Nagano, an energetic 19-year-old sailor who jumped ship in New Westminster in 1877. He fished for salmon on the Fraser River and worked as a longshoreman, merchant, salmon exporter and hotelier, setting the example for fellow countrymen who followed. Other settlers, mostly from southern Japan, struggled to make a living in fishing, farming, mining, in the timber trade and working on the railroad. Some enterprising immigrants built up good businesses. Arichika Ikeda headed north to what is now known as Ikeda Bay on Moresby Island where he developed a copper mine. Shinkichi Tamura built the New World Hotel on Powell Street and made a fortune exporting wheat and lumber to Japan. Y. Aoki—who employed 45 Japanese in his logging camp at Indian River—and other lumber barons in Port Moody and North Vancouver built up their businesses to nearly $ 1.2 million worth of timber exports by the mid-1930s.

At the turn of the century about 5,000 Japanese, mostly men, were living in British Columbia, mostly in the Lower Mainland. But Vancouverites resented the successes of entrepreneurial Asian immigrants and the fact that these Asians were paid half the wages that European-Canadians earned.

In 1907 whites rioted and plundered Chinatown, but when they hit the Japanese community on Powell Street they were met with flying rocks and fierce resistance. European-Canadians fought back with legislation limiting immigration of Japanese men but they neglected to mention women. So, Japanese men started bringing in "picture brides"—wives ordered from Japan, mostly through pictures shown to them by friends and relatives. One Japanese-Canadian employer of the time advised, "However goodlooking a wife may be, if she neglects her household duties by drinking tea or sightseeing or rambling on the hillside, she must be divorced." But the women worked as hard as the men, if not more so.

Although numerous Japanese fishing families lived in Steveston, the Japanese commercial centre for the province was Powell Street, which had developed because it was close to the Hastings Sawmill. There were Japanese shops, hotels and boarding houses, restaurants and ice cream parlors, a language school and a community hall, Buddhist and Christian churches and a sandlot for sports.

Some immigrants or *issei*, as they have come to be known, were realizing their dreams. During World War I a Japanese contingent fought for Canada, which had promised citizenship to the survivors. A monument to them stands near Lumbermen's Arch in Stanley Park. However, by the time citizenship was finally granted in 1931, only 80 of more than 200 soldiers were still living. They were the only Japanese in Canada with the right to vote.

The *issei* pioneers sent their children (the *nisei*) to school to study the professions but licences to practice were issued only to citizens on the voters list. At the start of World War II about 22,000 people of Japanese origin were living in the Lower Mainland. Some wanted to enlist to fight against Hitler but were refused.

Racism remained rampant. When, in December, 1941, the Japanese bombed Pearl Harbor in Hawaii, already half-way to North America, Canadians panicked. Fearing Vancouver might be next and that collaborators might be harbored aboard Japanese boats in Steveston, the Canadian government followed the American example and invoked the War Measures Act. Not only the entire fishing fleet, but also other businesses, radios, cameras and cars were confiscated. Newspapers were suppressed and language schools were closed.

Suspected spies and protesters were shipped to prisoner-of-war camps in Northern Ontario. The rest, about 21,000 in number, were moved from the West Coast inland to Kaslo, New Denver, Lemon Creek, Roseberry, Slocan City, Sandon, Popoff, Greenwood and Tashme, their dreams shattered. Families were forced to live in old mining shacks and rooming houses in overcrowded and humiliating conditions, cut off from the outside world and rejected by their chosen country.

Not a single Japanese-Canadian was ever charged with a treasonable offence, yet they remained undesirable aliens, unwelcome in most communities. In 1946, about 4,000 of the interned were sent back to Japan. British Columbians encouraged the others to relocate in other provinces. Many moved to Toronto although some did return to Vancouver.

Japanese-Americans had been allowed to return to the coast in 1945, before the war ended, but it wasn't until 1949 that the Canadian exile was actually over. That same year, the federal government finally granted Japanese-Canadians the right to vote. They had lived through years of hardship with perseverance and patience. Finally, they were free to rebuild their lives once more. And they did.

There are still fishing boats in Steveston, some belonging to Japanese-Canadians. The same smell of fish pervades as at the turn of the century but that's about the only thing that remains the same. The village has grown into sleek rows of big bold homes and cheek-by-jowl townhouses and condominiums, with a core of quaint boutiques, shops and fish and seafood restaurants. The Gulf of Georgia Cannery, located at 12138 Fourth Avenue, has become a national historic site and is open to the public (tel. 664-9009).

Powell Street has faded into a rundown remnant of the past, ripe for redevelopment. There are few Japanese here now except during the first weekend in August when resonant *takio* drumming announces the annual Powell Street Festival in Oppenheimer Park. *Issei, nisei* and *sansei* (third-generation Canadians) come from all over the country to celebrate their dual heritage. Now known as *nikkei*, Japanese-Canadians have been making the summer pilgrimage for the past 20 years to the first Canadian community of their ancestors.

There are now about 50,000 *nikkei* in Canada. About 16,000, along with 5,000 Japanese nationals, live in Greater Vancouver. The Vancouver Japanese Canadian Business Directory has 1,350 listings. TV and radio broadcast regularly in Japanese. The Japanese Consulate runs two Japanese movies every month. *The Vancouver Shinpo,* a weekly newspaper in Japanese, claims a circulation of 5,000. *The Bulletin* (circ. 2,500) is published monthly in English and Japanese by the Japanese Canadian Citizens Association. The JCCA, located at 511 East Broadway (tel. 874-8187), is the local communications, cultural and contact centre.

Nikkei Place, located at Kingway and Sperling in Burnaby, is scheduled for completion late 1997. The $25 million complex will comprise a 400-seat theatre for cultural events, a national museum and archives, various rooms for crafts and classes, a Japanese-Canadian garden, a seniors' residence and a health care home.

The *nikkei* no longer live clustered together but are scattered throughout the city and work in all walks of life. Some like to live in Richmond, while retired *nikkei* seem to prefer the North Shore. About 90 per cent of young *nikkei* marry people of other racial backgrounds. They shop at the local Safeways, buy their rice at Chinese shops and patronize such grocery stores as Fujiya on Clark Drive at Venables and Yaohan in Richmond for specialty items. City streets are filled with Honda, Mazda, Nissan and Toyota vehicles and almost every Vancouver home houses Japanese electronics in the form of telephones, tape decks, TVs and VCRs. B.C. imports from Japan run around $ 3.4 billion annually, while exports to Japan total around $ 5.6 billion. Japan receives 25 per cent of British Columbia's exports.

The first Japanese came for the salmon, salted it and shipped it back home. Salmon is still important to trade and to Japanese visitors.

Japanese fishing village, Steveston, 1905. cva

Indo-Canadians
Rattan Mall

A S MANY AS 130,000 Indo-Canadians in the Lower Mainland form a veritable multicultural society within the Canadian mosaic, drawn from such far-flung lands as Fiji, Guyana, Trinidad, East Africa, South Africa, Malaysia, Hong Kong and even Britain, bringing a fascinating mix of languages, religions and cultures.

Indo-Canadians are a vibrant and vital part of Lower Mainland society, occupying prominent positions in academia, business, politics and the legal, medical and other professions, besides forming a key component of the labor force. A rough break-up of Indo-Canadians in the Lower Mainland is 70,000 Punjabis (most of whom are Sikhs but also including members of other religions), 40,000 Fijians, 15,000 Ismailis, 5,000 Gujaratis and 2,000 Tamils and Telegus, as well as a variety of other groups.

Indo-Canadians have come a long way from 1897, when Sikh soldiers, then a part of the British Army, passed through Canada en route to India from London, where they had participated in Queen Victoria's Diamond Jubilee celebrations. Their stories of this gorgeous land led to 45 Indians in 1904 becoming the first immigrants from the Indian sub-continent.

In 1907 the B.C. legislature disenfranchised all "natives of India not of Anglo-Saxon parents" and barred them from logging on Crown lands and entering the legal and medical professions. The racist atmosphere was highlighted by the infamous *Komagata Maru* incident in 1914, when a Japanese freighter carrying 376 Indians (12 Hindus, 24 Muslims and 340 Sikhs) anchored in Burrard Inlet on May 23. Most of the passengers were denied entry and forced to depart on July 23.

It was only in 1947 that Indo-Canadians were given the right to vote. Moe Sihota (NDP—Esquimalt-Metchosin) became the first Indo-Canadian in Canada to be elected an MLA in 1986. He also became the first Indo-Canadian to be appointed a cabinet minister. In 1991 as many as four Indo-Canadian MLAs were elected: Sihota, Ujjal Dosanjh (NDP—Vancouver Kensington), who was appointed attorney general, has been a pioneer in the union movement, Harry Singh Lall (NDP—Yale-Lillooet) and Judy Tyabji (Liberal—Okanagan East), who later along with former Liberal leader Gordon Wilson (whom she married in 1994) formed the Progressive Democratic Alliance Party.

Among the prominent Liberal Party members are Dr. Gur Singh, former president of the B.C. Medical Association, and Gulzar Cheema, who was first elected as a Manitoba MLA in 1988. Indo-Canadians made their debut in federal politics in 1993, when Herb Dhaliwal was elected as a Liberal in Vancouver South and became a parliamentary secretary. Prem Vinning (Liberal—Surrey North) and Mobina Jaffer (Liberal—North Vancouver), who is also a prominent lawyer and social worker, made powerful though unsuccessful bids in 1993, and remain active in politics.

A slew of Indo-Canadian women play a prominent role in the professions. Suromitra Sanatani is the B.C. and Yukon provincial affairs director for the Canadian Federation of Independent Business. Tazeem Nathoo, senior vice president, operations, VanCity, is well known for community service. Raminder Dosanjh, wife of Ujjal Dosanjh, co-founded the India Mahila (Women's) Association in 1973 and is a famous human rights and women's rights activist. Shushma Datt established Rim Jhim—Canada's first Indo-Canadian radio station—in 1987 and broadcasts in Hindi and Punjabi. Another successful Indo-Canadian media venture has been that of Rajesh Gupta and Munish Katyal, who run the Indo-Canadian *Voice* weekly newspaper in English, *Voice Magazine* in English, *Awaaz* weekly newspaper in Punjabi and bring out an annual Indo-Canadian business directory. The *Link,* which in 1978 became the first Indo-Canadian English paper to be published in Vancouver, by Pramod Puri, is a twice-a-week publication. *Mehfil,* a glossy magazine brought out by Rana and Minto Vig in 1993 was the first of its kind. Among the Punjabi papers the most respected is the the *Indo-Canadian Times,* the first issue of which came out in 1978. Its editor, Tara Singh Hayer, was paralyzed when a Sikh extremist shot him in 1988. Other Punjabi papers include the *Charhdi Kala, Punjabi Tribune* and *Sangarsh.*

Indo-Canadians also figure in mainstream media. In TV there are Ian Hanomansingh, CBC national reporter for the past 11 years, Belle Puri, CBC reporter, Simi Sara, UTV associate producer and reporter, and Jaspreet Johal, BCTV reporter. In the print media, the best-known name is that of Salim Jiwa, who has been a reporter with the *Province* since 1983 and is known for his crime stories. Behind the scenes in the *Province* is Fabian Dawson, city editor.

Scores of Indians are now established in business. Many who started as laborers in saw and pulp mills or worked long hours picking berries now run their own mills and businesses. In the top rung are Herb Doman, Kewal Khosla, Asa Johal, who is also known for his charitable works, and Mohan Jawl, a Victoria-based businessman who was chair of the Pacific Racing Association (1993-95) that runs Hastings Park Race Course. Among other prominent businessmen are Firoz Rasul, who is also president of the Ismaili Council for B.C., Paul Dusanj,

Sikh Temple, Richmond, 1988. vs

Sadru Ahmed and Amir Ahamed.

Indo-Canadians have also made their mark in the world of higher learning and there are many Indo-Canadian professors at UBC and SFU. Prof. K.D. Srivatsava was vice president of UBC until 1994. Setty Pendakur, UBC professor of tranportation planning, was a Vancouver city councillor in 1973-74. The UBC chair of Sikh and Punjabi Studies was established in 1987 and Dr. Harjot Oberoi is the first incumbent. There is a Gandhi study section in the Institute for Humanity at SFU to which the Indian government donated 100 volumes and books of Mahatma Gandhi's writings and related works in 1995.

Two of the many Indo-Canadian doctors and dentists, Dr. Gur Singh and Dr. Arun Garg, have been presidents of the B.C. Medical Association. Among the many Indo-Canadian lawyers are two B.C. Supreme Court judges: Justice Wallace J. Oppal and Justice Tim Singh. Justice Oppal was commissioner of B.C.'s Royal Inquiry into Policing in 1992. The sole Indo-Canadian on the Provincial Court is Justice Gurmel Singh Gill.

With such a large Indo-Canadian labor force, there have been many Indo-Canadians in the forefront of the labor move-

ment. Besides Ujjal Dosanjh, other well-known figures are Raj Chouhan, Harinder Mahil, chair of the B.C. Council of Human Rights, and Charan Gill. Aziz Khaki has been president of the Committee for Racial Justice for the past 11 years.

Catering to a fast growing community are hundreds of Indo-Canadian restaurants and stores. Two main Indo-Canadian shopping complexes have appeared in South Vancouver—on Main Street from 48th to 51st avenues—and on the Surrey-Delta border—on Scott Road between 92nd and 96th avenues.

With Sikhs forming the majority of Indo-Canadians along with other Punjabis belonging to different religions, the Punjabi culture is naturally dominant. The latest craze in the pop culture scene is Bhangra Fusion. Bhangra is a Punjabi folk dance. Punjabi poets and writers include Ajmer Rode and his wife Surjit Kalsey, Ravinder Ravi, Kesar Singh, Gurcharan Rampuri, Sadhu Bining, R. Paul Dhillon and Phinder Dulai. Indo-Canadians are great fans of Hindi movies and Vancouver is constantly hosting dance and music shows of Hindi film personalities from India. In 1993 Salim Samji and Bob Jessa leased the Regal Theatre in Vancouver to start daily screening of Hindi movies.

Vancouver's first gurdwara (Sikh temple), built by the Khalsa Diwan Society, opened in 1908. Famous gurdwaras include the Nanak Sar Gursikh Temple and the Indian Cultural Centre of Canada, both in Richmond. The main religious event is the Baisakhi procession in South Vancouver organized by the Ross Street Gurdwara, built in 1969. Since 1994 the Sikhs in Surrey have an annual procession from the Guru Nanak Sikh Temple to mark Miri Piri. The Satnam Education Society of B.C. started the Khalsa School in Vancouver in 1986 and opened a branch in Surrey in 1992.

Surrey's Guru Nanak Temple was the scene January 11, 1997 of a riot between two opposing temple factions, described in the media as "moderates" and "fundamentalists." The RCMP had to be called in to quell the disturbance. An agreement was reached by the opposing factions a few days later to share the Temple's space, but in March 1997 the moderates announced plans to establish a temple of their own.

Hindus, the second-largest religious group, have several temples, including the Vishva Hindu Parishad Temple in Burnaby, which was built in 1973, the Hare Krishna Temple in Burnaby and the Mahalakhshmi Temple in Vancouver. The Ismailis have their own places of worship called Jamatkhanas, the main one being in Burnaby.

Chinese

Eleanor Yuen and P.K. Ip

THE CHINESE COMMUNITY of today is a heterogeneous, vibrant group blessed with diverse cultural, professional and social backgrounds. Between April 1994 and March 1995, the Community Airport Newcomers Network recorded a total of 18,200 new immigrants from Hong Kong, representing approximately 45 per cent of all newcomers landed during that period compared with 3,973 individuals from Taiwan and 3,921 from China, which together make up about 20 per cent. Continuing a trend started in the nineties, 70 per cent of them were destined for Vancouver, Richmond, Burnaby, Surrey, Delta and Coquitlam, in order of preference, ushering in British Columbia as the most favored Canadian prov- ince for Asian settlers. Today about 10 per cent of British Columbia's population is ethnic Chinese.

This so-called third wave of Chinese newcomers includes entrepreneurs, investors admitted under the Immigrant Investor Program and self-employed persons who invested substantially in real estate, hotels and the catering industries, manufacturing—especially in electronics and textiles—media and advertising. Much of the Hong Kong capital began to flow into the coffers of Vancouver in 1984, when the Sino-British Joint Declaration was signed and proclaimed the return of Hong Kong to China in 1997, whereas Taiwan investments surged significantly after Expo 86. Many were drawn by the beauty of the Vancouver region and the lifestyle.

The increasingly significant and diversified economic role played by the thriving Chinese here is well reflected by the establishment of official bodies such as Taipei Economic & Cultural Office and a new crop of business organizations which include the Vancouver Chinatown Merchants Association, Hong Kong Merchants Association of Vancouver, Taiwan Entrepreneurs & Investors Association, Hong Kong Canada Business Association, Richmond Asia Pacific Business Association, Sunbrite Business Association, Lower Mainland Independent Grocers Association and Canada China Business Council. Between them, they bring together businesspeople from the same region and companies with similar interests, and are instrumental in promoting local economies as well as international trade.

Once settled here, however, many do not find Vancouver an easy place in which to do business. A demanding and complicated tax system and government regulations nipped many Chinese businesses in the bud. Frustration is shared by professionals, artists, scholars and skilled workers whose credentials and life-long experiences are not recognized. Statistics Canada in June stated that 24 per cent of ethnic Chinese take up managerial or professional jobs, though a much higher percentage hold post-secondary qualifications.

Living in a new economic and cultural environment is very taxing for immigrants who have to re-establish their identity, cultivate new networks, adjust old practices and strive to have their credentials recognized. Some come to believe that a better life awaits them in their country of origin and return to Hong Kong and Taiwan, jump-starting a host of phenomena associated with "astronauts"—people who leave their families here to work in Asia, flying back and forth for occasional visits. Some simply uproot the whole family and return to their homeland. This is a far cry from the era of the gold rushes and the Canadian Pacific Railway construction of the last century when laborers, miners and tradesmen left their families in war-torn and impoverished Southern China to look for gold in the Fraser Valley or for back-breaking and poorly paid jobs with the CPR, returning home only one or two times in their entire lives to see their families.

The majority of Chinese immigrants rely on their own media for information and leisure ideas. There are three major newspapers, two radio stations and two television channels delivering their services in Chinese. Modern Asian shopping malls such as Aberdeen Centre in Richmond provide a comfort zone to those who are more at ease with their own mother tongue. Over the last ten years, new Chinatowns have emerged in Richmond, Burnaby and gradually even in Coquitlam, and are fast becoming colorful tourist and cultural attractions as well.

In the political arena Chinese play influential and active roles in municipal, provincial and federal elections. Looking back, numerous battles have been fought and hurdles overcome since 1923, when the Asiatic Exclusion Act was passed, stripping the Chinese of their voting rights. The Act was repealed in May 1947, after which Chinese Canadians were allowed to vote in federal elections, become citizens and take up professions such as medicine and law, from which they were previously barred. In 1993 further changes to the electoral act allowed all Canadians living overseas, including those who have returned to Hong Kong and Taiwan for fewer than five consecutive years, to vote in Canadian federal elections.

By and large there have been three major stages of Chinese immigration. Immigrants belonging to the second wave of the 1960s were of more diverse background and talents when compared with their predecessors. Many were well-educated, high-income profesionals, merchants and skilled workers from

The Hong Kong Merchants' Association of Vancouver was founded in 1968 by Dr. David C. Lam, with the main objective being to assist Hong Kong businessmen to establish themselves in the business and professional sector of Greater Vancouver. The Association, with 225 members, also endeavors to bridge cultural differences and cultivate a sense of belonging to the local community. They are encouraged to contribute their talents and services to society making Greater Vancouver a true multicultural society.

Chinese workers on the Canadian Pacific Railway, circa 1884. cva

Hong Kong who sought refuge here from the social and political instability back home. In 1961 there were 15,223 Chinese in Vancouver, doubling the number a decade earlier. It doubled again a decade later. As a result of Canadian multiculturalism policy, many began to engage in hot debates about their ethnic identity. The post-1967 era also brought about new forms of community associations with a more activist orientation. The establishment of the United Chinese Community Enrichment Services Society (SUCCESS) in 1973 and the Strathcona Property Owners and Tenants Associations (SPOTA), formed in response to urban redevelopment in the Strathcona region, are notable examples.

Since the post-war years, new generations of leadership have emerged. Alongside the old-style China-born leadership, the Canadian-born (tushang), along with new immigrants from Hong Kong, South East Asia and China, injected diversity and energy into the organizations and the leadership style. There have been healthy tensions and at times conflict in the community as a result.

Compared with the Chinese who came in 1967, when the government introduced an immigration policy based on merit, new immigrants of the last decade brought with them more sophisticated taste and greater consuming power, and retained close linkages with their homeland. New consumer trends such

Taiwan Entrepreneurs and Investors Association in British Columbia (TEIA) is the largest business association in the Taiwanese community. Established in Vancouver on March 29, 1992 TEIA has more than 300 members. TEIA's mandate is to consolidate individual strength and experience for business development, and to uphold the honor and rights of the Taiwanese business community in Canada.

as the so-called "mega house" and luxurious car fleets gradually emerged. So did other splendid facets, such as Chinese cultural and artistic programs.

In 1971 diplomatic relations with China triggered an influx of immigrants from Mainland China who came here mainly to join family members. This pattern, however, has been changing over the last few years, which have witnessed the arrival of a sizable number of investors who bring with them a good measure of investments. Canada-China trade has also been increasing substantially.

Though small in number, low-key and living a unique lifestyle, ethnic Chinese from South East Asian countries such as Singapore, the Philippines and Malaysia form part of the kaleidoscopic Chinese Canadian population. All in all, the Chinese community in Vancouver is a rich multi-cultural mix in its own right.

The metamorphosis from uneducated rural workers to sophisticated urbanites has spanned more than a century. The first Chinese settlers dated back to 1858, when the discovery of gold in the Fraser Valley lured them up from San Francisco. Between 1881 and 1885 a great influx of Chinese workers flocked to British Columbia to help build the British Columbian section of the CPR. Seventeen thousand Chinese came. They were paid half the wage their white counterparts received. About six hundred Chinese died during the construction of the railway.

With the completion of the CPR, the Chinese were out of work. Many were stranded in Vancouver, an environment fueled with racial hostility and suspicion. Many anti-Chinese organizations mushroomed. The extent of the discrimination was bared when more than 24 anti-Chinese items of legislation were promulgated in British Columbia between 1878 and 1913, including a law prohibiting Chinese from working on provincial government projects. Chinese immigrants were levied a head tax and by 1903 they were charged $500 per head. Chinese women were not allowed to immigrate to Canada unless they were married to white men, reducing the Chinese population to a pathetic bachelor society.

Amidst racial hostility and discrimination from the white majority, the Chinese formed voluntary associations such as the Chih-Kung Tong to fend for themselves. In 1906 the Chinese Benevolent Association (CBA) was officially established. As a community based association, CBA consistently lived up to its mandate to provide social services to the community, to help resolve conflicts and disputes, to represent the Chinese community in its struggle for social justice and, more importantly, to lobby the government for repeals to the discrimina-

tory laws which had been victimizing the community.

Anti-Chinese sentiments lingered on. In 1907, when a rumor was spread that a mass influx of Chinese, Japanese and East Indians would arrive in Vancouver to take up jobs in the forest industry and the construction of the Pacific Great Eastern Railway, widespread violence erupted. A racist organization called the Asiatic Exclusion League was formed. A rally was initiated by the organization and a mob rampaged through Chinatown, destroying property and goods. The Chinese protested by holding a three-day general strike. In 1919 the white farmers of British Columbia started a campaign to prohibit Chinese from owning or leasing farmland. In 1920 the Children's Protective Association initiated the removal of Chinese students from the classroom. In the thirties several Chinese cafés were closed because they employed white waitresses, in violation of a restrictive law. This hostility and the many campaigns waged against the Chinese culminated in the passing of the infamous 1923 Chinese Immigration Act by the federal government under which only four categories of Chinese immigrants were allowed: diplomats, children born in Canada, students and merchants. The act was effective in halting Chinese immigration to Canada and inhibiting the growth of the Chinese community for the next 25 years. Within this period, only 44 Chinese landed. The first of July, the date the act was enacted, was thereafter observed by Chinese as Humiliation Day.

During the war years, hostility towards the Chinese shifted to the Japanese. Events in China almost invariably impacted on the Chinese community. The Sino-Japanese War and World War II brought the Chinese community closer together. People continued to maintain close ties with China through their clan associations, sending cash remittances and shipping the remains of deceased members home. The wartime contributions of the community also helped to change white attitudes toward Chinese Canadians.

The repeal of the 1923 act renewed the growth of the community. From 1950 to 1959 an average of more than 2,000 Chinese came each year. Between 1947 and 1962, 24,000 arrived. Vancouver now had the largest Chinese community, and British Columbia the largest concentration of Chinese in Canada.

With hard work and resourcefulness the Chinese community continued to grow and prosper. Despite negative reactions from mainstream society, the values and contributions of the new immigrants were appreciated. Their considerable wealth, talents and business acumen, together with their efforts to assimilate into Canadian society, have set the stage for a dynamic future in Vancouver.

Vietnamese
Kevin Griffin

IT STARTED AS a trickle in the mid-1970s, but within a few years, the number of Southeast Asian refugees, most of them from Vietnam, had become a wave. During previous refugee crises since the end of World War II, the federal government had selected and brought in sponsored refugees. But this time the response was different. For the Boat People, as the Vietnamese refugees were called, Canadians for the first time opened their hearts and individually sponsored tens of thousands of refugees.

In Vancouver the first Vietnamese refugees began arriving in 1975, the year the U.S. finally decided to pull out of Vietnam and end its two-decade-long war against the Communist government in North Vietnam. With the Americans out and Vietnam united, the Communists started targeting the urban and professional middle and upper classes in South Vietnam, confiscating homes and businesses, and sending selected individuals off to re-education camps. As the repression intensified, the number of refugees increased.

A decisive turning point came in 1978. A rusty old freighter called the *Hai Hong* anchored off the coast of Malayasia that year, unable to unload its human cargo. Hung over the side of the boat was a sign in English: Please Rescue Us. Captured by TV news cameras, it was an image that showed up in living rooms in Europe, the U.S. and Canada. Images of hungry and homeless refugees stuck on what amounted to a floating casket tweaked the conscience of thousands of Canadians. Vancouverites were no different.

On a wet November in 1978 the first 15 Vietnamese refugees from the *Hai Hong* arrived in Vancouver. Former Saigon resident Tzee Kok Wu told of leaving in such secrecy that he was told of the boat's departure only an hour before it left. Wu and his four brothers and sisters made it in time but their parents were delayed a half hour and were left behind. Wu told of being so crowded aboard the boat he could only sit because there wasn't enough space to lie down. Of the 2,500 refugees crammed aboard the *Hai Hong,* about 600 arrived in Canada; 150 eventually arrived in Vancouver.

Throughout the late 1970s, stories about the Boat People continued to dominate international media coverage of Southeast Asia. Refugees told of paying exorbitant amounts to flee, only to find they were paying unscrupulous smugglers with no intention of providing safe passage. And if they managed to escape, they faced attacks from pirates who raped, looted and murdered defenceless refugees. Thousands are believed to have perished because their rickety boats sank in tropical storms. And if they managed to survive all that, many Southeast Asian countries were unwilling or unable to give them succor.

Locally the response reached its peak in 1979-80. In 1979 the provincial government, in part prompted by the situation facing refugees from Southeast Asia, passed a special act to help refugees resettle in British Columbia. In August the following year, Vancouver formed a special Task Force on the Boat People Rescue Project and opened a special refugee coordinating centre at 16th and Cambie. The centre wasn't so much a place for the refugees themselves to get help as much as it was for local residents to get information about sponsoring a Vietnamese refugee or to donate furniture, clothing or lend a hand. The City of North Vancouver declared September as Boat People Rescue Fund Month to focus attention on raising money for Vietnamese refugees and the GVRD sent letters to its member municipalities asking for funds and other support for the Boat People.

Eventually the arrival of the Boat People amounted to the largest single group of refugees ever accepted by Canada. Between 1975 and 1985 about 111,000 came to Canada, 14,000 of those to British Columbia. The peak year was 1980, when the province received almost 5,000 of the 35,000 that arrived in Canada. What was remarkable was that 30,000 were sponsored by individual Canadians, religious organizations and other non-profit groups. In fact the arrival of Vietnamese refugees marked the beginning of the country's private refugee sponsorship program.

Although most of the Boat People who fled Vietnam were Vietnamese, a significant minority—about 30 per cent—were Vietnamese of Chinese descent. Many of them Cantonese-speaking, they constituted the bulk of the middle and large business community in Saigon and other centres. The ethnic Chinese faced increasing discrimination in Vietnam beginning in 1976, when all those who registered their citizenship as Chinese lost jobs. Other Indo-Chinese refugees who arrived in the Lower Mainland include Laotians and Kampucheans (Cambodians), the latter fleeing the brutal regime of Pol Pot.

Within a few years of arriving in British Columbia, hard-working Vietnamese Canadians managed to open a variety of stores and restaurants throughout Vancouver, especially on the east side of the city around Kingsway and Fraser. The area is home to several Vietnamese clothing and food stores.

Other Asians
Ken Lundgren

THE PEOPLE OF Korea, Singapore, the Philippines, Malaysia, Indonesia and Brunei are represented in increasing numbers in the Greater Vancouver area. Some come to live, some to invest their wealth and many more come each year to visit.

KOREANS

In 1995 there were over 100,000 vacationers from Korea alone. The Korean consulate and the department of applied science at SFU promise this number will triple in the years to come.

There are also some 40 Korean churches, three Korean-language newspapers, a community centre and self help groups offering everything from language training to legal aid. The Korean community, which now numbers about 25,000 in the Lower Mainland, has established dozens of restaurants along with tour bus companies, hotels and retail stores. The relaxed trade agreement of 1994 between Korea and Canada, coupled with the economic growth that has propelled it from fourth poorest to twelfth richest nation in the past two decades, indicate it will become an even greater partner in Vancouver's future development.

FILIPINOS

In the mid 1950s, a handful of "pioneers" from the newly liberated Philippines found their way to British Columbia in search of an improved way of life and a means to help their families back home. In the sixties a first wave mainly consisted of nurses,

medical technologists, managers and engineers. Following them were clerical, sales, manufacturing and garment workers. Then, in the 1980s, desperate conditions under a state of martial law sent more than 30,000 Filipinos to work in Canada as domestics. Of these about 7,000 live in the Greater Vancouver region out of a total Canadian Filipino population of 45,000.

The Philippines is the third-largest English-speaking country in the world and boasts a literacy rate of 96 per cent. Many Filipinos still struggle to create a new home, far from a familiar culture and climate. They uphold a strong feeling of community, evidenced by the annual Filipino Days celebrations and active participation in cultural events. There are now Filipino television programs, newspapers, a Filipino-Canadian business directory and public-minded community groups. Discriminatory treatment of domestic workers and accreditation for professional qualifications are still a concern of many.

MALAYSIANS

There was very little immigration by Malaysians to Canada, or anywhere else for that matter, until the 1960s, when political stability and economic expansion made travel abroad not only practical but attractive. The Malaysian population in Vancouver is primarily of East Indian or Chinese descent and numbers about 7,000. They are mainly business and professional people and tend to keep to themselves even on national Malaysian holidays. As Malaysia continues to ride the crest of Southeast Asian prosperity, some are opting to return home for financial reasons.

SINGAPOREANS

If you've ever been to Singapore, you may be surprised to learn that the notorious Bugis Street in the nightlife district is named after one of the Malay peoples. (They don't particulary reflect the lifestyle of that street!) The Bugis and other ethnic Malays by and large make up the Lower Mainland's Singapor-ean contingent. There is an active Singapore and Malaysian Society and they often bring in entertainers from Asia.

INDONESIANS

Indonesia's economy is the largest in Southeast Asia thanks in part to huge natural resources such as mining, oil and gas, and also to recent growth in industry and manufacturing. Indonesia is also the country with the world's largest Muslim population.

As the diverse people of Southeast Asia and the similarly well concocted population of Greater Vancouver continue to mingle, we find ourselves in what has become anthropologically known as a "new growth circle." It means we shall be seeing a lot more of each other as these interesting times unfold.

facing page: Dancers practice for Year of the Rooster parade, 1993. vp

Latin Americans
Jacqueline Wood

LATIN AMERICANS are relatively recent arrivals to the region, but with steadily growing numbers they are becoming a significant group. The first big wave of Latin Americans to arrive were political refugees from Chile. They came following the overthrow of the Salvador Allende government in a military coup led by Augusto Pinochet in 1973. Many of the refugees had been tortured under the Pinochet regime, and although initially wary of others, the Chileans did much to spread the word here about human rights abuses in their homeland. While Chileans were the largest group to come in the 1970s, other South Americans who arrived during this period include Argentinians and Uruguayans.

Another large wave of refugees occurred in the 1980s when the military escalated its brutal war against the people of El Salvador. In 1983 the federal government introduced a special refugee program for Salvadorans, and in 1985 the community held its first public protest in front of the Vancouver Art Gallery. Other Central Americans who fled severe human rights abuses in their countries during the 1980s include Nicaraguans and Guatemalans.

Father Eduardo Diaz of the Hispanic Catholic Mission in Vancouver estimates that there are now about 20,000 Latin Americans living in the Lower Mainland. This diverse community also includes Colombians, Peruvians, Hondurans, Ecuadorans and Mexicans. The mission operates a number of assistance programs for Spanish-speaking refugees and immigrants, in conjunction with the Hispanic Community Centre. Diaz says they come here with a sense of being Chileans, for example, and not Latin Americans. One of the biggest challenges facing newcomers, he adds, is to feel they belong in Canada and won't be immigrants forever.

Although this is a loose-knit community, there is a festival in mid-September called Dia Alegre or Happy Day, when the people of several Central and South American countries celebrate their National Day.

Iranians
Hadani Ditmars

VANCOUVER'S IRANIAN POPULATION has tripled in the last five years. In certain areas of Lonsdale Quay in North Vancouver, shop signs in Farsi (Persian) are becoming the norm, and Persian restaurants, delicatessens and video shops are visible throughout the North Shore.

Prominent families such as the Khosrowshahis, who own Future Shop, have established themselves in the business community and Vancouver is now the home of well-known Iranian artists, architects and academics—many having arrived here in the last decade.

When asked to explain Vancouver's popularity with the nearly 30,000 Iranians who reside here, many recent immigrants point to Vancouver's natural beauty—and in particular the mountainous North Shore's resemblance to Northern Tehran—as a deciding factor.

Environmental factors aside, for many Iranians Vancouver represents a safe haven, far from both the political turmoil that brought the first major influx of immigrants here after the Iranian Revolution in 1979 and the post-revolutionary economic hardship and restrictions on personal freedoms that have encouraged a wave of emigration since the end of the 1980s.

A small Persian community did exist in Vancouver as early as the 1950s but it has really only been since the late Eighties that Iranians have come here in significant numbers. Although political tensions still cause some divisions within the Iranian community, a sense of cultural unity is slowly being fostered.

Schools, like Deh Khoda (named after a famous Persian philosopher) in North Vancouver, where children can study Farsi as well as Persian culture and history, and arts groups like Atash—a troupe that performs traditional Persian dances—are some examples of community projects that transcend politics.

Along religious lines, Vancouver's Iranian community is composed mainly of Muslims but it also contains a significant number of Bahais, as well as smaller minorities of Zoroastrians, Jews and Christians.

As there is only one Shia (the predominant form of Islam in Iran) mosque in the Vancouver area—the mosque in Richmond mainly frequented by Indo-Pakistani Muslims—efforts are underway to establish a new mosque where Farsi-speaking Muslims can hear sermons in their own language. In the interim worshippers meet for prayer every Friday at the Delbrook recreation centre in North Vancouver.

For many immigrants the transition from Tehran to Vancouver has not been an easy one. Culture shock and new social realities have particularly affected the adjustment process for women and young people.

But organizations like the Persian Independent Women's Group provide counselling and legal advice in Farsi, and North Vancouver Family Services runs a program for Iranian youth, many of whom experienced the trauma of being drafted into the Iran/Iraq war in the 1980s. In addition the Persian Immigrants and Refugee Association of B.C. acts as an advocacy group and human rights watchdog, monitoring cases of deportation.

The Vancouver Iranian community's developing cultural life is evidenced by publications such as *Daftar-E-Shenakht*, an international literary review published by North Vancouver-based novelist and poet, Payman Vahabzadeh. A recent performance of *Quest*, Morry Ghomshei's dramatic adaptation of classical Persian poetry, successfully premiered at the Vancouver East Cultural Centre. Vancouver-based artist Ali Koushkani, who plays the *santur* (a traditional Persian instrument), with often avant-garde invention, is internationally known. And Houshang Seyhoun, the renowned painter and architect who designed the famous Omar Khayyam mausoleum in Iran, has lived in West Vancouver for more than a decade.

A weekly Persian newspaper, *Shahrvand-e-Vancouver* (Citizens of Vancouver), was started in 1991 and has a national circulation of 20,000 (3,150 in B.C.) and a quarterly magazine aimed at the Zoroastrian community, *Pake-e Mehr* (Good News), has been in existence since 1994. In addition a weekly Persian show airs on Vancouver's Co-op Radio and *Byad-e-Iran* (Memory of Iran) is shown three times each week on Rogers Cable TV.

Restaurants such as North Vancouver's Casbah and the Caspian are known for their traditional Persian cuisine, and food for thought is available at Fruogh bookstore in Lonsdale, the only Persian bookstore in Vancouver.

Iranian architects like Foad Rafii, who designed the first buildings constructed on the north shore of False Creek after Expo 86 and the new mixed-use Woodward's building Downtown, have made and are continuing to make a significant impact on the changing face of Vancouver.

As Vancouver's new cosmopolitan attitude and natural beauty continue to attract Iranian immigrants, the Persian community will have an increasingly important role to play as *shahrvand-e-Vancouver* or citizens of Vancouver.

Africans

Zayed Gamiet

UNLIKE BLACK AMERICANS, whose migration into Canada can be traced back to the years of the Civil War in the 1860s, Africans from various parts of the African continent have emigrated to Canada and British Columbia on a significant scale only in the last 30-40 years.

The term "African" has a wider connotation than mere skin color. Africans identify themselves by nationality and not by the color of their skin, i.e., as Nigerians, Ugandans, Zambians, Ethiopians. Once they arrive in Canada they are usually identified as black, although South Africans describe themselves by their nationality, as South Africans, whether they are white, mixed-race, East Indian or black South Africans, or even Chinese South Africans, of whom there are a number in the Lower Mainland, mainly in the professions and business. Similarly do Zimbabweans, whether black or white, although there are undoubtedly hard-core white Zimbabweans who will never refer to themselves as anything but "Rhodesians." Indeed Africans are difficult to categorize racially, as, strictly speaking, Arabs in North African states such as Morocco, Tunisia, Egypt, Libya and Algeria are also Africans, although they identify themselves by nationality and not by race.

Another dimension to the African identity is that many Africans in Canada are from Francophone Africa, such as Gabon, Senegal, Chad, Zaire, Ivory Coast and Cameroon, fluent in French and in their own national languages. To add further to the complexity of the African identity, Africans in the former Portuguese colonies of Angola and Mozambique on the western and eastern coasts of Southern Africa are also fluent in Portuguese, having been ruled by Portugal for more than 400 years. Further, East Indians born and long settled in East Africa in Kenya, Uganda and Tanzania have migrated to Canada for well over 30 years. Hundreds came to Canada in the 1970s to escape persecution by the repressive regime of Idi Amin in Uganda, describing themselves as Ugandans and thereby identifying themselves as Africans.

Africa is a vast continent where many different languages and dialects are spoken. Swahili, the lingua franca of Africans in East Africa and part of Zaire, is not known in Central, West or Southern Africa. Indeed it is not unusual for Africans to have to use English, French or Portuguese to communicate with one another.

A number of Africans have come to Canada to escape natural disasters, wars and ethnic or political conflicts. Ethiopia, Biafra/Nigeria, Sudan, Somalia and Rwanda come to mind. The struggles against the minority regime in the former Rhodesia of Ian Smith and against apartheid and racism in South Africa and Namibia resulted in many Africans seeking refuge in Canada as political exiles, including a number of white South Africans, persecuted and harassed for active opposition to the oppressive system of apartheid.

However, most Africans seeking entry into Canada were not political exiles or refugees facing danger from dictatorial or racist regimes but were immigrants with skills and abilities who applied through the normal immigration channels, painstaking and laborious as these procedures often were, particularly for black and mixed-race Africans.

While most Africans entering Canada gravitated to Ontario and those from former French colonies to Montreal, the less rigorous climate on the Lower Mainland and more favorable economic conditions have attracted many Africans of all nationalities and ethnic identity, many of them professional or otherwise highly skilled persons. White South Africans and Zimbabweans have had little difficulty in adjusting to local conditions and finding positions suited to their professional and technical training, or starting their own practices as doctors, dentists and lawyers, after passing qualifying exams, or commencing business ventures.

Black South Africans, Zimbabweans and other Africans, however, have had to overcome resistance from private employers, government officials at provincial and municipal levels and public corporations, to secure employment commensurate with their qualifications and skills, and have faced rejection under the guise of lack of "Canadian experience," often a convenient cover for color and racial prejudice. Africans frequently have had to accept jobs well below their qualifications and experience to survive. Africans who have made the grade are to be found as teachers in schools, lecturers in universities or colleges, in technical and professional capacities in different levels of government, Crown Corporations such as B.C. Hydro and BC Transit, and in business enterprises, banks and other financial institutions.

Africans, estimated at some 20,000 to 30,000 in the Lower Mainland, tend to organize themselves into social and cultural groups based on their national origin. However, efforts have been made to organize them under a broader, single association embracing Africans from all over the African continent without regard to their race, nationality or ethnic or cultural backgrounds. In 1983 the African-Canadian Association of British Columbia was formed.

CODA PRINT COMMUNICATIONS

Tel 731-2126 Fax 733-3938

Cemeteries
Harald Gunderson

WHETHER IT BE FORT LANGLEY, Deadman's Island, Forest Lawn, Mountain View, Capilano View, New Westminster's Fraser Cemetery or Surrey's Victory Memorial, the cemeteries of the region provide a pastoral "pleasure ground" where visitors can escape the hustle and bustle of city life in an outdoor museum without walls. Here displayed are memorial stones, columbariums and mausoleums, and an attractive array of flora and fauna.

Early cemeteries reveal a forest of upright memorial stones, dedicated to those who were loved, while more recent burial grounds may call for memorials flush with the ground and special areas for inurnment of cremated remains.

As *B.C. Historical News* indicated: "Custom points to an interesting aspect of the sociology of death. It would appear that even in death, people prefer to congregate with those whom they share a common bond. The bond varies. It seems to be religion in the case of the Jewish people; nationality among the Chinese, Japanese, Greeks and Russians; membership in a lodge such as the Masons, Oddfellows or Knights of Pythias; or a disaster in which all died together as in shipwrecks or fires; or service to one's country such as the Royal Canadian Legion and their Fields of Honour." And there are the unannounced and rejected. Those who lie in unmarked pauper's graves or the 45 murderers who paid the supreme penalty.

The City of Vancouver's oldest and most controversial burial ground is Deadman's Island, a 2.8-hectare stretch of land surveyed by the Royal Engineers in 1863 and today the location of HMCS *Discovery*. In *The Stanley Park Explorer*, historian Richard M. Steele writes that both natives and non-natives used the island to bury their dead. Much earlier the Musqueam and Squamish peoples used the branches of the island's massive trees for their ornately carved funeral boxes. On the ground, simpler wood-slab tombs protected the remains of others, moss-covered and half-hidden by the ferns and salal.

Steele says smallpox appeared in the area in 1888, and by April of that year quarantine regulations were in effect. The epidemic raged for two years and a number of victims were buried on Deadman's Island despite the 1887 opening of the Mountain View cemetery. The epidemic's casualties "joined the bodies of British seamen, infants and suicides interred there," Steele writes. "To this day they remain on Deadman's Island; despite later developments none of the dead was exhumed."

Illinois-born Frank W. Hart and wife Amelia, who had started a small furniture factory, opened the city's first undertaking establishment in 1886 on Cordova Street. Hart also opened the city's first opera house and built Hart's Arch to welcome the first Canadian Pacific Railway train on May 23, 1887. He was well connected at city hall, being a pal of Mayor M.A. Maclean, and with help from the latter, Mountain View Cemetery was surveyed in November 1886 and opened in 1887 with Caradoc Evans, an infant, the first occupant. Since that time more than 135,000 deceased have been interred in Vancouver's only official burial ground.

Mountain View's manicured lawns and gentle slopes of today are a far cry from the early days. The *B.C. Historical News* recalled the Masonic funeral for Alderman Joseph Humphries: "To make a grim business even grimmer, the route to the cemetery was a steep, corduroy road, built over swampy land. When it rained heavily, parts of the road were under water and the timbers of which it was made tended to drift apart. On the Humphries' occasion, everyone except the deceased had to get out and walk across the swamp. Even then, one of the horses slipped between two of the timbers, the wheels of the hearse did likewise and the vehicle became mired in mud."

Superintendent Wayne Smith says there are 90,000 graves, many at double depth to hold two deceased, and the cemetery is spread over 42.5 hectares west of Fraser between 31st and 41st avenues. As many as 13,000 veterans are buried there, including five or six winners of the Victoria Cross. The city stopped selling plots in 1986, although there are 3,600 graves that have been bought but never used. Interments for indigents are Mountain View's main business today, but the city was said to be considering leasing the site to a private operator to cut the cemetery's annual deficit of more than $600,000.

It's little known that Vancouver started a second burial ground in Burnaby, about 1.5 kilometres north of the Lougheed Highway in the 1930s, with the burial of eight indigents. They were quietly exhumed in the 1970s. The burial ground was closed.

The Pioneer Cemetery is adjacent to St. George's Anglican Church at Fort Langley. Most of those buried there were Hudson's Bay Company employees or early settlers. A tablet on a large stone reads: "Among the many pioneers of the Langley district who are buried here are: Ovid Allard 1817-1874 and William H. Newton 1833-1875. Two faithful servants of the Hudson's Bay Company at its Port Fort Langley." The wrought iron cross attached to the church's western gable memorializes a Hawaiian-born employee and formerly stood in the cemetery. The first burial in the Fort Langley Cemetery was in 1882, when Robert Mackie, father of the municipality's first reeve, died. The cemetery is noted for its wrought iron grave enclosures, impressive marble and granite monuments, and mature landscaping.

The Royal Engineers started cemeteries in New Westminster at the corner of Agnes and Dufferin and between 8th Avenue and 10th Avenue, but these gave way to the 8-hectare Fraser Cemetery, opened in 1870 at 100 Richmond Street, located on a hill facing east and overlooking the Fraser River. Here you will find the earthly remains of such notables as "Gassy Jack" Deighton of Gastown, riverboat Captain William Irving, Raymond Burr of Perry Mason fame, and politicians and businessmen of yesteryear. Here you will also find special sections for members of the Masonic Order, the Oddfellows and the Church of England.

St. Peter's Roman Catholic Cemetery in New Westminster, opened in 1880, covers slightly more than 2 hectares.

New Westminster's Jewish Schara Tzedeck Cemetery is located at 23rd Street and Marine Drive on the boundary of New Westminster and Burnaby. There are many Jewish cemeteries spotted throughout the Lower Mainland.

And what of British Columbia's luckless ones? Those whose lives ended when a scaffold door gave way? In his book *Four Walls in the West—The Story of the B.C. Penitentiary,* Jack David Scott says there was one hanging at this institution, built in 1878 and closed in 1980. Prisoner Joseph Smith killed guard J.H. Joynson in 1912 and was executed January 31, 1913. Smith, and others who died of natural causes while incarcerated, were buried in a small cemetery across the glen from the top of the prison. Earl Anderson, author of *A Hard Place To Do Time—The Story of Oakalla Prison,* notes there were 44 hangings from the time the prison farm opened in 1912 to its close in 1991. Their remains would find a place in the pauper's section of Mountain View or Forest Lawn Cemetery, opened in 1924, or families would claim them.

"The Old Cemetery" on Lillooet Road in North Vancouver is located in a wilderness setting and was established in 1909 with the first interment in 1910. Its 9 hectares will allow for interments for years to come with more than 10,000 graves already in use.

West Vancouver's Capilano View Cemetery at 1490 3rd Street is another cemetery gem. Opened in the mid-1920s by the municipality, and with 7 of its 18 hectares fully developed, stone ruins have been used to form a columbarium wall with 502 rock and granite niches. Six satellite locations in a grove of mature trees offer the visitor a vista of great beauty.

Three corporations own four Greater Vancouver cemeteries.

Service Corporation International (Canada) operates Forest Lawn Memorial Park and Ocean View Burial Park in Burnaby. Forest Lawn was started by Albert F. Arnold in 1935 and is located at 3789 Royal Oak Avenue, while Ocean View primarily serves New Westminster and Vancouver's East End. Its location is 4000 Imperial Street, directly across from Burnaby's Central Park. Funeral homes occupy both sites, which were acquired by SCIC in 1969.

Spectacular, to say the least, is Ocean View's mausoleum, which underwent a $1.2 million addition in 1986. Perhaps one of Canada's largest mausoleums, it is adorned with a two-storey stained glass window and a marble statue carved from a single block weighing 2.5 tons and standing 183 centimetres high. There are approximately 4,500 entombments in the mausoleum as well as a large number of inurnments. The cemetery has 86,000 interments, with 30 of its 36 hectares developed.

Valley View Memorial Gardens, opened in 1954 by Arbor Memorial Services, is at 14660 72nd Avenue in Surrey. It also has a funeral home on site.

Opened in the late 1950s, the 13.8-hectare Victory Memorial Park has been a landmark, with its big white cross, in the South Surrey-White Rock area for nearly 40 years. Victory was acquired in 1984 by The Loewen Group, now the second-largest publicly owned funeral corporation in North America.

Newest cemetery in the Greater Vancouver district is at Whistler, opened in 1985 and comprising 1.3 hecatres, of which a fifth of a hectare has been developed for the community of 6,000. It's in a wood-like setting with a stream running by near Alta Lake Road on the west side of the resort municipality.

It is now 30 years since the Gardens of Gethsemani was opened by the Archdiocese of Vancouver. On May 10, 1965, work commenced on clearing a portion of a 23.4-hectare site in South Surrey. It was the first regional cemetery and mausoleum to serve the needs of Catholics and their families in the Lower Mainland. According to Rev. Msgr. Nunzio Defoe, executive director, there has been a recent addition of a second mausoleum with 190 crypts and 72 niches. There's also a full service Catholic chapel at Gethsemani.

There are other cemeteries just as important to their communities: Port Coquitlam at the top of Oxford Street, started in the 1950s; Surrey's municipally owned Hazelmere, Sunnyside Lawn and Surrey Centre; Maple Ridge's 6-hectare site at 21404 Dewdeny Trunk Road and the Burquitlam Municipal Cemetery, established in 1937.

All serve, and serve well. For as Longfellow wrote: "I like that ancient Saxon phrase, which calls the burial ground God's acre."

Catholic Churches
Ben D'Andrea

THE STORY of Greater Vancouver's Catholic churches begins with missionaries known as the Oblate Fathers. In 1858 the Oblates of Mary Immaculate (O.M.I.) established their first mission in British Columbia. St. Peter's, the church they built in New Westminster in 1860, became the offical centre of the Catholic Church. After the formation of the Archdiocese of Vancouver in 1908, the focal point of Catholicism in British Columbia shifted to the church that became Holy Rosary Cathedral.

St. Peter's in New Westminster is the oldest Catholic parish in Greater Vancouver. Soon after Father Leon Fouquet's arrival in New Westminster in 1860, O.M.I. cleared land to build one church for European colonists and another for the Indians. Unused for years, St. Charles Indian Church was demolished in 1910, but the parish of St. Peter's flourished.

Father Fouquet's original parish church was replaced by a cathedral in 1886. St. Peter's Cathedral on Blackwood Street was built in the Gothic style with wooden buttresses, pointed-arch stained glass windows and a 45-metre bell tower. In 1910, on the parish's 50th anniversary, the cathedral was enlarged. Decades later a powerful storm battered the cathedral beyond repair in 1934.

The present church of St. Peter's at the corner of Royal Avenue and Fourth Street was built for $35,000 in 1939 in the California mission style with a gabled tower and white walls. The church has statues that survive from the old cathedral—the Blessed Mother and Child, St. Joseph and Peter. The crucifix over the altar is also from the old cathedral. On the entrance floor the brass plate inscribed with the Oblate motto probably also came from the cathedral.

In 1908 the Archdiocese of Vancouver superseded the Diocese of New Westminster, and the Bishop of New Westminster, the Rt. Rev. Augustine Dontenwill, O.M.I., became Vancouver's first archbishop. As archbishop, Dontenwill approved the plan to build a new church for Holy Rosary Parish.

The Parish of Our Lady of the Holy Rosary is older than the cathedral that now stands on Dunsmuir Street in downtown Vancouver. Built in 1886, the parish's first church was also Vancouver's first Catholic church. Father Patrick Fay, the diocesan priest in charge of the parish, is believed to have pointed to the tallest tree on the hill above the waterfront and declared it the location of the new church.

When the Oblate Fathers assumed leadership of the growing parish, they decided to replace the small wooden church. Father J.M. McGuckin was appointed pastor and largely though his efforts construction began on a magnificent Gothic Revival church. Because of the parish's substantial debt, however, some parishioners opposed building a monumental church, which was dubbed "McGuckin's Folly." Father McGuckin died before his splendid "Folly" was declared a cathedral in 1916.

Opened in 1900, Holy Rosary Cathedral is the finest example of Gothic Revival architecture in Vancouver. Its asymmetrical towers are its most prominent feature, but its Gothic character is also reflected in the pointed arch of its windows and doorways, the vaulted ceiling, the sandstone carving decorating the cathedral exterior and the tracery stained glass windows. The stained glass window of the Church Triumphant in the Lady Chapel to the left of the altar is the cathedral's oldest. Made in Paris in 1896, this window predates the cathedral itself.

Of special note are the cathedral bells. Eight bells, tuned to a full octave, hang in the cathedral's 66-metre east tower. They are hung for change ringing, which means that the bells can be struck in varying sequences. Peal ringing consists of more than 5,000 continuous changes. Holy Rosary celebrated Dominion Day, 1911, by ringing the first peal ever heard in Canada.

The original wood-frame church of Holy Rosary Parish was the first Catholic church built in Vancouver. But the oldest surviving Catholic church in Greater Vancouver is St. Paul's Indian Church in North Vancouver. The Oblate Fathers established the Sacred Heart Mission for the Squamish Indians on the north shore of Burrard Inlet in 1863. Under the leadership of Father Fouquet and Chief Snat, a mission church was first built there in 1868. The present church was built in 1884. Added to the church in 1909 were the transepts and two 26-metre towers. New stained glass windows were also installed. The extensively reconstructed church was then renamed St. Paul's to honor the second Catholic Bishop of Vancouver, Paul Durieu, O.M.I.

St. Paul's was restored between 1980 and 1983. As a fine example of Gothic Revival architecture, St. Paul's has pointed-arch windows, a rose window and octagonal towers with dormers. The carved wood designs above the doors, however, are unique rather than Gothic in style. To further emphasize the parish's Indian orgins, a Coast Salish motif of geometric shapes has replaced the fleurs-de-lis around the church's interior arches. The church's original 250-kilogram bell of 1881, replaced when it developed a crack, is now displayed on the west lawn. St. Paul's is designated a National Historic Site.

Archbishop Dontenwill launched two new parishes in addition to Holy Rosary: Sacred Heart in Vancouver and St. Edmund's in North Vancouver. In 1905 the Oblate Fathers purchased the Protestant church on the corner of Campbell and Keefer in East Vancouver for $1,500. It became the Church of the Sacred Heart, Vancouver's second Catholic church. The present church was built in 1949.

St. Edmund's was built in 1908 on land provided by the Sisters of the Child Jesus. Father Edmund Peytavin, O.M.I., supervised the construction; consequently the church was named for Father Peytavin's patron, St. Edmund of Abingdon.

St. Edmund's was widened in 1949. Its side walls were moved out by three metres onto new foundations. Although redecorated in the 1960s, the sanctuary and its altars survive from the original church. In the 1970s a panel of icons was added to the sanctuary's back wall and medallions were painted along the wall of the nave. More recently two stained glass windows were found in the wall behind the altar and installed on either side of the sanctuary. Struck by lightning in 1988, the church's octagonal tower was subsequently repaired.

The Oblate Fathers built their third Vancouver church in Mount Pleasant. Built in the neo-classical revival style and opened in 1910, St. Patrick's had twin cupolas and a grand entry portico with Ionic columns. However, extensive repairs and restorations radically changed the church and, faced with financial problems, the parish sold almost all of the stained glass windows. Only one of the original windows remains: the window of the Sacred Heart of Jesus, made by the Standard Glass Company of Vancouver in 1912.

St. Andrew's Parish was established to serve the growing neighborhood south of St. Patrick's. Although the property was purchased in 1910, the first church of the Fraser area parish was probably not built until 1912. A new red brick church replaced the first church in 1954. St. Andrew's grew substantially in the post-war years, and the parish's third church was built in 1992.

New parishes were established to serve Vancouver's growing eastern neighborhoods. But the ten Catholic families living in Burnaby Heights also needed a church. The oldest Catholic parish in Burnaby is St. Helen's, and the parish's first church was built in 1912. Justice Kelly donated $6,000 toward construction costs, and at his request the church was consecrated in honor of St. Helen and in memory of his daughter.

A bigger church was built in 1956 to serve the expanding parish. The bell from the first church was moved to the new church. The parish's third church will be built in 1996 to meet the needs of nearly 1,500 Catholic families.

The Parish of Our Lady of Sorrows in the East Hastings area

Holy Rosary Cathedral, Vancouver, c 1900. cva

was the last Catholic parish established in Greater Vancouver before World War I. In 1913 the Servite Fathers used an unassuming building as both church and rectory. The parish initially consisted of 60 families, but by the 1950s this number had grown to nearly 500 and so a new church was built.

The largest Catholic church in Vancouver, the present church of Our Lady of Sorrows on Slocan Street, was built in 1959. The Servite crest was set in the floor of the sanctuary to honor the parish's founding fathers. A new parish hall was built in 1970, and when a 1971 fire destroyed the old rectory and church, a new rectory was built the following year. The church's original bell was installed in a remodelled bell tower in 1986.

The war ended the building of Catholic chuches, but only temporarily. Star of the Sea Parish in White Rock was established in 1923, St. Francis of Assisi in Vancouver's Grandview area in 1924, St. Augustine's in Kitsilano in 1931, Holy Spirit Church in New Westminster's Queensborough area in 1941, and St. Joseph's in Squamish in 1951. Today there are more than 60 Catholic churches in Greater Vancouver.

Protestant Churches
Lloyd Mackey

W HEN JOHN MORTON trekked through the forests of what would become Vancouver's West End in the 1860s, he little knew that his homesteading activity would impact for generations to come on the industrial, commercial—and spiritual—development of the new city.

One of the "Three Greenhorns," Morton, following the gold rush, had migrated west from England via New Westminster. With little knowledge of the virgin forest, but a good deal of courage, they were carving out a new life for their families on land where highrise towers would one day sprout.

As it happens, John Morton was a Baptist. For him, settling his 200 hectares also involved putting down spiritual roots. So he became one of the early members, in the 1880s, of Vancouver's little woodframe First Baptist Church.

The little congregation grew and, in 1911, built a towering new stone church at Nelson and Burrard, on property donated by Morton, kitty corner from the handsome tan-brick King George High School. They say that on Sunday mornings, you could clearly hear the church's bells away over on Kitsilano Beach.

In the early twenties the church was destroyed by fire. It was rebuilt by the fledgling Dominion Construction, headed by another Baptist, Charles Bentall, whose family eventually developed the Bentall Centre, a few blocks north.

In 1930 another new church was built across the street. It, too, was stone, but it was taller and longer. Its name, St. Andrew's-Wesley United, indicates it was a merger of two churches, one Presbyterian, the other Methodist, resulting from the formation of the United Church of Canada five years earlier.

Those West End Presbyterians who wanted no truck with the new church built themselves a small but impressive four-columned brown-brick church on the southwest corner of the St. Paul's hospital property just south of the two bigger churches. Then, in the 1980s, when the hospital needed more space, Central Presbyterian Church was replaced with a gleaming ten-storey hospital tower. Centralites moved across the street into a warm worshipper-friendly contemporary structure.

Closer to the city centre, the Anglicans had built their little cathedral at Burrard and Georgia at about the same time as First Baptist was settling in. "Little," we say, because it could have easily gotten lost on the altar of its mighty British 14th century forebears. But a cathedral it was, nevertheless. And some of the 1970s church pillars (of the human sort) were not about to let the younger and untaught leaders forget it. It was

about that time when developers wanted to pull down the cathedral and "bury" its congregation in an underground crypt molded sleekly into a tower dedicated to the god of commerce.

Throughout the years various downtown church properties were developed for other uses. Just a few years ago, developers tore down the Arts Club Theatre's former home at Seymour and Davie. In earlier years, it was the home of Seymour Street Gospel Hall.

As the downtown grew, a "holy huddle" developed across False Creek in the Mount Pleasant district, known in more recent years for clashes between residents and hookers. The huddle's most obvious landmark was the silvery spire of St. Giles Presbyterian Church, which successively became St. Giles United, Evangelistic Tabernacle and now an upscale condominium development retaining its heritage facade.

Across the street was the stubby stony structure of Mt. Pleasant Baptist Church. And within a few blocks could be found Tenth Avenue Alliance Metropolitan Tabernacle, Mt. Pleasant Presbyterian and Christ Lutheran. Today both the Baptists and Presbyterian buildings have largely immigrant congregations, from the Philippines and Korea respectively.

Across from city hall the Lutherans put up seniors' housing on their property a few years ago, incorporating their church into the housing complex design in a fashion the Anglicans had rejected in their downtown cathedral.

Various Protestant churches dotted the scene in and around Granville Street, stretching from Granville Bridge south to the Fraser River. At 12th and Hemlock stood the impressive domed Chalmers Presbyterian, later a United church and now the home of both Holy Trinity Anglican and Pacific Theatre, a Christian live drama troupe.

Redeemer Lutheran is a fifties structure in mid-Shaughnessy. A few blocks south is St. John's (Shaughnessy) Anglican, the place where Vancouver mayor Philip Owen worships, as did his late father, Lieutenant-Governor Walter Owen. Shaughnessy Heights United, just blocks south of St. John's and slightly to the west on 33rd, was until recently the home pulpit of Robert Smith, a brilliant orator and former United Church moderator.

Proceeding south, we encounter barbecue pit-like Granville Chapel and Trinity Baptist. Both churches are a contemporary blending of Asian and Caucasian worshippers. Many are younger people from Hong Kong who have chosen to assimilate rather than stay in Chinese churches.

facing page: St. James Anglican Church, Vancouver, 1954. Built in 1935-37 by English architect Adrian Gilbert Scott, the church is said to have been inspired by a cathedral in Cairo that Scott had designed. vs

Trinity, for its part, was a fifties merger of two churches. From the west came Kerrisdale worshippers, whose building was sold to the Christian Scientists. From the east were the folk from South Hill Baptist, a structure whose tall, square tower is still visible for kilometres from the 49th and Fraser area. South Hill's building has been subsequently occupied by two Chinese congregations, the most recent of Mennonite persuasion.

The last stop before the river is St. Stephen's United, formed in the sixties as one of the last of that denomination's rapid development of neighborhood congregations.

In other Vancouver neighborhoods, originally peopled mainly from British stock, Anglican, United and Presbyterian churches tended to dominate the ecclesiastical skyline. That was certainly true in Point Grey and the University area. Ryerson United, Kerrisdale Presbyterian, St. Helen's Anglican and University Hill United were among the best known. While the others stayed put, University Hill United moved to the Vancouver School of Theology at UBC, selling its building to University Chapel, a congregation with strong links to Regent College, an evangelical UBC affiliate.

On the North Shore many large, wealthy Protestant churches serve the affluent suburbs. West Vancouver and Highlands United are notable. St. Francis-in-the-Woods Anglican, with a scenic oceanside setting in Caulfeild, has become a favorite place for weddings. And so has West Vancouver Baptist, set among the tall evergreens just south of British Properties.

New Westminster, the mainland's oldest city, has maintained much of its British character long after other neighborhoods changed. And its churches reflected this. First Presbyterian, Queen's Avenue United, Olivet Baptist and St. Paul's Reformed Episcopal still have strategically located churches just uphill from the city centre, seemingly clustered around the more secular shrines, known as the Royal Towers Hotel, Douglas College and city hall.

Queen's Avenue United, with its white, fifties post-modern style sanctuary, was the crowning achievement of Will Wilding, the architect of some 150 Western Canadian post-war churches.

One New Westminster landmark for many years was the Loyal Protestant Orphan's Home, operated by the Orangemen of Irish Protestant fame. In due course, as the need for orphanages subsided, the site, adjacent to two large high schools, was taken over by a growing charismatic church, Royal City Christian Centre.

The civic governments of some of Vancouver's surrounding suburbs have attempted, in more recent years, to entice congregations into what may irreverently be called "church malls." In Burnaby, for example, Iglesia Ni Cristo (a Filipino-based group), the Evangelical Chinese Bible Church (with around 1,200 wor-

shippers) and the Hare Krishna (with a 12-metre high statue of their master) are clustered on Marine Way. And the city's leaders point out that there is room for more. Richmond has acted similarly adjacent to Highway 99, where Mennonite, Greek Orthodox, Islamic and Chinese religious edifices are clustered together, with some vacant properties still looking for spiritual buyers.

Most of Vancouver's suburbs have landmark churches—South Delta Baptist, near the highway to the ferry in Tsawwassen, Broadway Tabernacle in East Vancouver and Christian Life Assembly in Langley.

But tucked around the corners of most communities are tiny churches that development seemed to leave behind. Surrey has at least two—a Ukrainian Orthodox chapel, complete with onion-top tower, just steps from the Gateway SkyTrain station, and Christ Church Anglican in Surrey Centre. The latter is a rural congregation in south Surrey, not to be confused with Surrey City Centre, where the city's downtown is emerging.

Many Vancouver churches began as neighborhood congregations in the twenties and thirties. Congregants either wanted to walk to church or had to because they had no cars and the streetcar service was not the best on Sunday mornings. Over time some of those neighborhood churches died, merged or grew and moved onto larger and more generally accessible properties.

Consider the eastward migration of the Pentecostals. An enthusiastic and assertive Christian spinoff, the group had two neighborhood churches in Kitsilano, one at 4th and MacDonald, which was eventually replaced by a pub, the other at 6th and Fir, which gave way to an office building.

As more people took their cars to church, Broadway Tabernacle grew up. The church then moved south to Marine. Having moved, the tabernacle became, simply, Broadway Church. In the early nineties it outgrew its "new" 1,000 seat church and replaced it, across the street, with one holding 2,500 people.

Another different kind of Pentecostal church—Glad Tidings—was originally downtown, wedged between where the Queen Elizabeth Theatre and General Motors Place are now located. When it burned down in the fifties, its worshippers congregated for a while in a theatre near Joyce Street, then built a 1,000-seat edifice on Fraser, just south of Kingsway. Outgrowing that, too, they added a 2,500 seat high-tech worship centre, with the help of a $1 million contribution from their most famous member, businessman Jimmy Pattison.

South Hill Baptist Church's tall tower dominated a neighborhood that changed dramatically twice after World War II. The first change came when Henry and Arthur Block formed Block Brothers Realty, in part to sell houses being built by Mennonite developers in the south slopes areas. Many of those

homes were bought by Mennonites and others whose mother tongue was German—some Baptist, others Lutheran. Churches of those denominations multiplied. The Mennonite congregations included First, Fraserview and Killarney Park; the Baptists included Ebenezer, Bethany and Immanuel; and the Lutherans included First, Killarney Park and Prince of Peace. Large numbers of them came from Europe via the prairies or the Fraser Valley. The Blocks, themselves, grew up in Yarrow, a Mennonite community southwest of Chilliwack.

As more Asian people—both of Chinese and East Indian extraction—moved into those areas, the German-speakers scattered, many returning to the more distant suburbs close to the rural roots inhabited by their forebears.

Fraserview Mennonite Brethren, for example, moved across the Fraser into Richmond, where its cross-topped structure can be easily seen from Highway 99. Arthur, one of the Block brothers, still worships there. Its former south slope home became a Chinese Baptist church. While most of those Germanic-background churches have stayed put, some will move with time. Bethany Baptist, for example, has a new high-profile site between Queensborough and Alex Fraser bridges in east Richmond.

A more obvious example of the in-migration—and transformation—of the Fraser Valley Mennonite influence is Willingdon Church, just south of the B. C. Institute of Technology in Burnaby. Willingdon began as an ethnic Mennonite Brethren congregation of about 300 people in the fifties. It drew many of its members from the new subdivisions which sprouted at that time in west Burnaby and East Vancouver.

Its leadership determined to let it grow beyond its ethnic origins, however. It became attractive to people looking for a fair mix of evangelical belief and progressive educational programs, and has grown to a community of close to 3,000 people. Among them is a healthy Hispanic contingent of 300 and a singles organization of 50.

One family recalls being impressed by watching the Crystal Cathedral on television, then looking for a church like it in their neighborhood. Willingdon was their choice.

In the Fraser Valley's Bible Belt, churches often "hived off" as second and third generation worshippers looked for new ways of doing things. In Abbotsford the Mennonite Brethren and Christian Reformed churches (the latter of Dutch extraction) followed those modes. The first-generation immigrants were farmers and stayed in the original churches, while, in many cases, just down the street and around the corner, the younger teachers and business people developed new, more sophisticated churches. They did so while retaining their connections with the "mother churches."

Greater Vancouver's churches have sprung from many traditions. Vancouver is noted as being one of the most secular cities in North America, although the Fraser Valley Bible Belt provides a counter-balancing reputation.

It can be said of both Vancouver and the valley, however, that their churches are generally vibrant and outward looking, rather than being so heavenly minded that they are no earthly good.

above: Wesley Methodist Church (demolished) and Christ Church Cathedral (right) at Georgia and Burrard, Vancouver, c 1914. cva

Synagogues
David Berner

JEWS HAVE ALWAYS been wonderful about accommodating diversity. Why should Vancouver be different? From avant garde to Orthodox, from the most traditional to the most egalitarian and participatory, Ashkenazic, Sephardic and inventive congregations that are a creative mix of world traditions and modern needs, Greater Vancouver synagogues have it all.

Local Jewish historian Cyril Leonoff notes religious observance as early as 1887 in Mr. Zebulon Franks' hardware store and home on Water Street. Mr. Leonoff cites a Yom Kippur service in 1892 as the first documented public service. The local press took note and led with the headline, "God's Peculiar People."

Vancouver's first synagogue, built in 1911-12 on the southeast corner of Heatley Avenue and East Pender Street, was the B'Nai Yehudah (Sons of Israel). This wood-frame building was moved to the back of the lot and stuccoed over to match the new Schara Tzedeck when it was completed in 1921 at a cost of $65,000. Today that site is irreverently known as Beth Condo, since the old building became, as a part of the gentrification of the Strathcona neighborhood, a compact of privately owned apartments.

While the two great Oak Street synagogues, the Orthodox Schara Tzedeck and the Conservative Beth Israel stand within blocks of each other as public witnesses to the Jewish presence in Vancouver, synagogue life has never been more varied or vibrant in the Lower Mainland than it is today. There are fewer than 15,000 Jews but there are riches.

What do you want? Ultra-orthodox? The Heather Street Beth Hamidrash has become in its way the home of the Sephardic congregation. Reform? Temple Shalom, with 430 families, has the largest religious school in the city. Services in English and Hebrew are guided by "the Gates of Prayer" siddur. Women, called to the Torah and leading both services and policy meetings, are total participants.

Conservative Egalitarian? In Richmond? No problem. The Beth Tikvah, begun over 20 years ago, now boasts a new sanctuary, a Hebrew school, two choirs and a growing congregation of more than 300 families. Orthodox in Richmond? Eitz Chaim has grown from 11 families in 1977 to over 120 families and offers a full range of programs, including afternoon school.

The Beth Israel, with over 850 families, is both the largest congregation in Greater Vancouver and the largest Conservative synagogue west of Winnipeg. Like several local schuls, the B.I. strives to be a Bet Tefillah (House of Worship), a Bet Midrash (House of Study) and a Bet Knesset (House of Assembly).

Looking for a "traditional egalitarian Jewish alternative spiritual community in Vancouver?" Then look at Or Shalom in its new home on East 10th Avenue. Guitars, flutes, banners, tapestries, original songs, meditations and group aliyot are only the outward signs of a congregation that is not just different, but deeply committed to Jews of every kind. With over 200 members Or Shalom's immediately recognizable hallmarks are inclusiveness, warmth and a sense of community.

Remember also that there are congregations in Coquitlam, White Rock and West Vancouver. The Har El congregation on the North Shore is beginning construction on a beautiful new $3 million synagogue and community centre designed by architect Mark Ostry. The new facility will be located on the southwest corner of Taylor Way and the Trans-Canada Highway, amidst creek and towering trees and, with 170 families in membership, will strive to serve all Jews on the North Shore.

Many of the congregations listed, large and small, extend the full range of programs to members and public alike: daily minyan, Shabbat services, High Holidays, Bar/Bat Mitzvahs, weddings, funerals, youth programs, Hebrew studies, summer camps, social action groups, counselling and community outreach.

Beth Hamidrash *Sephardic Orthodox*
3231 Heather Street

Beth Israel *Conservative*
4350 Oak Street

Beth Tikvah *Conservative*
9711 Geal Road, Richmond

Burquest Jewish Community Association *Traditional*
New Westminster

Chabad House Kabbalah Centre *Chassidic*
3673 West Broadway

Chabad-Lubavitch *Chassidic*
5750 Oak Street

Eitz Chaim *Orthodox*
8080 Frances Road, Richmond

Har El *Conservative*
1735 Inglewood Avenue, West Vancouver

Lower Fraser Valley Jewish Community Centre
1349 Johnston Road, White Rock

Or Shalom *Traditional Egalitarian*
710 East 10th Avenue

Schara Tzedeck *Orthodox*
3476 Oak Street

Shaarey Tefilah *Traditional*
785 West 16th Avenue

Schaare Tzion *Orthodox*
8360 St. Albans Road

Temple Sholom *Reform*
7190 Oak Street

Eastern Religions
Deana Luchia

THE VAST PACIFIC OCEAN has proved to be a small obstacle for Asian migrants attracted to the promise of a new life in Vancouver. With this ongoing migration comes a rich variety of religious faiths practised in an array of shrines, temples and mosques throughout the Lower Mainland.

The largest Eastern religious community are the Sikhs, with more than 40,000 adherents. Many Sikhs began arriving in Vancouver from India at the beginning of the century (5,800 in 1906 alone), and they first established a place for worship in a rented house at 1866 West 2nd Avenue in 1906.

Another religion introduced from India is Hinduism, which is not as well established in the Vancouver area despite its widespread presence in Asia. Hindu workers first arrived in Vancouver in 1895 on the heels of a visit by Swami Vivekananda, India's spiritual ambassador.

Because of racist groups like the Asiatic Exclusion League, and legislation like the Canadian Immigration Act of 1910, which specifically barred immigrants from India, the number of arriving Hindus was a trickle compared to other ethnic communities. A formal association of Hindus was not founded until 1971 and today there are about 14,000 Hindus in the Lower Mainland.

Most Buddhists in the Vancouver area are followers of the Jodoshinshu school, which arrived in Canada from Japan at the turn of the century. The first Buddhist church (Bukkyo-kai) was opened in 1905, and operated out of the rented city hall until the following year, when a building was purchased at 32 Alexander Street.

Buddhism's influence grew steadily until World War II, when people of Japanese descent were forbidden to gather in groups and eventually forced to relocate to internment camps in the B.C. Interior. Their temples were sold, and when the war ended, most returned to Japan or went to Eastern Canada. Those that remained in Vancouver reopened services at the Hastings Auditorium, moving in 1954 to a site at 220 Jackson Avenue, where the Vancouver Bukkyo-kai continues to operate today. There are more than 31,000 Buddhists in Greater Vancouver, including many Chinese.

The first Muslim settlers came in the first few decades of this century, but most arrived after 1967, when immigration laws were relaxed. In 1971 John Norris wrote, in *Strangers Entertained*, "The three hundred Moslems in British Columbia are not an ethnic group in the proper sense of the word, but rather are members of a variety of groups, including Croats, Serbs, Albanians, Turks, Arabs, Iranians, Pakistanis, Indians, Chinese and Fijians.

Only the Pakistanis—numbering about a hundred—have more than a few representatives. Most live in the Greater Vancouver area." Today the 23,000 strong Muslim population is served by the Islamic Centre, established in 1964 at 655 West 8th Avenue, and by mosques in Richmond and Surrey.

SIKH
Khalsa Diwan Society
8000 Ross Street, Vancouver
Sikh Temple Sukhsager
347 Wood Street, New Westminster
Guru Nanak Sikh Temple
7050-120th Street, Surrey
India Cultural Centre of Canada
8600 No. 5 Road, Richmond
Nanak Sar Gursikh Temple
18691 Westminster Highway, Richmond
Akail Singh Sikh Temple
1890 Skeena Street, Vancouver
HINDU
Hare Krishna
5462 Marine Drive, Burnaby
Mahatakshima Temple
467 East 11th Avenue, Vancouver
Vishva Hindu Parshad
3885 Albert Street, Burnaby
Shiva Temple
1795 Napier, Vancouver
BUDDHIST
Buddha's Light International Association
6680-8181 Cambie Road, Richmond
Dharmadhatsu Buddhist Centre
3275 Heather Street, Vancouver
International Buddhist Society
9160 Steveston Highway, Richmond
Lions Gate Buddhist Priory
1745 West 16th Street, Vancouver
PPT Buddhist Society
514 Keefer Street, Vancouver
Universal Buddhist Temple
525 East 49th Avenue, Vancouver
Buddhist Churches of Canada
4680 Garry Street, Richmond
Tung Lin Kok Yuen Canadian Society
2495 Victoria Drive, Vancouver
Vancouver Buddhist Church
220 Jackson Avenue, Vancouver
World Vietnamese Buddhist Order
Chan Quang Temple
1795 East 1st Avenue, Vancouver
ISLAM
B.C. Muslim Association
12300 Blundell Road, Richmond.
Surrey Mosque
12407-72nd Avenue, Surrey
Pakistan Canada Association
655 West 8th Avenue, Vancouver

Education

GREATER VANCOUVER SCHOOLS are changing almost as fast as the rest of the region—largely because of upheavals elsewhere in the world. Vancouver Community College, for example, offers adult classes in English as a second language in the West End Community Centre; in 1995 they were full of students who had been TV producers, doctors, engineers, academics, actors and other professionals in pre-war Sarajevo.

Partly because China was about to resume possession of Hong Kong, Coquitlam schools in 1994-95 enrolled 1,333 students who had been born in the British colony. Thanks to Russian foreign policy at the end of the 1970s, Burnaby has 58 students born in Afghanistan. North Vancouver—which still remembers the Hallowe'en riot of 1965 as its worst incident of civil unrest—has 604 Iranian-born students whose families escaped something a bit rougher.

All told, Greater Vancouver public schools in the mid-1990s are dealing with a total student population of more than 260,000. Almost one-quarter of them were born elsewhere.

In Maple Ridge and Langley, the proportion is only five per cent. But the percentage of foreign-born students in West Vancouver is 22 per cent, in Burnaby 25 per cent, in Vancouver 31 per cent. In Richmond, just over one-third of all students were born elsewhere, including 4,000 from Hong Kong and another 1,000 from Taiwan.

But internal immigrants, especially from Ontario, are far more numerous than those from overseas, and a local baby boomlet is boosting enrolments. The ministry of education estimates that almost every Greater Vancouver school district will grow over the next decade, sometimes explosively.

In 1994, the total public school population of Greater Vancouver was 262,046. The ministry expects that number to rise to more than 307,000 by the year 2004, some 17 per cent.

Many districts will grow much more than that. Coquitlam will see a rise of almost 20 per cent. Maple Ridge will grow by 25 per cent. Surrey students will increase their numbers by 31 per cent, and Langley by a dramatic 50 per cent—from a bit over 18,000 to 25,000. At current class size (just over 23), that means Langley will have to find space for 275 new classes.

In the regional core, numbers will also increase. Vancouver's 13 per cent growth will mean serving an additional 7,567 students for a total of 63,551. Richmond will see another 2,600 students. Only neighboring Delta will lose students, with enrolments falling by 400 from current levels.

Greater Vancouver students are increasingly diverse. They come from almost every country in the world and bring both talents and disabilities. In 1994 programs for the gifted enrolled almost 13,000 Greater Vancouver students. Other programs served almost 14,000 children with moderate to severe physical and mental disabilities.

Almost 14,000 regular classroom teachers and department heads are working in Greater Vancouver schools in the mid-1990s. Thirty per cent of them have more than 20 years experience and are likely to retire within the next decade. We need to recruit and retain well over 5,000 new teachers to meet the demand in the growing schools of the next century.

A similar situation will arise in post-secondary education. Greater Vancouver colleges, institutes and universities currently enroll well over 100,000 students. Many post-secondary professors are now close to retirement, while growing numbers of students of all ages are seeking further education.

For the foreseeable future, Greater Vancouver schools, colleges and universities will deal with hundreds of thousands of students with highly individual backgrounds, needs, skills and ambitions. How well our schools (and our students) succeed will depend largely on the support, understanding and wisdom of the Greater Vancouver community.

—*Crawford Kilian*

facing page: Graduates at Simon Fraser University, 1990. vs
above: Computer class, Assumption School, 1993. vp

First Schools
Carolyn Bateman

FOR MOST ADULTS, the first day of school holds potent memories of chalk dust, bag lunches and new friends. But imagine if your first day of school was in the first school ever built in your area? And that to get there you had to cross forests full of animals or full-spate rivers, or at the very least trudge muddy, rutted trails? Getting to school was a daily adventure; one teacher's record book for the year 1899-1900 notes 475 tardies!

Still that first school day was one of immense pride for the pioneers who settled the dense woods of the Lower Mainland. A school meant permanency and learning, stability and culture. It meant they had arrived.

BURNABY—DOUGLAS ROAD SCHOOL, 1894
By 1892, when Burnaby became a municipality, about 250 people lived along two main roads, Kingsway and Douglas. So when the issue of a school arose, there was disagreement about where it should be. T.J. Trapp's offer of a free site on Douglas Road ended the stalemate and on January 22, 1894, 29 students and one young but enthusiastic teacher, Ethel LePage, entered the one-room school built for $975. Things went along smoothly for several weeks, but when a husky farm lad, objecting to LePage's disciplining, carried her bodily from the school, she resigned. She was replaced by Ellen Lister, a British school matron who sent those who misbehaved outside to chop wood.

COQUITLAM—PORT MOODY SCHOOL, 1884
The present school district of Coquitlam takes in a number of communities: Coquitlam, Port Coquitlam, Belcarra, Maillardville and Port Moody, whose future in 1879 seemed assured when it was named the terminus of the transcontinental railway (later this honor went to Vancouver). By 1884 the railway had brought boom times to the small town on Burrard Inlet and on May 1, 1884, a school opened with 25 children. Classes were held in Clarke's Hall, the upper storey of Tays' store. The first teacher, A.C. Dallas, received a salary of $50 a month. By July 4, 1885, a year before the first train reached Port Moody, the town had a four-room schoolhouse and attendance was more than 39.

DELTA—TRENANT PUBLIC SCHOOL, C. 1875
The first school in Delta, the Trenant Public School, was built by C.F. Green and A.R. Green about 1875. The neat, one-room structure was erected in the northwest corner of a 40-hectare land reserve over a kilometre from Ladner's Landing. Nellie Edwards was the first teacher and one can only imagine the job she had teaching children who had come from far away and were already tired by the time they reached the school. The Deas and Green children arrived by boat, often fighting waves in the sloughs to get there. But the department of education required a minimum average attendance to keep the school going, and in Delta in 1874 that average was sometimes difficult to maintain.

LANGLEY—FORT LANGLEY SCHOOL, C. 1867
By 1867 Fort Langley's importance as a military post had waned; land clearing and planting had replaced military drills and there were enough children to warrant a school. The first was built on a site donated by the Hudson Bay Company just west of the Old Fort near Derby Townsite (briefly considered as the colony's capital in the late 1850s). By 1872, when the first superintendent, John Jessop, visited the school on June 12, the teacher, James Kennedy, was in the process of being fired, school was about to close because of the mosquitoes, and there were no maps or blackboards. But by 1875 a new school had been built and the future of Langley's education was secure.

MAPLE RIDGE—MAPLE RIDGE SCHOOL, 1875
James William Sinclair, the first teacher in Maple Ridge, was 17 when he arrived with a suitcase and a map of the world. Maple Ridge's first school, built in 1875 on the north bank of the Fraser River near Nelson's Landing, was to see much service, both as a polling station and later as the municipal hall. School, delayed for two weeks because the mosquitoes were so fierce, opened with 16 pupils from six families. When Sinclair realized two families on the south side of the river were not sending their children, he bought a boat and ferried them back and forth every day. By 1877 it was the second-largest school on the mainland.

NEW WESTMINSTER—SAPPERTON SCHOOL, C. 1859
The first school in the Colony of British Columbia was in Sapperton, the Royal Engineers' camp near New Westminster townsite. On October 11, 1859, Governor James Douglas authorized a £160 grant and 28 children received lessons four hours a day from a soldier's daughter. New Westminster parents were not so fortunate. While there were more than 20 school-age children in the Royal City by 1860, Douglas did not act. It took the benevolent gesture of Presbyterian minister Robert Jamieson, who arrived in spring 1862, to get a school in the town: he taught 20 students in a cabin in his garden. By April 1863 Crown colony funds had arrived and the first public common school in New Westminster was opened, still in Rev. Jamieson's cabin but taught by James McIlveen.

Getting to school was a daily adventure. That first school day was one of immense pride for the pioneers who settled the dense woods of the Lower Mainland. A school meant permanency and learning, stability and culture. It meant they had arrived

NORTH VANCOUVER—MOODYVILLE SCHOOL, 1870

Education was a constant concern for Vancouver's early communities. Until the School Act passed in 1872, no public education was in place and parents relied on the fickle nature of the colonial government for money. In 1869 Moodyville received a $400 grant and a school was opened in August with 13 pupils and a school teacher, Laura Haynes of Bangor, Maine, in a cramped, ill-equipped classroom, hardly an auspicious beginning. School had to adjourn at noon for several months because of the choking smoke from the sawmill. But by 1876 a new and better located schoolhouse had a record number of 41 pupils outfitted with proper equipment. Education had come to Moodyville.

RICHMOND—ENGLISH SCHOOL, 1887

In Richmond the history of its schools and churches is entwined, for in these youthful communities, buildings served several purposes. In 1877, while the official-sounding North Arm School District had been formed, students attended classes not in a school but in the Methodist Church on the north side of the Fraser. Lulu Island students rowed across the river to attend classes taught by Miss Sexsmith, daughter of a school trustee. It wasn't until 10 years later that a school was established on the south arm of the Fraser for families in Steveston, the South Arm and east Richmond. Again the first school here, English School at London's Landing, had once been a church.

SURREY—CLOVER VALLEY SCHOOL, 1882

Sometimes one person can make a big difference. In Surrey that person was Henry T. Thrift, who arrived in Clover Valley in 1881. Thrift was always in a hurry. One day as he dashed along the road on foot he was overtaken by a man in a horse and buggy offering him a lift. "No thanks," said Thrift, "I'm in a hurry." Thrift didn't waste any time petitioning for a public school and on August 15, 1882, he organized a school meeting with two other trustees. They soon took possession of an old cedar shack close by and started making repairs and building desks. By 1883 the government built the first public school at Clover Valley on a site donated by Joe Shannon.

VANCOUVER—HASTINGS MILL SCHOOL, 1872

In the rugged community growing up around Hastings sawmill in 1870, there were only 11 school-age children. So it was a happy day for scholars when the Patterson family arrived with their four daughters. The men of the mill built the 5.5 by-12-metre schoolhouse in a stump-filled clearing 100 metres from the mill, well away from the noise and smoke. Georgia Sweeney, the musical daughter of the mill's master mechanic, was the first teacher and she made an impression on four-year-old Adelaide Patterson. "Before the day ended, Miss Sweeney had us singing songs and hymns with the aid of a tuning fork. I decided, then, I was going to enjoy school."

WEST VANCOUVER—HOLLYBURN SCHOOL, 1911

West Vancouver's first school owed much to the city's founder, John Lawson—its location, its name, even its unique existence. By 1910 the Lawson family, tired of the trek to Vancouver to attend church, donated land at 18th and Marine Drive for a church that was half wood structure, half tent. That first winter was harsh and the tent collapsed under the snow. A proper church was built, but to defray costs they rented it to the school board. While the building was the Presbyterian Church on evenings and weekends, on weekdays it was known as the Hollyburn School, named for the Lawson family's estate.

WHISTLER—ALTA LAKE SCHOOL, 1930

In the early part of this century Whistler centred not around skiing but fishing, not the mountains but Alta Lake. By 1930 there were several lodges, including the original—Alex and Myrtle Philip's Rainbow Lodge. Myrtle Philip was a pioneer of the first order. She helped run the lodge, kept a general store and was postmistress for 30 years. She was also instrumental in establishing the area's first school. When the government turned down her request for a school, she arranged to lease land from the railway and parents built their own. Myrtle was a board member until 1970, and when the municipality built a new school in 1976, it was named in her honor.

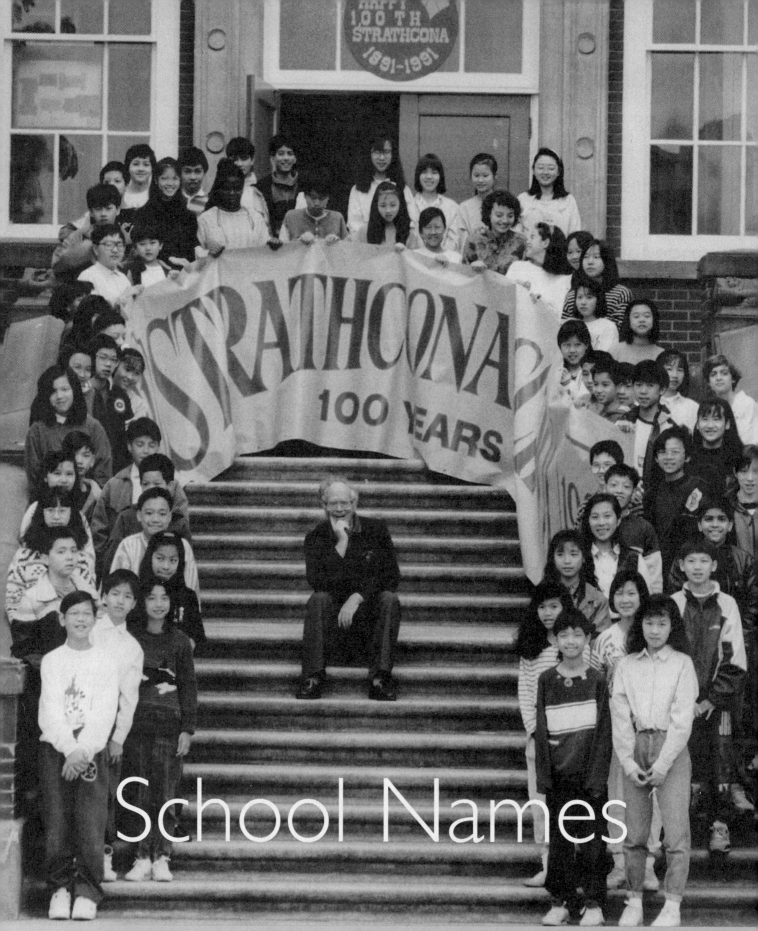

School Names

MacMillan Bloedel Limited

MacMillan Bloedel's roots go back to the early years of this century through its three founding companies: Bloedel, Stewart and Welch (primarily a logging operator); the Powell River Company (a newsprint manufacturer) and the H.R. MacMillan Co. (initially a lumber export brokerage). Today, as Canada's largest forest products company, we are proud of our contribution to the growth and prosperity of our province. On the following pages are a few milestones in British Columbia's forest industry history.

Origins of School Names
Laura Cozzens

MORE THAN 50 schools in Greater Vancouver responded to our invitation to have one or more of their students write a paragraph on the origin of their school's name. Laura Cozzens, herself a Grade 12 student at North Surrey Secondary, coordinated the student project. Uncredited material was adapted from *The Vancouver Book* (1976) assembled by a volunteer research team led by Mrs. Sherwood Lett.

BURNABY

CHAFFEY-BURKE ELEMENTARY Many people think our school name comes from the fact it's at the intersection of Chaffey Avenue and Burke Street. That is true, but there is more to the story. Chaffey Avenue was named after Charles F. Chaffey whose family home, Fir Grove, was constructed at Kingsway and Chaffey in the year 1902. Burke Street was named in a 1912 bylaw after William Burke whose family originally lived by Central Park. Chaffey-Burke School was going to be given a different name, but it was never altered. ELYSIA ALLEN age 13. Teacher: Ms. Cooke

COQUITLAM

MONTGOMERY ELEMENTARY Montgomery Elementary was named after British military leader Bernard Law Montgomery, first Viscount Montgomery of Alamein. He served in both world wars. During his years of service he gained numerous titles including commander of the British Eighth Army, chief of the Imperial General Staff and a deputy supreme commander of NATO. SARAH KNUDSON age 12

DELTA

GRAY ELEMENTARY Gray Elementary School was named after the Gray family which homesteaded on Gray Road (now 80th Avenue) in North Delta. The Gray family consisted of four members. Robert and Adeline were the parents who farmed the original homestead. The children, Robb and Samuel, were also actively involved in the farming activities. MATT MCLEAN age 10, grade 5

LANGLEY

NOEL BOOTH ELEMENTARY Noel Booth, born in 1897, was the owner-operator on one of the first general stores in Langley. His store also contained a post office, a travelling library and the only phone for miles. He was very active in local politics, being elected reeve, councillor, alderman and school trustee. Teacher: DOREEN MURPHY, on behalf of her grade 1 Class

facing page: Strathcona School centenary, 1991. vp

ALICE BROWN ELEMENTARY Alice Brown, 1906-75, was a student, teacher, librarian and principal in Langley from 1924-71.

ALEX HOPE ELEMENTARY A Langley school trustee, municipal councillor and reeve of Langley for eleven years before being elected to the B.C. Legislature for ten years. An instigator of the restoration of the National Historical Park of Fort Langley. Helped establish the British Columbia Insemination Centre for dairy cattle. His contributions to farming include chairmanship of the B.C. Coast Vegetable Marketing Board, B.C. Federation of Agriculture. KYLY FLETCHER grade 7, French Immersion, age 12

JAMES KENNEDY ELEMENTARY James Kennedy (1817-1902) was born in Ireland. Pioneer of New Westminster, B.C. Both an architect and a builder, he designed and constructed many of the city's first buildings. He also helped out by teaching, operating a ranch and building roads. His wife was the first white woman in New Westminster. CHRIS MADDOCKS age 12

D. W. POPPY SECONDARY David William Poppy is a second-generation pioneer and politician. Born in 1906 and currently living on the original homestead settled in 1886. His involvement in Langley municipal politics ranged from councillor to mayor during his 28 active years. In recognition of his dedication to the community, he was named Freeman of the Township of Langley in 1984. LAURIE POPPY age 17, grade 12

H.D. STAFFORD SECONDARY H. D. Stafford, 1904-78, was an educator who served the Langley area as district superintendent of schools for 19 years and the education system for 30 years. He was a graduate from the University of Alberta, who received an honorary life membership from the Canadian Education Association and the Canadian Association of School Administrators. MEGAN HELMER age 17, grade 12

NORTH VANCOUVER

HANDSWORTH SECONDARY The name Handsworth was given to our school because of its location on Handsworth Road. The name of the road, however, has a much more interesting origin. When the Capilano area was only a logging community, the workers lived in shacks near the Suspension Bridge east of the Capilano River and took ferries home on the weekend. These eventually became permanent homes and required street addresses. Residents, originally from Saskatchewan, applied to district council to name the street Handsworth, after their hometown, northeast of Weyburn and west of Moose Mountain. DANIEL GREEN age 13, grade 8

RICHMOND

J.N. BURNETT JR. SECONDARY John Napier Burnett, 1899-1989. Born in Fraserburgh, Scotland, moved to Vancouver in 1911. Served as lieutenant-colonel in World War II. Outstanding teacher, administrator and inspector of schools in the interior. President of British Columbia Teacher's Federation, member of UBC Senate. Named district superintendent for Richmond in 1955. LIVIA SURI age 16, grade 11

JOHN T. ERRINGTON ELEMENTARY J. T. Errington (from England, date unknown) was one of the first settlers in Richmond. His name appears on the petition for incorporation, and he was elected as one of Richmond's second council members. He was a principal owner of the Richmond Developing and Mining Company. NADIA PONA age 8, grade 3

TOMEKICHI HOMMA ELEMENTARY The time was 1865 and the place, Onigoye mura, Chibaken, Japan. Tomekichi Homma was born into an ancient Samurai family. Eighteen years later he came to Canada, settling in Steveston. From 1899 to 1900, he fought for the Japanese franchise in the district and supreme courts, winning both cases. The war years saw him evacuated to Slocan, but he was able to return to Vancouver during his later years. He passed away on October 28, 1945, at 80 years of age. HIDEMI UCHIAGE AND CANDIS MOORE, both grade 7.

ALEXANDER KILGOUR ELEMENTARY Alexander Kilgour was born in Fifeshire, Scotland and came to Canada with his family and lived in Quebec. He left his family to come to British Columbia which took a long time as there was no overland travel or Panama Canal. He settled in Richmond in 1862 and married Elizabeth Jane McDowell but had no children. Alexander Kilgour was a poet and philosopher and carried out the role of councillor from 1880-88. He died in 1908. The school opened on April 27, 1964. PAUL CHAMPNESS age 10, grade 5

DONALD E. MCKAY ELEMENTARY Donald E. McKay, 1884-1950. At 18, McKay arrived from Ontario and became one of Richmond's pioneers, farming in Steveston and along River Road. He contributed to the growth and development of Richmond as president of three agricultural organizations and through involvement in many business and community activities. He served as dyking commissioner and municipal councillor. LARA YULE age 11, grade 6

MATHEW MCNAIR SR. SECONDARY Mathew McNair (1889-1971) was an adventurous Scotsman who left his homeland and journeyed to Richmond at the age of 22. He donated much of his time to the Royal Canadian Army, the South Arm Church, the Kiwanis Club, and even founded the Richmond Christmas Hamper group. Named Richmond's Good Citizen of the Year in 1960, Mathew McNair's name carries with it a tradition of compassion and generosity. STEPHANIE CHUA age 16

HUGH MCROBERTS JR. SECONDARY Hugh McRoberts was a pioneer of Richmond. He was a talented road builder and he also applied dyking and draining techniques to help establish the Fraser Islands. In his later years, McRoberts devoted his time to agriculture and supporting the growth of the Richmond Municipality. He died in 1883 in New Westminster. ANNA LEGGO age 16, grade 11, EMILY TAN age 16, grade 11

R.C. PALMER JR. SECONDARY Robert C. Palmer was a Richmond city councillor from 1943-55 who was instrumental in the growth and development of the community. DIEGO DE MERICH grade 10

ROBERT J. TAIT ELEMENTARY Mr. Tait and his wife were pioneer farmers on Lulu and Sea islands. In the years 1908-10, Mr. Tait served as a councillor on Richmond's municipal council. In 1980 the current Robert J. Tait School was officially renamed and founded by the Hon. James A. Nielsen. KRYSTLE TAN age 12, grade 7

DANIEL WOODWARD ELEMENTARY Daniel Woodward, 1856-19??. In 1874 Daniel Woodward and his father settled on Lulu Island from Ontario. Settlers on Lulu Island and Sea Island decided to form a municipality in 1879, which happened on November 10, 1879. Some schools in the district were named after the settlers whose names appeared on the petition. It was then sent to the lieutenant-governor. Another memorial named after Daniel Woodward besides the school is Woodward's Landing. JULIE ASHIZAWA age 13, grade 7

SURREY

WM. BEAGLE JR. SECONDARY In 1954, Bill Beagle was a milkman for Dairyland, and a sax player. In the same year he was elected to the Surrey school board, a position he would hold for 16 years. He started the special education department. He also raised teachers' salaries. Beagle retired from B.C. School Trustees Association in 1972. JASMINE BAINS age 13, grade 8, RAVI GILL age 13, grade 8

BONACCORD ELEMENTARY One part of Surrey used to be called Bon Accord because there was a creek there called that. The creek is near the south end of the Port Mann Bridge, and local Indian people used to have their canoes on it. Bon Accord is French for "good agreement," so maybe there were some French people living there who became friends with the Indian people. Bonaccord School makes it one word. SEAN COCHLIN age 10, grade 4. (Thanks to Shirley Ripmeester for her assistance.)

HENRY BOSE ELEMENTARY Henry Bose was born in London, England in 1868. He moved to Surrey, B.C. in the 1890s where he farmed over 300 acres. Among many accomplishments Mr. Bose served one year on council, 35 as police magistrate and on December 3, 1965 schools doors opened honoring his name. OWEN BAXTER age 12, grade 7

In the 1860s, B.C.'s first big lumber camp was built at Jerry's Cove on English Bay—now Jericho Beach. Until then loggers had lived so near the timber that they could usually go home at night. So rich was the timber on English Bay that nine million board feet of Douglas fir were cut from 80 acres, including beams 112 feet by 28 inches used in the Imperial Palace in Peking.

CINDRICH ELEMENTARY Cindrich Elementary School first opened on September 9, 1993. The name of the school was selected to recognize the role of the Cindrich family in pioneering and homesteading this area in Surrey. The school presently consists of more than 475 children from kindergarten to grade seven. THE GRADE 5 CLASS

MARTHA CURRIE ELEMENTARY Martha Currie was a pioneer in the township of Cloverdale. She was loved by all because when new people moved into the area she would make them feel welcome, so she had many friends. The school district wanted to recognize her for her efforts and so named our school Martha Currie. DERRICK WILSON age 12, grade 7

WILLIAM F. DAVIDSON ELEMENTARY The name of our school came from a man named William F. Davidson who began his teaching career in 1938 in Surrey. William spent 3 years in the RCAF during World War II and later became a principal, supervisor, and director of instruction. He retired in 1976. KEVIN BALMER age 12, grade 7

FROST ROAD ELEMENTARY Frost Road Elementary is situated on land once owned by the Frost family. They owned 10 acres on Frost Road, now 162nd Street. The property was purchased by Surrey School District and the school opened in 1992. Today, over 225 children attend the school named in memory of the Frosts. KATHERINE BLANEY AND EMILY WIGHT both age 12 and in Mr. Sharma's grade 7 class

BETTY HUFF ELEMENTARY Ms. Huff was born in Chatham, Ontario. Her parents moved to Surrey when she was four. She began her teaching career in 1936 in Grandview Heights Elementary. After two years she moved to the old Simon Cunningham School. After a few years she transferred to White Rock where she became the primary Supervisor for Surrey. She also wrote a book on geometry called *Activities in Geometry.* In 1974 Ms. Huff retired; in 1976 the new elementary school was named after her. Since then Ms. Huff has been an active member of our school and she still is. AMANDA YU age 13, grade 7

JOHNSTON HEIGHTS SECONDARY James Johnston settled in the Sullivan area of Surrey in 1866. People called his 960-acre section the Johnston Settlement. It was located along 152nd Street, formerly known as Johnston Road. He built a house and cleared tall timber which took nearly three years to finish. Johnston Heights proudly bears his name because he was a hardworking pioneer and his spirit lives on in the students and staff who persevere and strive for success. TRACY CHU, age 15

KIRKBRIDE ELEMENTARY Neal Kirkbride and his wife, Estella May, were early pioneers in Surrey. They had six children. Mr. Kirkbride cut a trail, which became Kirkbride Road (122nd Street), into the woods so they could go to Kennedy School. In time, a school was built on the land that the Kirkbrides had pioneered. SONIA GREWAL, age 11, grade 6, CRYSTAL HALE, age 11, grade 6

LARONDE ELEMENTARY Mr. Louis Laronde (1882 - 1937) first owned the property that the school is on today. When he died, his two sons took over the property. They then decided to sell the property to the school district. When asking about names for the new school, Laronde Elementary was suggested. They decided it would be a good decision. RACHEL JAHNER age 12, grade 7

MCCLOSKEY ELEMENTARY McCloskey Elementary School was named for the pioneer McCloskey family who homesteaded near McCloskey Road (115th Street) and Gray Road (80th Avenue) in North Delta in the early 1900s. TINA MINHAS age 12, grade 7

EARL MARRIOTT SECONDARY Earl Marriott, (Feb. 24, 1906 - Nov. 16, 1992) former B.C. educator of 36 years and Surrey School District superintendent, was honored at his retirement in 1972. Mr. Marriott, keenly interested in "his" school, offered financial assistance to the graduation scholarship fund and the writing contest, both of which have been carried on by his family. SHELLEY A. TOMLINSON age 15, grade 10

SENATOR REID ELEMENTARY Senator Tom Reid came to Surrey from Scotland. He was a Liberal MP for New Westminster and later a senator. Tom Reid was a Surrey pioneer. He gave the municipality land that is now Bear Creek Park. The senator played the bagpipes, sometimes at special events in parliament. He died on October 11, 1968. Our elementary school opened in 1961. ADEL ASUNCION age 11, grade 6, TRUDY LE age 11, grade 6, PARIN PATEL age 11, grade 6

RAY SHEPHERD ELEMENTARY Ray Shepherd Elementary is proud to be named after a well-known White Rock pioneer named John Ray Shepherd. John was well-known for his 13 years of participation on the Surrey School Board, his establishment of the Pioneer Meat Market, and his many contributions to White Rock, and our community. NICOLETTE RIVERA grade 7

ERMA STEPHENSON ELEMENTARY After growing up in Rosetown, Saskatchewan, Erma Stephenson moved to Surrey, B.C. to teach at Fleetwood Elementary. As the primary consultant then later ranked up to primary supervisor, Ms. Stephenson accomplished excellent work for the school district. GILIAN ORTILLAN age 12, Mr. Beer's grade 7 class

TAMANAWIS SECONDARY The word "Tamanawis" is a Chinook word meaning one who teaches wisdom. Native people assumed that when they accomplished things, they did it through the empowering of their Tamanawis, which would make it an appropriate concept to be associated with a school. PARENT ADVISORY COUNCIL 1994

From 1912 to 1916, Harvey Reginald MacMillan (better known as H.R.) served as British Columbia's first Chief Forester with an annual salary of $3,000. He established the B.C. Forest Service and began a province-wide survey of the 100 million acres of forests to determine more accurately the size and nature of the resource—which he described in his first Annual Report as "unparalleled in any other country."

VANCOUVER

SIR MATTHEW BEGBIE ELEMENTARY Matthew Baillie Begbie was born on a ship sailing around the Cape of Good Hope, in the year 1819. He became a lawyer in England and arrived in Victoria, B.C. in the year 1858. He was its first judge. He travelled throughout New Caledonia on horseback. His courthouse was almost everywhere, one was a large tent. Mr. Begbie also had a nickname. He was called the "Hanging Judge" because he threatened to hang the juries, when they would not convict their friends. SOPHIA LEE age 9, grade 5, LESTER POON age 10, grade 5, CHRISTOPHER TUNG age 9, grade 5

GENERAL BROCK ELEMENTARY General Brock is generally agreed to be a war hero. He was mortally wounded at Queenston Heights on the Niagara frontier in the war of 1812, while defending Canada from American forces. He was born in 1769, and earned the titles of British major-general and administrator of Upper Canada before he died in 1812.

CARISBROOKE ELEMENTARY Carisbrooke Road was named in the early 20th century when the British-born members of city council changed many of the street names to old British names. Carisbrooke was one such road, renamed after the Carisbrooke family, who were lords of Carisbrooke Castle during Norman, Saxon and Medieval times. Carisbrooke School was named after this street. DEVON COOKE age 12, grade 7

SIR GUY CARLETON ELEMENTARY In 1910, the municipality of South Vancouver held a contest to rename its schools. Selkirk School won, suggesting the names of famous Canadians. Collingwood Heights was renamed Sir Guy Carleton in 1911. Carleton (1724-1808), first Baron Dorchester, British soldier and administrator, became lieutenant-governor and later governor of Quebec from 1766-78. He was governor-in-chief of British North America (1782-83, 1786-96). AMRIT TOOR age 12, grade 7

LORD CARNARVON COMMUNITY Lord Carnarvon, otherwise known as Henry Herbert, was a British Colonial secretary who introduced the British North America Act and helped smooth things over between B.C. and the Dominion Government during the years immediately following British Columbia's entry into the confederation. He died in 1890.

EMILY CARR ELEMENTARY Born in Victoria in 1871. Emily Carr followed her heart to the wilds of British Columbia where her bold and haunting artistic interpretations of native culture broke away from Canada's view of popular landscape paintings. Carr's unique style drew on the power of the land and the people. When age forced Carr to give up painting, she turned to a new canvas and created award-winning books. Emily Carr died in 1945. An elementary school was named in her honor on July 1, 1961. BONNIE MILLER age 10, grade 5

EDITH CAVELL ELEMENTARY World War I found this British nurse living life on the edge. Stationed in Belgium, she risked her life to help Allied soldiers escape to France or Holland. On October 11, 1915 she was arrested and shot by the Germans, becoming a heroine of the first world war.

CHAMPLAIN HEIGHTS ELEMENTARY This school owes its name to the "Father of New France," Samuel de Champlain (1570-1635). History remembers him as the French explorer, cartographer, colonizer, writer and founder of Quebec City.

SIR WINSTON CHURCHILL SECONDARY This school was named for the man who was Britain's Prime Minister during the years of World War II, and who, through his powerful oratory, kept his people's spirits up when the war was going badly for Britain and her allies. He lived from 1874 to 1965.

CAPTAIN JAMES COOK ELEMENTARY Captain James Cook (1728-79) is an British navigator and explorer credited for having made the first landing in the Pacific Northwest and the first chart of the coast line.

CROFTON HOUSE Crofton House School (established 1898) was named after the "Crofton Cottages" just outside Cambridge, which were used as overflow houses for women students, and in which the founder, Miss Jessie Gordon, had stayed while pursuing her studies in England. SIOBHAN CARROLL age 16, grade 11

G. T. CUNNINGHAM ELEMENTARY You may be familiar with Shopper's Drug Mart Stores. George T. Cunningham (1889-1965) founded Cunningham Drug Store and built it into a 52-store chain. The company later turned into Shopper's Drug Mart Stores. His parents left Guelph, Ontario travelling toward the Fraser Valley by cart. He was born during that trip, somewhere in North Dakota. His later accomplishments included being chairman of the Vancouver School Board, alderman for four years, and chairman of the UBC board of governors.

CHARLES DICKENS ELEMENTARY Charles Dickens (1812-70), was the most popular English novelist of his time. His powerful novels, such as *Oliver Twist,* hastened much needed social reforms. Dickens wrote *A Christmas Carol,* which introduced the famous character Ebenezer Scrooge.

SIR JAMES DOUGLAS ELEMENTARY Sir James (1803-77) was governor of the Colony of British Columbia. In 1843 he built Fort Camosun at Victoria. As first governor of the Crown Colony he was active in providing a road to the Interior during the gold rush of 1858.

SIR SANDFORD FLEMING ELEMENTARY If you decide to call your great-aunt in Toronto at 10 o'clock tonight and are dismayed when she informs you it is well past midnight by her clock, then you will be sure to remember Sir Sandford Fleming. He can be credited for the establishment of time zones across Canada. Postage stamp collectors will be interested to know that Sir Sandford, chief engineer of the Canadian Pacific Railway (1871-80), also designed the first Canadian stamp, a 3-penny Beaver issued in 1851.

SIR JOHN FRANKLIN COMMUNITY Sir John (1786-1847) was a British explorer in northern Canada. He surveyed a long stretch of Arctic shoreline and set out in 1845 to search for the Northwest Passage. All members of the expedition perished in the Arctic.

SIMON FRASER ELEMENTARY Simon Fraser was born to a family of United Empire Loyalists in the state of New York (not Vermont, as has sometimes been claimed) in 1776. His adventurous spirit led him in 1805 to establish the first trading post west of the Rockies, on Lake McLeod. Three years later, he followed the Fraser from Fort George to its outfall in the Pacific.

GARIBALDI ELEMENTARY Giuseppe Garibaldi (1807-82) was an Italian patriot and ardent republican who helped to secure the unification of Italy in 1861 by supporting the monarchy established under Victor Emmanuel II of Sardinia.

DAVID LLOYD GEORGE ELEMENTARY David Lloyd George School was named after the former prime minister of Britain who lived between 1863-1945. Prior to becoming prime minister, he also served as cabinet minister, chancellor and president of the board of trade. Lloyd George contributed a great deal to his country and in 1921 the Vancouver School Board named a school after him to celebrate his achievements. LEAH PELTON and CHANDEL BODNER both age 12, from Mr. Badchuk and Mr. Butchart's grade 7 classes

GLADSTONE SECONDARY William Ewart Gladstone (1809-98), prime minister of Britain four times.

GLEN EDEN SCHOOL The name Glen Eden School was made up by the names of two farms in Delta, where the school first started. The farms' names were Del Eden and Glenlivet. It's a good name too, because it's a place of new beginnings. Glen Eden is a school where kids can learn better. WILL DEMOOY age 12, grade 5, KEVIN SHERWOOD age 11, grade 6

GENERAL GORDON ELEMENTARY General Charles Gordon (1833-85) was a famous British soldier, noted for his part in the wars in China, the Egyptian Sudan and particularly in the siege of Khartoum, where he was killed.

SIR WILFRED GRENFELL ELEMENTARY Sir Wilfred was born in 1865 and chose to work as a medical missionary in the Newfoundland and Labrador area. He worked with Inuit and Labrador fishermen to build hospitals, nursing stations, agricultural centres, and libraries before his death in 1940.

ERIC HAMBER SECONDARY Eric Hamber (1880-1960) was president of B.C. Mills, Timber and Trading Company and later on, in 1913, Hastings Sawmills Co. He was director of the CPR and lieutenant-governor of B.C. 1936-41, and was chancellor of UBC from 1944-51.

HASTINGS ELEMENTARY Rear-admiral George Fowler Hastings was a popular man. Not only was the school named for him, but so were the street, the mill and the park. He was commander of the Royal Navy's Pacific squadron from 1867 to 1869. He visited what is now Vancouver harbor in 1867, after a seven-month voyage around the Horn from England to Esquimalt.

JOHN HENDERSON ELEMENTARY John Henderson (1880-1968) was a Vancouver school trustee for 21 years, beginning in 1943. He was named Vancouver's Good Citizen in 1961 because of his long service in a score of organizations and many personal deeds.

HENRY HUDSON ELEMENTARY Henry Hudson was an English navigator and explorer hired by English and Dutch companies to find the Northeast passage to the Orient. He also attempted to find the Northwest passage. What he eventually found in 1610 is known today as Hudson's Bay, which he initially assumed to be an ocean. His discoveries gave England her claim to the entire Hudson's Bay area.

ANNIE B. JAMIESON ELEMENTARY Dr. Jamieson is remembered as an outstanding Vancouver school teacher and vice-principal, school trustee and chair of the school board, chair of the senate and board of governors of UBC, and a founding member of the UBC Women's Club.

KERRISDALE ELEMENTARY Mr. and Mrs. William MacKinnon were asked to name a tram stop on the corner of 41st Avenue and Boulevard. They named it Kerrydale, in memory of their Scottish home town. Kerrydale means "little seat of the fairies." Kerrydale later became Kerrisdale and was adopted as the school's name.

KHALSA ELEMENTARY Khalsa means pure and this name was given to the Sikhs by Guru Bovind Singh Ji, the tenth Guru of the Sikhs. He initiated the Khalsa by administering the Amrit, nectar, to the Sikhs. The Amrit is made by the holy hymns of the Gurus. JAPMAN SINGH MALIK grade 6

KING GEORGE V British monarch, King George V, lived from 1865 to 1936 and won the deep respect of his subjects for his courage and devotion during World War I.

SIR CHARLES KINGSFORD-SMITH ELEMENTARY Sir Charles Edward Kingsford-Smith was an Australian aviator who, as a boy, lived with his family briefly in Vancouver. His skill and daring wrote an important chapter in the early history of long-distance flight. He captained the first flight across the Pacific

---

In 1938 Bloedel, Stewart and Welch (BS&W), founding company of MacMillan Bloedel Limited, became the first company in B.C. to plant seedlings in a logged-over area. By the late 1940s BS&W had been responsible for 70 per cent of all the reforestation carried out by private industry in the province. Today, MacMillan Bloedel plants about eight million seedlings a year.

Ocean. Kingsford-Smith flew with the Royal Air Force in World War I. His plane went down in the Indian Ocean in 1935 on a flight from London, England heading toward Australia, and he was never found.

LORD KITCHENER ELEMENTARY Earl Horatio Herbert Kitchener of Khartoum, to give him his full name and title, was born in 1850. He was a British statesman, field marshal and conqueror of the Sudan in 1898. As secretary of state for war he organized the British Army during World War I.

SIR WILFRID LAURIER ELEMENTARY Sir Wilfrid Laurier was a member of the House of Commons for 45 years. He was leader of the Liberal Party for 32 years. He was the first French-Canadian to become prime minster (1896-1911). Laurier promoted self-government for Canada. This excellent speaker spoke English and French fluently and worked to unite French and English speaking Canadians. ADRIENNE CHAN age 12, grade 7

L'ÉCOLE BILINGUE L'École Bilingue Elementary school is one of the first French bilingual schools of the province. Its English translation is "bilingual school." L'École Bilingue was originally named "Cecil Rhodes" after the British diamond miner who funded the Rhodes scholarship to Oxford University. The school's name was changed to L'École Bilingue in September 1977 because parents of Vancouver wanted a French immersion school.

LITTLE FLOWER ACADEMY Little Flower Academy is named after St. Theresa of Lisieux, the young Carmelite Sister canonized in 1925, noted for her childlike spirituality, she was given the title "The Little Flower of Jesus." In the ordinary routine of her simple life, she lived in faith, simplicity and love. DORIS TANG age 14, grade 9

DAVID LIVINGSTONE ELEMENTARY My school, David Livingstone Elementary, got its name from the Scottish explorer and missionary, Dr. David Livingstone. David Livingstone School opened in 1913 as an eight classroom school. Generally, up until now, it has gotten bigger. David Livingstone is a great school because of the friendly staff and hard-working students. It has great learning opportunities. STEFANIE ANTONIA DOIRON age 12, grade 7

DR. A. R. LORD ELEMENTARY Dr. Lord was born in Nova Scotia and became a prominent educator, British Columbia inspector of schools and principal of the Provincial Normal School. He was a member of the UBC senate (1936-50).

LORD BEACONSFIELD ELEMENTARY This school was named for the Earl of Beaconsfield, Benjamin D'Israeli (1804-81) who was twice British prime minister and thrice chancellor of the exchequer. Even so, he still had time to earn the title of English statesman and novelist!

LORD BYNG Julian Hedworth George, Viscount Byng of Vimy (1862-1935). He served in the South African war, commanded an army occupying Egypt in 1912 and took an active part in World War I. He was governor general of Canada from 1921-26. The National Hockey League's Lady Byng Trophy, awarded for sportsmanship combined with excellence, was donated in 1925 by Lord Byng's wife.

LORD NELSON ELEMENTARY Horatio Nelson was born in 1758 in Norfolk, England. After a distinguished naval career as admiral of the British fleet, he defeated the combined French and Spanish navies near Cape Trafalgar off the Spanish coast in 1805. This was his greatest victory and ended in his death. Nelson was loved for his devotion to God and his country. SANDY CHAN age 11, grade 6

LORD ROBERTS ELEMENTARY Lord Earl Frederick Sleigh Roberts was born in 1832 and went on to become a British field marshal, famous for service in India and Abysinnia (now Ethiopia). He died in 1914.

LORD SELKIRK ELEMENTARY Thomas Douglas Selkirk (1771-1820), the 5th Earl of Selkirk, laid the foundation for the settlement of the west. In 1811 he brought the first Scottish immigrants to settle in the Red River Valley, in an arrangement with the Hudson's Bay Co. The North West Co. almost destroyed the settlement at Point Douglas, but it survived as Fort Garry and eventually grew into the city of Winnipeg. Lord Selkirk died in France in 1820.

LORD STRATHCONA ELEMENTARY Donald Smith, Lord Strathcona (1820-1914), was the chief Montreal officer of the Hudson's Bay Co. in 1869. He became a member of Parliament in 1871, and drove "the last spike" of the CPR at Craigellachie in 1885. In 1886 he was knighted for his share in getting the CPR built. He also raised a regiment called the Lord Strathcona Horse for service in the Boer War.

LORD TENNYSON ELEMENTARY Lord Alfred Tennyson, a noted English poet who became poet laureate of England in 1850.

DR. H. N. MACCORKINDALE ELEMENTARY Dr. Hugh Neil Mac-Corkindale was a special kind of pioneer. He was a pioneer in novel educational concepts, a superintendent of Vancouver City Schools from 1933-54, a member of the UBC senate and an officer of the Canadian Education Association. A good person to be naming a school for!

SIR WILLIAM MACDONALD ELEMENTARY Sir William Christopher MacDonald, born in 1831, became a millionaire tobacco merchant. He was a chancellor and generous benefactor of McGill University. In Vancouver, he donated money for the establishment of two manual training courses for the school system.

In 1924 the H.R. MacMillan Export Co. established the Canadian Transport Company. Within a year of its formation the company had 14 ships under charter. Between 1929 and 1940 CTC was one of the world's biggest ship charter companies as it carried B.C. lumber and paper products to ports around the world.

SIR ALEXANDER MACKENZIE ELEMENTARY Sponsored by the North West Co., Mackenzie (1755-1820) was the first white man to make the journey overland across Canada to the Pacific in 1793. He reached the upper stretches of the Fraser River and the tidewaters at the mouth of the Bella Coola River.

SIR RICHARD MCBRIDE ELEMENTARY Sir Richard was a Canadian statesman elected in 1898 (as a Conservative) to the British Columbia Legislature. In 1903, at age 33, McBride became the youngest premier in the history of B.C. He served until 1915.

DR. R. E. MCKECHNIE ELEMENTARY Dr. Robert Edward McKechnie (1861-1944) settled in Vancouver in 1894 and became a distinguished surgeon. He was a member of the first congregation of UBC and was elected to the first senate of the university, later becoming a member of the board of governors. He became the second chancellor of the university in 1918 and retained that office until his death.

MAGEE SECONDARY This school was originally named King George, but so many people confused it with another school named King George in Vancouver that it was officially renamed in 1926. No one is really sure what year Hugh Crawford Magee was born, but we do know he was a successful pioneer farmer who took up land in Point Grey in 1867. He was the first farmer to settle the North Arm of the Fraser. He died in 1909.

CHIEF MAQUINNA ELEMENTARY Chief Maquinna was of the Haida Nootka Tribe and he welcomed Captain James Cook at Nookta in 1776.

WALTER MOBERLY ELEMENTARY Mr. Moberly (1832-1915) helped explore the Canadian Pacific Railway route across Canada, and built the Cariboo Road. The original school was built in 1911, but it burned down in 1945 and was rebuilt the following year.

FLORENCE NIGHTINGALE ELEMENTARY Known as the "Lady of the Lamp," this English nurse was the first woman to receive the British Order of Merit. She was influential in modernizing training for nurses and in 1854 organized a hospital unit for the Crimean War.

JOHN NORQUAY ELEMENTARY Mr. John Norquay (1841-89) was a memorable Canadian political figure. He was elected by acclamation to represent High Bluff, Manitoba in the first provincial assembly. He held many portfolios and eventually became the first premier of Manitoba in 1878.

JOHN OLIVER SECONDARY John Oliver, 1856-1927. Premier of British Columbia from 1918 until his death at age 71. Social legislation during his time included the Minimum Wage Law for Women and the Mothers' Pension Act. The village of Oliver, B.C. is named in honor of this former minister of agriculture and railways, who was nicknamed "Honest John." DONNA CHANG age 15, grade 10

DAVID OPPENHEIMER ELEMENTARY David Oppenheimer (1834-97) was the second mayor of Vancouver from 1887-91 and pioneered the development of transportation, lighting and water supplies. Some call him the "Father of Vancouver." He promoted trade and steamship communications between Canada and other countries. He established the park board, and officiated at the opening of Stanley Park.

SIR WILLIAM OSLER ELEMENTARY Sir William Osler, 1849-1919. The Canadian doctor known for changing the way medicine was taught. His students learned at hospital bedsides and became leaders of the profession. His *Principles and Practice of Medicine* (1892) was widely translated, including Chinese. JANICE TONG age 10, grade 5, JASMINE TONG age 10, grade 5

QUEEN ALEXANDRA ELEMENTARY Queen Alexandra, 1844-1925. Consort of Edward VII, whom she married in 1863 at age 19. She was from the royal Danish family. She had five children, two sons and three daughters. She was crowned queen in August 1903 in Westminster Abbey. Her husband died in 1910 one year after the school was built. She lived to be 81 years old. During her lifetime she liked wearing her jewelry, and enjoyed her pets. She was always dressed in a fashionable way. ROBERT NGUYEN age 10, grade 5

QUEEN ELIZABETH ELEMENTARY Named after the Queen Mother, a distinguished lady who was married to King George VI and is the mother of Queen Elizabeth II. In 1939 she visited Vancouver with King George and toured the whole area. They were among the first people to stay in today's Hotel Vancouver.

QUEEN MARY ELEMENTARY Queen Mary was the grandmother of Queen Elizabeth II. She was born in 1867, and a good way to remember that year is that it's the same year Canada was created. Queen Mary died in 1953, just two months before her granddaughter Elizabeth became queen.

QUEEN VICTORIA ANNEX Queen Victoria reigned in England for more than 60 years, from 1837-1901. The Victorian age was named for her, and she witnessed the rise and flowering of the British Empire. When early residents here were trying to decide on a name for the new capital of mainland British Columbia, it was Queen Victoria who decided. "Call it New Westminster," she said.

ÉCOLE JULES QUESNEL ELEMENTARY ("école" is French for school) is named for Jules Maurice Quesnel who lived from 1786 to 1842 and travelled with explorer Simon Fraser. He was a fur trader most of the time, and the river and town of Quesnel are also named for him. It was Fraser who named the river for Quesnel, after the latter explored it.

In 1962 MacMillan Bloedel launched an "Intensive Forestry Program" which involved not only replanting logged areas, but thinning new forests and getting rid of weed species. In 1974 MB established its "Land Use Planning Advisory Team" which recruited fisheries and wildlife biologists and other scientists to study ways in which logging could be carried out with minimum harm to the environment.

QUILCHENA ELEMENTARY In 1920, a little two-room school-house called Strathcona Heights was built on a rocky slope at 5300 Maple Street. This school house only enrolled grades one and two and a second three-roomer was built on the property in 1924. In 1925/26 a larger eight-room school was built and renamed "Quilchena"—the First Nations name for "land of many waters," due to the abundance of little rivers and bogs in the area. ALEXANDRA BOYD, age 12, grade 7, KATE DRANCE, age 12, grade 7, JENNIFER VAN ELK, age 12, grade 7

LAURA SECORD ELEMENTARY Laura Secord (1775-1868) was born to a family of United Empire Loyalists who came to Canada after the American Revolution. During the war of 1812 while American troops were billeted at her house in Queenston, she learned of their plans for a surprise attack on Beaver Dam. The 37-year-old heroine made her way through American lines to warn the garrison at Beaver Dam. She lived until she was 93.

J. W. SEXSMITH (COMMUNITY) ELEMENTARY Mr. John Wesley Sexsmith (1850-1920) was an important person and successful farmer in Richmond. He founded the first school in that area and spearheaded the building of the first bridge connecting Lulu Island to the mainland and Vancouver.

SHAUGHNESSY ELEMENTARY Lord Thomas George Shaughnessy (1853-1923), purchasing agent for the CPR in 1882 and president of the CPR from 1898-1918.

TECUMSEH ELEMENTARY Tecumseh was a Shawnee chief who fought beside General Brock in the War of 1812. He lived from 1768 to 1813.

TEMPLETON SECONDARY William Templeton was a merchant, a member of the Vancouver School Board and mayor of Vancouver (1893-95). He is not the William Templeton who was the first manager of the Vancouver Airport.

DAVID THOMPSON SECONDARY David Thompson (1770-1857) was a Welsh explorer, fur trader and geographer. He was the first white person to travel the Columbia River. The Thompson River, which he never saw, was named for him by explorer Simon Fraser.

THUNDERBIRD ELEMENTARY The name Thunderbird comes from First Nations people's beliefs. Some schools in Vancouver were named after First Nations chiefs, but our school was named after a powerful mythical bird. The Thunderbird is a huge bird believed to cause thunder and lightning. The First Nations people really respected the Thunderbird and that is why it appeared at the top of many totem poles and as our school name. MICHEAL HEADLEY age 12

TRAFALGAR ELEMENTARY Named for the street that was named for the battle that took place between Napoleon and Nelson on October 21, 1805. Napoleon was defeated.

After 1759 Quebec belonged to the British because General James Wolfe defeated French forces under General Montcalm on the Plains of Abraham near Quebec City on Sept. 13, 1759. Wolfe and Montcalm were killed. Rarely have both leaders of opposing sides in a battle been killed

SIR CHARLES TUPPER SECONDARY Sir Charles Tupper, born in 1821, grew up to be politically active. This outstanding Canadian statesman counts the following in his list of political achievements: he was prime minister of Nova Scotia from 1864-67, high commissioner for Canada in London from 1884-96, and was prime minister of Canada for three months in 1896. He was one of the Fathers of Confederation.

YORK HOUSE York House School was founded in 1932 by Lena Cotsworth Clarke, who called the school after her home town, the ancient cathedral city of York. York was named for the House of York whose symbol is the York Rose, which the school adopted as part of its crest. KRISTIN ARMSTRONG age 13, grade 8

GENERAL WOLFE ELEMENTARY After 1759 Quebec belonged to the British. This is because General James Wolfe, born in 1727, defeated French forces under General Montcalm in a battle on the Plains of Abraham near Quebec City on September 13, 1759. He was killed during the battle, as was Montcalm. It is very rare to have both leaders of opposing sides in a battle killed.

WEST VANCOUVER

COLLINGWOOD SCHOOL Baron Collingwood (1750-1810) was Nelson's vice-admiral during the Battle of Trafalgar (1805) and took command of the British Navy after Nelson's death. Collingwood was also the name given to Canada's first corvette of World War II which was captained by the father of the school's first chair of governors. ALEX HUDSON age 10, grade 5

In the 1970s MacMillan Bloedel researchers developed an engineered timber material known as Parallam that is stronger than the highest structural grades of conventional lumber. In 1988 Parallam's inventors received the prestigious Marcus Wallenberg Award, the world's highest prize in forest research.

Leadership Vancouver
Derlang Ansager

LEADERSHIP VANCOUVER—a program to develop, promote and encourage effective community leadership—sprang from a concept that began in the United States. That concept was, in turn, sparked by an horrific 1962 plane crash that killed virtually every major community and cultural leader in the city of Atlanta, Georgia. The grieving city eventually established a leadership program, a volunteer community effort "to foster successive generations of community leaders." The idea caught on in other American cities and in 1991 came to Vancouver, the first Canadian city to pick up the concept. Modelled after a highly successful Seattle program, Leadership Vancouver was a joint effort by Volunteer Vancouver and the Vancouver Board of Trade.

It is a non-profit society, governed by a board of directors, whose participants are selected through an application and interview process and provided with a nine-month curriculum that includes a three-day retreat, eight specific-issue days and numerous skills sessions and seminars directed by dedicated professionals. Participants, acting in project teams working on focussed community targets, interact with community leaders and experts through experiential sessions and site visits.

Leadership Vancouver has graduated more than 120 committed and qualified community leaders since its beginnings. Though it draws from more than 400 related programs, the Leadership Vancouver model was designed to meet the unique needs of the Lower Mainland.

One graduate, Rachelle Lee, an advertising and promotions specialist at BC Central Credit Union, wrote in 1996 to Leadership Vancouver about the results of her participation. She'd been a professional marketer for more than eight years but it wasn't until her graduation from LV, she wrote, "that I realized how the power of my business skills, added to the skills of people from other sectors, could begin to bring about positive social change within the community . . . Through the LV program I had the opportunity to work as a team with four others on a community action project. We paired up with Family Services of the North Shore, a local non-profit organization, to assist them in developing a policy on multiculturalism. I was able to offer my market research and business planning skills, while other team members provided expertise in many other different areas . . . Since that time I have put the lessons learned in the LV program to good use . . ." (One continuing project: Rachelle created a quarterly staff newsletter for North Shore Family Services.)

"The most valuable thing I learned is that everyone has the potential to become a leader if given the right training"

"To summarize the benefits I received from the program, they would be: a strong sense of what the key problem issues are in the Lower Mainland, what various sectors can do to provide possible solutions, first-hand experience working with the non-profit sector, a vast network of contacts including current community leaders and, above all, a personal sense of how I can work with others to make a difference. The most valuable thing I learned is that everyone has the potential to become a leader if given the right training."

The Leadership Vancouver program enjoys significant support from all sectors of the region and is financed through tuition of individuals and organizations, as well as scholarship money provided by foundations, corporations and individuals.

One example of Leadership Vancouver's philosophy was expressed in the June 12, 1995, graduation ceremony address by financier Milton K. Wong, when he told graduates that the intent of the program "is to sensitize you to a whole spectrum of social changes happening in our communities." Wong took as his theme multiculturalism "from a broad perspective of the whole community . . . I support multiculturalism wholeheartedly, but it would be dishonest for any of us to claim there are no problems with it at all." He went on to cite a 1994 poll conducted for the federal government that found that four in ten Canadians believe there are too many members of visible minorities in Canada. "Here in the Lower Mainland, 40 per cent of residents identified neither French nor English as their mother tongue in the last census. My question to you today is not what we can do for those 40 per cent. Instead I want to think about how the other 60 per cent feel about this. What about their wants, desires and envy—and especially, what about the underlying resentment among some of them? . . . The cornerstone of multiculturalism at its finest is open acceptance. But how much do we really share other cultures? Your challenge, as I see it, is to return to your communities with the responsibility of reaching out to those alienated groups . . . and then we need to find the courage to enter the debate. Only then will we arrive at an ongoing understanding among all parts of the community. The solution is in the process."

UBC

University of British Columbia
Iain Hiscoe

THE UNIVERSITY OF BRITISH COLUMBIA, the province's premier seat of higher learning, boasts the second largest library in Canada with significant holdings in areas of study ranging from Asian history, language and art to zoology and genetics. Research facilities abound, attracting first-rate scholars from around the world. Public events are various and manifold: lectures are sponsored, seminars convened. It is no exaggeration to say that UBC is the engine that drives cultural and economic life in the Lower Mainland. What makes this achievement so remarkable is that it has been accomplished in so little time—the first proposal for a publicly funded university in B.C. was made in 1887. It took, however, the better part of 30 years before that proposal bore fruit: UBC opened its doors in 1915.

Student activism has been a hallmark of the UBC experience (at least until recently) with the standard being set in the early '20s by the "Build the University" campaign. That endeavor generated a 56,000-name petition calling for the completion of the Point Grey campus and culminated in the historic "Great Trek" of 1922 from downtown Vancouver to the new site on the West Side. The government responded by authorizing a $1.5 million loan to resume construction. Rapid expansion of the physical infrastructure ensued in the years following and UBC officially took up residence at the new facilities in 1925.

The Great Depression forced the province to reduce funding to UBC by almost two-thirds in 1932. The university came perilously close to shutting down. Only another concerted, student-led publicity campaign saved it. Sustained expansion did not resume, though, until after World War II. Then buildings were erected and faculties founded, most notably those of Law, Graduate Studies, Pharmacy, Forestry, Education and Medicine. In 1954 the Department of Asian Studies, a key component of UBC's Pacific Rim focus, was established.

From the late '40s to the early '80s UBC enjoyed smooth sailing, fiscally speaking. The economy was growing and government allocations were stable and generous.

As post-war enrollees passed into professional life, their own children, the so-called "baby boomers," arrived to replace them. A number of successful fund-raising drives were undertaken and prominent graduates made bequests to fund chairs

facing page: The "Great Trek", 1922. cva

and scholarships, underwrite capital projects and expand library holdings. In 1972 the TRIUMF cyclotron, operated in conjunction with U Vic and the University of Alberta, was built at UBC. This facility, the largest of its kind in the world, continues to attract top-notch researchers despite recent funding cutbacks. The Museum of Anthropology, a definitive example of West Coast architecture and home to a number of outstanding collections of Northwest Coast First Nations art, opened in 1976. That same year, the Centre for Human Settlement was established in conjunction with the Habitat '76 conference.

After years of sustained growth the recession of 1982 rocked the fiscal foundation of the university and led to skyrocketing tuition fees, a trend which has continued unabated for the past 15 years. In 1985 then-president George Pedersen resigned to protest cuts in government funding. Pedersen was succeeded by David Strangway, a noted astrophysicist who once did research on moon rocks for NASA. While Strangway's administration was a controversial one, even his critics concede that he was a wildly successful fund-raiser. The four-year "World of Opportunity" program which he oversaw raised more than four times its $66 million target.

UBC has seen its share of strife over the years. In 1968 Yippie leader Jerry Rubin (who would later become a stockbroker) led a 22-hour sit-in at the university administration offices. More recently, the 1994 McEwan report on student harassment (which led to a freeze in graduate admissions to the Department of Political Science) sparked a furore debated in such lofty publications as the *Wall Street Journal* and the *Times,* of London.

On the other side of the coin, UBC has made contributions commensurate with its status as a major Canadian university. Notable graduates include journalist Allan Fotheringham, author Pierre Berton, senator Pat Carney, soprano Judith Forst, former prime ministers Kim Campbell and John Turner, and Texas Instruments co-founder Cecil B. Green. Distinguished Canadian poet Earle Birney helped found the Creative Writing department and George Woodcock, foremost authority on anarchist political theory and B.C.'s most prolific author until his death in 1995, taught history there. In 1971 UBC began offering the first credit courses in Women's Studies in Canada. In 1993 biochemist professor Dr. Michael Smith received the Nobel Prize for Chemistry.

From its humble beginnings, with a student body numbering in the hundreds, this "city within a city" has grown in size and influence to rival and sometimes even exceed the stature of many of its more venerable counterparts to the East and South. As of July, 1997 UBC's new president was Dr. Martha C. Piper.

UBC's Buildings
Mike Ecker

Please note: this material on some of UBC's more important buildings was adapted from information supplied us by the university's public affairs office and its campus planning and development office. Our thanks to the former, especially Connie Bagshaw, and to the latter, especially Imbi Harding, manager, facilities and resources.

Acadia Community Centre *(1989)* (Architects: Waisman, Dewar, Grout) Also known as the Common Block or Acadia/Fairview Common Block, this is a focal point for students living in the Acadia Park area of the UBC campus. The facility includes meeting space and activity rooms. The exterior appearance is similar to the nearby housing. The complex is managed by Student Housing and Conferences.

Advanced Materials & Process Engineering Laboratories (AMPEL) *(1995)* (Architects: Hemingway Nelson) This facility provides a setting for collaborative work between applied science disciplines. It brings together several departments in shared laboratories, fostering industrial research in the private sector. The light-sand-blasted concrete-frame building is enhanced with metal canopies, sunshades and a curved roof, and linked by second-storey bridges to the civil engineering, mechanical engineering and electrical engineering buildings.

Ambulance Station *(1991)* The station is operated by the provincial ministry of health, the lessee being the B.C. Buildings Corporation.

Henry Angus Building Faculty of commerce and business administration *(1965)* (Architects: Thompson, Berwick & Pratt) Known as UBC's first "skyscraper," the eight-storey Henry Angus building—the first fully air-conditioned building on campus—replaced 15 dilapidated army huts to house both commerce and all of the social sciences. At the corner of Main Mall and University Boulevard, the building was named after dean emeritus Henry F. Angus. The complex includes a four-storey classroom block. February 12, 1976 marked the opening ceremonies of the Earle Douglas MacPhee Executive Conference Centre and the Cyrus H. McLean Audio-Visual Theatre, the bottom and top floors (respectively) of the north wing of the building.

Applied Science The Faculty of Applied Science occupies a 15-acre site at the south end of the campus. It consists of the following buildings: Chemical Engineering (1961); Electrical Engineering (1964); Metallurgical Engineering (1968) - (Metals & Materials Eng.); Civil-Mechanical Laboratories (1972); Civil-Mechanical Building (1977). The faculty offers undergraduate and graduate programs in engineering, architecture and nursing. Seven departments and two boards of study offer programs in engineering: bio-resource engineering; chemical engineering; civil engineering; electrical engineering; geological engineering; mechanical engineering; metals and materials; engineering; mining and mineral process engineering; engineering physics.

Civil-Mechanical Rusty Hut Contains interesting testing equipment like the wind tunnel and wood strength testers. One potentially useful research project conducted here was on the shapes of fish boat hulls to discover a better shaped hull which would roll less easily in storms.

Aquatic Centre The Aquatic Centre indoor pool opened in 1980 at a cost of $5.4 million, largely paid by students, alumni and the community. The pool is Olympic size—50 metres long, 25 metres wide, 3'10" shallow, 13'6 deep—and holds three million litres (644,000 gallons) of water. Designed for recreational and competitive use, it holds up to 738 swimmers and allows several different activities to take place at one time. The centre also houses a well-equipped exercise room, physical fitness testing centre, two saunas and a whirlpool. The centre is open to all students, staff, faculty members and the general public.

Asian Centre *(1981)* (Interior design: Donald Matsuba) The purpose of the Asian Centre is to promote greater awareness and understanding of Asian cultures. The centre got its start when UBC religious studies professor, Shotaro Iida, went to Expo 70 in Osaka, Japan. The Sanyo Electric Company Exhibit building, he thought, would make a great Asian Centre for UBC after the fair. He asked Sanyo, and they donated the structure in honor of B.C.'s centennial. In addition to the Sanyo Corporation, sponsors included the Canadian and Japanese governments, business, industry and private individuals, many from Japan.

Since the cost of shipping the entire dismantled building would have been astronomical, only the supporting beams and girders were sent. UBC, however, did not know about the shipment and only learned of it when Canada Customs called saying they had some "white pipes" waiting to be picked up by UBC. The dismantled pieces were numbered to make reconstruction easy and efficient. Unfortunately, the beams were left on the site for a few years while UBC recruited sponsors for the construction, and when construction finally started, it was learned that rain had washed the numbers off. Putting the beams together was rather like trying to solve a 172-ton jigsaw puzzle. The puzzle did eventually materialize into the unique Asian Centre. Construction started January 8, 1974, and the building was officially opened June 5, 1981. When you enter, the white beams from the Sanyo Pavilion are immediately noticeable.

The Asian Centre houses the Asian Studies department and the Asian Library. Inside the building is an auditorium, a music room and several seminar rooms available for use by groups outside the university as well as within.

The department of Asian studies, founded in 1961, with 21 faculty members, offers both undergraduate and graduate degree programs. Total enrolment, including both undergrads and graduates, is about 1,500 students. The Asian Library is the largest Asian-languages library in Canada with more than 300,000 volumes in Chinese, Japanese, Urdu, Sanskrit and other Asian languages. It has an important collection of Chinese rare books and manuscripts dating as early as 986 A.D. It also has one of the best collections of Japanese woodblock and copper engraved maps of the Tokugawa Period (1600-1867) and an extensive collection of Chinese local gazetteers. These maps are in the special collections division of the Main Library.

Morris and Helen Belkin Art Gallery *(1995)* (Architects: Peter Cardew) The $3.3 million gallery, which received a Canadian Architect Yearbook Award, was a gift from Morris and Helen Belkin. It replaced inadequate gallery space located from 1923 to 1995 in the basement of the Main Library.

Jack Bell Building School of Social Work *(1992)* (Architects: Larry McFarland Architects Ltd.) This $3.9 million three-storey building was funded by a donation by philanthropist Jack Bell. The plan form encourages interaction between faculty and students, with the basement area functioning as a drop-in space for off-campus visitors.

Biological Sciences Building *(1948, with additions and alterations 1970, 1976, 1980, 1992 and 1993, with a south wing added in 1959)* (Architects: Thompson, Berwick & Pratt) This building is busy, used by the faculty of science, dean of science, and the departments of botany, chemistry, oceanography, science one program, zoology, Marine Biopods Inc. Biotechnology Laboratory, general university facilities, and by the faculty of forestry, the department of forest sciences and the faculty of medicine.

Biomedical Research Centre *(1988)* The centre is devoted to advancing the treatment of cancer and other diseases such as arthritis, allergies and asthma. The $23 million centre officially opened May 5, 1988 and is a joint project of the Terry Fox Medical Research Foundation and the Wellcome Foundation (funded by Burroughs-Wellcome, a pharmaceutical company). Supporting organizations include the University Hospital, the TRIUMF research laboratory and the Imaging Research Centre, all on campus.

Bio-Resource Engineering - Annex 2 *(1990)* A temporary building slated for removal after 1997.

UBC Bookstore *(1984)* The bookstore replaced a much smaller shop. It holds 3,250 sq. metres of selling space, with 250 tons of books sold each year, or 4.5 million volumes. Course books make up about half of that number. Leisure and other reading material for both children and adults make up the other half. The bookstore also sells a variety of other items, from computers to art supplies, from flashlights to bathing suits.

Botanical Gardens Centre *(1990)* (Architects: Downs Archambault) The $1.95 million centre has become a favorite spot for an increasing number of visitors, some arriving on tour buses. The project was made possible by a donation from David Lam, former lieutenant-governor of British Columbia and his wife Marjorie. Of post-and-beam and lumber frame construction, the three domestic-scale buildings are linked by a walkway which leads to the scenic lookout.

Brock Memorial Hall In 1939 UBC students provided nearly $80,000 to build the university's first student union building, a memorial to the late dean of applied science, Reginald W. Brock and his wife, killed in a 1935 airplane accident. Brock Memorial Hall originally housed a main lounge, snack bar, alma mater society (AMS) offices, club rooms, a committee room seating 200 people and general offices including the Mildred Brock Room for women students. In 1955 the AMS launched the Brock Hall Art Collection, which unfortunately suffered theft and vandalism. In 1973 measures were taken to increase security. However, $33,000 worth of paintings had already been lost. This collection may now be found in the Student Union Building Art Gallery and is continually added to by the AMS. An extension to Brock was built in 1957.

A huge mural, *Symbols for Education* by Lionel Thomas, was a gift to UBC by the graduating class of 1958.

The building now houses a variety of student services including student counselling and resources, campus employment centre, legal aid clinic, women students office, school and college liaison office and, in the annex, the Crane Resource Centre. Crane has an extensive collection of reading and resource material for visually impaired students. See its own entry.

Brock Memorial Hall - East Wing *(1993)* (Architects: Poon, Gardner, Garrett) This two-storey $7.4 million building, together with existing Brock Hall (1939/40), accommodates many student services in one central location. Users include the departments of awards and financial aid, financial services, registrar's office, student housing and conferences, student services and the Rick Hansen Disability Resource Centre.

Buchanan Building In 1958 the Buchanan Building—opened by Premier W.A.C. Bennett—became the new home of the liberal arts at UBC. Built at a cost of $2 million, the facility accommodates almost 8,000 students and 650 regular faculty members representing 19 departments and four schools. Most lectures in the faculty of arts are held here. A striking example of contemporary West Coast architecture, the building took 16 months to construct. The three units, surrounding an open-ended court, include a four-storey building for staff and faculty offices. To the south is a two-storey classroom wing, and to the west, the two-storey lecture theatre block. The name honors the late dean of arts and sciences, Daniel Buchanan, who died in 1950.

Buchanan Tower A 12-storey office/seminar room extension to the Buchanan Building. Completed in 1972 at a cost of just under $2.6 million, it is the tallest building on campus—45 metres high. It holds 267 faculty offices and nine seminar rooms.

Cecil Green Park House *(1912)* (Architect Samuel McClure) Built in 1912 by lawyer Edward P. Davis, who named it Kanakla—a native Indian word meaning "house on the cliff." In 1967 Kanakla was bought and donated to the university by Dr. Cecil and Mrs. Ida Green and became the "town and gown" meeting place for UBC. Ida Green died December 26, 1986, having bequeathed nearly $3 million to the university for the maintenance and upgrading of Cecil Green Park and for academic purposes such as the Cecil and Ida Green lecture series. Today Cecil Green Park houses offices of both the alumni association and the faculty women's club. It can be rented for private as well as university functions. The house is a favorite place for tourists with a view overlooking Georgia Strait and Howe Sound. The grand piano in the central foyer has an interesting history: famed pianist Ignacy Jan Paderewski had ended a world tour in Vancouver and put his piano up for sale. It was purchased by the Marquess of Anglessey who was establishing a utopian community at Walhachin in B.C.'s Thompson Valley. The community dwindled after World War I, but the piano remained there until the mid-1960s when it was entrusted to the university, then furnishing Cecil Green Park House. It is still played during weddings and gatherings.

Centre for Integrated Computer Systems Research *(1993)* (Architects: Chernoff Thompson) CICSR's three-storey-with-penthouse building provides space for interdisciplinary research in computer and related sciences. The $12.4 million building is used by CICSR and the departments of computer science, electrical engineering, mechanical engineering and by general university facilities.

Chan Centre for the Performing Arts *(1997)* Under construction as this book went to press, the Chan Centre—designed by Bing Thom Architects Inc., winner of the Governor General's Award for Architecture—will be a significant addition to Vancouver's art scene. It will house the 1,400-seat Chan Shun Auditorium (a concert hall), the 200-seat B.C. Tel studio theatre and the 150-seat Royal Bank Cinema. The $24 million project was largely funded by a $10 million gift from the Chan Foundation of Canada. Other major donors include B.C. Tel, the Royal Bank of Canada, Falconbridge Limited, Rheinzink Canada and the provincial government.

Chan Sun is the father of Drs. Tom and Caleb Chan. Members of a Vancouver family originally from Hong Kong, the Chans are business people with a long history of philanthropic giving and service to the community. In addition to the family's outstanding support for the building, they have made a generous contribution for the establishment of the Chan Endowment for the Performing Arts. The endowment will assist international and community groups who wish to perform at the Chan Centre.

Chemistry Building *(1925)* One of the oldest buildings on the UBC campus. Its modern Tudor style is reminiscent of buildings found at Oxford and Cambridge universities. Originally, all the university's buildings were to be done in this style, but the B.C. granite exterior was too expensive—and only three buildings were faced with this stone (Chemistry, Main Library and Hennings). Two wings were later added to the main structure, which together house senior undergraduate and graduate labs, offices and lecture halls.

Child Care Services Buildings *(1989)* (Architects: Larry McFarland Architects Ltd.) These five single-storey facilities replaced many army huts.

Child Study Centre *(1990)* (Architects: Larry McFarland Architects Ltd.) The focus of activities here is the study of early childhood development. Parents bring young children into a setting similar to a child-care setting, where the children are the focus of research through observation and other techniques. An exterior activity space is an essential component of the study function. Activity spaces are linked by a "street." The faculty of education runs this building, valued at $1 million.

C.K. Choi Building for the Institute of Asian Research *(1996)* (Architects: Matsuzaki and Wright) This building provides space for collaborative research and studies of five geographic regions of Asia. It is the first environmentally sensitive structure on the UBC campus; among other things, it is not connected to a sewer, but uses composting toilets. A significant portion of the building re-uses beams from the 1943 Armouries Building, demolished in the mid-1990s. The facing bricks are from Vancouver streets.

Crane Resource Centre The Charles Crane Memorial Library, a unit of the Disability Resource Centre, was formed as a reading room in 1968 with the donation of a personal collection of about 6,000 Braille books, belonging to the late Charles Allen Crane. Known as Charlie among friends, he was often referred to as "Canada's Helen Keller." Almost completely deaf and blind from birth, Charlie was a bright student at the Halifax and Jericho Hill schools for the deaf and a special student at UBC from 1934-37. He was also outstanding in athletics, particularly in wrestling. Due to lack of publicity and support, Charlie settled into a life of manual work and personal study. He became an avid Braille book collector, and with help from others created his own Braille books. After Crane's death in 1965, by his previous request, his collection was bequeathed to UBC to benefit blind and visually impaired students.

The Charles Crane Memorial Library is one of a kind in Canada. Since 1970 the library and its dedicated volunteers have recorded talking textbooks and background materials. A special disbursement was established in 1974 as a continuous funding base for the library, staff, book budgets and raw materials. By 1981, the centre had expanded to house nine sound-proof studios with state-of-the-art professional recording equipment and high-speed duplicating and editing equipment. Hundreds of cassettes can be copied per hour, serving 35 to 50 blind, visually impaired or print-handicapped UBC students per year. Through inter-library loans, the centre serves up to 500 students. In 1996 holdings were about 46,000 titles.

Talking books produced at the Crane Library are sold on a non-profit basis to libraries and schools in such places as New Zealand, Australia, Japan, Hong Kong, Papua New Guinea, Ghana, South Africa, the U.S. and Sweden. About 300 new Braille publications are purchased each year from commercial sources in Canada, the U.S., Great Britain and continental Europe. e-mail: crane@unixg.ubc.ca

George F. Curtis Building This 1945 law building is named for George F. Curtis, first dean of the faculty (1945-71). A 1976 addition contains the main lecture hall, which can be divided into three separate halls, faculty offices, a lounge and a library of more than 200,000 volumes. Law's first students were admitted in 1945. The faculty of law has almost 700 students and 45 to 50 faculty

members. Since 1976, the faculty has offered a native law program which has proved highly successful. The Curtis Building is home to the Moot Court Room, used for moots or mock courts, in which every law student must take part.

Engineering High Headroom Laboratory (1992) (Architects: Formwerks) This single-storey building is used by the department of mechanical engineering.

Environmental Services Facilities (1969, 1973, 1986, 1989) A collection of waste control and disposal facilities: solvent storage, chemical waste processing and storage, waste processing and storage and a $622,000 incinerator.

Faculty Club The faculty club and social centre, which opened in June 1959, was a gift from Mrs. Thea and Dr. Leon J. Koerner. As the campus residence for visiting royalty, the club—which, faced with financial insolvency, closed its doors in 1994—was honored by the presence of both Queen Elizabeth and Prince Charles. The faculty club, built at a cost of $750,000, had both public and private dining rooms, reading room, lounges, music room, snack bar, games room and four salons. It was the centre of social activity for UBC faculty. In 1968, an extension to the club (designed by architect Erickson Massey, who won architectural awards for it) was built with funds from membership fees. On October 24, 1968, the faculty club was the site of student unrest: American Jerry Rubin and a number of UBC students invaded and took it over for 22 hours, after which they left voluntarily. The club no longer exists although the building that houses it is still standing, unoccupied at this writing. Renovated and expanded it will be rechristened as the Liu Centre for International Studies, a comprehensive centre for teaching and research that will house the south-north studies program, the Institute for International Relations and the Centre for Human Settlements.

First Nations Long House (1993) (Architects: Larry McFarland Architects Ltd.) This $4.57 million development, much influenced by the architecture of a native long house, won the Governor General's Award in 1994. Well-established West Coast materials—cedar and glass— are extensively used, including the use of very large dressed logs. A waterfall screens a retaining wall facing the West Mall. Built near an historic arboretum, it provides a focus for the activities of various native Indian programs. Users include First Nations House, First Nations law, First Nations Library, First Nations health care and the native Indian teacher education program (NITEP) begun in 1974. Major donors were William and June Bellman, Jack Bell and James and Ilse Wallace. There is a child care facility here.

Forest Engineering Research Institute of Canada (1990) (Architects: Henry Hawthorne Architect Ltd.) Like the adjacent FORINTEK building, the striking three-storey FERIC facility was constructed to illustrate the use of wood in large scale/heavy construction buildings. It includes the use of newly developed wood structural components combined with concrete.

Forest Harvesting and Wood Science Trailer (1989) A temporary building, slated for removal following construction of the Forest Sciences Centre.

FORINTEK Western Research Facility (1990) (Architects: The Hulbert Group B.C.) This two-storey forestry research facility illustrates the use of wood in large scale/heavy construction buildings. The building is clad with aluminum, faced plywood panels and cedar siding. It is on land leased by UBC to FORINTEK and the Forest Engineering Research Institute of Canada.

Frederic Wood Theatre The Freddy Wood opened its doors September 19, 1963 with the English musical comedy *Salad Days*. Originally located in an old army hut along West Mall, the theatre now contains three 50-seat classrooms and a 400-seat theatre. It was built at a cost of $600,000, half of which was paid for by the Canada Council. The theatre's most striking feature is two revolving stages that permit complex scenery changes. All performances and directing are under the direction of UBC's fine arts department. The theatre was named for one of UBC's original faculty members, Frederic G.C. Wood, a professor of English. UBC theatre grads include John Gray, Richard Ouzounian, Larry Lillo, Eric Petersen, Goldie Semple, Jeremy Long and Bill Millerd. Ten of the theatre companies operating in Vancouver today were founded by UBC alumni, including Tamahnous, Touchstone and Green Thumb. The Dorothy Somerset Studio, named for another UBC theatre pioneer, located in the back of the building, is used for full-length productions, summer stock and one-act plays.

Gas Gun Facility (1989) This nondescript single-storey building is a research facility, run by the department of physics, used to investigate new materials through the use of an explosive device. The choice of site, and the design of the building, reflect due regard to safety requirements.

Geological Sciences Building (1972) This building is architecturally unique on campus. Made entirely of standard-sized pieces fitted together, it can be compared to a Meccano set. All of the interior walls are movable (except the dinosaur wall) enabling additions or changes to the building to be made quickly and relatively easily. In 1974 two of the panels were removed and a walkway added, then the panels were reattached to the office wing.

The UBC Geological Museum Named after M.Y. Williams, a Canadian geologist and former head of the UBC department of geology, the building is the outgrowth of a small collection started by Williams in 1924. The collection today includes an assortment of mineral and fossil specimens formed during the past 4.5 billion years. There are several displays of rocks, minerals and fossils for visitors to view. The highlight is the 80-million-year-old Lambeosaurus dinosaur, which extends 10 metres in length, found in Alberta's Red Deer Valley in 1913. On permanent loan since 1950 from the National Museum in Ottawa, Lamby stands 2.7 metres high, and (in his plaster frame) weighs approximately one ton.

UBC's department of geological sciences' more than 800 graduates have helped develop over $35 billion worth of mineral and petroleum resources.

Geophysics and Astronomy Building This building houses two observatories used to train astronomers. The observatories are too close to the city and too near sea level for new and original research to be possible. The UBC Observatory here is open for public viewing on clear Saturday nights from 8:00 to midnight. Geophysics is the science of the "physics of the earth" and includes such fields as oceanography, seismology, radioactivity and magnetism. In the lobby of the geophysics building are several seismographs (earthquake-measuring instruments). UBC seismologists have announced that we are long overdue for a major earthquake.

One seismograph here has sensors in the building itself: if people jump up and down in the lobby the resulting vibration is registered.

UBC astronomers made a discovery in 1987 providing evidence there are planets outside our solar system.

Graduate Student Centre Thea Koerner House *(1961)* (Architects: Thompson, Berwick & Pratt) The centre was the gift to UBC of Dr. Leon Koerner, the founder of Alaska Pine Co., and is named in memory of his wife who died in 1959. Dr. Koerner lived in the penthouse of the building during the summer months from the time the building was completed until his death in 1972. The building—which includes a 1971 extension paid for by graduates—serves as a social and cultural centre for students in graduate studies. The centre is very active during the school year, with events sponsored by the graduate student society. The original structure received the Massey Gold Medal for outstanding architecture. *Transcendence,* the fountain sculpture in front of the building, is by Jack Harman.

Green College *(1994)* (Architects: Birmingham and Wood with Paul Merrick) The college was funded by Sir Cecil Green, founder of Texas

Instruments, with a matching grant from the provincial government. The building's value is $7.3 million. It is a resident graduate college modelled after Green College in Oxford, England. The graduate students are limited in number but of high scholarship promise.

Green College - Principal's Residence *(1994)* (Architects: Birmingham and Wood with Paul Merrick) The principal's residence of Green College, funded by Dr. Cecil Green and a matching grant from the provincial government, is a feature of this college and a sister college in Oxford, England.

Hebb Building *(October 24, 1963)* Named in memory of Thomas Carlyle Hebb, a professor of physics at UBC (1916-38). Hebb was built as a teaching addition to the physics department. At a cost of $1.4 million, the building houses tutorial rooms, laboratories and the second largest lecture theatre on campus, seating 450 students (IRC 1 and 2 each seat 700 people).

Hennings Building The UBC Physics Building was opened in 1948 by Premier John Hart. In 1963 the building was dedicated in honor of Dr. A.E. Hennings, a UBC professor of physics for 29 years. An outstanding feature is the exterior granite columns. Many features of the design were incorporated from what were then ultra-modern physics labs in Sweden. Built at a cost of more than $700,000, the building houses lecture rooms (total capacity 400 students), classrooms, laboratories, research rooms and offices.

Imaging Research Centre The positron emission tomography (PET) scanner, located in the Imaging Research Centre, scans the brain to help identify stroke, Parkinson's disease, Alzheimer's disease and Huntington's chorea. It produces computerized cross-sectional images of biochemical activity in the brain through the use of radioactive tracers. The nuclear magnetic resonance (NMR) unit scans the body, monitoring tissue metabolism and distinguishing between normal and abnormal cells. There is also a computerized axial tomography (CAT) scanner, using narrow X-ray beams in two planes at various angles to produce computerized cross-sectional images of the body.

International Centre for Criminal Law Reform and Justice Policy *(1992)* A temporary portable building, adjacent to the UBC/IBM Law and Computer Centre/Legal Aid Clinic.

Douglas Kenny Building Psychology *(1984)* Named after Douglas T. Kenny, the 7th president of UBC (1975-83), the building houses the psychology department equipped with labs, offices and equipment. The Whaler's Pole outside the front entrance is noteworthy (an explanation of the pole is on the plaque) for people interested in North West Coast indigenous cultures. The

pole was made by the Nu-Cha-Nalth people and depicts a harpooner, assistant whaler, shaman, Puk-Up and Grey Whale.

Koerner Gallery Museum of Anthropology *(1990)* (Architects: Arthur Erickson) The gallery was an addition to the Museum of Anthropology, accommodating a unique collection of Czech, Slovak and Bohemian ceramics and tiles, donated by Dr. Walter Koerner. One feature is a 12th-century oven clad entirely in tiles. The use of massive concrete walls for the high headroom space continues the use of the material used in the museum itself.

Walter C. Koerner Library *(1996)* (Architects: Aitken Wregglesworth with Arthur Erickson) Completed in the summer of 1996, this striking new building will be the new Main Library. It will merge the collections of the Sedgewick Library and the divisions of humanities and social sciences, government publications and microforms, and the data library from the current Main Library. The Sedgewick Library will be fully incorporated into the Koerner.

Ladner Clock Tower The tower was built in 1968 and stands 37 metres high. Named after Dr. Leon J. Ladner, QC, it houses a 330-bell carillon once played during special occasions, such as UBC's May congregation. For the past several years, the bell has not sounded because of corrosion problems. The tower was not a popular structure when first built. Students of the university thought the money could have been better spent on just about anything else. Some of the names they bestowed on it were less than flattering, and it has been the butt of several engineering week pranks. One year a Volkswagen Beetle was put on top of the clock tower. No one knows how they got it up there, but we do know how it was brought down — the university rented a crane large enough to lift it off. There is a moral to this story: the engineering undergraduate society (EUS) had to pay for the rental of the crane. The Ladner Clock Tower is a good orienteering point for new students and lost visitors since it can be seen from most central points on campus.

David Lam Management Research Centre *(1992)* (Architects: Carlberg Jackson Partners) The four-storey centre is an $8.8 million addition to the 1965 Henry Angus Building. A glass tower linking the centre to Angus is also the main entrance. Exterior finishes are brick and glass. Focus of study is business issues related to the Pacific Rim. Building users include the faculty of commerce and business administration, commerce and professional programs, faculty development and institutional service, UBC food services, the centre for continuing education and the UBC library. The main floor accommodates

Trekker's Restaurant. Major donors were David and Dorothy Lam and many others.

Lasserre Building *(1962)* (Architects: Thompson, Berwick & Pratt) Designed in the "International" style of the 1950s and built at a cost of $1 million. One of the few UBC buildings with a podium, its louvre windows reflect a time when energy conservation was not critically practiced. The main floor contains four lecture halls. Fine arts and architecture studios occupy the second and third floors respectively. The schools of architecture and community and regional planning and the department of fine arts have offices on the fourth floor. Named after the head of the school of architecture (1936-61) who was killed in a 1961 mountain climbing accident.

Gerald McGavin Building *(1995)* (Architects: Chernoff Thompson) This three-storey-with-penthouse facility, a joint project by Discovery Parks and UBC Real Estate Corporation offers an opportunity for entrepreneurial research and development companies to establish commercial operations within the campus core. The faculties of science, applied science, medicine, dentistry and pharmaceutical sciences are all nearby.

H.R. MacMillan Building Forestry and Agriculture *(1967)* Dedicated to H.R. MacMillan who contributed more than $12 million to UBC, the building makes efficient use of space for two small faculties, forestry and agriculture, each of which requires a lot of research space. Both forestry and agriculture have their own wings for faculty and graduate student offices and labs. They share the centre wing containing classrooms, seminar rooms, a lecture hall and the combined forestry/agriculture branch of the library. The building has facilities for 550 undergraduates, 120 graduate students and 46 faculty.

Main Library *(1925)* As you open the doors to the Main Library, you see UBC's crest and motto engraved on the handle. The Latin motto, *Tuum Est,* means "it is yours." In the case of the library the motto is literally true. It is open to the public and people everywhere may borrow its books through interlibrary loan. The largest library in British Columbia, a north wing was added in 1948 and a south wing in 1960. The building holds approximately one million books. An additional 1.5 million volumes are located in the branch libraries listed below:

- Asian Studies Library
- Crane Resource Centre for the visually impaired
- Curriculum Laboratory
- Data Library, machine readable data
- Film Library
- Fine Arts Library
- Government Publications
- Law Library
- MacMillan Forestry/Agriculture Library
- Map Library
- Marjorie Smith Social Work Library
- Mathematics Library
- Music Library
- Special Collections, rare books, UBC archives, manuscripts, local history
- Wilson Recordings Collection
- Woodward Biomedical Library
- Biomedical Branch Library, Vancouver Hospital and Health Sciences Centre
- Hamber Library, B.C. Children's Hospital/Women's Hospital and Health Centre
- St. Paul's Hospital Library

In the main concourse on the 5th floor is an information referral centre for the entire library system. The decorative windows in the concourse show the crests of universities in Canada and Great Britain. The mural on the north wall, *Emergent Image,* on loan to the library, is the work of B.C. artist Jack Shadbolt.

Mathematics and Statistics Resource Centre *(1992)* A temporary portable building situated on the parking lot to the west of the Math Annex.

Museum of Anthropology *(1976)* The museum is a gift from the federal government to the people of B.C., to celebrate the 100th anniversary of B.C. entering Confederation in 1871. The building was designed by architect Arthur Erickson, once a professor at UBC, who received an honorary degree from UBC at Spring 1985 congregation. The Great Hall is reminiscent of Haida Indian longhouses (examples of which can be found behind the museum). Inside is an impressive collection of Northwest Coastal Indian artifacts and a remarkable research collection of anthropological artifacts from most of the Pacific cultures. These collections are kept in "open storage," displayed in glass cases and drawers where anyone can see them easily, instead of in closed storage where access for research or enjoyment in difficult. See also Kerry McPhedran's article in this book.

There is an admission fee (except on Tuesdays). Visitors enjoy a magnificent view from the water side of the museum.

Music Building *(January 12, 1968)* Part of the Norman Mackenzie Centre for Fine Arts, the building cost $2.5 million. The school of music was first headed by Dr. G. Welton Marquis, a master of music composition. Prior to 1968, the music department was located in army huts along West Mall. Within the building are large rooms for choir, band, opera and orchestra, as well as smaller rooms for lectures and individual practice. There are 36 teaching studios and a

recital hall seating 285 people. The pipe organ in the recital hall, purchased through an anonymous donation of $100,000, was installed November 14, 1967. The small music library on the fourth floor contains recordings (for library use only) and books. For more than 30 years, music students have pooled their talents for a year-end celebration called GRONK (no one seems to know where this term comes from). In the evening of the last day of classes, the students perform music, skits and other entertainment. This is the only opportunity they have to perform in the building without being marked and critiqued.

National Research Council - Institute for Machinery Research *(1995)* (Architects: Kasian Kennedy) A non-UBC building accommodating a federal government program. The space includes high headroom for research into heavy machinery and laboratories for electronics and computing research.

Networks of Centres of Excellence *(1991)* (Zoltan Kiss Architect) The two-storey $6.9 million facility is atop the UBC Bookstore and was designed to accommodate laboratories and offices. This is the building that housed Michael Smith's laboratory, and where he shared a champagne toast with colleagues the day it was announced he had won the 1993 Nobel Prize for chemistry. Dr. Smith, who was director of the biotechnology laboratory at the time, is the first British Columbian to win the Nobel Prize.

There remains additional development potential for laboratories. Cladding is precast concrete to match the bookstore. The two lab floors are linked to the biological sciences building north wing. Building users include animal science, biochemistry, biotech laboratory, faculty of pharmaceutical sciences, medical genetics, microbiology, immunology, NCE-bacterial, NCE-genetic, oceanography, zoology.

Nitobe Garden *(1960)* Named for Dr. Inazo Nitobe, a Japanese international educator who tried to bridge the gap between East and West. Dr. Nitobe was the Japanese representative to the League of Nations in the 1920s. Here he met Norman Mackenzie who later became President of UBC (1948-62). Dr. Nitobe died in Victoria in 1933 after attending a meeting in Banff of the Institute of Pacific Affairs. Designed by landscape architect Kanosuke Mori, it is considered the most authentic Japanese garden outside Japan. There are two parts: the Teahouse Garden, designed for peaceful contemplation with pleasant associations; and the Main Garden, illustrating the variety of nature and the journey of life. The garden follows traditional principles of yin and yang and its layout conforms to the map of the Milky Way. The teahouse in the tea garden was built in Japan, then dismantled and shipped to Canada and finally reassembled by two Japanese carpenters who came over with it. The flower arrangements inside are renewed weekly by members of the Ikebana Association. The irises were given to UBC by the Meiji Shrine, famous in Japan for its beautiful iris gardens.

The yatsu-hashi bridge in the iris garden has symbolic meaning. According to Japanese legend, devils can only walk in straight lines. To be rid of the devils following you, cross the zig-zaggy bridge and the devil will fall into the water. Since devils cannot stand the touch of water, you can carry on happily.

There are many fish in the pond. Originally, UBC brought in 1,000 goldfish. Unfortunately, the bald eagles and great blue herons living around UBC ate all the goldfish. UBC then acquired 100 expensive Japanese carp, or koi, much bigger than goldfish. Unfortunately, the brightly colored koi did not reproduce. Next a number of local Fraser River carp were introduced. They have reproduced and their numbers are now quite substantial (but great blue herons still come on occasion to fish for baby carp).

North Parkade *(1988)* (Engineers: N.D. Lea Engineers, with Zoltan Kiss, architect) The eight-level $7.7 million parkade can accommodate 1,003 vehicles. Some spaces are used by residents in the nearby Walter Gage Towers. All UBC parking structures, incidentally, are self-financing.

Old Barn Cafeteria *(1917)* An original UBC Point Grey Campus building. Initially a classroom for returning World War I soldiers, it later became the horticulture facility for generations of undergraduate students in agriculture. After a long battle to save this heritage building, it was converted in 1967 into a faculty, staff and student cafeteria. The Barn is at Main Mall and Agronomy Road and seats 148 people. While the building's original cost was just $5,250, the 1967 renovation cost more than $62,000.

Pacific Bell Tower The Pacific Bell, a 1983 gift to UBC by the Japanese government, was made and presented by master craftsman Masahiko Katori. Of his 105 bells, only two are in North America. The other, the Friendship Bell, is in San Diego. Katori was given the official title of living national treasure by the Japanese government for his skill in the declining art of fine metal casting and bell making. This is the highest and most prestigious title any Japanese artisan can hold for his skills. (Katori also made the Hiroshima Peace Bell.) The tower housing the bell is built of B.C. western yellow cedar—very similar to hiba, or Japanese yellow cedar. Its design dates back more than 800 years to the Kamakura period.

Prefabricated in Japan and assembled here, the structure—built at an estimated cost of $80,000—is held together without a single nail, with the exception of the eaves and the roof. Its location was chosen by Mr. Katori while on a visit to UBC, with special attention to the acoustics of the site. Construction costs were high because UBC imported skilled tradesmen from Japan to assemble the structure. The three characters on the bell mean "Clear thoughts lead to a tranquil mind."

Plant Operations: Exterior Storage Shed *(1992)* (Engineers: N.D. Lea, Engineers) Used for plant operations materials and equipment.

Plant Sciences Field Station and Garage *(1964)* (Architects: Morton Ramsey Associates) This domestic-scale building is adjacent to fields used for research by the plant science department of the faculty of agricultural sciences.

RESIDENCES ON CAMPUS

Student housing accommodates more than 4,000 single students and 450 families. The two family complexes are Fairview Crescent Residences and Acadia Park Residences. Acadia Park was finished in early 1989 at a cost of $7 million, the third and final phase of the project to upgrade student accommodation on campus. In 1985 a 187-unit townhouse, **Fairview Crescent Student Housing** was built with shared accommodation for 782 single students. This complex was leased to Expo during the 1986 exposition. An additional 158-unit complex for married students was opened in early 1987, the first family housing to be constructed on campus since 1967.

Acadia Family Housing - Phase II *(1988)* (Architects: Waisman, Dewar, Grout) The second phase following construction of Fairview Crescent Student Housing. The $12.8 million complex is managed by student housing and conferences.

Acadia Family Housing - Phase III (1989) (Architects: Waisman, Dewar, Grout) This final phase completed the plan for student housing begun in 1982, and eliminated a vast number of World War II army huts. Infill in the original 1967 development is still available if ever required. The $8.3 million complex is managed by student housing and conferences.

Acadia House Apartments *(1991)* (Architects: Eng and Wright) This four-storey complex is managed by Student Housing and Conferences.

Place Vanier (single students) This housing centre has ten houses; three are all-female, four all-male and three co-ed (more men tend to live in residence than do women). The Commons Block of Place Vanier won the Massey Silver Medal for Architecture in 1961.

Point Grey Apartments *(1993)* (Architects: Eng and Wright) Four storeys.

Sopron House Apartments *(1991)* (Architects: Eng and Wright) Four storeys.

Spirit House Apartments *(1993)* (Architects: Eng and Wright) A $4.4 million four-storey apartment block, managed by the department of student housing and conferences. A child-care unit is on the main floor.

Thunderbird Student Residences *(1995)* (Architects: Waisman, Dewar, Grout, Carter) A $13.3 million housing development at the south end of the Main Mall provides a mix of studio, one-, two- and four-bedroom units for a total of 403 units, including a companion development on the east side of Main Mall. The latter, designed by the same architects, was also constructed in 1995. Its current value is $11.6 million. Both complexes are managed by student housing and conferences.

Totem Park (single students) Located at the southwest end of the campus, Totem Park has six houses of six floors each. Each floor holds 30 students, and all of the students eat in a central cafeteria. Its name derived from a collection of totem poles next to the residence until the Museum of Anthropology opened in 1976. There is still a carving shed by Kwakiutl House, used by native carvers working on totem poles at UBC. All of the houses are co-ed, with alternating male/female floors.

Thunderbird Student Residences *(1995)* (Architects: Waisman, Dewar, Grout, Carter) A $13.3 million housing development at the south end of the Main Mall provides a mix of studio, one-, two- and four-bedroom units for a total of 403 units, including a companion development on the east side of Main Mall. The latter, designed by the same architects, was also constructed in 1995. Its current value is $11.6 million. Both complexes are managed by student housing and conferences.

UBC-Ritsumeikan House *(1992)* (Matsuzaki Wright Architects Inc.) This $4.9 million student residence houses 200 UBC and Ritsumeikan University students from Japan. Featuring a state-of-the-art language laboratory, the house is also used by the centre for continuing education and UBC/Ritsumeikan program.

Walter Gage Residence (single and married students) One thousand students live in three 17-floor towers and approximately 300 more live in Gage Lowrise, made up of smaller units for married couples. In the towers each floor contains four quads, with six students per quad (there are two male, two female quads on each floor). This is UBC's only housing where residents do their own cooking. Students can apply to live in Gage Towers if they are 19 or over and have been out of high school for two or more years. There is accommodation here for disabled students.

Rose Garden The Rose Garden covers half an acre and contains some 300 varieties of roses and 2,000 individual plants. Many of the roses (most of them hybrid tea roses) were collected from around the world and some are irreplaceable. Many faculty, staff and students go to the garden during a morning, afternoon or lunch break to take in the beautiful ocean view.

Rose Garden Parkade *(1994)* (Architects: Aitken Wreglesworth) The sandy sub-surface conditions of the UBC area made the construction of this massive—23,674 sq. metre—structure possible. The building takes advantage of the substantial change in grade levels between North West Marine Drive and the Main Mall. Built at a cost of $12.5 million, it provides parking for 900 cars, and room on the roof for UBC's much-loved Rose Garden.

Neville Scarfe Building Education *(Oct. 4, 1962; additional renovations 1965, 1972 and 1966)* (Architects: B.C. Department of Public Works. 1996: Hotson Bakker) In 1956, UBC took over the responsibility for training B.C.'s teachers, but there was no central facility for instruction. Six years later the hoped-for education building opened. Measuring 6,363 sq. metres, the Lecture Block, the first of three phases of the education complex, stands 16 metres tall, 70 metres long and 41 metres wide. The three-storey building is rectangular, housing seminar rooms, classrooms, laboratories, reading rooms, offices and a student lounge. Later in 1962 phase two was completed, consisting of two wing extensions at the north and south ends of the Lecture Block. The south wing contains specialized classrooms, the north wing faculty offices. The complex was completed with the addition of an auditorium seating 258 people. In 1973 the building was renamed to honor Neville V. Scarfe, former dean of the faculty.

The 1996 work on this building included seismic upgrading. The exterior was modified to be more consistent with the look of nearby buildings. A busy place, its users include the faculty of education, education computing services, education psychology/special education, mathematics and science education, psychology education resources and training, social and educational studies, teacher education and student, visual and performing arts, education undergraduate society, general university facilities, A/V and media services, library and food services. The 1995 value of the building: $21.5 million.

Neville Scarfe Building Library *(1995)* (Architects: Hotson Bakker) This $4.5 million three-storey (with penthouse) building provides replacement and additional space for the Education Library. It includes the teacher education office. The library is fully accessible via the interi-or of the Scarfe Building.

Neville Scarfe Children's Garden One of the highlights of 1987 was the creation of the Neville Scarfe Children's Garden. Created by students and faculty in education and landscape architecture, this unique garden was designed to be a model learning environment for children, as well as to serve as a beautiful retreat for faculty, staff and students. The West Coast forest grotto, clover meadow, stream, pond, vegetable and flower gardens appeal to daycare, pre-school and school groups of children. The 1.5 metre by 1.5 metre cedar carving of *Raven Bringing the Light* symbolizes the native indian teacher education program (NITEP), the department that donated this carving to the garden. Visitors are welcome to stroll through the garden at any time.

School of Family & Nutritional Sciences Building *(1983)* Officially opened by Queen Elizabeth II during her visit to UBC. The main foyer contains a tapestry created by faculty member Joanna Staniszkis.

The school itself, now part of the faculty of agricultural sciences, offers four undergraduate programs (dietetics; family science; home economics; human nutrition) and two graduate programs (human nutrition and family studies).

Students take courses interrelated with the arts, humanities and social, physical and biological sciences. Professional opportunities include work in dietetics, family research, home economics, teaching, extension services, community agencies and business and industry.

Sedgewick Undergraduate Library *(January 1973)* (Architects: Rhone and Iredale) Sedgewick Undergraduate Library—a name which will cease to exist when the renovation attaching it to the new Koerner Library is complete—is a popular area of study for new university students and a favorite tourist attraction for visitors. It is one of the largest branches in the UBC library system, and one of the most innovative in design. When the student population increased rapidly in the 1960s, UBC decided to construct a new library building devoted entirely to undergraduate needs. Students' traffic surveys indicated the best location would be the Main Mall, close to the Main Library. To preserve the area's open space, it was decided to build the new library partially underground. The eight magnificent oaks that had lined the Mall for decades were incorporated into the design.

The 10,497-sq.-metre library, built at a cost of $3.8 million, was named for Garnet Gladwin Sedgewick, a Shakespearean scholar and member of UBC's English department (1918-48). The collection includes all texts for undergraduate courses in arts and first and second year science and engineering. Sedgewick has 195,000 books, selected by the reference librarians and teaching faculty and subscribes to 350 magazines. It also has a newspaper clipping file, a pamphlet file and a paperback collection for browsing. Although only UBC library card holders may borrow books, anyone is welcome to read the books at Sedgewick. There are 1,200 study seats and 300 lounge seats.

Student Recreation Centre *(1995)* (Architects: Henriquez and Partners/IBI Group) This $7 million two-storey structure, on McInnes Field, was conceived as a companion piece to the 1951 War Memorial Gymnasium. A triple gymnasium on the upper floor can be fully opened for major events. Beneath are a dance studio, fitness centre, changing rooms, meeting rooms and office space. The building has potential for expansion (squash courts).

Student Union Building *(1968)* SUB is unique on campus: it is student-funded and run by the alma mater society (AMS). A new basement wing completed in the spring of 1985 was completely funded by the AMS, a non-profit student organization whose main objective is to develop, promote and coordinate the activities and interests of the UBC student body. AMS has a membership of more than 40,000 students and is one of the largest student employers in Canada, with 400 part-time student staff and 50 full-time staff on the payroll. AMS runs all food services in SUB except Subway Cafeteria. That includes the Pit Pub, Tortellini's, Gallery Lounge and Snack Attack.

Since 1918 AMS has been responsible for several publications, including the student newspaper, *The Ubyssey*. Since 1938 it has operated a low-power radio station, CITR. It is the parent organization for more than 185 clubs and nine service organization and also offers the following non-academic services: food and beverage outlets; copy centre; typing and word processing centre; ticket centre; concerts and speakers; art gallery; games room; sports facilities; Whistler Lodge; Joblink; used bookstore; outdoor equipment rentals.

SUB also houses 22 multi-purpose meeting rooms that accommodate 10 to 600 people for a wide variety of events.

UBC/IBM Law and Computer Centre/Legal Aid Clinic *(1991)* A temporary portable building.

University Services Centre Building *(1992)* (Architects: Howard Bingham Hill) This one-and-two-storey large-scale complex (nearly 9,000 sq. metres) houses UBC's plant operations and is also used by the centre for continuing education, campus mail and media services. The $10.7 million building screens a service yard to the east.

Vancouver School of Theology *(1927)* (Architects: Thompson, Berwick & Pratt) includes a 1989 library addition by architect Howard Yano. The buildings have a range of architectural character, with extensive use of granite and pitched roofs.

In 1920 the Anglican Theological College was formed, an amalgamation of Latimer Hall and St. Mark's Hall. The **Chancellor Building** was officially opened in 1927 to house the college. The opening of the centre and east residence wings followed in 1963, and the dedication of the Chapel of the Epiphany in 1966. Located in the Chancellor Building is the Vancouver school of theology dining room, women's resource centre, a resident lounge, Chapel of the Epiphany, an auditorium, study carrels, meeting rooms and a library reading room.

In 1927 Ryerson College, Westminster Hall and Congregational College amalgamated to form Union College. UBC gave the college five acres of land on a 999-year lease to house the school. In May 1927 the cornerstone of the **Iona Building** was laid. The west wing was built in 1927, the tower or "Castle" in 1935, and the east wing in 1960. The principal's home, 25 yards west of the Iona building, went up in the mid-1950s. It contains many of the distinctive touches of Ron Thom, then a young architect with Thompson, Berwick and Pratt.

Located in the Iona Building are faculty offices, residence rooms, administration offices, classrooms, a board room, conference room and chapel. The stained glass window in the chapel on the second floor was dedicated in 1943 to George Bell, a layman of the Methodist and United Church and long-time member of the board of governors of Union College. In the rotunda one finds plaques honoring the late W.J. Van Dusen, who contributed many gifts to the school, including the stone facing on the tower, the board room and the entire east wing.

In 1971 the Anglican Theological College, Union College (United Church) and the Ecumenical College amalgamated to form the Vancouver School of Theology (VST). There are approximately 120 VST dorms accommodating mostly undergraduates. Although there are also approximately 180 students attending VST, there is no corelation between those attending VST and those living in residence.

War Memorial Gymnasium (1951) Built with money raised by students and alumni, the War Memorial Gym is UBC's largest gymnasium. It is dedicated to the memory of those connected with UBC who died in either of the two world wars. Their names are listed on a large plaque in the lobby.

As a result of the vast seating space (3,000 in the bleachers and 800 on the floor), the gym is

Woodward Instructional Resources Centre, 1973. vs

used for conferences, concerts and congregation, as well as for athletic events. The rest of the athletic facilities, other than the Aquatic Centre, are located at the south end of the campus. They include a stadium, indoor and outdoor tennis courts, three ice rinks, a curling rink, squash and racquetball courts, several smaller gymnasia, as well as fields for grass sports such as grass hockey and soccer.

West Parkade (1992) (Engineers: N.D. Lea Engineers, with Zoltan Kiss, architect) The nine-level $9.7 million parkade can accommodate 1,200 vehicles. The architecture is described as an evolution of the pattern set by the 1982 Fraser River Parkade and the 1988 North Parkade by the same engineers and architects.

Wilson Recordings Collection The collection began in the mid-1930s with a donation of scores, books, records and a phonograph from the Carnegie Foundation. Many of the scores are now part of the Music Library. Located on the main floor of the Sedgewick Undergraduate Library, the collection has grown to more than 35,000 recordings of music, prose, drama and other spoken material. The bulk of the recordings are classical music and literature, but you can also find in the record collection a section of sound effects and—for the jazz buff—several records of Ella Fitzgerald, Louis Armstrong and Billie Holiday. There are 78 audio carrels.

The Wilson Recordings Collection is named after Mrs. Ethel Wilson and Dr. Wallace Wilson, long-time friends and supporters of the university in general and the library in particular. This library has many other friends who continually update the collection with donated recordings. The favorite composers are Bach, Mozart and Beethoven.

Wood Products Laboratory (1990) A temporary one-storey trailer-type building used by the department of wood science.

Woodward Instructional Resources Centre (IRC) The centre was named after Charles Woodward who founded the first pharmacy in B.C., as well as Woodward's department stores. The centre was completed in 1972 with money given to UBC by the P.A. Woodward Foundation. The centre comprises a biomedical library, five lecture halls with a seating capacity of 117 to 500, fourteen seminar rooms, health sciences deans' offices and the department of biomedical communications. Also located in IRC are two lecture theatres each with a seating capacity of 700 people.

This building is the heart of UBC's Health Sciences Centre. It houses the following: Health Sciences Centre Hospital, including an acute care unit (240 beds), an extended care unit (300 beds) and a psychiatric unit (60 beds); faculty of medicine; faculty of dentistry; faculty of pharmaceutical sciences; school of nursing rehabilitative sciences; school of audiology and speech sciences. UBC follows a health team concept, encouraging different disciplines to work together more fully.

Charles Woodward Memorial Reading Room This room is dedicated to pioneer physicians of British Columbia. It contains rare volumes in UBC's biomedical collection, books on the history of medicine and science, as well as Canada's leading collection of angling and game fish books, made possible by the Harry Hawthorn Foundation for the Inculcation and Propagation of the Principles and Ethics of Fly Fishing.

The large Gobelin tapestries, *Masters of the Spirit* and *Masters of Science*, were created in France and finished in 1948, each taking three years to complete. They were a gift to UBC by the P.A. Woodward Foundation. The upper tapestry is known as the *Neurological Tapestry*. The artist had a cerebral hemorrhage when he had completed the left half of the tapestry, but after his recovery he completed the work. Compare the left and right sides and note how they differ.

The Ubyssey: A Vile Rag, Fer Damshur
Tom Hawthorn

I N 1955 THE Reverend E.C. Pappert flipped through a copy of the *Ubyssey* before pronouncing it "the vilest rag you can imagine." Of course the student-staff of the offending journal merrily adopted the clergyman's slur as a motto. To this day it is used as a recruitment come-on.

For more than 75 years the student newspaper at the University of British Columbia has amused, outraged and offended its readers. On occasion it has even informed them. The *Ubyssey* has been called the best unofficial school of journalism in the country. Newsrooms are filled with assorted scribes and hangers-on who earned their first bylines in what continues to proclaim itself the best rag west of Blanca Avenue.

The paper has produced poets (George Bowering, Tom Wayman, Earle Birney) and politicians (John Turner, Pat Carney, Ray Perrault), judges (Nathan Nemetz, Les Bewley) and journalists (Pierre Berton, Allan Fotheringham). In fact *Ubyssey* alumni are common in most every field save one—academia. (Patricia Marchak, who became UBC arts dean, is a notable exception.)

First published under the unpromising title of *Anonymous* by Caroline P. Munday, the monthly became the *Ubi Cee,* a pun on the university's initials, in 1917. The *Ubyssey* ("The Odyssey of U.B.C.") first appeared on October 17, 1918, with the banner headline: "FRESHMAN RECEPTION: 'Frosh' Have the Privilege of Shaking Hands with Important Personages." It was a staid and sober weekly but that was soon to change.

By 1920 a letter writer was moved to declare the *Ubyssey* to be "a glorified gutter newspaper." It was the opening salvo in a battle that has continued to this day. Over the years the paper has been censored, seized and shut down. Publication was suspended entirely in free speech battles in 1931, 1951, 1959, 1961 and 1993. In 1931 the paper printed a fake funeral notice. The memorial read: "Sacred to the memory of Free Speech." Sixty-two years later the staff bought an obituary notice in one of the daily newspapers to make the same point.

In April, 1994, the paper was closed by its publisher, the Alma Mater Society, which operates as the student government. It did not reappear on campus until July 13, 1995, returning only after students voted to revive the newpaper as an independent publication. "We were away for so long," noted coordinating editor Siobhan Roantree, "that students forgot

facing page: The 1950s Buchanan Building, UBC is one of several modernist buildings on campus. rw

A 1920 letter writer declared the Ubyssey "a glorified gutter newspaper"

why they hated us so much."

The *Ubyssey's* tradition of irreverence has perhaps offended the most over the years. After all, one reader's satire is another's smut. On a newspaper known for both puerile pranks and snappy journalism, those most likely to be offended indeed become the target.

The *Ubyssey* has been called "squalid," *(Vancouver Sun),* and "irresponsible" *(the Province).* Judge Les Bewley, a former staffer, once suggested the paper should be "drenched in Lysol." Worst of all, humorist Hymie Koshevoy complained that his old paper had become "drab and portentous." In 1965 a *Sun* editorial called the paper "cheap, vulgar and nasty." Its offense: printing three four-letter words in a single edition. In an age of undergraduate rebellion, intemperate language seemed but a minor transgression.

The ferment of the 1960s was well-reflected in the paper's pages. When four photographs from *Playboy* magazine were ruled obscene, forcing the magazine from local newsstands, the *Ubyssey* reprinted the offending pictures as a protest against censorship. That was too much for crusty Margaret (Ma) Murray, legendary editor of the *Bridge River-Lillooet News.* She called the *Ubyssey* "a filthy rag" demanding it be suspended, "fer damshur."

While at times it has been as much social calendar as news source, the paper has a proud legacy of campaigning against injustice. It encouraged the protests that led to the Great Trek of 1922, a march that embarrassed the provincial government into building the long-promised Point Grey campus. That done the paper took up a crusade against fraternity hazing. The brutal practice was halted in 1924.

During World War II the *Ubyssey* defended the rights of Canadian-born students of Japanese ancestry to study on campus. In 1963 Keith Bradbury exposed undercover RCMP agents spying on student political groups.

The *Ubyssey* printed statements and commentary suppressed by other papers fearful of reprisals under the War Measures act during the October Crisis of 1970. More recently it has earned notoriety for a trailblazing approach to reporting on sexuality.

Those who learned the newspaper trade by publishing an annual hoax story on April Fools' Day followed by a year-end goon issue (featuring such parodies as Torts Illustrated, Rolling Clone, Scientific Armenian, Maclown's and the ProVice) lament losing that carefree sense of freedom of the press.

SFU

Simon Fraser University
Bruce Mason

SIMON FRASER UNIVERSITY keeps the pace, the faith and its unique place in this part of the world. Fifty thousand people earned academic credentials in the first 30 years after the main campus opened on Burnaby Mountain on September 9, 1965.

With more than 20,000 undergraduates and 2,500 graduate students, 650 faculty and 1,000 staff, it has become a significant economic and cultural force, as well as a major teaching and research university.

Harbour Centre—a downtown satellite campus that opened on May 5, 1989—was originally financed through private sector funding and designed to meet another major challenge: mid-career education in the emerging global, knowledge-based economy. Within its first five years of operation the busy "intellectual heart of the city" was serving more than 50,000 people annually, who take advantage of new opportunities in life-long learning.

From the beginning, and at both sites, innovation and accessibility are what it's all about. Consistent growth and achievement are a matter of record and the university ranks as one of Canada's very best comprehensive schools in *Maclean's* magazine's annual ratings. By any measure, it's quite a success story.

SFU pioneered the year-round trimester system—self-contained 16-week semesters—a radical departure from the traditional academic year, with new possibilities for work and study. It also developed the "Oxbridge" system of tutorials, in which students, guided by tutors, were left to their own resources. Large lectures are supplemented with small discussion groups.

Admission requirements were relaxed for bright high-schoolers and mature students. Whiz kids and grandparents have always shared classes. Proposed admission requirements look beyond grades—to non-academic success in community service and life circumstances—on some student applications.

Interdisciplinary studies were built in. Students choose freely from an extraordinary range of courses, and renowned research is conducted in a complex organizational weave and cluster of departments, centres and institutes. SFU's continuing studies offers about 2,000 credit and credit-free courses which have a combined enrolment of 60,000.

Distance education also developed into one of Canada's largest programs—offering more than 100 courses to some

facing page: The Academic Quadrangle, SFU, built 1963–65. vs

12,000 students—along with new disciplines, such as pestology, kinesiology, communications, gerontology, criminology, resource and environmental management and computing science. Co-operative education—which combines academic study with semesters of full-time, paid work experience—is a Canadian education hallmark and SFU has one of the largest, longest-running and most successful co-ops in the country.

In 1995 the SFU-led and -based TeleLearning Research Network (TL-RN) was established by the federal government. It is an unprecedented collection of more than 125 researchers at 28 universities and other organizations established to convert the information highway into a global cyberclassroom. Among other things, TL-RN will create the Virtual University, the first networked multimedia system in the world, specifically customized for teachers and learners.

From 365 metres above the river, also named for the fur trader and explorer, in "splendid isolation," 30 minutes east of downtown Vancouver, North America's only mountain top campus overlooks the city, its suburbs and Burrard Inlet, with a panoramic view of North Shore mountains, fjords, farmland or fog.

Outdoor convocation ceremonies, held in June and October, attract more than 20,000 visitors (occasionally huddled under blankets). At the cue of SFU's world championship pipe band, brightly-robed graduates and faculty proceed along "philosopher's walk," through a garden symbolizing Canada's geography, past the reflecting pond, to the grand stairway leading to convocation mall.

"No great event of our time in this province will surpass the lasting significance of this formal opening," Premier W.A.C. Bennett told a 1965 crowd of 5,000, the first of many to gather on the mall.

Standing before the library which would bear his name, he meant what he said and later left his papers to the archives. Even those who had labelled his decision to build a "university for B.C.'s working people" as "Bennett's folly" and a "Sacred monument" were agog at the instant, miracle university.

Only two years earlier a report had urged the government to build another university on the Lower Mainland "as soon as possible," before existing institutions became inevitably and hopelessly overcrowded. With the document still warm in his hands, Bennett called on Gordon M. Shrum—former head of physics at UBC (1937-60)—a 67-year-old "bulldozer in a blue serge suit" and who had earned a reputation in "retirement" as "a man to get things done."

Although he was co-chair of the giant B.C. Hydro—responsible for the $880 million Peace River Dam, Canada's largest single construction project after the St. Lawrence Seaway—Shrum also took on the job of founder and first chancellor.

The task Bennett assigned him was to find a site, construct a campus, hire staff and faculty, enroll students and develop an academic program, within two years!

Among other things, Shrum-the-physicist had discovered the liquefaction of helium, and invented a Geiger counter in his spare time. But he valued teaching above research and installed photo-radar beams which lit up "Late Again!" when tardy students arrived in his UBC classrooms. From his lectern Shrum-the-teacher gargled liquid air or filled his lungs with helium, producing unforgettable blasts of frozen fog and cartoon-like voices.

Shrum had scrounged huts from abandoned military bases when a wave of World War II veterans enrolled at UBC. The buildings of an entire airforce base were floated on barges from Tofino, on Vancouver Island. "I suppose you could say we stole them," he later recalled, "but sometimes its necessary to cut red tape to get the job done." He now seconded a small Hydro plan—under the pretense of surveying power lines and substations—to begin the search for a site. Municipal governments were keen and quick with offers of land—two sites in Surrey, two in Burnaby and one in Delta were proposed.

Decrying Burnaby Mountain as "too difficult" until Mayor Alan Emmott upped the ante from 16 to just over 400 hectares, Shrum then declared it "imaginative—a site, excelling UBC's Point Grey in natural amenity, with an immediate opportunity to achieve unique stature, unsurpassed grandeur, distinction and significance." The die was cast. SFU would be unlike any other university. Especially UBC.

Shrum announced an architectural competition—a two-year design project, with a four-week deadline—for a lightning fast-track megaproject of five buildings (library, theatre, gym, science and arts) where students could "navigate from one end to the other without going outside" to "look finished by September 1965."

From 71 entries (actually 72, but Mrs. Shrum stopped at the hairdresser before delivering it, too late), which included more than 200 drawings of walled cities and high rises, the international panel made a unanimous decision: a proposal by the virtually unknown Arthur Erickson and Geoffrey Massey.

Their proposal was bold and wildly imaginative, a low-lying interconnected concrete structure, linked by a common courtyard, with a classic quadrangle, "hugging the mountain summit." This integrated community, based on ancient models, became the contemporary model for the North American campus. "It seems presumptuous to put towers on a mountain top,

besides we want to merge people and disciplines," explained Erickson, a UBC associate architecture professor, who had built only houses, but studied, first-hand, the relationship between the physical plants and educational philosophies at the world's great universities. "I really like concrete," he enthused, "it's the marble of our time, the stone of our century, and a natural material in the earth."

Reaction to the design was swift and mixed—from "square doughnut" to "square halo." "Works perfectly as an environment and monumental piece of architecture," declared the *New York Times.* "Stirring," added *Time* magazine, "a series of exciting, constantly changing vistas, a turning point in Canada's architecture." "Cold," "glum," "sterile" and "smelly," students, staff and faculty would later argue. "Magnificent to look at, not to work in," insisted an instructor.

The winners went to work on "Main Street" (convocation mall) and a transportation centre with a unique glass rotunda, while four runners-up were responsible for five other projects: the library, academic quadrangle, gymnasium, theatre and science complex.

Shrum now seized the opportunity for a new beginning, academically as well as architecturally, based on "instant traditions." At his side was the first president, Patrick D. McTaggart-Cowan, former head of Canada's meteorological services, dubbed "McFog" and "the weatherman" by students.

"We're facing a population explosion, a cost explosion and a knowledge explosion," they warned. "Universities have to teach more students more things and they have to do it more efficiently." "We'll stop the brain-drain and muscle-hustle of students out of B.C.," promised Shrum, "even if we have to buy the best faculty."

"Microfilm in the library," and "Lectures on TV," reported a gleeful media who jotted down his spontaneous, unorthodox opinions on "egg-heads," "stay-in-schoolers," "waitresses with more than Grade 8" and new ideas such as using "housewives as tutors" and establishing a campus "baby sitting service."

The use of technology began with early innovations such as taped lectures (which now includes more than 300 courses). It led to the first computerized university library and student registration in the nation, a leading network of microcomputing facilities, video conferencing of courses with other campuses and to TL-RN, a leading player in Canada's knowledge-based society and economy.

Many "instant traditions" were controversial, including offering the first financial assistance for academically qualified athletes (endorsed decades later by other Canadian universities). SFU would also be the first and only Canadian university to compete in the U.S.-based National Association of Inter-collegiate Athletics (NAIA).

Meanwhile, a parade of trucks rumbled through Lower Mainland streets hauling seemingly endless loads of cement along steep, gravel access paths sliced through the forest. Construction crews brush-hammered vast expanses of concrete and laid thousands of tiles, while throngs of curious onlookers gathered at the edge of the clearing for a glimpse.

Supports for the library—which would house more than a million books and had to withstand earth tremors—were made from Saturna Island gravel, baked until it resembled popcorn. The 30 pre-cast beams for the gymnasium roof—the largest ever built in Western Canada—weighed 36 tons each and were carried individually on four tractor units with steering trailers, along roadways which the original city buses had to climb in reverse, until they were fitted with more powerful engines.

"The whole mountain is swarming with men and equipment," a reporter wrote in May 1964. "At 9 A.M. officials signed a contract to build the $1 million gym; at 10 A.M. the government granted approval to build the gym and a $3 million library; and at 11, they were pouring concrete for the footings."

The haste and two tough winters were later blamed for the ubiquitous leaks (Erickson had wanted different and more expensive grades of concrete). But there was only one real construction snafu—the mall is covered by 400 metres of glass, and the wrong size was ordered. After a heavy snowfall, nearly half the panels broke. Twice as many, half the original size, were later installed. In the shadow of the broken mall roof, however, the sky seemed to be falling and SFU's foundation began to shake and show cracks.

"I wanted an experimental university," said Shrum, "where new ideas would flourish and creative people would flock in." He got it.

Applications from acclaimed scholars and enthusiastic students poured into the unfinished offices of the "brand-new educational experiment" from around the world.

Even before SFU opened, there was a call for a freeze on fees. Students immediately "liberated" the staff-only elevators and the carpeted, wood-panelled faculty lounge. They called for a boycott of cafeteria food and held a "plant-in" at a proposed parking lot. "Shift Shell" protests concerned a campus gas station, which blocked the view of Indian Arm from popular hitch-hiking spots at the "commuter university." Winning what they considered token concessions—the mechanic's bays were moved to the back—students demanded a say.

Student Power had arrived and it would never really leave. At issue was a cheeky demand for student representation on sen-

ate and the board of governors. And for faculty: freedom and security. There were mall rallies and teach-ins, strike committees and anti-Vietnam War demonstrations, myriad coalitions, Black Power, Red Power and something called the Women's Caucus, a faint first whisper of feminism.

Five teaching assistants were fired by the board of governors in 1967 for supporting a student who had criticized a teacher at Templeton High School. The board recanted when the howl for academic freedom reached previously unheard-of decibels.

The political science, sociology and anthropology department, a madcap collection of brilliant New Left academics, included many devoted to democratizing universities by translating thought into action. They would butt heads and rhetoric with conservatives over hiring and firing, courses and conduct, for years to come.

A popular soap box—a Hyde Park-style podium—was a gift from Erickson, whose campus design worked better than even he could have imagined. This platform in the uncovered portion of the mall—which came to be called "Freedom Square"—attracted thousands to rallies, including journalists and photographers.

"Radical U," said TV anchors and crewcutted news people, who had visuals of wild-eyed, long-haired "weirdos" to prove it. "Hippie U," taxpayers wrote to editors and told the talk shows. "Ding-a-ling hill," barked a radio sportscaster.

Panty raids, Miss SFU contests, pep rallies and fraternities were quickly cast aside. *The Peak,* the student newspaper, published *Screw the System* and *The Student as Nigger* and students staged *The President's Other Ball.*

Some suggested that the major (concrete) access road, Gaglardi Way (named for Socred Highways Minister "Flyin'" Phil) be changed to "Ho Chi Minh Trail." Others suggested "Louis Riel U," in honor of the hanged Metis leader.

"Simon Fraser sought out these scholars," insisted the *Province.* "It searched around the world for young, questioning iconoclasts who wanted to set up a new order. It got them, now it can't cope with them or them with it." "More like Wreckers than Reformers," harrumphed the *Vancouver Sun.*

SFU students would eventually be first to win elected representation on senate and the board of govenors, followed by SFU alumni and staff. And the meetings of both bodies would be opened to the public.

In May 1968 the university was first censured by the Canadian Association of University Teachers (CAUT). The charge: interference in academic affairs by the board of governors. It was lifted in November but reinstated in October 1970, when seven faculty were dismissed from the PSA (the Political Science, Sociology and Anthropology department).

Eventually the PSA was broken into separate political science, sociology and anthropology, and archaeology departments, and the censure was finally removed in 1976.

SFU's community continues to win Rhodes Scholarships, Guggenheim fellowships, research and teaching awards, Orders of Canada and Olympic medals. Sociology professor Ernest Becker was given the Pulitzer Prize in non-fiction, posthumously, for *Denial of Death.* The English department's George Bowering has two Governor General's awards (poetry, fiction). Among the faculty is Birute Galdikas, world authority on the orangutan and "third angel" of famed anthropologist Louis Leakey, with Jane Goodall (chimpanzees) and the late Dian Fossey (gorillas).

Alumni include MPs and MLAs, lawyers and Queen's Counsels, arts and business leaders, such as journalist John Sawatsky, former CP Air head Ian Gray, former auditor-general Ken Dye, the former Margaret Trudeau and film-maker Terre Nash, who won an academy award in 1983 for *If You Love This Planet.*

Controversy was formally enshrined by the founder of SFU's School of Computing Science, Ted Sterling and his wife, Nora. Their annual Sterling Prize in support of controversy was first awarded, in 1994, to the original chair of economics Parzival Copes, who had been driven out of Newfoundland in the sixties for predicting that the cod fishery couldn't sustain the population. The second recipient, Russel Ogden, who studied euthanasia and AIDS, refused to break his promise of anonymity in Coroner's Court. He won his case and then sued the university for legal costs.

Opening day remains SFU's defining moment. In the shadows of unfinished buildings—the academic quadrangle had only three sides—the colorful flash of pomp and speechifying was highlighted by a standout performance. "As Anthony said, lifting the flap of Cleopatra's tent after travelling to Egypt to visit—'I didn't come here to talk,' " began Lord Lovat, dapper, graying war hero and 17th head of the Clan Fraser. Brandishing a broadsword, used in battles against the English and during Wolfe's capture of Quebec, he shouted through the applause, "Nous Sommes Frets" (We are ready), the clan motto, which was immediately adopted, along with a modified Fraser crest.

SFU's pipe band, formed to play at times of "great joy and great sadness," first won the world championships in Glasgow, in 1995. The university offers scholarships to the pipers and drummers who flock to the campus from around the world. So many, in fact, that a second-tier band has been formed, along with the Robert Malcolm Junior Memorial Band.

Although Simon Fraser himself never set foot in Scotland, his heritage also lives on in SFU's 17 varsity teams—The Clan. With 500 plus members in the NAIA, SFU is frequently judged as having the best female and male athletic programs and has won dozens of championships. It's the nation's training centre for soccer and wrestling, a training centre for middle distance running and throwing events, and host of one of the largest and most successful sports camp and summer programs in Canada.

More players than from any other institution have gone on to the Canadian Football League, including Dave Cutler, who kicked his way to a world record for points scored in pro football, and Lui Passaglia, who outdistanced even Cutler.

The major playing field is named in honor of Terry Fox, a junior varsity basketball player who lost a leg to cancer and raised millions of dollars for cancer research, despite dying before he completed his cross-country run, the Marathon of Hope. The Terry Fox humanitarian awards at SFU are funded by a $5 million dollar endowment, administered by Lorne Davies, who built SFU's highly regarded athletic department from scratch, over a 30-year period. The annual scholarship awards are given to about 20 students from across Canada for humanitarian work.

The eras at SFU are represented by those who have occupied the solitary president's house on Burnaby Mountain. Patrick McTaggart-Cowan (1964-68) shared responsibility for building and opening the university on schedule and chaired and endured "long, arduous and torn" meetings. "Faculty return home at 2 A.M., tell their spouse they were at a senate and are believed," one dean remarked. He would eventually lose the confidence of Shrum, the board of govenors and others in a community consumed by sixties' intellectual ferment.

Kenneth Strand (1968-74) used a bull-horn to warn students to end an occupation of the administration building (1968) over access to admission records. When 114 refused to comply, they were arrested by 200 RCMP he had summoned to campus. He also hammered out agreements on faculty promotion, renewal and tenure, and appointments of chairs and deans. A new administration building was named Strand Hall.

Pauline Jewett (1974-78)—Canada's first female university president—worked to have the CAUT censure lifted. And women's studies, a senior's program, distance education into the B.C. Interior, and an innovative child-care centre were established.

George Pedersen (1979-83) cooperated with BCIT to establish downtown classes in rented office space. During his tenure part-time studies for mature students and the school of engineering science, which concentrates on new technology, began.

William Saywell (1983-94) was greeted by cutbacks—the "worst financial crisis for universities since the depression"—and responded with painful, painstaking tuition increases, program and staff cuts, salary roll-backs and hiring freezes, but left enrolment unchanged. Saywell's legacy—the Bridge to the Future capital campaign—began in 1986 with a $33 million goal and surpassed $60 million, two-thirds of which went to the main campus, the remainder going to create high-tech Harbour Centre, inside what had once been Spencer's department store.

"I believe the collective wisdom of the community is what a president needs to tap, rather than imposing a particular view," says John Stubbs, current president and vice chancellor. An historian and consensus builder (who insists on teaching), he oversees a $150 million operating income, research grants totalling $18.5 million and donations, $10 million. SFU generates more than $400 million in economic activity in the GVRD.

Ongoing public readings, lectures, conferences and seminars take place in all SFU's five faculties—arts, education, sciences, applied sciences and business administration.

Public services include the library and archives, performances and exhibitions, often free, in theatre, dance, music, film and art. Noteworthy are the art gallery and archaeology museum. The public also has access to gyms, pools, fields and elite varsity competition.

Research is varied and specialized. The magnetic fields of the brain are measured on one of three scanners in the world. Engineers and dancers develop renowned choreography software, psychologists and criminologists join forces to fight crime, and economists and geographers actively work with communities struggling to survive.

The university is a world leader in chemical ecology and pest management, and in 1988 an SFU team synthesized a queen bee pheromone (message-carrying chemicals) that others had tried to replicate for 25 years. It's used to boost production in North America's $20 billion fruit and vegetable industries.

Burnaby Mountain is one of three B.C. Discovery Park research and development sites and has a university industry liaison office. Joint research facilities include Bamfield Marine Station and TRIUMF (Tri-University Meson Facility).

With UBC and the Society for the Reform of Criminal Law, SFU operates the International Centre for Criminal Law Reform and Criminal Justice Policy, one of only two such institutes in the United Nation's network of crime prevention and criminal justice.

In addition to many international affiliations and co-op placements, SFU has more than 30 student exchanges in 15 countries, field schools or group study tours in seven countries as well as development projects, primarily in Latin America and the Pacific Rim.

A partnership with the Secwepemc Cultural Education Society in Kamloops resulted in university-level courses oriented to the Shuswap people and the first full graduation ceremony in 1994.

Across the street from Harbour Centre an international conference centre—in the heritage Toronto-Dominion Bank building—will be unique in the Pacific Northwest, and among the best facilities of its kind anywhere.

"It was a centre of unrest, but they would solve their problems," said Erickson, "because there was no escaping them." He designed the west mall complex (1995), the largest single capital project since the university was built. The student services building (1996) consolidated myriad services previously scattered across campus. And yes it is possible (unlike UBC) to walk across the entire campus (the "human path") under cover from rain.

Despite his many accomplishments, SFU remained the "greatest joy" for Gordon Shrum, who died at 90 in 1985. The science wing carries his name, along with the popular crosstown football bowl and annual grudge match with UBC.

In 1995 the university agreed to convert 320 hectares of campus land on the mountain into public green space in exchange for a multi-million dollar endowment fund and greater flexibility in development of the remaining 140 hectares.

Construction cranes are part of the landscape and jackhammers batter the soundscape, as building and repairs go on.

The "commuter campus" now has more than 1,125 units for student residence, including townhouses, available for rent by the public during the summer semester. Plans are being made to create a "city on the hill." Eventually the campus will be connected to more housing, commercial services and sports facilities. Parking problems, like the weather, are a fact of life.

But as universities juggle increasing demands and decreasing funding, SFU, in its inimitable way, and true to its mandate, will continue to create innovations to further increase accessibility to education, including the most radical notion of all, education in cyberspace.

"It will make an elegant ruin," architect Bruno Freschi decided, back at the beginning.

Colleges

MODEL P50

Colleges

Ben D'Andrea

A MAJOR CHANGE IN this section since the original *Vancouver Book* appeared in 1976 is the emergence of Kwantlen University College. *The Greater Vancouver Book* is indebted to Charlie Giordano of Kwantlen's journalism department, many of whose students contributed time and energy to the research and writing of articles for the book.

VANCOUVER COMMUNITY COLLEGE

When it opened its King Edward Centre doors in September, 1965 Vancouver City College was the first two-year community college in Canada. The new college was formed by bringing together the Vancouver School of Art, established in 1925, the Vancouver Vocational Institute, established in 1949, and the King Edward Senior Matriculation and Continuing Education Centre, established in 1962. Vancouver City College became Vancouver Community College (VCC) when it separated from the Vancouver School Board in 1974.

The domed grey stone building of the King Edward Centre on Fairview Hill at 12th and Oak was in fact the old King Edward High School, built in 1905. The high school moved to another location when the new two-year college moved in. A connection between the old high school and the new college was preserved, however, in that the first principal of Vancouver City College, J.D. Newberry, was the former principal of King Edward High School.

Overcrowding soon became a problem at the King Edward campus and the new Langara campus at 49th and Ontario was opened in October of 1970 to house the college's academic and career programs. (When the Langara campus separated from VCC in April, 1994 it became Langara College.) The King Edward Centre became the special programs division and offered the college's core programs in English-as-a-second-language and remedial English.

The old King Edward building was less crowded after the Langara campus opened but it still presented many inconveniences. Its playing field served as the emergency landing site for Vancouver General Hospital helicopters. Bouncing too vigorously on the gymnasium floor was said to bring parts of the ceiling raining down. Then, on June 19, 1973, the special programs division was left homeless when a fire, assumed to have been caused by faulty wiring in the attic, gutted the building. Classes were temporarily held at the Langara campus until new

Facing page: Welding instruction, Vancouver Community College, 1988. vs

classrooms could be built on the playing field. By September the special programs division was once again being administered from the King Edward centre.

A new $26 million campus facility for the King Edward centre was finally built in the Mount Pleasant area at 1155 East Broadway and was officially opened in 1983. Its opening was marked by a trek—billed as "King Edward's Last Trek"—of more than a thousand students. Most of the students walked but a few made the trip from the old campus on Oak Street to the new campus on Broadway riding in a horse-drawn carriage. The stained glass window depicting King Edward VII from the original high school survived the 1973 fire and is now located on the second floor of the King Edward campus library.

Located in the block above Victory Square on land once occupied by the old Central Elementary School, Vancouver Vocational Institute (VVI) officially opened in November, 1949. In its first semester the institute enrolled 600 students in 23 different classes.

Like the old King Edward centre, VVI's downtown building was soon full to capacity. As student enrolment rapidly increased some of the institute's programs like plastering, bricklaying, drywalling and aircraft repair were forced to relocate to places such as the poultry and livestock buildings at the P.N.E. A $2 million addition to the downtown building in 1964 finally made it possible for all VVI classes to return to the downtown campus. In 1969 a multi-storey extension was built. Another major construction and renovation project was completed in 1983. (The Vancouver School of Art had by then become a separate institution and had moved to its new location on Granville Island.) In 1990 VVI was renamed the City Centre campus of Vancouver Community College.

Since the Langara campus separated from VCC to become Langara College, VCC has served its students on two campuses: the City Centre campus at 250 West Pender Street and the King Edward campus at 1155 East Broadway.

Today VCC, City Centre offers over 60 full-time and part-time career and technical programs to over 3,000 students each year. The programs in tourism and hospitality, business, health care and technical training are the centre's largest. Some of its programs such as jewellery art and design, and printing production are unique in Western Canada. One of its oldest training programs is practical nursing, a part of the centre's health division that in fact predates the founding of VVI.

The King Edward campus continues to serve primarily those students studying English-as-a-second-language. But a large number of students enrolled at King Edward are in the adult basic education program. The smaller careers division of the campus offers training in six different programs: auto mechanics, auto body, diesel mechanics, pharmacy technical assistant, institutional aide and music. More recently established was an international education program for overseas students planning to pursue university degrees in Canada and for Canadian students wishing to study in post-secondary schools in other parts of the world.

The continuing education division of VCC offers nearly 2,000 courses at both campuses to more than 27,000 adult students each year. Since 1979 it has offered a court interpreting program, the first of its kind in Canada. Starting in 1989 continuing education has expanded to offer several new certificate programs: small business management, office administration, local area network administration and telecommunications management. It now offers over 35 certificate programs as well as a wide range of non-certificate courses.

CAPILANO COLLEGE

On March 7, 1968 voters in the school districts of North and West Vancouver and Howe Sound decided overwhelmingly in favor of establishing a community college, the fourth two-year college approved in the province. Following the referendum a new college council was formed and at its inaugural meeting members voted on a name. From among forty names suggested by North Shore residents—including Evergreen, Alpine, Sunset, Muskrat, and Seagull—the clear winner was Capilano.

By the first day of classes on September 10, Capilano College had enrolled about 750 students, twice the anticipated number. Classes were held in temporary quarters at West Vancouver Senior Secondary School and later in several church basements, a warehouse and even a bowling alley. The college operated on an after-hours basis from 4:00 in the afternoon to 10:30 at night. Initially the college offered 23 courses in four different career and vocational programs. Fees were set at $100 per semester.

The first principal of Capilano was the Vancouver-born Alfred (Alf) H. Glenesk. Unaware of the job opening to head the new college Glenesk did not apply. But the fledgling college needed a man with Glenesk's background. His 22 years in education and his experience as vice-principal of another recently established two-year college, Vancouver City College, made Glenesk the ideal candidate. He was persuaded to take the job and served as principal of Capilano College from its inception to the spring of 1974.

Plans for a permanent campus began to take shape in the college's second year but it was not until 1972 that a 13.7-hectare site in the Lynnmour area of North Vancouver, between Lynn Creek and the Seymour River, was finally chosen. A bear was found hibernating in the region when work began on clearing the site for the college's first permanent facility. The Lynnmour area was originally logged in the early 1900s and has some trees that are nearly 100 years old. Capilano's new Lynnmour Centre, consisting of classrooms, media centre, library, science labs and cafeteria was officially opened in November, 1973. A couple of years later construction began on two new additions to the Lynnmour development.

As part of a later construction phase the Cedar Building, with three floors of classroom and office space as well as a 90-seat lecture theatre, was constructed in 1991. In the same year a sports complex was completed with facilities including a gymnasium with a seating capacity of 1,700, an aerobics gym and a weight and fitness centre. Construction of a new student and instructional services building with a 350-seat performance theatre, new cafeteria and book store is expected to be completed sometime in 1996. In spite of the college's expansion second-growth forest still covers nearly one-third of the campus.

Capilano College also serves students on a regional campus in Squamish, established in 1973, and another in Sechelt, established in 1977. A south campus in Sechelt was also established at the Sechelt Indian band's House of Hewhiwus. A new Squamish campus was officially opened in May, 1995.

In 1968 the original Capilano College library was a 3.4 metre by 30.5 metre portable unit erected on the grounds of West Vancouver Senior Secondary. Well before its 15,000 books were in place, however, the library was described as already "bulging at the seams." In 1993, the college's 25th anniversary year, a new $10.9 million library was opened. The three-storey building has a shelving capacity of 200,000 books and includes an audio-visual centre, a media production lab and an achievement resource center (ARC) that provides services and courses to help students develop their learning and study skills.

Capilano College currently offers credit and non-credit courses in five program areas: an academic or university-transfer program, career and vocational programs, a preparatory program, extension programs and, more recently introduced, post-baccalaureate programs. The academic program provides students with a wide range of courses leading to a two-year diploma at the university-transfer level. The career and vocational programs lead to diplomas and certificates in creative and applied arts, business and commerce, education, community health and applied science. The adult basic education program provides upgrading courses leading to both a provincial- level diploma and an advanced-level certificate. The extension program offers non-credit workshops and lectures. Capilano's new post-graduate programs are in Asia-Pacific management and environmental sciences. Since the early 1990s Capilano College has also offered courses leading to undergraduate degrees in jazz studies, music therapy and administrative studies.

One of the ten largest employers on the North Shore, Capilano College currently enrols about 6,000 credit students a year.

DOUGLAS COLLEGE

"YEAH COLLEGE!" was the slogan of the publicity campaign to persuade voters in the Fraser Valley West college district to support the founding of a two-year college. With nearly one third of British Columbia's population the district was the province's largest. In addition to thousands of bumper stickers the campaign included 300 one-metre by two-metre roadside billboards.

On March 8, 1969 voters in the school districts of New Westminster, Burnaby, Langley, Coquitlam, Delta, Richmond and Surrey decided in favor of establishing a regional college, the seventh in the province. Two years later the school district of Maple Ridge voted to join the college district. Shortly after the success of the first plebiscite the college steering committee named the new institution after B.C.'s first governor, Sir James Douglas. Fees were set at $100 per semester.

The first principal of Douglas College was George C. Wootton, dean of divisions at Seneca College of Applied Arts and Technology in North York, Ontario. Wootton was a graduate of North Vancouver High School and UBC. While earning his doctoral degree in engineering Wootton served as president of UBC's graduate student association. After graduating he worked for five years at the Canadian Atomic Energy Commission. He served as principal of Douglas College from August, 1969 to September, 1979.

In the rush to get the college campuses ready in time for classes, Wootton combined his official duties as principal with construction work such as clearing the parking lot site for the New Westminster campus. At a rally on September 24, 1970 Wootton addressed the college's charter students from the ice rink of Queen's Park Arena. Two years later Douglas College's first 175 graduates received their two-year diplomas in a ceremony at the Royal City Curling Club in New Westminster.

The college was officially opened by then-Premier W.A.C. Bennett on Douglas Day, November 19, the anniversary of the day in 1858 that Sir James Douglas was sworn in as governor. Opening day ceremonies included a speech by Bennett in the auditorium of New Westminster Senior Secondary and the unveiling of a plaque. Mud surrounding the New Westminster campus at Eighth Avenue and McBride interfered with plans for a tour of its buildings.

Even before classes were in full swing the college's music department managed to organize a band that performed at orientation week activities. In September, 1970 classes for Douglas College's first 1,600 students were temporarily held at the high school in the evenings. In late October and early November classes were transferred to the college's three campus sites: a remodelled warehouse on Minoru Boulevard near Westminster Highway in Richmond, a 6.4 hectare campus with 10 portable buildings at 92nd Avenue and 140th Street in Surrey, and an 3.2-hectare campus with 13 portable units at McBride and Eighth Avenue in New Westminster. These portable campuses earned Douglas College the name "trailer park university."

The Surrey campus in the Green Timbers area boasted a spacious 18-metre by 9-metre cafeteria made by combining three portable units. The library on each of the campuses consisted of two portable buildings. The Richmond warehouse campus contained all of the college's science laboratories. Later on, to accommodate new industrial and vocational programs, the Newton Campus, consisting of two buildings, was built in Surrey at 77th Avenue, just off the King George Highway.

By 1981, in response to the enormous growth of the student population in the college region, Douglas College had expanded to eight locations. The possibility of dividing the college district into two smaller and more manageable areas was raised as early as 1979. About a year later the college board decided to separate the college into two independent institutions, one for the north shore of the Fraser River and another for the south shore. The separation officially came into effect on April 1, 1981. Douglas College retained its campuses in New Westminster, Coquitlam and Maple Ridge. The new college—later named Kwantlen—took charge of the campuses in Langley, Surrey (including Newton) and Richmond.

In 1978 the Douglas College council approved a downtown New Westminster site for the college's first permanent campus. The campus at Royal Avenue and Eighth Street was completed in the fall of 1982 and officially opened the following spring. The $40 million facility includes a two-storey library, a double gymnasium, a dance studio, a 350-seat performance theatre and a studio theatre. Less than 10 years after the new campus opened, a $3.5 million expansion and renovation project added new lecture theatres, offices and seminar rooms.

On March 8, 1982 the move to the new campus was marked by a trek of students, teachers and administrators. Accompanied by a marching band they walked or drove from the Queen's Park campus at McBride and Eighth Avenue to the new downtown site. Leading the trek on his black motorcycle was the college's second president, William L. Day. A pine tree uprooted from the old campus and transported by wheelbarrow was replanted on the new campus. Also transported during the trek was the wooden college entrance sign. A few years later that sign was given legs and turned into a bench.

On the occasion of the college's 20th anniversary all 18 babies born at Maple Ridge, Burnaby, and Royal Columbian Hospitals on Douglas Day, November 19, 1990 received Douglas College entrance scholarships.

In the late 1980s Douglas College offered programs in two Maple Ridge locations: the Dewdney Trunk site and Maple Ridge Senior Secondary School. In the fall of 1992 the $19 million Thomas Haney centre opened in Maple Ridge, a campus facility that Douglas College shares with Thomas Haney Secondary and Continuing Education for School District 42. The building includes a civic arts centre and theatre as well as sports facilities.

In Coquitlam, Douglas College offered courses at Winslow School. With the opening of the permanent campus these courses were relocated to New Westminster. Douglas currently offers training programs at its Lincoln centre in Coquitlam. The new $35 million Pinetree Way campus near the Coquitlam town centre opened in the fall of 1996.

When it opened in 1970 Douglas College offered courses in three program areas: career and vocational training leading to a certificate or diploma, academic studies for university-bound students and community-oriented courses including skills upgrading. Today these program areas have evolved into three divisions: academic, applied programs and community programs and services.

The academic division offers students first- and second-year university transfer courses in six diploma programs: an associate in arts degree, a diploma in criminology, an associate in science degree, a diploma in performing arts, a diploma in print futures and a diploma in general studies. In recent years the college's university-transfer program has attracted the largest enrollment.

The applied programs division includes programs ranging from nursing to commerce and business administration. The community programs and services division offers courses in areas such as social services, CPR, multiculturalism and recreation. Douglas College also has a centre for international education that serves foreign students studying at the college.

Douglas College enrols about 6,500 students in credit courses and more than 12,000 in continuing education courses each year.

KWANTLEN UNIVERSITY COLLEGE

As noted above, Kwantlen College was established in 1981 when the Fraser Valley college district served by Douglas College was divided into two smaller ones. A contest was held to find a name for the new South Fraser region college. From over 200 names suggested—including Tillicum, Dogwood, Surdel-Langrich and Salish—Kwantlen was the clear winner. The winning entry was submitted by Stan McKinnon, news editor of the *Surrey Leader*. The name Kwantlen means "tireless runners" and refers to the First Nations people who lived in the South Fraser region. A second contest was held to select a logo that reflected the college's native name. A faculty member of the Douglas College graphic arts department drew the winning design. The logo's colors are blue and brown, representing water, sky and land.

The first principal of Kwantlen College was Anthony Wilkinson. The English-born Wilkinson came to Canada in the early 1950s, served in the air force from 1954 to 1957 and went on to teach at Ryerson Polytechnical Institute in Toronto. He spent 23 years at Ryerson and was one of its instructional division deans when he accepted the appointment as Kwantlen principal. Wilkinson served as principal from the summer of 1981 to June of 1986.

When Kwantlen College was established it had no permanent campus buildings. Except for a 10-hectare site in Langley and leaky 17-year old portable classrooms on 140th Street in Surrey, Kwantlen leased its property and buildings. Early in 1986 a petition was circulated to get support for a plan to build a permanent campus at 72nd Avenue and 128th Street. The goal was to present the ministries of education and finance with 10,000 signatures. That summer Kwantlen was finally granted the authority to borrow money for a permanent campus.

Kwantlen's new Surrey campus was built on a 8.9-hectare site that has a farmhouse and small orchard in its southwest corner. The house belongs to Margaret Westerman who sold her property to Kwantlen in exchange for the right to live there. In the summer of 1987, before construction began on the college, the 64-year-old widow dug the ditch for the pipes needed to connect her house to the municipal water supply. The well that had served the farm since 1916 was finally replaced.

The Surrey campus officially opened on August 23, 1990. The old Surrey campus closed for good and several divisions of Kwantlen's Newton campus also moved to the new site.

The Richmond campus, located at 5840 Cedarbridge Way, consisted of a converted warehouse first leased by Douglas College in the fall of 1976. In 1989 Kwantlen received approval to build a new $37 million Richmond campus on the 4-hectare site of the former Lansdowne Race Track at the corner of Garden City Way and Lansdowne Road. Construction began in March, 1991 and the campus officially opened in August, 1992. The earthquake-resistant facility features a centre for applied design studies with 20 design labs, computer labs and a darkroom suite. It also includes Kwantlen's first day care centre.

Kwantlen's $30.4 million Langley campus opened in September, 1993. Located on a 18.2-hectare site at the Langley Bypass and Glover Road the facility features the provincial horticulture training centre which includes a greenhouse and nursery. Other facilities include a 250-seat music performance auditorium, a library and a day care centre. Located on the southwest corner of the campus site and now owned and maintained by Kwantlen College is the turn-of-the-century Wark/Dumais House, designated a heritage building by the B.C. Heritage Society.

Kwantlen College offers an array of programs ranging from first- and second-year academic studies for university-bound students to technical and vocational programs. Students can earn course credits leading to an associate degree, a diploma, a certificate or a citation. A variety of courses is offered at each of Kwantlen's four campuses but each campus has a program-area focus: university-transfer courses at the Surrey campus, vocational and technical training at the Newton campus, university-transfer courses and applied programs at the Richmond campus and horticultural programs at the Langley campus.

On February 2, 1995 Kwantlen became Kwantlen University College, the fifth college in the province to be granted the authority to develop degree programs. In 1994-95 Kwantlen served more than 13,000 students through its programs and more than 16,000 students through its continuing education division.

BCIT

In 1961 the B.C. government approved a plan to establish the province's first technical training institute. Not until the spring of 1964, however, did the B.C. Institute of Technology in Burnaby open its doors to its first class of 37 medical laboratory technology students. By September, with the institute's first 17 two-year technology programs in place, about 645 more students were enrolled, fewer than half the number who had applied. BCIT's original three-storey building was designed to accommodate 1,200 students but first-year capacity was set at 750. First-year fees were between $150 and $190, second-year fees $60. The institute's first 400 graduates received the two-year national diploma of technology on June 17, 1966.

The $7 million institute contained classroom equipment valued at $2 million. Classrooms for the hotel, motel and restaurant management course were among the most unusual and included a complete hotel front office, a fully furnished hotel room, a motel room with kitchenette and even a mahogany cocktail bar. Facilities for other courses included a fully operational planetarium, a room-size crude oil refinery and a miniature pulp mill capable of churning out 11 kilograms of pulp a day. The boiler room also served as a classroom for teaching boiler plant procedures.

At BCIT's official opening on October 6, 1964 then-Premier W.A.C. Bennett promised to double the institute's size. His promise was fulfilled when a new laboratory and classroom building opened in September, 1967. Today the main campus of BCIT at 3700 Willingdon Avenue in Burnaby includes 55 permanent buildings and a few portable structures. BCIT also has a Sea Island campus at 5301 Airport Road in Richmond and a Pacific marine training campus at 265 West Esplanade in North Vancouver.

A new $32-million campus at 555 Seymour Street in downtown Vancouver was completed in late 1996 and replaced BCIT's Howe Street facility. The eight-storey Seymour centre includes a conference room, lecture halls, an electronic media centre and a library.

The first principal of BCIT was Edward Cecil "Cece" Roper. Roper came to BCIT from teaching in the commerce department at the UBC where he had obtained a masters of business administration after 20 years in the mining industry. After graduating from the University of Alberta in 1936 with a Bachelor of Science in mining engineering Roper worked as a miner at the Britannia copper mine near Vancouver and, ten years later, was appointed mine manger. In 1955 he joined the staff of the mine's parent company, Howe Sound Mining, first as executive vice-president and then as president in 1957. Roper served as principal of BCIT from June, 1962, when the institute was still being planned, to June, 1967.

Early members of the BCIT Student Association were instrumental in getting new facilities built on the Burnaby campus. With the construction of a new playing field and track in 1968 the association succeeded in reaching its first big goal. Student executives also eventually persuaded the government of the need for a multi-purpose building to serve as a student centre. The $1.5-million student activity centre was completed in the fall of 1970 and included a cafeteria, a gymnasium and several other recreational facilities. An extension to the centre was built in 1973. Today the centre has four racquetball/handball courts, two squash courts and a weight training room. Outdoor recreational facilities on the main campus include four tennis courts, two playing fields and a fitness trail.

For years students at BCIT were known as the best dressed college students in Greater Vancouver: the institute had a dress code requiring ties and jackets for men and dresses or skirts—no slacks—for women. Student opposition to the policy slowly developed in the late sixties.

In 1968 the student association began a long campaign for a campus residence to accommodate the growing number of out-of-town students. Success, however, did not arrive until September, 1973 when an unoccupied building, formerly the Willingdon Avenue School for Girls, was converted into a residence for about 100 BCIT students. Another temporary residence was found in the following year. Finally, in 1978, a permanent residence was built on campus. It consists of five low-rise houses and accommodates up to 250 students.

The first BCIT library occupied a cramped room in the original 1964 building. The need for additional space led to a proposal for a separate library building. The library moved into its new two-storey building in the summer of 1968.

The rapid growth of BCIT, particulary at its Burnaby campus, reflected the constant need to accommodate new and changing training programs. With the addition of a new building in 1967 BCIT added nine new technologies in its three program areas of business, engineering and health. In 1966 the institute set up the evening programs of its extension division. It also acquired new programs and campus space when it officially merged with the Pacific Vocational Institute on April 1, 1986.

BCIT currently offers certificate and diploma programs in six school divisions: business, computing and academic studies, electrical and electronic technology, engineering, health sciences and trades training. In 1994-95 the institute served more than 38,000 students.

LANGARA COLLEGE

Formerly one of three campuses of VCC, Langara became a separate college on April 1, 1994.

The search for a new campus to replace the crowded King Edward Centre of Vancouver Community (City) College began only two years after that college was established in 1965. Five portable classrooms had been set up on the centre's playing field and additional offices had been squeezed into its former auditorium. An eight-hectare site in the northeast corner of Langara golf course was purchased in 1967 and construction of a new eight-million dollar campus to serve about 5,000 students began in April, 1969. The Langara campus, consisting of a five-storey library block and a three-storey instructional block, was completed in September, 1970.

The move to the Langara campus was marked by a "great trek" on October 13. About 3,000 students, teachers and administrators walked or drove from the old King Edward Centre at Oak Street and 12th Avenue to the new campus at 100 West 49th Avenue. The trek was led by Vancouver's mayor, the provincial education minister, the student council president and included the Vancouver Firemen's Band.

In keeping with the activism of the time students at the new Langara campus started fighting for a crosswalk at the busy intersection of 49th and Ontario almost as soon as the campus opened. In February of 1971 they stopped traffic to paint their own crosswalk on the street. The city eventually gave in to the students' demands and installed two crosswalks. Another student contribution to the Langara campus was the totem-pole erected in 1979 near the college's main entrance. Its sculptor was Don Yeomans, a Haida native and a graduate of Langara's fine arts program.

Later additions to the Langara campus included a two-storey gymnasium and a student union building. A new three-storey classroom and administration building is scheduled for completion sometime in 1996.

While the King Edward campus retained the college's vocational and English-as-a-second-language programs the new Langara campus became the centre for VCC's academic and career programs. Journalism, accounting and nursing are some of Langara's oldest programs. Today Langara offers more than 30 two-year career programs and an expanded selection of first- and second-year arts and science courses in its university transfer program. Career programs are offered in the areas of art and applied arts, business administration and community services.

Students in the arts and science programs have the option of earning an associate of arts, associate of science or a college diploma in arts and science. Students in the career programs can earn either a two-year diploma or a one-year certificate.

Langara's theatre arts program is well known throughout Canada. Theatre students present plays on their own stage, Studio 58, located in the basement of the academic building. More recently introduced programs include Pacific Rim business, environmental studies and publishing technology. Langara also operates a co-operative education program, begun in 1980, that combines academic studies with practical work experience.

Langara College currently serves about 5,000 students in its academic program and about 1,500 in career programs each day. An additional 8,400 students are served through Langara's continuing education division.

facing page: Students, Langara College, 1993. vp

Emily Carr Institute of Art & Design
Jacqueline Wood

AFTER 70 YEARS of producing more than 4,000 artists and designers the Emily Carr Institute of Art and Design is now almost as famous as the painter it was named after. It's ironic, then, that Emily Carr was not everyone's first choice of a namesake.

The school was only named after the Victoria-born artist in 1978. At the time there was a lot of support for calling it the British Columbia College of Art to reflect its new provincial mandate. Painter Gordon Smith, a former student and teacher at the school, was among those who opposed naming it after Emily Carr. Smith was on the school's board at the time and says there had been some fear that no one would know who Carr was. Many students also opposed the idea and protested against it.

The provincial government obviously went ahead with the name change anyway. "In retrospect, I think it was a good idea," says Smith. "Emily Carr was one of the greatest artists in Canada. Her name has become synonymous with the school."

The genesis of the institute was in 1920 when a group of artists, educators and art patrons formed the British Columbia Art League to lobby the province and city for a school. On October 1, 1925 the league got its wish when the Vancouver School of Decorative and Applied Arts opened its doors. In its early years the school was administered by the Vancouver School Board and was housed on the top floor of the board's offices at Hamilton and Dunsmuir.

Charles H. Scott was appointed principal in 1926 and remained with the school until his retirement in 1952. The institution's first of several name changes occurred in 1933 when it became the Vancouver School of Art (VSA). The school quickly became the focus of cultural activity in Vancouver: its students and instructors organized exhibitions, promoted art education and documented the life of the city through their art. Others went on to establish design firms, influencing the city's architecture.

In 1952 Fred Amess became principal and immediately oversaw the school's merger with the Vancouver Vocational Institute which later became Vancouver Community College (VCC). The art school's affiliation with VCC signified its evolution into a post-secondary institution.

An experimental mood hit the VSA in the 1960s. The influence of the ideas of Marshall McLuhan and the growth of image technology meant practitioners of traditional approaches to art had to make room for multi-media productions and industrial design.

In 1978 the newly named Emily Carr College of Art regained its independence from VCC through the efforts of then-principal Robin Mayor (appointed in 1972). With increased enrolment and a new mandate to serve all of British Columbia, the college needed a new facility.

As part of a federal urban renewal project on Granville Island three abandoned industrial buildings on Johnston Street were transformed into the school's new premises and officially opened in October 1980. The words "and Design" were added to the college's name.

Within three years the number of students had exceeded the limit of the new facilities. When Alan Barkley became the school's first president in 1986 painting courses had to be housed in leased space just off Granville Island. In 1988 new design programs were added and they too had to be moved to the off-campus facility.

Nevertheless the school continued to grow in enrolment and reputation. In 1989 the college began offering bachelor's degrees in fine arts and design through the British Columbia Open University. Then, in the summer of 1994, the College and Institute Act was amended to allow select institutions to offer bachelor's degrees. Emily Carr was among them and its name changed once again, this time to reflect its new status. The Emily Carr Institute of Art and Design (ECIAD) is now one of only two art and design schools in Canada that grant degrees under their own name.

The phenomenal growth of the school meant it needed new facilities yet again. Building a major extension to the institute was not a popular idea with every member of the Granville Island Trust, an advisory body overseeing development on the island. Maurice Egan, chair of the trust at the time, says a minority felt any new building should bring a financial benefit to Granville Island. Egan, now chair of the ECIAD board, argued that the island should be a centre for both the arts and commerce. "Commerce [on Granville Island] subsidizes arts—to an extent—and the absence of the school would have weakened the arts side," he says. A balance was struck when it was agreed that a 255-stall visitors carpark would be incorporated into the school's design.

In September 1994 ECIAD opened its new building across the street from the main campus thereby consolidating its programs on one site. The school now teaches some 700 full-time and more than 1,500 part-time students each year. Degrees and four-year diplomas are offered in studio (drawing, painting, print-making, sculpture and ceramics), media (animation, film/video, photography, multi-media), and design (electronic

New block, Emily Carr Institute of Art & Design, 1994. vs

communication, graphic and industrial). The total cost of the 5,400 square-metre structure was about $14 million. It even has a retractible roof that, with the push of a button, transforms the interior concourse into an atrium within 45 seconds.

The institute should not be measured just by its burgeoning growth, however. The heart of the institute has always been its faculty: respected artists and designers from Canada, the U.S. and around the world. Included among past faculty members are F.H. Varley of the Group of Seven who taught when it was still called the Vancouver School of Decorative and Applied Arts, and B.C. Binning who was instrumental in reviving West

Coast architecture and designed the mosaic of blue, green and black tiles on the BC Electric Building (now the Electra) on Burrard Street.

This distinguished faculty has, in turn, encouraged the development of artists with national and international reputations. Well-known alumni include painter Jack Shadbolt, designer Martha Sturdy, cartoonist Lynn Johnston (*For Better or For Worse*), Academy Award-winning documentary filmmaker Terre Nash (*If You Love This Planet*), Douglas Coupland, well-known author of *Generation X*, fashion designer Simon Chang and painter Richard Atilla Lukacs.

Trinity Western University
Lloyd Mackey

LONG AGO, A FEW miles south of Fort Langley, stood the Seal Kap Dairy Farm. Its pastoral home was on the banks of the Salmon River and it was flanked on the east by a virgin forest. Through its southeast sector each day the milk trains and interurban trolleys rattled on their way between Vancouver and Chilliwack.

In the early 1960s the urban influences began to encroach. On the north side of the farm, the new four-lane freeway heading east into the mountains pushed itself past. The milk trains and interurbans had disappeared a few years before, replaced with the long, rumbling coal trains carrying their payload from British Columbia's interior to the coal port at Point Roberts.

Earlier in the century clusters of Scandinavian immigrants had settled across Western Canada and in the adjacent American states. Some of them were members of the Evangelical Free Church. In the communities where they settled they started new churches where they could worship in their own language and traditions.

Two generations later the descendants of those immigrants sensed the need for a college—a place where their children could receive an education which integrated the faith and values that they held dear. These folks wanted a liberal arts school—not a Bible institute like those dotting the prairies. Some of them even dreamed it might some day become a real university. They cast their eyes on Seal Kap farm and, in the early 1960s, bought it on the wings of faith and prayer.

Trinity Junior College began classes in 1962. Its dorms were portable housing units moved from a B.C. Hydro construction project in B.C.'s interior. The dining hall was the old Seal Kap farmhouse; the barn was converted into—you guessed it —the "barnasium." There were 17 students.

In the 1970s, with 300 students then enrolled, Trinity Junior became Trinity Western and adopted its first four-year degree-granting program. In the mid-1980s it became a full-fledged university and began developing its first graduate programs. Today more than 2,000 students are enrolled in a dozen degree programs, ranging from business to nursing, from education to communications, from fine arts to science.

Masters degrees in counselling and nursing are just one reflection of the school's "servant leadership" philosophy. Taking its Christian roots seriously, it attempts to develop leaders who will win their right to lead by serving the needs of the communities in which they eventually settle.

They cast their eyes on Seal Kap farm and, in the early 1960s, bought it on the wings of faith and prayer

Community standards to which students commit themselves require that they refrain from drinking, smoking and extra-marital sex.

Trinity Western's president for its first nine years was an American named Calvin Hanson. When he resigned the governors looked for a Canadian. They found Neil Snider in a Bible college in Manitoba, with a freshly-minted doctorate in educational administration. He has been there 21 years now and relishes the challenge of continuing to develop an increasingly complex institution.

Six years ago Ken Davis, who had been academic vice-president, moved across the campus to pioneer a consortium of theological seminaries. There are now more than 200 students in what is known on the campus as "seminary village" and the community's first doctoral program—a doctorate in ministry—is about to come on stream.

Succeeding Davis was Donald Page, who had been an external affairs senior policy advisor in Ottawa. His previous "bosses" had been people like Mitchell Sharp and Joe Clark. His Ottawa experience persuaded him Trinity Western was uniquely equipped to develop a new generation of Canadian leaders.

In the 1970s, one of the school's founders, Robert Thompson, a respected parliamentarian, spearheaded the funding for an environmental project which gave Trinity Western its lake, flanking the west side of the campus. The lake was created out of some of the marshland through which the Salmon River flows.

Trinity Western's voluntary daily chapel service consistently attracts more than 1,000 students. They are regularly involved in a range of service projects both near the campus and, often, overseas.

Trinity Western's best known alumna is Deborah Grey, the first Reform Party candidate ever elected to the House of Commons. She was one of the MPs who gave up the federal pension plan, and it cost her $1.4 million. To her that is economics TWU style—you do the right thing and work with God to take care of the rest.

Continuing Education in Vancouver
Marg Meikle

CINNAMON BUNS: The Really Big Kind; Hormones: Our Body's Messengers; First Aid for your Pet; On-line Research; Latin Dancing; Web Page Design—just a few offerings from thousands in the 1996 continuing education fly-ers. As we ease towards the millennium it is safe to say that somewhere in Vancouver there is a course on just about any-thing you ever wanted to learn. Adult or continuing education, now part of what is called "lifelong learning," has became part of our make-up. And Vancouver's got a history of folks getting out there to soak up something new. Whether it's salsa-making, sailing or shorthand we've got a thirst for knowledge and, for-tunately, a lot of excellent resources to satisfy that thirst.

Adult education in the Vancouver area has been around since around the time of the 1858 gold rush. Mechanics' institutes in New Westminster, Moodyville (North Vancouver) and Hast-ings Mill were created in the 1860s. Their activities included reading rooms, exhibitions, lectures, debating, an orchestra, etc. An Act Respecting Literary Societies and Mechanics' Insti-tutes was passed in 1871 and provided the basis for the province to give grants to these organizations.

The first evening instruction in specialties began in 1888, the same year that the Vancouver Reading Room—forerunner of the Vancouver Public Library—opened. By the next year the Vancouver Art Association was founded and gave art classes and organized exhibitions. B.C. Tel began training programs for its employees in 1890 and the Methodist church taught English language classes for Japanese immigrants starting in 1891. Commercial libraries and reading rooms were fairly com-mon at the time. Diplock's Book Store offered use of their 3,000 volume collection for $2.00 per quarter (borrowing three books at a time was the limit).

Beginning in 1887 the YMCA became an important education centre for the developing city. At first the classes were primarily religious. Things really took off with YMCA evening classes in 1893 when they moved into their new building. The curriculum was broad: writing, arithmetic, penmanship, bookkeeping, French, shorthand, architectural drawing, music and elocution. And they did the most teaching until the Vancouver School Board began to offer courses in 1909 (with 966 registrants). The YWCA was founded in 1898. By 1907 they were offering English literature, Bible study, French, shorthand, dressmaking, embroi-dery, physical training and choral music. The St. John Ambu-lance Association started first aid instruction in 1909.

Whether it's salsa-making, sailing or shorthand we've a thirst for knowledge and a lot of excellent resources to satisfy that thirst

Lectures were very popular in early Vancouver. In 1907 the Imperial Order of the Daughters of the Empire (IODE) offered a series on "imperial" topics. The first was "Track of the Empire" by Sir Charles Tupper. The Vancouver Institute was founded in 1916 to offer lectures during the winter term. It is still going strong.

McGill University College, a partner of Vancouver College, started evening courses in 1907. The University of British Columbia was established in 1915 and began adult education work in 1917. By 1923 technical high schools opened in Van-couver providing facilities for adult education. The Vancouver School of Decorative and Applied Arts (later the Vancouver School of Art, then Emily Carr Institute of Art and Design) was founded in 1925.

Considerable effort went into education programs in relief camps from 1931 to 1938. In 1934 the province began recreation and physical education programs which were hugely popular. They were replaced by the community programs branch in 1952.

Throughout the next four decades major changes took place. In 1965 Vancouver Community College and Capilano College were opened and Vancouver School Board night school enrol-ment increased rapidly. The 1980s brought us province-wide distance learning through the creation of what has became the Open Learning Agency (a merging of the Knowledge Net-work—B.C.'s educational broadcaster—and the Open Learning Institute—the Open University and Open College). Delivery of courses now ranges from print to television to the Internet (http://www.ola.bc.ca).

Today, as the school seasons start, mailboxes and communi-ty newspapers fill with Vancouver School Board tabloids, a combined community centre tabloid and continuing educa-tion booklets from community colleges, UBC and SFU. The best places to find all of these publications are branch libraries and community centres. The social sciences reference desk at the main branch of the public library carries reference copies of everything they can get their hands on. And check the Yellow Pages under Schools.

Some Theses on Greater Vancouver
Deborah Wilson

ARCHAEOLOGY

Burley, David Vincent Marpole: anthropological reconstructions of prehistoric Northwest Coast culture type. SFU, PhD diss.,1979, 656pp.

ARCHITECTURE

Gutstein, Donald I. Towards a model of the urban development process. UBC, MArch. thesis, 1972, 282pp.

Mok, Ru-Ping Use of Chinese geomancy in contemporary architectural design. UBC, MArch. thesis, 1978, 156pp.

Virdi, Nirbhai Singh Theatre Vancouver. UBC, MArch. thesis, 1977, 195pp.

BIBLIOGRAPHY

Freer, Katherine M. Vancouver, a bibliography compiled from material in the Vancouver Public Library and the Special Collections of the University of British Columbia Library. U of London, Dipl. Lib., 1962, 234pp.

BUSINESS ADMINISTRATION

Ball, Brian Kent Ownership of Vancouver's C.B.D. 1951-71. UBC, MSc thesis, 1974, 85pp.

Dobrovolny, Jerry W. Guidelines for the development of a water conservation program for the City of Vancouver, B.C. SFU, MBA research project, 1993, 79pp.

Duval, Jean-Marc Japanese joint ventures in British Columbia. UBC, MSc thesis, 1974, 151pp.

Ferguson, Bruce Effect of the Vancouver advanced light rapid transit system on single family property values. UBC, MSc (Bus Admin) thesis, 1984, 116pp.

Finlay, Stephen Benefits, costs and policy strategies for telecommuting in Greater Vancouver. SFU, MBA thesis, 1991, 105pp.

Greenstein, Howard Barry Business of prostitution in Vancouver: an empirical study with policy implications. SFU, MBA research project, 1984, 165pp.

Higginbottom, Edward N. The changing geography of salmon canning in British Columbia, 1870-1931. SFU, MA thesis, 1988

Jamieson, William Sinclair Analysis of growth of Vancouver's central business district. UBC, MBA thesis, 1972, 179pp.

Liivamagi, Peeter Road pricing: a Vancouver case study. SFU, MBA research project, 1986, 108pp.

Skowronski, Paul Vancouver FM radio feasibility study. SFU, MBA research project, 1985, 97pp.

Sommers, Michael James Renewed life for Gastown: an economic case study and evaluation of commercial rehabilitation in the old Granville Townsite, Vancouver B.C. UBC, MBA thesis, 1971, 279pp.

Stacey, Duncan Technological change in the Fraser River salmon canning industry, 1871-1912. UBC, MA thesis, 1977

Wiebe, Gary Bernard Density and income patterns of metropolitan Vancouver. UBC, MSc (Bus Admin) thesis, 1988, 106pp.

Yee, Paul Chinese Business in Vancouver 1886-1914. UBC, MA thesis, 1983

CIVIL ENGINEERING

Jones, Evan Lewis Survey of household hazardous waste generation and collection preferences in the City of Vancouver, British Columbia. UBC, MSc thesis, 1990, 242pp.

Wallis, Douglas Montague Ground surface motions in the Fraser delta due to earthquakes. UBC, MSc thesis, 1979, 199pp.

COMMERCE

Barclay, Herbert Richmond Review of the finances of the City of Vancouver. UBC, BCom essay, 1935, 65pp.

CRIMINOLOGY

Bernard-Butcher, Diane Crime in the third dimension: a study of burglary patterns in a high-density residential area. SFU, MA thesis, 1991, 128pp.

Coburn, Gordon Maxwell Bradley Patterns of homicide in Vancouver, 1980-1986. SFU, MA thesis, 1988, 146pp.

Coutts, Dorothy Mae An examination of the structure of the women's unit, Oakalla Prison Farm. UBC, MA thesis, 1961

Newlands, Malcolm John Mackay An analysis of burglary offence patterns in a Vancouver neighborhood. SFU, BA (Honours) thesis, 1983, 160pp.

Sands, Dale Ecological perspectives on street-walking: testing a model for predicting active settings of female heterosexual streetwalkers in Vancouver. SFU, MA thesis, 1985, 223pp.

Young, Michael G. The history of Vancouver youth gangs, 1900-1985. SFU, MA thesis, 1993, 151pp.

ECONOMICS

Basi, Raghbir Singh Vancouver Board of Trade: a study of its organization and role in the community. UBC, BA essay, 1953, 122pp.

Renzetti, Steven Joseph The economics of a seemingly abundant resource: efficient water pricing in Vancouver, Canada. UBC, PhD diss., 1990, 180pp.

EDUCATION

Earnshaw, A.P. Russell Experience of job insecurity for women university graduates in temporary and contract jobs in Vancouver. UBC, MA thesis, 1987, 212pp.

Elderton, Victor James Study of children's behavior in family groups in the Graham Amazon Gallery, Vancouver Public Aquarium. UBC, MA thesis, 1986, 116pp.

Gordon, Wendy Lorraine Study of mental health services provided to mentally retarded adults in a metropolitan area. UBC, MA thesis, 1980, 273pp.

Haig-Brown, Evelyn Celia Taking control: power and contradiction in First Nations adult education. UBC, PhD diss., 1991, 367pp.

Hannah, Jo-Ann Shelley Socio-economic status and the career plans of grade 12 girls. UBC, MA thesis, 1986, 109pp.

Heath, Jean Educational programs for lone parent families in the city of Vancouver. UBC, MA thesis, 1982, 111pp.

Ironside, Linda L. Chinese- and Indo-Canadian elites in Greater Vancouver: their views on education. SFU, MA thesis, 1985, 126pp.

James, Cathy L. "An opportunity for service": women of the Anglican Mission to the Japanese in Canada, 1903-1957. UBC, MA thesis, 1991, 173pp.

Joe, Delbert Thomas The problems of Chinese youth gangs in the schools and community in Vancouver's Strathcona-Britannia area. SFU, MA (Ed.) thesis, 1976, 244pp.

Lefkos, Patricia Mae The development and implementation of a wilderness experience program for inner city elementary school children: a case study. SFU, MEd research project, 1982, 92pp.

Pallett, Joanne Hendrika Relief systems of alcoholics and problem drinkers. UBC, MA thesis, 1983, 122pp.

Thaler, Carol-Lyn Sakata Development of an ethnocentrism scale for junior high school students in British Columbia. UBC, MA Thesis, 1985, 144pp.

Tufuor, Joseph Kwame Changes in students' attitudes towards conservation resulting from outdoor education: a case study. UBC, EdD thesis, 1982, 219pp.

Willms, Jon Douglas Retarded adults in the community: an investigation of neighborhood attitudes and concerns. UBC, MA thesis, 1978, 150pp.

Chung, Rosamond C. Underemployment and the Chinese immigrant of former professional status: a qualitative-exploratory study. UBC, MA thesis, 1988, 224pp.

Ota, Midori Japanese schools overseas: their development and a case study of a supplementary school in Vancouver, Canada. UBC, MA thesis, 1988, 174pp.

Dhaliwal, Baljeet Sikhs in the Vancouver region: a descriptive study of certain Sikhs' views of education since 1904. SFU, MA thesis, 1986, 78pp.

Chiang, Po-Yu Emmy The development of school principalship in Vancouver, 1886-1928.

UBC, MA thesis, 1990, 98pp.

ENGLISH

Richards, Donna Jean Prestige and standard in Canadian English: evidence from the survey of Vancouver English. UBC, PhD diss., 1988, 275pp.

FINE ARTS

Duncan, Alan Slater Planning strategy for public art: City of Vancouver. UBC, MA thesis, 1990, 387pp.

Munroe, Doris C. Public art in Vancouver. UBC, MA thesis, 1973, 33pp.

Thom, William Wylie Fine arts in Vancouver, 1886-1930: an historical survey. UBC, MA thesis, 1969, 198pp.

FOREST ENGINEERING

Flynn, James Emmett Early lumbering on Burrard Inlet, 1862-1891. UBC, BSc essay, 1942, 48pp.

GEOGRAPHY

Anderson, Kay "East" as "West": place, state and the institutionalization of myth in Vancouver's Chinatown, 1880-1980. UBC, PhD diss., 1987, 467pp.

Apps, Mindy Jeanne From isolation to suburbia: the urbanization of Bowen Island. UBC, BA essay, 1973, 76pp.

Biggs, Wayne Griffin Ecological and land use study of Burns Bog, Delta, British Columbia. UBC, MSc thesis, 1976, 171pp.

Carr, Adriane Janice Development of neighborhood in Kitsilano: ideas, actors and the landscape. UBC, MA thesis, 1980, 221pp.

Cho, George Chin Huat Residential patterns of the Chinese in Vancouver, British Columbia. UBC, MA thesis, 1970, 127pp.

Collett, Christopher William Congregation of Italians in Vancouver. SFU, MA thesis, 1983, 170pp.

Connolly, Philip H. A geographical analysis of historical events in the Maple Ridge District. Geography, BA essay, 1953

Dowling, Robyn Margaret Shopping and the construction of femininity in the Woodward's Department Store, Vancouver, 1945 to 1960. UBC, MA thesis, 1991, 175pp.

Fairclough, Terence John Gay community of Vancouver's West End: the geography of a modern urban phenomenon. UBC, MA thesis, 1985, 107pp.

Fujii, George Toshio Revitalization of the inner city: a case study of the Fairview slopes neighborhood, Vancouver, B.C. UBC, MA thesis, 1981, 191pp.

Gale, Donald Thomas Impact of Canadian Italians on retail functions and facades in Vancouver. SFU, BA essay, 1968

Galois, Robert Michael Social structure in space: the molding of Vancouver, 1886-1901. SFU, PhD diss., 1980, 506pp.

Gibson, Edward Mark Walter Impact of social relief on landscape change: a geographical study of Vancouver. UBC, PhD diss., 1972, 237pp.

Hall, Wayne Robert Spatial behavior in Victory Square: the social geography of an inner-city park. UBC, MA thesis, 1974, 145pp.

Holdsworth, Deryck William House and home in Vancouver: the emergence of a West Coast urban landscape, 1886-1929. UBC, PhD diss., 1981, 340pp.

Ivanisko, Henry I. Changing patterns of residential land use in the Municipality of Maple Ridge, 1930-1960. UBC, MA thesis, 1964

Jackson, Bradley Grant Social worlds in transition: neighborhood change in Grandview-Woodlands, Vancouver. UBC, MA thesis, 1984, 300pp.

Kahrer, Anna Gabrielle Logging and landscape change on the North Shore of Burrard Inlet, British Columbia, 1860s to 1930s. UBC, MA thesis, 1998, 158pp.

Kerr, Donald Peter Vancouver: a study in urban geography. U of T, MA thesis, 1943, 137pp.

Khan, Abul Monsur Mohammad Amantullah Manufacturing diversification in the Vancouver metropolitan area. SFU, MA thesis, 1982, 139pp.

McCririck, Donna Opportunity and the workingman: a study of land accessibility and the growth of blue collar suburbs in early Vancouver. UBC, MA thesis, 1981, 137pp.

McPhee, Don No place for the poor: restructuring and entrepreneurial redevelopment in downtown Vancouver, B.C. SFU, MA thesis, 1992, 193pp.

Martin, Ronald Bruce Faith without focus: neighborhood transition and religious change in inner-city Vancouver. UBC, MA thesis, 1989, 259pp.

Meyer, Ronald H. The evolution of roads in the Lower Fraser Valley. UBC, BA essay, 1967

Nightingale Berry, Ellen Janet Tourist's image of a city: Vancouver, B.C. UBC, MA thesis, 1980, 332pp.

Rees, Morriss Henry Watts Factors affecting the utilization of Indian Reserve lands: a comparative study of two Indian bands within metropolitan Vancouver. SFU, BA essay, 1968, 67pp.

Robertson, Angus Everett Pursuit of power, profit and privacy: a study of Vancouver's West End elite, 1886-1914. UBC, MA thesis, 1977, 328pp.

Smith, Christopher James The acoustic experience of place: an exploration of the soundscapes of three Vancouver area residential neighborhoods. SFU, PhD diss., 1993, 481pp.

Stobie, Peter William Private inner city redevelopment in Vancouver: a case of Kitsilano. UBC, MA thesis, 1979, 176pp.

GEOLOGICAL SCIENCES

Ashley, Gail Mowry Sedimentology of a freshwater tidal system, Pitt River - Pitt Lake, British

Columbia. UBC, PhD diss., 1977, 404pp.

Burwash, Edward Moore Jackson Geology of Vancouver and vicinity. U of Chicago, PhD diss., 1918, 106pp.

HEALTH SERVICES PLANNING

Wood-Johnson, Faith Alvanley Integration of selected groups of physically disabled men and women into the workforce in Greater Vancouver. UBC, MSc thesis, 1984, 277pp.

HISTORY

Adam, Robert David Myths and realities of Vancouver's oriental trade 1886-1942. Univ. of Victoria, MA thesis, 1980, 172pp.

Anderson, Robin John The Vancouver employment business, 1900-1915: sharks and white slavers? SFU, MA thesis, 1991, 120pp.

Andrews, Margaret Roberta Winters Medical services in Vancouver 1886-1920: a study in the interplay of attitudes, medical knowledge and administrative structures. UBC, PhD diss., 1979, 285pp.

Belshaw, John Douglas Administration of relief to the unemployed in Vancouver during the Great Depression. SFU, MA thesis, 1982, 161pp.

Bradbury, Bettina Road to receivership: unemployment and relief in Burnaby, North Vancouver City and District and West Vancouver, 1929-1933. SFU, MA thesis, 1976, 193pp.

Bray, Bonita Dawn The weapon of culture: working-class resistance and progressive theatre in Vancouver, 1930-1938. U of Victoria, MA thesis, 1990, 196pp.

Burkinshaw, Robert Kenneth American influence upon Canadian evangelicalism: Greater Vancouver as a test case, 1920-1980. UBC, BA essay, 1980, 89pp.

Flynn, James E. Early lumbering on Burrard Inlet, 1862-1891. UBC, BSc essay, 1942

Gerber, Jean Miriam Immigration and integration in post-war Canada: a case study of Holocaust survivors in Vancouver 1947-1970. UBC, MA thesis, 1989, 112pp.

Gibbard, John E. Early history of the Fraser Valley, 1808-1885. UBC, MA thesis, 1937

Gomery, Darrel History of early Vancouver. UBC, BA essay, 1936, 150pp.

Gough, Barry Morton Royal Navy on the Northwest Coast of North America, 1810-1914. UBC, PhD diss., 1971, 294pp.

Gumpp, Ruth Ethnicity and assimilation: German postwar immigrants in Vancouver, 1945-1970. UBC, MA thesis, 1989, 175pp.

McDonald, Margaret New Westminster, 1858-1871. UBC, MA thesis, 1947

McDonald, Robert Arthur John Business leaders in early Vancouver, 1886-1914. UBC, PhD diss., 1977, 502pp.

McKee, William Carey History of the Vancouver park system, 1886-1929. U of Victoria, MA thesis, 1977, 156pp.

MacKenzie, Ken Freeway planning and protests in Vancouver, 1954-1972. SFU, MA thesis, 1984, 136pp.

Ng, Wing Chung Ethnicity and community: southern Chinese immigrants and descendants in Vancouver, 1945-1980. UBC, PhD diss., 1993, 344pp.

Nilsen, Deborah The 'social evil': prostitution in Vancouver, 1900-1920. UBC, BA essay, 1976, 52pp.

Roy, Patricia E. Railways, politicians and the development of the city of Vancouver as a metropolitan centre 1886-1929. U of T, MA thesis, 1963, 276pp.

Smith, Andrea Barbara Origins of the NPA: a study in Vancouver politics 1930-1940. UBC, MA thesis, 1981, 95pp.

Sugimoto, Howard Hiroshi Japanese immigration, the Vancouver riots and Canadian diplomacy. U of Washington, MA thesis, 1966, 254pp.

Walden, Phyllis Sarah History of West Vancouver. UBC, MA thesis, 1947, 181pp.

Woodward-Reynolds, Kathleen Marjorie History of the City and District of North Vancouver. UBC, MA thesis, 1943, 168pp.

Young, David John Vancouver City Police Force, 1886-1914. UBC, BA essay, 1976, 95pp.

Zaharoff, William John Success in struggle: the Squamish people and Kitsilano Indian Reserve No. 6. Carleton, MA thesis, 1978, 198pp.

PLANNING

Adelman, Michael David Measuring selected neighborhood impacts of rapid transit. UBC, MA thesis, 1991, 170pp.

Atkins, Julian Francis Zoning in Vancouver: an expert system to assess development proposals. UBC, MA thesis, 1990, 153pp.

Bone, R.M. A land-use study of the Steveston District. UBC, BA essay, 1955

Bottomley, John Ideology, planning and the landscape: the business community, urban reform and the establishment of town planning in Vancouver, British Columbia. UBC, PhD diss., 1977

Buchan, Robert Bruce Gentrification's impact on neighborhood public service usage. UBC, MA thesis, 1985, 145pp.

Chao, Moses Chinatown, Vancouver; an analysis of its physical, social, and economic situation with recommendations for its improvement and future growth. U. of Oregon, MUP thesis, 1971, 145pp.

Foerstel, Hans-Joachim Fritz Otto Arthur Effectiveness of land use controls in curbing urban sprawl: a case study in Richmond, B.C. UBC, MSc thesis, 1964, 234pp.

Folkes, Sharon Elisabeth Citizen participation and the redevelopment of urban land: a case study of the north shore of False Creek. UBC,

MA thesis, 1989, 134pp.

Friesen, Brock Frederick James Study of the opportunities and costs of preserving recreation sites along the Lower Fraser River. UBC, MA thesis, 1974, 175pp.

Heir, Marlene F. Ethnicity and residential location. UBC, MA thesis, 1973, 114pp.

Hinds, Diane Beverley Evolution of urban public park design in Europe and America: Vancouver adaptation to 1913. UBC, PhD diss., 1979, 217pp.

Holmes, Robert James Industrial zoning in Vancouver. UBC, MA thesis, 1979, 117pp.

Huzel, Suzanne Zenovia Conflict and compromise: a case study of the decision-making process in the Downtown Eastside. UBC, MA thesis, 1982, 103pp.

Jensen, Jens Christian Urban land development, political process, and the local area: comparative study of Kitsilano and Grandview-Woodlands. UBC, MSc thesis, 1974, 104pp.

Johnson, Richard John Recreation and open space in urban waterfront redevelopments. UBC, MA thesis, 1984, 95pp.

Kopystynski, Adrian Daniel Potential of passenger ferries in an urban transit system. UBC, MSc thesis, 1979, 173pp.

Lazzarin, Celia Carlotta Rent control and rent decontrol in British Columbia: a case study of the Vancouver rental market, 1974-1989. UBC, MA thesis, 1990, 191pp.

Levesque, Ernest R. Impact of the Knight Street Bridge on the allocation of industrial land. UBC, MA thesis, 1974, 145pp.

McIntyre, James Lewis Mixed-used development along suburban Vancouver streets. UBC, MA thesis, 1985, 171pp.

MacLaren, Guy Planning for a multiple airport system in the Lower Mainland. UBC, MA thesis, 1991, 111pp.

Moodie, Robert James Gastown: past, present and future. UBC, MA thesis, 1971, 114pp.

Olds, Kristopher Nelson Planning for the housing impacts of a hallmark event: a case study of Expo 86. UBC, MA thesis, 1988, 269pp.

Patrinick, Steve Jay Sustainable development in the Vancouver-Seattle corridor: a system for transborder planning. UBC, PhD diss., 1994, 160pp.

Pednealt, Michael Maurice Peter Investigation of the issues and implications of floating homes: the Greater Vancouver region. UBC, MA thesis, 1977, 127pp.

Pettit, Barbara Ann Zoning and the single-family landscape: large new houses and neighborhood change in Vancouver. UBC, PhD diss., 1993, 254pp.

Read, Kim Alexander Continuity with change: an investigation of the "monster house" issue in

Vancouver's westside single-family neighborhoods. UBC, MA thesis, 1989, 120pp.

Roth, Heike Dagmar Neighborhood traffic management and community livability: three Vancouver case studies. UBC, MA thesis, 1986, 122pp.

Rowe, Greg Alan Cottaging and the cost of travel. UBC, MA thesis, 1977, 101pp.

Rye, Tom Bicycle policies and programmes in Vancouver, B.C. and Seattle, Washington: a comparison. UBC, MA thesis, 1991, 79pp.

Scott, Laura E. The imposition of British culture as portrayed in the New Westminster Capital Plan of 1859 to 1862. SFU, MA thesis, 1983.

Ulmer, Arno A comparison of land-use changes in Richmond, British Columbia. UBC, MA thesis, 1964.

Vanin, Daniel Legislating for urban aesthetics: a case study of the civic design panel Vancouver, B.C. UBC, MA thesis, 1972, 229pp.

Winter, Wayne Francis Alden Development of automated light rapid transit in Vancouver: the potential for significant community change. UBC, MA thesis, 1985, 103pp.

Young, Raymond Edgar Street of T'ongs: planning in Vancouver's Chinatown. UBC, MA thesis, 1975, 125pp.

Zeiss, Christopher Andrew Financial and social costs of solid waste disposal. UBC, MSc thesis, 1984, 212pp.

POLITICAL SCIENCE

Campbell, Michael Graeme Sikhs of Vancouver: a case study in minority-host relations. UBC, MA thesis, 1977, 128pp.

Ferguson, Thomas Francis Barry Formal cooperation among public agencies: a case study of Vancouver's police and community services project. UBC, MA thesis, 1979, 93pp.

Hightower, Jillian Kaye Bidmead Reserve land and irreconcilable objectives: a case study of political interaction between an urban Indian band and municipal governments. SFU, MA thesis, 1979, 197pp.

Miller, Fern Vancouver civic political parties: developing a model of party system change and stabilization. Yale, PhD research paper, 1972, 62pp.

Munton, Donald James Ecological analysis of voting behavior in Vancouver. UBC, MA thesis, 1969, 178pp.

Savas, Daniel Johnathan Interest group leadership and government funding: the Federation des Franco-Colombiens—community organization or government policy agent? UBC, PhD diss., 1988, 442pp.

Sharpe, Robin Study in the voting behavior of the Chinese community in Vancouver-Centre. UBC, BA essay, 1956, 75pp.

Walsh, Susan Equality, emancipation and a more just world: leading women in the British Columbia C.C.F. SFU, MA thesis, 1983

RESOURCE MANAGEMENT

Gorham, Richard Arthur All dredged up and no place to go: the disposal of contaminated dredged material from Greater Vancouver, British Columbia, into the neighboring Strait of Georgia. UBC, MSc thesis, 1985, 261pp.

Holfield, Julia Margaret Harvie Landslide hazard management in the Greater Vancouver Regional District. SFU, MRM research project, 1984, 146pp.

SOCIAL AND EDUCATIONAL STUDIES

Angell, Corinne Lois Residential alternatives for women on Vancouver's skid road. UBC, MA thesis, 1982

Chiu, Siu-Miu Luda Job transferability of Chinese immigrant women in Vancouver: their voices. UBC, PhD diss., 1994, 304pp.

Creese, Gillian Working class politics, racism, sexism: the making of a politically divided working class in Vancouver, 1900-1939. Carleton, PhD diss., 1986.

Foran, Sylvia Marie Use of the companion advertisements in Vancouver's main newspaper, 1900-1960. SFU, MA thesis, 1982

Friesen, Lloyd Out of the closets and into the street? The increasing visibility and openness of gay business in the urban landscape. UBC, undergraduate paper, 1986

Greenstein, Howard Barry The business of prostitution in Vancouver: an empirical study with policy implications. SFU, MBA thesis, 1984.

Kohlmeyer, Klaus Kim An ethnographic study of street prostitution in Vancouver, B.C. SFU, MA thesis, 1982.

Mogg, Monica The experience of bi-cultural conflict by adolescent Vietnamese girls in Greater Vancouver. SFU, MA thesis, 1991.

Read, John M. The pre-war Japanese Canadians of Maple Ridge: land ownership and the 'Ken-Tie. UBC, MA thesis, 1975

Weightman, Barbara The Musqueam reserve: a case study of the Indian social milieu in an urban environment. U of Washington, PhD diss., 1972

Wisenthal, Christine B. Insiders and outsiders: two waves of Jewish settlement in British Columbia, 1858-1914. UBC, MA thesis, 1987.

Wood Johnstone, Faith Integration of selected groups of physically disabled men and women into the workforce in Greater Vancouver. UBC, MA thesis, 1984

SOCIAL WORK

Chow, Lily Lucia Criminalization of the mentally ill: a study of psychiatric services within the Lower Mainland Regional Correctional Centre, Health Care Centre. UBC, MSW thesis, 1991, 134pp.

Ng, Chee Chiu Clement The Chinese Benevolent Association of Vancouver, 1885-1923: a

response to local conditions. U of Manitoba, MSW thesis, 1987, 293pp.

SOCIOLOGY AND ANTHROPOLOGY

Baxter, Kenneth Wayne Search for status in a Salish Indian community. UBC, MA thesis, 1967, 47pp.

Boulter, Alison Isabel Instituting ethnic difference: an ethnography of the Portuguese immigrant experience in Vancouver. UBC, MA thesis 1978, 120pp.

Bronsdon, Madeline Cohesion and competition: family structure in eleven Chinese households. UBC, MA thesis, 1966, 232pp.

Buckley, Patricia Lorraine Cross-cultural study of drinking patterns in three ethnic groups, Coast Salish Indians of the Mission Reserve, immigrant Italians and Anglo-Saxons of East Vancouver. UBC, MA thesis, 1968, 115pp.

Cassin, Marguerite Class and ethnicity: the social organization of working class East Indian immigrants in Vancouver. UBC, MA thesis (Sociology), 1977, 199pp.

Chadney, James Gaylord The Vancouver Sikhs: an ethnic community in Canada. Michigan State PhD diss., 1976.

Coutts, Dorothy Mae Examination of the social structure of the women's unit, Oakalla Prison Farm. UBC, MA thesis, 1961, 271pp.

Dossa, Parin Aziz Ritual and daily life: transmission and interpretation of the Ismaili tradition in Vancouver. UBC, PhD diss., 1985

Habinski, Avi Aharon Assimilation and residential location: Jews in Vancouver. SFU, MA thesis, 1973, 55pp.

Indra, Doreen Marie Ethnicity, social stratification, and opinion formation: an analysis of ethnic portrayal in the Vancouver newspaper press, 1905-1976. SFU, PhD diss., 1979, 581pp.

Joardar, Sourodyuti Emotional and behavioral responses of people to urban plazas: a case study of downtown Vancouver. UBC, PhD diss., 1977, 196pp.

Kuprowsky, Stephen George Practice of Chinese medicine in the contemporary urban context: herbalism in Vancouver's Chinatown. UBC, MA thesis, 1983, 141pp.

Lambrou, Yianna Greek community of Vancouver: social organization and adaptation. UBC, MA thesis, 1975, 178pp.

Lim, Bea Fung Prestige deprivation and responses: Chinese professionals in Vancouver. UBC, MA thesis, 1981, 115pp.

McCaskill, Donald Neil Urbanization of Canadian Indians in Winnipeg, Toronto, Edmonton and Vancouver: a comparative analysis. York, PhD diss., 1979, 532pp.

Malagueno, Marco Antonio Fractured mosaic: the split-labor market for Hispanic migrants in Vancouver, B.C., Canada. SFU, MA thesis, 1994,

230pp.

Nodwell, Evelyn "How do you integrate Indian culture into your life?": second generation Indo-Canadians and the construction of "Indian culture" in Vancouver, Canada. UBC, PhD diss., 1993, 369pp.

Persky, Stan Deathwork: ethnographic materials on the social organization of the Coroner's Office. UBC, MA thesis, 1972, 303pp.

Samis, Stephen Michael "An injury to one is an injury to all": heterosexism, homophobia, and anti-gay/lesbian violence in Greater Vancouver. SFU, MA thesis, 1995, 137pp.

Stiefel, Sheryl Kay Subsistence economy of the Locarno Beach culture (3300-2400 B.P.). UBC, MA thesis, 1985, 254pp.

Staaton, Karin Vivian Political system of the Vancouver Chinese community: associations and leadership in the early 1960s. UBC, MA thesis, 1974, 170pp.

Tarasoff, Koozma John Study of Russian organizations in the Greater Vancouver area. UBC, MA thesis, 1963, 271pp.

Weightman, Barbara Ann Musqueam Reserve: a case study of the Indian social milieu in an urban environment. U of Washington, PhD diss., 1972, 267pp.

WOMEN'S STUDIES

Braid, Kate Invisible women: women in non-traditional occupations in B.C. SFU, MA thesis, 1979

Hale, Linda Louise The B.C. woman suffrage movement, 1890-1917. UBC, MA thesis, 1978

Riddington, Jillian Botham Women in transition: a study of the Vancouver transition house as an agent of change. UBC, MA thesis, 1982

Rose, Ramona 'Keepers of Morale': The Vancouver Council of Women, 1939-1945. UBC, MA thesis, 1990

Weiss, Gillian M. As women and as citizens: clubwomen in Vancouver, 1910-1928. UBC, PhD diss., 1983

People
Helping
People

KITS MUSIC FEEDS THE FOOD BANK

PEOPLE HELPING PEOPLE? That's not what you usually hear when you hear about people these days. Usually, you hear about people hurting people, exploiting people, taking advantage of them, stealing from them, ignoring them, abusing them, insulting them.

What you hear about these days is apathy and alienation. Studies show, we are both angry and passive. Studies also show, violence is epidemic. We are isolated and scared. In our hurry to get to work we ignore car accident victims lying on the street. We resent the poor.

Boy! What bad and sad people!

Except . . . are we?

I asked myself that a few years ago, and took a big risk. Instead of looking for things that were wrong in our town, I started looking for things that were right. I thought this would be hard. If we were all isolated and angry, alienated and passive, where would I find positive social initiative? Where would I track down people who felt empowered enough to help their fellow human beings, and who could inspire the rest of us to do likewise?

Well! I found those people everywhere, from the Downtown East Side—not long ago distinguished as being the poorest postal code in Canada—to the slopes of posh, upper West Vancouver. I found them opening art schools for people with disabilities and giving aid to developing countries with fair trade and real partnerships. I found them launching vital and vibrant projects all by themselves, and I found them participating in long-established organizations, such as the YWCA or Volunteer Vancouver.

I couldn't believe it, frankly. Street people were trying to get themselves, and their peers, off welfare by starting little businesses close to home. Amnesty International volunteers were sitting in suburban kitchens spending years, maybe, trying to track down a political prisoner who had disappeared in a far, far away land.

On the one hand, it became clear that these helping people had always been with us. On the other hand, something new was growing: a revived sense of community and a sense of the importance and power that individual humans do have. Betrayed all too often by governments and the corporate agenda, people were starting to help people in the most wondrously various and imaginative ways.

Wanting to help the hungry and homeless, a group called The Quest discovered that by letting the homeless cook and serve meals for one another, everyone benefits. Realizing that people with terminal or life-threatening illnesses such as AIDS, cancer or lupus often have little or no emotional support, a group called Friends for Life formed to share the caring. To help curb violence in the suburbs, a group called Innerstart began to teach conflict resolution skills to young people. Everywhere in town neighborhood groups were forming, finding out how to be real neighbors again, and how to contend with social problems that faced them, from overdevelopment to prostitution and drug abuse.

People were realizing that the world, too, is a neighborhood —a global neighborhood, where many of the same principles, writ large, can apply.

I suppose at heart we do know these good things about people. It's wonderful, in these difficult times, to be reminded of them.

—Jeani Read

facing page: Kitsilano High School senior band raising money for the Food Bank, 1994. vp

above: Opening ceremony; the Salvation Army Harbour Light centre, 1953. vs

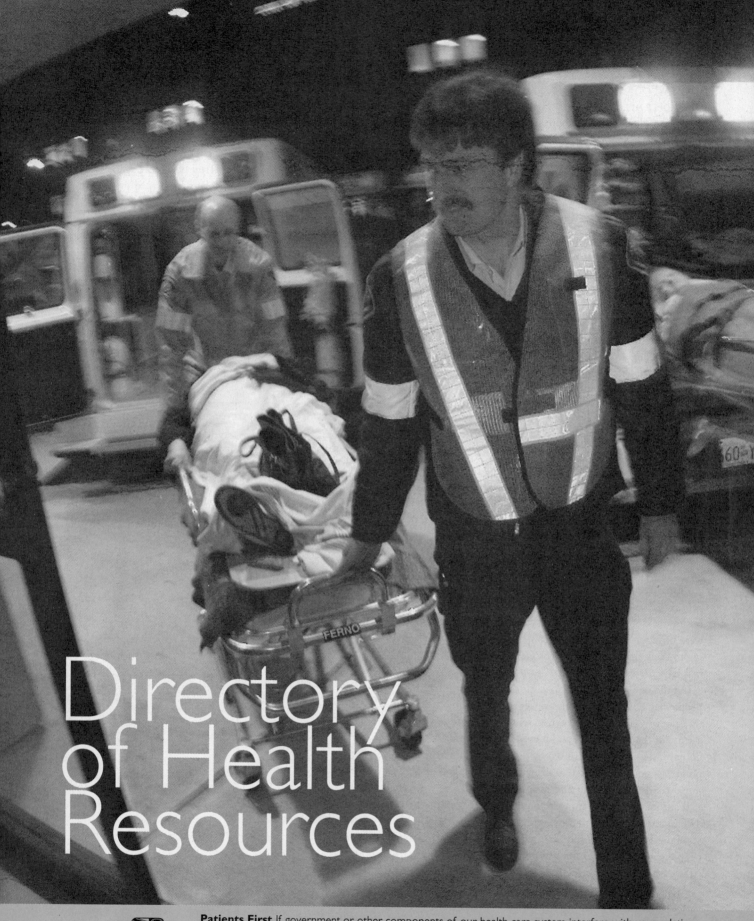

Directory of Health Resources

BRITISH COLUMBIA MEDICAL ASSOCIATION

Patients First If government or other components of our health care system interfere with your relationship with your doctor, then the quality of care is affected. This is why doctors speak out on important issues, putting patients first. It is the best way to make certain you are well taken care of in all aspects of your health.

Directory of Health Care Services
Al Arnason

THERE ARE PEOPLE and places that preserve and protect the health of the 1.8 million residents of Greater Vancouver. The people are our healers and planners. The places are our hospitals. Both are in the midst of a revolutionary reorganization to contain rising costs of health care in a time of faltering economies.

At this writing the health professions of British Columbia were all being reviewed by the Health Professions Council (HPC), a body appointed by the B.C. government to consider the scope of practice (what functions each profession is allowed by law to do) and the legislative framework (mainly how self-regulation is applied) under which each profession operates.

Although the general public may not notice many of the early changes they could be of immediate and critical importance to the professionals themselves, the employers of salaried professionals and especially the associations and trade unions that represent professionals, which could lose or gain members or self-regulated freedoms under revised legislation.

THE COLLEGE OF PHYSICIANS AND SURGEONS OF BRITISH COLUMBIA *1807 West 10th Avenue, Vancouver.*
The primary function of the college is to protect the public interest under terms of B.C.'s Medical Practitioners Act. The college is responsible for governing B.C.'s more than 8,000 medical doctors, including laboratory specialists, radiologists, researchers and physicians who work part-time. There are roughly 3,500 registered doctors in the Lower Mainland. Every physician who practises in the province must be a registered member of the college, created by provincial statute in 1886.

The college conducts an extensive search of records of training and conduct of all physicians before they are registered.

When a physician's competence is brought into question, the college investigates. If found incompetent a physician may be suspended until he or she successfully completes remedial education. When improper conduct is alleged, the facts are examined by full-time college investigators with RCMP experience. The executive committee or council decides whether charges should be laid. If charges are laid an inquiry committee is appointed to determine guilt or innocence under rules similar to those of courts of law. Physicians who by ill health or abuse of alcohol or drugs become unfit to practise may be suspend-

Facing page: Ambulance attendants bring patient in to emergency at Royal Columbian Hospital in New Westminster, 1997. vs

ed and not permitted to return to practice until objective evidence of continuing recovery is provided.

A council made up of 10 physicians elected by physicians from various regions of the province (three from the Lower Mainland region) is responsible for governing the college. Five public representatives who are not doctors are appointed to the council by the provincial cabinet.

THE BRITISH COLUMBIA MEDICAL ASSOCIATION (BCMA) *115 - 1665 West Broadway, Vancouver.*
The BCMA, founded in 1900, is the provincial division of the Canadian Medical Association (CMA). The BCMA is the voice of the profession in British Columbia. It negotiates and lobbies on behalf of doctors and provides member services, insurance services, financial planning, continuing medical education and a variety of publications and research information. It has 50 working committees and 23 specialty sections.

Members are served by two councils: the Council on Health Promotion (COHP) and the Council on Health Economics and Policy (CHEP).

The COHP, established in 1957, is comprised of 15 committees, each dealing with specific areas of community health and health promotion. Current issues of special concern to the COHP are violence in society, health education in school and community involvement in health promotion.

Examples of CHEP's work are the issues of regionalization, health care financing, physician supply and utilization and the problems facing rural physicians. CHEP's work helps determine future BCMA policy.

A major portion of the BCMA's communications program involves projects such as obtaining legislation for mandatory use of seatbelts and informing the public about the dangers associated with alcohol consumption during pregnancy.

The BCMA publishes a patient wellness newsletter, information pamphlets on medical and environmental topics, and has produced the television series *Doctor Doctor* which examines health on many levels. A speakers service, in place since 1985, involves doctors who volunteer to speak about medical issues in their communities.

B.C. doctors are active in municipal, provincial and federal politics either as politicians or working behind the scenes to ensure B.C. has the best health care system possible. The association also aligns itself in community partnerships such as promoting road safety and healthy living.

THE COLLEGE OF DENTAL SURGEONS OF B.C. *Suite 500-1765 West 8th Avenue, Vancouver.*
Since 1908 the College of Dental Surgeons of B.C. has governed dentistry in British Columbia under the Dentists Act.

BRITISH COLUMBIA MEDICAL ASSOCIATION

Aboriginal Health Doctors are taking steps to improve the health of aboriginal people in a variety of ways. These include supporting the training of aboriginal students for health careers, as well as educating the profession about the history and culture of aboriginal people. Focusing on the basic requirements for good health, doctors are working with governments to improve the social and economic conditions of aboriginal communities.

The mandate of the college is to protect the public interest in matters related to dentistry and to administer the Dentists Act. Its mandate extends also to supporting and serving its members because the college is also the professional association for dentists and certified dental assistants. All costs of the college are borne by its registrants.

The college is run by a council composed of 26 members of the dental profession representing ten dental electoral regions, plus 13 public representatives. An executive committee and regulatory quorum consisting of a smaller group of public representatives and members of the dental profession reports to council. Their responsibility is to carry out the business of the college between council meetings. These bodies are assisted by the efforts of 54 committees and sub-committees with focuses ranging from public education to hospital dental services.

All dentists and certified dental assistants in B.C. are regulated by the college to ensure high standards of dental care. In 1994 there were approximately 2,300 licensed dentists in practice in British Columbia, about 1,300 of them in the Vancouver-Fraser Valley district. At the same time, about 4,500 dental assistants were licenced.

Dental health studies were undertaken in 1986 and 1991 to assess the dental health of British Columbians. In each study more than 8,000 dental patients were screened in one day in dental offices. In the five-year period between the surveys there was a 19.75 per cent decrease in the number of decayed teeth, and a 31.03 per cent decrease in the number of missing teeth.

The college receives about 4,500 telephone calls a year for assistance in finding a new dentist, a second-opinion dentist or a low-cost treatment facility. Most of these calls come from the Greater Vancouver area. Where low-cost alternatives are sought, patients are referred to one of five dental clinics in Vancouver. Low-cost dental cleanings are also available through community colleges that offer dental-assistant or dental-hygiene training. Individuals requesting low-cost denture services are referred to the Academy of Dentistry which operates two denture clinics in Greater Vancouver supported by the College of Dental Surgeons.

An outside association, the Federation of Dental Societies of B.C., made up of 10 component societies across B.C., negotiates fees with governments and develops the annual fee guide used by dental offices.

The University of B.C. graduates approximately 40 new dentists per year.

THE COLLEGE OF PHARMACISTS OF B.C. *200-1675 West 8th Avenue, Vancouver*

The terms of how pharmacists function in British Columbia are changing. The B.C. government is changing the rules for pharmacists and other health professionals to make the professions more responsive to the public. The terms of Bill 61, the new bill to govern pharmacists, were given third reading by the provincial legislature in 1993 but are still being fine-tuned by the health ministry and the College of Pharmacists of British Columbia. The college is the licencing and regulatory body for the practice of pharmacy in B.C., obtaining its authority from the Pharmacists, Pharmacy Operations and Drug Scheduling Act. The mission of the college is to develop and maintain standards that ensure that all pharmacists in British Columbia provide safe and effective pharmacy services.

The objects of the college are: (a) to regulate the practice of pharmacy and to govern its members in accordance with this act, the bylaws and rules; (b) to establish, maintain and develop among its members standards of knowledge and skill, qualification and pharmaceutical practice; (c) to establish, maintain and develop standards for the entry into the profession, operation of pharmacies and distribution of drugs for human or animal use; (d) to establish, maintain and develop requirements for the ownership of pharmacies; (e) to administer this act and perform such other duties and exercise such other powers as are conferred on the college by or under any act, in order that the public interest may be served and protected.

Twelve councillors from all parts of the province are elected by the college membership for two-year terms. The new act requires that 30 per cent of councillors be non-pharmacists. Together with the registrar they carry out the mandate of the college.

Pharmacists are represented by the British Columbia Pharmacy Association, a voluntary association of 1,600 member pharmacists and more than 420 member pharmacies (1,067 members and 158 pharmacies in the Lower Mainland) which provides an active, unified voice for the concerns of the profession. Established in 1968 as the B.C. Professional Pharmacists Society, it changed to its current name in 1990. The association, registered under the Society Act, is distinct from the regulatory body.

The association's board of directors comprises 10 pharmacist directors elected by members to two-year terms from regions throughout the province and six appointed pharmacist directors from related groups—the Drug and Poison Information Centre, the Canadian Pharmaceutical Association, the Faculty of Pharmaceutical Sciences at UBC, the Chain Drug Store Association, B.C. Wholesalers and Long Term Care. The president and vice-president of the association are elected annually by board members.

The association office is at 150 - 3751 Shell Road, Richmond.

Alcohol and drugs As early as 1980 doctors were calling on the government to ensure that all products containing alcohol carried warning labels to educate consumers about the risks of drinking alcohol.

THE COLLEGE OF PSYCHOLOGISTS OF B.C. *404-1755 West Broadway, Vancouver*

Psychologists operate in many different contexts and specialty areas. The majority perform some combination of direct service, consulting, teaching, research and/or administration. Some conduct research and teach in colleges and universities; some are employees of government at all levels, administering and rendering diagnostic and healing services to the public in such areas as education, health and welfare, social services and corrections; others provide their services to adults, families, couples and children in individual or group private practices. The designated specialty areas in which psychologists are registered are: clinical counselling; school/educational; organizational/industrial; and academic/research. There are nearly 900 registered psychologists in B.C.

In recent years the terms of how psychologists function in B.C. have been undergoing significant change. Most changes have been designed to regulate psychologists as well as other health professionals to make them more responsive to the public.

The College of Psychologists of British Columbia is the regulatory body for the practice of psychology in B.C. Its duty at all times is to serve and protect the public and to exercise its powers and discharge its responsibilities under all enactments in the public interest.

The board is composed of nine members, six of whom are registered psychologists elected under the bylaws by members of the college for periods of up to three years, and three of whom are persons appointed by the minister of health. The board subsequently elects from its members a president and a secretary-treasurer.

Not all psychologists are registered and thus verified as to credentials and subject to the discipline of the college. Exempted from the terms of the Psychologists Act are psychologists who teach, lecture or engage in research under an appointment or program operated under the University Act, those acting in the course of employment by a provincial, federal or municipal government or government agency and those employed by a board of school trustees under the School Act where qualifications in psychology are a condition of employment.

Psychologists are represented by the British Columbia Psychological Association. This voluntary association of registered psychologists was reinstated in January, 1993 to give a separate voice to the concerns of the profession without compromising the public purposes of the original society after it was tasked by the province (and name changed to college) to register and regulate the activities of psychologists. The association promotes psychology as a profession and a science, provides a referral directory for the public, arranges continuing education training for psychologists and other interested health professionals, and has developed a network of registered psychologists to respond to community needs in the event of natural or other disasters.

The association is at 202-1755 West Broadway, Vancouver.

The British Columbia Psychological Association, which is registered under the Society Act, is the continuation of the original society formed in 1938 and is distinct from the regulatory body. The association represents more than 400 members.

NURSES

In the seven health regions in Greater Vancouver nearly 18,000 practising nurses represent the largest group of patient-care providers in the health care system. As with all the health care professions, nursing in 1995 is being measured by the government for organizational changes that might be little noticed by the general public but are potentially momentous for the nurses themselves, their professional associations, unions and employers.

At the time of writing nurses are generally classified in three major groups according to qualifications and job descriptions but both the scope of their practice and the legislative framework under which they operate are being re-evaluated by the HPC. Nearly 14,000 are registered nurses (RNs) and about 300 are licensed graduate nurses (LGNs). They are licensed and regulated together by the Registered Nurses Association of B.C. (RNABC) as a self-regulated profession under the provincial Nurses (Registered) Act.

Nearly 1,600 registered psychiatric nurses (RPNs) in Greater Vancouver are separately self-regulated as a profession by the Registered Psychiatric Nurses Association of B.C. (RPNABC) under the provincial Nurses (Registered Psychiatric) Act.

The education and training of psychiatric nurses is the critical difference between them and other nurses. The preparation and practice of psychiatric nurses focuses specifically on caring for clients who are mentally ill, mentally disabled or are suffering from a variety of dementias of the elderly. Prior to 1993 the RPNABC served as both a regulator to protect the public interest and an association to represent the interests of psychiatric nurses. Because of changes in legislation that focused RPNABC efforts on protection of the public only, psychiatric nurses are in the process of forming a separate association to represent their own interests.

Nearly 1,800 licensed practical nurses in Greater Vancouver (6,000 in B.C.) are regulated as a profession by the B.C. Council of Licensed Practical Nurses under the Nurses (Licensed Practical) act. The expectation in 1995 was that this Act would

Doctors' stop-smoking project A B.C. doctor-developed program to assess patients' smoking behaviors and guide them toward quitting smoking. Doctors have lobbied governments for years to increase tobacco taxes, to make cigarettes less available to young people, and to ban smoking in public places.

be repealed and a College of Licensed Practical Nurses would be established under the Health Professions Act.

Currently LPNs are represented in labor/management matters predominantly by the Hospital Employees Union (HEU). A small percentage was represented by a variety of other unions. LPNs may also be members of the Licensed Practical Nurses Association of B.C., a voluntary association formed in 1951 and incorporated in 1965. The association provides malpractice insurance coverage for all members as well as affiliate membership in the Canadian Association of Practical and Nursing Assistants (CAPNA).

In an official publication for its own members the RNABC lists its principles of regulating nursing practice. They are not dissimilar to those written for nurses in the other categories. The RNABC states:

"The Registered Nurses Association of British Columbia is the professional organization of all registered and licensed graduate nurses in the province. Everyone wishing to practice nursing in British Columbia and use the title 'registered nurse' or 'licensed graduate nurse' must be a member of the association. Founded in 1912, RNABC's mandate is to serve and protect the public."

REGISTERED NURSES

In the main, registered nurses are represented by the British Columbia Nurses Union (BCNU) whether they are employed in acute or community care or by provincial or municipal governments. The BCNU came into existence in 1981. Its predecessor, the Registered Nurses Association of B.C. (RNABC) obtained its first certification at St. Paul's Hospital in 1946. The BCNU has more than 22,600 members. The HEU and the BCNU have a jurisdictional agreement dated November 7, 1991 that the HEU will not organize RNs and the BCNU will not organize LPNs. The BCNU proposes a provincial bargaining unit of all RNs and RPNs to be represented by the BCNU. It suggests a province-wide representational vote for all RPNs and RNs.

REGISTERED PSYCHIATRIC NURSES

RPNs are represented by the Union of Psychiatric Nurses, HSA (Health Sciences Association of B.C.) and the BCNU. Most RPNs are employed by the provincial government and represented by the Union of Psychiatric Nurses (UPN) in the nurses unit under the Public Service Labor Relations Act. The HSA represents 400 or so RPNs in acute care hospitals. The BCNU represents a smaller and uncertain number in several employment situations. Some nurses are professionally "double registered" as RNs and RPNs.

The first school of psychiatric nursing opened in B.C. in 1930. The Psychiatric Nurses Association of B.C. (PNABC) was founded in 1947 and started to act as a bargaining agent in 1965. In 1980 the professional and union functions were split with the creation of the UPN.

The PNABC and the RNABC were jointly certified for the nurses unit under the Public Service Labor Relations Act in 1974. At that time RPNs outnumbered RNs in this unit 1,250 to 750. The mix has changed with the closure of mental health facilities and the growth of community health. Today the split is 1,850 to 1,070 in favor of BCNU over UPN. The balance will likely revert to the UPN's favor after regional restructuring.

LICENSED PRACTICAL NURSES

These nurses provide much of the hands-on basic bedside care to patients. B.C. history shows that, at certain labor cost threshold, LPNs will be replaced by RNs. (*Editor's note: By 1995 the reverse was happening, said LPN registrar Caroline Sams. As facilities downsized LPNs were being upgraded and increasingly utilized to provide nursing care in cooperation with other health care professionals and providers in a variety of settings.*)

Licensed Practical Nurses are represented by the HEU.

HOME SUPPORT WORKERS

Although home support workers are not nurses, they play an essential role in maintaining the elderly and disabled in their own homes as an alternative to having these clients admitted to care institutions.

Six trade unions represent home support workers employed by member employers of Health Employers Association of B.C. (HEABC). Approximately 95 per cent of the unionized home support workers are represented by the United Food and Commercial Workers Union (UFCW) and BCGEU.

Greater Vancouver Home Support Society handiDART services funded by B.C. Transit are covered by a collective agreement with ICTU (Independent Canadian Transit Union).

UFCW, Local 1518 with 23,000 members, began representing 57 home care workers in 1987 when the Service Office and Retail Workers Union (SORWUC) merged with it. Today UFCW represents 3,500 home-support workers whose employers are both in and outside of HEABC. The BCGEU represents approximately the same number of home support workers. Through collective bargaining, wage rates have increased from $5.00 an hour to a high of $16.00 in 1998, when the current collective agreement expires.

VANCOUVER HOSPITAL AND HEALTH SCIENCES CENTRE

(Formed from merger of Vancouver General Hospital and University Hospital - UBC Site in August 1993) 12th & Oak Pavilions (formerly VGH) -855 West 12th Ave., Vancouver. UBC Pavilions (formerly UH-UBC Site) - 2211 Westbrooke

First aid against AIDS Doctors were one of the first professions to publicly call for the use of condoms against the spread of the Acquired Immune Deficiency Syndrome (AIDS), long before governments or politicians were prepared to advocate the use of condoms.

Mall, Vancouver. (Statistics for each hospital can be found at the end of this article.)

Vancouver Hospital is B.C.'s largest hospital and the second largest in Canada. It is located on two sites. The larger (the 12th and Oak Pavilions) is in Vancouver's Fairview area, the smaller site (the UBC Pavilions) is on the UBC campus.

KEY SPECIALIZATION: Vancouver Hospital serves a continuum of patient needs ranging from community outreach programs to specialized tertiary care for the whole province. It is a referral centre for specialties such as Alzheimers disease, bone marrow transplant and leukemia, burns, magnetic resonance imaging, multiple sclerosis, oncology, organ transplantation, orthopedics, psychiatry, sleep disorders, spinal cord injury, sports medicine, trauma services and others. Research emphasis is on immunology and transplantation, neurosciences, oncology, and trauma and tissue repair.

HISTORY: Vancouver's first hospital was a tent set up by the Canadian Pacific Railway between Hawks and Heatley Streets north of Powell. It served the men laying rails to Burrard Inlet. 1886: a one-and-a-half-storey, nine-bed wooden structure is added to the tent. 1886: the City of Vancouver takes over the hospital. 1888: patients are moved to the first city hospital, a two-storey, 16-bed structure, costing nearly $8,000, on Beatty Street facing Cambie Street. 1893: the first operating room installed, leading eventually to construction of two more buildings and a move to the Fairview location. 1906: Heather Pavilion opens. 1946: second survey recommends expansion, beginning a decade of building and growth. 1959: the Centennial Pavilion, a cruciform-shaped, 12-storey building opens. 1968: UBC Health Sciences Centre opens on the UBC campus. 1970-1980: focus of hospital care shifts as smaller, specialized hospitals are created, including Grace Hospital (now B.C. Women's Hospital) for obstetrics, B.C. Children's Hospital for children's care, and G.F. Strong Centre for rehabilitation. At the same time, VGH becomes the major referral centre for the entire province. Changing function dictates changes to accommodate building a teaching hospital out of what was a community hospital. 1988: University Hospital comes into existence as a merger takes place between Shaughnessy Hospital, UBC Health Sciences Centre and George Derby Centre. This dissolved in 1993 with the closure of the Shaughnessy site and subsequent merger of the UBC site with VGH. 1989: phased construction of a $250 million, 17-storey, 90-metre-high acute care tower (known as the Laurel Pavilion) on the hospital site begins in January. The building, 60 per cent of its costs borne by the provincial government and 40 per cent by the Greater Vancouver Regional Hospital District, is being built in

stages with each stage being financed separately. Its outer shell, visible to the public but not in use for much of that time, is a source of confusion to many observers who are unaware of the phasing schedule. Phasing was decided on in hopes of reducing costs. In practice, construction over a shorter span of five years would have been cheaper overall by as much as $70 million, said hospital president Murray Martin in 1994. But he notes that the building will allow the hospital to consolidate its operations in eight buildings rather than 17. This will produce a $10 million annual saving, says Martin. A number of older structures are to be torn down. The lower floors of the Laurel Pavilion opened at the end of 1995. The tower portion of the building, more than 14,000 square metres of floor space, houses nursing units containing 540 beds to replace those in older buildings. Part of the overall plan for redevelopment of the hospital site is a two-hectare park bounded by Heather and Willow Streets and 10th and 12th Avenues. In the midst of planning and construction in 1994, the hospital has more than 400,000 patient visits. 1995: VHHSC is named one of the 80 best hospitals in North America by American authors John Wright and Linda Sunshine.

ST. PAUL'S HOSPITAL, *1081 Burrard Street, Vancouver.*

KEY SPECIALIZATION: St. Paul's is a tertiary, teaching and research hospital serving residents of Vancouver's downtown core and from across B.C. It is home, since 1992, to the B.C. Centre of Excellence in HIV/AIDS, the Canadian HIV Trials Network and B.C.'s Heart Centre. It offers adult services from community hospital services to tertiary and provincial services such as renal dialysis and transplantation, adult cystic fibrosis and critical care. The hospital is a site for academic research through the Health Research Centre, and academic training in cooperation with UBC and other post-secondary institutions. Unique programs are a community-based comprehensive clinic for downtown-south residents, and a native AIDS co-ordinator service. St. Paul's is committed to function as a Roman Catholic Christian institution.

(Four Sisters of Providence remain at the hospital where they once numbered about 40. But the Sisters of Providence remain active in the hospital's daily life—visiting patients, assisting volunteers and running the clothing supply depot. Moreover, the order still owns the land under the hospital and most of its buildings. The nuns, who live on the hospital's sixth floor, also are represented on the hospital's board.)

HISTORY: St. Paul's was founded in 1894 by the Sisters of the Charity of Providence, part of a Roman Catholic order founded in Montreal in 1843 by Mother Emilie Gamelin. Mother Mary Theresa, provincial superior to the then Oregon Province

Waiting lists Increasingly the government can't find enough money for the health care system to meet the needs of the public. Doctors want to work with the government and others to ensure that every dollar spent in the health care system is spent wisely and to decrease waiting lists.

St. Paul's Hospital, c 1910. cva

at Portland, Oregon, comes to Vancouver at the request of her bishop. She buys seven lots of land on which to build a small hospital on a dirt road to English Bay on the outskirts of Vancouver. 1894: construction begins on the 25-bed wood-frame building on May 16; admits first patient, a Mrs. Woodcock, about six months later on Nov. 21; begins selling prepaid annual plans to loggers and fishermen for $10 each. 1904: building expansion triples beds to 75. 1906: first X-ray machine in use. 1907: nursing school opens; 1912: construction starts on 120-bed hospital. American College of Surgeons begins North American campaign for medical staff organization, record management and improved clinical laboratory services. 1920: twenty-seven doctors invited to join visiting staff. 1921: invents machine that controls ether administration in operating room. 1940-50: major increases in senior government funding spurs growth of St. Paul's and other hospitals. 1959: hospital's first heart catheterization performed. 1960: opens B.C.'s first bio-medical engineering department. 1966: opens its intensive-care unit; federal passage of Medicare increases use of hospitals including St. Paul s. 1969: Sisters of Providence stand aside to allow a lay administrator and the medical staff to lead the hospital. 1959: cardiology department opens. 1960: first open-heart surgery performed. 1964: performs first heart valve replacement and double valve replacement. 1965: critical care department opens. 1975: opens first Drug and Poison Information Centre (DPIC) in Canada. 1976: implements Western Canada's first automated laboratory computer system. 1981: introduces computerized medication service that became model for other acute care hospitals. 1983: admits its first AIDS patient; Canada's first cochlear implant performed. 1985: opens B.C.'s only AIDS clinic. 1993: establishes North America's first Chair for AIDS research with funding from SPH Foundation and UBC. 1995: SPH is named one of the 80 Best Hospitals in North America by American authors John Wright and Linda Sunshine.

Road safety Doctors formed the B.C. Road Safety Alliance with the B.C. Automobile Association and 20 other high-profile organizations to fight for reforms in road safety, such as better education and graduated licensing for new drivers.

The question of how to deal with the AIDS epidemic, with a high concentration of illness in the city's West End, caused much soul searching by St. Paul's board members during the 1980s. Eventually, the matter was decided in a way that is now looked back on with intense pride. According to the hospital's president and CEO at the time, Ron Mulchey, one of the Sisters of Providence, whose order founded St. Paul's, took a stand on the issue. Mulchey, quoted in the hospital's newsletter, recalled: "One of the sisters told the board: 'Are these people not sick? Well, are we not here to look after sick people? "In a time of intense fear and ignorance about AIDS, St. Paul's began treating AIDS patients while many other hospitals were reluctant to do so. St. Paul's opened B.C.'s only AIDS clinic 2 years later

Now St. Paul's is said to have the most advanced AIDS program in Canada with a multi-disciplinary team of doctors, nurses, pharmacists, social workers, psychiatrists, home-care liaison nurses and other specialists.

BURNABY HOSPITAL *3935 Kincaid Street, Burnaby*
KEY SPECIALIZATION: A secondary referral facility offering specialized clinical services in obstetrics, ophthalmology, orthopedics and oncology, as well as community hospital services.
HISTORY: In 1943 a group of Burnaby citizens interested in building a local hospital met and formed a fund-raising committee; $6,000 was raised by door-to-door canvass (Burnaby population at the time was 35,000 and average weekly wage was $33.81). 1947: committee, now Burnaby Hospital Society, persuades municipal council to contribute $55,000 for hospital. 1949: council approves bylaw to raise $196,000 from public; public votes 80 per cent approval. 1952: health minister Eric Martin opens 125-bed facility, Canada's largest suburban hospital. 1957: construction starts on new 123-bed Centennial Wing; voters approve second money bylaw by 11-to-one. 1959: Centennial Wing opens; total now 250 beds, 63 bassinets. 1960: doubled in size, hospital operates near capacity. 1961: CANTEL communications tower erected on roof; 50,000th patient admitted. 1963: cardiac-arrest team forms; girls aged 16 to 18 form Candy Stripers group. 1965: up to 500 people on surgical waiting list; new staff hired, new operating room opens and new beds placed in corridor alcoves; province approves 340-bed expansion. 1966: operating room averages 510 cases monthly; full-time teacher appointed for pediatric patients. 1968: five-bed intensive care unit opens. 1970: 147-bed extended-care facility approved at $2.3 million. 1973: health minister Dennis Cocke opens extended-care wing. 1975: hospital bans cigarette sales. 1977: $29.4 million acute care facility opens with 422 beds. 1982: outpatient arthritis service and pacemaker clinic

established. 1985: cataract implant surgery up to 400 from 75 in 1984; knee and hip replacement surgery started. 1986: five-year-old foundation raises $600,000 for computed tomography (CT) scanner. Health ministry puts up $900,000. 1989: Christopher Erienbeck, B.C.'s 3-millionth citizen born. 1991: Customer Care, a self-initiated quality/service program, starts. 1994: Burnaby Hospital's Regional Cancer Centre opens. 1995: eight-bed palliative care unit opens; the hospital has been a popular site for about a decade for feature films, which included such stars as Katharine Hepburn and Burt Reynolds, as well as for made-for-TV movies and commercials.

Research started by Burnaby Hospital senior nurse Peg McIsaac in 1993 has created insights into the standard hospital policy of waking all long-term patients three times during night. Instead, nurses quietly checked all patients every half hour, giving assistance only to those awake and in need. Patients in the study responded to uninterrupted sleep with improved appetite and by exhibiting less agitation, belligerence and confusion during the day. Other hospitals that have adopted the system have praised it and the provincial health ministry has urged widespread adoption of the changes.

LIONS GATE HOSPITAL *231 East 15th Street, North Vancouver.*
KEY SPECIALIZATION: An acute, extended and ambulatory care hospital serving the North Shore communities and the Sunshine Coast and Garibaldi areas.
HISTORY: In her book, *The Story of Lions Gate Hospital, The Realization of a Pioneer Settlement's Dream, 1908-1980*, Sally Carswell says a citizens committee looked into building a hospital on the North Shore in 1908. It concluded that a 12-bed hospital would cost under $10,000. Running it would cost $600 a month. Later highlights: North Vancouver City Council (NVC) doesn't think a hospital is needed yet. It votes instead to rent a room that would be kept for emergency purposes. The committee responds by bringing the North Vancouver District Council (NVD) into the deliberations. Meanwhile, three nurses, Mina and Jenny Dawson and a widowed sister named Stevenson make a deal with the councils and open a two-storey, wood frame building as a hospital in May, 1908, on 15th Street, near St. Andrews Avenue. 1909: Vancouver General Hospital asks NVD Council to make a donation to the hospital because 22 NVD residents had been treated in the hospital the year before. NVD Council says Vancouver General received $1,100 in provincial aid for treating the NVD patients, which should have gone to the North Shore hospital. 1910: the hospital moves to a bigger 15-bed building at 151 East 12th Street. 1913: the provincial Hospitals Act states that municipalities are responsible for hospital costs when their residents

Infant car seats Doctors established the popular and life-saving New Year's Baby program. Each year parents of the first babies born in the New Year at each hospital throughout B.C. are given an infant car seat by doctors of B.C.

are treated in hospitals in other areas and cannot or will not pay directly. 1918: Mrs. S.D. Schultz opens private 12-room hospital. 1921: NVD's voters narrowly approve buying the Dawson Sisters Hospital which is improved and expanded to 23 beds. Oddly, the hospital, wholly owned by NVD, is located in NVC which pays an annual contribution. 1927: NVC and NVD voters approve new hospital bylaw. 1929: North Vancouver General Hospital opens on 13th Street. 1931: as the depression deepens, patients routinely leave hospital without paying. 1932: North Shore citizens donate shrubbery and plants from their own gardens to complete the new hospital grounds landscaping. 1932: NVD is bankrupt. 1933: NVC also bankrupt. Hospital avoids disaster by forcefully collecting unpaid patient bills. 1943: private hospital insurance scheme starts in B.C. 1945: at end of war NVC gets back its right to elect its government. 1948: NVD follows suit. The hospital, built for 65 beds, is crammed with 83. Senior government grants allow expansion to 108 beds. 1954: West Vancouver joins with the two other North Shore municipalities in the incorporation of the North and West Vancouver Hospital Society to equally share the cost of a new hospital. But West Vancouver council is reluctant and both North Vancouver councils actually refuse to put money bylaws for a $6 million hospital to the public. They suggest the hospital society raise the funds; 1955: 500 names on hospital waiting list, conditions cramped. 1957: all three councils agree to put a hospital bylaw to the public to raise funds that with federal and provincial grants would provide a new hospital. But the councils continue to delay money bylaws to raise the required $900,000 in each of the North Shore communities. 1958: public in all three municipalities overwhelmingly support building a new hospital. 1961: Lions Gate Hospital, currently the fifth largest in the Greater Vancouver Regional Hospital District, opens at its current site on April 22, with 285 beds. 1967: acute care beds now number 456. 1971: the original 169-bed extended-care unit (Evergreen House) opens. 1984: addition completed to add 125 extended-care beds.

ROYAL COLUMBIAN HOSPITAL *330 East Columbia Street, New Westminster.*

EAGLE RIDGE HOSPITAL *475 Guildford Way, Port Moody.*
Two hospitals run by a single management team, one president/CEO and one board of trustees under the name Fraser-Burrard Hospital Society.

KEY SPECIALIZATION, RHC: offers emergency, trauma, ambulatory and acute care referral service for the Fraser Valley; provides tertiary-level care in obstetrics, neonatology, cardiac services and neurosciences; provides regional laboratory and diagnostic support services; has one of busiest emergency

departments in B.C. with more than 60,000 visits annually not including ambulatory care visits.

KEY SPECIALIZATION, ERH: a community hospital, providing emergency, ambulatory care, long-term care and acute-care programs as well as innovative community health promotion and outreach services.

HISTORY, RCH: first opened in 1862 at Agnes and Clement in New Westminster, with 30 beds, at a cost of $3,396. 1889: moves to current location. 1908: adds 20-bed maternity cottage, three isolation cottages and a nurses residence. 1950: new building opens. 1978: HRH Prince Philip opens Health Care Centre. 1984: RCH and ERH amalgamated as the Fraser-Burrard Hospital Society. 1992: new 300-bed Columbia Tower opens. 1993: demolition of 1950 building.

HISTORY, ERH: 1984: Hospital opens and is amalgamated with RCH to form Fraser-Burrard Hospital Society (FBHS). 1993: Eagle Ridge Manor, a 75-bed extended-care facility opens.

THE RICHMOND HOSPITAL *7000 Westminster Highway, Richmond.*

KEY SPECIALIZATION: a community hospital providing primary, secondary and selected tertiary care services to the people of Richmond and surrounding areas including Vancouver International Airport and B.C. Ferry Service facilities.

HISTORY: 1953: three founding trustees of the Richmond Hospital Fund meet; total fund assets $1,011; two months later, 70 people at a public meeting approve formation of the Richmond Hospital Society. 1960: health ministry announces approval in principle for new hospital in Richmond. 1961: a site is acquired on five acres at Westminster Highway and Gilbert Road. 1963: a hospital auxiliary is formed. 1966: health minister Eric Martin opens the 132-bed Richmond General Hospital on Feb. 26, next to a cow pasture. The first patient is admitted March 17 and the hospital's first baby is born later that day. 1968: expansion to 154 beds plus 29 bassinets. 1972: a 74-bed extended-care unit completed on Westminster site; a second unit on Minoru Boulevard is acquired and converted, adding 36 beds. 1980: south tower is completed. 1991: on the hospital's 25th anniversary, the parkade opens and construction starts on 250-bed extended-care facility. 1992: name changes to The Richmond Hospital; the new south medical nursing unit opens. 1993: $3 million raised for hospital equipment. 1994: $18.5 million Minoru Residence extended-care facility opens with 200 beds and another 50 in reserve.

Since then the province and the GVRHD have approved the hospital's plans to serve up to 75 per cent of the current and projected community needs over the next few years.

Seatbelt legislation Countless lives and millions of dollars have been saved because of the doctors' aggressive campaign in 1975 that resulted in legislation requiring adults to wear seatbelts when they drive.

BRITISH COLUMBIA'S CHILDREN'S HOSPITAL *4480 Oak Street, Vancouver*

KEY SPECIALIZATION: this is British Columbia's major treatment, teaching and research centre for child health care, serving patients to age 16 from throughout the province, 65 per cent of whom are from outside the Vancouver area. It is the only centre in Western Canada where children receive bone-marrow transplants. The special-care nursery treats 900 premature infants and critically ill newborns annually and 87 kidney transplants have been performed at Children's since 1982.

HISTORY: 1910: associated Charities of Vancouver start a West End Crèche (as child-care facilities then were called). 1914: City of Vancouver takes over the crèche and moves it to a new building in the 1100-block Haro Street. 1917: crèche taken over by Vancouver General Hospital. 1921: ward for children opened at Mount St. Joseph Hospital. 1923: the Women's Institute, a province-wide group of community-minded women, sparks the idea of creating a Crippled Children's Hospital. 1925: funding efforts take on new name of Women's Institute Hospital Association for Crippled Children (WIHACC). 1927: WIHACC leases large house at 8264 Hudson Street for a 16-bed children's hospital and admits the first patient in January, 1928; in March, the hospital is officially opened by T. Dufferin Pattullo, then provincial secretary. 1931: city grants the Crippled Children's Hospital Society 3.4 acres of land between 59th and 60th Avenues and Manitoba and Columbia Streets. 1933: 25-bed hospital opens at 250 West 59th Avenue; the official opening ceremony is delayed by a scarlet fever outbreak until May 13, 1934 when acting Premier A. Wells Gray cuts the ribbon. 1944: new West Wing adds 20 beds and other facilities. 1947: hospital expands beyond its mainly orthopedic care into a general medical care facility for children and changes its name to Children's Hospital; East Wing adds another 28 beds. 1948: travelling clinic introduced; Hospital Insurance Act passed. 1956: realization of the traumatic psychological effects of separating children from their families during hospitalization spurs efforts to seek a unified children's facility where families are part of the treatment. 1969: Dr. Sydney Israels chairs joint board of directors, made up equally by the boards of Children's Hospital and Vancouver General Hospital's Health Centre for Children, which seeks integration of the two facilities in a new hospital. Greater Vancouver Regional Hospital District, responsible since 1967 for hospital planning and construction, expresses concern that a geriatric facility is needed more urgently. 1973: health minister Dennis Cocke announces that a new tertiary medical centre, including a children's hospital, is to be built on the Oak Street site. 1974: Care by Parent Unit opens. 1975: re-elected Social Credit government drops NDP hospital plan but commits to building a children's hospital somewhere in Vancouver. 1976: Oak Street is chosen for hospital. 1977: health minister Robert McClelland breaks ground at 28th Avenue and Oak Street. 1982: hospital completed at cost of $60 million, with 320,000 square feet of space and 250 acute care beds, an adolescent unit, a modern isolation facility, a rehabilitation unit, a 10-bed psychiatric unit and a 60-bed special care nursery. 1992: expansion and redevelopment plan for the hospital is approved by the GVRHD in an age of rapidly expanding population of the Vancouver area.

A little girl with a serious illness, a foster mother and a community women's group leader played key roles in creating the first children's hospital in Vancouver in the 1920s.

The girl was Othoa Scott, 12, of Hornby Island, suffering from a tubercular spine, but not qualified for treatment at Vancouver General Hospital because she was not a Vancouver resident. Her foster mother Mrs. Edith Scott made a plea for help to Mrs. V.S. MacLachlan, then provincial secretary of the British Columbia Women's Institute. In 1923 the institute persuaded VGH to admit Othoa, where she was treated for eight months and completely cured.

More notably, because of Othoa, who was to become a fundraising symbol, the women's institute set aside $2,000 in 1924 to establish a fund for a facility for crippled children. The fund, vigorously promoted by the institute, prospered.

Othoa, who by 1925 was nothing like the seriously ill child of her past, entered a contest for Queen of the Pacific National Exhibition. Although barely 13, she took second place and a stenography course that was her prize.

The Crippled Children's Hospital, a large, renovated house at 8264 Hudson Street—forerunner to today's B.C.'s Children's Hospital—admitted its first patient in January, 1928.

BRITISH COLUMBIA WOMEN'S HOSPITAL AND HEALTH CENTRE *4490 Oak Street, Vancouver*

KEY SPECIALIZATION: B.C.'s high-risk maternity centre combined with a full range of ambulatory, partnership (with other agencies) and health-promotion programs for women.

HISTORY: 1907: the Salvation Army opens its first hospital, the 30-bed Salvation Army Maternity Home, at Eighth and Birch. It will be there for 20 years. 1927: growing population leads to opening what is now called "old Grace Hospital" at 26th Avenue and Heather Street; cornerstone for that building is to be laid by Premier John Oliver, but he is ill that day; Vancouver banker Mayne D. Hamilton and architect Enoch Adams perform the ceremony Jan 22.

Infant car seat legislation Concerned about protecting lives, doctors also pushed for legislation, aided by a 94,000-name petition, to require that children under six years old were buckled up. Supported by their patients and the general public, the doctors, along with other concerned citizens, forced the government to act.

Later milestones: 1949: addition of a gynecological wing and X-ray department. 1957: births of its first triplets, all girls. 1959: Lt.-Gov. Frank Ross opens new 99-bed wing. 1960: celebrates its 50,000th birth. 1977: 100,000th birth. 1982: health minister James Nielsen opens 120-bed "New Grace Hospital" on the Oak Street site, April 2. 1993: 200,000th baby born August 27. 1994: Salvation Army announces it is handing control of the hospital to the provincial government. 1994: hospital established under its current name on March 31. It is now affiliated with the University of British Columbia as a major research and teaching hospital with 56,000 patient visits a year. It is also Canada's busiest obstetrical centre with 7,300 births annually.

RIVERVIEW HOSPITAL *500 Lougheed Highway, Port Coquitlam*
KEY SPECIALIZATION: to house and treat mentally ill patients.
HISTORY: first mental hospital on Lower Mainland opens in 1878 in Sapperton as New Westminster Asylum. 1883: Dr. R.I. Bentley appoints a medical superintendent and introduces work therapy for inmates. 1888: using mostly the labor of its 82 patients, the hospital's gardens produce 27 tons of fruit and vegetables. 1894: a commission of inquiry finds widespread maltreatment of patients; Dr. Bentley resigns. 1901: the principal causes of insanity listed as heredity, intemperance, syphilis and masturbation. 1904: a thousand acres of land is purchased at the future site of Essondale (current site plus Colony Farm) and 48 patients are transferred to satellite colony in Vernon, B.C. 1909: construction starts on the Hospital for the Mind at Mt. Coquitlam, later renamed Essondale/The Male Chronic Building/West Lawn Unit. 1911: Colony Farm is considered the best farm in Canada, producing more than 700 tons of crops and 20,000 gallons of milk. 1917: syphilis is the cause of the mental illness of 10 per cent of patients. 1923: influenza epidemic kills 11 patients at Essondale, 13 at New Westminster. 1924: new Acute Psychopathic Unit (later renamed Centre Lawn) opens at Essondale and the first RN at Essondale, Sarah Van Wyck, is appointed superintendent of nurses. 1925: patient #85 dies after being hospitalized for 50 years, nine months and 28 days. 1937: with more than 3,000 patients in care, insulin shock and Metrazol therapy (no longer used) is introduced; first full-time dentist appointed; new nurses home built and first psychologist appointed. 1942: 34 patients die from tuberculosis; electro-convulsive shock therapy (ECT) introduced. 1943: ECT given to 138 patients with good results claimed; sulpha drugs now available. 1945: psycho-surgery in vogue. 1946: first female physician appointed. 1950: New Westminster Mental Hospital renamed Woodlands. 1951: Principal treatments in vogue are individual and group psychotherapy, ECT, elec-

tronarcosis, somnolent and coma insulin and lobotomies; A survey finds up to 81.8 per cent overcrowding. 1953: Canadian Mental Health Association volunteer services organized. 1954: antipsychotic drug chlorpromazine and reserpine (no longer in use) available. 1957: tranquilizers used extensively; lobotomies less popular and some decline in use of ECT; new legislation separates geriatric and adult services. 1960: eighty patients are placed in boarding homes. Farms are transferred to agriculture ministry. 1961: last lobotomy is performed. 1962: coma insulin therapy slips in popularity while group and milieu therapy (pleasant peaceful surroundings) are popular; community care and aftercare increases. 1965: a new Mental Health Act consolidates mental health legislation; male and female nursing divisions are amalgamated; total inpatient population is 5,961, with 628 in boarding homes; anti-psychotic drug haloperidol and slow-release, intramuscular phenothyazines (anti-psychotics) are in use. 1972: 1,300 patients live in boarding homes; Vancouver Out-patient Service is opened on East Broadway. 1973: last class of psychiatric nurses graduates from Essondale. 1983: water intoxication (potentially fatal compulsive consumption of water) ward opens. 1986: Riverview and Valleyview Hospitals amalgamate. 1988: federal court rules mental patients eligible to vote in federal elections. 1993: Riverview celebrates its 80th anniversary. 1994: Hillside Unit is occupied by a patient from Forensic Psychiatric Institute; the Riverview Charter of Patients Rights is introduced and the Patient Empowerment Society officially started.

Riverview Hospital is a facility for patients with serious, long-term mental illnesses. It is within the geographical boundaries of the Greater Vancouver Regional Hospital District but has been operated outside the GVRHD system by the B.C. Mental Health Society since 1988.

In keeping with a 40-year trend in Western countries away from institutional care and toward community care, Riverview has been reducing its inpatient numbers. Patients are being switched to care in or through psychiatric departments in acute-care hospitals, in care-homes or by outreach services in the patients own communities.

An historical review of Riverview notes: "Whether the seriously mentally ill will profit in the long run from these changes will largely depend upon the degree of integration of the various components of this community model and the adequacy of their funding."

LANGLEY MEMORIAL HOSPITAL *22051 Fraser Highway, Langley*
KEY SPECIALIZATION: a community hospital providing primary services, selected secondary services and extended-care services

---

Bicycle helmet legislation Years of work by doctors paid off when government finally made it a law for cyclists to wear bicycle helmets. Thousands of injuries can now be prevented, and doctors are hoping that similar helmet legislation will be applied to skiers and in-line skaters.

and programs.

HISTORY: 1943: Langley Memorial Hospital is incorporated. 1948: the first "cottage" hospital opens with 35 beds on July 14. 1949: nurses' residence built and opened. (It is now the Marion Ward Pavilion, named in honor of LMH's first director of nursing, 1948-1977.) 1965: new 81-bed acute care hospital opens. 1968: "cottage" hospital becomes Cedar Hill Centre, a 50-bed extended care facility. 1975: Acute Care Hospital expands to 145 beds. 1978: new 75-bed extended-care facility opens (Cedar Hill Centre). 1979: First Cedar Hill Centre becomes Public Health/Mental Health unit. 1981: second 75-bed extended-care facility opens (Maple Hill Centre). 1988: Acute Care Hospital expands to 201 beds. 1993: third extended care facility opens (Extended Care Centre). 1995-1996: $13.4 million expansion to include new maternity, expanded physiotherapy, occupational therapy, addition of a histopathology section to the laboratory, a new cafeteria, and renovated ambulatory care and outpatient areas.

BRITISH COLUMBIA CANCER AGENCY *Vancouver Cancer Centre, 600 West 10th Avenue, Vancouver*

KEY SPECIALIZATION: the Vancouver Cancer Centre serves the Vancouver region and the province with specialized cancer-care services including prevention, early detection, diagnosis and treatment, research, supportive care, rehabilitation and palliative care. It is operated by the BC Cancer Agency which has a mandate to provide a comprehensive cancer-care program for the entire province. The agency, fully funded by the provincial government, is responsible for the administration of the BC Cancer Research Centre on the north side of 10th Avenue, the Screening Mammography Program, a cervical cytology program and cancer centres on Vancouver Island and in the Fraser Valley. It also works with community partners in regional clinics to help provide cancer care services for the province.

HISTORY: 1935: a special committee of the BC Medical Association is formed to investigate what can be done about an increasing incidence of cancer and lack of treatment facilities. The committee works with the Vancouver Board of Trade and the Greater Vancouver Health League. The first meeting is chaired by T.S. Dixon, president of the board of trade. Dr. C.W. Proud, a pioneer in treatment and research in cancer, set the objective of forming a cancer institute. The British Columbia Cancer Foundation is incorporated under the Canadian Societies Act. Borrowed funds are used to purchase 3.5 grams of radium, a precious commodity. Hon. Eric Hamber, Lt.-Gov. of B.C. agrees to pay the interest on the loan for two years. 1938: anonymous $50,000 donation allows the BC Cancer Foundation to establish a treatment centre, the

British Columbia Cancer Institute, where 288 patients are treated in the first year. First chairman of the board of governors is W. H. Malkin, who serves until 1945. Dr. A. Maxwell Evans is named head of the institute where he stays for 33 years. 1948: the foundation opens the Victoria Cancer Diagnostic Clinic (the predecessor of today's Vancouver Island Cancer Centre), operated by the agency. 1949: consult clinics open in Penticton, Kelowna and Kamloops, forerunners of today's network of regional clinics linked to the agency. 1950: training program for radiotherapy technicians is established at the BC Cancer Institute. 1952: new building opens, housing modern radiation therapy equipment. 1956: cervical screening program (the Pap smear program) is launched by Dr. H.K. Fidler and Dr. David Boyes, across the province, seeking to include all women in B.C. over the age of 20; the program becomes a model for other countries and continues 40 years later. 1974: arrangements are made with the ministry of health to create a comprehensive provincial cancer program and to change the name to Cancer Control Agency of BC. The BC Cancer Foundation continues to raise funds for cancer research and in 1995 still owns the BC Cancer Research Building on West 10th Avenue. 1977: Dr. David Boyes, a Vancouver obstetrician and gynecologist-turned-cancer researcher, is appointed executive director of the agency and serves for 10 years. He becomes a widely-honored world authority and advisor to nations on cytology screening programs and chairman of advisory groups including the Medical Ethics Committee to the B.C. government and the False Creek Toxic Waste Cleanup Committee. 1984: a new, six-storey building opens at 600 West 10th Ave. 1990: The agency changes its name to the BC Cancer Agency. 1995: The BC Cancer Agency operates the BC Cancer Research Centre and three facilities, the Vancouver, Vancouver Island and Fraser Valley Cancer Centres, the latter in Surrey. A fourth centre is to open in Kelowna early in 1998. The Vancouver Cancer Centre, built around an existing radiation therapy area, houses inpatient and outpatient chemotherapy facilities, a pharmacy, a bone marrow transplant program, a public and staff resource library, a radiation therapy department (including a physics department, electronics and machine shops and a mould room), diagnostic imaging and laboratory services, schools for radiation therapists and cytology technologists, a patient and family counselling department, a nutrition department and six specially-focused research programs —medical biophysics, cancer endocrinology, cancer imaging, epidemiology and cancer prevention, the Terry Fox Lab (hemotology) and medical oncology lab operations.

Environmental causes Doctors stopped the uranium mining in Clearwater, B.C., because of concerns about health hazards to workers and to the community. A Royal Commission resulted and a seven-year moratorium was imposed by the government.

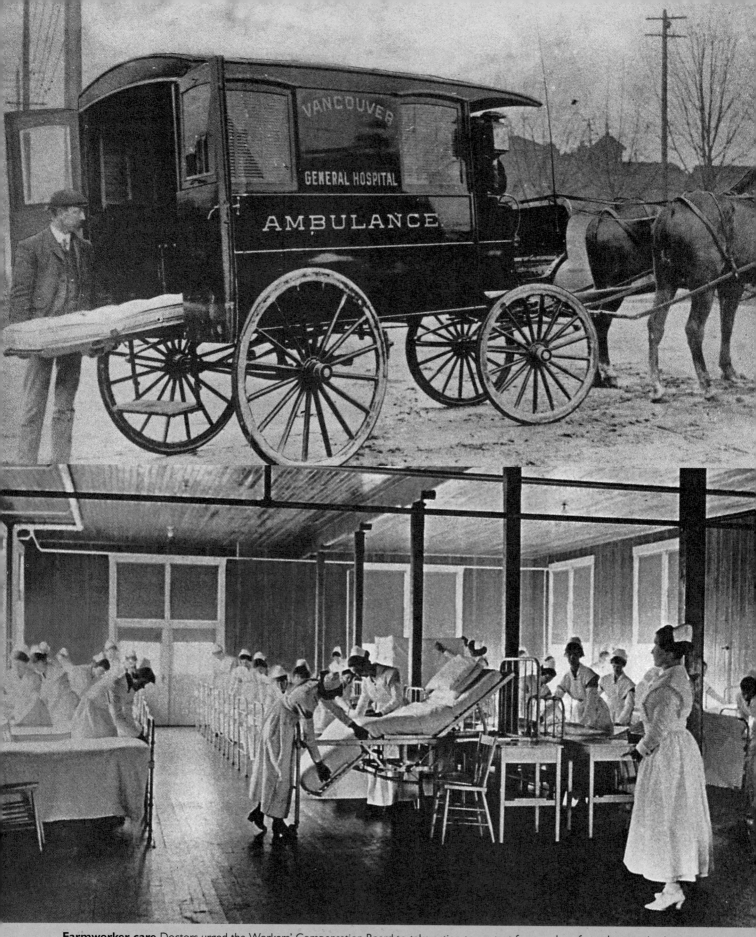

Farmworker care Doctors urged the Workers' Compensation Board to take action to protect farmworkers from the negative impacts of exposure to pesticides. This was followed by a joint education program on the safe handling of pesticides.

Vancouver Hospital and Health Sciences Centre
operating budget 1994-95: $400 million
admissions: 40,000
patient days: 447,675
total beds in use: 1,613 (includes extended care)
employees at both sites: 8,500 plus 1,400 physicians

St. Paul's Hospital
operating budget 1994-95: $162.5 million
annual admissions: 17,653
patient days: 172,806
beds in use: 538; total constructed: 632; future use: 602
occupancy: 85.4 per cent
full-time employees: 2,900 (staff physicians: 450, of whom 300 are physicians with admitting privileges; nurses: 1,000; others 1,450)
part-time and casual employees: 361

Burnaby Hospital
operating budget 1994-95: $76 million
annual admissions: 13,564; discharge planning and extended care: 367; newborn: 2,000
patient days: 90,022 acute care; 6,083 newborn; 70,313 extended care
total beds in use: 482; acute care: 248; extended care: 205; discharge planning unit: 29
occupancy: acute care: 99.44 per cent based on 248 operational beds; newborn: 53.76 per cent; extended care: 93.96 per cent; discharge planning unit 101.26
full-time employees: 1,139 full-time equivalent positions (1,688 actual employees full-time and part-time, including nurses; 165 private physicians have admitting privileges)

Lions Gate Hospital
projected operating budget 1994-95: $104.1 million.
annual admissions: 15,060 (acute care)
patient days: 235,550
total beds: 355 acute care; 294 extended care
occupancy: acute care : 90 per cent; 25-bed discharge planning ward: 100 per cent; 294-bed extended care unit: 100 per cent
employees on payroll: appr. 2,500 (full-time equivalent employees: 1,566; nurses: 799; others: 515; a total of 214 private physicians have admitting privileges)

The Richmond Hospital
operating budget 1994-95: $54 million
annual admissions: 13,054
patient days: 109,075
total beds in use: 470
occupancy: 88 per cent
full-time employees: 573 (registered and practical nurses: 166; food and housekeeping services: 266; physiotherapists, laboratory technicians and technologists: 81; physical plant: 11; non-contract: 42; executive: 7)
part-time and casual employees: 856 (registered

and practical nurses: 325; food and housekeeping services: 410; physiotherapists, laboratory technicians and technologists: 112; physical plant: 2; non-contract: 7; 180 private physicians have admitting privileges)

British Columbia's Children's Hospital
operating budget 1994-95: $130 million
annual admissions: 8,200
patient days: 66,750
total beds in use: 252, including 57 in the special care nursery
average occupancy: 83 per cent
full-time employees: 1,400
Part-time employees: 625

**British Columbia Women's Hospital
and Health Centre**
operating budget 1994-95: $50 million
annual admissions: 16,590
patient days: 57,993 (newborns and women)
total beds in use: 254; (120 maternity; 84 bassinets; 25 addiction treatment; 10 high-risk newborn; 15 delivery suites with home-like atmosphere)
occupancy: 85 per cent
full-time employees: 422 (nurses: 175; others: 247; private doctors with admitting privileges: 170)
part-time employees: 210 (nurses: 140; others: 78)
casual employees: 362 (nurses: 209; others: 153)

Riverview Hospital
operating budget 1994-95: $104.119 million
annual admissions: (not available)
patient days: 28,787
total beds set up: 871
occupancy: 90 per cent
full-time employees: 1,750 actual employees; 1,598 full-time equivalents (41 private admitting doctors; 604; nurses; 399 health care workers or practical nurses)
part-time and on-call employees: 150

Langley Memorial Hospital
operating budget 1994-95: $46,700,000
annual admissions: 9,606
patient days: 133,808. acute care: 57,689; newborn: 3,422; long term care: 5,023; extended care: 67,674
total beds in use: 451; acute care: 167 including medical: 77; medical short-stay: 10; surgical: 46; critical care: 7; psychiatric: 12; maternity: 16; pediatric 9; closed: 34; extended care: 225; transitional care: 25
employees: 1,200 individuals (710 full-time equivalent positions).
physicians: active staff: 114; visiting consultants/general practitioners: 67; visiting dentists: 23
volunteers: 190; candy-stripers: 100

British Columbia Cancer Agency

operating budget 1994-95: $60 million (includes operating funds for the BC Cancer Research Centre).
patients treated annually: 6,500
total beds in use: 50 (for inpatient care)
full-time and part-time employees: 1,400 (includes research centre)
total floor space: 40 square metres in both buildings and parking structure

facing page: top; Ambulance, 1902 vp
*bottom; Nursing class, Heather
Pavilion, 1918.* cva
*above: Vancouver General Hospital,
west wing, 1993.* vs

Patient wellness Produced by the doctors of B.C. Head to Toe is a popular wellness newsletter published quarterly for patients. Distributed throughout the province, Head to Toe offers practical health information to British Columbians.

Services for People with Disabilities
Lynn Atkinson

Every time I travel, coming home to Vancouver makes me appreciate how fortunate I am to live in one of the most accessible cities in the world.

As a wheelchair user I enjoy today the results of 20 years of advocacy by many Vancouverites with disabilities. Together with city councils in the Lower Mainland, elected officials and community organizations, they have tirelessly worked to remove physical and social barriers that in the past have prevented me and my disabled friends from enjoying the same rights and privileges accorded able-bodied people.

Both as a person with a disability and as publisher of a national newsletter for disabled travellers, covering accessible destinations worldwide, I have begun to get an appreciation of how far Vancouver has come, compared to other cities in Canada and the world.

At Independence '92, an international conference for people with disabilities held in Vancouver, over 3,100 delegates from 97 countries sampled what Vancouver had to offer and they didn't go home disappointed. Whether it's accessible transportation, progressive building codes, accessible leisure and recreation opportunities or innovative housing, the city leads the way in making the Lower Mainland a more liveable place for people with disabilities whether they use a wheelchair, a white cane, or a hearing aid.

"We've all seen dramatic changes not only architecturally, but in attitude," says Norman Haw, Executive Director of the B.C. Paraplegic Association. "My colleagues from back east, when they come out west, always comment on how well they are treated by businesses and people in the city. Hotels here often make extra effort to accommodate the needs of persons with disabilities."

And don't forget our mild climate, largely responsible for the fact that B.C. has the highest concentration (18-20%) of disabled people in Canada. It's true, fun in the sun usually turns into recreation in the rain, but at least we don't have the snow stopping us from getting where we want to go like the rest of Canada!

Here are just some of the reasons why Greater Vancouver is fast becoming a leader in facilitating ways to allow disabled people more freedom to move:

In 1990, Vancouver became the first city in Canada to provide scheduled bus service to people with disabilities. To date, B.C. Transit runs 277 lift-equipped buses on 76 of its 161 routes in the Greater Vancouver area, with an additional 40 low-floor accessible buses planned for 1995. Plans are to have all routes covered by 2007. All rapid transit SkyTrain stations except Granville Street are also wheelchair accessible. A new commuter rail system Westcoast Express, similar to SkyTrain, and designed for commuters between Mission and downtown Vancouver, is also accessible.

"B.C. Transit's commitment to have a totally accessible transit system within the next few years is a phenomenal one," says Rick Hansen, author, motivational speaker and former chairman of Independence '92. "It has huge implications for people who traditionally are restricted in how far out they can commute from unless they have their own vehicle."

Custom door-to-door transportation, Handy-DART, is provided in Vancouver and municipalities in the Lower Mainland by local agencies through individual operating contracts with B.C. Transit. Eligible users can book a ride up to four days in advance. A new fixed route transportation was also begun in 1994. It serves people along Oak and Cambie Streets between George Pearson Centre linking up with the east-west accessible bus routes on W. 49th and King Edward.

Vancouver and the Lower Mainland boast more wheelchair-accessible taxis than any other Canadian city. Vancouver Taxi runs 30 accessible cabs in Vancouver alone, with 18 taxi companies with accessible cabs serving the Lower Mainland. The service enables people who have difficulties using public buses to take spontaneous taxi trips at half the cost. Registered HandyDART users can buy coupon books with a HandyPass.

Although facilities for the deaf and hard of hearing are still very poor according to Trevor Thomas of the Western Institute for the Deaf and Hard of Hearing, more and more theatres are installing amplification systems and in the future, closed captioning at convention and meeting locations will become a reality.

The link between the disability community and the city has improved dramatically since B.C.'s first Advisory Committee on Disability Issues was established by the city in 1977.

In addition to seeing that past access problems are corrected, the Committee closely monitors new development projects. The 1995 completion of the new city library "which goes far beyond building code requirements," says a Committee member, is an example of how close co-operation between city and the disabled community has resulted in access for all.

Vancouver built its first curb ramps for wheelchair users in 1965. Since then about 90 per cent of the sidewalks in the downtown core have sloping ramps, called curb cuts, for easy access. In the rest of the city approximately 55 per cent of the curbed streets have curb cuts. Audible crosswalk signals have been installed at 69 intersections in the city. A distinctive sound lets blind pedestrians know when to cross the street. Textured high-contrast sidewalk finish in commercial areas also helps the visually impaired.

As parking is a major concern of persons with disabilities, in 1985 the city initiated a parking identification program run by SPARC to enable persons with mobility impairments to park in specially identified spaces in public and private lots.

Vancouver's building code was the blueprint for Section 3.7 of the B.C. Building Code, still considered the most advanced in Canada. Further evidence of this commitment to accessibility, came when the Ministry of Municipal Affairs created the new position of Access Advisor. The advisor works closely with Frank Jonasen, Director of the Provincial Office for Disability Issues. The office was established in 1994, to promote on-going communication between government and people with disabilities.

"We must be vigilant to ensure that new buildings meet the building code standard," says Jonasen. "Unfortunately, enforcement is left up to the municipalities, and inspectors often aren't aware of barrier-free design so the code can be misinterpreted." Bad news for wheelchair users who must do battle daily with inaccessible buildings, including those with the standard double doors into public washrooms. As a wheelchair user myself, I invariably get trapped in the middle, between the two doors, because there isn't enough space left to open the second door. Toilets with doors that open inward, so that when you're in the cubicle, the door can't be closed, are also another frustrating fact of my life.

In the area of social housing, the city has successfully integrated suburban group homes for people with disabilities into suburban settings. Special projects have been built for people with high lesion spinal cord injuries, psychiatric disabilities, mental handicaps, cerebral palsy and AIDS. Creekview and Noble House in False Creek are just two examples of unique housing projects, allowing ventilator-dependent quadriplegics to live independently.

Employment equity for people with disabilities is still not yet a reality, but the city is working towards achieving representative hiring and promotion of persons with disabilities. Unemployment among disabled people is six or seven times the national average. However, following a significant lobby by groups including the Special Advisory Committee on Disability Issues, the City's Equal Employment Opportunity Program

Fence at Crab Park, 1988. vs

(EEO) was established in 1977 and expanded in 1986. The EEO liaises with agencies to provide funding for special equipment or wage subsidies, and assists departments with job accommodation issues. In 1993, the Taskforce on Employment Equity for Persons with Disabilities was established although, to quote a member of the taskforce, "We're still looking for evidence of positive changes in this area."

A wide range of integrated leisure activities, including adaptive fitness and aquatic programs, have been opened up to disabled people in the Lower Mainland. Capital funds have been allocated to improve access to Park Board facilities and a fee-reduction program introduced. As well as municipal programs, there are several non-profit groups in the Lower Mainland offering leisure activities including: Pacific Riding for the Disabled, Disabled Sailing, and Disabled Skiers Association. Performing Arts Ticket discounts are also available from DISTIX.

RESOURCES
Transit

For information on accessible bus schedules and stops call B.C. Transit 521-0400.
For information about HandyDART, to apply for a HandyPass or to purchase Taxi Saver coupons, call the Accessible Transit Department 540-3400 or your local Handy-Dart office. In Vancouver call 430-2892.

Vancouver Taxi 255-5111
Disabled Parking Permits (SPARC)
Tel. 736 4367. Parking Exemption Decal Program: City Hall Tel. 873-7338.

Resource Groups

Advocacy information: Coalition of People with Disabilities, Tel. 875-0188; TDD 875-8835; Fax 875-9227. Accessible Vancouver guide book (1991) available from the Coalition.
Office for Disability Issues, Frank Jonasen director, 100-333 Quebec St, Victoria, B.C. V8V 1X4. Tel. 387-3813; TDD 387-3555; Fax 387-3114
B.C. Paraplegic Association, Tel. 324-3611
U.B.C. Disability Resource Centre, Tel. 822-5844; TTY/TDD 822-9049
Canadian Mental Health Association, Tel. 254-3211
Vancouver/Richmond Association for Mentally Handicapped People, Tel. 263-1931
B.C. Association for Community Living, Tel. 875-1119
Western Institute for the Deaf and Hard of Hearing, Tel. 736-7391; TDD 736-2527
Canadian National Institute for the Blind, Tel. 321-2311; TDD 321-5506
Coast Foundation Society helps people with psychiatric disabilities with vocational, social, and housing needs, Tel. 877-0033

Housing

Easter Seal Houses provide low-cost accommodation to children and families from outside the Lower Mainland
Greater Vancouver Housing Corporation disabled housing, Tel. 437-9611
For further information on housing see the MS Society book Resources Disability Benefits

Independent Living Aids

Neil Squire Foundation, Tel. 473-9363; Fax 473-9364
Tetra Development Society, Tel. 688-6464; Fax 688-6463
Kinsmen Rehabilitation Foundation of B.C. , Tel. 736-8841; TDD 738-0603; Fax 738-0015

Recreation/Travel

We're Accessible Newsletter for Wheelchair Travellers, Tel. 731-2197
Greyhound Lines of Canada for lift-equipped bus information, Tel. 662-3222
Airlines Attendant Fare Discount Air Canada, Tel. 688-5515 or Canadian Airlines Tel. 279-6611
Sport and Fitness Council for the Disabled, Tel. 737-3039
Disabled Sailing Association, Tel. 222-3004
Disabled Skiers Association, Tel. 738-7175
B.C. Parks Disabled Access Pass in Victoria, Tel. 387-5002

Directories of Disability Information

Vancouver, An Overview of City Programs & Services for People with Disabilities (1992) Available from the City Clerk's office, Tel. 873-7276
Surrey-Community Services ,Tel. 584-5811
Freedom in the 90's Access for All Committee, Tel. 574-7682
New Westminster-Burnaby Access Guidebook, Tel. 294-7400
Unlimited Access Awareness Society (Burnaby) Diane Dobson, Tel. 291-2392
Richmond Connections publishes Community Services Directory (incl. disability information) Tel. 279-7020
Richmond Committee on Disability Tel. 271-8302
North Shore disability Resource Centre Tel. 985-5371; Fax 985-7594
Port Coquitlam, Tel. 944-5411
Coquitlam Mayor's Committee for People with Disabilities, Tel. 664-1400
Port Moody-Recreation Centre, Tel. 461-4411
Seniors, Tel. 937-5541
Delta Assist, Tel. 946-9526

Terry Fox
Rita Woodman

Terry Fox was a super-achiever, yet a humble hero, a charismatic curly haired young man who, while illuminating a path of hope and encouragement to those suffering from cancer, became a legend. He was born Terrance Stanley Fox on July 28, 1958, in Winnipeg and moved to Port Coquitlam with his family in 1966. "He graduated from Port Coquitlam High School," says Leslie Scrivener in her book, *Terry Fox: His Story,* "with straight A's but for one B in English." Then he went on to Simon Fraser University to study kinesiology. He tried out for the junior varsity basketball team where his coaches noted that other players may have had better skills but young Terry Fox "out-gutted" them. He made the team.

He lost his right leg to osteogenic sarcoma on March 9, 1977, at age 18. While he was in hospital awaiting the operation Terry's basketball coach, Terri Fleming, gave him a sports magazine that included a profile on a one-legged runner named Dick Traum who had competed in the New York Marathon. The Traum story inspired Terry, on the night before the amputation of his leg, to take on a challenge that would eventually raise tens of millions of dollars for cancer research. *His goal was nothing less than to run across the country and receive one dollar in donations from every Canadian.*

"I don't know why I dreamed what I did. It's because I'm competitive. I'm a dreamer. I like challenges. I don't give up. When I decided to do it, I knew I was going to go all out." (That determination was shown by his participation in 1979 and 1980 on a wheelchair-basketball team, a slot he got after being recruited by Rick Hansen! Part of Terry's self-designed exercise routine was to push his chair along Gaglardi Way, a long, steep climb up Burnaby Mountain toward Simon Fraser University at the top.)

After the operation Terry began to run daily—painfully short distances at first but increasing steadily as he developed strength and technique. His running style was his own: two hops on his remaining leg then a long stride on his artificial leg while lifting his torso and shoulders for leverage. "It takes more courage to fight cancer than it does for me to run," said a determined Fox. Two years later he had obtained sponsorship and planned his route, and on April 12, 1980, he was in St. John's, Newfoundland. As he dipped his artificial leg in the Atlantic, then turned his face to the west to run across the nation, Terry's dream, the "Marathon of Hope," began.

When he died, he passed the torch to all of us
—Betty Fox

The quotations from the diary that Terry kept along his run, generously quoted in Leslie Scrivener's moving book, are a poignant reminder of this 21-year-old's indomitable spirit. (Scrivener was a writer with the *Toronto Star* at the time and accompanied Terry on part of his run.)

Initially there was little media attention but as he survived dangerous road hazards, semi-trailers that almost blew him into ditches, hailstones the size of golf balls, police barring him from parts of the Trans-Canada Highway and trouble with his artificial leg, the image of this courageous young man and the story of his crusade began to take hold of the public's imagination. Media excitement began to build. By the time he reached Ontario, Terry Fox was famous, a Canadian hero. He marked his 22nd birthday in Gravenhurst . . . a day on which he ran only 32 kilometres instead of the daily 42 he aimed for. The trickle of coins had become an outpouring of dollars—the Ontario division of the Canadian Cancer Society was getting 500 pledges and donations a day. On Terry's arrival in Toronto the Canadian media were overwhelmingly behind him. From the vantage point of this writer who was hosting a radio show in Toronto at the time, Terry Fox was the news of the day. As his popularity increased so did the crowds. School children would line the streets contributing their allowances and pledges. He overcame shyness and became an eloquent public speaker, raising even more money. "Knowing that there are people who care about what I'm doing," he said, "that I'm not just running across Canada, that there are people who are giving money to help fight the disease that took my leg and to help other people who are lying down in hospital beds all over the world, it's a reward."

But as his run continued westward through Ontario, Terry began to be bothered by a persistent cough. His last diary entry was made Sunday, August 31, 1980. On an early September day 18 miles outside Thunder Bay, Ontario, Terry's run came to a tearful end. "I tried as hard as I could, I said I'd never give up and I didn't." His cancer had metastasized and spread to his lungs. The pain was unbearable and he was hospitalized. He had run in constant pain for 143 days, averaging an unbelievable marathon (42 kilometres) a day, and raised $1.7 million for cancer research. Canadians flooded Terry with messages of love and support and continued to contribute money to his cam-

Terry Fox Memorial, BC Place, Vancouver, 1992. rw

paign. The Port Coquitlam post office reported that, during December, 1980, Terry got more mail than everyone else in town—residential and business—combined!

By the end of December, largely due to a CTV telethon, a total of more than $24 million had been raised. Terry's goal of one dollar for every Canadian had been reached and surpassed. He had, as Scrivener wrote, "more than doubled the National Cancer Institute of Canada's 1980 research allowance . . ."

Terry Fox died on June 28, 1981, one month before his 23rd birthday. His dedication, courage and selflessness are perpetuated through the annual Terry Fox Run and the Terry Fox Foundation. His parents, Betty and Rollie Fox, work today to keep the Marathon of Hope alive.

The first Terry Fox Memorial Run was held September 13, 1981, at 880 sites across Canada with more than 300,000 participants. They ran, walked, cycled, roller-bladed, swam and wheeled—and raised $3.5 million. Unique ways were invented to raise money. Residents of a Newfoundland rest home had a rocking chair "rockathon," raising money through pledges. One group of young people had jello bath "sit-ins." Beginning in the early 1990s a deaf man in Prince Rupert began going door-to-door annually for the cause; he collected more than $39,000 in 1994 and was up to nearly $47,000 in 1995. That year there were more than 275 runs in 50 countries, raising more than $10.5 million—history's most successful single-day fundraising event in the fight against cancer. To date more than $166 million has been raised, virtually all of which has remained in the country of origin to fund innovative cancer research in accordance with Terry's wishes.

Too numerous to mention in full Terry Fox's honors and awards include: Canadian of the Year; Companion of the Order of Canada, Canada's highest honor; Order of the Dogwood, British Columbia's highest award; the Sword of Hope, the American Cancer Society's highest award; and The Lou Marsh Award, for outstanding athletic accomplishment. The Canadian government created a $5 million endowment fund, The Terry Fox Humanitarian Award, to provide scholarships in his honor, and he was inducted into the Canadian Sports Hall of Fame. In 1983 Burrard-Yarrows Shipyard in North Vancouver built an ice-breaker named the MV *Terry Fox*. There is a Terry Fox Mountain and a Terry Fox Courage Highway running 83 kilometres between Thunder Bay and Nipigon, Ontario, commemorating the ending of the run. A Terry Fox stamp was issued. Terry Fox monuments have been erected at B.C. Place in Vancouver, Port Coquitlam, Rideau Square in Ottawa and in Thunder Bay. Many schools, parks and roads continue to be named after him.

Once in a while someone special comes along who awakens our consciousness to the needs of others. Terry Fox was such a man and now we carry the torch for him.

Rick Hansen–Man in Motion
Rick Hansen and Jim Taylor

O<small>N THE NIGHT</small> of June 27, 1973, on a road near Williams Lake, B.C., three young friends coming back from a weekend of fishing ran their truck off the road in the dark. They accepted a ride to Williams Lake in another truck from a man and his girlfriend. The driver, unfamiliar with the roads, ran his vehicle off the road and it flipped. One of the passengers, 15-year-old Rick Hansen, was severely injured, his spine irreparably damaged. Told he'd never walk again, the stubborn Hansen (who turned 16 in New Westminster's Royal Columbian Hospital) refused to be defeated. He began therapy at G.F. Strong Rehabilitation Centre, became involved in wheelchair sport, got into marathoning, and met and was inspired by other people in wheelchairs like Stan Stronge. In 1983 while training for the Los Angeles Olympics demonstration wheelchair race, Rick fell and injured his shoulder and met and later fell in love with his physiotherapist, Amanda Reid. Then, in March of 1985, Rick launched the dream that he'd had since shortly after his accident..

"I didn't wake up one day and decide that I was going to wheel around the world. The Man in Motion project began as an itch in the back of my mind back in the days after I left G.F. Strong and headed back to Williams Lake. At that time it had nothing to do with awareness or fundraising and everything to do with pure, physical challenge.

"At first it was one of those kid dreams where you lie on the grass staring up at the moon and imagining that you'll go there some day. Then, as I began to focus on marathoning and enjoyed some success, I realized I really was physically and emotionally strong enough to wheel around the world—if I wanted to. But so what . . . ?

"I was working on my Phys. Ed. degree and competing internationally in wheelchair sports. I didn't want to leave all that just so I could come home and say, 'Well, I wheeled around the world.' Big deal.

"And then, in 1980, my friend and basketball teammate Terry Fox set off on his Marathon of Hope. He was going to run across Canada to focus attention on the horrors of cancer and to raise funds for cancer research. He wanted nothing for himself. He'd had cancer, it had taken his leg, and now he was going to fight back. That's what it was: a personal fight between one young man and this terrible thing that had attacked him. He would battle it one-on-one. He would show people it could be beaten, and in the course of the battle he would raise funds and inspire other people so that they would be better equipped to join the fight that would someday stamp out cancer for good.

"I've heard and seen it written that cancer beat him. Not true. It only beat his body. It returned and raged through him this time, forcing a halt to his marathon after five months and finally taking his life. But it didn't win. In life and in death Terry did what he'd set out to do: he rallied Canadians to a common cause as never before. The money poured in and is still pouring in, because every year, through memorial walks and other fundraisers, people remember the fighter who wouldn't quit . . .

"What if I continued Terry's theme, made it the major focus of a wheelchair journey around the world in which I would be the catalyst or messenger, and as such help disabled people everywhere? The potential impact was staggering. And as an afterthought—and that's all it was—maybe I could raise money for people disabled through spinal cord injuries for research, rehabilitation and wheelchair sport and recreation programs. Right then, the tour ceased being something I *could* do and became something I *had* to do. I had my physical challenge, my mountain to climb."

Next, with the help and support of people like Marshall Smith, chair of the B.C. Wheelchair Sports Association; Doug Mowat, head of the B.C. Paraplegic Association; Denny Veitch, the one-armed organizer of the 1973 Canada Summer Games; Dr. Bob Hindmarch, a veteran sports administrator; Tim Frick, Rick's basketball coach; Don Alder, who was with Rick when he was injured and others, Rick began to plan the Man in Motion journey. The target: 40,163.79 kilometres, equal to the circumference of the earth. The beginning: March 21, 1985, at Oakridge Shopping Centre.

"I was wheeling, and operating on fumes and nerve ends. The send-off had been emotionally overwhelming: hundreds of people swarming around the chair, lured there by a morning fundraising blitz involving all the major radio stations in town. Disabled persons in wheelchairs of all types. Some disabled, who couldn't wheel and depended on operating the joystick of a motorized chair, were accompanied by parents and friends. They wanted to be a part of it. They wanted to see me off . . ."

Rick Hansen: Man in Motion next goes on to detail, in more than 100 wonderfully readable pages of triumph and frustration, rage and hilarity, hope and despair, boredom and spine-tingling adventure, the incredible journey that took Rick and his support crew through the Pacific states (where Rick heard for the first time a song, "St. Elmo's Fire," inspired by his crusade and written by Canada's David Foster, a song that was to become a major hit), across the southern U.S. to Miami—by which time total donations had reached just $6,000—by plane to Dublin, all through the United Kingdom, then through Western Europe, up into Scandinavia (Rick celebrated his 28th birthday in Finland), a side-trip by air to Russia, then by chair through Poland and Czechoslovakia, Switzerland, Spain, Portugal, Italy (where Rick met the Pope in Rome), Greece. He then wheeled through several places in the Arab world, went to Israel by plane and then went on to wheel through New Zealand and Australia (the halfway point, and the point when crew tensions, anger and frustration were highest). It was then over to Beijing by air to wheel south to Shanghai, during which Rick wheeled a portion of the Great Wall, through Japan from Sapporo to Tokyo, by plane to Miami for a gruelling wheel up the eastern seaboard to Boston and Bar Harbor, then finally into Canada again (where Rick's arrival was cause for a nation-wide burst of affection and respect), to wheel across Newfoundland, from Charlottetown through Fredericton, Quebec City, Montreal, Ottawa, Toronto, Winnipeg (entering the prairies in the winter of 1987), Regina, Calgary, Edmonton, then down the Yellowhead Highway and, finally, back into British Columbia where a huge crowd waited to welcome them home. Among the crowd there was a very special person.

"My mother had a yellow band tied around her arm, a yellow ribbon on her lapel. Everywhere I looked there were yellow ribbons, yellow balloons, yellow armbands—all bearing the same message: WELCOME HOME, RICK. The sounds of 'Tie a Yellow Ribbon 'Round the Old Oak Tree' blared out of the public address system . . .

"In our situation 'coming home' had several definitions: home to B.C., home to Williams Lake, home to Vancouver where the journey had begun. But I know the instant it happened. "Hello, son," my mother said, giving me a big hug. "Welcome home." Nobody would say it better than that ...

"Now it was time for the official welcome by Premier Bill Vander Zalm. I cocked both ears for that one. There was a lot riding on what he had to say. We knew the provincial government would be adding a substantial donation to the Legacy Fund. We knew that donations by the people of B.C. might be a staggering total indeed. The question was, would the premier announce a flat donation, a matching grant arrangement such as that in Alberta, with the government's half supporting other projects similar to ours within the province—or would he shoot the works, match the B.C. contributions and give it all to the Legacy Fund?

"It was a more than million-dollar question, and he came through with the answer we wanted. B.C.'s government would match B.C.'s people dollar for dollar from that moment until the tour ended, and he hoped it would cost him millions." As it turned out, it cost him $5.45 million."

Rick Hansen's 34-country journey, which began March 21, 1985, at Oakridge Mall in Vancouver and ended there 40,163.79 kilometres later on May 22, 1987, raised $24 million for the Man in Motion Legacy Fund. In the ten years since the tour $15 million has been dispersed for spinal cord research, rehabilitation and awareness programs, and the capital fund remains intact for future funding. And, through Rick's indomitable example, the consciousness of a nation was raised. On May 23, 1987, 50,000 people turned out at B.C. Place to welcome Rick back.

"There was a moment, someone else's moment, that told the story of Man in Motion as simply and as truly as it was possible to be told. Eighteen-year-old Kerris Huston, badly injured in a car accident two years earlier, pushed away the hand of a would-be helper and walked slowly and haltingly to the microphone.

"Her voice was slurred. She was obviously nervous. But she spoke to me, and she proved again that the effort was worth the prize: 'One year ago I was in a wheelchair. You showed me how to reach for the stars. You gave me that encouragement to be the best I can. I thank you for letting me share a part of your dream.' Then she walked back to her chair and sat down . . .

"It was a warm and wonderful celebration, a meaningful recognition of and commitment to the disabled of our province and our country. And when all the speeches were over, no one had said it better than Kerris did by walking unaided across that stage at Oakridge: 'Thank you for letting me share a part of your dream.'

The tour ended under a banner that said "The End is Just the Beginning." For Rick, life since the tour has been equally rewarding. Rick is executive director of the Rick Hansen Institute at UBC where he oversees the Disability Resources Centre, the Rick Hansen National Fellow Program, the Life Skills Motivation Centre, Rick Hansen Enterprises and the Man In Motion Foundation. He and Amanda are the proud parents of three daughters—Emma, Alana and Rebecca. Although his Man in Motion Tour is long over, Rick's message is still strong and his life an example to us all.

Excerpts from Rick Hansen: Man in Motion, *by Rick Hansen and Jim Taylor, were reprinted with permission of the authors and the publishers, Douglas & McIntyre.*

Ron Marcoux became president and CEO, Western Canada, for McDonald's Restaurants of Canada. His leadership and persistence helped McDonald's grow—and today its restaurants across Canada exceed 900 in number, with more than 300 in the west. Ron Marcoux's dedication to community support led to two meetings with Rick Hansen. During the second Ron said: "Okay! If anybody can do something as crazy as what you're undertaking, you can, Rick." And McDonald's became Rick's first sponsor for the Man in Motion tour.

Steve Fonyo
Carol Woodman

ON MAY 25, 1985 the "Journey For Lives" cavalcade rounded a bend of Highway 97, and 19-year-old Steve Fonyo hip-hopped into Kelowna. A group of us, waiting at a nearby golf course for tee times, paused to watch. His gait was awkward but there was an unmistakable aura of greatness about him. He was energized and the energy flowed from him, encompassing all of us. It was magic. We'll never forget that moment, or the hush that fell over the crowd. How privileged we felt watching a legend pass. We were awed by the sheer force of his determination, the endless smile, the friendly wave as he painstakingly jog-skipped down the last leg of his epic, cross-Canada marathon.

Fonyo, who lost his leg to cancer at the age of 12 was inspired by fellow one-legged runner Terry Fox. Cancer overtook Fox at Thunder Bay and he had to terminate his run. Fonyo wanted to finish it for his idol but later decided to do his own. Journey For Lives took two years to organize. Money for the venture, $26,500, was donated by the Pacific Pulmonary Research Society and private interests.

On March 31, 1984, in St. John's, Newfoundland, Steve Fonyo dipped his artificial leg into the Atlantic Ocean beginning the journey that would take him 14 months to complete. It ended similarly on May 31, 1985, on the shore of the Pacific Ocean in Victoria. Fonyo completed 7,924 kilometres, crossed ten provinces and raised over $13 million for cancer research. On the way he wore out six artificial legs and 17 pairs of running shoes.

His artificial leg cracked in Newfoundland and although he couldn't run because of the pain he continued walking to make his designated 32 kilometres per day. In New Brunswick the temperatures hit 32 degrees celsius causing him to run in the cooler mornings and evenings. He braved wind, sleet, blizzards and heat waves, all the while drinking copious quantities of Coke and munching on his favorite junk foods, cheesies and doughnuts. His travelling support team drove the motorhome at the snail's pace of seven kilometres an hour.

In Hamilton he was fitted with a special jogging leg, an experimental prosthesis the design of which had been suggested by Terry Fox. The limb had a spring-loaded mechanism in the heel to absorb the impact when the heel hit the ground. With the new device the Journey for Lives became a little easier.

The press kept Fonyo in the shadow of Terry Fox, comparing every accomplishment, every achievement, every painstaking

A Canadian of historic stature, a shining example of the true strength of the human spirit
—Brian Mulroney

mile. However Fonyo was, and is, his own person. When he was called a hero he said simply, "I'm just a 19-year-old who's had cancer." It wasn't until he'd passed Thunder Bay that the media and the Cancer Society really got behind the volatile and outspoken young runner. This superb athlete who was running across Canada, raising millions for cancer, finally came into his own.

To defy the freezing temperatures of a prairie winter he donned special jogging gear. The climate was frigid but the reception along the way kept heating up. Donations poured in as the momentum built. Children were allowed out of school to cheer the cavalcade as it passed.

In Vancouver a cheering crowd of 20,000 welcomed him. The band played *Chariots of Fire* as Fonyo ran into B.C. Place where a giant map of Canada was stretched over the football field. He had only 33 kilometres to go.

Thousands of fans lined the roadway as Steve Fonyo painfully hop-skipped the last 10 kilometres into Victoria. He dipped his artificial leg in the Pacific Ocean and emptied a vial of water from the Atlantic into it.

For a few months Fonyo recuperated, then ran in Britain, from the northern to the southern tip, raising money for the British Cancer Society. He completed this in May 1987.

Steve Fonyo started his journey at the age of 18. It was his first time away from home. By 20 he was a national hero. Then the fanfare died, promises of fame and fortune diminished and his accomplishments faded from public memory. The Fonyo headlines changed. Bouts with alcohol, speeding, and news of his volatile temper were dutifully reported. Fame was short-lived and public recognition for his incredible feat was forgotten. Steve Fonyo, the legend, the one-legged runner from Vernon, B.C., who with superhuman effort achieved a miracle, was demoted to antihero.

Despite his present problems, Fonyo's run achieved extraordinary results. As one youngster summed it all up, "I just think of what he's done for cancer."

Senior Citizens
Jenny Shaw

SEARCHING FOR THE PERFECT PLACE to retire? Vancouver has it all—just ask any one of those thousands of immigrants from the other provinces who have acted on their dream of spending the last third of their life in the only city in Canada where you will see the over-fifties playing tennis in their shorts on Christmas Day! (Well, not every Christmas Day, but I have seen them.) We have the best views of the mountains, the best harbor for sailing and the best trails for walking—not to mention the best and largest number of coffee bars, perfect for watching the rest of the world go by on its way to work.

According to the 1995 edition of *The Fact Book on Aging* (published by the SFU Gerontology Research Centre) at least one-third of the more than 200,000 seniors living in the Greater Vancouver Regional District reside in the City of Vancouver itself. Another 18 per cent live in Surrey and 11 per cent in Burnaby. In some communities, notably White Rock, New Westminster and Langley, the number of seniors far exceeded the provincial average of 12.9 per cent in 1991. And the numbers keep growing! If projections prove true and the boomers survive into their retirement years, we could have a population of half a million active post-boomers running (or roller-blading) along the seawall.

An interesting trend I am noticing here in the West End is that several people move from the city to more rural areas, only to move back again after ten or even 20 years. Why? For one thing our public transportation service is excellent (and that's only if you don't want to walk everywhere, which many of us do), the two major hospitals have been named among the best in America, and the many home-delivery restaurant services allow you to eat well and cheaply (and even entertain) without spending hours slaving over the proverbial hot stove.

If you're a senior who likes to volunteer in your community, there are opportunities through local organizations if you have an area of preference, or through Volunteer Vancouver (875-9144). Most senior centres have a great selection of ongoing drop-in programs ranging from crafts to computers if you want to learn new practical skills. Continuing education departments at all the universities and colleges have courses designed specifically for the older learner at minimum cost. Simon Fraser University's downtown campus offers a Senior's Certificate Program (291-5100) which has the largest alumni association (the Opsimaths) in the history of the university.

Vancouver, the only city in Canada where you will see the over-fifties playing tennis in their shorts on Christmas Day

Seniors are retiring with more skills now than ever before. They can, if they wish, pass some of this knowledge on to younger generations through volunteer mentoring and tutoring programs in the schools. The Vancouver School Board (731-1131) has a list of schools and their needs. The West End Seniors' Network (669-5051) has its own storytelling program, where seniors share stories related to their life experiences with students who are eager to learn first hand what is was like to live in Canada or Vancouver in the "early days." The network also offers computer courses and even a senior men's cooking class.

Among the many advantages of being in the third age of life are the discounts available. Restaurants, movies and other entertainments, pharmaceuticals and banks all offer special rates to seniors. Exploring new places, whether at home or abroad, is within reach for many older travellers who find they finally have time and money to spend. From Vancouver you can hop on a train to Banff, a plane to Reno or a ferry to Alaska, all for lower prices than apply to the rest of the population. If Vancouver Island or one of the many Gulf Islands is your choice, then you pay nothing at all—provided you travel with B.C. Ferries Monday through Thursday.

Vancouver has become a leading centre for gerontological research in Canada, thanks to the excellent leadership provided by Dr. Gloria Gutman and her staff at Simon Fraser University's Harbour Centre Campus (291-5062). The 1995 annual meeting of the Canadian Association on Gerontology was held at Vancouver's Hyatt Regency Hotel and the International Association of Gerontology's Convention (held every four years) will be at the Vancouver Trade and Convention Centre in 2001. Vancouver was chosen as the best site over five other countries at the 1993 meeting in Budapest. Over 5,000 professional gerontologists are expected to attend.

Belive it—Vancouver's the place to be at 73, or 84 or 95. It's warmer, friendlier, prettier and well, wetter than anywhere else in Canada (but everyone knows that rain is great for the skin).

Canuck Place
Jim Moodie

WALKING THROUGH CANUCK PLACE, Vancouver's hospice for terminally ill children, elicits strong emotions of admiration for the individuals and companies whose dedication and generosity have made this hospice real. The work that has gone into restoring the "Glen Brae" mansion and turning it into a functioning hospice, while retaining a sense of home, is truly inspiring.

Canuck Place contains welcoming sitting areas, generous fireplaces, restored wood panelling and colorful stained-glass windows throughout each of its three storeys. Just over the threshold is the wood-paneled Loewen Library which serves as the bereavement resource centre. The centre will make available across B.C. a wide range of bereavement support including resource materials and consultation for parents, teachers and health-care professionals. The centre will also provide telephone support and training for school and community staff to help them deal with the effects of grieving and loss.

The combined kitchen and dining room would be the envy of any chef. Pots and pans hang from the ceiling and low countertops accommodate junior bakers. A dining room table with seating for 16 presides over one corner of the room, brightened by the natural light that pours in from wide windows overlooking the gardens.

An oak staircase leads to a stained-glass window depicting a small cottage in the Scottish Highlands—a legacy from a previous owner. On the second floor are the children's bedrooms and nursing stations. The walls are lavender, peach or yellow—the colors of bedrooms, not hospital rooms. Bright quilts, wooden bed frames, toys, mobiles and posters create a home-like atmosphere and subdue the presence of the most current medical equipment. Special touches, like the bathrooms and Jacuzzi room which include mobile harnesses so a child in a wheelchair can bathe and shower unaided, are the culmination of consultation with families caring for a terminally ill child.

There are two family suites on the third floor so families can stay under the same roof as their children. There are no rules; parents can visit their kids in the middle of the night or, if possible, take them back to bed with them. Patients and their siblings can continue their education in the classroom/multimedia/computer room. They can also benefit from the "Snoezlen Room," a textured environment that stimulates all five sense through bubbling colored water, fibre-optic lights, fans and streamers, music and wall projections of the "Man in the Moon." A Canuck-themed Jacuzzi room and a soundproof, padded "volcano" room provide a safe outlet for stress and tension.

An unobtrusive staff of physicians, nurses, therapists, psychologists, social workers and all-faith clergy support the children and their families. Canuck Place can accommodate eight children (up to the age of 17) and two families with a combination of palliative and respite care.

Canuck Place is housed at "Glen Brae," a mansion bequeathed to the City of Vancouver by Julian and Elizabeth Wlosinski under the sole condition that the home be used for the good of the general public. With the aid of then-mayor Gordon Campbell, the Canuck Foundation, the *Vancouver Sun* and The Loewen Group, as well as the executor of the estate and its heirs, Canuck Place came into being. The city leased "Glen Brae" to the HUGS Children's Hospice Society for one dollar for 25 years. A major contributor and an innovative "sale" of small parcels of the garden enabled the purchase of the adjoining property for the children's garden. Committed financial, professional and volunteer support will ensure the continued success of Canuck Place in coming years.

Ornamental iron fence, Glen Brae. VS

THE LOEWEN GROUP INC.

The Loewen Group supports hospice care for children through its charitable organization—the Loewen Children's Foundation—and is grateful to be able to assist British Columbia children and their families through its support of Canuck Place.

Neighborhood Houses
Dave Adair

VANCOUVER'S NEIGHBORHOOD HOUSES have a rich history of community service in the more than 50 years that they have been a key part of Vancouver's neighborhoods. Today's Neighborhood Houses trace their roots back to the Settlement House movement that started with the establishment of Toynbee Hall in London, England, in 1884.

Vancouver's first Neighborhood House grew out of the Alexandra Orphanage in Kitsilano, one of the province's first non-profit societies. Incorporated in 1894 it was the 36th non-profit society in B.C. By the 1930s the orphanage was in decline; the trend was clearly toward foster homes rather than orphanages. In 1938 they closed down the facility in order to re-open a couple of months later as the Alexandra Neighborhood House. North Shore Neighborhood House opened in 1939 and Gordon House followed in the West End in 1942. The numbers continued to grow; today there are 11 Neighborhood Houses in Greater Vancouver.

In the 1960s three Houses formed an umbrella organization to reduce administrative duplication and expand services. Seven of Vancouver's Houses are now members of the Association of Neighborhood Houses. In addition to its role as a legal and administrative umbrella for its members it has also been involved in the development of low-cost housing in the city and administers the A.N.H. Home Support Services, providing homemaker services for seniors in their homes.

Over the years the Association has been involved in camping for children and families. Camp Alexandra at Crescent Beach was one of the first "fresh-air camps" in the province. It still operates on the original site with camping programs in the summer and as a Neighborhood House the rest of the year. Sasamat Outdoor Centre operates a year-round camping program and is used by all of the Neighborhood Houses. In cooperation with the Houses it runs the largest and most comprehensive leadership training program for teens in B.C.

An effective Neighborhood House is the true centre of the community. Here you will find a tremendous range of programs and services for all ages, a real community spirit and a great variety of opportunities for residents to work together to contribute to their community. Fundamental to the Neighborhood House concept is that each one is unique in that its programs and services reflect the needs of the people living in that community. This has been one of the key strengths of the Houses over the years as they were able to be flexible and responsive to emerging community needs. That response might include developing programs for a particular group, such as after-school day-care or a first-aid program, or it could be oriented more toward community development, like working with local residents on a local issue such as a need for more recreation facilities for children or low-cost housing for families and seniors.

Early Settlement Houses established a strong tradition of working with new immigrants to help them become established in their new homes. This tradition is central to today's Neighborhood Houses, located, as most of them are, in areas with high concentrations of new immigrants. For many of them the local Neighborhood House becomes a vital resource for starting their new life in Canada. This relationship is far from being a one-way street. Many of these new Canadians come from countries where "community" is extremely important, so they bring with them a deep understanding of the importance of community and a real willingness to contribute in whatever ways they can.

Vancouver's Neighborhood Houses are deeply rooted in their communities and the widespread support they enjoy can be seen in part in the recent substantial expansion of their facilities. In the past few years Kiwassa, Mount Pleasant and Collingwood Neighborhood Houses have all opened major new buildings and several other Houses are currently working on similar projects.

NEIGHBORHOOD HOUSES AND MEMBER UNITS

Cedar Cottage Neighborhood House
4065 Victoria Drive — 874-4231

Frog Hollow Neighborhood House
2131 Renfrew Street — 251-1225

Gordon Neighborhood House
1019 Broughton Street — 683-2554

Kitsilano Neighborhood House
2325 West 7th Avenue — 736-3588

Mount Pleasant Neighborhood House
800 East Broadway — 879-8208

South Vancouver Neighborhood House
6470 Victoria Drive — 324-6212

Home Support Services
#200 - 1820 Renfrew Street — 251-2078

Collingwood Neighborhood House*
5288 Joyce Street — 435-0323

Kiwassa Neighborhood House*
2425 Oxford Street — 254-5401

Little Mountain Neighborhood House*
3981 Main Street — 879-7104

North Shore Neighborhood House*
225 East 2nd Avenue, N. Vancouver — 987-8138

Sasamat Outdoor Centre
3302 Senkler Road, Belcarra — 939-2268

Crescent Beach Community Services
2916 McBride Avenue — 535-0015

*Independent Societies

Association of Neighborhood Houses: Mission Statement
We are a volunteer driven, community service agency. • Our mission is to make neighborhoods better places to live. • Our goal is to enable people to enhance their lives and strengthen their communities. • Our challenge is to work with communities to develop innovative programs and services that meet the changing needs of a diverse population.

Information and Referral in Greater Vancouver

Gil Evans; Compiled with input from Cynthia Crampton, Hazel Smith and Al Arnason

A caller has recently become widowed. She has a six-year-old daughter. Friends have been supportive but she would like to meet other widowed people with children.

Agency suggested: **Good Company for Kids**

A parent believes his child is very bright and wants to know how best to challenge and stimulate him.

Agency suggested: **Gifted Children's Association**

A caller has a daughter with anorexia nervosa and needs some support from other parents in the same situation.

Agency suggested: **Canadian Association for Anorexia Nervosa and Associated Disorders**

Help! I am up to my ears in debt. I have consolidated my debts and think I have things under control but need to join up with others in order to stay that way.

Agency suggested: **Debtors Anonymous**

There you have a typical cross-section of calls (real ones) that come in daily to Information Services Vancouver (ISV). People with problems call ISV and are referred to appropriate services. In 1995 more than 47,000 people found the assistance they were looking for through ISV, a nonprofit United Way agency governed by a volunteer board of directors and run by a staff of 22 under the directorship of Gil Evans.

It was in the U.S. during the 1920s that information and referral services were first established by the United Way. After World War II, there was significant growth in these services when government began sponsoring information centres for war veterans. Later, in the 1960s and '70s, there were more dramatic increases in information and referral services—this time fuelled by the anti-poverty movement and the advances in information technologies.

It is an odd quirk of fate that ISV, the Association of Neighbourhood Houses (ANH) and the Junior League of Vancouver (JLV) are neighbors on the second floor of Heritage Hall. In 1953 the Community Chest and Council (now the United Way), recognizing that it had become increasingly difficult to know where to turn for help with a problem, determined that Vancouver needed an information and referral service, a place where trained professionals could help people assess their situation and identify appropriate services to

meet their needs. A first year-budget of $7,300 was established. The Rotary Club promised $2,500 and there was a personal donation of $200. The Community Chest asked the Junior League for the remainder. The JLV had also received a request for the same money from ANH but decided to donate it to the Community Chest. And thus, on June 9, 1953 the Community Information Service, managed by Elaine Keene, was able to open its doors and its phones.

The Community Information Service became part of the Vancouver Crisis Centre in 1973, changed its name to the Community Information Centre (CIC) and began to shift its role from direct service to support for the 35 neighborhood information centres that had sprung up in the Lower Mainland. After 20 years of service Elaine Keene retired. (She would return as a volunteer from 1982-88.) In 1975 Gil Evans was hired as CIC coordinator. In 1977 it became an independent United Way agency and acquired yet another new name, the Greater Vancouver Information and Referral Service (GVIRS, pronounced 'Jeevers' by its friends) and, because the neighborhood centres had shrunk to just seven municipal/regional centres, went back to providing direct service to the public.

It was Charles Keast, the first president of GVIRS, who led an initiative to have the City of Vancouver buy the old Mount Pleasant Post Office from the federal government and turn it into Heritage Hall, a permanent home for five community service agencies including ANH, JLV and ISV. They moved into Heritage Hall, at 3102 Main St., in September 1985.

1985 brought more changes: an experimental public computer information service, Information Online; two new specialized services—Information Daycare and Information Seniors Housing — and; yes, a name change—Information Services Vancouver. (In March, 1996 the agency adopted a new look for its name. The emphasis is now on **Inform**ation Services with Vancouver taking a less prominent position—a move designed to show that ISV serves the whole of B.C. The bold emphasis on "inform" is a visual reminder of the work of the agency.) This was followed by the addition of a fee-based service to employees of large corporations, the Working Parents Daycare Assurance Plan. (Clients include Xerox, Royal Trust, American Express and Kodak.) It was the City of Vancouver which asked ISV to establish Information Seniors Housing which later became part of the Vancouver Housing Registry. Information Daycare became part of the Westcoast Child Care Resource Centre in 1989.

These four new services found other homes but their place was taken at ISV by two province-wide contract services for the provincial government:

the Victims Information Line (at the request of the attorney general) and the Alcohol and Drug Information and Referral Service (requested by the ministry of labor and consumer services). These agencies are both still operated by ISV. A regional association, the United Way established in 1978 as the Lower Mainland Alliance of Information and Services, has grown to become the B.C. Alliance of Information & Referral Services (BCAIRS), with 16 members in the Lower Mainland:

- Burnaby Information and Community Service
- Deltassist Information Centre
- Greater Coquitlam Crisis and Information Line
- Maple Ridge-Pitt Meadows Information and Referral
- North Shore Community Services
- Peace Arch Community Services
- Richmond Connections Information and Volunteer Society
- Surrey Community Services
- Legal Resource Centre
- 411 Seniors Centre
- Shalom Vancouver
- West End Seniors Centre
- Seniors Support Service
- YWCA Women's Information Centre
- Self-Help Resources Association
- Gay & Lesbian Centre

Each of these agencies provides special services to their respective constituents. BCAIRS was host in October 1995 to a conference of more than 150 information and referral people from "Cascadia," that is, Oregon, Washington, Idaho, Montana, British Columbia and Alaska.

THE RED BOOK

In 1957 the Community Information Service realized their comprehensive card catalogue of community services in the Lower Mainland would be useful to many other agencies and services and so began publishing, once every two years, the Directory of Services for Greater Vancouver. The first issue, edited by Elaine Keene, had 206 pages. It's now called the Directory of Services for the Lower Mainland. In 1974 the directory was published in a red three-ring binder and thus was born the Red Book. Due to the rapid change in information about services, the Red Book began annual publication in 1977 (70 per cent of the listings change each year.) Red Book sales now exceed 3,000 annually and it is used by everyone who provides services to the public, many of whom refer to it as our "bible." It is subscribed to by doctors, lawyers, educators, clergy, human resources staff, emergency services workers and others. Keeping up with the times, ISV began a computer version, the Electronic Red Book, in June 1996. More than 5,000 social, community and government agencies and services are listed in the data base.

Information
Services
Vancouver

Admin: (604) 875-6431
Fax: (604) 660-9415
Email: informbc@vcn.bc.ca
Website: http://www.vcn.bc.ca

Information and Referral: Bringing People and Services Together

Downtown Eastside, Vancouver, 1993. VS

**There are 38 major topical divisions
in the Red Book:**

- Advocacy and Rights Organizations
- Business Information and Assistance
- Child Abuse and Neglect
- Community Planning and Development
- Consumer Assistance
- Correctional and Rehabilitation Services
- Counselling Services
- Services for People with Disabilities
- Drugs, Alcohol, Addictions
- Education

- Employment
- Environment
- Financial Assistance and Information
- First Peoples
- Free and Low Cost Goods and Services
- Gay, Lesbian and Bisexual Community Services
- Health (dental)
- Health (medical)
- Health (mental)
- Home Support and Home Repair Services
- Housing and Accommodation
- Services for Immigrants
- Information Services
- Legal Services

- Men's Community Services
- Multicultural Services
- Non-profit Societies
- Parenting and Family Life
- Political Representation and Parties
- Professional Associations
- Services for Senior Citizens
- Social, Recreational and Cultural Resources
- Transportation Services
- Travel and Tourism
- Victims' Services
- Volunteer Centres
- Women's Community Services
- Youth Community Services

Service Clubs of Greater Vancouver
Barbara Rogers

Beta Sigma Phi

Beta Sigma Phi is an international women's organization founded in Abilene, Texas, in 1931. It now has 250,000 members in 32 countries. The first Canadian chapter was established in Vancouver in 1935. Today there are about ten area councils in the Lower Mainland with many chapters and several thousand members.

Beta Sigma Phi stands for life, learning and friendship. Their mandate includes social and cultural enhancement and community service. Each chapter supports its own projects. The Vancouver chapter's priority has been the arthritis centre recently renamed The Mary Pack Centre after a deceased honorary member who was its original founder. The Beta Sigma Phi were the first recipients of the Bentall Centre Service Award. In 1993 a scholarship fund for a student at Studio 58 was started.

Money is raised for the larger projects by holding casino and theatre nights, and craft fairs.

The Honorable Order of the Blue Goose, International

The Blue Goose Organization came to life in 1906 on the shore of Green Lake, Wisconsin, as a lark amongst insurance agents attending an annual meeting. Incredibly the idea took hold and grew into an international fraternity order with more than 9,000 members across North America. The British Columbia "pond," based in Greater Vancouver, was founded in 1917 and now has 140 members.

It has been described as the "fun side of the property and casualty insurance industry," and this approach is reflected in the delightful names given to the organizational structure and members. State or area chapters are called "ponds," members "ganders" and initiates "goslings." If an area has too few members to become a "pond," a "puddle" is formed. Officers of the various "ponds" bear titles such as "most loyal gander," "supervisor of the flock," "custodian of the goslings," "guardian of the pond," "keeper of the golden goose egg" (treasurer); the secretary is referred to as the "wielder of the goose quill." The international organization is called the "grand nest" and its officers add the prefix "grand" to the above titles.

Amusing names apart, the Blue Goose members are seriously dedicated to "character, charity and fellowship" and their mandate is to support worthy charitable causes. Each pond has its own projects but the official international goal is to support the Special Olympics. The B.C.

pond also contributes to worthy causes including the Salvation Army, the Food Bank and other agencies.

Funds are raised primarily through their own insurance industry members and special drives.

British Columbia Lions Clubs

The Vancouver Central Lions Club, founded in 1921, is the oldest Lions Club in British Columbia and the second oldest in Canada.

There are 26 Lions Clubs in Vancouver. Altogether in the Lower Mainland there are 55 clubs with about 1,500 members. As well there are approximately 25 Lions Ladies Clubs, the first of which was established in 1937.

Lions Clubs' goals are to take an active interest in the civic, cultural, social and moral welfare of their respective communities. Their motto is "we serve" and their mandate is to give assistance when and where needed for children, adults and seniors. Each club is autonomous in the selection of various projects but most support the Lions Society. "Give a Gift of Sight" is an annual eyeglasses collection and recycling program co-sponsored by the Lions Clubs. Originally they sponsored "The White Cane" and "Seeing-Eye Dogs for the Blind" programs; lately they sponsor "Sight First" an international project to aid people with sight problems.

Almost from its inception Vancouver Central has been very active in its support of equipment and facilities for the blind. It has also served the needs of the community in a variety of other ways. These include sponsoring and maintaining senior citizen's homes (the first Lions Club to do so); donating funds and equipment to St. Paul's and Vancouver General Hospitals and the Faculty of Medicine at UBC; inaugurating the School Person Patrol Safety Program in B.C.; and sponsoring glee club performances. Today it maintains a number of very important projects and services. Included in these are: The CARSCRAFT sheltered workshop which employs 26 people with disabilities; annual scholarships to King George Secondary School; an annual Christmas party for single-parent children; Food Bank drives; and helping to maintain the Banfield Pavilion for senior citizens. Financial support is also given to the Salvation Army, the Western Institute for the Deaf, C.A.R.E., L.C.I.F. and other charitable organizations.

Funds are raised through casinos and the sale of entertainment booklets. Funds to assist the Lions Society are raised provincially through Timmy's Christmas Telethon held on the first weekend in December. Four-and-a-half million dollars were raised last year.

The British Columbia Lions Society for Children with Disabilities

The Lions Society of B.C. was established in

1972 by the Lions Clubs as a registered charitable organization. It holds the Easter Seals franchise for the province of B.C. and is responsible for Easter Seal Services which include the Easter Seal houses, buses and camps. The society's 50 board members are Lions elected from across the province.

Their mandate is to provide services and programs that will directly benefit children with disabilities throughout British Columbia. Some of the services provided include: the Lion's Laser Skin Centre; Patient Care Grants Program which provides transportation needs, respite care, special equipment and prosthetics; and the Fraser Valley Child Development Centre in Abbotsford which offers therapy to more than 450 children.

Funds are raised through various activities such as special events, direct-mail campaigns and appeals as well as planned giving and bequests. These activities raise over $8.5 million annually.

The Canadian Daughters League (National Council)

This organization was established in 1923 with approximately 30 members. It is a fraternal and benevolent organization whose members believe in Canada and its people. Today it has about 300 members in British Columbia. There are three branches in the Lower Mainland with about 90 members.

Their mandate is in the field of education, art and music. They offer bursaries and scholarships for university and college students and also donate to the Kiwanis Music Festival.

Funds are raised for these projects with special teas, the sale of baked goods, raffles and garage sales.

The Canadian Progress Club—Greater Vancouver

Established in Toronto in 1922 the Canadian Progress Club is an all-Canadian service club dedicated to supporting those in need. Today it reaches from coast to coast with 45 chapters. There are three branches in Greater Vancouver (one in Vancouver and two in North Vancouver) with approximately 75 members. The men's Greater Vancouver club, based on the North Shore, was originally chartered in 1964. The men's Vancouver Downtown club, as well as the ladies Vancouver Evergreens in North Vancouver, were chartered in the early 1980s.

Each club is devoted to assisting those less fortunate and each club is committed to the best interests of its local community. Their objectives are to foster goodwill throughout Canada; to aid in uniting all the people of Canada into a nation that shall stand as one of the great and prosperous peoples of the world; and to show by leadership and example the pride of being a Canadian.

The Greater Vancouver club provided the first $40,000 to help the B.C. Special Olympics get its start in British Columbia. Other projects include: an annual scholarship for the UBC School of Audiology; providing funding for child amputees; childhood speech impairment treatments; and support for the Lions Gate Hospital neonatal unit. They currently support B.C. Special Olympics and two treatment centres for autism and learning disabilities.

Funds are raised by casinos, lotteries, raffles and the sale of a Christmas coloring book.

The Fraternal Order Of Eagles

The Fraternal Order of Eagles was established on February 6, 1898, by five theatre owners sitting on a pile of lumber in a Seattle shipyard. The first Canadian chapter "Aerie No. 6," was founded in Vancouver on March 3, 1899. There are about seven aeries in the Lower Mainland with approximately 2,000 members. The first of several ladies auxiliaries was founded in 1926. They are attached to but entirely independent of the men's aeries. In 1945 the B.C. Eagles broke away from their Washington roots to form the first provincial aerie.

The Order of Eagles has been described as "the poor man's Masons" since their beliefs are similar. But their rituals are quite different. The fraternity is very much a family affair and activities are encouraged that involve the family as a whole. The organization should get credit for the introduction of Mother's Day which they celebrate every year.

Their motto is "people helping people" and each aerie is autonomous although they sometimes work together on joint projects.

In 1943 a youth guidance program for emotionally disturbed youths was launched. Great crusaders, the Eagles in the past have fought for the worker's compensation act, mothers' pensions, old age pensions and social security laws. These efforts on behalf of others attracted members including such U.S. presidents as Roosevelt, Truman and Kennedy and entertainers Jimmy Durante and Bob Hope.

Locally the Eagles have taken an active role in the fight against arthritis. They have also raised thousands of dollars for heart/stroke, cancer, diabetes and Alzheimer's research, kidney dialysis, senior citizen projects, crippled children programs and many other worthy charities and community projects.

Funds are raised by members through dances, casinos, a Grey Cup party and various other events.

Vancouver Elks Lodge #I

The Elks of Canada is an order that has been in existence since 1912. The national governing body is called the Grand Lodge and its chartered branches are called lodges. There are approximately 340 lodges across Canada with about 34,000 members. In the Lower Mainland there are approximately 20 lodges with about 1,000 members. The organization has an Eastern influence in the titles of its different offices and the Elks regalia. Some of the former are called exalted ruler, leading, loyal and lecturing knights and inner guard. The regalia, which is only worn at lodge meetings and special functions, is not mandatory but encouraged. It consists of a purple fez and blazer with white shirt and pants. A white tassel denotes a regular member, or brother. A purple tassel denotes an exalted or past exalted ruler and a gold tassel represents a district deputy, grand lodge officer or regional representative.

The Elks is a fraternal and charitable organization promoting and supporting community needs through volunteer efforts. Each lodge chooses its own project. However the national charity of the Elks (The Elks Purple Cross Fund) provides funds to help children in need, regardless of the nature of their disease or physical disability, race, religion, creed or color. The Elks Purple Cross Deaf Detection and Development Program was founded in 1967 to help identify the earliest possible hearing impairment in children and to assure the best possible services in hearing and speech rehabilitation. Elks have also built three summer camps for underprivileged or handicapped children.

Funds are raised by holding casinos, raffles and flea markets.

The Royal Purple of Canada (Vancouver Lodge #I)

This is the women's auxiliary of the Elks, established on September 11, 1914. There are about 20 branches and approximately 750 members in the Lower Mainland. Their purpose is charitable and benevolent—their aim is to promote the principles of justice, charity, sisterly love and fidelity; to encourage the equality of women in society; to encourage and create opportunities for women to develop their leadership qualities; and to create a greater awareness of women and their contributions to their communities.

The Royal Purple not only helps finance the national fund but also takes an active part in serving their community, with special regard for children and senior citizens. The Elks Purple Cross Fund literary and poster contest provides opportunity to encourage Canadian youth in writing and art.

Fundraising activities include casinos, raffles and bake and craft sales.

Independent Order of Foresters

Established in 1874, the IOF is one of the world's oldest and largest family fraternal benefit societies, with headquarters in Toronto and over 1.5 million members in Canada, the U.S. and the U.K. In the Lower Mainland there are seven clubs (called courts) with about 14,500 members.

The order has nothing to do with the forest industry; it claims its origins date back to the time of Robin Hood in Sherwood Forest. Before the Magna Carta it was illegal for people to form groups. Afterwards people were able to form guilds, or friendly societies, to provide help for one another in times of distress. The Ancient Order of Forestry began to develop around 1830 in England, imitating to some degree the rituals and symbolism of Freemasonry. The organization soon spread to North America but when headquarters in England refused to grant home rule to the American Foresters in 1874, they broke away to form the Independent Order of Foresters. A further schism took place in 1881 when the Canadian contingent withdrew to incorporate under Ontario legislation. Within IOF there are three levels of government: the supreme and high courts, and members' local courts.

As well as providing their members with a variety of benefits and social activities, the IOF courts participate actively in various local charitable projects. Their mandate is to raise money which they channel into agencies that work with children. But IOF members have also raised money for the purchase of kidney machines and cancer research equipment as well as guide dogs for the blind and a mobile eye clinic. Each court is autonomous and chooses its own charity to support but they unite for some projects. Collectively they raise more than $1 million each year for Children's Hospital and on April 30, 1995, a donation of $21,900 was presented to Canuck Place. One of their most important goals is to help prevent child abuse. Since 1975 they have been supporting agencies aiding child abuse victims. Through the IOF's Foresters Against Child Abuse program informative booklets and educational films are distributed to hundreds of family service agencies, community groups and individuals.

Fundraising for the Children's Hospital is done through an event called Bowling for Miracles, an annual bowl-a-thon that teams the IOF with the Children's Miracle Network, sponsors of the world's largest telethon. Money for other charitable work is raised through member donations, casinos, fashion shows and community events.

The Freemasons

Freemasonry is inextricably interwoven with the history of British Columbia and the settlement of Greater Vancouver. Many of its members were among the politicians, civic leaders, business people and other historical figures who helped shape the province. Today several of those Freemasons are remembered by the communities, streets and buildings named in their honor.

Many of the first fur traders and explorers, including Captain James Cook, were Freemasons. It is not known whether explorer Simon Fraser was a Mason but his son, John Alexander Fraser, certainly was. The latter arrived in British Columbia when thousands of American miners, many of whom were Masons, were swarming into the new province in search of gold. Masonry was formally established in the province during this era. At John Fraser's Barkerville funeral in 1865 "his remains were borne to their last resting place by his Masonic brethren and by the largest concourse ever before assembled in the Cariboo for such a purpose."

The oldest Masonic Lodge in British Columbia, (Victoria-Columbia) was established in Victoria in 1860 in what was then known as the Colony of Vancouver Island. The second oldest (but first on the Mainland), Union Lodge, was established in 1861 at New Westminster in the new Colony of British Columbia. By the time British Columbia joined confederation in 1871 there were a total of nine lodges. These early founders faced almost insurmountable problems including the vast distance from the mother lodges in England and Scotland, and small populations separated by hundreds of miles of unbroken and almost impassable wilderness. The problems experienced by the small settlement at Moodyville on Burrard Inlet was a typical example.

In order to attend the meetings at the Union Lodge in New Westminster, the Masons of Moodyville were faced with an unenviable choice—either to take a ferry trip across Burrard Inlet, then attempt a rough ride through a dense forest over a marshy, broken, corduroy road or to take a four-hour steamer trip. By both means it usually meant an overnight stay which, being busy men, they could not afford. They decided to form their own lodge, which they built themselves at the present Park and Tilford Gardens location.

When the Grand Lodge of England refused to grant them a charter, saying there was already an adequate lodge in New Westminster, they promptly applied to the Grand Lodge of Scotland which immediately granted them the required charter. The new lodge, named Mount Hermon, was formally established in May, 1869, with 17 proud founding members. Included were Josias Charles Hughes, Sewell "Sue" Prescott Moody, George W. Haynes, George Black, William O. Allen and Philander Wheeler Swett. There are now 120 members.

Mount Hermon Lodge still practises the

ancient Scottish rituals which are the same as the American work. At least 35 lodges descended from this lodge practise the Scottish rituals. The other British Columbia lodges practise the modified English rituals now known as Canadian work. The original Mount Hermon Hall was used to shelter the victims of the Great Fire of 1886.

Canada does not have a national lodge like most countries. Instead each province has its own grand lodge and grand master. The Grand Lodge of British Columbia was established in 1871. It officially opened at its present location on August 24th, 1974. The grand lodge might be called the administrative body for the other lodges in British Columbia and it rents meeting space to about 25 lodges. Mount Hermon Lodge was the first lodge to hold a meeting in the new Freemason's Hall, its present home. The Grand Lodge does not undertake any large public projects itself but holds the constitution and regulations to which all 168 lodges (consisting of more than 18,000 members) in British Columbia and the Yukon must adhere. The grand master is the highest office and wields great power in the Freemasonry organization.

Freemasonry is the oldest, largest and most widely known fraternity in the world but is also one of the most misunderstood. In reality Freemasonry is anything but sinister or secret. There are many books on the subject in libraries. The only mystery is in its origins. Some believe Freemasonry began as far back as the Crusades, since there are certainly Eastern influences. However it is more generally accepted that its origins date back to the stonemasons who built the cathedrals and other great buildings in the Middle Ages. The stonemason's working tools, compass, square and aprons are still used symbolically in Freemasonry. The actual practices and procedures, observed worldwide, were formalized with the establishment of the Grand Lodge of England in 1717.

What is a Freemason? Basically Freemasonry is a philosophy to live by. It adheres to the old values of kindness and courtesy to others, honesty and dependability in work or business, and compassion and concern for the unfortunate. A Freemason strives to live this way of life by pledging to uphold the principles of justice, truth, integrity, honesty and charity. He believes in a greater power, of any faith, and binds himself to like-minded men in a brotherhood that transcends all ethnic, social, cultural and educational differences. Within that organization he enjoys the friendship and brotherhood of other Freemasons, not only in his community, but anywhere in the world. Far from joining the organization in the hope of some material gain or personal advancement, a Freemason strives to

serve mankind. In aspiring to make the world a better place, and in doing good for others, they strive to make themselves better than they are, not better than others. Freemasonry does not solicit new members. It believes that a man who joins of his own free will is more likely to become a better member.

In the Lower Mainland there are 75 lodges with about 11,000 members. Each lodge chooses, and is responsible for, their own particular humanitarian project. Each year the various lodges raise a substantial amount for charities including hospitals, homes for the needy and relief for people in distress. Masons provide necessary equipment for handicapped children, present scholarships for deserving students and support local community projects.

Female relatives of Freemasons may join the Order of the Eastern Star while girls can join the International Order of Job's Daughters and boys may join the Order of DeMolay.

The Order of the Eastern Star
There are about 69 chapters in British Columbia and the Yukon with approximately 8,000 members. About 12 of those chapters are in the Lower Mainland. To be a member one has to be a female relative of a Freemason. Again each chapter chooses their own humanitarian projects. For example one chapter raises funds for cancer research and makes cancer dressings which are donated to patients.

The Shriners (Gizeh Temple A.A.O.N.M.S.)
Many of the world's greatest charitable organizations are operated by Freemasons. Perhaps the best known are the Shriners with their circuses, their colorful parades and their work on behalf of crippled children. Less known is that each Shriner must be a Freemason before being admitted to the Shrine.

Once accepted as an Apprentice Mason of the Blue Lodge, each member works his way up through several degrees. To earn each degree a Mason must learn certain lessons and participate in a ceremony that illustrates them. At the third degree he reaches Master Mason and then can join either or both of two branches, the Scottish Rite or the York Rite. Should he reach the 32nd degree of the Scottish Rite or the Knights Templar in the York Rite, he may then petition to become a Noble of the Mystic Shrine. Members of the Ancient Arabic Order of Nobles of the Mystic Shrine for North America adhere to the principles of Freemasonry—brotherly love, relief and truth.

In contrast to the more conservative work of Freemasonry, Shriners are distinguished by an enjoyment of life in the interest of philanthropy. Their buoyant philosophy has been described as "pleasure without intemperance, hospitality without rudeness and jollity without coarseness." Anybody who has witnessed their parade antics on mini-bikes, dressed in colorful Eastern attire and red fez's can attest to their sense of fun. But it is "fun with a purpose." The most noticeable symbol of Shrinedom is the distinctive red fez that all Shriners wear at official functions. The Eastern theme was originally chosen to appeal to the public and to raise awareness of the organization. Today their red fezzes are recognized everywhere. Shriners are famous for their philanthropy and their hospitals for crippled children.

There are approximately 3,500 members of 45 clubs in B.C. and the Yukon. About ten of those clubs are in the Lower Mainland. All clubs in British Columbia and the Yukon come under the jurisdiction of the Gizeh Temple Shrine. Gizeh temple was founded on June 11, 1902, in Victoria. The name Gizeh was chosen in accordance with the Shrine rule that "every Temple shall select an Arabic or Egyptian name." It was an appropriate choice since no other temple had a name beginning with the letter "g," a letter which has important significance in Freemasonry. Gizeh is one of the most ancient and famous Egyptian pyramids. In 1942 Gizeh Temple was moved from Victoria to Vancouver. On November 23, 1969, after much ceremony, Gizeh Temple Shrine moved into its new headquarters at the present location.

Since the early 1930s Gizeh Temple has sponsored the popular circuses which continue today. Children's Hospital and various other local hospitals have greatly benefited from the financial assistance of the Gizeh Temple clubs.

The Shrine has always been involved in charitable endeavors. However, in the early 1920s, the membership decided to develop and support an official philanthropy by establishing hospitals for crippled children. In the early 1960s, the Shrine of North America established another first by building the three Shriner Burn Institutes, the first hospitals dedicated to treating children with severe burns. The Shrine now operates 19 orthopaedic hospitals and three burn institutes for crippled and burned children to receive free, specialized medical treatment until they reach the age of 18. Over $1 million per day is required to operate these hospitals. Since 1922 Shriners have substantially improved the quality of life for nearly 400,000 crippled and burned children. Millions more have benefited as recipients of treatments and techniques at Shriners' hospitals.

Children are substantially funded through the Shriners Hospitals for Crippled Children Endowment Fund, which is maintained through gifts, bequests and contributions. Additional income for Shriners hospitals is provided by an annual

hospital assessment paid by every Shriner as well as designated charitable fundraising events such as the colorful circuses. (From information provided by Jim Harrison.)

The Gyro Club of Vancouver

The Gyro Club was established in Vancouver in 1920 and now has 65 members. It is an international social and service club with its head office in Cleveland. (In North America there are 129 clubs with a total of 4,690 members. District four, which includes B.C., Washington and Oregon, has 29 clubs with 1,064 members.) There are seven branches in the Lower Mainland with approximately 400 members. Though it is a men's club there are many mixed functions.

Gyro comes from the Greek language and may be translated loosely as a well-balanced individual. The Gyro Club was founded to promote understanding through peace and friendship between like-minded men throughout the world. Members are men with unselfish ideals and an altruistic desire to improve the world, themselves and their fellow men. Their goal is to stimulate personal achievement. Each club sponsors its own projects supporting the smaller charities, charitable education work and institutions. The Paraplegic Association, Canuck House, a musical scholarship and many playgrounds in the Greater Vancouver area have benefited from their support.

Funds are raised through their charitable foundation as well as casinos and lotteries.

IODE—Provincial Chapter of B.C.

IODE is a Canadian women's charitable organization whose mission is to help improve the quality of life for children, youth and those in need through educational, social service and citizenship programs. The first B.C. chapter was established in 1902. Today there are 15 chapters in the Lower Mainland with approximately 350 members.

Each chapter raises funds for their own special projects. Funds raised have helped build the IODE Glaucoma Centre at Vancouver General Hospital, have provided amenities for B.C. seniors' residences and facilities, have supported diabetes research and cancer clinics and have been used to establish a bursary fund for students at the University of Northern B.C. Several programs related to citizenship, education and social services are also supported. To name but a few: annual awards to outstanding police officers and fire fighters and donations to food banks, women's centres and safe houses. Many needy students, at all levels, have benefited from the more than 133 bursaries, scholarships and awards provided by the tireless efforts of the ladies of IODE.

Fundraising activities include their annual

bazaar, garage sales, auctions, benefits, luncheons and fashion shows.

Kinsmen and Kinette Clubs

The association was established in 1920 by Hal Rogers in Hamilton, Ontario. The first club in B.C. (the fourth in Canada) was the Kinsmen Club of Vancouver founded in 1924. The first Kinette Club was established in 1942. An important resolution was passed at the national convention in 1994 permitting individual clubs to form mixed Kin Clubs. The Kinsmen Club of Vancouver re-chartered as a Kin Club in 1995. Today there are 1,100 clubs in Canada with 14,000 members. Seventeen of these clubs with about 350 members are in the Lower Mainland. There are 96 Kinsmen and Kinette Clubs in B.C., of which two are Kin Clubs.

The association's mandate is "fellowship, personal development and a concern for others less fortunate." Prime Minister Chretien best summed up their accomplishments in his congratulatory letter for the association's 75th anniversary. "For the past 75 years, communities across Canada have had cause to be grateful for the presence and active support of the Kinsmen and Kinette Clubs. Concrete signs of your work are everywhere: your fundraising and service projects have improved the quality of life of countless individuals, both young and old. Your unflagging efforts on behalf of the Canadian Cystic Fibrosis Foundation have given patients and their families new hope that a cure will someday be found . . ." Nationally they have raised more than $20 million to help combat this disease.

In 1952 the Vancouver Kinsmen Club was active in founding the Kinsmen Rehabilitation Foundation of B.C. to combat the polio epidemic. Supported by Kin Clubs throughout the province, the Kinsmen Mothers' March is the primary source of revenue for the KRF. Locally their accomplishments are many, ranging from well-organized events with the Vancouver Canucks and B.C. Lions to smaller events such as Christmas night at the Sunny Hill Children's Hospital. Each club is autonomous in supporting their own community projects. The Vancouver club was instrumental in establishing Operation Go Home, an organization dedicated to helping street youths from across the country return home. They also co-sponsor, with Forerunners, the St. Paddy's Day Fun Run. Proceeds go towards spinal cord research and other Kin charities.

Fundraising is taken seriously but there is also a commitment to fun. Events such as ski weekends, scavenger hunts like Walk in the Wild West End, the St. Paddy's Day Fun Run and the Dream Team dinner with the B.C. Lions help finance the various projects.

The Kinsmen Rehabilitation Foundation of British Columbia

The KRF was founded by the Kinsmen and Kinette service clubs of British Columbia in 1952. Its mandate is to provide programs, services and technologies that assist British Columbians with physical disabilities. These include providing technical aids to the severely disabled, a communication aid program, a public education program and information and client support services.

By focussing on handicapped people's abilities rather than their disabilities, the KRF helps people with physical disabilities attain a lifestyle of independence, at home whenever possible. Others with severe disabilities are assisted with electronic control systems which enable them to control standard electronic appliances in their homes. Through the communication aid program, people with physical disabilities are provided with aids to enable them to communicate with those around them. An educational puppetry program, "Kids on the Block," teaches awareness of disabilities through puppetry. It is designed to assist the integration of disabled children into schools by helping children and their parents overcome any attitudinal barriers.

Funds are raised for these programs by thousands of volunteers who participate in the Kinsmen Mothers' March (begun in 1953 in response to the devastating polio epidemic and now held every January 15-31.) Additional funds are raised by the "getaway" lotteries, memorial donations and bequests.

Kiwanis Club of Vancouver (Downtown Club)

Established in 1919, the Kiwanis Club of Vancouver is a private, voluntary, non-profit organization that is part of Kiwanis International. There are more than 330,000 members in more than 84 countries. In the Lower Mainland there are 17 branches with approximately 11,000 to 12,000 members, both male and female, who come from all walks of life.

The projects the Kiwanis support are many and varied but all help to make communities better places in which to live. Some past projects funded by the Kiwanis Club of Vancouver include: the B.C. Sports Hall of Fame; Vancouver's first public golf course; the world-famous rose garden in Stanley Park; Boys and Girls Clubs; the faculty of commerce and business administration at UBC; the Vancouver Tourist Bureau; and Crime Stoppers of Greater Vancouver.

Kiwanis has provided grants to organizations such as B.C. Children's Diabetic Clinic, the Kiwanis Music Festival which attracts more than 12,000 entrants, the UBC audiology department, B.C. Children's Hospital, Vancouver Community College, the John Howard Society and other community organizations. In addition Kiwanis bursaries and funds are awarded to students at secondary and post-secondary schools. Volunteering is encouraged through such programs as Volunteer Youth Recognition. Kiwanis has built summer camps enjoyed by hundreds of school children. Senior citizens are provided with safe, secure and affordable apartment buildings by several of the Kiwanis' branches who manage their own seniors' housing.

Each branch of the Kiwanis holds its own fundraising activities. For example those for the Vancouver club include the annual television auction, wine festival and bingo as well as numerous other activities throughout the year.

The Kiwassa Club of Vancouver

The Kiwassa Club of Vancouver was formed in 1934 by 100 wives of members of the Kiwanis Club of Vancouver. Kiwassa is an Indian name for "little sisters." Today there are 62 members, including one charter member. The Kiwassa Girls Club became a reality in 1949. An old city firehall, No. 5 on Vernon Drive, was their headquarters.

During the war years, service work included assisting the Red Cross. Today the Kiwassa Club assists the Kiwanis Club with the music festival. They also maintain strong ties to the Kiwassa Neighbourhood Services of East Vancouver. Their fundraising efforts helped establish the new Kiwassa Neighbourhood Service headquarters at 2425 Oxford Street, which offers many community services including daycare, housing, career advice and classes.

Fundraising activities include bridge luncheons and bake sales.

Knights of Columbus, Vancouver Council 1081

This is a fraternal organization for Catholics which originated in New Haven, Connecticut on March 29, 1882. Vancouver Council 1081, chartered on March 4, 1906, was the first Knights of Columbus council established west of Montreal. There are now 40 councils in the Lower Mainland with about 4,000 members.

Founded by Father McGivney to assist the families of men who died suddenly without leaving adequate support, the work of the organizaton has expanded, making it a worthy contribution to the community at large. The work of education and sports in Catholic schools has naturally been one of the the primary objectives of the order but by utilising the principles of charity, unity and fraternity, many other non-sectarian charities have benefited from their work and assistance. Each council is autonomous in the selection of projects it chooses to support. A few examples of such projects include the Special Olympics, Camp Laton and seniors' groups and residences.

Funds are raised through casino nights, fund drives, direct mail and many other activities.

The Knights of Pythias

The Knights of Pythias was established in Washington, D.C. on February 19, 1864, the first American order ever chartered by an act of the Congress of the United States. It now has more than 2,000 subordinate lodges in the U.S. and Canada. Though a fraternal order it is also a family organization. Pythian Sisters for wives, sisters and mothers was founded in 1889. Junior Order and Sunshine Girls are auxiliaries for boys and girls, respectively, from 12-18 years of age. There are two Knights of Pythias lodges in the Lower Mainland: Vancouver Lodge No. 3, instituted in 1886, and Royal Lodge No. 6, instituted in New Westminster the following year. Together they have about 40 members.

Pythian knighthood had its conception in the exemplification of the test of true friendship between Damon and Pythias. Its principles are friendship, charity and benevolence. The main goal is to help people suffering from cerebral palsy. In the Lower Mainland they have been directly involved with this charity and its various units and organizations since 1955. The Victoria Lodge was involved with the setting up of the G.F. Strong unit and the Royal Lodge with the Fraser Valley unit. Over the past two or three years more than $50,000 has been raised throughout B.C. to combat cerebral palsy.

Monies are raised almost exclusively through their own lodges and temples.

The Independent Order of Odd Fellows and Rebekahs

The North American Independent Order of Odd Fellows was founded in Baltimore, Maryland, in 1819. In British Columbia the Odd Fellows Association was formed in 1858 in Victoria during the Fraser River Gold Rush. The first actual lodge was instituted in Victoria on March 10, 1864. The first Rebekah Lodge was instituted in Victoria on December 16, 1887. The first Odd Fellows lodge on the Lower Mainland (No. 3.) was established on March 17, 1871. Vancouver's Lodge No. 8 was instituted in 1887. In 1875 there were 387 members. Today there are approximately 3,500 members in B.C. There are 27 branches in the Lower Mainland with about 1,750 members.

The origin of the name Odd Fellows goes back to 18th-century England when it was considered "odd" to find a group of men organized for the purpose of giving aid to those in need and dedicated to pursuing projects for the benefit of all humankind. The principles of Odd Fellowship are friendship, love, truth, faith, hope, charity and universal justice. Odd Fellowship is a world-wide fraternity which encompasses the whole family. The men meet at Odd Fellows lodges. The women's lodge is known as the Rebekahs. They hold their own meetings but work with the Odd Fellows in all their projects. The Boys Junior Lodge and Girls Theta Rho Club are for children between the ages of 8 and 21 years.

The order is neither sectarian nor political in character but all members are required to believe in a Supreme Being. It seeks to improve and elevate the character of humankind and to direct members' energies into channels of unselfish service. Members are encouraged to care for the physically and mentally disabled and do charitable work on various community projects. Each lodge is autonomous and chooses its own projects but they also support the order's joint projects.

Joint international projects include: the Educational Foundation; the Odd Fellows World Eye Bank; the Visual Research Foundation; the Rose Bowl Float Parade; the United Nations Pilgrimage for Youth; fighting world hunger; and disaster assistance, to name but a few. Special B.C. projects have included: a boarding residence at Newton; low-cost housing; home board assistance for the needy; college and university bursaries; eye equipment for Vancouver General Hospital; and wheelchair buses, as well as community projects throughout the province.

Fundraising activities include donations from members, bazaars and garage sales among other things.

The Rotary Club of Vancouver

The Rotary Club of Vancouver, chartered on April 23, 1913, with 94 founding members, was the first Rotary club in Vancouver and only the third in Canada. There are now 51 clubs in the Lower Mainland with a total membership of 2,450. Each club is independent and devoted to providing service in its community, in the spirit of the "service above self" motto. The Rotary club concept was started in 1905 by five men in Chicago to provide a friendly, non-sectarian forum where business and professional men could share their experiences and render badly needed community services. Since they rotated their meetings from one office to another they called themselves Rotarians. Today the Rotary Club of Vancouver is proud to bear the number 61 in the current world register of 27,173 rotary clubs in 151 countries.

It can be equally proud of its achievements, a list of which reads like a social history of the city. It began work with a fund for needy children. Forty-four members of the club served in World War I while others on the home front did all they could to support the war effort. In Septem-

ber, 1919, the new Rotary Clinic for Chest Diseases was officially opened to provide free medical care for children. This was an outpatient clinic for the treatment and prevention of tuberculosis, the dreaded "white death" so prevalent early in the century. A year later it was turned over to the city and the first fresh-air camp was established at Point Grey.

The aftermath of war brought the need for rehabilitation. New social programs emerged. The rehabilitation workshop of Vancouver General Hospital, Children's Hospital, Children's Aid Society, the Boy Scouts, the Community Chest, the Hastings Athletic Community Centre and Cancer Clinic—all received financial and moral support. In 1931 the Rotary Club joined with IODE to begin the Vancouver Preventorium for kids exposed to tuberculosis, the forerunner of Sunny Hill Hospital. The tuberculosis work continued until the late thirties, providing fresh-air camps for children, and family social services.

Service continued during World War II. Postwar work included launching a youth counselling service in cooperation with the YMCA. The Vancouver Epilepsy Centre, the Elizabeth Fry Society, the Missions to Seamen and other agencies too numerous to mention—all benefited from the Rotarian's assistance.

The flagship of Rotarians, the International Centre at UBC, was opened by Eleanor Roosevelt. People with low vision were helped at the Low Vision Clinic at the Vancouver General Eye Centre. More recently the club provided quarters to house the nuclear magnetic resonance scanner at UBC Hospital.

Funds to provide services are derived from many sources, the best known being the ice shows, sponsored by the Vancouver club, which began in 1924. Now in its 71st year, the much loved annual IceCapades has assisted countless agencies in the city. Each club has its own fundraising activities such as the popular "Duck Race" on the Capilano River, other lotteries, raffles and events. In March, 1950, the Oscar Olson Foundation was established to provide continuous funds for "charitable organizations and community enterprises." In 1969 the Rotary Foundation was established. All these fundraising methods enable the Rotarians to continue with their enviable record of community service.

The R.W.A. Inner Circle Society

In 1921 the women's auxiliary to the Rotary Clinic for Chest Diseases was formally established. For two years prior it had been an informal association of wives of Vancouver Rotary Club members who met weekly at the newly opened Rotary Clinic to make hospital garments and clothing for patients. There are now about 80 members.

In 1932 the name was changed to the Rotary Women's Auxiliary but it remained a separate entity, financially independent of the Rotary Club. In 1983 the R.W.A. incorporated under the societies act and officially changed its name to R.W.A. Inner Circle Society but the more familiar title, R.W.A., is still used.

During its 75 years of service, both the endeavors and fundraising have changed. Social aid was the main project during the Great Depression; World War II brought new challenges—members added a Red Cross unit to their other commitments, which they were officially recognised for after the war. Their service activities, post-war until the present day, include involvement in business, bursaries, summer "camperships" for less fortunate children, a crisis centre for battered wives, Literacy B.C. and the Vancouver Health Department. Funds previously raised by garden teas, bridge parties and golf tournaments are now raised through a casino, a fall fashion show, a February daffodil auction and by selling IceCapades programs.

Soroptomist International

Soroptomist International was established in 1921 in Oakland, California, and now has 100,000 members in 100 countries. The oldest of British Columbia's 16 clubs is Soroptomist International of Vancouver, established in 1926. There are nine clubs in the Lower Mainland with about 200 members.

Soroptomist was formed to foster the ideals of service and to improve the quality of life for all people. Its name was taken from the Latin *soror* (sister) and *optima* (best), and is loosely interpreted as "the best for women." This is an apolitical, non-sectarian international club for business and professional women who wish to give something back to their communities. Each club chooses projects it wishes to undertake in the local community or further afield. Projects include school-based mentor programs for "at risk" teens, literacy programs, housing for seniors, advocacy for the reduction of violence in the media, safe Halloween events, scholarships and grants to young people and women re-entering the work force, and the publication of an emergency services directory for "street kids." They also support the guide-dog program for the blind, homeless and battered women's shelters and various types of hospital projects. Clubs also support Western Canadian regional projects and joint international endeavors such as literacy programs and the establishing of eye clinics in developing countries.

Fundraising is as diverse as the clubs. They include operating ticket gates at fairs or events, a Mardi Gras, a speaker series, fashion shows, theatre evenings, seawall walks, murder mystery and

other fundraising dinners, casinos, raffles and the sale of entertainment books.

The Variety Club of British Columbia

Established in 1965 the Variety Club of British Columbia (Tent 47) is a member of Variety Clubs International, a global charity comprised of 54 chapters in 12 countries. Tent 47 has more than 400 members, both men and women, of all age groups and from all walks of life. The sole purpose of the Variety Club is to raise funds to provide equipment and services for B.C.'s children with special needs. Since its inception it has raised in excess of $66 million.

Funds raised are channelled into many worthy projects. The Variety Club primarily funds the projects of other charities, hospitals, development centres and the many other child-related organizations. One of the special projects is Canuck Place hospice for children suffering from progressive life-threatening illnesses. Other projects include the creation of child development centres; providing prosthetic limbs to children with limb deficiencies and talking computers for children who are unable to talk; and the creation of parks accessible to children with special needs (such as the water park at Lumberman's Arch and the Kids' Farmyard in Stanley Park).

Recently the Variety Club has placed its support behind the Children's Foundation, which provides a wide range of services to emotionally and physically abused children. Many fun outings and recreational events for children are sponsored throughout the year. More than 355 "sunshine coaches" have been purchased which provide "special children" safe and comfortable transportation to and from places of therapy, learning and recreation throughout B.C.

More than 600 groups around B.C. help raise funds by many different methods including bingos, paper recycling, special luncheons, golf tournaments, Cash for Kids, the Variety Club Auction and Gold Heart Day. In addition money is raised through the generosity of the many individual and corporate donors. Possibly the best known fundraiser is the Variety Club Telethon in partnership with BCTV. This televised marathon is not only the most successful annual fundraising event but is also a form of recognition for the 5,000-6,000 hard-working volunteers of the Variety Club and its thousands of sponsors.

The Zonta Club of Vancouver

Zonta was founded in Buffalo, New York, on November 8, 1919. The Zonta Club of Greater Vancouver is part of Zonta International. It is the only club in the Lower Mainland and boasts about 30 members. There are approximately 36,000 members in more than 1,100 clubs, located in 21 districts, in 61 countries. Districts are sub-divided into areas. Zonta of Vancouver is in district eight, area two.

Zonta International is the worldwide service organization of professional women working to improve the legal, political, economic and professional status of women. Zonta takes its name from the Sioux Indian word meaning "honest and trustworthy." The goals of Zontians are "world peace through understanding" and a commitment to personal growth through community and international service. As well as supporting Zonta's international projects, each club selects community projects as determined by local needs. Ninety per cent of the Vancouver club's fundraising goes to assist the women's shelter in Burnaby. Their other projects include supporting Parents in Crisis, adopting a family at Christmas and providing a small political science bursary at UBC. The clubs in district eight have also helped fund the Lester B. Pearson World College Scholarship, enabling one young woman each year to receive a two-year scholarship at the University of Victoria.

Funds are raised through casinos, the sale of entertainment books and a wine-tasting evening.

facing page: Publicizing the Variety Club telethon, Oak Street, 1987. vs
above: Sunshine Coach, 1990. vs

Media

↟Hemlock

Hemlock Printers Ltd. has been serving Greater Vancouver since 1968. Since then, the company has grown from four employees and $68,000 in sales to become the largest sheetfed printer in B.C. with rapidly growing export sales to the western United States. The Burnaby company and its Vancouver affiliate, Hemlock Express, offer a full range of separation, electronic prepress, press and bindery services. The Hemlock group specializes in advertising literature, corporate communications, publications and fine art reproduction.

Drinking too much, spending recklessly when he was in funds, always in debt, he was willing to use his pen for any purpose, even for writing trade puffs.

> —Hamilton Frye, of some journalist, almost any of his time in Sixty Years of Fleet Street, 1949.

DON'T ASK ME about newspapers, I might tell you. Take drink. Approximately 96 per cent of all newspaper legends rest on excessive drink. The *Vancouver Sun*'s Denny Boyd once drank. So did the *Province*'s patriarch, Jim Coleman. (He tells the story of the guy who habitually ate lunch perched on the toilet. "Why don't you just throw your lunch into the can," Coleman advised, "and save the expensive middleman?")

Photographers drank too. A few years ago, renovations at a certain paper revealed a fantastic treasureless trove—around 500 jugs—of empty bottles adjacent to the paper's darkroom. The dead and departed were official suspects. The living virtuously denied blame.

Radio people also drank. And harbored equally flagrant characters. One sat on a flagpole and later poisoned his wife. Job security in radio was of legendary precariousness. It is a hallowed and not extinct tradition that a radio staffer returning from holidays could reasonably expect to find himself workless.

Stars? In 1962 the *Sun*'s Jack Scott allegedly was paid $24,000 a year—pointedly, $1,000 less than boss Erwin Swangard, who also enjoyed a Cadillac provided by classically eccentric publisher Don Cromie—at a time when the guild wage was $128 a week. Up, coming and eventually surpassing Scott was Jack Wasserman (who once said of a rival whose name appears here "his every instinct is bad") at a reputed $17,000. Chuckle-inducing Barry Mather: $19,000. Awed whispers accompanied Jack Webster's reaching a hundred big ones on radio.

Names make news, they say. So many names, past and present, so much ability, which is bigger than talent—a kind of daily genius. Pierre Berton (who once boasted he'd write a story that would be the *Sun* line story every day for a week, and did). Art Jones, father of BCTV. Simma Holt. Rafe Mair. Alex MacGillivray. Lloyd Dykk. Pat Wallace. Stuart Keate. The beloved Harold Gray. Bruce Hutchison (still missed). Clancy Loranger. Ann Barling. The Bill Goods, senior and junior. Pete McMartin. Daphne Bramham. Hal Straight (who invented tough). Mike McRanor. Dave Abbott. Nicole Parton. Brian Kieran.

Moira Farrow (total integrity, fantastic output, a reporter's reporter—same with George Garrett). The Griffiths, especially Frank Sr. Archie McDonald. Len Lauk. Vaughn Palmer. Kay Alsop. Monty McFarlane. The sporting Jims, Taylor and Kearney. Bill Rea. Cliff MacKay. Thelma Hartin. Rob Hunter. Paul Grescoe. Pat Markley. Bob Bouchette. Dorwin Baird. Linda Hossie. Brian Kent. Kevin Evans. Olivia Ward. Tom Ardies. Doris Milligan (first woman city editor in these parts). Cartoonists Len Norris, Roy Peterson, Kerry Waghorn, and Dan Murphy. Frank Rutter. Cecilia Walters. Ted Byfield. Warren Barker. Maria Moreau. Ross and Hilda Mortimer. Vicki Gabereau. Earl Smith. Two tely Bobs, Quintrell and Fortune. CKNW twins Philip Till and Jon McComb. Items mongers Malcolm Parry and Joy Metcalfe (how do they do it?). Barry Broadfoot (who boasted, tried, and did). Doug Collins (what if, by and large, he's right?). And, without sycophancy, straight from the heart (I've cashed the cheque), he who begat the *Vancouver Book* and this successor in your hands, Chuck Davis.

And that's not even mentioning the craft and technical staff, who produce some of the wildest characters and quirkiest humor of all, as well as expertise. Thousands equally great have been left out. You know who you are.

> —*Trevor Lautens*

facing page: The World Building, 1911. Later known as the Sun Tower, it was the tallest building in the British Empire when completed in 1912. cva *above: First press run in the Sun Tower, 1938 (home of the Vancouver Sun 1937–65).* vs

Newspapers In Greater Vancouver
Douglas Sagi

THE MOODYVILLE TICKLER no longer exists and that is a pity because it was a wonderful name for a newspaper. It is remembered as the first newspaper on Burrard Inlet (before there was a Vancouver), appearing in 1878. Like many of British Columbia's early newspapers, it did not last long. A list of the dead is much longer than a list of survivors, though some of the survivors outlived many younger and feistier publications. The first newspaper in the province was the *Victoria Gazette,* founded in 1858, a few months before the *British Colonist,* ancestor of the present *Victoria Times-Colonist,* now the oldest daily newspaper in the province.

The *Province* newspaper was born as a weekly in Victoria but moved to Vancouver as a daily, beginning publishing March 26, 1898. The *Vancouver Sun* published its first edition the morning of February 12, 1912.

For years the *Province, Sun* and the old *News-Advertiser* (among others) faltered in competition with the powerful *Vancouver World,* founded as an evening paper in 1888 by J.C. McLagan. It was sold to the adventurous Louis Denison Taylor in 1905.

Taylor used the newspaper to attack Vancouver city council with enough vigor to get elected mayor in 1909 and 1910. He repeated as mayor in 1925-28 and 1931-32, long after he had seen his newspaper become one of the richest in the country and then fall into bankruptcy.

The *World* was the first newspaper in Canada to have a direct news telegraph to its building. At one time Taylor claimed the *World* carried more display advertising than any other newspaper in North America. He made a huge amount of money and built a huge monument to the newspaper and himself—the World Tower, now known as the Sun Tower on Beatty Street. When it opened in 1912 it was the tallest building in the British Empire, but it was far from the city centre and Taylor could not get adequate tenants other than his newspaper. The *World* went bankrupt but survived under different owners until finally being sold to the *Sun,* which closed it. (The World Tower had a short life as the Bekins Tower, named for the Seattle moving company, before the *Sun* bought it in 1937. The *Sun* published from the building until it moved to its present quarters in 1965.)

The *Sun* began life as a Liberal Party organ but later asserted its independence under the Cromie family. Robert Cromie acquired it during World War I. He also bought the *News-Advertiser* in 1917 and the *World* in 1924. The *Province* prospered to become the city's leading daily in the 1920s.

It was a lively time. In 1924 the *Evening Star* was created by Charles Campbell who had been a former *Sun* shareholder. The *Star* survived until 1932. A group of *Star* staffers formed a cooperative to publish the *News-Herald* in 1933. It managed a circulation of 10,000 in the face of the *Province's* 90,000-plus and the *Sun's* nearly 70,000.

The *News-Herald* was small and the staff not well paid, but the newspaper was lively. It insisted on supplying fresh "new" news every morning without rewriting anything that had appeared in the previous evening papers. Stories were short and politics rarely covered. The formula worked for a time and circulation grew to more than 40,000, though profits were sparse. The little paper was killed in 1957 by its last owner, the late Roy Thomson, who built the Thomson newspaper group but disliked direct competition.

Through the 1930s and 1940s the *Sun* and *Province* waged war. The *Sun* tried to be brighter and livelier with bigger pictures and snappier stories. The more conservative and grey *Province* retained its circulation bulge until being set back by a 41-month strike by its printing trade unions that ended November 4, 1949. The *Province* had continued to publish in the face of a labor movement boycott against a "scab" newspaper, but had fallen behind the unfettered *Sun.* The *Province* never regained superiority and the *Sun* flourished as Western Canada's largest daily throughout the 1950s and 1960s.

The *Sun* was a bold, brassy publication with a range of columnists that covered many viewpoints. Alan Fotheringham became the country's leading national affairs columnist. Jack Wasserman covered the city's nightlife. Bob Hunter, a radical defender of the environment in the 1960s, shared column space with Paul St. Pierre, the television dramatist and novelist who was elected a Liberal MP. The column stable included several women who covered more than mere "women's news." Simma Holt, a hard-working reporter, made a national reputation with articles on the Sons of Freedom Doukhobors; she also became a Liberal MP. Patricia Carney covered economics and wrote a business column before becoming a Conservative MP and cabinet minster, and later a senator.

The *Province* fought back by trying to become the city's newspaper of record, covering the provincial legislature with more detail and longer stories than the *Sun* preferred. Its strong legislative reporter, Paddy Sherman, rose to become editor, then publisher and eventually a senior Southam executive. Its columnists included the humorist and playwright Eric Nicol, the wry Himie Koshevoy and Lorne Parton. In the 1980s sev-

MacMillan Bloedel Limited

On April 12, 1912 hundreds of workers and their families watched horse-drawn wagons emerge from the Powell River Company, a parent company of MacMillan Bloedel (MB), carrying the first rolls of newsprint produced in British Columbia. Operating at speeds of 650 feet per minute, newsprint machines Numbers 1 and 2 were the fastest in the world and had a combined production capacity of 115 tons daily.

Vancouver Daily Province, 1931. vp

eral of the *Sun's* top writers—sports columinist Jim Taylor, legislative affairs reporter Brian Kieran and television critic Lee Bacchus—were lured away to the *Province.*

The *Province* also emulated the Toronto *Globe and Mail* with a powerful business section guided by the late Robert McMurray, who rose to become the newspaper's editor.

In 1994 Val Warren established the *Vancouver Times.* He attracted many bright, young journalists eager to compete with the *Sun* and *Province* but was unable to attract enough advertising. The *Times* died in infancy without marking a first birthday.

In New Westminster one of the province's oldest dailies, the *Columbia,* published without venturing to compete in Vancouver. It had been established in 1861 when New Westminster was a more important community than Vancouver. Then called the *British Columbian* it might have become the most important newspaper in the province but contented itself with suburban coverage. It struggled with growing costs including union pay-scales that closely matched rates paid in Vancouver. It declared bankruptcy in 1983 and published its last edition on November 15 of that year.

The two Vancouver dailies are no longer highly competitive rivals. In 1964 they established Pacific Press to print both newspapers from a single shared plant at 2250 Granville Street. The *Sun* was given exclusive jurisdiction as the evening newspaper and the *Province* became a morning daily when the old *News-Herald* was killed. There were two separate owners, Southam for the *Province* and, successively, Sun Publishing, FP Publications and, briefly, Thomson Newspapers for the *Sun.* The owners promised tough editorial competition. But advertising sales people, circulation staff and library staff worked for both newspapers. Reporters remained competitive (and continue to compete) although Southam bought outright ownership of the *Sun* on August 27, 1980. The *Sun* remained the most profitable of the two as long as Vancouverites, like other Canadians, preferred their newspapers for evening reading. As more and more readers turned to television, however, the *Sun* began suffering. Circulation began to decline despite the city's population increase. The *Province* made some gains after becoming a tabloid on August 2, 1983. The *Sun* became a morning daily on September 16, 1991.

Labor relations in Vancouver's newspaper industry were often troubled. In 1970 and 1978–79 both dailies were closed by strikes and lockouts for several months and the newspaper unions published a tabloid, the *Vancouver Express.* Though not a daily, the *Express* made money on both occasions, allowing the union to provide pay cheques. The strikes and strike-lockouts ended with Pacific Press employees winning contracts that put them among the best-paid newspaper workers on the continent. In the 1980s and 1990s the company said it was losing money because of its high labor costs.

The company denied rumors it would close or sell one of the newspapers but it reduced its labor costs by offering early retirements and contracting out its delivery service. The company says it intends to continue publishing both newspapers and has recently ordered new presses, but the days of swaggering newspapering in Vancouver are long past.

In 1997 Pacific Press moved to new quarters in the Granville Square building in Downtown Vancouver.

One of the first shipments went to the Vancouver Daily Province, which previously had been obliged to order newsprint from the United States. Today MB continues to not only supply many of Vancouver's newspapers, but many publications around the world. In 1995 MacMillan Bloedel became the first company in Western Canada to produce a lightweight coated paper for news magazines and catalogues.

History of Magazines
Sandra McKenzie

OF THE 183 million magazines that find their way into Canadian homes each year the vast majority are wholly domestic. *Maclean's, Chatelaine* and *Canadian Living,* for example, outsell any of their U.S. competitors by as much as two to one. We support about 1,400 home-grown titles of which more than 160 are produced, published and printed in the Lower Mainland.

The demographically elect who share postal codes that indicate a preferred level of affluence, or who subscribe to the right newspapers, receive such glossy titles as *Western Living, Vancouver Magazine, Homemaker* and *Saturday Night* free of charge.

Other, usually tabloid-style, magazines such as the *Georgia Straight, Common Ground, CityFood* and *Xtra West* are available free. A modem and access to the Internet gets you to the Swiftsure Cafe—the Web site of the BC Association of Magazine Publishers (located at http://www.swifty.com/becamp or http://www.bcamp.bc.ca/bcamp) where you can browse through a growing list of cyberzines.

Only about six per cent of our periodicals reach us through the newsstands. The rest arrive through controlled circulation (free, either through the mail, as a supplement to a newspaper, or as part of a package deal with another magazine), through subscription or through membership in a professional or fraternal association.

There is a local periodical for virtually every interest, political persuasion, lifestyle, vocation and avocation. These range from the iconoclastic *Adbusters Quarterly*—founded in 1989, with a mission to raise consumer alarms about the advertising industry, it is supported by 25,000 skeptical readers across North America—to the iconic bibles of West Coast style, *Western Living* and *Vancouver Magazine* (circulations 235,000 and 70,000 respectively.) Librarians and educators can hunker down with *Emergency Librarian;* film industry insiders and wannabes can scope out local productions through the pages of *Reel West;* the rest of us can explore our inner lives with *Common Ground.*

Defining a magazine was once simple but the distinctions have grown blurry over the years. The *Georgia Straight,* for example, began life in 1967 as a weekly newspaper but in 1986 morphed into a magazine that just looks like a newspaper. Though both *CityFood* and *Business in Vancouver* are printed on newsprint, *CityFood* counts itself a magazine while *Business in Vancouver* doesn't. And what about the recent proliferation of electronic publishing efforts?

"There are lots of different ways of defining a magazine," says Western Magazine Awards' coordinator Tina Baird, "but for the purposes of the awards we consider a magazine to be any periodical that has at least 60 per cent editorial content; the content is fundamentally reflective, rather than news-driven; and it has a contents page." Where there is a fine line—for instance, the Saturday Review section of the *Vancouver Sun*—the periodical may compete for either community newspaper awards or for Western Magazine Awards, at the discretion of the publisher. To date the awards committee has not defined a policy to encompass electronic efforts.

The distinctions were clearer in July, 1907, when William Blakemore and Percy Godenrath published the debut issue of *Western Ho! The British Columbia Magazine of Art, Literature, Criticism and Publicity* from their offices at 536 Hastings Street. The single-issue price of Vancouver's first magazine was ten cents; a yearly subscription was one dollar. That first issue stated the editorial policy thus: *"Western Ho!* will stand first, last, and all the time for an imperial policy, for the Motherland, for the flag and for the King."

Harbour and Shipping Journal (circulation 2,000) is the oldest continuing magazine in British Columbia. Owner/publisher Murray McLellan speculates it may be the oldest trade journal on the West Coast. Established in October, 1918, by McLellan's grandfather, the magazine covers the waterfront, with articles of interest to the deep-sea and coastal marine industries.

Our longest-running general-interest periodical is Arch-Way Publishers' *Playboard.* Started by Vienna-born theatre enthusiast Harold Schiel in 1966, *Playboard* began life as a program guide for the Vancouver Little Theatre. Over the years this little labor of love has become part of the theatre- and opera-going experience for Vancouverites, with its mix of movie industry news, theatrical trivia and guides to current productions. It has also been remarkably stable, with only three editors—James Barber, Mick Maloney and, currently, Chuck Davis—in its 30-year history.

More flamboyant has been the evolution of *Vancouver Magazine.* Its genesis goes back to 1967 and *Dick MacLean's Greater Vancouver Greeter Guide,* a digest-sized listing of clubs, restaurants, theatres and cinemas. The cumbersome title was eventually trimmed to *Vancouver Leisure Magazine.* By April, 1974, the magazine was on the verge of collapse. MacLean was fired by owner Agency Press and new editor Malcolm (Mac) Parry hired. The first issue under his guidance featured five

 Canada Wide Magazines & Communications Ltd. is the largest independent publishing company in Western Canada. Headquartered in Burnaby, with offices in Winnipeg and Toronto, Canada Wide publishes 13 titles (15 million magazines a year)—a mix of consumer, business, trade and contract publications that includes TV WEEK, BC Business, GROCER Today, Westworld BC, Westworld Alberta, Westworld Saskatchewan, Going Places, Leisureways, BC Pharmacy, Award, Pacific Golf, Cash for Kids and Super Camping Guide.

bylines—all of them Parry, in various disguises, including golfer/author Driver T. Niblick. By the second issue journalist Sean Rossiter joined Parry and, for the next two years, they produced most of the magazine's articles.

With Parry's arrival the magazine gained new vibrancy and insouciance though not, alas, new revenues. Disenchanted with publishing, Agency Press decided to focus attention instead on printing and declared the magazine defunct after just a few issues with Parry at the helm. They announced their decision on a Friday afternoon. Rossiter alerted journalists Paul and Audrey Grescoe and artists Iain and Ingrid Baxter of the magazine's imminent demise. They in turn approached lawyer Ron Stern and all mobilized their resources to purchase the magazine by the following Monday, with Paul Grescoe becoming the editorial director and Stern the publisher.

The late 1970s through the 1980s were, all participants agree, the glory days of magazine publishing in Vancouver. With copious advertising revenue behind it *Vancouver Magazine* gained a reputation as a springboard for new talent and a free-wheeling venue for maverick writers, photographers and artists. "For a decade most of the people who are publishing locally first wrote for *VanMag*," Parry claims. "We tried to use the most talented people we could find, then give them as much liberty as we could." (Gen-X pundit Doug Coupland and *CityFood* publisher Rhonda May were first published under Parry's regime.)

That freedom also extended to fiction—*Vancouver Magazine* published stories by Susan Musgrave, William Gibson, W.P. Kinsella and Jack Hodgkins. Jounalistic ventures included sending Ben Metcalfe to Switzerland to cover the murder trail of Cyril Belshaw. It remains, Parry points out proudly, the only Western-based, western-owned magazine to have ever won a National Magazine Award.

In 1982 Stern and the other investors sold *Vancouver Magazine* to Comac Communications, which had previously acquired *Western Living*. That publication had in turn evolved from *Western Homes and Living*—a gently domestic creation of the post-war boom, though even in its earliest days displaying a decided bias towards cutting-edge design and architecture and a tongue-in-cheek attitude. Both *Vancouver Magazine* and *Western Living* were subsequently sold to industry giant Telemedia in 1987.

In search of a new magazine Stern joined with journalist Harvey Southam to found *Equity Magazine,* a brash, take-no-prisoners business magazine with a gossipy flavor and no clearly discernible political bias. *Equity* roused ire and interest on left and right in equal measures, often with startling, photo-retouched covers, including one that depicted then-premier Mike Harcourt as a Nazi brownshirt. It garnered several Western Magazine Awards along the way, including Magazine of the Year. Stern sold *Equity* to Canada Wide Magazines, publishers of rival *BCBusiness,* in September, 1995. (*Equity* ceased publication in June, 1996.)

In 1987 Southam and Stern introduced *V,* a glossy, sophisticated city magazine distributed through the *Sun. Alas V to* couldn't compete with the better-established *Vancouver Magazine* and, despite being named Western Magazine of the Year in 1989, lasted only two years. A similar fate befell the *Globe & Mail's* urbane glossy effort, *West,* inaugurated in 1990, cited as Western Magazine of the Year in 1991 and pronounced dead in 1992. History repeated for a third time when *Step,* an independent arts magazine produced by neophyte pubishers Ray Dearborn and Philip Aw, was launched in 1991, then lauded as, yes, Western Magazine of the Year in 1992 before succumbing to recessionary forces in 1993.

While Peter Legge—owner of Canada Wide Magazines and publisher of 15 titles—is not a household name, the magazines he publishes are as familiar as your local supermarket check-out or dentist's office. *TV Week* and *BCBusiness* are the flagship publications of a growing empire that includes *Westworld* (in B.C., Alberta and Saskatchewan editions,) *Grocer Today* and *Award.* Cumulative annual circulation for all titles is about 15 million, Legge estimates.

Launched in 1972 by Joe Martin of Agency Press, *BCBusiness* has survived four ownerships, passing to Canada Wide in 1990 after a brief spell under the Jim Pattison umbrella. Almost as remarkable as the title's longevity is editor Bonnie Irving's stewardship—possibly the longest tenure of any general-interest editor in the Lower Mainland and conceivably in Canada. She has edited *BCBusiness* since 1982 when it was, she says, "remarkably dull and boring, with an emphasis on guys in suits standing next to their big corporate widgets." Working under each of its owners she has shepherded the title through two recessions and shifted the editorial stance from an initial emphasis on resource industries to entrepreneurial strategizing to its current role as a trends forecaster. "It's an exciting time to be editing a magazine, to be covering all those changes," she says. "But it's also very frightening. It's easy to lose sight of the fact that magazines actually touch people and change the way they see things."

Canada Wide is the publisher of record for nine Canadian Automobile Association clubs across Western Canada and Ontario. Although magazine publishing remains its core focus, Canada Wide has developed a number of communications-related tangents including production of special promotional magazines and inserts, event co-ordination, comprehensive mailing services, book publishing and organization of motivational/business seminars. The company also operates a highly successful in-house graphic design firm called The Art Department.

History of Radio
Chuck Davis

IN 1926 HENDERSON'S DIRECTORY listed six radio stations in Vancouver where there had been none listed the year before. Yet we know that CFQC (today's CFUN) went on the air in 1922, making it the oldest radio station in Western Canada. On December 5, 1923, radio was used for the first time in a Vancouver mayoralty election campaign: candidate W.R. Owen gave a ten-minute speech over station CJCE. In 1924 CFXC, founded by radio-shop owner Fred Hume, began broadcasting out of a tiny room in the back of his shop in New Westminster.

The six stations that made it into that 1926 directory were: CNRV, the Canadian National Railway Company's station operated from studios in the CNR station on Main Street (the CNR ran a radio service for its train passengers); CFYC, operated by a company called Commercial Radio; CFDC, owned by the Sparks Company; the aforementioned CFQC, a station operating out of the 16th floor at 500 Beatty, home of the Sprott Shaw Radio Company, a company that had already been in business for years teaching the technical aspects of radio (and would in 1928 change the name of CFQC to CKMO); a "United Churches" station called CKFC; and CKDC, owned by the *Province* newspaper (which began a second station, CHLS, in 1930). By 1927 CFXC changed its call letters to CJOR, destined to become the city's major station for many years. In 1933 it moved to 846 Howe and operated for years there out of the Devonshire Hotel's basement. The station became a real force in local radio in the 1930s with broadcasters like Ross and Hilda Mortimer, Dorwin Baird, the Bill Browns, Sr. and Jr. and Vic Waters. Waters would eventually become program director at 'OR, and hire future broadcasting stars like Red Robinson, Jack Webster and Brian "Frosty" Forst.

Arthur "Sparks" Holstead was granted a licence to operate a 10-watt radio station, CFDC, in Nanaimo on April 1, 1923. In 1925 he brought the station's transmitter to Vancouver in a suitcase and went on the air, but the federal government's broadcasting regulatory agency objected and ordered him off. Public petitions demanded the station's return and it signed back on. In 1928 Holstead changed its name to CKWX. Of all the call letters cited so far, that latter set is the only one that exists today. (Just before this book went to press 'WX changed to an all-news format, proving for the thousandth time that nothing is so permanent in the world of radio as change.) In 1934 a sta-

tion appeared called CRVC, on Station Street off Main. It had been CNRV, the CNR station, but now it was run by a new entity called the Canadian Radio Commission, which in 1936 would change yet again to the CBC, the Canadian Broadcasting Corporation.

What were people listening to in the earliest days? Well, many of the stations were tiny and often on the air for just a few hours a day. Shows were simple with such fare as poetry readings, recitations, amateur musicians, educational programs and preachers. On Fred Hume's CFXC, for example, the station's entire schedule consisted of a brief daily broadcast of Hume's singing sister and her pianist.

Not surprisingly most local listeners preferred American network radio, on which more polished drama, comedy and music could be heard. The Canadian Encyclopedia quotes a survey taken at the end of the 1920s showing that 80 per cent of radio programs listened to by Canadians originated in the U.S.

That began to change with the creation of a national radio network started, curiously, by the Canadian National Railway CNRV, the CNR's Vancouver station, produced Canada's first regular drama series on radio, beginning in 1927. Produced by Jack Gillmore, the CNRV Players lasted until 1932, heard across the country on the railway's network. Among their offerings were occasional plays by British Columbia writers. By 1936 the CN Radio network had transmogrified into the CBC, whose local call letters were CBR; it would soon have studios in the CNR Hotel at Georgia and Hornby, a building we know today as the Hotel Vancouver. A lot of the drama for which the public radio network became famous originated from the CBC's Hotel Vancouver studios. Radio drama still exists on CBC (local call letters are CBU today) but television and reduced budgets have dealt heavy blows to its scope and regularity.

A closed-circuit station, CITR, begun in 1950 at the University of British Columbia, was started by students who had been broadcasting on other stations since 1937. Alumni include Dorwin Baird, Pierre Berton, Ray Perrault and Lister Sinclair.

In the 1940s, thanks partly to a listening public hungry for news of Canadian troops, homegrown stations grew in popularity. Still, my own recollection of Vancouver radio in the 1940s was that, with the exception of Billy Brown's cheerful morning program on CJOR, virtually every show we listened to originated in the U.S.: Jack Benny, Fibber McGee and Molly, Lum and Abner, *Inner Sanctum, The Shadow, The Lone Ranger, The Great Gildersleeve,* and soap operas like *Ma Perkins* and *One Man's Family* . . . many of them relayed by local stations affiliated with American networks. CKWX, for example, became a Mutual affiliate in 1945. The CBC began an FM sta-

AM1320 CHMB is an ethno-cultural radio station broadcasting in 15 languages including Chinese (Cantonese and Mandarin), Japanese, Scottish, Irish, Italian, Indo-Canadian, Filipino, Greek, Tamil, Vietnamese, Jewish, Aboriginal, Portuguese, Iranian (Farsi) and Korean. More than 100 different radio shows are produced locally by AM1320's qualified team of more than 80 personalities.

tion (CBU-FM) in 1947.

By 1944 the newspaper listings for local radio showed that four stations had survived of the six listed in 1926. On Tuesday, August 15, 1944, you could choose from CBR, CJOR, CKWX and CKMO. Local programs included *Moments in Melody; Twiddle, Biddle and Bop;* and *The Royal Canadian Navy Presents.* U.S. network stations that Tuesday were bringing us Ginny Sims, Lum and Abner, George Burns and Gracie Allen, and the crime drama *Big Town.* Most stations featured live orchestras at night.

A new station that had signed on that day, one that was destined to change local radio dramatically, was not listed. As far as the newspapers were concerned the arrival on the scene of CKNW was a non-event. Part of the reason was its location in "far-off" New Westminster. But 'NW's owner Bill Rea, a 35-year-old Edmonton-born dance hall manager, band leader and radio time salesman (he'd quit CKMO to start his own station) had assembled an eager little group of people to staff his new station. And what did 'NW listeners hear? Cowboy music.

And a lot of it. No soap operas or cops-and-robbers dramas interrupted the flow. "I think cowboy songs are a whole lot better," Rea told his staff, "Such songs all tell a story—a clean, wholesome story about the outdoors." His new station had another distinction right from the start: a very strong emphasis on news. He'd guessed correctly that audiences would be eager for news of Canadian troops overseas. From its opening day 'NW broadcast news every hour on the hour. The importance given to news by CKNW has paid dividends to the station every day of its existence. More than 50 years after it signed on, it is still considered the leader in local radio news.

Sometime during 'NW's first day a young sailor stationed at Esquimalt on Vancouver Island was hunched over his ship's radio equipment and picked up the station. "Everyone used to listen to Seattle in those days," he recalled, "but I was roaming the dial and picked up this new station at 1230 kilocycles. I got rid of it instantly! Cowboy music! Yechhh!" The sailor's name was Jack Cullen. In October, 1996, Cullen would celebrate 50 years of broadcasting . . . virtually all of it on CKNW, with his gigantic collection of records and old radio shows and his encyclopedic memory for show biz minutiae, on a remarkable show called *The Owl Prowl.*

Big bands were a radio staple: Dal Richards, still active, led his band for many years in a weekly CBC Radio show broadcast nationally from the Panorama Roof of the Hotel Vancouver. In the early 1950s Monty McFarlane began a hugely popular and funny morning record show on CJOR.

Programming began to fragment, a phenomenon not unique

to Vancouver, as different audiences honed in on their favorite kinds of music or special programming. CKLG, which went on air in 1955 in North Vancouver (the LG stands for Lions Gate), was owned by the Gibson brothers, the logging family. In the summer of 1961 the station was taken over by new owners, who moved it to Vancouver. In 1964 'LG went rock and started an FM station that today is called C-FOX. In 1996 'LG was still rocking but it also carried Vancouver Grizzlies games.

Red Robinson became a meteoric favorite in the fifties, playing music by Elvis Presley, Buddy Holly, Chuck Berry and Motown, and thereby introducing that music to local audiences. After 40 years Red's still getting good numbers in the morning on Richmond's C-ISL and in 1995 he was inducted into the Rock and Roll Hall of Fame in Cleveland, Ohio.

CHQM, which started in 1959, began the trend to "easy listening," and launched CHQM-FM in 1960. The latter was the first privately-owned FM station in Vancouver. In 1960 it went "stereo," also a Vancouver first. Today CHQM has become CHMB, a station owned by, and broadcasting mainly in, Chinese. QM/FM, still with that name and programming "soft favorites," is owned by the same company that runs CFUN.

CKLG and CFUN went for younger listeners with rock while the country music fan had CKNW at first. When 'NW eased out of country its fans went to (now-vanished) CJJC in Langley—if they could pick it up—and later to CKWX. C-FUN, by the way, had been CKMO—the former CFQC—until February of 1955. In 1968 it changed owners and got its fourth name, CKVN, emphasizing news. In October, 1973, CKVN died and CFUN was reborn as a contemporary music station at the same spot on the dial. Today, country music fans tune into CJJR.

On December 1, 1967, French-language radio came to B.C. when the CBC's CBUF-FM signed on.

An early indication of the popularity of talk on local radio was the success of a Glasgow-born ex-newspaperman named Jack Webster. Webster, who'd worked for the *Sun* from 1947 to 1953, was lured away by CJOR in 1953 to do a show called *City Mike.* He was 35. His pugnacious style won him listeners quickly and his hard-hitting daily reports on the Mulligan police scandal made news themselves. (Webster, an expert in shorthand, pulled a pencil from his pocket as he sat in the courtroom and—no recording devices being allowed—scribbled down verbatim testimony.) In 1960 'WX started the kind of open-line broadcasting so popular in Greater Vancouver today. Barrie Clark was an early star. But the talk show as a local ratings phenomenon really had its beginning in 1964 on CJOR with the sudden and volcanic appearance of a man named Pat

AM1320 CHMB is an effective and extensive ethno-cultural radio in Canada. Not only does AM1320 CHMB strive to reach major population groups in their most proficient language, but also to provide programming which helps these groups to expand their interests and to become part of the mainstream life of Canadians. This station talks to the Chinese population about issues that reflect their concerns and events that will shape their future. Additionally AM1320 CHMB is heavily involved in community services and activities.

Burns. Burns wasn't new to radio; he'd been a news broadcaster for years. But when 'OR's Peter Kosick put Burns on air with his *Hotline* program, the change in local radio was convulsive. Within weeks seemingly everyone was listening to, as Webster described him, this "gruff-voiced, well-informed, first-class demagogue." In fact it was Burns' success on 'OR that sparked 'NW's counterattack with Jack Webster and talk radio has been a local radio staple ever since. Astonishingly the Burns phenomenon was over in little more than a year; by the end of 1965 he was released without explanation by CJOR's owners. He later returned to the talk-show format but his ratings never matched the earlier numbers. Webster on the other hand became hugely successful in the format for many years and later took it to television with BCTV. (Pat Burns died while this book was in production.)

Today CKNW's talk-show hosts include Rafe Mair, Bill Good, Gary Bannerman and the remarkable Dave Berner. Mair's show inherits (and adds to) a big audience from Brian "Frosty" Forst's morning show. Morning is radio's prime-time; news, weather, traffic and sports are presented with machine-gun speed, and competition is constant. In 1996 Forst was head of a pack that included CFUN's Dave Welch, CKKS's Fred Latremouille and Cathy Baldazzi, CBU's Hal Wake (who departed in March, 1997), C-ISL's veteran rocker Red Robinson, Stu Jeffries and Stu McAllister on CKLG and Larry and Willy on C-FOX. "The Fox," by the way, had started with an "easy-listening" format in 1964 as CKLG-FM

CKNW's decades-long success enabled them to move in 1995 to glossy new quarters taking up two floors of the Toronto-Dominion Tower in Downtown Vancouver. Part of the station's success comes from its coverage of Vancouver Canucks, Vancouver Grizzlies and B.C. Lions games. Its parentr company has a corporate relationship and part-ownership of GM Place where the Canucks and Grizzlies play their home games.

Vancouver Co-Operative Radio (CFRO-FM), a unique station—non-profit, community-based and run by its members—began broadcasting in 1975, and has an enthusiastic and eclectic audience. I turned on Co-Op Radio while typing this, and the host (named Parth, who was presenting a program of religious music from India) was thanking the host of the preceding Jewish program for covering for him for 15 minutes because he, Parth, had been stuck in a traffic jam! The station's like that: informal, lots of ethnic programming, public affairs, out-of-the-mainstream music.

CJVB, started by Jan Van Bruchem on June 18, 1972, carries on its multi-lingual programming under new owners. Most of its programming is in Cantonese and Mandarin. CHMB (once

CHQM) is now run by Chinese owners and carries many Chinese shows and a variety of programs in other languages. CHMB has a relationship with a Hong Kong broadcasting company and carries some programming from there.

With the advent of television, the increase in car radios and the upsurge in popularity of FM stations (there are now 10 AM and nine FM stations in the Lower Mainland) regular titled programs of drama and the like began to disappear on both public and private radio, and what took over was pretty much what we hear today: a mix of news, recorded music and talk shows. There are a few exceptions: CBU has the widest variety of programming; there are the two Chinese-owned stations; and CJOR, after a six-year stretch as CHRX playing "classic rock," changed call letters in 1994 to become 600 AM The Bridge (CKBD), Canada's first Christian music station.

Radio tends not to keep archives, so much of its interesting local past lives on only in the memories of oldtimers. And, in the absence of a detailed history, the names of radio stars like actor John Drainie, hosts Ross and Hilda Mortimer, musician John Avison, entertainer Barney Potts, "items" broadcaster Earle Bradford and sportscaster Bill Good, Sr. (a member of the CFL and the Canadian Curling Hall of Fame) may be fated to join their earlier counterparts in unrecorded obscurity.

AM

600	CKBD The Bridge
650	C-ISL
690	CBU (CBC)
730	CKLG
980	CKNW
1040	CKST Coast Radio
1130	CKWX
1320	CHMB (Chinese, multi-lingual)
1410	CFUN
1470	CJVB (Chinese, multi-lingual)

FM

92.9	CFMI
93.7	CJJR
95.3	Z
96.9	CKKS ("KISS FM")
97.7	CBUF-FM (French)
99.3	CFOX
102.7	Co-Op Radio
103.5	QM/FM
105.7	CBC Stereo

Additional research by Carrie Gillette, Kelly Bland, Sara Reeves and Nicole Smith.

Television
Lee Bacchus

EXPERIMENTAL TELEVISION COVERAGE of the opening of the 1939 New York World's Fair heralded the first network broadcast in North America, but the Lower Mainland wouldn't join the TV age until almost two decades later. Not surprisingly, and perhaps prophetically, when the first live television program arrived in British Columbia it was an American import.

On November 28, 1948, a ghostly image of a Seattle high school football game materialized on a 10-by-13 centimetre screen at a home in West Vancouver's British Properties. As reported in the Vancouver *Province* the following day, radio-shop proprietor E.A. Mullins had built the primitive set from a kit that cost $238, and about nine viewers gathered to watch the telecast from Seattle TV station KRSC—later to become KING-TV.

Two years later a few hundred rooftop TV aerials had sprouted in the Lower Mainland—mainly in south-facing, reception-friendly areas like the North Shore and the southern slopes of Burnaby, New Westminster and Vancouver. Early tube-technology sets were picking up grainy programming from Seattle where KING was transmitting shows like *Hopalong Cassidy, Arthur Murray's Dance Party* and professional wrestling.

The early black-and-white images may have been murky but viewers' reception was glowing. "This [TV] is one of the finest things that has come out in the way of entertainment," Vancouver resident Hugh Dick Jr. told the *Vancouver Sun* in 1950.

By 1951 that sparse grove of rooftop aerials was on the verge of becoming a forest. A few thousand homes in the Lower Mainland now included a Motorola (with "Sabre Jet Tuning"), an RCA or a Philco TV among their appliances and, according to the *Province,* "Housewives claimed TV paid for itself in money no longer dribbled away on outside entertainment, that it quieted their nerves, kept their families together and their children off the streets."

While the CBC launched its TV service in 1952 with two stations in Toronto and Montreal (Vancouver wouldn't get its station until the fall of 1953) the Lower Mainland received another station, KVOS (dubbed "Your Peace Arch Station"), from just across the border in Bellingham in the spring of 1953. A gutsy entrepreneur named Rogan Jones had snatched channel 12 from a frequency originally earmarked by the Canadian government for Chilliwack. Jones' "shoestring" station launched

its programming with kinescope coverage of the coronation of Queen Elizabeth II. The bulk of KVOS'S intitial news coverage, however, comprised still photographs accompanied by voice-over narration.

By now Greater Vancouverites were growing accustomed to their first TV celebrities. Cowboy heroes like Hopalong Cassidy and Cisco Kid became cult heroes. Film stars like Groucho Marx and Ray Bolger hosted shows. And a growing number of radio personalities like Jack Benny now were being watched as well as heard.

By late 1953 sales of TV sets (cost: about $500) were in the tens of thousands and residents with a $50 aerial or a deftly manipulated pair of "rabbit-ear" antennae could watch three U.S.-based stations: KING (channel 5), KVOS (channel 12) and KOMO (channel 4).

The TV boom combined with Greater Vancouver's mountainous and undulating topography posed a growing problem: the need for clear and consistent reception. Pioneers Stan and John Thomas strung the first community cable lines in Horseshoe Bay in 1954. At about the same time a Vancouver plumbing store owner named Syd Welsh, along with Bud Shepard and Garth Pither, founded Premier Cablevision which would later evolve through subsequent buyouts and mergers into Vancouver Cablevision and later Rogers Cable.

By December of that year Lower Mainlanders could also tune to their first Canadian programming. On December 16, 1953, CBC Vancouver affiliate CBUT (channel 2) was launched when CBC chair Davidson Dunton pushed a button at the station, a converted auto garage on West Georgia.

With words that others would echo with the same urgency 40 years later, Dunton said, "It is extremely important for Canada to have a strong system—it could make or break the national sense in the next generation." The station's inaugural broadcast was listed as *The BBC Show* which featured Vancouverites in Britain.

"In the early years everybody was flying by the seat of their pants," recalls Les Jackson, a former CBUT newsman. He says fast-breaking news in pre-video days was often delivered in film-negative form—and the polarity reversed on air. And portable sound? Jackson said technicians would hook a tape recorder or camera up to a car battery. "We were pioneers."

Finally Lower Mainlanders had their own TV station that was transmitting a modest schedule (five-and-a-half hours a day) to compete with American shows like *Howdy Doody, Ding-Dong School, Ozzie and Harriet* and *Dave Garroway.*

A year later CBUT helped CBC serve as host broadcaster for the 1954 Commonwealth Games and TV viewers around the world saw Roger Bannister and John Landy compete in the dramatic "Miracle Mile." In 1955 the station presented its first televised drama, a one-act tragedy by Pirandello called *The Vise.* It starred Derek Ralston, Peter Mannering, Valerie Cooter and Rae Brown, who would later go on to star along with Bruno Gerussi in the long-running CBC series *The Beachcombers.*

Among other series produced at CBUT were: *Leo and Me* (which starred Brent Carver and a young newcomer named Michael J. Fox), a local current-affairs show called *Hourglass, Lies from Lotus Land, Red Serge Wives, Northwood* and *Odyssey.* But by the late 1980s budget cuts squeezed most local productions and in-house drama became an endangered species.

In 1955 KCTS—an educational commercial-free station based in Seattle—began transmitting 20 hours of programming a week on channel 9. Eleven years later KCTS would join 75 other stations, forming National Educational Television, later re-named the Public Broadcasting Service (PBS)—home to *Sesame Street* and *Masterpiece Theatre.*

Vancouver didn't get its first private station until October, 1960, when a 34-year-old former newspaper photographer named Art Jones launched CHAN-TV (channel 8)—now better known as BCTV. Viewers could also watch *All-Star Wrestling* with Fred Asher and Brad Keene, *Ted Peck's Tides and Trails, Buddy Clyde's Dance Party,* a children's show with the avuncular Ron Morrier and a prime-time schedule weighted down with such U.S. series as *The Rifleman* and *77 Sunset Strip.* Originally housed Downtown at the corner of Richards and Davie, CHAN moved in May of 1961 to a sprawling complex in Burnaby's Lake City, where a strong news presence turned station personalities such as news anchors Tony Parsons and Pamela Martin, sports broadcasters Bernie Pascall, John McKeachie and Barry Houlihan, as well as weatherperson Norm Grohmann, into household names.

In 1969 Vancouver Cablevision (later Rogers Cable) initiated the Lower Mainland's first community cable channel. Radio man Vic Waters, along with partners Dave Liddell and Gerry Rose, operated the service on a shoestring budget—and the attitude was frighteningly casual. Martin Truax, who joined in 1970, recalls Waters getting calls from viewers who said they missed a show: "Vic would say, 'No problem. I'll just run it again for you right now!'"

In September 1976 a former CBC producer-director named Daryl Duke and his partner, a writer-producer named Norman Klenman, created CKVU, a small independent station located on West 2nd Avenue in Vancouver. Their flagship program was a five-day-a-week, live talk and entertainment potpourri called *The Vancouver Show,* and CKVU kicked off its broadcast on September 5, 1976, with the two-hour program hosted by Mike Winlaw (a former host of CBUT'S *Hourglass*) and Pia Shandel (a local actor).

"It was pretty hairy back then," says Ed Knight, the station's design director and charter staffer. "I was the eldest even back then. Most of the employees were very young people who had come from other media. We worked around the clock—of course there were no unions back then."

The year 1980 saw the creation of the Knowledge Network, a B.C. government funded educational channel that debuted in January 1981. During that year the Knowledge Network staff increased from one to 30.

Along with the 1980s came satellite technology and with it cable broadcasting entered a new phase, albeit gradually at first. Freed from over-the-air and land-line systems, satellites ushered in a new communications age marked by all-news networks, pay television and specialty channels.

It took a while for the regulatory bodies to agree but in 1983 the Canadian Radio-Television and Communication Commission licensed pay television—Superchannel and First Choice, both of them movie networks, obtained the first two licenses. Specialty cable channels such as MuchMusic, The Sports Network and CNN were added the following year.

Over the next 15 years more services were added and TV guides were growing fatter to accommodate YTV (a youth-oriented network), The Family Channel, a handful of American superstations, Arts and Entertainment, a multicultural channel, a multi-denominational religious station, CBC Newsworld, a home-shopping network and a weather channel.

By 1995 the CRTC had licensed another handful of specialty services that included Bravo!, Showcase, Life Network, Discovery and MovieMax as well as Canada's first pay-per-view channels. Lower Mainland viewers now could choose from among more than 60 listings. Digital technology and direct-to-home satellite services—scheduled to debut in 1996—are expected to push that number into the hundreds.

In February, 1997 it was announced that the CRTC had awarded a licence to CITY-TV, making it the first new TV station in the city in 20 years. CITV-TV aimed to sign on September 1, 1997. Principals included movie director Daryl Duke, impresario David Y.H. Lui and SFU professor Catherine Murray.

facing page: Yeltsin–Clinton summit, Vancouver, 1993. vs

Media Directory

The *Vancouver Sun* and *The Province* are members of the Southam Inc. group of newspapers, which has 32 daily newspapers published across the country. For the first time in Southam's history, the company's president and chief operating officer is based in Vancouver—he is Don Babick, publisher of *The Sun* and *Province*.

Media Directory for Greater Vancouver
Daniel Say

Adv: accepts advertising

PRINT MEDIA

AABC Newsletter • (1981) • Quarterly • Archives Association of B.C. • P.O. Box 78530, University Post Office, Vancouver, B.C. V6T 2E7 • Circ 1,300 • Membership newsletter • Adv

ANZA News • (1961) • Australia - New Zealand Association • Down-Under Publications • 3 W. 8th Ave., Vancouver, B.C. V5Y 1M8 • Circ 1,000 • News of Australia/NZ and happenings of the club.

Acropolis • (1956) • Text in English, Greek • 2122 W. 47th Ave., Vancouver, B.C. V6M 2M7 • Circ 7,000 • Adv • News of the Greek community.

Adbusters Quarterly • (1989) • Quarterly • Adbusters Media Foundation, 1243 W. 7th Ave., Vancouver, B.C. V6H 1B7 • E-mail: adbuster@wimsey.com • Circ 12,000 • Adv • For environmental, anti-commercial and media literacy groups, advertising executives and academics.

Advocate • (1943) • Bi-monthly • Vancouver Bar Association • 4765 Pilot House Rd., West Vancouver, B.C. V7W 1J2 • Circ 9,000 • Adv

AIDS Update • Quarterly • Ministry of Health, Centre for Disease Control • 828 W. 10th Ave., Vancouver, B.C. V5Z 1L8 • Government health publication.

Airports North America • (1993) • Quarterly • Baum International Media • 1625 Ingleton Ave., Burnaby, B.C. V5C 4L8 • Circ 20,000 • Adv

Alive-Canadian Journal of Health and Nutrition • (1975) • 12 times annually • Canadian Health Reform Products Ltd. • 7436 Fraser Park Dr., Burnaby, B.C. V5J 5B9 • Circ 170,000

Allies • Six times a year; free • 3622 Main Street, Vancouver, B.C. V5V 3N5 • "Our unique alliance includes 36 progressive, alternative, self-supporting publishing groups." Free at many drop points around the area, this tabloid includes all their publications under one cover.

Alpine Garden Club of British Columbia Bulletin • (1956) • Five times a year, membership only • Alpine Garden Club of British Columbia • Box 5161, Main Post Office, Vancouver, B.C. V6B 4B2 • Circ 700 • Contains articles on plants, especially alpines, occurrence in wild, club news, plant culture and more.

Alumni UBC Chronicle • (1941) • Quarterly • University of British Columbia, Alumni Association, Cecil Green Park, 6251 Cecil Green Park Rd., Vancouver, B.C. V6T 1Z1 • Circ 95,000 •

facing page: Linotype operator, Vancouver Province, circa 1940. vp

Adv • News of UBC and its graduates.

Amphora • (1967) • Quarterly • Alcuin Society • Box 3216, 8737 212th St., No. 150, Vancouver, B.C. V1M 2C • Circ 275 • Publishes articles on book art, book collecting, typography, private press publishing and related topics.

Angles: Magazine of Vancouver's Queer Voice • (1983) • Monthly • Lavender Publishing Society of British Columbia • 1170 Bute St., Vancouver, B.C. V6E 1Z6 • URL: http://www.anotherplace.com • Circ 18,000 • Adv • Community magazine offering a gay-lesbian perspective on contemporary events, politics, arts and entertainment.

Apartment & Building • (1971) • Six times a year • BKN Publications, Ltd. • 4580 Victoria Dr., Vancouver, B.C. V5N 4N8 • Adv

Aqua Scene • (1956) • Three times a year, membership • Vancouver Aquarium Association • Box 3232, Vancouver, B.C. V6B 3X8 • Circ 18,000 • Scholarly newsletter.

Aquaculture Today • (1988) • Quarterly • 831 Helmcken St., Vancouver, B.C. V6Z 1B1 • Circ 6,721 • Adv

Artichoke • Three times a year • 210 - 901 Jervis Street, Vancouver, B.C. V6E 2B6 • Circ 1,000 • Writings about art, emphasis on Western Canada.

Asian Dragon News • Weekly, free • In Chinese • Asian Dragon News, 537 Powell St., Vancouver, B.C. V6A 1G8 • Show-business personality news, community events. Free at various drop points around the community.

Association for Canadian Theatre Research: Newsletter (1976) • Semi-annual • Association for Canadian Theatre Research, c/o Department of Theatre and Film, University of British Columbia, Vancouver, B.C. V6T 1Z2 • E-mail: andrel@unixg.ubc.ca • Circ 250 • Contains a range of news items of interest to members.

Auto Trader • Weekly • 8 Auto Trader Centre, 1300 Woolridge Street, Coquitlam, B.C. V3K 6Y6 • Adv • Weekly advertiser with photo ads for cars. Editions include Domestic Auto, Import Auto, Light Truck, Commercial Truck, B.C. Bike, Boat and RV, Equipment trader, Old Car trader.

Automotive Retailer • (1947) • Monthly • Automotive Retailers' Publishing Co. Ltd. • 4281 Canada Way, Ste.120, Burnaby, B.C. V5G 4P1 • Circ 5,000 • Adv • Trade publication.

Award Magazine • (1987) • Five times a year • Canada Wide Magazines Ltd. • 4180 Lougheed Hwy., Ste. 401, Burnaby, B.C. V5C 6A7 • Circ 7,500 • Adv • Covers architectural and design trends, company and project profiles for architects, interior designers, landscape architects, general contractors, developers and engineers.

BC Bookworld • (1987) • Quarterly, free • 3516 W. 13th Ave., Vancouver, B.C. V6R 2S3 • Circ 100,000 • Book reviews and announcements with

emphasis on B.C. authors and publishers. Free to qualified personnel and at various drop points (libraries and bookstores) around the city.

BC Broker • (1949) • Bi-monthly • Insurance Agents' Association of British Columbia • Insurance Publications Ltd. • P.O. Box 3311, Vancouver, B.C. V6B 3Y3 • Circ 2,500 • Adv

BC Business • (1973) • Monthly • Canada Wide Magazines Ltd. • (Subscr. to: 401-4180 Lougheed Hwy., Burnaby, B.C. V5C 6A7) • Circ 26,000 • Adv • Covers prominent business leaders and key developments in the local area. Provides data on business trends and opportunities.

BC Business Examiner • (1985) • 10 times a year • Golden City Co. • 545 East Broadway, Vancouver, B.C. V5T 1X4 • Circ 25,000 • Adv

BCDNA News • Monthly • British Columbia Dietitians' and Nutritionists' Association • 1755 W. Broadway Ave., Ste. 402, Vancouver, B.C. V6J 4S5 • Circ 900 • Adv • Provides members with information on topics and events of interest.

BC Fellowship Baptist • (1927) • Monthly • Fellowship of Evangelical Baptist Churches of British. Columbia & Yukon • Box 800, Langley, B.C. V3A 8C9 • Circ 10,000

BC Home • (1992) • Six times a year • Canada Wide Magazines Ltd. • 4180 Lougheed Hwy., Ste. 401, Burnaby, B.C. V5C 6A7 • Circ 110,000 • Adv • Lifestyle magazine: home design, food, fashion, travel and recreation.

BCIT Update • Weekly, free • British Columbia Institute of Technology, Marketing & Development, Information & Community Relations • 3700 Willingdon Ave., Burnaby, B.C. V5G 3H2 • BCIT newletter.

BC Journal of Special Education • (1976) • Three times a year • Special Education Association, Dept. of Educational Psychology and Special Education, University of British Columbia, 10-550 West 6th Ave., Vancouver, B.C. V5Z 4P2 • Circ 800 • Adv • Devoted to reviews of research, case studies, surveys and reports on the effectiveness of innovative programs.

BCLA Reporter • (1957) • Five times a year, membership only • British Columbia Library Association • 6545 Bonsor Ave., Ste. 110, Burnaby, B.C. V5H 1H3 • E-mail: bcla@unixg.ubc.ca • Circ: 810 (controlled) • Reports on activities of B.C.L.A., policy and news pertaining to libraries in the province. Includes features on information retrieval and technology, library architecture, literacy, management, finance.

BC Naturalist • (1969) • Six times a year • Federation of British Columbia Naturalists • 321-1367 West Broadway, Vancouver, B.C. V6H 4A9 • Circ 6,000 • Adv • Newsletter.

BC Outdoors • (1945) • Eight times a year • OP Publishing Ltd. • 1132 Hamilton St., Ste. 202, Vancouver, B.C. V6B 2S2 • Circ 39,374 • Adv •

Covers fishing, hunting and outdoor recreation.

BC Professional Engineer • (1950) • 10 times a year • Association of Professional Engineers and Geoscientists of British Columbia • 210-6400 Roberts St., Burnaby, B.C. V5G 4C9 • Circ 16,500

B.C. Professional Forester • (1947) • Bi-monthly • Association of British Columbia Professional Foresters • 1201-1130 W. Pender St., Vancouver, B.C. V6E 4A4 • Circ 3,800 • Newsletter to members of the association and interested forestry groups on issues which impact foresters in their roles as professionals.

BC Runner • (1978) • Quarterly • Seawall Running Society • Box 4981, Vancouver, B.C. V6B 4A6 • Circ 3,000

BCSF A-ZINE • (1973) • Monthly • British Columbia Science Fiction Association • P.O. Box 35577, Vancouver, B.C. V6M 4G9 • Circ 135

BC Sport Fishing Magazine • Six times a year • 909 Jackson Crescent, New Westminster, B.C. V3L 4S1

BC Studies • (1969) • Quarterly • University of British Columbia • 2029 West Mall, Vancouver, B.C. V6T 1Z2 • Circ 1,000 • Adv • Focuses on all aspects of human history in British Columbia.

BC Woman • (1985) • Monthly • B.C. Woman to Woman Magazine Ltd. • 704 Clarkson Street, New Westminster, B.C. V3M 1E2 • Circ 29,000 • Women's lifestyles in British Columbia.

B.S.D.A. News • (1969) • Six times a year, free • Building Supply Dealers Association of British Columbia • 630 Columbia St., No. 101, New Westminster, B.C. V3M 1B2 • Circ 1,400 • Adv • Trade publication.

Beale's Industry Letter • (1972) • 26 times a year • Box 48651, Vancouver, B.C. V7X 1A3 • Circ 300 • Resource industry newsletter.

Belles-Lettres • Bi-monthly, membership • Vancouver Society of Letters and Correspondence • Box 86368, North Vancouver, B.C. V7L 4K6

Billington's Stock Focus II • (1987) • Editions in Chinese, English • Quarterly, free • Billington Securities Ltd. • 1660 Benson Rd., Pt. Roberts, WA 98281 (And: 1095 Jervis St., No. 1, Vancouver, B.C. V6E 2C2) • Circ 62,500

Bingo Caller News • Bi-monthly • Nielsens' Publications Corporation • 19607 88th Ave., Langley, B.C. V3A 6Y3 • Circ 10,000

Boat World • Monthly • 400-1200 West Pender Street, Vancouver, B.C. V6Z 2S9 • Circ 13,500 • Adv

Boating News • (1970) • Monthly • Tyrell Publishing • 1252 Burrard St., Ste. 201, Vancouver, B.C. V6Z 1Z1 • Circ 11,000 • Adv • Covers commercial and pleasure boating.

Bowen Island Undercurrent • (1975) • Weekly • 495 Mount Gardner Road, Bowen Island, B.C. • Circ 6,000 • Suburban community newspaper, distributed free to households in the area.

British Columbia Catholic • (1931) • Weekly • Vancouver Archdiocese • 150 Robson St., Vancouver, B.C. V6B 2A7 • Circ 20,000 • Adv

British Columbia Curling News • (1977) • Bi-monthly • R.C. Publishing Co. • Suite 212-20216 Fraser Highway, Langley, B.C. V3A 4E6

British Columbia Film News • (1989) • Monthly • Polo Holdings Ltd. • 3030 Lincoln Ave., Coquitlam, B.C. V3B 6B4 • Adv • News of filmmaking in the province.

British Columbia Genealogical Society Newsletter • Quarterly • British Columbia Genealogical Society • Box 88054, Richmond, B.C. V6X 3T6

British Columbia Historical News • (1968) • Quarterly • British Columbia Historical Federation • P.O. Box 5254, Sta. B, Victoria, B.C. V8R 6N4 • Circ 1,250 • Adv • British Columbian history: articles ranging from scholarly to anecdotal.

British Columbia Medical Association News • (1972) • Bi-monthly, membership • British Columbia Medical Association • 115-1665 West Broadway, Vancouver, B.C. V6J 5A4

British Columbia Medical Journal • (1959) • Monthly • British Columbia Medical Association • 115-1665 W. Broadway, Vancouver, B.C. V6J 5A4 • Circ 7,800 • Adv

British Columbia Mountaineer • (1917) • Biennial • British Columbia Mountaineering Club • P.O. Box 2674, Vancouver, B.C. V6B 3W8 • Circ 500 • Adv

British Columbia Report • (1989) • Weekly • British Columbia Report Magazine Ltd. • 535 Thurlow St., Ste. 600, Vancouver, B.C. V6E 3L2 • Circ 27,992 • Adv • B.C. news magazine.

British Columbia Thoroughbred • (1957) • Seven times a year • British Columbia Thoroughbred Breeders Society • 4023 E. Hastings St., Burnaby, B.C. V5C 2J1 • Circ 750 • Adv

Build and Green • Eight times a year • Build and Green, Studio D, 2922 West 6th Avenue, Vancouver, B.C. V6K 1X3 • E-mail: buildgrn@dowco.com • Gardening and home renovation. Free at various points around the area.

Burnaby News Leader • Weekly • 6569 Kingsway, Burnaby, B.C. V5E 1E1 • Circ 49,000 • Suburban community newspaper, distributed free to households in the area.

Burnaby NOW! • Wednesday and Sunday • 205A 3430 Brighton Avenue, Burnaby, B.C. V5A 3H4 • Circ 47,000 • Adv • Community newspaper, distributed free to households in the area.

Business in Vancouver • (1989) • Weekly • BIV Publications Ltd. • 1155 Pender St. W., Ste. 500, Vancouver, B.C. V6E 2P4 • Circ 14,000 • Adv • Covers business news in the Greater Vancouver area. Widely distributed in the Downtown area.

Butter-Fat • (1923) • Four times a year • Agrifoods International Cooperative Ltd. • P.O. Box 9100, Vancouver, B.C. V6B 4G4 • Circ 1,750 • Adv • Informs members of activities in the co-op and dairy industries.

CGA Magazine • (1967) • 12 times a year • Certified General Accountants' Association of Canada • 1188 W. Georgia St., Ste. 700, Vancouver, B.C. V6E 4A2 • Circ 48,000 • Adv • Covers accounting matters for Canadian professional accountants and financial executives.

Camera Canada • Twice a year • National Association for Photographic Art • 1140 South Dyke Road, New Westminster, B.C. V3M 5A2. • Circ 3,700 • Opinions and outlooks on photography.

Canada Japan Business Journal • (1990) • Six times a year • Text in English, Japanese • Van Network Ltd. • 220 Cambie St., Ste. 370, Vancouver, B.C. V6B 2M9 • Circ 10,858 • Adv

Canada Poultryman • (1912) • Monthly • Farm Papers Ltd. • 105B, 9547-152nd St., Surrey, B.C. V3R 5Y5 • Circ 8,530 • Adv • Incorporating: *Aviculteur Canadien* • (Text in English, French) • Provides information on poultry and the poultry industry, designed primarily for Canadian commercial poultry producers.

Canada Stockwatch: Western Edition • (1984) • Daily • Canjex Publishing • 609 Granville Street, Box 10371, Vancouver, B.C. V7Y 1J6 • Covers news issued that day or week by every company listed on the Vancouver and Alberta stock exchanges. (*Canada Stockwatch: Eastern Edition* covers daily news from every company listed on the Toronto and Montreal stock exchanges.)

Canada West Travel News • (1988) • 12 times a year • Host Resources Inc. • 1037 W. Broadway, Ste. 104, Vancouver, B.C. V6H 1E3 • Circ 24,000 • Adv

Canadian Critical Care Nursing Journal • (1984) • Four times a year • Health Media Inc. • 14453 29A Ave., White Rock, B.C. V4A 9K8 • Circ 3,000 • Adv

Canadian Environmental Protection • (1989) • Nine times a year • Baum Publications Ltd. • 1625 Ingleton Ave., Burnaby, B.C. V5C 4L8 • Circ: 23,393 (controlled) • Adv

Canadian Heavy Equipment Guide • (1986) • Nine times a year • Baum Publications Ltd. • 1625 Ingleton Ave., Burnaby, B.C. V5C 4L8 • Circ 31,093 • Adv • Describes new products and industry developments. Industry experts explain the best way to use and maintain heavy equipment.

Canadian Holistic Healing Association Newsletter • (1978) • Quarterly • Canadian Holistic Healing Association, c/o Vancouver Health Enhancement Centre, 2021 Columbia St., Vancouver B.C. V5Y 3C9 • Circ 1,800 • Adv

Canadian Journal of Botany—Revue Canadienne de Botanique • (1974) • Monthly • Text in English and French • c/o National Research Council Research Journals, 4186 University Boulevard,

Vancouver, B.C. V6T 1Z4 • Circ 1,600 • Adv • Academic journal on research in botany.

Canadian Journal of Civil Engineering—Revue Canadienne de Genie Civil • (1974) • Bi-monthly • Text in English and French • c/o National Research Council Research Journals, 4186 University Blvd., Vancouver, B.C. V6T 1Z4 • Circ 3,300 • Adv • Academic journal on research in civil engineering.

Canadian Journal of Communication • (1974) • Quarterly • Canadian Journal of Communication, c/o Communications, Harbour Centre, Simon Fraser University, 515 West Hastings St., Vancouver, B.C. V6B 5K3 • Circ 437 • Adv • Academic journal covering communications and tele-communications.

Canadian Journal of Mathematics • (1948) • Bi-monthly • c/o Canadian Mathematical Society, Dept of Mathematics, University of B.C., Vancouver, B.C. V6T 1Y4 • Circ 1,220 • Academic journal of mathematics.

Canadian Journal of Nursing Administration • (1988) • Quarterly • Health Media Inc. • 14453 29A Ave., White Rock, B.C. V4A 9K8 • Adv • For Canadian nurse administrators, managers, educators.

Canadian Literature / Litterature Canadienne: A Quarterly of Criticism and Review • (1959) • Quarterly • Text in English, French • University of British Columbia, 223-2029 West Mall, Vancouver, B.C. V6T 1Z2 • Circ 1,400 • Adv • Devoted to the study of all aspects of Canadian writing.

Canadian Mill Product News • (1990) • 69 times a year • Baum International Media Ltd. • 1625 Ingleton Ave., Burnaby, B.C. V5C 4L8 • Adv

Canadian Nursing Home Journal • (1985) • Quarterly • Health Media Inc. • 14453 29A Ave., White Rock, B.C. V4A 9K8 • Circ 4,000 • Adv

Canadian Operating Room Nursing Journal • (1983) • Four times a year • Operating Room Nurses Association of Canada • Health Media Inc. • 14453-29A Ave., White Rock, B.C. V4A 9K8 • Circ 4,020

Canadian Public Policy—Analyse de Politiques • (1975) • Quarterly • Text in English and French • Canadian Public Policy, c/o Simon Fraser University, Burnaby, B.C. V5A 1S6 • Circ 1,600 • Adv • Academic journal covering ideas and research on policy proposals.

Canadian School Executive • (1981) • 10 times a year • Xancor Canada Ltd. for The Canadian School Executive • P.O. Box 48265 Bentall Centre, Vancouver, B.C. V7X 1A1 • Circ 7,500 • Adv • Dedicated to promoting effective leadership, management and instruction in schools.

Canadian Traveller: An Altracs Publication for the Travel Industry • (1983) • Monthly • Canadian Traveller • 115-5200 Miller Rd., Richmond, B.C. V7B 1K5 • Circ 12,782 • Adv

Canadian Yearbook of International Law/Annuaire Canadien de Droit International • (1963) • Annual • University of British Columbia Press • 6344 Memorial Rd., Vancouver, B.C. V6T 1Z2 • Articles on international law, Canadian practice in international law, and a digest of Canadian cases in public international law and conflict of law.

Cancer Research News • (1984) • Semi-annual, Free • Canadian Cancer Society, B.C. and Yukon Division • 565 W. 10th Ave., Vancouver, B.C. V5Z 4J4 • Circ 7,500 • Bulletin summarizing current research into all aspects of cancer: causation, detection, prevention, treatment, epidemiology, survival.

Capilano Courier • (1968) • Weekly • Capilano College, Courier Publishing Society • 2055 Purcell Way, North Vancouver, B.C. V7J 3H5 • Circ 3,500 • Adv • Student publication: student news, opinion and letters.

Capilano Review • (1972) • Three times a year • Capilano Press Society • (Capilano College) • 2055 Purcell Way, North Vancouver, B.C. V7J 3H5 • Circ 1,000 • Adv • Journal of poetry, art and short fiction.

Captain Lillie's British Columbia Coast Guide and Radiotelephone Directory • (1936) • Biennial • Progress Publishing Co. Ltd. • Ste. 200, 1865 Marine Dr., West Vancouver, B.C. V7V 1J7

Chamber Comment and the Chamber Newsbulletin • (1977) • Monthly, free • British Columbia Chamber of Commerce • Box 30, 750 Pacific Blvd., Vancouver, B.C. V6B 5E6 • Circ 2,000 • Adv

Charhdi Kala • (1986) • Weekly • In Punjabi • Charhdi Kala Weekly Punjabi Newspaper • 7743 - 128th St., Unit 6, Surrey, B.C. V3W 4E6 • Circ 48,000 • Adv • Newspaper, free at many drop points in the community.

Chinatown News • (1953) • Semi-monthly • Text in English • Chinese Publicity Bureau Ltd. • 459 East Hastings St., Vancouver, B.C. V6A 1P5 • Circ 24,000 • Adv • Contains items of news and general interest to the Chinese community in North America.

Chinese Edition Lifestyle Magazine • (1988) • Monthly • Text in Chinese and English • Chinese Edition Publications, Ltd. • 960 Richards St., Ste. 206, Vancouver, B.C. V6B 3C1 • Circ 50,000 • Adv • Consumer lifestyle magazine directed at the Chinese market in Canada .

Chinese-Canadian Bulletin • (1961) • Monthly • Text in English and Chinese • Chinese-Canadian Press • 3289 Main St., Vancouver 10, B.C. • Adv

Christian Info News • (1982) • Monthly • Christian Info (Vancouver-Lower Mainland) Society • Ste. 200, 20316-56 Ave., Langley, B.C. V3A 3Y7. • Circ 27,000 • Adv

Coast: The Outdoor Recreation Magazine • Eight times a year, free • Glissade Publishing Ltd. • P.O.

Box 65837, Station F, Vancouver, B.C. V5N 5L3 • E-mail: coastmag@mindlink.net • Free at many drop points about the area. Sports in the outdoors for those who like to bicycle, hike or ski.

Collective Bargaining Information Monthly Summary • Monthly • Labour Relations Board • 1125 Howe St., Vancouver, B.C. V6Z 2K8 • (Subscr. to: Crown Publications, 521 Fort St., Victoria, B.C., V8W 1E7) • Contains information of wage settlement, work stoppages and collective agreement settlements.

College Institute Educators' Association: Profile • (1989) • Quarterly • College Institute Educators' Association • 301 - 555 W. 8th Ave., Vancouver, B.C. V5Z 1C6 • Circ 6,500 • Offers analysis and information on policy, labor relations and professional issues affecting community college and institute educators and the higher education system in general.

Common Ground • Ten times a year • Common Ground Publishing Corp. • 201-3091 West Broadway, Vancouver, B.C. • Mail: Box 34090 Station D, Vancouver, B.C. V6J 4M1 • Circ 80,000 • Adv • "Dedicated to health, ecology, personal/ professional development and creativity." Free at various points around the city.

Communique • (1986) • Bi-monthly, membership • Amyotrophic Lateral Sclerosis Society of B.C. • 411 Dunsmuir St., 2nd Fl., Vancouver, B.C. V6B 1X4 • Circ 875 • Studies ALS research, fundraising and coping mechanisms and services for families faced with the disease.

Community Digest • (1983) • Weekly • Community Digest Publications • 216-1755 Robson St., Vancouver, B.C. V69 3B7 • Circ 25,000 • Adv • Serves the South Asian, East African, Middle Eastern, aboriginal and black Canadian ethnic communities.

Computer Paper • (B.C. Edition) • (1988) • Monthly • Canada Computer Paper Inc., part of Telemedia Inc. • 503-425 Carrall Street, Vancouver, B.C., V6B 6E3 • E-mail: editorial@tcp.ca • URL: http://-tcp.ca • Circ 60,000 • Adv • For IBM, Macintosh, OS/2 and Unix end-users. Offers news, features and reviews. Free at various drop points around the city..

Computer Player • Monthly, free • In English with some Chinese • Our Computer Player Ltd. • 900-1788 West Broadway, Vancouver, B.C. V6J 1Y1 • E-mail: computer _player@computerplayer.com • or 66640,1756 on Compuserve • URL: http:// www.computer player.com./cp • BBS: 604-528-3500. Log on with name "Computer Player Guest" • Magazine on computers and computing. Found free at various drop points about the area.

Conspiracy! • (1994) • Cosmological Meditations Society • P.O. Box 515, 916 W. Broadway, Vancouver, B.C. V5Z 1K7 • Circ 200 • Adv • Presents satire of conspiracy theories, extraterrestrials, government and business.

Consulting Engineers of British Columbia: Commentary • (1978) • Quarterly, membership • . Consulting Engineers of British Columbia • 514-409 Granville St., Vancouver, B.C. V6C 1T2 • Circ: 2,000 (controlled) • Offers industry profiles, selection procedures, awards for engineering excellence, export activity, sector articles.

Cosmos Chinese Weekly • Weekly, free • In Chinese • Part of Sing Tao Group • 8872 Hudson Street Vancouver, B.C. V60 4M2 • Adv • Entertainment and show-business profiles, TV listings. Free at many drop points around the area.

El Contacto Directo • (1992) • Bi-weekly, free • El Contacto Directo, 141 West Broadway, Vancouver, B.C. V5Y 1P4 • News of the general Latin American community in Vancouver and Bellingham. One page in English.

Copper Toadstool • (1976) • Semi-annual • Soda Publications • 7500 Bridge St., Richmond, B.C. V6Y 2S7 • Literary magazine.

Coquitlam NOW! • Wednesday and Saturday • 1-2700 Barnet Hwy., Coquitlam, B.C. V3B 1B8. • Circ 47,000 • Suburban community newspaper, distributed free to households in the area.

Counterplay • (1984) • Six times a year • Counterplay Publishing Association • P.O. Box 4422, Vancouver, B.C. V6B 3Z8 • Circ 450 • Adv • Local chess games and news; includes occasional theory, "how-to-improve" articles and interviews.

Country Life in British Columbia • (1915) • Monthly • Country Life Ltd. • 3308 King George Hwy., Surrey, B.C. V4P 1A8 • Circ 9,060 • Adv • News and features concerning farming in B.C. Covers a wide spectrum of commodities such as beef, tree fruits and dairy.

Country Wave • Monthly • Country Wave, 101 - 9780 197B St., Langley B.C. V3A 4P8 • Circ 21,000 • Covers country and western music.

Coupler • (1957) • Bi-monthly, Free • BC Rail Ltd. • P.O. Box 8770, Vancouver, B.C. V6B 4X6 • Circ 4,000 • Company newsletter.

Critique: Getting to the Heart of the Matter (West Vancouver) • (1980) • Four times a year • Xanthyros Foundation • Box 91980, W. Vancouver, B.C. V7V 4S4 • Circ 25,000 • Adv • New Age publication.

Crux: A Quarterly Journal of Christian Thought and Opinion • (1966) • Quarterly • Regent College • 5800 University Blvd., Vancouver, B.C. V6T 2E4 • Circ 1,000 • Adv

Cycling: B.C. News • Monthly, membership • Cycling British Columbia • 332-1367 West Broadway, Vancouver, B.C. V6H 4A9

Dance International • (1984) • Quarterly • Vancouver Ballet Society • 1415 Barclay St., Vancouver, B.C. V6G 1J6 • Circ 3,000 • Adv • Provides national and international dance coverage.

Delta Optimist • (1922) • Wed., Fri., Sun. • (Sun-

day: *South Delta Today*) • Today Publishing Ltd. • 5485-48th Ave., Delta, B.C. V4K 1X2 • Circ: 15,000 • Adv • Suburban community newspaper, distributed free to households in the area.

Democrat • (1933) • 10 times a year • Democrat Publications, Ltd. • 3110 Boundary Road Burnaby, B.C. V5M 4A2 • Circ 30,000 • Adv • Newspaper of the New Democratic Party. Current events.

Democratic Commitment • (1967) • Bi-monthly • British Columbia Civil Liberties Association • 283 E. 11th Ave., Vancouver, B.C. • Circ 750

Diaspora Magazine: Black Consciousness and Culture • (1993) • Semi-annual • The Point Five Cultural Society • 4204 W. 14th Ave., Vancouver, B.C. V6R 2X8 • Circ 1,500 • Adv • Lists arts, ethnic interests, literary and political reviews.

Discorder Magazine • (1983) • Monthly • CITR-FM • 6138 SUB Boulevard, UBC, Vancouver, B.C. V6T 1Z1 • Adv • Free at various drop points around the city. Reports on alternative rock and other music played by the radio station.

Discovery • (1972) • Quarterly • Vancouver Natural History Society • Box 3021, Vancouver, B.C. V6B 3X5 • Circ 1,500 • Adv • Covers natural history topics such as herpetology, mycology, entomology, botany, mammalogy, ornithology, marine biology and conservation issues.

Discovery News • (1982) • Bi-monthly • Discovery Foundation • 400 The Station, 601 West Cordova St., Vancouver, B.C. V6B 1G1 • Circ 6,209 • Adv

Diver Magazine • (1975) • Nine times a year • Seagraphic Publications Ltd. • 295-10991 Shellbridge Way, Richmond, B.C. V6X 3C6 • E-mail: Diver@boardbob.tor250.org • (Subscr. to: P.O. Box 1312, Delta, B.C. V4M 3Y8) • Circ 30,000 • Adv • Contains Canadian and North American regional dive destination articles and travel features.

The Drive • (1995) • Monthly, free • The Drive, 1698 East 15th Ave., Vancouver, B.C. V5N 2G1 • E-mail: the.drive@star.ship.net • BBS: Arts Cascadia 604-299-4598 • Monthly community newspaper. Literature, commentary, articles about Commercial Drive in Vancouver.

East Side Revue • (1974) • Bi-weekly • 1736 East 33rd Ave., Apt A, Vancouver, B.C. • Adv • Community newspaper, distributed free to households in the area. Also free at various drop points.

The Echo • Weekly, free • 3355 Grandview Highway, Vancouver, B.C. V5M 1Z5 • URL: http://www.vannet.com/vanecho • Circ 56,000 • Suburban community newspaper, distributed free to households in the area.

Eclectic Muse • (1989) • Three times a year • 340 West 3rd St., Ste. 107, North Vancouver, B.C. V7M 1G4 • Circ 200 • Publishes poems, especially from women poets .

Eco d'Italia • (1955) • Weekly • Text in Italian, with English page • Zone Publishing Ltd. • 12-

3683 East Hastings, Vancouver, B.C. V5K 4S1 • Circ 5,900 • Adv • News of Italy and Italian speakers in Canada and B.C.

Education Leader: News and Views on Education • (1967) • Semi-monthly • British Columbia School Trustees Association • 1155 W. 8th Ave., Vancouver, B.C. V6H 1C5 • Circ 7,000 • Adv • Provides information about broad curriculum and policy issues and developments, and the latest trends in research.

Encore • (Arts Club Theatre) • (1984) • Monthly • Arts Club Theatre • 1585 Johnston St., Vancouver, B.C. V6H 3R9 • Adv

Enjoy • (1987) • Bi-monthly • Plymouth Publications, Inc. • 1685 Inglewood Ave., Burnaby, B.C. V5C 4L8

Ennui • (1980) • Bi-monthly • Ennui Publications • 4196 Main St., Ste. 4, Vancouver, B.C. V5V 3P7 • Art magazine.

Event • (1971) • Three times a year • Douglas College • P.O. Box 2503, New Westminster, B.C. V3L 5B2 • Circ 1,000 • Adv • Presents reviews, fiction and poetry.

Events Canada • Monthly • Events Canada, 1304 Hornby Street, Vancouver, B.C. V6Z 1W6 • Circ 50,000 • Entertainment and arts features and listings.

False Creek News • (1988) • Weekly • Creek Slopes Publications • 661A Market Hill, Vancouver, B.C. V5Z 4B5 • Circ 25,000 • Adv • Suburban community newspaper, distributed free to households in the area.

Fisherman • (1937) • Monthly • (United Fishermen and Allied Workers Union) • Fisherman Publishing Society • 111 Victoria Dr., No. 160, Vancouver, B.C. V5L 4C4 • Controlled Circ 10,500 • Adv

The Flag & Banner • (1987) • Semi-annual • J. Braverman Incorporated • 1755 W. 4th Ave., Vancouver, B.C. V6J 1M2 • E-mail: doreenb@ flagshop.ca • Circ 6,000 • Adv • Aims to enhance the public understanding of vexillology, the study of flags. Covers the protocol, history, controversy involving, and manufacture of flags.

Fraser Forum • (1985) • Monthly • Fraser Institute • 626 Bute St., Vancouver, B.C. V6E 3M1 • Circ 6,000 • Studies market solutions for public policy problems.

Full Tide • (1936) • Semi-annual, membership • Vancouver Poetry Society • c/o 4602 Prospect Rd., North Vancouver, B.C.

GRC News • (1990) • Semi-annual, free • Simon Fraser University, Gerontology Research Centre • 515 W. Hastings St., Vancouver, B.C. V6B 5K3 • E-mail: smithak@sfu.ca • URL: http://biblio.ucs .sfu.ca/gero/ • Circ 300 • Publishes news about the centre and senior citizens in British Columbia.

Gallerie: Women Artists Monographs • (1988) • Irregular • Gallerie Publications • 2901 Panorama

Dr., North Vancouver, B.C. V7G 2A4 • Circ 2,500 • Adv • Women artists from across North America discuss their art and concerns in a series of books.

Garage & Service Station News • (1934) • Monthly • Garage & Service Station News Publishing Co. • No. 204, 260 Raymur Ave., Vancouver 6, B.C. • Circ: Controlled • Adv

Gardens West • (1987) • Nine times a year • Cornwall Publishing Company Ltd. • Box 2680, Vancouver, B.C. V6B 3V7 • Circ 50,000 • Adv • Information for the home gardener in Western Canada.

Geist: The Canadian Magazine of Ideas and Culture • (1990) • Five times a year • Geist Foundation • 100 - 1062 Homer St., Vancouver, B.C. V6B 2W9 • Circ 5,000 • Adv • Commentaries on literature, society and the arts.

Georgia Straight • (1967) • Weekly • Vancouver Free Press Publishing Corp. • 1770 Burrard St., 2nd Fl., Vancouver, B.C. V6J 3G7 • E-mail: info@straight.com • Circ 97,000 • Adv • Covers news, arts, movies, music, travel, food, style, business. Free at many drop points around the city.

Geotechnical News • (1982) • Quarterly • BiTech Publishers Ltd. • 173 - 11860 Hammersmith Way, Richmond, B.C. V7A 5G1 • Circ 6,000 • Adv • News on geotechnical activities in Canada, the U.S., Mexico and Europe, including special sections on waste geotechnics and geosynthetics, geotechnical events and instrumentation.

Gladiolus, Dahlias • (1921) • Annual, membership • Canadian Gladiolus Society • 1274 129 A St., Surrey, B.C. V4A 3Y4 • Adv

Glasnik Hrvatske Seljacke Stranke • (1985) • Monthly • Text in Croatian • P.O. Box 82187, North Burnaby, B.C. V5C 5P2 • Circ 2,000 • News of Croatia and Croatian peoples in Canada and B.C.

Good Friends • (1977) • Monthly • Vancouver Canada-China Friendship Association • P.O. Box 4168, Vancouver, B.C. • Trips and features about the People's Republic of China.

Greater Vancouver Japanese-Canadian Citizens Association: Bulletin • Greater Vancouver Japanese-Canadian Citizens Association • *Geppo;* a monthly publication for and about the Japanese-Canadian Community • (1959) • Text in English, Japanese • Japanese-Canadian Citizens Association of Greater Vancouver • 511 E. Broadway, Vancouver, B.C. V5T 1X4 • (Subscr. to: Box 2108, Vancouver, B.C. V6B 3T5) • Circ 6,000 • Adv

Grocer Today Magazine • (1986) • 10 times a year • Canada Wide Magazines Ltd. • 4180 Lougheed Hwy., Ste. 401, Burnaby, B.C. V5C 6A7 • Circ 11,500 • Adv • Trade magazine for the food and beverage industry in Western Canada, serves independent grocers, brokers, importers, manufacturers, etc.

Hallelujah! • (Vancouver) • (1949) • Bi-monthly • Bible Holiness Movement • Box 223, Sta. A, Vancouver, B.C. V6C 2M3 • Circ 5,000 • Magazine of aggressive evangelical Christianity and social activism.

Harbour and Shipping • (1918) • Monthly • Progress Publishing Co. Ltd. • 1865 Marine Dr., Ste. 200, West Vancouver, B.C. V7V 1J7 • Circ 2,000 • Adv

Head to Toe • (1983) • Quarterly, free • British Columbia Medical Association • 115-1665 W. Broadway, Vancouver, B.C. V6J 5A4 • Circ 25,000 • News on public health.

Healthy Eating • Six times a year • Odyssey Publishing Inc. • 2135 W. 45th Ave., Vancouver, B.C. V6M 2J2 • Circ 125,000

Hellenic View • (1971) • Semi-monthly • Text in English and Greek • Box 2045, Vancouver, B.C. V6B 3R6 • Circ 2,249 • Adv • News of the Greek community in B.C. and Canada.

Hiballer Forest Magazine • (1948) • Monthly • H B Publishers Ltd. • 106 14th St., E., Ste. 11, N. Vancouver, B.C. V7L 2N3 • Circ 10,600 • Adv • Trade publication for the forestry industry.

Hollandse Krant • (1969) • Monthly • Text in Dutch • J.I. Timmer Publishing Co. Ltd. • 12-20505 Fraser Highway, Langley, B.C. V3A 4G3 • E-mail: holkrant@awinc.com • Paid Circ: 7,600 • Adv • News of Dutch speakers in B.C. and the Netherlands.

Hort West • (1982) • Bi-monthly • British Columbia Nursery Trades Association • 101 - 5830 176 A St., Surrey, B.C. • E-mail: jstock@B.C.nta.netwave.com • Circ 1,200 • Adv • Trade publication for the horticultural industry.

In Pharmation • (1968) • Monthly, membership • British Columbia Pharmacists' Society • 604-1200 W. 73rd Ave., Vancouver, B.C. V6P 6G5 • Circ 2,000 • Adv • Pharmacists' newsletter.

Independent Senior • (1990) • Monthly, 10 times a year • KW Publishing Ltd. • 1268 W. Pender St., Vancouver, B.C. V6E 2S8 • Circ 45,000 • Adv • Articles of interest for seniors 55 and over.

Indian Voice • (1969) • Monthly • Indian Homemakers Association • 429 East 6th Ave., Vancouver, B.C. V7L 1P8 • Circ 3,000 • Adv

Indo Canadian Times • (1978) • Weekly • Text in Punjabi • 12414-82 Ave., Ste. 103, Surrey, B.C. V3W 3E9 • Circ 15,200 • Adv • Suburban weekly in Punjabi. Free at various points around the area.

Indo-Canadian • (1964) • Quarterly • Text in Punjabi • Indo-Canadian Times Inc. • P.O. Box 2296, Vancouver, B.C. V6B 3W5

Indo-Canadian Phulvert • In Punjabi and English • Indo-Canadian Phulvert, 14891 Spencer Drive, Surrey, B.C. V3S 7K7 • News for the Punjabi community in B.C.

Institute of Chartered Accountants of British

Columbia: Communication • (1945) • 10 times a year, membership • Institute of Chartered Accountants of British Columbia •1133 Melville St., 6th Fl., Vancouver, B.C. V6E 4E5 • Circ 8,000 • Adv • Information for chartered accountants in British Columbia.

Interlog Quarterly Review • (1991) • Quarterly • Image Fast Productions Inc. • Box 601, Vancouver, B.C. V6C 2N5 • Circ 4,145 • Adv • Focuses on the common good and economic health of full-phase logging contractors, owner-operators and haulers.

International History Review • (1979) • Quarterly • Simon Fraser University, Burnaby, B.C. V5A 1S6 • E-mail: intl—hist—rev@stu.ca • Circ 800 • Adv • Examines relations between all states throughout history.

The Iranian • Bi-weekly • In Farsi • The Iranian, P.O. Box 37050, North Vancouver, B.C. V7N 4M0 • Circ 4,000.

Jewish Western Bulletin • (1929) • Weekly • Anglo-Jewish Publishers • 3268 Heather St., Vancouver, B.C. V5Z 3K5 • Circ: 2,402 (controlled) • Adv • Weekly news of the Jewish community in Vancouver.

Journal of Business Administration • (1969) • Semi-annual • University of British Columbia, Faculty of Commerce and Business Administration, Vancouver, B.C. V6T 1Z2 • Circ 400 • Adv

Journal of Commerce • (1911) • Monday and Wednesday • Journal of Commerce Ltd. • (Subsidiary of: Southam Information & Technology Group) • P.O. Box 82230, N. Burnaby, B.C. V5C 6E7 • Circ 5,124 • Adv • Reports on construction and building industry.

Journal of Human Justice • (1989) • Semi-annual • Human Justice Collective • Dept. of Anthropology and Sociology, U. of British Columbia, 6303 N.W. Marine Dr., Vancouver, B.C. V6T 2B2 • Offers a forum for progressive analyses of economic, gender, legal and political relations as they pertain to studies of social justice in Canadian society and abroad.

Just Wages: A Bulletin on Wage Discrimination and Pay Equity • (1991) • Quarterly • Trade Union Research Bureau • 111 Victoria Dr., No. 170, Vancouver, B.C. V5L 4C4 • Paid Circ: 370 • Adv

Karuna Society Newsletter • (1984) • Three times a year • Karuna Meditation Society • 25 West 10th Ave., Vancouver, B.C. V5Y 4G3 • Circ 2,000 • Adv • Provides articles related to meditation in daily life, the relationship between spiritual practice and social change and issues related to women and Buddhism.

Kinesis: News About Women That's Not in the Dailies • (1972) • 10 times a year • Vancouver Status of Women • 301-1720 Grant St., Vancouver, B.C. V5L 2Y6 • Circ 2,500 • Covers news from a feminist angle. Analyzes government policies, feminist theories and debates within the women's movement.

Kitsilano News • Weekly, free • Trinity Holdings, 103-2145 West Broadway, Vancouver, B.C. V6K 4L3 • Suburban community newspaper, distributed free to households in the area. Also free at various points about the area.

Langley Advance • (1931) • Wednesday and Friday • 20488 Fraser Hwy., Langley, B.C. V3A 4G2. • Circ 34,500 • Adv • Suburban community newspaper, distributed free to households in the area.

Leader • Wednesday and Sunday • Box 276, Surrey, B.C. V3T 4W8 • Circ 66,000 • Adv • Suburban North Delta/Surrey community paper, distributed free to households in the area.

Link (Burnaby) • (1966) • Weekly • British Columbia Institute of Technology, Student Association • 3700 Willingdon Ave., Burnaby, B.C. V5G 3H2 • Circ 5,000 • Adv • Student newspaper.

The Link (Vancouver) • (1973) • Twice Weekly • Link Communications Ltd. • 225 E. 17th Ave., Ste. 201, Vancouver, B.C. V5V 1A6 • Circ 10,000 • In English, with some Punjabi. Free at various drop points around the area.

Logger • (1990) • Bi-monthly • Westcoast Publishing Ltd. • 1496 West 72nd Ave., Vancouver, B.C. V6P 3C8 • Circ 12,000 • Adv • Trade publication for the logging industry.

Logging & Sawmilling Journal • (1968) • Monthly • 622 W. 22nd St., North Vancouver, B.C. V7M 2A7 • Circ 16,700 • Adv • Trade publication.

Logistics and Transportation Review • (1965) • Quarterly • University of British Columbia, Centre for Transportation Studies, Vancouver, B.C. V6T 1Z2 • Circ 1,000 • Adv

Maclean's Magazine • (Chinese Edition) • Bi-monthly • 900-1130 West Pender St., Vancouver, B.C. V6E 4A4 • Circ 80,000 • Adv • Chinese (Cantonese) edition of MacLean's news magazine with translations of earlier English-language stories. Distributed in a weekend edition of *Sing Tao* as well as on newstands.

Madison's Canadian Lumber Reporter • Weekly • Madison's Canadian Lumber Reporter • (1973) • Box 2486, Vancouver, B.C. V6B 3W7 • Devoted to North American lumber market activity.

Maple Ridge-Pitt Meadows News • Wednesday and Sunday • 22328-119th Ave., Maple Ridge, B.C. V2X 2X5 • Circ 24,000 • Adv • Suburban community newspaper, distributed free to households in the area.

Maple Ridge-Pitt Meadows Times • Wednesday and Sunday • 22334 Selkirk Ave., Maple Ridge, B.C. V2X 2X5 • Circ 23,000 • Adv

Marketing Edge • (1992) • Bi-monthly • Media West Publishing Inc. • 1497 Marine Dr., Ste. 300,

W. Vancouver, B.C. V7T 1B8 • Circ 5,000 • Adv • Helps marketing professionals learn and apply information as efficiently as possible in order to maintain a competitive edge.

Markwick Midden • (1982) • Semi-annual • 3506 Swansacre, Vancouver, B.C. V5S 4J8 • Circ 100 • Articles on heraldry.

Marpole Good Morning News • Weekly • 1496 West 72nd, Vancouver, B.C. V6P 3C8 • Adv • In English and Chinese • Community newspaper, distributed free to households in the area.

Maternal Health News • (1975) • Quarterly • Maternal Health Society • Box 46563, Sta. "G", Vancouver, B.C. V6R 4G8 • Circ 8,000

Maturity Magazine • (1984) • Bi-monthly • CYN Investments Ltd. • Box 397, New Westminster, B.C. V3L 4Y7 • Circ 175,000 • Adv • General interest for senior citizens. Includes finance, health, travel and lifestyle.

Mehfil Magazine • (1993) • Nine times a year • Text in English • VIG Communications Inc. • 301-1334 W. 6th Ave., Vancouver, B.C. V6H 1A7 • Circ 25,000 (controlled) • Adv • Multicultural and lifestyle magazine.

Mensageiro • Fortnightly • 6926 Tyne St., Vancouver, B.C. V5S 3M6 • Circ 3,500 • Adv • Spanish language news.

Metropolitan Pensioner • (1966) • Monthly • Metropolitan Pensioners Welfare Association • Box 2929, Vancouver 3, B.C. • Circ 4,800 • Adv

The Midden • (1969) • Five times a year • Archaeological Society of British Columbia • Box 520, Sta. A, Vancouver, B.C. V6C 2N3 • Circ 350.

Ming Pao • Daily • Text in Chinese • 44 East Pender St., Vancouver, B.C. V6A 3V6 • Daily with news of Vancouver and its parent newspaper in Hong Kong.

Monthly Stock Charts-Canadian Companies • (1984) • Quarterly • Independent Survey Co. Ltd. • P.O. Box 6000, Vancouver, B.C. V6B 4B9 • Charts the 12-year share price and volume for 1,000 Canadian resource and industrial companies.

Multifaith News • (1976) • Five times a year •. Multifaith Action Society • 385 Boundary Rd., Vancouver, B.C. V5K 4S1 • Circ 2,000 • Adv • An inter-faith publication aimed at promoting understanding between different faiths.

Music Research News • (1976) • Semi-annual, membership • Canadian Music Research Council, c/o Robert Walker, Simon Fraser University, Faculty of Education, Burnaby, B.C. • Circ 100

Musick • (1979) • Quarterly • Vancouver Society for Early Music • 1254 W. Seventh Ave., Vancouver, B.C. V6H 1B6 • E-mail: earlymusic@ mindlink.bc.ca • Circ 4,000 • Covers medieval, Renaissance, baroque and classical music.

National Radio Guide: Guide to CBC radio and CBC stereo • (1981) • Monthly • Core Group

Publishers Inc. • Box 48417, Bentall Centre, Vancouver, B.C. V7X 1A2 • Circ 40,000 • Adv

Native Issues Monthly • Monthly • 822 East 10th Ave., Vancouver, B.C., V5T 3B1 • Circ 300 • Adv

Native Voice • (1946) • Bi-monthly • Native Brotherhood of British Columbia • 319 Seymour Blvd., North Vancouver, B.C. V7L 4J5 • Circ 3,000 • Adv • Keeps members updated on events in the fishing industry.

New Republic • (1911) • Daily • Text in Chinese, English • New Republic Printing & Publishing Co. Ltd. • 531 Main St., Vancouver, B.C. V6A 2V1 • Ed. S.H. Hsu • Circ 2,679 • Adv

New Times • (1936) • Monthly • Institute of Economic Democracy • P.O. Box 2797, Vancouver, B.C. V6B 3X2 • Circ 4,000 • Examines teachings of C.H. Douglas and political and economic issues.

New West News • (New Westminster) • Wednesday and Sunday • 6569 Kingsway, Burnaby, B.C. V5E 1E1 • Circ 15,000 • Adv • Suburban community newspaper, distributed free to households in the area.

New Westminster NOW • Wednesday and Sunday • 418-6th Street, New Westminster, B.C. V3L 3B2 • Circ 15,000 • Adv • Suburban community newspaper, distributed free to households in the area.

North Delta Sentinel • (1973) • Bi-weekly • 10680-84th Ave., Delta, B.C. V4C 2L2 • Circ 12,000 • Adv • Suburban community newspaper, distributed free to households in the area.

North Shore News • Thrice weekly • 1139 Lonsdale Ave., North Vancouver, B.C. V7M 2H4. • Circ 59,000 • Adv • Community newspaper, distributed free to households in the area.

Nursing BC • (1968) • Five times a year • Registered Nurses Association of British Columbia • 2855 Arbutus St, Vancouver, B.C. V6J 3Y8 • Circ 35,000 • Adv • Contains news about nurses and nursing in Canada. Covers health issues.

On the March! • Quarterly • Bible Holiness Movement • Box 223, Sta. A, Vancouver, B.C. V6C 2M3 • Keeps friends and adherents informed. Contains prayer requests of the movement.

Online-Onward • (1978) • Irregular, approx. 8 times a year • Vancouver Online Users Group • P.O. Box 798, Station A. Vancouver, B.C. V6C 2N6 • Circ 100 • Events and information of interest to local librarians and others who work with computerized information retrieval and database management systems.

Opinion • Bi-weekly • In Greek and English • Opinion Magazine, 5042 Irmin Street, Burnaby, B.C. V5J 1Y5 • News and views of the Greek community.

Other Press • (1976) • Fortnightly, free • Other Publications Society • Douglas College, Box 2503,

700 Royal Ave., New Westminster, B.C. V3L 5B2 • Circ 5,000 • Adv • Student newspaper.

Outdoor Report • (1977) • Quarterly • Outdoor Recreation Council of B.C. • 334-1367 W. Broadway, Vancouver, B.C. V6H 4A9 • Circ 2,000 • Contains informative accounts of developments in outdoor recreation. Of interest to the council's members as well as elected officials, recreation managers, media and public libraries.

Outlook • (1963) • 10 times a year • Canadian Jewish Outlook Society • 6184 Ash St., Ste. 3, Vancouver, B.C. V5Z 3G9 • Circ 4,000 • Adv • Provides a Jewish secular humanist perspective on political and cultural issues.

Overseas Times • Bi-weekly • Foremost Publishing Co., 3 East Broadway, Suite 2033, Vancouver, B.C., V5T 1V5 • Circ 12,000 • News of the Indo-Canadian community.

PIBC News • (1959) • Five times a year • Planning Institute of British Columbia • 10551 Shellbridge Way, Ste. 20, Richmond, B.C. V6X 2W9 • Circ 600 • Adv • Presents articles and news of local events of interest to the practicing urban and regional planners of British Columbia.

Pacific Affairs: An International Review of Asia and the Pacific • (1927) • Quarterly • Pacific Affairs—University of British Columbia, 2029 West Mall, Vancouver, B.C., V6T 1Z2 • Paid Circ 3,000 • Adv • Scholarly journal dealing with Asia and the Pacific.

Pacific Currents: Life and Politics in B.C. • (1985) • Bi-monthly • Pacific New Directions Publishing Society • Box 34279, Sta. D, Vancouver, B.C. V6J 4P2 • E-mail: kotsopou@sfu.ca • Circ 1,600 • Adv • Political comment from the left. Articles with a progressive point of view.

Pacific Golf • (1994) • Six times a year • Canada Wide Magazines Ltd. • 401-4180 Lougheed Hwy., Ste 401, Burnaby, B.C. V5C 6A7 • Circ 16,000 • Adv

Pacific Hosteller • (1964) • Quarterly, membership • Canadian Hostelling Association, B.C. Region • 1515 Discovery St., Vancouver, B.C. V6R 4K5 • Circ: 10,000 (controlled) • Adv • News of the youth hostel movement and travel notes.

Pacific Report Newsletter • (1978) • Semi-annual, free • Canadian Cancer Society, B.C. and Yukon Division • 565 W. 10th Ave., Vancouver, B.C. V5Z 4J4

Pacific Trollers Association Newsletter • (1965) • Monthly, free • Pacific Trollers' Association • Box 94336, Richmond, B.C. • Circ 1,500 • Adv

Pacific Yachting • (1968) • Monthly • OP Publishing Ltd. • 1132 Hamilton St., Ste. 202, Vancouver, B.C. V6B 2S2 • Circ 17,141 • Adv

Paragraphic • (1957) • Quarterly, membership newsletter • Canadian Paraplegic Association, British Columbia Division • 780 S.W. Marine Dr., Vancouver, B.C. V6P 5Y7 • Circ 2,000 • Adv

Partners with Poland • Monthly • 1496 West 72nd Ave., Vancouver, B.C. V6P 3C8 • English news of the Polish community.

Pax Regis • (1942) • Semi-annual • Westminster Abbey Ltd. • Mission, B.C. V2V 4J2 • Circ 1,500 • Articles and news for alumni of the Seminary of Christ the King, and for those interested in Roman Catholic seminary education.

Pazifische Rundschau/Pacific Review • (1965) • Fortnightly • Text in German • Ackermann Advertising and News Service • B.P. 88047, Richmond, B.C. V6X 3T6 • Circ 15,000 • Adv • Newspaper covering German interests.

Peace Arch News • Wednesday and Saturday • 101-1440 George Street, White Rock, B.C. V4B 4A3 • Circ 28,000 • Adv • Community newspaper, distributed free to households in the area.

Peak • (1965) • 39 times a year • Peak Publications Society • Simon Fraser Univ., Burnaby, B.C. V5A 1S6 • Circ 10,000 • Adv • Student newspaper.

Peninsula Prime • (1989) • Monthly • Peace Arch Publications Ltd. • 1335 Johnston Rd., P.O. Box 75149, White Rock, B.C. V4A 9M4 • Circ 27,000

People's Voice • Monthly • 100-1726 East Hastings St., Vancouver, B.C. • Reports of peoples' movements across the country.

Periodico News • Weekly • In Portuguese • P.O. Box 56022, First Ave. Marketplace, Vancouver, B.C. V5M 4S9 • News of Azorean, Portuguese and Brazilian communities.

Pets Quarterly Magazine • (1992) • Quarterly • PQM • 151-8333 Jones Rd., Richmond, B.C. V6Y 1L5 • Paid Circ 38,600 (Controlled Circulation 31,400) • Adv • Features stories and photos on people and their pets. Subjects include training, play, adoption, health and nutrition, grooming, travel.

Philippine Chronicle • Bi-weekly • P.O. Box 41081, Port Coquitlam, B.C. V3C 3G1 • News for and about the overseas Filipino community.

Phulwari • Semi-monthly • Text in English, Punjabi. Phulwari Publications • 14199-72A Ave., Surrey, B.C. V3W 2R2.

Playboard: Professional Stage Magazine • (1967) • Monthly • Arch-Way Publishers Ltd. • 7560 Lawrence Dr., Burnaby, B.C. V5A 1T6 • Circ 50,000 • Adv • Theatre notes.

Popular Lifestyle and Entertainment • Monthly • P.O. Box 32520, Richmond, B.C. V6X 3L7 • Circ 45,000 • In Chinese • Leisure and personality notes with TV listings of Chinese-language television in Vancouver.

Prevention at Work • Quarterly • Workers' Compensation Board, Community Relations Department • 6951 Westminster Hwy., Richmond, B.C. V7C 1C6 • Circ 25,000 • Provides information on policies and operations of the WCB for employers and labor organizations.

Prism International: A Quarterly Journal of Contemporary Writing • (1959) • Quarterly • University of British Columbia, Creative Writing Department • E462-1866 Main Mall, Vancouver, B.C. V6T 1Z1 • E-mail: prism@unixg.ubc.ca • URL: http://www.arts.ubc.ca/crwr/prism/prism.html • Circ 1,100 • Adv

Professional Recreation Society of B.C. Newsletter • (1972) • Bi-monthly • Professional Recreation Society of B.C. • c/o 1600 West Broadway, Vancouver, B.C. V5N 1W1

Property Management News • (1992) • Bi-monthly • K-Rey Publishing Inc. • 789 W. Pender St., Ste. 920, Vancouver, B.C. V6C 1H2 • Circ 8,007 • Adv

Prospector Exploration & Investment Bulletin • (1980) • Six times a year • KW Publishing Ltd. • 1268 W. Pender St., Vancouver, B.C. V6E 2S8 • Circ 25,000 • Adv

Province • (1898) • Daily • Pacific Press, 2250 Granville Street, Vancouver, B.C. V6H 3G2 • URL: http://www.southam.com:80/vancouver-province/ • Circ: 158,500 daily, 192,300 Sunday • Adv • Morning daily English tabloid for Vancouver area.

Quincentario Hispano • Semi-monthly • Text in Spanish • 1836 W. 11th St., Vancouver, B.C. V6J 2C5 • Adv • News of the Spanish speaking world with emphasis on Latin America.

Ralph: Coffee, Jazz and Poetry • (1992) • Monthly • Text in: English, French, Italian • P.O. Box 505, 1288 Broughton St., Vancouver, B.C. V6G 2B5 • E-mail: ralpha6982@aol.com • Circ 3,500 • Featuring the poetry, opinions and reviews of editor Ralph Alfonso. Covers illustrations and themes revolving around Beatnik values of the fifties, sixties and the present.

Ranjeet • Bi-weekly • 6319 Main St., Vancouver, B.C. V5W 2V2 • In Punjabi and English • News of the local Punjabi community.

Recycling Product News • (1992) • Six times a year • Baum Publications Ltd. • 1625 Ingleton Ave., Burnaby, B.C. V5C 4L8 • Circ 15,000 • Adv

The Rez • Quarterly • All Right Production Ltd. • 443 W. 3rd St., N. Vancouver, B.C. V7M 1G9 • Children's magazine.

Richmond News • Wednesday and Sunday • 5731 No. 3 Road, Richmond, B.C. V6X 2C9 • Circ 41,000 • Adv • Suburban community newspaper, distributed free to households in the area.

Richmond Review • Wednesday and Saturday • 120-5851 No. 3 Road, Richmond, B.C. V6X 2C9 • Circ 42,000 • Adv • Community newspaper, distributed free to households in the area.

Robotronics Age Newsletter • (1983) • Monthly • Twenty-First Century Media Communications, Inc. • 548 Cardero St., Vancouver, B.C. V6N 2K3.

Room of One's Own: A Feminist Journal of Literature and Criticism • (1975) • Quarterly • Grow-

After 85 years as a broadsheet newspaper, The Province switched to its smaller and punchier tabloid format on August 2, 1983. In addressing readers at the time, then-publisher Gerald Haslam wrote: "There is nostalgia, some joy, some sadness, and a great sense of anticipation. We are embarking on an adventure filled with excitement."

ing Room Collective • Box 46160, Sta. D, Vancouver, B.C. V6J 5G5 • Paid Circ 1,000 • Adv • Publishes fiction, poetry, essays and reviews by, for and about women.

Rungh: A South Asian Quarterly of Culture, Comment and Criticism • (1993) • Quarterly • English • Rungh Cultural Society • Box 66019, Sta. F, Vancouver, B.C. V5N 1L4 • E-mail: rungh@helix.net•Web-site: http://www.helix .net/rungh • Provides a platform for South Asian writers, artists, musicians and other creative people, cultural administrators and decision-makers to articulate what it means to be South Asian within a Western context.

RV Times • Six times a year • Sheila Jones Publishing Ltd. • 33154 7th Ave., Mission, B.C. V2V 2E1 • Circ 45,000 • Adv • Includes events of interest in B.C. and Washington state, camping stories, repair tips and general RV and camping information.

Sacred Fire • (1990) • Four times a year • P.O. Box 91980, West Vancouver, B.C. V7V 4S4 • Circ 20,000 • Poetry magazine.

Sangharsh • Bi-weekly • In Punjabi and English • 5352 Joyce St., Vancouver, B.C. V5R 4H2 • News of the Punjabi community.

Scarlet & Gold • (1919) • Annual • Scarlet & Gold Enterprises • 1215 Alder Bay Walk, Vancouver, B.C. V6H 3T6 • Circ 2,500 • Adv • Articles about the mounted police, written mainly by veterans.

Sei Pao Monthly • Bi-weekly • Text in Chinese • Richmond Review • 5851 No. 3 Road, Unit 120, Richmond, B.C. V6X 2C9 • Circ 10,000 • Chinese-language newspaper distributed as part of *Richmond Review.*

Seniors Choice • Monthly • 19770-46A Street, Langley, B.C. V3A 3G6 • Circ 15,000

Sentinela • (1972) • Semi-monthly • Text in Portuguese • Box 65532, Station F, Vancouver, B.C. V5N 5K5 • Circ 3,000 • Adv • News of Portuguese-speaking community.

Shared Vision • Monthly • Ryane Publications Group Ltd., 1625 West 15th Ave., Vancouver, B.C. V6J 1N5 • E-mail: publisher@shared-vision.com • URL: http://www.shared-vision.com • New Age magazine. Free at various drop points around the community.

Shore Line • (1976) • Monthly • North Shore Numismatic Society • P.O. Box 86241, North Vancouver, B.C. V7L 4J8

Sing Tao Jih Pao • (1984) • Daily • Text in Chinese • Sing Tao Newspaper (Canada) Ltd. • 549 Main St., Vancouver, B.C. V6A 2V1 • Circ 15,000 • Daily with news from Vancouver and its parent newspaper in Hong Kong.

Single Minded • Bi-monthly • Box 4933, Vancouver, B.C. V6B 4A6 • Life as an unmarried person.

Ski Trails • (1966) • Eight times a year • Raipub Enterprises Ltd. • Suite 8, 2375 York St., Vancou-

ver, B.C. V6K 1C8 • Circ 50,000 • Adv

Slovak Heritage Live • (1993) • Quarterly, membership • Slovak Heritage and Cultural Society of British Columbia • 3804 Yale St., Burnaby, B.C. V5C 1P6 • E-mail: vlinder@direct.ca • Paid Circ 2,200 • Adv

Society of Management Accountants of British Columbia: Update • Bi-monthly, free • Society of Management Accountants of British Columbia • 1575-650 W. Georgia St., Box 11548, Vancouver, B.C. V6B 4W7 • For certified management accountants in British Columbia.

Softball B.C. Magazine: The Voice of the British Columbia Amateur Softball Association • (1980) • Quarterly • Softball British Columbia • P.O. Box 45570 Sunnyside Mall, Surrey, B.C. V4A 9N3 • Circ 7,000 • Adv • Contains membership information and articles of sport-related interest.

Soleil de Colombie • (1968) • Weekly • In French • 1645 W. 5th Ave., Vancouver, B.C. V5N 1S4 • Circ 2,800 • Adv • News about Francophonie in B.C. TV and radio schedules for several French broadcasters.

Sounding Board • (1935) • Monthly, 11 times a year • Board of Trade • World Trade Centre, Ste. 400, 999 Canada Pl., Vancouver, B.C. V6C 3E1 • Circ 12,000 • Adv .

Speak Up! • (1973) • Quarterly • Bible Holiness Movement • Box 223, Sta. A, Vancouver, B.C. V6C 2M3 • Circ 3,000 • Adv

Sportsvue • Weekly, 47 weeks a year • Twenty-first Century Communications • 200-873 Beatty St., Vancouver, B.C. V6B 2M6 • Circ 20,000 • Adv • All-sports weekly.

Sports Only • Weekly • Sports Only, Box 11103, Suite 2103, 1055 West Georgia St., Vancouver, B.C. V6E 3P3 • Adv • All-sports weekly.

Star Serviceman • (1946) • Monthly • Media Public Relations Ltd. • P.O. Box 2929, Vancouver, B.C. • Circ 2,410 • Adv • Veterans' news.

Sub-Terrain • (1988) • Four times a year • Anvil Press Publishers • P.O. Box 1575, Bentall Centre, Vancouver, B.C. V6C 2P7 • E-mail: subter@pic.com • Circ 2,500 • Adv • Provides a varied mix of fiction, poetry, art, photography and some commentary from Canadian, American and international writers and artists.

Supply Post • (1971) • Monthly • Ken Kenward Enterprises Ltd. • 19329 Enterprise Way, No.108, Surrey, B.C. V3S 6J8 • Circ 16,022 • Adv • Forestry magazine.

Surrey/North Delta NOW • Wednesday and Saturday • 201, 7889-132 St., Surrey, B.C. V3W 4N4 • Circ 102,300 • Adv • Suburban community newspaper, distributed free to households in the area.

Swedish Press/Nya Svenska Pressen • (1929) • Monthly • Text in English and Swedish • Swedish Press Inc. • 1294 W. 7th Ave., Vancouver, B.C.

V6H 1B6 • Circ 5,000 • Adv • News of Sweden, the ex-pat Swedish community and Scandanavia.

TV Guide • Weekly • Telemedia West, 300 Southeast Tower., 555 W. 12th Ave., Vancouver, B.C. V5Z 4L4 • Circ 185,000 for B.C. edition • Television magazine with listings and television-related features.

TV Week Magazine • (1976) • Weekly • Canada Wide Magazines Ltd. • 4180 Lougheed Hwy., Ste. 401, Burnaby, B.C. V5C 6A7 • Circ 80,000 • Adv • Television magazine with listings and television-related features.

Teacher • Monthly • B.C. Teachers' Federation • 100-550 W. 6th Ave., Vancouver, B.C. V5Z 4P2 • Newsletter of teachers' professional organization.

Terminal City • Weekly • 2nd Floor, 825 Granville St., Vancouver, B.C. V6Z 1K9 • E-mail: tcmag@vkool.com • Alternative music and entertainment news, and commentary. Free at many drop points around the area.

Thorn • (1983) • Semi-monthly, free • Thorn Publications Association • Box 9030, Kwantlen College, Surrey, B.C. V3T 5H8 • Circ 1,500 • Adv • Student paper.

Today's Times • (1958) • Monthly • Today's Times Publications • 100 Annex, 856 Homer St., Vancouver, B.C. V6B 2W5 • Circ 30,000 • Devoted to news and lifestyle topics aimed at people fifty and older.

Todistaja • In Finnish and Estonian • 1920 Argyle Street, Vancouver, B.C. V6- 2A8 • Circ 1,550 • Finnish Pentacostal Christian newsletter.

Transmitter • (1978) • Six times a year, free • Telecommunications Workers Union • 5261 Lane St., Burnaby, B.C. V5H 4A6 • Circ 13,000 • Telephone union newsletter.

Transportation & Materials Handling • (1975) • Monthly • Triad Publishing Co. Ltd. • 145-892 W. Pender St., Vancouver, B.C. V6C 1J9 • Adv

Tri-City News • (1985) • Wednesday and Sunday • Meadowridge Publications • 1405 Broadway, Port Coquitlam, B.C. V3C 5W9 • Circ 45,458 (controlled) • Adv • Free to households in the Coquitlam, Port Moody, and Port Coquitlam districts.

Truck World & Western Trucking News • (1984) • Monthly • Global Trade Publications Ltd. • 11-106 E. 14th St., North Vancouver, B.C. V7L 2N3 • Circ 30,000

Truck-West • (1975) • Monthly • T. P. Truck Publications Ltd. • 211-20216 Fraser Hwy., Langley, B.C. • Circ 5,000 • Adv • Transport news.

UBC Library News • (1968) • Quarterly, free • University of British Columbia Main Library, Vancouver, B.C. V6T 1Y3 • Circ 3,200

UBC Reports • Bi-weekly • 310-6251 Cecil Green Park Road, UBC, Vancouver, B.C. V6T 1Z1 • Adv • News and reports about UBC.

The spirit of Christmas prompts generosity and few have been more generous than Province readers who have kept The Empty Stocking Fund alive since 1918. Providing assistance at Christmas to families in need, it's now the oldest newspaper-run charity of its kind in Canada. Watch for stories in the paper starting each year in mid-November.

Ubyssey • (1918) • Twice weekly • 6138 SUB Boulevard, UBC, Room 245 K, S.U.B., Vancouver, B.C. V6T 1Z1 • Circ 12,000 • Adv • The student newspaper at UBC.

University of British Columbia Law Review • (1959) • Semi-annual • University of British Columbia Law Review Society, Faculty of Law, Vancouver, B.C. V6T 1Z2 • Circ 900 • Adv • Promotion of legal scholarship, with articles by judges, professors, practising lawyers.

Uptrend: Canadian Penny Market Newsletter • (1979) • Every three weeks • Yorkton Continental Securities Inc. • 1055 Dunsmuir St., 10th Fl., P.O. Box 49333, Bentall Four, Vancouver, B.C. V7X 1L4 • Circ 2,000 • Adv

Vancouver Art Gallery: Quarterly • Four times a year, membership • Vancouver Art Gallery • 750 Hornby St., Vancouver, B.C. V6Z 2H7 • Bulletin providing a schedule of events and exhibitions at the gallery.

Vancouver Buy and Sell Press • (1971) • Twice weekly • Buy and Sell Press • 350 Columbia Street, New Westminster, B.C. V3L 1A6 • Free Ad Line 604-280-1000 • URL: http://www.buy-sell.com • Circ 49,500 • Adv • Free classfied advertising, tabloid form.

Vancouver Courier • Twice weekly • 1574 West 6th Ave., Vancouver, B.C. V6J 1R2 • Circ 101,000 Sunday; 45,000 Wednesday • Adv • Suburban community newspaper, distributed free to households in the area.

Vancouver Magazine • (1968) • Monthly • Telemedia West • 300 Southeast Tower., 555 W. 12th Ave., Vancouver, B.C. V5Z 4L4 • Circ 70,000 • Adv • City lifestyle magazine; newsstand sales, and distributed free to certain areas.

Vancouver Prospector • (1988) • Monthly • Vancouver Prospector, Inc. • Box 3169, Blaine, WA 98230 • Covers speculative Vancouver stocks, especially penny and junior precious metals mining stocks poised for over 200 per cent profits in one to two years.

Vancouver Review • Quarterly • 2-8763 Ashgrove Crescent, Burnaby, B.C. V5A 4B8 • E-mail: vr@portal.ca • A literary magazine of "new writing," commentaries, reviews and essays.

Vancouver Stock Exchange Review • (1960) • Monthly • Vancouver Stock Exchange • Stock Exchange Tower, P.O. Box 10333, 609 Granville St., Vancouver, B.C. V7Y 1H1 • Circ 2,000 • Provides a summary of trading in equities and options. Includes trading statistics and cumulative figures, listing changes, financings and related topics.

Vancouver Studies in Cognitive Science • Irregular • (Simon Fraser University) • Oxford University Press • Walton St., Oxford OX2 6DP, England.

Vancouver Sun • (1886) • Daily • Pacific Press, 2250 Granville St., Vancouver, B.C. V6H 3G2 •

URL: http://www.southam.com:80/vancouversun/ • Circ: 252,00 daily, 253,000 Saturday • Adv • Morning daily English broadsheet for Vancouver area.

Voice • Weekly, September to April • Langara College, Journalism Department • Langara, 100 W. 49th Ave., Vancouver, B.C. V5Y 2Z6 • Circ 1,000 • Student news and writings.

Voice of Choice • Quarterly • Bible Holiness Movement, Religious Freedom Council of Christian Minorities • Box 223, Station A, Vancouver, B.C. V6C 2M3

WCEL News • (1977) • Bi-weekly • West Coast Environmental Law Research Foundation • 1001-207 W. Hastings, Vancouver, B.C. V6B 1H7 • Circ 600

WCRA News • (1961) • Monthly • West Coast Railway Association • Box 2790, Vancouver, B.C. V6B 3X2 • Circ 500 • Provides updates on association activities, rail stories of interest, rail travel and tours.

WIDHH News • (1967) • Quarterly, membership • Western Institute for the Deaf and Hard of Hearing • 2125 W. 7th Ave., Vancouver, B.C. V6K 1X9 • Circ 1,050 • Adv

Wandering Volhynians: A Magazine for the Descendants of Germans from Volhynia and Poland • Quarterly • Wandering Volhynian Group • 3492 W. 39th Ave., Vancouver, B.C. V6N 3A2 • Circ 600

Wargamer • (1973) • Bi-monthly • 8635 Gilley Ave., Burnaby, B.C. V5J 4Z1 • Circ 100

Watan • Quarterly • In Punjabi • P.O. Box 27132, Collingwood P.O., Vancouver, B.C. V5R 6A8 • Punjabi news.

Weekly Stock Charts-Canadian Industrial Companies • (1965) • Monthly • Independent Survey Co. Ltd. • P.O. Box 6000, Vancouver, B.C. V6B 4B9

Weekly Stock Charts-Canadian Resource Companies • (1965) • Monthly • Independent Survey Co. Ltd. • P.O. Box 6000, Vancouver, B.C. V6B 4B9 • Two-and-a-half-year record of weekly share price and volume for 1,200 Canadian resource companies.

West Coast Libertarian • (1978) • Bi-monthly • Greater Vancouver Libertarian Association • 922 Cloverley St., North Vancouver, B.C. V7L 1N3 • E-mail: lux-lucre@mindlink.bc.ca • Circ 300

West Coast Line: A Journal of Contemporary Writing and Criticism • (1966) • Three times a year • Simon Fraser University, West Coast Review Publishing Society • 2027 E. Academic Annex, Simon Fraser University, Burnaby, B.C. V5A 1S6 • Circ 750 • Adv • Contains contemporary poetry, fiction, essays, reviews of modern literature. International in scope but emphasis is on Canadian writing.

West End Times • Weekly • 201-1155 Robson

St., Vancouver, B.C. V6E 1B5 • Adv • Suburban community newspaper, distributed free to households in the area.

West Ender / Kitsilano News • (1923) • Weekly, free • Trinity Holdings, 103-2145 West Broadway, Vancouver, B.C. V6K 4L3 • Circ 59,000 • Suburban community newspaper, distributed free to households in the area. Also free at various drop points about the area.

West Side Revue • Bi-weekly • 1736 East 33rd Ave., Apt A, Vancouver, B.C. • Circ 7,500 • Adv • Suburban community newspaper, distributed free to households in the area. Also free at various points about the area.

Westbridge Art Market Report: The Newsletter for Fine Art Collectors and Investors • (1974) • Bi-monthly • Westbridge Publications Ltd. • 2339 Granville St., Vancouver, B.C. V6H 3G4 • Circ 500 • Adv

Westcoast Fisherman • (1986) • Monthly • Westcoast Publishing Ltd. • 1496 W. 72nd Ave., Vancouver, B.C. V6P 3C8 • Circ 12,000 • Adv • News for coast commercial fishers.

Westcoast Mariner • (1986) • Monthly • Westcoast Publishing Ltd. • 1496 W. 72nd Ave., Vancouver, B.C. V6P 3C8 • Circ 11,000 • Adv • For skippers and crews who work the Pacific Coast.

Western Canadian Lumber Worker • (1939) • Monthly • International Woodworkers of America • 1285 W. Pender St., 500, Vancouver, B.C. V6E 4B2 • Circ 34,000 • Adv • Union news.

Western Living • (1971) • 10 times a year • Telemedia West • 300 Southeast Tower., 555 W. 12th Ave., Vancouver, B.C. V5Z 4L4 • Circ 252,000 • Lifestyle magazine: home design, food, fashion, travel and recreation; distributed free to certain districts.

Western Star • Bi-weekly, free • In Chinese and English • 110- 2268 No. 5 Road, Richmond, B.C. • Adv • Suburban community newspaper, free at many drop points around the area.

Westworld British Columbia • Quarterly • Canada Wide Magazines Ltd. • 4180 Lougheed Hwy., Ste. 401, Burnaby, B.C. V5C 6A7 • Circ 450,000 • Magazine published on behalf of the B.C. Automobile Association. Features automative-related tips; club news; national and international travel articles.

Where Vancouver • (1969) • Monthly • Where Canada, Inc. • (Subsidiary of: Where Magazines International) • The Sixth Estate, 2208 Spruce St., Vancouver, B.C. V6H 2P3 • E-mail: 766312,716@compuserve.com • Circ 39,000 • News for tourists and visitors with articles about where to dine and shop. Found in hotels and tourist information offices.

Wildlife Rescue • (1979) • Quarterly, membership • Wildlife Rescue Association of British Columbia • 5216 Glencarin Dr., Burnaby, B.C.

V5B 3C1 • Circ 1,500 • Reviews the organization's activities in wildlife rehabilitation and education.

Windmill Herald: Western Edition • (1958) • Fortnightly • Text in Dutch and English • Vanderheide Publishing Co. Ltd., • P.O. Bag 9033, Surrey, B.C. V3T 4X3 • News and views from the Netherlands and ex-pat Dutch communities.

Women's Chronicle • (1989) • Six times a year • West Coast Women's Chronicle Inc. • 1120 Hamilton St., Ste. 206, Vancouver, B.C. V6B 2S2 • Circ 25,000 • Adv

Working Teacher • (1977) • Quarterly • Working Teacher Educational Society • Box 46534, Sta. G, 3760 W. 10th Ave., Vancouver, B.C. V6R 4G8

World Journal • Daily • In Chinese • 157 East Pender St., Vancouver, B.C. V6A 1S9 • Circ 10,000 • Adv • News from Vancouver and parent newspaper in Taipei.

World Market Perspective • (1968) • Monthly • ERC Publishing Co. • 210-1760 Marine Drive, West Vancouver, B.C. V7V 1J4 • Circ 12,000 • Business investment magazine.

World of Chabad • (1987) • Bi-monthly • Text in English, Hebrew, Russian • Lubavitch British Columbia • 5750 Oak St., Vancouver, B.C. V6M 2V9 • Circ 6,000 • Jewish religious and philosophical articles, stories and announcements.

Writing • (1980) • Three times a year • Box 69609, Station K, Vancouver, B.C. V5K 4W7 • Circ 750 • A journal of socially committed and experimental poetry and fiction from Canada, the United States and Great Britain.

XTRA West • Bi-weekly • Box 93642, Nelson Park P.O., Vancouver, B.C. V6E 4L7 • 1033 Davie St., Suite 5U • E-mail: xtrawest@web.net • Circ 27,500 • News of the gay and lesbian community. Free at many drop points around the area.

YMCA Weekly News • (Vancouver) • Vancouver Downtown Young Men's Christian Association • 955 Burrard St., Vancouver, B.C. V6Z 1Y2 • Circ 1,000

Your Health • (1918) • Semi-annual, free • British Columbia Lung Association • 2675 Oak St., Vancouver, B.C. V6H 2K2 • Circ 19,500 • Respiratory disease news.

Zhen Fo Bao/True Buddha News • (1991) • Semi-monthly • Text in Chinese • True Buddha Publication • 357 East Hasting St. Ste 200, Vancouver, B.C. V6A 1P3 • (Subscr. to: P.O. Box 88180, CPO, Vancouver, B.C. V6A 4A5) • Circ 210,000 • News and views of a Buddhist group. Found free at various drop points about the area..

TELEVISION STATIONS IN GREATER VANCOUVER
The TV stations below are arranged by their broadcast channels. But as more than 90 per cent of Greater Vancouver is connected to community antennas (Cable-TV), the cable companies move

some channels around to bring UHF channels to VHF channels. The cable companies also broadcast their own community-based programs. Various regions have different cable companies with slightly different programs and cable channel arrangements. Check TV listings in newspapers or specialty magazines for the relevant information..

CBUT-TV • Channel 2 • Regional station of the Canadian Broadcasting Corporation • CBC building, 700 Hamilton St., Vancouver, B.C. V6B 2R5 • URL: http://www.cbc.ca/ • (Many rebroadcast antennas around the province; also on satellite.)

CHAN-TV "BCTV" • Channel 8 • A member of the CTV network • British Columbia Television Broadcasting System Ltd. • 7850 Enterprise St., Burnaby, B.C. V5A 1V7 • URL: http://tv.bc.sympatico.ca/ • (Many rebroadcast antennas around the province; also on satellite.)

CKVU-TV "U.Tv" • Channel 21 • A member of the Canwest Global network • Canwest Pacific Television Inc. • 180 West 2nd Ave., Vancouver, B.C. V5Y 3T9

CBUFT • Channel 26 • The regional station of the Societé Radio-Canada (French-language network of CBC) • CBC building, 700 Hamilton St., Vancouver, B.C. V6B 2R5 • URL: http://www. cbc.ca/ • (In French) • (Many rebroadcast antennas around the province; also on satellite.)

OTHER TV CHANNELS DIRECTED AT GREATER VANCOUVER
KVOS "TV Twelve" • Channel 12 • KVOS-TV Inc. • 1151 Ellis St., Bellingham, Washington 98225 • Canadian office at: 1764 West 7th Ave., Vancouver, B.C. V6J 5A3

TELEVISION FROM VANCOUVER ON COMMUNITY CABLE
Channel 4 is the community station of the cable companies. Central offices are:

Rogers Cablesystems Ltd. • 1600-4710 Kingsway, Vancouver, B.C. V5H 4M5

Shaw Cable • 1471 Pemberton, North Vancouver, B.C.

Delta Cable Television • 5381 Ladner Trunk Road, Ladner, B.C.

Pacific Place Communications Ltd. • 289 Drake St., Vancouver, B.C.

TELEVISION ONLY ON CABLE
Fairchild Television Ltd. • 525 West Broadway, Suite B-8, Vancouver, B.C. V5Z 4K5 • URL: http://www.ftv.com/ • (In Chinese, predominantly in Cantonese, some Mandarin.)

Talent Tv • 525 West Broadway, Suite B-8, Vancouver, B.C. V5Z 4K5 • URL: http://www.ftv.com/talent/ (In Asian languages, predominantly Cantonese.)

Multicultural Television • 1600 - 4710 Kingsway, Vancouver, B.C. V5H 4M5.

Knowlege Network • Part of B.C. Open Learning Agency • 4355 Mathissi Place, Burnaby, B.C. V5G

4S8 (Teaching programs or programs that instruct for the Open Learning Agency and its institute and university.)

AM RADIO IN GREATER VANCOUVER
Many stations are on community television cable, shifted to an FM frequency by the cable company.

CKBD "The Bridge" • 600 kHz • A division of Great Pacific Industries • 1401 West 8th Ave., Vancouver, B.C. V6H 1C9 • Format: contemporary Christian.

CISL "C-Isle" • 650 kHz • A division of Standard Broacasting of Toronto • 20-11151 Horseshoe Way, Richmond, B.C. V7A 4S5 • URL: http://www.650cisl.com:80/index.html • Format: oldies, early rock.

CBU • 690 kHz • Regional station of the Canadian Broadcasting Corporation • CBC building, 700 Hamilton St., Vancouver, B.C. V6B 2R5 • URL: http://www.cbc.ca • Format: public affairs, music.

CKLG "LG 73" • 730 kHz • Shaw Radio Limited • 1006 Richards St., Vancouver, B.C. V6B 1S8 • Format: adult contemporary.

CKNW • 980 kHz • A division of Westcom Radio Group Ltd. • 2000-700 West Georgia St., Vancouver, B.C. V7Y 1K9 • URL: http://www. cknw. com • Format: news, talk.

CKST "Coast Radio" • 1040 kHz • Radio One Vancouver Corp. • 101-856 Homer St., Vancouver, B.C. V6B 2W5 • URL: http://www. am1040.com/ • Format: adult pop, variety, conversation.

CKWX • 1130 kHz • Rogers Broadcasting • 2440 Ash St., Vancouver, B.C. V5Z 4J6. • Format: news.

CHMB • 1320 kHz • Mainstream Broadcasting Corporation • 1200 West 73rd Ave., Suite 100, Vancouver, B.C. V6P 6G5 • URL: http://www.1320.com/ • Format: multilingual, multicultural.

CFUN • 1410 kHz • CHUM Western Ltd., Toronto • 300-380 West 2nd Ave., Vancouver, B.C. V56 1C8 • URL: http://www.cfun.com/ • Format: talk radio.

CJVB • 1470 kHz • Y.B.C. Holdings Ltd. • 101-814 Richards St., Vancouver, B.C. V6B 3A7 • Format: multilingual, multicultural.

AM STATIONS TARGETED AT GREATER VANCOUVER
KARI • 550 kHz • 5,000 watts • Box 75150 White Rock, B.C., V4A 9M4 • Blaine, Washington • Format: gospel, Christian music .

CKMA "Radio Max" • 850 kHz • 10,000 watts • Fraser Valley Radio Group • 2722 Allwood St., Abbotsford, B.C. V2T 3R8 • Format: carries play-by-play of the Vancouver Canadians baseball team as well as rock music.

SHORTWAVE
CKZU • 6160 kHz • 0.3 kilowatts • Regional station of the Canadian Broadcasting Corporation • CBC building, 700 Hamilton St., Vancouver, B.C. V6B 2R5 • Format: public affairs, music (rebroad-

---

Known for its irreverent, if not cheeky style, The Province newspaper has often delivered a belly laugh with its headlines. Some of the more memorable ones: See Expo and Di, (as in Diana, then Princess of Wales), Has Bins (on goodwill boxes being removed from grocery store lots), and the unforgettable Top Red Dead (on the death of Konstantin Chernenko, Soviet communist party secretary).

Graphic Artist, Vancouver Sun, 1993. vs

The Georgia Straight
Mark Leiren-Young

When the *Georgia Straight* hit the streets in 1967, Mayor Tom Campbell was determined to shut it down. Twenty years later, as the paper celebrated the release of its 1,000th issue, Mayor Gordon Campbell (no relation) declared May 5, 1987, *"Georgia Straight* Day."

It was quite the trip for Canada's original counterculture newspaper, which was dreamt up by a group of artists and poets (including publisher Dan McLeod) following a poetry reading by Leonard Cohen at the University of British Columbia. The name was chosen because marine forecasts were constantly referring to gale force winds from the Georgia Strait and the founders thought it couldn't hurt to get a free plug on every weather report.

Originally focussing on news written by and for Vancouver's "hippies," the paper outraged strait-laced Mayor Campbell who (with the help of the Vancouver Police Department) kept looking for new ways to close the *Straight* down, including criminal charges of obscenity, gross misconduct and "inciting to commit an indictable offense" (for an article on how to grow marijuana). The *Georgia Straight* fought the charges successfully (winning all their legal appeals), became a genuine 1960s phenomenon and responded to Campbell's attacks by once jokingly adding his name to their masthead as "Advertising Manager."

In the mid-seventies the *Straight* began a long struggle to redefine itself, eventually evolving into an entertainment publication focusing on music and movies. The *Straight* shifted direction again with the hiring of Charles Campbell (no relation to either Tom or Gordon) as managing editor in 1986. Under Campbell's guidance, the *Straight* expanded their coverage to focus on the entire arts and cultural scene. In 1991 it added news coverage and in-depth investigative feature stories.

With the hippie past a distant memory and circulation up to 100,000 the *Straight* (which is still published by founder Dan McLeod despite assorted attempted coups and buy-out offers) has become one of the most respected publications in Canada, winning dozens of national and regional magazine awards and maintaining a roster of contributors that reads like a who's who of B.C. journalists.

casts the AM network).

CKFX • 6080 kHz • 0.01 kilowatts • Rogers Broadcasting • 2440 Ash St., Vancouver, B.C. V5Z 4J6 • Format: news (rebroadcasts CKWX). The status of CKFX was unclear. The station was not on the air at this writing..

FM RADIO IN GREATER VANCOUVER

CFOX-FM • 93.3 MHz • 100,000 watts • Shaw Radio Limited • 1006 Richards St., Vancouver, B.C. V6B IS8 • URL: http://www.cfox.com/ • Format: rock.

CJJR-FM • 93.7 MHz • 75,000 watts • A division of Great Pacific Industries • 1401 West 8th Ave., Vancouver, B.C. V6H 1C9 • Format: new country.

CJSF • 93.9 MHz (Cable only) • 20 watts • Radio Simon Fraser • TC 216, Simon Fraser University, Burnaby, B. C. V5A 1S6 • Format: alternative rock. (A very low-power station heard only on cable outside of SFU housing; shifted to another frequency by the cable company.)

CKZZ "Z-95" • 95.3 MHz • 70,000 watts • A division of Standard Broacasting of Toronto • 20-11151 Horseshoe Way, Richmond, B.C. V7A 4S5 • Format: contemporary hit radio.

CKKS-FM "Kiss-FM" • 96.9 MHz •100,000 watts • Rogers Broadcasting • 2440 Ash St., Vancouver, B.C. V5Z 4J6 • Format: adult contemporary, soft hits.

CBUF-FM • 97.7 MHz (many repeaters around the province) • 50,000 watts • Regional station of the Société Radio-Canada (French-language network of CBC) • CBC building, 700 Hamilton St., Vancouver, B.C. V6B 2R5 • URL: http://www.cbc.ca/ • Format: public affairs, music.

CFMI-FM "Rock 101" • 101.1 MHz • 100,000 watts • A division of Westcom Radio Group Ltd. (WIC, Western International Communications Co.) • 2000-700 West Georgia St., Vancouver, B.C. V7Y 1K9 • URL: http://www.rock101.com/ • Format: classic rock.

CITR-FM • 101.9 MHz • 1,800 watts • 6138 SUB Boulevard, UBC, Vancouver, B.C. V6T 1Z1 • Format: alternative rock. (A very low-power station best heard on cable; shifted to another frequency by the cable company.)

CFRO-FM "Co-op Radio" • 102.7 MHz • 5500 watts • Vancouver Cooperative Radio • 337 Carrall St., Vancouver, B.C. V6B 2J4 • URL: http://www.vcn.ca/cfro/ • Format: varied; community and listener-supported radio.

CHQM-FM • 103.5 MHz • 100,000 watts • CHUM Western Ltd, Toronto • 300-380 West 2nd Ave., Vancouver, B.C. V56 1C8 • URL: http://www.chqm.com/ • Format: adult contemporary.

CFML-FM • 104.5 MHz • 20 Watts (at BCIT only) • CFML, BCIT: 3700 Willingdon St., Burnaby, B.C. V5G 3H2 • Format: adult contemporary, news.

CBU-FM • 105.3 MHz (many repeaters around the province) • 50,000 watts • Regional station of the Canadian Broadcasting Corporation • CBC building, 700 Hamilton St., Vancouver, B.C. V6B 2R5 • URL: http://www.cbc.ca/ • Format: public affairs, music.

FM STATIONS TARGETED AT GREATER VANCOUVER

KISM-FM • 92.1 MHz • 2219 Yew St., Bellingham, Washington

KLYN-FM • 106.5 MHz • Lynden, Washington • Format: contemporary Christian.

SUBCARRIER AUDIO RADIO.
Coded radio broadcast; requires a decoding radio set.

Radio Pabla Akashwani • 305-6569 Main St., Vancouver, B.C. • Format: Punjabi and Hindi-language music and news.

Radio Sangeet Sagar • 104-8334 128 St., Surrey, B.C. V3W 4G2 • Format: Punjabi and Hindi- language programs and music.

Are you someone who likes to read the back page first? That's not a problem with The Province. Since 1993, the popular tabloid has sported two front pages every day. The front of the paper features top news stories. Flip it over and the front page of Sports is the back page of the paper.

Transportation

Transportation—really our ability to get about—embraces both the best and worst aspects of life in Vancouver. Some things work wonderfully, even blissfully, well. Others are the pits. Consider the contrasts:

Walk or ride a bike on a summer evening around Stanley Park; board a SeaBus for a quick, comfortable trip across Burrard Inlet; make an efficient journey by SkyTrain from downtown Vancouver to New Westminster; fly on a float plane or helicopter from Coal Harbour to Victoria; cross False Creek on a tiny, bobbing ferry to shop Granville Island; ride a gondola up Grouse Mountain; pass swiftly through the Canada Place cruise ship terminal on your way to Alaska. Transportation is rarely as enjoyable; it doesn't get much better than this. (Perhaps a crowded SkyTrain isn't much fun, but it's efficient.)

But think too about highway and bridge congestion; the weary, frustrating, exhaust-choking hours drivers waste in traffic; motorists whose manners worsen each year, increasing numbers of whom routinely shoot red lights, execute illegal and hazardous U-turns and give the finger to other drivers whose conduct, however innocently, earns their censure. Behavioral scientists must have a ball observing the effect of highway stress. Think also of the hours people spend hanging about in the rain for buses that never seem to come. This unremitting daily tension, along with unhealthy, smelly automobile smog, is arguably the worst aspect of life in Vancouver.

There's an irony when Vancouverites fondly recall the success of Expo 86 an international showcase dedicated to transportation and related technologies. Greater Vancouver has since grown enormously, both in terms of population and the physical infrastructure that accommodates an expanding economy. But, while the past 25 years have seen the introduction of SkyTrain and SeaBus, the construction of the Arthur Laing, Alex Fraser and SkyTrain bridges and articulated buses, automobile congestion with its attendant air pollution is getting worse.

For a city with world-class aspirations Greater Vancouver's public transportation is woefully bad. Consider the excellent subway systems in London or Toronto or, better still, those operating in Hong Kong or Singapore. SkyTrain, an efficient people mover, offers only a fraction of the route system a vigorously expanding city requires.

Urban planning commentators frequently contrast Canadian cities with those to the south of us and argue how Toronto and Montreal and Vancouver have been spared the intrusive mid-city freeways which isolate communities. Obviously the answer to Vancouver's transportation problems isn't to increase the number of vehicles on our highways. They must be reduced by a combination of incentives and penalties: car pools, higher parking costs and so on. But commuters will never abandon the automobile unless they can depend on frequent and efficient public conveyance. A bus an hour when it's pouring down in November doesn't cut it.

Vancouver still fails to exploit its easy water access for the benefit of commuters. SeaBus has demonstrated how an efficient passenger ferry system can move large numbers of people efficiently and pleasantly between the downtown business district and the north shore. We need more. Why can't a similar publicly owned ferry system operate a fast service between the rapidly expanding City of Coquitlam at the eastern end of Burrard Inlet and downtown Vancouver? It's been tried privately, but the experiment didn't last long. It needs, at least initially, the backing of a publicly owned corporation. Once proven, the system could eventually be expanded to link the increasing population of the Sunshine Coast with downtown Vancouver.

Look to Hong Kong to see how an efficient ferry system can serve the needs of a major city.

—Jim Lyon

Lions Gate bridge, 1981. vp
facing page: SkyTrain bridge, New Westminster, 1990. vs

Railways

FIRST RUN ACROSS CANADA JULY 4, 1886

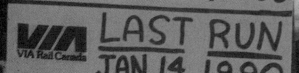

FIRST RUN 'The Canadian' APRIL 24, 1955

LAST RUN JAN. 14, 1990

Since the late 1800s, the rugged beauty of Western Canada has made travel from the Rocky Mountains to the coastal city of Vancouver one of the world's most impressive train trips. In order to attract travellers from around the world, railway companies constructed magnificent hotels to provide natural stopping points along the way.

Railways in Greater Vancouver
David Mitchell

VANCOUVER HAS ALWAYS been a railway town. This crucial fact may not be so apparent to residents of the city today, but it is no exaggeration to say that without railways there never would have been a Vancouver.

In the 19th century the European invention of the steam engine and the innovation of railroads radically changed ideas about travel. Both time and distances were dramatically abbreviated by the revolutionary process of laying steel rails upon the ground and running engines upon them, hauling both passengers and freight at then unimaginable speeds. When this new technology was transferred to North America, a young continent still in the early stages of European settlement, it held the promise of forging new lines of communication as well as new nations.

Indeed it was railways moving westward that gave rise to the dream of creating a transcontinental nation stretching from the Atlantic to the Pacific. That dream would be aggressively realized, first by the United States of America. Could it be repeated by the sparsely settled British colonies to the north? Most everyone agreed that only a transcontinental railway, linking the new Canadian confederation in the east with the small west coast colonies of Vancouver Island and British Columbia, could make such a bold dream come true. But that seemed extremely unlikely at the time.

In 1867, the year Canada was born, the United States purchased Alaska from Russia. More than simply a coincidence, this remarkable concurrence of events highlighted just how vulnerable British Columbia was, sandwiched now between American territories on the Pacific. Canada was a remote and fledgling nation of three and a half million souls on the other side of the continent. The United States, on the other hand, was rapidly emerging as a powerhouse, with a swelling population of more than 40 million and apparently intent on fulfilling its Manifest Destiny of incorporating all of North America within its boundaries. British Columbia at the time was a small cluster of frontier outposts with a non-native population of fewer than 10,000. Increasingly the colony found its trade and livelihood within the American orbit—its eventual absorption

facing page: top; Last run of "the Canadian", CN Station, Vancouver, 1990. rw

bottom; The CPR's chateau–style station (1898–99) and its neoclassical–style replacement (1912–14), Cordova Street, Vancouver. cva

into the United States seemed inevitable.

But it was not to be. Canada's "Fathers of Confederation" and British statesmen of the era conspired to frustrate what seemed like an insatiable appetite for territorial expansion on the part of the Americans. And, while immediate consolidation of half a continent was highly unlikely, events unfolded more quickly than almost anyone thought possible. Canada's first prime minister, John A. Macdonald, was criticized at the time for his bold ambition. However, he justified his plans for westward expansion: "I would be quite willing personally to leave the whole country a wilderness for the next half-century, but I fear if Englishmen do not go there, Yankees will."

In 1868 the British parliament passed an act allowing for the liquidation of the rights of the Hudson's Bay Company and the transfer to Canada of the huge area known as Rupert's Land (basically what today comprises the three prairie provinces and the Northwest Territories). In 1869 a new governor of British Columbia was appointed with explicit instructions to clear the way for the colony's entry into Canadian confederation. In 1870 British Columbia agreed upon the terms of union and sent a delegation to Ottawa to negotiate. They hoped to receive a commitment for a wagon road to be built from Canada, across the prairies, through the mountains and, eventually, to the Pacific Coast. They returned home triumphantly with a promise of a railway linking them ultimately to the Atlantic seaboard. The agreement was ratified by the colony in 1871, when British Columbia officially became a Canadian province.

A second transcontinental nation had been formed. It was, however, a tenuous union that defied both geography and economics. Only a railway, it seemed, could truly fulfil the promise of a new nation. But no one knew exactly what route such a rail line would follow or, indeed, if its construction over the immense western terrain was even feasible.

The challenges and difficulties which this project encountered were truly Herculean. The final terms of union with British Columbia stated that Canada would complete construction of the railway within a decade. But it was not to be. Opponents of the idea thought it more than simply impractical, they called it a "preposterous proposition" and an act of "insane recklessness." An exhaustive survey of potential routes through the mountains commenced and a half-hearted start on construction was made, but the project was stalled, first by political scandal, and then by economic recession. When it became clear that the railroad would not be completed on schedule, some British Columbians began to agitate for secession from Canada. In time, however, the remarkable feat of engineering and construction would be completed, but at great

So successful were these trains and hotels that, in some areas, entire communities developed to accommodate the number of tourists pouring off the trains. Years later, the advent of mass airline and automobile travel created strong competition for slower-paced train travel. Frequent train departures and a thriving network of lines became things of the past. Before long, the thunderous trains which had developed and brought wealth to the frontier had all but vanished from the western Canadian landscape.

cost of both money and human life.

One of the most significant debates of this era revolved around the difficult question of where the railroad company—the Canadian Pacific Railway—would locate its western terminus. As the rail line moved toward completion during the 1880s, this controversy fuelled hopes, dreams and rampant real estate speculation. Victoria and New Westminster were the only communities of any significance in British Columbia at the time. However, neither of them was deemed suitable for the CPR terminus. Several different locations along the Pacific Coast were considered before it was generally agreed that the railway would end at Burrard Inlet.

At first Burrard Inlet was synonymous with Port Moody, causing the small settlement at the head of the harbor to boom. But the CPR was anxious to develop a sizable new townsite as well as an ocean seaport to tap the lucrative trade with the Orient. In 1881 a CPR engineer visited the area and, in a secret report to railway headquarters, suggested that Port Moody was too cramped and lacked the deep-water anchorage required for a large port. An area farther to the west was recommended, at Granville (Gastown). Over the next couple of years the CPR shrewdly developed a plan to locate the railway terminus at either Coal Harbour or Kitsilano.

Of course there was no Vancouver yet. There were a couple of sawmills located on the shores of Burrard Inlet and a few hundred residents living in a rough and tumble setting variously referred to as Coal Harbour, Gastown or Granville. This crude frontier society was the nucleus of the future Vancouver.

As the railroad crept across the country, the CPR routinely decided on the location of towns and consolidated its position as a major landowner in each of them. This was a consequence of generous grants of property along the rail line's right-of-way. However, since the official Pacific terminus was to be at Port Moody, the railway's property entitlements from the government of Canada ended there. As a result, the CPR secretly entered into negotiations with the provincial government of British Columbia for Crown land on Burrard peninsula. An initial request for 4,452 hectares was rejected, but a counter-offer of 2,428 hectares was agreed upon, subject to an extension of the rail line from Port Moody to a new CPR terminus "in the immediate vicinity of Coal Harbour and English Bay." Very quietly railway executives began to plan a new city, which they decided should be named "Vancouver." The CPR would become the dominant private landowner in the new townsite which, at the time, was heavily wooded and almost bereft of settlement.

Naturally Port Moody residents and landowners were out-

raged when the decision was announced to move the terminus nearly 20 kilometres west. Civic pride was wounded and personal fortunes were lost on speculation. The rail line was completed to Port Moody on November 5, 1885—the seemingly impossible connection between Eastern Canada and the Pacific Coast was finally a reality. But it would take another year and a half to construct the extension to Vancouver. Why? Aggrieved and persistent Port Moody landowners sought an injunction preventing the CPR from crossing their lands. The Supreme Court of Canada eventually decided in favor of the railway and construction was allowed to proceed. On May 23, 1887, the first passenger train from Montreal arrived in Vancouver, heralded by a huge throng of people including civic dignitaries and CPR officials. The city would never look back.

For its first few decades Vancouver boomed as a company town. The influence of the CPR was everywhere evident. In addition to holding a monopoly on the city's rail connections with the rest of the continent, the CPR passenger station dominated the waterfront. The original Hotel Vancouver, the city's first opera house and a number of other edifices and amenities were built and owned by the railway company, which was by far the city's largest employer. A CPR land agent laid out the streets of downtown Vancouver in the 1880s, with several of them named after railway officials such as Abbott, Cambie, Hamilton and Beatty. Thomas Shaughnessy, who later rose to the position of CPR president, had an entire exclusive residential district named after him. The CPR earned a good return on all of its investments, including railways, shipping services, telegraphs, hotels and real estate. It is no wonder that early residents of the city were reputed to have remarked: "The government? The CPR's the government here!"

A little-known fact is that Vancouver's downtown core was not necessarily destined to be situated where it is today. Right from the outset, CPR officials were interested in building a branch line to English Bay and, with a bridge across False Creek, there was a vision of a large urban centre to be developed where Kitsilano is now located. Imagine massive wharves, industrial terminals and large grain elevators on the shores of Kitsilano beach with downtown skyscrapers sprawling towards Point Grey. It would have meant a very different Vancouver. Two key factors, however, dissuaded the CPR from pursuing this vision. First, the Coal Harbour site worked well from the outset and initial concerns about the First Narrows being too constricted for ocean-going vessels entering Burrard Inlet were unfounded. Secondly, a serious economic depression in the 1890s forced a temporary halt to further expansion via the English Bay branch line.

Then in 1988 VIA Rail Canada, the federally-owned national passenger-train carrier began a daylight service through the Rockies to capture the international tourism market which continued to thrive in Western Canada. Their efforts were met with less than expected results and the service was subsequently privatized.

Locomotive No. 374 arrives with the first passenger train from Montreal, 23 May 1887 (the engine is preserved at the Roundhouse Community Centre, Pacific Boulevard). cva

In spite of minor setbacks caused by the boom-and-bust nature of British Columbia's resource-based economy, Vancouver continued to grow and the CPR thrived with it. By the early years of the 20th century the city was becoming much less of a company town and more an emerging metropolis characterized by a diversified service sector economy. With a population of 38,000 in 1904, Vancouver was already the largest city in British Columbia and was growing at a rate of 20 per cent annually. And the CPR, with a near monopoly of rail transportation, had become highly unpopular. This provided an incentive for both civic and provincial governments to encourage competition.

Vancouver had a street railway in operation ever since 1890 and, shortly thereafter, an interurban line to New Westminster provided a popular service. With the aid of British capital, these services were amalgamated under the B.C. Electric Railway Company, which built numerous streetcar lines into new residential areas. Fairview, Kitsilano, Mount Pleasant and Grandview all had B.C. Electric streetcar service by 1907, as did North Vancouver, where streetcars ran from the ferry terminal up Lonsdale Avenue. In Vancouver B.C. Electric often used CPR rail lines, and the companies worked together close-

In 1990, a local tourism maverick and former motorcoach CEO, Peter Armstrong, created a team of tourism railway executives to form the privately-owned Great Canadian Railtour Company Ltd. Together they represented more than 120 years of combined railway experience. They set forth a vision to bring back the golden age of the passenger train in Western Canada.

ly to prevent other railways from entering their market.

The CPR actually lost its transcontinental rail monopoly in 1904, when the first bridge over the Fraser River at New Westminster was built. This enabled the Vancouver, Westminster and Yukon Railway to provide a link to the United States via the Great Northern's line (today Burlington Northern). The VW&YR trains entered Vancouver on a line north of B.C. Electric's New Westminster interurban, crossed False Creek on a trestle near Main Street, with a terminus in Chinatown at the corner of East Pender and Columbia.

After 1915 the CPR was no longer the sole Canadian transcontinental railway serving Vancouver. In that year the Canadian Northern Railway completed its rail line and its first through train from the east arrived in Vancouver on August 28. The CPR's monopoly may have ended, but its competitors found it almost impossible to enter the downtown area of the city, which was surrounded by CPR trackage. As a result the Canadian Northern was forced initially to use the VW&YR's Great Northern line and terminal. However, a solution to this predicament had to be found.

At the time False Creek was much larger than it is today. The Great Northern came up with a scheme to circumvent the CPR's blockade of the heart of Vancouver: create new land. Part of False Creek between Main Street and Clark Drive was filled in. Then, in 1915, the Canadian Northern received permission to fill in the remainder of the area. By 1919 both railways had completed their work. The Canadian Northern, which had fallen on hard times, had merged with the Grand Trunk Pacific and a number of smaller rail lines to become part of the new federal government-owned Canadian National Railways. The new CN station on Main Street continued to use Great Northern tracks on its approach into Vancouver.

Yet another railway arrived in Greater Vancouver during this era. The provincially chartered Pacific Great Eastern (today British Columbia Railway) opened a line between North Vancouver and Horseshoe Bay in 1914. This line was abandoned in 1928 but would later be revived as part of the province's recurring fascination with railways as aggressive agents of development.

In the years after 1920 there were few fundamental changes in rail patterns in Vancouver. The city was well served by its national and international rail connections and continued to grow rapidly as a result. But the era of steam locomotives soon gave way—first to diesel engines, then automobiles and airplanes. Railways still carried freight in an efficient manner, which helped fuel Western Canada's commodity-based economy. However, passenger rail travel declined as a consequence of the transportation revolution of the 20th century.

In 1962 the Great Northern abandoned its False Creek station, which was demolished in 1965. Using the CN terminal, the American railway continued to operate a Vancouver-Seattle train service for another 15 years. Meantime the large passenger terminal used by the CPR for more than half a century disappeared beneath the towering buildings of a busy Vancouver waterfront on Burrard Inlet. In the mid-1970s the CN station on Main Street became the only point of arrival and departure for train passengers in Vancouver. This coincided with the amalgamation of all Canadian passenger train service under the VIA Rail banner.

More than a century after the railway first came to town—and, indeed, created the town—Vancouver clearly owes a lot to its unique rail heritage. In the hustle and bustle of the modern city, railways are less visible but still influential. And in a new era marked by SkyTrain and commuter rail services, the CPR and CNR continue to make significant contributions to the local economy, especially to the thriving Port of Vancouver.

Change is ever-present in the world of railways. As the federal government privatizes CN and proposals are made for the sale of B.C. Rail by the provincial government to the private sector, no one can doubt that railways in Greater Vancouver are still going concerns and exciting businesses.

On top of all this is an apparent renaissance in passenger rail travel. Evidence of this includes the continuing popularity of the Royal Hudson steam train from North Vancouver to Squamish, the spectacular success of the Rocky Mountaineer train ride from Vancouver to Banff or Jasper, and the restoration of the Vancouver-Seattle passenger service by Amtrak.

Looking ahead to the 21st century, no one can predict what modes of transportation will carry us to our various destinations. Nor is it safe to predict how far into the future travel by steel wheels on steel rails will survive. But no one can deny the very special way that the railway has shaped the history of our city—and our country. And, as far as we can see ahead, it seems likely that railways will continue to shape Vancouver's unique identity.

facing page: clockwise from top left; Canadian National Station, Vancouver, c 1920; Locomotive No. 3716 (Royal Hudson back—up) at BC Rail Station, North Vancouver, 1994; Royal Hudson, BC Rail shops, North Vancouver, 1981. cva, vs, vs

Owned and operated by Great Canadian Railtour Company Ltd., Rocky Mountaineer Railtours offers a two-day, all-daylight train excursion connecting Vancouver with the Rockies resort towns of Jasper and Banff, or the foothills' cosmopolitan city of Calgary, Alberta. Guests aboard the Rocky Mountaineer train are treated to a unique combination of ever-changing scenery, individualized service and unequalled comfort.

Whether travelling eastbound or westbound, the Rocky Mountaineer spans more than 600 miles, crossing numerous mountain ranges and National Parks, raging rivers, trestled bridges and spiralling tunnels. Rocky Mountaineer Railtours continues to attract travellers from around the world, and was voted as one of *International Railway Traveler Magazine*'s top ten train trips in the world. It's no wonder so many have called this "The Most Spectacular Train Trip In The World."

The Pacific Great Eastern and B.C. Rail
David Mitchell

"Please Go Easy"
"Prince George Eventually"
"Province's Greatest Expense"
"Past God's Endurance"

THESE WERE BUT a few of the popular epithets used over the years to describe the long-running saga of British Columbia's PGE railway. The initials actually stood for Pacific Great Eastern and the railway's history is characterized by lofty ambitions, political intrigue and visions of northern empire.

Following the completion of the Canadian Pacific Railway line to the Pacific Coast in the 1880s, a kind of railway mania gripped British Columbia. At one point, 10 railways (most existing only on paper) were under construction or had been chartered. Various entrepreneurs, promoters and visionaries encouraged the construction of new railroads; very few, though, would actually be built.

By the time of World War I the Grand Trunk Pacific (today part of the Canadian National rail system) was completed across the northern part of the province to the purpose-built city of Prince Rupert. Conservative Premier Richard McBride expounded the benefits of a new provincial railway linking Vancouver with Fort George (today known as Prince George) and the Grand Trunk main line. It was hoped that such a railway could be eventually extended to the Peace River region, rich in agricultural potential. This was a popular idea in Vancouver at the time, for it was felt that the immediate construction of a railway would prevent the north and the Peace River district from falling into the commercial orbit of Edmonton. "Vancouver wholesalers complained," historian Patricia Roy has written, "that the lack of direct rail connections and discriminatory freight rates put them at a disadvantage relative to Calgary and Winnipeg in securing the trade of B.C.'s interior." Besides, the idea of opening up the province's interior and northern region conjured dreams of future greatness.

In 1912 the provincial government incorporated the Pacific Great Eastern Railway. Investment money for the project came from Great Britain; as a result the founders named the railway after Britain's Great Eastern Railway, in the hope of attracting more English investors. The PGE mandate was to construct and operate a railway along Howe Sound and northeasterly to a junction with the Grand Trunk Pacific at Prince George. That, said the visionaries, would provide the Cariboo with the long-desired outlet to the coast. (Premier McBride even talked of extending the line to Alaska.) However, it would take the railway more than four decades to get to Prince George, during which time the world would change considerably.

The PGE was to face severe difficulties from the start. World War I came at a critical time for the fledgling railway and a subsequent worldwide economic downturn further delayed the project. While surveyors worked their way through the rugged interior in an effort to chart a path for the pioneering railroad, early residents of West Vancouver petitioned to have the route diverted from the foreshore. Despite local concerns about the effect of a railway on waterfront property values, the government remained firm and the route was unchanged.

By 1914 there was regular passenger rail service between North Vancouver and Whytecliff, near Horseshoe Bay, a 20-kilometre stretch. (The station had been named White Cliff, but a land developer named Colonel Albert Whyte persuaded the railway to rename it!) Horseshoe Bay's first taxi service was started by Lew Hall, who met the trains in his Chevrolet touring car. A rail line was in operation by 1916 between Squamish and Clinton. During the economic depression of the late 1920s and the 1930s the railway was stalled, its tentative progress characterized by fits and starts and large financial losses. The provincial government took control of the bankrupt railway in 1918. By 1928 the line between North Vancouver and Whytecliff was no longer in operation. A twice-weekly run between Squamish and Quesnel was barely keeping the railway alive.

World War II brought increased business and economic activity to the interior of British Columbia which finally spurred the railway project into further action. The difficulties of construction over mountains and across rivers, however, prevented the line from reaching Prince George until 1952. In that year both freight and passenger service commenced on the PGE between Squamish and Prince George. The final task was to close the 64-kilometre gap between Squamish and North Vancouver. It was a daunting challenge, given the sheer cliffs and unforgiving topography of Howe Sound. And once again the residents of West Vancouver loudly protested the reopening of the rail line through their municipality. Premier W.A.C. Bennett, whose Social Credit government had never elected a member from West Vancouver, took a special delight in running his beloved railway across the back lawns of well-to-do West Vancouverites. (The residents were successful, however, in preventing the trains from sounding their whistles in Ambleside and Dundarave. That by-law is still in effect, although the Royal Hudson is exempt.) By 1956 the original charter of the PGE was fulfilled; the railway ran uninterrupted

BC Rail is a modern, rail-based, integrated transportation company, diversified to meet the needs of its customers. The company is the successor to the Pacific Great Eastern Railway (PGE), founded privately in 1912 to link developing, northern-based resource industries with the Port of Vancouver and the transcontinental rail system. It became the British Columbia Railway Company in 1972. In 1984 the railway operating subsidiary, BC Rail, was created. Today the BCR Group of companies has assets of more than $1.4 billion.

from the Port of Vancouver to Prince George. The extension from Squamish markedly increased North Vancouver's importance as a transshipment point.

By 1972, when the PGE changed its name to B.C. Rail, the railway was providing an economic spine through the centre of the province. Freight could be shipped from the Peace River region to Vancouver by the 1970s, and in the 1980s the railway would play a crucial role in developing the province's northeast coal deposits. By 1990 B.C. Rail's total length of track was 2,232 kilometres, making it the third-largest railway in Canada.

Present-day B.C. Rail is a modern, profitable, diversified company whose operations include a deep-sea terminal, real estate development and telecommunications. In a time when we have seen the privatization of CN Rail, it's no wonder there are now proposals from various quarters to transfer this successful provincial Crown corporation to the private sector.

Passenger rail travel has never been the primary focus of the PGE/B.C. Rail operations. In the 1940s, with the switch from steam to diesel, the romantic era of passenger rail would begin to fade into the past. However, B.C. Rail continues to run a Budd car dayliner service from various points within its system. And in 1974 the railway refurbished its famous 2860 steam engine, known as the Royal Hudson, and placed it back in service between North Vancouver and Squamish. Later, the similar 3716 was added to the service. Each summer, from mid-May through mid-September, the Royal Hudson hauls 1940s-style passenger coaches, baggage cars and a dining car through 60 kilometres of some of the most picturesque mountain and ocean scenery in Canada. This popular, historic excursion is enjoyed by as many as 70,000 passengers each season and has become a feature of British Columbia's booming tourism industry. The Royal Hudson got its name in 1939, when it drew King George VI and Queen Elizabeth across Canada. The King was very impressed with the huge, powerful locomotive and permitted the Hudson locomotives to bear the "Royal" designation. The Royal Hudson is a visible tribute to the trials and tribulations of the pioneers who waited during decades of frustration to finally see their dream become a reality.

BC Rail Dayliner; the PGE route, from North Vancouver up Howe Sound and on to Prince George, is one of the most scenic in Canada. vp

BC Rail carries a variety of British Columbian resources, including forest products, coal, minerals and metal concentrates to domestic, trans-border and overseas connecting points. Other strategic business units within the operating railway company are: Intermodal Services, which operates a fleet of piggyback equipment, road vehicles, warehouses and reload facilities; Passenger Services; Fleet Management; and International Rail Consultants. The company has 2,285 employees stationed in more than 20 communities throughout the province.

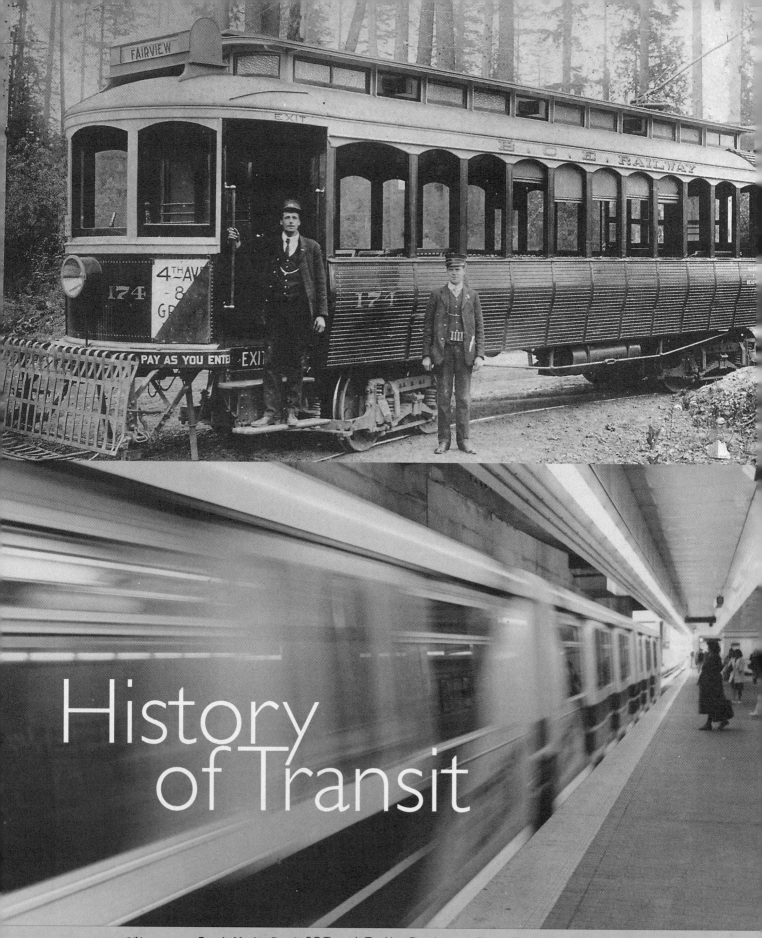

History of Transit

BC Transit 〰 Vancouver Regional Transit System · **People Moving People** BC Transit's Ten-Year Development Plan In Transit, People Moving People, announced by the provincial government in September 1995, calls for rapid bus systems, development of light transit, a 300-vehicle bus fleet expansion, replacement of 530 buses, new community bus, paratransit and shared taxi services. West Coast Express commuter rail service, 25 Compressed Natural Gas buses, 108 low-floor buses and 20 new SkyTrain cars were introduced to launch the Plan in 1995 and early 1996.

History of Transit
Brian L. Kelly

PUBLIC TRANSIT in Greater Vancouver traces its roots back to 1889. Following several attempts by various entrepreneurs a charter to build a street railway and to "carry passengers upon it by the force of animals or other such motive power" was granted to George Turner, Frederick Innes, J.W. Horne and C.D. Rand. Incorporating the Vancouver Street Railway, they began laying tracks to run horse cars. At this time a farsighted lawyer, Henry McKee, bought in and pointed out that even the rival city across the straits, Victoria, was planning an electric streetcar system. Electricity was the way of the future, not horses!

Fortunately the directors listened, and a merger was quickly initiated with the Vancouver Electric Illuminating Company. A large horse barn built on the south shore of False Creek at what is now Main Street and Terminal Avenue was sold off, and six electric cars ordered, four powered and two trailers.

The delay in ordering the conversion to electricity gave Victoria the honor of having their system start first, in February 1890. But Vancouver was not far behind. On June 26 motorman Aubrey Elliott and conductor Dugald Carmichael took car No. 14 out for a trial run over the system. Hundreds of people lined up to witness the novelty, so the directors put the rest of the cars out and gave everyone free rides until 6:00 P.M. Businesses and schools closed and every kid in town got a holiday! Two days later the whole system, 9.5 kilometres of track and two routes, was officially opened for service with a five cent fare.

Cars ran from the horse barn site north on Westminster Avenue (today Main Street), then via Powell, Carrall, Cordova, Cambie, Hastings and Granville to Drake. The second line went east on Powell to Campbell Avenue. Plans were immediately unveiled to extend up Granville, across Broadway through the Fairview district, and back down Westminster Avenue again.

This was a progressive city, now with electric lights and streetcars. Visitors climbing off the Canadian Pacific Railway's ships or trains and stepping out to see a streetcar with a number like No. 14 go sparking past couldn't help but marvel at the size of this magnificent city and its large transit system.

These street railway expansions were closely watched by the citizens of the old capital of British Columbia, New Westminster. The "Royal City," riverboat centre of the Fraser Valley, was connected to the outside world by steamboat, the CPR and was soon to have a new route south to Seattle and beyond with the Great Northern Railway.

It was the latter's construction that gave birth to an idea by the developers and brothers-in-law John Webster and Henry Edmonds. Why not a railway to connect New Westminster to Vancouver, develop the land in between, and carry connecting freight and passengers for the Great Northern? With the help of Benjamin Douglas and Vancouver's Mayor David Oppenheimer, they formed the Westminster and Vancouver Tramway Company to build a streetcar system in New Westminster and an electric railway through to Vancouver. Three small streetcars were ordered from an eastern builder, and seven large interurban cars from the famous J.G. Brill Company of Philadelphia.

On October 8, 1891, superstition was laid aside as car No. 13 made the inaugural run carrying a host of company and civic officials on what is widely recognized as North America's first true interurban railway. The next day service was opened to the public, two cars daily each way at 8:30 A.M. and 4:30 P.M., a 45-minute ride through virgin timber that would soon be the Municipality of Burnaby for 50 cents each way or 75 cents return. A self-propelled box car was added for freight.

The new street railways were firmly based, but trouble soon loomed. In the 1890s the province went into a recession, and the expected flood of new growth slowed to a trickle. Up to their ears in debt for new track and equipment, the street railways soon found they could barely cover daily operating expenses. The cities refused to take them over or grant funds, and within a few years all declared bankruptcy.

The Yorkshire Guarantee Company, holders of the Vancouver system, put their best man on the job, Sir Francis S. Barnard, son of the famous F.J. Barnard of BX Express fame, known for freight and passenger transportation throughout the Cariboo. Sperling and Company, an English firm holding the Victoria system, sent out one of their best, Robert Horne-Payne, to look over the situation.

It chanced that these two men were introduced by none other than Sir William Van Horne, president of Canadian Pacific Railway. When Barnard and Horne-Payne realized the similarity of their aims, a bold plan was formed. They would raise capital to take over the power, light and street railway system in Vancouver, Victoria and New Westminster. Both went to work raising funds, and on May 1, 1896, incorporated the

facing page: top; BC Electric 4th Avenue tram at Alma Street, circa 1910. cva

bottom; Skytrain, opened in 1986, brought high tech public transport to Greater Vancouver, 1990. vs

---

BC Transit's Ten-Year Development Plan has three fundamental goals: (1) to increase the number and proportion of people who use transit; (2) to shape urban growth and help reduce sprawl; (3) to ensure people are well served by transit, especially people who don't have cars or have difficulty getting around.

Consolidated Railway and Light Company, merging power and transportation as one utility for the first time.

Unfortunately success was to be short-lived. On May 26 an overcrowded streetcar plunged through Victoria's Point Ellice Bridge killing 55 people, a tragedy that still ranks as one of the worst ever on a transit system in North America. The financial backers, fearful of losing their ensuing lawsuits, quickly withdrew their support and the Consolidated went bankrupt.

Finally, when the dust had settled and the inquiries ended, it was deemed that the city, not the street railway, was mainly responsible for failing to maintain the bridge. Barnard and Horne-Payne set about raising new capital, mostly in England, and on April 15, 1897, organized a new company, the B.C. Electric Railway.

Under B.C. Electric the street railway grew rapidly. New routes were opened in Victoria and New Westminster, but it was Vancouver and its neighboring municipalities of South Vancouver and Point Grey that saw the greatest growth. New settlers were arriving daily, and the B.C. Electric was pushing streetcar tracks into the forests, clearing the land for subdivision, and offering reduced power rates and car fares to new home buyers. A popular slogan of the day was "In 1910, Vancouver then, will have 100,000 men." It must be presumed that women and children also counted in the prediction. By the middle of the decade tracks had been extended to Stanley Park, Davie, Robson, Main, Fraser, Commercial and Kitsilano. The system could now boast 48 cars.

With growth equally swift in Victoria and New Westminster, B.C. Electric faced another problem—they couldn't get new cars from the manufacturers fast enough. Under general manager Johannes Buntzen a bold solution was formed. In New Westminster, at the foot of the 12th Street hill, B.C. Electric erected huge car shops and began building its own streetcars. And well built they were, too, many surviving right to the end. The original barn at Main and Prior streets was now too small and a new larger one was built farther south at Main and 14th.

Over the next several years, right to the dark days of World War I, the B.C. Electric continued to experience tremendous expansion. As housing crept farther and farther south, east and west out of Vancouver, the tracks and power lines crept out along with them. Cars now travelled along Broadway, Hastings, 4th Avenue, Victoria, Kingsway, Oak, Dunbar, Nanaimo and even 41st through Kerrisdale. By 1914 the fleet had grown to 232 cars of all types and sizes in daily service.

Transit had invaded the North Shore as well, beginning on Labor Day, 1906, when little four-wheel car No. 25 crept up Lonsdale from the ferry wharf to the end of the line at 12th Street. Within five years larger streetcars had reached upper Lonsdale, Capilano and Lynn Valley. A few rolled away and plunged into the inlet, too, fortunately with no loss of life. And in West Vancouver a bus company operated by the municipality linked up with the West Van ferries, making the independent "blue bus" operation the oldest continuously operating bus company in North America.

Transporting the settlers, commuters and shoppers wasn't the only business either. In 1909 B.C. Electric had purchased plans for two open-air sightseeing cars from the Montreal Tramways Company for the magnificent sum of 25 cents and constructed them in their New Westminster shops. A young conductor worked one on short notice one day, and found himself a born showman. From that day on "Teddy Lyons and the observation car" were inseparable. His quick wit and nonstop humor became so well known that the company even published a book of Teddy Lyons jokes. "See that old Ford?" he would quip, "It's known as a Bolshevik. Two cranks and a revolution." "See that seagull? Richest one in Vancouver. Came by here the other day and made a deposit on a new Packard." It was corny, and the passengers loved it, almost as much as they loved the little groups of children who would sing at corners where the car stopped, or the long narrow souvenir photos of the passengers taken by photographer Harry Bullen and sold on every trip.

City streetcars were not the only arm of B.C.Electric's transportation division that was growing. The interurban line from Vancouver to New Westminster was double-tracked and officially entitled the "Central Park Line." Newer and larger cars, or "trams" as most people called them, as large and ornate as railway passenger coaches, were built in the New Westminster shops. In 1905 the company leased the CPR line from downtown Vancouver through Kerrisdale, West Boulevard, Marpole and on out to Richmond through to Steveston, and electrified it as their "Lulu Island Line." A branch was also built along the north side of the Fraser River from Marpole to New Westminster, where a new, large depot was built on Columbia Street to be the "hub" of the system.

By 1911 tracks had been laid through the centre of Burnaby, giving a second through route between Vancouver and New Westminster, the "Burnaby Lake Line." Today most of the freeway is over the right of way. On Vancouver Island trams ran from Victoria up to Sidney, and short routes were built to Fraser Mills and Sapperton. But by far and away the biggest undertaking was the line to Chilliwack, 102.6 kilometres in length, which opened in 1910. The company purchased even larger trams for passengers, freight and mail, many of them restroom

Customer-Focused Service Improvements To provide better customer service, attract new riders and support growth management strategies, the Plan proposes improvements in many areas, including: frequency of bus service, especially in medium-and high-density areas; safety and security through patrols and better lighting at stops and stations, and video surveillance; accessibility through widespread introduction of low-floor buses; customer service training for front-line personnel; passenger facilities such as bike lockers, Park & Rides and transit stations; information to customers on services.

equipped. Now residents could travel easily from the valley's rural areas to the city markets, and farmers could ship produce, meat and milk. The tram quickly became the lifeline and backbone of the entire valley. Industry opened, and B.C. Electric, using heavy electric freight locomotives, was soon switching and hauling long freight trains at night over all the interurban lines after the passenger service stopped until the morning.

In 1923, under general manager George Kidd, the first vehicle to challenge the supremacy of the electric streetcar arrived on the scene. To inaugurate a new route connecting Broadway and Commercial with the Grandview area at 22nd and Rupert, the company bought two 23-passenger buses from the White Motor Company, with bodies built locally by G.W. Ribchester. They were hand cranked, sported solid tires and were so successful that more buses were ordered, and within a few years were running along 10th Avenue to the new UBC, along Macdonald, Knight and Renfrew as well as to Spanish Banks.

But despite these upstart internal-combustion machines, development continued to rely on the streetcar. In one never-equalled move, master mechanic George Dickie arranged to have all the cars and tracks changed overnight when Vancouver switched from driving on the left to driving on the right precisely at the stroke of midnight on New Year's Eve, 1922. Not one accident was recorded, but not much has been written about people's confusion the following morning!

Vancouver was into the roaring "twenties." New steel streetcars were ordered from Eastern Canada, replacing some of the older B.C. Electric-built wooden cars. One-man cars were introduced, passengers had to board at the front door of cars painted with an "x" or bow tie pattern across the front and pay their fare to the "operator" rather then board at the back door to pay the conductor. The colors changed, too: after years of being painted a dark green, streetcars, trams and buses now sported the new colors of red with cream trim. You could read about it all, including schedules, events about town and even silly jokes, in the little company publication, the *Buzzer*.

It was a prosperous, exciting and innovative time, but it was not to last. As more and more families bought new-fangled "automobiles" and the spectre of depression loomed, ridership began to fall. As profits fell along with patronage, the street railways fought back. Tickets and weekly passes were introduced, better schedules became the rule, and lots of advertising was done. Then, on the eve of World War II, B.C. Electric took delivery of a new, ultra-modern, streamlined streetcar—the P.C.C. No more high steps and wooden or wicker seats, no more shake, rattle and roll, patrons were whisked to and fro on padded leather seats in quiet comfort. Thirty-five more P.C.C.s

BC Electric P.C.C. streetcar at Hastings and Granville, Vancouver, c 1945. vs

showed up over the next five years, and were it not for the war even more would have been ordered.

Unfortunately for the streetcar advocates, the P.C.C. didn't arrive in time or quantity to make a major difference. Neither did B.C. Electric's efforts to rebuild the older cars to make them more comfortable, nor the hiring for the first time of female "conductorettes" to keep the system fully operational while most young men were overseas. By the end of the war B.C. Electric officials faced a system more than 50 years old.

Tracks were worn, wooden car bodies were worn, overhead trolley wires were worn. A major decision had to be made. Buses had already replaced the streetcars in New Westminster and would soon do the same in North Vancouver and Victoria. The company could retrack, rewire and order hundreds of new cars, or it could seriously consider a newcomer to the transit industry—the trolley bus. It combined the flexibility of the bus with the clean, quiet efficiency of electricity, saved the cost of track laying, and utilized the company's ownership of the electrical system and its substantial investments in distribution. President W.G. Murrin and vice president E.W. Arnott considered all the possibilities and, after borrowing a trolley bus from neighboring Seattle for a test, chose the latter.

Trolley buses were built in Canada by Canadian Car and Foundry Brill, and over the next eight years B.C. Electric acquired the largest fleet in the country. Soon 44-passenger and

New Bus Service En Route In order to meet the growing and diverse needs of customers and provide customer-focussed transportation alternatives, the Ten-Year Development Plan outlines a major expansion of bus services. By the year 2006, the Vancouver Regional Transit System will see: more express bus routes utilizing low-floor, articulated buses; new suburb-to-suburb and crosstown services; new premium commuter services; new community-oriented services; new taxis and dial-a ride services.

later 48-passenger models, painted in the company's new cream colors and sporting the new B.C. Electric red "thunderbird" logo, were roaming streets once served by streetcars, and more. Finally on April 24, 1955, the last streetcar rolled off Hastings East, the last route, amidst flashbulbs and the tears of fans, to end 65 years of street railway service.

The streetcars weren't the only ones to fall either. Sleek diesel buses of the company's intercity bus division, Pacific Stage Lines, were now running to the suburbs and throughout the Fraser Valley, spelling the end of the handsome interurbans. One by one they closed until finally on February 27, 1958, the last tram clanked its way between Marpole and Steveston. Down came the electric wires and shiny new diesel locomotives took over the freight duties.

On August 1, 1961, B.C. Electric became a new provincial Crown corporation, B.C. Hydro and Power Authority. Within a few years buses sported the new B.C. Hydro white colors with blue and green stripes and the stylized "H" logo. Day in and day out they continued to serve patrons all over the Lower Mainland. But just as in the late 1920s the company was again facing declining ridership, albeit for a different reason.

The sixties were a decade of growth and a decade of change. New housing was springing up unheard of kilometres from the city centre, in far-off Delta, Surrey and Coquitlam. People drove faster, sportier, more powerful automobiles, and no longer relied on the transit system. All across the nation it was the same: public transit was going through recession and little money was available to improve it.

Growth of housing and auto ownership brought two of its own problems—traffic congestion and pollution. Slowly the pendulum began swinging back. By the early 1970s the provincial government had formed a new transit arm, the Urban Transit Authority, to oversee the operations of B.C. Hydro and other systems throughout the province and supply capital funds, planning and direction. New diesel buses were bought to replace older gas models, new colors of brown and orange stripes were introduced, and new routes were opened to the previously unserviced suburbs of Delta, Surrey, Coquitlam and the eastern side of North Vancouver.

Perhaps the most dramatic transit innovation of the era was the SeaBus, the two passenger-only transit ferries that whisk passengers between the North Shore and downtown Vancouver, relieving traffic congestion on the bridges. Fully integrated as part of the transit system, SeaBus provides both an important commuter link and a tourist attraction, and it's a unique way to see the harbor.

On April 1, 1980, B.C. Hydro split off its transit division and a new company, Metro Transit, was formed. Within a few years Metro Transit and the Urban Transit Authority joined forces to become BC Transit, the corporation responsible today.

Two major steps undertaken in the 1980s were designed to keep pace with the rapidly growing metropolitan area. First, at a time most cities had eliminated their trolley buses for more flexible new diesels, BC Transit considered the abundance of hydro-generated electricity in the province and the quiet pollution-free efficiency of the trolley bus, and opted to renew the fleet with trolleys in addition to extending several routes.

Even more dramatic was the opening of SkyTrain. After years of studies, reports and suggestions the province announced it would build a rapid transit line in time for the opening of Expo 86, the world's fair held in conjunction with the city's 100th birthday. And what a rapid transit line it was to be—Canadian built, both above ground and under it, and with driverless, automatic trains. The route was from New Westminster to Vancouver, echoing the need identified almost 100 years earlier for the Central Park interurban.

SkyTrain opened for Expo, and since has seen a farther extension deep into Surrey, crossing the Fraser River on a unique cable-supported bridge. The bus system continues to grow, too, with service now throughout the region as far south as White Rock and as far east as Aldergrove and Ruskin. Passengers can enjoy the fully integrated and easy-to-use system of SkyTrain, SeaBus, bus and trolley bus, and even West Van transit. And, in the fall of 1995, a new system came on line—commuter rail, the West Coast Express. Running full-size passenger trains along the CPR line from Mission to Vancouver, BC Transit now offers people a much faster, easier and more comfortable alternative than commuting by private automobile each day.

In celebrating the centennial of transit in 1990, the people of the Lower Mainland realized the major role their systems have played in growth and development over the century, and the major role transit will continue to play in the future. The region owes a geat deal to what motorman Elliott and conductor Carmichael began with little car No. 14 such a very, very long time ago.

facing page: BC Electric building, built at Hastings and Carrall, 1911–12. cva

Rapid Bus: A New Concept in Service Rapid bus service will operate along the Granville Street, Richmond-downtown Vancouver corridor by the year 1998. Rapid buses feature: limited-stop service; boarding through multiple doors; on-board voice and digital display next-stop announcements; low-floor, articulated buses. Rapid bus shelters will have: digital signs that count down the next-bus arrival time; improved signage and image; fare pre-payment ticket machines.

Light Rail Transit BC Transit is dedicated to implementing a high-quality light rail service on the Broadway-Lougheed-Coquitlam Centre corridor by 2005 and on to New Westminster by 2008. Light Rail Transit (LRT) can operate either on its own right-of-way, on street in mixed traffic, elevated, at-grade, depressed or underground. LRT is cost-effective, environmentally sound and meets regional planning objectives. Extensive public consultation, planning, engineering and land-use agreement work will take place before construction begins in 1998/99.

Road and Street Development
Andrew Scott

Greater Vancouver's street system got off to a jump start because British Columbia's earliest military personnel were excellent road-builders. Constructing public facilities was, in fact, their vocation. A troop of Royal Engineers, under the command of Col. Richard Clement Moody, arrived on the West Coast in 1858 with the express purpose of helping government hew the Empire's newest colony from the forest primeval.

In 1859 Col. Moody chose a site for the colony's first capital. For protection against possible American invasion and to guard the mouth of the Fraser, Moody selected "the first high ground on the north side after entering" the river, and Queen Victoria named it New Westminster. But the river sometimes froze, and the navy might have to supply or defend—or even evacuate—an ice-bound capital. A nearby saltwater anchorage was required, and the head of Burrard Inlet was deemed the best spot. The engineers built the region's first road from New Westminster to a landing on the inlet at Port Moody. (But from *A History of Coquitlam and Fraser Mills* by H.A.J. Monk and J. Stewart comes this: "On August 10th, 1858, a crew of men under the direction of A.C. Anderson, Director of Road Operations, started British Columbia's first road construction; a road from Tsawwassen Beach, south of Ladner overland to Fort Langley.") Today North Road forms the boundary between Burnaby and Coquitlam. In 1861, when the river did freeze, mail and passengers were hauled to New Westminster from Port Moody by sleigh.

Another early road recommended by Col. Moody was the False Creek Trail, cut through the forest in 1860 to provide a route to the military reserve at Stanley Park. It was only completed as far as False Creek, but would later be upgraded to a wagon road and become the forerunner of today's Kingsway. The North Arm Trail was built in 1861-62 from New Westminster to Marpole and Musqueam, where a number of early farmers had settled. It provided access to the Royal City when the river froze. Today parts of Marine Drive follow its course.

As capital of the colony, New Westminster was the hub for the region's first suburban thoroughfares. The Kennedy Trail, built in 1861 ran south to Mud Bay, while the Pitt River Road snaked eastwards in 1862. In 1865 the Kennedy Trail was extended to the U.S. border and became part of the Telegraph Trail, an ambitious but unsuccessful plan to connect Europe and North America by telegraph via Bering Strait.

In 1865, despite the difficult terrain and the bankruptcy of its contractor, another ambitious project was completed. This was the 20-kilometre Douglas Road, Vancouver's first real wagon route, which ended where New Brighton Park sits today at the north foot of Windermere Street. It gave New Westminster access to Burrard Inlet's new lumber mills—and to two early hotels that catered to weekend bathing parties and other visitors. Some sections are still called Douglas Road; others are known as Canada Way.

In 1872 the first bridge was built across False Creek at Westminster Avenue (now Main Street), connecting the sawmill community of Granville (Gastown) to the wider world. False Creek was longer then; the eastern end, between Main and Clark Drive, was filled in during World War I. In 1874 a trail was cut to link Marpole's farmers to Granville's market. It was replaced the following year by a "waggon" road (now Fraser Street), which joined the upgraded False Creek Road to New Westminster.

The 1870s also saw the construction of some important regional or trunk roads: the Yale Road (1874) from New Westminster to Hope and Yale at the head of the Fraser Valley, Ladner Trunk Road through Delta (1874), and Scott Road (1875) and McLellan Road (1876) in Surrey. All these early routes were often impassable—little more than muddy clearings through the bush. Useless after heavy rains, they "made up in depth what they lacked in width," according to one period description.

Vancouver was incorporated as a city in 1886, its boundaries extending south to 16th Avenue and from Trafalgar Street on the west to Nanaimo Street on the east—virtually all forest wilderness at the time. In 1885 the Canadian Pacific Railway's assistant land commissioner, Lauchlan A. Hamilton, had begun surveying, laying out and naming Vancouver's streets. Bridges were built and rebuilt: Granville Street in 1889, Bridge Street (now Cambie) in 1891, Westminster Avenue (now Main) in 1876 and 1888. The Fraser was bridged to Sea Island in 1890. By the turn of the century much of the city was crisscrossed with a grid of roadways, and Vancouver's first residential neighborhoods—the West End, Mount Pleasant and Fairview—flourished.

From 1900 until the start of World War I, the city's suburbs —especially South Vancouver, Point Grey, Coquitlam, North Vancouver, Burnaby and Richmond—grew quickly. Travellers still used horse-drawn rigs for short, local trips, and trains, trolleys and riverboats for longer journeys. The first automobiles were beginning to appear, but would not be popular enough until the 1920s and 1930s to warrant massive road

Hastings Street, looking east from Seymour Street, Vancouver, c 1889. cva

improvement projects. A network of suburban routes gradually developed, often providing the only means of communication between rural neighbors. The Dewdney Trunk Road along the north shore of the Fraser River was completed in 1900, and a major bridge across the Fraser constructed in 1904 at New Westminster.

In Vancouver most streets followed a rather dull rectangular grid inherited from the original Lower Mainland surveys of the 1870s, and either ran east-west or north-south. There were exceptions, however, like the CPR's Shaughnessy Heights subdivision, opened in 1909. In order to emphasize the exclusivity of the homes, a series of curving crescents was laid out to follow the natural contours of the land. Before asphalt paving, which became popular about this time, most roads were dirt or gravel. A few were surfaced with wooden blocks or lined with bricks, which allowed horses to get a better grip.

By the 1930s most of Vancouver's streets had been laid out. A few areas of empty land lingered along the city's southern and eastern fringes until the 1950s, while the area south of 41st Avenue and west of Cambie remained without a tight network of streets until the sixties. Vancouver's last undeveloped areas, like Champlain Heights in the extreme southeast corner of the city, were street-free until the late 1970s.

Patches of raw land still remain in the municipalities surrounding Vancouver, though urban pressures get heavier all the time, especially on the lower Fraser Valley's prime farmland. Much of Richmond is now covered by a dense street grid, also parts of Delta and Surrey, while in North and West Vancouver, the street system has climbed surprisingly high up the sides of the North Shore mountains.

Better roads to and from Vancouver came with the automobile age. The Fraser Highway (originally Yale Road), which heads east from New Westminster up the Fraser Valley, was greatly improved during the 1920s and became part of the Trans-Canada Highway in 1946. In 1923 the Pacific Highway, the first major road link to the U.S., was constructed. The first Second Narrows Bridge went up in 1925, the Pattullo Bridge in 1937 and the Lions Gate in 1938. By 1937 the Lougheed Highway was finished; by 1940 the King George Highway to the U.S. border was in place.

In the 1950s automobiles were already becoming a problem, forcing major expenditures on road projects. Highway 99 was built south to the U.S. at this time, complete with Oak Street Bridge (1957) and George Massey Tunnel (1959). The Upper Levels Highway to the Horseshoe Bay ferries was finished by 1958, and Highway 17 to the Tsawwassen ferries by 1960. Highway 1 (the Trans-Canada) and the Port Mann Bridge opened in 1964. Recent improvements have included several new bridges—the Georgia and Dunsmuir Viaducts (1972), Knight Street (1974), Arthur Laing (1975), Alex Fraser (1986) and No. 2 Road in Richmond (1994)—while Highway 91 (the Annacis Freeway) and SkyTrain rapid-transit system were built by 1986.

What of the future? In the nineties, rapid-transit is scheduled to expand to Coquitlam, while commuter rail has begun operating to Mission. A decision must soon be made on a new First Narrows crosssing. But Vancouver continues to grow faster than its infrastructure can expand. More people with more cars are creating ever more serious traffic and pollution problems, with no easy or popular solutions in sight. Most people agree, reluctantly, that the city's only options are to invest heavily in expensive public-transit schemes, build large inner-city residential highrises, develop suburban "town centres" and penalize single-occupancy vehicles and downtown auto commuters.

The Car

The Car In Greater Vancouver
Douglas Sagi

ON THE CARIBOO Mountain Road lies Jackass Mountain, remembered as the place where the first motor vehicle to travel a British Columbia "highway" got stuck in the mud. It was an enormous steam tractor brought from Scotland by Francis Jones Barnard, a man with a stage-coach company and a vision. It was 1871 and he thought the steam tractors would be as useful in B.C. wilderness as they were hauling sugar cane at his plantation in Java. The story is told in G.W. Taylor's book, *The Automobile Saga of British Columbia 1864-1914,* published in 1984 by Morriss Publishing of Victoria and available in the Vancouver Public Library. Barnard's experiment ended on Jackass Mountain. He shipped five of the six machines he had ordered back to Scotland, where they became part of the Glasgow transit system for the next 50 years, and turned the sixth into a logging locomotive on English Bay.

British Columbians stuck with railways and the horsepower of real horses until September 24, 1899, when the first automobile, a Stanley Steamer, appeared on a Vancouver street. It had been purchased for $650 from the Stanley Brothers factory in Newton, Mass. The first motorist was William Henry Armstrong, a contractor with an eye for new businesses. He took the mayor and other civic dignitaries for a ride on that late September day. According to one newspaper writer: "The beautiful horseless carriage answered the steering gear to a hair's breadth as with rubber tires it noiselessly rolled along the asphalt with a motor power entirely hidden from view like some graceful animal curving its way in and out of the traffic."

Armstrong tried to get an auto factory going but his Armstrong Morrison and Company made just one car, a steamer with a 30-horsepower motor that broke down several times on its first and only trial run. Taylor writes that the engine was too powerful for the converted wagonette that served as a chassis. Armstrong sold his Stanley to an adventurous Methodist minister, Rev. W.G. Tanner, who took it to his charge in Victoria and became the province's first mobile minister. (He later became religion editor of the *Vancouver Sun.*)

Thomas Plimley, patriarch of the family that operated a Vancouver auto dealership for more than 70 years, opened the first car dealership in the province in Victoria in 1900. The first car he sold was an Oldsmobile with all of four horsepower emanating from its single, internal combustion cylinder. Plimley's wife, Rhoda, was probably the first woman to learn to drive. She taught herself by piloting an Oldsmobile around the orchard of her home.

Vancouver's first car dealers were Ernest and Walter Stark who, like Plimley in Victoria, combined the selling of automobiles and bicycles. They opened the Vancouver Auto and Cycle Company in 1906. They were joined by three more dealers that year. By 1917 there were another 15.

There are now about 140 new car dealers in the Lower Mainland and another 200 throughout the province. There are also about 1,100 used car dealers, repair shops and towing companies in British Columbia.

The early dealers sold British as well as North American cars. A Spence's Bridge storekeeper, Art Climes, imported a Wolsley. He got it home after it arrived by ship in Vancouver despite the absence of decent roads and the fact that the engine was not powerful enough for many of the mountain grades.

Taylor says the first purchaser of a Cadillac was Capt. J.W. Troup, an executive of the Canadian Pacific Railway. Other leading business people followed, some buying more than one car. John Hendry, a paint manufacturer, is credited with hiring the first chauffeur, Harry Hooper, a champion bicycle rider. Hooper later established one of the first taxi businesses in the city. Old records for Stanley Park show 176 drivers toured the park on one Sunday in 1905. The number grew to just 191 in 1911, then 1,513 in 1917. Now there are fewer British Columbians without cars than with them and barely enough parking spaces to go around in the Lower Mainland. The Insurance Corporation of B.C. says more than one million vehicles are registered in the Lower Mainland and another 1.2 million more in the rest of the province.

The province did not start regulating motor vehicles until 1904 when the legislature passed "An Act to Regulate the Speed and Operation of Motor Vehicles on Highways." (The bill was modelled on legislation passed in 1903 in Ontario.)

Among the first horses to be displaced by motor vehicles were the powerful creatures that pulled Vancouver's firefighting equipment. Fire chief John Howe Carlisle persuaded the city to buy a steam-driven, self-propelled fire engine from the International Power Company for $12,768. A year later the city approved his recommendation for two gasoline-powered hose wagons and two chemical wagons. "As the maintenance of the automobile apparatus is 75 per cent less than the horse-drawn apparatus, I would recommend that all our future apparatus be self-propelling," Chief Carlisle wrote in his 1908 annual report.

At first British Columbians drove on the left, like the British

facing page: A Stanley Steamer, the first car in Vancouver, 1889. vs

in Mother England. The rest of North America, meanwhile, adopted the European practice (started by Napoleon's armies) of keeping to the right. A provincial decree was needed to get British Columbia onto the right and on New Year's morning, 1922, the province's motorists awoke, started their cars and, to the surprise of many, kept to the right without a single accident.

Reported the *Province* in its first post-holiday edition, Monday, January 3: "With the customary adaptability of the West and its attitude of studied calm in the presence of an approved reform or of anything which it does not understand, the City of Vancouver kept to the right at 6 A.M. on Sunday and has kept there ever since, just as if it had been doing it for centuries. It was supposed and prophesied by croakers that there would be a scene of wild confusion at all the great nerve centres of the traffic system, that there would be innumerable accidents, that people would be killed every ten minutes and the gods of all old customs would rise up and demand a continuous stream of human sacrifices. But there were no sacrifices and no confusion."

Love of Great Britain and its automobiles flourished after World War II. Britain exported Austins, Morrisses, Triumph Vanguards, Humber Super Snipes, Hillman Minxes, Sunbeams, General Motors Vauxhalls, British Ford Anglias and Prefects. Most were small sedans powered by four-cylinder engines. While other North American teens yearned for U.S. made muscle cars, young British Columbians piloted British sports cars. They were relatively cheap, economical to run and much of the time the Lower Mainland climate was similar to Britain's. Alas many of the little cars did not run well. It got colder at times than England and British cars, especially the low slung sporty kind with side curtains in place of windows, were notoriously poor performers in bad weather.

In the late 1950s the German "peoples' car" (Volkswagen) appeared, followed by Japanese Datsuns, Toyotas and rugged Swedish Volvos. Like the British cars they were cheap to buy and cheap to run. They were also reliable and soon began displacing big North American V8's as rapidly as they displaced the British cars.

Nevertheless one of the larger exhibitions of vintage British automobiles outside of England is held each year in VanDusen Gardens. Sponsored by the Olde British Car Society this world-class all-British field meet features more than 400 exhibits. Their owner-drivers sprawl on the grass beside their treasures to talk cars with the thousands who wander by to admire pristine MGs and Bentleys, Triumph TR3's and Jaguar XKE's.

Sponsored by the Olde British Car Society, this world-class all-British field meet features more than 400 exhibits

Some owners drive them home to await next year's show. Others drive them onto trailers to be towed home behind a sturdy Japanese compact truck.

Vancouverites love cars. In any given traffic jam—and these are "given" daily from dawn to midnight on some roadways—there are often vintage automobiles, possibly the exquisite old Jaguar bearing the vanity licence plate A GIFT, Volvos with Asian owners, Brits in scarves and cloth caps piloting Austin-Healeys and treasured Morgans, kids with boom boxes nearly as big as their Hondas, retired folk nursing their "last new car," spotless quarter-century-old Chevys or Fords.

The climate is the reason for the number of older cars. Newcomers from the east, where road salt may devour cars in half-a-dozen years, are surprised at the number of elderly, yet pristine vehicles around. On the warm and wet coast, there is only occasional need for road salt to melt winter ice and a rinsing rain is usually quick to arrive to wash down the streets and the cars on it.

The love affair continues despite concerns that the car is becoming a monster. There are more than 4,900 injuries and more than 500 deaths due to vehicle accidents in B.C. each year. ICBC pays claims of nearly $2 billion dollars annually. There are growing fears that the environment is an even larger casualty. The provincial government has introduced AirCare testing stations on the Lower Mainland and requires the owners of all licensed private vehicles to demonstrate that their vehicle exhausts are at an acceptable standard. Vehicle manufacturers will soon be required to meet standards already in effect in smog-polluted California. The Lower Mainland is not yet as bad as California but environmentalists argue that the danger rises every year. The thick, yellow haze that fills the Fraser Valley on summer days is evidence that the climate that is so kind to our cars may soon become poisonous for motorists to breathe.

facing page: A 1970 Morgan at the Olde British Car Society field meet, VanDusen Gardens, 1993. vp

Trust is best illustrated by the fact that more than 80 per cent of all Dueck new and used vehicle retail sales are to people who are past Dueck customers or have been referred to Dueck by a friend or relative. Many Dueck sales people have been with the company for more than a decade and three have received their 35-year pins. Their success is glowing tribute to the trust their customers have in them and in Dueck GM.

History of Bus Lines
Brian L. Kelly

FROM THE TURN of the century through to World War I, travel in, out of, and around Greater Vancouver was accomplished on the trains of the Canadian Pacific, Canadian Northern and Great Northern railways and the streetcars and interurbans of the B.C. Electric Company. During World War I the first serious competition arose to challenge rail-bound transportation, the jitney car. Owners of Model T's or other such "horseless carriages" began picking up passengers and charging fares until regulations were brought in banning jitneys, except in places not served well by rail. The field was now open.

It was from these early jitneys that the first true intercity bus companies were formed, even if those first "buses" were nothing more than stretched touring cars. One pioneer was Goodman Hamre who in 1914 began bus service between New Westminster and Aldergrove, expanding in 1915 from New Westminster to White Rock. By 1921 he'd expanded west to Vancouver and farther east to Abbotsford. Others had joined him, such as Tom Coldicott with his Blue Funnel line from New Westminster to Vancouver; White Star Motor from Vancouver to Ladner; Earle Moorehouse in the New Westminster, Surrey and Delta areas; Harold Gallagher in the Fraser Valley; Messrs. Stevens and Pringle in the Coquitlam, Haney and Mission areas; and William Pottruff operating from Mission to Harrison and eastwards. Even the mighty B.C. Electric formed its own intercity bus operation, B.C. Rapid Transit, in 1922, introducing for the first time true intercity buses built by both the Fageol and the White Motor Companies.

Onto this scene came another bus pioneer, Ivor W. Neil. In 1915 Neil operated a sightseeing bus and taxi service in Vancouver and in 1919 he took over Hamre's White Rock service, extending it to Vancouver in 1922 and renaming his company Pacific Stage Lines. Continuing to grow, and backed with B.C. Electric money, Neil expanded his operations to Bellingham and Seattle under the name Green Stage Lines, took over White Star Motor and other smaller companies such as Triangle Tours, Yellow Cabs, Circle Tours and Vancouver Transfer putting them all under a B.C. Electric holding company known as B.C. Motor Transportation. It wasn't long before B.C. Electric's other subsidiary, B.C. Rapid Transit, had taken over the last of Hamre's operations and Neil further expanded by taking over Smith, Pringle, Pottruff, Stevens and the others. By 1932 B.C. Motor and B.C. Rapid were merged under the umbrella of Pacific Stage Lines, a wholly owned B.C. Electric subsidiary and one of the largest intercity bus companies in Canada. PSL buses ran to North and West Vancouver, took over service to Horseshoe Bay when the first Pacific Great Eastern Railway line closed, went to Deep Cove, Chilliwack, Hope, up the Fraser Canyon and in fact virtually everywhere not served by the company's interurbans or streetcars.

Neil's success stemmed from his standardization of operations and his businesslike drive, earning him the nickname "Ivor the Driver." It was Neil who first established regular fares, regular schedules and regular stops or depots in various towns. In Vancouver the first depot was at 724 West Hastings where the sidewalk was the loading platform, the "longest bus platform in Canada" if you figured it ran from Burrard Street to Boundary Road! In 1926 a new depot was opened at Dunsmuir and Seymour with ticket offices, an inside bus bay for loading, restaurant, travel agency and more. And in one of the most successful moves of all, PSL became agents for Gray Line Sightseeing, the largest tour company of its kind in North America. Buses were now operating more than 1,600 kilometres per day of passenger service.

By now a new bus company was on the scene, a company destined to become the best known on the continent, if not in the world. Started in Montana in 1914 Greyhound had grown rapidly by taking over many smaller companies in their bid to become the first cross-continent bus organization. In B.C. Greyhound gradually absorbed all of the long-distance routes such as service to the Okanagan and Fraser Canyon, while PSL concentrated more on the Lower Mainland. By World War II the last of the private operators had been absorbed by PSL which then merged with Pacific Northwest Traction (PNT) to offer a service between Vancouver and Seattle. (Before it began, Seattle-bound passengers had to take a bus to Bellingham, the PNT interurban to Mount Vernon, a bus to Everett and the interurban again to Seattle!) When the PNT closed its interurban lines in the 1930s and renamed its bus operations North Coast Lines, PSL and NCL operated the Vancouver-Seattle service jointly as a "pool" line until just after World War II. NCL became part of the Greyhound empire also and PSL pulled out to concentrate on service expansion in the Fraser Valley.

By 1947 the depot at Dunsmuir and Seymour was outgrown so, a few blocks to the east, a city playing field known as Larwill Park was rebuilt as the most modern bus terminal in Canada. Into the new depot came buses of Pacific Stage Lines, Greyhound and new local operators like Sechelt Motor Transport, Squamish Coach Lines, Deep Cove Stage Lines and oth-

Greyhound bus at CN Station, Vancouver, circa 1950. vs

ers. The independent Airline Limousine Service, a subsidiary of C&C Taxi in Victoria, operated their bus service mainly to the airport from their depot on West Georgia. From 1,600 kilometres of service per day in 1926 to more than 16,000 in 1947—a ten-fold increase in just over 20 years.

It was a successful business but one not destined to last. Like all other forms of transportation, intercity bus service was hit hard by the 1950s and 1960s cult of the automobile. Services were cut back and some companies folded. New ones arrived, companies like Maverick that took over the Sechelt and Squamish operations. In cooperation with the Airline Limousine Company, Greyhound's largest U.S. competitor, Trailways, began a competitive Vancouver-Seattle service. But the ridership just wasn't there.

PSL combined again in a successful and busy pool service with Vancouver Island Coach Lines to operate buses to Victoria and Nanaimo on the new B.C. ferries starting in the 1960s. Grey Line sightseeing was still very popular but it was not

enough. The operations of PSL and VICL were merged into a new company, Pacific Coach Lines, before it too was split up and sold off.

Today the intercity bus business is strong once again but not in the local or suburban areas of Vancouver, as most of these areas are now covered by B.C. Transit with city bus service. Intercity bus companies such as International Stage concentrate on the growing tourism business with cruise ship transfers and sightseeing, or on long distance travel. Maverick operates to the Sunshine Coast and Squamish/Whistler as well as the old PSL Nanaimo route; Laidlaw runs Vancouver Island; Fraser Valley operates to Chilliwack; and Greyhound operates throughout the rest of the province and across Canada.

Go down to Pacific Central Station at Main and Terminal street today, climb aboard a modern restroom-equipped bus, sit back in air-conditioned comfort, grab your refreshments, and watch a movie. It's a long, long way from "Ivor the Driver" and a seven-passenger Pierce Arrow bumping along a gravel road.

Taxis in Greater Vancouver
Tom Hawthorn

THE RIGHT FOOT steps off the curb, the left remaining safely on the sidewalk. The right arm is raised, fingers extended. Sometimes, in the movies, a man in a fedora waves a rolled-up newspaper. The gesture is universal. In that most satisfying of urban experiences, a taxi cab has been hailed.

When it comes to taxis, the city remains stubbornly mired in the forties (except for fares). Dozens of curbside taxi stands are scattered around the city. Special telephones provide hot-line service to dispatchers.

"Vancouver is unique in the world," says Sig Weber, president and CEO of Black Top and Checker Cab, the province's largest taxi fleet. "It is a telephone city, rather than a flag city. In New York City, the taxis don't even have radios."

In New York City the drivers don't even have manners. Here they'll do just about anything for a passenger. On August 1, 1954, cabbie Dave King driving for B.C. Radio Cabs, was taking a young woman to West Vancouver. When the cab slowed in traffic on the Lions Gate Bridge, she jumped out and, to King's horror, began climbing the railing. He raced over, dragged her to safety, shoved her in the car, and raced back to her West End address. The would-be suicide paid her fare, he told police, and even tipped him 50 cents.

When a driver named Charles Harry Hooper offered himself and his wheezy, two-cylinder Ford for hire in 1903, he became Vancouver's first taxi driver. Seven years later, he opened Harry Hooper Ltd., the city's first taxi company. Born in Nepanee, Ontario, he arrived in Vancouver with his mother in 1886. His was a wanderer's soul, so he made busy by driving cattle in the Cariboo, by joining the Klondike Gold Rush, and by touring Asia with a troupe of professional cyclists. Handsome Harry, as he called himself, died after a lengthy illness on January 11, 1956. He was 81.

Yellow, the oldest company still in operation, began doing business here in 1920 with a single car owned by Roy Long, a lawyer. In 1930 the firm was taken over by B.C. Electric, which was operating Terminal City Cabs. In 1947 the Yellow fleet of 31 cars was sold to Walter P. Radford and Associates, which owned the similarly sized Star Cabs fleet. After seven years of negotiations, 110 owner-drivers of Yellow, Star and Checker Cabs bought the 85-car Yellow Cabs Co. in February 1958.

Yellow's rival is Black Top, which was formed as a cooperative by 12 war veterans, each of whom owned a single car, in March 1947. Its depot was an eight sq. metre hut. Thanks to the popularity of its radio-dispatched cabs, Black Top had grown to a 62-car fleet by April 1, 1960, when it amalgamated with 48-car Blue Cab to become the largest taxi operation in Western Canada. Blue Cab, founded in 1935 by A. Pashos, soon faded into memory, as all cars were painted in Black Top's distinctive cream-and-black scheme.

The last of the little taxi firms was swallowed by Yellow on August 17, 1977. Forum Empress Taxi, its 10 company and nine privately owned cars operating from a converted house at 2053 East Hastings Street, had formed when the Grandview, Forum, Empress and Hastings services merged in 1964.

Cab companies in the suburbs retain names chosen to highlight their neighborliness or sophistication: Bonny's, Bel-Air, Royal City, Queen City, Burnaby Select, Clover, Corby, Surdell-Kennedy, Executive, Delta Sunshine, and Semiahmoo ("Well-dressed drivers—many of whom you already know").

The industry has not been without its controversies. Drivers have been fired for forming unions. The battle over airport fares has at times threatened to degenerate into violence. The first steel-and-plastic shield, strong enough to stop a bullet from a .38-calibre revolver, was imported from New York by businessman Winston Malt in 1975 and used in a Yellow cab driven by John Adam.

Some cabbies even have law degrees, which can come in handy. In the thirties and forties it was common practice for customers to ask drivers to bring a bottle of hooch to the door. Some companies would make the delivery, others feared bootlegging charges. The matter even went to County Court (Rex vs. Paulson, 1939). On July 21, 1976, Black Top bowed to the B.C. Human Rights Branch and lifted a 9 P.M. ban on woman drivers that had been contested by owner-operator Terry Bellamy, a mother of three who needed to work nights.

In October 1951 city council agreed to a rate change, hiking the hourly rate to $3 from $2.50 The meter rate of 45 cents minimum plus 10 cents for each two-fifths of a mile was unchanged. In 1996 the hourly charge was a princely $21, while the "drop"—the ante for engaging a cab—was $2.10 with a charge of $1.20 a kilometre.

By 1996 the Yellow fleet stood at 146 cars with 230 owner-operators and about 600 drivers. Only Black Top, with 159 cars, was bigger, while MacLure's, Advance taxis and Vancouver divide the remaining 143 city licenses. Overall, that works out to about one cab for every 1,000 Vancouver residents. But you already know that if you've ever tried to flag a taxi in the rain.

In March, 1997 local cabbies were alarmed by an inspection crackdown that saw dozens of vehicles taken off the road because of safety defects. Rapid resolution was promised.

Vancouver International Airport

AIR CANADA With Vancouver's strategic location on the globe as the closest point between Asia and North America, Vancouver International Airport has become North America's gateway between Asia and the world. In recognition of the potential of the lucrative Asian marketplace, Air Canada had its Chinese name, "The Maple Leaf Airline", emblazoned in six-foot high Chinese characters, across both sides of a Boeing 747-400 aircraft serving the Vancouver-Hong Kong route.

Vancouver International Airport
Sean Rossiter

I T IS PART of Vancouver's aviation lore that Charles Lindbergh skipped the city on his triumphal tour of the continent (after his New York-to-Paris solo flight of 1927) because, as the Lone Eagle put it, "there's no airport there fit to land on." It is not as if Vancouver was totally inaccessible by air. But it was true that how safely you could land in Vancouver during the late 1920s depended on what kind of airplane you were flying. Lindbergh's Ryan NYP (for New York-to-Paris) was equipped with wheels. If you wanted to land in Vancouver at that time it helped to be flying a seaplane. Vancouver's runways were many, long and sometimes as smooth as glass. But almost all of them were liquid.

Most of the land flat enough for airfields on B.C.'s Lower Mainland is on the Fraser River delta. The first airplane ever seen in Vancouver, a Curtiss Pusher, made several flights over four days in late March, 1910, from the infield of Minoru Park Race Track, Richmond, near the present Lansdowne Mall. The pilot was a self-taught barnstormer named Charles K. Hamilton. He raced a car and a horse, losing to both. The scene was preserved in an account by William Templeton, who made it aloft himself a year later from the same field in a homebuilt, three-cylinder biplane, and who in 1931 became the first manager of Vancouver's new airport.

Templeton had to agree with Lindbergh when it came to the pasture next to the racetrack on Lulu Island that had been wishfully designated Vancouver Airport. "We had an airport," Templeton would explain, "but no night lighting, no traffic control, no weather bureau, no radio aids, and, of course, no business."

Still, B.C. Airways operated the biggest airliner in Canada, a Ford Trimotor, between Seattle and Vancouver starting in early August, 1928, from Lulu Island. But it crashed into Puget Sound on the 25th while trying to fly under the fog, after a passenger challenged the pilot for being reluctant to take off. All seven aboard, including a cocker spaniel, perished.

So there was truth in Lindbergh's remark, which only made it hurt more. His historic solo flight in a wheel-equipped airplane showed that the greater efficiency of landplanes was beginning to overcome the safety value of seaplanes on overwater flights. Lindbergh's streamlined Ryan monoplane, powered by the first reliable aero engine, the Wright Whirlwind

overleaf: Control tower and International Terminal with Air Canada 747. air canada photo

J-4, was less likely than most previous long-range aircraft to end up in the drink. Water and aviation were practically cause and effect in Vancouver, just as they were in one of aviation's world capitals, nearby Seattle.

The Boeing Airplane Company plants in both cities were former boatyards. The same trades built both boats and aircraft with the big difference that more sewing went into building an airplane. This made aircraft plants early equal-opportunity employers. Spruce was the main aircraft framing material and spruce is common in this part of the world.

Vancouver's first Boeing plant was the Hoffar-Beeching Shipyard at the foot of Cardero Street on Coal Harbour. The floats on seaplanes were where the boatbuilding art coincided with aeronautical engineering.

In fact that shipyard had been building aircraft as early as the winter of 1915, when the Hoffar brothers, Henry and Jimmie, fitted floats to the Curtiss Jenny belonging to Vancouver's first licensed pilot, Billy Stark. By the fall of 1916 the Hoffars were building a "hydroplane," as seaplanes were then called, designed to imitate a photo of an Avro Biplane they saw in the British periodical *Flight.* Jimmie taught himself how to fly it. The replica was sound enough for the first-ever flight over Downtown Vancouver on July 16, 1917, when Jimmie Hoffar took the *Province* sports editor up to 600 metres in the H-1.

Buoyed by their success, the Hoffars built a flying-boat—an aircraft with a hull-shaped fuselage for operation from water—the H-2. It crashed into the roof of Dr. J.C. Farish's house at 755 Bute Street after an engine failure at 450 metres, about halfway between Burrard Inlet and False Creek. This second test flight of the H-2, on September 4, 1918, ended moments before its Royal Air Force pilot, home on leave, regained consciousness in the doctor's bathroom.

As early as March 3, 1919, Vancouver's watery surroundings made it the site of a civil aviation milestone when Bill Boeing and his test pilot, Eddie Hubbard, completed the first international air-mail flight at the Royal Vancouver Yacht Club. It took them two days to get here. In his 1956 history of the company, *Vision,* former Boeing vice president Harold Mansfield tells the story:

"The Boeing 'C' was 50 minutes on the way to Vancouver when Hubbard tapped Boeing on the shoulder and pointed silently at blackening clouds ahead. In a moment, a change of wind hit them with a wild gallop. The sky closed about them, filling with snow. Wiping his goggles with his sleeve, Boeing looked back at Hubbard. Hubbard pointed down and pushed the stick forward, starting down. Boeing nodded. No ground outline appeared; no bottom. Groping downward, Hubbard

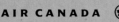 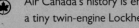 Air Canada's history is entwined with the growth of aviation in Vancouver. It began September 1, 1937, with a tiny twin-engine Lockheed 10A. Onlookers cheered as pilots Billy Wells and Maurice McGregor lifted off for Seattle. The first commercial flight of Trans-Canada Air Lines (TCA) was underway.

finally saw black water and levelled off above it. For twenty minutes, with blinding snow in their faces, they bucked along, watching a blurred shoreline to the right. Hubbard identified Anacortes and set the plane down on the bay. Boeing was pale when they climbed ashore. "Good job, Eddie," he said."

In 1925 the year-old Pacific Airways operated its upcoast fishery patrols from a flying-boat base at Jericho Beach. Its founder, Don MacLaren, was Vancouver's first aviation hero. A dapper, mustachioed man of many talents who became the third-ranking Canadian ace of World War I, MacLaren has been forgotten despite his 54 victorious air battles, a total he ran up in less than eight months of combat.

The Jericho base had been established by MacLaren as Vancouver's air harbor at the request of the Canadian Air Board, created in 1920 to govern aviation in Canada. The CAB operated ex-U.S. Navy Curtiss HS2L flying boats, all-wood aircraft built in 1916 that were known as the "flying cigar boxes" for their mahogany planking. One of these aircraft made the first flight up the B.C. coast in 1923.

So hazardous were flying conditions along the coastline and so crude was the equipment that in 1928, when a new Boeing B-1E went down between Butedale and Swanson Bay, the immediate replacement aircraft required by Pacific Airways' contract with the fisheries department itself crashed on its way to the Queen Charlotte Islands.

The same year Lindbergh snubbed Vancouver, the need for something better than the Minoru Park facility was pounded into the mayor's head. Louis D. Taylor, who built the Sun Building for his *Vancouver World* newspaper and who remains the city's longest-serving mayor, was on the first flight from Victoria to Vancouver. As a crowd assembled from the nearby racetrack, the Ford Trimotor arrived and taxied toward the throng. Mayor Taylor leaped out of the plane before its door was secured, ran forward toward the crowd and was struck by a propeller, suffering a skull fracture. "It sliced off the top of his head, you know, and [knocked] him unconscious," MacLaren would note many years later. "They said if he'd had an ounce more brains he'd have been a dead man."

In 1932 MacLaren and Canadian Airways introduced a luxurious eight-seat Sikorsky S-38 amphibian that made two or three flights a day to and from Victoria, at $20.00 a seat. Unfortunately the Sikorsky was not designed to withstand the effects of salt water. Within two years it was "just one gob of corrosion," according to maintenance engineer Rex Chandler, quoted in *Pioneering Aviation in the West.*

Although the seaplane's value along the north Pacific coast has outlasted its usefulness in most of the rest of the world, the fact that its days were numbered elsewhere meant that if Vancouver wanted to remain an important travel stop it would need a paved runway. Vancouver, which has often short-changed itself on its infrastructure, suddenly approved a $600,000 bond issue to finance the new airport. But the importance of the move was not fully understood for another generation. It was only after World War II that the city's motto, "By Land and Sea We Prosper," had "Air" added to it.

The site selection committee was headed by MacLaren and also included Templeton. Like MacLaren he had flown over the delta and thought Sea Island a pretty good place to build an airport. On the start of construction in 1930 he published a brochure that exclaimed: "The day is not far distant when giant airliners and dirigibles will leave this harbour for far-away China, Japan, and even Australia, while large multi-motored planes will carry the passengers and mails which arrive here from these distant countries . . . faster than the winds themselves and higher than the birds which fly."

If the word "harbour" sounds odd that is because the YVR of its time was named the City of Vancouver Airport and Seaplane Harbour. It was an impressive airdrome. Much of it remains in the form of today's South Airport, home to small-scale aircraft-repair industry and various coastal charter operations. Because of the importance to the aircraft of the time of taking off and landing into the wind, a radial runway system was installed. Runways ran off in five directions from a single hub. The harbor part was the Middle Arm of the Fraser River, where floatplanes still alight today.

Airports need airlines to succeed and, as well-planned and located as Vancouver Airport was, it had no airlines for the first three years of its opulent, if isolated, existence. It became known jokingly as "Templeton's Farm." Unofficial airport statistics for its first year show the overwhelming majority of passengers, 2,652, were there to embark on sightseeing flights. (Another 536 arrived there from other points on 309 incoming flights.)

It was Templeton who is said to have exercised some kind of inside influence in persuading Sewell Hall, United Airlines' Seattle superintendent, to give Vancouver a try. The first United flight arrived on Dominion Day, 1934. The move brought Vancouver air links with most of the continent and introduced the first modern airliner, the "three-mile-a-minute," all-metal Boeing 247.

In 1936 Canadian Airways decided to compete with United on the Seattle-Vancouver run. Canadian started with de Havilland Dragon Rapides—twin-engine biplanes that looked prehistoric beside United's Boeings. That year, though, MacLaren bought two new Lockheed 10 Electras—the fastest airliners in

The ten-passenger aircraft flew passengers and mail the 122 miles (196 kilometres) to Seattle in 50 minutes. Airfare was $7.90 one-way. Five years later the airline had a route network extending to Halifax and St. John's, Newfoundland.

the world at the time—and checked out two of his pilots, Billy Wells and Maurice McGregor, on the hot new ships. The run was considered a rehearsal for the transcontinental flights Canadian hoped to win.

But the federal government's conditions were unacceptable to Canadian's owners. So Trans-Canada Air Lines was founded by the federal government in 1937. Don MacLaren became the new airline's first employee and the Lockheed-10s its first aircraft. With the planes came their newly trained pilots and the Seattle-Vancouver route. When Wells and McGregor had completed their daily round-trip on September, 2 1937, they were informed that they were now part of TCA. The following year, 1938, runway lights were added.

The main changes to the airport during the war included construction of a new Boeing plant near the Fraser River, where a total of 362 Consolidated PBY flying boats and amphibians were built under license. Late in the war the plant switched to making bomb-bays for Boeing B-29s, examples of which dropped atomic bombs on Hiroshima and Nagasaki.

Early in the war the federal government became involved in running the airport for the first time. Ottawa underwrote the Sea Island Boeing plant in 1941. Two new one-and-a-half-kilometre (5,000-foot) runways were built. An RCAF Station and Number 8 Elementary Flight Training School appeared at the north end of the field. Canadian Pacific Airlines was born in 1942 and focused at first on servicing routes within the province from Sea Island. The airport was returned to civic control in 1946 and when Templeton retired three years later he was able to point out how critical the facility had been in supplying Fraser Valley communities during the great flood of 1948.

That same year CPA began its trans-Pacific flights in high-flying but noisy North Star aircraft, quickly replaced by larger types that required longer runways. Two de Havilland Comet jetliners were built for CPA during the early 1950s, the prospect of their introduction causing concern that the wartime runways were already obsolete and would have to be lengthened to "at least 7,500 feet," according to the city's *Forward Year Book* of 1950.

But design flaws in the Comet kept CPA from becoming a jet airline until 1958 when it bought turboprop Bristol Britannias. Both TCA and CPA bought pure-jet DC-8s in 1961. A major makeover was in store for YVR; perhaps $100 million would be required to bring Vancouver into the jet age. That was too rich for the city. In 1961 the city voted to sell its dwindling share of the airport to the federal government for $2.5 million.

The year 1986 may not have been the best time to finish a new terminal at the north end of Sea Island—a terminal designed to take Vancouver to the end of the 20th century. One year later the Boeing 747 Jumbo Jet would fly for the first time near Seattle, setting off a worldwide round of even more ambitious airport expansions. In 1970 and 1971 CP Air and Air Canada completed jet-sized hangars at YVR and in the latter year Transport Canada completed a new Air Traffic Control Centre in a low, windowless building among the old hangars at what had become known as the South Airport. By then Vancouver was being served by eight major airlines.

Despite the phenomenal growth, the $32 million 1968 terminal, designed by Zoltan Kiss on behalf of Vancouver's leading firm of architects, Thompson Berwick Pratt, had a beautiful sweeping, skylit concourse that adapted well to more and more intensive use until, during the early 1990s, Vancouver became the fastest-growing city north of the Sunbelt. Suddenly it seemed as if, once again, the city knew better what it needed in an airport than Ottawa did.

So YVR was back in the city's hands in 1990, being run by a locally appointed Vancouver International Airport Authority that was prepared to put $750 million into the facility—half-a-billion more than Transport Canada had planned to spend. Anyone who used the airport during the mid-1990s knew about snaking lineups occupying most of the old terminal's third floor check-in areas and the cramped, basement International Arrivals tunnels—Vancouver had outgrown its airport. Nevertheless the authority saw the airport expansion not as a limitless drain on its funds but as a profitable front door to Canada from the Pacific Rim.

YVR's new terminal and second major runway are the logical $350 million outcomes of that philosophy. The terminal extends north from the "old" one, which is not yet 30 years old. The entry to the new departure hall appears to have been designed almost solely to showcase Bill Reid's *Jade Canoe* sculpture, the masterpiece of the Haida arts revival that Reid pioneered. It dominates a mezzanine above the foyer and is surrounded with cool blue- and green-greys intended by Clive Grout and his architectural design team to evoke B.C.'s natural splendor. The terminal's grey tree-like columns have the same effect as do the light-green, photo-sensitive glass curtain walls that show off the mountains past the new third runway to the north.

William Templeton's stately vision of huge dirigibles moored at masts on Sea Island may not have come true exactly as he foresaw it. Speed has become more important than comfort aloft. So instead, today's big jets carry as many as 500 people at close to the speed of sound. In the new YVR, those passengers won't spend any more time standing around than they want to.

Then service across the Atlantic to the U.K. began. After the war TCA launched flights to sunny destinations like Florida and the Caribbean, and more European destinations were added.

Vancouver International Airport Authority
Chuck Davis

THE VANCOUVER INTERNATIONAL Airport Authority, which took over control of YVR on July 1, 1992, is a community-based, non-profit corporation. Its primary objective is to expand the contribution which Vancouver International Airport makes to local economic development and to improve the cost-effectiveness and commercial orientation of the airport. The board of directors is comprised of people with wide experience in areas such as finance, administration, law, engineering, organized labor, consumer interests and the air transportation, aviation and aerospace industries.

No elected officials or civil servants are eligible for appointment to the board. The authority has members appointed by the following jurisdictions: the cities of Vancouver and Richmond; the GVRD; the Vancouver Board of Trade; the Institute of Chartered Accountants of B.C.; the Association of Professional Engineers and Geoscientists of B.C.; the Law Society of B.C.; and seven appointees chosen from the community at large. There is an annual general meeting, open to the public at large.

In a June, 1996, *Equity* interview with writer Stuart McNish, David Emerson, the president and chief executive officer of the authority, explained the unpopular May 1, 1993, imposition of the "airport improvement fee." (The AIF fee is five dollars for passengers travelling to a destination within British Columbia or the Yukon; ten dollars for passengers travelling to other North American destinations, including Mexico, plus Hawaii; or $15 for passengers travelling to destinations outside North America. The fee must be paid by passengers departing from the airport. Children under two and passengers connecting through Vancouver on the same day—the latter accounting for about 30 per cent of all enplaning passengers—are not required to pay.)

Someone, Emerson explained, has to pay the $500 million for the airport's expansion and it was decided to make the fee visible so the public associates the money with the project. American airports, said Emerson, have similar fees buried within ticket prices. "Under our system," he continued, "it goes from your hand to the person in the green vest and in ten minutes it's been deposited in the Royal Bank and applied to the debt on the new terminal and runway." Once the additions are completed, he says, the fee will disappear and further expansion will likely be funded by 20-year bonds. (By June 1, 1996, the date the new International Terminal Building opened

for business, the AIF program had raised approximately $100 million towards the cost of the building.)

The cost to airlines of landing their jumbo jets and large cargo planes at YVR has dropped since the Airport Authority took over and that has led to an increase in the number of planes landing. And income from the airport's retail outlets—there are 58 shops in the new terminal alone—has jumped.

SCHEDULED AIRLINES SERVING YVR (SUMMER 1996)

MAJOR AIRLINES

Air Canada, Air China, Air New Zealand, Alaska Airlines, All Nippon Airways, American Airlines, America West Airlines, British Airways, Canadian Airlines, Cathay Pacific Airways, Delta Air Lines, Japan Airlines, KLM Royal Dutch Airlines, Korean Air, Lufthansa, Malaysia Airlines, Mandarin Airlines, Northwest Airlines, Qantas, Reno Air, Singapore Airlines, Swissair, United Airlines.

MAJOR REGIONAL AIRLINES

AirBC, Canadian Regional Airlines, Greyhound Air, Horizon Air, WestJet Airlines.

REGIONAL/LOCAL AIRLINES

Awood Air, Central Mountain Air, Hanna's Air Saltspring, Harbour Air, Helijet Airways, K.D. Air, North Vancouver Air, Pacific Coastal Airlines, Shuswap Air, Wilderness Airlines.

PASSENGERS (ARRIVING AND DEPARTING) AT VANCOUVER INTERNATIONAL AIRPORT

- 1974   *4,336,000*
- 1985   *7,017,850*
- 1986   *8,413,490*
- 1987   *7,822,500*
- 1988   *8,840,130*
- 1989   *9,143,850*
- 1990   *9,544,300*
- 1991   *8,996,140*
- 1992   *9,449,940*
- 1993   *9,677,570*
- 1994   *10,206,340*
- 1995   *11,290,000*
- 1996   *12,250,500*
- 1997   *12,915,200* (projected)
- 1998   *13,471,100* (projected)
- 1999   *14,015,700* (projected)
- 2000   *14,550,000* (projected)

Air Canada—the new name was born in the mid-sixties—continues to expand, with the most rapid growth for its Vancouver operation occurring in the mid-nineties when it became the fastest growing airline, with new flights from Vancouver to Korea, Japan, Hong Kong, New Delhi, Glasgow, Paris, Frankfurt, Zurich, Los Angeles and San Francisco.

Water Transportation
Jim Lyon

VANCOUVER, NAMED after a famous navigator, is a city defined by water—a gulf, a sound, straits, rivers, bays, inlets, lakes and dykes. Since the earliest times, when the forest—thick and formidable—precluded most land travel, water has furnished convenient highways.

Long before European settlement, British Columbia's native peoples traded (and fought) from impressive canoes. For instance, in 1828 about 500 Cowichan canoes were observed coming down the Fraser River over three days in September at the end of the fishing season. The Cowichan people from Vancouver Island seasonally occupied three fishing villages on the South Arm of the Fraser between the mouth and New Westminster. The explorer Simon Fraser described the canoes of the Coast Salish people. They were 4.6 to 9.1 metres long, he said. They had been adzed and burnt out of a single cedar half-log, and then stretched open.

Organized water traffic was thin and sporadic in the early 19th century. The first steamer to reach the Pacific Northwest coast—the 30.8-metre Hudson's Bay Company *Beaver,* built in England—arrived at Fort Vancouver (now Vancouver, Washington) in 1836. A decade earlier, carpenters from the Orkney Islands in northern Scotland had constructed the first vessel ever built on the Columbia River, the Hudson Bay schooner *Vancouver.* Another early vessel to trade up the coast was the *Cadboro* (after which Cadboro Bay in Victoria is named), built in England in 1827. These early vessels traded from the Hudson's Bay headquarters on the Columbia River at Fort Vancouver (moved to Victoria in 1843 by Gov. William Douglas) to company forts established at Fort Simpson on the Nass River and Fort McLoughlin near Bella Bella.

The Fraser River Gold Rush in the 1850s brought many new vessels to the area. In just a few months in 1858 thousands of would-be miners travelled from San Francisco to Victoria. An early ferry service was established to connect Victoria with Queensborough (now New Westminster). The pioneering vessel on the river in 1858—only 50 years after Simon Fraser descended the river bearing his name—was the 67-metre sidewheeler *Surprise.* She carried between five and six hundred prospectors on some 30 trips between Victoria and Hope.

The only passenger transportation available along Burrard Inlet in the 1880s was the Moodyville ferry and the *Union,* a small craft with an unreliable engine. Gerald A. Rushton, in his excellent account of the Union Steamship company, *Whistle up the Inlet,* relates the story of how on a stormy night in 1883 a Mrs. Patterson, with a native boatman, paddled in a dugout canoe to help the sick wife of the Point Atkinson lightkeeper. Burrard Inlet's north shore was then described as "a rocky terrain of trail-less forest and unfordable streams." Contrast that experience with the quick and comfortable trip today's SeaBus makes across Burrard Inlet!

In the 1880s the mail was rowed from the end of the road at Hastings across Burrard Inlet to Moodyville (now the site of the Saskatchewan Wheat Pool elevator) and to Gastown. One celebrated rower was a Norwegian named "Hans the Boatman," who, having lost a hand in an accident, rowed with the aid of an iron hook buckled onto his left arm.

By 1869 the Inlet had become a thriving seaport, with two sawmills working to capacity. A daily stagecoach from New Westminster connected with Captain James Van Bramer's little ferry, *Sea Foam,* the Inlet's first regular transit service. It ran from Brighton, near the site of the present Alberta Wheat Pool elevator, to Moodyville then back to Stamp's Mill (site of the present Vanterm container dock) and on to Brighton.

When the *Sea Foam* sank after an explosion in 1868, Captain Van Bramer operated a tiny craft, called the *Chinaman,* and then the vessels *Lillie* and *Leonora.* In 1880 he had a wooden vessel named *Senator* built for him. This ship, a steam-propelled vessel, could accommodate a dozen passengers in an enclosed cabin and many more on deck. Fares to cross the inlet in 1881 were 10 cents for a passenger and 50 cents for cattle. Wagons were sometimes towed behind on a scow. These vessels were the forerunners of many which conveyed passengers across the Inlet.

Vancouver's first home-controlled shipping company was the Union Steamship Co. It prospered from the Fraser River Gold Rush and built several fine passenger ships for operation to northern outports. Later the company became preeminent in the excursion trade out of Burrard Inlet. The line's headquarters was the Union Wharf at the foot of Carrall Street, just east of the Canadian Pacific Railway wharves. The red-funnelled Union steamers could be seen in the port until 1959, when the company was absorbed by Northland Navigation Co.

For more than half a century, ferries operated across Burrard Inlet between the Carrall Street wharf and the small communities of North and West Vancouver. Service to West Vancouver was doomed by the opening of the Lions Gate Bridge, and ended in 1947. The ferry continued to run across to the foot of Lonsdale Avenue in North Vancouver for several more years, until it too fell victim to the popularity of the automobile and ceased operation in 1958.

HBC ship Beaver *wrecked at Prospect Point, Stanley Park, 1888.* cva

As the population of the North Shore grew, so did the demand for some sort of "third crossing" of the Inlet to ease the pressure of traffic on the two bridges. In 1977 the harbor ferry reappeared in ultramodern dress as the SeaBus, a high-speed, marine passenger service. Built completely in British Columbia, the SeaBus is the first marine transit service of its kind in the world. Each of the catamaran-style SeaBus ferries is 34 metres long, with a capacity of 400 passengers. Constructed of lightweight aluminum, the vessels are powered by four diesel engines and have a cruising speed of 11.5 knots. Highly manoeuverable, the double-ended ferries can move in any direction and turn in their own length. A SeaBus ferry departs every 15 minutes during daytime from the floating terminals adjoining Lonsdale Quay in North Vancouver and from the old CP Rail station near Canada Place.

Coastal travel today is dominated by the BC Ferries system—one of the biggest and most sophisticated operations in the world. BC Ferries began life officially on June 15, 1960, as the awkwardly named B.C. Highways and Bridges Toll Authority Ferries. At first it had two vessels—the MV *Tsawwassen* and the MV *Sidney*—which shuttled on the one route between Tsawwassen and Swartz Bay. It then had 225 employees.

Throughout the 1960s, new construction, fleet acquisitions and route expansion continued until BC Ferries had reached the 24-ship mark. With more people using the service, a decision was made to enlarge the fleet—but in an unusual way. The first part of BC Ferries now famous "stretch and lift" program began in 1970, when four of its major vessels were cut across the middle so that a 25.6-metre midsection could be "spliced" in. Similar operations had been performed on smaller boats, but this was the first time BC Ferries' larger ships were subject to such extensive alterations.

The next expansion occurred in 1976, when a new generation of "jumbo ferries" was launched. By the early 1980s five of these new double-ended "Cowichan class" ships had been added to the fleet. Five years later, part two of the stretch and lift strategy was implemented. Four major vessels were hauled back into dry dock and sliced horizontally. The two halves were separated from each other so that new car decks could be slid into place, thus giving birth to the Victoria class ships. In each case the object was to meet constantly increasing passenger demand by creating more capacity.

By 1994 BC Ferries operated 40 vessels, serving 42 ports of call along 24 routes. During 1993-94 BC Ferries carried 21.53 million passengers and 8.38 million vehicles.

The ferries are an integral part of British Columbia's coastal transportation system, linking Greater Vancouver to many small islands of the Strait of Georgia and Vancouver Island. Three routes connect the Lower Mainland to Vancouver Island. (Service is also provided from Prince Rupert, on the province's north coast, to the Queen Charlotte Islands/Haida Gwaii and to northern Vancouver Island.)

In 1994 BC Ferries' workforce consisted of unionized (British Columbia Ferry & Marine Worker's Union) and management employees. The permanent workforce numbered about 2,700, augmented by approximately 1,400 casual workers.

The fleet ranges in size from the 33.8-metre *Nimpkish*, which carries 133 people and 16 vehicles, to the massive S-class vessels (*Spirit of British Columbia* and *Spirit of Vancouver Island*, launched in 1993 and 1994), which measure 167.6 metres long and can carry 2,000 passengers and 470 vehicles each.

In 1994 the provincial government announced an $800 million, ten-year capital plan for BC Ferries which included a new terminal in Nanaimo (Duke Point), continued expansion of facilities at major terminals, replacement of two older ferries and the introduction of fast ferries. It was noted that half of the ferry fleet was built either before or during the 1960s and, since the useful life of a ferry is generally only 40 years, there was a pressing need for a long-range vessel replacement program.

Tugs and Barges of Our Coast
Liz Bennett

THE FIRST TOW BOAT in Vancouver is thought to be the sidewheeler *Isabel,* delivered at Victoria in 1866 to escort ships to and from the Stamp and Moody mills on the shores of Burrard Inlet. She was not the first vessel to perform this duty in British Columbia waters—that honor goes to the *Beaver,* which was used for ship handling as early as 1836—but she was the first built specifically to perform this duty. The sailing ships that carried lumber and other export products from the new colony had a hard time making way against the tides and winds, so it was in the interest of the mill and wharf owners to ensure they had power launches available to tow them in and out of the harbor. Independent boat owners also vied for this ship-handling work, as well as carrying passengers and freight between the settlements springing up along Burrard Inlet and the Fraser River.

As the number of settlements grew, so did the coastal shipping industry, and some vessel operators began to specialize in towing. The tug and barge combination offers the advantage of keeping the capital-intensive motorized vessel, a tug, working while the low-tech cargo carrier, a scow or barge, is loaded or used for floating storage. The canneries up and down the coast also used tug and barge transportation. With the spread of ocean-going steamers and the development of the trans-Pacific trade, coal had to be barged from the mines at Nanaimo to bunker Canadian Pacific's fleet. When Lower Mainland mills exhausted the trees within easy reach, flat booms of logs were brought in from elsewhere, often by tugs owned or leased by the forest companies themselves. There was work enough as one century turned into the next to enable one-man, one-boat operations to grow into companies under the leadership of men such as Charles H. Cates, Capt. G.H. French, George McKeen and Harold Jones, to name only a few.

The first two decades of the century saw the formation of some of the precursor companies of the major players in today's towing industry. The list of companies who advertised in *Harbour & Shipping* magazine during its first year of publication (October 1918 through September 1919) included many names that are still remembered by those in the industry: Greer, Coyle & Co.; T.G. McBride & Co.; Vancouver Tug & Barge; Campion & White; Progressive Steamboat Co.; McNeill, Welch & Wilson; McKeen & Wilson (est. 1894), whose fleet consisted of scows; Gulf of Georgia Towing Co., then owned by the Walkem family; Fraser River Pile Driving Co., which still offers pile driving and towing services; and Victoria Tug Co. Competition within the industry was getting sophisticated. The B.C. Towboat Owners' Association, formed in the 1920s, included, at its peak, 52 towing firms who agreed to a schedule of rates and wages. Outside the BCTOA ranks were dozens of independent operators, some of whom became players to reckon with in the tough times to come.

The towing industry weathered the dirty thirties better than many; goods still had to be moved, and there was room to economize by cutting wages and crew size. Perhaps because tough times encourage change, the 1930s saw a shift toward diesel engines, which offered more power in less space. The steam-powered tugs of this decade had to be large to carry the coal that powered their engines, and the crew to keep the machinery going. For example, one of the first vessels built specifically for towing logs was the *Active,* 35.4 metres long, 6.4 metres in the beam, and powered with triple-expansion engines that developed 55 nominal horsepower. It could take her anywhere from two to six weeks to bring a boom of logs from an up-coast logging camp to Hastings Mill on Burrard Inlet. In 1936 the 1923-built *Sea Wave,* owned by Young & Gore Tugboat Co., had her 200 BHP steam plant replaced with a 350 BHP Union diesel, increasing her earning capacity by nearly 50 per cent. Ultimately most of the remaining tugs from the era of steam would be repowered, though one, the *Master,* is still in service with its steam plant intact. Gasoline and diesel engines were even manufactured in Vancouver by Vivian Engine Works and Easthope.

The decade also saw the introduction of log barges. Until this time logs had been made up into flat booms, or more compact Davis rafts, cigar-shaped bundles of logs held together with chains that could be towed across the open waters between the Queen Charlotte Islands and the inland passage between Vancouver Island and the mainland. The early log barges were stripped down sailing ships that had been displaced on the world's freight lanes by steamships. Today's log barges are purpose-built vessels with onboard cranes for loading, and a system of ballast tanks that permits the logs to be unloaded by tipping the vessel on its side until they slide into the water.

The formation of companies continued, as did the trend toward specialization. It was during the thirties that C.H. Cates & Sons began to specialize in ship handling in Burrard Inlet, while on the Fraser River Cooper & Smith Towing, started in 1919 by Tom Cooper, began to do the same, ultimately becoming, in 1932, Westminster Tug Boats. Competing for salvage contracts were Pacific Salvage Co., whose assets included tugs from 60 to 2,700 HP, and West Coast Salvage & Contracting Company with a "complete salvage plant ready at all times."

Seaspan International Ltd., Canada's largest tug and barge company, is a familiar sight along the coast of North America. In reliable service to British Columbia industries for almost one hundred years, Seaspan's modern fleet of tugs and barges is identified by distinctive colors, black hulls with red and white superstructure and the jaunty symbol of a seahorse.

Tug S.S. Master, 1993. vs

Marpole Towing, on the other hand, made "scow towing a specialty," while, in 1937, Sparkie New and George Ellis took on the problem of coastwise transport with Coastal Towing, predecessor to Coast Ferries, still owned by Sparkie's son Bill.

Then came the war. With West Coast shipyards building Liberty ships, there was lots of harbor work, and coastwise movement of goods continued. River Towing was formed in 1941 by Cecil Cosulich, whose father, Bob, was a noted skipper, but whose own attempts to form a company had failed. Cecil and his brother Norman, who shortly joined the company, had the business acumen, and their new enterprise prospered. However, a new era was about to begin. In 1942 Straits Towing was formed by Harold Elworthy and Stan McKeen out of the one-tug Preston-Mann fleet and McKeen's Standard Towing. The partnership between the two was relatively short-lived, but the trend was clear. For the next couple of decades the formation of new tugboat companies would slow, while established companies merged to achieve rationalization of scale.

During the thirties and forties few new tugs joined the B.C. fleet. Stout hulls were patched and re-engined, and new technologies, such as radios, fitted, but by the end of the war the fleet was severely in need of renewal. Cheap war surplus vessels provided the towboat industry with a ready-made supply of new vessels, including large sea-going tugs such as the *Sudbury*, that enabled a number of companies, like Island Tug & Barge, to branch out into deep-sea towing. Steel tugs were not unknown on the B.C. coast but like Canadian Fishing Company's *Kingsway* (later *LaPointe*), a former North Sea trawler, were imports. Local builders had continued to work in wood, which was plentiful and cheap. War-time construction provided a pool of expertise in steel-boat building, however, so when, in the 1950s, the industry began to look at constructing new vessels, a number of yards were ready and equipped to move to steel construction.

The modern towboat is a powerful and sophisticated vessel. Building and maintaining such a substantial capital asset has more or less forced the industry to develop large, sophisticated companies. In the 1950s there were five major companies: Island Tug and Barge, Vancouver Tug Boat Co., Gulf of Georgia Towing Co., Straits Towing and River Towing, each with its strengths. This pattern held for almost two decades, then in 1969 Straits and River Towing combined to form RivTow Straits. In 1970 Island Tug & Barge and Vancouver Tug Boat joined forces, forming the nucleus of Seaspan International. Gulf of Georgia Towing Co. remained independent until 1977, when it was bought by Genstar Corporation, then owner of Seaspan.

Seaspan International is the largest towboat company in Canada, and, though the main focus remains on serving B.C. forest companies, it operates world-wide with specialized tug and barge combinations to meet a myriad of needs including heavy lift and deep-sea towing and salvage. In 1994 Seaspan challenged the status quo in ship-handling by building two berthing tugs for use in Burrard Inlet.

C.H. Cates & Sons consolidated its monopoly on ship-berthing in Burrard Inlet by absorbing Seaforth Towing, and developed specialized vessels to match the type of deep-sea vessel using the port. Cates remained a family company until 1992, when it was bought by Washington Group of Missoula, Montana, who leave day-to-day operations in the hands of local management.

RivTow, still controlled by the Cosulich family, has become a highly diversified company, but still retains a strong connection with the towboat industry. Westminster Tug Boat still provides berthing services at Fraser Port as one of the operating units of the RivTow group.

In addition to these major players, there are a number of medium-sized companies, such as Pacific Towing Services, Catherwood Towing, Riverside Towing, Shields Navigation, Valley Towing and Squamish Tugboat—even the odd owner/operator—who manage to stay in business by balancing competition with cooperation.

Editor's note: our thanks to Harbour & Shipping Journal and editor Liz Bennett, for this article.

A highly diversified company with a colorful history, Seaspan has progressed and together with associated companies Vancouver Shipyards Co. Ltd., Vancouver Drydock Company, Vancouver Shipyards (Esquimalt) Ltd., SeaFuels Ltd. and Manly Marine Closures Ltd., will continue to meet the growing needs of the marine industry in the Pacific northwest.

Famous Boats

"TAGONITE"
— BUILT BY —
BOEING AIRCRAFT OF CANADA
LIMITED
YARD No 990
1930
VANCOUVER, CANADA

HARBOUR & SHIPPING
Established 1918

Canada's Premier Marine Trade Journal, providing Shipping and Transportation News and Features to Business and Industry.

Topics covered include maritime law, local and international company news and profiles, regulatory changes, shipping schedules, shipping statistics, new products and maritime history. Well-illustrated articles feature new tugboats, ferries and deep-sea vessels, including cruise ships. Published Monthly by Progress Publishing Co. Ltd. 200-1865 Marine Drive, West Vancouver, B.C. V7V 1J7 • Tel: (604) 922-6717 • Fax 922-1739

Famous Boats
Rob Morris and Leonard McCann

Beaver Wood-hulled, steam engined sidewheel freighter built in England in 1835 for Hudson's Bay Company service in the Pacific Northwest. *Beaver* was the first steamship to operate along the coast north of the equator. From 1862 to 1870 she served as a Royal Navy hydrographic survey ship and from 1874 to 1888 was in use as a towboat and freighter. Wrecked in 1888 at the entrance to Burrard Inlet. Now a heritage wreck site, the artifacts are in the Vancouver Maritime Museum.

Black Hawk This Robert Allan-designed speedster was built in 1935 by water taxi pioneer Lloyd Burns. *Black Hawk*, with her twin Liberty aircraft engines did a 45 mph top speed. Based in Coal Harbour, she carried loggers, RCMP officers and undertook many a medical emergency mission.

Burrard Otter This vessel and her sistership, *Burrard Beaver*, are B.C. Transit's SeaBuses, crossing Vancouver Harbour between Lonsdale Quay on the North Shore and the Vancouver waterfront in about 12 minutes. Since starting service in 1977, the two SeaBuses have carried well over 70 million passengers, averaging more than 15,000 passengers daily during the summer months.

Cape Beale With her high, rounded stern and deep, narrow hull the *Cape Beale* represents the classic Norwegian-influenced halibut boat of the 1920s and 1930s. She was built on a site where the present Burrard Bridge now stands by Edgar Arnet and John Berg in 1925 and made many trips to the halibut grounds of the Gulf of Alaska and the Bering Sea. *Cape Beale* was bought by John Gibson of logging family fame who chopped the traditional, small wheelhouse and replaced it with a large house, but *Cape Beale*'s beautiful hull is still intact.

Cassiar (I) Well known to her crew and passengers as the "Loggers' Palace," the Union Steamship Company's general freighter served the coastal communities and northern logging camps for 23 years, logging many miles with only one accident. *Cassiar* was originally built as a four-masted schooner in 1890, converted to steam power in 1892 and bought by the USS Co. in 1901. Retired in 1923, she ended her days as a

facing page: top; Canadian Pacific's Clydebuilt Empress of Asia *(one of the legendary "White Empress" liners) steaming into Vancouver, circa 1936.* cva *bottom; builder's brass plate on the* Taconite. vp

dance hall in Lake Washington.

Charles H. Cates The ex-*Gaviota*, ex-*Charles H. Cates III* was built for the founder of C.H. Cates Towing of North Vancouver in 1913. Bought in 1990 and faithfully restored by the family of Charles Cates' granddaughter, *Gaviola* was built by Andy Linton based on his pilot boat design. She first worked as a lines boat in Vancouver Harbour before becoming a pleasure boat, after WWII, available to Cates' employees for their summer holidays.

Clifford J. Rogers A steel freighter built in Montreal in 1955 for the White Pass and Yukon Railway Co. for service between Vancouver and Skagway. *Clifford J. Rogers* was the world's first purpose-built container ship. She carried 168 8x8x7-foot metal containers. Sold in 1966, the vessel underwent several name changes and areas of operation and in 1967 sank suddenly with some loss of crew in the vicinity of the Bermuda Triangle.

Dragon Boat Each June the dragon boats streak across the harbor, their 22 paddlers stroking in perfect unison to the beat of their drummer, guided by their steersman as they compete against one another. The Dragon Boat Festival celebrates a 2,000-year-old Chinese tradition. Built in Hong Kong, the 40-foot teak dragon boats are "brought to life" by the ancient "dotting of the eyes" ceremonial blessing before the races.

Empress of Japan (I) Built in England in 1891 for the Canadian Pacific Railway's initial trans-Pacific freight and passenger runs to the Orient. This steel steamer operated for 32 years without mishap including service as an armed merchant cruiser during WWI. Her original dragon figurehead is in the Vancouver Maritime Museum; a replica can be found in Stanley Park.

Empress of Japan (II) This was the Canadian Pacific Railway's finest trans-Pacific liner. Upon arrival in Vancouver in late 1930, she commenced regular crossings to the Orient via Honolulu. Requisitioned as a troop ship in 1939, her name was changed to *Empress of Scotland*. (where she was built) After WWII she returned to CPR service in the North Atlantic, was sold in 1958 and renamed *Hanseatic*. After fire damage she was scrapped in 1966.

Eva A well-preserved example of the small, Japanese-style salmon gillnetters which fished the Fraser River in the 1930s through 1950s. *Eva* was built by the Kishi Brothers in Steveston in 1939 for Henry Jacobson of Finn Slough and is still in the family. She fished up to 1993, still powered by her original 10-18 Easthope gas engine manufactured by Easthope Brothers on Coal Harbour, Vancouver.

Fort Wallace Launched in 1943 as the 200th

cargo ship out of Burrard Dry Dock, the *Fort Wallace* was a Victory-type ship named after Alfred "Andy" Wallace, founder of the shipyard. She carried war equipment and materials to beachheads in Europe, and made at least six trips to Normandy as a troop carrier. Sold in 1946, *Fort Wallace* passed through several owners before eventually being scrapped.

Graybeard Designed as an ocean racer/cruiser by Vancouver marine architect Peter Hatfield and owner Lol Killam, *Graybeard* embarked on an illustrious ocean racing career under the flag of the Royal Vancouver Yacht Club in 1970. That year she won the Swiftsure Lightship and Victoria-Maui races and went on to compete in the Sidney-Hobart, Capetown-Rio races and a near-disastrous TransPac before Killam began to cruise her throughout the Pacific. Humphrey Killam owns *Graybeard* now as a liveaboard and charter yacht. "Graybeards" are huge waves which circle Antarctica, occasionally capsizing freighters as they come ashore in the Straits of Magellan.

Greenhill Park A dry cargo Victory-type merchant ship built by Burrard Drydock Co. in 1945, *Greenhill Park* blew up March 6, 1945 while being loaded in Vancouver Harbour. Eight men were killed and the blast shattered downtown Vancouver windows. *Greenhill Park* was towed at great risk out into the harbor and later it was found that improper stowage of flammable cargo and explosives, plus flouting of safety regulations, all contributed to the disaster.

Haro This wood-hulled, steam-powered tug was built in Vancouver in 1910 for B.C. Mills (Hastings Mill) for its harbor service. In 1932 *Haro* was sold to M.R. Cliff and during WWII served as a RCN patrol boat off Victoria. In 1960 she was rebuilt as *LeBeau*; she was laid up in 1967 and scrapped a couple of years later.

Harold A. Jones A fine representative of the great post-WWII advances in tugboat construction technology with welded steel hulls, Kort nozzles and powerful, high-speed diesels. This Robert Allan-designed 136-foot towboat was built at Star Shipyards in New Westminster. She was the flagship of the Vancouver Tug Boat Company fleet, became *Seaspan Monarch*, and was totally refitted in 1995 as *Island Monarch* for Island Tug and Barge.

HMS Discovery See the separate article by W. Kaye Lamb.

Hollyburn For many years ferries were the only link between the North Shore municipalities and downtown Vancouver before bridges and wheeled public transportation rendered them "obsolete." *Hollyburn* was built in 1936 for the West Vancouver Municipal Ferry system, the last vessel to join the fleet. Sold to Harbour Navigation in 1945, *Hollyburn* has worked as an excursion vessel ever since, especially during Expo 86.

Imperial Skeena The last of the oil tankers servicing the coast, this 300-foot vessel was built by Burrard Dry Dock Company and runs from the Esso refinery at Ioco in Burrard Inlet. Capable of carrying eight different petroleum products, *Imperial Skeena* has delivered to Nanaimo and Victoria distribution points for 25 years.

Iron Blue A "Sea Skiff" model built by the Turner Boatworks on Coal Harbour, *Iron Blue* represents a class of popular fishing, camping, commuter boat used in Howe Sound and the Sunshine Coast area in the 1940s and 1950s. "Turner built" boats were clinker, or lapstrake, hulls from eight-foot dinghies to 36-foot cruisers, plus hundreds of wartime lifeboats. John Turner came from the U.K. and went into business in 1887 with another well-known Coal Harbour boatbuilder, Andy Linton. Turner Boatworks was opened about 10 years later and closed in 1957.

Isabel Built in Victoria in 1866 as a tug for Captain Edward Stamp, owner of what became Hastings Mill at the foot of Dunlevy Street. Probably the first tug in Burrard Inlet, *Isabel* was used largely for shiphandling and led an active and varied life which included coal and mail carriage, plus the odd stranding. Tied up in Esquimalt in 1898, *Isabel* was abandoned.

Island Commander This North Sea fishing trawler was built in Selby, England, in 1912 as *Andrew Kelly*. She came to fish out of Prince Rupert in 1914, and was converted to a tug in 1941 by Island Tug and Barge of Victoria and renamed *Island Commander*. In 1946 she towed the last sailing ship out of B.C waters, the *Pamir* with a load of coal for Australia. Rebuilt in 1956 as a salvage vessel, there is presently a proposal to return her to Britain as a heritage vessel—the last Grimsby trawler.

Ivanhoe is the last remaining large prototype tug in B.C. Wooden-hulled and originally steam-powered, she was built in 1907 for G.I. Wilson and sold in 1913 to Kingcome Navigation for general log towing. *Ivanhoe* is now a heritage vessel, owned and operated by a non-profit society, and has summer moorage at the Vancouver Maritime Museum.

J.H.Carlisle Built in 1928 at Burrard Dry Dock, this vessel was Vancouver's—or rather False Creek and Granville Island's—first fireboat. She actually made only two working forays into Vancouver Harbour. By 1972 the False Creek industries that had supported her commissioning had almost entirely disappeared, so *J.H.Carlisle* was disposed of and is now a workboat at Port Edward on the Skeena River.

Kestrel Built at Wallace Shipyard in Vancouver in 1903, *Kestrel* was a fisheries protection cruiser for the Dominion Government and made many appearances at public maritime events. In 1911 *Kestrel* was sold for official duties of various South Seas Island governments and, after fire damage, eventually reappeared in 1914 as a "blackbirder" or slave carrier. She disappeared a year later after calling at the Gilbert Islands.

Komogata Maru This freighter was built in 1890 in Glasgow for a German shipping line. In 1914 she was chartered from then Japanese owners to bring 400 "would-be" immigrants from India to Vancouver. When landing was denied, the passengers seized the ship; supplies and food ran out. Immigration authorities attempted boarding to enforce deportation but were driven off. A Royal Canadian Navy ship finally turned *Komogata Maru* and her hapless passengers back to India.

Lady Alexandra Does anyone remember the "Moonlight Cruises" to Bowen Island in the 1930s and 1940s? *Lady Alexandra* was the "Excursion Queen" of the Union Steamship Company fleet, carrying well over a million vacationers and daytrippers during her lifetime (1924-53), mainly to resorts and vacation spots at Bowen Island and along the southern B.C. coast. In 1959 *Alex* became a notable floating restaurant in Coal Harbour; she was drastically and unsuccessfully redesigned in 1970, before being towed in 1972 to Redonda Beach, California, to become a gambling hall. She was finally storm-damaged and scrapped in 1980.

Lady Van This R-class racing yacht was ordered by a syndicate of yachtsmen from the Royal Vancouver Yacht Club to compete for the Lipton Cup with their Seattle counterparts. *Lady Van* was built by Vancouver Drydock Co. in 1928 to a C.E. Nicholson design and won the cup the following year. She continued to compete under subsequent owners including B.C. Lt.-Gov. Eric Hamber and was sold to Seattle interests in the 1940s.

Lazee Gal Vancouver boat designer Thornton Grenfell opened a design shop on Coal Harbour in 1945, and a boatbuilding shop at 2nd Avenue and Fir in 1958. *Lazee Gal* is a beautifully maintained testimony to Grenfell's designs. Built in 1952 for Lee Dueck by the B.C. Millwork subsidiary of Dominion Construction, the 62-foot, twin-screw cruiser was eventually acquired by current owner Clarke Bentall, who owns Dominion Construction. *Lazee Gal* berths at the Royal Vancouver Yacht Club.

Mabel Brown Wood-hulled, five-masted auxiliary schooner built in North Vancouver in 1916 for the Canada West Coast Navigation Co. The Mabel Brown name was given to a class of 18 lumber-carrying sailing ships built on the Pacific Coast. *Mabel Brown* was uneconomic and was eventually sold to Norwegians. Damaged in a 1921 North Sea storm, the vessel was scrapped the following year.

Malahat A wooden, five-masted auxiliary schooner of the Mabel Brown class built in Victoria in 1917 as a lumber carrier. During the U.S. prohibition era she became known as the "Queen of Rum Row," sailing as a mothership out of Vancouver, often with 60,000 cases of liquor on board. She became a log barge (the first to be powered) for Gibson Brothers in 1933 and was wrecked in 1944.

Maple Leaf Built at Vancouver Shipyard in Coal Harbour in 1904 for lumber baron Alexander McLaren. This was the first vessel to fly the colors of the Royal Vancouver Yacht Club in an open race. Sold in 1916, this wooden, auxiliary schooner entered the halibut fishery under the names *Constance B* and *Parma*. In 1979 she was converted back to a sailing ship, her original name was restored and *Maple Leaf* now provides educational/environmental cruises between the Gulf of Georgia and Alaska. She is the oldest B.C. vessel in the Canada Registry of Ships.

Master Still powered with a triple-expansion steam engine, the wooden-hulled tug *Master* is the last surviving steam tug on the B.C. coast. She was built in 1922 in Arthur Moscrop's False Creek Shipyard. Presently maintained by an enthusiastic non-profit society, *Master* attends maritime festivals as a representative of the pioneering steam towboating era of the first half of this century and ties up at the Vancouver Maritime Museum in the summer.

Mastodon This bucket dredge, built in Scotland in 1910, started dredging the entrance to Vancouver Harbour in 1912 and continued on an around-the-clock basis, removing hazardous shoals until 1917. *Mastodon* then was moved to dredge the Fraser River and Port Alberni before ceasing operations in 1925 and remained tied up through the Depression. The dredge was converted to a RCN tanker in 1942 and was sold to Peruvian interests in 1947.

Melanope British-built in 1876 as an emigrant carrier to Australia, the fully rigged ship *Melanope* travelled the world's oceans always under a curse. Dismasted in a gale in 1906, she was converted to a log barge on the B.C. coast and in 1910 became well known in Vancouver Harbour as the Canadian Pacific Railway's coaling hulk servicing the Empress ships. *Melanope* now lies in the log booming grounds breakwater

facing page: Lumber schooner Mabel Brown, *circa 1916.* vancouver maritime museum

at Royston on Vancouver Island.

Norsal Originally built by Menchions Coal Harbour shipyard in 1922 for use by Powell River Company executives. *Norsal* was sold in 1946 to the J. Gordon Gibson lumbering family. Gibson changed the name in 1973 to *Maui Lu* prior to his notable trip to the Hawaiian Islands. Sold in 1977 and operated as a coastal charter vessel, *Norsal* sank in Hecate Strait in 1990.

North Vancouver No. 5 Built in False Creek in 1941 as the last car ferry for the North Vancouver Ferry system, a service which had commenced around 1900. *No. 5* ran from the foot of Lonsdale Avenue in North Vancouver to downtown Vancouver. Maintenance costs and post-war changes in auto transport such as the Lions Gate Bridge ended the service in 1958, but *No. 5* still serves the public in her old berth as the Seven Seas restaurant. Interestingly the harbor crossing service has been restored in the form of the SeaBus.

Oak II As far back as 1912, the B.C. Forest Service's boats were stationed all over the B.C. coast. Eleven of the 34-footers like *Oak II* successfully served as accommodation, office and patrol boat for district forest rangers. They were built and maintained by the Forest Service's marine depot on the Fraser River's North Arm and are nicknamed "blimps" after the rounded appearance of the 32-foot design which preceded them.

Pacific Princess Because of her "starring" role in *The Love Boat* TV series, *Pacific Princess* is probably the best-known passenger ship in the world. She and her sistership, *Island Princess* (a stand-in for at-sea film shoots), were based in Vancouver Harbour for 15 summers (1974 to 1991) in the Alaska cruise trade. The 20,000 ton vessels were built in Germany and are owned by P&O's Princess Cruises.

Point Ellice This tug was built in 1911 in North Vancouver as a dredge tender for the department of public works. Acquired by the Pacific Great Eastern Railway in 1920, she was put on a barge run between Vancouver and Squamish. Forty years later, after about 12,000 return trips, *Point Ellice* was scrapped in Victoria.

Powell River No. 1 and **No. 2** The self-dumping log barges are a uniquely British Columbia innovation. In order to bring upcoast wood cheaply, efficiently and without log losses down to the pulp and sawmills of the Lower Mainland, MacMillan Bloedel hired marine architect Robert

facing page: The Marine Building, and an Empress liner off Brockton Point, seen from the roof of the old Hotel Vancouver, 1931. cva

Allan to design a log barge from scratch. *Powell River No. 1* and *No. 2* became the prototypes for today's fleet of self-dumping log barges.

Prince George II When *Prince George* was built in Esquimalt in 1948, she was, at the time, the largest commercial vessel to have been built in Canada. She served regularly and uneventfully on the Canadian National Railway's tourist cruise run between Vancouver and Alaska. Sold in 1975, *Prince George* passed through a bewildering succession of owners and projected uses, some of which came to fruition, almost all of which lost heavily. Tied up in Britannia Beach in Howe Sound, she was totally gutted by fire in October 1995.

Prince Robert Built in 1930 for the Canadian National Railway's Vancouver-to-Alaska cruise service. *Prince Robert* carried the King and Queen from Victoria to Vancouver in 1939 and was converted by the Royal Canadian Navy to an armed merchant cruiser the same year. She seized the German freighter *Weser* off Manzanillo in 1940 and brought her to Esquimalt as a prize of war, and continued her wartime service around the world until 1945.

Princess Louise (II) Built in 1921 for the Canadian Pacific Railway's northern service by Wallace Shipyard. This was the only "Princess" to be designed and built in Vancouver. *Princess Louise* was on the run for 40 years without an incident, a record, before being sold in 1955 to become a restaurant in Long Beach, California, where she sank in 1990.

Princess Victoria Designed by Captain J.W. Troup to help establish the Canadian Pacific Railway's triangle route between Vancouver, Victoria and Seattle. *Princess Victoria* arrived in Vancouver from England in 1903 and, as a fast and luxurious liner, set the pattern for the B.C. Coast Steamship Service. In 1929 she was rebuilt as an auto ferry, was sold in 1952 and converted to a chip barge. She sank in a storm a year later.

Rivtow Lion The 147-foot oceangoing tug *Rivtow Lion* was built in 1940 in Selby, England, and joined the Rivtow Straits fleet in 1964. She worked the B.C. coast for 22 years, most often towing the 10,000-ton log barge *Rivtow Carrier*. Her original horn was contributed by Rivtow Straits to the Pacific Coliseum, where it resonated loudly each time the Vancouver Canucks hockey team scored a goal. The horn was returned to Rivtow when the Canucks moved into the new General Motors Place arena.

Samson V The Samson snagpuller vessels date back to 1884 and served primarily to keep the Fraser River's channels free of hazards, particularly the lifting of deadheads, and also to maintain the marker buoys and lights. Everyone along the river knew the Samsons and the cooks often

provided cookies and pie to visiting youngsters. *Samson V* was retired in 1980 and is now a New Westminster-berthed maritime museum, which portrays the history of the Fraser River.

Seaspan Commodore This 142-foot, 5750-bhp deep-sea tug is the flagship of the North Vancouver-based Seaspan International fleet. Built in 1974 at Vancouver Shipyards, she was soon involved in a North Sea anchor handling and towing joint venture. *Commodore* tows *Seaspan Forester,* the world's largest log barge, and barges of lumber, salt, gravel and clinker between Vancouver and Californian, Mexican and Alaskan ports.

Spirit of British Columbia One of two S-class superferries (470 cars; 2,100 passengers) built for the British Columbia Ferry Corporation, *Spirit of British Columbia* was launched in January 1993 and represents a new generation of ferries on the West Coast. The European design was built in five modules by three shipyards—Allied Shipbuilders and Pacific Rim Shipyards of Vancouver and Integrated Module Fabricators/Yarrows in Victoria—and then joined.

St. Roch Wooden-hulled and diesel engined, *St. Roch* was built in North Vancouver in 1928 as an RCMP patrol ship for Western Arctic operations. In 1940-42 she voyaged from Vancouver to Sydney, Nova Scotia, traversing the Northwest Passage. Returning two years later, she became the first vessel to navigate the Passage in both directions. When *St. Roch* sailed through the Panama Canal, she became the first vessel to circumnavigate the North American continent. She is permanently on view as a National Historic Ship at the Vancouver Maritime Museum.

Star Hoyanger A representative of the many carriers that frequent Vancouver Harbour with a wide variety of cargo, Star Shipping's *Star Hoyanger* was built in Korea in 1995. She is a state-of-the-art "open hatch bulk carrier" designed primarily to carry forest products. Her versatile, rail-mounted gantry cranes can load unitized bales of wood pulp, newsprint, lumber or containers and unload cargo with a clamshell grab. *Star Hoyanger* is 650 feet long and carries 45,000 tons of cargo.

Taconite A beautiful representative from a bygone era of splendid luxury yachts, the 125-foot, all-teak *Taconite* was built for William Boeing in 1929 by the Hoffar-Beeching Shipyard, adjacent to the Boeing aircraft plant on Coal Harbour. Current Vancouver owner, Gordon Levett, is continuing to maintain *Taconite* to fine yacht standards and runs coastal charters with her.

Thomas F. Bayard This two-masted schooner was built in New York in 1880 as a Delaware Bay pilot ship. It successively became a Gold

Rush freighter, running between Puget Sound and Alaska, 1898-1906; then a seal hunter out of Victoria, 1907-11; the *Sandheads #16* lightship at the mouth of the Fraser River, 1913-57. Eventually *Bayard* was purchased in 1978 by the Vancouver Maritime Museum and awaits major restoration.

Tyee Princess From her berth at the Coast Ferries' dock under the Knight Street Bridge, *Tyee Princess* departs on scheduled runs, dropping Vancouver-originating goods at numerous, isolated upcoast communities and logging camps as far north as Bella Bella and Klemtu. As such, *Tyee Princess* is one of the last freight-carrying coasters in operation on the B.C. coast.

Tymac No. 2 This classic water taxi was built in 1938 by Sam Tyson and Alex McKenzie (Tymac Launch Services) and in the 1940s and 1950s ran passengers from the foot of Columbia Street to Britannia Mines and church camps and summer resorts around Howe Sound. Fully restored by Tymac Launch, *Tymac No. 2* has continued to earn her keep, carrying 24 passengers as a False Creek ferry in 1984; a Vancouver Harbour tour boat 1986-89; and a tour boat out of Steveston in 1991.

William Irving A well-known, elegant stern-wheeler, one of hundreds that plied the Fraser River in the 1800s. *William Irving* was built in 1880 and named for the "King of the River," Capt. William Irving. A typically sleek representative (166 feet long and 34 feet beam) of the riverboats with their reputation for speed and service, the all-white *Irving* had ornate railings and superstructure and a carved eagle on her wheelhouse. She was lost when broken on a sandbar in 1894, but her engines and eagle went on to other vessels.

right: The Taconite's *telegraph.* vp
facing page: top; BC Ferries Spirit of British Columbia, *Vancouver, 1994.* vs
bottom; Crew on the Princess Louise, *1924.* vp

Business and Industry

The Vancouver Board of Trade was formed in 1887 by 31 merchants, lumbermen, bankers and manufacturers who met to organize the rebuilding of Vancouver after the Great Fire. For more than 100 years The Vancouver Board of Trade, as the city's chamber of commerce, has been representing the Vancouver business community, working in the enlightened interest of its members to promote, enhance and facilitate the development of the region as a Pacific centre for trade commerce and travel

THREE THINGS MAKE Vancouver's economy percolate: geography, natural resources and the uninterrupted inflow of people. Newcomers have built Canada but nowhere is this more true than in Vancouver, its youngest and most dynamic major city. Ever since the city's forefathers invited business to come and create a new town on the ashes of the first, burnt-out one, Vancouver has been a mecca for the ambitious and the job-hungry alike. Canadians have heard Vancouver's siren call for decades. They are the ones who piled onto the Canadian Pacific Railway to come west to make their fortunes. They erected sawmills along the city's shores, started banks and shipping companies and created a feisty stock exchange where they swapped shares in their mining companies. In record time they created the city's resource economy, still its bedrock today.

The shift of Canadians steadily west, particularly during bad times in their home provinces, has never really stopped. When I came here 20 years ago from hard-scrabble Winnipeg I came, like so many others, in pursuit of work. My friends and I didn't realize it then but Vancouver was on the brink of accelerated growth that would radically change the face of the city. The stream of newcomers to Vancouver was turning into a torrent. In the last ten years the pace of immigration, from Asia especially, has been explosive. Vast sums of money from overseas began quietly making its way downtown, buying towers and businesses. Then Mandarin International of Hong Kong built a hotel in downtown Vancouver, its first outside Southeast Asia and the most public display yet of off-shore commitment to the city.

The other watershed was Expo 86. Fraught with labor unrest, and almost cancelled, the world fair nevertheless succeeded in turning the international spotlight onto Vancouver. Investors saw a rarity—a peaceful, relatively undeveloped city in a democratic country—and they began doing business here.

Vancouver's attractions are obvious. But perhaps even more important than its natural gifts is its youth. Unlike older Canadian cities Vancouver is still a fluid democracy with no *ancien regime* or deep-rooted, impenetrable establishment. It still can offer opportunities like those that lured the first wave of entrepreneurs here almost a century ago.

It is a city where a man such as David Lam, with no particular connections, can emigrate and in 20 years make his fortune and be named the Queen's representative. Like many others Mr. Lam made his money in real estate, an industry that blossomed in the early 1970s when immigration pressures pushed land values to stratospheric levels. House prices here still are double the national average.

Real estate, tourism, financial services, technology, higher education and transportation have been added to the city's backbone of mining, fishing and lumber. They have fleshed out an economy once hostage to international resource prices. Resources remain the heartbeat of the city but its economy is now broad enough to avoid the wild gyrations of the boom or bust days. Mention the recession of the early 90s that wasted industrial Ontario and you get a blank stare. What recession?

Vancouver's other huge advantage is its geography. Poised on the edge of the Pacific, Vancouver is a neighbor to Asia whose economies are in explosive growth. Goods and people are moving through Vancouver in record volumes. And there will be more. The city's port has expanded hugely and the airport, almost bursting at the seams, has added a third terminal to deal with the vast increase in travellers it expects. Growth feeds on growth. The challenge now for Vancouver—with its embarrassment of riches—is to remain a dynamic city without sacrificing those qualities that brought us all here in the first place.

—*Catherine Gourley*

facing page: Construction of the Pacific Great Eastern Railway bridge across the Capilano River, 1955. vp

above: Granville Square, built 1971–73, was the only large structure to emerge from Project 200 (an ambitious waterfront development plan). vs

The Port of Vancouver

PORT OF VANCOUVER

The Vancouver Port Corporation (VPC) is the crown agency that administers the lands and waterways of the port of Vancouver. The port operates on the doorstep of nine municipalities. Our mission statement: To facilitate the efficient movement of maritime trade and passengers through the port of Vancouver in the best interests of Canadians with facilities and services that are competitive, safe, commercially viable, dependable and customer-oriented and which have broad public support.

The Port of Vancouver

Jim Lyon

IN JUNE 1792 the British navigator George Vancouver, meticulously surveying the North American Pacific Coast, stumbled upon one of the finest deep water harbors in the world which he named after his friend and former shipmate, Captain Sir Harry Burrard.

In November 1864, 72 years after Captain Vancouver's visit the harbor's first export cargo, a shipment of 277,750 board feet of lumber and 16,000 fence pickets for Australia, was shipped on board the barque Ellen Lewis from Moodyville in North Vancouver. It took almost two months to load the vessel. With today's equipment the job would take 48 hours.

At first the port catered exclusively to exports from local sawmills. In 1884, for example, a cargo of specially cut wooden beams—122 feet long, 28 inches square and without a knot—was shipped for the Imperial Palace in Beijing.

As Canada's economy matured and, most significantly, British Columbia was linked by rail with the continental hinterland, trade flourished.

In 1887 the newly completed Canadian Pacific Railway set records with a small shipment of tea. The tea left Yokohama, Japan on the Abyssinia on May 31 and arrived in English Bay on June 13. Canadian Pacific delivered it to New York by rail on June 21 and it was immediately transshipped to a vessel named the *City of Rome,* which arrived in London on June 29. The record time Yokohama to London was 29 days. An all water shipment from Yokohama to London—even by the fastest clipper vessel—would have taken two weeks longer.

Imports of silk from Japan and China, brought on board Canadian Pacific's White Empress vessels, enhanced the reputation of the port and CP in the 1890s and early 1900s. Speedy "silk trains" rushed the precious cargoes from Vancouver across the North American continent. The silk trains were specially designed for high speed, stopping only for fresh relays of locomotives and crews. Silk had priority over passengers. Even the future King George VI once had to wait in a siding somewhere in the Rockies. A Canadian Pacific Railway conductor told him: "We had to let a silk train go by. In Canada silk has rights over everything."

The first known wheat cargo exported from Vancouver was sent to London in 1895. Trial shipments of grain were sent to the United Kingdom during World War I to prove the feasibility of shipping from Vancouver via the Panama Canal

facing page: Cates tug and cruise ship, Canada Place, 1983. vs

(which had opened in 1914) without spoilage.

Today the port handles close to 10,000 vessel calls each year, of which 3,000 are by foreign ships, representing Canada's Pacific Coast trade with 90 nations. The jobs of 9,000 workers depend directly on moving cargo and cruise ship passengers.

For many years most trade passing through the port was with industrialised Europe. Today the port's commerce is focused predominantly on Asia, bulk resource exports dominating its cargoes.

The Port of Vancouver, including Burrard Inlet and Roberts Bank in the outer harbor, encompasses more than 276 kilometres of coastline. It has 29 terminals. Burrard Inlet, with a low-tide water depth of 15 metres at First Narrows, can accommodate vessels of 150,000 deadweight tonnes.

Most of the coal exports—the primary export commodity—are handled at Westshore Terminals coal facility at Roberts Bank. It can handle dry bulk vessels of 260,000 deadweight tonnes and holds the world record of 239,084 tonnes of coal loaded on the *Hyundai Giant* in May 1987. A Westshore spokesman says: "We don't know of any dry bulk carriers we can't handle." Oil tankers are built even bigger, but Westshore doesn't handle oil shipments.

On both its north and south shores Burrard Inlet has 28 kilometres of waterfront. There are forest products terminals; bulk handling facilities dedicated to the transport of coal, sulphur or potash; terminals specializing in cleaning, sorting and loading grain; and export facilities for chemicals and petrochemicals.

The Port is served by four railways—Canadian National, Canadian Pacific, British Columbia Railway and the American carrier Burlington Northern.

Forest products are loaded at four specialized cargo terminals. including Fibreco Export Inc., the world's largest woodchip storage and shipping terminal. Fibreco is owned by a consortium of 26 sawmill companies operating in the B.C. Interior.

Seaboard International Terminal is the largest volume throughput forest products terminal in the world. Seaboard, the port's primary lumber handler, can handle more than 900 million board feet of equivalent lumber and panel products a year. Forest products from Seaboard are shipped to all major world markets. Seaboard uses a fleet of ships that includes bulk carriers and custom-designed roll-on/roll-off (Ro/Ro) vessels.

The big grain elevators that ring Burrard Inlet—Saskatchewan Wheat Pool, Alberta Wheat Pool, Pacific Elevators Ltd., United Grain Growers—are all owned by farmers' cooperatives. Only one, Pioneer Grain, is owned privately.

Sulphur—brilliant yellow piles of it can be seen at Vancouver

PORT OF VANCOUVER

VPC is accountable to the Parliament of Canada through the Minister of Transport. It is financially self-sufficient and operates with a staff of 180, including Port Police. VPC owns and manages $410 million in physical assets, exclusive of land values. These assets include Canada Place. Port revenues are earned from leases, licenses, harbor dues, berthage, wharfage, cruise ship charges per passenger and investment income.

Wharves and at Pacific Coast Terminals—is extracted from natural gas at processing plants close to the well heads in British Columbia, Alberta and Saskatchewan and exported for use in agricultural fertilizers. About 35 per cent of the total world trade in sulphur is exported through Vancouver.

Potash, mined in Saskatchewan, is also shipped around the world as an important agricultural fertilizer.

Canadian mineral production—copper, lead, zinc, molybdenum, barite and so on—is also exported through Vancouver to serve industrial users around the world.

The most exciting—and potentially the most lucrative—traffic to pass through Vancouver, however, is the container trade, which has transformed international transportation over the past 40 years.

Each day a commercial armada races east across the Pacific at warship speed carrying Asian-manufactured goods North Americans take for granted: billions of dollars worth of computers, electronics, toys, motorcycles, skirts, shirts, auto parts.

The service between Asia and North America is now so well greased that the big steel containers—thousands of them, stacked as many as 12 deep on the vessels—have become surrogate warehouses carrying inventories for stores and factories dotted throughout this continent.

It is generally acknowledged that Vancouver stumbled badly over the container trade, allowing U.S. West Coast ports to handle massive volumes of business that ought to pass through our port. It's been estimated that 70 per cent of the container traffic from the Far East to Ontario and Quebec—business worth more than $150 million to the Canadian economy—was captured by U.S. ports and railroads.

For a number of years we lost traffic through union insistence that containers frequently be packed or unpacked on the docks rather than at a distant warehouse. The "destuffing clause" was eliminated in 1988.

Containerization actually began on Burrard Inlet. It was developed by The White Pass & Yukon Route, whose narrow-gauge railway connected Skagway on the Alaskan Panhandle with Whitehorse. In 1955 White Pass was the first company in the world to build a specialized cellular container ship and custom design rail cars to handle eight-cubic-foot containers.

While the container sector accounted for only 5.7 per cent of Vancouver's overall tonnage in the early 1990s it was a labor-intensive operation that supported more than 20 per cent of the total waterfront workforce. It also represented about 40 per cent of the value of all commerce transacted through the port. It is lucrative out of all proportion to its size. It's not unusual, for example, to find $3 million worth of herring roe in refrigerated containers waiting to be loaded for Japan.

Container ships are the oceans' high-value speedsters that dash in directly to berths, load and discharge cargoes rapidly—usually within 24 hours—and then make a high-speed exit for the next port.

Since the mid-1980s the Vancouver Port Corporation has devoted significant energy and money to keeping pace with customer demand in the container sector. It has improved terminal layouts, enlarged intermodal yards, bought new cranes and helped initiate an electronic data interchange system. This effort has paid off.

Even though we lost a big chunk of the trade to the U.S. over the years, Vancouver's container business has increased steadily. It became clear in the early 1990s that the two specialized terminals on Burrard Inlet would soon be unable to handle growing business. Construction begin in 1994 of a brand new container terminal, known as DeltaPort, alongside the Roberts Bank coal port. It opened in the Spring of 1997.

Deltaport will effectively double Vancouver's handling capacity. It will be slicker than the older, somewhat congested facilities in Burrard Inlet: it's nearer to the open ocean and road and rail access is simplified and more direct.

In touting its attractions to foreign shipping companies, Vancouver enjoys a number of clear advantages. For one the port is about a day's steaming closer to ports in the North Pacific than, say, Seattle or Tacoma. Canadian railways offer direct transcontinental services which the fragmented U.S. rail system cannot match.

Both Canadian National and Canadian Pacific Railway have made significant investments in recent years to speed and facilitate the rapid movement of containers to distant inland locations. They have developed highly efficient intermodal transfer facilities, acquired spine cars and spent many millions increasing the tunnel clearance of their tracks to accommodate double-stack container trains.

The port corporation has also established representative offices in Southeast Asia and Europe and now teams with railways, terminal operators and union representatives in regular visits to customers and potential customers throughout Asia.

Vancouver is a prized port of call for the cruise industry. Most days, between late May and early October, some of the largest and most luxurious cruise vessels afloat cast off from downtown terminals, slip under the Lion's Gate Bridge and head for Alaska.

Among the first ships dedicated specifically to Alaska cruising were former navy Corvettes, converted in the late 1940s by Union Steamships from their original role of escorting World War II

The Port of Vancouver is a safe, year-round, all-weather, deep water harbor, with 150 km of coastline. With more than 20 major cargo and marine-related facilities handling between 65 and 70 million tonnes annually, Vancouver is the top export port on the North American west coast. As the most diversified port in the Western Hemisphere, Vancouver handles coal, grain, potash, sulphur, mineral concentrates, petroleum products, liquid chemicals, lumber, pulp, paper, woodchips, containers and cruise ships.

Atlantic convoys. These northern summer cruises were a hit, but the economics of the operation were unsatisfactory to Union and the company didn't remain in the business long.

The great explosion of interest in Alaskan cruising did not occur until the 1970s. The international cruise companies have marketed the Alaska cruise vacation aggressively and efficiently: the romance of America's last frontier, the glamor of life aboard fun-oriented vessels (namely, the highly successful *Love Boat* television series), the comfort of sailing the Inside Passage —all contribute to today's thriving industry.

Vancouver's cruise business boomed in the late 1980s and early 1990s, and the port corporation sees cruise ship traffic growing significantly by the end of the first decade of the 21st century. By then, as many as a million cruise ship visitors could pass through the port annually. To handle increased demand, plans were in hand to construct two new berths at the Central Waterfront, just east of the Canada Place terminal, by 1996.

This article is largely a condensation of the book *The Port of Vancouver: Canada's Global Gateway* (Vancouver Port Corporation copyright).

Container terminal, Port of Vancouver, 1986. vp

Bulk cargoes like coal and grain represent 83 per cent of total port tonnage. General cargo like lumber and pulp accounts for one per cent, with containerized cargo the remaining six per cent. More than 60 per cent of exports flowing through the port come from Alberta, Saskatchewan and Manitoba. The Port of Vancouver is the premier west coast gateway to the world's fastest growing economies, the Asia Pacific. Japan, South Korea and China are the port's principal trading countries.

Pacific Rim Trade
Ashley Ford

WHEN THE OLD colonial trader *Ellen Lewis* slipped her moorings from a North Vancouver dock in 1864 and drifted out into Burrard Inlet heading for Adelaide, Australia, her skipper Captain Stephen Hector likely didn't realize he was navigating a new chapter in Canada's, and more specifically British Columbia and Vancouver's, business romance with the Pacific Rim.

Some 68 days later the *Ellen Lewis,* after a fairly uneventful passage, docked and unloaded a cargo of lumber and pickets for fences. It was the first commercial shipment out of the still unorganized Port of Vancouver.

Vancouver's era of Pacific trade was underway and 131 years later it shows absolutely no sign of decay. In fact the opposite is true. This enduring partnership is gathering strength. Today the world's most vibrant economic region is a major market for B.C. and Canadian goods, second only to our trade with the United States. If you roll the two together—after all the U.S. is also a Pacific Rim country—then the region is our most important trading area by far.

Two-way trade between the countries of Asia and Canada has grown consistently over the years but the major push has come since World War II, especially here on the West Coast, Canada's transportation gateway for the flow of goods to and from the Pacific Rim. Vancouver is now taking on a new persona. Rapid immigration from Hong Kong, Taiwan, China, The Philippines, Japan, South Korea, Malaysia and Singapore throughout the eighties and nineties has vastly increased Asian business ties and the city is becoming more of an international business centre because of them.

Sitting in a perfect time zone to deal both with Europe and Asia, and now armed with a critical mass of business expertise in both cultures, Vancouver over the next century is expected to become more than just a simple gateway for the passage of goods. And if the Pacific Rim is still largely misunderstood or unknown in other Canadian jurisdictions, it isn't in B.C. As one Central Canadian businessperson recently commented, "for us, Asia begins in Vancouver."

Indeed with Asians accounting for 30 per cent of the population, Vancouver is increasingly being seen as the first Asian city on the North American continent. This trend is being dramatically illustrated through the flow of business. Latest trading figures from the B.C. government show that 38 per cent of provincial exports now flow into the Pacific Rim compared with 48 per cent to the U.S. The remainder goes into Europe. The success of this trade surge can be seen in the fact that in 1994 fully 56.7 per cent of B.C. products were destined for the U.S. The Asian connection sets B.C. apart from every other province in Canada. Canada as a whole ships 81 per cent of its exports to the U.S. and only a trifling nine per cent to the Pacific Rim.

The benefits of this trade diversification are readily apparent. B.C. has suffered less from economic restructuring than any other region of the country and has enjoyed the best economic growth of any of the provinces for the past half-decade. The major reason is diversified trade.

In the first half of 1995 exports to the region grew by an astonishing 46 per cent over the same period for 1994 with the total value of exports soaring in value by $5 billion. Government statisticians were confident a new export record would be established in 1995. In 1994 the total value of B.C. exports into the region totalled $22.8 billion. By the end of the first six months of 1995 more than $13 billion worth of goods had already been exported and the second half of the year has traditionally been the more active trading period. The trade growth with B.C.'s major Asian trading partners over the first half of 1995 has been, to say the least, staggering. Exports to China climbed by 110 per cent to $259.1 million from $122.9 million in 1994. Even with Japan, B.C.'s major Asian client, still mired in recession, exports over the first half of the year climbed by 40.6 per cent to $3.05 billion from 1994's $2.4 billion. Anywhere one cared to look the performance was just as sparkling: South Korea up 70 per cent, Taiwan up 48 per cent, Hong Kong up 51 per cent, Australia up 25 per cent, India up 43.8 per cent and on and on.

Provincial government number-crunchers cannot attach any accurate job figures to the booming export trade but they estimate that more than 25 per cent of every job in the province is connected in some way to Pacific Rim trade.

While the same commodity that underpinned the first voyage of the *Ellen Lewis* remains one of the dominant exports, it has been joined by an ever-widening field of products. While commodities such as pulp, paper, coal and metals remain important, they are being joined by a growing list of manufactured and highly valued agri-food products. Sophisticated "conceived in B.C. and made in B.C." products such as submarines and ultra-deep-sea diving suits, state-of-the-art computer-mapping technology, aerospace equipment, electronic communication, battery technology, and trucks and other heavy equipment are making their presence felt in the economies of Asia. In 1994 value-added exports accounted for 13 per cent of the province's exports and that number will continue to grow.

BRITISH COLUMBIA

As part of the Ministry of Employment and Investment, the British Columbia Trade and Investment Office (BCTIO) is a service organization supporting B.C. exporters and investors in the province. By expanding export opportunities, and international and domestic investment in the province, the B.C. Trade and Investment Office effectively supports the Provincial Government's priority of job creation and economic growth.

Grain ships anchored in English Bay, 1991. vs

Someone once described Australia, which has many of the same attributes found in B.C., as the "lucky country." The same description has been attached to B.C. by others in Canada. They point out that geography has had as much to do with the growth of Pacific Rim trade as anything else. That's only partially true. To be sure Vancouver is the closest major seaport on the North American West Coast. But successive provincial governments, no matter their political stripe, have consistently followed a policy of expanding economic, cultural and business ties with the Pacific Rim.

For example, the recent expansion of Vancouver International Airport will make it a leading North American hub for the Pacific Rim. That coupled with major ongoing construction of port facilities at Roberts Bank will further cement Vancouver's claim as the continent's major West Coast transportation clearing house for imports and exports. The importance of Pacific Rim trade to the port can be seen from the tonnage numbers. In 1994 the Port of Vancouver's throughput totalled

67.6 million tonnes, an 11 per cent increase over 1993's 60.8 million tonnes. Tonnage increases were registered in virtually every cargo sector and container traffic increased by 14 per cent. Of the top ten destinations for goods, seven were Pacific Rim countries led by Japan, South Korea, China, Taiwan, Indonesia and Australia. On the import side Japan, Hong Kong, China, Taiwan, Australia, Thailand and Peru dominated the top ten. And on a total imports and exports basis, the top three port users were Japan, South Korea and China.

When people talk of the Pacific Rim they inevitably think of Asia. It is much more than that and a new era is about to dawn on the next major region on the Rim. The opening up of markets on the Pacific coast of South America holds huge promise for B.C. and the province has already indicated that this is the next major regional target for new economic opportunities.

While some may conclude that B.C.'s relationship with the Pacific Rim is reaching new levels of maturity, the reality is that, 131 years later, the adventure has hardly started.

The amalgamation of trade and investment under one umbrella capitalizes on the synergy between the two areas of activity. BCTIO develops sectoral trade opportunities in such areas as advanced manufacturing, knowledge-based industries, service industries and natural resources. In addition, it ensures a strong B.C. presence in international markets, particularly in the Asia Pacific region and other markets of like growth potential. At the same time, BCTIO promotes investment opportunities in the province and assesses strategic sectoral investments.

Some Large Companies

Some large companies in Greater Vancouver
Richard Von Kleist

Note: Revenues and net revenues are for 1995. Employees (empl:) are those in B.C. only.

MacMillan Bloedel • Forest products • revenue: $5.25 billion • net revenue: $279 million • assets: $5.271 billion • R.F. (Dick) Haskayne, Chairman; Robert B. Findlay, President and CEO • empl: 7,898 • 925 West Georgia Street • Vancouver, B.C. V6C 3L2 • Ph: (604) 661-8000 • Fax: (604) 661-8377

MacMillan Bloedel, Canada's largest forest products company, manages 2 million hectares of productive timberlands, about half of them in B.C. The products of MB and its affiliated companies are marketed throughout the world and include lumber, panelboards, engineered lumber, cement fibre roofing, kraft pulp, newsprint, groundwood printing papers, containerboard, corrugated containers and SpaceKraft.

Westcoast Energy Inc. • Natural gas distribution • rev: $4.165 billion • net rev: $197 million • assets: $9 billion • CEO: Michael (E.J.) Phelps • empl: 1,580 • 3400-666 Burrard Street • Vancouver, B.C. V6C 3M8 • Ph: 488-8000 • Fax: 488-8500

In September 1996 Westcoast Energy announced a plan to join The Coastal Corporation of Houston, Texas to form North America's fourth-largest marketer of natural gas and electricity. Westcoast's main pipeline subsidiary, Westcoast Energy Pipeline Division, owns the largest gas transportation system in B.C., comprising 5,600 kilometres of pipeline, seven gas-processing plants and four sulphur-recovery plants. Total corporate capital expenditures in 1995 exceeded $1 billion.

The Jim Pattison Group • Diversified; consumer oriented • rev: $3.4 billion • assets: $1.6 billion • Jim Pattison, CEO • empl: 17,000+ • 1055 W. Hastings Street • Vancouver, B.C. V6E 2H2 • Ph: 688-6764

The Jim Pattison Group is Canada's third largest privately held company and the largest private company held by one individual in Canada. Pattison earned a very high profile as the man who made Expo 86 work. His companies include food services, export services, manufacturing, communications/entertainment, transportation and leasing. The company began May 8, 1961 when Pattison purchased a GM dealership with

facing page: Neon sign, BC Electric (now BC Hydro) "Reddy Kilowatt" promotional character, 1961. vs

a $40,000 loan from the Royal Bank, using his home and life insurance policy as collateral. Pattison was appointed to the Order of Canada in April 1987 and the Order of British Columbia June 21, 1990.

BC Telecom • Telecommunications • rev: $2.391 billion • net rev: $234.8 million • assets: $4.61 billion • Brian A. Canfield, CEO• empl: 13,851 • 3777 Kingsway • Burnaby, B.C. V5H 3Z7 • Ph: 432-2151 • Internet: http://bctel.com

The first telephones in British Columbia were made sometime between 1876 and 1878 by a mechanic at the coal mining firm of Dunsmuir, Diggle and Co. in Wellington, near Nanaimo. William Wall used copper from the copper bands encircling the mine's kegs of blasting powder. He borrowed a magnet from a friend, and for the diaphragms cut out pieces of the thin photographic material known as tintype (cutting up a photograph of his wife for the purpose!). A line was established, using No. 14 gauge wire, between the mine and loading docks a few miles away. Success! This was the first telephone line placed in regular use in B.C. (For the first in Vancouver, see the article on Page 531.) Things have changed since Mr. Wall's handmade device. On March 13, 1990 in Vancouver the last two strands of a fibre-optic network were fused together, completing the longest land-based fibre-optic network in the world. (More than 7,000 kilometres from coast to coast.) The network was built by the ten member telephone companies of Telecom Canada, including B.C. Tel. It is the first and only system in the country capable of transmitting voice, data and video communication all on one network. (The entire *Encyclopaedia Britannica* could be sent across Canada in less than a second.) In August 1966 BC Telecom and the University of British Columbia announced they have entered into a relationship that will see a broadband, fibre-optic infrastructure linking sites throughout UBC's 400-hectare campus. The Campus Connectivity project will provide classrooms, laboratories, offices and student residences with high-speed access (up to 10 megabytes per second) to electronic mail and the World Wide Web. BC Telecom Inc. was incorporated under that name November 14, 1984.

B.C. Hydro (Crown corporation) • Electric utility • rev: $2.3 billion • assets: $10.4 billion • (Interim at this writing) Michael Costello, President and CEO • empl: 5,600 • 333 Dunsmuir Street • Vancouver, B.C. V6B 5R3 • Ph: 528-1600

B.C. Hydro's earliest corporate ancestor was the Victoria Gas Company, founded in 1860, which supplied Victoria with gas for street, office and domestic lighting. In 1883, also in Victoria, a young entrepreneur named Robert McMicking installed three electric streetlights in the city, the

first commercial electric lights in Canada. Three years later electric streetcars had come to B.C.'s capital and to the Lower Mainland. Similar companies began springing up. With financial backing from England, two entrepreneurs named Robert Horne-Payne and Frank Barnard began buying up electric lighting, streetcar firms and gas companies and formed the B.C. Electric Company. BCE began supplying power to the Lower Mainland in 1903. Montreal-based Power Corporation bought the company in 1928. Even into the 1940s many communities in B.C. had no electric power. In 1945 the provincial government created the B.C. Power Commission which began extending electricity into rural or isolated areas. Then in 1961 Premier W.A.C. Bennett bought B.C. Electric and a year later amalgamated it with the Power Commission to create a new Crown corporation: the B.C. Hydro and Power Authority. The Columbia River Treaty followed in 1964, and continues to generate income from sale of water to the United States. Construction of huge dams and extensive power lines followed. When the provincial government bought B.C. Electric, it got with it a gas company, transit companies and a freight railway system. In 1979 it sold its long-distance bus operations to Pacific Coach Lines, then during the next decade sold off its city bus operations. The gas and rail divisions were sold in 1988. Today, B.C. Hydro concentrates on power generation and sales, with its Power Smart initiative designed to help customers use power more efficiently.

ICBC Insurance Corporation of B.C. (Crown corporation) • Auto insurance • rev: $2.253 billion • Thom Thompson, CEO • empl: 3,923 • 151 W. Esplanade • North Vancouver, B.C. V7M 3H9 • Ph: 661-2100

ICBC is a provincial Crown corporation established in 1974 to provide universal vehicle-related insurance for British Columbia motorists. The corporation collects vehicle and driver premiums from more than two million motorists and invests the money to provide insurance benefits for its customers and for victims of crashes. ICBC operates on a non-profit, break-even basis. In 1995 ICBC wrote 2.39 million policies and incurred $1.96 billion in claim costs.

Weyerhaeuser Canada • Manufacturing/Forest products • rev: $2.2 billion • George A. Weyerhaeuser, Jr., CEO • empl: 1,900 • 25th floor, 1075 West Georgia Street • Vancouver, B.C. V6E 3C9 • Ph: 687-0431 • Fax: 691-2445 • Internet: http://biz.yahoo.com/profiles/wy.html

In 1964 Kamloops Pulp and Paper and Weyerhaeuser Company of Tacoma, Washington formed a partnership to build a pulp mill in Kamloops. Weyerhaeuser bought all the shares of Kamloops Pulp and created Weyerhaeuser Canada Ltd. In 1990 the company planted its 50

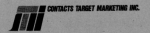

millionth seedling in B.C. (They reached the same plateau in Saskatchewan in 1993.) Weyerhaeuser is the world's largest private owner of softwood timber, with about six million acres of U.S. timberland and cutting rights to 18 million acres in Canada. The company is the largest supplier of wood pulp in the world.

Fletcher Challenge Canada Limited • Manufacturing/Forest products; retail merchandise • rev: $2.154 billion • net rev: $120 million • assets $2.931 billion • Douglas W.G. Whitehead, CEO • empl: 5,000 • P.O. Box 10058, Pacific Centre • 11th floor-700 West Georgia Street • Vancouver, B.C. V7Y 1J7 • Ph: 654-4000 • Fax: 654-4961

Fletcher Challenge Canada Limited was incorporated January 31, 1946. The company has the capacity to produce 2.2 million tonnes annually of newsprint, groundwood specialty papers, containerboard, coated paper and market pulp at three mills in B.C., and a coated paper mill in Minnesota. In October 1996 FC announced a scaling back of its B.C.-based operations by selling off its majority interest in TimberWest Forest Products, saying it saw no room for growth in the paper business in the province.

Canfor Corporation • Forest products (lumber, pulp, kraft paper, newsprint) • rev: $1.932 billion • net rev: $45.6 million • assets: $2.115 billion • Peter J.G. Bentley, O.C., Chairman; Arild S. Nielssen, President and CEO • empl: 5,700 (4,400 directly; 1,300 through affiliates) • P.O. Box 49420 Bentall Postal • 2900-1055 Dunsmuir Street • Vancouver, B.C. V7X 1B5 • Ph: 661-5241 • Fax: 661-5235

The company was founded in 1938 by Austrian immigrants Poldi Bentley and John Prentice, who opened the New Westminster-based Pacific Veneer plant. Bentley and Prentice acquired other companies to build a forest company that included sawmills, forest lands, pulp mills and building material distribution centres. As Canadian Forest Products, it also bought into other non-forestry interests. In 1985, now under the leadership of Poldi's son Peter, CFP was forced by a high debt load to restructure, went public and changed its name to Canfor. It began to shed non-forestry assets and non-performing forestry assets and to modernize mills. On March 31, 1988 it entered into a joint venture with New Oji Paper of Japan to create Howe Sound Pulp and Paper (see below).

Finning • Heavy equipment, sales and service • rev: $1.752 billion • net rev: $77 million • assets: $1.608 billion • James F. Shepard, Chairman and CEO; Dave Edwards, President • empl: 4,087 • 555 Great Northern Way, Vancouver, B.C. V5T 1E2 • Ph: 872-4444 • Fax: 872-2994

Finning Ltd., incorporated October 22, 1969 as Finning Tractor & Equipment, changed to its present name May 14, 1987. It is North America's largest Caterpillar dealer (earthmovers, diesel tractors, engines). It deals mainly with customers in forestry, mining and construction throughout B.C., Yukon and parts of the Northwest Territories.

Methanex • Methanol production • rev: $1.752 billion • net rev: $200.1 million (U.S.) • assets: $2.431 billion • Pierre Choquette, President and CEO • empl: 189 • 1800 Waterfront Centre • 200 Burrard Street • Vancouver, B.C. V6C 3M1 • Ph: 661-2600 • Internet: http://www.methanex.com

Methanol is a primary liquid petrochemical made from renewable and non-renewable fossil fuels containing carbon and hydrogen. (Formaldehyde is an important by-product.) It is used in solvents, recyclable packaging, printing inks, panelboard, and as a fuel and antifreeze. There is potential, says Methanex—the world's largest producer and marketer of methanol—for the use of methanol in fuel cells. Fuel cells convert hydrogen, of which methanol is a source, into electricity with zero emissions. Methanex—which has operations in North America, New Zealand and Chile—was incorporated in Alberta March 11, 1968.

Cominco • Mining • rev: $1.537 billion • net rev: $103.7 million • assets: $2.764 billion • David H. Thompson, CEO • empl: 5,743 • 500-200 Burrard Street • Vancouver, B.C. V6C 3L7 • Ph: 682-0611

Incorporated in 1906, Cominco's principal activities are mineral exploration, mining, smelting and refining. The company is the world's largest zinc concentrate producer. Other concentrates produced by Cominco include lead, copper, molybdenum, gold and germanium. It mines a wide variety of metals, including lead, copper, gold and silver, and produces many additional products like copper sulphate, sulphuric acid and fertilizer. Vancouver's Teck Corporation has been a major shareholder since 1987.

Hollinger Inc. • Newspaper and magazine publication • rev: $1.513 billion • net rev: $10.3 million • assets: $2.888 billion • Conrad M. Black, Chairman and CEO; David Radler, President • empl: 280 • 1827 West 5th Avenue • Vancouver, B.C. V6J 1P5 • Ph: 732-5638

Southam Inc., owned 40 per cent by the rapidly growing worldwide Hollinger empire, is Canada's largest publisher of daily newspapers. Among its 59 properties are *The Vancouver Sun* and *The Province*. Hollinger's *Electronic Telegraph*, launched on the Internet in November 1994 is the busiest European site on the World Wide

Web and was voted by users the best on-line newspaper. Hollinger Inc. was incorporated January 3, 1966. Conrad Black's Hollinger Inc. now controls more than 150 dailies and 350 weeklies in Canada, the United States, Britain, Israel and Australia. More than half of Canada's daily newspaper circulation is now in Black's hands. In October 1996 Hollinger made a bid for more of Southam's shares.

West Fraser Timber Co. Ltd. • Forest products, home improvement retail • net sales: $1.49 billion • net rev: $96 million • assets: $1.92 billion • CEO: Henry H. Ketcham, Jr., Chairman; Henry H. Ketcham III, President and CEO • empl: 5,099 • 1000-1100 Melville Street • Vancouver, B.C. V6E 4A6 • Ph: 895-2700 • Fax: 681-6061

The company began operations in 1955 with the purchase by three brothers—Henry, William and Samuel Ketcham—of a small planer mill in Quesnel, B.C. Today, it also owns and operates, through its wholly owned subsidiary Revelstoke Home Centres Ltd., a chain of 34 retail home improvement stores in Western Canada. Six of these are Revy full-service warehouse stores. In the years 1991 through 1995 West Fraser planted 88.4 million trees. It was incorporated under its present name May 7, 1986. On January 14, 1997 Revelstoke Home Centres bought the 17-store Lumberland chain to become the largest home improvement retailer in Western Canada.

B.C. Liquor Distribution (Crown Corporation) • Retail and distribution of liquor products • rev: $1.48 billion • assets: $69.7 million • John Nieuwenburg, CEO • empl: 3,400 • 2625 Rupert Street (admin) • Vancouver, B.C. V5M 3T5 • Ph: 252-3000

Government control of the sale of spirituous and malt liquors came into effect in British Columbia June 15, 1921. (There had been a brief and ineffective period of prohibition from 1917 to 1921.) A history of the Liquor Distribution Branch, written for it by Maurice Walford, explains the legislation provided for government-run liquor stores and permitted drinking in hotel rooms and private homes, but not in public places. Municipalities were to receive half the profits from the Liquor Control Board in exchange for enforcing the law. There were 51 stores by March 1922 including seven in Vancouver. No liquor was visible from the street, and the shop's windows were painted a dark green with a circle in gold lettered Government Liquor Store. Expo 86 opened the door to a new level of liquor service in the province. The government of the day adopted a more liberal attitude, and the archaic and paternalistic laws of the past began to change. In 1987 a Liquor Policy Review was launched. Among its recommendations: expand the present system, which was working well; finance alcohol-abuse programs;

As the Greater Vancouver business community has grown, so has Contacts' data base. In 1975 the company's data base for Greater Vancouver contained information on 21,132 companies and listed 30,000 executive contacts. By 1996 the Contacts data base for Greater Vancouver contained information on more than 90,000 companies and 120,000 key decision makers. A Greater Victoria business directory was created in 1987 and was expanded to include all of Vancouver Island in 1994.

improve the staff's knowledge of the product; and permit no beer or wine sales in supermarkets and corner stores. The branch actively promotes the responsible use of the products it sells. "It participates," writes Walford, "in many abuse-prevention programs, including an LDB-sponsored poster contest for high school students, in-store responsible- use messages, a moderation campaign aimed at college and university students, and other initiatives aimed at drinking drivers, underage drinking and fetal alcohol syndrome. By volume, 80 per cent of our consumption is beer, 10 per cent wine, six per cent spirits and four per cent ciders and coolers. Spirits provide more than 40 per cent of gross revenue.

Workers' Compensation Board (Crown corporation) • Workers' compensation • rev: $1.42 billion • assets: $5.27 billion •Dale G. Parker, CEO • empl: 2,536 • 6951 Westminster Highway, Richmond, B.C. V7C 1C6 • Ph: 273-2266

Serving more than 1.5 million workers and funded by 145,400 employers, the Workers' Compensation Board is a provincial statutory agency governed by a Panel of Administrators. The WCB is committed to a safe and healthy workplace and to providing safe, effective return-to-work rehabilitation and fair compensation to workers injured or suffering occupational disease in the course of their employment. In 1990 British Columbia had 6.7 injuries per 100 person-years of work. By 1995 that figure had been lowered to 5.3.

Placer Dome Inc. • Mining • rev: $1.4 billion • net rev: $74 million • assets: $3.525 billion • Robert M. Franklin, Chairman; John M. Willson, President and CEO • empl: 529 • 1600 Bentall IV 1055 Dunsmuir Street, Vancouver, B.C. V7X 1P1 • Ph: 682-7082 • Fax: 682-7092

Placer Dome had its origins in 1909 when a party of prospectors in northern Ontario literally stumbled over what would turn into one of the biggest gold finds of the century. One of the men slipped and fell, dislodging a piece of moss . . . under which was found a dome-shaped rock structure studded with gold. Hence the name Dome Mines Limited. The company has more than 8,000 employees world wide. In 1926 in Vancouver another, unrelated mining operation was incorporated as Placer Development Limited. The two companies merged in 1987 and, with the addition of Campbell Red Lake Mines Limited (Ont.), became Placer Dome.

Future Shop Ltd. • Retail • rev: $1.3 billion • net rev: $17.2 million • assets: $355 million • Mohammad Ziabakhsh, CEO • empl: 1,060 • 1400-1111 West Georgia Street • Vancouver, B.C. V6E 4M3 • Ph: 689-1804 • Fax: 681-9258

Future Shop Ltd. was incorporated December 2, 1983. An Iranian immigrant named Hassan Khos-

rowshahi—whose family had fled Iran in 1979 during the Ayatollah Khomeini unrest—began the venture with a small office equipment shop on West Broadway. In 1994 there were 43 Future Shop locations in Canada, eight in the U.S. northwest.

Weldwood of Canada Limited • Manufacturing/Forest products • rev: $1.135 billion • net rev: $275.6 million • assets: $1.296 billion • Thomas A. Buell, Chairman; George R. Richards, President and CEO • empl: 2,197 • 1055 West Hastings Street • Vancouver, B.C. V6B 3V8 • Ph: 687-7366 • Fax: 662-2798

Weldwood's manufacturing operations in British Columbia began in 1945 when a predecessor company, Western Plywood, began producing fir and poplar plywood in a Vancouver plant. Weldwood of Canada was incorporated March 17, 1964. Today, it's 83.7 per cent owned by Champion International of New York and has become a private company. One of Weldwood's subsidiaries is Babine Forest Products, formed in 1974 as a joint venture between Weldwood, West Fraser Timber Co. and the Burns Lake Native Development Corporation, an economic development organization created by five First Nations bands in the area.

Chevron Canada • Manufacturing/Petroleum products • rev: $1.07 billion • assets: $384 million • John S. Watson, CEO• empl: 434 (another 2,500 through retail and commercial networks) • 1500-1050 West Pender Street • Vancouver, B.C. V6E 3T4 • Ph: 668-5300

Chevron Canada Limited—which celebrated its 60th anniversary in British Columbia in 1995—is a B.C.-based company producing a wide range of petroleum products for use by industries in B.C. and Yukon. It began as Standard Oil of B.C. in 1935 with a small refinery built to run California crude. Today, Chevron's refinery processes about 50,000 barrels of B.C. and Alberta crude oil daily.

Interfor (International Forest Products Ltd.) • Forest products • rev: $930 million (1995) • assets: $743 million • CEO: William L. Sauder, Chairman, CEO; Robert M. Sitter, President, COO • empl: 3,500 • Suite 3500-1055 Dunsmuir Street • Vancouver, B.C. V7X 1H7 • Ph: 689-6800 • Fax: 688-0313

Interfor began in the 1930s with a sawmill in Whonnock, about 48 kilometres east of Vancouver. Today, the company has 58 logging operations and seven sawmills in the southern coastal region of British Columbia, and one logging operation and one sawmill in the Interior. In 1988 the company changed its name from Whonnock Industries Limited to International Forest Products Limited.

BC Gas • Gas utility • rev: $895 million • net rev:

$47.5 million • assets: $2.367 billion • Ron Cliff, Chairman; Stephen Bellringer, President and CEO • empl: 1,600+ • 1111 West Georgia Street • Vancouver, B.C. V6E 4M4 • Ph: 443-6500

BC Gas—which purchases natural gas from various energy companies whose gas comes primarily from wells in northeastern B.C. and Alberta—distributes that gas to 700,000 residential, commercial and industrial customers in more than 100 communities throughout British Columbia. The company was formed in 1988 when Inland Natural Gas (incorporated in 1952) bought the Mainland Natural Gas division of B.C. Hydro. BC Gas' pipeline system is 30,000 kilometres long. Starting in late 1995 the Vancouver Police Department began using police cars powered with natural gas. BC Gas says the boys in blue are happy with the switchover.

Dairyworld Foods • Food processing, marketing • rev: $888 million • David E. Coe, CEO • empl: 2,400 • 300 -3920 Norland Avenue • Burnaby, B.C. V5G 4K7 • Ph: 298-9600

B.C.'s largest dairy, owned by the Fraser Valley Milk Producers Co-Operative Association. The company produces about 600 products including cheese, yogurt, ice cream and juices. In August 1996 Dairyworld Foods announced a world first in milk packaging: a new lightweight four-litre milk container that collapses as the milk is used to save fridge space. Made with flexible plastic, the Store 'n Pour pouch was created in co-operation with Tetra Pak, a major manufacturer in liquid foods packaging. At press time, it was being market tested throughout the Lower Mainland.

Slocan Forest Products Ltd. • Manufacturing/Forest products (lumber, plywood, wood chips, pulp, newsprint and specialty papers) • rev: $862 million • net rev: $50.8 million • assets: $976 million • Irving K. Barber, Chairman, President and CEO • empl: 2,600 • 240-10451 Shellbridge Way • Richmond, B.C. V6X 2W8 • Ph: 278-7311 • Fax: 278-7316 • Internet: http://slocan.com

In 1996 Slocan was named one of the world's 200 fastest-growing companies. It placed 65th, and was one of just 15 Canadian companies on the list, compiled by Deloitte & Touche Consulting Group and Braxton Associates. Slocan also placed 15th on *BC Business* magazine's Top 20 Employers list, a continued testament, says the company, to its contribution to B.C.'s economy. Irving Barber was a 1994 finalist in Ernst & Young's Pacific Region Entrepreneur of the Year program.

Itochu Canada • Import/Export and Real Estate • rev: $836 million • assets: $51 million • Yushin Okazaki, CEO • empl: 18 • 770-999 Canada Place • Vancouver, B.C. V6C 3E1 • Ph: 683-5764 • Fax: 688-9293

The Fraser Valley was added to the Contacts Target Marketing Greater Vancouver data base in 1992 and the Squamish/ Whistler/Pemberton corridor completed in 1994. Kamloops and the Okanagan were added in 1995 and the rest of the Province will follow. When all research is completed, Contact will maintain a growing data base of approximately 180,000 British Columbia companies and more than 325,000 business owners, senior executives and professionals.

BC Sugar Refinery • Refinery/Holding company • rev: $825 million • assets: $460 million • William C. Brown, CEO • empl: 242 • P.O. Box 2150 • Vancouver, B.C. V6B 3V2 • Ph: 253-1131

The story of BC Sugar is really interesting; in fact, it's been told by John Schreiner in the book *The Refiners*. The company was incorporated March 26, 1890 by Benjamin Tingley Rogers, a 24-year-old Philadelphia-born go-getter who noted that the western terminus of the new trans-Canada railway was in Vancouver, right across the Pacific from Manila, source of most of Canada's sugar.

The Loewen Group • Funeral Services • rev: $821 million • assets: $3.1 billion • Raymond L. Loewen, CEO • empl: 430 • 4126 Norland Avenue • Burnaby, B.C. V5G 3S8 • 299-9321 • Fax: 473-7333

With more than 12,000 employees and more than 1,000 funeral home and cemetery locations across North America, the Loewen Group is the largest funeral service corporation in Canada and the second largest on the continent. In October 1996 Loewen was fighting a hostile take-over bid from the U.S. funeral home giant, Service Corporation.

Western Star Trucks Holdings Ltd. • Transportation production and retailing • rev: $727 million • assets: $247 million • Terrence E. Peabody, CEO • empl: 1,117 • 30586 South Fraser Way • Abbotsford, B.C. V2T 6L4 • Ph: 857-1987

Western Star Trucks Holdings Ltd. was incorporated October 22, 1990. The company builds heavy-duty trucks for the world market at its facility in Kelowna and transit buses in Ontario and New York state. They recently acquired a major U.K. truck builder, ERF.

Southland Canada Inc. • Retail/Convenience food (7-Eleven stores) • rev: $718 million • assets: $141 million • Frank V. Farr, CEO • empl: 1,500 • 3185 Willingdon Green • Burnaby, B.C. V5G 4P3 • 299-0711 • Fax: 293-5634 or 299-6700

Of Southland's 15,385 stores world-wide, 136 are in British Columbia. Southland—the largest operator, franchisor and licensor of convenience stores in the world—began operating in 1927, and the name 7-Eleven was adopted in 1946 to reflect the fact the stores were open from 7 a.m. to 11 p.m. Today, virtually all 7-Elevens are open 24 hours a day. • Motto: What they want, where and when they want it

Teck Corporation • Mining development and exploration • rev: $714 million • net rev: $89.6 million • assets: $1.99 billion • Robert J. Wright, Chairman; Dr. Norman B. Keevil, President and CEO • empl: 2,200 • 600-200 Burrard Street • Vancouver, B.C. V6C 3L9 • Ph: 687-1117 • Fax:

687-6100 • e-mail: info@teckcorp.ca

Teck Corporation produces gold, copper, zinc, lead, niobium, molybdenum, silver and metallurgical coal with working interests in 11 Canadian mines and one in Chile. Big news for Teck in 1995 was the nickel discovery at Voisey's Bay, and its early acquisition of 10.8 per cent of the company that made the find. By the end of the year that Teck investment of $108 million had increased in value to $309 million, and further investment since has increased that figure. Teck Corporation was incorporated under that name April 2, 1966. Norman Keevil was the 1996 Pacific Region Entrepreneur of the Year.

Daishowa-Marubeni International • Manufacturing/Forest products • rev: $662 million • Y. Yamamaka, CEO • empl: 473 • 1700-1095 West Pender Street • Vancouver, B.C. V6E 2M6 • Ph: 684-4326

Van Waters & Rogers • Wholesale chemical distribution • rev: $548 million • assets: $203 million • Larry Bullock, CEO• empl: 115 • 9800 Van Horne Way • Richmond, B.C. V6X 1W5 • Ph: 273-1441

Wajax Industries Ltd. • Retail/Mobile equipment, diesel engines and industrial components • rev: $521 million • net rev: $12 million • assets: $303 million • H. Gordon MacNeill, Chairman; John A. Powell, President and CEO • 8760 River Road • Delta, B.C. V4G 1B5 • Ph: 946-1171 • Fax: 946-1319

Wajax moved its head office to Vancouver from Montreal in 1996.

Howe Sound Pulp and Paper • Pulp and paper manufacturing • rev: $544 million • Gary Graham, CEO• empl: 799 • P.O. Box 49420 • Bentall Stn. • 1055 Dunsmuir Street • Vancouver, B.C. V7X 1B5 • Ph: 661-5269 • Division of Canfor.

Crestbrook Forest Industries • Manufacturing/Forest products • rev: $538 million • net rev: $20 million • assets: $1.02 billion • Masayasu Inoue, CEO • empl: 1,126 • 1200-1055 West Hastings Street • Vancouver, B.C. V6E 2E9 • Ph: 685-3221 • Fax: 685-1340

Crestbrook Forest Industries was incorporated February 2, 1967 as Crestbrook Timber. It changed to its present name May 1 of the same year.

Taiga Forest Products Limited • Lumber and building goods distribution • rev: $522 million • net rev: $2.3 million • assets: $110 million • Patrick E. Hamill, President • empl: 88 • 1000-4330 Kingsway • Burnaby, B.C. V5H 4G7 • Ph: 438-1471

Taiga is Canada's largest independent wholesale distributor of lumber, panel products and related building materials.

CanWest Gas Supply Inc. • Natural gas marketing • rev: $522 million • assets: $54 million • D.

Hugh Gillard, President and CEO • empl: 44 • 7th floor-1285 West Pender Street • Vancouver, B.C. V6E 4B1 • Ph: 661-3300

CanWest is the largest gas marketer in British Columbia, drawing from more than 2,000 wellhead supply sources and reserves. It is owned by more than 80 oil and gas producers, and supplies gas through 14 different pipelines in Western Canada and the United States.

Charlwood Pacific Group • Service franchiser • rev: $479 million • U. Gary Charlwood, CEO • empl: 1,300 • 900-1199 West Pender Street • Vancouver, B.C. V6E 2R1 • Ph: 662-3800 • Fax: 662-3878

The Charlwood Pacific Group is the majority owner of Century 21 Real Estate Canada Ltd., one of Canada's leading real estate franchise organizations; it has majority ownership of Uniglobe Travel, the world's largest franchisor of travel agencies with more than 1,100 outlets in Canada, the U.S., U.K., Japan, Belgium, Luxembourg, Germany and Austria. And it is the majority owner of Charlwood Pacific Properties, a property management and renovation company.

Repap British Columbia • Manufacturing/Forest products (pulp, lumber, coated and kraft papers) • rev: $475 million • Sr. exec in B.C.: Harry R. Papushka, Exec. VP • empl: 1,318 • 2300-666 Burrard Street • Vancouver, B.C. V6C 2X8 • Ph: 688-2225

Repap Enterprises Inc. (parent firm) was incorporated November 2, 1988. The company's coated papers are used by publishers like *Time, Sports Illustrated, The New Yorker* and *Canadian Living*. Repap exports more coated paper—46,000 tons in 1995—than any other North American producer.

Simons International • Consulting engineering, project management, industrial training • rev: $438 million • Tom Simons, Chairman and CEO; B.C. Bentz, President and COO • empl: 1,100 • 400-111 Dunsmuir Street • Vancouver, B.C. V6B 5W3 • Ph: 664-4315 • Fax:669-9516

Since its formation in Vancouver in 1944 by Howard Simons, this company—originally formed to serve the forest products industry—has completed more than 10,000 projects in more than 70 countries. Their range of products and services is very broad. Two interesting examples: (1) a newsprint machine developed by Simons for Howe Sound Pulp and Paper Limited at Port Mellon began working April 3, 1991—only one day later than had originally been scheduled three years earlier, and (2) The Vancouver Island Highway, involving a 120-kilometre route selection and the design of 37 bridges, nine interchanges, 28 grade separations, and nearly 30 kilometres of secondary roads. Among the company's awards is the Environmental Engi-

As Contacts moves into the 21st Century, online information service will be provided to customers from the company's web site at www.contactsbc.com. The company's e-mail address is contactsinfo@contactsbc.com. The Company maintains its Lower Mainland offices at 201-460 Nanaimo Street, Vancouver, B.C. V5L 4W3 and can be reached by telephone at (604) 253-1111 or 1-800-668-2864.

neering Design Award from the Association of Professional Engineers and Geoscientists of B.C. for the environmental upgrade of a B.C. pulpmill.

Pacific Forest Products Limited • Lumber manufacturing • rev: $434 million • net rev: $36.2 million • assets: $260 million • Paul E. Gagne, Chairman; Sandy M. Fulton, President and CEO • empl: 1,100 • 1000-1040 West Georgia Street • Vancouver, B.C. V6E 4K4 • Ph: 640-3400 • Fax: 640-3480

Pacific Forest Products Limited was incorporated under that name July 29, 1993.

BC Railway Company (Crown corporation) • Transportation • rev: $425 million • net rev: $47 million • assets: $1.56 billion • Paul J. McElligott, CEO • empl: 2,480 • 221 West Esplanade • North Vancouver, B.C. V7M 3J1 • Ph: 986-2012

"As taxpayers," BC Rail president Paul McElligott told the Vancouver Board of Trade in January 1996, "you'll be relieved to hear that we continue to stay out of the public purse. We don't take a dime from public coffers and in 16 years the only loss we've had was because of a write-off." BC Rail's net income for 1995 was 18 per cent better than that of 1994.

Tolko Industries • Lumber, plywood veneer manufacturing • rev: $425 million • J.A. Thorlackson, CEO • 200 Bridge Street • North Vancouver, B.C. V7H 1W7 • Ph: 929-3471

Canfor-Weldwood Distribution • Wholesale building materials distribution • rev: $423 million • Thomas J. Longworth, CEO: • empl: 112 • 301-4603 Kingsway • Burnaby, B.C. V5H 2B3 • Ph: 432-1400

WIC Western International Communications Ltd. • Broadcast, entertainment and communication • rev: $422 million • net rev: $15.2 million • assets: $713 million • G. Edmund King, Chairman; John S. Lacey, President and CEO • empl: 713 • 1960-505 Burrard Street • Vancouver, B.C. V7X 1M6 • Ph: 687-2844 • Fax: 687-4118 • e-mail: comments@wic.ca

WIC's revenues in 1995—which had almost doubled in five years—came 59 per cent from television (eight TV stations, including BCTV and Victoria's CHEK-TV), 18 per cent from satellite network services, 15 per cent from radio (12 stations, including CKNW and CFMI) and 8 per cent from pay television (Superchannel, MovieMax!, etc.). Other WIC activities include wireless distribution of video, voice and data signals and a satellite Direct-To-Home distribution and marketing service. WIC Western International Communications Ltd. was incorporated under that name June 24, 1983.

Shoppers Drug Mart • Retail drugstores • rev: $418 million • Terrance I. Morrison, CEO • empl: 2,000 • 6th floor-100 Park Royal South • West Vancouver, B.C. V7T 1A2 • Ph: 926-7821

BC Buildings (Crown corporation) • Real estate, property management and development • rev: $415 million • assets: $1 billion • Dennis Truss, CEO • empl: 850 • 500 Lougheed Highway • Coquitlam, B.C. V3C 4S2 • Ph: 528-3850

TCG International (TCGI) • Manufacturing/Retail household merchandise; high tech communications • rev: $404.6 million • net rev: $1.7 million • Arthur Skidmore, CEO • 27th floor-4710 Kingsway • Burnaby, B.C. V5H 4M2 • Ph: 438-1000 • Fax: 438-7414 • Internet: http://www.tcgi.com

In June 1995 the founders of TCGI, Arthur and Herbert Skidmore, received the Order of British Columbia for their entrepreneurial efforts in building a business from one automotive replacement glass store in 1946 to an international corporation. Apple Auto Glass (124 locations), Speedy Auto Glass (162 locations in Canada, 111 in the U.S.), and hundreds of NOVUS windshield repair and replacement franchises are among TCGI's activities. They are also heavily into satellite and cellular phones and paging systems. TCGI operates more than 300 corporate and franchise operations in Quebec. TCG International Inc. was incorporated under that name January 30, 1970. The company returned to private status in 1996.

Celgar Pulp • Bleached sulphate pulp manufacturer • rev: $399 million • assets: $757 million • Claude Janelle, CEO • empl: 450 • 3063-595 Burrard Street • Vancouver, B.C. V7X 1G4 • Ph: 681-7204 • Fax: 681-7230 • Internet: http://www.castlegar.com/celgar

In the 1960s the Celanese Corporation of America invested $50 million to build the first inland sulphate pulp mill at Castlegar, B.C. It also built a sawmill.

Brewers' Distributor • Beer distribution • rev: $394 million • assets: $31 million • Gary Clermont, CEO: • empl: 380 • 109 Briad Street • New Westminster, B.C. V3L 5T3 • Ph: 664-2300 • Fax: 664-2309

B.C. Packers • Salmon canning • rev: $392 million • Donald A. McLean, CEO • empl: 200 • P.O. Box 5000 • Vancouver, B.C. V6B 4A8 • Ph: 277-2212

B.C. Packers—western Canada's largest seafood company—has roots going back to 1870 when the first commercial salmon cannery in western British North America was opened at Annieville, on the south bank of the Fraser River near New Westminster. Alexander Ewan was one of the owners. Later Ewan began his own cannery and in 1902 when The British Columbia Packers Association began with the purchase of 42 canneries (including Ewan's), he became the first president. (The money to buy the operations was American.) A new company, British Columbia Packers Limited,

was incorporated May 18, 1928. Among its most famous products is Clover Leaf salmon, first sold under that name in 1889. Besides salmon, the company packs herring, tuna, clams, oysters and industrial fish meals and oils, and exports herring roe to Japan. It grows Atlantic salmon in hatcheries and "grow-out" sites around Vancouver Island. Its Prince Rupert fish cannery is the largest in the world. (Fast fact: The production of B.C. and Alaskan canned salmon exceeds North American consumption, so export markets are crucial.)

Pharmasave Drugs • Retail drug store franchise • rev: $375 million • Brad Bond, CEO • empl: 1,250 • 6350-203rd Street • Langley, B.C. V2Y 1L9 • Ph: 532-2250

Crown Packaging • Holding • rev: $370 million • assets: $275 million • Timothy F. Dwayne, CEO: • empl: 963 • P. O. Box 8930 • Vancouver, B.C. V6B 4P5 • Ph: 522-6889 • Fax: 522-0758

Tim Dwayne and partner Hans Koch began, says *BC Business* magazine, with a corrugated carton plant in Richmond in 1981. They went on to build a recycled paper and packaging products empire that stretches from northern California to Alaska and east to the Ontario border. Crown is now the largest consumer of recycled paper products in Western Canada. Tim Dwayne was a 1995 finalist in the Entrepreneur of the Year program.

Macl_an Capital • Corporate and real estate holding company • rev: $369 million • Harald H. Ludwig, CEO • empl: 3 • 940-1040 West Georgia Street • Vancouver, B.C. V6E 4H1 • Ph: 688-6668 • Fax: 688-6527

Homestake Mining Company • Mining • rev: $764.4 million • net rev: $30.3 million • Jack Thompson, President and COO • empl: 236 • Canada: Homestake Canada Inc. • 1000-700 West Pender Street • Vancouver, B.C. V6C 1G8 • Ph: 684-2345 • Fax: 684-9831 • Internet: http://www.homestake.com

The Homestake Mine in the Black Hills of the Dakota Territory opened in 1877. (Homestake has been on the New York Stock Exchange since 1879.) Besides its operations at Eskay Creek, B.C., Homestake has a stake in mining operations in, among other places, Ontario, Nevada, Australia, Chile and Bulgaria. The company owns 50.6 per cent of Prime Resources Group. Homestake's 1995 gold production was about 1.9 million ounces, 35 per cent of that from its Canadian operations.

Great Pacific Enterprises • Manufacturing • rev: $364 million • assets: $205 million • Jim Pattison, CEO • 1600-1055 West Hastings Street • Vancouver, B.C. V6E 2H2 • Ph: 688-6764 • Fax: 687-2601

With thanks to Bonnie Irving, editor of BC Business, for invaluable assistance.

Industrial Development
Michael Kluckner

VANCOUVERITES have always had a schizophrenic attitude towards industry. According to the Vancouver creed, jobs are wonderful, but jobsites have a tendency to spoil the view. Over the years, "eyesore" and "sewer" were two of the more polite words used to describe local industrial districts, and Vancouver has received most of its international attention due to what has happened on reclaimed industrial land—mainly on False Creek and along the downtown waterfront. Few tears have been shed for the loss of the old sheds during the de-industrialization of the modern city.

Vancouver has often been nicknamed the "Terminal City"—it is the movement of goods through, rather than from, Vancouver that has made it what it is today. Before Vancouver was even incorporated, Canada's population base had long been established in the east; with the railway completed, manufactured goods were easily moved across the country, while British Columbia's raw resources such as lumber and coal were shipped from Vancouver using lots of capital investment but relatively few workers. Thus Vancouver never developed the industrial potential envisioned by some of its early boosters, and the view towards the mountains remained relatively unspoiled until, in the decades since the 1960s, the world economy changed to the point that Vancouver has been able to evolve into a pristine "Executive City"—a centre of office buildings and white-collar jobs.

Historically, compared with the manufacturing centres of the Canadian east, Vancouver's economy has been on a roller-coaster ride. Its major industry in the 19th century, lumber milling, was dependent on the ups and downs of world demand, mainly from the United States and Australia, whose own economies were cyclically dependent on metal discoveries and population migrations. After a deep depression in the early 1890s which almost brought international trade to a halt, Vancouver recovered while outfitting participants in the Klondike Gold Rush, and then grew rapidly, buoyed by an influx of British and German capital and immigration.

Then, in 1913, the world once again sank into a depression. The Great War, which revived the industrial cities of the east, had little economic impact in far-away Vancouver, and it took much of the so-called Roaring Twenties for Vancouver to get roaring again. During World War II, local industry expanded quickly, but the great wartime industries—shipbuilding and airplane assembling—closed soon after. There were simply not enough people on the West Coast to create the sort of recession-proof manufacturing base on which southern Ontario, for example, thrived.

Throughout its existence, the mainstay of the Lower Mainland has been lumber milling. Beginning in the 1860s at Moodyville in North Vancouver and on Vancouver's waterfront just east of the foot of Main Street, lumber mills opened to exploit the stupendous stands of timber clothing the Burrard Inlet slopes. The greatest of the early lumber tycoons was John Hendry, who arrived on the West Coast in the 1870s and opened the Royal City Planing Mills. Subsequently he purchased the Moodyville and Hastings mills, and built one of the first sawmills on False Creek; he later consolidated these operations, including sash-and-door factories and a prefabricated-house plant, into the B.C. Mills, Timber & Trading Company.

The two original export-oriented sawmills—Moody's and Hastings Mill—closed many years ago, the former in 1901 and the latter in 1928. Although there were later generations of sawmills established on Burrard Inlet, including the Robert Dollar Company's lumber and shingle mill at Dollarton and the Pacific Coast Lumber Company mill on the Bayshore Hotel site around 1920, most of the big mills operated on the Fraser River and boomed their logs along the shore. The New Westminster waterfront, extending eastwards to Fraser Mills, was home to the largest collection of sawmills and plywood and paper plants. Shingle mills and sawmills also opened near the mouth of the river at Eburne, now Marpole, after the turn of the 20th century, and the completion of the B.C. Electric Railway's Marpole-New Westminster interurban line in 1909 gave workers and shippers access to other mill and general industrial sites along the North Arm, some of which survive today.

The False Creek mills, with smoke billowing from their distinctive beehive burners, were a feature of Vancouver through the 1950s. The fire on the south shore of False Creek in the summer of 1960, which began in B.C. Forest Products' spruce division and spread through nearby lumber yards and industrial operations, spelled the end of that part of Vancouver's industrial landscape, for the city chose to rezone the land for housing and parks. The last False Creek mill survived on the north shore, on the site of the Plaza of Nations, until 1985.

In the early days of New Westminster and Vancouver, when even modest houses had to be fashionably decorated with fancy shingling and fretwork, a large demand existed for decorative woodwork, and numerous small factories turned out complex and beautiful windows, doors and detailing to supply the demand. Simplified housing styles after World War I ensured

Finning has been associated with the industrial development of Greater Vancouver and the resource growth of British Columbia since 1933. That year Earl B. Finning, who came from Salinas, California in the 1920s as a partner with Morrison Tractor Equipment Ltd., formed Finning Tractor & Equipment Company Ltd., as Caterpillar equipment dealer for British Columbia. From a five-person sales office in downtown Vancouver Mr. Finning relocated to Station Street and began to expand a network of facilities throughout the province.

the end of that industry, but the recent revival of interest in heritage restoration has caused a few firms to open, in some cases using old tools and dies discovered in antique stores.

Another of the great early industries was salmon canning, first established on the South Arm of the Fraser River at Annieville in the early 1870s. Technological advances in processing fish and soldering cans, as well as in shipping them to distant markets such as England, helped the industry to thrive, so that by the time Vancouver was incorporated in 1886 there were dozens of canneries in the Lower Mainland, mainly on the Fraser River and along the Steveston waterfront.

Informally known as "Salmonopolis," Steveston was a significant city in the early years of the 20th century, with six hotels, an opera house, a theatre and, after 1902, an efficient and direct rail link with downtown Vancouver (which, in its own right, helped open up Marpole and the Kitsilano-Arbutus area to industrial development). Two of the great fortunes of early Vancouver—the Bell-Irvings' and R.V. Winch's—came from salmon. Henry Bell-Irving, in partnership with Captain R.G. Tatlow, purchased local canneries beginning around 1890 and, under the banner of the Anglo-British Columbia Packing Company, began exporting tinned salmon to England. Winch's achievement is reflected in the Winch Building, erected in 1908 at the northeast corner of Hastings and Howe in downtown Vancouver and now part of Sinclair Centre. After 1902, two-thirds of the Fraser River canneries and a number of others scattered along the B.C. coast operated as the British Columbia Packers Association.

Fishboats lined wharves along the Lower Mainland's waterways until quite recently; a sign of the decline of the industry was the closure in 1990 of the Campbell Avenue fisherman's wharf to the east of the B.C. Sugar Refinery. The main harbor for fishboats today is Steveston, home to a large B.C. Packers operation. A relic of fishing's glory days, the century-old Gulf of Georgia Cannery on the Steveston waterfront, was restored in the 1990s.

Just upstream from the restored cannery is the Britannia Heritage Shipyard, a survivor of another industry once prominent in the Lower Mainland. Opened originally in 1889 as a cannery, the owners converted it to boatbuilding after the Fraser River salmon run collapsed due to the 1913 Hell's Gate landslide. Following its abandonment in the 1980s, the site was donated to the City of Richmond which, with the help of the B.C. Heritage Trust and a group of volunteers, began its restoration. A new generation is now learning wooden-boat construction skills under the tutelage of "old Steveston hands." The other centre for small-boat construction, until the 1960s, was Coal Harbour.

By World War II the yards were an enormous operation, employing thousands of workers in the construction of merchant-marine "Victory" ships

Regrettably the Lower Mainland's other great boatbuilders have all but disappeared. The largest and most significant was the Wallace Shipyard just east of Lonsdale in North Vancouver, a business begun in 1892 on False Creek by Alfred Wallace, who gained a reputation for his wooden, molded-hull salmon boats. Wallace began producing steel-hulled steamers, and to obtain more land moved to North Vancouver shortly after the turn of the 20th century. By World War II the yards were an enormous operation, employing thousands of workers in the construction of merchant-marine "Victory" ships. However, after years of on-again-off-again government contracts and increasing competition from shipyards overseas, the firm, by then known as Versatile, closed forever in December 1991; the site is to be redeveloped with a mixture of commercial buildings and housing, possibly incorporating a few of the old shipbuilding structures.

The other large Lower Mainland yard was West Coast Shipbuilders on the south shore of False Creek just east of the Cambie Bridge. Like Wallace's, its glory days were World War II and the building of "Victory" ships. In its final incarnation as Canron, one large building survives under city ownership, while the surrounding land awaits a new, non-industrial use.

Buildings from both of these sites may survive into the future because of the credibility of Granville Island. A sandbar in False Creek until 1916, when it was filled with dredging spoil, Granville Island soon built up with small industrial firms—machine shops and factories—mainly producing specialized products for the lumber industry. The conversion of Granville Island's buildings into a market, shopping and entertainment area began in the 1970s. Nothing remains of the other heavy industries which lined the shores of False Creek, including the Vancouver Iron & Engineering Works and the aforementioned lumber companies; on the north shore of the Creek, only the historic Roundhouse, headquarters for locomotive maintenance for the Canadian Pacific Railway's western operations, survives amidst highrise towers

under the banner of "we service what we sell", which became the cornerstone of the business. In 1966, company headquarters moved to the 36-acre site on Great Northern Way and became a publicly-held company three years later. In 1987 the company's name changed to Finning Ltd. to better reflect its growing product and support capabilities. Today Finning operates as a Caterpillar dealer in western Canada, the United Kingdom, Poland and Chile, with more than 4,000 employees worldwide.

and parks as a community centre.

The City of Vancouver retains two large industrial districts—its shoreline on the Fraser River and the Burrard Inlet shoreline to the east of downtown. Most of the city's great early industries located along the latter. Among the largest was the B.C. Sugar Refinery, which opened in 1890. Scattered through the blocks of streets near the harbor, through which ran the CPR mainline and numerous small spur lines, were foundries including Mainland and the Ross & Howard Iron Works and factories such as the American Can Company on Alexander Street (since converted into a fashion factory and outlet). One of the most dramatic pieces on the industrial landscape is the Standard Oil refinery on Burrard Inlet east of the Second Narrows Bridge: it is tucked away "around the corner" from the main harbor, as is the Imperial Oil Company's storage facility at Ioco, across the water from Port Moody.

On the Vancouver waterfront, after the Panama Canal opened in 1914, grain terminals were erected for prairie wheat awaiting trans-shipment. The export of bulk goods expanded greatly after World War II to include potash, sulphur and wood pulp; together with containerized goods handling and cruiseships, bulk goods have made the Port of Vancouver the largest in Canada and the largest by tonnage on the Pacific Coast of North America. Freighters awaiting their turn at the port's wharves idle silently in English Bay. Other freighters use the Fraser/Surrey docks on the south arm of the river near New Westminster.

Coal is exported from the Roberts Bank terminal next to the Tsawwassen ferry causeway. Built in the 1960s, Roberts Bank is the region's only freight terminal facing directly onto the open sea. Plans to build ocean wharves that would avoid the navigational intricacies of First Narrows and the Fraser River date back to the 1880s, when the CPR drew up plans to establish a terminus on Kitsilano Point. The Vancouver Harbour and Dock Extension Company proposed an even more ambitious scheme in 1912 for wharves on Richmond's seafront, a rail line crossing Sea Island to Vancouver, and a tunnel extending beneath the city to the downtown area.

The arrival in Vancouver of the Great Northern and Canadian Northern railways during World War I years created some enduring industrial areas. Both approached the Lower Mainland from the south and southeast, and crossed the Fraser River at New Westminster. The spine of mixed industry along Winston Street and Still Creek in Burnaby, and in the Grandview-Boundary areas of Vancouver, date from those days, as do the businesses on the filled, eastern end of False Creek between Main Street and Clark Drive.

Since World War II the revolution in trucking—and the taxpayers' willingness to pay for major road infrastructure—has spread industrial Vancouver away from the watercourses and rail lines. Warehouses and small plants in downtown Vancouver, most notably in the Gastown area, were vacated in favor of the wide-open spaces of the suburbs. In 1946, for example, Kelly-Douglas abandoned the Gastown building now known as The Landing for warehouse space on Kingsway.

Annacis Island, which opened to industry in the 1950s, had a combination of water access and, more recently with the completion of Highway 91, excellent road access. Lake City Industrial Park along the Lougheed Highway in Burnaby is another early example; the Port Kells, North West Langley and Gloucester industrial areas are more recent, as are the Van Horne and Crestwood estates in Richmond, built on former farmland, and those in the Newton area of Surrey.

Many high-tech, clean industries, which contribute greatly to Vancouver's economy and international reputation, labor quietly in out-of-the-way bays of these industrial estates. All feature easy truck access to freeways, loading docks and warehouses combined with corporate offices, ample parking for employees' cars, anonymous buildings and pleasant landscaping—they are not landmarks like the industrial edifices of earlier generations.

Some of Vancouver's inner-city neighborhoods were designated for six-storey light industry in the 1930 Harland Bartholomew plan written for the Town Planning Commission. Strathcona residents protested so effectively in the late 1960s against plans to demolish their homes and relocate them into public-housing projects that Vancouver rethought its attitude towards its industrial land base. In the 1970s and 1980s, the city systematically converted industrial land to other uses—in some areas housing, to put more people closer to downtown white-collar jobs, in other cases to commercial uses, like the "big box" Superstore on Marine Drive at Main Street. Conversions to housing of some industrial land, such as the old Vancouver Brewery site on 12th Avenue in Kitsilano, proved to be controversial, as surrounding residents resisted attempts to infiltrate their neighborhoods with higher-density accommodation.

A counter-move began in the 1990s to save Vancouver's surviving industrial land-base, and the jobs that go with it. Some of the old industrial areas, built along rail lines and watercourses, are getting a second look as the newer industrial estates battle traffic congestion, and planners take a closer look at broadening the spectrum of available work within the city.

facing page: Launch of a "Victory" ship, North Vancouver, 1943. cva

Since its inception Finning has cared about the well-being of the communities it serves. The company and its employees support a wide range of charities, community organizations and social services. Among these is the United Way campaign in which the company matches dollar-for-dollar contributions by employees. In the Vancouver area Finning is the leading donor on a per capita basis. The "Power Tour," which Finning has sponsored for a number of years, visits schools in B.C. and Alberta, delivering its positive self-esteem, anti-substance-abuse presentation to thousands of elementary school students. The message is presented by two former Olympic wrestling contenders.

In addition, Finning contributes to a host of health, educational, cultural and environmental causes. Finning also matches contributions through its volunteer involvement fund to various charities and service endeavors by its employees, numbering more than 2,200 located in some 70 communities throughout Western Canada.

The Vancouver Stock Exchange
John Schreiner

BECAUSE OF A COLORFUL HISTORY that began with its founding in 1907, the Vancouver Stock Exchange is both famous and infamous: famed as one of the world's leading exchanges for junior or venture companies; infamous for the empty or fraudulent promotions that are a continual challenge to securities regulators. Important stock market reforms undertaken in the 1990s are attempting to curb the VSE's unruly culture while preserving its crucial economic role.

Now trading between five billion and six billion shares a year, the VSE has become North America's third busiest exchange by volume. Its reputation for technical excellence is based on its computer trading system; in 1990 the VSE became North America's first fully automated exchange. Its system has been sold to six other stock exchanges from Mexico to India. The VSE's almost 2,000 listings also have become increasingly international. Many of the listed junior mining companies are exploring outside North America with funds raised through the VSE. And in 1995 the VSE sought to capitalize on its Pacific Rim location by inaugurating its Asian Board—a trading category enabling companies based in Asia to use the VSE as their first North American stock exchange.

The various British Columbia gold and silver rushes in the last half of the 19th century spawned at least 15 ill-organized stock exchanges, including several short-lived ventures in Vancouver. After much of the trading in companies involved in the 1898 Rossland Gold Rush was done on the Spokane Stock Exchange, Vancouver business moved to repatriate this economic activity. In April, 1907, the legislature passed a private member's bill creating the VSE.

"The creation of the VSE was a psychological coup de grace to Victoria, once the premier city on the Pacific coast outside of San Francisco," wrote journalists David Cruise and Alison Griffiths in their critical 1987 book on the VSE, *Fleecing The Lamb.* Victoria "had already lost its control over trade, communications and industry in B.C. and, with the failure of the Victoria-based Bank of B.C. in the late 1890s and its absorption by the Canadian Bank of Commerce in 1900, lost its grip on finance as well."

The VSE started slowly, with only 14 companies listed by the end of 1908. However business improved amid the general economic boom that began in 1910 and lasted until the 1913 recession and the 1914 outbreak of World War I. When war started the VSE actually suspended trading for two months and then endured diffcult business conditions until stock markets across North America boomed in the frenzied 1920s. Trading volumes soared especially in 1928 and 1929, amid the first widespread market abuses. Cruise and Griffiths discovered that a VSE president was fined three times in 1926 and 1927, twice for not delivering stock on time and once for trading on behalf of a client without the client's permission. A police investigation of market abuses petered out with the market crash in October, 1929. However the VSE also launched some significant resources companies during the 1920s, among them Home Oil which went public in 1928 at two dollars, using the funds for exploration in Alberta that led to a major discovery.

Volume on the VSE plunged from 143 million shares in 1929 to 10 million shares in 1930. But trading revived sharply in 1933 with feverish speculation in gold shares. Bralorne Mines, which was to become one of British Columbia's largest gold mines, surged from 75 cents a share to $18. Unhappily not all of the issues were real. Huge trading volumes in a company called Wayside turned out to be artificial, with brokers selling the paper back and forth among themselves. That scandal killed VSE trading volumes until the Turner Valley oil discovery in 1936 triggered a boom market in the VSE's junior oils, with the volume reaching 120 million shares in 1937. Another scandal intervened, this one involving fraudulent assay results from a listed mining company, and trading collapsed to 30 million shares in 1938. With the outbreak of war the following year, the VSE entered the doldrums for six years. Volume bottomed at 11 million shares in 1944, with brokers devoting themselves to selling Canadian government Victory bonds. The VSE did not trade more than 100 million shares per year again until 1962.

The VSE was not the only exchange in Canada on which junior mines listed; the Toronto Stock Exchange was the exchange of choice for juniors, in part because so much mining exploration was then centered in Ontario and Quebec. Then in 1964 the TSE was rocked when Windfall Oil and Mines neglected to disclose worthless assays while its shares soared. The promoter was jailed and the regulators in Ontario so tightened regulation of penny mining stocks that these companies and associated promoters moved to the West Coast and the VSE. Because their arrival coincided with significant mineral discoveries in Western Canada, the VSE captured the juniors even when the properties being financed were in Toronto's backyard. That is why, for example, exploration of the Hemlo gold discovery in Ontario in the 1980s was financed on the VSE, through companies controlled by Murray Pezim, the most famous promoter driven from Toronto to Vancouver by the post-Windfall over-regulation. Soon the VSE was trading 300 million shares a year, then 500 million and ultimately 900 million in 1972. The value of trading exceeded $1 billion for the first time in 1969.

If Toronto became over-regulated, the VSE was grossly under-regulated; the exchange's horrific reputation became established amid the explosion of speculative trading that erupted in 1965. By 1973 the RCMP, in a report on commercial crime on the West Coast, said: "The law enforcement agencies have estimated that approximately 20 to 30 per cent of the mines and local, junior industrial stock listed on the Vancouver Stock Exchange are manipulated." Controversy like that, along with the negative impact on investor confidence of the NDP government's mining royalties caused VSE trading to dry up, with the exchange losing money in 1973 for the first time in almost 40 years. The trading volume in 1975, at 190 million shares, was the worst in 12 years.

The VSE regrouped in 1976 under a new president, tough-minded securities lawyer Robert Scott. "He created new regulations and saw to it that the old ones were enforced," Cruise and Griffiths wrote. The exchange was comparatively free of major scandals although in 1977 a VSE vice president fled to Britain to evade the RCMP investigation, who charged him with 94 counts of conspiracy and taking bribes.

This led into the remarkable events of the 1980s, arguably the blackest decade for the VSE. As the stature of the VSE grew, it attracted listings and money from investors in the United States and Europe; indeed the senior Vancouver brokerage firms specializing in junior issues opened offices in Europe, specifically to raise money for companies trading on the VSE. There has been a long tradition of Canadian companies being financed from Europe, with Canadian Pacific being a classic example. Unhappily not every junior floated on the VSE had real value.

Adnan Khashoggi, then known as the world's richest man, popped up in 1986 as a director of a VSE-listed company aptly named Skyhigh Resources; the shares went from 60 cents to $72 before evaporating. Two other Khashoggi companies—one claiming to be in the satellite launch business and the other claiming to be in search of King Solomon's mines—also took gullible investors for a ride. All three were hollow manipulations by the cash-strapped Khashoggi who brought the VSE world-wide attention, notably from investigative journalists. They found more grist for the mill. There was the Carter-Ward scandal, named after two promoters who bribed a Texas mutual fund manager to trade in worthless VSE companies, using accounts at most of the major brokerage firms in Vancouver.

This manipulation went on for 15 months, apparently undetected, before the regulators moved to shut it down. The promoters received jail sentences. About the same time there was another manipulation on the VSE, involving half-a-dozen companies, which blew up so suddenly on a Friday afternoon in October 1984, that $40 million in share value evaporated in less than an hour. Two of the promoters involved, who had sold worthless shares to German investors, got jail sentences.

A succession of events like that led to a new securities act in 1987 that set up a fully staffed securities commission to replace the bare bones and largely ineffective office of superintendent of brokers. Because market abuses continued—in spite of more aggressive policing both by the commission and the VSE—the provincial government in 1993 launched the first ever public inquiry into the British Columbia securities market in the VSE's history. Lawyer James Matkin, who headed the inquiry, observed that "the reputation of the VSE marketplace for sharp and dishonest practices is well-known." But he also found that "identical problems prevail in other markets . . . Much more money is lost because of swindling on other exchanges." He recommended substantial reforms of market regulation, acknowledging that it is in no-one's interest for the VSE to tolerate abuses even if these same abuses exist elsewhere. Many of the reforms were implemented, a number of which aim to hold the brokerage firms much more responsible than before for weeding out poor quality listings and market manipulations.

As a marketplace for junior companies, the VSE is destined to be a paradox. "Public financing of early stage ventures is acknowledged to be a high-risk undertaking with many failures," Matkin observed. Back in 1978 the British Columbia government asked Vancouver consultants Brown Farris & Jefferson to study how investors fared on the VSE. "The odds of losing, overall, are 84 per cent—about five times out of six," the study concluded. "The chances of investors doubling their money each year for more than four years by buying and holding an issue appear to be nil." What the study failed to acknowledge was that investors continue to speculate on VSE juniors for two reasons: some have mastered the art of profiting in trading stocks of companies that subsequently are not successful; others hope for the home run. In 1995, for example, the shares of Atna Resources soared from 30 cents to a high of $5.12 after a commercially significant ore body was found on the company's claims in the Yukon. "The principles of the free market have included the notion of 'caveat emptor' or 'let the buyer beware' since the days of Adam Smith," Matkin wrote. "'Caveat emptor' retains its wisdom."

Vancouver as an International Financial Centre
Michael A. Goldberg

DURING THE EARLY 1980s it became clear that British Columbia had to diversify its resource-based economy. There was also a pressing need to stimulate the B.C. economy to help lift the province out of the deep and protracted 1981-85 recession.

Options facing the province included broadening our trading patterns for existing resource products away from heavy reliance on the U.S. and delving into new products and services. Expo 86 sought to do both by exposing B.C. to the world and promoting our nascent tourism industry. Another important option that was pursued was the development of Vancouver as an "international financial centre" (IFC), in part to take advantage of the boom in international financial services that was occurring in the mid-1980s and in part to build on our existing financial infrastructure such as the Vancouver Stock Exchange (VSE) and our strong community of investment managers. This option spawned IFC Vancouver, the focus of this article.

IFCs are broadly-based financial service centres catering to foreign as opposed to domestic demand. They provide a more diverse set of services than more narrowly focused "international banking centres" (IBCs) which, as the name suggests, are domiciles for international banks. IBCs are frequently driven by tax and regulatory considerations. IFCs on the other hand rely much less on favorable legal treatment and much more for their viability on the presence of a large pool of financial professionals who provide specialized international financial services. IFCs thrive because of the breadth and depth of the specialized financial and associated knowledge resident in the IFC.

The idea of creating an international financial centre in Vancouver originated in the early 1980s. A coordinated effort by senior members of the business and academic communities resulted in the creation of the Society for IFC Vancouver in September 1986, the vehicle for the provincial government's IFC initiative. At the federal level Vancouver's potential as an IFC was given a boost when finance minister Michael Wilson announced in his February, 1986 budget speech that IBCs would be established in Vancouver and Montreal. In December, 1987 the federal government amended the Canadian Income Tax Act to designate Vancouver and Montreal as IBCs. This legislation permits financial institutions operating in these IBCs to be exempt from federal income tax on the profits earned from lending non-resident deposits to non-resident borrowers.

At the provincial level IFC legislation was passed as Bills 22 and 23 in May, 1988 and proclaimed on October 31, 1988. The enabling regulations followed a week later. Through the provincial legislation, firms (and their employees in special cases) carrying on a broad range of eligible international financial transactions are subject to a full refund of the tax paid on the profits earned from these transactions. Eligible transactions include dealing with non-residents in: insurance and reinsurance; stock and bond trading and underwriting; foreign exchange; trade finance; private banking; funds management; making loans; financial advising and; leasing.

IFC Vancouver opened its offices in Canada Place in September 1988. I served as its executive-director from then until 1991 when I returned to the faculty of commerce at UBC in July, 1991. I worked with an outstanding board of directors chaired by Don Hudson, president of the Vancouver Stock Exchange. Liam Hopkins, a career banker with decades of experience in the international and trade finance area, replaced me as executive-director. Under his direction IFC Vancouver has broadened its membership, developed a number of task forces and generally drawn into its operations a larger and more diverse group of supporters. I continue to serve on a broadened and expanded board and thus have participated in the continued evolution of IFC Vancouver and taken great joy in seeing Vancouver emerge as a significant international managerial and financial centre over the half dozen years since we opened our offices.

The goals of IFC Vancouver are: "to facilitate and hasten the development of Vancouver as an international financial centre and to promote and enhance Vancouver's locational attributes so that it is increasingly seen to be a preferred location for the conduct of international financial transactions."

To realize these goals we began by targeting six financial sectors where we felt that Vancouver had significant potential. These sectors were: private banking; asset management; securities underwriting; brokerage and advice; trade finance; insurance and reinsurance (particularly marine insurance and so-called "captive" insurance firms) and; trust and fiduciary services. Given these sectoral targets we then identified potential financial institution targets which we have sought to register for the provincial tax exemption. Under Liam Hopkins' leadership IFC Vancouver has sought to broaden its scope further by developing the concept of IFC Canada which would include potentially any jurisdiction in Canada, not just Vancouver and Montreal, under an expanded and more liberal set of federal IFC tax advantages. The organization continually seeks clarification of tax rulings so that greater certainty and advantage can be bestowed on those doing international financial transactions under the federal and provincial legislation. IFC Vancouver has also stepped up its information function with a strong program of seminars and written materials all aimed at encouraging IFC participants to take advantage of the favorable tax legislation that has been created.

During IFC Vancouver's half decade of operation a number of important successes can already be claimed. More than fifty financial firms here registered for the provincial tax exemption. Included here are foreign and domestic banks, trust companies, domestic and international investment dealers, and asset managers. Registrants engage in diverse activities such as taking and lending non-resident deposits, trade finance, securities brokerage and underwriting, merger and acquisition advice, corporate finance especially for smaller firms and asset management. We are particularly optimistic about the securities related areas and asset management given existing activities in these areas locally. Significant synergies are also seen in marine insurance and ship finance given the parallel growth of the International Maritime Centre in Vancouver which has attracted half a dozen shipping companies to locate head offices in Vancouver.

As the impact of the "Pacific century" becomes more widespread Vancouver's role will grow generally as a geographical, cultural and commercial mediator between Asia Pacific, North America and Europe. Financial services in particular can be expected to grow briskly in the Asia Pacific region with Vancouver's financial sector benefiting in the process from our significant strengths in dealing with that region, foremost among which are:

• political stability and the sanctity of contracts and law
• location on the Great Circle Route to Asia from the US West Coast
• median location and time zone between Europe and Asia
• gateway port and airport
• state-of-the-art telecommunications systems
• excellent public support services (schools, hospitals, parks, libraries, museums)
• availability of a broad range of private management and consulting services
• historical, cultural and business ties with both Asia and Europe
• strong and numerous post-secondary institutions.

Vancouver is rapidly becoming a truly international city. The Clinton-Yeltsin Summit, the new NBA franchise, the

As the impact of the "Pacific century" grows, so will our role as a geographical, cultural and commercial mediator

success of the Vancouver Canucks and the development of such international institutions as the International Commercial Arbitration Centre (ICAC), the International Maritime Centre (IMC), the Asia Pacific Foundation and the dramatic expansion of both the port and the airport all speak to this internationalization. In such an outward-looking setting Vancouver cannot help but attract the attention of the international financial community and thus take its place as an important node in the emerging global network of international financial centres.

Our future is very bright indeed. However, we cannot take it for granted. We must continue to expand our world view and reach. We must also be aware of caveats of growth and development. Livability is very much a key to our success as an IFC. Paradoxically our growth, which thrives on our superb livability, will inevitably threaten it. Thus we must acknowledge the potential trade-off between growth and living quality and guide our growth so we can reap its benefits (higher incomes, greater employment opportunities and stability of employment) while minimizing its potential costs. We will need to use both density and open space judiciously. Congestion needs to be minimized and access maximized, necessitating careful planning and acknowledgement of the links between urban economic and population growth and land use and transportation.

All this growth and change is stressful. It is also likely unavoidable. Thoughtful planning and guidance is a must to maintain livability, our ultimate attraction. Indeed we have made progress on this front already and I am optimistic that we will continue to do so. What is needed is energy and vision and a willingness to face our changing future, overcome our fears and seize the opportunities that the changing world holds for us.

In the "Pacific century" Vancouver is no longer at the back end of a continent. Rather it is in the centre of global commerce midway between Europe and Asia. I firmly believe that we are well on our way to capitalizing upon our advantages and overcoming our weaknesses. The time is not far off when it will be common knowledge that Vancouver is an influential international financial centre. Move over Toronto, and L.A. too!

by more than a dozen senior partners until June of 1996, when the company agreed to join the Hongkong Bank of Canada. The new association gives MKW access to a broad, existing distribution network as well as access to the expertise and views of money managers around the world. MKW provides discretionary, specialty and balanced fund management to pension funds, mutual and pooled funds, foundations, health and welfare trusts, endowment funds and individuals.

Banks in Greater Vancouver
Bruce Constantineau

VANCOUVER RESIDENTS never had the benefits of formal banking services until the Bank of British Columbia opened for business on West Cordova Street on September 1, 1886. The bank, headquartered in London, England, had opened a branch in New Westminster in October 1862 (it closed for 11 years in July 1887).

James Douglas—first governor of Vancouver Island and the mainland colony—urged British business leaders to create a new bank for the booming colony. Desperate gold miners at the time were literally burying their gold dust in order to protect their savings.

On April 26, 1862 a group of British bankers received a Royal charter to operate the Bank of British Columbia and the first branch opened in Victoria in July 1862. Bankers never saw the need for such a facility in Vancouver until 1886. Canadian Pacific Railway land commissioner Lauchlan Hamilton had invited the general manager of the Bank of Montreal to visit Vancouver to assess the value of opening a new branch. The banker came, but returned to Montreal unconvinced.

The manager of Vancouver's first Bank of British Columbia branch was James Cooper Keith, a native of Aberdeen, Scotland. He later became president of the Board of Trade and reeve of North Vancouver. Keith Road in North Vancouver was named after him.

The bank moved its premises in 1887 to 542 West Hastings Street and in 1891 moved to a corner site at Hastings and Richards on property it bought for $2,250. The decision to build a branch in Vancouver was quickly justified; by 1891 its net earnings exceeded those of the bank's San Francisco, Portland and Victoria branches. The bank, which opened two branches in the Cariboo gold fields in the 1860s (and three more Cariboo branches later), expanded to Nanaimo, Kamloops, Nelson, Kaslo, Rossland and the U.S.A. before the directors decided it was too difficult to run the growing operation from their English headquarters. In early 1901 the bank merged with the Canadian Bank of Commerce, which had opened its first provincial branch in Vancouver in 1898.

The Bank of Commerce, keen to establish a major presence in Western Canada, followed up the merger with many more acquisitions over the next several years. The Quebec-based Eastern Townships Bank, which had opened a Vancouver branch in 1905, amalgamated with the Commerce in 1912.

The Toronto-based Bank of Hamilton, which had expand-ed to several Vancouver area branches after opening its first in 1898, merged with the Commerce in 1923. The same year the Ontario-based Home Bank crashed, creating a major public crisis of confidence in Canadian banks in general. In 1928 the Commerce acquired the Standard Bank of Canada, which had opened a Vancouver branch in 1912, and in 1961 merged with the Imperial Bank of Canada, which had opened its first Vancouver branch in 1895. After the 1961 merger the bank became known as the Canadian Imperial Bank of Commerce.

Vancouver's boom-and-bust real estate market made it difficult for bankers to count on a steady income stream and several banking ventures never got off the ground. The Bank of Vancouver, for example, went into liquidation just five years after it was founded in 1910 because it could not attract a significant deposit base.

In 1909 real estate prices soared—an alley corner on Hastings Street was sold for $100,000 while one property owner refused an offer of $250,000 for a corner on Robson and Granville. Bank of Toronto officials at the time deplored "the wild speculation which has taken place in real estate." In 1911 the Bank of Toronto and The Dominion Bank, which eventu-

The Canadian Bank of Commerce at Hastings and Granville, 1908. cva

ally merged, each opened second branches in Vancouver. This was considered a major expansion, but they weren't the first banks to have such a presence in the city, as the Merchants' Bank of Halifax had two Vancouver branches in 1898—the only bank at the time to have two branches in the same city west of Toronto.

The Merchants' Bank changed its name in 1901 to The Royal Bank of Canada and by 1909 had 27 branches in British Columbia, compared with just 10 in Quebec and 31 in Ontario.

After dismissing the prospect of opening a Vancouver office years earlier, the Bank of Montreal set up its first branch in the city in a modest frame building on Hastings Street in July 1887. It was the bank's first branch west of the Rockies.

Bank manager Campbell Sweeney reported a profit of just $143.67 in the first month—about half his monthly salary. But within five years the branch stood tenth in loans and four-teenth in deposits among the Bank of Montreal's 36 Canadian branches.

The second Bank of British Columbia—the 1960s ver-sion—received its federal charter on December 14, 1966, exact-ly one year after the Senate banking committee rejected B.C. Premier W.A.C. Bennett's proposal to create a B.C.-based bank, with the provincial government as a major shareholder.

Bennett had long been disenchanted with Canada's eastern-based financial establishment and those feelings were shared by many in British Columbia, including Bennett's political oppo-nents. He felt financial institutions headquartered in Toronto and Montreal could not understand the pressing need to finance private development in the province. He even tried to convince one of the big chartered banks to move its head office to Vancouver.

"Vancouver is farther away from the head office of a char-tered bank than any other city of comparable size in the whole free world," Bennett told the banking committee in July 1964. But the committee was concerned about the undue influence the B.C. government, as the major shareholder, could have on the new bank, and turned Bennett down by a vote of 19 to 7.

However, the committee approved a different, totally pri-vate, proposal for a new Bank of British Columbia in March 1966, and the bank began full operations in 1968, with $34 mil-lion in assets.

For a while, the bank flourished, fuelled by the success of Western Canada's resource-based economy. It established a net-work of branches throughout British Columbia and Alberta and maintained offices in San Francisco, Hong Kong and the Cayman Islands. But the bank never fully recovered from the recession of the early 1980s, when real estate values plunged

and the oil industry collapsed. It never lived to see its twentieth birthday but it didn't go down without a fight.

Well-known Vancouver entrepreneur Edgar Kaiser Jr. be-came the faltering bank's new president and chief executive officer in October 1984, and the bank raised $153 million through a private placement and a public offering of bank shares. In February 1985 the bank bought the assets of a col-lapsed trust company—Pioneer Trust—and opened nine new branches in Alberta, Saskatchewan and Manitoba. But the fail-ures of two Alberta-based banks in late 1985—Northland Bank and the Canadian Commercial Bank—created a crisis of confi-dence in Western-based financial institutions and the Bank of British Columbia was doomed. Commercial depositors fled and the bank had to find a buyer or cease operations for good.

The Hongkong Bank of Canada bought substantially all the assets and liabilities of the Bank of British Columbia on November 27, 1986. The transaction was aided by a $200 mil-lion cash injection from the Canada Deposit Insurance Corp., to protect the Hongkong Bank from future losses resulting from the acquisition of the Bank of British Columbia assets.

Overnight the small Vancouver-based Hongkong Bank moved from being the twentieth largest to the ninth largest bank in Canada by adding $2.6 billion in assets and 41 branch-es in British Columbia and Alberta. The Hongkong Bank of Canada is a wholly owned subsidiary of HSBC Holdings, based in London, England. It received its federal charter on July 1, 1981 following changes to the Bank Act of Canada which allowed foreign-based banks to operate in Canada.

The new legislation prompted many foreign banks to set up shop in Vancouver but most sought only corporate business from commercial clients. After the Bank of British Columbia acquisition, the Hongkong Bank aggressively pursued a national branch network to serve commercial and retail clients across the country.

On May 20, 1988, it acquired all the assets of Midland Bank Canada and on May 29, 1990, it bought Lloyds Bank Canada. The two acquisitions added nearly $5 billion in assets and 53 new branches, mainly in Ontario and Quebec. By 1995 the Hongkong Bank of Canada had 109 branches, 3,200 employ-ees and more than $17 billion in assets to rank as the seventh largest bank in Canada.

Vancouver's newest bank is the Citizens Bank of Canada, a Vancouver City Savings Credit Union subsidiary. This is a branchless electronic bank, which customers will access by tele-phone, personal computer and automated teller machine. The bank's president, Linda Crompton, says assets are expected to grow to at least $1.5 billion by 2002.

and products to retail, agricultural, commercial, corporate and institutional clients. More than six million individuals and corporations rely on CIBC services. They are served by 40,000 employees through 1,400 branches across Canada, along with an extensive ABM network and telephone banking. The CIBC's ownership base is broad with some 93,000 shareholders.

Credit Unions In Greater Vancouver
Bruce Constantineau

THE CREDIT UNION MOVEMENT, with its then-revolutionary concept of cooperative banking, made its unofficial B.C. debut in Burnaby on August 22, 1936. The Army of the Common Good, a self-help group formed during the Great Depression, created the "Common Good Credit Unit" with six charter members and $10.25 in deposits.

The organization deliberately chose the word "unit" instead of "union," reflecting its practice of using "unit" to designate its various areas of activity. There was also no provincial legislation in place that would allow for the official formation of credit unions.

Within two months deposits at Common Good Credit Unit more than doubled to $25.10 and the operation's first loan, totalling $27, was made on May 22, 1937.

From that modest start the credit union system in B.C. has grown to become the largest locally owned and controlled financial organization in the province—with 1.3 million members and more than $17 billion in assets. More than half the members and about two-thirds of the system's assets are located in Greater Vancouver.

Credit unions trace their North American origins to Quebec's *caisse populaire* system of cooperative banking in the early 1900s. A 1938 letter from the Vancouver and District Cooperative Council, discussing B.C.'s first Credit Union Act, spells out exactly what credit union pioneers in the province wanted.

It said a credit union should be an association of persons, united by a common bond, working together for three main goals: to encourage thrift by providing a safe, convenient and attractive medium for the investment of members' savings; to promote industry, eliminate usury and increase the purchasing power of members by letting them borrow for productive purposes at a reasonable cost; to train members in business methods and self-government and bring them to a full understanding of the value of cooperation. The provincial government passed the Credit Union act in the fall of 1938, allowing for the official designation of chartered credit unions throughout B.C.

The act ensured each credit union would have an elected board of directors, with just one vote for each member, regardless of the amount of business they conducted with the credit union. The legislation also provided for annual general meetings, closed-bond credit unions based on working relationships and open-bond, community-based credit unions.

Canada's largest credit union, Vancouver City Savings Credit Union, received its provincial charter on October 11, 1946. More than 150 credit unions were already operating in B.C. at the time but they were all based on employment, ethnic or religious bonds, which excluded most people from joining

The first charter was awarded to Powell River Credit Union on June 9, 1939, and the credit union still exists by that name. The second charter was granted to Amalgamated Civil Servants Credit Union of Vancouver on July 3, 1939. It was prominent in the early days of the B.C. credit union movement, as its civil-servant members helped many other groups of volunteers form their own credit unions.

Amalgamated Civil Servants Credit Union was renamed Vanfed before it became part of Burnaby Credit Union in 1982. That organization was renamed Harbour Savings in 1985 before it was merged with North Shore Credit Union in 1986.

The Common Good Credit Unit received the province's third charter on July 22, 1939, and became known as Common Good Credit Union. It was renamed South Burnaby Credit Union in 1951 and Pioneer Credit Union in 1984, and now lives on as Burnaby Savings Credit Union.

In 1948 14 charter members signed a constitution, gathered $48 in assets, and started what is today Fraser Valley Credit Union. The FVCU closed the year with 53 members and assets of $2,441.35. Today it's the sixth largest credit union in the province, with nine branches, more than 40,000 members and more than $500 million in assets. In 1983 FVCU expanded into the insurance industry and now operates six insurance agencies from Surrey to Agassiz.

By 1961 there were 328 credit unions throughout B.C. The

explosive growth and quick success achieved by many credit unions showed they clearly filled a market niche, as many low-income savers and borrowers considered themselves poorly served by banks, trust companies and finance companies.

Many credit unions promoted consumer cooperatives and when housing became a serious social issue in the 1960s several credit unions actively supported the creation of cooperative housing. Some credit unions were formed on the basis of work associations while others were organized specifically to serve members of various ethnic communities. Edelweiss Credit Union, for example, was established in Vancouver on March 27, 1943 to serve the area's German community.

But the market recognized that 328 individual credit unions throughout B.C. were far too many to support on a long-term basis as several credit unions were often organized in areas large enough to support just one. Rationalization in the industry, often accelerated by economic downturns and financial problems at certain credit unions, brought the total number of credit unions in B.C. down to 101 by 1995.

Canada's largest credit union—Vancouver City Savings Credit Union—received its provincial charter on October 11, 1946. More than 150 credit unions were already operating in B.C. at the time but they were all based on employment, ethnic or religious bonds, which excluded most people from joining. VanCity's 14 founders envisioned an open-bond credit union to which anyone could belong, an unpopular concept at the time as many credit union pioneers felt the closed-bond approach was a surer road to success because members would know each other and work harder to ensure the organization succeeded. It was that approach which helped the North American credit union movement expand during the Great Depression of the 1930s when thousands of banks failed. But the VanCity founders persisted and history has clearly proven them right. In fact the innovative credit union has probably grown far beyond their wildest expectations. Assets at VanCity reached $1 million by 1954 and hit the $1 billion mark by 1980. By 1995 VanCity and its subsidiary —Citizens Trust—had combined assets of more than $4 billion and the credit union boasted more than 200,000 members throughout Greater Vancouver. In the fall of 1995 VanCity opened a new $25 million head office building that towers above the Main Street SkyTrain station near the Downtown core.

Part of VanCity's success can be attributed to a series of firsts it brought to the Canadian banking community. The credit union offered Canada's first open mortgage in 1959 and introduced North America's first daily-interest savings account —known as Plan 24—on June 1, 1967. It also offered Canada's first international automated teller machine network in 1983

and in February, 1986, it launched the country's first socially responsible mutual fund—the Ethical Growth Fund.

The fund, with more than $182 million in assets by 1995, has investment guidelines based on ethical principles. It cannot, for example, invest in companies which manufacture weapons or tobacco products and all companies with which it invests must maintain good labor relations and high environmental standards.

Canada's second largest credit union—Surrey Metro Savings— began operations on May 5, 1947. Surrey Metro started out as a closed-bond credit union, open only to members of the Surrey Cooperative, but it expanded to become a community credit union in 1983 and its assets topped the $1.5 billion mark by 1995.

While Surrey Metro enjoyed several years of strong growth after enduring a tough financial period during the mid-1980s, it became better known to some in the industry as B.C.'s maverick credit union—the one that liked to buck the trend.

It introduced a new share structure in 1992 and non-voting ownership shares began trading on the Toronto Stock Exchange on October 5, 1992. The move outraged many credit union traditionalists who fear control of credit unions could shift to out-of-province interests if such actions become a trend.

Surrey Metro president Lloyd Craig took even more flak in the fall of 1993 when his credit union proposed a merger with Chilliwack-based First Heritage Savings Credit Union. At the time Surrey Metro had $1.2 billion in assets while First Heritage had $600 million and Craig felt a merger made sense since a combined operation could achieve more economies of scale and be in a better position to compete against larger banks and trust companies. But First Heritage officials viewed the proposal as a hostile takeover and credit union members overwhelmingly rejected the deal—by a vote of 15,930 to 650—following a stormy meeting attended by an overflow crowd of 2,500 people at the Ag-Rec Centre in Chilliwack on October 22, 1993.

The failed merger/takeover attempt accentuates the dilemma facing B.C.'s credit union industry. Credit unions were created as smaller, local alternatives to big banks, but as the financial services industry becomes increasingly competitive, there's a growing feeling that the bigger you are, the better chance you have to survive.

Traditionalists feel the credit union system will naturally evolve into a more rationalized operation—with fewer, but larger, credit unions. Others argue that that will take too long and they risk losing ground to bigger, more efficient financial institutions. "A lot of people seem to be comfortable with the status quo but we don't live in a status quo world," said Surrey Metro's Lloyd Craig. "I know we don't live in a status quo industry."

Foundations
Sandra McKenzie

ACCORDING TO THE 1994–95 *Canadian Directory to Foundations* there are more than 70 active foundations in the Lower Mainland representing assets in excess of $500 million and supporting interests as diverse as animal rights, third-world hunger relief, ornithological research and the promotion of Norwegian culture. In 1994, the last year for which figures are available, foundations across British Columbia disbursed grants worth $42,953,311. The Vancouver Foundation, established in 1943, is the largest foundation in the province and the second largest nationwide, with total assets of $355,602,470. With 779 grants worth $22,001,209 (in 1994) supporting a wide range of charitable, educational and cultural activities, it ranks first in Canada in terms of the value of grants. The Jim Pattison Foundation with assets of $4,779,321 disbursed funds of $1,568,215 to 42 grant-seekers, primarily for the advancement of Christianity and the relief of poverty thus ranking fourth nation-wide for value of grants.

Foundations are the fastest growing form of philanthropy in North America according to Allan Ecclestone, founding director of the brand-new Surrey Foundation (established in May, 1995). With government purse-strings tightening across North America, city-based foundations provide irreplaceable support to museums, theatres, senior citizens' centres, recreational facilities, services to youth, enviromental programs, heritage sites, enviromental agencies, bursary and scholarship programs, sport teams and charitable organizations. Any citizen can pledge a tax-deductible gift, make a memorial bequest or name a foundation as the beneficiary of an insurance policy.

In the Lower Mainland the city-based foundations are:
MATSQUI-ABBOTSFORD FOUNDATION, 112-32868 Ventura Ave., #200, Abbotsford, v3s 6J3 (assets: $1,821,904; grants: $36,804; charities: $78,350)
CHILLIWACK FOUNDATION, P.O. Box 427, Chilliwack, v2P 6J7 (assets: $471,634; grants: $31,170)
MAPLE RIDGE FOUNDATION, 11995 Haney Pl., Maple Ridge, v2v 6A9 (assets: $150,000; grants: $0; charities: $35,237)
NORTH SHORE CHARITABLE FOUNDATION, 600 W. Queen's Rd. North Building, North Vancouver, (assets: $79,581; grants: $4,250; charities: $3,243)
RICHMOND FOUNDATION, 570-8100 Granville Ave., Richmond, v6Y 3T6 (assets: $195,327; grants $5,563)

SURREY FOUNDATION, P.O. Box 34089, Surrey, v3s 8C4 (assets not determined; no grants as yet)
VANCOUVER FOUNDATION (also agents for the W.J. VanDusen Foundation), 230-505 Burrard St., One Bentall Centre, Vancouver,v7x 1M3 (assets: $355,602,470; grants: $11,001,209)
WEST VANCOUVER FOUNDATION, P.O. Box 91447, West Vancouver, v7s 2Y6 (assets:$394,094; grants: $15,007)

In terms of assets the ten largest private foundations in Vancouver are:
CHAN FOUNDATION OF CANADA, 1800-1030 W. Georgia St., Vancouver v6B 2Y3 (assets: $26,364,400) Benefits educational institutes, charitable associations, Christian organizations, Chinese culture, social services and hospitals.
THE LAW FOUNDATION OF BRITISH COLUMBIA, 1340-605 Robson St., Vancouver, v6B 5J3 (assets: $23,626,759) Supports programs which advance and promote the rule of law and a just society.
MR. AND MRS. P.A. WOODWARD'S FOUNDATION, 305-1155 W. Pender St., Vancouver, v6E 2P4 (assets: $13,405,933) Benefits pioneer projects, especially clinical research in the health field, primarily for the betterment of the people of British Columbia.
THE DAVID AND DOROTHY LAM FOUNDATION, 400-576 Seymour St., Vancouver, v6B 3K1 (assets: $7,987,143) Benefits evangalism, arts and cultural education.
THE HAMBER FOUNDATION, 1055 Dunsmuir St., P.O. Box 49390, Vancouver, v7x 1P3 (assets: $8,067,612) Benefits arts, culture, health, education, sports and recreation.
THE DIAMOND FOUNDATION, 105 N. Commercial Dr., Vancouver, v5L 4V7 (assets: $6,571,292) Benefits general charitable purposes, Jewish organizations, hospitals, United Way, services to children and education.
THE JIM PATTISON FOUNDATION, 1600-1055 W. Hastings St., Vancouver, v6E 2H2 (assets: $4,779,321) Benefits general charitable purposes, particularly grants to Christian schools, for the advancement of Christianity and the relief of poverty.
THE LEON AND THEA KOERNER FOUNDATION, Box 39209, Point Grey Rd. Post Office, Vancouver, v6R 4P1 (assets: $4,000,000) Promotes arts and culture, higher education and public welfare in British Columbia.
BLOCK CHARITABLE FOUNDATION, 800-1030 W. Georgia St., Vancouver, v6E 3B9 (assets: $3,827,486) Benefits general charitable purposes, evangalism and social services.
JOHN HARDIE MITCHELL FAMILY FOUNDATION, 777 Dunsmuir St., P.O. Box 10426, Vancouver, v7Y 1K3 (assets: $3,465,703) Benefits hospitals, social services.

Notaries Public
Kayce White

GREATER VANCOUVER NOTARIES public have written a large part of our domestic legal history over the past century. Their hands and seals are imprinted on hundreds of thousands of documents ranging from property conveyances to last wills filed in public registries.

Notaries in Greater Vancouver hold more than one-third the 323 notarial appointments permitted by statute in 81 notary districts in British Columbia. While the total may appear small in a region of rapid growth, amendments to the Notaries Act which capped appointments in 1981 seemed to be the key to survial in a challanging legal community.

Lawyers who *ex officio* are notaries often view members of the Society of Notaries Public of B.C. as competition. Until 1981 the B.C. Supreme Court decided how many notaries were needed in a given area. While seldom more than 300 B.C. notaries were registered to practise at the same time, the number of practising lawyers quadrupled from fewer than 1,000 in 1947 to more than 4,000 in 1981. Over the years many *ad hoc* groups of lawyers had tried to block notarial appointments: they argued there was no need for independent notaries where lawyers were available.

Legislation in 1981 finally liberated notaries from the control of the Law Society of B.C. which previously had the power to block any appointment. The statute also wiped out a 25-year-old informal agreement between the law society and the notaries. The agreement originated in 1953 when Alex Matthew, an insurance-agent secretary of the notaries society and Socred MLA, drafted amendments to the Notaries Act eliminating the need clause. Disputatious lawyers and notaries swiftly united in opposition: both sides feared that unlimited appointments would curtail their earnings. On January 10, 1955 an agreement ratified by the notaries and the law society stipulated that the need for a notaries appointment would arise when a vacancy occurred through resignation, retirement or death. The agreement capped the number of notaries at 330, the number practising on January 31, 1955. Their seals now were anchored to designated districts.

Membership in the notaries society incorporated November 2, 1926, was optional until it became compulsory through statutory amendments in 1956. The same amendments gave the society full professional status with power to discipine members. Today British Columbia and Quebec are the only two Canadian provinces where notaries are organized in a statutory self-governing society. Although the number of statutory notarial appointments in B.C. has twice been reduced in the past 50 years, many seals remain vacant throughout the province.

By law and by training, B.C. notaries enjoy limited and distinct rights in the practice of non-contentious law, primarily in conveyancing, wills and attesting of various documents for public registration. Generally when no element of a contract or agreement is in dispute notaries public are regarded as an effective, lower-cost alternative to lawyers.

Notaries are required by law to meet standards of professionalism and practice equal to those required of lawyers. Each year, approximatley 20 candidates enroll in the two-year Notary Preparatory Program, a blend of distance education and classroom study of the theory and practise of law. This state-of-the-art program places an emphasis on contract and property law, conveyancing and mortgage law, and the law of wills and estates. With the cost of books and tuition increasing each year, few candidates undertake notary training without a reasonable expectation that a seal will be available to them after graduation.

The office of notary public and its forerunner, the scribes, may be traced back at least 2,000 years. *Notarius,* from the Latin, meant one who wrote from dictation. From the early days of the Roman Empire when few people knew how to write, the *notarii* were essential in recording private and public agreements, contracts and dispositions of property. They also compiled notes for magistrates and jurists. Even today, many jurisdictions refer to their notaries as scriveners, from the root of scribe. It is in honor of their rich history that notaries chose the *Scrivener* as the name of their quarterly legal journal, and to celebrate those aspects of a notary's role—accurately communicating, drafting and authenticating.

The B.C. colonial government officially recognized the need for notary services fewer than six years after the region became a Crown colony governed by English law. On May 4, 1864 Gov. Frederick Seymour signed an order providing for the appointment of notaries public.

The B.C. Legislature often reviewed notarial requirements after passing the first Notaries Public Appointment Act in 1872. In 1897 the act was amended to free notaries from political patronage and to set examinations for competency. A further amendment in 1924 defined notaries' rights and duties, provided for lifetime commissions and specified that future appointments be made on the basis of need for notary services in an area.

A Notary Public is a legal professional commissioned for life by the Supreme Court of British Columbia. Notaries specialize in land law, preparing and registering documents that define and protect your property interests. When you buy your first home or make a will, you want someone you can trust; someone who can advise of your rights and give you the personal attention you deserve. Your Notary Public is part of your neighborhood and is dedicated to ensuring that you receive fair, honest service of value.

Downtown Vancouver
Chuck Davis

THE CITY'S PLANNING department shows "Downtown" as north of False Creek and taking in everything west of Main to Burrard Street and, beyond Burrard, north of Georgia Street to Stanley Park. Those are the borders we'll use in this article. (They take in Chinatown and Gastown, treated in separate articles.)

Downtown moves. When Vancouver began in the 1880s downtown was a couple of short blocks of Cordova Street. Then it began moving up from the water. By September 1928 the city was testing automatic traffic lights (the city's first) at two intersections: Robson and Granville, and Main and Hastings. Parents brought their children down to see the newfangled invention. Today most people agree the epicentre of Downtown is the intersection of Granville and Georgia streets.

It was at that corner I began this article on a pleasant busy weekday afternoon in June 1996. I inject a personal note only because at the very moment I flipped open a notebook to jot down my first observations two big Canada geese suddenly, thrillingly, appeared overhead, honking and beating their wings, skimming swiftly between the office towers. They flew diagonally southeast just above the busy surge of traffic, bringing the pedestrians below to a momentary, grinning stop. Then they were gone.

So downtown can surprise—above and below. Did you know there are rivers under these busy streets? They're 24-inch steel pipes, actually, laid under the surface to provide a source of water to fight fires in the event of a major earthquake, up to 8.5 on the Richter scale, and capable of blasting out an endless supply of ocean water at 10,000 gallons a minute. The $40 million project, called DFPS (Dedicated Fire Protection System), was launched September 9, 1995 with the opening of the False Creek pumping station at Homer and Pacific Boulevard. The system was tested by aiming the water jets upward: they reached a height equivalent to the Marine Building. (The system's designed to deliver water to an individual fire fighter at standard pressure.) By 2002 there will be three pump stations linked to a network of pipelines in the downtown peninsula and Kitsilano. (The False Creek Pump station is also control centre for the city's water and sewer monitoring system.) The water in the pipes is fresh but, in the event of an emergency that disrupts the conventional water system, can be switched to take in salt water.

Birds aren't all you see if you look up. Downtown is an outdoor art gallery. The streets are rich with architectural and decorative oddities above eye-level: half-clad maidens, fiercely scowling gargoyles, floral and abstract designs, floating metal clouds, sealife, heroic workers and, a curious touch, on the Burrard Street side of the Hotel Vancouver two elegantly carved turkeys.

Downtown is crowded. This will not be news to you. What may be surprising is the extent to which it is planned to become more crowded: there is a great deal of development going on in this area but, oddly, relatively little of it is new offices and retail. It's mostly residential. "Our city," says Larry Beasley, Vancouver's director of central area planning, "is emerging as an unbelievably unique place. We have tens of thousands of citizens who have elected to move back into the city." It's expected that 1996 census figures will show a net increase in the area's population for the first time in decades. "Most of North America has an anti-urban philosophy. But here, people want to move into the downtown."

That desire led to a change in zoning regulations, creating a new entity called a "Choice of Use Area." Developers can now opt for either residential or office buildings; both are acceptable. And leeway has been awarded to the owners of designated heritage structures: they can now make whatever alterations they want inside their buildings—only the exteriors must remain unaltered.

The predicted population increase is large. Consider "Triangle West," the name given to a small neighborhood between Bute and Nicola, and between Alberni Street and Coal Harbour. The area is already home to several high-rise apartment towers. An estimated 4,000 additional residential units— already approved—will be going into this busy little wedge. New downtown neighborhoods include more than 200 acres on the north shore of False Creek (the Concord Pacific development) where an estimated 14,500 more people will eventually live; the Marathon development at Coal Harbour, to be home to an estimated 3,700 people, and the adjacent Bayshore Gardens development, where 1,800 more people will be added. Then there's Downtown South, with its spine along a revitalized Granville Street and expected to be home by 2021 to another 11,000 people; East False Creek (centered around the Main Street SkyTrain station) will be an eventual home to yet another 2,800 citizens, and, finally, Granville Slopes, on the land running down to False Creek between the Burrard and Granville bridges where an estimated 2,300 people will end up living. Add all those figures, and you get more than 40,000 residents to add to the 10,000 or so there now. (Remember, we're not including West End population figures.)

Downtown Vancouver is developing and changing more than any other Lower Mainland location. With this growth will come

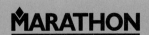

Georgia and Granville, looking west, 1992. vs

and the Georgia/Dunsmuir viaducts. On average, in the first three years of the 1990s a major new office building went up in Downtown Vancouver every 84 days. Then the pace slowed: in 1993 there was just one new tower (at 111 Dunsmuir), and in 1994 and 1995 there were none at all. As this book was going to press, an announcement was made that a new office tower, Ocean Golden Plaza, would be going up on Georgia Street with a completion date by late 1998, the first new office building in Downtown in years.

The "populations" of some of Downtown's big, familiar buildings are impressive. The building manager estimates nearly 3,000 people work inside the Toronto-Dominion Tower—there are nearly a thousand in the IBM Building—1,300 in Cathedral Place, the same at 1075 West Georgia (the old MacMillan Bloedel Building), more than 1,400 in the BC Gas Centre. The "population" of the four Bentall Buildings alone is nearly 5,000, equivalent in size to the city of Ladysmith on Vancouver Island.

Those workers use a lot of cars. Downtown's 25,000 parking spaces can accommodate a line of vehicles more than 115 kilometres long, and thousands more will be needed if car ownership continues to grow. The city is working on ways to increase the use of walkways, bicycle routes and public transit. The aim is to preserve our quality of life. "We're reclaiming the water," says planner Larry Beasley. "We're developing the best pedestrianized areas in the world, we're developing state-of-the-art bicycle routes. Places like Yaletown are springing up, where the 'inventors of the culture' gather." Granville Mall is changing. A determined group of retailers —including the fiercely energetic Blaine Culling, involved in a dozen projects along the Mall—aims to revitalize it and lure people back who had earlier avoided the strip with its army of street youths and panhandlers.

It was expected that a "cultural precinct" would develop around the city-owned Queen Elizabeth Theatre, which opened in 1959. It eventually did happen, but it took a lot longer—nearly 40 years—than had been anticipated. Today, the Queen E is within steps of the CBC's headquarters, the new home of the Vancouver Public Library, and the Ford Centre for the Performing Arts. B.C. Place Stadium and General Motors Place add a sporty element to the mix. Adds Beasley: "People adjust as the city grows. The city is elastic, robust, it has agility—the city will never be filled."

The downtown "office precinct" is gradually being made more compact and centred on transit. As the density of the downtown population increases, you can expect to see a lot more use of buses, SkyTrain and the SeaBus. Many of the thousands of new downtown residents expected will likely live close to their jobs, and might be able to walk to them.

new retail locations, hotels, parks, theatres, schools, community centres, walkways and bicycle routes. These amenities and much development activity can be seen in the north of the downtown peninsula, with the expansive waterfront development by Marathon. Adjacent to Coal Harbour to the west the Bayshore Developments is underway. Activity to the east includes the opening of the new Vancouver Public Library main branch, General Motors Place and the Ford Centre for the Performing Arts. Activity to the south includes the development of Yaletown and the vast Concord Pacific holdings on False Creek.

A lot of people work here already: about 120,000 in 1996. Total jobs in the area are expected to increase by another 40,000 by 2021. Downtown's "office precinct" is expanding to the east. There is 25 million square feet of office space in Downtown now (half the office space in Greater Vancouver), and the potential for another 25 million immediately adjacent to the east. Look for development from the waterfront to Nelson Street, and ultimately east (skirting south of Victory Square) to Beatty Street

Coal Harbour will include a community centre, an elementary school and day care centres. With more than 6.4 hectares of parks and open spaces, new recreational and commercial marinas and other community amenities, the site will ultimately house approximately 4,000 new residents. With the inclusion of more than 2 million square feet of commercial space Coal Harbour will also be viewed as a strong extension of the downtown business core, and will vastly improve Vancouver's industrial waterfront, already a considerable tourist attraction.

Science/Technology
Mark Wilson

THE SILVER ORB of Science World British Columbia, built for Expo 86, replaced a sawmill within a few minutes walk of Vancouver's central business district. The ridding of False Creek of mill-bound logs along with the erection of a geodesic dome devoted to the popularization of science are tokens of major change in the provincial economy. Faced with a shrinking fibre supply and galloping growth, B.C. is seeking to turn itself into a high-technology workshop. There is no other obvious course if wealth creation is to be sustained.

Vancouver is the seat of high-tech industry in the province. Victoria ranks next in importance and there are outcroppings in communities such as Kelowna and Nelson, but provincial statistics on this sector refer chiefly to activity in the Lower Mainland.

As of 1993 high-tech companies were estimated to number some 3,000, employing 37,000 workers and generating $4 billion in revenues. The information technologies (IT) sector was dominant with 1,876 companies, 23,246 workers and sales of $2.8 billion. But with companies averaging a dozen workers apiece, the bulk of them are quite small, suggesting others were too minuscule or too impermanent to gain notice in the official statistics. The software development sector in particular has always been very volatile.

IT companies include Burnaby-based MPR Teltech Ltd., which has a clutch of technologies related to telecommunications and advanced data transfer. MacDonald Dettwiler and Associates Ltd. (MDA) of Richmond is expert in earth observation from space and the handling of satellite data traffic at earth stations. Another Richmond enterprise, the mobile data division of Motorola, develops and supplies hardware for mobile wireless data transmission networks. Hughes Aircraft of Canada Ltd. in Richmond has drawn on the engineering and software talents of MDA to supply Canada with an advanced air traffic control system. (The scope of the $659 million program was narrowed in 1995 in an effort to regain lost time and stay within budget.)

PMC-Sierra Inc., a Burnaby semiconductor company, makes chips for ATM (asychronous transfer mode) switching of huge data flows over fibre optic networks. PMC-Sierra was spun off from MPR Teltech which had developed ATM switching technology to cope with traffic rates equivalent to 145 million words of text a minute. All of the above named companies are U.S. owned, indicating that foreign owners find

B.C. an acceptable place to do development and research as well as to engage in production.

One U.S. company that acquired a Vancouver software development laboratory and chose to uproot it was Microsoft Corp. which bought electronic mail specialist Consumer Software in 1991 and transferred its operation to Redmond, Washington in 1994. By contrast, MDA predicted it would be strengthening its Lower Mainland work force of 650 after agreeing in 1995 to an $87 million takeover by Virginia-based Orbital Science Corp.

The provincial government is encouraging the high-tech sector to stay home by developing infrastructure, joining with the private sector in funding start-up companies, supporting R&D, realigning the education system to better meet the needs of industry and showcasing local companies at a growing number of international trade shows held in Vancouver.

The province has had two grand development strategies. The first, fashioned in the immediate postwar period, emphasized infrastructure to support extractive resource industries. It petered out in the 1970s due to disappointing railways projects in the province's northern tier. The second strategy was formulated in the early 1990s and had a heavy tilt toward technology, with education as a central prop. In 1995, B.C. had the equivalent of 131,831 full-time students in government-funded, postsecondary education. Many of the courses being taken were of short duration or offered on a part-time basis, so the true number of students was much higher.

The number of students receiving technical training, in particular, is growing. In 1995 the government announced plans for a 3,300-student technical university to open in Surrey in 1999. This is in addition to 3,300 student places created at Kwantlen University College and the University College of the Fraser Valley since 1991. In 1994 the new University of Northern British Columbia was opened in Prince George. The campus is laid with a fibre optic communications cable connected to a provincial high-speed data network, another plank of the infrastructure program.

In 1995 the government-supported Research Networking Association of B.C. launched its broadband Rnet test bed to move data between selected research sites at a rate of 145 megabits per second. One of the connections is between Simon Fraser University and Vancouver's St. Paul's Hospital. The link allows the testing of medical conferencing between the two sites, accompanied by live broadcast-quality video and multiple information streams including X-rays and CAT scans. It was the pioneering role St. Paul's played in advanced communications in medicine that helped draw 3,500 medical informa-

Science World, Vancouver, 1985. VS

tion professionals to Vancouver in 1995 for a world convention. The event helped gain exposure for local software companies in the medical field.

Vancouver software companies have also taken advantage of three international conferences held in the city under the label Softworld. The conference organizers sought to bring together software producers and companies looking for products to invest in or distribute. Forty per cent of participants have forged strategic alliances.

The biennial Airshow Canada aerospace trade show at Abbotsford is another display window for B.C. industry. Aerospace ranks second in employment and revenues to IT in the high-tech field.

While Canadian Aircraft Products of Richmond and Ebco Aerospace of Ladner both do work for Boeing, among others, the biggest aerospace employer is Canadian Airlines International, with 6,000 employees in the Lower Mainland, half of them concerned with aircraft maintenance and repair. Work includes the rebuilding of gas turbines and overhauling the modified aero engines that power the Canadian Navy's latest class of frigates.

TECHNOLOGICAL INNOVATION

An armored diving suit with self-pressurizing oil seals at the limb joints is one product of Vancouver's subsea technology sector, which comprises dozens of small companies. The Newtsuit from Hard Suits Inc. allows divers to breathe unpressurized air when descending to depths as great as 300 metres. In 1995 the Newtsuit, a pun on the name of company chairman Phil Nuytten, allowed recovery of the ship's bell of the Great Lakes ore carrier *Edmund Fitzgerald*. The ship sank with the loss of all hands in 175 metres of water during a storm on Lake Michigan in 1975.

Ballard Power Systems Inc. of North Vancouver is best known for fuel-cell technology for powering highway vehicles. But it has ventured into the subsea field with a 40-kilowatt prototype power plant which could be scaled up tenfold to drive a submarine. Ballard has built three different sizes of power packs for prototype buses and is working with major car manufacturers in Europe and North America to develop pollution-free propulsion for cars. The company has developed fuel cells which produce electricity when they combine hydrogen and oxygen to make water. In 1995 Daimler-Benz announced that collaboration with Ballard had gone so well that it planned to offer fuel-cell propulsion in two planned cars.

The application of Ballard technology to submarines was first suggested by the Canadian government in 1990. Ballard claims its fuel cells offer endurance and very low heat and noise signatures, making them suitable for subsea stealth missions. Fuel cells are also offered for standby power generation on land.

Another North Vancouver company—Applied Power & Propulsion Ltd.—has collaborated with Allison Engine Co. of Indianapolis, Allied Signal Corp. of Los Angeles, and EDO Energy Corp. of New York to research the potential of powering railway locomotives with gas turbines burning compressed natural gas. Computer modelling done by BC Rail suggests this alternative power source could lower fuel costs by 37 per cent compared to diesel locomotives of matching output. BC Rail tested the performance characteristics of the theoretical design over a 1,364-kilometre coal train haul using a computerized track model supplied by Burlington Northern Railroad.

BC Rail has extended the life of its railway steel by grinding it at regular intervals prescribed by the National Research Council's Vancouver-based Machinery Research Institute. The institute's tribology department (which studies wear in moving parts) is a leader in developing preventive techniques to stop railway steel corrugating under wheel loads and so extend its life.

High-technology research in the Lower Mainland ranges from highly visible rail wear down to microscopic designer proteins for targeting defective cells and delivering corrective fragments of DNA to them. Inex Pharmaceuticals Corp. of Vancouver, is using protein delivery of remedial DNA to combat cystic fibrosis. Inex president James Miller was earlier associated with Vancouver-based Quadra Logic Technologies Inc., a pioneer in the development of light-activated drugs to combat a range of cancers and other ills. Drugs delivered to target cells through protein affinities are switched on by laser light to release destructive oxygen. QLT drugs have received various approvals for qualified or full commercial use in North America, Europe and Asia.

B.C. Research Incorporated
Chuck Davis

WHEN THE B.C. RESEARCH COUNCIL began on the campus of the University of British Columbia in 1944 it was a non-profit, government-subsidized research facility. It worked in a multitude of fields such as research and development for small business, environmental consulting and laboratory analyses for a range of private- and public-sector clients. When Har Gobind Khorana won the Nobel Prize for Medicine in 1968 (for the test tube synthesis of a gene and original work in DNA research) he acknowledged the importance of his work at this facility in 1952. B.C. Research incorporated as a private company in 1988 and revenues climbed to more than $10 million annually. But by 1992, on sales of $11 million, the company, employing more than 100 people, reported a loss of $700,000. In March of 1993 it was declared insolvent. The provincial government created a fund to keep it going and—while the employees stayed on without pay—looked for a buyer.

They found one three months later, a consortium of three companies (Terracy Inc., Noram Engineering and Constructors Ltd. and Stothert Group Inc.) that paid $2 million for the company's assets, including its 54,000-square-metre facility at 3650 Wesbrook Mall and previously-signed contracts. The president of the new company, christened BCRI, was Dr. Hugh Wynne-Edwards, Terracy's president. Wynne-Edwards, the head of UBC's geology department in the early 1970s, also had extensive experience in government and private industry, including an Alcan vice-presidency and the presidency of Moli Energy.

Today BCRI is profit-driven ("Our commitment is to generate wealth through innovation"), markets its services worldwide and concentrates on three main areas: biotechnology, advanced systems engineering, and environmental sciences and engineering. Wynne-Edwards told writer Wendy Stueck, "In the environmental area . . . we want to move into pollution prevention and remediation . . . We want to be a problem solver." (*Business in Vancouver*, May 10-16, 1994).

BCRI's scientists and engineers offer expertise few of their clients can match. One interesting example is the Clean Transportation Group. With increased government insistence on cleaner automobile exhaust emissions, this group plays an increasingly key role in the environmental sector and backs it with two decades of experience in alternative fuels, natural gas vehicle fuel system integration, the conversion of vehicles to alternative fuels, fleet maintenance and so on.

BCRI gets into the movies, too: a large wave basin (30.5 metres long) at the Ocean Engineering Centre has proven to be ideal as an aquatic sound stage! It includes a 29-tonne wave maker. "Here, accurate models of entire harbors and shorelines can be constructed and subjected to scaled-down tempests." Features filmed on location at the OEC include *The First Season, Jason Takes Manhattan* and *The Sea Wolf.* (The basin's water was warmed in the latter film for star Charles Bronson.) The centre opened in 1978 and is consulted frequently by naval architects and ship builders. They use the 67-metre-long towing tank here as an interactive design tool allowing them to optimize hull lines. Tests of models have examined the performance of tugs, barges, planing hulls, sailboats, offshore supply boats, hydrofoils, ferries, catamarans and even submarines.

In 1991 BCRI—using military volunteers—began a five-year study into human response to vibration and impact. Specifically, more information was wanted on health hazards of "whole-body" vibration and repeated impacts associated with off-road vehicles and heavy industrial equipment. The work was commissioned by the U.S. Army Aeromedical Research Laboratory which operates a multi-axis ride simulator at Fort Rucker, Alabama where the experiments for this research were carried out. With high-speed attack vehicles and personnel carriers being developed this will be essential information. "The challenge," says BCRI's Dan Robinson, of the Ergonomics and Human Factors Group, "was to look for early signs of damage to the body without damaging our volunteers! We did that through blood biochemistry, urine chemistry and biomechanical measures. We were looking for muscle fatigue, the effect on bones and on internal organs. That phase of the research is done, but we're continuing our studies in this area. Our volunteers were all male, as requested, but now with further integration of women into the army, we've been asked—if the army can find the funding—to extend the studies and replicate the research using female volunteers. We are also studying the influence of ship motion and extended crew shifts on search and rescue performance for the Canadian Coast Guard and the Transportation Development Centre."

Other BCRI projects include development of spruce seedlings to resist insect weevil depradation, work-space design, noise surveys, waste management, control and display layouts, human/computer interaction—important in jobs like air traffic control—and myriad other environmental, biotechnological and advanced systems engineering assignments.

Vancouver—Undersea Capital
Jim Lyon

Can–Dive miniature submarine in the Vancouver Aquarium, 1986. vs

VANCOUVER BOASTS a vigorous undersea industry. Equipment designed and manufactured here is used beneath most of the world's oceans and even under the Arctic ice. Vancouver firms supply state-of-the-art equipment for many of the world's navies; help build, inspect and fix underwater pipelines, bridge supports, oil wells and hydroelectric dams; and convey tourists though tropical reefs.

Almost a century ago local hard-hat divers were supplied with air by men working hand-crank pumps. They laid pipes across the floor of Burrard Inlet at First Narrows to carry water from the North Shore to Vancouver. Prior to World War I Japanese commercial divers also harvested abalone locally.

Hard-hat divers, who work at depths to about 30 metres, are always in demand in a big harbor. They handle salvage work and help in the construction of piers and other marine structures. Before the days of TV cameras, divers were most valued as underwater observers. Their skills included underwater cutting and welding, photography, rigging and diamond drilling, concrete work and the placing of sophisticated shape charges—explosives which cut with precision through seven-inch steel.

Phil Nuytten, chairman of Hard Suits Inc., Vancouver's best-known underwater expert, says: "Very few people are aware of the things that commercial divers do. Every time you drive across the Second Narrows or the First Narrows bridges remember that the supports and all of the underwater foundation work was done by divers. All the docks are maintained by divers. All of the sewage lines were installed by divers and all the water intakes were originally installed by divers. Virtually every marine structure of any size involves divers."

Nuytten started diving when he was only 12, designing his own scuba equipment. At 15 he opened a scuba diving store on Fourth Avenue in Vancouver—the first in Western Canada—and was making good money as a freelance diver even before he finished high school. He flew up and down the coast on lucrative diving assignments and earned his first million by age 31. He founded Can-Dive Marine Services in 1966 to supply divers to Shell Oil then searching for oil off the west coast of Vancouver Island. He then signed contracts with oil companies exploring in the Beaufort Sea and off the East Coast.

Even more than diving, Nuytten loves inventing. He worked for a decade to perfect a revolutionary diving suit he calls Newtsuit which allows divers to work at great depths on the ocean floor, pop up to the surface for lunch if they want to, and never have to face the long periods of decompression that were once required. More importantly, they no longer risk the potentially fatal bends. Newtsuits, made by Hard Suits Inc. of North Vancouver, carry price tags of up to $1 million each. Nuytten has supplied them to Australia, France, Germany, Italy, Korea, Japan and the United States. Following on this success he was developing a lightweight version which could be carried in a couple of sports bags. A Nuytten project just getting into production in the mid-1990s is a sleek one-person "sports car" submarine, retailing for under $100,000, which could go to 100 metres and stay there for six to 10 hours. It is targeted at scientists, fire departments, police forces and coast guards.

Another major player since 1975 in the Greater Vancouver undersea industry is International Submarine Engineering Ltd. (ISE) of Port Coquitlam. Run by James McFarlane, ISE is a world leader in the manufacture of unmanned civilian submersibles used to mine seabed minerals, to cap undersea oil well blowouts, to search for sunken treasure and to survey and map under water and ice. One of its most famous assignments was to help locate and map the wreckage of the Air India passenger aircraft in the Irish Sea in 1985.

Atlantis Submarines of Vancouver, run by Denis Hurd, was the first company in the world to design, build and operate passenger-carrying submarines. Since 1985 vessels built by Atlantis have carried tourists on dives at locations around the world, including Grand Cayman, Barbados, St. Thomas, Aruba, Kona, Maui, Oahu, Guam and the Bahamas. In the decade since it began operations in December 1985, Atlantis has carried more than three million passengers on more than 100,000 dives without a single safety-related incident. The Atlantis is a free swimming, self-propelled submersible capable of operating at a depth of 45 metres. It swims in and out through reef structures, providing passengers with exceptional views of fish, coral, plant life, wrecks and archaeological remains.

We are taught that 75 per cent of this world is underwater, but ours is the first generation to see Planet Earth from space and to realize, in the most graphic sense, that it should have been called 'Planet Ocean.' Now, and more so in the future, men and women will go undersea, to pursue their various endeavors. Hard Suits Inc. was founded on the premise that advanced technology will provide armor to protect us as we venture far beyond our 'original design specifications.'

Computing in Greater Vancouver
Linda Richards

THERE'S SOMETHING ABOUT our saltwater city that has always called to adventurers in every new field. It doesn't really seem to matter what it is—if it's hot and new and the least bit exciting, Vancouverites seem ready to jump aboard with both feet.

It hasn't been surprising to watch Vancouver grow comfortably through the high-tech age. To see this country's leaders in software, hardware and netware often hail from this city and even to witness a certain portion of the population resolutely refer to Vancouver as Silicon North brings no shock.

Two decades ago *The Vancouver Book* advised readers that there were 239 computers in the Greater Vancouver area, as well as a passionate computing community bringing Vancouver to the leading edge of the industry.

Some things change incredibly, don't they? Some things never change at all.

Today computer retailers in the Greater Vancouver area number in the thousands: from multi-outlet computer "superstores" to family-owned mom-and-pop electronic stores. Even certain drug stores sell computers in Vancouver these days, blurring the distinctions still further, as in "Mom, when you go to the store will you get me a tube of toothpaste, some deodorant and a Pentium 100?"

When 40 per cent of Canadians are reported to have computers at home and when it's rare to find a business or school that doesn't have one—or more likely several—it follows that it's just about impossible to measure the silicon in Vancouver. Add to that the fact that in the mid-1990s one in six Canadians is said to have some kind of connection to the Internet and you begin to get a feel for the incredible numbers we might be talking about. And don't forget the electronic beasties we don't generally think of as computers but that most certainly are: the automated tellers, electronic game devices, the computer-driven cameras. All of these are thrice as complex and talented as the computers we were crowing about back in the 1970s.

Today Vancouver boasts more than just a high computer population; the district also manufactures more than its share of software, hardware and peripherals. Computer-related services such as Internet provider services and computer and networking consultants and specialists are abundant.

The age of computing has arrived in a way that exceeds every early hacker's dreams and the power available to the owner of the most humble modern computer equals that of computers that helped whole countries make decisions not that long ago.

The thrust of computing has changed a lot as well. Two decades ago computers were the realm of only dedicated geeks, although many of the computing leaders reported in the original *Vancouver Book* remain influential in the mid-nineties. B.C. Telephone, B.C. Hydro, ICBC and the universities and colleges continue their roles as power-computing leaders. In addition, however, the home and small business computing sectors have made—and continue to make—their marks.

Two Richmond manufacturers, Seanix and Comtex Micro Systems, produce PCs that are recognized throughout the country by home and business users.

Many important software and peripheral companies had their start in Vancouver and some continue to be headquartered here. One name that is recognizable by many segments of the population is Burnaby-based Electronic Arts whose contributions to the world have included the fabulously successful NHL hockey series of games for both computers and home entertainment systems like Sega Genesis and Nintendo.

Advanced Gravis Computer Technology—also Burnaby-based—is recognized across North America for its contributions to the games people play. Their wildly popular series of PC sound cards, game cards and joysticks are as easily available and recognizable at computer dealers across the U.S. as they are here at home in Vancouver.

Digital Courier International, again of Burnaby, is developing a whole new area of computing, shipping digital audio "packages" to radio stations around North America—and potentially the world—via their own innovative system and network.

In the area of pure entertainment Vancouver and technology have not fallen behind either. The Discovery Channel aired a series of technology-related television shows in early 1995 and let viewers across Canada choose the one they enjoyed the most. The various series were produced by companies throughout Canada under the title *CyberWars*. The "winner" of the battle of high-tech shows was a Vancouver production called *Hi-Tech Culture*. Today *Hi-Tech Culture* airs every week on the Discovery Channel and their production offices remain right here in Vancouver.

Surrey's Destiny Software Productions is producing state-of-the-art computer games—including Dark Seed II, Blood Bowl and Sports Illustrated Baseball. These high-tech games have been winning industry awards and attracting fans around the globe. Surrey's Strategic Technologies produces computer systems used by correctional facilities across North America and Australia for electronic offender monitoring.

BC Transit SkyTrain computerized control room, 1990. VS

In Richmond VTech Electronics Canada produces brightly colored computer-type toys that let kids do everything from coloring on their television screens to learning basic reading skills.

The Vancouver-based *Computer Paper* has built a cross-Canada readership for its publication. With 14 editions across the country and offices in the major Canadian cities, the *Computer Paper*—and her sister publication *Canada Computes!*—have become the most influential mainstream computer publications in the country, with readers numbering in the millions. The head office can be found at the same location —just a few blocks from the beach—it has occupied since the company started eight years ago.

For every company I've mentioned there are another 20 worthy of inclusion. If you can think of an aspect of computer technology, it's likely a Greater Vancouver-based company has had an impact on, or input into, that particular field. This growth shows no signs of slowing down.

The private sector has grown and changed, leading the international computer industry in many ways, but public sector organizations have contributed an incalculable amount. These include large umbrella organizations such as the Science Council of B.C., whose programs and shepherding have been directly responsible for much that is good in computing in the province.

For example the Science Council has had a strong involvement with their computer recycling program called Computers for Schools. Working with retired B.C. Telephone employees and many volunteers from all walks of life, Computers for Schools takes the mostly outdated computers donated by industry, government agencies and the private sector, services them, upgrades them where possible and then sends them throughout the province to schools who've expressed a need for computers.

As well Vancouver-based non-profit organizations such as the Western Canadian Computer Distributors Society and the BBS Association of Vancouver are just two of the scores of clubs and organizations whose sole purpose is to forward the computing interests of their organizers. Known as SIGs (Special Interest Groups) these organizations alone likely number far more than the 239 computers here in the mid-seventies.

And things have come full circle. In the 1970s powerful mainframes were the only computing devices worthy of mention. Since then we've witnessed the personal computer revolution that has put PCs on the desks of millions of Canadians. The influence of the Internet, however, has put the focus back on the mega-system. Increasingly in the 1990s we'll see the network-as-the-system as a growing number of Vancouverites plug into the Internet and use the incredible storage and power available internationally to perform some of the larger tasks. Why duplicate locally what's available on a computer system across the street or on the other side of the globe?

From the Internet to local area networking; from children's software titles to programs that track the activities of prisoners; from hardware for the home to mega-systems for the corporate office, Greater Vancouver high-technology companies continue at the head of the column when it comes to blazing new trails . . . and finding the balancing place where the cutting edge meets the deep blue sea.

Greater Vancouver Online
Linda Richards

IN AN AGE THAT IS UNASHAMEDLY wired Vancouver is as wired as they come. Vancouver's online community had its beginnings on the hobby bulletin board services (BBSs) that still proliferate today. Vancouver first got online in a big way in the mid-1980s when the city's telephone systems began to be cluttered with a myriad of modem users—many of them in their mid-teens—who spent their nights cheerfully chatting with others of a similar bent on topics as stimulating as world peace and as inane as golden topping for popcorn and blue moss for nothing at all. Being online then largely meant dialing into one-line hobby BBS's, logging in under a pseudonym and chatting or reading messages until sleep or bedtime (whichever came first) overtook one.

Predictably many of these early onliners have gone on to get real lives. Therefore Sufboard's system operator (sysop) Doctor Benway is now revealed to be an art teacher at one of the city's more prominent colleges; the sysop of Nightline BBS, The Spark, is now a Victoria dentist: and The Wolfhound is now a Langley-based writer and editor. (If anyone knows what happened to Kidd Judo, Magic Mushroom, The Gerbil Master and some of the other prominent onliners of that time, drop me a line—Pink Knight would love to know.)

We were changed, however, through what had passed. We had discovered that online communication could touch us in a way that nothing had before. Sure it was electronic. Sure it involved computers. But we'd found that this seemingly impersonal medium could put an incredibly intimate spin on reaching out and touching someone. Gone were all the barriers we'd come to expect: race, age, looks, health. The only thing that mattered was intelligence. Stupid people were never tolerated for long in this environment. Vancouver's online community was reflecting what forward-thinking and electronically ready communities around the globe were moving toward. At the end of the 1980s a few of Vancouver's BBS's became multi-line systems, meaning communication was no longer limited to one caller at a time. Better still—or at least as good—some of the sysops brought in "feeds" from other places so that we could not only exchange silliness with people based in our own city, we could do it with others around the world.

By hook or by crook—but mostly by telephone line—the Internet came to Vancouver in the late 1980s. It did not come earthshakingly nor with the fanfare that would herald the popular media's discovery of it a few years later. What it meant for those of us already connected was smoother electronic mail exchanges and more cool stuff to look through and read. We could do what we'd been doing for the last half-decade or so but we could do it faster and with more global effect.

Today the Internet has so many people using it and so much information passing through it that we are still calculating the potential power of this sometime-toy-turned-tool. We are fairly confident that the number of people connected to the world via the Internet is in the millions. We have the same kind of confidence that in the Greater Vancouver area there are hundreds of thousands thus connected. We are confident but not certain. The most certain thing about it all is that it's pretty tough to be certain.

The Internet is a global undertaking. Electronic mail can be sent to Germany or Hong Kong as easily as it can across the city. With a Web site the Internet user is as likely to have someone in London or Dallas look at their home page as someone from North Vancouver. The Internet makes the world smaller; much smaller than the airplane or the automobile ever seemed to. The World Wide Web is the Internet service that perhaps shows this most clearly and with the least amount of high-tech squinting. Developed at CERN, a high-energy physics lab in Switzerland in 1988, the World Wide Web (Web) became the most used Internet service in early 1995. Since that time the Web has been growing incredibly.

The Web makes it possible to view—from anywhere—specially prepared "pages" of information stored on remote computers around the world, provided they are linked via the super-network known as the Internet. While using a piece of software known as a "browser" it is possible to see pictures, hear sound-bytes and even view little movies and animations on appropriately configured pages. Thus the Louvre has a Web site where you can see portions of the collection, as does the Smithsonian and even Molson Breweries.

Predictably Vancouverites have led the way and several Vancouver-based sites number among the "top" "first" and "historic" around the world. I've included a small cross-section of sites with this article. The number of Web sites in Vancouver defies actual calculation and—even if it didn't—the number grows daily. These will get you started on local sites and you'll find links on many of them to still more.

THE GOVERNMENT OF BRITISH COLUMBIA
http://www.gov.bc.ca/
The government of British Columbia home page has been growing and changing rapidly of late. At present you can get information on government special dates and events, find links to various ministries and even get headlines from late-breaking

stories. Like many factions of the non-geek community the B.C. government has spent a while scrambling to try to make a Web site that is actually useful. It looks as though they might have finally succeeded.

CIVICNET–B.C. MUNICIPALITIES ONLINE

http://www.civicnet.gov.bc.ca/

Links to city home pages around the province. At present only a smattering of B.C. cities actually have their own home pages, Vancouver and North Vancouver among them. The others, however, have CivicNet sponsored pages that offer basic information on the town in question. It's not the most intuitive site around but it'll get the job done with a bit of struggling.

DISTRICT OF NORTH VANCOUVER

http://www.district.north-van.bc.ca/

CITY OF VANCOUVER

http://www.city.vancouver.bc.ca/

THE ASIA PACIFIC FOUNDATION CANADA

http://www.apfnet.org/apfweb/

The foundation is based in Vancouver and has an entirely useful Web site for Canadian business people with an interest in the Asia Pacific regions.

BC FERRIES

http://bcferries.bc.ca/ferries/

People with places to go should take note of this Web site. It is possible to receive route, scheduling and cost information—and even information on the BC Ferries fleet—at any time of the day or night. You can learn, for instance, that the Saltspring Queen was built at Esquimalt in 1949 and is 44 metres long. You never would have thought to ask the prerecorded information tape that, now would you?

VANCOUVER INTERACTIVE

http://www.cyberstore.net/vi/vibe/marketplace/vip/main-bridge.html

An interesting and uniquely Vancouver project that marries high-tech and the arts in a kind of cyber literary magazine.

GREATER VANCOUVER TOURISM

http://tbcisb6.tbc.gov.bc.ca/tourism/regions/southwestern/vancouver/vancouver.html

From the home page: "Vancouver is home to some of the most breathtaking natural scenery in the world. Towering snow-capped mountains rise high above the city, adorned by ancient forests that tumble in evergreen splendor toward the sparkling blue Pacific."

Does it all sound a little like it came straight out of a tourism brochure? Well, good! Only this one is online. Check it and appropriately illustrated links.

GREATER VANCOUVER CRIME STOPPERS

http://kaos.deepcove.com/crime_stoppers/

Crime Stoppers on the web is the online—and therefore extended version—of what you see on television.

THE VANCOUVER HOME PAGES LIST

http://vancouver-webpages.com/url-list.shtml

It's free. It's growing. It's alphabetized. Well, mostly. And you can add your site to the list as well.

VANCOUVER PUBLIC LIBRARY

http://www.city.vancouver.bc.ca/library/vpli.html

You can search for a book from wherever you (and your Web connection) are, as well as find out lots of information about the Vancouver Public Library system.

THE GREATER VANCOUVER ART GALLERY

http://www.vanartgallery.bc.ca/index.html

A tour, hours of operation, what's going on: everything you need to know about the gallery before you get there.

Vancouver Public Library; wired behind the "Roman" exterior, 1995. vs

Energy Use
Jim Lyon

Vancouver's appetite for energy is prodigous. Energy to illuminate our homes, cook our food, run our TV sets and computers, warm us in winter, cool us in summer. We also need energy to transport us to work and energy to power our tools when we get there. We burn energy in the evenings too—whether we're mowing the lawn, watching hockey or messing about in a boat. Where does it all come from?

Vancouver uses two main fuel sources: hydrocarbons (oil, natural gas) and electricity. Getting it to us is complex and horrendously expensive. Vancouver's oil supplies come from Alberta. Much of the gasoline and diesel fuels consumed in the Lower Mainland are refined in Edmonton and shipped to the coast by the Trans Mountain Pipe Line Co. Ltd. Vancouver once had four active oil refineries—Petro-Canada, Chevron, Ioco and Shell— which processed crude oil. Petro-Canada, Esso and Shell decided, however, that these relatively small operations can't run efficiently. Their facilities in Vancouver are now used primarily as distribution terminals. Only the Chevron refinery in Burnaby continues to process crude oil into refined products. Chevron also supplies products to Shell. Refined products are also distributed on Vancouver Island and to remote coastal communities by small tankers and tug and barge units. Canadian crude oil is exported to Asia from the Westridge Marine Terminal in Burnaby which is also used to import jet turbine fuel.

While many homes in Greater Vancouver were once heated with oil, most now use natural gas, obtained from the northeast of the province, around Dawson Creek and Chetwynd. That area, incidentally, is one of the richest sources of natural gas in North America. The gas is delivered to homes, factories and offices by BC Gas, a publicly owned utility that was once part of B.C. Hydro. Gas supplies are delivered to BC Gas at the Huntingdon gate station near Sumas in the Fraser Valley by the mainline transmission carrier, Westcoast Energy, which pumps it under pressure (in 30-42 inch steel pipes) from the northeast using aircraft-style jet engines for the job.

Before the natural gas can be put into the pipeline it must be processed to remove water through dehydration. Also taken out are contaminants that would corrode the pipeline. This includes large quantities of sulphur. (The yellow piles of sulphur you see awaiting export shipment just east of the Lion's Gate Bridge in North Vancouver and in Port Moody have all been extracted from natural gas. Sulphur is an important ingredient in fertilizers.) BC Gas facilities are also used as a link through which gas from Westcoast Energy is moved from Huntingdon to the Pacific Coast Energy pipeline for onward transmission to Vancouver Island.

Natural gas, the cleanest-burning of all fossil fuels, heats our homes and fuels our appliances much more cheaply than oil or electricity. It isn't pollution free, but it is the most benign fossil fuel available to us today. The attraction of clean-burning natural gas, of course, is one of the big selling points of BC Gas' Natural Gas for Vehicles (NGV) program. Switching to NGV helps to cut dramatically the release of reactive hydrocarbons (which cause chemical smog). It also cuts emissions of carbon dioxide and sulphur dioxide. Stimulated by tough clean-air regulations in the United States, especially California, research is being pushed ahead into the use of natural gas for transportation. We can expect much greater use of this fuel in the coming decades.

BC Gas has to be prepared to supply its customers in Greater Vancouver on exceptionally cold days in winter when the pipeline system from the north cannot meet the extra demand of space heaters working overtime. To do this BC Gas operates a liquefied natural gas (LNG) plant at Tilbury Island in Delta, which provides fuel for those high-demand winter days. This is known in the jargon of the natural gas industry as "peak-shaving." The big tank is filled slowly during the summer when natural gas demand is low. The energy is then released to supplement normal pipeline deliveries when demand is high. LNG is ordinary natural gas that's been purified and refrigerated to about minus 162 °C. As a liquid the fuel requires only one six hundredth of the storage space it needs as gas. The Tilbury Island plant stores 28,000 cubic metres of LNG. For a few crucial days each winter it can supply a fifth of the Lower Mainland's natural gas needs. BC Gas also stores backup supplies of natural gas in underground reservoirs across the international boundary in Washington State.

More than 70 per cent of British Columbia's electrical power is generated by the crown corporation B.C. Hydro and Power Corporation from a series of hydro-electric generating stations on the Peace and Columbia rivers. These date from the 1960s and 1970s, an era of rapid industrial expansion in the province, when B.C. Hydro took on some of the most ambitious hydro-electric construction projects in the world.

The first phase of the Peace River development saw the 183 metre-high W.A.C. Bennett Dam completed in 1968, initially bringing 681,000 kilowatts of power on line. The first two dams on the Columbia were completed in 1967 (Duncan) and 1968 (Hugh Keenlyside), both of them for water storage. The

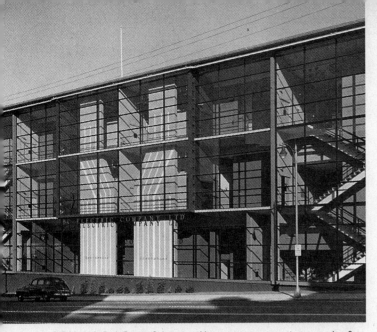

BC Hydro's Dal Grauer Substation, Vancouver, a progressive example of functional modern architecture when built, 1953–54. VS

third, the 198-metre-high Mica Dam, added 870,000 kilowatts to the B.C. Hydro system when it was commissioned in 1976.

To move this power to its distant customers in the late 1960s, B.C. Hydro pioneered the use of high-voltage systems as it built 500,000-volt transmission lines from the Peace project to the Lower Mainland, and from the mainland to Vancouver Island. By the end of the 1970s, the company's 500 kilovolt transmission lines had become the backbone of the province's integrated electrical grid, in which both generation and transmission were controlled by a sophisticated microwave system. By 1980, when power from the Peace Canyon project came on line, Hydro's province-wide capacity was 7,948,000 kilowatts (83 per cent of it hydro-electric), more than five times its capacity two decades earlier. Faced with the slowing of economic growth and intensifying environmental criticism over the practice of flooding valleys to provide hydro-electric generation, in the 1980s B.C. Hydro turned away from building more generating facilities. Instead, it sought to get the most out of its existing ones.

By the end of the 1980s total installed capacity had risen to 10,467,000 kilowatts (90 per cent hydro-electric). In 1989 B.C. Hydro launched its highly successful Power Smart conservation program aimed at consumer education. By 1994 Power Smart and the associated Resource Smart program (which enhanced existing production facilities) saved enough electricity to supply 233,200 homes.

The Power Smart concept became so successful that a separate company, Power Smart Inc. (PSI), was set up. PSI (whose ownership B.C. Hydro shared with several other Canadian utilities) promoted the use of the Power Smart brand name, product promotions and marketing expertise to more than 30 member utilities and governments in Canada and the United Kingdom, Mexico, the Caribbean and Eastern Europe. PSI ended operations in March 1997. The Resource Smart program (as its name so well implies) is concerned with extracting the most energy from existing Hydro production facilities—and delaying as long as possible the construction of new dams.

At times when the water level in the reservoirs is depleted because of abnormally light rainfall or snow, Hydro makes use of the Burrard Thermal generating plant at Port Moody. Some years much of Greater Vancouver's electricity (and about 12 per cent of total provincial supply) comes from Burrard Thermal. (You can recognize the six tall stacks emitting steam just west of the Ioco refinery on the north shore of Burrard Inlet.) The plant was completed in 1963 at a cost of $150 million. Thirty years later, its replacement value was estimated to be over $1.4 billion. Originally the plant was designed to burn either crude oil or natural gas, but a decision was made in 1978 to switch to natural gas only. High pressure steam is passed through turbines to generate electricity—almost 7,000 gigawatt-hours of electricity a year, enough for 700,000 homes, if needed.

Burrard Thermal was built as a backup facility, to supply electricity when water levels in the province's rivers and reservoirs are insufficient to supply the needed power. The plant is more expensive to operate than the province's hydro-electric generating stations, so it isn't used all the time. During the mid-1980s it was hardly used. However, as Vancouver continues to grow and Hydro seeks to avoid building major hydro-electric projects, Burrard Thermal will be run more often.

With this in mind, in the early 1990s BC Hydro began a $270 million program to upgrade the plant over eight years. It has cut down on the noise made by venting steam and is working to reduce nitrous oxide emissions, which contribute to urban smog.

Many people are unaware that more than 135 buildings in downtown Vancouver rely for heat, humidification and domestic hot water on steam provided to them by underground pipeline. The steam is supplied by Central Heat Distribution Ltd. (which incidentally also supplies steam free of charge to the world's first steam-powered chiming clock in Gastown). Central Heat has been in business since 1968. It was started to help improve Vancouver's air quality by eliminating building stacks and vents. Previously many downtown buildings had used oil or coal for building energy. The company uses natural gas to generate the steam which is distributed through several miles of underground steam line piping. Customers include hotels, office buildings, small manufacturers, condominiums, shopping centres and civic buildings.

Organized Labor in Greater Vancouver
Derlang Ansager

DURING THE EARLY decades of the 19th century many British craftsmen migrated to Canada, bringing with them the framework of the British trade union movement, but in British Columbia—especially in the Vancouver Island coal mining industry—there were few attempts at union organizing until the late 1870s and those were marked by clashes between workers and management.

A period of economic expansion accompanying the construction of the B.C. section of the Canadian Pacific Railway provided scope for organizing workers. By the time the terminus at Port Moody was completed in 1886, the U.S.-based Knights of Labor had organized local assemblies in Vancouver and New Westminster.

The Knights agitated for a general nine-hour work day. However, they were deeply involved in campaigns directed against imported Chinese workers, primarily because of the latter's willingness to accept low wages and unsafe working conditions on the CPR. There was a direct attempt by the union in 1887 to drive Chinese workers from Vancouver. The agitation subsided soon after the provincial government intervened. The Knights' influence declined with the growth of individual trade unions. The oldest craft union in Vancouver, still active today, is the Vancouver local of the International Typographical Union. The Stevedores Union was organized in 1888, followed by longshoremen, carpenters, painters, plasterers, bricklayers and masons.

On November 21, 1889 these unions and the Shaftesbury Local of the Knights of Labor met in the Sullivan Hall on Cordova Street to organize the Trades and Labour Council of Vancouver. The council lobbied for free libraries, evening and technical schools and access to English Bay beaches, then in danger of becoming privately-owned.

In *Working Lives Vancouver 1886-1986* (New Star Press, 1985), writer Randy Wick says the Trades and Labour Council "protested to city council against 'crimping' by local saloons which for $20 a head deliver drunken sailors to shipmasters who illegally pressed them as seamen."

By the mid-1890s a nation-wide depression halted the growth of the trade union movement in its tracks. However, one evidence of official recognition of organized labor was the designation, in 1894, of the first Monday in September as the Labour Day holiday.

By 1900 union organization was again on the rise. A partic-ularly significant development was the formation of unions in the fishing industry, and a subsequent strike. With the full support of the VTLC, a Vancouver local and a New Westminster local of fishermen, together with the Japanese Fishermen's Benevolent Society and an Indian band from Port Simpson, struck the B.C. canning industry for higher fish prices. That industry enlisted the aid of provincial police, strike-breakers and Pinkerton spies to try to break both the strike and the union, but failed. Although the settlement did not give the workers everything they had struck for, it nevertheless was a landmark in B.C. union history. It marks the beginning of a continuous thread of unionism in the fishing industry in the province. More important, it was the first major strike outside the mining industry: It also marked the emergence of radical socialist leadership on the industrial front. Unfortunately, it also marked the existence of racial tension between the Japanese and Caucasian strikers.

During this period offshoots of such groups as the International Workers of the World (Wobblies), the Western Federation of Miners and the American Labor Union were set up in B.C. in opposition to the Trades and Labour Congress (TLC). These radical organizations obtained their support mainly in the forestry, mining and railroad industries. Although they did not displace the craft-oriented unions, they did establish a pattern of militancy that was to reappear in the coming decades.

In 1902, Randy Wick writes, the Trades and Labour Council heard a complaint that a local hatmaker had employed a woman apprentice without pay for a year, then offered her $1 a week at a time men workers were making $10 to $15 and other women workers made $2. "No young woman could live a virtuous life on $2 a week," the labor council declared. The first union of women workers, a local of the Shirt, Waist and Laundry Workers International Union was formed in 1902. It lasted only a few years, but the more permanent Laundry Workers Union was organized locally in 1914.

The Vancouver council joined the Canadian Trades and Labour Council in 1909 and was affiliated with the American Federation of Labor. A questionnaire concerning the formation of a province-wide labor federation was circulated in *Western Wage Earner,* the Labour Council's own newspaper. The response was favourable, and in 1910 a convention was called to found the first B.C. Federation of Labour. Twenty-six delegates, mainly from the Lower Mainland, pledged the first federation to seeking the eight-hour day, favoured industrial unionism (the trademark of militant B.C. labor since the turn of the century) and endorsed socialism. With $50 borrowed from the VTLC, the "fed" began organizing under its first pres-

The British Columbia Federation of Labour is a voluntary association of affiliated unions, members of the national body, the Canadian Labour Congress. The "BC Fed" has a long and proud history of fighting to improve the well-being of all working people in B.C., a tradition exemplified by its motto: "What we desire for ourselves, we wish for all." The primary role of the Federation is to speak for more than 450,000 workers on a wide range of public policy issues.

Shipyard workers, North Vancouver, 1942. vp

ident, J. C. Watters, and first secretary, R. P. Pettipiece.

In 1915 the pre-war depression finally ended, and the following year the provincial government introduced a workers' compensation act. Labor's campaign for women's suffrage, led by Helena Gutteridge of the tailors' union, also achieved partial success when the issue was referred to a plebiscite.

Western Canadian unions (unlike some in Ontario) opposed conscription during World War I. A pacifist, Albert "Ginger" Goodwin, a former B.C. Federation president, was shot and killed by a police officer on Vancouver Island, allegedly for fleeing arrest for draft evasion. Union leaders claimed Goodwin was murdered. They said he should have been exempt from military service because of lung disease contracted in Vancouver Island coal mines.

Goodwin's death resulted in a provincewide general strike, Aug. 2, 1918, the first in Canadian history. The strike was called off in the face of a riot by returned soldiers who broke into the Labour Temple and badly beat up two men who were forced to kiss the flag.

The first B.C. Federation of Labour was disbanded in 1920 when workers across Western Canada joined the One Big Union, organized to represent everyone. The OBU had trouble keeping all factions together and the Vancouver National Labour Council was organized in 1926. While the trade unions in Vancouver were involved in a struggle to maintain the prevailing conditions in the organized industries, the major area of new and aggressive organization shifted to the unemployed. In 1929 the Vancouver Unemployed Worker's Association was formed. At that time the unemployed raided the city relief

office. Two of the leaders were accused of being Communist agitators and were arrested. This incident established a pattern of relations between the unemployed and the authorities which reached a peak in April 1935, when about 4,000 unemployed converged on Vancouver demanding work and wages and the abolition of military control of relief camps. After numerous clashes Mayor Gerry McGeer, standing at Victory Square at Hastings and Cambie, read the Riot Act. The demonstrators decided to march "On-to-Ottawa."

In another violent demonstration June 19, 1938, protesters at the Vancouver Art Gallery and at the main post office clashed with police. Harold Winch negotiated a settlement at the Art Gallery, but things were different at the post office. The demonstrators, led by Steve Brodie, were charged by mounted policemen, bombed and tear-gassed. Thirty-nine persons were injured, including five police officers. There were 22 arrests and damage totalled $30,000.

The Vancouver Labour Council grew rapidly during World War II, expanding from 16 locals and 1,373 members in 1940 to 38 locals and 28,000 members by 1944. Much of this growth was caused by the extraordinary rise in shipbuilding in the Vancouver area. In 1944, a second B.C. Federation of Labour was founded, succeeding the original organization which had disbanded in 1920. The new federation found its backing mainly among the industrial CLC unions.

The founding of the CCF, the Co-operative Commonwealth Federation, forerunner of the present New Democratic Party provided some labor supporters with a political arm. Union supporters Harold Winch and Robert Strachan headed the B.C. branch of the CCF, but failed to win power, although Winch came close just before the rise of W.A.C. Bennett's Social Credit party in the 1950s. The labor-supported Committee of Progressive Electors achieved some seats on Vancouver City Council, but COPE mayoralty candidates did not win office.

In the 1950s and '60s, British Columbia's unions faced a movement of employers to form unions of their own. The International Woodworkers Association, long accused of "whipsawing" by winning contracts with weaker forest companies that they extended throughout the industry, were confronted with Forest Industrial Relations Ltd., insisting on bargaining for the industry as a whole. Merchant seamen faced the B.C. Towboat Owners Association. Longshoremen on the docks of Vancouver and New Westminster began bargaining with the Maritime Employers Association. Building trade unions were confronted by the Construction Labour Relations Association.

These issues include labour law, workers compensation, occupational health and safety, pensions and benefits, economic development, environment, land use, aboriginal affairs, the equality of women and human rights. The BC Fed works with the CLC and its regional and community Labour Councils to implement education and social justice programs. Our members reflect B.C. society, working in virtually every industrial and service sector and occupation.

There was even a union of the employers' unions: the B.C. Employers Council, a direct counterpart to the B.C. Federation of Labour. Just as the Fed researched and lobbied governments on labor issues, the Council (now renamed the B.C. Business Council) did the same on behalf of businesses.

Following the defeat of the NDP government in 1975, Premier Bill Bennett's Social Credit government proposed laws that the B.C. Federation of Labour opposed. The bills would have cut social programs, doing away with the Rentalsman and Human Rights Commission and cutting the provincial public service by 25 per cent. The legislation fuelled the longheld enmity the labor movement felt for Social Credit. On July 15, 1983 the B.C. Federation of Labour announced the formation of Operation Solidarity. Federation President Art Kube promised a province-wide general strike, including school teachers, public servants and all other trade and craft unions in Federation jurisdiction, if Bennett did not back down.

There were rallies and marches through the summer. When the B.C. Government Employees Union contract expired Oct. 31, the union's 35,000 members went on strike. They were followed a week later by all but a few of the province's school teachers in November. More strikes were planned.

The showdown between organized labor and the provincial government was averted by Jack Munro, head of the province's largest private sector union, the 40,000-member International Woodworkers of America. The Fed had planned to order the IWA out on strike, but Munro personally felt his membership alone was responsible for when it would choose to strike.

"Munro had been saying all along that social issues could not be won on a picket line . . . Munro would be damned if he'd let community groups, feminists and church leaders make decisions about his members going on strike and losing wages," Jane O'Hara wrote in *Union Jack* (Douglas and McIntyre, 1988), the biography of Munro she wrote with him. Munro felt the labor movement looked bad in the final days of Solidarity's windup to a general strike. Other union leaders joined Munro in negotiations with the province. Munro felt the operation was bound to fail. "In my mind, if you call a general strike, you'd better be in good enough shape to win it—which means, basically overthrowing the government," Munro wrote.

The government was not going to be overthrown, but there was an awareness that a long, bitter confrontation would result in economic losses harmful to both sides.

Munro and Premier Bennett met in the premier's home in Kelowna late Sunday, Nov. 13 and agreed to a package that included no reprisals against those who went on strike. There would be no general strike.

When Bennett's successor Bill Vander Zalm brought in the Industrial Relations Act (Bill 19) in July 1987, the B.C. Federation of Labour instituted a province-wide boycott of the Act, describing it as "viciously anti-union." The Fed refused to appoint any of its members to the tribunal appointed to administer the Act—the Industrial Relations Council—and refused to attend the Council's hearings. (The only exception to the boycott was where an application to the IRC was deemed essential to protect worker rights.) The Act was repealed December 15, 1992 by the new Harcourt government, ending a period of bitter labor relations in the province.

Since the late 1980s the B.C. Federation of Labour has developed campaigns to stop racism and violence in the workplace, reminding its members unionism is based on a commitment to seek equality and justice for every working person. Along with the Canadian Labour Congress and Simon Fraser University, the Federation is a sponsor of the B.C. Summer Institute for Union Women. "The Institute is committed to building solidarity between women workers and overcoming obstacles and barriers, particularly those of race, culture and sexual orientation." In 1994 BC FORUM (British Columbia Federation Of Retired Union Members) was formed with support of the Fed. FORUM works to ensure that the "security, bargaining and political power of the union can benefit members even after retirement by putting the spotlight on issues of concern to retired workers."

In recent years there has been a move by unions toward more focused use of pension funds for the benefit of their members. In B.C., the Fed joined with some of its largest affiliates to pool pension assets to create one of the largest residential construction companies in Western Canada, Greystone Properties. And the Fed helped to set up a labor-sponsored venture capital fund to invest in the development of businesses in B.C. The Working Opportunity Fund now has more than $120 million in assets, has invested more than $40 million in B.C. companies, and has created more than 1,000 jobs in the province, generating over $34 million in annual payroll.

The 1995 B.C. Labour Directory counts more than 545,000 union members, about 35 per cent of the total work force in the province. (B.C. Federation of Labour affiliates represent 450,000 workers in British Columbia. As this book was going to press, the B.C. Teachers Federation was preparing for a vote among its members on the question of joining the Federation.) More than 58 per cent of male workers are organized and more than 40 per cent of female workers. The total membership, men and women, is among the highest ratios of union membership of any province, occasionally being exceeded only in Quebec.

For further information about the B.C. Federation of Labour, visit our site on the World Wide Web at <http://www.bcfed.com/>
For information about health and safety at work, or Workers Compensation, you can call us toll-free at 1-888-BCFL-NOW or, within Greater Vancouver, 434-1410. For general inquiries, including information on joining or forming a union, call us at 430-1421.

The History of Retail Trade in Greater Vancouver
Lisa Tant

IN JUST OVER a hundred years we have come a long way from the rag tag stores clustered along the fledgling city's two-block waterfront. Water and Cordova Streets dominated Vancouver's retail trade until the turn of the century. Built in 1865 the Hastings Mill Store was the city's first store—and meeting house, post office and church. Originally located at the foot of present-day Dunlevy Street it was one of the few buildings to survive the 1886 fire. It was moved to its present home on Alma Street in 1930.

Brothels and saloons clustered in the area around the Hastings Mill. John "Gassy Jack" Deighton built a saloon in 1867. "Portuguese Joe" Silvey opened his combination saloon and general store and others followed close behind. By 1882 the village of Granville boasted six general merchants, two shoemakers and a wine merchant.

Four years later a devastating fire razed the brand new city of Vancouver. Within the year the city was reconstructed and the Hudson's Bay Company opened its first store, a log building, on Cordova Street. Two years later, in 1888, the giant Canadian retailer opened its flagship store at Granville and Georgia. Its location across from the first Hotel Vancouver (where Eaton's is now) was regarded as the fringe of the new city. In 1913 Birks, the Montreal-based jewelry chain, moved from Hastings Street to a new location across from The Bay. That historic building was demolished in 1975 and replaced by a tower and squat store that could never match the exquisite terra-cotta facade. The accompanying public outrage helped form new heritage guidelines that would protect The Bay, now a designated heritage building, from a similar fate. The landmark four-sided Birks clock marked the spot until 1995 when the store moved back to a new location on Hastings Street, directly across from its original store. Bollum's Books, a 1,850 square-metre multimedia book store (with cafe), moved in to the vacant Granville Street building during the summer of 1995.

Closest to the waterfront, Cordova Street remained the central shopping area leaving Granville Street's new shops neglected. The dusty village jumped to town status with the extension of the Canadian Pacific Railway. In turn it was christened with a new name, Vancouver, but lost much of its surrounding land (an area that currently makes up today's central business district) to the CPR. The train's arrival in 1887 established the city as Canada's West Coast commercial centre and retail business exploded.

Granville Street merchants' fortunes soared at the turn of the century with the discovery of Klondike gold. Empty downtown lots filled and Granville became *the* shopping street. An electric streetcar line, built at the end of the 1880s, helped expand retail trade throughout the downtown core and surrounding neighborhoods. Shops sprang up along its route and continued to thrive long after its demise in 1955. Thirty years later its modern equivalent, Light Rapid Transit (more commonly known as the SkyTrain), had a similar effect on shops at stops along its route.

All that remains of Woodward's, one of Western Canada's retail institutions, is a forlorn red "W." The 1902 beacon that once towered over the city is now hidden by the towers springing up around it. Its flashing, rotating presence was extinguished after the chain's 100th anniversary celebration. Established by Charles Woodward in 1892 Woodward's started as a three-level store selling piece goods, men's clothing and footwear. In 1903 Woodward's moved from Main and Hastings Street over to Hastings and Abbott, site of a former swamp. As much a part of Vancouver as Gastown, the store attracted crowds to its annual automated Christmas windows and venerated $1.49 day sales.

Woodward's horse-drawn delivery wagons were a common sight during the early years. After World War I the store introduced a new concept to keep operating costs down—a self-service food floor that became the largest in the world under one roof. It spawned a new trend away from pricey specialty boutiques to middle-of-the-road shops. Woodward's established the busy Hastings retail community. In later years when the downtown core shifted south-west, the area slid into the nearby Skid Road district. Today the original store and much of the rest of the block sit destitute and boarded up, waiting for a promised rejuvenation.

Woodward's fell victim to a fast-paced retail market where being an institution became a liability rather than an asset. On December 11, 1992 the company filed for court protection from creditors who were owed more than $65 million. It collapsed with 26 department stores, 33 Woodwyn discount outlets, 20 travel agencies, four Abercrombie & Fitch specialty stores and three Commercial Interiors divisions in B.C. and Alberta. The following year it was purchased by Canadian retail institution The Hudson's Bay Company which quickly converted the old stores into new Bay or Zeller's outlets.

Another pioneering chain, Saba Brothers, opened near Woodward's in 1903 and closed in the mid-1980s. Founding brothers Alex and Mike Saba began importing Japanese silks and later expanded to fabric and fashion. In 1906 David Spencer opened a store on Hastings between Seymour Street and Richards Street that eventually expanded to eat up the entire block. In 1948 he was bought out by Eaton's. In 1973 the Edwardian buildings were demolished and Sears moved into the city's newest, tallest building (a 140-metre tower topped by a revolving restaurant). Today it's home to Simon Fraser University's downtown campus.

One of Vancouver's first fashion stores continues to set trends. Edward Chapman's 1890 store outfitted miners heading north to the Klondike Gold Rush. Chapman's assistant, Earnest Rea, bought into the company and expanded into women's wear after World War II. In the mid-fifties David Rea took over the business and split it into two stores. Today his nephew John Rea operates the women's stores while Hugh Chapman, the founder's grandson, owns the men's division.

Economic turbulence gave birth to the discount store. Selling ends of lines, overstocked inventory and bankruptcy close-outs, the first Army & Navy Department Store opened in the early 1930s on West Hastings and moved to its present Hastings location in 1939. With $800 in his pocket Joseph Segal founded Field's Stores in 1955. Today the mass-market chain operates more than 120 stores in Western Canada. Segal was also involved in many other companies including Vancouver's leading garment manufacturer, Mr. Jax Fashions, sold to Koret of Canada in 1995. This retail pioneer was named a 1992 recipient of the Order of British Columbia.

Economic fall-out from the high-flying 1980s spawned a similar retail revolution. Retailers now cater to extremes—the deep-pocketed luxury fan at one end and the cost-conscious average Joe at the other. Caught in between the department stores and mainstream retailers are feeling the squeeze. One-stop megastores and so-called "big box" retailers peddle everything from cut-rate groceries and tools to discounted designer fashions and running shoes. Many of these massive warehouse outlets, such as Costco, require consumers to become "members" through employers or associations. Six former Woodward's executives opened Points West Fashion Outlet in 1993. Their aim? To offer the prices of a discount outlet with the service of a specialty store and the assortment of a department store.

What was innovative in the 1950s is now old hat. Shopping malls are introducing day-care centres, markets and services to keep up the new retail pace. Vancouver's electric streetcar helped shift population growth to the suburbs and with it came the shopping centre. The first mall in Canada, West Vancouver's Park Royal Shopping Centre, was heralded as innovative

state-of-the-art shopping at its launch in 1945. Developed by British Pacific Properties it marked the concept of a major store as an anchor (in this case Woodward's) attached to a handful of smaller shops and surrounded by ample free parking. Over the years it underwent several expansions and a major addition across Marine Drive. Larco Investments purchased Park Royal in 1990 and gave it a $20 million facelift. New shops, a fashion galleria and a marketplace helped the granddaddy of malls to keep up with its seaside community, home to some of Canada's highest-average-income households (in excess of $80,000).

Oakridge, also anchored by Woodward's, opened in 1959 and other malls quickly sprouted around the city. Eaton's new store was built in 1970 and a year later Pacific Centre connected it to The Bay with an underground shopping network. An addition in the early 1990s stretched the mall over three city blocks.

Shopping malls catering to the thousands of new residents crowding Vancouver began to spring up all over the Lower Mainland. Welcome alternatives to the need to commute Downtown, malls in Coquitlam, Surrey and Richmond became the anchors for new communities and business districts. Whalley, in Surrey, is being developed to rival Downtown Vancouver as another Lower Mainland buisness centre.

A nineties trend in shopping malls reflects Vancouver's growing ethnic diversity. Vancouver's Chinatown, a protected historic area, has expanded into Richmond where Chinese and South Asian immigrants make up its largest market. Four malls—Yaohan Centre, featuring a 2,500 square-metre grocery store, Parker Place, President Plaza and Aberdeen Centre—showcase shops and restaurants geared towards the Asian market. Chinatown is currently being revitalized with new buildings and improved parking. Established by the Chinese who helped to build the railway, Vancouver's Chinatown is the third largest in North America after San Francisco's and New York's. Streets are packed on the weekends with shoppers inspecting barbecued ducks hanging in windows and exotic vegetables crammed on sidewalk stalls. An insurance agency sits in the world's narrowest (less than 2 metres wide) commercial building at Carrall and Pender Streets.

Asian tourists primarily from Japan and Hong Kong have helped establish Vancouver as an international destination. Some shops estimate that local and visiting Asian customers represent 85 per cent of their sales. After Expo 86 a booming economy and soaring tourism attracted scores of high-profile

facing page, clockwise from top: Hudson's Bay Company store, Vancouver, c. 1924; first HBC store, Gastown, c. 1887; second store, Georgia and Granville, c. 1893. cva

designer boutiques to the city. When Chanel opened its Vancouver location in 1990 Normand Pitre, president of Chanel Canada, called Vancouver "the Canadian city of the future." It appears that many other designers agreed. Names that fleck the pages of Vogue Magazine—Gianni Versace, Byblos, Escada, Sonia Rykiel and Valentino—flocked to the city.

The influx of designer boutiques has forever changed the once homey retail landscape. In downtown Vancouver Sinclair Centre, a post office in 1910, has been transformed into a high fashion pitstop with stores like Leone, Plaza Escada and Feastwear. The delicatessens and cafes of quaint Robsonstrasse have been replaced by Robson Street's slick, Euro-style coffee bars and global retailers such as Benetton, The Gap and Laura Ashley. In between the two lies Couture Corner, home to many of the city's most exclusive designer boutiques and shops that open and close by airline and tour bus schedules.

To cater to these global visitors Holt Renfrew, an eastern-based luxury chain, completed a $6 million expansion in 1994. A handful of chi-chi designer boutiques and an extra 1,400 square-metres were added to the Pacific Centre store.

The gritty underside to Vancouver's explosive retail growth is that many small family stores are being killed by high taxes and skyrocketing rents. Mom and Pop stores have been squeezed out of Robson Street and replaced by high-flying projects like the former Vancouver Public Library's transformation. In 1996 it reopened as an entertainment and retail centre showcasing a Virgin Records Superstore and Planet Hollywood, a restaurant fronted by stars Arnold Schwarzenegger, Bruce Willis and Sylvester Stallone. Future growth on Robson Street is expected to extend east towards the new Public Library, the Ford Centre and Yaletown.

However all is not lost. Many small stores are revitalizing shopping areas like West 4th Avenue, Commercial Drive and Yaletown. Most Vancouverites haven't discovered Yaletown, Vancouver's version of New York's Soho. Construction cranes tower over the southeast corner of Downtown (a two-block neighborhood bordered by Nelson and Davie Streets and Hamilton and Mainland Streets), the turn-of-the-century warehousing district. Neglected for decades, these heritage brick-and-beam warehouses are being transformed into artist's lofts, bistros, pool halls and boutiques.

Gastown underwent a similar revival in the 1970s. Declared a historic site in the late 1960s, Gastown was gussied up with cobblestoned streets and old-fashioned lamp standards. Today it's become a prime tourist attraction and many of the city's oldest buildings have been converted into chic urban lofts. Cordova Street is now a hot spot for local fashion designers'

Boboli fashion store's instant heritage—the doorway was found in Mexico City, 1993. vs

work and vintage clothing. Granville Street, once an opulent shopping street, has crumbled into a row of movie theatres and nightlife south of Pacific Centre.

Granville Island, a favorite shopping spot with both tourists and locals, lies under the Granville Street Bridge. In 1913 the area was dredged out of the False Creek mud flats to become the city's industrial heart. The federal government formed the Granville Island Trust in 1973 and opened a public market six years later. Today the tremendously successful Public Market has been joined by restaurants, theatres, Kids Only Market (a two-storey children's shopping complex) and the Emily Carr Institute of Art and Design (built in 1980 and expanded in 1994).

The success of Granville Island spawned similar suburban markets that combined fresh produce and groceries with upscale boutiques. Two of the most successful, Lonsdale Quay at the port to North Vancouver's Seabus and Westminster Quay at New Westminster's waterfront, were opened to coincide with Expo 86. Both feature a vibrant mix of fruit and veggie stands, upscale boutiques and restaurants.

Vancouver's metamorphosis from dusty frontier village to sparkling world-class city is far from complete. As the city speeds into the future expect more cranes and hard hats to dig in.

The Telephone
Carol Woodman

IN 1876 ALEXANDER GRAHAM BELL patented an invention that was to change our lives: the telephone. The first telephone in British Columbia, laughingly called a "talking box," was in Nanaimo. It connected the Dunsmuir mine to the dock at Departure Bay and was constructed by William H. Wall from instructions in *Scientific American*. A missionary working in a remote native village near Prince Rupert hung a line between the village store and the sawmill and a contractor working on the new Canadian Pacific Railway strung a line through the Fraser Canyon so he could talk to supervisors. A new industry was emerging.

B.C.'s first telephone company, the Victoria and Esquimalt, was established in 1880. The first telephone in Vancouver connected the new community of Granville (Gastown) with New Westminster and the first switchboard was located in a bookstore, which doubled as a concert hall, on Carrall Street. By the end of 1885 there were 35 subscribers. In 1904 the British Columbia Telephone Company was established and the task of building a province-wide network continued. It was dangerous, back-breaking, time-consuming labor. Gorges and rivers were spanned. Poles were secured on slippery mountainsides, through swamps and muskeg while the workers, often in protective netting, battled relentless hordes of mosquitoes and black flies.

In 1932 the "Copper Highway," a line from Vancouver to Halifax, was completed and the miracle of cross-Canada communication was a fact.

In 1958 came the "Invisible Skyway," a microwave relay system that revolutionized the telephone business and made B.C. Telephone a communications company. Microwave towers forwarding our calls can be seen on numerous mountaintops. The sixties continued the revolution with direct distance dialling, push-button phones and computers. The telephone was now our most important means of communication. In 1972 Telesat Canada launched the first domestic communications satellite—Anik 1.

Expo 86 was a showcase for technological advances in the communications field. "Card Phones" were introduced and events at Expo were broadcast to 86 countries using a high-tech lightguide system specially installed for the occasion. Two years later B.C. Telephone began construction of the Lightguide Transmission system and by 1990 had completed its portion of the cross Canada LTS—the world's longest terrestrial fibre-

optic network consisting of three million metres of fibre-optic cable. This allows British Columbians rapid interactive voice, data, image and video transmission on one circuit.

Until 1992 B.C. Telephone was our phone company. Then a decision by the CRTC, the governing body of the communications industry, opened the long-distance market to full competition. Now numerous competitors not only want our long-distance business, they also want us to purchase their sophisticated retail products and services such as pagers, cellular phones, fax phones and 800 and 900 numbers. The cable companies are also fighting the phone companies for exclusive rights to install and carry the latest technologies.

Innovative uses of emerging technologies are examples of the changing focus at BC Telecom. The high-speed fibre backbone network proven in medical, educational and government applications is gaining ground in business markets. Brokers at offices in B.C., Alberta and Ontario can provide instant stock quotations, transactions and account management. Banking and bill paying can be done by telephone. With the demand for more telephone lines and the growing use of mobile communications and modems, a new area code has been installed for the areas north and east of Hope and all of Vancouver Island.

In August, 1994, BC Telecom brought the XV Commonwealth Games in Victoria to the world. The integrated fibre-optic network, the first of its kind to carry video, voice and data for such an event, connected 17 games venues to an international broadcast centre. This enabled the host broadcaster and seven international TV networks to transmit live coverage around the world.

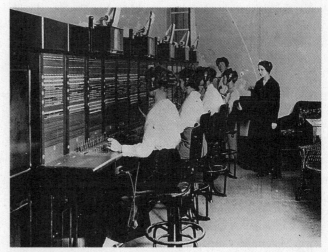

Switchboard, Hotel Vancouver, c 1904. cva

The Fashion Industry
Lisa Tant

OUTSIDERS CONSIDER Vancouver fashion an oxymoron. Fashion? In a city where hiking boots, cycling shorts and backpacks reign supreme? You bet. City- smart tailoring shapes Toronto fashion while vibrant colors and splashy glitz define Montreal's chic mode. In contrast, Vancouver style, on first glance, suggests an attitude so laid-back it's almost horizontal. But, in fact, the local fashion industry presents an eclectic potpourri of original internationally recognized designs.

Vancouver's fashion profile has only reached a global level in the past decade. Today the apparel industry is the sixth largest secondary (manufacturing) industry in the province, says Maureen Drew, executive director of Apparel BC, an industry trade group. The designer focus didn't kick in until 1979, when Drew and other industry leaders launched the Western Canadian Designers & Fashion Association. At that point, currently feted designers such as Zonda Nellis and Christine Morton were just emerging from their small home-based workshops.

Prior to that, Vancouver's fashion industry revolved around a handful of major manufacturers and cottage businesses. "The industry has grown through due diligence," says Harold Lennett, an apparel industry pioneer. "It wasn't practical to open major operations in Vancouver when all of the business contacts were centred in Eastern Canada."

Many of the original manufacturers, including Lennett, continue to flourish with worldwide customers. Yet others have been battered by economic cycles. Marjorie Hamilton, in existence for 49 years, and eight-year-old Style 1 Designs closed shop in 1995. Sadly one of the oldest manufacturers closed its doors in April 1996—Jantzen Canada was established in the 1920s by A.C. Cohen as the Universal Knitting Company, "Canada's Finest Knitwear." Jantzen in Portland, Oregon, granted Universal its first foreign franchise to make knitted garments 10 years later and then purchased the company in 1959. Today Jantzen is owned by VF Corporation, the American conglomerate that decided to close the Canadian subsidiary in spite of its profitable status.

Aero Garment Ltd. was founded in 1925 as Vancouver's largest privately-owned clothing manufacturer. Today the family operated sportswear manufacturer sells to more than 3,000 North American stores. A former sales agent, Lennett started the Gastown Mercantile Corporation, makers of Gassy Jack leather apparel, in 1970. Most of the city's manufacturers—including

Original Blouse, Aljean, Neto Leather and National Cloak—were located in Gastown, Vancouver's oldest neighborhood. Employees of National Cloak bought out the company and started Surrey Classics, which became one of the most successful outerwear companies in Canada. Surrey Classics was later bought by Joe Segal and Louis Eisman, who also spun Mr. Jax Fashions out of Lounge Fashions. A victim of the recession, Surrey Classics closed in 1994. Koret of Canada was established by its San Francisco-based parent company 35 years ago. Koret purchased the city's largest manufacturer, Mr. Jax Fashions, in 1995 and is now king of the local apparel castle (under the new West Coast apparel parent name) with annual sales topping $50 million.

Harold Lennett approached Levi Strauss to make leather jean jackets but was asked to produce denim instead. So, with a $5,000 loan for old Levi equipment, he launched Pimlico Apparel in 1979. With sons Gary and Howard, Lennett has turned Pimlico into North America's leading denim jacket producer, supplying Levi Strauss and The Gap from a brand-new 7,000 sq. metre factory.

One of North America's top lingerie manufacturers also calls Vancouver home. Adagio Lingerie crumbled into bankruptcy at its peak in 1992. Two years later, former designer Patricia Fieldwalker picked up the pieces and is quickly regaining her worldwide celebrity following (including *Vogue Magazine* and actors Sharon Stone and Julia Roberts) for luxurious silk undies.

Peter Fox and his kid's former babysitter, John Fluevog, joined forces in 1970 to open Vancouver's now legendary Fox and Fluevog Shoes. The pair sold skyscraping peacock platforms and over-the-knee patent leather boots at their Gastown boutique. Fifteen years later the partners amicably split, with Fox going upscale and Fluevog paving a wacky new route with fans such as Madonna. In 1995 Fox's son, Calvin, works for Fluevog and the company has five stores in North America and a successful catalogue business.

Fortunes turned in the early eighties when the major national department stores, Eatons and The Bay, moved their regional buying and advertising offices to centralized Toronto operations. "That shift impacted all aspects of the industry," says Maureen Drew, "from photographers who shot their advertising campaigns to local designers." 1993 saw the demise of the 101-year-old Woodwards, the only remaining regional department store and another key local fashion supporter.

After a recessionary dip, Vancouver's fashion rollercoaster appears to be riding up again. Apparel BC started with six members in February 1994 and currently sits at 35 (and grow-

Leone store, Vancouver, 1993. vp

After Expo, names that were as foreign as their countries of origin—Gianni Versace, Chanel, Byblos, Escada, Sonia Rykiel and Valentino—flocked to the city

fledged internationally recognized studios.

Where West Coast designers once struggled to have their work viewed seriously, today their work is showcased in North America's finest stores and the pages of influential fashion magazines. Yet Vancouver fashion isn't reserved for the wealthy or avant garde. Accessories to leather, appliqued wools to handwoven silks range in price and fashion sense.

Vancouver's maturing designer profile is mirrored by a similar evolution on the retail front. Edward Chapman opened one of the first fashion stores in 1890, outfitting men for the Klondike Gold Rush. In the fifties, the store branched into women's wear, which continues to be one of Vancouver's most respected boutiques. Today the men's and women's wear are separate companies.

After Expo, names that were as foreign as their countries of origin—Gianni Versace, Chanel, Byblos, Escada, Sonia Rykiel and Valentino—flocked to the city. Leone started from owner Alberto Leone's hair salon and has now grown into a high-fashion designer emporium. In 1995 the Leone family launched a new Vancouver-designed label, AWear, that they plan to franchise across Canada. The influx of designer boutiques has forever changed the once homey retail landscape. Vancouver streets are rapidly morphing into fashionable pitstops with slick Euro-style coffee bars, designer boutiques and global labels.

Internationally recognized fashion design schools and modelling agencies enhance the local industry. Three top design and technology programs are offered at Kwantlen University College, Helen Lefeaux School of Fashion Design and Vancouver Community College. Talent scouts from fashion capitals flock to local modelling agencies for the sought-after fresh West Coast look.

A city's soul is reflected by its attitude and culture. Vancouver's emerging world-class fashion image—from teenage models to multi-million dollar manufacturers—is helping shape a look that's uniquely West Coast.

ing weekly) with a newly established design division. In June 1995 three former executives of Mr. Jax Fashions, including popular designer Ron Leal, launched The Apparel Group (TAG). With his new line, Leal plans to retain his high fashion influence—a hybrid of New York sensibility, European sophistication and relaxed West Coast attitude. In the past five years, Vancouver has also become a North American hub for technical apparel—clothing for hiking, skiing, cycling and demanding outdoor sports. Labels such as Westbeach, Sugoi Cycle and Planet X are riding high on the backs of sports nuts worldwide.

The turning point for Vancouver's role as a Canadian fashion design centre was the World Exposition in 1986 (Expo 86). Shows by local designers captured global attention and the fashion industry began to blossom. Ten years later many of those small home-based businesses have flowered into full-

Food

Overwaitea began with the entrepreneurial spirit of a charismatic Irishman named Robert C. Kidd, who on March 8, 1915 opened a grocery store on Columbia Street in New Westminster. Kidd developed innovative merchandising techniques to draw customers to his store. One of the most famous was his practice of adding an extra two ounces to each pound of his best Indian and Ceylon-blended teas. His store soon became known as the "overweight-tea" store. Kidd condensed this to Overwaitea.

How Greater Vancouver Gets Its Food
Beverley Sinclair

EVERY YEAR, the 1.8 million residents of the GVRD fill their plates and glasses with more than $3 billion dollars worth of food and drink bought at grocery stores, restaurants, and farmers markets. Most of those food-buying dollars go to the superpowers of the retail food industry: Overwaitea/ Save On Foods, Safeway, Real Canadian Super Store, and Super-Valu. Like other North American cities, we have a three- or four-day supply of fresh foods at any given time in food warehouses and retail outlets' dairy cases, produce departments and meat counters.

Increasingly, those fresh foods are produced in British Columbia. The province's 19,000 farmers produce 250 different food commodities. Half of the 2,647 farms in the GVRD are in Langley, the rest are in Surrey, Richmond, Delta and Burnaby. Typical GVRD farms are much smaller than the B.C. average—13.7 hectares compared to 124.4—but they're hugely productive. Local farms occupy only 2 per cent of the province's farmland, but in 1993 they generated 23 per cent of total farm income. GVRD farms produce more than 80 different items totalling at least $300 million per year, including half the province's greenhouse vegetables, most farm-grown veggies, and the vast majority of cranberries, mushrooms and greenhouse flowers. Add in the food processing and distribution businesses, and the region's agricultural industry added about $3 billion to the economy in 1991.

The ministry of agriculture, fisheries and food says the average Vancouver family of four spends close to $10,000 on meals per year in Vancouver (1992). Here's where the basics come from, based on information from that ministry as well as the Greater Vancouver Regional District, Statistics Canada, various producer associations, provincial marketing boards, Farm Folk/ City Folk and food-industry businesses.

DAIRY PRODUCTS

Greater Vancouver residents gulp down about $350 million dollars worth of dairy products per year, almost all of it, except imported cheeses, from British Columbia dairy farms. Most of the 880 dairy farms are clustered around Chilliwack, Abbotsford and Matsqui, but there are several in Delta, Richmond, Langley and Surrey including Donia Farm Ltd. in South Surrey, one of the province's largest with more than 400 milking cows. Local farms provide about 12 per cent of the province's

facing page: Public market, Vancouver, 1987. VS

total dairy food production.

Milk: Stats Canada says the average person drinks 58 litres of 2 per cent milk every year, and 6 litres of skim milk. In both cases, that's double the amount consumed 25 years ago. Whole milk's popularity has gone down: we used to drink about three times as much as we do now. All told, we buy more than 300 million litres of milk per year in Greater Vancouver.

Butter: Vancouverites go through almost five million kilograms of butter every year, 30 per cent less than in 1981.

Cheeses: We're eating almost double the amount of cheese we did 25 years ago, largely because of the increase in availability and taste for speciality cheeses like Mozzarella and Parmesan. Local dairy cases are loaded up with almost 19 million kilograms of cheese every year for Vancouver cheese lovers.

Ice Cream: Ice cream is Greater Vancouver's dessert of choice: we scoop up almost 18 million litres each year. In spite of the incursion of exotic specialty flavors, vanilla and chocolate still top the charts.

Yogurt: The average person eats more than 3 litres of yogurt a year, the equivalent of more than 26 single-serving containers. Compare that to 1971 when yogurt was still on many people's weird-food list and most people didn't even make it through four of those small containers. Imagine 5.6 million litres of yogurt piled high—that's about how much Greater Vancouver residents eat now.

Eggs: Virtually all eggs on Greater Vancouver store shelves come from B.C. chickens, 80 per cent from farms in the Abbotsford and Langley areas. The province's 2.2 million commercial laying hens produce about 54 million dozen eggs every year, and about half become part of Greater Vancouver meals. The average person eats about 15 dozen eggs a year, down from 23 dozen in 1960.

VEGETABLES

B.C. farms produce 180 million kilograms of vegetables valued at $70 million dollars per year, more than half from GVRD farms. Imported veggies, $17 million worth, come primarily from California.

Beans: If all the beans produced in the province were piled on the field at half time during a B.C. Lions football game, they'd cover the ground with a bean blanket more than 2 metres deep. Most of the yearly 4 million kilograms harvest comes from the Lower Mainland and Fraser Valley. We eat the equivalent of the entire B.C. bean crop in the GVRD alone every year, and rely on imports from California, Washington, Belgium, Mexico and Thailand.

Broccoli: We eat almost 6 million kilograms of broccoli every year, up 150 per cent since 1981. Most imported broccoli

While the overweight-tea policy was later dropped because of skyrocketing tea prices, Kidd continued to develop innovative merchandising methods. He didn't round out prices to the nearest nickel, but began, for example, selling five bars of soap for 24 cents instead of 25. This infuriated his competitors, who put pressure on suppliers to withhold product from him. One bakery refused to sell Kidd bread until he raised the price. He responded by further reducing the price of bread!

comes from California, some from Mexico.

Cabbage: Cabbage consumption has gone down about 25 per cent, but we still eat almost 8 million kilograms. Much of that comes from local farms that produce almost three-quarters of the provincial crop. Put all the B.C. cabbages together and you'd fill 380 semi trailers. Imported cabbage comes from California, Texas, Arizona, Mexico, Taiwan and China.

Carrots: Imagine a pile of 15 million kilograms of carrots. That's what we eat every year, more than 9 kilograms each. Local veggie farms produce about 60 per cent of the province's eight million kilograms crop. The rest come from California, some from Mexico.

Cauliflower: Some 3.5 million kilograms of cauliflower are consumed in Greater Vancouver every year, most of it during the summer when local crops are ripe and considerably cheaper than the off-season imports from California.

Celery: GVRD vegetable farms produce 85 per cent of B.C.'s 2.2 million kilogram celery crop. That's not enough to feed us though. More than 4 kilograms each amounts to 7 million kilograms for local residents alone each year, so most of our celery comes from California.

Chinese Vegetables: The most popular Chinese greens are bok choy, choy sum, gai choy, Chinese cabbage, sui choy and gai lan. Virtually all 1.5 million kilograms of Chinese vegetables grown in B.C. come from farms between Vancouver and Hope.

Corn: We eat six million kilograms, on-the-cob and processed. B.C. farms produce 21 million kilograms of corn, and three-quarters of that is canned or frozen. Corn with a B.C. label on it comes from the Lower Mainland, Okanagan Valley and Vancouver Island; imported corn is from Washington, Florida and California.

Cucumbers: We eat almost 30 per cent more cukes than 10 years ago, about 5 million kilograms a year now. Approximately half comes from B.C. farms, the rest mainly from California, Florida, Mexico and Spain.

Lettuce: The average lettuce-eater goes through about 16 heads of iceberg lettuce a year. B.C. Place would probably be about the right size to hold a salad made of all the lettuce we eat in the GVRD—more than 27 million heads. Eighty per cent of the B.C. lettuce we buy comes from local farms, the rest is from Vancouver Island. In 1994, 13 million kilograms came to B.C. from California and Mexico, about half of it destined for Greater Vancouver kitchens.

Mushrooms: Statistics Canada says the average Canadian eats less than two kilograms of mushrooms a year, but we ate a lot more than that here—about 3.5 kilograms each, almost six million kilograms in the GVRD. All but the 5 per cent imported from Washington State are B.C. grown. In fact mushrooms are B.C.'s second most valuable edible crop, after apples. More that three-quarters of the mushrooms we buy come from farms within the GVRD, like Minh Hien Farm in Surrey which produces .5 million kilograms a year and Brothers Mushroom Farm in Langley with .7 million. Eight-five per cent of B.C. mushroom producers are associated with Money's Mushrooms, now making an aggressive push into Japan.

Onions: Most of the 14 million kilograms we eat come from Washington, Oregon, California, New Zealand and Australia. B.C. onions come from the Lower Mainland and Okanagan Valley which produce about six million kilograms per year.

Peas: You'd think this old standby would top the scales, but it doesn't. The average person only eats about 2.5 kilograms a year, mostly frozen. Virtually all peas grown in B.C. soil—9000 tonnes—are harvested from Lower Mainland and Fraser Valley farms. B.C. imports about 850,000 kilograms of fresh peas from California, Washington, Mexico, Guatemala and Taiwan.

Potatoes: Potatoes are the most popular vegetable by far. On average we eat almost 66 kilograms per person per year, about 112 million kilograms in the GVRD. The way we eat them has changed dramatically since the early eighties, assuming we've followed American eating habits relatively closely. The taste for processed and fast food potatoes used to outweigh fresh potatoes almost two to one. Now, it's the other way around. About half the potatoes we eat are grown here, most of the rest are from Washington, with some from California, Idaho, and Florida.

Tomatoes: We go through almost 100 million tomatoes (about 19 million kilograms) every year, largely from local greenhouses and farms. Imports come primarily from California, Mexico, and Florida, but also from Spain and the Netherlands.

MEAT

Beef: The amount of beef we eat has decreased from about 28 kilograms per person in 1986 to 23 in 1993. Current totals add up to more than 39 million kilograms of beef stir-fries, hamburgers and steaks in the GVRD. Although some of the beef we eat comes from B.C.'s Cariboo country ranches and American farms, the vast majority is imported from Alberta.

Chicken: We eat double the amount of chicken we ate 30 years ago, 40 per cent in the form of nuggets, fingers and other processed chicken foods. The GVRD's annual per capita consumption is about 28 kilograms, or more than 25 million chickens for the region. Virtually all of it comes from B.C. poultry farms, 80 per cent of which are in the Fraser Valley. Two of the

Robert Kidd's methods proved successful and he opened more stores. But by 1967, facing rising competition from more powerful, multi-national supermarket chains, Overwaitea realized it needed financial muscle to continue growing. In 1968 the directors sold controlling interest in the company to Jim Pattison. With Pattison's financial support and a commitment to stay ahead of the competition every store was upgraded. New departments were added and the range of general merchandise was expanded.

largest are in the GVRD: Dogwood Poultry in Langley and Clifford Pollen's farm in Surrey with combined quotas of more than one million chickens a year. Put a year's worth of B.C. chickens in a line, and it would stretch for more than 16,000 kilometres. When demand is greater than that, we import from other parts of Canada, particularly Alberta, Ontario, and Quebec.

Lamb: B.C. imports about 375,000 kilograms of lamb every year, about half for local dinner plates. Eighty-six per cent of the lamb we eat comes from New Zealand, Australia and Alberta, the largest lamb-producing province in Canada. The rest of the 1.5 million kilograms of lamb eaten locally comes from B.C. farms. The largest sheep farms—500 to 1,000 ewes—are in the Peace River area, but there are dozens on the Lower Mainland and Vancouver Island with 25 sheep or less.

Pork: About a third of our pork comes from B.C.'s 150 pork producers, mainly in the Fraser Valley. The largest producer is the Ritchie-Smith operation which has a herd of about 40,000 on several sites near Abbotsford. The rest of Vancouver's pork comes from the prairies and Ontario. All told, it adds up to an annual total of about 36 million kilograms of pork dinners and bacon with eggs in the GVRD.

Turkey: Eighty-five per cent of the turkey we carve up locally comes from B.C.'s 54 turkey farms. Most are in the Aldergrove/Abbotsford area, but there are a couple closer to home in Port Coquitlam and Richmond. Imported turkeys come from Ontario, Quebec and Manitoba. Greater Vancouver residents ate the equivalent of more than 1.5 million 7-kilograms (15 lb.) turkeys in 1994, whole or processed into rolls, burger, sausage and more.

Fish: Seventy per cent of Vancouver families eat fresh fish at least once a month, and more than a third eat it every week. A lot of that comes from B.C. waters—the province's 16,000 fishers, 90 salmon farms, 100 trout farms and more than 200 fish processing plants produce about $1 billion (wholesale value) of processed seafood per year. We also eat canned, frozen and fresh fish and seafood from many different countries including tuna from Japan, the Philippines, Indonesia and Thailand; salmon and halibut from the U.S. and Russia; shrimp and prawns from Hong Kong, Vietnam and China; herring from Denmark, and anchovies from Morocco. The average Vancouver family eats the equivalent of about eight salmon steaks a year—that's about 3.5 million steaks for Greater Vancouver—and spends $260 on all kinds of fish.

FRUIT

B.C. produces about $145 million worth of fruit, berries, and nuts per year, and imports $80 million more mainly from California.

Apples: It might take the Pacific Coliseum to hold all B.C. apples we eat in the GVRD, about 68 million a year. Although most comes from our orchards, the province imports 26 million kilograms, primarily from Washington, with some from New Zealand, Chile and China. On top of that, the average Vancouverite drinks more than 7 kilograms of juice in a year, made from apples of the Okanagan and Similkameen valleys, the U.S., Germany, South Africa and Argentina.

Bananas: More than 25 million kilograms are imported into Vancouver every year, particularly from Ecuador, Mexico, Panama, Peru, Colombia and Costa Rica.

Grapefruit: The average person in Greater Vancouver eats 2.5 kilograms a year, totalling more than 4 million kilograms for the region. Most of it comes from California, Florida, Thailand and China.

Oranges: About 35 million kilograms end up in Vancouver kitchens, half of it fresh, the rest as juice. Fresh oranges come from California, Florida, Australia, Mexico, Argentina and Portugal. The juice is imported from processors in the U.S., Brazil, Mexico, South Korea and Taiwan.

BERRIES

Blueberries: B.C. is one of the top three producers in the world, about nine million kilograms a year. Virtually all come from the more than 450 family farm operations in Richmond, Surrey, Pitt Meadows and Matsqui Prairie. Seventy per cent of the crop is frozen or processed into flavorings, jams etc.; the rest we eat fresh, including a couple of million kilograms that local blueberry fans buy at u-pick farms. No doubt they eat more than the two kilograms per year that Statistics Canada says the average person eats. Consumption has gone up 200 per cent in the last ten years or so.

Cranberries: About one-quarter of the world's cranberries are grown in B.C. by 53 growers who are almost all second-generation cranberry farmers. Eighty-five per cent of the average 17 million kilograms crop comes from the cranberry bogs of Richmond, Pitt Meadows and Fort Langley. Almost all the berries are sold to the grower-owned Ocean Spray Pool along with the crops from Wisconsin, Massachusetts, New Jersey, New York, Oregon and California, then processed into juices, jellies, etc. Fresh cranberries at Granville Market and other local markets are from B.C. too, but the ones in plastic bags at the supermarkets are likely from Wisconsin.

Strawberries: The numbers from Statistics Canada say the average person eats about 2.5 kilograms a year, but it's bound to be much higher in the Greater Vancouver area, fed by one of the prime strawberry growing areas in the country. Eighty per cent of the annual 3 million kilograms of B.C. strawberries come from fields from Ladner to Chilliwack. Seventy-five per cent are processed into such items as jam, sauces, yogurt and ice cream flavorings. Imported berries are from California and Florida; frozen imports come from California, Mexico and the Philippines.

MISCELLANEOUS

Alcohol: In 1994, the average Vancouverite downed about $550 worth of booze: 252 bottles of beer, 7.2 litres of spirits, and 15 litres of wine. British Columbians drink more of all types of alcohol than Canadians in any other province.

Chocolate: Based on the statistics, those who consider chocolate a separate food group may be right. Spokespeople for Purdy's Vancouver plant won't say how much chocolate they produce, but they figure we each eat about 9 kilograms of chocolate a year. That's more than 15 million kilograms in Greater Vancouver—way ahead of peas. See Sandra McKenzie's article.

Coffee: We buy almost eight million kilograms of coffee beans every year, imported mainly from Colombia, Mexico, Guatemala, Ethiopia, Kenya, Indonesia and Sumatra.

Flour: We eat more than 100 million kilograms of flour in the GVRD in a year, virtually all of it from the wheat fields of Saskatchewan and Alberta.

Honey: About half the honey we spread on our toast comes from the prairie provinces, particularly Alberta. The other half of the 1.7 million kilograms we gobble up in the GVRD comes from the province's 3,000 beekeepers and their 45,000 bee colonies, mainly in the Peace River area, Vancouver Island, and the stretch of fertile land from Richmond to Hope. The vast majority of registered B.C. beekeepers are hobbyists with two to 50 hives in their backyards, but there are a few big operations, notably Babe's Honey with 3,000 colonies on the Saanich Peninsula.

Restaurant meals: The average Vancouver family of four spends about $60 a week on restaurant meals. Tourism Vancouver adds that overnight visitors spent $451 million dollars dining out in Vancouver in 1994.

Soft drinks: Add up all the soft drinks we guzzle in a year and you end up with 153 million one-litre bottles. This is one of those items whose average consumption looks astronomical if you're not one of the consumers—90 litres per person per year.

Sugar: On average, we each eat about 43 kilograms a year, more than 73 million kilograms in the GVRD. In 1994, Rogers Sugar Ltd.'s Vancouver refinery processed raw cane sugar —mostly from Australia—into 160,000 metric tons of sugar. Seventy per cent of that went to B.C. markets.

above: Entrance to Granville Island—Parking protest (the mix of cars and people integrates the island and its market with city life), 1986. vs
facing page: top; Pacific salmon in cold storage, Vancouver, 1988. vs
bottom; Fraser Valley farmland, 1995. vs

In 1982 a brand-new Save-On-Foods was opened in North Delta and five existing stores were rechristened. Those six Save-On-Foods stores were the beginning of an enviably strong and trend-setting chain. Another head-turning unveiling came in September 1993 when all Overwaitea Foods stores in the Lower Mainland were simultaneously converted to Save-On-Foods stores, creating a total of 18 Save-On-Foods stores in B.C. Since then, two additional stores have opened in the Lower Mainland, bringing the total by 1996 to 20.

Next Overwaitea expanded to Alberta. The company built its first store (of nine) and purchased Associated Grocers, a well-established wholesaler serving more than 500 independent grocers in Alberta and B.C. Today, our interests are no longer restricted to Overwaitea and Save-On-Foods, but include a wholesale operation. With new stores opening regularly and new divisions being created, our new name, the Overwaitea Food Group, reflects the company's diversity. And it all began with "over-weight tea."

Restaurants in Greater Vancouver
Claire Hurley

In 1892 when my grandfather, Alfred W.H. Curtis and other members of the 1891-92 Vancouver rugby team (familiar names like Woodward, Alexander, Palmer, Horne and Akroyd), finished a game they probably headed off to quaff a few brew and eat in the Gastown area.

When dressed in their best bib-and-tucker there's no doubt that all the fine folk dined at the Canadian Pacific Railway-owned Hotel Vancouver, as the arrival of the railway brought with it the formal dining of rail cars: silver tableware, white linen tablecloths and napkins, silver tea and coffee services, crystal water goblets and wine glasses.

The history of the restaurants and ethnic cuisines in the Greater Vancouver area continues to follow the settlement patterns of the immigrants. As the Chinese settled in Chinatown, Chinese restaurants prospered. So, too, on Powell Street, where Japanese merchants opened stores and cooks created restaurants. French-Canadian restaurants flourished in Maillardville; Italian cuisine and Commercial Drive became synonymous. British fare was, and still is, popular everywhere.

Family scrapbooks provide insight into local history. My mother has an April, 1927, Orpheum Theatre program for Bizet's *Carmen* with ads for Scott's (formerly Picardy's) at 722 Granville, the Strand Cafe—"finest cafe in Vancouver"— at 29 West Hastings and the International Chop Suey Parlor at 143 Pender.

Nat Bailey opened the first drive-in White Spot restaurant at 67th and Granville in 1928 when that Marpole location was still outside Vancouver's city limits. The landmark log cabin was named White Spot Barbecue. In 1937 he replaced the Barbecue with the White Spot Restaurant and Drive-in. The next year he added the White Spot Dining Room. With its wonderful murals, the drive-in proved popular for decades while the dining room attracted the dress-up crowd.

Before World War II there were many excellent Japanese restaurants in Vancouver and Steveston. Unfortunately these were confiscated during the war and the buildings and their contents sold at public auction.

An interview with Vancouver city councillor Don Bellamy, recently retired from the post of executive director of the Restaurant and Foodservices Association of B.C., was a trip into Vancouver's history. Bellamy spoke of the Pall Mall building on Hastings which housed a huge restaurant on its main floor. The White Lunch on Hastings served as the central commissary restaurant and staff prepared and delivered meals to other restaurants along Hastings and West Pender, and up Granville and Howe.

After World War II Scott's, the Trocadero, Syd's Tamale House (Mexican food), the Peter Pan on Granville, Love's Skillet, and The Only near Carrall and Hastings were all well-known and thriving. The Only, established in 1912, was the only licensed restaurant that operated without any washrooms.

For many years liquor was not served in restaurants; old photos show an abundance of small brown bags under tables and a surprising amount of bottled mixers in plain view. Beer parlors had two rooms: one for men only, the other for ladies and escorts. Bottle clubs such as the Cave Theatre Restaurant, the Palomar Supper Club, the Mandarin Gardens, Isy's "highclass strip joint" as Bellamy called it, the Arctic Club and the Penthouse provided entertainment, buckets of ice, high-priced mixers and, in some cases, girls as company.

After World War II European-trained chefs arrived and restaurants began specializing: steak and lobster houses and ethnic establishments such as the Greek Village, Kobe Japanese Steak House, and Puccini's Italian were all well-received.

A copy of a 1978 issue of *Skyword*, the inflight magazine of Pacific Western Airlines, brought back memories of such well-known establishments as the Cavalier in the Hotel Georgia, whose ad boasted of "Fine dining midst the grace and elegance of Vancouver's first great restaurant." Chez Luba at the Queen Elizabeth Theatre promised exquisite French and Russian cuisine. Las Tapas Restaurante, the English Bay Cafe, Harbour House Revolving Restaurant atop Harbour Centre, Restaurant Toulouse-Lautrec, McQuiggans in the old mansion at 1119 Robson Street and the Hornby Street favorites of Hy's and, of course, the Cave Theatre Restaurant were all popular locales in the 1970s and early 1980s.

In 1971 George Tidball started the Keg Restaurants in North Vancouver. The restaurants capitalized on our love of beef. Their concept of casual dining with reasonably priced steaks, cheap bar prices, tempting salad bars and oh-so-friendly servers proved popular. In 1987 Tidball sold his empire of 76 restaurants to Whitbread PLC of London, England.

At about that time pasta and seafood replaced beef as consumer favorites. The Keg Boathouse restaurants, Roy's Seafood House, the Cannery and Steveston Seafood attracted crowds.

The producers of Expo 86 invited the world to come to Vancouver and, in the decade following, people from all over the world have immigrated to the Lower Mainland. As a result you'll find ethnic cuisine for gourmets and gourmands all over the Greater Vancouver region.

Chocolate
Sandra Mackenzie

IT MAY BE overstating the case to claim that Vancouver is the chocolate capital of North America—or maybe not. According to Tom Cinnamon, director of business operations for Purdy's Chocolates and a board member for the Retail Confectioners Institute of North America, informal research on the subject—a perusal of yellow page listings of confectioners in every city he visits—indicates that our per capita consumption of *theobroma* (literally, "the food of the gods") *cacao* is matched only by Salt Lake City's.

With no hard statistics to support Cinnamon's claim, the evidence is purely anecdotal. But local chocolatiers concur that Vancouver is a chocolate-loving city supporting, at last count, 20 confectioners specializing in decadent truffles and other trifles. What is indisputable is that local chocoholics have discerning tastes and a definite preference for Belgian chocolate—generally acknowledged as the world's finest.

For our educated palates we owe a debt of thanks to Ed Foley, the Vancouver godfather of chocolate. Now retired, Foley, who comes from a long line of confectioners in his native Ireland, was the first designated distributor for Callebeault chocolate in Canada. Since 1972 he has supplied pastry chefs and chocolatiers as far east as Montreal with the prized product, dubbed "the gold of Europe," and introduced local confectioners to European techniques and recipes.

Vancouver's passion for chocolate dates back to 1907 when Richard Cormon Purdy founded the firm that still bears his name today. Purdy sold his thriving enterprise to Hugh Forrester in 1925. Forrester, in turn, battled through the Great Depression and went into receivership at one point. Shortly after pulling the company out of debt the confectioner suffered another direct hit, this time in the form of sugar rationing during World War II. During the war years Forrester opened his shop at noon and limited his customers to a pound of chocolate apiece. In spite of this measure he was frequently sold out by 12:30 P.M.

By 1963 when Forrester sold the company to Charles Flavelle, the Purdy name was for many Vancouverites synonymous with chocolate, though the company's financial future was shaky. Under Flavelle's stewardship Purdy's regained its leadership role, growing from four stores to a chain of 45 located throughout British Columbia, Alberta and Washington. It is now the largest manufacturing retailer of chocolate in British Columbia and the second largest in Canada. The little factory kitchen on the Fairview Slopes, (dubbed "Choklit Park" by neighborhood children) has since moved to a 5,400-square-metre facility on Kingsway, where Purdy's turns out more than 100 varieties of chocolate, many based on techniques and recipes developed by R.C. Purdy.

While Purdy's is the oldest continuing manufacturer in Vancouver, it is only one of a long progression of chocolate purveyors who have fed our sweet tooth over the years. Charlie Sigurdsen, owner of Charlie's Chocolate Factory, researched the subject for a marketing thesis in 1953. He recalls that the stretch of Robson Street between Burrard and Granville was home to five chocolate shops during the fifties. Besides Purdy's there were Ziegler's, Debrett's, Pauline Johnson and Welch's. In addition each of the major department stores had thriving confectionery departments. According to Ed Foley by the mid-1960s there were 36 candy manufacturers in the city.

Today many of these once prominent names have passed into history and department stores no longer devote whole floors of retail space to candy sales. But Vancouver's passion for chocolate continues unabated, well served by wholesalers like Charlie Sigurdsen, Richard's Imported Foods (Ed Foley's import company, now owned by his sons) and Rene Rey. A wealth of smaller, boutique retailers like au Chocolat, Tout Sweet, Daniel Le Chocolat Belge, Rocky Mountain Chocolate Factory and Chocolate Arts dot virtually every shopping district in the Lower Mainland, bringing truffles (made of the finest Belgian chocolate, of course) to the masses.

But chocolate is more than a confection in the hearts and minds of Vancouverites. It's a social event and an artistic medium as well. No other city in North America can boast a chocolate buffet such as the one served up at the Sutton Place Hotel every Thursday, Friday and Saturday for the past ten years. "Death by Chocolate," chef John Bishop's intense contribution to our collective identity, is as indigenous a delicacy as Pacific salmon, or Saltspring Island lamb. And where else can you buy edible West Coast native sculpture but at Chocolate Arts? Owner Greg Hook combines a passion for chocolate and a love of native arts with moulds created by renowned Haida artist Robert Davidson. Combining chocolate's social and artistic merits is the Chocolate Extravaganza fundraiser to benefit Carousel Theatre and the Vancouver Museum. The brainchild of Carousel director Elizabeth Ball, the affair was an annual event during the early 1980s and was resurrected in 1995.

CHOCOLATES

In 1907 Richard Cormon Purdy opened his first chocolate shop in downtown Vancouver. Using family recipes brought with him from England, Mr. Purdy created fine hand-crafted chocolates that soon became a Vancouver favorite. Ninety years later, that tradition of quality continues. All of Purdy's 100 varieties are made with the freshest ingredients and the highest quality Belgian Chocolate. The same care and attention is given to every chocolate that comes out of the family-owned and operated kitchen.

Brewing
Mike Tytherleigh

Beer is as old as history. It was brewed in ancient Egypt, Mesopotamia and the monasteries of Europe, and both brew-pubs and microbreweries were common. (Witness the Bavarian Purity Law of 1516 becoming the standard for today's Granville Island Brewing Company.) In 1792—six years after John Molson, an immigrant from Lincoln, England, laid the foundation for today's multinational brewing company—Captain George Vancouver, charting Burrard's Canal, Point Grey and Howe Sound aboard the *Discovery*, wrote in his journal that Molson's brew was "a very salubrious and palatable beer."

European-style beers spread to the colonies through immigrants like Molson. Another was Tom Carling who arrived in Quebec City from Bristol, England, in 1818 and whose home-brew ale was in such demand that he set up a commercial brewery in London, Ontario. In 1883 John Labatt, an Irishman of French Huguenot stock who provided barley for a brewery and a son, John, founded Labatt Breweries in 1847. In fact brewing became one of the Dominion's first industries.

William Steinberger from California is reputed to be the first brewer in British Columbia, having set up a small log brewery near Victoria in 1858. He also built the Phoenix plant on Government Street and amalgamated the two into the Victoria Phoenix, later to become the Lucky Lager Breweries. Lucky Lager was acquired by Labatt 100 years later in 1958. Also in 1958 Labatt opened a new packaging and warehouse building at their New Westminster location. Since the late 1950s continued expansion and upgrading of the Labatt brewery has produced one of the most advanced brewing facilities in Western Canada, employing more than 200 people and featuring computerized can and bottle lines able to produce a combined total of 100,000 cans and bottles per hour. Today Labatt produces brands such as Labatt Genuine Draft, Labatt Blue, Labatt Ice and Lucky Lager in the New Westminster plant and distributes them to markets in Canada, the United States and Japan. Labatt's New Westminster brewery also brews, packages and distributes Budweiser, Guinness and Carlsberg through licensed brand agreements with these foreign breweries. Molson Breweries became a major player in B.C. also in 1958 when they bought out the American-owned Sick's Brewery and gained a plant at the south end of Burrard Bridge.

However this booming 20th century industry had more modest beginnings. At the time of incorporation in 1886 Vancouver was growing rapidly with 1,000 citizens, 12 hotels and several saloons to cater to its thirst. The pioneer brewery to slake that thirst was the whimsically named Red Cross Brewing Company built in 1882 on the waterfront at what was then the foot of Hastings Street. Originally a steam beer brewery it was overhauled, enlarged and fitted up as a lager brewing plant in 1892. It began shipping all over the province and was soon outselling the imported brands. The owners were John Williams and E.E. Barker, a pioneer who built the first residence in Mount Pleasant and developed much of that area.

The same year Charles Doering of Saxony, who had come to B.C. in 1879 and started the Vancouver Brewery on Seventh Avenue, about one block west of today's Main Street, joined with Otto Marstrand of Copenhagen in setting up a brewery eponymously named Doering and Marstrand. In 1900 they amalgamated with Red Cross and closed it down while taking on Williams as a partner. Marstrand dropped out and the name was changed to Vancouver Breweries which drew its water from Brewery Creek.

Founded in 1889 the Columbia Brewery at 1973 Powell Street (near Victoria Drive) grew out of the city's first beer garden, the Columbia Hall, which served 300 guests on opening day in 1886. There were no streetcars east of Victoria Drive so citizens going to Hastings Park for the livestock shows and harness racing had to walk there and back from the end of the line, making the beer garden a welcome refresher.

About the same time there was the Cedar Cottage Brewery at Knight and Kingsway (later converted into a private home by the owner, John Benson) and the Royal Brewery on Powell, near Woodland Drive. The Stanley Park Brewery was in a converted house on the south side of Lost Lagoon between Robson and Alberni, near today's tennis courts.

In 1910 through various mergers, Vancouver Breweries became part of a holding company, B.C. Breweries Ltd. A new brewery was built at 12th Avenue and Yew Street in 1912 on the wooded outskirts of the city, beside a creek flowing through a duck-filled marsh (now Connaught Park.) Other corporate changes followed with the brewery surviving financial problems caused by prohibition, recessions and war before expanding in 1946 and again in 1954. On May 1, 1957, the company became Carling Breweries (B.C.) which two years later became part of the larger Carling organization whose head office was in Toronto.

In 1986 the Australian conglomerate Elders IXL bought Carling to gain access to the North American market for its Foster's lager, brewing it at the 12th and Yew brewery.

Through a merger with Molson in 1989 the Carling name

Labatt Breweries of Canada is one of the world's leading brewing companies. Labatt and Belgian-based Interbrew S.A. together constitute the fourth largest brewer in the world with Labatt alone brewing more than 50 different brands, including Canada's best-selling Labatt Blue, and distributing in 40 countries internationally.

This photo is thought to be Vancouver's pioneer Gastown saloon keeper "Gassy Jack" Deighton but this is uncertain. cva

ceased to exist and the new company was able to close seven of its combined 16 breweries and still comply with the rule that beer had to be brewed in the province where it was sold. The brewery on 12th was one of the casualties and, in 1995, was destined to be demolished to make way for high-density housing.

The Australian buyout of Carling and the subsequent merger with Molson made Elders IXL and Molson equal partners in the Montreal company. In 1993 both sold 10 per cent of their interest to the giant Miller Brewing Company. Thus the Foster's Brewing Group, which also included the Courage Group, Britain's second largest brewer, had made a major strategic alliance to sell Molson's, Foster's and Miller beer in North America.

Despite this "multi-lagering" beer drinkers had other tastes. The Campaign for Real Ale, founded in Britain in 1971, was pushing for a more traditional approach to brewing and soon the demand for European-style beers "migrated" to Vancouver, particularly with the opening of neighborhood pubs. (The neighborhood pub concept was approved by the NDP government [1972–1975] and served to break the hotel industry's monopoly on the sale of draft beer.)

Today there are new kids on the block perpetuating an ancient tradition. Brew-pubs sell their own products; brew-it-yourself storefront breweries provide recipes and professional equipment; and several microbreweries are in business with listings at government liquor stores.

The latter range from the Bowen Island Brewing Company, the Horseshoe Bay Brewing Company and the Whistler Brewing Company (founded in 1989 and located at Function Junction in the tourist mecca), to the major micros—Granville Island Brewing and Shaftebury Brewing Company.

Local businessman Mitch Taylor opened the Granville Island brewery near the island's bustling marketplace in June, 1984, producing a premium, natural, unpasteurized Bavarian-style pilsner. Its success led to the production of more ales and beers, with a second brewery opening in Kelowna in 1994.

In 1987 two university students and part-time waiters, Paul Beaton and Timothy Wittig, decided to go into the specialty brewing business by producing British-style draft ales. When the first keg of their Shaftebury was tapped, Beaton was 22 years old and Wittig was 26. In 1994 their company was rated the eleventh fastest-growing company in B.C. The success of their ales, especially their cream ale, found them outgrowing their plant at 1973 Pandora Street; their new brewery opened in the Delta industrial park in November, 1995.

And so we see a poetic symmetry: about 100 years after the first small breweries opened in Vancouver, history is repeating itself.

During the past four decades since Labatt's arrival in the Lower Mainland, the company has not only produced beer but also played a key supporting role in amateur sporting and charity events such as the Labatt Brier and ski racing. Since 1979, the brewer has organized the Labatt 24 Hour Relay, a major fund-raiser with Vancouver's corporate community, which has raised millions of dollars for children with disabilities.

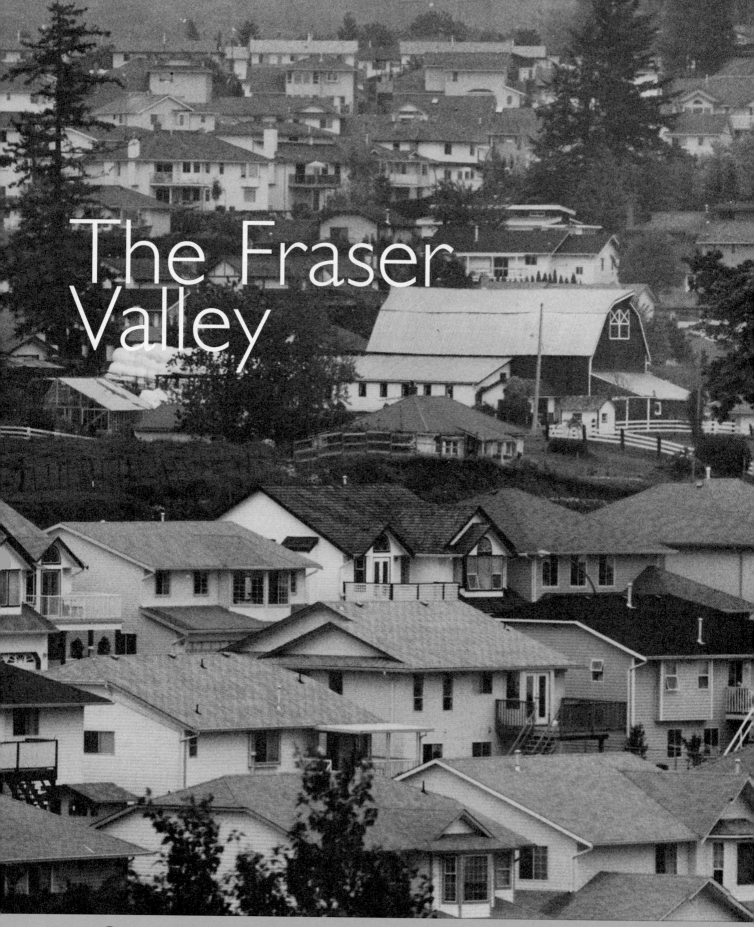

The Fraser Valley

Dairyworld
FOODS

In 1992 Fraser Valley Milk Producers Cooperative Association, better known as Dairyland, celebrated its 75th anniversary. Later that year it merged with two Alberta dairy cooperatives to form Agrifoods International Cooperative (Dairyworld Foods), one of the largest and most progressive food companies in Canada. In 1996, after consolidating, building and refining its operations, Dairyworld Foods merged with a dairy from Saskatchewan to form Canada's largest dairy cooperative and Western Canada's largest food company.

The Fraser Valley
Don Hunter

WHEN THE OREGON TREATY of 1846 awarded the United States undisputed possession of the Pacific Northwest territories south of the 49th parallel, the fur brigades of the Hudson's Bay Company needed fresh routes to the interior lands north of the new international border. Three years later the company began building Fort Hope. Less than a decade later an international army of men, burning with optimism and gold fever, would tramp through and drive their wagons and pack trains along its rutted streets. In 1858 the discovery of gold along the Fraser drew 25,000 prospectors to the scene, and more would arrive four years later on their way to the Cariboo gold fields. Fort Langley became a supply and jumping off point, with sidewheel paddle steamers transporting dreamers and their supplies through the treacherous sandbars as far as Fort Hope.

It is from the thriving town of Hope, where the Fraser River bursts free from the cliff walls of its canyon, that the lush Fraser Valley runs west over 160 kilometres to the Strait of Georgia. To the north of the river the valley reaches the feet of the towering Coast Mountains, to the south the American border.

Many of the gold-rush adventurers stayed and put down roots; many others who stayed with their families were men of the Royal Engineers, originally sent from Britain to build roads and bridges.

It is a rich, fruitful garden valley, producing annually millions of kilograms of vegetables, fruit, poultry and dairy products. Fully three-quarters of the province's dairy farmers live in the Fraser Valley, and the value of their output is approximately $200 million annually. Dairying, in fact, is the single largest contributor to the province's agricultural revenues. One of the great pleasures for Lower Mainland families each spring and summer is a trip to any of the many you-pick fields of strawberries and raspberries, where more than one farmer has considered weighing—in addition to the berry containers—crimson-mouthed and full-bellied children for comparison before and after the picking.

Travelling west on Highway 1 from Hope, the first major community is the Chilliwack-Sardis-Vedder area, with a population now well over 50,000, a largely rural and agricultural district, though changing as young families move away from the crowded city in search of affordable housing. Chilliwack was

facing page: Abbotsford, 1993 showing a traditional farm barn engulfed by new housing. vs

one of the first rural municipalities to be incorporated in British Columbia, in 1872, along with Langley, and one of the last to issue liquor licences. It is widely regarded as being the centre of the valley's so-called Bible Belt.

Dairy farms proliferate here, as do spring fields packed with hosts of golden daffodils, and in the late summer and early fall, row on marching row of incomparable Chilliwack corn. (Best way to enjoy it: Soak the cobs, silk, husks and all, in water for 30 minutes. Onto the barbecue on medium for about 20 minutes, turning every few minutes. Strip, butter, eat.)

Nearby Cultus Lake Provincial Park is a popular summer spot for camping and water sports. It was at this lakeside one day early this century that the great chief of the Chillwack people, Sepass, expressed his fears for the future of his tribe to the attentive Eloise Street, granddaughter of pioneer Methodist missionary Edward White, and asked her to record in writing the Chillwacks' myths and legends. Eloise and her mother spent the next four years in producing the Sepass Poems.

A few kilometres southeast of Chilliwack, in the Cascade Mountains, looms forbidding Mount Slesse, where on December 9, 1956, all 64 people aboard a Trans Canada Airlines North Star died when the plane slammed into the mountain. The dead included four members of the Saskatchewan Roughriders football team and one from the Winnipeg Bluebombers, heading home from a championship game in Vancouver. The plane remained hidden under deep snow, its disappearance a mystery for six months before the spring thaw revealed its presence. It was, at that time, the worst air crash in Canada's history, but government promises to dedicate the mountain as a permanent cemetery were abandoned until 1994, when families of the Slesse victims from around North America formed an organization and the B.C government responded with firm commitments.

Just east of Chilliwack, north of the river, are the villages of Agassiz and, a short drive on, Harrison Hot Springs. In a chilly late October in 1859 a canoe full of gold miners in search of a spot of rest and relaxation paddled toward the south end of Harrison Lake. The point man jumped into the shallows ready to pull the craft up onto the sand—and immediately flopped down into the water and entreated his companions to do the same. He had discovered the hot springs of Harrison, now a spa and vacation centre with a public pool and pools in a first class hotel offering the soaking pleasures of the natural mineral springs that still bubble up from the lake.

The Harrison-Agassiz area has a firm place in the storied history of the Sasquatch, or Bigfoot. Many reports of sightings and personal confrontations have come from the region, and

When Fraser Valley dairy farmers formed the Fraser Valley Milk Producers Association (predecessor to today's Dairyworld Foods) in 1913, they included some historic British Columbians, like John Oliver, who would go on to become premier, and W.J. Park, whose son and grandson would follow in his footsteps as leaders of the province's dairy industry. The Association, officially started in 1917, by 1922 had purchased its first dairy processing plant, and was on its way to becoming one of the leading food companies in Canada.

local native lore affirms belief in the mysterious creature's existence. One of the best-known researchers of the Sasquatch legend, John Green, lives in Harrison.

A short drive east of Agassiz, on Seabird Island, is one of the most architecturally impressive schools in British Columbia, the community school of the Sea Bird Island band of the Sto:lo ("people of the river") nation.

A traveller staying north of the river and heading west on Highway 7 (Lougheed Highway) would reach Harrison Mills, where the splendidly resurrected and re-created Kilby Historic Store and Farm, open from May to September, is a living history of pioneer life.

Continue west on the Lougheed and arrive at Mission, a town where much of the traditional economy has been based in the sawmills along the river and the tugboats scooting about on it. The town made its mark in history in September 1904, when the notorious but always courteous gentleman-bandit Bill Miner, 61, chose Silverdale, just west of the community, to stage Canada's first train robbery. He and his gang lifted $7,000 from the strongbox of the Canadian Pacific Railway's transcontinental and slipped away into the night, The event was recorded in the fine movie that echoed Miner's nickname—*The Grey Fox*.

If you pass by here on a Sunday there's a good chance you'll hear the pealing bells of the beautiful, serene Westminster Abbey, where Benedictine monks live and work on a 180-metre hilltop overlooking the Fraser. The abbey sits in 80 hectares of forest, lawns and garden, and conducts a seminary that includes a secondary school and a degree-granting arts and theological college. It is open to the public 1:30 to 4 P.M. Monday through Saturday and 2 P.M. to 4 P.M. on Sundays. The abbey, at 34224 Dewdney Trunk Road, will also accommodate groups, couples and singles seeking a retreat.

Farther west and north from Mission, in the wild country beyond the head of Pitt Lake, another character made his mark and left a legend that still tantalizes—the legend of Slumach's lost gold mine, and the curse laid on anyone trying to find it.

Slumach was a Katzie native who in the 1880s would appear intermittently in New Westminster looking for a good time and having the wherewithal, in the form of gold nuggets, to pay for it. Following each carousing, he would return to the mountains, each time taking with him a different and apparently amenable white woman—who would never again be seen alive. Molly Tynan was the ninth to leave with him. He was questioned when she was found later knifed to death, floating in the Fraser, but there was insufficient evidence for a charge. Slumach was hanged in 1841 for the murder of Louis Bee, whom he killed in a fight. He was said to have given a map of

his gold mine to a nephew—and to have warned that anyone trying to find his gold mine would die doing so. Versions of the map have turned up in various hands, and legend has it that more than 20 searchers have failed to return from that quest.

Directly south of Mission, back across the river, is Abbotsford, in recent years a town of exploding population growth and, since January 1, 1995, incorporating what was previously the separate district municipality of Matsqui. The town was named for Henry Abbott, a CPR superintendent.

Approaching Abbotsford, just off the highway that crosses through vast stretches of blueberry and dairy farms, sits the tiny village of Clayburn, named for the brick-making factory that supported the area in the early 1900s. The village and factory were built by Charles Maclure, brother of the renowned architect, Samuel, who transported the rare white clay from nearby Sumas Mountain, using a narrow-gauge steam railway. The Vancouver Hotel and Victoria's Royal Jubilee Hospital were built of Clayburn bricks, which became famous and by 1909 were being produced at the rate of 30,000 a day. (A visitor to Roche Harbor on Washington's San Juan Island will note that almost every other brick on the hotel walkways is marked Clayburn.)

The restored Clayburn Village Store retains the atmosphere of those early days when it sold everything from soap and sugar, to longjohns and life insurance, and when the back room was also the barbershop. Built in 1912 to service the brickworks employees, it is believed to have been the first "company store" in the province and has been lovingly restored, with many museum pieces, by the Haber family, who would like to see it again become the heart of the community it once was. The village sits in the shadow of the western slopes of Sumas Mountain, where new subdivisions now spread daily.

Had the residents of these new developments been there on two earlier occasions in the valley's history, they could have looked down on a river gone mad.

The first great flood experienced by white settlers happened in 1894. Heavy snow held in the grip of a cold winter suddenly thawed in an unusually warm spring, and at the end of May the Fraser rose like an angry beast, splintering and swallowing bridges in the canyon before rushing out and sweeping away houses, livestock, and stretches of railway track as it started down the valley. Thousands of farmland hectares were inundated. Families took to their rooftops, from where they were rescued and taken to higher ground. In Chilliwack, residents paddled canoes to church and tied the craft to pews while they prayed. In Fort Langley, determined clients tied their boats to the doors of the town's two hotels. When the waters subsided,

The Fraser Valley produces some of the best dairy products in the world. This is no idle claim—in 1994 Armstrong cheese, manufactured at Dairyworld Foods plant in Abbotsford, was named best cheddar in the world at the prestigious World Championship Cheese Competition in Green Bay, Wisconsin, outpointing entries from the top cheesemaking countries on the globe. And Fraser Valley milk also goes into the manufacture of a full range of ice cream products under highly respected brand names like Dairyland, Legend and Legend Sensation.

the citizens of Mission moved their whole settlement to high-er ground—a move for which their descendants no doubt were grateful 54 years later.

On the late May holiday weekend of 1948 the same conditions in the mountains prevailed after a winter of heavy snow. On May 18 the temperature leaped to over 26°C from under 3°C the previous day. By May 23 the Mission gauge showed the level just 1.5 metres lower than the high-water mark of 1894. In the pre-dawn hours of the next morning, the river breached its banks. In the days that followed, Agassiz was swamped and, farther down the river, so was Matsqui and thousands of hectares of farmland. A state of emergency was proclaimed as road and rail connections to the rest of Canada were severed. Up and down the river thousands of citizens and more than 3,000 troops labored together, filling sandbags, dumping gravel, transporting livestock, whatever it took to hold back the raging waters. When it was over, damage was estimated at almost $20 million, 10 people had died, and nearly 17,000 had had to flee their homes. More than 20,000 hectares of prime farm land was under water. The federal government helped with reclamation and repairs, and the Fraser's dykes received serious attention. Today mountain snow packs and the Mission gauge are monitored very closely each spring.

The fast-growing 233 sq. kilometre Abbotsford area, reaching south from the Fraser to the U.S. border, has a population in excess of 100,000 (estimated to be 173,000 by 2011). With one of the mildest climates in Canada, the area is at the heart of the valley's farming production, as well as being the home of an assortment of light industry.

The annual International Abbotsford Air Show draws as many as 300,000 spectators over three days in August. Every second year it includes an air trade show held in the vast Tradex complex, where the more than 11,000 sq. metres of exhibition floor space is the second biggest in the province.

Abbotsford is home to the main campus (of three) of the University College of the Fraser Valley, which has blossomed from a small community college into degree-granting status in recent years, providing valley students with welcome and increasing alternatives to the two bigger Lower Mainland universities. The school districts of Abbotsford and Mission have introduced ground-breaking programs involving the presence as counsellor-teachers in some secondary schools of selected inmates from the minimum-security Ferndale Institution, one of several prisons in the central valley.

On several weekends between spring and fall the Abbotsford-Aldergrove area is host to fascinating sight-hound, lure-coursing meets, where owners of a dozen types of purebred hounds from basenjis to afghans and whippets "slip" their dogs to chase a mechanical lure in a dazzling test of speed and agility.

Aldergrove, straddling the Fraser Highway, is a pleasant village whose residents consider it an entity to itself, although for municipal purposes it sits partly in Abbotsford and partly in Langley, the next district west. North of the village, the sight of elephants almost on the sidewalk announces the Greater Vancouver Zoological Centre on 264th Street. The complex draws more than 400,000 visitors a year to its 24 hectares and 115 animal species.

There are two Langleys—the City (10 sq. kilometres) and the surrounding Township (303 sq. kilometres) with a combined and growing total population of more than 100,000. The area is a comfortable blend of urban and rural life, with a busy airport and a city-sized mall.

Langley especially is horse country, with virtually every turn in the road presenting views of broad meadows occupied by sleek, muscled and pampered thoroughbreds and standardbreds in training for careers at any of dozens of racetracks in North America, including Vancouver's own Hastings Park. Equestrian centres abound, such as the Milner Downs Centre near Glover Road and 64th Avenue, where much of the TV series *The Adventures of the Black Stallion,* starring Mickey Rooney and young local actor Richard Cox, was shot. And there's the very special Pacific Riding for Disabled Centre, an almost wholly volunteer-run stable where people including those with the most profound disabilities enjoy the pleasures and therapy of riding. The Langley horse population is estimated at almost 7,000, and the industry is valued at $40 million annually.

Unique to Langley's agricultural base is the valley's only estate winery, Domaine de Chaberton Estate, on 216th Street, and, yes, they do have tastings.

Langley recently gained its second degree-granting campus in Kwantlen University College. Trinity Western University, which began in 1962 as a junior college and was upgraded to university status in 1985, stresses education in a Christian context.

The Township includes the village of Fort Langley, established by the Hudson's Bay Company in 1827 and named for a company director. The settlement became a vital economic and administrative centre for a developing British Columbia. Local native bands, drawn by the chance to trade salmon and sturgeon for tools and weapons, established permanent camp sites around the fort and were allowed inside the walls by day but sent out at nightfall. Interracial marriages were common and the first child of mixed blood, born to the native wife of a fort employee, on July 2, 1828, was named Louis Langley. Sir James Douglas, who

What really tells the tale of the Fraser Valley are the kilometres of dairy fields on every side. This is dairy country, and has been for more than a century. Settled by European (predominantly Dutch) immigrants in the late 1800s, the rich soil and agreeable climate of the valley proved ideal. These early families farmed their land the hard, old-fashioned way: milking the cows by hand and delivering the milk to the coast in horse-drawn wagons, ten-gallon cans sloshing about precariously in the back.

Chilliwack, 1873. cva

rose from company clerk to chief factor and eventually to governor and "father" of British Columbia, was married to Lady Amelia Douglas, herself of mixed native-white blood.

The fort was the rendezvous each July for the voyageurs who swept downstream, firing their rifles into the air, their bateaux weighed down with furs. Their arrival was the signal for the distribution of extra rum rations and the beginning of days and nights of raucous partying, dancing and general debauchery. Each year in August the arrival of the voyageurs is re-created for the pleasure of thousands of tourists. And every November 19, the anniversary of the day in 1858 when Queen Victoria proclaimed British Columbia a Crown colony, the province's premier and cabinet turn up in Fort Langley to watch "Sir James Douglas" being sworn in as governor.

The fort, now restored and looking down on the great river, remains a historic site popular with tourists and school groups. The village itself retains heritage character in the shops, homes and restaurants along Glover Road, its main street. At the north end of the village the provincial transportation ministry's *Albion* ferry runs 24 hours a day on the five-minute run across the Fraser to link up with the Lougheed Highway, which going west runs through Maple Ridge and Pitt Meadows, into the suburbs and City of Vancouver.

In 1910 a record time of two hours and 10 minutes was set for the drive (no roads as such, much axle-deep mud and water) from Chilliwack to New Westminster. On a Friday afternoon rush hour on Highway 1 today, it is tempting to contemplate the matter of progress.

Dairyworld Foods markets a complete line of dairy and related food products across Western Canada, with emerging markets in the Asia Pacific region, the United States and beyond. Today the Dairyland brand can be found from Vancouver Island to Toronto. Dairyworld Foods is becoming a global organization in a global food industry. At heart, however, it is still a dairy cooperative, owned and guided by the Fraser Valley's almost 500 cooperative farmers who still till the land and milk the cows.

Consumer Services
Marlaina Gayle

WHERE HAVE ALL the consumer activists gone? In the past 20 years Canada's and B.C.'s consumer movement has soared, stalled, split apart and now virtually faded away. While consumers increasingly find they are on their own when it comes to fighting the marketplace, they are also finding that if they can get together they are a powerful force.

Consumers (who are taxpayers, too) have no presence at the federal cabinet table. The federal department of consumer and corporate affairs has been swallowed up by Industry Canada and hidden among several bureaucracies.

In B.C. the consumer movement has fallen from government grace since the 1973 NDP government decided consumers were an important part of the financial equation. After having been buried inside the ministry of labor, consumers were tucked (by former NDP premier Mike Harcourt) into the ministry of housing, recreation and consumer services. Today's minister blames the low profile of consumer services on a lack of money.

The B.C. branch of the Consumers Association of Canada lost its funding in the mid-eighties. For years they lived on their savings and turned to charity casinos to keep their telephone mediation line alive. President Evelyn Fox, who has 20 years experience in the consumer mediation and investigation field, says more public consumer education is needed. "Consumers don't know their rights," says Fox. She says the provincial government doesn't always enforce its legislation and when it does it fails to tell consumers what the ministry has accomplished.

The Better Business Bureau of mainland B.C. is taking almost 500,00 consumer calls a year. General manager Valerie MacLean also complains there is no information sharing between the government and private agencies to warn consumers.

What are today's scams? Eerily the same as yesterday's scams updated by technology—telephones, fax machines and now the Internet. The B.C. government named telemarketing ripoffs as the number one consumer scam of 1994. Consumers are conned into buying junk by the promise of fabulous prizes.

There's a national task force mostly sponsored by Ontario to fight telemarketing scams, which mainly originate out of Montreal. Project Phonebusters' detective Barry Elliot says telephone fraud needs a concentrated, national approach. But most provinces including B.C. complain they are cash-strapped, choosing to let their constituents and the legitimate economy lose millions of dollars. But technology will also change the marketplace for the better. Through the Internet consumers will no longer be isolated in their complaints. They will be able to get first-hand buying information from like-minded consumers.

In the meantime too many British Columbians don't know the rules of the road. No law entitles a customer to a cash refund. All transactions are contracts. It's a customer service issue whether a merchant gives a refund, unless the product is defective. The Sale of Goods act says a merchant must replace the defective item, repair the item or refund the cost of the item. The merchant can choose the option.

There is no blanket cooling-off period on consumer purchases. But a seven day cooling-off period does apply to contracts of more than $50 signed in the home or away from the merchant's regular place of business and contracts for fitness studios, health spas and dance studios.

The greatest consumer myth of all is that consumers are entitled to a return of their deposit if they change their mind. A deposit encourages a retailer to order an item or prevent him from selling the item. If you change your mind the retailer may get damages for a lost sale. Only put down as much as you are prepared to lose.

Cases under $10,000 are heard in small-claims court. It costs $50 to launch a case valued at less than $5,000 and $100 for a case valued at more than $5,000. Despite the Consumer Protection act and the Trade Practices act, consumers should not expect the government to go to court on their behalf. The provincial government prefers to get restitution rather than police the marketplace.

The old consumer rules apply even more today in our fast paced, computer-driven marketplace: don't do anything in a rush. If the deal sounds too good to be true, it usually is. Buyer beware.

(The B.C. government's Consumer Investigations branch is at 660-3570. Industry Canada which deals with consumer issues involving labelling, packaging, textiles and precious metals is at 666-5000. Health Canada deals with product safety issues at 666-3350. Concerns about marketing practices, including advertising and pyramid schemes, can be voiced at 1-800-348-5358. The Consumers Association of Canada is at 682-3535. The Chinese Consumers Association of Vancouver is at 689-1218. Environmentally Sound Packaging Coalition deals with the consumer and the environment at 689-3770.)

Advertising
Michael McCullough

THE HISTORY OF advertising in Vancouver mirrors that of advertising in general—appearing as a profession around the turn of the century, growing first with print and then radio and television, peaking creatively and economically in the 1960s and 1970s and then succumbing to leaner times and the diversification of marketing media.

Companies that posted and otherwise distributed handbills appeared in Vancouver as early as 1893, but the first advertising agency in the modern sense—that is, offering media buying and creative and account services—was the Noble Advertising Agency founded around 1907. By that time there were also a handful of independent copywriters in the city as well as single-medium ad agencies such as Dominion Publishing and the Pacific Railways Advertising Company.

By the 1920s there were about 15 advertising agencies in the city, including Benwell Curran Atkins, which survives as the printing company Benwell Atkins, and Neon Products of Western Canada, then as now (under the name of Seaboard Advertising) the largest billboard firm in British Columbia. A handful of companies provided direct-mail services. There was even an agency specializing in movie trailers called Motion Skreenadz Limited.

Briefly merging with Burgess Advertising of Victoria, Crawford-Harris Advertising Service became the first Vancouver agency to boast a branch office. But established eastern firms had similar designs on Vancouver. McKim Advertising, Canada's oldest agency, set up a local office in 1926 and another Montreal-based agency, Cockfield, Brown & Company, appeared in 1930. Toronto's MacLaren Advertising arrived within the next decade and New York-based J. Walter Thompson followed in 1956.

Much of the business was still handled by either media outlets—newpapers mostly—or by the clients themselves: retailers, utilities and consumer products manufacturers. Spencer's department store, for example, had both its own advertising department and its own direct-mail advertising department as far back as the 1920s. It was there that Harold Merilees, Vancouver's first great ad man, got his start in 1925. Merilees moved on to the B.C. Electric Railway Company in 1931 and eventually became the firm's manager of public information. During World War II he was loaned to the National War Finance Committee to promote sales of Victory Bonds and combat absenteeism on the home front. In 1950 Merilees was elected

Billboards on Granville Street, 1972. vs

president of the Advertising Association of the West, a federation of 47 advertising clubs in 14 western states and provinces. He would devote his skills to public projects such as Vancouver's diamond jubilee celebrations in 1946, the British Empire Games in 1954 and the B.C. centennial in 1958. In 1962 as head of the Vancouver Tourist Association (precursor to Tourism Vancouver) he founded the Sea Festival. In 1969 he was elected as the Social Credit MLA for Vancouver-Burrard. He died in office in 1972.

Born in East Vancouver in 1909, just a few months after Merilees, was Jimmy Lovick, the true giant of Vancouver ad men. Lovick started his career teaching grade school on Annacis Island before joining the J.J. Gibbons agency at the age of 25. He later teamed up with V.L. (Pinky) Stewart to form Stewart Lovick. In 1948 he struck out on his own, boldly opening James Lovick & Company offices in Vancouver, Calgary, Toronto and Montreal. By 1958 James Lovick & Company was the largest agency in Canada, with additional offices in Edmonton, London (Ontario), Halifax, New York and San Francisco, not to mention its own custom-built headquarters at 1178 West Pender Street. The building still stands, now dwarfed by its neighbors.

Lovick himself seemed to live on airplanes, becoming the first customer of Trans-Canada Airways to log a million air miles. He captured national accounts that included Kelly Douglas (which owned the Super-Valu chain of supermarkets and Nabob Foods) and Nelson Laundries. He parlayed his Social Credit Party connections into major provincial government contracts. Lovick once flew to Toronto to pitch the Toronto-

As the legend goes, young Frank Palmer, in the early days of his fledgling agency, was talking to a very big client. Someone else's client. The client's new store opening, with radio station remote on site, had promised free hot dogs. The hot dogs didn't arrive. The client called his agency who told him, "We don't do hot dogs." Without missing a beat, Frank replied, "We do hot dogs." The next day, Palmer Jarvis had the very big account.

Dominion Bank account. In the middle of an Ontario snowstorm, wearing only his pinstripe suit, he drove down Bay Street in a rented convertible with the top down. Launching into his presentation to the bank's brass, he took off his trousers, opened a window and threw the pants out, trying to impress upon the bankers the need to change their pin-striped image. It worked. The agency from the ad world's wilderness won the Toronto-Dominion, of all accounts.

Unfortunately the agency could not long survive its founder's death in 1968. Two years later the head office moved to Calgary, then Toronto when it merged with Baker Advertising to form Baker Lovick. By the mid-1970s New York-based BBDO became BL's largest shareholder. In 1992 BBDO bought McKim and merged it with BL, creating the largest agency Canada had ever seen with billings in excess of half-a-billion dollars. BBDO's Vancouver office survives as one of the premier agencies in town, holding among others the coveted B.C. Telephone account.

Vancouver's chief contribution to today's multinational advertising industry began with the apprenticeship of Frank Anfield who came to the city in the 1960s to work in Nabob's marketing department. He would go on to manage the Vancouver office of McKim through the 1970s and early 1980s and, after a nine-year stint in Toronto, rise to the presidency of Young & Rubicam, one of the world's largest advertising agency networks, in New York in 1992.

Anfield's tenure in Vancouver would be fondly remembered as the golden age of advertising, a time when budgets were fat, staffs were big and creative departments had a free hand. The real business went on in the Hotel Vancouver's Timber Room over two-dollar double martinis served in a beaker. Ted Bethune of Cockfield, Brown reigned as the city's pre-eminent creative mind, winning international awards for his billboards for Babco Paint.

It was still pretty much a young man's game. One of the Lovick agency's best-remembered jingles sang the praises of "The girl at checkout number three." Only in the late 1970s, as women began appearing in their clients' brand manager positions, did agencies begin to hire women as more than support staff. The first to make her mark was Cassandra Gwilliam, a copywriter at McKim who penned the "Super, Natural British Columbia" tag line used by the provincial ministry of tourism to this day.

As the seventies became the eighties, however, a number of shocks hit the industry. The art of advertising was giving way to the science of marketing. Pollsters and market researchers proliferated and creative personnel could no longer base campaigns on their hunches. Agencies had to be accountable; campaigns had to produce results. The recession of the early 1980s hit Vancouver especially hard and major national accounts, including CP Air, IKEA Canada and Bridgestone Tires, left the city for Toronto and Calgary. The trend would continue right up to 1995 with the departure of Scott Paper. Other major advertisers, such as Eaton's and The Bay, took their advertising business in-house while Woodward's went bankrupt. The once huge Kelly Douglas account simply dried up as the company got out of the retail business.

As in Toronto, where the bulk of the Canadian advertising industry resides, most of the larger agencies were bought by multinational companies such as McCann-Erickson, Scali McCabe Sloves, Grey Advertising, FCB Communications and BBDO. Unlike Toronto the trend here has reversed somewhat in the 1990s, leaving all but a few agencies in the hands of Vancouverites once again.

In fact the single greatest success story of the last, leanest, 15 years has been locally owned Palmer Jarvis Communications. Formed as Trend Advertising by freelance art director Frank Palmer and Simons Advertising's Rich Simons in 1969, it welcomed radio man George Jarvis in the early 1970s and gradually built a roster of heavyweight accounts including Safeway Canada and McDonald's Restaurants of Western Canada. Surviving Woodward's collapse PJ became in 1995 the first Vancouver agency to bill $100 million. It remains the only Vancouver agency to boast several national accounts such as Clearly Canadian, Safeway Canada, Investors' Group and Health Canada.

Palmer Jarvis and other agencies that survived and prospered in this tight-belted environment increasingly offered "a la carte" services on a fee basis instead of the traditional 15 per cent commission. Meanwhile "boutique" agencies such as Glennie Stamnes Strategy, Ken Koo Creative Group, Lanyon Phillips Brink and Moreland & Associates came to challenge the big shops with their stripped-down, idea-centred approach. Palmer Jarvis vice-president Ron Woodall who masterminded much of the design of Expo 86 and former McKim copywriter Alvin Wasserman, now president of Wasserman & Partners, reign as the city's senior creative minds.

The advertising industry continues to fight a losing battle with competing forms of marketing, such as direct marketing, telemarketing, public relations, special events, database marketing and the new interactive media. Marketing consultants, PR firms, event promoters and in-house marketing departments prosper at the expense of old-fashioned ad agencies. But the memory of Jimmy Lovick and his convertible remains.

In advertising vernacular "we don't do hot dogs" means an agency accepts only prestigious high end work like national magazine ads and television commercials. Conversely, Palmer Jarvis has diversified into a complex of specialized, wholly-owned resource divisions capable of quickly providing virtually any client need. To this day, on Friday afternoons, Palmer does hot dogs when the entire PJ staff meet at the big hot dog machine in the creative department for "Frank's Franks".

Tourism

IT COMES AS no surprise that tourism is on a roll in Vancouver. Accented with a cityscape that blends architectural feats like the soaring five sails of Canada Place, towering skyscrapers and an eclectic mix of ethnic neighborhoods, the city scene complements Mother Nature's best. One can't help but marvel at the foresight of the city's forefathers back in 1886 when their first resolution was to purchase 405 hectares and declare it a park. Surely they had tourism on their minds. Today, Stanley Park is Canada's largest city park and a famous landmark. More than one international traveller has recalled Vancouver to me as "the city with the wonderful park in the middle."

Expo 86 was the turning point. Not only did the world's fair attendance surpass expectations—13 to 15 million visitors were projected and more than 20 million came—but visitors fell in love with the city. The love affair has continued. Today tourism is Greater Vancouver's largest industry, generating an overall economic impact of $3.52 billion, creating $800 million in tax revenues and supporting over 62,300 jobs. (In the province, tourism ranks second only to softwood lumber and pulp exports. Revenues have increased an average of four per cent over the last four years.)

What brings them? A city that bustles with kinetic energy and thrives on this energy, a city where people are the focal point whether they arrive on a cruise ship for a day's tour or book into a five-diamond hotel and "do the works" from Stanley Park to the Museum of Anthropology. Thanks to a mosaic of cultures, visitors are invited to imbibe in culinary feasts (from Thai to East Indian to Chinese and Greek, we have it all) and to participate in colorful events such as the International Dragon Boat Festival. Vancouver grabs attention, first with its dramatic setting then with its western hospitality. Our casual, West Coast lifestyle lends itself to a cheerful service industry where nothing is too much trouble. Most downtown hotels offer babysitting, can arrange dog walking and are adept at problem-solving. At the Waterfront Centre Hotel a concierge had a guest's pearls restrung in record time.

A good part of Vancouver's appeal is the meld of nature and commercial attractions. It has become a cliche that you can sail and ski in one day; you can also meander through an old growth forest, visit Science World, browse designer shops, take in an internationally acclaimed production at the Ford Centre for the Performing Arts and dine in an elegant restaurant in one day. Granted, a very busy day—but it is possible.

A Vancouver visitor will not soon forget a boat cruise into Indian Arm, a friendly coffee bar on Robson Street, a stroll on the seawall, or a perfect sunset on English Bay. Tourism will continue as a juggernaut because Vancouver, once discovered, is truly unforgettable.

—Judi Lees

facing page: Doorman, Hotel Vancouver, 1994. vs
above: The cruise ship Fair Princess, docked at Ballantyne Pier, 1993. vp

Visitor Attractions

Tourism Vancouver, established in 1904, is a non-profit association of 1,200 members working to promote Greater Vancouver in targeted markets worldwide. The tourism association creates opportunities for members and the community to share in the economic, environmental, social and cultural benefits that tourism brings. Tourism Vancouver's vibrant sectors include accommodation, transportation, tourist attractions, convention facilities/services, retailers, dining/night life, performing arts/events and the maritime industry.

Visitor Attractions in Greater Vancouver
Tom Poiker

For the last half century, when world travellers have been invited to name the most beautiful cities in the world, Vancouver has been among the top three. Still, about half of the top visitor attractions in Greater Vancouver were created within the last 25 years! Today, when asked for attractive places, we think not only about mountains, ocean and lakes, but also about trees and gardens, colorful streets and modern buildings, parks and beaches, good restaurants and interesting theatres, festivals, runs and parades.

This is certainly not an exhaustive list. There is too much going on in this corner of British Columbia! And, an important note: addresses and phone numbers change, so we've left them out. A call to Tourism Vancouver will get you information on any or all of these attractions.

Abbotsford Air Show On two weekends in August, the community of Abbotsford east of Vancouver swings into action. The first weekend provides hot-air balloon rides, model airplane contests, kite contests, etc. The second weekend is the one everybody talks about: the largest airshow in North America with the Biggest, the Fastest, the Loudest and the Bravest. Nothing beats the spectacle as Canada, the U.S., Britain, Russia and others put their newest aircraft through their paces. Abbotsford isn't really in Greater Vancouver, but most of the people coming here are from the Lower Mainland.

Ambleside Park A favorite beach-walking area with views of downtown Vancouver, Stanley Park and the Lions Gate Bridge, sailboats, freighters and tugboats . . . and occasionally the tourist-beloved Royal Hudson, the only steam locomotive in service in Canada. There are playing fields, a pavilion and concessions at the park.

Aquarium See article on Vancouver Aquarium

B.C. Place Stadium opened in 1983 as the world's largest air-supported Dome. With 60,000 seats it hosts the B.C. Lions CFL football team (from July to November), as well as major concerts, trade shows and other large gatherings. It was in this enormous building Queen Elizabeth II invited the world to Expo 86. The "Three Tenors" concert (Pavarotti, Domingo, Carreras) took place at B.C. Place December 31, 1996. The BC Sports Hall of Fame and Museum is housed within this giant structure. The Hall is dedicated to honoring the province's athletes,

facing page: Edwardian tourists on the Capilano Suspension Bridge, c 1905. cva

teams and builders. Hands-on displays and touch-screen computers show the lives and accomplishments of B.C.'s top sportsmen and women. The stadium neighborhood has experienced a boom of new buildings with General Motors Place next door (home to the NHL Vancouver Canucks and the NBA Vancouver Grizzlies), with the big new Vancouver Public Library and the Ford Centre for the Performing Arts a couple of blocks away.

B.C. Sugar Museum The company began in 1891, and displays here show interesting old sugar-processing machinery (some of it going back to the 18th century), advertisements, packaging and much else. Fascinating and free.

Britannia Beach Home of the B.C. Museum of Mining, open late May to early October.

Buddhist Temple The new wave of Chinese immigrants has taken a liking to Richmond where a large number of new immigrants have settled. Testimony of their commercial activity is the Aberdeen Shopping Centre. Their most impressive artistic symbol is the Buddhist Temple on Steveston Highway, a classic example of traditional Chinese architecture. Take your shoes off when you walk into the temple.

Burnaby Lake is a large, shallow lake, surrounded by wetland. A rowing pavilion, an equestrian centre, picnic areas and many kilometres of walking trails provide many activities. There is an abundance of wildlife, especially waterbirds. It is said there are more beavers in this lake than anywhere else in southwestern B.C.

Burnaby Mountain Park To the west of Simon Fraser University, the park slopes down to the suburb of Burnaby. It offers a splendid view of downtown and the Islands through the Playground of the Gods, a monument for Japanese-Canadian friendship, and of Indian Arm to the north. There is a rose garden, some interesting totem poles and a restaurant. Kids: it doesn't snow very often in Vancouver but when it does, this is the best sliding place in town, on anything from cardboards to high-tech toboggans.

Burnaby Village Deer Lake Park contains a multitude of attractions besides those of a city park on a lake. There is the Burnaby Village Museum, a turn-of-the-century village with real people at work in traditional trades, like blacksmithing; the Burnaby Art Gallery, housed in Ceperley Mansion, a stately old home; an arts centre; a theatre complex; a large garden, and a big, splendid vintage carousel with 36 wooden horses and a pony-drawn chariot. A place to come back to again and again. April to October 1st and December.

CN IMAX Theatre A five-storey-high screen in the Canada Place complex has regular showings of spectacular IMAX movies . . . taking

you out into space or right into a beaver's underwater home.

Canada Place was built as the Canadian contribution to Expo 86, the hugely successful world's fair held in Vancouver in 1986 (21 million visits.) It looks like a great ship with the Pan Pacific Hotel as the stack and the Vancouver Trade and Convention Centre under the sails. There is a public promenade around Canada Place that gives an excellent view of the Port of Vancouver, with many explanatory plaques.

Canadian Craft Museum A small gem of a building, and displays of highest-quality crafts. Even if you don't buy (the gift shop is pricey, as the best often is) you'll find this a visually rewarding experience.

Canadian Museum of Flight and Transportation At Langley Airport, a "walkman" tour takes you past a fascinating array of dozens of aircraft "from World War I through the jet age."

Capilano Suspension Bridge is the ultimate tourist attraction: wilderness a few minutes from downtown, the hair-raising sense of danger when you walk 70 meters (more than 200 feet) above the yawning chasm of the Capilano River on a 450-foot-long bridge that seems to respond to every step you make, photo stops, a souvenir shop, teahouse, native carving displays, etc. You can take fantastic photos to show the folks back home. The sheer granite cliffs of the Capilano Canyon were carved out more than a hundred centuries ago by natural water courses left behind by glacial action. The first version of the bridge went in in 1889. Nearby is the Capilano Fish Hatchery with excellent glass-windowed displays of the life cycle of the Pacific salmon. You look right into the river to see the living fish.

Chinatown in Vancouver is a visitor must. The third largest in North America (after San Francisco and New York City), it's located along several blocks of Pender Street, with more shops and restaurants on Keefer, one block away, and along Main Street. Chinatown is the centre of the old Chinese shopping and restaurant district. The scene of violent racism a century ago, Chinatown is now one of the city's liveliest areas for locals and tourists alike. Heritage buildings give the area a unique character of early century Chinese architecture, restaurants and specialty shops.

Cloverdale Rodeo Second in size only to the Calgary Stampede, this May event brings calf roping, bronco busting, bull throwing and more with cowboys from all around North America.

Cypress Provincial Park Walking up-up-up from Lighthouse Park will eventually get you to the top at Cypress Park. Driving up the mountain might be easier, and both routes give you sweeping views of Vancouver and the Islands. At the

Accommodation Vancouver was the first North American city to be awarded three five-diamond-rated hotels. New major hotels grace Vancouver's sleek skyline. Spectacular views, service and locations attract visitors to more than 15,000 rooms citywide. Visitors can choose from luxurious penthouse suites to more budget-conscious hotel, motel and hostel accommodation. Bed and Breakfast registries offer cozy family settings. Riverside RV sites are minutes from downtown.

Park you'll find an intricate network of trails for hiking, trails which turn into ski trails—both downhill and cross-country—in the winter.

English Bay beach stretches from the Vancouver Aquatic Centre to Stanley Park, offering something for everyone throughout the year: sunbathing in summer; kayak rentals; walking in the winter; watching the sun set over the freighters; an international fireworks competition during summer festival . . . and on New Year's Day, hundreds of foolhardy locals jump into the chilly water for the decades-long tradition of the Polar Bear Swim. English Bay gets its name because Capt. George Vancouver moored his ships here in 1792 while exploring local waters (like Burrard Inlet) at closer range. Watch for flying Frisbees, roller-bladers, joggers, skateboarders, cyclists, and elderly strollers!

Fantasy Garden World A Disneyish attraction in Richmond with gardens, rides, a miniature train, a "castle" from Coeverden, Holland and an Olde World Village. (Coeverden was home to George Vancouver's ancestors. His father was John Jasper van Coeverden.)

Fort Langley Where British Columbia began. A restored version of the third fort (shortly after the fort moved to this site in 1839 it burned down, and had to be rebuilt), active from mid-May to the end of October. Historic buildings and authentically costumed staff take you back to the 1850s, and there are demonstrations by artisans of old-time skills like blacksmithing. The Langley Centennial Museum and the B.C. Farm Machinery and Agricultural Museum are nearby.

Fraser Downs There's a certain charm to harness racing, and this handsome little park is the place to enjoy it. October to April. For flat racing, see the Hastings Park entry.

Gastown is where Vancouver started. This area might have ended as the local Skid Road with old warehouses and seedy hotels, had it not experienced a complete recovery and heritage-style Victorian renovation in the early 1970s, an initiative of Vancouver's Community Arts Council. The street is cobblestoned and bordered by young maple trees and antique street lamps. There are art galleries, souvenir shops, fine furniture stores, and a variety of restaurants and bars. Step into oddly-named side streets like Gaoler's Mews and Blood Alley, and admire the "flat-iron" architecture of the Europe Hotel. Don't miss the famous Gastown Steam Clock, likely the single most photographed object in Greater Vancouver, that pipes a tune every quarter of an hour. Gastown, by the way, was so nicknamed because of an early (1867 and on) saloon keeper, John Deighton, who talked so much he was called "Gassy Jack." Early Vancouver grew around his saloon. The famous statue of Gassy at Carrall

and Water Streets is a product of sculptor Vern Simpson's imagination: nobody knows what the famed saloon keeper looked like (except for a contemporary's description of him as having a "muddy purple" complexion). A photograph of a portly fellow with a beard was plucked at random from a pile of ancient photos by 1970s developers as someone who "looks as if he could be a Gassy Jack."

General Motors Place Guided tours of this newest of the city's sports halls are available. The NHL's Vancouver Canucks and the NBA's Vancouver Grizzlies play here.

Granville Island was once a dilapidated and ugly industrial region in the middle of Vancouver. But, thanks to an imaginative federal government scheme (who would have guessed?) the island—which was originally nothing more than a sandbar that disappeared at high tide, then was built up with silt taken from elsewhere—has been transformed since 1973 into a mecca for shopping and cultural activities. A caution: parking is sometimes virtually impossible. We recommend coming by foot, public transit, bike, taxi or ferry. (A fleet of stubby little Granville Island Ferries brings people over from the south foot of Hornby Street.) The heart of the Island—or perhaps we should say the stomach—is the big, always crowded, Public Market with dozens of stands selling fresh vegetables, meat, fish and the like, and lots of booths selling ready-to-eat goodies. The Market is surrounded by four dozen small shops for food, clothing, art, boating supplies, etc. Look for the unique Kids Only Market. There's a hotel, pubs, restaurants, bistros. Granville Island is also the seat for several theatre groups, making Vancouver one of the most interesting Canadian centres for the performing arts. Another tenant: the Emily Carr Institute of Art and Design, Vancouver's leading art school.

Grouse Mountain Should we call it urban skiing? You never get away from the view of the city and the inlet. It's like taking off from the slopes and flying over the town. A popular spot for local skiers for decades. You could have dinner at famed Grouse Nest with an unsurpassed view 1,100 meters (about 3,600 feet) above town. Or you could just go to a lookout and look over the city for a place to have dinner after a long walk. The famous gondolas lift you to mountaintop in six minutes, and when the skies are clear the views are jaw-dropping. Horse-drawn wagons are a visitor favorite. (The horses come up in the gondolas, too.) Grouse's Theatre In The Sky shows locally-themed videos.

Harbour Centre is one of the more interesting modern buildings in Vancouver, as if a flying saucer had landed on top of a high-rise. The two highest levels are an observation deck, called The

The Sam Kee Building, built in 1913 in Chinatown, "The Thinnest Commercial Building in the World", 1992. rw

Lookout, and a revolving restaurant called Top of Vancouver. The restaurant rotates 360 degrees in an hour. The Lookout has knowledgeable young guides and lots of plaques describing distant buildings and landmarks. You glide to the top of this 167-metre-high building, tallest in the city, in 50 seconds in glass-walled elevators on the outside of the building. Take your friends out for lunch for a glorious, panoramic view of the city and its mountains. The first two storeys of Harbour Centre were donated to Simon Fraser University as its Downtown Campus, the venue of many high-tech conferences with superb technical installations.

Hastings Park Raceway Thoroughbred racing from early April to early November. A covered grandstand and genuinely good food. There's been racing here from 1889, and since 1961 all Lower Mainland flat racing has been concentrated at Hastings Park. (For harness racing, see the article on Fraser Downs.)

Irving House Captain William Irving had this house built in New Westminster in 1865, when it was still the capital of the mainland colony of British Columbia, and furnished it opulently. It's been lovingly maintained, and looks as if the Captain had just moved out. (One odd feature: a crack in the wall caused by a 1946 earthquake.)

Lighthouse Park The North Shore is an area of parks, from the coast to the tip of the moun-

Vancouver's innovative transportation systems are recognized globally. A $360 million airport terminal and runway at Vancouver International Airport opened in 1996. Amtrak rail service leaves daily for Seattle. The elevated SkyTrain makes Greater Vancouver travel a self-guided tour. The inner-harbor SeaBus connects the North Shore with downtown. The Westcoast Express commuter train is a Fraser Valley link. Visitors can also travel by bike, boat, bus, helicopter, floatplane and rollerblade or walk the seawalls.

tains. This is where the story (true) originated that, in summer, you can ski Whistler or Blackcomb Mountain in the morning and, on your way back to Vancouver, go for a swim in the ocean on one of the North Shore's beaches - and dine at a fine restaurant in the evening. Lighthouse Park is 75 hectares of the most original and most rugged of the North Shore's parks. Stunning views, and more than 60 bird species have been spotted here. Hikes through one of the few remaining original forests in Greater Vancouver end at Point Atkinson with its lighthouse. The lighthouse has been staffed without interruption since 1875, although a recent trend toward unmanned stations may have now put an end to that tradition.

Lonsdale Quay A handsome shopping, restaurant and food market complex at the foot of North Vancouver's Lonsdale Street. A big seafood restaurant in the area was once a working ferry on the inlet. The SeaBus, which crosses Burrard Inlet every few minutes, docks here.

Lynn Canyon Park Lynn Canyon's Suspension Bridge, built in 1912, is 50 metres above scenic Lynn Creek, and it's free. There is a very pleasant Nature Walk through 250-hectare Lynn Canyon Park, past deep water pools. It starts with a fine introduction at the small Ecology Centre (interactive displays and educational programs), near the bridge. Scattered here and there throughout the park, the stumps of once-mighty forest giants, some with loggers' springboard notches still visible. The park began with a 12-acre donation of land by the logging McTavish brothers. For hardier hikers, Lynn Headwaters Regional Park beckons.

Maplewood Farm A year-round North Vancouver location, five acres of fun for the little ones: there are pony rides, milking demonstrations, and more than 200 domestic animals and birds to see.

Minter Gardens Another big, beautiful collection of themed gardens (11 of them), this 27-acre specimen is near Chilliwack, 65 kilometres east of Vancouver. There are witty topiary displays, a maze and—unique in North America—Penjing Rock Bonsai (dwarf plants).

Mount Seymour Provincial Park First, you have to drive 1,000 metres (about 3,300 feet) up. But stop at the two viewpoints, one overlooking Indian Arm and, on clear days, Washington State's Mount Baker, the other looking west towards downtown and the Islands. Then you arrive at a large parking lot to start some beautiful skiing in the winter and equally enchanting hiking in the summer.

The Museum of Anthropology If a city is lucky it gets something special, what we might call a gift of the gods. Vancouver has the Museum of

Anthropology at UBC. It is inspired—and inspiring—architecture, by Vancouver's Arthur Erickson. The museum is filled with some of the world's most beautiful and striking native art, and is surrounded by magnificent views. The building is a combination of concrete and glass creating an openness matching the grandeur of the native art inside. Centrepiece is Bill Reid's Raven and the First Men, a large carving—a masterpiece—depicting a native story of the creation of men. Don't have time to include this in your itinerary? Make time. You'll remember it forever.

Museum of the Royal Westminster Regiment A small museum devoted to the regiment is housed in an 1895 Armory gun room. Free, year-round.

Pacific National Exhibition This big annual late-summer fair was planning a move as our book was going to press. The 1997 PNE will be at its longtime home, Hastings Park. After that, who knows? See Mark Leiren-Young's article on the Exhibition.

Park & Tilford Gardens Eight separate theme gardens on the North Shore, created in 1968 by a privately-owned distillery. In the Rose Garden there are nearly 300 plants, in 24 varieties. Free admission and parking, and open seven days a week.

The Port of Vancouver is Greater Vancouver's bustling heart, one of the three largest North American harbors, and busiest on the Pacific coast of North America. It occupies much of Burrard Inlet west of the Second Narrows bridge. From docks for luxury liners to grain elevators, from large lumber loading areas to huge mountains of sulphur, there is everything that has to do with international shipping. The port can be viewed from many points in greater Vancouver, from Stanley Park to Burnaby Mountain and from the SeaBus Terminal to the North Shore Mountains.

Queen Elizabeth Park Greater Vancouver is a hilly place, and one of the most unique of the "hills" is this strikingly landscaped 150-metre (500-foot) high extinct volcano. Queen Elizabeth Park, named in 1939 for the Queen Mother (the present Queen's mother), is the public garden of the city. Once a rock quarry, now a riot of color, with flowers, shrubs, rare trees, and more on every side. A favorite for wedding parties, it's a great place to stroll around, and the views are magnificent wherever you are. Watch for a dramatic sculpture by world-famed Henry Moore. Also in the park, the Bloedel Conservatory, a year-round tropical paradise under a "triodetic" dome . . . with parrots and tiny tropical birds, more than 50 kinds, flitting between the exotic plants, and the soothing splash of waterfalls. Japanese carp glide beneath the waters. A bonus: it's warm year-round. Seasons Restaurant in the Park hosted a

summit lunch April 3, 1993 for U.S. President Bill Clinton and Russian President Boris Yeltsin.

Rainforest Reptile Refuge A year-round display in Surrey of more than 300 reptiles and amphibians.

Redwood Park This lovely 32-hectare Surrey park is rich in exotic trees from around the world. Two profoundly deaf and gently eccentric brothers, Peter and David Brown, owned this property and built themselves a multi-level treehouse in it where they could be away from the rest of the world. A "replica" (nothing like the rude original) of the treehouse can be seen. The Browns gathered seedlings of trees from other countries and planted them here.

George C. Reifel Bird Sanctuary This 850-acre sanctuary on Delta's Westham Island, 10 kilometres west of Ladner, is a resting place for thousands of migratory birds on their way south to warmer places in fall and their way back in spring. With three kilometres of hiking trails and a nature house, there is much to see—and hear— all year long. More than 1.5 million birds pass through here annually (240 species have been spotted!), many thousands just stopping to rest and feed, others to spend the winter. Some species make this their home year-round. Operated by the B.C. Waterfowl Society, a non-government, self-supporting non-profit organization. The Sanctuary has been called a "rural remnant of the once vast Fraser estuary marshes."

Robson Square Robson Square starts with the New Courthouse, a massive slope of glass covering the Law Courts. The Courthouse opens up into a public space with a waterfall, trees and many stairs - the gathering point of young people in the summer - that descend to a lower level with restaurants, conference rooms and a skating rink. Arthur Erickson, the complex's architect, showed the world with this structure that high-rises are not the only solution for inner cities. Robson Street, busiest pedestrian thoroughfare in Greater Vancouver, used to be called "Robsonstrasse" when it was more European-themed, but it's been homogenized in recent years. High energy street, and great for people-watching.

Roedde House Museum This little charmer is set in a West End block (bounded by Barclay, Nicola, Haro and Broughton Streets) called Barclay Heritage Square and featuring nine historic houses built between 1890 and 1908. Roedde House, built in 1893 for Vancouver's first bookbinder, Gustav Roedde, has been owned by the city since 1966. It's operated by the Roedde House Preservation Society, a non-profit volunteer group, and has been handsomely restored. There are guided tours and afternoon tea.

Royal Hudson Steam Train Canada's only steam-operated locomotives, the beautifully-restored 2860 and 3716, take travelers along more than 60

Tourist Attractions More than seven million visitors came to Vancouver in 1996. A healthy three per cent growth of tourism per year is predicted to continue. The city is famous for its traditional attractions of wilderness, sports, Native Art, pristine beaches and cultured Asian gardens. The city's urban sophistication includes an $8.6 million Pacific Space Centre offering visitors interactive space flights. Vancouver's dynamic downtown also includes a new Colosseum-style library, Pacific Place, trendy Robson Street, Yaletown and exotic Chinatown.

kilometres of spectacularly scenic Howe Sound from North Vancouver to Squamish. (The 2850 Hudson drew King George VI and Queen Elizabeth across Canada in 1939, and the King was so impressed with its power he gave his approval for the Hudson locomotives to carry the "Royal" designation.) At Squamish you can visit the West Coast Railway Heritage Museum, with more than 50 locomotives—including the only surviving Pacific Great Eastern Railway steam engine—and cars on display, one of them a handsomely restored Executive Business Car. Also in or near Squamish, the Howe Sound Brewing Co., logging shows and scenic Shannon Falls. To vary your trip, you can return by sea on the MV Britannia, or go up on the boat and return by rail. See also Page 450.

Science World Housed in what is sometimes nicknamed the "golf ball," this former Expo pavilion at the east end of False Creek is a delight for children of all ages. In three major galleries (biology, physics and sound) it presents a scientific view of the earth and life in B.C., with lots of hands-on displays to illustrate scientific concepts in fun ways. There's a Natural History Gallery, the "Mine Game," a 3D Laser Theatre, and the Omnimax Theatre, presenting spellbinding films on the world's largest domed screen.

Seymour Demonstration Forest See the article on the GVRD.

Simon Fraser University Just turned 30, with one of the livelier histories of any university in North America (a hotbed of student and faculty unrest in the turbulent Sixties), Simon Fraser is a dynamic centre of studies and research located atop Burnaby Mountain. The attraction here (for the non-student) is its architecture by the young Arthur Erickson, with partner Geoffrey Massey. The campus buildings hug the mountaintop in a dramatic sprawl.

SplashDown Park Three minutes from the Tsawwassen Ferry Terminal, this 13-slide 10-acre fun spot is Vancouver's only waterpark.

Stanley Park is the jewel of Vancouver, the envy of every city planner in the world. It is unique as a city park, not only for its size (408 hectares, or 1,000 acres) and its closeness to the downtown area but also for its beauty and the variety of amenities it offers, from the forest-like interior of the park (criss-crossed by safe walking trails), to the ocean beaches, to kids' playgrounds, to the built-up area of the world-famed Vancouver Public Aquarium. The park follows a wise rule of recreational planning: to protect an area from being overrun by users, set aside a small section and make it high-density, with intensive use. Of course, with nearly two million people able to use the park, not to mention out-of-area visitors, we cannot expect it to remain an untouched wilderness. By concentrating people in the southern reaches

and around the rim of the park, a large area has been kept in a relatively natural state. The park's walking trails, by the way, were originally "skid roads," used by early loggers who greased them with whale oil to permit teams of oxen to drag massive, felled trees to the water's edge. There are hour-long horse-drawn tours of the park's highlights, using teams of giant Clydesdales and other big horses, and look for the charming miniature railway and Children's Farmyard.

There are many attractions within the Park:

• The Seawall walkway, affording you one of the world's great walks, wraps entirely around the park, giving pedestrians and cyclists nine kilometres of breathtaking views of the city, the harbor and the mountains beyond. Stroll a portion, stroll it all.

• The hiking trails in the interior of the Park guide people through thick forests, with many chances to get out to the Seawall and join in with the crowd.

• The Stanley Park Causeway winds gently around the perimeter of the park, giving drivers (don't go too fast!!!) a general glimpse of what can be seen in detail, with many chances to stop and enjoy.

• The Nine O'Clock Gun. It's been in the park for a century, once used to signal the end of the day's legal fishing, but for decades now a famed nightly time signal. Ever since the gun was "kidnapped" by University of British Columbia engineering students (who returned it when a "ransom" was paid to the Children's Hospital), there has been a protective fence around it. The gun is fired electronically from the harbormaster's perch high atop a downtown skyscraper.

• Beaches and swimming pools.

• The Royal Vancouver Yacht Club with its myriad of boats

• Brockton Point with a famous old Lighthouse and picturesque (and genuine) totem poles

• Prospect Point with striking views of Lions Gate Bridge, the north shore and the mountains. No, they're not the Rockies! Those are a long way away to the east. These are the Coast Mountains.

• Ferguson Point and the Teahouse

• The Tennis Courts and Pitch and Putt area
. . . plus the Hollow Tree, Giant Checkerboard, and much, much more.

Steveston Village Once a centre of Japanese fishing activity before World War II, Steveston is home to a big, colorful commercial fishing harbor. Visitors buy the sea's bounty directly from the boats at the public fish sales dock. A series of shops and restaurants has developed on and near the wharf, making this a very pleasant outing throughout the year. A relic of fishing's glory days, the century-old Gulf of Georgia Cannery

on the Steveston waterfront, was restored in the 1990s and is now a National Historic Site; guided tours show how this important industry once operated. Nearby are the Britannia Heritage Shipyards, the oldest remaining structures on the Fraser River, weathered by a century of exposure to a silvery grey.

Dr. Sun Yat-Sen Classical Chinese Garden is a beautiful, quiet oasis in the heart of a busy city, a "refreshment for the heart." Behind the Chinese Cultural Centre, this first full-sized classical Chinese garden ever built outside China (created by experts flown in from that country) provides a glimpse into another world of symmetry of architecture, rocks, trees and water, unknown in the West. Every square inch of the space has been exquisitely designed . . . even the eaves on the roofs have been shaped to turn rain showers into beaded curtains of water. Handsome, porous "Taihu" rocks and jade green water add to the quiet, exotic beauty. The garden is a genuine must see. Docent-guided tours.

Trev Deeley Motorcycle Museum More than 200 classic and antique motorcycles, representing 43 makes, have been gathered at this Richmond site.

UBC Botanical Garden Seventy acres of plants from around the world, set in a coastal forest at the University of British Columbia. You'll find 400 species of rhododendron here, and a 16th century "Physick Garden." Established in 1916, this is the oldest university botanical garden in Canada.

The University of British Columbia is the oldest and largest university in the province. Its haphazard mix of architecture is one of its visitor attractions. Walk along the Main Mall, down to the rose garden, with its beautiful views across the Strait of Georgia, or go to the Asian Centre and the beautiful Japanese Nitobe Gardens, an authentic Japanese "Tea and Stroll" Garden. Don't miss the new Centre for Native Studies with its impressive and massive beam structure, look for the dramatic new Koerner Library and visit the world-famed Museum of Anthropology. The campus is adjacent to big (763 hectares), attractive and undeveloped Pacific Spirit Regional Park, and it's possible to climb down to the beach. (Caution! Wreck Beach is clothing optional.) There are 50 kilometres of walking/hiking trails in the park, 35 km of equestrian trails and another 35 km for cyclists. This area was logged by Hastings Sawmill from 1860 to 1923, then endowed to the university. You'll see second-growth Douglas fir, western red cedar, western hemlock and more.

Vancouver Aquarium is famous the world over, with pools for Orcas (killer whales), plump white Beluga whales, Steller sea lions and enclosures for sea otters, seals and other water animals of

Performing Arts and Events The Ford Centre for the Performing Arts is a new face in Vancouver's energetic arts community. Extravaganza musicals in the 1,824-seat venue join a respected host of contemporary cultural events and settings. Provincial, municipal and corporate funding help sponsor quality opera, symphony, live theatre, ballet, art and many other groups that make this city an international star. All-Jazz, Shakespeare, writers, women, dance, film, comedy, bluegrass, fireworks, poets and folk music enliven the mix.

the Pacific. The many galleries within, including an Indonesian Reef exhibit, feature hundreds of different species of Pacific marine life. Kids will enjoy the Graham Amazon Gallery, with its giant fishes and hourly rainstorms.

The Vancouver Art Gallery is a heritage building that once was the Courthouse. With the neo-classical exterior preserved, the new interior houses, among other Canadian and international artists, the largest collection of Emily Carr paintings anywhere in the world. The building's original architect, Thomas Rattenbury, also designed the Legislative Buildings and the Empress Hotel in Victoria. (p.s. Rattenbury was murdered by his wife's young lover.) Touring shows bring a mix of modern and traditional.

Vancouver East Cultural Centre A former church in an East Vancouver residential neighborhood, the "Cultch" offers a wide variety of theatre, music and dance, with a focus on contemporary performing arts. There are also special childrens' programs.

VanDusen Botanical Garden This relatively young, but already well respected, big botanical garden is a joy for everybody who likes plants. There is much to see, to learn and to do: 22 acres of beauty, tranquil ponds and great views. Right in the centre of the city, the garden (once a golf course) has areas representing different parts of the world. There are sculptures, and an Elizabethan hedge maze.

Vanier Park There is always something happening at Vanier Park when it's sunny, and often when it's not: the Beautiful People jogging along the beach; fighter kites rushing up to challenge airborne competitors; model sailboats chasing ducks and being chased by them in the pond; catamarans and sailboarders in the water; and in the summer, Bard on the Beach, a local professional Shakespeare company under artistic director Christopher Gaze offering, in a huge red-and-white tent, excellent productions of Will's classics. Overlooking all of this, and sharing the same distinctively-shaped building, are the Vancouver Museum and the Pacific Space Centre, which includes the H.R. MacMillan Planetarium. The shape of the building was inspired by the hats of Haida natives. The Planetarium has regular multimedia shows on its 20-metre domed screen on the planets, galaxies, comets and such. Nearby Gordon Southam Observatory (free) lets you look through telescopes at the heavens—when the weather cooperates. The Planetarium and Observatory are evolving into the Pacific Space Centre, being developed as this book went to press. "We will be renovating the Star Theatre," says president and chair Stephen J. Miller, "with sophisticated new control systems, video projection units and a live performance stage. We will

be offering a new exhibit hall with hands-on, interactive experiences and learning systems employing technologies developed right here in British Columbia. Our new Centre will also feature a Cosmic Simulator, taking visitors on explorations into outer space, and Groundstation Canada, a multi-screen theatre and demonstration lab for visitors and schoolchildren."

The gleaming crab fountain in front of the Museum/Planetarium was created by sculptor George Norris, and is worth a visit by itself. Also in this spacious park, the Maritime Museum and the Vancouver Academy of Music. The museum features exhibits highlighting this area's rich marine past, with a Children's Maritime Discovery Centre where kids can take the helm of a scale-model tugboat and "navigate" it around English Bay. Next door is a unique structure specially built to house the St. Roch, a ship built for the RCMP (nicknamed "horse sailors") which became the first to go through the Northwest Passage in both directions, and was also the first ship to circumnavigate North America. There are regular tours. In the western reaches of Vanier park, the Vancouver City Archives, a huge and fascinating collection of material from the city's past.

West End This has been called the most populated square kilometre in North America, but that's not quite true: there are areas in New York City that are considerably more packed. Still, the population is high for such a small area. More to the point is that Vancouver's West End is one of the most livable areas in Canada for singles and couples. Even though crammed with highrises, two- and four-storey apartment buildings and (a very few) family houses, there are still trees, parks and playgrounds and a lot of neat shopping and entertainment. The West End is a great place to live, bordered by the great Stanley Park, lively English Bay, the city's energetic downtown and the busy harbor. There is a large gay population. Take a walk along English Bay, have tea in the old-world Sylvia Hotel, go shopping on crowded Robson Street and on Davie Street see The Mansion, a fine old home converted to a popular restaurant.

Westminster Quay Shops, restaurants, a broad boardwalk, an authentic paddlewheeler, and excellent views of the working Fraser River: tugboats, log booms, barges, freighters and more. One of New Westminster's real attractions.

Whistler Village Ski magazine named Whistler the number one ski resort in North America, and Snow Country Magazine gave it the same title four years running. Golf magazine chimes in by rating it "one of the best golf resorts in the world." There are four courses here, three with designers even duffers have heard of: Arnold

Palmer, Robert Trent Jones, Jr., and Jack Nicklaus. Whistler, 120 kilometres north of Vancouver, with 1,600 metres of vertical drop, highest on the continent, is a gateway to skiing on a grand scale. Two adjacent mountains, Whistler and Blackcomb attract skiers from all over the world. But a first class ski resort cannot exist on natural attributes alone. Whistler has developed an excellent infrastructure: eating, lodging and shopping locations are all within easy walking distance in the no-car village. If it's good (and expensive) the Village has it. Snowboarding and cross-country skiing in the winter, hiking, mountain biking and water sports in the summer are offered to the energetic visitor. And for everybody else, there are conventions and festivals galore, with symphony concerts in summer right at the top of the skiing area. B.C. Rail has train service there.

White Rock A favorite summer resort for Vancouverites since the turn of the century, White Rock is now a busy and attractive suburb. Thanks to its beautiful waterfront location, it brings Vancouverites and foreigners to enjoy a day at the beach, a swim in the ocean or merely a leisurely stroll along the shore. A famous old (1914) pier here was once a landing dock for coastal steamships, now offers scenic strolling and fishing. White Rock was once the site of an international Sandcastle competition (cancelled because of rowdyism) in the summer that lured hundreds to the broad expanse of the beach here to try their hand at sand sculptures. The town is named for a huge (486.63 ton) white rock on the beach, deposited millennia ago by a glacier.

Wreck Beach Vancouver is blessed with about 56 kilometres (35 miles) of beaches, all of them public, most of them developed. They are all worth visiting, but Wreck Beach, just some hundred steps below the University of British Columbia, is the most beautiful, the least developed and the most controversial because it is clothing optional. On sunny days more than a thousand naked sun worshipers can congregate here. The beach's name was given it for the now vanished hulk of a wrecked vessel here.

Yaletown was a Vancouver warehouse district only a decade ago, but has now evolved into an attractive quarter of sophisticated cafes, restaurants and upscale shops. A favorite locale for the growing film industry. The name comes from the nickname for this area a century ago, from CPR workers (who had come down from the railway town of Yale) who moved here in the mid-1880s to help bring the railway into Vancouver.

Additional material provided by Kirstin Brundin and by Heather Chapman, Elvira Quarin and Tracey Corbett of Tourism Vancouver.

Convention Facilities/Events Convention delegates to Vancouver arrive from Europe, Pacific Asia and North America. A continuing trend of delegates, flocking to meet and to be entertained in Vancouver, has seen the city play host to health care workers, academics, Shriners, law enforcement officers and scientists. A joint provincial and city announcement has called for proposals to build, by the year 2000, an expanded or new convention centre with 250,000 sq. ft. of exhibition space and an attached hotel with up to 1,000 rooms.

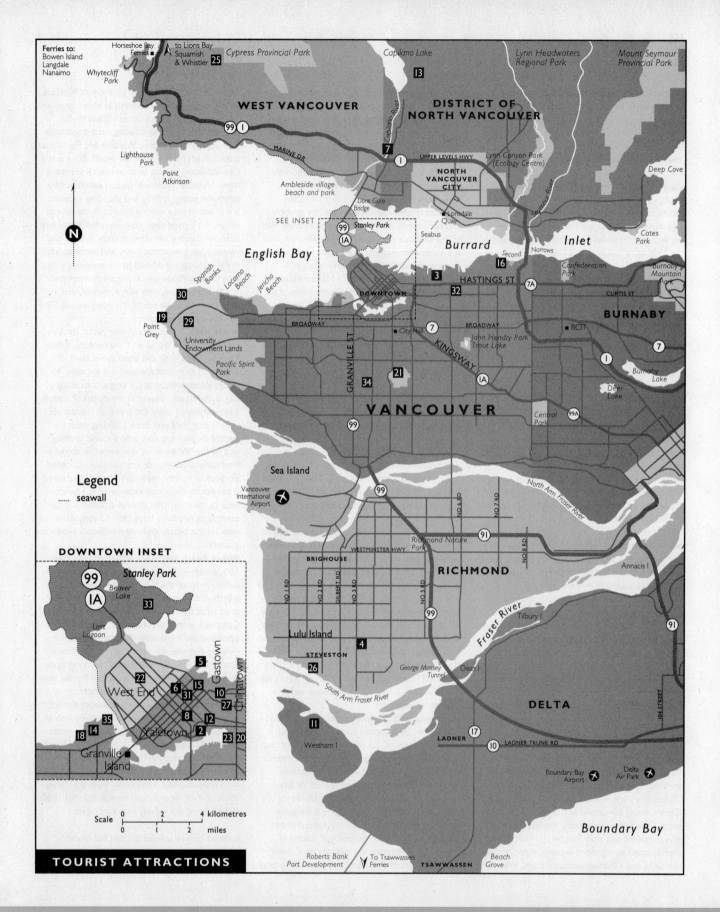

Ferries to:
Bowen Island
Langdale
Nanaimo

Horseshoe Bay Ferries ■

to Lions Bay Squamish & Whistler **25**

Cypress Provincial Park

Capilano Lake

Lynn Headwaters Regional Park

Mount Seymour Provincial Park

13

Whytecliff Park

WEST VANCOUVER

DISTRICT OF NORTH VANCOUVER

Lighthouse Park

99 **1**

MARINE DR

Capilano River

UPPER LEVELS HWY

7

NORTH VANCOUVER CITY

Lynn Canyon Park (Ecology Centre)

Seymour River

Deep Cove

Point Atkinson

Ambleside village beach and park

1

Cates Park

Lions Gate Bridge

Lonsdale Quay

Seabus

Burrard

Inlet

Confederation Park

Burnaby Mountain Park

SEE INSET

99
1A

Stanley Park

Second Narrows

16

English Bay

Spanish Banks

Locarno Beach

Jericho Beach

DOWNTOWN

3

HASTINGS ST

7A

CURTIS ST

BURNABY

30

32

19

29

Point Grey

University Endowment Lands

BROADWAY

GRANVILLE ST

■ City Hall

7

BROADWAY

John Hendry Park Trout Lake

■ BCIT

7

Pacific Spirit Park

KINGSWAY

34

21

1A

1

Burnaby Lake

VANCOUVER

Deer Lake

Central Park

99A

99

Sea Island

North Arm Fraser River

Vancouver International Airport ✈

99

91

NO. 6 RD

NO. 7 RD

NO. 8 RD

Annacis I

WESTMINSTER HWY

Richmond Nature Park

Legend

...... seawall

BRIGHOUSE

NO. 1 RD

NO. 2 RD

GILBERT RD

NO. 3 RD

NO. 5 RD

RICHMOND

91

DOWNTOWN INSET

99
1A

Stanley Park

Beaver Lake

33

99

Fraser River

Tilbury I

Lost Lagoon

5

Gastown

Chinatown

Lulu Island

4

22

6 **15**

31

10

27

West End

STEVESTON

26

George Massey Tunnel

Deas I

DELTA

35

8

12

104 STREET

18 **14**

2

23 **20**

Yaletown

11

17

LADNER

10

LADNER TRUNK RD

Granville Island

Westham I

Scale
0   2   4 kilometres
0   1   2   miles

Boundary Bay Airport ✈

Delta Air Park ✈

Boundary Bay

TOURIST ATTRACTIONS

Roberts Bank Port Development

To Tsawwassen Ferries

TSAWWASSEN

Beach Grove

Dining and Night Life Vancouver's more than 60 cultural groups have created a multicultural cuisine with European, African, First Nations, Asian and North America influences. Visitors can eat dim sum in Chinatown, sushi in Little Japan, salmon in a First Nation's restaurant or sip B.C. wine in Little Italy. Cappuccino bars and brew pubs offer premium coffees and beers. Vancouver's club scene is a whirlwind of jazz, rock, blues, Caribbean, folk and Latino rhythms. Comedy clubs and karaoke bars are also popular.

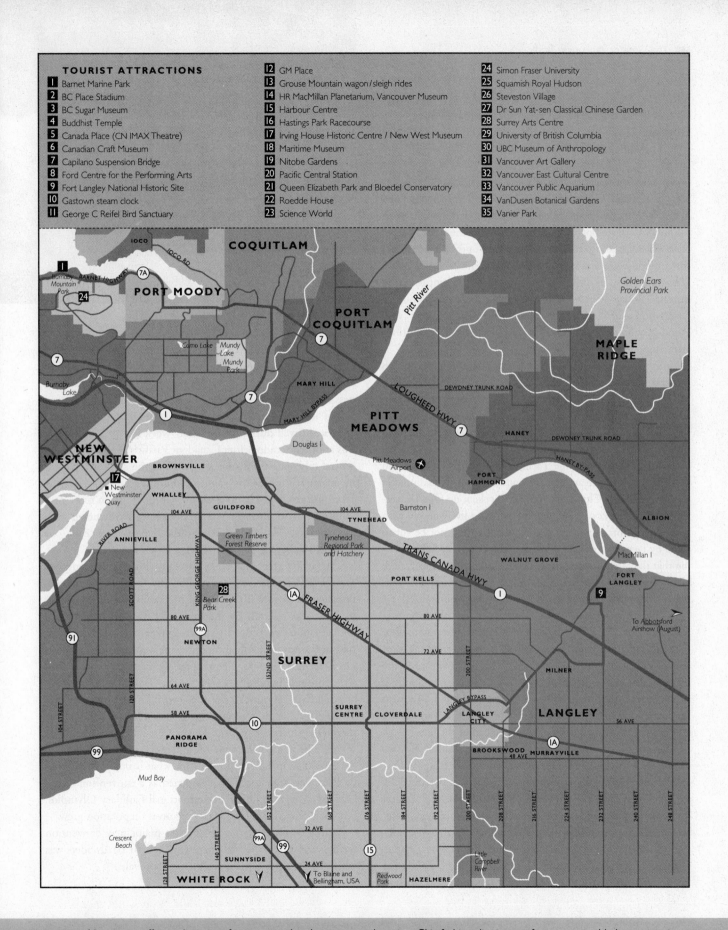

Retailers Vancouver offers a diversity of international and west coast shopping. Chic fashion districts, craft centres, world-class art, regional specialty shops and markets cater to a thriving urban and world-wide clientele. Robson Street and Yaletown offer fashionable, busy downtown boutiques and bistros. Historic Gastown is an energetic mix of aboriginal crafts, souvenir shops, cafes and smart clothing stores. Granville Island is an imaginative shopping area with an indoor market, kid's market, cafes, galleries and microbrewery.

Greater Vancouver Convention and Visitors Bureau

Alan Daniels

Canada Place, 1991. vs

A NEWSPAPER ADVERTISEMENT PLACED by the newly formed Vancouver Tourist Association in 1902 stated "Vancouver has excellent accommodation and a large number of private boarding houses. Rates are the same as other coast cities." A photo taken two years later outside the bureau's first office at 439 Granville Street shows a shingle which reads: "Headquarters for vistors and tourists—free information bureau." Today Vancouver is one of North America's hottest destinations, attracting 6.5 million overnight visitors who spend $1.7 billion each year. The city hosted 328 conventions attracting 148,000 delegates in 1994.

Vancouver's potential for creating wealth and jobs through tourism was identified as early as 1929 when members of the Vancouver Publicity Bureau concluded that "money expended to advertise the tourist attractions of the city brought better returns than that expended on advertising for new industries." Inspired by a report that 99,495 automobiles carrying 354,015 passengers had entered B.C. over the Pacific Highway at Douglas and Huntingdon, the bureau took city council members to dinner at the Terminal City Club and promptly hit them up for an advertising grant of $35,000. The request sparked a lively debate with some councillors arguing that the bureau should not be subsidized by taxpayers' dollars. However Mayor W.H. Malkin, noting that the ratepayers get the benefit of every dollar spent, said: "I am anxious that we should develop the modern spirit of looking at things in a big way and not with a village outlook."

In 1935 the *Vancouver Sun* campaigned for a convention bureau. Hotel Devonshire manager Karl de Morest pointed out that Bellingham hosted three times as many meetings as Vancouver and alderman J.J. Mcrae said: "Our merchants need the business that conventions bring, and our city can stand a little of the cheer that throngs of visitors bring to the city." By 1950 the convention business had started to grow despite Vancouver's geographic disadvantage of being "at the end of the line."

Vancouver Tourist Association and the B.C. Automobile Association were run by a common executive board, but in 1952 they split. Vancouver's "happiest marriage," as it was described by VTA president Fred Brown, ended by common consent at noon on January 12. Three years later the bureau became the Greater Vancouver Tourist Association and in November, 1963, after moving to new premises at 650 Burrard, it got a new name: Greater Vancouver Visitors and Convention Bureau. This lasted until 1973 when it became the Greater Vancouver Convention and Visitors Bureau. Perhaps it couldn't decide where the emphasis was. In any event from 1986 the agency has been known simply as Tourism Vancouver and the convention business was turned over to crown-owned B.C. Pavilions Corp.

Not altogether by chance, Vancouver's millionth convention delegate arrived during Convention Week in April 1967 but it was another decade before Canadian Pacific's Pier B-C, on the central city waterfront, was suggested as the site for a Downtown convention centre. Tourism minister Grace McCarthy asked former B.C. Hydro chair Dr. Gordon Shrum to be project director. Shrum, who was then 82, must have known what was coming. "As long as it's within the next 10 years," he remarked with a cynicism that proved well-founded.

The facility, to be funded by three levels of government, was initally projected to cost $25 million. By 1980, with construction not yet begun, it had soared to $52 million, then, within months, $80 million. By the time steel was ordered, in September, 1981, it was $100 million. A year later, in November 1981, it was $135 million and politicians were starting to panic. On December 8, 1981, Premier Bill Bennett postponed construction indefinitely.

Then Expo 86 came to the rescue with Prime Minister Pierre Trudeau's dramatic announcement that Ottawa would fund the Pier B-C development to be the Canada Pavilion at Expo. It would be 9,000 square metres under one roof, room enough for 10,000 people. The final cost for what is now called Canada Place was $144.8 million. It opened as a convention centre on July 9, 1987, to host the International Culinary Olympics, but soon proved inadequate as Vancouver's reputation grew.

As this book was going to press, a major new convention facility was projected. All that remained to be decided was which of the three bidders would get approval.

In 1888, George Grant Mackay, a civil engineer and land developer, left Scotland and moved his family to the young city of Vancouver. Mackay purchased 6,000 acres of dense forest on either side of Capilano River and built a cabin on the very edge of the canyon wall. Assisted by two local native men and a team of horses. Mackay suspended a hemp rope and cedar plank bridge across the river to his property on the other side.

Major Conventions 1997 to 2002

Please note: many more large (1,000+ delegates) conventions will be added as time goes on. Thanks to the Vancouver Trade and Convention Centre, and to Tourism Vancouver for their assistance.

(number of delegates)

May 2 to May 4, 1997 (3,000)
Wolgamott Leadership Seminar 97

May 10 to May 18, 1997 (1,500)
Particle Accelerator Conference

May 11 to May 14, 1997 (1,000)
Rendez-Vous Canada

May 19 to May 20, 1997 (1,000)
Travel Trade Magazine

May 20 to May 23, 1997 (3,200)
NAFSA: Assn. of Int'l Educators

May 24 to May 27, 1997 (2,000)
In Vitro Fertilization Congress

June 6 to June 10, 1997 (1,200)
Canadian Anaesthetists Society

June 9 to June 13, 1997 (1,500)
International Association of Psychosocial
   Rehabilitation Services

June 15 to June 20, 1997 (9,000)
International Council of Nurses

June 27 to July 3, 1997 (2,000)
World Council of Credit Unions Inc.

July 16 to July 19, 1997 (2,500)
Nat'l Assn. of Federal Credit Unions

July 21 to July 25, 1997 (1,500)
Int'l Foster Care Organization

July 27 to July 30, 1997 (1,400)
American Society of Plant Physiologists

August 10 to August 14, 1997 (1,000)
National Automobile Aerospace Transportation
   and General Workers Union

August 20 to August 24, 1997 (1,100)
National Society of Public Accountants

August 25 to August 28, 1997 (1,200)
4th World Chinese Entrepreneurs Convention

September 1 to September 5, 1997 (3,000)
International Congress of Pharmaceutical
   Sciences - FIP

September 11, 1997 (700)
Merisel Canada Softeach 97

Sept. 13 to Sept. 17, 1997 (3,500)
Int'l City Management Association

Sept. 18 to Sept. 19, 1997 (1,000)
ACTA B.C. (Travel agents)

Sept. 19 to Sept. 22, 1997 (1,200)
IMAX Corporation

Sept. 20 to Sept. 22, 1997 (1,200)
International Space Theater Consortium

Sept. 25 to Sept. 28, 1997 (4,000)
Royal College of Physicians and Surgeons

October 3 to October 7, 1997 (3,500)
Association of School Business Officials
   International

October 20 to October 24, 1997 (1,600)
Union of British Columbia Municipalities 1997

October 24 to October 29, 1997 (7,000)
International Foundation of Employee Benefit
   Plans

November 2 to November 4, 1997 (1,200)
Deloitte & Touche

March 18 to March 20, 1998 (1,800)
Globe 98

March 26 to March 29, 1998 (2,500)
International Emergency Medicine

May 24 to May 28, 1998 (2,000)
International Federation of Societies for Surgery
   of the Hand

June 10 to June 13, 1998 (1,500)
American Academy of Cosmetic Dentistry

June 22 to June 25, 1998 (1,500)
Int'l Assn. on Water Quality

August 14 to August 21, 1998 (3,000)
WASP (World Association For Social Psychiatry)

Sept. 12 to Sept. 19, 1998 (5,000)
International Bar Association

September 27 to October 1, 1998 (2,500)
Communications, Energy and Paperworkers
   Union

October 30 to November 5, 1998 (1,500)
Canadian Association of Broadcasters

January 24 to 26, 1999 (2,200)
Meeting Professionals International

March 5 to March 9, 1999 (3,000)
American Assn. of Dental Schools

March 10 to March 14, 1999 (4,500)
Int'l Assn. for Dental Research

April 23 to May 1, 1999 (5,000)
17th World Orchid Conference

May 5 to May 8, 1999 (1,500)
Medical Users Software Exchange

May 17 to May 19, 1999 (1,800)
Canadian Cable Television Association

June 5 to June 11, 1999 (3,000)
International Conference on Communications-IEEE

August 17 to August 20, 1999 (2,000)
Int'l Psychogeriatric Assn.

August 30 to September 3, 1999 (5,000)
Pan American Congress of Gastroenterology

Sept. 14 to Sept. 17, 1999 (3,000)
Int'l Federation Of Bee Keepers

Sept. 22 to Sept. 25, 1999 (1,500)
International Federation of Business and
   Professional Women

October 6 to 10, 1999 (1,000)
American Association of Electrodiagnostic
   Medicine

October 16 to October 19, 1999 (1,600)
Canadian Real Estate Association

March 14 to March 18, 2000 (2,000)
Teachers of English to Speakers of Other
   Languages

April 5 to April 9, 2000 (3,500)
Council for Exceptional Children

May 6 to May 10, 2000 (2,000)
Medical Library Association

June 10 to June 16, 2000 (2,000)
International Patent Lawyers

June 19 to June 22, 2000 (2,500)
World Congress of Medical Technologists

July 14 to July 18, 2000 (1,200)
International Society of Clinical Physiology

July 19 to July 23, 2000 (6,000)
Canadian Square and Round Dance Society

October 4 to October 6, 2000 (1,200)
International Society of Naval Architects

October 25 to October 27, 2000 (1,400)
Canadian Cardiovascular Society

May 5 to May 9, 2001 (1,500)
Society of Cardiovascular Anesthesiology

May 11 to May 13, 2001 (1,200)
American Society of Regional Anesthesia

June 4 to June 15, 2001 (2,000)
International Hospital Federation

July 1 to July 5, 2001 (5,000)
Int'l Congress on Gerontology

March 2 to March 5, 2002 (1,200)
Grain Elevator and Processing Society

July 20 to July 23, 2002 (1,500)
National Association of College and University
   Business Officers

October 14 to October 16, 2002 (1,000)
National Association of College Auxiliary Services

George Mackay's bridge became a popular destination for adventurous friends and Capilano Suspension Bridge, Vancouver's first visitor attraction, was born! With its majestic mountain backdrop, the 22-acre historic park's progress over the past century has not infringed on the site's heritage or natural surroundings and offers visitors to the city an unmatched West Coast experience.

Cruise Ships
Gary Bannerman

Vancouver has become one of the most significant ports in the passenger-shipping world, home base for what is the industry's most profitable market on a per-passenger basis.

In a mass movement of people and ships not seen since the Klondike Gold Rush of a century ago, vacationers, predominantly Americans, sail the Inside Passage of British Columbia each summer to the 50th state.

Some of the largest and most luxurious ships afloat make Vancouver a regular port of call between May and October. In 1995, 25 different ships made over 270 separate sailings, carrying more than 600,000 passengers. They collectively spent $140 million in Canada. The economic impact, measured in provisions, ship servicing, employment and other spin-offs may be double that amount.

Passenger travel along the coast has been a factor of every chapter of British Columbia history. Vessels owned by Canadian Pacific, Canadian National Railway, Union Steamship Company and other competitors have worked the British Columbia-Alaska trade.

Several of Canadian Pacific's renowned and beloved White Empresses were based here, postcard sights as they made their way through First Narrows. This evolved in later years into a CP partnership with Union Steamships of New Zealand, marketed as The Australasian Line, transporting passengers and cargo from Vancouver to the Orient.

But Vancouver was never a major port of the world passenger liner business. Immigrant ships of all shapes and sizes occasionally stopped here. During World War II several of the passenger ships conscripted into troop-carrying modes went into B.C. yards for refit. One of these was the original *Queen Elizabeth,* in her dull naval grey, which dropped anchor in English Bay en route to Yarrows Shipyard in Victoria.

In 1954, when the Orient Line included Vancouver in a pioneering Pacific itinerary with the ships *Oronsay, Orcades* and *Orsova,* a new era dawned. The British giant P&O Lines, which would ultimately absorb the Orient Line, began its association with the arrival of *Himalaya* in 1958.

This occurred amidst the death throes of pan-oceanic passenger shipping, as the great lines tried to compete with aircraft. Many famous corporate names disappeared during the 1960s. Venerable firms such as P&O, Cunard and Holland America flirted with vacation travel and managed to survive, but the modern cruise industry was the creation of newcomers.

One of these was a Canadian-born Seattle businessman, Stan McDonald, who had developed a taste for cruising with a charter ship serving the 1962 Seattle World's Fair.

Following that event, McDonald looked for another ship. He was aware that Canadian Pacific's small coastal steamer *Princess Patricia,* although busy each summer from Vancouver to Alaska, was idle in the winter. He chartered her for two seasons, the first Mexican Riviera cruises from Los Angeles. Princess Patricia lent her name to what would become one of passenger shipping's most famous firms, Princess Cruises.

McDonald chartered two larger Italian ships in 1966 and set about building his company to serve Alaska in the summer, Mexico in the winter. At first, he competed only with the small Canadian railway ships, but he soon attracted company.

P&O diverted 28,000-ton *Arcadia* into seasonal Alaska service. When McDonald acquired the 20,000-ton *Island Princess,* majestic by 1970 standards, P&O responded by purchasing a 17,000-ton Scandinavian vessel, and called her *Spirit of London* (subsequently renamed *Sun Princess*), the first purpose-built cruise ship ever to enter the fleet. Holland America, the historic Dutch firm, and the super-luxury fleet of Royal Viking Line came next.

The Port of Vancouver processed 22,800 cruise passengers in 1971. The total passed 170,000 in 1981; 423,000 in 1991 and a staggering total of 600,000 in 1995.

Canada Place, a cruise port, hotel, office and convention centre complex, was built in advance of the Expo 86 world fair. The five sails have become the most identifiable landmark on Canada's West Coast. The facility's ocean terminal was designed to handle as many as five ships at a time but when Canada Place opened in 1986, it faced a difficult reality: the average cruise ship had doubled in size and even bigger ones were planned. The modern port could often serve only two of these new giants at any one time. While 20,000-ton vessels were still dominant in 1980, a few ships in the 70,000-ton range now make Vancouver their summer home.

Ballantyne Pier, a cargo terminal in Vancouver's East End, was temporarily put into service for cruise passengers in 1983. It has been in continuous service ever since. The Port of Vancouver recently invested $46 million to give it permanent life as a convertible facility for pulp and paper products in the winter and cruise ship passengers in the summer.

The Port of Vancouver expects to serve more than one million passengers a year by the turn of the century, a volume that would require additional terminal capacity.

Hotels in Greater Vancouver
Claire Hurley

The second Hotel Vancouver, built 1905–16 (demolished 1948). cva

T HE COLONIAL HOTEL, built by the Grelley brothers on Columbia Street in New Westminster around 1860, was the first hotel in the Greater Vancouver area. In those days New Westminster was connected to Burrard Inlet by a meandering Douglas Road. In 1865, at the Inlet end of the road, Oliver Hocking and Fred Houston opened the Brighton Hotel with beautiful grounds, picturesque walks and a floating wharf. The hotel attracted vacationers from New Westminster who, starting in 1867, could take a weekly stagecoach to get there. Maximilien Michaud, who had walked to the Pacific coast from Eastern Canada, bought the place in 1869 and renamed it the Hastings Hotel. Other early hotels of note were Mansion House in New Westminster (1868), the Deighton Hotel (built by Gassy Jack Deighton of Gastown fame in 1870) and the Granville Hotel (1874). The latter two were destroyed in the Great Fire on June 13, 1886. With great speed new hotels were built: in 1886 the Terminus Hotel at 30 Water Street featured projecting bay windows on the upper floors; rooms at the opulent Alhambra Hotel, built in 1886-87 at 2 Water Street, went for more than a dollar per night!

The Canadian Pacific Railway built the first Hotel Vancouver which opened May 16, 1887, at Georgia and Granville Streets. Its location, far from the centre of town, was ridiculed by some. However the site afforded fabulous views and its luxurious style ensured its success. The timely arrival of the first CPR passenger train a week later boosted business. The first banquet of the Vancouver Board of Trade was held in the hotel March 5, 1889—at a cost of $12.50 per plate, which included a quart bottle of Mumm's Extra Dry Champagne. And Vancouver's Canadian Club held its inaugural luncheon there September 25, 1906, with Governor General Earl Grey as guest of honor, an event marked by the first public singing of the "Buchan version" of "O Canada."

Vancouver experienced rapid growth between 1908 and 1913. The flatiron building at 43 Powell Street, the Hotel Europe (1908-09), is one survivor of this period. Other early hotels and buildings in Gastown and neighboring Chinatown remain intact because of the B.C. government's 1971 decision to designate these areas as historical sites, thereby preventing demolition. A splendid new Hotel Vancouver, the second, was built in 1916 on the same site as the first. It was a building still fondly recalled by oldtimers for its grandly ornate exterior, but it was not well-built and deteriorated over time. The first convocation (1916) for the conferring of degrees by the Universtiy of British Columbia was held there. The Georgia Hotel, still active, opened May 7, 1927.

In 1928 the Canadian National Railway began building a chateau-style hotel at Georgia and Hornby Streets but the depression halted construction in 1932. The building stood uncompleted for five years, until the CNR reached a joint-operation agreement with the CPR—whose second hotel was proving too costly to maintain—and construction resumed. Still it was seven more years before the grand new structure opened. The new (the third and present) Hotel Vancouver was hastily completed in time for the royal visit of King George VI and Queen Elizabeth. The official opening took place May 25, 1939. In 1962 CP Hotels, unwilling to spend more money on a hotel it didn't own, decided not to renew its contract. CN contracted the hotel's management to Hilton but then resumed sole management in 1983. Finally, in 1988, the hotel's ownership came full circle as Canadian Pacific Hotels once again acquired the Hotel Vancouver. The famed hotel's steep green copper roof (used to dramatic effect in the 1975 film, *Russian Roulette*), ornate dormer windows, menacing gargoyles and notched machicolations evoke memories of medieval French castles.

Some fondly recalled hotels live on only in memory: on December 10, 1962, the old Union Steamship Hotel on Bowen Island—once a favorite gathering spot for leisure-minded locals—was demolished and the resort closed down. And, on a more dramatic note, on July 5, 1981, the Devonshire Hotel was brought down by a controlled explosion. New hotels blossomed in the 1980s in anticipation of Expo 86 and to meet the increasing demands of the convention trade. Following Expo, offshore investors bought, sold and built hotel properties at a fast pace. More hotel development is inevitable following the construction of a new convention centre in Vancouver, a facility whose location was not yet announced at this writing.

Granville Island
Catherine Gourley

GRANVILLE ISLAND, the jewel of False Creek, has sparked more passion, greed and love in its short history than perhaps any other chunk of real estate around. Today it is the crowning glory of the government of Canada, perhaps the most successful real estate deal undertaken by Ottawa.

In its original, natural state, however, Granville Island was neither an island nor particularly valuable. What would one day be the most popular public park in Canada was originally two seaweed-laden sandbars lying half-submerged at the entrance to False Creek. Rich with fish and wildlife, they were the winter fishing grounds of the Squamish Indians.

With the arrival of the fortune-seeking Europeans, the quiet sandbars took on a glamor and attraction few could resist. And when a bridge linking the north and south shores of False Creek was erected in 1889, the sandbars lying on either side of the bridge's southern end figured even larger in men's minds.

First to make a grab for them were three local contractors who set about encircling the sandbars with stakes, planning to seek approval for a sawmill and booming grounds there later. The Canadian Pacific Railway scared them off with a court injunction but their actions were to trigger a decades-long squabble over foreshore and water rights between the CPR, the provincial government, city officials, local business people and the federal marine ministry.

Each of them came up with grandiose plans for the twin mudflats, from a massive rail terminal to a $10 million seaport. But the sandbars lay tantalizingly undisturbed for years as industry built up around them. Then, in 1911, Vancouver had a new voice in Ottawa—Conservative MP Harry Stevens whose far-ranging vision for the city included a fully developed harbor. The sandbars fit into that plan.

In 1915 the newly created Harbour Commission gave Ottawa one dollar for the sandbars and received clearance to reclaim the land. The commission then raised $300,000 to cover the cost of railway tracks and a wooden roadway to False Creek's southern shore.

More than 760,000 cubic metres of sea mud were sucked from False Creek's bed and poured within the island's wooden walls. The mud flats finally transformed into an island and Stevens was able to say, "I had everything to do with the creation of Granville Island."

Officially called "Industrial Island," it opened for business in 1916. It was 14.5 hectares in size, three metres above the high-water mark, had 80 lots and rents were $1,200 to $3,700 per hectare, per year.

The island was a success from day one. Keen to locate close to the creek's sawmills and next to shipping channels, businesses signed up quickly. The first tenant was B.C. Equipment at the island's northwest corner. Then came Vulcan Ironworks, Wallace Shipyards, National Machinery, Diethers Coal and Shipping, Pacific Roofing, Wright's Canadian Ropes, Tyee Machinery and Arrow Transport.

They built long, skinny, corrugated tin plants with their fronts facing the rail tracks and their backs abutting wharves leading to the creek. Barges ringed the island, boxcars cluttered the rail tracks and noise and filth were everywhere.

By 1930 about 1,200 people worked in the island's factories, churning out steel rivets, band saws, anvils, bolts, cement, paint, barrels, rope, boilers and chains. They worked six days a week, trying to satisfy their two big customers—the forestry and mining industries.

This frenzied activity stopped suddenly with the Depression. Business on the island got even quieter when a few big customers along the creek were eliminated by financial troubles or fire.

But in September, 1939, when Prime Minister William Lyon Mackenzie King declared that Canada was at war, Granville Island's role was clear. As the industrial heart of the city, it began to go full-blast, working around the clock and producing defense equipment such as anti-torpedo nets, minesweeping ropes and rigging ropes for the merchant fleet.

For the first time women were hired at the factories, filling in for those at the Front. Granville Island was declared crucial to the war effort and, by 1942, was closed to the public to "guard island industries against saboteurs."

The real danger to island life was fire. The oily, junk-littered factories were classic firetraps but Granville Island's sole water supply was a 20-centimetre main often clogged with sand or slush. Fire had already wiped out a number of factories on the island, including a sawmill. Many owed their existence to the False Creek fireboat, the *J.H. Carlisle*.

"There is not an area between Frisco and Prince Rupert which has so much valuable property and is so poorly served," Major Chutter, longtime president of British Wire Ropes and unofficial mayor of Granville Island, complained to authorities.

Ultimately, though, it was change throughout the entire False Creek basin that spelled the end to the island as an industrial centre. After the war many of the island's biggest customers had moved out of False Creek, seeking more and cheaper land,

Granville
Island

Granville Island has seen a world of change since the days of the great sandbar and the wooden fishing traps. Today, the Island is home to more than 250 artistic, educational, commercial and industrial businesses and facilities, brought together under the ambitious waterfront redevelopment plan championed by the Federal Government's Canada Mortgage and Housing Corporation.

and preferring truck transport to water.

With their departure the fortunes of the Granville Island businesses fell. Many decided it would be easier to move to better sites than fix up their grimy, decades-old plants.

Then two longtime islanders, Wright's Ropes and Pacific Bolts, were wiped out by separate, spectacular fires. The loss of two big mainstays was a body blow to the island. Tenants started moving out, following their customers to better quarters. Once the object of such ambition and greed, Granville Island was now a squalid little island suffering from neglect.

It had even lost its status as an island. When a fishermen's terminal was built to the west, the dredging fill was dumped between the island and False Creek's south shore, turning it into a peninsula. This was the first part of a five-stage plan to fill in the entirety of False Creek, a plan later abandoned as too costly.

Nothing much was going to happen to Granville Island until its landlord, the National Harbours Board, took an active interest in it. But the change in public thinking about the future of False Creek inevitably brought similar change to Granville Island. After much debate, those who favoured remaking False Creek into a more people-friendly urban area won the day.

Urban geographer Walter Hardwick completed a land economics study of the creek and discovered that the CPR charged such low rents that plants had no incentive to move. He saw the area as ideal for an urban mix of housing and public use.

The civic battle was on. In 1972 the proponents for change, led by Art Phillips, swept to power at city hall and began transforming False Creek. Change for Granville Island was inevitable.

Ron Basford, a senior cabinet minister whose riding included Granville Island, knew this and began agitating for a new role for the island. Agreeing with an architectural report that viewed the island as a "people place," Basford saw his chance in 1973. He shifted responsibility for Granville Island from the National Harbours Board to his ministry, Canada Mortgage and Housing Corp., a body already heavily involved in the redevelopment of False Creek.

Ottawa granted $25 million for the island's renewal and consultants were hired to come up with a new design. They already had imaginative examples in Bill Harvey and Mitch Taylor who, sensing the island's potential, bought the old Monsanto building and its lease, re-applied tin cladding so it would look like its neighbors and leased it out again. This new "old" building set the tone for the island's future revamping.

Granville Island would be a "key urban amenity," the consultants said, a description that met with howls of derision and led to cynical refrences to "Basford's Bay" or the "Purple Lagoon" as a new sinkhole for taxpayers' money.

Through the Granville Island Trust, authorities made a commitment to open up the island for a variety of public uses while preserving the industrial character of the old buildings. Russell Brink had the job of buying up the remaining leases and overseeing the island's heart surgery. Rail ties were ripped up, tin cladding taken off and re-applied, foundations reinforced. Old buildings became new.

In July, 1979, the Granville Island public market opened for business to instant success. It encouraged others to come. Today Granville Island is an urban stew whose appeal remains undiminished. It is totally self-supporting and all profits go back into the operation of the island.

Its remarkable consistency of architecture has won design awards for Hotson Bakker Architects, the coordinating architects, and others who worked on projects.

The island owes much of its success to its unique relationship with the people of Vancouver. Its lifeblood comes from those who have made Granville Island part of their routine. They have made the Granville Island market the most successful public market in North America.

Hundreds of others come down regularly for the theatres, the art school, Arts Umbrella, the community centre and work. And with 2,500 people working there, Granville Island retains its roots as a place of productivity.

Public Market, Granville Island, 1993. vs

As a destination for seven to nine million visitors a year, a workplace for more than 2,000 Vancouverites and home to the internationally acclaimed Granville Island Public Market, the Island is a "must do" experience for anyone visiting the city. For more information about Granville Island contact our Information Centre at (604) 666-5784 or visit our website at http://www.granvilleisland.bc.ca

False Creek
Catherine Gourley

IN LESS THAN A century, False Creek has been transformed from the sleepy fishing grounds of the Squamish nation into a showcase of sophisticated urban living. Its metamorphosis is a drama that embraces some of the biggest land deals and most powerful players in British Columbia's history. The Canadian Pacific Railway, Ottawa, local authorities and Hong Kong investors all took part in re-shaping the creek.

Before the Europeans arrived here False Creek was a shallow arm of the ocean, teeming with fish and wildlife, and about five times the size it is today. The Squamish traditionally wintered on the creek's south shore, placing nets and weirs on the great sandbar where Granville Island now stands.

But this idyllic life changed in 1859 when Captain George Richards nosed his ship into the huge tidal basin. Richards was conducting a hydrographic survey of the northwest coast shoreline for the Royal Navy. On entering the creek he expected to discover a water link to coal deposits he had noticed in Burrard Inlet. When he met a dead end he gave the basin the mundane name of False Creek. Captain Richards did not know then that forestry, not coal, would be the dominant industry of the new colony. Nor that the inlet that disappointed him so much would play a crucial role in the province's economy.

Captain Edward Stamp, Sewell Moody, Jeremiah Rogers and others erected mills and used False Creek for easy access to the immense Douglas fir stands in Shaughnessy, and for their vast booming grounds. Shipping prime B.C. lumber throughout the world, they prospered mightily. But the village that would be Vancouver remained a two-bit, hard-drinking, one-road town surrounded by bog and blackberry brambles.

Three events that would affect False Creek forever then happened in quick succession. First, the mighty Canadian Pacific Railway unexpectedly announced it would not stop at Port Moody but would extend to the open waters of English Bay. That decision gained it more than 2,400 hectares of land in the pioneer town. Then squatters who fled the Great Fire of 1886 chose to remain on False Creek's south shore and settle it rather than return to the town's devastated peninsula. The CPR was soon razing the trees on the slope and offering lots for sale.

And finally, in 1889, a bridge spanning the creek's two shores was built, the first of three Granville Street bridges.

These developments turned the focus of the new town south to False Creek. Businesses gravitated to it. Soon its banks were lined with sawmills and plants, transforming the tidal basin into the industrial heart of town. William Van Horne, head of the CPR and the most powerful figure in town, built extensive railway yards on False Creek's north shore, enticed by the offer of 20 tax-free years. This district became known as "Yaletown" after the CPR workers who settled there. They had worked at Yale, on the railway's line.

During World War 1 two railways, the Great Northern and the Canadian Northern Pacific Railway, contracted to have the east end of False Creek (from Main Street to Clark Drive) filled in to provide space for their yards and terminals. The CNPR's station—still there and known today as Pacific Central Station —went in in 1915, the Great Northern's was there from 1917 to 1965. By the 1890s False Creek was criss-crossed with bridges. Its waters were clogged with log booms, raw sewage, industrial waste, barges. Its banks were littered with smoke-belching sawmills, greasy wharves, rats and finally, in the Depression, with squatters. With fire such a hazard, the businesses commissioned the *J.H. Carlisle,* a fireboat, for exclusive False Creek service.

World War II was a boom time for the creek. But by the time it ended False Creek had become a seedy eyesore. The dream of its becoming Vancouver's secondary harbor was fading; large ships could not enter it, navigation was bad and the large industries were moving out. By 1950 many thought it should be filled-in, a suggestion Van Horne had made 60 years earlier. False Creek was a "filthy ditch" good for nothing but a sewage line down the centre. Those sentiments continued until consultants came up with a cost for draining the creek: an impossible $50 million.

"What To Do With False Creek" remained a favorite civic debate. By the 1960s, however, there was a change in public thinking and a group of local politicians began pushing for a clean-up of the creek. Accomplishing that required the cooperation of the Canadian Pacific Railway which, since Van Horne's day, had effective control of two-thirds of the creek land. The CPR had been leasing it to marginal customers who used its rail lines. Urban planner Walter Hardwick was given the job of approaching the CPR and the provincial government; their talks resulted in the biggest land swap in the city's history. The CPR, the province and the city basically threw their individual land holdings into a pot and re-arranged their ownership. The CPR returned control of 35 hectares on the creek's south side to the province which promptly flipped it to the city for $400,000 and a city-owned site in Burnaby that the province wanted for Simon Fraser University.

Now that it was in possession of False Creek's south shore the city began to act on its renewal plans. It announced that 1970 would be the common expiry date for leases along the creek's

Sawmills on the south shore of False Creek, circa 1920. vs

south shore, ending the decades-long tenure of many industries. The debate now was over what the next generation of False Creek tenants would be like. The controversy boiled into a furious public debate that split city council into two camps: the old school seeing secondary industry as the creek's only salvation and others like Hardwick who saw a future beyond industry. The pro-change group won the day and in 1972, led by Art Phillips, they swept to power at city hall.

Granville Island, as the centre of the city's industrial basin, inevitably was at the core of the entire creek's revitalization plan. Consultants working on the city-ordered False Creek study were asked by the federal government to include the island in their thinking. They recommended that False Creek become an urban mix of housing and public space and that Granville Island become an "urban park." City hall adopted this daring plan and set about cleaning up the industrial sludge along the creek, gouging out bays, lining the shore with a seawall and dividing the land among dozens of groups for residential development. With strict density and car limits, False Creek South blossomed into a remarkable mix of people and housing with a large, waterside park and a school in the middle. It remains one of the city's most popular districts.

An even more drastic change was destined for the CPR's former railyards on the creek's north side. The province took it as the future site of Expo 86. Despite immense opposition from the media, continuous labour disputes and last-minute haggling among countries, Expo 86 under the stewardship of

Jim Pattison turned out to be one of the most successful world's fairs ever.

At first, the provincial government, under Premier Bill Bennett, expected a crown corporation would develop this spectacular site, using False Creek's south shore as a model. But Bennett's successor, William Vander Zalm had other thoughts. He offered the entire 84-hectare site as one package to private developers. In spring, 1988, it was announced that Hong Kong billionaire, Li Ka-shing, one of the richest men in the world, was the top bidder, paying $320 million over 15 years. The local outcry was immediate. Vancouverites felt the deal of the century had been made too cheaply, too quickly and under great secrecy. "Mystery Unanswered, Questions Remain," a newspaper headline read more than a year after the deal closed.

Amid this storm of controversy Li Ka-shing's company, Concord Pacific, began drawing up blueprints for the huge area, in consultation with city officials. When finally presented, the official development plan revealed the largest development scheme in North America, an ambitious $3 billion re-designing of the entire shore. It shows a series of neighborhoods strung along the waterfront with 40 highrise towers, four parks, schools, marinas and a three-kilometre seawall. And as a salute to the area's industrial past, the CPR's Roundhouse has been preserved and is slated for use as a community centre. By 2010, when the last building is finished and sold, Concord Pacific should be home to 15,000 people and the north shore of False Creek at last open to all the residents of Vancouver.

Science World

Gillian Lunde

Camera trickery shows the science world building admired by two young fans. science world photo

A UNIQUE EXPERIENCE awaits visitors to Science World British Columbia. The centre, located in an Expo 86 legacy building at the eastern edge of False Creek, uses interactive exhibits and entertaining presentations to introduce people of all ages to the wonders of science and technology. This landmark silver geodesic dome building opened as Science World on May 6, 1989, but the centre's history is much older.

Under the leadership of Barbara Brink, the Junior League of Greater Vancouver and the City of Vancouver, the dream of establishing a science centre began in 1977. A set of hands-on exhibits known as the "Extended I" was displayed in venues around Vancouver prior to the opening of the Arts, Sciences & Technology Centre on January 15, 1982. Over six years, the temporary centre at the corner of Granville and Dunsmuir attracted more than 600,000 visitors. Another 400,000 benefited from the centre's outreach programs which travelled around the province. The demand for a permanent venue was clear; the only obstacles which stood in the way were finding a location and securing funding. Following Expo 86, an intensive lobbying campaign was launched to secure the Expo Centre for Science World. With three levels of government backing its proposal, the Arts, Sciences and Technology Centre succeeded in persuading the provincial government to designate the fair's famous "golf ball" as the new facility. The announcement was made in September 1987. A massive fund-raising campaign ensued, with donations from the federal, provincial and municipal governments, the GVRD, the private sector, foundations and individuals contributing $19.1 million to build an addition to the Expo Centre, redesign the interior and construct exhibits.

The public's first chance to see inside the new building came in the summer of 1988, with a four-month preview featuring *Dinosaurs! A Journey Through Time*. More than 350,000 visitors saw this blockbuster exhibition during its run. The centre closed during refurbishment, then permanently reopened with five new galleries filled with hands-on exhibits and the largest Omnimax screen in the world on May 6, 1989.

Today Science World is one of British Columbia's most popular educational family attractions with attendance of more than half a million visitors every year (including 60,000 children on school field trips). An additional 150,000 people enjoy its provincial outreach programs annually. Exhibitions such as *Star Trek Federation Science, Backyard Monsters: The World of Insects* and *The Return of the Dinosaurs* captivated the imagina-

tions of thousands, as did the Omnimax films *Blue Planet, Beavers* and *Antarctica*. The Omnimax theatre holds 401 people.

"Science About Us"—the science we experience every day—became an important focus for Science World exhibits in 1994. Issues which have special relevance for British Columbians, from the Lions Gate Bridge to how a building is erected over a SkyTrain station, were explored in a number of exhibits both inside and outside the centre. Also in 1994, Science World opened Mine Games, a major exhibition about the impact of mining on British Columbia. This exhibition was the first in a series on the theme of *The Living Planet*.

Among the centre's most popular exhibits are a crawl-through beaver lodge, a giant hollow walk-in red cedar tree, a busy beehive, a walk-on synthesizer, a shadow wall, a plasma ball that lights up when you touch it and a giant bubble sheet. Science World also features demonstrations in its Centre Stage area, on topics as diverse as water, fire, kinetic engineering and liquid nitrogen. In November 1995 the centre added an additional experience: the 3D Laser Theatre. Here educational presentations are made using state-of-the-art laser technology.

Over the years, Science World has played host to many dignitaries. Queen Elizabeth II dedicated the Expo Centre as "Science World. A science centre for the people of British Columbia" in October 1987. Former president of the Soviet Union Mikhail Gorbachev participated in a student forum at the centre prior to speaking at a fund-raising dinner for Science World in March 1993. Dr. Stephen Hawking, the physicist, visited in June 1993 to talk with some 150 disabled students about how he manages his disability—the life-threatening disease amyotrophic lateral sclerosis (ALS). Science World is a non-profit organization which raises more than 90 per cent of its annual operating budget. The balance of funds is generated through grants, donations and special fund-raising events.

Gastown
Chuck Davis

THE MOST WIDELY ACCEPTED VIEW is that Gastown— Vancouver in embryo—gets its name from its most famous resident, "Gassy Jack" Deighton. A competing, although weaker, claim is that a small pocket of natural gas in the area resulted in the name. The story of Deighton and of how his first saloon—built at a spot called Luck-Lucky ("grove of maple trees") next to Stamp's Mill in 24 hours on September 30/October 1, 1867—became the nucleus of the tiny settlement is told on Page 48.

Gastown started slowly. Sewell Moody's mill on the north shore had been going since 1862 and was doing well. In 1868 some 33 export cargoes left the inlet, with Moody's Mill— which produced three times as much wood as Stamp's Mill— claiming most. The steamer *Sea Foam* was transferred from Fraser River service to run as a ferry between Moody's Mill, Stamp's Mill and New Brighton (a resort at the north end of Douglas Road from New Westminster). And in 1869 Colonial Governor Frederick Seymour, visiting Burrard Inlet, included Gastown on his itinerary. But it was not a beehive of activity in the early years. "When customers were gone," wrote Raymond Hull and Olga Ruskin in *Gastown's Gassy Jack,* "Luck-Lucky was quiet. There were the Three Greenhorns a mile to the west, the mill half-a-mile east, a few lights across the inlet at Moodyville and, on three sides, the thick forest."

The BC and VI Mill manager, Edward Stamp, frequently argued with his partners and on January 2, 1869 ceased to be manager. The mill's business faltered. So, of course, did business at Gassy's saloon. Stamp's successor, Captain John Raymur, arrived to look over the mill, then strode over to Gastown. He stopped in horror, cast an alarmed eye over the muddy, squalid little settlement, then delivered himself of one of our local history's more pithy remarks: "What is the meaning of this aggregation of filth?"

Gastown could be a tense and dangerous place, with lots of drinking, fighting and theft. As well, many local native people were resentful of the intrusion into their land. In July of 1969 a man named Alfred Perry was axed to death by a native man named Stackeye, who confessed and was hanged. In *Making Vancouver* (published in 1996), Robert A.J. Mac-Donald writes interestingly of racial, economic and social levels in Gastown.

In February 1870 San Francisco-based owners bought the BC and VI Mill, which had closed, and changed its name to Hastings Mill (in honor of Admiral G. F. Hastings, commander of the British naval squadron at Esquimalt). The lumber market was so depressed the new owners delayed reopening. Only the busy mill across the inlet kept Gastown going.

A six-acre townsite—bounded by today's Water, Carrall, Hastings and Cambie streets, and including Gastown within it —was surveyed by the Crown and named Granville after the colonial secretary of the time. Many people continued to call it Gastown, and British Admiralty charts showed "Gastown" well into the 1880s. Gassy successfully bid $135 on one of the lots, half in cash, and built a larger establishment called Deighton House. Two storeys high, it included a hotel and billiard parlor. In August the Hastings Mill re-opened and Granville/Gastown was back at full throttle.

The entry of British Columbia into Canada on July 20, 1871 caused less of a stir in the townsite than the appointment the same year of its first constable. Jonathan Miller, who would go on to hold several other posts including customs collector and postmaster, and who lived in a cottage with a small lockup in the backyard, next to Deighton House. The two-cell log-built jail had no locks on the doors. Gaoler's Mews, in modern Gastown, recalls that early lockup. Then another indicator of stability appeared: at a public meeting residents agreed to start a private school. It opened the next year, called at first the Hastings Mill School, then, eventually, Granville School. Its students may have been among the crowd on April 24, 1872 when Gassy climbed to the roof of Deighton House and hoisted the first Canadian flag to fly in Burrard Inlet. The year 1872 also saw the establishment of the Granville Post Office, set up in the Hastings Mill Store. Then Polish-born Louis Gold arrived at Granville, and he and his wife Emma rented premises from Gassy and opened a general merchandise and grocery store. George Black started a butcher shop, built out over the water so meat could be lowered to customers who came by boat. New roads were connecting Granville to distant places like Hastings Townsite, Eburne (Marpole) and the Fraser Valley. It was still a rough, humble spot—and a small one: the 1873 population was 75. New Westminster's was about 1,500 at the time.

On May 29, 1875 the long-ailing Gassy Jack Deighton died. He was 44.

The tiny settlement's first church was established in 1876 by Methodist missionaries at water's edge at the northwest corner of Water and Abbott streets. Most of the parishioners were native mill workers which, says *Making Vancouver,* made non-natives reluctant to go. They attended Anglican services in the

PITMAN
BUSINESS COLLEGE **P**

Situated on the third floor of Birks Place, the College occupies 12,000 square feet of ultra-modern space and is equipped with state-of-the-art computers serviced by a 100-station Novell network and a Windows NT LAN with Windows 95 and the Internet.

Masonic Hall on the north shore until St. James Anglican (sponsored by the filth-detesting James Raymur) began services in 1881.

The end of Gastown/Granville came suddenly. By the time William Van Horne, the Canadian Pacific Railway's hard-nosed general manager, visited in August of 1884 it was known that Port Moody was out as the railway's terminus and that Granville—more precisely, Coal Harbour—was in. During his visit Van Horne was taken on a rowboat tour of the area by the CPR's local land commissioner, Lauchlan Hamilton. Looking around, Van Horne became excited. "Hamilton," he said, "this is destined to be a great port, and it must have a name commensurate with its greatness. And Vancouver it shall be, if I have a say in the matter." A word in the right ears in Ottawa and Victoria, and Granville vanished as a name. There was an explosion of real-estate activity in this place called "Vancouver." Lots bought for $66 before the news broke sold for $2,000 after.

Lauchlan Hamilton began laying out the Vancouver townsite in 1885, and on January 15, 1886 there appeared the first issue of the *Vancouver Weekly Herald and North Pacific News.* People were calling it Vancouver already, with incorporation as a city still three months away.

The old, the original, Gastown had disappeared after 29 years of life. As the years passed and the city grew, its centre of activity moved west and south. Beginning around the time of World War I the old area, which had become a warehouse district, started to sink into a slow decline. As Gastown observer Marc Denhez has written, "Gastown was being left alone—and thus began a 50-year journey on the slippery slope of economic stagnation and social decline. The warehouses gradually emptied, and the hotels often became home for Vancouver's skid-roaders."

The story of the fight to save the area—at a time when the civic, provincial and federal levels of government were in favor of demolishing it for massive redevelopment—is practically a book in itself. (In fact, Denhez wrote several chapters about it in *Heritage Fights Back,* published by Fitzhenry and Whiteside, 1978.) The campaign began as early as the late 1950s. Said Garry Marchant, writing in *The Review:* " . . . a small group of Gastown property owners had already started renovating their buildings and had launched a clean-up campaign in that part of the city. They were joined in the campaign—by an unusual coalition of 'urban rebels'—young businessmen and professionals, even younger street-corner entrepreneurs who sold crafts

facing page: Turn-of-the-century warehouses, Water Street, 1980. vp

Vancouver's Community Arts Council sponsored a walking tour to point out Gastown's charming buildings and colorful past. More than 700 people showed up in the rain

from stalls, academics, the Community Arts Council, architects, planners, and university professors, the Chinese community and various citizens' groups concerned with Vancouver's heritage." On September 22, 1968 Vancouver's Community Arts Council, which had been showing heritage film and slide shows on the area for years, sponsored a walking tour to point out Gastown's charming buildings and colorful past. More than 700 people showed up in the rain. The CAC organized more tours, and the prospect of Gastown's demolition began to fade. The Old Spaghetti Factory opened on Water Street in 1970, and its funky ambience drew big crowds to the area. Then in February 1971 the provincial government designated Gastown an historic site, and that ensured the old brick buildings would be saved from demolition.

The city joined in the beautification of Gastown in 1972. Next the federal government gave money, then the provincial. Utility wires were buried, trees were planted, and old-fashioned street lights, modeled somewhat after the originals, were installed. Subtle, unobtrusive touches were added: the chain-linked bollards between the sidewalks and the roadways are there to discourage jay-walking. That they happen to look good is a bonus. The streets were paved with brick. The city's planner for Gastown then, Jon Ellis, said it was the first time a North American city had torn up good streets to rebuild them in the old style. (Ellis, incidentally, is the man who conceived of Gastown's famous steam clock, created by Raymond Saunders and dedicated September 24, 1977.) When Gastown threw a party in September 1975 to celebrate the reopening of Water Street some 200,000 people showed up.

Today's Gastown is a lively collection of shops, art galleries, antique stores, offices, studios and ethnic restaurants housed in dozens of restored and refurbished heritage buildings. It is a magnet for thousands of tourists and locals.

Chinatowns in Greater Vancouver
Eleanor Yuen

VANCOUVER HAS THE biggest Chinatown in Canada, boasting a history of more than a century. When the City of Vancouver was incorporated in 1886 a small Chinese settlement had already developed at Shanghai Alley near what is now Pender and Carrall Streets. Soon, it started to develop along the shores of False Creek adjacent to Gastown. Though Victoria was the port-of-call then, Vancouver was dubbed "Salt Water City" by the Chinese and was their favorite city for settlement. Smaller groups of Chinese laborers, farmers and merchants were also found in Nanaimo and New Westminster.

The typical Chinatown building at that time was a two-storey wooden structure with a storefront on the ground floor and the residence and meeting rooms tucked in on the second floor. The area was often cramped, run-down and dirty. Many of the buildings now standing in the commercial and tourist centre were built by different clan associations in the early 1980s. The architecture of these three-storey brick buildings with recessed balconies and decorative metal railings were modeled after structures in Southern China.

In 1971 the municipal government quelled the growth of Chinatown by declaring it an historical area where all old buildings of significant value were to be preserved and new development strictly controlled. This designation was a blessing in those years as it helped fight proposals for a freeway across the heart of the area. A decade later, however, the heritage classification turned into a curse by stalling development in the district. Meanwhile Chinatown underwent two "beautification projects". New lampposts, phone booths with oriental designs and colorful banners added festive charm to Chinatown while modern shopping arcades such as the Golden Crown Centre and the Golden Gate shopping mall gave the area a face-lift.

Today Chinatown is a lively cultural centre frequented by the Vancouver Chinese community and tourists alike during weekends and Chinese festivals. To many of its patrons it is also a commercial hub with its 13 financial institutions and numerous professional services where business can be carried out in the mother tongue. Both the Sun Yat-sen Garden, a major attraction featuring classical Ming Dynasty garden architecture, and the Chinese Cultural Centre which hosts a variety of cultural events, were built with support from the city. Plans for a new wing in the centre to house a museum, library and retail stores are now in the pipeline. Restaurants offering savory cuisines, shops specializing in famous Southern Chinese barbecue meat, Chinese herbs, health foods, seafood, groceries and articrafts, and theatres showing Chinese opera and film line the busy streets bounded by Hastings, Georgia, Jackson and Carrall. Shopping in Chinatown is always enjoyable because of the great variety of commodities, its self-containment and its century-old traditions. Toishanese, Cantonese, Mandarin and English mingle freely in the hustle-and-bustle of everyday business. Chinese from many different parts of the world come here for a taste of their old traditions. To this day clan and locality associations, tongs and cultural societies still attract the ethnic Chinese community, even when pitted against the modern Concord Pacific project to the immediate east of the area.

The Chinatown Merchants Association worked very hard to maintain its vitality in the mid 1980s when suburbs such as Richmond, Burnaby and Coquitlam started to develop into major Chinese settlement areas, drawing substantial business away from their merchants. Its greatest task in the last decade has been fighting for the construction of a 100-car parkade (which materialized in 1995), part and parcel of a huge development plan funded by local and offshore investments. Other major milestones in the rejuvenation of Chinatown are the new Chinatown Plaza which accommodates the largest Chinese restaurant in Canada, seating 1,000 people in total, and the new Wayfoong House which houses Hongkong Bank's Chinatown branch serving about 20,000 clients. Their business catchment area will no doubt be further broadened with residential projects in the neighborhood such as the International Village. Citygate, General Motors Place and 84 residential units with retail outlets in the 200-block East Georgia are complete. It should also draw a good mix of upscale residents who used to shun the area because of its proximity to the Downtown Eastside.

Meanwhile the quality of life in Chinatown in general has been enhanced by the redevelopment of Block 17 which includes new quarters for SUCCESS, a 100-bed intermediate care facility and hundreds of units of social and market housing. The presence of a community police storefront and security personnel hired by merchants help make Chinatown a safer place to live and visit. Even the neighborhood's notoriously high taxes started to level off in 1994 and gave merchants some much needed breathing space. In view of all these favorable factors, Chinatown is now charged for another boom and enjoys a rosy vista despite the squeeze from Richmond and its new Chinatown.

Demographic changes in Chinatown were once a significant sign-post in Chinese immigration trends. After 1947 the rate of immigration was bolstered by family reunification and some

Lee Building, Chinatown, showing the recessed balconies typical of the area's architecture. cva

sitting on the mouth of the Fraser River.

In 1961 there were only 298 ethnic Chinese in Richmond. By 1994 about 25 per cent of its population was ethnic Chinese from Hong Kong, Taiwan, mainland China and the Philippines. They are served by social services centres such as the Caring Place and community groups like the Richmond Chinese Community Society. Chinese specialty food markets, Asian malls, the President Hotel and numerous restaurants offering a broad variety of Chinese cuisines sprawl along No. 3 Road. Aberdeen Centre, Parker Place, Yaohan and the T&T shopping mall form the longest stretch of modern Chinese shopping arcades in North America. It is also said to have attracted the highest concentration of good Chinese cooks in overseas Chinatowns. To accommodate the rapid influx of population, city council plans to encourage high density housing in its town centre area which lies between Blundell and Bridgeport on both sides of No. 3 Road. The Chinese propensity to stay where their language is spoken started the snowball effect, making Richmond the new Chinatown for the middle class. Traditional festivals are celebrated in Richmond with the same fervor displayed at shows by pop singers flown in fresh from their homeland. Two Chinese language radio stations, CHMB AM 1320 and CJVB AM 1470, and the *Ming Pao* newspaper have all chosen to set up offices here. With all this prosperity and rapid ethnic change, however, come problems such as huge ESL (English-as-a-second-language) classes, traffic jams, changes in neighborhood character, pressure on services and higher property prices, to name just a few. Nevertheless, the new dynamic of the city has come from some fundamental changes in the nature of Chinese business which are now dominated by large scale food retailing, professional services, corporate investments and realty. Richmond's outskirts, on the other hand, have been rapidly taken up by manufacturing industries and have become a satellite of the town itself, whereas farmland on Steveston Highway east of No. 4 Road and a five-hectare nursery site right in the downtown core have given way to new residential and commercial developments. Even the fishermen's quay has been quick to respond to the delicate Chinese taste for live seafood. Residentially, Richmond tends to attract many affluent or professional Chinese immigrants.

Within the last two decades the Chinese have helped change Richmond from a sleepy fishermen's village into a city of over 140,000 people. Together with the old Chinatown on the eastside of downtown Vancouver they house about 270,000 Chinese and will surely go down in the history of Canada as models of historical and modern Chinatowns.

newcomers moved into the adjacent Strathcona region. In the 1960s Strathcona was targeted for redevelopment and the McLean Park housing project was built under the city urban renewal plan. In response, the Strathcona Property Owners and Tenants Association (SPOTA) was formed to ensure preservation of the character of the neighborhood. Many elderly Chinese prefer to live in a familiar environment and senior housing built by the Chow Lun Association at Keefer and Gore and other projects along Hastings and Main became their home.

Many locally born Chinese who came of age in the 1980s, along with overseas immigrants with a taste for more spacious houses, have chosen to settle in new suburbs in the south and east. This factor coupled with its proximity to the Vancouver International Airport and the United States helped kick off the speedy development of Richmond, a small piece of flat land

Sport

THERE IS A SCIENCE fiction story of an alien race poring for generations over a piece of film from a long-deserted planet Earth, puzzling over the beings in it and writing speculative essays on how they must have lived. The last line on the film reads A Walt Disney Production.

Should the aliens get around to studying the ancient sporting culture of the planet's western quadrant of the northern half of one of its continents, they might find a sign just as puzzling: (INSERT NAME) MUST GO!

"Go where?" they'll ask, as they struggle to break the linguistic code. "And what kind of a name is INSERT?" Maybe they'll write essays and argue it over whatever they drink, or ingest, or pour over their mandibles. But they'll never understand those four words that have been the driving force of Vancouver sport since Pandora opened the idiot box and unleashed the demons of home TV.

Until then, sport was an activity watched by those with the gumption to go into rinks or sit in open stadiums or tramp the fairways to see the action firsthand. Television offered the joys and frustrations of fandom without ever leaving the living room. And it didn't just make them fans, it made them instant coaches. Three losses into any season—and over the years, Vancouver teams have done more losing than winning—they knew that they could do it better than the jerk who was doing it now.

They couldn't get the job, but they could damned well demand that the teams get rid of the incumbents. They could write letters, phone talk shows, hang signs from the concourse at the rink or stadium. With luck ("Hi, Mom!") they might even get on TV themselves. And the beauty of it was that with football, basketball, hockey, soccer and baseball operating professional franchises, discontent was never out of season. Only the names changed.

The modern Vancouver sports fan, the aliens might discover, was divided into several sub-species:

Jockophis Invisibles: Surfaces as disembodied voice on radio program. Answers to name like Ben From Burnaby and Sam From Surrey. Known for distinctive cry: "Hi, Dan, Howyadooon? Like, I was wundrin—how come Canucks don't trade for Mario Lemieux?"

Memoribiliacus Collectus: Scavenger. Buys photos, cards, balls and sticks used and signed by athletes. Takes them to lair and slobbers over them. Believes he has a life.

Trivias Incurabilis: Full-throated, tiny-brained collector of useless information. Known to turn violent: "Hey, yoose guys didn't run the collective career batting averages of red-headed, left-handed shortstops in the Pacific Coast League pre-war seasons. A lotta people wanna know this stuff. Smarten up!"

Poolsharkis Knowitallis (male): Lives to choose players who get more points in their sport than players chosen by all the other Poolocrats. Cry: "Who-cares-who-wins? . . . Who-cares-who-wins? . . . Who-got-points? . . . Who-got-points?"

Poolsharkis Knowitallis (female): Employed by male counterpart to collect pool information. Haunts sports departments, calling in to plead, "Uh, could you give me all the goals and assists and penalty things in all the games tonight? The boss has to have them before 8 A.M. so he'll know whether to go to the office and crow, or call in sick . . . ?

Post-Lobotomis Idiotus: Psychologically incapable of leaving for hockey game without equipment check. ("Octopus? Check. Rubber chicken? Check. Live white mouse? Check. Pennies for heating and throwing on ice? Check. Referee Sucks sign? Check.") Known for driving half-way to rink, turning, and coming home. Forgot tickets.

All these things the aliens could probably pick up over a few centuries—and yet, like the Disney cartoon, they would not begin to tell the whole story. They would overlook the common denominator, the single thread that runs through Vancouver's sporting culture and always will. It is (blush) love.

The Vancouver sports fan in all his, hers or its diverse forms is wildly, covertly and sometimes ashamedly in love with the teams he shells out money to see in person, or spends the hours at home or in the pub watching on TV and knocking back a few with fellow addicts. Always has been, always will be. Don't talk to them ozone layers, unemployment, oil slicks, fire, flood, pestilence, politics or the GST. That stuff's for later, when the game's over and they've figured out which coach to fire next.

—Jim Taylor

facing page: Vancouver Canadians vs Tucson, Nat Bailey Stadium, 1994. vs
above: Nat Bailey Stadium, 1991. vp

Hockey

Mark Leiren-Young

THERE WERE JUST 1.6 SECONDS left in game seven of the 1994-95 Stanley Cup finals and the Canucks were trailing the New York Rangers by a score of 3-2. Vancouver coach Pat Quinn sent Pavel Bure out to take the face-off. The Canucks needed a miracle and as the leading goal scorer in the playoffs, "The Russian Rocket" was the team's designated miracle worker. But when the puck dropped, Craig MacTavish won the draw and a series many hockey observers believe was the most exciting Stanley Cup final ever had come to an end.

Although it was the Rangers who sipped champagne from Lord Stanley's mug there was no doubt in anyone's mind that the Canucks were also winners. Over the course of 24 playoff games the team had electrified the hockey world. Until the day they bring the Cup to the city for the first time since the Vancouver Millionaires won it in 1915, the 1994-95 playoffs will stand as the franchise's finest hours.

When the Pacific Coliseum opened its doors in 1968, Vancouver civic chaplain George Turpin offered the prayer: "Please God, bring us the NHL." In 1970 his prayers were answered when the Canucks were admitted to the league along with the Buffalo Sabres at a seemingly outrageous expansion fee of $6 million (three times what the cost had been when six teams joined in 1967). The original applicants balked at the price and the franchise was purchased by Minneapolis entrepreneur Tom Scallen. (In 1974 Scallen found himself in deep financial—and legal—trouble and sold the team for $9 million to Frank Griffith's Vancouver-based telecommunication's company, Western Broadcasting.)

In order to determine who would have first choice at the expansion draft a wheel of fortune was spun at the Queen Elizabeth Hotel in Montreal. The Sabres won, choosing future Hall of Famer Gilbert Perreault. The Canucks took Dale Tallon who racked up 137 points in three seasons as a Canuck but never became the franchise player the team had hoped for (although he was later traded to Chicago for Jerry Korab and franchise player Gary "Suitcase" Smith, the goalie who almost single-handedly carried the Canucks to their first-ever division title in 1975, winning 32 games with six shutouts).

After more than 20 years as a Western Hockey League franchise (1948 to 1970), the Canucks played their first NHL game on October 9, 1970, losing 3 to 1 to the Los Angeles Kings with the lone Canuck goal scored in the third period by defense man Barry Wilkins. The team's first captain, their second pick in the expansion draft, was Orland Kurtenbach, who later coached the Canucks. Their fourth pick was defense man Pat Quinn, who took over the team in 1987. The first coach was Hal Laycoe and general manager was Norman (Bud) Poile.

The Canucks revamped their uniforms in 1978 changing the team colors from the original blue, green and white (with hockey stick logo) to a yellow, orange and black outfit that looked like a bad set of pajamas. A San Francisco marketing firm claimed it would strike fear into the hearts of opponents, but all it induced was giggles and they soon switched to a more subdued uniform—although they did keep the speeding skate logo.

The year 1982 witnessed "the miracle on Renfrew Street." Under interim coach Roger Neilson (who was filling in for Harry Neale who had been suspended after getting into a fight in the stands in Quebec) and with the heroic goaltending of "King" Richard Brodeur, the Canucks trounced Calgary 3-0 in the first round, then took out Los Angeles 4-1 but ran into trouble in game two of the Campbell conference final against the Chicago Blackhawks. The Canucks were losing 3-1 in the third period and were frustrated by a series of calls by referee Bob Myers—including a disallowed goal—so Neilson showed his dismay by raising a white towel. Players Gerry Minor and Tiger Williams joined in and towel power was born. Although the Canucks received a bench penalty and went on to lose the game, the sarcastic gesture galvanized the team and when they returned to Vancouver the loyal fans were all waving white towels.

Between towel power and the home fans chants of "Na Na Na Hey Hey Good-bye" the Canucks won the next three games, knocking off the Hawks before running into the then-unstoppable New York Islanders. Vancouver fans were so proud of their team that despite losing the final in four straight games, half-a-million people lined Burrard Street for a joyous victory parade.

The next milestone was 1987 when the Canucks hired Pat Quinn away from the L.A. Kings bringing him back to Vancouver as president, general manager and some-time coach.

In 1988, Quinn's first draft pick was future captain Trevor Linden. Linden was voted Hockey News Rookie of the Year that season and in 1996 became the Canucks iron-man after passing Don Lever's record of 437 consecutive games.

In 1989 the Canucks took the Calgary Flames to the seventh game of the first playoff round before losing on a disputed overtime goal (it was kicked dammit!) by Joel Otto that sent the Flames on to their first-ever Stanley Cup. Then on June 7, 1989 the Canucks made possibly the best sixth-round pick in

The warm and welcoming ambience of the Beatty St. Bar & Grill— with cherry stained woodwork, abundant natural light and a sophisticated lighting system—sets the right mood, day or night. Fifteen big-screen satellite TV's let people keep their eye on the ball, the puck or their favorite sporting event. A billiards table awaits those who would rather play than watch.

NHL history when they chose Pavel Bure. In order to be eligible for the draft a Russian player needed 11 games at the elite level and the stats claimed Bure had only played 10. The Canucks scouts disagreed and an investigation by the NHL proved they were right.

The move paid immediate dividends when Bure jumped on the ice for his first NHL game, November 5, 1991 against the Winnipeg Jets. He stunned fans and players alike with his dazzling speed prompting *Sun* reporter Iain McIntyre to label him "the Russian Rocket." Despite joining Vancouver 16 games into the season Bure won the NHL's Calder trophy for Rookie of the Year becoming the first Canuck player ever to win an NHL award. Pat Quinn also received silverware that season when the NHL awarded him his second Jack Adams Trophy as Coach of the Year (he'd previously won in Philadelphia).

In 1992 and 1993 the Canucks finished at the top of the Campbell conference but were unable to get past the second round in the playoffs. Then, in 1994, after a mediocre season, the Canucks caught fire against the Flames. Trailing in the first-round best-of-seven series by three games to one the Canucks won three consecutive overtime games to advance to the conference finals. The most miraculous moment came at 11:40 in overtime when goalie Kirk McLean, who had been spectacular throughout the series (and would remain so for the entire playoff run), made a seemingly impossible stop on Robert Reichel. Dubbed "the save of the century," McLean stole the Flames spark and gave Bure the opportunity to beat Calgary goalie Mike Vernon in the second overtime period to win the series.

The Canucks disposed of their next opponent, the Dallas Stars, in five games and went on to win national gloating rights and the conference championship by knocking out the Toronto Maple Leafs in five.

For their second trip to the finals the Canucks were again faced with a seemingly unstoppable team from New York. Led by gritty superstar Mark Messier the Rangers took a three-game-to-one lead before the Canucks stunned the hockey world by taking the series to seven games.

Off the ice the big news came the following season when controlling interest in the Canucks parent company Northwest Entertainment was sold to Seattle cellular phone moguls John and Bruce McCaw who created a new company, Orca Bay Sports and Entertainment, which operates the Canucks and the NBA Grizzlies.

In 1995-96 the Canucks left the Coliseum (which they leased) to move to their new downtown home, General Motors Place, Orca Bay's 19,000-seat, state-of-the-art facility which cost more than $160 million (including real estate). They also made one of the most dramatic signings in the team's history, apparently stealing Russian superstar Alexander Mogilny from the Buffalo Sabres in exchange for a first round draft pick, Mike Peca and Mike Wilson.

So far the team has only one retired number—12—worn by Stan "The Steamer" Smyl. The former captain is the team's all-time leading scorer with 262 goals and 411 assists during his team-leading 896 games in a Canuck uniform and joined the team as an assistant coach after retiring in 1991. The only Canucks in the Hockey Hall of Fame are Frank Griffiths (1917-94) the team's long-time owner and former NHL governor who is honored in the builders category, and "the voice of the Vancouver Canucks," play-by-play man Jim Robson honored in the media category.

Off the ice the Canucks' biggest achievement is the creation of Canuck Place, a hospice for terminally ill children that opened in Vancouver in 1994. Canuck Place was set up through the work of the Canuck Foundation, their community fundraising organization which was incorporated in 1986.

Vancouver Canucks vs New York Rangers, Stanley Cup Playoffs, 1994. vs

Football
Jim Kearney

FOOTBALL, CANADIAN STYLE—12 men, three downs, a 110-yard field and 25-yard end zones—did not, as many believe, make its Vancouver debut with the birth of the B.C. Lions in 1954.

While the early history of the game here is a little vague, its probable start can be traced back to Nov. 11, 1924 when two teams, one junior and the other senior, were put together at UBC. The juniors were the first into the field of play January 17, 1925, beating a team named the Tillicums, 17-5. The seniors followed a week later, losing, 7-6, to St. Mark's, the campus theological college.

By 1928 the Thunderbirds won the provincial championship under their pioneer coach Dr. Gordon Burke and were 12-1 losers to Regina Roughriders when they challenged for the Western Canada title. Two years later, in 1930, they made history of sorts in Athletic Park at 5th and Hemlock, the first sports ground in Canada to be equipped with floodlights. An exhibition game against Hamilton Tigers was the first football game in the country to be played under lights.

They made history again in 1933, once more at Athletic Park, in the first-ever football game in Canada to be called on account of fog. A contemporary report said the fog was so thick that at one point the two reporters covering the game—Don Tyerman of the *Province* and Hal Straight of the *Sun*—walked onto the field and stuck their heads into the UBC huddle in an effort to find out was going on.

The University of Alberta Golden Bears were leading, 8-3, when the referee stopped the game because nobody could find the ball. As it happened, a visiting player, Pete Rule, had tucked it inside his jersey and was crawling, on hands and knees, along the far sidelines, hoping he wouldn't be noticed until he crossed the UBC goal line 50 yards away.

Two days later the game was replayed in bright sunshine and the Thunderbirds won, 12-5. The losing quarterback, Reg Moir, later moved to Vancouver, worked as a night side reporter at the *Province* while earning a law degree at UBC and eventually became a provincial court judge in Kelowna.

During the 1930s UBC, along with the Meralomas, the Vancouver Athletic Club and the North Shore Lions, formed the senior Big Four League. The calibre of play was a considerable cut below the product being played on the prairies in the Western Interprovincial Football Union (WIFU).

Indeed, it was so unsophisticated a 1934 photo in the Vancouver Archives shows the Meralomas, most of them playing without helmets, in the process of losing to the completely helmeted Roughriders from Regina.

The advent of World War II put an end to the Big Four but ironically, brought professional football to the city for the first time. When Calgary Broncs, as they were then known, suspended operations for the duration before the start of the 1941 season, WIFU was in need of another city to join Regina and Winnipeg.

Led by Vancouver engineer and restaurant owner I.A. (Tiny) Rader, and *Province* sports columnist Jim Coleman, a group of local enthusiasts brought in the remains of the Calgary team, merged them with the best of the local players and named the team the Grizzlies.

They were hardly as fearsome as the kings of the bear family, winning only once in an eight-game schedule. To add to their miseries, every one of their home games was visited by a torrential downpour. After one season the Grizzlies were no more. The Lions came along 13 years later.

But between the death of the Grizzlies and the birth of the Lions, Vancouver won its first-ever national championship—at the junior level. The Vancouver Blue Bombers, coached by Ranjit Mattu and quarterbacked by Lorne Cullen, beat Hamilton here to win the 1924 Canadian title.

While the Lions weren't born until 1954, the gestation period started three years earlier, on the evening of November 19, 1951, to be precise. A column by then-*Sun* sports editor Andy Lyttle, chastising Vancouver for not joining Canada's other major cities in pro football inspired a meeting at the Pender Auditorium, where 400 "average fans" appointed an organizing committee headed once more by Tiny Rader.

Their initial attempts to get Vancouver into WIFU at first were rebuffed, but when the decision was made to build a new stadium to house the 1954 Commonwealth Games, the lure of 25,000 seats in Canada's third-largest city brought official acceptance by Edmonton, Calgary and Regina in 1953. Winnipeg voted against admitting the team to be known as the Lions.

Their first season was 1954. From a rocky 1-15 start they went on to five Grey Cup appearances and three national championships in the next 40 years. Just over a decade after their founding they won the first of their Grey Cups, in 1964. The others came in 1985 and 1994.

On the junior scene it was another 35 years after the 1947 Blue Bombers before the national title returned to Greater Vancouver. Renfrew Trojans were the 1982 winners. Richmond Raiders (1984) and Surrey Rams (1992) were losing finalists.

The Lions also had two losing trips to the national final—in

BC Lions win the Grey Cup, BC Place, 1994. vp

1963 and 1983. Their 34-24 win over Hamilton Tigercats in the 1964 final was, in terms of national respect, the most important event in the team's history. This was their first championship. The first in anything tends to be the most defining moment, the most memorable event.

The day after their historic win, the following appeared in the *Vancouver Sun:* "Eleven years and eight months after the event, it's almost impossible to believe the circumstances into which this team was born. The Lions became flesh and blood with the hiring of their first employee, Vida Scott, on All-Fools Day, 1953. In light of future antics, no more appropriate starting day could have been selected.

"They opened up shop in one room at 411 West Hastings. It was lighted by a 60-watt bulb, at the top of a long and sagging flight of stairs in a tumbledown building which has long since been razed. Even at that time the premises were condemned, which was the reason they were able to get office space at $25 a month. Until Annis Stukus was hired later in the month as the team's first coach, Vida had the place to herself.

"When payday rolled around every two weeks, she and Stuke would phone up some of the club's 24 directors and remind them. They in turn would hit the streets and sell enough $20 memberships to meet the payroll for another fortnight.

"And that's how the Lions existed for almost a year before they announced the signing of Arnie Weinmeister (an All-Pro from the NFL New York Giants) the day they opened their first-ever season ticket campaign. It was the first time in pro football history a defensive tackle sold 9,000 season tickets and put a club in business."

Weinmeister was long gone when they won their first championship. To this day the three most memorable names from that historic moment are quarterback Joe Kapp, running back Willie Fleming and middle linebacker Tom Brown. They were the foundation on which this championship team was built.

Quarterback Roy DeWalt and wide receiver Mervyn Fernandez provided the offense for the 1985 champions and 20-year veteran place kicker Lui Passaglia was the 1994 hero, kicking the winning field goal on the final play of the first Canada-U.S. final, against Baltimore Stallions, at B.C. Place Stadium. It was the Lions' first title win before a home crowd.

At the college level, UBC Thunderbirds won the only two national championships to date, in their 70-year existence, during the 1980s. Coached by Frank Smith, the 'Birds best the University of Western Ontario Mustangs in 1982 and again in 1986. They were losing finalists in 1978 and 1987.

When Simon Fraser University opened in 1965, it was the only university in Canada to offer athletic scholarships for academically qualified students. Instead of playing Canadian football the Clansman opted to play American football in the small college National Association of Intercollegiate Athletics (NATA). The only Canadian school in NATA, Simon Fraser University has sent more players into the Canadian Football League than any other university in Canada—more than 150 by the eve of the new century.

Soccer
Jack Keating

SOCCER HAS A RICH and storied history in Vancouver. But the same has also had more ups-and-downs than the PNE rollercoaster. Undoubtedly soccer's grandest time was the glory days of the Vancouver Whitecaps, who won the hearts of the city with a remarkable couple of years.

It was the late 1970s and the Whitecaps "turned on" the city. At the height of the euphoria they were greeted by an estimated 100,000 people who turned out, into, and around Robson Square on September 9, 1979 to celebrate the victory that made the team the champions of the North American Soccer League (NASL).

The Whitecaps, on two goals by Trevor Whymark, defeated the Tampa Bay Rowdies 2-1 to win the coveted Soccer Bowl on September 8, 1979 at Giants Stadium in East Rutherford, N.J.

But the Soccer Bowl victory was set up by an astounding upset victory over the powerful New York Cosmos led by Franz Beckenbauer, Giorgio Chinaglia, Johan Neaskans and a raft of other international stars.

Goals by Willie Johnston and Whymark gave the Whitecaps a 2-0 first-leg win over the Cosmos before 32,875 fans at Empire Stadium.

The Cosmos won the second leg 3-1 and after the so-called mini-game ended in a 0-0 tie there was an NASL shootout. Bobby Lenarduzzi, Carl Valentine and Derek Possee scored for Vancouver while goalkeeper Phil Lofty Parkes out-dueled his New York counterpart. The Whitecaps emerged victorious at Giants Stadium and advanced to the aforementioned final.

Earlier, the Whitecaps beat Dallas Tornado and Los Angeles Aztecs in the first two rounds of the playoffs for a crack at the mighty Cosmos. After losing the first game at Pasadena's Rose Bowl, the Whitecaps faced the difficult task of beating L.A. twice on the same night at Empire.

The victory over the Johan Cruyff-led Aztecs resulted from Kevin Hector's goal in a dramatic 1-0 win before a chanting, singing crowd of 32,379 at Empire Stadium. "This town has never had a night to match it," wrote veteran *Province* sports columnist Eric Whitehead.

The Soccer Bowl triumph followed on the heels of an NASL best 24-6 first-place finish in 1978, highlighted by an NASL-record 13-game winning streak of 13 games to finish the regular season. That was the year the Whitecaps were drawing crowds of close to 30,000 at Empire Stadium, a far cry from the team's early days after its "berth" in 1974 following in the tracks of the

city's first professional team, the Vancouver Royals, who played one season in the NASL in 1968.

The NASL and the Whitecaps folded after the 1984 season and sadly Empire Stadium, which opened in 1954, was torn down by short-sighted politicians in 1993. It was the second soccer venue torn down by short-sighted politicians, who in 1971 demolished Callister Park.

Out of the ashes of the Whitecaps rose the Vancouver 86ers in 1987. While the Whitecaps were a glamor team playing in American Major League cities like New York, Chicago, Boston and Los Angeles against international stars such as Pele, Beckenbauer, Cruyff, and English stars like George Best, Rodney Marsh et al., the 86ers relied on local talent to take on the best of Canada in cities such as Edmonton, Calgary, Winnipeg, Toronto, Hamilton, North York, Ottawa and Montreal.

Under the direction of coach Bobby Lenarduzzi, the 86ers rapidly became the most successful soccer team in Canada, rarely tasting defeat in the Canadian Soccer League (CSL). The 86ers captured four consecutive CSL championships from 1988 to 1991 and set a raft of records along the way, including an incredible 46-game (37-0-9) streak without a defeat from June 8, 1988 to August 8, 1989.

Dominating Canadian pro soccer the 86ers added to their remarkable record, winning a fourth consecutive CSL championship with a 5-3 win over the Toronto Blizzard on October 6, 1991.

Vancouver's Domenic Mobilio became the most prolific goal scorer in the Canadian Soccer League, including a CSL record of 25 goals in 28 games earning him most valuable player honors in 1991. Mobilio scored 93 career goals making him the all-time CSL goal-scoring leader when the league folded and the 86ers moved to the American Professional Soccer league in 1993.

Mobilio, John Catliff and Dale Mitchell were outstanding Vancouver-born players with the 86ers and Canada's national team. Catliff scored 80 goals in the CSL and was a member of five CSL championship teams (four with Vancouver and one with Calgary). "British Columbia starts with the excellent youth soccer system and grows from there," said Dick Mosher, head coach of the UBC soccer Thunderbirds, winners of five of six Canadian Intercollegiate Athletic Association championships from 1989 to 1994.

Dozens of players from the Lower Mainland became fulltime professional players with the 24-NASL teams, including the Whitecaps. With experience from the pro ranks, Canada reached the World Cup for the first time in 1986 in Mexico. Coached by former Whitecaps coach and West Vancouver resident Tony Waiters, the Canadian team included Vancouver's Bobby Lenarduzzi and Dale Mitchell, Richmond's Randy Samuel, Coquitlam's Bruce Wilson, David Norman and Paul Dolan, and Manchester-born Carl Valentine. The team reached the World Cup finals with a dramatic 2-1 win over Honduras in St. John's, Nfld.

The groundwork for the success of the Whitecaps both on and off the field was really hatched by the rich history of the game in the Vancouver-based Pacific Coast Soccer League or Coast League as it was commonly called. "The records will show that British Columbia won the national championship more than any other province. We've always had a good calibre of soccer," said Dave Fryatt, who has a total of 32 years of service to the B.C. Soccer Association, including 18 years as president. In fact, our teams have won the Canadian championship 37 times, including 29 by Greater Vancouver-based teams, in the 72-year history of the Canadian amateur senior men's championship.

For more than five decades soccer's legendary home was Callister Park, formerly known as Con Jones Park, across from the PNE grounds. Bounded by Renfrew, Oxford, Kaslo and Cambridge streets it was built by Con Jones in 1912 as a showpiece for his Vancouver field lacrosse team and its newly signed star player Newsy Lalonde. The old wooden stands, which completely surrounded the field, burned down in the 1930s; the rebuilt version lasted until the stadium was torn down in 1971. Jones, an ex-bookie from Australia turned tobacco-and-sports entrepreneur was known for the slogan "Don't argue Con Jones sells fresh tobacco" on Vancouver's first neon sign. He died in 1942 and the park reverted to Mrs. Ada Stevenson, who deeded it to the city on the condition that it be renamed for her uncle, John Callister. The PNE abused Callister Park, allowing a rodeo in 1960 and then demolition car derbys that destroyed the grass field. All the while it allowed the stadium to deteriorate.

Goalkeeper Ken Pears; backs Dave Stothard, Buster Cairns; half-backs Jack Steele, Pat Philley, Doug Greig; right wing Gordie Top; inside right Brian Phillay; centre forward Art Hughes; inside left Gordon "Gogie" Stewart; and outside left Normie McLeod were among the big names at Callister in the fifties and sixies. The aforementioned players formed Canada's starting team against Mexico and the U.S. for the World Cup in Sweden.

Starting in the early 1900s, soccer was also played at Recreation Park at Homer and Smithe and at Athletic Park. The latter was located at West 6th and Hemlock under what is now the on-ramp to the Granville Street Bridge, The local soccer scene was spiced by touring teams from the United Kingdom that came to play the Vancouver and B.C. All-Stars at Callister Park and, from the mid-fifties at Empire Stadium.

The records will show that British Columbia won the national championship more than any other province. We've always had a good calibre of soccer

Although there were some touring games in the 1920s and 1930s, they became a regular feature a few years after World War II. In June of 1956 Vancouver had what was termed its first Dream Game between two professional teams rather than a professional against an amateur all-star team. Aberdeen played Everton to a 3-3 draw at Empire Stadium attracting 18,000 in the pouring rain. Moscow Lokomotive also came here in 1956 to play the Vancouver All-Stars, the first sports group to come to North America from the Soviet Union. Real Madrid, Leningrad, Liverpool, Wolverhampton, Rangu of Brazil and Red Star Belgrade were among the glamor teams who came in the sixties.

After Nanaimo won this province's first two national titles in 1923 and 1927, the New Westminster Royals, known as the Westminsters Royals, captured the Lower Mainland's first national title in 1928. They won again in 1930, 1931, 1936, 1953, 1955, 1958 and 1960. Vancouver Firefighters, winners of four Canadian championships, have also won a record 11 Province Cups, followed by North Shore United with nine.

Dave Turner, who played nine years as inside forward with the Royals in the twenties and thirties was named Canada's player of the half century. He was inducted into the B.C. Sports Hall of Fame as well as the Canadian Sports Hall of Fame. Originally from Scotland, Turner resided in Vancouver. The Royals were owned by Fred Hume, a wealthy electrical contractor, who became mayor of New Westminster and Vancouver.

Aubrey Sanford, another Royals player, is also in the B.C. Sports Hall of Fame. Austin Delaney of the Royals was also a top player of the same period. Les Wilson, who grew up in South Vancouver, played nine years with Wolverhampton in the sixties and early seventies. Coquitlam's Craig Forrest is now a goalkeeping star with England's Ipswich.

As former UBC football coach Frank Smith once quipped, "You can shake any tree in B.C. and 11 soccer players fall out."

Ball, Thou Art Mine
Tom Hawthorn

ON DOMINION DAY, 1900, a Victoria batter hit a routine pop fly just over the infield at the Powell Street Grounds. Billy Holmes, Vancouver's handsome and popular infielder, settled beneath the ball, pointed skyward, and announced: "Thou art mine."

The ball settled softly in his hands, before dropping to the ground. "The general public are warned," the Vancouver *Daily World* reported the next day, "that it is 'quite' unnecessary to repeat the words 'Thou art mine' to the genial Billy."

It comes as a surprise to most to learn that Vancouver—a city associated with hockey's Canucks, basketball's Grizzlies and football's Lions—has a rich baseball history. Yet, every summer, thousands press into tiny Nat Bailey Stadium, drawn not so much by the fortunes of the local team as by the simple pleasures of the summer game.

Even in the early days, base ball—it was more often spelled as two words then—was a less popular sport than cricket, lacrosse or even bicycle races.

To mark Queen Victoria's 69th birthday on May 24, 1888, the amateur Vancouver baseball club travelled to New Westminster to accept a challenge from the Royal City nine. The Vancouver side ordered for the occasion new uniforms of white flannel shirts and knickerbockers. New Westminster led 9-8 after five innings, at which time the players had to surrender the grounds for a cricket match.

The city's first diamond was carved out in the 1880s on what became known as the Cambie Street Recreation Grounds. It was a "slope imperfectly levelled of lumps and hollows, and with quantities of loose stones lying everywhere," city archivist James S. Matthews later recalled. The lot—a city block bounded by Beatty, Dunsmuir, Cambie and Georgia—was cleared with help from the chain gang.

In 1905 the city got its first enclosed ballpark and its first professional team. Recreation Park at the southeast corner of Smithe and Homer cost a princely $25,000 to build. It was owned by the Canadian Pacific Railway, but leased to a syndicate, which in turn rented it out. Admission to the grounds was 25 cents when it opened on May 11, 1905. Vancouver beat Victoria 4-2 before 3,070 fans (*Daily World*) or nearly 4,000 (*Daily News-Advertiser*) or 4,750 (*Daily Province*).

The Vancouver club in the four-city Northwestern League was known as the Vets and the Horse Doctors. They concluded the season with 45 wins and 52 defeats, finishing 15 games behind

It was a slope imperfectly levelled of lumps and hollows, and with quantities of loose stones lying everywhere
—James S. Matthews

Washington's pennant-winning Everett Smokestackers. In 1908 the city enjoyed its first pennant when the ball team, since renamed the Beavers, won the last 10 games of the season.

One of the visiting players over the years at Recreation Park was a hard-charging, red-haired infielder by the name of Bob Brown. Ruby Robert, as he was called, had played football for Notre Dame University in South Bend, Ind., and had been a volunteer cavalry private during the Spanish-American War. He played for and managed the Black Cats in Aberdeen, Washington, where he ran a shoe store on the side. In 1910 the man who was to become known here as Mr. Baseball bought the Vancouver Beavers for $500. He was the club's owner, president, manager and shortstop. Brown brought with him a reputation for parsimony. Hal Straight, a left-handed pitcher who doubled as a *Vancouver Sun* sports reporter, once wrote: "Bob came to Vancouver from that shoe store in Aberdeen and he brought one of the shoe strings with him. He did business on it every year afterwards."

Brown built a splendid wooden ballpark on the edge of False Creek at the southeast corner of Fifth and Hemlock. Athletic Park opened its doors to pro ball on April 17, 1913, as 6,000 fans filled every seat to watch the Beavers beat the Tacoma Tigers 8-4.

The Beavers claimed pennants in 1911, 1913 and 1914, before falling on hard times. The club disbanded at the end of the 1922 season, and the city was without pro ball for 15 years. But competition was fierce in the popular Senior League, a local semi-professional circuit.

A few hours at Athletic Park was cheap entertainment in the Depression days. A young man named Nat Bailey, the son of a carney and a former circus barker himself, patrolled the stands as a vendor, shouting in his telltale tenor: "A loaf of bread, a pound of meat, and all the mustard you can eat . . ."

On July 3, 1931, Athletic Park was the site of the first night game to be played in the Dominion, not to mention west of the Mississippi.

facing page: Scoreboard, Nat Bailey Stadium, 1987. vp

Since before 1900, amateur clubs had played at the Powell Street Grounds, where a modest four-bench wooden grandstand hugged the southeast corner of Dunlevy and Powell. Located in the heart of the Little Tokyo neighborhood, the park's most popular tenants were the Asahi ("Asa" for morning, "hi" for sun), a club composed of Japanese-Canadians that was formed in 1914. The Asahi played their final game on Sept. 18, 1941. In the offseason, following the Japanese attack on Pearl Harbor, the Little Tokyo community was banished to exile on farms and internment camps. The Asahi never played again.

Amateur ball of a different sort was played at Centre Park, a 1,200-seat softball diamond at Broadway and Fir that opened in 1937 and was razed in 1950. Marg and Helen Callaghan went on to play baseball in the U.S. Midwest in the All-American Girls Professional Baseball League. Helen was so fine a hitter on the circuit—immortalized by the movie *A League of Their Own*—that reporters called her the "female Ted Williams." Her son, Casey Candaele, became a major leaguer.

Pro baseball returned to Vancouver in 1937, when the Maple Leafs of the Western International League played at Con Jones Park (today known as Callister Park). Before the 1939 season, Bob Brown took over the franchise and moved it to Athletic Park. The club was named the Capilanos after the Capilano Brewery, a sponsor owned by the beer magnate Emil Sick of Seattle. In 1944 Sick bought the park, which was renamed Capilano Stadium.

The Caps played until 1942, the year they won the pennant. Wartime travel restrictions brought the league to a halt, but play resumed in 1946. The Capilanos won the pennant in '47, but disbanded for good when the league folded in 1954, a victim, like so many other minor leagues, of television. The Caps bowed out in grand style as Western International League champions.

They had moved into a new home three years earlier. After 38 seasons, including extensive repairs following fires in 1927 and 1945, Athletic Park was destroyed to make way for the elevated Hemlock Street ramp onto the new Granville Street Bridge.

The final game in the old ballyard was played on June 7, 1951, when Vancouver beat Washington's Wenatchee Chiefs 10-8 in 11 innings. Only about 2,000 fans braved a chilly night to bid adieu and sing "Auld Lang Syne" in place of the traditional "Take Me Out to the Ball Game."

A week later, on June 15, more than 8,000 eager fans paid to enter the new park on six-and-a-half hectares near Thirtieth and Ontario in the lee of Little Mountain. The park boasted 7,500 seats, so some spectators stood along the foul lines to watch the Caps beat the Salem Senators 10-3. Top tickets cost $1.35, although a child could sit in the left-field bleachers for just 15 cents. The concrete and steel Capilano Stadium, a replica of Sick's Stadium in Seattle, cost $550,000 to build. It was financed by a bond issue.

Before the 1956 season, the Oakland Oaks franchise of the Pacific Coast League was moved to Vancouver, where the team was renamed the Mounties. (Among the rejected nicknames: Totems and Evergreens.) On April 27, 8,149 fans watched the new team lose 2-1 to the San Francisco Seals in the club's home debut. The Mounties would finish dead last (pitcher Ernie Funk was 1-19) in the eight-city circuit.

At the end of the season, the Mounties were sold for $150,000 to a syndicate of businessmen, including Nat Bailey, the vendor who had become a successful restaurateur with his White Spot chain of drive-ins. Shares in the club cost $25. Among the shareholders was Premier W.A.C. Bennett.

The Mounties never did win the championship and folded on November 29, 1962. They returned for the 1965 season. The darkest day of the new franchise occurred when the Mounties' Santiago Rosario hit catcher Merritt Ranew of the Seattle Rainiers in the head with a baseball bat during an on-field brawl on May 11, 1966. The club folded for good at the end of the 1969 season.

That the city had a team even for that long depended on Nat Bailey's deep pockets. Five days after he died on March 28, 1978, at age 76, the park board voted to rename the ball park Nat Bailey Stadium.

The name change occurred in time for the return of professional baseball after an eight-year absence. Harry Ornest, an entrepreneur, snagged a PCL franchise in the fall of 1977. The ball park had fallen into decrepitude; its facelift cost nearly as much as did the original construction in 1951. Rud Haar, a local groundskeeper, needed a full month to get the field in shape for the Vancouver Canadians' home debut on April 26, 1978. They beat the San Jose Missions 9-4 before a crowd of 7,128.

The C's won PCL championships in 1985 and '89, the season in which left-hander Tom Drees pitched no-hitters on May 23, May 29 and August 16.

Vancouver is also home to the Canadian Baseball Institute, a training ground for college-age players with an eye on the majors.

The Seattle Mariners of the American League have flirted with the idea of becoming a regionally-based major league club with the possibility of scheduling some home games under the dome at B.C. Place Stadium. In the fall of 1994 the United Baseball League—a rival to the American and National Leagues—announced plans to locate a future team here. If major-league baseball ever arrives at the dome, the games will be played just four short blocks from the site of the city's original pro ball park.

Basketball
Howard Tsumura

I N RELATIVE TERMS, Vancouver's basketball history is just past the fine print. For generations it has been a game tied predominantly to the scholastic experience, played in the high schools, colleges and universities of this province. But now, in letters big and bold enough to capture the interest of even the most casual observer, the NBA has come to town, set to write new, ground-breaking chapters that will define the game's evolution in British Columbia.

The National Basketball Association's 29th franchise, the Vancouver Grizzlies, opened their inaugural season in November 1995 at the new 20,000-seat General Motors Place. The team has been built by former New York Knicks head coach Stu Jackson, who was hired in July 1994 by team CEO Arthur Griffiths as the Grizzlies' director of basketball operations. Jackson oversaw the drafting of seven-foot, 292-pound college star Bryant "Big Country" Reeves from Oklahoma State University, as well as the acquisition of veterans like Byron Scott of the Indiana Pacers, Gerald Wilkins of the Cleveland Cavaliers and Greg Anthony of the Knicks. Jackson hired Brian Winters from the Atlanta Hawks to be the team's first head coach. (But on January 24, 1997, after a disastrous string of losses, Winters was fired and Jackson took over the coaching slot until a replacement could be found.) And like a new expressway opening in the middle of rush hour traffic, the mere presence of an NBA team in Vancouver promises to do more in a couple of years for the advancement of the game then the combined efforts of the preceding half-century.

Suddenly, the game's brightest stars like Michael Jordan and Shaquille O'Neal are not just the property of television. They are real, flesh-and-blood characters coming to this city to play actual games. There is simply no other way to describe the overall impact the Grizzlies will have on the local hoop community. Awareness of the game will jump, more children will play, and the overall skill level of the individual player will rise.

For some, like former mens national team head coach Ken Shields and Mike Hind, the executive director of Basketball B.C., the NBA has come so fast that there's barely been time to catch a collective breath. Nothing more then a hot rumor in late February 1993, it became reality 27 months later when the league officially accepted the terms of the Grizzlies' $125-million U.S. expansion fee. "I think it's the most significant basketball development in my lifetime," says Shields, the country's most successful collegiate coach who enjoyed unprecedented prosperity as head coach of the men's team at the University of Victoria. Adds Hind: "This is the biggest, other than the day maybe, when James Naismith invented the game." Naismith, of course, was a Canadian. And he invented basketball in 1891.

In the Greater Vancouver area, the real history of the sport actually began a full year before the formation of the NBA. The first B.C. boys high school championships, an invitational affair, were staged in 1946 at the New Westminster YMCA. Vancouver College went on to win the first tournament, beating city rival King George, 25-21. College and Victoria's Oak Bay have each won five titles, but the dominant program has been the one established in Richmond by head coach Bill Disbrow. The Colts have won four times, finished second five times and placed in the final four in 11 of their 15 trips to the event. Tournament finals, which have been guaranteed sellouts, have been played at War Memorial Gymnasium at UBC, the Pacific Coliseum and PNE Agrodome. The tournament moved to the home of the Grizzlies, G.M. Place.

On the university scene, UBC's men's team has won four national championships, the last coming in 1972, while the women's team, which represented Canada in 1930, won a world championship. The women's team from Simon Fraser University has been a model of consistency under head coach Allison McNeill. Her Clan teams have qualified for six NAIA championship tournaments. And while there are no Canadian-born player on the Grizzlies roster this season, one native son—Steve Nash of Victoria—was slated as a top 20 pick in the 1996 NBA college draft. Nash is a senior point guard at Santa Clara University.

The only British Columbia-born and schooled player to ever suit up in the NBA was Lars Hansen, a 6-foot-10 centre from Coquitlam's Centennial Secondary. After leading his high school to the B.C. title in 1972, Hansen went on to play four seasons at the University of Washington in Seattle, where he had opportunity to play against Stu Jackson's University of Oregon team. Hansen later played 15 games for the Seattle SuperSonics during the 1978-79 season, averaging just over five points per contest. Seattle went on to win the NBA title that season; however, Hansen did not play in any of the playoff games.

But Hansen has proved to be the rarest of exceptions. In 50 years of high school basketball in British Columbia, he is the only player from this province that has ever gone on to play in the NBA.

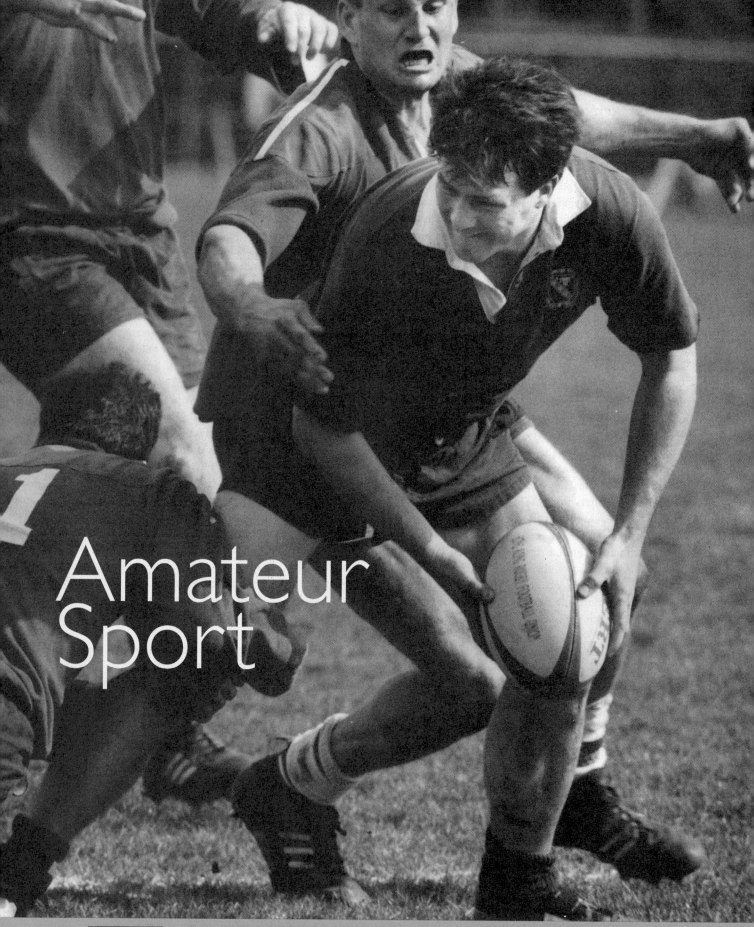

Amateur
Sport

Amateur Sports
Jim Kearney

THE FIRST AMATEUR sports event in what is now Greater Vancouver was held on the Queen's birthday, May 24, 1859, at Queensborough. A track and field meet, the events included foot and hurdle races, shot put, hammer throw, high and long jumps and tossing the caber.

The first amateur sports competition in Vancouver after the city was incorporated in 1886 was a rugby match, in which Vancouver beat New Westminster, on a cleared but muddy piece of ground on Cambie Street. A few years later it was named Larwill Park, after Al Larwill, who lived there in a shed filled with sports equipment, which he loaned out for countless rugby, soccer, lacrosse, cricket and baseball games.

The first event was to have been a track and field meet, scheduled for Dominion Day, 1886. But when Vancouver burned to the ground two weeks earlier, it was cancelled.

From these humble beginnings, the Lower Mainland sports scene embraces 88 amateur associations—alphabetically, from archery to wrestling—under the aegis of Sport B.C., the umbrella agency for all amateur sport in the province. The total membership amounts to 750,000 recreational and competitive athletes, the bulk of them in the Lower Mainland.

With half the 6,000 registered teams and 90,000 players in B.C. playing on the Lower Mainland, softball is the most widely played sport of all. Soccer comes second with 75,000 registered players of all ages, with nearly half of them in the Greater Vancouver area. Hockey comes third with 50,000 registered and another 20,000 unregistered adult recreation players. The 33 hockey associations on the Lower Mainland represent approximately 50 per cent of the registered players.

Add in all the unregistered recreational excercisers who jog and swim, play fun golf and tennis and generally pay homage to fitness. Sport B.C. estimates one of every two adults in Greater Vancouver is physically active. Add to this more than 40,000 volunteers between Vancouver and Chilliwack who, in various capacities, support the entire amateur sports apparatus.

A far cry from July 20, 1871, when the scattering of residents along Burrard Inlet celebrated B.C.'s entry into Confederation with a day of races and sports. Or four years later when the first horseshoe pitching competition in Canada was staged by the Horseshoe Flinging Club in Gastown.

At the time Gastown was about to become Vancouver, the only good playing field in the area belonged to George Black, proprietor of the Brighton Hotel at Hastings Townsite, which was not yet part of Vancouver.

This was the first Hastings Park and the Vancouver rugby side played its games there. Spectators arrived by excursion steamer from the foot of Carrall, by horse and carriage and by special CPR day coach (25 cents return) or by streetcar.

Inasmuch as the line ended at Powell Street and Victoria Drive, spectators had to walk a mile through the forest to the park. They didn't complain, because this intersection—known as Cedar Cove—was the home of the Columbia Brewery. Coming and going, they were able to fuel up with big five-cent schooners of beer.

Looking for a field closer to home, the rugby players obtained a lease at Brockton Point from the Parks Board and formed the Brockton Point Amateur Athletic Association in 1890. They hired a contractor to clear the land that is now Brockton Oval.

It has been Vancouver's rugby headquarters ever since and arguably is the most scenic rugby pitch in the world. Certainly that's how Don Bradman, the legendary Australian cricketer, described the adjoining cricket pitch when he played there in 1930.

With its rickety headquarters the longest surviving structure in Coal Harbor, the Vancouver Rowing Club (VRC) is the oldest sports club in Vancouver. Its genesis was in 1886 as the Vancouver Boating Club. Rowers representing the VRC have been Olympic and Commonwealth Games' medalists from 1924 until 1964, after which Canada was represented by national, rather than club, crews.

Still functioning and still winning and just as old, is the New Westminster Salmonbellies lacrosse club, born in 1890 and so uniquely named as a result of derision on the part of Vancouver fans, who called the hated enemy from New Westminster "fish bellies." The salmon-canning industry was big in the Royal City at the time, so the club gladly adopted the prejorative and substituted "salmon" for "fish."

Under this name they have won more Canadian championships than any other team in any sport anywhere in the country—24 Mann Cup wins in all, up to and including 1994. The game moved indoors and became box lacrosse in 1933, but the Salmonbellies' home address remains the same, Queens Park, the first athletic ground in British Columbia. The Royal Engineers, stationed at nearly Sapperton, built the park in 1859.

The first B.C. athlete to challenge for a world title was Bob Johnston of Vancouver, who lost in 1898 by two lengths to world single-sculls champion Jake Gaudaur of Hamilton over a three-mile course in Vancouver harbor. A charter member of the B.C. Sports Hall of Fame, he died in 1951.

The first sports event of the 20th century in British Columbia took place at Brockton Oval on New Year's Day, 1900, a rugby game between the high school team and the Selects. The Selects won.

Compared with the late 20th century, women's sport was virtually non-existent in Vancouver's swaddling days. Nonetheless, young Vancouver women made history in 1896, forming the Vancouver Ladies Club and playing the first recorded field hockey match in Canada. Six years later, in 1902, when the first provincial table tennis championships were played in Vancouver, women, as well as men and boys, competed.

While professional sport—hockey, lacrosse and baseball—dominated the Vancouver sports scene from the turn of the century until the outbreak of World War I in 1914, amateur sport made news on two fronts.

British Columbia hosted its first international rugby match when an Anglo-Welsh 15 played at Brockton Oval in 1908 before a packed house. Newspaper accounts of the day reported that when the referee blew his whistle to start the game, all the Welsh immigrants in the crowd started to sing the Welsh hymn, *Land of My Fathers*.

As the Welsh players immediately stood to attention, the locals went down the field and scored a converted try for five points. But they paid for their sneak attack. The tourists won the match, 61-5. Not until half a century later in 1958, did a British Columbia team best one of the established rugby powers in Vancouver—an 11-8 win over Australia's Wallabies.

In 1912, a 250-pound Vancouver policeman, Duncan Gillis, became the first Olympic medal winner from B.C., winning silver at Stockolm as runner-up in the hammer throw.

Athletes from Greater Vancouver didn't start making the Olympic gold standard until 1928, when Percy Williams won the 100- and 200-metre sprints at the Amsterdam Games. As Canada heads into the 21st century, his victories remain the greatest accomplishment by a single Canadian athlete since the Olympics began in 1896.

It was also the most surprising accomplishment. Unknown and unrated outside Canada and unprepossessing in physique (he weighed only 125 pounds), Williams became the first and, so far, only Canadian to win two gold medals in the Olympics main event, track and field.

While he put Vancouver on the world athletic map for the first time, he was a reluctant hero, a man who never wanted to be a runner, who never sought public acclaim, who later turned his back on the sport that made him famous and lived much of his later life as a virtual recluse.

Williams gave all the credit for his success to Bob Granger, a coach of all-sports at King George high school, who saw this speedy teenager running for King Edward high and spotted the ingredients of greatness. They didn't take long to develop. Williams was only 20 when he stole the show at Amsterdam. Not so well known are a couple of additional accomplishments: the winter following the Olympics he won 21 of 22 races on the indoor circuit. And in 1930 he set a world record of 10.3 seconds for the 100 metres that lasted until 1941.

Also in 1930 he won the 100 yards in the first-ever British Empire Games at Hamilton, Ontario, a race which effectively ended his career. Just before reaching the tape he tore a large thigh muscle. It was not properly repaired and while he did compete in the 1932 Olympics, he didn't make it out of the heats.

Gold-medal Olympians from the Vancouver area since Williams' 1928 double are:

1932 Duce McNaughton, a Magee high school grad who led his school to the first ever provincial boys' basketball championship, won the high jump at the Los Angeles Olympics.

1956 The coxless fours crew, representing not only Canada but also the University of British Columbia-Vancouver Rowing Club racing program, won their event at Melbourne, Australia. The gold medal four were: Archie McKinnon, Lorne Loomer, Walter D'Hondt and Don Arnold. The UBC-VRC eight won the silver medal.

1964 George Hungerford and Roger Jackson teamed to win double sculls gold at the Tokyo Olympics.

1984 The first Olympics in which athletes based in Vancouver won gold in totally separate sports. Lori Fung, Vancouver's first ever gold medallist, was the winner in rhythmic gymnastics. UBC medical student Hugh Fisher teamed with Quebecer Alwyn Morris to win the two-man, 1,000-metre kayak final.

Athletes from this area also have won gold in world championship events:

1930 The UBC women's team won the world basketball championship at the Women's World Games in Prague, beating France, 18-14, in the final. The crystal vase representing the world title is still on display in a trophy case at UBC.

1953 Doug Hepburn won the world heavyweight weightlifting championship at Stockholm. Totally self-taught, he overcame the handicap of a club foot and built himself from a scrawny 145-pounder to a 275-pound global champion. A year later he won another gold at the British Empire and Commonwealth Games in Vancouver.

1959 There was no formal competition as such, but Stan Leonard, formerly the pro at the Marine Drive Golf Club, was named World Golfer of the Year by his peers.

1964 The Lyall Dagg rink of Vancouver won the World Curling Championship, played in Calgary. His team mates, also from Greater Vancouver, were Leo Hebert, Fred Britton and Barry Naimark.

1969 Dorothy Lidstone of North Vancouver won the world archery championship at Valley Forge, Pa. She beat a field of 40 women from 27 countries with a record 2,361 points, 110 points more than the previous world record.

1973 Runnerup for gold behind American star Mark Spitz at the 1972 Olympics, Bruce Robertson won gold in the 100-metre butterfly at the World Aquatic Championships in Belgrade.

Karen Magnussen (Cella) of North Vancouver, silver medallist at both the Olympics and the Worlds a year earlier, won the World Figure Skating Championship at Bratislava, Slovakia. A new community arena in North Vancouver was named for her.

1990 A Vancouver laboratory technician who bowls one night a week, Jean Gordon bowled a 198 average through 47 games to finish 45 pins ahead of her nearest competitor while winning the Women's World Cup of tenpin bowling at Jakarta, Indonesia.

1994 Allison Sydor of North Vancouver won the World Mountain Bike Championship at Vail, Colorado. Greg Streppel of Vancouver won the 25-kilometre marathon in the World Aquatic Championships at Rome.

In terms of world records, Harry Jerome of North Vancouver was the finest sprinter Canada ever produced. For four years in the 1960s he was co-holder of the world record in both the 100-yard and 100-metre sprints (9.1 seconds and 10.0 seconds). Gold medallist at the 1966 Commonwealth Games and the 1967 Pan-American Games, he won bronze at the 1964 Tokyo Olympics.

For medals won and world records broken, Elaine Tanner of West Vancouver remains Canada's finest-ever woman swimmer. Her four golds and three silvers at the 1966 Commonwealth Games set an individual games record for women that still stands.

At only 15, she was the youngest person ever named as Canada's Athlete of the Year. A year later at the Pan-American Games she won two golds and three silvers, a big buildup to the biggest letdown in her athletic life. She went to the 1968 Olympics in search of two golds, but had to settle for two silvers.

For world class longevity, Debbie Brill, who learned to high jump as a school girl in Maple Ridge, may hold the Canadian record. She never won an Olympic medal. Her only global gold medal came in the World Cup of track and field at Montreal in 1978. And she never held a world record.

But she won gold as a 17 year old at the 1970 Commonwealth Games in Edinburgh, again at the same games at Brisbane,

In terms of world records, Harry Jerome of North Vancouver was the finest sprinter Canada ever produced

Australia, in 1982, and for a third time when the games returned to Edinburgh in 1986.

In team sport, the Salmonbellies are the only amateur club side in Greater Vancouver that can be characterized as a dynasty. Another New Westminster team, the soccer Royals, likely come in second, with four national championships between 1928 and 1936. In amateur basketball, Vancouver Cloverleafs won four national titles in five years during the later forties and early fifties. Neither club exists anymore.

Aside from the Vancouver Rowing Club, Vancouver's oldest functioning amateur sports organization is the Meralomas, founded in 1923 as the Mermaid Swim Club. It soon progressed into other sports, motivating the 12 founding members to find a new name.

They combined "mer" from mermaids with "al" from alpha and "om" from omega. Then they added an "a" at the end to make it more phonetically pleasing. Freely translated—very freely—Meraloma means "mermaids from beginning to end."

It its time the club has run the gamut of strenuous living from swimming through rugby, baseball, softball, basketball, lacrosse, track and field, tennis, wrestling, weightlifting, table tennis and chess. The Meralomas clubhouse is situated at Connaught Park in Kitsilano.

Vancouver has played host to many significant amateur sports events, but the biggest—and most historic—of all remains the British Empire and Commonwealth Games of 1954. It was here, at now-razed Empire Stadium, where the world's first two sub-four-minute milers, Dr. Roger Bannister of England and John Landy of Australia, ran their famous duel. It was the first mile run in history where both the winner (Banister) and runnerup (Landy) completed the race in under four minutes.

This was the infant television industry's first-ever international sports challenge, the first international sports event broadcast live to all of North America. The race attracted media from all over the world and it was the lead story in the first-ever issue of *Sports Illustrated*. Never before (and seldom since) had Vancouver been accorded such world-wide exposure.

Provincial sport & recreation organizations

Archery	980-6848
Athletics	688-6266
Badminton	737-3030
Ball Hockey	291-0628
Baseball	737-3031
Basketball	737-3032
Baton Twirling	241-1205
Blind Sports	737-3035
Bodybuilding	748-7576
Bowling Federation	522-2990
Bowling-Lawn	224-4407
Boxing	291-7921
Broomball	859-3234
Canoe Sport	275-6651
Canoe-Flatwater	737-3129
Canoe-Whitewater Kayaking	275-6651
Cerebral Palsy	599-5240
Coaches	737-3120
Colleges	527-5005
Cricket	327-5819
Curling	737-3040
Cycling	7373034
Dancing	433-0010
Deaf Sports	737-3041
Disabled Sports	737-3039
Diving	737-3043
Dog Sport-Fido	277-3158
Equestrian-House Council	576-2722
Fencing	737-3044
Field Hockey-Men's	737-3045
Field Hockey-Women's	737-3046
Figure Skating	737-3047
Football	583-9363
Golf	294-1818
Golf-Ladies	294-6664
Gymnastics	737-3049
Gymnastics-Rhythmic	737-6043
Handball-Team	734-2611
Hang Gliding	980-9566
Hockey	477-9551
Horseshoe	525-4375
Judo	737-3050
Karate	737-3051
Lacrosse	421-9755
Lifesaving	664-6468
Luge	737-3030
Motorsport	737-3052
Netball	293-1820
Orienteering	737-3000
Outward Bound	737-3093
Parachuting	939-8340
Parks & Recreation	257-8492
Pentathlon	327-7559
Racquetball	931-4944
Ringette	737-3106

Roller Hockey	253-6439
Rowing	737-3064
Rugby	737-3065
Sailing	737-3113
School Sports	737-3035
Shooting Sports	527-1345
Skiing-Alpine	737-3070
Skiing-Cross Country	545-9600
Skiing-Disabled	737-3042
Soaring	574-4141
Soccer	299-6401
Soccer-Youth	299-6401
Softball	531-0044
Special Olympics	737-3078
Speed Skating	737-3063
Sports Hall of Fame	687-5520
Squash	737-3084
Swimming	734-7946
Swimming-Summer	734-7411

Swimming-Synchro	732-7962
Table Tennis	737-3012
Taekwondo	588-4434
Tennis	737-3086
Triathlon	736-3176
Underwater Hockey	327-6011
Volleyball	737-3087
Water Polo	734-3310
Water Safety	431-4209
Water Ski	861-2285
Weightlifting	737-3089
Wheelchair Sports	737-3090
Women in Sport	737-3092

above: The Abbotsford Air Show, a bi-annual highlight for sport flyers, 1984. vp
facing page: Empire Pool, British Empire Games, 1954. vp

Leisure

WHILE MOST GREAT cities of the world are defined by their buildings, monuments and other man-made ephemera, what distinguishes Greater Vancouver above all else is its sublime natural setting.

The mountains, ocean, forests, lakes, rivers and streams that make up our backyard shape the psyche of the region and, in turn, us. That's especially true when it comes to how we spend our leisure time, since those same natural endowments also make for a perfect playground.

In no other major metropolitan area in the world can you hike through old growth forest in the morning, ski mountain slopes in the afternoon and end the day with a seaward paddle into the sunset.

We're as close to an urban paradise as one could ever get. And each municipality has its own unique pocket of heaven.

Within the confines of the City of Vancouver alone, it's possible to wander trails through the lush forests of Stanley Park or make a circular tour via the seawall on foot, rollerblade or bicycle. Mountain bikes explore the more rugged terrain of Pacific Spirit Regional Park, and share some of those trails with walkers, horseback riders and people just out to encounter some of the varied flora and fauna to be found.

Down at the seaside, sailors, kayakers and windsurfers gambol among the waves, while others enjoy recreational pursuits on land with beach volleyball, croquet and the region's most popular leisure activity—walking.

A vast system of municipal, regional and provincial parks provides similar opportunities throughout the Lower Mainland.

In spring, rock-climbers begin to clamber the cliffs at Lighthouse Park in West Vancouver. In summer, scuba divers explore rich undersea worlds in places such as Belcarra and Indian Arm. Families set up a home away from home in campgrounds such as those nestled in the forests of Golden Ears provincial park or along the shores of Cultus Lake. In autumn, fishers cast about the rivers, lakes and streams for trout and salmon. In winter, the North Shore mountains become a veritable wonderland for snowshoers, snowboarders and skiers of both the cross-country and downhill varieties.

From parks as tiny and perfect as Deas Island with its 71 hectares of Delta riverfront, marshland and historic buildings, to the vaster expanses of Cypress Provincial Park with its 3,000 hectares of ancient forests, jewel-like lakes and lofty peaks, Greater Vancouver provides limitless opportunities to play and to relax among world-class scenery.

We're also the gateway to the wilder wonders offered by the rest of British Columbia. Kayakers come from all over the world to ply the coastal fjords. Mountaineers gather to face the challenges of the Coast Range, and rock-climbers head for the granite mecca called the Stawamus Chief. Paragliders set their sights on the peaks of Mount Cheam and Blackcomb Mountain.

Our backyard attracts more and more visitors each year. With outdoor publications such as *Outside, Bicycling, Rock and Ice* and travel magazines such as *National Geographic* and *Escape* letting the world in on our secrets, it is more important than ever to ensure that these special places are set aside as a legacy of our natural endowments.

Some of our parks are already being pushed to capacity and the demand can only increase. Preserving the best of Greater Vancouver—our natural spaces—is essential to preserving the best of who we are.

In its vision statement, the Outdoor Recreation Council sees the future thus: "People from all over the world view B.C. as a prime locale for some of the world's best outdoor recreation. By the year 2001, outdoor recreation ought to be recognized as a cultural trademark of British Columbians, in the same way that Swedes are known for their physical fitness."

—Dawn Hanna

Cypress Bowl, 1969. vs
facing page: Snowboarding, 1995. vp

Skiing
Steven Threndyle

To the downhill skier, the lights of Grouse Mountain, Cypress Bowl and Mount Seymour have offered an irresistible "come hither" since they were installed in the 1960s. Hundreds of thousands of Lower Mainland skiers have taken lessons after work or school in conditions ranging from starry twilight to dreadful downpours.

But the history of skiing on the North Shore mountains goes way back before the lights were plugged in, indeed, to a time when the the only way to the top of the mountain was under your own power. The first four decades of skiing on the North Shore have far more in common with wilderness backcountry skiing than the lift-assisted commercial recreation that exists today.

Being the closest and smallest of the North Shore mountains, it's only logical that Grouse Mountain (1,211 metres) was the focus of early skiing in Vancouver. The first skis to touch snow on Grouse likely belonged to a Swedish immigrant, one Rudolph Verne, who would later open a sporting-goods shop and promote this new form of winter recreation to residents of the young city. His account of a 1911 trip to Grouse with an unnamed partner first appeared in Polly Pogue's *Hiker and Skier* magazine in 1933 as part of a four-part series on the history of skiing in the Dominion of Canada. Verne recounts that one of the members of the party had a ski run away into the trees before its owner had the opportunity to attach it.

Like hikers and climbers in the summer, skiers had to take the ferry from Stanley Park, then follow a crude trail from the end of the Lonsdale Street streetcar line up the flanks of the mountain. The first expeditions took three days; two days to reach the summit and another day to get back down. A small shelter known as Trythall's cabin supplied hikers and climbers with soft drinks and candy. In winter, it was reported that a person could ski down to the streetcar in about three hours. One of the first cabins was completed in 1922 by the Outdoor Club, a forerunner of UBC's Varsity Outdoor Club.

Grouse Mountain's commercial recreation potential was recognized as early as 1911, with a scheme to run an incline-railway from Capilano Lodge upstream and around the mountain to the summit. That dream was derailed by World War I but skiing and cabin building began in earnest after the construction of a toll road known as Skyline Drive in 1924. A full-service chalet offering accommodation, meals and even dogsled rides opened a year later. A young Grouse summer employee,

17 year-old Lindsay Loutit, formed the Grouse Mountain Ski Club in 1927 to provide new skiers with lessons and equipment rentals.

The hyperbole which often surrounds tourist attractions and winter resorts is evident in an early Grouse brochure: "Patrons may indulge to their heart's content in skiing, tobogganing, bobsled riding, and curling under climatic conditions and at an altitude similar to those of the most-noted Swiss mountain resorts, about one hour's trip by auto, which will transport the visitor from the winter rains at water level to a climate that is keen and bracing and exhilarating." Perhaps the freezing level was lower back then.

What really put Grouse on the map was the construction of the first double chairlift in North America by Joseph Wepsela in 1949. The lift started at the end of Skyline Drive in North Vancouver and went up to the Ski Village (at the base of the present-day Cut chairlift) where the original 1926 chalet was built. Two years later, a second chairlift (known as the Cut chair) was completed and the downhill boom was on. The *Vancouver Sun* started offering free skiing lessons in 1952; later that year Grouse hosted the Canadian Amateur Ski Championships. By this time, hundreds of cabins, some privately owned, others owned by ski clubs, had been built.

In 1962, the original Grouse Mountain chalet burned down. Development shifted away from the Village to the current site, where the Grouse Nest restaurant and Theatre In The Sky are located. The Village chairlift from Skyline Drive became obsolete with the construction of the Blue Skyride, and later, the 125-passenger Grouse SuperSkyride aerial tramway.

Although Grouse Mountain was a good ski hill, the immigrant Scandinavian loggers who had brought the new sport over from Northern Europe felt that Hollyburn Ridge above West Vancouver was superior. The aforementioned Rudolph Verne was a major proponent of Hollyburn skiing.

By the early 1920s, logging on the lower slopes of Hollyburn was finished. The Naismith Mill on the mountain's lower slopes had fallen into disuse, and in 1925 Verne and his Norwegian friends occupied the logger's bunkhouses and established a ski camp. That first season, skis rented for ten cents a day, and you could bunk down for the night on a mattress of balsam and hemlock boughs for 50 cents. But the Naismith mill site proved unworkable because of its low elevation, and Verne and company hauled the bunkhouse by horse cart to First Lake, 500 metres higher.

The trail to the camp, known as Fred Furfield's Road, was often a muddy quagmire, but interest in skiing was strong. Verne himself proved to be an indefatigable promoter. In 1927 he formed the first ski club in western North America, the Hollyburn Pacific Ski Club. In its charter, members boasted that [the club is] "fortunate in having within its radius the finest territory for cross-country skiing in the Dominion." The first organized ski competition was held from April 15-17, 1927. Soon after, the Vancouver Ski Club was created, and an intense rivalry took hold that manifested itself not only in ski competitions, but in seeing which club could get the most members out for work parties on the trails and cabins.

When the Great Depression put many of the Scandinavian loggers-cum-skiers out of work, they turned their talents to cabin building. They lived year-round on Hollyburn within metres of their beloved trails and ski jumps, in a sense becoming the West Coast's first ski bums. The logs cut to make trails were perfect for cabins, which were enjoyed by the loggers and Vancouverites alike. People coming up from the city would often be loaded down with building materials, food, or even, in one case, a grand piano. A 1933 copy of *Hiker and Skier* reports that "there seemed to be no end of the hikers that came up the trail every day and the ski runs and nursery slopes were lively with planksters, even in the rain." Almost 4,000 passengers were ferried from the city to the trailhead at the Ambleside ferry dock on a single day in January 1934.

You wouldn't have known that a Depression was in full swing on Hollyburn Ridge in the 1930s. The hills were packed with over 300 cabins tucked in beside the trails. Two large hostel-style lodges were the focal point for après-ski parties: the Saturday night dance over at Hollyburn Lodge drew 600 participants. To get in on the action skiers would often rush from work on Saturday afternoon to catch the last Ambleside ferry and hike up in the dark.

The Jack Pratt Memorial Ski Jump was named after one of Hollyburn's top skiers, and became the focal point for many competitions. At Westlake Lodge, several rope-tows were built to take the pain out of skiing uphill. Novices did their first turns on Paradise, moved over to Graveyard as they improved and progressed to Suicide once they became experts. Competition between skiers of the Grouse Mountain Ski Club, the Hollyburn Pacific Ski Club and the Vancouver Ski Club was particularly fierce during this time.

Access to the slopes of Hollyburn and Westlake improved dramatically in 1950 with the completion of one of the longest chairlifts in North America. A one-way trip from the starting point at Roseberry Avenue in West Vancouver to the Hi-View Lodge was now reduced to 14 minutes. Hollyburn, Grouse and newcomer Mount Seymour battled for the hearts (not to mention the pocketbooks) of Vancouver skiers. In 1965 Hollyburn suffered a double-whammy when the chairlift shut down and Hi-View Lodge was destroyed by fire. Downhill skiing would not take place in earnest again until the provincial government took over the ski area following the Valley Royal logging/development scandal. Hollyburn was privatized in 1983. It now features four chairlifts and a beginner's rope-tow.

With its more easterly location, ski development on Mount Seymour was slower than on Grouse or Hollyburn. First climbed by a B.C. Mountaineering Club party in 1908, the mountain saw no winter activity until 1929, when two members of the rival Alpine Club, Mr. and Mrs. R.J. Shaich, made the first ski foray to Seymour. Their club built a cabin for its members and immediately popularized the area. Although its development was preceded on Grouse and Hollyburn by almost two decades, James Sinclair did a survey of the North Shore mountains for the provincial government, identifying Mount Seymour as having "the highest amount of recreation potential." It was dedicated as a provincial park in 1937.

In 1938 the government granted money for road access, but funding was cut during the war. Nevertheless, skiing was still popular at this time. One of the early clubs known as The Hikers and Skiers of Dog Mountain, was later rechristened the Mount Seymour Ski Club. When construction resumed nine years later, much of the roadbed was overgrown.

Access improved greatly after the first eight miles of road was upgraded, though skiers still had to walk to the slopes from the parking lot at the Giant Mushroom. By 1953, five rope tows were taking skiers on to slopes that even today are not serviced by chairlifts. The frenzy of lift building on the North Shore was such that the motto of the Mount Seymour Ski Club became "for every lift Grouse gets, we get one, too!" Not to be outdone by Grouse or Hollyburn, Mount Seymour boasted its own Suicide Run as well as Manning run (after E. C. Manning, a chief forester of the B.C. Forest Service) and the Northlands run. By 1954 over 150 cabins had been completed. The Vancouver Section of the Alpine Club of Canada still had a presence there, as did UBC's Varsity Outdoor Club.

As time passed, not all of the great plans for Mount Seymour panned out. A half-million-dollar, gondola-type ski lift proposed by Mount Seymour operator Earl Pletsch never materialized. Currently, the downhill ski area features four double-chairlifts and two small rope-tows.

By the mid-1960s, several groups of Vancouver skiers were tired of the local mountains and started looking at potential ski sites north of Squamish. Most interesting of all was a peak known as London Mountain, a place that later generations of skiers (and the rest of the world) would come to know as Whistler. But that's another story.

Backcountry Skiing
Charles Montgomery

SOMEWHERE BEYOND the lift lines and crowded cross-country trails of Vancouver's mountain resorts are the backcountry skiers. They seek out untouched powder and pristine alpine, using specialized equipment to trudge uphill and carve graceful turns back down in solitude.

The abundance of downhill and cross-country ski facilities within easy reach of Vancouver leads us to forget skiing's more adventurous beginnings. In the early part of the century, there were regular ski ascents of Grouse, Seymour, Hollyburn and Mount Strachan.

As early as 1910, mountaineers were trying a sturdy cousin of today's cross-country equipment on their winter attempt to reach the Lions. They found the gear no match for such rugged terrain. But in 1930, Vancouver mountaineers Don and Phyllis Munday used skis to explore the immense snowfields of Mount Waddington, the highest peak wholly within British Columbia. This marked the beginning of widespread ski exploration in the Coast Range.

Meanwhile, local clubs were building cabins on the North Shore mountains. In 1931 Mount Seymour's first ski mountaineering hut was built.

By the seventies, logging roads had found their way up most of the valleys near Vancouver. This access, combined with improvements in backcountry gear, put vast expanses of alpine within the skier's reach. Intrepid locals continued to push back the high frontiers of the southern Coast Range. John Clarke is renowned for his explorations, travelling on skis for weeks at a time in the remote glaciated ranges north of Vancouver.

Today, the sport is gaining popularity with a decidedly thick-skinned breed of weekend recreationalist, as the challenges of the Coast Range include notoriously temperamental weather and variable snow conditions. Rain and whiteouts are common even at high elevations, and avalanches are a constant concern. Occasionally the hardy are rewarded with deep powder and unparalleled views of a relentlessly rugged land.

The North Shore mountains boast excellent backcountry access, but skiers are limited by steep terrain and the boundaries of the Greater Vancouver watershed. Consequently, local backcountry skiers have claimed much of the southern Coast Range as their backyard. Dozens of day and weekend mountain ski tours within reach of Vancouver are outlined in John Baldwin's comprehensive guide *Exploring the Coast Mountains on Skis.*

Occasionally the hardy are rewarded with deep powder and unparalleled views of a relentlessly rugged land

Here are five of Vancouver's closest backcountry trips:

CYPRESS PROVINCIAL PARK Trails lead from the nordic parking lot, around the west edge of the cross-country ski area up to Hollyburn Mountain. Mount Strachan can be reached by descending west from Hollyburn Mountain and climbing its easy southern slopes. Beware! A lift pass is needed when travelling on Cypress Bowl's marked ski runs or Hollyburn's cross-country tracks.

MOUNT SEYMOUR These summits offer spectacular views of the Coast Range, though surrounding steep, cliffy terrain and avalanche hazards require caution. A well-used trail leads north from the ski area parking lot along the west edge of downhill ski runs. Tourers continue north past the chair lifts to reach Seymour's three successively higher peaks.

GROUSE MOUNTAIN From the top of Grouse Mountain Skyride, a road leads around the west side of Grouse to the edge of the ski area. Ridges and open forest lead north to several minor summits though steep slopes below the ridges pose a safety hazard. Traditionalists can avoid the skyride by hiking up one of several trails from North Vancouver.

DIAMOND HEAD This is the most popular backcountry destination near Vancouver. A gravel road leads from Squamish to a trailhead high on Paul Ridge at the south end of Garibaldi Park. Skiers follow a marked trail through the forest to alpine meadows, with wonderful views of mounts Garibaldi and Mamquam. After a tough 11 kilometres skiers can relax or camp overnight at the popular Elfin Lakes hut.

SKY PILOT Although road access to Howe Sound's Sky Pilot area has deteriorated over the years, the ambitious are rewarded with pretty open bowls under several craggy peaks and a primitive cabin at Mountain Lake. Roads lead east from Highway 99 up both Furry and Britannia creeks towards the alpine. These roads are locked, so skiers are in for a long hike or an interesting combination mountain bike/ski tour.

Before planning a trip, it is important to remember that all backcountry skiing involves potential dangers. The Federation of Mountain Clubs of B.C. (737-3053) offers several essential mountain skills courses.

Mountaineering
Charles Montgomery

THE HISTORY of mountaineering in Vancouver is in fact the recent history of the exploration of the Coast Range. Mountaineers were pioneers in a country unexplored by Europeans, and explorers became mountaineers in the region's spectacularly rugged terrain.

Settlers in the Lower Mainland began recording conquests of nearby peaks in the late 1800s. Most early first ascents, however, were carried out by prospectors, hunters, surveyors and others who didn't consider themselves climbers. The crags of the nearby Chilliwack and Skagit valleys, for example, were traversed by international border-surveying parties as far back as 1857. And too often we forget the local native Indians, who had quietly climbed some of them hundreds of years earlier. The Indians were mentioned as guides on several early expeditions, but rarely as members of mountaineering parties.

One notable exception was Chief Joe Capilano, who accompanied Dr. Duncan Bell-Irving on a hunting trip in 1889. The hunters followed goats to the summit of the west Lion. Both the Lions were considered an impossible feat at the time, but one of Capilano's youths, stripped naked, raced up and down the pinnacle in 20 minutes. The following year, Capilano led an expedition to the source of the river which now bears his name.

Meanwhile, the disappearance of a pair of explorers north of Squamish resulted in the most fantastic mountaineering journey of that time. The provincial police dispatched local Stanley Smith to find the missing men in 1893. While Smith and his partner, a "Mr. Doolittle of Maple Ridge," found only a tweed cap, their decidedly thorough search took them through the unexplored heart of the Coast Range. Without maps, rope or provisions, the men traversed the glaciers and passes of the Lillooet ice cap, enduring days of snow blindness and near starvation before reaching Chilko Lake.

The pair finally concluded that their quarry in fact never left the Squamish Valley, and turned west. They built canoes and paddled down the Klinaklini river towards Knight Inlet, dining on whatever they could club or shoot. Smith and Doolittle reached the coast after nearly three months and hundreds of miles of travel.

This adventure serves to illustrate the nature of local mountaineering over the next half century. While climbers elsewhere were searching for new routes up familiar peaks, local clubs had not yet begun to explore the Coast Range. These early moun-

taineers soon realized their greatest challenge: thrashing through miles of tangled coastal undergrowth just to reach high country. Even the North Shore mountains demanded a full day's bushwhack from the city's edge. But by 1908 ascents had been recorded on all of them.

The first recorded ascent of Grouse was in 1894. Sidney Williams and Phil Thompson are said to have shot blue grouse on Grouse, noticed the old Capilano dam on Mount Dam, and shot two goats on Goat Mountain, hence the names. The following year, jagged Crown Mountain was reportedly climbed by a group led by G.W. Edwards, president of the Vancouver Pioneers Association. An imaginative story was printed in the *Vancouver World,* claiming the party had seen an avalanche and "one of The Lions fallen off!"

Melodramatic accounts of mountain adventure flourished at the time. A.T. Dalton declared Mount Garibaldi "one terrible monarch of the skies not to be approached by man." In 1907 Dalton led the first ascent of Garibaldi, then considered the highest peak in the southern Coast Range. His account describes a route "that sickened the bravest of us, on the edge of a thin toppling precipice of rotten lava overhanging a horrible green glacier a thousand feet below."

In contrast is the bumbling account of three brothers who climbed both Lions in 1903. Admittedly wet behind the ears, the young Latta brothers carried 50 feet of manila rope, "having seen pictures of mountain climbers tied together with it." After several entanglements the rope was jettisoned halfway up the east Lion, though the threesome managed to argue and claw their way on to the summit.

The Vancouver Mountaineering Club was formed in 1907 and evolved into the B.C. Mountaineering Club (BCMC). Club members were recording first ascents of many nearby peaks, from the bramble-clogged rims of the Lynn headwaters and the alpine knobs of Mount Seymour, to the inaccessible crest of Cathedral Mountain deep within what is now the Greater Vancouver Watershed.

Several names stood out in the early club's years. Basil Darling was a pioneer of winter climbing, trudging up a frozen Capilano River to battle the ice and snow of the Lions. Darling went on to explore the Tantalus Range, the jagged mass of glaciers and rock now visible west of the Sea-to-Sky Highway north of Squamish.

Tom Fyles was the first to complete a winter ascent of the Lions, in 1922. Described in the city as a quiet, unimpressive postman, Fyles shone in the mountains, making a name for himself as the province's finest rock climber. While he led many BCMC expeditions, several of Fyles' greatest achieve-

ments were made alone. His daring solo climbs included first ascents of Black Tusk's north peak and the notorious crumbling Table Mountain, both in Garibaldi Provincial Park.

In 1925, a friend invited Don and Phyllis Munday to hike on Vancouver Island. Phyllis followed her usual drill of stashing her skirt in the bushes and donning knickers, and the group climbed Mount Arrowsmith. From the summit they spied a huge peak in the distant northeast, towering above all its neighbors. Their resolution to reach the mystery mountain resulted in years of expeditions around what is now called Mount Waddington, at 4,016 metres the highest point wholly within British Columbia. Driven by a fascination with the area's flora, fauna, geology and glaciation, the pair battled some of the harshest terrain on earth, claiming dozens of first ascents in the remote ranges east of Knight and Bute inlets.

The Mundays were both active in the community, but Phyllis was an inspiration to all. She won the Order of Canada for her promotion of mountaineering, conservation and work with the Girl Guides. The first woman to stand on the summit of Mount Robson, she was one of the great mountaineers of her time, when such behavior was unheard of in her gender. Before she died in 1990 she wrote, "My spirit belongs to all of the mountains, for this to me is heaven."

But Phyllis Munday wasn't the only woman in knickers and hiking boots. From the beginning, many local mountaineering expeditions were mixed, especially in the egalitarian BCMC. Over the next few decades many women made their mark on the Coast Range. Elfrida Pigou led the female climbers of the fifties, though her adventures ended in the path of an avalanche on Mount Waddington in 1961. She was followed by the likes of Esther Kafer and Alice Purdey. Kafer explored the remote icecaps northwest of Whistler on skis, while Purdey led technically difficult alpine climbs. She was part of a group that climbed the great Mount Saint Elias on the Alaskan border, becoming the first Canadian to do so.

Purdey married Dick Culbert, the leader of a new generation of mountaineers in the sixties and seventies.

Climbing was a new game in the latter half of the century, shaped by several developments. The first was the creep of logging roads into previously remote regions. Climbers gained access to entire ranges without the brutally long approaches suffered by their predecessors. And in the forties a new style emerged with American Fred Beckey's technical ascents of spectacular peaks in the nearby Cascades. With better access, tools and techniques, locals challenged tougher routes throughout Southwestern British Columbia.

Then in 1961 the highway to Squamish opened. Vancouver climbers suddenly had access to the exceptional granite cliffs of the Stawamus Chief. The Culberts and their peers polished technical skills on the Chief in preparation for increasingly difficult alpine routes. The new generation passed their time clinging to sheer rock faces in the high alpine from Pemberton to Hope.

Today, almost every peak within a weekend's reach of Vancouver has been climbed. Mountaineers amuse themselves finding new routes up the hardest faces of familiar peaks like Mount Slesse in the Chilliwack Valley, ascended by a dozen different routes on its infamous dark walls and buttresses.

Rather than joining the siege on accessible summits, a hardy few have gone back to the basics of West Coast mountaineering. Vancouver's John Clarke is their inspiration. Since the 1970s he has been trekking through the vast unexplored regions of the Coast Range, often alone. Clarke hikes or skis for weeks on end across untouched ridges and glaciers, reaching peak after unclimbed peak. He has complained that after leaving his phone number under cairns on dozens of such peaks, he is still looking for climbing partners. In the last 20 years, Clarke has claimed the first ascent of more alpine peaks than perhaps anyone alive.

Now climbers have taken to ice climbing on glaciers and frozen waterfalls with specialized ice axes and crampons. "Sticky" slippers are enabling them to traipse up rock faces that Basil Darling could only have kicked at in his old spiked boots. Mountain gear is getting lighter, more efficient and certainly more colorful as the pastime-turned-sport becomes increasingly popular.

Some say the local peaks are becoming too popular: they actually meet other climbers on their expeditions. But compared to elsewhere in the world where dozens of mountaineers may converge on favorite summits every weekend, Vancouver is fortunate. One need only look to the adventures of John Clarke to be reassured that our city does indeed still lie on the edge of a fierce and lonely wilderness.

Vancouver boasts a growing, friendly mountaineering community. For information on the UBC Varsity Outdoor Club, Vancouver's chapter of the Alpine Club of Canada, or the B.C. Mountaineering Club, contact the Federation of Mountain Clubs of B.C. (phone 737-3053). The federation also offers a variety of mountain skills courses. Several excellent guidebooks are available, of which Bruce Fairley's *Guide to Climbing in Southwestern B.C.* is the most complete.

Rock Climbing
Charles Montgomery

VANCOUVER SITS only 60 kilometres from Squamish, one of the world's great rock-climbing meccas. The focus is on the Stawamus Chief, a granite monolith towering 650 metres above Howe Sound, with a multitude of clean rock bluffs around the town used as training areas.

Since the Squamish highway opened in 1961 rock climbing has seen a tremendous surge in popularity. The sport has gone from being the religion of a few eccentric adventurers to the yuppie trend of the nineties. On dry weekends, Squamish merchants and shoppers see the nearby Little Smoke Bluffs transform into a vertical gymnasium draped in ropes and dotted with neon-clad acrobats, struggling up the bluffs' cracks and near-blank faces.

With all the hubbub in Squamish, it's easy to forget that much of Vancouver's rock-climbing history lies closer to home. Although the North Shore's famous Lions have been climbed via their easiest routes since the turn of the century (see the article on Mountaineering), climbers have since conquered their most challenging faces. The first focus for difficult rock climbing, however, was a lofty granite rock blade known as The Camel. Its distinctive blocky shape can be seen from most of Vancouver: a dark silhouette on the north-east shoulder of jagged Mount Crown.

In 1908 F.W. Hewton led a party up the Camel's back to its hump. In the next few decades, Alec Dalgleish pioneered several routes up its daunting vertical flanks, using the Camel as a training area for more distant adventures. The beast has been rediscovered by modern rock enthusiasts, drawn to its spectacularly exposed profile with sheer cliffs falling away more than 300 metres to Hanes Creek in Lynn Headwaters Park. Climbers tame the Camel by climbing its back (about 40 metres), rappelling down to the neck, then delicately ascending the head slab. A tough hike up to the base from Grouse Mountain or Lynn Creek ensures solitude.

Though at a humbler altitude, Siwash Rock is another crag with some history. The famous 13-metre sea-stack rises from the surf along Stanley Park's seawall near Third Beach. While the crag (actually the petrified body of Skalsh the Unselfish, according to Indian legend) has seen many ascents over the centuries, such actions are currently illegal. The rock sports a sign threatening climbers with prosecution. However, several climbing guidebooks note that the sign makes an excellent foothold.

Also within city limits is Juniper Point. Set in West Vancouver's Lighthouse Park, the area is arguably the prettiest local climbing venue. Between lush old growth forest and crashing waves are rough cliffs marked with cracks, dykes and overhangs. Bolt anchors above several routes enable novices to top-rope, that is to climb with the protection of a rope leading up through the anchor and back down to a belay partner. The point is a favorite for training and after-work climbing.

In Deep Cove, near the east end of the famous Baden-Powell hiking trail, are a series of bluffs overlooking Indian Arm. Climbers return periodically to fight an ongoing battle with several of the area's mossy walls. One clean, blocky cliff has been used as a teaching area, making use of the solid anchor provided by a steel B.C. Hydro tower.

Local climbers continue to explore other nooks and crannies of the North Shore in search of vertical challenges. At least one popular route has been established in the deep, dark gorges of Capilano Canyon.

When they run out of high cliffs, climbing fanatics resort to bouldering. This game consists of climbing or traversing huge rocks or low walls where a fall would be relatively painless without the protection of ropes. Such bouldering can be found on the granite outcrops of North Vancouver's Greenwood Park, and all along West Vancouver's seashore.

Of course the city's most desperate rock fiends will stop at nothing to climb. When thwarted by wet weather, lack of transportation or time, they take bouldering a step further to buildering on man-made structures. Various cathedrals, Park Royal's rockery, the walls of UBC—none are safe from the climber's rubber soles and chalk-dusted hands. In fact, a guide to the best in low level stonework is said to have been circulated among UBC's vertically inclined.

Fortunately, with the rise of climbing's popularity has come a new industry to serve them. In recent years, entrepreneurs have converted cavernous warehouses into simulated rock playgrounds. Artificial walls complete with corners, overhangs and bolted-on holds feature dozens of routes of varying difficulty. Indoor climbing gyms have opened in Richmond, North Vancouver and False Creek, proving that locals need not trek to the wilderness to climb. But the people of Squamish have known that for years.

Rock climbing involves obvious potential dangers. One would be crazy to try it without basic instruction. Fortunately, the Federation of Mountain Clubs of B.C. (737-3053) offers excellent courses on climbing methods and safety, as well as further information on local climbing and clubs.

Hiking
Charles Montgomery

As VANCOUVER GROWS into a sprawling metropolis, we turn to our peaks, rainforest and waterways for refuge from the urban din. Many years after his first ascent of the east Lion, veteran climber John Latta said: "Their unchanging serenity is a tonic to the souls of those who, in their perplexity, wonder what it is all about and how it all will end."

Right on our doorstep, we can find hiking to challenge all levels of ability. The ancient forest begins just steps away from downtown's concrete and steel. Vancouver boasts large natural urban parks, wild seashores and protected marshland. Hikers descending from the alpine backcountry in the North Shore mountains are moments away from the comfort of a cold beer or streetside espresso.

URBAN REFUGE

While expanses of wilderness are within easy reach of Vancouver, two jewels lie right in the heart of the city. Stanley Park, a short walk from the business district is still, for the most part, a wild park. A visit to the Stanley Park Nature House transforms a hike on the park's extensive trail network (or a walk on the seawall) into an exploration of natural history.

On Vancouver's west side the University of British Columbia's Endowment Lands became Pacific Spirit Park in 1989. Thirty-four multiple-use trails traverse coniferous and deciduous forests, ancient bogland, ravines and the Point Grey foreshore. Rock and cobblestone beaches lead one west from Spanish Banks until surrounded only by cliffs, surf and distant mountains.

FOREST AND ALPINE

Vancouver has always been in love with those mountains. Once considered the domain of deer, bear, and only the hardiest of mountaineers, all of the North Shore's peaks had been climbed by 1908. Today's hikers can reach almost all the remote corners of the North Shore on an excellent trail system. For that they can thank German-born Paul Binkert, whose passion for the mountains spawned the successful volunteer trail maintenance program. Binkert has been building mountain trails near Vancouver since the 1960s, and the gruelling route from Lions Bay up to the Lions bears his name.

In Cypress Provincial Park a network of marked paths lead from the ski lodge (at 1,000 metres) up Black, Strachan and Hollyburn mountains. The Howe Sound Crest Trail follows the old mountaineers' route north from Cypress Bowl, 10.5 kilometres to the mighty Lions (1,646 metres) and on to Deeks Lake and the Sea-to-Sky Highway. One day this trail will join

Most of the Capilano, Seymour and Coquitlam watersheds are off limits to hikers, to protect Greater Vancouver's drinking water

with others along Howe sound all the way to Squamish.

Further east, the now-popular trip up Grouse Mountain once meant a three-day epic, starting with a ferry ride to North Vancouver. Fred Hinckleton built the first shack on Grouse in 1909. It quickly became a rendezvous point for hikers demanding food and refreshments. The Hinckletons good-natured attempts at catering ended on a stormy July 4th weekend, after packing in nearly 90 kilograms of food for an expected crowd of 75 who failed to materialize.

Several trails meander their way up 1,224-metre Grouse Mountain and across to nearby Mount Fromme. A spectacular but well-travelled path leads from Grouse along subalpine Dam and Goat ridges. Mount Crown's dizzying, knife-edged summit (1,503 metres) can be reached by crossing Crown Pass, a toilsome 300-metre gap to the north.

Most of the Capilano, Seymour and Coquitlam watersheds are off limits to hikers, in order to protect Greater Vancouver's drinking water. However, access has recently improved. The lower Seymour Valley was opened to recreationalists (for the first time in 59 years) in 1987, with the creation of Seymour Demonstration Forest. Hikers may run into cyclists, fishers and foresters, not to mention deer or the occasional bear.

The creation of Lynn Headwaters Regional Park in 1985 meant 4,685 hectares of watershed suddenly accessible to hikers. This rugged wilderness park offers 40 kilometres of marked and backcountry trails right in North Vancouver's backyard. Explorers can wander along rushing creeks, through deep rainforest and up surrounding peaks, including those of the Grouse/Crown area.

Meanwhile, the all-weather highway to Mount Seymour (1,450 metres) provides the quickest access to alpine near Vancouver. While the knobby summits and meadows beyond Seymour's ski area are unquestionably beautiful, they are the site of the most backcountry mishaps in the province. Bluffs, gullies and fog seem to swallow unprepared hikers regularly.

Joining most North Shore routes together is the 41-kilometre Baden-Powell Trail. Built in 1971 by an assortment of Boy

Scout and Girl Guide troops, the trail was named in honor of the scouting movement's founder. It cuts a wandering line from Horseshoe Bay to Indian Arm, sampling all the delights of the North Shore: from Black Mountain's magnificent views of Howe Sound through dark forests and rushing canyons all the way to the quiet waters of Deep Cove.

Perhaps the most challenging local hike is the trek from Alouette Lake up to the Golden Ears, at 1,706 metres. The double summit is the highest of the rugged group that dominates Maple Ridge's northern skyline, and offers the best chance to see mountain goats locally. Adjoining Golden Ears Park is UBC's research forest, with much easier trails leading to small lakes and pleasant views.

The gentlest of summit objectives is Burnaby Mountain, now capped by Simon Fraser University. Trails circle the mountain under thick second-growth stands.

CREEK AND SHORELINE

Capilano and Lynn Canyon parks cradle waterways alternately delicate and furious, with trails winding along their forested rims. In Maple Ridge, the Greater Vancouver Regional District continues to acquire forest, meadow and marshland along Kanaka Creek. A 12-kilometre trail is under construction, running from the Fraser River to the creek's headwaters. Burnaby Lake Park, a 300-hectare nature preserve, offers over ten kilometres of level walking trails in the heart of suburbia. West Vancouver's Lighthouse Park is a special gem, with shorter trails leading through salal and shadowy old growth Douglas fir to surf-beaten sea cliffs. (Some say it's the only place to enjoy sunsets!)

A varied network of trails has been cut north of Port Moody near the tiny villages of Anmore and Belcarra. From Belcarra Park and Buntzen Lake Recreation Area, hikers follow rugged shorelines pocketed with cozy beaches and tidal mud flats or climb past Sasamat and Buntzen lakes. Routes lead to steep forest-clad ridges high above Indian Arm.

Another chance to hike from sea to sky is on quiet Bowen Island. Trails from the ferry dock at Snug Cove lead right up to the island's apex, 727-metre Mount Gardner.

ALONG THE GREAT RIVER

Though the Fraser River dominates much of the local landscape, for years it was treated as the city's dirty back door, abused by industry and largely ignored by recreationalists. However in 1985 with the birth of the Fraser Estuary Management Program, government and industry began working together to preserve the Fraser's natural wetlands. The public now has access to miles of easy trails along the river's channels, islands and tidal backwaters.

An extensive dyke network protects various valley communities from floodwaters. The city of Richmond is completely surrounded by dykes. An excellent trail follows them around the western shores of Lulu Island, from the marinas and sandbars of the Fraser's Middle Arm, past the tidal marshes of Sturgeon Bank, all the way south to Steveston.

Other stretches of dyke have become popular with hikers. These include the north shore of Sea Island, others along Roberts Bank in Ladner, and nearly ten kilometres along the crescent of Boundary Bay. The latter's trails offer superb birdwatching on the bay's unique saltmarsh. Long dyke trails also follow both shores of the Pitt River on its journey from Pitt Lake, through Coquitlam and Pitt Meadows to the Fraser. The trails join others winding through Pitt Polder's marsh, with mountains rising from its edge. (Polder is the Dutch settlers' name for wetlands reclaimed by dykes.)

The Fraser's eclectic blend of industry and wildlife can be sampled from a number of riverside walks. Access can be found along the North Arm in Vancouver's Southlands, Killarney and Kerrisdale neighborhoods, and in Burnaby's Fraser Foreshore Park. Along the South Arm, explorers will need a boat to reach Steveston's Shady Island and lush Don and Lion, two undeveloped floodplain islands further east. Delta's Deas Island Park has several kilometres of trails through forest and meadow. Perhaps the largest remaining area of undyked, natural river shoreline in the Lower Mainland is the Surrey Bend area. Adjacent to the Barnston Island ferry dock in Surrey, the wetlands offer trails and an oasis of biological diversity. Hawks and herons, duck, geese and swallows, deer, muskrat, otters, foxes and beavers all await the marsh hiker.

Vancouver's hikes are but a taste of what Southwestern B.C. has to offer. A few hours travel in any direction by highway, logging road or ferry opens up hundreds of opportunities. Fortunately, several excellent guidebooks cover the area.

SOME USEFUL PHONE NUMBERS

- B.C. Parks—South Coast Region: 929-1291.
- Federation of Mountain Clubs of B.C.—for information on hiking clubs, outdoor safety and skills courses: 737-3053.
- Fraser River Estuary Management Program—for information on river access and trails: 525-1047.
- Greater Vancouver Regional District—Parks Department: 432-6350.
- Mountain Weather Forecast: 664-9021.
- Stanley Park Nature House (at Lost Lagoon) —for park natural history, maps and occasional walking tours: 685-7314.

Over the years Mountain Equipment Co-op has contributed hundreds of thousands of dollars to environmental causes, funding projects such as trail building, maintenance and clean-ups throughout Canada. MEC's largest single grant to date has been a $100,000 contribution to the purchase of B.C.'s Jedediah Island, now preserved as a marine park. In 1993 MEC created the Endowment Fund for the Environment to finance long-term environmental projects. For more information, contact Julie Davidson at our head office (604) 732-1989.

Bicycling

Faith Bloomfield

A bicycle does get you there and more and there is always the thin edge of danger to keep you alert and comfortably apprehensive. Dogs become dogs again and snap at your raincoat; potholes become personal. And getting there is all the fun.

—Bill Emerson, The Saturday Evening Post, July 29, 1967

CARS AND THEIR drivers become foes, you become an expert in wind currents and POPS (probability of precipitation), and you start to really notice differences between car and bus exhaust. Once you arrive at your destination, your ability to sponge bathe in all-too-public washrooms while maintaining your decency becomes not only a necessity, but a matter of pride. But I complain not, after all "getting there is all the fun."

There are many reasons to commute by bicycle—your health, the environment, the satisfaction. But there are several more convincing excuses not to. Commuting by bike takes a lot of pre-planning: a safe, direct route, proper equipment and adequate end-of-trip facilities.

The Greater Vancouver Regional District's strategic planning division spent three years compiling a comprehensive commuter cycling map. This map clearly marks out difficult areas and intersections. Recommended routes are defined and graded. Commuters travelling between municipalities face additional obstacles such as highways, tunnels and bridges, which the map tries to clarify.

Existing and proposed regional bike routes are highlighted throughout the map, including the City of Vancouver's unique bikeway system, which modifies main corridors to create traffic-calmed roadways. The City of Surrey, in its *Bicycle Blueprint,* details plans to spend more than $5 million in cycling improvements. Joint projects are in the works for a number of other areas. The city and district of North Vancouver linked up on several proposed bikeways as did the districts of Maple Ridge and Pitt Meadows. The City of Richmond has had bike lanes on a number of streets for more than a decade; the No. 2 Road bridge integrated cyclists into its recent construction.

It's not impossible to commute to and from work. You are limited only by your ability and traffic know-how. The fact that most commuting trips begin early in the morning—when motivation is at its lowest—is yet another deterrent. It's hard enough getting up some mornings without needing to prepare for a bike ride. Many will recognize the excuses: "I rode twice this week already . . . It looks like it might rain . . . I'm tired."

Though enjoyable, the bicycle commute is not a joy ride. Cyclists must follow the same rules of the road as drivers. Cycling B.C. and BEST (Better Environmentally Sound Transportation) offer several informative courses that teach appropriate traffic procedures and increase both your confidence and your ability to be knowledgeable and aggressive. Try out different bike routes beforehand, find a safe and expedient route, and allow yourself time for wash-up and dressing. Common sense, preparation and road smarts equal an alert cyclist. In 1994 there were six fatalities in British Columbia. That's six in approximately two per cent of all commuters. Clothing selection can also make or break the commute. Essential gear such as goggles, gloves and helmets increase the safety factor, as do the appropriate water- and wind-repellent, bright-colored clothing. In September 1996 helmets became compulsory under the ministry of transportation. Although not mandatory, anyone cycling without a rear reflector and front light risks not being seen.

The idea of integrating cycling with other forms of transportation is also being realized. The SeaBus now allows cyclists to bring their bikes aboard for the regular fare and the new rush-hour West Coast Express from Mission City to Waterfront Station is also bicycle-friendly. For an extra dollar, riders can transport their "vehicle" onto the train, which can accommodate two bicycles per train car. Although there is still no SkyTrain access, BC Transit installed more than 100 secure bike lockers at selected park-and-ride stations. As well, three bus routes traversing the Massey Tunnel are equipped with vehicle-mounted bicycle racks: the 351 and 601 from Burrard Station to White Rock and the 404 from the airport to Ladner.

In a further effort to encourage this healthy and environmentally friendly mode of transportation, a number of municipalities are providing end-of-trip facilities. New building codes and by-laws requiring showers, lockers and safe bike locations have been passed in Vancouver and the district of Pitt Meadows. The town centre of Richmond and the city and district of North Vancouver are in the process of creating similar standards.

The first time is always the hardest, physically and mentally. You'll be surprised how much easier it becomes. Commuting ten kilometres or less takes almost the same time by bike as by car. One "extreme" cyclist racked up 12,000 commuting kilometres last year, travelling between Port Coquitlam and Richmond every day. In the hour-and-a-quarter it takes him by bike, he gets his daily quota of exercise and reduces his stress level. Even when it rains, he says he knows the cycling is going to be the best part of his day.

Motor Racing
Gordon McIntyre

Molson Indy Vancouver, 1990. VS

Vancouver's choked downtown streets hadn't seen anything like it. Methanol-propelled IndyCar racing cars made their debut in Vancouver's commercial core in the summer of 1990, zipping along residential lanes, through long shadows thrown by office towers and under SkyTrain rails at speeds of up to 370 kilometres per hour.

Many downtown and West End residents weren't impressed —three days of high-pitched hell gave them an idea of what it must be like to live beside an airport runway. But tourism and economic officials were gleeful: millions of people worldwide watching the race live, giving Vancouver a free ad the tourism board couldn't afford to pay for; $25 million in economic spin-off pumped into local coffers; 25,000 out-of-town visitors.

Each year, there are about 16 IndyCar races, in Australia, Brazil, the United States, Toronto and Vancouver. The Vancouver race began in 1990. By 1996 it drew more than 70,000 people to race day Sunday and more than 170,000 in total for the three days of practice qualifying and racing.

Because the Molson Indy Vancouver track is a temporary road circuit—it gets rebuilt each year for the late August race—its dimensions change a bit each year. Roughly speaking, the boomerang-shaped course is about 2.5 kilometres around. The cars drive clockwise, taking about 50 seconds to complete a lap (10 or 11 corners) and average about 160 kilometres per hour on a dry, sunny day.

It takes 340 truckloads of asphalt (5,000 tonnes) to make the track, which is ringed by 2,000 steel-reinforced concrete barriers, each 3.65 metres long, .8 metres high, .6 metres wide and weighing 3,175 kilograms. There's also 3,048 metres of three-metre-high chain link fence to prevent debris from crashing cars from flying into the stands, and 487 metres of tires stacked five-high to help keep drivers from getting injured in a crash.

The IndyCar vehicles themselves are open-wheel race cars powered by turbo-charged engines that produce 800 horsepower with top speeds of 370 kilometres per hour. The chassis, made by two English companies unless a race team is rich enough to build its own from scratch, cost more than $500,000, and that's without extras. For your half mill, you get the body, suspension and steering systems, and aerodynamic wings. You don't get an engine. You don't even get a dashboard, tires, electronics or turbocharger. You do get a 181-litre fuel tank, but then the cars only average 2.8 kilometres per litre.

The Vancouver course is notorious among drivers. It's short, narrow and has tight turns, making it extremely hard to pass. To quote the IndyCar fan magazine, "Vancouver is one of IndyCar racing's most challenging circuits. Molson Indy Vancouver means slam-bang action. In just seven years, the Molson Indy Vancouver has developed a reputation as the roughest race on the schedule, the result of a circuit where overtaking is an undertaking and staying out of the walls is sometimes hard for even the most precise drivers."

The Molson Indy Vancouver didn't get off to a good start. In the inaugural race, volunteer worker Jean Patrick Heir was killed when struck by the car driven by Willy T. Ribbs. Heir had jumped on the track to push the stalled car of Vancouver driver Ross Bentley, in a tight corner known as a chicane. Ribbs hadn't time to see Heir on the track when he rounded the tight turn.

The Vancouver circuit has had its fair share of driver controversy. As the IndyCar fan magazine points out, there have been several crashes. None were as colorful as the fender-bender between two old friends and former Formula One champions, Brazilian Emerson Fittipaldi and Brit Nigel Mansell.

As the two grizzled veterans came around the final turn into the homestretch in the 1993 race, both cars vied for the same line to the finish, though neither was in contention for a podium spot. The drivers had a law of physics reconfirmed—two material objects can't occupy the same space and time. They left the track shaking their fists at each other after the crash.

"Nigel tried to use my brakes to slow his car," Fittipaldi said. "My car is not a ghost. There was no space between my car and the wall, yet he tried to pass me where no space existed."

The best story of the Molson Indy Vancouver was Al Unser Jr. winning the 1994 race. Unser, winner of four of the first six Molson Indy Vancouver races (Michael Andretti won the other two), was diagnosed with serious food poisoning the day before the race, yet he fought off the sickness, fatigue and weight loss to earn the checkered flag.

Development of the Concord Pacific property squeezed the Indy out, forcing a search for a new location. In early April, 1997, no new site had yet been announced.

Thoroughbred Racing
Jim Coleman

Photo finish; Treasure's Glory nips One–Eyed Admiral in first heat of Derby Trial, Exhibition Park, 1968. vp

THOROUGHBRED RACING in Vancouver is almost as old as the city. Racing first was conducted here in 1889 with the opening of a half-mile track at East Park, later Hastings Park. Vancouver's first one-mile track, named Minoru Park in honor of King Edward VII's horse, Minoru, which won the 1909 Epsom Derby, opened on Lulu Island in 1909. Shut down during World War I, it re-opened in 1924, under the name Brighouse Park. Another one-mile track, Lansdowne Park, opened in 1924 immediately adjacent to Brighouse. In that era, federal laws restricted each track to 14 days of racing with pari-mutuel betting in each calendar year. The province had ten separate seven-day meetings, beginning with Hastings Park in May and concluding with Victoria's The Willows and Colwood in September.

British Columbia horsemen of that period were noted for colorful individuality, rather than wealth. However, two gentlemen of means who operated extensive stables were Austin C. Taylor and Eric W. Hamber, later lieutenant-governor. Hamber bred and raced horses under the nom de course, Greencroft Stable. From England, he imported Papworth, son of Derby-winning Papyrus, and a court of well-bred mares. He never enjoyed huge success on the track but Papworth and those foundation-mares left a profound imprint on British Columbia racing. Taylor was much more adventurous than Hamber. He raced and bred horses on a lavish scale under the name ACT Stock Farm. He imported American trainers and employed a stable jockey, Henry Palaez. Taylor was well known on California tracks where he raced with notable success. In 1936 he took a shot at the Kentucky Derby with Indian Broom, a three-year-old purchased during the winter from Mrs. Isabel Dodge Sloan. Indian Broom finished third to Bold Venture. Major Taylor's other successful horses included Special Agent and Whichcee.

However, the Taylors and Hambers were comparative rarities. The public was intrigued by horsemen such as C.C. (Gyp) Emmert, Asah (Cougar) Smith, George Addison, Mrs. Jessie Mackenzie and Herb Fullerton, who was also internationally famous as the proprietor of one of North America's most formidable stables of fighting-cocks. Mrs. Mackenzie was a rare lady: when failing health and financial insolvency overtook her, she lived in a shack at Brighouse Park and kept her old thoroughbred bread-winner, Jim Rogan, in a nearby stall until he died at 39.

One person who assured respectability for British Columbia racing was Robert F. Leighton, a courtly English gentleman and presiding steward for many years. Distinguished by birth and education, Judge Leighton nevertheless was jobless and out of funds shortly upon arrival here. He doffed his Bond Street finery and to support his wife and children took a job as bartender in the Bodega Hotel on Cordova. Of the highest personal integrity, he was also famously compassionate, realizing that many of the horsemen racing under his jurisdiction were no better than God had intended them to be.

Vancouver enthusiasm for racing peaked in the 1930s when both evening newspapers (*Province* and *Sun*) published racing extras which were sold on the street less than 20 minutes after the completion of each afternoon's final race. The racing extras carried complete form-charts of the entire day's racing.

After World War II, there was a sharp consolidation of racing. Brighouse, The Willows and Colwood were closed. In 1961, Lansdowne Park was sold for real estate development and all Lower Mainland racing was concentrated at Hastings Park. The B.C. Jockey Club was operated by Jack Diamond and the three sons of S.W. Randall. The senior Randall, in partnership with Sam Levy, operated Hastings back in the era when the province had seven tracks. Diamond and the Randalls ran Hastings until their lease expired in 1993. They were supplanted by a new organization, the B.C. Racing Association.

The post-World War II period produced the best horse ever foaled in Western Canada. George Royal, bred by Wilson Dunn at Aldergrove, was bought and raced by E.C. Hammond and Robert W. Hall. George Royal went on to win 21 races, including two consecutive runnings of the San Juan Capistrano Handicap at Santa Anita and two consecutive runnings of the Canadian International Championship at Woodbine in Toronto.

Exciting, live thoroughbred racing at Hastings Park Racecourse is conducted on 126 days between mid-April and early November. Hastings Park, at the same location since 1889, and owned by the Pacific Racing Association, offers unique venues for individual or group entertainment with a range of restaurants, bars, concession facilities, private entertainment rooms and, of course, totalizator betting. Hastings Park also offers live simulcast coverage of racing from Hong Kong and all major racetracks in California.

Harness Racing
Gary Bannerman

THE GRAND OPENING of Fraser Downs in the Cloverdale area of Surrey on October 5, 1996, was a landmark event in the harness racing life of British Columbia. On the same site, on opening day January 1, 1976, Cloverdale Raceway became one of the premier harness racing centres in North America. Lengthened from one-half to five-eighths of a mile, and modernized throughout the complex, Fraser Downs promises to provide the most exciting racing the region has ever seen.

"We needed modern sports lounges and television technology to maximize the potential of today's multi-dimensional product," said Chuck Keeling, the general manager of Fraser Downs. "We not only bring in simulcast racing and other sports from abroad, we beam our signal around the continent." He said the technology parallels the improvement in horses. "As horses became better and faster, our half-mile track became, figuratively speaking, smaller. We want racing as competitive as any in the world, and this new track should give it to us."

The Cloverdale track and the sport's summer venue at Sandown Raceway near Victoria combine to present about 160 days of horse racing and over 1,600 races annually. The parimutuel wagering, incorporating teletheatres around British Columbia, surpassed $75 million in 1996, generating purses in excess of $7 million. There are 2,500 registered standardbred horses in the province and an active breeding industry. The industry generates thousands of full-time and part-time jobs and an economic impact of $60 million per year in the province.

Photographs of ice racing in Vernon in 1897 (the horses specially shod) provide evidence of the sport's roots in the province, but it remained somewhat of a country fair and occasional curiosity until the early 1970s. In 1975, James Keeling Sr., the proprietor of Orangeville Raceway and other businesses in Ontario, struck a deal with the Surrey Fair Board and Cloverdale Raceway went into business. Millions were invested in grandstands, barns and public amenities. The principal executive who built the business was James Keeling Jr., the founder's son, who tragically died on May 18, 1996 in a boating accident. His 24-year-old son Chuck succeeded him.

Harness racing operates in 48 countries of the world. It is rare when a major stakes race runs anywhere in North America, not to have prominent Canadian representation among owners, trainers and drivers.

Heading for the backstretch, Fraser Downs, 1996. tracy holmes

Fraser Downs features a seasonal harness racing schedule of 110 live race-days from October through April. The additon of simulcasting full race cards from world-class harness and thoroughbred tracks has boosted seasonal attendance to 450,000. Amenities include a "Finish Line" Sports Lounge and Clubhouse Buffet Restaurant. Just 30 minutes from Vancouver and 10 minutes from the U.S. border, Fraser Downs provides harness racing entertainment via televised signal to Sandown Raceway in Sidney, and to teletheatres in communities throughout B.C.

Golfing
Don Harrison

GOLF AND CANADA have never made much sense, at least from a meteorological point of view. All that snow and ice, rain and fog couldn't, however, stop expatriate Britons from starting the first club in North America (Royal Montreal, 1873) or from smacking the first tee shot west of the Mississippi River (Victoria Gold Club, 1893, also Canada's first 18-hole course in 1895). Our willful weather, notes the authoritative Canadian Golf Foundation, also hasn't kept more Canadians from playing the game—per capita—than our large, latitudinally blessed neighbor to the south.

Vancouver has always managed to out-manoeuver its edge-of-North America location relative to the world's golfing circuits with bright lures of great fishing and scenic splendor. Most of the greatest names to strike a dimpled ball have played in Vancouver: Bobby Jones, Joyce Wethered, Byron Nelson, Babe Didrikson, Ben Hogan, Arnold Palmer, Jack Nicklaus, Nancy Lopez, Nick Faldo, Bernhard Langer and others.

The Greater Vancouver Open announced January 15, 1997 that the purse for the '97 tournament, August 21 to 24 at Surrey's Nothview club, would be $1.5 million U.S., with the winner's share being $270.000.

Furthermore, 1996 saw the city return for the first time in 30 years to a place on the world's No. 1 professional circuit, the U.S. PGA Tour, when the men tackled the new Palmer-designed Northview Golf Club in Surrey in the $1-million U.S.-Greater Vancouver Open. It was the richest tournament held west of Toronto or north of California.

On what was undoubtedly a damp, chilly night in November 1892 at 524 West Cordova, a man with a good pioneer Vancouver name, Dr. Duncan Bell-Irving, called the first meeting to form the city's first club, the Vancouver Golf Club (VGC). The site chosen for the club was what is now Jericho Park and the military base across 4th Avenue west of Alma.

The Victoria Golf Club actually got up and running in 1893 before the nine-hole Vancouver club, the latter hampered by being accessible only by boat or a tortuous trek through the bush. Vancouver's delay certainly could not have been caused by the time needed to construct an elaborate clubhouse. The facility that was built for the princely sum of $35 had neither a wooden floor nor, crucially, a place to store the drinks for the 19th hole.

The cruel sea would show no mercy to that low-lying first Vancouver club, rendering the course unplayable under the frequent tidal deposits of rocks, sand and logs that first winter. The VGC members decamped to a more convenient location near Brockton Point in Stanley Park.

Sadly uncelebrated by the current owners, the Vancouver Park Board, 1995 marked the centenary of golf in Stanley Park with today's players enjoying the picturesque pitch-and-putt facility and putting green near Ceperley Park.

Golf at Brockton soon became problematic, however, as nearby archers, cricketers and lacrosse players gave a different meaning to the term "Fore." Three years later, Stanley Park was abandoned, first for an ill-fated move near to the current foot of Lonsdale in North Vancouver. Again, accessibility proved a problem for members who lived on the south side of Burrard Inlet.

The VGC, and organised golf, ceased to exist in Vancouver from 1899 until the Jericho course was revived in 1907. In November of that year, the area's first pro, Albert Kam, was hired by the VGC. He was succeeded by the inimitable Alex Duthie in 1910. Alex remained at the Jericho course until the Canadian military doomed the facility to the history books with the outbreak of World War II.

The century's second decade would begin a golf boom in the region that lasted until the grip of World War II rendered the game a frivolity, a benefit only for raising money for the war effort.

The region would open its second course in 1911, as the B.C. Golf Club was founded on the old Austin farmsite in Coquitlam. Today, the course is known as the Vancouver Golf Club, host of two of the LPGA's three official tournaments held in Western Canada. The first was won in 1988 by South African Sally Little and in 1991 by American Nancy (Brown) Scranton. The current VGA is the second oldest course in the province.

The original Shaughnessy course, known properly as the Shaughnessy Heights Golf Club, opened in 1912. It was a further inducement by Canadian Pacific Railway to have the well-to-do move from Vancouver's West End to its large, English-style mansions in the new community between the current 16th and 25th avenues and Oak and East Boulevard.

Other courses followed before World War II such as Point Grey and Marine Drive (both 1923), Hastings (opened 1924, killed in 1954 by the British Empire Games); Quilchena (1925, killed for Prince of Wales High School and housing, 1955) Langara (1926); Gleneagles and Peace Portal (1977); University (1930); Beach Grove (1933); Fraserview (1934); and Capilano (1937).

But it was Shaughnessy that scaled the heights, attracting the first big exhibition when thousands turned out in 1913 to

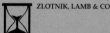

watch the immortal Harry Vardon—the only six-time winner of the British Open. The big show would soon be a Shaughnessy trademark.

"The Haig," dapper Walter Hagen followed in 1924 before appearing at Langara in 1928 and 1929, called at the time "unrivalled as a public course on the West Coast of North America."

Bobby Jones, considered along with Jack Nicklaus the century's best male players, appeared in 1934. Byron Nelson had the title of the 1936 Golden Jubilee Open celebrating the city's half-century birthday stolen by an astonishing eight-under-par 29 on Shaughnessy's final nine by Vancouver amateur Ken Black.

Ben Hogan did a wartime fundraiser at Shaughnessy in 1944, while Sam Snead and South African Bobby Locke wowed the crowds in 1945 and 1947, respectively. The first Canadian Open staged west of Toronto went to Shaughnessy Heights in 1948 with Tacoma's Chuck Congdon taking the top prize.

Hall-of-Famer Carol Mann would win her fourth straight tour title when she captured the Canadian Open at the new Shaughnessy in 1969, the LPGA's first official event in Western Canada. Nine years later, Lanny Watkins would win the Canadian PGA Championship at Shaughnessy by 12 strokes over a field that included Faldo and Langer in what remains the European super-duo's only tournament appearances in Canada.

Across town, Englishwoman Joyce Wethered, still considered the best female player of all time, broke the course record at Jericho in 1935 with a 73.

In 1964, a man whose name always surfaces when discussing this country's best player, Toronto's George Knudson, drew 5,000 fans to Capilano for a filming of the popular *Shell's Wonderful World of Golf*.

But no name game of great stars would be complete without a tip of the cap to Vancouver's—and certainly British Columbia's, at least—greatest player, Stan Leonard. Born in 1915 of immigrant parents from Aberdeen, Leonard would caddie at Shaughnessy Heights for 50 cents a round in the late 1920s. A good wage for kids, but remember, this was before the 14-club limit. At least 20 clubs was not uncommon. By 1932, Leonard was B.C. Amateur champion, a title he would hold once more, along with four B.C. Open crowns.

It wasn't until he was 40 years old in 1955 that Leonard felt he could try the U.S. PGA tour fulltime. He would win three times: the Greater Greensboro in 1957; the Tournament of Champions in 1957 and the Western Open in 1960. In 1959 he was voted player of the year by the Golf Writers' Association in the U.S., the only Canadian to be so honored. Since then, career amateur Doug Roxburgh of Marine Drive and pro Dave Barr of Richmond have come forward as best men.

Roxburgh has won four Canadian Amateur championships to go with his Canadian record of 12 B.C. Amateur titles. Barr has consistently been the country's top touring pro for more than a decade. He's finished second in a U.S. Open, led Canada to wins in the World Cup and in 1994 helped bring home this nation's greatest trophy by winning the Dunhill Cup at St. Andrews with B.C. teammates Rick Gibson and Ray Stewart.

The women, when they haven't been fighting the long battle for equal rights at Vancouver's private clubs (also known in the past for policies that forced the establishment of a Jewish club, the new Quilchena in 1957), have seen the likes of star Violet Pooley Sweeny. The Jericho member won a record of nine provincial Amateur championships, the last in 1929, and is in the B.C. Hall of Fame.

There are now 70 courses of bigger than pitch-and-putt size from Whistler to Hope. The building boom of the later 1980s and the first half of the 1990s has stopped, but the period has left the region with works of agronomical art by the likes of marquee Americans, Nicklaus (Nicklaus North), Palmer (Northview, Whistler GC), Robert Trent Jones Jr. (Chateau Whistler), Lee Trevino (Swan-e-Set Bay), while Canadian Les Furher (Mayfair Lakes, Riverway and Meadow Gardens) and Tom McBroom (new Langara and Morgan Creek) have followed in the traditions of excellence left by the likes of Stanley Thompson (Capilano) and A.V. Macan (both Shaughnessys and Marine Drive).

With such a distinguished timeline, it's not surprising that Vancouver has the only golf museum in Canada, save the Royal Canadian Golf Association headquarters at Glen Abbey in Toronto.

Museum executive director Dorothy Brown, with her Scottish brogue, seems perfectly suited to the task of handling the large library and equipment collections. The old University Golf Club clubhouse was saved from demolition and the refurbished building is the home for Golf House. Dave Barr officially christened the facility on May 6, 1989 when he hit a feathery ball with a 1750 track iron.

The museum, all the new courses, tournaments like the Canadian Tour's B.C. Tel Pacific Open, the John Daly-led West Coast Classic and the Greater Vancouver Open have signalled a golfing rebirth. They bond the public's enthusiasm to play the game to a calculated appreciation for the sports' position in Vancouver as recreation, a source of pride, and valuable business.

Curling
Gordon McIntyre

Vancouver has lester and Frank to thank for introducing curling to the shores of the West Coast. The roarin' game arrived in Vancouver when the hockey-mogul Patrick brothers pilled up stakes out east in 1910. They formed the Pacific Coast Hockey Association (PGHA) to represent the West's interests in pursuit of the Stanley Cup against the National Hockey Association, the precursor to the NHL. The Patricks built the Denman Arena (known as The Pile) on the north end of Denman Street for their PCHA Vancouver Millionares. Curlers, mostly ex-patriates from Manitoba, immediately took to the ice and formed the Vancouver Curling Club in 1912.

From its beginnings in the late 1800s in the Interior's mining towns, where engineers of mostly Scottish descent brought the game with them, curling had taken Vancouver by storm by the 1930s, after a lull forced by the outbreak of World War I. Curling didn't regain its popularity until the Depression years, but according to Murray Soder, chaiman of the B.C. curling 100th anniversary committee, "a strong contingent of former Manitobans in Vancouver made the city a curling power during the 1930s."

An Olympic sport for the first time in Chamonix, France, in 1924, curling was introduced to The Forum in 1931. The arena's 10 sheets of curling ice made it the biggest curling rink in the world at the time. By 1932, the Vancouver Club had affiliated with The Forum.

The first provincial championship was contested in 1935. Joe Dundas of Vancouver won, but chose not to compete in the Brier, the Canadian championship. The next year, Vancouver skip Billy Whalen and his rink (team) won the B.C. Consols, as the provincial championship was called. They paid their own train fare and travelled to Toronto for the Brier, where they finished fourth with a respectable 6-3 record (legendary Ken Watson won representing Manitoba).

In 1950, the Vancouver Club hosted the city's first Brier, held at Kerrisdale Arena. The Northern Ontario rink, skipped by Tim Ramsay, won the event. The following year, the B.C. Ladies Curling Association was formed. Velma Lyttle of Vancouver was the first president.

B.C. had won one Brier—Frenchy D'Amour's Trail rink won in 1948—but Lyall Dagg's rink became the first Vancouver foursome to win the Brier. Dagg followed his Canadian success in Charlottetown by going on to win the Scotch Cup, the world curling championship, in Calgary.

Canada vs Norway, BC Place, 1987. vs

Other Lower Mainland clubs include: Tunnel Town (opened four sheets of ice in a Boundary Bay air hangar in 1958, moved to Tswassassen in 1971); Valley (opened 1954 in Cloverdale, but well water wouldn't freeze so Vancouver water was trucked in, opened new bulding in 1980); Arbutus (Vancouver, 1964); Heather (Surrey, 1970); Hollyburn Country Club (West Vancouver, 1963); North Vancouver Recreation Centre (1966); Royal City (New Westminster, 1965); UBC Thunderbird Winter Sports Centre (1963 as host of Point Grey Club, which folded in 1985 because of dwindling membership); Langley (1973, claim to fame is providing rocks for 1987 world championship held at Vancouver's B.C. Place Stadium); and Port Moody (1975).

Bowling
Gordon McIntyre

YOU COULD ARGUE that Greater Vancouver's first bowler was Sir Francis Drake, who sailed past what's now British Columbia on his round-the-world tour of 1577–80. How serious a bowler he was is beyond dispute: informed during a game of bowls that the Spanish Armada was approaching, he calmly finished up before going out to defeat it.

Canada carved its niche in bowling lore in 1908 when Toronto alley owner Tom Ryan invented five-pin. The customers at his snack bar found 10-pin too demanding during their short lunch breaks, so he came up with the smaller balls and lower pin number. Today, five-pin is a $300-million industry in Canada.

Variations of bowling are recorded in Vancouver as early as 1890 with U.S. prospectors introducing 10-pin around 1900. Five-pin was introduced to the Lower Mainland in 1920 and by the end of World War II it overtook 10-pin as a participation sport. It's estimated that 30,000 Greater Vancouver bowlers visit a lane every week. About 20,000 people in the Lower Mainland are registered in leagues. There are 35 alleys in Greater Vancouver with about 300 lanes dedicated to five-pin and 60 lanes to 10-pin.

The grand-daddy of them all, Commodore Lanes and Billiards in the basement at 838 Granville is a great place to capture some of the atmosphere of bowling's early years in Vancouver. The Commodore wasn't the first alley constructed in the Lower Mainland (which was is disputed), but it's the oldest surviving bowling centre in Canada. Frank Panvin opened the lanes on September 7, 1930, an event that made the papers.

Today, women make up as much as two-thirds of league members, but in the roaring twenties bowling was almost exclusively a male sport. Panvin changed that. He introduced a promotion that allowed women to bowl free in the mornings and he was the first to rent out shoes. Panvin also had an important employee: Mitz Nozaki. Nozaki began his association with bowling as a pin boy at Panvin's Abbott Bowling Alleys (Panvin owned several, including the long-gone Universe Alleys and the Abbott) in 1927 at the age of 13. He enjoyed watching the patrons bowl and hang out at the bar drinking beer and whiskey.

But the pins didn't have rubber bands around them in those days. When struck they turned into erratic, dangerous missiles without flight patterns. "We risked our necks," Nozaki says. When Panvin offered him a job as a cashier in his spanking new alley, with its 12 lanes for both five- and 10-pin, its black-and-white checkered linoleum floors and state-of-the-art

Canada carved its niche in bowling lore in 1908 when alley owner Tom Ryan invented five-pin. The customers at his snack bar found 10-pin too demanding for a short lunch break

Brunswick equipment, the young Japanese-Canadian jumped at the chance. From opening day in 1930, until Panvin's death in 1962, the only time Nozaki spent away from the alley was when the Canadian government interned him at Shuswap Lake with other Japanese-Canadians during World War II.

When Panvin died, Nozaki bought the place. He watched some of Vancouver's great bowlers—Frank (Mr. Bowling) Lavigne; Joan (Rocco) Haines, chosen the world's best female bowler in 1965; even his son Frank, winner of several Western and Canadian championships—roll countless balls down his polished wood lanes. He hosted the likes of Clark Gable, Jack Benny, Marion Davies (William Hearst's companion) and Buster Crabbe as they bowled at the centre with its famous motto Where Pleasant Days May Be Spent. Roy Rogers rode Trigger down the steep stairs one day, a stunt to promote the cowboy and local female bowling star Jean Hodson.

Today, the duck pins and 10-pins are gone. But 12 of the original 20 lanes survive along with 18 pool tables and several pinball machines. You can still order a beer while scouting for Greater Vancouver's next Mr. or Mrs. Bowling.

It's not like the fifties and sixties when bowling reached its peak. Back then, there were waiting lists with 100 names on them, right up to closing time at midnight. Now with the steady gentrification of the downtown, nearby Yaletown and developing Concord Pacific lands, bowling's on the rebound at the Commodore, if not throughout the Lower Mainland.

Nozaki retired in 1990 and sold the Commodore to Al Rose. It was Rose who renovated the joint to make it as much like it was during the 1930s as possible. During the renovations, heaps of pictures, directories and old trophies were dug up. They adorn Rose's office and the walls of the alley, making the Commodore a living museum. At this writing both Mitz Nozaki and Frank Lavigne are still steady fixtures at the lanes.

Boxing
Jim Coleman

THE VANCOUVER HISTORY of professional pugilism, although extensive and blood-spattered, is highlighted by two unrelated bits of trivia.

1—Tommy Burns (Noah Brusso), the only Canadian ever to win the world heavyweight title, died while visiting a Vancouver friend on May 10, 1955. He is buried in Oceanview Cemetery. Only two people attended his funeral and his grave went unmarked for six years.

2—Jimmy McLarnin, two-time world welterweight champion, was raised in Vancouver after coming from Belfast, Ireland, when he was nine. He never fought a professional bout in Vancouver but after he invaded California in 1923, he returned to this city frequently.

Tommy Burns, who stood only seven inches over five feet and weighed only 175 pounds, was born in Hanover, Ont. He won the heavyweight title with a 20-round decision over Marvin Hart at Los Angeles in 1906. He held the crown until December 26, 1908 when Jack Johnson—who was five inches taller and 25 pounds heavier—caught up with him at Rushcutter's Bay, Australia. Johnson beat Burns so unmercifully that the police stopped the bout in the 14th round.

Vancouver was the scene of Jack Johnson's first ring appearance after beating Burns. The champion arrived here by steamship from Australia on March 9, 1909. The next night at the Vancouver Athletic Club, he boxed a six-round exhibition with Victor McLaglen, a 26-year-old actor-longshoreman on his way to Hollywood. Later, McLaglen won an Academy Award for his performance in *The Informer.*

Jimmy McLarnin was the most successful pugilist ever to come out of Vancouver. His father Sam McLarnin, came to Vancouver from Ireland opened a second-hand furniture shop and sired 12 children. Charles "Pop" Foster, a former English carnival boxer and part-time stevedore, was Sam McLarnin's crony. One day, as the older men watched Jimmy play, Foster said, "I could make a boxer of that boy—a champion!" When Jimmy was 16, Foster took him to California to launch a professional career.

Ten years later, on May 29, 1933, Jimmy won the world welterweight championship, kayoing Young Corbett. Later, he fought three memorable title-bouts with Barney Ross: losing the championship in May 1934, regaining it in September 1934, and losing it, again, in May 1935.

McLarnin retired at 28, completely unmarked and with $300,000 in the bank. As these words are written, McLarnin, 85, and in full possession of his faculties, lives with his son in Richland, Washington.

Boxing's early homes in Vancouver were low-ceilinged, smoky establishments such as the Vancouver Athletic Club where Jack Johnson and Victor McLaglen sparred in 1909.

Vancouver didn't have a semi-permanent promoter of fight-shows until 1918 when Jack Allen, an American, arrived by steamer from Anchorage, Alaska. U.S. authorities had cut short his promising career as an Anchorage bootlegger.

Allen was in and out of Vancouver for the next 20 years; promoting fight-shows, managing fighters and presiding over a 24-hour gambling club. The most successful boxers he managed locally were Vic Foley, Billy Townsend and Gordon Wallace. Allen took Townsend to New York where he fought headline-bouts at Madison Square Garden.

Vancouver was "a bit too far from the beaten track" to attract many championship bouts. Nevertheless, Muhammad Ali was defending the North American Boxing Federation heavyweight championship when he won a 12-round decision over George Chuvalo at the Pacific Coliseum on May 1, 1972. Michael Spinks was world light-heavyweight champ when he kayoed Oscar Rivandeneyra in the same Coliseum in November 1983.

Two heavyweight ex-champions made Vancouver ring-appearances. Jack Dempsey was on one of his comeback tours when he boxed three men in two-round exhibitions at the old Vancouver Arena, at Georgia and Denman, on August 28, 1931.

Promoter Jack Allen persuaded his boyhood friend, manager Ancil Hoffman, to bring Max Baer to Vancouver for a bout on August 19, 1936. As an opponent, Allen signed an unknown, James J. Walsh, who billed himself as The Alberta Assassin. Walsh lasted only one punch.

Later that night, the Vancouver Arena was destroyed by fire. Promoter Allen, deprived of a major facility for staging fight-shows, moved to Toronto, accompanied by a group of Vancouver's most active pugilists, including Gordon Wallace, Alan Foston, Eddie Troll, Julius Troll and Katsumi Moriaki.

While space-limitations will result in some regrettable omissions, following is a partial list of those who contributed to the local scene as boxers, coaches, managers and promoters: Bud Davies, Arnold Bertram, Al Principe, Jackie Turner, Stan Almond, Frank Almond, Jimmy Langston, Kenny Lindsay, Dave Brown, Phil Palmer, Angelo Branca, Len Walters, Gordon Racette and Micheal Olajide. A man who deserves a special word was George Paris, a black middleweight, who arrived here at the turn of the century and, until he died at a great age, trained police constables on Main Street.

History Of Chess
Nathan Divinsky

Vancouver was once frontier town, more famous for its sawmills than its ballet. Nevertheless it seems to have had more of an artistic seed than other towns of the Pacific Northwest.

"The Vancouver Chess Club on May 20, 1905 gave an interesting exhibition of living chess at the Drill Hall. The games were played by J. Cameron and P. Dunne, versus A.C. Brydon-Jack and W. Francis. The kings were young men but the other pieces were young ladies. . . as they stood facing each other they might well have posed for a tableau of King Arthur's court in towered Camelot. The places of the pawns were taken by boys of the Christ Church brigade" (*Lasker's Chess Magazine* June, 1905).

"...there is hardly anything doing in Portland, Seattle, Tacoma or Spokane. I could not hear of a chess club in any of these cities, although there may be a small club or two which I did not locate" (*American Chess Bulletin* November, 1912).

"At Seattle, the Y encourages chess, and there are several rather clever players . . . but I was told that there is a flourishing club up at Vancouver. One can always find chess where there are Englishmen" (*Knight Errant*).

"On April 21-25, the first congress was held of the new British Columbia Chess Association, the venue being Vancouver. The winner of the tournament is entitled to be called the Chess Champion of British Columbia and holds the championship shield, besides taking a gold medal as first prize" (*British Chess Magazine Annual* 1916).

Mr. J.M. Ewing, a Scot by birth, was the winner on this first occasion (with 6-1). R.G. Stark, B.A. Yates and H. Butler tied for second (4.5-2.5), Stark winning the playoff. A. Stevenson (4-3), C.F. Millar (2.5-4.5), A. Tree (2-5) and E. Thompson (0-7) were the other competitors.

A large number of chess-playing immigrants came to Canada after World War II and some ended up in Vancouver. Partly as a result of this chess enrichment, the first Canadian championship held in Vancouver took place at the Hotel Vancouver August 24 - September 1, 1951.

Paul Vaitonis who came to Canada (Hamilton) from Lithuania in 1949 won the title (10.5-1.5) just ahead of Toronto's Frank Anderson (10-2). The Vancouver entries, Jursevskis, Taylor and Millar finished 6th, 8th and 13th. Millar is the very same C.F. Millar who played in the 1916 B.C. championship. He was born in Ontario in 1883, won the B.C. title 4 times but in 1951, at the age of 68, won only one game—against your present writer (who came fifth with 6.5-5.5).

> At Seattle, the Y encourages chess, and there are several rather clever players ...but I was told that there is a flourishing club up at Vancouver. One can always find chess where there are Englishmen
> —*Knight Errant*

One of the most influential immigrants to the Vancouver chess scene was John Prentice (1907-1987). He came from Vienna in the late 1930s and founded a lumber empire —Canadian Forest Products. He had a deep passion for chess and acted as president of the Chess Federation of Canada from 1955 to 1971 as well as representing Canada at the World Chess Federation (FIDE) from 1957 to 1987. His financial support for international competion and his organizational ability made it possible for Canada to send teams to almost every international chess olympiad (held every two years) during the '60s, '70s and '80s. Although not a chess master himself, Prentice was a strong, knowledgeable player who gave even accredited masters a struggle. For 30 years he *was* "Mr. Chess" in Canada.

Professor Elod Macskasy (1919-1990) came to Vancouver from Hungary in 1956. He taught mathematics at UBC for over 30 years and was B.C.'s top chess player for most of that time. He won the Canadian Open Championship in 1958 and had a great influence on young B.C. chessplayers. He played on a number of Canadian Olympic chess teams and always with distinction.

In the late '50s and early '60s, he often could be found at the old Heidelberg Restaurant on RobsonStrasse, the hangout for European immigrants. Macskasy was a gentle, artistic man with almost no poison in him. He was a wonderful friend.

Vancouver has produced two grandmasters of chess: Peter Biyiasas and Duncan Suttles. Biyiasas has since moved to the U.S. Suttles lives in Vancouver and runs a computer business.

Boating

Boating in Greater Vancouver
Susan MacDonald

VANCOUVER IS ARGUABLY the best boating venue in the world: English Bay for an afternoon or evening outing; Howe Sound, the Sunshine Coast, the Gulf Islands for a day or a weekend; one of the world's most spectacular coastlines for extended cruising; and the Fraser River for water-skiing or jet sports. Yet for hundreds of thousands in the Lower Mainland, boating is a trip on the SeaBus or by BC Ferries. And boating visitors complain, with cause, that it's almost impossible to pay a call to Vancouver because transient moorage or anchorage is just about non-existent.

Nobody—not Coast Guard, Ship's Registry, Canada Customs or any provincial government ministry—really knows how many recreational boats there are out there. The figure everyone uses comes from the Canadian Allied Boating Association—approximately 408,000 recreational boats in British Columbia, most of them outboard powerboats. Going by the population ratio, that means about 100,000 craft in the Greater Vancouver area or one for every 18 people. That's about the same number as reported in the first edition of *The Vancouver Book* some 20 years ago. What's changed is that in the early seventies, boaters favored sail over power—and many of those sailors were keen racers. Today, powerboats are more popular, even among ex-sailors who have decided that the destination is more important than how they get there.

In 1991, according to BC Parks, 28 per cent of British Columbians participated in powerboating, nine per cent in sailing and 20 per cent in canoeing or kayaking. As well, more than 50,000 visiting U.S. boaters cruise our waters annually, a figure that is increasing every year.

The leading reason people buy boats is to go fishing. However, bad news about salmon stocks resulted in 1995 being the first flat year in sales of small (under six metres) boats in more than 10 years. But in general, boating as a recreation is not keeping pace with growth in population and in the economy. People with small children and big mortgages don't have the disposable income or time to invest in boating. Many of the new Canadians swelling the population of the Lower Mainland don't have a background in boating.

Still, there are hot spots. Small boats sell well because people want boats they can trailer, and so avoid moorage costs. Large boat—more than 12 metres—sell well to people for whom

facing page: Yacht racing, 1995. vs

financing isn't a problem. Interest in kayaking and canoeing is burgeoning, as are sales of personal watercraft.

MOORAGE

There are nearly 10,000 marina or yacht club berths in the Greater Vancouver area. They range in size from Point Roberts Marina (Point Roberts, Washington, south of Tsawwassen) with 950 berths, Thunderbird (West Vancouver) with 860 and Reed Point (Port Moody) with 859, down to the informality of one or two boats tied up to a fishboat dock along the Fraser River. Finding moorage is generally not a problem, except for large boats. Burrard Civic Marina, for instance, with 500 slips on False Creek, has space for boats under six metres, but will be reconfiguring its docks to make a few bigger berths.

Marinas are increasingly expensive to build as all levels of government take an interest, particularly in their impact on shoreline and marine environments. One of the few new marinas opened in recent years is the Union Steamship Co. Marina with 150 slips in Snug Cove, Bowen Island.

Big changes will come to the Vancouver boating scene with Concord Pacific's massive residential development on False Creek and another by Marathon Developments on Coal Harbour. Concord Pacific is reported to be planning three marinas to berth a total of 400 boats. In Coal Harbour, Marathon will have a series of new facilities, including a 200-300 berth public marina at the west end of its property, and is providing for liveaboard boats and a few float homes.

The big need in Vancouver, say those in the business, is moorage for big boats, especially transient moorage for "superyachts" of 30 metres or more. These boats and their big-spending owners are bypassing Vancouver—because of the lack of facilities—in favor of Vancouver Island destinations such as Victoria and Nanaimo which extend more of a welcome.

CLUBS

The oldest yacht club in the area is Royal Vancouver, which started in 1903 and caters to both power and sail, with outstations in the Gulf Islands and up the coast for cruisers, and a busy program for the racing crowd. Burrard YC, Eagle Harbor YC and West Vancouver YC, which celebrated its 50th anniversary in 1995, are well-established but newer clubs. There are a number of smaller groups, with or without clubhouse or docks or both. Some emphasize racing, such as Kitsilano YC, which dates from the 1930s, or the informal Tiddly Cove YC (there really is a Tiddly Cove—it's not just a figment of cartoonist Len Norris' imagination), which has a clause in its constitution stating it will never own property. One of the newest clubs is False Creek, with clubhouse and moorage on the creek's north shore, opposite Granville Island. Other clubs are social, among them Airport and Richmond YCs in the Middle Arm of the Fraser. Vancouver Rowing Club recently completed a major renovation to its Stanley Park clubhouse and is planning to add dinghy sailing to its rowing lessons.

The biggest success story of the past two decades, however, has been the Jericho Sailing Centre, operated at Jericho Beach since 1974 by a non-profit, self-supporting association, under the aegis of the city park board. Completely land-based, the centre has 3,000 members, 13 affiliated clubs, four schools, and last year saw 90,000 launchings of kayaks, canoes, sailboards and sailboats up to about six metres. A unique affiliate is the Disabled Sailing Association whose members take to the water in specially modified boats. The centre is seeing a decline in the numbers of board and dinghy sailors, but an increase in paddle and rowing sports participants. Racing at Jericho has picked up in the past five years with the introduction of a rookie program, and the club hosts more regattas every year.

In recent years, a number of specialty clubs have sprung up, including the Vancouver Wooden Boat Society which stages the Vancouver Wooden Boat Show at Granville Island in late August. The Oarlock and Sail Club helps members learn to build small boats. The Bluewater Cruising Association is for those who have sailed offshore—or want to. The Britannia Heritage Shipyard Society is restoring the historic Steveston shipyard. Projects include the building and sailing of tiny Fraser River skiffs, once used to gillnet salmon.

MARINE INDUSTRY

Recreational boating, along with the commercial marine industries, supports a wide range of suppliers, as well as repair and maintenance specialists and boat brokers.

More than 40,000 people attend the February Vancouver Boat Show at B.C. Place, staged in part by the B.C. Marine Trades Association. For the past couple of years, the association has keyed its boat show promotion particularly to potential new boaters.

While local manufacturers Double Eagle, Hourston Glascraft and Monaro continue to do well with their day-fishing boats and small cruisers, Vancouver has gained a substantial reputation for building luxury yachts. McQueen's, Crescent Beach, Westbay Sonship and Queenship are constantly busy on boats worth from $250,000 to $2 million-plus, mainly for U.S. customers. Most are powerboats, although Queenship is also doing large sailboats. Sceptre Yachts (1993) Ltd. builds its Sceptre 43, starting at $275,000, and Martin Yachts, with a production of 50 up-to-eleven-metre sailboats yearly, is selling mainly to the U.S. and Japan. Martin is carving a niche with a new high-tech eleven-metre racer.

Faced with a shortage of skilled workers, the industry is working with the provincial government to establish a boat-building apprenticeship program.

CHARTERING

A boat costs money and time to keep shipshape. Consequently, many who want a boating holiday without the investment are simply chartering—some estimates say 80 per cent of charterers were once owners. Cooper Boating Centre on Granville Island is the largest charter firm/sailing school in Canada with 2,000 charter dispatches a year and 2,500 sailing students. Next to locals, Albertans are the biggest customers, but others are coming here from the eastern U.S., California and Germany. Bareboat charter operators are working through the Marine Trades Association to push for better marina facilities for cruising customers and also for more support in marketing British Columbia.

PERSONAL WATERCRAFT

Over the past five years Kawasaki, Yamaha and Bombardier have each sold a half-million of these often-controversial water versions of snowmobiles across North America.

In the Lower Mainland, the sales count is 700-1,000 in total yearly for the past three years, with another 300 pre-owns changing hands each year. Costing under $10,000, complete with lifejackets and trailer, they are becoming the entry-level family boat, says Jeff Smith, director of the Jet Sport Safety and Rescue Training Centre. That's the B.C. branch of the national association dedicated to improving the image of jet sports.

Once available only for a single stand-up rider, some PWCs are now three metres long and can carry three people plus picnic or camping gear for longer trips. Clubs, often spearheaded by dealers, have sprung up, including the Thursday Night Ride which takes place in the Deas Slough area of the Fraser River. The small craft can be rented at a number of locations around the Lower Mainland. Smith's group also holds workshops for police, coast guard and other enforcement officers.

LIVEABOARDS

Then there are those who choose to live on their boats, a coastal tradition that's almost as old as the province itself. Again, no one really knows how many there are since historically liveaboards have not been openly acknowledged. However, guesstimates suggest at least 1,000 live here and there throughout the Lower Mainland's waterways, from the relative grandeur of False Creek's Spruce Harbour Co-op to the down-and-dirty of a Fraser River reach.

Now that's really using the boat!

facing page: Marina, False Creek, 1994. vs

The Royal Vancouver Yacht Club
George Cran

THE VANCOUVER YACHT CLUB was formed in 1903, just 17 years after Vancouver was incorporated. The club set up its first headquarters in a small rented house at the foot of Thurlow Street in Coal Harbour. There were 18 yachts in its fleet. First elected Commodore was Walter E. Graveley, a real estate dealer whose racing credits included sailing in the Canadian challenger for the America's Cup, the *Countess of Dufferin*, in 1876.

The club soon built a two-storey floating clubhouse on a leased waterlot just west of the foot of Bute Street. Early in 1905 it was towed to a new site in the shelter of Deadman's Island, close to the present Coal Harbour location. This same building was subsequently hoisted onto the beach in Stanley Park and continued in use as a spar shed until 1977.

In 1905 the club included 187 members, and 43 flew its burgee (nautical pennant)—a Cambridge blue burgess with a black diamond in the centre. That same year application was made for a Royal Charter, and in 1906 permission was granted to use the prefix "Royal," and for members to fly the Blue Ensign. The present R.V.Y.C. burgee, incorporating the Royal Crown, was designed that year. During this time several members took advantage of $50 life memberships offered by the club.

The club continued to expand, and in 1927 a permanent clubhouse was officially opened at Jericho on English Bay. In 1978 the club completed further expansion and modification work as membership continued to increase. By 1996 another very substantial enlargement, taking more than ten months to complete, prepared the clubhouse for the 21st century.

Between the years 1960 and 1993 the club acquired seven properties used as Offshore Stations. Tugboat Island, a 28-acre park at Silva Bay, was purchased in 1960. Alexandra Island, in Centre Bay of Gambier Island, was purchased in 1965. The membership approved the acquisition of 400 feet of waterfront at Secret Cove in 1972, and the spring of 1977 saw the addition of the first "complete" marina at Scott Point on Salt Spring Island. Colorful Wigwam Inn, located in Indian Arm, was acquired in 1985 and in October 1989 the club took possession of its second "full service" marina at Garden Bay in Pender Harbour. In the fall of 1993 the club purchased 18 acres in Cortes Bay, on Cortes Island, with approximately 1,300 feet of waterfront.

At the end of 1996 there were 1,630 Active and Associate Members, 290 Intermediate Members and 400 Junior Members. In addition, there were 384 Non-Resident Members, 1,250 Affiliate Spouses, and 350 Special, Honorary, Honorary Life and Life Members. The fleet numbers 470 sailing yachts and 505 power yachts, berthed variously at Coal Harbour and Jericho Stations or moored elsewhere.

left: Graybeard raced under the flag of the Royal Vancouver Yacht Club, 1970. mm
facing page: top; Kitsilano Beach, 1897. cva
bottom; English Bay, c1915. cva

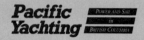

In its 28-year existence Vancouver-based Pacific Yachting has grown, evolved and matured in step with the community of B.C. boaters, who think of it as their magazine. Today, its circulation exceeds 19,000, primarily in B.C. but with healthy bases in neighboring Alberta and Washington, as well as in surprisingly far-flung corners of Canada and the U.S. Today, under B.C. ownership, the magazine is once again in growth mode and a key player on the West Coast boating scene.

PY has witnessed and participated in the explosive growth of pleasure boating in the 1970s, then survived ups and downs affecting the local economy and boating industry in the '80s. As always, PY focuses on wet-berthed boats from 20' up, with cruising accommodation. What has changed since the 1970s is a greater emphasis on power over sail, following the shift in interest among boaters and readers. Today, about 55 per cent of readers are powerboaters, 45 per cent sailors.

Beaches Of Greater Vancouver
Lisa Tant

To some, the ideal beach starts with palm trees gracing white sands that drift into warm turquoise waters. To me, the perfect beaches lie in the nine kilometres around Vancouver. Sure the sands are often rocky and the water will turn your toes blue even in the summer, but local beaches provide their own beachcomber's paradise.

As a kid, I seemed to walk for miles across the rippling sands of Spanish Banks without getting wet above my knees. I felt I could walk a few more feet and climb aboard the sea-battered freighter steaming into the harbor—across to Dundarave Pier on the opposite West Vancouver shore. I spent countless lazy days captivated by the tidepools and sandcastle cities framed by logs. Other days, I was happily shipped off to summer camp at Belcarra Regional Park where we hurled our lily-white bodies off the tire swing and into warm Sasamat Lake at White Pine Beach.

Vancouverites love water. We have to—we're surrounded by it and often drenched by it. Some of us even seem to have developed webbed toes. Protected from the open ocean by Vancouver Island, the city's coastline is dotted with tiny coves and bordered by endless parks and walkways. Many of these beaches provide picnic areas, lifeguards (on duty from Victoria Day to Labour Day) and swimming beaches. Summer temperatures only reach an average of 21 degrees Celsius—so it's not Acapulco but, as we natives like to brag wherever we travel, it is Lotus Land.

The seeds for Vancouver's glorious beach heritage were planted in September 1888 with the first park committee meeting. Over the years, the Vancouver Park Board has acquired, developed and managed a network of city beaches that are crowded year-round. Tanners blanket the beach during the summer while walkers, cyclists and now roller bladers cherish the walkways 365 days a year.

WEST VANCOUVER

WHYTECLIFF PARK Named for its white cliffs, secluded Whytecliff Park features a protected sandy beach tucked away on the western tip of the North Shore. A popular scuba diving area, it was designated as one of Canada's first undersea parks. The park's grassy playing fields, rustic trails and views of Howe Sound make it a favorite family spot.

HORSESHOE BAY PARK This small wading beach and playground are nestled in Horseshoe Bay's cove adjacent to the BC Ferries terminal. Visitors may watch the sleek ferries come and go or explore the nearby marina and boutiques.

CAULFEILD PARK Residents keep these wide sandy beaches a secret. The shoreline park with low cliffs is reached by a trail from Marine Drive. Skunk Cove, at the park's western tip, provides a government wharf for temporary moorage.

DUNDARAVE BEACH This delightful beachfront park and pier lies at the foot of 25th Street at picturesque Dundarave Village. The pier marks the spot of the Beachside Restaurant, formerly Peppi's, a legendary West Vancouver landmark, and also presents spectacular views of Vancouver, Mount Baker and Vancouver Island.

JOHN LAWSON PARK Children love the sandy beach, playground and wooden pier at the foot of 17th Street. Named for John Lawson, the second mayor of the community, the pier is the former home of a ferry service to Vancouver.

AMBLESIDE PARK A popular meeting place, Ambleside Beach features a pitch 'n' putt, fitness circuit, dog path and bird sanctuary. The Vancouver Symphony Orchestra has played in the park in past summers and the Ferry Building, a heritage gallery, exhibits local artists' work year-round. During the summer, the vintage steam locomotive, The Royal Hudson, chugs past twice daily. As summer moves into fall, members of the local Burrard Indian band fish for salmon in the rushing Capilano River. West Vancouver's shoreline Centennial Seawalk starts at Ambleside and features a panoramic view of freighters and cruise ships travelling past the beach and under Lions Gate Bridge.

NORTH VANCOUVER

PANORAMA PARK Tucked in Deep Cove at the entrance to Indian Arm, this shoreline family park is popular as a gathering place for picnics, open-air concerts, and lookout for the carol ships, the annual Christmas boat parade.

CATES PARK Bordering the protected waters of Indian Arm, this sandy beach park is marked by native totem poles and heritage remnants of the old Dollar Mill, a former lumber mill.

VANCOUVER

SPANISH BANKS Jericho and Locarno Beach and Spanish Banks are strung together three kilometres along the Point Grey shoreline. The warm shallow water edging Spanish Banks is perfect for paddling, exploring tidepools and beach sports.

LOCARNO BEACH Mixing old with new, Locarno is the site of an old Indian village and Vancouver's current board sailing centre. A designated quiet area (leave the boom box at home), it's a favorite family beach.

JERICHO BEACH At Point Grey's eastern edge lies Vancouver's second largest park and sandy beach. Originally called Jerry's Cove, after logger Jeremiah Rogers, who ran a local logging operation. In the past, the area was the former site of the Jericho Aerodome for seaplanes and, in 1976, of Habitat, the United Nations Conference on Human Settlements. Today it hosts the annual Vancouver Folk Festival, a youth hostel in a former military barracks, a duck pond and bird sanctuary, and a shoreline sailing centre.

WRECK BEACH Hidden around the corner from Spanish Banks, this is a popular nudist retreat. Nude sunbathers and beach vendors have flocked to the six-kilometre strip since the 1920s. On a bright summer's day, an estimated 10,000 sun worshippers will visit Vancouver's only civic beach where nudity is overlooked.

PACIFIC SPIRIT PARK Formerly part of the University Endowment Lands, this 800-hectare wilderness park/beach around Point Grey's shoreline was a gift from the province in 1989. Thankfully, the park designation prevented continuing controversy about developing the land. Leisurely walking trails through second-growth forest are shared by strollers, cyclists, dogs and horses.

KITSILANO BEACH In the summer, this trendy hang-out turns into a giant human skillet for suntanning, swimming and people watching. Originally called Greer's Beach, it was renamed in 1905 by the Canadian Pacific Railway in honor of Chief Khahtsahlano of the Squamish Indian Band. Built in 1931 and later renovated in 1979, Kitsilano Pool was the largest salt water pool in the British Empire. The Kitsilano Showboat, an outdoor stage hosting amateur performances, has become an annual summer tradition since 1935. Kits Beach is known for its sandy beach, playing fields and packed tennis courts. During July's Sea Festival, it's also the final destination for the 61-kilometre bathtub ocean race from Nanaimo across Georgia Strait.

HADDEN PARK This quiet cove with a small sandy beach is tucked between Kitsilano Beach and Vanier Park. A number of festivals and Bard on the Beach, a series of Shakespeare plays presented in a tent, take place every summer.

ENGLISH BAY & SUNSET BEACHES This stretch of sandy beach was a Squamish Indian fishing camp known as Eeyulshun (good footing). Sunset Beach starts under the Burrard Street Bridge and drifts into English Bay Beach which carries on around to the entrance of Stanley Park. Sunset Beach has a bicycle path and wading beach that isn't suitable for non-swimmers.

Crowds throng to English Bay year-round from January 1st for the annual Polar Bear swim, (a hangover cure since 1927) to the Sea Festival in July and the Symphony of Fire in early August. The popular beach pier is no longer there but the bandstand and English Bay bathhouse, built in 1931 and refurbished 55 years later, is now home to a windsurfing rental business. Seraphim "Black Joe" Fortes, a Jamaican seaman, was English Bay's self-appointed lifeguard and police until his death in 1922. He taught many Vancouverites how to swim and today, a branch library and noted Robson Street oyster bar are named in his honor.

STANLEY PARK BEACHES: SECOND BEACH & THIRD BEACH Follow the seawall around English Bay (First Beach) and you'll reach

Jantzen staff volunteers clean city beaches, Vancouver, 1996. Jantzen

Second Beach. A new playground and summertime outdoor ballroom (folk and square dancing) sit across from the sandy beach. Next to it, the seaside pool built in 1932 recently received a high-tech face lift with the latest in rapid sand filtration, automatic chlorinators and waterslides. Around the seawall lies Third Beach with its wide sandy shores and The Teahouse Restaurant.

NEW BRIGHTON PARK One of the only beaches on the city's east side, New Brighton Park was the site of the first road and ferry. The open grassy park with a wading beach and freshwater heated pool provides a view of busy port activities.

BELCARRA REGIONAL PARK A native fishing area, this collection of tiny beach coves along Indian Arm and the northeast shore of Burrard Inlet was developed into a city retreat in the 1920s. Now you'll find a picnic area, playing field, long wooden dock and a trail leading to White Pine Beach on Sasamat Lake.

BARNET MARINE PARK At this North Burnaby seaside park, children play on the concrete remnants of the sawmill destroyed by fire in 1946. In 1982, Burnaby Parks and Recreation opened the site as a marine park and grassy space.

The company name was later changed to Jantzen Knitting Mills of Canada Ltd. By 1949 the Universal brand was dropped and the Jantzen brand was made exclusively. Ten years later, Jantzen Canada Inc. became a subsidiary of Jantzen (USA). Today Jantzen is a familiar worldwide name operating in many countries, and manufacturing a wide variety of garments, easily recognized by the familiar Red Diving Girl Emblem.

Swimming Pools and Scuba Diving
Vesta Giles

FEW COULD ARGUE that Vancouver is a wet place. Yet despite outbursts lamenting this wetness, Vancouverites are known to seek out any and all watery pursuits from the shallowest of local pools to the deep waters of the Pacific Ocean.

In Greater Vancouver there are no fewer than 40 indoor and 40 outdoor public swimming pools (not counting wading pools and waterslides). These include therapeutic and university pools, Y's and municipal pools. And for deep water enthusiasts the Greater Vancouver area boasts some of the finest scuba diving in the world.

Pools like New Westminster's Canada Games Pool and the Vancouver Aquatic Centre serve as both community recreation centres and sites for internationally sanctioned swimming and diving competitions. Many serve as training grounds for some of Canada's most talented nationally and internationally ranked swimmers, synchronized swimmers and divers.

Local pools have been a haven for recreational swimmers and learners of all ages since the early 1900s. Besides the multitude of local wading pools, there are many larger pools suited to small children and people with special swimming needs. Some, like East Vancouver's New Brighton Pool, have gently sloping shallow ends making water play less threatening for children. Others, like the Canadian Memorial Pool on West 16th Street, maintain warmer temperatures to make swimming easier for small children and babies.

Vancouver also hosts some unusual swimming opportunities in leisure centres like the Newton Wave Pool. The surf's been up in Newton since November 1987, with waves ranging from gentle ripples to one-metre breakers. One of the most famous local pools, the legendary Kitsilano Swimming Pool, opened for the first time on July 1, 1931, as the largest saltwater pool in North America. However, by 1979, maintaining saltwater pools had become too difficult and later that year the current, smaller, self-contained Kits Pool reopened.

Of course, with all the pools come lessons. Since the turn of the century, swimming lessons have been big news. For some, the name "Joe Fortes" still brings images of swimming lessons to mind (instead of seafood). In September 1900 Joe was the first swimming instructor hired by the City of Vancouver. Over the years he taught thousands of eager locals to swim. Swimming lessons later made news and newspapers from the 1940s through early 1970s as both the Vancouver *Sun* and *Province*

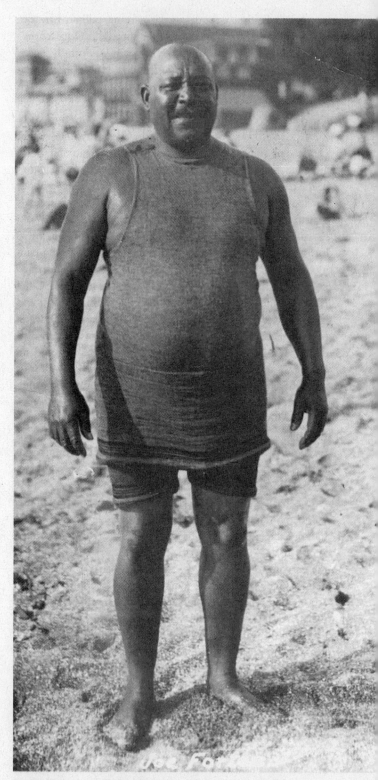

Joe Fortes, famed Vancouver lifeguard, at English Bay, c 1900. cva

offered free lessons in an aquatic popularity contest.

Farther down, in the depths of the local aquatic world, you'll find the scuba divers!

With nearly 200 kilometres of prime, rugged coastline, Vancouver boasts some of the world's finest scuba diving opportunities. Divers can see abundant marine life in an extraordinary underwater landscape (including shipwrecks) all within the Greater Vancouver limits. Divers of any experience level can choose from easy access shore dives to boat dives from the north shore of Howe Sound and Burrard Inlet.

Dive shops, great for details on local resources and finding partners, abound. Around the Lower Mainland you'll also find several dive clubs, including the Artificial Reef Society, Pacific Northwest Scuba Challenge Association (for the physically challenged), the Underwater Archaeological Society of B.C., the Marine Life Sanctuary Society, as well as regional clubs.

Dive planning is a must. Diving is restricted in the harbor, and if you're diving in Indian Arm, let the Harbor Master know (666-2405/666-6011). Be aware that areas like Whytecliff Park are strictly marine reserves protecting marine life within their boundaries. Because the Northern Pacific is just a little nippy (average water temperature 8°C with some variations according to depth, season and location), extra hypothermia precautions are necessary. Wet or dry suits are a must and can be rented or purchased from local dive shops. In order to get air tanks filled, divers must show proper certification (for example, PADI, NAUI, ACUC, NASDS, YMCA, SSI). Although there is no surf in Vancouver and no extremely dangerous currents or tides, specific conditions including weather forecasts should be checked thoroughly as part of the dive planning process.

There are also many local books and magazines covering all aspects of Vancouver's diving environment. Locally published *Diver Magazine* covers diving sites and news across Canada and regularly features British Columbia's best diving locations. Most publications are available at libraries, newsstands and dive shops. The Vancouver Aquarium and the department of fisheries and oceans are also resources on local marine life.

With Vancouver's abundance of swimming and scuba diving opportunities, it must be concluded that nothing, except perhaps a lack of water, will dampen the spirits of thousands of local swimming and diving enthusiasts!

Nudist Clubs
Vancouver Sunbathing Association

SOCIAL NUDISM in Canada began in 1939 with the founding of the Van Tan nudist club. From its scenic vantage point 457 metres feet up Grouse Mountain, it continues to be the granddaddy of all such clubs.

One of its founders, Ray Connett, had the opportunity to visit several leading nudist clubs in England during the war. On his return to Canada in 1945, he set out to write about social nudism and invited interested people across the country to register with him in confidence. By the fall of 1947 a group of dedicated nudists gathered in a rented hall in Vancouver and drafted a constitution for the Canadian Sunbathing Association. Guidelines were laid down to ensure that member clubs adhered to strict moral codes. Social nudism involves a natural way of life, a place for families where children could grow up without shame about their bodies.

Faced with having to pay tolls on both the Pattullo and Lion's Gate bridges, some Van Tan members broke away in 1948 to create the Border Tans in Langley Prairie. They gave an open invitation to the police to stop by at any time. They had nothing to hide. The club ran successfully for a few years but folded when the health of the couple looking after it failed.

The Sunny Trails Club was founded in Surrey in 1952, again with the assistance of Ray Connett. The club had a number of "firsts" including a sign on the Trans Canada Highway and live radio broadcasts on the CBC. Many cabins were built, initially as summer havens but later as year-round residences. Tent spaces, RV and trailer hook-ups, a nudist restaurant, swimming, volleyball, hiking through the forest and many other activities were available to nudists from around the world. They could visit Vancouver during the day and spend their evenings and nights enjoying all the club offered. Sunny Trails remained there until 1992, when it moved to Lake Errock to make way for the expansion of Tynehead Park.

The Meadowbrook Sun Club was located in Aldergrove. They had an in-ground pool, a sauna and numerous campsites. In their clubhouse, they held "open house" days where they put on plays and provided musical entertainment. It was quite successful until the seventies when the property owner raised the rent too high.

An off-shoot of that club was the Hyperion Club, which has recently changed its name to the Vancouver Sunbathing Association. Pot-luck dinners, hot-tub nights, camp-fires and a relaxed atmosphere are the highlights.

Sport Fishing
Tony Eberts

THERE ARE TWO kinds of people in this world: those who fish and those who really ought to. There are two kinds of fish too—those that will bite and those that won't. Now that the scientific stuff's taken care of let it be known that there may be no other urban area in the world with better access to varied fishing opportunities than Greater Vancouver. We boast several species of salmon, all of them powerful gamefish, noble sea-run trout and many lesser beasties to test your patience, skill and tackle. On one side of us lies the infinitely varied salt water of the Gulf of Georgia and the vast Pacific Ocean. On the other, the salmon-rich Fraser River, smaller rivers and scores of lakes of all sizes. You can put on chest waders and pit yourself against the current of a rushing stream or you can doze in a folding chair with a bell on your rod to tell you if a fish strikes. You can stand quietly on a lakeshore or go down to the sea in boats.

More than a million British Columbians go fishing every year and the lure of good fishing is a mainstay of our booming tourist industry. There's nothing wrong with food-fishing for the likes of flounder, sole, rockfish and halibut, but most sports anglers spend most of their time pursuing the salmonids—salmon and trout. They are the stars of our piscatorial theatre. One of the wonderful things about such fish is that they almost always inhabit lovely places—pools like great bowls of lime Jello, blue ocean currents, lakes that mirror tall trees and high mountains. Even if the action is slow and the catch slight, you can hardly call a day wasted when it's spent in such surroundings.

The sport of angling can be pursued at many levels. You can ease into it with practically no skill and no effort or you can read books and take lessons and study the life cycles of certain insects and become expert at catching trout on dry flies that you tie yourself. If you're new to fishing and to this favored part of the world the best way to start would be to go out with a friend who's experienced and has all the right tackle and equipment. Otherwise once you've decided whether you want to try salt water or fresh, hire a professional guide.

Let's go salt for starters. You will be fishing for salmon: depending on the time of year, for chinook (AKA king, spring, or, if 14 kilograms or more, tyee); coho (AKA silver, blueback or northern); sockeye; or pink (AKA humpy). Favorite fishing spots in Vancouver area ocean waters include Point Atkinson and the mouth of the Capilano River along the North Shore; the south end of Bowen Island at the entrance to Howe Sound; and off the North Arm of the Fraser River. There are two main methods—trolling and mooching. Mooching means fishing with bait, often live herring, from a boat that is anchored, drifting or with only occasional use of the motor. It can be pleasantly quiet on a calm day but if dogfish (small sharks) get after your bait, you might as well move on. Usual tackle is a long, flexible mooching rod and an ounce or two of lead to sink the herring or anchovy, which is attached with two small hooks, single or treble. Often the best fish lie just above the sea bottom.

Trolling is the more common method. Unless there are salmon feeding on or near the surface you use a downrigger (a lead ball on a wire cable, mounted on a small windlass affair) to get bait or a lure down to fish that are often more than 30 metres deep. When a salmon strikes, your line snaps away from the downrigger so you can play the fish with little interference. In this way you can use very light, sporty tackle. Trollers use bait and an assortment of artificial lures such as little, octopus-like, soft plastic "hootchies," torpedo-shaped plugs and metal spoons. Large, shiny "flashers" are often located some distance ahead of the lures to get the attention of salmon at a distance.

The biggest salmon are the chinook which may average close to nine kilograms and have been caught in the 45-kilogram range. They can be found in the area at any time of the year. Considered the sportiest by most are the coho, which habitually jump and fight like trout. They are caught in late spring and early summer as bluebacks (immature fish of one to three kilograms); in late summer or fall the "northerns" arrive, and may get as big as nine kilograms. Perhaps the best table salmon is the sockeye, averaging three kilograms and usually plentiful when heading to spawning runs up the Fraser in late summer and early fall. Pinks are similar in size but not as tasty.

Your tidal-waters permit allows you to fish the Fraser as far up as the Abbotsford-Mission bridge. Check the regulations carefully for what species can be legally caught at any given time. Above that bridge, and on any Fraser tributaries, it's necessary to have a licence for non-tidal waters. There's a fairly long open season for pinks and coho in the Fraser and shorter openings for chinook and sockeye. The most popular angling method along the Fraser's banks and sandspits is bar fishing (no, it has nothing to do with catching cocktails). Any local sports shop can provide the terminal tackle which calls for a lead weight at the end and one or two wire-stiffened leaders and lures above. Armed with "spin-'n'-glo" lures and cured roe or worms, this rig is put out into deep water with sturdy rods and level-wind (bait-casting) or spinning reels. Set the rod on

facing page: The de Havilland Beaver—designed as a bush plane and used for fishing charters. rw

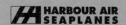

downtown Vancouver to downtown Victoria, and Vancouver to the Gulf Islands. Sightseeing tours are also very popular and a wide range are offered, from the "Vancouver Panorama," a 20 minute introductory flight, to wilderness exploration flights and "fly 'n dine" picnics and dinner flights. Two other important markets are forestry flights, flying "log-buyers" to inspect log booms in the Fraser River or in Howe Sound, and sports fishing flights, flying fishers to remote resorts north of Campbell River for salmon fishing.

Dragon Boat racing, False Creek, 1989. vp

its holder, attach its bell and get comfortable. You might catch a coho or chinook, a rainbow trout, a steelhead (which you release) or maybe just a whitefish or bullhead.

If you want to fish one of the lakes open to the public the simplest way is with a float and worm and a light spinning outfit. And, if you're casting a fly or other artificial lure, a small boat helps you cover the water. Fishing lakes near Vancouver include: Deer Lake in Burnaby; Como Lake in Coquitlam (restricted to children and seniors); LaFarge Lake behind Coquitlam Centre; Sasamat and Buntzen Lakes north of Ioco in Port Moody; Mike Lake, in Golden Ears Provincial Park north of Maple Ridge; Mill Lake in Abbotsford.

The Chilliwack/Vedder River, crossed by Highway 1 about 100 kilometres east of Vancouver, is a very special waterway beloved of fisherfolk of all persuasions as well as canoeists, kayakers, rafters, swimmers, naturalists and more. Swift runs, deep pools, quiet channels—every type of water is there and there are fish for every season and every kind of tackle. There is an impressive winter run of steelhead, for example, with some of the bruisers weighing more than nine kilograms. In the fall runs of coho abound and there's always a chance of rainbow trout. Anglers try for steelhead and salmon with floats and bait, artificial flies, spoons and spinners. Because of heavy clearcut logging in the watershed, the Chilliwack/Vedder is sometimes damaged by high water that scours out trout and salmon eggs and muddies the river, but time and new growth are lessening the problem.

While the Fraser carries a heavy load of effluent from towns and mills along its banks, public awareness of the problem is growing and plans are being laid to contain or neutralize harmful substances. At any rate the river's water quality remains good enough for the famous runs of salmon. The greatest danger to the salmon seems to come from overfishing by the commercial net fleet and that, in turn, is partly the fault of poor fishery management by bureaucrats. As well as the threats to water quality and fish stocks in many of our streams, however, there are some heartening examples of waterways once thought to be virtually beyond hope. The Brunette River, which runs from Burnaby Lake to the Fraser at the north end of New Westminster, is a fine example of what can be accomplished by the hard work of volunteers. A couple of decades ago it was polluted and barren but members of the local fish and game club have brought back populations of salmon and trout.

To get the most out of your fishing experience set your personal rules as high as possible—that is, use the lightest tackle you feel comfortable with, try to go with artificial lures instead of bait, consider barbless hooks and learn about catch-and-release. Find out how to let a fish go with the least possible harm and then come back and try to catch it again next year when it's much bigger. Real sportsmanship is the best hope for preserving high-quality fishing. Funny thing is—it's the most fun that way, too. Good luck!

If you're new to the area or to fishing, call: For tips on Fraser River and other non-tidal angling, Fishin' Mission at 826-0337; for salt water, Sewell's Marina at 921-3474.

The de Havilland Beaver seaplane is a mainstay of Harbour Air's fleet. The plane first flew in 1947. 1,800 were built in Toronto, the majority of which are still flying. The plane flies at 110 miles per hour and can comfortably carry six passengers and gear. The unique sound of the engine is legendary. The "Flying Beaver Bar and Grill" at Vancouver Airport - South, which takes its name from the aircraft, is the hangout for aviation enthusiasts.

Paddling and Kayaking
Charles Montgomery

VANCOUVER'S UNIQUE CLIMATE and geography combine to make it the envy of whitewater paddlers from across the country. While kayakers and canoeists elsewhere are frozen out in winter and dried out in summer, most local rivers can be run all year. Runoff from Vancouver's mountainous watershed boils through its canyons all winter, but alpine snowmelt makes springtime flows particularly wild. And while droughts can tame the wild rivers, many still provide worthwhile summer paddling.

Vancouver's most famous paddler was, of course, Simon Fraser, who ran the river which now bears his name in 1808. He reached the Fraser delta after enduring the furious whitewater of the Fraser canyon, only to be chased scurrying back up river by angry Musqueam Indians.

Since their arrival on the coast, local native Indians like the Musqueam had depended on the dugout canoe for hunting, transport, fishing and trading. The Lower Fraser saw thousands of natives arriving by canoe every summer, drawn from as far as northern Vancouver Island by the river's bountiful fishery.

Not until the 1960s did paddling for recreation gain popularity. People took to the water as a means of reliving history and escaping the din of urban life. More recently, sealed river kayaks have enabled paddlers to run wildwater far too turbulent for the traditional open canoe. River runners seek out monstrous waves, rollercoaster rapids, and turbulent holes to play in, while adventure tour companies have taken to bouncing down the province's larger rivers in inflatable rafts. Vancouver has become the ideal base for canoeists, kayakers and rafters who crave the mix of excitement and solitude that natural waterways offer.

Of dozens of streams and rivers around Greater Vancouver, several deserve mention for their value to paddlers:

North Vancouver's Capilano River is famous for its suspension bridge, spawning salmon and rainforest. But this oasis of solitude—just minutes from downtown—is a treat for paddlers as well. The river rages violently in winter and spring for expert kayakers, and subsides to provide a training ground for novices in summer.

The Seymour River, which enters Burrard Inlet at the Second Narrows Bridge, sees paddlers along its lower four kilometres. The stretch is usually an ideal training ground for beginners, who can navigate its rock gardens while drifting past quiet neighborhoods down to the sea. The Seymour can be run most of the year, with occasional high water for the advanced paddler.

The Coquitlam River is transformed from a rocky trickle into a turbulent playground for experienced kayakers, canoeists and rafters when either the Coquitlam Dam releases excess water or the coast is blessed with torrential rains.

The North and South Alouette rivers emerge from the mountains of Golden Ears Park, joining to flow into the tidal lower Pitt River. The North Alouette flows through UBC's wildlife-rich research forest, and offers more playful rapids than its gentle southern sister.

Winding through Maple Ridge to the Fraser River is Kanaka Creek, named for the Hawaiians who settled in the area in the 1800s. Paddlers follow the delicately sculpted canyon of the mid-Kanaka down to its tidal estuary on the Fraser River. A minor monsoon is required for summer travel on the creek.

Some of the West Coast's best paddling lies within the reach of daytrippers. The Chilliwack, Squamish, Elaho and Cheakamus rivers all rage turbulently, inspired by their landscape of towering peaks and glaciers.

The popularity of the sea kayak has spawned a rebirth of interest in local flatwater paddling. There's so much to choose from. Several islands—from McMillan and Barnston upstream to Shady and Wood in the estuary—sit amid the boiling murk of the Fraser River. The delta's many marshes and tributaries invite the curious bows of paddlecraft.

Vancouver's harbors and fjords also await explorers. False Creek, Burrard Inlet and Port Moody offer an eclectic mix of industry, wildlife and seaside neighborhoods. Indian Arm and Pitt Lake cut into the wild heart of the mountains, right from the city's edge. On calm days paddlers venture from the rocky headlands of West Vancouver across to Bowen Island in Howe Sound.

A note of caution: whitewater paddling is a dangerous sport by nature. None of the routes should be attempted by novices without a guide, and some only by experts. Variable flows and hazards—from logjams and sweeping deadfalls to trapping undercurrents—must be assessed. On the Fraser, the harbors and ocean, paddlers must watch for larger craft, barges, log booms and tricky tides.

Information on Vancouver's various paddle sport clubs, commercial outfitters and instructors is available from Brian Creer at Canoe Sport B.C. (275-6651). Mr. Creer is 80 and still running rivers. Two good local guidebooks available are: *Whitewater Trips* by Betty Pratt-Johnson, and Richard and Rochelle Wright's *Canoe Routes: British Columbia*.

Civic Parks

The two most beautiful parks in Vancouver include among their attractions two distinctive restaurants. In world-famed Stanley Park, overlooking historic Ferguson Point, is The Teahouse Restaurant. The Teahouse has been a favorite with visitors and local residents for more than 40 years. Then, looking out over the city, in beautifully landscaped Queen Elizabeth Park, is elegant Seasons in the Park Restaurant with stunning views of the City of Vancouver, the North Shore mountains, Burrard Inlet and distant Howe Sound.

The Parks of Vancouver
Kerry McPhedran

In January 1996 the City of Vancouver could claim 176 "parks." The largest and first is West End's 405-hectare Stanley Park; the smallest is Pigeon Park—a well-used .03 hectares in the Downtown Eastside. Vancouver's parks include stadiums, beaches, seawalls, botanical gardens, golf courses and as yet unnamed "Park Sites." The following list is a glimpse of some favorite neighborhood parks. Some are frequented by visitors, too.

The first Park Board was appointed by City Council in 1888 and entrusted with the task of providing recreation and leisure for the citizens of Vancouver. After Stanley Park was opened September 27, 1888 the system of parks began to grow almost immediately. A piece of land was donated by E.J. Clark and named Clark Park after him in 1889. At the same time, the provincial government gave Hastings Park to the city. In 1911 the Vancouver Park Board, realizing the importance of playgrounds, set aside MacLean Park. It was the city's first supervised playground. Ceperley Playground in Stanley Park was the second and, today, one of the busiest.

After World War II there was a move to include community recreation centres in parks. In the 1970s a system of mini-parks set in West End streets was developed to control through-traffic while providing a quiet space for West Enders. Scattered along the waterfront in Point Grey are other small, grassy spaces: parks the width of one or two houses which, for a while, the city could afford to buy and remove. In 1985 the 23-kilometre-long B.C. Parkway began linking some 30 parks, following the Sky-Train route between downtown Vancouver and New Westminster.

Currently, planners intend to provide or improve urban parks in neighborhoods lacking in parks—often on the east side—and in new areas of the city growing rapidly near Yaletown. Small portside parks now allow eye-level views of the city's harbor traffic. A future city-wide waterfront walkway/bikeway route is planned for parks already linked like Fraser Lands Riverfront Park and Gladstone Park. Commemorative benches have proved the most popular recent park program. Since the program started in the Expo year of 1986, nearly 720 benches have been given to the park system by the public.

facing page: Summer profusion in Queen Elizabeth Park, 1996. vance hanna

VANCOUVER

Alexandra Park & English Bay Beach
(Beach and Davie)
Named in honor of Queen Alexandra, the wife of King Edward VII who reigned when this park was acquired, this tiny triangle is only .4 hectares of lawn and trees. But combined with the larger white crescent that is English Bay Beach it forms a favored part of Vancouver's West End and one end of the Stanley Park Seawall. Swimmers first flocked here in the 1890s; now board-sailors do. A simple drinking fountain near the Beach Avenue entrance celebrates beloved Barbados-born seaman Joe Fortes, lifeguard, swimming teacher and special constable. The bronze plaque reads "Little Children Loved Him." His cottage was moved up beside the bandstand in the park, to stay as long as Joe lived. He died in 1922. Traditional events include free Sunday concerts from the Edwardian bandstand and New Year's Day Polar Bear Club swim. There's prime viewing here for the July international fireworks competition, Symphony of Fire.

Andy Livingstone Park
(International Village; Keefer Street)
One of Vancouver's newest parks, with artificial turf, opened in the spring of 1995 as part of Concord Pacific's False Creek development. It was named for a long-time Vancouver park commissioner. A pedestrian-only Carrall Street land-bridge divides the park into two halves, one for leisurely use, the other for active sports.

Barclay Heritage Park
(Barclay and Broughton)
Early examples of West End residential architecture have been preserved in a unique blend of restored heritage houses and park space. Roed-de House, built by Vancouver's first book binder, Gustav Adolph Roedde in 1893, operates as a museum in this full square block of heritage.

David Lam Park
(Pacific Boulevard and Drake)
A treeless approach to this new urban park west of the heritage Canadian Pacific Railway Round-house (in the heart of the Yaletown development) protects water views of False Creek while honoring British Columbia's former lieutenant-governor.

Devonian Harbour Park
(Georgia Street at Stanley Park entrance)
Angry citizens protested high-rise development just metres from Stanley Park's entrance in the late 1960s. Activists set up a tent city lasting nine months, planting an "All Seasons Park" until city council and the developers backed down. Today, strollers enjoy four hectares of rose gardens, ponds, a stone bridge, plazas and footpaths, funded in part by the Calgary-based Devonian Group of Charitable Foundations.

False Creek Water Playground
(Granville Island)
A summertime water facility for children, built with artifacts from the island's past.

Fraser RiverPark
(75th Avenue and Angus Drive)
A 100-metre-long wooden pier juts almost to the log booms from this long, skinny park hugging the natural shoreline of the Fraser River. It provides a unique chance to watch endless river traffic and aircraft at Vancouver International Airport across the river on Sea Island. Interpretive signs are scattered along a wheelchair-accessible boardwalk that bridges riverside ponds and marshy areas.

Grandview Park
(Commercial and Cotton drives at William and Charles streets)
A well-loved neighborhood park with benches, majestic trees and views of downtown, the mountains and the harbor. This is a key site for Commercial Drive's community celebrations, like August's La Quena Fiesta.

Hadden Park
(Ogden Avenue; Chestnut to Maple Streets)
Sandwiched between Vanier Park and Kitsilano Beach, Hadden Park, donated by Harvey Hadden, leads to tiny Elsje Point for a view of the West End, or down a few steps to a small sandy cove near the Maritime Museum. Queen Elizabeth II owns the original of the replica 30.5-metre-high Kwakiutl totem pole carved in 1958 for British Columbia's centennial by Mungo Martin, Henry Hunt and David Martin. The original stands in England's Windsor Great Park.

Hastings Mill Park (also Pioneer Park)
(Alma and Point Grey roads)
This block-square grassy park, popular for kite flying, is home to Vancouver's oldest building. The Old Hastings Mill Store, built c. 1867, is now a museum, barged to this quiet spot from the foot of Dunlevy Street in July 1930. The park is close to the Royal Vancouver Yacht Club, with unlimited, grand views of the North Shore mountains and English Bay.

Jericho Beach Park
(Trimble, 4th Avenue, west of Wallace Street)
This great 45-hectare stretch of family park with endless sandbars is one of Vancouver's gems. "Jericho" is a shortened version of "Jerry's Cove," named for Jeremiah Rogers who logged here in the late 1800s. Jericho was also the site of Vancouver's first Golf and Country Club, and until the 1970s was a base for the Department of National Defense. The 1976 United Nations' Habitat Forum happened here. The park includes seasonal concessions and lifeguards, mature trees shading picnickers, ponds for migrating birds, and—in a former barracks—a youth hostel for

Stanley Park is the site of Vancouver's most historic restaurant—and one of its most scenic—The Ferguson Point Teahouse. It was originally built as a World War II garrison and officers' mess when Ferguson Point was a military installation. The building comprised what is now the entrance area and the "Tea Room" or middle section of the restaurant. After the war, the house was briefly used as a military residence. In the 1950s it opened during the summers as a Teahouse.

migrating youth. The annual Vancouver Folk
Music Festival is held here.

John Hendry Park
(13th and 19th avenues; Victoria and Templeton
drives)
Also known as Trout Lake, this East Vancouver
park is named for John Hendry, part-owner of
the old Hastings Mill and father of Mrs. E.W.
Hamber, who donated most of the land. The
trout-stocked lake, that also draws model boat
enthusiasts, was once a.source of water for the
mill.

Jonathan Rogers Park
(7th and 8th avenues; Columbia to Manitoba
streets)
Jonathan Rogers, a Park Board member for 22
years, bequeathed money for this Fairview park.
His ideals are mirrored in this delightful park
which has athletic and playground facilities for
small children.

Kerrisdale Centennial Park
Centennial Park is the centre of organized recreation in Kerrisdale. Two blocks away, Kerrisdale
Park houses Kerrisdale Arena where, in 1956, Bill
Haley and the Comets brought—in the words of
the *Vancouver Sun,* "the ultimate in musical
depravity."

Kitsilano Beach Park
(Cornwall waterfront; Trafalgar to Maple streets)
Named for Chief Khahtsahlahno, head of the
Squamish tribe who settled at Chaythoos
(Prospect Point in Stanley Park), this park is better known as Kits Beach. Home to Vancouver's
largest saltwater outdoor pool, beach volleyball,
windsurfing, tennis and the Kitsilano Showboat
—a summer tradition since 1935.

Locarno Beach
(Waterfront west of Trimble Street to Blanca)
Named after the Swiss town that hosted the
1925 European Peace Conference, this popular
beach park (a smaller continuation from Jericho)
has a much older First Nations name: Eyalmo,
meaning "good spring water." People lived here
at least 2,400 years ago, in one of Vancouver's
oldest First Nations villages. Development in the
1950s destroyed the midden here. There are
spectacular views of the Coast Range mountains,
Stanley Park and the West End.

MacLean Park
(Heatley and Hawks avenues, East Georgia and
Keefer streets)
In 1960 this block-square park replaced the original park at Union and Jackson, taken over for
Vancouver's first urban renewal housing. Named
in 1912 after Vancouver's first mayor, J.A.
MacLean, it was the first supervised playground
for children in Vancouver. Today, seniors use the
"new" park—where houses, apartments and a
bakery once stood—for daily tai chi.

Raccoons, Stanley Park, 1994. vs

Maple Grove Park
(Yew, 51st Avenue and Marine Drive)
A well-known Kerrisdale family park with wading
pool, horseshoes, soccer and softball, it's at its
peak in fall when mature maple trees blaze. In
1960 the park was the site of Vancouver's first
recreation program for blind children.

Marpole Park
(Cartier Street and 72nd Avenue)
Originally the site of the great Fraser Midden
used for generations by the Musqueam Indian
band. The park was named for Richard Marpole,
a superintendent of the CPR.

Memorial Park South
(41st Avenue and Prince Albert Street)
Memorial Park West
(Dunbar and 33rd Avenue)
Both parks were named as memorials to soldiers
of World War I. At "South" park a cenotaph set
in the centre boulevard lists those from the district who gave their lives. The cenotaph, the first
in Canada, originally stood at the South Vancouver municipal hall site at 41st Avenue and Prince
Albert. At "West" park, four city blocks in size,
you'll find the local community centre.

Musqueam Park
(Marine Drive and Crown Street)
The name of this large (24-hectare), lushly treed
site—formerly known as Georgia Park—is taken
from the Musqueam Indian band and its reserve,
which the park overlooks. The Musqueams
turned back explorer Simon Fraser after his journey down the Fraser River to the Pacific in 1808.
A trail allows hikers and riders from the Fraser
River trail to link with trails in Pacific Spirit
Regional Park.

New Brighton Park
(Windermere, Nootka and waterfront)
This park was the location of Hastings Townsite,
one of the earliest communities in the Lower
Mainland. The area can claim many other firsts,
detailed on a plaque by the swimming pool: the
first cricket ground, first pier, first store, and first
hotel—which advertised itself as the most fashionable watering place in the province. Close to
railways tracks and the Ironworkers Memorial
Second Narrows Bridge, this large urban park
with its pier never forgets Vancouver is a busy
port.

Oppenheimer Park
(Powell, Cordova, Dunlevy and Jackson streets)
Born as the Powell Street Grounds—the first
official playing fields in Vancouver—this park was
later renamed for David Oppenheimer, the city's
second mayor. It became a staging point for
Depression-era rallies. In 1936 the Vancouver
Park Board recognized the obvious, declaring
Oppenheimer the only park where political, reli-
gious or other views could be publicly voiced.
Today it remains the only park within the Down-
town-Eastside.

Pigeon Park
(Hastings and Carrall streets)
Vancouver's smallest park, also known as Pigeon
Square, was once part of an old CPR right-of-
way connecting the False Creek railyards with
the main line on Burrard Inlet. It is a favorite
gathering spot for local residents.

Portside (CRAB) Park
(Main Street Overpass)
Eastside residents who fought and squatted here
for three months for a waterfront park between

The building—badly in need of repair—was closed down by the city in 1976. In 1978 the present owner, Brent Davies, leased the building
from the Parks Board, thoroughly repaired and refurbished it and opened for business as The Ferguson Point Teahouse, keeping the historic name. In 1980 the now famous glass conservatory was added to the southeast side of the restaurant, and in 1982 the elegant drawing room was built onto the northwest side.

Second Narrows Bridge and Stanley Park on what was National Harbours Board land saw their dream come true in 1987. Local people still call this Crab Park (Create a Real Available Beach). A grand view of bustling port activity and mountains. A small pavilion here reflects Northwest Coast design on a site known as luk'luk'i by Coast Salish.

Queen Elizabeth Park
(29th and 37th; Cambie and Ontario streets)
(see article below)

Ravine Park
(33rd and 36th avenues west of Arbutus)
A long, leafy haven from the bustle of West Boulevard, this ancient salmon stream bed that once drained into English Bay has a paved path wide enough for wheelchairs and strollers.

Stanley Park
(entrances at Georgia Street and Beach Avenue)
(see article below)

Tatlow Park
(Point Gray Road, Third Avenue, Macdonald & Bayswater streets)
One of the city's oldest parks, Tatlow was also one of Vancouver's first film locations. Robert Altman filmed Sandy Dennis here in *That Cold Day in the Park*. There is a tranquil English feel, thanks to a canopy of mature trees, weeping willows, lawns, a small creek and wooden bridges. The name honors R.G. Tatlow who served for the first 18 years of the Park Board.

Vanier Park
(Chestnut Street to Kitsilano Railway trestle)
Prime kite-flying at this former Royal Canadian Air Force station and Sun'ahk Squamish settlement, now on a 99-year lease to the city. Named after former Governor General Georges P. Vanier, the 15 hectares of open grassy spaces, ponds and pathways are home to the Vancouver Museum and H.R. MacMillan Planetarium, Burrard Civic Marina, the City of Vancouver Archives and the Coast Guard station. In mid-May, the Vancouver Children's Festival blossoms in tents.

Victory Square
(Cambie and Hamilton, Hasting and Pender streets)
The Province newspaper originally donated funds to develop this park. Known as Courthouse Square until the provincial law courts were demolished in 1918, it was the official public gathering place for such occasions as the visit of the future King George V in 1901. Civic Remembrance Day services are still held here at the cenotaph built to Vancouver citizens who fell in World War I. It reads: *"Their name liveth for ever more/ Is it nothing to you—All ye that pass by."*

West Point Grey Park
(8th Avenue and Trimble Street)

Sweeping views from Burnaby Mountain to West Van's Lighthouse Park for lawn bowlers and soccer players. Best viewpoint is from 8th Avenue and Discovery Street, the latter named after Captain George Vancouver's ship.

BEYOND VANCOUVER
Half the population of British Columbia uses Greater Vancouver Regional District parks. The City of Surrey has the most parkland per capita in Greater Vancouver. Here is a small sampling of parks in some of the municipalities and electoral areas that make up the metropolitan area of the GVRD.

BURNABY

Burnaby Mountain Park
(Centennial Way off Gaglardi Way)
A great view from this North Burnaby high spot. A surprising mix of totem poles by Salish artists and Japanese Nuburi and Shusei Toko, featuring symbols of the Ainu, Japan's aboriginal people.

Central Park
(Kingsway and Boundary Road)
This big park was once a naval reserve set aside as a source of masts and spars for ships of the Royal Navy. A landmark since 1891, when the 90-hectare wooded park was named to honor Mrs. David Oppenheimer, the New York-born wife of Vancouver's second mayor. Attractions include the award-winning Variety Park Playground and lakes for ducks and hobbyists with remote-controlled boats.

Deer Lake Park
(Canada Way and Sperling Avenue)
As much cultural centre as city park, Deer Lake —once a large Indian encampment—is home to the Burnaby Art Gallery, the new Shadbolt Centre for the Arts, formal 1967 Century Gardens, Burnaby Village Museum and heritage Hart House. The movie *Cousins* and scenes from TV's *MacGyver* have been shot here.

Fraser Foreshore Park
(down Byrne Road off Marine Way)
A riverside park that runs by industrial and farming areas. A favorite with fishing parties, its maples and cottonwoods are colorful in fall.

Barnet Marine Park
(follow signs on Barnet Road)
David McLaren of Quebec built his mill here in 1889 and named it Barnet, his wife's maiden name. Fire destroyed the mill in 1946, but kids love clambering around the remains of the scrap burner.

Confederation Park
(off E. Hastings Street at Willingdon and Penzance)
Cleared during the Depression by Burnaby residents earning their relief scrip, this is a true community park. Formal on one side, rustic on the other, this was originally named Queen's Park but was changed in 1913 to honor Canada's

1867 Confederation.

Robert Burnaby Park
(off First Avenue)
A large (48 hectares) but well-kept local hillside secret named after Robert Burnaby, secretary to Colonel Richard Moody of the Royal Engineers.

COQUITLAM

Coquitlam River Park
(entrances off Shaughnessy and Pipeline streets)
The park embraces both sides of the river. Spawning salmon return in fall, using fish-enhancing weirs.

Mundy Park
(between Como Lake and Austin avenues, east of Mariner Road)
Woodchip trails meander past two lakes in this 192-hectare jewel of a large urban park. Deciduous and coniferous second-growth mature forests cover 80 per cent of the park.

Town Centre Park
(new City Centre)
An active park in Coquitlam's new City Centre, complete with Olympic-grade synthetic running track, bike trails, a fishing lake and tennis courts.

NEW WESTMINSTER

Byrne Creek Ravine
(access from Ron McLean Park)
Now cleaned of dumped cars and sofas, the Ravine is arguably the most distinctive landscape feature along the North Arm of the Fraser. A pocket rainforest ecosystem set in the deepest gorge from New Westminster to Point Grey.

Hume Park
(foot of Holmes Street at Columbia Street)
Constructed as a relief project during the Great Depression, this park is named for former New Westminster (and Vancouver) mayor Fred Hume.

Moody Park
(between 8th and 10th streets, south of 8th Avenue)
Set aside in 1863 to honor Colonel Moody of the Royal Engineers, Moody Park has very large trees. Some have bird houses.

Queens Park
(off First Street)
Colonel R.C. Moody set aside this park in 1859 while establishing New Westminster as British Columbia's capital. It's still the community's hub, with imaginative playgrounds. The Royal Agricultural and Industrial Exhibition here even attracted Winston Churchill in 1929, the event's last year. This was the site of the 1973 Canada Summer Games.

NORTH VANCOUVER

Cates Park
(Dollarton Highway)
Great family picnic park with gentle forest walks, historical remains of Dollar Lumber Mill, a sandy beach and a 15-metre Indian war canoe—a gift

The Teahouse's owner continues to keep the restaurant constantly fresh by adding new colors, updating amenities for the guests, and enlarging the gardens. In the summer of 1994 the Teahouse added a 50-seat patio to the front of the restaurant, overlooking the waters of busy English Bay. The patio has been the site of some beautiful wedding ceremonies since! The Teahouse has hosted many interesting events from theatre production wraps to gala events for heads of state.

of the late Chief Henry Peter George of Burrard Indian Band. Malcolm Lowry Walk recalls the celebrated author of *Under the Volcano*. He lived here with his wife in a squatters' shack from 1940 to 1954.

Lynn Canyon Park

(Lynn Valley Road)

Devotees of Lynn Canyon's gorge have been drawn since 1912 by 250 hectares of forest, natural trails, the Ecology Centre, tempting but treacherous pools and an 82-metre-high suspension bridge. Free now; tourists originally paid ten cents. Lynn Creek (named, with a slight change, after Royal Engineer John Linn who came to B.C. in 1859) is the only major watershed on the North Shore not controlled by a dam.

RICHMOND

Garry Point Park

(south end of 7th Avenue, Steveston)

Ocean and river meet in this peninsula park bounded by the Fraser River and historic remains of fishing canneries. The small Japanese garden is a gift of Wakayama, Japan, Richmond's sister city. Ten kilometres of dike paths head out from here.

McDonald Park

(north end of McDonald Road)

A thin shoreline river park with excellent bird and boat watching. A well-kept secret.

Minoru Park

(Granville Avenue)

A popular racetrack in the 1920s and 1930s, 2.7-hectare Minoru is named for one of King Edward's VII's famous racehorses. A hub of Richmond family life—starting with weddings in tiny Minoru Chapel in the park.

Richmond Nature Park

(No. 5 Road)

More than 3,000 years ago, all of Richmond was one dank peat bog. Opened in 1976 to preserve the last remaining section of the Greater Lulu Island bog, this park encourages observation of wildlife along a series of trails and boardwalks.

SURREY

Bear Creek Park

(King George Highway and 88th Avenue)

Home to the Surrey Art Centre as well as salmon and great blue herons standing in the shallows. Meadows and forest are laced with walking trails and bridges.

Green Timbers Park

(146th Street and 96th Avenue)

Completely logged of its 70-metre-high trees by 1930, this area became the birthplace of reforestation in B.C. In 1931, the government dedicated the site to remain treed in perpetuity. There is a forest education centre here.

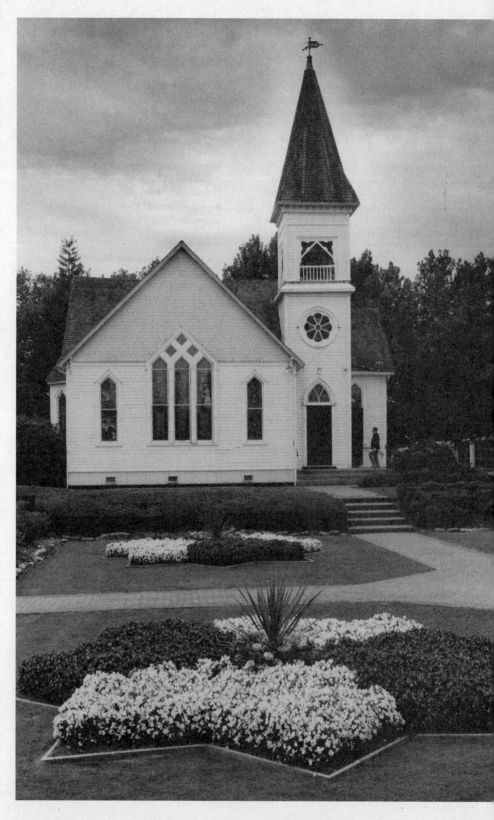

Minoru Chapel, Minoru Park, Richmond, 1994. vs

It's not uncommon to see movie and television stars among the diners at the Ferguson Point Teahouse. Vancouver is, after all, the versatile backdrop to many feature films and TV productions. Locals dine here year round, too, driving through the scenic Stanley Park or walking or biking along the park's seawall from Vancouver's West End. The Teahouse has always had an excellent reputation for its West Coast cuisine. Fresh local ingredients are prepared with creative imagination.

Redwood Park

(179 Street and 20th Avenue)

The deaf sons of original homesteaders replanted the logged area with exotic tree species from around the world. A reconstruction of the tree house in which they lived for many years stands among the trees they planted.

WEST VANCOUVER

Ambleside Park and Seawall

(Marine Drive from 11th to 29th)

Around 1912, John Nesbitt's cattle grazed on the swamp lands that are now Ambleside Park. Half this beachside 16-hectare park is on Squamish Indian Band land. An interconnecting and well-used seawalk from Lions Gate Bridge to 25th Ave—about 15 blocks—links two villages of Ambleside and Dundarave. En route: two piers, an exercise circuit, pitch-and-putt, duck ponds and dog beach, massive wooden sculptures by Robert Behrens and Chung Hung, playing fields, an historic ferry building and pioneer John Lawson Park. In summer, the Royal Hudson Steam Train chuffs through.

Cypress Falls Park

(off Woodgreen Place, Upper Levels)

Trails cut through old growth stands of huge cedar and fir trees (up to 2.3 metres in diameter) and past waterfalls (2-kilometre circular route) in this little known gem of a wilderness park that allows dogs.

Lighthouse Park

(Marine Drive & Beacon Lane)

These 75 hectares of rugged, virgin forest are home to some of the largest remaining stands of Douglas firs in Vancouver. A trail network leads to the lighthouse at Point Atkinson, first charted and named by Captain George Vancouver in 1792.

Whytecliff Park

(Horseshoe Bay)

Named originally for the white cliffs, but changed by land developer Colonel Albert Whyte in 1914, Whytecliff Park contains B.C.'s only underwater reserve.

WHITE ROCK

Semiahmoo Park

(western end of Campbell River Road)

Warm shallow water and a picnic area ideal for families.

Admiralty Reserve

(south of Belcarra)

This undeveloped 76 hectares at Admiralty Point on Burrard Inlet was set aside as a military reserve. The park, under lease from the federal government for park purposes is, in fact, still subject to use by the Armed Forces should the necessity arise.

Queen Elizabeth Park
Kerry McPhedran

EXPLORING QUEEN ELIZABETH Park's beginnings is like peeling an onion. Officially known as Little Mountain (and still called that by many Vancouverites), the 53-hectare park was renamed to commemorate the 1939 royal visit by King George VI and Queen Elizabeth (now the Queen Mother). The site of Vancouver's third largest park and one of its prettiest began life as a volcanic outcropping—something of an anomaly in the surrounding flat delta setting left by a retreating glacier. As a result, Queen Elizabeth Park is the highest point in Vancouver at 150 metres above sea level. Conveniently, the park rises smack in the centre of the city, providing grand 360 degree views.

Earlier citizens were quicker to quarry the rock for many of the city's first roads than to appreciate the view. Now glorious gardens, bursting with newlyweds and their photographers, spill gently down the rocky slopes of the two abandoned quarries, thanks in part to the CPR. The City of Vancouver and the (then) municipalities of Point Grey and South Vancouver took up the option jointly. It wasn't until 1929 that final purchase arrangements were made, following the amalgamation of the city with the two municipalities.

In 1948, a start was made on the selective clearing of the northwest side of the proposed park. The Canadian Pulp and Paper Association kicked in $5,000 a year over the next 10 years to spur development. On October 22, 1949 acting mayor R.K. Gervin planted the first official tree of the future garden and civic arboretum—Canada's first. Princess Elizabeth went one better when she brought—and planted—her own English oak from Windsor Great Park in 1951.

Landscaping on the largest quarry was completed in 1954, and a copper box buried beneath Century Rock—a time capsule to be opened in July 2054. The second quarry was finished in 1961—just in time for Vancouver's 75th anniversary.

One of the city's most popular parks, Queen Elizabeth Park serves the Little Mountain neighborhood but really belongs to the city, the region and visiting tourists. The rolling eastern slopes—filled with brilliant rhododendrons and azaleas in spring and tobogganers when the snow falls—are really a botanical gallery of every native tree and shrub in British Columbia.

The Bloedel Conservatory, a gift to the city from the Bloedel family in 1969, sits atop Little Mountain. Inside the triodetic plexiglass dome, some 500 species of jungle and desert plants bloom year round in the moist heat that's home to tropical birds. Canadian Pulp and Paper came through with yet another $5,000 to build the wooden pedestrian bridge which spans a 16-metre-high waterfall. Henry Moore's abstract bronze sculpture *Knife Edge-Two Pieces* sits on the plaza. A life-size bronze family, *Photo Session,* by American artist Seward Johnson, has proved to be a photo op itself.

There are three parks close by: Riley Park and adjoining Hillcrest Park and Nat Bailey Stadium. Local baseball fans know the volcanic slopes of Q.E. Park provide the ultimate cheap seats overlooking a Triple A game in one of North America's classic outdoor stadiums. Once described as a Norman Rockwell painting in three dimensions, the pillar-free 1940s stadium was named for the founder of another Vancouver legend, the White Spot restaurants. Nat Bailey got his start bagging peanuts at baseball games. For those who'd rather do than watch, the Queen E, as locals call it, offers pitch-and-putt, lawn bowling and Vancouver's only frisbee golf course.

Seasons in the Park Restaurant is the crown jewel of the highest geographic point in Vancouver. Also known as Little Mountain, Queen Elizabeth Park has panoramic views of Vancouver, the North Shore Mountains, Burrard Inlet and Howe Sound. The windows of Seasons in the Park allow guests dining throughout to see the lights of the city and the sometimes snow-capped mountains. Built in 1968, this was originally The Quarry House, named for the rock quarry that became this lovely park.

Stanley Park
Kerry McPhedran

STANLEY PARK—Vancouver's first—is one of the world's great parks. Described by columnist Allan Fotheringham as a "1000-acre therapeutic couch," the park was created from a federal military reserve set aside in the mid-1800s to guard the entrance to Vancouver harbor from feared American aggression.

Today Stanley Park is a community park for the West End, a city-wide park for Vancouverites, a regional park for the entire Lower Mainland and Vancouver's most popular tourist draw. The largest urban park in Canada and one of the largest in North America, Stanley Park covers 405 hectares. The layout is based on the planning principles of Frederick Law Olmsted who designed New York City's Central Park.

Each year some three million visitors travel by foot, car, roller blades, bike and bus through and around the park. Activity is concentrated at the two entrances to the park. Chess, pitch-and-putt, lawnbowling, highland dancing, tennis, beaches, a children's playground and restaurants are found near the English Bay entrance while the Georgia Street entrance is near the aquarium, children's zoo and miniature train. Each locomotive is an authentic replica, including Engine 374 from Canada's first transcontinental train in 1887. On summer evenings, there is TUTS (Theatre Under The Stars) live at Malkin Bowl.

There's a dreamy, Edwardian feel to the nearby Rose Garden and Elizabethan plantings of the Shakespeare garden. The chalet-style dining pavilion by the World War II Garden of Remembrance to Commonwealth flyers and the Tudor-inspired Vancouver Rowing Club (of which the Duke of Edinburgh is patron) both date from 1911. Monuments to Robbie Burns, Queen Victoria and Lord Stanley seem at home here. Even the duck ponds date from the turn of the century.

From here the Stanley Park drive runs counter-clockwise around the park, and through much of Vancouver's early history. Highlights along the way: land-locked freshwater Lost Lagoon (once a tidal basin) named by celebrated Mohawk poet Pauline Johnson, "Tekahionwake," whose ashes are buried near Third Beach. (The earlier narrow isthmus may explain why Captain Vancouver charted the area as an island in 1792.) Salvation Army prayers no longer echo from Hallelujah Point, site of totem poles and the 200-year-old canoe of August Jack Khahtsahlano, but the Nine O'Clock Gun still booms. Once used to set ships' chronometers and to mark a fishing curfew, with the exception of the World War II years and a brief period when it was "kidnapped" by UBC engineering students, it has fired every night since 1894.

Deadman's Island was the site of a massacre of 200 warriors by a northern tribe, according to First Nations' legends. Today navy reserves train in the building HMCS *Discovery.*

Close by today's cricket and rugby matches at Brockton Oval, pioneers were once buried at Brockton Point. Just beyond, a reproduction of the Empress of Japan figurehead recalls the great steamships which joined Canada and the Orient from 1891 to 1922. At Lumberman's Arch, a Douglas fir replacement of the earlier 1913-47 arch, the Salish people built the first permanent longhouse in the mid-19th century, although it was an ancient seasonal camping ground. In 1888 ss *Beaver,* first steam vessel on the Pacific coast, ran aground off Prospect Point. At 64 metres Prospect is the highest point in the park. A horse trough at the picnic grounds is a reminder that the park's history began before the car, and that city police are still part of a mounted force patrolling the trails.

Geologists explain Siwash Rock ("Nine Pin Rock" on Admiralty Charts of 1864) as volcanic andesite, millions of years old. Squamish legend tells of a virtuous father transformed into rock as a symbol for his people. Just past Third Beach, Ferguson Point was armed with a gun emplacement during World War II. The former officer's mess remains as part of the Teahouse Restaurant. Further along the drive, Ceperley Park honors realtor Henry Ceperley who bequeathed Vancouver's second supervised playground in 1918.

But for many, the biggest attraction is the carless pleasure of travelling the seawall that surrounds most of Stanley Park or walking the trails through the great, peaceful forest that covers most of the park. Even Vancouverites are surprised to learn the imposing, mature Douglas firs and cedars are mostly second growth. (Today's trails retrace the old skid roads use by small companies that logged actively here from the 1860s to the 1880s.)

Of the low-level parklands in GVRD, Stanley Park contains the largest remnant of old-growth forest. The National Geographic society believes one red cedar, almost 30 metres around, is the largest of its kind in the world. It grows near Stanley Park's Hollow Tree, 30 metres along the trail to Third Beach. The tallest Douglas fir ever recorded in the park was 99 metres tall. It toppled in 1926. In 1962, Typhoon Frieda blew down 3,000 trees in a few hours with winds approaching 90 kilometres an hour.

It took 60 years to build the nine-kilometre-long Stanley Park seawall, much-loved by walkers, joggers, cyclists and rollerbladers. Unemployed after the Great War, 2,300 men in the early 1920s were set to work building the wall, heaving 46-kilogram blocks of granite into place, often waist-deep in freezing water. In 1968 the $70,0000 allotment bought over 1,200 lineal feet; in 1969, only 350. Sadly, master stonemason Jimmy Cun-

Seasons' current owner took over in 1989 and major renovations were performed, taking more than a year-and-a-half. The Gazebo was added during the renovations. The restaurant's elevated and spacious glass-enclosed dining room is an extraordinarily popular meeting place. Seasons in the Park is surrounded by the world-renowned gardens of Queen Elizabeth Park with a myriad of trees on every side and flowers blooming year round. The Bloedel Floral Conservatory is popular with visitors and locals and is just a few steps away.

ningham who supervised work even after retirement until his death at 85, died 17 years before the seawall was completed. His ashes are buried in an unmarked place in the wall that meant so much to him. The seawall links English Bay to Coal Harbour, named for the soft coal discovered there in 1859 by the surveying ship HMS *Plumper*.

Stanley Park continues to change with the times. The public continues to resist. In 1927 aghast citizens rejected a proposed causeway to link with a new bridge to the North Shore. The causeway went through. One happy note: each spring, daffodils bloom along the causeway—a gift of 60,000 bulbs from a grateful Holland in 1948 to Canadian soldiers. The Vancouver Park Board introduced pay tennis in 1985. Pay parking followed in 1993. As "exotic" animals like the polar bears died off, so has public support for the small Zoological Garden which began with one black bear tied to a tree and grew to include penguins. Soon only the Children's Farmyard of domestic animals and the miniature train will remain.

Georgia Street entrance to Stanley Park, 1898. cva

On April 3rd, 1993 Seasons in the Park played host to its most famous visitors when President Bill Clinton of the United States and President Boris Yeltsin of Russia dined there during the US/Russia Summit. Their very special menu is on view at the restaurant. Seasons in the Park has won much recognition and many awards for its food. It is open for lunch, dinner and weekend brunches year round, and there is all-day patio dining in the summer.

Gardens

Gardens
Dagmar Hungerford

PARKS AND GARDENS are an essential ingredient in making a city liveable. In the Greater Vancouver area they are an extension of the natural beauty. Most of our parks and gardens have a view of mountains—and sometimes ocean—or they include the magical silhouettes of tall western red cedars.

Land set aside for parks and gardens is often the result of the foresight of a few people. Many of our gardens were slated for development at one time or another, either for housing or freeways, but a few dedicated people took the time and made the effort to save land for green spaces.

In the Greater Vancouver area there is no shortage of parks and gardens. Many are situated in residential areas and are easily accessible by foot or public transportation.

CAMOSUN BOG
PUBLIC SPIRIT REGIONAL PARK, 19TH AND CAMOSUN

This 12,000-year-old bog was saved from development and has now become a protected area for many unusual plants. The wet, poorly drained soil is home to many varieties of native water plants and birds. Sphagnum moss; round-leaved sundews (a carnivorous plant that traps and eats insects); cloudberry, a plant long used by the area's earliest inhabitants for food; and the lodgepole pine, one of our most adaptable native trees, all inhabit the bog area. Visitors year-round find it interesting to see this ancient ecosystem at work, especially in late spring when the air is filled with the sound of frogs and birds. A boardwalk for visitors has been built over the entire bog area.

DAVIDSON ARBORETUM
RIVERVIEW HOSPITAL SITE, 500 LOUGHEED HIGHWAY, COQUITLAM

This 98.7-hectare site surrounding the hospital was landscaped in 1912 with the help of provincial botanist John Davidson. It was the first botanical garden and arboretum to be built in British Columbia. In the years 1916-1917 more than 25,000 plants, including 900 different species, were moved to the new site of the University of British Columbia to help landscape the new campus. Many of the trees, however, were left on the original site. Today the hospital grounds are home to more than 1,500 mature trees in more than 150 different varieties. Many of the trees are labelled. This garden is a wonderful place for a stroll and picnic. Tours are available.

facing page: Ornamental screen, Dr. Sun Yat–Sen Garden, 1987. vp

DR. SUN YAT-SEN CLASSICAL GARDEN
578 CARRALL STREET, VANCOUVER

The first authentic Suzhou-style classical garden to be built outside of China is located on one hectare in the heart of Vancouver's Chinatown. The garden is modeled after private classical gardens built during the Ming dynasty (1368-1644). A team of 52 artisans from China assembled the garden using tools, materials and techniques similar to those used centuries ago. Traditionally the elements of classical Chinese gardens are simple and symbolic. They include four main elements: buildings, rocks, water and plants. Inside the whitewashed walls in the Dr. Sun Yat-Sen Garden, a zigzag-shaped colonnade with pavilions, courtyards and lookouts allows the visitor to stroll through the garden at a leisurely pace. The garden is meant to be a microcosm of nature; carefully placed rocks, trees, shrubs and pools of water create a series of compact, exquisite vistas. Large pitted limestone rocks represent mountains and the rugged landscape. Rocks form the structure of the garden. They are hard and unmoving and form the masculine or yang element of the garden. On the other hand, reflective pools of water and gentle streams represent the yin or feminine element. The Taoist philosophy of yin and yang plays an important role in Chinese classical gardens. Everything is designed to be balanced and in harmony.

Planting material is restricted and each tree and shrub has a meaning and symbolic place within the garden. Chosen plants create different moods giving each area in the garden a unique feeling. The placement of plants is of great importance. Open spaces in the rockeries are planted with strong plants such as pine and cypress; in other areas more delicate plants such as bamboo and miniature rhododendrons are used. Symbolically the most famous group of plants are the three "friends of winter," pine, bamboo and winter-flowering plum. The pine is associated with strength and eternity, the bamboo symbolizes resiliency amid adversity and the plum blossom represents rebirth. These three plants are located in the shallow courtyard to the north of the scholar's study.

The peaceful atmosphere within the enclosed walls of the garden is conducive to quiet contemplation and meditation in an otherwise busy, noisy world. Guided tours are available year-round.

FANTASY GARDEN WORLD (FORMERLY BOTA GARDENS)
10800 NO. 5 ROAD, RICHMOND

This four-hectare garden is more of a European-style entertainment and amusement park than a serious botanical garden. It includes a family fun park, miniature railways, restaurants and shops. In the spring it has a wonderful collection of spring bulbs in bloom. There is also a garden centre on site.

JAPANESE FRIENDSHIP GARDEN

NEW WESTMINSTER

This garden was created in 1962 as a tribute to New Westminster's sister city, Mariguchi, Japan. One hundred ornamental flowering cherry trees have been planted in this informal Japanese-style garden. Waterfalls, ponds and streams add to the charm of the park.

MINTER GARDENS

52892 BUNKER ROAD, ROSEDALE

From Vancouver, the trip to Minter Garden takes about 90 minutes by car along Highway 1. Exit at the Harrison Hot Springs exit (exit 135). Where the rich Fraser River Valley farmland meets the mountains—at the base of 2,134 metre Mt. Cheam—the Minter family has converted 10.9 hectares of woodland into a garden with something for everyone to enjoy. There are 11 theme gardens, all connected by concrete pathways. The visitor is led through a rose garden, fragrance garden, native trails, an evergreen maze for children and much more. The showcase of summer annual bedding plants is spectacular. Highlights include hanging baskets, a floral maple leaf and topiary sculpture.

NITOBE MEMORIAL GARDEN

UNIVERSITY OF BRITISH COLUMBIA

The garden was opened in 1960 in memory of Dr. Inazo Nitobe, a Japanese scholar, educator, diplomat and publicist. It was designed by Professor Kannosuke Mori, a well-known Japanese landscape architect. For visitors the garden offers one hectare of gravel and moss pathways with vistas of man-made waterfalls, mountains and forests. Large cedar trees, native plants including vine maples, Douglas firs, huckleberries, kinnikinnick and Oregon grape create a West Coast interpretation of a classical Japanese garden and a year-round inspiration for gardeners. Each tree, shrub and plant is carefully chosen, cared for and pruned to perfection. The garden also has a large pond and a teahouse. Behind the teahouse is a little enclosed garden, a perfect example of a beautiful garden created in a very small space.

PARK AND TILFORD GARDENS

333 BROOKSBANK AVENUE, NORTH VANCOUVER

Commissioned by Park and Tilford Distillers as a centennial year beautification project in 1967, this small space has a native woodland garden, a rose garden, a herb collection, an oriental- style garden and a greenhouse with tropical plants. During the summer months there is a very good collection of bedding plants. In December the garden is magically converted to a winter wonderland with more than 50,000 lights strung throughout the trees, shrubs and plants on its 1.2 hectares. Landscape horticulture students from Capilano College learn the practical side of their studies in this garden. They also help with the upkeep.

In December the garden is magically converted to a winter wonderland with more than 50,000 lights

QUEEN ELIZABETH PARK AND BLOEDEL CONSERVATORY

33RD AVENUE AT CAMBIE STREET, VANCOUVER

The top of the garden is 152 metres above sea level. It has a beautiful view of Vancouver, the mountains and the ocean. To reach the top you can stroll along a number of woodland paths from 33rd Avenue and Cambie Street. There is a parking lot at the top. The park has many rhododendrons, azaleas and a fine collection of trees and shrubs. In the spring the flowering bulbs are a must-see and in summer a large selection of annual bedding plants replace the bulbs. There are tennis courts and a pitch-and-putt. In winter when the snow flies people flock to the park to sled down the many hills and in the summer it is a popular place to picnic.

The Bloedel Conservatory is situated at the top of the park.

STANLEY PARK

VANCOUVER

Stanley Park is a 404.7-hectare combination of gardens, wilderness and recreational areas. The majority of the land is undeveloped, with hundreds of wilderness trails running through it, and is home to many animals and birds. The towering Douglas fir, western red cedars, vine maples and other native plants are in sharp contrast to the Downtown skyline. The park is surrounded by ocean on three sides, and around the edge of the park the famous seawall draws walkers, bikers and rollerbladers from all over the Lower Mainland. English Bay, Burrard Inlet and Coal Harbour seen from the seawall offer spectacular views of Vancouver Island, the Port of Vancouver and the city skyline.

The arbored rose garden is a favorite site for many visitors. In June and July the roses are at their best. Close by are large perennial and annual borders filled with colorful flowers from spring through fall. For rhododendron and azalea enthusiasts the Ted and Mary Grieg rhododendron collection, located close to the park office and next to the pitch-and-putt area, is not to be missed. In late spring and early summer thousands of rhododendrons and azaleas are in bloom and visitors can walk along woodland paths to see ferns, hostas, daylilies and many interesting trees.

Stanley Park is also home to the Vancouver Public Aquarium,

the miniature railway, bowling greens, tennis courts, a pitch-and-putt, an outdoor theatre and numerous restaurants. Lost Lagoon Nature House located underneath the Lost Lagoon concession houses exhibits of Stanley Park's history, park attractions, examples of the intertidal shoreline surrounding the park and information on the forest, wildlife and birds living in the park. For up to date information, agendas and reports regarding the park, the e-mail address is http:/www. wimseycom/~nmills/.

UNIVERSITY OF BRITISH COLUMBIA BOTANICAL GARDEN
6804 S.W. MARINE DRIVE, VANCOUVER

Visitors to the garden will see a large variety of plants including trees, shrubs, native plants, alpines, perennials, herbs and vegetables growing on 44.5 hectares of land within the university area. The garden is divided into many different sections, with the starting point the David Lam Asian Garden. It encompasses 12.1 hectares of wooded area and holds the largest collection of woody Asian plants in North America. Imported trees and shrubs combined with native plants make this area a very special part of the garden. The collection of many imported rhododendrons, azaleas, magnolias and other trees and shrubs growing in the company of the western red cedar, vine maples, ferns and mosses best displays the variety of plant material that can be grown in this region of Canada. Bald eagles perched on tree-tops are a common sight.

The E.H. Lohbrunner Alpine Garden, situated on the other side of the "walk-through tunnel" is the largest alpine garden in North America. Volcanic rock and limestone brought in from the Interior form the base. The garden is laid out in pathways enabling the visitor to walk through various continents and alpine regions of the world. Africa, South America, Australia, Asia, North America and Europe are all well-represented by more than 12,000 alpine plants.

For many visitors to Canada the Native Garden is interesting as it includes one-third of the native trees and plants grown in various areas of B.C. Bark mulch trails lead the visitor through various growing regions of the province. This part of the garden encompasses about 3.2 hectares. The vegetable area is a highlight for many visitors. In this enclosed area many varieties of vegetables and berries are grown. Recently the garden has experimented with winter vegetable gardening and in the middle of winter cauliflowers, kale and other hardy vegetables can be seen. Vegetables are labelled. This area also has a wide variety of espaliered fruit trees. The garden combines teaching, research and public service; its Plant Introduction Scheme has provided new and unusual plants to gardeners since the 1980s.

Associated with the garden is a group of hard working volunteers called Friends of the Garden (FOGS) They run the shop,

> ## The garden is laid out in pathways enabling the visitor to walk through various continents and alpine regions of the world—Africa, South America, Australia, Asia, North America and Europe

harvest seeds, label plants, organize an annual plant sale, act as guides and run a plant information line called the Hortline.

The Shop-in-the-Garden located at the entrance sells a variety of plants, books, pots and other garden accessories.

VANDUSEN BOTANICAL DISPLAY GARDEN
5251 OAK STREET, VANCOUVER

Situated on the former grounds of Shaughnessy Golf Course, VanDusen Garden has become a very well-respected botanical garden in a relatively short period of time. Collections of plant groupings such as hollies, bamboos, magnolias, rhododendrons and azaleas are easily accessible by paved pathways, and the plants in these areas are well labelled. For visitors the rhododendron walk in late spring is very popular; in winter the holly walk attracts visitors from all over.

There are various theme gardens within the 22 hectares, including large formal and informal perennial borders, a children's garden and a large cedar maze, a rose garden and a lakeside garden. The newest addition is the Canadian Heritage Garden. Here native plants from across Canada are grown and well-labelled. Many of the plants were used to clothe, feed and house the first natives to inhabit this area. The garden also has large lawns and an interesting collection of outdoor sculpture. This vast grassy area is the site for the annual VanDusen Flower and Garden Show which takes place at the end of May or the beginning of June.

Volunteer guides give walking tours year-round. Electric carts are available for visitors who have difficulty walking. The pathways around the garden are paved and most areas of the garden are easily accessible. There is a restaurant and giftshop on site. (Take a look at the large kiwi vine growing along the outside wall of the restaurant.) Education programs run year-round and VanDusen is the home for the Master Gardens' group in Vancouver. There is an extensive public botanical library and many horticultural clubs hold their annual meetings in Floral Hall.

Bloedel Conservatory
Stephanie Davis and Alex Downie

V ANCOUVER IS A beautiful city nestled below striking mountains and bordered by the blue waters of the Pacific. Most of its inhabitants speak proudly of its natural attributes yet many do not spend as much time as they would like enjoying its beauty. What a treat it is then to visit the Bloedel Floral Conservatory in Queen Elizabeth Park, 153 metres above sea level. The conservatory is a dome containing a simulated tropical forest. Stepping inside one is immediately struck by the sounds, smells, sights and even the humidity of a tropical paradise. Inside the large dome (42 metres in diameter, 21 metres high, enclosing 1,430 square metres) beautiful plants from all over the world surround you, small waterfalls drop into ponds where Japanese Koi carp swim and colorful birds fill your field of vision with motion. There are approximately 40 different kinds of tropical birds, including Australian finches, Indian and African weavers, waxbills and South African whydahs, all of them amazing in their variety and charm. In total there are about 160 tropical birds flying about freely. Macaws, cockatoos and Amazon parrots preen themselves and—if they desire—respond to your greetings. Children delight in seeing the charming miniature Button quail forage at ground level among the foliage.

Three simulated ecological zones are re-created within the conservatory: tropical rainforest, subtropical and desert. Temperatures are maintained within a range of 18-25 degrees Celsius throughout the year. Eight individual heating and cooling units provide controlled conditions for the cultivation of a wide range of plants. Heat is supplied by two 50-hp gas-fired boilers. The cooling system is supplied by city water. A mist humidification system is used to increase humidity in the rainforest exhibit area. Plant and animal care is carried out by three full-time staff. Plant watering is done entirely by hand to provide the precise control required. Predatory insects are used to provide insect control, making the use of pesticide sprays unnecessary.

The tropical display, in a setting of pools and a waterfall, includes 500 species of plants from Africa, Mexico, Australia, South America, Asia, the southern United States and the West Indies. In addition plants of economic value such as the banana, coffee, coconut palm, papaya and citrus trees are displayed. The desert exhibit contains several unusual and bizarre plants such as the dragon's blood tree, candelabra cactus, century plant, old man cactus and barrel cactus. The permanent plantings are complemented by ever-changing floral displays themed

Stepping inside one is immediately struck by the sounds, smells, sights and even the humidity of a tropical paradise

to coincide with the time of year. In January early spring bulbs and azaleas are on display; in March, Easter lilies; in April, Asiatic lilies. From May through September subtropical flowers are featured. October and November feature chrysanthemums and December brings out the poinsettias and Christmas plants.

The Bloedel Conservatory opened on December 6, 1969, a generous gift of Virginia and Prentice Bloedel to the Vancouver Board of Parks and Recreation. The gift included the striking Henry Moore sculpture, *Knife Edge-Two Piece,* which can be seen in the conservatory plaza. Vancouver's conservatory is Canada's largest single-structure conservatory. Its domed design is based on the geodesic principle, which utilizes a structural space-frame to support the roof, enabling a large interior volume to be enclosed without the need for internal supporting columns. The conservatory dome consists of 2,324 pieces of extruded aluminum tubing each 12.5 centimetres in diameter, and 1,490 plexiglas "bubbles."

The covered walkways, plazas and fountains, and the large parking area, are at the top of the Little Mountain water reservoir, an important part of Vancouver's water supply. Within the beautifully landscaped 53-hectare Queen Elizabeth Park is a large collection of native and exotic trees and shrubs, the jewel-like Quarry Gardens (created from an old rock quarry), the rose garden, 20 tennis courts, a pitch-and-putt golf course and a lawn-bowling club. The conservatory is built atop the highest point within the City of Vancouver and panoramic views of the Downtown skyline and North Shore mountains can be enjoyed from the plaza. A restaurant in the park, Seasons, was the scene of a 1993 summit lunch with U.S. president Bill Clinton and Russian president Boris Yeltsin.

The Bloedel Conservatory was proclaimed a heritage building by order of Vancouver city council in 1994, 25 years after its completion. More than seven million visitors have enjoyed the conservatory in its first quarter-century.

The conservatory is open seven days a week and is fully wheelchair-accessible. A gift shop featuring souvenirs and gift items is contained within the conservatory.

The Story of the Pacific National Exhibition
Mark Leiren-Young

ONE OF THE FEW common experiences shared by everyone who grew up in Vancouver in the 20th century is their first childhood trip to the Pacific National Exhibition. The cotton candy-scented memories of the PNE are an indelible part of life in the Lower Mainland.

The Pacific National Exhibition is actually the title of a 17-day agricultural fair, but the name has been synonymous with the event's location—Hastings Park—and the 69.6-hectare site which houses the exhibition, a carnival style midway, the Pacific Coliseum and the thoroughbred race track.

The Vancouver Exhibition Association (VEA) was founded in 1907 by a group of Vancouver businessmen who met in the office of realtor Thomas Duke to discuss the creation of a Vancouver-based fair. The minutes of the preliminary meeting on May 31, 1907 read: "In the opinion of this meeting the time has arrived for the establishment of an Exhibition Association for Vancouver to embrace Fat Stock, horses, dogs, poultry, also Horticulture, Agricultural and industrial interests and also for the object of maintaining the City of Vancouver in that leading position she by right should occupy."

Opposition to the establishment of a Vancouver exhibition came from groups concerned with hurting attendance at New Westminster's Royal Agricultural Fair. Because of the lack of public transportation facilities between the two communities, the pro-exhibition forces prevailed, arguing that it would be good to have an exhibition site that people could reach for the cost of a five-cent streetcar ride.

Ironically, the exhibition that in the late 20th century was often criticized for harming the neighborhood was originally responsible for creating it. Streetcar service, extended to the area because of the exhibition encouraged growth. During the early years the site was also accessible by both CPR train and boat, with docking facilities at nearby Brighton Beach.

The VEA decided to develop Hastings Park, given to the city by the provincial government in 1889 and already home to a small racetrack. Despite opposition from the track operators, a lease was arranged. However, the VEA was initially unable to secure government funding for their plan—the provincial government, led by Premier Richard McBride remained concerned about harming the fair in New Westminster—and initial money was raised through the sale of "life memberships." A public awareness campaign eventually convinced Vancouver taxpayers to allow the city to invest $50,000 in the creation of

PNE rollercoaster, 1973. vs

the flashy but badly constructed Industrial Building (demolished in 1936) and a grandstand. The VEA's first president was J.G.V. Field-Johnson, a journalist who had also been involved with the establishment of the Winnipeg Exhibition. George Miller (later a Vancouver mayor) served as president from 1908 -1922 and is credited with inspiring the formation of the VEA.

On August 16, 1910 Prime Minister Wilfrid Laurier officially opened the first Vancouver Exhibition—although in the finest tradition of visiting dignitaries from Ottawa, the actual opening date was August 15. Attendance on the official first day, the 16th, was 5,000. A mini riot ensued as people crowded to see the prime minister.

The poster for what was billed as "Vancouver's First Exhibition" advertised twice-daily band concerts, free vaudeville shows, "Wrestling competitions, Foolish House, Push House,

Snake Charmers, Plantation Shows, Dancing Girls and all the Fun of the Fair."

Overall attendance for the six-day event was 68,000 people. The exhibition grossed $41,996 which gave the operators a surplus of $8,825. The admission fee was 50 cents, a price that remained in place until the 1960s.

By 1915 the exhibition had become a permanent fixture in Hastings Park, housing nearly a dozen buildings and an athletic field. The 1915 exhibition also had a new feature—"50,000 in prizes." During World War I, the exhibition concentrated on military themes; in its off-months the grounds were used as military facilities.

In the 1920s the exhibition expanded, averaging crowds of 200,000. The VEA faced criticism for monopolizing so much land for a week-long event. It responded by attempting to provide facilities available to the public on a year-round basis including convention buildings, a permanent carnival midway known as "Happyland" (the big attractions were two roller coasters known as The Giant and Baby Dippers and a water ride called Shoot-the-Chutes), a campground, an aquarium, a zoo and Vancouver's first public golf course. One specific condition of the 1923 lease was that the VEA would also build and run a gas station.

During the Depression, the exhibition's attendance continued to rise hitting 377,000 in 1936. This may have been partly due to the collapse of the competition. The New Westminster Exhibition closed in 1930 encouraging the expansion of the Vancouver Exhibition's agricultural component. The VEA also built an ice hockey arena known as The Forum in 1930. The new arena boasted the largest artificial ice surface in North America—although it was briefly transformed into the world's largest snowcone when the roof collapsed in 1935 due to record snowfalls. This was also the year of the first annual exhibition parade.

The 1940s provide the most shameful memories in the PNE's history. In 1942 Hastings Park was closed to the public as bunks and toilets were built for what was euphemistically referred to as "a processing centre" for more than 8,000 Japanese Canadians ordered evacuated to the interior of British Columbia by the federal government. After the evacuation was complete the site served as a military facility until 1946 when it was renamed Exhibition Park. The Vancouver Exhibition was also renamed, becoming the Pacific National Exhibition.

The first official PNE took place for eight days in 1947 and drew close to 600,000 visitors. Headline acts included come-

facing page: PNE amusement park ride, 1988. vp

dian Jimmy Durante and ventriloquist Edgar Bergen.

After Vancouver won the right to host the 1954 British Empire Games the PNE opened Canada's largest sporting facility, Empire Stadium, built on the site of the public golf course. The arena soon had a permanent place in sporting history when Englishman Roger Bannister (who had set a world record earlier with a sub-four-minute mile) and Australian John Landy both broke the four-minute mile on August 7, 1954. Although it is now common for world-class athletes to run a mile in less than four minutes, in the 1950s the phenomenon of two racers breaking the mark was considered as unthinkable as a trip to the moon. The "miracle mile" made news around the world.

The construction of Empire Stadium also allowed Vancouver to add a Canadian Football League franchise, the B.C. Lions, in 1954. The facility was considered the finest in the country and in 1955 Vancouver played host to the first of many Grey Cup games. The stadium was also home to the Vancouver Whitecaps, the North American Soccer League franchise that formed in 1973, won the Soccer Bowl in 1979 and folded in 1985. After the construction of B.C. Place in 1983, Empire Stadium fell into disuse and was demolished in 1993.

Since 1962 the PNE's attendance has consistently passed the one million mark. Meanwhile, federal, provincial and municipal governments joined forces to build the Pacific Coliseum. Opened in 1968, the $6-million 15,600-seat arena was a state-of-the-art facility best known as the home of the Vancouver Canucks. The team's first game at Pacific Coliseum was on October 9, 1970; it moved to General Motors Place at the start of their 1995-96 season. Prior to the construction of the coliseum, Exhibition Park was home to the Western Hockey League Vancouver Canucks. They played in The Forum from 1948 to 1970.

Politically the biggest year of the PNE was 1973. After a conflict over the use of The Forum (between minor hockey and a boat show) became a front page controversy, the provincial government took over. The event was transformed from a Vancouver Exhibition into a provincial one and resulted in two decades of high-profile political manoeuvres.

In the mid-1990s, the fair's fortunes began to suffer—there was agitation to move the exhibition out in order to create more parkland, and in 1996 the PNE parade was cancelled.

On January 1, 1997 the site, once again called Hastings Park, became the property of the City of Vancouver and will be transformed into East Vancouver's largest park. Meanwhile, the Pacific National Exhibition will relocate in 1998, likely to one of Greater Vancouver's rural suburbs.

Expo 86
Kerry McPhedran

VANCOUVERITES STILL REMEMBER 1986 as the year when summer was six months long. Expo 86 was Vancouver's 100th birthday party and B.C. wanted to "Invite the World" to join our celebration. The Queen herself issued the invitation and the world came. Vancouver has never been the same.

On May 2, a retired couple who'd driven their trailer from Newfoundland clicked through the turnstile to become Expo's first visitors. By October 13 another 22,111,576 visitors from 44 countries had followed. For $20 per day or $160 for a season's pass (for 165 magical days), people stepped through the four gateways into a "world city-within-a-city," rising from Vancouver's old railyards. Expo's slender site has been likened to a five-kilometre-long string of pearls lying along the north side of False Creek, strung with 62 pavilions, plazas, countless theatres, bandstands, cabarets and amusement rides. The Canada Pavilion—the longest ever built—sat on a satellite site on Burrard Inlet, four-minutes away by the new SkyTrain. The world's largest flag flew over it.

Expo 86 was rife with superlatives, offering the "world's largest" hockey stick (62 metres), flagpole, Swatch watch and Omnimax screen. It was itself the largest "specialized" world exposition ever staged, with 54 countries participating. (Unlike less frequent, larger "universal" expositions, "specialized" expositions have focussed themes, and the host country must provide pavilions for other countries, while corporations, provinces and states design and build their own.) The smallest country to participate was tiny Nauru from the South Pacific. The real coup? Signing up the benchmark troika of China, the U.S. and the USSR. Taiwan and South Africa were not invited, although made-in-Taiwan souvenirs showed up in the China Pavilion gift shop.

Expo 86's "World in Motion, World in Touch" theme focused on transportation and communications, and served as a showcase for the achievements of these 54 countries plus seven provinces, two territories, three states and 41 corporations. Appropriately Expo's 70 hectares encompassed the world's largest barrier-free integrated environment.

Expo 86 was also the first world exposition to hold three academic symposia on the transportation and communications themes; 14 specialized "theme" periods, from polar transportation to search and rescue, were demonstrated. From an operational point of view, Expo 86 was the first to have construction

Pavilions offered everything from a ride on Japan's high speed HSST train to Cuban cigar-rolling demonstrations

95 per cent complete six months before opening and the first to exceed its budgeted attendance of 13.75 million by pre-selling 15 million visits before the gates ever opened. Its corporate support of $175 million was larger than the Los Angeles Olympics, a previous benchmark.

Pavilions offered everything from a ride on Japan's high speed HSST train to Cuban cigar-rolling demonstrations; and every form of film from Omnimax to 3-D Imax and Showscan was presented. Real (U.S. space shuttle, Great Wall of China, Pakistan bazaar) or replica (Paris Metro, Temple of Karnak), it was there. Surprise hits emerged: the quirky Roundhouse theme pavilion designed by the Czechs, the low-budget Northwest Territories' entry and General Motors' Spirit Lodge.

But the best "pavilion" was the site itself, with non-stop national day celebrations, free street entertainment, the RCMP Musical Ride, the Scream Machine roller coaster, a 1907 carousel, 9,000 seats for the foot-weary and UFO water fountains for kids of all ages. Everyone from explorer Thor Heyerdahl, Margaret Thatcher, Princess Margaret and Countess Mountbatten of Burma to Lee Iacocca and Lillian Gish wandered past the 30-metre-high nose cone of a Boeing 747, clambered through boats and over the undulating life-size sculpture "Highway 86" before plunging into the Land Plaza's international traffic jam. Both the Concorde and a replica of France's 18th century Montgolfier hot-air balloon flew over the site. Special events brought the largest gathering of operating steam locomotives assembled since Chicago's world fair in the 1940s, followed by, on June 7, the largest flyover of DC-3's since World War II.

Art being the ultimate communication, about 70,000 performers entertained at Expo 86 presenting some 260 performances a day. Folklife's singing coalminers Men of the Deep, Rita McNeil, England's Bloolips and France's avant-garde Urban Sax, Norway's Dollie Deluxe Rock Opera, Fats Domino, k.d. lang, Mikhail Baryshnikov and Company, Bob Hope, Loretta Lynn and Wynton Marsalis all took bows. The Royal Bank's off-site World Festival brought the likes of the Kirov Ballet, La Scala's *I Lombardi,* Japan's all-male *Medea* and Beijing People's Art Theatre's *Teahouse.*

Everyone got into the act. Six couples were married by Shin-

to priests at the Kodak Theatre. The calendar of on-site events alone was 61-pages long. Ninety-six committees in towns throughout B.C. planned Expo events. Cowboy wannabes mounted up for a trail ride from 100 Hundred Mile House. Two French swimmers swam through the Fraser River's Hell's Gate to Expo 86. Wheelchair athlete Rick Hansen missed Expo 86 but his round-the-world "Man in Motion" (Expo's original motto, thought too sexist) wheelchair tour, which began in Vancouver in March 1985 and ended there in May 1987, raised $18 million for spinal cord research. Even the Vancouver Aquarium's three orcas Hyak, Bjossa and Finna joined the Vancouver Bach Choir in a Celebration of Whales.

By opening day newly elected Mayor Mike Harcourt—who had earlier convinced recession-ridden Vancouver not to help the provincial and federal governments fund Expo 86—and most of the city had been won over. The Prince and Princess of Wales did the honors in B.C. Place Stadium. (Diana would later do an even greater service by fainting in the California Pavilion, generating massive media coverage and many subsequent visits by Californians.) It was exactly 135 years and one day after Prince Charles' great-great-grandmother Queen Victoria opened the first world exposition in London's Crystal Palace.

Expo 86 was born in London on a fall day in 1978, thanks to three British Columbians sipping coffee in the anteroom of the Cavalry Club. Social Credit cabinet minister Grace McCarthy wanted "something dramatic" for Vancouver's centennial (could we borrow the *Mona Lisa,* she first wondered). Lawrie Wallace, agent general for British Columbia, knew that the third person—Ambassador Patrick Reid, then running Canada House—was also president of the Paris-based International Bureau of Expositions which gave Expo 67 to Montreal. "Why couldn't Vancouver have one?"

Eight years and $1.5 billion later—despite loud nay-sayings (columnist Denny Boyd wrote urging "Kill it, Mr. Premier, Kill it") and union strikes during construction in 1984 that nearly cancelled the whole event—what began as Transpo 86 could claim success as Expo 86.

Success was due to another uneasy troika of top management. As Expo 86's commissioner general, Patrick Reid winced at the term "world fair," fought for international participation, for dignity for developing nations and for more than lip service to the theme. He understood Queen Victoria's vision of "this peace festival uniting the industry and art of all nations of the world." (Reid credits another "old expo warrior," Frank Mayrs, who preceded Ron Woodall as chief designer, created the Expo 86 logo and, along with architect Bruno Freschi, set the ship on

the right course.) American Michael Bartlett brought theme-park know-how to the job until he was replaced as Expo chairman by bottom-liner Jimmy Pattison (who took the job for one dollar per year).

His "strict attendance to the discipline of money" paid off. Expo exceeded its original visitors projection by 9 million. Given the $700-million plus in government revenues, Lotto 6/49 happily paid off the $300-or-so million debit.

There were no scams and no terrorism but there were tragedies. A nine-year-old girl died when she was crushed by a moving wall in Canada's rotating theatre one week after opening. An 88-year-old Downtown Eastside resident, Olaf Solheim, evicted to make room for more lucrative Expo 86 visitors, committed suicide. Folksinger Pete Seeger held a free concert in memory of Solheim.

There were 15,000 volunteers and 15,000 staff (with a turnover of 70 per cent, some 37,000 people ultimately worked for the Expo 86 Corporation). For many—including Patrick Reid—the singular event that captured the heart and soul of Expo 86 was the final performance of the World Drum Festival. On July 27, 140 percussionists from 17 nations—from Inuit with caribou drums to an Indonesian gamelan orchestra to American drummer Steve Gadd—jammed to standing ovations.

As for Expo 86 itself, press coverage from the 10,000 journalists from 60 countries—from the *London Times* to *Entertainment Tonight* and *Newsweek*—was almost embarrassingly positive. Americans raved. Ironically the only consistently sour notes came from Eastern Canada. Robert Fulford, writing for *Saturday Night,* found Expo 86 a dream that never came true: "at its core, American . . . unremarkable . . ." while E.J. Kahn Jr. countered in his July 14, 1986, *New Yorker* Letter from Vancouver, "It's not so much Expo 86's substance that accounts for its charm as it is its style. You feel good just walking around."

So good that on October 12—Expo's last day but one—a record 341,806 visitors (120,000 was the daily average) showed up for one last walk. As cab dispatcher Harold Smith put it, "We invited the world and on Sunday they all showed up." After the nightly fireworks Vancouver turned into one gridlocked parking lot.

Another 60,000 jammed B.C. Place Stadium for the closing ceremonies to sing "Something's Happening Here" and "This is My Home" one last time. The American and Soviet flag-bearers exchanged flags; others followed and the tears flowed. Expo 86 was over. A week later *Sun* columnist Vaughn Palmer wrote, "So long, beautiful. We'll miss you." Ten years later, we still do.

Vancouver Aquarium
Murray A. Newman

THE AQUARIUM IN Stanley Park is Canada's largest marine life exhibit and has been recognized by the federal government as Canada's Pacific National Aquarium. Its displays are organized according to regions: Western Canada, Arctic Canada, the Amazon Basin and the tropical Pacific. Over the years it has grown slowly from modest beginnings to an internationally recognized institution that features major aquatic mammals and significant research and education programs.

Its history started in 1951 when a private non-profit society, the Vancouver Public Aquarium Association, was formed with downtown businessman, Carl L.A. Lietze, as the first president. Capital funds ($300,000) were obtained from the three governments, and the aquarium opened on June 15, 1956. It was the first public aquarium to be built in the country.

When it opened, the Vancouver Aquarium was a simple, cedar-sided, one-floor building with saltwater intake pipe running to a pump house at the beach and out into the harbor. Within the 1,858-square-metre building were glass-fronted tanks arranged according to four water systems: warm and cool saltwater, and warm and cool freshwater.

From opening day, the aquarium drew great crowds. As the skates, dogfish and salmon were put on display it proved to be a great success but far too small.

In 1960 Murray Newman, the Vancouver Aquarium's first director, attended the first International Aquarium Congress in Monaco, and visited the Berlin Aquarium and the British Museum of Natural History. From these observations plus visits to Marine Studios in Florida came the concept of a new kind of facility, a living aquatic museum which would tell the story of the aquatic habitats of Western Canada from the open ocean to the headwaters of the Fraser River.

The new exhibits would be symbolized by a sculptured replica of a killer whale in the fashion of the replicas in the British Museum of Natural History. An expedition was launched to capture a killer whale off Saturna Island and one was accidentally caught alive in the summer of 1964. It was the first killer whale ever to be studied alive in captivity and it became known as Moby Doll.

The lieutenant governor, the Honorable George Pearkes and the president of the Vancouver Aquarium Association, Ralph M. Shaw, opened the enlarged aquarium, tripled in size, in the spring of 1967. There was a large glassed foyer within which

The first killer whale in captivity became known as Moby Doll

were giant Pacific Ocean forms including Moby Doll, the killer whale. Nearby was a dolphin pool which introduced a gallery with a sequence of exhibits showing first the marine fishes and invertebrates of the region, and then the freshwater species. The old building was redeveloped into the H.R. MacMillan Tropical Gallery.

The two killer whales, Skana and Hyak, beginning in 1967, were famous performers for 13 years under chief trainer Klaus Michaelis. In 1971 Prime Minister Pierre Trudeau and his wife Margaret, opened the new 2.3-million-litre whale pool.

This was followed by the Finning Sea Otter Pool in 1973 and the Gordon and Mary Russell Seal Pool in 1975. In 1981 the research areas were consolidated at the north end of the building into the VanDusen Aquatic Science Centre.

Reflecting extensive research conducted during several expeditions to South America, the Graham Amazon Gallery was opened in 1983 at the front of the aquarium. The opening ceremony was assisted by Her Majesty Queen Elizabeth II together with aquarium president Ron Basford and aquarium patrons Jim and Isabelle Graham. In 1984 Bill Reid's magnificent bronze killer whale was unveiled in the presence of Lieutenant-Governor Robert Rogers at the aquarium entrance. As part of the Vancouver Expo 86 celebrations the aquarium completed the Max Bell Marine Mammal Centre which brought together the marine mammal exhibits and doubled the size of the killer whale pool.

Although the aquarium had been studying Arctic marine mammals in the Lancaster Sound Area of Baffin Island since 1968, the Arctic Canada Pavilion was not opened until 1990. This included a two-million-litre beluga whale pool and the Jean MacMillan Southam Arctic Gallery looking into the beluga habitat. The gallery features the sounds of Arctic marine mammals.

With the completion of the Earl B. Finning Indo-Pacific Reef and the Forest Angus Giant Amazon Fish exhibits, the Aquarium became home to more than 8,000 species of aquatic life. It is now the largest aquarium in Canada and one of the largest in North America. More than 800,000 people visit annually. Director Murray Newman retired in 1993 and was succeeded by the aquarium's second director, Dr. John Nightingale, formerly deputy director of the New York Aquarium.

Abbotsford Air Show
Don Hunter

I<small>T'S A PLANE</small>, it's a . . . In the second week of August people in southwestern B.C. find themselves glancing skyward and pondering the identity of yet another exotic flying object. "It must be the air show," they say, and no one needs to ask which one.

Since its inception in 1962, when 40 enthusiastic members of the Abbotsford Flying Club passed the hat and came up with $700 to put on the first one, the Abbotsford International Air Show has acquired an enviable reputation as one of the world's premium flying and aviation-technology extravaganzas, attracting increasing numbers of participants from all parts of the world. Since 1970 it has been officially Canada's National Air Show.

That first event in 1962 attracted 15,000 spectators. In recent years an average of between 250,000 and 300,000 have turned out during the show's three-day run at Abbotsford International Airport, 80 kilometres east of Vancouver in the heart of the verdant Fraser Valley.

The airport is the designated alternate to the busy Vancouver International Airport, and with its two runways of 2,438 metres and 1,524 metres is capable of handling all commercial and private aircraft, day and night.

The event is one of 400 airshows taking place in North America each year, which draw a total of 20 million spectators.

Any given year at Abbotsford you will thrill to the sights and sounds of the finest of international military formation flying teams, including our own Canadian Armed Forces Snowbirds, the USAF Thunderbirds, and the USN Blue Angels, Italy's Frecce Tricolori, Brazil's Esquadrilha da Fumaca and the Chilean Halcones.

In 1989 Abbotsford was selected by organizers of the first Soviet Union group of planes to visit North America. The Soviets showed off their sleek MiG 29s, an IL-76 and the enormous AN-225, the world's biggest aircraft. Canadian Armed Forces Major Bob Wade became the first Western pilot to fly the MiG 29. The Soviets attracted so much interest that 60,000 would-be spectators were turned away.

In 1991 the first public air-show appearance of the exotic American F-117 Stealth took place at Abbotsford, and two years later the air show rang up another prize with the only Canadian appearance of the fabled Russian Knights SU-27 demonstration team.

And all of that is to say nothing of an annual wealth of heart-

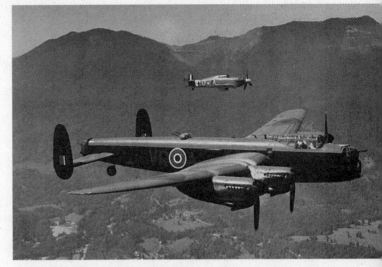

Avro Lancaster bomber and above it a Hawker Hurricane fighter of the Canadian Warplane Heritage of Hamilton, Abbotsford, 1990. vp

stopping "civilian" wing walking and aerobatics, pin-point accuracy sky-diving displays, races between 36,000 horsepower jet-propelled trucks and aircraft and, in 1995, flights through a 60-storey-high wall of fire. As well each year there is a static display of around 100 aircraft representing just about everything that flies.

In 1989 the Airshow Society created Airshow Canada which every second year in the nearby Tradex exhibition centre operates Canada's only aerospace trade show. The show presents the newest in the world of aviation business and developing technology.

The Abbotsford show is very much a community affair. All profits from the concession and souvenir stands go directly to non-profit local groups, such as the Boy Scouts and the Lions Club, who run them. In 1994 that contribution to the community surpassed $130,000.

It's advisable to start out early for the show, especially if you're approaching from the Vancouver area or from Washington State. A shuttle bus service runs from the metro-Vancouver area to the show. The gates open at 7:30 A.M., flying events usually begin well before noon, and the show ends at 5 P.M. Special handicapped parking and seating is available. In addition to gate admission, box seating is a reserved and very popular public viewing area, where you're nose to nose with the action, the heat and the thunder. Private viewing areas are available for corporate and group entertainment. The Air Show provides camping facilities and complimentary shuttle bus service in the local area.

Crafts
Carolyn Bateman

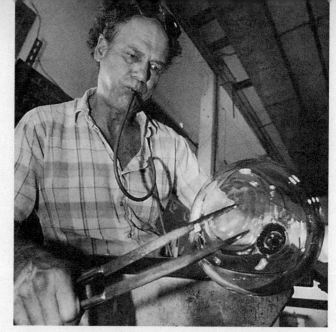

Glass blower, Granville Island, 1991. vp

I S IT OUR CITY'S RICH NATURAL BEAUTY, something that has inspired artists since the beginning of time, that has made Greater Vancouver a centre for some of the finest craft work being done in Canada? Whatever the reason, Vancouver craftspeople are experiencing a renaissance.

"Craft provides an intimate link with what it means to be human," says Vancouver fibre artist Jean Kares speaking from her studio on Granville Island. "I think as life becomes more hectic, we want and need that link." Kares is a quiet yet forceful spokesperson for a community of craftspeople working in clay, glass, wood, metal and fibre and creating work of both a high technical and artistic maturity. It seems fitting that she is the current national president of the Canadian Craft Council.

Proof of this astonishing talent is everywhere in the city. Go to Robert Held's Kitsilano glass studio, where a line of high-quality, internationally sold studio glass originates. Or go to Cathedral Place's remarkable Canadian Craft Museum or Granville Island's tiny perfect Crafthouse gallery. Granville Island is the heart of the city's craft community. Here you will find colorful, busy studios such as Pat Cairns and Jean Kares' TextileContexT and the Daniel Materna and Zuzy Vacek Ceramic Studio. The island is also home to Circle Craft, a cooperative gallery and store that represents many fine B.C. craftspeople. "There has been an explosion of craft in the 13 years since I came from Sweden," says executive director Helena Wennerstrom. As if still hot and liquid, Morna Tudor's lush orange glass vases and bowls glow in the late afternoon sun. Tudor's work typifies the nineties approach to craft: technically still bowls and vases ready to receive fruit or flowers, they are also unmistakable works of art.

Is it art or is it craft? It's a question many craftspeople grapple with and while not exactly shunning the term craft, many are gently moving away from it. "We're still very aware of what makes craft craft," says fibre artist Anne Love, a past president of the Vancouver Guild of Fabric Arts. "We're still aware of the value of useable objects in daily life." But as modern craftspeople enter into a time of perfected craftsmanship they are "pushing the envelope," says Love. Many include political and social messages in their work.

Wennerstrom believes the very act of making beautiful objects by hand has a social message. She has seen customers come into the gallery store over and over again to simply stand and admire a piece. "We are tiring of the 'buy-and-throw-away' consumer society," she says with feeling. "It goes against the grain of human character, against our basic instinct as human beings."

Yet the craftsperson, who traditionally honors the past, must still survive in this time of increasing technology, speed and disposability, a paradox people like glass artist Robert Studer are very aware of. Studer, president of the Vancouver Glass Arts Association, practises the ancient art of glassmaking yet is very much a modern craftsperson. "The pace of society is picking up," says Studer. "Government funding is gone. We have to become more street smart, we have to develop more business sense. Otherwise we'll be left behind." Studer says glass art has experienced incredible growth since the formation of the association in 1988. "We've banded together for workshops and exhibits, spreading knowledge and inspiration." Studer notes that glass artists have resisted the traditionally isolated nature of the craftsperson and started working directly with designers to create one-of-a-kind windows, sculptures and other pieces for clients.

The trend Studer describes is taking hold throughout the Vancouver craft community. The Craft Association of B.C., based in the city, has become more aggressive in marketing its talented members, networking with international craft associations to gain exposure for the province's world-class artists. The arrival of the Canadian Craft Museum in May, 1992, gave craft a well-deserved legitimacy, helping it gain more recognition in the public eye. Guest curator Sam Carter's inaugural exhibit set the tone: 30 of the 198 pieces selected for the exhibit came from Vancouver area craftspeople including Martha Sturdy's resin bowl and platter, Brian Baxter's leaded-glass *Red Square,* Judson Beaumont's *Waterfall* cabinet and Tam Irving's celadon vase. Within the museum's elegant spaces craft is displayed in a setting that befits its beauty and integrity.

Hobbies

Carolyn Bateman

HAVE A SUDDEN yen to pull a rabbit out of a hat? Don't suppress it. Join the Vancouver Magic Circle. Do you have a shrine to Sir Arthur Conan Doyle on your bookshelves? Don't hide it. Take in a meeting of the Stormy Petrels of B.C. Got a sneaking suspicion you would be better suited to life in the Middle Ages? Try the Northern Society for Creative Anachronisms.

There are hundreds of hobby clubs and societies all over the Lower Mainland, and they run the gamut from more traditional clubs like quilting, stamp and coin collecting, photography and gardening to esoteric delights such as the Vancouver Canary Club, the Association of Reptile Keepers, and the Paper Folders Around the Lower Mainland.

The Vancouver Public Library has an excellent online community services directory organized by category. Many groups meet in community centres, libraries and other neighborhood facilities such as lawn bowling clubs or seniors' centres. Give them a call to see what clubs may be meeting, sharing and having fun right around the corner from you.

NATURE
- Vancouver Natural History Society. 738-3177
- B.C. Council of Garden Clubs. Rose Bancroft, 522-2094
- Royal Astronomical Society, Vancouver Centre. 738-2855
- Vancouver Canary Club. Roak Citroen, 437-6824
- Fraser Valley Racing Pigeons. James Steenson, 589-1928
- Fraser Valley Allbreed Cat Club, (affiliated with the Cat Fanciers Association) Myrtle Youmans, 576-2305
- B.C. Falconry Association. Muriel Galicz, 599-6873
- Association of Reptile Keepers. 521-1817

COMPUTERS
- MacWest Computer Society. 268-9530
- Commodore Computer Club. Ray Norman, 589-7199

CRAFT AND ART
- Vancouver Lace Club. 263-0378
- Burnaby Embroiderers' Guild. Shirley McLellan, 439-1343
- Vancouver Sketch Club. Bert Pepin, 266-9231
- Tri-City Photographic Society. Len Waddell, 942-0708
- Paper Folders Around the Lower Mainland. Lisa David, 662-7131
- Westcoast Calligraphy Society. Margo Ferris, 430-8626
- Kensington Pottery Club. Mary Dunai, 589-9124

PERFORMING ARTS
- Vancouver Guild of Puppetry. Karen Eskilson, 255-9946
- West Vancouver Seniors' Choir. Betty Downing, 929-8098
- Vancouver Magic Circle. David Wilson, 467-7887
- Vancouver Storytelling Festival. Helen O'Brian, 876-2272

COLLECTING
- Minoru Spoon Club. 231-6440
- British Columbia Philatelic Society. Roger Packer, 685-1826
- Miniature Club of B.C. Marilyn Conibear, 738-4580
- Vintage Car Club of Canada, Golden Ears Chapter. Art Halfnights, 467-2921 (w); 467-6658 (h)
- Fraser Valley Bottle and Collectables Club. Pat McNamara, 939-4874
- Vancouver Numismatic Society. 266-8331

READING AND WRITING
- Jane Austen Society of North America. Eileen Sutherland, 988-0479
- West End Writers' Club. Ruth Kozak, 251-9776; Dr. Glen Wheeler, 874-1336
- International Pen Friend, B.C. Chapter. John Wood, 271-3270
- Stormy Petrels of B.C. (Sherlock Holmes Society). Len Haffenden, 985-4613

HISTORY
- Northern Society for Creative Anachronisms, Barony of Lions Gate. Gerry and Nancy Stevens, 988-0304
- Vancouver Genealogical Society Margaret Hannay, 325-0374

GAMES AND OTHER ACTIVITIES
- Burnaby Duplicate Bridge Club. Hazel Dressler, 524-4445
- B.C. Kite Fliers Association. Bruce Darroch, 879-1267
- Burnaby Amateur Radio Club. Harry Curtis, 530-3962
- North Shore Scrabble Club. Alan Burwell, 987-7610
- Vancouver Chess Club. David Hunter, 588-2560

MODELS AND MODELLING
- Vancouver Gas Model Club. A.B. Duncan, 855-7295
- B.C. Society of Model Engineers. Lindsay McDonnell, 420-1778
- B.C. Meccano Club. Neil Wilkie, 926-2706
- British Railway Modellers of North America. Neil Wilkie, 926-2706

WINE AND FOOD
- Vancouver Amateur Winemaker's Association. Gary Armanini, 420-6041
- Vancouver American Wine Society. Jim Robertson, 669-8988; Gordon Wilcox, 872-8621
- Confrérie de la Chaine des Rôtisseurs. Bert J. Phillips, 985-6255

Arts and Entertainment

The CN IMAX® Theatre, located at Canada Place, originally opened as part of the Canada Pavilion at Expo 86. The theatre re-opened in May of 1987, becoming the first theatre in the world to offer films in the "ultra real" IMAX® 3D format on a year-round basis. Spectacular IMAX® and IMAX® 3D features celebrate such themes as Canadian wildlife, historical flights and natural wonders. Audiences are continuously thrilled, entertained and educated by "The Ultimate Film Experience."

SUMMER 1989: Angus Reid Takes a Poll. A Vancouver newspaper is in decline, bleeding money in gushes. Time for a poll. For the purpose, Angus Reid Associates, carves the Lower Mainland into six mentalities: Literate Inquisitors • Post-Literate Hedonists • Competitive Acquisitors • Homebodies • Middle-Class Joiners • The Insular Forlorn. Applying this grid they discover that the one cultural category unserved by Vancouver media is the Literate Inquisitor.

SUMMER 1996: THE LITERATE INQUISITOR ON THE RUN.

Literate Inquisitors emerge—haggard, squinting, starved for culture. Forsaken by the entertainment industry, they impersonate Middle-Class Joiners at fireworks displays, performances of *Show Boat* and other spectacles comprehensible to the whole family—and to the family dog as well. In an era of government cutbacks, anyone who attempts to cater to the Literate Inquisitor without full backing from a cigarette manufacturer will quickly find himself among the Insular Forlorn.

SUMMER 1936: THE KITSILANO SHOWBOAT IS BORN.

Built for Vancouver's 50th anniversary, the pool at Kits Beach features a 36-metre tower for Hawaiian cliff divers. The event leaves behind a set of concrete bleachers with nothing to look at but the pool—a magnet for Post-Literate Hedonists of the most sordid kind. Bert Emery, an alderperson and Competitive Acquisitor, orders a stage built across from the bleachers. At the Kitsilano Showboat (a backdrop is added), homebodies and Middle-Class Joiners perform Broadway melodies in the electric sun, in a city that traditionally holds culture at a distance; like the Queen Elizabeth Theatre complex or our two universities, the Kitsilano Showboat presents culture as a foreign object to be showcased in a concrete structure surrounded by water, trees or government.

SUMMER 1940: THE RISE OF THE LITERATE INQUISITOR.

Middle-Class Joiners have taken to roller skating in a big way, on the pier at English Bay. Meanwhile on Hastings Street, Competitive Acquisitors play games of chance, Post-Literate Hedonists eye the bearded ladies and Homebodies ride the Ferris wheel at "Happyland." Scorned by roller rink and midway, Literate Inquisitors wander about, Insular and Forlorn, until Mr. Malkin, a food wholesaler, agrees to finance an outdoor amphitheatre in Stanley Park. The cry goes up throughout the Lower Mainland: Shakespeare! Outdoors!

Theatre Under the Stars is launched with *As You Like It* and *A Midsummer Night's Dream,* starring Alan Young, performed before 10,000 Literate Inquisitors at Brockton Point Oval. (Two complete casts are necessary—one to broadcast the dialogue from a sound booth, the other to lip sync onstage.) But the Literate Inquisitors' triumph is short-lived as the economics of the Competitive Acquisitor prevail. Theatre Under the Stars becomes a venue for remounts of Broadway musicals and as an amateur showcase—not unlike, yes, the Kitsilano Showboat. Alan Young will find immortality as television's Mr. Ed.

SUMMER 1968: ATTACK OF THE POST-LITERATE HEDONIST.

At Scott's Restaurant on Granville Street, Homebodies and Middle-Class Joiners take high tea before watching each other sing "Old Man River" at the Kitsilano Showboat. Suddenly the hippies descend! Post-Literate Hedonists loiter, promiscuous and unwashed, where Competitive Acquisitors compete and Homebodies shop. Plainclothesmen from The Bay use a garden hose, a Canadian version of the water cannon, to clear the sidewalk.

In retaliation hippies open the Colonial Magic Theatre— the Kitsilano Showboat on acid—and Vancouver splits into enemy camps: which consumer group will define the Downtown core? The Colonial Magic Theatre is demolished and replaced by a marble wall with no shelter from the rain. Nobody but the Insular Forlorn remains. The Kitsilano Showboat wins again.

SUMMER, 1996.

At the grand opening of the Ford Centre for the Performing Arts (near General Motors Place) where Broadway hits will be produced by a multinational impresario, Homebodies, Competitive Acquisitors, Middle-Class Joiners and Post-Literate Hedonists pay tribute to Brent Carver, the Tony Award-winning Vancouverite, prior to the opening of *Show Boat.*

All but the most Insular Forlorn applaud this fellow citizen who crossed the moat and stepped onto the platform, into the electric sun.

It's the Kitsilano Showboat all over again.

—*John MacLachlan Gray*

above: Stage sign, Kitsilano Showboat bandshell, 1992. vs
facing page: Kids wear 3–D glasses for planetarium show, 1987.
planetarium photo.

Artists of Greater Vancouver: The First Three Generations
Tony Robertson

The following list presents twelve significant artists in each of the first three generations of B.C. artists. The fourth generation is presently at work and it is probably too soon to tell about them. Several of the second and most if not all of the third generation are still hard at work, but they've been at it long enough for there to be some consensus as to their place in our art history. All lists are exclusionary and this list is no exception. Many artists who would have been on even a slightly longer list, let alone a comprehensive one, are not here. Also absent are the gallery directors and owners, patrons, critics, interested parties, connectors and facilitators without whom art history does not happen.

It seems only fair to give a partial and random list of the significant unlisted in all categories: Tony Emery, Alvin Balkind, Abraham Rogatnik, Doug Christmas, Doris Shadbolt, Nan Cheney, Roy Kiyooka, Iian Baxter, Marguerite Pinney, Claude Breeze, Al Neil, Joan Lowndes, Joe Plaskett, Ian Wallace, Evelyn Roth, Molly Lamb Bobak, Mildred Valley Thornton, Jack Wise, Beatrice Lennie, Scott Watson, Leslie Poole, Jill Pollack, Gerry Tyler, Al McWilliams, Sherry Grauer, J.A. Morris, Lyle Wilson, Don Jarvis, Art Perry, Paul Goranson, Ed Varney, Ann Rosenberg, Beau Dick, Luke Rombout.

THE FIRST GENERATION
(born before 1900)

Charles Edenshaw *1839-1920* Best known of the North Pacific coast carvers and the first professional Haida artist. His uniquely individualist and innovative work, especially in gold and silver jewelry and argillite carvings, demonstrates his ability to move outside the familiar forms of traditional native art. As an authority on Haida art and culture his extensive contacts with anthropologists and collectors had a strong influence on how native art was received and understood in the non-native world.

Emily Carr *1871-1945* Her unique vision of the "rhythm of life" in the coastal forest, the result of a long and determined effort to understand and print what she had struggled to see in new ways, and her discovery of a new personal and artistic sense of the wilderness, forever changed the way we see and understand the coastal landscape in art and life. She is also noted for her celebration and interpretation of northwest coast native art and culture.

Charles Marega *1879-1939* A sculptor and teacher at the Vancouver School of Art and a very active arts facilitator in the community, Marega is best known for his public sculptures, among them the carved lions on the Lions Gate Bridge and the busts of Michelangelo and Leonardo which flanked the entrance to the old Vancouver Art Gallery on Georgia Street. His teaching, support and encouragement of the city's growing arts community in the 1920s and 1930s had a much greater impact.

W.P. Weston *1879-1967* A painter and teacher who did for the mountains what Carr had done for the coastal forests. His paintings dramatized the vital forces of nature, drawing their form and structure from what he had learned to see in the anatomy of mountains and trees. Like Carr and other contemporaries, Weston was concerned with the universality of nature and man's spiritual response to it, discoverable through art whose purpose was to heighten man's awareness of the cosmos.

Mungo Martin *1881-1962* A man of great dignity and simplicity, he was the most influential Kwakiutl master carver, noted for his massive totem poles. He devoted most of his working life to preserving the past by copying the best examples of earlier tribal totems before they were lost. As a teacher he trained successive generations of carvers such as the Hunts and Bill Reid, and did much to interpret his culture and its traditions to those interested in learning about them.

F.H. Varley *1881-1969* A painter, teacher and former member of the Group of Seven, he had such a powerful influence in the ten years he lived and worked in Vancouver that few of his students were able to shake off the dominance of his vision. He loved and painted the landscape with passionate intensity. His work, striking in its distinctive use of a luminous emerald green all his own, conveys an intense feeling for the inner meaning of the landscape.

John Vanderpant *1884-1939* A photojournalist, portraitist and active arts catalyst in the 1920s and 1930s. His European education and background gave him a wider cultural knowledge and experience than most. In his photography studio he exhibited the paintings of his Vancouver contemporaries and held musicales and discussions about modern art, life and culture with his fellow artists and students. His own work, his religious and artistic beliefs, and his practical support had an important influence on the Vancouver art world.

Lawren Harris *1885-1970* Painter, intellectual and theosophist, and a founding member of the Group of Seven, Harris was the single most influential, important and often controversial figure in this generation. He dominated the period of the 1940s and early 1950s in Vancouver with his broad experience, curiosity, ideas, energy and enthusiasm. With his rigorous critical standards and vital, assertive personality he was responsible for taking the Vancouver Art Gallery from a largely amateur to a fully professional institution.

Charles H. Scott *1886-1964* A painter but most important historically in his role as a teacher and administrator at the Vancouver School of Applied and Decorative Art. Like many of his contemporaries Scott was preoccupied with finding new and more effective ways of seeing and depicting the landscape to reveal the true essence that an earlier and more scenic style obscured in its fidelity to realistic detail. His own pictures are characterized by a very personal and expressive lyrical moodiness.

Paul Rand *1896-1970* A landscape painter and a commercial artist for most of his working life. His pictures have a strong and dramatic sense of regional identity and their own very distinctive clear and clean style. Rand wanted to make painting accessible to ordinary people, using recognizable images presented in an easily understood manner. He also painted people at work in a style reminiscent of the social realism of the Mexican muralists and other B.C. painters working in Vancouver.

J.W.G. Macdonald *1897-1960* He was originally a designer and teacher brought to Vancouver by C.H. Scott and encouraged by Scott and Varley to turn to painting. Again, like many of his contemporaries, Macdonald was very interested in and involved with discovering the spiritual values of the landscape and the power of revelation in their artistic depiction. He was unable to remain in B.C. but never lost his love for the landscape, particulary the mountainous area around Garibaldi Park.

Sybil Andrews *1898-1992* A color linocut artist, printmaker and teacher, she spent the first half of her life in Britain, the second in Campbell River. Her highly stylized work is characterized by its bold simplicity, dramatic clarity and vivid enthusiasm for the ordinary world of everyday life. She was interested in depicting the shapes, rhythms and patterns of people and machines at work, using the formal elements of early modern art in a very distinctive and personal manner.

THE SECOND GENERATION
(born before 1940)

Maxwell Bates *1906-1980* An architect and expressionist figurative painter, he was the central influence in a Calgary group of expressionist painters in the years after World War II. The last and most productive twenty years of his life were spent in Victoria painting brightly colored, witty and satirical comments on the ways of the world and human follies and pretensions. His sharp, ironic, irreverent, humorous, engaging and sometimes savage work expresses his largely pessimistic vision.

B.C. Binning *1909-1976* A painter, teacher and founder of the Fine Arts Department at UBC, he was as important for his influence as a teacher as for his work as a painter fully at ease with the mid-century move from representational to abstract art. Associated with the Art in Living movement of the 1940s and 1950s, his witty and good-humored early abstracts play with the forms and shapes of familiar objects; his later work is purely abstract.

Jack Shadbolt *1909-* A painter, a teacher for more than thirty years and the dominant figure in his generation as Emily Carr was in hers. He has been an active presence in the B.C. art world for more than sixty years, engaged on many different levels. His work is noted for the continual experimentation and exploration of themes, ideas and media as it has moved from social realism to abstraction, and for the imaginative and challenging use of native images and motifs.

E.J. Hughes *1913-* A "realistic" landscape painter with an inimitable style and distinctive vision of place pursued with single-minded determination for more than forty years. His subject matter is almost exclusively the southwest coastal area of B.C. His paintings explore and describe a seemingly fabled or mythic world along the edges where man and nature meet, depicted with a seemingly naive simplicity in crisp and telling detail of landscape and the human artifacts of boats, docks and houses.

John Koerner *1913-* A painter best known for his distinctive and spiritually resonant evocations of the landscape, which incorporate both man-made geometric forms and the rhythmic forms of nature in several series of paintings—most notably the *Pacific Gateway* and *Balcony* series. Cultivated and cosmopolitan in background and education, he has produced strong and sure work that at the same time conveys warmth, feeling, intelligence and philosophical serenity.

Gordon Smith *1919-* An abstract painter and teacher who turned to landscape, he described himself as concerned with paint and color rather than with recording place as such. The landscape is not so much described or defined as referred to, metaphorically as well as literally, in lyrical, painterly expressionist abstractions. His work, inward-looking, controlled, astringent, open in composition, using clear, lightly saturated colors, has been more literal as of late. Smith is the best known of the Vancouver abstract expressionists of his generation.

Bill Reid *1920-* The preeminent Haida artist of his generation, working within and sometimes innovatively adapting his people's traditional forms in several media. He was the first native artist to have a retrospective exhibition at the Vancouver Art Gallery. The Museum of Anthropology holds the world's largest collection of his work including the famous cedar sculpture *Raven and the First Men*. Reid has also been a teacher and very active spokesperson for B.C. native art and culture.

Elza Mayhew *1916-* An abstract sculptor, most of whose works—some huge and some small enough to smooth and caress in the palm of the hand—are cast in bronze. Her work has echoes of Greece and Egypt, the Orient, Central and Latin America, and the totemic poles of her native northwest coast. While consistently and clearly expressing a singularly personal, intimate and unmonumental vision, her sculptures display the sense of the sacred that is at the heart of her vision.

Henry Hunt *1923-* An artist of Tlingit ancestry who brought a distinctly northern influence to otherwise Kwakiutl designs and whose life and work exemplify the generational continuity of tradition in native art. He carried on the important totem preservation work of his father-in-law, Mungo Martin, at the Victoria Museum for some years and he has also done a prodigious amount of distinguished contemporary work of his own, both for the commercial art market and for traditional ceremonial use.

Toni Onley *1928-* A painter who began as an abstract collagist and then turned to the coastal landscape. His style and vision are as personal and immediately recognizable as Hughes' or Carr's. Retaining many of the abstract elements of his earlier work in moody visions of islands, mountains, cloud and mist, his spare but sensual images reveal a place whose texture is found in the expression of feelings rather than a precise or detailed depiction of any given locale.

Gathie Falk *1928-* A teacher, painter, sculptor, ceramicist and multimedia performance and installation artist, she is noted for the variety, versatility and imagination of her work, much of which makes us think hard about our relationship to ordinary things and places. She brings together the mundane and the bizarre in charming and usually provocative ways, making her own rules for her own work and remaining open to new ideas and new directions.

Alan Wood *1935-* A landscape painter, abstract expressionist, sculptor and installation artist whose work responds energetically to the toughness and physicality of the landscape by breaking it up and reassembling it in massive structures and concepts of a piece with the

place that generates them. His best work, the multidimensional *Ranch Project*, depicts the scale, texture and color of the western landscape and its related artifacts of buildings, tools and machinery in a 130-hectare walk-in art work.

THE THIRD GENERATION
(born before 1962)

Michael Morris *1942-* A painter, art activist, catalyst and rebel with international interests and contacts who invigorated the Vancouver art scene from the late Sixties through the Seventies. He was very involved in the Western Front, the Image Bank and Intermedia and the whole alternative avant-garde art culture that evolved as a protest against the art establishment of the commercial galleries and the "system." A ubiquitous, elegant and often outrageous figure.

Tony Hunt *1942-* A Kwakiutl carver and grandson of Mungo Martin who continued the totem preservation work of his father and grandfather at the Victoria Museum. He also opened the Arts of the Raven Gallery to facilitate the production and sale of quality northwest coast art and to train young artists in carving and design through the B.C. Indian Arts and Crafts Society. He continues to carve and is actively recording the history of the southern Kwakiutl tribal style.

Robert Davidson *1946-* A Haida carver, painter and printmaker, great-grandson of Charles Edenshaw and apprentice to Bill Reid. His *Eagle of the Dawn* was the second solo exhibition at the Vancouver Art Gallery by a native artist. Immersed in his culture and aware of the importance of sustaining and renewing the strength of its traditions, his work also explores innovative ways to transform and elaborate the conventions of Haida art to give them ongoing vitality and fresh meaning.

Jeff Wall *1946-* An artist, dramatist, cinematographer, filmmaker and storyteller best known for his back-lit Cibachrome transparencies of carefully composed, mannered and controlled dramatic scenes and disturbing narrative vignettes. These present sharp social criticism of our urban myths, illusions and our pretensions to civility and well-being, and are not simply a record of a landscape or a situation. His disturbing, subversive, sophisticated and challenging work is full of ironic references and allusions to classical art.

Roy Vickers *1946-* A native artist in the Tsimshian tradition who began as a commercial artist and who has become a leading wildlife painter and environmentalist. He takes traditional native designs, images and symbols and extends their range by combining them with European and native styles and Christian iconography to form a unique and very appealing personal style. His paintings and

scenes, and equally vivid and distinctive landscapes and still lifes with flowers, fruit, vegetables and objects found in her studio, reveal her
sharp intelligence, energy, passion and humor.
Her work is about place and paint, and is more
concerned with what she sees and depicts than
what it might mean. Her vibrant landscapes are
almost a return to the sources and preoccupa-
tions of the first generation of B.C. artists.

Jim Hart *1952-* A Haida artist and great-great-
grandson of Charles Edenshaw. He worked
with Robert Davidson on an Edenshaw memorial in Masset and spent four years in apprenticeship with Bill Reid. Since then he has worked in
many traditional forms but is best known for his
large carvings, including totems, a huge, elaborate carved and painted red cedar screen, old-
style Haida houses on Haida Gwaii and a
massive cedar sculpture of the creation of
the Frog Crest.

Julie Duschenes *1953-* A painter whose work,
largely still lifes and landscapes in a combination
of geometric abstraction and simplified representation, detaches and dislocates the viewer into a
new world by breaking down the conventions of
sight and response, making us reassess how and
what we see. Functional objects like plates and
bowls—the typical landscape of a table top after
a meal—normally taken for granted in their utilitarian state, become metaphorical structures in
her spare and telling depiction.

Paul Wong *1955-* A video and performance
artist interested in and obsessed by popular culture and the narcissism of the consumer society
in a world whose perceptions are dominated by
the electronic media. His work is immediate and
raw and yet carefully rehearsed and controlled in
every detail. He has been one of the most active
promoters and energizers of the video art form;
he challenges our understanding of a medium
that we take for granted more than any other.

Allan Storey *1960-* A sculptor, inventor, installation and mixed-media artist working mostly in
large and fanciful moving constructions, the best
known of which is the pendulum in Vancouver's
Hongkong Bank building. His work is playfully
serious and seriously playful. His comic machines
—toys or objects out of their expected places
and roles—exist in a machine-mad world where
they nevertheless function beautifully and gracefully in ceaseless motion, commenting whimsically on the wonders of our material and
technological world.

prints depict the powerful spiritual qualities of
the connection between the land and its
original peoples.

Richard Prince *1949-* A sculptor noted for his
visionary machines and equally visionary symbolic
landscapes, his work is full of charm, humor and
fantasy, mocking, celebrating and wondering in
the same breath. The world is managed by making it small and containing it in boxes that are
somehow more than the sum of their parts.
Many of his pieces either move with the wind or
express the idea of movement produced by the
wind, thereby giving form to the invisible.

Susan Point *1952-* A Coast Salish artist who
uses the form and meaning found in traditional
art to create innovative and original work in a
variety of mediums. Out of her study of the
motifs of traditional Coast Salish art she has
formulated a language of design that is both
authentic and contemporary. Her art displays
her distinctive personal style and the energy of
her commitment to integrate the two elements
of her work and continue the evolution of
native art.

Vicki Marshall *1952-* A painter whose vivid,
exuberant, expressionistic cityscapes and

above left: Alan Storey's pendulum,
Hong Kong Bank, 1988. vs

facing page: Gordon Smith in his studio, 1996. vs

Vancouver Art Gallery
Tony Robertson

THE VANCOUVER ART GALLERY is located in the heart of the Downtown core in the old Vancouver Provincial Courthouse, designed by Francis Rattenbury more than 90 years ago and renovated by noted architect Arthur Erickson in 1983. The gallery offers both historical and contemporary exhibitions of painting, sculpture, graphic arts, photography and video by distinguished regional, national and international artists. A portion of the permanent collection, which covers four centuries and includes works from two centuries of Canadian art as well as Dutch paintings from the 17th and 18th centuries and modern British paintings and sculpture from 1930-1955, is always on view, together with paintings and drawings by Emily Carr from the largest permanent collection of her work in Canada. Since 1983 the Vancouver Art Gallery has focused its acquisitions endowment on art from British Columbia since 1900 and on contemporary international art. There are regularly scheduled tours, lectures and family workshops. The gallery also contains a 25,000 volume (non-circulating) reference library, a restaurant and a gift and book shop.

The Vancouver Art Gallery opened for business at 3:00 P.M. on Monday, October 5, 1931 at its first home on Georgia Street. The city provided the land. The founders supplied the building and the art.

Led by businessman Henry Athelstan Stone and some like-minded friends with familiar Vancouver names like Malkin, Spencer, Rogers, Southam and Farrell, the founders deeded the building and its contents to the city for "the perpetual enjoyment of its citizens." The founders pledged $100,000 to buy the nucleus of a collection of the best of British art from the previous hundred years. This was to be balanced with the ongoing purchase of the best of contemporary Canadian art. It all seemed like a perfect prescription for what the *Vancouver Sun* had earlier described in an article on art and education as "the machinery of happiness."

Nothing is ever that simple and the Vancouver Art Gallery's history since that bright day has had at least its share of controversy and outright warfare. Enjoyment and the gallery often have been at odds in the minds and hearts of many people.

A year after the glorious founding Stone resigned in protest at the city's failure to provide needed operating funds. Around the same time critic J.A. Radford laid into the Canadian content. He denounced the painters in an exhibition of Canadian works as "prolific producers of artificialities, grotesque fantasies, gruesome hallucinations, morbid conceits and paranoiac monstrosities."

Those sentiments have since been echoed and elaborated many times as artists, gallery staff and the public have struggled with the perennial questions. What is art? What should it cost? Who should pay for it? Does a certain work belong in the Vancouver Art Gallery in the first place?

In 1938, for instance, the gallery board refused to buy an Emily Carr picture, priced at $400, because it wasn't art as they understood it. They were eventually persuaded it was and paid up. By 1983, when the gallery moved into the old courthouse, the Carr collection, grown mightily from that first purchase to include her 1942 donation of 145 paintings and sketches, and subsequent donations by patrons and further acquisitions, was showcased in a permanent exhibition in a large room on the main floor. Then-director Luke Rombout said, "I wanted the main floor to say something about ourselves. The best of what we stand for: city, province, people." The Emily Carr permanent exhibition has since moved to the third floor. And the old maid in the attic has lately come in for some critical, feminist and culturalist slagging, her once bright flame flickering and dimming a little.

Lawren Harris, a member of the Group of Seven and "an emphatic, modern and impatient spirit," liked Carr's work a lot and was instrumental in acquiring it for the gallery. Although never more than an appointed member of the VAG board, Harris was the dominant presence in the Vancouver art world for about ten important years as the gallery became a professional organization. Harris insisted on leaving amateurism and good intentions behind. Exacting critical standards and dedication to "only the best of regional art" were the rule. Doris Shadbolt began her long association with the gallery when she was hired to set up a public education program to encourage public taste to rise to meet the new standards.

There was some resistance to the new ideas about art and appreciation. Much of it centered around the annual and always controversial B.C. Artists' Exhibition, to which many submitted though few were chosen. Critic and painter of native portraits, Mildred Valley Thornton, and landscape painter Denton Burgess led an assault on Harris and curator J.A. Morris, accusing them of being a "modernist clique" who delighted in "thumbing down" representational art because it didn't suit their agenda.

Modernism, the definition depending on who had the floor in the debate, was definitely a problem for the gallery. The public did not come along on it as quickly or as far as the professionals. William Dale, the gallery's first formal director,

Cleaning the Art Gallery (former courthouse) lions, 1990. vp

announced in 1959 that there were only two or three works of art worth the name in the permanent collection and none of them were among the best of British art purchased by the founders, much as the public may have liked them. William Jarvis, a former National Gallery director, excepting Emily Carr, called the permanent collection "pitiful."

On the other side the Vancouver papers characterized the VAG as elitist, clique-ridden and riddled with dissension. The modern shows were keeping people away, resulting in the gallery's ongoing financial problems. The public might not have known much about art but they knew what they liked and they weren't getting it. VAG board president Aubrey Peck told a city council meeting in 1963 that there had been too much emphasis on art and not enough on business. He promised that the art of business would have something to say about the business of art in gallery affairs.

Vancouver caught up with the sixties late in the decade and not long after perhaps the greatest moment in the gallery's history—The Arts of the Raven: 450 Northwest Indian Masterworks exhibition, curated by then acting director Doris Shadbolt in 1967—brought the gallery international recognition and general attention to the most important art of the region. In that same year Tony Emery became director of the VAG and the sixties really arrived. He lasted seven years before being "non-renewed," proving the adage that you can tell the pioneers by the bullets in their backs.

The Emery years are thought of by many as the golden age of the Vancouver Art Gallery. They were lively and interesting years, and probably neither as wonderful nor as terrible as many remember them being. Emery's ideas about the gallery were close to what the founders had imagined themselves creating—a vital public centre of art and education, the visibly turning cogs and wheels of the machinery of happiness at work.

The VAG became Canada's most active community arts centre. Art, music, theatre, dance and that sixties thing, the Happening, went on day and night. Mother Tucker's Yellow Duck,

the Anna Wyman Dance Company and John Juliani's Savage God Theatre, among many others, played the gallery. There were satellite galleries at the racetrack and Capilano Stadium to spread the joy around town. Established artists like Jack Chambers and Christopher Pratt had major exhibitions, and there was a Jack Shadbolt retrospective covering 30 years of his work. Doris Shadbolt organized The Sculpture of the Inuit exhibition with an impact similar to her Arts of the Raven show.

But critics on and off the board argued that there was too much Op and Pop going on at the VAG. Membership was down and the people with money and art to donate were withholding both in unprecedented quantities. What was needed was a return to the visual arts and a new building. The old and original premises had expanded once already in 1951. True to gallery tradition, there was controversy over eviction of tenants from buildings demolished to make more space for the gallery. The tenants' supporters argued that human beings were more important than "a bunch of old paintings."

After an immensely successful fundraising campaign to "take the art gallery to court"—$8 million raised, twice the intended target and more than any other arts organization had ever raised in the city—the new Vancouver Art Gallery opened on October 15, 1983, in Arthur Erickson's renovation of Francis Rattenbury's 1912 courthouse. Four blocks east of the original site and 52 years after the founding, the Vancouver Art Gallery at last stood right in the heart of the heart of the city. There was money in the bank and pictures on the walls. Emily Carr was there on the main floor; the Masterworks from the National Gallery exhibition was there; and the Vancouver Art and Artists 1931-1983 exhibit was there too.

But anyone familiar enough with the gallery to harken back to the great days of the annual B.C. Artist's Exhibition would have known that the blush would soon be off the rose.

Masterworks from anywhere are mostly above and beyond reproach and those were the days when Emily Carr was still sacrosanct. But not so Vancouver Art and Artists 1931-1983. The ends of the ribbon cut by Governor General Ed Schreyer to open the new gallery had scarcely hit the floor before charges of elitism and modernism and denial of representationalism were once again flying around. What else could something like *Reindeer Discipline,* which offered Santa Claus holding an ax and some bloody reindeer parts, demonstrate but that the VAG was biased in favor of modernism? Lots of people, many but not all of them B.C. artists whose work hadn't been accepted for the show, took exception to much of the work exhibited. And while it was one thing for an artist to be excluded from the old gallery, it was a much sharper and seemingly more discriminatory cut not to be seen by so many more people at the new place.

Still and all the new era began pretty well. Gallery membership was at an all-time high and the VAG was a presence in the city in a way it had not been for some time.

But only a few months later, director Luke Rombout cancelled an exhibition titled *Confused/Sexual Views* by video artist Paul Wong. It consisted of 27 people having frank sexual conversations on video. Rombout denied "aesthetic merit" to the show. Critics claimed he was too concerned about the sensibilities of the 20,000 VAG members. Others wondered if the exhibition was art and where the VAG was going. Paul Wong charged censorship and literally took the gallery to court. The various cases went on for several years before Wong's charge was eventually dismissed as "vexatious and frivolous."

Then there was all that money that had been raised. There was so much left over that the city was able to take $4 million and put it into an acquisitions endowment fund. This gave the VAG the largest dedicated endowment budget of any gallery in the country and a wonderful new source of potential controversy. Who was going to get the money? And, more importantly, who was not? And what would they have to say and do about it?

At the same time the gallery cost much to operate and the ongoing funding from all three levels of government was either being frozen, decreased or realigned. Some shows were cancelled and some drew meager audiences. Critics and commentators wondered aloud about direction or the lack of it as curators came and went and directors resigned. The VAG seemed at cross-purposes with itself, confused, confounded, frustrated and just barely ahead of its operating deficits.

Local artists increased their demands for space on the walls and on the board, gaining a little but never enough. If there ever had been a truly collective artistic voice in the community, it was now increasingly fragmented, its various elements equally vociferous but mutually contradictory.

For a while what went on outside of the gallery often appeared to be more lively and significant than inside. The south stairs facing onto Robson Street and the plaza on Georgia Street, with its lawns and fountain, became very much public spaces and centres for rallies and demonstrations for causes of all sorts. The area has a centrality and "feel" the old building never had. This has helped to connect what is happening inside the gallery to what is happening outside, although the building's somewhat formidable exterior implies a distinct separation between the two.

And there were still the artists and critics who kept on pointing out that there was very much an inside and an outside, and that the rules of admission were rigged. The "innies" got everything and the "outies" looked on enviously. One art teacher described the gallery as "a restaurant of visual malnutrition," and said the permanent collection was "no good." Critic Jill Pollack wrote that the VAG "still doesn't seem to know whether it's leading or following" as it headed into the nineties. Artists criticized the number of exhibitions being given to artists who had served on the board and there were louder allegations of favoritism and insider trading. Doubt was cast on the artistic meritocracy supposedly driving exhibition policy.

Public funding from all levels of government became still more problematic leading to ongoing financial crises of varying intensity. This led a prominent collector and former board member, Ian Davidson, to ask artists on the board to make way for fund-raisers and to call for more "popular" shows. Others countered that the VAG's exhibition policy played it too safe and wasn't cutting edge enough. Director Willard Holmes said that a "populist fix" might cast doubt on the gallery's long term stability and credibility in the larger artistic community.

Artist Toni Onley, a member of the VAG acquisitions committee, charged that quality local art was being ignored by the committee. He said that "none of its purchased works would be accepted as art outside the narrow context of extreme avant garde galleries, museums and aficionados."

Other Vancouver artists decried the intellectualization trend in which "academics suck out art's emotional guts." Onley resigned from the board saying, among other things, that if too few people go to the VAG its operational polices and programming needed to be fairly re-evaluated. He accused the gallery of lacking "any sense of responsibility to the people of Vancouver now and in the future." The acquisitions committee operated with a "KGB-like secrecy," he said.

At about the same time, a group called the Artist's Coalition for Local Color picketed the opening of a show called Fabled Territories, consisting of photography by a dozen south Asian artists living in Britain. The picket protested VAG manipulation of discourse by people of color and the delay of much-needed changes in the gallery's exclusionary policies. The ACLC called for two people of color on every VAG committee and two on the board itself.

The gallery did point with pride to a highly successful 1993 show of the work of native artist Robert Davidson. Critics replied that it was only the second VAG retrospective of the work of a native artist, Bill Reid being the first with a show

facing page: Jack Shadbolt, 1994. vs

Our grand hotel places the financial and business districts within easy reach. (And the Vancouver Art Gallery is right next door.) The city's finest shopping and dining, and unforgettable attractions are all very close. Below the hotel, more than 200 fine shops and services in Pacific Centre await you. In the heart of a spectacular and vibrant city, Four Seasons, Vancouver.

organized several years before by Doris Shadbolt, and that there were lots of other native artists around whose work merited an exposure they weren't getting from the VAG.

The 1993 annual meeting was an almost perfect microcosm of the VAG's history and the continuing travails of public art in Vancouver. It was Willard Holmes' last meeting as director, after serving for five years, and J. Brooks Joyner's first meeting as the incoming director. The presiding spirits could easily have been those of the late Mildred Valley Thornton and her allies past and present in the struggle against modernism on the one side, and Lawren Harris and his modernist associates past and present on the other. Not much had changed in 50 years.

On the one hand was artist Ed Varney, spokesperson for a group called Friends of the Vancouver Art Gallery. The group had a slate of candidates for the board and a series of motions accusing the VAG of "ignoring parts of the local art community, especially women and minority artists," and of spending exorbitant sums on the works of others, notably photo-based artists such as Jeff Wall and Ian Wallace. Varney said that the VAG was seen as "a fossilized institution." He wanted to see the gallery become "more inclusive and less cliquey."

On the other hand was Holmes who, in his final report, warned of those who would turn the VAG into "a sandbox of a local culture or a regional culture or a national culture." The gallery was being pressured to "relinquish its international significance and high standards" in favor of "something that might be more comfortable or recognizable." Holmes did not think this was a good thing. The VAG, he said, "was the only game in town" in its ability to "validate artists' work critically and support it financially. Some artists are disappointed when they don't get the support they think they deserve."

And on yet another hand was the new director, J. Brooks Joyner, who may possibly see the VAG through the rest of the century.

Joyner described himself as a consensus-builder and said that local artists will have a place in that process. "The relationship between the gallery and the community can and should evolve into something that is mutually beneficial." He knew that the local art community "would like to see more local artists, more women, more marginalized [read aboriginal, gay, Asian etc.] artists and more young artists represented at the gallery." He believed that this could be done "without compromising the professionalism or the integrity of the museum." Joyner would "like the artists in this community to look on the Vancouver Art Gallery with respect and pride."

In the year or so since that bright beginning gallery operations have delivered a modest surplus and a balanced budget,

and the once very lively dissidents have been lying lowish. Some people are still asking what the VAG is really for, why it doesn't seem to be for the things they think it should be for and why it doesn't show as many women artists as it could if it really wanted to. The new five-year plan for the gallery delivered in 1995 contains no stunning prospects, with the possible exception of trying to find a way to use the imposing Georgia Street entrance. There wasn't even a suggestion of some radical programming to liven the place up, although a new chief curator and artistic stirrer-upper was more or less promised by late 1996. Perhaps a good start would be to find a way to harness the "unexplained energy force" which periodically manifests itself in the building. This is thought to be the spirit of William Charles Hopkinson, an immigration officer murdered in the old courthouse in 1914. He, or it, seems to demonstrate at least some of the vitality required of a chief curator, now and into the new millennium.

In the meantime B.C. artists remain generally frustrated by what they see as VAG indifference to their work. And while the gallery has identified 20 contemporary B.C. artists—establishing off-the-top a long exclusionary list of artists who will probably take issue with the choices made—at least some of whom it wants to show in a 1996 survey exhibition, director Joyner cautioned that the gallery "is not just an exhibition centre. As a museum/gallery, we have to produce something that has substance to it."

The recent Andy Warhol exhibition, of artistic substance or otherwise, did very well at the gate and that factor will continue to be a very important consideration at the VAG. After all, the cogs and wheels of the "machinery of happiness" are oiled and driven by money as well as art.

The VAG is open Monday through Saturday, 10:00 A.M. until 5:00 P.M. and on Sundays from noon until 5:00 P.M. On Thursdays the doors remain open until 9:00 P.M. Between October 1 and May 31 the gallery is closed on Tuesdays. Children under 12 enter for free when accompanied by an adult. On Thursday nights admission is pay-what-you-can. The Gallery Shop and Gallery Cafe are open daily.

POSTSCRIPT: OCTOBER 1996

J. Brooks Joyner has been replaced as director of the VAG by Alf Bogusky, late of the Edmonton Art Gallery. In many ways the history of the VAG suggests that, in the broadest sense, the more things change the more they stay the same. Whatever individual touches he brings to the direction of the Vancouver Art Gallery, Mr. Bogusky's problems and potential solutions will likely be much the same as those of his predecessors.

Museums
Kerry McPhedran

MUSEUM OF ANTHROPOLOGY
6393 Northwest Marine Drive, Vancouver

Queen Elizabeth II and Prince Charles have visited. So have Queen Silvia of Sweden, Boris Yeltsin, Bill Clinton and Pierre Elliot Trudeau. This year another 170,000 visitors from around the world will show up to visit the museum that was designated "Tourist Attraction of the Year—Canada" in 1989.

Year after year MOA remains one of Vancouver's and Canada's best-loved museums on the basis of its award-winning Arthur Erickson building, one of the world's finest collections of northwest coast First Nations art and active programming (over 100 events a year) that has effectively mixed clowns with totem poles.

Most museums display less than five per cent of their collections. As a research museum MOA pioneered open storage that would make over 50 per cent of their objects available to visitors. MOA's visible storage galleries allow it to show more of its collection to the public than any major museum in Canada.

And MOA's got the goodies to show—30,000 cultural objects and 200,000 archaeological specimens. Almost half originated with First Nations but MOA has other surprising areas of excellence, including one of the oldest and largest collections of Cantonese opera costumes. A data base provides detailed information on the exhibits. Visitors, who once grumbled about the minimalist approach to labelling specimens, are now offered a free guide to the various galleries.

MOA was a pioneer in both visible storage and the use of natural light. The Great Hall that houses the great totem poles is almost all glass. Both innovations, now widely copied, were controversial at first.

The University of British Columbia had been collecting ethnographic material since 1927. MOA was founded in 1947 to preserve and display existing material, while continuing to collect archaeological and ethnographic artifacts from British Columbia and the rest of the world. For almost 50 years the collection remained in the basement of the Main Library, directed and curated by Dr. Harry Hawthorn and Audrey Hawthorn.

In 1976 the collection came out of the basement and moved into its 6,500-square-metre home on the bluffs of Point Grey overlooking Howe Sound and the mountains. The new director, Dr. Michael Ames, a professor in the department of anthropology and sociology, was appointed in time to play a role in the building's final design, to the benefit of

all. Inspired by yet another centennial (B.C.'s 1871 entry into confederation), Erickson's award-winning concrete-and-glass structure is based on the post-and-beam houses of northwest coast First Nations. It leaked, but would anyone have traded that form for better function?

The outdoor Haida House complex created in 1962 includes a large 19th-century family dwelling and a smaller mortuary house that would have been present in a 19th-century Haida village, as well as ten poles. The works of some of the finest contemporary First Nations artists of the northwest coast are here—Bill Reid, Douglas Cranmer, Norman Tait, Walter Harris, Joe David, Jim Hart and the late Mungo Martin.

The museum also has the world's largest collection of works by Haida artist Bill Reid, whose famous sculpture, *The Raven and the First Man,* was commissioned by Walter and Marianne Koerner. Carved from a four-tonne block of yellow cedar formed from 106 beams, it was unveiled by Prince Charles in 1980. Haida people brought the sand at the base of the sculpture from the beach where the trickster raven is said to have made his discovery of the first humans, huddled in a clam shell. The equally entrancing boxwood prototype, small enough to fit snugly into a person's hand, is now in a permanent display of Reid's smaller work.

In 1990 MOA received 600 pieces of rare European ceramics collected by Dr. Walter C. Koerner over 80 years, making MOA a unique ceramic resource in Canada. Now displayed in a new wing, the tranquil Koerner Ceramics Gallery remains one of Vancouver's best kept secrets. (MOA might well be called The Koerner Museum. The Koerners' 1975 gift of their extensive Northwest Coast art collection was instrumental in getting government support for MOA's building.)

As the largest teaching museum in Canada, MOA also offers special training programs and internships for First Nations peoples. Through the Native Youth Program, high school students learn to act as cultural interpreters for museum visitors. The Aboriginal Cultural Stewardship Program trains communities to manage and/or develop their own cultural and interpretive centres.

Some of the more provocative exhibits are temporary shows curated by museum students. But most visitors are stunned by the great achievements of the First Nations of the northwest coast, of whom 100,000 now live in British Columbia. "This is the true beauty of Canada," wrote one Tokyo visitor, "Not its advertised 'supernatural' hype." Ouch!

VANCOUVER MUSEUM
1100 Chestnut Street, Vancouver

Where to begin? Vancouver's oldest museum has much to be proud of since its founding on

April 17, 1894. There are now 100,000 objects packed away in the 1,000 square metres or so of vault space at Kits Point. There are 5,500 toy soldiers in the Cecil Akrigg Collection. There are some 250 dolls; Cantonese opera figures from the late 18th century; impressive northwest coast Indian regalia; one million uncatalogued seashells in the Newton Drier Collection; forty local neon signs (Vancouver once claimed more neon footage per capita than any other city in the world).

This permanent collection is now the largest administered and interpreted collection of any civic museum in Canada. Large and small exhibits of international quality have been produced. Yet last year, more Vancouverites made the trek to Victoria to see the Genghis Khan exhibition at the Royal B.C. Museum than went to the Vancouver Museum.

Since moving from the former Carnegie Library building at Main and Hastings to its present custom-built quarters in Vanier Park in 1967, the civic museum has been bedeviled with operational problems.

Ironically the culmination came in a six-month-long strike protesting a 65 per cent layoff of staff, that drastically cut attendance to 100 Years, A Million Stories, a new exhibition celebrating the museum's 100th anniversary. When the dust settled, 65 per cent of the staff was still laid off, the education school program was cancelled and 120 docents were gone. There was even discussion about renting out or selling parts of the collection.

The bitter wrangling went on for two years. An independent report concluded that the museum was an "institution in crisis," and recommended the director be "let go." Cultural institutions rallied, urging the city to save the museum. In February, 1996, the city announced that the museum association was to revert to its original form as a volunteer-support organization. A five-member appointed commission would take over the operation of the exhausted museum.

Poor H.J. De Forest, the first curator of the Arts, Historical and Scientific Association from 1894 to 1911, must be spinning in his grave. An artist, De Forest worked "for love of the museum and a pittance somewhere between $25 and $75 per month as funds permitted."

The 1982 exhibition Cabinets of Curiosities captured the spirit and history of that earlier museum, where collections had grown "somewhat randomly." The result was both fascinating and eclectic. Vancouverites loved the hodge-podge.

The exhibition offered up a nostalgic selection from the very first donation—a stuffed white swan —to First Nations poet Pauline Johnson's performance costume and the beloved Egyptian mummy, displayed for 30 years as "Diana" until X-rays in 1951 proved "Diana" was really a ten-year-old

Award–winning architecture; Museum of Anthropology, 1994. vs

boy. "If you put out the mummy, they will come," could well be any museum's mission statement.

The museum always collected actively. Regular purchasing began in 1898; early buys included West Coast First Nations artifacts and Japanese sword guards. In the early 1900s, active association supporter and anthropologist Charles Hill-Tout sparked important digs at the great Marpole midden, adding hundreds of artifacts.

When the library moved from Main and Hastings to new quarters on Burrard Street in 1957, the museum happily moved into the old Carnegie building. By 1958 the museum, along with the Maritime Museum, had become a city department under the control of a civic museum board with the association represented on the board.

The collections were still treated as one unit. In 1967 the re-named Centennial Museum, re-housed in the first building designed and built for it, created four curatorial departments: archaeology, ethnology, history and natural history. By 1979 the focus was clearly on the Lower Mainland and its heritage. A new department, Decorative and Applied Arts, produced The Look of Music, the most ambitious exhibit to date.

But it was 100 Years, A Million Stories that plucked the heartstrings of those few who saw it. Unlike the Cabinets of Curiosities, concentration was on the stories connected with artifacts. Curator Al Bowen's rules were simple. He selected one item received by the museum in each year since its founding. The items had to be unique or unusual and accompanied by an interesting story—like the wolf eel, eaten only by shamans of the Queen Charlotte Islands; or the passenger pigeon (last sighted in Langley in 1859). Vancouver's first gas pump and Louis Riel's rifle were on display. Easy to say. It took Bowen almost two years to make his selections. The exhibition showed us our own history. It was great stuff; more's the pity it was seen by so few.

VANCOUVER MARITIME MUSEUM
1905 Ogden Avenue, Vancouver.

Fittingly housed in a building that's far enough below the waterline to require a pump, the Maritime Museum specializes in unbelievable true stories, with an emphasis on Burrard Inlet and coastal B.C. Its finest hour with respect to attendance? The temporary exhibit focussing on the *Titanic*. The museum had its genesis in a local movement to preserve and restore the *St. Roch*, which was built by Burrard Shipyard in North Vancouver in 1928 as the RCMP's floating detachment and Arctic base. The sturdy auxiliary schooner and her ten-man crew, the first to make the Northwest Passage both ways (1940-

42 and 1944), became a national historic site, frozen in time, complete with howling wind and husky sounds (Inuit guides' teams), jaunty 1940s tunes and the smell of crew members' socks soaking in their cramped quarters. It has been in dry-dock since the museum was built in 1958 as a B.C. centennial project. Parks Canada handed over control of this tourist draw in the fall of 1995.

The museum holds a large model collection, a reference library of books, photographs and documents as well as maritime artifacts. Choice items include: track charts made during Captain James Cook's third voyage of exploration and a chronometer used by Captain George Vancouver while he charted this coast in the 1790s. The slightly oversize replicated forecastle of his good ship *Discovery* is permanently on exhibit.

The tugboat wheelhouse replica in the children's step-aboard Maritime Discovery Centre is as close as you can get to the real thing, right down to the hum of the engine, buzz of the radio and rumble of the floor. The museum also maintains a heritage harbor which serves as a base for vintage vessels, mostly privately owned. The historic steam tug *Master* docks every summer and B.C.'s oldest sailing vessel, *Maple Leaf*, joins the harbor community every winter.

Community Museums
Kerry McPhedran

Greater Vancouver is bursting with museums, interpretive centres and heritage sites. Artifacts range from road kills to 18th-century lingerie. Some reflect private passions; others are civic institutions with international reputations. Most are community museums, from Anmore to West Vancouver. (In Canada community museums account for 35 per cent of all museums—the largest single group of museums.) There's a shift away from the "attic" approach. New professionals—some products of Canada's largest teaching museum, the Museum of Anthropology—are looking for creative solutions as traditional funding is cut. Here's a sampling of who's looking after our past and looking out for our future.

ANMORE MUSEUM
2697 Sunnyside Road, Anmore
Housed in the former home of feisty homesteader and newspaper woman Margaret "Ma" Murray.

B.C. FARM MACHINERY AND
AGRICULTURAL MUSEUM
9131 King, Fort Langley
A two-headed stuffed calf and the first double-wing crop-dusting plane (1941 Tiger Moth) are big draws in this collection, circa 1830-1960. Check out historical methods of beekeeping and dairy production. On Mondays, staff and volunteers restore and operate machines.

B.C. GOLF MUSEUM
2545 Blanca, Vancouver
The original 1931 UBC golf clubhouse houses Canada's only provincial golf museum. Classic clubs, old trophies and prints from early days of golf. Library and archives (1,200 books and 100 volumes of clippings and photos). Video footage of great B.C. golf moments, including Ben Hogan in 1967 Masters. Nifty gift shop.

B.C. MUSEUM OF MEDICINE
1665 West Broadway, Vancouver
Some 1,500 historic medical artifacts, most of which relate to private practice in B.C., plus some ethnographic material.

B.C. MUSEUM OF MINING
Britannia Beach
Originally a small museum on leased land in 1975, the B.C. Museum of Mining has grown into a national historic site and B.C. historic landmark. Britannia Copper Mine was the largest copper producer in the British Empire from 1930-1935. The museum has expanded to cover building restoration (22 mine buildings) and land management programs. Guided underground tours that include demonstrations of diamond drilling give you new respect for the "men of the deep."

B.C. SPORTS HALL OF FAME AND MUSEUM
B.C. Place Stadium, 777 Pacific Boulevard
South, Vancouver
Go for the gold! Hands-on experience where visitors can literally spring, row, climb and throw, or "time travel" through the history of sport in B.C. and learn more about local heroes such as Rick Hansen and Terry Fox.

B.C. SUGAR MUSEUM
123 Rogers Street, Vancouver
Benjamin Tingley Rogers made enough money from his sugar refinery (built in 1891) to build his elegant West End "Gabriola" mansion. Sugar-making equipment on display dates back to 1715, but the sweetest treat is a tour of the raw sugar sheds capable of holding 18,000 tonnes when full.

BEATLES MUSEUM
203-525 Seymour Street, Vancouver
Original Beatles' paraphernalia, from wallpaper to posters, draws Fab Four fans to this by-appointment-only collection that's also for sale. Around $100 will buy you an original 45 "flexi" recording of the Beatles press conference held in Vancouver.

BIBLICAL MUSEUM OF CANADA
5800 University Boulevard, Regent
College, Vancouver
Michelangelo, Dürer and Rembrandt are here, depicting great biblical events, along with a LANDSAT 5 Satellite view of the Holy Land. Educational focus is on "humanity's search for meaning throughout history, from the stone-age to the space-age."

BRITANNIA HERITAGE SHIPYARD
3811 Moncton Street, Steveston
Now a national historic site, the oldest remaining shipyard on the Fraser features nine restored buildings. Britannia in its glory days was both cannery (1889) and boat repair facility (1919). The *Silver Ann,* the last vessel built at the site, rolled down the ways in 1968. Japanese-Canadians (and their internment) are part of the story. The three-room Murakami house was home to the 11-member family that built two boats each winter. Visitors can stroll the boardwalk, help build traditional Fraser River skiffs or watch old Steveston hands pass on skills through an apprentice program.

BURNABY VILLAGE MUSEUM
6501 Deer Lake Avenue, Burnaby
Once an Indian encampment, this living museum is a throwback to the Burnaby tram stop town- site of a century ago, complete with costumed school marm, town printer, blacksmith and Chinese herbalist who double as interpreters. Kids of all ages get a kick out of ordering sarsaparilla at the ice cream parlor and squeezing into small school desks. Includes a general store, pharmacy, steam sawmills, tram and church.

CANADIAN CRAFT MUSEUM
639 Hornby Street, Vancouver
A "bonus" spin-off from Cathedral Place, this architectural delight is just off Hornby. Readers of *Vancouver Magazine* voted the museum shop "best gift shop." Shows by Canada's master artisans range from erotic jewelry to knitted symbols of Vancouver.

CANADIAN LACROSSE HALL OF FAME
65 East 6th Avenue, New Westminster
Canada's national summer sport is "the fastest game on two feet," as New Westminster's Salmonbellies can attest. Trophies, jerseys, equipment and the scoop on its inductees.

CANADIAN MUSEUM OF FLIGHT AND TRANS-
PORTATION
Hangar 3, 5333-216th Street, Langley
Airport
After years in Crescent Beach, it now has a hangar of its own. Volunteers don't come much more enthusiastic than those who have donated, restored and even flown "artifacts" in from across Canada. On the tarmac and indoors: everything from homebuilts and World War II trainers to the TF-104 that reached twice the speed of sound.

DELTA MUSEUM AND ARCHIVES
4858 Delta, Ladner
1912 Tudor-style former municipal hall and jail. The six furnished Victorian rooms are fun, but the "real" Ladner is downstairs with True Haviland Oliver, "painter, builder and renowned Canada Goose Hunter," and his trusty bicycle. Good, affordable First Nations art in the gift shop.

FORT LANGLEY NATIONAL HISTORIC SITE
23433 Mavis Avenue, Fort Langley
Fort Langley's population of Scots, French-Canadians, Metis and Indians moved, lock, stock and barrel to the current living museum location in 1939 to be closer to its farm. It was built by the Hudson's Bay Company in 1827 as a supplier for inland forts and a deterrent to pushy Americans trading along the coast. Briefly, in 1858, Fort Langley was the government capital for the mainland.

GULF OF GEORGIA CANNERY MUSEUM
12138-4th Avenue, Steveston
A new 40-seat Boiler House Theatre uses multimedia to tell the story of the "monster cannery" here in the sockeye capital of the world. The best parts of the 1894 cannery-turned-historic-site (designated 1994) are the herring reduction equipment—used to press herrings from 1940 to 1979—and the net-making demonstrations.

IRVING HOUSE HISTORIC CENTRE / NEW WESTMINSTER MUSEUM / ARCHIVES
302 Royal, New Westminster

". . . the handsomest, the best and most home-like house of which British Columbia can yet boast" was how the *British Columbian* newspaper described Captain William Irving's new home—located high on the hill in New Westminster and boasting a cornice shaped like a ship's hawser—in April, 1865. Tucked behind Irving House, the New Westminster Museum is loaded with the history of Canada's oldest city west of the Great Lakes, including the Royal Engineers' china teacups! Lots of programs, from cemetery tours to the November 23 "Bullet Hole Re-enactment" are available.

LANGLEY CENTENNIAL MUSEUM AND NATIONAL EXHIBITION CENTRE
9135 King Street, Fort Langley

As a National Exhibition Centre, Langley Centennial Museum qualifies for major travelling exhibitions from the likes of the Canadian Museum of Civilization. Scenes from pioneer living are what you'd expect. Unexpected: wonderful collection of First Nations artifacts and a partial replica of a Coast Salish house.

MUSEUM OF EXOTIC WORLDS
3561 Main Street, Vancouver

Not your average museum. Harold and Barbara Morgan invite visitors into their turquoise building to take a gander at their strange and wonderful memorabilia and photos of trips to 45 count- ries. Tapes of fighting baboons are gone ("they slowed people up") but a 12-centimetre-long insect labelled "Your Guess is as Good as Mine" is still there. Best of all are Harold's stories.

NORTH VANCOUVER MUSEUM AND ARCHIVES
333 Chesterfield, North Vancouver

The Lower Mainland's first museum was in Moodyville. When the mill closed in the 1870s the collection was "dispersed." North Vancouver Museum and Archives picked up the ball in 1972. Outstanding early photos and changing exhibits of lively social and industrial life, including shipyards that fitted out 70 per cent of World War II Victory ships. Largest artifact: PGE railway station, moved near to its original location in lower Lonsdale in summer of 1996.

OLD HASTINGS MILL STORE MUSEUM
1575 Alma Street, Vancouver

Vancouver's oldest building was one of few to escape the fire of 1886. Built in 1865 to serve the settlement at Vancouver's first mill, it was barged over from Centennial Pier in 1930 to Pioneer Park. Volunteers from the Native Daughters of B.C. operate the museum and annual fall bazaar and spring tea.

PACIFIC SPACE CENTRE
1100 Chestnut Street, Vancouver

The epitome of planetariums when it opened in 1968, the H.R. MacMillan Planetarium (funded by Vancouver's lumber baron) re-invents itself in the summer of 1997 as the $9 million Pacific Space Centre. Visitors can morph themselves into aliens, ride the Cosmic Simulator and check out GroundStation Canada, an experimental theatre. Still home to Canada's premier laser light shows and the place to call with UFO sightings. Gordon MacMillan Southam Observatory (in memory of H.R.'s grandson) invites photographers to "Shoot the Moon" through an enormous half-metre Cassegrain telescope.

RICHMOND MUSEUM
280-7700 Minoru Gate, Richmond

This is L.A.A.M.A. land! The library, archives, arts centre, museum and art gallery all housed at Richmond's Library/Cultural Centre joined forces to develop programs that fit well with this new breed of community museum. Emphasis is on changing exhibits, programs and research projects. "We're not just about the 'olden' days" says curator/director Lana Panko. "Everything we do has to relate to where we are today."

ROEDDE HOUSE PRESERVATION SOCIETY
1415 Barclay, Vancouver

Vancouver's first bookbinder Gustav Anton Roedde has two reasons to be proud. G.A. Roedde Bookbinder, Stationer and Printer survives today as B.C.'s eighth oldest business. And his modest 1893 West End home, attributed to family friend and renowned architect Francis Mawson Rattenbury, is Vancouver's first restored house-museum. Fully restored down to the wallpaper, Roedde House is the cornerstone of Barclay Heritage Square—the Vancouver Park Board's unique collection of nine homes. You can rent Mr. Roedde's house, complete with 1893 Steinway, exuberant Queen Anne tower and porch, for your very own private party.

ROYAL WESTMINSTER REGIMENT MUSEUM
530 Queens Avenue, New Westminster

The 100-year-old wooden armory alone is worth the trip. The museum, housed in the old gun room, traces the proud history of B.C.'s oldest regiment back to the red-jacketed Royal Engineers who laid out New Westminster in the 1860s. Among the nifty exhibits: scale diorama of World War II vehicles; ceremonial War World I snare drums and a memorial to Trooper Timlick, the only volunteer of 29 not to return from the Boer War.

SAMSON V MARITIME MUSEUM
Westminster Quay, New Westminster

Museum sinkings, other than fiscal, are rare. But late in 1995 the *Samson V*, permanently moored since 1983 as New Westminster's own show boat of river history, went glub-glub in the Fraser. Resurrected before she went under completely, the last steam-powered paddle wheeler to operate on the Fraser River is now better than ever.

SCIENCE WORLD
1455 Quebec Street, Vancouver

Vancouver's most hands-on exhibits are housed in the geodesic dome built as an Expo 86 theme pavilion that housed Omnimax, then the world's largest dome screen. (There are now two the same size, in Paris and New Jersey). Most popular exhibit: Search Gallery, a treasure trove of natural history with a walk-in cedar tree, crawl-in beaver dam, human skeletons and road-kill critters. A 3-D laser theatre opened November 25, 1995.

STEVESTON MUSEUM
3811 Moncton, Richmond

A visitor left a note that he felt "definite vibrations" of ghosts in this 1905 heritage building. An early pre-fab built in four-foot sections in New Westminster for the Northern Bank, Richmond's first. Ground floor now houses a working post office alongside the original bank manager's office.

SURREY MUSEUM AND ARCHIVES
6022-176th Street, Surrey

B.C.'s third largest community history museum houses Surrey's oldest public building, the small 1881 municipal hall. Exhibits emphasize early business and homelife in the 1900s and 1920s. Northwest coast materials include Coast Salish archaeological finds and fine basketry. The museum operates Stewart Farm, an 1890s heritage homestead on the banks of the Nicomekl River.

VANCOUVER HOLOCAUST EDUCATION CENTRE
50-950 West 41st Avenue, Vancouver

B.C. survivors of the Holocaust created this teaching museum, with a Yizkor Buch (memory book) collection, as a legacy devoted to Holocaust-based anti-racism programs. Many have recorded eye-witness testimonials since the November, 1994, opening. Among the heroes celebrated in changing exhibits: a Japanese diplomat in Lithuania in 1939 who defied orders, issuing visas that saved the lives of many Jews.

VANCOUVER POLICE CENTENNIAL MUSEUM
240 East Cordova, Vancouver

Kids would give this museum their highest praise: "Gross!" Not for the faint of heart, but fascinating, from wanted posters to forensic pathology exhibit of a preserved larynx fractured by a fatal karate chop. Housed in the old Coroner's Court Building, the museum was created in 1986 to commemorate the centennial of the city's police force. You can view the old morgue and autopsy room where actor Errol Flynn ended up in 1959. Also, see the crime scene re-creation of "Babes in the Woods," a 1953 murder still unsolved.

Former PNE carousel, preserved at Burnaby Village Museum, 1993. vs

WEST VANCOUVER MUSEUM AND ARCHIVES
680-17th Street, West Vancouver
With over 500 members in the West Vancouver Historical Society, there are more members than there are artifacts housed in the Gertrude Lawson heritage house. That's because this innovative new community museum which opened July 1, 1994, is determined to "actively collect [through a data base], but not own" artifacts. West Vancouverites are encouraged to

keep heirlooms, lending as needed. Curator Jacqueline Gijssen sees the museum not as a community attic, but a cultural facilitator. All exhibits are temporary and 90 per cent of artifacts are borrowed. Ethnic communities are encouraged to tell their own stories. Until she died in 1989, Gertrude Lawson rented out apartments in her beautiful stone house (built in 1939 from stones used as ships' ballast) to "young women in need."

Commercial Galleries
Tony Robertson

For art and artists to survive art must be seen and bought by ordinary individuals as well as public galleries, museums, private collectors and corporations. The best place to do this is in commercial art galleries. Their place in the art world is often criticized and sometimes condemned. They are necessary to the survival of art and of artists who hope to make any kind of a living at what they do. This is a selective listing of some commercial galleries in Greater Vancouver. With few exceptions these galleries encourage you to walk right in and see what is on the walls. (Space limitations dictate that only some of the artists represented by the various galleries can be listed below.)

A Walk Is *976 Denman* St. Work by contemporary B.C. artists Joe Average, Jim Cummins, Manwoman, Robin Konstabaris and others.

Acme Animation Art Gallery *2003 Park Royal South, West Vancouver.* All kinds of animation art from Disney and Warner Brothers.

Alex Fraser Galleries *2027 W. 41st Ave.* Canadian, British and traditional Quebec works by Vladimir Horik, Claude Langevin, Gilles Pelletier, Pauline Paquin, Peter Ewart, Janice Robertson, Robert Genn, Alan Wylie, Jennifer Dickson, Francine Noreau.

The Art Emporium *2928 Granville St.* Canadian and international works by Jack Shadbolt, Pablo Picasso, the Group of Seven, Ebe Kuckein, Ron Hedrick, Geoffrey Rock, Montague Dawson.

Art Image Gallery *5892 Cambie St.* Original paintings and limited-edition prints by Nancy O'Toole, Fred Buchwitz and others.

Art Speak *401-112 W. Hastings St.* A non-profit, artist-run gallery. Original art by young Canadian artists in ten four-week shows each year.

Art Works *225 Smithe St.* Paintings, sculpture, prints, multimedia by Ken Prescott, Joyce Kamikura, Roberta Nadeau, Vern Simpson, Helen Zenith, Irmgard Benedict, Derek Houston.

Atelier Gallery *2421 Granville St.* Contemporary Canadian, American and European paintings, drawings, prints and photographs by Al Neil, Barbara Milne, Esther Devenyi, Herbert Siebner, Enn Erisalu, Barbara Hepworth, Christopher Wool, Andreas Gursky, Henry Moore, Graham Sutherland and Michael Young.

Baird Delano Gallery *101-1445 Commercial Dr.* Contemporary originals in oil, acrylic, watercolors and pastels by Joy Anson, Tim White, Donald Catton.

Bau-Xi Gallery *3045 Granville St.* Contemporary Canadian work by Bonifacho, Don Jarvis, Sherry Grauer, Joseph Plaskett, Ken Wallace, Jack Shadbolt, Sylvia Tait, Pat O'Hara, Norman Rich, Tom Smith.

Buschlen-Mowatt Gallery *111-1445 W. Georgia St.* Contemporary Canadian works by Pat Service, Helen Frankenthaler.

Canadian Craft Museum *639 Hornby St.* Regional, national and international crafts.

Canada West Antiques *3607 West Broadway.* Canadian folk art by Paul Burke, Walter Myette, Jim Brown, Charlie Schlase.

Catriona Jefferies Fine Art Gallery *3149 Granville St.* Contemporary Canadian and international work in sculpture and photographs by Ian Wallace, Alan Wood, Christos Dikeakos.

Caulfeild Gallery *9347 Headland Dr., West Vancouver.* Original paintings, limited-edition prints, etchings by Canadian and European artists Ela Kowallek, Sopena, Michael Tickner, Jack Yeats.

CC Arts Gallery *20 East Pender St.* Original local and Southeast Asian and Chinese art and calligraphy by various artists.

Cedar Root Gallery *1607 E. Hastings St.* A cornucopia of North American native art in many media by many artists.

Chief's Mask *73 Water St.* First Nations arts and crafts by many different artists.

Chinese Impression Art Gallery *4548 W. 10th Ave.* Chinese art, brush drawings featuring the work of various schools of Chinese artists.

Circle Craft Co-op *1666 Johnston St.* Juried glass, jewelry, fibre, clay, metal, wood and ceramic art by many B.C. artists.

Coast Salish Arts *3917 W. 51st Ave.* Salish wood, jewelry, glass, acrylics and prints by Susan Point, Kelly Canhell.

Cobblestone Gallery *731 Columbia St., New Westminster.* Original paintings, limited-edition prints, pottery and needlework by Robert Bateman, Terry Isaac, Carol Evans, Keith Hiscock.

Crafthouse *1386 Cartwright St.* Juried work in ceramics, glass, fibre, wood and papier-maché by B.C. artists belonging to the B.C. Craft Association.

Crown Gallery *1017 Cambie St.* Painting, sculpture and original prints by Canadian artists Leslie Poole, Dianne Ostroich, Rob Wilson, Maboru Sawai, Wayne Leidenfrost, Marcello Niccoli.

Diane Farris Gallery *1565 W. 7th Ave.* Contemporary work by David Bierk, Angela Grossman, Hanneline Rogeberg, Gu Xiong, Sam Lam, Lionel Doucette, John Korner, Gloria Masse, Attila Richard Lukàcs, Frank Mayrs, Chris Woods, David Robinson, Paul Kuhn, Jack Darcus, Kathryn Jacobi.

Douglas Reynolds Gallery *103-1926 W. 4th Ave.* Northwest coast First Nations art and jewelry and Inuit sculpture by Gerry Marks, Alvin Adkins, Larry Rosso.

Douglas Udell Gallery *1558 W. 6th Ave.* Canadian and international works by Vic Cicansky, Dorothy Knowles, Natalka Husar, Joe Fafard.

Downstairs Gallery *260-1425 Marine Dr., West Vancouver.* Signed and numbered original prints, silkscreens, etchings, embossing by Ted Harrison, Jurgen Gorte, Barb Wood.

Equinox Gallery *2321 Granville St.* Contemporary Canadian painting, sculpture and prints by Gathie Falk, Richard Prince, Mary Pratt, Gordon Smith, Takao Tanabe, Paterson Ewen, Terence Johnson, Al McWilliams.

Exposure Gallery *851 Beatty St. Gallery* of the Vancouver Association of Photographic Art.

Federation of Canadian Artists Gallery *1241 Cartwright St.* Works in all media and styles by B.C. artists George Bates, Mike Svob, Jeane Duffey, Robert Bateman, Brent Heighton, Ann Zielinski, Alessandra Bitelli, Daniel Izzard, Kiff Holland.

First Peoples Art *102-12 Water St.* First Nations art including carvings, masks, jewelry and paintings by Doug Harper, Demsey Willie, Beau Dick, Donald Peters, Joe Binnie.

Focus Gallery *3578 W. 4th Ave.* Jewelry, photography, pottery and glass by Norman Tate, David Olson, Trudy and Stan Grief-Zolowsk.

Folk Art Interiors *3715 W. 10th Ave.* Folk art, wood carvings and sculpture by Don Thompson and many other folk artists.

Foto Base Gallery *231 Carrall St.* Photography by Ed Olson, Tom Bowen, Mandy Williams.

Gallery Gachet *1134 Granville St.* Paintings, sculpture, collage and mixed-media, the work of approximately forty artists who are consumers or survivors in the mental health community.

Gallery of B.C. Ceramics *1359 Cartwright St.* Sculptural and functional work by Wayne Ngan, Vincent Massey, Meg Buckley, Elaine Brewer-White, Penny Birnbaum.

Gallery of Tribal Art *2329 Granville St.* Contemporary art in all media by First Nations artists Robert Davidson, George Littlechild, Joane Cardinal-Schubert, Richard Hunt, Lawrence-Paul Yuxweluptun, Rick Bartow, Jim Logan, Fred Davis, Stephen Bruce, Henry Green, Richard Sumner, Don Yeomans.

Gallery of Woman in Art *342 Water St.* Vancouver's only permanent erotic art gallery displaying the female form as interpreted by Tom Luscher, Paul Butvila, Brian Ward.

Graham Sayell Galleries *2416 Granville St.* Limited-edition prints by Stephen Lyman, Carol Evans, Bev Doolittle, Robert Bateman.

Grosvenor Fine Arts *822 Howe St.* Canadian and international art in various media by Robert McVittie, Alex Sutherland, Dale Byhre, Jack Lee McLean, Denis Walliser, Andre Szasz.

grunt gallery *116-350 E. 2nd Ave.* A non-profit, artist-run gallery featuring the work of many local artists in various media.

Gulf of Georgia Galleries 5-3500 Moncton, Richmond. Contemporary original watercolors and oils by John M. Horton, Rod Charlesworth, Santo DeVita.

Harrison Galleries 2932 Granville St. and 1471 Marine Dr., West Vancouver. Traditional and contemporary art by George Bates, Wilson Chu, Daniel Izzard, Jose Trinidad and other major B.C. artists.

Heffel Gallery 2247 Granville St. American, British, Canadian and European contemporary art, and classic Canadian work by Joe Andoe, Tony Scherman, Guido Molinari, Leslie Poole, Vicky Marshall, Werner Liebmann, Alex Colville, David Blackwood and others, and the estates of B.C. Binning, Lawren Harris and W.P. Weston.

Hill's Indian Crafts 165 Water St. First Nations art by many artists in many media.

Homer Arts L200/L20 1-560 Beatty St. By appointment only. An underground gallery of new age/contemporary/chaos-fractal work by Jason McCelvey, Hugh Chapman, Mitzi, Joanne Probyn, Murray Reichmuth, Joanna Liv, Tanya Fader, Milan Radovanovic, Terry Kozick, Arthur Shimizu, Amitava Bhowmick.

Humberston Edwards Fine Srt 1360 Marine Dr., West Vancouver. Contemporary Canadian art by Robert Genn, Allen Sapp, Ken Kirkby, Bruce Muir.

Image One 940 Richards St. Glass, metal and wood sculpture by various artists.

Images for a Canadian Heritage 164 Water St. Northwest coast First Nations and Inuit carvings and graphics by the Hunt family and various Inuit artists.

Inuit Gallery of Vancouver 345 Water St. Inuit soapstone sculpture and northwest coast First Nations masks, prints and drawings by Joe David, Beau Dick, Kiawak Ashoona, Ken McNeil, Norman Jackson, Stan Bevan, Kinquak Ashevak, Axanqayu.

Iron Works Studio 235 Alexander St. Terry Cosick's open studio also exhibits group shows focussing on environmental aspects of art and art in support of environmental causes.

Jack Gibson Gallery 8740 River Rd., Richmond. Contemporary painting and sculpture by Lew Waitlin, Brent Heighton, Karl Nobles, Rick McDirmid, Bonny Roberts, Alex Fang, April White, Ron Hedrick, Linda Stewart.

Jamm Original Art 1601 W. Georgia St. Woodcarvings, prints, silver and gold jewelry by various First Nations artists.

Joan Dean Gallery 227 Carrall St. Mixed-media work by Dana Zoe Coop, Margot Pear, Mad Dog.

John Ramsay Gallery 1065 Cambie St. Contemporary work in several media by Patrick Amiot,

Jamie Evrard, Louis de Niverville, Robert Suder, Kathryn Young.

Joyce Williams Antique Prints and Maps 346 W. Pender St. Antique maps and prints and modern prints in traditional forms by Naoko Matsubara, Laurent Schkolnyk, Joseph Therien, Edie Miller, Colin Paynton, W.J. Phillips, Charles Van Sandwyk.

Keith Alexander Gallery 647 Howe St. Paintings, sculpture and original prints by Bill Reid, Amanda Watt, Yehouda Chaki, Z.Z. Wei, Toko Shinoda, Helen Frankenthaler, Bernard Gantner, Bernard Cathelin.

Kinsalang Gallery 857 Hamilton St. First Nations artists including Bill Reid and Don Yeomans, jewelry by Alvin Adkins.

Leona Lattimer 1590 W. 2nd Ave. Northwest coast First Nations art by Robert Davidson, Reg Davidson, Jim Edenshaw, Kelvin Thompson.

Lyle Sopel Studio 322 E. Esplanade, North Vancouver. Jade sculpture by Lyle Sopel.

Marion Scott Gallery 481 Howe St. Canadian Inuit and northwest coast First Nations art by Alexander Schick, Michael Lord, Brent Gelaude.

Macewen Arts 560 Beatty St. First Nations art and folk-art carvings by Gordon Tobacco, Jerry Whitehead, Phillip Melvin, Norval Morriseau.

Monte Clark Gallery 1727 W. 3rd Ave. Canadian and American contemporary painting, sculpture and prints by Peter Aspell, Graham Gillmore, Gayle Ryon, Drew Shaffer, Allan Switzer, Jason Young.

New-Small & Sterling Studio Glass 1440 Old Bridge St. Glass works by Lisa Samphire, Mornie Tudor, Gary Bolt, Naoko Takanouchi, David New-Small.

Paperworks Gallery 1650 Johnston St. Contemporary watercolors, drawings, graphics and limited-edition prints by Pauline Pike, J. Yaworski, Edi Miller.

Petley Jones Gallery 2245 Granville St. Early and contemporary Canadian and British works by Michael Kluckner, Don Li-Leger, Doris Livingstone, Dale Ketcheson, Vallie Travers, Cynthia Nugent, Diana Zoe Coop, Colin Graham, Nic de Grandmaison.

Pitt Gallery 317 W. Hastings St. Contemporary works by Carel Moiseiwitsch, Oraf.

Potlatch Arts 100-8161 Main St. Northwest coast First Nations art by Robert Davidson, Don Yeomans, Glen Rabena.

Prior Editions Gallery 206 Carrall St. Contemporary Canadian works on paper by Doug Biden, Brian Musson, Jack Shadbolt, David Ostrem, Torrie Groening, Jamie Evrard, Carel Moiseiwitsch.

Rendez-Vous Art Gallery 1009 Cambie St. Canadian and international contemporary art by Gaston Rebry, Claude Langevin, Lise Lacaille, Ron

Stacy, Patrick Chiming Leung.

Sarah Dobbs Gallery 1767 W. 3rd Ave. International contemporary art by Manuel Neri, Robert Kelly, Ron Pokrasso, Andrew Cripps, Juan Kelly, Linda Kooluris Dobbs, Julie Richard, Shawn Westlaken.

Stoodeo 2nd Floor, 1045 Mainland St. Contemporary work by Sheryl McDougald, Joe Average, Chris Catalano, Jamie Griffiths.

Talking Stick Cafe and Gallery 221 Carrall St. Contemporary paintings, acrylics and photographs by Sarah Berges, Daniel Lockwood.

TexTileContext Studio 1420 Old Bridge St. Contemporary textile art by Pat Cairns, Jean Kares.

Torres Gallery 2255 W. Broadway. Contemporary abstract, representational and pop art by Pnina Granirer, Gregg Simpson, Kitty Blandy.

Uno Langmann 2117 Granville St. North American, British and European art of the 18th, 19th and early 20th centuries.

Vancouver Chinese Art Gallery B-123 E. Pender St. Chinese paintings by artists from China, Taiwan, Hong Kong, the U.S. and Vancouver.

Van Vort Visuals 1300-666 Burrard St. By appointment. Contemporary Canadian photography and original illustrative work by Stephan Schulhof, Stuart McCall, Gary Taxall.

Vincent Lee Fine Arts Gallery 1040 W. Georgia St. Vincent Lee Fine Arts Galleries in Vancouver, Hong Kong, U.S., Japan, etc. specialize in the works of international contemporary artists including Yankel Ginzburg, Frank Licsko, Ball Mack, Dario Campanile.

Westbridge Fine Art 2339 Granville St. Nineteenth and early 20th-century and contemporary work by H.E. Kuckein, Tammy Rosenblatt, Leonard Brett, Dora Hornung.

White Rock Gallery 1565 George St., White Rock. Traditional and 20th century work, contemporary landscapes in all media by Bill Saunders, Keith Hiscock, Michael Tickner, Victor Santos.

Wickaninnish Gallery 14-1666 Johnston St. Traditional and contemporary northwest coast First Nations art by Correen Hunt, Derek Wilson, Norman Bentley, Don Lancaster.

World of Animation 1140 Robson St. Animation art from such studios as Disney, Hanna-Barbera, Universal, Nickelodeon, Warner Brothers.

Other Art Galleries of Greater Vancouver
Tony Robertson

THE BURNABY ART GALLERY is located in the Ceperley Mansion in Deer Lake Park and is adjacent to the arts complex of the City of Burnaby. The Burnaby Art Gallery maintains an active exhibition program showing local and regional work as well as national and international art. The gallery offers educational programming and special events for both adults and children and there are guided tours available for every age and interest group. The gallery provides outreach programs for the community and organizes travelling exhibitions for communities in British Columbia and beyond. There is also an art rental service for gallery members.

Burnaby Art Gallery, 6450 Deer Lake Avenue, Burnaby, B.C. V5G 2J3, (604) 291-9441. Hours of operation: Tuesdays through Fridays, 9 A.M. – 5 P.M. First Thursday of every month, 9 A.M. – 9. P.M. Saturdays, Sundays, holidays, 12 P.M. – 5 P.M. Closed Mondays. Office Hours: Mondays through Fridays, 9 A.M. – 5 P.M. Admission: $2.00, family membership $5.00, members and children under 12 free.

THE RICHMOND ART GALLERY is located in the Richmond Library and Cultural Centre where the Richmond Museum, archives, library, arts centre and gallery shop are located.

The Richmond Art Gallery presents approximately 40 exhibitions a year of contemporary art by local and international artists in the main galleries, and another 18 at its outreach gallery at the Gateway Theatre. The gallery maintains a permanent collection of more than 200 works by such artists as Toni Onley, Bonifacho and Noboru Sawai.

The Richmond Art Gallery offers an art rental service which promotes the work of local artists. It also has public programs with hands-on workshops for children and adults which offer access to established artists with international recognition. Gallery space is available to community art groups.

Richmond Art Gallery, 180-7700 Minoru Gate, Richmond, B.C. V6Y 1R9, (604) 231-6440. Hours of operation: Weekdays, 9 A.M. – 9 P.M. Weekends, 10 A.M. – 5 P.M. Admission: Free.

THE SURREY ART GALLERY is located in the Surrey Arts Centre in Bear Creek Park. It has three exhibition halls and a permanent collection of contemporary art. The gallery's mandate is to provide exhibitions and events which address issues, provoke dialogue and educate the public in contemporary art.

The Surrey Art Gallery promotes emerging B.C. and Canadian artists with important provincial and national exhibitions; it also shows the work of international artists. Most exhibitions are accompanied by lectures, workshops, panel discussions, tours and films designed to foster the development of community awareness, appreciation and understanding of contemporary visual art.

The Surrey Art Gallery, 13750-88th Avenue, Surrey, B.C. V3W 3L1, (604) 596-7461; fax (604) 597-2588. Hours: Monday to Thursday, 9 A.M. – 9 PM. Friday, 9 AM. – 4:30 P.M. Saturday and Sunday, 1 P.M. – 5 P.M. Closed statutory holidays. Admission: By donation.

THE MUSEUM OF ANTHROPOLOGY holds one of the world's finest collections of Northwest Coast native art on the campus of the University of British Columbia.

The museum's Great Hall displays poles, feast dishes and canoes of the Kwakwaka'wakw, Nishga'a Gitskan, Haida and Coast Salish. The sculpture complex includes two Haida houses and ten poles, and features the work of some of the finest contemporary native artists. The museum has the largest collection of works by Haida artist Bill Reid, among them the large sculpture in cedar, *The Raven and the First Men*. The Koerner Ceramics Gallery displays a collection of 15th to 19th century European ceramics, as well as ceramics and textiles specially commissioned from contemporary Vancouver artists.

The Museum of Anthropology, 6393 N.W. Marine Drive, Vancouver, B.C. V6T 1Z2, (604) 822-3825. Hours of operation: 11 A.M. – 5 P.M. Tuesday to 9 p.m. Seven days a week July & August; closed Mondays Sept. 7 to May 18. Admission: Adults $5.00, students/seniors $2.50, children under six free.

THE CONTEMPORARY ART GALLERY is a non-profit public gallery supported by its members, and by the three levels of government, particularly the City of Vancouver. The gallery administers a collection of several thousand art works which belong to the city and are displayed in various civic offices. It is one of the premier exhibition spaces for contemporary art in Vancouver and presents seven exhibitions a year by regional, national and international artists, of works in all media, from painting to installations to video. The gallery generally offers the work of young artists.

Contemporary Art Gallery, 555 Hamilton Street, Vancouver, B.C. V6B 2R1, (604) 691-2700; fax (604) 683-2710. Hours of operation: Tuesday through Saturday, 11 A.M. – 5 P.M. Admission: Free.

THE VANCOUVER MARITIME MUSEUM is located in Vanier Park in Kitsilano. It holds marine artifacts, maritime art, memorabilia and historical paraphernalia chronicling the maritime heritage of the city and the province.

The museum houses the RCMP schooner *St. Roch* in drydock. Several other historic vessels are berthed in its Heritage

The Raven and the First Men, by Bill Reid; Museum of Anthropology,

Harbour on English Bay. There is a large collection of ship models and the Claridge Gallery features outstanding models of the Canadian Pacific Railway's coastal fleet that formed an important part of British Columbia maritime history.

The museum holds a collection of maritime paintings by noted artists and a recently acquired collection of early Inuit carvings. The museum also has an extensive maritime reference library.

Vancouver Maritime Museum, 1905 Ogden Avenue, Vancouver, B.C. V6J 1A3, (604) 257-8300. Hours of operation: Victoria Day to Labour Day, 10 A.M. – 5 P.M. Closed Mondays Labour Day to Victoria Day. Admission: Adults $5.00, seniors and students $2.50, children under five free, family (2 adults, four children) $10.00. Seniors' Tuesdays free. Groups of ten or more half price. Memberships available.

THE CHARLES H. SCOTT GALLERY is part of the Emily Carr Institute of Art and Design which opened its Granville Island campus in 1980. The gallery presents eight to 10 exhibitions a year, including the institute's graduating exhibition in May.

The Charles H. Scott Gallery has an ongoing educational mandate to involve the public in the institute's role as an active centre for the production, discussion, teaching and exhibition of art and design through regional, national and international exhibition focusing largely on contemporary work in the institute's range of disciplines. The mandate also includes modern and historical exhibitions, and discussion of past, present and future developments in art and design through symposiums, lectures, publications and exhibition catalogues.

Charles H. Scott Gallery, 1399 Johnston Street, Granville Island, Vancouver, B.C. V6H 3R9, (604) 844-3809; recorded information, (604) 844-3811. Hours of operation: Monday to Friday 12 P.M. – 5 P.M. Saturday and Sunday, 10 A.M. – 5 P.M. Admission: Free.

THE MORRIS AND HELEN BELKIN ART GALLERY opened in June 1995 on the campus of the University of British Columbia. Peter Cardew's award-winning building provides a stunning new home for the university's gallery.

The gallery mounts exhibitions of contemporary art and also acts as a research centre with its own collection and archives.

The Morris And Helen Belkin Art Gallery, The University of British Columbia, 1872 Main Mall, Vancouver, B.C. V6T 1Z2, (604) 822-2759. Hours of operation: Tuesday to Friday, 10 A.M. – 5 P.M. Saturday, 12 P.M. – 5 P.M. Admission: By donation. Students: Free with student card.

THE SIMON FRASER GALLERY was established at Simon Fraser University in 1983 to support and enhance the academic excellence and well-being of the students, faculty, staff and the general public through the gallery's ongoing collection and exhibitions programs.

The Simon Fraser Collection holds over 2,500 works of art, mostly contemporary Canadian and Inuit, and includes a collection of B.C. art second only to that of the Vancouver Art Gallery. The exhibition program involves four rotating exhibition spaces and the permanent installation of more than 100 works of art at both the Burnaby Mountain and Harbour Centre campuses.

The Simon Fraser Gallery, Academic Quadrangle 3004, Simon Fraser University, Burnaby, B.C. V5A 1S6, (604)291-4266. Hours of operation: Monday, 12 P.M.-6 P.M. Tuesday to Friday, 10 A.M. – 4 P.M. Admission: Free.

PRESENTATION HOUSE GALLERY is located in the Presentation House Art Centre and specializes in exhibiting contemporary Canadian, international and historical photography and photo-related work.

Presentation House Gallery, 33 Chesterfield Avenue, North Vancouver, B.C. V7M 3G9, (604) 986-1351; fax. (604) 986-5380. Hours of operation: Wednesday to Sunday, 12 P.M. – 5 P.M. Thursdays, 12 P.M. – 9P.M. Admission: $2.14, students/seniors $1.14. Members: Free.

Public & Office Building Art in Greater Vancouver
Elizabeth Godley

STANLEY PARK

Bust of David Oppenheimer Beach Ave. exit, Charles Marega, bronze on granite pedestal, 1911. Oppenheimer was Vancouver's second mayor (1888-92). $4,519.03 was collected for the bust, of which $3,600 was paid to the artist.

Pauline Johnson Memorial Ferguson Point, James McLeod Hurry, natural rock, 1922. In 1913, the Women's Canadian Club began raising funds for this cairn, which marks the resting place of the Mohawk poet's ashes. Johnson specifically decreed in her will that no memorial be raised.

Harding Memorial Malkin Bowl, Charles Marega, bronze and granite, 1925. Commemmorates the 1923 visit to Vancouver of Warren G.Harding, first U.S. president to visit Canada.

Robert Burns across from the Vancouver Rowing Club, artist unknown, bronze and granite, 1928. Cast from the original statue in Burns' s native town of Ayr, Scotland. Cost was $5,000, including shipping, plus $2,000 for the pedestal.

Japanese-Canadian War Memorial Stanley Park, James Benzie, 1932. Commemorates Japanese-Canadians who fought in World War I.

Totem poles Brockton Oval. In 1912, an area in the park was set aside for an "Indian village" and two poles and the thunderbird house-posts were donated at the time. More poles were purchased for Vancouver's Jubilee in 1936. They include: *Wakius pole*, Kwakiutl, Alert Bay, 1899; *Yakdzi pole*, Kakiutl, Rivers Inlet, 1894 (replica); *Tsa-wee-noh house post*, Kwakiutl, Kingcome Inlet, carved by Charlie James of Alert Bay and restored in 1963 by his granddaughter, Ellen Neel; *Nhe-is-bik pole*, Kwakiutl, Rivers Inlet, 1892 by See-wit of Blunden Harbor; *Si-sa-kau-laus pole*, Tlingit, Kingscome Inlet; *Skedans mortuary pole*, Haida, Queen Charlotte Islands, 1879.

Killer Whale near Vancouver Aquarium, Bill Reid, bronze, 1984.

Chehalis Cross Brockton Point, erected in memory of eight who died on the steam-tug *Chehalis* in 1906.

Girl in Wetsuit sculpture, Elek Imredy, 1972. "She represents Vancouver's dependence on the sea and the necessity to use the sea for the benefit of all," according to Peggy Imredy, the artist's widow.

Empress of Japan Figurehead next to Lumberman's Arch, installed c. 1923. The *Empress of Japan* sailed into Vancouver harbor many times between 1891 and 1922. In 1960 the original was given to the Vancouver Maritime Museum for safekeeping and replaced with this fibreglass

reproduction. The museum has restored the much more impressive original work.

Thunderbird Dynasty Pole Prospect Point, carved by Chief Joe Capilano of North Vancouver. Erected to commemorate the meeting of the Squamish people and Capt. Vancouver near the mouth of the Capilano River on June 12, 1792. Dedicated 1936.

Lord Stanley statue Sydney March, bronze/granite, 2.4 m, 1960. In 1950, Major J.S. Matthews, then Vancouver's archivist, discovered a letter dated Oct. 19, 1889 promising a suitable monument would be erected to commemorate the naming and dedication of Stanley Park. Matthews gathered donations to pay English sculptor March.

Solo Devonian Park, Natalie McHaffie, stainless steel, 12 m x 4.5 m, 1986. McHaffie, a Toronto artist, created this piece for the City Shapes project to celebrate Vancouver's centennial. She says the piece evokes mountains, cargo cranes, airplanes and "the fluid elements of wind and water."

WEST END

George Cunningham Memorial Sun Dial near foot of Denman at English Bay, Gerhard Class, bronze/granite,1967. Cunningham Drug Stores commissioned the artist to commemorate the "three greenhorns" who settled in the West End around 1867, as well as the first drugstore built in the area in 1911.

Sculpture 1255 Bidwell, Egon Milinkovich, limestone, 1959. Commissioned by Tom Campbell, mayor of Vancouver from 1967 to 1972.

Swimmer 1050 Beach (outside aquatic centre), George Norris, sculpture, welded stainless steel, 1977.

Inukshuk English Bay, 6 m, 31,500 kg. A large version of an ancient symbol of Inuit culture, traditionally used as a landmark and navigational aid. Built roughly in human form, Inukshuks are symbols of northern hospitality. This one, part of the NWT's Expo 86 pavilion, was moved here in 1987.

Art-glass windows at Weeks House 1459 Barclay, Brian Baxter,1995. The artist donated these designs, a variation on the "*tree of life*" theme that celebrates diversity, to this "wellness centre" for people with life-threatening diseases, run by Friends for Life Society.

Gathering Place Seymour and Helmcken (northwest corner), Debbie Bryant.

DOWNTOWN

Gargoyles Hotel Vancouver, artists unknown, Haddington Island stone, 1929. According to a 1956 article in the *Province*, many of the figures were adaptations or reproductions of 11th or 12th century cathedral carvings.

Spring Robson Square, Alan Chung Hung, red

metal.The same artist who created the *Gateway* at Vanier Park.

Mural 1025 West Georgia (Royal Bank, interior), carved by artists in 'Ksan, near Hazelton, nine wooden panels, 36 m x 2.4 m.

Cloudscape 666 Burrard (Park Place, lobby), Joanna Staniszkis, tapestry, plexiglass/silk ribbon, four panels, each 1.2 m x 3 m, 1986.

Builders Discovery Park (Burrard and Dunsmuir), B. Joyce McDonald, black Quebec granite, 1986. A tribute to Vancouver's pioneers, this piece was part of the City Shapes project for the city's centennial. Another City Shapes creation in this park is *Vessel* (red/green Quebec granite/steel cable), by Dominique Valade of Quebec, which evokes a ship anchored to the earth.

Lions Vancouver Art Gallery, 750 Hornby, John Bruce, granite, 1910. Modelled after those in London's Trafalgar Square, by Sir Edwin Landseer. Each weighs 15 tonnes; cost was about $8,000 for the pair.

Placed Upon the Horizon (Casting Shadows) 750 Hornby (Robson Street facade), Lawrence Weiner, 35 cm high yellow-cedar letters, 4.2 m x 12. 6 m, 1990. Weiner, an American artist whose work is based on the use of written language as object, created this installation specifically for the VAG.

Bird of Spring Robson Square (on stairway near art gallery), Etungat, an Inuit artist, bronze, installed 1979. This sculpture is a recreation of a tiny 14 cm original.

Bronze 1111 West Georgia (B.C. Gas), Abraham Anghik, 1992. Anghik, who won an open competition, says his work represents the birds and animals of B.C.

The Ridge 1090 West Georgia, Joanna Staniszkis, wall hanging, perforated plexiglas/silk ribbons, 1987.

Space Ribbon 1040 West Georgia, Roy Lewis, cast bronze, 4 m, 1985.

The Treasures 1040 West Georgia (lobby), Joanna Staniszkis, tapestry, 3 m x 5 m, 1985.

Primavera 1075 West Georgia (formerly MacMillan Bloedel Building), Jack Shadbolt, mural, painted plywood, 3 x 6 m, 1987. A similar mural by Shadbolt was installed in the Cineplex Odeon, 855 Granville St., the same year.

Ice Skater 1075 West Georgia (lobby), Giacomo Manzu, bronze sculpture, 1957.

Pendulum 995 West Georgia (Hongkong Bank), Alan Storey, steel, 1986. This kinetic sculpture is one of the best examples of art that enhances its surroundings. Also in the lobby is *Wings of Prey*, a granite sculpture by George Schmerholz, weighing three tonnes and standing two metres.

Horse 475 West Georgia (former B.C. Turf Building), Jack Harman, bronze, 1976. This is one of the few of Harman's sculptures that he did not cast himself.

Untitled painting 888 Dunsmuir (lobby), Joe Plaskett, 1990.

Courtly Evanescence 840 Howe (Robson Court, lobby), Lutz Haufschild, art-glass window, 1986.

Clouds 983 Howe (upper-level balcony), Alan Chung Hung, 1992. Instead of trellises, the building's architect, Bing Thom, commissioned this piece which pokes gentle fun at the notion of a skyscraper and celebrates Vancouver's soggy climate.

Symbols from the Cuneiforms 750 Burrard (former Vancouver Public Library), Lionel Thomas, exterior wall sculpture, bronze/plexiglas, 4.5 m x 5 m, 1961. Seventy-five citizens contributed $4,500 and the library board ponied up $2,000 from a revenue surplus for this work, illuminated from behind by low-voltage automobile lights.

External mosaic decoration Burrard and Nelson (Electra Condominiums originally the B.C. Electric, then B.C. Hydro Building), designed by Thompson, Berwick, Pratt Architects, who commissioned Bert Binning to decorate the exterior, 1957. "A main theme was beaten out, a sort of basic tune or rhythm which we enriched with overtones of form, pattern and color," Binning said. "[T]his mural cannot be viewed by itself but only as a part of the larger and whole architectural scheme."

Salute to the Lions of Vancouver Canada Place, Gathie Falk, aluminum, 9 m, 1991. This piece, which includes a bronze plaque commemorating poet Pauline Johnson, was commissioned from Falk by the architects after a cross-Canada competition failed to turn up anything they liked. The artist's original scheme, comprising eight dogs leaping through rings of fire ("I wanted it to be a real salute") was modified considerably.

Relief work Marine Building, James Watson, C. Young and J.D. Hunter, then on staff of McCarter, Nairne & Partners Architects, terra cotta, stone, brick and plaster, 1930, The designs were executed in terra cotta by Gladding, McBean in Seattle.

Stained glass Marine Building, Joel Berman, 1989. This $25,000 window was installed as part of renovations for the 60th anniversary of this building. At the same time the lobby floor was redone in marble.

Bust of Charles Bentall 595 Burrard (Bentall Building), Jack Harman, bronze, 1977. Bentall founded Dominion Construction Co.

Transformation 1140 West Pender (rear plaza), Abraham Archer, an Inuit artist, sculpture.

Bronze lions 1155 West Pender, E. Schulte Beecham, bronze commissioned in 1914. The lions were installed in 1920 but sent to New York to be stored in 1962. They were replaced

in 1969.

Muse figures 576 Seymour (exterior), artists unknown. The four muses shown are Calliope, Erato, Euterpe and Clio.

Caryatids 100 West Pender (Sun Building originally World Building), Charles Marega, terra cotta, 1912. Originally 12 in number, three began to crumble and were removed.

Birds in Flight 700 West Pender, Robert Dow Reid, metal, 1976.

GRANVILLE STREET

Wood sculpture 200 Granville (Granville Square), Michael Phifer, 1973. Commissioned by the Canadian Pacific Railway and Marathon Realty.

Mural 499 Granville (Toronto-Dominion Bank), Charles Fraser Comfort, linen on plaster, 3 x 19 m, 1951. "My composition deals largely with discovery and development, then and now; the West Coast Indians and their artifacts, the Spaniards, the French, the British," Comfort told *Canadian Art* magazine in 1951. Emily Carr is also depicted, representing culture, while labor is symbolized by a logger.

Painted window panels 600 Granville (former B.C. Electric showroom), Terry Howard, Tamara Arden, Dwayne Bigsby, Paolo Majano and Gail Ouellette, 1994. These panels were commissioned by the Downtown Vancouver Business Improvement Assoc. to replace glass broken in the 1993 riot that took place after a hockey game.

Granville Street Mural 600-block Granville, Tangjun Zhao, L.E. Wakelin, Madeleine Wood and Eric Scholtz, coordinated by Gail Ouellette, 1992. Commissioned by DVBIA to decorate hoardings on buildings awaiting redevelopment.

Mural 580 Granville (CIBC, interior), B.C. Binning, mosaic and marble, 3 m x 13 m, 1958.

Untitled sculpture Orpheum Theatre's West-coast Hall, Judi Young, stainless steel/copper tubing, 3.6 m, 1986. Created for the City Shapes project, this work pays homage to the "strength and manual labor of the early pioneers."

Waterfront Centre Hotel 900 Canada Place Way. This hotel, opened in 1991, boasts a major collection of about 50 works by B.C. artists and others. An art tour is available by arrangement. Some highlights include *Voyage of Discovery* by Peggy Vanbianchi and Emily Standley; *Marsh Breeze* by Rebecca Perehudoff; untitled acrylic on canvas by Audrey Capel-Doray; *Stanley Park* by Leslie Poole; *Sun Flowers* by Vaughn Neville; *Epiphany I, II and III* by Jack Shadbolt; and *Portrait of Artist at Work* by J.C. (Carl) Heywood.

G.M. Place Vancouver's newest sports arena officially opened in 1995. According to city policy, one per cent of the construction cost was to be used to purchase a work of art. The commission

went to one of Canada's most enigmatic artists, Liz Magor. Titled *Game,* Magor's work consists of seven steel and seven aluminum balls, all 152 cm in diameter, cast bronze medallions and pavement signs. The steel balls weigh about 270 kg each and the aluminum ones 106 kg.

CONCORD PACIFIC DEVELOPMENT

Work commissioned and installed in 1995:

Password Alan Storey. A series of four 4-letter stainless-steel word groups mounted within the air-vent grilles for the underground parking system; can be seen from the pedestrian walkway opposite David Lam Park. Designed to rotate at different speeds, they create various combinations.

A Memory of Place, Passage of Time Gwen Boyle, footnotes. Consists of 57 pieces of unpolished black Indian granite set into the pedestrian walkway on Pacific Blvd. between Homer and Drake. This site-specific work refers to the history of False Creek's north shore.

Collection Mark Lewis. Six pieces installed along Homer St. between Drake and Pacific, consists of two parts: three stainless-steel wedge-shaped refuse collectors, each equipped with internal receptacles for garbage, are mounted on concrete bases, seemingly cracked by the force of the steel and inscribed with the word "refuse"; and three sealed steel containers enclosing a variety of discarded objects. On the surface of each is a list of the objects they contain. The word "collection" is inscribed on the concrete bases.

HASTINGS STREET

Sculptures 1111 West Hastings, McLeary Drope, 1967. Architect Allan Waisman chose these works by this Winnipeg artist.

Relief 900 West Hastings (Bank of Canada), Eliza Mayhew, cast bronze, 4 m, 1968. Architect W.W. Rennie commissioned this work, which cost $30,000, after seeing photographs of the artist's work in *Canadian Art.*

Celebration 757 West Hastings (Sinclair Centre, interior), John Hooper, sculpture, 1986. Hooper, a New Brunswick artist, created this work for City Shapes.

The Fathomless Richness of the Seabed 1055 West Hastings (Guinness Tower, lobby), Jordi Bonet, ceramic mural, 5.4 m x 9.6 m, 1968. Architect Charles Pine commissioned this work by Bonet. Inspired by sea life, it beautifully complements the facade of the Marine Building, just around the corner.

Vancouver Skyline 999 West Hastings, Joanna Staniszkis, tapestry, 9 m x 4.5 m, 1980.

DOWNTOWN, EAST OF GRANVILLE

Angel of Victory 601 West Cordova, Couer de Lion MacCarthy, war memorial, bronze on marble and stone base, 1922. A jury of CPR officials chose the Ottawa artist from a cross-Canada competition. The sculpture depicts an angel carrying a dead soldier heavenwards, and initially commemorated CPR employees who died in World War I. Later, the dates of World War II were added. Identical statues were placed outside CPR stations in Montreal and Winnipeg.

Gassy Jack Vern Simpson, bronze sculpture, date unknown. This statue of Capt. John Deighton standing on a beer barrel commemorates the founder of Gastown, the settlement from which Vancouver grew.

The Postman 300-block West Georgia (main post office, Homer Street facade), Paul Huda, relief, red granite, 1956.

Mural 349 West Georgia (main post office, Homer St. entrance), Orville Fisher, 1957. This mural features the figure of Mercury, god of messages and glad tidings.

Women's Monument Thornton Park, 1300-block Main, Beth Alber, 1996. The design for this monument was chosen from 98 entries in a cross-Canada competition and commemorates the 14 women slain in Montreal in 1989. Alber teaches jewelry at the Ontario College of Art in Toronto.

Sculptured murals Queen Elizabeth Theatre, Gordon Smith, metal and enamel, 1959. Smith, one of the Vancouver art community's "grand old men," had to learn to weld to produce this piece.

Cycle of Flowering Queen Elizabeth Theatre Restaurant, Jack Shabdolt, mural, 1.2 m x 5 m, 1959.

The Golden Opportunity Queen Elizabeth Theatre, Pieter Wiegersma, stained glass window, 1.5 m x 2 m, 1959. Gift from the Dutch-Canadian community.

Rainforest Queen Elizabeth Theatre (plaza), Gordon Ferguson, steel, 4 m x 2 m x 2.5 m, 1986. Created for the City Shapes project.

Florentine Door and Wall #3 Queen Elizabeth Playhouse (plaza), Frank Perry, bronze sculpture, 1967.

Mural Queen Elizabeth Playhouse, Toni Onley, canvas collage, 3 m x 65 m, 1962. This work sparked a storm of controversy when it was installed, with one outraged citizen claiming it was "a communist plot" in a 1962 letter to the *Province.* Onley was paid $3,000.

Terry Fox Memorial Robson and Beatty, (B.C. Place), Franklin Allen, baked enamel/concrete/tile/fibreglass, 1984, . Ten per cent commission on total sum of $300,000. This monument to Terry Fox, the young Port Coquitlam man who died before he could complete a cross-Canada marathon to raise awareness about cancer, has been the focus of anger and controversy since its unveiling. Allen's design was chosen by a nine-person jury that included architect Arthur Erickson. Note the wall decoration, 788 Beatty St. (facing Terry Fox Plaza), a brick and mosaic design by Xavier Bellprat Rob Leshgold, c. 1988.

Bridge Marker west end of east-bound section of Georgia Viaduct, George Norris, liquid-filled glass sphere designed to reflect traffic patterns, 2.4 m (poorly maintained), 1972.

Cenotaph Victory Square, Hastings and Cambie, granite obelisk, dedicated 1924.

Sculpture Victory Square (SE corner), Gerhard Class, cast aluminum/granite, 1.5 m, 1967. The artist cast this work using Styrofoam and sand. It commemorates a donation by the *Province* newspaper, which had offices for 67 years in the vicinity, to landscape and fence the grounds, left vacant after Vancouver's original court house moved to Georgia St.

WEST SIDE (Vancouver)

Beautiful British Columbia Multi-Purpose Thermal Blanket 1441 Creekside (B.C. Central Credit Union, lobby), Gathie Falk, painted canvas, 5.4 x 4.8 m, 1980.

Girl Waiting for a Bus Burrard & Cornwall (Edward Apt), cement fondu, 1961.

Wind-Blown Mounds W. 13th and Fir, Lutz Haufschild, fibreglass, 1975. These yellow mounds are all but obscured by greenery.

Seven columns Granville Island, Ron Rule, painted steel, 5.4 m, 1986. These columns, now covered with clematis and ivy, were commissioned by the park board to draw the eye away from nearby electrical and sewage equipment.

Mural Jericho beach, north wall of utility building, by five Mexican artists (Alexandro Mojica, Carlos Kunte, Estrella Ubando, Poluqui, and J. Aguirrez) here on a 1992 cultural exchange, 35 metres. The exchange was organized by Vancouver's Art In Action group.

Salmon Wall Southlands Elementary, 5351 Camosun, 1995. This project was created under the city's community-art initiative.

Knife Edge (Two Piece) placed in plaza at Queen Elizabeth Park in 1969. Henry Moore, bronze sculpture, 1962 Moore authorized three castings of this work. The first stands on Nelson Rockefeller's New York estate and the second outside the House of Lords, London, England. *Knife Edge* was the first non-commemorative sculpture accepted by Vancouver's park board. Prentice Bloedel purchased the piece and donated it along with the conservatory and funds for landscaping.

Five "game tables" (and 10 stools) Talmud Torah Hebrew School (playground), Bill Pechet, cast concrete, 61m x 36 m x 46 cm, 1995. Commissioned by landscape architect Cornelia Oberlander.

Bas-reliefs 2695 Granville, Lionel Thomas, 1965. One is a copper relief, the other an enamelled glass panel. Architect C.B.K. Van Norman commissioned the work.

Family Group Surrey, (Pacific Press), Jack Harman, sculpture, bronze/marble, 1966. "The work is intended to depict the role of a newspaper in the family and the importance of the family in the community," Harman said. The figures are elongated to lend them a spiritual quality. In 1997 the sculpture was moved to the Pacific Press printing plant in Surrey.

Spirit of Communication Granville Square (lobby), George Norris, sculpture, copper/brass, 1966. The artist used old newspaper from Vancouver's history as well as foreign-language papers to form a decorative collage in the form of typographical plates. These collages were then photo-engraved in copper. In 1997 the sculpture was moved to the new Pacific Press editorial offices in Granville Square.

Earth art 1363 West Broadway (rear plaza), Judson Beaumont, sculpture of steel mesh sprayed with liquid concrete, 1988. This extremely subtle piece doubles as a bench and retaining wall in a plaza designed by landscape architect Ron Rule.

Frieze 2405 Pine (Postal Station D), George Norris, cast-in-situ concrete, 1.5 x 28.5 m,1966. This design was commissioned by architect Ian Davidson.

Capt. George Vancouver 453 West 12th, (City Hall), Charles Marega, bronze and granite, 1936. This statue of the explorer was erected to commemorate the city's golden jubilee.

Bust of Gerald Grattan McGeer 453 West 12th (City Hall), Yanka Brayovitch, bronze and granite, 1948. Vancouver's most famous mayor.

Relief Vancouver Labour Temple, 307 West Broadway, Beatrice Lennie, cast stone, 2 m x 6 m, 1949. The Dominion Construction Co. commissioned the artist, who created an abstracted wheel of industry with figures clustered around it. Lennie, a student of Charles Marega, was one of the first women to graduate from the Vancouver School of Art. Also by her are *Hippocrates,* relief sculpture, Academy of Medicine, 1807 West 10th Ave., cement/marble dust/sand, 5.7 m x 1.2 m; 1951, relief murals, Shaughnessy Hospital, composite stone, 2.4 x 1.5 m, 1941, and relief work at Ryerson United Church.

Exterior/interior decoration Holy Name Church, 4925 Cambie, George Norris, 1963.

Sunbow Grounds of B.C.'s Children's Hospital, 4480 Oak St., Art Lucs.

Gate to the North West Passage Kitsilano Point near Vancouver Museum, Alan Chung Hung, corten steel, 1980.

Centennial Pole Kitsilano Point near Maritime Museum, by renowned Kwakiutl carver Chief Mungo Martin, a replica of a pole created for

Queen Elizabeth, dedicated 1958.

Anchor Spanish Banks, Christel Fuoss-Morre, 4.5 m x 3.6 m x 1.8 m. This concrete work, created for Vancouver's Centennial in 1986, marks the point of arrival of the first European to sail into Burrard Inlet, Jose Maria Narvaez, 1791.

Wall-mounted sculpture 6350 Nanaimo (Corpus Christi Church), Jack Harman, bronze, 1962. Harman also created bronze relief murals inside.

Horizons 888 S.E. Marine Drive (Wilkinson Steel Co.), Gerhard Class, corten steel sculpture, 1970. Commissioned ($5,000) for the company's 60th anniversary.

Ironworkers' Memorial south end of Second Narrows Bridge, since 1994 officially known as Ironworkers Memorial Bridge. This memorial, designed by an engineer with Swan Wooster (now Sandwell Inc.), commemorates the workers killed when the bridge collapsed during construction in June, 1958.

EAST VANCOUVER

Gargoyles 233 Main, Ken Clarke, painted fibreglass, 1992. Clarke, a sculptor whose studio is at this address, created this frieze of heads to enliven the Downtown Eastside.

Flower Totems Kingsway and King Edward, Sam Carter, steel, 1980. Funds came from a neighborhood improvement project for the Kensington area.

V6A Art 528 Powell, 1995. This mural was created by people with mental-health problems, coordinated by Therasa Gaiters.

Mapping the Future Trout Lake, Paula Jardine, 1995.

Personalizing 19th and Fleming, Corinna Dallin, 1995.

Relief 803 East Hastings (Gulf & Fraser Fishermen's Credit Union), Leonhard Epp, precast concrete, 1968. Architect Robert Harrison chose Epp's work in a closed competition.

Mural Four Sisters Housing Co-op, Richard Tetrault, 1990. Tetrault also created the *Street Performance* mural at the Firehall Arts Centre (1987); *Summer City Street* mural at Carnegie Community Centre (1980); and coordinated murals at Charles Dickens Elementary, Beaconsfield Elementary, Lord Strathcona Elementary, General Gordon elementary and Queen Alexandra Elementary schools. The city commissioned him to paint the mural on the Keefer St. overpass (1994).

Untitled archway CRAB Park (north foot of Main), Volker Steigemann, red cedar/stones, 1986. Created for the City Shapes project, this work honors the city's multicultural aspect where people from all over the world are "joined together like an old hand-hewn log cabin."

Community Fence 8th and Fraser, 1994. This fence consists of about 400 red-cedar pickets, each one hand-carved by someone living and/or working in Mount Pleasant. The fence surrounds a community garden and the project was initiated by artists connected with the grunt gallery, a storefront, artist-run centre.

Monument to Old Hastings Mill 50 Dunlevy (adjacent to Missions to Seamen Building, formerly the National Harbours Board Building), Gerhard Class, B.C. granite, 1966. The Vancouver Historical Society commissioned the monument for $1,500 as a centennial project.

Set of Five Pencils Britannia Community Centre, Josef Holy, 1992. This rather phallic sculpture doubles as playground equipment.

Signature Commercial Drive railway overpass, Susan Schuppli, 1995. This work, part of the city's community-art initiative, consists of a collection of signed tiles embedded in the sidewalk.

Bird Feeders Woodland Drive railway overpass, Rick Gibson, 1995.

Bridging/Healing Victoria Drive railway overpass, Janice Bowley and Oliver Kelhammer, 1996.

Stained glass 3927 Knight (Kensington library), Brian Baxter, two panels.

Wall-mounted installation 2969 East 22nd, (Renfrew library, entrance), Brian Baxter and Markian Olynyk, glass/metal, 1995. This new branch library was designed by Hughes Baldwin Architects. The installation takes its theme from a diagram and quotation from Leonardo da Vinci's notebooks: "All our knowledge is based on our perception."

Gates Kensington Park, 36th and Knight, Douglas Senft, steel, 1986. Situated on the second-highest hilltop in Vancouver, this piece was created for Vancouver's centennial and pays homage to the city's mountain backdrop.

Bannister-Landy sculpture East Hastings near Cassiar, Jack Harman, bronze, 1967. Denny Boyd, then sports columnist at the *Vancouver Sun,* put forward Jack Harman's name for this work, which commemorates Bannister's narrow victory in the "Miracle Mile", the four-minute mile run at the British Empire Games in Vancouver in 1952. Both Bannister and Landy attended the sculpture's unveiling in 1967.

VANDUSEN GARDENS

Eleven pieces of stone sculpture were created on site during the 1975 International Stone Sculpture Symposium:

Travertine Sculpture 75 David Marshall, Vancouver, travertine

Guardian Mathias Hietz, Austria, marble

Earth, Air and Sea Joan Gambioli, Vancouver, travertine

Woman Kiyoshi Takahashi, Japan, marble

For the Botanical Garden Hiromi Akiyama, France, travertine

Horizontal Column the Kubach-Wilmsen team, Germany, marble

Meta Morphosis Olga Jancic, Yugoslavia, marble

Observing Your Society David Ruben, aka Piqtoukun, North West Territories, marble

Between Adolf Ryszka, Poland, travertine

Landscape 75 Jiro Sugawara, Italy, marble

Developing Form Michael Prentice, France, marble

Also in the garden:

Throne of Nezahualcoyotl Sebastian, Mexico, Depicts the Aztec prince Nezahualcoyotl who found inspiration in flowers; presented by the Mexican government in 1978.

Boy With Dolphin Andrea del Verrochio, Italy. This bronze is a reproduction of the original.

Birds in Flight Patsy Macdonald (aka Pat Ryan), bronze.

Fisherman Gerhard Juchim, cast cement.

Jade George Norris, nephrite (B.C. jade).

Sundial Gerhard Class, bronze/jade.

Al of the Gispudwada Arthur Sterritt, Gitksan, totem pole.

Mosquito Earl Muldoe, Gitksan, totem pole,

Three Botanists Jack Harman, depicts Carolus Linnaeus, Archibald Menzies and David Douglas, a gift of Schenley of Canada.

UNIVERSITY OF BRITISH COLUMBIA

Mother and Child George Norris, bronze,1955.

Three Forms Robert Clothier, cast concrete, 1956.

Hanging sculpture St, Mark's Theological College, (west wall), Lionel Thomas, bronze and gold leaf.

Statue of King George VI Woodward Biomedical Library, Sir Charles Wheeler, 1958. A gift of P.A. Woodward to the Vancouver Branch of the War Amputations of Canada who presented it to UBC. Originally located at the War Memorial Gymnasium. The second casting of this statue stands near Buckingham Palace, London.

Hanging sculpture Buchanan Building, Gerhard Class, 1958.

Asiatic Head Near Frederic Wood Theatre, Otto Fischer-Credo, 1958.

Mosaic mural Brock Hall, Lionel and Patricia Thomas, 1960.

Fertility Lasserre Building, Jack Harman, bronze, 1960.

Relief sculpture Education Building (north wall), Paul Deggan, welded copper, aluminum and brass, 1965.

Thunderbirds Thunderbird Stadium, Zeljko Kujundzic, concrete, 1967.

Figure Forestry and Agriculture Building (courtyard), George Norris, granite, 1967.

Three free-standing sculptures Frederic Wood Theatre (plaza), Germain Bergeron, iron, 1967. This piece, donated to UBC, was commissioned by Expo 67 and sponsored by Seagram.

Reclining Figure Lasserre Building (north side), Jan Zach, red sandstone. 1967. Zach presented this work to Walter Koerner, who gave it to UBC.

Tuning Fork Music Building (plaza), Gerhard Class, corten steel, 7.2 m, 1968. Alfred Blundell donated this work, which cost $5,000, to UBC.

Mural Metallurgy Building, George Norris and John Fraser, brick, 6 m x 16.5 m, 1968,

The Pacific Rim Student Union Building, Lionel Thomas, painted mural, 3 m x 4.7 m. Commissioned by graduating class.

VANCOUVER INTERNATIONAL AIRPORT

Spirit of Haida Gwai A major work of art by Haida artist Bill Reid was created in 1994 for the Canadian Embassy in Washington, D.C. This is the second and final casting.

"Spindle whorl" Susan Point (Musqueam), carved in cedar, 5 m.

Two Salish welcome figures Shane Point, red cedar, 5 m.

Salish-style woven wall hangings Deborah Sparrow, Robyn Sparrow, Krista Point and Gina Grant, 4.8 x 1.5 m.

Great Wave Lutz Haufschild, glass installation, 39 m x 10 m.

THE FUTURE

Four major pieces of public art are scheduled to be installed by Concord Pacific at the Roundhouse in 1996 and 1997:

Geometry Richard Prince

Welcome to the Land of Light Henry Tsang

Street Light Bernie Miller and Alan Tregebov

Brush with Illumination Buster Simpson

Also to come, as part of Vancouver's community art projects, are:

Sahilli Pillars in Mount Pleasant

Mosaic Creek in a new park at Charles and Maclean

BURNABY

Kamui Mintara—Playground of the Gods Burnaby Mountain Park, Naburi Toko and Shusei Toko, father and son of Ainu descent (Japan's aboriginal people), wood, 1990. This installation commemorates 25 years of goodwill between Burnaby and sister city Kushiro and refers to the Ainu creation myth.

Mural Burnaby Mountain Park, (Sports Plaza), Ken Rainford, mosaic tile, 6 m x 9 m, created to raise funds for the 1973 Canada Games.

Untitled Deer Lake Park, Bodo Pfeifer, 1970. This installation (poorly maintained) consists of nine slanting concrete blocks, each topped with reflective steel plate, designed to reflect light to the Burnaby Art Gallery.

Arrow in Tree artist unknown. Created for the 1977 outdoor sculpture symposium held at Deer Lake Park, this piece was a last-minute entry and

was not included in the catalogue. Ironically, it is the only work left in the park from the symposium.

The Viking 750 Hammarskjold Way, metal, 1994. This large bust was created by welding teacher John Clarke and his students at Burnaby North Senior Secondary.

Un, Deux, Trois 4550 Lougheed Hwy. (car dealership), Jim Willer. This work was originally created for Expo 67.

Birds Metrotown Mall (north side), Gerry Gladstone, aluminum.

Mythic Messengers 3033 Beta (Teleglobe Canada), Bill Reid, 1984. This bronze relief was inspired by a Haida ritual, "exchange of tongues", whereby power was transferred from one entity to another.

SIMON FRASER UNIVERSITY

Bear Mother and Cub artist unknown, small unpainted totem pole, cedar.

Celebration of Man and Nature Hannah Franklin, newspaper/acrylic, 2.4 m x 1.8 m, 1986. This piece by a Montreal artist was created for the City Shapes project.

Northern Light Lynn Vardeman, polyester resin (set in outdoor pond), 1983 .

(Negative #1) Adam/Eve D'Arcy Henderson, cast fibreglass, wall sculpture.

The Faces vs Edges Series Chung Hung, corten steel, five pieces, 1981.

Bust of Mahatma Ghandi cast by Wagh Bros. Fine Arts Studio, Bombay, installed 1969.

Guardian II Elize Mayhew, cast bronze, 1963.

Untitled Gordon Smith, mosaic, 1964.

Energy Alignment Sculpture: Pyramid in the Golden Section Bridge Beardslee, tubular steel, 1976.

North Burnaby Cenotaph 250 Willingdon, B.C. granite. Erected in 1953 by Canadian Legion members, it was designed by F.J. Brisdon.

NORTH VANCOUVER

Integrated Plane City Hall (upper plaza), 141 West 14th, Barry Cogswell, corten steel, 2.5 m x 2.5 m x 1.2 m, 1975. Purchased for $4,800 by the Community Arts Council and the City of North Vancouver, this piece refers to the mountains, sea and forest.

Tapestry 121 West 14th, Library (interior), Setsuko Piroche, 1975.

Ribbons North Vancouver District Hall, 355 West Queens (atrium), Doug Senft, aluminum, 1996. This spectacular piece, commissioned as part of the district's centennial celebrations in 1991, evokes the swift-flowing rivers of the North Shore.

Untitled sculpture Carson Graham Secondary School (courtyard), 2145 Jones, David Marshall, Nelson Island granite. Nearby is a sculpture by Joan Gambioli.

Totem pole Lonsdale Quay, Leonard and Mark George of the Burrard band, wood, 9 metres.

Memorial to Frank Rivers Mosquito Creek Marina, Stan Joseph, totem pole, 6 m, 1977. Rivers, the marina's first manager, died in 1976.

North Shore Rhapsody and Joe Bustemente Trumpet two sculptures by Richard Wojciechowski, cast concrete, 1992. *North Shore Rhapsody*, in Rogers Plaza near the Keg Restaurant on Esplanade, symbolizes the female spirit who lures seafarers into danger and takes the form of a harpist. One side of the harp is played by the wind, the other is a traditional instrument for people to strum. *Joe Bustemente Trumpet*, on a balcony overlooking Esplanade near Waterfront Park, commemorates an early North Van resident, Chilean by birth. According to the story, this one-armed musician for years played his trumpet to help ferry captains negotiate the docks in fog and storms.

Cathedral Waterfront Park, Douglas Senft, steel/fluorescent lights, 1985. This piece is known as "the spider" to people on the North Shore, but according to the artist, a Capilano College instructor, the shape refers to the Capilano River, Howe Sound, and the North Shore mountains. For someone standing underneath the piece, the arches resemble a cathedral's vaults.

Your Ancient Scribe Pioneer Park, Lynn Valley Rd. and Mountain Hwy., Kevin Head, bronze, 1986. This life-size portrait of Walter Draycott, considered the "Father of Lynn Valley" and author of a book about North Shore history, was cast at Jack Harman's foundry. At the time of the commission the artist was a student at Emily Carr Institute of Art and Design.

Fish forms Carrie Cates Park, Gerald Gladstone, metal and stones.

Timesline Mahon Park, 18th and Jones, Tom Osborne, sculpture, concrete, 4.2 m x 4.8 m, 1971. This work, commissioned to commemorate B.C.'s entry into Confederation, consists of large wedge-shaped concrete pieces laid on the ground around a central grassy area.

Gahlgihl Masganihl Gat (Children of the People) and Naawokow Kiikinskw (Grizzly Bear Coming to the Village) Capilano Mall, both by Norman Tait, wood totems.

RICHMOND

Dymaxion World Map Sculpture International Business Park, 4611 Viking Way, Sam Carter, stainless steel/concrete/jade/granite, 1995. This work is a tribute to engineer/architect/philoso-

facing page: Metal sculpture, Waterfront Park, North Vancouver, 1995. vp

pher Buckminster Fuller who invented the dymaxion map in the '30s. Carter, an instructor at Emily Carr Institute of Art and Design, studied with Fuller in the late '60s and remained fascinated by the way Fuller's projection represents the world as one island.

Soo Gee Ghet (New Generation) Richmond Cultural Centre, 7700 Minoru Gate, Victor H. Reece (Tsimshian), carved wooden pole, 1993. This pole was created by the Richmond Carvers Society under Reece's direction and donated to the cultural centre in 1994. It tells the story of a father passing on history and expertise to his son.

SURREY

A Project for Surrey Foot of 130th near public fishing dock. Micah Lexier, installation, 1991. Commissioned by the Surrey Art Galley. Lexier, a Toronto artist, has created works for communities across Canada. This one, a gateway form made of logs, stands near a mill that ships lumber to Japan and includes the phrase, "As you were."

City Plaque Project: The first public art project for Surrey City Centre was unveiled Sep 9, 1995. Artist Ken Walters's plaque was the first in a series to be installed in the sidewalk of City Parkway (135th Street), commemorating the arrival of SkyTrain in 1994.

Untitled sculpture George Norris, metal, 13 m, 1974. This piece, which once graced the outside of the Vancouver Eaton's store at Granville and Georgia, is currently stored in Surrey's works yard. It was purchased in 1974 by Pacific Centre and removed in 1987. In a 1981 guide book Terry Noble described the piece as "a majestic, glistening, glinting dragonfly, bowing gracefully to all who pass."

Surrey Taxation Centre, 9755 King George Hwy. In consultation with a representative from the federal government the architects of this building, Carlberg Jackson Partners of New Westminster, invited numerous artists to submit proposals for this building. The proposals were judged by a panel that included two artists. The selected artists then worked closely with the architect to develop works that would enhance the building:

Homage to Salish Weavers Katherine Dickerson. This weaving in the traditional twining method hangs in the cafeteria. The pattern was derived from an 1854 trading blanket

Structured Dolmen 2 Barry Cogswell. This outdoor earthwork refers to massive stone tombs found at Avebury Ring, Silbury Hill and other prehistoric sites in England

Untitled David Toresdahl. This colorful ceramic wall mural is installed at the west entrance

Stainless Steel Abacus Tom Burrows. This 2.4 metre work outside the rear entrance was inspired by a Delhi desk clerk who used an abacus to tally Burrows' hotel bill.

WEST VANCOUVER

Mural 2496 Marine Dr., (west wall of Capers), Jim Mackenzie, a Gulf Islands artist, created this scene of the Vancouver area as it might have appeared before Europeans arrived.

Giant concrete chairs Ambleside Park pier, and wall ornamented with concrete soccer balls, airplanes and baseballs at Ambleside Park, were created by Bill Pechet. The chairs were first exhibited at the Charles H. Scott Gallery on Granville Island then purchased by West Vancouver's parks department in 1992. The "ball wall" was commissioned in 1991 as part of renovations to the changing rooms.

The Woods Columbarium Capilano View cemetery, off Mathers in the British Properties. Bill Pechet, river rock/granite/concrete with text, 13,000 sq m, 1993. Cremated remains are stored here. The word derives from the Latin for "dovecote." Also in the cemetery, by Pechet, is a 7.5 m x 6 m stone/concrete/galvanized aluminum/granite monument dedicated to the 50th anniversary of the end of the World War II, unveiled 1995. The first phase of a larger memorial to the war's veterans to be completed by the year 2000.

Turtle Patsy Macdonald (aka Patsy Ryan), reinforced concrete, mid-1960s. This piece was commissioned by the Vancouver Garden Club and originally placed in the grounds of the Jericho Hill School for the Deaf. In 1995, when the school was dismantled, the piece was moved to its present site near Dundarave Beach.

Myth of the Bear People West Van Aquatic Centre, Chief William Jeffrey, pole, 12 m, 1976. In 1977, West Vancouver and the Park Royal Shopping Centre hosted "Wood Sculpture of the Americas", a symposium that included ten sculptors from Canada, the U.S. and South America. The resulting works can be found in various locations:

Two Columns in Space No. 5 Klee Wyck House, 200 Keith, Barry Cogswell, North Vancouver

Burrard Piece and Vancouver Piece •Park Royal (south mall), Joseph DeAngelis, Ontario, together with *Caracas 77* by Domenico Casasanta, Venezuela

An Enclosed Line Forming Three Planes Perpendicular to Each Other in a Symmetrical Order Ambleside Park, Alan Chung Hung, Vancouver, and *Standing Wave* by Robert Behrens, *Colorado*

Raven and the Sun West Vancouver Municipal Hall, 750-17th St., Calvin Hunt, Victoria

Symposium Piece for Eva West Vancouver Municipal Hall, 750-17th St., Hayden Davies, Toronto

Bicycles municipal library, 1950 Marine Drive, Fumio Yoshimura, New York

Mr. and Mrs. Carver Plumtree municipal library, 1950 Marine Drive, Barbara Spring, California

Tropical Woman municipal library, 1950 Marine Dr., Hernando Tejada, Colombia

Wooden sculptures on Ambleside Beach Cathy Matheson, Wood Symposium, 1977

History of the Tsimshian Indian Nation Horseshoe Bay, Chief William Jeffrey, pole, 14 m, 1975

Kwakiutl Bear Pole Horseshoe Bay, Tony Hunt, 4 m, 1966

COQUITLAM

The collection of 27 sculptures and other work by B.C. artists at Coquitlam Centre, 2929 Barnet Hwy., puts many an art museum to shame. Opened in 1979, the shopping centre won the Governor-General's Award for Excellence in Architecture in 1982 for Edmonton architect B. James Wensley. Waisman Dewar Grout Architects carried out renovations in 1989.

Stained glass works commissioned from Ray Friend, Anna Gustavson and Lutz Haufschild.

Sculpture includes work by David Marshall, George Rammell, George Schmerholz and Greg Stephenson

Granite sculptures Blue Mountain Park, remain there from a 1986-87 symposium arranged by sculptor Patrick Sullivan. The other artists involved were Barry Holmes and Carl Sam; assistants were Bea Bullshields, K. Moore and K. Rose.

PORT COQUITLAM

Statue of Terry Fox Terry Fox Library, 2470 Mary Hill, George Pratt, Nelson Island granite, 1983.

SQUAMISH

Four sculptures, a bench and a sign all in B.C. granite, were installed in 1994 in Squamish Junction Park by artist Patrick Sullivan.

Chamber Music
Ray Chatelin

Put three musicians in the same room and you have instant chamber music. This is a city awash in wonderful musicians playing in small and large ensembles in churches and a variety of other small venues as well as at the Orpheum Theatre.

While the Vancouver Women's Musical Club is the oldest of local music organizations (formed in 1905 and the practical starting point for concentrated musical life in the region) music in this city goes back a lot farther. The first bands, not surprisingly, were military, with the musical life of New Westminster (then Queensborough) centering around the activities of the Royal Engineers in the 1860s.

By comparison to choral and band music, chamber music in the Lower Mainland is a Johnny-come-lately, really getting underway only with the advent of the Vancouver Academy of Music, organized in 1897 as the first private conservatory in Vancouver. (No relation to the current music facility by the same name.)

The largest of Vancouver's chamber ensembles—and arguably the best known—is the CBC Vancouver Orchestra, the last of many CBC in-house orchestras that once dotted the Canadian musical landscape. Founded in 1938, the orchestra annually plays a series of concerts at the Orpheum under the banner of the Avison Series, named in honor of its first conductor, John Avison. The orchestra has hosted virtually every major Canadian soloist at one time or another and has a long list of major guest conductors including Raffi Armenian, Monica Huggett, Sir Ernest MacMillan and Jon Washburn. And, in its most important role, it has staged premieres of more than 200 compositions from 80 Canadian composers.

The region is also blessed with a wide variety of small ensembles and umbrella organizations that cater to the ever-expanding local chamber audience. Among them is the venerable Friends Of Chamber Music (FOCM) whose 10 concerts a season at the Vancouver Playhouse feature leading ensembles from around the world. Formed in 1948, the organization also sponsors an annual Young Musicians Competition.

The FOCM's position as the only major local chamber music organization has changed over the years as other organizations like Masterpiece Music, the Vancouver Recital Society, Music In The Morning, and the Pacific Baroque Orchestra, among others, have staked out positions in the community.

Masterpiece Music is the Vancouver East Cultural Centre's in-house organization and produces Sunday afternoon and evening concerts throughout the season, drawing its talents from the Vancouver Symphony Orchestra, the CBC Vancouver Orchestra and freelance musicians.

The Vancouver Recital Society, meanwhile, has evolved from presenting only the best of young unknowns, to a mix of stars and unknowns, bringing in superstars like mezzo-soprano Cecilia Bartoli, cellist Yo-Yo Ma, soprano Jessye Norman and violinist Itzhak Perlman. It also stages the Vancouver Chamber Music Festival for two weeks in July on the campuses of St. George's and Crofton House schools as well as at the Bard on the Beach tent in Vanier Park.

Music in the Morning has carved itself a niche in Vancouver's music scene by becoming a morning institution. Changing work habits and technology meant that more people had time in the mornings rather than during the usual evening concert hours. So, in 1985, June Goldsmith stepped into the void with a combination lecture and concert series at the Vancouver Academy of Music in Vanier Park across from the planetarium. It now stages three performances of eight concerts annually. Start time is 10:30 A.M.

The Pacific Baroque Orchestra was founded in 1990 by a group of West Coast musicians experienced in the performance of classical and baroque music on instruments of the period. Led by violinist Marc Destrube the ensemble not only plays instrumental concerts but collaborates with choirs.

Other notable chamber groups include the Vetta Chamber Music and Recital Society, Curio, the Deep Cove Chamber Soloists, the Pacific Arts Ensemble, the Ramcoff Concerts and the Little Chamber Music Series.

- CBC Vancouver Orchestra, P.O. Box 4600, Vancouver, v6b 4a2
- Friends of Chamber Music, P.O. Box 74636, Kitsilano Post Office, Vancouver, v6k 4p4
- Masterpiece Music, c/o Vancouver East Cultural Centre, 1895 Venables St., Vancouver, v5l 2h6
- Music in The Morning, P.O. Box 62013, Arbutus Post Office, Vancouver, v6j 1z1
- Pacific Baroque Orchestra, 5115 Keith Rd., West Vancouver, v7w 2m9
- Vancouver Recital Society, P.O. Box 35605, Station E, Vancouver, v6m 4g9

Choral Groups
Ray Chatelin

GIVE THEM MUSIC and they will sing! The choral tradition in Vancouver and environs has never been richer. The principal 19th century choral organization was the New Westminster Choral Union, founded in 1882 by Bishop Acton Windeye Sillitoe, with the first concert—consisting of songs and glees—on May 10, 1882.

Today, in a region that has always had many wonderful choirs, the numbers are staggering—some 140 in Greater Vancouver ranging from the large 150-member Vancouver Bach Choir to the 12-member Pandora's Vox. The numbers consist of church, male, female, ethnic and general performance choirs. Among these choirs are several whose quality and seasons have drawn audiences for years—the Vancouver Bach Choir, the Vancouver Cantata Singers, the Vancouver Chamber Choir and the Phoenix Chamber Choir—each of whom also have several compact discs to their credit.

There are also several choirs whose quality and longevity have made them a force within the choral community, although they may not perform with the regularity of the biggest choirs. Among these are the Vancouver Men's Chorus, the Elektra Women's Choir, the Chor Leone Men's Choir and Pandora's Vox.

With 130 members, the largest and oldest of the Vancouver-area choirs is the Vancouver Bach Choir, formed in 1930 by Herbert Mason. Its repertoire is grand, consisting of major works by Beethoven, Britten and Mahler and the like, performed with the Vancouver Symphony Orchestra. Led by Bruce Pullan, the choir is often heard nation-wide on the CBC.

The Vancouver Cantata Singers are an international award-winning 40-member ensemble of auditioned members led by conductor and artistic director, James Fankhauser who celebrated his 20th season with the choir in 1994. Performing a regular season from September to May, their repertoire is wide-ranging but leans to the baroque and early classical periods. It also commissions new works by Canadian composers.

The Vancouver Chamber Choir, led by founder/conductor/music director Jon Washburn, was formed in 1971 as one of only two professional choirs in Canada. It immediately made an impact: in 1973 it was the first Canadian choir to ever win a first-place award in the prestigious BBC Let The People Sing competition. Its Vancouver season emphasizes short works and Canadian compositions, but the group is also a major international force, touring the world both independently and for Canada's external affairs ministry.

The Phoenix Chamber Choir, formed in 1983 by conductor Cortland Hultberg, is among the newest of Vancouver's major choirs. It immediately established itself as one of the finest of Canada's choirs, winning first-place in the contemporary and chamber choir categories of the CBC choral competitions in 1984 and again in 1994. Since 1984 it has won a total of seven first-place awards at both the BBC and CBC annual competitions. In 1989 they took the coveted BBC award for best overall performance. In addition to presenting three Vancouver concerts every year the choir continues an active broadcast and recording schedule under its new conductor Ramona Luengen.

- Phoenix Chamber Choir, 10560 River Dr. Richmond, V6X 1Z4
- Vancouver Bach Choir, 5730 Seaview Rd., West Vancouver, V7W 1P8
- Vancouver Cantata Singers, 5115 Keith Rd., West Vancouver, V7W 2M9
- Vancouver Chamber Choir, 1254 W. 7th Ave., Vancouver, VGH 1B6

Vancouver Chamber Choir with conductor Jon Washburn at the Museum of Anthropology, 1996. vcc

Pop Music
Jeff Batemen

THE 1950S. ELVIS PRESLEY'S seismic arrival launched a blue-suede revolution. CJOR staged an April, 1957, competition to find a local Elvis. The winner by audience decision: Jimmy Morrison. Later that year Morrison and the Stripes (who originally featured Ian Tyson of Ian and Sylvia fame) recorded "Singin' the Blues" backed with "Your Cheatin' Heart," a 45 that's regarded as the city's first rock 'n' roll recording. Other rockabilly contenders included Les Vogt, whose band The Prowlers was named after Jack Cullen's radio show *The Owl Prowl,* and Stan Cayer.

THE 1960S
A kaleidoscopic decade began with Vogt scoring a local number one hit with "The Blamers," written by Surrey milkman Al Parker (aka Sipson P. Kloop). The Chessmen emerged in 1963 with Terry Jacks, who would lead The Poppy Family to a U.S. number two smash with "Which Way You Goin' Billy" in 1969. Other Beatlemania-era pop attractions included the Hi-Fives, The Valentines and teen idol Terry Black. Clubs like Oil Can Harry's fostered a popular rhythm and blues scene spearheaded by The Nocturnals, Little Daddy and the Bachelors (featuring comedian Tommy Chong of Cheech and Chong renown) and Night Train Revue.

The Vancouver scene in the mid-sixties was showcased on the CBC-TV shows *Let's Go* and *Music Hop.* One *Let's Go* regular, Tom Northcott, blended folk with rock and landed a contract with Warner Brothers in Los Angeles. The kings of the Kitsilano hippie scene were The Collectors, a quintet famous for its psychedelic light show and half-hour instrumental jams; the band later evolved into Chilliwack, one of Canada's top acts of the Seventies. Such 4th Avenue heroes as The United Empire Loyalists, The Seeds of Time, The Northwest Company, Spring and Mother Tucker's Yellow Duck drew crowds at the Retinal Circus and Village Bistro but failed to crack the big time.

THE 1970S
Canadian content regulations ensured radio airplay for homegrown artists and the music scene went into overdrive. Two local songs became huge international smashes: "Seasons in the Sun," the Terry Jacks adaptation of a Jacques Brel song; and "Wildflower" by the group Skylark. The Hometown Band, featuring Valdy and Shari Ulrich, tapped into the peaceful folk-rock scene. Bachman Turner Overdrive rumbled out of Vancouver in 1974 and were followed soon after by Heart, founded by Seattle-born

Bryan Adams began his ascent to superstardom with the popular albums *Cuts like a Knife* and *Reckless*

sisters Ann and Nancy Wilson. Touring on a breakneck schedule, Prism, Trooper and Jerry Doucette became leading concert draws in Canada. A new generation of angry, politically aware bands—D.O.A., The Pointed Sticks, The Subhumans and Young Canadians included— brought the thrash and burn of punk rock to the city late in the decade.

THE 1980S
Bryan Adams began his ascent to superstardom with the albums "Cuts Like a Knife" (1983) and "Reckless" (1985); Adams, songwriting partner Jim Vallance and producer David Foster co-wrote "Tears Are Not Enough," an all-star recording that in 1986 spearheaded Canada's aid for Ethiopia campaign. Loverboy, featuring Vancouver native Paul Dean, arose from the west to sell ten million albums internationally. The Payola$ looked eastward in becoming the nation's best-received new wave band, while 54-40 went south and secured an American record deal. The beloved Doug and the Slugs toured relentlessly from coast to coast. Britain's electro-pop sound was represented locally by Images in Vogue, led by Dale Martindale. Another member, Kevin Compton, formed the pioneering industrial rock ensemble Skinny Puppy. Young guitar whiz Colin James relocated from Regina, while the Grapes of Wrath brought their jingle-jangle sound from Kelowna. Spirit of the West's blend of folk, rock and Celtic music won fans at the Railway and Savoy clubs.

THE 1990S
It's been the decade of the diva as Albertan k.d. lang, Halifax's Sarah McLachlan and Brandon, Manitoba native Mae Moore conduct their international careers from the Lower Mainland. 54-40 solidified its position as the city's top band with the album "Dear Dear" (1993), selling over 100,000 copies in Canada. The Odds, Spirit of the West and Barney Bentall have strong followings nationwide, while Moist is the most successful of a mid-nineties crop of new groups that includes Rose Chronicles, Pure, Zumpano, Ginger, Econoline Crush, Cub, Mecca Normal, Rhymes With Orange and Salvador Dream.

Red's Rock
Red Robinson

IN THE FIFTIES the adult world looked upon us as a rebellious generation. As a part of that rebellion we had discovered the merits and talents of black singers. To buy a record by Lloyd Price, Ruth Brown, Wynonie Harris or Laverne Baker you had to go to a record store and ask for it by title and artist. The record clerk would bring it from the back of the store or from under the counter in a plain brown sleeve. They were called "race records" and were not featured on the racks along with all the nice lily-white recording artists of the day. This in itself was an attraction to the young; it was our feeling that if it was "bad" it just had to be "good." The popular music slush of the era was not to our liking. Singers such as Frankie Laine, Vaughn Monroe, Patti Page, Eddie Fisher and the Four Aces were older cats and not singing to us. Teenage music as we know it hadn't been invented at this point.

There was a radio show for Vancouver teens in 1953 called *Theme For Teens,* an hour-long show on CJOR hosted by Al Jordan. Jordan played the standard hits of the day and invited listeners down to the studio to take part in the show. He also accepted phone calls. I got up enough nerve one day to call him and impersonate actor James Stewart. Stewart was in town at the time and I thought it would be great fun to phone Jordan's radio show and spoof him. I must have done a convincing job because Jordan put me on the air and thought I really was James Stewart. I forget how the dialogue went but I do remember it was brief and I hung up quickly. It was a few weeks before I could work up enough nerve to call his program again. This time I called in the voice of actor Peter Lorre. This time it clicked with Jordan that someone was doing impressions and he stopped me midway through my call and asked who I was. I identified myself and he invited me down to the show.

Prior to this I had been collecting every magazine available on recording artists and deejays and decided to create an interesting "show business" name for myself. There were two reasons: one, to create a name people would remember and two, to hide my identity from my school pals if and when I ever made it behind a microphone. I chose "Red" Robinson because of my hair—and it's significant that the initials were also the initials of the new music form. I visited the Al Jordan show after school one day and stayed on to join in the fun each afternoon. I created a daily skit called "Rod Gat," a parody on the then-current Mike Hammer books. The mail this skit drew was unbelievable, and all the while Jordan was taking time to

show me the ropes in radio. He eventually allowed me to take over the controls and engineer his program for him.

As *Theme for Teens* grew I became more and more involved and less and less interested in school work. I had decided radio was going to be my full-time career. In the fall of 1954 Al Jordan left the show and program manager Vic Waters, a great deejay in his own right, asked me if I would like to try to maintain it. I jumped at the chance. Without question the first day on the air by myself was the most hectic and nervous time of my life. I knew this was it; I was going to get a quick start toward my goal as a career deejay or I was going to blow it entirely. I hit the air and kept on moving records through a full hour, on nervous energy alone. At the end of the hour the control room door flew open and Waters said the show was mine. He said the telephone reaction was great and he could live with what he had heard. What he had heard was a very immature voice—but it was a voice belonging to a young man whose enthusiasm overcame a lack of announcing ability. I was totally hooked. I skipped school to learn everything there was to learn about broadcasting.

While employed at CJOR I was also attending a University of British Columbia course on broadcasting. During the day it was high school but after school until midnight or one o'clock in the morning I was totally immersed in radio. Having the freedom of expression and the stewardship of my own program allowed me to start playing those Lloyd Price records. In 1954 I moved swiftly to offering the music my high school peers were searching the dial to hear. I read every article in *Cash Box* and *Billboard*. I learned that Alan Freed was holding theatre parties at the Paramount in New York. I wanted to do the same. Nothing was really happening in Canada but in the United States rock 'n' roll was on fire. I was determined to bring this new fad to my audience. In September, 1954, while other stations were playing hits like "Hey There" by Rosemary Clooney I was playing "Sh-Boom" with the Crew Cuts and the Chords. Pop stations were featuring "The High and The Mighty" with Victor Young and his Orchestra and "Little Things Mean a Lot" by Kitty Kallen. I was playing "Shake, Rattle and Roll" by Joe Turner and a forbidden record by Clyde McPhatter and the Drifters called "Honey Love."

The message was obvious to the youth of British Columbia and northwest Washington. Here was a young, high-voiced rapid-patter deejay playing their kind of music. It all came together when a Decca recording landed on my desk in July of 1955 . . . it was Bill Haley's "Rock Around The Clock" and it changed the music world forever. I had graduated from high school the month before and this record holds a lot of signifi-

---

The first song was heard May 1st, 1980 from a little radio station in Riverside Industrial Park in Richmond. What is now Oldies 650 CISL began as CISL AM 940 Radio. Owned and operated by local businessman Michael Dickinson, CISL broadcast locally to Richmond, Delta, Surrey and White Rock. Four years later CISL changed both its frequency and format.

cance for me. It launched rock but it also stabilized my career; from that moment on it was clear sailing. The skyrocket had taken off and was soaring. The music world would never be the same again. Radio would never be the same again.

The radio station sent me out on a remote around this time and it was a rampage. The remote was at a record store and the line-ups filled the street. At one remote at a shoe store so many teenagers turned up that they broke all the showcases with just the mass of their bodies. The shock of these events hit parents hard and it was apparent by the letters to the editors of local newspapers. One columnist referred to me as "The Platter Prince of the Pimply Set." A writer referred to me as "The Pied Piper of Sin." All of this of course added to the popularity of my show and the music. Everyone hated it—except the teens—and the show grew. I wasn't about to let my new found discovery die. I took the records to high schools and parades. I rented airplanes and flew throughout British Columbia and Washington, taking the music with me. At first I appeared with records at "sock hops" but these graduated to gigs featuring local rock 'n' roll bands and then imported stars from the U.S. I would appear anywhere a young crowd was gathered: theatres, ball parks, even at the beach for outdoor sessions.

Radio was increasingly available in automobiles but the big break came with the invention of the transistor. Now you could take radio with you wherever you went. This mobility allowed radio to grow and grow. It had not died, as many had suggested it would, with the coming of television. Records and radio were the entertainment art forms for youth; only movies and drive-ins provided competition. All that was needed now was a musical form. "Rock Around The Clock" became the teenage world's national anthem.

The success of this record told the producers that a new form had been born. Some radio stations, either out of desperation to stay alive or because of an imaginative deejay, started playing this new brand of music called "rock 'n' roll." But success required a deejay who was tuned in to the tastes of the times. I was "of" that generation. I understood the music, the audience and the excitement of a new discovery. And it was exciting. New artists, new music, new areas to enjoy. It was dance hops, live performances, new dances, new movies—and it was totally ours.

Every major act played this city during the fifties, either in night clubs like the Cave or at one of the halls at the Pacific National Exhibition. The PNE was one reason Vancouver was on the list for all major acts. It was one of the biggest annual fairs in North America and was always on the touring circuit of the major booking agencies. And the Queen Elizabeth Theatre was a fine facility. Acts that worked up and down the Pacific

> At one remote at a shoe store so many teenagers turned up that they broke all the showcases with just the mass of their bodies. The shock of these events hit parents hard, apparent by the letters to the editors of local newspapers

coast always stopped off in Vancouver as part of their West Coast tour. Over the years I had met every major act in the music world when many did not stop to play cities such as Seattle or Portland. My American friends couldn't understand how these celebrities always seemed to find time in their schedules to perform in our city but play here they did (and still do).

When I started my deejay work on CJOR it was Western Canada's first 5,000-watt radio station. The radio dial then wasn't jammed up as it is today and you could hear CJOR over most of Washington and clear to Alaska. When I moved in 1957 to CKWX it was Western Canada's first 50,000-watt radio station and at night the signal could be heard in Northern California.

The benchmark years for rock 'n' roll were 1954 through 1957. I am proud to say the first regularly scheduled rock 'n' roll radio show in Canada was *Theme For Teens* in 1953. Realizing the power of the radio show and its gigantic following, concert promoters started booking acts into this city starting with Bill Haley and the Comets in 1956. They were followed by the famous touring shows of rock 'n' roll featuring all the main singers of the genre such as Chuck Berry, Little Richard, Fats Domino, Buddy Holly, Sam Cooke and so on. But the main event came in August of 1957 when Elvis Presley appeared at Empire Stadium. After this Vancouver was firmly established as a major destination for every rock 'n' roll act that followed.

Cleveland lays claim as the first American city to feature rock 'n' roll on the radio with the deejay who coined the phrase, Alan Freed. Vancouver was the first city in Canada to launch the brand new music form. Vancouver is Canada's pioneer rock 'n' roll city and proud of it. The tradition began here.

Moving to 650 on the AM dial and becoming Canada's first "Oldies" radio station proved to be a lucrative move. Since 1984 CISL has grown to become the Lower Mainland's biggest music station on the AM band, today a part of the Standard Radio chain, with a loyal listening audience that stretches from Campbell River to Abbotsford and south across the Canadian border.

The Jazz Scene
Renee Doruyter

THERE ARE A half-dozen establishments in Vancouver that feature jazz consistently and perhaps an equal number that present jazz once or twice a week. Vancouver also plays host to an annual International Jazz festival, produced by the Coastal Jazz and Blues Society in two dozen venues, including the Vogue Theatre, the Vancouver East Cultural Centre, and the Western Front. The festival usually runs the last week of June and finishes with two days of free concerts at the Plaza of Nations on the July 1 weekend. CJBS, formed in 1985 by Ken Pickering, Bob Kerr and John Orysik, also presents mainstream and creative improvisers in concert throughout the year and invites visitors to call the jazz hotline (682-0706) for information on upcoming events.

The Casbah Jazzbah at 175 West Pender, Rossini's (1525 Yew Street) and the Blue Note (2340 West 4th) are restaurants presenting easy-listening or "dinner jazz" most nights, usually featuring some of the world-class talent that chooses to live here, with occasional imports.

The Glass Slipper was a favorite haunt, run by musicians and volunteers, and presenting an eclectic mix of music. Unfortunately it burned down just before Christmas 1996. At press time, a campaign was under way to reopen.

For fans of traditional and swing music the Hot Jazz Club (2120 Main), also run by volunteers, is open Fridays and Sundays and has a dance floor. There's also an annual trad jazz festival, the Vancouver Classic Jazz Band Ball, which takes place in a downtown hotel in mid-November. New on the scene, the Purple Onion (15 Water Street) offers an intimate jazz lounge and a larger room that doubles as a disco. At the Georgia Hotel there's Chameleon Urban Lounge downstairs, and the Georgia Street Bar and Grill upstairs.

The Alma Street Cafe, on West Broadway at Alma, Bistro! Bistro! and Steam Works in Gastown, and Sortino's, Santos, the Latin Quarter and Cafe Deux Soleils in the Commercial Drive area also feature live jazz, mostly on weekends.

Jelly Roll Morton spent some time living in Vancouver in the 1940s, but Vancouver's jazz history really begins in the 1950s, when clubs such as the Press Club, the Cellar and the Quadra Club presented such soon-to-be-famous artists as Oscar Peterson, Art Pepper and the Montgomery Brothers and such local luminaries as Chris Gage, Eleanor Collins and Kenny Colman. Colman, a fine singer, is heard at the Casbah Jazzbah with potent trios and quartets made up of top-notch locals.

In the 1960s the jazz scene revolved around the Flat Five, an earlier Blue Note, and the big bands at Isy's and the Cave, where Bobby Hales, Stew Barnett, Fraser MacPherson, Doug Parker and a host of other talented players entertained. The after-hours action was at Neil Longton's Espresso Coffee House, where local and visiting musicians could and would play until dawn. Among them were a couple of Vancouver's best-known exports, the internationally renowned composer, arranger and instrumentalist Don Thompson, now living in Toronto, and one of the most musical drummers on the scene, Terry Clarke, now based in New York. Sadly the Espresso closed after a fire in 1968.

The late 1960s and early 1970s saw the arrival of mega-clubs such as Oil Can Harry's and Dirty Sal's Cellar (which was upstairs) and a funky little coffee house in Gastown called the Classical Joint, which by the time it closed in 1989 had became Vancouver's oldest jazz club. Touring big bands still played at the Commodore Ballroom regularly but disco was hurting the live clubs in a big way.

Vancouver's jazz scene revived in the late 1970s. The Landmark Jazz Bar at the Sheraton Plaza on Robson Street, under the guidance of the late Patric Brown, became the hot club in town with a lively mix of local and imported talent: Skywalk (one of the best fusion bands in the country and still around), Mose Allison, Freddie Hubbard and Larry Coryell are among those who made an impression there.

Sam Yehia also brought fabulous blues and jazz artists to Vancouver in this period, first to his intimate Robson Street restaurant, Cafe New York, then to Plazazz! at the International Plaza Hotel in North Vancouver. B.B. King, Ella Fitzgerald, Betty Carter, the Modern Jazz Quartet, Wynton Marsalis, Stephane Grappelli, Dizzy Gillespie and Oscar Peterson are among the stars that played there.

The Hotel Vancouver had jazz in the Red Barrel Room, featuring talented up-and-comers such as pianist Renee Rosnes, now living in New York, and Bob Murphy, whose recent recordings are finally bringing him some well-deserved attention. Maximilian's Symphony Hall brought people like Anita O'Day and Teddy Wilson to town, but opened and closed in the same year. Longtime Woody Herman saxophonist Roy Reynolds started a regular Thursday afternoon gig at Annabelle's, then at the disco in the Four Seasons Hotel, a tradition that continues today at the Fairview on Broadway.

Other important venues still sorely missed include the Three Greenhorns and Cafe Django. And there are too many wonderful musicians in town to even begin to name names.

In 1959, after owning and operating a six-store chain called A.B.C. Television, Colin Ryan and wife Lola changed the name of the company to J. Collins Furniture Gallery and opened two very large upscale stores, one in Burnaby, the other in downtown Vancouver. Son Dennis Ryan joined the company in 1970 and worked his way up to President. Colin retired in 1995 and Dennis wound up the business in April, 1996. Says jazz fan Colin, "I'm enjoying my retirement!"

Country Music
John P. McLauglin

COUNTRY MUSIC, A billion-dollar, 90s pop phenomenon, began modestly at a 1927 field recording session in Bristol, Tennessee. There Jimmie Rodgers and The Carter Family first put their dusty, unadorned songs to wax. Within a year both acts would boast million-selling records though it took a decade or so for their homespun sounds to waft up our way.

Still discernable in the Vancouver fog of time are CJOR radio stars like Billy Blinkhorn and the singing, slapstick-y Sleepy and Swede. They were steeped in vaudeville traditions which still had currency in the thirties and forties and were among the first in a long line—up to Elmer Tippe in the early Nineties—of performer/broadcasters in local country radio.

Over on CKMO in the late forties bassist Andy Fraser would sing on air when he wasn't spinning the latest discs while Bill Rea, a young dreamer from Saskatchewan, tuned in and made plans. The mercurial and irascible Rea would soon found the mighty CKNW where country music became the staple. He regularly invited local talent to his Bill Rea's Roundup—the Beckett Brothers, Evan Kemp (later a big name in Canada and the States) and the Rhythm Pals, who went on to work on national TV in Toronto, all performed.

The biggest hit the Rhythm Pals never had was called "My Home By The Fraser," recorded in 1947. Written by one Keray Regan the song was a local hit until the Fraser River overran its banks that year, carrying off homes and dreams. Suddenly tributes to the mighty, muddy Fraser seemed vaguely irrelevant. Later Evan Kemp hosed off the song, made it a hit and kept it in his repertoire for years.

Songwriter Keray Regan's brother was Bob Regan, a partner with Lucille Starr in the Canadian Sweethearts. The two had a serious run of success locally and south of the border but their marriage would later crumble in rancor over Lucille's solo stardom, a stardom that peaked with her mid-sixties international hit, "The French Song."

A big novelty number from the same time came from "Spade" Carl Neilsen and the Gamblers with their hilarious "(That's The Way) The Pickle Squirts" which not only became a big regional hit but was extremely popular on American Armed Forces bases down the East Coast. Neilsen himself was known for his skits and quick wit on stage. When he later became a realtor—he would eventually become president of Block Brothers Realty—Neilsen rewarded his top sales people at a Christmas party one year with turkeys, fully plumed and very much alive.

"My Home By The Fraser," was a local hit until the Fraser River overran its banks carrying off homes and dreams

The local country scene was coming into its own by 1964 when entrepreneur Jim Howe began running a West Burnaby club called the Lamplighter. While local music thrived in the legions, here's where you went to catch Waylon and Bobby Bare. And in an era when nightlifers still packed illicit bottles, the Lamplighter boasted B.C.'s first liquor license. Howe was also an early promoter of a B.C. country legend, Ray McAuley. Working with guitarist/songwriter Ed Molysky and managed by fifties Vancouver rocker Les Vogt and, later, Jim Howe, McAuley had a pending international RCA record contract when he died young and suddenly of a brain aneurism in the mid-Seventies.

Through the latter Seventies and into the Eighties country music in Vancouver diverged. On the one hand CKWX's Super Country man, fiddling Elmer Tippe, maintained the traditional, cozy feel of the genre, playing records and interviewing visiting Nashville glitterati and emerging local stars like Laurie Thain, Jess Lee and Rocky Swanson. On the other hand the eighties saw the rise of hip, left-of-centre acts like Denny Mack's Cement City Cowboys and the Billy Cowsill/Ray O'Toole-led Blue Northern, harmonizing on their memorable "Can't Make No Sense Out Of Loving You."

When entrepreneur Jimmy Pattison's JR Country FM began broadcasting in the mid-Eighties a friendly rivalry with 'WX emerged and local country singers, musicians, songwriters and producers won unprecedented attention and support. Bootleg and Alibi were two big bands of the time, the latter managed by Claude Lelievre and Diana Kelly, organizers of the massive Merritt Mountain Music Festival summer gala. Both have also been enthusiastic presidents of the B.C. Country Music Association.

The brainchild of a woman named Charlie Galbraith, the non-profit BCCMA was conceived in 1975 as an awards vehicle for local country music and today holds an annual conference and awards show every June. It has encouraged and jump started national and international careers for the likes of the Moffatt Brothers, Patricia Conroy, Lisa Brokop and One Horse Blue.

The once-dominant CKWX switched to all-news in 1996 and "new country" JR-FM is Vancouver's country music home now. Meanwhile clubs like Coquitlam's Boone Country and Gabby's in Langley keep the pedal steel weeping for the live crowd.

The Performing Arts

Vancouver Symphony Orchestra
Michael Scott

T HE VANCOUVER WE love today—this city of teeming
streets and manicured parks, of international chic,
Pacific Rim style—grew out of a single, sobering fact:
120 years ago there was nothing here but a sawmill at the
water's edge and a scattering of native Indian villages. Back
then, New Westminster and Victoria were the region's big
towns, bustling communities that had been growing for a generation. Port Moody was expected to be the terminus of the
transcontinental railway, and our link to Canada 3,000 miles
away. In 1880, Vancouver was still forest.

It doesn't matter how many shiny new office towers we
build, or how many ocean-view condo developments sprout
along False Creek, we live in a town so close to the frontier that
understanding anything about our cultural past means remem-
bering how far we've come in such little time. When the first
flood of European settlers arrived, just over a century ago, the
musical culture they brought with them consisted of a straggle
of brass players working on transcriptions of Bach in the shadows of the rainforest; and of loggers and grocers taking up their
fiddles and horns after supper for an hour of Brahms.

There was music here from the start of course, in the form of
choirs and ad hoc orchestras. But unlike the grown-up cities on
the other side of the continent—where the arts offered a lens
through which the citizens could observe and understand their
world—in Vancouver the arts were a diversion from the real business of beating back the frontier. That attitude of nature first, arts
second continues to stalk us even today, when deciding on concert tickets frequently means checking the weather report first.

It's been 77 years since a dodgy New Zealander and a sugar
baron's wife established the organization we still call the Vancouver Symphony Orchestra (VSO): an institution that has
yawed from insolvency to triumph again and again. Without
question, it has been an uphill battle all the way, waged by a
cadre of committed music lovers whose names and faces have
changed over the course of three-quarters of a century, but
whose message has stayed the same: a city without a symphony orchestra is a town without a musical heart.

That the VSO has survived at all is a testament to their
determination. When the shady Henry Green (who never
answered personal questions and refused to have his photograph taken) convinced Mary Isabella Rogers to help under-

facing page: Vancouver Symphony Orchestra, 1921. cva

write his subscription orchestra in the summer of 1919, they
launched what has become Western Canada's most enduring
cultural institution. Green and Mrs. Rogers also set the pattern
for the financial woes that have dogged the VSO ever
since—after 27 concerts in two seasons, the fledgling orchestra
collapsed in a welter of debt. Green slipped out of town one
spring night in 1921, never to be heard from again.

It wasn't until 1930 that the VSO reappeared, still championed by Mrs. Rogers, but now led by a professional musician,
Dutch violist Allard de Ridder. The next decade was a golden
age for Vancouver and its orchestra, with de Ridder's famous
friends trooping out to the Pacific coast as guest conductors,
among them Sir Ernest MacMillan, Sir John Barbirolli, Sir
Thomas Beecham and Arthur Benjamin. During the war, with
de Ridder gone off to Toronto, the orchestra ran along on a
series of guest conductors, Beecham and Barbirolli, Antal
Dorati, Eugene Goossens and Otto Klemperer among them. In
fact, Klemperer was hired as principal conductor for the
1946/47 season but performed only two concerts before his
deteriorating mental health forced him to cancel his contract.
It was under the rambunctious direction of Polish conductor
Jacques Singer—a temperamental protégé of Leopold Stokows-
ki—from 1947 to 1950 that the orchestra finally went professional, with a full-time administrative staff and 26-week
contracts for the musicians.

Reading histories of the VSO such as John Becker's 1989 *Discord: The Story of the Vancouver Symphony Orchestra,* or Dale
McIntosh's *History of Music in British Columbia: 1850 to 1950,* it
becomes clear that the Furies that have beset the orchestra have
remained constant over the decades. Money problems, quarrel-
some boards, controversial conductors and a tough-minded
musicians' union have plagued the VSO in one combination or
another right from the beginning. In 1938 Mary Rogers wondered why only 100 people in a city of 250,000 contributed to
the VSO's coffers. Were she still alive today, she might well ask
a similar question.

For most of us, the history of the VSO is indelibly colored
by the collapse and bankruptcy of 1987-88, when the orchestra
actually cancelled half its season and stung its subscribers and
other creditors for millions of dollars. There were days and
weeks in the spring of 1988 when it wasn't clear if the orchestra
would ever play again—or even whether it should.

That was probably as close as we've ever come to losing the
VSO. In the eight years since, after wildly generous bail-outs
from provincial and federal governments, the orchestra continues to lurch back and forth along the precipice.

One of the reasons is that whatever the situation was in 1919,

VSO performs on Blackcomb Mountain, 1988. vs

the VSO in 1996 no longer holds a monopoly on the musical life of the city. There are other orchestras, among them the CBC Vancouver Orchestra and the Vancouver Opera Orchestra, either of which could be expanded into a full-scale organization within a few seasons, given the will and the right music director.

Nor is there any longer a clear cultural imperative in this town for European high art—witness the fact that fewer than half the children in Vancouver schools speak English as their first language. High-fidelity recordings can summon up the finest orchestras in the world. And in the academic sphere, music schools would continue to find good teachers regardless of whether there were a symphony here or not.

Choosing to spend our leisure hours somewhere other than The Orpheum does not make us uncivilized or uncultivated. It's not that musical Vancouver has grown heartless, it's that as a community we've become more diverse. Like it or not, an 80-member orchestra is no longer a *sine qua non* of civilized urban life: it needs to earn its keep. These days it is the cultural institution that must adapt to the changing metropolis, not vice versa.

And so the VSO is learning, sometimes a little awkwardly, to reach out to new markets and new communities, to ask itself what it can sell that audiences want to buy, and how it can deploy its forces in new and attention-catching ways. As with any large 19th-century institution (daily newspapers and department stores included) the VSO is notoriously slow to change. Where small subscription series like the Friends of Chamber Music and the Vancouver Recital Society can narrowcast to their audiences, the VSO is still broadcasting, trying to be all things to all people. But it is working to change, slowly, like a giant ocean liner coming around in the water.

One of the brightest reasons for hope is the orchestra's music director, Sergiu Comissiona, who since coming here in 1990 has presided over a musical rebirth at the VSO. The band is playing better than it has in memory, thanks to Comissiona, who is as exacting in the rehearsal room as he is charming to the public.

For 77 years the VSO has fought a good fight, and it's not over yet. As tempting as it might be to invent a warm, halcyon past for the orchestra at the edge of the rainforest, the truth is that it's been tough to keep the music playing. Let's hope that the VSO continues to find the balance of public enthusiasm and government generosity it needs to keep going.

On January 10, 1997 an announcement was made that the VSO would merge with Vancouver Opera. But opposition led by VO orchestra members led to the proposal being shelved.

Early Music
Ray Chatelin

THE FIRST PIANO to arrive in the Lower Mainland is said to have belonged to Emmaline Jane Todd who first brought it to Victoria in 1856 and then to the mainland a year later. The first pipe organ, by comparison, was a second-hand instrument (a Karn-Warren) bought for Holy Trinity Cathedral of New Westminster in 1899.

Both of those instruments would today be the envy of Early Music Vancouver (EMV), by far the leading presenter of period music in the Lower Mainland. (Its formal name is the Vancouver Early Music Society.) The once-large number of groups in the 1970s that specialized in the form have narrowed considerably although the audience has not. Now the genre is included in the repertoire of many organizations with even Mozart currently being defined as "early."

Formed in 1969 by Jon Washburn, Ray Nurse, David Skulsky, Hans-Karl Piltz and Cuyler Page, EMV's purpose was and is to foster interest in medieval, renaissance and baroque music. But since then its interests have expanded—even to the point of having joint concerts with Vancouver New Music.

Besides having 10 main concert series during the season the society also hosts a joint summer program with the UBC music department offering a series of workshops and concerts. Its collection of 20 accurate replicas of old instruments—built by Vancouver-area craftsmen—is among the finest in the country.

The society also sponsors the Vancouver Early Music Festival which recruits teachers from their workshops and a variety of musicians from Canada, the U.S. and Europe.

- Early Music Vancouver, 1254 W. 7th Ave., Vancouver

> Vancouver, always a hotbed of Canadian contemporary composition, is today home to some of Canada's leading composers, spanning all musical forms and generations

New Music
Ray Chatelin

CONTEMPORARY MUSIC has a permanent home in Vancouver in the form of the Canadian Music Centre where you'll find a complete music and informational library of 300 British Columbian and Canadian composers. One of five CMC offices across Canada, the extensive libraries hold about 12,000 published and unpublished scores by Canadian composers. And you can buy books, records, CDs and tapes of many of these works and composers there .

Vancouver, always a hotbed of Canadian contemporary composition, is today home to some of Canada's leading composers, spanning all musical forms, generations and fashions. Styles range from the traditional, romantic orchestrations of Jean Coulthard by the Vancouver Symphony, to taut, contemporary experimentation played by young musicians on computers or computer-acoustic instruments in a variety of venues.

The Vancouver New Music Society is Vancouver's leading exponent of international and local contemporary music. Artistic director Owen Underhill, himself a composer, often leads pickup ensembles in performances of Canadian and international works, mainly at the Vancouver East Cultural Centre.

Underhill is also associated with the new music ensemble, Magnetic Band, the former Days, Months, and Years To Come Ensemble. Stationed at SFU the group plays in several venues.

Vancouver Pro Musica specializes in the music of Vancouver composers although it also stages works by international names. It has its own in-house ensemble, Standing Wave, made up of musicians devoted to the very new and unusual in acoustic music.

But Vancouver's new music scene doesn't end with only those organizations specializing in the genre. In fact, many of Vancouver's most established institutions include contemporary music in their main-stage programs and often have in-house composers. The CBC Vancouver Orchestra, Music in The Morning, the Vetta Chamber Music and Recital Society, Curio, the Vancouver Chamber Choir, the Vancouver Cantata Singers and the Vancouver Recital Society, as well as individual performers, help keep Greater Vancouverites in constant contact with the new, the unusual and the mainstream of late-20th-century music creation.

- Canadian Music Centre, 200-2021 W. 4th Ave., Vancouver
- Magnetic Band, School For The Contemporary Arts, SFU, Burnaby
- Vancouver New Music Society, 400-873 Beatty St., Vancouver
- Vancouver Pro Musica, 4755 Commercial St., Vancouver

Opera
Ray Chatelin

O NE MIGHT BELIEVE that opera came to Vancouver as early as the late 1880s with the opening of Hart's Opera House. Alas, this grandly named establishment was but a plank-sided building of exceeding plainness. Once a skating rink in Port Moody, it was eventually moved to Vancouver where it was home to minstrel shows, Salvation Army meetings and raucous comedies with features like live horses —one of which fell through the stage.

The real thing began February 9, 1891 with the grand opening of the 2,000-seat CPR-built Vancouver Opera House on Granville Street. The first production was Wagner's *Lohengrin,* starring the famed Vienna-born soprano Emma Juch, whose company it was. (Frau Juch was so impressed with the city she bought several local lots.) Dame Nellie Melba performed in concert there in 1905. This building, too, was used for much besides opera: on April 21, 1912 a public memorial service was held at the opera house in aid of widows and orphans of the seamen of the *Titanic,* lost on April 14. The Opera House was renamed the Orpheum—no connection to the current theatre of that name—and on March 17, 1913 began showing vaudeville acts. Then, as tastes changed further, on July 26, 1935 it became a cinema called the Lyric. The Lyric closed in December of 1960 before being demolished for the development of Pacific Centre.

So, when conductor Irwin Hoffman gave the downbeat and the VSO played the first notes of the overture to Bizet's opera, *Carmen,* on April 2, 1960, no one knew if Vancouver was really ready for its own opera company.

Not quite four decades later, Vancouver Opera has not only survived but is thriving. Through good years and bad the company has grown from one-opera-a-season into a multi-million dollar enterprise that is in economic and artistic good health and is giving every indication it will stay that way.

Originally incorporated as The Vancouver Opera Association, the founding artistic director was Irving Guttman who eventually also established companies in Edmonton, Winnipeg and Regina. The first season was an outgrowth of the Vancouver International Festival of 1958 in which a collection of musical stars (conductor Herbert von Karajan among them) gave Vancouverites a taste of high-calibre music.

While the festival drowned in a sea of financial losses, its most visible outgrowth was the fledgling opera company. Guttman's talent was in bringing together voices that meshed on stage: Vancouver soon found itself host to a lot of up-and-coming talent.

The real thing began February 9, 1891 with the opening of the 2,000-seat CPR-built Vancouver Opera House. The first production was Wagner's *Lohengrin,* starring the famed Vienna-born soprano Emma Juch

The October 1963 production of *Norma* had a young Joan Sutherland and Marilyn Horne singing together with Sutherland's husband, conductor Richard Bonynge, in the pit. Horne again sang in the March 1965 production of *An Italian Girl in Algiers,* in the 1966 staging of *Il Trovatore* and in 1968's *Barber of Seville.* Sutherland returned for *Lucia Di Lammermoor* (1967), and made her Lucrezia Borgia debut in 1972. She would later be a regular at Vancouver opera when Bonynge took over from Guttman as artistic director in 1974-75. By then, Sutherland was a superstar, one of the great voices of the 20th century. A then-unknown Spanish tenor, Placido Domingo, sang twice under Guttman, in *Tosca* (1968) and *Manon* (1969). During that time the company also staged recitals that featured Sutherland and Montserrat Caballe, among others, a tradition that continues.

Currently, Vancouver Opera stages a recital series in conjunction with other music organizations like the Vancouver Recital Society, bringing in such international opera stars as Jessye Norman, Kathleen Battle, Dmitri Hvorostovsky, Ben Heppner and Samuel Ramey.

The Bonynge years—1974 to 1978—began with great promise and ended with the last half of the 1977-78 season being cancelled because of mounting debt. Bonynge, though often mired in controversy about finances and programming, changed the direction of the company. He created his own orchestra and established a resident training program, both of which are foundations of the current operation. He was succeeded by Hamilton McClymont, formerly of the Canada Council, whose primary objective was to bring the operation back into financial stability.

After McClymont left in 1982 came Brian McMaster of the Welsh National Opera Company—following an interim season by Guttman who had returned as consulting director. (Guttman had also acted briefly as interim-director immediately after Bonynge left.) It was McMaster who defined the modern company in his six year tenure, giving Vancouver audiences unusual, controversial and mainstream-with-a-difference operatic productions. His off-the-wall production of *Carmen* set in a Central American banana republic and with contemporary dialogue was one of the highlights of Expo 86.

Current general director Robert Hallam and music director David Angler oversee a music organization with a multi-million dollar annual budget and that is broadening its outreach programs to fit Vancouver's changing cultural character.

The company's attendance figures continue to run at about 90 per cent and its education program reaches more than 70,000 school children in British Columbia. In fact, its Opera In The School program is the largest of its kind in Canada with some 176 performances in the Lower Mainland and the Interior. It's a company within a company, having an 18-week season with four singers (tenor, baritone and two sopranos), a stage manager and a pianist on a keyboard/synthesizer. Singers in the educational program also sing in the main-stage productions.

Established in 1972 by the Vancouver Opera Guild it is designed as an introduction to opera for children in grades 1 to 7. And since the program is the first experience that children have with the art form, it is designed to bridge any high-brow barriers. Young people are given 50-minute adaptations of originals after teachers prep them with targeted educational kits. Reflecting that style was a recent production entitled *Magic Flute: The Space Tour,* adapted by local singer/writer Sandy Winsby from Mozart's opera *The Magic Flute.*

The main-stage company's programming has come a long way since its first season of *Carmen,* followed the next year by *La Boheme* and *La Traviata.* Not only does the company now have a five-opera program with 28 performances, it often goes outside the mainstream for its stagings with productions like Stravinsky's *The Rake's Progress,* Handel's *Alcina* and Bizet's *Pearl Fishers,* giving audiences opera with a difference. In 1994 the company staged its first-ever commission, *The Architect,* by composer David MacIntyre and librettist Tom Cone. It was staged in front of 85 per cent-capacity houses. The company has also commissioned another new work, *Alternate Visions,* by Vancouver composer John Oliver.

Greater Vancouver's most well-known home-grown opera name is likely Coquitlam-born Judith Forst. Awarded a five-year contract with the Metropolitan Opera Association of New York in 1969, she went on to become a world-renowned mezzo-soprano. She is still active.

From Carmen's Spain to China, opera in Greater Vancouver is varied; above, a member of the Richmond-based Lee Siu Wah Opera at the Plaza of Nations for Chinese New Year, 1997. vs

The company's founders instilled an appreciation for nature's gifts with an environmental ethic that is a foundation of today's operations. The company has been a leader in the development of innovative logging and sustainable forestry practices, industrial processes and total utilization of the wood fibre resources of the province.

Musicals and Revues
Mark Leiren-Young

O N NOVEMBER 2, 1995, Vancouver entered a new era of musical theatre when Brent Carver took the stage to perform his one-man show at the Ford Centre for the Performing Arts. Created by Toronto entrepreneur Garth Drabinsky to house Broadway-style mega-musicals, the $24.5 million Ford Centre redefined the city's theatre landscape.

Just a few days earlier Jeff Hyslop appeared at the Vogue Theatre in his one-man musical revue, *Feet First,* and the message was inescapable—Vancouver's musical theatre scene was all grown up.

Both Carver and Hyslop are local performers who have won accolades on Broadway. Carver, who was born in Cranbrook, received a 1993 Tony Award for his starring role in *Kiss of the Spiderwoman* and Hyslop, who was the first North American to play the title role in *Phantom of the Opera,* starred in the international touring production of *A Chorus Line* and was the lead dancer in Norman Jewison's film version of *Jesus Christ Superstar.*

Both men have proven themselves repeatedly over lengthy careers and both started those careers in Vancouver, taking some of their first professional dance steps with Theatre Under the Stars, a professional company founded in 1940 by Gordon Hilker. The debut season of TUTS featured *The Geisha, As You Like It* and *A Midsummer Night's Dream*; reserved tickets sold for fifty cents with unreserved seats available for a quarter. Since then TUTS has operated almost continuously, presenting approximately 150 musicals primarily at Malkin Bowl in Stanley Park. TUTS suspended operations in 1963 but was revived as a semi-professional company in 1969.

In addition to providing both training and recognition to such well-known local performers as Hyslop, Carver, Rex Downey, Roma Hearn and Ruth Nichol, TUTS also helped launch the musical career of Robert Goulet. Vancouver impresario Hugh Pickett who served as a manager (and later press agent) for TUTS recalls the company bringing Goulet out for *Gentlemen Prefer Blondes* before the actor's career had taken off "and everybody liked him." During much of the 20th century TUTS has been the only professional company presenting homegrown musical theatre productions.

Many TUTS alumni actually received their start through Mussoc (the University of British Columbia Musical Theatre Society), formed in 1916.

Two of the most important players in the history of both organizations were director Jimmy Johnston and choreographer Grace MacDonald, who acclaimed Canadian director Richard Ouzounian described as "the grand lady of the UBC Musical Society and Theatre Under the Stars." Ouzounian recalls making his Mussoc debut in a production of *Fiddler on the Roof* with a cast that included Ruth Nichol, Jane Mortifee and a crew member named Brent Carver. Other Mussoc alumni include Hyslop, Patrick Rose, Ann Mortifee, Victor Young, David Y.H. Lui and Margot Kidder. MacDonald, who died in 1987 at the age of 71, choreographed Mussoc's productions for more than 30 years.

Another major musical event to come from UBC was the smash hit *In the Rough.* Produced in 1964 and 1965 at the Frederic Wood Theatre, the topical revue was directed by John Brockington, starred Jimmy Johnston, Daphne Goldrick, Norman Young, Pat Rose and Louise Glennie and featured sketches and songs by such writers as Dave Brock and Eric Nicol. *In the Rough* was so successful that the show was revived in 1967 to tour the province as part of Canada's centennial celebrations.

The TUTS torch as the bright light of Vancouver musical theatre was taken over by the Arts Club Theatre in 1972 when the musical *Jacques Brel is Alive and Well and Living in Paris*—a co-production with David Y.H. Lui—launched the current era of Vancouver's professional theatre scene. *Brel* originally starred Leon Bibb, Ruth Nichol, Ann Mortifee and Pat Rose (and featured Brent Carver in his first professional role). The show was so popular it drew 40,000 people to the Arts Club Seymour Street Theatre—even selling out 11:00 A.M. Sunday matinees—and provided a new local definition for the word "hit" that has shaped programming at the Arts Club and throughout the city ever since. Since the opening of *Brel* the Arts Club has produced nearly 70 musicals.

In 1983 the Arts Club opened a new theatre designed specifically for musicals and revues. The Arts Club Revue Theatre kicked off with *An Evening with Ruth and Leon* starring *Brel* alumni Ruth Nichol and Leon Bibb. The Revue Theatre's biggest hits included *Ain't Misbehavin',* (a collection of Fats Waller tunes) and the punk musical *Angry Housewives.* Both productions ran for over 1,000 performances. The Revue Theatre was transformed into a more traditional theatre space in 1995 but the Arts Club is set to open a new revue theatre in the old Stanley movie house. The Arts Club's repertoire of long-running hit musicals also includes *Pippin, A Closer Walk With Patsy Cline, El Grande De Coca Cola* and *Reflections on Crooked Walking* (created for the Arts Club by Ann Mortifee).

Although the Arts Club has been the main home for made-in-Vancouver musical productions, there were a few major pro

 Howe Sound Pulp and Paper Ltd., jointly owned by Canfor and New Oji Paper Co. Ltd. of Japan, was the first pulp and paper mill in Canada capable of producing totally chlorine-free bleached pulp. Canfor's Research and Development Centre in Vancouver has played a critical role in the company's efforts to develop new products and processes.

ductions that got their start in some of Vancouver's other theatres. *Billy Bishop Goes to War,* playwright-composer John Gray's two-man musical about Canada's World War I flying legend, opened at the Vancouver East Cultural Centre in 1978 and eventually played all over the world.

Gray, who was declared "a national treasure" by the *Toronto Star's* Gina Mallet, was actually raised in Nova Scotia but studied theatre at UBC and began his career with Tamahnous Theatre, a company he helped found in 1971. Gray's other major musicals include *18 Wheels, Rock and Roll* and *Don Messer's Jubilee.* The Vancouver East Cultural Centre was also the launching pad for the 1982 comedy musical *Last Call!,* a "postnuclear cabaret" marking the arrival of the duo—Morris Panych and Ken MacDonald—that helped define Vancouver theatre through the 1980s and into the 1990s. The two co-created and starred in the acclaimed Tamahnous Theatre production. Panych went on to become a Governor-General's Award winner as a playwright as well as one of Vancouver's most successful stage actors, while MacDonald has shown himself to be one of Canada's most innovative set designers.

The Vancouver Playhouse company was formed in 1963 and has produced numerous musicals over the years, the most notable being its production of George Ryga's *Grass and Wild Strawberries,* the 1969 musical about hippie culture that featured live music by The Collectors (who later became nationally famous as Chilliwack). The show was a pop-culture phenomenon with many Playhouse subscribers leaving the theatre at intermission and local hippies flocking to the empty seats to watch the second act. Other homegrown musical highlights have included *Piaf, Her Songs, Her Loves.* Directed by the late Ray Michal and starring Joelle Rabu, the musical ran offand-on throughout the 1980s at the now-defunct City Stage.

With the creation of the modern mega-musical in the 1980s the entire concept of musical theatre changed worldwide, as the genre became synonymous with big-budget, big-spectacle productions. The first show to prove that Vancouver could sustain a long run for a mega-musical was *Cats,* which was also the first time a Canadian company had ever been granted the rights to produce a made-in-Canada version of a Broadway musical hit. Produced by Tina VanderHeyden and Marlene Smith *Cats* opened at the Queen Elizabeth Theatre June 29, 1987, and ran until September 12, grossing $8 million and convincing entrepreneurs that Vancouver was ripe for commercial theatre productions. *Cats* returned a year later with a new litter that played another month and paved the way for *Phantom of the Opera.* Co-produced by VanderHeyden and Garth Drabinsky's Livent, Inc. the latter show spooked audiences for six

months in 1991 and ultimately led to VanderHeyden's decision to move back to Vancouver with her production company (Headquarters Entertainment) and Drabinsky's decision to build the Ford Centre which opened with the musical that has made the most impact in Vancouver's history. Livent Inc.'s production of the classical American musical *Show Boat* featured a cast of 73 (including George Grizzard and Cloris Leachman), a 30-piece orchestra and a backstage crew of 37. It opened on December 3, 1995, to rave reviews including one in the *Province* proclaiming that the production will "change Vancouver theatre forever."

It will. And that's why each ticket comes with a surcharge that will be donated to Vancouver's other theatres to help make sure they're not run over by the Ford.

However *Show Boat* wasn't the biggest musical in Vancouver's history. As far back as the late 1800s Vancouver hosted touring productions from around the world and at the turn of the century there was a taste for spectacles even more spectacular in their day than *Show Boat* or *Phantom of the Opera.*

A 1908 touring production of *Ben Hur* that played Vancouver featured a cast of 275 and onstage chariot races. Many other productions of that era also called for live animals to appear onstage alongside all the modern marvels of the day ranging from cars and trains to full-scale blast furnaces.

Phantom of the Opera souvenir shop, 1991. VS

Drama

Anne Tempelman-Kluit

THEIR NAMES ARE LEGENDARY: Sarah Bernhardt, Ellen Terry, Henry Irving, Mark Twain—they performed in London, Paris, New York and . . . Vancouver. More than a century ago, when Vancouver barely had running water, we had an Opera House where the international greats of show business appeared.

Vancouver's love affair with the theatre began when the city was just a few months old. Keefer Hall was one of the first new structures built after the city was razed by fire in June, 1886. It doubled as a skating rink and theatre. But Vancouver's cultural scene was truly launched by Shakespeare's *Richard III* starring William Lloyd at the Imperial Theatre in December, 1889. The new theatre was on Beatty Street near Cambie, then the heart of Downtown. Downtown, uptown, out-of-town—Vancouver's citizens and Shakespeare have flirted with each other ever since.

When the Canadian Pacific Railway rolled into Vancouver in 1887 the first Hotel Vancouver was built to accommodate its passengers. To enhance the surroundings the CPR built the 2,000-seat Vancouver Opera House in 1891, across from the hotel at Georgia and Granville. In February, in a snow storm, the $100,000 Opera House's opening presentation was *Lohengrin* starring Emma Juch. Declared by some to be the best theatre on the continent, it saw many revered actors tread its boards. Mark Twain appeared in 1895 to rave reviews despite a severe head cold. The Opera House, later renamed the Lyric, became a movie theatre in 1935 and demolished in the 60s to make way for Eaton's.

The city's growth continued unabated and to appease the demand for entertainment, theatres—the Savoy, the Lyric, the Orpheum, the Empress, the Alcazar, the Beacon, the Royal—were built and flourished. The Empress presented *Romeo and Juliet,* Nijinsky danced with the Ballet Russe at the Opera House in 1917 and Sarah Bernhardt appeared at the Orpheum in 1918. The best seats were 80 cents, the cheapest 15 cents.

The Vancouver Shakespeare Society was formed in 1916. *Hamlet, The Merchant of Venice, Julius Caesar* and *Romeo and Juliet* entranced audiences and always played to full houses.

In the 1930s Shakespeare's plays were again the star attraction at Stanley Park's Malkin Bowl. Actors on the stage performed the motions while other actors off-stage said the words into a microphone. In the same Malkin Bowl, Theatre Under the Stars came into being in 1940 but closed in 1963. Resurrected in 1969 by local enthusiasts TUTS continues to thrive. Every summer (weather permitting) musicals are performed under starry skies.

More formal theatre came to Vancouver with the opening of the Vancouver Playhouse in 1963. The first production was Brendan Behan's scandalous work, *The Hostage.* The first original Canadian play produced was Eric Nicol's *Like Father, Like Fun* in the 1965 season. In 1967 George Ryga's landmark play about the abuse of native women, *The Ecstasy of Rita Joe,* with Chief Dan George and Ann Mortifee, electrified audiences with its strong message. The intimate Playhouse has always given Canadian plays priority. The late Larry Lillo wooed Vancouver audiences with "modern, slightly off-beat works" as well as the comfortably familiar during his tenure as artistic director from 1988 to 1993. Audiences should be challenged as well as entertained, Lillo said. Some theatre-goers "wanted to see plays with meat on their bones."

Shakespeare competes with the matchless setting of the city, ocean and mountains visible from Bard on the Beach's open-ended candy-striped tent at Vanier Park. Artistic director Christopher Gaze mounted the first year's production of *A Midsummer Night's Dream* in 1990 with financing from "my dentist, my insurance man, anyone. We raised $36,000 and cleared $1,300 at the end of the season."

Bard on the Beach is also at the whim of the weather, although sometimes the weather steals the show. Gaze recalls a violent thunder storm during *A Midsummer Night's Dream* which stopped the play. "You couldn't hear a thing. Oberon ran to the back of the stage and as he leapt off, he was silhouetted by a huge lightning flash. We couldn't have staged it better if we'd tried." A Cathay Pacific vice-president in the audience was so impressed he immediately offered sponsorship. In a 1995 production of *Hamlet* the actor playing Laertes was hit by a car enroute to the theatre and had his leg broken. Gaze quickly dressed as Laertes and played the role reading from the script! Storms, fog horns, broken legs, fireworks . . . the Bard goes on.

There was nothing spectacular about the Arts Club Theatre's venue on Seymour Street—located above a former auto repair shop and gospel hall—but it became an instant theatrical institution when Yvonne Firkins opened it in 1964. The first production, Moss Hart's *Light Up the Sky,* won high praise. Now the largest regional theatre in Western Canada, the Arts Club expanded to Granville Island where it opened a main stage and a revue theatre. The shabby, cozy Seymour Street venue continued to flourish until 1991 when the building was sold.

Now the Arts Club with its emphasis on 20th century productions is taking another giant leap of faith. The Stanley, the lovely old movie theatre on Granville Street, will reopen as the Arts Club at the Stanley. Bill Millerd, artistic and managing director of the Arts Club Theatre since 1972, reflects that local theatre has traditionally favored productions it feels comfortable with but

Figures originally mounted on the cornice of Pantages Theatre (1908), displayed in the Vancouver Museum, 1986. VS

that change is inevitable. "We've been reluctant to adapt," Millerd comments, "but we're being challenged by outside forces."

One major outside force is the $24.5 million Ford Centre for the Performing Arts which opened in November, 1995, with the mega-musical *Show Boat*. It was the first time a Broadway-style production was staged in Vancouver on a long-term basis.

While musical extravaganzas will always find an audience, small play companies, many under the umbrella of the Vancouver Professional Theatre Alliance, continue to survive, even flourish. The Firehall Theatre's searing production of *Whale Riding Weather* played to packed houses for weeks. To paraphrase W.P. Kinsella, "perform it and they will come."

The Dance Scene
Max Wyman

THE EARLIEST public professional dancing that happened in Vancouver was, not surprisingly, imported. Busy building a city, the new Vancouverites had other things on their minds than the urge to trip the light fantastic. But they were enthusiastic audiences and they liked what they saw to have a touch of the exotic about it.

Vancouver was just ten years old when the U.S. dancer Loie Fuller did her *Fire Dance*—an extravagance of swirling fabrics that used the new electric lighting to great effect—before a capacity audience at the Vancouver Opera House in 1896. Vancouver was Anna Pavlova's only Canadian port of call during her first North American tour in 1910 and she returned three times. Ruth St. Denis and Ted Shawn, two of the pioneers of U.S. modern dance, showed Vancouver their Oriental exotica on frequent visits on the vaudeville circuit between 1914 and 1924. The Diaghilev Ballets Russes, an emigré troupe of Russian dancers, choreographers and artists whose tours showed North American audiences an entirely new way of looking at ballet, made Vancouver its only Canadian engagement, in 1917 (with Vaslav Nijinsky dancing).

The cultural development of Vancouver in the 1920s and 1930s was stimulated by Edinburgh-born Lily Laverock, a Vancouver newspaper woman who set up as an impresario in 1921, seeking out whatever she felt might best benefit and interest the city's audiences. (Two promoters inherited her entertain-and-educate traditions—Hugh Pickett, whose Famous Artists served the dance audience through the 1950s and 1960s, and David Y.H. Lui, a Chinese-Canadian promoter who brought Vancouver most of the international ballet and modern dance companies of the 1970s).

In the late 1920s and early 1930s North America teemed with itinerant Russian dance-master emigrés, all of them basking in the reflected glory of the internationally famed Russian companies. Nicholas Rusanoff, who claimed to have been with the Imperial Russian Ballet in Moscow, taught in Vancouver in 1927 before moving to Victoria. In the same period Nikolas Merinoff shared a Vancouver studio with Charlotte del Roy. Kazan-educated Boris Novikoff taught alongside his sister, Tatiana Platowa. Novikoff established the Russian-American Ballet Company here and performed extensively around southern B.C. before settling in the U.S. with his Seattle-based brother, Ivan.

In 1934 June Roper, a teacher from Rosebud, Texas, settled in Vancouver after a distinguished career as a dancer in Europe. Roper understood the style the Russian companies preferred: big, flamboyant, flashy. It was a significant ingredient of her success. In 1938 two of her teenage students were accepted as members of the de Basil Ballet Russe, a hybrid of up-and-coming young dancers and leftovers from Diaghilev's troupe, and both were given Russian names. Rosemary Deveson, 16, became Natasha Sobinova. Patricia Meyers, 15, was Alexandra Denisova. They were the first of more than 60 dancers that June Roper sent from Vancouver to international ballet companies and to Hollywood: Ian Gibson, who danced in North America's first *Coppélia* (in Victoria, in 1936) went to New York's Ballet Theatre. Peggy Middleton went to the movies—as Yvonne de Carlo. Sixty dancers: the cream of the B.C. crop. *Dance Magazine* called June Roper North America's greatest star-maker.

At that time success for a Vancouver dancer was measured by the ability to find work with a professional company elsewhere. Everyone went away . . . usually under an assumed name. Indigenous professional ballet was short-lived. Companies from here went to most of the Canadian Ballet Festivals of the late 1940s and early 1950s: a program from the 1953 festival carries a photo of a Vancouver 14-year-old described by New York critics as "one of the joys of the festival." Her name was Lynn Springbett. She went away as well—and she, too, went away under an assumed name: Lynn Seymour.

In 1961 the Vancouver Ballet Society (established in 1946) launched a workshop in classical repertoire with the intention of developing a Vancouver ballet company as a joint endeavor by the city's teachers. Until the late 1960s the VBS workshop mounted substantial productions featuring many dancers who went on to professional careers (including Reid Anderson, eventually the head of the National Ballet of Canada). What they did not produce, however, was a company.

Not that others didn't try. Modern dancer-choreographer Norbert Vesak joined ballet teacher Joy Camden to launch Pacific Dance Theatre; its early performances were welcomed warmly by the press but the company never became financially viable. Two years later Beth Lockhart, who had settled in Vancouver after a career in Hollywood and Toronto, teamed up with former Royal Ballet dancer Peter Franklin White for an abortive attempt at a year-round Ballet B.C. And in 1971 five former Royal Winnipeg Ballet dancers launched Ballet Horizons here. It lasted a year.

The individual who finally made a ballet company happen in Vancouver was Maria Lewis who established Pacific Ballet Theatre in 1969 after a career as a dancer in Montreal and

Toronto. The company grew slowly to semi-professional regional status dancing a repertoire of small works in the classical style. Lewis was succeeded in 1980 by Kamloops-born Renald Rabu and in 1985 the company was renamed Ballet British Columbia, under the artistic direction of former Grands Ballets Canadiens principal Annette av Paul.

In 1987 av Paul passed the reins to Reid Anderson who used his extensive European connections (19 years with the Stuttgart Ballet) to give the company a contemporary-ballet look. He also brought in Natalia Makarova for a gala featuring a duo from the Kirov Ballet—the first time in 17 years that Makarova had danced on the same stage as dancers from her home company.

Anderson moved to Toronto in 1989 and was succeeded briefly by Patricia Neary, a former New York City Ballet principal, before Barry Ingham took over in 1990. John Alleyne, a Barbados-born National Ballet School alumnus with extensive performing experience in Germany, became artistic director following Ingham's death in 1992. Building on a repertoire that mixes his own work with that of some of Europe's most influential ballet innovators, Alleyne has given Ballet B.C. a style unique in Canada: lean, daring, off-kilter. Meanwhile teacher Choo Chiat Goh was working to establish the Goh Ballet, featuring senior students in classical ballet and traditional Chinese movement. Goh's daughter, Chan Hon Goh, has become a much-admired principal with the National Ballet of Canada.

If, however, ballet had a hard time becoming established, modern dance has thrived. At several points in modern dance history Vancouver has been the nation's creative hotbed. Some of the earliest activities were centred round the Bohemian sisters Gertrud and Magda Hanova, who studied ballet and modern dance in Vienna and Berlin, and Indian dance styles and yoga in India, before bringing their mix of these influences to Vancouver in the late 1950s. Many of Vancouver's modern dance pioneers studied with the Hanovas. Others studied with Norbert Vesak, the lone B.C. participant in Canada's first national modern dance festival (in Toronto in 1963) and Vancouver's first modern dance professional.

Born in Port Moody in 1936, he trained in modern dance and ballet in the U.S. and England, and in the early 1960s returned to Vancouver with a mission—to teach modern dance based on a technical system rather than merely an interpretive method. In 1970 he launched his own company, Western Dance Theatre. Lynn Seymour came back to dance with him as a guest; hopes grew for the establishment of Canada's fourth major dance company. But the organizational and financial pressures, combined with negative commentary on Vesak's

There was a brief flaring up of activity in Vancouver in the early 80s as the solo, independent, experimental dancer became prominent

artistic judgment, became intolerable and the company closed midway through its second season. The next day Vesak was invited to make *The Ecstasy of Rita Joe* for the Royal Winnipeg Ballet. It became one of that company's most popular ballets. Vesak later resettled in California and developed a busy international career as a choreographer and director. He was another who went elsewhere to succeed.

Developments at the two Lower Mainland universities were crucial in helping modern dance get its footing here. U.S.-trained Iris Garland arrived at Simon Fraser University in 1965 and developed a dance program that showcased leading U.S. modernists. Echoes of these influences were seen for years in the companies created by SFU alumni. Even earlier Helen Goodwin was serving a similar function at the University of British Columbia (her experimental group, The Co., founded in 1964, took part in many of UBC's contemporary arts festivals).

The earliest properly established modern dance group in Vancouver was created by Paula Ross in 1965. A former student of ballet teacher Mara McBirney, Ross worked as a "specialty dancer" and chorine in the U.S. and Canada before returning to Vancouver in the early 1960s to teach the city's show-dancers and chorus girls a modern technique of her own devising. Her troupe, which suspended operations in 1987, was a showcase for her own "visual poetry," which expressed the passion of a driven and socially committed artist.

Anna Wyman was another who drew on a mixed ballet and modernist background. Born in Austria, she moved to Vancouver in 1967 and in 1968 began to present student performances. Initially based on improvisation, her style evolved into a theatrical abstract linearity. A regular at the Vancouver Art Gallery's noon concerts in the early 1970s, her company opened the Vancouver East Cultural Centre with a two-week residency in 1973. Subsequently the company undertook numerous tours (including the first tour of China by any modern dance troupe).

Stimulated in part by government make-work funding, several other modern companies sprang up in the 1970s. Former

members of the Vesak company set up Synergy and the same year Jamie Zagoudakis, another Vesak alumnus and former Synergy co-head, created Contemporary-Jazz Dance Theatre. He was joined as co-director in 1975 by Gisa Cole and, as Prism Dance Theatre, the company became a popular producer of entertainment dance.

SFU provided some of the most significant companies of that period. Mountain Dance Theatre began as Burnaby Mountain Dance Company in 1973 and moved off-campus in 1975 under the joint direction of Mauryne Allan and Freddie Long. Allan became sole head in 1979 and the company survived until 1987. It was reincarnated in 1988 as DanceCorps with Cornelius Fischer-Credo as director. Active in the same period was Ernst and Carole Eder's two-person troupe, Tournesol.

A company with long-term significance for movement-making in Vancouver was Terminal City Dance (launched in 1976). A product of a collaboration between (initially) two former Garland students, Karen Rimmer and Savannah Walling, and (eventually) three other dancers, its focus was experiment and exploration. In 1983 the ensemble broke up with Karen Rimmer reverting to her maiden name, Karen Jamieson, and establishing a company of her own, and Walling and Terry Hunter creating Special Delivery Dance/Music/Theatre (now known as Vancouver Moving Theatre, specializing in transcultural exploration of mask, mime and myth). Jamieson has remained broadly within the Western dance tradition, creating uncluttered, energy-focussed movement that allows her to address problems of the human condition. In recent years she has been investigating collaborations with Northwest Coast native artists.

Judith Marcuse, born in Montreal in 1947, danced in modern and classical companies in Europe, Israel and North America and began to choreograph in 1976, the year she moved to Vancouver. She launched her own company in 1980 as a repertory for modern choreography and later turned her attention to projects integrating dance with other arts.

In 1982 a diverse group of young independent dance-makers created another influential modernist collective, EDAM (Experimental Dance and Music), exploring issues ranging from contact improvisation to dance of the absurd. The group began to splinter in 1987 and by 1989 EDAM was directed by contact improviser Peter Bingham. Jay Hirabayashi and Barbara Bourget broke away to create Kokoro Dance, using raw, emotional movement that blends Western styles with elements of Japanese butoh techniques. Another EDAM co-founder who has had her own company since 1989 is Jennifer Mascall, a radical explorer of less predictable modern dance. EDAM original Lola MacLaughlin set up a company the same year as a showcase for her own

Dance Magazine called Vancouver's June Roper North America's greatest star-maker

thoughtful, witty movement meditations. Interdisciplinary adventure has marked much new dance. Lee Eisler's Jumpstart, launched in the early 1980s by poet Nelson Gray and former Olympic athlete Eisler, is dedicated to exploring the new technology, stressing language and vocal performance.

From the late 1970s through the mid-1980s the West Coast modern dance scene moved into a lull. Money began to dry up, people's attention moved to other things and the focus of modern dance in Canada shifted—first to Toronto, then Montreal, where social upheaval spawned a generation of highly politicized artists. There was a brief flaring-up of activity in Vancouver in the early 1980s as the solo, independent, experimental dancer became prominent—a phenomenon fostered in part by the steady drying-up of funding for the arts—but the economic problems that had stemmed the flow of funding were bringing about a new conservatism on the part of audiences: experiment was out, safety was in. By the mid-1990s the dance community was reshaping itself yet again in response to changing economic forces. Many younger creators found themselves forced to evolve new means of survival—primarily through collaboration. A dance community that once had been little more than a geographic region found itself unified by adversity. Times have never been so tough yet, conversely, the sense of mutual support has never been so great.

Today it's no longer necessary for anyone to leave town. We have a more mature dance community than ever. The establishment of the Vancouver Dance Centre and the Vancouver Cultural Alliance means that dancers talk to each other and to other artists. Ballet dancers work with modern choreographers. Independent artists pop up everywhere. We have well-established and well-respected schools. We have a generation of creatively mature modernist choreographers turning out work that is consistently as interesting as anything from the rest of Canada. We have dancers who dazzle the eye. (Awards and accolades have been showered on Vancouver dancers and choreographers: the Chalmers and Lee choreographic awards, the country's top prizes, regularly come this way.) We have one of the country's most exciting annual modern dance festivals (Dancing on the Edge at the Firehall Theatre). We have a ballet company with an international reputation.

All that's missing is the audience.

Amateur and Little Theatre

Mark Leiren-Young

IN 1985 A SMALL COMPANY called TheatreSpace (led by artistic director Joanna Maratta) produced the first annual Vancouver Fringe Festival—a non-juried performing arts smorgasbord that provides the venue, technical support and publicity so that anyone who wants to put on a show can. Modelled after the Edmonton Fringe Festival (one of North America's largest theatre events) acts of all types are admitted from Vancouver—and around the world—on a first-come first-serve basis and the only qualification for admission is the ability to afford the entrance fee.

Although some Fringe participants are professional actors and a handful of shows are produced by professional companies, the majority of the productions are staged by amateur groups or ad hoc troupes formed to produce a play they believe in. Because of the high profile of the event and the relatively low cost of mounting a Fringe production, the festival (which runs for two weeks each September) has become Greater Vancouver's premiere launching pad for amateur theatre. Originally located in the Mount Pleasant area the Fringe moved to Commercial Drive in 1995.

On a year-round basis Greater Vancouver is also home to numerous amateur companies—some of which have been operating for decades. Theatre B.C., an umbrella organization for community theatre companies throughout British Columbia, listed over two dozen active amateur companies in the GVRD in 1995, including a variety of groups with mandates to serve specific ethnic communities.

The Vancouver Little Theatre Association, possibly Canada's oldest continuously operating community theatre company, was formed in 1921, producing its first play, *Lonesome Like* (directed by Frederick Wood) in a 200-seat auditorium at Templeton Hall at Pender and Templeton. Two years later it purchased the Alcazar Theatre (now The York), but its most recent home opened in 1985, when the VLTA created a new venue at Vancouver's Heritage Hall—the aptly named Vancouver Little Theatre, which comfortably seats 71 people (if no one inhales). In 1989 the VLTA switched its focus from producing plays to managing its venue (and changed its name to the Vancouver Little Theatre Alliance), but it is still involved in mounting the occasional production and the theatre has become one of the city's most popular rental venues for small companies.

Among the other seniors on the community theatre circuit are the Vagabond Players in New Westminster, which formed

> Acts of all types are admitted from Vancouver, and around the world, on a first-come first-serve basis, and the only qualification for admission is the ability to afford the entrance fee

in 1937 and operates out of the Vagabond Theatre; the White Rock Players (1944), which also runs the White Rock Playhouse; Theatre West Van (formerly the West Vancouver Little Theatre Association), which started in 1944; the United Players, which was created in 1960 by the St. James United Church Women as the St. James Drama Group and performs at the Jericho Arts Centre; the North Vancouver Community Players (1946), which works out of Hendry Hall; and the Metro Theatre, which began life as the Metropolitan Theatre Co-operative, an organization of various local community theatre companies. The Metro opened its first theatre on 4th Avenue in Kitsilano in 1962 and the next year moved to a new home at 1370 S.W. Marine Drive, where it's been located ever since.

Vancouver also has a tradition of high quality amateur musical theatre with the two most influential companies being Mussoc and Theatre Under The Stars. TUTS has been producing musicals at Stanley Park's Malkin Bowl each summer since 1940 with a tradition of working with both professional and amateur performers. Mussoc (the University of British Columbia Musical Theatre Society) was formed in 1916.

The UBC Player's Club was also born in 1916 and was one of the city's only theatre troupes for much of our early history. UBC also runs a well-respected theatre program as does Simon Fraser University, which has been training people in the performing arts since its campus opened in 1965. SFU has developed a national reputation for innovative work that frequently blends a variety of artistic disciplines. The Langara Campus of Vancouver Community College also has a well-respected theatre program known as Studio 58 which—like much of the work done by student and community groups—is frequently as "professional" as any theatre in the city.

Big Bands
Jeff Bateman

Mart Kenney band, 1939. vp

Swing was once king in Vancouver. From the bleak days of the Great Depression through the Diefenbaker years, the city's popular dance bands plied their terpsichorean trade in hotel ballrooms, community halls and nightclubs that ranged from the swank to the seedy. Ensembles of six-to-12 musicians followed the cues of their celebrity leaders as they elegantly played the popular chart hits of the day. Their audiences, young and stylishly dressed, would swarm the dancefloor to jitterbug, jive and waltz the night away.

A fair percentage of the musicians were graduates of the famed Kitsilano Boys Band. Founded at General Gordon school in 1928 and conducted with legendary discipline for a half-century by one-time Salvation Army trumpet player Arthur W. Delamont, this biggest of big bands (as many as 70 pieces) routinely toured overseas, released 78's on top jazz labels and won over 200 competitive awards. Alumni included musicians Dal (Dallas) Richards and Bobby Gimby, business mogul Jim Pattison and former MacMillan-Bloedel president Ray Smith.

Vancouver was first base for Mart Kenney and His Western Gentlemen, Canada's leading dance band of the pre- and post-war period ("I was the Bryan Adams of 1944," Kenney once said). The Kerrisdale-bred saxophonist was a member of the CJOR and Len Chamberlain orchestras in the late 1920s before fronting his own group at the Alexandra Ballroom beginning in 1931. National renown stemmed from a series of CBC Radio programs, notably the Sunday night favorite *Sweet and Low* (broadcast live during its inaugural 1935-37 run from the original Hotel Vancouver's ritzy Spanish Grill). His booming career took him east to Toronto, though he returned with wife Norma Locke (his longtime vocalist on such hits as "The West, a Nest and You, Dear") in the late 1960s to settle in Mission.

Mandolin and banjo wizard George Calangis was a contemporary of Kenney's, leading the CKCD Radio orchestra and performing on the CBC shows *Music from the Pacific* and *Continental Varieties*. When Kenney left town, however, it was Dal Richards who stepped lightly to the fore. His sax and clarinet were first heard in the Sandy DeSantis and Stan Paton bands. On May 1, 1940, Richards, his 11-piece band and a then-unknown 13-year-old singer named Juliette were booked to replace Kenney at the new Hotel Vancouver's Panorama Roof Ballroom. An initial six-week contract stretched into 25 years of regular performances and broadcasts at "The Roof." When work dried up in the mid-1960s, Richards went into hotel

management but continued to perform regularly. In 1982-1983 he recorded a pair of well-received swing revival albums. Then-mayor Mike Harcourt declared February 3, 1984, Dal Richards Day in Vancouver.

The Hotel Vancouver was by no means the only dance palace in town. The Palomar Ballroom, the Beacon Theatre and the Cave Supper Club, a landmark nightspot that operated from 1937-81 and featured the bands of Chuck Barber, Bobby Reid, Lance Harrison and Chris Gage among others, all prospered. The granddaddy of city clubs was the Commodore Ballroom, which originally opened in December, 1929, as the Commodore Cabaret. Owners Nick Kogas and John Dillias began a tradition of showcasing local bands and international touring artists that continued under their successors Doug Gurley and, from 1969, Drew Burns. For a one-dollar-per-person cover charge, Vancouverites in the 1930s and 1940s could spend Saturday nights at the Commodore dining on chicken á la king, sneaking drinks from their own flasks (the club finally acquired a liquor licence in 1970) and tripping the light fantastic on a spring-loaded hardwood dance floor. Ole Olsen and His Commodores were the house band in the early 1940s, and such local jazzmen as Doug Kirk, Dave Robbins, Carse Sneddon, Fraser MacPherson and Bobby Hales all fronted dance bands at the club over the years. Innumerable big names graced the Commodore's stage during the swing era, among them Tommy Dorsey, Count Basie, Cab Calloway, Rudy Vallee and Stan Kenton. An era ended in July, 1996, with the closing of the Commodore and its alteration for other forms of entertainment.

One key non-musical figure in this story is the late Bob Smith, the broadcaster and longtime *Vancouver Sun* columnist. The city's first jazz disc jockey, he began playing big-band 78's as a teenager on the CJOR program *Hilites* in 1937. Jazz fans nationally tuned religiously to his CBC Radio program *Hot Air*, which he hosted for 30 years beginning on February 1, 1947. A who's who of Vancouver musicians paid their respects to Smith at an October, 1988, tribute concert at the Commodore.

Photographer David Roels was born and raised in Vancouver. (His grandfather arrived in Vancouver in May, 1887 aboard the first train into the city.) David specializes in black-and-white portraiture of political and business leaders, and in corporate photography—but he also took the cover shot for the Bachman Turner Overdrive 11 album. David's work has been published worldwide, and displayed across Canada and in eleven European countries. His work is in the permanent collection of the Canadian Archives in Ottawa.

Comics and Clubs
Mark Leiren-Young

FROM THE MOMENT Neanderthal man told the first joke about why the brontosaurus crossed the road there have always been comedians, but the idea of clubs devoted entirely to comedy is a relatively recent phenomenon.

Punchlines, Western Canada's original comedy club, got its first laugh in 1978. Originally located in the basement of the Queen Elizabeth Theatre in what later became the Vancouver Media Club, Punchlines was so poor (how poor was it?) that comics used to borrow the chairs from the restaurant next door. Founder Rich Elwood decided it was time to stop fooling around and moved to Gastown where Punchlines generated giggles until its last laugh in 1995.

No one else got serious about comedy until 1986 when Expo organizers invited the legendary Second City Theatre to take over an on-site cabaret called The Flying Club. Second City's new Vancouver troupe featured a handful of Vancouver's top performers and was successful enough to convince local impresarios Bruce Allen, Roger Gibson and Lou Blair to take over the space and rename it The Comedy Club.

Yuk Yuks funnyman-in-chief Mark Breslin had always wanted a Vancouver venue for his Toronto-based comedy chain; he opened a club on Davie Street in 1988 but wasn't amused by the location. He took over the old Expo real estate in 1989.

Despite a number of short-lived attempts to start clubs outside of Vancouver the only full-time comedy venue to succeed is Lafflines (formerly Punchlines) in New Westminster, which was opened in 1991 by Bernie Stoelzle.

The stand-ups, writers and actors who helped kick start their careers in Vancouver's clubs include Jan Derbyshire, Rick Duccomun, Johnny "Bagpipes" Johnston, Ryan Stiles, Frank Van Keeken and the late Colin Campbell who many comedians believe could have been a huge star. Says comedian Mark Dennison, "He did verbally what Gary Larson did with cartoons —we called him the Chief."

Vancouver also has its own answer to Second City—the internationally acclaimed Vancouver TheatreSports League. The ever-changing cast of improvisational comedians (which has included such successful performers and/or writers as Jay Brazeau, Garry Chalk, Roger Frederichs, Dean Haglund, Christine Lippa, Colin Mocherie, Louise Moon, Morris Panych and Veena Sood) began by performing late-night shows on weekends at the now defunct City Stage in 1980. The group gradually developed a devout following and in 1986 took over

Punchlines, Western Canada's original comedy club, was so poor that comics used to borrow the chairs from the restaurant next door

the space for themselves, renaming their venue The Back Alley Theatre. Unfortunately the landlords didn't get the joke and rising downtown rental costs forced TheatreSports to exit the Alley in 1994 and create a new theatre (as yet unopened) at the Stanley Theatre on Granville Street.

Vancouver's best known comedy troupe throughout the 1970s was Dr. Bundolo's Pandemonium Medicine Show. The CBC radio sketch troupe began as Ted Stidder, Steve Woodman, Marla Gropper and the Don Clark Band. Bill Reiter joined midway through the first year, Stidder was replaced by Bill Buck and Norm Grohmann joined in 1974, replacing Woodman who was seriously injured in a car accident. The Bundolos recorded their shows in front of live audiences (mostly at UBC's Student Union Building) complete with live sound effects by Lars Eastholm. Bundolo was produced by Don Kowalchuk, written by Jeffrey Groberman and Dan Thatchuk (now Colin Yardley) and ran from 1972 to 1980 before moving to CBC Television for two seasons. The troupe reunited briefly for Expo 86.

Vancouver is also home to impressionists Bob Robertson and Linda Cullen who created their weekly radio series *Double Exposure* for the CBC in 1987 and quickly became national comedy institutions. The radio show is produced by Tod Elvidge and written by Cullen and Robertson, who have also published a book and starred in several TV specials. CBC also launched the musical-comedy duo Local Anxiety (Mark Leiren-Young and Kevin Crofton) stars of Vancouver's annual Year in Revue, a satirical tradition on Granville Island since 1992.

Each summer the city hosts the Vancouver International Comedy Festival. Founded in 1987 by Chris Wootten and Jane Howard Baker, the festival was inspired by the success of the street performers at Expo 86. Although the Granville Island-based festival—which is now run by Karen Carotenuto and Alan Scales—still features some of the world's best buskers, they also present a diverse collection of local and international comedy acts at theatres and clubs throughout Vancouver.

Music Industry
Jeff Bateman

WHILE CANADA'S $1.2 billion music industry is primarily based in Toronto, Vancouver has routinely produced more than its demographic share of rock and pop artists. Entrepreneurs have tapped this wellspring of musicians, singers and songwriters through a myriad of talent-oriented companies over four decades. Many have been run by fans and enthusiasts whose ambitions were quickly undermined by a lack of capital and expertise. Yet a handful of key businesses and individuals have survived and prospered over the long haul. Their trailblazing success has created the foundation of a bona fide music industry, one that looks as much towards Asia for its future as traditional markets in the United States, Europe and Eastern Canada.

RECORDING STUDIOS
Vancouver is widely regarded as a world-class centre for studio recording. That reputation is built in large part on Little Mountain Sound, the West 7th Avenue facility that prior to its 1994 bankruptcy hosted such foreign hard-rock stars as Aerosmith, Bon Jovi and AC/DC. Advertising agency Griffiths Gibson Ramsay Productions and the Western International Broadcasting Company invested $500,000 to open Little Mountain in 1974. Under the direction of Bob Brooks, the studio purchased a state-of-the-art recording console in 1985 and began attracting star clientele. Little Mountain's appeal was bolstered considerably by its two world-class producers, Bruce Fairbairn and Bob Rock.

The city's first "studio" appears to have been a booth in Spencer's department store circa World War II that Vancouverites used to tape personal greetings. Aragon Recording opened in 1945 at 615 West Hastings. One of its founding partners, broadcaster and musician Al Reusch, acquired sole ownership of the three-room space in 1954 and over the ensuing 15 years established Aragon as the premier facility in town—particularly after its move to a spacious new site at 1234 West 6th Avenue in 1965. Aragon evolved into Mushroom Studios under current owner Charlie Richmond and today remains a favorite haunt of Jane Siberry, Sarah McLachlan and some persistent ghosts that have spooked more than a few artists and producers.

Al Reusch faced little competition until the post-Beatles boom in pop music spurred ventures like Vancouver Recording Services (run by Robin Spurgin), PBS Studios (Brent Jaybush and Steve Grossman) and Studio 3 (Ralph Harding and Tom Northcott). In the 1980s a new generation of rooms—Geoff

Every imaginable icon of the rock era has performed in Vancouver, from Elvis Presley (August 31, 1957, Empire Stadium) and The Beatles (August 22, 1964, PNE) to such contemporary giants as U2, REM and Pink Floyd

Turner's Pinewood, Tom Lavin's Blue Wave and Ken Morrison's Ocean Sound included—were combining album production with soundtrack work for film and television. Today approximately 50 recording studios operate in Greater Vancouver, many of them specializing in film, TV and video postproduction. Filling the high-end void left by Little Mountain's closure are Armoury Studios (opened in 1993 by songwriter Jim Vallance) and The Greenhouse (formerly S.B. Vancouver Studios).

TALENT MANAGEMENT
Few rock managers anywhere have the clout and experience of Bruce Allen, the ever-quotable showman whose 68 Water Street office is wallpapered in the gold and platinum sales plaques of his superstar client Bryan Adams. Born in Vancouver in 1945, Allen began his managerial career at 23 with Five Man Cargo. Bachman Turner Overdrive sold ten million albums from 1973-1978 under his direction, and he reached similar heights with Loverboy (co-managed by Lou Blair). His greatest success has come with Adams, the North Vancouver singer who hounded Allen in 1978 until he agreed to manage him.

While Allen casts a long shadow, a number of managers from Vancouver have made their mark. Their ranks include Allen's business partner Sam Feldman (The Chieftains, Trooper, Headpins), Janet Forsyth (Spirit of the West), Terry McBride (Sarah McLachlan), Keith Porteous (54-40, Mae Moore), Cliff Jones (The Hometown Band, Payola$), Laurie Mercer (DOA, NoMeansNo) and Steve Macklam (Colin James).

CONCERT PROMOTION AND TALENT BOOKING

Every imaginable icon of the rock era has performed in Vancouver, from Elvis Presley (August 31, 1957, Empire Stadium) and The Beatles (August 22, 1964, PNE) to such contemporary giants as U2, REM and Pink Floyd. Some homegrown entrepreneurs have tried their hand at concert promotion—Hugh Pickett, Roger Schiffer, Paul Mercs, Craig McDowall and Peter McCulloch are among the more successful—but prior to 1977 most major touring artists were brought to town by Seattle promoters Concerts West, John Bauer and Northwest Releasing. This stranglehold was broken by Perryscope Concert Productions, founded by Norman Perry. Today Perryscope and MCA Concerts Canada present the lion's share of concerts in the Lower Mainland. Control of the ticketing business has resided in local hands. Concert Box Office, founded by Gary Switlo and Tom Worrall, sold tickets to rock shows beginning in 1971. CBO merged with its chief competitor, Vancouver Ticket Centre, in 1987 and established a virtual monopoly as a TicketMaster franchise in the 1990s. Sam Feldman has been just as dominant in the talent booking sector. Launching S.L. Feldman & Associates in 1972, the one-time doorman has traditionally commanded the majority of club and concert business west of the Manitoba/Ontario border. In recent years S.L.F.A. has diversified and expanded nationally, becoming Canada's leading full-service entertainment agency.

RECORD LABELS

The Canadian arms of the "big six" foreign-owned record companies—BMG, EMI, MCA, Mercury/Polydor, Sony and Warner—all have offices in Vancouver. In the early years of rock 'n' roll, however, the major labels of the day used regional distributors like the Taylor, Pearson and Carson group to circulate recordings. Local point men such as RCA Victor's Knox Coupland were on the scene but it was mainly independently owned labels that put Vancouver's music on wax.

The pioneer was Aragon Records, an ancillary of Al Reusch's studio. Aragon's first releases in 1948 were by Scottish piper William Barrie, but it quickly became known as a country label with Keray Regan's national hit "My Home by the Fraser" and early recordings by Canada's "pet," Juliette. Reusch's label was also the first to record "There's a Bluebird on Your Windowsill" (written by Vancouver nurse Elizabeth Clarke); Aragon's version was sung by Don Murphy, the first of many people to record it. "Bluebird" is said to be the first song by a Canadian to sell one million copies. The Rhythm Pals had the big Canadian hit version, but it was later recorded by Doris Day, Frankie Carle, Bing Crosby and others. By 1956 Aragon had dipped into rock 'n' roll with The Prowlers and Jimmy Morrison and the Stripes. Singles at the time were also released by Arctic Records, run by teen broadcaster Red Robinson and singer Les Vogt, and Stan Cayer's S.G.M. Records.

The arrival of Imperial Records, Western Canada's first modern vinyl mastering and pressing plant, in 1968 helped spur a generation of new labels. Many were custom imprints created by musicians to release their own music—just as Tom Northcott had done with Syndrome Records in 1965. One ambitious label of note, Coast Records, scored regional hits with Spring, The Seeds of Time and the Northwest Company from 1969 through 1972.

Another studio offshoot, Mushroom Records, was founded in 1974 by brothers Wink and Dick Vogel. An early Mushroom album, "Dreamboat Annie" by the rock group Heart, sold an astronomical four million copies. The label declared bankruptcy in 1980, a year after the death of its energetic vice president and creative sparkplug, Shelly Siegel.

Quintessence Records was an outgrowth of Ted Thomas' Kitsilano record store of the same name. In 1978 it was a focal point for the emerging punk and new wave scene, releasing fiery bands like The Pointed Sticks and Young Canadians. The do-it-yourself tenor of the times also produced vinyl 45s by such raw basement labels as Pinned, Sudden Death, Full Friction and Useful. When Quintessence folded in December, 1981, staffer Grant McDonagh carried on with Zulu Records in the same Kitsilano shop. He also created Zulu, the record label, which is now distributed nationally by PolyGram.

Label activity continued in the 1980s with MoDaMu (short for "Modern Dance Music"), Penta and Parallel One. The one venture to stick, however, was the stylish Nettwerk Productions. Terry McBride, Mark Jowett, Cal Stephenson and Tom Ferris created the company as a vehicle for Moev, a band that McBride managed and the other partners performed in. Nettwerk celebrated its tenth anniversary in 1995 as one of Canada's leading indie labels. Buoyed by its million-selling artist Sarah McLachlan, Nettwerk serves as inspiration to an emerging generation of new companies spearheaded by Mint, Scratch and Bang On.

PACIFIC MUSIC INDUSTRY ASSOCIATION

The P.M.I.A. was incorporated in 1990 to address key issues and stimulate activity and employment in the B.C. music business. It sponsors the annual Demo-Listen Derby, the latest incarnation of a battle-of-the-bands tradition in Vancouver that dates back to the 1950s. The association also backs Music West, a high-profile international conference, festival and exhibition that has been produced annually since 1991 by Maureen Jack and Laurie Mercer.

Arts Umbrella
Faith Bloomfield

THE SOUNDS OF children squealing with delight and the bustle of happy activity are what Vancouver's Arts Umbrella is all about. In one class (Sculpture, Painting and Drawing) paper clouds, the result of a project long-completed, float from the ceiling while groups of four-to-six-year-olds work on their next creations.

The atmosphere is one of encouragement but despite an unstructured appearance there is a definite purpose to the class. Instructors are there to help and suggest as the children work independently with paper and colors. Results are all personal and unique to each junior artist.

Promoted as "Canada's visual and performing arts institute for young people," the Arts Umbrella takes off where traditional schooling ends, supplementing the three R's of education. There is no right or wrong way of creating at Arts Umbrella and through osmosis the organization provides an education applicable to all aspects of learning.

"The sense of training, of concentration, of learning, the creative thinking—all are transferable to the rest of their education. They learn different ways of thinking, different ways of perceiving material and resourcing for themselves. In the arts you don't fail. And you bring that sense of success to the rest of your life," says Carol Henriquez, co-founder and current executive director of Arts Umbrella.

Since it first opened its doors in 1979 Arts Umbrella has empowered thousands of children. It's the ideal vehicle for young people to gain self-esteem and confidence through creative activity and self-exploration.

The organization's first minuscule budget of $250 and humble registration of 45 kids divided among four classes has grown by leaps and bounds. Currently there are 23,000 annual participants—aged two to 18—attending more than 150 weekly in-house classes. And with budgetary requirements increasing to keep up with this growth, Arts Umbrella raised more than $500,000 in 1995.

A non-profit registered charity, Arts Umbrella takes pride in not relying on government funding. It receives support from the community and a variety of large corporate sponsors. In addition to financial support, supplies and materials are also donated. About 75 per cent of the children involved require—and receive—financial assistance through an extensive bursary program.

From two mobile vans—Van Go for the visual arts, and Stage Coach for the performing arts—Arts Umbrella's Outreach Program provides free cross-cultural programs for approximately 13,000 children. Every week during the school year the vans go to public schools in less advantaged areas throughout the Lower Mainland. The idea is to teach drawing, painting, print-making and theatre to kids who might not otherwise have access to these courses.

"It's really important in their lives, really important for the teachers," says Henriquez, adding that it is also immensely popular. "The programs are offered on a first-come, first-served basis and are literally filled for the entire year in the first week of September."

In room after room of the 1,400-square-metre facility located on Granville Island, sounds of creativity and encouragement abound and the selection of programs and classes is diverse. In fact the name itself came from one of the very first grass-roots discussions about putting the organization together. It was decided there was a need within the community to form an organization where all the arts would be under one roof, one arts umbrella.

There are eight different types of dance classes featured at Arts Umbrella while theatre programs range from Dress-Up Drama to the Arts Umbrella Theatre Company with both junior and senior troupes. Visual arts selections include animation and movie-making; architecture, jewelry and accessory design, the culturally enriching Asian Kingdoms program and a course on fibre arts are some of the other available areas of study. All of these give young people the opportunity to create and experiment with their imaginations and abilities. New courses are often initiated by the participants and their parents, such as the recent addition of stagecraft and singing classes.

But creating isn't the only thing being manifested in Arts Umbrella courses. Students graduate skilled, confident and proud. As artists and performers their work is constantly being validated. Final creations hang on a wall and productions are performed on stage. There is an annual film and animation festival, an exhibit at a local gallery, dance and theatre performances, the summer sandcastle competition and constant presentations to parents arriving at the end of classes.

There are always things for kids to see and do at Arts Umbrella at any time of the year. There are three sessions of classes from September to June and a summer camp that continues through July.

Hollywood North
Lynne McNamara

IT WAS ABOUT one hundred years ago that American film-makers began their love affair with British Columbia. A cameraman named Robert K. Bobine was sent to northern B.C. by the Edison Manufacturing Company of New Jersey to shoot footage of fortune-hunting miners migrating to the Klondike Gold Rush. A few years later (in 1907) the American Mutoscope and Biograph company produced a one-reel film called *An Acadian Elopement,* the first story on film about life north of the 49th parallel.

In the next fifty years Hollywood made hundreds of movies about Canada, portraying its citizens as igloo-inhabiting, snowshoeing, blubber-eating Mounties and lumberjacks. Some of these pictures were shot in Canada but most were shot in Arizona or California, with burning desert disguised as the frozen north.

Looking for authenticity Anna May Wong came to B.C. in 1924 to shoot *The Alaskan.* Richard Arlen and Lilli Palmer shot *Silent Barriers* here in 1935. But American movie-makers really began to flow here in the early 1930s, when the British government implemented a quota on their own distributors and exhibitors, making room for productions from anywhere in the British Empire to be shown on screens in Britain. American producers immediately began shooting low-budget movies in Canada for release in Britain, and the "quota quickie" was born.

Hollywood siren Rita Hayworth starred in *Across the Border* and *Convicted,* quota quickies shot here in the late 1930s. In 1936 MGM boss Louis B. Mayer convinced the RCMP in Vancouver to let him shoot some footage for his classic movie, *Rosemarie* (with Jeanette MacDonald and Nelson Eddy), the story of the daring rescue of a damsel in distress by an heroic Mountie after she is robbed and left stranded in the woods by an evil trapper. (The scene of singing Mounties galloping in formation on horseback down a shallow stream is said to have been shot in North Vancouver's Capilano Canyon.)

A few Hollywood movies were shot here in the forties and fifties but until the mid-1960s American producers found that, apart from the scenery, there was no real advantage to shooting in Canada. Over the years, however, with the gradual weakening of the Canadian dollar and the growing expertise of British Columbia crews, Americans again began to shuffle their money and their movies northward.

In 1969 film production began here in earnest with Robert Altman's *That Cold Day in the Park* (starring Sandy Dennis) and Bob Rafelson's *Five Easy Pieces* (Jack Nicholson and Karen Black). In 1970 Altman returned to shoot *McCabe and Mrs. Miller* (with Warren Beatty and Julie Christie), Mike Nichols shot *Carnal Knowledge* (Jack Nicholson, Candice Bergen, Art Garfunkel, Ann-Margret, Rita Moreno) and Universal shot *The Groundstar Conspiracy* (George Peppard and Michael Sarrazin).

In the 1970s production grew steadily and, in 1978, the B.C. Film Commission was formed to promote and market B.C. to the world as a film, television and commercials location, and to promote the use of our skilled professionals. The B.C. Film Commission reports to the ministry of small business, tourism and culture and maintains extensive photo files of locations, assists producers with budgeting and production scheduling, acts as a liaison for production companies and handles inquiries from the public. (To register your home or vehicle, or for more information, call the commission at 660-2732.)

The film industry has grown by leaps and bounds since 1978. Today it has an army of highly trained industry workers and is capable of assembling more than 20 crews at a time.

Film production now brings in over $400 million to the province annually; we're one of the top five production centres in North America, shooting an average of a dozen television series, forty television movies-of-the-week, many features and several pilots each year. (Television series shot here in 1995 were: *The X-Files, Strange Luck, Sliders, Profit, Poltergeist, The Marshal, Outer Limits, The Sentinel, Robin's Hoods, The Commish, Highlander, University Hospital, M.A.N.T.I.S, Hawkeye* and *Madison.)*

And although the low Canadian dollar makes B.C. an attractive place to shoot, budget-wise, that factor may no longer be the major one. In addition to fabulous scenery and locations Vancouver is now capable of supplying a depth of technical and performing talent as well, and return business is surely a sign of satisfaction. The industry, dubbed "Hollywood North" by some, often takes criticism for merely providing services for American producers; while that may be true to some extent, our own indigenous industry is gradually developing.

Approximately 6,000 British Columbians are employed in the film industry today. Hundreds of film and video companies have sprung up and there are more than 40 talent agencies, approximately 36 post-production facilities, several distributors and more than a dozen shooting stages including Canada's largest film and television studio, North Shore Studios. The Bridge Studios in Burnaby have the largest special effects stage in North America.

North Shore Studios was built by Hollywood writer-producer Stephen J. Cannell in 1989 and contains seven soundstages, production offices, on-site shooting facades and technical production services. The studio now houses two Fox-TV series, *The X-Files* and *Strange Luck,* and was home to TV's *The Commish* and *21 Jump Street* and the features *Little Women* and *Intersection.*

The Bridge Studios, former home to the TV series *MacGyver,* was the old home of the Dominion Bridge Steel Company and began its use as a makeshift soundstage after the closing of an earlier facility, West Vancouver's Panorama Studio, in the early 1980s. The Bridge's huge soundstage was used for the features *Bird On A Wire, Timecop, Look Who's Talking, Stay Tuned* and the big-budget Robin Williams picture *Jumanji.* As well many former industrial warehouses throughout the city, though their exteriors remain nondescript, have interiors outfitted as shooting stages.

Our locations are top-notch too. American producers say we have the most "shootable" alleys in North America—you can see them in the *Stakeout* movies. Jodie Foster and Kelly McGillis shot their courtroom scenes for *The Accused* in the Vancouver Art Gallery. You can see "The Hollies," a mega-million-dollar mansion on the Crescent in Shaughnessy, in scores of locally shot films. St. Paul's Hospital was host to the Linda Fiorentino/Ray Liotta film *Unforgettable.* Lord Byng and Kitsilano Secondary can both be seen in the Rick Moranis/Tom Arnold film *Big Bully.* Alexander Street in Gastown was transformed into Helena, Montana, circa 1915, for *Legends of the Fall* with Brad Pitt and Anthony Hopkins. Manhattan Apartments on Thurlow Street is home to Kirstie Alley and John Travolta in the *Look Who's Talking* movies. Versatile Shipyards on the North Vancouver waterfront is often host to film noir gangster gunfights. The GVRD watershed area in the North Shore mountains, only 20 minutes away from the city, is perfect for those wilderness scenes so loved by American viewers.

Much of the post-production work on locally shot American movies is still taken south for completion, even though many Vancouver studios are equipped to do sophisticated state-of-the-art post work. In fact a few have such an international reputation that they are attracting post-production work on movies shot elsewhere. Many actors shooting movies in Vancouver spend their free time in Vancouver sound studios "looping" (recording for sound mixing) for their previously shot film, which may be in the editing process in Los Angeles or New York.

As a result of their work in the Vancouver film industry over the years, a few Vancouverites have developed important contacts and credibility with American producers and networks. Some have launched their own film companies here and travel south to pitch their own projects and scripts to the U.S. television networks, then bring them home to shoot. Some local producers rely on government bodies such as B.C. Film and Telefilm Canada to help fund their projects while others find private investors. Some finance their projects with both public and private monies.

A sampling of some of the most successful local companies today producing feature films and/or television movies for the American cable networks would include: Pacific Motion Pictures (headed by Tony Allard, Matthew O'Connor and Tom Rowe); Crescent Entertainment (Harold Tichenor, Gordon Mark, Jeff Cohen, Jayme Pfahl); Shavick Entertainment (Los Angeles-based producer James Shavick); Keystone Entertainment (the Vince Brothers, Robert and William, and their sister Lynn), Forefront Productions (Mickey Rogers, Teri Woods-McArter, Gillian Lindsay, Helena Cynamon); Movie Vista Productions (Robert Frederick); New City Productions (Colleen Nystedt); Soapbox Productions (Nick Orchard); Cactus Pictures (Ron French, Scott Kennedy); Everest Films International (John Curtis); and North American Pictures (Lloyd Simandl).

Many local actors are beginning to make a name for themselves in the business today—without setting foot in Hollywood. Eventually, of course, if they want to make it big they'll probably have to re-locate to Los Angeles or New York, but certainly they can get their feet very wet in the business right here at home.

Hundreds of commercials are shot here every year—including many toy commercials and that means lots of work for local kids flogging Barbies and G.I. Joes. From commercials they may go on to small speaking roles in movies, then to larger parts like former locals Jason Priestley and Cameron Bancroft did when they landed in Hollywood on the TV series *Beverly Hills 90210.*

If business continues as it has, local film professionals predict a billion-dollar movie industry in British Columbia by the end of the century.

facing page: Alexander Street, Gastown, transformed into Helena, Montana (circa 1915) for Legends of the Fall, *1993.* vs

Movies

Since 1978 the British Columbia Film Commission has promoted the province as a great place to make movies. In the same time zone and only a two hour flight from Los Angeles, British Columbia is a convenient and economical treasure trove of locations for filmmakers. Besides actively encouraging producers to plan their shoots here, the Film Commission provides information to the community, ensuring cooperation from the most important element of any location—its owners and residents.

Movies Made in Greater Vancouver
Michael Walsh

WE'RE NUMBER TWO!

"Vancouver has become the second largest motion picture production centre in North America, after Los Angeles," says Hollywood's Universal Pictures. This remarkable news item appears in the press package the studio issued to promote its 1994 feature *Timecop,* a Jean-Claude Van Damme feature filmed in and around Vancouver.

Alas, like so much of the news out of Hollywood, it's not quite true. In Toronto direct spending on film and video projects amounted to $501 million in 1994, while Vancouver-based production accounted for only $402 million. Even so the Hollywood hyperbole pays tribute to the generations of creative professionals who have worked to make this city a movie-making metropolis . . . they've earned our applause.

Twenty years ago our original *Vancouver Book* peek at local feature filmmaking was a story of huge hopes and largely unfulfilled dreams. Today the movie business (which includes television production) is British Columbia's fourth largest industry, employing more than 8,500 people. An expanding universe of artists, administrators, deal-makers and craftspeople, it is supported by a sophisticated infrastructure of talent agencies (44 at last count), studios (offering 15 soundstages), mobile services and post-production facilities that can compete with the best in the world.

Numbers? More than 200 theatrical features and about 100 made-for-TV movies have been shot in whole or in part in the Greater Vancouver area. (Not to mention at least 36 television pilots and episodes for more than 60 small-screen series. But that is another story.) In celebration of these achievements, then, we welcome you to . . .

THE GREATER VANCOUVER BOOK'S FEATURE FILM FESTIVAL

What follows is your program guide to a series of 20 festival-style movie retrospectives. Taken together, they include all of the theatrical feature films made in Vancouver and in release as of June, 1995. Not included are the many made-for-TV productions. (Though we've tried to make our program as complete as possible,

facing page: Granville Street's glory days—more movie theatres per block than Broadway, the 1940's neon still shone when this picture was taken in 1973. vs

we've almost certainly missed a few. If you know of any that are not mentioned here, please let us know.)

Notes for each picture include its title (and any alternate titles), year of release, the director's name, the cast and a brief description.

VANCOUVER FEATURE FILM FIRSTS

Canada's first permanent movie house, John Schuberg's Edison Electric, opened on Cordova Street in 1902 and offered the latest in novelty entertainment —short, silent pictures that moved and occasionally told stories. Soon the movies grew to feature length, spinning yarns that took an hour or more to view. Eventually feature filmmakers discovered Vancouver. Among the city's production landmarks are its:

First Dramatic Feature

The Winds of Change (1925; Frank Lloyd) The tradition of Hollywood producers filming on location in Vancouver begins with this gold-rush melodrama in which Capilano Canyon stands in for the Klondike.

First Canadian-Made Feature

Policing the Plains (1927; A.D. "Cowboy" Kean) A frontier romance made to honor the men and traditions of the RCMP, Kean's feature was a passionate attempt to found a domestic film industry.

First Sound Feature

Rose Marie (1936; W.S. Van Dyke) Though stars Jeanette MacDonald and Nelson Eddy did all their singing on California soundstages, background exteriors for MGM's famous Mountie operetta were shot in Capilano Canyon.

First Color Feature

The Trap (1964; Sidney Hayers) Another wilderness romance, this Anglo-Canadian co-production features a burly trapper (Oliver Reed) carrying a mute orphan (Rita Tushingham) into an Eastmancolor North Shore rainforest.

First Made-for-Television Feature

Waiting for Caroline (1967; Ron Kelly) Pioneering the movie-of-the-week format, this NFB-CBC co-production offered a bi-cultural domestic drama set in Vancouver and Quebec City.

First Feature Directed by a Woman

Madeleine Is . . . (1970; Sylvia Spring) Reflecting the militant, mystic 1960s, Torontonian Spring created a feminist fantasy about a runaway Quebecoise (Nicola Lipman) who finds personal fulfillment clowning around Kitsilano.

First Box Office Megahit

First Blood (1982; Ted Kotcheff) American pop culture icon John Rambo (Sylvester Stallone) got his start with a rampage shot on location in Hope, B.C. and on the soundstages of Burnaby's Bridge Studios.

First 3-D Feature

Spacehunter: Adventures in the Forbidden Zone

(1983; Lamont Johnson) Bat men and barracuda women are among the stereoscopic shocks a galactic mercenary (Peter Strauss) encounters on forbidden planet Terra Eleven, all created on soundstages at the Bridge Studios.

First Academy Award Winner

The Accused (1988; Jonathan Kaplan) Actress Jodie Foster earned her first Oscar playing a rape victim who seeks justice through the courts, a performance filmed on location in Vancouver.

First IMAX 3-D Feature

Wings of Courage (1995; Jean-Jacques Annaud) Vancouver stands in for 1930s Buenos Aires in the world's first non-documentary made in the IMAX stereoscopic format, a dramatization of the true story of Andes plane crash survivor Henri Guillaumet (Craig Sheffer).

GOD'S COUNTRY

First called "God's Country" by American adventure novelist James Oliver Curwood, B.C.'s spectacular wilderness vistas blinded early generations of Hollywood filmmakers to Vancouver's own charms. Vancouver Island or the Interior mountains were the preferred shooting locations. Even so a few outdoors films have used the Lower Mainland's ability to simulate rugged landscapes, including:

The Wilderness Patrol (1928; J.P. McGowan) Made to sidestep British film quota legislation, this quickie silent Western featured Winnipeg-born screen cowboy Bill Cody riding the North Vancouver range.

Mother Lode (1982; Charlton Heston) The woods above North Vancouver's Cleveland Dam stand in for a Cassiar forest in this adventure-thriller starring director Heston in a dual role as sinister, gold-obsessed twins.

Clan of the Cave Bear (1986; Michael Chapman) After filming in Cathedral Park and the Nahanni Valley, actress Daryl Hannah completed work as a Cro-Magnon beauty on Bridge Studios sets.

Distant Thunder (1988; Rick Rosenberg) The Seymour watershed doubled as Washington State's Olympic Peninsula for the story of a "bush vet" (John Lithgow), a troubled Vietnam war survivor in self-imposed wilderness exile.

First Season (1990; Ralph Thomas) A hull-shattering storm simulated at Vancouver's Ocean Engineering Centre was the action highlight in a drama about a mother (Kate Trotter), daughter (Christianne Hirt) and their North Coast commercial fishing boat.

The Russia House (1990; Fred Schepisi) Though most of this espionage thriller was filmed on actual Russian locations, the key meeting between British and American spymasters (Sean Connery, Roy Scheider) takes place at a safe house on Bowen Island.

K2 - Journey to the Top of the World (1992; Franc

BRITISH COLUMBIA FILM COMMISSION

In 1995 more than 140 scripts were submitted to the B.C. Film Commission by producers considering B.C. for their film and TV projects. The Locations department at the Film Commission prepares a synopsis of the script and a breakdown of locations suitable to the script. From this research, a package of photo files is then sent to the producers. If we are successful in convincing producers to come to B.C. to take a closer look, we offer a personalized location survey to suit their needs and to assess possibilities.

Roddam) Vancouver plays Seattle and Black-comb stands in for the "Savage Mountain" of the Himalayas that challenges the endurance of rival climbers (Michael Biehn, Matt Craven).

Alive (1993; Frank Marshall) Though exteriors were filmed on the Delphine glacier and in the Bugaboo Mountains, this re-creation of the Andes cannibals incident included air flight and crash footage shot at the Bridge Studios.

Legends of the Fall (1994; Edward Zwick) That's Gastown dressed to look like 1920s Helena, Montana, the only urban setting seen in this big skies family saga starring Brad Pitt, Anthony Hopkins and Aidan Quinn.

Arctic Blue (1995; Peter Masterson) A dedicated ecologist (Dylan Walsh) and a traditional frontiersman (Rutger Hauer) overcome their differences to survive in an Alaskan wilderness filmed on North Vancouver locations.

CYBERCITY

When superspies and spacemen replaced cowboys as popular screen heroes, Vancouver finally came into its own. Its fresh look and cutting-edge architecture fit right into tales of near-future worlds full of technological wonders and worries. Science-fiction features shot here include:

The Groundstar Conspiracy (1971; Lamont Johnson) A CIA spymaster (George Peppard) uses an amnesiac scientist (Michael Sarrazin) to trap the foreign agents responsible for blowing up a U.S. space research centre (SFU).

Food of the Gods (1976; Bert I. Gordon) When growth hormones from outer space turn Bowen Island rats into monster rodents, a vacationing B.C. Lion football player (Marjoe Gortner) calls the plays like a professional exterminator.

Iceman (1984; Fred Schepisi) Frozen for millennia in the high Arctic, an ancient Inuit (John Lone) is reawakened by cryobiologists (Timothy Hutton, Lindsay Crouse) working in high-tech labs built on Panorama Studios soundstages.

Runaway (1984; Michael Crichton) Urban future-cops (Tom Selleck, Cynthia Rhodes) specialize in fighting the robot criminals devised by a 21st-century techno-terrorist (Gene Simmons).

Quarantine (1988; Charles Wilkinson) A young rebel (Beatrice Boepple) recruits a scientist (Garwin Sanford) to fight the government's use of a health crisis to enslave its people.

Beyond the Stars (1989; David Saperstein) A young space scientist (Christian Slater) makes some shocking discoveries about the Apollo 11 moon mission and his personal idol, a retired astronaut (Martin Sheen).

Time Runner (1993; Michael Mazo) A fugitive from the future (Mark Hamill) is pursued by aliens preparing for an invasion of the Earth.

Tomcat (aka *Dangerous Desires*, 1993; Paul Donovan) In this health-care crisis thriller, the treatment a genetic researcher (Maryam D'Abo) prescribes for her patient (Richard Grieco) has ferociously feline side-effects.

Timecop (1994; Peter Hyams) An incorruptible near-future lawman (Jean-Claude Van Damme) faces danger in the past to thwart a crooked politician (Ron Silver) with a plan to hijack the U.S. presidency.

Crying Freeman (1995; Christope Gans) Adapted from a Japanese *manga* (comic book), this story of an artist (Mark Dacascos) programmed to kill by the Yakuza makes use of Vancouver's Tokyo-like locations.

Cyberjack (1995; Robert Lee) An ex-cop (Michael Dudikoff) providing security for a 21st century bio-research centre must stop a high-tech thief (Brion James) who's out to steal an experimental virus.

Cyberteens in Love (1995; Brett Dowler) The addictive power of illicit brain implants threatens the fragile happiness of an orphan (Justine Priestly) and her streetwise boyfriend (Martin Cummins) in this Vancouver-based production.

Starlight (1995; Jonathan Kay) A beautiful extra-terrestrial geneticist (Deborah Wakeham) awakens love in a suicidal youth (Billy Wirth) who turns out to be the half-alien son of a starman.

DOCUMENTARY FEATURES

Canada's non-fiction films are world famous. With its legendary standard of excellence, our National Film Board collects Oscars for its documentary shorts with satisfying regularity. Made in the public interest, NFB productions are most often seen in schools, on television and in festival settings. Rare, by contrast, are documentary features made for commercial theatrical release. Vancouver examples include:

The Royal Visit (1939; Canadian Government Motion Picture Bureau) The Canadian Pacific Railroad's Hudson series locomotives won the right to be called Royal for their service during this cross-Canada tour, a journey that ends with King George VI and Queen Elizabeth enjoying a Vancouver welcome.

Greenpeace—Voyages to Save the Whales (1977; Michael Chechik, Fred Easton, Ron Precious) Don Francks narrates the story of the good ship *Phyllis Cormack* and its crew of Vancouver environmentalists as they face down Soviet whalers on the high seas, an encounter captured by SFU Film Workshop alumni.

Hookers on Davie (1984; Janice Cole, Holly Dale) Torontonians Cole and Dale record the stories told to them by four prostitutes and three transsexuals in Vancouver's West End.

Stripper (1986; Jerome Gary) Gary follows dancers Kimberly "Danyel" Holcomb, Loree "Mouse" Menton and Lisa "G.O." Saurez from Vancouver, home of "the best strip bars in the world," to Las Vegas for a strippers competition.

YOUTHQUAKES

The majority of moviegoers are between the ages of 16 and 30 years old, a statistic that accounts for the production of a lot of pictures by, for and about the young. For beginning filmmakers, it's often a matter of filming what they know. Youthful anxieties and anxious youths are featured in such Vancouver-made movies as:

The Bitter Ash (1963; Lawrence Kent) Made with a University of British Columbia student cast and crew, Kent's debut drama upset censors across Canada with its despairing portrait of a would-be playwright (Alan Scarfe) lost in a world of sex and drugs.

Sweet Substitute (aka *Caressed*, 1964; Lawrence Kent) Reuniting his UBC team Kent filmed the story of an intense, randy high school graduate (Robert Howay) and the girl he leaves pregnant (Carol Pastinsky).

When Tomorrow Dies (1965; Lawrence Kent) Moving on to melodrama Kent cast Pat Gage as an unhappy matron who attempts to regain her youth by returning to school and having an affair with her English teacher.

Explosion (1970; Jules Bricken) An American draft dodger (Gordon Thompson) meets a Vancouver hippie (Don Stroud), an association that ends in robbery and murder.

The Life and Times of Chester Angus Ramsgood (1970; David Curnick) A love-smitten teen (Robert Matson) develops elaborate schemes to impress the ultra-Scottish parents of his would-be girlfriend (Mary-Beth McGuffin) in this Vancouver West Side farce.

Carnal Knowledge (1971; Mike Nichols) Vancouver is Middle America in a drama about guys (Jack Nicholson, Art Garfunkel) who spend their lives chasing girls and talking about sex.

In Pursuit of . . . (1972; Richard Walton) Private school girlfriends (Cecilia Smith, Celine La Freniere) learn about life and love in this upbeat, mildly moralistic romantic comedy.

Ladies And Gentlemen, The Fabulous Stains (aka *All Washed Up*, 1982; Lou Adler) All-girl punk rock band members Diane Lane and Laura Dern find fame, endure shame and play Seymour Street's Penthouse, all in the name of artistic rebellion.

Out of the Blue (aka *Ce Be*, 1982; Dennis Hopper) *The Easy Rider* director used East Side locations for the story of a disturbed, abused teen (Linda Manz) who must face the bitter fact that her parents (Sharon Farrell, Dennis Hopper) are terminally dysfunctional.

Housekeeping (1987; Bill Forsyth) Given into the care of an eccentric aunt (Christine Lahti), orphan sisters (Sara Walker, Andrea Burchill) are faced with a choice between freedom and conformity in this gentle serio-comic fable.

First established as Film British Columbia, this arm of the Provincial Ministry of Small Business, Tourism and Culture has helped the film industry grow in earnings from $12 million to more than $400 million annually. While this growth is a great boost to the general economy, the presence of a film crew can be disruptive. Neighborhood residents can direct enquiries and concerns to the Film Commission, which acts as liaison with production companies to maintain a friendly film environment.

Cafe Romeo (1991; Rex Bromfield) A dental student (Jonathan Crombie) decides that he loves his cousin's wife (Catherine Mary Stewart) and managing his family's bistro more than college.

Crooked Hearts (1991; Michael Bortman) Domesticity in the 1980s is seen through the eyes of a Tacoma college dropout (Peter Berg) appalled by his once close-knit family's self-destructive behavior.

This Boy's Life (1993; Michael Caton-Jones) A sensitive kid (Leonardo Di Caprio) can't wait to escape his overbearing stepfather (Robert De Niro) and small-town life in late1950s Washington State.

The Air up There (1994; Paul M. Glaser) Vancouver was a location stop for globe-trotting director Glaser during the making of this comedy about a basketball coach (Kevin Bacon) recruiting hoop talent in Africa.

Little Women (1994; Gillian Armstrong) Victoria locations and North Shore Studios interior sets were used for the Winona Ryder-Susan Sarandon remake of Louisa May Alcott's cozy tale of sisterhood on the U.S. Civil War home front.

Double Happiness (1995; Mina Shum) An aspiring actress (Sandra Oh) is caught between the expectations of a traditional Chinese family and her own career ambitions in modern Vancouver's film industry.

Gold Diggers (1995; Kevin J. Dobson) Summering in small-town Washington, a city kid (Christina Ricci) finds a friend and confidant in the local wild child (Anna Chlumsky).

LOVELY COUPLES

Though Vancouver has yet to be the subject of a great love song, filmmakers know that romance in all its forms thrives in our rainforest. Among the many meaningful relationships played out before their cameras are those depicted in the following films:

McCabe and Mrs. Miller (1970; Robert Altman) A drifter (Warren Beatty) becomes enamored of a frontier madam (Julie Christie) in director Altman's second Vancouver-made feature, a Western that he shot in a specially built North Shore mining town.

A Man, a Woman and a Bank (1979; Noel Black) A caper comedy set in Gastown about two high-tech robbers (Donald Sutherland, Paul Mazursky) and the non-technical distractions provided by a local beauty (Brooke Adams).

By Design (1981; Claude Jutra) Director Jutra broke new ground thematically with his comic tale of same-sex lovers (Patty Duke Astin, Sara Botsford) seeking a man (Saul Rubinek) to father a baby for them.

The Boy Who Could Fly (1986; Nick Castle) Making friends with an autistic classmate (Jay Underwood), a lonely teenaged girl (Lucy Deakins)

discovers her mate's amazing powers in this coming-of-age fantasy filmed at Vancouver's Lord Byng Secondary.

Fire with Fire (1986; Duncan Gibbons) Vancouver's St. George's school plays an Oregon Catholic girls academy, home to a rebellious teen (Virginia Madsen) who becomes involved with a local prison inmate (Craig Sheffer).

Cousins (1989; Joel Schumacher) In a domestic comedy that makes Vancouver look like a lover's paradise, in-laws (Ted Danson, Isabella Rossellini) keep romance within the family by pretending to cheat on their unfaithful spouses.

Immediate Family (1989; Jonathan Kaplan) Maternity and married love are examined in this drama about an infertile Seattle couple (James Woods, Glenn Close) who agree to care for an unwed, pregnant teen (Mary Stuart Masterson) in exchange for her baby.

The Crush (1993; Alan Shapiro) Nasty problems ensue when a sexy Shaughnessy teen (Alicia Silverstone) becomes psychotically obsessed with her parents' handsome tenant (Cary Elwes).

Bulletproof Heart (aka *Killer*, 1994; Mark Malone) A hitman (Anthony LaPaglia) endangers his own life as well as his professional standing when he falls in love with a woman (Mimi Rogers) he's been hired to kill.

Bad Company (1995; Damian Harris) Working undercover a CIA operative (Laurence Fishburne) with an attitude problem is seduced by an attractive enemy agent (Ellen Barkin).

Tokyo Cowboy (1995; Kathy Garneau) In this cultural re-adjustment comedy a young Japanese (Hiromoto Ida) arrives in Vancouver hoping to fulfill his Western fantasies and discovers that his dream girl (Christianne Hirt) is living with a dream girl (Janne Mortil) of her own.

ENCORE

In the motion picture business, success breeds sequels. Although the originals were made elsewhere, these follow-on features provided work and professional credits for Vancouver film folk:

The Other Side of the Mountain, Part 2 (1978; Larry Peerce) Overcoming her fear of commitment, paraplegic Jill Kinmont (Marilyn Hassett) marries a sensitive truck driver (Timothy Bottoms) and passes through Vancouver on her way to a Vancouver Island honeymoon.

Rocky IV (1985; Sylvester Stallone) The Pacific National Exhibition's Agrodome stands in for a Soviet sports palace where the Red Army's steroidal best (Dolph Lundgren) takes a beating from the American champ (Stallone).

The Fly II (1989; Chris Walas) The monstrous mutations continue on a huge Bridge Studios laboratory set as profit-driven scientists experiment upon the original Fly's son (Eric Stoltz).

Friday the 13th Part VIII: Jason Takes Manhattan (1989; Rob Hedden) The hockey-masked slasher adds 19 notches to his machete, dispatching victims on locations that include a SkyTrain dressed to look like the New York subway.

Xtro II (1990; Harry Bromley-Davenport) An American scientist (Jan-Michael Vincent) battles a hideous, violent thing from another world in an isolated subterranean military research lab.

Ernest Rides Again (1994; John R. Cherry III) UBC plays the Virginia college where the comic handyman (Jim Varney) helps an obsessed professor (Ron K. James) find a lost Revolutionary War cannon.

Red Scorpion II (1994; Michael Kennedy) With the Soviet Union gone, Russia's finest female commando (Jennifer Rubin) finds work infiltrating a gang of American neo-Nazis plotting a presidential assassination.

Ernest Goes to School (1995; Coke Sams) Lord Byng Secondary plays a U.S. high school with a custodian (Jim Varney) who becomes an instant genius with a little help from the science teacher's brain-boosting machine.

SELF-PORTRAITS

Versatility is the key to Vancouver's popularity as a film location. Though the ability to pass for Seattle, New York or Nagoya, Japan, attracts business, it's also a sore point with civic boosters. "Vancouver is never Vancouver in the movies," goes an oft-heard complaint. But it is. Some examples:

Johnny Stool Pigeon (1949; William Castle) International drug dealers are tracked to their Downtown Vancouver lair by a heroic U.S. Treasury agent (Howard Duff).

The Sweet and the Bitter (1962; James Clavell) Intent on avenging the death of her father (Dale Ishimoto), a Japanese fisherman interned during the war, a dutiful daughter (Yoko Tani) comes to Vancouver looking for the Scots businessman (Torin Thatcher) who stole her father's boats.

Russian Roulette (1975; Lou Lombardo) In a suspense thriller based on newsman Tom Ardies' novel, an RCMP corporal (George Segal) uncovers a plot to assassinate Soviet premier Alexei Kosygin during his 1971 state visit to Vancouver.

Cold Front (1990; Allan "Paul Bnarbic" Goldstein) A U.S. drug enforcement agent (Martin Sheen) works with an RCMP partner (Michael Ontkean) to stop a renegade Soviet assassin at large in Vancouver.

Skip Tracer (1979; Zale Dalen) Death threats prompt some serious lifestyle changes for a hard-driving Vancouver repo man (David Petersen).

Shoot to Kill (1988; Roger Spottiswoode) Tracking a deranged killer (Clancy Brown) to Vancouver, an FBI agent (Sidney Poitier) stakes out Robson Square, leads a hot pursuit through Downtown and shoots it out aboard a B.C. ferry.

The Burning Season (1993; Harvey Crossland) Bored with her life in the Vancouver suburbs, a young Indo-Canadian matron (Akesh Gill) has a passionate affair with her college instructor (Ayub Khan Din), a dashing Rajput prince.

Impolite (1993; David Hauka) A boozy reporter (Robert Wisden) manages the extra legwork necessary to cover Howe Street and get a big scoop for the Vancouver *Gazette*.

Intersection (1994; Mark Rydell) Richard Gere plays a Vancouver architect with an Arthur Erickson-like style and a personal life complicated by the demands of a wife (Sharon Stone) and a lover (Lolita Davidovich).

ENCORE II

Did we mention that films shot in Vancouver also return for their sequels? These include:

The Neverending Story (1984; Wolfgang Petersen) Though the imaginary world of Fantasia exists only on a Bavarian Studios soundstage, pre-teen explorer Bastian (Barret Oliver) enters it from the "real" world of Vancouver's Gastown. The producers returned for . . .

The Neverending Story II (1990; George Miller) A new Bastian (Jonathan Brandis) finds the antiquarian bookshop still in business. His adventures continued in . . .

The Neverending Story III (1995; Peter MacDonald) The teen-aged Bastian (Jason-James Richter) discovers that Fantasia's Childlike Empress (Julie Cox) is no longer a child.

My American Cousin (1985; Sandy Wilson) Shot on location in Penticton, Vancouver writer-director Wilson's winning tale of Sandy Wilcox (Margaret Langrick), an Okanagan 12-year-old who comes of age in the 1950s, was followed by . . .

American Boyfriends (1989; Sandy Wilson) At 17, Sandy (Langrick) is a first-year SFU student who cuts classes to attend her cousin's wedding in Oregon.

Empire of Ash II (1987; Michael Mazo, Lloyd Simandl) Starting this series of post-holocaust adventures with the second chapter, producer Simandl shot his story of Danielle (Melanie Kigour), a female road warrior, in and around Squamish. Then came . . .

Empire of Ash III (1988; Michael Mazo, Lloyd Simandl) Filmed in the Abbotsford area, the battle continues as Danielle (Kigour) deals with a warlord bent on ruling what's left of the world.

Stakeout (1987; John Badham) The B.C. Penitentiary and the Campbell Avenue Fish Wharf are among the distinctive locations used in this comedy-thriller about Seattle cops (Richard Dreyfuss, Emilio Estevez) on surveillance duty. They returned for . . .

Another Stakeout (1993; John Badham) A female prosecutor (Rosie O'Donnell) joins the team for a suburban Seattle undercover operation filmed on Bowen Island.

Look Who's Talking (1989: Amy Heckerling) Downtown doubles for Manhattan in this courtship comedy cutely narrated by the infant son of a single mom (Kirstie Alley). The chatter continues in . . .

Look Who's Talking Too (1990: Amy Heckerling) With two infants to handle the narration, the young marrieds (Alley, John Travolta) experience separation and a reconciliation that results in . .

Look Who's Talking Now (1993: Tom Ropelewski) The family's bantering dogs report on another marital crisis, one that ends on Christmas Eve in a blizzard filmed on Bowen Island.

Ski School (1991; Damian Lee) Speaking of snow, Whistler provided the scenery and party rooms for this winter sports comedy starring Dean Cameron. A reunion was held in . . .

Ski School II (1995; David Mitchell).

LOCAL HEROES

Big screens need big stories. It's no surprise, then, that filmmakers find inspiration in the larger-than-life deeds of famous figures. Among the Vancouver-made features celebrating outstanding individuals (both real and imagined):

Another Smith for Paradise (1971; Tom Shandel) In this fictional examination of ethnic ambition, a dynamic Ukrainian-Canadian stock promoter (Henry Ramer) plans a grand gesture to impress Vancouver's WASP Establishment.

Klondike Fever (1979; Peter Carter) The young Jack London (Jeff East) encounters such legendary characters as Northwest Mounted Policeman Sam Steele (Lorne Greene) during his real-life Yukon Gold Rush odyssey.

Eureka (1981; Nicolas Roeg) Gene Hackman plays a misanthropic millionaire in this fictionalized look at the last days of Canadian mining tycoon Sir Harry Oakes, murdered in the Bahamas in July, 1943.

The Grey Fox (1982; Phillip Borsos) Richard Farnsworth has the title role in the true story of Bill Miner, the "gentleman bandit" who robbed trains in turn-of-the-century B.C.

Star 80 (1983; Bob Fosse) Mariel Hemingway stars in the tragic story of Dorothy Stratten, the Vancouver beauty who became a *Playboy* model and a Hollywood murder victim.

The Terry Fox Story (1983; Ralph Thomas) Eric Fryer plays the one-legged Port Coquitlam runner who ignored his cancer and inspired the nation with his 1980 Marathon of Hope.

Walls (1985; Tom Shandel) A charismatic convict (Winston Rekert) draws public attention to barbaric prison conditions in a drama inspired by a 1979 B.C. Penitentiary hostage-taking incident.

Roxanne (1987; Fred Schepisi) In a comic reworking of Cyrano de Bergerac, Nelson's great-hearted fire chief (Steve Martin) learns that his large nose is no impediment to romance.

Chaindance (1991; Allan A. Goldstein) Based on actual penal reform proposals from the 1970s, this period prison drama focusses on a social worker (Rae Dawn Chong) with a plan to turn a convict (Michael Ironside) into a care-giver.

The Legend of Kootenai Brown (1991; Allan Kroeker) A fictional Scots villain (Donnelly Rhodes) adds a serio-comic note to the tale of real-life Irish adventurer John George Brown (Tom Burlinson), a gold-seeker tried for murder in pre-confederation B.C.

Whale Music (1994; Richard J. Lewis) Rock idealism is recalled in this story of a retired, mildly mad pop star (Maury Chaykin) who hides out in his seaside villa composing symphonic works for passing whale pods.

Magic in the Water (1995; Rick Stevenson) A radio talk-show host (Mark Harmon) gets to know his kids during a vacation spent searching for Orky, a mythical aquatic monster inspired by Okanagan Lake's Ogopogo.

DIRECTORIAL TRIBUTE–JACK DARCUS

Vancouver's ranking auteur Jack Winston Darcus (born February 22, 1941) has created a distinctive body of work in his own hometown. A successful painter as well as a filmmaker, Darcus has written and directed six feature dramas that reflect his personal vision as a B.C.-born artist. In each he creates complex and allegorical social relationships that illuminate moments in the maturation of the Canadian West Coast experience.

Great Coups Of History (1969) A single mom (Delphine Harvey) reminisces about a life spent trading on her female charms, while her teenaged daughter (Jani Cassie) struggles with her own budding sexuality.

Proxyhawks (1971) A coastal farm couple (Jack Darcus, Susan Spencer) experience deepening sexual tensions in their relationship when the man becomes obsessed with falconry.

The Wolfpen Principle (1974) A holocaust survivor (Vladimir Valenta) joins a young Coast Salish mystic (Laurence Brown) in a plot to free the Stanley Park wolves.

Deserters (1982) An idealistic Canadian immigration officer (Dermot Hennelly) and his wife (Barbara March) find themselves at odds with a U.S. Army sergeant (Alan Scarfe) who is using them to get at Vietnam war resisters.

Kingsgate (1989) A selection of tragicomic relationships are on view when a university professor (Duncan Fraser) and his young lover (Elizabeth Dancoes) visit her feuding parents (Christopher Plummer, Roberta Maxwell).

The Portrait (1992) Commissioned to paint a

wealthy woman's portrait, a desperate artist (Alan Scarfe) must resolve the conflict between his ideals and his survival instincts.

THE B-LIST

In the days of the double-feature, B pictures were the ones that played the bottom of the bill. They were often action melodramas made on tight budgets by craftspeople for whom movies were a business. In Vancouver B productions were a way to break in and, perhaps, break through to commercial success. Hopes as well as dollars were invested in such features as:

One Minute Before Death (1973; Rogelio Gonzales) Producing entertainment with an American look for the Mexican market, director Gonzales filmed Wanda Hendrix and Giselle McKenzie in an old Shaughnessy mansion. Together they starred in this occult murder mystery and in . .

The Oval Portrait (1973; Rogelio Gonzales) A haunted-house thriller based on the Edgar Allan Poe short story.

Christina (1974; Paul Krasny) Planning to make his home here, producer Trevor (*Groundstar Conspiracy*) Wallace found backers for both this mystery romance, a vehicle for Vancouver-born actress Barbara Parkins, and . . .

Journey into Fear (1975; Daniel Mann) Sam Waterston, Yvette Mimieux, Vincent Price, Shelley Winters, Zero Mostel and Donald Pleasence were among the stars assembled for a remake of the 1942 suspense thriller, with Vancouver playing various Mediterranean ports of call.

Dead Wrong (1984; Len Kowalewich) A debt-ridden Vancouver commercial fisherman (Winston Rekert) gets involved with drug runners and an attractive undercover cop (Britt Ekland) in an action feature developed by a BCTV production team.

Ladies of the Lotus (1986; Douglas C. Nicolle, Lloyd Simandl) Sinister forces are at work in this tale of a West Coast fashion studio whose models begin disappearing after the installation of a sophisticated surveillance system.

High Stakes (1987; Larry Kent) On a return visit Vancouver film pioneer Kent cast local broadcasting legend Jack Webster as a television anchor in an action-comedy about newsgathering and a lost Nazi treasure.

Malone (1987; Harley Cokliss) Vacationing in rural Oregon (played by Hedley and suburban Vancouver), an ex-CIA agent (Burt Reynolds) happens upon a white supremacist (Cliff Robertson) conspiring to overthrow the government.

Silhouette (1990; Lloyd Simandl) In an urban mystery from prolific Vancouver director Simandl, a murder investigation brings an idealistic attorney (Tracy Scoggins) into conflict with ruthless corporate executives.

Home Movie (1992; Fred Frame) A comedy, this low-budget feature about low-budget feature filmmaking works to blur the line between art made on the run and reality.

Exquisite Tenderness (1994; Carl Schenkel) Blamed for the death of a patient by her former lover (Sean Haberlem), a dedicated surgeon (Isabel Glasser) experiences self-doubts in this psychological thriller filmed in Riverview Hospital's Crease Clinic.

Hard Evidence (1994; Michael Kennedy) Framed for the murder of his mistress (Cali Timmins), a philandering developer (Gregory Harrison) finds an unexpected ally in his wife (Joan Severance).

Crash (aka *Dirty Money*, 1995; Charles Wilkinson) Computer disks unlock the secrets of a criminal empire for an undercover agent (Leilani Sarelle) and her partner (Michael Biehn).

Power of Attorney (1995; Howard Himelstein) Shot in New Westminster's law courts, this suspense drama is the story of a former prosecutor (Elias Koteas) with his own reasons for defending a notorious mobster (Danny Aiello).

THINGS THAT GO BUMP IN THE NIGHT

Fright-night features are a film industry staple. Since a hint of the supernatural is enough to induce shivers, Vancouver has played host to its share of wraiths, entities and ectoplasmic emanations. The list includes:

A Name for Evil (aka *The Grove*; *The Face of Evil*, 1970; Bernard Girard) An architect (Robert Culp) inherits an 18th-century mansion and is driven to extremes when his wife (Samantha Eggar) is seduced by the resident ghost.

Shadow of the Hawk (1976; George McCowan) The Vancouver grandson (Jan-Michael Vincent) of a tribal shaman (Chief Dan George) is summoned to his ancestral home to deal with a demonic entity.

The Changeling (1979; Peter Medak) Vancouver plays a Gothic-looking Seattle in this tale of a restless spirit attempting to communicate with a grieving widower (George C. Scott).

Prophecy (1979; John Frankenheimer) Though caused by industrial pollution, the horrific mutations that an environmental scientist (Robert Foxworth) encounters in the Maine woods also fulfill local Native American legends.

The Resurrected (aka *The Tomb of Charles Dexter Ward*, 1992; Dan O'Bannon) Chris Sarandon has a dual role in this adaptation of the H.P. Lovecraft novel in which a scientist messes with things man was not meant to know.

Needful Things (1993; Fraser Heston) Gibsons plays Stephen King's Castle Rock, a Maine community visited by Old Nick (Max Von Sydow), a storekeeper in the market for souls.

Hideaway (1995; Brett Leonard) A near-death experience forges a psychic link between a family man (Jeff Goldblum) and a serial killer (Jimmy Sisto) who preys upon unwary young women.

The Hunted (1995; J.F. Lawton) Aided by the ghost of a gangster's murdered mistress (Joan Chen), an American business person (Christopher Lambert) in Japan does battle with her Ninja killer (John Lone).

Jumanji (1995; Joe Johnston) Monsoons, simulated in B.C. Research Institute tanks, are among the trials endured by an unlucky game-player (Robin Williams), who escapes from a magic dimension to seek help in his struggle with its savage forces.

Susie Q (1995; John Blizek) A lonely child (Justin Whalen) helps a friendly ghost (Amy Jo Johnson) solve an old mystery in this family fantasy.

CABIN FEVER DREAMS

Not everything that frightens us lives outside. The mind is capable of creating its own demons and is the source of countless screen obsessives, compulsives and dangerously deranged villains. Consider, for example, Vancouver's own psycho-thriller caseload:

The Mad Room (1969; Bernard Girard) A remake of 1941's *Ladies in Retirement,* this is the story of a lady's companion (Stella Stevens) whose teenaged siblings are suspects in the murder of her employer (Shelley Winters).

That Cold Day in the Park (1969; Robert Altman) In director Altman's first Vancouver feature, a lonely, delusional spinster (Sandy Dennis) picks up a young drifter (Michael Burns) in Kitsilano's Tatlow Park.

The Keeper (1976; Tom Drake) In this tongue-in-cheek look at institutional bedlam, it's hard to tell the patients from the administrator (Christopher Lee) of the Underwood Asylum.

Mr. Patman (1980; John Guillermin) Insanity proves contagious for a Vancouver psychiatric orderly (James Coburn), an Irish charmer who identifies too closely with his patients.

Abducted (1986; Boon Collins) Vancouver Island writer-director Collins used North Vancouver wilderness locations for the story of a pretty marathon runner (Roberta Weiss) kidnapped by a mad mountain man (Lawrence King Philip).

Blood Link (1986; Alberto De Martino) Troubled by violent nightmares, a doctor (Michael Moriarty) discovers that he's tuned into the misdeeds of his separated Siamese-twin brother.

The Stepfather (1987; Joseph Rubin) "Father knows best—or else" is the shock message in this tale of a domestic disciplinarian (Terry O'Quinn) who marries into, then murders, whole families.

Until Death (1987; Lloyd Simandl, Michael Mazo) A woman (Sharlene Martin) discovers that her intense suitor (John R. Johnston) is the psychotic killer terrorizing the city.

American Gothic (1988; John Hough) Bowen

Island provides splendid rural isolation for a family of recreational murderers (Yvonne De Carlo, Rod Steiger), until an innocent-looking ex-mental patient (Sarah Torgov) comes calling.

Matinee (1990; Richard Martin) When the local movie house books a Halloween horror festival, a Fraser Valley girl (Beatrice Boepple) learns that serial killing runs in her family.

Deep Sleep (1990; Patricia Gruben) An unbalanced West Vancouver girl (Megan Follows) and an East Side musician (Damon D'Oliveira) uncover secrets about U.S.-Asian relations.

Deadly Ambition (1995; Harvey Frost) Left alone with an unhinged weekend guest (Wolf Larson), an attractive matron (Kelly LeBrock) becomes the object of his unwanted sexual attentions.

Malicious (1995; Ian Corson) Breaking training for an after-hours adventure, a rookie baseball star (Patrick McGaw) becomes the obsessive love object of a dangerous, demanding Nat Bailey Stadium fan (Molly Ringwald).

No Fear (1995; James Foley) Urban tribalism rules when a grunge rocker ("Markie Mark" Wahlberg) stalks a 16-year-old Seattle girl (Reese Witherspoon), bringing his posse along to lay siege to her parents' seaside home.

LAW AND ORDER

In the movies the conflict between good and evil is most often expressed in terms of cops versus killers. Men with badges stand against violent forces in these Vancouver-made features:

Year of the Dragon (1985; Michael Cimino) A restaurant massacre filmed in Vancouver's Chinatown is a key moment in the story of a relentless New York cop (Mickey Rourke) and his war on an international drug trader (John Lone).

The Hitman (1991; Aaron Norris) Vancouver doubles as Seattle, the home of an undercover cop (Chuck Norris) posing as a killer to thwart the planned union of Italo-American and French-Canadian mobsters.

Jennifer Eight (1992; Bruce Robinson) Vancouver urban exteriors and North Shore Studios interiors complement California locations as a homicide cop (Andy Garcia) tracks a madman attempting to kill a blind girl (Uma Thurman).

Beyond Suspicion (1993; Paul Ziller) A corrupt police officer (Jack Scalia) involved with an amnesiac photographer (Stephanie Kramer) becomes the object of a departmental internal affairs investigation.

Knight Moves (1993; Carl Schenkel) A police chief (Tom Skerritt) suspects a chess champ (Christopher Lambert) when a psycho goes on a killing spree during a major international chess tournament.

Edge of Deception (1994; George Mihalka) A tabloid drama unfolds when an investigative reporter (Mariel Hemingway) finds a subject

(Stephen Shellen) for her story about "cops who fall in love with killers."

Suspicious Agenda (1994; Clay Borris) A pair of tightly wound cops (Richard Grieco, Nick Mancuso) assigned to a homicide task force become prime suspects in a series of unsolved murders.

Crackerjack (1995; Michael Mazo) A neo-Nazi terrorist (Christopher Plummer) takes control of a remote mountain hotel, upsetting the vacation plans of a notoriously short-tempered Chicago cop (Thomas Ian Griffith).

Deadly Sins (1995; Michael Robison) A small-town sheriff (David Keith) works with a young nun (Alyssa Milano) to solve a brutal murder in a convent school.

Dream Man (1995; Rene Bonniere) Sexual fantasies foreshadow a dangerous involvement for a policewoman (Patsy Kensit) who dreams of making love to a man (Andrew McCarthy) later accused of murdering his wealthy wife.

Midnight Heat (1995; Harvey Frost) A police detective (Steve Mendel) investigates his old college buddy, a professional football player (Tim Matheson) suspected of killing his team's owner.

Someone to Die For (1995; Clay Borris) When two cops die violently, police suspect one of their own officers (Corbin Bernsen), a grieving dad known to have blamed the murdered men for the death of his daughter.

TERMINAL CITY COMEDY CLUB

Being funny is no joke and providing audiences with comic relief is one of the hardest jobs in show business. Fortunately filmmakers keep trying. Among the made-just-for-laughs Vancouver features are:

Reno and the Doc (1984; Charles Dennis) Whistler is the scenic setting for this ski lodge comedy in which two forty-something buddies (Kenneth Welsh, Henry Raymer) establish a telepathic link.

Home Is Where the Hart Is (1987; Rex Bromfield) Old jokes abound in this tale of elderly twins (Eric Christmas, Ted Stidder) who call in the sheriff (Leslie Nielsen) when their 104-year-old dad runs off with his nurse (Valri Bromfield).

Experts (1989; Dave Thomas) Something of a cinematic Chinese puzzle, SCTV veteran Thomas' feature is set in a Soviet-built replica of an American town where a pair of New York hipsters (John Travolta, Arye Gross) are duped into teaching the KGB all about U.S. pop culture.

Who's Harry Crumb? (1989; Paul Flaherty) Hired to find a kidnapped California heiress, an inept, disguise-happy private eye (John Candy) bumbles about in a Vancouver disguised as Los Angeles.

Short Time (1990; Gregg Champion) Thinking he's terminally ill, a Seattle cop (Dabney Coleman) risks all in the hope of winning death-in-

the-line-of-duty benefits for his family.

Mystery Date (1991; Jonathan Wacks) In this mistaken identity farce, a college kid (Ethan Hawke) poses as his older brother to impress a girl (Teri Polo) and then runs into all of his shady sibling's worst enemies.

Stay Tuned (1992; Peter Hyams) Commercial broadcasting is the satirical target in this look at Satan's own cable service, its promise of 666 channels and the suburban couple (John Ritter, Pam Dawber) condemned to its "hellvision."

Man of the House (1995; James Orr) A mean little kid (Jonathan Taylor Thomas) makes his divorced mom's beau (Chevy Chase) work hard to win his approval in an action-comedy shot in that bit of Vancouver that's forever Seattle.

Big Bully (1995; Steve Miner) This domestic comedy poses the question "do they ever grow up?" with the story of a writer (Rick Moranis) who returns to his hometown for a rematch with his childhood nemesis (Tom Arnold).

MAN'S BEST FRIENDS

Human actors haven't a chance when they have to share the screen with Vancouver scenery and a scene-stealing animal actor. Locally filmed pictures in which pets play major roles include:

Dogpound Shuffle (aka *Spot,* 1975; Jeffrey Bloom) A pair of bickering buskers (Ron Moody, David Soul) work Davie Street for enough change to free their beloved dancing dog (Scruffy) from the pound.

The Journey of Natty Gann (1985; Jeremy Kagan) Vancouver is dressed to look like the Depression-era U.S. for this story of an abandoned girl (Meredith Salenger) who makes a cross-country trek accompanied by a protective wolf (Jed).

Watchers (1988; Jon Hess) A trusting teen (Corey Haim) discovers that his new golden retriever (Sandy) is the friendly half of an escaped living-weapons system; the killer half is at large in the woods.

Bingo (1991; Matthew Robbins) In a remake of 1958's The *Littlest Hobo,* an adventurous mutt (Bingo) crosses the country to find his family (Cindy Williams, David Rasche).

Andre (1994; George Miller) Released into the wild, an orphan seal (Tory) returns to his adopted human family (Keith Carradine, Tina Majorino) in that corner of West Vancouver that looks like coastal Maine.

White Fang 2: Myth of the White Wolf (1994; Ken Olin) The husky hero (actually five different dogs) helps a Haida village protect its caribou herds from a greedy mining company in this sequel to the 1991 feature.

Far from Home: The Adventures of Yellow Dog (1995; Phillip Borsos) A brave dog (Dakotah) helps his best buddy (Jesse Bradford) survive three weeks in the Vancouver Island wilderness.

The B.C. Film Commission and industry stakeholders created a new position, Communities Affairs Manager, in 1995 to troubleshoot issues related to location filming. Equally funded by public and private monies, this position is the key communications link between the film industry and B.C. communities, particularly in and around Vancouver. The mandate is not only to help manage the effective use of B.C. locations but to seek out communications opportunities that will enhance general understanding of industry impact and ensure a mutually beneficial relationship.

IN OTHER WORDS

Not every film shot here is shot in English. A cosmopolitan community, Vancouver attracts artists from across the country and over the sea who have come here to make movies for their home markets. In the 1990s we took our place on the Pacific Rim as a production centre for Chinese films. Among the non-English language features made in and around Vancouver:

J'ai Mon Voyage (1973; Denys Heroux) Taking a comic look at Canada's "two solitudes," Quebecois director Heroux chronicles the problems of a French-speaking family (Dominique Michel, Jean Lefebvre, Rene Simard) during a cross-country trip to Vancouver.

La Menace (aka *Flashback*, 1977; Alain Corneau) A co-production with France, this mystery-thriller ends with Vancouver truckers chasing a suspected killer (Yves Montand), a man on the run from his violent past in Europe.

Virus (1980; Kinji Fukasaku) Local backgrounds supplement the Antarctic footage featured in this Japanese-made disaster drama that follows the fate of the 858 survivors of a global holocaust.

Return Engagement (1989; Tung Joe Cheung) In this Chinese-language thriller, a family man (Alan Tang) is framed by mobsters, serves a prison term and then seeks revenge on the hired killers who murdered his wife and daughter.

Black Cat (1991; Stephen Shin) Chinese is the operative language for this action feature's heroine (Jade Leung), an urban survivor programmed by CIA scientists to kill for America.

Never-Ending Summer (1991; Lawrence Cheng) Domestic complications are played for laughs in this tale of a Hong Kong immigrant (Lawrence Cheng) who arrives in Vancouver to discover his wife (Do Do Cheng) living with a non-Asian.

Black Cat II (1992; James Fung, Stephen Shin) On assignment in Russia, the CIA's computer-enhanced female asset (Jade Leung) battles a terrorist mutant under orders to kill Boris Yeltsin.

Saviour of the Soul II (1992; David Lai, Kong Man Yun) Vancouver doubles as Alaska in this romantic fantasy about a Chinese dreamer (Andy Lau) searching for the legendary beauty (Rosemund Kwan) who sleeps in suspended animation in an ice cave.

Swallow in the Rain (1992; Kong Man Yun, David Lai) Betrayed by their Hong Kong lovers, a policewoman (Chang Man Yee) and a young druggie (Guo Tamara) join forces while fleeing for their lives in urban America.

Young Offenders (1993; Elizabeth Wong) This locally produced drama tells the story of a Taiwanese teen (Danny Wang), living in Vancouver with too much money and too little supervision, who has the misfortune to cross some professional Chinese mobsters.

Rumble in the Bronx (1994; Stanley Tong) Vancouver plays New York for martial arts superstar Jackie Chan, cast here as a dutiful nephew who beats up the street gangsters causing trouble for his honest, entrepreneurial uncle.

MIDNIGHT MADNESS

Though every filmmaker is a visionary, some cinematic visions play best after hours. Not intended for mass audiences, these films are either too personal, too quirky, too explicit or too outrageous for mainstream filmgoers. Possible Vancouver-made candidates for cult film status are:

The Plastic Mile (aka *The Finishing Touch; She's a Woman*, 1969; Morrie Ruvinsky) The story of an unhinged director (Jace Vander Veen) who rapes his leading lady (Pia Shandel) during the making of his magnum opus, this controversial "art movie" added new sex scenes to each successive version.

Master of Images (1972; Byron Black) Puckish conceptual artist Black offered his personal take on the state of cinema with this non-linear tale of a young woman (Lulu Ulul) who flees the city for some karmic readjustment and experiences a kaleidoscopic 1960s-style happening.

Sexcula (1973; John Holbrook) Aimed at the then-new American market for hardcore porn, this sexually explicit fantasy features a nymphomaniacal scientist who seeks help from her cousin the vampire when her male monster fails to function.

The Holy Assassin (1974; Byron Black) Adding a science-fiction twist to his visual experimentation, director Black's second feature involves a metaphysical criminal from another dimension hiding out in a local hippie commune.

Big Meat Eater (aka *The Butcher of Burquitlam*, 1980; Chris Windsor) Cannibalism and small appliance repair are featured in this deliberate attempt by SFU Film Workshop alumni to create a suburban midnight movie musical.

Terminal City Ricochet (1989; Zale Dalen) Full-volume rock music and a newsboy's rebellion contribute to the chaos in this vision of urban derangement designed for inner-city cult crowds.

Flesh Gordon Meets the Cosmic Cheerleaders (1991; Howard T. Ziehm) In this sex-comedy sequel to the 1972 softcore serial spoof, the intergalactic hero (Vince Murdocco) is drafted by scantily clad aliens who need him to restore pleasure to their planet.

ON THE ROAD AGAIN

Freedom, symbolized by the open road, is at the heart of what's known as "the American dream." In common with our U.S. neighbors, Canadians enjoy the idea of personal mobility. The movies invite us to share in the freedom fantasy with various kinds of road, escape and pursuit pictures. And so, we conclude *The Greater*

Vancouver Book's Feature Film Festival with a look down some local highways.

The Supreme Kid (1975; Peter Bryant) Anticipating Generation X, SFU Film Workshop graduate Bryant sent three young drifters (Frank Moore, Jim Henshaw, Don Granberry) on an ill-fated search for adventure in and out of town.

Certain Fury (1985; Stephen Gyllenhaal) In a female rerun of 1958's *The Defiant Ones*, a racially mixed pair of fugitives (Tatum O'Neal, Irene Cara) are at large in the city and at odds with one another.

We're No Angels (1989; Neil Jordan) An entire 1930s town was built near Stave Lake Falls for this comic adventure of escaped convicts (Robert De Niro, Sean Penn) masquerading as itinerant priests.

Bird on a Wire (1990; John Badham) A real exercise in illusion, this tale of lovers (Mel Gibson, Goldie Hawn) on the run has Victoria and Lower Mainland locations doubling for six different eastern U.S. cities.

Narrow Margin (1990; Peter Hyams) Hired assassins pursue a U.S. district attorney (Gene Hackman) and a murder witness (Anne Archer) aboard a Via Rail train in a thriller filmed on B.C. Rail's Howe Sound line.

Run (1990; Geoff Burrowes) Park Royal plays a New England shopping mall in the story of an accidental killer (Patrick Dempsey) one step ahead of vengeance-seeking mafiosi.

Pure Luck (1991; Nadia Tass) Vancouver provides the urban locations for a buddy comedy about a klutzy guy (Martin Short) who helps a detective (Danny Glover) find a missing heiress (Sheila Kelley) in the Mexican jungle.

Leaving Normal (1992; Edward Zwick) On the run without guns, female buddies (Christine Lahti, Meg Tilly) follow their dream of Alaskan independence.

North of Pittsburgh (1992; Richard Martin) Local back roads substitute for mid-1970s Pennsylvania in this tale of a small-timer (Jeff Schultz) pursuing a widow's compensation cheque for his iron-willed granny (Viveca Lindfors).

Harmony Cats (1993; Sandy Wilson) An unemployed Vancouver Symphony violinist (Kim Coates) takes up bull-fiddling and goes on tour with a country and western band.

The Raffle (1994; Gavin Wilding) To create a unique lottery two Vancouver dreamers (Nicholas Lea, Bobby Dawson) set out in search of its intended prize, the world's most beautiful woman.

B.C. has been host to many noteworthy productions over the years. At least 20 productions are filming in and around the Vancouver area at any given time. The worldwide hit TV series The X-Files has shot here for five consecutive years. Reboot and Madison were created and shot in B.C. for the past several years. Feature film credits for 1995/96 include: Jumanji, Carpool, Big Bully, Excess Baggage, Free Willy III, The Sixth Man, Alaska, Firestorm and over forty more titles.

Movie Houses of Greater Vancouver
Casey Lazecki

THROUGHOUT THE ENTIRE history of motion pictures, the citizens of Greater Vancouver have always loved attending the movies.

Hastings Street from the 100-block west to the 300-block east, Vancouver's first prominent theatre district in the 1910s and 1920s, was originally called the "great white way." By the 1930s the vaudeville and various other live entertainments that had supported the eight theatres along the street had all but disappeared. Possibly the most beautiful theatre ever built in Vancouver, the Pantages Theatre at 20 West Hastings, carried on under new owners and a new name, the Beacon, with vaudeville and second-run movies. Other important theatres on Hastings such as the Rex and Columbia soldiered on as best they could during the Great Depression. The fortunes of Hastings Street continued to decline however, and by the mid-1930s the main theatre district of Vancouver was definitely considered to be Granville Street.

Granville Street was aptly named "theatre row." In its heyday the street boasted ten theatres within a five-block radius. In addition to being the home of two grand movie palaces, the Capitol and the Orpheum, Granville Street also offered the Colonial, the Lyric (the former Vancouver Opera House), the Paradise (later remodelled as the Coronet), the Studio (now the Paradise), the Plaza, the Vogue, the Dominion (now the Caprice) and the Strand (at the corner of Georgia and Seymour). The street was awash in brilliant neon and lineups often stretched to the end of the block.

Unlike the Pantages and Orpheum theatres which were built to house vaudeville and live theatre, the Capitol Theatre at 820 Granville was a pure movie palace. Opened in the silent movie era in 1921, it was a lush facility that originally seated 2,500. Like the Orpheum, the Capitol was equipped with a huge Wurlitzer organ to accompany the movies. The Capitol also had the privilege of premiering Vancouver's first talking picture, *Mother Knows Best,* on October 18, 1928. Today, the theatre is a multiplex, known as the Capitol 6.

The Orpheum is Vancouver's only surviving movie palace from the 1920s. Opened in November, 1927, the grand old theatre has been host to a who's who of legendary performers as well as memorable movie premieres, including *Gone with the Wind* on February 16, 1940. The late, longtime manager Ivan Ackery was considered a master of movie promotion for his attention-getting stunts and contests. In fact Ackery and the

The classy old Stanley Theatre on Granville is destined to come back to life as a live theatre

late Charlie Doctor of the Capitol held a friendly showmanship rivalry for years.

The Vogue, the Odeon theatre chain's "prestige" movie house on Granville, was opened in 1941 as competition for the Capitol and Orpheum, both operated by Famous Players. The Vogue was very eye-catching, becoming the first Canadian theatre to win a "Perfect 36" award for architectural merit from the *Annual Theatre Catalogue* of the United States.

While the Downtown theatres received the first-run movies and the largest audiences, neighborhood theatres were an essential component of the movie-going experience for most of Greater Vancouver during the 1930s, 1940s and 1950s. In the era before television, these theatres had a large, regular base of patrons who lived nearby and enjoyed everything from weekend children's matinees to Saturday night double-features. Of the dozens of neighborhood theatres that existed in Greater Vancouver, most are now gone, having been demolished or converted to other uses.

Longtime Vancouver residents may recall departed old favorites from a partial list that includes the Windsor, the Rio, the Cambie, the Kerrisdale, the Alma, the Kitsilano, the Grandview, the Fraser, the Circle, the Star and the Roxy theatres. Burnaby residents may recall the art-deco splendor of the Oak Theatre, or the Kingcrest, Regent or Dolphin theatres. In North Vancouver the Nova (later the Totem), the Lonsdale and the Odeon theatres were popular, while Richmond had the Lulu and the Steva theatres. New Westminster was home to the elegant Columbia, the Paramount, the Fox (later Odeon), the Metro and the Sapperton theatres.

Despite the loss of some fine theatres many have survived these many years and indeed continue to flourish. The classy old Stanley Theatre on Granville is destined to come back to life as a live theatre, while the Hollywood, the Ridge, the Park, the Dunbar and the Varsity theatres continue to remain popular fixtures in their neighborhoods. Indeed the Hollywood—built by the Fairleigh family in 1935—has been owned and operated by the Fairleighs ever since .

In the 1930s general attendance at movie theatres, especially the palaces like the Capitol and the Orpheum, dropped off due to the Great Depression, a fact contrary to the popular conception that people spent a considerable amount of time at the movies as a means of escaping the harsh economic reality of the times. Theatres held on during these times by offering double- and triple-features and by running such audience-building promotions as "Foto-Nite" and kitchenware giveaways.

World War II not only cured the economy, it brought customers back to the theatres in droves. The time between 1940 and 1946 was the most lucrative era in Vancouver movie theatre history. Citizens packed Downtown theatres to participate in the war effort. Newsreels offered the latest news of the war, while war-bond drives were held by the theatres on a regular basis. The renewed boom times for local theatre owners would not last much longer however.

In the late 1940s a rapid decline in movie attendance was felt, and unlike previous drops in attendance, this one was permanent. The public would never again return to the movie theatres in the numbers experienced before the end of World War II. There were two main reasons for the decline, particularly between 1947 and 1955. First of all the flight to the suburbs by returning veterans had a devastating impact on Vancouver's urban theatres. There were simply fewer and fewer people living in the city to attend the theatres. Across Canada nearly 50 per cent of the theatres being used in 1948 were out of service by 1970.

However the biggest blow to the movie theatres came from the introduction of television in the late 1940s and early 1950s. Money that used to be spent going to the movies every week was now being diverted towards the purchase of a television set where "free" entertainment was now available.

The motion picture industry tried to respond to the popularity of television by improving its technology. Enlarged screens and improved vision formats such as Cinemascope, Cinerama, Todd A-O and 3-D brought some of the customers back, but not on a permanent basis. Greater Vancouver lost over two dozen theatres during the 1950s including many neighborhood theatres. Almost no new theatres were built in the 1950s, the only notable exception being the Ridge Theatre on Arbutus in Vancouver, a smart, stripped-down example of international-style architecture. Theatres were again being built in the 1960s—but not in Vancouver.

Theatre chains had followed the population to the suburbs and multi-screen cinemas were being constructed in malls everywhere throughout the 1960s and 1970s. Parking was free and plentiful, and the suburbs were considered "safer" than the city. Dwindling patronage, rising land values and a lack of heritage protection led to the loss of several of the best theatres in Vancouver between 1967 and 1975, including the old Pantages (Majestic) Theatre (which remains a parking lot to this day) on West Hastings, the Strand on Georgia and Seymour (the Scotia Tower site), the Capitol on Granville (now the Capitol 6), and very nearly the Orpheum. Original plans called for the Orpheum to be carved up into a seven-screen complex before the public and various forms of government came through with the money to buy the theatre from Famous Players and restore it for live performances.

More competition arose for the theatre industry during the early 1980s as the introduction of home video again took business from the theatres. By this time the Downtown theatre business was dominated by multiplexes, the largest including the Capitol 6, the Granville 7, and the Royal Centre (ten small theatres). With the exception of the Royal Centre, the theatres have held on and we have also seen a revitalization of neighborhood theatres by individuals such as Leonard Schein (the Park, the Varsity and the Fifth Avenue Cinemas), Ray Mainland (the Ridge) and David Fairleigh, Sr. (the Hollywood). The dedicated film enthusiasts also have the excellent Pacific Cinematheque on Howe Street to serve their needs.

During the 1990s the closing of the Stanley Theatre by Famous Players was a huge disappointment. Leonard Schein's recently opened Fifth Avenue Cinemas (with five screens) will help fill the void left by the Stanley's closing and the shuttering of the Royal Centre. Vancouver has seen movies expand from storefronts to multiplexes and today several of the theatres from the golden era remain, including the Vogue, the Stanley, the Caprice (formerly the Dominion), the Paradise, the Plaza, and of course, the Orpheum.

1940's neon, Stanley Theatre, 1993. VS

Theatres of Greater Vancouver
Mark Leiren-Young

I T IS VIRTUALLY IMPOSSIBLE TO do a comprehensive theatre listing for a book because immediately you publish it, it will be out of date. Small theatres open, close and change management faster than actors can change costumes. In a few months prior to the publication of this book, the Station Street Arts Centre closed after seven exciting years, the Starlight Theatre reverted back to its origins as a movie theatre and the Arts Club Revue Theatre underwent a substantial redesign. Meanwhile the Arts Club and the Vancouver TheatreSports League are slated to transform the Stanley Theatre into a live venue and the Vancouver Opera is building a new home next to the Queen Elizabeth Theatre.

It's also tough to define a proper "theatre" as almost every community centre and school in the lower mainland houses at least one space suitable for live performance. Some venues such as the Norman Rothstein theatre at the Jewish Community Centre or the Michael J. Fox Auditorium in Burnaby are used for public performances on a regular basis. Others are used more sporadically.

So instead of a comprehensive listing of every theatre space in the Lower Mainland the following is a collection of some of Greater Vancouver's more venerable venues. All were chosen because they seated over 150 people and they'd either been around a while or seemed likely to remain a part of the city scene. However if you're looking for a place to put on a show it's important to remember legendary director Peter Brook's advice that all you really need to create theatre is an actor, an audience and an empty space.

THE ARTS CLUB REVUE THEATRE
1585 Johnston Street, Granville Island, Vancouver
Flexible seating: maximum 225
Originally built as a cabaret venue the Revue opened in 1983 with the show "An Evening with Ruth and Leon" (a collection of songs performed by local stars Leon Bibb and Ruth Nichol). In 1995 the Arts Club Theatre cleared out the tables and bar stools and turned the space into an intimate "black box" style theatre focussing on modern Canadian drama.

THE ARTS CLUB THEATRE: MAINSTAGE
1585 Johnston Street, Granville Island, Vancouver
460 seats
Since forming back in 1964 when it ran out of a theatre on Seymour Street, the Arts Club has been one of Vancouver's foremost theatre companies. When this building opened in 1979 it became one of the earliest landmarks on Granville Island and a personal triumph for managing director Bill Millerd who had always dreamed of having a theatre on the waterfront. With three theatres and an adjoining lounge the theatre is home base for a company that regularly tours their shows throughout the province.

CENTENNIAL THEATRE CENTRE
2300 Lonsdale Avenue, North Vancouver
718 seats
One of many theatres built across Canada as part of the country's centennial celebrations, the Centennial officially opened in 1966. Home to the North Shore Light Opera, the North Shore Chorus and the Greater Vancouver Operatic Society, the Centennial offers diverse programming as the North Shore's official cultural centre.

FIREHALL ARTS CENTRE
280 East Cordova Street, Vancouver
Flexible seating: maximum 200
Vancouver's second firehall, although it is often designated as the city's first, started answering alarms back in 1906. The last fire truck drove away in 1975 and a group called Actor's Workshop attempted to turn it into a theatre but ended up folding. After brief rumblings about the building being demolished, it was saved by the Vancouver Playhouse which turned it into a home for their theatre school, sharing the space with Axis Mime (now Axis Theatre Company), Touchstone and La Troupe de la Seizieme. Axis hired freelance director Donna Spencer to help turn the building into a theatre and in 1982 the Firehall Theatre— which is still run by Spencer— opened its doors. The Firehall is home to Touchstone Theatre, Axis, the Firehall's own theatre company, the Dancing on the Edge Festival and a small gallery.

THE FORD CENTRE FOR THE PERFORMING ARTS
777 Homer Street, Vancouver
1,824 seats
This state-of-the-art $24.5 million theatre opened in November, 1995. Designed by architect Moshe Safdie (who also designed Vancouver's main library located right across the street) the theatre was created by Toronto entrepreneur and impresario Garth Drabinsky and his company Livent Inc. to house long-running mega-musicals starting with the acclaimed revival of *Show Boat.*

JAMES COWAN THEATRE
6450 Deer Lake Avenue, Burnaby
285 seats
Named for Burnaby arts patron James Cowan, the theatre is part of Burnaby's Shadbolt Centre for the Arts which also has a 157-seat recital hall and a new studio theatre which seats up to 200 people. Originally built in the 1940s as a retreat for Benedictine monks, it was converted into a theatre in 1970.

MALKIN BOWL
Stanley Park, Vancouver
1,200 seats
Canada's original permanent open-air theatre was originally built in 1934 by Mayor W.H. Malkin in memory of his wife, Marian. Originally intended for concerts, the Bowl (which closed briefly from 1963 to 1969) became home to Theatre Under the Stars (TUTS) in 1940 and the group has been producing popular musicals there almost every summer since.

MASSEY THEATRE
735-8th Avenue, New Westminster
1,260 seats
Opened in 1949 as an auditorium for both the community and New Westminster Secondary School, the Massey is now the home of the Royal City Musical Theatre, the second home for the Vancouver Symphony Orchestra and a rental hall that also presents a variety of touring artists.

METRO THEATRE CENTRE
1370 S.W. Marine Drive, Vancouver
366 seats
Opened in 1963 as the home to a variety of community theatre groups, the Metro Theatre

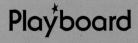

became the permanent home of the Metropolitan Co-op Theatre Society in 1966. They began producing their own work and have been one of Vancouver's most prominent community theatre companies ever since, producing an average of ten shows per season.

THE NEW YORK THEATRE
639 Commercial Drive
425 seats
One of the first theatres built in Vancouver, the New York (formerly the York) opened November 3, 1913, as the Alcazar Theatre with the comedy *Too Much Johnson*. The long-time home of the Vancouver Little Theatre Association, it also spent time as a movie house and is now a rental hall for live acts, primarily rock bands.

THE ORPHEUM THEATRE
884 Granville Street, Vancouver
2,780 seats plus eight wheelchair spaces
The largest theatre in Canada when it opened as a vaudeville house called the New Orpheum in 1927 at a cost of $500,000, the Orpheum was purchased by the City of Vancouver for $3.9 million in 1974 and then renovated for an additional $3.2 million (after Famous Players had revealed plans to transform the heritage building into a multiplex cinema). The Orpheum, which hosts various touring shows, is now home to the Vancouver Symphony Society, the Bach Choir, the Vancouver Chamber Choir and the B.C. Entertainment Hall of Fame.

PERFORMANCE WORKS
1218 Cartwright Street, Granville Island, Vancouver
Flexible seating: maximum 500 (for a standing reception)
This long-derelict warehouse was transformed into a multipurpose facility in 1992 by the Canada Mortgage and Housing Corporation which administers Granville Island. Depending on how it is set up—the renters determine the layout—Performance Works can be anything from a theatre to a reception hall. The venue's regulars include Playwrights Theatre, the Judith Marcuse Dance Project Society, Kinesis Ballet British Columbia and Arts Umbrella.

PRESENTATION HOUSE ARTS CENTRE
333 Chesterfield Avenue, North Vancouver
158 seats
Originally built as a school in 1902, it later became North Vancouver city hall, housing not only politicians but a courtroom and jail cells. The facility was transformed into Presentation House in 1977. Operated by the Presentation House Cultural Society, the building is primarily a rental facility although the society does have its own community theatre company called Presentation House Players. Presentation House is also home of the Presentation House Gallery, which specializes in photo-based exhibits, the North

Shore Museum and Archives and the North Vancouver Arts Council.

THE QUEEN ELIZABETH THEATRE
Hamilton at Dunsmuir, Vancouver
2,930 seats plus six wheelchair spaces
Built by the City of Vancouver and opened in July, 1959, the Queen Elizabeth Theatre was long the place to see big touring shows and visiting stars. The ideal setting for Broadway musicals, the "Queen E" has played host to long runs of such blockbuster shows as *A Chorus Line, Cats, Les Miserables* and *Phantom of the Opera*. It is also home to Ballet British Columbia and the Vancouver Opera.

RICHMOND GATEWAY THEATRE
6500 Gilbert Road, Richmond
561 seats, 110 seats in Studio theatre
Opened in 1984 by the City of Richmond, and run by the Gateway Theatre Society, the Gateway houses two theatres, an art gallery and a photo gallery. The Gateway Theatre Society produces an annual season of professional productions and also attempts to actively present material geared towards a multicultural audience. Other home companies include Ballet B.C., the Greater Vancouver Operatic Society and Richmond Community Concerts.

THE STANLEY THEATRE
ARTS CLUB
2700 block Granville Street, Vancouver
Two theatres: 450 seats and 220 seats—was slated to open in fall, 1996
During the 1991 provincial election there seemed to be only one issue that candidates from all three major parties agreed on—the Stanley must be saved. The former movie theatre (which was originally built as a vaudeville house in 1930) was slated to be turned into retail space but successful lobbying and funding from all levels of government helped transform it into a new home for the Vancouver Theatre Sports League and the third theatre in the Arts Club Theatre's mini-empire.

SURREY ARTS CENTRE
13750 - 88th Avenue, Surrey
405 seats
Located in Bear Creek Park this theatre, which serves as a home for a variety of Surrey's community arts organizations, was originally built in 1967 as a federal centennial project at a cost of $225,000. In 1981 the theatre, which was originally quite Spartan, was rebuilt by the municipality and the province at a cost of $2.1 million.

VANCOUVER EAST CULTURAL CENTRE
1895 Venables, Vancouver
"The Cultch" as it's known to its friends opened in 1906 as the Grandview Methodist Church. In the early 1920s it became a United Church and in 1968 the building was born again as the home

to Inner City Services which included the Vancouver Free University and storefront legal offices for such tenants as B.C.'s future premier, Mike Harcourt. In 1973 Chris Wootten, then an Opportunities for Youth Art Projects officer, and political shakers Darlene Marzari, Jonathan Baker and Gary Lauk succeeded in remaking the building into one of the country's most beautiful theatres. Although it has been home to a number of groups, the Cultch is now primarily a roadhouse—and a presenter—with an emphasis on programming top performers from across Canada and around the world.

VANCOUVER PLAYHOUSE THEATRE
Hamilton at Dunsmuir, Vancouver
668 seats plus six wheelchair spaces
Best known as the home of the Vancouver Playhouse Theatre Company, the first curtain went up in 1963 with a production of *The Hostage* by Brendan Behan. Built by the City of Vancouver to provide a facility for local arts groups, the Playhouse is also home to the Friends of Chamber Music, the Festival Concert Society and the Vancouver Recital Society.

THE VOGUE
918 Granville Street, Vancouver
1,178 seats
Built in the style of a vaudeville house—although it was always intended for use as a movie theatre—the Vogue opened in 1941 with the film *I See Ice* and performances by local legends Dal Richards and Juliette. The Vogue was one of the flagships of the Odeon (later Cineplex Odeon) movie chain until 1987 when it was sold to a development company. It remained closed until 1992 when it was reopened as a live performance venue. In 1994 the Vogue was taken over by Granville Entertainment and former Prism drummer Rocket Norton became the theatre's general manager. Resident companies for this rental venue include ABC Productions which primarily sponsors live music events.

WATERFRONT THEATRE
1410 Cartwright Street, Granville Island, Vancouver
240 seats
Opened in 1979 the Waterfront was originally the home of Carousel Theatre, the New Play Centre (now Playwrights Theatre) and the now-defunct Westcoast Actors. The Waterfront is now primarily a rental venue and the home to Carousel, which produces three shows for family audiences each year.

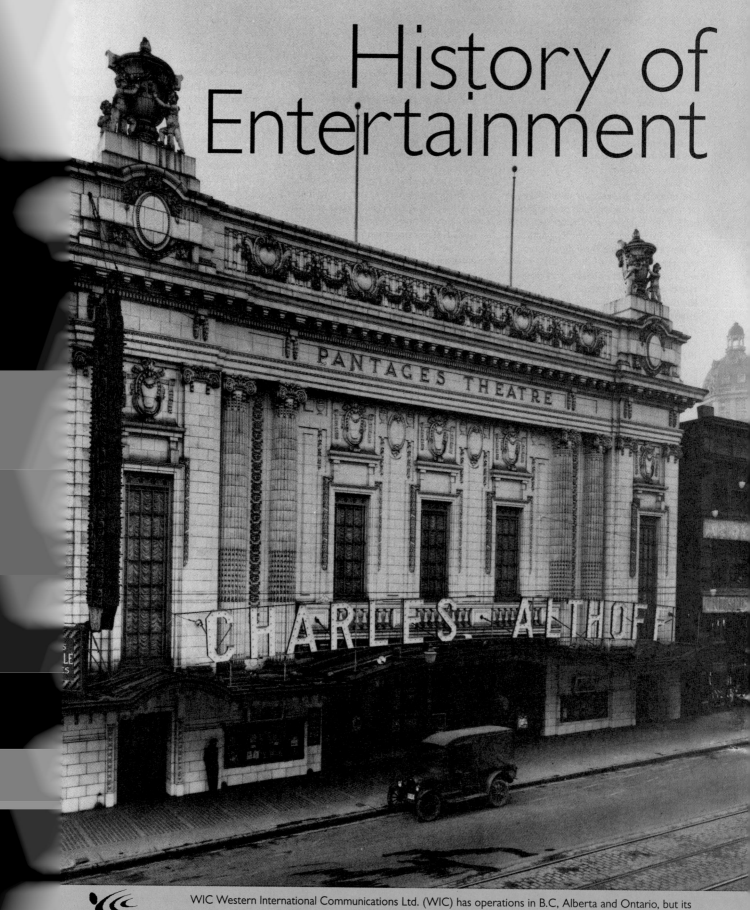

History of Entertainment

WIC Western International Communications Ltd. (WIC) has operations in B.C, Alberta and Ontario, but its roots lie in Greater Vancouver. In 1956 the company was born when Frank A. Griffiths purchased radio station CKNW in New Westminster. WIC's founder and former chairman, a chartered accountant when he entered the broadcast business, was a visionary at heart. He saw great potential for the radio and television broadcast businesses and anticipated tremendous growth for the communications industry.

History of Entertainment
Mark Leiren-Young

LULU ISLAND WAS named after a show girl—which probably explains why the place is now referred to as Richmond. Even in Vancouver, a place where people are proud of leaving work early Friday afternoons to play on the mountains or by the ocean, entertainment and entertainers never seem to get much respect. But that doesn't mean people don't need to be entertained.

Vancouver's first theatre, Hart's Opera House, began its life as a roller rink in Port Moody. After the Great Fire, Frank Hart bought the roller rink and in 1887 he moved it to what is now the corner of Carrall and Pender Streets (then known as Dupont) where it became a home for amateur theatricals and recitals. Popularly called "the skating rink" it could hold an audience of 800, had 250 pairs of roller skates available for rent and had the extra bonus of padded walls to protect roller skaters from banging their knees. Hart's remained open until the end of the century when it was transformed into a furniture warehouse.

In 1890 Vancouver's first professional theatre, the Imperial Opera House, was opened on Pender Street and became home to the Vancouver Philharmonic. A year later the Canadian Pacific Railway opened the Vancouver Opera House at the then mind-boggling cost of $100,000 and the Imperial—unable to compete with the new theatre—soon closed, becoming the city's first drill hall in 1896. Located on Granville Street next to the original Vancouver Hotel, the Vancouver Opera House was considered the finest theatre west of the Great Lakes and featured such legendary acts as Thomas Keene, Sir Henry Irving, the Gaiety Burlesque, John L. Sullivan, Ellen Terry, Anna Pavlova and Sarah Bernhardt.

One audience favorite of the era was Blind Tom whose special skills included a photographic memory and impressions of lightning storms. The Grand Theatre on Carrall Street (which later became the Savoy) was the Opera's most serious competitor—the Grand specialized in vaudeville performances and magic lantern slide shows which were the precursor to moving pictures. The Opera House was sold to the Orpheum Theatre circuit in 1912 and the Grand moved on from magic lanterns to become the city's first movie theatre.

Other events prior to 1900 included summer open air concerts

facing page: Pantages Theatre, circa 1914—"possibly the most beautiful theatre ever built in Vancouver." vancouver public library photo

One audience favorite of the era was Blind Tom whose special skills included a photographic memory and impressions of lightning storms

by the Vancouver Music Club or the Glee and Madrigal Society and, in 1895, the Great Syndicate and Paris Hippodrome arrived, providing Vancouver with the first visit by a genuine three-ring circus complete with clowns, acrobats and elephants.

At the turn of the century Vancouver audiences—like audiences around the world—were fascinated by spectacles that still sound spectacular next to modern mega-musicals like *Show Boat, Cats* and *Miss Saigon,* and there were almost as many major theatres in the city as there are a century later. The city was home to 10 major theatres early in the 20th century—the Vancouver Opera House, the Alhambra (which later became the People's Theatre and was bought by the Orpheum chain at the turn of the century), the Savoy (later renamed the Grand and now the Woodward's parking lot), the Empress, the first Pantages on Hastings Street (later the State, the Queen, the Avon, the Royal, City Nights and now the Sun Sing Theatre), the second Pantages, the Lyric, the Avenue, the Imperial (now a porn theatre on Main Street) and the Palace and many of these theatres had their own stock companies producing a variety of different entertainments.

One of the prime forces on the theatre scene was actor-manager George B. Howard who ran the Empress stock company and had managed the original Lyric. He had also previously run the Imperial and the Avenue. When Howard suffered a stroke on stage in 1921 while playing the lead in the popular melodrama *Cappy Rick's* the headline for the *Vancouver Sun* obituary read: "The Great Flyman of the Universe Lowers the Curtain on George B. Howard." There was also a collection of small theatres, the most prominent of which was the National, that specialized in writing musicals around popular songs.

The Alhambra at Pender and Howe was modelled after the Alhambra in San Francisco and featured a sliding roof that allowed for open-air performances. During its lifetime it evolved from a low-class vaudeville house to a high-class vaudeville house to a peanut wholesaler to the site of the Vancouver

Stock Exchange where it played host to many of Vancouver's finest dramatic performances. Among the acts that appeared there were Stan Laurel and Charlie Chaplin (who played there three times). Local legend has it that Mack Sennet signed Chaplin while he was playing at the Alhambra (then the Orpheum) and launched his career in pictures.

The first Pantages opened its doors with a performance featuring British lion tamer Frank Hall and his lion, Wallace, and the second Pantages, which seated 1,825, brought such acts as Stan and Mae Laurel to Vancouver.

Between World War I and 1930 the picture show was the most popular force on the entertainment scene and Vancouver's favorites included *Birth of a Nation*—which played the Orpheum annually during World War I—and a melodrama called *The Whip*, about villains trying to kill a race horse during a train wreck.

In 1915 Freddie Wood founded the Player's Club at the University of British Columbia. The theatre troupe produced their own very popular shows in downtown Vancouver. At the same time UBC also started a musical society known as Mussoc. In 1952 UBC honored Wood's memory by opening the Frederic Wood Theatre on campus.

A brief entertainment fad of the early 1920s was college debating. Not surprisingly this was out of vogue by the end of the decade. Another short-lived fad consisted of events called "smokers" where men would receive a cheap pipe, tobacco, a bottle of beer and an apple and then watch—or participate in—an evening of community singing, skits, music and perhaps boxing.

The era also featured visits by Broadway shows as Vancouver was a regular stop on the summer circuit. There was also some cross-border entertainment shopping as many locals would visit Bellingham to hear Bing Crosby perform. Meanwhile legendary American jazz artist Jelly Roll Morton moved to Vancouver to start a band that soon failed. He then created a trio at the St. Regis featuring Horace Eubanks on the clarinet and helped launch the city as a jazz hotbed in North America. Vancouver also inherited the San Francisco Light Opera Company which defected from San Francisco to Vancouver in search of a bigger audience in the early 1920s.

The most popular local entertainers of the 1920s and 1930s included The Dumbells, who served as the concert party of the Third Canadian Division in France and Flanders from 1916-1919 and toured Canada until the 1930s.

During the Depression Vancouverites were also caught up in the craze of dance marathons. The marathons, which were held at the Lyric, could last as long as four months as exhausted dancers vied for cash prizes. Bike marathons were also popular

Another short-lived fad consisted of events called "smokers" where men would receive a cheap pipe, tobacco, a bottle of beer and an apple and then watch, or participate in, an evening of community singing, skits, music and perhaps boxing

and the 10,000 seat Arena (which burned down in 1936) would hold "races" that could last six days. The Arena also had a live band which would accompany ice skaters as they sped around what was then the largest indoor ice surface in the world.

Theatre Under the Stars began with an ad hoc production of *A Midsummer Night's Dream* at Brockton Point in 1939 which played to 10,000 people on opening night and was performed in the trees at Stanley Park. TUTS began performing formally as a professional company the following year when they started appearing at Malkin Bowl in Stanley Park. A professional company which specialized in Gilbert and Sullivan operettas, TUTS was a vital part of the city's cultural scene until folding in 1963. In 1969 TUTS was revived as a semi-professional company that continues the tradition of producing musicals in Malkin Bowl each summer.

A few of the international stars that came out of Vancouver prior to World War II included Bill Pratt, a remittance man from England, who spotted a help-wanted ad and decided to join the Russell Players during their stint in Kamloops. His career went on the upswing after he changed his name to Boris Karloff. Jack Benny's wife, Mary Livingstone, was originally Sadie Marks of Vancouver and Vancouver acting teacher Joan Miller became the first big star of BBC Television.

One of the entertainment phenomena that started in the 1930s and thrived through to the 1970s were supper clubs like the Palomar (run by Sandy DeSantis), the Cave (opened as part

facing page: Ivan Ackery and Louis Armstrong, circa 1942, Orpheum theatre. vs

WIC is active in satellite network services through its 53.7 per cent ownership of Cancom, a name long synonymous with satellite distribution of signals to cable systems and directly to homes in small and remote communities beyond the reach of ordinary signal delivery methods. Increasingly, Cancom is also becoming synonymous with versatile and cost-effective data networks for business communications. WIC and Cancom together own an equity interest in Express Vu Inc., a Canadian satellite television direct-to-home distribution company set to launch in the near future.

of a small Western Canadian chain and run by Ken Stauffer) and Isy's (located on Georgia Street and run by Isy Walters who got his show business start running the midway at the PNE). The clubs were popular venues for some of the world's top acts. The Palomar, which was located at Alberni and Georgia, featured such performers as George Burns and Gracie Allen.

In addition to bringing out touring entertainers Isy's was also indirectly responsible for the creation of one of Vancouver's most respected dance companies. Paula Ross was working as a showgirl at Isy's when she decided to form her own modern dance company in 1965. The first Paula Ross Company was made up of other dancers from Isy's who wanted lessons from the classically trained Ross. Her company was a vital part of the local dance scene until suspending operations in 1987.

Foremost among the clubs was the Cave which let Vancouverites see "name" acts ranging from Mitzi Gaynor, Milton Berle, Lena Horne, Henny Youngman and Louis Armstrong to Eric Burdon and the Animals and The Doors. The Cave closed its doors July 20, 1981, with a farewell performance by the Bobby Hales Orchestra; the club was demolished the next day.

The nightclub phenomenon was chronicled—and nurtured—by *Sun* columnist Jack Wasserman who became a local legend for the way he helped convey a sense of excitement and action to a city that still felt like a small town. The nightclub scene became so well associated with Wasserman that when he died in 1977 the section of Hornby Street that was then home to the Cave (near the Hotel Vancouver where local legend Dal Richards would lead his orchestra at the Panorama Roof) was officially renamed "Wasserman's Beat."

The B.C. centennial of 1958 was commemorated by the construction of the Queen Elizabeth Theatre (which opened in 1959). The centennial also saw the premiere of the Vancouver International Festival, a world-class performing arts showcase mixing local and international acts. It remained an annual event for the next decade.

The Queen Elizabeth got a new neighbor in 1963 with the construction of the Vancouver Playhouse which was inhabited by the Playhouse Theatre company. Meanwhile the Arts Club Theatre was being formed by Yvonne Firkins who ran her company out of a Gospel Hall on Seymour Street (Bill Millerd became the theatre's artistic and managing director in 1972) and a new and much improved Frederic Wood Theatre was opening at UBC.

The Canadian centennial celebration of 1967 was a milestone year for entertainment in Vancouver as everybody in the city decided to put on a show. Among the acts that played Vancouver in 1967 were Marilyn Horne, Don Ho, Petula Clark,

The nightclub scene became so well associated with Wasserman that when he died in 1977 the section of Hornby Street that was then home to the Cave was officially renamed "Wasserman's Beat"

Danny Kaye, Maureen Forrester, Wayne Newton, Victor Borge, the National Ballet of Canada, the American Ballet Theatre, the Royal Winnipeg Ballet, the New York Ballet and the New York Philharmonic under Leonard Bernstein. There were so many international acts visiting Vancouver in 1967 that the Centennial Vancouver Festival was actually criticized for having a "mediocre line-up" when they announced shows including the Mermaid Theatre of London, *The Sound of Music* starring Dorothy Collins (a Canadian-born U.S. TV star), classical pianist Van Cliburn and the Royal Ballet featuring Rudolph Nureyev and Margot Fonteyn.

In 1970 *Sun* critic Christopher Dafoe posed the question "is Vancouver big enough to support two professional theatre companies?" Soon the question was answered as companies began springing up all over the city courtesy of a federal program called Local Initiatives Project Opportunities for Youth Programs (popularly known as LIP grants). The program provided the initial funding that started many Vancouver theatre companies including the New Play Centre (renamed Playwrights Theatre in 1995); City Stage (which started running lunch-hour theatre out of a donut shop in 1972) and Westcoast Actors.

Vancouver was also home to two of Canada's cutting edge experimental theatre companies, Tamahnous (another LIP company) and Savage God, which was started in 1966 by director John Juliani who, according to the *Province* "pioneered experimental theatre in Vancouver during his days as theatre head at Simon Fraser University." Savage God's productions were so notorious that one local critic accused Juliani of corrupting innocent youth.

facing page: Bryan Adams outside the Marine Building, 1989. vp

WIC has applied to the Canadian Radio-television and Telecommunications Commission to provide an enhanced pay-per-view service called edd - Electronic Digital Delivery. Best described as an electronic video rental service, edd will provide consumers with access to an extensive inventory of video store-type programming.

The next milestone on the entertainment scene was Expo 86 which had arguably the biggest effect on Vancouver's cultural scene since the Great Fire. The world's fair hit Vancouver's theatres like a neutron bomb—although the buildings remained standing there was nobody left inside them. City Stage folded, other theatres cut back or cancelled their seasons and Vancouver's attitude towards culture shifted as Expo's World Stage Festival created a taste for "world-class" productions which can best be defined as anything that got great reviews in America.

The city proved to be such a lucrative market for big shows and mega-musicals that in 1995 Toronto entrepreneur Garth Drabinksy opened a new theatre designed to stage long-running Broadway-style shows. The Ford Centre for the Performing Arts opened in 1995 with a production of the classic American musical, *Show Boat*.

In the 1980s Vancouver also began laying claim to the title of Hollywood North because of all of the movies and TV shows being filmed locally. Then in the 1990s the name switched to Brollywood, as what had appeared to be a temporary industry now seemed to be staying. And beginning in the mid-1980s Vancouver audiences were able to stay at home and watch Vancouver performers on such popular American shows as *21 Jump Street, MacGyver* and *Wiseguy.*

One way of tracing Vancouver's cultural history is to look at the events taking place at the Pacific National Exhibition. Modern readers may wince at hearing a review of the entertainment at the first exhibition that appeared in the August 16, 1910, edition of the *Vancouver Daily News-Advertiser.* "Petrified women, sacrificial crocodiles from the sacred river Ganges; chickens that lay eggs and dusky negroes who dodge swiftly thrown baseballs, to say nothing of the numerous Salome dancers, Spanish Carmens, Dutch comedians and chorus girls are some of the attractions being offered the visitors at the fair this week.

"To do the Skid Road properly would take at least half a day. To witness each show, see all the dancing attractions, throw baseballs at each of the African dodgers, ride the merry-go-rounds and be entertained at the half hundred other resorts, would require a sum of money not less than $5."

Other popular attractions throughout the fair's history included "freak" shows and, of course, dancing girls in various stages of dress. In the 1940s scantily clad women were featured at an attraction known as "the nudist village." Nude shows were later to become a Vancouver specialty as the city has long been famous, or notorious, for having some of the most explicit strip clubs in North America. The title of rock group Bon Jovi's best-selling 1986 album "Slippery When Wet" was apparently inspired by the band's numerous visits to a local strip bar where

onstage showers were a popular part of the routine.

After 1947, when the fair reopened after being used as a military base and an internment camp for Japanese-Canadians during World War II, the PNE attempted to re-establish itself as the place to be by bringing in big-name headline acts like Jimmy Durante and Edgar Bergen, a tradition that has continued ever since with the exhibition annually presenting some of the top acts in the world. Throughout the 1950s the PNE also regularly featured the Shrine-Polack Brothers Circus (later known as the Shrine Circus). In the 1970s the PNE added what has become one of their most popular features, the Demolition Derby.

There were also a number of important players behind the scenes who were responsible for bringing out some of the big-name acts. Hugh Pickett and David Y.H. Lui were two Vancouver "impresarios" who helped shape the local cultural scene.

Lui opened his own venue, the David Y.H. Lui Theatre, in 1975 (it closed in 1979 and soon became the popular nightclub Richard's on Richards) and brought out various major classical acts such as Dame Joan Sutherland, Martha Graham, the National Ballet of Canada and the Royal Winnipeg Ballet.

Pickett, who managed the original Vancouver International Festival and TUTS, started his company Famous Artists in 1947 and was responsible for bringing in a steady stream of world-class performers for four decades (Pickett officially retired from Famous Artists in 1985). Pickett's tastes as a promoter were completely eclectic ranging from the Joffrey Ballet and Igor Stravinsky to Frank Sinatra, Elvis Presley and the Rolling Stones. After his alleged retirement Pickett continued to be an active force on the city's cultural scene joining with longtime Vancouver theatre practitioner and UBC professor Norman Young to create the B.C. Entertainment Hall of Fame and the Starwalk (which is located outside the Orpheum Theatre).

As the 21st century approaches Vancouver seems poised on the cutting edge of the world's entertainment scene. The city seems intent on exploring and exploiting the information superhighway which will be either the biggest thing in the history of entertainment or the 21st century's answer to dance marathons.

And what about poor, forgotten Lulu? Lulu Island was named for dancer Lulu Sweet of a touring company known as The Potter Troupe. When she performed in New Westminster in 1860 the Royal Engineer's Colonel R.C. Moody (namesake of Port Moody) was so smitten by her performance that he named the island after her.

facing page: Hugh Pickett on Granville Street's Starwalk, 1994. vp

WIC and all of its operations have a long tradition of community service, a quality instilled by Mr. Griffiths. Each of the WIC stations donates air-time and supports fund-raising and charitable efforts in its community. In Vancouver, BCTV's Variety Club Telethon raises millions of dollars each year for children throughout the Lower Mainland. CKNW's Orphan's Fund helps Vancouver's underprivileged and disabled children. In 1996 WIC was awarded the Variety Clubs International's prestigious Corporate Award, recognizing the company's significant, on-going contribution to the Variety Club's fundraising efforts.

WIC is a dynamic broadcast, communications and entertainment company whose mandate is to be Canada's leading creator, packager and supplier of entertainment, news and information through the electronic media and to ensure the public has access to that content.

Hugh Pickett
Agnes Thom

FACTS FIRST: BORN APRIL 11, 1913, Vancouver, B.C. Named Hugh Frank Digby Pickett. Attended Magee High School in Vancouver. Destiny led him at 15 years old to his first summer job at the Colonial Theatre, where he saw Marlene Dietrich in *The Blue Angel* five times a day for six weeks. At 18 he worked for his father at Dingwall Cotts and Company, steamship agents, and at 21 he went around the world for 18 months, spending some time in Hollywood where he played tennis with young unknowns like Ginger Rogers. In 1939 he helped Elsa Maxwell raise money to build two Spitfires and in 1941 he joined the army for four years. After the war he lived in Los Angeles for a time, meeting more unknowns who would later become very famous artists as well as lifelong friends. He returned to Vancouver to work for Hilker Attractions Concert Agencies where he handled publicity for Theatre Under the Stars from 1946 to 1964. He took over the business in 1950 with partner Holly Maxwell and they managed Famous Artists Limited until 1982 when the company was sold to Jerry Lonn of Seattle. Pickett received the Order of Canada in 1986; the committee in charge of the awards was startled to receive recommendations from close Pickett friends such as Marlene Dietrich, Lillian Gish, Mitzi Gaynor, Katharine Hepburn, Ginger Rogers, Leontyne Price, Carlos Montoya, Sir Laurence Olivier, Vincent Price, Phyllis Diller and others.

Pickett is on the Board of Civic Theatres in Vancouver. He is active in Orpheum Theatre projects and is often at the theatre conducting tours or on stage as a commentator. "I spent half my youth at the Orpheum," he says, "and now I'm spending half my old age there. I bought a ticket to *The Wise Wife* on the day it opened in 1927—I was 14—and I bought the last ticket sold by Famous Players on the day it closed as a movie house." Pickett judges talent at the Pacific National Exhibition in Vancouver and fosters young talent wherever he finds it throughout the province, attending plays and performances in many remote venues. Pickett calls his years with Famous Artists "Forty years of jerks and geniuses" and dubs his close friends Marlene Dietrich, Miriam Hopkins, Mary Martin and Mitzi Gaynor "the four M's." Great names are a part of his daily life. Not only did he travel with Dietrich for 12 years as her man-

ager and tour with Laurence Olivier as his manager across Canada, but Pickett also formed long-lasting relationships with many of the stars he booked: names like Katharine Hepburn, Dorothy Kirsten, Lillian Gish, Ginger Rogers, Leontyne Price, Phyllis Diller and Arthur Rubenstein (whose name, Pickett says, was really "Arthur," and not "Artur." The "Artur" was the idea of Sol Hurok who thought it would attract attention). Pickett brought every great act of the time to Vancouver: Katherine Cornell, Ruth Draper, Frank Sinatra, Helen Hayes, Bette Davis, Charles Laughton, Elsa Lanchester, Beatrice Lillie, Ethel Barrymore, Sylvia Sydney, Pearl Bailey, Jimmy Durante, Mae West, Maurice Evans, Sir John Gielgud, Johnny Mathis, Judy Garland, Billie Holiday, Oscar Levant, Alexandra Danilova, Jeanette MacDonald, Grace Moore, Sir Laurence Olivier, Bette Midler, the Rolling Stones, Elvis, Van Cliburn, Nureyev, Margot Fonteyn, Jack Benny, Carlos Montoya, Lucille Ball and many more.

His anecdotes about the stars would fill several books (as would his columns in Vancouver's weekly newspaper the *West Ender*). "I've never worked a day in my life," says Pickett. "None of the money I ever earned was 'hard-earned.' It was all showbiz money, starting with my first summer job when I worked from eleven in the morning until eleven at night and loved every minute of it."

This love was returned again and again by the "showbiz" people he later managed. Pickett says, "I was privileged to know them. I didn't have any illusions I had as a kid shattered. The people I didn't know as a kid—but admired—all turned out to be human beings like anybody else when I met them, and most of them were wonderful people." They called him a "lovable, irritating, marvellous, one-of-a-kind, red-necked dinosaur" at his 80th birthday party held at the Orpheum to raise funds for the B.C. Entertainment Hall of Fame. Pickett is known for his lifelong loyalty to his friends be they rich or poor, famous or not. His home base is the same suburban house he's lived in since he was 11 years old and his local reputation as an acid wit is matched by his unending kindness and generosity to local showbiz talent he has helped discover, and whom he promotes as enthusiastically as he promoted world-famous figures in the past. A man who rarely talks about himself, Pickett is a walking, talking encyclopedia of first-hand experiences covering more than 50 years of show business in America.

facing page: Hugh Pickett with a wall of memorabilia, 1987. vs

Literary
Vancouver

Duthie Books Ltd. was established in 1957 by Bill Duthie at the corner of Robson and Hornby Streets where the flagship store stands today. Bill Duthie was a literate, convivial and often sardonic bookseller. The tone he set for Duthie Books remains much the same now throughout the company—good stock, extensive research facilities, and knowledgeable staff.

A Personal View of Literary Vancouver
David Watmough

THE FIRST INTIMATION I had of our city's strenuous literary history was the fierce debate prior to the official pronouncement of a name for what is now the Queen Elizabeth Playhouse. As a relative newcomer to the town when the theatre opened in 1963, I was guardedly neutral but I recall ardent partisans for the name of the part-native Indian poet, Pauline Johnson, whose statue (probably as a result of her retiring here in 1909, rather than the calibre of her verse), is the earliest of a writer ever erected in Vancouver and which stands today in Stanley Park.

A primary literary reference for me in the sixties was my initial encounter with Ethel Wilson (born Ethel Bryant in South Africa and related to the Malkin family). She was the first major Vancouver author I was to meet and still, in my opinion, a fiction writer of truly international stature.

I recalled her name readily for, as a small boy in pre-war Cornwall, I had started precociously reading her stories in the British weekly *New Statesman & Nation*. The sense of literary networking in our town was forcibly brought home to me in 1964, when I chatted with her at the book party for Jane Rule's first novel, *The Desert of the Heart*. Mrs. Wilson turned out to be a friend of Jane's—as she was indeed of numerous writers scattered about the city in those days.

Jane Rule introduced me to many authors and literary figures such as Canada's most prolific man of letters, the late George Woodcock, the Governor General's Award winning poet Phyllis Webb, and Bill and Alice McConnell, the former a barrister and founder of Klanak Press in 1958, and an original member of an informal but important literary discussion group dating back to the 1930s.

In fact Jane Rule and her companion, Helen Sonthoff, presented the nearest thing to a literary salon Vancouver has ever boasted. At a time when social life was relatively fragmented and isolated, their social gatherings were an invaluable social adjunct to all the arts. Thirty-five years ago social contacts between writers and kindred soul-mates were often enacted in one another's homes at dinner-parties or just plain drinking sessions. Then there were far fewer restaurants or civilized bars at which to congregate for gossip or to exchange rumors of job opportunities.

Too few know how much the literary cohesion of Vancouver

facing page: MacLeod's Books, Vancouver, 1997. rw

At a time when social life was relatively fragmented and isolated, their social gatherings were an invaluable social adjunct to all the arts

owes to those two women cultural pioneers. Visitors like the shy novelist Brian Moore, who won a Governor General's Award in 1960 for his *The Luck of Ginger Coffey* (but had produced a far superior book in 1955 with *The Lonely Passion of Judith Hearne*), and Canada's major novelist, the prairie-born, Margaret Laurence, who was to become a firm friend of mine and faithful correspondent on her return to Lakefield, Ontario in 1962.

I recall first meeting in that Rule household local resident Audrey Thomas (who shocked much local male taste by centring on basic female physiology with her first novel, *Mrs. Blood*, in 1970). There were also social encounters with poets like George Bowering and the ebullient and mirthful Marya Fiamengo, who imparted to me a lively sense of her Vancouver childhood and whose poems about nature I have always found captivating.

Stan Persky—later to find fame with the erotic if hard-to-classify *Buddies*—was another young writer I met through Jane Rule, as was the unduly neglected poet and professor Robin Blaser—both the above, part of the highly significant and invaluable American literary contingent which made its way up the West Coast from San Francisco in the mid-sixties.

The British-born playwright and short-story writer Margaret Hollingsworth was also a regular guest at the Rule/Sonthoff menage when she was a graduate student in the Creative Writing department of UBC. She, too, has also subsequently become a firm friend and frequent visitor to my own Kitsilano cottage.

It was back in the early sixties that I first met the novelist Robert Harlow, who was then head of CBC Radio and beavering away at his first novel, *Royal Murdoch*—to be eventually succeeded by some half dozen more. This leads me to the singular role the CBC has played in the literary history of Vancouver over the course of the past 35 years.

The Corporation's contribution to local literary letters was twofold—from within its salaried structure and from the freelance contributors it supported. Apart from Bob Harlow it employed as producer the far from loquacious Norman Newton who (I discovered almost by accident) had written, among other books and plays, such intriguing historical novels as *The House of Gods* and *The One True Man.*

Historical biography was to be served in a similar context by Hugh Palmer, then head of CBC-TV and subsequently author of a fascinating biography of his engineer father, *Circumnavigating Father.* By sheer coincidence, his family were neighbors during my first decade in the city.

Not a writer himself but a crucial midwife to the literary scene whose support touched not only myself but the likes of George Woodcock, the poet Phyllis Webb, and literally dozens of others, was the late Robert Patchell, onetime supervisor in public affairs at CBC and one of those unsung heroes of Can Lit particularly here on the West Coast in the blossoming mid-century period.

Some of the most talented authors and convivial personalities I met as a fellow free-lancer for the CBC in the 1960s and 1970s included the novelist and playwright Betty Lambert, who gave us a stream of brilliant plays, many for radio, and the novel *Crossings* before death tragically took her far too early in a still evolving career. Another major talent, in my opinion, who shared free-lancing chores with me is the playwright Michael Mercer, author of the prize-winning play *Goodnight Disgrace* invoking the historical relationship between Malcolm Lowry and the American poet Conrad Aiken, and one of the few Canadian writers of superior TV drama who has had substantial financial success both here at home and in the United States.

It was the same Liverpool-born Mercer who was told in Toronto by some TV honcho that if he wanted to be taken seriously as a writer he had better pull up stakes in Vancouver and remove to the big T . . . Apart from extended stints in 1994 to southwestern Alberta on behalf of the TV series *Lonesome Dove,* he is still happily living in our midst.

On the back stairs of the Hotel Vancouver leading to the offices of various CBC producers I would often bump into critics, commentators and documentary writers who, while not going on to fame and fortune as men and women of letters, nevertheless helped to provide that overall literary climate which made Vancouver a highly congenial place for the rest of us to ply our trade. These included the Hungarian-born Peter Hay who introduced me to Talonbooks before he departed for Los Angeles and a wholly different career.

There were others such as playwrights John Lazarus and John Gray, still very much with us and still very literarily active, who were also grateful for the bounty derived from "Mother Corp" as we call the CBC with considerably less than respect!

The stairway off Hornby Street also saw a bevy of free-lance

Nor can anyone living the "literary life" during Vancouver's mid-century forget the gossip and excitement attending the famous battles between the two personal arch-rivals of the UBC campus, the professor-poet Earle Birney of *David* fame, and English department head and also poet, the late Roy Daniells

writers associated with UBC—and later the SFU campus—who likewise supplemented their incomes from the CBC. I think of social historian Peter Buitenhuis, and the late Stanley Cooperman, a fiery Jewish counter-culture poet who loved to wear the full regalia of beads, rings and ankhs—both then SFU faculty.

Nor can anyone living the "literary life" during Vancouver's mid-century ever forget the gossip and excitement attending the famous battles between the two personal arch-rivals of the UBC campus, the professor-poet Earle Birney of *David* fame, and English department head and also poet, the late Roy Daniells.

But that leads to a consideration of those authors whose presence in the city's midst we owe primarily to the existence of our various academic institutions, including the subsequent new community colleges, that grew apace in the late sixties.

A major constituent of that scene were the various English departments, although they were not exclusive nurseries of neither neophyte literary talents nor the only sustenance of poets, playwrights and fiction writers who came here because of their faculty teaching positions.

Still adding to the overall literary picture of Greater Vancouver is Ulster-born poet and fiction writer George McWhirter, who incidentally received the most unfair review of a novel I have ever seen penned here for his excellent book *Paula Lake*

In honor of Bill Duthie, the Canadian Booksellers' Association inaugurated an annual lecture, the ultimate event at The Vancouver International Writers Festival. The lecture has been delivered by such luminaries as Margaret Atwood, Timothy Findley, Robertson Davies, Mordecai Richler, Carol Shields and Michael Ignatieff. The Bill Duthie Booksellers' Award was established in his memory and is presented at the annual B.C. Book Awards.

in 1984. And Crawford Kilian at Capilano College, who boasts an impressive international reputation under the broad and even misleading heading of science fiction. These are still highly active members of the Vancouver literary community and therefore part of its future.

Considering the lack of mainstream appeal for later 20th century poetry, it is hardly surprising that the campus has provided a source of livelihood for high profile poets such as George Bowering and the quietly effective John Pass, who spins his verse from a world which includes gentle but profound meditations on the mundane.

The academic infrastructures have also helped to promote and nurture gender equality from within the reservoir of local literary talent. So that we can celebrate, among others, the Australian-born Daphne Marlatt with her Vancouver-based historical novel *Ana Historic,* and the Vancouver Island sea stories of Gladys Hindmarch entitled *The Watery Part of the World.*

The house I have dwelled in for the past 20 years was previously owned by the novelist and Simon Fraser English professor, John Mills, author of *The Land of Is, The October Men* and the 1978 novel *Skevington's Daughter,* which I found a somewhat soggy satire in the light of its lively predecessors.

The literary world of Vancouver as I have experienced it since 1959 obviously shares traits with other cities of comparable size and relative remoteness. For instance, writers drawing their livelihood from academe tend to relate especially to fellow campus dwellers in other fields. Whereas those of us who have taken the downtown free-lance route to sustain our creative habit generally find our literary friendships in comparable venues.

There are always exceptions to the rule, however, and one such was Simon Gray, the British playwright. I had reviewed his novel *Colmain* when he was unhappily teaching at UBC. In the early 1960s he spent much of his time knocking the mediocrity of UBC, the unfriendliness of Vancouver and the awfulness of British Columbia generally. He was also much exercised by his poverty.

But Simon was also rather eccentric—as I discovered when he airily informed me that he took a taxi daily to campus from his West End apartment off Beach Avenue so that he would not have to endure fellow passengers on the buses. So much for poverty . . .

His return to London, brought him fame and fortune as one of Britain's leading playwrights of the mid-century with such works as *Butley* and *Otherwise Engaged.*

Something that happily dented our local penchant for "ghettoizing" the literary scene into "town" and "gown" was The Writers' Union of Canada when it opened a Vancouver-based

Canada's literary "superstar" Margaret Atwood knew Vancouver in 1964-65 where as a UBC English department lecturer she wrote the first draft of her novel *The Edible Woman*

provincial branch. That was the way, for instance, I became friends with fellow-novelist Jan Drabek, the only Vancouverite who went from teaching high school here to becoming ambassador of the new Czech Republic to the Republic of Kenya.

Among those who left after a sustained stint here was Carol Shields in 1980. The Governor General Award holder and internationally acclaimed novelist is the author of *The Stone Diaries,* which was the runner-up for Britain's prestigious Booker Prize, winner of the 1994 fiction prize of the U.S. National Book Critics Circle and the 1994 Pulitzer Prize for fiction.

Canada's literary "superstar" Margaret Atwood knew Vancouver in 1964-65 where as a UBC English department lecturer she wrote the first draft of her novel *The Edible Woman* and was yet another of those I encountered through the generous hospitality of Jane Rule and Helen Sonthoff.

The overly lionized Malcolm Lowry, author of the internationally acclaimed *Under the Volcano* written during his lengthy sojourn here which included World War II, also produced much uneven writing but mercifully offset by such brilliantly evocative stories as "The Forest Path to the Spring."

But an increasing number of Vancouver natives such as anthologist and travel-writer Keath Fraser have returned from elsewhere—he from London and Calgary—or just never left.

A variant on this theme is represented by the Governor General's Award winner (for her biography of painter Emily Carr), the art-historian and author of the superior fiction collection *Breaking the Cycle,* Maria Tippett. The Victoria-born Tippett virtually commutes between the University of Cambridge and her home on Bowen Island.

Another writer I have known over the years and whom I count a crucial linchpin in the evolution of what we might call "Vancouver Letters" is the author-editor Alan Twigg, a fellow contributor to this opus. From the start I was impressed by this hometown literary pioneer who exhibited his confidence in the quality of our literary life by founding the highly acclaimed *BC Book World* back in the 1980s as a vigorous and impressive manifestation of that faith.

Keeping the banner of superb writing and gentle humor flying for us is Bill Richardson. I am neither a gambler nor a prophet but I confidently predict that the author of the Stephen Leacock medal winner in 1993 for his novel *Bed & Breakfast,* and the volume of comic verse *Queen of all the Dustballs* a year earlier, will yet produce works of international calibre and universal acclaim.

I now come to a more sombre aspect of this largely personal account of literary life in our town. Immortal work may well have been produced here but that doesn't obviate the fact of the eventual mortality of its creators. Some of the most impressive literature I have encountered anywhere was composed by people known to me in varying degree who have since died. Their names are perhaps not legion but the roster of them is surely impressive.

George Ryga, the playwright, lived for the most part in Summerland but in later years, when teaching at UBC's Creative Writing Department, maintained an apartment in the West End. George was the creator of the excellent first novel *The Hungry Hills* but reached the pinnacle of fame with his play *The Ecstasy of Rita Joe.*

One of the most lovable as well as professionally impressive authors I have ever encountered came about through my editing *Vancouver Fiction* for the city's centennial in 1986. The writer in question was D.M. Fraser, author of the novels *Class Warfare* and *The Voice of Emma Sachs.* Both brilliant works I urge all to read.

The city and its environs have been peculiarly blessed, I think, by the calibre of writers for young people who have resided here. One of the most distinguished I have been privileged to know is veteran Christie Harris, who started writing her children's books in 1927. They include *Raven's Cry,* which draws inspiration from the history of the Haida nation and which I think is one of those works that in years ahead progressively find adult appeal, as has happened so often in the past history of work originating for young folk.

Anne Cameron (Cam Hubert), who lived for a while in New Westminster but is now in Powell River, is another author who has drawn on native Indian matter for her children's books, *How Raven Freed the Moon* and *How the Loon Lost Her Voice.* In her non-juvenile fiction she is also a vigorous feminist voice but distinguished from so many of that genre by a persistent sense of humor.

And finally in the category of the lamented deceased there persists the memory of the craggy-featured, veteran author Hubert Evans, who would be well over a hundred were he still with us. As he did so redolently in his own person, his books provided that sense of historical continuity which perhaps a fictional literature does better than anything else.

A further example of fiction which proves a worthy conduit for history is the 1929 novel, *The Eternal Forest Under Western Skies,* which is set in Whonnock, B.C., in the 1913-16 era and has recently (1994) been re-issued by Godwin Books under the title of *The Eternal Forest.* This fascinating work includes a superlative introduction by George Woodcock—one of the last major contributions from his busy pen.

So much of the past, what of the future? I often recall the following experience. In 1990 I was invited to talk with the 11th and 12th grade students interested in creative writing at a high school in the east part of Vancouver. The majority of those eager young faces were Indo-Canadian or Chinese. I told them that of the baker's dozen included in my anthology, *Vancouver Fiction,* in 1985, all were by Caucasians. But from what I have already read since that date, I am confident that for the second centennial that will certainly no longer be the case. Among a growing contingent of new voices we already have poet and memoirist Evelyn Lau, whose erotic accounts delight some while offending others; novelist Sky Lee with her account of several generations of a Vancouver Chinese family—and Denise Chong who gained the City of Vancouver Book Award in 1994 for her fascinating memoir *The Concubine's Children.*

There is already a healthy promise of young writers who will reflect the creative diversity that now nudges the contemporary social and cultural scene in Vancouver. It cannot be too strongly emphasized that this fresh wave of literary talent currently shaping about us issues both from a diversity of races and cultures and from the new verbal explicitness surrounding the gender experiences of gays and lesbians and our native peoples.

Indeed, the verbal weave of tomorrow's Vancouver literary fabric will be much more diverse than what the city has seen to date. My hope is that the pinnacles of future excellence in all the literary genres will be found worthy of the finest that has already been bequeathed to us. Without that insistence on matching the finest aspects of our literary past, both the statistically "more" and an expanding cultural and racial "diversity" won't really signify very much.

facing page: Famous scribes are featured on the Edwardian stained glass window, Carnegie Library, Hastings and Main Streets, Vancouver, 1980. vs

In 1980 Duthie Books began to publish The Reader, a quarterly of book reviews and announcements that drew on staff and customers for recommendations. This publication was distributed through the Duthie stores and other independent bookstores across Canada and the U.S. In 1996 we began a second series of The Reader called The New Reader which will be distributed only through Duthie Books and the World Wide Web.

Book Publishing in Greater Vancouver
Kayce White

VANCOUVER'S FIRST BOOK—that is, the first book published and printed in the city—entitled *City of Vancouver, Terminus of the Canadian Pacific Railway, British Columbia Handbook,* appeared in 1887. The 88-page handbook was "compiled by M. Picken, and published and printed at the *Daily News* office." For the next 80 years of the city's life the local book-publishing scene was quiet. For several decades before and after 1909, when Percy F. Goldenrath's name appeared as the sole publisher in the Vancouver telephone book, Lower Mainland book publishers would have had no problem holding a convention in a phone booth. By 1911 even Mr. Goldenrath had disappeared from the directory and the publishing scene remained languid until the mid-'30s when five publishers appeared, three of them branch offices of Eastern Canadian firms.

The local book-publishing trade didn't really begin to make an impression until the 1970s. In 1976 *The Vancouver Book* listed more than 35 local book publishers with an annual total of 100 new titles, including books on poetry, yoga, metric conversion as well as educational, medical and music textbooks. Vancouver's Mitchell Press published books on B.C. history, travel and the outdoors; Sono Nis Press in Delta (since moved to Victoria) published Canadian poetry, fine art and literature titles; Tad Publishing (1973) Ltd. produced a pictorial *Canada Calling* series; Tantalus Research Ltd. published technical and academic books and a B.C. geographical series, and Trendex Products in North Vancouver produced history titles. With its magazine, *Raincoast Chronicles,* being an immediate success, Harbour Publishing began to produce books in 1974 with titles on dulcimer tuning and floor loom design. In November, 1974 it published *Raincoast Chronicles First Five,* a collection of the first issues of the magazine. Harbour's publisher, Howard White, is unique in that he co-authors many of his house's titles, like Jim Spilsbury's best-selling autobiographies *Spilsbury's Coast* and *The Accidental Airline.* Harbour's authors include Hubert Evans, Ethel Wilson and Anne Cameron. A huge success for Harbour was Edith Iglauer's *Fishing With John,* which told of the writer's marriage to salmon fisherman John Daly of Pender Harbour. Harbour has continued a fine—and prize-winning—tradition of publishing good regional books.

A few firms published specialty fiction, including Press Gang Publishers Ltd. which began life in 1975, at a time when the women's movement was gathering momentum, as a printing

With its magazine, *Raincoast Chronicles,* being an instant success, Harbour Publishing began to produce books in 1974 and has continued a fine, prize-winning, tradition of publishing good regional books

collective staffed entirely by women. The 1970s also saw the birth of Pulp Press (later, Arsenal Pulp), which sought out new B.C. writing, Prism Books at UBC which published fiction and poetry by Canadian writers and Talonbooks, offering Canadian plays, fiction and poetry. International Self-Counsel Press was publishing do-it-yourself legal, work and business books. And although the firm of J.J. Douglas in North Vancouver (now Douglas & McIntyre in Vancouver) was gaining recognition as a national trade book publisher, many of the more than 300 writers listed in *The Vancouver Book* were published by firms outside B.C.

Between 1974 and 1995 the number of B.C. publishers increased tenfold, from five to 50. In 1970 the entire provincial book publishing industry earned $350,000 in sales. By 1992, through the continuous creation of a huge range of chiefly regional books priced at under $30, total provincial book revenue climbed to $25 million, more than 70 times the 1970 figure, achieving what publisher Scott McIntyre called a "critical mass"—a self-sustaining industry.

The leading publisher here of trade books (those directed at the general public) is Douglas & McIntyre, the largest English-language, Canadian-owned house outside of Toronto. Company president Scott McIntyre believes his firm has defied all odds by not only staying in business but by gaining stature in international circles since producing its first two books in 1971. "Surviving in this business for 25 years beats the odds. Doing it from the West Coast beats additional odds," said McIntyre, who believes a large part of the company's success lies in "defiantly resisting trendiness."

The company produces about 80 new titles annually in three publishing divisions: Douglas & McIntyre and Greystone

Books, both based in Vancouver, and Douglas & McIntyre Children's Books in Toronto. Their impressive list includes Canadian biography, native studies and anthropology, art, architecture, photography, food and wine. As this book was in production, D&M popped the champagne cork for its 25th anniversary celebration, and had yet another best seller: former B.C. Premier Mike Harcourt's memoirs, *A Measure of Defiance.* With more than $10 million in annual sales, about 20 per cent of which is derived from international sales, D&M's history of best sellers is enough to bring joy to any writer's heart: Crawford Kilian's *Icebreak* sold 250,000 copies, all in the export market; *Rick Hansen, Man in Motion,* by Jim Taylor and Rick Hansen sold 125,000 copies; Doris Shadbolt's *The Art of Emily Carr* sold 50,000 copies; Jack Webster's *Memoirs* sold 60,000 copies.

Also in the big leagues is Self-Counsel Press and International Self-Counsel Press which in two decades have become the largest and most successful publishers of self-help books in Canada. These firms have a list of more than 190 books dealing with business, law, reference and psychology for lay people.

Raincoast Books, established in 1979, is a three-pronged company: they're publishers, national distributors and regional wholesalers. As this book went to press, Mark Stanton of Raincoast was excited about a book of paintings and stories about Vancouver entitled *Michael Kluckner's Vancouver,* and a history by Paul Grescoe of the romance-novel company, Harlequin Publishing, entitled *The Merchants of Venus.*

Many Lower Mainland publishing houses were built from humble beginnings. Talonbooks grew out of a small poetry magazine that began in 1963. The company published its first book in 1967 and publisher Karl Siegler recalls the early days when staff members met once or twice a month in people's basements to read and vote on what work to accept for publication. By 1996 Talonbooks was well established as a literary press, producing a list or more than 200 books in non-fiction, adult fiction, drama and literary criticism.

Also rated as leaders in their own specialized fields are: Whitecap Books of North Vancouver, incorporated in 1977, publishers of scenic and natural history books, regional guides, gardening, history and children's non-fiction, with more than 140 books in print, and UBC Press with 229 titles in print, including Canadian and native studies, political science and resource studies. Scholarly books on Canadian history and political science turned out by UBC Press, educational books for the college market produced by VCC Press and children's fiction published by Pacific Educational Press at UBC total more than 360 titles in print.

In 1970 the entire provincial book publishing industry earned $350,000 in sales. By 1992, total provincial book revenue climbed to $25 million

Heritage House Publishing in Surrey has more than 50 titles on history, the outdoors and travel in B.C. Arsenal Pulp Press lists 125 titles in fiction, humor, native and regional history and poetry. A famous annual event initiated by Arsenal Pulp is the Three-Day Novel Contest in which people are challenged to write a complete novel in three days. Polestar Book Publishers, founded in the early 1980s in Victoria, is now in Vancouver with Michelle Benjamin as owner and publisher. Polestar publishes Canadian literary fiction and poetry, sports books, children's fiction and general non-fiction. Authors include poets Kate Braid and Gregory Scofield, sports journalists Wendy Long and Eric Dwyer, historian Geoffrey Molyneux and children's writer Ellen Schwartz. In June, 1996 Polestar launched a new imprint called Sirius—all the books of which celebrate dogs! (Sirius is the Dog Star.)

The newest entry into local book publishing, The Linkman Press, began by publishing the book you're reading. *The Greater Vancouver Book,* an urban encyclopedia of more than 900 pages, is the biggest general-trade book in B.C. publishing history. Linkman's owners, Chuck Davis and John Cochlin, have ambitious plans for many local, regional and international titles.

New Star Books (publisher: Rolf Maurer) annually adds about eight titles to an existing list of 78 books on regional social issues, politics and literature. "Regional books are popular. People want to read about themselves and life around them," says Maurer.

Publishers in the Greater Vancouver area are a diverse, highly motivated group, affiliated through membership in the Association of Book Publishers of B.C. Their common goal is to promote a healthy local book-publishing industry, B.C.-owned and controlled. The association was founded by five book publishers in 1974. Today, out of more than 50 members, the 18 based in the Greater Vancouver area cover every type of book-publishing, including literary, poetry, educational, scholarly and a full range of trade books.

Some Greater Vancouver Authors
Alan Twigg

(Alan Twigg's original manuscript named about four times as many authors as we have been able to include. It's a wonderful piece of work and we sorely regret not having the space to include it all. See his book Vancouver and its Writers *and blame the publishers for omissions in this collection.)*

Paul Adam spent ten years exploring the Whistler region as a guide. His *Whistler and Region Outdoors* (1994) is a guide to the best places to hike, bike, kayak, canoe, swim, fish, climb and ski between Squamish and Lillooet.

Helen Akrigg and George Philip Akrigg, retired UBC professors, wrote two widely used B.C. histories, *British Columbia Chronicle: 1778-1846* and *British Columbia Chronicle: Vol. II 1847-1871,* and produced a bestseller, *British Columbia Place Names.* They were pioneers in self-publishing under their imprint, Discovery Press. He also wrote as a Shakespearean scholar; she has contributed essays on B.C. history.

Sue Alderson (Sue Ann Alderson) succeeded George McWhirter as head of the UBC creative writing department. She is most widely known for her "Bonnie McSmithers" series of kids' books. She was the initiator of UBC's Writing for Children program and was directly influential in encouraging Shirley Sterling to write her award-winning *My Name is Seepeetza.*

John Atkins has published a series on Vancouver walking tours for the Vancouver Community Arts Council and co-authored *Heritage Walks Around Vancouver* (1992) with Michael Kluckner. He lives in an 1898 heritage house in Strathcona. His second book: *Strathcona: Vancouver's First Neighborhood.*

Keith Baldrey, as a *Vancouver Sun* political reporter based in Victoria, co-authored *Fantasyland: Inside the Reign of Bill Vander Zalm* (1989) with the *Sun's* former Victoria bureau chief Gary Mason.

Gary Bannerman is an open-line radio host (CKNW) and a former reporter for the *Province.* He has written *Gastown, The 107 Years* and books on cruise ships and BC Ferries.

Nick Bantock of Bowen Island, a British-raised graphic designer and artist, achieved international success with the 1991 art novel, *Griffin & Sabine,* which details a bizarre correspondence. It was followed by *Sabine's Notebook* and *The Golden Mean.* Bantock has also produced an interpretation of *Solomon Grundy, The Egyptian Jukebox* and numerous other titles. *Sabine's Notebook* received the Bill Duthie Booksellers' Choice Award in 1993.

Jean Barman is the author of *The West Beyond The West: A History of British Columbia* and *Growing Up British in British Columbia: Boys in Private School.* She co-edited *Vancouver Past: Essays in Social History* with UBC professor Robert A.J. McDonald and *Indian Education in Canada* with Don McCaskill. With Linda Hale she co-produced a bibliography of B.C.'s local history books for B.C. Heritage Trust.

Sheila Baxter is an anti-poverty activist who first published *No Way to Live: Poor Women Speak Out,* based on her interviews with poor Vancouver women in 1986. To recognize the plight of the homeless she released *Under the Viaduct* (1991), which publicized life in skid road hotels, under bridges and on the streets. It won the first VanCity Book Prize for best B.C. book on women's issues. Her third book, *A Child Is Not A Toy* (1993), concerns children and poverty.

John Becker wrote *Discord: The Story of the Vancouver Symphony Orchestra.* The book chronicles the soul-searching, dissension, acrimony and public begging in 1988 and 1989 that accompanied the financial troubles of Canada's sixth largest cultural institution.

Elizabeth Bell-Irving (O'Kiely) traced the history of Vancouver's best-known private school for girls in *Crofton House: The First Ninety Years,* which covers 1898-1988.

Guy Bennett is the author of *Guy's Guide to the Flipside,* an offbeat but acerbically truthful view of Vancouver's less-known attractions, self-published in 1988, and re-issued by Pulp Press in 1992.

Don Benson's history (in verse) of the telephone in B.C., *Wiresong,* emanates from his career with B.C. Telephone. Written in the style of Robert Service, the book celebrates historical characters and engineering feats.

Earle Birney (Alfred Earle Birney) is one of B.C.'s most seminal literary figures. He was renowned as a prolific and often experimental poet who influenced many writers as the founder of UBC's creative writing department, the first such department in Canada. Also a novelist, he wrote a Vancouver-based Depression story of his Trotskyite days, *Down the Long Table,* and a picaresque military novel, *Turvey.* He earned many awards and led a complex life described by Elspeth Cameron in a comprehensive 1994 biography, *Earle Birney: A Life.* Birney died in 1995.

Lisa Birnie of Bowen Island is a journalist, foreign correspondent and author. After serving on the National Parole Board she wrote *Inside the Parole Board: The Truth About Canada's Criminal Justice System.* She chronicled the life and death of ALS sufferer Sue Rodriguez in *Uncommon Will.*

Ann Blades, one of Canada's leading illustrators of children's books, began her career by writing *Mary of Mile 18* in 1971, based on her experiences as a teacher in the B.C. Interior. She illustrated many books such as Betty Waterton's *Salmon for Simon,* Ainslie Manson's *A Dog Came, Too* and Michael Macklem's *Jacques the Woodcutter.* She lives in Crescent Beach, the setting for her *The Cottage at Crescent Beach.*

Lilian Boraks-Nemetz of Vancouver, a child-survivor from the Warsaw Ghetto, wrote *The Old Brown Suitcase* (1994), a novel about a 14-year-old girl, Slava, who comes here from Poland after World War II. Boraks-Nemetz has taught creative writing at UBC.

David Boswell, born in London, Ontario, came to Vancouver in 1977 to contribute cartoons to the *Georgia Straight.* Eclipse Comics of California distributes his comic books about *Laszlo, Great Slavic Lover* and *Reid Fleming, The World's Toughest Milkman.*

George Bowering has published more than 40 books and has twice received the Governor General's Award, once for poetry and once for fiction. Raised in the Okanagan, he was a leading member of the informal TISH literary movement at UBC and now teaches English at SFU. His witty historical novel *Burning Water* recalled Captain George Vancouver; *Caprice* is an offbeat Okanagan "western" with an emancipated female heroine.

Denny Boyd, a longtime *Vancouver Sun* columnist, was born in the now-vanished B.C. mining town of Anyox. His books are *The History of Hockey in B.C., Pros and Cons: The Vancouver Canucks Story* (a light-hearted look at the first three years of the franchise) and a cookbook, *Man on the Range.* His 1995 autobiography is titled *In My Own Words.*

Robert Bringhurst, born in Los Angeles in 1946, is a typography expert, editor and poet who collaborated with photographer Ulli Steltzer on *The Black Canoe: Bill Reid and the Spirit of Haida Gwai,* (Bill Duthie Booksellers Choice Award, 1992.) He wrote a history of fine art publishing in B.C. called *Ocean/Paper/Stone,* published by William Hoffer, and released a major poetry collection, *Pieces of Map, Pieces of Music,* in 1986. He received the Macmillan Prize for poetry in 1975.

Constance Brissenden succeeded Daniel Francis as president of the Federation of B.C. Writers in 1994, the same year her third book, *Whistler, Featuring Sea to Sky Country,* was published.

Anne Broadfoot wrote the text for two coffee-table books, *Vancouver Island* and *Through Lions Gate,* with photos by Ted Czolowski. She wrote a history of the Real Estate Board of Greater Vancouver, for which she worked for many years.

Paula Brook, born in Saskatoon in 1952, is the managing editor of *Western Living* magazine. *Backyard Adventures* is a source book for games, toys, projects and safe activities suited to the backyard. She also wrote *Vancouver Secrets* and *Vancouver Rainy Day Guide.*

Liz Bryan and husband **Jack Bryan** were the

founding (1971) publishers and editors of *Western Living* magazine. Among other titles, Liz Bryan wrote *Country Roads of B.C. and Southwestern Alberta*, plus a perennial bestseller, *Backroads of British Columbia*, both accompanied by Jack Bryan's photos.

Sally Carswell of West Vancouver has recounted the development of library service in West Vancouver over a 70-year period with *Fulfilling A Dream.* She wrote *The Story of the Lions Gate Hospital.*

John Cherrington, born and raised in Vancouver, now lives in Fort Langley where he sits on the board of the Fort Langley Legacy Foundation. He followed his first book, *Mission On The Fraser* (1974) with a comprehensive overview of the Fraser Valley, *The Fraser Valley: A History* (1992).

Curley Chittenden, a veteran logger and musician, co-wrote an illustrated history of logging and sawmilling in the Fraser Valley, *Fraser Valley Challenge,* with Arnold M. McComb. Chittenden's grandfather, Newton Chittenden, published two of B.C.'s first travel books in 1882 and 1884.

Denise Chong received the City of Vancouver Book Prize in 1994 for *The Concubine's Children,* a memoir tracing her return to China with her mother and the bittersweet family reunion that ensued.

Jack Christie is a Vancouver-based travel writer who writes about the Lower Mainland. His first book was *Daytrips From Vancouver.*

James Clavell, who died in 1994, had a home in West Vancouver from 1963 to 1972. His international bestsellers include *King Rat* (1962), *Tai-Pan* (1966), *Shogun* (1975), *Noble House* (1981) and *Whirlwind.*

Doug Collins, an outspoken and controversial journalist for the *North Shore News,* has written *Immigration: The Destruction of English Canada* and *P.O.W.,* an account of his escape from a German prisoner-of-war camp.

David Corcoran, born in Toronto in 1953, edited *Prism International* and wrote an historical novel for the Vancouver centennial, *The West Coasters,* which skillfully includes research into Vancouver's origins.

Judy Corser's romance *Man of Steele,* written under her pen name Judith Bowen, is the story of a petite deckhand on a troller east of Bella Bella. The Richmond author says she was inspired by reading Edith Iglauer's *Fishing with John.*

Douglas Coupland's *Generation X* is the acerbic, satirical story of three young refugees from the world of "yuppie wannabeism" who are underemployed, overeducated and intensely private. Coupland writes for *Vancouver* magazine and has studied architecture. His subsequent works: *Shampoo Planet, Life After God* and *Microserfs.*

Mike Cramond, born in Alberta and raised in West Vancouver, was outdoors editor of the *Province* for 24 years. His books include *Fishing Holes of the West, Hunting and Fishing in North America, A Bear Behind* and *Killer Bears.*

Marion Crook's *The Body Image Trap* is "for the 92 per cent of women who don't fit the idealized frame." She is a nurse and author of a series of mysteries for juveniles, plus stories about 11-year-olds named Megan and Ricky, *The Hidden Gold Mystery* and *Crosscurrents.* Crook co-wrote and published *How To Self-Publish and Make Money* with Nancy Wise of Kelowna and has published two books about teenagers, *The Face in the Mirror: Teenagers Talk About Abortion* and *Every Parent's Guide to Understanding Teenagers and Suicide.*

Cordell Cross of Vancouver is a retired Major who has written a novel about seven boys who attend a Vernon army cadet camp in the 1950s, *Stand By Your Beds!* (1992). His sequel is called *Form Three Ranks On The Road.*

Jeff Cross, as a *Province* sports journalist, co-wrote *Karen: The Karen Magnussen Story.*

Chuck Davis, born in Winnipeg in 1935, began his broadcasting career in 1956. As a radio host, quizmaster and newspaper columnist, he has consistently popularized Vancouver and area history. Among his books are *Reflections* (a history of the District of North Vancouver) and a history of CKNW radio, *Top Dog!* With John Cochlin, he founded The Linkman Press, publishers of *The Greater Vancouver Book* (1997).

Roma Dehr is a Vancouver environmentalist and educator. Her information guide and action book for kids, *Good Planets Are Hard To Find,* co-written by Ronald M. Bazar and illustrated by Nola Johnston, promotes the belief that everyone can make a difference for the planet.

Paul Delany is an SFU English professor who edited *Vancouver: Representing The Postmodern City* (1994), a collection of essays evaluating Vancouver's cultural and social life. He has authored and edited eight previous books.

James Delgado, director of the Vancouver Maritime Museum, is an underwater archaeologist and author of numerous maritime titles such as *Pearl Harbor Recalled: New Images of the Day of Infamy.*

Eleonore Dempster's centennial history of the Capilano Suspension Bridge, *The Laughing Bridge,* traces the origins of the bridge to 1889 when August Jack Khahtsahlano strung a hemp rope across the Capilano Canyon.

William Deverell, born in Regina in 1937, is a lawyer and former president of the B.C. Civil Liberties Association. His bestselling thrillers, some of which are based on his cases, include *Needles* (for which he won the Seal Book Prize), *High Crimes, Mecca, The Dance of Shiva, Platinum Blues* (about the music industry) and *Mindfield,* which probes the CIA-financed brainwashing experiments in Montreal's Allan Memorial Institute. In 1994 he published *Kill All The Lawyers* and became chair of the Writers Union of Canada.

Art Downs (Arthur George Downs), originator of *B.C. Outdoors* magazine and publisher of Surrey-based Heritage House books, has written numerous B.C. historical books such as *Paddlewheels on the Frontier, Wagon Road North* and *The Hope Slide Story,* and edited *Pioneer Days in British Columbia.*

Barry Downs, a Vancouver architect, celebrated B.C.'s early churches in *Sacred Places* (1980). It received an Eaton's B.C. Book Prize.

Jan Drabek, born in Prague, Czechoslovakia, in 1935, came to Canada in 1965. He has recalled his upbringing in a memoir, *Thirteen,* written numerous thrillers including *Report on the Death of Rosenkavalier, What Happened to Wenceslas?, The Lister Legacy* and *The Statement,* and penned a Canadian guide to retirement, *The Golden Revolution.* He temporarily returned to Czechoslovakia upon its reversion to democracy and was appointed ambassador to Kenya until 1994.

Ken Drushka wrote *Against Wind and Weather,* a history of the B.C. towboating industry, and *Stumped,* a study of the B.C. forest industry. He collaborated with Ian Mahood, a professional forester for more than 50 years, for *Three Men and a Forester,* an "insider's expose" of how B.C.'s forest industry has been mishandled.

Adrian du Plessis is a critic of the Vancouver Stock Exchange whose collaboration with artist Carel Moisiewitsch resulted in *Sideshow: The Howe Street Carnival.* He is a former VSE floor trader.

Gregory Edwards photographed and researched the architectural details and motifs that grace Victoria and Vancouver's older buildings for *Hidden Cities,* which features more than 350 photos.

Katie Ekroth's son Matthew underwent one of the world's first heart and lung transplants prior to his seventh birthday in 1986. Since Matthew's death she has become an active member of the Pacific Organ Retrieval for Transplantation Program, and wrote a memoir of her son's four-year battle for life, *Lionheart.* She lives in Tsawwassen.

Arthur Erickson is Vancouver's most renowned architect and the designer of Simon Fraser University, Robson Square and the Museum of Anthropology. His *The Architecture of Arthur Erickson* examines and celebrates his career up to 1988.

Henry Ewert, an English teacher, rode the Vancouver streetcars on their final day of service in 1955 and rode the interurbans on their final day in 1958. He published *The Story of the B.C. Electric Railway Company* in 1986.

Bruce Fairley's *A Guide to Climbing and Hiking in Southwestern British Columbia* in 1986 was conceived as a successor to Dick Culbert's *Alpine*

Guide to Southwestern British Columbia of 1974. Fairley (born 1951) is a lawyer who has been a climber since joining the UBC Outdoor Club.

Vicki Gabereau, born in Vancouver, was sent to live with the family of Pierre Berton, a friend of her father, at age 19. After driving taxi and running for mayor of Toronto in 1974 as Rosie the Clown, she joined CBC Radio and hosts the national Gabereau program. Her 1988 collection of interviews and autobiographical glimpses is This Won't Hurt A Bit. In 1994 she published a cookbook culled from her guests' recipes, Cooking Without Looking.

Anne Garber, a consumer columnist and broadcaster, has written several shopping and eating guides pertaining to the Lower Mainland, including one illustrated by filmmaker Marv Newland.

Karie Garnier, a White Rock photographer, self-published a tribute to native elders called Our Elders Speak (1991).

Steve Gatensbury, born in New Westminster in 1923, started work in the sawmill industry at 16. His "fly on the wall" approach to B.C. logging history, Once, To Learn It, is a light-hearted look at his 50 years of work. His Queensborough: Images of an Old Neighborhood recalls New Westminster.

Daniel Gawthrop, the former editor of Xtra West, wrote Affirmation: The AIDS Odyssey of Dr. Peter (1994) which traces the life and death of Dr. Peter Jepson-Young, whose 111 instalments of his "AIDS diary" on the CBC Evening News were later edited into a documentary film nominated for an Oscar.

William Gibson, born in North Carolina in 1948, came to Vancouver in 1972 and sold his first science-fiction story to Omni magazine in 1981. Since then he has won the Nebula, Hugo and Philip K. Dick awards for his first novel, Neuromancer, and completed his "cyberspace" trilogy with Count Zero and Mona Lisa Overdrive. After a collection of short stories, Burning Chrome, he collaborated with Bruce Sterling for a Victorian novel, The Difference Engine, partly about how computers evolved. His 1994 novel is Virtual Light.

Terry Glavin, after ten years on the native affairs beat for the Vancouver Sun, wrote Death Feast at Dimlahamid which telescopes the history of the Gitskan and Wet'suwet'en tribes into his observations on a three-and-a-half-week roadblock. In 1994 Glavin became editor of a new B.C. history series of "Transmontanus" titles beginning with his A Ghost in the Water. It examines the endangered giant white sturgeons of the Fraser River.

Michael Goldberg, while a UBC professor of urban land policy, interviewed 80 Chinese real estate investors and their related Pacific Rim advisors for The Chinese Connection, a 1985 analysis of the economic growth of the Pacific Rim.

Chuck Gosbee, former director of communica-

tions for the Vancouver School Board, and Leslie Dyson, a VSB publications editor, co-wrote Glancing Back: Reflections and Anecdotes on Vancouver Public Schools. The book begins with the first school, which opened in 1872 with 15 students.

Jurgen Gothe was born in Berlin, raised in Medicine Hat and now hosts CBC-FM's Disc Drive program. A restaurant and wine critic, he recommended 91 Vancouver restaurants in First Rate and has also published Good Gothe, which collects "the enthusiasms of an airwaves connoisseur."

Laurence Gough, born in Vancouver, is best known for his Vancouver-based detective novels about the investigative team of Alec Willows and Claire Parker. The first, The Goldfish Bowl, won the Arthur Ellis Crime Writers of Canada Award for best first novel. Death on a No. 8 Hook, Hot Shots (Ellis Award for best Canadian crime novel), Serious Crimes, Accidental Deaths, Fall Down Easy and Killers followed. The latter opens with a dead body in the killer whale pool of the Vancouver Aquarium.

Catherine Gourley, journalist and former stringer for Reuters and the Wall Street Journal, wrote Island in the Creek, a history of Granville Island.

Donald Graham, a political scientist and lightkeeper at Lighthouse Park, spearheaded the campaign to curtail replacement of manned lighthouses with strictly automated signals. His Keepers of the Light and Lights of the Inside Passage reveal that many of B.C.'s lightkeepers have been underpaid working-class heroes. The first title won a Haig-Brown B.C. Book Prize.

John Gray, born in Nova Scotia, attended UBC and co-founded Tamahnous Theatre. He is most widely known as the composer of Billy Bishop Goes to War, winner of the Governor-General's Award for drama in 1982. His other musicals 18 Wheels, Rock 'n' Roll and Don Messer's Jubilee comprise the 1987 anthology Local Boy Makes Good. His comic novel of Vancouver's hippie era is Dazzled. He is an outspoken nationalist and a frequent CBC commentator. In 1994 he published a collection of essays about Canadians, Lost in North America, and a book on tattoos.

Nancy Greene published an autobiography co-written with Jack Batten, Nancy Greene, and Alpine Skiing with Nancy Greene and Al Raine, co-written with her husband. Since winning her Olympic medal she has been involved in ski resort developments, primarily at Whistler.

Ruth Greene recalls 34 distinctive ships and their crews in Personality Ships of British Columbia. It includes a section on Union Steamships by Gerald Rushton.

Mike Grenby was a popular Sun columnist for many years. His first book, My Darling Dollar, has been followed by many others about personal finance.

Paul Grescoe, born in Winnipeg in 1939, commenced a mystery series about Ukrainian-Canadian detective Dan Rudnicki with Flesh Wound, set in Vancouver. Rudnicki appears again in Blood Vessel. A career journalist, Grescoe's business-related books include Jimmy, an autobiography of Jimmy Pattison. (See also Russell Kelly.)

Kevin Griffin, a Sun reporter, provided brief local histories of ethnic groups and introduced their customs in Vancouver's Many Faces (1993).

Donald Gutstein, born in 1938, grew up in Toronto and received a degree in architecture from UBC before his first book of investigative journalism, Vancouver Ltd., examined the corporate structure of Vancouver. In The New Landlords he probed the climate for Asian investment in Canadian real estate. (Also see Michael Goldberg.)

Norman Hacking is one of B.C.'s most important maritime historians. For many years he was marine editor with the Province. His publications include The Two Barneys, a memoir about a father and son who both served as well-known captains on the B.C. coast, and Royal Vancouver Yachting Annals 1903-1965, a history of the yacht club that reviews sail and power boating in Burrard Inlet, English Bay and the Gulf of Georgia. With W. Kaye Lamb he also wrote The Princess Story.

Alan Haig-Brown, son of Roderick Haig-Brown, was the executive editor of Westcoast Logger, Westcoast Fisherman, Westcoast Aviator and Westcoast Mariner magazines in Vancouver before returning to a career as a freelancer. Raised in Campbell River with experience as a commercial fisherman, he wrote The Suzie A, a juvenile novel which traces the life of a wooden fishboat launched at Steveston in 1927, and won the 1994 Bill Duthie Booksellers' Choice Award for Fishing for a Living (1993). He lives in New Westminster.

Linda Hale, born in 1949, has identified 1,044 local history titles in British Columbia Local Histories: A Bibliography, a 1991 project undertaken with Jean Barman and Brian Owen under the auspices of the B.C. Library Association, with the sponsorship of B.C. Heritage Trust.

David Hancock, who operates Hancock House publishing in Surrey, is a pilot and biologist. His books include Adventures with Eagles, Introducing the Birds of North America and Some of the Common and Uncommon Birds of British Columbia, co-authored with David Stirling.

Rick Hansen pushed his wheelchair more then 40,000 kilometres through 34 countries to raise $26 million for spinal cord research and wheelchair sport. With Jim Taylor he co-authored Rick Hansen: Man in Motion. In 1994 he co-wrote a self-help guide with California psychologist Dr. Joan Laub, Going the Distance: 7 Steps to Personal Change.

Walter Hardwick is an urban geographer who has

been a deputy minister of education in B.C. With J. Lewis Robinson he co-authored *British Columbia: One Hundred Years of Geographical Change.*

Christie Harris, born in New Jersey (1907) but raised on a B.C. farm, started writing children's stories in 1927. She published the first of her 20 children's books at age 50. She has incorporated native mythology into many stories, most notably *Raven's Cry* (1966) which relates the history of the Haida from 1775. She is a member of the Order of Canada and a recipient of numerous awards. A longtime Vancouver resident, she moved to Victoria in the early 1990s and released a new children's book, *Something Weird Is Going On*, in 1994.

Jurgen Hesse was born in Germany in 1924 and came to Canada in 1958. He has received awards for his radio documentaries and written two self-help titles, *The Radio Documentary Handbook* and *Mobile Retirement Handbook.* In *Voices of Change: Immigrant Writers Speak Out,* he interviewed 15 immigrant writers.

Art Hister was the first full-time doctor at Kitsilano's Pine Free Clinic in the 1960s. Now a newspaper columnist and host of a television program on health, he published *Dr. Art Hister's Do-It-Yourself Guide to Good Health.*

Peggy Hodgins is a Vancouver freelance writer who co-authored *Rockbound* with longtime Vancouver deejay Red Robinson. The book details Red's memories of Vancouver's rock 'n' roll days.

Irene Howard, born in Prince Rupert, taught at UBC and wrote the first book underwritten by the Vancouver Historical Society, *Vancouver's Svenskar: A History of the Swedish Community in Vancouver.* She also wrote *Bowen Island 1872-1972,* published by the Bowen Island Historians in 1973. *The Struggle for Social Justice,* her biography of progressive Vancouver city councillor Helena Gutteridge, earned a B.C. Book Prize nomination and a UBC biography medal.

Jeff Howlett of Vancouver visited 160 golf courses for *B.C. Golf: The Authoritative, Complete Guide to British Columbia Golf Courses.* Golf writer Arv Olson and retired English professor Alan Dawe have also published golfing guides.

Don Hunter compiled his fictional columns in the *Province* about a Gulf Islands community into a book, *Spinner's Inlet.* In 1972 he co-wrote Swiss-born Rene Dahinden's summary of 20 years' research into the Sasquatch for *Sasquatch.*

Christopher Hyde, born in Ottawa in 1949, is a Vancouver-based screenwriter and television journalist who has written 11 thrillers, including *The Icarus Seal* and *Hard Target. Abuse of Trust* is Hyde's 1991 study of UBC psychiatrist Dr. James Tyhurst, who was convicted of sexual and common assault on female patients, then later released on appeal.

Peggy Imredy, born in Vancouver, produced *A*

Guide to Sculpture in Vancouver in 1980. For research she incorporated the files of her husband, sculptor Elek Imredy. An independent summary of Elek Imredy's career was published in 1993, prior to his death in 1994.

Damian Inwood, born in London, England in 1950, co-wrote *The Olson Murders* with fellow ex-Brit journalist, Jon Ferry. (See also Ian Mulgrew.) Inwood later wrote *Fort Steele: The Golden Era* as well as a history of Deep Cove.

Carole Itter is a poet whose works include *The Log's Log* and *Word Work.* With Daphne Marlatt she co-authored an oral history book about Strathcona in *Vancouver, Opening Doors.*

Jack James, a lawyer, founded one of B.C.'s largest publishing companies, International Self-Counsel Press, currently operated by his former wife, Diana Douglas. He self-published *B.C. Incorporation Guide* and *Canadian Income Tax Law.*

Robert Jarvis, born in Vancouver in 1942, was widely travelled before settling in Chilliwack. He helped found the B.C. Free Speech League and has published *The Workingman's Revolt: The Vancouver Asiatic Exclusion Rally Of 1907.* He also wrote *The Komagata Maru Incident: A Canadian Immigration Battle Revisited.*

Norm Jewison, editor of the Vancouver Canucks fan magazine *Breakaway,* assembled anecdotes, statistics and more than 100 photos by Bill Cunningham for *Vancouver Canucks: The First Twenty Years.*

Salim Jiwa, as a reporter with the *Province,* investigated extremist minorities within B.C.'s Sikh community to write *The Death of Air India Flight 182,* a 1986 study that examines India's political tensions and the terrorist bombing that ripped open a jumbo jet over the Irish Sea, murdering 329 people in 1985.

Hugh Johnston of SFU's history department, is co-author with Robin Fisher of a biography of Captain Cook. To mark the incident's 75th anniversary he re-published *The Voyage of the Komagata Maru: The Sikh Challenge to Canada's Colour Bar.*

Lynn Johnston grew up in Vancouver and studied at the Vancouver School of Art. Her cartoon strip *For Better or For Worse* appears in 1,400 daily and Sunday newspapers, and her books based on the series have sold more than half-a-million copies.

Terry Julian of New Westminster chronicles the story of why the capital of British Columbia was moved from New Westminster to Victoria in *A Capital Controversy* (1994). He is also the author of *Book Collecting For Everyone.*

Harold Kalman worked for 15 years on his two-volume *A History of Canadian Architecture,* the most comprehensive book on the subject. He operates the Vancouver office of Commonwealth Historic Resource Management, a heritage con-

sulting firm, and works on projects across Canada. He also wrote *Exploring Vancouver, Reviving Main Street* and *Exploring Ottawa.*

Jim Kearney, born in 1922, was sports columnist for the *Sun* for 18 years before becoming manager of publications for Sport B.C. His *Champions: A British Columbia Sports Album* recalls the forgotten greatness of Olympic hammer thrower Duncan Gillis, the Stanley Cup champion Victoria Cougars, Olympic double-gold medalist Percy Williams, Penticton's Ted Bowsfield—the only major leaguer from B.C. to have earned a baseball pension—and many other B.C. sports figures.

Betty Keller, born in Vancouver in 1930, has been the only coordinator of the Sechelt Festival of the Written Arts, established in 1983 as the first ongoing B.C. literary festival. Her books include a biography of Pauline Johnson, for which she received the Canadian Biography Award, and *On The Shady Side,* a light-hearted look at the seamier side of Vancouver from 1886-1914.

Brian Kelly was born in Belfast in 1947 and came to Canada when he was six. A former bus driver, he researched the history of B.C. transit for ten years to co-write *Transit in British Columbia* with Daniel Francis. His self-published books are *Farewell to Brill* (1984), the story of Vancouver's trolley bus operations. He has one of the largest collections of transit memorabilia in B.C.

Russell Kelly, born in Toronto in 1949, came to Vancouver in 1982. He wrote *Pattison: Portrait of a Capitalist Superstar* (1986). In 1991 he became editor of *B.C. BookWorld.*

Eileen Kernaghan operates Neville Books in Burnaby with her husband and fellow writer, Patrick. She was born in Grindrod, B.C. in 1939, grew up on a farm, came to Burnaby in 1963 and completed her Grey Isles trilogy of pre-history novels, *Journey to Aprilioth, Songs from the Drowned Lands* and *The Sarsen Witch.*

Catherine Kerr contributed the text for photographer Ulli Steltzer's *Coast of Many Faces* and Steltzer's *Indian Artists at Work.* Born in Vancouver in 1945, she studied languages and pedagogy at UBC, was a child-care worker and teacher, and then an editor for Douglas & McIntyre.

Crawford Kilian, a Capilano College English professor, wrote a 1985 critique of B.C. education, *School Wars.* Born in New York in 1941, he emigrated to Vancouver in 1967. In 1979 he published the first novel in his Chronoplane Wars trilogy, *Empire of Time,* and a non-fiction book on B.C.'s black pioneers, *Go Do Some Great Thing.* Two natural disaster novels, *Icequake* and *Tsunami,* were followed by a mystical West Coast fantasy, *Eyas,* the futuristic *Brother Jonathan* (republished in 1996), the science-fiction novel *Lifter* and the Chronoplane novels *The Fall of the Republic, Rogue Emperor* (in which the 21st century battles the 1st century in ancient Rome) and *Gryphon.* A 1995 title: *2020 Visions: The Future of Canada.* In September, 1996: *The Communications Book: Writing for the Workplace.*

W.P. Kinsella (William Patrick Kinsella) of White Rock was born in Edmonton in 1945 and raised on a remote Alberta homestead. In 1967 he moved to Victoria where he learned from UVic's W.D. Valgardson. His Indian stories, mostly set on the Hobbema reserve, have resulted in *Dance Me Outside, Scars, Born Indian, The Moccasin Telegraph, The Fencepost Chronicles* (winner of the Leacock Medal for Humour, 1987) and a final collection, *Brother Frank's Gospel Hour.* His baseball-related stories are *Shoeless Joe* (made into the movie *Field of Dreams*), *The Iowa Baseball Confederacy* and *The Further Adventures of Slugger McBatt.* His nostalgic Alberta novel is *Box Socials.*

Anne Kloppenborg prepared *Vancouver's First Century* with her *Urban Reader* colleagues Alice Niwinski and Eve Johnson in 1977. More than 300 photos and advertisements were complemented with excerpts from newspapers, memoirs and an introduction by the late David Brock. Supplementary versions appeared in 1985 and 1991, titled *Vancouver: A City Album.*

Michael Kluckner, born in Vancouver, won the Bill Duthie Booksellers Choice Award in 1990 for his collection of watercolors and heritage architecture commentary, *Vanishing Vancouver.* He has also written detailed architectural histories of Vancouver, Victoria and Toronto, plus *Paving Paradise,* which contains his ideas on how cities have gone awry. He also self-published a collection of his artwork in 1993, *British Columbia in Watercolour.*

Rolf Knight grew up on the Vancouver waterfront. He has worked mostly outside the academic scene to produce six books of working-class history, mainly relying on first-hand interviews. These are *Stump Ranch Chronicles, A Man of our Times* (with Maya Koizumi), *A Very Ordinary Life, Work Camps and Company Towns in Canada and the U.S., Indians at Work* and *Along the No. 20 Line* (reminiscences of the Vancouver waterfront). *A Very Ordinary Life* chronicles the far-from-commonplace life of the author's Berlin-born mother, Phyllis Knight, who died in Burnaby at age 76. He received a B.C. Book Prize nomination in 1993 for co-authoring the memoirs of fishing union leader Homer Stevens. In 1992 Knight received a Canadian Historical Association Career Contribution Award.

Joy Kogawa, daughter of an Anglican minister, was born Joy Nozonie Nokayama in Vancouver in 1935. Her award-winning 1981 novel *Obasan,* a memoir of Japanese-Canadian internment, followed in 1992 by *Itsuka,* a novel which recounts the same central character's reconciliation with Canada against the backdrop of the redress

movement.

Andrew Lamb, a West Vancouver biologist, and Phillip Edgell, a fisheries biologist and former staff photographer for the Vancouver Aquarium, co-authored *Coastal Fishes of the Pacific Northwest,* a comprehensive field guide to all the saltwater fish in B.C. waters.

W. Kaye Lamb (William Kaye Lamb), B.C.'s pre-eminent archivist, was born in New Westminster in 1904. His books and many publications include *Empress to the Orient,* a revised and lavishly illustrated reprinting of articles Lamb wrote between 1937 and 1948 about the CPR's Empress service to the Orient. The first national librarian of Canada, he has ten honorary doctorates and is past president of the Canadian Historical and Canadian Library Associations.

Evelyn Lau was an honor student when she ran away from her parents at 14 and became a teenage prostitute. Her memoir *Runaway: Diary of a Street Kid* received much publicity and became the basis for a critically acclaimed CBC movie. At 20 she won the Milton Acorn Memorial 1990 People's Poetry Award for *You Are Not Who You Claim,* her first book of poetry. She has published more poetry and a collection of fiction, *Fresh Girls and Other Stories.* A novel, *Other Women,* appeared in 1996.

SKY Lee [sic], born in Port Alberni in 1952, came to Vancouver in 1967. She worked for *Makara* magazine and illustrated Paul Yee's *Teach Me To Fly, Skyfighter!* before releasing her novel, *Disappearing Moon Cafe,* about four generations of the Wong family in Vancouver. It received the City of Vancouver book award. A registered nurse, she has also published a 1994 collection of short fiction, *Bellydancer.*

Mark Leier's *Where the Fraser River Flows* is a history of Industrial Workers of the World within B.C. It reveals the "Wobblies" were not only pitted against bosses and government, but also against conservative elements within the labor movement. He recounts IWW's glory days in 1912 when the dream of establishing "one big union" was becoming a force for revolution in B.C.

Cyril Leonoff combined a lavish collection of photos by B.C.'s most important photographer of the century, Leonard Frank, with a biography of Frank for *An Enterprising Life,* covering 1895 to 1944. The book won numerous awards including the City of Vancouver Heritage Award and a B.C. Historical Association Award. Leonoff, an engineer by profession, has been active with the Jewish Historical Society, Vancouver Historical Society and Vancouver Heritage Advisory Committee. His preceding book was a pictorial history of B.C. and Yukon Jewish communities, *Pioneers, Peddlars and Prayer Shawls.*

Mary Macaree and **David Macaree's** *103 Hikes in Southwestern B.C.* is into its third edition. The Macarees' other book is *109 Walks in B.C.'s Lower Mainland,* also in its third printing. A companion volume is Jean Cousins and Heather Robinson's *Easy Hiking Around Vancouver,* revised for a third edition in 1990. Also see Bruce Fairley.

Bruce Macdonald, born in Vancouver in 1948, got the idea for *Vancouver: A Visual History* in the summer of 1984. The 1992 book (10,000 hours of work for the author) comprises a series of maps showing the development of Vancouver in ten-year increments from the 1850s to the 1980s, with accompanying text. Other maps show ethnic heritage, religious affiliation, etc.

Donald MacKay, born in Nova Scotia in 1925, lives in Montreal but wrote a company history of MacMillan Bloedel, *Empire of Wood,* plus *Heritage Lost: The Crisis in Canada's Forests.* His social history *Lumberjacks* was nominated for a Governor General's Award and he detailed the race between the Grand Trunk Pacific and Canadian Northern railways to reach Vancouver and commence a Pacific Rim link in *The Asian Dream.*

Lee Maracle's *I Am Woman* describes her struggle to "climb the mountain of racism" as a West Coast native. Her autobiographical *Bobbi Lee, Indian Rebel* recounts her travels within B.C. in the 1960s and 1970s, her time with California farmworkers and her brief presence on the counter-cultural drug scene in Toronto. *Sojourner's Truth* is a story collection of native oral forms and traditional stories. *Ravensong* is a novel about life on a North Vancouver Indian reserve in the 1950s. Her novel *Sundogs* is a first-person narrative reflecting the impact of political events such as the Oka stand-off on the daily lives of a Vancouver native family.

Daphne Marlatt, born in Melbourne in 1941, spent much of her childhood in Malaysia before emigrating in 1951. Since 1968 she has written two prose narratives, *Zocolo* (set in Mexico) and *Ana Historic* (an historical novel set in Vancouver); two oral histories for Sound Heritage (about Steveston and Strathcona); an evocation of Steveston with photographer Robert Minden; and numerous poetry books.

Ralph Maud edited the four-volume collection, *The Salish People,* including the 1895-1911 field work of ethnologist Charles Hill-Tout. Maud's biography and bibliography in volume IV show why Hill-Tout became president of the Anthropological Section of the Royal Society of Canada. Maud, who has been a teacher of English and Indian oral tradition at SFU, also wrote *A Guide to B.C. Indian Myth and Legend.*

Glen McDonald recalled his most interesting cases as Vancouver's coroner in *How Come I'm Dead?,* a memoir co-written with John Kirkwood, a weekly newpaper columnist in Vancouver.

Robert A.J. McDonald teaches in UBC's department of history. With Jean Barman, he co-edited *Vancouver Past: Essays in Social History*. In 1996 UBC Press published his *Making Vancouver: 1863-1913*, an economic and social examination of the city's first years.

Pixie McGeachie is the co-author of *Archdeacon on Horseback*. A biography of an early B.C. missionary, it doubles as a history of Lytton and Anglican schools in the Fraser Canyon. (Also see Cyril Williams.) McGeachie's other books are *Adventures in Canada* and *Bygones of Burnaby*. She lives in Burnaby where she has been president of the historical society.

Geoff Meggs became editor of the UFAWU's *The Fisherman* in 1978 , the oldest and largest circulation West Coast fishing publication, then became editor of *Pacific Current*, a new left-wing magazine, in 1994. His *Salmon: The Decline of the British Columbia Fishery* reveals how the drive for short-term profit has proven ruinous for a threatened industry. It won a Lieutenant-Governor's Medal for B.C. history.

Marg Meikle appears on CBC Radio's *Gabereau* program to answer listeners' quirky questions, collected in *The Answer Lady*.

Roy Miki, a third-generation Japanese-Canadian, was born in 1942, six months after his parents had been shipped from Haney to a sugar beet farm in Manitoba. Now an SFU English professor, he and his father Art Miki were at the forefront of the successful redress movement which Roy Miki has chronicled with Cassandra Kobayashi in *Justice in Our Time*. He authored an extensive bibliography of George Bowering's work, edited an essay collection about bp Nichol and was editor of *This Is My Own: Letters to Wes and other Writings on Japanese Canadians, 1941-1948* by Muriel Kitagawa.

David Mitchell was elected as a Liberal MLA for West Vancouver-Garibaldi in the 1991 provincial election. He is a former B.C. archivist with the Sound Heritage series, a political commentator and author of *W.A.C. Bennett and the Rise of British Columbia,* one of the most important volumes of B.C. history. His follow-up book on the reshaping of the Social Credit party was *Succession* in 1987. He was born in Montreal and educated at SFU. In 1996 he produced *All Aboard! Through the Canadian Rockies by Train*.

Geoffrey Molyneux is a former editor with the *Province*. Born in London, England, he arrived in Vancouver to work for the *Sun* in 1952. He served as chief western writer and researcher for *Chronicle of Canada*. Currently at work on a history of Pacific Press, he has compiled *British Columbia: An Illustrated History*.

Alan Morley wrote *The Romance of Vancouver* in 1940, followed by *Vancouver: From Milltown to Metropolis* in 1961. Morley, who died in 1982, was a veteran *Vancouver Sun* journalist.

Ian Mulgrew came to Vancouver in the early 1980s as West Coast bureau chief for the *Globe and Mail,* then joined the *Province* in 1986. His *Unholy Terror: The Sikhs and International Terrorism* was followed by *Final Payoff: The True Price of Convicting Clifford Robert Olson*. He contributed to the writing of Jack Webster's autobiography.

Jack Munro headed the largest union for Canada's $2.5 billion forest industry, the International Woodworkers of America, for 16 years. He was persuaded to co-write (with Jane O'Hara) his memoir *Union Jack*, by Auto Workers president Bob White. Born in Lethbridge in 1931, the only son of Scottish immigrants, Munro was raised on a relief farm near Calgary and came to work in Nelson, B.C. as a mechanic in the early 1950s.

Derik Murray, along with his partner Marthe Love and Whitecap Books publisher Michael Burch, was responsible for one of the bestselling and most successful books ever produced in B.C., *The Expo Celebration*. Murray/Love Productions also produced *Share The Flame: The Official Retrospective of the Olympic Torch Relay*. He was born in 1956 in Vancouver, where he works as a photographer and packager of book projects including a hardcover tribute to NHL greats.

Isabel Nanton, born in Kenya, is a travel writer who speaks five languages. She teaches travel writing at UBC and has co-authored a guide, *Adventuring in British Columbia,* with Mary Simpson, an avid cross-country skier and West Coast sailor.

W.H. New (William "Bill" Herbert New) was born in Vancouver in 1938. He took over as editor of *Canadian Literature* in 1977 from George Woodcock and in the process edited *A Political Art: Essays and Images in Honour of George Woodcock* and the book, *Native Writers and Canadian Writing*. He has taught English at UBC since 1965 and serves on the advisory panel for McClelland & Stewart's reprint series of Canadian classics with Guy Vanderhaege and Alice Munro.

Peter Newman of Deep Cove was born in Vienna in 1929. Editor of *Macleans* magazine from 1971 to 1982, he is most widely known for his books on Canada's business elite, such as *The Canadian Establishment* and *The Acquisitors*. His trilogy on the Hudson's Bay Company and earlier books on Canadian politics have made him one of Canada's most successful writers.

Eric Nicol, B.C.'s best-known humorist, is a three-time winner of the Leacock Medal for Humour for *The Roving I, Shall We Join the Ladies?* and *Girdle Me a Globe*. His many other books include a 1978 history of Vancouver, several comical views of sports and a spoof about Charles Dickens' son in the RCMP, *The Astounding Long-Lost Letters of Dickens of the Mounted*. A longtime columnist for the *Province*, Nicol was also one of B.C.'s first successful playwrights. "Anarchist in theory, liberal in practice," he was born in Kingston, Ontario in 1919 but grew up in Vancouver. He served three years with the RCAF and studied French at the Sorbonne.

Alice Niwinski. See Anne Kloppenborg.

Timothy Oke was born in Devon, emigrated in 1963 and came to UBC to teach in 1970. He was head of the geography department until 1996; he is co-editor with Graeme Wynn of *Vancouver and its Region,* an overview by 19 UBC geographers. The author of *Boundary Layer Climates* and *The Climate of Vancouver,* Oke is a Fellow of the Royal Society of Canada and the Royal Canadian Geographic Society.

Steve Osborne, co-founder of Pulp Press in 1971, is a writer, book publisher, desktop publishing consultant and publisher of *Geist* magazine. Illustrated by his brother J.T. Osborne, his *Social Credit for Beginners* is a history of the Social Credit movement from 1917 in England through to the government of Bill Vander Zalm. With Mary Schendlinger he edited a pocket-sized bestseller, *Quotations of Chairman Zalm;* he has also edited the fiction of D.M. Fraser. Osborne was born in 1947 in Pangnirtung on Baffin Island.

Rick Ouston born in 1955, cites Allan Fotheringham's maxim "News isn't news unless someone else doesn't want it told" to introduce *Getting the Goods: Information in B.C.,* a guide to finding people and information in B.C. A former *Sun* journalist and an adoptee, Ouston documented the search for his birth mother and an older sister in *Finding Family* (1994).

Stephani Paine (Stephani Hewlett Paine) of Ladner was employed by the Vancouver Aquarium from 1972 until 1991 as a curatorial assistant, staff biologist and manager of public affairs. Born in Vancouver in 1946, she has written *Sea Life of the Pacific Northwest* and *Beachwalker: Sea Life of the West Coast*. As a media personality, consultant and writer on marine biology she has been most widely known as Stephani Hewlett.

T.W. Paterson (Thomas William) has produced ten volumes of popular history since *Treasure, British Columbia* in 1971 and *Shipwreck! Piracy and Terror in the Northwest* in 1972. Other titles from the 1970s and 1980s are *Encyclopedia of Ghost Towns and Mining Camps of B.C.* and *British Columbia: The Pioneer Years*.

George Payerle was born in Vancouver of Hungarian-Canadian parents in 1945. He studied and taught creative writing at UBC and followed a short, 1970 experimental novel, *The Afterpeople,* with *Unknown Soldier,* a fictional portrait of a 59-year-old, ex-sergeant who still suffers psychological after-affects from World War II. Payerle has been active in writers' politics and lives in Vancouver.

E.G. Perrault (Ernie), older brother of Senator Ray Perrault, is a Penticton-born (1922) novelist and screenwriter who also worked in advertising and public relations. He wrote a thinly disguised biographical novel about the early days of rogue B.C. timber baron Gordon Gibson Sr., *The Kingdom Carver*, a 1968 forerunner to Gibson's own memoir, *Bull of the Woods*. Perrault's second novel, *The Twelfth Mile* (1972) is a suspenseful tale about a West Coast towboat operator. Perrault wrote the corporate history of Seaboard Lumber and Shipping, *Wood and Water*. He also wrote a 1975 suspense novel, *Spoil!*, based on his five years in the Arctic making documentary films.

Stan Persky, born in Chicago in 1941, co-founded *Georgia Straight Writing Supplements* which led to the formation of New Star Books by Lanny Beckman. Now a sociology professor at Capilano College, and a well-known leftist media commentator and *Vancouver Sun* columnist, Persky first gained wide attention for his popular political books, *Son of Socred* (1979), *The House That Jack Built* (1980) and *Bennett II* (1983). *At the Lenin Shipyard* explored Polish politics; *America: The Last Domino* examined U.S. foreign policy. His autobiographical meditations on homosexuality, *Buddy's*, received an Evans B.C. Book Prize nomination and marked a return to Perksy's literary roots. His most recent book, *Fantasy Government*, scrutinized Bill Vander Zalm's premiership.

Helen Potrebenko, born in Grand Prairie, Alberta in 1940, fictionalized a female cabbie's struggle to earn a living in the novel, *Taxi* (1975). Drawing upon her own background she completed *No Streets of Gold*, a social history of Ukrainian-Canadians in Alberta. Proud of the dignity in working-class lives, particularly women's, she produced a collection of fiction and non-fiction, *A Flight of Average Persons* and *Two Years on the Muckamuck Line*, about her experiences as a picketer. Four other Potrebenko titles are *Walking Slow*, *Sometimes They Sang*, *Live, Love and Unions* and *Hey Waitress and Other Stories*.

Margaret Powers (Margaret Fishback Powers) composed a meditative poem called *Footprints* in 1964 during a troubled period in her life. It was illegally reprinted and became known to millions as an inspirational message on plaques, calendars, posters and cards. *Footprints: The Story Behind the Poem* chronicles her creation, loss and legal recovery of the material, interwoven with the author's life experiences.

Betty Pratt-Johnson's authoritative guide to scuba and skin diving in B.C. and Washington, *141 Dives*, was re-released in two volumes in 1994. She has written two books on whitewater trips

for kayakers, canoeists and rafters. Born in the Midwestern U.S. in 1930, she lives in Vancouver.

Marie Putnam had attended Oakridge Special School for 14 years prior to the publication of her moving, autobiographical novel about a young mentally handicapped person looking for love, *Mentely Handicapped Love*. Her illuminating story —packaged and presented as Putnam submitted it—is a testament to the dignity of a young handicapped woman's yearnings and perceptions.

Bill Richardson, born in Winnipeg in 1955, is a humorist and self-dubbed "Poet Laureate of Canada," who hosts a musical program on CBC Stereo titled *As You Like It*. He won the 1994 Stephen Leacock Humour Medal for *Bachelor Brothers' Bed & Breakfast*, a series of lighthearted remembrances from fifty-something twins Hector and Virgil who manage a Gulf Islands retreat. He also writes for the *Sun* and *Georgia Straight*. His 1988 collection of memoirs, observations and poems is *Canada Customs*. He published humor and poetry in *Queen of the Dustballs* (1992).

Anthony Robertson (Tony) is a Vancouver screenwriter and critic whose 1984 appreciation of the life and works of Roderick Haig-Brown, *Above Tide*, describes and assesses the range of Haig-Brown's output.

Martin Robin, an SFU political scientist, explored the roots of extreme right-wing and racist groups in Canada between 1920 and 1940 in *Shades of Right*. His other books are *The Saga of Red Ryan, The Bad and the Lonely* and *Pillars of Profit: The Company Province* 1934-1972, the latter being one of the few critical views of W.A.C. Bennett's premiership. See David Mitchell.

Spider Robinson, a winner of the Hugo and Nebula Awards for science-fiction, was born in New York City in 1948. Like the protagonist in his novel *Stardance*, he came to Canada and fell in love with the Bay of Fundy; then he married dancer and choreographer Jeanne Robinson. The couple left Halifax after nine years and moved to Vancouver in 1987. They co-authored *Stardance*, in which a dancer realizes her dream of dancing in space with zero gravity. His best-known work is *Callaghan's Crosstime Saloon*.

Red Robinson. See Peggy Hodgins.

Fred Rogers is a Vancouver-born shipwreck historian whose 20 years of research for *Shipwrecks of British Columbia* in 1973 resulted in a B.C. bestseller that chronicles more than 100 shipwrecks and their discoveries. His 1992 follow-up is *More Shipwrecks of British Columbia*.

Gary Ross was born in Toronto in 1948 and settled in B.C. in 1989. He has twice won National Magazine Awards and created books from his research. *At Large*, his 1992 story of how American Murray Hill and two elephants were fugitives from the FBI, is slated to become a movie. His

Arthur Ellis Crime Writers Award-winning *Stung* chronicles the remarkable gambling addiction of embezzler Brian Molony, and has also attracted prospective movie producers. His other books are *Tears of the Moon* and a 1980 novel about gambling, *Always Tip The Dealer*.

Sinclair Ross received the Order of Canada in 1992. He is revered for his 1941 love story, *As For Me And My House*, about a preacher and his wife during the dustbowl days of the Depression. His other works include two short-story collections and three novels. Born on a homestead near Prince Albert, Saskatchewan in 1908, Ross worked on farms before turning to a banking career that lasted until his retirement in 1968 (interrupted only by four years in the Canadian army, 1942-46). Hampered by Parkinson's Disease, he has resided in Vancouver in relative obscurity since 1982. The 50th anniversary of the publication of *As For Me And My House* was marked by a symposium in Ottawa.

Sean Rossiter, born in Halifax in 1946, came to B.C. in 1972. He has been a freelance expert on Vancouver civic affairs for many years, while also teaching journalism. His essays on the history of aviation in *Legends of the Air* are drawn from 22 aircraft types housed in Seattle's Museum of Flight. He assisted CBC's Phil Reimer with the text for Reimer's *B.C. Weather Book*.

Sorelle Saidman is a Vancouver music industry columnist and freelance writer who has worked in the music business as a promoter, consultant and publicist. From 1984 to 1987 she produced fan club newsletters, press kits and program copy for Bryan Adams and Loverboy. Her biography, *Bryan Adams: Everything He Does* (1993), provides a straightforward account of Adams' rise to fame as one of the world's most popular rock stars.

John Schreiner, western editor of the *Financial Post* for 16 years, wrote *The World of Canadian Wine* and a company history of the Rogers Sugar Co., *The Refiners*, which details the rise of the first major B.C. industry not based on fishing or logging. In 1994 Schreiner also published an evaluative guide, *The Wineries of British Columbia*.

Andreas Schroeder was born into a Mennonite family in Germany in 1946 and emigrated in 1951. His early interest in surrealism and experimental writing at UBC was interrupted by an acclaimed non-fiction memoir of prison life, *Shaking It Rough*. His major novel *Dustship Glory* is loosely based on the true story of the quixotic Finnish-Canadian farmer Tom Sukanen who spent seven years building an ocean-going freighter in Saskatchewan. A former chair of the Writers' Union of Canada, Schroeder led the successful campaign to convince Ottawa to create the Public Lending Rights program which compensates Canadian authors for public use of their books in libraries.

Doris Shadbolt's *Emily Carr* is a thematic and definitive look at the art of Emily Carr with 125 photos of Carr's work. She wrote a critical study, *Bill Reid,* and co-created a fund to support young B.C. artists with Jack Shadbolt, her husband. Born and educated in Ontario, Doris Shadbolt divides her time between Hornby Island and Burnaby.

Michael Slade is two people, Vancouver lawyers Jay Clarke and John Banks, who teamed up (originally with a third lawyer, Richard Covell) in 1981 to write a crime thriller titled *Headhunter.* It was a success, so Clarke and Banks, while carrying on their respective law practices, also continued their literary collaboration. A 1996 entry is titled *Evil Eye.*

Ian Slater was born in Toowoomba, Australia, in 1941, and worked for the Australian Navy and Australian Intelligence. He published an acclaimed study of George Orwell, *Orwell: The Road to Airstrip One,* and edits *Pacific Affairs* at UBC, where he teaches. His string of prophetic novels about ecological and technological disasters began with *Firespill,* foreseeing an oil-tanker disaster on the West Coast, followed by *Sea Gold, Air Glow Red, Deep Chill, World War III: Rage of Battle* and *Forbidden Zone. MacArthur Must Die* (1994), is a thriller based on a fictional plot by War Minister Tojo to assassinate General Douglas MacArthur.

Michael Sone edited one of the most ambitious local histories ever undertaken in B.C., *Pioneer Tales of Burnaby* (1987). See also George Green's *History of Burnaby and Vicinity* (1947), and the entry on Pixie McGeachie.

Gordon Soules became an author after he and his wife Christine prepared an extensive sociological and economic study with Raymond Hull in 1974, *Vancouver's Past.* While operating Gordon Soules Book Publishers, which publishes books and also distributes independently prepared titles, he wrote *Vancouver at Your Feet.*

Jim Spilsbury, a West Coast renaissance man, was raised on Savary Island where he pioneered coastal radio communication. His first bestselling memoir, *Spilsbury's Coast,* was followed by his recollections of establishing Queen Charlotte Airlines as Canada's third largest airline in the 1950s, *The Accidental Airline* (both co-written with Howard White). His vast archive of photographs, now stored at UBC's Special Collections, is the basis of *Spilsbury's Album*—to be followed by a book featuring Spilsbury's coastal paintings. As a raconteur, inventor, entrepreneur, historian, painter and pioneer, he's the subject of a documentary film called *Spilsbury's Coast.* Born in England in 1905, he lives in West Vancouver.

Paul St. Pierre of Fort Langley and Sinaloa, Mexico is a former Liberal MP and columnist. His Chilcotin-based stories of ranchers and Indians in collections such as *Boss of the Namko Drive,* *Breaking Smith's Quarter Horse, Chilcotin Holiday* and *Smith and Other Events* arose from his 1950s CBC television series *Cariboo Country* (which launched the acting career of Chief Dan George). Mexican-based stories dominate his *Chilcotin and Beyond.* His other titles are *Sister Balonika* and a coffee-table book, *British Columbia Our Land.* Born in Chicago in 1923, he grew up in Nova Scotia and came to Vancouver in 1945. He is the first Canadian to receive the Western Writers of America Spur Award.

Ulli Steltzer's photography and Robert Bringhurst's text for *The Black Canoe* received the Bill Duthie Booksellers' Choice Award in 1992. Steltzer has also collaborated with writer Catherine Kerr for *Coast of Many Faces,* which continued Steltzer's concern for photographing people "in a culture gap." Following two years in the Canadian Arctic she produced *Inuit.* Other Steltzer titles are *Indian Artists at Work* and *The New Americans.* Steltzer was born in Frankfurt, Germany, in 1923, emigrated to the U.S. in 1953 and moved to Vancouver in 1972.

Hilary Stewart of Quadra Island and Vancouver is an authority on northwest Indian art and culture. Her *Cedar* examines the ways native cultures have utilized cedar; *John R. Jewitt, Captive of Maquinna* is another retelling of the famous captivity of the stranded English sailor. Both received B.C. Book Prizes. Other titles include *Indian Artifacts of the Northwest Coast, Indian Fishing, Robert Davidson: Haida Printmaker* and *Totem Poles.* She was born in St. Lucia, West Indies, in 1924, educated in England and came to Canada in 1951.

Randy Stoltmann, who died while this book was in production, was a hiker and photographer whose *Hiking Guide to the Big Trees of Southwestern British Columbia* was released in 1987 to help stimulate the preservation of forests. He claimed that 81.2 per cent of B.C.'s land was covered by provincial forests and tree farm licences; parks comprised 5.4 per cent and ecological reserves comprised 0.1 per cent. (The Western Canada Wilderness Committee, under Paul George, has released numerous other forest ecology titles such as Joan E. Vance's *Tree Planning: A Guide to Public Involvement in Forest Stewardship* from the B.C. Public Interest Advocacy Centre.)

Gerald Straley has written six books on B.C. vegetation. His *Trees of Vancouver* identifies 470 varieties of trees. He is a research scientist at the UBC Botanical Garden who has co-authored the four-volume ministry of forests series which catalogues all the plants in the province.

Peter Stursberg, born in China in 1913, has written books about prime ministers Diefenbaker and Pearson, Governor General Roland Michener, Gordon Shrum and *The Golden Hope,* which chronicles Anglican missions in China from 1890 to 1950. His journalism career started in 1934 with the *Victoria Daily Times.* For the Sound Heritage series he wrote a history of early Vancouver and Victoria journalism, *Extra! When The Papers Had The Only News.* He lives in West Vancouver.

David Suzuki, Canada's best-known scientist, says he has lost faith in the power of television to create change after hosting CBC's *The Nature of Things* since 1974. Increasingly turning to books, the UBC-based geneticist has produced *Inventing the Future, Wisdom of the Elders* (with Peter Knudtson), *It's A Matter of Survival* (with Anita Gordon), *Genethics* (with Peter Knudtson) and a bestselling autobiography, *Metamorphosis: Stages in a Life,* plus numerous educational titles for children. Born in Vancouver in 1936, he was interned for three years with his family during World War II, then grew up in Leamington, Ontario before attending universities in the U.S. Partly because he was repelled by racial tensions in the U.S., he returned to Canada to teach at the University of Alberta and UBC, where he gained an international reputation for his work on fruit-fly genetics.

Joe Swan, a retired Vancouver police staff-sergeant, once operated the Vancouver Police Centennial Museum and wrote an historical crime column for the West Ender. His accounts of murder cases are reprinted in *Century of Service: Vancouver Police 1886-1986* and *Police Beat: 24 Vancouver Murders.*

Ben Swankey was born in Steinbach, Manitoba, in 1913 and moved to Vancouver in 1957. As owner of Heritage Biographies, he has devoted much of his life to history and economic analysis from a left-wing perspective. *Man Along The Shore* is a Vancouver waterfront history. *The Fraser Institute* evaluates the right-wing think-tank.

Robert Swanson wrote Robert Service-like verse about oldtime logging in the 1940s and 1950s, selling 80,000 copies of his books. The best of his poems have been collected in *Bard of the Woods.* He was also one of the world's leading sound technicians and sound inventors. Swanson's steam whistles and musical horns are used around the world. They include the noon "Oh Canada" serenade (for many years atop the B.C. Hydro building) and the Gastown steam clock whistle. He was born in Reading, England, in October of 1905 and died in Vancouver in October of 1994.

David Tarrant, host of CBC-TV's *The Canadian Gardener,* has been education coordinator at UBC's Botanical Garden since 1974. His books include *David Tarrant's Pacific Gardening Guide, Highrise Horticulture* and *A Year in Your Garden.* In 1994 he published *David Tarrant's Canadian Gardens.* (The West Coast's best-known gardener in the 1970s and early 1980s was Bernard Moore, whose publications include *Pruning with Bernard Moore* (1981) from Intermedia Press. See also Bill

Vander Zalm.)

Jim Taylor is B.C.'s most widely read sports columnist. His 1987 chronicle of Rick Hansen's wheelchair journey, *Man In Motion,* had a record first printing for a B.C. book. In addition to Taylor's books on Wayne Gretzky, Debbie Brill and B.C. Lion Jim Young (*Dirty Thirty*), Taylor was recently credited with the rewrite of a Soviet journalist's biography of Igor Larionov.

Audrey Thomas was the first winner of the Ethel Wilson B.C. Fiction Prize for her 1984 novel *Intertidal Life.* She was born in 1935, raised in New York state, emigrated in 1959 and attended UBC. Her short-story collections include *Ladies and Escorts, Two in the Bush and Other Stories, Real Mothers, Goodbye Harold, Good Luck* and *The Wild Blue Yonder,* for which she also won the Wilson Prize in 1991. Other novels are *Blown Figures* and *Latakia.* She lives on Galiano Island.

Phil Thomas, B.C.'s leading folk-music historian, was forced to take a remote teaching job in Pender Harbour in 1949 when he was suspected of being a Communist by the Delta School Board. In Pender Harbour Thomas met legendary B.C. author and fisherman Bill Sinclair who inspired Thomas to collect distinctly British Columbian songs. Thomas' books are *Songs of the Pacific Northwest* and *Twenty-five Songs for Vancouver 1886-1986.* His archives are in the Royal B.C. Museum and he remains active as a banjo player, singer and composer in the Vancouver Folk Song Circle which he, his wife Hilda and others founded in 1959. He was born in Victoria.

Peter Trower, formerly known as B.C.'s "voice from the bunkhouse," was born in St. Leonard's, England, in 1930 and came to Canada in 1940. He studied for two years at Vancouver School of Art and worked for 22 years as a logger. A writer since 1971, he was the subject of a 1976 CBC film, *Between the Sky and the Splinters,* also the title of his 1974 poetry collection, and collaborated with logging illustrator Bus Griffiths for *Bush Poems. Ragged Horizons* in 1978 was a retrospective collection of earlier works, followed by *Goosequill Snags, The Sliding Back Mountains* and *Unmarked Doorways.* Trower contributed one of the best bibliographic articles on logging-related literature, *Caulk-Boot Legacy: Logging Poetry in B.C.,* which appeared in *Raincoast Chronicles.* His novel loosely based on Minstrel Island, *Grogan's Cafe,* appeared in 1993. A 1996 novel is titled *Dead Man's Ticket.*

Michael Turner formed the hillbilly recording group Hard Rock Miners after acquiring an anthropology degree from UVic. Having spent his summers working in a fish cannery on the Skeena River, he wrote a first book of poems, *Company Town,* which records a year in the life of a northern B.C. cannery called Raspaco. His second book, *Hard Core Logo,* was an amalgam of short pieces

about the reunion of a rock band (recently made into a feature film). Turner is widely publicized for coordinating readings at the Railway Club in Vancouver and the Malcolm Lowry Room in Burnaby. He was born in North Vancouver in 1962.

Robert Turner, chief of historical collections at the Royal B.C. Museum, is the leading historical expert on B.C. transportation. Born (1947) into a pioneer B.C. family, Turner began publishing in 1973 with *Vancouver Island Railroads,* followed by *Logging by Rail, The Pacific Princesses, The Pacific Empresses, Sternwheelers and Steam Tugs* and *West of the Great Divide* which won the Canadian Railroad Historical Association's Book Award in 1987.

Alan Twigg is the publisher of *B.C. BookWorld,* founded in 1978. His *Vancouver and Its Writers* is the first book-length overview of B.C. authors. *For Openers: Conversations with 24 Canadian Writers* and *Strong Voices: Conversations with 50 Canadian Authors* were interspersed with a 1985 biography, *Hubert Evans: The First Ninety-Three Years.* He also wrote the first critical book on Bill Vander Zalm in 1986, *Vander Zalm: From Immigrant to Premier,* and published *Twigg's Directory of 1,001 B.C. Authors* in 1992. He co-founded the B.C. Book Prizes and the VanCity Book Prize. He produced a documentary film, *Spilsbury's Coast,* which aired on CBC, and in 1994 organized events honoring George Woodcock. Born in 1952, Twigg grew up in West Vancouver.

Freda Van der Ree's comprehensive guidebook to 51 of the most enticing boating areas in the Strait of Georgia and Puget Sound, *Exploring the Coast by Boat,* has had numerous printings since 1979.

Peter Vassilopoulos was born in Capetown, South Africa, in 1940. An avid boater and scuba diver, he came to B.C. in 1973 and began a series of articles for *Pacific Yachting.* His resulting book on old B.C. vessels is *Antiques Afloat.* He lives in Tsawwassen and has published *Diver Magazine,* a national publication, since the late 1970s.

Eleanor Wachtel was host of *The Arts Tonight* on CBC Radio, and a frequent interviewer of authors. She co-edited *The Expo Story* with SFU communication professor Robert Anderson, an anthology of essays expressing criticism of Expo 86. She was born in Montreal in 1947.

Jill Wade teaches B.C. history in the university program at the Open Learning Agency in Burnaby. Her book, *Houses for All* (1994), is the story of the struggle for social housing in Vancouver between 1919 and 1950.

Tamio Wakayama was born in New Westminster in 1941 and spent his early childhood in an internment camp at Tashme, B.C. He studied journalism and philosophy in Toronto and joined the civil rights movement in the U.S. in 1963. His sixth book, *Kikyo: Coming Home to Powell Street,* documents the history of the Powell Street Festival

with his photographs and testimony from 80 people who have been involved in the annual event.

Michael Walsh, longtime film critic for the *Province,* wrote *The Canadian Movie Quiz Book* in 1979 and contributed the section on Vancouver-made films in this book. Born in Toronto in 1945, he came to B.C. in 1969.

Peter Ward, born in 1943, won the 1990 Certificate of Merit from the Social Sciences Federation of Canada for *White Canada Forever,* his study of anti-Asian attitudes and policies in B.C. A UBC history professor, he is also the author of *Courtship, Love and Marriage in Nineteenth-Century Canada.*

Robin Ward was born in Glasgow in 1950. He worked for Hudson's Bay trading posts and as a miner in northern Manitoba before returning to Scotland to study graphic design at the Glasgow School of Art. He subsequently published three books on Scottish architecture. Formerly a design manager for the BBC in London, he fulfilled a longtime ambition to live in Vancouver (which he visited briefly as a young man) and now writes a regular column on architecture for the *Vancouver Sun.* His drawings and commentaries comprise *Robin Ward's Vancouver.* He co-wrote, designed and photographed *Exploring Vancouver.* His most recent book is *Echoes of Empire,* the story of Victoria's buildings. He designed *The Greater Vancouver Book.*

David Watmough has written numerous connected works of fiction about his fictional counterpart, Davey Bryant, who is also a Cornish-raised author, an immigrant to Vancouver and a homosexual in a long-standing relationship. *Thy Mother's Glass* in 1993 followed such works as *Ashes for Easter, No More Into the Garden, Fury Vibrations in Time, The Year of Fears* and *Families.* He was born in London in 1926 and moved to the U.S. in 1952, living first in New York and then in San Francisco. He moved to Vancouver in 1960 and became a Canadian citizen in 1967. His readings are available on a CD called *Vibrations.* His 1994 novel is *The Time of the Kingfishers.*

Scott Watson's biographical study of Jack Shadbolt, *Shadbolt,* won the 1991 Evans Non-fiction Prize. A signed, limited edition of the book with 190 illustrations was also made available at $575, making it one of the most expensive books ever produced in B.C. A former curator of the Vancouver Art Gallery and the UBC Fine Arts Gallery, Watson is also an arts critic who contributed the text for the book-length catalogue accompanying bill bissett's VAG exhibit. A slim collection of five stories from Watson, *Stories,* appeared in 1974.

Jack Webster has been B.C.'s best-known broadcaster, switching from radio to television in 1978. His autobiography, *Webster!,* looks beyond his celebrated media career to reveal personal struggles as a family man in West Vancouver. The son of a Glasgow ironworker, he married his teenaged sweetheart after persuading her to give up their child. Thirty-six years later, she successfully traced her long-lost child's whereabouts. He is retired, with property on Saltspring Island.

Terri Wershler wrote *The Vancouver Guide*, which has so far sold more than 100,000 copies, and works as a freelance production coordinator and book packager. She was born in Winnipeg in 1950 and came to B.C. in 1969.

Howard White, born in Abbotsford in 1945, spent part of his childhood on Nelson Island. After attending UBC, he started the regional journal *Raincoast Chronicles* in 1972, which led to the founding of Harbour Publishing. His labor biography, *A Hard Man To Beat,* replicates the voice of Bill White (no relation) and he has co-authored the bestsellers *Spilsbury's Coast* and *The Accidental Airline* with Jim Spilsbury. He has written two books of poems and a children's book, *Patrick and the Backhoe*. In 1991 White received the Stephen Leacock Medal for Humour for *Writing in the Rain,* a collection of stories and articles.

Bill Wolferstan's four-volume *Cruising Guides to B.C.* is the most ambitious canon of coastal guides available. Born in Vancouver in 1942, Wolferstan was a lieutenant in the Royal Canadian Signal Corps and then a geography master in Bournemouth, England, before returning to study at SFU. He has been a government researcher since 1973 and director of the SALT Society since 1983. In 1986 he edited *The Pacific Swift,* about building and sailing a tall ship. He lives in Victoria. (As well, Victoria's Shirley Hewett has two books related to sailing, *Swiftsure, The First 50 Years* and *Down The Hatch, Royally.*)

Paul Wong is a multimedia artist who edited *Yellow Peril Reconsidered,* a collaborative art book by 25 Asian-Canadian artists which examined cultural and personal relations between Asian-Canadians and Canadian society as a whole.

George Woodcock was B.C.'s most distinguished and prolific man of letters. Born in Winnipeg on May 8, 1912, and raised in England, he never attended university. As a conscientious objector during World War II he befriended writers such as Herbert Read, George Orwell and Julian Symons. His first book was *Aphra Behn: The English Sappho,* a study of a free-spirited British female novelist. As an anarchist he was inspired by the Doukhobors to return to Canada in 1949. He briefly homesteaded on a farm near Sooke with his wife Ingeborg. They settled in Vancouver with the assistance of Earle Birney and their longtime friends, Jack and Doris Shadbolt. He wrote and edited most of his approximately 150 books on the same black Underwood typewriter in a modest home in Kerrisdale. His biography of George Orwell is *The Crystal Spirit*. He has written books on Gabriel Dumont, Pierre-Joseph Proudhon,

Thomas Merton, Oscar Wilde and Amor De Cosmos (to name a few). His 1962 history, *Anarchism,* is a definitive text, as is his fair-minded *The Doukhobors,* co-written with Ivan Avakumovic. Other books on B.C. include his travel narrative *Ravens and Prophets* from 1952, *People of the Coast* and *British Columbia: A History of the Province.* At UBC he was the founding editor of *Canadian Literature,* the first publication exclusively devoted to the study of Canadian literature. Collections of poems include *Tolstoy at Yasnaya Polyana* and *The Cherry Tree on Cherry Street.* His books on China include *Caves in the Desert* and *Voices from Tiananmen Square.* He and Ingeborg Woodcock raised money for India and Tibet by establishing independent relief agencies and publishing two books based on writing contests, *The Dry Wells of India* and *The Great Canadian Anecdote Contest.* Later books include an iconoclastic review of how history has been recorded through the ages, *The Monk and his Message* and *A Social History of Canada.* In 1994 he became the first writer in Vancouver's history to receive Freedom of the City. The largest gathering of authors in Canada's history occurred in his honor on George Woodcock Day, May 7, 1994, at the Vancouver law courts. His oldest friend, Julian Symons, wrote, "I know of nobody who has been of more generous help to others, or has pursued good ends in life more unswervingly." Woodcock died January 28, 1995.

Alan Woodland, a native of New Westminster, published *New Westminster: The Early Years, 1858-1898* while he was the city's chief librarian. The 1973 book contains 118 photos dating back to when the "Royal City" was the capital of the Colony of British Columbia.

L.R. Wright (Laurali "Bunny" Wright) is Canada's leading female author of mysteries. Born in Saskatoon in 1939 and raised in Abbotsford, she left a newspaper job in Mission to work for major newspapers in the prairies. She received the Alberta First Novel Award in 1979 for *Neighbours,* which was followed by two more realistic novels, *The Favorite* and *Among Friends.* Her set-in-Sechelt tale about an 80-year-old committing murder, *The Suspect,* received the Mystery Writers of America Edgar Allan Poe Award for best novel in 1985. Its success has prompted a string of popular, low-key Sechelt mysteries: *Sleep While I Sing, A Chill Rain in January, Fall From Grace, Prized Possessions, A Touch of Panic* and *Mother Love.* The latter won the 1996 Arthur Ellis Award for the best Canadian crime novel of the year. All seven books feature a slow-brewing romance between the town librarian, Cassandra, and RCMP inspector Karl Alberg. Her 1988 novel about a middle-aged relationship is *Love in the Temperate Zone.* She lives in Burnaby.

Max Wyman (b. 1939) of Lions Bay is an English-

born journalist who moved to Vancouver from London in 1967. A long-serving arts critic for the *Vancouver Sun* and the *Province,* he is the book editor for the *Sun's* Saturday Review. He has served as a national assessor of dance companies for the Canada Council since 1976. His books include *The Royal Winnipeg Ballet: The First Forty Years, Dance Canada: An Illustrated History* and *Evelyn Hart: An Intimate Portrait.* With the support of Vancouver businessman David Lemon, Wyman edited a 1992 collection of essays by Vancouver artists, *Vancouver Forum I: Old Powers, New Forces.*

Michael Yates, founder of Sono Nis Press, is one of Canada's most determinedly experimental writers. He was born in Fulton, Missouri, in 1938, educated at the universities of Missouri and Michigan, and joined UBC's creative writing faculty from 1966 to 1971. He has written many books of poetry and prose works such as *man in the glass octopus* and *the abstract beast.* Formerly an SFU Ph.D candidate in criminology, he worked in the 1980s as a prison guard and wrote a well-received memoir, *Line Screw* (1993).

Paul Yee is the first recipient of the Vancouver Book Award for his illustrated history of Vancouver's Chinese community, *Saltwater City.* His collection of New World folktales illustrated by Simon Ng, *Tales from Gold Mountain,* received the Egoff Children's Prize. He was born in Spalding, Saskatchewan, in 1956 but moved to Vancouver shortly thereafter, where he grew up in Chinatown. Formerly an archivist for the City of Vancouver, he left Vancouver to become multicultural coordinator for the Archives of Ontario.

Poet and novelist Peter Trower, 1986
bc bookworld photo

Bookstores in Greater Vancouver
John Cochlin

Albany Books
1319B-56th Street, Delta, 943-2293

Albion Books
532 Richards Street, Vancouver, 662-3113

Amber Bookshop Ltd
2460A Marine Drive, West Vancouver, 926-1133

Anvil Book Store
706 Sixth Street, New Westminster, 526-3311

Arcanum Book Shop
3740 Hastings Street, Burnaby, 294-9311

Ariana's Books & Benefits
9248C Main Street, Chilliwack, 729-8923

Banyen Books
2671 Broadway West, Vancouver, 732-7912

Better Buy Books
4443 West 10th Avenue, Vancouver, 224-4144

Black Bond Books
Guildford Town Centre, 1381 Guildford Town Centre, Surrey, 589-3680
Haney Place Mall, 141-11900 Haney Place, Maple Ridge, 463-8624
Scottsdale Mall, 7023-120th St, Delta, BC, 591-8757
2381 Surrey Place Mall, P.O. Box 2769, Surrey, 583-1282
Willowbrook Shopping Centre, 442-19705 Fraser Hwy, Langley, 533-7577
21-32700 S. Fraser Way, Abbotsford, 859-7701

Black Sheep Books
2742 West 4th Avenue, Vancouver, 732-5087

Blackberry Books
2855 West Broadway, Vancouver, 739-8477
1663 Duranleau Street, Vancouver, 685-4113

Bollum's Books
710 Granville Street, Vancouver, 689-1802

Bonanza Books & Video
1123 Granville Street, Vancouver, 684-3775

Bonjour Books
2135-11821 Horseshoe Way, Richmond, 271-2665

Book Company
650 West 41st Avenue, Oakridge Centre, Vancouver, 264-9245
2929 Barnet Highway, Coquitlam, 944-0799
100 Park Royal North, West Vancouver, 922-5125

Book Warehouse
19559 Fraser Highway, Surrey, 532-5711
2388 West 4th Avenue, Vancouver, 733-5721
Unit M 163-4820 Kingsway, Burnaby, 434-5711
1150 Robson Street, Vancouver, 685-5711
632 West Broadway, Vancouver, 872-5711

Booktique
2960 Granville Street, Vancouver, 736-3727

Burnaby Books
4435 Hastings Street, Burnaby, 298-0038

Burquitlam Books
552C Clarke Road, Coquitlam, 939-6366

Carolyn's Book Store
120-22441 Dewdney Trunk Rd, Maple Ridge, 463-2122

Chapters
1174-4700 Kingsway, Burnaby, 431-0463
8171 Ackroyd Road, Richmond, 303-7392

Cloverdale Books
5667-176th Street, Surrey, 576-9476

Coast Bookstore
277 Gower Place-Box 520, 886-7744

Cody Books
3200 East 54th Avenue, Vancouver, 437-5553
810 Front Street, New Westminster, 525-9850
2 3000 Lougheed Highway, Port Coquitlam, 464-5515

Coles Bookstore
948 Park Royal South, Park Royal Shopping Centre, West Vancouver, 926-6216
12R-6060 Minoru Blvd, Richmond, 273-811
33H-777 Dunsmuir Street, Pacific Centre Mall, Vancouver, 688-3231
9855 Austin Avenue, Lougheed Mall, Burnaby, 421-0312
20-1199 Lynn Valley Road, Lynn Valley Shopping Centre, North Vancouver, 980-5429
2100-2929 Barnet Hwy, Coquitlam Centre, Coquitlam, 464-5815
1206 Guildford Town Centre, Surrey, 584-8044
102-4800 Kingsway, Metrotown Centre, Burnaby, 435-3910
956-5300 No. 3 Road, Lansdowne Park Shopping Centre, Richmond, 270-2032
223A-4567 Lougheed Highway, Brentwood Mall, Burnaby, 294-2922
75-935 Marine Drive, Capilano Mall, North Vancouver, 985-2001
C-19705 Fraser Highway, Langley, 530-2244
2082 Surrey Place Mall, Surrey Place Shopping Centre, Surrey, 581-0800
209-610 Sixth Street, Royal City Centre Shopping Centre, New Westminster, 540-1782

Copper Beach Books
121B 13745 72nd Avenue, Surrey, 594-2627

Cottage Books Ltd
8266-160th Street, Surrey, 597-3653

Dead Write Books
4374 West 10th Avenue, Vancouver, 228-8223

Duthie Books
919 Robson Street, Vancouver, 684-4496
2239 West 4th Avenue, Vancouver, 737-5344
4255 Arbutus Street, Vancouver, 738-1833
4444 West 10th Avenue, Vancouver, 224-7012
205-345 Robson Street, Vancouver, 602-0610
1701 West 3rd Avenue, Vancouver, 732-1448

Eaton's-Book Deptartment
701 Granville Street, Vancouver, 685-7112 Ext. 4567

Family Book Shoppe
c/o 7761 Barrymore Drive, Delta, 594-4428

Gold Bond Books City Square
555 West 12th Avenue, Vancouver, 872-5554

Granville Book Company
850 Granville Street, Vancouver, 687-2213

Hager Books
2176 West 41st Avenue, Vancouver, 263-9412

Haney Book & Novelties
22330 Dewdney Trunk Road, Maple Ridge, 467-4913

Imperial Book Store
617 Main Street, Vancouver, 669-8638

Imperial Books
4924 Imperial Street, Burnaby, 432-9940

Iwase Books
2535-3700 No. 3 Road, Richmond, 231-0701

Jane Ross Books
129-1711 152nd Street, White Rock, 531-1716

Kidsbooks In The Village
3040 Edgemont Blvd., North Vancouver, 986-6190

Kidsbooks On Broadway
3083 West Broadway, Vancouver, 738-5335

Kirkwood Books
8662 Granville Street, Vancouver, 263-4660

Lady Rose Book Store
P.O. Box 41, Bowen Island, 947-2929

Little Sisters Books & Art
1221 Thurlow Street, Vancouver, 669-1753

Lunsford Books
711-207 West Hastings Street, Vancouver, 681-6830

Macleod's Books
435 West Pender Street, Vancouver, 681-7654

Mallard Books
184-8120 No. 2 Road, Richmond, 275-3825

The West Coast has been home to many writers over the years, and British Columbians are the most avid readers in the country. Vancouver's flourishing literary community is well served by the city's many bookstores, which cater to a diverse population and an increasing tourist trade. Besides offering the best books from around the world, Vancouver bookstores have always supported local writers and featured books which celebrate our region.

Manhattan Books & Magazines
1089 Robson Street, Vancouver, 681-9074

McNews
1460 Lonsdale Avenue, North Vancouver, 984-9412

Michael Thompson Bookseller
1111-510 Hastings St, Vancouver, 682-6885

Murdoch Book Shoppe
33078 1st Avenue, Mission, 826-9229

Mystery Merchant Book Store
1952 West 4th Avenue, Vancouver, 734-4311

Northshore Books
140 East 14th Street, North Vancouver, 983-9855

Odin Books
1522 West Broadway, Vancouver, 739-8804

Oscar's Art Books
1533 West Broadway, Vancouver, 731-0553

Pacific Books
1144 Lonsdale Avenue, North Vancouver, 980-2121

Page One Books
3980 Main Street, Vancouver, 877-7766

Pathfinder Book Store
3967 Main Street, Vancouver, 872-8343

People's Co-op Book Store
1391 Commerical Drive, Vancouver, 253-6442

Royal Book Mart
600 Agnes Street, New Westminster, 521-3332

Save-On Foods
Book Dept., 6100 McKay Avenue, Burnaby, 433-2774
Book Dept., 9014-152nd Street, Surrey, 930-1133
Book Dept., 7015-120th Street, North Delta, 596-2944
Book Dept., 8200 Ackroyd Road, Richmond, 278-3933
Book Dept., 333 Brooksbank Avenue, North Vancouver, 983-3033
Book Dept., 2991 Lougheed Highway, Coquitlam, 464-9111
Book Dept., 1250 Marine Drive, North Vancouver, 986-0463
Book Dept., 1641-152nd Street, White Rock, 536-4522
Book Dept., 300-32700 S. Fraser Way, Clearbrook, 854-5318
Book Dept., 46020 Yale Road, Chilliwack, 792-7520

Simon Fraser University Bookstore
Simon Fraser University, Burnaby Mountain, Burnaby, 291-3656
Harbour Centre Campus, 515 W. Hastings Street, Vancouver, 291-5048

Smithbooks
924 Park Royal South, West Vancouver, 922-0033
Seven Oaks Mall, 32900 S. Fraser Way, Abbotsford, 859-6440
595 Burrard Street, Box 49156-Bentall Centre, Vancouver, 689-8231
1230-6551 No. 3 Road, Richmond Centre, Richmond, 273-7114
212-5300 No. 3 Road, Lansdowne Shopping Centre, Richmond, 273-3557
700 W. Georgia Street, Box 10163-Pacific Centre, Vancouver, 669-9311
Vancouver Int'l Airport, Richmond, 270-1421
4567 Lougheed Hwy., Brentwood Mall, Burnaby, 298-2825

Sophia Bookstore Ltd
725 Nelson Street, Vancouver, 684-4032

Spartacus Books
311 W. Hastings Street, Vancouver, 688-6138

SRS Book Boutique & Gifts Inc.
1616-152nd Street, White Rock, 538-6226

Stairways Bookshop
104-20560 56th Avenue, Langley, 530-9528

Steveston Book Store
3760 Moncton Street, Richmond, 274-3604

Stillman Books
1321 Kingsway, Vancouver, 877-1712

Superior Book Store Co Ltd
166 E. Pender Street, Vancouver, 669-6288

Talewind Books
Box 919, 5494 Trail Avenue, Sechelt, 885-2527

UBC Bookstore
6200 University Boulevard, UBC, Vancouver, 822-2665

Vine & Fig Tree Books
4109 Macdonald Street, Vancouver, 734-2109

Whitby's Bookstore
14837 Marine Drrive, White Rock, 536-3711

White Dwarf Books Ltd
4368 West 10th Avenue, Vancouver, 228-8223

White Rose New & Used Books
1481 Johnston Road, White Rock, 531-7353

Williams Books
3007 Granville Street, Vancouver, 733-1326

Women in Print
3566 West 4th Avenue, Vancouver, 732-4128

Zebra Books
1095 Hornby Street, Vancouver, 331-0033

A man will turn over half a library to make one book
—*Samuel Johnson*

Never read any book that is not a year old
—*Ralph Waldo Emerson*

When a new book is published, read an old one
—*Samuel Rogers*

A good book is the best of friends, the same today and for ever
—*Martin Tupper*

Public Libraries of Greater Vancouver

BRITISH COLUMBIA

The Library Services Branch of the Ministry of Municipal Affairs and Housing, Province of B.C., provides financial assistance and special programs for Greater Vancouver public library boards. The Branch also helps fund InterLINK, a partnership of twelve library boards providing free access to public library service throughout the region. Through its Burnaby office, the Branch produces audiobooks for people with visual or neurological impairments and provides access to special materials for libraries with special needs clients.

Vancouver Public Library
Sandra McKenzie

ON MAY 26, 1995, THE LATEST, and possibly most contentious, chapter in the history of the Vancouver Public Library began. Proudly on-time and on-budget, Library Square comprises a seven-storey central library and a federal office complex wrapped in an elliptical colonnade. It occupies a city block bounded by Hamilton, Robson, Homer and Georgia. At $100 million, this is the single largest civic project ever undertaken in Vancouver. The $30 million, 35,150 sq. metre library boasts twice the space of its predecessor and, with 1,200 chairs, seats four times as many patrons.

There was never any serious question that a new central library was in order for Canada's most literate city. The old facility, built in 1957 at Robson and Burrard, was designed to accommodate 750,000 volumes, with seating for 300 patrons. In the intervening years the VPL's collection, which numbers over 1.4 million items, and public demand for the library's services, swelled well past this capacity. Despite seconding the auditorium, several meeting rooms and much of the seating space to shelf space, nearly a third of the collection was stored in the basement, while more than 5,000 patrons a day scrambled for scarce chairs.

On November 10, 1988, then-mayor Gordon Campbell promised a program that would lead to a new central library. The news came none too soon. On August 19, 1988, a high-pressure water main broke, flooding the basement of the old library, imperiling 200,000 items, and forcing a one-day closure. Workers mopped up much of the mess, using 2,000 kilograms of newsprint to blot the moisture out of the less severely damaged items. Another 3,500 items were rescued when BC Ice and Cold Storage froze the books to prevent mildew until they could be shipped to BMS Catastrophe Ltd., in Fort Worth, Texas. There the books were freeze-dried, and the resultant ice crystals removed, preserving fragile paper and bindings. Losses included 400 books, as well as several art periodicals printed on clay-coated paper stock that turned to muck in the flood. Also lost was a complete, bound collection of *Vancouver Sun* and *Province* newspapers dated from 1939 to 1961.

By January 11, 1989, the freeze-dried books were back on the shelves. In November 1990 close to 70 per cent of the city's voters endorsed capital spending for a new library facility, raising a capital fund of about $36 million.

The controversy began when City Council elected to hold a

facing page: Library Square, Vancouver, 1995. vs

limited architectural competition for this lucrative and important civic commission. From among a field of 27 consortia of local and international architects, the VPL selection committee culled three teams, all working in a joint venture with local firms: Toronto's Kuwabara Payne McKenna Blumberg, with James Cheng and Musson Cattel Mackey; Los Angeles' Hardy Holzer Pfeiffer, with Waisman Dewar Grout, and Boston's Moshe Safdie, with Downs/Archambault. Frozen out of the competition were home-grown favorites Arthur Erickson and Richard Henriquez.

The finalists submitted elaborate models of their visions to public scrutiny in February 1992. Moshe Safdie's great ellipse, strikingly reminiscent of an ancient Roman amphitheatre, was the overwhelming popular favorite. Of the 7,000 citizens who submitted remarks, approximately 70 per cent favored the Colosseum, as the proposal was promptly dubbed.

While the public input was not binding on the decision-makers, there was a risk that the people would endorse a scheme that the jury, which included Mayor Campbell and two councillors, simply could not recommend. In the end, the judges unanimously approved Safdie's design, noting its ability to "function as an efficient and enjoyable library, as well as an important symbolic centre of learning." They awarded the commission with the proviso that the architects resolve the structural and financial shortcomings.

On June 16 the architects presented a revised model to city council. To the architecturally uninitiated, the edited version is virtually indistinguishable from the original. The only visible change is the site of the office tower, originally placed on the southeast corner, now flipped to the northwest, thus bringing a wash of natural light into the heart of the library. If these changes compromise the earlier vision, those concessions are well hidden.

While the architecture leaves room for a wide variety of opinions, there is no argument that the facility itself is a high-tech harbinger of the 21st century. Among the innovations are scanners for self-serve book borrowing, a $3 million on-line catalogue system, 216 in-house terminals and ten modem telephone lines, as well as CD-ROMs, card-operated printers and plans for Internet hook-ups. Computer-toting patrons can plug into carrels wired for full access to the VPL's internal data base. New (and controversial) user-fees for such specialized services as corporate research will help pay for these and other amenities.

In its time the Robson and Burrard main branch was hailed as the most modern library on the continent. In 1957 the sleek, modernist structure, Vancouver's first glass curtain building, designed by architects H.N. Semmens and D.C. Simpson, was awarded the Massey Medal, Canada's highest architectural honor. However, the years, and public taste, were not kind to

Sponsored by the Ministry of Municipal Affairs and Housing, Province of British Columbia.

its once-shimmering street presence. After nearly four decades of use, its transparent facade was gray and grimy, and the well trodden interior was scarcely worth preserving. Despite preservationists' interest in its architectural significance, there was little public sympathy for the building's fifties-style modernism. The Library Board, concerned with realizing fair market value for this site, took no partisan stand in its fate. Fortunately, the forces for heritage preservation won out, and the building has gained a second life. After extensive renovations, the old building reopened with a music megastore at street level, and a restaurant upstairs.

Vancouver's long and often stormy relationship with its libraries dates back over a century, with competing Mechanics Institutes claiming the distinction of being the area's first library. On the north side of Burrard Inlet, on January 23, 1869, Sewell P. Moody, manager of the Vancouver Island Spar, Lumber and Sawmill Hastings Mill (later renamed Hastings Mill) started the New London Mechanics Institute, complete with reading room, for his mill's employees.

In 1886 Rev. Henry G. Fiennes-Clinton spearheaded a movement to establish a permanent library. In December 1887, with a donation of 400 volumes for the old Hastings Mill collection, Fiennes-Clinton, aided by a small committee, opened the Vancouver Reading Room above Thomas Dunn's Hardware Store at 136 Cordova Street. The first librarians were George Pollay, a cooper, and his wife, who served without pay until 1889. The free circulating library survived, thanks in large part to the Pollays, and to grants from city council. The first grant of $250 was awarded in 1888.

The next year Edwin Machin, a young English lawyer, succeeded Pollay. For a wage of $65 a month, Machin acted as janitor and librarian. In 1893 the library relocated to the YMCA building at 169 West Hastings Street. Machin fought for a dedicated building to house the expanding collection, which by 1894 numbered 2,500 books and several periodicals. As the city's population grew, so did its library. By 1903 there were more than 8,000 books and circulation figures reached 44,000.

In 1901 US Steel magnate and philanthropist Andrew Carnegie offered the city a grant of $50,000 to build a new library on condition that the city commit $5,000 yearly to its maintenance and expansion. The city accepted the offer and, after much debate about the proposed site, assigned architect G.W. Grant to supervise construction. Edwin Machin's dream of a real library opened its great doors at Westminster (now Main) and Hastings in November 1903.

Machin resigned as librarian in 1910. The following year R.W. Douglas of Toronto was appointed librarian. Criticized for his poor judgement in acquiring rare and beautiful books at the expense of the library as a whole, Douglas resigned in 1924. He left a legacy of acquisitions that would grow into the library's treasured special collections.

The new librarian, Edgar Stewart Robinson, took charge of a collection of 60,000 books, reorganized the main branch to include a bindery, promoted the concept of branch libraries, and began dreaming of a new building. Alas, the Great Depression intervened, and budget cuts forced a drastic reduction in the library's staff, operating hours and services.

With the end of the Second World War in 1945, Robinson renewed his battle for more money, more books, more staff and a new building. In 1952 the city acquiesced, purchasing the Robson and Burrard site. Semmens and Simpson were commissioned to design the new facility in 1954. On November 1, 1957—a week after Robinson died of a heart attack—the new central library opened.

Today the VPL system is the most heavily used in Canada. The central library serves a network of 20 branches including the Carnegie Reading Room, open 365 days a year, from 10 A.M. to 10 P.M. There are more than 300,000 VPL cards in circulation. Card holders check out more than 5.5 million books a year—about 15 books per patron. Current chief librarian Madge Aalto estimates that library staff members field about 450 phone enquiries every hour.

Early visionaries like Sewell Moody and James Raymur, Edwin Machin and Andrew Carnegie might be puzzled by bar codes and scanners, the hum of computer hard drives, or the whine of modem connections, but they can rest assured that the library continues to function as an indispensable and democratic conduit for knowledge.

Vancouver Public Library, main branch, 1960. vs

 **BRITISH COLUMBIA**   Sponsored by the Ministry of Municipal Affairs and Housing, Province of British Columbia.

Branch Libraries
Sandra McKenzie

Carnegie Library, Vancouver, 1964. vs

WITH AN ANNUAL operating budget of close to $30 million Vancouver's library system comprises a central library, 20 branches plus an outreach service for homebound patrons. The fourth largest municipal service (in terms of budget) the public library serves 330,000 borrowers who check out nearly seven million items a year.

The city's first branch library opened in Kitsilano at 2375 West 4th Avenue in February, 1927. Built at a cost of $12,000 the pretty little stucco building was to be the first in a series of neighborhood libraries. Three more branches were planned for Hastings Street and Lakewood Drive, Commercial Drive and East 3rd Avenue, and Kingsway and Fraser with a fourth site in Fairview to be purchased. In its first year of operation the Kitsilano branch, with 7,000 books, attracted 6,000 cardholders and lent 128,000 volumes. In its opening weeks the library registered as many as 80 new users a day. Despite the success of this neighborhood amenity the Great Depression and the Second World War, stalled plans to develop the system for another 20 years.

In 1945 the city agreed to provide $1 million for a new main library to replace the 1901 Carnegie Building. At the same time citizens approved a ten-year plan to expand the branch network. The first post-war branch, located in the West End at Gordon House, opened that same year. The Kerrisdale branch followed, opening in 1948. Hastings and South Hill gained new libraries in 1949 followed by Dunbar in 1950 and Collingwood in 1951. By 1951 the library board had embarked on an ambitious building and acquisitions program. The system boasted seven branches and had plans for another six or seven libraries for Renfrew, Victoria Drive, Marpole, Sasamat, Fairview, Mount Pleasant and possibly the Downtown Eastside. As well, the city was committed to building a modern new facility to replace the shabby, outdated old Carnegie Library at Hastings and Main. To that end council authorized the library board to divert $250,000 from the branch system to buy an appropriate property.

The choice of a site proved contentious. While one faction advocated building east of Granville the other argued for Robson and Burrard, pointing out that this site would eliminate the need for a new West End branch, thus saving the board about $65,000 in capital costs plus $30,000 a year in operating expenses. This pragmatic argument won over the skeptics and the West End branch continued to operate out of Gordon House until the completion of the new central library 1957.

Over the years as the city grew, the VPL added more branches to the system, often tying them to existing community facilities such as Oakridge shopping centre (1959), and Killarney Secondary School (1968). The Strathcona Boys' and Girls' Library, in conjunction with Strathcona Elementary School, opened in 1972. The West End regained its own library, the Joe Fortes Branch, in 1976. In 1980 the old Carnegie Library was resurrected as the Carnegie Reading Room, open seven days a week, 12 hours a day, 365 days each year. The newest additions, Hastings at Nanaimo (1989) and Renfrew (1994) complete the system. With about 70,000 items and 1,530 square metres of space the Renfrew library is the largest branch, followed by Oakridge. Riley Park and Kensington Community Libraries, at 180 square metres and between two and three thousand volumes each, are the smallest.

Traditionally the branches have offered a good selection of popular reading material with some limited information services. In the past the card-holder who needed in-depth research and reference sources and services or simply wanted to cruise the stacks had to make the trip downtown to the central library. Now, with computer terminals in each branch, patrons anywhere in the city can browse electronically, order a title from the central collection then pick it up from and return it to their neighborhood library. Since dropping its 50¢ surcharge for 'holds' in 1990 the library, which now allows 24 free 'holds' per user per year, has seen a tenfold increase in transfers—nearly 700,000 in 1994, the most recent year for which figures are available.

With 20 branches, a central library and an outreach service, Vancouver is well served by its existing library system, according to VPL chief librarian Madge Aalto. Though there are no plans for expansion, technology will continue to alter the patterns of use, she predicts. What will not change, one hopes, is Vancouver's long history of a personal and intimate relationship with this very democratic and civilized institution.

BRITISH COLUMBIA — Sponsored by the Ministry of Municipal Affairs and Housing, Province of British Columbia.

Regional Libraries
Sandra McKenzie

IN THE INFORMATION AGE library walls have all but crumbled into insignificance and municipal borders are disappearing altogether. In recent years two powerful agents have been instrumental in this tectonic shift: the computer, which makes a library without walls possible, and shifting population patterns, which makes it necessary.

The libraries of the Lower Mainland and Fraser Valley are in the forefront of this revolution with a unique program called InterLINK. Twelve libraries—Burnaby, Coquitlam, New Westminster, North Vancouver, North Vancouver District, Port Moody, Richmond, Surrey, Vancouver, and West Vancouver municipal libraries, the Fraser Valley Regional Library (FVRL) and Bowen Island Public Library—have joined forces to provide free access to library materials and services from Bowen Island to Boston Bar. This cooperative effort, inaugurated in April, 1994 to replace the Greater Vancouver Library Federation, (GVLF) brought four additional libraries—Fraser Valley, Bowen Island, Coquitlam and Surrey—under its umbrella and more than doubled the population served by the GVLF.

InterLINK comprises 68 branches and a collection of six million items. In 1995, the most recent year for which figures are available, the total InterLINK circulation reached 24.5 million, serving a population of 1.9 million. Nearly 800,000 Lower Mainlanders crossed municipal borders to borrow nearly three million items from libraries other than their own. A further 22 per cent of all reference questions fielded by librarians came from non-resident users.

Here's how InterLINK works: residents of the Lower Mainland can borrow materials from any library which belongs to the network, have them delivered to any convenient branch then return the borrowed articles to any other branch in the system. For example, a computer user in Abbotsford can conduct a title search from home, locate the material in Burnaby, arrange to pick it up in Port Coquitlam, then return it to a branch in Whistler. There is one cumbersome aspect to the system: because the libraries don't share membership data bases our hypothetical user may have to keep track of twelve separate library cards. The long-term plan is to merge the systems but until then a member must have a valid card for each library he or she borrows from.

For serious library users InterLINK offers the obvious advantages of convenience and access to a vast collection of materials. For the libraries it's a cost-efficient collaboration,

allowing individual libraries to maintain autonomy while sharing and distributing services and resources equitably regardless of surrounding population or location. The ministry of municipal affairs, through the library services branch, picks up 69 percent of the costs and the balance is shared among the members.

Among the services InterLINK oversees is the acquisition and circulation of "audio-books." These two-track tapes, mostly popular fiction and biographies narrated by professional actors and broadcasters, are provided for library users with visual, perceptual or physical disabilities. While some audiobooks are purchased from the CNIB or commercial producers, the bulk of the collection is produced locally by the B.C. Library Services Branch at its production facility in Burnaby. As a producer of taped books exclusively for public library use the library services branch is unique in Canada.

Since its beginnings in 1974 as Vancouver Taped Books, a project funded by a Local Initiatives Project grant, Audiobooks has produced about 5,000 tapes and adds about another 250 titles a year. While the selection lists heavily towards light romance, westerns and historical fiction, the library services branch has recently signed an agreement with the Canadian Copyright Licensing Agency to record works by well-known Canadian authors including Alice Munro, Margaret Atwood, Robertson Davies and Bill Richardson. Among the planned non-fiction audio-books are selections by and about Jean Chretien, Pierre Trudeau and Preston Manning. About 5700 people throughout British Columbia use this service yearly.

One of five regional library districts in the province (the others are: Vancouver Island, the Okanagan, the Cariboo, and the Thompson-Nicola district) the FVRL district is the largest in the province. With 21 branches plus a regional headquarters it serves a population of about 550,000 people spread from Delta to Hope, with a small jog into the GVRD and Barnston Island.

In the beginning the FVRL was an experiment—the first of its kind in Canada—in providing library services to a rural population. In 1929 the provincial public library commission applied for and received a grant of $100,000 from the Carnegie Corporation to test the idea for five years. The project, known as the Fraser Valley Public Library Demonstration, started on March 1, 1930 with Dr. Helen Gordon Stewart as director. Dr Stewart, the first trained librarian west of Toronto, promoted, organized and guided the project through the demonstration years. By all reports a dynamo, Stewart's professional experience had included training at the New York Public Library, the directorship of the Victoria Public Library, five years with the provincial public library commission and two years as head the

 Sponsored by the Ministry of Municipal Affairs and Housing, Province of British Columbia.

department of sociology at Wells College, Aurora, New York.

The beginnings of the Fraser Valley demonstration were humble. The first book van was dispatched from Chilliwack to service the 24 communities and schools of the Fraser Valley scattered over 4,100 square kilometres. Among the van's regular stops were seven "branches," most of which were located in rented quarters which ranged from a former jail to a corner of a plumbing supply shop. Only Abbotsford had a dedicated library—attached to the municipal hall—bought, built and furnished for less than $900.

Despite the modest circumstances demand was brisk from the outset. According to Dr. Stewart, the first request she handled was for a book on Gregorian chants, the second for the last two volumes of *The Intimate Papers of Colonel House.* By the end of the first year the little library possessed 10,000 volumes—about one per registered user, Steward estimated.

In a progress report dated February 5, 1931 and addressed to F.P. Keppel, president of the Carnegie Corporation, Stewart plays shamelessly on big-city heartstrings with a letter that could have been cribbed from Mark Twain: "I enclose $1.00 Per Capita on Public Libraries," the letter begins. "I was a deaf boy till a few years ago now I kin hear good and talk but I find it hard to learn everything what a man should know . . . I am not got a good education but living in a small place and pore this will be my only hope if you kin send me the right book."

While that letter may have been an invention Stewart was undoubtedly sincere about the importance of this venture to an agricultural community, writing, " . . . doubtless God could have made a better place for a library experiment, but doubtless He never did."

In 1933 electors in 20 of the 24 municipalities and school districts voted to support the cooperative service once the demonstration finished. In June, 1934 the demonstration became the Fraser Valley Union Library District—the first regional library in North America—with headquarters in Abbotsford. The per capita tax rate was set at 35¢—miserly even by depression standards though the financial hardship for the nascent system was offset by an agreement among the participating communities to provide rent-free space. The rate wasn't raised until 1950 when it was increased to 40¢.

Dr. Stewart went on to organize similar library districts in the Okanagan and Vancouver Island. The National Film Board recognized the union library's pioneering role in 1944 with *Library on Wheels,* a 16mm film used as a teaching aid in library schools throughout the English-speaking world to illustrate a model rural library. By the end of World War II the Fraser Valley's population had grown, providing the union library with a budget of $37,000—enough to build a new bookmobile and purchase a new delivery truck to service the branches and schools.

In 1951 an amendment to the Public Libraries Act changed the name of the library to the Fraser Valley Regional Library. By 1955, with the inclusion of Richmond, the FVRL district covered an area of 10,000 square kilomtres extending from Richmond to Hope, from Port Coquitlam to Agassiz and from the international border to the mountains north of the Fraser River. In 1970 the system boasted two bookmobiles, each carrying 2,000 volumes, serving 206 stops every two weeks.

In 1931 Dr. Helen Stewart worried that she was pushing the issue by ordering her first stock of books for the new library "on the assumption that life in every normal community gives rise to a mental curiosity both wide and varied." Today the FVRL has a collection of nearly 900,000 volumes plus another 27,000 newspaper and magazine subscriptions, audio and video cassettes and audio-books, and a budget of $10 million. Serving a population of 500,000 it is the largest library in the province.

Author George Woodcock, 1994. vs

 **BRITISH COLUMBIA**   Sponsored by the Ministry of Municipal Affairs and Housing, Province of British Columbia.

Festivals

Ernie Fladell

Symphony of Fire, 1990. vs

AFTER 11 STAR-studded years, when the elegant Vancouver International Festival, debt-ridden and desperate, died of embarrassment in 1969, conventional wisdom decreed that there would never be another professional performing arts festival produced in Greater Vancouver. Currently, there are 33.

The greening of our once bleak festival scene is a story that starts the very year (1976) the first *Vancouver Book* was published. At that time, the editors could find only two arts festivals worth mentioning and neither was alive. One was the aforementioned Vancouver International Festival, which had died seven years earlier. The other, Festival Habitat, was still waiting to be born as Vancouver's contribution to the massive United Nations Conference on Human Habitation (aka Habitat) to be hosted by Ottawa in Vancouver in June 1976.

At the behest of city council, Festival Habitat was to be organized by social planner Ernie Fladell: to create a friendly and festive civic atmosphere for visitors; to give the Vancouver public, few of whom would be admitted to the formal conference, a sense of participation in an historic event; and to showcase Vancouver artists and other talented Canadians. Eclipsed by Habitat's galaxy of international eco-stars and Al Clapp's controversial forum facilities built at Jericho Beach, at first the festival excited little interest. So little, in fact, that it barely seemed to be happening. To make matters worse, the people who knew everything about everything said that Canadians would not pay to see other Canadians perform, and definitely not during an off-season month, i.e. June. Festival Habitat, it seemed, was doomed to disappear without a trace. But, a funny thing happened on the way to oblivion—almost every show sold out.

Later, after the official downtown conference was over, after Clapp's constructions along with the old World War II hangars that housed the unofficial forum at Jericho were demolished, there was not much left of Habitat to remember. Even the terrorism scare associated with the PLO presence, turned out to be nothing, which in a word seemed to sum up the public perception of what the conference had accomplished. It was then, with no small sense of satisfaction that city officials viewed the considerable accomplishments of its own Festival Habitat. Maurice Egan, the director of social planning and his planner-cum-festival producer especially savored a surprising surplus of $40,000. At the urging of music critic Ian Docherty they wasted little time in planning an encore. Renamed the Heritage Festival and organized in cooperation with the VSO and CBC Radio in June of 1977 the event once again succeeded in attracting large audiences for music, drama and dance—creating yet another surplus. Vancouver summer entertainment, which previously revolved around the PNE and Theatre Under The Stars, was never to be the same again.

The next year Heritage Festival invented the trail-blazing Vancouver Children's Festival. During that same summer of 1978, at Heritage Festival's invitation, music maven Mitch Podolak aided by Gary Cristall and a cadre of Winnipeg Folk Festival veterans produced the first Vancouver Folk Music Festival. By 1980 the federal department of communications established the Cultural Initiatives Program which unlike the Canada Council could provide popular arts festival funding. In 1982 Leonard Schein initiated The Vancouver Film Festival. In 1985 Joanna Maratta gave us the Vancouver Fringe Festival and Leila Getz created the Vancouver Chamber Music Festival. Next year the Vancouver International Jazz Festival was co-produced by Ken Pickering and Bob Kerr.

That was 1986, the year we invited the world to Expo. "Cultural Tourism" was the name of the game. And as one corporate convert put it, "thar's gold in them thar frills." Except, they don't call them "frills" anymore, not as long as professional arts and arts festivals, like those listed below, entertain audiences by the tens of thousands and collectively generate revenue in the tens of millions.

 Sponsored by the Ministry of Municipal Affairs and Housing, Province of British Columbia.

GREATER VANCOUVER CALENDAR OF PROFESSIONAL ARTS FESTIVALS:

january, february and march The *Women in View* festival celebrates the creative contributions of women, beginning the last week of January at the Firehall Arts Centre, Gastown. The *New Play Festival* highlights a first look at new works by outstanding Canadian authors. It starts in the second week in March at Performance Works on Granville Island.

april The *Story Telling Festival* brings wonderfully told tales for all ages for three days in early April at Barclay Square in Vancouver's West End. *La Fete Colombienne des Enfants* presents songs and stories for young students of French, in mid-April at the Coquitlam Arena. *Dancing on the Edge* is where leading companies present the new and different in dance. The event runs for 11 days, commencing the third Monday in April at the Firehall Arts Centre in Gastown.

may *Mayworks* festival performers celebrate the workplace on the first weekend in May at the Vancouver East Cultural Centre. The *Blue Grass Festival* at Granville Island brings lots of bands, lots of old timey tunes, lots of fun, daily at noon, during the first three weeks of May. *Music West* is a pop and rock celebration during the second weekend in May in downtown clubs. The *Jewish Film Festival* presents comedy, drama and dilemma, in mid-May, at the Rothstein Arts Centre, Vancouver Jewish Community Centre, 41st and Oak, Vancouver. The *Chinese Film Festival* is a fascinating mix of subjects and styles in mid-May at the Chinese Cultural Centre and Cinematheque. Another *Mayworks* features performers donating their professional talents for a student fête in the third weekend in May at the King Edward Campus, 1155 East Broadway. The *Vancouver Children's Festival* was the first and is still the finest festival of its kind with the best theatre, music and movement the world has to offer. It runs for seven days starting on the last Monday in May in Vanier Park.

june *Out on Screen* shows films and videos depicting lesbian and gay culture, from early June at Cinematheque, Video Inn, Emily Carr Institute of Art and Design and Caprice. The *Jewish Festival of the Arts* is two days of arts, crafts and performance celebrating *yiddishkite,* mid-June, Granville Island. The *International Dragon Boat Festival* features colorful Dragon Boat races and international teams, with performances and food pavilions at the Plaza of Nations in mid-June. The *International Jazz Festival* includes many free performances all over town. *La Fête* highlights Quebec performers on St. Jean Baptiste Day, June 24 at Granville and 7th Avenue in Vancouver.

july *Harrison Festival* is an internationally themed arts and performance event held during the second week in July at Harrison Lake. An exhilarating non-stop mix of great music, the *Vancouver Folk Music Festival* is held on the third weekend in July at Vancouver's Jericho Park. The *Chamber Music Festival* is Vancouver's premiere classical music event. It runs over six days, July into August at King George School and/or Crofton House. Medieval to Baroque, classics as they were meant to be heard are performed at the *Early Music Festival* from mid-July to August at UBC. Weird, wacky and wonderful performers populate Granville Island for the *International Comedy Festival* from the end of July to early August. At the *Symphony of Fire,* international fireworks artists compete in half-hour shows on three Wednesdays in late July to August at English Bay.

august Splendid music in a splendid setting are features of the *Mission Folk Festival* on the second weekend in August in Mission's Heritage Park. *Harmony Arts Festival* highlights concerts, art, fun and games in the second week in August in West Vancouver. Political sensibilities share centre stage with a variety of performers at the *Under the Volcano Festival* on the second Sunday in August at Cates Park in North Vancouver. For traditional Japanese food, music, dance and arts catch the *Powell Street Festival* over the B.C. Day weekend at Oppenheimer Park in Vancouver. Also in August, *Luminaries,* Public Dreams Society's artful lantern parade on B.C. Day in Vancouver's East Side and *StreetFare,* a gathering of two dozen buskers around the Vancouver Art Gallery on the last weekend of the month.

september In 1995 the *Vancouver Fringe Festival* moved to Commercial Drive. Performing arts companies by the bushel perform in ten venues for ten days, starting the second week in September. The *Vancouver International Film Festival* is a film buff's dream: 400 screenings of 250 films from 40 countries over 17 days from the end of September to mid-October in various city theatres. *Word on the Street* features readings and performance in the cause of literacy in Vancouver's Library Square.

october Leading literati lead workshops and read their works for five days at the *Vancouver International Writers Festival* during the third week in October at various Granville Island venues.

Note: The events listed above are primarily oriented toward professional presentations. However, Greater Vancouver also boasts a number of popular community events which celebrate local physical attributes, culture and history, featuring non-professional and student presentations. These include some of the region's most noteworthy annual events such as the Fraser River Festival, New Westminster Hyack Festival, North Vancouver Folk Festival, Steveston Salmon Fest, Surrey Dance Festival, Vancouver Kiwanis Art Festival, Vancouver Sea Festival and Vancouver Canada Day Celebration.

Omnium
Gatherum

essay

Rarely does one come across a place so ideally suited to the act of bumbering as the city of Vancouver. Bumbering? It's a totally made-up verb, and a darned useful one at that. Bumbering is onomatopoeia at its best—it's ambling, sauntering, wandering, exploring and enjoying. Likely the word is a bad and unintentional malapropism of bunburying from Oscar Wilde's play *The Importance of Being Ernest.* But maybe not. When it comes to living in Vancouver, a little bumbering is the perfect balm for our often goal-oriented, clock-watching, deadline-obsessed lives. Easterners think we are laid back, but we all know that's a myth. There are lots of folks here who work all the time zones. In that driven state, we can easily drive right by the good stuff.

Bumbering celebrates serendipity, and embraces tangents, two activities that can only enhance one's life in Vancouver. Consider these guidelines for very happy bumbering:

- Open yourself up to possibilities, and try not to make a set plan. If you must have a plan, abandon it at the slightest hint of a better idea. Let whimsy be your guide. There's always a festival or exhibit to explore right around the corner, or a new coffee shop you ought to try. Get out of your groove.
- Whenever there's a road along the water or a route with a better view, take it. If you can ride a bicycle, even better.
- Never pass up the opportunity to round a corner.
- Give yourself lots of time. Try not to bumber to a deadline, it makes for a far happier day if getting back home is as serendipitous as the rest of the excursion.
- Talk to people. The best reviews, tips and ideas come from folks in movie line-ups, ferry line-ups or out bumbering themselves.

When you don't notice the mountains or the ships in the harbor you are in trouble. When you don't take the time to really use the city and to explore the good bits, drastic action (in a gentle sort of way) is needed. Whether you see remedial bumbering as an excuse for an urban adventure, or you look to bumbering as a lifestyle to embrace, it's a useful tool for seeing things in the city you might otherwise miss.

Like Alan Storey's giant, spinning, silver public art project known as Password on Pacific Street between Drake and Homer. Four sets of four letters are inset into exhaust airduct vent grills exiting from the parking garage below. The words come from four subject areas: active: work, rest, play; architectural: post, beam, wall; social change: city, park, yard; and weather: wind, rain, smog. Air spins the letters, and as you drive by (or better yet walk), you will see thousands of different word combinations.

That's one example of one detail on one street. You don't want to pass by entire areas, like Hastings around Nanaimo, home of fabulous Italian food and multinational breads.

Excellent bumbering staples. These are not the trendy-West-Side-$4.00-a-loaf-bread-experiences. No, these are the authentic articles—Portuguese buns for $2.00 a dozen, bagels with a heft unmatched, Chinese buns, Italian loafs and Slavic deli delights.

Bianca Maria at 2469 East Hastings is a tiny shop I was happy to discover. Filled to the brim with Italian foods, it is run by two women who will almost take you by the hand and teach you to cook. An open can of sardines on the counter scents the place; samples of cheeses are there to delight the uninitiated.

And Chinatown—it's a bumberer's haven. Remember to look up to see intriguing architectural details like dragons on roofs. Look down too, because there are a number of shops (including two large grocery stores) tucked away underground. My favorite building is the 1909 home of the Chinese Benevolent Society at 108 East Pender. Look closely too at 123 East Pender. You'll see a remarkable, tall piece of stained glass with inset Chinese characters.

When it rains, I am particularly keen on the Dr. Sun Yat-Sen Gardens, at 575 Carrall. The roof tiles were specially designed to catch the rain and cause it to drip artistically into the garden. It's a lovely place to catch your breath or to finish your wander for the day.

—Marg Meikle

above: Photographer at work, Quality Inn, Vancouver, 1993. vp
facing page: Plant sale purchase, VanDusen Botanical Garden, 1993. vp

A Few Firsts for Greater Vancouver
Diane Sturgess

These were plucked from articles in this book. For more information check individual articles.

Abbotsford Air Show, 1962.

Advertising agency, Noble Advertising, c. 1907.

Advertising agency to bill $100 million, Palmer Jarvis

AIDS organization, AIDS Vancouver, 1983.

AIDS patient at St. Paul's Hospital, 1983

Airmail (it went to Seattle), Mar. 3, 1919.

Airplane flight west of Winnipeg, Mar. 25, 1910.

All-Chinese-language school, Feb. 1940.

Aquarium, Private, Oct. 11, 1939.

Aquarium, Public, June 15, 1956.

Archbishop, Rt. Rev. Augustine Dontenwill, 1908.

Arthur Laing Bridge traffic, May 15, 1976.

Artificial ice rink in Canada, Dec. 20, 1911.

Arts Club Theatre show, Light Up the Sky, 1964.

Ascent of Grouse Mountain, 1894.

Ascent of Mount Seymour, 1908

Assizes, Nov. 15, 1892.

Automobile, A Stanley Steamer, Sept. 24, 1899.

Automobile dealer, 1904, Frank and Fred Begg.

Automobile, gasoline-powered, 1904

Aviation firsts, Richmond has several: B.C.'s first passenger flight (1912), first female passenger, first flight over the Rockies left from there.

B.C. Lions season, 1954, first Grey Cup, 1964.

Bank Sep. 1, 1886.

Bar, Globe Saloon, owned by Gassy Jack, 1867.

Bard on the Beach production, A *Midsummer Night's Dream,* 1990.

Baseball team, professional, 1905.

Bathtub Race, July 30, 1967

Bell peal at Holy Rosary Cathedral, July 1, 1911

Boat Show, Apr. 26, 1948.

Boat to circumnavigate North America, *St. Roch,* Book printed, 1887.

Border crossing at Douglas, July 1, 1891.

Bridge across Burrard Inlet, 1925

Bridge across False Creek, Oct. 2, 1872.

Bridge across First Narrows, Nov. 12, 1938..

Bridge across Fraser in Lower Mainland, 1904.

Bridge across Second Narrows, Sep. 7, 1925.

B.C. High Schools Olympiad, Aug. 7, 1930.

B.C. Place event, June 19, 1983.

Buddhist church (Bukkyo-kai), 1905.

"Buzzer" Transit newsletter, June 2, 1916.

CBC war correspondent to cover Canadian troops in action, Peter Stursberg, World War II.

CNR train, Aug. 28, 1915.

Cable television, Horseshoe Bay,1954.

Cable television community channel, 1969.

Canadian woman newspaper editor, Sara Anne McLagan, Vancouver Daily World, 1901.

Capitol Theatre shows, Mar. 25, 1921.

Catholic church, The Parish of Our Lady of the Holy Rosary, 1886.

Cemetery, Mountain View, 1887.

Census, 1881.

Chancellor, Simon Fraser University: Dr. Gordon Shrum.

Chancellor, University of British Columbia: Francis Carter-Cotton

Chess Championship, Canadian Aug. 24,1951.

Children's Festival, 1978.

Children's Hospital, 1927.

Chinese settlers, 1858.

Christian service for non-natives, Methodist service, at Moody's Mill, June 19, 1865.

Church at Granville (Gastown), 1876, Methodists' Indian mission church.

Circus, Great Syndicate Paris Hippodrome, 1895.

City Archivist, Major James Skitt Matthews

City council meeting, May 10, 1886.

City librarian, James Machin, 1892.

Civic arboretum Queen Elizabeth Park, 1939.

Civic election May 3, 1886.

Classes, Simon Fraser University Sept. 9, 1965.

Classes, University of B.C. Sept. 30, 1915.

Classes, downtown campus of SFU May 5, 1989.

Cocktail bar, July 1954 Sylvia Hotel.

Comedy club, Punchlines, 1978.

Conductor, CBC Orchestra John Avison, 1938.

Consulate, Chile opened an office in 1892.

Cows, 1853, McLean farm on the Pitt River.

Creative writing department in Canada, UBC, 1963.

Curb ramps for wheelchair users, 1965.

Dal Richards band at Hotel Vancouver, May 1, 1940.

Dean of women UBC, Mary Louise Bollert, 1921-41

Massey Tunnel traffic, May 23, 1959.

Direct distance dialing, June 5, 1961.

Drama series on radio, 1927 on CNRV.

Driving on the right, Jan. 1, 1922.

Earthquake recorded, 1872 near White Rock

Election, civic May 1886.

Electricity, Feb. 4, 1882 at Moodyville.

Electric lights in Vancouver, Aug. 8, 1887.

Empress ship, Apr. 28, 1891 Empress of India.

Escalators (two-way), Apr. 14, 1948, Hudson's Bay store.

European starlings sighted, four, in Surrey, 1949.

European to see Vancouver, Narvaez, 1791

Execution at Oakalla Prison Farm, Aug. 29, 1919.

Exhibition, Aug. 15, 1910, became the PNE. First PNE Parade was 1935.

Expo 86 paying visitors, May 2, 1986.

Faculty appointee, UBC Leonard Klinck, 1914.

Farmers, McCleery brothers, Sep. 1862.

Ferry across Burrard Inlet (casual), 1866, "Navvy Jack" Thomas' rowboat.

Ferry across Burrard Inlet (regular), 1900.

Ferry across the Fraser K de K, Mar. 17, 1884.

Films, see Michael Walsh article.

Fireboat The J.H.Carlisle, built in 1928.

Fire chief, John Howe Carlisle, 1889.

Fire engine July 30, 1886.

Flight over Vancouver, July 16, 1917.

Fort Langley Construction, Aug. 1, 1827.

French-language radio, Dec. 1, 1967.

Fully-automated stock exchange in North America, Vancouver Stock Exchange, 1990.

Funeral parlor, Hart's, 1886.

Gasoline sold for motorcar, c. 1905, by Imperial Oil.

Gas pipeline to Vancouver, 1957.

Gas station, c. 1907 (also first in Canada)

General strike, Aug. 2, 1918.

Georgia Street viaduct, July 1, 1915.

Golf club, Vancouver Golf Club, Nov. 1892.

Golf course, Public Fraserview, 1935.

Governor General's visit, Sep. 14, 1876.

Grain export Jan. 7, 1909.

Grain export via Panama Canal, May 18, 1918.

Gramophone demonstration, Sep. 21, 1891.

Granville Island industry, 1915.

Granville Island Market, July 12, 1979.

Granville Mall traffic closure, Jan. 22, 1975.

Granville Street Bridge, Jan. 4, 1889.

Granville Street Bridge (present), Feb. 4, 1954.

Grey Cup game played in Vancouver, Nov. 26, 1955 Montreal Alouettes vs. Edmonton Eskimos.

Grocery wholesaler, Oppenheimer Bros.,1886.

Grouse Mountain Chalet November, 1926.

Grouse Mountain skyride, Dec. 15, 1966.

Hindu workers, 1895.

Home mail delivery, 1895.

Hospital CPR tent, before 1888.

Hotel Vancouver, May 16, 1887.

Hungarian refugees, Dec. 5, 1956.

Ice hockey, winter of 1861.

Indian immigrants, 1904.

Industrial park in Canada, Annacis Island, 1952.

Inmate at Oakalla Prison Farm, Sep. 2, 1912.

Interurban railway run, Oct. 8, 1891.

Ismailia Jamatkhana Centre, 1985.

Japanese immigrant, Manzo Nagano, 1877.

Jazz disc jockey, Bob Smith, 1937.

Jewish religious leader, Zebulon Franks, fl 1880s.

Killer whale, "Moby Doll," 1964.

Kindergarten, 1894

Kitsilano Showboat, summer, 1935.

Knight Street Bridge traffic, Jan. 15, 1974.

Letterboxes, 1895.

Library in Vancouver, Dec. 14, 1887.

Lifeguard, Joe Fortes, 1892, formalized 1901.

Lighthouse Point Atkinson, 1874.

Locomotive, Oct.1883. It arrives by ship!

Long-distance telephone, Mar. 28, 1898.

Lumber cargo, to New Westminster, 1863.
Magazine Western Ho!, July 1907.
Map of City, 1886.
Mayor Malcolm Alexander MacLean, 1886.
Mayor born in Vancouver, William Rathie
May Queen, New Westminster May 4,1870.
Mechanized logging in B.C. forest industry, on Little Mountain by Jeremiah Rogers, 1874.
Mega-musical in Vancouver Cats, June 29, 1987.
Mental Hospital, New Westminster Asylum, 1878.
Miracle Mile, Aug. 7, 1954. Also first sports event broadcast live to all of North America.
Missionary Catholic priest, Father Modeste Demers at Fort Langley, Sep. 1841.
Molson Indy, Labor Day, 1990.
Motorized fire department in Canada, 1917.
Movie seen in Vancouver, Aug. 2, 1897.
Movie theatre in Canada, Oct. 7, 1898.
Movie theatre (permanent), Edison Electric 1902
Museum ,1894
NASL Championship, Sep. 8, 1979.
Native Indian voters, Mathias Joe Capilano, Squamish chief and carver, and wife Ellen, 1949.
Neighborhood House, 1938.
Newspaper, Vancouver Weekly Herald and North Pacific News, Jan. 15, 1886.
Newspaper firsts, The News-Advertiser (1887) first to classify advertising in Vancouver, first on the continent with electric-powered press, first with machine-set type.
Newspaper on Burrard Inlet, July 20, 1878.
Nine O' Clock Gun firing, 1894.
O Canada, First singing of Feb. 9, 1910.
Olympic gold medalist, Percy Williams, 1928.
Olympic medal winner, Duncan Gillis, 1912.
Opera locally produced, Carmen, Apr. 2, 1960.
Opera commissioned by Vancouver Opera, The Architect, 1994.
Orpheum as home of the Vancouver Symphony Orchestra, Apr. 2, 1977.
Orpheum Theatre show, Nov. 8, 1927.
PNE Parade, 1935.
Papal visit, Pope John Paul II Sep. 18, 1984.
Parachute jump in Canada, May 24, 1912.
Park Board chair, Alfred Graham Ferguson, 1888.
Passenger flight in B.C., Apr. 24, 1911.
Patient at St. Paul's Hospital, Nov. 21, 1894.
Pay telephones, Aug. 6, 1898 at English Bay.
Peace Arch, Sep. 6, 1921
Peace march, Apr. 24, 1982.
Polar Bear Club swim, Jan. 1, 1920 or 1921.
Police department, 1886.
Policeman mounted (city), 1909 in Stanley Park.
Policeman killed, Constable Lewis Byers, shot and killed by a drunk Mar. 25, 1912.
Policewomen, 1912.
Port Mann Bridge traffic, June 12, 1964.

Postage meter 1927, Hudson's Bay Co.
Postal zones, 1951.
Postmaster, Henry Harvey.
Post office (official), Apr., 1874 at Granville.
Post office (unofficial), July 2, 1869.
President SFU, Dr. Patrick D. McTaggart-Cowan, 1965
President UBC, Frank Wesbrook, 1913.
President of Russia to visit, Boris Yeltsin in 1993.
President of the U.S. to visit, Warren G. Harding
Priest of the 2nd Avenue gurdwara (Sikh temple), Balwant Singh Atwal. Son Hardial, born Aug. 28, 1912, was first Canadian-born Sikh.
Prisoners at the B.C. Penitentiary, 1878
Province (daily), Mar. 26, 1898.
Racing, harness, 1975, Cloverdale.
Racing, thoroughbred, 1889, East Park.
Radio used in mayoralty campaign, Dec. 5, 1922 .
Real estate transaction, George Black bought waterfront Lot 26 for $25 down, $25 later. 1886.
Rental housing, low-income, 1953.
Road North Arm Trail, 1859.
Road link to U.S., Major Pacific Highway, 1923.
Rock 'n Roll concert, June 27, 1956, Bill Haley and the Comets, Kerrisdale Arena.
Rock 'n Roll DJ, Red Robinson. 1953/54
"Royal Hudson" run, June 21, 1975.
Royal visit, Duke and Duchess of Cornwall and York Sep. 30, 1901.
Safety Patrol Program in North America (likely the world), 1935, as the School Boy Patrol.
Salmon shipped to Britain, Sep. 28, 1889
Salmon cannery in B.C., 1870 at Annieville.
Sawmill on north shore Burrard Inlet, 1863.
Sawmill on south shore Burrard Inlet, 1867.
Scheduled overseas airline, Australian National Airways (now called Qantas), 1946.
Schools, See the article First Schools.
Science World attendance, May 6, 1989.
SeaBus trip, June 17, 1977.
Sea Festival, summer 1963.
Sermon on Burrard Inlet, 1865.
Ship to the Klondike gold fields, July 22, 1897.
Sikh place of worship, 1906.
Ski club, Hollyburn Pacific Ski Club, 1927.
Skiing on Grouse Mountain, 1911.
Skiing on Mount Seymour, 1929.
Ski lift at Whistler Feb. 15, 1966.
Skyscraper, The Dominion Trust Building, 1909.
SkyTrain run, Dec. 11, 1985.
Sliced bread, July 19, 1937.
Solicitor, Alfred St. George Hamersley, 1888
Stanley Cup, Vancouver Millionaires,1915.
Streetcar (electric), run June 26, 1890.
Suffrage convention, 1911.
Sugar, 1890, 250 tons from the Philippines.
Sunday opening, major store, Woodwards, 1984.
Sun Free Salmon Derby, Aug. 26, 1940.

Suzhou-style classical Chinese garden, The Dr. Sun Yat-Sen Classical Garden
Swimming at Kits Pool, July 1, 1931.
Synagogue, B'Nai Yehudah,1911-12.
Talkie, "Mother Knows Best," Oct.1928.
Taxi, 1903.
Technical training institute, British Columbia Institute of Technology (BCIT), 1964.
Telegraph line, Apr. 18, 1865.
Telephone, 1885.
Televised drama, locally produced 1955, CBUT. Television seen locally, Nov. 28, 1948, Seattle
Television station, public, CBUT, 1953.
Television station, private CHAN-TV, 1960.
Terry Fox Memorial Run, Sep. 13, 1981.
Theatre, The Imperial Opera House, 1890.
Theatre, Amateur Hart's Opera House, 1887.
Theatre Under the Stars, Aug. 6, 1940.
Traffic lights, 1928.
Train to Burrard Inlet, July 4, 1886, Port Moody.
Train into Vancouver, May 23, 1887.
Transcontinental flight arrival, Oct. 17, 1920.
Transcontinental passenger air service, Apr. 1, 1939, TCA (Vancouver to Montreal).
Transit buses, 1923.
Tug in Burrard Inlet, The Isabel, 1866.
Ubyssey, 1917 as Anonymous
Vancouver Art Gallery, Oct. 5, 1931.
Vancouver Book Award winner, Paul Yee, 1988.
Vancouver Canadians game, April 14, 1978 in Hawaii, at home, April 26, 1978.
Vancouver Canucks game, Oct. 9, 1970.
Vancouver Folk Music Festival, summer of 1978
Vancouver Fringe Festival, 1985.
Vancouver Grizzlies game, Nov. 3, 1995, at Portland, home game Nov. 5, 1995.
Vancouver Little Theatre production, Lonesome Like, 1921.
Vancouver Playhouse production, Brendan Behan's The Hostage, 1963. First Canadian play, Eric Nicol's Like Father, Like Fun, 1965.
Vancouver Sun, Feb. 12, 1912.
Vancouver Symphony Orchestra July 8, 1934
Vietnamese refugees, 1975.
Voting by native Indian people, June 18, 1962 .
Water piped into Vancouver, Mar. 26, 1889.
West End apartment block, Manhattan, 1908.
Wheat export to London, 1895.
White boy born at Burrard Inlet, Dec. 13, 1873.
White girl born at Burrard Inlet, Apr. 29, 1875.
White Spot drive-in June, 1928 at Granville and West 67th by Nat Bailey.
Woman president of UBC, Martha Piper, July 1997
Woman on city council, Helena Gutteridge, 1937.
Woman judge in B.C., Helen MacGill, 1917.
Woman M.P., Grace MacInnis, 1965.
Woman president of a major Canadian university (SFU), Pauline Jewett,1974.
Woodward's store, Mar. 3, 1892.

Today, there are 45 White Spots throughout British Columbia, making it the largest full-service restaurant chain in B.C. White Spot serves more than 35,000 people daily, or about 13 million every year. Breakfast, lunch or dinner guests can be sure they will get the same great taste no matter which White Spot Restaurant they visit.

Some Famous Visitors
David Spaner

NO PLACE LIKE HOBOKEN. That's what a lonely young member of the Hoboken Four, a group of "singing and dancing fools," wrote home in the wee hours of the morning after playing Vancouver in 1936. To Frank Sinatra, Vancouver may have been no Hoboken, New Jersey, but it has been the place where many visitors' lives have been permanently rearranged.

In March 1892 Rudyard and Carrie Kipling's honeymoon stopped long enough for the writer to buy "20 acres of a wilderness called North Vancouver." After paying taxes on the land for years, he discovered it belonged to someone else.

In 1909 Vancouver hosted a heavyweight title bout between one of boxing's all-time bests and a future Oscar winner. Jack Johnson, the first black heavyweight champ, who had just won the title, agreed in Vancouver to an exhibition match with a boxer from Tacoma, Washington, a last-minute replacement for Denver Ed Martin. The boxer turned out to be Victor McLaglen, who would go on to win a best-actor Academy Award in 1935 for his role in *The Informer*. But on March 10, 1909, MacLaglen was a little-known, awkward brawler who was knocked down in the first round. From that point, Johnson toyed his way to victory, joking with the Vancouver audience.

The next year, an itinerant young Englishman Boris Karloff arrived. In those pre-Hollywood North days, the acting hopeful was unsuccessful in his show biz job hunt, and wound up working construction on what would be the Pacific National Exhibition. The 10-hour days and blistered hands were horrifying to the future movie monster, so Karloff tried his hand at selling real estate. "Probably one of the greatest things that happened to me was in Vancouver when I was 22 years old," Karloff would recollect. "Someone offered me a half interest in a gold mine for 100 pounds. I had the money, too. I asked the advice of a banker friend and he said, 'No'. That mine was subsequently sold for three million pounds. But imagine what would have happened to me. It would have ruined me." Imagine a world without *Abbott and Costello Meet Frankenstein*.

Bill Clinton met Boris Yeltsin in Vancouver in 1993. Before that event, Warren Harding had been the only U.S. president to visit the city. You would never know by looking at the one lasting memorial to Harding's 1923 visit, near Malkin Bowl, that Vancouver may have been the beginning of the end for that American head of state. He arrived July 26 and the first

hint of trouble came after a luncheon as Harding played the old Shaughnessy golf course. He played the first six holes, then was so fatigued he moved directly to the 17th. He returned to the Hotel Vancouver, rested for an hour, then delivered a listless speech, the first by a U.S. president on Canadian soil. After standing for 25 minutes in the main ballroom shaking hands he excused himself before the long line had passed. By the time Harding returned to the U.S. on July 29, it was clear he'd had a cardiac collapse. He also had pneumonia. He died August 2, 1923.

"He had ptomaine poisoning in Vancouver," one of Harding's aides, a Colonel Miller, said. "Why did he have that ptomaine poisoning? He didn't eat anything that all the rest of the party were not eating."

There were more questions the night Benny Kubelsky met Sadie Marks. In 1922 Kubelsky, a vaudeville comedian, was playing the Orpheum with the Marx Brothers. Zeppo Marx brought Kubelsky to a Passover seder at the home of a family named Marks. In his autobiography, Kubelsky would write that during dinner the four traditional Passover questions were asked, "the first of which I should have heeded: 'Why is this night different from all other nights?' It was the most important night of my life, but I didn't know it." At that dinner at 1649 Nelson Street, Benny Kubelsky, who later changed his name to Jack Benny, meet Sadie Marks, who changed her name to Mary Livingstone. They would marry and become one of Hollywood's legendary comedy teams.

Vancouver was a popular stop on the vaudeville circuit, and in October 1933 Texas Guinan played the Beacon Theatre. The singer-entertainer, who was also a nightclub owner famous for flouting U.S. prohibition laws, reportedly looked forward to some time off in the city after performing on Saturday, Oct. 28. "It will be the first Sunday we've rested for many years. I like these Canadian Sundays," she said. She was too ill to perform on Monday and was booked into Vancouver General Hospital. On Nov. 5—a Canadian Sunday—Guinan died from a massive abdominal infection. The hospital contacted the nearest priest, from St. Patrick's church on East 12th, to minister to her. Her parents would show their appreciation by donating a tabernacle which is still in the church.

Three decades later another controversial performer appeared in Vancouver. In July 1962, Lenny Bruce, author of *How To Talk Dirty and Influence People* opened to a packed house at Isy's Supper Club. In the next day's *Vancouver Sun*, Jack Wasserman attacked Bruce's caustic performance. That evening the morality squad showed up at Isy's, and after the show informed Bruce and club owner Isy Walters that the show was finished, citing a bylaw against "any lewd or immoral performance or exhibition." Walters was told his operating licence would be suspended unless Bruce was cancelled, and he killed the balance of the engagement. The operator of the Inquisition Coffee House stepped forward with an offer to present the remainder of the performances. Bruce agreed, but the city's licensing boss announced the Inquisition's licence would be lifted if he performed. Bruce, who would be remembered as a hugely influential, ground-breaking comic, finally threw up his hands, vowing never again to perform in Vancouver.

Elvis Presley also riled local morality buffs when he played Empire Stadium in 1957. Presley's Northwest U.S. tour had gone relatively quietly, but when he started shaking his pelvis at Empire Stadium the crowd gave a thundering roar and vaulted the barricades. During the 35-minute show, youths repeatedly charged a police line protecting the stage. And when Elvis' performance ended rock 'n' rollers tossed bottles and went toe-to-toe with police.

Other visiting rockers would leave marks in Vancouver, from the mania surrounding the Beatles visit in 1964 to the riot outside the Rolling Stones concert in 1972.

In 1972, another visitor drew cameras to a Vancouver hotel. That year, billionaire Howard Hughes, who had not been photographed for years, arrived at the Bayshore Inn in broad daylight, and in what amounted to reckless abandon for the recluse, sauntered through the hotel lobby in a bathrobe, then stood at his penthouse window to watch a seaplane land. The last time Hughes had viewed the harbor was 1945 when he piloted Vancouver actress-turned-Hollywood star Yvonne deCarlo on a flight over Vancouver. This time local photographers began a stakeout but without success because Hughes was soon ensconced in a blacked-out bedroom. His refuge in Vancouver lasted from July to September.

In 1968 a less-conventional writer visited the city. "I got invited to Vancouver to give three speeches, and there I experienced a breakthrough," Yippie Jerry Rubin would recall in one of his autobiographies, noting that his speechmaking reached new highs during his visit. At UBC on Oct. 24, Rubin ignited an occupation of the faculty club. "People were rolling joints in five- and ten-dollar bills. Some people took off their clothes and jumped into the faculty pool."

West Coast civilization had tangled with another American a couple of decades earlier when Paul Robeson—opera singer, Shakespearean actor, writer, movie star, social critic, folk singer, all-American football player, lawyer—was barred from giving a concert presented by the miners' union in Vancouver. In January 1952 (the McCarthy era) Robeson was stopped when he arrived by car at the Blaine, Washington border crossing. The U.S. State Department used legislation enabling it—during a "national emergency"—to prevent the departure of U.S. citizens. Robeson returned to Seattle and the following day used a long-distance telephone hookup to sing to trade unionists at the Vancouver convention. The union voted to organize a concert at the Peace Arch and in May, Robeson sang at the border park to 25,000 to 30,000 spectators on the Vancouver side of the line, and 5,000 on the U.S. side.

Crossing the border was also troubling for Brooks Robinson, the only member of baseball's hall of fame to play for a Vancouver team. Robinson was demoted to the Pacific Coasts league's Triple A Vancouver Mounties by the Baltimore Orioles in 1959. "My ego was really hurt," he later said. Yet it turned out to be the best thing that could have happened to me. . . . I was brought back at the All Star break. I had more confidence and also I had gotten stronger physically, so I was no longer overmatched."

More than 30 years later, another visiting athlete wasn't overmatched. Then again, Mike Tyson was only scrapping with members of the media. In 1989 the boxer arrived in Vancouver where his estranged wife Robin Givens was shooting a TV movie called *The Penthouse.* When he arrived at her lodgings, the Hotel Vancouver, he was greeted by media cameras. He grabbed one from a *Sun* photographer and threw it against the wall, then lunged at a BCTV camera, ripping away its viewfinder and smashing it to the floor. Tyson tried to grab the TV camera, but the cameraman escaped through a revolving door, with only minor injuries.

Malcolm Lowry was the visitor least anxious to leave. Lowry arrived in Vancouver in July 1939. He lived at several Vancouver addresses and wrote periodically for the *Province,* but he wasn't comfortable in the area until he moved to a $10-a-month beach cottage in North Vancouver's Dollarton village. There he would work on his classic novel *Under the Volcano.* The book includes just a passing reference to Vancouver, a place "where they eat sausage meals from which you expect the Union Jack to appear at any minute."

Errol Flynn had a more enthusiastic view. "Vancouver is one of the most beautiful places in the world," he told a friend hours before he died here Oct. 14, 1959. Flynn had been in the city six days bar-hopping with his 17-year-old companion Beverly Aadland and was at a West End apartment (1310 Burnaby) regaling partygoers when he asked to be excused to lie down for awhile. At the bedroom door, he turned and pronounced, "I shall return." He didn't. Flynn was dead at 50 of a massive heart attack.

Sounds of Greater Vancouver
Sandra McKenzie

MORE THAN MOST cities, Vancouver can boast a distinctive soundscape of auditory artifacts and acoustic conditions. For most of us the Nine O'clock Gun, the *O Canada* horn and the ships' whistles in the harbor are welcome reminders of our unique, coastal urban environment. Less welcome is the cacophony of traffic. In Vancouver traffic noise is a classic, good-news/bad-news scenario. The good news is that the roar of traffic hasn't actually gotten worse over the past decade; the bad news is that that's because our aural environment is already saturated with street noise. Here's a brief overview of what makes Vancouver sound the way it does.

THE HARBOR
According to Capt. Geoff Drewery, deputy harbormaster for the Vancouver Port Authority, the city's harbor is as quiet as international marine law will allow. By law all ships are required to blast their whistles in warning when leaving their berths although, with the exception of the Seabuses which pull out from a blind slip, this is honored more in the breach than in the observance, says Drewery.

One strictly observed regulation requires a mandatory lifeboat drill, marked by seven short blasts followed by one long blast, for all passenger ships before entering harbor—the cause of most noise complaints from nearby office workers. Other distinctive harbor sounds include the rhythmic beating of drums during the dragon boat races, the angry little blasts from creekside ferries as they dodge boating traffic and the sounds of the 13,000 helicopters and seaplanes that take off and land in the harbor each year. Blessedly missing from our maritime soundscape is the noise of sea-doos, banned from Vancouver's harbors.

POINT ATKINSON LIGHTHOUSE FOG HORN ("OLD WAHOO")
Fog in Vancouver will never "sound" the same again. Since 1912 two blasts and a grunt from "Old Wahoo" aided mariners and comforted the landlocked. One of Vancouver's oldest auditory artifacts, this familiar "soundmark" is no more, silenced by a budgetary decision of the ministry of fisheries and oceans. (A "soundmark" is the auditory equivalent to an architectural landmark.) Early in June, 1996 the diesel-powered air chimes, whose sound carried eight to sixteen kilometres, were replaced by a solar-powered electronic signal rated for three kilometres—"like replacing an oboe with a penny whistle," according to Capt. Drewery. Actually, "Old Wahoo" itself was a modern innovation that came in for its share of criticism when introduced in 1974 as a replacement for the original, bellows-operated diaphone foghorns.

NOON HORN
From June, 1967 until Febuary, 1994 Vancouverites knew it was 12:00 noon by the first four notes of *O Canada* which blasted through 10 cast aluminum horns mounted on top of the old B.C. Hydro building. When the building was sold for development as condominiums the horns, designed by engineer and sound specialist Robert Swanson as a centennial project, fell silent for eight months until a permanent home could be found for them.

Eventually the horns were relocated to Canada Place. The first test in their new home came on October 13, 1994 at 2:00 P.M., timed to coincide with a memorial service for Swanson who died, at age 89, on October 4. A month later, on November 8, the familiar horns once again marked the noon hour, as they have ever since, although now their four-note melody, generating 115 decibels (db) of sound, plays towards the harbor rather than the downtown core.

THE BELLS OF HOLY ROSARY CATHEDRAL
The glorious peal of church bells that ring out from Holy Rosary Cathedral on Richards Street every Sunday morning between 10:30 and 11:00 are the only English-hung (that is, free-swinging) church bells in the city. There are eight bells and, besides the Sunday service, they are called into use for ceremonial occasions including weddings, funerals and ordinations. They rang for the first time on July 1, 1911 to commemorate the coronation of King George V. Aspiring bell-ringers are invited to join the group of 20 to 30 volunteers who meet for practice sessions every Tuesday at 7:00 P.M.

NINE O' CLOCK GUN
The Nine O' Clock Gun near Hallelujah Point is one of Vancouver's most colorful (so to speak) soundmarks and its oldest. The copper, tin and antimony gun was installed at Brockton Point, near its present location, in 1894.

There are two commonly held theories on the tradition of firing a time signal from a cannon, both wrong. The first story holds that the gun signalled a curfew for fishing boats, the second that it was a public chronometer for the citizens of Vancouver.

According to information provided by the park board, the time signal was intended to help sailors in port synchronize their chronometers so they could take accurate tide readings. It replaced the earlier, more nerve-wracking method of detonating a stick of dynamite dangled over the water each night. The gun's sound was incidental to this function, reports the first lighthouse keeper, William D. Jones. It was the flash that counted—a ship's captain would never wait for the sound to reach him.

The gun was moved to its present granite and wire-mesh cupola in January, 1954. With few exceptions—breaks for repair, the duration of World War II when it was silenced for fear of alarm-

Nine O'Clock Gun, 1988. vs

ing the public, and the brief "kidnapping" by engineering students in 1969—the gun has been fired every evening since 1894.

TRAFFIC

The first recorded complaint about traffic noise comes from ancient Sumer according to acoustical researcher Barry Truax, a professor in the School of Communication and Contemporary Arts at Simon Fraser University. Evidently the Sumerian gods, kept awake by late-night street revels and commerce, retaliated by unleashing the Great Flood. Their reaction may have been extreme but modern-day Vancouverites might well sympathize.

In February, 1996 Vancouver city council appointed the Urban Noise Task Force with a mandate to develop a systematic approach to the causes and eradication of noise pollution in the city. A member of the UNTF, Truax (who was also involved with Soundscape Vancouver '96, a 25-year retrospective of the city's ambient sounds) has been conducting an inventory of the city's soundmarks and the sources and levels of urban noise. Eventually, he hopes, the group will also identify acoustic sanctuaries—the increasingly rare quiet corners of the city.

How noisy is Vancouver's traffic? At an average of about 80-plus db, not much worse than it was 10 years ago when architect Roger Kemble conducted a series of sound readings around the city. That level rises to 95 db when diesel buses, emergency vehicles and trucks pass by. For comparison, 50 to 60 db is a comfortable conversational level while less than 30 db is recommended for sleep. The Workers Compensation Board identifies a level of 85 db as a significant risk for hearing loss and municipal noise by-laws cap intermittent noises at a limit of 75 db. (At 115 db, the *O Canada* horns are allowed an exemption because they predate the by-law.) According to a noise survey conducted by one of Truax's students, the only time when noise levels in the West End fall significantly below the average of 80 db is between 4:00 and 5:00 A.M.

Truax speculates that the intersection of Georgia and Burrard is the noisiest point in the city, exacerbated by the "canyon effect" in which noise is trapped and amplified by the surrounding buildings, making normal conversation at street level inaudible. Because of the space limitations of the streets the noise level itself hasn't worsened. But, he points out, as the city grows and more traffic comes into the downtown core, more traffic arteries open up, spreading high levels of traffic noise to formerly tranquil, outlying neighborhoods.

To date, sound pollution has not been part of the general agenda of environmental and development considerations, a serious omission when one considers the very real stresses and health risks of exposure to a more or less constant barrage of sound. The World Forum for Acoustic Ecology is one international organization concerned with restoring balance to the sonic environment. In Vancouver the WFAE can be reached at Simon Fraser University, School of Communication, Burnaby, v5a 1s6. Fax: (604) 291-4024; e-mail: wfae@sfu.ca, or, on the World Wide Web at http://Interact.uoregon.edu/MediaLIt/-WFAE Home Page.

Maps of Greater Vancouver
Tom Hawthorn

ABBREVIATIONS
BCLL: B.C. Legislative Library
NLC: National Library of Canada
PABC: Provincial Archives of B.C.
PAC: Public Archives of Canada
VCA: Vancouver City Archives
VPL: Vancouver Public Library

Each map entry shows publisher, date of publication (where known), map scale in inches (where available), where it can be seen. Maps may be available in other collections.

Maps identified as in possession of SFU are in the W.A.C. Bennett Library. Maps identified as located at UBC are in the Map and Special Collections Library unless otherwise noted. UBC has the most extensive collection of maps in Greater Vancouver.

Of great benefit in preparing these listings was the extensive cartobibliography by Frances M. Woodward contained in the Vancouver Centennial Bibliography: A Project of the Vancouver Historical Society, vol. 1, compiled by Linda L. Hale.

Aerial View, GVRD
Aero Surveys Ltd., 1957 • 1:35,700 • VCA

Agricultural Land Reserve
GVRD Planning Dept., 1973 • 1:63,000 • SFU

Atlas of the City of Vancouver
Chas. E. Goad Co., 1912 • 1:600 • VCA

Atlas of the City of Vancouver
Chas. E. Goad Co., 1913 • 1:2,400 • UBC

Atlas of Vancouver, Cities of North Vancouver and New Westminster and Adjoining Municipalities
Ricketts, Taschereau & Co., 1912 • VCA, PAC

Base Map
City of Vancouver Planning Dept., 1965 • 1:13,800 • PAC

Base Map
City of Vancouver Planning Dept., 1966 • 1:12,000 • PAC

Bird's Eye View of Vancouver
Dawson & Elliot, 1925 • VCA

Bird's Eye View of Vancouver
Greater Vancouver Real Estate Board, 1969 • UBC, UBC Dept. of Geography

Business Section of Vancouver
Nirenstein's National Realty Map Co., c. 1954 • 1:1,500 • UBC, BCLL

Cedar Cottage
Goddard & Son, 1911 • 1:9,087 • UBC

Civil Defense Subdivisions, Vancouver
Vancouver City Engineer's Office, 1937 • 1:22,000 • VCA

City of Vancouver Canadian Pacific Townsite
Canadian Pacific Railway Co., Land Dept., 1887, 1889 • 1:7,200 • UBC, SFU, VCA, PABC

Coal Harbour Area Map
Vancouver Harbour Commission, 1927 • 1:2,400 • PAC

Commercial Map of Greater Vancouver
Colonist Litho., 1921 • 1:31,680 • PAC

Commercial Map of Greater Vancouver and District
Vancouver Map and Blue Print Co. Ltd., 1921, 1927, c.1928, 1930, 1950 • (scales vary) • UBC, VCA, PAC (not all available at each location)

Composite Industrial Map, Lower Mainland
B.C. Dept. of Industrial Development, Trade and Commerce, 1958 • 1:50,000 • SFU, UBC, UBC Dept. of Geography

Consumer Culture
Vancouver: A Visual History, Talonbooks, Vancouver, 1992 • 1:50,000 • UBC, VPL, VCA

Downtown Business District and West End
Town Planning Commission, Vancouver, 1947 • 1:2,410 • UBC Dept. of Geography

Drainage Areas Outfalls and Trunk Sewers, Burrard Inlet
Burrard Peninsula Joint Sewerage Committee, 1913 • UBC

Electoral Districts, B.C., 1966 Redistribution
British Columbia Chief Electoral Officer, 1966 • 1:31,680 • UBC

Electoral Districts, City of Vancouver
Dept. of Mines and Technical Surveys, Canada, 1966 • 1:25,344 • PAC

Electoral Districts, Vancouver Dominion
Office of the Surveyor General, Canada, 1948 • 1:23,000 • UBC Dept. of Geography

Electric Light, Gas and Power Services
British Columbia Electric Railway Co., Ltd., 1905 • 1:9,600 • VCA

Ethnic Heritage
Vancouver: A Visual History, 1992 • 1:150,000 • UBC, VPL, VCA

Existing Development
GVRD Planning Dept., 1970 • BCLL

False Creek Plan of Suggested Improvements
Vancouver Gas Co., 1913 (shows area previously dredged, dredging required for gas works and navigation, and waterfront companies south of Keefer St.) • 1:2,400 • UBC

Fire Insurance Map
Dakin Publishing Co., 1889 (series of maps) • 1:600 • UBC, UBC Dept. of Geography, VCA

Fire Insurance Plan
Plan Dept., British Columbia Fire Underwriters Assn., 1924, 1925, 1927, 1930, 1936 (series of maps covering Vancouver, South Vancouver, Point Grey and the harbor) • 1:600 • UBC, VCA

Fire Insurance Plans
Plan Dept. Fire Branch, B.C. Insurance Underwriters Assn., 1927-1964 (series of sheets covering Point Grey, Burnaby, City and District of North Vancouver and West Vancouver) • 1:6,000 • UBC

First Composite Photomap of the Entire Lower Mainland
Vancouver Province, 1954 • 1:63,360 • UBC

Gender
Vancouver: A Visual History, Talonbooks, 1992 • 1:150,000 • UBC, VPL, VCA

Generalized Land Use
GVRD Planning Dept., 1980 • 1:50,000 • UBC Library

Geological & Development Map
Geological Dept., British American Oil Co. Ltd., 1950 • 1:63,360 • UBC

Geological History
Vancouver: A Visual History, 1992 • 1:500,000 • UBC, VPL, VCA

Grandview and East End
Dow Fraser & Co. Ltd., 1909 • VCA

Granville, B.C.
Sanborn Map and Publishing Co., Ltd., 1885 (reprinted in the *Vancouver Daily World,* June 20, 1886) • 1:600 • VPL, UBC, VCA

Granville Island: Plan of Subdivision
Vancouver Harbour Commissioners, 1925 (photocopy) • 1:2,400 • PAC

Granville Town Plan
Lands and Works Office, Victoria, 1870 • 1:792 • PAC

Great Vancouver Fire of 1886
VCA (by J.S. Matthews, city archivist), 1972-73 • PAC, Hastings Hill Store Museum

Greater Vancouver Street Atlas
Canadian Cartographics Ltd., Burnaby, 1991, 1992 • 1:200,000 (key plan) • UBC

Greater Vancouver Street Guide
Natural Color Productions Ltd., 1977 • UBC Library

Greater Vancouver "Street Wise" Map Book
Westport Publishing Co. Ltd., Victoria, 1993 • 1:176,000 (key plan) • UBC

Guide Map of Greater Vancouver
Woodwards Dept. Stores, B.C. Motels & Resorts Assn., 1976 • UBC

Guide Map of Vancouver, New Westminster, Burnaby and North Shore Municipalities
City Map and White Print Co., 1935 • 1:38,400 • VPL, VCA, PAC

Guide Map of Vancouver and Suburbs
Vancouver Map and Blue Print Co. Ltd., 1908, 1910, 1911, 1912, 1913, 1920, 1923, 1924 (scales vary, some photocopies) • VPL, PAC, SFU, UBC, UBC Library, VCA

Hastings Townsite
George Herbert Dawson, 1907 • 1:10,200 • UBC, SFU, PAC

Hastings Townsite
Archibald Moir & Co., 1911 (photocopy) •
1:4,800 • UBC

Historical Trek
Downtown Vancouver Assn., 1984 • UBC, VPL

History of Vancouver
Vancouver: A Visual History, 1992 (series of 14
maps) • 1:50,000 • UBC, VPL, VCA

Housing Prices, 1986
Vancouver: A Visual History, 1992 • 1:500,000 •
UBC, VPL, VCA

Hydrographic Charts
Hydrographic Office of the Admiralty, London,
England, 1849-1905 (includes charts based on
drawings and surveys from Capt. G. Vancouver, 1793, Capts. D. Galiano and C. Valdes,
1792, H.B.C. schooner *Cadboro*, 1827, H.M.
surveying ship *Plumper*, 1859-60, some photocopies) • UBC, VPL, VCA, PABC

**Hydrographic Chart, First Narrows, Burrard
Inlet, Canada,**
Dept. of Public Works, Canada 1904, (photo-
copy) • 1:2,400 • VCA

Hydrographic Charts, Vancouver Harbor
Canadian Hydrographic Service, 1958, 1965, 1966
• UBC Library, PAC

Indian Villages and Landmarks
Mary Jessiman • VCA

**Indian Villages and Landmarks: Burrard Inlet
and English Bay Before the White Man Came**
VCA (compiled by J.S. Matthews, City Archivist),
1932 • VCA

**Indian Villages and Landmarks: Burrard Inlet and
Howe Sound Before the White Man Came**
VCA (compiled by J.S. Matthews and August Jack
Khaatsalano), 1937 • VCA

**It Might Have Been Albert City: Vancouver his-
torical notes and obsolete names**
VCA, (compilation and drawing by J.S. Matthews),
1943 • UBC, VPL, VCA, PAC

Insurance Plan of Vancouver
Chas. E. Goad Co., 1910 (series of sheets, some
photocopies) • 1:600 • UBC, VPL Historic
Photo Collection, VCA

Land and Infrastructure, Vancouver
Canada, Central Mortgage and Housing Corp.,
B.C. Regional Office, 1978 • 1:88,704 • VPL

**Lots To Be Sold At Auction by Chief
Commissioner of Lands and Works, Hastings,
Burrard Inlet**
B.C. Dept. of Lands and Works, 1884 • 1:3,168 •
VPL

**Low Density Multiple Housing Projects, Suburban
Vancouver**
City of Vancouver Planning Dept., 1967 • UBC
Library

Lower Mainland Street Atlas
Great Pacific News, Richmond, 1990 •
1:34,000 (key plan) • UBC

Marinas
The Vancouver Book, J.J. Douglas Ltd., North Van-
couver, 1976 • UBC, SFU, VCA, VPL, PABC,
BCLL, NLC

Metropolitan Area, Lower Mainland
Technical Committee for Metropolitan Highway
Planning, Vancouver, 1955 • 1:19,200 • UBC
Library

Mining Claims
Cartwright Matheson & Co., 1917 • 1:52,272 •
PAC

Municipal-Owned Lands to be Sold, Point Grey
Office of the Municipal Engineer, 1925 • VCA

Musqueam Indian Reserve No. 2
David H. Burnett & Associates, 1965-1978 •
1:2,400 • VCA

Neighborhoods
The Vancouver Book, 1976 (series of 23 maps) •
UBC, SFU, VPL, VCA, PABC, BCLL, NLC.

Neighborhoods
Vancouver: A Visual History, 1992 • 1:50,000 •
UBC, VPL, VCA

New Westminster District
D.R. Harris, 1905 (roads, railroads, townships and
district lots, canneries, stations) • 1:63,360 •
UBC

New Westminster District
Lowenberg, Harris & Co., 1898 (photocopy) •
1:126, 720 • PAC

North Shore Hikes
H. Blackadder, British Columbia Electric Railway
Co. Ltd., 1936 (1 map : part. col., spot heights;
24.2 x 31.5 cm.) • • UBC

North Shore Hikes
British Columbia Electric Railway Co, Ltd., 1936,
1945 • UBC

Official City Map of Vancouver
Free Press Lith., London, Ont., 1886 • 1:4,800 •
UBC, VCA, PAC

Panoramic View of Vancouver
Vancouver World Printing and Publishing Co. Ltd.,
1898 • UBC, SFU, VPL, VCA, PAC

**Perspective of Greater Vancouver From Grouse
Mountain** (elevation 12,000 metres.)
Vancouver Map and Blue Print Co. Ltd., 1926 •
scale indeterminable • UBC

Physical Geography
Vancouver: A Visual History, 1992 • 1:50,000 •
UBC, VPL, VCA

Plan of the City of Vancouver
Thomson Stationery Co., Ltd, 1902, 1907 •
1:4,800 • UBC, VCA

Plan of Greater Vancouver
H.T. Devine Co. Ltd., 1911 • 1:15,600 • VCA,
UBC Dept. of Geography

**Plan of North Vancouver, Burnaby, South Vancou-
ver and Coquitlam**
Thomson Stationery Co. Ltd., 1905 • 1:63,360 •
UBC, VPL, PAC

**Plan of Portions of False Creek (Kitsilano) Indian
Reserve Required for Burrard Street Bridge
Right-Of-Way**
Vancouver City Engineer's Office, 1930 (photo-
copy) • 1:2,400 • VCA

Pocket Map of Vancouver
Allan Kilbee Stuart, 1893 • 1:180,080 • VCA

Point Grey District Map
Harland Bartholomew and Associates, 1927 •
1:25,200 • UBC, VPL

Point Grey (Kerrisdale) Lots For Sale
Harry K. Windle, 1910 • 1:2,880 • UBC

Point Grey Municipality
Clarke and Stuart Co., 1922-1924 • 1:10,800 •
UBC

Point Grey And Kitsilano
Coast Map and Blue Print Co., 1914 • 1:23,424 •
UBC

Point Grey Riding Trails
The Vancouver Book, 1976 • 1:27,600 • UBC, SFU,
VPL, VCA, PABC, BCLL, NLC

Politics
Vancouver: A Visual History, 1992 • 1:150,000 •
UBC, VPL, VCA

Polling Districts, Vancouver
Vancouver City Clerk, 1937 (photocopy) • VCA

Polling Divisions, City of Vancouver
Vancouver City Engineer's Office, 1936 • VCA

Port of Vancouver
W.A.C. Currie, 1935 • 1:16,800 • VPL

Port of Vancouver
The Vancouver Book, 1976 • UBC, UBC Library,
VPL, VCA, PABC, BCLL, SFU, NLC

Portion of the Town of Granville Burrard
John Jane, 1875 (photocopy) • PAC

**Proposed Dam, Locks and Wharves, Second
Narrows, Burrard Inlet**
Kilmer and Holland, 1910 • 1:2,400 • VCA

**Proposed Interurban Canal from Port Moody to
Pitt River**
Coquitlam, B.C. Engineer's Office, 1910 • VCA

**Provincial Government Lands to be Sold at
Auction in Vancouver**
J. Rankin and Arthur J. Ford, Auctioneers, 1906 •
VCA

**Provincial Government Property to be Sold at
Auction**
J.P. Davies & Co. Auctioneers, 1890 • 1:3,600 •
VCA

**Rail Lines, City and Suburban, Vancouver and
New Westminster**
British Columbia Electric Railway Co. Ltd., c.
1931-1940 • 1:95,040 • PAC

Rail Lines, Freight
British Columbia Electric Railway Co. Ltd. 1941 •
1:63,360 • VPL

Rail Lines, Inter-Urban
British Columbia Electric Railway Co., Ltd., 1986
(photocopy) • 1:79,200 • UBC

Rail Route, Proposed, Vancouver to Mission
British Columbia Electric Railway Co. Ltd., 1912 (photocopy) • 1:253,440 • UBC

Railway and Transmission Lines, Westminster Chilliwack
British Columbia Electric Railway Co. Ltd., 1908 (photocopy) • 1:253,440 • UBC

Railways, Proposed and in Operation, Burrard Inlet
Canadian Pacific Railway Co., Land Dept., 1893 • 1:2,400 • VCA

Recycling Directory
SPEC, 1981 • UBC

Religion
Vancouver. A Visual History, 1992 • 1:150,000 • UBC, VPL, VCA

School Locations, Greater Vancouver
B.C. Dept. of Education, 1925 • 1:47,520 • UBC, PABC

Sectional Map and Street Directory, Vancouver and adjacent areas
Dominion Map Ltd., 1972 • 1:95,040 • UBC Library, PAC

Sectional Map and Street Directory
Sectional Map and Street Directory Co., 1933, 1935, 1936, 1938, 1941 • 1:95,040 • UBC

Sectional Maps
Vancouver City Engineering Dept., 1945, 1953, 1954, 1970 • (scales vary) • UBC Library, UBC

Settlement Pattern
Lower Mainland Regional Planning Board, 1967 • 1:40,800 • VCA

Shaughnessy Heights
Canadian Pacific Railway Co., Land Dept., 1917, 1930 (photocopies) • 1:4,800 • UBC, VCA

Sociology Maps of Vancouver
UBC Dept. of Sociology 1936-1944 (18 maps, compiled by students in Sociology laboratory courses, photocopy) • • UBC

South Vancouver Municipality
Coast Map and Blue Print Co., 1913 • 1:11,880 • VCA

Squatters, Stanley Park
Vancouver Park Board, 1923 (photocopy) • 1:1,584 • VCA

Stanley Park Grounds and Zoo
Cartwright Matheson & Co., 1910 (photocopy) • 1:633 • VCA

Stanley Park
Vancouver Board of Park Commissioners, 1911 (drawn by Thomas A. Mawson, landscape architect, includes pedestrian and horse trails, circumference of large trees, photocopy.) • 1:4,800 • VCA

Stanley Park Topographical Plan
Vancouver Board of Park Commissioners, 1913 • VCA

Street Map
Vancouver: A Visual History, 1992 • 1:50,000 • UBC, VPL, VCA

Street Map of Greater Vancouver
Challenger Cartographers Ltd., 1951 • 1:36,115 • UBC

Street Map, Vancouver and Surrounding Municipalities
David Spencer Ltd., Vancouver, 1942 • • UBC

Street Map, Vancouver
Vancouver Town Planning Commission, 1944 • 1:21,600 • UBC

Street Map, Greater Vancouver
Evergreen Press, 1958 • 1:36,000 • UBC Library

Street Map
GVRD Planning Dept., 1964, 1965 • 1:24,000 • SFU

Streetcar Lines, Vancouver
British Columbia Electric Railway Co., Ltd., 1910 (photocopy) • 1:9,600 • UBC

Streets and Principal Buildings, Vancouver
Chas. E. Goad Co., 1897 • 1:1,200, 1:600 • PAC

Survey of Coast Line Around Coal Peninsula
Vancouver City Engineer's Office, 1923 (photocopy) • VCA

Timber Claims of A.B.C. Mill Co.
F.W. Green, 1870 • 1:31,680 • UBC

Topography
Canada Geological Survey, Ottawa, 1919 • • UBC

Topography
Geological Survey of Canada, 1921, 1923 (series of maps of Burrard Inlet, Fraser Delta and North Arm of the Fraser River.) • 1:12,000 • UBC, UBC Library

Tourist Map and Street Guide to Vancouver
Croydon Publishing Co., 1940 • 1:31,680 • UBC

Tourist Guide Map
Garden, Hermon & Burwell, 1898 • 1:14,400 • VCA, PAC

Town of Granville, Burrard Inlet
B.C. Dept. of Lands, 1876, 1927 (photocopies) • 1:1,560, 1:4,752 • PAC

Transit Map of Greater Vancouver
Challenger Cartographers Ltd. (prepared for B.C. Electric), 1949, 1954 • 1:36,115, 1:36,000 • UBC, UBC Library, VPL, VCA

Transit System Map, Greater Vancouver
B.C. Electric, 1957 • 1:36,115 • UBC, VCA, VPL

Transportation Network and Industrial Sites, Lower Mainland
Canadian Pacific Railway Co., Dept. of Industrial Development, 1975 • 1:63,360 • SFU

UBC Campuses, 1923
G.W.H.(Hal) Norman, 1976 • UBC

Vancouver and Vicinity
British American Oil Co. Ltd., 1959 • 1:48,000 • UBC Library, VPL

Vancouver and Region Street Directory
Mainland Magazine Service, Langley, 1986 (includes Expo 86 site) • 1:30,000 (key plan) • UBC

Vancouver Area
Lands and Works Dept., Victoria, 1874-75 • 1:31,680 • UBC

Vancouver During The Depression
VCA, (compiled by J.S. Matthews, shows houses of people on relief during the Depression),1943 • VCA

Vancouver Parks and Recreation Map
Vancouver Board of Parks and Recreation, 1971 • 1:63,360 • UBC

Vancouver's Origins
F.G.H. Brooks, 1952 • 1:48,000•UBC

Vegetation of the Southwest Fraser Lowland
Environment Canada, Lands Directorate, 1979 • 1:50,000 (horizontal); 1:120 (vertical) • SFU, UBC, UBC Library, UBC Dept. of Geography

Visitors Map of Greater Vancouver and South-western B.C.
Mainland Southwest Tourist Ass., 1972 • 1:79,200 • VCA

Ward System Before 1935, Vancouver
Vancouver Province, 1968 • UBC Library

Warehouse and Store Sites on Alexander Street
Mahon McFarland & Mahon Ltd., 1909 • VCA

Water Pipes, Hydrants, etc, Locations
Vancouver City Engineer's Office, 1888-1909 • 1:2,400 • VCA

Water Supply Sources and Systems
Engineering Institute of Canada, 1952 (map of Greater Vancouver Water District in 13 sheets, photocopy) • 1:120,000 • VCA

Water Supply Sources and Systems
Greater Vancouver Water District, 1931, 1963 • 1:190,080; 1:253,440 • VCA, UBC

Weather
Vancouver: A Visual History, 1992 • 1:500,000 • UBC, VPL, VCA

Where You Vote Tomorrow
Vancouver Sun, 1934 • UBC Library

Zoning and Development Sectional Maps
City of Vancouver Planning Dept., 1976 • 1:5,100 • UBC Library

Zoning Diagram, Vancouver
Dominion Map and Blue Print Co., 1942 • 1:33,000 • VCA

facing page: Portion of Department of Marine chart, 1898, showing Burrard Inlet and the Fraser River delta. cva

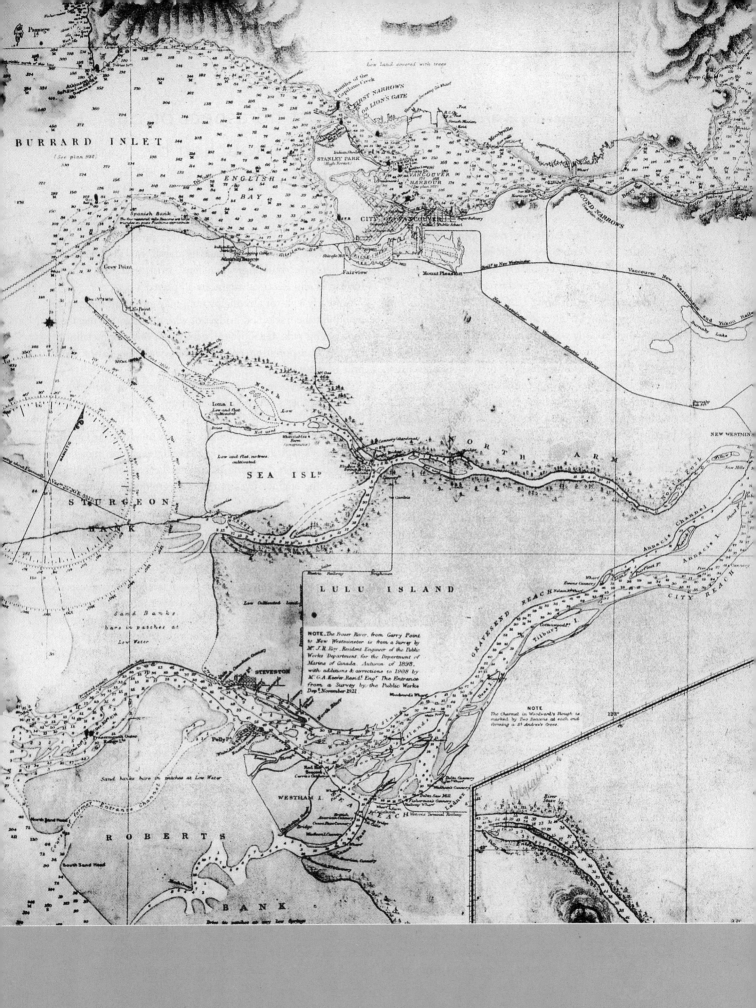

The History of Engineering in Greater Vancouver

Jim Lyon

WHAT FIRST POPS into mind when you think of engineering? For me, two things. A landmark and a prank. The landmark: the stunningly elegant, albeit geriatric, Lions Gate Bridge, built in 1938 so the Guinness brewing family of Ireland could exploit their land holdings in the British Properties in West Vancouver.

The prank: exuberantly daring UBC engineering grads (in the 1970s) suspending a Volkswagen Beetle under the bridge's centre span when nobody was looking. Nice that they didn't let it drop on a cruise ship. But they knew what they were about.

When lay people think of engineering their attention is usually claimed by the big, obvious chunks of hardware its practitioners scatter across the landscape: bridges; SkyTrain; B.C. Place with its inflatable roof that looks like a pin cushion; the odd-looking Westcoast Energy building on West Georgia.

In fact the ubiquitous products of the engineer's discipline (or rather disciplines, as the profession boasts many sub-branches) affect our lives in ways not intuitively obvious.

Much of the engineering expertise resident in Greater Vancouver derives from the imperatives of British Columbia's geography and economy. Because we're on the water, we build and repair ships and boats and we develop expertise in underwater engineering. Because our economy still depends primarily on the forest industry, we become skilled in designing and building sawmills and pulp and paper mills, and export that knowledge around the world. Forests catch fire and burn so we develop skills putting them out. Polluting pulp mills spawn expertise in environmental engineering.

Since British Columbia is geologically immature and hillsides sometimes collapse on people, we develop know-how in soil stability.

We've also learned how to transport British Columbia's abundant supply of natural gas over vast distances and use it to heat our homes and offices, and cook our meals without the gas blowing us up.

Because Canada, defined by its sprawling geography, has to overcome immense distances, we have also developed superb telecommunications skills.

Almost no aspect of our lives is untouched by engineering. We drive to work by car. An automotive engineer had much to do with that. The road under our wheels is there only because the civil engineer surveyed and built it. Flying home from a

Almost no aspect of our lives is untouched by engineering

vacation, we may give a passing thought to aerospace engineers but do we think of who created and transported the electricity to guide the plane in, announce its arrival, run the machinery and light the buildings and signs? Structural, mechanical, industrial and electrical engineers all played a part.

Similarly a visitor arriving by train may give scant thought to who built the tracks and bridges or who provided the metal for the shining rails. Geophysical, geological, mining, metallurgical and transportation engineers were with the visitor every mile of the way.

And so it goes on: every day we are affected by the work of unseen engineers—chemical, petroleum, nuclear, agricultural, biomedical.

In this limited space, though, we can only hint at Greater Vancouver's rich diversity of engineering expertise, inevitably neglecting much deserving of tribute. Let's glance quickly at some of the engineering innovations employed by Vancouver firms.

Mining giant Placer Dome taps images from spy satellites to help locate ore bodies. This method has become a valuable tool in the search for mineral wealth.

Macdonald Dettwiler & Associates of Richmond is a world-leader in developing computer-based systems for areospace ventures, resource management and electronics manufacturing. Clients include NASA, the European Space Agency, the Australian department of transportation, the U.S. Jet Propulsion Laboratory, the U.S. Air Force and the Canadian government.

MacMillan Bloedel spent $45 million over 20 years on research and development of parallel strand lumber which it now markets under the trade name Parallam. This engineered lumber creates large beams out of small trees. An efficient sawmill may only recover 15 per cent of a log as highgrade lumber and another 35-40 per cent in lower-grade lumber products. The rest of the log becomes wood chips or fuel. With Parallam, MB uses 70-80 per cent of a log to produce a super lumber product. Parallam is manufactured by bonding long strands of wood, under pressure, into uniform structural beams with a waterproof adhesive. The bonding resin is cured with microwave energy—somewhat like cooking in a kitchen microwave. MB began producing Parallam at a pilot plant on

Annacis Island in Vancouver in 1981. In 1987, when it was satisfied it had a viable product, it decided to spend $100 million to bring the Annacis Island plant into full commercial production and to build a similar plant in Georgia.

A small Vancouver company, International Telepresence Corporation, builds a three-dimensional vision system that doctors attach to surgical instruments when they perform "belly-button" or laparoscopic surgery. ITC has also built vision systems to give three-dimensional depth perception to remote submarines working more than 4,800 metres under water and to robots dismantling IRA parcel bombs in Britain. Same technology, different application.

Engineers played a distinguished role in the early history of British Columbia. Responding to a request in 1858 from British Columbia's first governor, Sir James Douglas, the British colonial secretary sent 150 non-commissioned officers and men in a company of sappers and miners to B.C. under the command of an officer of the Royal Engineers, Colonel R.C. Moody. Gov. Douglas sought to preserve British influence in the face of a large influx of American gold-seekers. He argued that the new colony needed the underpinnings of settlement: mechanisms to raise and collect revenue; construction of roads, trails and bridges; and exploration and development, including the charting of settlement patterns and townsites, and the surveying and mapping of land.

The first trail built by the sappers in 1859 was the North Road which ran straight north from the engineers' camp in New Westminster to Burrard Inlet. Its purpose was to give the soldiers an alternate supply route should the Americans attack via the Fraser River.

In the summer of 1859 the company surveyed and laid out the town of New Westminster, the temporary capital of B.C. The military engineers also surveyed the towns of Yale, Hope and Douglas. They were also responsible for the building of the Cariboo Road, one of Canada's greatest early engineering achievements. The engineers and sappers erected many of the buildings of the emerging communities: schools, churches, a library, a hospital and an observatory. It was Moody who made the enlightened decision to preserve the tract of original forest that became known as Stanley Park. When the company was disbanded in 1863 (following a dispute over the payment of costs), 130 of the 150 engineers stayed on as civilian settlers.

Engineers were responsible for Canada's first interurban electric tramway which began running between New Westminster and Vancouver in 1891.

Greater Vancouver's hydro-electric generating potential was tapped early in the 20th century. Engineers created a tunnel to

divert water from Coquitlam Lake to Buntzen Lake and then by penstocks to two powerhouses on Indian Arm. The original plant was placed in service in 1903 and a second plant began operating in 1914. Nearly all the inflow into Buntzen Lake comes from Coquitlam Lake through the diversion tunnel. In 1911 power was also produced from a concrete dam and 52.5 megawatt powerhouse located at the outlet of Stave Lake.

During World War I the Imperial Munitions Board placed many orders with Canadian shipyards. During the war British Columbia shipyards built 20 wooden schooners, 69 wooden steamers and 43 steel steamers to further the war effort.

But no period of engineering activity can have been more exciting for Vancouver than the period during World War II. Then the Port of Vancouver was host to a frenzied ship building boom. Responding to the national crisis, Vancouver's shipyards turned out hundreds of cargo vessels and warships, and by the peak year of 1943 the work force had grown to more than 25,000. This number did not include several thousand people employed in support industries such as boilermaking and the manufacture of steering engines and winches. In just four years West Coast yards built almost three million tonnes of new shipping and repaired, converted and refitted a similar amount. In 1943 alone Burrard Drydock completed 33 cargo vessels, North Vancouver Ship Repairs completed 15, West Coast Ship Builders turned out 17 and the remaining yards in British Columbia launched four. The vessels, of 9,000 tonnes and 4,200 tonnes, were produced at remarkable speed, some completed in just 65 days.

Greater Vancouver's bridges each represent significant engineering accomplishments and are worthy monuments to the engineer's art: Burrard, Granville, Cambie, Oak Street, Arthur Laing, Alex Fraser, Second Narrows, Port Mann, the Georgia Viaduct, Pattulo, Lions Gate. Second Narrows collapsed during construction in 1958, killing 18 workers and a diver. The Port Mann Bridge, built as an essential link in the Trans-Canada Highway in the 1960s, represented the first use of orthotropic steel decking in North America. When it opened it was the longest bridge of its type in the world.

Bridge statistics are staggering. One of the latest river crossings to be built in Greater Vancouver is the SkyBridge which went into service in 1990 to carry the SkyTrain light rapid transit system across the Fraser River into Surrey. The 616-metre long structure was part of a $179 million, three-kilometre SkyTrain extension. The bridge, which carries trains 50 metres above the Fraser, is the world's longest cable-stayed bridge designed solely for rapid transit. The 104 deck sections, eight weighing 100 tonnes, were built in Richmond, barged up the

research into sustainable engineering practices in the forest industry, B.C.'s engineers and geoscientists are applying new technology to meet the needs of a vibrant and growing community. When it comes to professionalism and integrity, the designations P.Eng. and P.Geo. are the hallmarks of creativity, experience and excellence.

Even scaffolding has to be engineered; workers erect temporary stands for the Molson Indy Vancouver, 1993. vs

Fraser and then lifted into place by heavy equipment. Thirty-five thousand cubic metres of concrete (4,000 mix truckloads), 13.5 kilometres of stay cables and 13 kilometres of steel pilings were used in the construction.

In the 1990s Georgia Street in Vancouver acquired several stunning new buildings: General Motors Place, the new Van-couver Public Library building and the Ford Theatre. But a quarter of a century after its construction the Westcoast Build-ing at the other end of West Georgia near Stanley Park remained the city's most eye-catching construction. Its earth-quake-resistant design is the imaginative work of Vancouver engineer Bogue Babicki (who, incidentally, also engineered the striking "golf ball" that now houses Science World at the east-ern end of False Creek).

Dr. Babicki noticed that trees usually escape earthquake damage. Although a tree may sway violently the branches that radiate out from the trunk move freely without causing dam-age. He decided to apply his observations to a building of unusual design. Strong steel cables attached to the central core of the Westcoast building support the rest of the structure. Dr. Babicki has since built ten cable-suspended office towers in the earthquake-prone region of Cagliari, Sardinia using the same principle.

Engineering of a far different type has been undertaken by engineers at the Medical Engineering Research Unit at Shaugh-nessy Hospital in Vancouver.

James Foort and his colleagues have used CAD/CAM tech-niques (computer assisted design/computer assisted manufac-turing) to help design and make properly fitting prostheses to replace missing limbs. The techniques developed by the Shaughnessy Hospital team have replaced the traditional trial-and-error process of fitting artificial limbs. (Three-dimension-al imaging is used to produce a computerized map of the patient's stump. A full-scale model is then carved for use in making the plastic socket connecting the stump to the artificial limb. Using computer technology the system eliminates much of the hit-and-miss adjustments traditionally used to ensure that a prosthesis fits comfortably.)

The widespread influence of engineering on the lives of B.C. citizens—only a small portion of which has been conveyed in this short history—requires that engineers follow the highest standards of professional conduct. The Association of Profes-sional Engineers of British Columbia was formed through the Engineers act of 1921 to establish the qualifications necessary to practise. Some seven decades later this self-regulating body operates as the 17,000 member Association of Professional Engineers and Geoscientists of British Columbia (APEGBC), mandated under the Engineers and Geoscientists act to regis-ter and license its membership in the interests of safeguarding public health, safety and welfare.

For information about the engineering profession, contact the Association of Professional Engineers and Geoscientists of B.C. at (604) 430-8035.

SERVIRE CREARE PERMANERE

Vancouver: City in Chaos (A View from 2020)
Frank Ogden (Doctor Tomorrow)

Our city looked a lot different just prior to Expo 86. "The village on the edge of the rain forest" boasted few of the sophisticated restaurants found in other major cities. Today we have thousands of these Epicurean centres—many match those found anywhere. In a time of roaring technological development nothing was to stay the same. Ninety per cent of everything we interacted with by the year 2005 had changed. This tsunami of change carried Vancouver into the 21st century in better shape than most other cities.

Our location on the Pacific Rim, although less a factor than it would have been during the 19th century, did help somewhat, especially during the early part of the Communications Age, which took off back around 1970. Asia, long known as the Far East, quickly became the Near West to Vancouverites during the 1990s. Immigrants from Hong Kong, Japan, Taiwan, China, Singapore, India, Sri Lanka and Vietnam mixed with the continuing stream of Europeans, Mexicans and Central and South Americans. Even in the mid-1990s if you listened closely you could hear 50 different frequently spoken languages in the Lower Mainland. We definitely had a large number of world-wide fans, many flying in aboard Boeing 18-hour non-stop 747-400 series airplanes. Our growing television, movie and CD-ROM industries spread the word and fueled the fame of this beautiful city on what was then Canada's West Coast.

The Communications Age exploding at the speed of light disrupted many institutions that had become comfortable with a life in the past. Vancouver Public Library, erected at a cost well in excess of $100 million and so far the last major library to be built in North America, opened in 1995. Before that year ended it was short of funds for repairs, purchases and subscriptions to newspapers and magazines. The sale of the old library location brought much less revenue than anticipated.

The new library came on the scene just as optical storage came on stream. Some found out that the entire library contents, one million books, could be stored on one 12-inch disc called a SEROD. Some were already calling SEROD obsolete. No land, no building, no equipment, no books and basically no staff required to disseminate disc information worldwide—at less cost than it then took to park a car to enter the library.

This was a weather vane point in the new Age of Chaos, as traditional institutions, large and arthritic as elderly elephants, could not move fast enough to compete in a world gone glob-

Library Square opening, 1995. vs

al. What the establishment saw as chaos was, to the electronically liberated, a garden of creativity, freeing the adventurous to follow more exciting and colorful lifestyles than available to humankind in the past. Vancouverites began walking faster than urbanites in other North American cities. The Asian influence of energy, willingness to study and work harder, and longer, and risk time and capital in new ventures fueled even more radical change.

The population of Greater Vancouver (1.8 million in 1995) rose rapidly around 1997, as another surge of Hong Kong immigrants saw insurance value in planting wealth and energy here rather than leaving it all to potential risk back home. Other Southeast Asians found reasons to move family members to the North American west coast and created further two-way business arrangements that benefitted all sides of the Vancouver/Hong Kong/Southeast Asia golden triangle. Chaos, once considered dangerous by many North Americans, turned into the yin/yang of Chinese legend—danger and opportunity. Immigrants from the Near West saw creative opportunity where many contented Canadians, comfortable in Lotus Land and unwilling to change or be disturbed, saw only danger.

Now in 2020 what was once known as the Lower Mainland has become an economically independent state like Singapore. Culture changed as a hyperglut of philosophies, religions, ideas and global change built an efficient and exciting new age. "The village on the edge of the rainforest" is now home to seven million people.

Vancouver is a cosmopolis of opportunity, a successful city state among the empires of the mind.

Clocks of Greater Vancouver
Faith Bloomfield

There are steam clocks and moving clocks, street clocks and tower clocks, small clocks and big clocks. The Vancouver Block clock is one of the big clocks.

Crowning the building 17 storeys above the ground, each of the tower clock's four faces is approximately nine metres in diameter, and the almost-three-metre long minute hands move 15 centimetres a minute. When the clock was first built more than 80 years ago (the cornerstone at the top of the clock has 1911 carved on it but the Vancouver Block was officially opened in 1912), each face was made of glass and the hands of a heavy tin. Over the years the glass became brittle and most has been replaced with wood. Except for one hand and a couple of bits and pieces, the clock is still made up of its original parts.

Despite modern buildings towering around its Granville Street location, the clock is still visible from several points around the city. (Northbound over the Granville Street Bridge provides an ideal view of the majestic timepiece.) And the clock is also visible at night, illuminated since the late 1920s by red and blue neon tubing. Judging by the dimensions of the clock, one would think the works would be proportionally large. They aren't. Until the 1950s the clock's gears, crank and shaft were battery-operated. Located in the hub of the clock, the works are still contained on their original 61-centimetre-square stand. A .25 h.p. 60-cycle motor and transformer have been added, and three tiny timers keep the whole thing in sync.

Virtually maintenance-free, the clock has stopped few times in almost a century of timekeeping: as a result of earthquakes—December 7, 1918, and June 23, 1946—and about twelve years ago when only weeks of patience and tinkering got it running again. In late December, 1952, the clock broke down and was set at twelve o'clock with New Year's Eve in mind. Not only did the clock welcome in 1953 at midnight on December 31, but it continued to usher in the new year until it was finally repaired 16 days later!

There have been many antics involving the clock—around 1980 UBC engineering students suspended a Volkswagen from the top of the tower—and intrigue as well. Eight or nine years ago when maintenance engineer Wayne Yarwood went up to check the clock, he saw that the door leading to the roof of the clock was missing. Mysteriously, it was never found and at no time did anyone report being hit by a flying door on Granville Street.

In 1983 Yarwood noticed a hole, almost eight centimetres in diameter, at the two o'clock position on the south face. He thought it might be a bullet hole, but never heard anything to back up this theory. Then in 1994 carpenters replacing the north face glass with wood discovered an unexplained rifle shell!

The tower clock located at 757 West Hastings (the Sinclair Centre) has been there since 1909, as part of the main post office. In 1985 the clock's works were replaced by a tiny electronic mechanism and the four clock fronts received face-lifts to replace the glass and dials. The original parts—the winding mechanism and old bell—were restored and are displayed in the Centre's atrium.

The Sinclair Centre tower clock is a *big* clock. The minute hand alone weighs 91 kilograms and it used to take three days for the controlling weights to completely travel the tower's 21-metre shaft.

There are only two mechanical clocks left in the area. The Heritage Hall clock tower, or Little Ben (named after its London cousin also built by J.B. Joyce and Company of Whitchurch, England) is wound once a week and ticks only 48 times each minute. Each face is almost two metres in diameter, the swinging pendulum is one-and-a-half metres long and its 91 centimetre, almost two-tonne bronze bell still sounds every hour, between 9:00 a.m. and 9:00 p.m. The B.C. chapter of the National Association of Clock and Watchmakers maintains the clock in exchange for its monthly meeting space.

Appropriately named, the Beast is Maple Ridge's answer to the *big* clock. Although surrounded by controversy, the Beast was welcomed to its municipal hall location in 1989. People walking by can't help but notice the imposing grandeur of the clock and statue. If they pass on the hour, they catch the Beast doing its thing: in a process lasting 12 minutes, the Beast rears up, its front legs fluttering, its tail beating the air.

At no cost to the municipality Don Brayford funded his "beastly" dream through a GoBC grant, donations and his own pockets. After a three-year search, Brayford compiled the Beast's design from several horse "visions." The production took three more years to build—two years of that devoted to the mechanics and problem solving.

What is the Beast? Well, as legend has it (there is in fact a detailed, copyrighted legend), the Beast was a horse that ran free in Maple Ridge "from the beginning of time in perfect harmony with the environment." That is, until man and technology destroyed nature. The Beast came back as a statue and is a constant reminder to all who see it of the destruction of the earth.

The materials used to create this almost seven-and-a-half-metre clock (the horse brings the height to more than ten metres, 12 metres when it is activated) are recycled parts, metals and bevelled gears from an out-of-service municipal secondary sewage treatment plant, and used farm and mill machinery.

A big old Commodore Vic 64 computer controls the 54 hydraulic valves in the horse's belly, giving the Beast its kick. Every quarter-hour Westminster chimes ring out from a household clock, amplified by two speakers from within the statue.

The district covers the costs of running the Beast and Brayford takes care of maintaining the computer, the hydraulics and the motor.

There are dozens of other public clocks in Greater Vancouver, all with their own histories and meanings to the people who look at them. The Gastown Steam Clock and the relocated Birks clock are just two that spring to mind as integral parts of Vancouver's history.

Seventy-one years before the 1977 construction of the Gastown landmark, jeweller George E. Trorey erected Vancouver's first public clock on the northeast corner of West Hastings and Granville. The following year, in 1907, Henry Birks and Sons took over the location and the Birks clock became an icon of the store and city. In 1913 the store moved to its newly built Birks Building at the corner of West Georgia and Granville, where the clock marked time and stood as a meeting place for more than eight decades.

It was moved twice, temporarily, before being relocated to its original site (albeit across the street) when Birks moved into a heritage building on October 23, 1994.

The clock was built in November, 1905, and the original wooden movement still keeps it going. Sharing the distinction with Little Ben, the clock is still hand-wound every Tuesday morning.

Despite the relative "youthfulness" of Ray Saunders' steam clock, it is an oft-cited and popular attraction. There are always people waiting at the Water Street and Cambie location to hear the hourly Westminster chimes or to see the almost-five-metre-high cast-bronze clock "blow off steam" every 15 minutes.

Saunders is one of a small number of experts in public clockmaking. He considers himself an artist and advisor as well as a watch and clock technician. Besides the Gastown Steam Clock, 12 other public clocks throughout Greater Vancouver were built by Saunders. There are other steam clocks: one in Whistler that blows a cloud of steam and gongs every hour and a miniature replica of the Gastown clock in the restaurant area of Vancouver International Airport. There are the street clocks located in Kerrisdale on West 41st Avenue at Yew Street and the Mount Pleasant clock at Main and East 50th that he was commissioned to do. There are the several standard (four-dial) tower clocks all over the region: the Granville and Broadway tower, Bill Chow Jewellers, Bridgepoint Market tower, Westminster Quay tower, Trenton Park tower and a rare three-faced clock at Lacollage on West 4th, near Cypress Street.

More unusual clocks created by Saunders include the waterclock in Nanaimo Mall and the world's largest functioning lunar/tide clock at the Bridgeport Market in Richmond.

There are other unusual methods of keeping track of time in the area including the nine o'clock gun, the horns at Canada Place that toot the first four notes to "Oh Canada" at noon and the federal debt clock that shows how time flies and money flies out the window. Then there is the sundial at North Vancouver's Waterfront Park. Unfortunately due to the often inclement weather—North Vancouver may not be the ideal place for a timepiece needing sun for accuracy—the time may not always be exact.

The clock at Vancouver's city hall deserves mention as well, as a clock steeped in civic history and aesthetic beauty. The four-faced clock is visible from a wide radius during the day or at night when the red neon dials are aglow. Built into the tower when it was first erected in 1936, the clock figures prominently in the city hall logo and has become a distinct symbol of Vancouver.

The old Vancouver Main Post Office, built 1905–10 at Hastings and Granville, showing the prominent 43m-high clock tower. cva

Manufactured by E. Howard & Company of Boston, Massachusetts, this four-sided clock is constructed of cast-iron and features foliated capitals, columns, friezes and cornices, a reflection of Victorian fascination with ornamental detail. A plaque on the clock is dedicated to the generations of people who have met, and will continue to meet, at the Birks Clock. It reads "Dedicated this 2nd Day of November, 1994 by The Birks Family Foundation and The City of Vancouver Heritage Conservation Foundation."

Stained Glass in Greater Vancouver
Faith Bloomfield

WITH THE ESTABLISHMENT of Henry Bloomfield & Sons in 1890, art arrived in British Columbia in the form of stained-glass windows. Their glass shop produced creative pieces of quality at a time when the only other works available were of inferior calibre. Before bringing his family from England in 1887, Henry Bloomfield was a trained plumber with extensive experience using lead. Because of this skill he became a "master in the art" of stained glass by re-leading old church windows at Oxford University.

Today there are many companies specializing in stained glass in Greater Vancouver. While many artisans use computer-aided designs and calculations, others still rely on some of the same techniques used by the Bloomfields. Stained-glass windows are again fashionable and newer styles of glass art are also much in demand.

The Bloomfields settled in New Westminster in 1889. Through the early 1890s business was slow for Henry and his sons James and Charles due to an economic depression suffered by the construction industry. Nevertheless until the turn of the century they produced many works using the Gothic and Victorian revival methods. The windows consisted of geometric patterns of both bright and muted colors held together with heavy lead canes and encircled painted-image centrepieces. The images were floral, heraldic and literary, and these works came to represent a new movement in art and stained glass for that day in British Columbia.

In 1896 Bloomfield & Sons (without James, who left B.C. in 1895) was asked to work on stained glass for the new parliament buildings in Victoria—its largest contract to date. Shortly after completion of this project the Bloomfield house, studio and workshop were destroyed in the huge fire that swept New Westminster in 1898. The family relocated to Vancouver's Mount Pleasant area at the corner of West 10th and Columbia, and took up residence in a building still standing and now considered a heritage landmark.

When James left in 1895 he sought new design techniques. He returned in 1899 highly influenced by the art-glass styles in vogue in the U.S. and Europe. The glasswork produced by his father and brother for Victoria would not have been progressive enough for James and, in fact, on a world scale might have been considered mediocre.

However the family continued to produce works for private homes, churches and other public buildings, many of which remain intact. Holy Trinity Cathedral on Carnarvon in New Westminster features a number of pieces produced by the Bloomfields in 1900. Also produced by the Bloomfields are the windows at St. Paul's Reformed Episcopal Church at 628 Royal, a window with the city's coat of arms displayed at the present city hall and a dome made in 1910 for lumber baron J. B. Wilson's home "Melrose" (now part of a collection at the Vancouver Museum). A 1901 memorial to Queen Victoria still remains at Vancouver's St. Paul's Anglican Church on Jervis and the 1901 entrance transom and several panes originally produced for "Gabriola"—the West End home of sugar magnate B. T. Rogers—are still installed at their original location, now Romano's Macaroni Grill.

James brought back with him a more modern technique of design. No longer restricted to geometric shapes, the art nouveau offered a more honest interpretation of natural settings and images. Now the centrepiece was also produced in a mosaic with individual glass pieces leaded together, instead of the former painted and fired images. The new art allowed the designer to be true to an area's indigenous nature. Instead of tulips or roses, James used British Columbia's wildflowers— dogwood, trillium and even skunk cabbage—in his designs.

Together with architects who followed this same honest interpretation, James Blomfield (he dropped the "o" as a tribute to his ancestors in England) went on to create even more art glass— stained glass and murals—incorporating aboriginal and natural designs. His artistic and design abilities eventually caught the eye of Governor General Lord Aberdeen. Aberdeen commissioned James to work on a modified version of Vancouver's coat of arms and in 1902 he presented this work to the visiting Duke and Duchess of Cornwall.

Bloomfield and Sons closed shortly thereafter and the sons went out on their own. Charles, to keep up with the growing competition, started the Standard Glass Company and in the 1920s was part of a group of several artisans commissioned to work on glass paintings for the heraldic windows in the University of British Columbia library.

With a surge in urban development, stained-glass windows of geometric and floral designs were starting to appear in public and private clubs, heraldic symbols incorporating coats-of-arms and shields were being produced for academic and governmental buildings, and Vancouver's new lowrise apartment buildings were replacing plain glass with art nouveau-designed windows— many of which still remain in the Kitsilano and south Granville areas.

Throughout time churches used stained-glass windows to display religious figures and events. The Sanctuary and Chancel

Memorial Windows at St. John's Shaughnessy Anglican Church at Nanton and Granville Streets in Vancouver are made from 11th century glass salvaged from Canterbury Cathedral windows after they were shattered during a 1942 air raid. The fragments were given to wartime parishioner Archdeacon Greig, who later settled in Vancouver. They were taped together by matching the colors, and the windows, measuring 61 centimetres by two metres, are now installed in the sanctuary above the choirstalls.

Many religious works produced in the early part of the century have survived, including those in several West End churches: the 1901 St. Paul's memorial to Queen Victoria; several memorial pieces at Christ Church Cathedral; and a series of biblical depictions at St. Andrew's Wesley Church.

Several heraldic and literary designs are still installed at a number of Vancouver academic institutions. The glass paintings Charles Bloomfield was involved with for the UBC Great Hall consist of coats of arms of Canadian and English universities. The Bromsgrove Guild designed another piece for the hall—a centrepiece consisting of the British Columbia coat of arms hangs in the west window. The window depicting the coats of arms of the other provinces hangs in the stairwell of the library. In the senior building of Lord Strathcona School on East Pender Street an early 1900s stairwell window contains many literary figures, including Robert Burns, and at Carnegie Public Library 1903 depictions of Spenser, Milton and Shakespeare, and a shield of B.C. overhang the staircase leading to the third floor.

In the late 1960s a resurgence in arts and crafts brought forth a whole new interest in stained and art glass and in 1965 students at Sir William MacDonald Elementary School on East Hastings created a 14-window art project.

Langara Chapel at St. Vincent's Hospital on West 62nd Avenue in Vancouver features two wall-sized windows depicting an open book complete with religious artifacts and icons. The technique used for this monumental piece by Studio One Art Glass is called *dalle de verre* (or slab glass) because of the thickness of the glass panes. Each window consists of six separate windows bound together with an epoxy-concrete instead of traditional lead. The glass is two centimetres thick, six times thicker than usual stained-glass windows.

Yves Trudeau of Studio One is not simply an artisan, but considers himself an "architectural glass designer." Besides the *dalle de verre,* Trudeau creates traditional stained-glass pieces as well as using modern techniques of sandcarving, fused and kiln-formed glass and lamination. Although some are still done manually, most of the designs and firings are now computer-generated.

No longer just an artistic way to dress up a window, these techniques also create free-standing works of art. An example of

Stained glass (circa 1900), B.T. Rogers mansion, Vancouver 1988. vs

sandblasted and fused laminated glass can be found at the entrance to the Fujian Church on Blundell Road in Richmond. The doors were completed by Studio One in 1994.

At the entrance of the council chambers in the main foyer of Delta municipal hall stands a majestic example of glasswork mosaic. "Delta Legacy" incorporates a site-specific design and many precious metals found in the area including silver, gold and platinum. Within a glass canvas, the nine-metre-by-three-metre multilayered piece shows Delta surrounded by its neighboring municipalities, its fields and waters, and Mount Baker. The work is a collage of different metals and glass pieces and its intricacies further exemplify the technological road art glass has taken.

Gambling
Paul Manning

IN THE LAST 25 years gaming has become a big, big industry in British Columbia. Government-sanctioned or legal gambling—including lotteries and lottery machines, "charitable" casino operations, horse racing and off-track betting, "Sports Action" betting, bingo and other games of chance—is a $1.5 billion annual business in British Columbia.

While legal horse racing and illegal Irish Sweepstakes lottery tickets have been available in the Lower Mainland for decades, gaming didn't really get rolling until the provincial government gained legal control of it.

Prior to 1969 the criminal code prohibited public gaming with the exception of pari-mutuel wagering on horse races, small lottery schemes for charitable purposes and limited gaming at agricultural fairs.

In 1969 the criminal code was amended to permit public gaming by the provinces as well as the federal government. In 1970 B.C.'s attorney general began licensing gaming conducted by charitable and religious groups and at fairs and exhibitions. In 1974 British Columbia enacted the Lottery act and began conducting lotteries. The next ten years also saw the establishment of charitable casinos and bingo halls.

In 1985 control of public gaming, with the exception of pari-mutuel wagering, was ceded to the provinces. In 1987 the B.C. Gaming Commission was established to carry out licensing and policy-making functions.

Current gaming in British Columbia falls into three categories: charitable gaming, lotteries and pari-mutuel wagering on horse races. The total gaming "win" (amount wagered minus prizes paid out) for 1994-95 was $622 million. The win was divided as follows: lotteries 61 per cent; bingo and casinos 29 per cent; pari-mutuels six-and-a-half per cent; raffles and others three-and-a-half per cent.

Charitable casinos, first permitted in 1978, evolved from temporary events into today's 18 permanent casinos, half of which are located throughout the Lower Mainland.

The charitable casinos are a uniquely British Columbian partnership between charitable organizations and government-sanctioned gaming. Qualifying organizations provide a total of 30,000 volunteers to operate the cash on designated casino nights and take fifty per cent off the top for their organizations. These casinos raised $42 million for charitable and non-profit organizations in 1994-95. Charitable gaming events—including bingo games and ticket raffles as well as the casino nights—provide revenues to over 4,700 charitable and religious organizations annually.

In 1994-95 charitable proceeds from bingo were $64 million, from casinos $42 million and from ticket raffles $1.5 million. About 20 per cent was distributed to poverty or disadvantaged groups and roughly one-and-a-half per cent to each of the following: service clubs, cultural and arts groups, public safety programs and facilities, amateur sport and education. Religious organizations took in roughly five per cent. Revenue to the provincial government from this form of legal gaming approached $15 million.

But lotteries are by far the biggest game going. With over two-thirds of British Columbians playing on a regular basis, lottery ticket sales were $780 million in 1994-95. Net revenues go to the provincial government. Since 1992 half of these revenues have been spent on health care and the remainder allocated to the general budget. The net revenues to the provincial government from lotteries alone was $302 million in 1994-95.

Additional revenue comes from gaming at agricultural fairs and exhibitions, gaming at genuine social clubs and horse racing. In 1993-94, revenues to the horse-racing industry from pari-mutuel wagering were $33 million from purses and operations. Provincial government revenues were $5.8 million. In recent years the provincial government has also taken control of the horse-racing industry and set up off-track betting at teletheatres.

In 1994 the provincial government considered, and rejected, an expansion of gaming which would have permitted "for profit" casinos. Taxes would have been paid to the provincial government but projects would have been financed and operated by private companies.

The Seaport Centre project proposed for Vancouver's central waterfront would have more than doubled the convention and cruise ship capacity at Canada Place, and would have been privately financed through a 1,000-room resort hotel with an entertainment complex and casino gaming.

Following its 1994 gaming policy review the NDP government opted to maintain the status quo while considering some further expansion in charitable and First Nations' casino gaming. Proposals to permit video lottery terminals in licensed establishments were abandoned in the face of strong opposition from municipalities.

Vancouver Secrets
Robin Ajello

THE MARINE BUILDING, the art deco masterpiece that went a million dollars over budget when it was completed in 1930, boasts a secret penthouse. The Guinness family's Canadian representative A.J. Taylor lived there with his wife—until Mrs. Taylor complained about vertigo and limited elevator access. The penthouse, currently leased as office space, has two levels, a 360-degree view, a black marble-faced fireplace, a full kitchen and two washrooms. It would have been a somewhat lonely experience for the Taylors; thanks to the Depression only four floors were occupied until the early 1930s. Moreover in those days the Marine Building was unfashionably far from the Downtown business core.

At first glance the building that houses the MacMillan Bloedel Planetarium and the Vancouver Museum might be said to resemble a spaceship. Actually architect Gerald Hamilton designed the structure to resemble a Haida hat. As for the George Norris-designed crab fountain out front: it was chosen because the building sits on the site of an old Haida village and according to native folklore the crab is guardian of the harbor.

The Vancouver Museum's collection includes an Egyptian mummy with an unusual past. Before Egyptologist D.G. Kidd donated the exhibit he kept it in his West End apartment until, that is, his wife gave him an ultimatum: me or the mummy. For a time the mummy suffered from gender confusion. The curators at the museum nicknamed it "Princess Diana" since an Egyptian medical school had identified the mummy as a high-ranking female. The truth was revealed when a 1951 X-ray showed the mummy to have been a boy and a murdered boy at that, complete with a cracked skull. Mysteriously etched on his chest in Greek script is the name Panechates, son of Hatres.

New Westminster Senior Secondary School sits atop an old cemetery where pioneers, Caucasian and Chinese alike, were buried between 1860 and 1914. Apparently not all the bodies were properly exhumed. Also in New Westminster, rumor has it that under Columbia Street are the storefronts of hotels and shops, survivors of the fire of 1898 that destroyed most of downtown.

Chinatown still supports at least two old-style gambling halls, where locals bet on mahjong. One den is located at Columbia and Main Streets, another next to the Shanghai barber shop on Columbia and North Pender. A building that once stood next to the headquarters of S.U.C.C.E.S.S. held a cache of guns intended for the army of Dr. Sun Yat-Sen. The Chinese leader never received the armaments; they were discovered when the building burned down in 1990. Like many buildings in Chinatown, the Wong Association clan house at 123-A East Pender Street boasts a secret storey, the second, built to foil turn-of-the-century tax inspectors who based taxation on a structure's number of floors.

It took George Challenger seven years and a million hand-cut pieces of plywood to construct a relief map of British Columbia. Completed in 1954, the map resided for years in the Pacific National Exhibition's B.C. Pavilion. So did the ashes of George. A small panel concealed by a plaque on the Pacific Ocean opened to reveal his urn.

The Tunstall Bay area was rocked in the 1900s by no fewer than four unplanned explosions at Western Explosives, which opened a factory on Bowen Island in 1909. The first explosion occurred in August of that year; all the workers died, most of them Japanese and Chinese. Four months later a second blast rocked the region. In 1910 a man lit a pipe in the warehouse's vicinity and . . . kaboom. The final big bang occurred later that year and was so percussive that Nanaimo residents heard it. A subsequent inquiry determined that Chinese and Japanese employees couldn't read the safety manuals, which were printed in English. Solution: print manuals in Chinese. In 1911 Canadian Explosives bought the company and three years later moved the warehouse by scow to a new location at James Bay. Retired contractor George Adams bought the Tunstall Bay site in the 1930s. In the early 1970s he sold the land to former *Vancouver Sun* publisher Donald Cromie, who floated a plan to create 450 lots with underground wiring, a swimming pool and clubhouse. To appease visiting environmental watchdogs—aka the Island Trust—Cromie planted rows of trees, which died before the concerned citizens arrived. According to historians he sprayed the trees green and no one was the wiser.

The Dominion Building at 207 West Hastings Street has a tragic secret. The man who designed the terracotta-clad landmark, J.S. Helyer, stumbled on the treads of his prized trapezoidal staircase and tumbled to his death. Built in 1910 the Dominion was once the tallest building in the British Empire—until it was eclipsed by the nearby World Tower, known now as the old Sun Tower. The Sun Tower's signature green copper roof is one of Vancouver's most impressive faux finishes. The cladding is not really copper, as it appears, but an artful coat of green paint.

The Vancouver Aquarium boasts two little-known architectural flourishes. One is the killer whale boardroom which looks onto orcas cavorting behind glass. Upstairs is the shark penthouse, actually the office of the aquarium's Tim Low. A short distance to the left of Low's desk is an open pool full of sharks.

English Doulton terra–cotta bison and moose heads on the old Hotel Vancouver; they vanished when the hotel was demolished, (date unknown). cva

Nine metres below VanDusen Botanical Gardens is an enormous abandoned reservoir that was built in 1912. Its rust-stained concrete vaults once held almost 14 million litres of city drinking water. The reservoir was abandoned and sealed in the early 1970s.

The Vancouver Art Gallery's collection includes a putative ghost named "Charlie." He haunts the catacombs where the holding cells of the former courthouse were located. Charlie is said to be the spirit of William Charles Hopkinson, an immigration officer who was murdered by an immigrant while waiting to give evidence against the same man. Security guards swear they've heard Charlie "moving things around."

The Royal Vancouver Yacht Club's Eight Bells Club was formed in 1928 by club members seeking a burial at "sea"— actually just off the RVYC's Point Grey location. Family and friends of the deceased sail out and pour the ashes into the bay.

Afterwards they return to the club and have an informal social. Names of the deceased are engraved on a bell that hangs in the yacht-club bar. Eight bells are traditionally rung at the end of a watch, thus the name. In 1995 the club had some 200 members.

The Burrard Street Bridge was supposed to have an elevator. Until not long ago the mock castle structure over the span's center housed the equipment for a lift that was to take passengers down to what is today's seawall on the north side. The rails for the intended elevator remain inside pier four. For reasons unknown, the lift was never used. Stairs inside the piers at the south end were completed, but were bricked off after incidents of late-night crime. Graffiti artists who manage to penetrate bridge defences will discover circa-1930 railings and stair treads made from brass.

"Page House" at 330 West Pender Street is home to a wholesale jewelry supplier today. But the elegant Beaux-Arts-style structure, built in 1907, started life as the headquarters of the British Columbia Permanent Loans Company. The architectural *piece-de-resistance* is an oval, Tiffany-style, stained-glass dome that bears an autumnal maple leaf motif. At each end of the mezzanine gallery are stained-glass panels featuring both B.C.'s and Great Britain's coats of arms. In 1935 the Bank of Canada moved in. Back then bank robberies were a popular craze so the bank had a machine gun installed to defend the enlarged vault that, at one time, held all of the bank's B.C. assets. Cash was safely lugged in and out along a since-walled-off tunnel that ran underground to West Hastings Street.

At Hastings Park racetrack, there's a room perched high above the action that was the former haunt of track czar Jack Diamond. The room, which holds about 30, boasts monitors to watch the races, a wet bar and a small patio. Now that the track is government-owned and non-profit, Diamond's former aerie can be rented by groups.

If Stanley Park seems to resemble Central Park, it's because it should. The design of Vancouver's most famous park was based on the planning principles of Frederick Law Olmsted, who designed New York's most famous park. Moreover every single great grey squirrel in Stanley Park is descended from eight pairs given to Vancouver by New York in 1909. Also in Stanley Park is the little-known *National Geographic* tree, a red cedar almost 30 meters in diameter that the venerable organization believes is the largest of its kind in the world. The centuries-old giant can be found near the well-known Hollow Tree—off to the left, some 30 metres along the trail to Third Beach. When Stanley Park was commandeered as a military headquarters during World War II, a young recruit and future famous artist painted the Tea House sky blue and then added some clouds. Jack Shadbolt reportedly couldn't abide olive drab.

Gay and Lesbian Life in Greater Vancouver
Daniel Gawthrop

O N AUGUST 4, 1990, 20,000 people marched into B.C. Place Stadium for the opening ceremonies of Celebration 90: Gay Games III and Cultural Festival. Celebration 90 was much more than a week-long tourist bonanza ($15 million according to some estimates); it was also the world's largest sporting and cultural event that year, with 8,500 participants in 29 sports and 14 cultural events.

For Vancouver gays and lesbians, the Games also marked a turning point in the community's development. With a single event, "queer culture" became more visible in politics, media, entertainment and advertising than ever before. This would have been unthinkable ten years earlier when Vancouver city council voted down a Committee of Progressive Electors' proposal to proclaim Gay Unity Week.

Until homosexuality was decriminalized in Canada in 1969 gay and lesbian "communities" were largely underground. The stigma of being gay or lesbian made it impossible to be out of the closet without suffering the various consequences. Even the educated middle class was vulnerable: after UBC English instructor Jane Rule published her first novel with a lesbian narrator in the mid-1960s, she was shunned by closeted colleagues at social gatherings.

During the 1960s there were few places to gather in public. For working-class men there was the Castle on Granville Street or Gastown's New Fountain; women hung out at the Vancouver Hotel beer parlor. But these places, gay clientele notwithstanding, were straight-owned and maintained a strict, no-touching policy.

In 1964 a group of academics and feminists began the first gay and lesbian discussion group in the country, the Association for Social Knowledge (ASK). Seven years later a group of radical activists from the Gay Liberation Front held a "kiss-in" to defy the Castle's no-touching policy. That demonstration and a later march at the courthouse steps by the Gay Alliance Toward Equality (GATE) were two of Canada's first organized gay protests.

In the mid-1970s GATE took the *Vancouver Sun* to the Supreme Court of Canada when the *Sun* refused to run a two-line classified ad promoting the *Gay Tide* newspaper. (The supreme court ruled in the *Sun's* favor on May 22, 1979.) GATE also prompted a young alderperson, Michael Harcourt, to condemn the Vancouver police for their "Elliot Ness-style raids" on gay bars and bathhouses in 1974.

In the 1980s Vancouver's gay community was hit hard by the devastating effects of AIDS. In 1983 AIDS Vancouver became the first AIDS organization in the country. Much of the community's resources and political energies since then have gone toward fighting AIDS, but this was by no means the only issue.

Since the Gay Games in 1990, Vancouver has made several contributions to gay and lesbian rights. Local activist organizations such as the December 9 Coalition were instrumental in pressuring the federal government to amend the human rights act to prohibit descrimination based on sexual orientation. The amendment was announced on May 9, 1996.

In 1992, Christine Morrissey launched the first successful challenge of Canadian immigration law prohibiting sponsorship of same sex partners, Doug Saunders became the first openly gay man to address the United Nations on human rights issues and United Church Minister Tim Stevenson became the first openly gay man to be ordained by a mainstream church in Canada. Four years later he and Whistler Mayor Ted Nebbeling became the first openly gay men elected to the B.C. legislature.

In 1993 Betty Baxter became the first openly lesbian candidate in a federal election when she ran for the New Democrats in Vancouver Centre (following Svend Robinson's lead as Canada's first openly gay MP). And in 1994 Little Sister's Book and Art Emporium finally saw its challenge of Canada Customs border harassment brought before a supreme court judge after four years of postponements. The upshot? Canada Customs was ordered to cease detaining items at the Vancouver Mail Centre and pay $175,000.

By 1996 Vancouver's gay and lesbian communities were not all that different from any other self-confident ethnic group divided by the usual class distinctions. The West End—long established as a comfortable neighborhood for gay men—had begun attracting more lesbians. The reverse was true on Commercial Drive where an increasing number of politicized gay men had become attracted to a culturally rich neighborhood often associated with lesbians. The Gay and Lesbian Business Association of Greater Vancouver boasted 280 members, a large enough advertising base to support two gay newspapers, *Angles* and *Xtra West*.

Events like the annual Whistler Gay Ski Week attract major corporate sponsors; in the alternative art scene, gay themes find expression at places like the Western Front and Video In.

Community celebrations include the Stonewall Festival in Grandview Park and the Pride Society parade at English Bay.

Population Statistics
Richard von Kleist

POPULATION CENTRES (Incorporation Date)	1881	1891	1901	1911	1921	1931	1941	1951	1961	1971	1981	1991	1996 (est.)
Anmore (1987)											423	741	900
Belcarra (1979)											430	586	650
Bowen Island										350	1,125	1,791	2,245
Burnaby (1892)		300	750	13,300	12,873	25,564	30,328	58,376	100,157	125,660	136,494	158,858	175,811
Coquitlam (1891)				1,226	2,374	4,871	7,949	15,697	29,053	53,073	61,080	84,035	100,946
Fraser Mills (1971)					600	616	562	369	165	157	(annexed 1971)		
Delta (1879)			2,000		2,839	3,709	4,287	6,701	14,597	45,860	74,771	89,428	96,870
Langley-City (1955)								2,025*	2,365	4,680	15,124	19,765	22,750
Langley-Township (1987)					4,881	5,537	7,769	12,267	14,585	21,935	44,617	66,040	80,708
Lions Bay (1971)										396	1,078	1,328	1,414
Maple Ridge (1874)					3,772	4,932	6,476	9,891	16,748	24,480	32,232	48,422	59,830
New Westminster (1860)	1,500	6,678	6,499	13,199	14,495	17,524	21,967	28,639	33,654	42,835	38,550	43,585	47,016
North Vancouver-City (1907)				5,196	7,652	8,510	8,914	15,687	23,656	31,847	33,952	38,436	41.584
North Vancouver-District (1891)		250	365	3,000	3,800	4,788	5,931	14,467	38,971	57,861	64,904	75,157	81,848
Pitt Meadows (1914)					595	832	1,119	1,434	2,187	2,770	6,209	11,147	14,500
Port Coquitlam (1913)					1,178	1,312	1,539	3,232	8,111	19,560	27,535	36,773	41,845
Port Moody (1913)		250 (1885)			1,030	1,260	1,512	2,246	4,789	10,778	14,917	17,712	20,459
Richmond (1879)	200				4,825	8,182	10,370	19,186	43,323	62,121	96,154	126,624	150,000
Surrey (1979)				4,802	5,814	8,388	14,840	33,670	70,838	96,601	147,138	245,173	294,000
Vancouver (1886)	1,000	13,709	27,010	100,401	117,217	246,593	275,353	344,833	384,522	426,256	413,952	471,844	521,048
Point Grey (1908)				4,320	13,736 (Amalgamated 1929)								
South Vancouver (1892)		500	1,500	16,126	32,482 (Amalgamated 1929)								
University Endowment Lands						575	636	2,120	3,272	3,536	3,674	4,534	5,503
West Vancouver (1912)					2,434	4,786	7,769	13,990	25,454	36,440	35,728	38,783	41,778
White Rock (1957)									6,453	10,349	13,550	16,314	17,603

* 1955

Note: rather than have this page bristling with footnotes for the source of every figure, we'll tell you that from 1921 on Statistics Canada is the usual source, using information from the Canadian census. Figures prior to that come from a variety of places, including the census. It is difficult to get accurate early population figures. The Linkman Press would welcome additions, corrections and refinements of these figures for the next printing of this book. Thanks to Bruce Macdonald for his assistance.

Ethnic Restaurants
Jurgen Gothe

Kingsway, 1994. vs

After the mushrooms on toast and the first happily caloric brush with Triple-Os, and the Vi's steaks and the Iaci's spaghetti what else was there to eat in Vancouver in 1960 when I got here from Medicine Hat? Oh, there were Ding Ho drive-ins, and there was The Beachcomber, culturally muddled Tahitian. There was the odd little place with red-checked tablecloths purveying pizza and baked meatball spaghetti. There were some mysterious eateries in Chinatown. That seems to have been it, so far as I can remember. There were steak spots of dubious repute, and some places the cab drivers hung out late at night; and restaurants in the department stores, plus the occasional fish place that deep-fried everything in elderly oil and you could just tell by the smell as far as the parking lot.

There were a great many coffee shops, but surprisingly few doughnut parlors. There were burger drive-ins, but not as many as now. I still remember my first vision of a golden arch, I think it was in Richmond, but that came later.

Food, it seemed to me then, was not something you did much in public. Now look at us: thousands of eateries from the hautest to the coolest, the most elegant to the most retrofunky. Ethnic isn't even in—it just is. Food is, regardless of where it originated and how—it's here and now. It's all around and we're all for it. Italian and French came first, as I recall. After Chinese, of course.

Then everybody started piling in: Indian, Greek, Japanese, Spanish. Thai came relatively late: eighties, anyway—and then the ubiquitous "Mediterranean." Soon, it started to fuse and that's the best part.

Chinese cuisine especially has flowered here. Much of it better than in Hong Kong, I'm told by my foodie friends and well-versed culinary journalistic colleagues who hang out on the shores of the South China Sea. More variety, better freshness, quality, style, imagination; the new elbowing the old out of the way and creating something fabulous and original in the doing.

Sushi? If that's your idea of culinary expression (to me, it simply seems like artful arranging, rather than cookery) there is none better than in this town. Certainly better than in most of Tokyo, give me a break.

Umberto Menghi put Italian cooking on the map for us, and on the tables. Thank you; we all thank you: my kid, my cat, my waistline. Gildo Casadei showed us there was a whole world of imaginative departures from the Italian launch-pad. The three great cuisines of the world, according to me? Italian, French, Chinese, and in that order.

Afghan may have proved to be a turning point for further-afield explorations. Ethiopian, for goodness' sake! Caribbean and Malaysian. Danish, Swiss, Ukrainian, Persian, the beat goes on. Better Greek food than you'll find in any of the isles. Hotter, anyway, and fresher. Chefs came and brought with them ingredients and methods; old recipes, or just made new ones to fit with the stuff we had at hand. We're all richer for it. Starred chefs are stirring the pots and stirring up the creations.

We have, in Vancouver, the best available ingredients in the world: fish and fowl, meat and dairy, greens and grains, the lot. And now the locals are cooking it. In the heady early days of ethnic eating the chefs were all named Andre, Giovanni, Weng Chu or Karlheinz. Now there's Blair and Scott and Steve and Dan, Karen and Corinne and Carol and Anne.

We have cooking schools, so chefs can study here, then travel on to gather knowledge, coming back to throw all their own energies and ideas into the pot. The old days are gone forever; fusion is no longer novelty, it's the way of life. The best fusioneer in town, as I write this, may well be Simon Chin, at Sonoma on 4th.

Diversity, creativity, cooking of the world, for the world—I know it's been said before, and with better harmony, but we are the world. And I've said this for years now, I'll say it one more time, because it's even better, more true if I can bend the envelope of an absolute: you can eat as well in Vancouver, British Columbia, Canada as you can anywhere—everywhere—in the world.

Mind you, that shopping list is a killer: from abalone to poblanos, wintermelon, kaffir lime leaf, chanterelles, arugula, mahi mahi, garam masala, chevre, enoki, quinoa, green papaya, fish sauce, balsamic vinegar. Not bad. Have fun seeking them all out. *Vielen dank und guten appetit.*

Some other Place Names
Barbara-Anne Eddy

The Lower Mainland has attracted people from many places for thousands of years. Not surprisingly, place names in this area reflect the diversity of peoples who have sailed by, passed through, and settled here.

The following is a partial list of regional names used in various parts of the Lower Mainland, with their origins as far as I have been able to determine them.

For more on Greater Vancouver place names see the article by G.P.V. and Helen B. Akrigg.

Albion (Maple Ridge): a name suggested by a resident, in honor of England. (The Romans gave England the name, from the Latin for "white," because of the dazzling white cliffs of Dover.)

Aldergrove (Langley): Philip Jackman, reeve of Langley from 1895-1897, suggested the name Aldergrove for the settlement, originally called Shortreed, because of the many alders growing in the area.

Ardley (Burnaby): named for a station on the B.C. Electric Railway. Originally named Burrard, the name was changed to Ardley in 1909.

Capitol Hill (Burnaby): realtor G.A. Barret & Co. advertised houses in a subdivision it called "Capitol Hill" in the early 1900s. The company sued a rival realtor for using the name, and the rival then changed the spelling in its advertising to "Capital Hill." Because of the association of the name with the original Capitoline Hill in Rome, the spelling "Capitol" has survived.

Cascades Village (Burnaby): named for the Cascades Drive-in Theatre, Canada's first drive-in theatre, which stood on the site from 1946 until 1980.

Clayton (Surrey): John George, an early settler, gave the name to the area. It was at one time a station on the New Westminster Southern Railway.

Colebrook (Surrey): the early settlers found "cool brooks" in the area.

Connaught Heights (New Westminster): named for the Duke of Connaught, governor-general of Canada, who visited the Lower Mainland area, and laid the cornerstone for a school. When the school was demolished to make way for the New Westminster City Hall, a new school took the name of the old one, and the area took the name of the school.

Elgin (Surrey): after a store and hotel in the area, which had been named for Scottish soldier and politician Lord Elgin.

Kanaka Creek (Maple Ridge): Some members of James McMillan's (see McMillan Island) group of explorers came from Hawaii, having served as sailors on Hudson's Bay Company ships. These Kanakas, as they were called, helped to

Albion: The Romans gave England the name, (Latin for "white,") because of the dazzling white cliffs of Dover

build Fort Langley, the first capital of the colony; later, some of them settled near a creek which became known as Kanaka Creek.

Kelvin (New Westminster): named after Lord Kelvin School, which in turn was named for the renowned Scottish scientist Thomson, Lord Kelvin.

Kennedy Heights (Delta): named for James Kennedy, an early settler. He also built the Kennedy Trail, along which the area's first telegraph line was built in 1865.

Lochdale (Burnaby): Mrs. Eudora Jane Lochead owned a general store and the first post office in the area. She named the settlement "Loch" from her own name, and "dale," meaning "valley."

Murrayville (Langley): originally called Murray's Corners, it was named for an Irish immigrant, Paul Murray, who first settled the area.

Port Kells (Surrey): named after Henry Kells, who laid out a townsite in the area in 1890.

Ruskin (Maple Ridge): takes its name from the English writer John Ruskin. A group of young men bought land in the area in 1886 as part of a socialist experiment, planning to run a sawmill and other businesses communally. The experiment ended in disaster three years later.

Sullivan (Surrey): T. J. Sullivan and his brother Henry acquired limber limits in about 1903, and the town of Sullivan grew up around the mill.

Terra Nova (Richmond): Henry Youdall brought five families from Newfoundland to settle on land he had acquired from the government in 1886. In the course of a legal dispute over the ownership of the land, the residents of "Terra Nova" (Latin for "new land") petitioned for and won title to their homes.

Tucks (Richmond): named for a station on the interurban railway.

Victory Heights (New Westminster): named because housing was developed in the area for soldiers returning from World War II.

Whonnock (Maple Ridge): means "place of the hump-backed salmon" in the Halkomelen (Coast Salish) language.

The Vancouver Institute
Peter Nemetz

The Vancouver Institute, a free educational forum, began in 1916. Lectures are held on the campus of the University of British Columbia during the fall and spring academic terms.

Overflow audiences are common for our main auditorium of 500 seats. A second closed-circuit lecture theatre is available. On several occasions, extra rooms and the large lobby have all been used. We have had as many as an estimated 4,000 people come out for our regular lectures.

Many Nobel laureates have addressed us, and people like French academician Claude Levi-Strauss and Singapore's Prime Minister Lee Kuan Yew, as well as distinguished speakers from Britain, continental Europe, Asia, the United States and, of course, Canada. Our most celebrated speaker was the Dalai Lama, who attracted about 10,000 people, most of whom could not be seated.

The Vancouver Institute is the most successful public forum in North America

The appreciation of the audience for the evening's lecture is the only reward that the enthusiastic, all-volunteer executive wants. The speakers are not paid by The Vancouver Institute although their travelling expenses are covered by us. The institute has been fortunate enough to co-sponsor speakers with several lectureship committees, including Cecil and Ida Green, Leon and Thea Koerner, Dal Grauer, J.V. Clyne, E. S. Woodward, the *Vancouver Sun* and External Affairs Canada.

We feel we have achieved something very special in Canada—an educational public forum that reaches between 20,000 and 30,000 people directly and many more indirectly each year. Some of the programs are later broadcast and our speakers are regularly interviewed and discussed in the news media. Books and reports have been published nationally and internationally quoting lectures given at The Vancouver Institute. Our speakers from various parts of the world have told us that The Vancouver Institute is by far the most successful public forum in North America.

Community Centres in the GVRD
Richard von Kleist

Note: This information was supplied by the listed centres.

BURNABY

Burnaby Parks and Recreation
101-4946 Canada Way, Burnaby, B.C. V5G 4H7 • 294-7450

Bonsor Recreation Complex
6550 Bonsor Avenue • 439-1860 fax: 439-5513
Racquetball and squash courts, weight room, snooker room, banquet hall, restaurant, child-minding (daycare), meeting and activity rooms, seniors' lounge, fitness dance studio, sauna, whirlpool, leisure pool, pool. Pool built 1973, new features 1988. Wheelchair accessible.

Burnaby Lake Arena
3676 Kensington Avenue • 291-1261
Ice rink, lacrosse, snack bar, meeting and activity rooms. Built 1965.

C.G. Brown Pool
3702 Kensington Avenue • 299-9374
Pool, sauna, whirlpool, leisure pool, waterslide, weight room. Named for Clifton G. Brown, educator and councillor. He was principal of Burnaby's first high school, Burnaby South, in 1922. Appointed inspector of Burnaby schools 1936. He served on council 1956-60.

Cameron Recreation Centre
9523 Cameron Street • 421-5225 fax: 421-6387
Racquetball, squash, indoor tennis, weight room, pro shop, library, refreshment counter, banquet hall, meeting, activity and party rooms.

Confederation Seniors Centre
4585 Albert Street • 294-1936 fax: 299-3161
Seniors' lounge, snooker room, strength training room, arts and crafts rooms, craft store, weekly hot lunch program, computer room, meeting and activity room rentals, banquet hall (capacity 200).

Eastburn Community Centre
7435 Edmonds Street • 525-5361
Games room, gymnasium, weight room, banquet hall, meeting, activity and party room, child minding. Opened in 1980.

Edmonds Community Centre for Older Adults
7282 Kingsway • 525-1671 fax: 540-7936
Lounge and activity room, meeting rooms, banquet hall, snooker, food service, arts and crafts room. Opened April 25, 1973.

Eight Rinks
6501 Sprott Street • 291-0626
Recreational hockey, public skating, eight skating rinks, pro shop, restaurant, lounge, Canucks practice rink. Originally four rinks, additions and expansion December 1995.

Eileen Dailly Leisure Pool and Fitness Centre
240 Willingdon Avenue • 298-SWIM (7946) fax: 298-9036
Water slide, children's water play area, weight room, child minding, multipurpose room, whirlpool, sauna, steam room, cafe. Wheelchair accessible. Eileen Dailly is a former MLA, cabinet minister and community activist. The centre opened May 16, 1993.

Kensington Park Arena and Community Recreation Office
6159 Curtis Street • Arena: 299-8354; Office: 298-5027; fax: 294-3245
Ice rink, roller rink, snackbar. Opened in 1973.

Willingdon Heights Community Centre
1491 Carleton Avenue • 299-1446
Weight room, games room, cardio room, banquet hall, meeting and activity rooms. Built in 1964, renovated 1981.

Club Metro Youth Centre
4585 Imperial Street • 433-6032
Games room, entertainment room, computer room. Opened June 7, 1991.

COQUITLAM

Coquitlam Leisure and Parks Services
633 Poirier Street, Coquitlam B.C. V3J 6B1 • 933-6000 fax: 933-6099,

City Centre Aquatic Complex
1210 Pinetree Way • 927-6999
Fitness centre, aerobics, child minding, pool, sauna, steam room, Jacuzzi, waist-pool.

Chimo Indoor Swimming Pool
620 Poirier Street • 933-6027
Pool, weight room, Jacuzzi, sauna, children's pool. Also in the complex: social recreational centre, sports centre, Dogwood Pavilion.

Coquitlam Sports Centre
633 Poirier Street • 933-6000
Two ice rinks, curling rink, sports lounge. Also in the complex: Chimo Pool (see above).

Dogwood Pavilion
624 Poirier Street • 933-6098
Activity room, lounge, computers, library, crafts, woodworking, lapidary, games, kitchen. A seniors (50+) centre. Also Coquitlam Sports Centre and Chimo Pool (see above).

Place Maillardville Neighbourhood House
1200 Cartier Avenue • 933-6051
Billiards, games, meeting rooms, drop-in centre. Hall rentals.

Social Recreation Centre
630 Poirier Street • 933-6090
Meeting rooms, program rooms.

Town Centre
1290 Pipeline Road • 927-6960
Children's programs, preschool day trips. For adults: tai chi, yoga.

DELTA

Delta Parks and Recreation
4500 Clarence Taylor Crescent, Delta, B.C. V4K 3E2 • 946-3293 or 946-4141 fax: 946-4693

Winskill Aquatic Centre
5575 9th Avenue • 943-1151 fax: 943-1370
Children's pool, weight room.

South Delta Recreation Centre
1720 56th Street • 943-0267 fax: 943-6324
Hall rentals, ice rink, curling rink, lounges, gymnastics hall.

North Delta Recreation Centre
11415 84th Avenue • 596-1547 or 590-INFO (4636) fax: 943-6324
Aerobics, ice rink, curling rink, multipurpose rooms, lounge.

Sungod Aquatic Centre
7815 112th Street • 591-5566 fax: 943-6324
Pool, sauna, fitness centre, children's pool, weight room, child minding.

Sungod Arena
7815 112th Street • 591-5566 fax: 943-6324
Ice rink, concession stand, skate shop, etc.

Pinewood Leisure Centre
11807 Pinewood • 590-2616 fax: 943-6324
Room rentals, hall rentals.

Kennedy House
11760 88th Avenue • 594-2717
Dancing, arts and crafts, snooker, cards, cafeteria, lunch service, library, gift shop. Seniors (55+) recreation centre.

McKee House
4705 Arthur Drive • 946-1411
Table tennis, snooker, cards, arts and crafts. Seniors (55+) recreation centre.

Phoenix Club
6062 16th Avenue • 943-1340
Various activities designed for seniors 55+.

Ladner Leisure Centre
4600 Clarence Taylor Crescent • 946-0211 fax: 946-8614
Weight room, leisure pool, fitness centre, sauna, whirlpool, children's pool, child minding.

Ladner Community Centre
4734 51st Street • 946-9226 fax: 943-6324
Hall rentals, multipurpose rooms.

LANGLEY CITY

City of Langley Parks and Recreation
5549 204th Street, Langley, B.C. V3A 1Z4 • 530-3131

Al Anderson Memorial Pool
4949 207th Street • 534-3017
Pool, outdoor pool. Al Anderson was a member of Langley town council; he died in an automobile accident on the Hope-Princeton Highway.

Douglas Recreation Centre
20550 Douglas Crescent • 530-3131
Gymnasium, multipurpose room, preschool

room, games room. Built in 1974, the centre underwent reconstruction in 1996.

LANGLEY TOWNSHIP

Langley Civic Centre
20699 42nd Avenue, Langley • 530-1323
fax: 530-9372
Ice arena, concession stand, multipurpose rooms, curling rinks, cafe and lounge.

Walnut Grove Community Centre
8889 Walnut Grove Drive • 882-0408
fax: 882-0361
Social lounge, fitness room, games room, multi-purpose room, library, conference room, flexi-hall, child minding, indoor tennis courts.

W. C. Blair Recreation Centre
22200 Fraser Highway • 533-6170 fax: 533-6178
Free-form wave pool, sauna, whirlpool, weight room, multipurpose room, kitchen facilities, sportswear store. W.C. Blair was mayor of the township 1981-1985.

MAPLE RIDGE AND PITT MEADOWS

Ridge Meadows Parks and Leisure Services (Maple Ridge Office)
11995 Haney Place • Maple Ridge, • 467-7346
fax: 467-7393

Ridge Meadows Parks and Leisure Services (Pitt Meadows Office)
12007 Harris Road • Pitt Meadows, • 465-2452
fax: 465-2404

Maple Ridge Leisure Centre
11925 Haney Place • 467-7322 or 467-7373
Pool, leisure pool, gymnasium, weight room, sauna, whirlpool, children's pool, multipurpose rooms.

Cam Neely Arena
11995 Haney Place • 467-7322 or 465-2452
Ice rink, arena. Named for the NHL right winger, formerly with the Vancouver Canucks, now the Boston Bruins.

Yennadon Community Centre
12854 232nd Street.

Hammond Community Centre
20601 Westfield Avenue • 465-8515

Pitt Meadows Recreation Hall
12460 Harris Road

NEW WESTMINSTER

New Westminster Parks and Recreation Office
600 Eighth Street, New Westminster, • 526-4811 fax: 526-6358

Moody Park Arena
701 Eighth Avenue • 525-5301 fax: 525-5307
Ice rink, skate shop, concession stand.

Queensborough Community Centre
920 Ewen Avenue • 525-7388 fax: 525-5934
Rental facility, gymnasium, weight room, preschool, spray pool, multipurpose rooms.

Centennial Community Centre and Fitness
65 East 6th Avenue • 526-2751 fax: 526-2753

Fitness classes, children's programs, multipurpose rooms, home of the Lacrosse Hall of Fame.

Canada Games Pool and Fitness Centre
65 East 6th Avenue • 526-4281 fax: 521-8465
Pool, Nautilus, hammer-strength and full fitness centre, whirlpool, sauna, wading pool, water slide.

Century House
620 Eighth Street • 526-2733 fax: 526-6358
Seniors' centre: cards, snooker, dancing for 50+ seniors, kitchen, painting, pottery, soapstone carving.

Queen's Park Arenex
Corner of 1st Street and 3rd Avenue • 525-0485
Arena: 524-9796 fax: 524-0942
Gymnasium, gymnastics program, floor hockey, volleyball, basketball. Complex includes spray pool, petting farm.

Queen's Park Facilities
Queen's Park-Corner of 1st Street and 3rd Avenue • (all facilities) phone: 524-9796 fax:524-0942

Queen's Park Arena
Ice rink, concession stand, seats 3,500+

Queen's Park Stadium
Softball, soccer field, seats 2,000

Centennial Lodge
Banquet Facility, seats 135, Vagabond Playhouse

NORTH VANCOUVER CITY

Lonsdale Recreation Centre
123 East 23rd Street, North Vancouver, • 987-7529; programs: 983-6411, 983-6417, 983-6416
Pool, weight rooms, curling rink, outdoor tennis courts.

Memorial Recreation Centre
Address and phone numbers same as Lonsdale Recreation Centre. Gymnasium, dance studio, multipurpose rooms, arts and crafts rooms, outdoor tennis courts.

Mickey McDougall Recreation Centre
address and phone numbers as for Lonsdale Recreation Centre. Gymnasium, activity room, dance studio, outdoor tennis courts. The late Mickey McDougall was principal of North Vancouver High School, the building which is now the recreation centre.

NORTH VANCOUVER DISTRICT
123 East 23rd Street, North Vancouver, • 987-7529 fax: 987-9275

Ron Andrews Recreation Centre
931 Lytton Street • 987-7529 Programs: 983-6509
Pool, weight rooms, sauna, whirlpool, activity room, dance programs, martial arts, preschool programs.

William Griffin Recreation Centre
851 West Queens Road • 987-7529 Programs: 983-6541 or 983-6535
Pool, weight room, steam room, sauna,

whirlpool, youth centre, multipurpose rooms, gymnasium. William Griffin was a North Vancouver alderman.

Lynn Valley Recreation Centre
3590 Mountain Highway • 987-7529
Meeting rooms, preschool, fitness classes, yoga, martial arts.

Seylynn Recreation Centre
605 Mountain Highway (at Fern) • 987-7529
Gymnasium, martial arts, dance groups, aerobics.

Karen Magnussen Recreation Centre
2300 Kirkstone Road • 987-7529 Programs: 983-6557 or 983-6556
Wave pool, ice arena, multipurpose rooms, weight room, steam room, whirlpool, therapy pool, games pool. Karen Magnussen is the silver medallist Olympic Games skater, and former world champion.

North Shore Neighborhood House
225 East 2nd Street • 987-7529 Programs: 987-8138
Daycare (integrated), community social recreation for all age groups, preschool program, family support services, adolescent special needs, aerobics, seniors' programs, peer counselling, food bank, health clinic.

Centennial Theatre Centre
2300 Lonsdale Avenue • 987-7529 Programs: 983-6453
Theatre, concession stand, festival bookings, family festival, theatre rental. Seats 718.

Delbrook Recreation Centre
600 West Queens Road • 987-7529 Programs: 983-6326
Gymnasium, squash, racquetball, arts and crafts.

PORT COQUITLAM

City of Port Coquitlam Parks and Recreation
2253 Leigh Square, Port Coquitlam • 927-7900

Hyde Creek Indoor Pool
1379 Laurier • 927-7946 fax: 927-7984
Pool, weight room, racquetball courts, gymnasium, aerobics studio.

PoCo Recreation Centre
2150 Wilson • 927-7933 fax: 927-7931
Ice rink, lacrosse, roller blading.

Wilson Centre
2150 Wilson • 927-7970
Seniors' centre.

PORT MOODY

Port Moody Parks and Recreation Centre
300 Ioco Road, Port Moody, • 469-4555
fax: 469-4560

Arena and Curling Rink
Address and phone numbers as above. Ice rink, curling rink, and in summer dry floor rentals.

Kyle Recreation Centre
125 Kyle Street • 469-4561 fax: 931-6954
For seniors: activity rooms, craft rooms, games

room, snooker, library/lounge, kitchen facilities.
Social Recreation Centre
300 loco Road • 469-4556 fax: 469-4560
Meeting rooms, activity rooms.
The Alley Youth Centre
2732 St. Johns Street • 936-9000 fax: 931-6954
Pool, table tennis, video and arcade games, television.
RICHMOND
Richmond Community Service
5911 No. 3 Road • 276-4107 fax: 276-4132
Cambie Community Centre
4111 Jacombs Road • 273-3394 fax: 278-2609
Gymnasium, basketball, floor hockey, preschool, badminton, tennis, hall rentals, multipurpose rooms.
City Centre Community Association
7700 Minoru Gate • 231-6440 fax: 231-6423
Various programs for people of all ages. A non-profit organization formed by Richmond residents to cultivate an atmosphere of community in the city centre.
Hamilton Community Centre
5140 Smith Drive • 524-0631 fax: 524-8149
Hall and room rentals, preschool, various programs for people of all ages.
Sea Island Community Centre
7140 Miller Road • 278-5820 fax: 276-4561
Community hall rental, Burky's Preschool, other varied programs.
South Arm Community Centre
8880 Williams Road • 277-1157 fax: 277-2962
Gymnasium, preschool, flag football, softball, basketball, badminton, tennis, other varied programs. Aerobics room, fitness centre, weight room, racquetball, squash, seniors' programs.
Steveston Community Centre
4111 Moncton Street • 277-6812 fax: 272-5126
Gymnasium, badminton, basketball, preschool, child minding, fitness centre, weight room, aerobics, seniors' programs, racquetball, squash, tennis.
Thompson Community Centre
5151 Granville Avenue • 272-5338 fax: 272-1670
Preschool, fitness centre, weight room, aerobics, gymnasium, seniors' programs.
West Richmond Community Centre
9180 No. 1 Road • 277-9812 fax: 277-9877
Gymnasium, badminton, floor hockey, basketball, volleyball, preschool, fitness centre, weight room, aerobics, racquetball, squash, tennis.
Minoru Aquatic Centre (Richmond Aquatic Services)
7560 Minoru Gate • 278-3178 fax: 278-3564
24-hour public swim info line: 276-4383.
Five pools, fitness centre, hydro pools, weight room, sauna.
Minoru Place Seniors' Centre
7660 Minoru Gate • 273-1975 fax: 278-1071

Cards, billiards, cafeteria, many programs designed for seniors.
Minoru Arenas (Richmond Arena Services)
7551 Minoru Gate • Public Skate & Drop-In Hockey Info: 276-4353. Skate lessons: 278-9704. Ice Rental: 274-7465 fax: 278-7357
2 ice rinks, one with 1,600 seat capacity, public skating, dry floor in spring and summer, available for special events.
Richmond Ice Centre (Richmond Arena Services)
14140 Triangle Road • Ice Rental: 274-7465, Fax: 275-2736 (other info numbers as for Minoru Arenas)
6 ice rinks, year-round ice, 2 dry floors in summer, daily drop-in hockey, pro shop, restaurant, meeting rooms.
Minoru Pavilion (Richmond Fitness Association)
7191 Granville Avenue • 270-3636 fax: 244-1630
Fitness centre, weight room, aerobics, child minding, circuit training.
Richmond has two outdoor pools: South Arm Pool, 277-3900 and Steveston Pool, 277-4333.
SURREY
SURREY PARKS AND RECREATION
7452 132nd Street, Surrey B.C. V3W 4M7 • 501-5050
COMMUNITY RECREATION OFFICES:
Cloverdale Community Recreation Office
6220 184th Street • 543-3400 fax: 543-3401
A variety of recreation programs for children and adults in the Cloverdale area, as well as rooms for meetings and banquets.
Fleetwood Community Recreation Office
15996 84th Avenue • 501-5030 fax: 501-5031
A variety of recreation programs for children and adults in the Fleetwood area, as well as providing child minding for participants in aerobics classes. Weight room, and several rooms that can be rented for public use.
Guildford Community Recreation Office
15105 105th Avenue • 930-3860
A variety of recreation programs for children and adults in the Guildford area. Several halls can be booked for public use.
Newton Community Recreation Office
7120 136B Street • 501-5040 fax: 501-5041
A variety of recreation programs for children and adults in the Newton area.
South Surrey Recreation Office
2199 148th Street • 541-3210 fax: 541-3201
A variety of recreation programs for children and adults in the South Surrey area, as well as several facilities for public use.
Whalley Community Recreation Office
10275 135th Street • 930-3840
A variety of recreation programs for children

and adults in the Whalley area.
POOLS
South Surrey/White Rock Indoor Pool
14655 17th Avenue • 541-3220 fax: 541-3221
This is a 37-metre pool with sauna, whirlpool, free weights, universal gymnasium, exercise bikes, children's pool, diving boards and slides.
North Surrey Indoor Pool
10275 135th Street • 930-3900
This is a 37-metre pool with sauna, whirlpool, free weights, universal gymnasium, exercise bikes, children's pool, diving boards, slides and rope swing.
Newton Wave Pool
13730 72nd Avenue • 501-5540 fax: 501-5541
The Wave Action Leisure Pool features two water slides, play lagoon, kids' pool, steam room, whirlpool, weight room, free usage of two fooseball tables, ping pong table, licenced lounge, cafe and concession.
ARENAS
Note: These arenas have one sheet of ice, except for North Surrey Arena, which has two, and offer public skating, skating lessons, recreational hockey, ice and equipment rentals.
Cloverdale Arena
6090 176th Street • 543-3410 fax: 543-3411
Newton Arena
7120 136B Street • 501-5044 fax: 501-5041
North Surrey Arena
10275 135th Street • 930-3900 fax: 930-3901
South Surrey Arena
2199 148th Street • 541-3200 fax: 541-3201
SENIORS' CENTRES
These centres offer a wide range of recreation activities from education, social and physical, as well as crafts, games and services.
Cloverdale Seniors' Centre
17671 56th Avenue • 543-3433 fax: 543-3434
Cloverdale Seniors' Centre is noted for its commitment to wellness and its warm welcome.
Newton Seniors' Centre
13775 70th Avenue • 501-5010 fax: 501-5011
Sunrise Pavilion
10341 135th Street • 930-3880 fax: 930-3881
Youth Centres (These centres offer a variety of programs and events for ages 12 to 18.)
Cloverdale Youth Centre
6228 184th Street • 543-3420
Guildford Youth Centre
10310 154th Street • 930-3890
Newton Youth Centre
13355 68th Avenue • 501-5533
South Surrey Youth Centre
14601 20th Avenue • 541-3241
Whalley Youth Centre
10665 135th Street • 930-3870

VANCOUVER

Vancouver Board of Parks and Recreation
2099 Beach Avenue, Vancouver, B.C. V6G 1Z4 •
257-8400

Barclay House
1447 Barclay Street • 257-8349
Heritage house, available for use by service
groups, seniors, etc.

Britannia Community Services Centre
1661 Napier Street • 253-4391
Ice rink (arena), racquetball courts, indoor
swimmng pool, fitness centre, gynmnasium,
library.

Carnegie Centre
401 Main Street • 665-2220
Library, photography, computers, weight room,
dancing, kitchen, arts and crafts, native cultural
activities. This building was once the main branch
of the Vancouver Public Library.

Champlain Heights Community Centre
3350 Maquinna Drive • 437-9115
Fitness centre, racquetball courts, squash court,
gymnasium

Douglas Park Community Centre
810 West 22nd Avenue • 257-8130
Two sports fields, crafts studio, gymnasium,
weight room, aerobics.

Dunbar Community Centre
4747 Dunbar Street • 224-1374
Weight room and fitness centre, racquetball and
squash courts, multipurpose rooms.

False Creek Community Centre
1318 Cartwright Street • 257-8195
Aerobics, weight room, sauna, preschool.

Hastings Community Centre
3096 East Hastings Street • 255-2606
Racquetball courts, weight room, outdoor tennis
courts, gymnasium, auditorium, preschool.

Kensington Community Centre
5175 Dumfries Street • 327-9401
Fitness centre, weight room, racquetball courts,
indoor pool.

Kerrisdale Community Centre
5851 West Boulevard • 257-8100
Ice rink (arena), indoor pool, gymnasium, auditorium, weight room.

Killarney Community Centre
6260 Killarney Street • 434-9167
Ice rink (arena), indoor pool, multipurpose
rooms, preschool, seniors' centre.

**Kitsilano War Memorial Community
Centre**
2690 Larch Street • 257-6976
Ice rink (arena), fitness centre, weight room, aerobics, gymnasium, multipurpose rooms.

Marpole-Oakridge Community Centre
990 West 59th Avenue • 257-8180
Fitness centre, weight room, racquetball courts,
sauna, whirlpool, etc.

Mount Pleasant Community Centre
3161 Ontario Street • V5T 2Z1
Weight room, fitness centre, racquetball courts,
multipurpose rooms, outdoor pool.

Ray Cam Cooperative Centre
920 East Hastings Street • 251-2141
Gymnasium, weight room, seniors' programs,
daycare.

Renfrew Park Community Centre
2929 East 22nd Avenue • 257-8388
Weight room, fitness centre, indoor pool, gymnasium, sauna, whirlpool.

Riley Park Community Centre
50 East 30th Avenue • 257-8545
Weight room, fitness centre, ice rink (arena),
gymnasium, multipurpose rooms. Percy Norman
Pool: Indoor pool named for the well-known
Canadian swimmer.

Strathcona Community Centre
601 Keefer Street • 254-9496
Weight room, fitness centre, gymnasium, aerobics.

Sunset Community Centre
404 East 51st Avenue • 325-1202
Ice rink (arena), outdoor pool, gymnasium.

Thunderbird Neighborhood Community Centre
2311 Cassiar Street • 254-0427
Weight room, gymnasium, preschool, daycare,
seniors' and children's programs, Chinese
seniors' groups, ESL for women, food bank.

Trout Lake Community Centre
3350 Victoria Drive • 257-6955
Fitness centre, ice rink (arena), racquetball
courts, multipurpose rooms.

West End Community Centre
870 Denman Street • 257-8333
Fitness centre, ice rink (arena), racquetball
courts.

West Point Grey Community Centre
4397 West 2nd Avenue • 257-8140
Weight room, gymnasium, arts and crafts rooms,
multipurpose rooms.

POOLS

Vancouver Aquatic Centre
1050 Beach Avenue • 665-3412
Fitness centre, indoor pool.

Lord Byng Pool
3990 West 14th Avenue • 228-9734
Indoor pool, sauna, whirlpool, fitness centre.

Templeton Park Pool
700 Templeton Drive • 253-7101
Indoor pool, weight room, sauna, whirlpool.

WEST VANCOUVER

West Vancouver Parks and Recreation
750 17th Street, West Vancouver, B.C. V7V 3T3
• 925-7200

Aquatic Centre
776 22nd Street • 925-7210 fax: 925-5944
Weight room, pool, sauna, Jacuzzi, children's

pool. The centre opened April 3, 1976.

Arena
786 22nd Street • 925-7250 fax: 925-5949
Skating rink, snack bar.

Recreation Centre
780 22nd Street • 925-7270 fax: 925-5952. The
centre opened in 1958.

Seniors' Centre
695 21st Street • 925-7280 fax: 925-5935
Cafeteria, snooker room, woodwork room, over
100 programs geared to seniors.

WHITE ROCK

White Rock Leisure Services
15322 Buena Vista, White Rock, B.C. V4B 1Y6 •
541-2161 fax: 541-2168

Centennial Arena and Pavilion
14600 North Bluff • 541-2171 fax: 541-2176
Skating rink, meeting rooms, concession stand
during hockey games.

Senior Citizen's Activity Centre
1475 Kent Street • 541-2231 fax: 541-2239
Auditorium, library, snooker, coffee shop,
instructional classes and day trips. The centre
opened May 19, 1973.

Canada's First Service Station
Chuck Davis

THE FIRST HORSELESS carriage in Vancouver, a steam-driven auto, was introduced to the city in 1899 by W.H. Armstrong. It was followed in 1904 by the first auto dealership in Vancouver—started by brothers Frank and Fred Begg—and the appearance of the first gasoline-powered car, bought by sawmill industrialist John Hendry. (Thomas Plimley had opened a dealership in Victoria in 1901.) The first licence plates were required that year, as well, and plate number one was issued to John Barnsley, manager of the Union Steamship Company.

Automobiles caught on quickly. A local club held an 11-car race around Stanley Park in 1905 and on one pleasant day that same year 176 autos were counted driving through the park. (It's possible some of them were repeaters.) By 1906 there were four listings in the Vancouver city directory for "automobile livery."

It isn't easy to find, but if you search long enough near the southeast corner of Cambie and Smithe in Vancouver, you'll find a plaque—installed in September of 1955 to commemorate the 75th anniversary of Imperial Oil—that marks the location of Canada's first service station. It may have been the world's first.

The station opened, says the plaque, "in or before 1907."

James Skitt Matthews, in his late twenties at the time, was an employee of Imperial Oil under local manager C.M. Rolston. In a 1955 speech Matthews, who was by then the city archivist, recalled how that station began.

"There had arrived in Vancouver a queer-looking vehicle called an automobile. We had read about them in magazines. One day the telephone rang. The call came from the Hastings Sawmill and the speaker asked me if we had any gasoline which could be used in automobiles.

"The office boy replied that we had three kinds: one was '74'-brand Baume gasoline and was supplied to drug stores, who sold it to ladies for cleaning their gloves; the second kind was deodorized stove gasoline, used in plumber's firepots for heating soldering irons; and the third kind was benzine, used for dissolving lacquer in the salmon canneries along the Fraser to prevent the salmon cans from rusting.

"The office boy went to the warehouse and told the foreman, Bud Mulligan, to send a four-gallon [18-litre] can of '74' down to John Hendry, manager of the mill. That can was the first gasoline ever sold in British Columbia for motorcar use.

"Some time later, when the number of automobiles in Vancouver had leaped ahead (Matthews: "Ultimately, automobiles

Ultimately, automobiles became more numerous and the number in Vancouver grew to seven or eight
—Major Matthews

became more numerous and the number in Vancouver grew to seven or eight . . ."), it was decided that the method of fuelling them—using pails dipped into a large wooden barrel of gasoline—was inefficient and dangerous. So a 13-gallon (59-litre) kitchen hot-water tank was procured and a length of rubber garden-hose attached to it.

That was the equipment. Now an attendant was needed. The company's night watchman, J.C. Rollston, had been in poor health and his cohorts believed he would improve in the sun and open air.

"We got a barroom chair," Matthews recalled, "and my wife made a cushion." A corrugated tin shed was built for shelter and Rollston was installed as attendant. The "service station" was ready for business. "The fresh air and the sunshine soon banished the pallor from Mr. Rollston's cheeks," Matthews recalled, "and, ofttimes as I passed and waved good morning, he would call out, 'I've been busy this morning!'

"'How many?' I would call, and he would answer back, 'Three cars this morning!'"

Two local bicycle shops began selling gasoline, which they bought from Imperial for five cents a litre and sold for ten. Word of this new way of delivering gasoline to cars spread. "A dealer in Florida," says Matthews, "wrote asking details." (The Florida people had been using garden watering-cans.)

There's some dispute over whether Imperial's Vancouver service station is, as some have claimed, the world's first. Seattle and Dallas both claim a 1907 start, although Matthews says that Seattle got the idea from Vancouver. St. Louis, Missouri, claims a station in 1905. The 1904 date for Hendry's first car seems a good argument for setting the opening date of the Vancouver station well before 1907, since it's unlikely that three years would pass before the dangerous dipped-out-of-a-barrel system was discarded! Perhaps in the future someone will find a reference to a specific opening date in a newspaper or other document of the day.

There's no doubt, however, that Vancouver's first service station was also Canada's first.

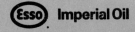

Alternative Medicine
Ronit Cohen

The doctor of the future will give no medicine, but will interest his patients in the care of the human frame, in diet, and in the cause and prevention of disease. —Thomas Edison

ALTERNATIVE MEDICINE HAS become a catch-all phrase for healing methods outside of the traditional western "open-up-and-say-aah" approach. Years ago in the Lower Mainland only a few such practices existed, such as naturopathic medicine, herbalism, chiropractic and massage therapy. Now there are dozens of different therapies to choose from, thanks to some brave pioneers, many of whom suffered from diseases labelled incurable by traditional western medicine. Because of their persistent search for answers the Vancouver natural health scene has burgeoned.

Every new industry has pioneers that make things happen. In this story a Latvian herbalist, a controversial talk show host and a housewife with a rare genetic disease are key players.

One of the first naturopathic physicians in Vancouver was Dr. Herbert Nowell. Prior to 1918 he spent most of his time teaching herbal medicine to doctors. In 1926 he founded the Dominion Herbal College. Now located in Burnaby it's the oldest college of its kind in North America.

The college has changed hands over the years. In the late 1950s it was taken over by Edward Moxey. Edward was famous for keeping fluorides out of Vancouver water and for founding Nature's Path Health Foods, one of the city's first natural food stores. (The store eventually closed but not without inspiring Arron Stephens to borrow the name for his successful natural food company).

When Edward decided to return to England in 1962 a gifted herbalist, Ella Birzneck, took over the school. She brought with her a legacy of herbal knowledge passed down from her Latvian relatives along with her training in physiotherapy, massage therapy and chiropractic medicine. Ella totally revamped the college's curriculum, adding a herbal textbook that she herself wrote and that her daughter Nancy illustrated. (Her other daughter Judy is a naturopathic physician, chiropractor and herbalist who is currently president of the school. Ella's son Art, a chiropractor, is dean and vice-president and his wife Bernice is the registrar.)

During the time Ella was reorganizing Dominion College a pharmacist named Stephen Kripps kept getting a lot of colds. Realizing that his ailments would be bad for business he decided to follow the example of Linus Pauling, the famous Nobel Prize winning chemist, and began taking vitamin C to ward off his colds. It worked, so he started passing on the advice to his customers who kept coming back for more. Soon his clients began asking him for additional vitamins. Relying on his background as a chemist he began creating supplements for his clientele.

When radio talk show host Pat Burns tried some of Stephen's "Mega-4" B complex vitamins he raved about it on the air. That's when business at Kripps Pharmacy took off. The fame gave Stephen the momentum to develop even more potent and effective supplements, minerals and herbal medicines that made his pharmacy a cornucopia of alternative remedies.

Known for his controversial style, Burns continued focusing attention on alternative medicine into the 1970's. This media attention contributed to a growing awareness of natural medicine and influenced, among others, Ida Lecomte, a fiery and determined housewife afflicted by a rare but crippling genetic disease. Dissatisfied with traditional medicine's limitations she formed CAPOM, the Canadian Association for Preventive and Orthomolecular Medicine, whose purpose was to educate its members about disease prevention and vitamin therapies. The group survived for about 7 years. After Ida's death members of the community began looking for a new organization with a different focus, one that was stable and that would empower people to make informed health choices.

One February evening in 1982 individuals who had been members of CAPOM joined with members of another defunct group, the Coalition for Alternative Therapy. They gathered in pregnant ex-CAPOM member Lorna Hancock's basement to decide on a name for a new organization. Lorna went into labor and politely excused herself from the meeting. While Lorna delivered her daughter Lorill, the group gave birth to a new organization, the Health Action Network Society (HANS). Today HANS has moved out of Lorna's basement into a 180-square-metre Burnaby office. It has over 4,000 members and serves as an international resource for information on alternative health choices.

These are but a few of the individuals who have contributed to making the Lower Mainland a place where alternative approaches to health care are readily available. For those who are seeking methods to complement allopathic treatments HANS can provide you with resources to make informed choices about your health.

Health Action Network Society: (604) 435-0512
Dominion Herbal College: (604) 521-5822
Kripps Pharmacy: (604) 687-2564

Greater Vancouver Food Banks
Barbara-Anne Eddy

A CONTINENT-WIDE RECESSION in the late 1970s and early 1980s hit British Columbia's resource-based economy especially hard. In response to the needs of laid-off workers, churches, trade unions and other socially aware organizations started to collect food from persons who were better off to distribute to those in need. Thus food banks were born.

In December 1982 a group called Canadian Ecumenical Action, meeting in the basement of Chalmers United Church (now Holy Trinity Anglican Church), on Hemlock at West 12th, established the Greater Vancouver Food Bank Society. The group included Reverend Val Anderson, and the first executive director of the food bank, Sylvia Russell. Within a few months, the food bank had moved into its own warehouse, and was distributing supplies each week through five depots.

Despite difficulties resulting from charges of misuse of funds that led to Sylvia Russell leaving her post (she was later completely exonerated), and the resignation a short time later of Russell's succesor, Jill van Dijk, as well as chronic shortages of both food and funds, the Vancouver Food Bank has endured. It now serves needy residents of Vancouver, Burnaby and the North Shore. Through 14 distribution centres, it provides supplemental food aid to more than 6,000 recipients weekly. In 1993-94 it collected and distributed more than 1,134,000 kilograms of food.

In 1991 the Vancouver Food Bank began an associated program, Food Runners. Specially equipped trucks collect excess perishable food from restaurants, hospitals, catering firms and event organizers, and transport it directly to missions, soup kitchens and meal programs. In 1994 Food Runners collected more than 60 tonnes of food, distributing it to agencies which provide between 30,000 and 40,000 meals and snacks per month.

The Greater Vancouver Food Bank Society is located at 311 East 6th Ave., Vancouver. Phone: 876-3601 Fax: 876-7323.

OTHER FOOD BANKS IN THE LOWER MAINLAND INCLUDE:

COQUITLAM/PORT COQUITLAM/PORT MOODY

Share Family Services opened in 1983 and serves approximately 200 families weekly in the above municipalities, as well as in Anmore and Belcarra. Share Family and Community Services also offer counseling services, operate a thrift store and provide a range of other programs and services. Share Food Bank: 2403A Spring St., Coquitlam. Phone: 931-2451 Fax: 931-1868.

LANGLEY

Since 1989, the Langley District Help Network has operated the Langley Food Bank, currently helping more than 600 people weekly. The Help Network also operates a furniture bank, a laundromat, and a free store. Langley Food Bank, 20561 Logan Ave., Langley. Phone: 533-0671 Fax: 530-9632.

NEW WESTMINSTER

The New Westminster and District Labour Council founded the Unemployment Action Centre in 1982. Seeing that claimants often needed food, the action centre, with the help of local labor unions, established the New Westminster Food Bank in that same year. The food bank currently assists 1,000 people monthly. Unemployment Action Centre/Food Bank, 1111-16th St., New Westminster. Phone: 525-9628 Fax: 524-4681.

RICHMOND

Founded as a committee of St. Alban's Anglican Church in 1983, the Richmond Food Bank is now a separate society assisting 250 families weekly. It also provides food to other community organizations, including a women's shelter and a family drop-in centre. Richmond Food Bank Society, #135-12417 No. 2 Rd., Richmond. Phone 271-5609.

SURREY

The Surrey Self-Help Society for the Under-Employed was formed in June 1983 after the Surrey Co-ordinating Centre, the United Way and other groups joined to address the growing problem of hunger in Surrey. The Surrey Food Bank Society now helps 5,600 residents of Surrey and North Delta monthly. It operates community kitchens, in which people cook quantities of food which they then divide up and take home, and food buying clubs, which allow members to buy food in bulk at substantial savings. Other successful Surrey Food Bank projects include a cable TV show, *The Thrifty Kitchen,* a recipe book of the same name, and four recyling deports. Surrey Food Bank, 10732-135th St., Surrey. Phone: 581-5443 Fax: 588-8697.

WHITE ROCK

The White Rock-South Surrey Food Bank began in a small room in a church basement in 1982. Now housed in a storefront in central White Rock, the food bank serves approximately 350 White Rock and South Surrey residents weekly. White Rock-South Surrey Food Bank, 882 Maple St., White Rock. Phone: 531-6226 Fax: 531-2316.

Volunteer Vancouver
Craig Brett

PEOPLE WITH A DESIRE to make their community a little happier and healthier might want to take a look at volunteer work. There is no better place to start than the Vancouver Volunteer Centre, also known as Volunteer Vancouver. From spending a quiet afternoon with a senior citizen to tramping up and down river banks collecting garbage, the centre has information on more than enough activities to fill up someone's free time.

Formed in 1943, it was initially charged with mobilizing women for the war effort and providing accommodation for children evacuated from Britain and for those whose mothers worked on the assembly line.

The Women's Voluntary Service, as it was known at the time, began by helping 37 agencies and registering 267 volunteers. By the end of the war approximately 10,000 volunteers were involved.

Despite the war's end many of these volunteers were willing to continue contributing their services to the community. As a result the Volunteer Bureau was established in 1946.

Over the years the range and magnitude of the bureau's activities has grown rapidly. Today Volunteer Vancouver is a nerve centre responsible for linking roughly 400 non-profit groups with 7,000 volunteers in the Vancouver area.

A large number of these volunteers are young people. By the 1980s more than 65 per cent of new volunteers were under the age of thirty.

These changing demographics reflect Volunteer Vancouver's attention to the student community through the establishment of a volunteer centre at the University of British Columbia and through the student volunteer certificate program. This program has rewarded more than 10,000 students with the presentation of certificates at school assemblies along with academic and athletic awards.

Young people increasingly see volunteering as a means to gain valuable experience and references before entering the job market. Recognizing this trend, Volunteer Vancouver participated in career fairs where hundreds were introduced to the concept that voluntary work leads to employment.

As the make-up of the volunteer work force changes so has the face of the recipients of voluntary assistance. In 1989 a survey of the Lower Mainland showed an increase in the number of senior citizens and a growing multicultural population.

A three-year federal grant helped set up a senior's talent bank which matched the skills and experience of the senior community with its requirements.

One member of Volunteer Vancouver that utilizes seniors is the Volunteer Grandparents Society which attempts to provide a grandparent figure for families that have none. The society has more requests than volunteers at its branches in Vancouver, Abbotsford, Prince George and Kelowna.

In order to increase volunteerism among ethnic communities, Volunteer Vancouver initiated the Volunteerism in Multicultural Society project. This initiative provided volunteer opportunities, training and services to people from the Chinese, Indo-Canadian, Latin American and other communities.

While some of these communities already have strong volunteer networks Volunteer Vancouver seeks to inform members of the opportunities available elsewhere.

If you're interested in searching for information on the subject, check with Volunteer Vancouver's resource centre. It contains the largest collection of information on voluntary action and non-profit management in Canada. Research data can be obtained in person or by computer modem.

The centre is open from 9:00 A.M. to 4:00 P.M. Monday to Friday except Wednesday when it's open from 5:00 P.M. to 7:00 P.M.

Interviews are available for those who prefer assistance in their search for volunteer opportunities. Appointments usually must be made a week in advance.

FOR MORE INFORMATION CONTACT
Volunteer Vancouver
#301-3102 Main Street
Vancouver, B.C. V5T 3G7
Tel: 875-9144 Fax: 875-0710

DERA
Jim Green

Jim Green, 1990. vp

THE DOWNTOWN EASTSIDE was Vancouver's original townsite, the economic and financial centre of the city, home of Canada's deep-sea merchant fleet, shipyard workers, fish processors, sawmill workers and marine workers, many of whom lived in the community. Then the financial district moved west and the downtown core became neglected. Many residents, mainly single men employed in the resource industry, made the single room occupancy (SRO) hotels of the Downtown Eastside their permanent homes.

By the early 1970s the community held about 15,000 men, their average age in the mid to late fifties. Most were of European extraction, but there were aboriginal peoples and others from all walks of life and heritages. Missions, churches and sandwich lines could be found, and most residents lived on fixed incomes. Most paid more than 50 per cent of their income for a 10 by 10 room with no facilities. The room might contain a sink, but the communal washroom facilities were down the hall and usually there was no cooking allowed. This is a very poor community—in fact, it is Canada's poorest and one that was without a democratic voice until the early 1970s.

Community decisions were being made by city council or the province, church groups or planners. Most, if not all the organizations, had boards composed entirely of people from outside the community. The residents themselves had no voice. In 1973, with the support of the Social Planning Department of the City of Vancouver, this situation changed. Planner Peter Davies was sent to deal with some of the problems in the area. (Among the worst were concerns about the health of the residents. The area had one of the highest incidences of tuberculosis in the country, and its women had an extremely short life span compared with women in other communities.) Davies decided what was needed was a democratic organization to permanently alter the situation. The fact that many residents were single, elderly men was considered by many to be a negative component, but it became the strongest because many of those same men had experienced the Dirty Thirties, and had been in unemployment organizations such as the Single Men's Unemployment Association, the Relief Camp Workers Union and various other anti-poverty organizations that were very strong at that time.

Davies met a retired member of the Canadian Seaman's Union who had lived in the Downtown Eastside for many years. Although Bruce Eriksen had no formal education, he was very knowledgeable about the conditions and people in the neighbor-

hood. Bruce began to organize community meetings to identify the problems of the community. One early accomplishment was the lighting of lanes to prevent robberies and beatings by people hiding in unlit corners. This early success provided the residents with evidence of the organization's collective abilities and power.

In 1973 Bruce Eriksen and a handful of others set up the Downtown Eastside Residents' Association to build a democratic voice and bring pride and self-esteem to the people of the community. DERA required its members to be residents of the community. The first order of business was to name the area, which for many years had been known as Skid Road. It had never been recognized as a community of human beings. DERA named it "The Downtown Eastside."

Libby Davies, Peter's daughter, joined DERA as a community worker. Soon after, Jean Swanson, a bar waitress from the Patricia Hotel, joined the group. Another key player was Anna Wong, who came by the DERA office about the same time as a group of Chinese seniors were complaining of poor treatment in the East Hotel. Anna began working for DERA and started to organize around the East Hotel. There were court cases and huge battles about living conditions in the hotel, which eventually shut down without compensating any of its tenants. This was the beginning of one of DERA's most powerful aspects: the unity between the neighborhood's non-Chinese Canadians and low-income Chinese-Canadians. From the beginning, DERA has been bilingual, with everything conducted in both languages. At other times hundreds of Chinese-Canadians were on picket lines and in other types of demonstrations carrying bilingual DERA banners and signs. This diversity gave DERA added strength.

One important struggle of the early 1970s was the fight for fire-sprinkler bylaws. Neither the province nor the city made it mandatory for SRO hotels to have sprinkler systems. Approximately 25 people died every year, 40 in 1973. DERA worked hard to have the bylaw changed. The struggle was ignored by the city and fought against by the landlords who threatened to close permanently if they were required to put sprinkler systems in. The fire deaths of five people in the Commercial Hotel on Cambie Street allowed Bruce Eriksen to corner the mayor at the site of the burning building in front of the media and demand he bring in sprinkler laws to stop the unnecessary deaths. This incident led to the passing of the Fire Sprinkler Bylaw, responsible for the saving of many lives over the past 20 years.

Until DERA came into being, the only two places to socialize in the Downtown Eastside were bus stop benches and the beer parlors. Alcoholism was a serious problem as was a complete lack of social alternatives such as libraries. It required a seven-year battle to create Carnegie Community Centre at the corner of Main and Hastings. Carnegie had been the centre of many unemployment activities during the 1930s and was a museum until 1967. Bruce, Libby and Jean struggled with the City of Vancouver to have it made into a community centre—and to save a valuable heritage building. The battle was won: Carnegie is one of the most successful community organizations in Canada, as well as one of the most-used community spaces in the city. It contains the largest collection of Chinese paperbacks and is the most-frequented branch library in the system.

In the late 1970s and early 1980s DERA was having trouble keeping its funding. The forces of civic politics and the Social Credit government made it extremely difficult for DERA to keep going. During that time both Bruce Eriksen and Libby Davies were elected to city council. (Jean Swanson went on to work in the trade union movement.) With no funding, DERA was forced to close the office, but Anna Wong kept the spirit alive. With Libby and Bruce on council and other supporters such as Harry Rankin and Mike Harcourt, DERA was eventually able to obtain the funding to hire an organizer. In late 1980 Jim Green was hired.

Soon after, DERA entered into a construction phase. The organization started to work not only to make the slum lords keep their premises liveable, but to build alternatives. (It was also an effective method of preventing unwanted development!) The first project was the DERA Co-op in 1984, an outstanding example of community development. This co-op, in which 50 per cent of members do not speak English and 50 per cent are over 65, has never had staff. It is run entirely by its members, a powerful example of the abilities of low-income peoples.

Projects like the Four Sisters Housing Co-operative put forward the concept of "architecture of opportunity," using the development process to empower people. Residents gained new skills and self-esteem from the construction of millions of dollars worth of housing while working co-operatively with people from many backgrounds. There are numerous cultures and heritages in the Four Sisters—and more than 30 languages. The project houses 90 children, seniors, aboriginals, disabled persons and a myriad of others from different walks of life.

In 1986 the community braced itself for its biggest challenge: Expo 86, a world's fair to be held right in the middle of the Downtown Eastside. DERA feared Expo would be destructive.

It proved to be just that. Hundreds of units were torn down to build new structures such as office towers, shopping malls and parking garages. Perched on the edge of Expo, they were to be used as a catalyst for other business opportunities. The Social Credit government and its allies on city council fought against any bylaws that would allow SRO hotels to remain as living units for the people of the community. One thousand people were evicted from their homes. Eleven people died in the first month of the evictions including Olaf Soldheim who, according to the city's medical health officer, died as a direct result of being evicted from his residence of 62 years. It was a devastating period. Networks and social relations were destroyed that to this date have never been rebuilt.

Expo could have been a great opportunity for the community if it had offered opportunities to leverage people from welfare into working on the Expo site. There was no attempt to do this. When DERA put the idea forward, those in control refused to listen. As a result, thousands of people who lived within a few hundred metres of the site were never given the opportunity to work. There was no positive Expo legacy for the people of the Downtown Eastside.

This was not the end of the community. Although wounded, it has survived. More housing was built, about 600 units in all, including Pendera on Pender Street and Olaf Soldheim Place—also known as Sun Lai Lau—in Chinatown. All of DERA's housing work attempts to create safe conditions for people, to allow them to seek employment and generally make better lives for themselves. An early city hall at 16 East Hastings Street, a nine-storey early high-rise, was converted from an office tower in disrepair to a heritage award-winning project now on the designated list, and named after one of the great people of the community, Gerry Tellier. Pendera, although a new structure, won a heritage award for revitalizing a heritage area.

DERA is a grass roots organization working to give the people of its community a voice in their own future and an organization that works hard to unite people of diverse backgrounds for common causes. DERA has shown that people in low-income neighborhoods can be the masters of their own destiny. It is a lesson many others could learn and one that brings pride to the people of the Downtown Eastside and the City of Vancouver.

The Peace Arch
Nicole Smith

On tuesday, september 6, 1921, more than 10,000 people attended a ceremony held to commemorate 100 years of peace between two great countries. Both Canada and the United States joined on this day to dedicate a Peace Arch on the international boundary.

The Peace Arch, standing 20.4 metres high with a base equal to its height, was an idea turned into a reality by one man. Samuel Hill, an American railroad builder, Harvard graduate and world traveller, was the creator of the arch itself. He constructed it to commemorate the peace and harmony established by the Treaty of Ghent, signed at Ghent, Belgium, in 1814 to end the War of 1812 between the British and the U.S. The arch also honors the Rush-Bagot Agreement, which led to the demilitarization of the Great Lakes.

The building of the Peace Arch began with land clearing in 1919. The actual construction began in July, 1920, and in honor of this a brass medallion was struck bearing symbols and legends of the monument on one side and "Belgium, England, France, U.S.A." on the other.

Without the contributions of school children from both sides of the border the park may never have existed. They collected dimes, nickels and even pennies to help purchase privately owned property for park use. Each child received a certificate for their contribution to the "Great Arch" project. In this certificate it stated, "_____ 's name has been added to the great roll which is sealed in the Peace Arch on the International Boundary Line between the Dominion of Canada and the U.S. and that (he/she) has resolved to dedicate (his/her) life to the advancement of peace throughout the world."

The Peace Arch also contains historic documents that describe the pleasant relations between the U.S. and Canada, and a film called *The Sacred Faith of a Scrap of Paper* shows scenes from Europe and America, depicting the Treaty of Ghent story. Behind two bronze tablets lie great historical pieces. Behind the one on the Canadian side bearing the picture of the historical ship, the *Beaver*, lies a relic of that boat, the first steam-propelled vessel to navigate the North Pacific (in June, 1838). And on the American side is a picture of the *Mayflower*, behind which lies a relic of the boat that brought the Pilgrims to New England in 1620.

Workers from both sides of the border toiled together on the arch. Three-thousand-five-hundred sacks of cement were processed to produce 611 cubic metres of concrete all of which was framed with approximately 45 tonnes of steel. The foundation was made practically earthquake-proof in order to guarantee permanency. The building project, directed by W.E. Simmons of Vancouver, B.C., had to be stopped between November 1920 and June 1921 to allow time for the concrete to set. Many of the materials for the arch were donated.

The designer and landscape director was John Booth of New Westminster who recalled that they had to haul the rockeries from other parts of Surrey. The garden on the American side was initiated in 1930 by Washington and covers 10.5 hectares. The Canadian side started with six hectares and increased to more than nine hectares. The work, done by the B.C. government, began in 1938 and was completed in two years.

On the American side of the monument are the words "Children of a Common Mother" and on the side facing Canada are the words "Brethren Dwelling Together in Unity." Within the arch are two iron gates turned back against the walls. Inscribed over one is "1814—Open One Hundred Years—1914" and above the other is a prayer which says "May These Gates Never Be Closed." These inscriptions "declare that the doorway of social and commercial communication now open, shall never be shut and that those who dedicate it as children of a common mother, will live together in perpetual unity."

Many important persons attended the dedication ceremony. Princess Patricia and then-premier John Oliver came from Victoria by boat and anchored in Blaine with 383 passengers, and a train came from Vancouver with a large crowd. The ceremony consisted of the playing of the American anthem by the 72nd Seaforth Highlanders from Victoria while the Bellingham Elks band played the British national anthem. The mayor of Blaine presented Premier Oliver with a key to the city, and a plaque dedicated to Samuel Hill was laid.

Mayor R.H. Gale of Vancouver said in his speech, "Let this arch, more glorious than a frowning fort or arsenal bristling with weapons of destruction, symbolize for all time that the United States, Canada and Great Britain stand today united as Anglo-Saxons of justice, liberty and universal peace."

The Peace Arch today is used for various international gatherings and is a popular spot for tourists. It was declared international territory so citizens of both countries may meet there on occasion without going through the formality of crossing the border. Celebrations include the exchange of flags between 2,000 Canadian and American school children each year. It is also known by American and Canadian war veterans as an impressive memorial to peace.

Some Books of Local Interest
Jean Barman

Burnaby centennial anthology: stories of early Burnaby Produced for the Burnaby Heritage Advisory Committee by Harry Pride, et al. (Rev. ed., June 1994)

A Tapestry of cultures: voices from Burnaby's ethnic communities *Clelie Rich, editor.* Burnaby Multicultural Society (1992)

Burnaby: a proud century: a historical commemoration of Burnaby's centennial *Pixie McGeachie with additional writing by Jim Wolf.* Opus Productions (1991)

Pioneer tales of Burnaby: early Burnaby as recalled by the settlers themselves *Editor: Michael Sone* Corporation of the District of Burnaby (1987)

Mountain memories: a history of Burke *Norma K. Campbell* Metaphoric Media (1991)

Harvesting the Fraser: an early history of Delta *Terrence Philips; edited and designed Susan Buckley* Delta Museum and Archives (1988)

Mosaic fragments: from the memoirs of T. Ellis Ladner (1871-1958) *Edited by Edna G. Ladner* G. Ladner (1980)

The Delta Centenary, 1879-1979 Corporation of Delta (1979)

Above the sand heads: first hand accounts of pioneering in the area which, in 1879, became the Municipality of Delta, British Columbia *Narrated by T. Ellis Ladner; prepared for publication by Edna G. Ladner* (1979)

It's up to you: women at UBC in the early years *Lee Stewart* UBC Academic Women's Association (1990)

The way we were: a celebration of our UBC heritage *Philip Akrigg, et al.* University of British Columbia Alumni Association (1987)

Lord of Point Grey: Larry MacKenzie of U.B.C. *P.B. Waite* UBC Press (1987) Biography of UBC president Norman MacKenzie

Bowen Island, 1872-1972 *Irene Howard* Bowen Island Historians (1973)

The Langley story illustrated: an early history of the municipality of Langley *Donald E. Waite* (1977)

Fort Langley, birthplace of British Columbia *B.A. McKelvie, annotated by Charles Lillard* Porcepic Press (1991)

Queensborough: images of an old neighborhood *Steve Gatensbury; illustrations by Charlene Kamachi Janzen* Sedge Pub. (1991)

The Natural history of New Westminster *Dana Anderson, et al.* Douglas College: Challenge '85 (1985)

New Westminster, the real story of how it all began *Hellen C. Pullem* Hawkscout Group (1985)

Once in the Royal City: the heritage of New Westminster *Jack David Scott* Whitecap Books (1985)

Reflections: one hundred years: a celebration of the District of North Vancouver's centennial *Chuck Davis* Opus Productions (1990)

Echoes across the inlet *Dawn Sparks and Martha Border; edited by Damian Inwood* Deep Cove and Area Heritage Association (1989)

Early history of Port Moody *D.M. Norton* Hancock House (1987)

Richmond: secrets & surprises *Co-edited by Jacqueline Lee Son and Dona Sturmanis;* Yorklin & Associates (1994)

Steambox, boardwalks, belts and ways: stories from Britannia *Compiled and edited by Marie Bannister and Marilyn Clayton* Britannia Heritage Shipyards (1992)

Richmond, Child of the Fraser *Leslie J. Ross* Richmond '79 Centennial Committee (1979)

Richmond, child of the Fraser, 1979-1989 *Leslie J. Ross* Friends of the Richmond Archives (1989)

Exploring ethnic Vancouver *Anne Garber, John T. D. Keyes; Lorraine Gannon, research associate* Serious Publishing (1995)

Underlying vibrations: the photography and life of John Vanderpant *Sheryl Salloum* Horsdal & Schubart (1995)

In my own words (Autobiography of a *Vancouver Sun* columnist.) *Denny Boyd* Douglas & McIntyre (1995).

Vancouver voters, 1886: a biographical dictionary *Edited & compiled by Peter S.N. Claydon and Valerie A. Melanson, et al.* British Columbia Genealogical Society (c1994)

Strathcona: Vancouver's first neighbourhood *John Atkin* Whitecap Books (1994)

Vancouver: representing the postmodern city *Edited by Paul Delany* Arsenal Pulp Press (1994)

Vancouver the way it was *Michael Kluckner* Whitecap Books (1993)

Vancouver: a visual history *Bruce Macdonald* Talonbooks (1992)

Vancouver and its region *Edited by Graeme Wynn and Timothy Oke* UBC Press (1992)

Vancouver, a city album (Title of first two editions: **Vancouver's first century**) *Editors: Anne Kloppenborg, Alice Niwinski, Eve Johnson.* Douglas & McIntyre (1991, 3rd edition)

Collingwood pioneers: memories of a Vancouver district *Barbara Nielsen* Collingwood Pioneers (1990)

Robin Ward's Vancouver *Robin Ward* Harbour Pub. (1990)

Vanishing Vancouver *Michael Kluckner* Whitecap Books (1990)

The Natural History of Stanley Park *Edited by Valentin Schaefer and Angela Chen; compiled and illustrated by members of the Vancouver Natural History Society* (1988)

Running tough: the story of Vancouver's Jack Diamond *Gareth Sirotnik* Diamond Family (1988)

Saltwater City: an illustrated history of the Chinese in Vancouver *Paul Yee* Douglas & McIntyre (1988)

Hastings and Main: stories from an inner city neighborhood *Laurel Kimbley, Jo-Ann Canning-Dew* New Star Books (1987)

First class: four graduates from the Vancouver School of Decorative And Applied Arts, 1929: Lilias Farley, Irene Hoffar Reid, Beatrice Lennie, Vera Weatherbie Women in Focus (1987)

M.I. Rogers, 1869-1965 *Mary Isabella Rogers* Compiled and edited by Michael Kluckner J. Gudewill (1987) (Excerpts from Mary Isabella Rogers' diary and reminiscences of family and friends of wife of B.C. Sugar founder.)

Distant neighbors: a comparative history of Seattle and Vancouver *Norbert MacDonald* University of Nebraska Press (1987)

Lucky to live in Cedar Cottage: Memories of Lord Selkirk Elementary School and Cedar Cottage neighbourhood, 1911-1963 *Seymour Levitan, editor; Carol Miller, editor* Vancouver School Board (1986)

On the shady side: Vancouver, 1886 to 1914 *Betty Keller* Horsdal & Schubart (c1986) Tongue-in-cheek look at crime and criminals

Vancouver past: essays in social history: Vancouver centennial issue of BC studies *Edited by Robert A.J. McDonald and Jean Barman* UBC Press (1986) Includes: **Cottages and castles for Vancouver home-seekers,** *Deryck W. Holdsworth;* **Working class Vancouver, 1886-1914,** *Robert A. McDonald;* **Sam Kee: a Chinese business in early Vancouver,** *Paul Yee;* **Neighborhood and community in interwar Vancouver:** *Jean Barman;* **The confinement of women:** childbirth and hospitalization in Vancouver, 1919-1939, *Veronica Strong-Boag & Kathryn McPherson;* **The triumph of "formalism":** elementary schooling in Vancouver from the 1920s to the 1960s, *Neil Sutherland;* **The incidence of crime in Vancouver during the great depression,** *James P. Huzel;* **The Mother's Council of Vancouver:** holding the fort for the unemployed, 1935-1938, *Irene Howard;* **"A Palace for the Public":** housing reform and the 1946 occupation of the old Hotel Vancouver, *Jill Wade;* **A half century of writing on Vancouver's history,** *Patricia Roy*

Working lives: Vancouver 1886-1986 *The Working Lives Collective* New Star Books (1985)

Exploring Vancouver's past: an informal guide to researching local and family history in Vancouver *History Resource Committee, Vancouver Centennial Commission* (1984)

False Creek: history, images, and research

From modest West Coast roots, general trade publisher Douglas & McIntyre has grown over the past 25 years to pass $10,000,000 in annual revenue, producing 75 new Canadian titles per year, with a total of some 1,500 books published and several million units sold, in addition to enjoying a strong national and international presence. Douglas & McIntyre is the largest English-language Canadian-owned house headquartered outside of Toronto.

sources *Robert K. Burkinshaw* City of Vancouver Archives (1984)

Fond memories: recollections of Britannia High School's first 75 years, 1908-1983 *Editor: Clive Cocking* Britannia High School Diamond Jubilee Reunion Committee (1983)

A place of excellence: a chronicle of West Vancouver, 1912-1987 *Bruce Ramsey* District of West Vancouver (1986)

The struggle for social justice in British Columbia: Helena Gutteridge, the unknown reformer *Irene Howard* UBC Press (1992)

Mayor Gerry: the remarkable Gerald Grattan McGeer *David Ricardo Williams* Douglas & McIntyre (1986)

The refiners: a century of BC Sugar *John Schreiner* Douglas & McIntyre (1989)

Woodwards: the story of a distinguished B.C. family *Douglas E. Harker* Mitchell Press (1976)

Vancouver: an illustrated history *Patricia E. Roy* J. Lorimer (1980)

Along the no. 20 line: reminiscences of the Vancouver waterfront *Rolf Knight* New Star Books (1980)

Opening doors: Vancouver's East End *Compiled and edited by Daphne Marlatt and Carole Itter* Sound heritage.— Vol. 8, no. 1-2

Vancouver *Eric Nicol* Doubleday (1978, revised edition)

The enterprising Mr. Moody, the bumptious Captain Stamp: the lives and colourful times of Vancouver's lumber pioneers *James Morton* J.J. Douglas (1977)

Vancouver, from milltown to metropolis *Alan Morley* Mitchell Press (1974, 3rd ed.)

The Vancouver Book *Chuck Davis, general editor* J.J. Douglas (1976) Predecessor to **The Greater Vancouver Book**

Coquitlam 100 Years: Reflections of the Past District of Coquitlam (1990)

The Ladners of Ladner: By Covered Wagon to the Welfare State *Leon J. Ladner* Mitchell Press Ltd. (1972)

The Surrey Story *G. Fern Treleaven* Surrey Museum and Historical Society (1978)

The Surrey Pioneers *Richard V. Whiteside* Evergreen Press Ltd. (1974)

Tynehead Memories Tynehead Historical Society (1982) History of a Surrey neighborhood

Along the Way: An Historical Account of Pioneering White Rock and Surrounding District in British Columbia *Margaret A. Lang* (1967, reprinted 1970)

Houses for all: the struggle for social housing in Vancouver, 1919-50 *Jill Wade* UBC Press (1994)

Exploring Vancouver: the essential architectural guide *Harold Kalman, Ron Phillips, Robin Ward; photographs and book design Robin Ward; additional photography Ron Phillips* UBC Press (1993)

Trees of Vancouver *Gerald B. Straley* UBC Press (1992)

Making Vancouver: Class, Status, and Social Boundaries, 1863-1913 *Robert A.J. McDonald* UBC Press (1996)

Saints: the story of St. George's School for Boys *Douglas E. Harker* Mitchell Press (1979)

Crofton House School, the first ninety years, 1898-1988 *Elizabeth Bell-Irving* Crofton House School (1988)

West Coast Chinese boy *Sing Lim* Tundra Books (1979)

The curses of third uncle *Paul Yee; illustrated by Don Besco* Lorimer (1986)

Teach me to fly, Skyfighter! and other stories *Paul Yee; illustrated by SKY Lee* Lorimer (1983)

Runaway: diary of a street kid *Evelyn Lau* Harper & Collins (1989)

The Vancouver Club first century, 1889-1989 *Reginald Roy* Vancouver Club (1989)

Red flags and red tape: the making of a labour bureaucracy *Mark Leier* University of Toronto Press (1995)

The climate of Vancouver *Tim Oke and John Hay* UBC Press (1994, 2nd ed.)

Discord: the story of the Vancouver Symphony Orchestra *John Becker; foreword by Max Wyman* Brighouse Press (1989)

Fleecing the lamb: the inside story of the Vancouver Stock Exchange *David Cruise & Alison Griffiths* Douglas & McIntyre (1987)

Hidden cities: art & design in architectural details of Vancouver & Victoria *Text and photographs by Gregory Edwards* Talonbooks (1991)

The concubine's children: portrait of a family divided *Denise Chong* Viking (1994) Recollections of a Chinese family

Glancing back: reflections and anecdotes on Vancouver public schools *Edited by Chuck Gosbee and Leslie Dyson* Vancouver School Board (1988)

This is my own: letters to Wes & other writings on Japanese Canadians, 1941-1948 *Muriel Kitagawa, Roy Miki, ed.* Talonbooks (1985)

New Westminster, the Royal City *Barry Mather and Margaret McDonald* J.M. Dent and the City of New Westminster (1958)

The boom years: G.G. Nye's photographs of North Vancouver 1905-1909 *Donald J. Bourdon* Hancock House (1981)

Vancouver Ltd. *Donald Gutstein* J. Lorimer (1975) Economic study of Vancouver

Inverted pyramid *Bertrand William Sinclair* Frederick D. Goodchild (1924)

The architecture of Arthur Erickson *Arthur Erickson* Douglas & McIntyre (1988)

Seven stones: a portrait of Arthur Erickson, architect *Edith Iglauer* Harbour Pub. (Vancouver); University of Washington Press (1981)

Ron Thom: the shaping of an architect *Douglas Shadbolt* Douglas & McIntyre (1995)

Vancouver fiction *Edited and with an introduction by David Watmough* Polestar Press (1985)

Paving paradise: is British Columbia losing its heritage? *Michael Kluckner* Whitecap Books (1991)

The innocent traveller *Ethel Wilson* Macmillan (1960, first edition published 1949)

Vancouver's Chinatown: racial discourse in Canada, 1875-1980 *Kay J. Anderson* McGill-Queen's University Press (1991)

Kingsway *Michael Turner* Arsenal Pulp Press (1995) Poetry expressing the mood of this historic thoroughfare

Hotel Europe, Gastown—from Exploring Vancouver, *1993.* rw

Douglas & McIntyre operates from growing and electronically integrated offices in both Toronto and its hometown. Douglas & McIntyre has published many distinguished Vancouver authors and many have been bestsellers: Doris Shadbolt's book The Art of Emily Carr has sold 30,000 copies and A Salmon for Simon, written by Betty Waterton and illustrated by Ann Blades, has sold more than 100,000 copies around the world.

Book of Days

EVERYTHING THAT EVER happened happened on a date. That simple fact is good to know, and useful, and you can see and hear the evidence daily: when a disc jockey celebrates Bryan Adams' birthday by playing one of his songs, when a columnist muses on the 60th anniversary of the opening of the Burrard Bridge, when a store like The Bay or Chapman's has an anniversary sale, when kids don scary masks on October 31, or their parents lift a jovial glass as midnight ushers in New Year's Day.

Forty years in broadcasting and nearly 30 (concurrent!) in writing have led me to a fondness for observing the anniversaries of significant events. They are excellent generators of ideas, and a great source of the often-overlooked or unremembered. Take November 23. Among the events listed in my files for that date is the birth of actor Boris Karloff. Now, thanks to one of this book's writers, David Spaner, any disc jockey, columnist or historian on November 23 can mention that back around 1907 when Boris Karloff was a young actor, using his real name William Pratt, he spent some time acting in British Columbia with a travelling Okanagan theatre troupe and worked part-time as a carpenter during the construction of the Vancouver Exhibition, later renamed the Pacific National Exhibition. Think of that: Frankenstein's monster helped to build the PNE!

You'll find in the pages that follow several hundred events in our local past. Emphasis is given to the specific date on which the event occurred, which means that disc jockeys, columnists or historians will find something on every day of the year to spark an ad lib, or an idea for a column, or even a book. (If Proust could be moved to write a multivolumed masterpiece of a novel as a result of memories stirred by the aroma of a fragment of pastry, think how much more potent a solid thing like a date could be!)

I can think of no more engaging way to illustrate the diversity of our past than to present it to you in bite-sized date-linked morsels. Note the date on which you read this little essay, then check in the following pages for the event noted on that day. It may be news to you, so reading it will make a small contribution to your expanding knowledge of Greater Vancouver. Or see which event we chose to coincide with your birthday or your marriage. Wouldn't it be interesting to know you were born the same day (February 2) on which the Grouse Mountain skyride opened or that you were married on the very day (December 11) SkyTrain began?

Date collecting can perform another function, too: it can link us to the outside world in ways that fix the events more firmly in our memories. When the wheel was invented in the Tigris-Euphrates basin more than 8,000 years ago there were already people living, hunting and fishing in what we now call Greater Vancouver. In 1792, the year George Vancouver explored Burrard Inlet, the French Revolution was raging, Robbie Burns was writing those immortal words, "Flow gently, Sweet Afton, among thy green braes ..." and Eli Whitney invented the cotton gin.

Dates can remind us that our own modern history is modestly brief: when Vancouver, a dusty collection of ramshackle wooden shacks, was incorporated in 1886, Toronto, older by more than 50 years, already boasted a substantial Conservatory of Music.

The remembrance of dates can spark ideas, bring back memories, initiate recurring rituals, increase our knowledge or merely entertain us.

Want a date? Turn the page.

—*Chuck Davis*

Opening of Canadian Pacific Piers B and C, July 4, 1927. vs
facing page: Babe Ruth at the Pantages Theatre, Nov 29, 1926.
Vancouver Public Library photo

The Greater Vancouver Book of Days
John Cochlin

JANUARY

January 1 *1922* At 6 a.m., all drivers in B.C. move over to the right side of the road.

January 2 *1891* Electric street lights are switched on in New Westminster from a power plant fuelled by sawdust.

January 3 *1897* Vancouver city chain gang goes on strike protesting work on clearing lanes.

January 4 *1889* The first Granville Street bridge opened.

January 5 *1912* The first professional hockey game is played in Vancouver at the Denman Arena, with the Vancouver Millionaires versus New Westminster Royals. Vancouver wins 8-3.

January 6 *1903* Vancouver Business College opens with four students.

January 7 *1909* The first shipment of grain is exported from Vancouver.

January 8 *1950* Tom Alsbury is sworn in as Vancouver's mayor, the first to have been born in the 20th century (1904).

January 9 *1972* The second Georgia Viaduct opens in Vancouver.

January 10 *1861* Col. Moody names Lulu Island for Miss Lulu Sweet, a touring actress.

January 11 *1965* The *Vancouver Times*, started to take advantage of a strike at the city's other two dailies, names Victor Odlum as publisher.

January 12 *1973* MP Ron Basford announces that Central Mortgage and Housing Corporation has acquired Granville Island, and redevelopment will commence immediately.

January 13 *1836* Samuel Brighouse, one of the Three Greenhorns, is born in Lindley, England. He farmed on Lulu Island, and the Brighouse name becomes familiar in Richmond.

January 14 *1961* Gertrude Guerin is the first woman to be elected chief of the Musqueam Indian Band.

January 15 *1886* Vancouver's first newspaper, the *Herald*, appears. It will last less than two years. *1917* The famed ballet star Nijinsky appears with the Ballet Russe at Vancouver's Opera House. *1974* New Knight Street Bridge officially opened.

January 15 1986 Dome Advertising is formed in Vancouver. Today, this major firm is known as Dome FCB.

January 16 *1894* Volunteer soldiers from Vancouver parade for the first time, before going off to the Boer War in South Africa. *1953* Police raid the Avon Theatre on Hastings Street, showing *Tobacco Road,* and arrest the cast for an allegedly indecent performance.

January 17 *1894* Maj. T.O. Townley administers oath to men at theatre on Pender Street, inaugurating No. 5 company of B.C. Brigade of Garrison Artillery.

January 18 *1973* An old brewery is renovated, becomes the Creekhouse, first building on Granville Island to be converted from industrial use.

January 19 *1869* The New London Mechanics Institute is founded at Hastings Mill as a meeting and reading room, counted by some as Vancouver's first library.

January 20 *1902* The Royal Brewing Company begins brewing at Cedar Cottage.

January 21 *1935* The roof of the Hastings Park Forum collapses under a heavy snowfall. *1864* The first session of the Legislative Council of the mainland colony of British Columbia is held in New Westminster.

January 22 *1974* Granville Street closes to automobile traffic for conversion to a pedestrian mall.

January 23 *1939* Sculptor Charles Marega's lions are placed at the south end of the brand-new Lions Gate Bridge.

January 24 *1918* Mary Ellen Smith is elected first woman MLA in British Columbia, winning in Vancouver Centre.

January 25 *1918* Samuel Patrick Cromie is born in Vancouver. One of the newspaper publishing Cromies, elected a city alderman in 1946 at age 28, youngest in the city's history to that time.

January 26 *1856* Henry Ogle Bell-Irving is born in Lockerbie, Scotland. He formed the Anglo-British Columbia Packing Co. in 1891, became Canada's biggest salmon exporter.

January 27 *1933* Blackburns Farmers' Market opens at Seymour and Robson.

January 28 *1912* Vancouver alderman Pettipiece addresses crowd at Powell Street grounds on unemployment. The meeting is broken up by mounted police.

January 29 *1870* Boat race between Inlet and New Westminster crews over a two-and-a-half mile course between Moody's Mill and Hastings Mill.

January 30 *1919* The Native Daughters of B.C. form. The group's objective is to pay tribute to the pioneers and history of the province.

January 31 *1941* The first orders are given to west coast shipyards for 10,000-ton cargo ships to convey war material and food to a war-torn Europe.

FEBRUARY

February 1 *1969* Stanley Park's Nine O'Clock Gun is "kidnapped" by UBC engineering students, who return the 1,500-pound cannon for a "ransom" donated to the Children's Hospital.

February 2 *1917* After an unsuccessful attempt Jan. 20, the *Mabel Brown* is launched at Wallace Shipyards, first ship built in Greater Vancouver. *1947* At a sod-turning ceremony for the new Schara Tzedeck synagogue at 19th and Oak, the ground is dedicated to Jewish veterans of World War II. *1966* The gondola is opened on Grouse Mountain.

February 3 *1920* The harbor police are formed. *1978* To mark the opening of its new cultural centre, the Italian community stages its first Carnevale Italiano.

February 3 1983 Earl's Restaurants begins! Today, there are 15 Earl's Restaurants in Greater Vancouver.

February 4 *1954* The present Granville Street Bridge is opened; a million cars will cross over the bridge in the first month.

February 5 *1946* One of Vancouver's showbiz institutions, Calvin Winter, dies. His orchestra—Calvin Winter and his Capitolians—played at the 1921 opening of the Capitol Theatre.

February 6 *1868* William Grafton, a Bowen Island pioneer, is born in London, England. Around 1887 he began the first ferry service on Howe Sound.

February 7 *1929* Movies in color (not tinted) come to Vancouver for the first time.

February 8 *1990* Richard Loney sings two versions of *O Canada* (the one we know and an early version by Vancouver's Ewing Buchan) at a Vancouver meeting of the Canadian Club.

February 9 *1910* A Vancouver banker, Ewing Buchan, has his version of *O Canada* sung at a meeting of the Canadian Club. *1976* Prime Minister Trudeau officially commissions the TRIUMF nuclear accelerator at UBC.

February 10 *1947* An era ends as the last ferry across Burrard Inlet, No. 6, runs to West Vancouver, then returns to the downtown terminal. Not until the SeaBus in 1977 will ferry service return.

February 11 *1966* The Right Reverend James Francis Carney is the first Vancouver-born Catholic to be named a bishop.

February 12 *1873* Granville Townsite (Gastown) gets its first school. *1978* Vancouver's Variety Club Telethon raises $1,152,000, a world record for any telethon sponsored by Variety.

February 13 *1861* The first issue of New Westminster's *British Columbian* newspaper appears.

February 14 *1859* Governor James Douglas begins to build a new colonial capital at Queensborough—today's New Westminster. *1915* The first trans-Canada telephone call, between Vancouver and Montreal, is placed. *1950* Nancy Hodges of Vancouver is the first woman in the British Empire to be named Speaker of the Legislature. *1978* Harry Ornest announces his new Pacific Coast League baseball team will be called the Vancouver Canadians.

February 15 *1915* The Imperial Theatre opens a brand-new musical comedy, *Fifty Years Forward.* Among its predictions for 1965: a lady mayor in Vancouver. *1965* The new Canadian flag rises at 6 a.m. at Vancouver City Hall, perhaps the first appearance of the flag in Canada after its official proclamation. *1968* Skier Nancy Greene wins gold in the Winter Olympics.

February 15 *1922* Odlum Brown is incorporated, and in 1997 celebrates 75 years in business in British Columbia.

February 16 *1881* A land grant of 25,000 acres (10,120 hectares) of land is given to the CPR in exchange for its extending its line to Vancouver. *1913* Dr. F. F. Wesbrook, dean of the medical college at the University of Minnesota, is named the first president of UBC. *1937* The CBC begins broadcasting over radio station CRVC. *1977* Marjorie Cantryn becomes a judge, the first native Indian woman to attain the post.

February 17 *1965* Testimonial dinner for W.A.C. Bennett at Hotel Vancouver on occasion of his becoming longest serving premier in B.C.'s history.

February 17 Happy Birthday Edna Davis!

February 18 *1922* Brothers M.J. Lannon and P.J. Ryan found Vancouver College.

February 19 *1986* The Lions Gate Bridge is illuminated, a gift from the Guinness family who built the bridge.

February 20 *1833* James Murray Yale takes command of Fort Langley and a Hudson's Bay Company farm is established at Langley Prairie.

February 21 *1977* North Vancouver's Carrie Cates dies. Married to John Henry Cates of the famed tugboat firm, she was elected mayor of North Vancouver three times.

February 22 *1936* The Seaforth Highlanders Regimental Band is formed.

February 23 *1887* Tilly Jean Rolston is born in Vancouver. In the 1952 provincial election, she won her SC seat in Point Grey and became education minister in the W.A.C. Bennett government, the first woman in Canada to hold a cabinet post with portfolio.

February 24 *1939* The first Fireman's Dance is held in Burnaby, admission $1 a couple. It becomes an annual event.

February 25 *1915* Israel Wood Powell dies. He was the first Masonic Grand Master of the Grand Lodge of B.C., donated the site for Vancouver's first city hall, and has Powell Street named for him.

February 26 *1962* The Queen Elizabeth Playhouse opens.

February 27 *1911* North Vancouver Ferry No. 3 is launched from Wallace Shipyards - the first self-propelled boat of any size to be built in North Vancouver.

February 28 *1910* A new Main Post Office for Vancouver opens at Hastings and Granville. Today it's Sinclair Centre.

February 29 *1940* The *Sun* merges its radio station with CKWX and the station's power is increased to reach nearly all parts of B.C.

MARCH

March 1 *1866* A customs collector is established on Burrard Inlet, making it possible for ships to leave harbor without their captains having to walk through the forest to the customs office in New Westminster. *1870* The Granville Townsite is registered; most continue to call it Gastown. *1978* Capilano Stadium is renamed Nat Bailey Stadium.

March 2 *1954* The first edition of the *Chinese Free Press,* Canada's first bilingual newspaper, is published.

March 3 *1892* Charles Woodward opens his first store near today's Main and Hastings—a dry goods shop. *1919* The first commercial seaplane takes off from Vancouver, carrying airmail for Seattle. There is a passenger, too: William Boeing.

March 4 *1971* Prime Minister Pierre Trudeau, 57, marries Margaret Sinclair, 22, at St. Stephens Catholic Church in Lynn Valley, North Vancouver.

March 5 *1889* The first banquet of The Vancouver Board of Trade is held in the Hotel Vancouver. The $12.50 cost per diner gets them a full dinner, plus a quart bottle of champagne.

March 6 *1918* "Honest John" Oliver, a farmer from Delta, is elected premier. He holds the office until his death in 1927. *1991* The new Bob Prittie Metrotown Branch of the Burnaby Public Library officially opens.

March 7 *1955* Margaret Jean Gee is the first woman of Chinese descent to be called to the British Columbia bar.

March 8 *1901* The Carnegie Foundation offers $50,000 to Vancouver for a library. *1974* The Dover Arms, Vancouver's first neighborhood pub, opens in the West End.

March 9 *1983* The royal yacht *Britannia* sails into Vancouver harbor, bringing the Queen and Prince Philip. Her Majesty opens the Graham Amazon Gallery at the Aquarium ... and caps the day by appearing on a special satellite hookup, inviting the world to attend Expo 86.

March 10 *1903* Fraser River Sawmills company is formed in Port Coquitlam, grows to become the largest lumber shipper in the British Empire.

March 11 *1913* Port Moody is incorporated as a city. *1924* The *Vancouver Sun* buys the *World,* and moves into both morning and evening markets.

March 12 *1968* The inaugural meeting of The Elector's Action Movement (TEAM) is held; they will go on to become a force in civic politics.

March 13 *1913* The Municipality of Fraser Mills secedes from Coquitlam. In 1971 it will become part of Port Coquitlam.

March 14 *1889* Real Estate Board formed in Vancouver.

March 15 *1912* The Municipality of West Vancouver is incorporated. It had once been the western portion of the District of North Vancouver. *1930* B.C.'s first "forest plantation" opens when Green Timbers is dedicated in Surrey with the planting of 120 baby trees. *1955* Langley City is incorporated as a separate municipality.

March 16 *1959* The first ship docks at the new Centennial Pier.

March 17 *1875* Edwin and Ann Woodward arrive at the Point Atkinson Light as the first lightkeepers. *1884* The *K de K* steam ferry, built for $2,000, begins the first ferry service between New Westminster and Brownsville (now part of Surrey).

March 18 *1943* Construction begins on the *Fort Columbia,* first of the Victory ships to be built by Burrard Dry Dock. The company builds 34 of the World War II ships in a little over two years.

March 19 *1923* The B.C. Electric Railway inaugurates a motorbus line on Grandview Highway; the bus runs from Commercial and Broadway to Rupert and East 22nd.

March 20 *1907* C.B.K. Van Norman, an important Vancouver architect, is born in Meaford, Ontario. He built mansions for the city's business leaders, designed the Burrard Building, the Maritime Museum and much of Park Royal.

March 21 *1985* Rick Hansen, paralyzed as the result of an accident, begins his around-the-world Man In Motion tour by wheelchair.

March 22 *1922* The *Weekly Optimist* begins publishing in Delta. It becomes the *Delta Optimist.*

March 23 *1937* Helena Gutteridge becomes the first woman elected to Vancouver city council in the city's 51-year history.

March 24 *1966* Bob Dylan performs at the Agrodome.

March 25 *1910* The first airplane flight west of Winnipeg takes place at Minoru Park in Richmond. *1921* The Capitol Theatre opens on Granville Street.

March 26 *1915* The Vancouver Millionaires win the Stanley Cup.

March 27 *1993* The restored Parker Carousel, built in 1912 in Kansas, is set in motion at Burnaby's Village Museum

March 28 *1898* Vancouver's first long-distance telephone installed in *Daily Province.* *1952* Retiring director Charles H. Scott officially opens the Vancouver Art School at Dunsmuir and Hamilton.

March 29 *1909* Greater Vancouver longshoremen strike for higher pay. They want 35 cents an hour for day work, 40 cents an hour for night work.

March 30 *1912* The Vancouver local of the International Longshoremen's Association is formed, with 60 charter members.

March 31 *1969* Vancouver is granted its present coat of arms.

APRIL

April 1 *1874* Henry Harvey becomes Vancouver's first official postmaster. *1968* Joachim Foikis, armed with a grant from the Canada Council, becomes Vancouver's Town Fool. *1981* Kwantlen College opens in Richmond.

April 2 *1977* A performance by the Vancouver Symphony Orchestra marks the official opening of the beautifully refurbished Orpheum Theatre. *1982* Premier Bill Bennett announces that Vancouver will host a world exposition in 1986 to mark Vancouver's centennial, and that a trade and convention centre will be built.

April 3 *1956* One robber dies and a police officer is wounded in a shootout following a Coquitlam robbery in which the bad guys used a machine gun for the first time in Greater Vancouver crime history. *1993* Vancouver hosts a summit meeting between U.S. President Bill Clinton and Russian President Boris Yeltsin.

April 4 *1952* *Bwana Devil* plays at the Plaza, Greater Vancouver's first 3D movie.

April 5 *1917* Women are now allowed to vote in British Columbia.

April 6 *1886* The City of Vancouver is incorporated. *1975* Sixty-one orphans arrive in Vancouver from Vietnam.

April 7 *1970* Jana Jorgensen, an 18-year-old Centennial High student from Coquitlam, wins the Miss Teen Canada contest.

April 8 *1912* The West Vancouver ferry service is taken over by the municipality. It runs at a loss until 1924.

April 9 *1920* The memorial to Japanese Canadians who died in World War I is dedicated in Stanley Park.

April 9 1917 The B.C. and Yukon Hotels Association is incorporated.

April 10 *1899* Historian Frederick Hubert Soward is born in Minden, Ont. Described as the "boy wonder" of UBC's history department, he taught from 1922-66, headed the department from 1953-63.

April 11 Burrard Inlet's first telegraph message goes out from Moody's Mill on the North Shore to New Westminster.

April 11 1860 The eminent B.C. architect Samuel Maclure is born at Sapperton, the first white male child born in that area. At 21 he was a telegraph operator in Granville (Gastown). Much of his architectural work—about 30 buildings—is visible in Vancouver today, a story told in the book *Samuel Maclure Architect*, by Janet Bingham. This remembrance of Maclure is sponsored by Janet and Alec Bingham.

April 12 *1907* The Vancouver Stock Exchange is incorporated.

April 13 *1932* Paderewski performs in recital at the Vancouver Arena.

April 14 *1918* Daylight Saving Time is introduced to Vancouver. *1975* Vancouver Co-Operative Radio, CFRO-FM, goes on the air.

April 14 1864 Alexandre Joseph Prefontaine is born in Beloeil, Quebec to a family whose ancestors have lived in the region since 1865. In 1890-91 Alexandre, his wife Clara, and his young family travel to Vancouver, where he opens the Montreal Bakery on the site where the Marine Building now stands. Many of his descendants still live and work in Greater Vancouver today. Friend of the Book: Gerry P. Prefontaine.

April 15 *1881* The maiden voyage of the *Senator*, a steam tug built at Moodyville, that ferried passengers, mail and cattle across Burrard Inlet. *1957* The City of White Rock, which had broken away from Surrey, is incorporated.

April 16 *1856* Governor Douglas announces the discovery of gold in British Columbia. All gold found is declared to be the property of the British Crown.

April 17 *1894* The forerunner of the Vancouver Museum opens. The first donation was a stuffed white swan. Now there are more than 100,000 items. *1913* Baseball's Athletic Park opens its doors to professional baseball in Vancouver. Six thousand fans watch the Beavers defeat the Tacoma Tigers 8-4.

April 17 1915 Friend of the Book Sharon Furlotte-Unruh is happy to sponsor this date as a tribute to Melvin Unruh, her fiance's father, born on this day.

April 18 *1913* Port Coquitlam celebrates its incorporation as a city. Also *1913* Athletic Park is dedicated, and will become the home of Capilano Stadium. *1953* Vancouver's last streetcar runs on Oak Street.

April 18, 1995 The incorporation date of Captain Billy's Magical Tours Ltd., organizers of unique and personalized tours of the Vancouver area.

April 19 *1958* Professional baseball tickets are sold on Sunday in Vancouver for the first time, after a years-long fight.

April 20 *1864* Governor Douglas' successor, Frederick Seymour, arrives in New Westminster to take up residence as governor of the mainland colony. *1910* A man is arrested in Surrey for speeding at 12 mph in his 1907 Marion. He is fined $10.

April 21 *1916* The first congress of the new British Columbia Chess Association opens in Vancouver.

April 22 *1961* North Vancouver's Lions Gate Hospital opens at its current site with 285 beds.

April 23 *1935* Mayor Gerry McGeer reads the Riot Act in Victory Square as relief camp men riot in Vancouver. *1976* The Four Seasons Hotel officially opens with a benefit to raise funds for the Vancouver Symphony Orchestra.

April 24 *1912* Pilot Billy Stark makes the first passenger flight in British Columbia. Reporter James Hewitt is flown six miles in eight minutes riding on a board strapped to the lower wing. *1933* The *Vancouver News Herald* publishes its first edition.

April 25 *1858* Some 450 wild-eyed gold prospectors arrive by ship from San Francisco, the first of a flood of 25,000.

April 25 1907 The Vancouver Stock Exchange is established.

April 26 *1873* The District of Langley is incorporated.

April 27 *1956* The Vancouver Mounties play the San Francisco Seals at Cap Stadium in the inaugural game of baseball's Pacific Coast League. *1960* The Percy Norman Memorial Pool is dedicated.

April 27 1993 Opening of Red's Classic Cafe in Coombs, on Vancouver Island, by Don & Linda Cassie, Operators/Owners.

April 28 *1911* William Templeton becomes the first person to fly an airplane over Vancouver.

April 29 *1875* Mabel Ellen Boultbee (nee Springer) is born in Moodyville, the first white child born on Burrard Inlet. She will be a journalist here for 30 years.

April 30 *1945* Fire destroys Capilano Stadium. *1970* The first computer-commanded coal train from Alberta reaches the new Roberts Bank superport in Delta.

MAY

May 1 *1859* St. John the Divine Anglican Church is consecrated at Derby, near Fort Langley, the first permanent church in the new colony of British Columbia. *1886* The Hastings Mill post office changes its name to the Vancouver Post Office.

May 1 1996 The official opening of the New International Terminal building at Vancouver International Airport.

May 2 *1984* The Mandarin Hotel opens in downtown Vancouver, a $41 million structure owned by a Hong Kong chain.

May 3 *1886* The first election is held in Vancouver and Malcolm MacLean becomes the city's first mayor. *1974* The Aquatic Centre, built to replace Crystal Pool, is officially opened. Swimmers start using it May 6.

May 3 1974 Jeff Veniot is pleased to sponsor this day as a tribute to the Aquatic Centre. Jeff is even more pleased that he was the first paying swimmer to use the centre's pool on May 6th, 1974. He was 18 at the time.

May 4 *1974* Professional soccer comes to town as the Vancouver Whitecaps play their opening game at Empire Stadium against the San Jose Earthquakes.

May 5 *1988* Simon Fraser University opens a downtown Vancouver campus in the historic Spencer Building on West Hastings Street. *1983* Alderman Rita Johnston is elected an MLA for Surrey. She will later become the first woman to be a provincial premier in Canada.

May 6 *1912* The King Edward VII Memorial Fountain is unveiled in Stanley Park. Today it's beside the Vancouver Art Gallery. *1959* The official opening of Oakridge Shopping Centre.

May 6 1989 Science World opens in the former Expo Centre.

May 7 *1945* Air raid sirens ring at 7:04 a.m. to mark VE Day (Victory in Europe).

May 8 *1847* Alexander Mitchell is born in Masham County, Que. He moves to B.C. in 1877 and becomes Richmond's first farmer. *1912* George Woodcock, B.C.'s most distinguished and prolific man of letters, is born in Winnipeg.

May 8 1949 The Ace Cycle Shop becomes the first to introduce imported European ten-speed bicycles to the British Columbia market.

May 9 *1927* The Hotel Georgia opens.

May 10 *1886* The first Vancouver City Council meeting is held; its first decision is to ask Ottawa for a grant of an adjacent 1,000-acre military reserve; that's today's Stanley Park. *1947* Local school children circulate a petition calling for an end to wartime taxes on candy; in July prices are lowered to seven cents from eight for a chocolate bar.

May 11 *1907* The University Women's Club of Vancouver is founded by eight graduates, headed by Mrs. J.W. deB. Farris.

May 12 *1900* The ferry *North Vancouver* begins operation as the first ferry with regular service between North Vancouver and the south shore of the Inlet.

May 12 1990 Roedde House opens as a museum in Vancouver's West End.

May 13 *1907* The City of North Vancouver is incorporated.

May 14 *1978* George Tocher and a navigator set out for Hawaii from West Vancouver in a native-style log canoe Tocher has made to prove Hawaiians could have originated in British Columbia.

May 15 *1886* CPR surveyor Lauchlan Hamilton begins to survey what will become Granville Street. *1959* Vancouver's Harry Jerome breaks the world record for the 220-yard dash.

May 16 *1982* The New York Islanders defeat the Vancouver Canucks in four straight games to win the 1982 Stanley Cup, despite "White Towel Power."

May 17 *1869* Chris (Christopher) Spencer, department store heir, is born in Victoria. After his father David's death, he was president of Spencer Stores until the company's purchase by the T. Eaton Co. in 1948. *1917* The *War Dogs* is launched by Wallace Shipyards, their first steel steamer, and the first steel ocean-going freighter to be built on Burrard Inlet.

May 18 *1918* The first grain shipment from Vancouver via the Panama Canal departs; five ships take 800,000 bushels of wheat to Europe. *1937* The *Vancouver Sun* purchases the Bekins Tower (originally the World Building), which becomes the Sun Tower. *1980* Mount St. Helen's erupts in Washington State

May 19 *1952* A major exhibition of work by Picasso opens at the Vancouver Art Gallery.

May 20 *1904* A small school house is opened in Lynn Valley, with 18 pupils.

May 21 *1934* First sod is turned for the construction of Malkin Bowl in Stanley Park.

May 22 *1808* Simon Fraser sets out on the perilous and famous descent down the river that will come to bear his name. *1987* Rick Hansen's 34-country Man in Motion tour ends as he wheels into Oakridge Mall in Vancouver. *1937* The Common Good Credit Unit (sic) makes its first loan ($27) and begins the Credit Union movement in British Columbia.

May 23 *1887* The first CPR passenger train arrives in Vancouver from Montreal. *1914* The *Komogata Maru* arrives in Vancouver.

May 24 *1912* The first parachute jump in Canada is made in Richmond's Minoru Park by Charles Saunders. *1921* The grand opening of the largest dance pavilion in B.C., at the Union Steamship Company's resort on Bowen Island. It could accommodate 800 people.

May 25 *1868* The capital of British Columbia is moved from New Westminster to Victoria. *1939* The present Hotel Vancouver opens on its present site, more than 10 years after the beginning of construction.

May 26 *1939* The Lions Gate Bridge, which has been open to traffic since November 1938, is officially opened by King George V and Queen Elizabeth. *1995* The new Central Branch of the Vancouver Public Library opens its doors.

May 27 *1948* First refugees from serious flooding in the Fraser Valley arrive in Vancouver aboard a special CPR rescue train.

May 28 *1886* Vancouver's first fire department, Volunteer Hose Company Number One, is formed.

May 29 *1875* Grumbling at a dog barking outside his home, where he lies ill, John "Gassy Jack" Deighton dies. *1922* The *Norsal*, built to carry Powell River Co. executives to the company's mill, makes her maiden voyage from Vancouver.

1939 King George VI and Queen Elizabeth visit Vancouver. They officiate at the formal opening of the Lions Gate Bridge. *1978* The first Vancouver Children's Festival is held in big colorful tents in Vanier Park.

May 30 *1963* The University Women's Club of Vancouver holds its first meeting in its elegant new home, Hycroft.

May 31 *1907* A dozen Vancouver businessmen meet and form an Exhibition Association that will lead to what is today the Pacific National Exhibition. *1949* The new Labour Temple opens on West Broadway. *1976* UBC's Museum of Anthropology moves into its stunning new home. *1985* Steve Fonyo ends his 14-month cross-country run at the Pacific Ocean. Inspired by Terry Fox, Fonyo raises $13 million in the fight against cancer.

JUNE

June 1 *1905* L.D. Taylor and others buy the *World* newspaper from Sara McLagan. *1954* Vancouver acquires the pioneer McCleery farm for a golf course. *1967* Vancouver businessman Harry Con publishes the first history of Canada written in Chinese.

June 2 *1972* A disturbance breaks out at a Rolling Stones concert at the Pacific Coliseum and 21 police are injured.

June 3 *1935* One thousand unemployed men board freight cars in Vancouver to begin the On to Ottawa trek protesting conditions for the unemployed. *1955* CP Airlines inaugurates the first service between Vancouver and Amsterdam. The 4,825-mile journey over the North Pole takes 18 hours.

June 3 1961 Charlie and Mary Mayrs are married. Happy anniversary!

June 4 *1847* Francis Carter-Cotton is born in Yorkshire, England. He will launch the *News-Advertiser*, the first Vancouver newspaper to carry classified advertising, the first in North America with an electric-powered press and the first with machine-set type.

June 5 *1961* Direct distance telephone dialling begins in Vancouver.

June 6 *1865* Tomekichi Homma is born in Onigoshi-mura, Japan. He organized the Japanese fisherman's union here, and began the first Japanese-language newspaper.

June 7 *1951* The last game of baseball is played in Athletic Park before it's torn down to make way for the Hemlock Street entrance ramp to the Granville Street Bridge. *1989* The Vancouver Canucks make a sixth-round pick, a young Russian player named Pavel Bure.

June 8 *1963* The Agrodome, a domed exhibition hall, is opened at the PNE. *1977* Vancouver Centre is officially opened, at 198 metres (651 feet) the tallest building yet built in the city.

June 9 *1933* A city by-law amendment allows men to wear bathing trunks on city beaches and dispense with body-length suits.

June 10 *1925* Inaugural services at St. Andrews Presbyterian Church mark the formation of the United Church. *1957* Douglas Jung becomes Canada's first member of parliament of Chinese descent, becoming PC member for Vancouver Centre.

June 11 1930 Airplane and boat builder W.E. Boeing launches his luxury yacht *Taconite* **in Vancouver; today it's owned by W. Gordon Levett.**

June 12 *1891* The Ross McLaren Sawmills at Millside (later known as Fraser Mills), built in 1889, finally begin operations.

June 12 1950 Ray Greenwood, Vancouver's "Mr. Fireworks," is born.

June 13 *1792* Capt. George Vancouver, his two ships anchored in the Gulf of Georgia, begins exploring local waters in two small skiffs . . . and names Point Grey and Burrard Inlet. *1859* Report is made of the discovery of coal on the south shore of Burrard Inlet, today's Coal Harbour. *1886* The Great Fire destroys virtually all of the two-month-old City of Vancouver. **Friend of the Book: Sharon Furlotte-Unruh, who sponsors this day (June 13 was the birthdate of her mother, Jean Furlotte-Howard) as a tribute to her mother, "who was definitely the 'wind beneath my wings' when I had hard times."**

June 14 *1880* Lily Laverock is born in Edinburgh; she will become an impresario in Vancouver during the 1920s and 1930s, bringing in scores of famed classical performers.

June 15 *1846* The 49th parallel is decided on as the Canadian-U.S. border west of the Rockies (it already was to the east). *1931* The B.C. government takes over the sale of liquor.

June 15 1956 The opening day of the Vancouver Aquarium.

June 16 *1928* Nat Bailey opens a drive-in barbecue stand at Granville and 67th Avenue. That marks the beginning of the White Spot chain.

June 16 1988 The Roxy Cabaret opens!

June 17 *1917* The Beacon Theatre (later called the Pantages) opens on Hastings Street and is proclaimed one of the continent's best vaudeville houses. *1918* Famed actress Sarah Bernhardt appears in Vancouver; costliest ticket is 85 cents. *1958* The Second Narrows Bridge, under construction, collapses. Eighteen men die.

June 18 *1867* Edward Stamp begins to cut wood at the mill he manages; it will become a very successful operation under his leadership. *1962* B.C.'s native Indian people vote for the first time in a federal election.

June 19 *1967* Air chimes designed by Robert Swanson are placed atop the B.C. Hydro Building at Burrard and Nelson. They play the first four notes of *O Canada*. *1983* Premier Bill Bennett opens the 60,000-seat B.C. Stadium, the first domed stadium in Canada.

June 20 *1983* In the first event at B.C. Place Stadium, the Vancouver Whitecaps defeat the Seattle Sounders.

June 21 *1974* B.C. Rail's Royal Hudson makes its inaugural run to Squamish. The big, beautiful locomotive is an instant hit with locals and tourists alike.

June 22 *1792* English explorer George Vancouver and Spanish explorer Dionisio Galiano are startled to meet in what is now English Bay. They hit it off.

June 23 *1973* The opening of False Creek Park marks the official start to redeveloping False Creek.

June 24 *1911* The first nine holes of the Vancouver Golf Club in Coquitlam are opened for play.

June 25 *1994* The Gulf of Georgia Cannery in Steveston celebrates its 100th birthday, and reopens to the public with new exhibits commemorating the fishing industry.

June 26 *1890* The first streetcar in Vancouver runs a test route down Cordova Street.

June 26 1967 Griffiths Gibson Productions begins. By 1972 it expands as Griffiths Gibson & Ramsay Productions Limited, and goes on to become one of Canada's leading commercial jingle studios.

June 27 *1956* Red Robinson hosts Vancouver's first rock and roll concert as Bill Haley and the Comets blow 'em away at Kerrisdale Arena. *1976* The first Greek Days Festival is held on West Broadway, sponsored by the Hellenic Community Association.

June 28 *1890* The first streetcar in Vancouver begins a regular route, a rectangular journey along Main, Cordova, Granville and Pender streets. *1972* The present Georgia/Dunsmuir Viaduct opens. *1981* Terry Fox dies, one month before his 23rd birthday and Canada mourns a genuine, and a beloved, hero.

June 29 *1878* The *Moodyville Tickler*, Burrard Inlet's first newspaper, appears; it has a short, tongue-in-cheek existence.

June 29 1993 John Cochlin and Chuck Davis enter into a partnership to establish The Linkman Press, publishers of *The Greater Vancouver Book.*

June 30 *1858* The last fur brigade arrives at Fort Langley. Thereafter, brigades travel to steamers at Hope.

JULY

July 1 *1867* Confederation. (British Columbia's membership is still four years away). *1911* Canada's first "peal," in which the bells of Holy Rosary Cathedral in Vancouver ring through more than 5,000 changes without a break—it takes three hours. *1915* The original Georgia Viaduct opens. *1957* The Oak Street Bridge is officially opened.

July 1 1993 On Canada's 126th birthday, The Westbrook Hotel was renamed The Landis Hotel & Suites.

July 2 *1808* Simon Fraser arrives at Musqueam at the mouth of the Fraser River, then he and his men are chased back up the river by angry natives. *1954* Vancouver's first cocktail bar is opened on the main floor of the Sylvia Hotel.

July 3 *1906* Chief Capilano goes to London to meet King Edward VII and Queen Alexandra. *1931* Canada's first baseball game played under lights is held at Athletic Park.

July 4 *1927* The CPR opens piers B and C as part of the celebrations marking the Diamond Jubilee of Confederation. *1967* A crowd of more than 30,000 at Empire Stadium is moved to silence when Chief Dan George recites a Lament for Confederation mourning the passing of the Indian's way of life. *1979* The *Vancouver Courier* begins as a daily.

July 5 *1791* Spanish explorer Don José Maria Narvaez, the first European to see the site of the future city of Vancouver, anchors west of Point Grey.

July 6 *1936* Telegraph wires link Vancouver to London. *1967* Jack Harman's statuary group *The Family* is unveiled at the Pacific Press Building.

July 7 *1917* Vancouver Fire Department firefighters go on strike for better pay and conditions. City Council grumbles, but agrees to their demands.

July 8 *1934* Malkin Bowl opens in Stanley Park with a performance by the Vancouver Symphony Orchestra. **Geoffrey Dodds of Buckley Dodds Chartered Accountants is pleased to sponsor this tribute to Malkin Bowl.**

July 9 *1940* The first of thousands of children evacuated from Britain for the duration of World War II begin to arrive in Vancouver. *1953* The Davis Cup tournament, the "world championship" of tennis, opens at the Vancouver Lawn and Tennis Club. The club was chosen because the Japanese team insisted on playing on grass courts, and none were available in the U.S.

July 10 *1888* John B. Rivet, blacksmith and wheelwright, opens a shop in Trounce Alley.

July 11 *1911* Wallace Shipyards in North Vancouver is destroyed by fire. It is rebuilt almost immediately.

July 12 *1913* The Pacific Highway is opened, running from the Fraser River bridge to the U.S. border. *1930* A city market opens at Main and Pender streets. *1979* Granville Island Public Market opens.

July 13 *1886* Vancouver council passes a by-law requiring bicyclists not to exceed 8 mph. *1934* Coquitlam councillor Thomas Douglas is shot dead at his North Road gas station.

July 14 *1986* The *New Yorker's* E.J. Kahn, Jr., writes "It's not so much Expo 86's substance that accounts for its charm as it is its style. You feel good just walking around."

July 15 *1952* The present-day Lumberman's Arch is dedicated in Stanley Park, replacing an earlier version. *1959* Queen Elizabeth II presides at the opening of the Deas Island Tunnel, today called the George Massey Tunnel, and attends a performance at the brand-new Queen Elizabeth Theatre, named for her.

July 16 *1899* The cornerstone of Vancouver's Holy Rosary Cathedral is laid. *1860* The City of New Westminster is incorporated. *1966* Elaine Tanner is named female swimmer of the year by the Canadian Amateur Swimming Association.

July 17 *1860* New Westminster is incorporated as a municipality, making it the oldest in Canada west of the Great Lakes.

July 18 *1868* The first marriage among the non-native population of Burrard Inlet: the Rev. Edward White marries Ada Young and Peter Plant at Moody's Mill. *1968* The Bank of British Columbia, Canada's tenth chartered bank, opens in Vancouver.

July 19 *1917* Helen McGill becomes the first woman to be appointed a judge of the juvenile court. *1937* Sliced bread comes to Greater Vancouver. *1958* Chief Mungo Martin presents to Queen Elizabeth a 100-foot totem pole he has carved to mark B.C.'s centennial. A replica stands by the Maritime Museum.

July 20 *1859* Queensborough's name is changed to New Westminster. *1871* British Columbia joins Confederation. Over his saloon, John "Gassy Jack" Deighton raises a Canadian flag, the first to be seen in Greater Vancouver.

July 21 *1954* A time capsule is buried beneath Centuries Rock in Queen Elizabeth Park. It is to be opened in 2054. (Future readers take note!)

July 21 *1995* **Air Transat Holidays begins regular low-cost flights from Vancouver to the U.K.**

July 22 *1931* Vancouver Airport and Seaplane Harbor officially opens.

July 23 *1904* The first bridge to span the lower Fraser River is opened. Costing $1 million, it links New Westminster with Brownsville (now in Surrey).

July 24 *1899* Chief Dan George is born in North Vancouver. After a career including leading a small music band, longshoring and logging, he becomes a hugely successful actor. *1912* The B.C. Electric Railway Co. holds its first annual picnic at Hastings Park.

July 25 *1879* Gustav Konstantin "Alvo" von Alvensleben is born in Neu Gettersleben, Germany. He arrives in Vancouver in 1904 to begin an incredible career as realtor, inn owner and suspected spy. *1891* The City of Coquitlam is incorporated. *1905* Grace McInnis is born in Winnipeg. In 1965 she will become the first woman to be a British Columbia Member of Parliament.

July 26 *1923* U.S. President Warren Harding visits Vancouver, first to do so. He dies in the United States shortly after his visit, and the Kiwanis Club initiates a drive for a grand memorial to him in Stanley Park. *1924* Nanny Janet Smith is found murdered in the Shaughnessy home of her employers; it is the city's most famous unsolved murder.

July 27 *1929* Charles Lindbergh refuses an invitation to fly into Vancouver because the city lacks an adequate airport; that spurs the drive to build a new one.

July 28 *1930* The old Hastings Mill Store is towed to Alma Park (now Pioneer Park) as a museum; it's still there.

July 29 *1938* Anne Mindigel becomes the first person to swim from Vancouver to Bowen Island. *1969* Arthur Clarke becomes the first black man to become a Vancouver police officer.

July 30 *1865* The first religious service is held on Burrard Inlet, conducted for the men of Moodyville by the Rev. Ebenezer Robson, a Methodist. *1915* The famed White Rock Pier is officially opened.

July 31 *1913* Visiting American aviatrix Alys Bryant is the first woman to make a solo flight in Canada; location is Richmond's Minoru Race-track.

AUGUST

August 1 *1907* The Vancouver Stock Exchange opens at 849 West Pender, with 12 charter members. *1928* Runner Percy Williams wins a gold medal at the Amsterdam Olympics. The city plans a civic parade.

August 2 *1918* The Vancouver Trades and Labor Council conducts an almost completely successful 24-hour general strike in memory of martyred labor leader Albert "Ginger" Goodwin. *1985* The light at the Stanley Park war memorial commemorating Japanese-Canadian soldiers who fought in World War I, which had been extinguished December 8, 1941, is relighted.

August 3 *1939* Radio telephones are installed in Vancouver's police cars.

August 4 *1923* Southam assumes control of the very successful *Vancouver Daily Province*. *1945* Froth on beer glasses is limited by law to half an inch.

August 5 *1920* Fire destroys much of downtown Port Coquitlam. It apparently started in the fire chief's living quarters.

August 6 *1866* The Crown colonies of Vancouver Island and British Columbia are united under the name British Columbia. *1940* Theatre Under The Stars, the famous TUTS, begins its decades-long history of entertainment at Malkin Bowl.

August 7 *1954* The "Miracle Mile" is run at Exhibition Park, when Roger Bannister and John Landy both finish in under four minutes.

August 8 *1887* The first electric lights are turned on in Vancouver.

August 9 *1902* The IODE (Imperial Order Daughters of the Empire) is formed in Vancouver on Edward VII's coronation day.

August 10 *1914* Dr. Leonard S. Klinck, dean of agriculture, is the first faculty member appointed by UBC.

August 11 *1925* Radio CNRV begins broadcasting from a studio in the CNR train station.

August 12 *1977* A plaque by artist Stjepan Pticek dedicates a section of Hornby Street as "Wasserman's Beat" in memory of the late *Sun* columnist. *1979* The *Province* first appears on a Sunday.

August 13 *1920* Garibaldi Park is officially opened.

August 13 *1977* **The Lookout! opens high atop Vancouver's Harbour Centre Tower. Neil Armstrong, first man on the moon, ascends to the top in one of the building's famed outdoor glassed-in elevators and leaves his footprints as an official memento of the opening. The Lookout! celebrates 20 years of fabulous city-wide views in 1997.**

August 14 *1907* The first newspaper reference to the Vancouver Police Department's first automobile. *1944* Odessa in the USSR is adopted as Vancouver's sister city. To mark the occasion, the VSO gives a concert of Russian music. *1945* The end of World War II is celebrated wildly in Greater Vancouver.

August 15 *1931* Kitsilano Pool officially opens. *1944* Radio station CKNW unofficially signs on; the official date will be September 1st. *1949* Kingsway becomes a six-lane highway between Vancouver and New Westminster.

August 16 *1910* The PNE is officially opened by Prime Minister Wilfrid Laurier. (It had opened unofficially the day before). *1965* Johnny Longden rides his 6,000th winner at Exhibition Park. *1980* Vancouver's Lois Wilson is the first woman to be named moderator of the United Church of Canada.

August 17 *1977* The last of Vancouver's little cab companies goes, when the 10-car Forum Empress Taxi Co. is purchased by Yellow Cab.

August 18 *1981* Delegates from Vancouver's sister city, Odessa, in the Ukrainian SSR, visit Vancouver.

August 19 *1936* The boxing Baer Brothers, Max

Original Lumberman's Arch erected at Pender and Hamilton for the September 19, 1912 visit of the Duke and duchess of Connaught. cva

and Buddy, put on an exhibition match in Vancouver, the first time they appeared in the ring together. *1988* A watermain in the Main Library (at Burrard and Robson) breaks and thousands of books and other items are damaged.

August 20 *1936* Fire destroys the Auditorium and Denman Arena. Also *1936* The statue of Capt. George Vancouver is unveiled at City Hall.

August 21 *1909* Minoru Race Track, named for King Edward's Epsom Derby winner, opens in Richmond.

August 21 *1886* **C. H. Cates & Sons, whose tugboats have long been a familiar part of the Greater Vancouver scene, has its origins when Charles Henry Cates starts business.**

August 22 *1974* Granville Street Mall opens.

August 23 *1990* The Surrey campus of Kwantlen College officially opens.

August 24 *1929* Boeing of Canada opens a plant on Coal Harbour.

August 25 *1960* Premier W.A.C. Bennett officially opens the Second Narrows Bridge.

August 26 *1903* The Vancouver Museum is created out of The Art, Historical and Scientific Association. *1939* Local militia stand by guns at

First Narrows in North Vancouver as world war threatens. *1957* One-way streets begin at midnight in downtown Vancouver.

August 27 *1929* The Graf Zeppelin visits Coal Harbour. *1975* The Arthur Laing Bridge, speeding traffic to and from the airport, opens to traffic. *1980* Southam acquires ownership of the *Vancouver Sun,* now owns both dailies in the city.

August 28 *1915* The first Canadian Northern Pacific Railway train (the CNPR will eventually be absorbed by the CNR) arrives in Vancouver.

August 28 *1950* **Sev Morin and Pauline Morin tie the knot. They'll celebrate 47 years of marriage in 1997. Sev, a well-known restaurateur and showbiz buff, says, "The big song back then was Frank Loesser's *Slow Boat to China*."**

August 29 *1921* The CPR's *Princess Louise,* the largest passenger ship ever built in B.C., is launched. *1936* Governor General Tweedsmuir officiates at the opening of the Seaforth Armories (Tweedsmuir, whose name was John Buchan, was the author of a best-selling mystery, twice filmed, titled *The Thirty-Nine Steps*).

August 30 *1936* The first service is held in the present-day St. James Anglican Church, at Gore

and Cordova in Vancouver. *1953* Vancouver's Doug Hepburn wins the world heavyweight weightlifting championship.

August 31 *1957* Elvis Presley performs one song at Empire Stadium, leaves the stage when fans begin to battle with police. He returns to sing four more songs—none are heard over the screaming.

SEPTEMBER

September 1 *1917* Robert Cromie buys the *News Advertiser,* amalgamates it with his *Morning Sun.*

September 1 *1979* **Barry Downs and Richard Archambault, architects, go into business as Downs Archambault & Partners.**

September 2 *1927* The Rogers Building at Pender and Granville is sold to General "One-Arm" Sutton for $1 million, the city's largest real estate transaction to that time.

September 3 *1906* Streetcars begin operation in North Vancouver, will serve the area for 40 years. *1923* A banquet is held to commemorate the completion of cement surfacing of the Pacific Highway.

September 3 *1975* **Irene Croden establishes Croden Personnel Consulting Services Inc. "Committed to your Success."**

September 4 *1923* West Vancouver High School opens in the Hollyburn Elementary School building.

September 5 *1900* River frontage lots go on sale in Surrey at $105 per lot, "irrespective of acreage." The lots range from 10 to 13 acres.

September 6 *1909* The first Granville Street Bridge opens.

September 7 *1976* B.C. Tel inaugurates direct distance dialling overseas; Mayor Art Phillips calls the mayor of Kings Lynn in Norfolk, England, birthplace of George Vancouver.

September 8 *1979* The Vancouver Whitecaps win the North American Soccer League Championship, defeating Tampa Bay Rowdies 2-1.

September 9 *1908* The incorporation of the British Columbia Refining Company, located in Port Moody. It refines oil shipped from California. *1918* The Surrey Board of Trade is established. *1965* Simon Fraser University opens on Burnaby Mountain.

September 10 *1949* Gloria Cranmer, the first native Indian woman to attend UBC, registers for pre-medicine.

September 11 *1898* The entire downtown section of New Westminster burns and hundreds are left homeless.

September 12 *1902* Woodward's Department Store opens at Hastings and Abbott streets

September 13 *1966* The H.R. MacMillan Planetarium opens in Vancouver, a gift from the lumber company executive.

September 14 *1912* Lynn Canyon Park is opened in North Vancouver and the 6th Field Engineers make their first appearance as the honour guard. *1980* The first phase of Vancouver's Chinese Cultural Centre opens.

September 15 *1911* Thieves make off with more than a quarter-of-a-million dollars in a New Westminster bank vault heist. It is the greatest bank robbery in North America to that time.

September 16 *1884* CPR President William Van Horne asks the railway's directors to choose Granville (Gastown), not Port Moody, as the terminus. *1972* DeCosmos Village, Vancouver's first co-op housing development, opens at 49th and Boundary.

September 17 *1950* The last run of the famous B.C. Electric "observation cars," roofless streetcars in which tourists and locals alike toured the city.

September 18 *1984* Pope John Paul II makes the first visit by a pope to Greater Vancouver.

September 19 *1912* The visiting Duke and Duchess of Connaught open the Connaught Bridge. Everyone calls it the Cambie Street Bridge.

September 20 *1908* The Rev. W. A. Davis conducts Sunday service in John Lawson's North Vancouver home for a group of Presbyterians, Methodists, Baptists and Congregationalists.

September 21 *1947* Mon Keong School, a high school to teach Chinese language, literature and music, opens in Chinatown; it is unique in Canada. *1957* Leon Koerner begins the Thea and Leon Koerner Foundation which will give millions to good causes

September 22 *1968* Vancouver's Community Arts Council sponsors a walking tour of Gastown to promote interest in developing the historical, but badly deteriorated, area. *1986* The Alex Fraser Bridge is opened linking Delta with New Westminster.

September 23 *1941* Beloved *Province* columnist Jimmy Butterfield, whose daily column, *The Common Round,* had appeared for 18 years, dies.

September 24 *1956* Little Richard is mobbed by fans and a near riot erupts during his show at Kerrisdale Arena.

September 25 *1906* The Vancouver Canadian Club has its inaugural luncheon. Governor General Grey is the guest of honor. *1969* Lougheed Mall opens.

September 26 *1862* The McCleery family become the first settlers in what is today's Vancouver on what is today's McCleery Golf Course.

September 27 *1888* Stanley Park is opened. Mayor David Oppenheimer officiating.

September 28 *1889* The windjammer *Titania* departs Steveston with canned salmon for direct shipment to Britain, the first ship to do so. *1909* The first contingent of 110 French Canadians from Quebec's lumber industry arrive by train to work at Fraser Mills. Their residential community becomes known as Maillardville, after Father Maillard, a community leader.

September 29 *1984* Richmond's Gateway Theatre is opened.

September 30 *1867* John "Gassy Jack" Deighton, a garrulous Fraser River pilot, arrives at Burrard Inlet to open a saloon. *1915* The University of British Columbia opens for classes in a temporary structure at 10th and Laurel.

OCTOBER

October 1 *1903* The Vancouver Public Library moves into the Carnegie Building at Main and Hastings. *1913* Kingsway, "a broad magnificent road," is completed.

October 1 *1996* Benndorf Verster becomes Ikon Office Solutions. (Benndorf Verster itself had been formed from a 1976 merger between Benndorf Office Equipment and Verster Business Machines.)

October 2 *1872* The first bridge is opened over False Creek; it's where Main Street is today. *1927* Grace Hospital opens. *1936* UBC Stadium opens. *1942* Vancouver's Colonel Cecil Merritt becomes the first Canadian in World War II to win the Victoria Cross.

October 2 *1989* The Canadian Tour Guide Association of B.C. is formed. Friends of the Book: Jeff Veniot and Bill Sampson.

October 3 *1948* Hallelujah Point in Stanley Park is officially named to commemorate the work of the Salvation Army, which often held services there. *1950* The first section of Totem Park at UBC opens; the park will eventually represent works of every carving tribe in British Columbia.

October 4 *1897* Port Moody is named the official terminus of the CPR's transcontinental railway. Later the railway will change its mind.

October 5 *1918* Spanish influenza arrives in Vancouver, hundreds begin to die. *1930* The Vancouver Symphony Orchestra holds its first concert at the Orpheum. *1931* Lt.-Gov. Fordham Johnson officiates at the opening of the Vancouver Art Gallery.

October 6 *1909* Vancouver's first motorized ambulance is taken out for a test drive and runs over and kills an American tourist.

October 7 *1898* Canada's first motion picture theatre opens on Cordova Street in Vancouver.

October 8 *1983* The official opening of the *Samson V* Maritime Museum.

October 9 *1944* The RCMP schooner *St. Roch* arrives in Vancouver after a two-way trip through the Northwest Passage to Halifax and back. *1970* The Vancouver Canucks play their first game, losing 3 to 1 to Los Angeles in the Pacific Coliseum.

October 10 *1931* West Vancouver agrees to sell 4,000 acres to a syndicate called British Pacific Properties. *1957* Vancouver's Elsworth McAuley Searles is the first black man called to the B.C. bar.

October 11 *1939* UBC President Leonard Klinck officially opens the city's first public aquarium, at the old English Bay Bathhouse. The star attraction: Oscar the Octopus. *1962* Typhoon Frieda slams into Vancouver. "Trees in Stanley Park fall like matchsticks."

October 12 *1894* A party of hikers climb a North Vancouver mountain; on shooting a blue grouse there they decide to call it Grouse Mountain. *1915* The UBC Alma Mater Society forms.

October 13 *1986* Expo 86 closes, with a total paid attendance of 22 million.

October 14 *1912* Thomas Wilby and his driver F.V. Haney arrive in Vancouver, the first to go across Canada in an automobile (a 1912 Reo). *1959* Movie star Errol Flynn dies at 50 in Vancouver.

October 15 *1964* The UBC coxless rowing pairs win a gold medal at the Tokyo Olympics. *1953* The Trans-Mountain oil pipeline from Edmonton to Vancouver is completed.

October 16 *1940* King George VI Highway is named and officially opened; it runs from the Pattullo Bridge to the U.S. border. *1944* The RCMP ship St. Roch arrives in Vancouver from Halifax via the Northwest Passage, first ship to complete the route in both directions.

October 17 *1920* The first trans-Canada flight, piloted by two RCAF pilots, ends in Vancouver.

October 18 *1928* Vancouver gets its first traffic light, at Main and Hastings. People bring their children down to see it. (There is also a claim for Hastings and Carrall.)

October 19 *1967* A parade is held on Pender Street to protest a proposed freeway through Chinatown; it is successful, and the project is cancelled.

October 20 *1928* Greater Vancouver gets its first "talkie" when *Mother Knows Best* premieres at the Capitol Theatre. *1951* Greater Vancouver welcomes Princess Elizabeth and Prince Philip on their first trip to Canada.

October 21 *1944* HMCS *Discovery* is officially opened on Deadman's Island. *1949* A dogwood is planted in Queen Elizabeth Park to mark the beginning of Canada's only arboretum.

October 22 *1962* Scuba divers find the drive shaft of the SS *Beaver,* sunk more than 70 years earlier.

October 23 *1953* The Burnaby Lake interurban tram line closes after 42 years and is replaced by a bus service.

October 24 *1899* Seventeen Vancouver volunteers are among 60 men from B.C. who leave by train to join the Canadian contingent going to fight in the Boer War. *1969* Yippie Jerry Rubin and supporters "liberate" the Faculty Club at UBC.

October 24 *1957* Alan Walker arrives in Vancouver on board the P & O ship, Orsova, at CPR's Pier B.C. (now Canada Place). Nobody notices.

October 25 *1968* Vancouver's new International Airport terminal is opened. It becomes the "old" terminal in 1996 when a new one is added.

October 26 *1896* Vancouver council sets 25 as the maximum number of cows per owner within city limits.

October 27 *1914* Port Coquitlam City Hall is opened (with additions and renovations, it's still in use, but a replacement was being planned as this book went to press.)

October 28 *1922* The Great Trek, in which UBC students (stuck in the "Fairview Shacks") march to protest delays in building a decent campus.

October 29 *1889* Governor General Lord Stanley dedicates Stanley Park during the first visit of a GG to Vancouver. *1953* The movies fight television as big-screen Cinemascope comes to Vancouver with the motion picture *The Robe.*

October 30 *1985* To mark Orpheum manager Ivan Ackery's 86th birthday, the lane behind the theatre is titled Ackery Alley as a tribute to the master showman.

October 31 *1902* The Pacific Cable opens. Mayor Neelands sends greetings to King Edward VII via cable. *1918* Harry Gardiner, the "Human Fly," climbs up the World Building (known today as the old *Sun* tower). *1961* Vancouver's first private television station, CHAN-TV, begins broadcasting (It's known today as BCTV).

NOVEMBER

November 1 *1894* The Art, Historical and Scientific Association begins in Vancouver, the forerunner of the Vancouver Museum. *1914* The Twenty-Ninth Vancouver Battalion CEF, known as Tobin's Tigers, forms at Hastings Park with 1,100 recruits. *1919* The CNR station opens on Main Street. It's known today as Pacific Central Station. *1968* Central Heat Distribution Ltd. begins supplying steam to downtown Vancouver offices through underground pipes.

November 2 *1983* The first Grey Cup game played at B.C. Place sees the B.C. Lions lose 18-17 to the Toronto Argonauts.

November 3 *1862* John Morton, Samuel Brighouse and William Hailstone file a claim for the land that is today Vancouver's West End.

November 4 *1864* The first shipment of lumber to a foreign port leaves Burrard Inlet, bound for Australia. *1892* The first New Westminster Farmers Market opens.

November 5 *1939* Vancouver gets its first dial telephones.

November 6 *1945* Vancouver City Council withdraws the order that set separate swimming days at Crystal Pool for "colored" and Orientals. *1982* The B.C. Lions play their last game at Empire Stadium (and defeat the Montreal Alouettes).

November 7 *1925* The first Second Narrows Bridge opens.

November 8 *1909* The West Vancouver Transportation Company begins a ferry service across the Inlet with the 35-passenger *West Vancouver.*

November 9 *1864* Burrard Inlet Mills ships 277,500 feet of lumber to Australia, the first export of lumber from Vancouver to a foreign port. *1927* The new Anglican Church College building is opened at UBC.

November 10 *1879* The municipalities of Surrey and Delta, and the Township of Richmond, are all incorporated. *1961* A graduate students' centre is opened at UBC, a gift from Leon Koerner in memory of his wife Thea.

November 11 *1918* Armistice Day, signifying the end of The Great War, jams the streets of Vancouver with thousands of celebrants. *1938* Lions Gate Bridge opens.

November 12 *1890* The first shipment of raw sugar arrives fron the Philippines for the B.C. Sugar refinery.

November 13 *1974* Arbutus Village Square opens.

November 14 *1938* The Lions Gate Bridge is opened to traffic without ceremony; the official opening will occur May 29, 1939 by King George VI and Queen Elizabeth (the Queen Mother). *1964* The Marco Polo, first Chinese nightclub in Canada, opens. *1982* The teflon roof on B.C. Place Stadium is inflated in just over one hour.

November 15 *1935* A young schoolboy named John Cullen buys (for 35 cents) his first record, a song called *Don't Give Up the Ship.* Today, Jack Cullen's collection of records, transcriptions and discs is one of the world's largest. *1937* Premier Duff Pattullo officiates at the opening of a new bridge across the Fraser. Linking New Westminster to Surrey, the bridge is named for him. *1949* Vancouver's first underground parking lot opens on Hornby Street. Rate: 15 cents an hour.

November 16 *1984* Michael Jackson performs the first of three shows at B.C Place, the most successful entertainment event in Vancouver's history to that time: the gross is nearly $5 million.

November 17 *1910* The internationally famed dancer Anna Pavlova performs in Vancouver and the town goes gaga.

November 18 *1903* The first military cadet corps in Vancouver, the Vancouver High School Cadet Corps, is gazetted to the militia as a unit.

November 19 *1858* British Columbia is proclaimed a British Crown Colony; site of the proclamation is the Big House at Fort Langley. *1964* The New Westminster Museum is opened.

November 20 *1982* Vancouver is declared a "nuclear free zone" in a plebiscite, and voters also okay Sunday shopping. Also *1982* UBC Thunderbirds win football's Vanier Cup, defeating the University of Western Ontario 39-14.

November 21 *1930* "Lillibet" dolls, modelled after four-year-old Princess Elizabeth, become available in B.C.

November 22 *1894* St. Paul's Hospital opens. *1930* A letter appears in the *Daily Province* suggesting it would be a good idea to have traffic lights at Main and Kingsway.

November 23 *1910* HMCS *Rainbow,* Canada's first cruiser on the Pacific Coast, makes her maiden voyage into Vancouver. *1916* A provincial election is held, including a referendum on whether women should get the vote. They do.

November 24 *1992* More than 900 people attend the funeral in Vancouver of "Dr. Peter," Dr. Peter Jepson-Young, whose 111 instalments of his *AIDS Diary* on CBC-TV were made into an Oscar-nominated documentary.

November 24 *1992* A group of women who have recently completed their doctorates through UBC's clinical psychology program meets for dinner to maintain the mutual support and friendship they developed during graduate school. At this, the first of many such evenings, they christen themselves the "Psychobobs." Friend of the Book: Georgia L. Tiedemann, Ph. D., R. Psych.

November 25 *1858* Col. Richard Moody arrives from England with an advance party of "sappers" (engineers) to build fortifications and roads. *1948* Television is first seen in the Lower Mainland in a broadcast by Seattle's KRSC-TV.

November 26 *1955* The Edmonton Eskimos play the Montreal Alouettes in the first Grey Cup game played in Vancouver.

November 27 *1994* The B.C. Lions defeat Baltimore 26 to 23 to win the Grey Cup, their third Grey Cup victory in 40 years.

November 28 *1956* Fred Hume is elected Vancouver's mayor for a fourth consecutive time, first to do that.

November 29 *1926* Baseball's Babe Ruth hams it up on stage in Vancouver during a personal appearance tour of North America.

November 30 *1976* Virginia Briant and Elspeth Alley are ordained as Anglican priests at Christ Church Cathedral.

DECEMBER

December 1 *1949* The first section of the Grouse Mountain chair lift opens. *1967* The Powell Street Dugout opens as a day centre for homeless men in the area. *1969* Vancouver is awarded an NHL franchise. *1975* The new Vanterm container terminal goes into operation.

December 2 *1983* Vancouver-based Future Shop Ltd. is incorporated, and grows to become one of Canada's major electronics retailers.

December 3 *1867* William John Bowser is born in Rexton, New Brunswick. He came to Vancouver to practise law, became attorney general in 1907, premier in 1915. *1995* A hugely successful touring revival of the musical *Show Boat* opens in Vancouver at the brand-new Ford Centre for the Performing Arts.

December 4 *1928* Construction begins on the present Hotel Vancouver. *1936* Vancouver's new City Hall at 12th and Cambie is officially opened.

December 5 *1956* The first Hungarian refugees arrive in Vancouver aboard CP Air's *Freedom Express.*

December 6 *1930* Air mail is first shipped to the Orient via Vancouver.

December 7 *1918* An earthquake stops the clock atop the Vancouver Block (just as another will do in 1946). *1982* A Hong Kong bank opens a branch in Chinatown, operates in both Chinese and English.

December 8 *1930* Construction begins on the Burrard Bridge.

December 9 *1953* The inaugural meeting of the Chinese Lions Club marks the formation of the first Chinese Lions Club in North America. *1962* Bill Rathie is elected mayor, the first to have been born in Vancouver.

December 10 *1962* The old Union Steamship hotel on Bowen Island is demolished and the resort closed.

December 11 *1950* Elizabeth Rogers donates priceless art from China, Egypt and the Haida Band to the Vancouver Museum. *1985* The opening of SkyTrain, Vancouver's Advanced Light Rapid Transit system.

December 12 *1883* The first local telephone call is made; it's between Port Moody and New Westminster. *1967* Canada's largest library for the visually impaired opens at UBC. The Charles Crane Library is named for the first deaf-and-blind person to attend university in Canada.

December 13 *1934* Gerry McGeer is swept into the mayor's office with the largest lead in Vancouver history: 25,000 votes out of 44,000 cast. *1972* Art Phillips leads his TEAM players to a big win in city council: Phillips is joined by eight TEAM aldermen, ending 35 years of NPA domination. (In 1996 the NPA wins the mayoralty and all 10 council seats.)

December 14 *1966* Tom Campbell is elected mayor of Vancouver, serves a couple of turbulent terms.

December 14 *1930* **Beatrice M. "Bunny" Parton is born in Vancouver. Bunny has been in business (real estate and insurance) in Kitsilano since 1956. "I love my city!"**

December 15 *1918* Vancouver establishes its first traffic department. Constables directing traffic wear white gloves.

December 16 *1863* Grocer John Oscar Smith buys the Pioneer Mills in Vancouver and changes its name to Burrard Inlet Mills. *1953* The CBC's Davidson Dunton pushes a button to put CBUT (Channel 2), Vancouver's first TV station, on the air.

December 17 *1903* Transmission of electricity to Vancouver begins from BCER's hydro plant on Indian Arm. *1929* Unemployed men raid the city relief office.

December 18 *1929* Burnaby's first ornamental street lighting is turned on: Hastings Street from Boundary to Gilmore.

December 19 *1916* On the day before Prohibition is imposed in B.C., Vancouver's Strand Hotel sets an all-time record for bar receipts.

December 20 *1912* The Rex Theatre, described in the papers as "the most modern movie house in the world," opens on Hastings.

December 21 *1910* Hastings Townsite ratepayers vote to join Vancouver.

December 21 *1994* **Vancouver band leader Dal Richards gets a splendid Christmas present with a letter from the Secretary to Governor General Romeo LeBlanc informing him he has been appointed a Member of the Order of Canada. Dal and other inductees attend a glittering award ceremony at Rideau Hall, Ottawa on May 3, 1995.**

December 22 *1873* Moody's mill on the North Shore burns to the ground, but is quickly rebuilt with lumber and bricks purchased from the Hastings Mill, its competitor across the inlet.

December 23 *1884* The incorporation of Pioneer Lumber Company of Port Moody, the first mill to operate in the area.

December 24 *1920* Walter Cameron Nichol, editor and proprietor of the *Daily Province,* becomes lieutenant-governor of British Columbia.

December 25 *1885* Dominic Charlie is born (or baptized) near Jericho Beach. He will become locally famous for his ability to forecast the weather. He and his half-brother collect Squamish legends for publication. *1932* Greater Vancouverites listen to the first Christmas radio message from the sovereign as George V speaks from Sandringham.

December 26 *1871* The Masons' Grand Lodge of British Columbia opens. *1908* Boxer Tommy Burns, who dies in Vancouver in 1955, loses his world heavyweight title to Jack Johnson.

December 27 *1965* The *Sun* and *Province* begin publication in new Pacific Press premises at 2250 Granville Street. They move out and head downtown in 1997.

December 28 *1857* Governor James Douglas of Vancouver Island proclaims the Crown's control of mineral rights on the mainland.

December 28 *1929* **Harland Bartholomew submits his plans for the future of Vancouver. Christopher Richardson, FCA, is pleased to sponsor this remembrance of Mr. Bartholomew.**

December 29 *1970* Chief Dan George is named best supporting actor by New York film critics for his role in *Little Big Man,* and will be nominated for an Academy Award. *1972* The Vancouver City Archives, named for the late archivist Major J.S. Matthews, are officially opened by Mayor Tom Campbell.

December 30 *1883* Lester Patrick is born in Drummondville, Que. He and his brother Frank brought professional hockey to Canada's West Coast and built the Denman Arena.

December 31 *1971* *Province* publisher Fred Auger buries a time capsule near the reception desk in the editorial department. It's to be opened on British Columbia's 200th birthday.

Hall of Fame

ANNA PAVLOVA DANCED here; Caruso and Josephine Baker sang; Lunt and Fonteyn acted; Marlene Dietrich simply appeared. Rudyard Kipling passed through. Jack Dempsey and Mike Tyson fought their way through, Tyson outside the ring. Stravinsky premiered a symphony; Bill Haley and the Comets brought "the ultimate in musical depravity" to the Kerrisdale Arena. Ethel Barrymore smoked a cigar in the lobby of the first Hotel Vancouver, and Elsa Maxwell donated a cabochon ruby to a World War II Spitfire fundraiser. The Prince of Wales waved his hat to an adoring but well-mannered crowd.

In Vancouver we accept the famous easily. The privilege of being pestered by strangers is no burden here.

But our refusal to adopt a paparazzi approach to the visiting famous does not imply we do not take pride in nor claim our own. *The Greater Vancouver Book*'s Hall of Fame celebrates 500 local citizens. They share two distinctions. First, they are all dead. A good start, according to man of letters Harold Brodkey, who says "I associate being recognized with being dead." This also explains the absence of so many missing, albeit happily, from the list.

Second, they all played a noteworthy part in our history. Doctors, lawyers, Indian chiefs, rum runners and 100-metre sprinters, railway barons and immigrants, premiers and poets, activists and racists, suffragettes and artists, heroes and heroines. These are people more deserving of fame then merely being famous.

Some put us on the map. Olympians Harry Jerome and Percy Williams both tied world records for the 100-yard dash. Fred Cyclone Taylor remains a hockey legend. And we can claim two of the Group of Seven painters: Frederick Varley taught at the Vancouver School of Art; Lawren Harris lived and died here.

I like to think of these 500 gathered at a giant celestial cocktail party, with Jack Wasserman scouting items for his *About Town* column, and Claud Detloff taking candid shots. (Because Vancouver is one of a few large cities in the world so young that the invention of photography preceded the arrival of the city's first European settlers, we are in the curious and enviable position of being able to literally look almost all of our past luminaries in the face.)

The party would include train robber Bill Miner a.k.a. The Grey Fox and Mandrake the Magician; Count Alvo von Alvensleben who arrived penniless, became a millionaire and was frozen out as an enemy alien; SFU president Pauline Jewitt and writer Julia Henshaw who, despite receiving the Croix de Guerre in World War I, and being the only woman listed in the pre-war *Canadian Who's Who*, still strongly opposed the right of women to vote. Teddy Lyons, from B.C. Electric's open air observation car, could try out his one-liners on Sister Frances Redmond, first public health nurse and Joe Quoy, the Chinese jockey.

What a guest list! Court interpreter Tadaichi Nagao, Penthouse owner Joe Philliponi and murdered Scottish nanny Janet Smith; golfer Violet Sweeny and cycleman Cap Hobbis; First Nations chief, actor, writer and longshoreman Dan George and poet Pauline Johnson; Earle Birney and Malcolm Lowry; explorer José Maria Narvaez and archivist Major James Skitt Matthews. Then there are the namesakes, Francis Annance (Annacis Island), Robert Burnaby, Chief Joe Capilano and Manoah Steves (Steveston), among others. The rich and influential also have their place: the Bell-Irvings, Reifels, Gibsons, MacMillans and Koerners et al. Those like Dr. Peter, who died too young, and Sergeant Masumi Mitsui who defied life's cruel twists to live to 99. Self-appointed lifeguard Joe Fortes could rub shoulders with some of the 100-plus lives he saved at English Bay. And our more recent loss, but the celestial party's obvious gain, writer and editor George Woodcock, described as "quite possibly the most civilized man in Canada."

Jonathan Swift's longitude-latitude setting for his mythical Brobdignag, written when the existence of the North American coast was still unknown to Europeans, puts his Land of the Giants just off British Columbia's coast. Turn the pages of the Hall of Fame to meet our own giants.

—Kerry McPhedran

facing page: top row; Captain George Vancouver (navigator), Charles Marega (sculptor), Cornelius Van Horne (railway baron). cva, vp,vs
middle row; Leon Mandrake (magician), Masumi Mitsui, (war hero), Lorraine McAllister (singer). vp, cva, vs
bottom row; Nat Bailey (baseball promoter), Constantin Alvo von Alvensleben (businessman and suspected spy), Chief Dan George (First Nations leader and actor). vp cva, vs

Greater Vancouver Hall of Fame

Constance Brissenden with additional research by *Larry Loyie*

The Greater Vancouver Hall of Fame represents several hundred of the many thousands of people who have contributed to the history of the Lower Mainland. They come from all walks of life, all cultural backgrounds and all occupations. All of the Hall of Famers are now deceased, and we are proud to include a brief record of their accomplishments here. For the first time, the Lower Mainland has a biographical directory that includes individuals from communities overlooked in the past. If a name appears in capitals within a biography, it means that person has a separate entry. This material will form the nucleus of a Hall of Fame book planned by Linkman Press.

Abbreviations

CCF: Co-operative Commonwealth Federation
CNR: Canadian National Railway
CPR: Canadian Pacific Railway
HS: High School
Lib.: Liberal
MLA: Member of Legislative Assembly
MP: Member of Parliament
NDP: New Democratic Party
PC: Progressive Conservative
SC: Social Credit

A

Henry Braithwaite Abbott *CPR executive* b. June 14, 1829, Abbotsford, Que.; d. Sept. 13, 1915, Vancouver. Studied civil engineering at McGill. Throughout his career, he held important positions in Eastern Canadian railway systems, before appointment as CPR superintendent. Present at the laying of The Last Spike (Nov. 8, 1885), at Craigellachie; rode the first train from Montreal to Port Moody with Lord Strathcona and CPR president Sir William Van Horne. In March 1886 let the contract for the clearing of the townsite of Vancouver (pop. 500). A mountain in the Selkirks and Vancouver's Abbott St. are named for him.

Ivan (Ivor Frederick) Ackery *Movie promoter* b. Oct. 30, 1899, Bristol, Eng.; d. Oct. 29, 1989, Vancouver, on the eve of his 90th birthday. Moved to Vancouver in 1914. As manager of the Orpheum Theatre (1935-69), was known as Mr. Orpheum, Atomic Ack and Little Orpheum Ackery. Promotional stunts earned him two Motion Picture Quigley Awards, the theatre promoters' equivalent of an Oscar. Paraded a cow down Granville carrying a sign: "There's a great show at the Orpheum and that's no bull." Biblio: *Fifty Years on Theatre Row.*

Harry Adaskin *Musician* b. Oct. 6, 1901, Riga, Latvia; d. April 7, 1994, Vancouver. A child prodigy, he played the violin from age seven. Founding member of the Hart House Quartet (1924). In 1946 moved to Vancouver. Established musical faculty at UBC, retiring in 1973. Known for his efforts to popularize classical music. Received Order of Canada (1975); LL.D (UBC, 1980). Biblio: *A Fiddler's World; A Fiddler's Choice.*

Hy Aisenstat *Restaurateur* b. April 28, 1926, Calgary; d. Aug. 11, 1988, Vancouver. Son of a Russian émigré wholesale grocer in Calgary. Hy worked in sales, then owned a small oil company. In 1955 with wife Barbara opened Hy's Steak House in Calgary with a $3,000 loan. Moved to Vancouver (1960) and opened Hy's at The Sands, The Mansion and Hy's Encore. By 1968 Hy's of Canada united 12 companies, with restaurants across Canada, and in Chicago, Honolulu, Palm Springs and Beverly Hills. Called his restaurants "saloons" and smoked 10 Havana cigars daily. Host to Bob Hope, Marlene Dietrich, Louis Armstrong and other stars.

Henry Osborne Alexander *First white male born on Burrard Inlet, judge* b. Dec. 13, 1873, Hastings Mill; d. April 18, 1920, Vancouver. His father was RICHARD ALEXANDER. Educated at St. Paul's College, Esquimalt. Called to the bar in 1896 and practised in Vancouver. On Jan. 10, 1908, when two South Vancouver neighbors came to court over ownership of a rooster, Magistrate Alexander ordered the bird turned loose on the street to decide for itself where it belonged. An early, active member of the Royal Vancouver Yacht Club.

Richard Henry Alexander *Hastings Mill storekeeper* b. March 26, 1844, Edinburgh, Scotland; d. Jan. 29, 1915, Seattle. In 1855 emigrated to Toronto with his parents. In 1862 joined an overland party to the Fraser gold fields. Kept a diary of his journey, now in the Vancouver City Archives. Reaching New Westminster, he odd-jobbed until 1870, when he took over the Hastings Mill Store. Quickly rose to mill accountant, later manager on the death of Captain JAMES RAYMUR. Served as justice of the peace, member of the Granville school board, and on other public bodies.

Tom Alsbury *Mayor of Vancouver, 1959-62* See Mayors of Vancouver.

Robert Alexander Anderson *Mayor of Vancouver, 1894* See Mayors of Vancouver.

Margaret Grant Andrew *Arts activist* b. Mar. 19, 1912, Kingston, Ont.; d. July 30, 1982, Vancouver. Daughter of William L. Grant, history professor and principal of Upper Canada College. Graduated from McGill (BA, economics and political science, 1933). Worked in a bank, then joined CBC when it started in 1936. Vancouver School Board trustee (1975-76); chair (1977-79). A popular figure in the artistic and academic community, she was active in B.C. Arts in Education Council, Vanier Institute of the Family, Vancouver Art Gallery, Family Service Association and University

Women's Club. Husband Geoffrey was vice president of UBC and director of Association of Universities and Colleges in Canada (d. 1987).

Henry Forbes Angus *UBC dean* b. April 19, 1891, Victoria; d. Sept. 17, 1991, Vancouver. BA (McGill U., 1911), MA (Oxford, 1919). In 1919 joined UBC as assistant professor of economics. Head of economics, political science and sociology (1930-56). First dean of graduate studies (1949-56); Dean Emeritus (1956-91). One of the few public voices to oppose internment of Japanese-Canadians. LL.D (UBC, 1956). His wife, Anne Margaret (b. Anatolia, Turkey) was a diplomat's daughter, UBC graduate (1923), president of the University Women's Club and a child welfare activist. She wrote the first UBC student play (*The High Priest*, 1922) performed by the University Players' Club and received an LL.D (UBC, 1933).

Francis (François Noel) Annance *Explorer* b. 1789, St. Francis, Richelieu Valley, Que.; d. c. 1851, St. Francis. Son of an Abenaki Indian interpreter he went to Moor's Indian Charity School in New Hampshire. Joined North West Co. (1810); supported the British in the War of 1812. Chosen for difficult expedition from Fort George to the Fraser (1824), establishing Fort Langley (1827). After conflicts with Hudson's Bay Co. chief factor John McLoughlin, over a lack of promotion (said to be due to his native heritage), Francis resigned but he was forced to complete his contract. Returned to St. Francis (1845) as a Protestant school teacher. Annacis Island, originally Annance's Island, is named for him.

James William Armstrong *Flour and sawmill owner, politician* b. Oct. 31, 1826, Peterborough, Ont.; d. Dec. 18, 1915, New Westminster. Came to B.C. in 1858. First white settler in New Westminster; first merchant (general store, 1859-73). Built first house on the Fraser and first flour mill (1867-71). Elected one of first town councillors (1860-73). From 1873-76 he was B.C. minister of finance and agriculture under Amor DeCosmos. In 1881 named provincial secretary. In 1883 appointed sheriff of Westminster County.

William Henry Armstrong *Bridge builder, first B.C. car owner* b. Sept. 18, 1857, Stratford, Ont.; d. March 31, 1922, Vancouver. At 16 worked as a railway switchman, later in bridge construction. From 1877-83 he was a master mechanic in Winnipeg. Moved to Victoria 1883; worked for CPR until 1887. After 1902 his firm, Armstrong, Morrison & Balfour, built the Fraser River bridge at New Westminster, Great Northern Railway bridge across False Creek, and Granville and Main street bridges. Began seven bridges in August 1912, all completed in May 1913. Paved many of Vancouver's streets. He purchased the first car to appear in Vancouver, a Stanley Steamer bought in Boston in 1899.

Balwant Singh Atwal *Sikh priest* b. 1882, Punjab, India; d. March 16, 1917, Lahore, India. Well-respected in the Sikh community, he was the first priest of the 2nd Ave. gurdwara (temple). His son, Hardial Singh Atwal, born at the temple (Aug. 28, 1912; d. Sept. 25, 1996, Duncan. B.C.) was the first Canadian-born Sikh. After his wife Kartar Kaur became ill, the family moved back to India. En route, Atwal was jailed in Singapore as a revolutionary. A letter from the temple confirming his position was never received by the authorities. He was hanged in Lahore on charges of sedition and political agitation against the British government. Biblio: *Becoming Canadians: Pioneer Sikhs in Their Own Words* by Sarjeet Singh Jagpal.

Jack (John Henry Patrick) Avison *Orchestra conductor* b. April 25, 1914, Vancouver; d. Nov. 30, 1983, Vancouver. Played his first piano concert at age six at Grandview Elem.; at 11 was a pianist-announcer at local radio station. Awarded BA (UBC, 1935), B.Mus (U. of Washington, 1936). Studied with Paul Hindemith at Juilliard. Pianist with Vancouver Symphony Orchestra. "Big John" was founder and conductor of 35-piece CBC Vancouver Chamber Orchestra. In 1971 conducted the Canadian Arctic's first orchestral concert. Produced more than 40 recordings. Noted for his support of Canadian composers. He "belonged to the last generation of the pioneers of music in Canada." Twice received Order of Canada.

B

Nat (Nathaniel Ryal) Bailey *White Spot Restaurant founder* b. Jan. 31, 1902, Saint Paul, Minn.; d. March 27, 1978, Vancouver. His itinerant family arrived from Seattle in 1911. At 18 Nat moved his peanut stand to Athletic Park; later served Sunday drivers at Lookout Point from a 1918 Model T truck. A customer's shout, "Why don't you bring it to us?" inspired first White Spot drive-in (opened June 1928, Granville and 67th). From 1930-60s his second wife, Eva (Ouelette), co-managed his restaurants. Thirteen White Spots and other interests were sold to General Foods for $6.5 million (1968). A lifelong promoter of local baseball; Nat Bailey Stadium is named for him. Biblio: *Triple-O, The White Spot Story* by Constance Brissenden.

Frank Madill Baker, *Restaurateur* b. June 24, 1922, Vancouver; d. Nov. 21, 1989, Vancouver. Opened Baker's Catering (25th and Kingsway) and Spring Gardens (41st and Boulevard) in 1946. With partner Frank Bernard opened two restaurants in Georgian Towers and bought Park Royal Hotel. After the partnership ended, opened The Attic (1968) in West Vancouver, with 1,200 seats. Guests were entertained by Lance Harrison and His Dixieland Band. A showman, Frank played the trumpet (learned with the Four Square Gospel

Church) and always wore a trademark white suit. Outside The Attic, he showcased the Aston Martin driven in the James Bond movie *Goldfinger*.

Russell Francis Baker *Pioneer bush pilot* b. Jan. 31, 1910, Winnipeg, Man.; d. Nov. 15, 1958, West Vancouver. Early bush pilot for Western Canada Airways and Canadian Pacific. In 1946 began Central B.C. Airways with a B.C. Forest Service fire-patrol contract. Took over airlines in B.C. and Alberta to create an independent airline to serve Western communities. In 1953 the company name was changed to Pacific Western Airlines. It grew to be the largest Western regional air carrier. PWA bought CP Air in 1987.

Alvin Balkind *Curator* b. March 28, 1921, Baltimore, Maryland; d. Dec. 21, 1992, Vancouver. Attended Sorbonne. Came to Vancouver in 1954. His New Design Gallery, founded in 1955 in Vancouver, was a centre for the avant-garde. Curator of UBC Fine Arts Gallery (1962-73); chief curator at Vancouver Art Gallery (1975-78). Won first $50,000 VIVA award (Vancouver Institute for Visual Arts) in 1992.

Frank (Francis Stillman) Barnard *Streetcar system founder, lieutenant-governor* b. May 16, 1856, Toronto, Ont.; d. April 11, 1936, Esquimalt, B.C. A founder of Vancouver's streetcar system (opened June 28, 1890), he was one of B.C.'s four richest people. President, Consolidated Railway (1894), later managing director (1896-1906) after sale to British financiers (renamed B.C. Railway). MP, Cariboo (1888-96); lieutenant-governor (1914-19). Knowing war was near, he signed a special $1-million warrant approving Premier McBride's purchase of two submarines. Knighted in 1918 by King George V. "A living link of the industrialized B.C. with that of the pre-railroad and Crown colony days."

Sam Bass *Pharmacist* b. April 25, 1915, on a Winnipeg farm; d. Nov. 8, 1990, Vancouver. Son of Kiev area immigrant farmers. Sam and brother Jack became pharmacists; brother Paul received a PhD in pharmacology. Graduated from U. of Manitoba (1939). After serving in WWII as Royal Canadian Air Force pharmacist, he was en route to California when he settled in Vancouver. In 1945, on a loan, he bought Schoff's Drug Store (Main and Union), and renamed it London Drugs. A pioneer in his field, he created the first modern drug store in B.C. and was the first pharmacy discounter. A strong supporter of Jewish charities and community affairs. "He took his profit in pennies."

Truman Smith Baxter *Mayor of Vancouver, 1913-14* See Mayors of Vancouver.

Daniel Loftus Beckingsale *First port doctor* b. Nov. 18, 1846, Isle of Wight; d. c. Feb. 14, 1929, London, Eng. Graduated MB, CM (Edinburgh U., 1872); MD in 1874. Served on several London hospital staffs. Came to Vancouver in June 1886.

First port doctor and early health officer. Formed the Vancouver Reading Room, predecessor of the first public library. Moved to Interior because of ill health, residing in Nelson in 1894. Lived in San Francisco (1905-06) and survived the big earthquake. In 1916 he was practising in Wales.

Frank Ross Begg *Auto dealer* b. Lindsay, Ont.; d. Sept. 16, 1958, Vancouver. Arrived in Vancouver in 1898. From 1904-06, with brother Fred (Frederick Bruce) Begg (b. Lindsay, Ont.; d. May 11, 1939, Vancouver), he operated a garage on Hastings. They soon opened Begg Motor Co., Vancouver's first auto dealership. Frank left an estate of nearly $2 million. Fred was president of the Vancouver Motor Dealers Association when he died. He left an estate of $187,056. His wife, Ethel Mae, later willed $375,000 for medical purposes. As a result, the Vancouver Preventorium, which housed young tuberculosis cases, was rebuilt and renamed the F.R. Begg Memorial Preventorium.

Duncan Bell-Irving *Aviator* b. Aug. 28, 1894, Vancouver; d. April 24, 1965, Vancouver. Son of HENRY OGLE BELL-IRVING. Canada's first WWI flying ace. As a member of the RFC, shot down six planes and a balloon. A lifelong supporter of the Canadian Air Force. During WWII he commanded a Royal Canadian Air Force training school at Trenton, Ont. Biblio: *Gentleman Air Ace* by Elizabeth O'Kiely.

Henry Ogle Bell-Irving *Salmon canner* b. Jan. 26, 1856, Lockerbie, Dumfrieshire, Scotland; d. Feb. 19, 1931, Vancouver. Arrived in Vancouver in 1885. Formed Anglo-British Columbia Packing (ABC) in 1891. Owned canneries along the coast to become largest exporter of tinned salmon. ABC was a major player in the coastal canning industry from 1891-1969.

Alice Helena Berry (née Miller) *Publisher* b. Oct. 10, 1869, New Westminster; d. 1919, Vancouver. Daughter of JONATHAN MILLER. Married on June 24, 1890, second wife of Harry (Henry Azariah) Berry (b. 1862, Jersey Islands, Wales; d. Sept. 20, 1899, Vancouver), head of H.A. Berry & Co. transfer agents. After his death, she taught piano and was "lady manager" of Mutual Life Insurance of Canada. A founder of The World Printing and Publishing (1905). Purchased, with her father's help, the *World* (1911), a newspaper established Sept. 25, 1888, and became the only woman managing director of a Canadian daily. The *World* was the first Canadian paper to bypass C.P. Telegraph and get its news from U.S. press associations. One of her partners was L.D. TAYLOR, whom she later married (June 9, 1916).

Alexander Bethune *Mayor of Vancouver, 1907-08* See Mayors of Vancouver.

Bertram Charles Binning *Artist* b. Feb. 10, 1909, Medicine Hat, Alta.; d. March 16, 1976, Vancouver. His family moved to Vancouver in 1913.

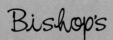

Bishop's, called by many the finest restaurant in Vancouver, opened December 13, 1985 at 2183 West 4th Avenue. John Bishop set a standard then of fresh, clean and simple presentation. "I hope the restaurant's feel," John says, "is casual, but elegant, without being stuffy." Some of that elegance is on the walls, created by local artists, but the true heart of Bishop's is in its contemporary North American cooking, using the best and freshest ingredients. (p.s. Look for Bishop's Restaurant: The Cook Book)

Attended Vancouver School of Art (VSA), and art schools in Oregon, Greenwich Village and London, Eng. Joined UBC school of architecture (1949) after teaching at VSA. A founder and head of UBC fine arts department (1955-68); instructor (1968-73). Developed UBC's Fine Arts Gallery, launched Brock Hall Canadian art collection and founder/director of the Festival of Contemporary Arts. Order of Canada Medal of Service (1971); D.Litt (UBC, 1974). "One of the first real abstract artists on the scene."

Earle Alfred Birney *Poet* b. May 13, 1904, Calgary, Alta.; d. Aug. 27, 1995, Toronto, Ont. An English graduate (UBC, 1926; PhD, U of T, 1938), he wrote seriously from the late 1930s. Won two Governor General's poetry awards (1942, 1945) and the Leacock Medal for Humor. Taught literature at UBC (1946-65). Founded UBC's creative writing department, the first in Canada (1963). Published more than 30 books (*Rag and Bone Shop; Ghost in the Wheels: Selected Poems; Turvey* (dramatized)). CBC broadcaster, critic, literary editor of *Canadian Forum*, editor of *Canadian Poetry Magazine*. Officer of the Order of Canada. D.Litt (UBC, 1987). Biblio: *Earle Birney: A Life* by Elspeth Cameron.

Davey (David Lambie) Black *Golfer* b. 1884, Troon, Ayrshire, Scotland; d. March 26, 1974, Vancouver. The "Wee Scot" began his career as an apprentice club maker in Scotland. After working at Outremont and Rivermeade golf clubs (1905-20), he moved west as golf pro at Shaughnessy Golf Club (1920-45). Won four national titles, the first in 1913; in 1928 won first B.C. Open. In 1929, with Duncan Sutherland, beat Walter Hagen and Horton Smith at the Point Grey Golf Club; in 1935, again with Sutherland, bested the great Bobbie Jones partnered with Davey's son, B.C. amateur champion Kenny Black (b. July 23, 1912, Montreal, Que.; d. Nov. 25, 1995, Oakville, Ont.). Inducted into B.C. Sports Hall of Fame (1966); Canadian Golf Hall of Fame (1972).

George Black *Butcher, hotelier* b. 1831, Aberdeen, Scotland; d. Dec. 21, 1896, Vancouver. In 1866 bought waterfront Lot 26 for $25 down, $25 later. Built a slaughterhouse and supplied meat to Hastings, Moodyville, Stamp's Mill and ships in harbor. Built two-storey New Brighton Hotel at Hastings where New Westminster Rd. met Burrard Inlet, a popular resort rivalled only by Harrison Hot Springs. The "laird of Hastings" was an "ardent Scotsman, who always wore Highland dress to dances, and also imported the area's first race horses." He built Vancouver's first roller rink.

Henry Blair *One of Vancouver's "fathers of incorporation"* b. May 24, 1861, Ont.; d. March 24, 1949, Vancouver. Came to the Cariboo in 1880. Mined to 1881, then moved on to coast. Chairman of H.B. Smith's survey party, making first

map of City of Vancouver in 1886. Later logged on the North Arm of the Fraser River. The last survivor of 125 signatories to petition the legislature for the incorporation of Vancouver.

Julius Harold Bloedel *Lumberman* b. March 1864, Fond du Lac, Wisconsin; d. Sept. 20, 1957, Seattle, Wash. After his mother's death, he was raised by an aunt. Said to have paid for his first bike by renting it to friends. At 17 entered civil engineering (U. of Michigan), but left due to money problems. Bloedel worked on the Wisconsin railway, then developed real estate in Sheboygan. With $10,000 profit, moved west (1886). In 1890 opened Samish Logging in Bellingham Bay, Wash. In 1911 began logging in B.C. Retired in May 1942 as president of Bloedel, Stewart & Welch in favor of son Prentice Bloedel (b. Aug. 13, 1900, Bellingham, Wash.; d. June 15, 1996, Seattle, Wash.) but continued as board chair. "His business philosophy was to own timber. It was a passion that dominated his life." Julius' archives were donated to UBC; Prentice was lifelong supporter of B.C. Council of Boy Scouts (Vancouver Coast Region) and won a Silver Wolf Award in 1951 for "exceptional service to Scouting."

Mary Louise Bollert *UBC's first dean of women* b. 1884, Guelph, Ont.; d. Aug. 1, 1945, Vancouver. Graduate, U of T (BA, 1906); Columbia U. (MA, 1908). Director of women's education and social welfare programs in Toronto, then dean of women at Regina College (1914-21). Appointed first dean of women at UBC (1921-41), officially "advisor to women students," with a salary far below that of male deans. A founder of B.C. Teachers Federation. Delegate to many international women's conferences; one of 12 deans of women invited to tour Japan (1934). President, Confederation of University Women (1929-30). Biblio: *"It's Up to You:" Women at UBC in the Early Years* by Lee Stewart.

Charles Edward Borden *Archaeologist* b. May 15, 1905, New York City; d. Dec. 25, 1978, Vancouver. "Grandfather of B.C. archaeology." Grew up in Germany. Graduated from U. of California in German Literature (PhD, 1937). Formed UBC's department of archaeology (1939) and also taught German. In 1945 served as archaeological resident with a small, privately funded dig in Point Grey, followed by major B.C. studies. In 1949 appointed lecturer in archaeology and taught the first courses at UBC. In the mid-1950s began studies in the Fraser Canyon. Wrote some three dozen publications on B.C. and Fraser River archaeology. D.Litt (UBC, 1975).

Phillip Borsos *Film director* b. May 5, 1953, Hobart, Tasmania, Aust.; d. Feb. 2, 1995, Vancouver. Moved to Vancouver at age five. Made three short films of which *Nails* was nominated for an Oscar in 1980. Feature movies included *One*

Magic Christmas (1985), *The Mean Season* (1985), *Bethune* (1991). *The Grey Fox* (1982), the story of train robber BILL MINER, was nominated for Best Film at the Golden Globe Awards (1983). *Nails* and *The Grey Fox* won Genie Awards. His last movie was *Far From Home: The Adventures of Yellow Dog* (1995). "Demanding, exasperating and one of the best film directors in Canada." Died of acute myeloid leukemia.

Bob (Robert Errol) Bouchette *Columnist* d. June 12, 1938, Vancouver. Wrote *Vancouver Sun* column *Lend Me Your Ears*. Harangued the 1930s' establishment to do more about poverty, joblessness, relief camps. "The champion of the underdog . . . a shining knight out of time in the harsh world of the Depression." Death by drowning off Second Beach.

Mabel Ellen Boultbee (née Springer) *Columnist* b. April 29, 1875, Moodyville; d. Feb. 2, 1953, Ritz Hotel, Vancouver. The first white child born on Burrard Inlet, she was the daughter of Mary Frances Miller (sister of JONATHAN MILLER) and Benjamin Springer, manager of Moody's Sawmill. A divorcee, she briefly ran a school with her sister, Eva, in the 1890s. A journalist for 30 years, she wrote the *Vancouver Sun*'s women's pages until just before her death. A prominent citizen and member of the Georgian Club, her apartment (shared with Eva) was "famed among the social elite of the 1930s and 1940s."

Francis Bowser *Point Grey pioneer* b. Sept. 13, 1858, Kingston (now Rexton), NB; d. Sept. 26, 1929, Vancouver. "Trail blazer of Point Grey." At 17 went to sea for five years, then came overland to Victoria (1883). He joined Dominion Customs Service (1888-1908) as chief landing officer to 1908. His first home was at Macdonald between 43rd and 44th avenues (1907); his second at Trafalgar and 45th (1926). Reeve of Point Grey. Oldest brother of W.J. BOWSER.

William John Bowser *Premier* b. Dec. 3, 1867, Rexton, NB; d. Oct. 25, 1933, Vancouver. A Dalhousie graduate and criminal law specialist, he came to Vancouver in 1891. Retained in nearly all murder cases tried in Vancouver. In 1900 named Queen's Counsel. PC MLA (1903-24); became attorney general (1907). He replaced Richard McBride as premier on Dec. 15, 1915. Party politics and bad management led to his defeat in the 1916 B.C. election. Led Opposition (1916-24). After retirement, campaigned in 1933 as leader of independent non-partisan group. Died delivering a speech at the Hotel Vancouver.

Hugh Boyd *Richmond's first reeve* b. 1842, County Down, Ire.; d. Nov. 22, 1931, Bangor, Ire. Came to B.C.'s Cariboo Gold Rush in 1862 but failed to find gold. Bought Section 19, Sea Island, on March 7, 1865, with Alexander Kilgour. Settled at Rosebrook Farm. Richmond reeve (1880-86). Left for

Ireland (1887) to live near Belfast. His farm was purchased by the Mackie brothers in 1890. Crisscrossed Pacific Ocean 12 times after his retirement. Richmond was named in honor of his wife Mary A. McColl Boyd's birthplace in Yorkshire.

Angelo Ernest Branca *Judge* b. March 21, 1903, Mount Sicker, B.C.; d. Oct. 3, 1984, Vancouver. Canadian amateur middleweight boxing champion. Began practising law in Vancouver in 1926 as leading defence attorney. Defended high profile cases, including more than 60 murderers. "Lost only two . . . to the hangman." At 36 he was B.C.'s youngest Crown prosecutor ever. A judge with the B.C. Supreme Court (1963-66) and B.C. Court of Appeal (1966-78). Leader in Italian community. A Christopher Columbus statue on Clark was erected by the Italian community in his honor. "A dear friend of the little guy." Biblio: *Angelo Branca, Gladiator of the Courts* by Vincent Moore.

William John Brewer *First reeve of South Vancouver* b. c. 1841, Truro, Cornwall, Eng.; d. June 24, 1931, Vancouver. Arrived in 1870 after living in Australia. In 1884 purchased 10.5 hectares in Cedar Cottage district. Moved to South Vancouver area after the Great Fire of 1886 destroyed his Granville St. business. In 1889 elected Ward 4 alderman. First reeve of new municipality of South Vancouver (April 30, 1892). Described as "irascible," he sided with local residents who "preferred bad roads to good debts."

Samuel Brighouse *Vancouver and Lulu Island pioneer* b. Jan. 13, 1836, Lindley, Huddersfield, Eng.; d. July 31, 1913, Huddersfield. Arrived in New Westminster in June 1862. With partners JOHN MORTON and William Hailstone, "The Three Greenhorns." They bought 222 hectares of land in today's West End and started a brick factory which soon failed. He later farmed on Lulu Island, returning to Vancouver in 1881. Ran for alderman in civic election of 1887 after helping to obtain city charter. In 1911 he returned to England. His son Michael W. Brighouse (d. 1932) was one of Lulu Island's largest landowners.

Dave (David Hamilton) Brock *Columnist, broadcaster* b. 1910, Ottawa, Ont.; d. Sept. 8, 1978, West Vancouver. Son of REGINALD W. BROCK. Came to Vancouver at age four. Attended UBC and Harvard. Called to B.C. bar but never practised. Best known for CBC radio and TV shows, talks and documentaries, notably the *Seven O'Clock Show*. Wrote a column for *Victoria Times* in the 1960s. His barbs were directed at people in power and politicians. Regularly published in *Punch, Saturday Night, Atlantic Monthly* in the late 1930s and 1940s.

Reginald Walter Brock *Geologist, UBC dean* b. Jan. 10, 1874, Perth, Ont.; d. July 30, 1935, Alta Lake, B.C. One of Canada's leading geologists. Graduated from Queens (MA, Geology). Worked as geologist with Dawson Survey of B.C. (1897). Chair of geology at Queens (1902-07). Director of Geological Survey of Canada (1907-14). One of the first four teachers chosen by UBC president F.F. Wesbrook. In 1914 named dean of applied science but served in WWI before resuming his duties. Brock and his wife were killed in a plane accident. Brock Hall is named for him. Father of DAVE BROCK.

Bernice R. Brown (née Dickhoff) *Refugee activist* b. April 11, 1905, San Francisco, Calif.; d. Dec. 15, 1971, West Vancouver. Worked at the *San Francisco News,* then married and settled in Vancouver in 1930. Early editor, *Jewish Western Bulletin.* In 1939 organized a Red Cross unit to enable Jewish women to do war work. In addition to providing supplies for use overseas, the unit resettled refugees and opened their homes to servicemen of all faiths. Bernice received a Canadian Red Cross Distinguished Service Award (1946). The unit continued until 1947, collecting clothes for Holocaust survivors. Through the media, she urged Parliament to change immigration policy and accept orphans of the Holocaust. She was later an active member of the Canadian Institute of International Affairs.

Bob (Robert Paul) Brown *Baseball promoter* b. July 5, 1876, Glencoe, Iowa; d. June 17, 1962, Vancouver. "Mr. Baseball's" career spanned 60 years. A successful athlete at Notre Dame in 1890s, he was a pro ball player (1900-09) in Montana, Oregon and Washington state, leading Spokane Indians to Pacific Coast League pennant win in 1908. A shoestring operator and shrewd promoter, he built Vancouver's Athletic Park (opened April 18, 1913). He was owner/manager, Vancouver Beavers (renamed Vancouver Canadians). Introduced Canada's first night games played under lights. First inductee to B.C. Baseball Hall of Fame.

Brent (Brenton Samuel) Brown *Insurance manager, backroom political force* b. Dec. 25, 1881, Stanley Bridge, PEI; d. Nov. 20, 1944, Vancouver. Educated in Vancouver. Joined Equitable Life (1899). Provincial manager of Crown Life Insurance's B.C. office (1908-Nov. 1937). President of Liberal Association for 25 years. Numerous directorships. Local sports supporter. Polish consulate. Died from injuries in a car accident. "One of the most powerful political personalities in the province," yet a "retiring figure." At his funeral, thousands paid their respects.

Buda Hosmer Brown (née Jenkins) *MLA* b. June 10, 1894, Bellingham, Wash.; d. Aug. 12, 1962, Vancouver. Taught school in Washington state, then married Donald Cameron Brown (b. Feb. 22, 1812, Winchester, Ont.; d. Oct. 26, 1963, Vancouver), a businessman who was elected twice as Coalition MLA (1945,1949). In 1958 was elected Social Credit MLA (Vancouver Point Grey). In 1960 elected without portfolio in W.A.C. Bennett's cabinet as minister at large, the first woman in a Bennett cabinet since TILLY ROLSTON. Interests included traffic safety and youth fields. In 1961, when UBC first-year female students received a survey *Is Chastity Outmoded?* Brown protested in the House, saying it was "too indecent to show the legislature." A parks commissioner, she was the first woman president of the International Northwest Parks Association.

Roy W. Brown *Journalist* b. c. 1880, New Brunswick; d. Sept. 4, 1954, Vancouver. Came to Vancouver as a small boy. At 11 was the youngest pupil to enrol in Vancouver High School. In 1898, worked as office boy for the *News-Advertiser,* later as cub reporter for the *World.* In 1899, scooped the *Daily Province* on property losses from the New Westminster fire. Retired in 1938 as editor of the Vancouver *Province;* appointed editorial director and vice president of *Vancouver Sun* on Sept. 3, 1938. His biggest scoop was the 1918 sinking of CPR's *Princess Sophia* off Alaska with 398 lives lost.

John Bruce *Sculptor* b. 1863, Dundee, Scotland; d. 1952, Calif. One of the first architectural sculptors to come to North America (1988). Moved to Seattle (1889), then to Oakland (1901). In 1908 he carved the two lions on the steps of Vancouver courthouse, op. in 1912. Said to have halted stonecutting when the money ran out, leaving mane, nose and ears of the 13.6 tonne lions unfinished. On Nov. 3, 1942, the rear of one was cracked in an isolated bomb incident. Also carved "Old Leo" in plaster of Paris over a steel frame, used for displays by Spencer's department store.

Johan (Johannes) Buntzen *First general manager, B.C. Electric Railway* b. Dec. 16, 1859, Copenhagen, Denmark; d. Sept. 1922, Copenhagen. Came to Vancouver in early 1890s. Worked as bookkeeper with Ross and Ceperley, handling electric railway company affairs. Managed early development of B.C. Electric Railway from 1897. Supervised Buntzen Lake engineering and electrical work. He was in charge of Old No. 1, the Lake Coquitlam powerhouse that provided Vancouver's electricity for 47 years. Resigned from B.C. Electric Railway, Jan. 20, 1909, as managing director. Retired to Copenhagen.

Frank (Francis James) Burd *Publisher* b. Jan. 7, 1870, Muskegon, Mich.; d. Jan. 6, 1962, Vancouver. At 13 he sold newspapers in Winnipeg, working days as an apprentice printer. At 18 hired as circulation manager of *Winnipeg Free Press.* In 1899 moved to Vancouver. Unable to find work, he moved to Yukon with brother Richard Burde (sic) and began the *Whitehorse Tribune* in a tent. In 1901, after eight months, returned to Vancouver. Hired by FRANK CARTER-COTTON at *News-Advertiser.* Later joined Vancouver *Province* as circulation manager. He was founder of Canadian Press (1917). In 1933 named president of the *Province*, retiring in 1935.

Robert Burnaby *Surveyor* b. Nov. 30, 1828, Woodthorpe, Leicestershire, Eng.; d. Jan. 10, 1878, Loughborough, Eng. Arrived in B.C. in 1858, was secretary to Col. RICHARD MOODY. Worked on survey of New Westminster. A leading businessman, mainly in Victoria, until failing health caused him to return to England in 1874. More landmarks named for him than any other B.C. pioneer.

Raymond (William Stacy) Burr *Actor* b. May 21, 1917, New Westminster; d. Sept. 12, 1993, Dry Creek, Calif. Nicknamed Fatso as a child. At six years, moved with mother to Vallejo, Calif. Grew orchids at age 12, eventually shipping 3,000 varieties worldwide. As a young stage actor, worked in Toronto, NY and England. Served in the navy during WWII, then worked in Hollywood films. Famous for his television roles, Perry Mason (1957-66, late 1980s-93) and Ironside (1967-75). A philanthropist and art collector, especially in Fiji, where he owned a home and properties.

John Francis Bursill (pen name Felix Penne) *Columnist, poet* b. 1848, London, Eng.; d. Feb. 8, 1928, Burnaby. From 1865 he worked as a Fleet Street journalist. Nearing 60, he came to Vancouver in 1905 to join his eldest son in East Collingwood, a working class suburb. He founded Coll- ingwood Free Library (1911-53); founder, The Vancouver Dickens Fellowship and The Shakespeare Society. Well-known *Vancouver Sun* columnist in 1920s under pen name Felix Penne. Wrote and staged the musical *How a Forest Becomes a City*. His best-known poem, *I Shall Not Cease*, began, "Tis infamy to die and not be missed." Bursill St. is named for him.

Frederick Buscombe *Mayor of Vancouver, 1905-06* See Mayors of Vancouver.

Jimmy (James) Butterfield *Columnist* b. c. 1879, London, Eng.; d. Sept. 23, 1941, Penticton, B.C. Began writing in England for *Exchange, Telegraph, London Echo, Westminster Gazette*. Freelanced in the Balkans after graduating from Cambridge and Heidelberg. Ranched in Kootenays to 1910. In 1914 he went overseas with 122nd Battalion, Kootenay Regiment. Recuperated from tuberculosis at Balfour Sanatorium. Wrote a daily column, *The Common Round* in the Vancouver *Daily Province* (1923-41). "He launched a dangerous but rarely poisonous shaft against nearly everything, but especially against smugness and pseudo-respectability."

C

Angelo Calori *Hotelier* b. c. 1860, Italy; d. May 7, 1940, Burnaby. Arrived in Victoria in 1882; moved to Vancouver in 1886. Built and managed Vancouver's premier example of a flatiron building, the Europe Hotel at Alexander and Powell. Erected in 1908-09, the building still stands in Gastown, with fine stonework, glass and marble main floor. Building claimed to be "absolutely fireproof . . . with all outside rooms." Its slogan was, "Our autobus meets all trains and boats." A founder (with restaurateur Agostino Ferrera) of the Sons of Italy.

Henry John Cambie *Railway engineer* b. Oct. 25, 1836, Tipperary, Ire.; d. April 23, 1928, Vancouver. Came to Canada in 1852, working for Grand Trunk Railway until 1859. Joined Sandford Fleming exploring the Chilcotin for a route to Bute Inlet. In charge of CPR surveys (1876-80). His survey from Yellowhead Pass to Port Moody set the route to the Lower Fraser. In 1879 surveyed the north for a third route from Prairies to coast. From 1880-83 supervised laying of tracks from Emory Bar to Boston Bar via Fraser Canyon; next supervised Savona to Shuswap Lake. In 1903 moved to Vancouver; retired in 1921. Cambie Street is named for him.

Agnes Deans Cameron *Teacher, travel writer* b. Dec. 20, 1863, Victoria; d. May 13, 1912, Victoria. In 1882-83, teaching at Hastings Mill School, she posted a notice on the schoolhouse door: "Irate parents will be received after 3 p.m." First woman high school teacher and first woman principal in the Vancouver area (1894). After being fired for allowing students to use a ruler during a drawing exam, she became a popular travel writer. In 1908 voyaged 16,000 kilometres up the MacKenzie to the Arctic Circle with niece Jesse Cameron Brown. Illustrated her book with her niece's photos. Later wrote about an amusing bicycle tour she also photographed. Biblio: *The New North: An Account of a Woman's 1908 Journey Through Canada to the Arctic*.

I. Glen Campbell *Pioneer oculist* b. c. 1868, Montreal, Que.; d. Sept. 27, 1949, Vancouver. As a youth, one of the fastest milers in Canada. After McGill and Royal London Ophthalmic Hospital, came to Vancouver in 1899. Established Vancouver Medical Association (president, 1906-07). One of the city's first eye, ear, nose and throat specialists, practising for more than 50 years. In 1902, introduced children's eye exams in city schools; in 1932, began sight-saving classes. President of B.C. Medical Association and B.C. College of Physicians and Surgeons. Wife H. Kathleen Campbell and daughter Margaret A. Campbell were graduates of the VGH School of Nursing.

Joe Capilano *Squamish chief, carver* b. 1840, North Shore; d. March 11, 1910, North Vancouver. With wife MARY CAPILANO welcomed first missionaries to Capilano Band. Responsible for building a church on reserve. Visited King Edward VII in 1906 to present a petition on Indian rights. On his return was threatened with being charged with "inciting the Indian to revolt" for reporting certain statements alleged to have been made by King Edward. A friend of PAULINE JOHNSON.

Mary Agnes Joe Capilano (Lay-kho-lote, also Lahullette, La-yulette) *Squamish matriarch* b. 1836, Potlatch Creek, Howe Sound; d. Dec. 15, 1940, Capilano Indian Reserve, North Vancouver, at 104. Her grandfather, George Mathias, welcomed George Vancouver off Point Grey on June 13, 1792; her father was Chief Skakhult. Known as the "Indian Princess of Peace." An authority on the genealogy of coastal tribes, she was a great orator in her language. Married to JOE CAPILANO, they were visited by dignitaries from England and other countries. Throughout her life she travelled by dugout canoe across dangerous First Narrows between the reserve and the city.

Mathias Joe Capilano *Squamish chief, carver* b. c. 1885, North Shore; d. Dec. 12, 1966, Vancouver. Son of CHIEF JOE and MARY CAPILANO. A prominent leader and internationally famed carver. Attended coronations of both George V and Elizabeth II, "wearing full tribal regalia." Lifelong campaigner for the rights of native people. In 1949, with wife Ellen (d. 1959), cast the first native ballots in B.C.

John Howe Carlisle *First Vancouver fire chief* b. Nov. 4, 1857, Hillsboro, NB; d. Nov. 28, 1941, Burnaby. Educated in Alberta; arrived in Vancouver in 1886. Joined volunteer fire brigade in May, just before the Great Fire of June 13. In 1887 made brigade chief. By 1889 he was chief of the Vancouver Fire Department with eight "full paid" men and 12 "call men." By 1906 there were 35 full paid men, two engines, plus a 23-metre aerial truck and village truck, three two-horse hose wagons, two chemical two-horse wagons, two combined two-horse hose and chemical wagons and 15 firehalls. Chief for 42 years. First to be awarded Vancouver's Good Citizen Award (1922). Carlisle St. is named for him.

Emily Carr *Artist, writer* b. Dec. 13, 1871, Victoria; d. March 2, 1945, Victoria. In 1899 travelled to Ucluelet on Vancouver Island, the first of many trips to paint native sites. After travels to Europe, Toronto and the Cariboo, moved to Vancouver (January 1906), renting a studio at 570 Granville. Taught art classes (1908-10). After travels in B.C. and abroad, returned to Vancouver (1912), renting a studio at 1465 W. Broadway. In March 1912 exhibited her French paintings. In April 1913 rented Vancouver's Drummond Hall and showed 200 paintings before returning to Victoria to live on family property. Later in life, she wrote books including *Klee Wyck* and *The Book of Small*. D.Lib (UBC, 1945). Biblio: *Dear Nan; Letters of Emily Carr; Nan Cheney and Humphrey Toms* edited by Doreen Walker.

Frank (Francis Lovet) Carter-Cotton *Publisher* b.

June 4, 1847, Yorkshire, Eng.; d. Nov. 20, 1919, Vancouver. Arrived in Vancouver after the Great Fire of 1886. Merged *Advertiser* with *News* to form *News-Advertiser* (1887), the first paper to classify advertising in Vancouver, first on continent with electric-powered press, first with machine-set type. From 1880-1900 served as Vancouver's PC MLA. Appointed to cabinet as minister of finance and chief commissioner of lands and works. Defeated in 1900; returned as Richmond MLA (1903). President, executive council, in McBride administration (1904-10). UBC's first chancellor (1912-18). First chair, Vancouver Harbour Commission (1913). Drowned himself in English Bay over financial difficulties, "crisply attired in business suit and hat, and carrying a neatly furled umbrella."

Charles Henry Cates *Marine Captain* b. Dec. 15, 1859, Machias, Maine; d. Oct. 14, 1938, North Vancouver. Brother of GEORGE EMERY CATES. Engaged in similar activities on coast from 1886. Hauled stone from Gibson and Squamish quarries to help rebuild Vancouver after the Great Fire (June 13, 1886). Built first wharf on the North Shore. In 1913 formed C.H. Cates towing, later Charles H. Cates & Son (1921), one of the oldest and largest towage and "lightering" firms on Burrard Inlet. His eldest son and partner, John Henry Cates (b. July 13, 1896, North Vancouver; d. Oct. 1986, North Vancouver), was Lib. MLA (North Vancouver, 1945-52) and labor minister. John Henry's wife, Carrie (Caroline), b. 1905, Canoe, B.C.; d. Feb. 21, 1977, Vancouver, was elected mayor of North Vancouver in 1964, defeating three male candidates, and was re-elected in 1965 and 1967.

George Emery Cates *Shipbuilder* b. Dec. 6, 1861, Machias, Maine; d. March 27, 1936, Vancouver. Worked from the age of nine. After learning shipbuilding in New York City, he was employed on a schooner as a cook. Arrived in Vancouver in 1896 and started Cates Shipyards; built 500-ton steamship *Britannia*, Klondike scows and a 500-horsepower electric plant. His son, John A. Cates, "a big, friendly man who loved boats and dogs and people," developed Bowen Island as a summer resort, opening Hotel Monaco and Terminal Hotel. In 1902 John launched Terminal Steamship ferry fleet. In 1920 Union Steamships bought the company and built its own excursion fleet to Bowen Island.

Francis William Caulfeild *Land developer* b. England; d. 1934, London, Eng., at age 94. Travelling through Canada, Caulfeild was attracted by the beauty of the B.C. coast. In 1899 purchased waterfront property east of Point Atkinson (former Skunk Cove). Renamed it Caulfeild and developed it as a "charming Old World community." The village was laid out to follow land con-

tours, with broad paths (later roads) and a quarter mile of waterfront parkland. Although he never lived in B.C., Caulfeild visited often, making his last trip in 1926.

Henry Tracy Ceperley *Realtor* b. Jan. 10, 1850, Oreonto, NY; d. Dec. 14, 1929, Coronado Beach, Calif. Arrived in Vancouver around 1885. Ceperley Rounsefell & Co. (est. 1886) became one of B.C.'s largest real estate/insurance firms. In 1887 company renamed Ross and Ceperley Real Estate, Insurance and Financial Agents. In partnership with Arthur Wellington Ross, successfully speculated in land ventures. Developed Stanley Park concept, encouraging CPR's WILLIAM VAN HORNE to promote it in Ottawa. The park, which includes Ceperley Playground, opened Sept. 27, 1889. His Deer Lake home is now the Burnaby Art Gallery.

Francis Millar Chaldecott *Point Grey settler* b. Oct. 10, 1863, Chertsey, Surrey, Eng.; d. Jan 24, 1949, Vancouver. Came to Canada in 1890. In 1891, admitted to B.C. bar; practised law in Vancouver until 1941 retirement. Owned 43 hectares in South Vancouver and half interest in 97 hectares in Point Grey. Member of B.C. Game Association with a special interest in game bird introduction. A local owner of Hong Kong-based yacht *Minerva*; also an officer of the Cricket Club. Chaldecott Road and Chaldecott Park are named for him.

Dominic Charlie (Tsee-Qawl-Tuhn) *Squamish leader, weather forecaster* b. or baptized Dec. 25, 1885, near Jericho Beach; d. Sept. 9, 1972, North Vancouver. Hereditary Squamish chief and teacher of Indian history and language. Son of JERICHO CHARLIE and half-brother of AUGUST JACK KHAHTSAHLANO. Renowned for his weather predictions, he was often consulted by the newspapers. To promote Salish language studies, Dominic and August Jack collected their stories and legends and allowed them to be transcribed and printed as *Squamish Legends . . . the First People*. At 85 enrolled in a grade one class to learn to read and write in English.

Jericho Charlie (Chin-nal-set) *Squamish freighter* In the late 1880s he canoed camp supplies, including hay and oats for horses and oxen, to Jerry Rogers' logging camp on Point Grey peninsula. His canoe, Houmiltichesen, was purchased from AUGUST JACK KHAHTSAHLANO, his stepson, by the B.C. Loggers' Association and the Consolidated Red Cedar Shingle Association of B.C. The two associations presented it to the City of Vancouver in March 1943.

Nan (Anna Gertrude Lawson) Cheney *Portrait painter, UBC medical artist* b. June 22, 1897, Windsor, NS; d. Nov. 3, 1985, Vancouver. B.C. portrait painter and the first UBC medical artist, she met and corresponded with many Canadian artists. Cheney enjoyed a close relationship with EMILY

CARR in the period before Carr's work gained general acceptance. She collected material about Emily Carr until December 1979. Biblio: *Dear Nan; Letters of Emily Carr; Nan Cheney and Humphrey Toms* edited by Doreen Walker.

Harry Lin Chin (aka Chin Chuck Lin) *Florist, community leader* b. Oct. 28, 1905, Foo Chung, China; d. April 1, 1995, Vancouver. Worked for his grandfather in a Denman St. grocery, then founded Keefer Wholesale Florist in the 1930s. Supported a Union St. home for bachelors from Foo Chung and paid for their Forest Lawn burial plots. A founder of the Chinese Cultural Centre, Golden Age Court Seniors Home, Harry Lin Chin Charitable Foundation and others. Endowed UBC's Asian Centre library with important books from China. Received City of Vancouver Distinguished Pioneer Award, Chinese Benevolent Association Award and others. Kept detailed records of 29 Chin generations (700 years) with additional records going back 2,000 years. Biblio: *History of the Struggles of an Overseas Chinese*.

Chung Chuck *Potato farmer* b. c. 1898, China; d. Dec. 8, 1986, Ladner. Came to Vancouver at 13 and farmed with his father. Worked as CPR laborer, then farmed near Ladner's Delta dyke. In 1934, to control Chinese farmers, the B.C. Coast Vegetable Marketing Board began a crack down. With Ladner farmer Mah Lai, Chung appealed to the Supreme Court. In January 1937 the Privy Council ruled the laws invalid. White farmers protested "unfair Chinese competition" and blocked Vancouver bridges. Chung attempted to cross, later charging seven men with assault. "He believed if he fought for his rights under the law, he would eventually win. And boy, did he fight." Biblio: *Saltwater City* by Paul Yee.

John Arthur Clark *Lawyer, brigadier general* b. June 8, 1886, Dundas, Ont.; d. Jan. 18, 1976, Vancouver. Graduated from U of T (BA, 1906; Bachelor of Law, 1909; Osgoode Hall, 1909). Joined 77th Regiment of Volunteers in Dundas (1903-09). In 1910 appointed captain of Seaforth Highlanders of Canada. In 1911 came to Vancouver. Opened law firm of Lennie & Clark (1911-29). During WWI commanded Vancouver's 72nd Battalion; then 7th Canadian Infantry Brigade, fighting at all major battles. Wounded once; awarded Companion of The Order of St. Michael and St. George, Distinguished Service Order with two bars. PC MP, Vancouver-Burrard (1921-26). LL.D (UBC, 1952).

Ernest Albert Cleveland *Water engineer* b. May 12, 1874, Alma, NB; d. Jan. 8, 1952, North Vancouver. Came to Vancouver in 1890; worked as a federal surveyor (1896). After graduation from U. of Washington, DC (1904), worked as an engineer. In 1910 opened the large engineering and surveying firm of Cleveland and Cameron. He was appointed first chief commissioner of the

Greater Vancouver Water District (1926-52). His work was considered so important that when it came to retirement in 1940, special legislation was passed allowing him to continue on the job. LL.D (UBC, 1936). The Cleveland Dam on the Capilano River is named for him.

Jack (John Valentine) Clyne *Supreme Court judge* b. Feb. 14, 1902, Vancouver; d. Aug. 22, 1989, Vancouver. Worked as cowboy, sawmill laborer, deckhand and placer gold miner. Entered UBC (1919). After graduation (1923), studied marine law at London School of Economics. Called to B.C. bar, Jan. 8, 1927; practised in Prince Rupert. Appointed to B.C. Supreme Court (1950). In 1957 named a director of MacMillan Bloedel; later chairman and CEO until retirement (1973). Leading role in three Royal commissions and creation of Canadian Institute for Advanced Legal Studies. Knighted (Order of St. John, 1959); Companion of Order of Canada (1972). Elected to UBC senate (1951-60); UBC chancellor. LL.D (UBC, 1984). Established J.V. Clyne Lecture Program.

Samuel Joseph Cohen *Army & Navy founder* b. Oct. 12, 1897, San Francisco, Calif.; d. Dec. 21, 1966, Vancouver. At 19 acquired his first stock by buying out a men's clothing store in Kamloops. Opened Army & Navy as a surplus store at 300 block W. Hastings (1919) with his father Jacob Solomon Cohen and brothers Joseph and Henry, eventually owning five stores. Shunned the limelight, saying, "If I want any advertising, I'll pay for it." A&N was cash only, offering "no credit cards, deliveries or fancy store fixtures." His motto was "Get the goods sold—there's always more to follow." He was an avid fisherman. A generous philanthropist, especially to children's charities.

Henry Collins *Mayor of Vancouver, 1895-96* See Mayors of Vancouver.

Fred Cope *Mayor of Vancouver, 1892-93* See Mayors of Vancouver.

Jonathan W. Cornett *Mayor of Vancouver, 1941-46* See Mayors of Vancouver.

George Henry Cowan *Author, public speaker* b. 1858, Watford, Canada West; d. Sept. 20, 1935, Vancouver. Arrived in Vancouver in 1893. Formed Cowan and Shaw, later C. Kappele & McEvoy law firms. Appointed Queen's Counsel (Dominion government, 1896); King's Counsel (B.C. government, 1905). Anti-Asian, he drafted the Chinese Head Tax law. Author of *Better Terms for British Columbians* (1904). Founder, Vancouver's Conservative Association. Solicitor for City and municipalities (1907-10). MP for Vancouver, 1908-11, when he chose not to seek re-election. Bought 1,000 acres of land on Bowen Island (Point Cowan), built cottages for visitors and ran a 12-acre farm raising purebred Ayrshires.

Alice Frances Crakanthorp (née Patterson) *Pioneer student* b. Feb. 26, 1864, Alberni, B.C.; d. Oct. 9, 1961, Haney, B.C. First white girl born in Alberni area. Moved to Hastings Mill shanty town with parents at age nine. Last surviving student of the first class at the mill school, located at what is now the foot of Dunlevy Street. Her mother, Emily Susan Patterson, first nurse of Burrard Inlet, was "the heroine of Moodyville" for her part in caring for some of the Gastown refugees after the Great Fire (June 13, 1886) destroyed Vancouver. Alice's dancing slippers, worn to the opening ball of the first Hotel Vancouver, were donated to Vancouver City Archives.

William Marr Crawford *Master mariner* b. 1883, Limekilns, Fife, Scotland; d. May 20, 1942, Vancouver. Apprenticed on sailing ships, entering steam in 1904. Came to Canada in 1911. Joined Empire Stevedoring, B.C.'s largest waterfront employer, as manager. In 1923 named president and managing director. Launched *The Fyfer*, "the finest private yacht on the Pacific" (1930). In 1941 donated it to Canadian Navy for war use. Sponsored Crawford Pipe Band, which piped the Duke of Sutherland to his yacht, *Sans Peur*, in Victoria Harbor on Aug. 5, 1939, the opening of the 53rd Annual Caledonian Games. In WWI, Captain Crawford served as marine master to ministry of shipping without pay; served in the same role in a civilian capacity in WWII.

Robert James Cromie *Vancouver Sun founder* b. July 4, 1887, Scotstown, Que.; d. May 11, 1936, Victoria. Worked as a bellhop in Winnipeg's Mariaggi Hotel where he met General J.W. STEWART. Hired in 1906 by Stewart's Vancouver firm of Foley, Welch and Stewart. Bought debt-ridden *Sun*, with little money and no experience, and absorbed the *News-Advertiser* (1917). Purchased the *World* (1924) and *News-Herald* (later sold to Thomson chain). Died suddenly and sons Donald, Peter and SAMUEL took over. Donald Cameron Cromie (b. Oct. 16, 1915, Vancouver) sold *Sun* to the Sifton family's FP Publications in 1963, leaving Vancouver with no locally owned newspaper.

Samuel Patrick Cromie *Newspaper publisher* b. Jan. 25, 1918, Vancouver; d. Feb. 16, 1957, Halfmoon Bay, B.C. "One of Canada's best-known newspaper men." Was third son of ROBERT JAMES CROMIE. Worked his way up from circulation department and pressman. Joined Royal Canadian Air Force in February 1942. Returned to *Vancouver Sun* as mechanical superintendent (Nov. 1, 1945) and was soon made vice president. In 1946, at 28, he was elected youngest alderman (Non-Partisan Association) and youngest acting mayor in Vancouver history (to the time of his death). Vice president/assistant publisher of Sun Publishing (1955). Drowned in a boating accident at Halfmoon Bay.

Everett Crowley *Avalon Dairy founder* b. June 3, 1909, Vancouver; d. Nov. 25, 1984, Vancouver. Family of 12 came from Newfoundland's Avalon Peninsula in 1906. Their South Vancouver farm delivered milk by dog and wagon, and registered Avalon Dairy before 1915. He graduated from South Vancouver HS; after the 1929 crash, too poor to go to university, he returned to the dairy. During WWII, opposed poll tax on non-property owners; served three days in jail. Elected Vancouver alderman but, after six weeks, a recount gave opponent Arthur Phillips a 37-vote lead. Later he served on park board (1961-67). Launched Collingwood Pioneers Reunion. Ev Crowley Park is named for him (1985). Lee Crowley, his youngest son, now runs Avalon Dairy.

Won Alexander Cumyow *Court interpreter* b. March 27, 1861, Fort Douglas on Harrison Lake; d. Oct. 6, 1955, Vancouver. First Chinese-Canadian born in Canada. Moved to New Westminster as a boy and attended same school as first B.C. premier, Richard McBride. Studied law. Appointed court interpreter (1888); official Vancouver City Police court interpreter (1904-36). Spoke several Chinese dialects, also Chinook. A community leader with the Chinese Empire Reform Association and other groups. President of the Chinese Benevolent Society. Cast his first vote in 1890. Saw the vote taken away but lived to see it returned to Chinese residents in 1947.

George Torrance Cunningham *Druggist* b. 1889, North Dakota; d. March 7, 1965, Palm Springs, Calif. Born on ox cart trail, arriving in New Westminster (1891). In 1904 hired as apprentice druggist at Woodward's; later worked at William M. Harrison's "classy" drug store/post office. Graduate, Ont. College of Pharmacy (1909); studied in New York and Chicago. At 21, in February 1911, opened "No. 1" Cunningham Drug Store (Denman and Nelson), a community drugstore. Bought Vancouver Drug Store (September 1939), increasing chain from 12 to 35 stores. Named Man of the Year (1948) by Independent Retail Drug Association. Elected alderman (1955-57) with most votes of any candidate. Chair, UBC Board of Governors. LL.D (UBC, 1965).

Jimmy (James) Cunningham *Stonemason* b. 1878, Isle of Bute, Scotland; d. Sept. 29, 1963, Vancouver. Came from Scotland in 1910, then served in WWI with Canadian Expeditionary Force. Worked extensively as a stonemason, including UBC, pools at Lumberman's Arch, 2nd and Kitsilano beaches, Empress and Banff Springs hotels. In 1917 began building Stanley Park seawall. In 1931 named master stonemason for Vancouver park board to secure Stanley Park's shores. Began at Brockton, supervising the building of the lighthouse and seawall. Retired in 1955 but supervised the wall until his death, completing almost five kilometres. The remaining 2.4 kilometres in the Siwash Rock area were completed in 1980.

Plaque at Siwash Rock erected in his memory. His ashes are in an unmarked spot in the seawall.

D

Annie Charlotte Dalton *Poet* b. Dec. 9, 1865, Birkby (Huddersfield), Eng.; d. Jan. 12, 1938, Vancouver. Arrived in B.C. in 1904 from Huddersfield with husband Willie Dalton (married 1891). Her home was a meeting place for writers and readers. President, Vancouver Poetry Club; executive member, Lower Mainland Branch Canadian Authors' Association and Dominion Council. Left partially deaf by a childhood illness, she was known as the "Poet Laureate of the Deaf" for her work on their behalf. Member, Order of the British Empire, the only woman poet honored at the time (1935). Biblio: *The Marriage of Music; Flame and Adventure; Lilies and Leopards.*

Josephine A. Dauphinee *Special education pioneer, women's activist* b. Nov. 15, 1875, Liverpool, NS; d. Dec. 6, 1977, Vancouver. In 1908, when she arrived in New Westminster to work for her uncle Dr. G.E. Drew, she was a trained nurse and teacher. After training in Seattle, she taught at Central HS and was soon supervisor of special classes for mentally challenged children. Travelled across the U.S., observing teaching methods. By her retirement (1941) the number of special classes had grown to 27. A founder of the Vancouver Business and Professional Women's Club (1922); president (1928-29). Helped establish Canadian Federation of Business and Professional Women's Clubs in 1930; president, 1932-35.

John Davidson *Botanist, conservationist* b. Aug. 6, 1878, Aberdeen, Scotland; d. Feb. 10, 1970, Vancouver. Son of a cabinet maker, he was hired as a boy in U. of Aberdeen's botany department. By 29 he was in charge of its botanical museum. In 1908 lack of formal education and class blocked his way to an assistant professorship. After a near-fatal flu/pneumonia attack (1909), advised to move to "more merciful" climate. Chose Vancouver, leaving April 1911. Hired by H.E. YOUNG as provincial botanist. Started gardens at Essondale (now Riverview) and UBC. "Botany John" joined UBC (1912); botany instructor and professor (1916-48). Founder, Vancouver Natural History Society (1918). Biblio: *The Vancouver Natural History Society, 1918-1933* by Jim Peacock.

John Sullivan Deas *Pioneer fish packer/canner, black entrepreneur* b. South Carolina, probably Charleston, c. 1838; d. July 22, 1880, Portland, Ore. Trained as a tinsmith. Searched for gold in California. In 1862 moved to Victoria. Ran a business in Yale (1866-68) during the gold rush, then returned to Victoria. By 1871 began canning Fraser salmon for Captain EDWARD STAMP. On Stamp's death, Deas continued canning, and in April 1873 preempted Deas Island and built his own cannery. He was the top canner until 1877.

That same year, wife Fanny bought a rooming house in Portland, Ore. Deas sold out and joined her. Died at 42, leaving wife and seven children.

Fred Deeley Sr. *Motorcycle dealer* b. 1881, Bromsgrove, Eng.; d. May 9, 1970, Vancouver. After 10 years in business in England, he first visited B.C. in 1913, representing the Birmingham Small Arms, manufacturer of BSA motorcycles. Bought out BSA and opened Fred Deeley Ltd. (1914) in a 3.7 metre wide store at 1075 Granville. In 1916 acquired the Harley-Davidson franchise, becoming its second oldest dealership. By 1925 he owned a motorcycle shop, bicycle shop, and one of Canada's larger car dealerships. Company included son Fred Jr. and grandson Trev (b. 1920) of Trev Deeley Motorcycles. Biblio: *Motorcycle Millionaire* by Trev Deeley.

"Gassy Jack" (John) Deighton *Innkeeper* b. 1830, Hull, Eng.; d. May 29, 1875, Gastown. At 14 went to sea, eventually arriving on the West Coast. First opened the Globe Saloon in New Westminster. When it failed, he canoed with his native wife (m. 1863) to Burrard Inlet, Sept. 29, 1867, and opened a saloon. When his wife died, he married her niece Madeline (birth name Qua-hail-ya or Qwahalia, d. Aug. 10, 1948, at age 90, buried in the Squamish Reserve Cemetery). A year later his son Richard Mason was born but died soon after Gassy Jack's death at age 45. Madeline was disinherited, and later married a Squamish man. Gassy Jack's voluble personality is said to have prompted his nickname.

Arthur William Delamont *Band leader* b. Jan. 23, 1892, Hereford, Eng.; d. Sept. 11, 1982, Vancouver. As a youth active in the Salvation Army Band in Moose Jaw, Sask., with father and four brothers. Survivor of 1914 sinking of *Empress of Ireland* in St. Lawrence. Came to Vancouver in 1922. Played trumpet at Pantages vaudeville theatre. For five decades, from January 1928, "Mr. D" conducted the Kitsilano Boys Band. Won first place in the Toronto Exposition (1931); performed at Chicago's Century of Progress Exposition and NY World's Fair (1939). Long-time Pacific National Exhibition performers. "Raised the status of youth bands to an art." Received Vancouver's Good Citizen Award (1946).

Adam Urias dePencier *Anglican priest* b. Feb. 9, 1866, Burritts Rapids, Ont.; d. May 30, 1949, Vancouver. Ordained 1890. Obtained BA, U. of Trinity College (Toronto, 1895). After various posts in other provinces, accepted rectorship of St. Paul's, Vancouver. Elected Bishop of New Westminster in June 1910. In 1911 U. of Trinity College awarded him DD (honoris causa). Chaplain in WWI, later Archbishop of New Westminster (1925-40) and Metropolitan. President, Anglican Theological College. On Nov. 12, 1918, Order of the British Empire from King George V. Original member of

UBC senate. LL.D (UBC, 1940).

Allard de Ridder *VSO conductor* b. 1887, Dordrecht, Holland; d. May 13, 1966, Vancouver. Received music education in Holland and Cologne Conservatory. Guest conductor in Arnhem, The Hague and Amsterdam. Conductor of Amsterdam's National Opera and Boston Symphony Orchestra. First Vancouver Symphony Orchestra conductor (1930). Put up his $3,000 life savings to cover musician's wages for first concert. Left California to become a citizen of Vancouver. In 1941 joined Hart House String Quartet (Toronto). Taught at Royal Conservatory of Music before founding Ottawa Philharmonic Orchestra in 1944. Retired in Vancouver in 1951.

Alexander Campbell Des Brisay *Chief justice* b. 1888, Winnipeg, Man.; d. Nov. 30, 1963, Vancouver. Elected president, Vancouver Bar Association (1941); treasurer, B.C. Law Society (1953-55); chief justice of B.C. Court of Appeal (1958). Head of one-man royal commission on workmen's compensation (1962). When he died, he had produced 6,000 pages of transcripts for the as-yet unfinished enquiry. His wife, Ella Helen, died the following morning (Dec. 1, 1963, Vancouver) of a heart attack. LL.D (UBC, 1959).

Dett (Claude P.) Dettloff *Photographer* b. 1899, Chippewa Falls, Wisc.; d. July 18, 1978, Vancouver. Started career with *Minneapolis Journal* in 1923. Worked 11 years with *Winnipeg Tribune*. Joined Vancouver *Daily Province* (1936), becoming chief photographer. *Wait for Me, Daddy*, his memorable WWII photo of a boy running after his marching dad, was shot Oct. 1, 1940, as the New Westminster brigade went overseas. Photo appeared Oct. 2, 1940, in the Vancouver *Daily Province*. Named one of 10 best pictures of the 1940s by *Life Magazine*. The unposed shot was taken at nine metres with a 3-1/4 by 4-1/4 Speed Graphic and a 13.5 C.M. Zeiss lens. Exposure was 1/200 of a second at F.8, using Agfa film.

Harry (Henry Torkington) Devine *Photographer* b. July 28, 1865, Manchester, Eng.; d. Dec. 17, 1938, Vancouver. His father, John Devine, was the first city auditor. Harry started his career in Brandon, Man. (1884), in partnership with J.A. Brock (1885). Moved to Vancouver (1886). The work of Brock & Co. has been called the "visual legends" of Vancouver. After the Great Fire of 1886, he photographed the first city council and first police department in front of a tent. He worked again as a photographer from 1895-97, when he ended his photography career.

Dick (Richard Alan) Diespecker *Radio announcer, writer* b. March 1, 1907, Adstock, Eng.; d. Feb. 11, 1973, San Francisco, Calif. Came to Canada as a baby; to Victoria in 1927. In 1940 joined artillery, later radio liaison. First book of poems, *Between Two Furious Oceans*, published in 1944. In 1948

DOUGLAS LAKE RANCH Douglas Lake Cattle Company Ltd. is one of the world's largest ranches. Established in 1874, it was purchased in 1957 by the Woodward family, who continue an active involvement. Although the Ranch's main business is beef production, running some 20,000 head, it also harvests timber on a sustainable basis. Additional activities include farming and agri-products sales. A recreational business has been developed, which includes a fishing resort and access to lakes boasting some of the continent's largest Kamloops trout.

won Columbus Award for a three-part radio documentary *Destination Palestine*. Wrote over 400 radio plays for CBC, BBC, South African Broadcasting Corp. Columnist with *Victoria Colonist, Vancouver News-Herald, Daily Province*. Was former *Province* radio director. Wrote a novel (*Elizabeth*, based on the life of his pioneer mother), as well as a pageant for 1958 Centenary. In 1958 moved to San Francisco to join a public relations firm.

Ira Dilworth *Scholar, broadcaster* b. March 25, 1894, High Bluff, Man.; d. Nov. 23, 1962, Vancouver. Came to Okanagan as a boy. From 1915-34, taught English at Victoria HS; principal (1926). A poetry expert, he was a popular UBC associate professor of English (1934-38). From 1938-40 directed Bach Choir. First president, Vancouver Community Arts Council (1945), the first of its kind in North America. From 1938 onward rose in CBC ranks to director of all CBC English networks (1956). A friend of Emily Carr, he encouraged her to write books. LL.D (UBC, 1948).

William Carey Ditmars *First car buyer* b. Nov. 12, 1865, St. Catherines, Ont.; d. Dec. 7, 1960, Vancouver. He arrived in Vancouver from Toronto (1891); worked as accountant for John Doty Engine. Moved back to Toronto (1894-97), then joined a new Vancouver bridge building firm, Armstrong & Morrison. In 1903 became a full partner, building Granville, Cambie and Fraser street bridges. Laid substructure for Lions Gate Bridge (1937). President, Vancouver Granite, supplying granite facing for bridge piers. In Feb. 1899 bought a tiller-steered Stanley Steamer for partner W.H. ARMSTRONG, the first car in Canada. Cost f.o.b. Vancouver was about $1,000. He received Vancouver's Good Citizen Award (1928).

Joseph Dixon *Carpenter* b. Oct. 2, 1860, Cumberland County, Eng.; d. Sept. 15, 1926, Vancouver. Opened his first shop in a basement on Seymour with partner Richard Lyte. In 1894, with new partner George Murray, established Dixon and Murray, a pioneer West End fixture store and manufacturer. Fire destroyed the building in 1907; in 1908 the firm relocated to 1052 Eveleigh, a three-story building torn down in the early 1960s, eventually moving to 925 Odlin Rd. in Richmond. The firm equipped most of Vancouver's palatial homes. President of Carpenter's Union (1889).

Charles (Carl Gottfried) Doering *Brewer* b. Jan. 10, 1856, Leipzig, Germany; d. April 15, 1927, Vancouver. Educated in Germany as a machinist. Established Doering & Marstrand Brewery in Mt. Pleasant, later sold to Vancouver Breweries. Alderman, Ward 6 (1890-91). His Mt. Pleasant home was the first built south of False Creek after the 1886 Great Fire. His saloon, Stag & Pheasant, was on Water St. Later years spent with second wife, Mary Ann Joan Gerrie Reid, a noted horsewoman, at their Hat Creek cattle ranch in the

Cariboo.

Robert Dollar *Steamship lines president* b. 1844, Falkirk, Scotland; d. May 16, 1932, San Rafael, Calif. Came to Eastern Canada at 14; by 19 was an experienced lumberjack. Moved to California (1888) and bought *Newsboy*, the first in a shipping empire of over 100 vessels. In 1902 made first China trip. In 1912 established Canadian Robert Dollar Co. in Vancouver to run the fleet of Dollar Steamship Line of California. Timber stands, bought from the B.C. government, supplied his sawmill on Burrard Inlet. The Dollar flag, a white dollar sign on a red background, was known worldwide. "Pacific's Grand Old Man."

Charles S. Douglas *Mayor of Vancouver, 1909* See Mayors of Vancouver.

Violet Alice Dryvynsyde *Educator, author* b. Nov. 4, 1899, Port Fairy, Australia; d. Oct. 29, 1969, Vancouver. Came to Vancouver with family in 1930. After husband's death in 1940 she founded the private Athlone School for Boys with six students. By 1969 the school at 49th and Arbutus had 230 students. In 1952 her novel *Provoke the Silent Dust* won third prize in a literary competition sponsored by the Australian government. The novel's plot involved a pioneering girl who went to Australia determined to avenge slights on her character by English society.

Wilson Duff *Anthropologist* b. March 23, 1925, Vancouver; d. Aug. 8, 1976, Vancouver. His entire career centred on the study of Northwest Coast Indians. Educated at UBC (BA, 1949), U. of Washington (MA, 1951). Curator of anthropology at provincial museum (1950-65). Moved to Vancouver to teach and research at UBC department of anthropology and sociology. Founding member of the B.C. Museum Association. Helped preserve the last remaining totem poles at Kitwancool and villages in Queen Charlotte Islands in the 1950s. Wrote *The Indian History of British Columbia* and *Arts of the Raven: Masterworks by the Northwest Coast Indians*. Biblio: *The World Is as Sharp as a Knife: An Anthology in Honor of Wilson Duff* edited by Donald N. Abbott.

Charles Trott Dunbar *Pioneer real estate developer* b. 1861, Rhode Island; d. April 15, 1927, Vancouver. A general agent for Union Land Co. of St. Paul, Minn., he arrived in Vancouver in 1888. Promoted development of Dunbar Heights, "selling like hotcakes" in 1906. As a marketing device, he gave away 1907 calendars. In 1909 planned a logging railway to his timber limits on the Mamquam River near Squamish. On Feb. 3, 1910, he won approval of B.C. legislature to incorporate The Port Moody, Indian Arm & Northern Railway. By 1911, 100 men were employed grading the CPR line from Port Moody to the north side of Burrard Inlet opposite Barnet, along his proposed route.

Nora M. Duncan *Poet* b. c. 1883, Vermont, Clari-

na, County Limerick, Ire.; d. May 31, 1946, aboard a CPR train near Moose Jaw, Sask. Came to London, Ont., as a child with her father, the Reverend Preceptor Alfred Dann. Educated at Bishop Strachan School, Toronto. After marriage to Wallace Craig Duncan at London, Ont., in June 1908, she spent a number of years on the prairies before coming to Vancouver. Wrote two books of poems, *Down to the Sea* and *Rainbow Reveries*. Organizer of the radio program *The Lyric West*.

Bill (Wilfred John) Duthie *Bookseller* b. April 8, 1920, Weston, Ont.; d. April 7, 1984, Vancouver. Came to Vancouver in 1952 as the first regional book representative on the West Coast. Opened Duthie Books in 1957. He dedicated an entire floor to paperback books, a marketing move unprecedented at the time. He was especially encouraging to emerging Canadian writers. The Bill Duthie Memorial Lecture is delivered annually at the Vancouver International Writers Festival.

E

Harry (William Henry) Eburne *Storekeeper, postmaster* b. c. 1856, Eng.; d. June 20, 1924, South Vancouver. In Feb. 1875 came to B.C. with foster parents, the year the Fraser River froze from early February to mid-March. Worked for FITZGERALD McCLEERY, before preempting 65 hectares. A poor farmer, he opened the first general store and post office at the Sea Island end of the Fraser (1881). Originally named North Arm, the settlement was renamed Eburne, and later Marpole in 1916. In 1881 he admonished horse-trading Rev. George Ditchman, the first rector of St. James Church, saying, "No man can swap horses and remain Christian."

Henry Valentine Edmonds *Mount Pleasant founder* b. Feb. 14, 1837, Dublin, Ire.; d. June 14, 1897, Vancouver. Arrived in New Westminster in 1862. In 1880 named sheriff of New Westminster; elected mayor in 1883. Speculated in real estate and promoted railways. A founder of Howe Sound Silver Mining and Fraser River Beet Sugar companies. Developed Mount Pleasant in 1888 on land purchased in 1870. Backed the Interurban between Vancouver and New Westminster (1891). When the Interurban went bankrupt, he lost most of his money.

John Emerson *Actor, pianist* b. March 13, 1911, Vancouver; d. May 2, 1968, Vancouver. Eldest of seven, son of a music-loving lawyer. After WWI the family home became the impetus for the Vancouver Symphony Orchestra. Attended UBC where he acted with the University Players' Club. From 1930-64 he was a popular pianist and musical arranger. Promoted local talent; discovered 13-year-old Mimi Hines in the East End. Noted for reading poetry on his national CBC radio show; wrote and performed in radio plays. From 1954-56 staged popular "capsule musicals" at the Arctic

Club. "Versatility is a euphemism for doing all the things I have to do to earn a living." ACTRA gives an annual scholarship in his name, honoring his "help to his fellow man."

Percy W. Evans *Cement and fuel supplier* b. Eng.; d. Oct. 21, 1943, Los Angeles, Calif. With brother Ernest and cousin George Coleman, came to B.C. from England in 1888. Opened a fuel and cement firm, Evans, Coleman and Evans, on Columbia. Built city's first deep sea dock. Firm was sold in 1910 to a group of prominent business people including WILLIAM FARRELL and FRANK BARNARD. With brother, also owned Vancouver's Stanley and Manitoba hotels with interest in the Plaza Theatre building. A director of B.C. Telephone and other communications concerns.

Alexander Ewen *Fraser River salmon canner* b. Nov. 22, 1832, Aberdeen, Scotland; d. July 8, 1907, New Westminster. Arrived in B.C. in 1864. Opened his first cannery in 1871 at Annieville; in 1884 established Ewen and Co., and built up the largest cannery on the Fraser River at Lion Island. A successful operator in the 1890s, in 1901 he merged with B.C. Packers' Association and served as president until his death. One of the giants of the boom years of the Fraser River canning industry. Described as "a dour Scot and extremely canny" with a hot temper.

F

Gordon Samuel Fahrni *General Surgeon, creator of iodized table salt* b. April 13, 1887, Gladstone, Man.; d. Nov. 3, 1995, Vancouver. Following graduation in medicine (U. of Manitoba), he built a distinguished career as a surgeon, specializing in thyroid diseases in Winnipeg and Vancouver and creating iodized table salt. Served in the Canadian Army in both world wars; senior consulting surgeon (rank of colonel) in WWII. A founder of the B.C. Housing Foundation, which established several low rent housing units for senior citizens. Member of the Order of Canada (1987). At the time of his death, he was the oldest living Shriner in North America.

William Farrell *B.C. Telephone Company's first president* b. c. 1854, Huddersfield, Eng.; d. Sept. 12, 1922, Vancouver. With wife Jessie Maude and infant son Gordon, he came to Vancouver in 1891 and, together with associates, formed the nucleus of B.C. Telephone, becoming its first president. Built 18-metre yacht *Sheileena,* named for his three daughters, Sheila, Kathleen and Nora. It was eventually renamed *Kitchener* and used in WWII by the Canadian army. Gordon (b. March 14, 1890, Huddersfield, Eng.; d. Aug. 21, 1979, Vancouver), served in the Royal Naval Air Force in WWI. He joined B.C. Telephone in 1919 as treasurer, rising to president (1928-58), and holding numerous directorships. In 1948 the William Farrell Building (Seymour and Robson) was built as B.C. Tele-

phone's head office. In 1963, due to a by-law he introduced barring B.C. Telephone directors over 72, Gordon was forced to retire as chair.

Evlyn Fenwick Keirstead Farris *Women's education activist* b. Aug. 21, 1878, Windsor, NS; d. Nov. 5, 1971, Vancouver. A minister's daughter and graduate of Acadia U. (MA, 1898) with first class honors. From 1899-1905 taught history at a Connecticut high school. At 28 a founder of UBC's University Women's Club (1907) to "stimulate intellectual activity." Club president, 1907-09, 1925-26. When the first UBC board was elected, women were excluded. In 1917 she was elected first woman on the board, serving more than 20 years (LL.D, Acadia and UBC, 1942). Wife of J.W. DEBEQUE FARRIS. "Clever, elegant, idealistic . . . made things happen."

John Wallace deBeque Farris *Crown prosecutor, attorney general* b. Dec. 3, 1878, White's Cove, NB; d. Feb. 25, 1970, Vancouver. His father was NB minister of agriculture. Attended Acadia U. and U. of Pennsylvania. Came to Vancouver in 1903 as city's first Crown prosecutor. Took more appeals to the British Privy Council than any other Canadian. Elected MLA (1917-22); attorney general and B.C.'s first labor minister. Counselled major corporations but she also defended society's outsiders, such as a group of Chinese charged with gaming. The imposing Liberal senator was called a radical by his opponents, "a term which pleased him." LL.D (UBC, 1938). His brother Wendell was chief justice of the B.C. Supreme Court.

Alfred Graham Ferguson *First chair, Vancouver park board* b. c. 1844, U.S.A.; d. June 2, 1903, San Francisco, Calif. A civil engineer, he was a wealthy CPR tunnel contractor. Built Ferguson Block, initially of wood. After the Great Fire (1886) he rebuilt it with brick. Also owned other significant city properties. Served as a park commissioner for several years in 1880s. An alien, "his swearing-in ceremony was tactfully omitted." Ferguson Point is named for him.

John George Ventris Field-Johnson *Agriculturalist, newspaper writer* b. Eng.; d. Nov. 23, 1908, Vancouver. Supported concept of Pacific National Exhibition. In 1908 called a meeting in a real estate office on New Westminster Ave., now Main St., and drew up a constitution. Some felt a Vancouver exhibition would detract from New Westminster's Royal Agricultural Show; others wanted a site within a five-cent ticket ride of Vancouver. A by-election defeated a $25,000 grant to the Hastings Park site so memberships were sold and building began. The Pacific National Exhibition opened in 1910.

Charles Edward Findlater *Choir master* b. 1893, Buckinghamshire, Eng.; d. Aug. 7, 1975, Vancouver. A bookkeeper, he came to Vancouver in 1918

to teach voice and piano. Founded Wesley Sunday School Choir (1924), later Elgar Choir (1934). Choir made 13 overseas tours (1924-74). Known as the frying pan choir during the 1930s because of its tight budget. During WWII travelled nationally raising money for wartime charities. In 1960 the choir was the first Canadian cultural group to visit the USSR; in 1963 made a world tour. Assisted by wife, Amy, a choirmaster's daughter. Over 6,000 teens were members. "Mr. F" was "plain-speaking, straight-thinking and dressed in sturdy plaids."

James Findlay *Mayor of Vancouver, 1912* See Mayors of Vancouver.

Yvonne Millicent Firkins *Theatre producer, director* b. Worcester, Eng.; d. Jan. 6, 1966, Vancouver in her 70s. During WWI lived in Birmingham, where she was introduced to theatre. Came to Vancouver in 1920. Her husband, magistrate Walter H.C. Firkins, was a police court clerk for 31 years. Founding member, Vancouver Little Theatre, Vancouver Ballet School and Vancouver Dance Festival. President, B.C. Drama Association; founder, B.C. Dance Festival; member, Community Arts Council; director, Theatre Under the Stars. From 1939-45 production manager of service shows for Pacific Command. In 1964 opened Arts Club Theatre with the controversial *Who's Afraid of Virginia Woolf.* "B.C.'s first lady of the theatre."

Betsy (Elizabeth) Flaherty *Private pilot* b. c. 1878; d. June 1965, Vancouver. A buyer for Spencer's department store, she was a passenger on Trans-Canada Airlines' first cross-Canada flight. She was over 50 when she received her licence on Dec. 16, 1931, the oldest female pilot in Canada. In 1936 she was the oldest founder of The Flying Seven Canadian Women Pilots, flying out of Sea Island, "the forerunners of a splendid air movement." During WWII the club members trained women in parachute packing, fabric work and other aspects of airplane care. Some trainees joined Boeing's Vancouver plant or the RAF's women's division. Biblio: *Daring Lady Flyers* by Joyce Spring; *No Place for a Lady* by Shirley Render.

Richard Samuel Ford *Newspaper writer* b. c. 1872, Petrolia, Ont.; d. Aug. 19, 1950, Ganges, B.C. Moved to Vancouver in 1907. One of three founders, with brother-in-law John P. "Black Jack" McConnell, of *Saturday Sunset,* later the *Morning Sun* (1912). The newspaper was in receivership (1916-17) when it was saved by Foley, Welch and Stewart, builders of the PGE railway. Trying to break its railway contract, the firm used the *Vancouver Sun* to embarrass the B.C. government. It then dropped the paper, later bought by ROBERT CROMIE. Ford later opened a wholesale dry goods firm. One of Kerrisdale's early residents, his home, Huron Lodge, was built in 1909 (45th and E. Boulevard).

North America's first retail specialty flag store, The Flag Shop is known worldwide. A family business founded more than 20 years ago by Doreen Braverman and now managed by daughter Susan, The Flag Shop is more than flags! It carries flag poles, hardware, pins, crests, decals—everything for the patriot. Custom banners are its specialty. The experienced staff gives personal service and all workmanship is guaranteed. Today, there are also Flag Shops in Victoria, Calgary, Edmonton, Winnipeg, Ottawa and Dartmouth.

Joe (Seraphim) Fortes *Beach guard* b. 1865, Barbados; d. Feb. 4, 1922, Vancouver. Came to Vancouver in 1885 and became a regular at English Bay, teaching children to swim. Appointed Vancouver's first official lifeguard in 1901; credited with saving more than 100 lives. Lived in a cottage near the Alexandra Park bandstand. In 1986 the Vancouver Historical Society named him Citizen of the Century. The Joe Fortes Branch of the Vancouver Public Library is named for him.

Pop (Charles) Foster *Boxing promoter* b. c. 1874, Leeds, Eng.; d. May 5, 1956, Glendale, Calif. His father ran a carnival fight booth in England; his uncle was a lightweight champion. Fought in Boer War and WWI with Canadian Railway Construction Corp. Almost lost his legs in an explosion at Poperinge, Belgium. Ex-fighter and stevedore. In 1923 discovered future world welterweight champion Jimmy McLarnin (b. Dec. 17, 1905, Ire.), selling newspapers in Vancouver. At 21 McLarnin was defeated for the lightweight title. At 26 came back to win world welterweight title. Foster's protégé was "the greatest fighter, pound for pound, in the prize ring today."

Terry Fox *Cancer crusader* See Terry Fox profile.

Sister Frances (Mrs. Fanny Dalrymple Redmond) *First public health nurse* b. c. 1852, Eng.; d. April 13, 1932, Vancouver. Arrived after Vancouver's Great Fire (1886). Nurse at St. James Church. Called the "Florence Nightingale of the City" for her nursing care during the smallpox epidemic of the 1890s.

Leonard Juda Frank *Master photographer* b. July 3, 1870, Berne, Germany; d. Feb. 23, 1944, Vancouver. He came seeking gold, arriving in Victoria in 1894. Served as postmaster in Port Alberni (1903-17). Began taking pictures with a crude camera won in a mining camp raffle. Moved to Vancouver to become its leading industrial and commercial photographer with a shop and lab at 553 Granville. His logging photos are judged the best ever taken; his photos of Vancouver people and places are "an impressive visual record . . . between wars." Took more than 33,000 of the photos in the Vancouver Public Library historic collection.

Zebulon Franks *Storekeeper, first Jewish religious leader in Vancouver* b. c. 1864, Odessa, Ukraine; d. 1926, Vancouver. Son of a High Rabbi, he had a deep knowledge of Judaism. At 17 survived a pogrom that murdered his family. Met wife, Esther, on his escape across Europe; they went to Winnipeg in 1882 and Vancouver in 1887. A "junk merchant," he opened a general hardware store at 42 Water St. The city's first active Jewish leader, he held the first Orthodox services in his home and store. President, Sons of Israel (B'nai Yehuda) in 1907, later the Schara Tzedeck Synagogue, with services held at 14 W. Cordova.

Simon Fraser *Explorer* See Simon Fraser profile.

Julius Martin Fromme *Father of Lynn Valley, North Vancouver* b. Nov. 26, 1857, Fox Harbour, Nova Scotia; d. Nov. 15, 1941, North Vancouver. He arrived Port Moody in 1883. In 1896 was named superintendent of the Hastings Mill shingle board camp (known as Shaketown) and settled in Lynn Valley. In 1899 preempted 65 hectares and built Lynn Valley's first home. In 1903 he persuaded the company to open a lumber mill on Mill Rd. in Lynn Valley. When the mill closed in 1906, he bought it with partner Thomas Allan Sr., renaming it Lynn Valley Lumber Company. Ran mill 1906-21. District of North Vancouver reeve for seven consecutive one-year terms (1924-30). Mount Fromme and Fromme Road are named for him.

G

Chris Gage (born Christian Geisinger) *Jazz pianist, composer* b. Dec. 12, 1927, Regina, Sask.; d. Dec. 27, 1964, North Vancouver. At four stood on tiptoes to play family pump organ; at six played Regina radio; at 11 performed all-nighters with adult band; at 14 had his own six-piece band. Came to Vancouver at 17. Played CBC radio, over 100 TV appearances, Vancouver clubs and with Louis Armstrong. Arrested for drunkenness, harassment of ex-wife; died of barbiturate overdose. "Peter Pan, rushing headlong toward disaster." Chris Gage Memorial Award established by Bob Smith Scholarship Fund (1990).

Walter H. Gage *Mathematics professor, UBC president* b. March 5, 1905, South Vancouver; d. Oct. 3, 1978, Vancouver. Educated at Tecumseh Elem. and John Oliver HS; UBC (BA, 1921-25; MA, 1926); graduate studies in math (U. of Chicago; California Institute of Technology). A scholar and revered instructor, he taught from 1927-33 at Victoria College, a UBC affiliate, then at UBC until 1968. Won UBC's 1953 Great Trekker Award and 1968 Master Teacher award. LL.D (UBC, 1958). Sixth president of UBC (1969-75). Order of Canada, 1971. Retired in 1975.

R. Harry Gale *Mayor of Vancouver, 1918-21, 1937* See Mayors of Vancouver.

James F. Garden *Mayor of Vancouver, 1898-1900* See Mayors of Vancouver.

Mae Garnett *Senior court reporter* b. 1897, London, Ont.; d. May 26, 1984, West Vancouver. Moved to Winnipeg in early 1900s as CPR public relations officer, transferring to the Calgary Exhibition and Stampede. One of the first female general news reporters in Western Canada, writing for the *Albertan, Edmonton Bulletin* and *Vancouver News-Herald*, joining the *Vancouver Sun* in 1930. In 1962 retired as senior court reporter covering B.C. Supreme Court and county courts. One of the first women to get a mortgage from Central Mortgage and Housing. "Known for championing women's rights at least two generations before the rise of the women's movement."

Dan George (born Teswahno) *Actor, writer* b. July 24, 1899, North Vancouver; d. Sept. 12, 1981, Vancouver. Longshoreman and logger. In 1959 began acting career. Appeared in first production of *The Ecstasy of Rita Joe* by George Ryga (1967). Films included *Little Big Man* (1970) (Oscar nomination) and *The Outlaw Josey Wales* (1975). Chief of Squamish Band (1951-63), he embodied the dignified elder. Biblio: *My Heart Soars* (1974); *My Spirit Soars* (1982).

Bruno Gerussi *Actor* b. May 7, 1928, Medicine Hat, Alta.; d. Nov. 21, 1995, Vancouver. Raised in New Westminster. Attended Banff School of Fine Arts before joining the Stratford Festival Theatre in 1954. A leading Shakespearean actor in the 1950s. Host of his own CBC radio show for four years, and later hosted CBC's *Celebrity Cooks*. Performed for 18 years in *The Beachcombers*, CBC's popular TV series, as gruff Nick Adonidas, a log salvager on the B.C. coast. His last public performance was in the play *Breaking Legs*, at the Vancouver Arts Club Theatre (1994).

Gordon (James Gordon) Gibson Sr. *Lumberman* b. Nov. 28, 1904, Goldbottom Creek, Yukon; d. July 18, 1986, West Vancouver. Left school at 12 to work in fishing and logging. Nicknamed "The Bull" as a young man. In 1939, with father W.F. Gibson and three brothers, started logging. From 1948-52 owned or participated in many related businesses. Lib. MLA (Lillooet, 1952); later elected in North Vancouver. He led a stormy political career, once accusing Premier W.A.C. Bennett of thinking he was God. A MacMillan Bloedel shareholder and director, he opposed expansion in mid-1960s. Biblio: *Bull of the Woods*.

Rachel Goldbloom *Philanthropist* b. c. 1865, New York; d. April 1931. Married William Goldbloom in 1882 and moved from New York to Fort Garry. Nell, their daughter, was the first Jewish girl born in Winnipeg. In the mid-1900s they moved to Vancouver; their home at 540 Burrard became the centre of Jewish community life, with almost every Jewish organization of that time said to have started there. The Hadassah's second Vancouver chapter was named for her during her lifetime. A "one-woman philanthropic organization."

William Grafton *Bowen Island pioneer* b. Feb 6, 1868, London, Eng.; d. Dec. 9, 1957, West Vancouver. Came to Vancouver with two brothers in 1885. One of Bowen Island's first settlers, preempting 640 acres (259 hectares) at $1 an acre. Farming on Bowen was difficult but salmon was abundant; he boiled cod, shark and dogfish livers on the beach in a 273-litre sugar kettle to extract the valuable oil. Also sold game to the Hotel Vancouver. About 1887 launched first Howe Sound ferry service with a four-ton sloop. From 1917-34 worked as a janitor. Bowen's Grafton Lake and Grafton Bay are named for him.

Walter Henry Grassie *Jeweller* b. Jan. 22, 1861, Seaforth, Ont.; d. April 3, 1941, Vancouver. Educated in Seaforth, he entered the jewelry business there. In 1882 moved to Port Arthur, Ont. Arrived in Port Moody in July 1886, coming to Vancouver by boat. Erected wooden building on Cordova; later moved to lower Cambie Street. Five years later moved business to final site on Cambie, north of Hastings St. His store was "particularly favored by railway men."

Dal (Albert Edward) Grauer *President, B.C. Electric Railway* b. Jan. 21, 1906, Sea Island; d. July 28, 1961, Vancouver. He was sixth son of pioneer John (Jacob) Grauer (b. 1861; d. 1936). Attended King Edward HS; UBC (BA, Economics, 1925); PhD (Berkeley); Rhodes Scholar (1927); BA (Oxford). As a young professor and head of social sciences at U of T, he assisted Bank of Canada and Rowell-Sirois Commission. Appointed secretary, B.C. Electric Railway (1939). Later, as president, he took the company (now B.C. Hydro) through major expansion. Chairman, Vancouver General Hospital; president, Vancouver Symphony Society; member of Gordon Commission. UBC chancellor (1957); LL.D (UBC, 1958). His daughter is artist Sherry Grauer.

Walter Edward Graveley *Pioneer realtor* b. Aug. 7, 1854, Cobourg, Ont.; d. June 30, 1939, Vancouver. Came west from Cobourg in 1883, moving to Gastown (1885). His real estate business profited from the 1912 boom. Purchased a lot at Oyster Bay (Carrall and Cordova) for business premises when CPR was extended from Port Moody to Vancouver. A founder of the Royal Vancouver Yacht Club in 1903, he owned many yachts and won "scores of trophies." His ashes were scattered over English Bay.

Sam Greer *Farmer* b. 1843, Northern Ire.; d. April 6, 1925, Vancouver. In 1882 "Gritty" preempted 65 hectares at Kitsilano Beach (popularly known as Greer's Beach), part of 2,428 hectares given by B.C. to the CPR in 1884. In 1887, New Westminster sheriff Thomas Armstrong tried to remove Gritty, his wife and six children. Gritty shot several times, hitting the sheriff and his deputy. After a second posse arrived, he gave himself up and his farm was razed. In 1891 convicted by Judge Begbie of wounding a sheriff, he served a term in the New Westminster jail, where he often ate lunch on the beach. His daughter JESSIE HALL was a leading Vancouver socialite.

Peter Greyell *White Rock builder* b. Ont.; d. June 1, 1919, White Rock. A local resident, he built a 50-room, four-storey hotel in White Rock in the east end of the settlement. It opened July 1, 1912, with a lunch for 300 guests. He also built the first bakery and tea room. The hotel was sold in 1913 and renamed The Tourist Hotel. Later, as the White Rock Hotel, it hosted concerts and local

talent to mid-October 1977, when it was torn down for development. Greyell died from a fall while building a pier restaurant.

John Grove *Lighthouse keeper* b. 1864, London, Eng.; d. March 21, 1935, Vancouver. He served as lighthouse keeper at Prospect Point, later at Brockton Point (1895-1930). From 1888, lived in a cottage on the rocks until the station was electrified in January 1926. One of the lowest paid workers in Vancouver, he received $25 per month but his station was coveted for its free housing and use of two acres in Stanley Park. To make extra money, Grove ran a lemonade stand for tourists until the park board closed it down.

Frank Armathwaite Griffiths *Radio and TV station owner, sportsman* b. Dec. 17, 1916, Burnaby; d. April 7, 1994, Vancouver. A professional accountant, he bought CKNW in 1956 and made it the cornerstone of a broadcasting empire. Formed Western Broadcasting (later Western International Communications), which included radio and TV cable services. From 1974, owner of the Vancouver Canucks. Member of Hockey Hall of Fame; Canadian Business Hall of Fame.

Helena Rose Gutteridge *Suffragette* b. c. 1880, London, Eng.; d. Oct. 3, 1960, Vancouver. "Feminist, trade unionist, tailor, socialist, politician." Immigrated to B.C. in 1911. Organized B.C. Women's Suffrage League. Her interest in the working class woman led to trade union activities. Soon took a leading role on Vancouver Trades and Labor Council. Joined the Co-operative Commonwealth Federation (CCF). In 1937, she was elected Vancouver's first woman alderman.

H

Harvey Hadden *Millionaire, philanthropist* b. Eng.; d. February 1931, London, Eng. First visited Vancouver in 1891, becoming a major property owner before 1913. Said to have made more than $1 million on his Vancouver real estate holdings. Owned former Birks site (Hastings and Granville). Bought 65 hectares in Capilano Canyon, sight unseen from architect S.M. Eveleigh. Built Hadden Hall (1903), "a sort of Garden of Eden in the forest" (now Capilano Golf and Country Club). Hadden Park at Kitsilano Beach was donated in 1928, dedicated in 1952. He bequeathed $500,000 to Vancouver parks. In 1957 parks at Georgia, Adanac, Woodland and McLean were purchased with his bequest.

Jessie Columbia Hall (née Greer) *Philanthropist* b. 1872, Jack-of-Clubs Creek, B.C.; d. June 22, 1949, Vancouver. Daughter of SAM GREER; first white child born in the Cariboo. In 1893 married James Z. Hall, Vancouver's first notary public and first volunteer soldier. In 1908 built Kitsilano's Killarney mansion and entertained high society. Volunteer with the Children's Aid Society, Vancouver Welfare Federation, Women's Auxiliary of Christ

Church and others. During WWI provided supplies for a French field hospital. First woman to serve as a member of a Vancouver jury. President, Burrard Women's Conservative Club (1931) and Victorian Order of Nurses. First past grand factor of Post No. 1, Native Daughters of B.C. Received Vancouver's Good Citizen Award (1934).

Ida Halpern (née Ruhdorfer) *Musicologist* b. July 17, 1910, Vienna, Austria; d. Feb. 7, 1987, Vancouver. Immigrated with chemist husband Georg to Vancouver in 1939. A force on the local music scene, she was the first person to study the music of West Coast Indians. Produced four albums of First Nations' songs. Director of the Academy of Music. *Province* music critic (1952-57). Member, Order of Canada (1978).

Eric Werge Hamber *Executive, lieutenant-governor* b. April 21, 1880, Winnipeg, Man.; d. Jan. 10, 1960, Vancouver. Star rower as a young man. Came to Vancouver as manager, Dominion Bank (1907). Married Aldyen Irene Hendry, daughter of JOHN HENDRY in 1912. A captain in the 72nd Seaforth Highlanders. Worked for B.C. Mills, Timber and Trading; appointed president in 1916. B.C. lieutenant-governor (May 1, 1936-41); LL.D (UBC, 1939); UBC chancellor (1944-51). The Hambers were prominent in society and philanthropic circles. Eric Hamber HS named for him.

Alfred St. George Hamersley *Vancouver's first solicitor, soldier* b. Oct. 8, 1848, Oxfordshire, Eng.; d. Feb. 25, 1929, Bournemouth, Eng. Educated at Marlborough, Woolwich. Played in first rugger international in 1871 and four times internationally for England. Called to the bar in 1873. Practised law in New Zealand, arriving in Vancouver in 1888. Legal advisor to Vancouver City Corporation and CPR. Active in local business and athletics. Sold some Mt. Pleasant property to fellow Freemason, the poet Rudyard Kipling. In 1906 returned to Rycot, Eng., and was elected Lib. MP (1910-18). Commanded a battery (1917) and a heavy artillery group.

Lauchlan Alexander Hamilton *Surveyor, city councillor* b. Sept. 20, 1852, Penetanguishene, Ont.; d. Feb. 11, 1941, Toronto, Ont. As CPR land commissioner and surveyor, established Prairie townsites and surveyed Canada/U.S. border. Arrived in Vancouver in 1883. Surveyed and named Vancouver streets. In 1885 surveyed CPR grant from English Bay to Hastings St. Resurveyed "Liverpool" (West End) after the Great Fire of June 13, 1886. As Vancouver city councillor (1886-87), proposed Stanley Park and laid out its perimeter. A noted amateur photographer. Hamilton St. was named for (and by) him.

Ellen Harris *Radio broadcaster* b. 1904, Winnipeg, Man.; d. June 15, 1967, Vancouver. Came to Vancouver in 1930. From 1920s onward, active in children's theatre. A prominent radio broadcaster

with *Morning Visit,* a CBC women's show (1944-52). In early 1950s involved in CBC school broadcasts. President, Vancouver Ballet Society; chair, building committee of UBC's International House. Public relations officer for B.C. Automobile Association and Health Centre for Children for many years. From the 1950s active in Vancouver Zonta Club and International Zonta Club.

Lawren Stewart Harris *Painter* b. Oct. 23, 1885, Brantford, Ont.; d. Jan. 29, 1970, Vancouver. Member of the famed Group of Seven painters (1920-31). Moved to Vancouver in 1940 and lived here until his death. One of Canada's greatest painters of the 20th century. LL.D (UBC, 1946).

Frank (Francis) E. Harrison *Postmaster* b. Feb. 1, 1861, Stratford, Ont.; d. July 5, 1934, Vancouver. First worked in the Ontario postal service (1876), later Railway Mail Service (RMS). Calgary's acting postmaster during the Riel Rebellion (1885). On the day of Riel's capture he returned to RMS. In 1889 came to B.C. on special duty; opened the Mainland's first RMS office. When the Vancouver Post Office was placed on a city basis (Jan. 7, 1895), he became assistant postmaster under JONATHAN MILLER. Passed over as postmaster when R.G. Macpherson, an ex-MP and outsider, was appointed. After 25 years as assistant postmaster, finally succeeded Macpherson on Jan. 10, 1920. Retired in 1928.

Frank William Hart *Theatre entrepreneur* b. June 1, 1856, Rock Island or Galesburg, Ill.; d. May 4, 1935, Prince Rupert, B.C. Hart's Swedish family immigrated from the U.S. In Dec. 1887 he built Vancouver's first theatre, Hart's Opera House on Carrall St., presenting amateur shows, touring companies, variety and vaudeville. Dubbed "the skating rink," the 15-metre by 40-metre arena housed 800 theatregoers or 250 roller skaters. When the Imperial Opera House opened (April 1889), Hart's closed. The building became a furniture warehouse. By 1912 Hart moved to Prince Rupert, selling furniture.

Uncle Billy (William George) Hassell *Children's program announcer* b. 1893, Bath, Eng.; d. Dec. 14, 1966, Vancouver. Moved to Vancouver in 1919 after serving as wireless operator in Royal Navy. In 1922 founded CHLS, one of the first radio stations on the coast (renamed CKCD and run by the *Daily Province*). In 1941 CKCD merged with CKWX. First Canadian newscaster to sign off with his own name; possibly the first to make a singing radio commercial. Known as Uncle Billy on his kid's program, *Squareshooters.* In 1946 retired to breed collies in Langley, B.C., becoming one of the world's top collie breeders. Biography: *The Hassells of Early Radio* by Alan D. Hassell.

Arthur Helps *Radio pioneer* b. Nov. 5, 1912, Toronto, Ont.; d. April 4, 1995, Surrey, B.C. Director and host of ground-breaking radio show

Town Meeting in Canada. An Armed Forces veteran, he was inspired by a similar U.S. broadcast. In 1947 engineered a dual broadcast with the show's U.S. counterpart, with an audience estimated at eight million. A conciliator, he drafted a resolution to invite veterans from Commonwealth countries to celebrate Remembrance Day at the Newton Legion. This led to some Legion members denying the entrance of Sikh veterans wearing turbans. In spite of this setback, Arthur continued to forge ties with his Sikh counterparts. His efforts inspired a successful community building workshop that included legion members and Sikh locals.

John Hendry *Lumberman* b. Jan. 20, 1843, Gloucester County, NB; d. July 17, 1916, Vancouver. Arrived in B.C. in September 1872, later working in a Seabeck, Wash., sawmill. By 1874, as foreman of Moodyville mill, he rebuilt it after a fire. Opened a sash and door factory in Nanaimo, B.C., later in New Westminster (1876). Built Kaslo & Slocan Railway, and Vancouver, Westminster & Yukon Railway. In 1878 elected to New Westminster city council. Elected mayor but quit after six months due to conflict of interest over his railway projects. In 1889/90 bought Hastings Mill, renaming it B.C. Mills, Timber and Trading. By 1914 it was the oldest and largest company of its kind in the Northwest with 2,000 employees, shipping doors, sashes and blinds. John Hendry Park is named for him.

Julia Willmothe Henshaw *Botanist, novelist* b. 1869, Durham, Eng.; d. Nov. 18, 1937, Caulfeild, West Vancouver. She followed in her naturalist father's footsteps, photographing mountain wildflowers. Settled in Vancouver c. 1887 with husband Charles Grant Henshaw, son of United Empire Loyalists. Editor of the *Province* and *Vancouver Sun* columnist. An internationally known novelist; *Hypnotized* (1898) was called Book of the Year. The prominent couple drove the first car across the Rockies (1914). She wrote several important plant studies, including *Mountain Wildflowers of Canada* (1906) and *The Wild Flowers of B.C.* (1908). Won Croix De Guerre as ambulance driver in France during WWI.

Stanley E. Higgs *Anglican minister* b. 1904, Warwickshire, Eng.; d. April 16, 1983, Vancouver. Served overseas with Royal Canadian Corps of Chaplains (1941-46) and 14 years in the Cariboo. Assisted at Christ Church Cathedral, then served as rector of St. Michael's (May 30, 1949-60). In 1957 he charged that general manager Cedric Tallis of the Vancouver Mounties would be in contempt of law if he pursued Sunday ball games. Track judge at the British Empire Games, Vancouver (1954), and in April 1958, in Cardiff, Wales. From 1960-68 chaplain of Haney Correctional Institute; in Sept. 1968 named executive head of Vancouver's Central City Mission. Retired in April

1974 after 47 years of service.

Harry Mackenzie Hilker *Haberdasher, impresario* b. c. 1880, Bruce County, Ont.; d. March 26, 1969. With son, Gordon (John Gordon) Hilker (b. Sept. 19, 1913, Vancouver; d. April 28, 1991, North Vancouver), formed Vancouver's first concert agency, Hilker Attractions. From 1936-50 imported more than 1,000 performers including Yehudi Menuhin, Paul Robeson, Isaac Stern. In 1946 Gordon erected the continent's biggest stage at Stanley Park's Brockton Oval for Vancouver's Diamond Jubilee. "The city, brave as only the frightened can be, agreed to his ideas." The company went bankrupt on Sept. 26, 1950. Gordon was later artistic director, Vancouver Festival (1961-67) and director, Expo 67 World Festival of Entertainment.

Georgina Hill (Lady Reid) *First president, Vancouver Council of Women* b. Halifax, NS. Wife of Sir John Watt Reid (m. July 6, 1863), she was a founder and the first president of the Vancouver Council of Women (1894). The original group of 16 women was dedicated to "further the application of the Golden Rule to Society, Custom and Law." An early campaign was for government control of the importation of opium, processed in local factories. The Reids built Fairview House (1151 W. 8th), in 1894 and lived there to 1898 (now a designated heritage building). John Reid (b. May 10, 1823, Edinburgh, Scotland; d. Feb 25, 1909, Eng.), director general of the Royal Navy medical department (1880) and honorary physician to Queen Victoria (1881), was knighted in 1882. In 1901 he returned to England as honorary physician to King Edward VII.

Charles Hill-Tout *Ethnologist* b. Sept. 28, 1858, Buckland, Eng.; d. June 30, 1944, Vancouver. Came to Canada in 1880s, arriving in Vancouver in 1890. He surveyed and wrote on the famous Marpole Midden. Acting principal of Dr. Whetlam's College before founding his own school, Buckland College. Settled in the Fraser Valley. A devoted amateur anthropologist, he focused on the Salish Indians of B.C. Elected to Royal Society of Canada (1913), later president of its anthropological section. His field reports were collected as *The Salish People* by Ralph Maud (1978). Asked by the CPR to name a new subdivision in Vancouver, he suggested Kitsilano, a modification of the name of the chief of the Squamish Band. Biblio: *The Native Races of British North America: The Far West* (1907).

Cap (Gerald) Hobbis *Bicycle store owner* b. Aug. 1, 1918, Vermilion, Alta.; d. Aug. 25, 1995, New Westminster. Traded a bunch of old magazines in 1932 for his first bicycle. He repaired it in his basement and sold it to his first customer, for $10. After working in a cedar mill, opened first Cap's Bicycle store in New Westminster in 1940. At first he sold everything from baby carriages to bicycles. With his two brothers and later their sons, established 11 more stores and a museum of unusual bicycles. The family's collection of antique and comic bikes was a crowd-pleaser in the annual Pacific National Exhibition parade from 1947.

Oliver M. Hocking *Hotelier* In 1885, in partnership with Fred Houston, he built the Brighton Hotel at what is now the foot of Windermere St., with a wharf for bathers. Three stages stopped daily, and a coachman announced arrivals with a bugle blast. Mill workers and loggers used the wharf en route to mills along Burrard Inlet. On March 1, 1866, he was appointed deputy collector of customs at Burrard Inlet, making it possible for captains to fill out their papers without walking through the woods to New Westminster. In March 1869 the partners sold the hotel to MAXIE MICHAUD.

Reinhart (or Reinhard) Hoffmeister *Electrical engineer* b. 1866, Wellington County, Ont.; d. July 9, 1948, Vancouver. The "Pioneer of Power" came to Vancouver in 1888 with dynamo castings of his own design and set up the city's first electrical shop (Davie and Howe). At 22 built the first dynamo (electric generator) to power the False Creek mill. Installed electrical plants at B.C. Sugar Refinery, Trail Smelter and original Hotel Vancouver. Patented designs for an electrical gold mining machine and a combined brake and foot rest for bicycles. Converted to electric power the presses of the newspapers which merged into the *Vancouver Sun*.

William Matthew Holden *Realtor and builder* b. Feb. 7, 1872, Sterling, Ont.; d. June 1, 1947, Vancouver. Brought up on a farm, later a salesman. Lived in B.C. after 1898. Manager, Federal Life Insurance (Western Canada); worked as an independent realtor and general finance broker (1905-12). In 1912 became a finance broker. His extensive city realty dealings led the press to write that "he made Granville Street." Purchased terminal lands on False Creek for Great Northern Railway. Built "the magnificent Holden Building" on E. Hastings in 1911, leased by city council (1929-36) as temporary city hall.

William Holmes *Pioneer settler* b. Jan. 4, 1813, Kilkenegh, Ire.; d. Sept. 10, 1907, Sapperton, B.C. Holder of the first certificate of title to land in B.C., dated March 5, 1860 (Lot 1 in Block 1). One of Burnaby area's earliest settlers, he built on the banks of the Brunette River close to today's North Rd. His property was located in the area between Sapperton St. and North Rd., from Holmes to Rochester. He named the Brunette River because of its dark brown water, colored by peat near the river's source.

Joseph Attwood Reynolds Homer *Sheriff* b. Aug. 1827, Barrington, NS; d. Sept. 20, 1886, New Westminster. Came to B.C. in 1858 via San Francisco and was one of the first sawmill owners in New Westminster. In 1860 elected to first New Westminster city council. Signed petition to the Colonial office from the Hope Convention (1861) for a separate Mainland government. From 1864-66 represented New Westminster in the Crown Colony of B.C.'s first legislative council. As High Sheriff (1866) read the Royal proclamation of Nov. 19, 1866, uniting the two Crown colonies. PC MP, New Westminster (1882). After incorporation of City of Vancouver (April 2, 1886), elected first MP but died after six months.

Tomekichi Homma *Civil rights activist* b. June 6, 1865, Onigoshi-mura, Chiba-ken, Japan; d. Oct. 28, 1945, Slocan, B.C. In May 1899, with TADAICHI NAGAO, he began contracting laborers to the CNR. Fished the Fraser from 1892, at first in an open Columbia boat. Organized Steveston Japanese fishermen's union (1899); first chair. Started first Japanese newspaper in Vancouver. In 1893 he tried unsuccessfully to have his name added to the voter's list. Relocated to Slocan, B.C., internment camp with his wife, Matsu (d. Jan. 7, 1951). An elementary school in Richmond is named for him. Biblio: *Stories of My People* by Roy Ito.

James Welton Horne *Land investor, politician* b. Nov. 3, 1853, Toronto, Ont.; d. Feb. 21, 1922, Vancouver. A successful Manitoba businessman before moving to Coal Harbour in March 1885. Invested in real estate, profiting when CPR approached. As founder of B.C. Electric Railway, he developed the street railway and interurban between New Westminster and Vancouver. Elected to Vancouver city council (1888); in the 1889/90 council election, he received the largest vote cast since incorporation. PC MLA, Vancouver (1890-94). Chairman of Board of Park Commissioners for six years.

Frederick William Howay (born Howie) *Judge, historian* b. Nov. 25, 1867, London, Ont.; d. Oct. 4, 1943, New Westminster. His father moved to B.C. in 1869; joined by wife and three children in 1870. Frederick practised law, becoming a county court judge (1907-37). Wrote books and articles establishing him as the leading B.C. historian of his generation. President, Art, Historical and Scientific Association of Vancouver (1910-15). Member, Historic Sites and Monuments Board Canada (1923-43). UBC senator (1915-42). Biblio: *British Columbia From Earliest Times to the Present* (1914), the standard history of B.C. into the 1950s.

Josias Charles Hughes *Mt. Hermon Masonic Lodge founder* b. May 5, 1843, Omeme, Upper Canada; d. Nov. 8, 1886, New Westminster. On Sept. 21, 1861, at 18, sworn in as poll clerk in Peterborough, Ont. Came to B.C. in 1862, joined lumber firm of Moody, Dietz and Nelson as a clerk. Elect-ed MLA (1871). Returned to New Westminster as government collector, soon appointed B.C. government agent. A founder of Mt. Hermon Lodge (1869); he was the first Right Worshipful Master (Jan. 15, 1869). Elected lodge honorary life member on Sept. 6, 1884, and to the office of Senior Grand Warden in 1886, but did not live to complete his term of office. Biblio: *Mount Hermon Lodge No. 7, 1869-1994* by Jim Harrison.

Fred J. Hume *Mayor of New Westminster and Vancouver, 1951-58* See Mayors of Vancouver

Bishan Kaur Hundal *Sikh woman pioneer* b. India; d. 1937, Vancouver. Because of racist immigration law excluding wives and children, Bishan's married son Hakim Singh Hundal came to Canada alone c. 1910, becoming a director of Guru Nanak Mining and Trust Company. On his wife's death, he attempted to bring Bishan and his four sons to Canada. He was allowed to re-enter, but his family was detained in Hong Kong (1911-13) by Canadian immigration. After appeals to all levels of government, the family was allowed to enter on humanitarian grounds. His mother thus became one of the first Sikh women to live in Canada.

Chung Hung *Sculptor* b. Feb. 8, 1946, Canton, China; d. July 21, 1994, Vancouver. Studied civil engineering in Hong Kong before immigrating to Canada in 1969. In 1973 graduated in sculpture at Vancouver School of Art. Specialized in monumental public steel sculptures, including *Gate to the North-West Passage* (Vanier Park) and *Steam Columns* (938 Howe). Co-creator, *Goddess of Democracy* (UBC, 1991). Permanent sculptures also in Hong Kong, Spain. Received Dal Grauer Memorial Award (1974); won eight competition-awarded commissions. Promoted awareness of Chinese artists in Vancouver.

Bruce (William Bruce) Hutchison *Journalist* b. June 5, 1901, Prescott, Ont.; d. Sept. 14, 1992, Victoria. Began lifelong career in journalism as sports reporter for the *Victoria Times* in 1918. Worked for Vancouver newspapers and *Winnipeg Free Press* 1927-50. LL.D (UBC, 1950). Editor, *Victoria Times* (1950-63); editor, *Vancouver Sun* (1963 to retirement). A leading political reporter. The author of 15 books, he won three Governor General's Awards. Appointed to Privy Council. Coined "Lotusland" to describe B.C. Biblio: *The Far Side of the Street*.

I

Elek Imredy *Sculptor* b. April 13, 1912, Pest, Hungary; d. Oct. 22, 1994, Vancouver. Came to Vancouver in 1957 after 1956 Hungarian uprising. Sculptures exhibited in Canada, U.S., Europe, including lifesize statue of prime minister Louis St. Laurent at Ottawa's Supreme Court. His most famous work is *Girl in Wetsuit* in Stanley Park, commissioned in 1972 by Vancouver lawyer Douglas McK. Brown. Created bust of archivist J.S.

MATTHEWS at City of Vancouver Archives and *Lady of Justice* (Vancouver Law Courts). Member, Sculptor's Society of Canada, the Sculptor's Society of B.C. and Vancouver Historical Society. Biblio: *The Sculpture of Elek Imredy* by Terry Noble.

John Benjamin Ireland *Actor* b. Jan. 30, 1915, Vancouver.; d. March 21, 1992, Santa Barbara, Calif. Left Vancouver at age seven after his father died in a horse racing accident. His first acting job, with the Free Theatre (New York), paid one cent a day. First of over 200 films was *A Walk in the Sun* (1945). Nominated for 1949 Oscar (best supporting actor in *All the King's Men*), which Dean Jagger won. Movies: *Spartacus, Red River*. Directors: Hawks, Ford, Kubrick. "A tough, cynical hero" in his films, he paid almost $2,000 in 1987 for an industry newspaper ad, "I'm an actor, PLEASE . . . let me act," which led to role of Ben Cartwright's brother in *Bonanza: The Next Generation*.

John Irving *Boat builder* b. Nov. 24, 1854, Portland, Ore.; d. Aug. 10, 1936, Vancouver. Son of Captain WILLIAM IRVING. Came to New Westminster in 1858. At 16 joined father's steamboat business; took over on father's death (1872). In 1883 active head of Canadian Pacific Navigation, a consolidation of the Irving and Hudson's Bay Company lines. In 1890 launched Columbia and Kootenai Steam Navigation, buying and building boats. In 1901 the line was absorbed by CPR's water service as B.C. Coast Service steamer fleet. John Irving Navigation was sold in 1906 to White Pass Railway. An MP for eight years.

William Irving *Pioneer boatbuilder* b. March 3, 1816, near Annan, Dumfriesshire, Scotland; d. Aug. 28, 1872, New Westminster. Began seagoing career as a boy. Came to B.C. in 1858 after selling Oregon steamboat interests. Joined old partner Alexander S. Murray and built *Governor Douglas*, the first B.C.-built steamer; also built the *Captain Moody*, making the first successful trip up the Fraser to Yale in 1861. He sold out in 1862. From 1862-64 built Irving House, New Westminster's first official heritage building, now a museum. In 1865 launched *Onward*, "the utmost in steamship luxury." Known as "King of the River." Father of JOHN IRVING.

J

Annie (Anna Bruce) Jamieson *Education activist* b. 1871, Leeds, Que.; d. Jan. 23, 1952, Vancouver. Graduate, U. of Manitoba in philosophy (1904). Taught in Manitoba before coming to Vancouver's Dawson School (1907). From 1908-27 taught at King Edward HS (vice principal for 10 years). Continuously elected to the Vancouver School Board (1929-46). Member, UBC senate; member, Board of Governors (1936-42). LL.D (UBC, 1942). Life member of the B.C. Library Association and 30-year library board member. Founding member,

University Women's Club. An elementary school is named for her. Born a Tory, she said she would "die a cynic where politics are concerned."

Laura Emma Jamieson (née Marshall) *Juvenile court judge* b. Dec. 29, 1883, Park Head, Ont.; d. June 29, 1964, Vancouver. Graduate, U of T (1908). In 1911 married lawyer J. Stewart Jamieson (d. 1926). Active member, University Women's Club and suffragette groups. In 1921 organized a branch of the Women's International League for Peace and Freedom. When her two children reached school age, she joined the B.C. Parent/Teacher Federation (president, 1925-26). On her husband's death, she succeeded him as Burnaby juvenile court judge, the first B.C. woman in this position (1926-38). Joined CCF party (1939); elected MLA, Vancouver Centre. Re-elected (1941) but lost her seat in 1945. In 1947 elected as Vancouver alderman.

Robert Jamieson *Presbyterian missionary* b. Oct. 18, 1829, N. Ire.; d. Sept. 6, 1893, New Westminster. B.C.'s first Presbyterian minister arrived on Dec. 10, 1861, reaching New Westminster in 1862. Preached first sermon Sunday, March 16, 1862, in the pulpit of the Methodist church. Until March 1863 his flock met in the courthouse. Built St. Andrew's Church on grant of land from Gov. Douglas (Carnarvon and Blackwood). Opened first school in the area, as well as Fraser Valley churches. In July 1870, on a borrowed horse, rode and preached 1,125 kilometres. After 1871 focused on St. Andrew's. In 1884 illness forced his resignation. He later recovered and was named first prison chaplain.

Thomas John Janes *Stagecoach owner, driver* b. April 16, 1855, Cornwall, Eng.; d. Oct. 14, 1926, Vancouver. Worked as a butcher in Seaforth, Ont., arriving in Granville (later Vancouver) on Oct. 31, 1883. Ran a butcher shop, then began operating Janes Stage, the first stagecoach line to carry passengers between New Westminster and Vancouver along Westminster Avenue (now Kingsway).

Harry Winston Jerome *Sprinter* b. Sept. 30, 1940, Prince Albert, Sask.; d. Dec. 7, 1982, North Vancouver. Began running at North Vancouver HS; member, Optimist Striders Track Club. Won a scholarship to U. of Oregon. Was the first male sprinter to simultaneously hold world records for 100-metre and 100-yard events. Bronze medal, 1964 Olympics; gold medals at 1966 Commonwealth Games and 1967 Pan-American Games. Competed in Olympics, Mexico City (1968), retiring the same year. He was inducted into B.C. Sports Hall of Fame (1966), Canadian Amateur Athletic Hall of Fame (1967), Canada's Sports Hall of Fame (1971). One of only a few blacks to receive Order of Canada (1970). Administered Premier Sports Award for athletic achievement in

B.C. elementary schools. Died of stroke.

Pauline Jewett *Political scientist, politician* b. Dec. 11, 1922, St. Catharines, Ont.; d. July 5, 1992, Ottawa, Ont. Came west as president of SFU (1974-78). Elected Lib. MP (1963-65). Switched to NDP, and was elected for New Westminster-Coquitlam (1979-88). First female president of a major Canadian university (SFU). Appointed to Privy Council in 1992. Chancellor of Carleton U. Biblio: *Faces of Canada* by George Lonn.

Charles Gardner Johnson *Shipping pioneer* b. Feb. 8, 1857, near Dunblane, Scotland; d. Jan. 19, 1926, Vancouver. In 1870, at 10, went to South Seas for a four-year apprenticeship. In the 1880s left seafaring to farm in Souris River, Manitoba. On Sept. 5, 1885, broke and married, arrived in Vancouver; worked for CPR as a laborer. In 1886 opened a shipping and insurance agency, the first in the city. C. Gardner Johnson & Co. (Hastings and Granville) became one of the city's major shipping agents. Addressed as Major because he served with local militia. "Father of Vancouver's shipping industry."

Pauline Johnson (Tekahionwake) *First Nations writer, stage performer* b. March 10, 1861, Six Nations Reserve, Brantford, Ont.; d. March 7, 1913, Vancouver. Her father was a Mohawk chief. Dressed as an Indian princess, she began performing her poetry in 1892, the start of an 18-year touring career. One of the most popular stage performers of her generation, many of her poems and stories were about Vancouver. Lost Lagoon, where she loved to canoe, was named from one of her poems. Retired to Vancouver (1909). A memorial to her was erected in 1922 near Third Beach. Biblio: *White Wampum* (1895); *Canadian Born* (1903); *Legends of Vancouver* (1911); *Flint and Feather* (1912).

Bob (Robert) Johnston *Rower* b. 1868, Elmsville, Charlottetown, NB; d. Aug. 9, 1951, Vancouver. Known as the "grand old man of rowing." A boat builder, he moved to West Vancouver (1888) and started rowing (1889). Rowing was at its height of popularity and he competed before thousands. Best known for challenging world champion Jake Gandaur of Hamilton, Ont., to a three-mile race in Coal Harbour (1898) but lost the $2,500 purse by two lengths. In his final race won the $1,000 purse by beating former world champion John Hackett by 4.5 lengths. Coached the Vancouver Rowing Club to a bronze medal in the 1932 Olympic double sculls event. Inducted into B.C. Sports Hall of Fame (1966). "A keen, cigar-chewing coach of champions."

Charles Jones *Mayor of Vancouver, 1948* See Mayors of Vancouver.

K

Stu (James Stuart) Keate *Journalist* b. Oct. 13, 1913, Vancouver; d. March 1, 1987, Vancouver.

Graduated from UBC (1935) and went into journalism. Sports writer for the *Daily Province, Toronto Star, Time* and *Life*. Information officer in North Atlantic and Pacific theatres (1942-45). After the war, served as bureau chief of Time Inc. in Montreal. Publisher of *Victoria Daily Times* (1951-64); publisher of *Vancouver Sun*, from 1964 until retiring in 1978. LL.D (UBC, 1985). Biblio: *Paper Boy.*

George Henry Keefer *Contractor* b. 1865, Bowling Green, Ont.; d. Dec. 8, 1957, Cobble Hill, Vancouver Island. Prominent in B.C. railway construction for 50 years. A railway contractor in 1886, he cleared the CPR right of way from Port Moody to English Bay, mostly with Stikine Indians. On June 12, 1886, looking for a camp site near today's Granville Bridge, he saw some dry brush and set it on fire to clean it up. On June 13 the Great Fire levelled Vancouver. He admitted his mistake many years later. (Some say his story is apocryphal.) Worked on railway lines in Washington state and B.C. before serving in WWI. Later a contractor for the Capilano Waterworks. Keefer St. is named for him.

Hugh Llewellyn Keenleyside *Diplomat* b. July 7, 1898, Toronto, Ont.; d. Sept. 27, 1992, Saanich, B.C. Graduated from UBC (1920). Diplomat (1928-47). Opposed internment of Japanese in WWII. LL.D (UBC, 1945). Worked for UN in 1950s. Chair, B.C. Power Commission (1959-61). Co-chair, B.C. Hydro (1961-69). Chancellor, Notre Dame (1969-77). Companion, Order of Canada (1969). Winner of Vanier Medal (1962); Pearson Peace Medal (1982). Biblio: *Memoirs of Hugh L. Keenleyside.*

Robert Kelly *Grocer* b. 1862, Russell, Ont.; d. June 22, 1922, Vancouver. Came to Vancouver in 1890; worked at Oppenheimer Bros' grocery. His first business, Braid and Kelly, folded during the 1893-94 depression. Co-founder of pioneer Kelly Douglas wholesale grocery firm on Water St. in Gastown (1896). Outfitted gold seekers in 1898. In 1901 his partner Frank Douglas drowned en route from Skagway to Vancouver when ship hit an iceberg and sank. His brother, Edward Douglas, took over his role in the company. Coffee was introduced in 1896, and its trade name, Nabob, became a household word.

August Jack Khahtsahlano (also 'Haatsalano, Khahtsahlanough, etc.) *Squamish chief* b. July 16, 1867, Sun'ahk (below Burrard Bridge); baptized Feb. 12, 1879; d. June 14, 1967, Vancouver. Buried at Squamish. Son of Khaytulk (Supple Jack) of Chaythoos and grandson of Chief Khahtsalanough of Sun'ahk. Worked in a sawmill. In 1900 he gave a potlatch to honor the receiving of his grandfather's name some years earlier. At the feast he gave out more than 100 blankets. On Aug. 26, 1938, by deed poll, he adopted name August Jack Khahtsahlano. The English name of

his wife, Swanamia, was Mary Ann.

Jim (James) Kinnaird *President, B.C. Federation of Labor* b. Jan. 5, 1933, Edinburgh, Scotland; d. Feb. 17, 1983, Vancouver. Son of working class parents, he left school at 14. Arrived in Vancouver in 1956. Joined International Brotherhood of Electrical Workers; elected business manager, Local 213 (1967). President, B.C. and Yukon Building Trades Council. In 1972 appointed assistant deputy minister of labor by NDP. Elected president, B.C. Federation of Labor (1978), uniting the divided body. Served three terms as leader of 250,000 unionized workers. Died suddenly of a heart attack. "Disliked flamboyance and public shouting matches but was not above them."

Roy Kenzie Kiyooka *Poet, photographer* b. Jan. 18, 1926, Moose Jaw, Sask.; d. Jan. 15, 1994, Vancouver. Moved from Moose Jaw to Calgary until 1943. Spent the war years at a farm in Northern Alberta. From 1956-49 attended art school in Calgary, then began teaching. Came to Vancouver in 1960. Taught fine arts at UBC (1973-91). A founder of TISH poets and the Western Front. His book *Pear Tree Pomes* was nominated for a Governor General's Award in 1988. Heavily involved in the Japanese-Canadian community.

Leonard Sylvanus Klinck *Agriculturalist, UBC president* b. Jan. 20, 1877, Victoria Square, Ont.; d. March 27, 1969, West Vancouver. Graduate, Ontario Agricultural College (1903); Iowa State College (1905). Took over cereal husbandry department at McGill. Visited Vancouver in 1914 to consult with UBC President FRANK WESBROOK. Appointed dean of agriculture, the first appointee to UBC. After Wesbrook's sudden death (1918), he was UBC's second president (1919-44). LL.D (UBC, 1944). "Supervised UBC's growth from its early Fairview campus days, the war-delayed move to Point Grey, the controversies of the 1930s, and the trying times of WWII."

Edmund Shorey Knowlton *Pioneer druggist* b. c. 1868, Newboro, Ont.; d. Dec. 25, 1943, Vancouver. Came to B.C. in 1896. Opened Knowlton's Drug Store (1897), located at several sites on Westminster (now Main St.) and Hastings until settling in at 15 E. Hastings (1911). Managing director (to 1944), when he was replaced by Bruce B. Knowlton. By 1948 the company opened a second drug store in West Vancouver. In 1965 the name was changed to Knowlans Drugs, but its original name was restored in 1970. A Pacific National Exhibition director. President, Pharmaceutical Association of B.C.

Albert O. Koch *"Father" of Congregation Beth Israel* b. May 1, 1894, Long Island, NY; d. April 16, 1969, crossing the Mediterranean. Came to Vancouver in 1925 from New York via Montreal and launched National Dress Co., Vancouver's first garment manufacturing plant, and later Lauries

dress store chain (1940). Founder and second president (1933-34, 1938-51) of Beth Israel Synagogue at 4350 Oak; a founder of Beth Israel Cemetery (consecrated July 28, 1946). Sold Lauries on Jan. 31, 1969. On his retirement trip to Israel with wife Henrietta, he suffered a stroke and died aboard ship.

Leon Joseph Koerner *Forestry executive* b. May 24, 1892, Novy Hrozenkova, Moravia; d. Sept. 26, 1972, Vancouver. Executive in J. Koerner Timber Industry (1912-38). A forestry industry innovator and executive. A creative philanthropist, he was particularly generous to UBC's faculty club and graduate student centre. With wife Thea established the Leon and Thea Koerner Foundation with a capital grant of one million dollars and further bequests in their wills. The foundation serves culture and the creative arts, social services and higher education. LL.D (UBC, 1957).

L

Leon Johnson Ladner *Lawyer, MP* b. Nov. 29, 1884, Ladner, B.C.; d. April 12, 1978, Vancouver. His father THOMAS LADNER and uncle WILLIAM LADNER founded Ladner. After BA (1907), LL.B (U of T, 1909), admitted to bar in 1910. In 1912 began his Vancouver law practice. A founder of UBC convocation (1912). Founder of Ladner, Downs, one of Vancouver's largest law firms. Liberal Conservative MP, Vancouver South (1921-30). UBC senator (1955-61). In 1957 elected to UBC's board of governors. Reappointed in 1963; retired in 1966. Honorary lecturer, faculty of law. Donated Ladner Carillon and Clock Tower to UBC in honor of B.C. pioneers. LL.D (UBC, 1967). Active in Conservative party.

Thomas Ellis Ladner *Farmer, salmon canner* b. Sept. 8, 1837, Trenant Park, Cornwall, Eng.; d. April 24, 1922, Vancouver. Came to B.C. in 1858. In 1868, with brother WILLIAM LADNER, was first to preempt land on site of Ladner, eventually owning 485 hectares. A successful farmer and pioneer salmon canner at Ladner's Landing (later Ladner). Owner of Delta Canning. Moved to Vancouver in 1909.

William Henry Ladner *Farmer* b. Nov. 28, 1826, Trenant Park, Cornwall, Eng.; d. Nov. 1, 1907, Ladner, B.C. Came to B.C. on May 15, 1858, on steamer *Brother Jonathan*, arriving May 30 at Fort Langley by skiff to avoid custom duties at mouth of Fraser River. Left Langley for Hope on June 1, 1858, to work as a miner and trader. Appointed customs agent and government officer. First Mainland constable. Ran a pack train to the Interior to 1865. In 1868 built a large home, Frogmore, at Ladner's Landing (later Ladner), to farm and raise stock. In 1872 named justice of the peace. First reeve of Delta (1880). His daughter, Delta Mary, was the first white child born in Ladner.

Arthur Laing *Politician* b. Sept. 9, 1904, Eburne,

June 3, 1953. A pioneer-spirited broadcaster named Rogan Jones launches KVOS TV, first to bring television to the area. Billed as "Your Peace Arch Station," its inaugural broadcast was a BBC kinescope of the Coronation ceremonies of Queen Elizabeth II. A host of TV "legends" debuted over TV 12, including *The Ed Sullivan Show, M*A*S*H* and *60 Minutes*. Incorporated in Canada in 1955, KVOS TV 12 today enjoys dual citizenship, unique in North American broadcasting.

B.C.; d. Feb. 13, 1975, Vancouver. Elected first Lib. MP for Vancouver South (June 1949) after two attempts. In 1953 resigned from federal office to become B.C. Liberal leader; elected MLA. Retired in 1959, then ran again federally in June 1962. One of only two B.C. members in Lester Pearson's cabinet after 1962 election. As head of Indian affairs, he occasionally raised the ire of native bands. After the 1968 election he was transferred to public works. On his 70th birthday, the bridge between South Vancouver and Sea Island was named in his honor by Prime Minister Pierre Trudeau.

Lily J. Laverock *Theatre impresario, reporter* b. Edinburgh, Scotland; d. Dec. 2, 1969, Duncan, B.C., at 89. First woman to graduate in moral philosophy from McGill. First woman reporter in Vancouver with the *World*. Two years later, she was assigned women's editor of *News-Advertiser*. In 1909 founded Vancouver branch of Canadian Women's Press Club. An avid arts supporter, she promoted her first Celebrity Concert in 1921. Brought in world-famed performers like Kreisler, Heifetz, Melba, Gigli, Casals; packed the Denman Arena with acts like the Ballet Russe de Monte Carlo and Belgian Royal Symphonic Band. WWII ended her impresario efforts. "Her pen was ever ready in the cause of women's suffrage."

John Lawson *West Vancouver's first permanent white settler* b. April 15, 1860, Cheltenham, Ont.; d. March 8, 1954, Vancouver. Arrived in B.C. in 1887. After 21 years as a railroad worker, bought property in West Vancouver area in 1903. Planted holly trees by "burn" (stream), coining the name Hollyburn. Second reeve of West Vancouver (1913). Developed ferry service to Vancouver (1909) aboard the 35-foot launch, *West Vancouver*. The *Seafoam*, a 60-footer, replaced it. Established the first school at Capilano, was first postmaster and telephone agent. "The history of West Vancouver is the history of John Lawson." In 1939 his daughter, Gertrude, a teacher, was one of the first B.C. women to get a mortgage.

Ronald Bick Lee (born Yat Yee Lee) *Businessman, community leader* b. 1892, Ong Sum Village, Toisan, Guangdong Province, China; d. Dec. 22, 1994, Vancouver. Arrived in Victoria at 17; worked as a dishwasher. In 1914 returned to China to marry Gin King Choon from a nearby village. From 1916 worked at White Lunch on Hastings and Castle Hotel on Granville. In 1921 founded Foo Hung Co., a leading importer of Asian goods. Active in politics and a philanthropist. Chairman, Vancouver Chinese Public School; chair, Lee's Association of North America. Charter member, Vancouver Chinatown Lion's Club. His son, Robert H. Lee, a UBC graduate, developer and philanthropist served as UBC chancellor, June 25, 1993 to June 25, 1996.

Wallis Walter Lefeaux *Barrister, socialist* b. Sept. 19, 1881, London, Eng.; d. Nov. 24, 1972, West Vancouver. After clerking in England, arrived in Canada in 1901. Worked as fur trader, grocer, real estate agent. In 1912 ran for CCF MLA (Interior) but lost. In 1918 became a lawyer and defended objectors to military training. In 1919 defended the worker leaders of Winnipeg Strike. "Offered classes in economics in which *Das Kapital* was taught." An original CCF member, elected CCF president for three consecutive terms. In 1936 visited Europe and Asia, including Moscow. MLA, Vancouver Centre (1941-45). Declined requests to run for a federal seat.

John Matthew Lefevre *Surgeon, businessman* b. Oct. 12, 1853, Brockville or Belleville, Ont.; d. Sept. 15, 1906, Vancouver. Graduate of McGill (1879); later studied with Sir William Osler. Came to Vancouver with wife LILY LEFEVRE in 1886, as surgeon general, CPR's Pacific Division. The couple crossed the Rockies by rail before the division's official opening. Member of first city council (1886); alderman (1887-89). In 1888 built the Empire Building (603 W. Hastings), site of his original cottage. With WILLIAM FARRELL, co-founded B.C. Electric Railway, and Burrard Inlet and New Westminster Telephone (later B.C. Telephone).

Lily Alice Lefevre (née Cooke) *Poet, hostess, philanthropist* b. April 5, 1853, Kingston, Ont.; d. Oct. 17, 1938, Vancouver. As a girl, won a medal for best descriptive poem of a Montreal carnival. Wrote many of her "loveliest verses" about Vancouver. Married J.M. LEFEVRE in 1883. Organized first Imperial Order of Daughters of the Empire in Vancouver on Edward VII's coronation, Aug. 9, 1902. A founder of the Vancouver Art Gallery; active member, Canadian Authors' Association. The Lefevre's home, Langaravine (6101 N.W. Marine), was a social centre for more than 50 years. In 1934 presented a $5,000 scholarship and gold medal to UBC in her husband's memory. Biblio: *The Lions' Gate* (1895; republished 1936 for Vancouver's jubilee); *A Garden by the Sea*.

Harry Farnham Germain Letson *Soldier* b. Sept. 26, 1896, Vancouver; d. April 11, 1992, Ottawa, Ont. First graduate of mechanical engineering at UBC. Won Belgian Military Cross (1917). From 1923-36 he was a member of UBC's mechanical and electrical engineering department. Between wars served with Duke of Connaught's Own 13th Armored Regiment, Canadian Officers Training Corps at UBC and 23rd Infantry Brigade. Named commander in 1927. In WWII held posts as Canadian military attache and commander of Canadian Army staff in Washington, DC, and adjutant-general in Ottawa. In 1944 donated 150,000 engineering books and periodicals to UBC. LL.D (UBC, 1945). In 1949, as the Governor General's secretary, he was named honorary

lieutenant-colonel. Order of the British Empire (1949).

Sherwood Lett *Judge* b. Aug. 1, 1895, Iroquois, Ont.; d. July 24, 1964, Vancouver. After distinguished service in both world wars, named first Canadian representative (1954-55) on International Control Commission to oversee the ceasefire and disengagement of French forces in North Vietnam and the country's political stabilization. Chief justice of B.C. (1955-64). In 1963 ruled expropriation of a private company, B.C. Electric Railway, by the provincial government's B.C. Hydro and Power Authority, to be illegal. The province was forced to pay far more to acquire B.C. Electric. LL.D (UBC, 1945).

Larry Lillo *Theatre director* b. Sept. 20, 1946, Kinuso, Alta.; d. June 2, 1993, Vancouver. Attended Royal Roads Military College (NS); BA (St. Francis Xavier). Studied at U. of Washington, then in New York. Received MA in directing (UBC). Co-founder, director and actor with Tamahnous Theatre (1971-81). Freelance theatre director, 1981-85. Artistic director, Grand Theatre, London, Ont. (1986), and Vancouver Playhouse (1988). Under his leadership Playhouse subscriptions rose from 5,800 (1988) to nearly 12,000 (1992/93). Winner of a Jessie (Vancouver) and Dora (Toronto) for directing *A Lie of the Mind*. Developed many new Canadian plays. His partner, John Moffat (d. May 16, 1995, Vancouver, at 39), was an award-winning actor.

John Linn *Stonemason* b. July 12, 1821, Corstorphine near Edinburgh, Scotland; d. April 18, 1876, Lynn Valley, North Vancouver. One of Colonel Moody's sappers (Royal Engineers), he came to B.C. in 1859 to build the Cariboo Rd. After the unit was disbanded in 1863, the officers returned to England. Most of the men, including Linn, remained in B.C. On Feb. 10, 1871, he received a 60-hectare Crown military grant and settled with wife and six children at the mouth of Lynn Creek, a misspelling of his name. "A strapping Scottish stonemason."

Marianne Linnell *Civic leader* b. 1914, Calgary, Alta.; d. June 6, 1990, Vancouver. A Vancouver NPA alderman, first elected in 1961, she served five terms to 1974. The only woman member of Canada's Centennial Commission. Chair of many committees from the Queen Elizabeth Theatre to sewers. In 1963, as chair of B.C. Aviation Council, she banned backyard burning. Director and columnist, The Sun's *Edith Adams' Cottage*. Rejected SC and ran for PC MLA (Vancouver-Point Grey, 1972) but was defeated by Garde Gardom. PC spokesperson for small business, municipal affairs and "that forgotten individual, the housewife." Described as "more rare steak than asparagus souffle."

Mary Livingstone (born Sadie Marks) *Radio per-*

In its more than 40 years of life Lisogar Construction changed the city's skyline. One example: the Fraser Villa, Vancouver's first low-rent family-apartment complex. Then there's Hycroft Mews, called the most deluxe condominium in B.C.; the Century Plaza Hotel and the Burrard Health Centre. Today, Roy Lisogar's family manage the company's two hotels (the Century Plaza and New Westminster's Royal Towers) while Roy enjoys retirement. Total value of the projects built by Lisogar Construction: more than $100 million.

former b. c. 1906-09, Seattle, Wash.; d. June 30, 1983, Hollywood, Calif. Lived in Vancouver as a child. Her father, David Marks, was a founder and president of Schara Tzedeck synagogue. Met Benny Kubelsky (Jack Benny), a vaudeville performer, at a Passover seder at her family's home, Ferrara Court (504 E. Hastings), in 1922. Met him again in 1926 while working at The May Co. in Los Angeles; they married in 1927. Played his wise-cracking partner for 21 years on his radio show.

Eudora Jane Lochead *Pioneer store owner, poet* d. Feb. 2, 1937, North Vancouver. Her (estranged) husband, James, was a logging contractor. She opened Hastings Grove Store, the first general store in the area, on Curtis in Burnaby in 1911. Above the store she ran a rooming house with 20 bedrooms (tents outside housed the overflow); the dining room sat 60 boarders. Two cousins, Marion and Emma, and son William (d. WWI) assisted. Concerts were held fortnightly with Eudora playing the violin. Her next store, in an area now called Lochdale, opened in 1913 at Sperling and Hastings, with a post office added March 1, 1914. A poet, her best-known work is *Would Life Be Worth Living*.

Alexander Russell Lord *Educator* b. June 27, 1885, Merigomish, NS; d. Sept. 18, 1961, Vancouver. Attended Queen's (BA, 1910). Principal of Kelowna Elem. (to 1916), then school inspector for Prince Rupert/Peace River districts, Okanagan and Vancouver. Joined Vancouver Normal School (1924-50), retiring as principal. Special lecturer, College of Education (1950-58). Member, UBC senate (1936-50). LL.D (UBC, 1948). President, Canadian Educational Association (1948-49) and Children's Aid Society. Educational advisor to the UN. Awarded Fergusson Memorial Award (1950) for "outstanding contribution to education in B.C." LL.D (UBC, Queens). An elementary school is named for him.

Malcolm (Clarence Malcolm) Lowry *Novelist* b. July 28, 1909, New Brighton, Eng.; d. June 27, 1957, Ripe, Eng. Lived in a shack at Dollarton, on the north shore of Burrard Inlet (1940-54), where he finished his master work, *Under the Volcano*, and wrote other books published posthumously. *Under the Volcano* is considered one of the great books of modern literature. He also wrote *October Ferry to Gabriola; Dark as the Grave Where My Friend Is Laid; Hear Us O Lord From Heaven Thy Dwelling Place*.

Pat (Patricia Louise) Lowther *Poet* b. July 29, 1935, Vancouver; d. Sept. 24, 1975, Vancouver. A respected poet, she wrote four books of poetry. Elected co-chair of League of Canadian Poets (1974) and to B.C. Arts Council. Her disappearance in 1975 led to a conviction of murder by her husband Roy. The League of Canadian Poets presents an annual prize named for her. Biblio: *The*

Difficult Flowering; The Age of the Bird; Milk Stone; A Stone Diary.

Teddy (Thadeous Sylvester) Lyons *B.C. Electric Railway conductor* b. c. 1887, Portage La Prairie, Man.; d. Feb. 27, 1955, Vancouver at 68. Came to Vancouver as a boy. At 14 left school and worked at odd jobs. In 1910 hired as a B.C. Electric conductor. Served for 40 years, 39 as a "spieler" announcing Vancouver highlights aboard Observation Car #124. In all, toured more than 930,000 kilometres around the city. In 1944 a wartime manpower and electric shortage caused B.C. Electric to halt operations for one summer. The tour, which sometimes included animal acts, ended September 1950; Teddy retired in 1951.

Mc

Lorraine McAllister *Singer, actor* b. April 15, 1922, Saskatoon, Sask.; d. April 27, 1984, Vancouver. Singing star of radio and TV in 1950s, headlining CBC Toronto's *Holiday Ranch* and Vancouver's *Burn's Chuckwagon, Some of Those Days* and *Meet Lorraine*. Headline performer for Theatre Under the Stars. Performed in Johnny Holmes' orchestra with Oscar Peterson as pianist and Maynard Ferguson as lead trumpet player. Wife of bandleader Dal Richards; sang with his orchestra at the Panorama Roof of the Hotel Vancouver (1950-65). "One of the glamorous performers whose warmth and charm make her a favorite."

Malcolm Peter McBeath *Mayor of Vancouver, 1916-17* See Mayors of Vancouver.

Fitzgerald McCleery *Farmer* b. Oct. 15, 1838, County Down, Ire.; d. April 18, 1921, Vancouver. Arrived in Esquimalt, B.C. (April 27, 1862), via the West Indies. Failed as a Cariboo prospector. With brother Samuel built the trail from New Westminster to Point Grey for a salary of $30/month. Worked for uncle, HUGH McROBERTS. In September 1862 the brothers were the first to farm the Fraser delta lands. Their first 15 head of cattle were shipped by sloops and scows from Oregon. Dairy products were canoed to New Westminster and carried by steamer to Fraser logging camps. His home, at the foot of Macdonald (1873), escaped the Great Fire (1886). His diary of life in B.C. is in the Vancouver City Archives.

Hugh Neil MacCorkindale *Educator* b. 1888, Owen Sound, Ont.; d. Jan. 17, 1977. A graduate of U of T, "Dr. Mac" first taught in Ontario (1906). Came to Vancouver in 1914. Served as an artillery officer in France from 1916-18. Taught at South Vancouver HS (now John Oliver). First principal of new Point Grey Junior HS (1928-33); superintendent of Vancouver City schools until retirement in 1954. In his 40 years with the school board and 21 years as superintendent, he pioneered concepts in education. Member, UBC senate. LL.D (UBC, 1954).

Anne Elizabeth Macdonald *Arts advocate* b.

March 18, 1930, Vancouver; d. July 10, 1993, North Vancouver. Established North Vancouver's Presentation House Arts Centre. Saved the historic Church of St. John the Evangelist as a recital hall (Anne Macdonald Hall, 1977). Founded North Vancouver Community Arts Council and B.C. Arts and Crafts Fair. As first executive director of Vancouver Community Arts Council, set up Assembly of B.C. Arts Councils. Sat on many boards and commissions including UBC senate, North Vancouver School District and Canadian Conference of the Arts. Member, Order of B.C. Received YWCA Woman of Distinction Award for Community Service (1990).

Blanche Macdonald (née Brillon) *Entrepreneur, native rights activist* b. May 11, 1931, Faust, Alta.; d. June 8, 1985, Vancouver. Her First Nations and French ancestry was a source of pride. Championed native causes and feminist ideals. A housewife and mother of two, she opened a modelling agency and self-improvement school (1960), later expanded into fashion, esthetics and make-up artistry training. As CEO, Native Communications Society of B.C., launched a journalism program for native students. Founding member, Vancouver's First Woman's Network; board member, Better Business Bureau, Modelling Association of America, Professional Native Woman's Association and Vancouver Indian Centre. Received YWCA Woman of Distinction Award for Business and the Professions (1985).

Jock (James Williamson Galloway) MacDonald *Artist* b. May 31, 1897, Thurso, Scotland; d. Dec. 3, 1960, Toronto, Ont. Lived in Vancouver (1926-46). A leading exponent of modern art as teacher and painter. Taught at Vancouver School of Decorative and Applied Arts and B.C. College of Arts (1933-35), which he co-founded with FRED VARLEY. One of the first abstract painters in Canada.

James M. McGavin *McGavin Bakeries founder* b. Dec. 28, 1882, Galston, Scotland; d. April 17, 1969, Vancouver. Learned his trade in Scotland. Bakery manager, Darvel Co-operative Society, Ayrshire. Came to Canada in 1913, joined Edmonton firm of J.A. Stinson. Bought the company in 1914. In 1928 incorporated as A. and J. McGavin, with brother Allan McGavin Sr. (b. c. 1893, Kilmarnock, Scotland; d. Aug. 29, 1955, Vancouver). Moved to Vancouver in 1924. President, McGavin Bakeries (1929-47). Built eight Western plants; also founded Bee Cee Honey (Vancouver); Peace River Honey (Dawson Creek) and Barbara Ann Baking (Los Angeles).

Gerry (Gerald Grattan) McGeer *Mayor of Vancouver, 1935-36, 1947* See Mayors of Vancouver.

Helen Gregory MacGill *Juvenile court judge* b. Jan. 7, 1864, Hamilton, Ont.; d. Feb. 27, 1947, Chicago, Ill. Her mother was a suffragette. In 1888 Helen was the first female graduate of Toronto's

U. of Trinity College (BA, MA, BMus). The first woman judge in B.C., she presided over Vancouver's juvenile court (1917-28), fighting for legal changes to benefit women and children. In 1934 named to B.C. board of industrial relations. On May 12, 1938, she was the first woman to receive an honorary LL.D from UBC. A journalist, her publication *Juvenile Courts in Canada* was accepted as a standard at Geneva. Her daughter, Elsie MacGill, was the world's first female aeronautical engineer. Biblio: *My Mother the Judge* by Elsie Gregory MacGill.

William J. McGuigan *Mayor of Vancouver, 1904* See Mayors of Vancouver.

George Albert McGuire *Pioneer dentist, MLA* b. April 7, 1871, Mount Forest, Ont.; d. July 2, 1955, Vancouver. Graduate, Royal College of Dental Surgeons (Toronto) and U. of Maryland (DDS, 1892). Practised dentistry in Vancouver (1892-1912), then moved into real estate and investments. President, B.C. section of the Conservative Association of Canada (1903). In 1907 elected Vancouver MLA, launching a long political career. As minister of education influenced the creation of UBC. Last survivor of the famous "Solid Five" Conservatives, representing Vancouver under B.C. premiers Richard McBride and WILLIAM J. BOWSER.

Angus MacInnis *Politician* b. Sept. 2, 1884, Glen William, PEI; d. March 2, 1964, Vancouver. As a teenager ran the family farm after his father's death. Arrived in Vancouver in 1908. Drove a milk wagon; later became a streetcar conductor (1910). He studied economics and politics and helped found the CCF. Worked for three years as business agent for Street Railwaymen's Union. In 1921 was elected to the school board. City councillor (1926-30). Vancouver MP (Vancouver East), 1930-56. LL.D (UBC, 1956). MacInnis Park in E. Vancouver was named for Angus and wife GRACE MacINNIS on Sept. 10, 1994. "A brilliant orator and champion of the little man."

Grace (Winona Grace) MacInnis (née Woodsworth) *Politician* b. July 25, 1905, Winnipeg, Man.; d. July 10, 1991, Vancouver. Daughter of J.S. Woodsworth, organizer of the CCF party in the 1930s, she was a lifelong socialist activist in CCF/NDP. Elected MLA (1941-45). She "emerged from the backrooms" to win the Vancouver-Kingsway seat for the federal NDP (1965-74), becoming B.C.'s first woman MP. LL.D (UBC, 1977). Her husband was ANGUS MacINNIS.

Thomas Robert McInnes *Physician, lieutenant-governor* b. Nov. 5, 1840, Lake Ainslie, NS; d. March 19, 1904, Vancouver. Graduated from Rush Medical College, Chicago, Ill. In 1874 came to New Westminster to practise medicine. Elected mayor (1877-78). Surgeon, Royal Columbian Hospital; superintendent, B.C. Insane Asylum. Elected MP

(1879). In 1881 appointed a Canadian senator. Sixteenth lieutenant-governor of B.C. (1897-1900). In July 1898 he dismissed the Turner ministry, and in 1900 the Semlin government. In June 1900 Sir Wilfrid Laurier dismissed Lt.-Gov. McInnes. In 1903 he was defeated as an independent candidate in a Vancouver by-election.

Robert Edward McKechnie *Surgeon, UBC chancellor,* b. April 25, 1861, Brockville, Ont.; d. May 24, 1944, Vancouver. Graduate of McGill U. in medicine. Spent 10 years in Nanaimo as surgeon with Vancouver Coal. In 1893 moved to Vancouver to practise surgery. First president, B.C. Medical Association. Member, Council of the College of Physicians and Surgeons of B.C. Consulting surgeon at Vancouver General Hospital. At its first convocation he was elected to the UBC senate; member of UBC board of governors; chancellor (1918-44). Companion of The Order of the British Empire, LL.D (McGill, UBC, 1925).

Larry (Norman Archibald MacRae) MacKenzie *International advisor, UBC president* b. Jan. 5, 1894, Pugwash, NS; d. Jan. 26, 1986, Vancouver. Worked on family farm (1909-13). Spent WWI in active service with military honors. Studied at Dalhousie U.; later Harvard and Cambridge in international law. Called to Nova Scotia bar (1926). Taught law at U of T (1926-39). Worldwide influence with organizations such as the League of Nations and War Information Board (1943-45). President, UBC (1944-62). On the Massey Commission, he favored federal grants to universities (1949-51). LL.D (UBC, 1968). Biblio: *Lord of Point Grey: UBC's Larry MacKenzie* by P.B. Waite.

John (James Campbell) McLagan *Newspaper publisher* b. July 22, 1838, Strathardle, Scotland; d. April 11, 1901, Vancouver. He first managed the *Guelph Mercury*. Moved west, settling in Winnipeg. Late in 1883 moved to Victoria, dealt in real estate and filed stories with *Toronto Globe*. From 1884-88 operated *Victoria Times*. From September 1887 to his death he published *Vancouver Daily World*. In his last months, he managed the newspaper from his bed. Also wrote plays and novels. See SARA ANNE McLAGAN.

Sara Anne McLagan (née Maclure) *First Canadian woman newspaper editor* b. 1855, near Belfast, Ire.; d. March 20, 1924, Vancouver. Her father, Sergeant John C. Maclure, came to New Westminster in 1858 with the Royal Engineers. Sara was educated in New Westminster. A co-founder of *Vancouver Daily World* with husband JOHN C. McLAGAN. After his death she continued as president and editor, publishing with brother Frederick S. Maclure (b. c. 1864, New Westminster; d. Nov. 25, 1941, Iona Island).

Malcolm Alexander MacLean *First mayor of Vancouver, 1886-87* See Mayors of Vancouver.

Samuel Maclure *Architect* b. April 11, 1860, New

Westminster; d. Aug. 8, 1929, Victoria. Brother of SARA ANNE McLAGAN. Most gifted of early B.C. architects. Designed some 150 buildings either alone, with his firm or in partnership with others, including The Temple Building (Victoria, 1893); Murray House (403 St. George St., New Westminster, 1900). He designed many Shaughnessy Heights homes before WWI. Biblio: *Samuel Maclure: Architect* by Janet Bingham; *The Architecture of Samuel Maclure* by Leonard K. Eaton.

Harvey Reginald MacMillan *Lumber magnate* b. Sept. 9, 1885, Newmarket, Ont.; d. Feb. 9, 1976, Vancouver. Attended Ontario Agricultural College and Yale Forestry School. In 1908 hired as assistant inspector, Western Canada forest reserves, but first spent two years in a tuberculosis sanitorium. In 1912 named chief B.C. forester. During WWI worked for federal timber-trade commissioner and Imperial Munitions Board. In 1919, backed by British timber merchant Montague Meyer, launched H.R. MacMillan Export. His manager (later partner) was W.J. VANDUSEN. During WWII chair of Wartime Shipping Ltd., a Crown corporation. LL.D (UBC, 1950). Merged with Bloedel, Stewart and Welch (1951). Resigned as chair in 1956; resigned as a director in 1970. Biblio: *H.R.* by Ken Drushka.

Alexander Duncan McRae *Brigadier-general* b. Nov. 17, 1874, Glencoe, Ont.; d. June 26, 1946, Ottawa. After selling a busy insurance firm in Duluth, Minn. (1895-1903), he bought 500,000 acres (202,350 hectares) in Saskatchewan from the Dominion government at $1 an acre, making a healthy profit. Arrived in Vancouver (1907); pursued lumber and fishing interests. As director, supply and transportation, for Western Canada, went overseas with 2nd Division, Canadian Expeditionary Force (April 1915). Brigadier-general, Canadian forces. He ran ministry of information under Lord Beaverbrook. PC MP (1926-30). Canadian senator (1931). In 1941 national chair, Canadian War Services Fund. Entertained high society at Hycroft (1489 McRae). In WWII he donated Hycroft to the department of health and pensions, and moved to Qualicum Beach, B.C.

Hugh McRoberts *Sea Island pioneer* b. 1816, Belfast, Ire.; d. July 11, 1883, New Westminster. After immigrating to Australia, he searched for gold in California (1849) and Yale (1858). Joined William Powers, an Englishman, building a trail from Yale to Boston Bar. Also built the McRoberts Trail from New Westminster to Musqueam. First settler on McRoberts' Island (later Sea Island) in 1861. Preempted a claim on the north bank of the Fraser on April 24, 1862, and transferred two lots to his nephews, Samuel and FITZGERALD McCLEERY. Later sold his farm and moved to New Westminster, establishing a dairy business.

George McSpadden *First assessor* b. Nov. 3, 1865,

near Bryansford, Ire.; d. May 22, 1920, Vancouver. An experienced building contractor, he was Vancouver's first building inspector and city assessor. Systemized operations, added new departments and gathered statistics. In 1900 took a census of Vancouver's population (just over 23,000). Elected city alderman by a large majority. McSpadden St. and McSpadden Park are named for him.

M

James Edwin Machin *First librarian, Carnegie Library* b. c. 1833, Leamington, Eng.; d. March 31, 1910, Vancouver. From 1892-1910 he served as Vancouver's second librarian, after Mrs. George Pollay (1887-92). Eliza, his wife (b. c. 1855, Eng.; d. Dec. 22, 1916, Vancouver), and daughter also worked with him. Lacking funds, they "begged books from their friends in England and in this country." The new library (Main and Hastings) was sponsored by U.S. industrialist Andrew Carnegie. The cornerstone was laid March 29, 1902. Eliza was choir mother of Christ Church Cathedral for 27 years, a founder of the Operatic Society and supporter of local musicians. She introduced Christmas dinners at the Carnegie Library, a tradition that continues today at the Carnegie Community Centre.

Charles Cleaver Maddams *Mount Pleasant settler* b. 1855, Eng.; d. 1928. In 1883 moved to Victoria as steward for B.C.'s third lieutenant-governor, Clement Francis Cornwall. Later worked as assistant to HENRY ABBOTT, remaining with CPR to 1901. In 1888 bought two hectares on the south shore of False Creek in Mt. Pleasant; in 1890 built Maddams Ranch (aka Maddams Orchard). Because of nearby Chinese farms, he named the area China Creek. In 1923 transferred the ranch to the park board to cover his taxes. "The ranch was the pride of the community in its day." Maddams St. is named for him.

Hugh Crawford Magee *Pioneer Point Grey farmer* b. 1858, Ont.; d. Dec. 2, 1936, Vancouver. Came to Vancouver at 24. First farmer to settle the North Arm of the Fraser River, taking up land in Point Grey in 1867. Associated with mining ventures, at one time in partnership with Dr. R.E. McKECHNIE. Magee Secondary School is named for him.

Edmond Maillard *Fraser Mills confessor* d. August 3, 1966, Ste.-Foy-Les-Lyon, France. On Sept. 22, 1909, some 30 families (110 people) left Montreal by special CPR train to work in Fraser Mills in the southwestern part of Coquitlam. Father Maillard, a young Roman Catholic Oblate from France, arrived with them. Lived in baggage cars for two weeks while homes were built by new employers. First service held in a room above a store. Opened Our Lady of Lourdes Church on Dec. 10, 1910. When it burned down on Feb. 26, 1912, he rebuilt it. After he left the community in

1912, the post office adopted the name Maillardville (1913). In 1937 he returned to France to teach at a Franco-Canadian College in Rhone.

W. H. Malkin *Mayor of Vancouver, 1929-30* See Mayors of Vancouver.

Mandrake the Magician (Leon Mandrake) *Entertainer* b. April 11, 1911, New Westminster; d. Jan. 28, 1993, Surrey. Raised in New Westminster. At eight performed at Edison vaudeville theatre and New Westminster's Civic National Exhibition. From 1927 toured North America with his magic show. By the 1940s he was a top box-office draw. Married Velvet, his wife and partner/assistant, in Chicago in 1947. Toured worldwide, setting the trend for large, elaborate illusion shows; was the first magician to play nightclubs. In the 1950s he had two TV series and performed on the CBC. Lectured at Canadian universities in the 1970s. Inspired a cartoon strip, *Mandrake the Magician*.

Joseph Mannion *Unofficial first mayor of Vancouver* b. March 17, 1839, County Mayo, Ire.; d. Sept. 12, 1918, Lillooet, B.C. Left priestly studies to hunt for gold in the Cariboo, arriving in New Westminster on April 19, 1862. From 1864 he worked as a stevedore, telegraph company employee, miner and logger. In 1874 bought a half interest in the Granville Hotel (later sole proprietor). In 1881 his two sons drowned when their canoe was swamped on English Bay. Known as "the mayor of Granville" before the first official mayor, M.A. MacLEAN, was elected. Elected alderman (1888) but resigned and moved to 65 hectares on Bowen Island. "Settled into the life of a country squire."

Charles (Carlos) Marega *First professional B.C. sculptor* b. Sept. 24, 1871, Genoa, Italy; d. March 27, 1939, Vancouver. Arrived in Vancouver in 1909. In addition to sculpting, he also taught art. His work can still be seen in Vancouver, including a statue of Captain GEORGE VANCOUVER at City Hall and twin lions at the south end of Lions Gate Bridge. See profile of Charles Marega in this book.

Richard Marpole *CPR executive* b. Oct. 8, 1850, Wales; d. June 8, 1920, Vancouver. At age 16 he joined Northern Railway of Canada. From 1881 he moved up in CPR ranks as a contractor, assistant manager of construction, and superintendent, construction and operation. Transferred to Pacific Division (1886) and was named general superintendent (1897-1907); B.C. general executive assistant (1914). Vice president, Esquimalt and Nanaimo Railway. He was manager when the first passenger trains crossed Canada and the first in North America to prepare timetables based on a 24-hour system. Member of the posse to catch BILL MINER (May 14, 1906) after Miner's second train robbery. Marpole is named for him.

Leonard Charles Marsh *Social scientist* b. Sept. 24, 1906, London, Eng.; d. May 10, 1982, Vancouver. He attended London School of Economics, then

moved to Canada to direct a social science research program at McGill (1930-41). Supported League for Social Reconstruction. A writer and editor, he contributed to the League's influential book, *Social Planning for Canada* (1935). His book *Canadians In and Out of Work* (1940) studied social class. Research advisor, federal committee on post-war reconstruction (1941-44). Published Report on Social Security for Canada (1943). His programs led to today's social security system. Welfare adviser to UN (1944-46); director of research, UBC school of social work (1948-64); professor, educational sociology (1964-72). Retired in 1973.

"Fighting Joe" (Joseph) Martin *Premier* b. Sept. 24, 1852, Milton, Ont.; d. March 2, 1923, Vancouver. Worked as a telegraph operator and teacher, then practised law. In 1883 elected as Manitoba MLA; minister of education and attorney-general. In 1893, elected MP. Practised law in Vancouver (1897), becoming one of the city's largest landowners. Elected B.C. MLA (1898). After Premier Semlin was forced to resign by Lt.-Gov. THOMAS R. MCINNES in February 1900, Joe became acting premier, with six supporters. Four months later he was defeated by James Dunsmuir. Moved to England (1908); elected to British House of Commons (1910). Back in Vancouver, he failed to get elected as Asiatic Exclusion League candidate, to become mayor, and to start an evening paper (1914-22).

James Skitt Matthews *Archivist* See profile.

Ranjit Mattu *Star athlete* b. July 17, 1916, Jullunder, Punjab, India; d. March 23, 1989, Malibu, Calif. He came to Vancouver in 1924. Graduated with a BA from UBC as a star athlete in rugby as well as football, "the Gretsky of his time." He coached high school football and later jr. football (to 1949). His team, the Vancouver Blue Bombers, were the Dominion Champions of 1947, the first such championship won by Vancouver. Joined his father's firm, Best Fuels; later established various business interests including Ocean City Sawmills (renamed Hem-fir Lumber) on Mitchell Island. A community leader, he was Indian Prime Minister Pandit Nehru's organizer and host when Nehru visited B.C. in 1949.

Thomas Hayton Mawson *English landscape architect* b. May 5, 1861, Scorten, Eng.; d. 1933. An influential landscape theorist, he taught at Liverpool University. Travelling across North America on a speaking tour, he was given several commissions in Vancouver. Offered designs for reclamation of Coal Harbour and Stanley Park (1912-13). His Vancouver office, T.H. Mawson and Sons, located in the Rogers Building in 1914, was represented by son John W. Mawson. Famous clients included Andrew Carnegie and Cecil Rhodes. Biblio: *The Life and Work of an English Landscape*

Architect.

George Ritchie Maxwell *Presbyterian cleric, labor party founder* b. Jan. 11, 1857, Stonehouse, Scotland; d. Nov. 17, 1902, Vancouver. Arrived in Vancouver in 1890 to take over first Presbyterian church. A "social gospel" clergyman, he helped create the Nationalist Party, B.C.'s first labor party, in 1894. Served as Liberal-Labor MP for Burrard riding from 1896 until his death.

Susanna Gertrude Clarke Mellon *Supporter of arts and worthy causes* b. c. 1844, London, Eng.; d. June 17, 1926, Vancouver. Family moved to Ontario in 1851. She convinced her husband, Captain Henry Augustus Mellon (b. May 22, 1840, Nottingham, Eng.), to move from Winnipeg to B.C. in 1886, arriving just after the Great Fire of June 13. Fundraiser for local arts groups; founder, Historical and Scientific Society (April 3, 1894). In 1901 they "pressed that Lord Strathcona be asked to help provide a museum building." The Carnegie Library building was proposed as an alternate site. Member of the PAULINE JOHNSON Fund committee to publish her works.

Maxie (Maximilian) Michaud *Hotelier, Francophone pioneer* b. c. 1838-40, Kamarouska, Que.; d. Dec. 22, 1882, Hastings Townsite. Walked across Canada to the Pacific. He bought the Brighton Hotel (located at the foot of today's Windermere St. in Vancouver) in March 1869 from OLIVER HOCKING. He changed name to Hastings Hotel (1871), promising "Travellers can be accommodated at all hours with good beds and meals. A good stock of liquors and cigars." It became a popular spot with holidayers from New Westminster. He was "not exactly married" to his companion, Frisadie, who "charms all sojourners at the 'End of the Road.'"

George Miller *Mayor of Vancouver, 1937-38* See Mayors of Vancouver.

Jonathan Miller III *Vancouver's first postmaster* b. Sept. 5, 1834, Middlesex, Ont.; d. Dec. 6, 1913, Vancouver. Came to B.C. from Ontario in 1862. Settled in New Westminster, "engaged in mercantile pursuits," later logging in 1865. About 1871 hired as tax collector/constable of Granville. Lived in Gaolers's Mews police station (Water and Carrall) until 1886, a small government-built log cottage facing Cordova. Two small cells had doors but no locks. On May 3, 1886, he became postmaster for the newly incorporated City of Vancouver, a position he held to 1909.

Bill Miner ("The Grey Fox," alias Bill Edwards) *Train robber* b. 1842 or 1847, Bowling Green, Kentucky; d. Sept. 2, 1913, Georgia State Penitentiary. Pulled Canada's first train robbery, in Silverdale, 64 kilometres east of Vancouver on Sept. 10, 1904. Described by Pinkerton Detective Agency as a "master criminal of the American West," he spent 28 years in San Quentin. After a second train robbery (May 8, 1906), in Ducks near Kamloops, he received a life sentence in the B.C. Penitentiary but escaped Aug. 9, 1907. On Feb. 24, 1911, he attempted the first train robbery in Georgia, was caught, convicted and died in prison. Called "the gentleman robber."

Alexander Mitchell *First farmer in Greater Vancouver* b. May 8, 1847, Masham County, Que.; d. May 16, 1931, Mitchell Island, B.C. Arrived in B.C. in April 1877; his wife and two small children arrived shortly after. Settled in Moodyville, later took out squatter's rights as a pioneer resident of Richmond's small Mitchell Island. Active in municipal politics, he represented Ward 3 of South Vancouver as councillor. Secretary of the school board, later councillor for Richmond's Ward 5. Promoted the Fraser Ave. bridge. His second wife also died, but his third wife survived him.

Alex (Alexander) Mitchell *Owner, Stanley Park stables* b. 1866, Bruce County, Ont.: d. April 1, 1948, Vancouver. Arrived in Vancouver on May 24, 1887. Hired as warehouseman and shipping clerk by Thomas Dunn and Co., a wholesale retail hardware store at 8 Cordova. In 1899 decided to start his own business. Bought Stanley Park Stables (Seymour and Dunsmuir), the taxi business of his day, with 86 horses, 40 rigs, seven hacks and two tallyhos. WWI and the popularity of the automobile led to bankruptcy in 1914. Worked for an ice delivery company in management until retirement.

Masumi Mitsui *WWI hero* b. Oct. 7, 1887, Japan; d. April 22, 1987, Vancouver. One of 196 local Japanese residents who volunteered for WWI. Of these, 145 men were killed or wounded. After leading his troop up Vimy Ridge, Sergeant Mitsui received the Military Medal for Bravery (April 1917), one of 12 Japanese to receive the honor in WWI. In 1942 his family was moved from their seven-hectare Port Coquitlam chicken farm and new house to an internment camp in Greenwood, B.C. In Aug. 1985 Masumi was the honored guest at the relighting of the lantern in the Japanese Canadian War Memorial (built in 1925) in Stanley Park. The light was extinguished during the Pacific war.

Masajiro Miyazaki *Doctor, community activist* b. Nov. 24, 1899, Minamiaoyanaji-Mura, Inukamigun (now Hikone City), Japan; d. July 24, 1984, Kamloops, B.C. Arrived in Vancouver on June 29, 1913. Took part in UBC's Great Trek (Oct. 22, 1922). Practised medicine in Vancouver until 1942 internment in Bridge River-Lillooet area. Served as doctor for 1,000 internees. In 1945 Lillooet petitioned for his release to replace its deceased doctor. The Miyazakis rented the main floor of Lillooet's historic Casper Phair home. After Japanese residents were legally able to buy property, he bought the house. Awarded Scouting's Medal of Merit (1970) and Order of Canada (1977). In 1983 he donated the Phair house as a heritage site. Biblio: *My Sixty Years in Canada*.

Richard Clement Moody *Engineer, colonel* b. Feb. 13, 1813, St. Anne's Garrison, Barbados; d. March 31, 1887, Bournemouth, Eng. Graduate of Royal Military Academy. Arrived in B.C. in Jan. 1859, in command of Columbia Detachment of Royal Engineers to lay out townsites, roads, etc. Chose New Westminster as site for the capital. Worked on major trails and Cariboo Rd. Owned Mayfield, a model farm near New Westminster. Established townsite at Hastings (later absorbed into Vancouver). Returned to England on Nov. 11, 1863, when his detachment was recalled.

Sew (Sewell Prescott) Moody *Sawmill owner* b. c. 1835, Hartland, Maine; d. Nov. 4, 1875, at sea, near Victoria. "The father of North Vancouver." After logging near New Westminster, he bought a Burrard Inlet sawmill on the North Shore in 1865, around which sprang up the community of Moodyville. Drowned when SS *Pacific* sank off Victoria on its way to San Francisco. "Sewell Moody was not an ostentatious man, to everyone, great and small, he was simply Sew Moody." His only son was also Sewell Prescott Moody (b. c. 1874, Victoria; d. 1949, Victoria). See Captain JAMES VAN BRAMER.

William Moore *Panoramic photographer* b. Dec. 11, 1887, Bryson, Que.; d. Oct. 30, 1963, Burnaby. Came to Vancouver in 1912 from Banff, where he worked with photographer Byron Harmon. Set up a studio at home on E. 21st; later on Sophia. One of two panoramic photographers in the city, he specialized in photos 20 centimetres high and up to 2.5 metres wide. Took hundreds of views (1913-53) including English Bay, sporting events and city scapes. From 1920-46 he photographed annual New Westminster May Day celebrations. His camera was a Kodak No. 8 Cirkut. He donated 370 Cirkut images to the Vancouver City Archives.

Alan Morley *Journalist* b. Aug. 15, 1905, Vancouver; d. Oct. 6, 1982, North Vancouver. Born in Vancouver but grew up in Armstrong and Penticton. First worked with father Harry, manager of the Sally Dam, in the Kettle Valley, as mucker and miner. Put himself through UBC in early 1930s writing for the *Vancouver Sun*. Wrote for 21 other newspapers before returning to the *Sun* in 1957 until retirement in 1970. Author of *Vancouver, From Milltown to Metropolis* (1961).

John Morton *Pioneer settler* b. April 16, 1834, Lindley, Eng.; d. April 18, 1912, Vancouver. Landed at English Bay on Oct. 16, 1862, lured by tales of rich coal deposits. Instead found "a forest of husky timber standing along Burrard Inlet." Built a brickyard with partners SAMUEL BRIGHOUSE and William Hailstone (b. May 18, 1830, Bridlington, Eng.; d. July 12, 1912, Newcastle-on-Tyne, Eng.), together derisively nicknamed "The Three Green-horns." Used local clay, making him the first resident to manufacture a product in the area. The factory soon closed. With partners bought 550 acres (222.5 hectares) in what is now the West End, at $1 an acre. When the CPR arrived, "the Morton Ranch" proved a bonanza. On his death his estate was worth $700,000.

Ruth Morton (née Mount) *Early settler* b. March 17, 1848, Yorkshire, Eng.; d. Dec. 14, 1939, Vancouver. Arrived in 1884 to marry JOHN MORTON, was the first white woman to settle in the area. When she arrived in New Westminster, the Burrard Inlet site of John Morton's business activities was an almost untracked wilderness. Their first home was on English Bay. The Ruth Morton Memorial Baptist Church was named for her.

Don (Walter Alfred Donald) Munday *Mountaineer* b. March 16, 1890, Portage la Prairie, Man.; d. June 12, 1950, Vancouver. Climbed more B.C. mountains than any other mountaineer in his 40-year career. A war hero, he was wounded in his left arm in WWI and permanently disabled. He met his equally daring wife PHYLLIS MUNDAY scaling a peak. Married in 1920. They discovered Mt. Waddington, B.C.'s highest peak, in 1923, and made four attempts to reach the top, coming within 18 metres in 1926. Took part in many mountain rescue operations. Member, Alpine Club of Canada. President, Canadian Authors Association. His books include *The Unknown Mountain*.

Phyllis Munday (née James) *Mountaineer* b. 1895, Sri Lanka; d. April 11, 1990, Nanaimo, B.C. Came to Vancouver in 1901; climbed Grouse Mountain at 10. With husband DON MUNDAY she did early backbreaking explorations of B.C. coastal mountains. Made many first ascents of highest peaks in Coast Range. First woman to climb Mt. Robson (1924). A Girl Guider (1910-45), she began Vancouver's first company (1910) with her mother. In 1924 founded the Lone Guides for girls in isolated areas. After retiring, named B.C.'s woodcraft and nature advisor. Awarded Bronze Cross for carrying an injured man down Grouse Mountain. LL.D (U of Victoria); member, Order of Canada (1975).

William George Murrin *B.C. Electric Railway president* b. Aug. 27, 1875, London, Eng.; d. July 25, 1964, Vancouver. Worked with City of London Electric Lighting (1894-1901); London United Tramways (1901-03). Joined B.C. Electric Railway in 1913 as mechanical superintendent; president (1929-46). Active in the community, he received the Silver Acorn from the Greater Vancouver and District Boy Scout Council and was a life member of the Salvation Army (1958). A governor of UBC; LL.D (1957). President, Vancouver Art Gallery Assoc., Vancouver Little Theatre Assoc.; member, Vancouver Symphony Society.

N

Jack Manzo Nagano *Pioneer Japanese immigrant* b. March 27, 1855, Kuchinotsu (near Nagasaki), Japan; d. May 21, 1924, Kuchinotsu. At 23 worked as a cabin boy from Nagasaki to New Westminster on a British ship, arriving in 1877 as the first Japanese immigrant in B.C. and possibly in Canada. Fished for salmon on the Fraser and later worked on the Gastown docks. Travelled to and from Japan several times. Ran businesses in Yokohama, Seattle and Victoria. Pursued several ventures, including a hotel for Japanese immigrants. Prospered by exporting salted salmon. In 1977 a mountain in Rivers Inlet area was named for him in honor of the Japanese Canadian centennial.

Tadaichi Nagao *Court interpreter* b. c. 1866, Tokyo, Japan; d. January 1950, New Denver, B.C. After studying in San Francisco, he arrived in Vancouver in 1889, the 12th Japanese national to settle in Vancouver. Worked in a Hastings sawmill, Steveston cannery, and sold sundries in the old Hotel Vancouver. By 1893 there were some 250 Japanese in the city, many brought in by Dunsmuir Coal of Nanaimo. From 1900-07 Japanese immigration increased, including some families. Tadaichi helped them find jobs with the CPR and Hastings Mill. Employed as a court interpreter for 40 years. In WWII he relocated to New Denver, where he died after 66 years in Canada. "A student and philosopher, he made his life work the Canadianization of the Japanese in Canada."

Edward Gilbert Nahanee *Longshoreman, Native Brotherhood of B.C. organizer* b. April 9, 1897, Moodyville, B.C.; d. April 3, 1989, North Vancouver. His heritage was Kanaka (Hawaiian aboriginal) and Squamish native. His grandfather, Joe Nahano (d. c. 1874, Burrard Inlet), arrived in Oregon in 1842 to work for the Hudson's Bay Co., eventually migrating to B.C., where he married Squamish native Mary Seeamia. His father, longshoreman William Nahanee Sr. (b. March 19, 1873, Kanaka Ranch at the foot of today's Denman St.; d. Dec. 10, 1946, North Vancouver), also married a Squamish wife, Cecilia. Ed, famed as a pitcher for the North Shore Indians baseball team, worked on the docks from age 14. Active in the longshoreman's union after WWI until violent clashes with RCMP and company police in 1923 broke the union. From 1946 served as business agent for the Native Brotherhood of B.C. Awarded Canada Confederation Medal (1967) for his work with native people. His brother, William Nahanee Jr. (b. July 26, 1903, Moodyville; d. March 19, 1987, North Vancouver,) was the first employee of the Squamish Indian Band and active in the Totem Athletic Club. There are currently 600 descendants of Joe and Mary Nahano. Biblio: *Kanaka: The Untold Story of Hawaiian Pioneers in British Columbia* by Tom Koppel.

José Maria Narvaez *Spanish explorer* b. 1756, Spain; d. 1840 or later, possibly Guadalajara, Mexico. In 1791 José, a master sailor with a Spanish expedition led by Francisco Elisa, explored the coast in the *Santa Saturnina*, the first white man known to have explored the Strait of Georgia. In July 1791, anchored near today's Point Grey (which he named Islas de Langara, thinking it was an island), and mapped the shoreline. His crew were Mexican Indians; a small Musqueam party traded with the ship. Running out of food, he left without finding the Fraser or exploring Burrard Inlet. Narvaez Bay, on the east point of Saturna Island, is named for him.

Thomas Fletcher Neelands *Mayor of Vancouver, 1902-03* See Mayors of Vancouver.

Hugh Nelson *Sawmill manager, lieutenant-governor* b. May 25, 1830, Larne, Ire.; d. March 3, 1893, London, Eng. Came to B.C. during 1858 Gold Rush as agent for Wells Fargo. Elected MP (District of New Westminster) in B.C.'s first federal election. Voted out in 1874. Became a co-owner of the Moodyville Sawmill in 1875, taking over on partner SEW MOODY's death. Developed the milltown of Moodyville, entertaining at the "Big House." Named lieutenant-governor (1887). In 1890 appointed Dr. ISRAEL WOOD POWELL chancellor of UBC. Appointed to Canadian senate (1879). Nelson St. and the City of Nelson are named for him.

Walter Cameron Nichol *Publisher, lieutenant-governor* b. Oct. 15, 1866, Goderich, Ont.; d. Dec. 19, 1928, Victoria. In Toronto founded *Saturday Night* magazine (1887). Moved to Victoria in 1897 and edited the *Province*, which he transferred to Vancouver in 1898. Bought the paper and owned it until the 1920s. Lieutenant-governor of B.C. (1920-26), the only journalist so honored.

Nick (Leo) Nicholson *Sportscaster* b. 1896, Winnipeg, Man.; d. Oct. 28, 1947, Vancouver. Flew with WWI Royal Naval Air Service. In the early 1920s worked in Hollywood as an agent and director. Began sportscasting with LA stations KNX and KFI. Moved to Vancouver c. 1930. Gained attention with *Big Brother Bill*, a children's show. Announced thousands of athletic events, including six-day bicycle races at Athletic Park. Known as the "Voice of Box Lacrosse." In 1941 aired home games of Montreal Canadiens but returned to call the 1942 box lacrosse opener in Vancouver. In 1942 left broadcasting briefly as sports editor of the *News-Herald*. A tireless supporter of Christmas charity shows and war bond drives. Inducted into Builders Category, Canadian Lacrosse Hall of Fame (1967).

Percy Norman *Swimmer* b. March 14, 1904, New Westminster; d. May 26, 1957, Vancouver. Started career as a promising marathon swimmer but chose to coach instead. Considered Canada's top swimming and diving coach for many years.

Coached the 1936 Canadian Olympic and 1954 British Empire and Commonwealth Games swim teams, winning six medals. Head coach, Vancouver Amateur Swim Club at Crystal Pool (1931-55). Inducted into B.C. Sports Hall of Fame (1967). Many of his swimmers are members of the B.C. Sports Hall of Fame. In 1960 the Vancouver park board named a pool for him.

O

Phillip Oben *Storekeeper* b. Nov. 15, 1856, St. Saviour's Parish, Jersey Channel, Eng.; d. July 4, 1933, Vancouver. Early settler in the Renfrew-Collingwood area of South Vancouver. Opened the area's first store, close to Central Park. In 1890 cleared the forest of the western section of the West End. Oben St. is named for him.

Edward Faraday Odlum *Scientist* b. Nov. 27, 1850, Tullamore, Ont.; d. May 4, 1935, Vancouver. Grew up on a farm. Taught in Ontario and Japan; president of a Tokyo college with 600 students (1886-89). Came to Vancouver (April 15, 1889). Built first electric arc light (used for football games) and first public telephone. An extensive landowner. In 1892 elected Vancouver alderman. From 1903-04 toured Britain lecturing on immigration. Re-elected alderman on return. Studied ethnology, botany and geology in central and northern Europe (1905). Wrote *A History of British Columbia* (1906). Supported the British Israelite movement. President, Arts and Science Association of Vancouver. Father of VICTOR ODLUM.

Victor Wentworth Odlum *Soldier, publisher* b. Oct. 21, 1880, Cobourg, Ont.; d. April 4, 1971, Vancouver. Arrived in Vancouver in 1889 with father, EDWARD ODLUM. Served in the Boer War and WWI. Between wars, worked as a journalist with several newspapers, including the *Vancouver Daily Star* as editor-in-chief. MLA (1924-28). *Star* publisher (1924-32). In the late 1930s served on CBC board. A brigadier-general, he commanded the 2nd Canadian Division (1940-41). Released as high commissioner to Australia and Canada's first ambassador to China (1943-46). Ambassador to Turkey (1947-52). LL.D (UBC, 1954). Publisher (1964) of short-lived *Vancouver Times*.

Paul L. (Tsunenojo) Okamura *Photographer* b. 1865, Japan; d. March 26, 1937, New Westminster. Arrived in Vancouver in 1891, moved to New Westminster. In 1895 he was listed as a professor of drawing at St. Louis College, New Westminster, a boy's school founded by the Oblate fathers (1865). He may have began his photography career as an amateur before 1900. Active as an artist, teacher and photographer. Biblio: *Camera workers: The B.C. Photographers Directory, 1858-1900* by David Mattison.

John Oliver *Premier* b. July 31, 1856, Hartington, Eng.; d. Aug. 17, 1927, Victoria. Moved to Ontario in 1870; to B.C. in 1877 to farm in Delta.

After serving in local politics, elected Lib. MLA (1900). Leader of the opposition, losing his seat in 1909. Re-elected in the sweeping 1916 Liberal victory; appointed minister of agriculture and railways. On Premier Harlan Brewster's death in 1918, "Honest John" became premier. Governed B.C. during the economic stagnation of the early 1920s. Promoted Okanagan orchards. Oliver, B.C., and Vancouver's John Oliver High School are named for him. Died in office.

David Oppenheimer *Mayor of Vancouver, 1888-91* See Mayors of Vancouver.

Ike (Isaac Cella) Oppenheimer *Businessman* b. 1835, Frankfort-on-the-Rhine, Blieskastel, Bavaria; d. Dec. 21, 1922, Spokane, Wash. Brother and partner of DAVID OPPENHEIMER. Left Germany in 1848 for U.S. gold fields with brothers Godfrey, Charles and David. In 1856 opened a Yale dry goods business and later another in Barkerville. In the fall of 1885 he moved to Vancouver. In 1886 opened a wholesale grocery warehouse in the Oppenheimer Bros. Building (Powell and Columbia), now owned by musician Bryan Adams. It became B.C.'s largest business of its type. Alderman, 1887-89. For years the courtly Oppenheimer brothers lived in the old Hotel Vancouver. Left Vancouver in 1901 to travel in Europe and U.S. Later lived with eldest son, Dr. Sidney Oppenheimer, in Spokane, Wash.

William Reid Owen *Mayor of Vancouver, 1924* See Mayors of Vancouver.

P

Mary Pack *Arthritis campaigner* b. Oct. 9, 1904, Ampthill, Eng.; d. May 11, 1992, Vancouver. The "angel of mobility" devoted her life to arthritis and rheumatism care and research. A teacher of physically handicapped children for the Vancouver school board. In 1945, dismayed by lack of services, she started the B.C. Spastic Society, which led to the B.C. Division of the Canadian Arthritis and Rheumatism Society (Jan. 1948), of which she was executive secretary. Received Queen's Coronation Medal (1953), Post No. 2 Native Sons of B.C. Good Citizen Award (1956), Order of Canada, LL.D (UBC, 1974). In 1990 the Mary Pack-Arthritis Society Chair in Rheumatology was established at UBC.

Peter Basil Pantages *Polar Bear Club founder* b. Nov. 15, 1901, Andros, Greece; d. May 4, 1971, Hawaii. Ran the Peter Pan Cafe with his three brothers from the early 1920s. Founder (1920) and director (for 51 years) of the Polar Bear swimming club, promoting New Year's Day outdoor swimming. Member, Canadian Restaurant Association. An ardent fisherman; member of Canadian Wildlife Association and Royal Lifeguard Association. He swam every day, no matter where he travelled. Son Basil remains president of the Polar Bear Club.

Lorne Parton *Journalist* b. May 23, 1931, New Westminster; d. Jan. 26, 1995, Vancouver. After service in the Royal Canadian Air Force, he joined the *Province* as a reporter and columnist (1952-89) until he suffered a major stroke. A sensitive writer with a broad knowledge of cars, planes, the film industry and Vancouver's power elite, he was noted for his careful use of language. A peer of fellow journalists JACK WASSERMAN, Jack Webster, Allan Fotheringham and Pierre Berton, "he moved with ease among politicians and paupers." Remembered for his rapier wit. Married (1974-95) to journalist Nicole Parton .

Florence Paterson *Actress* b. Nov. 3, 1927, St. John's, Nfld.; d. July 23, 1995, Vancouver. A child actor in radio skits written by her father. Performed in amateur theatre in St. John's, winning five best actress awards. Began acting professionally at 44 with Halifax's Neptune Theatre, playing memorable roles such as Mary Mercer in *Leaving Home* and "the missus" in *John and the Missus*. Starred in the CBC series *Backstretch* and in *Little Women* opposite Susan Sarandon. In 1989 Flo and husband John moved to Vancouver to be near family. Her last Vancouver role was in *Mother Miracle* (Arts Club Theatre, 1994). Received Arts Council Life Achievement Award. "One was always astonished by the honesty, the humor, the intensity and humanity she invested in every character she played."

Frank Alexis Patrick *Hockey player, builder* b. Dec. 21, 1885, Ottawa, Ont.; d. June 29, 1960, Vancouver. Moved to Nelson, B.C., with family in 1909. With brother Lester, he brought professional hockey to the West Coast. The brothers built the first two artificial ice rinks in Canada. See LESTER PATRICK and LYNN PATRICK. Inducted into B.C. Sports Hall of Fame (1966) and Canadian Sports Hall of Fame.

Lester (Curtis Lester) Patrick *Hockey player, builder* b. Dec. 30, 1883, Drummondville, Que., d. June 1, 1960, Victoria. With brother FRANK PATRICK, he brought professional hockey to the West Coast, constructed indoor ice rinks and developed NHL rules, including unrestricted passing in the central zone, the blue line and the penalty shot. Conceived the play-off series. Continued to influence NHL hockey as manager of New York Rangers (1926-39) and as coach in 1946. Inducted into B.C. Sports Hall of Fame (1966) and Canadian Sports Hall of Fame.

Lynn (Joseph Lynn) Patrick *Hockey player* b. Feb. 3, 1912, Victoria; d. Jan. 26, 1980, St. Louis, Miss. Member of 1933 Canadian Championship basketball team, the Victoria Blue Ribbons. In 1934 signed with Winnipeg Blue Bombers. In the first game he set season's record with 68-yard touchdown reception. In 1943 he joined New York Rangers, coached by father LESTER PATRICK, scor-

---

Orpheum   Home to the Vancouver Symphony Orchestra, the Orpheum is a beautifully restored 2,780-seat heritage theatre operated by Vancouver Civic Theatres, a department of the City of Vancouver. Superb acoustics make it the venue of choice for many musical and celebrity performances, while its magnificent architecture makes it a favorite location for film shoots. Home of the B.C. Entertainment Hall of Fame, the Orpheum boasts Starwalk, plaques in the sidewalk along Granville, and Starwall, a photo gallery of members.

ing 13 goals in his first season. During 10 years with the Rangers, he scored 145 goals, 190 assists in 455 games. Twice led the team in scoring and played with them to a 1940 Stanley Cup win. Coached and managed the Boston Bruins (1950-55). General manager, St. Louis Blues (1967), taking team to Stanley Cup play-offs in their first three seasons. Retired in 1977 as vice president, St. Louis Hockey Club. Inducted into B.C. Sports Hall of Fame (1968).

Charlie Pawlett *Band leader* b. 1902, Nanaimo, B.C.; d. Aug. 21, 1981, Vancouver. Began playing trumpet and violin in Vancouver clubs in 1920s; from 1936-39, as Commodore Ballroom band leader, his shows were broadcast on CJOR radio. The weekly music program opened with "And now Charlie Pawlett plays for you." Played in Royal Canadian Air Force band during WWII. Played at The Strand Theatre, Howden Ballroom, Arcadian Ballroom and Second Narrows Supper Club. He was playing with Jackie Borne in Peter Pan Ballroom when he retired at 68 years of age.

Torchy (William John) Peden *Cyclist* b. April 16, 1905, Victoria; d. Jan. 26, 1980, Northbrook, Ill. A "flame-haired youth that led the pack like a torch," he was famed during the Depression as "a six-day immortal" bicycle racer, winning Vancouver's first such event in 1931. With brother James Douglas Peden, won races across North America, setting a world record of 38 victories that lasted 28 years. Brother Ernie and cousin Rusty also raced. A crowd pleaser, he received a gold-plated bicycle in honor of his years aboard his CCM Flyer. Inducted into B.C. Sports Hall of Fame (1966) and Canadian Sports Hall of Fame.

Dr. Peter (Peter William Jepson-Young) *AIDS diarist* b. June 8, 1957, New Westminster; d. Nov. 15, 1992, Vancouver. A medical doctor, he began a weekly diary of his AIDS illness on CBC evening news in Sept. 1990. Until his death he continued to educate viewers, becoming Canada's leading HIV/AIDS spokesperson. The documentary of these diaries, *The Broadcast Tapes of Dr. Peter*, won many awards including an Academy Award nomination. The Dr. Peter AIDS Foundation (Box 63635, Capilano P.O., North Vancouver, B.C. V7P 1S3) continues his work to create a care centre for people with HIV/AIDS. Biblio: *Affirmation: The AIDS Odyssey of Dr. Peter* by Daniel Gawthrop.

Parm (Richard Parmater) Pettipiece *Labor union organizer, printer* b. 1875, Ont.; d. Jan. 10, 1960, Vancouver. Calgary's first newsboy, he began his printing career in 1890. In 1894 appointed editor and printer of *South Edmonton News*. In 1896 began a Revelstoke weekly but soon sold it and started the *Lardeau Eagle* in Ferguson, B.C. Came to Vancouver in 1901, joined Vancouver *Province* (1903-54). Editor, *B.C. Federationist*, a labor publication (1912-20). Served several terms on city

council. A director of Vancouver General Hospital for 27 years. Four-term president, International Typographical Union, founded in 1897.

Joe Philliponi (born Filippone) *Nightclub owner* b. Jan. 1, 1913, S. Italy; d. Sept. 18, 1983, Vancouver. Came to Vancouver in early 1930s and started Eagle-Time Delivery Systems (1934), later acquiring taxi cabs. Opened The Penthouse dinner club in 1945 at 1019 Seymour. Presented big names like Sammy Davis Jr. and George Burns. On Dec. 31, 1975, the club was closed by the vice squad; in 1977 he was charged with living off the avails of prostitution, but the conviction was quashed. His business licence was withdrawn but re-approved by city council in 1979. His murder in 1983 was linked to a robbery attempt. Some 800 "Supreme Court justices, businessmen and dancers" attended his funeral. The Penthouse is now managed by nephew Danny Filippone.

Elmore Philpott *Journalist, MP* b. May 1, 1896, Toronto, Ont.; d. Dec. 9, 1964, Penticton, B.C. A *Vancouver Sun* columnist (1943-61). Educated in Ontario, excelling in athletics. Crippled in WWI, he received the Military Cross. In 1922 entered journalism and also married. Writer and associate editor, *Toronto Globe*, for five years. Lost bids for provincial seat in West Hamilton, Ont. (1931, 1935). After a brief involvement with CCF, he returned to Liberal party. Moved to B.C. (1937), joined the *Vancouver Sun* (1943). Much travelled, he was an expert on China. In 1953 elected MP (Vancouver South); defeated in 1957. Continued writing for the *Sun* to 1961.

Thomas Plimley *Pioneer auto dealer* b. 1871, Walsall, Eng.; d. 1929, Victoria. Started a bicycle business in Victoria in 1893, the year he arrived from England. Sold the first car in Victoria, a tiller-steered Oldsmobile, in 1901. His wife Rhoda was the first woman driver in Victoria. Sold the Swift, Coventry, Humber, Rover, two-cylinder Buick and air-cooled Franklin. Plimley Motors on Howe was one of B.C.'s largest dealerships. His eldest son, Horace (Thomas Horace) Plimley (b. March 5, 1895, Victoria; d. March 21, 1985, Vancouver) opened a British car dealership in Vancouver (1936). From 1957-86 grandson Basil (b. June 21, 1924, Victoria) was one of the few third generation executives of a B.C. business. The Plimley companies closed in 1991, after 98 years.

Barney Potts *Entertainer* b. April 25, 1910, Hargate, Eng.; d. Feb. 6, 1993, Vancouver. Led bands in the 1930s in Vancouver nightspots such as Alma Academy, Happyland, Cinderella Ballroom, Quadra Club, Mandarin Gardens, Odyssey Room and the Second Narrows Supper Club. Performed in musicals in 1940s. Spent 12 years with Theatre Under the Stars. Accompanied by wife, singer Thora Anders (b. Sept. 12, 1913, Victoria), Potts played radio and TV (such as a Juliette special with

Robert Goulet), nightclubs and concert halls. Album: *Barney Potts, Live—Just Barely*, released in 1980. Inducted into Orpheum Theatre's Entertainment Hall of Fame (1990).

Israel Wood Powell *Surgeon, politician* b. April 27, 1836, Port Colburne, Ont.; d. Feb. 25, 1915, Victoria. Graduated in medicine (McGill, 1860). In 1862 moved to Colony of Vancouver Island; MLA (1863). In 1865 set up system of free public schools. Supported union of the colonies of Vancouver Island and B.C.; also entry of B.C. into Confederation, an unpopular stand that lost him the 1866 election. First Masonic Grand Master of the Grand Lodge of B.C., which opened Dec. 26, 1871, in Vancouver. Superintendent, Indian affairs (1872-90). Passed B.C. Medical Act (1886). In 1887 assisted in birth of Simon Fraser Tolmie, first B.C.-born premier. He named Vancouver streets for provinces from Columbia to Prince Edward. Donated site of first Vancouver city hall. Vancouver's Powell St. and town of Powell River named for him.

Bill (William Arthur) Pritchard *Labor activist* b. 1889, Salford, Eng., of Welsh parentage; d. Oct. 24, 1982, Los Angeles, Calif. Came to Vancouver in May 1911. Head, Vancouver Longshoremen's Union; executive member, Vancouver Trades and Labor Council; member, Socialist Party of Canada; organizer of One Big Union. After speaking at the Winnipeg Strike on June 12, 1919, he was arrested, found guilty of seditious conspiracy (March 28, 1920) and spent a year in jail. "His speech to the jury was a famous illustration of working-class oratory." Reeve of Burnaby (1930-32); president, Union of B.C. Municipalities. Ran as CCF MLA (1933) and PC MLA (1937) but lost both times, then worked as a baker. A musician, he organized youth orchestras, choirs and operatic productions.

Q

Juan Francisco de la Bodega Y Quadra (Y Mollinado) *Navigator* bap. June 3, 1743, Lima, Peru; d. March 26, 1794, Mexico City. His navigation studies began in Spain. Fought in Cuba, Honduras and Malvinas during the seven-year war between England and Spain. From 1775-79 made two expeditions from San Blas, Mexico. His final expedition, to Vancouver Island, began in 1792. He explored all the Northwest coast of North America. Catalogued more than 400 species of flora and fauna, studied aboriginal population and vocabulary. A friend of Captain GEORGE VANCOUVER, he suggested that Vancouver Island be named for him. Died of a seizure while walking on the street.

John Qualen *Actor* b. Dec. 8, 1899, Vancouver; d. Sept. 12, 1987, Los Angeles, Calif. His father, Olaus Peter Qualen, was pastor of First Scandinavian Church on Prior from 1898-1900. Spent his childhood travelling in Canada and U.S. Went into acting against his father's wishes. Performed in more than 120 films; his first was *Street Scene* (1931). Portrayed the father in three movies about the Dionne quintuplets. Noteworthy roles in *Casablanca, The Country Doctor, Reunion, Five of a Kind.* Played Muley in *The Grapes of Wrath.* His last movie was *Frasier, the Sensuous Lion,* made in 1973.

Joe Quoy *Jockey* b. 1866, New Westminster; d. Jan. 7, 1942, New Westminster. His parents came from California following the gold rush. Father ran a store in New Westminster, and owned several horses. The first horse races in New Westminster were held on Columbia, then unpaved. Joe was 12 years old and 40.8 kilograms when he launched his career. Rode at tracks in B.C., including Langley and Nanaimo, and in Seattle, Portland and Walla Walla. After putting on weight, he turned to sulky riding. Also supported lacrosse and rowing. Ran a small New Westminster tobacco store burnt out by the fire of 1898. He "announced 'Business as Usual' inside of two days."

R

Sam (S.W.) Randall *Thoroughbred race promoter* b. Sept. 25, 1882, near Toronto, Ont.; d. Nov. 2, 1961, Vancouver. In 1908 left Toronto for Vancouver with wife Sarah Catharine (d. 1951). Worked for Canada Pride Range, a home appliance company. Two friends got him involved in racing; he took over Exhibition Park in 1920. Operated Lansdowne Park on Lulu Island (1924-45); managed Victoria's Willows Track until 1947. For 35 years president and director, Ascot Jockey Club and Vancouver Thoroughbred Association. First Canadian track owner to adopt photo finish; first Western manager to install electric starting gate. Sold Lansdowne Park and Randall Building (535 W. Georgia) in 1945, reportedly for $1 million. Founder, S.W. Randall Plate. Inducted into B.C. and Canadian sports halls of fame.

William George Rathie *Mayor of Vancouver, 1963-66* See Mayors of Vancouver.

Francis Mawson Rattenbury *Architect* b. Oct. 11, 1867, Leeds, Eng.; d. March 28, 1935, Bournemouth, Eng. After arriving in B.C. in 1892, he designed Victoria's Legislature Buildings. In 1901 was named CPR western architect (to 1908). Designed Empress Hotel, Crystal Garden, banks and mansions and, in Vancouver, the Courthouse (now Vancouver Art Gallery). In 1924 his affair with Alma Victoria Clark Dolling Pakenham, who was 30 years younger, led to being outcast by polite society. The couple moved to England, where he was murdered. Alma and her lover George Stoner were charged. George was sentenced to life but released; Alma committed suicide. Biblio: *Rattenbury* by Terry Reksten.

James A. Raymur *Sawmill operator* b. 1823, Halifax, NS; d. July 31, 1882, Victoria. Captain Ray-

mur replaced Captain STAMP as manager of the Hastings Mill in 1869 and tried to transform it into a model town. Astounded by its filth, he set out to clean it up. "A devout, upright man, scornful of the excesses and haphazard ways of the pioneers." On Jan. 23, 1869, he built a meeting room and library for mill employees. In March its name was changed to The Hastings Literary Institute after Rear Admiral Hastings.

Bill (William) Rea Jr. *Radio pioneer* b. Dec. 27, 1908, Edmonton, Alta.; d. April 4, 1983, Santa Barbara, Calif. Began radio career in Edmonton with children's program; also aired a cooking program with his sister. In 1937 made commercial manager, CJAT, Trail, B.C. That same year came to Vancouver, worked at CJOR and CKMO (later CFUN). Founded CKNW in New Westminster (1944). Known for his five-musician hillbilly band as the leader, singer and bass player. At CKNW launched Roving Mike interview and the Orphans Fund. Moved to California in 1954 due to health problems. Sold CKNW in 1955. Later bought KBBO and KBBY-FM in Ventura, Calif.

James Inglis Reid *Butcher* b. 1874, Scotland; d. Nov. 16, 1952, Vancouver. Came to Vancouver in 1906. His meat store at 559 Granville (opened 1915) sold Scottish specialties, including haggis. In 1917 his employee, Scottish immigrant H. Nelson Menzies, introduced Reid's famous sausages. The shop's slogan was "We hae meat, that ye can eat." Charter member and president, Vancouver Scottish Society. In 1926 set up $25,000 fund for Vancouver General Hospital as memorial to his teenaged son Knox, who drowned off Bowen Island. The fund was used for therapeutic services for boys. His final estate was valued at $343,362.

Thomas Reid *Politician* b. April 18, 1886, Cambuslang, Scotland; d. Oct. 11, 1968, Surrey, B.C. Came to Canada in 1909 and farmed in Newton, B.C. Elected Surrey councillor (1922); Surrey reeve (1924-34). Twice head of Union of B.C. Municipalities. Lib. MP (New Westminster, 1930-49). Fought for railway freight reductions and natural resources issues. In 1937 helped form the Fisheries Commission, retiring as chair in 1967. Devoted to rehabilitation of Fraser salmon run. In 1958, as a result of his efforts, the run had its best year since 1905, with B.C. packing more than one million cases. Canada's only bagpipe-playing senator, appointed in 1949.

Henry Reifel *Brewer* b. April 2, 1869, Spiyer, Bavaria; d. Sept. 8, 1945, Vancouver. Emigrated to U.S. in 1886, brewing in Portland and San Francisco. Came to Vancouver in 1888, began a brewery at Main and 16th on Brewery Creek. By 1908 built Canadian Brewing and Malting (11th and Yew), later amalgamating several companies into Vancouver Breweries (sold to Carling O'Keefe). Developed technique to produce malt from rice

and opened Anglo-Japanese Brewing in Japan. He sold his brewing interests on retirement (1933). Donated property for the original Vancouver Art Gallery on Georgia.

George Conrad Reifel *Brewmaster* b. May 15, 1893, Vancouver; d. March 9, 1973, Vancouver. Eldest son of HENRY REIFEL, he was a New Westminster brewmaster and distiller. During Prohibition, he sailed his liquor down the coast. Brother Harry (Henry) Frederick (b. Dec. 3, 1895, Vancouver; d. July 20, 1958, Vancouver) raised purebred Jerseys in Milner, B.C. They built and owned Commodore Block on Granville (1929) and Vogue and Studio theatres in the 1940s. Grandson George Henry (b. July 22, 1922, Vancouver; d. March 7, 1992, Palm Desert, Calif.) farmed the 348-hectare Reifel Farms, and developed a way to grow sugar beet seed during WWII. In 1972 George Henry donated a portion of Reifel Island to the Crown to maintain the George C. Reifel Migratory Bird Sanctuary. George Henry's wife, Norma Eileen (b. Oct. 7, 1926, Calgary, Alta.; d. Oct. 20, 1995, Point Roberts, Wash.), led the fundraising campaign. Biblio: *Slow Boat on Rum Row* by Miles Fraser.

George Henry Richards *Sailor* b. 1820, England; d. c. 1898-1910, England. Joined the British Royal Navy in 1833. Served in the Opium Wars against China; in South America, Falkland Islands, New Zealand and Australia. Second commissioner in the British Boundary Commission (Pacific to the Rockies), and served as hydrographer on the coast (1856-63). From Dec. 23, 1860 to 1863, he surveyed the B.C. coast and Burrard Inlet aboard the HMS *Plumper* and HMS *Hecate.* Named geographical features such as False Creek. In 1859, after his engineer Francis Brockton found a vein of coal, he named the area Coal Harbour. Knighted in 1877. Retired as rear admiral in 1879.

Sydney John Risk *Theatre pioneer* b. May 26, 1908, Vancouver; d. Sept. 5, 1985, Vancouver. Early years spent training with Old Vic Theatre School (London, Eng.), and working as a professional actor. Returned to Canada (1938); taught drama at U. of Alberta and Banff School of Fine Arts, completing his MA at Cornell. Head of the Banff school for six summers. In 1946 founded Vancouver's Everyman Theatre, the first professional company in Western Canada, and toured Canadian plays from B.C. to Manitoba until 1953. From 1954 worked as field drama supervisor of UBC's extension department. Founder, Holiday Theatre for children (1952). "A charming man, absolutely dedicated to the theatre." The Sydney J. Risk Foundation, established in his honor, offers annual awards for acting, directing and playwriting.

John Robson *Newspaper editor, premier* b. March 14, 1824, Perth, Ont.; d. June 19, 1892, London, Eng. He arrived in B.C. in 1859; worked in the

Operated by Vancouver Civic Theatres, the modern 2,931-seat Queen Elizabeth Theatre is at the centre of Vancouver's entertainment district. Home to Vancouver Opera and Ballet B.C., it is also the favorite venue for spectacular musicals, feature ballets, multi-cultural shows and rock concerts. Next door, in the intimate 668-seat Vancouver Playhouse, The Vancouver Playhouse Theatre Company stages its six-play season, while the Friends of Chamber Music, Vancouver Recital Society and others present music, dance and more.

Cariboo. He was editor of the *British Columbian* in New Westminster (1861-66). Elected member, New Westminster council (1864); later president. New Westminster MLA (1867-70). In 1869 he moved to Victoria. In 1879 he returned to New Westminster's *Dominion Pacific Herald*, renaming it *British Columbian*. From 1882 began his political climb; elected premier in 1887. Re-elected in general elections (1886, 1890). A leading politician but ineffective as B.C. premier. Died in office.

Andrew Roddan *United Church minister* b. July 6, 1882, Hawick, Scotland; d. April 25, 1948, Vancouver. Served as lay minister in Gibraltar; later ordained in Winnipeg, serving in Saskatchewan, Winnipeg and Port Arthur. In 1929 appointed to Vancouver's First United Church, "the church of the open door." An early advocate of low rent and housing projects in the East End, welfare services for the poor and a fresh air camp on Gambier Island. Rev. Dr. Roddan's strong Scottish accent was heard weekly on Sunday radio sermons. A painter and charter member of the Vancouver Art Gallery, he assisted local artists. Exhibited his own works in 1942.

Gustav Roedde *Printer, bookbinder* b. Jan. 7, 1860, Gros Bodingin, Nordhausen, Germany; d. Nov. 24, 1930, Vancouver. Studied bookbinding before emigrating to Cleveland in 1881. Came to Vancouver via San Francisco and Victoria and opened the city's first bookbindery in 1886. Built homes in Vancouver and Horseshoe Bay, where he hosted an annual employees' picnic. His house in the West End was sold to H.W. Jeffreys in 1927, and later became a boarding house, the "Oehlerking Rooms." The City of Vancouver bought the building in 1966. As Roedde House, it is now used for community activities.

Benjamin Tingley Rogers *Sugar manufacturer* b. Oct. 21, 1865, Philadelphia, Penn.; d. June 17, 1918, Vancouver. Studied sugar chemistry, working in his father's New Orleans refinery until the latter's death in 1883. Worked in New York at the Havemeyer and Elder Refinery. In 1889, at age 24, moved to Vancouver, opening B.C. Sugar Refinery with $80,000 in investments from Sir WILLIAM VAN HORNE and associates. The small refinery, the first industry in B.C. not related to natural resources, produced its first sugar on March 26, 1890. The company is now Canada's largest sugar supplier, the third largest in North America. On June 1, 1995, it adopted its founder's name to become Rogers Sugar Ltd.

Jeremiah Rogers *Logger* b. 1818, NB; d. Oct. 24, 1878, Jericho Beach, Vancouver. Arrived in B.C. in 1860 to log at Port Alberni. Moved to English Bay in 1865 and established camp at Jericho Beach ("Jerry's Cove"). Logged most of Kitsilano designing much of his own equipment. Was probably the first to use mechanized power (instead of ani-

mals) to haul logs in B.C. Has been called "the greatest woodsman of them all."

Jonathan Rogers *Park commissioner, contractor* b. July 30, 1865, "Plas Onn," Denbighshire, Wales; d. Dec. 8, 1945, Vancouver. Born on a farm; learned English at 16. Arrived on the first passenger train to Vancouver, was first to step down onto platform (May 23, 1887). A painter, later builder and contractor. Built up more than 300 metres of frontage along Granville and Hastings including the Rogers Building (Granville and Pender, 1911). City of Vancouver alderman (1906, 1911). As a Vancouver park commissioner and chair (1908-43), he maintained Stanley Park in its natural state. Left $100,000 to develop new parks. An arts patron and world traveller, he loaned paintings from his collection to the Vancouver Art Gallery.

Charles Merle Rolston *Creator of Canada's first gas station* b. c. 1869. London. Ont.; d. March 1, 1947, Vancouver. After attending school in Ontario, he was hired by his uncle, H.E. Sharp, manager of Imperial Oil in Winnipeg. In 1896 he established the company's B.C. branch at the foot of Dunlevy. In 1902 JOHN HENDRY, manager of Hastings Sawmill, telephoned for gas for his new car. Rolston provided it in four-gallon (18-litre) cans, a first for the city. Around 1907 he opened the first gas station in Canada and perhaps the world (Smythe and Cambie), hiring another uncle, J.C. Rollston (sic), as the first attendant. An open shed of corrugated iron housed a 13-gallon (59-litre) kitchen hot water tank. To fill up, J.C. used a 3-metre length of garden hose with no nozzle. Charles remained with Imperial Oil for 40 years. JAMES S. MATTHEWS, his young assistant, was Vancouver's first archivist.

Tilly Jean Rolston *First Canadian woman with a cabinet post with portfolio* b. Feb. 23, 1887, Vancouver; d. Oct. 12, 1953, Vancouver. Entered politics as a PC MLA (1941). In 1951 sat as an independent for the remainder of the session. In the 1952 B.C. election in Vancouver-Port Grey she was elected as a Social Credit candidate and named education minister. Advocated education for every child in B.C. She "frequently blasted the government and said she would not be bound by party lines."

Gerald Arnold Rushton *Author, historian* b. July 20, 1898, Liverpool, Eng.; d. Nov. 12, 1993, Tsawwassen, B.C. His interest in marine history began in 1913 after winning a scholarship to Liverpool Collegiate School. Took officer training (1915-19), learning world trade shipping. Of the 12,000 students who trained with him, 9,000 died in WWI. After working with his father, a senior manager in Liverpool's J.H. Welsford Co., Gerald emigrated to B.C. in 1920 and joined a subsidiary, Union Steamship. His 38 years with the company and his knack for research made him a sought-after

expert on the coast's maritime heritage. Married MARGARET RUSHTON in 1930. Biblio: *Whistle up the Inlet*; *Echoes of the Whistle*.

Margaret Elinor Rushton *Holiday Theatre founder* b. Sept. 28, 1907, Wigan, Eng.; d. Aug. 13, 1977, White Rock. Came to Canada in 1930. Joined Vancouver Little Theatre, serving as president (1949-54). Her interest in children's theatre led her to Holiday Theatre, where she was tour coordinator. When Holiday Theatre became part of the Playhouse Theatre Centre, Margaret was public relations officer and organized B.C. tours. Member, Dominion Drama Festival national executive; president, B.C. Drama Association. Retired in 1971. Wife of GERALD RUSHTON.

Edward John Ryan *Builder* b. Sept. 7, 1884, Mille Isle, Que.; d. July 8, 1952, Vancouver. Entered construction in Vancouver (1909). His military career began in WWI with Irish Fusiliers 121st Battalion and 102nd Battalion in France and continued as the commander of Vancouver's Irish Fusiliers (1919-25). In 1919 he opened E.J. Ryan Contracting, one of Canada's largest contractors, in the Fairfield Building on Granville. Built the Hotel Vancouver (1926), Marine Building, Harrison Hot Springs Hotel, roads and bridges. In 1942 the firm was charged by the Vancouver Labor Council with importing underage boys from the prairies, paying them 18 cents an hour, then firing them without return fare. In 1943 the firm filed for bankruptcy.

S

Michael Saba *Silk merchant* b. c. 1861, Beirut, Lebanon; d. July 10, 1955, Los Angeles. The Saba family arrived in Nanaimo, B.C., in 1888, then moved to Vancouver. Mike opened Saba Brothers on W. Hastings with younger brother Alexander (b. c. April 7, 1881, Beirut, Lebanon; d. 1970, Vancouver) in November 1903. Two years later, the store moved to the 500 block Granville. Mike retired in 1921, selling his shares to Alex. By 1940 Saba's was the largest retail house in Western Canada specializing in silks. Although hit by shortages in WWII, the business survived. In 1942 there was a riot when 500 women stampeded the store to buy 300 pairs of nylon stockings (no one was hurt). In 1947 the company built a new five-storey $250,000 store at 622 Granville. In 1954 opened a Victoria outlet. Alex's three sons, Edgar, Clarence and Arnold, later managed the business.

Yip Sang (aka Yip Chun Tien) *Chinatown pioneer* b. Sept. 6, 1845, Canton, China; d. July 21, 1927, Vancouver. An orphan, he sailed at 19 by junk from Hong Kong to San Francisco's gold rush. Worked 17 years as dishwasher, cook, cigar maker. Came to Canada in 1881, settling in Vancouver's Chinatown. Established Wing Sang Co. (1888). In early 1900s, as a CPR contractor, supplied laborers in B.C. and Alberta and sold rail and

steam tickets. In 1889 built Wing Sang Building (51-67 E. Pender), the oldest standing structure in Chinatown. Married Lee Shee in China (1886). After her death, he remarried three times. His family included 19 sons and 4 daughters, and is now in its seventh generation in B.C. Father of KEW GHIM YIP and Yip Mow (b. 1890 on Chinese New Year, Canton, China; d. Nov. 17, 1951, Vancouver), who took over his father's business. Yip Mow chaired the Vancouver branch of the Chinese Nationalist League.' Chiang Kai-Shek sent a message of condolence on his death. Biblio: *Biography of Yip Sang* by the Yip Sang Family.

Darshan A. Sangha (aka Darshan Singh Canadian) *Activist* b. 1917, Langeri, Punjab, India; d. Sept. 25, 1986, Punjab, India. After arriving in Vancouver, his uncle lobbied to get him a job at Dominion Sawmills. As a result the uncle was fired and Darshan hired at 5 cents less an hour. In 1942 he was the first person in the Hindustani community to be drafted. As organizer of the International Woodworkers of America (1942-46), fought for the rights of B.C.'s East Indian woodworkers. Led IWA strikers on a march to Victoria in 1946. After 11 years in Canada returned to India (1948) and changed his surname to "Canadian." Represented Communist Party for three terms in the Punjabi state legislature. After speaking out against Sikh extremism was murdered by unknown attackers.

Koichiro Sanmiya *Cowboy, entrepreneur* b. c. 1880, Sendai, Japan; d. March 11, 1931, Vancouver. Arrived in Vancouver in 1907 and rode the range, herding cattle. Owned the Strand Hotel restaurant; later established K. Sanmiya Co. (importer/exporter of Japanese goods) and *Canada Daily Newspaper,* a Japanese-language paper published until 1921. In the 1920s started Vancouver Malt and Sake Co., and was issued the only distiller's license in B.C. Sponsored the Asahi baseball team. A founder and president of the Canadian Japanese Association (Nipponjin Kai, now the Japanese Canadian Association). Sold war bonds to raise the War Memorial in Stanley Park, donated on April 9, 1920.

Tsutae Sato *Educator* b. 1891, Tanekura, Fukushima-ken, Japan; d. May 23, 1983, Vancouver. Arrived in Canada on July 2, 1917, to teach at the Nippon Kokumin Gakko (Japanese Citizens School) on Alexander. His wife, Hanako Awaka (m. 1921; d. May 4, 1983, Vancouver), was also a teacher. Together they ran the Vancouver Japanese Language School (1906-1942). Due to growth in the number of Japanese residents, the Japanese Hall was built at 475 Alexander and dedicated March 19, 1928, for community activities and the school. In 1979 the Satos established scholarships in Japanese studies at UBC. Tsutae was awarded the Order of Canada (1978).

Nicolai C. Schou (pronounced "scow") *Burnaby reeve* b. c. 1857, Manchester, Eng.; d. Dec. 25, 1903, Burnaby (or Victoria). An English solicitor, he arrived in Burnaby area in early 1890s. Editor/feature writer for *News-Advertiser;* writer for *Commonwealth,* a New Westminster-based farm journal. An up-and-coming politician, he moved on July 25, 1892, that the new municipality be called Burnaby. It was carried unanimously. First reeve of Burnaby elected by ballot (1893-1903); also a Vancouver alderman (1896) while serving as reeve. Had just accepted a job with the *Victoria Colonist* when he died suddenly.

Garnett Gladwin Sedgewick *CBC broadcaster, professor* b. May 20, 1882, Musquodoboit, NS; d. Sept. 4, 1949, Vancouver. After attending Dalhousie College (1898-1903), he taught high school in Nanaimo and Vancouver before attending Harvard U. to study English (MA, 1911; PhD, 1913). From 1918-48 taught at UBC. In 1920 named head of English. A popular teacher, acclaimed for his Shakespeare and Chaucer lectures. CBC broadcasts and a weekly column spread his influence. The UBC undergraduate library and Sedgewick Lectures, sponsored by the English department, are named for him.

John Wesley Sexsmith *Richmond reeve* b. May 10, 1830, Lennox, Ont.; d. c. Sept. 22, 1920, Richmond, B.C. After running a cheese factory in Ontario, he came to Moodyville in 1876. Crossed the Fraser and settled in what is now Richmond. Built a cheese factory and expanded land holdings to 770 hectares. Ran a boat service on the North Fraser to New Westminster, a salmon cannery and flour mill. Responsible for building the first bridges connecting Marpole, Sea Island and Lulu Island. Founded Sexsmith Community School, Richmond's first school.

Frederick Seymour *B.C. governor* b. Sept. 6, 1820, Belfast, Ire.; d. June 10, 1869, Bella Coola. Spent his time as governor (1864-69) "blithely going his own way, entertaining lavishly, generally drifting." Given the cold shoulder by the upright citizens of Victoria. A bachelor at 43, he went to England in 1865 to marry, returning with his bride. Obstructed Confederation "by stalling and subterfuge." He preferred New Westminster to Victoria, but when Victoria was made the capital in 1868, he was forced to move there. Died suddenly, cruising aboard HMS *Sparrowhawk* off Bella Coola as he was about to be replaced as governor. Mt. Seymour is named for him.

Thomas George Shaughnessy *CPR president* b. Oct. 6, 1853, Milwaukee, Wisc.; d. Dec. 9, 1923, Montreal. An American railroader, he was recruited in 1882 over a glass of beer as general purchasing agent for the CPR. President of CPR (1898-1918). Knighted in 1901. In Sept. 1909 he bought property in Shaughnessy Heights, named in his honor, to build his mansion. Became the first Baron Shaughnessy of Montreal in 1916.

Charles R. Shaw *First Burnaby reeve* b. Aug. 20, 1834, Great Grimsby, Eng.; d. 1916, Ann Arbor, Mich. After a college education, he emigrated to Toronto in 1869 with his wife and two children. A Wesleyan Methodist preacher, he declined ordination. In 1889 he moved to New Westminster, building a home at 4th St. and 3rd Ave. Worked as a decorator, paperhanger and painter. On Oct. 8, 1892, the local property owners unanimously appointed him first reeve of Burnaby (pop. under 200). With his ailing wife, he moved to Kamloops in 1894. After her death, moved to Ann Arbor.

Kosaburo Shimizu *United Church minister* b. Sept. 13, 1893, Tsuchida, Shiga-ken, Japan; d. June 29, 1962, Winnipeg, Man. He immigrated to B.C. c. 1906. At Royal City HS in New Westminster (1910-11) he won a gold medal for the highest average of a first-year student. Entered UBC (1915-19); later Harvard (MA, 1924). Ordained by the United Church (1927), serving Vancouver's Christian community. Committed to bridging first and second generation Japanese-Canadians and Anglo-Saxons and Japanese-Canadians. During WWII relocated to Kaslo, B.C., internment camp. In 1945 transferred to Toronto and organized Japanese United Church work. Received DD from Union College (now the Vancouver School of Theology). Died while chairing a conference of Japanese ministers.

Shin Shimotakahara (née Kusama) *Community leader* b. c. 1891, Japan; d. Sept. 12, 1972, Toronto, Ont. A prominent woman in the Vancouver Japanese community before WWII. With husband, Dr. Kozo Shimotakahara (b. c. 1886, Japan; d. Nov. 30, 1951, Kaslo, B.C.), she ran a tuberculosis hospital and clinic for Japanese immigrants. Her husband arrived in Vancouver in 1900 and lived in the Japanese Methodist Church dormitory. He enrolled in Strathcona Elem. at 14; later studied medicine at U. of Chicago. They met in Seattle while he was studying for his medical license exams (first class honors). They corresponded in English until their marriage on June 5, 1916. During WWII the family was interned in Kaslo, B.C., where they remained. He practised medicine until the day of his death. From the late 1950s she lived with her daughter in Toronto.

Jack (John Richard Collister) Short *Racing broadcaster* b. Dec. 28, 1908, Victoria; d. Aug. 4, 1992, Victoria. At 15 rode bush tracks from Vancouver to Tijuana. "Too tall, too lanky," he failed as a jockey. In 1933 announced race results on CFUN radio. From 1934-76 called nearly 50,000 races at Exhibition Park and broadcast live for CJOR radio. He invariably signed off his broadcasts with the famous catch phrase, "Adios amigos!" Lifetime member, B.C. Thoroughbred Breeding Society; member, B.C. Racing Commission. Promoted

The Old Spaghetti Factory was established in 1970. The first restaurant opened at 53 Water Street in Gastown in a former coffee and tea packing plant that was built in 1907. The centrepiece of the restaurant is an authentic 1904 trolley car which travelled the streets of Vancouver for many years. All of our restaurants are living museums full of fascinating antiques, furnishings and memorabilia. There are now seven locations nationwide.

native Indian sports through the North Shore Totem Athletic Club. Broadcast Performer of the Year Award (1976). Named to B.C. Horse Racing Hall of Fame (1980) and the Canadian Horse Racing Hall of Fame (Nov. 4, 1988).

Gordon Merritt Shrum *First SFU chancellor* b. June 14, 1896, Smithville, Ont.; d. June 20, 1985, Vancouver. Grew up on a farm. Attended Hamilton Collegiate with Lester Pearson. He fought at Passchendaele. Graduate, U of T (BA, math, 1920; PhD, 1923). At 29 crossed Canada in a Model T to teach at UBC. Head of UBC physics department (1938-61); dean of graduate studies (1956-61). As SFU chancellor (1962-68) pushed through construction of "Berkeley North" in 18 months. Forced to retire at 65, he chaired the B.C. Energy Board. Oversaw projects such as Vancouver museum/planetarium complex, the courthouse, and waterfront convention centre. Order of the British Empire (1946); LL.D (UBC, 1961); Order of Canada (1967).

"Portuguese Joe" Silvey (born Joseph Silvia Simmons) *Storekeeper* b. 1836, Piepika Island, Portugal; d. Jan. 17, 1902, Reid Island, B.C. Son of a Scotsman and Spanish mother. Jumped ship in 1852 from a Portuguese whaler; rowed ashore to Point Roberts. Searched for gold, later ran Gassy Jack's competition, a combined saloon and grocery store. Pioneered Vancouver shipbuilding with the fishing sloop *Morning Star,* built at Brockton Point. Married Khaaltinaht, descendant of Chief Keyaplanough. Their daughter, Elizabeth Marion Silvey (b. July 4, 1868; d. Aug. 1, 1945, Ladysmith, B.C.) was the first child of European heritage born on the south shore of Burrard Inlet. Left a widower with two daughters, he married Kwatleemmatt, known as Lucy (b. c. 1857-59, Tsonei, B.C.; d. Aug. 13, 1934, Reid Island), in Tsonei, near Sechelt, Sept. 20, 1872. They had seven children. Granted fishing rights from Sansum Narrows to the western tip of Mudge Island (1872).

James Sinclair *Federal cabinet minister* b. May 26, 1908, Banff, Scotland; d. Feb. 7, 1984, West Vancouver. An outstanding UBC athlete. Attended Oxford (Rhodes Scholar, 1928) and London U., studying math and engineering. Taught at West Vancouver HS, then studied at Princeton. In 1935, appointed assistant to education minister G.M. WEIR; later secretary to B.C. mines minister. At 31 elected Lib. MP (Coast Capilano), later Vancouver North (1940-58). During WWII enlisted in Royal Canadian Air Force. On his return in 1945, he was re-elected. Fisheries minister in St. Laurent government (1952-57). Daughter Margaret married Pierre Trudeau in 1971.

Louie Gim (Gum) Sing (aka Loy Sum Sing, Lum Gim Sing) *Pioneer Chinese builder* b. June 6, 1850, China; d. Dec. 31, 1957, Vancouver. Left job in Hong Kong to work as foreman of a CPR Chinese crew. Arrived in Victoria on June 25, 1884. Helped lay the last track into Vancouver, survived the Great Fire, and helped rebuild the city. Fought to preserve the rights of Chinese workers before the courts. In later years took up truck farming on Lulu Island before settling in Chinatown. He was the oldest Chinese resident of Canada when he died at 107.

Gurdit Singh *Komagata Maru organizer* b. India. In 1890, to challenge an unfair federal immigration law that stopped immigration by anyone from India, Singh chartered the *Komagata Maru,* bringing with him to B.C. 376 South Asian passengers. The ship arrived in Burrard Inlet on May 23, 1914. Only 20 of the passengers, those who already had resident status, were allowed to disembark. The rest were sent back on July 23, 1914. Back in India, a riot following the ship's return resulted in the deaths of over 50 Sikhs and imprisonment for 200 more.

Jagdish Kaur Singh *Trucking company president* b. July 12, 1912, Mesopor, Punjab, India; d. Aug. 5, 1991, Chilliwack, B.C. She arrived in Canada on Nov. 19, 1929, settling in Abbotsford, B.C., at a time when fewer than 2,000 East Indians lived in Canada. Her husband, a Sikh priest, Giani Harnam Singh (d. 1956), ran a pioneer lumber business and helped found the Akali Singh Sikh Temple. After his death, she started a gravel truck business in Chilliwack (G.H. Singh & Sons Trucking). Director of Dhillon Holdings and owner of several dairy farms and land holdings in Chilliwack and Langley area. A staunch supporter of Sikhism, she donated to charities worldwide.

Mewa Singh *Sikh martyr* b. Punjab, India; d. Jan. 11, 1915, New Westminster. After the 1914 *Komagata Maru* incident (see GURDIT SINGH), tensions arose among members of Vancouver's Sikh community. They blamed William Hopkinson, formerly with the Calcutta Police Force, sent to B.C. by the British in 1908 as a spy. Mewa, a supporter of India's independence movement and the *Komagata Maru,* shot Hopkinson to death at the Vancouver provincial court house in 1914. He was sentenced to hang and is revered as a Sikh martyr. The langar (dining) hall of the Ross St. Sikh Temple is named in his honor.

Teja Singh *Teacher, community leader* b. India. Educated at Punjab U. and Harvard (MA). Taught at Khalsa College in Amritsar, Punjab. Invited by the Sikh community to aid their fight for human rights. Arrived in 1908 in Vancouver from the U.S., where he taught. His wife and two children came with him, possibly the first Asian family to come to Canada. Professor Singh emerged as a community leader, presenting a public image that contradicted media stereotypes. Dealt with many levels of government, including Ottawa.

Bob (Robert Norman) Smith *Columnist, broadcaster* b. Jan. 15, 1920, Winnipeg, Man.; d. May 16, 1989, Vancouver. Heard first jazz recording at 13, a clarinet piece from a Noel Coward play on the *British Empire* program on CKMO (later CFUN). Attended King Edward HS. Joined Royal Canadian Air Force, later served with U.S. forces in South Pacific. For more than 30 years from Saturday, Feb. 1, 1947, he was host of Vancouver's longest-running jazz radio show *Hot Air.* From 1954 hi-fi columnist; from 1962 *Vancouver Sun* jazz columnist. From 1971-79 host of Vancouver edition of CBC's *That Midnight Jazz.* "An encyclopedia of jazz, jazz musicians and records."

Janet Smith *Murdered nanny* b. June 25, 1902, Perth, Scotland; d. July 26, 1924, Vancouver. Employed in the home of a wealthy Shaughnessy businessman, she was mysteriously murdered. A sensational case followed "involving the city's elite, political corruption and widespread racism." A Chinese houseboy, Wong Foon Sing, was accused but acquitted. The murderer was never found. See article: Who Killed Janet Smith?

Mary Ellen Smith (née Spear) *Politician, feminist* b. Oct. 11, 1863, Tavistock, Eng.; d. May 3, 1933, Vancouver. First female B.C. MLA and the first woman cabinet minister in the British Empire. As an independent she won the January 1918 Vancouver by-election called after the death of her husband, Ralph Smith, finance minister in B.C.'s Liberal government. Re-elected as a Liberal in 1920 and 1924. Served as minister without portfolio, March to Nov. 1921. An advocate of B.C.'s first mother's pension and Female Minimum Wage acts.

Dorothy Somerset *Theatre director* b. June 9, 1900, Perth, Australia; d. Aug. 11, 1991, Vancouver. Studied at Radcliffe College (BA); moved to Vancouver in 1921. Actor/director with Vancouver Little Theatre; director, University Players' Club (1934-38). In 1937 joined UBC's extension department; in 1938 founded its Summer School of Theatre; in 1946 taught UBC's first theatre credit courses. Received Canadian Drama Award (1952). In 1958 helped found UBC's drama department. The Dorothy Somerset Scholarship Fund was set up in 1965. D.Litt (UBC, 1965). In June 1991 she won a Jessie Award for "humanity, integrity and encouragement of young talent in the theatre."

Law A. Soong *Merchant* b. Jan. 2, 1880, Canton, China. Arrived in New Westminster in 1889. Attended school for six years before being hired by Ying, Tai and Co., first as secretary, then as manager. Appears in *British Columbia From the Earliest Times to the Present* (Vol. IV), published in 1914, the only Asian included in this series of biographies.

Jung Jin Sow (aka Jang Jin Few) *Inventor of a Chinese perpetual calendar* b. c. 1889, Canton, China;

d. Oct. 2, 1948, Vancouver. Taught math in a Chinese high school for two years; later in Nanaimo and Vancouver. In the 1930s ran a restaurant. He was active in Chinese Benevolent Society (elected president in 1939). Grand Master, Chinese Freemasons. Superintendent of Kwong Chee (or Gee) Chinese school. As a youth he began analyzing a possible Chinese perpetual calendar, eventually developing one from 1 BC to 9999 AD, the first of its kind. A copy of the calendar was presented to the Vancouver Archives in 1937. Publisher, *Chinese Times* (1940-48).

Frederick Hubert Soward *Historian* b. April 10, 1899, Minden, Ont.; d. Jan. 1, 1985, Vancouver. Smart enough to enter high school at 10, he had to wait two years. Won scholarship to U of T but after two years went overseas with 48th Highlanders. After WWI studied at Oxford, where he began a lifelong friendship with Lester Pearson. The "boy wonder" of UBC's history department, he taught from 1922-66. During WWII adviser to external affairs and assistant to the secretary of state. Head, UBC history department (1953-63); LL.D (UBC, 1964); dean of graduate studies (1961-65). Famed on campus for his international affairs lectures. Biblio: *Empires and Nations,* essays by 14 Canadians published in his honor (1969) with a preface by Lester Pearson.

Chris (Christopher) Spencer *Department store heir* b. May 17, 1869, Victoria; d. May 31, 1953, Vancouver. Son of DAVID SPENCER. Educated at Victoria HS. Entered David Spencer Ltd. in 1882. In 1907 established the Vancouver branch. After his father's death he was president until purchase of Spencer stores by the T. Eaton Co. (Dec. 1, 1948). "Mr. Chris" was known for his public spirit and generosity. An early supporter of UBC; appointed to board of governors (1921-36). LL.D (UBC, 1952). Established Chris Spencer Foundation to assist worthy students. The first awards were made in Oct. 1950.

David Spencer Sr. *Department store founder* b. Aug. 9, 1837, St. Athan, Wales; d. March 3, 1920, Victoria. A farmer's son, he apprenticed to a dry-goods merchant in Wales and came to Victoria in 1862. After selling books and stationery, he bought a dry-goods store in Victoria (1873) which became David Spencer Ltd. Established branches in Nanaimo (1889), Vancouver (1906) and other B.C. centres. A lay preacher for the Methodist Church, he co-founded first temperance society on Vancouver Island. A benefactor to Victoria's Protestant Orphanage and other philanthropies. His son, CHRIS SPENCER, the eldest of 13 children, continued in the business.

Tim (Rochfort Henry) Sperling *Electrical engineer* b. Feb. 9, 1876, Yorkshire, Eng.; d. July 5, 1956, Vancouver. Studied at Eton and Faraday House. Came to B.C. in 1896 and joined B.C. Electric

Railway (1897); general manager (1905-14). General manager of Vancouver Gas, Victoria Gas, Vancouver Power, and Vancouver Island Power. Replaced coal burning plants with hydro-electric systems on Mainland and Vancouver Island. In April 1912 set a 5¢ fare for united tram lines in South Vancouver-Vancouver-Burnaby-Point Grey. Returned to England (1914); active in aircraft production. Moved to Drummondville, Que., as vice president of Canadian Celanese Ltd. Later he returned to live in Vancouver. Burnaby's Sperling St. is named for him.

Anna Ethel Sprott *Radio school founder, alderman* b. c. 1879, Norwood, Ont.; d. Oct. 9, 1961, Vancouver. Attended U of T. Came to Vancouver as a young widow in 1911 and attended Sprott-Shaw Schools of Commerce, Radio and Telegraphy. In 1918 married its founder, R.J. Sprott. After his death (1943) became president. Founder of West Coast Radio School. First woman candidate, civic Non-Partisan Association. Elected Vancouver alderman. Served on the council (1949-59) longer than any woman in city history; first woman alderman re-elected for three terms. First woman to serve as acting mayor (Sept. 1953). On retirement admitted to writing secret letters on council's behalf to those celebrating 50th and 60th anniversaries as well as 90th and 100th birthdays.

Edward Stamp *Sawmill operator* b. November 1814, Alnwick, Eng.; d. Jan. 17, 1872, London, Eng. Arrived in Victoria in 1858. Operated first export sawmill in B.C. at Port Alberni (1861-63). In 1865 opened B.C. and Vancouver Island Spar, Lumber and Sawmill (known as Hastings Mill) on Burrard Inlet, destined to be the city's largest industrial complex. It began production in 1867 and was the focus of Granville (later Vancouver). Company was sold in 1869 to Dickson, De Wolf and Co. of San Francisco for $20,000. In 1890 JOHN HENDRY and Associates, owners of the Royal City Planing Mills, bought the mill. In 1891 it was renamed the B.C. Mills, Timber and Trading.

Bobbie (Roberta) Steen *Leader in sport administration* b. April 9, 1946, North Vancouver; d. Nov. 12, 1995, Burnaby. A tireless promoter of B.C. and national sporting opportunities for women, she was founding chair and executive director of Promotion Plus (1990), the B.C. organization for girls and women in sport and physical activity. Chair, Canadian Association for the Advancement of Women and Sport and Physical Activity; co-chair, B.C. Games Society. In 1994 she was named volunteer of the year by the Canadian Sport Council, the first time that the national sport community recognized an individual for increasing opportunities for girls and women.

Pearl Steen (née Soper) *Women's activist* b. 1893, Victoria; d. 1988, Vancouver. Educated in Vancouver. President of National Council of Women,

Vancouver Council of Women and Vancouver Women's Canadian Club. Joined Canadian Federation of Professional and Business Women's Club; president (1935). President, Point Grey Conservative Association (1936-37). Spent six years on Vancouver school board (1947-52); elected chair in 1950. Member, B.C. Centennial Committee (1958). Sole Canadian woman delegate to UN General Assembly in 1960. The only woman director of the Pacific National Exhibition (1960-68). Member, B.C. Human Rights Council. Received Vancouver's Good Citizen Award (1967).

Dorothy Gretchen Steeves (née Biersteker) *Socialist* b. May 26, 1895, Amsterdam, Holland; d. May 9, 1978, Vancouver. Law graduate, Leyden U. During WWI served as legal advisor to Netherlands government. In 1918 married Rufus Palmer Steeves (b. 1892, Woodstock, NB; d. June 1960, Cloverdale, B.C.), a Canadian officer and former prisoner of war. He was later principal of Gen. Gordon HS and co-founder, Kitsilano Boys Band. Dot was a founder of the Co-operative Commonwealth Federation (1932), later the NDP. Served as CCF MLA (North Vancouver, 1934-45), one of seven original CCF members in B.C. In May 1948 elected CCF president (B.C./Yukon). "A fiery member . . . in the headlines much of the time."

Alexander Maitland Stephen *Poet* b. 1882, Hanover, Ont.; d. July 1, 1942, Vancouver. In his early years he tried ranching and mining, as well as rural teaching. Wounded in WWI. Back in Vancouver, he opened an engineering company. A well-known progressive social activist. Nationally known critic and author of two novels, plays, romances and poetry. His 1934 poem *Vancouver* was widely anthologized. Biblio: *The Verse of Pan; Land of Singing Waters; Brown Earth and Bunch Grass; Verendrye: A Poem of the New World.*

Harry (Henry Herbert) Stevens *Businessman, founder of political party* b. Dec. 8, 1878, Bristol, Eng.; d. June 14, 1973, Vancouver. Settled in Vancouver in 1902. Clerked for $12 a week at City Grocery (Main and Pender). Alderman, Ward 5 (1910). PC MP (Vancouver, 1911-30) and later for Kootenay East. "Saw threat in Asia's millions" and lobbied for the Oriental Exclusion Act. Member of Arthur Meighen's cabinet in the 1920s. Controversial politician in 1930s; founder of Reconstruction Party, which failed with voters, ending his political career. Succeeded in getting improvements to Vancouver Harbour, False Creek and Granville Island. LL.D (UBC, 1932).

Manoah Steves *Lulu Island settler* b. Dec. 18, 1828, Coverdale, NB; d. Dec. 7, 1897, Steveston, B.C. Arrived in B.C. in 1877, purchasing 300 (later 400) acres on Lulu Island. In 1878 his wife and six children arrived, the first white family to permanently settle the area. In 1879 Manoah was one of 25 Lulu Island residents to petition for incorporation of Municipality of Richmond. Elected to first council. In 1881 imported B.C.'s first purebred Holsteins. His second son, Joseph Moore Steves (d. Sept. 1, 1934, Steveston), developed B.C.'s largest Holstein herd, supplying milk for Vancouver until the cattle were sold during the Depression. The farm is now run by Richmond councillor Harold Steves (b. May 29, 1937, Vancouver), fourth generation on the original site. He lives in Joseph's 1917 house, which replaced Manoah's house built in 1877. Biblio: *Salmonopolis* by Duncan Stacey.

William Herbert Steves *Steveston founder* b. 1860, NB; d. May 27, 1899, Victoria. Eldest son of MANOAH STEVES. Began buying land on Lulu Island in 1880. In 1887 he purchased Steveston townsite and by 1889 had laid out a portion of "Steves" in lots. In 1890 the southwest corner of Lulu Island was renamed Steveston. Started the *Steveston Enterprise* newspaper to promote investment in his development as a potential major seaport terminal. In 1890 built Steveston Opera House. When the fishers were in town, up to 10,000 people strolled the boardwalks above the mud on a Saturday night. Died of heart disease at 39 years.

John Malcolm Stewart *Police chief* b. c. 1838, PEI; d. July 15, 1906, Agassiz, B.C. Vancouver's first official police chief, appointed after the Great Fire of June 13, 1886 for a one-year term, along with a sergeant and two constables. Between 1897-1900 he was engaged in logging.

John William Stewart *Railway builder, general* b. 1862, Assynt, Sutherlandshire, Scotland; d. Sept. 24, 1938, Vancouver. Arrived in Canada in 1882. Surveyed line of Granville St. in 1885. A partner in Foley, Welch and Stewart, the largest North American railway contracting firm. Built much of Grand Trunk Pacific Line. Began Pacific Great Eastern and parts of Canadian National Railway. In WWI commanded 13 battalions, organized railway troops and built railways in France. Sponsored J.W. Stewart Cup for pipe bands. "Shy and retiring . . . nevertheless one of the most powerful and wealthy men in B.C." Ardvar, his home on Angus Dr. was visited by the dukes of Windsor and Kent.

Edith McConnell Stewart-Murray *Journalist* b. 1900, Montreal, Que.; d. Nov. 22, 1965, Victoria. Lived in Vancouver from 1904-58, when she moved to Victoria. Her father, John P. (Black Jack) McConnell, with brother-in-law T.S. Ford, founded the *Morning Sun,* the forerunner of the *Vancouver Sun* (1912). A columnist and women's page editor of the *Sun* and *Vancouver News-Herald* for 40 years. Her best known column was *Let's Go Shopping.* Life member, Canadian Women's Press Club.

Randy Stoltmann *Environmentalist* b. Sept. 28, 1962, Vancouver; d. May 22, 1994, Kitlope River area, B.C. Over a 12-year period, made a painstaking exploration of mountain country within 200 kilometres of Vancouver. In April 1994 drew up a formal proposal to preserve the Elaho-Upper Lillooet wilderness under the B.C. government's protected area strategy. The 260,000-hectare roadless area is known as the Randy Stoltmann Wilderness. Killed in an avalanche while skiing through remote ranges west of the Kitlope River. Biblio: *Written by the Wind* by Randy Stoltmann.

George Frederic Strong *Heart specialist* b. Feb. 22, 1897, St. Paul, Minn.; d. Feb. 26, 1957, Montreal, Que. Graduate, U. of Minnesota (MD). He interned at Vancouver General Hospital (1922-23), then served on the staff for 34 years. Known internationally as a heart specialist. Chair, VGH medical board; a founder of B.C. Cancer Foundation, Western Society for Rehabilitation, B.C. Medical Research Institute, Vancouver Community Chest & Council and Family Welfare Bureau. A clinical professor and founder of UBC's faculty of medicine. LL.D (UBC, 1954). In 1955 named president, American College of Physicians and Surgeons. Died en route to a meeting of the National Heart Foundation. G.F. Strong Centre is named for him (May 1957).

Elizabeth Chang Suey *First Chinese girl born in B.C.* b. May 5, 1871, New Westminster; d. Feb. 8, 1951, Vancouver. Daughter of B.C. pioneer Won Luen Cumyow; sister of WON ALEXANDER CUMYOW. Born in New Westminster after parents moved from Fort Douglas at head of Harrison Lake. As a child, saw gold miners leaving Fort Douglas to prospect in the Cariboo. Family then moved back to New Westminster, where Suey went to school. From 1908 lived in Vancouver. Her husband Charles (d. 1947) was active in the Chinese community.

Anne Sugarman (née Wodlinger) *Organizer* b. 1895, Winnipeg; d. May 1973, Toronto. Daughter of pioneers, she attended a Winnipeg college. Married Ephraim R. Sugarman, a lawyer, in 1916. They lived in Vancouver from 1919-42, founding the Reform Jewish Sunday School (1922). First president, Vancouver Council of Jewish Women (1924). The couple founded Congregation Beth Israel (1932). During WWII she founded and chaired the Red Cross Salvage Scheme, copied across Canada. She was responsible for the first seeing-eye dog program in North America. During the Canadian Bill of Rights hearings, she presented a brief on women's rights. Biblio: *Pioneers, Pedlars, and Prayer Shawls* by Cyril E. Leonoff.

Erwin Michael Swangard *Journalist Pacific National Exhibition president* b. May 11, 1908, Munich, Germany; d. May 5, 1993, Vancouver. He emigrated to Canada in 1930. As a freelance sports reporter,

he covered the 1936 Olympic Games. He was *Province* foreign editor (1944-49). Worked his way up in *Vancouver Sun;* appointed managing editor (1959). Founded Tournament of Soccer Champions for juvenile soccer. Promoted the British Empire and Commonwealth Games in Vancouver (1954) and first Grey Cup final outside Toronto (1955). One of seven founders of B.C. Lions. Raised almost $1 million to build Swangard Stadium, opened in 1969. "Mr. PNE" was appointed president in January 1977, a position he held for 13 consecutive annual terms. Member, Order of Canada (1989).

Robert Eugene Swanson *Steam engineer, poet* b. Oct. 26, 1905, Reading, Eng.; d. Oct. 4, 1994, Vancouver. He arrived in Vancouver as a child. Trained as a steam engineer; worked in logging camps and wrote popular folksy poems about logging life. Born Robert Swanson, he added Eugene because it sounded dignified. After inventing the air horn for trains, he became internationally known as a maker of tuned whistle systems. Designed the horn that played *O Canada* at noon in downtown Vancouver. Called the "Bard of the Woods" for his poetry. Biblio: *Robert Swanson: Rhymes of a Western Logger.*

Leo (Michael Leo) Sweeney *Cooper* b. April 17, 1886, London, Ont.; d. Sept. 18, 1977, Vancouver. Came to Victoria in 1888, where his father founded Sweeney Cooperage, a barrel-making firm. He became managing director (1912). Two years after buying Canadian Western Cooperage (1921), he moved to Vancouver. Served on many civic boards and committees. As president of the Vancouver Tourist Association, he wore a straw boater when it rained "to prove it was liquid sunshine." The company operated at the foot of Smithe until 1981, when the land was expropriated for B.C. Place and the cooperage, one of the oldest industries in False Creek, was torn down.

Violet Pooley Sweeny *Golfer* b. Dec. 18, 1886, Victoria; d. March 19, 1965, West Vancouver. The "Queen of Northwest Golf" first played at eight. In 1905 she won the first of seven Pacific Northwest and nine B.C. championships. Moved to Vancouver, and in 1915 married Bimbo (Sedley Campbell) Sweeny (b. Oct. 16, 1888, Vancouver; d. Feb. 12, 1966, West Vancouver), a famed rugby player and rower. She sold cars for Consolidated Motors on W. Georgia, then demonstrated the basics of the golf swing at McLennan, McFeeley & Prior sports and hardware store. "She didn't hesitate to raise eye brows and hemlines . . . she simply did her own thing." B.C. Sports Hall of Fame (1974). Biblio: *Backspin, 100 Years of Golf in B.C.* by Arv Olson.

Lulu Sweet *Actress* b. c. 1844. On a performance tour to Victoria with the Potter Troupe, the 16-year-old performing star toured the Fraser River with a smitten Col. RICHARD CLEMENT MOODY on Jan. 12, 1860. She asked Moody the name of a particular island; he replied that since it had no name, he would call it Lulu Island in her honor. Little else is known of Lulu Sweet's career or life.

Georgia Sweney *Hastings Mill's first teacher.* d. Sept. 4, 1940, Santa Paulo, Calif. Graduate of girl's seminary in Victoria. An accomplished musician and artist, her admirers noted that she could also "milk a cow." Her pencil sketches are in the Vancouver City Archives. Circa 1872-73 she taught the first classes at Hastings Mill School, which was also used as a community church. Her daughter, Esther J. Cummings, reported to J.S. MATTHEWS in 1941 that Georgia was also the church soloist. After moving to San Francisco, she married John Franklin Cummings in the early 1880s.

T

William Lamont Tait *Lumberman, financier* b. March 1850, Scotland; d. 1921, Vancouver. Arrived in Vancouver on Feb. 13, 1891. Opened Rat Portage Lumber, a shingle and sawmill on False Creek (1902-1910). His luxurious Shaughnessy mansion, Glen Brae, built in 1910, had one of the city's first elevators. In 1925 the mansion housed the B.C. branch of the KKK until a by-law prohibited mask wearing. Also built Manhattan Apartments (Thurlow and Robson) and Orillia Block (Robson and Seymour, 1903). One of the first to hire workers from False Creek Indian Reserve and East Indians. Today Glen Brae is Canuck Place, a hospice for children.

Warren Tallman *Teacher, literary critic* b. Nov. 17, 1921, Seattle, Wash.; d. July 1, 1994, Vancouver. Arrived in Vancouver in 1956 to teach, with wife Ellen (b. Nov. 9, 1927, Berkeley, Calif.), at UBC English department. Their home was a centre of modern poetry in the city and introduced a generation of young writers to modernism. Revered teacher and critic of modern poetry from 1960s. Starting in 1963, he organized major poetry conferences in Vancouver and the U.S. Biblio: *The God-Awful Streets of Man; New American Poetics* (with Don Allen); *In the Midst.*

Shinkichi Tamura *Banker, builder* b. 1863, Osaka, Japan; d. 1936, Japan. Arrived in Vancouver in 1888, first working at a sawmill. Established Sien Ban Co., which, among other things, exported lumber and wheat to Japan. Built the New World Hotel (Powell and Dunlevy). He controlled the Japan and Canada Trust Savings, making him Japantown's foremost banker. Canada's first trade commissioner to Japan. Listed in *Who's Who in Western Canada* (1911), the only Japanese represented. In the mid-1920s returned to his homeland and was elected to parliament. Member, Japanese House of Peers.

Charles Montgomery Tate *Methodist missionary* b. Nov. 5, 1852, Blyth, Northumberland, Eng.; d.

Feb. 28, 1933, Vancouver. Came to B.C. in 1870 and searched for gold in the Cariboo. In Aug. 1879 ordained as Methodist priest. Published translations of the scriptures in Chinook. Established boarding school for native children at Sardis (later known as Coqualeetza Institute, a residential school) with wife Sarah Tate (b. 1842, Eng.; d. May 3, 1916). Missionary to first church in Vancouver built by native residents (1876). Affiliated with St. Andrews Wesley-United Church. Celebrated jubilee of his ministry in 1929. "He studied in the saddle and canoe."

Robert Garnett Tatlow *Capitalist* b. Sept. 6, 1855, Scarva, County Down, Ire.; d. April 11, 1910, Victoria. He worked with HENRY OGLE BELL-IRVING in shipping. Made fortune in real estate and insurance (Tatlow & Spinks on Cordova). Married HENRY CAMBIE's eldest daughter. PC MLA; minister of finance in Premier McBride's cabinet. A founder of B.C. Telephone. Died after falling off a carriage when a car frightened his horse. In Dec. 1935 his daughter Mrs. R.G. (Helen) Wilson died in a similar accident, also in Victoria. Tatlow Park is named for him.

A.J.T. (Alfred James Towle) Taylor *Capitalist* b. Aug. 4, 1887, Victoria; d. July 20, 1945, New York, NY. Founded Taylor Engineering in 1912 which built large B.C. projects. Promoted development of British Properties and construction of Lions Gate Bridge in the 1930s. Worked for British ministry of aircraft production in London during WWII. Taylor Way is named for him.

Austin Cottrell Taylor *Financier* b. Jan. 17, 1889, Toronto, Ont.; d. Nov. 1, 1965, Vancouver. Came to B.C. in 1917. In 1930s he was an owner of Bralorne gold mine and one of the city's wealthiest people. Raised race horses at A.C.T. stock farm in Langley. His horse, Indian Broom, placed third in Kentucky Derby (1936). Owned Shannon Estate (Granville and 57th), now townhouses. During WWII worked for war minister C.D. Howe for one dollar a year. In 1942 chaired B.C. Security Commission, which interned the Japanese. Awarded Companion of the Order of the British Empire (1947) for wartime service. He chaired B.C. Emergency Flood Committee after WWII, fundraising for victims of Fraser flood. His daughter married William F. Buckley.

Cyclone (Frederick) Taylor *Hockey player* b. June 24, 1883, Tara, Ont.; d. June 9, 1979, Vancouver. Won first Stanley Cup with Ottawa Senators in 1909; won again with Vancouver Millionaires in 1915. When he joined the Pacific Coast Hockey Association in 1913, it gave the new league the credibility it needed. Played for Vancouver (1913-21) until retirement. One of the great hockey players, he scored 194 goals in 186 games.

Louis Denison Taylor *Mayor of Vancouver, 1910-11, 1915, 1925-26, 1927-28, 1931-34* See May-

ors of Vancouver.

J. Lyle Telford *Mayor of Vancouver, 1939-40* See Mayors of Vancouver.

William Templeton *Mayor of Vancouver, 1897* See Mayors of Vancouver.

Charles E. Thompson *Mayor of Vancouver, 1949-50* See Mayors of Vancouver.

Stephen Joseph Thompson *Photographer* b. May 27, 1864, Baillieboro, Ont.; d. Aug. 7, 1929, Vancouver. He arrived in New Westminster, possibly from New York. Opened a studio partnership as Thompson & Bovill (December 1897). By 1889 ran his own studio in New Westminster until it was destroyed by fire (Sept. 11, 1898). Also in 1898 he accompanied an official expedition to Northern B.C. with the deputy minister of marine and fisheries, Louis Coste. Described as "prolific and versatile" in both portraits and landscapes. A major subject was CPR lines in the 1890s.

Mildred Valley Thornton *Artist, art critic* b. 1890, Dresden, Ont.; d. July 27, 1967, Vancouver. Studied art in U.S. before moving to Vancouver from Saskatchewan in 1934. In the 1920s, with her two sons, she spent summers with Saskatchewan's Plains Cree people. Created more than 300 paintings of ceremonies, dances and native people. *Vancouver Sun* art critic for 16 years to 1959, when she retired. Executive member, Canadian Women's Press Club; member, Vancouver Poetry Society and Canadian Authors' Association. In 1960 made a Fellow, Royal Academy of Arts. Biblio: *Indian Lives and Legends.*

Charlie (Lim Foon) Ting *Chinatown spokesperson* d. Feb. 9, 1939, Vancouver. Known as "Charlie the Christian" because of his benevolence, "his was the religion of the helping hand." President, Chinese Benevolent Association. His funeral, at the Oriental Theatre, was attended by more than 500 people in 200 cars, and crowds filled the streets. "No resident of Chinatown was ever given such lavish rites." At the time residents of Chinatown numbered approximately 36,000.

Charles Edward Tisdall *Mayor of Vancouver, 1922-23* See Mayors of Vancouver.

Peter Claude Toigo *Entrepreneur* b. Sept. 9, 1932, Powell River, B.C.; d. Oct. 6, 1993, Los Angeles, Calif. His parents came from N. Italy. At seven, sold eggs door-to-door in Powell River. In 1949, at 17, bought Wildwood Grocery and worked as a butcher. In 1950 married his childhood sweetheart, Elizabeth Rowher, and completed first major land transaction. In 1960 bought downtown Powell River from MacMillan Bloedel; built its first shopping centre. In mid-1970s his company, Shato Holdings, almost went bankrupt but it survived and expanded, buying the White Spot restaurant chain (Dec. 1982). An intensely private man, he was dogged by controversy on labor issues and SC party connections.

Frederick Laughton Townley *Architect, designer* b. 1887, Winnipeg, Man.; d. Oct. 17, 1966, Vancouver. Son of mayor, T.O. TOWNLEY. Attended Point Grey Jr. HS; apprenticed at 14 as an architect. In 1910 graduated from U. of Pennsylvania. One of only five architects in Vancouver when he set up practice in 1911. Founding member, Architectural Institute of B.C. Designed Vancouver city hall ("a proud, modern, 1936 streamlined building") and more than 1,000 buildings. These include Great Northern Railway station, Capitol Theatre, Vancouver General Hospital, Vancouver Stock Exchange Building and Canadian National Institute for the Blind Building.

Thomas Owen Townley *Mayor of Vancouver, 1901* See Mayors of Vancouver.

Chang Toy *Businessman* b. c. 1856, China; d. China on a business trip, c. June 1920. A farmer's son, he arrived in B.C. at 17. Established the Sam Kee Co. c. 1888. (The company name was often used as the name of a person.) Sam Kee produced charcoal, contracted Chinese labor, ran a Nanaimo herring saltery, imported and exported food products and acted as agent for Blue Funnel Steamship Line. Bought land at 8 Pender in 1906. In 1926 it was expropriated by the city, leaving him a 1.8-metre-wide strip. To spite city hall, he built the world's narrowest commercial building, still in use. His older sons, Chang Yat Jun and Chang Yat Leong, were active in the firm.

Ethlyn Trapp *Radiologist* b. July 18, 1891, New Westminster; d. July 31, 1972, Vancouver. Daughter of THOMAS TRAPP. Graduate of McGill (BA, 1913), then worked in WWI military hospitals. MD (McGill, 1927). Studied in Europe, then practised in Vancouver. Using her own money, set up a centre to prove the benefits of radiotherapy (1937). Director, B.C. Cancer Institute (1939-44). First woman president, B.C. Medical Association (1946-47); first woman president, National Cancer Institute of Canada (1952); president, Federation of Canadian Medical Women. Delivered Osler Lecture (1952) to Vancouver Medical Association. LL.D (UBC, 1954). Awarded citation from Canadian Medical Association (1963) for cancer research. Medal of service, Order of Canada (1968). An art collector, she deeded her home, Klee Wyck (named for friend EMILY CARR), to West Vancouver as an arts centre.

Thomas John Trapp *Businessman* b. June 4, 1842, Waltham Abbey, Essex, Eng.; d. Jan. 19, 1933, New Westminster. Came to Canada in 1872. Joined Cassiar gold rush, managed an Athabasca CPR survey depot, ranched in Nicola Valley. In 1880, after a severe winter, moved to New Westminster with brother Samuel. Soon opened T.J. Trapp and Co., a wholesale and retail hardware firm. Built Trapp Block on Columbia (1912-13), easily noted from SkyTrain. Three of his four sons

died in action in WWI; one of his three daughters was Dr. ETHLYN TRAPP. Instrumental in building New Westminster Southern Railway. Member, Ancient Order of United Workmen and Woodmen of the World.

U

Eileen (Margaret Eileen Stuart) Underhill (née George) *Badminton champion* b. April 1, 1889, Moosomin, Sask.; d. July 31, 1988, Vancouver. Moved to Vancouver in 1910. Considered to be B.C.'s all-time best female badminton player, she dominated the sport from 1927-36. With husband, Jack (John Edward) Underhill (b. Sept. 3, 1902, Vancouver; d. July 14, 1974, Vancouver), won National Doubles Championship for three consecutive years. Five times B.C. mixed doubles champions (1928-31, 1935). Jack was Canada's top male badminton star (1925-47), winning numerous B.C. and national championships. The Underhills were the first husband-and-wife team in the B.C. Sports Hall of Fame (1970).

V

James Van Bramer (also Bremer, Braemer) *Ferry captain* b. U.S.; d. Jan. 9, 1895, Santa Barbara, Calif. Partner of sawmill owner SEW MOODY. Both were Masons, founders of Mount Hermon Lodge in 1869. His steam tug, *Sea Foam*, Burrard Inlet's first regular transit service, ran from Brighton, near the site of today's Alberta Wheat Pool elevator, to Moodyville, Stamp's Mill and back. On Nov. 5, 1869, its upper decks were destroyed by fire. In 1888 built the Springer-Van Bramer Block (Cordova and Cambie), home to Mount Hermon and Cascade Masonic lodges. In early 1890s backed a treasure hunt to Cocos Island aboard his vessel, *Eliza Edward*. Retired to Santa Barbara.

George Vancouver *Explorer* See Captain George Vancouver.

John Vanderpant *Photographer* b. Jan. 11, 1884, Alkmaar, Netherlands; d. July 24, 1939, Vancouver. Arrived in New Westminster in 1919. Ran a commercial portrait studio and promoted arts locally, especially Group of Seven. An innovator, he was known for his interpretive photography and pictorialism, the application of painterly techniques. His experimental works, including close-ups of vegetables and cement surfaces, were internationally known. The Vanderpant Gallery on Robson was a centre of intellectual life in the city from 1926-39. Biblio: *Underlying Vibrations: The Photography of John Vanderpant* by Sheryl Salloum.

Whitford Julian VanDusen *Lumber magnate* b. 1889, Tara, Ont.; d. Dec. 15, 1978, Vancouver. In 1912 at U of T he met H.R. MACMILLAN, who pushed him to study forestry (BSc, 1912). From 1913 through WWI worked as a B.C. forester. In the fall of 1919 joined H.R. MacMillan Export as manager; senior vice president (1945-49). Follow-

ing merger with Bloedel, Stewart and Welch, named vice chair (1949-56). Remained on board of MacMillan Bloedel until he retired (1969). Involved in philanthropic works, including Vancouver Foundation (1943). Donated the purchase amount for the Shaughnessy Golf Course, now the VanDusen Botanical Gardens.

William Cornelius Van Horne *CPR executive* b. Feb. 3, 1843, Chelsea, Ill.; d. Sept. 11, 1915, Montreal. Began work at 14 with Illinois Central Railroad. By 1880 was general superintendent of the Milwaukee Road. Two years later joined CPR as general manager. Managed railway construction from Winnipeg to Calgary (to Aug. 1883). Visited Granville on Aug. 6, 1884; advocated renaming it Vancouver. Pushed rapid completion of main line from Montreal to Port Moody. Named CPR president in 1888. He launched the Empress line of Pacific steamships (1891) from Vancouver to Hong Kong. Knighted in 1894.

C.B.K. (Charles Burwell Kerrins) Van Norman *Architect* b. March 20, 1907, Meaford, Ont.; d. Sept. 13, 1975, Vancouver. Graduated in architecture (U. of Manitoba, 1927). Came to Vancouver in 1928. From 1930 his work included mansions for General A.D. McRAE, H.R. MacMILLAN and F. Ronald Graham. Designed Customs House, Burrard Building, Maritime Museum, Eagle Crest Lodge at Qualicum Beach. Specialized in post-WWII schools and pre-fab homes. Design consultant, Royal Centre (Burrard and Georgia); designed many of Park Royal's stores. After convincing the city to allow wider balconies than previously permitted, he won the Canadian Housing Design Council's Centennial Award for Beach Towers (1600 Beach).

Frederick Horsman Varley *Artist* b. Jan. 2, 1881, Sheffield, Eng.; d. Sept. 8, 1969, Toronto, Ont. Attended Sheffield School of Art (1892-1900) and Academie royale des beaux-arts in Antwerp, Belgium (1900-02). Immigrated to Canada in 1912. A hometown friend, artist Arthur Lismer, found him a job in Toronto as a commercial illustrator. Later met Tom Thomson and Frank Carmichael. Acclaimed for war paintings commissioned by Canadian War Records. A founder of the Group of Seven (May 1920). Taught at Vancouver School of Decorative and Applied Arts from 1926. In 1933, with J.W.G. MacDonald, opened the B.C. College of Arts.

Alvo (Gustav Konstantin) von Alvensleben *Realtor, suspected spy* b. July 25, 1879, Neu Gettersleben, Germany; d. 1965, Seattle, Wash. Son of Count Werner von Alvensleben, Alvo resigned from the army and left Hamburg, arriving in Vancouver in June 1904. A busy entrepreneur, he is said to have brought $10 million of German investment to Western Canada. Bought Wigwam Inn at Indian River Park, launched with a party for

600. Rumored to be a spy in 1914; said to have left Vancouver in women's clothes on a night train to Seattle. His Canadian assets were taken by the Custodian of Enemy Property. Interned in 1917 near Salt Lake City. Moved to Seattle after WWI; became a U.S. citizen (1939). A possible submarine base was found at the Pacofi Bay site of his Pacific Coast Fishing Co. in the 1930s. He denied he had ever been a spy.

W

George Alexander Walkem *Shipbuilder* b. July 8, 1872, Montreal, Que.; d. Dec. 13, 1936, Burnaby, B.C. After graduating from McGill, he joined the Royal Engineers, serving in Egypt and Palestine. Moved to Vancouver in 1898. President of West Coast Shipbuilders, Vancouver Iron Works, West Coast Salvage and Construction, and Gulf of Georgia Towing. Reeve, Point Grey (1923-24); MLA, Richmond-Point Grey (1924-28) and Vancouver from 1933 for a total of nine years. In 1946 he lobbied B.C. "to improve the quality of cooking for public consumption" in order to increase tourism. His ashes were scattered over English Bay from the tug *George A. Walkem*.

Andy (Alfred) Wallace *Burrard Shipyards founder* b. 1865, Moricetown, Eng.; d. Jan. 1, 1929, North Vancouver. Son of a master shipbuilder, he first worked in Owen Sound, Ont. In 1894 started a small False Creek shipyard. By 1906 operated on the North Shore as Wallace Shipyards. By 1910 Burrard Drydock was well established. In 1921 built *Princess Louise* for CPR fleet, the first contract awarded to a local firm. During WWI built merchant and naval vessels. Son, CLARENCE WALLACE, continued expansion. The company was one of the largest shipyards on the B.C. coast. In 1928 built *St. Roch*, now exhibited in Marine Museum, Vanier Park.

Clarence Wallace *Shipbuilder, lieutenant-governor* b. June 22, 1893, Vancouver; d. Nov. 12, 1982, Palm Desert, Calif. On leaving college, joined family business (see ANDY WALLACE). Served overseas (1914-16); wounded at Ypres. In 1918 secretary-treasurer of Burrard Drydock; in 1929 named president. During WWII built North Sands and Victory ships and converted vessels for war use. Awarded CBE (1946). Acquired Yarrows Ltd. of Esquimalt (1946), Pacific Drydock (1951) and shipbuilding operations of Victoria Machinery Depot (1967). In 1972 the Wallace family sold Burrard Drydock to Cornat Industries of Vancouver. Lieutenant-governor (1950-55).

Jack Wasserman *Columnist* b. Feb. 17, 1927, Winnipeg, Man.; d. April 6, 1977, Vancouver. Came to Vancouver in 1935. Dropped out of law school to take reporter's job with *Ubyssey*. Graduated from UBC (1949); joined *Vancouver Sun*, becoming a police reporter. His biggest scoop was the death of Errol Flynn in a West End apartment. Longtime

gossip and self-described "saloon reporter" columnist. Hosted an open line program with CJOR; later hosted *Hourglass* on CBC TV. Fired by the *Sun* (1967) for hosting his radio show but rehired 18 months later. A governor of the National Film Board. Died of a heart attack while speaking at the Hotel Vancouver during a roast for GORDON GIBSON SR.

Rebecca Belle Watson *Community activist* b. c. 1911, Kitsilano; d. April 7, 1976, Vancouver. Taught in the Cariboo, then trained as a nurse at Vancouver General Hospital. In 1958, as spokesperson for Save Our Parklands Association, rescued the Shaughnessy Golf Course from development. Ran unsuccessfully as independent alderman (1961, 1962). Elected to Vancouver park board (1968). Executive member, TEAM; president, PC Party of B.C. (1971). A West End resident, she was active in its community associations. Named to Vancouver Civic Merit Board of Honor (the 22nd inductee in its 34-year history).

Rick (Richard Alan) Watson *Disabled rights activist, writer* b. April 14, 1953, Bowmanville, Ont.; d. April 30, 1994, Vancouver. Disabled by cerebral palsy, he was a *Province* columnist from Sept. 1991, pecking out one letter at a time with a wand attached to a headband. Won a Canada 125 medal for his work for the disabled and a B.C. Newspaper Award for a column critical of telethons, one of which he had appeared on as a child. Assigned to write on services for the disabled for *The Greater Vancouver Book*, but died suddenly. Active in B.C. Coalition of People with Disabilities (BCCPD) as founding editor. Also wrote poetry. "His sense of humor offset the rage and despair he occasionally felt."

Agnes Watts *Telethon angel* b. 1899, Bunzlau, Germany; d. Oct. 30, 1989, Vancouver. At 19 came to Victoria as a nanny. Married a logger, and moved to Powell River; later divorced. Moved to Vancouver, married Isaac Watts in 1944 (d. 1952). First female employee of Scott Paper's New Westminster mill, "rolling toilet paper" for 22 years. She became a millionaire from stocks and real estate investments such as West End rooming houses. A patron of the Variety Club of B.C., she donated over $500,000 to children's projects. Received Variety Club Humanitarian Award from Prince Philip in London, Eng., in 1987. "Children were her great love."

William Watts *Boat builder* b. 1862, Collingwood, Ont.; d. May 8, 1954, West Vancouver. Came to Vancouver in 1887 with partner Edward Trott. For three summers, they ferried miners up Harrison Lake. In 1889 they opened a boat building business, Watts and Trott (later Vancouver Shipyards). Their firm built the city's first steamboat. A record-breaking rower, sailor, sport fisher and driver. In 1890 he won the B.C. rowing champi-

onship in a shell he built himself. "One of B.C.'s most colorful personalities."

Gertrude Weinrobe *First Jewish child born in Vancouver* b. May 12, 1893, Vancouver; d. Aug. 9, 1975, Vancouver. Daughter of Barney Weinrobe, a Russian, and Sara Sarbesky, a German (m. Montreal, Jan. 1884). In 1893 the family rode by train to Vancouver. On Feb. 13, 1893, three weeks after arriving, their eight-year-old son, Nathan, died of diphtheria, the first child buried in Mountain View's pioneer Jewish cemetery (Fraser and 37th). Gertrude, the first Jewish baby born in Vancouver, grew up in Vancouver Island mining towns where Barney ran stores. She received the 1971 B.C. Pioneer Centennial Medal. She was also buried in Mountain View.

George Moir Weir *Education innovator* b. May 10, 1885, Stonewall, Man.; d. Dec. 4, 1949, Vancouver. Entered politics in 1933 as a Lib. MLA. Named minister of education, serving for nearly a decade; also provincial secretary. In 1936 he advocated health insurance coverage for those living on $1,800 a year or less. Although not passed because of opposition by doctors, it was the basis of the B.C. Hospital Insurance Act. Left politics in 1941; returned as minister of education (Vancouver Burrard, 1946), supervising radical changes in school curricula. Head of UBC education department. LL.D (UBC, 1948). George M. Weir School is named for him.

Frank Fairchild Wesbrook *Bacteriologist, founding president of UBC* b. July 12, 1868, Brant County, Ont.; d. Oct. 20, 1918, Vancouver. Graduated from U. of Manitoba (1890), followed by studies in London, Dublin and Marburg. Awarded a studentship at Cambridge (1892). At 27 he was asked to head the U. of Minnesota's pathology department; later dean of medicine (1906). Published hard-hitting papers on medical and general university education. A forerunner of F.G. Banting in diabetes research. Founding president of UBC (1913-18). Suffered a recurring illness attributable to Bright's disease.

Thomas Moore Whaun *Political activist* b. Oct. 22, 1893, Toisan, Canton, China; d. March 5, 1985, West Vancouver. One of the first Asian residents of West Vancouver; second Chinese-Canadian graduate of UBC (BA, 1927). Emigrated to Canada in 1907. Worked in the newspaper industry as advertising manager for *Canada Morning News* and *New Republic Daily*, two of Vancouver's Chinese newspapers. Known for his nationwide letter-writing protest against the Chinese Exclusion Act. An altruist, he was committed to helping others. He became a Canadian citizen in 1950.

Edward White *Pioneer Methodist cleric* b. Nov. 11, 1822, Philadelphia, Penn; d. June 16, 1872, Montreal, of smallpox. Arrived from Smithville, Ont., on Friday, April 1, 1859, on the steamer *Elisa*

Anderson. On Sunday, April 3, preached his first sermon, by the Fraser in Queensborough (New Westminster), with "The Lord, our God made a covenant with us in Horeb" as text. One woman (Mrs. James Kennedy) and 50 men were present. An "expert axman," Rev. White built a shack at 6th and Carnarvon, site of Queen's Ave. United Church. Served as minister (1859-62; 1865-67). His son, Newton Arthur White, was the first white child born in New Westminster (b. July 29, 1859; d. July 31, 1899, New Westminster).

Arthur Bryan Williams *Game and forest warden* b. c. 1867, County Clare, Ire.; d. Feb. 16, 1946, Vancouver. Came to B.C. in 1888 from London, Eng. In 1905 became a game and forest warden. Later, as game commissioner, he formulated B.C.'s game preservation and hunting laws, including one copied worldwide that protected a trapper's personal trap line from encroachment. Published *Game Trails of British Columbia* and *Rod and Creel in B.C.* and wrote a series of articles for the Vancouver *Daily Province,* c. 1926. An expert guide and "dean of B.C. hunters."

Percy Alfred Williams *Sprinter* b. May 19, 1908, Vancouver; d. Nov. 29, 1982, Vancouver. Canada's leading track athlete of the 1920s; only Canadian to win two Olympic gold medals in track. He graduated from King Edward HS. Won 1928 Olympics in both the 100-metre and 200-metre races; world record holder 100 metre (1930-40); last ran in 1932 Olympics. After retirement he ran an insurance business in Vancouver until his death by suicide.

Ethel Davis Wilson (née Bryant) *Writer* b. Jan. 20, 1888, Port Elizabeth, South Africa; d. Dec. 22, 1980, Vancouver. An orphan, she came to Vancouver in 1898 to live with her grandmother. Taught in public schools (1907-20). In 1921 married Dr. Wallace Wilson. Began writing in 1937; in 1947 her first novel, *Hetty Dorval,* was published. From 1947-57, she wrote four more novels, best known being *Swamp Angel. Mrs. Golightly and Other Stories,* her last published work, appeared in 1961, the year she received a special Canada Council medal for contributions to Canadian literature. Awarded D.Litt (UBC, 1955); Lorne Pierce Medal (Royal Society of Canada, 1960); Order of Canada Medal of Service (1970). B.C.'s top fiction prize is named for her.

Harold Edward Winch *Politician* b. June 18, 1907, Loughton, Eng.; d. Feb. 1, 1993, Vancouver. Son of labor leader Ernest Winch. Arrived in B.C. in 1910. Elected CCF MLA for working class riding of Vancouver East (1933-53). Leader of CCF (1938-53). Leader of the opposition (1941-53). Came close to being premier in 1952-53. A bitter rival of W.A.C. Bennett, he coined the nickname "Wacky." Served as CCF/NDP MP, Vancouver East (1953-72). LL.D (UBC, 1973).

Richard Vance Winch *Cannery pioneer* b. 1862, Cobourg, Ont.; d. July 31, 1952, Vancouver. Ran away from home at 16, herded cattle and worked on CPR, arriving in B.C. in 1893. Established Canadian Packers Canning on the Fraser. In 1895 shipped first trainload of canned salmon from B.C. and sold first B.C. halibut in New York. In 1895 opened Queen Charlotte Fisheries. Owned seven canneries and a sawmill, valued at $1.6 million. Erected the Winch Building (739 W. Hastings) in 1909. Wife Isabelle Jane (b. Cobourg, Ont; d. Dec. 5, 1939, Vancouver) assisted his business activities for more than 50 years.

Calvin Winter *Orchestra leader, theatre manager* b. Auburn, Indiana; d. Feb. 5, 1946, Vancouver. He arrived in 1919 to play in Hotel Vancouver orchestra. Was one of the first radio conductors in the early 1920s. His band, Calvin Winter and His Capitolians, played for the Capitol Theatre opening in 1921. Operated Nelson's civic theatre, Vancouver's Music Box and Marpole Theatre in succession from 1936. Best known as conductor of Home Gas Sunday Symphony Hour at Malkin Memorial Bowl before WWII.

Gordon Sylvester Wismer *Lawyer, attorney general* b. March 23, 1888, Sutton, Ont.; d. Dec. 28, 1968, Victoria. Worked his way west, arriving in Vancouver in 1907. Began law practice in 1913 with GERALD G. McGEER. From 1922 ran his own firm, becoming one of B.C.'s best-known criminal lawyers. Elected Lib. MLA (Vancouver Centre, 1933). Served as attorney general under Pattullo from July 5, 1937; under Hart from April 4, 1946; and under Johnson until defeat of coalition government in 1952. Established New Haven Borstal School for Young Offenders (1938) and disbanded B.C. Police Force (1950), transferring policing duties to the RCMP.

Foon Sien Wong (aka Wong Mon Poo) *Spokesperson for Chinese rights* b. c. late 1890s, Canton; d. July 31, 1971, Vancouver. At 10 his family came to Vancouver Island and became well-off Cumberland, B.C., merchants. In 1911 met and was influenced by Dr. Sun Yat-Sen. Graduated from UBC; worked as legal interpreter and translator. In 1937 named publicity agent of Chinese Benevolent Association's (CBA) aid-to-China program during Sino-Japanese War. In 1945 pushed for vote for Chinese residents after war service. As president of Vancouver CBA (1947-59) pursued human rights issues, especially immigration laws. In the 1960s led fight to stop the bulldozing of Strathcona's Chinese homes. "The unofficial mayor of Chinatown."

Freddie (Frederic Gordon Campbell) Wood *University Players' Club founder* b. Jan. 26, 1887, Victoria; d. June 3, 1976, Vancouver. McGill graduate (1910). Taught in Victoria, then attended Harvard (MA, 1915). First B.C.-born educator at UBC

when it opened in 1915, retiring in 1950. Founded and directed University Players' Club (1915-31). Annually toured a student show across B.C., the only live theatre seen in many towns, Wife Beatrice (b. Nov. 29, 1899, Vancouver, d. July 18, 1992, Vancouver) was the daughter of Lieutenant-Governor John William Fordham-Johnson (1931-36). University Players' Club disbanded in 1966 after the launch of UBC's theatre department. D.Litt (UBC, 1971). Co-founder, Vancouver Little Theatre with E.V. Young. Frederic Wood Theatre is named for him.

George Woodcock *Writer* b. May 18, 1912, Winnipeg, Man.; d. Jan. 28, 1995, Vancouver. A literary intellectual in London, Eng., 1930s-40s. Moved to B.C. in 1949. Taught at UBC. Founder/editor, *Canadian Literature* (1959-77). A prolific author of over 150 books, including *The Crystal Spirit: A study of George Orwell* and *British Columbia, A History of the Province.* Winner, Governor General's Award (1966). D.Litt (UBC, 1977). First writer made Freeman of the City of Vancouver (1994). With his wife, Ingeborg, a Jewish refugee from the Third Reich, supported refugee causes and founded Tibetan Refugee Aid Society. Biblio: *Letters to the Past; Beyond the Blue Mountains.*

Steve (Stephen Francis) Woodman *Entertainer* b. Aug. 24, 1927, Saskatoon, Sask.; d. March 13, 1990, Vancouver. The "man of 1,000 voices" on popular radio and TV shows from CKUA Edmonton to WNBC New York. Interviewed Bing Crosby, the Beatles and the chimp, J. Fred Muggs. The first Ronald McDonald in L.A., where he hosted a TV show and performed in movies and award-winning commercials with legendary Mel Blanc. Moved to Vancouver in 1971. Appeared on network CBC as "Squeaky the Milk Elf" and wacky Dr. Bundolo (recorded live at UBC's student union building). Hosted CKWX's *Steve's Place* and Vancouver Variety Club telethons. After a 1974 telethon a car accident on black ice nearly took his life and ended his career.

Frank Everett Woodside *"Mining's Grand Old Man"* b. Dec. 8, 1874, Hamilton, PEI; d. Oct. 14, 1954, Vancouver. A sixth generation Canadian, he left home at 16 to mine in Colorado and Rossland, B.C. As secretary, Western Federation of Miners, helped pass B.C.'s eight-hour-day bill (1898). Came to Vancouver in 1903. In 1910 lobbied to end Hastings Townsite's ties with Burnaby and join Vancouver. The vote was held at 2598 Eton, adjacent to Frank's home (2594 Eton, now a heritage site). First alderman for Hastings Townsite area (1911-28). Charter member, B.C. Chamber of Mines (1912); president (1920). In 1922 Big Frank began a winter night school for prospectors. Appointed first manager in 1928, retiring after a 60-year mining career. A mountain in the Fraser Valley is named for him.

Charles A. Woodward *Department store founder* b. July 19, 1852, on a farm near Hamilton, Ont.; d. June 2, 1937, Vancouver. His first business venture was in a log cabin on Manitoulin Island, Ont. In 1891 visited Vancouver and bought two lots for a store, moving west in 1892. Woodward's drug department opened in 1895. In 1901 he took an option on a lot at 101 Hastings and incorporated as Woodward's Department Stores. The first store opened in Nov. 1903. In 1910 the store held its first one-price sale day, 25 Cents Day, a forerunner of $1.49 Day. Named to Canadian Business Hall of Fame (1966). Biblio: *The Woodwards* by Douglas Harker.

Chunky (Charles Nanby Wynn) Woodward *Retailer* b. March 23, 1924, Vancouver; d. April 27, 1990, Vancouver. Grandson of CHARLES A. WOODWARD and son of W.C. WOODWARD. In 1946 joined Woodward's Department Stores. Fought in WWII with 12th Manitoba Dragoons. In Oct. 1956 named president of Woodward's B.C. and Alberta chain. Involved in B.C. Place Stadium and Whistler developments. Worked with horses at his 220,000-hectare Douglas Lake ranch; established rodeo circuits across Western Canada. Received W.A.C. Bennett Award for sports contributions from B.C. Sports Hall of Fame (1986). Resigned as Woodward's president in 1988. The firm was purchased by The Bay in 1993.

William Culham Woodward *Retailer, lieutenant-governor* b. April 24, 1885, Gore Bay, Manitoulin Island, Ont.; d. Feb. 24, 1957, Hawaii. Son of CHARLES A. WOODWARD. At 16 he worked as a $15/month Royal Bank clerk. In 1908 joined Woodward's as bookkeeper. Served with First Canadian Heavy Artillery, then with Occupation forces (1916-18). Honorary colonel of 15th Field Regiment, 1932. During WWII served without pay as executive assistant to munitions and supply minister C.D. Howe. Lieutenant-governor (1941-46). Ran Woodward's with his brother, Percival Archibald Woodward, to 1956, the year his son CHUNKY WOODWARD became president. That same year, named colonel at large of the militia, a rank created for him by defence minister Ralph Campney.

George Harvey Worthington *Drug store chain founder* b. c. 1876, on a farm near Guelph, Ont.; d. May 13, 1954, Vancouver. Ontario College of Pharmacy graduate (1898). Spent a year in New York as a drug clerk, then opened pharmacies in Guelph and Toronto. Graduated in medicine (U of T, 1908). Came to Vancouver in 1909 working as a doctor to 1919, when he established Vancouver Drug Co. Alderman for Ward Six (1924-26); he founded the Vancouver Water District. In 1926 ran for mayor but lost to L.D. TAYLOR. Alderman (1940-44). Ran again for mayor but lost to J.W. Cornett. Retired in 1939, selling 23 drugstores to

Cunningham's. In memory of two sons killed in WWII, he willed $100,000 to UBC.

Ben Wosk *Furniture merchant* b. March 19, 1913, Vradiavka (near Odessa), Russia; d. Jan. 24, 1995, Honolulu, Hawaii. Arrived at Vancouver in 1929 with his family. By 1932 was dealing in old stoves from a small shop on Granville. Founded Wosk's Ltd., which owned and operated furniture and appliance stores, hotels and apartment buildings. With brother Abram (Abe) Wosk, the president of Schara Tzedeck synagogue, he chaired the Burn the Mortgage campaign in 1953. For his work with the B.C. Heart Foundation, Vancouver Epilepsy Centre, Boy Scouts and others, The Native Sons of B.C. named him Good Citizen of the Year (1975). Member, Order of Canada (1978).

Y

Yasutaro Yamaga *Laborer,* b. 1886, Toyohama-mura, Hiroshima-ken, Japan; d. Aug. 24, 1971, Beamsville, Ont. Came to B.C. from Seattle in 1907. After working as a CPR laborer, bought four hectares near Haney, B.C. (1908). Spoke English well and understood the Canadian way of life. Organized Japanese social clubs in Haney; imported Japanese schoolbooks from the U.S. to replace Japanese government textbooks. Led Fraser Valley's Japanese Farmers' Union. After WWII internment in Tashme, B.C., ran a sawmill at 70 Mile House, then moved to Beamsville. Established Nipponia Home, the first Japanese-Canadian senior citizen's home in Canada.

Yasushi Yamazaki *Publisher* b. May 11, 1871, Toyama, Japan; d. 1947, Japan. Came to B.C. in 1893; worked as logger, fisher, miner. Secretary, Japanese Fishermen's Union in Steveston (1900). Active in Japanese fishermen's strike (1900-01). Began publishing in Seattle in 1902; in 1908, started Vancouver's *Tairiku Nippo Sha* (*Continental Daily News*). Led a campaign against the prostitution of Japanese women. President, Canadian Japanese Association (1909-17). Organized Canadian Japanese Volunteer Corp (WWI) hoping it would lead to the vote, but the corps of 200 was rejected as too small. From 1917-33 editor of a newspaper in Japanese-held Manchuria. "His life was a full but lonely one."

Kew Ghim Yip *Physician* b. Jan. 16, 1902, Vancouver; d. Dec. 13, 1968, Vancouver. Son of YIP SANG. One of first Chinese general practitioners in Vancouver. He attended Central Elem., King George HS, and Queen's. Interned as a doctor in Ann Arbor, Mich., because of B.C. restrictions on Asian hospital interns. Practised in Chinatown (1927-68). In the days before medical coverage, he conducted a free weekly clinic at Main and Hastings for old age pensioners and others. Doctor with Mount St. Joseph Hospital on Campbell Ave., and helped raise funds for its Prince Edward site. Active in the Chinese community; known for

his philanthropic work.

Frederick McBain Young *Judge, Masonic leader* b. Oct. 30, 1863, English River, Que.; d. May 31, 1937, Vancouver. Brother of Dr. HENRY YOUNG. He was Grand Master of the Grand Lodge of B.C. Masons (1901, 1902). Laid the cornerstone of Vancouver's Carnegie Library (March 29, 1902), receiving an engraved trowel from the city. First judge of the county court of Atlin, B.C. (1905). Served 28 years as judge in Prince Rupert county court (from 1907). Retired and returned to Vancouver (Jan. 1933).

Henry Esson Young *Father of UBC* b. Feb. 24, 1867, English River, Que.; d. Oct. 24, 1939, Victoria. Graduate of Queen's and McGill. Practised medicine in the U.S.; served as houseman to Sir William Osler; joined the gold rush. Elected MLA (Atlin, 1903). As minister of education and provincial secretary in Premier McBride's cabinet (1907-16), he founded UBC. LL.D (UBC, 1925). Created Metropolitan Health Board with Rockefeller Foundation funds. Essondale Mental Hospital in Coquitlam was named for him. Met wife, Rosalind (b. c. 1874; d. February 1962, Victoria), a gold medallist at McGill, in the Cariboo researching her MA thesis (m. 1904). She was Victoria's first university graduate female HS teacher and introduced girl's grass hockey.

Z

Wanda Bianca Selma Ziegler (née Muller) *Candy store chain president* b. 1874, Ballersted, Prussia; d. March 3, 1967, Fort Langley, B.C. Came to Vancouver in 1911 with husband Fritz (b. Germany) and two children. Her father was reeve of Ballersted, an office passed on in the family since the 15th century. Fritz established Ziegler Chocolate Shops in 1921. When he died in 1923, there were three shops. Wanda became president, developing the chain to 11 stores. Her son, Fritz Alfred Wilhelm (b. Feb. 12, 1902, Wittenberge, Germany), served as managing director. She retired in 1956, after 33 years, and the shops closed.

1995-1997 . . . and stuff keeps right on happening

Shane McCune

PICKING UP AT the point where Hilary Blair's chronology ends in this book, the years 1995 and 1996 saw a number of Notable Events in This Part of the World.

In late 1996 Statistics Canada made it official: Fewer than half of Vancouver residents speak English at home. The changing linguistic makeup is most keenly felt in the schools, where English as a second language programs have long passed the crisis point. A *Province* newspaper report in November 1996 revealed that 49 percent of Vancouver students needed ESL instruction. In Richmond, ESL enrolment rose from 324 in 1987 to 10,108 in 1996. And education minister Moe Sihota candidly admitted, "there is no ESL policy," leaving schools to run their own programs with varying quality. Teachers and sociologists warn that today's linguistically alienated kids are tomorrow's violent misfits, yet budgetary restraints and a backlash among English-speaking citizens seem to guarantee that area schools will be hard-pressed to maintain order, let alone educate, as more students understand less of their lessons.

The Stanley Theatre, an empty husk since its screening of Fantasia on Sept. 25, 1991 will go forward into its past as a home to live theatre . . . soon . . . we think. Plans to redevelop the old vaudeville palace as a residential-commercial complex were shelved in favor of a joint bid from the Arts Club and TheatreSports, an improvisational comedy troupe. But the hoped-for opening date of "fall of '96" recently changed to "fall of '97."

The new Justice Institute of B.C. complex arose at 8th and McBride in New Westminster. *Vancouver Sun* architecture critic Robin Ward wrote: "Richard Henriquez's quirky style, a combination of artistry and functionality, enriches but does not dominate the design. Library Square, by comparison, is a monument not to enlightenment (as it should have been) but to civic boosterism and architect Moshe Safdie's overblown ego." Safdie said petty jealousy was behind the drubbing his new library took from many local architects and pundits. Certainly the public embraced the building, doubling library usage within a month of its opening.

The old library at Robson and Burrard was designated a heritage site, but it was uncertain how much of it would survive the conversion to a retail space housing Canada's first Planet Hollywood restaurant and a huge Virgin Records store.

The 50-year-old neon sign that adorned Dunn's Tailors store on West Hastings Street was saved when Dunn's moved to the Rogers Building at Granville and Pender.

The Port of Vancouver converted the run-down Ballantyne Pier to a transport of delight—a general cargo and cruise ship terminal—even though only one of its original four neo-Georgian facades was saved.

The Vancouver Trade and Convention Centre, a waterfront legacy of Expo 86, is already bursting at the seams. Wheels in the tourism biz agree Vancouver needs another convention centre—but they are divided on who should build what where. Marathon Developments (which had been Marathon realty until it was sold in 1996 by Canadian Pacific) proposes a new facility to the west of the current centre while the Vancouver Port Corp. wants to build to the east. Naturally, Gastown merchants favor the latter proposal. And Concord Pacific proposes a titanic complex of more than 92,900 sq. metres with up to 65,030 sq. metres of it buried under a theme park nestled next to the Queen Elizabeth Theatre, B.C. Place Stadium and GM Place. Whatever happens, Marathon is well into a massive, multi-billion redevelopment of Coal Harbour, which will see most of the city waterfront west of Burrard turned into condos for the Benz bunch, with a sidewalk and a clump of grass for the bootless and unhorsed to shuffle from Burrard to Stanley Park.

Another indicator of the city's booming hospitality industry was the opening in 1995 of the 275-suite Rosedale hotel at Robson and Hamilton, the first new downtown Vancouver inn since the Wall Centre Garden Hotel the previous year. The Rosedale was officially opened Oct. 18 by Chow Yei Ching, chairman of Chevalier International Holdings of Hong Kong.

Engineers agree the Lions Gate Bridge, erected in 1938, will be unsafe, statistically speaking, by 1999, but they disagree on what to do about it. Some say a new, wider roadbed would do the trick. A 1995 government report recommended replacing the bridge with twin tunnels at a cost of $350 million. As of autumn, 1996, the provincial government was facing unforecast deficits and didn't even want to think about the First Narrows crossing.

Traffic around the Oak Street and Arthur Laing bridges was snarled all day on Saturday April 27, 1996 as 42,000 Lower Mainlanders jammed an open house at the Vancouver International Airport's new $260-million international terminal. Four years in the planning, the 116,000 sq. metre (1.25 million sq. foot) terminal will allow six million more travelers per year to visit Vancouver. The old main terminal, opened in 1968, will serve only domestic flights. Despite years of opposition from nearby homeowners, the airport opened its new runway in November. Complaints of noise mushroomed. Led by Olympic gold medalist Donovan Bailey and wheelchair athlete

Rick Hansen, 10,000 ticketholders jogged down the new $100 million runway at Vancouver International Airport during its official opening Saturday, Nov. 2. The runway is 3,030 metres long, 60 metres wide and 38 centimetres thick.

In September 1995 Premier Mike Harcourt promised a new light-rail-transit line along the Broadway-Lougheed corridor from Granville Street to Coquitlam Centre, to be up and running by 2005. A year later there was little talk of the new line.

In March, Bjossa the killer whale gave birth at the Vancouver Aquarium to her third calf. Like the other two, it soon died, renewing calls to free the whales. On July 23, 1995 Aurora, a beluga whale, gave birth to a 70-kilogram baby dubbed Qila, bringing the aquarium's cetacean population to nine: two orcas, six belugas and a dolphin. On Sept. 30, 1996 the NPA-dominated Vancouver board of parks and recreation defeated a COPE motion that would have prohibited the practice. Instead, the board ordered the aquarium to restrict its capture program to sick, stranded or endangered animals. The aquarium may still acquire whales from other aquariums.

In November 1996 the Stanley Park Zoo's 22 Humboldt penguins were flown to the Brookfield Zoo in Chicago. That left the dilapidated zoo empty save for Tuk, a 34-year-old polar bear deemed too old to move. When Tuk dies, the zoo dies.

On Dec. 3, 1995 the curtain rose on *Show Boat,* the first production at the Ford Centre for the Performing Arts, the brainchild of Garth Drabinsky's Livent Inc.

Director Hal Prince's version of the Jerome Kern-Oscar Hammerstein II musical featured George Grizzard (later replaced by Ned Beatty) as Cap'n Andy and Cloris Leachman as his wife Parthy. The show closed Aug. 24, 1996. *Sunset Boulevard,* starring Diahann Carroll as Norma Desmond, began a 16-week run starting Dec. 1, preceded by six preview evenings.

Keeping up with its flashy new neighbor, the Queen Elizabeth Theatre was host to *Kiss of the Spider Woman,* in the summer of 1995, and *Miss Saigon* and *Tommy* in 1996.

In the film world, Babz Chula won the 1995 Vancouver Film Festival Woman of the Year Award for her work in *Live Bait* by Bruce Sweeney.

The youngest members of B.C.'s young film industry did well in 1995. Ashleigh Aston Moore, 14, landed a role in the Demi Moore feature, *Now and Then.* Gregory Smith, 12, starred with Rosie O'Donnell in *Harriet the Spy.* Jewel Staite, 13, filmed four episodes of *Fast Forward* for Disney, another TV series called *Space Cases,* and an episode of the *X-Files.*

Fine art's biggest splash since *Jack the Dripper* set down his buckets was 1995's *Andy Warhol: Images* show at the Vancouver Art Gallery. Opening night was a warm evening in June with 5,000 serious schmoozers wedging themselves into the line for free martinis and a glimpse of some of Warhol's best-known icons. Conceived and curated in Vancouver, the exhibition drew almost 100,000 visitors in its three-month run—the most popular in the VAG's history.

Northwest Sport president Arthur Griffiths wanted a new home for the Canucks, and he didn't want to rent it. But the Canucks alone couldn't pay for a new downtown stadium, so he bid for a National Basketball Association franchise.

The building became GM Place, built on a chunk of the Expo 86 lands at a cost of $163.5 million, and the franchise became the Grizzlies, founded after the NBA, the Cadillac of pro sport leagues, collected its franchise fee of $125 million U.S. (After conversion to Canadian funds, the franchise cost more than the arena.)

The cost to Griffiths was steep. By March of 1995 majority ownership of Orca Bay, the holding company controlling the Canucks, the Grizzlies and GM Place, passed to Seattle cell phone magnates John and Bruce McCaw. In November 1996 Griffiths sold his last shares in Orca to John McCaw, ending the Griffiths family's 22-year run as Vancouver's preeminent sport impresarios.

A shaky team in a shaky league, the B.C. Lions went from The Brick to the Orlick in 1995-96. After three unprofitable seasons, Edmonton-based Bill Comrie, owner of The Brick furniture stores, decided it was time to hand off the CFL franchise to a new quarterback. Having rescued it from one mercurial Vancouver promoter (Murray Pezim) in 1992 he handed it to another (Nelson Skalbania) in March 1996. All too predictably that house of cards collapsed five months later. In August, Hamilton businessman David Braley stepped gingerly into the breach. Braley, 55, owner of Orlick Industries Ltd. and former owner of the Hamilton Tiger Cats, offered to take over the Lions—but only if the team sold 15,000 season tickets by Dec. 31. Otherwise, team brass warned, the Leos would be put down in January. The target was not met, but Braley bought the team anyway. Head coach Joe Paopao left, and Adam Rita took his place.

In October 1995 the Surrey Glaciers folded after just one season in the Western Baseball League, leaving part-owner Stu Kehoe in personal bankruptcy and the municipality stuck with the Stetson Bowl—a $2.3-million white elephant that didn't meet safety standards.

On July 8, 1995 the Canucks announced they had acquired Alexander Mogilny, Pavel Bure's old Soviet National teammate, from the Buffalo Sabres in exchange for Mike Peca, Mike Wilson and a first-round draft pick. No. 89 scored 55 goals and 52 assists in the 1995-96 season. But he did much of that without Pavel Bure's help. On Nov. 9, 1995 a check by Chicago Blackhawks defenceman Steve Smith injured right winger Bure's right knee. He did not don his Canuck jersey again until an exhibition game Sept. 17, 1996—when he tallied two assists en route to 6-0 routing of the Phoenix Coyotes. A month later investigators told a U.S. congressional committee that Bure was suspected of links to the Russian mafia.

Maple Ridge's Greg Moore, 20, was a heavyweight on the Indy Lights circuit in 1995, winning 10 races to eclipse the former mark of nine victories in a single season held by fellow-Canadian Paul Tracy. In October, Moore announced he would replace Indianapolis 500 winner Jacques Villeneuve on the top Indy circuit, as Villeneuve moved to Formula One.

In August 1995 owners and breeders celebrated the inaugural of B.C. Cup Day at Hastings Park with B.C. breds Overtime Victory, Sales Model, Martini Rose, Whatchadointonight and Columbia King winning their respective races.

Charmaine Crooks, the North Vancouver middle-distance runner who has competed for Canada since 1980, was Canada's flag-bearer at the Atlanta Olympics. It was her fifth Olympiad —the most ever for a female track athlete.

There were 68 B.C. athletes at the games, and the Greater Vancouver contingent included rower Kathleen Heddle of Vancouver who, with Marnie McBean of Toronto, won a gold medal—a record third—in double sculls. Silver medalists included North Vancouver rower Jessica Monroe-Gonin of the women's eight crew; North Vancouver mountain biker Alison Sydor; Delta cyclist Brian Walton, who rebounded from knee surgery to take silver in the men's individual points race; synchronized swimmers Janice Bremmer of North Vancouver and Christine Larsen of Coquitlam. Heddle was also on the bronze-winning quad sculls team. Runner Leah Pells of Coquitlam didn't take the podium, but was rightly proud to finish fourth in the 1,500 metres.

Runners who didn't make the Olympics can opt for the Vancouver International Marathon. In 1997, the event marks its twenty-sixth year, with an expected 5,500 marathon and half-marathon competitors.

With exquisite timing, the CBC chose April 13, 1995—Jack Webster's 77th birthday—to announce the cancellation of *Front Page Challenge* after 38 years on the air. Webster, fellow panelists Allan Fotheringham, Pierre Berton and Betty Kennedy, and moderator Fred Davis had taped the last three seasons of North America's longest-running network TV show in Vancouver, under the direction of former BCTV wunderkind Cameron Bell. Davis died July 5, 1996 at age 74.

There were unkinder cuts to come for the network itself: $44 million (4.4 per cent) from its 1995 budget, with the warning that another $262 million must go by 1998. On Sept. 19, 1996 CBC president Perrin Beatty announced the corps would shed up to 2,500 jobs nationwide.

In April, 1997 CKNW decided to switch to an all talk format. Pacific Press, Southam-owned publisher of the *Province* and the *Vancouver Sun,* announced in 1996 it will move to new downtown offices at Granville Square in July 1997. Each paper's newsroom will occupy one large floor in the building, just east of Canada Place. Pacific Press will also lease six floors of 200 Granville's 28-floor business tower, for a total of about 11,148 sq. metres. Production of the *Province* and the *Vancouver Sun* at a new Surrey printing plant was to begin in the summer of 1997, on new presses worth more than $140 million.

Michael Pezim took over his father's business affairs in August 1996 after flamboyant VSE wheel Murray Pezim was diagnosed with delirium and "chronic evolving dementia." Pezim said his father, who had moved to Scottsdale, Arizona, "has a complex cardiovascular disorder with drug interactions which left him with only an intermittent ability to function."

The B.C. Securities Commission ruled in August 1996 that former B.C. premier Bill Bennett, his brother Russell and Herb Doman were guilty of insider trading of Doman Industries shares. Russell Bennett and Doman said they would appeal, but the former Socred leader did not.

It's full steam—or rather, gas—ahead for Ballard Power Systems of Burnaby, a world leader in proton exchange membrane fuel cell power systems. In November 1996 the federal government announced a $30-million investment in Ballard's $94-million bid to commercialize fuel cell power plants. The zero-emission fuel cell converts natural gas, methanol or hydrogen into electricity without combustion. Ballard's cell for cars has won contracts from firms including General Motors, Volkswagen, Volvo, Honda, Daimler-Benz and Hitachi.

Hard Suits Inc. of North Vancouver succumbed in October 1996 to a $16.5 million hostile takeover bid by Louisiana-based American Oilfield Divers Inc. The company evolved from Can-Dive, founded by diver Phil Nuytten in 1965. Its best-known product is the Newtsuit, which allows divers to work at 300-metre depths without having to undergo decompression after resurfacing.

There may be no Pacific National Exhibition in 1998. At the end of its 1997 run the annual fair was to leave Hastings Park in Vancouver, its home since Prime Minister Wilfrid Laurier opened it in 1910. But as 1996 ended the PNE did not have a new home lined up. Surrey council voted in 1995 to reject overtures from the PNE board. In the 1996 civic elections, mayoral candidates in Burnaby and Coquitlam campaigned on promises of luring the $200-million-to-$300-million facility to their respective boroughs—and lost. The fair's executives said a decision would have to be made by early 1997 if the cotton candy was to be spinning by the summer of 1998.

At the western end of Vancouver, occupying 14 square, lush kilometres of primo real estate, sit the University Endowment Lands—and the big bad city is baying at the gates. Officially governed by the province, the UEL has links to the GVRD (one UEL representative), the City of Vancouver (fire department, school board) provincial highways ministry, the RCMP and, of course, the University of B.C. Still, many of the 2,750 eligible voters of the area like to imagine they are roughing it, administratively speaking, and in March of 1995 a referendum on municipal status was defeated 599 to 318. So it came as a shock when, the next fall, the university announced it might just build housing on 30 per cent of its land. If new developments maintain the density of recent projects, that could mean as many as 18,000 new neighbors for the unincorporated UEL. "It is about time that they take some responsibility for themselves," grumbled GVRD chairman Greg Halsey-Brandt.

On Nov. 26 the B.C. Institute of Technology opened its $35 million downtown Vancouver campus—Western Canada's first "smart building," bristling with such hi-tech doodads as video-conference facilities, state-of-the-art multimedia and seminar rooms, electronic library and a fully integrated computer and fibre-optic cabling system (whew!) connecting it to other campuses and organizations. By 2000, the campus is expected to serve up to 10,000 part-time students a year.

On Aug. 8, 1995, Ottawa closed the Fraser River commercial salmon fishery to protect fish stocks. In September the federal fisheries department went further, allowing fewer fishing days for the aboriginal food fishery and banning sport sockeye fishing from the mouth of the Fraser to the Coquihalla River.

Former football great Emery Barnes, house speaker and NDP MLA for Vancouver Burrard, retired from politics in 1996 after 23 years and, at age 66, started training for the senior Olympics.

Acting on the recommendations of an independent report, Vancouver city council sacked the board of directors of the Vancouver Museum in early 1996. The museum had been the scene of bitter wrangling for two years, after a new board developed a business plan that resulted in layoffs for half the staff and cancellation of the museum's school education programs. Those moves in turn prompted a six-month strike and a backlash among the museum's membership.

Tree lovers say too many Lower Mainland homeowners are playing Paul Bunyan in the front yard to improve the view, maintain tradition or simply avoid raking leaves. In July 1996 Vancouver City Hall staff drafted a bylaw proposing to ban the cutting of trees wider than 20 centimetres without permission from the city. But council watered down the bylaw, settling for a limit of one large tree per home per year—no questions asked.

Everybody complains about local traffic, but nobody wants to give up his car. In 1995 the provincial government began work to widen the Trans-Canada, with a promise that major construction would begin in the summer (tourist season) of 1997. On Nov. 1 the first West Coast Express commuter train pulled into downtown Vancouver from Maple Ridge—and a year later its $7 fare was still $50 short of the cost per passenger.

Vancouver city council threw a few pylons on the Burrard Bridge to create a bike lane during the first week of June 1996 but furious commuters raised such a ruckus that the idea of a permanent bike lane on the bridge was parked indefinitely. In the fall, cash-strapped BC Transit announced plans for reduced bus service around the Lower Mainland—and morning rush hour on Highway 1 is stretching into the afternoon.

The well-hyped "Three Tenors" concert December 31, 1996 turned into a major embarrassment when slow ticket sales—mostly caused by high ticket prices—led promoter Tina VanderHeyden to try to cancel the show. But Pavarotti, Domingo and Carreras showed up to sing at B.C. Place when their producers ponied up money (reportedly $1 million) to pay some of the show's administrative costs. Then the three singers disappointed the audience by not staying on stage until midnight and the new Year.

UBC spent much of 1995 and 1996 mired in sexual politics. In June 1995 Vancouver lawyer Joan McEwen submitted a report alleging systemic racism and sexism in the university's political science department—and a bill for $240,000. Admissions to graduate studies in the department were immediately closed, then reopened in October after a firestorm of controversy. A year later the UBC board came under fire when its search for a successor to president David Strangway included an advertisement stating the university "especially" welcomed applications from women, ethnic minorities and disabled persons. On Nov. 19, 1996 UBC announced the new boss was Dr. Martha C. Piper, vice-president of research and external affairs at the University of Alberta.

And 1996 went out in a blizzard of Christmas white when the Lower Mainland was hit by the snowiest spell of winter since weather records began more than a century ago.

Epilogue
Stephen Hume

Dawn will come to Vancouver as always, slipping a pearly wedge between the crumpled edge of the continent and the restless dark of the Pacific where an unknowable future stirs.

Sun and tide may seem an odd way to begin a rumination about what lies ahead, but these are the mechanisms on which we base our whole endeavour. They are now, perhaps, the only things to be predicted with any certainty.

Change is the other certainty, of course. Our political, social and economic cultures in British Columbia teeter at the brink of a metamorphosis as profound as any we've seen.

Deep currents of pessimism now charge the psychological landscape. A third of us think the country won't survive. A third of us would refuse a blood transfusion for fear of tainted blood. One person in three worries that she—or a family member—faces losing a job.

This anxiety feeds on constant talk of downsizing to lower labor costs and the demonization of public services—as though fear were a good motivator, human resources a liability rather than an asset and wealth redistribution simply robbery. Growing numbers worry that if they do lose a job they'll be on their own, that community safety nets are being dismantled.

Meanwhile traditional assumptions of status based on ethnicity, race, language, age, economic expectation and opportunity—norms we establish to create an illusion of permanence—all shift under us. Nowhere is this more evident than in demographic patterns. If Pacific tides are harbingers of coming environmental change—at present rates they will rise a metre in a few generations—the human flood reshapes the planet beyond our visible horizons.

In Vancouver the tide of people is running strong. Rapid population expansion is obvious; demographic implications are less clear. Like an iceberg the bulk of the promised change is submerged, waiting to be fully charted by the sonar of statistical extrapolation.

As of January 1, 1996, the first baby boomers born between 1946 and 1964 began turning 50. In metro Vancouver this accelerating trend to middle-aged angst will affect close to 250,000 people. A baby boomer will reach that psychological milestone every seven-and-a-half seconds. With pressures to shed workers expected into the next century, these older employees will be vulnerable, not venerated. They will be anxious and—sooner or later—deeply resentful.

Like an iceberg the bulk of the promised change is submerged, waiting to be fully charted by the sonar of statistical extrapolation

Behind these social trends lie the great natural mechanisms on which our economic structures depend, processes so large we are able to perceive only segments of them. When they change, everything does.

Global warming is underway—the scientific consensus is now indisputable—and we play a significant role. In the last decade B.C.'s carbon dioxide emissions from burning fossil fuels increased 34 per cent. On average we produce 25 tonnes of greenhouse gases each, four times the global average and the worst per capita performance of industrial democracies. This output seems unlikely to decline soon. From Portland to Vancouver there are now more vehicles than drivers. Our commitment to mass public transit remains questionable. Government promises billions for transit upgrades while subsidizing air pollution with vast transfers to maintain automobile infrastructure and low gasoline taxes. In the Lower Mainland, public employees get free parking worth $26 million a year.

Global warming means melting ice caps and rising sea levels. The Pacific is now rising almost a half-centimetre per year. This rate may be accelerating. Imperceptible to the human eye, it is of great significance in a graduated estuary like the Fraser's. As tides reach farther upstream water tables will rise. Dikes offer limited protection. Over the next decade we could see severe downward pressure on the values of now-prized waterside property.

At the same time old social institutions rooted in European colonialism are crumbling while new ones are thrust up. By the end of this decade the Lower Mainland will be home to half-a-million immigrants, 60 per cent of whom will have arrived since 1981. Almost half will be of Asian origin, although cultures from Oceania, Africa, the West Indies, Central and South America already complement immigration from Europe and the U.S.

All eyes are on Asia yet no one should underestimate the rising importance of South and Central America. Think of South America as a new China next door, a continent where population—and markets—will be close to a billion when the 1996

New Year's baby enters the work force.

In the next decade look for a new entrepreneurial elite to emerge, surfing the high-flux, high-tech trends of what some economists are calling the turbo-charged capitalism of the 21st century. Chinese and East Indian business and professional leaders, members of communities which in the last decade have surpassed Germans, Italians and French in numbers, will help forge a new hybrid of rank and privilege.

Six per cent of Canada's population and one in two British Columbians will soon inhabit the Fraser River flood plain. Between now and 2000 the population there will grow by almost 200,000—adding a city the size of Regina to the suburbs every five years. We persuade ourselves to view growth as prosperity. It does expand retail and labor markets and increase real estate values. But population growth also represents a net drawdown on our most vital environmental capital. Traditional accounting methods fail to measure this. Expect growing public insistence on "green accounting" in business plans.

Lower Mainland growth means paving more precious agricultural land. Some estimate that in the last decade we've withdrawn from the agricultural land reserve about ten per cent of the richest food-producing soil on the planet. Why should we worry? Food is plentiful and cheap.

Worldwide the ratio of mouths to arable land increases at a disturbing rate. More than 200,000 square kilometres of the world's prime farmland have been lost to desertification alone. If the people of China develop a taste for beer that approaches North American consumption patterns, it alone would consume their entire grain production each year. And worldwide grain production is falling, not rising. Our arable land, a tiny fraction of B.C., may prove of immense strategic worth.

Exploding population means more lethal runoff and greater stress on salmon habitats, degrading yet another of our great sustainable protein-producing systems. It means more cars and more tonnes of pollution spewing into what is already some of the most polluted air on the continent. Fraser Valley crop yields are thought to be depressed by 20 per cent because of air pollution. Mortality spikes accompany Lower Mainland air quality that is sometimes worse than Mexico City's.

Clean-air initiatives notwithstanding, this problem will get worse. Business, locked into management perceptions that lag behind technological possibilities, has not fully awakened to the remedial potential of the modem. Too many managers still demand that workers commute to offices located where they cannot afford to live.

In addition to mass transit we need corporate commitment to more telecommuting, job-sharing and satellite offices—anything that reduces commuter numbers. JALA International, a Los Angeles management consulting firm, estimates a company can save $12,000 a year for each person who telecommutes at least two days a week.

We now spend $1.4 billion each year on 60,000 kilometres of roads. We subsidize Greater Vancouver drivers to take a tonne of steel and plastic to work each morning and park it for eight hours in a space that remains unused for the other 16 hours. In the process they pump 400,000 kilograms of toxic crud into the air each year

When I left the coast 31 years ago this summer I couldn't wait to get the stewed cabbage stench of pulp mills out of my nostrils. The political nostrum of the day was, "That's jobs you smell." To me the place seemed suffocatingly parochial, psychologically inbred, deferential, intellectually colonized. The smug grin of Social Credit seemed unassailable. Municipal politics was dominated by caricatures who thought Stanley Park would be perfect for condos.

When I returned I found an astonishing cultural transformation.

More interesting even than the surge in visible minorities is the half-a-million people who define themselves as multi-ethnic in origin. They exemplify a human desire to stretch the old constraints of tradition, conformity and social stratification. These people represent profound growth in the intellectual and cultural inventory of the community. They represent a remarkable confluence in history, the first wholly voluntary merging of global cultures in a social environment predicated on pluralism and tolerance.

This introduces a powerful new dynamic to the social intercourse that drives both the world of commerce and the life of the mind. Consider the British genius for administration fusing with the commercial acumen of the Chinese. Consider the marriage of India's knowledge, which profoundly influenced the course of Western thought, and the "Just do it!" pragmatism of American business culture. Consider Germanic efficiency framed by aboriginal teachings suggesting that we are part of nature and nature must be part of us. This ebullient, creative, hybrid vigor, I believe, yields our single greatest cause for optimism.

As a boy I knew men who remembered when no Vancouver lights shone across Georgia Strait. Tonight the habitation glow creates a celestial arc from Seattle to West Vancouver. This conurbation—"city" sheds its meaning in our age of megalopolis, mass transit and neural networks of fibre-optics—approaches a critical mass of self-sustaining economic and cultural evolution. Within it the convergence of cultures already triggers a transforming chain reaction.

Vancouver is evolving beyond its self-conception as the end of the line, the far outpost of Toronto's corporate culture, the place where drifters stop because they can't go further. We are increasingly aware that the city is now self-defining, a source rather than a hinterland, a centre of gravity rather than a satellite.

Geography dictates that Vancouver's future lies in its role as Canada's strategic gateway to the Orient. Every other major city in Canada is naturally orientated to the east and south.

Edmonton, Calgary and Winnipeg are physically connected by their rivers to the Atlantic and by the descending stairway of the Great Plains to the Gulf of Mexico. But our rivers flow west, arteries that propel our imaginations outward and into a different world.

Vancouver's umbilical connection to Asia has been evident since its beginning. The first Europeans came seeking a route to Cathay. Our first ecological catastrophe born of greed—the destruction of the sea otter—stemmed from the fur trade with China. Living men and women still remember the tea clippers and the silk express.

When I left B.C. the value of trade between Canada and the United Kingdom was double the value of trade with Japan. Today our trade is almost four times as valuable with Japan as with the U.K. In fact trade into the Asia-Pacific zone now exceeds by a third the value of trade with the big six of Europe. Much of this commerce travels through the Port of Vancouver.

So a powerful new role seems likely for British Columbia in the coming debate over what Canada is and should become, although it remains to be seen whether we can rise above our adolescent arrogance.

A know-it-all, boisterous, juvenile energy marks this emerging culture. Like most adolescents poised in the doorway of the wider world, contempt for parental authority mingles with a lingering reluctance to let go of the security that accompanies old deferences. Yet adolescents do not, cannot, stay at home forever. They must find their way to maturity on their own terms. In healthy families we educate one another; independence is not bought at the expense of loving relationships.

One test of British Columbia's maturity must be the way in which we deal with the unresolved grievances of the aboriginal peoples who occupied this place for 10,000 years before all others arrived. Too often we frame this discussion in material terms, reducing it to a squabble over how to divide the pie. In reality it is no more a material argument than a potlatch is about how much stuff you can acquire. This dispute is over moral, legal and spiritual obligations.

Are we open to a world which insists the debate must address

Vancouver's umbilical connection to Asia has been evident since its beginning. The first Europeans came seeking a route to Cathay

the problem's spiritual dimensions? I think we are. Surveys show 80 per cent of us believe we are spiritual people and have become even more so over the last few years. Why shouldn't this transfer to dealing with legitimate aboriginal grievances?

Elders in the aboriginal community say they have faith in the common people. Our own judicial elders have made it clear that we have a fiduciary obligation to assist in helping to preserve, protect and strengthen those distinct cultures and languages that pre-date our arrival.

Aboriginal grievances leave us faced with decisions that will determine the ethical shape of the society our children will evolve. If Canada is a model for the kind of state we must evolve in an over-populated world capable of self-destruction, B.C. is the model for Canada.

"The challenge," says Nu-cha-nulth leader George Watts, "is whether British Columbia can live side by side with a people who possess a world view, values, laws and institutions that are different from—and at times at odds with—the Euro-Canadian experience. The real test is whether mainstream Canadian society is able to embrace and accommodate the entire human experience of First Nation peoples. All of us in this journey will need to act with a great deal of tolerance, respect and civility."

Once, in the northern bush, hands bloody in the ruin of his kill, a young native hunter looked up at me and laughed at my question about land claims. "You white guys, you think we want to own this land. We can't own the land. The land owns us."

That may prove the most enduring prediction for the years ahead.

The Greater Vancouver Book–
A Serendipitous Adventure
Chuck Davis

> One of the advantages of being disorderly is that one is constantly making exciting discoveries
>
> —A.A. Milne

I SHOULD HAVE CALLED this article "Junk Mail Changed My Life." It really did, and it led directly to this book. Every book has its own story to tell. *The Greater Vancouver Book* has several. To use an old-fashioned phrase, they may be of interest to the reader.

The book is an expansion of *The Vancouver Book,* published by J.J. Douglas Ltd. in 1976. The original idea had come nine years before that (in July 1967) and I excitedly scribbled it and the date on a scrap of paper: "Should do urban almanac on Vancouver." I threw the note into a chaotic filing cabinet and forgot about it. Eight years later I came across the note and got enthusiastic all over again. (As A.A. Milne said, "One of the advantages of being disorderly is that one is constantly making exciting discoveries.")

Something wonderfully serendipitous then happened: a man named Ernie Fladell came to be interviewed on a CBC Radio show I was hosting at the time. He was there to talk about a Vancouver city hall division he worked at called the Social Planning Department. They were a lively group of people who wanted to, among many other things, promote and encourage cultural activities in the city. As Ernie, one of the brightest and most original thinkers it has ever been my privilege to meet, talked about what Social Planning was doing around the city I began to think he and they might be interested in my book idea. After the interview I invited him for coffee and bent his ear for more than an hour about my notion for an "urban almanac." The result was Social Planning commissioned me to do it. My gratitude to Ernie and to Maurice Egan, then the director of the department, will be understood. That original book was dedicated to Ernie who has been a good friend now for more than 20 years . . . and, you will note, is a contributor to the present version.

The 1976 book was a success; all the copies were sold and it became a standard reference work on the city . . . and J.J. Douglas Ltd. (which has metamorphosed into Douglas & McIntyre) vowed never to do it again! It was a huge undertaking, expensive, time-consuming and exhausting. It took guts for them to do that book and, like everything Scott McIntyre and his staff do, it was damned well done. (Scott, incidentally, named the book.) I heartily agreed with the decision not to attempt it again and carried on with my broadcasting career, and with other books. Still, it was gratifying to be told by the Vancouver Public Library that in 1976 *The Vancouver Book* was the second most frequently stolen book in their system. I counted that as a great testimony to its usefulness. (I asked, of course, what the most frequently stolen book was and learned it was *Mein Kampf* by Adolf Hitler. When I mentioned that curious fact to Denny Boyd, he cracked, "Thank God the other guy isn't doing a sequel.")

My determination never to repeat that 1976 effort was fated to end. I must have been asked a thousand times—an average of once a week for 20 years sounds about right—if there would ever be an update of *The Vancouver Book,* and had always said no. Then, again, serendipity struck.

This time it came through a side door via a completely unrelated writing assignment. In 1992 I'd been commissioned by John Plul, vice president of promotion at CKNW, to write a book on the station's 50th anniversary—which would occur in 1994. It happens that I'd just bought a fancy new computer, with a 486 co-processor, 500-mb hard-drive, eight megs of RAM, an internal CD-ROM and nine-port tower . . . and couldn't get it to work because I remain a computer klutz even after working with them for more than 20 years. (I asked my business partner to give me that technical description.)

I began to write the CKNW book by hand. Then on February 8, 1993 (I'm thinking of having a plaque made), in the morning's packet of junk mail that I was just about to pitch into the fireplace, I noted a small garishly colored flyer poking out of the stack. It was headlined Got a New Computer? . . . Need Help? The company, Kara Data Centre, was a few blocks from our home. I phoned for a consultation and the next morning the entire company—John Cochlin and his wife Kathy—showed up on our doorstep. Within 24 hours, thanks to them, I was happily tapping away at my new computer and finished the CKNW book (titled *Top Dog*) on it. I'm writing this on it.

The Cochlins and I developed a rapport. We liked working with each other. And one day Kathy Cochlin said, "Why don't you do *The Vancouver Book* again?"

It was gratifying to be told by the Vancouver Public Library that in 1976 The Vancouver Book was the second most frequently stolen book in their system

To which I replied after a few seconds' thought, "Okay."

Never in the history of literature have so many written so much for so tiny a word. That "okay" led to more than three years of unremitting labor, hundreds of conversations with local writers, hundreds of visits to potential sponsors, nearly two thousand letters, countless thousands of telephone calls, faxes sufficient to wrap B.C. Place, many visits to libraries, museums and city halls, interviews, typing, transcribing, converting from one computing platform to another, agonizing over the design, the weight of the paper . . . and on and on and on.

Fin Anthony, a longtime friend I roped in to handle sponsorships, suggested the new name. I'd intended using the original title. "It isn't about Vancouver," Fin insisted, "it's about Greater Vancouver!" Fin was later joined in handling sponsorships by the bracingly energetic Patricia Prince.

From the beginning I'd wanted Julian Beder (rhymes with "reader") as senior editor. Julian had handled an earlier book of mine, published by New Star Books, and I never forgot his punctiliousness and care. When the trickle of submissions turned into a flood, Julian was joined by Jack Vermee, Iain Hiscoe and Constance Brissenden. Julian found us Lawrence Boxall, who became the book's production manager and is responsible, second only to the prodigiously energetic and imaginative John Cochlin, for it coming out at all.

Robin Ward heard about the project and we agreed—during a long afternoon of pacing in my office (we're both pacers)—that he'd design it. And soon John and I began hearing words like pica, kerning, drop caps, pull quotes, footers, screens, Garamond and Gill sans serif fonts and more. Another old friend, Jim Rimmer—who designed the very first book I ever wrote, a *1973* guide to Vancouver—created Linkman's colophon in one inspired afternoon.

Then even more serendipity happened. At a meeting of the Friends of the Vancouver Archives, I was chatting with fellow members Bruce Macdonald and his wife Gail McDermott.

Bruce is the author of that fabulous book, *Vancouver: A Visual History* and, happily, is a contributor to this book. Apropos of nothing in particular, I was droning on about a fantasy I'd long enjoyed of commissioning a composer to write me a concerto or a symphony.

Gail thought I was talking about The Project.

"Yeah," she said, "that would be a nice way to launch the book." I gaped at her in amazement for a moment . . . and the very next day went to see Michael Conway Baker, whose music I had long enjoyed, and asked him to write a concerto to celebrate the publication of the book and Greater Vancouver itself. Because I'm fond of the oboe, I asked for an oboe concerto. Michael wrote a beauty. I'm listening to it as I write this. It's titled *Vancouver Variations* (after a suggestion from contributor Ben D'Andrea) and it's going to become a standard.

A CD of Michael's music containing *Variations,* played by the CBC Vancouver Orchestra under Bruce Rodney Dunn and featuring soloists Roger Cole, oboe, and Linda Lee Thomas, piano, appeared in the spring of 1996. A live concert (a benefit for Literacy B.C., sponsored by the *Vancouver Sun* and CBC Stereo), highlighted by the world premiere of Michael's concerto, featuring the same performers and produced by CBC's Karen Wilson, was held April 30, 1996, at the splendid old Orpheum Theatre. So far as we know that was the first time a book's publication was celebrated with a specially commissioned orchestral work. It was terrific to have many of the book's writers in the audience. My wife Edna and daughter Stephanie (Steph was going on four when the original book appeared) were there. So were John and Kathy, of course, and their three sons, Christian, Jared and Sean. My sister Donna Carlbom and her husband Ernie flew in from their home in Hawaii to attend the show. Longtime buddy Norm Grohmann —we were grade 7 classmates at Maple Ridge Junior High— spoke from the stage. So did Denny Boyd who read a portion of his essay from this book. Judy Taylor, vice chair of the Vancouver Public Library board, spoke. Jurgen Gothe was master of ceremonies, and the music was recorded for later national broadcast on CBC Stereo. It was a fine evening.

The original plan for the concert was to introduce the book during it but, alas, its 900-plus pages weren't ready. They are now.

acknowledgements . . . continued from page xiii

Ken Bagshaw of Ladner Downs; Jonathan Baker; Ron Barker, old buddy and tour business info guru; Diana Barkley and Mary Lou Gazely of the Barkley-Gazely Group; Bertie Beiser, longtime friend and entertainment-and-culture maven; Peter Bentley, a sponsor who went the distance and more, and Darrell Mawhinney at CanFor; Karel Birkman, consul general of the Netherlands; Gerry Blitstein, CD-ROM shepherd; Peter McMullen and David Brown at B.C. Hydro, two patient men; Brian Calder, who does a little of everything; J. Brooks Joyner and Donna Call of the Vancouver Art Gallery; Brian Campbell, head of systems at Vancouver Public Library and FreeNet pioneer; Dan Charette of Statistics Canada; Liz Chase at Island Paper; friend of 30 years Al Clapp and Geraldine; John Collison of the Vancouver Area Newspaper Network for a real good deal; Chris Cornwall, formerly with Bentall Development and unearther, for us, of a fascinating treasure trove of old construction photos; Ian Davidson, artist's patron; Sid Fancy, Vancouver Economic Development office; Carol Ferreira, indexer who gave terrific advice; Norman Frizzle, novelist; John Furlong of the Club Association; Hoot Gibson, composer, songwriter, book lender; Ed Gifford, friend and photographer; Paul and Audrey Grescoe, for their unstinting support and also for giving B.C. son Taras, one of our writers; Tom Haibeck of the Haibeck Group; Internet maven Todd Maffin; Shirley Hartwell, tour guide, actress and one hell of a southern belle; Wendy Heath of Vancouver Up Close and Personal; Dr. Bob Hindmarch of UBC for some excellent contacts; John Keirstead, for talks about Masons; Diana Lam, friend and contact-pointer-outer; Dave Laundy, then with the Vancouver Stock Exchange, who opened a nifty door; Paul Le Branche of the Building Owners and Managers Association; Jane MacDonald and Michael Francis at the Vancouver International Film Festival; Charlie Mayrs and Brad Philley at Dome Advertising; Jeremy Meharg at Burnaby South Secondary; Peggie Merlin; the late Dean Miller of Miller Leonard, thanks, old pal; John Mills of Sport BC who thought of the right guy; Howard Mitchell, Mitchell Press; Kyle Mitchell, Vancouver Public Library Board; Geoff Molyneux, who was working on his history of Pacific Press when we last lunched; Sev Morin for that invitation to the opening of the Michael J. Fox Theatre.

Thanks to Fred Morley for good advice about real estate research; to Gary Morrey, of Morrey Nissan, who cast the net wider; to Myles Murchison, whose sponsors' notes for Bentall Developments were as interesting as the article they made possible; to *Province* photograper Jon Murray for the photo of Ye Olde Editor; to Bess Narod for a great luncheon; editor Anne Norman; to Can-Dive's Phil Nuytten, one of the handful of people in this city whose biography I'd like to write; Lorna and Willard Persson, of St. Giles United Church, for organizing such a pleasant audience to hear a fat old man talk about a fat new book; Roy Peterson, cartoonist (cartoonist? hell, no, artist!); John Poser, of Signs Now; Laurie Roggeman of the Friends of the Library; Keith Sacre of MacNeill Library Service; Ashok Sarkar, who wants to make that movie; Daniel Say, who should write that book; Harry and Irene Schiel of *Playboard* magazine; Parjeet Singh, teacher and author; Della Smith, of Quay Strategies; Miriam Smith, the "walking tour lady;" Duart Snow, *Pacific Yachting* magazine; and Jon Steeves, many thanks! (Buy Jon's game, Moot. It's word-lovers' heaven.)

Thanks, too, to Norman Stowe at the Pace Group; to lawyer Alex Szibbo, Tosh Tanaka at the consulate general for Japan; Phil Thomas and Barry Hall for good music, and especially Phil for a good book idea; Greg Tjosvold of CD-ROM fame; the Vancouver Historical Society; to Ron Meyer and Rick Watson in memoriam, two old friends who didn't live to make their contributions to the book; Louise Whitney of *Where* magazine; Ron Woodall of Palmer Jarvis for his always funny, stimulating and helpful comments and conversation; to Marilyn Wright and Brenda Jackson at the Vancouver Public Library Capital Fund office; and to Mike Yazzolino, who designed the first book 21 years ago and happened to visit as we finished the second.

Very special thanks to Charles (Sonny) Widen for his valuable support.

Penultimately, a word of gratitude to all the people who helped us and whose names, whether through ineptitude or my chronic disorganization, did not make it onto this list. The days ahead will be peppered with moments where I smite my brow and say, "Ohmigod, I forgot to mention . . ." (Another mea culpa: since the preparation of these acknowledgements we've been helped by many people whose names don't appear here. They will be acknowledged on the CD-ROM version.)

Finally, and most importantly of all, thanks to my wife of 32 years, Edna and my daughter of 24 years, Stephanie. For four of those years, they have put up with an awful lot.

—*Chuck Davis, April 14, 1997*

Index

A note about the Index: if we had an entry for every person, building, boat, natural feature, performance, company, street name and so on in this book the index would be more than 100 pages long. We've attempted to restrict entries to those that give information not found elsewhere. For example, the reference in the Chronology of Greater Vancouver to Vancouver's Great Fire of 1886 is not shown in the index because there is a complete article on that subject. In addition, some minor events and personalities are not indexed. For researchers, students, librarians, etc., for whom a complete index would be useful, send a cheque or money order for $5 to obtain a printed version of the complete index to:

Index,
Linkman Press,
15032 97th Avenue,
Surrey, B.C. V3R 8K2

If you have access to the Internet you'll find the complete index at www.discovervancouver.com.